50¢

HARRAP'S

Student
French
Dictionary

plus
French grammar

D0725794

HARRAP'S

Student French Dictionary

plus French grammar

HARRAP

EDINBURGH   NEW YORK   TORONTO

Distributed in the United States by

PRENTICE
HALL
PRESS

Dictionary edited by Michael Janes
French Consultant:
Fabrice Antoine
English Consultants:
Hazel Curties and Stuart Fortey

Grammar compiled by LEXUS
with Raymond Perrez, Noel Peacock and
Sabine Citron

First published in this combined edition
in Great Britain 1991
by HARRAP BOOKS Ltd
43-45 Annandale Street
Edinburgh EH7 4AZ

Dictionary © Harrap Books Ltd 1988
Grammar © Harrap Books Ltd 1987

Reprinted 1992

ISBN 0 245-60295-X
In the United States ISBN 0-13-377631-X

TRADEMARKS

Printed and bound in Denmark
by Nørhaven Rotation

Preface

This dictionary is an entirely new publication designed to provide an up-to-date, practical and concise work of reference giving translations of the most useful French and English vocabulary.

The aim has been to achieve a work of great clarity of equal value to French and to English speakers, whether students, tourists, businessmen or -women or general readers, and to produce a text offering the maximum amount of guidance in pinpointing and understanding translations. Equal importance has been given to the presentation of French and English. Different translations of the same word or phrase are clearly labelled by means of bracketed context indicators and/or style and field labels. A single translation of a word is also often labelled as an additional aid to the user (e.g. **hedgehog** n (*animal*) hérisson m; **ungainly** a (*clumsy*) gauche; **béotien, -ienne** nmf (*inculte*) philistine). The user is helped by having indicators and labels in French in the French section and in English in the English section of the dictionary.

Style and field labels follow bracketed indicators (e.g. **grid** n . . . . (*system*) El réseau m; **bidule** nm (*chose*) Fam thingummy). In the event of more than one translation within a grammatical category being qualified by the same style or field label, the label may then precede (see **calé, liquidizer, trucker**).

The user will find in the text important abbreviations, useful geographical information such as names of countries, and a wide coverage of American words and usage. The vocabulary treated includes French and English colloquialisms and slang, and important technical jargon. Comparatives and superlatives of English adjectives are also indicated.

In order to save space, derived words are usually included within the entry of a headword. All such words are highlighted by means of a lozenge. Derivatives may be written in full or abbreviated, as is usually the case for important derived forms (such as English **-ly** or French **-ment**).

An oblique stroke in bold is used to mark the stem of a headword at which point the derived ending is added. A bold dash stands for a headword or the portion of a headword to the left of the oblique stroke (e.g. **awkward** a . . . ◆**—ly** adv . . . ◆**—ness** n . . . ; **boulevers/er** vt . . . ◆**—ant** a . . . ◆**—ement** nm).

An oblique stroke within an entry is another space-saving device. It is used to separate non equivalent alternative parts of a phrase or expression matched exactly in French and English (e.g. **les basses/hautes classes** the lower/upper classes is to be understood as: **les basses classes** the lower classes and **les hautes classes** the upper classes; **to give s.o./sth a push** pousser qn/qch as: **to give s.o. a push** pousser qn and **to give sth a push** pousser qch).

A further typographical device, a filled square, may be used to introduce a string of English phrasal verbs (see **come, take**).

In common with other Harrap dictionaries, when a headword appears in an example in the same form, it is represented by its initial letter. This applies whether the headword starts a new line (e.g. **advance** n |in a. of s.o. avant qn) or appears within an entry, either in full form (e.g. ◆**arterial** a a. road route f principale), or in abbreviated form (e.g. ◆**—ed** stands for **advanced** ◆**—ed** a a. in years âgé).

The pronunciation of both English and French is shown using the latest symbols of the International Phonetic Alphabet. Pronunciation is given for headwords at the start of an entry, and, as an additional help to the user, for a word within an entry where the correct pronunciation may be difficult to derive from the form of the word (e.g. ◆**aristocratie** [-asi]; ◆**aoûtien, -ienne** [ausjɛ̃, -jɛn]; ◆**rabid** [ˈræbɪd]; ◆**prayer** [preər]).

Stress in English is indicated for headwords and for derived words in which stress differs from that of a headword (e.g. **civilize** [ˈsɪvɪlaɪz] and ◆**civili'zation**). American English pronunciation is listed wherever it is considered to differ substantially from that of British English (e.g. **aristocrat** [ˈærɪstəkræt, Am əˈrɪstəkræt], **quinine** [ˈkwɪniːn, Am ˈkwaɪnaɪn]). American spelling is also given if considered sufficiently different (e.g. **tire** and **tyre, plow** and **plough**).

An original feature of this dictionary is its semantic approach to the order and arrangement of entries. An approach whereby the meaning of words is allowed to influence the structure of entries is felt to be of particular benefit to the user in his or her understanding of language.

Important semantic categories have been indicated by bold Arabic numerals within an entry (see **bolt**, **tail**, **général**) or have been entered as separate headwords (see **bug¹** and **bug²**, **draw¹** and **draw²**, **start¹** and **start²**). Note that grammatical categories, apart from the first, have been marked by a dash.

Words are entered under the headword from which they are considered to derive (e.g. **approfondi**, abbreviated as ◆—i follows **approfond/ir**; ◆**astronomer** and ◆**astro'no-mical** follow **astronomy**). Present and past participles (used adjectivally) are felt to be closely associated in meaning and form with the infinitive from which they derive. They are entered, usually in abbreviated form, within an entry immediately after the infinitive, any other derivatives there may be following in alphabetical order (e.g. **exalt/er** vt ... ◆—ant a ... ◆—é a ... ◆**exaltation** nf; **accommodat/e** vt ... ◆—ing a ... ◆**accommo'dation** n; **expir/e** vi ... ◆—ed a ... ◆**expi'ration** n ... ◆**expiry** n).

Derived words and compounds are felt to be semantically distinct and are, wherever possible, grouped together alphabetically and listed separately from each other (e.g. **base** n ... ◆—**less** a ... ◆—**ness** n ... ◆**baseball** n ... ◆**baseboard** n; **bouton** nm ... ◆**b.-d'or** nm ... ◆**b.-pression** nm ... ◆**boutonner** vt ... ◆**boutonneux**, **-euse** a ... ◆**boutonnière** nf). Compounds may be listed in the place within an entry where they are felt best to belong by virtue of meaning.

The author wishes to express his gratitude to Monsieur F. Antoine, Mrs H. Curties and Mr S. Fortey for their advice and help, to Mrs R. Hillmore for her assistance with proofreading, and to Mr J.-L. Barbanneau for his support and encouragement.

M. Janes
London, 1988

Abbreviations

Abréviations

adjective	*a*	adjectif
abbreviation	*abbr, abrév*	abréviation
adverb	*adv*	adverbe
agriculture	*Agr*	agriculture
American	*Am*	américain
anatomy	*Anat*	anatomie
architecture	*Archit*	architecture
slang	*Arg*	argot
article	*art*	article
cars, motoring	*Aut*	automobile
auxiliary	*aux*	auxiliaire
aviation, aircraft	*Av*	aviation
biology	*Biol*	biologie
botany	*Bot*	botanique
British	*Br*	britannique
Canadian	*Can*	canadien
carpentry	*Carp*	menuiserie
chemistry	*Ch*	chimie
cinema	*Cin*	cinéma
commerce	*Com*	commerce
conjunction	*conj*	conjonction
cookery	*Culin*	cuisine
definite	*def, déf*	défini
demonstrative	*dem, dém*	démonstratif
economics	*Econ, Écon*	économie
electricity	*El, Él*	électricité
et cetera	*etc*	et cetera
feminine	*f*	féminin
familiar	*Fam*	familier
football	*Fb*	football
figurative	*Fig*	figuré
finance	*Fin*	finance
feminine plural	*fpl*	féminin pluriel
French	*Fr*	français
geography	*Geog, Géog*	géographie
geology	*Geol, Géol*	géologie
geometry	*Geom, Géom*	géométrie
grammar	*Gram*	grammaire
history	*Hist*	histoire
humorous	*Hum*	humoristique
indefinite	*indef, indéf*	indéfini
indicative	*indic*	indicatif
infinitive	*inf*	infinitif
interjection	*int*	interjection
invariable	*inv*	invariable
ironic	*Iron*	ironique
journalism	*Journ*	journalisme
legal, law	*Jur*	juridique
linguistics	*Ling*	linguistique
literary	*Lit, Litt*	littéraire
literature	*Liter, Littér*	littérature

masculine	*m*	masculin
mathematics	*Math*	mathématique
medicine	*Med, Méd*	médecine
carpentry	*Menuis*	menuiserie
meteorology	*Met, Mét*	météorologie
military	*Mil*	militaire
masculine plural	*mpl*	masculin pluriel
music	*Mus*	musique
noun	*n*	nom
nautical	*Nau*	nautique
noun feminine	*nf*	nom féminin
noun masculine	*nm*	nom masculin
noun masculine and feminine	*nmf*	nom masculin et féminin
pejorative	*Pej, Péj*	péjoratif
philosophy	*Phil*	philosophie
photography	*Phot*	photographie
physics	*Phys*	physique
plural	*pl*	pluriel
politics	*Pol*	politique
possessive	*poss*	possessif
past participle	*pp*	participe passé
prefix	*pref, préf*	préfixe
preposition	*prep, prép*	préposition
present participle	*pres p*	participe présent
present tense	*pres t*	temps présent
pronoun	*pron*	pronom
psychology	*Psy*	psychologie
past tense	*pt*	prétérit
	qch	quelque chose
	qn	quelqu'un
registered trademark	®	marque déposée
radio	*Rad*	radio
railway, *Am* railroad	*Rail*	chemin de fer
relative	*rel*	relatif
religion	*Rel*	religion
school	*Sch, Scol*	école
singular	*sing*	singulier
slang	*Sl*	argot
someone	*s.o.*	
sport	*Sp*	sport
something	*sth*	
subjunctive	*sub*	subjonctif
technical	*Tech*	technique
telephone	*Tel, Tél*	téléphone
textiles	*Tex*	industrie textile
theatre	*Th*	théâtre
television	*TV*	télévision
typography, printing	*Typ*	typographie
university	*Univ*	université
United States	*US*	États-Unis
auxiliary verb	*v aux*	verbe auxiliaire
intransitive verb	*vi*	verbe intransitif
impersonal verb	*v imp*	verbe impersonnel
pronominal verb	*vpr*	verbe pronominal
transitive verb	*vt*	verbe transitif
transitive and intransitive verb	*vti*	verbe transitif et intransitif

Pronunciation of French

TABLE OF PHONETIC SYMBOLS

Vowels

[i]	vite, cygne	[y]	cru, sûr
[e]	été, donner	[ø]	feu, meule
[ɛ]	elle, mais	[œ]	œuf, jeune
[a]	chat, fameux	[ə]	le, refaire
[ɑ]	pas, âgé	[ɛ̃]	vin, plein, faim
[ɔ]	donne, fort	[ɑ̃]	enfant, temps
[o]	dos, chaud, peau	[ɔ̃]	mon, nombre
[u]	tout, cour	[œ̃]	lundi, humble

Consonants

[p]	pain, absolu	[z]	cousin, zéro
[b]	beau, abbé	[ʃ]	chose, schéma
[t]	table, nette	[ʒ]	gilet, jeter
[d]	donner, sud	[l]	lait, facile
[k]	camp, képi	[r]	rare, rhume
[g]	garde, second	[m]	mon, flamme
[f]	feu, phrase	[n]	né, canne
[v]	voir, wagon	[ɲ]	campagne
[s]	sou, cire	[ŋ]	jogging
		[']	hanche (*i.e. no liaison or elision*)

Semi-consonants

[j]	piano, voyage
[w]	ouest, noir
[ɥ]	muet, lui

PART 1
French-English

A

A, a [ɑ] *nm* A, a.

a [a] *voir* avoir.

à [a] *prép* (à + le = **au** [o], à + les = **aux** [o]) **1** (*direction: lieu*) to; (*temps*) till, to; **aller à Paris** to go to Paris; **de 3 à 4 h** from 3 till *ou* to 4 (o'clock). **2** (*position: lieu*) at, in; (*surface*) on; (*temps*) at; **être au bureau/à la ferme/au jardin/à Paris** to be at *ou* in the office/on *ou* at the farm/in the garden/in Paris; **à la maison** at home; **à l'horizon** on the horizon; **à 8 h** at 8 (o'clock); **à mon arrivée** on (my) arrival; **à lundi!** see you (on) Monday! **3** (*description*) **l'homme à la barbe** the man with the beard; **verre à liqueur** liqueur glass. **4** (*attribution*) **donner qch à qn** to give sth to s.o., give s.o. sth. **5** (*devant inf*) **apprendre à lire** to learn to read; **travail à faire** work to do; **maison à vendre** house for sale; **prêt à partir** ready to leave. **6** (*appartenance*) **c'est** (*son livre*) **à lui** it's his (book); **c'est à vous de** (*décider, protester etc*) it's up to you to; (*lire, jouer etc*) it's your turn to. **7** (*prix*) for; **pain à 2F** loaf for 2F. **8** (*poids*) by; **vendre au kilo** to sell by the kilo. **9** (*moyen, manière*) **à bicyclette** by bicycle; **à la main** by hand; **à pied** on foot; **au crayon** with a pencil, in pencil; **au galop** at a gallop; **à la française** in the French style *ou* way; **deux à deux** two by two. **10** (*appel*) **au voleur!** (stop) thief!

abaiss/er [abese] *vt* to lower; **a. qn** to humiliate s.o.; — **s'a.** *vpr* (*barrière*) to lower; (*température*) to drop; **s'a. à faire** to stoop to doing. **◆—ement** [-εsmɑ̃] *nm* (*chute*) drop.

abandon [abɑ̃dɔ̃] *nm* abandonment; surrender; desertion; *Sp* withdrawal; (*naturel*) abandon; (*confiance*) lack of restraint; **à l'a.** in a neglected state. **◆abandonner** *vt* (*renoncer à*) to give up, abandon; (*droit*) to surrender; (*quitter*) to desert, abandon; — *vi* to give up; *Sp* to withdraw; — **s'a.** *vpr* (*se détendre*) to let oneself go; (*se confier*) to open up; **s'a. à** to give oneself up to, abandon oneself to.

abasourdir [abazurdir] *vt* to stun, astound.

abat-jour [abaʒur] *nm inv* lampshade.

abats [aba] *nmpl* offal; (*de volaille*) giblets.

abattant [abatɑ̃] *nm* leaf, flap.

abattis [abati] *nmpl* giblets.

abatt/re* [abatr] *vt* (*mur*) to knock down; (*arbre*) to cut down, fell; (*animal etc*) to slaughter; (*avion*) to shoot down; (*déprimer*) to demoralize; (*épuiser*) to exhaust; — **s'a.** *vpr* (*tomber*) to collapse; (*oiseau*) to swoop down; (*pluie*) to pour down. **◆—u** *a* (*triste*) dejected, demoralized; (*faible*) at a low ebb. **◆—age** *nm* felling; slaughter(ing). **◆—ement** *nm* (*faiblesse*) exhaustion; (*désespoir*) dejection. **◆abattoir** *nm* slaughterhouse.

abbaye [abeji] *nf* abbey.

abbé [abe] *nm* (*chef d'abbaye*) abbot; (*prêtre*) priest. **◆abbesse** *nf* abbess.

abcès [apsɛ] *nm* abscess.

abdiquer [abdike] *vti* to abdicate. **◆abdication** *nf* abdication.

abdomen [abdɔmɛn] *nm* abdomen. **◆abdominal, -aux** *a* abdominal.

abeille [abɛj] *nf* bee.

aberrant [aberɑ̃] *a* (*idée etc*) ludicrous, absurd. **◆aberration** *nf* (*égarement*) aberration; (*idée*) ludicrous idea; **dire des aberrations** to talk sheer nonsense.

abhorrer [abɔre] *vt* to abhor, loathe.

abîme [abim] *nm* abyss, chasm, gulf.

abîmer [abime] *vt* to spoil, damage; — **s'a.** *vpr* to get spoilt; **s'a. dans ses pensées** *Litt* to lose oneself in one's thoughts.

abject [abʒɛkt] *a* abject, despicable.

abjurer [abʒyre] *vti* to abjure.

ablation [ablasjɔ̃] *nf* (*d'organe*) removal.

ablutions [ablysjɔ̃] *nfpl* ablutions.

abnégation [abnegasjɔ̃] *nf* self-sacrifice, abnegation.

abois (aux) [ozabwa] *adv* at bay.

abolir [abɔlir] *vt* to abolish. **◆abolition** *nf* abolition.

abominable [abɔminabl] *a* abominable, obnoxious. **◆abomination** *nf* abomination.

abondant [abɔ̃dɑ̃] *a* abundant, plentiful. **◆abondamment** *adv* abundantly. **◆abondance** *nf* abundance (de of); **en a.** in abundance; **années d'a.** years of plenty. **◆abonder** *vi* to abound (en in).

abonné, -ée [abɔne] *nmf* (*à un journal, au téléphone*) subscriber; *Rail Sp Th* season ticket holder; (*du gaz etc*) consumer.

◆**abonnement** *nm* subscription; (*carte d'*)a. season ticket. ◆**s'abonner** *vpr* to subscribe (à to); to buy a season ticket.

abord [abɔr] **1** *nm* (*accès*) **d'un a.** facile easy to approach. **2** *nm* (*vue*) **au premier a.** at first sight. **3** *nmpl* (*environs*) surroundings; **aux abords de** around, nearby. ◆**abordable** *a* (*personne*) approachable; (*prix, marchandises*) affordable.

abord (d') [dabɔr] *adv* (*avant tout*) first; (*au début*) at first.

aborder [abɔrde] *vi* to land; – *vt* (*personne*) to approach, accost; (*lieu*) to approach, reach; (*problème*) to tackle, approach; (*attaquer*) Nau to board; (*heurter*) Nau to run foul of. ◆**abordage** *nm* (*assaut*) Nau boarding; (*accident*) Nau collision.

aborigène [abɔriʒɛn] *a & nm* aboriginal.

about/ir [abutir] *vi* to succeed; **a. à** to end at, lead to, end up in; **n'a. à rien** to come to nothing. ◆**—issants** *nmpl voir* **tenants.** ◆**—issement** *nm* (*résultat*) outcome; (*succès*) success.

aboyer [abwaje] *vi* to bark. ◆**aboiement** *nm* bark; *pl* barking.

abrasif, -ive [abrazif, -iv] *a & nm* abrasive.

abrég/er [abreʒe] *vt* (*récit*) to shorten, abridge; (*mot*) to abbreviate. ◆**—é** *nm* summary; **en a.** (*phrase*) in shortened form; (*mot*) in abbreviated form.

abreuver [abrœve] *vt* (*cheval*) to water; – **s'a.** *vpr* to drink. ◆**abreuvoir** *nm* (*récipient*) drinking trough; (*lieu*) watering place.

abréviation [abrevjɑsjɔ̃] *nf* abbreviation.

abri [abri] *nm* shelter; **à l'a. de** (*vent*) sheltered from; (*besoin*) safe from; **sans a.** homeless. ◆**abriter** *vt* (*protéger*) to shelter; (*loger*) to house; – **s'a.** *vpr* to (take) shelter.

abricot [abriko] *nm* apricot. ◆**abricotier** *nm* apricot tree.

abroger [abrɔʒe] *vt* to abrogate.

abrupt [abrypt] *a* (*versant*) sheer; (*sentier*) steep, abrupt; (*personne*) abrupt.

abrut/ir [abrytir] *vt* (*alcool*) to stupefy (*s.o.*); (*propagande*) to brutalize (*s.o.*); (*travail*) to leave (*s.o.*) dazed, wear (*s.o.*) out. ◆**—i, -ie** *nmf* idiot; – *a* idiotic.

absence [apsãs] *nf* absence. ◆**absent, -e** *a* (*personne*) absent, away; (*chose*) missing; **air a.** faraway look; – *nmf* absentee. ◆**absentéisme** *nm* absenteeism. ◆**s'absenter** *vpr* to go away.

abside [apsid] *nf* (*d'une église*) apse.

absolu [apsɔly] *a & nm* absolute. ◆**—ment** *adv* absolutely.

absolution [apsɔlysjɔ̃] *nf* absolution.

absorb/er [apsɔrbe] *vt* to absorb. ◆**—ant** *a* absorbent; **travail a.** absorbing job. ◆**absorption** *nf* absorption.

absoudre* [apsudr] *vt* to absolve.

abstenir* (s') [sapstənir] *vpr* to abstain; **s'a. de** to refrain *ou* abstain from. ◆**abstention** *nf* abstention.

abstinence [apstinãs] *nf* abstinence.

abstraire* [apstrɛr] *vt* to abstract. ◆**abstrait** *a & nm* abstract. ◆**abstraction** *nf* abstraction; **faire a. de** to disregard, leave aside.

absurde [apsyrd] *a & nm* absurd. ◆**absurdité** *nf* absurdity; **dire des absurdités** to talk nonsense.

abus [aby] *nm* abuse, misuse; over-indulgence; (*injustice*) abuse. ◆**abuser 1** *vi* to go too far; **a. de** (*situation, personne*) to take unfair advantage of; (*autorité*) to abuse, misuse; (*friandises*) to over-indulge in. **2 s'a.** *vpr* to be mistaken.

abusi/f, -ive [abyzif, -iv] *a* excessive; **emploi a.** Ling improper use, misuse. ◆**—vement** *adv* Ling improperly.

acabit [akabi] *nm* **de cet a.** Péj of that ilk *ou* sort.

acacia [akasja] *nm* (*arbre*) acacia.

académie [akademi] *nf* academy; Univ = (regional) education authority. ◆**académicien, -ienne** *nmf* academician. ◆**académique** *a* academic.

acajou [akaʒu] *nm* mahogany; **cheveux a.** auburn hair.

acariâtre [akarjɑtr] *a* cantankerous.

accabl/er [akable] *vt* to overwhelm, overcome; **a. d'injures** to heap insults upon; **accablé de dettes** (over)burdened with debt. ◆**—ement** *nm* dejection.

accalmie [akalmi] *nf* lull.

accaparer [akapare] *vt* to monopolize; (*personne*) Fam to take up all the time of.

accéder [aksede] *vi* **a. à** (*lieu*) to have access to, reach; (*pouvoir, trône, demande*) to accede to.

accélérer [akselere] *vi* Aut to accelerate; – *vt* (*travaux etc*) to speed up; (*allure, pas*) to quicken, speed up; – **s'a.** *vpr* to speed up. ◆**accélérateur** *nm* Aut accelerator. ◆**accélération** *nf* acceleration; speeding up.

accent [aksã] *nm* accent; (*sur une syllabe*) stress; **mettre l'a. sur** to stress. ◆**accentuation** *nf* accentuation. ◆**accentuer** *vt* to emphasize, accentuate, stress; – **s'a.** *vpr* to become more pronounced.

accepter [aksɛpte] *vt* to accept; **a. de faire**

to agree to do. ◆**acceptable** *a* acceptable.
◆**acceptation** *nf* acceptance.
acception [aksɛpsjɔ̃] *nf* sense, meaning.
accès [aksɛ] *nm* access (à to); (*de folie, colère, toux*) fit; (*de fièvre*) attack, bout; *pl* (*routes*) approaches. ◆**accessible** *a* accessible; (*personne*) approachable. ◆**accession** *nf* accession (à to); (à un traité) adherence; a. à la propriété home ownership.
accessoire [aksɛswar] *a* secondary; – *nmpl* Th props; (*de voiture etc*) accessories; **accessoires de toilette** toilet requisites.
accident [aksidɑ̃] *nm* accident; a. d'avion/de train plane/train crash; par a. by accident, by chance. ◆**accidenté, -ée** *a* (*terrain*) uneven; (*région*) hilly; (*voiture*) damaged (in an accident); – *nmf* accident victim, casualty. ◆**accidentel, -elle** *a* accidental. ◆**accidentellement** *adv* accidentally, unintentionally.
acclamer [aklame] *vt* to cheer, acclaim. ◆**acclamations** *nfpl* cheers, acclamations.
acclimater [aklimate] *vt*, – **s'a.** *vpr* to acclimatize, Am acclimate. ◆**acclimatation** *nf* acclimatization, Am acclimation.
accointances [akwɛ̃tɑ̃s] *nfpl* Péj contacts.
accolade [akɔlad] *nf* (*embrassade*) embrace; Typ brace, bracket.
accoler [akɔle] *vt* to place (side by side) (à against).
accommod/er [akɔmɔde] *vt* to adapt; Culin to prepare; **s'a.** à to adapt (oneself) to; **s'a.** de to make the best of. ◆**—ant** *a* accommodating, easy to please. ◆**—ement** *nm* arrangement, compromise.
accompagner [akɔ̃paɲe] *vt* (*personne*) to accompany, go *ou* come with, escort; (*chose*) & Mus to accompany; **s'a.** de to be accompanied by, go with. ◆**accompagnateur, -trice** *nmf* Mus accompanist; (*d'un groupe*) guide. ◆**accompagnement** *nm* Mus accompaniment.
accompl/ir [akɔ̃plir] *vt* to carry out, fulfil, accomplish. ◆**—i** *a* accomplished. ◆**—issement** *nm* fulfilment.
accord [akɔr] *nm* agreement; (*harmonie*) harmony; Mus chord; être d'a. to agree, be in agreement (avec with); d'a.! all right! ◆**accorder** *vt* (*donner*) to grant; Mus to tune; Gram to make agree; – **s'a.** *vpr* to agree; (*s'entendre*) to get along.
accordéon [akɔrdeɔ̃] *nm* accordion; en a. (*chaussette etc*) wrinkled.
accoster [akɔste] *vt* to accost; Nau to come alongside; – *vi* Nau to berth.

accotement [akɔtmɑ̃] *nm* roadside, verge.
accouch/er [akuʃe] *vi* to give birth (de to); – *vt* (*enfant*) to deliver. ◆**—ement** *nm* delivery. ◆**—eur** *nm* (**médecin**) a. obstetrician.
accouder (s') [sakude] *vpr* **s'a.** à to lean on (with one's elbows). ◆**accoudoir** *nm* armrest.
accoupl/er [akuple] *vt* to couple; – **s'a.** *vpr* (*animaux*) to mate (à with). ◆**—ement** *nm* coupling; mating.
accourir* [akurir] *vi* to come running, run over.
accoutrement [akutrəmɑ̃] *nm* Péj garb, dress.
accoutumer [akutyme] *vt* to accustom; – **s'a.** *vpr* to get accustomed (à to); comme à l'accoutumée as usual. ◆**accoutumance** *nf* familiarization (à with); Méd addiction.
accréditer [akredite] *vt* (*ambassadeur*) to accredit; (*rumeur*) to lend credence to.
accroc [akro] *nm* (*déchirure*) tear; (*difficulté*) hitch, snag.
accroch/er [akrɔʃe] *vt* (*déchirer*) to catch; (*fixer*) to hook; (*suspendre*) to hang up (on a hook); (*heurter*) to hit, knock; – *vi* (*affiche etc*) to grab one's attention; – **s'a.** *vpr* (ne pas céder) to persevere; (se disputer) Fam to clash; **s'a.** à (se cramponner etc) to cling to; (s'écorcher) to catch oneself on. ◆**—age** *nm* Aut knock, slight hit; (*friction*) Fam clash. ◆**—eur, -euse** *a* (*personne*) tenacious; (*affiche etc*) eyecatching, catchy.
accroître* [akrwatr] *vt* to increase; – **s'a.** *vpr* to increase, grow. ◆**accroissement** *nm* increase; growth.
accroup/ir (s') [sakrupir] *vpr* to squat *ou* crouch (down). ◆**—i** *a* squatting, crouching.
accueil [akœj] *nm* reception, welcome. ◆**accueill/ir*** *vt* to receive, welcome, greet. ◆**—ant** *a* welcoming.
acculer [akyle] *vt* a. qn à qch to drive s.o. to *ou* against sth.
accumuler [akymyle] *vt*, – **s'a.** *vpr* to pile up, accumulate. ◆**accumulateur** *nm* accumulator, battery. ◆**accumulation** *nf* accumulation.
accus/er [akyze] *vt* (*dénoncer*) to accuse; (*rendre responsable*) to blame (de for); (*révéler*) to show; (*faire ressortir*) to bring out; a. réception to acknowledge receipt (de of); a. le coup to stagger under the blow. ◆**—é, -ée 1** *nmf* accused; (*cour d'assises*) defendant. **2** *a* prominent. ◆**accusateur, -trice** *a* (*regard*) accusing;

(*document*) incriminating; — *nmf* accuser. ◆**accusation** *nf* accusation; *Jur* charge.

acerbe [asɛrb] *a* bitter, caustic.

acéré [asere] *a* sharp.

acétate [acetat] *nm* acetate. ◆**acétique** *a* acetic.

achalandé [aʃalɑ̃de] *a* **bien a.** (*magasin*) well-stocked.

acharn/er (s') [aʃarne] *vpr* **s'a. sur** (*attaquer*) to set upon, lay into; **s'a. contre** (*poursuivre*) to pursue (relentlessly); **s'a. à faire** to struggle to do, try desperately to do. ◆**—é, -ée** *a* relentless; — *nmf* (*du jeu etc*) fanatic. ◆**—ement** *nm* relentlessness.

achat [aʃa] *nm* purchase; *pl* shopping.

acheminer [aʃmine] *vt* to dispatch; — **s'a.** *vpr* to proceed (**vers** towards).

achet/er [aʃte] *vti* to buy, purchase; **a. à qn** (*vendeur*) to buy from s.o.; (*pour qn*) to buy for s.o. ◆**—eur, -euse** *nmf* buyer, purchaser; (*dans un magasin*) shopper.

achever [aʃve] *vt* to finish (off); **a. de faire qch** (*personne*) to finish doing sth; **a. qn** (*tuer*) to finish s.o. off; — **s'a.** *vpr* to end, finish. ◆**achèvement** *nm* completion.

achoppement [aʃɔpmɑ̃] *nm* **pierre d'a.** stumbling block.

acide [asid] *a* acid, sour; — *nm* acid. ◆**acidité** *nf* acidity.

acier [asje] *nm* steel. ◆**aciérie** *nf* steelworks.

acné [akne] *nf* acne.

acolyte [akɔlit] *nm Péj* confederate, associate.

acompte [akɔ̃t] *nm* part payment, deposit.

à-côté [akote] *nm* (*d'une question*) side issue; *pl* (*gains*) little extras.

à-coup [aku] *nm* jerk, jolt; **sans à-coups** smoothly; **par à-coups** in fits and starts.

acoustique [akustik] *a* acoustic; — *nf* acoustics.

acquérir* [akerir] *vt* to acquire, gain; (*par achat*) to purchase; **s'a. une réputation**/*etc* to win a reputation/*etc*; **être acquis à** (*idée, parti*) to be a supporter of. ◆**acquéreur** *nm* purchaser. ◆**acquis** *nm* experience. ◆**acquisition** *nf* acquisition; purchase.

acquiesc/er [akjese] *vi* to acquiesce (**à** to). ◆**—ement** *nm* acquiescence.

acquit [aki] *nm* receipt; **'pour a.'** 'paid'; **par a. de conscience** for conscience sake. ◆**acquitt/er** *vt* (*dette*) to clear, pay; (*accusé*) to acquit; **s'a. de** (*devoir, promesse*) to discharge; **s'a. envers qn** to repay s.o. ◆**—ement** *nm* payment; acquittal; discharge.

âcre [ɑkr] *a* bitter, acrid, pungent.

acrobate [akrɔbat] *nmf* acrobat. ◆**acrobatie(s)** *nf*(*pl*) acrobatics. ◆**acrobatique** *a* acrobatic.

acrylique [akrilik] *a* & *nm* acrylic.

acte [akt] *nm* act, deed; *Th* act; **un a. de** an act of; **a. de naissance** birth certificate; **prendre a. de** to take note of.

acteur, -trice [aktœr, -tris] *nmf* actor, actress.

actif, -ive [aktif, -iv] *a* active; — *nm Fin* assets; **à son a.** to one's credit; (*vols, meurtres*) *Hum* to one's name.

action [aksjɔ̃] *nf* action; *Fin* share. ◆**actionnaire** *nmf* shareholder. ◆**actionner** *vt* to set in motion, activate, actuate.

activer [aktive] *vt* to speed up; (*feu*) to boost; — **s'a.** *vpr* to bustle about; (*se dépêcher*) *Fam* to get a move on.

activiste [aktivist] *nmf* activist.

activité [aktivite] *nf* activity; **en a.** (*personne*) fully active; (*volcan*) active.

actuaire [aktɥer] *nmf* actuary.

actualité [aktɥalite] *nf* (*d'un problème*) topicality; (*événements*) current events; *pl TV Cin* news; **d'a.** topical.

actuel, -elle [aktɥel] *a* (*présent*) present; (*contemporain*) topical. ◆**actuellement** *adv* at present, at the present time.

acuité [akɥite] *nf* (*de douleur*) acuteness; (*de vision*) keenness.

acupuncture [akypɔ̃ktyr] *nf* acupuncture. ◆**acupuncteur, -trice** *nmf* acupuncturist.

adage [adaʒ] *nm* (*maxime*) adage.

adapter [adapte] *vt* to adapt; (*ajuster*) to fit (**à** to); **s'a. à** (*s'habituer*) to adapt to; (*tuyau etc*) to fit. ◆**adaptable** *a* adaptable. ◆**adaptateur, -trice** *nmf* adapter. ◆**adaptation** *nf* adaptation.

additif [aditif] *nm* additive.

addition [adisjɔ̃] *nf* addition; (*au restaurant*) bill, *Am* check. ◆**additionnel, -elle** *a* additional. ◆**additionner** *vt* to add (**à** to); (*nombres*) to add up.

adepte [adɛpt] *nmf* follower.

adéquat [adekwa] *a* appropriate.

adhérer [adere] *vi* **a. à** (*coller*) to adhere *ou* stick to; (*s'inscrire*) to join; (*pneu*) to grip. ◆**adhérence** *nf* (*de pneu*) grip. ◆**adhérent, -ente** *nmf* member.

adhésif, -ive [adezif, -iv] *a* & *nm* adhesive. ◆**adhésion** *nf* membership; (*accord*) support.

adieu, -x [adjø] *int* & *nm* farewell, goodbye.

adipeux, -euse [adipø, -øz] *a* (*tissu*) fatty; (*visage*) fat.

adjacent [adʒasɑ̃] a (contigu) & Géom adjacent.

adjectif [adʒɛktif] nm adjective.

adjoindre* [adʒwɛ̃dr] vt (associer) to appoint (s.o.) as an assistant (à to); (ajouter) to add; **s'a.** qn to appoint s.o. ◆**adjoint, -ointe** nmf & a assistant; **a. au maire** deputy mayor.

adjudant [adʒydɑ̃] nm warrant officer.

adjuger [adʒyʒe] vt (accorder) to award; **s'a. qch** Fam to grab sth for oneself.

adjurer [adʒyre] vt to beseech, entreat.

admettre* [admɛtr] vt (laisser entrer, accueillir, reconnaître) to admit; (autoriser, tolérer) to allow; (supposer) to admit, grant; (candidat) to pass; **être admis à** (examen) to have passed.

administrer [administre] vt (gérer, donner) to administer. ◆**administrateur, -trice** nmf administrator. ◆**administratif, -ive** a administrative. ◆**administration** nf administration; **l'A.** (service public) government service, the Civil Service.

admirer [admire] vt to admire. ◆**admirable** a admirable. ◆**admirateur, -trice** nmf admirer. ◆**admiratif, -ive** a admiring. ◆**admiration** nf admiration.

admissible [admisibl] a acceptable, admissible; (après un concours) eligible (à for). ◆**admission** nf admission.

adolescent, -ente [adɔlesɑ̃, -ɑ̃t] nmf adolescent, teenager; − a teenage. ◆**adolescence** nf adolescence.

adonner (s') [sadɔne] vpr **s'a. à** (boisson) to take to; (étude) to devote oneself to.

adopter [adɔpte] vt to adopt. ◆**adoptif, -ive** a (fils, patrie) adopted. ◆**adoption** nf adoption; **suisse d'a.** Swiss by adoption.

adorer [adɔre] vt (personne) & Rel to worship, adore; (chose) Fam to adore, love; **a. faire** to adore ou love doing. ◆**adorable** a adorable. ◆**adoration** nf worship.

adosser [adose] vt **a. qch à** to lean sth back against; **s'a. à** to lean back against.

adouc/ir [adusir] vt (voix, traits etc) to soften; (boisson) to sweeten; (chagrin) to mitigate, ease; − **s'a.** vpr (temps) to turn milder; (caractère) to mellow. ◆**—issement** nm **a. de la température** milder weather.

adrénaline [adrenalin] nf adrenalin(e).

adresse [adrɛs] nf **1** (domicile) address. **2** (habileté) skill. ◆**adresser** vt (lettre) to send; (compliment, remarque etc) to address; (coup) to direct, aim; (personne) to direct (à to); **a. la parole à** to speak to;

s'a. à to speak to; (aller trouver) to go and see; (bureau) to enquire at; (être destiné à) to be aimed at.

Adriatique [adriatik] nf **l'A.** the Adriatic.

adroit [adrwa] a skilful, clever.

adulation [adylɑsjɔ̃] nf adulation.

adulte [adylt] a & nmf adult, grown-up.

adultère [adyltɛr] a adulterous; − nm adultery.

advenir [advənir] v imp to occur; **a. de** (devenir) to become of; **advienne que pourra** come what may.

adverbe [advɛrb] nm adverb. ◆**adverbial, -aux** a adverbial.

adversaire [advɛrsɛr] nmf opponent, adversary. ◆**adverse** a opposing.

adversité [advɛrsite] nf adversity.

aérer [aere] vt (chambre) to air (out), ventilate; (lit) to air (out); − **s'a.** vpr Fam to get some air. ◆**aéré** a airy. ◆**aération** nf ventilation. ◆**aérien, -ienne** a (ligne, attaque etc) air-; (photo) aerial; (câble) overhead; (léger) airy.

aérobic [aerɔbik] nf aerobics.

aéro-club [aerɔklœb] nm flying club. ◆**aérodrome** nm aerodrome. ◆**aérodynamique** a streamlined, aerodynamic. ◆**aérogare** nf air terminal. ◆**aéroglisseur** nm hovercraft. ◆**aérogramme** nm air letter. ◆**aéromodélisme** nm model aircraft building and flying. ◆**aéronautique** nf aeronautics. ◆**aéronavale** nf = Br Fleet Air Arm, = Am Naval Air Force. ◆**aéroport** nm airport. ◆**aéroporté** a airborne. ◆**aérosol** nm aerosol.

affable [afabl] a affable.

affaiblir [afeblir] vt, − **s'a.** vpr to weaken.

affaire [afɛr] nf (question) matter, affair; (marché) deal; (firme) concern, business; (scandale) affair; (procès) Jur case; pl Com business; (d'intérêt public, personnel) affairs; (effets) belongings, things; **avoir a. à** to have to deal with; **c'est mon a.** that's my business ou affair ou concern; **faire une bonne a.** to get a good deal, get a bargain; **ça fera l'a.** that will do nicely; **toute une a.** (histoire) quite a business.

affair/er (s') [safere] vpr to busy oneself, run ou bustle about. ◆**—é** a busy. ◆**affairiste** nm (political) racketeer.

affaiss/er (s') [safese] vpr (personne) to collapse; (plancher) to cave in, give way; (sol) to subside, sink. ◆**—ement** [afɛsmɑ̃] nm (du sol) subsidence.

affaler (s') [safale] vpr to flop down, collapse.

affamé [afame] *a* starving; **a. de** *Fig* hungry for.

affect/er [afɛkte] *vt•(destiner)* to earmark, assign; *(nommer à un poste)* to post; *(feindre, émouvoir)* to affect. ◆—é *a (manières, personne)* affected. ◆**affectation** *nf* assignment; posting; *(simulation)* affectation.

affectif, -ive [afɛktif, -iv] *a* emotional.

affection [afɛksjɔ̃] *nf (attachement)* affection; *(maladie)* ailment. ◆**affectionn/er** *vt* to be fond of. ◆—é *a* loving. ◆**affectueux, -euse** *a* affectionate.

affermir [afɛrmir] *vt (autorité)* to strengthen; *(muscles)* to tone up; *(voix)* to steady.

affiche [afiʃ] *nf* poster; *Th* bill. ◆**affich/er** *vt (affiche etc)* to post *ou* stick up; *Th* to bill; *(sentiment)* Péj to display; **a. qn** Péj to parade s.o., flaunt s.o. ◆—**age** *nm* (bill-)posting; **panneau d'a.** hoarding, *Am* billboard.

affilée (d') [dafile] *adv (à la suite)* in a row, at a stretch.

affiler [afile] *vt* to sharpen.

affilier (s') [safilje] *vpr* **s'a. à** to join, become affiliated to. ◆**affiliation** *nf* affiliation.

affiner [afine] *vt* to refine.

affinité [afinite] *nf* affinity.

affirmatif, -ive [afirmatif, -iv] *a (ton)* assertive, positive; *(proposition)* affirmative; **il a été a.** he was quite positive; – *nf* **répondre par l'affirmative** to reply in the affirmative.

affirmer [afirme] *vt* to assert; *(proclamer solennellement)* to affirm. ◆**affirmation** *nf* assertion.

affleurer [aflœre] *vi* to appear on the surface.

affliger [aflize] *vt* to distress; **affligé de** stricken *ou* afflicted with.

affluence [aflyɑ̃s] *nf* crowd; **heures d'a.** rush hours.

affluent [aflyɑ̃] *nm* tributary.

affluer [aflye] *vi (sang)* to flow, rush; *(gens)* to flock. ◆**afflux** *nm* flow; *(arrivée)* influx.

affol/er [afɔle] *vt* to drive out of one's mind; *(effrayer)* to terrify; – **s'a.** *vpr* to panic. ◆—**ement** *nm* panic.

affranch/ir [afrɑ̃ʃir] *vt (timbrer)* to stamp; *(émanciper)* to free. ◆—**issement** *nm* **tarifs d'a.** postage.

affréter [afrete] *vt (avion)* to charter; *(navire)* to freight.

affreux, -euse [afrø, -øz] *a* hideous, dreadful, ghastly. ◆**affreusement** *adv* dreadfully.

affriolant [afriɔlɑ̃] *a* enticing.

affront [afrɔ̃] *nm* insult, affront; **faire un a. à** to insult.

affront/er [afrɔ̃te] *vt* to confront, face; *(mauvais temps, difficultés etc)* to brave. ◆—**ement** *nm* confrontation.

affubler [afyble] *vt Péj* to dress, rig out *(de* in).

affût [afy] *nm* **à l'a. de** *Fig* on the look-out for.

affûter [afyte] *vt (outil)* to sharpen, grind.

Afghanistan [afganistɑ̃] *nm* Afghanistan.

afin [afɛ̃] *prép* **a. de** (+ *inf)* in order to; – *conj* **a. que** (+ *sub)* so that.

Afrique [afrik] *nf* Africa. ◆**africain, -aine** *a & nmf* African.

agac/er [agase] *vt (personne)* to irritate, annoy. ◆—**ement** *nm* irritation.

âge [ɑʒ] *nm* age; **quel â. as-tu?** how old are you?; **avant l'â.** before one's time; **d'un certain â.** middle-aged; **l'â. adulte** adulthood; **la force de l'â.** the prime of life; **le moyen â.** the Middle Ages. ◆**âgé** *a* elderly; **â. de six ans** six years old; **un enfant â. de six ans** a six-year-old child.

agence [aʒɑ̃s] *nf* agency; *(succursale)* branch office; **a. immobilière** estate agent's office, *Am* real estate office.

agenc/er [aʒɑ̃se] *vt* to arrange; **bien agencé** *(maison etc)* well laid-out; *(phrase)* well put-together. ◆—**ement** *nm (de maison etc)* lay-out.

agenda [aʒɛ̃da] *nm* diary, *Am* datebook.

agenouiller (s') [saʒnuje] *vpr* to kneel (down); **être agenouillé** to be kneeling (down).

agent [aʒɑ̃] *nm* agent; **a. (de police)** policeman; **a. de change** stockbroker; **a. immobilier** estate agent, *Am* real estate agent.

aggloméré [aglɔmere] *nm & a (bois)* chipboard, fibreboard.

agglomérer (s') [saglɔmere] *vpr (s'entasser)* to conglomerate. ◆**agglomération** *nf* conglomeration; *(habitations)* built-up area; *(ville)* town.

aggraver [agrave] *vt* to worsen, aggravate; – **s'a.** *vpr* to worsen. ◆**aggravation** *nf* worsening.

agile [aʒil] *a* agile, nimble. ◆**agilité** *nf* agility, nimbleness.

agir [aʒir] **1** *vi* to act; **a. auprès de** to intercede with. **2 s'agir** *v imp* **il s'agit d'argent**/*etc* it's a question *ou* matter of money/*etc*, it concerns money/*etc*; **de quoi s'agit-il?** what is it?, what's it about?; **il s'agit de se dépêcher**/*etc* we have to

hurry/*etc*. ◆**agissant** *a* active, effective.
◆**agissements** *nmpl Péj* dealings.

agit/er [aʒite] *vt* (*remuer*) to stir; (*secouer*)
to shake; (*brandir*) to wave; (*troubler*) to
agitate; (*discuter*) to debate; — **s'a.** *vpr*
(*enfant*) to fidget; (*peuple*) to stir. ◆**—é** *a*
(*mer*) rough; (*malade*) restless, agitated;
(*enfant*) fidgety, restless. ◆**agitateur,
-trice** *nmf* (political) agitator. ◆**agitation**
nf (*de la mer*) roughness; (*d'un malade etc*)
restlessness; (*nervosité*) agitation; (*de la
rue*) bustle; *Pol* unrest.

agneau, -x [aɲo] *nm* lamb.

agonie [agɔni] *nf* death throes; **être à l'a.** to
be suffering the pangs of death.
◆**agoniser** *vi* to be dying.

agrafe [agraf] *nf* hook; (*pour papiers*)
staple. ◆**agrafer** *vt* to fasten, hook, do up;
(*papiers*) to staple. ◆**agrafeuse** *nf*
stapler.

agrand/ir [agrɑ̃dir] *vt* to enlarge; (*grossir*)
to magnify; — **s'a.** *vpr* to expand, grow.
◆**—issement** *nm* (*de ville*) expansion; (*de
maison*) extension; (*de photo*) enlargement.

agréable [agreabl] *a* pleasant, agreeable,
nice. ◆**—ment** [-əmɑ̃] *adv* pleasantly.

agré/er [agree] *vt* to accept; **veuillez a. mes
salutations distinguées** (*dans une lettre*)
yours faithfully. ◆**—é** *a* (*fournisseur,
centre*) approved.

agrégation [agregɑsjɔ̃] *nf* competitive examination for recruitment of *lycée* teachers.
◆**agrégé, -ée** *nmf* teacher who has passed
the *agrégation*.

agrément [agremɑ̃] *nm* (*attrait*) charm;
(*accord*) assent; **voyage d'a.** pleasure trip.
◆**agrémenter** *vt* to embellish; **a. un récit
d'anecdotes** to pepper a story with anecdotes.

agrès [agrɛ] *nmpl Nau* tackle, rigging; (*de
gymnastique*) apparatus.

agresser [agrese] *vt* to attack. ◆**agresseur** *nm* attacker; (*dans la rue*) mugger;
(*dans un conflit*) aggressor. ◆**agressif,
-ive** *a* aggressive. ◆**agression** *nf* (*d'un
État*) aggression; (*d'un individu*) attack.
◆**agressivité** *nf* aggressiveness.

agricole [agrikɔl] *a* (*peuple*) agricultural,
farming; (*ouvrier, machine*) farm-.

agriculteur [agrikyltœr] *nm* farmer.
◆**agriculture** *nf* agriculture, farming.

agripper [agripe] *vt* to clutch, grip; **s'a. à** to
cling to, clutch, grip.

agronomie [agrɔnɔmi] *nf* agronomics.

agrumes [agrym] *nmpl* citrus fruit(s).

aguerri [ageri] *a* seasoned, hardened.

aguets (aux) [ozagɛ] *adv* on the look-out.

aguich/er [agiʃe] *vt* to tease, excite.
◆**—ant** *a* enticing.

ah! [a] *int* ah!, oh!

ahur/ir [ayrir] *vt* to astound, bewilder.
◆**—i, -ie** *nmf* idiot.

ai [e] *voir* **avoir**.

aide [ɛd] *nf* help, assistance, aid; — *nmf*
(*personne*) assistant; **à l'a. de** with the help
ou aid of. ◆**a.-électricien** *nm* electrician's
mate. ◆**a.-familiale** *nf* home help.
◆**a.-mémoire** *nm inv Scol* handbook (*of
facts etc*).

aider [ede] *vt* to help, assist, aid (**à faire** to
do); **s'a.** to make use of.

aïe! [aj] *int* ouch!, ow!

aïeul, -e [ajœl] *nmf* grandfather, grandmother.

aïeux [ajø] *nmpl* forefathers, forebears.

aigle [ɛgl] *nmf* eagle. ◆**aiglon** *nm* eaglet.

aiglefin [ɛgləfɛ̃] *nm* haddock.

aigre [ɛgr] *a* (*acide*) sour; (*voix, vent, parole*)
sharp, cutting. ◆**a.-doux, -douce** *a*
bitter-sweet. ◆**aigreur** *nf* sourness; (*de
ton*) sharpness; *pl* heartburn.

aigrette [ɛgrɛt] *nf* (*de plumes*) tuft.

aigr/ir (s') [segrir] *vpr* (*vin*) to turn sour;
(*caractère*) to sour. ◆**—i** [egri] *a* (*personne*)
embittered, bitter.

aigu, -uë [egy] *a* (*crise etc*) acute; (*dents*)
sharp, pointed; (*voix*) shrill.

aiguille [egɥij] *nf* (*à coudre, de pin*) needle;
(*de montre*) hand; (*de balance*) pointer; **a.
(rocheuse)** peak.

aiguill/er [egɥije] *vt* (*train*) to shunt, *Am*
switch; *Fig* to steer, direct. ◆**—age** *nm*
(*appareil*) *Rail* points, *Am* switches.
◆**—eur** *nm Rail* pointsman, *Am*
switchman; **a. du ciel** air traffic controller.

aiguillon [egɥijɔ̃] *nm* (*dard*) sting; (*stimulant*) spur. ◆**aiguillonner** *vt* to spur (on),
goad.

aiguiser [eg(ɥ)ize] *vt* (*affiler*) to sharpen;
(*appétit*) to whet.

ail [aj] *nm* garlic.

aile [ɛl] *nf* wing; (*de moulin à vent*) sail; *Aut*
wing, *Am* fender; **battre de l'a.** to be in a
bad way; **d'un coup d'a.** (*avion*) in continuous flight. ◆**ailé** [ele] *a* winged. ◆**aileron**
nm (*de requin*) fin; (*d'avion*) aileron;
(*d'oiseau*) pinion. ◆**ailier** [elje] *nm Fb*
wing(er).

ailleurs [ajœr] *adv* somewhere else, elsewhere; **partout a.** everywhere else; **d'a.** (*du
reste*) besides, anyway; **par a.** (*en outre*)
moreover; (*autrement*) otherwise.

aïoli [ajɔli] *nm* garlic mayonnaise.

aimable [ɛmabl] *a* (*complaisant*) kind;

(*sympathique*) likeable, amiable; (*agréable*) pleasant. ◆—**ment** [-əmɑ̃] *adv* kindly.

aimant [ɛmɑ̃] **1** *nm* magnet. **2** *a* loving. ◆**aimanter** *vt* to magnetize.

aimer [eme] *vt* (*chérir*) to love; **a.** (**bien**) (*apprécier*) to like, be fond of; **a. faire** to like doing *ou* to do; **a. mieux** to prefer; **ils s'aiment** they're in love.

aine [ɛn] *nf* groin.

aîné, -e [ene] *a* (*de deux frères etc*) elder, older; (*de plus de deux*) eldest, oldest; — *nmf* (*enfant*) elder *ou* older (child); eldest *ou* oldest (child); **c'est mon a.** he's my senior.

ainsi [ɛ̃si] *adv* (*comme ça*) (in) this *ou* that way, thus; (*alors*) so; **a. que** as well as; **et a. de suite** and so on; **pour a. dire** so to speak.

air [ɛr] *nm* **1** air; **en plein a.** in the open (air), outdoors; (*de deux*) flanquer en l'a. *Fam* (*jeter*) to chuck away; (*gâcher*) to mess up, upset; **en l'a.** (*jeter*) (up) in the air; (*paroles, menaces*) empty; (*projets*) uncertain, (up) in the air; **dans l'a.** (*grippe, idées*) about, around. **2** (*expression*) look, appearance; **avoir l'a.** to look, seem; **avoir l'a. de** to look like; **a. de famille** family likeness. **3** (*mélodie*) tune; **a. d'opéra** aria.

aire [ɛr] *nf* (*de stationnement etc*) & *Math* area; (*d'oiseau*) eyrie; **a. de lancement** launching site.

airelle [ɛrɛl] *nf* bilberry, *Am* blueberry.

aisance [ɛzɑ̃s] *nf* (*facilité*) ease; (*prospérité*) easy circumstances, affluence.

aise [ɛz] *nf* **à l'a.** (*dans un vêtement etc*) comfortable; (*dans une situation*) at ease; (*fortuné*) comfortably off; **aimer ses aises** to like one's comforts; **mal à l'a.** uncomfortable, ill at ease. ◆**aisé** [eze] *a* (*fortuné*) comfortably off; (*naturel*) free and easy; (*facile*) easy. ◆**aisément** *adv* easily.

aisselle [ɛsɛl] *nf* armpit.

ait [ɛ] *voir* **avoir.**

ajonc(s) [aʒɔ̃] *nm(pl)* gorse, furze.

ajouré [aʒure] *a* (*dentelle etc*) openwork.

ajourn/er [aʒurne] *vt* to postpone, adjourn. ◆—**ement** *nm* postponement, adjournment.

ajout [aʒu] *nm* addition. ◆**ajouter** *vti* to add (à to); **s'a. à** to add to.

ajust/er [aʒyste] *vt* (*pièce, salaires*) to adjust; (*coiffure*) to arrange; (*coup*) to aim; **a. à** (*adapter*) to fit to. ◆—**é** *a* (*serré*) close-fitting. ◆—**ement** *nm* adjustment. ◆—**eur** *nm* (*ouvrier*) fitter.

alaise [alɛz] *nf* (*waterproof*) undersheet.

alambic [alɑ̃bik] *nm* still.

alambiqué [alɑ̃bike] *a* convoluted, over-subtle.

alanguir [alɑ̃gir] *vt* to make languid.

alarme [alarm] *nf* (*signal, inquiétude*) alarm; **jeter l'a.** to cause alarm. ◆**alarmer** *vt* to alarm; **s'a. de** to become alarmed at.

Albanie [albani] *nf* Albania. ◆**albanais, -aise** *a* & *nmf* Albanian.

albâtre [albatr] *nm* alabaster.

albatros [albatros] *nm* albatross.

albinos [albinos] *nmf* & *a inv* albino.

album [albɔm] *nm* (*de timbres etc*) album; (*de dessins*) sketchbook.

alcali [alkali] *nm* alkali. ◆**alcalin** *a* alkaline.

alchimie [alʃimi] *nf* alchemy.

alcool [alkɔl] *nm* alcohol; (*spiritueux*) spirits; **a. à brûler** methylated spirit(s); **lampe à a.** spirit lamp. ◆**alcoolique** *a* & *nmf* alcoholic. ◆**alcoolisé** *a* (*boisson*) alcoholic. ◆**alcoolisme** *nm* alcoholism. ◆**alcootest®** *nm* breath test; (*appareil*) breathalyzer.

alcôve [alkɔv] *nf* alcove.

aléas [alea] *nmpl* hazards, risks. ◆**aléatoire** *a* chancy, uncertain; (*sélection*) random.

alentour [alɑ̃tur] *adv* round about, around; **d'a.** surrounding; — *nmpl* surroundings, vicinity; **aux alentours de** in the vicinity of.

alerte [alɛrt] **1** *a* (*leste*) agile, spry; (*éveillé*) alert. **2** *nf* alarm; **en état d'a.** on the alert; **a. aérienne** air-raid warning. ◆**alerter** *vt* to warn, alert.

alezan, -ane [alzɑ̃ -an] *a* & *nmf* (*cheval*) chestnut.

algarade [algarad] *nf* (*dispute*) altercation.

algèbre [alʒɛbr] *nf* algebra. ◆**algébrique** *a* algebraic.

Alger [alʒe] *nm ou f* Algiers.

Algérie [alʒeri] *nf* Algeria. ◆**algérien, -ienne** *a* & *nmf* Algerian.

algue(s) [alg] *nf(pl)* seaweed.

alias [aljas] *adv* alias.

alibi [alibi] *nm* alibi.

alién/er [aljene] *vt* to alienate; **s'a. qn** to alienate s.o. ◆—**é, -ée** *nmf* insane person; *Péj* lunatic. ◆**aliénation** *nf* alienation; *Méd* derangement.

align/er [aline] *vt* to align, line up; **les a.** *Arg* to fork out, pay up; — **s'a.** *vpr* (*personnes*) to fall into line, line up; *Pol* to align oneself (**sur** with). ◆—**ement** *nm* alignment.

aliment [alimɑ̃] *nm* food. ◆**alimentaire** *a* (*industrie, produit etc*) food-. ◆**alimentation** *nf* feeding; supply(ing); (*régime*) diet, nutrition; (*nourriture*) food; **magasin d'a.** grocer's, grocery store. ◆**alimenter** *vt* (*nourrir*) to feed; (*fournir*) to supply (**en** with); (*débat, feu*) to fuel.

alinéa [alinea] *nm* paragraph.

alité [alite] *a* bedridden.

allaiter [alete] *vti* to (breast)feed.

allant [alɑ̃] *nm* drive, energy, zest.

allécher [aleʃe] *vt* to tempt, entice.

allée [ale] *nf* path, walk, lane; (*de cinéma*) aisle, **allées et venues** comings and goings, running about.

allégation [alegasjɔ̃] *nf* allegation.

alléger [aleʒe] *vt* to alleviate, lighten.

allégorie [alegɔri] *nf* allegory.

allègre [alɛgr] *a* gay, lively, cheerful. ◆**allégresse** *nf* gladness, rejoicing.

alléguer [alege] *vt* (*excuse etc*) to put forward.

alléluia [aleluja] *nm* hallelujah.

Allemagne [almaɲ] *nf* Germany. ◆**allemand, -ande** *a & nmf* German; — *nm* (*langue*) German.

aller* [ale] **1** *vi* (*aux* **être**) to go; (*montre etc*) to work, go; **a.** (*convenir à*) to suit; **a. avec** (*vêtement*) to go with, match; **a. bien/mieux** (*personne*) to be well/better; **il va savoir/venir/etc** he'll know/come/*etc*, he's going to know/come/*etc*; **il va partir** he's about to leave, he's going to leave; **va voir!** go and see!; **comment vas-tu?, (comment) ça va?** how are you?; **ça va!** all right!, fine!; **ça va (comme ça)!** that's enough!; **allez-y** go on, go ahead; **j'y vais** I'm coming; **allons (donc)!** come on!, come off it!; **allez! au lit!** come on *ou* go on to bed!; **ça va de soi** that's obvious; — **s'en aller** *vpr* to go away; (*tache*) to come out. **2** *nm* outward journey; **a. (simple)** single (ticket), *Am* one-way (ticket); **a. (et) retour** return (ticket), *Am* round-trip (ticket).

allergie [alɛrʒi] *nf* allergy. ◆**allergique** *a* allergic (**à** to).

alliage [aljaʒ] *nm* alloy.

alliance [aljɑ̃s] *nf* (*anneau*) wedding ring; *Pol* alliance; *Rel* covenant; (*mariage*) marriage.

allier [alje] *vt* (*associer*) to combine (**à** with); (*pays*) to ally (**à** with); — **s'a.** *vpr* (*couleurs*) to combine; (*pays*) to become allied (**à** with, to); **s'a. à** (*famille*) to ally oneself with. ◆**-é, -ée** *nmf* ally.

alligator [aligator] *nm* alligator.

allô [alo] *int Tél* hullo!, hallo!, hello!

allocation [alɔkasjɔ̃] *nf* (*somme*) allowance; **a. (de) chômage** unemployment benefit. ◆**allocataire** *nmf* claimant.

allocution [alɔkysjɔ̃] *nf* (short) speech, address.

allong/er [alɔ̃ʒe] *vt* (*bras*) to stretch out; (*jupe*) to lengthen; (*sauce*) to thin; — *vi* (*jours*) to get longer; — **s'a.** *vpr* to stretch out. ◆**-é** *a* (*oblong*) elongated.

allouer [alwe] *vt* to allocate.

allum/er [alyme] *vt* (*feu, pipe etc*) to light; (*électricité*) to turn *ou* switch on; (*désir, colère*) Fig to kindle; — **s'a.** *vpr* to light up; (*feu, guerre*) to flare up. ◆**-age** *nm* lighting; *Aut* ignition. ◆**allume-gaz** *nm inv* gas lighter. ◆**allumeuse** *nf* (*femme*) teaser.

allumette [alymɛt] *nf* match.

allure [alyr] *nf* (*vitesse*) pace; (*de véhicule*) speed; (*démarche*) gait, walk; (*maintien*) bearing; (*air*) look; *pl* (*conduite*) ways.

allusion [alyzjɔ̃] *nf* allusion; (*voilée*) hint; **faire a. à** to refer *ou* allude to; to hint at.

almanach [almana] *nm* almanac.

aloi [alwa] *nm* **de bon a.** genuine, worthy.

alors [alɔr] *adv* (*en ce temps-là*) then; (*en ce cas-là*) so, then; **a. que** (*lorsque*) when; (*tandis que*) whereas.

alouette [alwɛt] *nf* (sky)lark.

alourd/ir [alurdir] *vt* to weigh down; — **s'a.** *vpr* to become heavy *ou* heavier. ◆**-i** *a* heavy.

aloyau [alwajo] *nm* sirloin.

alpaga [alpaga] *nm* (*tissu*) alpaca.

alpage [alpaʒ] *nm* mountain pasture. ◆**Alpes** *nfpl* **les A.** the Alps. ◆**alpestre** *a*, ◆**alpin** *a* alpine. ◆**alpinisme** *nm* mountaineering. ◆**alpiniste** *nmf* mountaineer.

alphabet [alfabɛ] *nm* alphabet. ◆**alphabétique** *a* alphabetic(al). ◆**alphabétiser** *vt* to teach to read and write.

altercation [alterkasjɔ̃] *nf* altercation.

altérer [altere] *vt* (*denrée, santé*) to impair, spoil; (*voix, vérité*) to distort; (*monnaie, texte*) to falsify; (*donner soif à*) to make thirsty; — **s'a.** *vpr* (*santé, relations*) to deteriorate. ◆**altération** *nf* deterioration, change (**de** in); (*de visage*) distortion.

alternatif, -ive [alternatif, -iv] *a* alternating. ◆**alternative** *nf* alternative; *pl* alternate periods. ◆**alternativement** *adv* alternately.

altern/er [alterne] *vti* to alternate. ◆**-é** *a* alternate. ◆**alternance** *nf* alternation.

altesse [altɛs] *nf* (*titre*) Highness.

altier, -ière [altje, -jɛr] *a* haughty.

altitude [altityd] *nf* altitude, height.

alto [alto] *nm* (*instrument*) viola.

aluminium [alyminjɔm] *nm* aluminium, *Am*

aluminum; **papier a.**, *Fam* **papier alu** tin foil.

alunir [alynir] *vi* to land on the moon.

alvéole [alveɔl] *nf* (*de ruche*) cell; (*dentaire*) socket. ◆**alvéolé** *a* honeycombed.

amabilité [amabilite] *nf* kindness; **faire des amabilités à** to show kindness to.

amadouer [amadwe] *vt* to coax, persuade.

amaigr/ir [amegrir] *vt* to make thin(ner). ◆**—i** *a* thin(ner). ◆**—issant** *a* (*régime*) slimming.

amalgame [amalgam] *nm* amalgam, mixture. ◆**amalgamer** *vt*, **— s'a.** *vpr* to blend, mix, amalgamate.

amande [amɑ̃d] *nf* almond.

amant [amɑ̃] *nm* lover.

amarre [amar] *nf* (mooring) rope, hawser; *pl* moorings. ◆**amarrer** *vt* to moor; *Fig* to tie down, make fast.

amas [amɑ] *nm* heap, pile. ◆**amasser** *vt* to pile up; (*richesse, preuves*) to amass, gather; **— s'a.** *vpr* to pile up; (*gens*) to gather.

amateur [amatœr] *nm* (*d'art etc*) lover; *Sp* amateur; (*acheteur*) *Fam* taker; **d'a.** (*talent*) amateur; (*travail*) *Péj* amateurish; **une équipe a.** an amateur team. ◆**amateurisme** *nm Sp* amateurism; *Péj* amateurishness.

amazone [amazɔn] *nf* horsewoman; **monter en a.** to ride sidesaddle.

ambages (sans) [sɑ̃zɑ̃baʒ] *adv* to the point, in plain language.

ambassade [ɑ̃basad] *nf* embassy. ◆**ambassadeur, -drice** *nmf* ambassador.

ambiance [ɑ̃bjɑ̃s] *nf* atmosphere. ◆**ambiant** *a* surrounding.

ambigu, -guë [ɑ̃bigy] *a* ambiguous. ◆**ambiguïté** [-gɥite] *nf* ambiguity.

ambitieux, -euse [ɑ̃bisjø, -øz] *a* ambitious. ◆**ambition** *nf* ambition. ◆**ambitionner** *vt* to aspire to; **il ambitionne de** his ambition is to.

ambre [ɑ̃br] *nm* (*jaune*) amber; (*gris*) ambergris.

ambulance [ɑ̃bylɑ̃s] *nf* ambulance. ◆**ambulancier, -ière** *nmf* ambulance driver.

ambulant [ɑ̃bylɑ̃] *a* itinerant, travelling.

âme [ɑm] *nf* soul; **â. qui vive** living soul; **état d'â.** state of mind; **â. sœur** soul mate; **â. damnée** evil genius, henchman; **avoir charge d'âmes** to be responsible for human life.

améliorer [ameljɔre] *vt*, **— s'a.** *vpr* to

improve. ◆**amélioration** *nf* improvement.

amen [amen] *adv* amen.

aménag/er [amenaʒe] *vt* (*arranger, installer*) to fit up, fit out (**en** as); (*bateau*) to fit out; (*transformer*) to convert (**en** into); (*construire*) to set up; (*ajuster*) to adjust. ◆**—ement** *nm* fitting up; fitting out; conversion; setting up; adjustment.

amende [amɑ̃d] *nf* fine; **frapper d'une a.** to impose a fine on; **faire a. honorable** to make an apology.

amender [amɑ̃de] *vt Pol* to amend; (*terre*) to improve; **— s'a.** *vpr* to mend *ou* improve one's ways.

amener [amne] *vt* to bring; (*causer*) to bring about; **— s'a.** *vpr Fam* to come along, turn up.

amenuiser (s') [samənɥize] *vpr* to grow smaller, dwindle.

amer, -ère [amɛr] *a* bitter. ◆**amèrement** *adv* bitterly.

Amérique [amerik] *nf* America; **A. du Nord/du Sud** North/South America. ◆**américain, -aine** *a & nmf* American.

amerrir [amerir] *vi* to make a sea landing; (*cabine spatiale*) to splash down.

amertume [amɛrtym] *nf* bitterness.

améthyste [ametist] *nf* amethyst.

ameublement [amœbləmɑ̃] *nm* furniture.

ameuter [amøte] *vt* (*soulever*) to stir up; (*attrouper*) to gather, muster; (*voisins*) to bring out; **— s'a.** *vpr* to gather, muster.

ami, -e [ami] *nmf* friend; (*des livres, de la nature etc*) lover (**de** of); **petite amie** girlfriend; **— a.** friendly.

amiable (à l') [alamjabl] *a* amicable; **— adv** amicably.

amiante [amjɑ̃t] *nm* asbestos.

amical, -aux [amikal, -o] *a* friendly. ◆**—ement** *adv* in a friendly manner.

amicale [amikal] *nf* association.

amidon [amidɔ̃] *nm* starch. ◆**amidonner** *vt* to starch.

amincir [amɛ̃sir] *vt* to make thin(ner); **— vi** (*personne*) to slim; **— s'a.** *vpr* to become thinner.

amiral, -aux [amiral, -o] *nm* admiral. ◆**amirauté** *nf* admiralty.

amitié [amitje] *nf* friendship; (*amabilité*) kindness; *pl* kind regrds; **prendre en a.** to take a liking to.

ammoniac [amɔnjak] *nm* (*gaz*) ammonia. ◆**ammoniaque** *nf* (*liquide*) ammonia.

amnésie [amnezi] *nf* amnesia.

amnistie [amnisti] *nf* amnesty.

amocher [amɔʃe] *vt Arg* to mess up, bash.

amoindrir [amwɛ̃drir] *vt*, **— s'a.** *vpr* to decrease, diminish.

amoll/ir [amɔlir] *vt* to soften; (*affaiblir*) to weaken. **◆—issant** *a* enervating.

amonceler [amɔ̃sle] *vt*, **— s'a.** *vpr* to pile up. **◆amoncellement** *nm* heap, pile.

amont (en) [ãnamɔ̃] *adv* upstream.

amoral, -aux [amɔral, -o] *a* amoral.

amorce [amɔrs] *nf* (*début*) start; *Pêche* bait; (*détonateur*) fuse, detonator; (*de pistolet d'enfant*) cap. **◆amorcer** *vt* to start; (*hameçon*) to bait; (*pompe*) to prime; **— s'a.** *vpr* to start.

amorphe [amɔrf] *a* listless, apathetic.

amort/ir [amɔrtir] *vt* (*coup*) to cushion, absorb; (*bruit*) to deaden; (*dette*) to pay off; **il a vite amorti sa voiture** his car has been made to pay for itself quickly. **◆—issement** *nm* Fin redemption. **◆—isseur** *nm* shock absorber.

amour [amur] *nm* love; (*liaison*) romance, love; (*Cupidon*) Cupid; **pour l'a. de** for the sake of; **mon a.** my darling, my love. **◆a.-propre** *nm* self-respect, self-esteem. **◆s'amouracher** *vpr Péj* to become infatuated (de with). **◆amoureux, -euse** *nmf* lover; **—** *a* amorous, loving; **a. de** (*personne*) in love with; (*gloire*) *Fig* enamoured of.

amovible [amɔvibl] *a* removable, detachable.

ampère [ɑ̃pɛr] *nm Él* amp(ere).

amphi [ɑ̃fi] *nm Univ Fam* lecture hall.

amphibie [ɑ̃fibi] *a* amphibious; **—** *nm* amphibian.

amphithéâtre [ɑ̃fiteatr] *nm Hist* amphitheatre; *Univ* lecture hall.

ample [ɑ̃pl] *a* (*vêtement*) ample, roomy; (*provision*) full; (*vues*) broad. **◆amplement** *adv* amply, fully; **a. suffisant** ample. **◆ampleur** *nf* (*de robe*) fullness; (*importance, étendue*) scale, extent; **prendre de l'a.** to grow.

amplifier [ɑ̃plifje] *vt* (*accroître*) to develop; (*exagérer*) to magnify; (*son, courant*) to amplify; **— s'a.** *vpr* to increase. **◆amplificateur** *nm* amplifier. **◆amplification** *nf* (*extension*) increase.

amplitude [ɑ̃plityd] *nf Fig* magnitude.

ampoule [ɑ̃pul] *nf* (*électrique*) (light) bulb; (*aux pieds etc*) blister; (*de médicament*) phial.

ampoulé [ɑ̃pule] *a* turgid.

amputer [ɑ̃pyte] *vt* **1** (*membre*) to amputate; **a. qn de la jambe** to amputate s.o.'s leg. **2** (*texte*) to curtail, cut (**de** by).

amputation *nf* amputation; curtailment.

amuse-gueule [amyzgœl] *nm inv* cocktail snack, appetizer.

amus/er [amyze] *vt* (*divertir*) to amuse, entertain; (*occuper*) to divert the attention of; **— s'a.** *vpr* to enjoy oneself, have fun; (*en chemin*) to dawdle, loiter; **s'a. avec** to play with; **s'a. à faire** to amuse oneself doing. **◆—ant** *a* amusing. **◆—ement** *nm* amusement; (*jeu*) game. **◆amusette** *nf* frivolous pursuit.

amygdale [amidal] *nf* tonsil.

an [ɑ̃] *nm* year; **il a dix ans** he's ten (years old); **par a.** per annum, per year; **bon a., mal a.** putting the good years and the bad together; **Nouvel A.** New Year.

anachronisme [anakrɔnism] *nm* anachronism.

anagramme [anagram] *nf* anagram.

analogie [analɔʒi] *nf* analogy. **◆analogue** *a* similar; **—** *nm* analogue.

analphabète [analfabet] *a* & *nmf* illiterate. **◆analphabétisme** *nm* illiteracy.

analyse [analiz] *nf* analysis; **a. grammaticale** parsing. **◆analyser** *vt* to analyse; (*phrase*) to parse. **◆analytique** *a* analytic(al).

ananas [anana(s)] *nm* pineapple.

anarchie [anarʃi] *nf* anarchy. **◆anarchique** *a* anarchic. **◆anarchiste** *nmf* anarchist; **—** *a* anarchistic.

anathème [anatɛm] *nm Rel* anathema.

anatomie [anatɔmi] *nf* anatomy. **◆anatomique** *a* anatomical.

ancestral, -aux [ɑ̃sɛstral, -o] *a* ancestral.

ancêtre [ɑ̃sɛtr] *nm* ancestor.

anche [ɑ̃ʃ] *nf Mus* reed.

anchois [ɑ̃ʃwa] *nm* anchovy.

ancien, -ienne [ɑ̃sjɛ̃, -jɛn] *a* (*vieux*) old; (*meuble*) antique; (*qui n'est plus*) former, ex-, old; (*antique*) ancient; (*dans une fonction*) senior; **a. élève** old boy, *Am* alumnus; **a. combattant** ex-serviceman, *Am* veteran; **—** *nmf* (*par l'âge*) elder; (*dans une fonction*) senior; **les anciens** (*auteurs, peuples*) the ancients. **◆anciennement** *adv* formerly. **◆ancienneté** *nf* age; (*dans une fonction*) seniority.

ancre [ɑ̃kr] *nf* anchor; **jeter l'a.** to (cast) anchor; **lever l'a.** to weigh anchor. **◆ancrer** *vt Nau* to anchor; (*idée*) *Fig* to root, fix; **ancré dans** rooted in.

andouille [ɑ̃duj] *nf* sausage (*made from chitterlings*); **espèce d'a.!** *Fam* (you) nitwit!

âne [ɑn] *nm* (*animal*) donkey, ass; (*personne*) *Péj* ass; **bonnet d'â.** dunce's cap; **dos d'â.** (*d'une route*) hump; **pont en dos d'â.** humpback bridge.

anéant/ir [aneãtir] *vt* to annihilate, wipe out, destroy; **— s'a.** *vpr* to vanish. **◆—i** *a* (*épuisé*) exhausted; (*stupéfait*) dismayed; (*accablé*) overwhelmed. **◆—issement** *nm* annihilation; (*abattement*) dejection.

anecdote [anɛkdɔt] *nf* anecdote. **◆anecdotique** *a* anecdotal.

anémie [anemi] *nf* an(a)emia. **◆anémique** *a* an(a)emic. **◆s'anémier** *vpr* to become an(a)emic.

anémone [anemɔn] *nf* anemone.

ânerie [ɑnri] *nf* stupidity; (*action etc*) stupid thing. **◆ânesse** *nf* she-ass.

anesthésie [anɛstezi] *nf* an(a)esthesia; a. générale/locale general/local an(a)esthetic. **◆anesthésier** *vt* to an(a)esthetize. **◆anesthésique** *nm* an(a)esthetic.

anfractuosité [ãfraktɥozite] *nf* crevice, cleft.

ange [ãʒ] *nm* angel; **aux anges** in seventh heaven. **◆angélique** *a* angelic.

angélus [ãʒelys] *nm* Rel angelus.

angine [ãʒin] *nf* sore throat; **a. de poitrine** angina (pectoris).

anglais, -aise [ãglɛ, -ɛz] *a* English; — *nmf* Englishman, Englishwoman; — *nm* (*langue*) English; **filer à l'anglaise** to take French leave.

angle [ãgl] *nm* (*point de vue*) & Géom angle; (*coin*) corner.

Angleterre [ãglətɛr] *nf* England.

anglican, -ane [ãglikã, -an] *a* & *nmf* Anglican.

anglicisme [ãglisism] *nm* Anglicism. **◆angliciste** *nmf* English specialist.

anglo- [ãglɔ] *préf* Anglo-. **◆anglonormand** *a* Anglo-Norman; **îles a.-normandes** Channel Islands. **◆anglophile** *a* & *nmf* anglophile. **◆anglophone** *a* English-speaking; — *nmf* English speaker. **◆anglo-saxon, -onne** *a* & *nmf* Anglo-Saxon.

angoisse [ãgwas] *nf* anguish. **◆angoissant** *a* distressing. **◆angoissé** *a* (*personne*) in anguish; (*geste, cri*) anguished.

angora [ãgɔra] *nm* (*laine*) angora.

anguille [ãgij] *nf* eel.

angulaire [ãgylɛr] *a* **pierre a.** cornerstone. **◆anguleux, -euse** *a* (*visage*) angular.

anicroche [anikrɔʃ] *nf* hitch, snag.

animal, -aux [animal, -o] *nm* animal; (*personne*) Péj brute, animal; — *a* animal.

animer [anime] *vt* (*inspirer*) to animate; (*encourager*) to spur on; (*débat, groupe*) to lead; (*soirée*) to enliven; (*regard*) to light up, brighten up; (*mécanisme*) to actuate, drive; **a. la course** Sp to set the pace; **animé de** (*sentiment*) prompted by; **— s'a.** *vpr* (*rue etc*) to come to life; (*yeux*) to light up, brighten up. **◆animé** *a* (*rue*) lively; (*conversation*) animated, lively; (*doué de vie*) animate. **◆animateur, -trice** *nmf* TV compere, Am master of ceremonies, emcee; (*de club*) leader, organizer; (*d'entreprise*) driving force, spirit. **◆animation** *nf* (*des rues*) activity; (*de réunion*) liveliness; (*de visage*) brightness; Cin animation.

animosité [animozite] *nf* animosity.

anis [ani(s)] *nm* (*boisson, parfum*) aniseed. **◆anisette** *nf* (*liqueur*) anisette.

ankylose [ãkiloz] *nf* stiffening. **◆s'ankylos/er** *vpr* to stiffen up. **◆—é** *a* stiff.

annales [anal] *nfpl* annals.

anneau, -x [ano] *nm* ring; (*de chaîne*) link.

année [ane] *nf* year; **bonne a.!** Happy New Year!

annexe [anɛks] *nf* (*bâtiment*) annex(e); — *a* (*pièces*) appended; **bâtiment a.** annex(e). **◆annexer** *vt* (*pays*) to annex; (*document*) to append. **◆annexion** *nf* annexation.

annihiler [aniile] *vt* to destroy, annihilate.

anniversaire [anivɛrsɛr] *nm* (*d'événement*) anniversary; (*de naissance*) birthday; — *a* anniversary.

annonce [anɔ̃s] *nf* (*avis*) announcement; (*publicitaire*) advertisement; (*indice*) sign; **petites annonces** classified advertisements, small ads. **◆annoncer** *vt* (*signaler*) to announce, report; (*être l'indice de*) to indicate; (*vente*) to advertise; **a. le printemps** to herald spring; **s'a. pluvieux/difficile**/*etc* to look like being rainy/difficult/*etc.* **◆annonceur** *nm* advertiser; Rad TV announcer.

annonciation [anɔ̃sjɑsjɔ̃] *nf* Annunciation.

annoter [anote] *vt* to annotate. **◆annotation** *nf* annotation.

annuaire [anɥɛr] *nm* yearbook; (*téléphonique*) directory, phone book.

annuel, -elle [anɥɛl] *a* annual, yearly. **◆annuellement** *adv* annually. **◆annuité** *nf* annual instalment.

annulaire [anɥlɛr] *nm* ring or third finger.

annuler [anɥle] *vt* (*visite etc*) to cancel; (*mariage*) to annul; (*jugement*) to quash; — **s'a.** *vpr* to cancel each other out. **◆annulation** *nf* cancellation; annulment; quashing.

anoblir [anɔblir] *vt* to ennoble.

anodin [anɔdɛ̃] a harmless; (*remède*) ineffectual.

anomalie [anɔmali] nf (*irrégularité*) anomaly; (*difformité*) abnormality.

ânonner [anɔne] vt (*en hésitant*) to stumble through; (*d'une voix monotone*) to drone out.

anonymat [anɔnima] nm anonymity; **garder l'a.** to remain anonymous. ◆**anonyme** a & nmf anonymous (person).

anorak [anɔrak] nm anorak.

anorexie [anɔrɛksi] nf anorexia.

anormal, -aux [anɔrmal, -o] a abnormal; (*enfant*) educationally subnormal.

anse [ɑ̃s] nf (*de tasse etc*) handle; (*baie*) cove.

antagonisme [ɑ̃tagɔnism] nm antagonism. ◆**antagoniste** a antagonistic; – nmf antagonist.

antan (d') [dɑ̃tɑ̃] a Litt of yesteryear.

antarctique [ɑ̃tarktik] a antarctic; – nm l'A. the Antarctic, Antarctica.

antécédent [ɑ̃tesedɑ̃] nm Gram antecedent; pl past history, antecedents.

antenne [ɑ̃tɛn] nf TV Rad aerial, Am antenna; (*station*) station; (*d'insecte*) antenna, feeler; **a. chirurgicale** surgical outpost; Aut emergency unit; **sur** ou **à l'a.** on the air.

antérieur [ɑ̃terjœr] a (*précédent*) former, previous, earlier; (*placé devant*) front; **membre a.** forelimb; **a.** à prior to. ◆**antérieurement** adv previously. ◆**antériorité** nf precedence.

anthologie [ɑ̃tɔlɔʒi] nf anthology.

anthropologie [ɑ̃trɔpɔlɔʒi] nf anthropology.

anthropophage [ɑ̃trɔpɔfaʒ] nm cannibal. ◆**anthropophagie** nf cannibalism.

antiaérien, -ienne [ɑ̃tiaerjɛ̃, -jɛn] a (*canon*) antiaircraft; (*abri*) air-raid.

antiatomique [ɑ̃tiatɔmik] a **abri a.** fallout shelter.

antibiotique [ɑ̃tibjɔtik] a & nm antibiotic.

antibrouillard [ɑ̃tibrujar] a & nm (**phare**) **a.** fog lamp.

anticancéreux, -euse [ɑ̃tikɑ̃serø, -øz] a **centre a.** cancer hospital.

antichambre [ɑ̃tiʃɑ̃br] nf antechamber, anteroom.

antichoc [ɑ̃tiʃɔk] a inv shockproof.

anticip/er [ɑ̃tisipe] vti **a. (sur)** to anticipate. ◆**-é** a (*retraite etc*) early; (*paiement*) advance; **avec mes remerciements anticipés** thanking you in advance. ◆**anticipation** nf anticipation; **par a.** in advance; **d'a.** (*roman etc*) science-fiction.

anticlérical, -aux [ɑ̃tiklerikal, -o] a anticlerical.

anticonformiste [ɑ̃tikɔ̃fɔrmist] a & nmf nonconformist.

anticonstitutionnel, -elle [ɑ̃tikɔ̃stitysjɔnɛl] a unconstitutional.

anticorps [ɑ̃tikɔr] nm antibody.

anticyclone [ɑ̃tisiklon] nm anticyclone.

antidater [ɑ̃tidate] vt to backdate, antedate.

antidémocratique [ɑ̃tidemɔkratik] a undemocratic.

antidérapant [ɑ̃tiderapɑ̃] a non-skid.

antidote [ɑ̃tidɔt] nm antidote.

antigel [ɑ̃tiʒɛl] nm antifreeze.

Antilles [ɑ̃tij] nfpl **les A.** the West Indies. ◆**antillais, -aise** a & nmf West Indian.

antilope [ɑ̃tilɔp] nf antelope.

antimite [ɑ̃timit] a mothproof; – nm mothproofing agent.

antiparasite [ɑ̃tiparazit] a **dispositif a.** Rad suppressor.

antipathie [ɑ̃tipati] nf antipathy. ◆**antipathique** a disagreeable.

antipodes [ɑ̃tipɔd] nmpl **aux a.** (*partir*) to the antipodes; **aux a. de** at the opposite end of the world from; Fig poles apart from.

antique [ɑ̃tik] a ancient. ◆**antiquaire** nmf antique dealer. ◆**antiquité** nf (*temps, ancienneté*) antiquity; (*objet ancien*) antique; pl (*monuments etc*) antiquities.

antirabique [ɑ̃tirabik] a (anti-)rabies.

antisémite [ɑ̃tisemit] a anti-Semitic. ◆**antisémitisme** nm anti-Semitism.

antiseptique [ɑ̃tisɛptik] a & nm antiseptic.

antisudoral, -aux [ɑ̃tisydɔral, -o] nm antiperspirant.

antithèse [ɑ̃titɛz] nf antithesis.

antivol [ɑ̃tivɔl] nm anti-theft lock ou device.

antonyme [ɑ̃tɔnim] nm antonym.

antre [ɑ̃tr] nm (*de lion etc*) den.

anus [anys] nm anus.

Anvers [ɑ̃vɛr(s)] nm ou f Antwerp.

anxiété [ɑ̃ksjete] nf anxiety. ◆**anxieux, -euse** a anxious; – nmf worrier.

août [u(t)] nm August. ◆**aoûtien, -ienne** [ausjɛ̃, -jɛn] nmf August holidaymaker ou Am vacationer.

apais/er [apeze] vt (*personne*) to appease, calm; (*scrupules, faim*) to appease; (*douleur*) to allay; – **s'a.** vpr (*personne*) to calm down. ◆**—ant** a soothing. ◆**—ements** nmpl reassurances.

apanage [apanaʒ] nm privilege, monopoly (de of).

aparté [aparte] nm Th aside; (*dans une réunion*) private exchange; **en a.** in private.

apartheid [aparted] nm apartheid.

apathie [apati] nf apathy. ◆**apathique** a apathetic, listless.

apatride [apatrid] nmf stateless person.

apercevoir* [apersəvwar] vt to see, perceive; (brièvement) to catch a glimpse of; **s'a. de** to notice, realize. ◆**aperçu** nm overall view, general outline; (intuition) insight.

apéritif [aperitif] nm aperitif. ◆**apéro** nm Fam aperitif.

apesanteur [apəzãtœr] nf weightlessness.

à-peu-près [apøprɛ] nm inv vague approximation.

apeuré [apœre] a frightened, scared.

aphone [afɔn] a voiceless.

aphorisme [afɔrism] nm aphorism.

aphrodisiaque [afrɔdizjak] a & nm aphrodisiac.

aphte [aft] nm mouth ulcer. ◆**aphteuse** af fièvre a. foot-and-mouth disease.

apiculture [apikyltyr] nf beekeeping.

apit/oyer [apitwaje] vt to move (to pity); **s'a. sur** to pity. ◆**—oiement** nm pity, commiseration.

aplanir [aplanir] vt (terrain) to level; (difficulté) to iron out, smooth out.

aplat/ir [aplatir] vt to flatten (out); — **s'a.** vpr (s'étendre) to lie flat; (s'humilier) to grovel; (tomber) Fam to fall flat on one's face; **s'a. contre** to flatten oneself against. ◆**—i** a flat. ◆**—issement** nm (état) flatness.

aplomb [aplɔ̃] nm self-possession, self-assurance; Péj impudence; **d'a.** (équilibré) well-balanced; (sur ses jambes) steady; (bien portant) in good shape; **tomber d'a.** (soleil) to beat down.

apocalypse [apɔkalips] nf apocalypse; **d'a.** (vision etc) apocalyptic. ◆**apocalyptique** a apocalyptic.

apogée [apɔʒe] nm apogee; Fig peak, apogee.

apolitique [apɔlitik] a apolitical.

Apollon [apɔlɔ̃] nm Apollo.

apologie [apɔlɔʒi] nf defence, vindication. ◆**apologiste** nmf apologist.

apoplexie [apɔplɛksi] nf apoplexy. ◆**apoplectique** a apoplectic.

apostolat [apɔstɔla] nm (prosélytisme) proselytism; (mission) Fig calling. ◆**apostolique** a apostolic.

apostrophe [apɔstrɔf] nf 1 (signe) apostrophe. 2 (interpellation) sharp ou rude remark. ◆**apostropher** vt to shout at.

apothéose [apɔteoz] nf final triumph, apotheosis.

apôtre [apotr] nm apostle.

apparaître* [aparɛtr] vi (se montrer, sembler) to appear.

apparat [apara] nm pomp; **d'a.** (tenue etc) ceremonial, formal.

appareil [aparɛj] nm (instrument etc) apparatus; (électrique) appliance; Anat system; Tél telephone; (avion) aircraft; (législatif etc) Fig machinery; **a. (photo)** camera; **a. (auditif)** hearing aid; **a. (dentier)** brace; **qui est à l'a.?** Tél who's speaking?

appareiller [apareje] **1** vi Nau to get under way. **2** vt (assortir) to match (up).

apparence [aparãs] nf appearance; (vestige) semblance; **en a.** outwardly; **sous l'a. de** under the guise of; **sauver les apparences** to keep up appearances. ◆**apparemment** [-amã] adv apparently. ◆**apparent** a apparent; (ostensible) conspicuous.

apparent/er (s') [aparãte] vpr (ressembler) to be similar ou akin (à to). ◆**—é** a (allié) related; (semblable) similar.

appariteur [aparitœr] nm Univ porter.

apparition [aparisjɔ̃] nf appearance; (spectre) apparition.

appartement [apartəmã] nm flat, Am apartment.

appartenir* [apartənir] **1** vi to belong (à to); **il vous appartient de** it's your responsibility to. **2 s'a.** vpr to be one's own master. ◆**appartenance** nf membership (à of).

appât [apa] nm (amorce) bait; (attrait) lure. ◆**appâter** vt (attirer) to lure.

appauvrir [apovrir] vt to impoverish; — **s'a.** vpr to become impoverished ou poorer.

appel [apɛl] nm (cri, attrait etc) call; (demande pressante) & Jur appeal; Mil call-up; **faire l'a.** Scol to take the register; Mil to have a roll call; **faire a. à** to appeal to, call upon; (requérir) to call for.

appel/er [aple] vt (personne, nom etc) to call; (en criant) to call out to; Mil to call up; (nécessiter) to call for; **a. à l'aide** to call for help; **en a. à** to appeal to; **il est appelé à** (de hautes fonctions) he is marked out for; (témoigner etc) he is called upon to; — **s'a.** vpr to be called; **il s'appelle Paul** his name is Paul. ◆**—é** nm Mil conscript. ◆**appellation** nf (nom) term; **a. contrôlée** trade name guaranteeing quality of wine.

appendice [apɛ̃dis] nm appendix; (d'animal) appendage. ◆**appendicite** nf appendicitis.

appentis [apãti] nm (bâtiment) lean-to.

appesantir (s') [apəzãtir] vpr to become heavier; **s'a. sur** (sujet) to dwell upon.

appétit [apeti] nm appetite (de for); **mettre**

qn en a. to whet s.o.'s appetite; **bon a.!** enjoy your meal! ◆**appétissant** *a* appetizing.

applaud/ir [aplodir] *vti* to applaud, clap; a. à (*approuver*) to applaud. ◆**—issements** *nmpl* applause.

applique [aplik] *nf* wall lamp.

appliqu/er [aplike] *vt* to apply (**à** to); (*surnom, baiser, gifle*) to give; (*loi, décision*) to put into effect; **s'a. à** (*un travail*) to apply oneself to; (*concerner*) to apply to; **s'a. à faire** to take pains to do. ◆**—é** *a* (*travailleur*) painstaking; (*sciences*) applied. ◆**applicable** *a* applicable. ◆**application** *nf* application.

appoint [apwɛ̃] *nm* contribution; **faire l'a.** to give the correct money *ou* change.

appointements [apwɛ̃tmã] *nmpl* salary.

appontement [apɔ̃tmã] *nm* landing stage.

apport [apɔr] *nm* contribution.

apporter [apɔrte] *vt* to bring.

apposer [apoze] *vt Jur* to affix. ◆**apposition** *nf Gram* apposition.

apprécier [apresje] *vt* (*évaluer*) to appraise; (*aimer, percevoir*) to appreciate. ◆**appréciable** *a* appreciable. ◆**appréciation** *nf* appraisal; appreciation.

appréhender [apreãde] *vt* (*craindre*) to fear; (*arrêter*) to apprehend. ◆**appréhension** *nf* apprehension.

apprendre* [aprãdr] *vti* (*étudier*) to learn; (*événement, fait*) to hear of, learn of; (*nouvelle*) to hear; **a. à faire** to learn to do; **a. qch à qn** (*enseigner*) to teach s.o. sth; (*informer*) to tell s.o. sth; **a. à qn à faire** to teach s.o. to do; **a. que** to learn that; (*être informé*) to hear that.

apprenti, -ie [aprãti] *nmf* apprentice; (*débutant*) novice. ◆**apprentissage** *nm* apprenticeship; **faire l'a. de** *Fig* to learn the experience of.

apprêt/er [aprete] *vt*, **— s'a.** *vpr* to prepare. ◆**—é** *a Fig* affected.

apprivois/er [aprivwaze] *vt* to tame; **— s'a.** *vpr* to become tame. ◆**—é** *a* tame.

approbation [aprɔbasjɔ̃] *nf* approval. ◆**approbateur, -trice** *a* approving.

approche [aprɔʃ] *nf* approach. ◆**approch/er** *vt* (*chaise etc*) to bring up, draw up (**de** to, close to); (*personne*) to approach, come close to; **— vi** to approach, draw near(er); **a. de, s'a. de** to approach, come close(r) *ou* near(er) to. ◆**—ant** *a* similar. ◆**—é** *a* approximate. ◆**—able** *a* approachable.

approfond/ir [aprɔfɔ̃dir] *vt* (*trou etc*) to deepen; (*question*) to go into thoroughly; (*mystère*) to plumb the depths of. ◆**—i** *a* thorough. ◆**—issement** *nm* deepening; (*examen*) thorough examination.

approprié [aprɔprije] *a* appropriate.

approprier (s') [saprɔprije] *vpr* **s'a. qch** to appropriate sth.

approuver [apruve] *vt* (*autoriser*) to approve; (*apprécier*) to approve of.

approvisionn/er [aprɔvizjɔne] *vt* (*ville etc*) to supply (with provisions); (*magasin*) to stock; **— s'a.** *vpr* to stock up (**de** with), get one's supplies (**de** of). ◆**—ements** *nmpl* stocks, supplies.

approximat/if, -ive [aprɔksimatif, -iv] *a* approximate. ◆**—ivement** *adv* approximately. ◆**approximation** *nf* approximation.

appui [apɥi] *nm* support; (*pour coude etc*) rest; (*de fenêtre*) sill; **à hauteur d'a.** breast-high. ◆**appuie-tête** *nm inv* headrest. ◆**appuyer** *vt* (*soutenir*) to support; (*accentuer*) to stress; **a. qch sur** (*poser*) to lean *ou* rest sth on; (*presser*) to press sth on; **— vi a. sur** to rest on; (*bouton etc*) to press (on); (*mot, élément etc*) to stress; **s'a. sur** to lean on, rest on; (*compter*) to rely on; (*se baser*) to base oneself on.

âpre [ɑpr] *a* harsh, rough; **a. au gain** grasping.

après [aprɛ] *prép* (*temps*) after; (*espace*) beyond; **a. un an** after a year; **a. le pont** beyond the bridge; **a. coup** after the event; **a. avoir mangé** after eating; **a. qu'il t'a vu** after he saw you; **d'a.** (*selon*) according to, from; **— adv** after(wards); **l'année d'a.** the following year; **et a.?** and then what?

après-demain [apredmɛ̃] *adv* the day after tomorrow. ◆**a.-guerre** *nm* post-war period; **d'a.-guerre** post-war. ◆**a.-midi** *nm ou f inv* afternoon. ◆**a.-shampooing** *nm* (hair) conditioner. ◆**a.-ski** *nm* ankle boot, snow boot.

a priori [aprijɔri] *adv* at the very outset, without going into the matter; **— nm inv** premiss.

à-propos [aprɔpo] *nm* timeliness, aptness.

apte [apt] *a* suited (**à** to), capable (**à** of). ◆**aptitude** *nf* aptitude, capacity (**à, pour** for).

aquarelle [akwarɛl] *nf* watercolour, aquarelle.

aquarium [akwarjɔm] *nm* aquarium.

aquatique [akwatik] *a* aquatic.

aqueduc [akdyk] *nm* aqueduct.

aquilin [akilɛ̃] *a* aquiline.

arabe [arab] *a & nmf* Arab; **— a & nm** (*langue*) Arabic; **chiffres arabes** Arabic

numerals; **désert** a. Arabian desert.
◆**Arabie** nf Arabia; **A. Séoudite** Saudi
Arabia.

arabesque [arabɛsk] nf arabesque.

arable [arabl] a arable.

arachide [araʃid] nf peanut, groundnut.

araignée [arɛɲe] nf spider.

arbalète [arbalɛt] nf crossbow.

arbitraire [arbitrɛr] a arbitrary.

arbitre [arbitr] nm Jur arbitrator; (maître
absolu) arbiter; Fb referee; Tennis umpire;
libre a. free will. ◆**arbitr/er** vt to arbi-
trate; to referee; to umpire. ◆**—age** a
arbitration; refereeing; umpiring.

arborer [arbɔre] vt (insigne, vêtement) to
sport, display.

arbre [arbr] nm tree; Aut shaft, axle.
◆**arbrisseau, -x** nm shrub. ◆**arbuste**
nm (small) shrub, bush.

arc [ark] nm (arme) bow; (voûte) arch; Math
arc; **tir à l'a.** archery. ◆**arcade** nf
arch(way); pl arcade.

arc-boutant [arkbutɑ̃] nm (pl
arcs-boutants) flying buttress.
◆**s'arc-bouter** vpr s'a. à ou contre to
brace oneself against.

arceau, -x [arso] nm (de voûte) arch.

arc-en-ciel [arkɑ̃sjɛl] nm (pl arcs-en-ciel)
rainbow.

archaïque [arkaik] a archaic.

archange [arkɑ̃ʒ] nm archangel.

arche [arʃ] nf (voûte) arch; **l'a. de Noé**
Noah's ark.

archéologie [arkeɔlɔʒi] nf arch(a)eology.
◆**archéologue** nmf arch(a)eologist.

archer [arʃe] nm archer, bowman.

archet [arʃe] nm Mus bow.

archétype [arketip] nm archetype.

archevêque [arʃəvɛk] nm archbishop.

archicomble [arʃikɔ̃bl] a jam-packed.

archipel [arʃipɛl] nm archipelago.

archiplein [arʃiplɛ̃] a chock-full,
chock-a-block.

architecte [arʃitɛkt] nm architect.
◆**architecture** nf architecture.

archives [arʃiv] nfpl archives, records.
◆**archiviste** nmf archivist.

arctique [arktik] a arctic; – nm **l'A.** the
Arctic.

ardent [ardɑ̃] a (chaud) burning, scorching;
(actif, passionné) ardent, fervent;
(empressé) eager. ◆**ardemment** [-amɑ̃]
adv eagerly, fervently. ◆**ardeur** nf heat;
(énergie) ardour, fervour.

ardoise [ardwaz] nf slate.

ardu [ardy] a arduous, difficult.

are [ar] nm (mesure) 100 square metres.

arène [arɛn] nf Hist arena; (pour taureaux)
bullring; pl Hist amphitheatre; bullring.

arête [arɛt] nf (de poisson) bone; (de cube
etc) & Géog ridge.

argent [arʒɑ̃] nm (métal) silver; (monnaie)
money; **a. comptant** cash. ◆**argenté** a
(plaqué) silver-plated; (couleur) silvery.
◆**argenterie** nf silverware.

Argentine [arʒɑ̃tin] nf Argentina. ◆**argentin, -ine** a & nmf Argentinian.

argile [arʒil] nf clay. ◆**argileux, -euse** a
clayey.

argot [argo] nm slang. ◆**argotique** a
(terme) slang.

arguer [argɥe] vi **a. de qch** to put forward
sth as an argument; **a. que** (protester) to
protest that. ◆**argumentation** nf argumentation, arguments. ◆**argumenter** vi
to argue.

argument [argymɑ̃] nm argument.

argus [argys] nm guide to secondhand cars.

argutie [argysi] nf specious argument, quibble.

aride [arid] a arid, barren.

aristocrate [aristɔkrat] nmf aristocrat.
◆**aristocratie** [-asi] nf aristocracy.
◆**aristocratique** a aristocratic.

arithmétique [aritmetik] nf arithmetic; – a
arithmetical.

arlequin [arləkɛ̃] nm harlequin.

armateur [armatœr] nm shipowner.

armature [armatyr] nf (charpente) framework; (de lunettes, tente) frame.

arme [arm] nf arm, weapon; **a. à feu** firearm; **carrière des armes** military career.
◆**arm/er** vt (personne etc) to arm (de
with); (fusil) to cock; (appareil photo) to
wind on; (navire) to equip; (béton) to reinforce; – **s'a.** vpr to arm oneself (de with).
◆**—ement(s)** nm(pl) arms.

armée [arme] nf army; **a. active/de métier**
regular/professional army; **a. de l'air** air
force.

armistice [armistis] nm armistice.

armoire [armwar] nf cupboard, Am closet;
(penderie) wardrobe, Am closet; **a. à
pharmacie** medicine cabinet.

armoiries [armwari] nfpl (coat of) arms.

armure [armyr] nf armour.

armurier [armyrje] nm gunsmith.

arôme [arom] nm aroma. ◆**aromate** nm
spice. ◆**aromatique** a aromatic.

arpent/er [arpɑ̃te] vt (terrain) to survey;
(trottoir etc) to pace up and down. ◆**—eur**
nm (land) surveyor.

arqué [arke] a arched, curved; (jambes)
bandy.

arrache-pied (d') [daraʃpje] adv unceasingly, relentlessly.

arrach/er [araʃe] vt (clou, dent etc) to pull out; (cheveux, page) to tear out, pull out; (plante) to pull up; (masque) to tear off, pull off; a. qch à qn to snatch sth from s.o.; (aveu, argent) to force sth out of s.o.; a. un bras à qn (obus etc) to blow s.o.'s arm off; a. qn de son lit to drag s.o. out of bed. ◆—age nm (de plante) pulling up.

arraisonner [arezɔne] vt (navire) to board and examine.

arrang/er [arɑ̃ʒe] vt (chambre, visite etc) to arrange, fix up; (voiture, texte) to put right; (différend) to settle; a. qn (maltraiter) Fam to fix s.o.; ça m'arrange that suits me (fine); — s'a. vpr (se réparer) to be put right; (se mettre d'accord) to come to an agreement ou arrangement; (finir bien) to turn out fine; s'a. pour faire to arrange to do, manage to do. ◆—eant a accommodating. ◆—ement nm arrangement.

arrestation [arestasjɔ̃] nf arrest.

arrêt [arɛ] nm (halte, endroit) stop; (action) stopping; Méd arrest; Jur decree; temps d'a. pause; à l'a. stationary; a. de travail (grève) stoppage; (congé) sick leave; sans a. constantly, non-stop.

arrêté [arete] nm order, decision.

arrêt/er [arete] vt to stop; (appréhender) to arrest; (regard, jour) to fix; (plan) to draw up; — vi to stop; il n'arrête pas de critiquer/etc he doesn't stop criticizing/etc, he's always criticizing/etc; — s'a. vpr to stop; s'a. de faire to stop doing. ◆—é a (projet) fixed; (volonté) firm.

arrhes [ar] nfpl Fin deposit.

arrière [arjɛr] adv en a. (marcher) backwards; (rester) behind; (regarder) back; en a. de qn/qch behind s.o./sth; — nm & a inv rear, back; — nm Fb (full) back; faire marche a. to reverse, back.

arrière-boutique [arjɛrbutik] nm back room (of a shop). ◆a.-garde nf rearguard. ◆a.-goût nm aftertaste. ◆a.-grand-mère nf great-grand-mother. ◆a.-grand-père nm (pl arrière-grands-pères) great-grand-father. ◆a.-pays nm hinterland. ◆a.-pensée nf ulterior motive. ◆a.-plan nm background. ◆a.-saison nf end of season, (late) autumn. ◆a.-train nm hindquarters.

arriéré [arjere] 1 a (enfant) (mentally) retarded; (idée) backward. 2 nm (dette) arrears.

arrimer [arime] vt (fixer) to rope down, secure.

arriv/er [arive] vi (aux être) (venir) to arrive, come; (réussir) to succeed; (survenir) to happen; a. à (atteindre) to reach; a. à faire to manage to do, succeed in doing; a. à qn to happen to s.o.; il m'arrive d'oublier/etc I happen (sometimes) to forget/etc, I (sometimes) forget/etc; en a. à faire to get to the point of doing. ◆—ant, -ante nmf new arrival. ◆—ée nf arrival; Sp ·(winning) post. ◆—age nm consignment. ◆arriviste nmf Péj social climber, self-seeker.

arrogant [arɔgɑ̃] a arrogant. ◆arrogance nf arrogance.

arroger (s') [sarɔʒe] vpr (droit etc) to assume (falsely).

arrond/ir [arɔ̃dir] vt to make round; (somme, chiffre) to round off. ◆—i a rounded.

arrondissement [arɔ̃dismɑ̃] nm (d'une ville) district.

arros/er [aroze] vt (terre) to water; (repas) to wash down; (succès) to drink to. ◆—age nm watering; Fam booze-up, celebration. ◆arrosoir nm watering can.

arsenal, -aux [arsənal, -o] nm Nau dockyard; Mil arsenal.

arsenic [arsənik] nm arsenic.

art [ar] nm art; film/critique d'a. art film/critic; arts ménagers domestic science.

artère [artɛr] nf Anat artery; Aut main road. ◆artériel, -elle a arterial.

artichaut [artiʃo] nm artichoke.

article [artikl] nm (de presse, de commerce) & Gram article; (dans un contrat, catalogue) item; a. de fond feature (article); articles de toilette/de voyage toilet/travel requisites; à l'a. de la mort at death's door.

articuler [artikyle] vt (mot etc) to articulate; — s'a. vpr Anat to articulate; Fig to connect. ◆articulation nf Ling articulation; Anat joint; a. du doigt knuckle.

artifice [artifis] nm trick, contrivance; feu d'a. (spectacle) fireworks, firework display.

artificiel, -elle [artifisjɛl] a artificial. ◆artificiellement adv artificially.

artillerie [artijri] nf artillery. ◆artilleur nm gunner.

artisan [artizɑ̃] nm craftsman, artisan. ◆artisanal, -aux a (métier) craftsman's. ◆artisanat nm (métier) craftsman's trade; (classe) artisan class.

artiste [artist] nmf artist; Th Mus Cin performer, artist. ◆artistique a artistic.

as [as] nm (carte, champion) ace; a. du volant crack driver.

ascendant [asɑ̃dɑ̃] *a* ascending, upward; — *nm* ascendancy, power; *pl* ancestors. ◆**ascendance** *nf* ancestry.

ascenseur [asɑ̃sœr] *nm* lift, *Am* elevator.

ascension [asɑ̃sjɔ̃] *nf* ascent; **l'A.** Ascension Day.

ascète [asɛt] *nmf* ascetic. ◆**ascétique** *a* ascetic. ◆**ascétisme** *nm* asceticism.

Asie [azi] *nf* Asia. ◆**Asiate** *nmf* Asian. ◆**asiatique** *a & nmf* Asian, Asiatic.

asile [azil] *nm* (*abri*) refuge, shelter; (*pour vieillards*) home; *Pol* asylum; **a. (d'aliénés)** *Péj* (lunatic) asylum; **a. de paix** haven of peace.

aspect [aspɛ] *nm* (*vue*) sight; (*air*) appearance; (*perspective*) & *Gram* aspect.

asperge [aspɛrʒ] *nf* asparagus.

asperger [aspɛrʒe] *vt* to spray, sprinkle (**de** with).

aspérité [asperite] *nf* rugged edge, bump.

asphalte [asfalt] *nm* asphalt.

asphyxie [asfiksi] *nf* suffocation. ◆**asphyxier** *vt* to suffocate, asphyxiate.

aspic [aspik] *nm* (*vipère*) asp.

aspirant [aspirɑ̃] *nm* (*candidat*) candidate.

aspirateur [aspiratœr] *nm* vacuum cleaner, hoover®; **passer (à) l'a.** to vacuum, hoover.

aspir/er [aspire] *vt* (*respirer*) to breathe in, inhale; (*liquide*) to suck up; **a. à** to aspire to. ◆**—é** *a Ling* aspirate(d). ◆**aspiration** *nf* inhaling; suction; (*ambition*) aspiration.

aspirine [aspirin] *nf* aspirin.

assagir (s') [sasaʒir] *vpr* to sober (down), settle down.

assaill/ir [asajir] *vt* to assault, attack; **a. de** (*questions etc*) to assail with. ◆**—ant** *nm* assailant, attacker.

assainir [asenir] *vt* (*purifier*) to clean up; *Fin* to stabilize.

assaisonn/er [asɛzɔne] *vt* to season. ◆**—ement** *nm* seasoning.

assassin [asasɛ̃] *nm* murderer; assassin. ◆**assassinat** *nm* murder; assassination. ◆**assassiner** *vt* to murder; (*homme politique etc*) to assassinate.

assaut [aso] *nm* assault, onslaught; **prendre d'a.** to (take by) storm.

assécher [aseʃe] *vt* to drain.

assemblée [asɑ̃ble] *nf* (*personnes réunies*) gathering; (*réunion*) meeting; *Pol Jur* assembly; (*de fidèles*) *Rel* congregation.

assembl/er [asɑ̃ble] *vt* to assemble, put together; — **s'a.** *vpr* to assemble, gather. ◆**—age** *nm* (*montage*) assembly; (*réunion d'objets*) collection.

asséner [asene] *vt* (*coup*) to deal, strike.

assentiment [asɑ̃timɑ̃] *nm* assent, consent.

asseoir* [aswar] *vt* (*personne*) to sit (down), seat (**sur** on); (*fondations*) to lay; (*autorité, réputation*) to establish; **a. sur** (*théorie etc*) to base on; — **s'a.** *vpr* to sit (down).

assermenté [asɛrmɑ̃te] *a* sworn.

assertion [asɛrsjɔ̃] *nf* assertion.

asserv/ir [asɛrvir] *vt* to enslave. ◆**—issement** *nm* enslavement.

assez [ase] *adv* enough; **a. de pain/de gens** enough bread/people; **j'en ai a.** I've had enough; **a. grand/intelligent/etc** (*suffisamment*) big/clever/etc enough (**pour** to); **a. fatigué/etc** (*plutôt*) fairly *ou* rather *ou* quite tired/etc.

assidu [asidy] *a* (*appliqué*) assiduous, diligent; **a. auprès de** attentive to. ◆**assiduité** *nf* assiduousness, diligence; *pl* (*empressement*) attentiveness. ◆**assidûment** *adv* assiduously.

assiég/er [asjeʒe] *vt* (*ville*) to besiege; (*guichet*) to mob, crowd round; (*importuner*) to pester, harry; **assiégé de** (*demandes*) besieged with; (*maux*) beset by. ◆**—eant, -eante** *nmf* besieger.

assiette [asjɛt] *nf* **1** (*récipient*) plate; **a. anglaise** *Culin* (assorted) cold meats, *Am* cold cuts. **2** (*à cheval*) seat; **il n'est pas dans son a.** he's feeling out of sorts.

assigner [asiɲe] *vt* (*attribuer*) to assign; *Jur* to summon, subpoena. ◆**assignation** *nf Jur* subpoena, summons.

assimiler [asimile] *vt* to assimilate; — **s'a.** *vpr* (*immigrants*) to assimilate, become assimilated (**à** with). ◆**assimilation** *nf* assimilation.

assis [asi] *a* (*sitting* (down), seated; (*caractère*) settled; (*situation*) stable, secure.

assise [asiz] *nf* (*base*) *Fig* foundation; *pl Jur* assizes; *Pol* congress; **cour d'assises** court of assizes.

assistance [asistɑ̃s] *nf* **1** (*assemblée*) audience; (*nombre de personnes présentes*) attendance, turn-out. **2** (*aide*) assistance; **l'A. (publique)** the child care service; **enfant de l'A.** child in care. ◆**assist/er 1** *vt* (*aider*) to assist, help. **2** *vi* **a. à** (*réunion, cours etc*) to attend, be present at; (*accident*) to witness. ◆**—ant, -ante** *nmf* assistant; — *nmpl* (*spectateurs*) members of the audience; (*témoins*) those present; **assistante sociale** social worker; **assistante maternelle** mother's help.

associ/er [asɔsje] *vt* to associate (**à** with); **a. qn à** (*ses travaux, profits*) to involve s.o. in; **s'a. à** (*collaborer*) to associate with, become associated with; (*aux vues ou au chagrin de qn*) to share; (*s'harmoniser*) to combine with. ◆—é, -ée *nmf* partner, associate; — *a* associate. ◆**association** *nf* association; (*amitié, alliance*) partnership, association.

assoiffé [aswafe] *a* thirsty (**de** for).

assombrir [asɔ̃brir] *vt* (*obscurcir*) to darken; (*attrister*) to cast a cloud over, fill with gloom; — **s'a.** *vpr* to darken; to cloud over.

assomm/er [asɔme] *vt* (*animal*) to stun, brain; (*personne*) to knock unconscious; (*ennuyer*) to bore stiff. ◆—**ant** *a* tiresome, boring.

assomption [asɔ̃psjɔ̃] *nf* Rel Assumption.

assort/ir [asɔrtir] *vt*, — **s'a.** *vpr* to match. ◆—**i** *a* **bien** *a*. (*magasin*) well-stocked; — *apl* (*objets semblables*) matching; (*fromages etc variés*) assorted; **époux bien assortis** well-matched couple. ◆—**iment** *nm* assortment.

assoup/ir [asupir] *vt* (*personne*) to make drowsy; (*douleur, sentiment etc*) Fig to dull; — **s'a.** *vpr* to doze off; Fig to subside. ◆—**i** *a* (*personne*) drowsy. ◆—**issement** *nm* drowsiness.

assoupl/ir [asuplir] *vt* (*étoffe, muscles*) to make supple; (*corps*) to limber up; (*caractère*) to soften; (*règles*) to ease, relax. ◆—**issement** *nm* **exercices d'a.** limbering up exercises.

assourd/ir [asurdir] *vt* (*personne*) to deafen; (*son*) to muffle. ◆—**issant** *a* deafening.

assouvir [asuvir] *vt* to appease, satisfy.

assujett/ir [asyʒetir] *vt* (*soumettre*) to subject (**à** to); (*peuple*) to subjugate; (*fixer*) to secure; **s'a. à** to subject oneself to, submit to. ◆—**issant** *a* (*travail*) constraining. ◆—**issement** *nm* subjection; (*contrainte*) constraint.

assumer [asyme] *vt* (*tâche, rôle*) to assume, take on; (*emploi*) to take up, assume; (*remplir*) to fill, hold.

assurance [asyrɑ̃s] *nf* (*aplomb*) (self-)assurance; (*promesse*) assurance; (*contrat*) insurance; **a. au tiers/tous risques** third-party/comprehensive insurance; **assurances sociales** = national insurance, *Am* = social security.

assur/er [asyre] *vt* (*rendre sûr*) to ensure, *Am* insure; (*par un contrat*) to insure; (*travail etc*) to carry out; (*fixer*) to secure; **a. à qn que** to assure s.o. that; **a. qn de qch, a. qch à qn** to assure s.o. of sth; — **s'a.** *vpr* (*se procurer*) to ensure, secure; (*par un contrat*) to insure oneself, get insured (**contre** against); **s'a. que/de** to make sure that/of. ◆—**é, -ée** *a* (*succès*) assured, certain; (*pas*) firm, secure; (*air*)

(self-)assured, (self-)confident; — *nmf* policyholder, insured person. ◆—**ément** *adv* certainly, assuredly. ◆**assureur** *nm* insurer.

astérisque [asterisk] *nm* asterisk.

asthme [asm] *nm* asthma. ◆**asthmatique** *a* & *nmf* asthmatic.

asticot [astiko] *nm* maggot, worm.

astiquer [astike] *vt* to polish.

astre [astr] *nm* star.

astreindre* [astrɛ̃dr] *vt* **a. à** (*discipline*) to compel to accept; **a. à faire** to compel to do. ◆**astreignant** *a* exacting ◆**astreinte** *nf* constraint.

astrologie [astrɔlɔʒi] *nf* astrology. ◆**astrologue** *nm* astrologer.

astronaute [astrɔnot] *nmf* astronaut. ◆**astronautique** *nf* space travel.

astronomie [astrɔnɔmi] *nf* astronomy. ◆**astronome** *nm* astronomer. ◆**astronomique** *a* astronomical.

astuce [astys] *nf* (*pour faire qch*) knack, trick; (*invention*) gadget; (*plaisanterie*) clever joke, wisecrack; (*finesse*) astuteness; **les astuces du métier** the tricks of the trade. ◆**astucieux, -euse** *a* clever, astute.

atelier [atəlje] *nm* (*d'ouvrier*) workshop; (*de peintre*) studio.

atermoyer [atɛrmwaje] *vi* to procrastinate.

athée [ate] *a* atheistic; — *nmf* atheist. ◆**athéisme** *nm* atheism.

Athènes [atɛn] *nm ou f* Athens.

athlète [atlɛt] *nmf* athlete. ◆**athlétique** *a* athletic. ◆**athlétisme** *nm* athletics.

atlantique [atlɑ̃tik] *a* Atlantic; — *nm* **l'A.** the Atlantic.

atlas [atlas] *nm* atlas.

atmosphère [atmɔsfɛr] *nf* atmosphere. ◆**atmosphérique** *a* atmospheric.

atome [atom] *nm* atom. ◆**atomique** [atɔmik] *a* atomic; **bombe a.** atom *ou* atomic bomb.

atomis/er [atɔmize] *vt* (*liquide*) to spray; (*région*) to destroy (*by atomic weapons*). ◆—**eur** *nm* spray.

atone [atɔn] *a* (*personne*) lifeless; (*regard*) vacant.

atours [atur] *nmpl* Hum finery.

atout [atu] *nm* trump (card); (*avantage*) Fig trump card, asset; **l'a. est cœur** hearts are trumps.

âtre [ɑtr] *nm* (*foyer*) hearth.

atroce [atrɔs] *a* atrocious; (*crime*) heinous, atrocious. ◆**atrocité** *nf* atrociousness; *pl* (*actes*) atrocities.

atrophie [atrɔfi] *nf* atrophy. ◆**atrophié** *a* atrophied.

attabl/er (s') [satable] *vpr* to sit down at the table. ◆—**é** *a* (seated) at the table.

attache [ataʃ] *nf* (*objet*) attachment, fastening; *pl* (*liens*) links.

attach/er [ataʃe] *vt* (*lier*) to tie (up), attach (à to); (*boucler, fixer*) to fasten; **a. du prix/un sens à qch** to attach great value/a meaning to sth; **cette obligation m'attache à lui** this obligation binds me to him; **s'a. à** (*adhérer*) to stick to; (*se lier*) to become attached to; (*se consacrer*) to apply oneself to. ◆—**ant** *a* (*enfant etc*) engaging, appealing. ◆—**é, -ée** *nmf* (*personne*) *Pol Mil* attaché. ◆—**ement** *nm* attachment, affection.

attaque [atak] *nf* attack; **a. aérienne** air raid; **d'a.** in tip-top shape, on top form. ◆**attaqu/er** *vt*, **s'a. à** to attack; (*difficulté, sujet*) to tackle; – *vi* to attack. ◆—**ant, -ante** *nmf* attacker.

attard/er (s') [satarde] *vpr* (*chez qn*) to linger (on), stay on; (*en chemin*) to loiter, dawdle; **s'a. sur** ou **à** (*détails etc*) to linger over; **s'a. derrière qn** to lag behind s.o. ◆—**é** *a* (*enfant etc*) backward; (*passant*) late.

atteindre* [atɛ̃dr] *vt* (*parvenir à*) to reach; (*idéal*) to attain; (*blesser*) to hit, wound; (*toucher*) to affect; (*offenser*) to hurt, wound; **être atteint de** (*maladie*) to be suffering from.

atteinte [atɛ̃t] *nf* attack; **porter a. à** to attack, undermine; **a. à** (*honneur*) slur on; **hors d'a.** (*objet, personne*) out of reach; (*réputation*) unassailable.

attel/er [atle] *vt* (*bêtes*) to harness, hitch up; (*remorque*) to couple; **s'a. à** (*travail etc*) to apply oneself to. ◆—**age** *nm* harnessing; coupling; (*bêtes*) team.

attenant [atnɑ̃] *a* **a. (à)** adjoining.

attend/re [atɑ̃dr] *vt* to wait for, await; (*escompter*) to expect (**de** of, from); **elle attend un bébé** she's expecting a baby; – *vi* to wait; **s'a. à** to expect; **a. d'être informé** to wait to be informed; **a. que qn vienne** to wait for s.o. to come, wait until s.o. comes; **faire a. qn** to keep s.o. waiting; **se faire a.** (*réponse, personne etc*) to be a long time coming; **attends voir** *Fam* let me see; **en attendant** meanwhile; **en attendant que** (+ *sub*) until. ◆—**u** *a* (*avec joie*) eagerly-awaited; (*prévu*) expected; – *prép* considering; **a. que** considering that.

attendr/ir [atɑ̃drir] *vt* (*émouvoir*) to move (to compassion); (*viande*) to tenderize; – **s'a.** *vpr* to be moved (**sur** by). ◆—**i** *a* compassionate. ◆—**issant** *a* moving. ◆—**issement** *nm* compassion.

attentat [atɑ̃ta] *nm* attempt (*on s.o.'s life*); murder attempt; *Fig* crime, outrage (**à** against); **a. (à la bombe)** (bomb) attack. ◆**attenter** *vi* **a. à** (*la vie de qn*) to make an attempt on; *Fig* to attack.

attente [atɑ̃t] *nf* (*temps*) wait(ing); (*espérance*) expectation(s); **une a. prolongée** a long wait; **être dans l'a. de** to be waiting for; **salle d'a.** waiting room.

attentif, -ive [atɑ̃tif, -iv] *a* (*personne*) attentive; (*travail, examen*) careful; **a. à** (*plaire etc*) anxious to; (*ses devoirs etc*) mindful of. ◆**attentivement** *adv* attentively.

attention [atɑ̃sjɔ̃] *nf* attention; *pl* (*égards*) consideration; **faire** ou **prêter a. à** (*écouter, remarquer*) to pay attention to; **faire a. à/que** (*prendre garde*) to be careful of/that; **a.!** look out!, be careful!; **a. à la voiture!** mind ou watch the car! ◆**attentionné** *a* considerate.

atténu/er [atenɥe] *vt* to attenuate, mitigate; – **s'a.** *vpr* to subside. ◆—**antes** *afpl* **circonstances a.** extenuating circumstances.

atterrer [atere] *vt* to dismay.

atterr/ir [aterir] *vi* *Av* to land. ◆—**issage** *nm* *Av* landing; **a. forcé** crash ou emergency landing.

attester [ateste] *vt* to testify to; **a. que** to testify that. ◆**attestation** *nf* (*document*) declaration, certificate.

attifer [atife] *vt* *Fam Péj* to dress up, rig out.

attirail [atiraj] *nm* (*équipement*) *Fam* gear.

attir/er [atire] *vt* (*faire venir*) to attract, draw; (*plaire à*) to attract; (*attention*) to draw (**sur** on); **a. qch à qn** (*causer*) to bring s.o. sth; (*gloire etc*) to win ou earn s.o. sth; **a. dans** (*coin, guet-apens*) to draw into; – **s'a.** *vpr* (*ennuis etc*) to bring upon oneself; (*sympathie de qn*) to win; **a. sur soi** (*colère de qn*) to bring down upon oneself. ◆—**ant** *a* attractive. ◆**attirance** *nf* attraction.

attiser [atize] *vt* (*feu*) to poke; (*sentiment*) *Fig* to rouse.

attitré [atitre] *a* (*représentant*) appointed; (*marchand*) regular.

attitude [atityd] *nf* attitude; (*maintien*) bearing.

attraction [atraksjɔ̃] *nf* attraction.

attrait [atrɛ] *nm* attraction.

attrape [atrap] *nf* trick. ◆**a.-nigaud** *nm* con, trick.

attraper [atrape] *vt* (*ballon, maladie, voleur, train etc*) to catch; (*accent, contravention etc*) to pick up; **se laisser a.** (*duper*) to get taken in *ou* tricked); **se faire a.** (*gronder*) *Fam* to get a telling off. ◆**attrapade** *nf* (*gronderie*) *Fam* telling off.

attrayant [atrejã] *a* attractive.

attribuer [atribɥe] *vt* (*donner*) to assign, allot (à to); (*imputer, reconnaître*) to attribute, ascribe (à to); (*décerner*) to grant, award (à to). ◆**attribuable** *a* attributable. ◆**attribution** *nf* assignment; attribution; (*de prix*) awarding; *pl* (*compétence*) powers.

attribut [atriby] *nm* attribute.

attrister [atriste] *vt* to sadden.

attroup/er [atrupe] *vt*, — **s'a.** *vpr* to gather. ◆**—ement** *nm* gathering, (disorderly) crowd.

au [o] *voir* à.

aubaine [obɛn] *nf* (**bonne**) **a.** stroke of good luck, godsend.

aube [ob] *nf* dawn; **dès l'a.** at the crack of dawn.

aubépine [obepin] *nf* hawthorn.

auberge [obɛrʒ] *nf* inn; **a. de jeunesse** youth hostel. ◆**aubergiste** *nmf* innkeeper.

aubergine [obɛrʒin] *nf* aubergine, eggplant.

aucun, -une [okœ̃, -yn] *a* no, not any; **il n'a a. talent** he has no talent, he doesn't have any talent; **a. professeur n'est venu** no teacher has come; — *pron* none, not any; **il n'en a a.** he has none (at all), he doesn't have any (at all); **plus qu'a.** more than any(one); **d'aucuns** some (people). ◆**aucunement** *adv* not at all.

audace [odas] *nf* (*courage*) daring, boldness; (*impudence*) audacity; *pl* daring innovations. ◆**audacieux, -euse** *a* daring, bold.

au-dedans, au-dehors, au-delà *voir* **dedans** *etc*.

au-dessous [odsu] *adv* (*en bas*) (down) below, underneath; (*moins*) below, under; (*à l'étage inférieur*) downstairs; — *prép* **au-d. de** (*arbre etc*) below, under, beneath; (*âge, prix*) under; (*température*) below; **au-d. de sa tâche** not up to *ou* unequal to one's task.

au-dessus [odsy] *adv* above; over; on top; (*à l'étage supérieur*) upstairs; — *prép* **au-d. de** above; (*âge, température, prix*) over; (*posé sur*) on top of.

au-devant de [odvãdə] *prép* **aller au-d. de** (*personne*) to go to meet; (*danger*) to court; (*désirs de qn*) to anticipate.

audible [odibl] *a* audible.

audience [odjãs] *nf Jur* hearing; (*entretien*) audience.

audio [odjo] *a inv* (*cassette etc*) audio.

◆**audiophone** *nm* hearing aid. ◆**audio-visuel, -elle** *a* audio-visual.

auditeur, -trice [oditœr, -tris] *nmf Rad* listener; **les auditeurs** the audience; **a. libre** *Univ* auditor, student allowed to attend classes but not to sit examinations. ◆**auditif, -ive** *a* (*nerf*) auditory. ◆**audition** *nf* (*ouïe*) hearing; (*séance d'essai*) *Th* audition; (*séance musicale*) recital. ◆**auditionner** *vti* to audition. ◆**auditoire** *nm* audience. ◆**auditorium** *nm Rad* recording studio (*for recitals*).

auge [oʒ] *nf* (feeding) trough.

augmenter [ɔgmãte] *vt* to increase (de by); (*salaire, prix, impôt*) to raise, increase; **a. qn** to give s.o. a rise *ou Am* raise; — *vi* to increase (de by); (*prix, population*) to rise, go up. ◆**augmentation** *nf* increase (de in, of); **a. de salaire** (pay) rise, *Am* raise; **a. de prix** price rise *ou* increase.

augure [ɔgyr] *nm* (*présage*) omen; (*devin*) oracle; **être de bon/mauvais a.** to be a good/bad omen. ◆**augurer** *vt* to augur, predict.

auguste [ɔgyst] *a* august.

aujourd'hui [oʒurdɥi] *adv* today; (*actuellement*) nowadays, today; **a. en quinze** two weeks today.

aumône [omon] *nf* alms.

aumônier [omonje] *nm* chaplain.

auparavant [oparavã] *adv* (*avant*) before(hand); (*d'abord*) first.

auprès de [oprɛdə] *prép* (*assis, situé etc*) by, close to, next to; (*en comparaison de*) compared to; **agir a. de** (*ministre etc*) to use one's influence with; **accès a. de qn** access to s.o.

auquel [okɛl] *voir* **lequel**.

aura, aurait [ora, orɛ] *voir* **avoir**.

auréole [ɔreɔl] *nf* (*de saint etc*) halo; (*trace*) ring.

auriculaire [ɔrikylɛr] *nm* **l'a.** the little finger.

aurore [ɔrɔr] *nf* dawn, daybreak.

ausculter [ɔskylte] *vt* (*malade*) to examine (*with a stethoscope*); (*cœur*) to listen to. ◆**auscultation** *nf Méd* auscultation.

auspices [ospis] *nmpl* **sous les a. de** under the auspices of.

aussi [osi] *adv* **1** (*comparaison*) as; **a. sage que** as wise as. **2** (*également*) too, also, as well; **moi a.** so do, can, am *etc* I; **a. bien que** as well as. **3** (*tellement*) so; **un repas a. délicieux** so delicious a meal, such a delicious meal. **4** *conj* (*donc*) therefore.

aussitôt [osito] *adv* immediately, at once; **a. que** as soon as; **a. levé, il partit** as soon as he was up, he left; **a. dit, a. fait** no sooner said than done.

austère [ɔstɛr] *a* austere. ◆**austérité** *nf* austerity.

austral, *mpl* **-als** [ɔstral] *a* southern.

Australie [ɔstrali] *nf* Australia. ◆**australien, -ienne** *a & nmf* Australian.

autant [otɑ̃] *adv* **1 a. de . . . que** (*quantité*) as much . . . as; (*nombre*) as many . . . as; **il a a. d'argent/de pommes que vous** he has as much money/as many apples as you. **2 a. de** (*tant de*) so much; (*nombre*) so many; **je n'ai jamais vu a. d'argent/de pommes** I've never seen so much money/so many apples; **pourquoi manges-tu a.?** why are you eating so much? **3 a. que** (*souffrir, lire etc*) as much as; **il lit a. que vous/que possible** he reads as much as you/as possible; **il n'a jamais souffert a.** he's never suffered as *ou* so much; **a. que je sache** as far as I know; **d'a. (plus) que** all the more (so) since; **d'a. moins que** even less since; **a. avouer/etc** we, you *etc* might as well confess/*etc*; **en faire/dire a.** to do/say the same; **j'aimerais a. aller au cinéma** I'd just as soon go to the cinema.

autel [otɛl] *nm* altar.

auteur [otœr] *nm* (*de livre*) author, writer; (*de chanson*) composer; (*de procédé*) originator; (*de crime*) perpetrator; (*d'accident*) cause; **droit d'a.** copyright; **droits d'a.** royalties.

authenticité [otɑ̃tisite] *nf* authenticity. ◆**authentifier** *vt* to authenticate. ◆**authentique** *a* genuine, authentic.

autiste [otist] *a*, **autistique** *a* autistic.

auto [oto] *nf* car; **autos tamponneuses** bumper cars, dodgems.

auto- [oto] *préf* self-.

autobiographie [otobjɔgrafi] *nf* autobiography.

autobus [otobys] *nm* bus.

autocar [otokar] *nm* coach, bus.

autochtone [ɔtɔktɔn] *a & nmf* native.

autocollant [otokɔlɑ̃] *nm* sticker.

autocrate [otokrat] *nm* autocrat. ◆**autocratique** *a* autocratic.

autocuiseur [otokɥizœr] *nm* pressure cooker.

autodéfense [otodefɑ̃s] *nf* self-defence.

autodestruction [otodestryksjɔ̃] *nf* self-destruction.

autodidacte [otodidakt] *a & nmf* self-taught (person).

autodrome [otodrom] *nm* motor-racing track.

auto-école [otoekɔl] *nf* driving school, school of motoring.

autographe [otograf] *nm* autograph.

automate [ɔtɔmat] *nm* automaton. ◆**automation** *nf* automation. ◆**automatisation** *nf* automation. ◆**automatiser** *vt* to automate.

automatique [ɔtɔmatik] *a* automatic; – *nm* **l'a.** *Tél* direct dialling. ◆**—ment** *adv* automatically.

automne [otɔn] *nm* autumn, *Am* fall. ◆**automnal, -aux** *a* autumnal.

automobile [otɔmɔbil] *nf & a* (motor)car, *Am* automobile; **l'a.** *Sp* motoring; **Salon de l'a.** Motor Show; **canot a.** motor boat. ◆**automobiliste** *nmf* motorist.

autonome [otonɔm] *a* (*région etc*) autonomous, self-governing; (*personne*) *Fig* independent. ◆**autonomie** *nf* autonomy.

autopsie [ɔtɔpsi] *nf* autopsy, post-mortem.

autoradio [otoradjo] *nm* car radio.

autorail [otoraj] *nm* railcar.

autoris/er [ɔtɔrize] *vt* (*habiliter*) to authorize (à faire to do); (*permettre*) to permit (à faire to do). ◆**—é** *a* (*qualifié*) authoritative. ◆**autorisation** *nf* authorization; permission.

autorité [ɔtɔrite] *nf* authority. ◆**autoritaire** *a* authoritarian; (*homme, ton*) authoritative.

autoroute [otorut] *nf* motorway, *Am* highway, freeway.

auto-stop [otostɔp] *nm* hitchhiking; **faire de l'a.** to hitchhike. ◆**autostoppeur, -euse** *nmf* hitchhiker.

autour [otur] *adv* around; – *prép* **a. de** around.

autre [otr] *a & pron* other; **un a. livre** another book; **un a.** another (one); **d'autres** others; **as-tu d'autres questions?** have you any other *ou* further questions?; **qn/personne/rien d'a.** s.o./no one/nothing else; **a. chose/part** sth/somewhere else; **qui/quoi d'a.?** who/what else?; **l'un l'a., les uns les autres** each other; **l'un et l'a.** both (of them); **l'un ou l'a.** either (of them); **ni l'un ni l'a.** neither (of them); **les uns . . . les autres** some . . . others; **nous/vous autres Anglais** we/you English; **d'un moment à l'a.** any moment (now); **. . . et autres . . .** and so on. ◆**autrement** *adv* (*différemment*) differently; (*sinon*) otherwise; (*plus*) far more (**que** than); **pas a. satisfait/etc** not particularly satisfied/*etc*.

autrefois [otrəfwa] *adv* in the past, in days gone by.

Autriche [otriʃ] *nf* Austria. ◆**autrichien, -ienne** *a* & *nmf* Austrian.

autruche [otryʃ] *nf* ostrich.

autrui [otrɥi] *pron* others, other people.

auvent [ovã] *nm* awning, canopy.

aux [o] *voir* à.

auxiliaire [ɔksiljɛr] *a* auxiliary; − *nm Gram* auxiliary; − *nmf* (*aide*) helper, auxiliary.

auxquels, -elles [okɛl] *voir* lequel.

avachir (s') [savaʃir] *vpr* (*soulier, personne*) to become flabby *ou* limp.

avait [avɛ] *voir* avoir.

aval (en) [ãnaval] *adv* downstream (*de* from).

avalanche [avalãʃ] *nf* avalanche; *Fig* flood, avalanche.

avaler [avale] *vt* to swallow; (*livre*) to devour; (*mots*) to mumble; − *vi* to swallow.

avance [avãs] *nf* (*marche, acompte*) advance; (*de coureur, chercheur etc*) lead; *pl* (*galantes*) advances; **à l'a., d'a., par a.** in advance; **en a.** (*arriver, partir*) early; (*avant l'horaire prévu*) ahead (of time); (*dans son développement*) ahead, in advance; (*montre etc*) fast; **en a. sur** (*qn, son époque etc*) ahead of, in advance of; **avoir une heure d'a.** (*train etc*) to be an hour early.

avanc/er [avãse] *vt* (*thèse, argent*) to advance; (*date*) to bring forward; (*main, chaise*) to move forward; (*travail*) to speed up; − *vi* to advance, move forward; (*montre*) to be fast; (*faire saillie*) to jut out (*sur over*); **s'en â. âge** to be getting on (in years); − **s'a.** *vpr* to advance, move forward; (*faire saillie*) to jut out. ◆**−é** *a* advanced; (*saison*) well advanced. ◆**−ée** *nf* projection, overhang. ◆**−ement** *nm* advancement.

avanie [avani] *nf* affront, insult.

avant [avã] *prép* before; **a. de voir** before seeing; **a. qu'il (ne) parte** before he leaves; **a. huit jours** within a week; **a. tout** above all; **a. toute chose** first and foremost; **a. peu** before long; − *adv* before; **en a.** (*mouvement*) forward; (*en tête*) ahead; **en a. de** in front of; **bien a. dans** (*creuser etc*) very deep(ly) into; **la nuit d'a.** the night before; − *nm & a inv* front; − *nm* (*joueur*) *Sp* forward.

avantage [avãtaʒ] *nm* advantage; (*bénéfice*) *Fin* benefit; **tu as a. à le faire** it's worth your while to do it; **tirer a. de** to benefit from. ◆**avantager** *vt* (*favoriser*) to favour; (*faire valoir*) to show off to advantage. ◆**avantageux, -euse** *a* worthwhile, attractive; (*flatteur*) flattering; *Péj* conceited; **a. pour qn** advantageous to s.o.

avant-bras [avãbra] *nm inv* forearm. ◆**a.-centre** *nm Sp* centre-forward. ◆**a.-coureur** *am* a.-coureur de (*signe*) heralding. ◆**a.-dernier, -ière** *a* & *nmf* last but one. ◆**a.-garde** *nf Mil* advance guard; **d'a.-garde** (*idée, film etc*) avant-garde. ◆**a.-goût** *nm* foretaste. ◆**a.-guerre** *nm ou f* pre-war period; **d'a.-guerre** pre-war. ◆**a.-hier** [avãtjɛr] *adv* the day before yesterday. ◆**a.-poste** *nm* outpost. ◆**a.-première** *nf* preview. ◆**a.-propos** *nm inv* foreword. ◆**a.-veille** *nf* **l'a.-veille (de)** two days before.

avare [avar] *a* miserly; **a. de** (*compliments etc*) sparing of; − *nmf* miser. ◆**avarice** *nf* avarice.

avarie(s) [avari] *nf(pl)* damage. ◆**avarié** *a* (*aliment*) spoiled, rotting.

avatar [avatar] *nm Péj Fam* misadventure.

avec [avɛk] *prép* with; (*envers*) to(wards); **et a. ça?** (*dans un magasin*) *Fam* anything else?; − *adv* **il est venu a.** (*son chapeau etc*) *Fam* he came with it.

avenant [avnã] *a* pleasing, attractive; **à l'a.** in keeping (**de** with).

avènement [avɛnmã] *nm* **l'a. de** the coming *ou* advent of; (*roi*) the accession of.

avenir [avnir] *nm* future; **d'a.** (*personne, métier*) with future prospects; **à l'a.** (*désormais*) in future.

aventure [avãtyr] *nf* adventure; (*en amour*) affair; **à l'a.** (*marcher etc*) aimlessly; **dire la bonne a.** à qn to tell s.o.'s fortune. ◆**aventur/er** *vt* to risk; (*remarque*) to venture; (*réputation*) to risk; − **s'a.** *vpr* to venture (**sur** on to, **à faire** to do). ◆**−é** *a* risky. ◆**aventureux, -euse** *a* (*personne, vie*) adventurous; (*risqué*) risky. ◆**aventurier, -ière** *nmf Péj* adventurer.

avenue [avny] *nf* avenue.

avér/er (s') [savere] *vpr* (*juste etc*) to prove (to be); **il s'avère que** it turns out that. ◆**−é** *a* established.

averse [avɛrs] *nf* shower, downpour.

aversion [avɛrsjɔ̃] *nf* aversion (**pour** to).

avert/ir [avɛrtir] *vt* (*mettre en garde, menacer*) to warn; (*informer*) to notify, inform. ◆**−i** *a* informed. ◆**−issement** *nm* warning; notification; (*dans un livre*) foreword. ◆**−isseur** *nm Aut* horn; **a. d'incendie** fire alarm.

aveu, -x [avø] *nm* confession; **de l'a. de** by the admission of.

aveugle [avœgl] *a* blind; − *nmf* blind man, blind woman; **les aveugles** the blind. ◆**aveuglément** [-emã] *adv* blindly.

◆**aveugl/er** *vt* to blind. ◆**—ement**
[-əmɑ̃] *nm* (*égarement*) blindness.
aveuglette (à l') [alavœglɛt] *adv* blindly;
chercher qch à l'a. to grope for sth.
aviateur, -trice [avjatœr, -tris] *nmf* airman,
airwoman. ◆**aviation** *nf* (*industrie,
science*) aviation; (*armée de l'air*) air force;
(*avions*) aircraft; **l'a.** *Sp* flying; **d'a.** (*terrain,
base*) air-.
avide [avid] *a* (*rapace*) greedy (**de** for); **a.
d'apprendre**/*etc* (*désireux*) eager to
learn/*etc*. ◆**—ment** *adv* greedily. ◆**avidité** *nf* greed.
avilir [avilir] *vt* to degrade, debase.
avion [avjɔ̃] *nm* aircraft, (aero)plane, *Am*
airplane; **a. à réaction** jet; **a. de ligne**
airliner; **par a.** (*lettre*) airmail; **en a., par a.**
(*voyager*) by plane, by air; **aller en a.** to fly.
aviron [avirɔ̃] *nm* oar; **faire de l'a.** to row,
practise rowing.
avis [avi] *nm* opinion; *Pol Jur* judgement;
(*communiqué*) notice; (*conseil*) & *Fin*
advice; **à mon a.** in my opinion, to my
mind; **changer d'a.** to change one's mind.
avis/er [avize] *vt* to advise, inform; (*voir*)
to notice; **s'a. de qch** to realize sth suddenly; **s'a. de faire** to venture to do.
◆**—é** *a* prudent, wise; **bien/mal a.**
well-/ill-advised.
aviver [avive] *vt* (*couleur*) to bring out;
(*douleur*) to sharpen.
avocat, -ate [avɔka, -at] **1** *nmf* barrister,
counsel, *Am* attorney, counselor; (*d'une
cause*) *Fig* advocate. **2** *nm* (*fruit*) avocado
(pear).
avoine [avwan] *nf* oats; **farine d'a.** oatmeal.
avoir* [avwar] **1** *v aux* to have; **je l'ai vu** I've
seen him. **2** *vt* (*posséder*) to have; (*obtenir*)
to get; (*tromper*) *Fam* to take for a ride; **il a**
he has, he's got; **qu'est-ce que tu as?** what's
the matter with you?, what's wrong with
you?; **j'ai à lui parler** I have to speak

to her; **il n'a qu'à essayer** he only has to
try; **a. faim/chaud/*etc*** to be *ou* feel
hungry/hot/*etc*; **a. cinq ans/*etc*** to be
five (years old)/*etc*; **en a. pour longtemps** to
be busy for quite a while; **j'en ai pour dix
minutes** this will take me ten minutes; (*ne
bougez pas*) I'll be with you in ten minutes;
en a. pour son argent to get *ou* have one's
money's worth; **en a. après *ou* contre** to
have a grudge against. **3** *v imp* **il y a** there is,
pl there are; **il y a six ans** six years ago; **il
n'y a pas de quoi!** don't mention it!;
qu'est-ce qu'il y a? what's the matter?,
what's wrong? **4** *nm* assets, property; (*d'un
compte*) *Fin* credit.
avoisin/er [avwazine] *vt* to border on.
◆**—ant** *a* neighbouring, nearby.
avort/er [avɔrte] *vi* (*projet etc*) *Fig* to
miscarry, fail; (**se faire**) **a.** (*femme*) to have
ou get an abortion. ◆**—ement** *nm* abortion; *Fig* failure. ◆**avorton** *nm* *Péj* runt,
puny shrimp.
avou/er [avwe] *vt* to confess, admit (**que**
that); **s'a. vaincu** to admit defeat; – *vi*
(*coupable*) to confess. ◆**—é** *a* (*ennemi, but*)
avowed; – *nm* solicitor, *Am* attorney.
avril [avril] *nm* April; **un poisson d'a.** (*farce*)
an April fool joke.
axe [aks] *nm* *Math* axis; (*essieu*) axle; (*d'une
politique*) broad direction; **grands axes**
(*routes*) main roads. ◆**axer** *vt* to centre; **il
est axé sur** his mind is drawn towards.
axiome [aksjom] *nm* axiom.
ayant [ejɑ̃] *voir* **avoir**.
azalée [azale] *nf* (*plante*) azalea.
azimuts [azimyt] *nmpl* **dans tous les a.** *Fam*
all over the place, here there and everywhere; **tous a.** (*guerre, publicité etc*) all-out.
azote [azɔt] *nm* nitrogen.
azur [azyr] *nm* azure, (sky) blue; **la Côte
d'A.** the (French) Riviera.
azyme [azim] *a* (*pain*) unleavened.

B

B, b [be] *nm* B, b.
babeurre [babœr] *nm* buttermilk.
babill/er [babije] *vi* to prattle, babble.
◆**—age** *nm* prattle, babble.
babines [babin] *nfpl* (*lèvres*) chops, chaps.
babiole [babjɔl] *nf* (*objet*) knick-knack;
(*futilité*) trifle.
bâbord [babɔr] *nm* *Nau Av* port (side).

babouin [babwɛ̃] *nm* baboon.
baby-foot [babifut] *nm inv* table *ou* miniature football.
bac [bak] *nm* **1** (*bateau*) ferry(boat). **2** (*cuve*)
tank; **b. à glace** ice tray; **b. à laver** washtub.
3 *abrév* = **baccalauréat**.
baccalauréat [bakalɔrea] *nm* school leaving certificate.

bâche [baʃ] *nf* (*toile*) tarpaulin. ◆**bâcher** *vt* to cover over (*with a tarpaulin*).

bacheller, -ière [baʃəlje, -jɛr] *nmf* holder of the *baccalauréat*.

bachot [baʃo] *nm abrév* = **baccalauréat**. ◆**bachoter** *vi* to cram (*for an exam*).

bacille [basil] *nm* bacillus, germ.

bâcler [bɑkle] *vt* (*travail*) to dash off carelessly, botch (up).

bactéries [bakteri] *nfpl* bacteria. ◆**bactériologique** *a* bacteriological; **la guerre b.** germ warfare.

badaud, -aude [bado, -od] *nmf* (*inquisitive*) onlooker, bystander.

baderne [badɛrn] *nf* **vieille b.** *Péj* old fogey, old fuddy-duddy.

badigeon [badiʒɔ̃] *nm* whitewash. ◆**badigeonner** *vt* (*mur*) to whitewash, distemper; (*écorchure*) *Méd* to paint, coat.

badin [badɛ̃] *a* (*peu sérieux*) light-hearted, playful. ◆**badin/er** *vi* to jest, joke; **b. avec** (*prendre à la légère*) to trifle with. ◆—**age** *nm* banter, jesting.

badine [badin] *nf* cane, switch.

bafouer [bafwe] *vt* to mock *ou* scoff at.

bafouiller [bafuje] *vti* to stammer, splutter.

bâfrer [bɑfre] *vi Fam* to stuff oneself (with food).

bagage [bagaʒ] *nm* (*valise etc*) piece of luggage *ou* baggage; (*connaissances*) *Fig* (fund of) knowledge; *pl* (*ensemble des valises*) luggage, baggage. ◆**bagagiste** *nm* baggage handler.

bagarre [bagar] *nf* brawl. ◆**bagarrer** *vi Fam* to fight, struggle; **— se b.** *vpr* to fight, brawl; (*se disputer*) to fight, quarrel.

bagatelle [bagatɛl] *nf* trifle, mere bagatelle; **la b. de** *Iron* the trifling sum of.

bagne [baɲ] *nm* convict prison; **c'est le b. ici** *Fig* this place is a real hell hole *ou* workhouse. ◆**bagnard** *nm* convict.

bagnole [baɲɔl] *nf Fam* car; **vieille b.** *Fam* old banger.

bagou(t) [bagu] *nm Fam* glibness; **avoir du b.** to have the gift of the gab.

bague [bag] *nf* (*anneau*) ring; (*de cigare*) band. ◆**bagué** *a* (*doigt*) ringed.

baguenauder [bagnode] *vi*, **— se b.** *vpr* to loaf around, saunter.

baguette [bagɛt] *nf* (*canne*) stick; (*de chef d'orchestre*) baton; (*pain*) (long thin) loaf, stick of bread; *pl* (*de tambour*) drumsticks; (*pour manger*) chopsticks; **b. (magique)** (magic) wand; **mener à la b.** to rule with an iron hand.

bah! [bɑ] *int* really!, bah!

bahut [bay] *nm* (*meuble*) chest, cabinet; (*lycée*) *Fam* school.

baie [bɛ] *nf* **1** *Géog* bay. **2** *Bot* berry. **3** (*fenêtre*) picture window.

baignade [bɛɲad] *nf* (*bain*) bathe, bathing; (*endroit*) bathing place. ◆**baign/er** *vt* (*immerger*) to bathe; (*enfant*) to bath, *Am* bathe; **b. les rivages** (*mer*) to wash the shores; **baigné de** (*sueur, lumière*) bathed in; (*sang*) soaked in; **— vi b. dans** (*tremper*) to soak in; (*être imprégné de*) to be steeped in; **— se b.** *vpr* to go swimming *ou* bathing; (*dans une baignoire*) to have *ou* take a bath. ◆—**eur, -euse 1** *nmf* bather. **2** *nm* (*poupée*) baby doll. ◆**baignoire** *nf* bath (tub).

ball, *pl* **baux** [baj, bo] *nm* lease. ◆**bailleur** *nm Jur* lessor; **b. de fonds** financial backer.

bâill/er [bɑje] *vi* to yawn; (*chemise etc*) to gape; (*porte*) to stand ajar. ◆—**ement** *nm* yawn; gaping.

bâillon [bɑjɔ̃] *nm* gag. ◆**bâillonner** *vt* (*victime, presse etc*) to gag.

bain [bɛ̃] *nm* bath; (*de mer*) swim, bathe; **salle de bain(s)** bathroom; **être dans le b.** (*au courant*) *Fam* to have got into the swing of things; **petit/grand b.** (*piscine*) shallow/deep end; **b. de bouche** mouthwash. ◆**b.-marie** *nm* (*pl* **bains-marie**) *Culin* double boiler.

baïonnette [bajɔnɛt] *nf* bayonet.

baiser [beze] **1** *vt* **b. au front/sur la joue** to kiss on the forehead/cheek; **— nm** kiss; **bons baisers** (*dans une lettre*) (with) love. **2** *vt* (*duper*) *Fam* to con.

baisse [bɛs] *nf* fall, drop (**de** in); **en b.** (*température*) falling.

baisser [bese] *vt* (*voix, prix etc*) to lower, drop; (*tête*) to bend; (*radio, chauffage*) to turn down; **— vi** (*prix, niveau etc*) to drop, go down; (*soleil*) to go down, sink; (*marée*) to go out, ebb; (*santé, popularité*) to decline; **— se b.** *vpr* to bend down, stoop.

bajoues [baʒu] *nfpl* (*d'animal, de personne*) chops.

bal, *pl* **bals** [bal] *nm* (*réunion de grand apparat*) ball; (*populaire*) dance; (*lieu*) dance hall.

balade [balad] *nf Fam* walk; (*en auto*) drive; (*excursion*) tour. ◆**balader** *vt* (*enfant etc*) to take for a walk *ou* drive; (*objet*) to trail around; **— se b.** *vpr* (*à pied*) to (go for a) walk; (*excursionner*) to tour (around); **se b.** (*en voiture*) to go for a drive. ◆**baladeur** *nm* Walkman®. ◆**baladeuse** *nf* inspection lamp.

balafre [balafr] *nf* (*blessure*) gash, slash;

(*cicatrice*) scar. ◆**balafrer** *vt* to gash, slash; to scar.

balai [balɛ] *nm* broom; **b. mécanique** carpet sweeper; **manche à b.** broomstick; *Av* joystick. ◆**b.-brosse** *nm* (*pl* **balais-brosses**) garden brush *ou* broom (*for scrubbing paving stones*).

balance [balɑ̃s] *nf* (*instrument*) (pair of) scales; (*équilibre*) *Pol Fin* balance; **la B.** (*signe*) Libra; **mettre en b.** to balance, weigh up.

balanc/er [balɑ̃se] *vt* (*bras*) to swing; (*hanches, tête, branches*) to sway; (*lancer*) *Fam* to chuck; (*se débarrasser de*) *Fam* to chuck out; **b. un compte** *Fin* to balance an account; **— se b.** *vpr* (*personne*) to swing (from side to side); (*arbre, bateau etc*) to sway; **je m'en balance!** I couldn't care less! ◆**—é a bien b.** (*phrase*) well-balanced; (*personne*) *Fam* well-built. ◆**—ement** *nm* swinging; swaying. ◆**balancier** *nm* (*d'horloge*) pendulum; (*de montre*) balance wheel. ◆**balançoire** *nf* (*escarpolette*) swing; (*bascule*) seesaw.

balayer [baleje] *vt* (*chambre, rue*) to sweep (out *ou* up); (*enlever, chasser*) to sweep away; **le vent balayait la plaine** the wind swept the plain. ◆**balayette** [balejɛt] *nf* (hand) brush; (*balai*) short-handled broom. ◆**balayeur, -euse** [balejœr, -øz] *nmf* roadsweeper.

balbutier [balbysje] *vti* to stammer.

balcon [balkɔ̃] *nm* balcony; *Th Cin* dress circle.

baldaquin [baldakɛ̃] *nm* (*de lit etc*) canopy.

baleine [balɛn] *nf* (*animal*) whale; (*fanon*) whalebone; (*de parapluie*) rib. ◆**baleinier** *nm* (*navire*) whaler. ◆**baleinière** *nf* whaleboat.

balise [baliz] *nf Nau* beacon; *Av* (ground) light; *Aut* road sign. ◆**balis/er** *vt* to mark with beacons *ou* lights; (*route*) to signpost. ◆**—age** *nm Nau* beacons; *Av* lighting; *Aut* signposting.

balistique [balistik] *a* ballistic.

balivernes [balivɛrn] *nfpl* balderdash, nonsense.

ballade [balad] *nf* (*légende*) ballad; (*poème court*) & *Mus* ballade.

ballant [balɑ̃] *a* (*bras, jambes*) dangling.

ballast [balast] *nm* ballast.

balle [bal] *nf* (*de tennis, golf etc*) ball; (*projectile*) bullet; (*paquet*) bale; *pl* (*francs*) *Fam* francs; **se renvoyer la b.** to pass the buck (to each other).

ballet [balɛ] *nm* ballet. ◆**ballerine** *nf* ballerina.

ballon [balɔ̃] *nm* (*jouet d'enfant*) & *Av* balloon; (*sport*) ball; **b. de football** football; **lancer un b. d'essai** *Fig* to put out a feeler. ◆**ballonné** *a* (*ventre*) bloated, swollen. ◆**ballot** *nm* (*paquet*) bundle; (*imbécile*) *Fam* idiot.

ballottage [balɔtaʒ] *nm* (*scrutin*) second ballot (*no candidate having achieved the required number of votes*).

ballotter [balɔte] *vti* to shake (about); **ballotté entre** (*sentiments contraires*) torn between.

balnéaire [balneɛr] *a* **station b.** seaside resort.

balourd, -ourde [balur, -urd] *nmf* (clumsy) oaf. ◆**balourdise** *nf* clumsiness, oafishness; (*gaffe*) blunder.

Baltique [baltik] *nf* **la B.** the Baltic.

balustrade [balystrad] *nf* (hand)rail, railing(s).

bambin [bɑ̃bɛ̃] *nm* tiny tot, toddler.

bambou [bɑ̃bu] *nm* bamboo.

ban [bɑ̃] *nm* (*de tambour*) roll; (*applaudissements*) round of applause; *pl* (*de mariage*) banns; **mettre qn au b. de** to cast s.o. out from, outlaw s.o. from; **un b. pour . . .** three cheers for . . . .

banal, mpl -als [banal] *a* (*fait, accident etc*) commonplace, banal; (*idée, propos*) banal, trite. ◆**banalisé** *a* (*voiture de police*) unmarked. ◆**banalité** *nf* banality; *pl* (*propos*) banalities.

banane [banan] *nf* banana.

banc [bɑ̃] *nm* (*siège, établi*) bench; (*de poissons*) shoal; **b. d'église** pew; **b. d'essai** *Fig* testing ground; **b. de sable** sandbank; **b. des accusés** *Jur* dock.

bancaire [bɑ̃kɛr] *a* (*opération*) banking-; (*chèque*) bank-.

bancal, mpl -als [bɑ̃kal] *a* (*personne*) bandy, bow-legged; (*meuble*) wobbly; (*idée*) shaky.

bande [bɑ̃d] *nf* **1** (*de terrain, papier etc*) strip; (*de film*) reel; (*de journal*) wrapper; (*rayure*) stripe; (*de fréquences*) *Rad* band; (*pansement*) bandage; (*sur la chaussée*) line; **b. (magnétique)** tape; **b. vidéo** videotape; **b. sonore** sound track; **b. dessinée** comic strip, strip cartoon; **par la b.** indirectly. **2** (*groupe*) gang, troop, band; (*de chiens*) pack; (*d'oiseaux*) flock; **on a fait b. à part** we split into our own group; **b. d'idiots!** you load of idiots! ◆**bandeau, -x** *nm* (*sur les yeux*) blindfold; (*pour la tête*) headband; (*pansement*) head bandage. ◆**band/er** *vt* (*blessure etc*) to bandage; (*yeux*) to blindfold; (*arc*) to bend; (*muscle*) to tense. ◆**—age** *nm* (*pansement*) bandage.

banderole [bɑ̃drɔl] *nf* (*sur mât*) pennant, streamer; (*sur montants*) banner.

bandit [bɑ̃di] *nm* robber, bandit; (*enfant*) *Fam* rascal. ◆**banditisme** *nm* crime.

bandoulière [bɑ̃duljɛr] *nf* shoulder strap; **en b.** slung across the shoulder.

banjo [bɑ̃(d)ʒo] *nm* *Mus* banjo.

banlieue [bɑ̃ljø] *nf* suburbs, outskirts; **la grande b.** the outer suburbs; **de b.** (*magasin etc*) suburban; (*train*) commuter-. ◆**banlieusard, -arde** *nmf* (*habitant*) suburbanite; (*voyageur*) commuter.

banne [ban] *nf* (*de magasin*) awning.

bannière [banjɛr] *nf* banner.

bann/ir [banir] *vt* (*exiler*) to banish; (*supprimer*) to ban, outlaw. ◆**—issement** *nm* banishment.

banque [bɑ̃k] *nf* bank; (*activité*) banking.

banqueroute [bɑ̃krut] *nf* (fraudulent) bankruptcy.

banquet [bɑ̃kɛ] *nm* banquet.

banquette [bɑ̃kɛt] *nf* (bench) seat.

banquier [bɑ̃kje] *nm* banker.

banquise [bɑ̃kiz] *nf* ice floe *ou* field.

baptême [batɛm] *nm* christening, baptism; **b. du feu** baptism of fire; **b. de l'air** first flight. ◆**baptiser** *vt* (*enfant*) to christen, baptize; (*appeler*) *Fig* to christen.

baquet [bakɛ] *nm* tub, basin.

bar [bar] *nm* **1** (*lieu, comptoir, meuble*) bar. **2** (*poisson marin*) bass.

baragouin [baragwɛ̃] *nm* gibberish, gabble. ◆**baragouiner** *vt* (*langue*) to gabble (a few words of); — *vi* to gabble away.

baraque [barak] *nf* hut, shack; (*maison*) *Fam* house, place; *Péj* hovel; (*de forain*) stall. ◆**—ment** *nm* (makeshift) huts.

baratin [baratɛ̃] *nm* *Fam* sweet talk; *Com* patter. ◆**baratiner** *vt* to chat up; *Am* sweet-talk.

barbare [barbar] *a* (*manières, crime*) barbaric; (*peuple, invasions*) barbarian; — *nmf* barbarian. ◆**barbarie** *nf* (*cruauté*) barbarity. ◆**barbarisme** *nm* *Gram* barbarism.

barbe [barb] *nf* beard; **une b. de trois jours** three days' growth of beard; **se faire la b.** to shave; **à la b. de** under the nose(s) of; **rire dans sa b.** to laugh up one's sleeve; **la b.!** enough!; **quelle b.!** what a drag!; **b. à papa** candyfloss, *Am* cotton candy.

barbecue [barbəkju] *nm* barbecue.

barbelé [barbəle] *a* barbed; — *nmpl* barbed wire.

barb/er [barbe] *vt* *Fam* to bore (stiff); — **se**

b. *vpr* to be *ou* get bored (stiff). ◆**—ant** *a* *Fam* boring.

barbiche [barbiʃ] *nf* goatee (beard).

barbiturique [barbityrik] *nm* barbiturate.

barbot/er [barbɔte] **1** *vi* (*s'agiter*) to splash about, paddle. **2** *vt* (*voler*) *Fam* to filch. ◆**—euse** *nf* (*de bébé*) rompers.

barbouill/er [barbuje] *vt* (*salir*) to smear; (*peindre*) to daub; (*gribouiller*) to scribble; **avoir l'estomac barbouillé** *Fam* to feel queasy. ◆**—age** *nm* smear; daub; scribble.

barbu [barby] *a* bearded.

barda [barda] *nm* *Fam* gear; (*de soldat*) kit.

bardé [barde] *a* **b. de** (*décorations etc*) covered with.

barder [barde] *v imp* **ça va b.!** *Fam* there'll be fireworks!

barème [barɛm] *nm* (*des tarifs*) table; (*des salaires*) scale; (*livre de comptes*) ready reckoner.

baril [bari(l)] *nm* barrel; **b. de poudre** powder keg.

bariolé [barjɔle] *a* brightly-coloured.

barman, *pl* **-men** *ou* **-mans** [barman, -mɛn] *nm* barman, *Am* bartender.

baromètre [barɔmɛtr] *nm* barometer.

baron, -onne [barɔ̃, -ɔn] *nm* baron; — *nf* baroness.

baroque [barɔk] **1** *a* (*idée etc*) bizarre, weird. **2** *a & nm* *Archit Mus etc* baroque.

baroud [barud] *nm* **b. d'honneur** *Arg* gallant last fight.

barque [bark] *nf* (small) boat.

barre [bar] *nf* bar; (*trait*) line, stroke; *Nau* helm; **b. de soustraction** minus sign; **b. fixe** *Sp* horizontal bar. ◆**barreau, -x** *nm* (*de fenêtre etc*) & *Jur* bar; (*d'échelle*) rung.

barr/er [bare] **1** *vt* (*route etc*) to block (off), close (off); (*porte*) to bar; (*chèque*) to cross; (*phrase*) to cross out; *Nau* to steer; **b. la route à qn, b. qn** to bar s.o.'s way; **'rue barrée'** 'road closed'. **2 se b.** *vpr* *Arg* to hop it, make off. ◆**—age** *nm* (*sur une route*) roadblock; (*barrière*) barrier; (*ouvrage hydraulique*) dam; (*de petite rivière*) weir; **le b. d'une rue** the closure of a street; **tir de b.** barrage fire; **b. d'agents** cordon of police. ◆**—eur** *nm* *Sp Nau* cox.

barrette [barɛt] *nf* (*pince*) (hair)slide, *Am* barrette.

barricade [barikad] *nf* barricade. ◆**barricader** *vt* to barricade; — **se b.** *vpr* to barricade oneself.

barrière [barjɛr] *nf* (*porte*) gate; (*clôture*) fence; (*obstacle, mur*) barrier.

barrique [barik] *nf* (large) barrel.

baryton [baritɔ̃] *nm* baritone.

bas¹, basse [ba, bas] *a* (*table, prix etc*) low; (*âme, action*) base, mean; (*partie de ville etc*) lower; (*origine*) lowly; **au b. mot** at the very least; **enfant en b. âge** young child; **avoir la vue basse** to be short-sighted; **le b. peuple** *Péj* the lower orders; **coup b.** *Boxe* blow below the belt; – *adv* low; (*parler*) in a whisper, softly; **mettre b.** (*animal*) to give birth; **mettre b. les armes** to lay down one's arms; **jeter b.** to overthrow; **plus b.** further *ou* lower down; **en b.** down (below); (*par l'escalier*) downstairs, down below; **en** *ou* **au b. de** at the foot *ou* bottom of; **de haut en b.** from top to bottom; **sauter à b. du lit** to jump out of bed; **à b. les dictateurs/etc!** down with dictators/*etc*!; – *nm* (*de côte, page etc*) bottom, foot; **du b.** (*tiroir, étagère*) bottom.

bas² [ba] *nm* (*chaussette*) stocking; **b. de laine** *Fig* nest egg.

basané [bazane] *a* (*visage etc*) tanned.

bas-bleu [bablø] *nm Péj* bluestocking.

bas-côté [bakote] *nm* (*de route*) roadside, shoulder.

bascule [baskyl] *nf* (**jeu de**) **b.** (game of) seesaw; (**balance à**) **b.** weighing machine; **cheval/fauteuil à b.** rocking horse/chair. ◆**basculer** *vti* (*personne*) to topple over; (*benne*) to tip up.

base [baz] *nf* base; (*principe fondamental*) basis, foundation; **de b.** (*salaire etc*) basic; **produit à b. de lait** milk-based product; **militant de b.** rank-and-file militant. ◆**baser** *vt* to base; **se b. sur** to base oneself on.

bas-fond [bafɔ̃] *nm* (*eau*) shallows; (*terrain*) low ground; *pl* (*population*) *Péj* dregs.

basilic [bazilik] *nm Bot Culin* basil.

basilique [bazilik] *nf* basilica.

basket(-ball) [basket(bɔl)] *nm* basketball.

basque [bask] **1** *a* & *nmf* Basque. **2** *nfpl* (*pans de veste*) skirts.

basse [bas] *1 voir* **bas¹. 2** *nf Mus* bass.

basse-cour [baskur] *nf* (*pl* **basses-cours**) farmyard.

bassement [basmɑ̃] *adv* basely, meanly. ◆**bassesse** *nf* baseness, meanness; (*action*) base *ou* mean act.

bassin [basɛ̃] *nm* (*pièce d'eau*) pond; (*piscine*) pool; (*cuvette*) bowl, basin; (*rade*) dock; *Anat* pelvis; *Géog* basin; **b. houiller** coalfield. ◆**bassine** *nf* bowl.

basson [basɔ̃] *nm* (*instrument*) bassoon; (*musicien*) bassoonist.

bastingage [bastɛ̃gaʒ] *nm Nau* bulwarks, rail.

bastion [bastjɔ̃] *nm* bastion.

bastringue [bastrɛ̃g] *nm* (*bal*) *Fam* popular dance hall; (*tapage*) *Arg* shindig, din; (*attirail*) *Arg* paraphernalia.

bas-ventre [bavɑ̃tr] *nm* lower abdomen.

bat [ba] *voir* **battre**.

bât [ba] *nm* packsaddle.

bataclan [bataklɑ̃] *nm Fam* paraphernalia; **et tout le b.** *Fam* and the whole caboodle.

bataille [bataj] *nf* battle; *Cartes* beggar-my-neighbour. ◆**batail/er** *vi* to fight, battle. ◆**—eur, -euse** *nmf* fighter; – *a* belligerent. ◆**bataillon** *nm* battalion.

bâtard, -arde [batar, -ard] *a* & *nmf* bastard; **chien b.** mongrel; **œuvre bâtarde** hybrid work.

bateau, -x [bato] *nm* boat; (*grand*) ship. ◆**b.-citerne** *nm* (*pl* **bateaux-citernes**) tanker. ◆**b.-mouche** *nm* (*pl* **bateaux-mouches**) (*sur la Seine*) pleasure boat.

batifoler [batifole] *vi Hum* to fool *ou* lark about.

bâtiment [batimɑ̃] *nm* (*édifice*) building; (*navire*) vessel; **le b., l'industrie du b.** the building trade; **ouvrier du b.** building worker. ◆**bât/ir** *vt* (*construire*) to build; (*coudre*) to baste, tack; **terrain à b.** building site. ◆**—i** *a* **bien b.** well-built; – *nm* *Menuis* frame, support. ◆**bâtisse** *nf Péj* building. ◆**bâtisseur, -euse** *nmf* builder (**de** of).

bâton [batɔ̃] *nm* (*canne*) stick; (*de maréchal, d'agent*) baton; **b. de rouge** lipstick; **donner des coups de b. à qn** to beat s.o. (with a stick); **parler à bâtons rompus** to ramble from one subject to another; **mettre des bâtons dans les roues à qn** to put obstacles in s.o.'s way.

batterie [batri] *nf Mil Aut* battery; **la b.** *Mus* the drums; **b. de cuisine** set of kitchen utensils.

batt/re* [batr] **1** *vt* (*frapper, vaincre*) to beat; (*blé*) to thresh; (*cartes*) to shuffle; (*pays, chemins*) to scour; (*à coups redoublés*) to batter, pound; **b. la mesure** to beat time; **b. à mort** to batter *ou* beat to death; **b. pavillon** to fly a flag; – *vi* to beat; (*porte*) to bang; **b. des mains** to clap (one's hands); **b. des paupières** to blink; **b. des ailes** (*oiseau*) to flap its wings; **le vent fait b. la porte** the wind bangs the door. **2 se b.** *vpr* to fight. ◆**—ant 1** *a* (*pluie*) driving; (*porte*) swing-. **2** *nm* (*de cloche*) tongue; (*vantail de porte etc*) flap; **porte à deux battants** double door. **3** *nm* (*personne*) fighter. ◆**—u** **chemin** *ou* **sentier b.** beaten track. ◆**—age** *nm* (*du blé*) threshing; (*publicité*) *Fam*

publicity, hype, ballyhoo. ◆**—ement** *nm*
(*de cœur, de tambour*) beat; (*délai*) interval;
battements de cœur palpitations. ◆**—eur**
nm (*musicien*) percussionist; **b. à œufs** egg
beater.

baudet [bodɛ] *nm* donkey.

baume [bom] *nm* (*résine*) & *Fig* balm.

baux [bo] *voir* **bail**.

bavard, -arde [bavar, -ard] *a* (*loquace*) talkative; (*cancanier*) gossipy; – *nmf* chatterbox; gossip. ◆**bavard/er** *vi* to chat, chatter; (*papoter*) to gossip; (*divulguer*) to blab.
◆**—age** *nm* chatting, chatter(ing);
gossip(ing).

bave [bav] *nf* dribble, slobber; foam; (*de
limace*) slime. ◆**baver** *vi* to dribble, slobber; (*chien enragé*) to foam; (*encre*) to
smudge; **en b.** *Fam* to have a rough time of
it. ◆**bavette** *nf* bib. ◆**baveux, -euse** *a*
(*bouche*) slobbery; (*omelette*) runny.
◆**bavoir** *nm* bib. ◆**bavure** *nf* smudge;
(*erreur*) blunder; **sans b.** perfect(ly), flaw-
less(ly).

bazar [bazar] *nm* (*magasin, marché*) bazaar;
(*désordre*) mess, clutter; (*attirail*) *Fam*
stuff, gear. ◆**bazarder** *vt* *Fam* to sell off,
get rid of.

bazooka [bazuka] *nm* bazooka.

béant [beɑ̃] *a* (*plaie*) gaping; (*gouffre*)
yawning.

béat [bea] *a Péj* smug; (*heureux*) *Hum* blissful. ◆**béatitude** *nf Hum* bliss.

beau (*or* **bel** *before vowel or mute h*), **belle**,
pl **beaux, belles** [bo, bɛl] *a* (*femme, fleur
etc*) beautiful, attractive; (*homme*) handsome, good-looking; (*voyage, temps etc*)
fine, lovely; **au b. milieu** right in the
middle; **j'ai b. crier/essayer/etc** it's no use
(my) shouting/trying/*etc*; **un b. morceau** a
good *or* sizeable bit; **de plus belle** (*recommencer etc*) worse than ever; **bel et bien**
really; – *nm* **le b.** the beautiful; **faire le b.**
(*chien*) to sit up and beg; **le plus b. de**
l'histoire the best part of the story; – *nf*
(*femme*) beauty; *Sp* deciding game.

beaucoup [boku] *adv* (*lire etc*) a lot, a great
deal; **aimer b.** to like very much;
s'intéresser b. à to be very interested in; **b.**
de (*livres etc*) many, a lot *ou* a great deal of;
(*courage etc*) a lot *ou* a great deal of, much;
pas b. d'argent/etc not much money/*etc*;
j'en ai b. (*quantité*) I have a lot; (*nombre*) I
have many; **b. plus/moins** much
more/less; many more/fewer; **b. trop**
much too much; many too many; **de b.** by
far; **b. sont . . .** many are . . . .

beau-fils [bofis] *nm* (*pl* **beaux-fils**) (*d'un*

précédent mariage) stepson; (*gendre*)
son-in-law. ◆**b.-frère** *nm* (*pl*
beaux-frères) brother-in-law. ◆**b.-père**
nm (*pl* **beaux-pères**) father-in-law; (*parâ-
tre*) stepfather.

beauté [bote] *nf* beauty; **institut** *ou* **salon de**
b. beauty parlour; **en b.** (*gagner etc*)
magnificently; **être en b.** to look one's very
best; **de toute b.** beautiful.

beaux-arts [bozar] *nmpl* fine arts.
◆**b.-parents** *nmpl* parents-in-law.

bébé [bebe] *nm* baby; **b.-lion/etc** (*pl*
bébés-lions/etc) baby lion/*etc.*

bébête [bebɛt] *a Fam* silly.

bec [bɛk] *nm* (*d'oiseau*) beak, bill; (*de
cruche*) lip, spout; (*de plume*) nib; (*bouche*)
Fam mouth; *Mus* mouthpiece; **coup de b.**
peck; **b. de gaz** gas lamp; **clouer le b. à qn**
Fam to shut s.o. up; **tomber sur un b.** *Fam*
to come up against a serious snag.
◆**b.-de-cane** *nm* (*pl* **becs-de-cane**) door
handle.

bécane [bekan] *nf Fam* bike.

bécarre [bekar] *nm Mus* natural.

bécasse [bekas] *nf* (*oiseau*) woodcock;
(*personne*) *Fam* simpleton.

bêche [bɛʃ] *nf* spade. ◆**bêcher** *vt* 1
(*cultiver*) to dig. **2** *Fig* to criticize; (*snober*)
to snub. ◆**bêcheur, -euse** *nmf* snob.

bécot [beko] *nm Fam* kiss. ◆**bécoter** *vt,* —
se b. *vpr Fam* to kiss.

becquée [beke] *nf* beakful; **donner la b. à**
(*oiseau, enfant*) to feed. ◆**becqueter** *vt*
(*picorer*) to peck (at); (*manger*) *Fam* to eat.

bedaine [bədɛn] *nf Fam* paunch, potbelly.

bedeau, -x [bədo] *nm* beadle, verger.

bedon [bədɔ̃] *nm Fam* paunch. ◆**bedonnant** *a* paunchy, potbellied.

bée [be] *a* **bouche b.** open-mouthed.

beffroi [befrwa] *nm* belfry.

bégayer [begeje] *vi* to stutter, stammer.
◆**bègue** [bɛg] *nmf* stutterer, stammerer;
– *a* **être b.** to stutter, stammer.

bégueule [begœl] *a* prudish; – *nf* prude.

béguin [begɛ̃] *nm* **avoir le b. pour qn** *Fam* to
have taken a fancy to s.o.

beige [bɛʒ] *a & nm* beige.

beignet [bɛɲɛ] *nm Culin* fritter.

bel [bɛl] *voir* **beau**.

bêler [bele] *vi* to bleat.

belette [bəlɛt] *nf* weasel.

Belgique [bɛlʒik] *nf* Belgium. ◆**belge** *a &*
nmf Belgian.

bélier [belje] *nm* (*animal, machine*) ram; **le**
B. (*signe*) Aries.

belle [bɛl] *voir* **beau**.

belle-fille [bɛlfij] *nf* (*pl* **belles-filles**) (*d'un* *précédent mariage*) stepdaughter; (*bru*) daughter-in-law. ◆**b.-mère** *nf* (*pl* **belles-mères**) mother-in-law; (*marâtre*) stepmother, ◆**b.-sœur** *nf* (*pl* **belles-sœurs**) sister-in-law.

belligérant [beliʒerã] *a & nm* belligerent.

belliqueux, -euse [belikø, -øz] *a* warlike; *Fig* aggressive.

belvédère [belvedɛr] *nm* (*sur une route*) viewpoint.

bémol [bemɔl] *nm Mus* flat.

bénédiction [benediksjɔ̃] *nf* blessing, benediction.

bénéfice [benefis] *nm* (*gain*) profit; (*avantage*) benefit; **b.** (**ecclésiastique**) living, benefice. ◆**bénéficiaire** *nmf* beneficiary; – *a* (*marge, solde*) profit-. ◆**bénéficier** *vi* **b. de** to benefit from, have the benefit of. ◆**bénéfique** *a* beneficial.

Bénélux [benelyks] *nm* Benelux.

benêt [bənɛ] *nm* simpleton; – *am* simple-minded.

bénévole [benevɔl] *a* voluntary, unpaid.

bénin, -igne [benɛ̃, -ip] *a* (*tumeur, critique*) benign; (*accident*) minor.

bénir [benir] *vt* to bless; (*exalter, remercier*) to give thanks to. ◆**bénit** *a* (*pain*) consecrated; **eau bénite** holy water. ◆**bénitier** [-itje] *nm* (holy-water) stoup.

benjamin, -ine [bɛ̃ʒamɛ̃, -in] *nmf* youngest child; *Sp* young junior.

benne [bɛn] *nf* (*de grue*) scoop; (*à charbon*) tub, skip; (*de téléphérique*) cable car; **camion à b. basculante** dump truck; **b. à ordures** skip.

béotien, -ienne [beɔsjɛ̃, -jɛn] *nmf* (*inculte*) philistine.

béquille [bekij] *nf* (*canne*) crutch; (*de moto*) stand.

bercail [berkaj] *nm* (*famille etc*) *Hum* fold.

berceau, -x [berso] *nm* cradle.

berc/er [berse] *vt* (*balancer*) to rock; (*apaiser*) to lull; (*leurrer*) to delude (**de** with); **se b. d'illusions** to delude oneself. ◆**—euse** *nf* lullaby.

béret [berɛ] *nm* beret.

berge [bɛrʒ] *nm* (*rivage*) (raised) bank.

berger, -ère [berʒe, -er] **1** *nm* shepherd; **chien (de) b.** sheepdog; – *nf* shepherdess. **2** *nm* **b. allemand** Alsatian (dog), *Am* German shepherd. ◆**bergerie** *nf* sheepfold.

berline [berlin] *nf Aut* (four-door) saloon, *Am* sedan.

berlingot [berlɛ̃go] *nm* (*bonbon aux fruits*) boiled sweet; (*à la menthe*) mint; (*emballage*) (milk) carton.

berlue [berly] *nf* **avoir la b.** to be seeing things.

berne (en) [ãbern] *adv* at half-mast.

berner [berne] *vt* to fool, hoodwink.

besogne [bəzɔn] *nf* work, job, task. ◆**besogneux, -euse** *a* needy.

besoin [bəzwɛ̃] *nm* need; **avoir b. de** to need; **au b.** if necessary, if need(s) be; **dans le b.** in need, needy.

bestial, -aux [bestjal, -o] *a* bestial, brutish. ◆**bestiaux** *nmpl* livestock; (*bovins*) cattle. ◆**bestiole** *nf* (*insecte*) creepy-crawly, bug.

bétail [betaj] *nm* livestock; (*bovins*) cattle.

bête[1] [bɛt] *nf* animal; (*bestiole*) bug, creature; **b. de somme** beast of burden; **b. à bon dieu** ladybird, *Am* ladybug; **b. noire** pet hate, pet peeve; **chercher la petite b.** (*critiquer*) to pick holes.

bête[2] [bɛt] *a* silly, stupid. ◆**bêtement** *adv* stupidly; **tout b.** quite simply. ◆**bêtise** [betiz] *nf* silliness, stupidity; (*action, parole*) silly *ou* stupid thing; (*bagatelle*) mere trifle.

béton [betɔ̃] *nm* concrete; **en b.** concrete-; **b. armé** reinforced concrete. ◆**bétonnière** *nf*, ◆**bétonneuse** *nf* cement *ou* concrete mixer.

betterave [betrav] *nf Culin* beetroot, *Am* beet; **b. sucrière** *ou* **à sucre** sugar beet.

beugler [bøgle] *vi* (*taureau*) to bellow; (*vache*) to moo; (*radio*) to blare (out).

beurre [bœr] *nm* butter; **b. d'anchois** anchovy paste. ◆**beurrer** *vt* to butter. ◆**beurrier** *nm* butter dish.

beuverie [bøvri] *nf* drinking session, booze-up.

bévue [bevy] *nf* blunder, mistake.

biais [bjɛ] *nm* (*moyen détourné*) device, expedient; (*aspect*) angle; **regarder de b.** to look at sidelong; **traverser en b.** to cross at an angle. ◆**biaiser** [bjeze] *vi* to prevaricate, hedge.

bibelot [biblo] *nm* curio, trinket.

biberon [bibrɔ̃] *nm* (feeding) bottle.

bible [bibl] *nf* bible; **la B.** the Bible. ◆**biblique** *a* biblical.

bibliobus [biblijɔbys] *nm* mobile library.

bibliographie [biblijɔgrafi] *nf* bibliography.

bibliothèque [biblijɔtɛk] *nf* library; (*meuble*) bookcase; (*à la gare*) bookstall. ◆**bibliothécaire** *nmf* librarian.

bic® [bik] *nm* ballpoint, biro®.

bicarbonate [bikarbɔnat] *nm* bicarbonate.

bicentenaire [bisɑ̃tner] *nm* bicentenary, bicentennial.

biceps [bisɛps] *nm Anat* biceps.

biche [biʃ] *nf* doe, hind; **ma b.** *Fig* my pet.

bichonner [biʃɔne] vt to doll up.

bicoque [bikɔk] nf Péj shack, hovel.

bicyclette [bisiklɛt] nf bicycle, cycle; **la b. Sp** cycling; **aller à b.** to cycle.

bide [bid] nm (ventre) Fam belly; **faire un b.** Arg to flop.

bidet [bidɛ] nm (cuvette) bidet.

bidon [bidɔ̃] **1** nm (d'essence) can; (pour boissons) canteen; (ventre) Fam belly. **2** nm **du b.** Fam rubbish, bluff; – a inv (simulé) Fam fake, phoney. **◆se bidonner** vpr Fam to have a good laugh.

bidonville [bidɔ̃vil] nf shantytown.

bidule [bidyl] nm (chose) Fam thingummy, whatsit.

bielle [bjɛl] nf Aut connecting rod.

bien [bjɛ̃] adv well; **il joue b.** he plays well; **je vais b.** I'm fine ou well; **b. fatigué/souvent/etc** (très) very tired/often/etc; **merci b.!** thanks very much!; **b.! fine!,** right!; **b. du courage/etc** a lot of courage/etc; **b. des fois/des gens/etc** lots of ou many times/people/etc; **je l'ai b. dit** (intensif) I did say so; **c'est b. compris?** is that quite understood?; **c'est b. toi?** is it really you?; **tu as b. fait** you did right; **c'est b. fait (pour lui)** it serves him right; – a inv (convenable) all right, fine; (agréable) nice, fine; (compétent, bon) good, fine; (à l'aise) comfortable, fine; (beau) attractive; (en forme) well; (moralement) nice; **une fille b.** a nice ou respectable girl; – nm (avantage) good; (capital) possession; **ça te fera du b.** it will do you good; **le b. et le mal** good and evil; **biens de consommation** consumer goods. **◆b.-aimé, -ée** a & nmf beloved. **◆b.-être** nm wellbeing. **◆b.-fondé** nm validity, soundness.

bienfaisance [bjɛ̃fəzɑ̃s] nf benevolence, charity; **de b.** (société etc) benevolent, charitable. **◆bienfaisant** a beneficial.

bienfait [bjɛ̃fɛ] nm (générosité) favour; pl benefits, blessings. **◆bienfaiteur, -trice** nmf benefactor, benefactress.

bienheureux, -euse [bjɛ̃nœrø, -øz] a blessed, blissful.

biennal, -aux [bjenal, -o] a biennial.

bien que [bjɛ̃k(ə)] conj although.

bienséant [bjɛ̃seɑ̃] a proper. **◆bienséance** nf propriety.

bientôt [bjɛ̃to] adv soon; **à b.!** see you soon!; **il est b. dix heures/etc** it's nearly ten o'clock/etc.

bienveillant [bjɛ̃vejɑ̃] a kindly. **◆bienveillance** nf kindliness.

bienvenu, -ue [bjɛ̃vny] a welcome; – nmf

soyez le b.! welcome!; – nf welcome; **souhaiter la bienvenue à** to welcome.

bière [bjɛr] nf **1** (boisson) beer; **b. pression** draught beer. **2** (cercueil) coffin.

biffer [bife] vt to cross ou strike out.

bifteck [biftɛk] nm steak; **gagner son b.** Fam to earn one's (daily) bread.

bifurquer [bifyrke] vi to branch off, fork. **◆bifurcation** nf fork, junction.

bigame [bigam] a bigamous; – nmf bigamist. **◆bigamie** nf bigamy.

bigarré [bigare] a (bariolé) mottled; (hétéroclite) motley, mixed.

bigler [bigle] vi (loucher) Fam to squint; – vti **b. (sur)** (lorgner) Fam to leer at. **◆bigleux, -euse** a Fam cock-eyed.

bigorneau, -x [bigɔrno] nm (coquillage) winkle.

bigot, -ote [bigo, -ɔt] nmf Péj religious bigot; – a over-devout, fanatical.

bigoudi [bigudi] nm (hair)curler ou roller.

bigrement [bigrəmɑ̃] adv Fam awfully.

bijou, -x [biʒu] nm jewel; (ouvrage élégant) Fig gem. **◆bijouterie** nf (commerce) jeweller's shop; (bijoux) jewellery. **◆bijoutier, -ière** nmf jeweller.

bikini [bikini] nm bikini.

bilan [bilɑ̃] nm Fin balance sheet; (résultat) outcome; (d'un accident) (casualty) toll; **b. de santé** checkup; **faire le b.** to make an assessment (de of).

bilboquet [bilbɔkɛ] nm cup-and-ball (game).

bile [bil] nf bile; **se faire de la b.** Fam to worry, fret. **◆bilieux, -euse** a bilious.

bilingue [bilɛ̃g] a bilingual.

billard [bijar] nm (jeu) billiards; (table) billiard table; Méd Fam operating table; **c'est du b.** Fam it's a cinch.

bille [bij] nf (d'un enfant) marble; (de billard) billiard ball; **stylo à b.** ballpoint pen, biro®.

billet [bijɛ] nm ticket; **b. (de banque)** (bank)note, Am bill; **b. aller, b. simple** single ticket, Am one-way ticket; **b. (d')aller et retour** return ticket, Am round trip ticket; **b. doux** love letter.

billion [biljɔ̃] nm billion, Am trillion.

billot [bijo] nm (de bois) block.

bimensuel, -elle [bimɑ̃sɥɛl] a bimonthly, fortnightly.

bimoteur [bimɔtœr] a twin-engined.

binaire [binɛr] a binary.

biner [bine] vt to hoe. **◆binette** nf hoe; (visage) Arg mug, face.

biochimie [bjoʃimi] nf biochemistry.

biodégradable [bjɔdegradabl] *a* biodegradable.
biographie [bjɔgrafi] *nf* biography.
◆**biographe** *nmf* biographer.
biologie [bjɔlɔʒi] *nf* biology. ◆**biologique**
a biological.
bip-bip [bipbip] *nm* bleeper.
bipède [biped] *nm* biped.
bique [bik] *nf Fam* nanny-goat.
Birmanie [birmani] *nf* Burma. ◆**birman,
-ane** *a & nmf* Burmese.
bis¹ [bis] *adv* (*cri*) *Th* encore; *Mus* repeat; **4
bis** (*numéro*) 4A; — *nm Th* encore.
bis², **bise** [bi, biz] *a* greyish-brown.
bisbille [bisbij] *nf* squabble; **en b. avec** *Fam*
at loggerheads with.
biscornu [biskɔrny] *a* (*objet*) distorted,
misshapen; (*idée*) cranky.
biscotte [biskɔt] *nf* (*pain*) Melba toast;
(*biscuit*) rusk, *Am* zwieback.
biscuit [biskɥi] *nm* (*salé*) biscuit, *Am*
cracker; (*sucré*) biscuit, *Am* cookie; **b. de
Savoie** sponge (cake). ◆**biscuiterie** *nf*
biscuit factory.
bise [biz] *nf* **1** (*vent*) north wind. **2** (*baiser*)
Fam kiss.
biseau, -x [bizo] *nm* bevel.
bison [bizɔ̃] *nm* bison, (American) buffalo.
bisou [bizu] *nm Fam* kiss.
bisser [bise] *vt* (*musicien, acteur*) to encore.
bissextile [bisɛkstil] *af* **année b.** leap year.
bistouri [bisturi] *nm* scalpel, lancet.
bistre [bistr] *a inv* bistre, dark-brown.
bistro(t) [bistro] *nm* bar, café.
bitume [bitym] *nm* (*revêtement*) asphalt.
bivouac [bivwak] *nm Mil* bivouac.
bizarre [bizar] *a* peculiar, odd, bizarre.
◆**—ment** *adv* oddly. ◆**bizarrerie** *nf*
peculiarity.
blabla(bla) [blabla(bla)] *nm* claptrap,
bunkum.
blafard [blafar] *a* pale, pallid.
blague [blag] *nf* **1** (*à tabac*) pouch. **2**
(*plaisanterie, farce*) *Fam* joke; *pl*
(*absurdités*) *Fam* nonsense; **sans b.!** you're
joking! ◆**blagu/er** *vi* to be joking; — *vt* to
tease. ◆**—eur, -euse** *nmf* joker.
blair [blɛr] *nm* (*nez*) *Arg* snout, conk.
◆**blairer** *vt Arg* to stomach.
blaireau, -x [blero] *nm* **1** (*animal*) badger. **2**
(*brosse*) (shaving) brush.
blâme [blɑm] *nm* (*réprimande*) rebuke;
(*reproche*) blame. ◆**blâmable** *a* blameworthy. ◆**blâmer** *vt* to rebuke; to blame.
blanc, blanche [blɑ̃, blɑ̃ʃ] **1** *a* white; (*page
etc*) blank; **nuit blanche** sleepless night;
voix blanche expressionless voice; — *nmf*

(*personne*) white (man *ou* woman); — *nm*
(*couleur*) white; (*de poulet*) white meat,
breast; (*espace, interligne*) blank; **b. (d'œuf)**
(egg) white; **le b.** (*linge*) whites; **magasin de
b.** linen shop; **laisser en b.** to leave blank;
chèque en b. blank cheque; **cartouche à b.**
blank (cartridge); **saigner à b.** to bleed
white. **2** *nf Mus* minim, *Am* half-note.
◆**blanchâtre** *a* whitish. ◆**blancheur** *nf*
whiteness.
blanchir [blɑ̃ʃir] *vt* to whiten; (*draps*) to
launder; (*mur*) to whitewash; *Culin* to
blanch; (*argent*) *Fig* to launder; **b. qn**
(*disculper*) to clear s.o.; — *vi* to turn white,
whiten. ◆**blanchissage** *nm* laundering.
◆**blanchisserie** *nf* (*lieu*) laundry.
◆**blanchisseur, -euse** *nmf* laundryman,
laundrywoman.
blanquette [blɑ̃kɛt] *nf* **b. de veau** veal stew
in white sauce.
blasé [blaze] *a* blasé.
blason [blazɔ̃] *nm* (*écu*) coat of arms;
(*science*) heraldry.
blasphème [blasfɛm] *nf* blasphemy.
◆**blasphématoire** *a* (*propos*) blasphemous. ◆**blasphémer** *vti* to blaspheme.
blatte [blat] *nf* cockroach.
blazer [blazœr] *nm* blazer.
blé [ble] *nm* wheat; (*argent*) *Arg* bread.
bled [blɛd] *nm Péj Fam* (dump of a) village.
blême [blɛm] *a* a sickly pale, wan; **b. de colère**
livid with anger.
bless/er [blese] *vt* to injure, hurt; (*avec un
couteau, une balle etc*) to wound; (*offenser*)
to hurt, offend, wound; **se b. le** *ou* **au
bras/etc** to hurt one's arm/*etc*. ◆**—ant**
[blesɑ̃] *a* (*parole, personne*) hurtful. ◆**—é,
-ée** *nmf* casualty, injured *ou* wounded
person. ◆**blessure** *nf* injury; wound.
blet, blette [blɛ, blɛt] *a* (*fruit*) overripe.
bleu [blø] *a* blue; **b. de colère** blue in the
face; **steak b.** *Culin* very rare steak; — *nm*
(*couleur*) blue; (*contusion*) bruise; (*vêtement*) overalls; (*conscrit*) raw recruit; **bleus
de travail** overalls. ◆**bleuir** *vti* to turn
blue.
bleuet [bløɛ] *nm* cornflower.
blind/er [blɛ̃de] *vt Mil* to armour(-plate).
◆**—é** *a* (*train etc*) *Mil* armoured; **porte
blindée** reinforced steel door; — *nm Mil*
armoured vehicle.
bloc [blɔk] *nm* block; (*de pierre*) lump,
block; (*de papier*) pad; (*masse compacte*)
unit; *Pol* bloc; **en b.** all together; (*serrer
etc*) tight, hard; **travailler à b.** *Fam*
to work flat out. ◆**b.-notes** *nm* (*pl*
blocs-notes) writing pad.

blocage [blɔkaʒ] *nm* (*des roues*) locking; *Psy* mental block; **b. des prix** price freeze.

blocus [blɔkys] *nm* blockade.

blond, -onde [blɔ̃, -ɔ̃d] *a* fair(-haired), blond; — *nm* fair-haired man; (*couleur*) blond; — *nf* fair-haired woman, blonde; (**bière**) **blonde** lager, pale *ou* light ale. ◆**blondeur** *nf* fairness, blondness.

bloquer [blɔke] *vt* (*obstruer*) to block; (*coincer*) to jam; (*grouper*) to group together; (*ville*) to blockade; (*freins*) to slam *ou* jam on; (*roue*) to lock; (*salaires, prix*) to freeze; **bloqué par la neige/la glace** snowbound/icebound; **— se b.** *vpr* to stick, jam; (*roue*) to lock.

blottir (se) [səblɔtir] *vpr* (*dans un coin etc*) to crouch; (*dans son lit*) to snuggle down; **se b. contre** to huddle *ou* snuggle up to.

blouse [bluz] *nf* (*tablier*) overall, smock; (*corsage*) blouse. ◆**blouson** *nm* (waist-length) jacket.

blue-jean [bludʒin] *nm* jeans, denims.

bluff [blœf] *nm* bluff. ◆**bluffer** *vti* to bluff.

boa [bɔa] *nm* (*serpent, tour de cou*) boa.

bobard [bɔbar] *nm Fam* fib, yarn, tall story.

bobine [bɔbin] *nf* (*de fil, film etc*) reel, spool; (*pour machine à coudre*) bobbin, spool.

bobo [bobo] *nm* (*langage enfantin*) pain; **j'ai b., ça fait b.** it hurts.

bocage [bɔkaʒ] *nm* copse.

bocal, -aux [bɔkal, -o] *nm* glass jar; (*à poissons*) bowl.

bock [bɔk] *nm* (*récipient*) beer glass; (*contenu*) glass of beer.

bœuf, *pl* **-fs** [bœf, bø] *nm* (*animal*) ox (*pl* oxen), bullock; (*viande*) beef.

bohème [bɔem] *a & nmf* bohemian. ◆**bohémien, -ienne** *a & nmf* gipsy.

boire* [bwar] *vt* to drink; (*absorber*) to soak up; (*paroles*) *Fig* to take *ou* drink in; **b. un coup** to have a drink; **offrir à b. à qn** to offer s.o. a drink; **b. à petits coups** to sip; — *vi* to drink.

bois¹ [bwa] *voir* **boire**.

bois² [bwa] *nm* (*matière, forêt*) wood; (*construction*) timber; (*gravure*) woodcut; *pl* (*de cerf*) antlers; *Mus* woodwind instruments; **en** *ou* **de b.** wooden; **b. de chauffage** firewood; **b. de lit** bedstead. ◆**boisé** *a* wooded. ◆**boiserie(s)** *nf(pl)* panelling.

boisson [bwasɔ̃] *nf* drink, beverage.

boit [bwa] *voir* **boire**.

boîte [bwat] *nf* box; (*de conserve*) tin, *Am* can; (*lieu de travail*) *Fam* firm; **b. aux** *ou* **à lettres** letterbox; **b. de nuit** nightclub; **mettre qn en b.** *Fam* to pull s.o.'s leg. ◆**boîtier** *nm* (*de montre etc*) case.

boiter [bwate] *vi* (*personne*) to limp. ◆**boiteux, -euse** *a* lame; . (*meuble*) wobbly; (*projet etc*) *Fig* shaky.

bol [bɔl] *nm* (*récipient*) bowl; **prendre un b. d'air** to get a breath of fresh air; **avoir du b.** *Fam* to be lucky.

bolide [bɔlid] *nm* (*véhicule*) racing car.

Bolivie [bɔlivi] *nf* Bolivia. ◆**bolivien, -ienne** *a & nmf* Bolivian.

bombard/er [bɔ̃barde] *vt* (*ville etc*) to bomb; (*avec des obus*) to shell; **b. qn** *Fam* (*nommer*) to pitchfork s.o. (**à un poste** into a job); **b. de** (*questions*) to bombard with; (*objets*) to pelt with. ◆**—ement** *nm* bombing; shelling. ◆**bombardier** *nm* (*avion*) bomber.

bombe [bɔ̃b] *nf* (*projectile*) bomb; (*atomiseur*) spray; **tomber comme une b.** *Fig* to be a bombshell, be quite unexpected; **faire la b.** *Fam* to have a binge.

bomb/er [bɔ̃be] **1** *vi* (*gonfler*) to bulge; — *vt* **b. la poitrine** to throw out one's chest. **2** *vi* (*véhicule etc*) *Fam* to bomb *ou* belt along. ◆**—é** *a* (*verre etc*) rounded; (*route*) cambered.

bon¹, bonne¹ [bɔ̃, bɔn] *a* **1** (*satisfaisant etc*) good. **2** (*charitable*) kind, good. **3** (*agréable*) nice, good; **il fait b. se reposer** it's nice *ou* good to rest; **b. anniversaire!** happy birthday! **4** (*qui convient*) right; **c'est le b. clou** it's the right nail. **5** (*approprié, apte*) fit; **b. à manger** fit to eat; **b. pour le service** fit for service; **ce n'est b. à rien** it's useless; **comme te semble** as you think fit *ou* best; **c'est b. à savoir** it's worth knowing. **6** (*prudent*) wise, good; **croire b. de** to think it wise *ou* good to. **7** (*compétent*) good; **b. en français** good at French. **8** (*valable*) good; **ce billet est encore b.** this ticket's still good. **9** (*intensif*) **un b. moment** a good while. **10** **à quoi b.?** what's the use *ou* point *ou* good?; **pour de b.** in earnest; **tenir b.** to stand firm; **ah b.?** is that so? **11** *nm* **du b.** some good; **les bons the good**.

bon² [bɔ̃] *nm* (*billet*) coupon, voucher; (*titre*) *Fin* bond; (*formulaire*) slip.

bonasse [bɔnas] *a* feeble, soft.

bonbon [bɔ̃bɔ̃] *nm* sweet, *Am* candy. ◆**bonbonnière** *nf* sweet box, *Am* candy box.

bonbonne [bɔ̃bɔn] *nf* (*récipient*) demijohn.

bond [bɔ̃] *nm* leap, bound; (*de balle*) bounce; **faire faux b. à qn** to stand s.o. up, let s.o. down (*by not turning up*). ◆**bondir** *vi* to leap, bound.

bonde [bɔ̃d] *nf* (*bouchon*) plug; (*trou*) plughole.

bondé [bɔ̃de] *a* packed, crammed.

bonheur [bɔnœr] *nm* (*chance*) good luck, good fortune; (*félicité*) happiness; **par b.** luckily; **au petit b.** haphazardly.

bonhomie [bɔnɔmi] *nf* good-heartedness.

bonhomme, *pl* **bonshommes** [bɔnɔm, bɔ̃zɔm] 1 *nm* fellow, guy; **b. de neige** snowman; **aller son petit b. de chemin** to go on in one's own sweet way. 2 *a inv* good-hearted.

boniment(s) [bɔnimɑ̃] *nm(pl)* (*bobard*) claptrap; (*baratin*) patter.

bonjour [bɔ̃ʒur] *nm* & *int* good morning; (*après-midi*) good afternoon; **donner le b. à, dire b. à** to say hello to.

bonne² [bɔn] *nf* (*domestique*) maid; **b. d'enfants** nanny.

bonnement [bɔnmɑ̃] *adv* **tout b.** simply.

bonnet [bɔnɛ] *nm* cap; (*de femme, d'enfant*) bonnet; (*de soutien-gorge*) cup; **gros b.** *Fam* bigshot, bigwig. ◆**bonneterie** *nf* hosiery.

bonsoir [bɔ̃swar] *nm* & *int* (*en rencontrant qn*) good evening; (*en quittant qn*) goodbye; (*au coucher*) good night.

bonté [bɔ̃te] *nf* kindness, goodness.

bonus [bɔnys] *nm* no claims bonus.

bonze [bɔ̃z] *nm Péj Fam* bigwig.

boom [bum] *nm Écon* boom.

bord [bɔr] *nm* (*rebord*) edge; (*rive*) bank; (*de vêtement*) border; (*de chapeau*) brim; (*de verre*) rim, brim, edge; **au b. de la mer/route** at *ou* by the seaside/roadside; **b. du trottoir** kerb, *Am* curb; **au b. de** (*précipice*) on the brink of; **au b. des larmes** on the verge of tears; **à bord (de)** *Nau Av* on board; **jeter par-dessus b.** to throw overboard. ◆**border** *vt* (*vêtement*) to border, edge; (*lit, personne*) to tuck in; **b. la rue/etc** (*maisons, arbres etc*) to line the street/*etc*. ◆**bordure** *nf* border; **en b. de** bordering on.

bordeaux [bɔrdo] *a inv* maroon.

bordée [bɔrde] *nf* (*salve*) *Nau* broadside; (*d'injures*) *Fig* torrent, volley.

bordel [bɔrdɛl] *nm* 1 *Fam* brothel. 2 (*désordre*) *Fam* mess.

bordereau, -x [bɔrdəro] *nm* (*relevé*) docket, statement; (*formulaire*) note.

borgne [bɔrɲ] *a* (*personne*) one-eyed, blind in one eye; (*hôtel etc*) *Fig* shady.

borne [bɔrn] *nf* (*pierre*) boundary mark; *Él* terminal; *pl* (*limites*) *Fig* bounds; **b. kilométrique** ≈ milestone; **dépasser** *ou* **franchir les bornes** to go too far. ◆**born/er** *vt* (*limiter*) to confine; **se b. à** to confine oneself to. ◆**—é** *a* (*personne*) narrow-minded; (*intelligence*) narrow, limited.

bosquet [bɔskɛ] *nm* grove, thicket, copse.

bosse [bɔs] *nf* (*grosseur dorsale*) hump; (*enflure*) bump, lump; (*de terrain*) bump; **avoir la b. de** *Fam* to have a flair for; **rouler sa b.** *Fam* to knock about the world. ◆**bossu, -ue** *a* hunchbacked; **dos b.** hunchback; – *nmf* (*personne*) hunchback.

bosseler [bɔsle] *vt* (*orfèvrerie*) to emboss; (*déformer*) to dent.

bosser [bɔse] *vi Fam* to work (hard).

bot [bo] *am* **pied b.** club foot.

botanique [bɔtanik] *a* botanical; – *nf* botany.

botte [bɔt] *nf* (*chaussure*) boot; (*faisceau*) bunch, bundle. ◆**botter** *vt* (*ballon etc*) *Fam* to boot. ◆**bottier** *nm* bootmaker. ◆**bottillon** *nm,* ◆**bottine** *nf* (ankle) boot.

Bottin® [bɔtɛ̃] *nm* telephone book.

bouc [buk] *nm* billy goat; (*barbe*) goatee; **b. émissaire** scapegoat.

boucan [bukɑ̃] *nm Fam* din, row, racket.

bouche [buʃ] *nf* mouth; **faire la petite** *ou* **fine b.** *Péj* to turn up one's nose; **une fine b.** a gourmet; **b. de métro** métro entrance; **b. d'égout** drain opening, manhole; **b. d'incendie** fire hydrant; **le b.-à-b.** the kiss of life. ◆**bouchée** *nf* mouthful.

bouch/er¹ [buʃe] 1 *vt* (*évier, nez etc*) to block (up), stop up; (*bouteille*) to close, cork; (*vue, rue etc*) to block; **se b. le nez** to hold one's nose. ◆**—é** *a* (*vin*) bottled; (*temps*) overcast; (*personne*) *Fig* stupid, dense. ◆**bouche-trou** *nm* stopgap. ◆**bouchon** *nm* stopper, top; (*de liège*) cork; (*de tube, bidon*) cap, top; *Pêche* float; (*embouteillage*) *Fig* traffic jam.

boucher² [buʃe] *nm* butcher. ◆**boucherie** *nf* butcher's (shop); (*carnage*) butchery.

boucle [bukl] *nf* 1 (*de ceinture*) buckle; (*de fleuve etc*) & *Av* loop; (*de ruban*) bow; **b. d'oreille** earring. 2 **b.** (*de cheveux*) curl. ◆**boucl/er** 1 *vt* to fasten, buckle; (*travail etc*) to finish off; (*enfermer, fermer*) *Fam* to lock up; (*budget*) to balance; (*circuit*) to lap; (*encercler*) to surround, cordon off; **b. la boucle** *Av* to loop the loop; **la b.** *Fam* to shut up. 2 *vt* (*cheveux*) to curl; – *vi* to be curly. ◆**—é** *a* (*cheveux*) curly.

bouclier [buklije] *nm* shield.

bouddhiste [budist] *a* & *nmf* Buddhist.

bouder [bude] *vi* to sulk; – *vt* (*personne, plaisirs etc*) to steer clear of. ◆**bouderie** *nf* sulkiness. ◆**boudeur, -euse** *a* sulky, moody.

boudin [budɛ̃] *nm* black pudding, *Am* blood pudding.

boue [bu] *nf* mud. ◆**boueux, -euse** 1 *a*

muddy. **2** *nm* dustman, *Am* garbage collector.

bouée [bwe] *nf* buoy; **b. de sauvetage** lifebuoy.

bouffe [buf] *nf Fam* food, grub, nosh.

bouffée [bufe] *nf* (*de fumée*) puff; (*de parfum*) whiff; (*d'orgueil*) fit; **b. de chaleur** *Méd* hot flush. ◆**bouff/er 1** *vi* to puff out. **2** *vti* (*manger*) *Fam* to eat. ◆**—ant** *a* (*manche*) puff(ed). ◆**bouffi** *a* puffy, bloated.

bouffon, -onne [bufɔ̃, -ɔn] *a* farcical; – *nm* buffoon. ◆**bouffonneries** *nfpl* antics, buffoonery.

bouge [buʒ] *nm* (*bar*) dive; (*taudis*) hovel.

bougeotte [buʒɔt] *nf* **avoir la b.** *Fam* to have the fidgets.

bouger [buʒe] *vi* to move; (*agir*) to stir; (*rétrécir*) to shrink; – *vt* to move; — **se b.** *vpr Fam* to move.

bougie [buʒi] *nf* candle; *Aut* spark(ing) plug. ◆**bougeoir** *nm* candlestick.

bougon, -onne [bugɔ̃, -ɔn] *a Fam* grumpy; – *nmf* grumbler, grouch. ◆**bougonner** *vi Fam* to grumble, grouch.

bougre [bugr] *nm* fellow, bloke; (*enfant*) *Péj* (little) devil. ◆**bougrement** *adv Arg* damned.

bouillabaisse [bujabɛs] *nf* fish soup.

bouillie [buji] *nf* porridge; **en b.** in a mush, mushy.

bouill/ir* [bujir] *vi* to boil; **b. à gros bouillons** to bubble, boil hard; **faire b. qch** to boil sth. ◆**—ant** *a* boiling; **b. de colère/etc** seething with anger/etc. ◆**bouilloire** *nf* kettle. ◆**bouillon** *nm* (*eau*) broth, stock; (*bulle*) bubble. ◆**bouillonner** *vi* to bubble. ◆**bouillotte** *nf* hot water bottle.

boulanger, -ère [bulɑ̃ʒe, -ɛr] *nmf* baker. ◆**boulangerie** *nf* baker's (shop).

boule [bul] *nf* (*sphère*) ball; *pl* (*jeu*) bowls; **b. de neige** snowball; **faire b. de neige** to snowball; **perdre la b.** *Fam* to go out of one's mind; **se mettre en b.** (*chat etc*) to curl up into a ball; **boules Quiès®** earplugs. ◆**boulet** *nm* (*de forçat*) ball and chain; **b. de canon** cannonball. ◆**boulette** *nf* (*de papier*) pellet; (*de viande*) meatball; (*gaffe*) *Fam* blunder.

bouleau, -x [bulo] *nm* (silver) birch.

bouledogue [buldɔg] *nm* bulldog.

boulevard [bulvar] *nm* boulevard.

boulevers/er [bulvɛrse] *vt* (*déranger*) to turn upside down; (*émouvoir*) to upset deeply, distress; (*vie de qn, pays*) to upset. ◆**—ant** *a* upsetting, distressing. ◆**—ement** *nm* upheaval.

boulon [bulɔ̃] *nm* bolt.

boulot, -otte [bulo, -ɔt] **1** *a* dumpy. **2** *nm* (*travail*) *Fam* work.

boum [bum] **1** *int* & *nm* bang. **2** *nf* (*surprise-partie*) *Fam* party.

bouquet [bukɛ] *nm* (*de fleurs*) bunch, bouquet; (*d'arbres*) clump; (*de vin*) bouquet; (*crevette*) prawn; **c'est le b.!** that's the last straw!

bouquin [bukɛ̃] *nm Fam* book. ◆**bouquiner** *vti Fam* to read. ◆**bouquiniste** *nmf* second-hand bookseller.

bourbeux, -euse [burbø, -øz] *a* muddy. ◆**bourbier** *nm* (*lieu, situation*) quagmire, morass.

bourde [burd] *nf* blunder, bloomer.

bourdon [burdɔ̃] *nm* (*insecte*) bumblebee. ◆**bourdonn/er** *vi* to buzz, hum. ◆**—ement** *nm* buzzing, humming.

bourg [bur] *nm* (small) market town. ◆**bourgade** *nf* (large) village.

bourgeois, -oise [burʒwa, -waz] *a* & *nmf* middle-class (person); *Péj* bourgeois. ◆**bourgeoisie** *nf* middle class, bourgeoisie.

bourgeon [burʒɔ̃] *nm* bud. ◆**bourgeonner** *vi* to bud; (*nez*) *Fam* to be pimply.

bourgmestre [burgmɛstr] *nm* (*en Belgique, Suisse*) burgomaster.

bourgogne [burgɔɲ] *nm* (*vin*) Burgundy.

bourlinguer [burlɛ̃ge] *vi* (*voyager*) *Fam* to knock about.

bourrade [burad] *nf* (*du coude*) poke.

bourrasque [burask] *nf* squall.

bourratif, -ive [buratif, -iv] *a* (*aliment*) *Fam* filling, stodgy.

bourreau, -x [buro] *nm* executioner; **b. d'enfants** child batterer; **b. de travail** workaholic.

bourrelet [burlɛ] *nm* weather strip; **b. de graisse** roll of fat, spare tyre.

bourr/er [bure] **1** *vt* to stuff, cram (full) (**de** with); (*pipe, coussin*) to fill; **b. de coups** to thrash; **b. le crâne à qn** to brainwash s.o. **2 se b.** *vpr* (*s'enivrer*) *Fam* to get plastered. ◆**—age** *nm* **b. de crâne** brainwashing.

bourrique [burik] *nf* ass.

bourru [bury] *a* surly, rough.

bourse [burs] *nf* (*sac*) purse; *Scol Univ* grant, scholarship; **la B.** the Stock Exchange; **sans b. délier** without spending a penny. ◆**boursier, -ière 1** *a* Stock Exchange-. **2** *nmf Scol Univ* grant holder, scholar.

boursouflé [bursufle] *a* (*visage etc*) puffy; (*style*) *Fig* inflated.

bousculer [buskyle] *vt* (*heurter, pousser*) to

jostle; (*presser*) to rush, push; **b. qch** (*renverser*) to knock sth over; **b. les habitudes**/*etc* to turn one's habits/*etc* upside down. ◆**bousculade** *nf* rush, jostling.

bouse [buz] *nf* **b. de vache** cow dung.

bousiller [buzije] *vt Fam* to mess up, wreck.

boussole [busɔl] *nf* compass.

bout [bu] *nm* end; (*de langue, canne, doigt*) tip; (*de papier, pain, ficelle*) bit; **un b. de temps/chemin** a little while/way; **au b. d'un moment** after a moment; **à b.** exhausted; **à b. de souffle** out of breath; **à b. de bras** at arm's length; **venir à b. de** (*travail*) to get through; (*adversaire*) to get the better of; **à tout b. de champ** at every turn, every minute; **à b. portant** point-blank.

boutade [butad] *nf* (*plaisanterie*) quip, witticism.

boute-en-train [butɑ̃trɛ̃] *nm inv* (*personne*) live wire.

bouteille [butɛj] *nf* bottle; (*de gaz*) cylinder.

bouteur [butœr] *nm* bulldozer.

boutique [butik] *nf* shop; (*d'un grand couturier*) boutique. ◆**boutiquier, -ière** *nmf Péj* shopkeeper.

boutoir [butwar] *nm* **coup de b.** staggering blow.

bouton [butɔ̃] *nm* (*bourgeon*) bud; (*pustule*) pimple, spot; (*de vêtement*) button; (*poussoir*) (push-)button; (*de porte, de télévision*) knob; **b. de manchette** cuff link. ◆**b.-d'or** *nm* (*pl* boutons-d'or) buttercup. ◆**b.-pression** *nm* (*pl* boutons-pression) press-stud, *Am* snap. ◆**boutonner** *vt*, — **se b.** *vpr* to button (up). ◆**boutonneux, -euse** *a* pimply, spotty. ◆**boutonnière** *nf* buttonhole.

bouture [butyr] *nf* (*plante*) cutting.

bouvreuil [buvrœj] *nm* (*oiseau*) bullfinch.

bovin [bɔvɛ̃] *a* bovine; — *nmpl* cattle.

bowling [bolin] *nm* (tenpin) bowling; (*lieu*) bowling alley.

box, *pl* **boxes** [bɔks] *nm* (*d'écurie*) (loose) box; (*de dortoir*) cubicle; *Jur* dock; *Aut* lockup *ou* individual garage.

boxe [bɔks] *nf* boxing. ◆**boxer** *vi Sp* to box; — *vt Fam* to whack, punch. ◆**boxeur** *nm* boxer.

boyau, -x [bwajo] *nm Anat* gut; (*corde*) catgut; (*de bicyclette*) (racing) tyre *ou Am* tire.

boycott/er [bɔjkɔte] *vt* to boycott. ◆**—age** *nm* boycott.

BP [bepe] *abrév* (*boîte postale*) PO Box.

bracelet [braslɛ] *nm* bracelet, bangle; (*de montre*) strap.

braconner [brakɔne] *vi* to poach. ◆**braconnier** *nm* poacher.

brader [brade] *vt* to sell off cheaply. ◆**braderie** *nf* open-air (clearance) sale.

braguette [bragɛt] *nf* (*de pantalon*) fly, flies.

braille [braj] *nm* Braille.

brailler [braje] *vti* to bawl. ◆**braillard** *a* bawling.

braire* [brɛr] *vi* (*âne*) to bray.

braise(s) [brɛz] *nf(pl)* embers, live coals. ◆**braiser** [breze] *vt Culin* to braise.

brancard [brɑ̃kar] *nm* (*civière*) stretcher; (*de charrette*) shaft. ◆**brancardier** *nm* stretcher-bearer.

branche [brɑ̃ʃ] *nf* (*d'un arbre, d'une science etc*) branch; (*de compas*) leg; (*de lunettes*) side piece. ◆**branchages** *nmpl* (cut *ou* fallen) branches.

branch/er [brɑ̃ʃe] *vt Él* to plug in; (*installer*) to connect. ◆**-é a** (*informé*) *Fam* with it. ◆**-ement** *nm Él* connection.

brandir [brɑ̃dir] *vt* to brandish, flourish.

brandon [brɑ̃dɔ̃] *nm* (*paille, bois*) firebrand.

branle [brɑ̃l] *nm* impetus; **mettre en b.** to set in motion. ◆**b.-bas** *nm inv* turmoil. ◆**branl/er** *vi* to be shaky, shake. ◆**—ant** *a* shaky.

braqu/er [brake] **1** *vt* (*arme etc*) to point, aim; (*yeux*) to fix; **b. qn contre qn** to set *ou* turn s.o. against s.o. **2** *vti Aut* to steer, turn. ◆**—age** *nm Aut* steering; **rayon de b.** turning circle.

bras [bra] *nm* arm; **en b. de chemise** in one's shirtsleeves; **b. dessus b. dessous** arm in arm; **sur les b.** *Fig* on one's hands; **son b. droit** *Fig* his right-hand man; **à b. ouverts** with open arms; **à tour de b.** with all one's might; **faire un b. d'honneur** *Fam* to make an obscene gesture; **à b.-le-corps** round the waist. ◆**brassard** *nm* armband. ◆**brassée** *nf* armful. ◆**brassière** *nf* (*de bébé*) vest, *Am* undershirt.

brasier [brazje] *nm* inferno, blaze.

brasse [bras] *nf* (*nage*) breaststroke; (*mesure*) fathom; **b. papillon** butterfly stroke.

brasser [brase] *vt* to mix; (*bière*) to brew. ◆**brassage** *nm* mixture; brewing. ◆**brasserie** *nf* (*usine*) brewery; (*café*) brasserie. ◆**brasseur** *nm* **b. d'affaires** *Péj* big businessman.

bravache [bravaʃ] *nm* braggart.

bravade [bravad] *nf* **par b.** out of bravado.

brave [brav] *a & nm* (*hardi*) brave (man); (*honnête*) good (man). ◆**bravement** *adv* bravely. ◆**braver** *vt* to defy; (*danger*) to brave. ◆**bravoure** *nf* bravery.

bravo [bravo] *int* well done, bravo, good show; – *nm* cheer.

break [brɛk] *nm* estate car, *Am* station wagon.

brebis [brəbi] *nf* ewe; **b. galeuse** black sheep.

brèche [brɛʃ] *nf* breach, gap; **battre en b.** (*attaquer*) to attack (mercilessly).

bredouille [brəduj] *a* **rentrer b.** to come back empty-handed.

bredouiller [brəduje] *vti* to mumble.

bref, brève [brɛf, brɛv] *a* brief, short; – *adv* (**enfin**) **b.** in a word.

breloque [brələk] *nf* charm, trinket.

Brésil [brezil] *nm* Brazil. ◆**brésilien, -ienne** *a* & *nmf* Brazilian.

Bretagne [brətaɲ] *nf* Brittany. ◆**breton, -onne** *a* & *nmf* Breton.

bretelle [brətɛl] *nf* strap; (*voie de raccordement*) *Aut* access road; *pl* (*pour pantalon*) braces, *Am* suspenders.

breuvage [brœvaʒ] *nm* drink, brew.

brève [brɛv] *voir* **bref.**

brevet [brəvɛ] *nm* diploma; **b.** (**d'invention**) patent. ◆**brevet/er** *vt* to patent. ◆**—é** *a* (*technicien*) qualified.

bréviaire [brevjɛr] *nm* breviary.

bribes [brib] *nfpl* scraps, bits.

bric-à-brac [brikabrak] *nm inv* bric-à-brac, jumble, junk.

brick [brik] *nm* (*de lait, jus d'orange etc*) carton.

bricole [brikɔl] *nf* (*objet, futilité*) trifle. ◆**bricol/er** *vi* to do odd jobs; – *vt* (*réparer*) to patch up; (*fabriquer*) to put together. ◆**—age** *nm* (*petits travaux*) odd jobs; (*passe-temps*) do-it-yourself; **salon/rayon du b.** do-it-yourself exhibition/department. ◆**—eur, -euse** *nmf* handyman, handywoman.

bride [brid] *nf* (*de cheval*) bridle; **à b. abattue** at full gallop. ◆**brider** *vt* (*cheval*) to bridle; (*personne, désir*) to curb; *Culin* to truss; **avoir les yeux bridés** to have slit eyes.

bridge [bridʒ] *nm* (*jeu*) bridge.

brièvement [brievmɑ̃] *adv* briefly. ◆**brièveté** *nf* brevity.

brigade [brigad] *nf* (*de gendarmerie*) squad; *Mil* brigade; **b. des mœurs** vice squad. ◆**brigadier** *nm* police sergeant; *Mil* corporal.

brigand [brigɑ̃] *nm* robber; (*enfant*) rascal.

briguer [brige] *vt* to covet; (*faveurs, suffrages*) to court.

brillant [brijɑ̃] *a* (*luisant*) shining; (*astiqué*) shiny; (*couleur*) bright; (*magnifique*) *Fig* brilliant; – *nm* shine; brightness; *Fig* brilliance; (*diamant*) diamond. ◆**brillamment** *adv* brilliantly.

briller [brije] *vi* to shine; **faire b.** (*meuble*) to polish (up).

brimer [brime] *vt* to bully. ◆**brimade** *nm* *Scol* bullying, ragging, *Am* hazing; *Fig* vexation.

brin [brɛ̃] *nm* (*d'herbe*) blade; (*de corde, fil*) strand; (*de muguet*) spray; **un b. de** *Fig* a bit of.

brindille [brɛ̃dij] *nf* twig.

bringue [brɛ̃g] *nf* **faire la b.** *Fam* to have a binge.

bringuebaler [brɛ̃gbale] *vi* to wobble about.

brio [brijo] *nm* (*virtuosité*) brilliance.

brioche [brijɔʃ] *nf* **1** brioche (*light sweet bun*). **2** (*ventre*) *Fam* paunch.

brique [brik] *nf* brick. ◆**briquette** *nf* (*aggloméré*) breezeblock.

briquer [brike] *vt* to polish (up).

briquet [brikɛ] *nm* (*cigarette*) lighter.

brise [briz] *nf* breeze.

bris/er [brize] *vt* to break; (*en morceaux*) to smash, break; (*espoir, carrière*) to shatter; (*fatiguer*) to exhaust; – **se b.** *vpr* to break. ◆**—ants** *nmpl* reefs. ◆**brise-lames** *nm inv* breakwater.

britannique [britanik] *a* British; – *nmf* Briton; **les Britanniques** the British.

broc [bro] *nm* pitcher, jug.

brocanteur, -euse [brɔkɑ̃tœr, -øz] *nmf* secondhand dealer (*in furniture etc*).

broche [brɔʃ] *nf* *Culin* spit; (*bijou*) brooch; *Méd* pin. ◆**brochette** *nf* (*tige*) skewer; (*plat*) kebab.

broché [brɔʃe] *a* **livre b.** paperback.

brochet [brɔʃɛ] *nm* (*poisson*) pike.

brochure [brɔʃyr] *nf* brochure, booklet, pamphlet.

broder [brɔde] *vt* to embroider (**de** with). ◆**broderie** *nf* embroidery.

broncher [brɔ̃ʃe] *vi* (*bouger*) to budge; (*reculer*) to flinch; (*regimber*) to balk.

bronches [brɔ̃ʃ] *nfpl* bronchial tubes. ◆**bronchite** *nf* bronchitis.

bronze [brɔ̃z] *nm* bronze.

bronz/er [brɔ̃ze] *vt* to tan; – *vi*, – **se b.** *vpr* to get (sun)tanned; **se (faire) b.** to sunbathe. ◆**—age** *nm* (sun)tan, sunburn.

brosse [brɔs] *nf* brush; **b. à dents** toothbrush; **cheveux en b.** crew cut. ◆**brosser** *vt* to brush; **b. un tableau de** to give an outline of; **se b. les dents/les cheveux** to brush one's teeth/one's hair.

brouette [bruɛt] *nf* wheelbarrow.

brouhaha [bruaa] *nm* hubbub.

brouillard [brujar] *nm* fog; **il fait du b.** it's foggy.

brouille [bruj] *nf* disagreement, quarrel. ◆**brouiller 1** *vt* (*papiers, idées etc*) to mix up; (*vue*) to blur; (*œufs*) to scramble; *Rad* to jam; — **se b.** *vpr* (*idées*) to be *ou* get confused; (*temps*) to cloud over; (*vue*) to blur. **2** *vt* (*amis*) to cause a split between; — **se b.** *vpr* to fall out (*avec with*). ◆**brouillon, -onne 1** *a* confused. **2** *nm* rough draft.

broussailles [brusaj] *nfpl* brushwood.

brousse [brus] *nf* **la b.** the bush.

brouter [brute] *vti* to graze.

broyer [brwaje] *vt* to grind; (*doigt, bras*) to crush; **b. du noir** to be (down) in the dumps.

bru [bry] *nf* daughter-in-law.

brugnon [bryɲɔ̃] *nm* (*fruit*) nectarine.

bruine [brɥin] *nf* drizzle. ◆**bruiner** *v imp* to drizzle.

bruissement [brɥismɑ̃] *nm* (*de feuilles*) rustle, rustling.

bruit [brɥi] *nm* noise, sound; (*nouvelle*) rumour; **faire du b.** to be noisy, make a noise. ◆**bruitage** *nm Cin* sound effects.

brûle-pourpoint (à) [abrylpurpwɛ̃] *adv* point-blank.

brûl/er [bryle] *vt* to burn; (*consommer*) to use up, burn; (*signal, station*) to go through (without stopping); **b. un feu (rouge)** to jump *ou* go through the lights; **ce désir le brûlait** this desire consumed him; — *vi* to burn; **b. d'envie) de faire** to be burning to do; **ça brûle** (*temps*) it's baking *ou* scorching; — **se b.** *vpr* to burn oneself. ◆**—ant** *a* (*objet, soleil*) burning (hot); (*sujet*) *Fig* red-hot. ◆**—é 1** *nm* **odeur de b.** smell of burning. **2** *a* **cerveau b.**, **tête brûlée** hothead. ◆**brûlure** *nf* burn; **brûlures d'estomac** heartburn.

brume [brym] *nf* mist, haze. ◆**brumeux, -euse** *a* misty, hazy; (*obscur*) *Fig* hazy.

brun, brune [brœ̃, bryn] *a* brown; (*cheveux*) dark, brown; (*personne*) dark-haired; — *nm* (*couleur*) brown; — *nmf* dark-haired person. ◆**brunette** *nf* brunette. ◆**brunir** *vt* (*peau*) to tan; — *vi* to turn brown; (*cheveux*) to go darker.

brushing [brœʃiŋ] *nm* blow-dry.

brusque [brysk] *a* (*manière etc*) abrupt, blunt; (*subit*) sudden, abrupt. ◆**brusquement** *adv* suddenly, abruptly. ◆**brusquer** *vt* to rush. ◆**brusquerie** *nf* abruptness, bluntness.

brut [bryt] *a* (*pétrole*) crude; (*diamant*) rough; (*sucre*) unrefined; (*soie*) raw; (*poids*) & *Fin* gross.

brutal, -aux [brytal, -o] *a* (*violent*) savage, brutal; (*franchise, réponse*) crude, blunt; (*fait*) stark. ◆**brutaliser** *vt* to ill-treat. ◆**brutalité** *nf* (*violence, acte*) brutality. ◆**brute** *nf* brute.

Bruxelles [brysɛl] *nm ou f* Brussels.

bruyant [brɥijɑ̃] *a* noisy. ◆**bruyamment** *adv* noisily.

bruyère [bryjɛr] *nf* (*plante*) heather; (*terrain*) heath.

bu [by] *voir* **boire**.

buanderie [bɥɑ̃dri] *nf* (*lieu*) laundry.

bûche [byʃ] *nf* log; **ramasser une b.** *Fam* to come a cropper, *Am* take a spill. ◆**bûcher 1** *nm* (*local*) woodshed; (*supplice*) stake. **2** *vt* (*étudier*) *Fam* to slog away at. ◆**bûcheron** *nm* woodcutter, lumberjack.

budget [bydʒɛ] *nm* budget. ◆**budgétaire** *a* budgetary; (*année*) financial.

buée [bɥe] *nf* condensation, mist.

buffet [byfɛ] *nm* (*armoire*) sideboard; (*table, restaurant, repas*) buffet.

buffle [byfl] *nm* buffalo.

buis [bɥi] *nm* (*arbre*) box; (*bois*) boxwood.

buisson [bɥisɔ̃] *nm* bush.

buissonnière [bɥisɔnjɛr] *af* **faire l'école b.** to play truant *ou Am* hookey.

bulbe [bylb] *nm* bulb. ◆**bulbeux, -euse** *a* bulbous.

Bulgarie [bylgari] *nf* Bulgaria. ◆**bulgare** *a* & *nmf* Bulgarian.

bulldozer [byldozœr] *nm* bulldozer.

bulle [byl] *nf* **1** bubble; (*de bande dessinée*) balloon. **2** (*décret du pape*) bull.

bulletin [byltɛ̃] *nm* (*communiqué, revue*) bulletin; (*de la météo*) & *Scol* report; (*de bagages*) ticket, *Am* check; **b. de paie** pay slip; **b. de vote** ballot paper.

buraliste [byralist] *nmf* (*à la poste*) clerk; (*au tabac*) tobacconist.

bureau, -x [byro] *nm* **1** (*table*) desk. **2** (*lieu*) office; (*comité*) board; **b. de change** bureau de change; **b. de location** *Th Cin* box office; **b. de tabac** tobacconist's (shop). ◆**bureaucrate** *nmf* bureaucrat. ◆**bureaucratie** [-asi] *nf* bureaucracy. ◆**bureautique** *nf* office automation.

burette [byrɛt] *nf* oilcan; *Culin* cruet.

burlesque [byrlɛsk] *a* (*idée etc*) ludicrous; (*genre*) burlesque.

bus [bys] *nm Fam* bus.

bus [by] *voir* **boire**.

busqué [byske] *a* (*nez*) hooked.

buste [byst] *nm* (*torse, sculpture*) bust. ◆**bustier** *nm* long-line bra(ssiere).

but [by(t)] *nm* (*dessein, objectif*) aim, goal;

(*cible*) target; *Fb* goal; **de b. en blanc** point-blank; **aller droit au b.** to go straight to the point; **j'ai pour b. de . . .** my aim is to . . . .

but² [by] *voir* boire.

butane [bytan] *nm* (*gaz*) butane.

but/er [byte] **1** *vi* **b. contre** to stumble over; (*difficulté*) *Fig* to come up against. **2 se b.** *vpr* (*s'entêter*) to get obstinate. ◆**-é** *a* obstinate.

butin [bytɛ̃] *nm* loot, booty.

butiner [bytine] *vi* (*abeille*) to gather nectar.

butoir [bytwar] *nm Rail* buffer; (*de porte*) stop(per).

butor [bytɔr] *nm Péj* lout, oaf, boor.

butte [byt] *nf* hillock, mound; **en b.** à (*calomnie etc*) exposed to.

buvable [byvabl] *a* drinkable. ◆**buveur, -euse** *nmf* drinker.

buvard [byvar] *a* & *nm* (**papier**) **b.** blotting paper.

buvette [byvɛt] *nf* refreshment bar.

C

C, c [se] *nm* C, c

c *abrév* centime.

c' [s] *voir* ce¹.

ça [sa] *pron dém* (*abrév de* cela) (*pour désigner*) that; (*plus près*) this; (*sujet indéfini*) it, that; **ça m'amuse que . . .** it amuses me that . . . ; **où/quand/ comment/etc ça?** where?/when?/how?/ *etc*; **ça va (bien)?** how's it going?; **ça va!** fine!, OK!; **ça alors!** (*surprise, indignation*) well I never!, how about that!; **c'est ça** that's right; **et avec ça?** (*dans un magasin*) anything else?

çà [sa] *adv* **çà et là** here and there.

caban [kabã] *nm* (*veste*) reefer.

cabane [kaban] *nf* hut, cabin; (*à outils*) shed; (*à lapins*) hutch.

cabaret [kabarɛ] *nm* night club, cabaret.

cabas [kaba] *nm* shopping bag.

cabillaud [kabijo] *nm* (fresh) cod.

cabine [kabin] *nf Nau Av* cabin; *Tél* phone booth, phone box; (*de camion*) cab; (*d'ascenseur*) car, cage; **c. (de bain)** beach hut; (*à la piscine*) cubicle; **c. (de pilotage)** cockpit; (*d'un grand avion*) flight deck; **c. d'essayage** fitting room; **c. d'aiguillage** signal box.

cabinet [kabinɛ] *nm* (*local*) *Méd* surgery, *Am* office; (*d'avocat*) office, chambers; (*clientèle de médecin ou d'avocat*) practice; *Pol* cabinet; *pl* (*toilettes*) toilet; **c. de toilette** bathroom, toilet; **c. de travail** study.

câble [kabl] *nm* cable; (*cordage*) rope; **la télévision par c.** cable television; **le c.** *TV* cable. ◆**câbler** *vt* (*message*) to cable; **être câblé** *TV* to have cable.

caboche [kabɔʃ] *nf* (*tête*) *Fam* nut, noddle.

cabosser [kabɔse] *vt* to dent.

caboteur [kabɔtœr] *nm* (*bateau*) coaster.

cabotin, -ine [kabɔtɛ̃, -in] *nmf Th* ham actor, ham actress; *Fig* play-actor. ◆**cabotinage** *nm* histrionics, play-acting.

cabrer (se) [səkabre] *vpr* (*cheval*) to rear (up); (*personne*) to rebel.

cabri [kabri] *nm* (*chevreau*) kid.

cabrioles [kabriɔl] *nfpl* **faire des c.** (*sauts*) to cavort, caper.

cabriolet [kabriɔlɛ] *nm Aut* convertible.

cacah(o)uète [kakawɛt] *nf* peanut.

cacao [kakao] *nm* (*boisson*) cocoa.

cacatoès [kakatɔɛs] *nm* cockatoo.

cachalot [kaʃalo] *nm* sperm whale.

cache-cache [kaʃkaʃ] *nm inv* hide-and-seek. ◆**c.-col** *nm inv*, ◆**c.-nez** *nm inv* scarf, muffler. ◆**c.-sexe** *nm inv* G-string.

cachemire [kaʃmir] *nm* (*tissu*) cashmere.

cacher [kaʃe] *vt* to hide, conceal (à from); **je ne cache pas que . . .** I don't hide the fact that . . . ; **c. la lumière à qn** to stand in s.o.'s light; **— se c.** *vpr* to hide. ◆**cachette** *nf* hiding place; **en c.** in secret; **en c. de qn** without s.o. knowing.

cachet [kaʃɛ] *nm* (*sceau*) seal; (*de la poste*) postmark; (*comprimé*) tablet; (*d'acteur etc*) fee; *Fig* distinctive character. ◆**cacheter** *vt* to seal.

cachot [kaʃo] *nm* dungeon.

cachotteries [kaʃɔtri] *nfpl* secretiveness; (*petits secrets*) little mysteries. ◆**cachottier, -ière** *a* & *nmf* secretive (person).

cacophonie [kakɔfɔni] *nf* cacophony.

cactus [kaktys] *nm* cactus.

cadastre [kadastr] *nm* (*registre*) land register.

cadavre [kadavr] *nm* corpse. ◆**cadavéri-**

que a (*teint etc*) cadaverous; **rigidité c.** rigor mortis.

caddie® [kadi] nm supermarket trolly *ou Am* cart.

cadeau, -x [kado] nm present, gift.

cadenas [kadna] nm padlock. ◆**cade-nasser** vt to padlock.

cadence [kadɑ̃s] nf rhythm; *Mus* cadence; (*taux, vitesse*) rate; **en c.** in time. ◆**cadencé** a rhythmical.

cadet, -ette [kadɛ, -ɛt] a (*de deux frères etc*) younger; (*de plus de deux*) youngest; — nmf (*enfant*) younger (child); youngest (child); *Sp* junior; **c'est mon c.** he's my junior.

cadran [kadrɑ̃] nm (*de téléphone etc*) dial; (*de montre*) face; **c. solaire** sundial; **faire le tour du c.** to sleep round the clock.

cadre [kadr] nm 1 (*de photo, vélo etc*) frame; (*décor*) setting; (*sur un imprimé*) box; **dans le c. de** (*limites, contexte*) within the frame-work *ou* scope of, as part of. 2 (*chef*) *Com* executive, manager; pl (*personnel*) *Mil* officers; *Com* management, managers.

cadr/er [kadre] vi to tally (**avec with**); — vt (*image*) *Cin Phot* to centre. ◆**—eur** nm cameraman.

caduc, -uque [kadyk] a (*usage*) obsolete; *Bot* deciduous; *Jur* null and void.

cafard, -arde [kafar, -ard] 1 nmf (*espion*) sneak. 2 nm (*insecte*) cockroach; **avoir le c.** to be in the dumps; **ça me donne le c.** it depresses me. ◆**cafardeux, -euse** a (*personne*) in the dumps; (*qui donne le cafard*) depressing.

café [kafe] nm coffee; (*bar*) café; **c. au lait, c. crème** white coffee, coffee with milk; **c. noir, c. nature** black coffee; **tasse de c.** cup of black coffee. ◆**caféine** nf caffeine. ◆**cafétéria** nf cafeteria. ◆**cafetier** nm café owner. ◆**cafetière** nf percolator, coffeepot.

cafouiller [kafuje] vi *Fam* to make a mess (of things). ◆**cafouillage** nm *Fam* mess, muddle, snafu.

cage [kaʒ] nf cage; (*d'escalier*) well; (*d'ascenseur*) shaft; **c. des buts** *Fb* goal (area).

cageot [kaʒo] nm crate.

cagibi [kaʒibi] nm (*storage*) room, cubby-hole.

cagneux, -euse [kaɲø, -øz] a knock-kneed.

cagnotte [kaɲɔt] nf (*tirelire*) kitty.

cagoule [kagul] nf (*de bandit, pénitent*) hood.

cahier [kaje] nm (*carnet*) (note)book; *Scol* exercise book.

cahin-caha [kaɛ̃kaa] adv **aller c.-caha** to jog along (with ups and downs).

cahot [kao] nm jolt, bump. ◆**cahot/er** vt to jolt, bump; — vi (*véhicule*) to jolt along. ◆**—ant** a, ◆**cahoteux, -euse** a bumpy.

caïd [kaid] nm *Fam* big shot, leader.

caille [kaj] nf (*oiseau*) quail.

cailler [kaje] vti, — **se c.** vpr (*sang*) to clot, congeal; (*lait*) to curdle; **faire c.** (*lait*) to curdle; **ça caille** *Fam* it's freezing cold. ◆**caillot** nm (*blood*) clot.

caillou, -x [kaju] nm stone; (*galet*) pebble. ◆**caillouté** a gravelled. ◆**caillouteux, -euse** a stony.

caisse [kɛs] nf (*boîte*) case, box; (*cageot*) crate; (*guichet*) cash desk, pay desk; (*de supermarché*) checkout; (*fonds*) fund; (*bureau*) (paying-in) office; *Mus* drum; *Aut* body; **c. (enregistreuse)** cash register, till; **c. d'épargne** savings bank; **de c.** (*livre, recettes*) cash-. ◆**caissier, -ière** nmf cash-ier; (*de supermarché*) checkout assistant.

caisson [kɛsɔ̃] nm (*de plongeur*) & *Mil* caisson.

cajoler [kaʒɔle] vt (*câliner*) to pamper, pet, cosset. ◆**cajolerie(s)** nf(pl) pampering.

cajou [kaʒu] nm (*noix*) cashew.

cake [kɛk] nm fruit cake.

calamité [kalamite] nf calamity.

calandre [kalɑ̃dr] nf *Aut* radiator grille.

calcaire [kalkɛr] a (*terrain*) chalky; (*eau*) hard; — nm *Géol* limestone.

calciné [kalsine] a charred, burnt to a cinder.

calcium [kalsjɔm] nm calcium.

calcul [kalkyl] nm 1 calculation; (*estima-tion*) calculation, reckoning; (*discipline*) arithmetic; (*différentiel*) calculus. 2 *Méd* stone. ◆**calcul/er** vt (*compter*) to calcu-late, reckon; (*évaluer, combiner*) to calcu-late. ◆**—é** a (*risque etc*) calculated. ◆**calculateur** nm calculator, computer. ◆**calculatrice** nf (*ordinateur*) calculator.

cale [kal] nf 1 (*pour maintenir*) wedge. 2 *Nau* hold; **c. sèche** dry dock.

calé [kale] a *Fam* (*instruit*) clever (**en qch at sth**); (*difficile*) tough.

caleçon [kalsɔ̃] nm underpants; **c. de bain** bathing trunks.

calembour [kalɑ̃bur] nm pun.

calendrier [kalɑ̃drije] nm (*mois et jours*) calendar; (*programme*) timetable.

cale-pied [kalpje] nm (*de bicyclette*) toe-clip.

calepin [kalpɛ̃] nm (*pocket*) notebook.

caler [kale] 1 vt (*meuble etc*) to wedge (up); (*appuyer*) to prop (up). 2 vt (*moteur*) to stall; – vi to stall; (abandonner) Fam give up.

calfeutrer [kalføtre] vt (avec du bourrelet) to draughtproof; **se c. (chez soi)** to shut oneself away, hole up.

calibre [kalibr] nm (diamètre) calibre; (d'œuf) grade; **de ce c.** (bêtise etc) of this degree. ◆**calibrer** vt (œufs) to grade.

calice [kalis] nm (vase) Rel chalice.

calicot [kaliko] nm (tissu) calico.

califourchon (à) [akalifurʃɔ̃] adv astride; **se mettre à c. sur** to straddle.

câlin [kɑlɛ̃] a endearing, cuddly. ◆**câliner** vt (cajoler) to make a fuss of; (caresser) to cuddle. ◆**câlineries** nfpl endearing ways.

calleux, -euse [kalø, -øz] a callous, horny.

calligraphie [kaligrafi] nf calligraphy.

calme [kalm] a calm; (flegmatique) calm, cool; (journée etc) quiet, calm; – nm calm(ness); **du c.!** keep quiet!; (pas de panique) keep calm!; **dans le c.** (travailler, étudier) in peace and quiet. ◆**calm/er** vt (douleur) to soothe; (inquiétude) to calm; (ardeur) to damp(en); **c. qn** to calm s.o. (down); – **se c.** vpr to calm down. ◆**—ant** nm sedative; **sous calmants** under sedation.

calomnie [kalɔmni] nf slander; (par écrit) libel. ◆**calomnier** vt to slander; to libel. ◆**calomnieux, -euse** a slanderous; libellous.

calorie [kalɔri] nf calorie.

calorifère [kalɔrifɛr] nm stove.

calorifuge [kalɔrifyʒ] a (heat-)insulating. ◆**calorifuger** vt to lag.

calot [kalo] nm Mil forage cap.

calotte [kalɔt] nf Rel skull cap; (gifle) Fam slap; **c. glaciaire** icecap.

calque [kalk] nm (dessin) tracing; (imitation) (exact ou carbon) copy; (papier-)c. tracing paper. ◆**calquer** vt to trace; to copy; **c. sur** to model on.

calumet [kalymɛ] nm **c. de la paix** peace pipe.

calvaire [kalvɛr] nm Rel calvary; Fig agony.

calvitie [kalvisi] nf baldness.

camarade [kamarad] nmf friend, chum; Pol comrade; **c. de jeu** playmate; **c. d'atelier** workmate. ◆**camaraderie** nf friendship, companionship.

cambouis [kɑ̃bwi] nm grease, (engine) oil.

cambrer [kɑ̃bre] vt to arch; **c. les reins** ou **le buste** to throw out one's chest; – **se c.** vpr to throw back one's shoulders. ◆**cambrure** nf curve; (de pied) arch, instep.

cambriol/er [kɑ̃brijɔle] vt to burgle, Am burglarize. ◆**—age** nm burglary. ◆**—eur, -euse** nmf burglar.

came [kam] nf Tech cam; **arbre à cames** camshaft.

camée [kame] nm (pierre) cameo.

caméléon [kameleɔ̃] nm (reptile) chameleon.

camélia [kamelja] nm Bot camellia.

camelot [kamlo] nm street hawker. ◆**camelote** nf cheap goods, junk.

camembert [kamɑ̃bɛr] nm Camembert (cheese).

camer (se) [səkame] vpr Fam to get high (on drugs).

caméra [kamera] nf (TV ou film) camera. ◆**caméraman** nm (pl -mans ou -men) cameraman.

camion [kamjɔ̃] nm lorry, Am truck. ◆**c.-benne** nm (pl camions-bennes) dustcart, Am garbage truck. ◆**c.-citerne** nm (pl camions-citernes) tanker, Am tank truck. ◆**camionnage** nm (road) haulage, Am trucking. ◆**camionnette** nf van. ◆**camionneur** nm (entrepreneur) haulage contractor, Am trucker; (conducteur) lorry ou Am truck driver.

camisole [kamizɔl] nf **c. de force** straitjacket.

camomille [kamɔmij] nf Bot camomile; (tisane) camomile tea.

camoufl/er [kamufle] vt to camouflage. ◆**—age** nm camouflage.

camp [kɑ̃] nm camp; **feu de c.** campfire; **lit de c.** camp bed; **c. de concentration** concentration camp; **dans mon c.** (jeu) on my side; **ficher** ou **foutre le c.** Arg to clear off. ◆**camp/er** vi to camp; – vt (personnage) to portray (boldly); (chapeau etc) to plant boldly; – **se c.** vpr to plant oneself (boldly) (devant in front of). ◆**—ement** nm encampment, camp. ◆**—eur, -euse** nmf camper. ◆**camping** nm camping; (terrain) camp(ing) site. ◆**camping-car** nm camper.

campagne [kɑ̃paɲ] nf 1 country(side); **à la c.** in the country. 2 (électorale, militaire etc) campaign. ◆**campagnard, -arde** a country-; – nm countryman; – nf countrywoman.

campanile [kɑ̃panil] nm belltower.

camphre [kɑ̃fr] nm camphor.

campus [kɑ̃pys] nm Univ campus.

camus [kamy] a (personne) snub-nosed; **nez c.** snub nose.

Canada [kanada] nm Canada. ◆**canadien, -ienne** a & nmf Canadian; – nf fur-lined jacket.

canaille [kanɑj] nf rogue, scoundrel; – a vulgar, cheap.

canal, -aux [kanal, -o] nm (*artificiel*) canal; (*bras de mer*) & TV channel; (*conduite*) & *Anat* duct; **par le c. de** via, through. ◆**canalisation** nf (*de gaz etc*) mains. ◆**canaliser** vt (*rivière etc*) to canalize; (*diriger*) Fig to channel.

canapé [kanape] nm **1** (*siège*) sofa, couch, settee. **2** (*tranche de pain*) canapé.

canard [kanar] nm **1** duck; (*mâle*) drake. **2** Mus false note. **3** (*journal*) Péj rag. ◆**canarder** vt (*faire feu sur*) to fire at ou on.

canari [kanari] nm canary.

cancans [kɑ̃kɑ̃] nmpl (malicious) gossip. ◆**cancaner** vi to gossip. ◆**cancanier, -ière** a gossipy.

cancer [kɑ̃sɛr] nm cancer; **le C.** (*signe*) Cancer. ◆**cancéreux, -euse** a cancerous; – nmf cancer patient. ◆**cancérigène** a carcinogenic. ◆**cancérologue** nmf cancer specialist.

cancre [kɑ̃kr] nm Scol Péj dunce.

cancrelat [kɑ̃krəla] nm cockroach.

candélabre [kɑ̃delabr] nm candelabra.

candeur [kɑ̃dœr] nf innocence, artlessness. ◆**candide** a artless, innocent.

candidat, -ate [kɑ̃dida, -at] nmf candidate; (*à un poste*) applicant, candidate; **être ou se porter c. à** to apply for. ◆**candidature** nf application; Pol candidacy; **poser sa c.** to apply (à for).

cane [kan] nf (female) duck. ◆**caneton** nm duckling.

canette [kanɛt] nf **1** (*de bière*) (small) bottle. **2** (*bobine*) spool.

canevas [kanva] nm (*toile*) canvas; (*ébauche*) framework, outline.

caniche [kaniʃ] nm poodle.

canicule [kanikyl] nf scorching heat; (*période*) dog days.

canif [kanif] nm penknife.

canine [kanin] **1** af (*espèce, race*) canine; **exposition c.** dog show. **2** nf (*dent*) canine.

caniveau, -x [kanivo] nm gutter (in street).

canne [kan] nf (walking) stick; (*à sucre, de bambou*) cane; (*de roseau*) reed; **c. à pêche** fishing rod.

cannelle [kanɛl] nf Bot Culin cinnamon.

cannelure [kanlyr] nf groove; Archit flute.

cannette [kanɛt] nf = **canette**.

cannibale [kanibal] nmf & a cannibal. ◆**cannibalisme** nm cannibalism.

canoë [kanɔe] nm canoe; Sp canoeing. ◆**canoëiste** nmf canoeist.

canon [kanɔ̃] nm **1** (big) gun; Hist cannon; (*de fusil etc*) barrel; **c. lisse** smooth bore; **chair à c.** cannon fodder. **2** (*règle*) canon.

◆**canoniser** vt to canonize. ◆**canonnade** nf gunfire. ◆**canonnier** nm gunner.

cañon [kanɔ̃] nm canyon.

canot [kano] nm boat; **c. de sauvetage** lifeboat; **c. pneumatique** rubber dinghy. ◆**canot/er** vi to boat, go boating. ◆**—age** nm boating.

cantaloup [kɑ̃talu] nm (*melon*) cantaloup(e).

cantate [kɑ̃tat] nf Mus cantata.

cantatrice [kɑ̃tatris] nf opera singer.

cantine [kɑ̃tin] nf **1** (*réfectoire*) canteen; **manger à la c.** Scol to have school dinners. **2** (*coffre*) tin trunk.

cantique [kɑ̃tik] nm hymn.

canton [kɑ̃tɔ̃] nm (en France) district (*division of arrondissement*); (en Suisse) canton. ◆**cantonal, -aux** a divisional; cantonal.

cantonade (à la) [alakɑ̃tɔnad] adv (*parler etc*) to all and sundry, to everyone in general.

cantonn/er [kɑ̃tɔne] vt Mil to billet; (*confiner*) to confine; – vi Mil to be billeted; — **se c.** vpr to confine oneself (dans to). ◆**—ement** nm (*lieu*) billet, quarters.

cantonnier [kɑ̃tɔnje] nm road mender.

canular [kanylar] nm practical joke, hoax.

canyon [kanɔ̃] nm canyon.

caoutchouc [kautʃu] nm rubber; (*élastique*) rubber band; pl (*chaussures*) galoshes; **en c.** (*balle etc*) rubber-; **c. mousse** foam. ◆**caoutchouter** vt to rubberize. ◆**caoutchouteux, -euse** a rubbery.

CAP [seape] nm abrév (*certificat d'aptitude professionnelle*) technical and vocational diploma.

cap [kap] nm Géog cape, headland; Nau course; **mettre le c. sur** to steer a course for; **franchir** ou **doubler le c. de** (*difficulté*) to get over the worst of; **franchir** ou **doubler le c. de la trentaine**/etc to turn thirty/etc.

capable [kapabl] a capable, able; **c. de faire** able to do, capable of doing. ◆**capacité** nf ability, capacity; (*contenance*) capacity.

cape [kap] nf cape; (*grande*) cloak.

CAPES [kapɛs] nm abrév (*certificat d'aptitude professionnelle à l'enseignement secondaire*) teaching diploma.

capillaire [kapilɛr] a (*huile, lotion*) hair-.

capitaine [kapitɛn] nm captain.

capital, -ale, -aux [kapital, -o] **1** a major, fundamental, capital; (*peine*) capital; (*péché*) deadly. **2** a (*lettre*) capital; – nf (*lettre, ville*) capital. **3** nm & nmpl Fin capital. ◆**capitaliser** vt (*accumuler*) to build up; – vi to save up. ◆**capitalisme** nm capitalism. ◆**capitaliste** a & nmf capitalist.

capiteux, -euse [kapitø, -øz] a (vin, parfum) heady.

capitonn/er [kapitɔne] vt to pad, upholster. ◆**—age** nm (garniture) padding, upholstery.

capituler [kapityle] vi to surrender, capitulate. ◆**capitulation** nf surrender, capitulation.

caporal, -aux [kapɔral, -o] nm corporal.

capot [kapo] nm Aut bonnet, Am hood.

capote [kapɔt] nf Aut hood, Am (convertible) top; Mil greatcoat; c. (**anglaise**) (préservatif) Fam condom. ◆**capoter** vi Aut Av to overturn.

câpre [kapr] nf Bot Culin caper.

caprice [kapris] nm (passing) whim, caprice. ◆**capricieux, -euse** a capricious.

Capricorne [kaprikɔrn] nm le C. (signe) Capricorn.

capsule [kapsyl] nf (spatiale) & Méd etc capsule; (de bouteille, pistolet d'enfant) cap.

capter [kapte] vt (faveur etc) to win; (attention) to capture, win; (eau) to draw off; Rad to pick up.

captif, -ive [kaptif, -iv] a & nmf captive. ◆**captiver** vt to captivate, fascinate. ◆**captivité** nf captivity.

capture [kaptyr] nf capture, catch. ◆**capturer** vt (criminel, navire) to capture; (animal) to catch, capture.

capuche [kapyʃ] nf hood. ◆**capuchon** nm hood; (de moine) cowl; (pèlerine) hooded (rain)coat; (de stylo) cap, top.

capucine [kapysin] nf (plante) nasturtium.

caquet [kake] nm (bavardage) cackle. ◆**caquet/er** vi (poule, personne) to cackle. ◆**—age** nm cackle.

car [kar] 1 conj because, for. 2 nm coach, bus, Am bus; c. **de police** police van.

carabine [karabin] nf rifle, carbine; c. **à air comprimé** airgun.

carabiné [karabine] a Fam violent; (punition, amende) very stiff.

caracoler [karakɔle] vi to prance, caper.

caractère [karaktɛr] nm 1 (lettre) Typ character; **en petits caractères** in small print; **caractères d'imprimerie** block capitals ou letters; **caractères gras** bold type ou characters. 2 (tempérament, nature) character, nature; (attribut) characteristic; **aucun c. de gravité** no serious element; **son c. inégal** his ou her uneven temper; **avoir bon c.** to be good-natured. ◆**caractériel, -ielle** a (trait, troubles) character-; – a & nmf disturbed (child). ◆**caractériser** vt to characterize; **se c. par** to be characterized by. ◆**caractéristique** a & nf characteristic.

carafe [karaf] nf decanter, carafe.

carambol/er [karɑ̃bɔle] vt Aut to smash into. ◆**—age** nm pileup, multiple smash-up.

caramel [karamɛl] nm caramel; (bonbon dur) toffee.

carapace [karapas] nf (de tortue etc) & Fig shell.

carat [kara] nm carat.

caravane [karavan] nf (dans le désert) caravan; Aut caravan, Am trailer; c. **publicitaire** publicity convoy. ◆**caravaning** n, ◆**caravanage** n caravanning.

carbone [karbɔn] nm carbon; (**papier**) c. carbon (paper). ◆**carboniser** vt to burn (to ashes), char; (substance) Ch to carbonize; **être mort carbonisé** to be burned to death.

carburant [karbyrɑ̃] nm Aut fuel. ◆**carburateur** nm carburettor, Am carburetor.

carcan [karkɑ̃] nm Hist iron collar; (contrainte) Fig yoke.

carcasse [karkas] nf Anat carcass; (d'immeuble etc) frame, shell.

cardiaque [kardjak] a (trouble etc) heart-; **crise c.** heart attack; **arrêt c.** cardiac arrest; – nmf heart patient.

cardinal, -aux [kardinal, -o] 1 a (nombre, point) cardinal. 2 nm Rel cardinal.

Carême [karɛm] nm Lent.

carence [karɑ̃s] nf inadequacy, incompetence; Méd deficiency.

carène [karɛn] nf Nau hull. ◆**caréné** a Aut Av streamlined.

caresse [karɛs] nf caress. ◆**caress/er** [karese] vt (animal, enfant etc) to stroke, pat, fondle; (femme, homme) to caress; (espoir) to cherish. ◆**—ant** a endearing, loving.

cargaison [kargɛzɔ̃] nf cargo, freight. ◆**cargo** nm freighter, cargo boat.

caricature [karikatyr] nf caricature. ◆**caricatural, -aux** a ludicrous; **portrait c.** portrait in caricature. ◆**caricaturer** vt to caricature.

carie [kari] nf **la c.** (**dentaire**) tooth decay; **une c.** a cavity. ◆**carié** a (dent) decayed, bad.

carillon [karijɔ̃] nm (cloches) chimes, peal; (horloge) chiming clock. ◆**carillonner** vi to chime, peal.

carlingue [karlɛ̃g] nf (fuselage) Av cabin.

carnage [karnaʒ] *nm* carnage.

carnassier, -ière [karnasje, -jɛr] *a* carnivorous; – *nmf* carnivore.

carnaval, *pl* **-als** [karnaval] *nm* carnival.

carné [karne] *a* (*régime*) meat-.

carnet [karnɛ] *nm* notebook; (*de timbres, chèques, adresses etc*) book; **c. de notes** school report; **c. de route** logbook; **c. de vol** *Av* logbook.

carnivore [karnivɔr] *a* carnivorous; – *nm* carnivore.

carotte [karɔt] *nf* carrot.

carotter [karɔte] *vt Arg* to wangle, cadge (à qn from s.o.).

carpe [karp] *nf* carp.

carpette [karpɛt] *nf* rug.

carquois [karkwa] *nm* (*étui*) quiver.

carré [kare] *a* square; (*en affaires*) *Fig* plain-dealing; – *nm* square; (*de jardin*) patch; *Nau* messroom; **c. de soie** (square) silk scarf.

carreau, -x [karo] *nm* (*vitre*) (window) pane; (*pavé*) tile; (*sol*) tiled floor; *Cartes* diamonds; **à carreaux** (*nappe etc*) check(ed); **se tenir à c.** to watch one's step; **rester sur le c.** to be left for dead; (*candidat*) *Fig* to be left out in the cold. ◆**carrel/er** *vt* to tile. ◆**—age** *nm* (*sol*) tiled floor; (*action*) tiling.

carrefour [karfur] *nm* crossroads.

carrelet [karlɛ] *nm* (*poisson*) plaice, *Am* flounder.

carrément [karemɑ̃] *adv* (*dire etc*) straight out, bluntly; (*complètement*) downright, well and truly.

carrer (se) [səkare] *vpr* to settle down firmly.

carrière [karjɛr] *nf* **1** (*terrain*) quarry. **2** (*métier*) career.

carrosse [karɔs] *nm Hist* (horse-drawn) carriage. ◆**carrossable** *a* suitable for vehicles. ◆**carrosserie** *nf Aut* body(work).

carrousel [karuzɛl] *nm* (*tourbillon*) *Fig* whirl, merry-go-round.

carrure [karyr] *nf* breadth of shoulders, build; *Fig* calibre.

cartable [kartabl] *nm Scol* satchel.

carte [kart] *nf* card; (*de lecteur*) ticket; *Géog* map; *Nau* Mét chart; *Culin* menu; *pl* (*jeu*) cards; **c. (postale)** (post)card; **c. à jouer** playing card; **c. de crédit** credit card; **c. des vins** wine list; **c. grise** *Aut* vehicle registration; **c. blanche** *Fig* free hand.

cartel [kartɛl] *nm Écon Pol* cartel.

carter [kartɛr] *nm* (*de moteur*) *Aut* crankcase; (*de bicyclette*) chain guard.

cartilage [kartilaʒ] *nm* cartilage.

carton [kartɔ̃] *nm* cardboard; (*boîte*) cardboard box, carton; **c. à dessin** portfolio; **en c.-pâte** (*faux*) *Péj* pasteboard; **faire un c. sur** *Fam* to take a potshot at. ◆**cartonn/er** *vt* (*livre*) to case; **livre cartonné** hardback. ◆**—age** *nm* (*emballage*) cardboard package.

cartouche [kartuʃ] *nf* cartridge; (*de cigarettes*) carton; *Phot* cassette. ◆**cartouchière** *nf* (*ceinture*) cartridge belt.

cas [kɑ] *nm* case; **en tout c.** in any case *ou* event; **en aucun c.** on no account; **en c. de besoin** if need(s) be; **en c. d'accident** in the event of an accident; **en c. d'urgence** in (case of) an emergency; **faire c. de/peu de c. de** to set great/little store by; **au c. où elle tomberait** if she should fall; **pour le c. où il pleuvrait** in case it rains.

casanier, -ière [kazanje, -jɛr] *a & nmf* home-loving (person); (*pantouflard*) *Péj* stay-at-home (person).

casaque [kazak] *nf* (*du jockey*) shirt, blouse.

cascade [kaskad] *nf* **1** waterfall; (*série*) *Fig* spate; **en c.** in succession. **2** *Cin* stunt. ◆**cascadeur, -euse** *nmf Cin* stunt man, stunt woman.

case [kɑz] *nf* **1** pigeonhole; (*de tiroir*) compartment; (*d'échiquier etc*) square; (*de formulaire*) box. **2** (*hutte*) hut, cabin.

caser [kaze] *vt Fam* (*ranger*) to park, place; **c. qn** (*dans un logement ou un travail*) to find a place for s.o.; (*marier*) to marry s.o. off; – **se c.** *vpr* to settle down.

caserne [kazɛrn] *nf Mil* barracks; **c. de pompiers** fire station.

casier [kazje] *nm* pigeonhole, compartment; (*meuble à tiroirs*) filing cabinet; (*fermant à clef, à consigne automatique*) locker; **c. à bouteilles/à disques** bottle/record rack; **c. judiciaire** criminal record.

casino [kazino] *nm* casino.

casque [kask] *nm* helmet; (*pour cheveux*) (hair) dryer; **c. (à écouteurs)** headphones; **les Casques bleus** the UN peace-keeping force. ◆**casqué** *a* helmeted, wearing a helmet.

casquer [kaske] *vi Fam* to pay up, cough up.

casquette [kaskɛt] *nf* (*coiffure*) cap.

cassation [kasasjɔ̃] *nf* **Cour de c.** supreme court of appeal.

casse¹ [kɑs] *nf* **1** (*action*) breakage; (*objets*) breakages; (*grabuge*) *Fam* trouble; **mettre à la c.** to scrap; **vendre à la c.** to sell for scrap. **2** *Typ* case; **bas/haut de c.** lower/upper case.

casse² [kas] *nm* (*cambriolage*) *Arg* break-in.

casse-cou [kasku] *nmf inv* (*personne*) *Fam* daredevil. ◆**c.-croûte** *nm inv* snack. ◆**c.-gueule** *nm inv Fam* death trap; – *a* (*rue*) perilous. ◆**c.-noisettes** *nm inv,* ◆**c.-noix** *nm inv* nut-cracker(s). ◆**c.-pieds** *nmf inv* (*personne*) *Fam* pain in the neck. ◆**c.-tête** *nm inv* **1** (*massue*) club. **2** (*problème*) headache; (*jeu*) puzzle, brain teaser.

cass/er [kase] *vt* to break; (*noix*) to crack; (*annuler*) *Jur* to annul; (*dégrader*) *Mil* to cashier; – *vi*, – **se c.** *vpr* to break; **il me casse la tête** *Fam* he's giving me a headache; **elle me casse les pieds** *Fam* she's getting on my nerves; **se c. la tête** *Fam* to rack one's brains; **c. la figure à qn** *Fam* to smash s.o.'s face in; **se c. la figure** (*tomber*) *Fam* to come a cropper, *Am* take a spill; **ça ne casse rien** *Fam* it's nothing special; **ça vaut 50F à tout c.** *Fam* it's worth 50F at the very most; **il ne s'est pas cassé** *Iron Fam* he didn't bother himself *ou* exhaust himself. ◆**—ant** *a* (*fragile*) brittle; (*brusque*) curt, imperious; (*fatigant*) *Fam* exhausting. ◆**—eur** *nm Aut* breaker, scrap merchant; (*manifestant*) demonstrator who damages property.

casserole [kasrɔl] *nf* (sauce)pan.

cassette [kaset] *nf* (*pour magnétophone ou magnétoscope*) cassette; **sur c.** (*film*) on video; **faire une c. de** (*film*) to make a video of.

cassis 1 [kasis] *nm Bot* blackcurrant; (*boisson*) blackcurrant liqueur. **2** [kasi] *nm Aut* dip (*across road*).

cassoulet [kasule] *nm* stew (*of meat and beans*).

cassure [kasyr] *nf* (*fissure, rupture*) break; *Géol* fault.

castagnettes [kastaɲɛt] *nfpl* castanets.

caste [kast] *nf* caste; **esprit de c.** class consciousness.

castor [kastɔr] *nm* beaver.

castrer [kastre] *vt* to castrate. ◆**castration** *nf* castration.

cataclysme [kataklism] *nm* cataclysm.

catacombes [katakɔ̃b] *nfpl* catacombs.

catalogue [katalɔg] *nm* catalogue. ◆**cataloguer** *vt* (*livres etc*) to catalogue; **c. qn** *Péj* to categorize s.o.

catalyseur [katalizœr] *nm Ch & Fig* catalyst.

cataphote® [katafɔt] *nm Aut* reflector.

cataplasme [kataplasm] *nm Méd* poultice.

catapulte [katapylt] *nf Hist Av* catapult. ◆**catapulter** *vt* to catapult.

cataracte [katarakt] *nf* **1** *Méd* cataract. **2** (*cascade*) falls, cataract.

catastrophe [katastrɔf] *nf* disaster, catastrophe; **atterrir en c.** to make an emergency landing. ◆**catastrophique** *a* disastrous, catastrophic.

catch [katʃ] *nm* (all-in) wrestling. ◆**catcheur, -euse** *nmf* wrestler.

catéchisme [kateʃism] *nm Rel* catechism.

catégorie [kategɔri] *nf* category. ◆**catégorique** *a* categorical.

cathédrale [katedral] *nf* cathedral.

catholicisme [katɔlisism] *nm* Catholicism. ◆**catholique** *a & nmf* Catholic; **pas (très) c.** (*affaire, personne*) *Fig* shady, doubtful.

catimini (en) [ākatimini] *adv* on the sly.

cauchemar [koʃmar] *nm* nightmare.

cause [koz] *nf* cause; *Jur* case; **à c. de** because of, on account of; **et pour c.!** for a very good reason!; **pour c. de** on account of; **en connaissance de c.** in full knowledge of the facts; **mettre en c.** (*la bonne foi de qn etc*) to (call into) question; (*personne*) to implicate; **en c.** involved, in question.

caus/er [koze] **1** *vt* (*provoquer*) to cause. **2** *vi* (*bavarder*) to chat (**de** about); (*discourir*) to talk; (*jaser*) to blab. ◆**—ant** *a Fam* chatty, talkative. ◆**causerie** *nf* talk. ◆**causette** *nf* **faire la c.** *Fam* to have a little chat.

caustique [kostik] *a* (*substance, esprit*) caustic.

cauteleux, -euse [kotlø, -øz] *a* wily, sly.

cautériser [koterize] *vt Méd* to cauterize.

caution [kosjɔ̃] *nf* surety; (*pour libérer qn*) *Jur* bail; **sous c.** on bail; **sujet à c.** (*nouvelle etc*) very doubtful. ◆**cautionn/er** *vt* (*approuver*) to sanction. ◆**—ement** *nm* (*garantie*) surety.

cavalcade [kavalkad] *nf Fam* stampede; (*défilé*) cavalcade. ◆**cavale** *nf* **en c.** *Arg* on the run. ◆**cavaler** *vi Fam* to run, rush.

cavalerie [kavalri] *nf Mil* cavalry; (*de cirque*) horses. ◆**cavalier, -ière 1** *nmf* rider; – *nm Mil* trooper, cavalryman; *Échecs* knight; – *af* **allée cavalière** bridle path. **2** *nmf* (*pour danser*) partner, escort. **3** *a* (*insolent*) offhand.

cave [kav] **1** *nf* cellar, vault. **2** *a* sunken, hollow. ◆**caveau, -x** *nm* (*sépulture*) (burial) vault.

caverne [kavɛrn] *nf* cave, cavern; **homme**

des cavernes caveman. ◆**caverneux,
-euse** *a* (*voix, rire*) hollow, deep-sounding.
caviar [kavjar] *nm* caviar(e).
cavité [kavite] *nf* cavity.
CCP [sesepe] *nm abrév* (*Compte chèque
postal*) PO Giro account, *Am* Post Office
checking account.
ce[1] [s(ə)] (c' *before e and* é) *pron dém* **1**
it, that; **c'est toi/bon/demain**/*etc* it's *ou*
that's you/good/tomorrow/*etc*; **c'est mon
médecin** he's my doctor; **ce sont eux qui
. . .** they are the ones who . . . ; **c'est à elle
de jouer** it's her turn to play; **est-ce que tu
viens?** are you coming?; **sur ce** at this
point, thereupon. **2 ce que, ce qui** what; **je
sais ce qui est bon/ce que tu veux** I know
what is good/what you want; **ce que c'est
beau!** how beautiful it is!
ce[2]**, cette,** *pl* **ces** [s(ə), sɛt, se] (**ce** *becomes*
cet *before a vowel or mute h*) *a dém* this,
that, *pl* these, those; (+ -**ci**) this, *pl* these;
(+ -**là**) that, *pl* those; **cet homme** this *ou*
that man; **cet homme-ci** this man; **cet
homme-là** that man.
ceci [səsi] *pron dém* this; **écoutez bien c.**
listen to this.
cécité [sesite] *nf* blindness.
céder [sede] *vt* to give up (à to); *Jur* to
transfer; **c. le pas à** to give way *ou* precedence to; – *vi* (*personne*) to give way, give
in, yield (à to); (*branche, chaise etc*) to give
way.
cédille [sedij] *nf Gram* cedilla.
cèdre [sɛdr] *nm* (*arbre, bois*) cedar.
CEE [seøø] *nf abrév* (*Communauté économique européenne*) EEC.
ceindre [sɛ̃dr] *vt* (*épée*) *Lit* to gird on.
ceinture [sɛ̃tyr] *nf* belt; (*de robe de chambre*)
cord; (*taille*) *Anat* waist; (*de remparts*) *Hist*
girdle; **petite/grande c.** *Rail* inner/outer
circle; **c. de sécurité** *Aut Av* seatbelt; **c. de
sauvetage** lifebelt. ◆**ceinturer** *vt* to seize
round the waist; *Rugby* to tackle; (*ville*) to
girdle, surround.
cela [s(ə)la] *pron dém* (*pour désigner*)
that; (*sujet indéfini*) it, that; **c. m'attriste
que . . .** it saddens me that . . . ; **quand/
comment**/*etc* **c.?** when?/how?/*etc*; **c'est c.**
that is so.
célèbre [selɛbr] *a* famous. ◆**célébrité** *nf*
fame; (*personne*) celebrity.
célébrer [selebre] *vt* to celebrate.
◆**célébration** *nf* celebration (**de** of).
céleri [sɛlri] *nm* (*en branches*) celery.
céleste [selɛst] *a* celestial, heavenly.
célibat [seliba] *nm* celibacy. ◆**célibataire**
a (*non marié*) single, unmarried; (*chaste*)

celibate; – *nm* bachelor; – *nf* unmarried
woman, spinster.
celle *voir* **celui**.
cellier [selje] *nm* storeroom (*for wine etc*).
cellophane® [selɔfan] *nf* cellophane®.
cellule [selyl] *nf* cell. ◆**cellulaire** *a* (*tissu
etc*) *Biol* cell-; **voiture c.** prison van.
celluloïd [selylɔid] *nm* celluloid.
cellulose [selyloz] *nf* cellulose.
celtique *ou* **celte** [sɛltik, sɛlt] *a* Celtic.
celui, celle, *pl* **ceux, celles** [səlɥi, sɛl, sø,
sɛl] *pron dém* **1** the one, *pl* those, the ones;
c. de Jean John's (one); **ceux de Jean**
John's (ones), those of John. **2** (+ -**ci**) this
one, *pl* these (ones); (*dont on vient de
parler*) the latter; (+ -**là**) that one, *pl* those
(ones); the former; **ceux-ci sont gros** these
(ones) are big.
cendre [sɑ̃dr] *nf* ash. ◆**cendré** *a*
ash(-coloured), ashen. ◆**cendrée** *nf Sp*
cinder track.
Cendrillon [sɑ̃drijɔ̃] *nm* Cinderella.
censé [sɑ̃se] *a* supposed; **il n'est pas c. le
savoir** he's not supposed to know.
censeur [sɑ̃sœr] *nm* censor; *Scol* assistant
headmaster, vice-principal. ◆**censure** *nf*
la c. (*examen*) censorship; (*comité, service*)
the censor; **motion de c.** *Pol* censure
motion. ◆**censurer** *vt* (*film etc*) to
censor; (*critiquer*) & *Pol* to censure.
cent [sɑ̃] ([sɑ̃t] *pl* [sɑ̃z] *before vowel and mute
h except* **un** *and* **onze**) *a & nm* hundred; **c.
pages** a *ou* one hundred pages; **deux cents
pages** two hundred pages; **deux c. trois
pages** two hundred and three pages; **cinq
pour c.** five per cent. ◆**centaine** *nf* **une c.**
a hundred (or so); **des centaines de** hundreds
of. ◆**centenaire** *a & nmf* centenarian; –
nm (*anniversaire*) centenary. ◆**centième**
a & nmf hundredth; **un c.** a hundredth.
◆**centigrade** *a* centigrade. ◆**centime**
nm centime. ◆**centimètre** *nm* centimetre;
(*ruban*) tape measure.
central, -aux [sɑ̃tral, -o] **1** *a* central;
pouvoir c. (power of) central government. **2**
nm **c. (téléphonique)** (telephone) exchange.
◆**centrale** *nf* (*usine*) power station.
◆**centraliser** *vt* to centralize. ◆**centre**
nm centre; **c. commercial** shopping centre.
◆**c.-ville** *nm inv* city *ou* town centre.
◆**centrer** *vt* to centre. ◆**centrifuge**
a centrifugal. ◆**centrifugeuse** *nf* liquidizer, juice extractor.
centuple [sɑ̃typl] *nm* hundredfold; **au c.** a
hundredfold. ◆**centupler** *vti* to increase a
hundredfold.

cep [sɛp] *nm* vine stock. ◆**cépage** *nm* vine (plant).

cependant [səpɑ̃dɑ̃] *conj* however, yet.

céramique [seramik] *nf* (*art*) ceramics; (*matière*) ceramic; **de** *ou* **en c.** ceramic.

cerceau, -x [sɛrso] *nm* hoop.

cercle [sɛrkl] *nm* (*forme, groupe, étendue*) circle; **c. vicieux** vicious circle.

cercueil [sɛrkœj] *nm* coffin.

céréale [sereal] *nf* cereal.

cérébral, -aux [serebral, -o] *a* cerebral.

cérémonie [seremɔni] *nf* ceremony; **de c.** (*tenue etc*) ceremonial; (*inviter, manger*) informally; **faire des cérémonies** *Fam* to make a lot of fuss. ◆**cérémonial,** *pl* **-als** *nm* ceremonial. ◆**cérémonieux, -euse** *a* ceremonious.

cerf [sɛr] *nm* deer; (*mâle*) stag. ◆**cerf-volant** *nm* (*pl* **cerfs-volants**) (*jouet*) kite.

cerise [s(ə)riz] *nf* cherry. ◆**cerisier** *nm* cherry tree.

cerne [sɛrn] *nm* (*cercle, marque*) ring. ◆**cerner** *vt* to surround; (*problème*) to define; **les yeux cernés** with rings under one's eyes.

certain [sɛrtɛ̃] **1** *a* (*sûr*) certain, sure; **il est** *ou* **c'est c. que tu réussiras** you're certain *ou* sure to succeed; **je suis c. de réussir** I'm certain *ou* sure I'll succeed; **être c. de qch** to be certain *ou* sure of sth. **2** *a* (*imprécis, difficile à fixer*) certain; *pl* certain, some; **un c. temps** a certain (amount of) time; – *pron pl* some (people), certain people; (*choses*) some. ◆**certainement** *adv* certainly. ◆**certes** *adv* indeed.

certificat [sɛrtifika] *nm* certificate. ◆**certifi/er** *vt* to certify; **je vous certifie que** I assure you that. ◆**-é** *a* (*professeur*) qualified.

certitude [sɛrtityd] *nf* certainty; **avoir la c. que** to be certain that.

cerveau, -x [sɛrvo] *nm* (*organe*) brain; (*intelligence*) mind, brain(s); **rhume de c.** head cold; **fuite des cerveaux** brain drain.

cervelas [sɛrvəla] *nm* saveloy.

cervelle [sɛrvɛl] *nf* (*substance*) brain; *Culin* brains; **tête sans c.** scatterbrain.

ces *voir* ce².

CES [seɑɛs] *nm abrév* (*collège d'enseignement secondaire*) comprehensive school, *Am* high school.

césarienne [sezarjɛn] *nf Méd* Caesarean (section).

cessation [sɛsasjɔ̃] *nf* (*arrêt, fin*) suspension.

cesse [sɛs] *nf* **sans c.** incessantly; **elle n'a**

(**pas**) **eu de c. que je fasse . . .** she had no rest until I did . . . .

cesser [sese] *vti* to stop; **faire c.** to put a stop *ou* halt to; **il ne cesse (pas) de parler** he doesn't stop talking. ◆**cessez-le-feu** *nm inv* ceasefire.

cession [sɛsjɔ̃] *nf Jur* transfer.

c'est-à-dire [sɛtadir] *conj* that is (to say), in other words.

cet, cette *voir* ce².

ceux *voir* celui.

chacal, pl -als [ʃakal] *nm* jackal.

chacun, -une [ʃakœ̃, -yn] *pron* each (one), every one; (*tout le monde*) everyone.

chagrin [ʃagrɛ̃] **1** *nm* sorrow, grief; **avoir du c.** to be very upset. **2** *a Lit* doleful. ◆**chagriner** *vt* to upset, distress.

chahut [ʃay] *nm* racket, noisy disturbance. ◆**chahut/er** *vi* to create a racket *ou* a noisy disturbance; – *vt* (*professeur*) to be rowdy with, play up. ◆**-eur, -euse** *nmf* rowdy.

chai [ʃe] *nm* wine and spirits storehouse.

chaîne [ʃen] *nf* chain; *TV* channel, network; *Géog* chain, range; *Nau* cable; *Tex* warp; (*pl liens*) *Fig* shackles, chains; **c. de montage** assembly line; **travail à la c.** production-line work; **c. haute fidélité, c. hi-fi** hi-fi system; **c. de magasins** chain of shops *ou Am* stores; **collision en c.** *Aut* multiple collision; **réaction en c.** chain reaction. ◆**chaînette** *nf* (small) chain. ◆**chaînon** *nm* (*anneau, lien*) link.

chair [ʃɛr] *nf* flesh; (*couleur*) **c.** flesh-coloured; **en c. et en os** in the flesh; **la c. de poule** goose pimples, gooseflesh; **bien en c.** plump; **c. à saucisses** sausage meat.

chaire [ʃɛr] *nf Univ* chair; *Rel* pulpit.

chaise [ʃez] *nf* chair, seat; **c. longue** (*siège pliant*) deckchair; **c. d'enfant, c. haute** high-chair.

chaland [ʃalɑ̃] *nm* barge, lighter.

châle [ʃal] *nm* shawl.

chalet [ʃale] *nm* chalet.

chaleur [ʃalœr] *nf* heat; (*douce*) warmth; (*d'un accueil, d'une voix etc*) warmth; (*des convictions*) ardour; (*d'une discussion*) heat. ◆**chaleureux, -euse** *a* warm.

challenge [ʃalɑ̃ʒ] *nm Sp* contest.

chaloupe [ʃalup] *nf* launch, long boat.

chalumeau, -x [ʃalymo] *nm* blowlamp, *Am* blowtorch; *Mus* pipe.

chalut [ʃaly] *nm* trawl net, drag net. ◆**chalutier** *nm* (*bateau*) trawler.

chamailler (se) [səʃamaje] *vpr* to squabble, bicker. ◆**chamailleries** *nfpl* squabbling, bickering.

chamarré [ʃamare] *a* (*robe etc*) richly coloured; **c. de** (*décorations etc*) *Péj* bedecked with.

chambard [ʃɑ̃bar] *nm Fam* (*tapage*) rumpus, row. ◆**chambarder** *vt Fam* to turn upside down; **il a tout chambardé dans** he's turned everything upside down in.

chambouler [ʃɑ̃bule] *vt Fam* to make topsy-turvy, turn upside down.

chambre [ʃɑ̃br] *nf* (bed)room; *Pol Jur Tech Anat* chamber; **c. à coucher** bedroom; (*mobilier*) bedroom suite; **c. à air** (*de pneu*) inner tube; **c. des Communes** *Pol* House of Commons; **c. d'ami** guest *ou* spare room; **c. forte** strongroom; **c. noire** *Phot* darkroom; **garder la c.** to stay indoors. ◆**chambrée** *nf Mil* barrack room. ◆**chambrer** *vt* (*vin*) to bring to room temperature.

chameau, -x [ʃamo] *nm* camel.

chamois [ʃamwa] **1** *nm* (*animal*) chamois; **peau de c.** chamois (leather), shammy. **2** *a inv* buff(-coloured).

champ [ʃɑ̃] *nm* field; (*domaine*) *Fig* scope, range; **c. de bataille** battlefield; **c. de courses** racecourse, racetrack; **c. de foire** fairground; **c. de tir** (*terrain*) rifle range; **laisser le c. libre à qn** to leave the field open for s.o. ◆**champêtre** *a* rustic, rural.

champagne [ʃɑ̃paɲ] *nm* champagne; **c. brut** extra-dry champagne.

champignon [ʃɑ̃piɲɔ̃] *nm* **1** *Bot* mushroom; **c. vénéneux** toadstool, poisonous mushroom; **c. atomique** mushroom cloud. **2** *Aut Fam* accelerator pedal.

champion [ʃɑ̃pjɔ̃] *nm* champion. ◆**championnat** *nm* championship.

chance [ʃɑ̃s] *nf* luck; (*probabilité de réussir, occasion*) chance; **avoir de la c.** to be lucky; **tenter** *ou* **courir sa c.** to try one's luck; **c'est une c. que...** it's a stroke of luck that ...; **mes chances de succès** my chances of success. ◆**chanceux, -euse** *a* lucky.

chancel/er [ʃɑ̃sle] *vi* to stagger, totter; (*courage*) *Fig* to falter. ◆**—ant** *a* (*pas, santé*) faltering, shaky.

chancelier [ʃɑ̃səlje] *nm* chancellor. ◆**chancellerie** *nf* chancellery.

chancre [ʃɑ̃kr] *nm Méd & Fig* canker.

chandail [ʃɑ̃daj] *nm* (thick) sweater, jersey.

chandelier [ʃɑ̃dəlje] *nm* candlestick.

chandelle [ʃɑ̃dɛl] *nf* candle; **voir trente-six chandelles** *Fig* to see stars; **en c.** *Av Sp* straight into the air.

change [ʃɑ̃ʒ] *nm Fin* exchange; **le contrôle des changes** exchange control; **donner le c. à qn** to deceive s.o. ◆**chang/er** *vt* (*modifier, remplacer, échanger*) to change; **c. qn**

en to change s.o. into; **ça la changera de ne pas travailler** it'll be a change for her not to be working; **– vi** to change; **c. de voiture/d'adresse/etc** to change one's car/address/*etc*; **c. de train/de place** to change trains/places; **c. de vitesse/de cap** to change gear/course; **c. de sujet** to change the subject; **— se c.** *vpr* to change (one's clothes). ◆**—eant** *a* (*temps*) changeable; (*humeur*) fickle; (*couleurs*) changing. ◆**—ement** *nm* change; **aimer le c.** to like change. ◆**—eur** *nm* moneychanger; **c. de monnaie** change machine.

chanoine [ʃanwan] *nm* (*personne*) *Rel* canon.

chanson [ʃɑ̃sɔ̃] *nf* song. ◆**chant** *nm* singing; (*chanson*) song; (*hymne*) chant; **c. de Noël** Christmas carol. ◆**chant/er** *vi* to sing; (*psalmodier*) to chant; (*coq*) to crow; **si ça te chante** *Fam* if you feel like it; **faire c. qn** to blackmail s.o.; **– vt** to sing; (*glorifier*) to sing of; (*dire*) *Fam* to say. ◆**—ant** *a* (*air, voix*) melodious. ◆**—age** *nm* blackmail. ◆**—eur, -euse** *nm* singer.

chantier [ʃɑ̃tje] *nm* (building) site; (*entrepôt*) builder's yard; **c. naval** shipyard; **mettre un travail en c.** to get a task under way.

chantonner [ʃɑ̃tɔne] *vti* to hum.

chantre [ʃɑ̃tr] *nm Rel* cantor.

chanvre [ʃɑ̃vr] *nm* hemp; **c. indien** (*plante*) cannabis.

chaos [kao] *nm* chaos. ◆**chaotique** *a* chaotic.

chaparder [ʃaparde] *vt Fam* to filch, pinch (à from).

chapeau, -x [ʃapo] *nm* hat; (*de champignon, roue*) cap; **c.!** well done!; **donner un coup de c.** (*pour saluer etc*) to raise one's hat; **c. mou** trilby, *Am* fedora. ◆**chapeller** *nm* hatter.

chapelet [ʃaple] *nm* rosary; **dire son c.** to tell one's beads; **un c. de** (*saucisses, injures etc*) a string of.

chapelle [ʃapɛl] *nf* chapel; **c. ardente** chapel of rest.

chaperon [ʃaprɔ̃] *nm* chaperon(e). ◆**chaperonner** *vt* to chaperon(e).

chapiteau, -x [ʃapito] *nm* (*de cirque*) big top; (*pour expositions etc*) marquee, tent; (*de colonne*) *Archit* capital.

chapitre [ʃapitr] *nm* chapter; **sur le c. de** on the subject of. ◆**chapitrer** *vt* to scold, lecture.

chaque [ʃak] *a* each, every.

char [ʃar] *nm Hist* chariot; (*de carnaval*)

float; *Can Fam* car; **c. à bœufs** oxcart; **c. (d'assaut)** *Mil* tank.

charabia [ʃarabja] *nm Fam* gibberish.

charade [ʃarad] *nf (énigme)* riddle; *(mimée)* charade.

charbon [ʃarbɔ̃] *nm* coal; *(fusain)* charcoal; **c. de bois** charcoal; **sur des charbons ardents** like a cat on hot bricks. ◆**charbonnages** *nmpl* coalmines, collieries. ◆**charbonnier, -ière** *a* coal-; – *nm* coal merchant.

charcuter [ʃarkyte] *vt (opérer) Fam Péj* to cut up (badly).

charcuterie [ʃarkytri] *nf* pork butcher's shop; *(aliment)* cooked (pork) meats. ◆**charcutier, -ière** *nmf* pork butcher.

chardon [ʃardɔ̃] *nm Bot* thistle.

chardonneret [ʃardɔnrɛ] *nm (oiseau)* goldfinch.

charge [ʃarʒ] *nf (poids)* load; *(fardeau)* burden; *Jur Él Mil* charge; *(fonction)* office; *pl Fin* financial obligations; *(dépenses)* expenses; *(de locataire)* (maintenance) charges; **charges sociales** national insurance contributions, *Am* Social Security contributions; **à c.** *(enfant, parent)* dependent; **être à c. à qn** to be a burden to s.o.; **à la c. de qn** *(personne)* dependent on s.o.; *(frais)* payable by s.o.; **prendre en c.** to take charge of, take responsibility for.

charg/er [ʃarʒe] *vt* to load; *Él Mil* to charge; *(passager) Fam* to pick up; **se c. de** *(enfant, tâche etc)* to take charge of; **c. qn de** *(impôts etc)* to burden s.o. with; *(paquets etc)* to load s.o. with; *(tâche etc)* to entrust s.o. with; **c. qn de faire** to instruct s.o. to do. ◆**-é, -ée** *a (personne, véhicule, arme etc)* loaded; *(journée etc)* heavy, busy; *(langue)* coated; **c. de** *(arbre, navire etc)* laden with; – *nmf* **c. de cours** *Univ* (temporary) lecturer. ◆**-ement** *nm (action)* loading; *(objet)* load. ◆**-eur** *nm (de piles)* charger.

chariot [ʃarjo] *nm (à bagages etc)* trolley, *Am* cart; *(de ferme)* waggon; *(de machine à écrire)* carriage.

charité [ʃarite] *nf (vertu, secours)* charity; *(acte)* act of charity; **faire la c.** to give to charity; **faire la c. à** *(mendiant)* to give to. ◆**charitable** *a* charitable.

charivari [ʃarivari] *nm Fam* hubbub, hullabaloo.

charlatan [ʃarlatɑ̃] *nm* charlatan, quack.

charme [ʃarm] *nm* **1** charm; *(magie)* spell. **2** *(arbre)* hornbeam. ◆**charm/er** *vt* to charm; **je suis charmé de vous voir** I'm delighted to see you. ◆**-ant** *a* charming.

◆**-eur, -euse** *nmf* charmer; – *a* engaging.

charnel, -elle [ʃarnɛl] *a* carnal.

charnier [ʃarnje] *nm* mass grave.

charnière [ʃarnjɛr] *nf* hinge; *Fig* meeting point (**de** between).

charnu [ʃarny] *a* fleshy.

charogne [ʃarɔɲ] *nf* carrion.

charpente [ʃarpɑ̃t] *nf* frame(work); *(de personne)* build. ◆**charpenté** *a* **bien c.** solidly built. ◆**charpenterie** *nf* carpentry. ◆**charpentier** *nm* carpenter.

charpie [ʃarpi] *nf* **mettre en c.** *(déchirer)* & *Fig* to tear to shreds.

charrette [ʃarɛt] *nf* cart. ◆**charretier** *nm* carter. ◆**charrier 1** *vt (transporter)* to cart; *(rivière)* to carry along, wash down *(sand etc)*. **2** *vti (taquiner) Fam* to tease.

charrue [ʃary] *nf* plough, *Am* plow.

charte [ʃart] *nf Pol* charter.

charter [ʃartɛr] *nm Av* charter (flight).

chas [ʃa] *nm* eye *(of a needle)*.

chasse [ʃas] *nf* **1** hunting, hunt; *(poursuite)* chase; *Av* fighter forces; **de c.** *(pilote, avion)* fighter-; **c. sous-marine** underwater (harpoon) fishing; **c. à courre** hunting; **tableau de c.** *(animaux abattus)* bag; **faire la c. à** to hunt down, hunt for; **donner la c. à** to give chase to; **c. à l'homme** manhunt. **2** **c. d'eau** toilet flush; **tirer la c.** to flush the toilet.

châsse [ʃas] *nf* shrine.

chassé-croisé [ʃasekrwaze] *nm (pl* chassés-croisés) *Fig* confused coming(s) and going(s).

chass/er [ʃase] *vt (animal)* to hunt; *(papillon)* to chase; *(faire partir)* to drive out *ou* off; *(employé)* to dismiss; *(mouche)* to brush away; *(odeur)* to get rid of; – *vi* to hunt; *Aut* to skid. ◆**-eur, -euse** *nmf* hunter; – *nm (domestique)* pageboy, bellboy; *Av* fighter; **c. à pied** infantryman. ◆**chasse-neige** *nm inv* snowplough, *Am* snowplow.

châssis [ʃasi] *nm* frame; *Aut* chassis.

chaste [ʃast] *a* chaste, pure. ◆**chasteté** *nf* chastity.

chat, chatte [ʃa, ʃat] *nmf* cat; **un c. dans la gorge** a frog in one's throat; **d'autres chats à fouetter** other fish to fry; **pas un c.** not a soul; **ma (petite) chatte** *Fam* my darling; **c. perché** *(jeu)* tag.

châtaigne [ʃatɛɲ] *nf* chestnut. ◆**châtaignier** *nm* chestnut tree. ◆**châtain** *a inv* (chestnut) brown.

château, -x [ʃato] *nm (forteresse)* castle; *(palais)* palace, stately home; **c. fort** fortìfied castle; **châteaux en Espagne** *Fig* castles in the air; **c. d'eau** water tower; **c. de cartes** house of cards. ◆**châtelain, -aine** *nmf* lord of the manor, lady of the manor.

châtier [ʃɑtje] *vt Litt* to chastise, castigate; *(style)* to refine.

châtiment [ʃɑtimɑ̃] *nm* punishment.

chaton [ʃatɔ̃] *nm* **1** *(chat)* kitten. **2** *(de bague)* setting, mounting. **3** *Bot* catkin.

chatouill/er [ʃatuje] *vt (pour faire rire)* to tickle; *(exciter, plaire à) Fig* to titillate. ◆**—ement** *nm* tickle; *(action)* tickling. ◆**chatouilleux, -euse** *a* ticklish; *(irritable)* touchy.

chatoyer [ʃatwaje] *vi* to glitter, sparkle.

châtrer [ʃɑtre] *vt* to castrate.

chatte [ʃat] *voir* chat.

chatteries [ʃatri] *nfpl* cuddles; *(friandises)* delicacies.

chatterton [ʃatertɔn] *nm* adhesive insulating tape.

chaud [ʃo] *a* hot; *(doux)* warm; *(fervent) Fig* warm; **pleurer à chaudes larmes** to cry bitterly; **–** *nm* heat; warmth; **avoir c.** to be hot; to be warm; **il fait c.** it's hot; it's warm; **être au c.** to be in the warm(th); **ça ne me fait ni c. ni froid** it leaves me indifferent. ◆**chaudement** *adv* warmly; *(avec passion)* hotly.

chaudière [ʃodjer] *nf* boiler.

chaudron [ʃodrɔ̃] *nm* cauldron.

chauffard [ʃofar] *nm* road hog, reckless driver.

chauff/er [ʃofe] *vt* to heat up, warm up; *(métal etc) Tech* to heat; **–** *vi* to heat up, warm up; *Aut* to overheat; **ça va c.** *Fam* things are going to hot up; **– se c.** *vpr* to warm oneself up. ◆**—ant** *a (couverture)* electric; *(plaque)* hot-; *(surface)* heating. ◆**—age** *nm* heating. ◆**—eur** *nm* **1** *(de chaudière)* stoker. **2** *Aut* driver; *(employé, domestique)* chauffeur. ◆**chauffe-bain** *nm*, ◆**chauffe-eau** *nm inv* water heater. ◆**chauffe-plats** *nm inv* hotplate.

chaume [ʃom] *nm (tiges coupées)* stubble, straw; *(pour toiture)* thatch; **toit de c.** thatched roof. ◆**chaumière** *nf* thatched cottage.

chaussée [ʃose] *nf* road(way).

chausser [ʃose] *vt (chaussures)* to put on; *(fournir)* to supply in footwear; **c. qn** to put shoes on (to) s.o.; **c. du 40** to take a size 40 shoe; **ce soulier te chausse bien** this shoe fits (you) well; **– se c.** *vpr* to put on one's shoes. ◆**chausse-pied** *nm* shoehorn. ◆**chausson** *nm* slipper; *(de danse)* shoe; **c. (aux pommes)** apple turnover. ◆**chaus-**

sure *nf* shoe; *pl* shoes, footwear; **chaussures à semelles compensées** platform shoes.

chaussette [ʃosɛt] *nf* sock.

chauve [ʃov] *a & nmf* bald (person).

chauve-souris [ʃovsuri] *nf (pl chauves-souris) (animal)* bat.

chauvin, -ine [ʃovɛ̃, -in] *a & nmf* chauvinist.

chaux [ʃo] *nf* lime; **blanc de c.** whitewash.

chavirer [ʃavire] *vti Nau* to capsize.

chef [ʃɛf] *nm* **1** **de son propre c.** on one's own authority. **2** leader, head; *(de tribu)* chief; *Culin* chef; **en c.** *(commandant, rédacteur)* in chief; **c'est un c.!** *(personne remarquable)* he's an ace!; **c. d'atelier** (shop) foreman; **c. de bande** ringleader, gang leader; **c. d'entreprise** company head; **c. d'équipe** foreman; **c. d'État** head of state; **c. d'état-major** chief of staff; **c. de famille** head of the family; **c. de file** leader; **c. de gare** stationmaster; **c. d'orchestre** conductor. ◆**chef-lieu** *nm (pl chefs-lieux)* chief town *(of a département)*.

chef-d'œuvre [ʃɛdœvr] *nm (pl chefs-d'œuvre)* masterpiece.

chemin [ʃ(ə)mɛ̃] *nm* **1** road, path; *(trajet, direction)* way; **beaucoup de c. à faire** a long way to go; **dix minutes de c.** ten minutes' walk; **se mettre en c.** to start out, set out; **faire du c.** to come a long way; *(idée)* to make considerable headway; **c. faisant** on the way; **à mi-c.** half-way. **2** **c. de fer** railway, *Am* railroad. ◆**chemin/er** *vi* to proceed; *(péniblement)* to trudge (along) on foot; *(évoluer) Fig* to progress. ◆**—ement** *nm Fig* progress. ◆**cheminot** *nm* railway *ou Am* railroad employee.

cheminée [ʃ(ə)mine] *nf (sur le toit)* chimney; *(de navire)* funnel; *(âtre)* fireplace; *(encadrement)* mantelpiece.

chemise [ʃ(ə)miz] *nf* shirt; *(couverture cartonnée)* folder; **c. de nuit** nightdress. ◆**chemiserie** *nf* men's shirt (and underwear) shop. ◆**chemisette** *nf* short-sleeved shirt. ◆**chemisier** *nm (vêtement)* blouse.

chenal, -aux [ʃənal, -o] *nm* channel.

chenapan [ʃ(ə)napɑ̃] *nm Hum* rogue, scoundrel.

chêne [ʃɛn] *nm (arbre, bois)* oak.

chenet [ʃ(ə)nɛ] *nm* firedog, andiron.

chenil [ʃ(ə)ni(l)] *nm* kennels.

chenille [ʃ(ə)nij] *nf* caterpillar; *(de char) Mil* caterpillar track.

cheptel [ʃɛptɛl] *nm* livestock.

chèque [ʃɛk] *nm* cheque, *Am* check; **c. de voyage** traveller's cheque, *Am* traveler's check. ◆**c.-repas** *nm* (*pl* **chèques-repas**) luncheon voucher. ◆**chéquier** *nm* cheque book, *Am* checkbook.

cher, chère [ʃɛr] **1** *a* (*aimé*) dear (**à** to); − *nmf* **mon c.** my dear fellow; **ma chère** my dear (woman). **2** *a* (*coûteux*) dear, expensive; (*quartier, hôtel etc*) expensive; **la vie chère** the high cost of living; **payer c.** (*objet*) to pay a lot for; (*erreur etc*) *Fig* to pay dearly for. ◆**chèrement** *adv* dearly.

cherch/er [ʃɛrʃe] *vt* to look for, search for; (*du secours, la paix etc*) to seek; (*dans un dictionnaire*) to look up; **c. ses mots** to fumble for one's words; **aller c.** to (go and) fetch *ou* get; **c. à faire** to attempt to do; **tu l'as bien cherché!** it's your own fault!, you asked for it! ◆**—eur, -euse** *nmf* research worker; **c. d'or** gold-digger.

chér/ir [ʃerir] *vt* to cherish. ◆**—i, -ie** *a* dearly loved, beloved; − *nmf* darling.

chérot [ʃero] *am Fam* pricey.

cherté [ʃɛrte] *nf* high cost, expensiveness.

chétif, -ive [ʃetif, -iv] *a* puny; (*dérisoire*) wretched.

cheval, -aux [ʃ(ə)val, -o] *nm* horse; **c.** (**vapeur**) *Aut* horsepower; **à c.** on horseback; **faire du c.** to go horse riding; **à c. sur** straddling; **à c. sur les principes** a stickler for principle; **monter sur ses grands chevaux** to get excited; **c. à bascule** rocking horse; **c. d'arçons** *Sp* vaulting horse; **c. de bataille** (*dada*) hobbyhorse; **chevaux de bois** (*manège*) merry-go-round. ◆**chevaleresque** *a* chivalrous. ◆**chevalier** *nm* knight. ◆**chevalin** *a* equine; (*boucherie*) horse-.

chevalet [ʃ(ə)valɛ] *nm* easel; *Menuis* trestle.

chevalière [ʃ(ə)valjɛr] *nf* signet ring.

chevauchée [ʃ(ə)voʃe] *nf* (horse) ride.

chevaucher [ʃ(ə)voʃe] *vt* to straddle; − *vi*, − **se c.** *vpr* to overlap.

chevet [ʃ(ə)vɛ] *nm* bedhead; **table/livre de c.** bedside table/book; **au c. de** at the bedside of.

cheveu, -x [ʃ(ə)vø] *nm* **un c.** a hair; **les cheveux blancs** white hair; **couper les cheveux en quatre** *Fig* to split hairs; **tiré par les cheveux** (*argument*) far-fetched. ◆**chevelu** *a* hairy. ◆**chevelure** *nf* (head of) hair.

cheville [ʃ(ə)vij] *nf Anat* ankle; *Menuis* peg, pin; (*pour vis*) (wall)plug; **c. ouvrière** *Aut & Fig* linchpin; **en c. avec** *Fam* in cahoots with. ◆**cheviller** *vt Menuis* to pin, peg.

chèvre [ʃɛvr] *nf* goat; (*femelle*) nanny-goat. ◆**chevreau, -x** *nm* kid.

chèvrefeuille [ʃɛvrəfœj] *nm* honeysuckle.

chevreuil [ʃəvrœj] *nm* roe deer; *Culin* venison.

chevron [ʃəvrɔ̃] *nm* (*poutre*) rafter; *Mil* stripe, chevron; **à chevrons** (*tissu, veste etc*) herringbone.

chevronné [ʃəvrɔne] *a* seasoned, experienced.

chevroter [ʃəvrɔte] *vi* to quaver, tremble.

chez [ʃe] *prép* **c. qn** at s.o.'s house, flat *etc*; **il est c. Jean/c. l'épicier** he's at John's (place)/at the grocer's; **il va c. Jean/c. l'épicier** he's going to John's (place)/to the grocer's; **c. moi, c. nous** at home; **je vais c. moi** I'm going home; **c. les Suisses/les jeunes** among the Swiss/the young; **c. Camus** in Camus; **c. l'homme** in man; **une habitude c. elle** a habit with her; **c. Mme Dupont** (*adresse*) care of *ou* c/o Mme Dupont. ◆**c.-soi** *nm inv* **un c.-soi** a home (of one's own).

chialer [ʃjale] *vi* (*pleurer*) *Fam* to cry.

chic [ʃik] **1** *a inv* stylish, smart; (*gentil*) *Fam* decent, nice; − *int* **c.** (**alors**)**!** great!; − *nm* style, elegance. **2** *nm* **avoir le c. pour faire** to have the knack of doing.

chicane [ʃikan] **1** *nf* (*querelle*) quibble. **2** *nfpl* (*obstacles*) zigzag barriers. ◆**chicaner** *vt* to quibble with (*s.o.*); − *vi* to quibble.

chiche [ʃiʃ] **1** *a* mean, niggardly; **c. de** sparing of. **2** *int* (*défi*) *Fam* I bet you I do, can *etc*; **c. que je parte sans lui** I bet I leave without him.

chichis [ʃiʃi] *nmpl* **faire des c.** to make a lot of fuss.

chicorée [ʃikɔre] *nf* (*à café*) chicory; (*pour salade*) endive.

chien [ʃjɛ̃] *nm* dog; **c. d'arrêt** pointer, retriever; **un mal de c.** a hell of a job; **temps de c.** filthy weather; **vie de c.** *Fig* dog's life; **entre c. et loup** at dusk, in the gloaming. ◆**c.-loup** *nm* (*pl* **chiens-loups**) wolfhound. ◆**chienne** *nf* dog, bitch.

chiendent [ʃjɛ̃dɑ̃] *nm Bot* couch grass.

chiffon [ʃifɔ̃] *nm* rag; **c.** (**à poussière**) duster. ◆**chiffonner** *vt* to crumple; (*ennuyer*) *Fig* to bother, distress. ◆**chiffonnier** *nm* ragman.

chiffre [ʃifr] *nm* figure, number; (*romain, arabe*) numeral; (*code*) cipher; **c. d'affaires** *Fin* turnover. ◆**chiffrer** *vt* (*montant*) to assess, work out; (*message*) to cipher, code; − *vi* to mount up; **se c. à** to amount to, work out at.

chignon [ʃiɲɔ̃] *nm* bun, chignon.

Chili [ʃili] *nm* Chile. ◆**chilien, -ienne** *a* & *nmf* Chilean.

chimère [ʃimɛr] *nf* fantasy, (wild) dream. ◆**chimérique** *a* fanciful.

chimie [ʃimi] *nf* chemistry. ◆**chimique** *a* chemical. ◆**chimiste** *nmf* (research) chemist.

chimpanzé [ʃɛ̃pɑ̃ze] *nm* chimpanzee.

Chine [ʃin] *nf* China. ◆**chinois, -oise** *a* & *nmf* Chinese; – *nm* (*langue*) Chinese. ◆**chinoiser** *vi* to quibble. ◆**chinoiserie** *nf* (*objet*) Chinese curio; *pl* (*bizarreries*) *Fig* weird complications.

chiner [ʃine] *vi* (*brocanteur etc*) to hunt for bargains.

chiot [ʃjo] *nm* pup(py).

chiper [ʃipe] *vt Fam* to swipe, pinch (à from).

chipie [ʃipi] *nf* **vieille c.** (*femme*) *Péj* old crab.

chipoter [ʃipɔte] *vi* **1** (*manger*) to nibble. **2** (*chicaner*) to quibble.

chips [ʃips] *nmpl* (potato) crisps, *Am* chips.

chiquenaude [ʃiknod] *nf* flick (of the finger).

chiromancie [kirɔmɑ̃si] *nf* palmistry.

chirurgie [ʃiryrʒi] *nf* surgery. ◆**chirurgical, -aux** *a* surgical. ◆**chirurgien** *nm* surgeon.

chlore [klɔr] *nm* chlorine. ◆**chloroforme** *nm* chloroform. ◆**chlorure** *nm* chloride.

choc [ʃɔk] *nm* (*heurt*) impact, shock; (*émotion*) & *Méd* shock; (*collision*) crash; (*des opinions, entre manifestants etc*) clash.

chocolat [ʃɔkɔla] *nm* chocolate; **c. à croquer** plain *ou Am* bittersweet chocolate; **c. au lait** milk chocolate; **c. glacé** choc-ice; – *a inv* chocolate(-coloured). ◆**chocolaté** *a* chocolate-flavoured.

chœur [kœr] *nm* (*chanteurs, nef*) *Rel* choir; (*composition musicale*) & *Fig* chorus; **en c.** (all) together, in chorus.

choir [ʃwar] *vi* **laisser c. qn** *Fam* to turn one's back on s.o.

chois/ir [ʃwazir] *vt* to choose, pick, select. ◆**—i** *a* (*œuvres*) selected; (*terme, langage*) well-chosen; (*public*) select. ◆**choix** *nm* choice; (*assortiment*) selection; **morceau de c.** choice piece; **au c. du client** according to choice.

choléra [kɔlera] *nm* cholera.

cholestérol [kɔlesterɔl] *nm* cholesterol.

chôm/er [ʃome] *vi* (*ouvrier etc*) to be unemployed; **jour chômé** (public) holiday. ◆**—age** *nm* unemployment; **en** *ou* **au c.** unemployed; **mettre en c. technique** to lay off, dismiss.

chope [ʃɔp] *nf* beer mug, tankard; (*contenu*) pint.

choqu/er [ʃɔke] *vt* to offend, shock; (*verres*) to clink; (*commotionner*) to shake up. ◆**—ant** *a* shocking, offensive.

choral, -als [kɔral] *a* choral. ◆**chorale** *nf* choral society. ◆**choriste** *nmf* chorister.

chorégraphe [kɔregraf] *nmf* choreographer. ◆**chorégraphie** *nf* choreography.

chose [ʃoz] *nf* thing; **état de choses** state of affairs; **par la force des choses** through force of circumstance; **dis-lui bien des choses de ma part** remember me to him *ou* her; **ce monsieur C.** that Mr What's-his-name; **se sentir tout c.** *Fam* (*décontenancé*) to feel all funny; (*malade*) to feel out of sorts.

chou, -x [ʃu] *nm* cabbage; **choux de Bruxelles** Brussels sprouts; **mon c.!** my pet!; **c. à la crème** cream puff. ◆**c.-fleur** *nm* (*pl* **choux-fleurs**) cauliflower.

choucas [ʃuka] *nm* jackdaw.

chouchou, -oute [ʃuʃu, -ut] *nmf* (*favori*) *Fam* pet, darling. ◆**chouchouter** *vt* to pamper.

choucroute [ʃukrut] *nf* sauerkraut.

chouette [ʃwɛt] **1** *nf* (*oiseau*) owl. **2** *a* (*chic*) *Fam* super, great.

choyer [ʃwaye] *vt* to pet, pamper.

chrétien, -ienne [kretjɛ̃, -jɛn] *a* & *nmf* Christian. ◆**chrétienté** *nf* Christendom. ◆**Christ** [krist] *nm* Christ. ◆**christianisme** *nm* Christianity.

chrome [krom] *nm* chromium, chrome. ◆**chromé** *a* chromium-plated.

chromosome [krɔmozom] *nm* chromosome.

chronique [krɔnik] **1** *a* (*malade, chômage etc*) chronic. **2** *nf* (*annales*) chronicle; *Journ* report, news; (*rubrique*) column. ◆**chroniqueur** *nm* chronicler; *Journ* reporter, columnist.

chronologie [krɔnɔlɔʒi] *nf* chronology. ◆**chronologique** *a* chronological.

chronomètre [krɔnɔmɛtr] *nm* stopwatch. ◆**chronométr/er** *vt Sp* to time. ◆**—eur** *nm Sp* timekeeper.

chrysanthème [krizɑ̃tɛm] *nm* chrysanthemum.

chuchot/er [ʃyʃɔte] *vti* to whisper. ◆**—ement** *nm* whisper(ing). ◆**chuchoteries** *nfpl Fam* whispering.

chuinter [ʃwɛ̃te] *vi* (*vapeur*) to hiss.

chut! [ʃyt] *int* sh!, hush!

chute [ʃyt] *nf* fall; (*défaite*) (down)fall; **c. d'eau** waterfall; **c. de neige** snowfall; **c. de pluie** rainfall; **c. des cheveux** hair loss. ◆**chuter** *vi Fam* to fall.

Chypre [ʃipr] *nf* Cyprus. ◆**chypriote** *a* & *nmf* Cypriot.

ci [si] **1** *adv* par-ci par-là here and there. **2** *pron dém* comme ci comme ça so so. **3** *voir* ce², celui.

ci-après [siaprɛ] *adv* below, hereafter. ◆**ci-contre** *adv* opposite. ◆**ci-dessous** *adv* below. ◆**ci-dessus** *adv* above. ◆**ci-gît** *adv* here lies (*on gravestones*). ◆**ci-inclus** *a*, ◆**ci-joint** *a* (*inv before n*) (*dans une lettre*) enclosed (herewith).

cible [sibl] *nf* target.

ciboulette [sibulɛt] *nf Culin* chives.

cicatrice [sikatris] *nf* scar. ◆**cicatriser** *vt*, — **se c.** *vpr* to heal up (*leaving a scar*).

cidre [sidr] *nm* cider.

Cie *abrév* (*compagnie*) Co.

ciel [sjɛl] *nm* **1** (*pl* ciels) sky; à c. ouvert (*piscine etc*) open-air; **c. de lit** canopy. **2** (*pl* cieux [sjø]) *Rel* heaven; juste c.! good heavens!; sous d'autres cieux *Hum* in other climes.

cierge [sjɛrʒ] *nm Rel* candle.

cigale [sigal] *nf* (*insecte*) cicada.

cigare [sigar] *nm* cigar. ◆**cigarette** *nf* cigarette.

cigogne [sigɔɲ] *nf* stork.

cil [sil] *nm* (eye)lash.

cime [sim] *nf* (*d'un arbre*) top; (*d'une montagne*) & *Fig* peak.

ciment [simã] *nm* cement. ◆**cimenter** *vt* to cement.

cimetière [simtjɛr] *nm* cemetery, graveyard; **c. de voitures** scrapyard, breaker's yard, *Am* auto graveyard.

ciné [sine] *nm Fam* cinema. ◆**c.-club** *nm* film society. ◆**cinéaste** *nmf* film maker. ◆**cinéphile** *nmf* film buff.

cinéma [sinema] *nm* cinema; faire du c. to make films. ◆**cinémascope** *nm* cinemascope. ◆**cinémathèque** *nf* film library; (*salle*) film theatre. ◆**cinématographique** *a* cinema-.

cinglé [sɛ̃gle] *a Fam* crazy.

cingl/er [sɛ̃gle] *vt* to lash. ◆—**ant** *a* (*vent, remarque*) cutting, biting.

cinoche [sinɔʃ] *nm Fam* cinema.

cinq [sɛ̃k] *nm* five; — *a* ([sɛ̃] *before consonant*) five. ◆**cinquième** *a* & *nmf* fifth; un c. a fifth.

cinquante [sɛ̃kɑ̃t] *a* & *nm* fifty. ◆**cinquantaine** *nf* about fifty. ◆**cinquantenaire** *a* & *nmf* fifty-year-old (person); – *nm* fiftieth anniversary. ◆**cinquantième** *a* & *nmf* fiftieth.

cintre [sɛ̃tr] *nm* coathanger; *Archit* arch.

◆**cintré** *a* arched; (*veste etc*) tailored, slim-fitting.

cirage [siraʒ] *nm* (shoe) polish.

circoncis [sirkɔ̃si] *a* circumcised. ◆**circoncision** *nf* circumcision.

circonférence [sirkɔ̃ferɑ̃s] *nf* circumference.

circonflexe [sirkɔ̃flɛks] *a Gram* circumflex.

circonlocution [sirkɔ̃lɔkysjɔ̃] *nf* circumlocution.

circonscrire [sirkɔ̃skrir] *vt* to circumscribe. ◆**circonscription** *nf* division; **c.** (**électorale**) constituency.

circonspect, -ecte [sirkɔ̃spɛ(kt), -ɛkt] *a* cautious, circumspect. ◆**circonspection** *nf* caution.

circonstance [sirkɔ̃stɑ̃s] *nf* circumstance; pour/en la c. for/on this occasion; de c. (*habit, parole etc*) appropriate. ◆**circonstancié, -iel, -ielle** *a* detailed. ◆**circonstanciel, -ielle** *a Gram* adverbial.

circonvenir [sirkɔ̃vnir] *vt* to circumvent.

circuit [sirkɥi] *nm Sp Él Fin* circuit; (*périple*) tour, trip; (*détour*) roundabout way; *pl Él* circuitry, circuits.

circulaire [sirkylɛr] *a* circular; — *nf* (*lettre*) circular. ◆**circulation** *nf* circulation; *Aut* traffic. ◆**circuler** *vi* to circulate; (*véhicule, train*) to move, travel; (*passant*) to walk about; (*rumeur*) to go round, circulate; faire c. to circulate; (*piétons etc*) to move on; circulez! keep moving!

cire [sir] *nf* wax; (*pour meubles*) polish, wax. ◆**cir/er** *vt* to polish, wax. ◆—**é** *nm* (*vêtement*) oilskin(s). ◆—**eur** *nm* bootblack. ◆—**euse** *nf* (*appareil*) floor polisher. ◆**cireux, -euse** *a* waxy.

cirque [sirk] *nm Th Hist* circus.

cirrhose [siroz] *nf Méd* cirrhosis.

cisaille(s) [sizaj] *nf*(*pl*) shears. ◆**ciseau, -x** *nm* chisel; *pl* scissors. ◆**ciseler** *vt* to chisel.

citadelle [sitadɛl] *nf* citadel.

cité [site] *nf* city; **c.** (**ouvrière**) housing estate (*for workers*), *Am* housing project *ou* development; **c. universitaire** (students') halls of residence. ◆**citadin, -ine** *nmf* city dweller; – *a* city-, urban.

citer [site] *vt* to quote; *Jur* to summon; *Mil* to mention, cite. ◆**citation** *nf* quotation; *Jur* summons; *Mil* mention, citation.

citerne [sitɛrn] *nf* (*réservoir*) tank.

cithare [sitar] *nf* zither.

citoyen, -enne [sitwajɛ̃, -ɛn] *nmf* citizen. ◆**citoyenneté** *nf* citizenship.

citron [sitrɔ̃] *nm* lemon; **c. pressé** (fresh)

lemon juice. ◆**citronnade** *nf* lemon drink, (still) lemonade.

citrouille [sitruj] *nf* pumpkin.

civet [sive] *nm* stew; **c. de lièvre** jugged hare.

civière [sivjɛr] *nf* stretcher.

civil [sivil] **1** *a* (*droits, guerre, mariage etc*) civil; (*non militaire*) civilian; (*courtois*) civil; **année civile** calendar year. **2** *nm* civilian; **dans le c.** in civilian life; **en c.** (*policier*) in plain clothes; (*soldat*) in civilian clothes. ◆**civilité** *nf* civility.

civiliser [sivilize] *vt* to civilize; **— se c.** *vpr* to become civilized. ◆**civilisation** *nf* civilization.

civique [sivik] *a* civic; **instruction c.** *Scol* civics. ◆**civisme** *nm* civic sense.

clair [klɛr] *a* (*distinct, limpide, évident*) clear; (*éclairé*) light; (*pâle*) light(-coloured); (*sauce, chevelure*) thin; **bleu/vert c.** light blue/green; **il fait c.** it's light *ou* bright; **—** *adv* (*voir*) clearly; **—** *nm* **c. de lune** moonlight; **le plus c. de** the major *ou* greater part of; **tirer au c.** (*question etc*) to clear up. ◆**—ement** *adv* clearly. ◆**claire-voie** *nf* à **c.-voie** (*barrière*) lattice-; (*caisse*) open-work; (*porte*) louvre(d).

clairière [klɛrjɛr] *nf* clearing, glade.

clairon [klɛrɔ̃] *nm* bugle; (*soldat*) bugler. ◆**claironner** *vt* (*annoncer*) to trumpet forth.

clairsemé [klɛrsəme] *a* sparse.

clairvoyant [klɛrvwajɑ̃] *a* (*perspicace*) clear-sighted. ◆**clairvoyance** *nf* clear-sightedness.

clam/er [klame] *vt* to cry out. ◆**—eur** *nf* clamour, outcry.

clan [klɑ̃] *nm* clan, clique, set.

clandestin [klɑ̃dɛstɛ̃] *a* secret, clandestine; (*journal, mouvement*) underground; **passager c.** stowaway.

clapet [klapɛ] *nm* Tech valve; (*bouche*) Arg trap.

clapier [klapje] *nm* (rabbit) hutch.

clapot/er [klapɔte] *vi* (*vagues*) to lap. ◆**—ement** *nm*, ◆**clapotis** *nm* lap(ping).

claque [klak] *nf* smack, slap. ◆**claquer** *vt* (*porte*) to slam, bang; (*gifler*) to smack, slap; (*fouet*) to crack; (*fatiguer*) Fam to tire out; (*dépenser*) Arg to blow; **se c. un muscle** to tear a muscle; **faire c.** (*doigts*) to snap; (*langue*) to click; (*fouet*) to crack; **—** *vi* (*porte*) to slam, bang; (*drapeau*) to flap; (*coup de revolver*) to ring out; (*mourir*) Fam to die; (*tomber en panne*) Fam to break down; **c. des mains** to clap one's hands; **elle claque des dents** her teeth are chattering.

claquemurer (se) [səklakmyre] *vpr* to shut oneself up, hole up.

claquettes [klakɛt] *nfpl* tap dancing.

clarifier [klarifje] *vt* to clarify. ◆**clarification** *nf* clarification.

clarinette [klarinɛt] *nf* clarinet.

clarté [klarte] *nf* light, brightness; (*précision*) clarity, clearness.

classe [klɑs] *nf* class; **aller en c.** to go to school; **c. ouvrière/moyenne** working/middle class; **avoir de la c.** to have class.

class/er [klɑse] *vt* to classify, class; (*papiers*) to file; (*candidats*) to grade; (*affaire*) to close; **se c.** to rank *ou* be classed among; **se c. premier** to come first. ◆**—ement** *nm* classification; filing; grading; (*rang*) place; Sp placing. ◆**—eur** *nm* (*meuble*) filing cabinet; (*portefeuille*) (loose leaf) file. ◆**classification** *nf* classification. ◆**classifier** *vt* to classify.

classique [klasik] *a* classical; (*typique*) classic; **—** *nm* (*œuvre, auteur*) classic. ◆**classicisme** *nm* classicism.

clause [kloz] *nf* clause.

claustrophobie [klostrofɔbi] *nf* claustrophobia. ◆**claustrophobe** *a* claustrophobic.

clavecin [klavsɛ̃] *nm* Mus harpsichord.

clavicule [klavikyl] *nf* collarbone.

clavier [klavje] *nm* keyboard.

clé, clef [kle] *nf* key; (*outil*) spanner, wrench; Mus clef; **fermer à c.** to lock; **sous c.** under lock and key; **c. de contact** ignition key; **c. de voûte** keystone; **poste/industrie c.** key post/industry; **clés en main** (*acheter une maison etc*) ready to move in; **prix clés en main** (*voiture*) on the road price.

clément [klemɑ̃] *a* (*temps*) mild, clement; (*juge*) lenient, clement. ◆**clémence** *nf* mildness; leniency; clemency.

clémentine [klemɑ̃tin] *nf* clementine.

clerc [klɛr] *nm* Rel cleric; (*de notaire*) clerk. ◆**clergé** *nm* clergy. ◆**clérical, -aux** *a* Rel clerical.

cliché [klife] *nm* Phot negative; Typ plate; (*idée*) cliché.

client, -ente [klijɑ̃, -ɑ̃t] *nmf* (*de magasin etc*) customer; (*d'un avocat etc*) client; (*d'un médecin*) patient; (*d'hôtel*) guest. ◆**clientèle** *nf* customers, clientele; (*d'un avocat*) practice, clientele; (*d'un médecin*) practice, patients; **accorder sa c. à** to give one's custom to.

cligner [kliɲe] *vi* **c. des yeux** (*ouvrir et fermer*) to blink; (*fermer à demi*) to screw up one's eyes; **c. de l'œil** to wink.

◆**clignot/er** vi to blink; (lumière) to flicker; Aut to flash; (étoile) to twinkle. ◆**—ant** nm Aut indicator, Am directional signal.

climat [klima] nm Mét & Fig climate. ◆**climatique** a climatic. ◆**climatisation** nf air-conditioning. ◆**climatiser** vt to air-condition.

clin d'œil [klɛ̃dœj] nm wink; **en un c. d'œil** in the twinkling of an eye.

clinique [klinik] a clinical; − nf (hôpital) (private) clinic.

clinquant [klɛ̃kɑ̃] a tawdry.

clique [klik] nf Péj clique; Mus Mil (drum and bugle) band.

cliqueter [klikte] vi to clink. ◆**cliquetis** nm clink(ing).

clivage [klivaʒ] nm split, division (de in).

cloaque [klɔak] nm cesspool.

clochard, -arde [klɔʃar, -ard] nmf tramp, vagrant.

cloche [klɔʃ] nf 1 bell; **c. à fromage** cheese cover. **2** (personne) Fam idiot, oaf. ◆**clocher** 1 nm bell tower; (en pointe) steeple; **de c.** Fig parochial; **esprit de c.** parochialism. **2** vi to be wrong ou amiss. ◆**clochette** nf (small) bell.

cloche-pied (à) [aklɔʃpje] adv **sauter à c.-pied** to hop on one foot.

cloison [klwazɔ̃] nf partition; Fig barrier. ◆**cloisonner** vt to partition; (activités etc) Fig to compartmentalize.

cloître [klwatr] nm cloister. ◆**se cloîtrer** vpr to shut oneself away, cloister oneself.

clopin-clopant [klɔpɛ̃klɔpɑ̃] adv **aller c.-clopant** to hobble.

cloque [klɔk] nf blister.

clore [klɔr] vt (débat, lettre) to close. ◆**clos** a (incident etc) closed; (espace) enclosed; − nm (enclosed) field.

clôture [klotyr] nf (barrière) enclosure, fence; (fermeture) closing. ◆**clôturer** vt to enclose; (compte, séance etc) to close.

clou [klu] nm nail; (furoncle) boil; **le c. (du spectacle)** Fam the star attraction; **les clous** (passage) pedestrian crossing; **des clous!** Fam nothing at all! ◆**clouer** vt to nail; **cloué au lit** confined to (one's) bed; **cloué sur place** nailed to the spot; **c. le bec à qn** Fam to shut s.o. up. ◆**clouté** a (chaussures) hobnailed; (ceinture, pneus) studded; **passage c.** pedestrian crossing, Am crosswalk.

clown [klun] nm clown.

club [klœb] nm (association) club.

cm abrév (centimètre) cm.

co- [kɔ] préf co-.

coaguler [kɔagyle] vti, − **se c.** vpr to coagulate.

coaliser (se) [səkɔalize] vpr to form a coalition, join forces. ◆**coalition** nf coalition.

coasser [kɔase] vi (grenouille) to croak.

cobaye [kɔbaj] nm (animal) & Fig guinea pig.

cobra [kɔbra] nm (serpent) cobra.

coca [kɔka] nm (Coca-Cola®) coke.

cocagne [kɔkaɲ] nf **pays de c.** dreamland, land of plenty.

cocaïne [kɔkain] nf cocain.

cocarde [kɔkard] nf rosette, cockade; Av roundel. ◆**cocardier, -ière** a Péj flag-waving.

cocasse [kɔkas] a droll, comical. ◆**cocasserie** nf drollery.

coccinelle [kɔksinɛl] nf ladybird, Am ladybug.

cocher[1] [kɔʃe] vt to tick (off), Am to check (off).

cocher[2] [kɔʃe] nm coachman. ◆**cochère** af **porte c.** main gateway.

cochon, -onne [kɔʃɔ̃, -ɔn] **1** nm pig; (mâle) hog; **c. d'Inde** guinea pig. **2** nmf (personne sale) (dirty) pig; (salaud) swine; − a (histoire, film) dirty, filthy. ◆**cochonnerie(s)** nf(pl) (obscénité(s)) filth; (pacotille) Fam rubbish.

cocktail [kɔktɛl] nm (boisson) cocktail; (réunion) cocktail party.

coco [kɔko] nm **noix de c.** coconut. ◆**cocotier** nm coconut palm.

cocon [kɔkɔ̃] nm cocoon.

cocorico [kɔkɔriko] int & nm cock-a-doodle-doo; **faire c.** (crier victoire) Fam to give three cheers for France, wave the flag.

cocotte [kɔkɔt] nf (marmite) casserole; **c. minute®** pressure cooker.

cocu [kɔky] nm Fam cuckold.

code [kɔd] nm code; **codes, phares c.** Aut dipped headlights, Am low beams; **C. de la route** Highway Code. ◆**coder** vt to code. ◆**codifier** vt to codify.

coefficient [kɔefisjɑ̃] nm Math coefficient; (d'erreur, de sécurité) Fig margin.

coéquipier, -ière [kɔekipje, -jɛr] nmf team mate.

cœur [kœr] nm heart; Cartes hearts; **au c. de** (ville, hiver etc) in the heart of; **par c.** by heart; **ça me (sou)lève le c.** that turns my stomach; **à c. ouvert** (opération) open-heart; (parler) freely; **avoir mal au c.** to feel sick; **avoir le c. gros ou serré** to have a heavy heart; **ça me tient à c.** that's close to my heart; **avoir bon c.** to be kind-hearted; **de bon c.** (*offrir*) with a good heart, willingly; (*rire*) heartily; **si le c. vous en dit** if you so desire.

coexister [kɔɛgziste] *vi* to coexist. ◆**coexistence** *nf* coexistence.

coffre [kɔfr] *nm* chest; (*de banque*) safe; (*de voiture*) boot, *Am* trunk; (*d'autocar*) luggage *ou Am* baggage compartment. ◆**c.-fort** *nm* (*pl* **coffres-forts**) safe. ◆**coffret** *nm* casket, box.

cogiter [kɔʒite] *vi Iron* to cogitate.

cognac [kɔɲak] *nm* cognac.

cogner [kɔɲe] *vti* to knock; **c. qn** *Arg* (*frapper*) to thump s.o.; (*tabasser*) to beat s.o. up; **se c. la tête**/*etc* to knock one's head/*etc*.

cohabiter [kɔabite] *vi* to live together. ◆**cohabitation** *nf* living together; *Pol Fam* power sharing.

cohérent [kɔerɑ̃] *a* coherent. ◆**cohérence** *nf* coherence. ◆**cohésion** *nf* cohesion, cohesiveness.

cohorte [kɔɔrt] *nf* (*groupe*) troop, band, cohort.

cohue [kɔy] *nf* crowd, mob.

coiffe [kwaf] *nf* headdress.

coiff/er [kwafe] *vt* (*chapeau*) to put on, wear; (*surmonter*) *Fig* to cap; (*être à la tête de*) to head; **c. qn** to do s.o.'s hair; **c. qn d'un chapeau** to put a hat on s.o.; **— se c.** *vpr* to do one's hair; **se c. d'un chapeau** to put on a hat. ◆**—eur, -euse** [1] *nmf* (*pour hommes*) barber, hairdresser; (*pour dames*) hairdresser. ◆**—euse** [2] *nf* dressing table. ◆**coiffure** *nf* headgear, hat; (*arrangement*) hairstyle; (*métier*) hairdressing.

coin [kwɛ̃] *nm* (*angle*) corner; (*endroit*) spot; (*de terre, de ciel*) patch; (*cale*) wedge; **du c.** (*magasin etc*) local; **dans le c.** in the (local) area; **au c. du feu** by the fireside; **petit c.** *Fam* loo, *Am* john.

coinc/er [kwɛ̃se] *vt* (*mécanisme, tiroir*) to jam; (*caler*) to wedge; **c. qn** *Fam* to catch s.o., corner s.o.; **— se c.** *vpr* (*mécanisme etc*) to get jammed *ou* stuck. ◆**—é** *a* (*tiroir etc*) stuck, jammed; (*personne*) *Fam* stuck.

coïncider [kɔɛ̃side] *vi* to coincide. ◆**coïncidence** *nf* coincidence.

coin-coin [kwɛ̃kwɛ̃] *nm inv* (*de canard*) quack.

coing [kwɛ̃] *nm* (*fruit*) quince.

coke [kɔk] *nm* (*combustible*) coke.

col [kɔl] *nm* (*de chemise*) collar; (*de bouteille*) & *Anat* neck; *Géog* pass; **c. roulé** polo neck, *Am* turtleneck.

colère [kɔlɛr] *nf* anger; **une c.** (*accès*) a fit of anger; **en c.** angry (**contre** with); **se mettre**

en c. to lose one's temper. ◆**coléreux, -euse** *a*, ◆**colérique** *a* quick-tempered.

colibri [kɔlibri] *nm* hummingbird.

colifichet [kɔlifiʃɛ] *nm* trinket.

colimaçon (en) [ɑ̃kɔlimasɔ̃] *adv* **escalier en c.** spiral staircase.

colin [kɔlɛ̃] *nm* (*poisson*) hake.

colique [kɔlik] *nf* diarrh(o)ea; (*douleur*) stomach pain, colic.

colis [kɔli] *nm* parcel, package.

collaborer [kɔlabɔre] *vi* collaborate (**avec** with, **à** on); **c. à** (*journal*) to contribute to. ◆**collaborateur, -trice** *nmf* collaborator; contributor. ◆**collaboration** *nf* collaboration; contribution.

collage [kɔlaʒ] *nm* (*œuvre*) collage.

collant [kɔlɑ̃] **1** *a* (*papier*) sticky; (*vêtement*) skin-tight; **être c.** (*importun*) *Fam* to be a pest. **2** *nm* (pair of) tights; (*de danse*) leotard.

collation [kɔlasjɔ̃] *nf* (*repas*) light meal.

colle [kɔl] *nf* (*transparente*) glue; (*blanche*) paste; (*question*) *Fam* poser, teaser; (*interrogation*) *Scol Arg* oral; (*retenue*) *Scol Arg* detention.

collecte [kɔlɛkt] *nf* (*quête*) collection. ◆**collect/er** *vt* to collect. ◆**—eur** *nm* collector; (**égout**) **c.** main sewer.

collectif, -ive [kɔlɛktif, -iv] *a* collective; (*hystérie, démission*) mass-; **billet c.** group ticket. ◆**collectivement** *adv* collectively. ◆**collectivisme** *nm* collectivism. ◆**collectivité** *nf* community, collectivity.

collection [kɔlɛksjɔ̃] *nf* collection. ◆**collectionn/er** *vt* (*timbres etc*) to collect. ◆**—eur, -euse** *nmf* collector.

collège [kɔlɛʒ] *nm* (secondary) school, *Am* (high) school; (*électoral, sacré*) college. ◆**collégien** *nm* schoolboy. ◆**collégienne** *nf* schoolgirl.

collègue [kɔlɛg] *nmf* colleague.

coller [kɔle] *vt* (*timbre etc*) to stick; (*à la colle transparente*) to glue; (*à la colle blanche*) to paste; (*affiche*) to stick up; (*papier peint*) to hang; (*mettre*) *Fam* to stick, shove; **c. contre** (*nez, oreille etc*) to press against; **c. qn** (*embarrasser*) *Fam* to stump s.o., catch s.o. out; (*consigner*) *Scol* to keep s.o. in; **être collé à** (*examen*) *Fam* to fail, flunk; **se c. contre** to cling (close) to; **se c. qn/qch** *Fam* to get stuck with s.o./sth; **—** *vi* to stick, cling; **c. à** (*s'adapter*) to fit, correspond to; **ça colle!** *Fam* everything's just fine! ◆**colleur, -euse** *nmf* **c. d'affiches** billsticker.

collet [kɔlɛ] *nm* (*lacet*) snare; **prendre qn au c.** to grab s.o. by the scruff of the neck; **elle**

est/ils sont c. monté she is/they are prim and proper *ou* straight-laced.

collier [kɔlje] *nm (bijou)* necklace; *(de chien, cheval)* & *Tech* collar.

colline [kɔlin] *nf* hill.

collision [kɔlizjɔ̃] *nf (de véhicules)* collision; *(bagarre, conflit)* clash; **entrer en c. avec** to collide with.

colloque [kɔlɔk] *nm* symposium.

collusion [kɔlyzjɔ̃] *nf* collusion.

colmater [kɔlmate] *vt (fuite, fente)* to seal; *(trou)* to fill in; *(brèche)* *Mil* to close, seal.

colombe [kɔlɔ̃b] *nf* dove.

colon [kɔlɔ̃] *nm* settler, colonist; *(enfant)* child taking part in a holiday camp. ◆**colonial, -aux** *a* colonial. ◆**colonie** *nf* colony; **c. de vacances** (children's) holiday camp *ou Am* vacation camp.

coloniser [kɔlɔnize] *vt Pol* to colonize; *(peupler)* to settle. ◆**colonisateur, -trice** *a* colonizing; – *nmf* colonizer. ◆**colonisation** *nf* colonization.

côlon [kɔlɔ̃] *nm Anat* colon.

colonel [kɔlɔnɛl] *nm* colonel.

colonne [kɔlɔn] *nf* column; **c. vertébrale** spine. ◆**colonnade** *nf* colonnade.

color/er [kɔlɔre] *vt* to colour. ◆**—ant** *a* & *nm* colouring. ◆**—é** *a (verre etc)* coloured; *(teint)* ruddy; *(style, foule)* colourful. ◆**coloration** *nf* colouring, colour. ◆**coloriage** *nm* colouring; *(dessin)* coloured drawing. ◆**colorier** *vt (dessin etc)* to colour (in). ◆**coloris** *nm (effet)* colouring; *(nuance)* shade.

colosse [kɔlɔs] *nm* giant, colossus. ◆**colossal, -aux** *a* colossal, gigantic.

colporter [kɔlpɔrte] *vt* to peddle, hawk.

coltiner [kɔltine] *vt (objet lourd) Fam* to lug, haul; – **se c.** *vpr (tâche pénible) Fam* to take on, tackle.

coma [kɔma] *nm* coma; **dans le c.** in a coma.

combat [kɔ̃ba] *nm* fight; *Mil* combat. ◆**combatif, -ive** *a (personne)* eager to fight; *(instinct, esprit)* fighting. ◆**combatt/re*** *vt* to fight; *(maladie, inflation etc)* to combat, fight; – *vi* to fight. ◆**—ant** *nm Mil* combattant; *(bagarreur) Fam* brawler; – *a (unité)* fighting.

combien [kɔ̃bjɛ̃] **1** *adv (quantité)* how much; *(nombre)* how many; **c. de** *(temps, argent etc)* how much; *(gens, livres etc)* how many. **2** *adv (à quel point)* how; **tu verras c. il est bête** you'll see how silly he is. **3** *adv (distance)* **c. y a-t-il d'ici à . . . ?** how far is it to . . . ? **4** *nm inv* **le c. sommes-nous?** *(date) Fam* what date is it?; **tous les c.?** *(fréquence) Fam* how often?

combine [kɔ̃bin] *nf (truc, astuce) Fam* trick.

combin/er [kɔ̃bine] *vt (disposer)* to combine; *(calculer)* to devise, plan (out). ◆**—é** *nm (de téléphone)* receiver. ◆**combinaison** *nf* **1** combination; *(manœuvre)* scheme. **2** *(vêtement de femme)* slip; *(de mécanicien)* boiler suit, *Am* overalls; *(de pilote)* flying suit; **c. de ski** ski suit.

comble [kɔ̃bl] **1** *nm* **le c. de** *(la joie etc)* the height of; **pour c. (de malheur)** to crown *ou* cap it all; **c'est un** *ou* **le c.!** that's the limit! **2** *nmpl (mansarde)* attic, loft; **sous les combles** beneath the roof, in the loft *ou* attic. **3** *a (bondé)* packed, full.

combler [kɔ̃ble] *vt (trou, lacune etc)* to fill; *(retard, perte)* to make good; *(vœu)* to fulfil; **c. qn de** *(cadeaux etc)* to lavish on s.o.; *(joie)* to fill s.o. with; **je suis comblé** I'm completely satisfied; **vous me comblez!** you're too good to me!

combustible [kɔ̃bystibl] *nm* fuel; – *a* combustible. ◆**combustion** *nf* combustion.

comédie [kɔmedi] *nf* comedy; *(complication) Fam* fuss, palaver; **c. musicale** musical; **jouer la c.** *Fig* to put on an act, play-act; **c'est de la c.** *(c'est faux)* it's a sham. ◆**comédien** *nm Th* & *Fig* actor. ◆**comédienne** *nf Th* & *Fig* actress.

comestible [kɔmɛstibl] *a* edible; – *nmpl* foods.

comète [kɔmɛt] *nf* comet.

comique [kɔmik] *a (style etc) Th* comic; *(amusant) Fig* comical, funny; **(auteur) c.** comedy writer; – *nm* comedy; *(acteur)* comic (actor); **le c.** *(genre)* comedy; *Fig* the comical side of (of).

comité [kɔmite] *nm* committee; **c. de gestion** board (of management); **en petit c.** in a small group.

commande [kɔmɑ̃d] **1** *nf (achat)* order; **sur c.** to order. **2** *nfpl* **les commandes** *Av Tech* the controls; **tenir les commandes** *(diriger) Fig* to have control.

command/er [kɔmɑ̃de] **1** *vt (diriger, exiger, dominer)* to command; *(faire fonctionner)* to control; – *vi* **c. à** *(ses passions etc)* to have control over; **c. à qn de faire** to command s.o. to do. **2** *vt (acheter)* to order. ◆**—ant** *nm Nau* captain; *(grade) Mil* major; *(grade) Av* squadron leader; **c. de bord** *Av* captain. ◆**—ement** *nm (autorité)* command; *Rel* commandment. ◆**commando** *nm* commando.

commanditaire [kɔmɑ̃ditɛr] *nm Com* sleeping *ou* limited partner, *Am* silent partner.

comme [kɔm] **1** *adv* & *conj* as, like; **un peu**

c. a bit like; **c. moi** like me; **c. cela** like that; **blanc c. neige** (as) white as snow; **c. si** as if; **c. pour faire** as if to do; **c. par hasard** as if by chance; **joli c. tout** *Fam* ever so pretty; **c. ami** as a friend; **c. quoi** (*disant que*) to the effect that; (*ce qui prouve que*) so, which goes to show that; **qu'as-tu c. diplômes?** what do you have in the way of certificates? **2** *adv* (*exclamatif*) **regarde c. il pleut!** look how it's raining!; **c. c'est petit!** isn't it small! **3** *conj* (*temps*) as; (*cause*) as, since; **c. je pars** as I'm leaving; **c. elle entrait** (just) as she was coming in.

commémorer [kɔmemɔre] *vt* to commemorate. ◆**commémoratif, -ive** *a* commemorative. ◆**commémoration** *nf* commemoration.

commenc/er [kɔmɑ̃se] *vti* to begin, start (**à faire** to do, doing; **par** with; **par faire** by doing); **pour c.** to begin with. ◆**—ement** *nm* beginning, start.

comment [kɔmɑ̃] *adv* how; **c. le sais-tu?** how do you know?; **et c.!** and how!; **c.?** (*répétition, surprise*) what?; **c.!** (*indignation*) what!; **c. est-il?** what is he like?; **c. faire?** what's to be done?; **c. t'appelles-tu?** what's your name?; **c. allez-vous?** how are you?

commentaire [kɔmɑ̃tɛr] *nm* (*explications*) commentary; (*remarque*) comment. ◆**commentateur, -trice** *nmf* commentator. ◆**commenter** *vt* to comment (up)on.

commérage(s) [kɔmeraʒ] *nm*(*pl*) gossip.

commerce [kɔmɛrs] *nm* trade, commerce; (*magasin*) shop, business; **de c.** (*voyageur, maison, tribunal*) commercial; (*navire*) trading; **chambre de c.** chamber of commerce; **faire du c.** to trade; **dans le c.** (*objet*) (on sale) in the shops. ◆**commercer** *vi* to trade. ◆**commerçant, -ante** *nmf* shopkeeper; **c. en gros** wholesale dealer; *— a* (*nation*) trading, mercantile; (*rue, quartier*) shopping-; (*personne*) business-minded. ◆**commercial, -aux** *a* commercial, business-. ◆**commercialiser** *vt* to market.

commère [kɔmɛr] *nf* (*femme*) gossip.

commettre* [kɔmɛtr] *vt* (*délit etc*) to commit; (*erreur*) to make.

commis [kɔmi] *nm* (*de magasin*) assistant, *Am* clerk; (*de bureau*) clerk, *Am* clerical worker.

commissaire [kɔmisɛr] *nm Sp* steward; **c. (de police)** police superintendent *ou Am* chief; **c. aux comptes** auditor; **c. du bord** *Nau* purser. ◆**c.-priseur** *nm* (*pl* commissaires-priseurs*) auctioneer. ◆**commis-**

sariat *nm* **c. (de police)** (central) police station.

commission [kɔmisjɔ̃] *nf* (*course*) errand; (*message*) message; (*réunion*) commission, committee; (*pourcentage*) *Com* commission (**sur** on); **faire les commissions** to do the shopping. ◆**commissionnaire** *nm* messenger; (*d'hôtel*) commissionaire; *Com* agent.

commod/e [kɔmɔd] **1** *a* (*pratique*) handy; (*simple*) easy; **il n'est pas c.** (*pas aimable*) he's unpleasant; (*difficile*) he's a tough one. **2** *nf* chest of drawers, *Am* dresser. ◆**—ément** *adv* comfortably. ◆**commodité** *nf* convenience.

commotion [kɔmɔsjɔ̃] *nf* shock; **c. (cérébrale)** concussion. ◆**commotionner** *vt* to shake up.

commuer [kɔmɥe] *vt* (*peine*) *Jur* to commute (**en** to).

commun [kɔmœ̃] **1** *a* (*collectif, comparable, habituel*) common; (*frais, cuisine etc*) shared; (*action, démarche etc*) joint; **ami c.** mutual friend; **peu c.** uncommon; **en c.** in common; **transports en c.** public transport; **avoir** *ou* **mettre en c.** to share; **vivre en c.** to live together; **il n'a rien de c. avec** he has nothing in common with. **2** *nm* **le c. des mortels** ordinary mortals. ◆**—ément** [kɔmynemɑ̃] *adv* commonly.

communauté [kɔmynote] *nf* community. ◆**communautaire** *a* community-.

commune [kɔmyn] *nf* (*municipalité française*) commune; **les Communes** *Br Pol* the Commons. ◆**communal, -aux** *a* communal, local, municipal.

communi/er [kɔmynje] *vi* to receive Holy Communion, communicate. ◆**—ant, -ante** *nmf Rel* communicant. ◆**communion** *nf* communion; *Rel* (Holy) Communion.

communiqu/er [kɔmynike] *vt* to communicate, pass on; (*mouvement*) to impart, communicate; **se c. à** (*feu, rire*) to spread to; *— vi* (*personne, pièces etc*) to communicate. ◆**—é** *nm* (*avis*) *Pol* communiqué; (*publicitaire*) message; **c. de presse** press release. ◆**communicatif, -ive** *a* communicative; (*contagieux*) infectious. ◆**communication** *nf* communication; **c. (téléphonique)** (telephone) call; **mauvaise c.** *Tél* bad line.

communisme [kɔmynism] *nm* communism. ◆**communiste** *a & nmf* communist.

communs [kɔmœ̃] *nmpl* (*bâtiments*) outbuildings.

commutateur [kɔmytatœr] *nm* (*bouton*) *Él* switch.

compact [kɔpakt] *a* dense; (*mécanisme, disque, véhicule*) compact.

compagne [kɔpaɲ] *nf* (*camarade*) friend; (*épouse, maîtresse*) companion. ◆**compagnie** *nf* (*présence, société*) & *Com Mil* company; **tenir c. à qn** to keep s.o. company. ◆**compagnon** *nm* companion; (*ouvrier*) workman; **c. de route** travelling companion, fellow traveller; **c. de jeu/de travail** playmate/workmate.

comparaître* [kɔparɛtr] *vi Jur* to appear (in court) (**devant** before).

compar/er [kɔpare] *vt* to compare; **— se c.** *vpr* to be compared (**à** to). ◆**—é** *a* (*science etc*) comparative. ◆**—able** *a* comparable. ◆**comparaison** *nf* comparison; (*Littér* simile. ◆**comparatif, -ive** *a* (*méthode etc*) comparative; **–** *nm Gram* comparative.

comparse [kɔpars] *nmf Jur* minor accomplice, stooge.

compartiment [kɔpartimã] *nm* compartment. ◆**compartimenter** *vt* to compartmentalize, divide up.

comparution [kɔparysjɔ̃] *nf Jur* appearance (in court).

compas [kɔpa] *nm* **1** (*pour mesurer etc*) (pair of) compasses, *Am* compass. **2** (*boussole*) *Nau* compass.

compassé [kɔpase] *a* (*affecté*) starchy, stiff.

compassion [kɔpasjɔ̃] *nf* compassion.

compatible [kɔpatibl] *a* compatible. ◆**compatibilité** *nf* compatibility.

compat/ir [kɔpatir] *vi* to sympathize; **c. à** (*la douleur etc de qn*) to share in. ◆**—issant** *a* sympathetic.

compatriote [kɔpatrijɔt] *nmf* compatriot.

compenser [kɔpɑse] *vt* to make up for, compensate for; **–** *vi* to compensate. ◆**compensation** *nf* compensation; **en c. de** in compensation for.

compère [kɔper] *nm* accomplice.

compétent [kɔpetɑ̃] *a* competent. ◆**compétence** *nf* competence.

compétition [kɔpetisjɔ̃] *nf* competition; (*épreuve*) *Sp* event; **de c.** (*esprit, sport*) competitive. ◆**compétitif, -ive** *a* competitive. ◆**compétitivité** *nf* competitiveness.

compiler [kɔpile] *vt* (*documents*) to compile.

complainte [kɔplɛt] *nf* (*chanson*) lament.

complaire (se) [səkɔplɛr] *vpr* **se c. dans qch/à faire** to delight in sth/in doing.

complaisant [kɔplezɑ̃] *a* kind, obliging; (*indulgent*) self-indulgent, complacent. ◆**complaisance** *nf* kindness, obligingness; self-indulgence, complacency.

complément [kɔplemɑ̃] *nm* complement; **le c.** (*le reste*) the rest; **un c. d'information** additional information. ◆**complémentaire** *a* complementary; (*détails*) additional.

complet, -ète [kɔplɛ, -ɛt] **1** *a* complete; (*train, hôtel, examen etc*) full; (*aliment*) whole; **au (grand) c.** in full strength. **2** *nm* (*costume*) suit. ◆**complètement** *adv* completely. ◆**compléter** *vt* to complete; (*ajouter à*) to complement; (*somme*) to make up; **— se c.** *vpr* (*caractères*) to complement each other.

complexe [kɔplɛks] **1** *a* complex. **2** *nm* (*sentiment, construction*) complex. ◆**complexé** *a Fam* hung up, inhibited. ◆**complexité** *nf* complexity.

complication [kɔplikasjɔ̃] *nf* complication; (*complexité*) complexity.

complice [kɔplis] *nm* accomplice; **–** *a* (*regard*) knowing; (*silence, attitude*) conniving; **c. de** *Jur* a party to. ◆**complicité** *nf* complicity.

compliment [kɔplimɑ̃] *nm* compliment; *pl* (*éloges*) compliments; (*félicitations*) congratulations. ◆**complimenter** *vt* to compliment (**sur, pour** on).

compliqu/er [kɔplike] *vt* to complicate; **— se c.** *vpr* (*situation*) to get complicated. ◆**—é** *a* complicated; (*mécanisme etc*) intricate; complicated; (*histoire, problème etc*) involved, complicated.

complot [kɔplo] *nm* plot, conspiracy. ◆**comploter** [kɔplɔte] *vti* to plot (**de faire** to do).

comport/er [kɔpɔrte] **1** *vt* (*impliquer*) to involve, contain; (*comprendre en soi, présenter*) to contain, comprise, have. **2 se c.** *vpr* to behave; (*joueur, voiture*) to perform. ◆**—ement** *nm* behaviour; (*de joueur etc*) performance.

compos/er [kɔpoze] *vt* (*former, constituer*) to compose, make up; (*musique, visage*) to compose; (*numéro*) *Tél* to dial; (*texte*) *Typ* to set (up); **se c. de, être composé de** to be composed of; **–** *vi Scol* to take an examination; **c. avec** to come to terms with. ◆**—ant** *nm* (*chimique, électronique*) component. ◆**—ante** *nf* (*d'une idée etc*) component. ◆**—é** *a* & *nm* compound. ◆**compositeur, -trice** *nmf Mus* composer; *Typ* typesetter. ◆**composition** *nf* (*action*) composing, making up; *Typ* typesetting; *Mus Littér Ch* composition; *Scol* test, class exam; **c. française** *Scol* French essay *ou* composition.

composter [kɔ̃pɔste] vt (billet) to cancel, punch.

compote [kɔ̃pɔt] nf stewed fruit; **c. de pommes** stewed apples, apple sauce. ◆**compotier** nm fruit dish.

compréhensible [kɔ̃preɑ̃sibl] a understandable, comprehensible. ◆**compréhensif, -ive** a (personne) understanding. ◆**compréhension** nf understanding, comprehension.

comprendre* [kɔ̃prɑ̃dr] vt to understand, comprehend; (comporter) to include, comprise; **je n'y comprends rien** I don't understand anything about it; **ça se comprend** that's understandable. ◆**compris** a (inclus) included (**dans** in); **frais c.** including expenses; **tout c.** (all) inclusive; **y c.** including; **c. entre** (situated) between; **(c'est) c.!** it's agreed!

compresse [kɔ̃prɛs] nf Méd compress.

compresseur [kɔ̃prɛsœr] a **rouleau c.** steam roller.

comprim/er [kɔ̃prime] vt to compress; (colère etc) to repress; (dépenses) to reduce. ◆**—é** nm Méd tablet. ◆**compression** nf compression; (du personnel etc) reduction.

compromettre* [kɔ̃prɔmɛtr] vt to compromise. ◆**compromis** nm compromise. ◆**compromission** nf compromising action, compromise.

comptable [kɔ̃tabl] a (règles etc) bookkeeping-; – nmf bookkeeper; (expert) accountant. ◆**comptabilité** nf (comptes) accounts; (science) bookkeeping, accountancy; (service) accounts department.

comptant [kɔ̃tɑ̃] a **argent c.** (hard) cash; – adv **payer c.** to pay (in) cash; **(au) c.** (acheter, vendre) for cash.

compte [kɔ̃t] nm (comptabilité) account; (calcul) count; (nombre) (right) number; **avoir un c. en banque** to have a bank(ing) account; **c. chèque** cheque account, Am checking account; **tenir c. de** to take into account; **c. tenu de** considering; **entrer en ligne de c.** to be taken into account; **se rendre c. de** to realize; **rendre c. de** (exposer) to report on; (justifier) to account for; **c. rendu** report; (de livre, film) review; **demander des comptes à** to call to account; **faire le c. de** to count; **à son c.** (travailler) for oneself; (s'installer) on one's own; **pour le c. de** on behalf of; **pour mon c.** for my part; **sur le c. de qn** about s.o.; **en fin de c.** all things considered; **à bon c.** (acheter) cheap(ly); **s'en tirer à bon c.** to get off lightly; **avoir un c. à régler avec qn** to have a score to settle with s.o.; **c. à rebours**

countdown. ◆**c.-gouttes** nm inv Méd dropper; **au c.-gouttes** very sparingly. ◆**c.-tours** nm inv Aut rev counter.

compt/er [kɔ̃te] vt (calculer) to count; (prévoir) to reckon, allow; (considérer) to consider; (payer) to pay; **c. faire** to expect to do; (avoir l'intention de) to intend to do; **c. qch à qn** (facturer) to charge s.o. for sth; **il compte deux ans de service** he has two years' service; **ses jours sont comptés** his ou her days are numbered; – vi (calculer, avoir de l'importance) to count; **c. sur** to rely on; **c. avec** to reckon with; **c. parmi** to be (numbered) among. ◆**—eur** nm Él meter; **c. (de vitesse)** Aut speedometer; **c. (kilométrique)** milometer, clock; **c. Geiger** Geiger counter.

comptoir [kɔ̃twar] nm **1** (de magasin) counter; (de café) bar; (de bureau) (reception) desk. **2** Com branch, agency.

compulser [kɔ̃pylse] vt to examine.

comte [kɔ̃t] nm (noble) count; Br earl. ◆**comté** nm county. ◆**comtesse** nf countess.

con, conne [kɔ̃, kɔn] a (idiot) Fam stupid; – nmf Fam stupid fool.

concave [kɔ̃kav] a concave.

concéder [kɔ̃sede] vt to concede, grant (à to, que that).

concentr/er [kɔ̃sɑ̃tre] vt to concentrate; (attention etc) to focus, concentrate; – **se c.** vpr (réfléchir) to concentrate. ◆**—é** a (solution) concentrated; (lait) condensed; (attentif) in a state of concentration; – nm Ch concentrate; **c. de tomates** tomato purée. ◆**concentration** nf concentration.

concentrique [kɔ̃sɑ̃trik] a concentric.

concept [kɔ̃sɛpt] nm concept. ◆**conception** nf (d'idée) & Méd conception.

concern/er [kɔ̃sɛrne] vt to concern; **en ce qui me concerne** as far as I'm concerned. ◆**—ant** prép concerning.

concert [kɔ̃sɛr] nm Mus concert; (de louanges) chorus; **de c.** (agir) together, in concert.

concert/er [kɔ̃sɛrte] vt to arrange, devise (in agreement); – **se c.** vpr to consult together. ◆**—é** a (plan) concerted. ◆**concertation** nf (dialogue) dialogue.

concession [kɔ̃sesjɔ̃] nf concession (à to); (terrain) plot of land). ◆**concessionnaire** nmf Com (authorized) dealer, agent.

concev/oir* [kɔ̃səvwar] **1** vt (imaginer, éprouver, engendrer) to conceive; (comprendre) to understand; **ainsi conçu** (dépêche etc) worded as follows. **2** vi (femme) to conceive. ◆**—able** a conceivable.

concierge [kɔ̃sjɛrʒ] *nmf* caretaker, *Am* janitor.

concile [kɔ̃sil] *nm Rel* council.

concili/er [kɔ̃silje] *vt* (*choses*) to reconcile; **se c. l'amitié**/*etc* **de qn** to win (over) s.o.'s friendship/*etc.* **◆—ant** *a* conciliatory. **◆conciliateur, -trice** *nmf* conciliator. **◆conciliation** *nf* conciliation.

concis [kɔ̃si] *a* concise, terse. **◆concision** *nf* concision.

concitoyen, -enne [kɔ̃sitwajɛ̃, -ɛn] *nmf* fellow citizen.

conclu/re* [kɔ̃klyr] *vt* (*terminer, régler*) to conclude; **c. que** (*déduire*) to conclude that; – *vi* (*orateur etc*) to conclude; **c. à** to conclude in favour of. **◆—ant** *a* conclusive. **◆conclusion** *nf* conclusion.

concombre [kɔ̃kɔ̃br] *nm* cucumber.

concorde [kɔ̃kɔrd] *nf* concord, harmony. **◆concord/er** *vi* (*faits etc*) to agree; (*caractères*) to match; **c. avec** to match. **◆—ant** *a* in agreement. **◆concordance** *nf* agreement (*de situations, résultats*) similarity; **c. des temps** *Gram* sequence of tenses.

concourir* [kɔ̃kurir] *vi* (*candidat*) to compete (**pour** for); (*directions*) to converge; **c. à** (*un but*) to contribute to. **◆concours** *nm Scol Univ* competitive examination; (*jeu*) competition; (*aide*) assistance; (*de circonstances*) combination; **c. hippique** horse show.

concret, -ète [kɔ̃krɛ, -ɛt] *a* concrete. **◆concrétiser** *vt* to give concrete form to; **— se c.** *vpr* to materialize.

conçu [kɔ̃sy] *voir* **concevoir**; **– a c. pour faire** designed to do; **bien c.** (*maison etc*) well-designed.

concubine [kɔ̃kybin] *nf* (*maîtresse*) concubine. **◆concubinage** *nm* cohabitation; **en c.** as husband and wife.

concurrent, -ente [kɔ̃kyrɑ̃, -ɑ̃t] *nmf* competitor; *Scol Univ* candidate. **◆concurrence** *nf* competition; **faire c. à** to compete with; **jusqu'à c. de** up to the amount of. **◆concurrencer** *vt* to compete with. **◆concurrentiel, -ielle** *a* (*prix etc*) competitive.

condamn/er [kɔ̃dane] *vt* to condemn; *Jur* to sentence (**à** to); (*porte*) to block up, bar; (*pièce*) to keep locked; **c. à une amende** to fine. **◆—é, -ée** *nmf Jur* condemned man, condemned woman; **être c.** (*malade*) to be doomed, be a hopeless case. **◆condamnation** *nf Jur* sentence; (*censure*) condemnation.

condenser [kɔ̃dɑ̃se] *vt*, **— se c.** *vpr* to condense. **◆condensateur** *nm Él* condenser. **◆condensation** *nf* condensation.

condescendre [kɔ̃dɛsɑ̃dr] *vi* to condescend (**à** to). **◆condescendance** *nf* condescension.

condiment [kɔ̃dimɑ̃] *nm* condiment.

condisciple [kɔ̃disipl] *nm Scol* classmate, schoolfellow; *Univ* fellow student.

condition [kɔ̃disjɔ̃] *nf* (*état, stipulation, rang*) condition; *pl* (*clauses, tarifs*) *Com* terms; **à c. de faire, à c. que l'on fasse** providing *ou* provided (that) one does; **mettre en c.** (*endoctriner*) to condition; **sans c.** (*se rendre*) unconditionally. **◆conditionnel, -elle** *a* conditional. **◆conditionn/er** *vt* **1** (*influencer*) to condition. **2** (*article*) *Com* to package. **◆—é** *a* (*réflexe*) conditioned; **à air c.** (*pièce etc*) air-conditioned. **◆—ement** *nm* conditioning; packaging.

condoléances [kɔ̃dɔleɑ̃s] *nfpl* condolences.

conducteur, -trice [kɔ̃dyktœr, -tris] **1** *nmf Aut Rail* driver. **2** *a & nm* (*corps*) **c.** *Él* conductor; (*fil*) **c.** *Él* lead (wire).

condu/ire* [kɔ̃dɥir] **1** *vt* to lead; *Aut* to drive; (*affaire etc*) & *Él* to conduct; (*eau*) to carry; **c. qn à** (*accompagner*) to take s.o. to. **2 se c.** *vpr* to behave. **◆conduit** *nm* duct. **◆conduite** *nf* conduct, behaviour; *Aut* driving (**de** of); (*d'entreprise etc*) conduct; (*d'eau, de gaz*) main; **c. à gauche** (*volant*) left-hand drive; **faire un bout de c. à qn** to go with s.o. part of the way; **sous la c. de** under the guidance of.

cône [kon] *nm* cone.

confection [kɔ̃fɛksjɔ̃] *nf* making (**de** of); **vêtements de c.** ready-made clothes; **magasin de c.** ready-made clothing shop. **◆confectionner** *vt* (*gâteau, robe*) to make.

confédération [kɔ̃federasjɔ̃] *nf* confederation. **◆confédéré** *a* confederate.

conférence [kɔ̃ferɑ̃s] *nf* conference; (*exposé*) lecture. **◆conférencier, -ière** *nmf* lecturer. **◆conférer** *vt* (*attribuer, donner*) to confer (**à** on).

confess/er [kɔ̃fese] *vt* to confess; **— se c.** *vpr Rel* to confess (**à** to). **◆—eur** *nm* (*prêtre*) confessor. **◆confession** *nf* confession. **◆confessionnal, -aux** *nm Rel* confessional. **◆confessionnel, -elle** *a* (*école*) *Rel* denominational.

confettis [kɔ̃feti] *nmpl* confetti.

confiance [kɔ̃fjɑ̃s] *nf* trust, confidence; **faire c. à qn, avoir c. en qn** to trust s.o.; **c. en soi** (self-)confidence; **poste/abus de c.** position/breach of trust; **homme de c.** reliable man; **en toute c.** (*acheter*) quite confidently; **poser la question de c.** *Pol* to ask for a vote of confidence. ◆**confiant** a trusting; (*sûr de soi*) confident; **être c. en** ou **dans** to have confidence in.

confidence [kɔ̃fidɑ̃s] *nf* (*secret*) confidence; **en c.** in confidence; **il m'a fait une c.** he confided in me. ◆**confident** *nm* confidant. ◆**confidente** *nf* confidante. ◆**confidentiel, -ielle** a confidential.

confier [kɔ̃fje] *vt* **c. à qn** (*enfant, objet*) to give s.o. to look after, entrust s.o. with; **c. un secret/etc à qn** to confide a secret/etc to s.o.; **— se c.** *vpr* to confide (**à qn** in s.o.).

configuration [kɔ̃figyrasjɔ̃] *nf* configuration.

confin/er [kɔ̃fine] *vt* to confine; **– vi c. à** to border on; **— se c.** *vpr* to confine oneself (**dans** to). ◆**–é** a (*atmosphère*) stuffy.

confins [kɔ̃fɛ̃] *nmpl* confines.

confire [kɔ̃fir] *vt* (*cornichon*) to pickle; (*fruit*) to preserve.

confirmer [kɔ̃firme] *vt* to confirm (**que** that); **c. qn dans sa résolution** to confirm s.o.'s resolve. ◆**confirmation** *nf* confirmation.

confiserie [kɔ̃fizri] *nf* (*magasin*) sweet shop, *Am* candy store; *pl* (*produits*) confectionery, sweets, *Am* candy. ◆**confiseur, -euse** *nmf* confectioner.

confisquer [kɔ̃fiske] *vt* to confiscate (**à qn** from s.o.). ◆**confiscation** *nf* confiscation.

confit [kɔ̃fi] a **fruits confits** crystallized ou candied fruit. ◆**confiture** *nf* jam, preserves.

conflit [kɔ̃fli] *nm* conflict. ◆**conflictuel, -elle** a *Psy* conflict-provoking.

confluent [kɔ̃flyɑ̃] *nm* (*jonction*) confluence.

confondre [kɔ̃fɔ̃dr] *vt* (*choses, personnes*) to confuse, mix up; (*consterner, étonner*) to confound; (*amalgamer*) to fuse; **c. avec** to mistake for; **— se c.** *vpr* (*s'unir*) to merge; **se c. en excuses** to be very apologetic.

conforme [kɔ̃fɔrm] a **c. à** in accordance with; **c. (à l'original)** (*copie*) true (to the original). ◆**conform/er** *vt* to model, adapt; **— se c.** *vpr* to conform (**à** to). ◆**–ément** *adv* **c. à** in accordance with. ◆**conformisme** *nm* conformity, conformism. ◆**conformiste** a & *nmf* conformist. ◆**conformité** *nf* conformity.

confort [kɔ̃fɔr] *nm* comfort. ◆**confortable** a comfortable.

confrère [kɔ̃frɛr] *nm* colleague. ◆**confrérie** *nf Rel* brotherhood.

confronter [kɔ̃frɔ̃te] *vt Jur etc* to confront (**avec** with); (*textes*) to collate; **confronté à** confronted with. ◆**confrontation** *nf* confrontation; collation.

confus [kɔ̃fy] a (*esprit, situation, bruit*) confused; (*idée, style*) confused, jumbled, hazy; (*gêné*) embarrassed; **je suis c.!** (*désolé*) I'm terribly sorry!; (*comblé de bienfaits*) I'm overwhelmed! ◆**confusément** *adv* indistinctly, vaguely. ◆**confusion** *nf* confusion; (*gêne, honte*) embarrassment.

congé [kɔ̃ʒe] *nm* leave (of absence); (*avis pour locataire*) notice (to quit); (*pour salarié*) notice (of dismissal); (*vacances*) holiday, *Am* vacation; **c. de maladie** sick leave; **congés payés** holidays with pay, paid holidays; **donner son c. à** (*employé, locataire*) to give notice to; **prendre c. de** to take leave of. ◆**congédier** *vt* (*domestique etc*) to dismiss.

congeler [kɔ̃ʒle] *vt* to freeze. ◆**congélateur** *nm* freezer, deep-freeze. ◆**congélation** *nf* freezing.

congénère [kɔ̃ʒenɛr] *nmf* fellow creature. ◆**congénital, -aux** a congenital.

congère [kɔ̃ʒɛr] *nf* snowdrift.

congestion [kɔ̃ʒɛstjɔ̃] *nf* congestion; **c. cérébrale** *Méd* stroke. ◆**congestionn/er** *vt* to congest. ◆**–é** a (*visage*) flushed.

Congo [kɔ̃go] *nm* Congo. ◆**congolais, -aise** a & *nmf* Congolese.

congratuler [kɔ̃gratyle] *vt Iron* to congratulate.

congrégation [kɔ̃gregasjɔ̃] *nf* (*de prêtres etc*) congregation.

congrès [kɔ̃grɛ] *nm* congress. ◆**congressiste** *nmf* delegate (*to a congress*).

conifère [kɔnifɛr] *nm* conifer.

conique [kɔnik] a conic(al), cone-shaped.

conjecture [kɔ̃ʒɛktyr] *nf* conjecture. ◆**conjectural, -aux** a conjectural. ◆**conjecturer** *vt* to conjecture, surmise.

conjoint [kɔ̃ʒwɛ̃] **1** a (*problèmes, action etc*) joint. **2** *nm* spouse; *pl* husband and wife. ◆**conjointement** *adv* jointly.

conjonction [kɔ̃ʒɔ̃ksjɔ̃] *nf Gram* conjunction.

conjoncture [kɔ̃ʒɔ̃ktyr] *nf* circumstances; *Écon* economic situation. ◆**conjoncturel, -elle** a (*prévisions etc*) economic.

conjugal, -aux [kɔ̃ʒygal, -o] a conjugal.

conjuguer [kɔ̃ʒyge] *vt* (*verbe*) to conjugate; (*efforts*) to combine; **— se c.** *vpr* (*verbe*) to be conjugated. ◆**conjugaison** *nf Gram* conjugation.

conjur/er [kɔ̃ʒyre] *vt* (*danger*) to avert; (*mauvais sort*) to ward off; **c. qn** (*implorer*)

to entreat s.o. (**de faire** to do). ◆**—é, -ée**
nmf conspirator. ◆**conjuration** *nf*
(*complot*) conspiracy.

connaissance [kɔnɛsɑ̃s] *nf* knowledge;
(*personne*) acquaintance; *pl* (*science*)
knowledge (en of); **faire la c. de qn, faire c.
avec qn** to make s.o.'s acquaintance, meet
s.o.; (*ami, époux etc*) to get to know s.o.; **à
ma c.** as far as I know; **avoir c. de** to be
aware of; **perdre c.** to lose consciousness,
faint; **sans c.** unconscious. ◆**connaisseur** *nm* connoisseur.

connaître* [kɔnɛtr] *vt* to know; (*rencontrer*)
to meet; (*un succès etc*) to have; (*un
malheur etc*) to experience; **faire c.** to make
known; **— se c.** *vpr* (*amis etc*) to get to
know each other; **nous nous connaissons
déjà** we've met before; **s'y c. à** *ou* **en qch** to
know (all) about sth; **il ne se connaît plus**
he's losing his cool.

connecter [kɔnɛkte] *vt* *Él* to connect.
◆**connexe** *a* (*matières*) allied. ◆**con-
nexion** *nf* *Él* connection.

connerie [kɔnri] *nf* *Fam* (*bêtise*) stupidity;
(*action*) stupid thing; *pl* (*paroles*) stupid
nonsense.

connivence [kɔnivɑ̃s] *nf* connivance.

connotation [kɔnɔtasjɔ̃] *nf* connotation.

connu *voir* **connaître;** **— a** (*célèbre*)
well-known.

conquér/ir* [kɔ̃kerir] *vt* (*pays, marché etc*)
to conquer. ◆**—ant, -ante** *nmf* conqueror.
◆**conquête** *nf* conquest; **faire la c. de**
(*pays, marché etc*) to conquer.

consacrer [kɔ̃sakre] *vt* (*temps, vie etc*) to
devote (**à** to); (*église etc*) *Rel* to consecrate;
(*coutume etc*) to establish, sanction, consecrate; **se c. à** to devote oneself to.

conscience [kɔ̃sjɑ̃s] *nf* **1** (*psychologique*)
consciousness; **la c. de qch** the awareness
ou consciousness of sth; **c. de soi** self-
awareness; **avoir/prendre c. de** to
be/become aware *ou* conscious of; **perdre
c.** to lose consciousness. **2** (*morale*)
conscience; **avoir mauvaise c.** to have a
guilty conscience; **c. professionnelle**
conscientiousness. ◆**consclemment**
[kɔ̃sjamɑ̃] *adv* consciously. ◆**consciencieux, -euse** *a* conscientious.
◆**conscient** *a* conscious; **c. de** aware *ou*
conscious of.

conscrit [kɔ̃skri] *nm* *Mil* conscript. ◆**conscription** *nf* conscription.

consécration [kɔ̃sekrasjɔ̃] *nf* *Rel* consecration; (*confirmation*) sanction, consecration.

consécuti/f, -ive [kɔ̃sekytif, -iv] *a* consecu-

tive; **c. à** following upon. ◆**—vement** *adv*
consecutively.

conseil [kɔ̃sɛj] *nm* **1 un c.** a piece of advice,
some advice; **des conseils** advice;
(**expert-**)**c.** consultant. **2** (*assemblée*) council, committee; **c. d'administration** board of
directors; **C. des ministres** *Pol* Cabinet;
(*réunion*) Cabinet meeting. ◆**conseiller¹**
vt (*guider, recommander*) to advise; **c. qch à
qn** to recommend sth to s.o.; **c. à qn de faire**
to advise s.o. to do. ◆**conseiller², -ère**
nmf (*expert*) consultant; (*d'un conseil*)
councillor.

consent/ir* [kɔ̃sɑ̃tir] *vi* **c. à** to consent to;
— vt to grant (**à** to). ◆**—ement** *nm*
consent.

conséquence [kɔ̃sekɑ̃s] *nf* consequence;
(*conclusion*) conclusion; **en c.** accordingly;
sans c. (*importance*) of no importance.
◆**conséquent** *a* logical; (*important*) *Fam*
important; **par c.** consequently.

conservatoire [kɔ̃sɛrvatwar] *nm* academy,
school (*of music, drama*).

conserve [kɔ̃sɛrv] *nf* **conserves** tinned *ou*
canned food; **de** *ou* **en c.** tinned, canned;
mettre en c. to tin, can.

conserv/er [kɔ̃sɛrve] *vt* (*ne pas perdre*) to
retain, keep; (*fruits, vie, tradition etc*) to
preserve; **— se c.** *vpr* (*aliment*) to keep.
◆**—é a bien c.** (*vieillard*) well-preserved.
◆**conservateur, -trice 1** *a* & *nmf* *Pol*
Conservative. **2** *nm* (*de musée*) curator; (*de
bibliothèque*) (chief) librarian. **3** *nm*
(*produit*) *Culin* preservative. ◆**conservation** *nf* preservation; **instinct de c.** survival
instinct. ◆**conservatisme** *nm* conservatism.

considér/er [kɔ̃sidere] *vt* to consider (**que**
that); **c. qn** (*faire cas de*) to respect s.o.; **c.
comme** to consider to be, regard as; **tout
bien considéré** all things considered.
◆**—able** *a* considerable. ◆**considération** *nf* (*motif, examen*) consideration;
(*respect*) regard, esteem; *pl* (*remarques*)
observations; **prendre en c.** to take into
consideration.

consigne [kɔ̃siɲ] *nf* (*instruction*) orders;
Rail left-luggage office, *Am* baggage checkroom; *Scol* detention; *Mil* confinement to
barracks; (*somme*) deposit; **c. automatique**
Rail luggage lockers, *Am* baggage lockers.
◆**consignation** *nf* (*somme*) deposit.
◆**consigner** *vt* (*écrire*) to record;
(*bouteille etc*) to charge a deposit on;
(*bagages*) to deposit in the left-luggage
office, *Am* to check; (*élève*) *Scol* to keep in;

(soldat) Mil to confine (to barracks); (salle) to seal off, close.

consistant [kɔ̃sistɑ̃] a (sauce, bouillie) thick; (argument, repas) solid. ◆**consistance** nf (de liquide) consistency; **sans c.** (rumeur) unfounded; (esprit) irresolute.

consister [kɔ̃siste] vi **c. en/dans** to consist of/in; **c. à faire** to consist in doing.

consistoire [kɔ̃sistwar] nm Rel council.

console [kɔ̃sɔl] nf Tech Él console.

consoler [kɔ̃sɔle] vt to console, comfort (**de** for); **se c. de** (la mort de qn etc) to get over. ◆**consolation** nf consolation, comfort.

consolider [kɔ̃sɔlide] vt to strengthen, consolidate. ◆**consolidation** nf strengthening, consolidation.

consomm/er [kɔ̃sɔme] vt (aliment, carburant etc) to consume; (crime, œuvre) Litt to accomplish; — vi (au café) to drink; **c. beaucoup/peu** (véhicule) to be heavy/light on petrol ou Am gas. ◆—**é 1** a (achevé) consummate. **2** nm clear meat soup, consommé. ◆**consommateur, -trice** nmf Com consumer; (au café) customer. ◆**consommation** nf consumption; drink; **biens/société de c.** consumer goods/society.

consonance [kɔ̃sɔnɑ̃s] nf Mus consonance; pl (sons) sounds.

consonne [kɔ̃sɔn] nf consonant.

consortium [kɔ̃sɔrsjɔm] nm Com consortium.

consorts [kɔ̃sɔr] nmpl **et c.** Péj and people of that ilk.

conspirer [kɔ̃spire] vi **1** to conspire, plot (**contre** against). **2 c. à faire** (concourir) to conspire to do. ◆**conspirateur, -trice** nmf conspirator. ◆**conspiration** nf conspiracy.

conspuer [kɔ̃spɥe] vt (orateur etc) to boo.

constant, -ante [kɔ̃stɑ̃, -ɑ̃t] a constant; — nf Math constant. ◆**constamment** adv constantly. ◆**constance** nf constancy.

constat [kɔ̃sta] nm (official) report; **dresser un c. d'échec** to acknowledge one's failure.

constater [kɔ̃state] vt to note, observe (**que** that); (vérifier) to establish; (enregistrer) to record; **je ne fais que c.** I'm merely stating a fact. ◆**constatation** nf (remarque) observation.

constellation [kɔ̃stelasjɔ̃] nf constellation. ◆**constellé** a **c. de** (étoiles, joyaux) studded with.

consterner [kɔ̃sterne] vt to distress, dismay. ◆**consternation** nf distress, (profound) dismay.

constip/er [kɔ̃stipe] vt to constipate. ◆—**é**

a constipated; (gêné) Fam embarrassed, stiff. ◆**constipation** nf constipation.

constitu/er [kɔ̃stitɥe] vt (composer) to make up, constitute; (être, représenter) to constitute; (organiser) to form; (instituer) Jur to appoint; **constitué de** made up of; **se c. prisonnier** to give oneself up. ◆—**ant** a (éléments) Pol component, constituent; (assemblée) Pol constituent. ◆**constitutif, -ive** a constituent. ◆**constitution** nf (santé) & Pol constitution; (fondation) formation (**de** of); (composition) composition. ◆**constitutionnel, -elle** a constitutional.

constructeur [kɔ̃stryktœr] nm builder; (fabricant) maker (**de** of). ◆**constructif, -ive** a constructive. ◆**construction** nf (de pont etc) building, construction (**de** of); (édifice) building, structure; (de théorie etc) & Gram construction; **de c.** (matériaux, jeu) building-.

construire* [kɔ̃strɥir] vt (maison, route etc) to build, construct; (phrase, théorie etc) to construct.

consul [kɔ̃syl] nm consul. ◆**consulaire** a consular. ◆**consulat** nm consulate.

consulter [kɔ̃sylte] **1** vt to consult; — **se c.** vpr to consult (each other), confer. **2** vi (médecin) to hold surgery, Am hold office hours. ◆**consultatif, -ive** a consultative, advisory. ◆**consultation** nf consultation; **cabinet de c.** Méd surgery, Am office; **heures de c.** Méd surgery hours, Am office hours.

consumer [kɔ̃syme] vt (détruire, miner) to consume.

contact [kɔ̃takt] nm contact; (toucher) touch; Aut ignition; **être en c. avec** to be in touch ou contact with; **prendre c.** to get in touch (**avec** with); **entrer en c. avec** to come into contact with; **prise de c.** first meeting; **mettre/couper le c.** Aut to switch on/off the ignition. ◆**contacter** vt to contact.

contagieux, -euse [kɔ̃taʒjø, -øz] a (maladie, rire) contagious, infectious; **c'est c.** it's catching ou contagious. ◆**contagion** nf Méd contagion, infection; (de rire etc) contagiousness.

contaminer [kɔ̃tamine] vt to contaminate. ◆**contamination** nf contamination.

conte [kɔ̃t] nm tale; **c. de fée** fairy tale.

contempler [kɔ̃tɑ̃ple] vt to contemplate, gaze at. ◆**contemplatif, -ive** a contemplative. ◆**contemplation** nf contemplation.

contemporain, -aine [kɔ̃tɑ̃pɔrɛ̃, -ɛn] a & nmf contemporary.

contenance [kɔ̃tnɑ̃s] *nf* **1** (*contenu*) capacity. **2** (*allure*) bearing; **perdre c.** to lose one's composure.

conten/ir* [kɔ̃tnir] *vt* (*renfermer*) to contain; (*avoir comme capacité*) to hold; (*contrôler*) to hold back, contain; **— se c.** *vpr* to contain oneself. **◆—ant** *nm* container. **◆—eur** *nm* (freight) container.

content [kɔ̃tɑ̃] **1** *a* pleased, happy, glad (**de faire** to do); **c. de qn/qch** pleased *ou* happy with s.o./sth; **c. de soi** self-satisfied; **non c. d'avoir fait** not content with having done. **2** *nm* **avoir son c.** to have had one's fill (**de** of). **◆content/er** *vt* to satisfy, please; **se c. de** to be content with, content oneself with. **◆—ement** *nm* contentment, satisfaction.

contentieux [kɔ̃tɑ̃sjø] *nm* (*affaires*) matters in dispute; (*service*) legal *ou* claims department.

contenu [kɔ̃tny] *nm* (*de récipient*) contents; (*de texte, film etc*) content.

cont/er [kɔ̃te] *vt* (*histoire etc*) to tell, relate. **◆—eur, -euse** *nmf* storyteller.

conteste (sans) [sɑ̃kɔ̃tɛst] *adv* indisputably.

contest/er [kɔ̃tɛste] **1** *vt* (*fait etc*) to dispute, contest. **2** *vi* (*étudiants etc*) to protest; **— vt** to protest against. **◆—é** *a* (*théorie etc*) controversial. **◆—able** *a* debatable. **◆contestataire** *a* **étudiant/ ouvrier c.** student/worker protester; **—** *nmf* protester. **◆contestation** *nf* (*discussion*) dispute; **faire de la c.** to protest (against the establishment).

contexte [kɔ̃tɛkst] *nm* context.

contigu, -uë [kɔ̃tigy] *a* **c. (à)** (*maisons etc*) adjoining. **◆contiguïté** *nf* close proximity.

continent [kɔ̃tinɑ̃] *nm* continent; (*opposé à une île*) mainland. **◆continental, -aux** *a* continental.

contingent [kɔ̃tɛ̃ʒɑ̃] **1** *a* (*accidentel*) contingent. **2** *nm* Mil contingent; (*part, quota*) quota. **◆contingences** *nfpl* contingencies.

continu [kɔ̃tiny] *a* continuous. **◆continuel, -elle** *a* continual, unceasing. **◆continuellement** *adv* continually.

continuer [kɔ̃tinɥe] *vt* to continue, carry on (**à** *ou* **de faire** doing); (*prolonger*) to continue; **— vi** to continue, go on. **◆continuation** *nf* continuation; **bonne c.!** *Fam* I hope the rest of it goes well, keep up the good work! **◆continuité** *nf* continuity.

contondant [kɔ̃tɔ̃dɑ̃] *a* **instrument c.** *Jur* blunt instrument.

contorsion [kɔ̃tɔrsjɔ̃] *nf* contortion. **◆se**

contorsionner *vpr* to contort oneself. **◆contorsionniste** *nmf* contortionist.

contour [kɔ̃tur] *nm* outline, contour; *pl* (*de route, rivière*) twists, bends. **◆contourn/er** *vt* (*colline etc*) to go round, skirt; (*difficulté, loi*) to get round. **◆—é** *a* (*style*) convoluted, tortuous.

contraception [kɔ̃trasɛpsjɔ̃] *nf* contraception. **◆contraceptif, -ive** *a* & *nm* contraceptive.

contract/er [kɔ̃trakte] *vt* (*muscle, habitude, dette etc*) to contract; **— se c.** *vpr* (*cœur etc*) to contract. **◆—é** *a* (*inquiet*) tense. **◆contraction** *nf* contraction.

contractuel, -elle [kɔ̃traktɥɛl] **1** *nmf* traffic warden; **—** *nf Am* meter maid. **2** *a* contractual.

contradicteur [kɔ̃tradiktœr] *nm* contradictor. **◆contradiction** *nf* contradiction. **◆contradictoire** *a* (*propos etc*) contradictory; (*rapports, théories*) conflicting; **débat c.** debate.

contraindre* [kɔ̃trɛ̃dr] *vt* to compel, force (**à faire** to do); **— se c.** *vpr* to compel *ou* force oneself; (*se gêner*) to restrain oneself. **◆contraignant** *a* constraining, restricting. **◆contraint** *a* (*air etc*) forced, constrained. **◆contrainte** *nf* compulsion, constraint; (*gêne*) constraint, restraint.

contraire [kɔ̃trɛr] *a* opposite; (*défavorable*) contrary; **c. à** contrary to; **—** *nm* opposite; **(bien) au c.** on the contrary. **◆—ment** *adv* **c. à** contrary to.

contrari/er [kɔ̃trarje] *vt* (*projet, action*) to thwart; (*personne*) to annoy. **◆—ant** *a* (*action etc*) annoying; (*personne*) difficult, perverse. **◆contrariété** *nf* annoyance.

contraste [kɔ̃trast] *nm* contrast. **◆contraster** *vi* to contrast (**avec** with); **faire c.** (*mettre en contraste*) to contrast.

contrat [kɔ̃tra] *nm* contract.

contravention [kɔ̃travɑ̃sjɔ̃] *nf* (*amende*) *Aut* fine; (*pour stationnement interdit*) (parking) ticket; **en c.** contravening the law; **en c. à** in contravention of.

contre [kɔ̃tr] **1** *prép & adv* against; (*en échange de*) (in exchange) for; **échanger c.** to exchange for; **fâché c.** angry with; **s'abriter c.** to shelter from; **il va s'appuyer c.** he's going to lean against it; **six voix c. deux** six votes to two; **Nîmes c. Arras** *Sp* Nîmes versus Arras; **un médicament c.** (*toux, grippe etc*) a medicine for; **par c.** on the other hand; **tout c.** close to *ou* by. **2** *nm* (*riposte*) *Sp* counter.

contre- [kɔ̃tr] *préf* counter-.

contre-attaque [kɔ̃tratak] *nf* counterattack. ◆**contre-attaquer** *vt* to counterattack.

contrebalancer [kɔ̃trəbalɑ̃se] *vt* to counterbalance.

contrebande [kɔ̃trəbɑ̃d] *nf* (*fraude*) smuggling, contraband; (*marchandise*) contraband; **de c.** (*tabac etc*) contraband, smuggled; **faire de la c.** to smuggle; **passer qch en c.** to smuggle sth. ◆**contrebandier, -ière** *nmf* smuggler.

contrebas (en) [ɑ̃kɔ̃trəba] *adv & prép* **en c. (de)** down below.

contrebasse [kɔ̃trəbɑs] *nf* *Mus* doublebass.

contrecarrer [kɔ̃trəkare] *vt* to thwart, frustrate.

contrecœur (à) [akɔ̃trəkœr] *adv* reluctantly.

contrecoup [kɔ̃trəku] *nm* (indirect) effect *ou* consequence; **par c.** as an indirect consequence.

contre-courant (à) [akɔ̃trəkurɑ̃] *adv* against the current.

contredanse [kɔ̃trədɑ̃s] *nf* (*amende*) *Aut Fam* ticket.

contredire* [kɔ̃trədir] *vt* to contradict; — **se c.** *vpr* to contradict oneself.

contrée [kɔ̃tre] *nf* region, land.

contre-espionnage [kɔ̃trɛspjɔnaʒ] *nm* counterespionage.

contrefaçon [kɔ̃trəfasɔ̃] *nf* counterfeiting, forgery; (*objet imité*) counterfeit, forgery. ◆**contrefaire** *vt* (*parodier*) to mimic; (*déguiser*) to disguise; (*monnaie etc*) to counterfeit, forge.

contreforts [kɔ̃trəfɔr] *nmpl Géog* foothills.

contre-indiqué [kɔ̃trɛ̃dike] *a* (*médicament*) dangerous, not recommended.

contre-jour (à) [akɔ̃trəʒur] *adv* against the (sun)light.

contremaître [kɔ̃trəmɛtr] *nm* foreman.

contre-offensive [kɔ̃trɔfɑ̃siv] *nf* counteroffensive.

contrepartie [kɔ̃trəparti] *nf* compensation; **en c.** in exchange.

contre-performance [kɔ̃trəpɛrfɔrmɑ̃s] *nf Sp* bad performance.

contre-pied [kɔ̃trəpje] *nm* **le c.-pied d'une opinion/attitude** the (exact) opposite view/attitude; **à c.-pied** *Sp* on the wrong foot.

contre-plaqué [kɔ̃trəplake] *nm* plywood.

contrepoids [kɔ̃trəpwa] *nm Tech & Fig* counterbalance; **faire c. (à)** to counterbalance.

contrepoint [kɔ̃trəpwɛ̃] *nm Mus* counterpoint.

contrer [kɔ̃tre] *vt* (*personne, attaque*) to counter.

contre-révolution [kɔ̃trərevɔlysjɔ̃] *nf* counter-revolution.

contresens [kɔ̃trəsɑ̃s] *nm* misinterpretation; (*en traduisant*) mistranslation; (*non-sens*) absurdity; **à c.** the wrong way.

contresigner [kɔ̃trəsiɲe] *vt* to countersign.

contretemps [kɔ̃trətɑ̃] *nm* hitch, mishap; **à c.** (*arriver etc*) at the wrong moment.

contre-torpilleur [kɔ̃trətɔrpijœr] *nm* (*navire*) destroyer, torpedo boat.

contrevenir [kɔ̃trəvnir] *vi* **c. à** (*loi etc*) to contravene.

contre-vérité [kɔ̃trəverite] *nf* untruth.

contribu/er [kɔ̃tribɥe] *vi* to contribute (**à** to). ◆**—able** *nmf* taxpayer. ◆**contribution** *nf* contribution; (*impôt*) tax; *pl* (*administration*) tax office; **mettre qn à c.** to use s.o.'s services.

contrit [kɔ̃tri] *a* (*air etc*) contrite. ◆**contrition** *nf* contrition.

contrôle [kɔ̃trol] *nm* (*vérification*) inspection, check(ing) (**de** of); (*des prix, de la qualité*) control; (*maîtrise*) control; (*sur bijou*) hallmark; **un c.** (*examen*) a check (**sur** on); **le c. de soi(-même)** self-control; **le c. des naissances** birth control; **un c. d'identité** an identity check. ◆**contrôl/er** *vt* (*examiner*) to inspect, check; (*maîtriser, surveiller*) to control; — **se c.** *vpr* (*se maîtriser*) to control oneself. ◆**—eur, -euse** *nmf* (*de train*) (ticket) inspector; (*au quai*) ticket collector; (*de bus*) conductor, conductress.

contrordre [kɔ̃trɔrdr] *nm* change of orders.

controverse [kɔ̃trɔvɛrs] *nf* controversy. ◆**controversé** *a* controversial.

contumace (par) [parkɔ̃tymas] *adv Jur* in one's absence, in absentia.

contusion [kɔ̃tyzjɔ̃] *nf* bruise. ◆**contusionner** *vt* to bruise.

convainc/re* [kɔ̃vɛ̃kr] *vt* to convince (**de** of); (*accusé*) to prove guilty (**de** of); **c. qn de faire** to persuade s.o. to do. ◆**—ant** *a* convincing. ◆**—u** *a* (*certain*) convinced (**de** of).

convalescent, -ente [kɔ̃valesɑ̃, -ɑ̃t] *nmf* convalescent; — *a* **être c.** to convalesce. ◆**convalescence** *nf* convalescence; **être en c.** to convalesce; **maison de c.** convalescent home.

conven/ir [kɔ̃vnir] *vi* **c. à** (*être approprié à*) to be suitable for; (*plaire à, aller à*) to suit; **ça convient** (*date etc*) that's suitable; **c. de** (*lieu etc*) to agree upon; (*erreur*) to admit; **c. que** to admit that; **il convient de** it's advisable to; (*selon les usages*) it is proper *ou* fitting to. ◆**—u** a (*prix etc*) agreed. ◆**—able** a (*approprié, acceptable*) suitable; (*correct*) decent, proper. ◆**—ablement** *adv* suitably; decently. ◆**convenance** *nf* **convenances** (*usages*) convention(s), proprieties; **à sa c.** to one's satisfaction *ou* taste.

convention [kɔ̃vɑ̃sjɔ̃] *nf* (*accord*) agreement, convention; (*règle*) & *Am Pol* convention; **c. collective** collective bargaining; **de c.** (*sentiment etc*) conventional. ◆**conventionné** a (*prix, tarif*) regulated (by voluntary agreement); **médecin c.** = National Health Service doctor (*bound by agreement with the State*). ◆**conventionnel, -elle** a conventional.

convergent [kɔ̃vɛrʒɑ̃] a converging, convergent. ◆**convergence** *nf* convergence. ◆**converger** *vi* to converge.

converser [kɔ̃vɛrse] *vi* to converse. ◆**conversation** *nf* conversation.

conversion [kɔ̃vɛrsjɔ̃] *nf* conversion. ◆**convert/ir** *vt* to convert (à to, en into); **— se c.** *vpr* to be converted, convert. ◆**—i, -ie** *nmf* convert. ◆**convertible** a convertible; **—** *nm* (*canapé*) c. bed settee.

convexe [kɔ̃vɛks] a convex.

conviction [kɔ̃viksjɔ̃] *nf* (*certitude, croyance*) conviction; **pièce à c.** *Jur* exhibit.

convier [kɔ̃vje] *vt* to invite (à une soirée/*etc* to a party/*etc*, à faire to do).

convive [kɔ̃viv] *nmf* guest (*at table*).

convoi [kɔ̃vwa] *nm* (*véhicules, personnes etc*) convoy; *Rail* train; **c. (funèbre)** funeral procession. ◆**convoy/er** *vt* to escort. ◆**—eur** *nm Nau* escort ship; **c. de fonds** security guard.

convoiter [kɔ̃vwate] *vt* to desire, envy, covet. ◆**convoitise** *nf* desire, envy.

convoquer [kɔ̃vɔke] *vt* (*candidats, membres etc*) to summon *ou* invite (to attend); (*assemblée*) to convene, summon; **c. à** to summon *ou* invite to. ◆**convocation** *nf* (*action*) summoning, convening; (*ordre*) summons (to attend); (*lettre*) (written) notice (to attend).

convulser [kɔ̃vylse] *vt* to convulse. ◆**convulsif, -ive** a convulsive. ◆**convulsion** *nf* convulsion.

coopérer [kɔɔpere] *vi* to co-operate (à in, avec with). ◆**coopératif, -ive** a co-operative; **—** *nf* co-operative (society). ◆**coopération** *nf* co-operation.

coopter [kɔɔpte] *vt* to co-opt.

coordonn/er [kɔɔrdɔne] *vt* to co-ordinate. ◆**—ées** *nfpl Math* co-ordinates; (*adresse,*

téléphone) *Fam* particulars, details. ◆**coordination** *nf* co-ordination.

copain [kɔpɛ̃] *nm Fam* (*camarade*) pal; (*petit ami*) boyfriend; **être c. avec** to be pals with.

copeau, -x [kɔpo] *nm* (*de bois*) shaving.

copie [kɔpi] *nf* copy; (*devoir, examen*) *Scol* paper. ◆**copier** *vti* to copy; *Scol* to copy, crib (sur from). ◆**copieur, -euse** *nmf* (*élève etc*) copycat, copier.

copieux, -euse [kɔpjø, -øz] a copious, plentiful.

copilote [kɔpilɔt] *nm* co-pilot.

copine [kɔpin] *nf Fam* (*camarade*) pal; (*petite amie*) girlfriend; **être c. avec** to be pals with.

copropriété [kɔprɔprijete] *nf* joint ownership; (*immeuble en*) c. block of flats in joint ownership, *Am* condominium.

copulation [kɔpylasjɔ̃] *nf* copulation.

coq [kɔk] *nm* cock, rooster; **c. au vin** coq au vin (*chicken cooked in wine*); **passer du c. à l'âne** to jump from one subject to another.

coque [kɔk] *nf* **1** (*de noix*) shell; (*mollusque*) cockle; **œuf à la c.** boiled egg. **2** *Nau* hull.

coquelicot [kɔkliko] *nm* poppy.

coqueluche [kɔklyʃ] *nf Méd* whooping-cough; **la c. de** *Fig* the darling of.

coquet, -ette [kɔkɛ, -ɛt] a (*chic*) smart; (*joli*) pretty; (*provocant*) coquettish, flirtatious; (*somme*) *Fam* tidy; **—** *nf* coquette, flirt. ◆**coquetterie** *nf* (*élégance*) smartness; (*goût de la toilette*) dress sense; (*galanterie*) coquetry.

coquetier [kɔktje] *nm* egg cup.

coquille [kɔkij] *nf* shell; *Typ* misprint; **c. Saint-Jacques** scallop. ◆**coquillage** *nm* (*mollusque*) shellfish; (*coquille*) shell.

coquin, -ine [kɔkɛ̃, -in] *nmf* rascal; **—** *a* mischievous, rascally; (*histoire etc*) naughty.

cor [kɔr] *nm Mus* horn; **c. (au pied)** corn; **réclamer** *ou* **demander à c. et à cri** to clamour for.

corail, -aux [kɔraj, -o] *nm* coral.

Coran [kɔrɑ̃] *nm* **le C.** the Koran.

corbeau, -x [kɔrbo] *nm* crow; **(grand) c.** raven.

corbeille [kɔrbɛj] *nf* basket; **c. à papier** waste paper basket.

corbillard [kɔrbijar] *nm* hearse.

corde [kɔrd] *nf* rope; (*plus mince*) (fine) cord; (*de raquette, violon*) string; **c. (raide)** (*d'acrobate*) tightrope; **instrument à cordes** *Mus* string(ed) instrument; **c. à linge** (washing *ou* clothes) line; **c. à sauter** skipping rope, *Am* jump rope; **usé jusqu'à**

la c. threadbare; **cordes vocales** vocal cords; **prendre un virage à la c.** *Aut* to hug a bend; **pas dans mes cordes** *Fam* not my line. ◆**cordage** *nm Nau* rope. ◆**cordée** *nf* roped (climbing) party. ◆**cordelette** *nf* (fine) cord. ◆**corder** *vt* (*raquette*) to string. ◆**cordon** *nm* (*de tablier, sac etc*) string; (*de soulier*) lace; (*de rideau*) cord, rope; (*d'agents de police*) cordon; (*décoration*) ribbon, sash; (*ombilical*) *Anat* cord. ◆**c.-bleu** *nm* (*pl* **cordons-bleus**) cordon bleu (cook), first-class cook.

cordial, -aux [kɔrdjal, -o] *a* cordial, warm; – *nm Méd* cordial. ◆**cordialité** *nf* cordiality.

cordonnier [kɔrdɔnje] *nm* shoe repairer, cobbler. ◆**cordonnerie** *nf* shoe repairer's shop.

Corée [kɔre] *nf* Korea. ◆**coréen, -enne** *a* & *nmf* Korean.

coriace [kɔrjas] *a* (*aliment, personne*) tough.

corne [kɔrn] *nf* (*de chèvre etc*) horn; (*de cerf*) antler; (*matière, instrument*) horn; (*angle, pli*) corner.

cornée [kɔrne] *nf Anat* cornea.

corneille [kɔrnɛj] *nf* crow.

cornemuse [kɔrnəmyz] *nf* bagpipes.

corner [kɔrne] **1** *vt* (*page*) to turn down the corner of, dog-ear. **2** *vi* (*véhicule*) to sound its horn. **3** [kɔrnɛr] *nm Fb* corner.

cornet [kɔrnɛ] *nm* **1** c. (**à pistons**) *Mus* cornet. **2** (*de glace*) cornet, cone; **c.** (**de papier**) (paper) cone.

corniaud [kɔrnjo] *nm* (*chien*) mongrel; (*imbécile*) *Fam* drip, twit.

corniche [kɔrniʃ] *nf Archit* cornice; (*route*) cliff road.

cornichon [kɔrniʃɔ̃] *nm* (*concombre*) gherkin; (*niais*) *Fam* clot, twit.

cornu [kɔrny] *a* (*diable etc*) horned.

corollaire [kɔrɔlɛr] *nm* corollary.

corporation [kɔrpɔrasjɔ̃] *nf* trade association, professional body.

corps [kɔr] *nm Anat Ch Fig etc* body; *Mil Pol* corps; **c. électoral** electorate; **c. enseignant** teaching profession; **c. d'armée** army corps; **garde du c.** bodyguard; **un c. de bâtiment** a main building; **c. et âme** body and soul; **lutter c. à c.** to fight hand-to-hand; **à son c. défendant** under protest; **prendre c.** (*projet*) to take shape; **donner c. à** (*rumeur, idée*) to give substance to; **faire c. avec** to form a part of, belong with; **perdu c. et biens** *Nau* lost with all hands; **esprit de c.** corporate spirit. ◆**corporel, -elle** *a* bodily; (*châtiment*) corporal.

corpulent [kɔrpylɑ̃] *a* stout, corpulent. ◆**corpulence** *nf* stoutness, corpulence.

corpus [kɔrpys] *nm Ling* corpus.

correct [kɔrɛkt] *a* (*exact*) correct; (*bienséant, honnête*) proper, correct; (*passable*) adequate. ◆**—ement** *adv* correctly; properly; adequately. ◆**correcteur, -trice 1** *a* (*verres*) corrective. **2** *nmf Scol* examiner; *Typ* proofreader. ◆**correctif, -ive** *a* & *nm* corrective.

correction [kɔrɛksjɔ̃] *nf* (*rectification etc*) correction; (*punition*) thrashing; (*exactitude, bienséance*) correctness; **la c. de** (*devoirs, examen*) the marking of; **c. d'épreuves** *Typ* proofreading. ◆**correctionnel, -elle** *a* **tribunal c.,** – *nf* magistrates' court, *Am* police court.

corrélation [kɔrelasjɔ̃] *nf* correlation.

correspond/re [kɔrɛspɔ̃dr] **1** *vi* (*s'accorder*) to correspond (**à** to, with); (*chambres etc*) to communicate; **c. avec** *Rail* to connect with; – **se c.** *vpr* (*idées etc*) to correspond; (*chambres etc*) to communicate. **2** *vi* (*écrire*) to correspond (**avec** with). ◆**—ant, -ante** *a* corresponding; – *nmf* correspondent; (*d'un élève, d'un adolescent*) pen friend; *Tél* caller. ◆**correspondance** *nf* correspondence; (*de train, d'autocar*) connection, *Am* transfer.

corrida [kɔrida] *nf* bullfight.

corridor [kɔridɔr] *nm* corridor.

corrig/er [kɔriʒe] *vt* (*texte, injustice etc*) to correct; (*épreuve*) *Typ* to read; (*devoir*) *Scol* to mark, correct; (*châtier*) to beat, punish; **c. qn de** (*défaut*) to cure s.o. of; **se c. de** to cure oneself of. ◆**—é** *nm Scol* model (answer), correct version, key.

corroborer [kɔrɔbɔre] *vt* to corroborate.

corroder [kɔrɔde] *vt* to corrode. ◆**corrosif, -ive** *a* corrosive. ◆**corrosion** *nf* corrosion.

corromp/re* [kɔrɔ̃pr] *vt* to corrupt; (*soudoyer*) to bribe; (*aliment, eau*) to taint. ◆**—u** *a* corrupt; (*altéré*) tainted. ◆**corruption** *nf* (*dépravation*) corruption; (*de juge etc*) bribery.

corsage [kɔrsaʒ] *nm* (*chemisier*) blouse; (*de robe*) bodice.

corsaire [kɔrsɛr] *nm* (*marin*) *Hist* privateer.

Corse [kɔrs] *nf* Corsica. ◆**corse** *a* & *nmf* Corsican.

cors/er [kɔrse] *vt* (*récit, action*) to heighten; **l'affaire se corse** things are hotting up. ◆**—é** *a* (*vin*) full-bodied; (*café*) strong; (*sauce, histoire*) spicy; (*problème*) tough; (*addition de restaurant*) steep.

corset [kɔrsɛ] *nm* corset.

cortège [kɔrtɛʒ] nm (défilé) procession; (suite) retinue; **c. officiel** (automobiles) motorcade.

corvée [kɔrve] nf chore, drudgery; Mil fatigue (duty).

cosaque [kɔzak] nm Cossack.

cosmopolite [kɔsmɔpɔlit] a cosmopolitan.

cosmos [kɔsmɔs] nm (univers) cosmos; (espace) outer space. ◆**cosmique** a cosmic. ◆**cosmonaute** nmf cosmonaut.

cosse [kɔs] nf (de pois etc) pod.

cossu [kɔsy] a (personne) well-to-do; (maison etc) opulent.

costaud [kɔsto] a Fam brawny, beefy; – nm Fam strong man.

costume [kɔstym] nm (pièces d'habillement) costume, dress; (complet) suit. ◆**costum/er** vt **c. qn** to dress s.o. up (en as). ◆**-é** a **bal c.** fancy-dress ball.

cote [kɔt] nf (marque de classement) mark, letter, number; (tableau des valeurs) (official) listing; (des valeurs boursières) quotation; (évaluation, popularité) rating; (de cheval) odds (de on); **c. d'alerte** danger level.

côte [kot] nf **1** Anat rib; (de mouton) chop; (de veau) cutlet; **à côtes** (étoffe) ribbed; **c. à c.** side by side; **se tenir les côtes** to split one's sides (laughing). **2** (montée) hill; (versant) hillside. **3** (littoral) coast.

côté [kote] nm side; (direction) way; **de l'autre c.** on the other side (de of); (direction) the other way; **de ce c.** (passer) this way; **du c. de** (vers, près de) towards; **de c.** (se jeter, mettre de l'argent etc) to one side; (regarder) sideways, to one side; **à c.** close by, nearby; (pièce) in the other room; (maison) next door; **la maison (d')à c.** the house next door; **à c. de** next to, beside; (comparaison) compared to; **passer à c.** (balle) to fall wide (de of); **venir de tous côtés** to come from all directions; **d'un c.** on the one hand; **de mon c.** for my part; **à mes côtés** by my side; **laisser de c.** (travail) to neglect; **(du) c. argent/etc** Fam as regards money/etc, moneywise/etc; **le bon c.** (d'une affaire) the bright side (de of).

coteau, -x [kɔto] nm (small) hill; (versant) hillside.

côtelé [kotle] a (étoffe) ribbed; **velours c.** cord(uroy).

côtelette [kotlɛt] nf (d'agneau, de porc) chop; (de veau) cutlet.

cot/er [kɔte] vt (valeur boursière) to quote. ◆**-é** a **bien c.** highly rated.

coterie [kɔtri] nf Péj set, clique.

côtier, -ière [kotje, -jɛr] a coastal; (pêche) inshore.

cotiser [kɔtize] vi to contribute (à to, pour towards); **c. (à)** (club) to subscribe (to); — **se c.** vpr to club together (pour acheter to buy). ◆**cotisation** nf (de club) dues, subscription; (de pension etc) contribution(s).

coton [kɔtɔ̃] nm cotton; **c. (hydrophile)** cottonwool, Am (absorbent) cotton. ◆**cotonnade** nf cotton (fabric). ◆**cotonnier, -ière** a (industrie) cotton-.

côtoyer [kotwaje] vt (route, rivière) to run along, skirt; (la misère, la folie etc) Fig to be ou come close to; **c. qn** (fréquenter) to rub shoulders with s.o.

cotte [kɔt] nf (de travail) overalls.

cou [ku] nm neck; **sauter au c. de qn** to throw one's arms around s.o.; **jusqu'au c.** Fig up to one's eyes ou ears.

couche [kuʃ] nf **1** (épaisseur) layer; (de peinture) coat; Géol stratum; **couches sociales** social strata. **2** (linge de bébé) nappy, Am diaper. **3** **faire une fausse c.** Méd to have a miscarriage; **les couches** Méd confinement.

couch/er [kuʃe] vt to put to bed; (héberger) to put up; (allonger) to lay (down ou out); (blé) to flatten; **c. (par écrit)** to put down (in writing); **c. qn en joue** to aim at s.o.; — vi to sleep (avec with); — **se c.** vpr to go to bed; (s'allonger) to lie flat ou down; (soleil) to set, go down, — nm (moment) bedtime; **c. de soleil** sunset. ◆**-ant** a (soleil) setting, — nm (aspect) sunset; **le c.** (ouest) west. ◆**-é** a **être c.** to be in bed; (étendu) to be lying (down). ◆**-age** nm sleeping (situation); (matériel) bedding; **sac de c.** sleeping bag. ◆**couchette** nf Rail sleeping berth, couchette; Nau bunk.

couci-couça [kusikusa] adv Fam so-so.

coucou [kuku] nm (oiseau) cuckoo; (pendule) cuckoo clock; Bot cowslip.

coude [kud] nm elbow; (de chemin, rivière) bend; **se serrer ou se tenir les coudes** to help one another, stick together; **c. à c.** side by side; **coup de c.** poke ou dig (with one's elbow), nudge; **pousser du c.** to nudge. ◆**coudoyer** vt to rub shoulders with.

cou-de-pied [kudpje] nm (pl **cous-de-pied**) instep.

coudre* [kudr] vti to sew.

couenne [kwan] nf (pork) crackling.

couette [kwɛt] nf (édredon) duvet, continental quilt.

couffin [kufɛ̃] nm (de bébé) Moses basket, Am bassinet.

couic! [kwik] *int* eek!, squeak! ◆**couiner** *vi Fam* to squeal; (*pleurer*) to whine.

couillon [kujɔ̃] *nm* (*idiot*) *Arg* drip, cretin.

coul/er¹ [kule] *vi* (*eau etc*) to flow; (*robinet, nez, sueur*) to run; (*fuir*) to leak; **c. de source** *Fig* to follow naturally; **faire c. le sang** to cause bloodshed; − *vt* (*métal, statue*) to cast; (*vie*) *Fig* to pass, lead; (*glisser*) to slip; **se c. dans** (*passer*) to slip into; **se la c. douce** to have things easy. ◆−**ant** *a* (*style*) flowing; (*caractère*) easygoing. ◆−**ée** *nf* (*de métal*) casting; **c. de lave** lava flow. ◆−**age** *nm* (*de métal, statue*) casting; (*gaspillage*) *Fam* wastage.

couler² [kule] *vi* (*bateau, nageur*) to sink; **c. à pic** to sink to the bottom; − *vt* to sink; (*discréditer*) *Fig* to discredit.

couleur [kulœr] *nf* colour; (*colorant*) paint; *Cartes* suit; *pl* (*teint, carnation*) colour; **c. chair** flesh-coloured; **de c.** (*homme, habit etc*) coloured; **en couleurs** (*photo, télévision*) colour−; **téléviseur c.** colour TV set; **haut en c.** colourful; **sous c. de faire** while pretending to do.

couleuvre [kulœvr] *nf* (grass) snake.

coulisse [kulis] *nf* **1** (*de porte*) runner; **à c.** (*porte etc*) sliding. **2 dans les coulisses** *Th* in the wings, backstage; **dans la c.** (*caché*) *Fig* behind the scenes. ◆**coulissant** *a* (*porte etc*) sliding.

couloir [kulwar] *nm* corridor; (*de circulation*) & *Sp* lane; (*dans un bus*) gangway.

coup [ku] *nm* blow, knock; (*léger*) tap, touch; (*choc moral*) blow; (*de fusil etc*) shot; (*de crayon, d'horloge*) & *Sp* stroke; (*aux échecs etc*) move; (*fois*) *Fam* time; **donner des coups à** to hit; **c. de brosse** brush(-up); **c. de chiffon** wipe (with a rag); **c. de sonnette** ring (on a bell); **c. de dents** bite; **c. de chance** stroke of luck; **c. d'État** coup; **c. dur** *Fam* nasty blow; **sale c.** dirty trick; **mauvais c.** piece of mischief; **c. franc** *Fb* free kick; **tenter le c.** *Fam* to have a go *ou* try; **réussir son c.** to bring it off; **faire les quatre cents coups** to get into all kinds of mischief; **tenir le c.** to hold out; **avoir/attraper le c.** to have/get the knack; **sous le c. de** (*émotion etc*) under the influence of; **il est dans le c.** *Fam* he's in the know; **après c.** after the event, afterwards; **sur le c. de midi** on the stroke of twelve; **sur le c.** (*alors*) at the time; **tué sur le c.** killed outright; **à c. sûr** for sure; **c. sur c.** (*à la suite*) one after the other, in quick succession; **tout à c., tout d'un c.** suddenly; **à tout c.** at every go; **d'un seul c.** in one go; **du premier c.** *Fam* (at the) first go; **du c.** suddenly; (*de ce fait*) as a result; **pour le c.** this time. ◆**c.-de-poing** *nm* (*pl* **coups-de-poing**) **c.-de-poing (américain)** knuckle-duster.

coupable [kupabl] *a* guilty (**de** of); (*plaisir, désir*) sinful; **déclarer c.** *Jur* to convict; − *nmf* guilty person, culprit.

coupe [kup] *nf* **1** *Sp* cup; (*à fruits*) dish; (*à boire*) goblet, glass. **2** (*de vêtement etc*) cut; *Géom* section; **c. de cheveux** haircut. ◆**coup/er** *vt* to cut; (*arbre*) to cut down; (*vivres etc*) & *Tél* to cut off; (*courant etc*) to switch off; (*voyage*) to break (off); (*faim, souffle etc*) to take away; (*vin*) to water down; (*morceler*) to cut up; (*croiser*) to cut across; **c. la parole à** to cut short; − *vi* to cut; **c. à** (*corvée*) *Fam* to get out of; **coupez pas!** *Tél* hold the line!; − **se c.** *vpr* (*routes*) to intersect; (*se trahir*) to give oneself away; **se c. au doigt** to cut one's finger. ◆−**ant** *a* sharp; − *nm* (cutting) edge. ◆−**é** *nm Aut* coupé.

coupe-circuit [kupsirkɥi] *nm inv Él* cutout, circuit breaker. ◆**c.-file** *nm inv* (*carte*) official pass. ◆**c.-gorge** *nm inv* cut-throat alley. ◆**c.-ongles** *nm inv* (finger nail) clippers. ◆**c.-papier** *nm inv* paper knife.

couperet [kuprɛ] *nm* (meat) chopper; (*de guillotine*) blade.

couperosé [kuproze] *a* (*visage*) blotchy.

couple [kupl] *nm* pair, couple. ◆**coupler** *vt* to couple, connect.

couplet [kuplɛ] *nm* verse.

coupole [kupɔl] *nf* dome.

coupon [kupɔ̃] *nm* (*tissu*) remnant, oddment; (*pour la confection d'un vêtement*) length; (*ticket, titre*) coupon; **c. réponse** reply coupon.

coupure [kupyr] *nf* cut; (*de journal*) cutting, *Am* clipping; (*billet*) banknote.

cour [kur] *nf* **1** court(yard); (*de gare*) forecourt; **c.** (*de récréation*) *Scol* playground. **2** (*de roi*) & *Jur* court. **3** (*de femme, d'homme*) courtship; **faire la c. à qn** to court s.o., woo s.o.

courage [kuraʒ] *nm* courage; (*zèle*) spirit; **perdre c.** to lose heart *ou* courage; **s'armer de c.** to pluck up courage; **bon c.!** keep your chin up! ◆**courageux, -euse** *a* courageous; (*énergique*) spirited.

couramment [kuramã] *adv* (*parler*) fluently; (*souvent*) frequently.

courant [kurã] **1** *a* (*fréquent*) common; (*compte, année, langage*) current; (*eau*) running; (*modèle, taille*) standard; (*affaires*) routine; **le dix/etc c.** *Com* the tenth/*etc* inst(ant). **2** *nm* (*de l'eau, élec-*

trique) current; **c. d'air** draught; **coupure de
c.** *Él* power cut; **dans le c. de** (*mois etc*)
during the course of; **être/mettre au c.** to
know/tell (**de** about); **au c.** (**à jour**) up to
date.

courbature [kurbatyr] *nf* (muscular) ache.
◆**courbaturé** *a* aching (all over).

courbe [kurb] *a* curved; – *nf* curve.
◆**courber** *vti* to bend; – **se c.** *vpr* to bend
(over).

courge [kurʒ] *nf* marrow, *Am* squash.
◆**courgette** *nf* courgette, *Am* zucchini.

cour/ir* [kurir] *vi* to run; (*se hâter*) to rush;
(*à bicyclette, en auto*) to race; **en courant**
(*vite*) in a rush; **le bruit court que . . .**
there's a rumour going around that . . . ;
faire c. (*nouvelle*) to spread; **il court encore**
(*voleur*) he's still at large; – *vt* (*risque*) to
run; (*épreuve sportive*) to run (in); (*danger*)
to face, court; (*rues, monde*) to roam;
(*magasins, cafés*) to go round; (*filles*) to run
after. ◆**—eur** *nm Sp etc* runner; (*cycliste*)
cyclist; *Aut* racing driver; (*galant*) *Péj*
womanizer.

couronne [kurɔn] *nf* (*de roi, dent*) crown;
(*funéraire*) wreath. ◆**couronn/er** *vt* to
crown; (*auteur, ouvrage*) to award a prize
to. ◆**—é** *a* (*tête*) crowned; (*ouvrage*) prize-.
◆**—ement** *nm* (*sacre*) coronation; *Fig*
crowning achievement.

courrier [kurje] *nm* post, mail; (*transport*)
postal *ou* mail service; (*article*) *Journ*
column; **par retour du c.** by return of post,
Am by return mail.

courroie [kurwa] *nf* (*attache*) strap; (*de
transmission*) *Tech* belt.

courroux [kuru] *nm Litt* wrath.

cours [kur] *nm* **1** (*de maladie, rivière, astre,
pensées etc*) course; (*cote*) rate, price; **c.
d'eau** river, stream; **suivre son c.** (*déroulement*) to follow its course; **avoir c.**
(*monnaie*) to be legal tender; (*théorie*) to be
current; **en c.** (*travail*) in progress; (*année*)
current; (*affaires*) outstanding; **en c. de
route** on the way; **au c. de** during; **donner
libre c. à** to give free rein to. **2** (*leçon*) class;
(*série de leçons*) course; (*conférence*)
lecture; (*établissement*) school; (*manuel*)
textbook; **c. magistral** lecture. **3** (*allée*)
avenue.

course [kurs] *nf* **1** (*action*) run(ning);
(*épreuve de vitesse*) & *Fig* race; (*trajet*) journey, run; (*excursion*) hike; (*de projectile
etc*) path, flight; *pl* (*de chevaux*) races; **il
n'est plus dans la c.** *Fig* he's out of touch;
cheval de c. racehorse; **voiture de c.** racing
car. **2** (*commission*) errand; *pl* (*achats*)

shopping; **faire une c.** to run an errand;
faire les courses to do the shopping.

coursier, -ière [kursje, -jɛr] *nmf* messenger.

court [kur] **1** *a* short; **c'est un peu c.** *Fam*
that's not very much; – *adv* short; **couper
c. à** (*entretien*) to cut short; **tout c.** quite
simply; **à c. de** (*argent etc*) short of; **pris de
c.** caught unawares. **2** *nm Tennis* court.
◆**c.-bouillon** *nm* (*pl* courts-bouillons)
court-bouillon (*spiced water for cooking
fish*). ◆**c.-circuit** *nm* (*pl* courts-circuits)
Él short circuit. ◆**c.-circuiter** *vt* to
short-circuit.

courtier, -ière [kurtje, -jɛr] *nmf* broker.
◆**courtage** *nm* brokerage.

courtisan [kurtizɑ̃] *nm Hist* courtier.
◆**courtisane** *nf Hist* courtesan. ◆**courtiser** *vt* to court.

courtois [kurtwa] *a* courteous. ◆**courtoisie** *nf* courtesy.

couru [kury] *a* (*spectacle, lieu*) popular;
c'est c. (**d'avance**) *Fam* it's a sure thing.

couscous [kuskus] *nm Culin* couscous.

cousin, -ine [kuzɛ̃, -in] **1** *nmf* cousin. **2** *nm*
(*insecte*) gnat, midge.

coussin [kusɛ̃] *nm* cushion.

cousu [kuzy] *a* sewn; **c. main** handsewn.

coût [ku] *nm* cost. ◆**coût/er** *vti* to cost; **ça
coûte combien?** how much is it?, how much
does it cost?; **ça lui en coûte de faire** it
pains him *ou* her to do; **coûte que coûte** at
all costs; **c. les yeux de la tête** to cost the
earth. ◆**—ant** *a* **prix c.** cost price.
◆**coûteux, -euse** *a* costly, expensive.

couteau, -x [kuto] *nm* knife; **coup de c.**
stab; **à couteaux tirés** at daggers drawn
(*avec with*); **visage en lame de c.** hatchet
face; **retourner le c. dans la plaie** *Fig* to rub
it in.

coutume [kutym] *nf* custom; **avoir c. de
faire** to be accustomed to doing; **comme de
c.** as usual; **plus que de c.** more than is
customary. ◆**coutumier, -ière** *a* customary.

couture [kutyr] *nf* sewing, needlework;
(*métier*) dressmaking; (*raccord*) seam;
maison de c. fashion house. ◆**couturier**
nm fashion designer. ◆**couturière** *nf*
dressmaker.

couvent [kuvɑ̃] *nm* (*pour religieuses*)
convent; (*pour moines*) monastery;
(*pensionnat*) convent school.

couv/er [kuve] *vt* (*œufs*) to sit on, hatch;
(*projet*) *Fig* to hatch; (*rhume etc*) to be
getting; **c. qn** to pamper s.o.; **c. des yeux**
(*convoiter*) to look at enviously; – *vi*
(*poule*) to brood; (*mal*) to be brewing;

(*feu*) to smoulder. ◆—**ée** *nf* (*petits*) brood; (*œufs*) clutch. ◆**couveuse** *nf* (*pour nouveaux-nés, œufs*) incubator.

couvercle [kuvɛrkl] *nm* lid, cover.

couvert [kuvɛr] **1** *nm* (*cuiller, fourchette, couteau*) (set of) cutlery; (*au restaurant*) cover charge; **mettre le c.** to lay the table; **table de cinq couverts** table set for five. **2** *nm* **sous (le) c. de** (*apparence*) under cover of; **se mettre à c.** to take cover. **3** *a* covered (*de* with, in); (*ciel*) overcast. ◆**couverture** *nf* (*de lit*) blanket, cover; (*de livre etc*) & *Fin Mil* cover; (*de toit*) roofing; **c. chauffante** electric blanket; **c. de voyage** travelling rug.

couvre-chef [kuvrəʃɛf] *nm Hum* headgear. ◆**c.-feu** *nm* (*pl* -x) curfew. ◆**c.-lit** *nm* bedspread. ◆**c.-pied** *nm* quilt.

couvr/ir* [kuvrir] *vt* to cover (**de** with); (*voix*) to drown; — **se c.** *vpr* (*se vêtir*) to cover up, wrap up; (*se coiffer*) to cover one's head; (*ciel*) to cloud over. ◆—**eur** *nm* roofer.

cow-boy [kobɔj] *nm* cowboy.

crabe [krab] *nm* crab.

crac! [krak] *int* (*rupture*) snap!; (*choc*) bang!, smash!

crach/er [kraʃe] *vi* to spit; (*stylo*) to splutter; (*radio*) to crackle; → *vt* to spit (out); **c. sur qch** (*dédaigner*) *Fam* to turn one's nose up at sth. ◆—**é** *a* **c'est son portrait tout c.** *Fam* that's the spitting image of him *ou* her. ◆**crachat** *nm* spit, spittle.

crachin [kraʃɛ̃] *nm* (fine) drizzle.

crack [krak] *nm Fam* ace, wizard, real champ.

craie [krɛ] *nf* chalk.

craindre* [krɛ̃dr] *vt* (*personne, mort, douleur etc*) to be afraid of, fear, dread; (*chaleur etc*) to be sensitive to; **c. de faire** to be afraid of doing, dread doing; **je crains qu'elle ne vienne** I'm afraid *ou* I fear *ou* I dread (that) she might come; **c. pour qch** to fear for sth; **ne craignez rien** have no fear. ◆**crainte** *nf* fear, dread; **de c. de faire** for fear of doing; **de c. que** (+ *sub*) for fear that. ◆**craintif, -ive** *a* timid.

cramoisi [kramwazi] *a* crimson.

crampe [krɑ̃p] *nf Méd* cramp.

crampon [krɑ̃pɔ̃] **1** *nm* (*personne*) *Fam* leech, hanger-on. **2** *nmpl* (*de chaussures*) studs.

cramponner (se) [səkrɑ̃pɔne] *vpr* **se c. à** to hold on to, cling to.

cran [krɑ̃] *nm* **1** (*entaille*) notch; (*de ceinture*) hole; **c. d'arrêt** catch; **couteau à c. d'arrêt** flick-knife, *Am* switchblade; **c. de**

sûreté safety catch. **2** (*de cheveux*) wave. **3** (*audace*) *Fam* pluck, guts. **4 à c.** (*excédé*) *Fam* on edge.

crâne [krɑn] *nm* skull; (*tête*) *Fam* head. ◆**crânienne** *af* **boîte c.** cranium, brain pan.

crâner [krɑne] *vi Péj* to show off, swagger.

crapaud [krapo] *nm* toad.

crapule [krapyl] *nf* villain, (filthy) scoundrel. ◆**crapuleux, -euse** *a* vile, sordid.

craqueler [krakle] *vt*, — **se c.** *vpr* to crack.

craqu/er [krake] *vi* (*branche*) to snap; (*chaussure*) to creak; (*bois sec*) to crack; (*sous la dent*) to crunch; (*se déchirer*) to split, rip; (*projet, entreprise etc*) to come apart at the seams, crumble; (*personne*) to break down, reach breaking point; — *vt* (*faire*) **c.** (*allumette*) to strike. ◆—**ement** *nm* snapping *ou* creaking *ou* cracking (sound).

crasse [kras] **1** *a* (*ignorance*) crass. **2** *nf* filth. ◆**crasseux, -euse** *a* filthy.

cratère [kratɛr] *nm* crater.

cravache [kravaʃ] *nf* horsewhip, riding crop.

cravate [kravat] *nf* (*autour du cou*) tie. ◆**cravaté** *a* wearing a tie.

crawl [krol] *nm* (*nage*) crawl. ◆**crawlé** *a* **dos c.** backstroke.

crayeux, -euse [krɛjø, -øz] *a* chalky.

crayon [krɛjɔ̃] *nm* (*en bois*) pencil; (*de couleur*) crayon; **c. à bille** ballpoint (pen). ◆**crayonner** *vt* to pencil.

créance [kreɑ̃s] *nf* **1** *Fin Jur* claim (*for money*). **2 lettres de c.** *Pol* credentials. ◆**créancier, -ière** *nmf* creditor.

créateur, -trice [kreatœr, -tris] *nmf* creator; — *a* creative; **esprit c.** creativeness. ◆**créatif, -ive** *a* creative. ◆**création** *nf* creation. ◆**créativité** *nf* creativity. ◆**créature** *nf* (*être*) creature.

crécelle [kresɛl] *nf* (*de supporter*) rattle.

crèche [krɛʃ] *nf* (*de Noël*) *Rel* crib, manger; *Scol* day nursery, crèche. ◆**crécher** *vi* (*loger*) *Arg* to bed down, hang out.

crédible [kredibl] *a* credible. ◆**crédibilité** *nf* credibility.

crédit [kredi] *nm* (*influence*) & *Fin* credit; *pl* (*sommes*) funds; **à c.** (*acheter*) on credit, on hire purchase; **faire c.** *Fin* to give credit (**à** to). ◆**créditer** *vt Fin* to credit (**de** with). ◆**créditeur, -euse** *a* (*solde, compte*) credit-; **son compte est c.** his account is in credit, he is in credit.

credo [kredo] *nm* creed.

crédule [kredyl] *a* credulous. ◆**crédulité** *nf* credulity.

créer [kree] *vt* to create.

crémaillère [kremajɛr] *nf* **pendre la c.** to have a house-warming (party).

crématoire [krematwar] *a* **four c.** crematorium. ◆**crémation** *nf* cremation.

crème [krɛm] *nf* cream; (*dessert*) cream dessert; **café c.** white coffee, coffee with cream *ou* milk; **c.** Chantilly whipped cream; **c. glacée** ice cream; **c. à raser** shaving cream; **c. anglaise** custard; – *a inv* cream(-coloured); – *nm* (*café*) white coffee. ◆**crémerie** *nf* (*magasin*) dairy (shop). ◆**crémeux, -euse** *a* creamy. ◆**crémier, -ière** *nmf* dairyman, dairywoman.

créneau, -x [kreno] *nm Hist* crenellation; (*trou*) *Fig* slot, gap; *Écon* market opportunity, niche; **faire un c.** *Aut* to park between two vehicles.

créole [kreɔl] *nmf* Creole; – *nm Ling* Creole.

crêpe [krɛp] **1** *nf Culin* pancake. **2** *nm* (*tissu*) crepe; (*caoutchouc*) crepe (rubber). ◆**crêperie** *nf* pancake bar.

crépi [krepi] *a & nm* roughcast.

crépit/er [krepite] *vi* to crackle. ◆**—ement** *nm* crackling (sound).

crépu [krepy] *a* (*cheveux, personne*) frizzy.

crépuscule [krepyskyl] *nm* twilight, dusk. ◆**crépusculaire** *a* (*lueur etc*) twilight-, dusk-.

crescendo [kreʃɛndo] *adv & nm inv* crescendo.

cresson [kresɔ̃] *nm* (water) cress.

crête [krɛt] *nf* (*d'oiseau, de vague, de montagne*) crest; **c. de coq** cockscomb.

Crète [krɛt] *nf* Crete.

crétin, -ine [kretɛ̃, -in] *nmf* cretin; – *a* cretinous.

creus/er [krøze] **1** *vt* (*terre, sol*) to dig (a hole *ou* holes in); (*trou, puits*) to dig; (*évider*) to hollow (out); (*idée*) *Fig* to go deeply into; **c. l'estomac** to whet the appetite. **2 se c.** *vpr* (*joues etc*) to become hollow; (*abîme*) *Fig* to form; **se c. la tête** *ou* **la cervelle** to rack one's brains. ◆**—é** *a* **c. de rides** (*visage*) furrowed with wrinkles.

creuset [krøze] *nm* (*récipient*) crucible; (*lieu*) *Fig* melting pot.

creux, -euse [krø, -øz] *a* (*tube, joues, paroles etc*) hollow; (*estomac*) empty; (*sans activité*) slack; **assiette creuse** soup plate; – *nm* hollow; (*de l'estomac*) pit; (*moment*) slack period; **c. des reins** small of the back.

crevaison [krəvɛzɔ̃] *nf* puncture.

crevasse [krəvas] *nf* crevice, crack; (*de glacier*) crevasse; *pl* (*aux mains*) chaps. ◆**crevasser** *vt*, – **se c.** *vpr* to crack; (*peau*) to chap.

crève [krɛv] *nf* (*rhume*) *Fam* bad cold.

crev/er [krəve] *vi* (*bulle etc*) to burst; (*pneu*) to puncture, burst; (*mourir*) *Fam* to die, drop dead; **c. d'orgueil** to be bursting with pride; **c. de rire** *Fam* to split one's sides; **c. d'ennui/de froid** *Fam* to be bored/to freeze to death; **c. de faim** *Fam* to be starving; – *vt* to burst; (*œil*) to put *ou* knock out; **c. qn** *Fam* to wear *ou* knock s.o. out; **ça (vous) crève les yeux** *Fam* it's staring you in the face; **c. le cœur** to be heartbreaking. ◆**—ant** *a* (*fatigant*) *Fam* exhausting; (*drôle*) *Arg* hilarious, killing. ◆**—é** *a* (*fatigué*) *Fam* worn ou knocked out; (*mort*) *Fam* dead. ◆**crève-cœur** *nm inv* heartbreak.

crevette [krəvɛt] *nf* (*grise*) shrimp; (*rose*) prawn.

cri [kri] *nm* (*de joie, surprise*) cry, shout; (*de peur*) scream; (*de douleur, d'alarme*) cry; (*appel*) call, cry; **c. de guerre** war cry; **un chapeau/etc dernier c.** the latest hat/etc. ◆**criard** *a* (*enfant*) bawling; (*son*) screeching; (*couleur*) gaudy, showy.

criant [krijɑ̃] *a* (*injustice etc*) glaring.

crible [kribl] *nm* sieve, riddle. ◆**cribler** *vt* to sift; **criblé de** (*balles, dettes etc*) riddled with.

cric [krik] *nm* (*instrument*) *Aut* jack.

cricket [krikɛt] *nm Sp* cricket.

crier [krije] *vi* to shout, cry (out); (*de peur*) to scream; (*oiseau*) to chirp; (*grincer*) to creak, squeak; **c. au scandale/etc** to proclaim sth to be a scandal/etc; **c. après qn** *Fam* to shout at s.o.; – *vt* (*injure, ordre*) to shout (out); (*son innocence etc*) to proclaim; **c. vengeance** to cry out for vengeance. ◆**crieur, -euse** *nmf* **c. de journaux** newspaper seller.

crime [krim] *nm* crime; (*assassinat*) murder. ◆**criminalité** *nf* crime (in general), criminal practice. ◆**criminel, -elle** *a* criminal; – *nmf* criminal; (*assassin*) murderer.

crin [krɛ̃] *nm* horsehair; **c. végétal** vegetable fibre; **à tous crins** (*pacifiste etc*) out-and-out. ◆**crinière** *nf* mane.

crique [krik] *nf* creek, cove.

criquet [krikɛ] *nm* locust.

crise [kriz] *nf* crisis; (*accès*) attack; (*de colère etc*) fit; (*pénurie*) shortage; **c. de conscience** (moral) dilemma.

crisp/er [krispe] *vt* (*muscle*) to tense; (*visage*) to make tense; (*poing*) to clench; **c. qn** *Fam* to aggravate s.o.; **se c. sur** (*main*) to grip tightly. ◆**—ant** *a* aggravating. ◆**—é**

a (*personne*) tense. ◆**crispation** nf (*agacement*) aggravation.

crisser [krise] vi (*pneu, roue*) to screech; (*neige*) to crunch.

cristal, -aux [kristal, -o] nm crystal; pl (*objets*) crystal(ware); (*pour nettoyer*) washing soda. ◆**cristallin** a (*eau, son*) crystal-clear. ◆**cristalliser** vti, **— se c.** vpr to crystallize.

critère [kriter] nm criterion.

critérium [kriterjɔm] nm (*épreuve*) Sp eliminating heat.

critique [kritik] a critical; — nf (*reproche*) criticism; (*analyse de film, livre etc*) review; (*de texte*) critique; **faire la c. de** (*film etc*) to review; **affronter la c.** to confront the critics; — nm critic. ◆**critiqu/er** vt to criticize. ◆**—able** a open to criticism.

croasser [krɔase] vi (*corbeau*) to caw.

croc [kro] nm (*crochet*) hook; (*dent*) fang. ◆**c.-en-jambe** nm (*pl crocs-en-jambe*) = **croche-pied**.

croche [krɔʃ] nf Mus quaver, Am eighth (note).

croche-pied [krɔʃpje] nm **faire un c.-pied à** qn to trip s.o. up.

crochet [krɔʃɛ] nm (*pour accrocher*) & Boxe hook; (*aiguille*) crochet hook; (*travail*) crochet; (*clef*) picklock; Typ (square) bracket; **faire qch au c.** to crochet sth; **faire un c.** (*route*) to make a sudden turn; (*personne*) to make a detour ou side trip; (*pour éviter*) to swerve; **vivre aux crochets de qn** Fam to sponge off ou on s.o. ◆**crocheter** vt (*serrure*) to pick. ◆**crochu** a (*nez*) hooked.

crocodile [krɔkɔdil] nm crocodile.

crocus [krɔkys] nm Bot crocus.

croire* [krwar] vt to believe; (*estimer*) to think, believe (**que that**); **j'ai cru la voir I** thought I saw her; **je crois que oui I** think ou believe so; **je n'en crois pas mes yeux I** can't believe my eyes; **à l'en c.** according to him; **il se croit malin/quelque chose he** thinks he's smart/quite something; — vi to believe (**à, en in**).

croisé¹ [krwaze] nm Hist crusader. ◆**croisade** nf crusade.

crois/er [krwaze] vt to cross; (*bras*) to fold, cross; **c. qn** to pass ou meet s.o.; — vi (*veston*) to fold over; Nau to cruise; **— se c.** vpr (*voitures etc*) to pass ou meet (each other); (*routes*) to cross, intersect; (*lettres*) to cross in the post. ◆**—é²**, **-ée** a (*bras*) folded, crossed; (*veston*) double-breasted; **mots croisés** crossword; **tirs croisés** crossfire; **race croisée** crossbreed; — nf (*fenêtre*)

casement; **croisée des chemins** crossroads. ◆**—ement** nm (*action*) crossing; (*de routes*) crossroads, intersection; (*de véhicules*) passing. ◆**—eur** nm (*navire de guerre*) cruiser. ◆**croisière** nf cruise; **vitesse de c.** Nau Av & Fig cruising speed.

croître* [krwatr] vi (*plante etc*) to grow; (*augmenter*) to grow, increase; (*lune*) to wax. ◆**croissant 1** a (*nombre etc*) growing. **2** nm crescent; (*pâtisserie*) croissant. ◆**croissance** nf growth.

croix [krwa] nf cross.

croque-mitaine [krɔkmiten] nm bogeyman. ◆**c.-monsieur** nm inv toasted cheese and ham sandwich. ◆**c.-mort** nm Fam undertaker's assistant.

croqu/er [krɔke] **1** vt (*manger*) to crunch; — vi (*fruit etc*) to be crunchy, crunch. **2** vt (*peindre*) to sketch; **joli à c.** pretty as a picture. ◆**—ant** a (*biscuit etc*) crunchy. ◆**croquette** nf Culin croquette.

croquet [krɔkɛ] nm Sp croquet.

croquis [krɔki] nm sketch.

crosse [krɔs] nf (*d'évêque*) crook; (*de fusil*) butt; (*de hockey*) stick.

crotte [krɔt] nf (*de lapin etc*) mess, droppings. ◆**crottin** nm (*horse*) dung.

crotté [krɔte] a (*bottes etc*) muddy.

croul/er [krule] vi (*édifice, projet etc*) to crumble, collapse; **c. sous une charge** (*porteur etc*) to totter beneath a burden; **faire c.** (*immeuble etc*) to bring down. ◆**—ant** a (*mur etc*) tottering; — nm (*vieux*) Fam old-timer.

croupe [krup] nf (*de cheval*) rump; **monter en c.** (*à cheval*) to ride pillion. ◆**croupion** nm (*de poulet*) parson's nose.

croupier [krupje] nm (*au casino*) croupier.

croupir [krupir] vi (*eau*) to stagnate, become foul; **c. dans** (*le vice etc*) to wallow in; **eau croupie** stagnant water.

croustill/er [krustije] vi to be crusty; to be crunchy. ◆**—ant** a (*pain*) crusty; (*biscuit*) crunchy; (*histoire*) Fig spicy, juicy.

croûte [krut] nf (*de pain etc*) crust; (*de fromage*) rind; (*de plaie*) scab; **casser la c.** Fam to have a snack; **gagner sa c.** Fam to earn one's bread and butter. ◆**croûton** nm crust (*at end of loaf*); pl (*avec soupe*) croûtons.

croyable [krwajabl] a credible, believable. ◆**croyance** nf belief (**à, en in**). ◆**croyant, -ante** a **être c.** to be a believer; — nmf believer.

CRS [seeres] nmpl abrév (*Compagnies républicaines de sécurité*) French state security police, riot police.

cru [kry] *voir* **croire.**

cru [kry] **1** *a* (*aliment etc*) raw; (*lumière*) glaring; (*propos*) crude; **monter à c.** to ride bareback. **2** *nm* (*vignoble*) vineyard; **un grand c.** (*vin*) a vintage wine; **vin du c.** local wine.

cruauté [kryote] *nf* cruelty (**envers** to).

cruche [kryʃ] *nf* pitcher, jug.

crucial, -aux [krysjal, -o] *a* crucial.

crucifier [krysifje] *vt* to crucify. ◆**crucifix** [krysifi] *nm* crucifix. ◆**crucifixion** *nf* crucifixion.

crudité [krydite] *nf* (*grossièreté*) crudeness; *pl Culin* assorted raw vegetables.

crue [kry] *nf* (*de cours d'eau*) swelling, flood; **en c.** in spate.

cruel, -elle [kryɛl] *a* cruel (**envers, avec** to).

crûment [krymɑ̃] *adv* crudely.

crustacés [krystase] *nmpl* shellfish, crustaceans.

crypte [kript] *nf* crypt.

Cuba [kyba] *nm* Cuba. ◆**cubain, -aine** *a* & *nmf* Cuban.

cube [kyb] *nm* cube; *pl* (*jeu*) building blocks; *– a* (*mètre etc*) cubic. ◆**cubique** *a* cubic.

cueillir* [kœjir] *vt* to gather, pick; (*baiser*) to snatch; (*voleur*) *Fam* to pick up, run in. ◆**cueillette** *nf* gathering, picking; (*fruits cueillis*) harvest.

cuiller, cuillère [kɥijɛr] *nf* spoon; **petite c., c. à café** teaspoon; **c. à soupe** table spoon. ◆**cuillerée** *nf* spoonful.

cuir [kɥir] *nm* leather; (*peau épaisse d'un animal vivant*) hide; **c. chevelu** scalp.

cuirasse [kɥiras] *nf Hist* breastplate. ◆**se cuirass/er** *vpr* to steel oneself (**contre** against). ◆**–é** *nm* battleship.

cuire* [kɥir] *vt* to cook; (*à l'eau*) to boil; (*porcelaine*) to bake, fire; **c. (au four)** to bake; (*viande*) to roast; *– vi* to cook; to boil; to bake; to roast; (*soleil*) to bake, boil; **faire c.** to cook. ◆**cuisant** *a* (*affront, blessure etc*) stinging. ◆**cuisson** *nm* cooking; (*de porcelaine*) baking, firing.

cuisine [kɥizin] *nf* (*pièce*) kitchen; (*art*) cooking, cuisine, cookery; (*aliments*) cooking; (*intrigues*) *Péj* scheming; **faire la c.** to cook, do the cooking; **livre de c.** cook(ery) book; **haute c.** high-class cooking. ◆**cuisin/er** *vti* to cook; **c. qn** (*interroger*) *Fam* to grill s.o. ◆**cuisinier, -ière** *nmf* cook; *– nf* (*appareil*) cooker, stove, *Am* range.

cuisse [kɥis] *nf* thigh; (*de poulet, mouton*) leg.

cuit [kɥi] **1** *voir* **cuire;** *– a* cooked; **bien c.** well done *ou* cooked. **2** *a* (*pris*) *Fam* done for.

cuite [kɥit] *nf* **prendre une c.** *Fam* to get plastered *ou* drunk.

cuivre [kɥivr] *nm* (*rouge*) copper; (*jaune*) brass; *pl* (*ustensiles*) & *Mus* brass. ◆**cuivré** *a* copper-coloured, coppery.

cul [ky] *nm* (*derrière*) *Fam* backside; (*de bouteille etc*) bottom. ◆**c.-de-jatte** *nm* (*pl* **culs-de-jatte**) legless cripple. ◆**c.-de-sac** *nm* (*pl* **culs-de-sac**) dead end, cul-de-sac.

culasse [kylas] *nf Aut* cylinder head; (*d'une arme à feu*) breech.

culbute [kylbyt] *nf* (*cabriole*) sommersault; (*chute*) (backward) tumble; **faire une c.** to sommersault; to tumble. ◆**culbuter** *vi* to tumble over (backwards); *– vt* (*personne, chaise*) to knock over.

culinaire [kyliner] *a* (*art*) culinary; (*recette*) cooking.

culmin/er [kylmine] *vi* (*montagne*) to reach its highest point, peak (**à** at); (*colère*) *Fig* to reach a peak. ◆**–ant** *a* **point c.** (*réussite, montagne etc*) peak.

culot [kylo] *nm* **1** (*aplomb*) *Fam* nerve, cheek. **2** (*d'ampoule, de lampe etc*) base. ◆**culotté** *a* **être c.** *Fam* to have plenty of nerve *ou* cheek.

culotte [kylɔt] *nf Sp* (pair of) shorts; (*de femme*) (pair of) knickers *ou Am* panties; **culottes (courtes)** (*de jeune garçon*) short trousers *ou Am* pants; **c. de cheval** riding breeches.

culpabilité [kylpabilite] *nf* guilt.

culte [kylt] *nm* (*hommage*) *Rel* worship, cult; (*pratique*) *Rel* religion; (*service protestant*) service; (*admiration*) *Fig* cult.

cultiv/er [kyltive] *vt* (*terre*) to farm, cultivate; (*plantes*) to grow, cultivate; (*goût, relations etc*) to cultivate; *– se c.* *vpr* to cultivate one's mind. ◆**–é** *a* (*esprit, personne*) cultured, cultivated. ◆**cultivateur, -trice** *nmf* farmer. ◆**culture** *nf* (*action*) farming, cultivation; (*agriculture*) farming; (*horticulture*) growing, cultivation; (*éducation, civilisation*) culture; *pl* (*terres*) fields (under cultivation); (*plantes*) crops; **c. générale** general knowledge. ◆**culturel, -elle** *a* cultural.

cumin [kymɛ̃] *nm Bot Culin* caraway.

cumul [kymyl] *nm* **c. de fonctions** plurality of offices. ◆**cumulatif, -ive** *a* cumulative. ◆**cumuler** *vt* **c. deux fonctions** to hold two offices (at the same time).

cupide [kypid] *a* avaricious. ◆**cupidité** *nf* avarice, cupidity.

Cupidon [kypidɔ̃] *nm* Cupid.

cure [kyr] nf **1** (course of) treatment, cure. **2** (fonction) office (of a parish priest); (résidence) presbytery. ◆**curable** a curable. ◆**curatif, -ive** a curative. ◆**curé** nm (parish) priest.

curer [kyre] vt to clean out; **se c. le nez/ les dents** to pick one's nose/teeth. ◆**curedent** nm toothpick. ◆**cure-ongles** nm inv nail cleaner. ◆**cure-pipe** nm pipe cleaner.

curieux, -euse [kyrjø, -øz] a (bizarre) curious; (indiscret) inquisitive, curious (de about); **c. de savoir** curious to know; – nmf inquisitive ou curious person; (badaud) onlooker. ◆**curieusement** adv curiously. ◆**curiosité** nf (de personne, forme etc) curiosity; (chose) curiosity; (spectacle) unusual sight.

curriculum (vitæ) [kyrikylɔm(vite)] nm inv curriculum (vitae), Am résumé.

curseur [kyrsœr] nm (d'un ordinateur) cursor.

cutané [kytane] a (affection etc) skin-. ◆**cuti(-réaction)** nf skin test.

cuve [kyv] nf vat; (réservoir) & Phot tank. ◆**cuvée** nf (récolte de vin) vintage.

cuver vt **c. son vin** Fam to sleep it off. ◆**cuvette** nf (récipient) & Géog basin, bowl; (des cabinets) pan, bowl.

cyanure [sjanyr] nm cyanide.

cybernétique [sibεrnetik] nf cybernetics.

cycle [sikl] nm **1** (série, révolution) cycle. **2** (bicyclette) cycle. ◆**cyclable** a (piste) cycle-. ◆**cyclique** a cyclic(al). ◆**cyclisme** nm Sp cycling. ◆**cycliste** nmf cyclist; – a (course) cycle-; (champion) cycling; **coureur c.** racing cyclist. ◆**cyclomoteur** nm moped.

cyclone [siklon] nm cyclone.

cygne [siɲ] nm swan; **chant du c.** Fig swan song.

cylindre [silɛ̃dr] nm cylinder; (de rouleau compresseur) roller. ◆**cylindrée** nf Aut (engine) capacity. ◆**cylindrique** a cylindrical.

cymbale [sɛ̃bal] nf cymbal.

cynique [sinik] a cynical; – nmf cynic. ◆**cynisme** nm cynicism.

cyprès [siprε] nm (arbre) cypress.

cypriote [siprijɔt] a & nmf Cypriot.

cytise [sitiz] nf Bot laburnum.

D

D, d [de] nm D, d.

d' [d] voir de [1,2].

d'abord [dabɔr] adv (en premier lieu) first; (au début) at first.

dactylo [daktilo] nf (personne) typist; (action) typing. ◆**dactylographie** nf typing. ◆**dactylographier** vt to type.

dada [dada] nm (manie) hobby horse, pet subject.

dadais [dadε] nm (grand) d. big oaf.

dahlia [dalja] nm dahlia.

daigner [deɲe] vt d. faire to condescend ou deign to do.

daim [dɛ̃] nm fallow deer; (mâle) buck; (cuir) suede.

dais [dε] nm (de lit, feuillage etc) canopy.

dalle [dal] nf paving stone; (funèbre) (flat) gravestone. ◆**dallage** nm (action, surface) paving. ◆**dallé** a (pièce, cour etc) paved.

daltonien, -ienne [daltɔnjɛ̃, -jεn] a & n colour-blind (person). ◆**daltonisme** nm colour blindness.

dame [dam] nf **1** lady; (mariée) married lady. **2** Échecs Cartes queen; (au jeu de dames) king; **(jeu de) dames** draughts, Am checkers. ◆**damer** vt (au jeu de dames) to crown; **d. le pion à qn** to outsmart s.o. ◆**damier** nm draughtboard, Am checkerboard.

damner [dane] vt to damn; **faire d.** Fam to torment, drive mad; – **se d.** vpr to be damned. ◆**damnation** nf damnation.

dancing [dɑ̃siŋ] nm dance hall.

dandiner (se) [sədɑ̃dine] vpr to waddle.

dandy [dɑ̃di] nm dandy.

Danemark [danmark] nm Denmark. ◆**danois, -oise** a Danish; – nmf Dane; – nm (langue) Danish.

danger [dɑ̃ʒe] nm danger; **en d.** in danger ou jeopardy; **mettre en d.** to endanger, jeopardize; **en cas de d.** in an emergency; **en d. de mort** in peril of death; 'd. de mort' (panneau) 'danger'; **sans d.** (se promener etc) safely; **être sans d.** to be safe; **pas de d.!** Fam no way!, no fear! ◆**dangereux, -euse** a dangerous (pour to). ◆**dangereusement** adv dangerously.

dans [dɑ̃] prép in; (changement de lieu) into; (à l'intérieur de) inside, within; **entrer d.** to go in(to); **d. Paris** in Paris, within Paris;

d. un rayon de within (a radius of); **boire/prendre/etc d.** to drink/take/etc from ou out of; **marcher d. les rues** (à travers) to walk through ou about the streets; **d. ces circonstances** under ou in these circumstances; **d. deux jours/etc** (temps futur) in two days/etc, in two days'/etc time; **d. les dix francs/etc** (quantité) about ten francs/etc.

danse [dɑ̃s] nf dance; (art) dancing. ◆**dans/er** vti to dance; **faire d. l'anse du panier** (domestique) to fiddle on the shopping money. ◆**—eur, -euse** nmf dancer; **en danseuse** (cycliste) standing on the pedals.

dard [dar] nm (d'abeille etc) sting; (de serpent) tongue. ◆**darder** vt Litt (flèche) to shoot; (regard) to flash, dart; **le soleil dardait ses rayons** the sun cast down its burning rays.

dare-dare [dardar] adv Fam at ou on the double.

date [dat] nf date; **de vieille d.** (amitié etc) (of) long-standing; **faire d.** (événement) to mark an important date, be epoch-making; **en d. du . . .** dated the . . .; **d. limite** deadline. ◆**datation** nf dating. ◆**dater** vt (lettre etc) to date; – vi (être dépassé) to date, be dated; **d. de** to date back to, date from; **à d. de** as from. ◆**dateur** nm (de montre) date indicator; – a & nm (tampon) d. date stamp.

datte [dat] nf (fruit) date. ◆**dattier** nm date palm.

daube [dob] nf **bœuf en d.** braised beef stew.

dauphin [dofɛ̃] nm (mammifère marin) dolphin.

davantage [davɑ̃taʒ] adv (quantité) more; (temps) longer; **d. de temps/etc** more time/etc; **d. que** more than; longer than.

de¹ [d(ə)] (d' before a vowel or mute h; de + le = du, de + les = des) prép 1 (complément d'un nom) of; **les rayons du soleil** the rays of the sun, the sun's rays; **la ville de Paris** the town of Paris; **le livre de Paul** Paul's book; **un pont de fer** an iron bridge; **le train de Londres** the London train; **une augmentation/diminution de** an increase/decrease in. 2 (complément d'un adjectif) digne de worthy of; **heureux de partir** happy to leave; **content de qch** pleased with sth. 3 (complément d'un verbe) **parler de** to speak of ou about; **se souvenir de** to remember; **décider de faire** to decide to do; **traiter de lâche** to call a coward. 4 (provenance: lieu & temps) from; **venir/dater de** to come/date from; **mes amis du village** my friends from the village, my village friends; **le train de Londres** the train from London. 5 (agent) **accompagné de** accompanied by. 6 (moyen) **armé de** armed with; **se nourrir de** to live on. 7 (manière) **d'une voix douce** in ou with a gentle voice. 8 (cause) **puni de** punished for; **mourir de faim** to die of hunger. 9 (temps) **travailler de nuit** to work by night; **six heures du matin** six o'clock in the morning. 10 (mesure) **avoir six mètres de haut**, **être haut de six mètres** to be six metres high; **retarder de deux heures** to delay by two hours; **homme de trente ans** thirty-year-old man; **gagner cent francs de l'heure** to earn one hundred francs an hour.

de² [d(ə)] art partitif some; **elle boit du vin** she drinks (some) wine; **il ne boit pas de vin** (négation) he doesn't drink (any) wine; **des fleurs** (some) flowers; **de jolies fleurs** (some) pretty flowers; **d'agréables soirées** (some) pleasant evenings; **il y en a six de tués** (avec un nombre) there are six killed.

dé [de] nm (à jouer) dice; (à coudre) thimble; **les dés** the dice; (jeu) dice; **les dés sont jetés** Fig the die is cast; **couper en dés** Culin to dice.

déambuler [deɑ̃byle] vi to stroll, saunter.

débâcle [debakl] nf Mil rout; (ruine) Fig downfall; (des glaces) Géog breaking up.

déball/er [debale] vt to unpack; (étaler) to display. ◆**—age** nm unpacking; display.

débandade [debɑ̃dad] nf (mad) rush, stampede; Mil rout; **à la d.** in confusion; **tout va à la d.** everything's going to rack and ruin.

débaptiser [debatize] vt (rue) to rename.

débarbouiller [debarbuje] vt **d. qn** to wash s.o.'s face; **se d.** to wash one's face.

débarcadère [debarkadɛr] nm landing stage, quay.

débardeur [debardœr] nm 1 (docker) stevedore. 2 (vêtement) slipover, Am (sweater) vest.

débarqu/er [debarke] vt (passagers) to land; (marchandises) to unload; **d. qn** (congédier) Fam to sack s.o.; – vi (passagers) to disembark, land; (être naïf) Fam not to be quite with it; **d. chez qn** Fam to turn up suddenly at s.o.'s place. ◆**—ement** nm landing; unloading; Mil landing.

débarras [debara] nm lumber room, Am storeroom; **bon d.!** Fam good riddance! ◆**débarrasser** vt (voie, table etc) to clear (de of); **d. qn de** (ennemi, soucis etc) to rid s.o. of; (*manteau etc*) to relieve s.o. of; **se d. de** to get rid of, rid oneself of.

débat [deba] *nm* discussion, debate; *pl Pol Jur* proceedings. ◆**débattre*** *vt* to discuss, debate; **— se d.** *vpr* to struggle ou fight (to get free), put up a fight.

débauche [deboʃ] *nf* debauchery; **une d. de** *Fig* a wealth ou profusion of. ◆**débauch/er** *vt* **d. qn** (*détourner*) *Fam* to entice s.o. away from his work; (*licencier*) to dismiss s.o., lay s.o. off. ◆**—é, -ée** *a* (*libertin*) debauched, profligate; **—** *nmf* debauchee, profligate.

débile [debil] *a* (*esprit, enfant etc*) weak, feeble; *Péj Fam* idiotic; **—** *nmf Péj Fam* idiot, moron. ◆**débilité** *nf* debility, weakness; *pl* (*niaiseries*) *Fam* sheer nonsense. ◆**débiliter** *vt* to debilitate, weaken.

débiner [debine] **1** *vt* (*décrier*) *Fam* to run down. **2 se d.** *vpr* (*s'enfuir*) *Arg* to hop it, bolt.

débit [debi] *nm* **1** (*vente*) turnover, sales; (*de fleuve*) (rate of) flow; (*d'un orateur*) delivery; **d. de tabac** tobacconist's shop, *Am* tobacco store; **d. de boissons** bar, café. **2** (*compte*) *Fin* debit. ◆**débiter** *vt* **1** (*découper*) to cut up, slice up (**en** into); (*vendre*) to sell; (*fournir*) to yield; (*dire*) *Péj* to utter, spout. **2** *Fin* to debit. ◆**débiteur, -trice** *nmf* debtor; **—** *a* (*solde, compte*) debit-; **son compte est d.** his account is in debit, he is in debt.

déblais [deblɛ] *nmpl* (*terre*) earth; (*décombres*) rubble. ◆**déblayer** *vt* (*terrain, décombres*) to clear.

débloquer [debloke] **1** *vt* (*machine*) to unjam; (*crédits, freins, compte*) to release; (*prix*) to decontrol. **2** *vi* (*divaguer*) *Fam* to talk through one's hat, talk nonsense.

déboires [debwar] *nmpl* disappointments, setbacks.

déboît/er [debwate] **1** *vt* (*tuyau*) to disconnect; (*os*) *Méd* to dislocate. **2** *vi Aut* to pull out, change lanes. ◆**—ement** *nm Méd* dislocation.

débonnaire [debonɛr] *a* good-natured, easy-going.

débord/er [deborde] *vi* (*fleuve, liquide*) to overflow; (*en bouillant*) to boil over; **d. de** (*vie, joie etc*) *Fig* to be overflowing ou bubbling over with; **l'eau déborde du vase** the water is running over the top of the vase ou is overflowing the vase; **—** *vt* (*dépasser*) to go ou extend beyond; (*faire saillie*) to stick out from; *Mil Sp* to outflank; **débordé de travail/de visites** snowed under with work/visits. ◆**—ement** *nm* overflowing; (*de joie, activité*) outburst.

débouch/er [debuʃe] **1** *vt* (*bouteille*) to open, uncork; (*lavabo, tuyau*) to clear, unblock. **2** *vi* (*surgir*) to emerge, come out (**de** from); **d. sur** (*rue*) to lead out onto, lead into; **d.** to lead up to. ◆**—é** *nm* (*carrière*) & *Géog* opening; (*de rue*) exit; (*marché*) *Com* outlet.

débouler [debule] *vi* (*arriver*) *Fam* to burst in, turn up.

déboulonner [debulone] *vt* to unbolt; **d. qn** *Fam* (*renvoyer*) to sack ou fire s.o.; (*discréditer*) to bring s.o. down.

débours [debur] *nmpl* expenses. ◆**débourser** *vt* to pay out.

debout [d(ə)bu] *adv* standing (up); **mettre d.** (*planche etc*) to stand up, put upright; **se mettre d.** to stand ou get up; **se tenir** ou **rester d.** (*personne*) to stand (up), remain standing (up); **rester d.** (*édifice etc*) to remain standing; **être d.** (*levé*) to be up (and about); **d.!** get up!; **ça ne tient pas d.** (*théorie etc*) that doesn't hold water ou make sense.

déboutonner [debutone] *vt* to unbutton, undo; **— se d.** *vpr* (*personne*) to undo one's buttons.

débraillé [debraje] *a* (*tenue etc*) slovenly, sloppy; **—** *nm* slovenliness, sloppiness.

débrancher [debrɑ̃ʃe] *vt El* to unplug, disconnect.

débrayer [debreje] *vi* **1** *Aut* to declutch, release the clutch. **2** (*se mettre en grève*) to stop work. ◆**débrayage** (*grève*) strike, walk-out.

débridé [debride] *a* (*effréné*) unbridled.

débris [debri] *nmpl* fragments, scraps; (*restes*) remains; (*détritus*) rubbish, debris.

débrouiller [debruje] **1** *vt* (*écheveau etc*) to unravel, disentangle; (*affaire*) to sort out. **2 se d.** *vpr* to manage, get by, make out; **se d. pour faire** to manage (somehow) to do. ◆**débrouillard** *a* smart, resourceful. ◆**débrouillardise** *nf* smartness, resourcefulness.

débroussailler [debrusaje] *vt* (*chemin*) to clear (of brushwood); (*problème*) *Fig* to clarify.

débusquer [debyske] *vt* (*gibier, personne*) to drive out, dislodge.

début [deby] *nm* start, beginning; **au d.** at the beginning; **faire ses débuts** (*sur la scène etc*) to make one's debut. ◆**début/er** *vi* to start, begin; (*dans une carrière*) to start out in life; (*sur la scène etc*) to make one's debut. ◆**—ant, -ante** *nmf* beginner; – *a* novice.

déca [deka] *nm Fam* decaffeinated coffee.

deçà (en) [ãd(ə)sa] *adv* (on) this side; – *prép* **en d. de** (on) this side of; *(succès, prix etc) Fig* short of.

décacheter [dekaʃte] *vt (lettre etc)* to open, unseal.

décade [dekad] *nf (dix jours)* period of ten days; *(décennie)* decade.

décadent [dekadã] *a* decadent. ◆**décadence** *nf* decay, decadence.

décaféiné [dekafeine] *a* decaffeinated.

décalaminer [dekalamine] *vt (moteur) Aut* to decoke, decarbonize.

décalcomanie [dekalkɔmani] *nf (image)* transfer, *Am* decal.

décal/er [dekale] *vt* **1** *(avancer)* to shift; *(départ, repas)* to shift (the time of). **2** *(ôter les cales de)* to unwedge. ◆**—age** *nm (écart)* gap, discrepancy; **d. horaire** time difference.

décalque [dekalk] *nm* tracing. ◆**décalquer** *vt (dessin)* to trace.

décamper [dekãpe] *vi* to make off, clear off.

décanter [dekãte] *vt (liquide)* to settle, clarify; **d. ses idées** to clarify one's ideas; **— se d.** *vpr (idées, situation)* to become clearer, settle.

décap/er [dekape] *vt (métal)* to clean, scrape down; *(surface peinte)* to strip. ◆**—ant** *nm* cleaning agent; *(pour enlever la peinture)* paint stripper. ◆**—eur** *nm* **d. thermique** hot-air paint stripper.

décapiter [dekapite] *vt* to decapitate, behead.

décapotable [dekapɔtabl] *a (voiture)* convertible.

décapsul/er [dekapsyle] *vt* **d. une bouteille** to take the cap *ou* top off a bottle. ◆**—eur** *nm* bottle-opener.

décarcasser (se) [sədekarkase] *vpr Fam* to flog oneself to death **(pour faire** doing).

décathlon [dekatlɔ̃] *nm Sp* decathlon.

décati [dekati] *a* worn out, decrepit.

décavé [dekave] *a Fam* ruined.

décéd/er [desede] *vi* to die. ◆**—é** *a* deceased.

déceler [desle] *vt (trouver)* to detect, uncover; *(révéler)* to reveal.

décembre [desãbr] *nm* December.

décennie [deseni] *nf* decade.

décent [desã] *a (bienséant, acceptable)* decent. ◆**décemment** [-amã] *adv* decently. ◆**décence** *nf* decency.

décentraliser [desãtralize] *vt* to decentral-

ize. ◆**décentralisation** *nf* decentralization.

déception [desɛpsjɔ̃] *nf* disappointment. ◆**décevoir*** *vt* to disappoint. ◆**décevant** *a* disappointing.

décerner [deserne] *vt (prix etc)* to award; *(mandat d'arrêt etc) Jur* to issue.

décès [desɛ] *nm* death.

déchaîn/er [deʃene] *vt (colère, violence)* to unleash, let loose; **d. l'enthousiasme/les rires** to set off wild enthusiasm/a storm of laughter; **— se d.** *vpr (tempête, rires)* to break out; *(foule)* to run amok *ou* riot; *(colère, personne)* to explode. ◆**—é** *a (foule, flots)* wild, raging. ◆**—ement** [-ɛnmã] *nm (de rires, de haine etc)* outburst; *(de violence)* outbreak, eruption; **le d. de la tempête** the raging of the storm.

déchanter [deʃãte] *vi Fam* to become disillusioned; *(changer de ton)* to change one's tune.

décharge [deʃarʒ] *nf Jur* discharge; **d. (publique)** (rubbish) dump *ou* tip, *Am* (garbage) dump; **d. (électrique)** (electrical) discharge, shock; **recevoir une d. (électrique)** to get a shock; **à la d. de qn** in s.o.'s defence. ◆**décharg/er** *vt* to unload; *(batterie) Él* to discharge; *(accusé) Jur* to discharge, exonerate; **d. qn de** *(travail etc)* to relieve s.o. of; **d. sur qn** *(son arme)* to fire at s.o.; *(sa colère)* to vent on s.o.; **— se d.** *vpr (batterie)* to go flat; **se d. sur qn du soin de faire qch** to unload onto s.o. the job of doing sth. ◆**—ement** *nm* unloading.

décharné [deʃarne] *a* skinny, bony.

déchausser [deʃose] *vt* **d. qn** to take s.o.'s shoes off; **se d.** to take one's shoes off; *(dent)* to get loose.

dèche [dɛʃ] *nf* **être dans la d.** *Arg* to be flat broke.

déchéance [deʃeãs] *nf (déclin)* decline, decay, degradation.

déchet [deʃɛ] *nm* **déchets** *(résidus)* scraps, waste; **il y a du d.** there's some waste *ou* wastage.

déchiffrer [deʃifre] *vt (message)* to decipher; *(mauvaise écriture)* to make out, decipher.

déchiquet/er [deʃikte] *vt* to tear to shreds, cut to bits. ◆**—é** *a (drapeau etc)* (all) in shreds; *(côte)* jagged.

déchir/er [deʃire] *vt* to tear (up), rip (up); *(vêtement etc)* to tear, rip; *(ouvrir)* to tear *ou* rip open; *(pays, groupe)* to tear apart; **d. l'air** *(bruit)* to rend the air; **ce bruit me déchire les oreilles** this noise is ear-splitting; **— se d.** *vpr (robe etc)* to tear, rip. ◆—ant a (navrant) heart-breaking; (aigu) ear-splitting. ◆—ement nm (souffrance) heartbreak; pl (divisions) Pol deep rifts. ◆déchirure nf tear, rip; d. musculaire torn muscle.

déchoir [deʃwar] vi to lose prestige. ◆déchu a (ange) fallen; être d. de (ses droits etc) to have forfeited.

décibel [desibɛl] nm decibel.

décid/er [deside] vt (envoi, opération) to decide on; d. que to decide that; d. qn à faire to persuade s.o. to do; — vi d. de (destin de qn) to decide; (voyage etc) to decide on; d. de faire to decide to do; — se d. vpr (question) to be decided; se d. à faire to make up one's mind to do; se d. pour qch to decide on sth ou in favour of sth. ◆—é a (air, ton) determined, decided; (net, pas douteux) decided; c'est d. it's settled; être d. à faire to be decided about doing ou determined to do. ◆—ément adv undoubtedly.

décilitre [desilitr] nm decilitre.

décimal, -aux [desimal, -o] a decimal. ◆décimale nf decimal.

décimer [desime] vt to decimate.

décimètre [desimɛtr] nm decimetre; double d. ruler.

décisif, -ive [desizif, -iv] a decisive; (moment) crucial. ◆décision nf decision; (fermeté) determination.

déclamer [deklame] vt to declaim; Péj to spout. ◆déclamatoire a Péj bombastic.

déclarer [deklare] vt to declare (que that); (décès, vol etc) to notify; d. coupable to convict, find guilty; d. la guerre to declare war (à on); — se d. vpr (s'expliquer) to declare one's views; (incendie, maladie) to break out; se d. contre to come out against. ◆déclaration nf declaration; (de décès etc) notification; (commentaire) statement, comment; d. de revenus tax return.

déclasser [deklase] vt (livres etc) to put out of order; (hôtel etc) to downgrade; d. qn Sp to relegate s.o. (in the placing).

déclench/er [deklɑ̃ʃe] vt (mécanisme) to set ou trigger off, release; (attaque) to launch; (provoquer) to trigger off, spark off; d. le travail Méd to induce labour; — se d. vpr (sonnerie) to go off; (attaque, grève) to start. ◆—ement nm (d'un appareil) release.

déclic [deklik] nm (mécanisme) catch, trigger; (bruit) click.

déclin [deklɛ̃] nm decline; (du jour) close; (de la lune) wane. ◆décliner 1 vt (refuser) to decline. 2 vt (réciter) to state. 3 vi (forces etc) to decline, wane; (jour) to draw to a close.

déclivité [deklivite] nf slope.

décocher [dekɔʃe] vt (flèche) to shoot, fire; (coup) to let fly, aim; (regard) to flash.

décoder [dekɔde] vt (message) to decode.

décoiffer [dekwafe] vt d. qn to mess up s.o.'s hair.

décoincer [dekwɛ̃se] vt (engrenage) to unjam.

décoll/er [dekɔle] 1 vi (avion etc) to take off; elle ne décolle pas d'ici Fam she won't leave ou budge. 2 vt (timbre etc) to unstick; — se d. vpr to come unstuck. ◆—age nm Av takeoff.

décolleté [dekɔlte] a (robe) low-cut; — nm (de robe) low neckline; (de femme) bare neck and shoulders.

décoloniser [dekɔlɔnize] vt to decolonize. ◆décolonisation nf decolonization.

décolor/er [dekɔlɔre] vt to discolour, fade; (cheveux) to bleach. ◆—ant nm bleach. ◆décoloration nf discolo(u)ration; bleaching.

décombres [dekɔ̃br] nmpl ruins, rubble, debris.

décommander [dekɔmɑ̃de] vt (marchandises, invitation) to cancel; (invités) to put off; — se d. vpr to cancel (one's appointment).

décomposer [dekɔ̃poze] vt to decompose; (visage) to distort; — se d. vpr (pourrir) to decompose; (visage) to become distorted. ◆décomposition nf decomposition.

décompresser [dekɔ̃prese] vi Psy Fam to unwind.

décompression [dekɔ̃presjɔ̃] nf decompression.

décompte [dekɔ̃t] nm deduction; (détail) breakdown. ◆décompter vt to deduct.

déconcerter [dekɔ̃sɛrte] vt to disconcert.

déconfit [dekɔ̃fi] a downcast. ◆déconfiture nf (state of) collapse ou defeat; (faillite) Fam financial ruin.

décongeler [dekɔ̃ʒle] vt (aliment) to thaw, defrost.

décongestionner [dekɔ̃ʒɛstjɔne] vt (rue) & Méd to relieve congestion in.

déconnecter [dekɔnɛkte] vt Él & Fig to disconnect.

déconner [dekɔne] vi (divaguer) Fam to talk nonsense.

déconseiller [dekɔ̃seje] vt d. qch à qn to advise s.o. against sth; d. à qn de faire to advise s.o. against doing; c'est déconseillé it is inadvisable.

déconsidérer [dekɔ̃sidere] vt to discredit.

décontaminer [dekɔ̃tamine] *vt* to decontaminate.

décontenancer [dekɔ̃tnɑ̃se] *vt* to disconcert; **— se d.** *vpr* to lose one's composure, become flustered.

décontracter [dekɔ̃trakte] *vt*, **— se d.** *vpr* to relax. ◆**décontraction** *nf* relaxation.

déconvenue [dekɔ̃vny] *nf* disappointment.

décor [dekɔr] *nm Th* scenery, decor; *Cin* set; (*paysage*) scenery; (*d'intérieur*) decoration; (*cadre, ambiance*) setting; **entrer dans le d.** (*véhicule*) *Fam* to run off the road.

décorer [dekɔre] *vt* (*maison, soldat etc*) to decorate (**de** with). ◆**décorateur, -trice** *nmf* (interior) decorator; *Th* stage designer; *Cin* set designer. ◆**décoratif, -ive** *a* decorative. ◆**décoration** *nf* decoration.

décortiquer [dekɔrtike] *vt* (*graine*) to husk; (*homard etc*) to shell; (*texte*) *Fam* to take to pieces, dissect.

découcher [dekuʃe] *vi* to stay out all night.

découdre [dekudr] *vt* to unstitch; — *vi* **en d.** *Fam* to fight it out; **— se d.** *vpr* to come unstitched.

découler [dekule] *vi* **d. de** to follow from.

découp/er [dekupe] *vt* (*poulet etc*) to carve; (*article etc*) *Journ* to cut out; **se d. sur** to stand out against. ◆**—é** *a* (*côte*) jagged. ◆**—age** *nm* carving; cutting out; (*image*) cut-out. ◆**découpure** *nf* (*contour*) jagged outline; (*morceau*) piece cut out, cut-out.

découplé [dekuple] *a* **bien d.** (*personne*) well-built, strapping.

décourag/er [dekuraʒe] *vt* (*dissuader*) to discourage (**de** from); (*démoraliser*) to dishearten, discourage; **— se d.** *vpr* to get discouraged *ou* disheartened. ◆**—ement** *nm* discouragement.

décousu [dekuzy] *a* (*propos, idées*) disconnected.

découvrir [dekuvrir] *vt* (*trésor, terre etc*) to discover; (*secret, vérité etc*) to find out, discover; (*casserole etc*) to take the lid off; (*dévoiler*) to disclose (**à** to); (*dénuder*) to uncover, expose; (*voir*) to perceive; **d. que** to discover *ou* find out that; **— se d.** *vpr* (*se dénuder*) to uncover oneself; (*enlever son chapeau*) to take one's hat off; (*ciel*) to clear (up). ◆**découvert 1** *a* (*terrain*) open; (*tête etc*) bare; **à d.** exposed, unprotected; **agir à d.** to act openly. **2** *nm* (*d'un compte*) *Fin* overdraft. ◆**découverte** *nf* discovery; **partir** *ou* **aller à la d. de** to go in search of.

décrasser [dekrase] *vt* (*éduquer*) to take the rough edges off.

décrépit [dekrepi] *a* (*vieillard*) decrepit.

◆**décrépitude** *nf* (*des institutions etc*) decay.

décret [dekre] *nm* decree. ◆**décréter** *vt* to order, decree.

décrier [dekrije] *vt* to run down, disparage.

décrire [dekrir] *vt* to describe.

décroch/er [dekrɔʃe] **1** *vt* (*détacher*) to unhook; (*tableau*) to take down; (*obtenir*) *Fam* to get, land; **d. (le téléphone)** to pick up the phone. **2** *vi Fam* (*abandonner*) to give up; (*perdre le fil*) to be unable to follow, lose track. ◆**—é** *a* (*téléphone*) off the hook.

décroître [dekrwatr] *vi* (*mortalité etc*) to decrease, decline; (*eaux*) to subside; (*jours*) to draw in. ◆**décroissance** *nf* decrease, decline (**de** in, of).

décrotter [dekrɔte] *vt* (*chaussures*) to clean *ou* scrape (the mud off). ◆**décrottoir** *nm* shoe scraper.

décrypter [dekripte] *vt* (*message*) to decipher, decode.

déçu [desy] *voir* **décevoir**; — *a* disappointed.

déculotter (se) [sədekylɔte] *vpr* to take off one's trousers *ou Am* pants. ◆**déculottée** *nf Fam* thrashing.

décupler [dekyple] *vti* to increase tenfold.

dédaigner [dedɛɲe] *vt* (*personne, richesse etc*) to scorn, despise; (*repas*) to turn up one's nose at; (*offre*) to spurn; (*ne pas tenir compte de*) to disregard. ◆**dédaigneux, -euse** *a* scornful, disdainful (**de** of). ◆**dédain** *nm* scorn, disdain (**pour, de** for).

dédale [dedal] *nm* maze, labyrinth.

dedans [d(ə)dɑ̃] *adv* inside; **de d.** from (the) inside, from within; **en d.** on the inside; **au-d. (de), au d. (de)** inside; **au-d.** *ou* **au d. de lui-même** inwardly; **tomber d.** (*trou*) to fall in (it); **donner d.** (*être dupé*) *Fam* to fall in; **mettre d.** *Fam* (*en prison*) to put inside; (*tromper*) to take in; **je me suis fait rentrer d.** (*accident de voiture*) *Fam* someone went *ou* crashed into me; — *nm* **le d.** the inside.

dédicace [dedikas] *nf* dedication, inscription. ◆**dédicacer** *vt* (*livre etc*) to dedicate, inscribe (**à** to).

dédier [dedje] *vt* to dedicate.

dédire (se) [sədedir] *vpr* to go back on one's word; **se d. de** (*promesse etc*) to go back on. ◆**dédit** *nm* (*somme*) *Com* forfeit, penalty.

dédommag/er [dedɔmaʒe] *vt* to compensate (**de** for). ◆**—ement** *nm* compensation.

dédouaner [dedwane] *vt* (*marchandises*) to clear through customs; **d. qn** to restore s.o.'s prestige.

dédoubl/er [deduble] vt (classe etc) to split into two; **d. un train** to run an extra train; **— se d.** vpr to be in two places at once. **◆—ement** nm **d. de la personnalité** Psy split personality.

déduire* [deduir] vt (retirer) to deduct (de from); (conclure) to deduce (de from). **◆déductible** a (frais) deductible, allowable. **◆déduction** nf (raisonnement) & Com deduction.

déesse [deɛs] nf goddess.

défaill/ir* [defajir] vi (s'évanouir) to faint; (forces) to fail, flag; **sans d.** without flinching. **◆—ant** a (personne) faint; (témoin) Jur defaulting. **◆défaillance** nf (évanouissement) fainting fit; (faiblesse) weakness; (panne) fault; **une d. de mémoire** a lapse of memory.

défaire* [defɛr] vt (nœud etc) to undo, untie; (bagages) to unpack; (installation) to take down; (coiffure) to mess up; **d. qn de** to rid s.o. of; **— se d.** vpr (nœud etc) to come undone ou untied; **se d. de** to get rid of. **◆défait** a (lit) unmade; (visage) drawn; (armée) defeated. **◆défaite** nf defeat. **◆défaitisme** nm defeatism.

défalquer [defalke] vt (frais etc) to deduct (de from).

défaut [defo] nm (faiblesse) fault, shortcoming, failing, defect; (de diamant etc) flaw; (désavantage) drawback; (contumace) Jur default; **le d. de la cuirasse** the chink in the armour; **faire d.** to be lacking; **le temps me fait d.** I lack time; **à d. de** for want of; **en d.** at fault; **prendre qn en d.** to catch s.o. out; **ou, à d....** or, failing that ....

défaveur [defavœr] nf disfavour. **◆défavorable** a unfavourable (à to). **◆défavoriser** vt to put at a disadvantage, be unfair to.

défection [defɛksjɔ̃] nf defection, desertion; **faire d.** to desert; (ne pas venir) to fail to turn up.

défectueux, -euse [defɛktɥø, -øz] a faulty, defective. **◆défectuosité** nf defectiveness; (défaut) defect (de in).

défendre [defɑ̃dr] 1 vt (protéger) to defend; **— se d.** vpr to defend oneself; **se d. de** (pluie etc) to protect oneself from; **se d. de faire** (s'empêcher de) to refrain from doing; **je me défends (bien)** Fam I can hold my own. 2 vt **d. à qn de faire** (interdire) to forbid s.o. to do, not allow s.o. to do; **d. qch à qn** to forbid s.o. sth. **◆défendable** a defensible.

défense [defɑ̃s] nf 1 (protection) defence, Am defense; **sans d.** defenceless. 2

(interdiction) **'d. de fumer'** 'no smoking'; **'d. d'entrer'** 'no entry', 'no admittance'. 3 (d'éléphant) tusk. **◆défenseur** nm defender; (des faibles) protector, defender. **◆défensif, -ive** a defensive; **— nf sur la défensive** on the defensive.

déférent [deferɑ̃] a deferential. **◆déférence** nf deference.

déférer [defere] 1 vt (coupable) Jur to refer (à to). 2 vi **d. à l'avis de qn** to defer to s.o.'s opinion.

déferler [defɛrle] vi (vagues) to break; (haine etc) to erupt; **d. dans** ou **sur** (foule) to surge ou sweep into.

défi [defi] nm challenge; **lancer un d. à qn** to challenge s.o.; **mettre qn au d. de faire** to defy ou dare ou challenge s.o. to do.

déficient [defisjɑ̃] a Méd deficient. **◆déficience** nf Méd deficiency.

déficit [defisit] nm deficit. **◆déficitaire** a (budget etc) in deficit; (récolte etc) Fig short, insufficient.

défier¹ [defje] vt (provoquer) to challenge (à to); (braver) to defy; **d. qn de faire** to defy ou challenge s.o. to do.

défier² (se) [sədefje] vpr **se d. de** Litt to distrust. **◆défiance** nf distrust (de of). **◆défiant** a distrustful (à l'égard de of).

défigur/er [defigyre] vt (visage) to disfigure; (vérité etc) to distort. **◆—ement** nm disfigurement; distortion.

défil/er [defile] vi (manifestants) to march (devant past); Mil to march ou file past; (paysage, jours) to pass by; (visiteurs) to keep coming and going, stream in and out; (images) Cin to flash by (on the screen); **— se d.** vpr Fam (s'éloigner) to sneak off; (éviter d'agir) to cop out. **◆—é** nm 1 (cortège) procession; (de manifestants) march; Mil parade, march past; (de visiteurs) stream, succession. 2 Géog gorge, pass.

défin/ir [definir] vt to define. **◆—i** a (article) Gram definite. **◆définition** nf definition; (de mots croisés) clue.

définitif, -ive [definitif, -iv] a final, definitive; **— nf en définitive** in the final analysis, finally. **◆définitivement** adv (partir) permanently, for good; (exclure) definitively.

déflagration [deflagrasjɔ̃] nf explosion.

déflation [deflasjɔ̃] nf Écon deflation.

déflorer [deflɔre] vt (idée, sujet) to spoil the freshness of.

défonc/er [defɔ̃se] 1 vt (porte, mur etc) to smash in ou down; (trottoir, route etc) to dig up, break up. 2 **se d.** vpr (drogué) Fam to get high (à on). ◆—é a 1 (*route*) full of potholes, bumpy. 2 (*drogué*) *Fam* high.

déform/er [deforme] *vt* (*objet*) to put *ou* knock out of shape;· (*doigt, main*) to deform; (*faits, image etc*) to distort; (*goût*) to corrupt; — **se d.** *vpr* to lose its shape. ◆—é a (*objet*) misshapen; (*corps etc*) deformed, misshapen; **chaussée déformée** uneven road surface. ◆**déformation** *nf* distortion; corruption; (*de membre*) deformity; **c'est de la d. professionnelle** it's an occupational hazard, it's a case of being conditioned by one's job.

défouler (se) [sədefule] *vpr Fam* to let off steam.

défraîchir (se) [sədefreʃir] *vpr* (*étoffe etc*) to lose its freshness, become faded.

défrayer [defreje] *vt* **d. qn** to pay *ou* defray s.o.'s expenses; **d. la chronique** to be the talk of the town.

défricher [defriʃe] *vt* (*terrain*) to clear (for cultivation); (*sujet etc*) *Fig* to open up.

défriser [defrize] *vt* (*cheveux*) to straighten; **d. qn** (*contrarier*) *Fam* to ruffle *ou* annoy s.o.

défroisser [defrwase] *vt* (*papier*) to smooth out.

défroqué [defrɔke] a (*prêtre*) defrocked.

défunt, -unte [defœ̃, -œ̃t] a (*mort*) departed; **son d. mari** her late husband; — *nmf* **le d., la défunte** the deceased, the departed.

dégag/er [degaʒe] *vt* (*lieu, table*) to clear (**de** of); (*objet en gage*) to redeem; (*odeur*) to give off; (*chaleur*) to give out; (*responsabilité*) to disclaim; (*idée, conclusion*) to bring out; **d. qn de** (*promesse*) to release s.o. from; (*décombres*) to free s.o. from, pull s.o. out of; **cette robe dégage la taille** this dress leaves the waist free and easy; — *vi Fb* to clear the ball (down the pitch); **d.!** clear the way!; — **se d.** *vpr* (*rue, ciel*) to clear; **se d. de** (*personne*) to release oneself from (*promise*); to get free from, free oneself from (*rubble*); **se d. de** (*odeur*) to issue *ou* emanate from; (*vérité, impression*) to emerge from. ◆—é a (*ciel*) clear; (*ton, allure*) easy-going, casual; (*vue*) open. ◆—**ement** *nm* **1** (*action*) clearing; redemption; (*d'odeur*) emanation; (*de chaleur*) emission; release; freeing; *Fb* clearance, kick; **itinéraire de d.** *Aut* relief road. **2** (*espace libre*) clearing; (*de maison*) passage.

dégainer [degene] *vti* (*arme*) to draw.

dégarn/ir [degarnir] *vt* to clear, empty; (*arbre, compte*) to strip; — **se d.** *vpr* (*crâne*) to go bald; (*salle*) to clear, empty. ◆—I a

(*salle*) empty, bare; (*tête*) balding; **front d.** receding hairline.

dégâts [degɑ] *nmpl* damage; **limiter les d.** *Fig* to prevent matters getting worse.

dégel [deʒɛl] *nm* thaw. ◆**dégeler** *vt* to thaw (out); (*crédits*) to unfreeze; — *vi* to thaw (out); — *v imp* to thaw; — **se d.** *vpr* (*personne, situation*) to thaw (out).

dégénér/er [deʒenere] *vi* to degenerate (**en** into). ◆—é, -ée a & *nmf* degenerate. ◆**dégénérescence** *nf* degeneration.

dégingandé [deʒɛ̃gɑ̃de] a a gangling, lanky.

dégivrer [deʒivre] *vt Aut Av* to de-ice; (*réfrigérateur*) to defrost.

déglingu/er (se) [sədeglɛ̃ge] *vpr Fam* to fall to bits. ◆—é a falling to bits, in bits.

dégobiller [degɔbije] *vt Fam* to spew up.

dégonfl/er [degɔ̃fle] *vt* (*pneu etc*) to deflate, let down; — **se d.** *vpr* (*flancher*) *Fam* to chicken out, get cold feet. ◆—é, -ée a (*pneu*) flat; (*lâche*) *Fam* chicken, yellow; — *nmf Fam* yellow belly.

dégorger [degɔrʒe] *vi* (*se déverser*) to discharge (**dans** into); **faire d.** (*escargots*) *Culin* to cover with salt.

dégot(t)er [degɔte] *vt Fam* to find, turn up.

dégouliner [deguline] *vi* to trickle, drip, run.

dégourd/ir [degurdir] *vt* (*doigts etc*) to take the numbness out of; **d. qn** *Fig* to smarten *ou* wise s.o. up, sharpen s.o.'s wits; — **se d.** *vpr* to smarten up, wise up; **se d. les jambes** to stretch one's legs. ◆—I a (*malin*) smart, sharp.

dégoût [degu] *nm* disgust; **le d. de** (*la vie, les gens etc*) disgust for; **avoir un** *ou* **du d. pour qch** to have a (strong) dislike *ou* distaste for sth. ◆**dégoût/er** *vt* to disgust; **d. qn de qch** to put s.o. off sth; — **se d. de** to take a (strong) dislike to, become disgusted with. ◆—**ant** a disgusting. ◆—é a disgusted; **être d. de** to be sick of *ou* disgusted with *ou* by *ou* at; **elle est partie dégoûtée** she left in disgust; **il n'est pas d.** (*difficile*) he's not too fussy; **faire le d.** to be fussy.

dégrad/er [degrade] **1** *vt* (*avilir*) to degrade; (*mur etc*) to deface, damage; — **se d.** *vpr* (*s'avilir*) to degrade oneself; (*édifice, situation*) to deteriorate. **2** *vt* (*couleur*) to shade off. ◆—**ant** a degrading. ◆—é *nm* (*de couleur*) shading off, gradation. ◆**dégradation** *nf* (*de drogué etc*) & *Ch* degradation; (*de situation etc*) deterioration; *pl* (*dégâts*) damage.

dégrafer [degrafe] *vt* (*vêtement*) to unfasten, unhook.

dégraisser [degrese] *vt* **1** (*bœuf*) to take the

fat off; (*bouillon*) to skim. **2** (*entreprise*) *Fam* to slim down, trim down the size of (*by laying off workers*).

degré [dǝgre] *nm* **1** degree; **enseignement du premier/second d.** primary/secondary education; **au plus haut d.** (*avare etc*) extremely. **2** (*gradin*) *Litt* step.

dégrever [degrǝve] *vt* (*contribuable*) to reduce the tax burden on.

dégriffé [degrife] *a* **vêtement d.** unlabelled designer garment.

dégringoler [degrɛ̃gɔle] *vi* to tumble (down); **faire d. qch** to topple sth over; – *vt* (*escalier*) to rush down. ◆**dégringolade** *nf* tumble.

dégriser [degrize] *vt* **d. qn** to sober s.o. (up).

dégrossir [degrosir] *vt* (*travail*) to rough out; **d. qn** to refine s.o.

déguerpir [degɛrpir] *vi* to clear off *ou* out.

dégueulasse [degœlas] *a Fam* lousy, disgusting.

dégueuler [degœle] *vi* (*vomir*) *Arg* to puke.

déguis/er [degize] *vt* (*pour tromper*) to disguise; **d. qn en** (*costumer*) to dress s.o. up as, disguise s.o. as; **– se d.** *vpr* to dress oneself up, disguise oneself (**en** as). ◆**–ement** *nm* disguise; (*de bal costumé etc*) fancy dress.

déguster [degyste] **1** *vt* (*goûter*) to taste, sample; (*apprécier*) to relish. **2** *vi* (*subir des coups*) *Fam* to cop it, get a good hiding. ◆**dégustation** *nf* tasting, sampling.

déhancher (se) [sǝdeɑ̃ʃe] *vpr* (*femme etc*) to sway *ou* wiggle one's hips; (*boiteux*) to walk lop-sided.

dehors [dǝɔr] *adv* out(side); (*à l'air*) outdoors, outside; **en d.** on the outside; **en d. de** outside; (*excepté*) apart from; **en d. de la ville/fenêtre** out of town/the window; **au-d. (de), au d. (de)** outside; **déjeuner/jeter/etc d.** to lunch/throw/etc out; – *nm* (*extérieur*) outside; *pl* (*aspect*) outward appearance.

déjà [deʒa] *adv* already; **est-il d. parti?** has he left yet *ou* already?; **elle l'a d. vu** she's seen it before, she's already seen it; **c'est d. pas mal** that's not bad at all; **quand partez-vous, d.?** when are you leaving, again?

déjeuner [deʒœne] *vi* (*à midi*) to (have) lunch; (*le matin*) to (have) breakfast; – *nm* lunch; **petit d.** breakfast.

déjouer [deʒwe] *vt* (*intrigue etc*) to thwart, foil.

déjuger (se) [sǝdeʒyʒe] *vpr* to go back on one's opinion *ou* decision.

delà [d(ǝ)la] *adv* **au-d. (de), au d. (de), par-d.,**

par d. beyond; **au-d. du pont/etc** beyond *ou* past the bridge/etc; – *nm* **l'au-d.** the (world) beyond.

délabr/er (se) [sǝdelabre] *vpr* (*édifice*) to become dilapidated, fall into disrepair; (*santé*) to become impaired. ◆**–ement** *nm* dilapidation, disrepair; impaired state.

délacer [delase] *vt* (*chaussures*) to undo.

délai [dele] *nm* time limit; (*répit, sursis*) extra time, extension; **dans un d. de dix jours** within ten days; **sans d.** without delay; **à bref d.** at short notice; **dans les plus brefs délais** as soon as possible; **dernier d.** final date.

délaisser [delese] *vt* to forsake, desert, abandon; (*négliger*) to neglect.

délass/er [delase] *vt*, **– se d.** *vpr* to relax. ◆**–ement** *nm* relaxation, diversion.

délateur, -trice [delatœr, -tris] *nmf* informer.

délavé [delave] *a* (*tissu, jean*) faded; (*ciel*) watery; (*terre*) waterlogged.

délayer [deleje] *vt* (*mélanger*) to mix (with liquid); (*discours, texte*) *Fig* to pad out, drag out.

delco [delko] *nm Aut* distributor.

délect/er (se) [sǝdelɛkte] *vpr* **se d. de qch/à faire** to (take) delight in sth/in doing. ◆**–able** *a* delectable. ◆**délectation** *nf* delight.

délégu/er [delege] *vt* to delegate (**à** to). ◆**–é, -ée** *nmf* delegate. ◆**délégation** *nf* delegation.

délest/er [delɛste] *vt Él* to cut the power from; **d. qn de** (*voler à qn*) *Fam* to relieve s.o. of. ◆**–age** *nm Aut* relief; **itinéraire de d.** alternative route (*to relieve congestion*).

délibér/er [delibere] *vi* (*réfléchir*) to deliberate (**sur** upon); (*se consulter*) to confer, deliberate (**de** about). ◆**–é** *a* (*résolu*) determined; (*intentionnel*) deliberate; **de propos d.** deliberately. ◆**–ément** *adv* (*à dessein*) deliberately. ◆**délibération** *nf* deliberation.

délicat [delika] *a* (*santé, travail etc*) delicate; (*question*) tricky, delicate; (*geste*) tactful; (*conscience*) scrupulous; (*exigeant*) particular. ◆**délicatement** *adv* delicately; tactfully. ◆**délicatesse** *nf* delicacy; tact(fulness); scrupulousness.

délice [delis] *nm* delight; – *nfpl* delights. ◆**délicieux, -euse** *a* (*mets, fruit etc*) delicious; (*parfum, parfum etc*) delightful.

délié [delje] **1** *a* (*esprit*) sharp; (*doigts*) nimble; (*mince*) slender. **2** *nm* (*d'une lettre*) (thin) upstroke.

délier [delje] *vt* to untie, undo; (*langue*) *Fig*

to loosen; **d. qn de** to release s.o. from; — **se d.** *vpr* (*paquet etc*) to come undone *ou* untied.

délimiter [delimite] *vt* to mark off, delimit; (*définir*) to define. ◆**délimitation** *nf* demarcation, delimitation; definition.

délinquant, -ante [delɛ̃kɑ̃, -ɑ̃t] *a & nmf* delinquent. ◆**délinquance** *nf* delinquency.

délire [delir] *nm Méd* delirium; (*exaltation*) *Fig* frenzy. ◆**délir/er** *vi Méd* to be delirious; (*dire n'importe quoi*) *Fig* to rave; **d. de** (*joie etc*) to be wild with. ◆**—ant** *a* (*malade*) delirious; (*joie*) frenzied, wild; (*déraisonnable*) utterly absurd.

délit [deli] *nm* offence, misdemeanour.

délivrer [delivre] *vt* **1** (*prisonnier*) to release, deliver; (*ville*) to deliver; **d. qn de** (*souci etc*) to rid s.o. of. **2** (*billet, diplôme etc*) to issue. ◆**délivrance** *nf* release; deliverance; issue; (*soulagement*) relief.

déloger [deloʒe] *vi* to move out; — *vt* to force *ou* drive out; *Mil* to dislodge.

déloyal, -aux [delwajal, -o] *a* disloyal; (*concurrence*) unfair. ◆**déloyauté** *nf* disloyalty; unfairness; (*action*) disloyal act.

delta [dɛlta] *nm* (*de fleuve*) delta.

deltaplane® [dɛltaplan] *nm* (*engin*) hangglider; **faire du d.** to practise hanggliding.

déluge [delyʒ] *nm* flood; (*de pluie*) downpour; (*de compliments, coups*) shower.

déluré [delyre] *a* (*malin*) smart, sharp; (*fille*) *Péj* brazen.

démagogie [demagɔʒi] *nf* demagogy. ◆**démagogue** *nmf* demagogue.

demain [d(ə)mɛ̃] *adv* tomorrow; **à d.!** see you tomorrow!; **ce n'est pas d. la veille** *Fam* that won't happen for a while yet.

demande [d(ə)mɑ̃d] *nf* request; (*d'emploi*) application; (*de renseignements*) inquiry; *Écon* demand; (*question*) question; **d. (en mariage)** proposal (of marriage); **demandes d'emploi** *Journ* situations wanted. ◆**demander** *vt* to ask for; (*emploi*) to apply for; (*autorisation*) to request, ask for; (*charité*) to beg for; (*prix*) to charge; (*nécessiter, exiger*) to require; **d. un nom/le chemin/l'heure** to ask a name/the way/the time; **d. qch à qn** to ask s.o. for sth; **d. à qn de faire** to ask s.o. to do; **d. si/où** to ask *ou* inquire whether/where; **on te demande!** you're wanted!; **ça demande du temps/une heure** it takes time/an hour; **se d. en mariage** to propose (marriage) to; — **se d.** *vpr* to wonder, ask oneself (**pourquoi** why, **si** if).

démanger [demɑ̃ʒe] *vti* to itch; **son bras le** *ou* **lui démange** his arm itches; **ça me démange de...** *Fig* I'm itching to.... ◆**démangeaison** *nf* itch; **avoir des démangeaisons** to be itching; **j'ai une d. au bras** my arm's itching.

démanteler [demɑ̃tle] *vt* (*bâtiment*) to demolish; (*organisation etc*) to break up.

démantibuler [demɑ̃tibyle] *vt* (*meuble etc*) *Fam* to pull to pieces.

démaquill/er (se) [sədemakije] *vpr* to take off one's make-up. ◆**—ant** *nm* make-up remover.

démarcation [demarkasjɔ̃] *nf* demarcation.

démarche [demarʃ] *nf* walk, step, gait; (*de pensée*) process; **faire des démarches** to take the necessary steps (**pour faire** to do).

démarcheur, -euse [demarʃœr, -øz] *nmf* *Pol* canvasser; *Com* door-to-door salesman *ou* saleswoman.

démarquer [demarke] *vt* (*prix*) to mark down; **se d. de** *Fig* to dissociate oneself from.

démarr/er [demare] *vi* (*moteur*) *Aut* to start (up); (*partir*) *Aut* to move *ou* drive off; (*entreprise etc*) *Fig* to get off the ground; — *vt* (*commencer*) *Fam* to start. ◆**—age** *nm* *Aut* start; **d. en côte** hill start. ◆**—eur** *nm* *Aut* starter.

démasquer [demaske] *vt* to unmask.

démêl/er [demele] *vt* to disentangle; (*discerner*) to fathom. ◆**—é** *nm* (*dispute*) squabble; *pl* (*ennuis*) trouble (**avec** with).

démembrer [demɑ̃bre] *vt* (*pays etc*) to dismember.

déménag/er [demenaʒe] *vi* to move (out), move house; — *vt* (*meubles*) to (re)move. ◆**—ement** *nm* move, moving (house); (*de meubles*) removal, moving (**de** of); **voiture de d.** removal van, *Am* moving van. ◆**—eur** *nm* removal man, *Am* (furniture) mover.

démener (se) [sədemne] *vpr* to fling oneself about; **se d. pour faire** to spare no effort to do.

dément, -ente [demɑ̃, -ɑ̃t] *a* insane; (*génial*) *Iron* fantastic; — *nmf* lunatic. ◆**démence** *nf* insanity. ◆**démentiel, -ielle** *a* insane.

dément/ir [demɑ̃tir] *vt* (*infirmer*) to belie; (*nouvelle, faits etc*) to deny; **d. qn** to give the lie to s.o. ◆**—i** *nm* denial.

démerder (se) [sədemɛrde] *vpr* (*se débrouiller*) *Arg* to manage (by oneself).

démesure [deməzyr] *nf* excess. ◆**démesuré** *a* excessive, inordinate.

démettre [demɛtr] *vt* **1** (*os*) to dislocate; **se d. le pied** to dislocate one's foot. **2 d. qn de**

to dismiss s.o. from; **se d. de ses fonctions**
to resign one's office.
demeurant (au) [odəmœrɑ̃] *adv* for all that,
after all.
demeure [dəmœr] *nf* **1** dwelling (place),
residence. **2 mettre qn en d. de faire**
to summon *ou* instruct s.o. to do.
◆**demeur/er** *vi* **1** (*aux être*) (*rester*) to
remain; **en d. là** (*affaire etc*) to rest there. **2**
(*aux avoir*) (*habiter*) to live, reside. ◆**—é** *a*
Fam (mentally) retarded.
demi, -ie [d(ə)mi] *a* half; **d.-journée**
half-day; **une heure et demie** an hour and a
half; (*horloge*) half past one; − *adv* (**à**) **d.**
plein half-full; **à d. nu** half-naked; **ouvrir à**
d. to open halfway; **faire les choses à d.** to
do things by halves; − *nmf* (*moitié*) half; −
nm (*verre*) (half-pint) glass of beer; *Fb*
half-back; − *nf* (*à l'horloge*) half-hour.
demi-cercle [d(ə)misɛrkl] *nm* semicircle.
◆**d.-douzaine** *nf* **une d.-douzaine (de)**
a half-dozen, half a dozen. ◆**d.-finale**
nf Sp semifinal. ◆**d.-frère** *nm* stepbrother. ◆**d.-heure** *nf* **une d.-heure** a
half-hour, half an hour. ◆**d.-mesure** *nf*
half-measure. ◆**d.-mot** *nm* **tu compren-**
dras à d.-mot you'll understand without my
having to spell it out. ◆**d.-pension** *nf*
half-board. ◆**d.-pensionnaire** *nmf* day
boarder, *Am* day student. ◆**d.-saison** *nf*
de d.-saison (*vêtement*) between seasons.
◆**d.-sel** *a inv* (*beurre*) slightly salted;
(*fromage*) **d.-sel** cream cheese. ◆**d.-sœur**
nf stepsister. ◆**d.-tarif** *nm & a inv* (*billet*)
(**à**) **d.-tarif** half-price. ◆**d.-tour** *nm* about
turn, *Am* about face; *Aut* U-turn; **faire**
d.-tour to turn back.
démission [demisjɔ̃] *nf* resignation.
◆**démissionnaire** *a* (*ministre etc*) outgoing. ◆**démissionner** *vi* to resign.
démobiliser [demɔbilize] *vt* to demobilize.
◆**démobilisation** *nf* demobilization.
démocrate [demɔkrat] *nmf* democrat; − *a*
democratic. ◆**démocratie** [-asi] *nf*
democracy. ◆**démocratique** *a* democratic.
démod/er (se) [sədemɔde] *vpr* to go out of
fashion. ◆**—é** *a* old-fashioned.
démographie [demɔgrafi] *nf* demography.
demoiselle [dəmwazɛl] *nf* (*célibataire*)
spinster, single woman; (*jeune fille*) young
lady; **d. d'honneur** (*à un mariage*) bridesmaid; (*de reine*) maid of honour.
démolir [demɔlir] *vt* (*maison, jouet etc*) to
demolish; (*projet etc*) to shatter; **d. qn**
(*battre, discréditer*) *Fam* to tear s.o. to

pieces. ◆**démolition** *nf* demolition; **en d.**
being demolished.
démon [demɔ̃] *nm* demon; **petit d.** (*enfant*)
little devil. ◆**démoniaque** *a* devilish,
fiendish.
démonstrateur, -trice [demɔ̃stratœr, -tris]
nmf (*dans un magasin etc*) demonstrator.
◆**démonstratif, -ive** *a* demonstrative.
◆**démonstration** *nf* demonstration; **d. de**
force show of force.
démonter [demɔ̃te] *vt* (*assemblage*) to
dismantle, take apart; (*installation*) to take
down; **d. qn** (*troubler*) *Fig* to disconcert
s.o.; **une mer démontée** a stormy sea; − **se**
d. *vpr* to come apart; (*installation*) to come
down; (*personne*) to be put out *ou* discon-
certed.
démontrer [demɔ̃tre] *vt* to demonstrate,
show.
démoraliser [demɔralize] *vt* to demoralize;
− **se d.** *vpr* to become demoralized.
◆**démoralisation** *nf* demoralization.
démordre [demɔrdr] *vi* **il ne démordra pas**
de (*son opinion etc*) he won't budge from.
démouler [demule] *vt* (*gâteau*) to turn out
(*from its mould*).
démunir [demynir] *vt* **d. qn de** to deprive
s.o. of; **se d. de** to part with.
démystifier [demistifje] *vt* (*public etc*) to
disabuse; (*idée etc*) to debunk.
dénationaliser [denasjɔnalize] *vt* to denationalize.
dénatur/er [denatyre] *vt* (*propos, faits etc*)
to misrepresent, distort. ◆**—é** (*goût, père*
etc) unnatural.
dénégation [denegasjɔ̃] *nf* denial.
déneiger [deneʒe] *vt* to clear of snow.
dénicher [denife] *vt* (*trouver*) to dig up, turn
up; (*ennemi, fugitif*) to hunt out, flush out.
dénier [denje] *vt* to deny; (*responsabilité*) to
disclaim, deny; **d. qch à qn** to deny s.o. sth.
dénigr/er [denigre] *vt* to denigrate, disparage. ◆**—ement** *nm* denigration, dispar-
agement.
dénivellation [denivelasjɔ̃] *nf* unevenness;
(*pente*) gradient; *pl* (*accidents*) bumps.
dénombrer [denɔ̃bre] *vt* to count, number.
dénomm/er [denɔme] *vt* to name. ◆**—é,**
-ée *nmf* **un d. Dupont** a man named
Dupont. ◆**dénomination** *nf* designation,
name.
dénonc/er [denɔ̃se] *vt* (*injustice etc*) to
denounce (**à** to); **d. qn** to inform on s.o.,
denounce s.o. (**à** to); *Scol* to tell on s.o. (**à**
to); − **se d.** *vpr* to give oneself up (**à** to).
◆**dénonciateur, -trice** *nmf* informer.
◆**dénonciation** *nf* denunciation.

dénoter [denɔte] *vt* to denote.

dénouer [denwe] *vt* (*nœud, corde*) to undo, untie; (*cheveux*) to undo; (*situation, intrigue*) to unravel; (*problème, crise*) to clear up; — **se d.** *vpr* (*nœud*) to come undone *ou* untied; (*cheveux*) to come undone. ◆**dénouement** *nm* outcome, ending; *Th* dénouement.

dénoyauter [denwajote] *vt* (*prune etc*) to stone, *Am* to pit.

denrée [dɑ̃re] *nf* food(stuff); **denrées alimentaires** foodstuffs.

dense [dɑ̃s] *a* dense. ◆**densité** *nf* density.

dent [dɑ̃] *nf* tooth; (*de roue*) cog; (*de fourche*) prong; (*de timbre-poste*) perforation; **d. de sagesse** wisdom tooth; **rien à se mettre sous la d.** nothing to eat; **manger à belles dents/du bout des dents** to eat whole-heartedly/half-heartedly; **faire ses dents** (*enfant*) to be teething; **coup de d.** bite; **sur les dents** (*surmené*) exhausted; (*énervé*) on edge; **avoir une d. contre qn** to have it in for s.o. ◆**dentaire** *a* dental. ◆**dentée** *af* **roue d.** cogwheel. ◆**dentier** *nm* denture(s), (set of) false teeth. ◆**dentifrice** *nm* toothpaste. ◆**dentiste** *nmf* dentist; **chirurgien d.** dental surgeon. ◆**dentition** *nf* (*dents*) (set of) teeth.

dentelé [dɑ̃tle] *a* (*côte*) jagged; (*feuille*) serrated. ◆**dentelure** *nf* jagged outline *ou* edge.

dentelle [dɑ̃tel] *nf* lace.

dénud/er [denyde] *vt* to (lay) bare. ◆**-é** *a* bare.

dénué [denye] *a* **d. de** devoid of, without.

dénuement [denymɑ̃] *nm* destitution; **dans le d.** poverty-stricken.

déodorant [deɔdɔrɑ̃] *nm* deodorant.

dépann/er [depane] *vt* (*mécanisme*) to get going (again), repair; **d. qn** *Fam* to help s.o. out. ◆**-age** *nm* (emergency) repair; **voiture/service de d.** breakdown vehicle/service. ◆**-eur** *nm* repairman; *Aut* breakdown mechanic. ◆**-euse** *nf* (*voiture*) *Aut* breakdown lorry, *Am* wrecker, tow truck.

dépareillé [depareje] *a* (*chaussure etc*) odd, not matching; (*collection*) incomplete.

déparer [depare] *vt* to mar, spoil.

départ [depar] *nm* departure; (*début*) start, beginning; *Sp* start; **point/ligne de d.** starting point/post; **au d.** at the outset, at the start; **au d. de Paris**/*etc* (*excursion etc*) departing from Paris/*etc.*

départager [departaʒe] *vt* (*concurrents*) to decide between; **d. les votes** to give the casting vote.

département [departəmɑ̃] *nm* department.

◆**départemental, -aux** *a* departmental; **route départementale** secondary road.

départir (se) [sədepartir] *vpr* **se d. de** (*attitude*) to depart from, abandon.

dépass/er [depase] *vt* (*durée, attente etc*) to go beyond, exceed; (*endroit*) to go past, go beyond; (*véhicule, bicyclette etc*) to overtake, pass; (*pouvoir*) to go beyond, overstep; **d. qn** (*en hauteur*) to be taller than s.o.; (*surclasser*) to be ahead of s.o.; **ça me dépasse** *Fig* that's (quite) beyond me; — *vi* (*jupon, clou etc*) to stick out, show. ◆**-é** *a* (*démodé*) outdated; (*incapable*) unable to cope. ◆**-ement** *nm Aut* overtaking, passing.

dépays/er [depeize] *vt* to disorientate, *Am* disorient. ◆**-ement** *nm* disorientation; (*changement*) change of scenery.

dépecer [depəse] *vt* (*animal*) to cut up, carve up.

dépêche [depɛʃ] *nf* telegram; (*diplomatique*) dispatch. ◆**dépêcher** *vt* to dispatch; — **se d.** *vpr* to hurry (up).

dépeign/er [depeɲe] *vt* **d. qn** to make s.o.'s hair untidy. ◆**-é** *a* **être d.** to have untidy hair; **sortir d.** to go out with untidy hair.

dépeindre* [depɛ̃dr] *vt* to depict, describe.

dépenaillé [depənaje] *a* in tatters *ou* rags.

dépend/re [depɑ̃dr] **1** *vi* to depend (**de** on); **d. de** (*appartenir à*) to belong to; (*être soumis à*) to be dependent on; **ça dépend de toi** that depends on you, that's up to you. **2** *vt* (*décrocher*) to take down. ◆**-ant** *a* dependent (**de** on). ◆**dépendance 1** *nf* dependence; **sous la d. de qn** under s.o.'s domination. **2** *nfpl* (*bâtiments*) outbuildings.

dépens [depɑ̃] *nmpl Jur* costs; **aux d. de** at the expense of; **apprendre à ses d.** to learn to one's cost.

dépense [depɑ̃s] *nf* (*action*) spending; (*frais*) expense, expenditure; (*d'électricité etc*) consumption; (*physique*) exertion. ◆**dépenser** *vt* (*argent*) to spend; (*électricité etc*) to use; (*forces*) to exert; (*énergie*) to expend; — **se d.** *vpr* to exert oneself. ◆**dépensier, -ière** *a* wasteful, extravagant.

déperdition [deperdisjɔ̃] *nf* (*de chaleur etc*) loss.

dépér/ir [deperir] *vi* (*personne*) to waste away; (*plante*) to wither; (*santé etc*) to decline. ◆**-issement** *nm* (*baisse*) decline.

dépêtrer [depetre] *vt* to extricate; — **se d.** *vpr* to extricate oneself (from).

dépeupl/er [depœple] *vt* to depopulate. ◆**-ement** *nm* depopulation.

dépilatoire [depilatwar] *nm* hair-remover.

dépist/er [depiste] *vt* (*criminel etc*) to track down; (*maladie, fraude*) to detect. ◆**—age** *nm Méd* detection.

dépit [depi] *nm* resentment, chagrin; **en d. de** in spite of. ◆**dépiter** *vt* to vex, chagrin; **— se d.** *vpr* to feel resentment *ou* chagrin.

déplac/er [deplase] *vt* to shift, move; (*fonctionnaire*) to transfer; **— se d.** *vpr* to move (about); (*voyager*) to get about, travel (about). ◆**—é** *a* (*mal à propos*) out of place; **personne déplacée** (*réfugié*) displaced person. ◆**—ement** *nm* (*voyage*) (business *ou* professional) trip; (*d'ouragan, de troupes*) movement; **les déplacements** (*voyages*) travel(ling); **frais de d.** travelling expenses.

déplaire* [depler] *vi* **d. à qn** to displease s.o.; **cet aliment lui déplaît** he *ou* she dislikes this food; **n'en déplaise à** *Iron* with all due respect to; *– v imp* **il me déplaît de faire** I dislike doing, it displeases me to do; **— se d.** *vpr* to dislike it. ◆**déplaisant** *a* unpleasant, displeasing. ◆**déplaisir** *nm* displeasure.

dépli/er [deplije] *vt* to open out, unfold. ◆**—ant** *nm* (*prospectus*) leaflet.

déplor/er [deplore] *vt* (*regretter*) to deplore; (*la mort de qn*) to mourn (over), lament (over); **d. qn** to mourn (for) s.o.; **d. que** (+ *sub*) to deplore the fact that, regret that. ◆**—able** *a* deplorable, lamentable.

déployer [deplwaje] *vt* (*ailes*) to spread; (*journal, carte etc*) to unfold, spread (out); (*objets, courage etc*) to display; (*troupes*) to deploy; **— se d.** *vpr* (*drapeau*) to unfurl. ◆**déploiement** *nm* (*démonstration*) display; *Mil* deployment.

dépoli [depoli] *a* **verre d.** frosted glass.

déport/er [deporte] *vt* **1** (*exiler*) *Hist* to deport (to a penal colony); (*dans un camp de concentration*) *Hist* to send to a concentration camp, deport. **2** (*dévier*) to veer *ou* carry (off course). ◆**—é, -ée** *nmf* deportee; (concentration camp) inmate. ◆**déportation** *nf* deportation; internment (in a concentration camp).

dépos/er [depoze] *vt* (*poser*) to put down; (*laisser*) to leave; (*argent, lie*) to deposit; (*plainte*) to lodge; (*armes*) to lay down; (*gerbe*) to lay; (*ordures*) to dump; (*marque de fabrique*) to register; (*projet de loi*) to introduce; (*souverain*) to depose; **d. qn** *Aut* to drop s.o (off), put s.o. off; **d. son bilan** *Fin* to go into liquidation, file for bankruptcy; *– vi Jur* to testify; (*liquide*) to leave a deposit; **— se d.** *vpr* (*poussière, lie*) to

settle. ◆**dépositaire** *nmf Fin* agent; (*de secret*) custodian. ◆**déposition** *nf Jur* statement; (*de souverain*) deposing.

déposséder [deposede] *vt* to deprive, dispossess (**de** of).

dépôt [depo] *nm* (*d'ordures etc*) dumping, (*lieu*) dump; (*de gerbe*) laying; (*d'autobus, de trains*) depot; (*entrepôt*) warehouse; (*argent*) deposit; (*de vin*) deposit, sediment; **d. (calcaire)** (*de chaudière etc*) deposit; **laisser qch à qn en d.** to give s.o. sth for safekeeping *ou* in trust.

dépotoir [depotwar] *nm* rubbish dump, *Am* garbage dump.

dépouille [depuj] *nf* hide, skin; (*de serpent*) slough; *pl* (*butin*) spoils; **d. (mortelle)** mortal remains. ◆**dépouill/er** *vt* (*animal*) to skin, flay; (*analyser*) to go through, analyse; **d. de** (*dégarnir*) to strip of; (*déposséder*) to deprive of; **se d. de** to rid *ou* divest oneself of, cast off; **d. un scrutin** to count votes. ◆**—é** *a* (*arbre*) bare; (*style*) austere, spare; **d. de** bereft of. ◆**—ement** *nm* (*de document etc*) analysis; (*privation*) deprivation; (*sobriété*) austerity; **d. du scrutin** counting of the votes.

dépourvu [depurvy] *a* **d. de** devoid of; **prendre qn au d.** to catch s.o. unawares *ou* off his guard.

dépraver [deprave] *vt* to deprave. ◆**dépravation** *nf* depravity.

dépréci/er [depresje] *vt* (*dénigrer*) to disparage; (*monnaie, immeuble etc*) to depreciate; **— se d.** *vpr* (*baisser*) to depreciate, lose (its) value. ◆**dépréciation** *nf* depreciation.

déprédations [depredasjɔ̃] *nfpl* damage, ravages.

dépression [depresjɔ̃] *nf* depression; **zone de d.** trough of low pressure; **d. nerveuse** nervous breakdown; **d. économique** slump. ◆**dépressif, -ive** *a* depressive. ◆**déprime** *nf* **la d.** (*dépression*) *Fam* the blues. ◆**déprim/er** *vt* to depress. ◆**—é** *a* depressed.

depuis [dəpɥi] *prép* since; **d. lundi** since Monday; **d. qu'elle est partie** since she left; **j'habite ici d. un mois** I've been living here for a month; **d. quand êtes-vous là?** how long have you been here?; **d. peu/longtemps** for a short/long time; **d. Paris jusqu'à Londres** from Paris to London; *– adv* since (then), ever since.

députation [depytasjɔ̃] *nf* (*groupe*) deputation, delegation; **candidat à la d.** parliamentary candidate. ◆**député** *nm* delegate, deputy; (*au parlement*) deputy, = *Br* MP, = *Am* congressman, congresswoman.

déracin/er [derasine] *vt* (*personne, arbre etc*) to uproot; (*préjugés etc*) to eradicate, root out. ◆**—ement** *nm* uprooting; eradication.

déraill/er [deraje] *vi* **1** (*train*) to jump the rails, be derailed; **faire d.** to derail. **2** (*divaguer*) *Fam* to drivel, talk through one's hat. ◆**—ement** *nm* (*de train*) derailment. ◆**—eur** *nm* (*de bicyclette*) derailleur (gear change).

déraisonnable [derezɔnabl] *a* unreasonable. ◆**déraisonner** *vi* to talk nonsense.

dérang/er [derɑ̃ʒe] *vt* (*affaires*) to disturb, upset; (*estomac*) to upset; (*projets*) to mess up, upset; (*vêtements*) to mess up; (*cerveau, esprit*) to derange; **d. qn** to disturb *ou* bother *ou* trouble s.o.; **je viendrai si ça ne te dérange pas** I'll come if that doesn't put you out *ou* if that's not imposing; **ça vous dérange si je fume?** do you mind if I smoke?; — **se d.** *vpr* to put oneself to a lot of trouble (**pour faire** to do), (*se déplacer*) to move; **ne te dérange pas!** don't trouble yourself!, don't bother! ◆**—ement** *nm* (*gêne*) bother, inconvenience; (*désordre*) disorder; **en d.** (*téléphone etc*) out of order.

dérap/er [derape] *vi* to skid. ◆**—age** *nm* skid; (*des prix, de l'inflation*) *Fig* loss of control (**de** over).

dératé [derate] *nm* **courir comme un d.** to run like mad.

dérégl/er [deregle] *vt* (*mécanisme*) to put out of order; (*estomac, habitudes*) to upset; (*esprit*) to unsettle; — **se d.** *vpr* (*montre, appareil*) to go wrong. ◆**—é** *a* out of order; (*vie, mœurs*) dissolute, wild; (*imagination*) wild. ◆**dérèglement** *nm* (*de mécanisme*) breakdown; (*d'esprit*) disorder; (*d'estomac*) upset.

dérider [deride] *vt*, — **se d.** *vpr* to cheer up.

dérision [derizjɔ̃] *nf* derision, mockery; **tourner en d.** to mock, deride; **par d.** derisively; **de d.** derisive. ◆**dérisoire** *a* ridiculous, derisory, derisive.

dérive [deriv] *nf* *Nau* drift; **partir à la d.** (*navire*) to drift out to sea; **aller à la d.** (*navire*) to go adrift; (*entreprise etc*) *Fig* to drift (towards ruin). ◆**dériv/er** *vi* *Nau Av* to drift; **d. de** (*venir*) to derive from, be derived from; — *vt* (*cours d'eau*) to divert; *Ling* to derive (**de** from). ◆**—é** *nm* *Ling Ch* derivative; (*produit*) by-product. ◆**dérivatif** *nm* distraction (**à** from). ◆**dérivation** *nf* (*de cours d'eau*) diversion; *Ling* derivation; (*déviation routière*) bypass.

dermatologie [dermatɔlɔʒi] *nf* dermatology.

dernier -ière [dernje, -jɛr] *a* last; (*nouvelles, mode*) latest; (*étage*) top; (*degré*) highest; (*qualité*) lowest; **le d. rang** the back *ou* last row; **ces derniers mois** these past few months, these last *ou* final months; **de la dernière importance** of (the) utmost importance; **en d.** last; — *nmf* last (person *ou* one); **ce d.** (*de deux*) the latter; (*de plusieurs*) the last-mentioned; **être le d. de la classe** to be (at) the bottom of the class; **le d. des derniers** the lowest of the low; **le d. de mes soucis** the least of my worries. ◆**d.-né**, ◆**dernière-née** *nmf* youngest (child). ◆**dernièrement** *adv* recently.

dérob/er [derɔbe] *vt* (*voler*) to steal (**à** from); (*cacher*) to hide (**à** from); — **se d.** *vpr* to get out of one's obligations; (*s'éloigner*) to slip away; (*éviter de répondre*) to dodge the issue; **se d. à** (*obligations*) to shirk, get out of; (*regards*) to hide from; **ses jambes se sont dérobées sous lui** his legs gave way beneath him. ◆**—é** *a* (*porte etc*) hidden, secret; **à la dérobée** *adv* on the sly, stealthily. ◆**dérobade** *nf* dodge, evasion.

déroger [derɔʒe] *vi* **d. à une règle/etc** to depart from a rule/etc. ◆**dérogation** *nf* exemption, (special) dispensation.

dérouiller [deruje] *vt* **d. qn** (*battre*) *Arg* to thrash *ou* thump s.o.; **se d. les jambes** *Fam* to stretch one's legs.

déroul/er [derule] *vt* (*carte etc*) to unroll; (*film*) to unwind; — **se d.** *vpr* (*événement*) to take place, pass off; (*paysage, souvenirs*) to unfold; (*récit*) to develop. ◆**—ement** *nm* (*d'une action*) unfolding, development; (*cours*) course;

dérouter [derute] *vt* (*avion, navire*) to divert, reroute; (*candidat etc*) to baffle; (*poursuivant*) to throw off the scent.

derrick [derik] *nm* derrick.

derrière [derjɛr] *prép & adv* behind; **d. moi** behind me, *Am* in back of me; **assis d.** (*dans une voiture*) sitting in the back; **de d.** (*roue*) back, rear; (*pattes*) hind; **par d.** (*attaquer*) from behind, from the rear; — *nm* (*de maison etc*) back, rear; (*fesses*) behind, bottom.

des [de] *voir* **de**[1,2], **le**.

dès [dɛ] *prép* from; **d. cette époque** (as) from that time, from that time on; **d. le début** (right) from the start; **d. son enfance** since *ou* from (his *ou* her) childhood; **d. le**

sixième siècle as early as *ou* as far back as the sixth century; **d. l'aube** at (the crack of) dawn; **d. qu'elle viendra** as soon as she comes.

désabusé [dezabyze] *a* disenchanted, disillusioned.

désaccord [dezakɔr] *nm* disagreement. ◆**désaccordé** *a* Mus out of tune.

désaccoutumer (se) [sədezakutyme] *vpr* **se d. de** to lose the habit of.

désaffecté [dezafɛkte] *a* (*école etc*) disused.

désaffection [dezafɛksjɔ̃] *nf* loss of affection, disaffection (**pour** for).

désagréable [dezagreabl] *a* unpleasant, disagreeable. ◆**—ment** [-əmã] *adv* unpleasantly.

désagréger [dezagreʒe] *vt*, **— se d.** *vpr* to disintegrate, break up. ◆**désagrégation** *nf* disintegration.

désagrément [dezagremã] *nm* annoyance, trouble.

désaltér/er [dezaltere] *vt* **d. qn** to quench s.o.'s thirst; **se d.** to quench one's thirst. ◆**—ant** *a* thirst-quenching.

désamorcer [dezamɔrse] *vt* (*obus, situation*) to defuse.

désappointer [dezapwɛ̃te] *vt* to disappoint.

désapprouver [dezapruve] *vt* to disapprove of; **— vi** to disapprove. ◆**désapprobateur, -trice** *a* disapproving. ◆**désapprobation** *nf* disapproval.

désarçonner [dezarsɔne] *vt* (*jockey*) to throw, unseat; (*déconcerter*) Fig to nonpluss, throw.

désarm/er [dezarme] *vt* (*émouvoir*) & Mil to disarm; **— vi** Mil to disarm; (*céder*) to let up. ◆**—ant** *a* (*charme etc*) disarming. ◆**—é** *a* (*sans défense*) unarmed, Fig helpless. ◆**—ement** *nm* (*de nation*) disarmament.

désarroi [dezarwa] *nm* (*angoisse*) distress.

désarticuler [dezartikyle] *vt* (*membre*) to dislocate.

désastre [dezastr] *nm* disaster. ◆**désastreux, -euse** *a* disastrous.

désavantage [dezavɑ̃taʒ] *nm* disadvantage, handicap; (*inconvénient*) drawback, disadvantage. ◆**désavantager** *vt* to put at a disadvantage, handicap. ◆**désavantageux, -euse** *a* disadvantageous.

désaveu, -x [dezavø] *nm* repudiation. ◆**désavouer** *vt* (*livre, personne etc*) to disown, repudiate.

désaxé, -ée [dezakse] *a* & *nmf* unbalanced (person).

desceller [desele] *vt* (*pierre etc*) to loosen; **— se d.** *vpr* to come loose.

descend/re [desɑ̃dr] *vi* (*aux* **être**) to come *ou* go down, descend (**de** from); (*d'un train etc*) to get off *ou* out, alight (**de** from); (*d'un arbre*) to climb down (**de** from); (*nuit, thermomètre*) to fall; (*marée*) to go out; **d. à** (*une bassesse*) to stoop to; **d. à l'hôtel** to put up at a hotel; **d. de** (*être issu de*) to be descended from; **d. de cheval** to dismount; **d. en courant/flânant**/*etc* to run/stroll/*etc* down; **— vt** (*aux* **avoir**) (*escalier*) to come *ou* go down, descend; (*objets*) to bring *ou* take down; (*avion*) to bring *ou* shoot down; **d. qn** (*tuer*) Fam to bump s.o. off. ◆**—ant, -ante 1** *a* descending; (*marée*) outgoing. **2** *nmf* (*personne*) descendant. ◆**descendance** *nf* (*enfants*) descendants; (*origine*) descent.

descente [desɑ̃t] *nf* (*action*) descent; (*irruption*) raid (**dans** upon); (*en parachute*) drop; (*pente*) slope; **la d. des bagages** bringing *ou* taking down the luggage; **il fut accueilli à sa d. d'avion** he was met as he got off the plane; **d. à skis** downhill run; **d. de lit** (*tapis*) bedside rug.

descriptif, -ive [deskriptif, -iv] *a* descriptive. ◆**description** *nf* description.

déségrégation [desegregasjɔ̃] *nf* desegregation.

désemparé [dezɑ̃pare] *a* distraught, at a loss; (*navire*) crippled.

désemplir [dezɑ̃plir] *vi* **ce magasin**/*etc* **ne désemplit pas** this shop/*etc* is always crowded.

désenchant/er [dezɑ̃ʃɑ̃te] *vt* to disenchant. ◆**—ement** *nm* disenchantment.

désencombrer [dezɑ̃kɔ̃bre] *vt* (*passage etc*) to clear.

désenfler [dezɑ̃fle] *vi* to go down, become less swollen.

déséquilibre [dezekilibr] *nm* (*inégalité*) imbalance; (*mental*) unbalance; **en d.** (*meuble etc*) unsteady. ◆**déséquilibrer** *vt* to throw off balance; (*esprit, personne*) Fig to unbalance.

désert [dezɛr] *a* deserted; **île déserte** desert island; **— nm** desert, wilderness. ◆**désertique** *a* (*région etc*) desert-.

déserter [dezɛrte] *vti* to desert. ◆**déserteur** *nm* Mil deserter. ◆**désertion** *nf* desertion.

désespér/er [dezɛspere] *vi* to despair (**de** of); **— vt** to drive to despair; **— se d.** *vpr* to (be in) despair. ◆**—ant** *a* (*enfant etc*) that drives one to despair, hopeless. ◆**—é, -ée** *a* (*personne*) in despair, despairing; (*cas, situation*) desperate, hopeless; (*efforts, cris*) desperate; **— nmf** (*suicidé*) person driven to despair *ou* desperation. ◆**—ément** *adv* desperately. ◆**désespoir** *nm* despair; **au d.** in despair; **en d. de cause** in desperation, as a (desperate) last resort.

déshabiller [dezabije] *vt* to undress, strip; **— se d.** *vpr* to get undressed, undress.

déshabituer [dezabitɥe] *vt* **d. qn de** to break s.o. of the habit of.

désherb/er [dezɛrbe] *vti* to weed. ◆**—ant** *nm* weed killer.

déshérit/er [dezerite] *vt* to disinherit. ◆**—é** *a* (*pauvre*) underprivileged; (*laid*) ill-favoured.

déshonneur [dezɔnœr] *nm* dishonour, disgrace. ◆**déshonor/er** *vt* to disgrace, dishonour. ◆**—ant** *a* dishonourable.

déshydrater [dezidrate] *vt* to dehydrate; **— se d.** *vpr* to become dehydrated.

désigner [dezine] *vt* (*montrer*) to point to, point out; (*élire*) to appoint, designate; (*signifier*) to indicate, designate; **ses qualités le désignent pour** his qualities mark him out for. ◆**désignation** *nf* designation.

désillusion [dezilyzjɔ̃] *nf* disillusion(ment). ◆**désillusionner** *vt* to disillusion.

désincarné [dezɛ̃karne] *a* (*esprit*) disembodied.

désinence [dezinɑ̃s] *nf* Gram ending.

désinfect/er [dezɛ̃fɛkte] *vt* to disinfect. ◆**—ant** *nm & a* disinfectant. ◆**désinfection** *nf* disinfection.

désinformation [dezɛ̃fɔrmasjɔ̃] *nf* Pol misinformation.

désintégrer (se) [sədezɛ̃tegre] *vpr* to disintegrate. ◆**désintégration** *nf* disintegration.

désintéress/er (se) [sədezɛ̃terese] *vpr* **se d. de** to lose interest in, take no further interest in. ◆**—é** *a* (*altruiste*) disinterested. ◆**—ement** [-esmɑ̃] *nm* (*altruisme*) disinterestedness. ◆**désintérêt** *nm* lack of interest.

désintoxiquer [dezɛ̃tɔksike] *vt* (*alcoolique, drogué*) to cure.

désinvolte [dezɛ̃vɔlt] *a* (*dégagé*) easy-going, casual; (*insolent*) offhand, casual. ◆**désinvolture** *nf* casualness; offhandedness.

désir [dezir] *nm* desire, wish. ◆**désirable** *a* desirable. ◆**désirer** *vt* to want, desire; (*convoiter*) to desire; **je désire venir** I would like to come, I wish *ou* want to come; **je désire que tu viennes** I want you to come; **ça laisse à d.** it leaves something *ou* a lot to be desired. ◆**désireux, -euse** *a* **d. de faire** anxious *ou* eager to do, desirous of doing.

désist/er (se) [sədeziste] *vpr* (*candidat etc*) to withdraw. ◆**—ement** *nm* withdrawal.

désobé/ir [dezɔbeir] *vi* to disobey; **d. à qn** to disobey s.o. ◆**—issant** *a* disobedient. ◆**désobéissance** *nf* disobedience (**à** to).

désobligeant [dezɔbliʒɑ̃] *a* disagreeable, unkind.

désodorisant [dezɔdɔrizɑ̃] *nm* air freshener.

désœuvré [dezœvre] *a* idle, unoccupied. ◆**désœuvrement** *nm* idleness.

désol/er [dezɔle] *vt* to distress, upset (very much); **— se d.** *vpr* to be distressed *ou* upset (**de** at). ◆**—ant** *a* distressing, upsetting. ◆**—é** *a* (*région*) desolate; (*affligé*) distressed; **être d.** (*navré*) to be sorry (**que** (+ *sub*) that, **de faire** to do). ◆**désolation** *nf* (*peine*) distress, grief.

désolidariser (se) [sədesɔlidarize] *vpr* to dissociate oneself (**de** from).

désopilant [dezɔpilɑ̃] *a* hilarious, screamingly funny.

désordre [dezɔrdr] *nm* (*de papiers, affaires, idées*) mess, muddle, disorder; (*de cheveux, pièce*) untidiness; *Méd* disorder; *pl* (*émeutes*) disorder, unrest; **en d.** untidy, messy. ◆**désordonné** *a* (*personne, chambre*) untidy, messy.

désorganiser [dezɔrganize] *vt* to disorganize. ◆**désorganisation** *nf* disorganization.

désorienter [dezɔrjɑ̃te] *vt* **d. qn** to disorientate *ou Am* disorient s.o., make s.o. lose his bearings; (*déconcerter*) to bewilder s.o. ◆**désorientation** *nf* disorientation.

désormais [dezɔrmɛ] *adv* from now on, in future, henceforth.

désosser [dezɔse] *vt* (*viande*) to bone.

despote [dɛspɔt] *nm* despot. ◆**despotique** *a* despotic. ◆**despotisme** *nm* despotism.

desquels, desquelles [dekɛl] *voir* **lequel.**

dessaisir (se) [sədesezir] *vpr* **se d. de qch** to part with sth, relinquish sth.

dessaler [desale] *vt* (*poisson etc*) to remove the salt from (*by soaking*).

dessécher [deseʃe] *vt* (*végétation*) to dry up, wither; (*gorge, bouche*) to dry, parch; (*fruits*) to desiccate, dry; (*cœur*) to harden; **— se d.** *vpr* (*plante*) to wither, dry up; (*peau*) to dry (up), get dry; (*maigrir*) to waste away.

dessein [desɛ̃] *nm* aim, design; **dans le d. de faire** with the aim of doing; **à d.** intentionally.

desserrer [desere] *vt* (*ceinture etc*) to loosen, slacken; (*poing*) to open, unclench;

(*frein*) to release; **il n'a pas desserré les dents** he didn't open his mouth; **— se d.** *vpr* to come loose.

dessert [desɛr] *nm* dessert, sweet.

desserte [desɛrt] *nf* **assurer la d. de** (*village etc*) to provide a (bus *ou* train) service to. ◆**desservir** *vt* **1** (*table*) to clear (away). **2 d. qn** to harm s.o., do s.o. a disservice. **3 l'autobus/*etc* dessert ce village** the bus/*etc* provides a service to *ou* stops at this village; **ce quartier est bien desservi** this district is well served by public transport.

dessin [desɛ̃] *nm* drawing; (*rapide*) sketch; (*motif*) design, pattern; (*contour*) outline; **d. animé** *Cin* cartoon; **d. humoristique** *Journ* cartoon; **école de d.** art school; **planche à d.** drawing board. ◆**dessinateur, -trice** *nmf* drawer; sketcher; **d. humoristique** cartoonist; **d. de modes** dress designer; **d. industriel** draughtsman, *Am* draughtsman. ◆**dessiner** *vt* to draw; (*rapidement*) to sketch; (*meuble, robe etc*) to design; (*indiquer*) to outline, trace; **(bien) la taille** (*vêtement*) to show off the figure; **— se d.** *vpr* (*colline etc*) to stand out, be outlined; (*projet*) to take shape.

dessoûler [desule] *vti Fam* to sober up.

dessous [d(ə)su] *adv* under(neath), beneath, below; **en d.** (*sous*) under(neath); (*agir*) *Fig* in an underhand way; **vêtement de d.** undergarment; **drap de d.** bottom sheet; **— *nm* underneath**; *pl* (*vêtements*) underclothes; **d. de table** backhander, bribe; **les gens du d.** the people downstairs *ou* below; **avoir le d.** to be defeated, get the worst of it. ◆**d.-de-plat** *nm inv* table mat.

dessus [d(ə)sy] *adv* (*marcher, écrire*) on it; (*monter*) on top (of it), on it; (*lancer, passer*) over it; **de d. la table** off *ou* from the table; **vêtement de d.** outer garment; **drap de d.** top sheet; **par-d.** (*sauter etc*) over (it); **par-d. tout** above all; **— *nm* top**; (*de chaussure*) upper; **avoir le d.** to have the upper hand, get the best of it; **les gens du d.** the people upstairs *ou* above. ◆**d.-de-lit** *nm inv* bedspread.

déstabiliser [destabilize] *vt* to destabilize.

destin [dɛstɛ̃] *nm* fate, destiny. ◆**destinée** *nf* fate, destiny (*of an individual*).

destin/er [dɛstine] *vt* **d. qch à qn** to intend *ou* mean sth for s.o.; **d. qn à** (*carrière, fonction*) to intend *ou* destine s.o. for; **se d. à** (*carrière etc*) to intend *ou* mean to take up; **destiné à mourir/*etc** (*condamné*) destined *ou* fated to die/*etc*. ◆**destinataire** *nmf* addressee. ◆**destination** *nf* (*usage*)

purpose; (*lieu*) destination; **à d. de** (*train etc*) (going) to, (bound) for.

destituer [dɛstitɥe] *vt* (*fonctionnaire etc*) to dismiss (from office). ◆**destitution** *nf* dismissal.

destructeur, -trice [dɛstryktœr, -tris] *a* destructive; **– *nmf** (*personne*) destroyer. ◆**destructif, -ive** *a* destructive. ◆**destruction** *nf* destruction.

désuet, -ète [desɥɛ, -ɛt] *a* antiquated, obsolete.

désunir [dezynir] *vt* (*famille etc*) to divide, disunite. ◆**désunion** *nf* disunity, dissension.

détach/er[1] [detaʃe] *vt* (*ceinture, vêtement*) to undo; (*nœud*) to untie, undo; (*personne, mains*) to untie; (*ôter*) to take off, detach; (*mots*) to pronounce clearly; **d. qn** (*libérer*) to let s.o. loose; (*affecter*) to transfer s.o. (on assignment) (**à** to); **d. les yeux de qn/qch** to take one's eyes off s.o./sth; **— se d.** *vpr* (*chien, prisonnier*) to break loose; (*se dénouer*) to come undone; **se d. (de qch)** (*fragment*) to come off (sth); **se d. de** (*amis*) to break away from, grow apart from; **se d. (sur)** (*ressortir*) to stand out (against). ◆**—é** *a* **1** (*nœud*) loose, undone. **2** (*air, ton etc*) detached. ◆**—ement** *nm* **1** (*indifférence*) detachment. **2** (*de fonctionnaire*) (temporary) transfer; *Mil* detachment.

détach/er[2] [detaʃe] *vt* (*linge etc*) to remove the spots *ou* stains from. ◆**—ant** *nm* stain remover.

détail [detaj] *nm* **1** detail; **en d.** in detail; **le d. de** (*dépenses etc*) a detailing *ou* breakdown of. **2 de d.** (*magasin, prix*) retail; **vendre au d.** to sell retail; (*par petites quantités*) to sell separately; **faire le d.** to retail to the public. ◆**détaill/er** *vt* **1** (*vendre*) to sell in small quantities *ou* separately; (*au détail*) to (sell) retail. **2** (*énumérer*) to detail. ◆**—ant, -ante** *nmf* retailer. ◆**—é** *a* (*récit etc*) detailed.

détaler [detale] *vi Fam* to run off, make tracks.

détartrer [detartre] *vt* (*chaudière, dents etc*) to scale.

détaxer [detakse] *vt* (*denrée etc*) to reduce the tax on; (*supprimer*) to take the tax off; **produit détaxé** duty-free article.

détecter [detɛkte] *vt* to detect. ◆**détecteur** *nm* (*appareil*) detector. ◆**détection** *nf* detection.

détective [detɛktiv] *nm* **d. (privé)** (private) detective.

déteindre* [detɛ̃dr] *vi* (*couleur ou étoffe au lavage*) to run; (*au soleil*) to fade; **ton**

tablier bleu a déteint sur ma chemise the blue of your apron has come on(to) my shirt; **d. sur qn** (*influencer*) to leave one's mark on s.o.

dételer [detle] *vt* (*chevaux*) to unhitch, unharness.

détend/re [detɑ̃dr] *vt* (*arc etc*) to slacken, relax; (*situation, atmosphère*) to ease; **d. qn** to relax s.o.; **— se d.** *vpr* to slacken, get slack; to ease; (*se reposer*) to relax; (*rapports*) to become less strained. **◆—u** *a* (*visage, atmosphère*) relaxed; (*ressort, câble*) slack. **◆détente** *nf* **1** (*d'arc*) slackening; (*de relations*) easing of tension, *Pol* détente; (*repos*) relaxation; (*saut*) leap, spring. **2** (*gâchette*) trigger.

déten/ir* [detnir] *vt* to hold; (*secret, objet volé*) to be in possession of; (*prisonnier*) to hold, detain. **◆—u, -ue** *nmf* prisoner. **◆détenteur, -trice** *nmf* (*de record etc*) holder. **◆détention** *nf* (*d'armes*) possession; (*captivité*) detention; **d. préventive** *Jur* custody.

détergent [detɛrʒɑ̃] *nm* detergent.

détériorer [deterjɔre] *vt* (*abîmer*) to damage; **— se d.** *vpr* (*empirer*) to deteriorate. **◆détérioration** *nf* damage (**de** to); (*d'une situation etc*) deterioration (**de** in).

détermin/er [detɛrmine] *vt* (*préciser*) to determine; (*causer*) to bring about; **d. qn à faire** to induce s.o. to do, make s.o. do; **se d. à faire** to resolve *ou* determine to do. **◆—ant** *a* (*motif*) determining, deciding; (*rôle*) decisive. **◆—é** *a* (*précis*) specific; (*résolu*) determined. **◆détermination** *nf* (*fermeté*) determination; (*résolution*) resolve.

déterrer [detere] *vt* to dig up, unearth.

détest/er [detɛste] *vt* to hate, detest; **d. faire** to hate doing *ou* to do, detest doing. **◆—able** *a* awful, foul.

détonateur [detɔnatœr] *nm* detonator. **◆détonation** *nf* explosion, blast.

détonner [detɔne] *vi* (*contraster*) to jar, be out of place.

détour [detur] *nm* (*de route etc*) bend, curve; (*crochet*) detour; **sans d.** (*parler*) without beating about the bush; **faire des détours** (*route*) to wind.

détourn/er [deturne] *vt* (*fleuve, convoi etc*) to divert; (*tête*) to turn (away); (*coups*) to ward off; (*conversation, sens*) to change; (*fonds*) to embezzle, misappropriate; (*avion*) to hijack; **d. qn de** (*son devoir, ses amis*) to take *ou* turn s.o. away from; (*sa route*) to lead s.o. away from; (*projet*) to talk s.o. out of; **d. les yeux** to look away,

avert one's eyes; **— se d.** *vpr* to turn aside *ou* away; **se d. de** (*chemin*) to wander *ou* stray from. **◆—é** *a* (*chemin, moyen*) roundabout, indirect. **◆—ement** *nm* (*de cours d'eau*) diversion; **d.** (*d'avion*) hijack(ing); **d.** (*de fonds*) embezzlement.

détraqu/er [detrake] *vt* (*mécanisme*) to break, put out of order; **— se d.** *vpr* (*machine*) to go wrong; **se d. l'estomac** to upset one's stomach; **se d. la santé** to ruin one's health. **◆—é, -ée** *a* out of order; (*cerveau*) deranged; **–** *nmf* crazy *ou* deranged person.

détremper [detrɑ̃pe] *vt* to soak, saturate.

détresse [detrɛs] *nf* distress; **en d.** (*navire, âme*) in distress; **dans la d.** (*misère*) in (great) distress.

détriment de (au) [odetrimɑ̃də] *prép* to the detriment of.

détritus [detritys] *nmpl* refuse, rubbish.

détroit [detrwa] *nm* *Géog* strait(s), sound.

détromper [detrɔ̃pe] *vt* **d. qn** to undeceive s.o., put s.o. right; **détrompez-vous!** don't you believe it!

détrôner [detrone] *vt* (*souverain*) to dethrone; (*supplanter*) to supersede, oust.

détrousser [detruse] *vt* (*voyageur etc*) to rob.

détruire* [detrɥir] *vt* (*ravager, tuer*) to destroy; (*projet, santé*) to ruin, wreck, destroy.

dette [dɛt] *nf* debt; **faire des dettes** to run *ou* get into debt; **avoir des dettes** to be in debt.

deuil [dœj] *nm* (*affliction, vêtements*) mourning; (*mort de qn*) bereavement; **porter le d., être en d.** to be in mourning.

deux [dø] *a & nm* two; **d. fois** twice, two times; **tous (les) d.** both; **en moins de d.** *Fam* in no time. **◆d.-pièces** *nm inv* (*vêtement*) two-piece; (*appartement*) two-roomed flat *ou Am* apartment. **◆d.-points** *nm inv* *Gram* colon. **◆d.-roues** *nm inv* two-wheeled vehicle. **◆d.-temps** *nm inv* two-stroke (engine).

deuxième [døzjɛm] *a & nmf* second. **◆—ment** *adv* secondly.

dévaler [devale] *vt* (*escalier etc*) to hurtle *ou* race *ou* rush down; **– vi** (*tomber*) to tumble down, come tumbling down.

dévaliser [devalize] *vt* (*détrousser*) to clean out, strip, rob (of everything).

dévaloriser [devalɔrize] **1** *vt*, **— se d.** *vpr* (*monnaie*) to depreciate. **2** *vt* (*humilier etc*) to devalue, disparage. **◆dévalorisation** *nf* (*de monnaie*) depreciation.

dévaluer [devalɥe] *vt* (*monnaie*) & *Fig* to devalue. **◆dévaluation** *nf* devaluation.

devancer [d(ə)vãse] *vt* to get *ou* be ahead of; *(question etc)* to anticipate, forestall; *(surpasser)* to outstrip; **tu m'as devancé** *(action)* you did it before me; *(lieu)* you got there before me. ◆**devancier, -ière** *nmf* predecessor.

devant [d(ə)vã] *prép & adv* in front (of); **d. (l'hôtel/etc)** in front (of the hotel/etc); **marcher d. (qn)** to walk in front (of s.o.) *ou* ahead (of s.o.); **passer d. (l'église/etc)** to go past (the church/etc); **assis d.** *(dans une voiture)* sitting in the front; **l'avenir est d. toi** the future is ahead of you; **loin d.** a long way ahead *ou* in front; **d. le danger** *(confronté à)* in the face of danger; **d. mes yeux/la loi** before my eyes/the law; **—** front; **de d.** *(roue, porte)* front; **patte de d.** foreleg; **par d.** from *ou* at the front; **prendre les devants** *(action)* to take the initiative. ◆**devanture** *nf* *(vitrine)* shop window; *(façade)* shop front.

dévaster [devaste] *vt* *(ruiner)* to devastate. ◆**dévastation** *nf* devastation.

déveine [deven] *nf Fam* tough *ou* bad luck.

développ/er [devlɔpe] *vt* to develop; *Phot* to develop, process; **— se d.** *vpr* to develop. ◆**—ement** *nm* development; *Phot* developing, processing; **les pays en voie de d.** the developing countries.

devenir* [dəvnir] *vi (aux être)* to become; *(vieux, difficile etc)* to get, grow, become; *(rouge, bleu etc)* to turn, go, become; **d. un papillon/un homme/etc** to grow into a butterfly/a man/etc; **qu'est-il devenu?** what's become of him *ou* it?, where's he *ou* it got to?; **qu'est-ce que tu deviens?** *Fam* how are you doing?

dévergond/er (se) [sədevergɔ̃de] *vpr* to fall into dissolute ways. ◆**—é** *a* dissolute, licentious.

déverser [deverse] *vt* *(liquide, rancune)* to pour out; *(bombes, ordures)* to dump; **— se d.** *vpr* *(liquide)* to empty, pour out (**dans** into).

dévêtir [devetir] *vt,* **— se d.** *vpr Litt* to undress.

dévier [devje] *vt (circulation, conversation)* to divert; *(coup, rayons)* to deflect; **— vi** *(de ses principes etc)* to deviate (**de** from); *(de sa route)* to veer (off course). ◆**déviation** *nf* deflection; deviation; *(chemin)* bypass; *(itinéraire provisoire)* diversion.

deviner [d(ə)vine] *vt* to guess (**que** that); *(avenir)* to predict; **d. (le jeu de) qn** to see through s.o. ◆**devinette** *nf* riddle.

devis [d(ə)vi] *nm* estimate *(of cost of work to be done)*.

dévisager [deviʒaʒe] *vt* **d. qn** to stare at s.o.

devise [d(ə)viz] *nf* *(légende)* motto; *pl* *(monnaie)* (foreign) currency.

dévisser [devise] *vt* to unscrew, undo; **— se d.** *vpr (bouchon etc)* to come undone.

dévoiler [devwale] *vt* *(révéler)* to disclose; *(statue)* to unveil; **— se d.** *vpr (mystère)* to come to light.

devoir*[1] [d(ə)vwar] *v aux* **1** *(nécessité)* **je dois refuser** I must refuse, I have (got) to refuse; **j'ai dû refuser** I had to refuse. **2** *(forte probabilité)* **il doit être tard** it must be late; **elle a dû oublier** she must have forgotten; **il ne doit pas être bête** he can't be stupid. **3** *(obligation)* **tu dois l'aider** you should help her, you ought to help her; **il aurait dû venir** he should have come, he ought to have come; **vous devriez rester** you should stay, you ought to stay. **4** *(supposition)* **elle doit venir** she should be coming, she's supposed to be coming, she's due to come; **le train devait arriver à midi** the train was due (to arrive) at noon; **je devais le voir** I was (due) to see him.

devoir*[2] [d(ə)vwar] **1** *vt* to owe; **d. qch à qn** to owe s.o. sth, owe sth to s.o.; **l'argent qui m'est dû** the money due to *ou* owing to me, the money owed (to); **se d. à** to have to devote oneself to; **comme il se doit** as is proper. **2** *nm* duty; *Scol* exercise; **devoir(s)** *(travail à faire à la maison) Scol* homework; **présenter ses devoirs à qn** to pay one's respects to s.o.

dévolu [devɔly] **1** *a* **d. à qn** *(pouvoirs, tâche)* vested in s.o., allotted to s.o. **2** *nm* **jeter son d. sur** to set one's heart on.

dévor/er [devɔre] *vt (manger)* to gobble up, devour; *(incendie)* to engulf, devour; *(tourmenter, lire)* to devour. ◆**—ant** *a* *(faim)* ravenous; *(passion)* devouring.

dévot, -ote [devo, -ɔt] *a & nmf* devout *ou* pious (person). ◆**dévotion** *nf* devotion.

dévou/er (se) [sədevwe] *vpr* *(à une tâche)* to dedicate oneself, devote oneself (**à** to); **se d. (pour qn)** *(se sacrifier)* to sacrifice oneself (for s.o.). ◆**—é** *a* *(ami, femme etc)* devoted (**à qn** to s.o.); *(domestique, soldat etc)* dedicated. ◆**—ement** [-umã] *nm* devotion, dedication; *(de héros)* devotion to duty.

dévoyé, -ée [devwaje] *a & nmf* delinquent.

dextérité [dɛksterite] *nf* dexterity, skill.

diabète [djabɛt] *nm* *Méd* diabetes. ◆**diabétique** *a & nmf* diabetic.

diable [djɑbl] *nm* devil; **d.!** heavens!; **où/pourquoi/que d.?** where/why/what the devil?; **un bruit/vent/etc du d.** the devil of a noise/wind/*etc*; **à la d.** anyhow; **habiter au d.** to live miles from anywhere. ◆**diablerie** *nf* devilment, mischief. ◆**diablesse** *nf* c'est une d. *Fam* she's a devil. ◆**diablotin** *nm* (*enfant*) little devil. ◆**diabolique** *a* diabolical, devilish.

diabolo [djabɔlo] *nm* (*boisson*) lemonade *ou* *Am* lemon soda flavoured with syrup.

diacre [djakr] *nm Rel* deacon.

diadème [djadɛm] *nm* diadem.

diagnostic [djagnɔstik] *nm* diagnosis. ◆**diagnostiquer** *vt* to diagnose.

diagonal, -aux [djagɔnal, -o] *a* diagonal. ◆**diagonale** *nf* diagonal (line); **en d.** diagonally.

diagramme [djagram] *nm* (*schéma*) diagram; (*courbe*) graph.

dialecte [djalɛkt] *nm* dialect.

dialogue [djalɔg] *nm* conversation; *Pol Cin Th Littér* dialogue. ◆**dialoguer** *vi* to have a conversation *ou* dialogue.

dialyse [djaliz] *nf Méd* dialysis.

diamant [djamɑ̃] *nm* diamond.

diamètre [djamɛtr] *nm* diameter. ◆**diamétralement** *adv* **d. opposés** (*avis etc*) diametrically opposed, poles apart.

diapason [djapazɔ̃] *nm Mus* tuning fork; **être/se mettre au d. de** *Fig* to be/get in tune with.

diaphragme [djafragm] *nm* diaphragm.

diapositive, *Fam* **diapo** [djapozitiv, djapo] *nf* (colour) slide, transparency.

diarrhée [djare] *nf* diarrh(o)ea.

diatribe [djatrib] *nf* diatribe.

dictateur [diktatœr] *nm* dictator. ◆**dictatorial, -aux** *a* dictatorial. ◆**dictature** *nf* dictatorship.

dict/er [dikte] *vt* to dictate (à to). ◆**—ée** *nf* dictation. ◆**dictaphone**® *nm* dictaphone®.

diction [diksjɔ̃] *nf* diction, elocution.

dictionnaire [diksjɔnɛr] *nm* dictionary.

dicton [diktɔ̃] *nm* saying, adage, dictum.

didactique [didaktik] *a* didactic.

dièse [djɛz] *a & nm Mus* sharp.

diesel [djezɛl] *a & nm* (**moteur**) **d.** diesel (engine).

diète [djɛt] *nf* (*jeûne*) starvation diet; **à la d.** on a starvation diet. ◆**diététicien, -ienne** *nmf* dietician. ◆**diététique** *nf* dietetics; – *a* (*magasin etc*) health-; **aliment** *ou* **produit d.** health food.

dieu, -x [djø] *nm* god; **D.** God; **D. merci!** thank God!, thank goodness!

diffamer [difame] *vt* (*en paroles*) to slander; (*par écrit*) to libel. ◆**diffamation** *nf* defamation; (*en paroles*) slander; (*par écrit*)

libel; **campagne de d.** smear campaign. ◆**diffamatoire** *a* slanderous; libellous.

différent [diferɑ̃] *a* different; *pl* (*divers*) different, various; **d. de** different from *ou* to, unlike. ◆**différemment** [-amɑ̃] *adv* differently (**de** from, to). ◆**différence** *nf* difference (**de** in); **à la d. de** unlike; **faire la d. entre** to make a distinction between.

différencier [diferɑ̃sje] *vt* to differentiate (**de** from); **— se d.** *vpr* to differ (**de** from).

différend [diferɑ̃] *nm* difference (of opinion).

différentiel, -ielle [diferɑ̃sjɛl] *a* differential.

différ/er [difere] **1** *vi* to differ (**de** from). **2** *vt* (*remettre*) to postpone, defer. ◆**—é** *nm* **en d.** (*émission*) (pre)recorded.

difficile [difisil] *a* difficult; (*exigeant*) fussy, particular, hard *ou* difficult to please; **c'est d. à faire** it's hard *ou* difficult to do; **il (nous) est d. de faire** ça it's hard *ou* difficult (for us) to do that. ◆**—ment** *adv* with difficulty; **d. lisible** not easily read. ◆**difficulté** *nf* difficulty (**à faire** in doing); **en d.** in a difficult situation.

difforme [difɔrm] *a* deformed, misshapen. ◆**difformité** *nf* deformity.

diffus [dify] *a* (*lumière, style*) diffuse.

diffuser [difyze] *vt* (*émission, nouvelle etc*) to broadcast; (*lumière, chaleur*) *Phys* to diffuse; (*livre*) to distribute. ◆**diffusion** *nf* broadcasting; (*de connaissances*) & *Phys* diffusion; (*de livre*) distribution.

digérer [diʒere] *vt* to digest; (*endurer*) *Fam* to stomach; – *vi* to digest. ◆**digeste** *a,* ◆**digestible** *a* digestible. ◆**digestif, -ive** *a* digestive; – *nm* after-dinner liqueur. ◆**digestion** *nf* digestion.

digitale [diʒital] *af* **empreinte d.** fingerprint.

digne [din] *a* (*fier*) dignified; (*honnête*) worthy; **d. de qn** worthy of s.o.; **d. d'admiration/etc** worthy of *ou* deserving of admiration/*etc*; **d. de foi** reliable. ◆**dignement** *adv* with dignity. ◆**dignitaire** *nm* dignitary. ◆**dignité** *nf* dignity.

digression [digresjɔ̃] *nf* digression.

digue [dig] *nf* dyke, dike.

dilapider [dilapide] *vt* to squander, waste.

dilater [dilate] *vt,* **— se d.** *vpr* to dilate, expand. ◆**dilatation** *nf* dilation, expansion.

dilatoire [dilatwar] *a* **manœuvre** *ou* **moyen d.** delaying tactic.

dilemme [dilɛm] *nm* dilemma.

dilettante [diletɑ̃t] *nmf Péj* dabbler, amateur.

diligent [diliʒɑ̃] *a* (*prompt*) speedy and efficient; (*soin*) diligent. ◆**diligence** *nf* 1 (*célérité*) speedy efficiency; **faire d.** to make haste. 2 (*véhicule*) *Hist* stagecoach.

diluer [dilɥe] *vt* to dilute. ◆**dilution** *nf* dilution.

diluvienne [dilyvjɛn] *af* **pluie d.** torrential rain.

dimanche [dimɑ̃ʃ] *nm* Sunday.

dimension [dimɑ̃sjɔ̃] *nf* dimension; **à deux dimensions** two-dimensional.

diminuer [diminɥe] *vt* to reduce, decrease; (*frais*) to cut down (on), reduce; (*mérite*, *forces*) to diminish, lessen, reduce; **d. qn** (*rabaisser*) to diminish s.o., lessen s.o.; − *vi* (*réserves*, *nombre*) to decrease, diminish; (*jours*) to get shorter, draw in; (*prix*) to drop, decrease. ◆**diminutif, -ive** *a* & *nm Gram* diminutive; − *nm* (*prénom*) nickname. ◆**diminution** *nf* reduction, decrease (**de** in).

dinde [dɛ̃d] *nf* turkey (hen), *Culin* turkey. ◆**dindon** *nm* turkey (cock).

dîner [dine] *vi* to have dinner, dine; (*au Canada, en Belgique etc*) to (have) lunch; − *nm* dinner; lunch; (*soirée*) dinner party. ◆**dînette** *nf* (*jouet*) doll's dinner service; (*jeu*) doll's dinner party. ◆**dîneur, -euse** *nmf* diner.

dingue [dɛ̃g] *a Fam* nuts, screwy, crazy; − *nmf Fam* nutcase.

dinosaure [dinozɔr] *nm* dinosaur.

diocèse [djɔsɛz] *nm Rel* diocese.

diphtérie [difteri] *nf* diphtheria.

diphtongue [diftɔ̃g] *nf Ling* diphthong.

diplomate [diplɔmat] *nm Pol* diplomat; − *nmf* (*négociateur*) diplomatist; − *a* (*habile*, *plein de tact*) diplomatic. ◆**diplomatie** [-asi] *nf* (*tact*) & *Pol* diplomacy; (*carrière*) diplomatic service. ◆**diplomatique** *a Pol* diplomatic.

diplôme [diplom] *nm* certificate, diploma; *Univ* degree. ◆**diplômé, -ée** *a* & *nmf* qualified (person); **être d. (de)** *Univ* to be a graduate (of).

dire* [dir] *vt* (*mot, avis etc*) to say; (*vérité*, *secret, heure etc*) to tell; (*penser*) to think (**de** of, about); **d. des bêtises** to talk nonsense; **elle dit que tu mens** she says (that) you're lying; **d. qch à qn** to tell s.o. sth, say sth to s.o.; **d. à qn que** to tell s.o. that, say to s.o. that; **d. à qn de faire** to tell s.o. to do; **dit-il** he said; **dit-on** they say; **d. que oui/non** to say yes/no; **d. du mal/du bien de** to speak ill/well of; **on dirait un château** it looks like a castle; **on dirait du Mozart** it sounds like Mozart; **on dirait du cabillaud** it tastes like cod; **on dirait que it**

would seem that; **ça ne me dit rien** (*envie*) I don't feel like *ou* fancy that; (*souvenir*) it doesn't ring a bell; **ça vous dit de rester?** do you feel like staying?; **dites donc!** I say!; **ça va sans d.** that goes without saying; **autrement dit** in other words; **c'est beaucoup d.** that's going too far; **à l'heure dite** at the agreed time; **à vrai d.** to tell the truth; **il se dit malade**/*etc* he says he's ill/*etc*; **ça ne se dit pas** that's not said; − *nm* **au d. de** according to; **les dires de** (*déclarations*) the statements of.

direct [dirɛkt] *a* direct; (*chemin*) straight, direct; (*manière*) straightforward, direct; **train d.** through train, non-stop train; − *nm* **en d.** (*émission*) live; **un d. du gauche** *Boxe* a straight left. ◆**-ement** *adv* directly; (*immédiatement*) straight (away), directly.

directeur, -trice [dirɛktœr, -tris] *nmf* director; (*d'entreprise*) manager(ess), director; (*de journal*) editor; *Scol* headmaster, headmistress; − *a* (*principe*) guiding; **idées** *ou* **lignes directrices** guidelines.

direction [dirɛksjɔ̃] *nf* 1 (*de société*) running, management; (*de club*) leadership, running; (*d'études*) supervision; (*mécanisme*) *Aut* steering; **avoir la d. de** to be in charge of; **sous la d. de** (*orchestre*) conducted by; **la d.** (*équipe dirigeante*) the management; **une d.** (*fonction*) *Com* a directorship; *Scol* a headmastership; *Journ* an editorship. 2 (*sens*) direction; **en d. de** (*train*) (going) to, for.

directive [dirɛktiv] *nf* directive, instruction.

dirig/er [diriʒe] *vt* (*société*) to run, manage, direct; (*débat, cheval*) to lead; (*véhicule*) to steer; (*orchestre*) to conduct; (*études*) to supervise, direct; (*conscience*) to guide; (*orienter*) to turn (**vers** towards); (*arme*, *lumière*) to point, direct (**vers** towards); **se d. vers** (*lieu, objet*) to make one's way towards, head *ou* make for; (*dans une carrière*) to turn towards. ◆**-eant** *a* (*classe*) ruling; − *nm* (*de pays, club*) leader; (*d'entreprise*) manager. ◆**-é** *a* (*économie*) planned. ◆**-eable** *a* & *nm* (**ballon**) **d.** airship. ◆**dirigisme** *nm Écon* state control.

dis [di] *voir* **dire**.

discern/er [disɛrne] *vt* (*voir*) to make out, discern; (*différencier*) to distinguish. ◆**-ement** *nm* discernment, discrimination.

disciple [disipl] *nm* disciple, follower.

discipline [disiplin] *nf* (*règle, matière*) discipline. ◆**disciplinaire** *a* disciplinary. ◆**disciplin/er** *vt* (*contrôler, éduquer*) to discipline; **— se d.** *vpr* to discipline oneself. **◆—é** *a* well-disciplined.

disco [disko] *nf Fam* disco; **aller en d.** to go to a disco.

discontinu [diskɔ̃tiny] *a* (*ligne*) discontinuous; (*bruit etc*) intermittent. **◆discontinuer** *vi* **sans d.** without stopping.

disconvenir [diskɔ̃vnir] *vi* **je n'en disconviens pas** I don't deny it.

discorde [diskɔrd] *nf* discord. **◆discordance** *nf* (*de caractères*) clash, conflict; (*de son*) discord. **◆discordant** *a* (*son*) discordant; (*témoignages*) conflicting; (*couleurs*) clashing.

discothèque [diskɔtɛk] *nf* record library; (*club*) discotheque.

discours [diskur] *nm* speech; (*écrit littéraire*) discourse. **◆discourir** *vi Péj* to speechify, ramble on.

discourtois [diskurtwa] *a* discourteous.

discrédit [diskredi] *nm* disrepute, discredit. **◆discréditer** *vt* to discredit, bring into disrepute; **— se d.** *vpr* (*personne*) to become discredited.

discret, -ète [diskrɛ, -ɛt] *a* (*personne, manière etc*) discreet; (*vêtement*) simple. **◆discrètement** *adv* discreetly; (*s'habiller*) simply. **◆discrétion** *nf* discretion; **vin/etc à d.** as much wine/etc as one wants. **◆discrétionnaire** *a* discretionary.

discrimination [diskriminasjɔ̃] *nf* (*ségrégation*) discrimination. **◆discriminatoire** *a* discriminatory.

disculper [diskylpe] *vt* to exonerate (**de** from).

discussion [diskysjɔ̃] *nf* discussion; (*conversation*) talk; (*querelle*) argument; **pas de d.!** no argument! **◆discut/er** *vt* to discuss; (*familièrement*) to talk over; (*contester*) to question; **ça peut se d., ça se discute** that's arguable; **— vi** (*parler*) to talk (**de** about, **avec** with); (*répliquer*) to argue; **d. de** *ou* **sur qch** to discuss sth. **◆—é** *a* (*auteur*) much discussed *ou* debated; (*théorie, question*) disputed, controversial. **◆—able** *a* arguable, debatable.

disette [dizɛt] *nf* food shortage.

diseuse [dizœz] *nf* **d. de bonne aventure** fortune-teller.

disgrâce [disgras] *nf* disgrace, disfavour. **◆disgracier** *vt* to disgrace.

disgracieux, -euse [disgrasjø, -øz] *a* ungainly.

disjoindre [disʒwɛ̃dr] *vt* (*questions*) to treat separately. **◆disjoint** *a* (*questions*) unconnected, separate. **◆disjoncteur** *nm* *Él* circuit breaker.

disloquer [disbke] *vt* (*membre*) to dislocate; (*meuble, machine*) to break; **— se d.** *vpr* (*cortège*) to break up; (*meuble etc*) to fall apart; **se d. le bras** to dislocate one's arm. **◆dislocation** *nf* (*de membre*) dislocation.

dispar/aître* [disparɛtr] *vi* to disappear; (*être porté manquant*) to be missing; (*mourir*) to die; **d. en mer** to be lost at sea; **faire d.** to remove, get rid of. **◆—u, -ue** *a* (*soldat etc*) missing, lost; **— nmf** (*absent*) missing person; (*mort*) departed; **être porté d.** to be reported missing. **◆disparition** *nf* disappearance; (*mort*) death.

disparate [disparat] *a* ill-assorted.

disparité [disparite] *nf* disparity (**entre, de** between).

dispendieux, -euse [dispɑ̃djø, -øz] *a* expensive, costly.

dispensaire [dispɑ̃sɛr] *nm* community health centre.

dispense [dispɑ̃s] *nf* exemption; **d. d'âge** waiving of the age limit. **◆dispenser** *vt* (*soins, bienfaits etc*) to dispense; **d. qn de** (*obligation*) to exempt *ou* excuse s.o. from; **je vous dispense de** (*vos réflexions etc*) I can dispense with; **se d. de faire** to spare oneself the bother of doing.

disperser [disperse] *vt* to disperse, scatter; (*efforts*) to dissipate; **— se d.** *vpr* (*foule*) to disperse; **elle se disperse trop** she tries to do too many things at once. **◆dispersion** *nf* (*d'une armée etc*) dispersal, dispersion.

disponible [disponibl] *a* available; (*place*) spare, available; (*esprit*) alert. **◆disponibilité** *nf* availability; *pl Fin* available funds.

dispos [dispo] *a* fit, in fine fettle; **frais et d.** refreshed.

dispos/er [dispoze] *vt* to arrange; (*troupes*) *Mil* to dispose; **d. qn à** (*la bonne humeur etc*) to dispose *ou* incline s.o. towards; **se d. à faire** to prepare to do; **— vi d. de qch** to have sth at one's disposal; (*utiliser*) to make use of sth; **d. de qn** *Péj* to take advantage of s.o., abuse s.o. **◆—é** *a* **bien/mal d.** in a good/bad mood; **bien d. envers** well-disposed towards; **d. à faire** prepared *ou* disposed to do. **◆disposition** *nf* arrangement; (*de troupes*) disposition; (*de maison, page*) layout; (*humeur*) frame of mind; (*tendance*) tendency, (pre)disposition (**à** to); (*clause*) *Jur* provision; *pl* (*aptitudes*) ability, aptitude (**pour** for); **à la d. de qn** at s.o.'s disposal; **prendre ses** *ou* **des dispositions** (*préparatifs*) to make arrangements, prepare; (*pour l'avenir*) to

make provision; **dans de bonnes disposi-tions à l'égard de** well-disposed towards.
dispositif [dıspozitif] *nm* (*mécanisme*) device; **d. de défense** *Mil* defence system; **d. antiparasite** *Él* suppressor.
disproportion [disprɔpɔrsjɔ̃] *nf* dispropor-tion. ◆**disproportionné** *a* disproportion-ate.
dispute [dispyt] *nf* quarrel. ◆**disputer** *vt* (*match*) to play; (*terrain, droit etc*) to contest, dispute; (*rallye*) to compete in; **d. qch à qn** (*prix, première place etc*) to fight with s.o. for *ou* over sth, contend with s.o. for sth; **d. qn** (*gronder*) *Fam* to tell s.o. off; **— se d.** *vpr* to quarrel (**avec** with); (*match*) to take place; **se d. qch** to fight over sth.
disqualifier [diskalifje] *vt Sp* to disqualify; **— se d.** *vpr Fig* to become discredited. ◆**disqualification** *nf Sp* disqualification.
disque [disk] *nm Mus* record; *Sp* discus; (*cercle*) disc, *Am* disk; (*pour ordinateur*) disk. ◆**disquaire** *nmf* record dealer. ◆**disquette** *nf* (*pour ordinateur*) floppy disk.
dissection [diseksjɔ̃] *nf* dissection.
dissemblable [disɑ̃mblabl] *a* dissimilar (**à** to).
disséminer [disemine] *vt* (*graines, mines etc*) to scatter; (*idées*) *Fig* to disseminate. ◆**dissémination** *nf* scattering; (*d'idées*) *Fig* dissemination.
dissension [disɑ̃sjɔ̃] *nf* dissension.
disséquer [diseke] *vt* to dissect.
disserter [diserte] *vi* **d. sur** to comment upon, discuss. ◆**dissertation** *nf Scol* essay.
dissident, -ente [disidɑ̃, -ɑ̃t] *a & nmf* dissi-dent. ◆**dissidence** *nf* dissidence.
dissimuler [disimyle] *vt* (*cacher*) to conceal, hide (**à** from); **–** *vi* (*feindre*) to pretend; **— se d.** *vpr* to hide, conceal oneself. ◆**—é** *a* (*enfant*) *Péj* secretive. ◆**dissimulation** *nf* concealment; (*dupli-cité*) deceit.
dissiper [disipe] *vt* (*brouillard, craintes*) to dispel; (*fortune*) to squander, dissipate; **d. qn** to lead s.o. astray, distract s.o.; **— se d.** *vpr* (*brume*) to clear, lift; (*craintes*) to disappear; (*élève*) to misbehave. ◆**—é** *a* (*élève*) unruly; (*vie*) dissipated. ◆**dissipa-tion** *nf* (*de brouillard*) clearing; (*indi-cipline*) misbehaviour; (*débauche*) *Litt* dissipation.
dissocier [disɔsje] *vt* to dissociate (**de** from).
dissolu [disɔly] *a* (*vie etc*) dissolute.
dissoudre* [disudr] *vt*, **— se d.** *vpr* to

dissolve. ◆**dissolution** *nf* dissolution. ◆**dissolvant** *a & nm* solvent; (*pour vernis à ongles*) nail polish remover.
dissuader [disɥade] *vt* to dissuade, deter (**de qch** from sth, **de faire** from doing). ◆**dissuasif, -ive** *a* (*effet*) deterrent; **être d.** *Fig* to be a deterrent. ◆**dissuasion** *nf* dissuasion; **force de d.** *Mil* deterrent.
distant [distɑ̃] *a* distant; (*personne*) aloof, distant; **d. de dix kilomètres** (*éloigné*) ten kilometres away; (*à intervalles*) ten kilome-tres apart. ◆**distance** *nf* distance; **à deux mètres de d.** two metres apart; **à d.** at *ou* from a distance; **garder ses distances** to keep one's distance. ◆**distancer** *vt* to leave behind, outstrip.
distendre [distɑ̃dr] *vt*, **— se d.** *vpr* to distend.
distiller [distile] *vt* to distil. ◆**distillation** *nf* distillation. ◆**distillerie** *nf* (*lieu*) distil-lery.
distinct, -incte [distɛ̃, -ɛ̃kt] *a* (*différent*) distinct, separate (**de** from); (*net*) clear, distinct. ◆**distinctement** *adv* distinctly, clearly. ◆**distinctif, -ive** *a* distinctive. ◆**distinction** *nf* (*différence, raffinement*) distinction.
distinguer [distɛ̃ge] *vt* (*différencier*) to distinguish; (*voir*) to make out; (*choisir*) to single out; **d. le blé de l'orge** to tell wheat from barley, distinguish between wheat and barley; **— se d.** *vpr* (*s'illustrer*) to distinguish oneself; **se d. de** (*différer*) to be distinguishable from; **se d. par** (*sa gaieté, beauté etc*) to be conspicuous for. ◆**—é** *a* (*bien élevé, éminent*) distinguished; **senti-ments distingués** (*formule épistolaire*) *Com* yours faithfully.
distorsion [distɔrsjɔ̃] *nf* (*du corps, d'une image etc*) distortion.
distraction [distraksjɔ̃] *nf* amusement, distraction; (*étourderie*) (fit of) absent-mindedness. ◆**distraire*** *vt* (*diver-tir*) to entertain, amuse; (*détourner*) to distract s.o. (from); **— se d.** *vpr* to amuse oneself, enjoy oneself. ◆**dis-trait** *a* absent-minded. ◆**distraitement** *adv* absent-mindedly. ◆**distrayant** *a* entertaining.
distribuer [distribɥe] *vt* (*répartir*) to distribute; (*donner*) to give *ou* hand out, distribute; (*courrier*) to deliver; (*eau*) to supply; (*cartes*) to deal; **bien distribué** (*appartement*) well-arranged. ◆**distri-buteur** *nm Aut Cin* distributor; **d.** (*automa-tique*) vending machine; **d. de billets** *Rail* ticket machine; (*de billets de banque*) cash

dispenser *ou* machine. ◆**distribution** *nf* distribution; (*du courrier*) delivery; (*de l'eau*) supply; (*acteurs*) *Th Cin* cast; **d. des prix** prize giving.

district [distrikt] *nm* district.

dit [di] *voir* **dire**; – *a* (*convenu*) agreed; (*surnommé*) called.

dites [dit] *voir* **dire**.

divaguer [divage] *vi* (*dérailler*) to rave, talk drivel. ◆**divagations** *nfpl* ravings.

divan [divã] *nm* divan, couch.

divergent [divɛrʒã] *a* diverging, divergent. ◆**divergence** *nf* divergence. ◆**diverger** *vi* to diverge (**de** from).

divers, -erses [divɛr, -ɛrs] *apl* (*distincts*) varied, diverse; **d. groupes** (*plusieurs*) various *ou* sundry groups. ◆**diversement** *adv* in various ways. ◆**diversifier** *vt* to diversify; – **se d.** *vpr Écon* to diversify. ◆**diversité** *nf* diversity.

diversion [divɛrsjɔ̃] *nf* diversion.

divert/ir [divɛrtir] *vt* to amuse, entertain; – **se d.** *vpr* to enjoy oneself, amuse oneself. ◆**—issement** *nm* amusement, entertainment.

dividende [dividãd] *nm Math Fin* dividend.

divin [divɛ̃] *a* divine. ◆**divinité** *nf* divinity.

diviser [divize] *vt*, – **se d.** *vpr* to divide (**en** into). ◆**divisible** *a* divisible. ◆**division** *nf* division.

divorce [divɔrs] *nm* divorce. ◆**divorc/er** *vi* to get ou be divorced, divorce; **d. d'avec qn** to divorce s.o. ◆**—é, -ée** *a* divorced (**d'avec** from); – *nmf* divorcee.

divulguer [divylge] *vt* to divulge. ◆**divulgation** *nf* divulgence.

dix [dis] ([di] *before consonant*, [diz] *before vowel*) *a & nm* ten. ◆**dixième** [dizjɛm] *a & nmf* tenth; **un d.** a tenth. ◆**dix-huit** [dizɥit] *a & nm* eighteeen. ◆**dix-huitième** *a & nmf* eighteenth. ◆**dix-neuf** [diznœf] *a & nm* nineteen. ◆**dix-neuvième** *a & nmf* nineteenth. ◆**dix-sept** [disset] *a & nm* seventeen. ◆**dix-septième** *a & nmf* seventeenth.

dizaine [dizɛn] *nf* about ten.

docile [dɔsil] *a* submissive, docile. ◆**docilité** *nf* submissiveness, docility.

dock [dɔk] *nm Nau* dock. ◆**docker** [dɔkɛr] *nm* docker.

docteur [dɔktœr] *nm Méd Univ* doctor (**ès**, **en** of). ◆**doctorat** *nm* doctorate, = PhD (**ès**, **en** in).

doctrine [dɔktrin] *nf* doctrine. ◆**doctrinaire** *a & nmf Péj* doctrinaire.

document [dɔkymã] *nm* document. ◆**documentaire** *a* documentary; – *nm*

(*film*) documentary. ◆**documentaliste** *nmf* information officer.

document/er [dɔkymãte] *vt* (*informer*) to document; – **se d.** *vpr* to collect material *ou* information. ◆**—é** *a* (**bien** *ou* **très**) **d.** (*personne*) well-informed. ◆**documentation** *nf* (*documents*) documentation, *Com* literature; (*renseignements*) information.

dodeliner [dɔdline] *vi* **d. de la tête** to nod (one's head).

dodo [dodo] *nm* (*langage enfantin*) **faire d.** to sleep; **aller au d.** to go to bye-byes.

dodu [dɔdy] *a* chubby, plump.

dogme [dɔgm] *nm* dogma. ◆**dogmatique** *a* dogmatic. ◆**dogmatisme** *nm* dogmatism.

dogue [dɔg] *nm* (*chien*) mastiff.

doigt [dwa] *nm* finger; **d. de pied** toe; **à deux doigts de** within an ace of; **montrer du d.** to point (to); **savoir sur le bout du d.** to have at one's finger tips. ◆**doigté** *nm Mus* fingering, touch; (*savoir-faire*) tact, expertise. ◆**doigtier** *nm* fingerstall.

dois, doit [dwa] *voir* **devoir** [1,2].

doléances [dɔleɑ̃s] *nfpl* (*plaintes*) grievances.

dollar [dɔlar] *nm* dollar.

domaine [dɔmɛn] *nm* (*terres*) estate, domain; (*sphère*) province, domain.

dôme [dom] *nm* dome.

domestique [dɔmɛstik] *a* (*animal*) domestic(ated); (*de la famille*) family-, domestic; (*ménager*) domestic, household; – *nmf* servant. ◆**domestiquer** *vt* to domesticate.

domicile [dɔmisil] *nm* home; *Jur* abode; **travailler à d.** to work at home; **livrer à d.** (*pain etc*) to deliver (to the house). ◆**domicilié** *a* resident (**à, chez** at).

domin/er [dɔmine] *vt* to dominate; (*situation, sentiment*) to master, dominate; (*être supérieur à*) to surpass, outclass; (*tour, rocher*) to tower above, dominate (*valley, building etc*); – *vi* (*être le plus fort*) to be dominant, dominate; (*être le plus important*) to predominate; – **se d.** *vpr* to control oneself. ◆**—ant** *a* dominant. ◆**—ante** *nf* dominant feature; *Mus* dominant. ◆**dominateur, -trice** *a* domineering. ◆**domination** *nf* domination.

dominicain, -aine [dɔminikɛ̃, -ɛn] *a & nmf Rel* Dominican.

dominical, -aux [dɔminikal, -o] *a* (*repos*) Sunday-.

domino [dɔmino] *nm* domino; *pl* (*jeu*) dominoes.

dommage [dɔmaʒ] *nm* **1** (**c'est**) **d.!** it's a

pity *ou* a shame! **(que** that); **quel d.!** what a pity *ou* a shame! **2** *(tort)* prejudice, harm; *pl (dégâts)* damage; **dommages-intérêts** *Jur* damages.

dompt/er [dɔ̃te] *vt (animal)* to tame; *(passions, rebelles)* to subdue. ◆**—eur, -euse** *nmf (de lions)* lion tamer.

don [dɔ̃] *nm (cadeau, aptitude)* gift; *(aumône)* donation; **le d. du sang/etc** (the) giving of blood/*etc*; **faire d. de** to give; **avoir le d. de** *(le chic pour)* to have the knack of. ◆**donateur, -trice** *nmf Jur* donor. ◆**donation** *nf Jur* donation.

donc [dɔ̃(k)] *conj* so, then; *(par conséquent)* so, therefore; **asseyez-vous d.!** *(intensif)* will you sit down!, sit down then!; **qui/quoi d.?** who?/what?; **allons d.!** come on!

donjon [dɔ̃ʒɔ̃] *nm (de château)* keep.

donne [dɔn] *nf Cartes* deal.

donner [dɔne] *vt* to give; *(récolte, résultat)* to produce; *(sa place)* to give up; *(pièce, film)* to put on; *(cartes)* to deal; **d. un coup à** to hit, give a blow to; **d. le bonjour à qn** to say hello to s.o.; **d. à réparer** to take (in) to be repaired; **d. raison à qn** to say s.o. is right; **ça donne soif/faim** it makes you thirsty/hungry; **je lui donne trente ans** I'd say *ou* guess he *ou* she was thirty; **ça n'a rien donné** *(efforts)* it hasn't got us anywhere; **c'est donné** *Fam* it's dirt cheap; **étant donné** *(la situation etc)* considering, in view of; **étant donné que** seeing (that), considering (that); **à un moment donné** at some stage; *– vi* **d. sur** *(fenêtre)* to look out onto, overlook; *(porte)* to open onto; **d. dans** *(piège)* to fall into; **d. de la tête contre** to hit one's head against; *– se d. vpr (se consacrer)* to devote oneself (à to); **se d. du mal** to go to a lot of trouble **(pour faire** to do); **s'en d. à cœur joie** to have a whale of a time, enjoy oneself to the full. ◆**données** *nfpl (information)* data; *(de problème)* (known) facts; *(d'un roman)* basic elements. ◆**donneur, -euse** *nmf* giver; *(de sang, d'organe)* donor; *Cartes* dealer.

dont [dɔ̃] *pron rel (= de qui, duquel, de quoi etc) (personne)* of whom; *(chose)* of which; *(appartenance: personne)* whose, of whom; *(appartenance: chose)* of which, whose; **une mère d. le fils est malade** a mother whose son is ill; **la fille d. il est fier** the daughter he is proud of *ou* of whom he is proud; **les outils d. j'ai besoin** the tools I need; **la façon d. elle joue** the way (in which) she plays; **voici ce d. il s'agit** here's what it's about.

doper [dɔpe] *vt (cheval, sportif)* to dope; *–*

se d. *vpr* to dope oneself. ◆**doping** *nm (action)* doping; *(substance)* dope.

dorénavant [dɔrenavɑ̃] *adv* henceforth.

dor/er [dɔre] *vt (objet)* to gild; **d. la pilule** *Fig* to sugar the pill; **se (faire) d. au soleil** to bask in the sun; *– vi Culin* to brown. ◆**—é** *a (objet)* gilt; *(couleur)* golden; *– nm (couche)* gilt. ◆**dorure** *nf* gilding.

dorloter [dɔrlɔte] *vt* to pamper, coddle.

dormir* [dɔrmir] *vi* to sleep; *(être endormi)* to be asleep; *(argent)* to lie idle; **histoire à d. debout** tall story, cock-and-bull story; **eau dormante** stagnant water. ◆**dortoir** *nm* dormitory.

dos [do] *nm* back; *(de nez)* bridge; *(de livre)* spine; **voir qn de d.** to have a back view of s.o.; **à d. de chameau** (riding) on a camel; **'voir au d.'** *(verso)* 'see over'; **j'en ai plein le d.** *Fam* I'm sick of it; **mettre qch sur le d. de qn** *(accusation)* to pin sth on s.o. ◆**dossard** *nm Sp* number *(fixed on back)*. ◆**dossier** *nm* **1** *(de siège)* back. **2** *(papiers, compte rendu)* file, dossier; *(classeur)* folder, file.

dose [doz] *nf* dose; *(quantité administrée)* dosage. ◆**dos/er** *vt (remède)* to measure out the dose of; *(équilibrer)* to strike the correct balance between. ◆**—age** *nm* measuring out *(of dose)*; *(équilibre)* balance; **faire le d.** **de** = **doser**. ◆**—eur** *nm* **bouchon d.** measuring cap.

dot [dɔt] *nf* dowry.

doter [dɔte] *vt (hôpital etc)* to endow; **d. de** *(matériel)* to equip with; *(qualité)* *Fig* to endow with. ◆**dotation** *nf* endowment; equipping.

douane [dwan] *nf* customs. ◆**douanier, -ière** *nm* customs officer; *– a (union etc)* customs-.

double [dubl] *a* double; *(rôle, avantage etc)* twofold, double; *– adv* double; *– nm (de personne)* double; *(copie)* copy, duplicate; *(de timbre)* swap, duplicate; **le d.** **(de)** *(quantité)* twice as much (as). ◆**doublage** *nm (de film)* dubbing. ◆**doublement** *adv* doubly; *– nm* doubling. ◆**doubler** **1** *vt (augmenter)* to double; *(vêtement)* to line; *(film)* to dub; *(acteur)* to stand in for; *(classe)* *Scol* to repeat; *(cap)* *Nau* to round; **se d. de** to be coupled with; *– vi (augmenter)* to double. **2** *vti Aut* to overtake, pass. ◆**doublure** *nf (étoffe)* lining; *Th* understudy; *Cin* stand-in, double.

douce [dus] *voir* **doux.** ◆**doucement** *adv (délicatement)* gently; *(à voix basse)* softly; *(sans bruit)* quietly; *(lentement)* slowly; *(sans à-coups)* smoothly; *(assez bien)* *Fam* so-so. ◆douceur *nf* (*de miel etc*) sweetness; (*de personne, pente etc*) gentleness; (*de peau etc*) softness; (*de temps*) mildness; *pl* (*sucreries*) sweets, *Am* candies; en d. (*démarrer etc*) smoothly.

douche [duʃ] *nf* shower. ◆doucher *vt* d. qn to give s.o. a shower; — se d. *vpr* to take *ou* have a shower.

doué [dwe] *a* gifted, talented (en at); (*intelligent*) clever; d. de gifted with; il est d. pour he has a gift *ou* talent for.

douille [duj] *nf* (*d'ampoule*) *Él* socket; (*de cartouche*) case.

douillet, -ette [dujɛ, -ɛt] *a* (*lit etc*) soft, cosy, snug; il est d. (*délicat*) *Péj* he's soft.

douleur [dulœr] *nf* (*mal*) pain; (*chagrin*) sorrow, grief. ◆douloureux, -euse *a* (*maladie, membre, décision, perte etc*) painful.

doute [dut] *nm* doubt; *pl* (*méfiance*) doubts, misgivings; sans d. no doubt, probably; sans aucun d. without (any *ou* a) doubt; mettre en d. to cast doubt on; dans le d. uncertain, doubtful; ça ne fait pas de d. there is no doubt about it. ◆douter *vi* to doubt; d. de qch/qn to doubt sth/s.o.; d. que (+ *sub*) to doubt whether *ou* that; se d. de qch to suspect sth; je m'en doute I suspect so, I would think so. ◆douteux, -euse *a* doubtful; (*louche, médiocre*) dubious; il est d. que (+ *sub*) it's doubtful whether *ou* that.

douve(s) [duv] *nf*(*pl*) (*de château*) moat.

Douvres [duvr] *nm ou f* Dover.

doux, douce [du, dus] *a* (*miel, son etc*) sweet; (*personne, pente etc*) gentle; (*peau, lumière, drogue etc*) soft; (*émotion, souvenir etc*) pleasant; (*temps, climat*) mild; en douce on the quiet.

douze [duz] *a & nm* twelve. ◆douzaine *nf* (*douze*) dozen; (*environ*) about twelve; une d. d'œufs/etc a dozen eggs/etc. ◆douzième *a & nmf* twelfth; un d. a twelfth.

doyen, -enne [dwajɛ̃, -ɛn] *nmf Rel Univ* dean; d. (d'âge) oldest person.

draconien, -ienne [drakɔnjɛ̃, -jɛn] *a* (*mesures*) drastic.

dragée [draʒe] *nf* sugared almond; tenir la d. haute à qn (*tenir tête à qn*) to stand up to s.o.

dragon [dragɔ̃] *nm* (*animal*) dragon; *Mil Hist* dragoon.

drague [drag] *nf* (*appareil*) dredge; (*filet*) drag net. ◆draguer *vt* 1 (*rivière etc*) to dredge. 2 *Arg* (*racoler*) to try and pick up;

(*faire du baratin à*) to chat up, *Am* smooth-talk.

drainer [drene] *vt* to drain.

drame [dram] *nm* drama; (*catastrophe*) tragedy. ◆dramatique *a* dramatic; critique d. drama critic; auteur d. playwright, dramatist; film d. drama. ◆dramatiser *vt* (*exagérer*) to dramatize. ◆dramaturge *nmf* dramatist.

drap [dra] *nm* (*de lit*) sheet; (*tissu*) cloth; dans de beaux draps *Fig* in a fine mess.

drapeau, -x [drapo] *nm* flag; être sous les drapeaux *Mil* to be in the services.

draper [drape] *vt* to drape (de with). ◆draperie *nf* (*étoffe*) drapery.

dresser [drese] 1 *vt* (*échelle, statue*) to put up, erect; (*piège*) to lay, set; (*oreille*) to prick up; (*liste*) to draw up, make out; — se d. *vpr* (*personne*) to stand up; (*statue, montagne*) to rise up, stand; se d. contre (*abus*) to stand up against. 2 *vt* (*animal*) to train; (*personne*) *Péj* to drill, teach. ◆dressage *nm* training. ◆dresseur, -euse *nmf* trainer.

dribbler [drible] *vti Fb* to dribble.

drogue [drɔg] *nf* (*médicament*) *Péj* drug; une d. (*stupéfiant*) a drug; la d. drugs, dope. ◆droguer *vt* (*victime*) to drug; (*malade*) to dose up; — se d. *vpr* (*personne*) to take drugs, be on drugs; (*malade*) to dose oneself up. ◆—é, -ée *nmf* drug addict.

droguerie [drɔgri] *nf* hardware shop *ou Am* store. ◆droguiste *nmf* owner of a droguerie.

droit[1] [drwa] *nm* (*privilège*) right; (*d'inscription etc*) fee(s), dues; *pl* (*de douane*) duty; le d. (*science juridique*) law; avoir d. à to be entitled to; avoir le d. de faire to be entitled to do, have the right to do; à bon d. rightly; d. d'entrée entrance fee.

droit[2] [drwa] *a* (*ligne, route etc*) straight; (*personne, mur etc*) upright, straight; (*angle*) right; (*veston*) single-breasted; (*honnête*) *Fig* upright; — *adv* straight; tout d. straight *ou* right ahead. ◆droite[1] *nf* (*ligne*) straight line.

droit[3] [drwa] *a* (*côté, bras etc*) right; — *nm* (*coup*) *Boxe* right. ◆droite[2] *nf* la d. (*côté*) the right (side); *Pol* the right (wing); à d. (*tourner*) to (the) right; (*rouler, se tenir*) on the right(-hand) side; de d. (*fenêtre etc*) right-hand; (*politique, candidat*) right-wing; à d. de on *ou* to the right of; à d. et à gauche (*voyager etc*) here, there and everywhere. ◆droitier, -ière *a & nmf* right-handed (person). ◆droiture *nf* uprightness.

drôle [drol] *a* funny; **d. d'air/de type** funny look/fellow. ◆**—ment** *adv* funnily; (*extrêmement*) *Fam* dreadfully.

dromadaire [drɔmadɛr] *nm* dromedary.

dru [dry] *a* (*herbe etc*) thick, dense; – *adv* **tomber d.** (*pluie*) to pour down heavily; **pousser d.** to grow thick(ly).

du [dy] = **de + le.**

dû, due [dy] *a* **d. à** (*accident etc*) due to; – *nm* due; (*argent*) dues.

dualité [dyalite] *nf* duality.

dubitatif, -ive [dybitatif, -iv] *a* (*regard etc*) dubious.

duc [dyk] *nm* duke. ◆**duché** *nm* duchy. ◆**duchesse** *nf* duchess.

duel [dyɛl] *nm* duel.

dûment [dymɑ̃] *adv* duly.

dune [dyn] *nf* (*sand*) dune.

duo [dyo] *nm Mus* duet; (*couple*) *Hum* duo.

dupe [dyp] *nf* dupe, fool; – *a* **d. de** duped by, fooled by. ◆**duper** *vt* to fool, dupe.

duplex [dyplɛks] *nm* split-level flat, *Am* duplex; (*émission en*) **d.** *Tél* link-up.

duplicata [dyplikata] *nm inv* duplicate.

duplicateur [dyplikatœr] *nm* (*machine*) duplicator.

duplicité [dyplisite] *nf* duplicity, deceit.

dur [dyr] *a* (*substance*) hard; (*difficile*) hard, tough; (*viande*) tough; (*hiver, leçon, ton*) harsh; (*personne*) hard, harsh; (*brosse, carton*) stiff; (*œuf*) hard-boiled; **d. d'oreille** hard of hearing; **d. à cuire** *Fam* hard-bitten, tough; – *adv* (*travailler*) hard; – *nm Fam* tough guy. ◆**dureté** *nf* hardness; harshness; toughness.

durant [dyrɑ̃] *prép* during.

durc/ir [dyrsir] *vti*, – **se d.** *vpr* to harden. ◆**—issement** *nm* hardening.

durée [dyre] *nf* (*de film, événement etc*) length; (*période*) duration; (*de pile*) *Él* life; **de longue d.** (*disque*) long-playing. ◆**dur/er** *vi* to last; **ça dure depuis . . .** it's been going on for . . . . ◆**—able** *a* durable, lasting.

durillon [dyrijɔ̃] *nm* callus.

duvet [dyvɛ] *nm* **1** (*d'oiseau, de visage*) down. **2** (*sac*) sleeping bag. ◆**duveté** *a*, ◆**duveteux, -euse** *a* downy.

dynamique [dinamik] *a* dynamic; – *nf* (*force*) *Fig* dynamic force, thrust. ◆**dynamisme** *nm* dynamism.

dynamite [dinamit] *nf* dynamite. ◆**dynamiter** *vt* to dynamite.

dynamo [dinamo] *nf* dynamo.

dynastie [dinasti] *nf* dynasty.

dysenterie [disɑ̃tri] *nf Méd* dysentery.

dyslexique [dislɛksik] *a* & *nmf* dyslexic.

E

E, e [ə, ø] *nm* E, e.

eau, -x [o] *nf* water; **il est tombé beaucoup d'e.** a lot of rain fell; **e. douce** (*non salée*) fresh water; (*du robinet*) soft water; **e. salée** salt water; **e. de Cologne** eau de Cologne; **e. de toilette** toilet water; **grandes eaux** (*d'un parc*) ornamental fountains; **tomber à l'e.** (*projet*) to fall through; **ça lui fait venir l'e. à la bouche** it makes his *ou* her mouth water; **tout en e.** sweating; **prendre l'e.** (*chaussure*) to take water, leak. ◆**e.-de-vie** *nf* (*pl* eaux-de-vie) brandy. ◆**e.-forte** *nf* (*pl* eaux-fortes) (*gravure*) etching.

ébah/ir [ebair] *vt* to astound, dumbfound, amaze. ◆**—issement** *nm* amazement.

ébattre (s') [sebatr] *vpr* to frolic, frisk about. ◆**ébats** *nmpl* frolics.

ébauche [eboʃ] *nf* (*esquisse*) (rough) outline, (rough) sketch; (*début*) beginnings. ◆**ébaucher** *vt* (*projet, tableau, œuvre*) to sketch out, outline; **e. un sourire** to give a faint smile; – **s'é.** *vpr* to take shape.

ébène [ebɛn] *nf* (*bois*) ebony.

ébéniste [ebenist] *nm* cabinet-maker. ◆**ébénisterie** *nf* cabinet-making.

éberlué [ebɛrlye] *a Fam* dumbfounded.

éblou/ir [ebluir] *vt* to dazzle. ◆**—issement** *nm* (*aveuglement*) dazzling, dazzle; (*émerveillement*) feeling of wonder; (*malaise*) fit of dizziness.

éboueur [ebwœr] *nm* dustman, *Am* garbage collector.

ébouillanter [ebujɑ̃te] *vt* to scald; – **s'é.** *vpr* to scald oneself.

éboul/er (s') [sebule] *vpr* (*falaise etc*) to crumble; (*terre, roches*) to fall. ◆**—ement** *nm* landslide. ◆**éboulis** *nm* (mass of) fallen debris.

ébouriffant [eburifɑ̃] *a Fam* astounding.

ébouriffer [eburife] *vt* (*cheveux*) to dishevel, ruffle, tousle.

ébranl/er [ebrɑ̃le] *vt* (*mur, confiance etc*) to shake; (*santé*) to weaken, affect; (*personne*) to shake, shatter; **— s'é.** *vpr* (*train, cortège etc*) to move off. **◆—ement** *nm* (*secousse*) shaking, shock; (*nerveux*) shock.

ébrécher [ebreʃe] *vt* (*assiette*) to chip; (*lame*) to nick. **◆ébréchure** *nf* chip; nick.

ébriété [ebrijete] *nf* drunkenness.

ébrouer (s') [sebrue] *vpr* (*cheval*) to snort; (*personne*) to shake oneself (about).

ébruiter [ebrɥite] *vt* (*nouvelle etc*) to make known, divulge.

ébullition [ebylisjɔ̃] *nf* boiling; **être en é.** (*eau*) to be boiling; (*ville*) *Fig* to be in turmoil.

écaille [ekɑj] *nf* **1** (*de poisson*) scale; (*de tortue, d'huître*) shell; (*résine synthétique*) tortoise-shell. **2** (*de peinture*) flake. **◆écailler 1** *vt* (*poisson*) to scale; (*huître*) to shell. **2 s'é.** *vpr* (*peinture*) to flake (off), peel.

écarlate [ekarlat] *a & nf* scarlet.

écarquiller [ekarkije] *vt* **é. les yeux** to open one's eyes wide.

écart [ekar] *nm* (*intervalle*) gap, distance; (*mouvement, embardée*) swerve; (*différence*) difference (**de** in, **entre** between); **écarts de** (*conduite, langage etc*) lapses in; **le grand é.** (*de gymnaste*) the splits; **à l'é.** out of the way; **tenir qn à l'é.** *Fig* to keep s.o. out of things; **à l'é. de** away from, clear of. **◆écart/er** *vt* (*objets*) to move away from each other, move apart; (*jambes*) to spread, open; (*rideaux*) to draw (aside), open; (*crainte, idée*) to brush aside, dismiss; (*carte*) to discard; **é. qch de qch** to move sth away from sth; **é. qn de** (*éloigner*) to keep *ou* take s.o. away from; (*exclure*) to keep s.o. out of; **— s'é.** *vpr* (*s'éloigner*) to move away (**de** from); (*se séparer*) to move aside (**de** from); **s'é. de** (*sujet, bonne route*) to stray *ou* deviate from. **◆—é** *a* (*endroit*) remote; **les jambes écartées** with legs (wide) apart. **◆—ement** *nm* (*espace*) gap, distance (**de** between).

écartelé [ekartəle] *a* **é. entre** (*tiraillé*) torn between.

ecchymose [ekimoz] *nf* bruise.

ecclésiastique [eklezjastik] *a* ecclesiastical; *— nm* ecclesiastic, clergyman.

écervelé, -ée [esɛrvəle] *a* scatterbrained; *— nmf* scatterbrain.

échafaud [eʃafo] *nm* (*pour exécution*) scaffold.

échafaudage [eʃafodaʒ] *nm* (*construction*) scaffold(ing); (*tas*) heap; (*système*) *Fig* fabric. **◆échafauder** *vi* to put up scaf-

folding *ou* a scaffold; *— vt* (*projet etc*) to put together, think up.

échalas [eʃala] *nm* **grand é.** tall skinny person.

échalote [eʃalɔt] *nf Bot Culin* shallot, scallion.

échancré [eʃɑ̃kre] *a* (*encolure*) V-shaped, scooped. **◆échancrure** *nf* (*de robe*) opening.

échange [eʃɑ̃ʒ] *nm* exchange; **en é.** in exchange (**dé** for). **◆échanger** *vt* to exchange (**contre** for). **◆échangeur** *nm* (*intersection*) *Aut* interchange.

échantillon [eʃɑ̃tijɔ̃] *nm* sample. **◆échantillonnage** *nm* (*collection*) range (of samples).

échappatoire [eʃapatwar] *nf* evasion, way out.

échapp/er [eʃape] *vi* **é. à qn** to escape from s.o.; **é. à la mort/un danger**/*etc* to escape death/a danger/*etc*; **ce nom m'échappe** that name escapes me; **ça lui a échappé (des mains)** it slipped out of his *ou* her hands; **laisser é.** (*cri*) to let out; (*objet, occasion*) to let slip; **l'é. belle** to have a close shave; **ça m'a échappé** (*je n'ai pas compris*) I didn't catch it; **— s'é.** *vpr* (*s'enfuir*) to escape (**de** from); (*s'éclipser*) to slip away; *Sp* to break away; (*gaz, eau*) to escape, come out. **◆—é, -ée** *nmf* runaway. **◆—ée** *nf Sp* breakaway; (*vue*) vista. **◆—ement** *nm* **tuyau d'é.** *Aut* exhaust pipe; **pot d'é.** *Aut* silencer, *Am* muffler.

écharde [eʃard] *nf* (*de bois*) splinter.

écharpe [eʃarp] *nf* scarf; (*de maire*) sash; **en é.** (*bras*) in a sling; **prendre en é.** *Aut* to hit sideways.

écharper [eʃarpe] *vt* **é. qn** to cut s.o. to bits.

échasse [eʃas] *nf* (*bâton*) stilt. **◆échassier** *nm* wading bird.

échauder [eʃode] *vt* **être échaudé, se faire é.** (*déçu*) *Fam* to be taught a lesson.

échauffer [eʃofe] *vt* (*moteur*) to overheat; (*esprit*) to excite; **— s'é.** *vpr* (*discussion*) & *Sp* to warm up.

échauffourée [eʃofure] *nf* (*bagarre*) clash, brawl, skirmish.

échéance [eʃeɑ̃s] *nf Com* date (due), expiry *ou Am* expiration date; (*paiement*) payment (due); (*obligation*) commitment; **à brève/longue é.** (*projet, emprunt*) short-/long-term.

échéant (le cas) [ləkazeʃeɑ̃] *adv* if the occasion should arise, possibly.

échec [eʃɛk] *nm* **1** (*insuccès*) failure; **faire é. à** (*inflation etc*) to hold in check. **2 les**

échecs (*jeu*) chess; **en é.** in check; **é.!** check!; **é. et mat!** checkmate!

échelle [eʃɛl] *nf* **1** (*marches*) ladder; **faire la courte é. à qn** to give s.o. a leg up. **2** (*mesure, dimension*) scale; **à l'é. nationale** on a national scale. **◆échelon** *nm* (*d'échelle*) rung; (*de fonctionnaire*) grade; (*dans une organisation*) echelon; **à l'é. régional/national** on a regional/national level. **◆échelonner** *vt* (*paiements*) to spread out, space out; **— s'é.** *vpr* to be spread out.

écheveau, -x [eʃvo] *nm* (*de laine*) skein; *Fig* muddle, tangle.

échevelé [eʃəvle] *a* (*ébouriffé*) dishevelled; (*course, danse etc*) *Fig* wild.

échine [eʃin] *nf Anat* backbone, spine.

échiner (s') [seʃine] *vpr* (*s'évertuer*) *Fam* to knock oneself out (**à faire** doing).

échiquier [eʃikje] *nm* (*tableau*) chessboard.

écho [eko] *nm* (*d'un son*) echo; (*réponse*) response; *pl Journ* gossip (items), local news; **avoir des échos de** to hear some news about; **se faire l'é. de** (*opinions etc*) to echo. **◆échotier, -ière** *nmf Journ* gossip columnist.

échographie [ekografi] *nf* (ultrasound) scan; **passer une é.** (*femme enceinte*) to have a scan.

échoir* [eʃwar] *vi* (*terme*) to expire; **é. à qn** (*part*) to fall to s.o.

échouer [eʃwe] **1** *vi* to fail; **é. à** (*examen*) to fail. **2** *vi*, **— s'é.** *vpr* (*navire*) to run aground.

éclabousser [eklabuse] *vt* to splash, spatter (**de** with); (*salir*) *Fig* to tarnish the image of. **◆éclaboussure** *nf* splash, spatter.

éclair [eklɛr] **1** *nm* (*lumière*) flash; **un é.** *Mét* a flash of lightning. **2** *nm* (*gâteau*) éclair. **3** *a inv* (*visite, raid*) lightning.

éclairc/ir [eklɛrsir] *vt* (*couleur etc*) to lighten, make lighter; (*sauce*) to thin out; (*question, mystère*) to clear up, clarify; **— s'é.** *vpr* (*ciel*) to clear (up); (*idées*) to become clear(er); (*devenir moins dense*) to thin out; **s'é. la voix** to clear one's throat. **◆—ie** *nf* (*dans le ciel*) clear patch; (*durée*) sunny spell. **◆—issement** *nm* (*explication*) clarification.

éclair/er [eklere] *vt* (*pièce etc*) to light (up); (*situation*) *Fig* to throw light on; **é. qn** (*avec une lampe etc*) to give s.o. some light; (*informer*) *Fig* to enlighten s.o.; **— vi** (*lampe*) to give light; **— s'é.** *vpr* (*visage*) to light up, brighten up; (*question, situation*) *Fig* to become clear(er); **s'é. à la bougie** to use candlelight. **◆—é** *a* (*averti*) enlightened; **bien/mal é.** (*illuminé*) well/badly lit.

◆—age *nm* (*de pièce etc*) light(ing); (*point de vue*) *Fig* light.

éclaireur, -euse [eklɛrœr, -øz] *nm Mil* scout; **— *nmf*** (boy) scout, (girl) guide.

éclat [ekla] *nm* **1** (*de la lumière*) brightness; (*de phare*) *Aut* glare; (*du feu*) blaze; (*splendeur*) brilliance, radiance; (*de la jeunesse*) bloom; (*de diamant*) glitter, sparkle. **2** (*fragment de verre ou de bois*) splinter; (*de rire, colère*) (out)burst; **é. d'obus** shrapnel; **éclats de voix** noisy outbursts, shouts. **◆éclat/er** *vi* (*pneu, obus etc*) to burst; (*pétard, bombe*) to go off, explode; (*verre*) to shatter, break into pieces; (*guerre, incendie*) to break out; (*orage, scandale*) to break; (*parti*) to break up; **é. de rire** to burst out laughing; **é. en sanglots** to burst into tears. **◆—ant** *a* (*lumière, couleur, succès*) brilliant; (*bruit*) thunderous; (*vérité*) blinding; (*beauté*) radiant. **◆—ement** *nm* (*de pneu etc*) bursting; (*de bombe etc*) explosion; (*de parti*) break-up.

éclectique [eklektik] *a* eclectic.

éclipse [eklips] *nf* (*du soleil*) & *Fig* eclipse. **◆éclipser** *vt* to eclipse; **— s'é.** *vpr* (*soleil*) to be eclipsed; (*partir*) *Fam* to slip away.

éclopé, -ée [eklope] *a & nmf* limping *ou* lame (person).

éclore [eklor] *vi* (*œuf*) to hatch; (*fleur*) to open (out), blossom. **◆éclosion** *nf* hatching; opening, blossoming.

écluse [eklyz] *nf Nau* lock.

écœur/er [ekœre] *vt* (*aliment etc*) to make (s.o.) feel sick; (*au moral*) to sicken, nauseate. **◆—ement** *nm* (*répugnance*) nausea, disgust.

école [ekɔl] *nf* school; (*militaire*) academy; **aller à l'é.** to go to school; **é. de danse/dessin** dancing/art school; **faire é.** to gain a following; **les grandes écoles** *university establishments giving high-level professional training*; **é. normale** teachers' training college. **◆écolier, -ière** *nmf* schoolboy, schoolgirl.

écologie [ekɔlɔʒi] *nf* ecology. **◆écologique** *a* ecological. **◆écologiste** *nmf Pol* environmentalist.

éconduire [ekɔ̃dɥir] *vt* (*repousser*) to reject.

économe [ekɔnɔm] **1** *a* thrifty, economical. **2** *nmf* (*de collège etc*) bursar, steward. **◆économie** *nf* (*activité économique, vertu*) economy; *pl* (*pécule*) savings; **une é. de** (*gain*) a saving of; **faire une é. de temps** to save time; **faire des économies** to save (up); **é. politique** economics. **◆économique** *a* **1** (*doctrine etc*) economic; **science é.** economics. **2** (*bon marché*, *avantageux*) economical. ◆**économiquement** *adv* economically. ◆**économiser** *vt* (*forces, argent, énergie etc*) to save; – *vi* to economize (**sur** on). ◆**économiste** *nmf* economist.

écoper [ekɔpe] **1** *vt* (*bateau*) to bail out, bale out. **2** *vi Fam* to cop it; **é. (de)** (*punition*) to cop, get.

écorce [ekɔrs] *nf* (*d'arbre*) bark; (*de fruit*) peel, skin; **l'é. terrestre** the earth's crust.

écorcher [ekɔrʃe] *vt* (*animal*) to skin, flay; (*érafler*) to graze; (*client*) *Fam* to fleece; (*langue étrangère*) *Fam* to murder; **é. les oreilles** to grate on one's ears; – **s'é.** *vpr* to graze oneself. ◆**écorchure** *nf* graze.

Écosse [ekɔs] *nf* Scotland. ◆**écossais, -aise** *a* Scottish; (*tissu*) tartan; (*whisky*) Scotch; – *nmf* Scot.

écosser [ekɔse] *vt* (*pois*) to shell.

écot [eko] *nm* (*quote-part*) share.

écouler [ekule] **1** *vt* (*se débarrasser de*) to dispose of; (*produits*) *Com* to sell (off), clear. **2 s'é.** *vpr* (*eau*) to flow out, run out; (*temps*) to pass, elapse; (*foule*) to disperse. ◆**—é** *a* (*années etc*) past. ◆**—ement** *nm* **1** (*de liquide, véhicules*) flow; (*de temps*) passage. **2** (*débit*) *Com* sale, selling.

écourter [ekurte] *vt* (*séjour, discours etc*) to cut short; (*texte, tige etc*) to shorten.

écoute [ekut] *nf* listening; **à l'é.** *Rad* tuned in, listening in (**de** to); **être aux écoutes** (*attentif*) to keep one's ears open (**de** for). ◆**écouter** *vt* to listen to; (*radio*) to listen (in) to; – *vi* to listen; (*aux portes etc*) to eavesdrop, listen; **si je m'écoutais** if I did what I wanted. ◆**—eur** *nm* (*de téléphone*) earpiece; *pl* (*casque*) headphones, earphones.

écrabouiller [ekrabuje] *vt Fam* to crush to a pulp.

écran [ekrɑ̃] *nm* screen; **le petit é.** television.

écraser [ekraze] *vt* (*broyer*) to crush; (*fruit, insecte*) to squash, crush; (*cigarette*) to put out; (*tuer*) *Aut* to run over; (*vaincre*) to beat (hollow), crush; (*dominer*) to outstrip; **écrasé de** (*travail, douleur*) overwhelmed with; **se faire é.** *Aut* to get run over; – **s'é.** *vpr* (*avion, voiture*) to crash (**contre** into); **s'é. dans** (*foule*) to crush *ou* squash into. ◆**—ant** *a* (*victoire, nombre, chaleur*) overwhelming. ◆**—é** *a* (*nez*) snub. ◆**—ement** *nm* crushing.

écrémer [ekreme] *vt* (*lait*) to skim, cream; (*collection etc*) *Fig* to cream off the best from.

écrevisse [ekrəvis] *nf* (*crustacé*) crayfish.

écrier (s') [sekrije] *vpr* to cry out, exclaim (**que** that).

écrin [ekrɛ̃] *nm* (jewel) case.

écrire* [ekrir] *vt* to write; (*noter*) to write (down); (*orthographier*) to spell; **é. à la machine** to type; – *vi* to write; – **s'é.** *vpr* (*mot*) to be spelt. ◆**écrit** *nm* written document, paper; (*examen*) *Scol* written paper; *pl* (*œuvres*) writings; **par é.** in writing. ◆**écriteau, -x** *nm* notice, sign. ◆**écriture** *nf* (*système*) writing; (*personnelle*) (hand)writing; *pl Com* accounts; **l'É. Rel** the Scripture(s). ◆**écrivain** *nm* author, writer.

écrou [ekru] *nm Tech* nut.

écrouer [ekrue] *vt* to imprison.

écrouler (s') [sekrule] *vpr* (*édifice, projet etc*) to collapse; (*blessé etc*) to slump down, collapse. ◆**—ement** *nm* collapse.

écru [ekry] *af* **toile é.** unbleached linen; **soie é.** raw silk.

écueil [ekœj] *nm* (*rocher*) reef; (*obstacle*) *Fig* pitfall.

écuelle [ekɥɛl] *nf* (*bol*) bowl.

éculé [ekyle] *a* (*chaussure*) worn out at the heel; *Fig* hackneyed.

écume [ekym] *nf* (*de mer, bave d'animal etc*) foam; *Culin* scum. ◆**écumer** *vt Culin* to skim; (*piller*) to plunder; – *vi* to foam (**de rage** with anger). ◆**écumoire** *nf Culin* skimmer.

écureuil [ekyrœj] *nm* squirrel.

écurie [ekyri] *nf* stable.

écusson [ekysɔ̃] *nm* (*emblème d'étoffe*) badge.

écuyer, -ère [ekɥije, -ɛr] *nmf* (*cavalier*) (horse) rider, equestrian.

eczéma [ɛgzema] *nm Méd* eczema.

édenté [edɑ̃te] *a* toothless.

édicter [edikte] *vt* to enact, decree.

édifice [edifis] *nm* building, edifice; (*ensemble organisé*) *Fig* edifice. ◆**édification** *nf* construction; edification; enlightenment. ◆**édifier** *vt* (*bâtiment*) to construct, erect; (*théorie*) to construct; **é. qn** (*moralement*) to edify s.o.; (*détromper*) *Iron* to enlighten s.o.

Édimbourg [edɛ̃bur] *nm ou f* Edinburgh.

édit [edi] *nm Hist* edict.

éditer [edite] *vt* (*publier*) to publish; (*annoter*) to edit. ◆**éditeur, -trice** *nmf* publisher; editor. ◆**édition** *nf* (*livre, journal*) edition; (*diffusion, métier*) publishing. ◆**éditorial, -aux** *nm* (*article*) editorial.

édredon [edrədɔ̃] *nm* eiderdown.

éducation [edykasjɔ̃] *nf* (*enseignement*) education; (*façon d'élever*) upbringing, education; avoir de l'é. to have good manners, be well-bred. ◆**éducateur, -trice** *nmf* educator. ◆**éducatif, -ive** *a* educational. ◆**éduquer** *vt* (*à l'école*) to educate (*s.o.*); (*à la maison*) to bring (*s.o.*) up, educate (*s.o.*) (*à faire qch*) (*esprit*) to educate, train.

effac/er [efase] *vt* (*gommer*) to rub out, erase; (*en lavant*) to wash out; (*avec un chiffon*) to wipe away; (*souvenir*) *Fig* to blot out, erase; — **s'e.** *vpr* (*souvenir, couleur etc*) to fade; (*se placer en retrait*) to step *ou* draw aside. ◆—**é** *a* (*modeste*) self-effacing. ◆—**ement** *nm* (*modestie*) self-effacement.

effar/er [efare] *vt* to scare, alarm. ◆—**ement** *nm* alarm.

effaroucher [efaruʃe] *vt* to scare away, frighten away.

effectif, -ive [efɛktif, -iv] **1** *a* (*réel*) effective, real. **2** *nm* (*nombre*) (total) strength; (*de classe*) *Scol* size, total number; *pl* (*employés*) & *Mil* manpower. ◆**effectivement** *adv* (*en effet*) actually, effectively, indeed.

effectuer [efɛktɥe] *vt* (*expérience etc*) to carry out; (*paiement, trajet etc*) to make.

efféminé [efemine] *a* effeminate.

effervescent [efɛrvesã] *a* (*mélange, jeunesse*) effervescent. ◆**effervescence** *nf* (*exaltation*) excitement, effervescence; (*de liquide*) effervescence.

effet [efɛ] *nm* **1** (*résultat*) effect; (*impression*) impression, effect (sur on); faire de l'e. (*remède etc*) to be effective; rester sans e. to have no effect; à cet e. to this end, for this purpose; en e. indeed, in fact; il me fait l'e. d'être fatigué he seems to me to be tired; sous l'e. de la colère (*agir*) in anger, out of anger. **2** e. de commerce bill, draft.

effets [efɛ] *nmpl* (*vêtements*) clothes, things.

efficace [efikas] *a* (*mesure etc*) effective; (*personne*) efficient. ◆**efficacité** *nf* effectiveness; efficiency.

effigie [efiʒi] *nf* effigy.

effilé [efile] *a* tapering, slender.

effilocher (s') [sefiloʃe] *vpr* to fray.

efflanqué [eflãke] *a* emaciated.

effleurer [eflœre] *vt* (*frôler*) to skim, touch lightly; (*égratigner*) to graze; (*question*) *Fig* to touch on; e. qn (*pensée etc*) to cross s.o.'s mind.

effondr/er (s') [sefɔ̃dre] *vpr* (*projet, édifice, personne*) to collapse; (*toit*) to cave in, collapse. ◆—**ement** *nm* collapse; *Com* slump; (*abattement*) dejection.

efforcer (s') [seforse] *vpr* s'e. de faire to try (hard) *ou* endeavour *ou* strive to do.

effort [efor] *nm* effort; sans e. (*réussir etc*) effortlessly; (*réussite etc*) effortless.

effraction [efraksjɔ̃] *nf* pénétrer par e. (*cambrioleur*) to break in; vol avec e. housebreaking.

effranger (s') [sefrãʒe] *vpr* to fray.

effray/er [efreje] *vt* to frighten, scare; — **s'e.** *vpr* to be frightened *ou* scared. ◆—**ant** *a* frightening, scary.

effréné [efrene] *a* unrestrained, wild.

effriter [efrite] *vt*, — **s'e.** *vpr* to crumble (away).

effroi [efrwa] *nm* (*frayeur*) dread. ◆**effroyable** *a* dreadful, appalling. ◆**effroyablement** *adv* dreadfully.

effronté [efrɔ̃te] *a* (*enfant etc*) cheeky, brazen; (*mensonge*) shameless. ◆**effronterie** *nf* effrontery.

effusion [efyzjɔ̃] *nf* **1** e. de sang bloodshed. **2** (*manifestation*) effusion; avec e. effusively.

égailler (s') [segaje] *vpr* to disperse.

égal, -ale, -aux [egal, -o] *a* equal (à to); (*uniforme, régulier*) even; ça m'est é. I don't care, it's all the same to me; — *nmf* (*personne*) equal; traiter qn d'é. à é. *ou* en é. to treat s.o. as an equal; sans é. without match. ◆—**ement** *adv* (*au même degré*) equally; (*aussi*) also, as well. ◆**égaler** *vt* to equal, match (en in); (*en quantité*) *Math* to equal. ◆**égalisation** *nf Sp* equalization; levelling. ◆**égaliser** *vt* to equalize; (*terrain*) to level; — *vi Sp* to equalize. ◆**égalitaire** *a* egalitarian. ◆**égalité** *nf* equality; (*régularité*) evenness; à é. (de score) *Sp* equal (on points); signe d'é. *Math* equals sign.

égard [egar] *nm* à l'é. de (*concernant*) with respect *ou* regard to; (*envers*) towards; avoir des égards pour to have respect *ou* consideration for; à cet é. in this respect; à certains égards in some respects.

égarer [egare] *vt* (*objet*) to mislay; é. qn (*dérouter*) to mislead s.o.; (*aveugler, troubler*) to lead s.o. astray, misguide s.o.; — **s'é.** *vpr* to lose one's way, get lost; (*objet*) to get mislaid, go astray; (*esprit*) to wander.

égayer [egeje] *vt* (*pièce*) to brighten up; é. qn (*réconforter, amuser*) to cheer s.o. up; — **s'é.** *vpr* (*par la moquerie*) to be amused.

égide [eʒid] *nf* sous l'é. de under the aegis of.

églantier [eglãtje] *nm* (*arbre*) wild rose. ◆**églantine** *nf* (*fleur*) wild rose.

église [egliz] *nf* church.
égocentrique [egɔsɑ̃trik] *a* egocentric.
égoïne [egɔin] *nf* (**scie**) é. hand saw.
égoïsme [egɔism] *nm* selfishness, egoism.
◆**égoïste** *a* selfish, egoistic(al); – *nmf* egoist.
égorger [egɔrʒe] *vt* to cut *ou* slit the throat of.
égosiller (s') [segɔzije] *vpr* to scream one's head off, bawl out.
égotisme [egɔtism] *nm* egotism.
égout [egu] *nm* sewer; **eaux d'é.** sewage.
égoutter [egute] *vt* (*vaisselle*) to drain; (*légumes*) to strain, drain; – *vi*, – **s'é.** *vpr* to drain; to strain; (*linge*) to drip. ◆**égouttoir** *nm* (*panier*) (dish) drainer.
égratigner [egratiɲe] *vt* to scratch. ◆**égratignure** *nf* scratch.
égrener [egrəne] *vt* (*raisins*) to pick off; (*épis*) to shell; **é. son chapelet** *Rel* to count one's beads.
Égypte [eʒipt] *nf* Egypt. ◆**égyptien, -ienne** [-sjɛ̃, -sjɛn] *a & nmf* Egyptian.
eh! [e] *int* hey!; **eh bien!** well!
éhonté [eɔ̃te] *a* shameless; **mensonge é.** barefaced lie.
éjecter [eʒɛkte] *vt* to eject. ◆**éjectable** *a* **siège é.** *Av* ejector seat. ◆**éjection** *nf* ejection.
élaborer [elabɔre] *vt* (*système etc*) to elaborate. ◆**élaboration** *nf* elaboration.
élaguer [elage] *vt* (*arbre, texte etc*) to prune.
élan [elɑ̃] *nm* **1** (*vitesse*) momentum, impetus; (*impulsion*) impulse; (*fougue*) fervour, spirit; **prendre son é.** *Sp* to take a run (up); **d'un seul é.** in one bound. **2** (*animal*) elk.
élanc/er [elɑ̃se] **1** *vi* (*dent etc*) to give shooting pains. **2 s'é.** *vpr* (*bondir*) to leap *ou* rush (forward); **s'é. vers le ciel** (*tour*) to soar up (high) into the sky. ◆**—é** *a* (*personne, taille etc*) slender. ◆**—ement** *nm* shooting pain.
élargir [elarʒir] **1** *vt* (*chemin*) to widen; (*esprit, débat*) to broaden; – **s'é.** *vpr* (*sentier etc*) to widen out. **2** *vt* (*prisonnier*) to free.
élastique [elastik] *a* (*objet, caractère*) elastic; (*règlement, notion*) flexible, supple; – *nm* (*tissu*) elastic; (*lien*) elastic *ou* rubber band. ◆**élasticité** *nf* elasticity.
élection [elɛksjɔ̃] *nf* election; **é. partielle** by-election. ◆**électeur, -trice** *nmf* voter, elector. ◆**électoral, -aux** *a* (*campagne, réunion*) election-; **collège é.** electoral college. ◆**électorat** *nm* (*électeurs*) electorate, voters.
électricien [elɛktrisjɛ̃] *nm* electrician. ◆**électricité** *nf* electricity; **coupure d'é.**

power cut. ◆**électrifier** *vt* Rail to electrify. ◆**électrique** *a* (*pendule, décharge*) electric; (*courant, fil*) electric(al); (*phénomène, effet*) *Fig* electric. ◆**électriser** *vt* (*animer*) *Fig* to electrify. ◆**électrocuter** *vt* to electrocute.
électrode [elɛktrɔd] *nf* El electrode.
électrogène [elɛktrɔʒɛn] *a* **groupe é.** El generator.
électroménager [elɛktrɔmenaʒe] *am* **appareil é.** household electrical appliance.
électron [elɛktrɔ̃] *nm* electron. ◆**électronicien, -ienne** *nmf* electronics engineer. ◆**électronique** *a* electronic; (*microscope*) electron-; – *nf* electronics.
électrophone [elɛktrɔfɔn] *nm* record player.
élégant [elegɑ̃] *a* (*style, mobilier, solution etc*) elegant; (*bien habillé*) smart, elegant. ◆**élégamment** *adv* elegantly; smartly. ◆**élégance** *nf* elegance.
élégie [eleʒi] *nf* elegy.
élément [elemɑ̃] *nm* (*composante, personne*) & *Ch* element; (*de meuble*) unit; (*d'ensemble*) *Math* member; *pl* (*notions*) rudiments, elements; **dans son é.** (*milieu*) in one's element. ◆**élémentaire** *a* elementary.
éléphant [elefɑ̃] *nm* elephant. ◆**éléphantesque** *a* (*énorme*) *Fam* elephantine.
élévateur [elevatœr] *am* **chariot é.** forklift truck.
élévation [elevasjɔ̃] *nf* raising; *Géom* elevation; **é. de** (*hausse*) rise in.
élève [elɛv] *nmf* *Scol* pupil.
élev/er [elve] *vt* (*prix, objection, voix etc*) to raise; (*enfant*) to bring up, raise; (*animal*) to breed, rear; (*âme*) to uplift, raise; – **s'é.** *vpr* (*prix, montagne, ton, avion etc*) to rise; **s'é. à** (*prix etc*) to amount to; **s'é. contre** to rise up against. ◆**—é** *a* (*haut*) high; (*noble*) noble; **bien/mal é.** well-/bad-mannered. ◆**—age** *nm* (*de bovins*) cattle rearing; **l'é. de** the breeding *ou* rearing of. ◆**—eur, -euse** *nmf* breeder.
élider [elide] *vt* Ling to elide.
éligible [eliʒibl] *a* Pol eligible (à for).
élimé [elime] *a* (*tissu*) threadbare, worn thin.
éliminer [elimine] *vt* to eliminate. ◆**élimination** *nf* elimination. ◆**éliminatoire** *a* & *nf* (*épreuve*) é. *Sp* heat, qualifying round.
élire* [elir] *vt* Pol to elect (à to).
élision [elizjɔ̃] *nf* Ling elision.
élite [elit] *nf* elite (**de** of); **d'é.** (*chef, sujet etc*) top-notch.
elle [ɛl] *pron* **1** (*sujet*) she; (*chose, animal*) it;

pl they; **e. est** she is; it is; **elles sont** they are. **2** (*complément*) her; (*chose, animal*) it; *pl* them; **pour e.** for her; **pour elles** for them; **plus grande qu'e./qu'elles** taller than her/them. ◆**e.-même** *pron* herself; (*chose, animal*) itself; *pl* themselves.

ellipse [elips] *nf Géom* ellipse. ◆**elliptique** *a* elliptical.

élocution [elɔkysjɔ̃] *nf* diction; **défaut d'é.** speech defect.

éloge [elɔʒ] *nm* praise; (*panégyrique*) eulogy; **faire l'é. de** to praise. ◆**élogieux, -euse** *a* laudatory.

éloign/er [elwaɲe] *vt* (*chose, personne*) to move *ou* take away (**de** from); (*clients*) to keep away; (*crainte, idée*) to get rid of, banish; (*date*) to put off; **é. qn de** (*sujet, but*) to take *ou* get s.o. away from; — **s'é.** *vpr* (*partir*) to move *ou* go away (**de** from); (*dans le passé*) to become (more) remote; **s'é. de** (*sujet, but*) to get away from. ◆**—é** *a* far-off, remote, distant; (*parent*) distant; **é. de** (*village, maison etc*) far (away) from; (*très différent*) far removed from. ◆**—ement** *nm* remoteness, distance; (*absence*) separation (**de** from); **avec l'é.** (*avec le recul*) with time.

élongation [elɔ̃gasjɔ̃] *nf Méd* pulled muscle.

éloquent [elɔkɑ̃] *a* eloquent. ◆**éloquence** *nf* eloquence.

élu, -ue [ely] *voir* **élire**; — *nmf Pol* elected member *ou* representative; **les élus** *Rel* the chosen, the elect.

élucider [elyside] *vt* to elucidate. ◆**élucidation** *nf* elucidation.

éluder [elyde] *vt* to elude, evade.

émacié [emasje] *a* emaciated.

émail, -aux [emaj, -o] *nm* enamel; **en é.** enamel-. ◆**émailler** *vt* to enamel.

émaillé [emaje] *a* **é. de fautes/etc** (*texte*) peppered with errors/*etc*.

émanciper [emɑ̃sipe] *vt* (*femmes*) to emancipate; — **s'é.** *vpr* to become emancipated. ◆**émancipation** *nf* emancipation.

émaner [emane] *vi* to emanate. ◆**émanation** *nf* emanation; **une é. de** *Fig* a product of.

emball/er [ɑ̃bale] **1** *vt* (*dans une caisse etc*) to pack; (*dans du papier*) to wrap (up). **2** *vt* (*moteur*) to race; **e. qn** (*passionner*) *Fam* to enthuse with, thrill s.o.; — **s'e.** *vpr* (*personne*) *Fam* to get carried away; (*cheval*) to bolt; (*moteur*) to race. ◆**—é** *a Fam* enthusiastic. ◆**—age** *nm* (*action*) packing; wrapping; (*caisse*) packaging; (*papier*) wrapping (paper). ◆**—ement** *nm Fam* (sudden) enthusiasm.

embarcadère [ɑ̃barkadɛr] *nm* landing place, quay.

embarcation [ɑ̃barkasjɔ̃] *nf* (small) boat.

embardée [ɑ̃barde] *nf Aut* (sudden) swerve; **faire une e.** to swerve.

embargo [ɑ̃bargo] *nm* embargo.

embarqu/er [ɑ̃barke] *vt* (*passagers*) to embark, take on board; (*marchandises*) to load (up); (*voler*) *Fam* to walk off with; (*prisonnier*) *Fam* to cart off; **e. qn dans** (*affaire*) *Fam* to involve s.o. in, launch s.o. into; — *vi*, — **s'e.** *vpr* to embark, (go on) board; **faire une e.** (*aventure etc*) *Fam* to embark on. ◆**—ement** *nm* (*de passagers*) boarding.

embarras [ɑ̃bara] *nm* (*malaise, gêne*) embarrassment; (*difficulté*) difficulty, trouble; (*obstacle*) obstacle; **dans l'e.** in difficulty; **faire des e.** (*chichis*) to make a fuss. ◆**embarrass/er** *vt* (*obstruer*) to clutter, encumber; **e. qn** to be in s.o.'s way; (*déconcerter*) to embarrass s.o., bother s.o.; **s'e. de** to burden oneself with; (*se soucier*) to bother oneself about. ◆**—ant** *a* (*paquet*) cumbersome; (*question*) embarrassing.

embauche [ɑ̃boʃ] *nf* (*action*) hiring; (*travail*) work. ◆**embaucher** *vt* (*ouvrier*) to hire, take on.

embaumer [ɑ̃bome] **1** *vt* (*cadavre*) to embalm. **2** *vt* (*parfumer*) to give a sweet smell to; — *vi* to smell sweet.

embell/ir [ɑ̃belir] *vt* (*texte, vérité*) to embellish; **e. qn** to make s.o. attractive. ◆**—issement** *nm* (*de ville etc*) improvement, embellishment.

embêt/er [ɑ̃bete] *vt Fam* (*contrarier, taquiner*) to annoy, bother; (*raser*) to bore; — **s'e.** *vpr Fam* to get bored. ◆**—ant** *a Fam* annoying; boring. ◆**—ement** [-ɛtmɑ̃] *nm Fam* **un e.** (some) trouble *ou* bother; **des embêtements** trouble(s), bother.

emblée (d') [dɑ̃ble] *adv* right away.

emblème [ɑ̃blɛm] *nm* emblem.

embobiner [ɑ̃bɔbine] *vt* (*tromper*) *Fam* to hoodwink.

emboîter [ɑ̃bwate] *vt*, — **s'e.** *vpr* (*pièces*) to fit into each other, fit together; **e. le pas à qn** to follow on s.o.'s heels; (*imiter*) *Fig* to follow in s.o.'s footsteps.

embonpoint [ɑ̃bɔ̃pwɛ̃] *nm* plumpness.

embouchure [ɑ̃buʃyr] *nf* (*de cours d'eau*) mouth; *Mus* mouthpiece.

embourber (s') [sɑ̃burbe] *vpr* (*véhicule*) & *Fig* to get bogged down.

embourgeoiser (s') [sɑ̃burʒwaze] *vpr* to become middle-class.

embout [ãbu] *nm* (*de canne*) tip, end piece; (*de seringue*) nozzle.

embouteill/er [ãbuteje] *vt Aut* to jam, congest. ◆—**age** *nm* traffic jam.

emboutir [ãbutir] *vt* (*voiture*) to bash *ou* crash into; (*métal*) to stamp, emboss.

embranch/er (s') [sãbrãʃe] *vpr* (*voie*) to branch off. ◆—**ement** *nm* (*de voie*) junction, fork; (*de règne animal*) branch.

embras/er [ãbraze] *vt* to set ablaze; — **s'e.** *vpr* (*prendre feu*) to flare up. ◆—**ement** *nm* (*troubles*) flare-up.

embrasser [ãbrase] *vt* (*adopter, contenir*) to embrace; **e. qn** to kiss s.o.; (*serrer*) to embrace *ou* hug s.o.; — **s'e.** *vpr* to kiss (each other). ◆**embrassade** *nf* embrace, hug.

embrasure [ãbrazyr] *nf* (*de fenêtre, porte*) opening.

embray/er [ãbreje] *vi* to let in *ou* engage the clutch. ◆—**age** *nm* (*mécanisme, pédale*) *Aut* clutch.

embrigader [ãbrigade] *vt* to recruit.

embrocher [ãbrɔʃe] *vt Culin & Fig* to skewer.

embrouiller [ãbruje] *vt* (*fils*) to tangle (up); (*papiers etc*) to muddle (up), mix up; **e. qn** to confuse s.o., get s.o. muddled; — **s'e.** *vpr* to get confused *ou* muddled (**dans** in, with). ◆**embrouillamini** *nm Fam* muddle, mix-up. ◆**embrouillement** *nm* confusion, muddle.

embroussaillé [ãbrusaje] *a* (*barbe, chemin*) bushy.

embruns [ãbrœ̃] *nmpl* (sea) spray.

embryon [ãbrijɔ̃] *nm* embryo. ◆**embryonnaire** *a Méd & Fig* embryonic.

embûches [ãbyʃ] *nfpl* (*difficultés*) traps, pitfalls.

embuer [ãbɥe] *vt* (*vitre, yeux*) to mist up.

embusquer (s') [sãbyske] *vpr* to lie in ambush. ◆**embuscade** *nf* ambush.

éméché [emeʃe] *a* (*ivre*) *Fam* tipsy.

émeraude [emrod] *nf* emerald.

émerger [emɛrʒe] *vi* to emerge (**de** from).

émeri [emri] *nm* **toile (d')é.** emery cloth.

émerveill/er [emɛrveje] *vt* to amaze; — **s'e.** *vpr* to marvel, be filled with wonder (**de** at). ◆—**ement** *nm* wonder, amazement.

émett/re* [emɛtr] *vt* (*lumière, son etc*) to give out, emit; *Rad* to transmit, broadcast; (*cri*) to utter; (*opinion, vœu*) to express; (*timbre-poste, monnaie*) to issue; (*chèque*) to draw; (*emprunt*) *Com* to float. ◆—**eur** *nm* (*poste*) é. *Rad* transmitter.

émeute [emøt] *nf* riot. ◆**émeutier, -ière** *nmf* rioter.

émietter [emjete] *vt*, — **s'é.** *vpr* (*pain etc*) to crumble.

émigr/er [emigre] *vi* (*personne*) to emigrate. ◆—**ant, -ante** *nmf* emigrant. ◆—**é, -ée** *nmf* exile, émigré. ◆**émigration** *nf* emigration.

éminent [eminã] *a* eminent. ◆**éminemment** [-amã] *adv* eminently. ◆**éminence** *nf* **1** (*colline*) hillock. **2** **son É.** *Rel* his Eminence.

émissaire [emisɛr] *nm* emissary.

émission [emisjɔ̃] *nf* (*programme*) *TV Rad* broadcast; (*action*) emission (**de** of); (*de programme*) *TV Rad* transmission; (*de timbre-poste, monnaie*) issue.

emmagasiner [ãmagazine] *vt* to store (up).

emmanchure [ãmãʃyr] *nf* (*de vêtement*) arm hole.

emmêler [ãmele] *vt* to tangle (up).

emménag/er [ãmenaʒe] *vi* (*dans un logement*) to move in; **e. dans** to move into. ◆—**ement** *nm* moving in.

emmener [ãmne] *vt* to take (**à** to); (*prisonnier*) to take away; **e. qn faire une promenade** to take s.o. for a walk.

emmerd/er [ãmɛrde] *vt Arg* to annoy, bug; (*raser*) to bore stiff; — **s'e.** *vpr Arg* to get bored stiff. ◆—**ement** *nm Arg* bother, trouble. ◆—**eur, -euse** *nmf* (*personne*) *Arg* pain in the neck.

emmitoufler (s') [sãmitufle] *vpr* to wrap (oneself) up.

emmurer [ãmyre] *vt* (*personne*) to wall in.

émoi [emwa] *nm* excitement; **en é.** agog, excited.

émoluments [emɔlymã] *nmpl* remuneration.

émotion [emosjɔ̃] *nf* (*trouble*) excitement; (*sentiment*) emotion; **une é.** (*peur*) a scare. ◆**émotif, -ive** *a* emotional. ◆**émotionné** *a Fam* upset.

émouss/er [emuse] *vt* (*pointe*) to blunt; (*sentiment*) to dull. ◆—**é** *a* (*pointe*) blunt; (*sentiment*) dulled.

émouv/oir* [emuvwar] *vt* (*affecter*) to move, touch; — **s'é.** *vpr* to be moved *ou* touched. ◆—**ant, -ante** *a* moving, touching.

empailler [ãpaje] *vt* (*animal*) to stuff.

empaler (s') [sãpale] *vpr* to impale oneself.

empaqueter [ãpakte] *vt* to pack(age).

emparer (s') [sãpare] *vpr* **s'e. de** to seize, take hold of.

empât/er (s') [sãpate] *vpr* to fill out, get fat(ter). ◆—**é** *a* fleshy, fat.

empêch/er [ãpeʃe] *vt* to prevent, stop; **e. qn de faire** to prevent *ou* stop s.o. (from) doing; **n'empêche qu'elle a raison** *Fam* all

the same she's right; **n'empêche!** *Fam* all
the same!; **elle ne peut pas s'e. de rire** she
can't help laughing. ◆**—ement** [-ɛʃmɑ̃]
nm difficulty, hitch; **avoir un e.** to be un-
avoidably detained.

empereur [ɑ̃prœr] *nm* emperor.

empeser [ɑ̃pəze] *vt* to starch.

empester [ɑ̃pɛste] *vt* (*pièce*) to make stink,
stink out; (*tabac etc*) to stink of; **e. qn** to
stink s.o. out; — *vi* to stink.

empêtrer (s') [sɑ̃petre] *vpr* to get entangled
(**dans** in).

emphase [ɑ̃faz] *nf* pomposity. ◆**emphatique** *a* pompous.

empléter [ɑ̃pjete] *vi* **e. sur** to encroach upon. ◆**emplétement** *nm* encroachment.

empiffrer (s') [sɑ̃pifre] *vpr Fam* to gorge *ou*
stuff oneself (**de** with).

empil/er [ɑ̃pile] *vt*, **— s'e.** *vpr* to pile up (**sur**
on); **s'e. dans** (*personnes*) to pile into
(*building, car etc*). ◆**—ement** *nm* (*tas*) pile.

empire [ɑ̃pir] *nm* (*territoires*) empire;
(*autorité*) hold, influence; **sous l'e. de** (*peur
etc*) in the grip of.

empirer [ɑ̃pire] *vi* to worsen, get worse.

empirique [ɑ̃pirik] *a* empirical. ◆**empirisme** *nm* empiricism.

emplacement [ɑ̃plasmɑ̃] *nm* site, location;
(*de stationnement*) place.

emplâtre [ɑ̃plɑtr] *nm* (*onguent*) *Méd* plaster.

emplette [ɑ̃plɛt] *nf* purchase; *pl* shopping.

emplir [ɑ̃plir] *vt*, **— s'e.** *vpr* to fill (**de** with).

emploi [ɑ̃plwa] *nm* **1** (*usage*) use; **e. du
temps** timetable; **mode d'e.** directions (for
use). **2** (*travail*) job, position, employment;
l'e. (*travail*) *Écon Pol* employment; **sans e.**
unemployed. ◆**employ/er** *vt* (*utiliser*) to
use; **e. qn** (*occuper*) to employ s.o.; **— s'e.**
vpr (*expression etc*) to be used; **s'e. à faire** to
devote oneself to doing. ◆**—é, -ée** *nmf*
employee; (*de bureau, banque*) clerk, employee; **e. des postes**/*etc* postal/*etc* worker; **e. de magasin** shop assistant, *Am* sales
clerk. ◆**employeur, -euse** *nmf* employer.

empocher [ɑ̃pɔʃe] *vt* (*argent*) to pocket.

empoigner [ɑ̃pwaɲe] *vt* (*saisir*) to grab,
grasp; **— s'e.** *vpr* to come to blows, fight.
◆**empoignade** *nf* (*querelle*) fight.

empoisonn/er [ɑ̃pwazɔne] *vt* (*personne,
aliment, atmosphère*) to poison; (*empester*) to
stink out; (*gâter, altérer*) to trouble, bedevil; **e. qn** (*embêter*) *Fam* to get on s.o.'s
nerves; **— s'e.** *vpr* (*par accident*) to be
poisoned; (*volontairement*) to poison oneself. ◆**—ant** *a* (*embêtant*) *Fam* irritating.

◆**—ement** *nm* poisoning; (*ennui*) *Fam*
problem, trouble.

emport/er [ɑ̃pɔrte] *vt* (*prendre*) to take
(away) (**avec soi** with one); (*enlever*) to take
away; (*prix, trophée*) to carry off; (*décision*)
to carry; (*entraîner*) to carry along *ou*
away; (*par le vent*) to blow off *ou* away;
(*par les vagues*) to sweep away; (*par la
maladie*) to carry off; **l'e. sur qn** to get the
upper hand over s.o.; **se laisser e.** *Fig* to get
carried away (**par** by); **— s'e.** *vpr* to lose
one's temper (**contre** with). ◆**—é** *a* (*caractère*) hot-tempered. ◆**—ement** *nm* anger;
pl fits of anger.

empoté [ɑ̃pɔte] *a Fam* clumsy.

empourprer (s') [sɑ̃purpre] *vpr* to turn
crimson.

empreint [ɑ̃prɛ̃] *a* **e. de** stamped with, heavy
with.

empreinte [ɑ̃prɛ̃t] *nf* (*marque*) & *Fig* mark,
stamp; **e. digitale** fingerprint; **e. des pas**
footprint.

empress/er (s') [sɑ̃prese] *vpr* **s'e. de faire**
to hasten to do; **s'e. auprès de qn** to busy
oneself with s.o., be attentive to s.o.; **s'e.
autour de qn** to rush around s.o. ◆**—é** *a*
eager, attentive; **e. à faire** eager to do.
◆**—ement** [-ɛsmɑ̃] *nm* (*hâte*) eagerness;
(*auprès de qn*) attentiveness.

emprise [ɑ̃priz] *nf* ascendancy, hold (**sur**
over).

emprisonn/er [ɑ̃prizɔne] *vt Jur* to imprison; (*enfermer*) *Fig* to confine. ◆**—ement**
nm imprisonment.

emprunt [ɑ̃prœ̃] *nm* (*argent*) *Com* loan;
(*mot*) *Ling* borrowed word; **un e. à** *Ling* a
borrowing from; **l'e. de qch** the borrowing
of sth; **d'e.** borrowed; **nom d'e.** assumed
name. ◆**emprunt/er** *vt* (*obtenir*) to borrow (**à qn** from s.o.); (*route etc*) to use;
(*nom*) to assume; **e. à** (*tirer de*) to derive *ou*
borrow from. ◆**—é** *a* (*gêné*) ill-at-ease.

empuantir [ɑ̃pɥɑ̃tir] *vt* to make stink, stink
out.

ému [emy] *voir* **émouvoir**; — *a* (*attendri*)
moved; (*apeuré*) nervous; (*attristé*) upset;
une voix émue a voice charged with emotion.

émulation [emylasjɔ̃] *nf* emulation.

émule [emyl] *nmf* imitator, follower.

en [ɑ̃] **1** [ɑ̃] *prép* **1** (*lieu*) in; (*direction*) to; **être en
ville/en France** to be in town/in France;
aller en ville/en France to go (in)to
town/to France. **2** (*temps*) in; **en été** in
summer; **en février** in February; **d'heure en
heure** from hour to hour. **3** (*moyen, état etc*)
by; in; at; on; **en avion** by plane; **en groupe**

in a group; **en mer** at sea; **en guerre** at war; **en fleur** in flower; **en congé** on leave; **en vain** in vain. **4** (*matière*) in; **en bois** wooden, in wood; **chemise en nylon** nylon shirt; **c'est en or** it's (made of) gold. **5** (*comme*) as; **en cadeau** as a present; **en ami** as a friend. **6** (+ *participe présent*) **en mangeant/chantant/*etc*** while eating/singing/*etc*; **en apprenant que . . .** on hearing that . . . ; **en souriant** smiling, with a smile; **en ne disant rien** by saying nothing; **sortir en courant** to run out. **7** (*transformation*) into; **traduire en** to translate into.

en² [ɑ̃] *pron & adv* **1** (= *de là*) from there; **j'en viens** I've just come from there. **2** (= *de ça, lui, eux etc*) **il en est content** he's pleased with it *ou* him *ou* them; **en parler** to talk about it; **en mourir** to die *ou* from it; **elle m'en frappa** she struck me with it. **3** (*partitif*) some; **j'en ai** I have some; **en veux-tu?** do you want some *ou* any?; **je t'en supplie** I beg you (to).

encadr/er [ɑ̃kadre] *vt* (*tableau*) to frame; (*entourer d'un trait*) to box in; (*troupes, étudiants*) to supervise, train; (*prisonnier, accusé*) to flank. **◆—ement** *nm* (*action*) framing; supervision; (*de porte, photo*) frame; (*décor*) setting; (*personnel*) training and supervisory staff.

encaissé [ɑ̃kese] *a* (*vallée*) deep.

encaisser [ɑ̃kese] *vt* (*argent, loyer etc*) to collect; (*effet, chèque*) *Com* to cash; (*coup*) *Fam* to take; **je ne peux pas l'e.** *Fam* I can't stand him *ou* her. **◆encaissement** *nm* (*de loyer etc*) collection; (*de chèque*) cashing.

encapuchonné [ɑ̃kapyʃɔne] *a* hooded.

encart [ɑ̃kar] *nm* (*feuille*) insert. **◆encarter** *vt* to insert.

en-cas [ɑ̃ka] *nm inv* (*repas*) snack.

encastrer [ɑ̃kastre] *vt* to build in (**dans** to), embed (**dans** into).

encaustique [ɑ̃kostik] *nf* (wax) polish. **◆encaustiquer** *vt* to wax, polish.

enceinte [ɑ̃sɛ̃t] **1** *af* (*femme*) pregnant; **e. de six mois/*etc*** six months/*etc* pregnant. **2** *nf* (*muraille*) (surrounding) wall; (*espace*) enclosure; **e. acoustique** (loud)speakers.

encens [ɑ̃sɑ̃] *nm* incense. **◆encensoir** *nm* *Rel* censer.

encercler [ɑ̃sɛrkle] *vt* to surround, encircle.

enchaîner [ɑ̃ʃene] *vt* (*animal*) to chain (up); (*prisonnier*) to put in chains, chain (up); (*assembler*) to link (up), connect; – *vi* (*continuer à parler*) to continue; – **s'e.** *vpr* (*idées etc*) to be linked (up). **◆enchaînement** *nm* (*succession*) chain, series; (*liaison*) link(ing) (**de** between, of).

enchant/er [ɑ̃ʃɑ̃te] *vt* (*ravir*) to delight, enchant; (*ensorceler*) to bewitch, enchant. **◆—é** *a* (*ravi*) delighted (**de** with, **que** (+ *sub*) that); **e. de faire votre connaissance!** pleased to meet you! **◆—ement** *nm* delight; enchantment; **comme par e.** as if by magic. **◆—eur** *a* delightful, enchanting; – *nm* (*sorcier*) magician.

enchâsser [ɑ̃ʃɑse] *vt* (*diamant*) to set, embed.

enchère [ɑ̃ʃɛr] *nf* (*offre*) bid; **vente aux enchères** auction; **mettre aux enchères** to (put up for) auction. **◆enchér/ir** *vi* **e. sur qn** to outbid s.o. **◆—isseur** *nm* bidder.

enchevêtrer [ɑ̃ʃvetre] *vt* to (en)tangle; – **s'e.** *vpr* to get entangled (**dans** in). **◆enchevêtrement** *nm* tangle, entanglement.

enclave [ɑ̃klav] *nf* enclave. **◆enclaver** *vt* to enclose (completely).

enclencher [ɑ̃klɑ̃ʃe] *vt* *Tech* to engage.

enclin [ɑ̃klɛ̃] *am* **e. à** inclined *ou* prone to.

enclore [ɑ̃klɔr] *vt* (*terrain*) to enclose. **◆enclos** *nm* (*terrain, clôture*) enclosure.

enclume [ɑ̃klym] *nf* anvil.

encoche [ɑ̃kɔʃ] *nf* notch, nick (**à** in).

encoignure [ɑ̃kwaɲyr] *nf* corner.

encoller [ɑ̃kɔle] *vt* to paste.

encolure [ɑ̃kɔlyr] *nf* (*de cheval, vêtement*) neck; (*tour du cou*) collar (size).

encombre (sans) [sɑ̃zɑ̃kɔ̃br] *adv* without a hitch.

encombr/er [ɑ̃kɔ̃bre] *vt* (*couloir, pièce etc*) to clutter up (**de** with); (*rue*) to congest, clog (**de** with); **e. qn** to hamper s.o.; **s'e. de** to burden *ou* saddle oneself with. **◆—ant** *a* (*paquet*) bulky, cumbersome; (*présence*) awkward. **◆—é** *a* (*profession, marché*) overcrowded, saturated. **◆—ement** *nm* (*embarras*) clutter; *Aut* traffic jam; (*volume*) bulk(iness).

encontre de (à l') [alɑ̃kɔ̃trədə] *adv* against; (*contrairement à*) contrary to.

encore [ɑ̃kɔr] *adv* **1** (*toujours*) still; **tu es e. là?** are you still here? **2** (*avec négation*) yet; **pas e.** not yet; **ne pars pas e.** don't go yet; **je ne suis pas e. prêt** I'm not ready yet, I'm still not ready. **3** (*de nouveau*) again; **essaie e.** try again. **4** (*de plus*) **e. un café** another coffee, one more coffee; **e. une fois** (once) again, once more; **e. un** another (one), one more; **e. du pain** (some) more bread; **que veut-il e.?** what else *ou* more does he want?; **e. quelque chose** something else; **qui/quoi e.?** who/what else?; **chante e.** sing some more. **5** (*avec comparatif*) even, still; **e. mieux** even better, better still. **6** (*aussi*) also. **7 si e.** (*si seulement*) if only; **et e.!** (*à peine*) if that!, only just! **8 e. que** (+ *sub*) although.

encourag/er [ãkuraʒe] *vt* to encourage (à faire to do). ◆—**eant** *a* encouraging. ◆—**ement** *nm* encouragement.

encourir* [ãkurir] *vt* (*amende etc*) to incur.

encrasser [ãkrase] *vt* to clog up (with dirt).

encre [ãkr] *nf* ink; **e. de Chine** Indian ink; **e. sympathique** invisible ink. ◆**encrier** *nm* inkwell, inkpot.

encroûter (s') [sãkrute] *vpr Pej* to get set in one's ways; **s'e. dans** (*habitude*) to get stuck in.

encyclique [ãsiklik] *nf Rel* encyclical.

encyclopédie [ãsiklɔpedi] *nf* encyclop(a)edia. ◆**encyclopédique** *a* encyclop(a)edic.

endémique [ãdemik] *a* endemic.

endetter [ãdete] *vt* **e. qn** to get s.o. into debt; — **s'e.** *vpr* to get into debt. ◆**endettement** *nm* (*dettes*) debts.

endeuiller [ãdœje] *vt* to plunge into mourning.

endiablé [ãdjable] *a* (*rythme etc*) frantic, wild.

endiguer [ãdige] *vt* (*fleuve*) to dam (up); (*réprimer*) Fig to stem.

endimanché [ãdimãʃe] *a* in one's Sunday best.

endive [ãdiv] *nf* chicory, endive.

endoctrin/er [ãdɔktrine] *vt* to indoctrinate. ◆—**ement** *nm* indoctrination.

endolori [ãdɔlɔri] *a* painful, aching.

endommager [ãdɔmaʒe] *vt* to damage.

endorm/ir* [ãdɔrmir] *vt* (*enfant, patient*) to put to sleep; (*ennuyer*) to send to sleep; (*soupçons etc*) to lull; (*douleur*) to deaden; — **s'e.** *vpr* to fall asleep, go to sleep. ◆—**i** *a* asleep, sleeping; (*indolent*) Fam sluggish.

endosser [ãdose] *vt* (*vêtement*) to put on, don; (*responsabilité*) to assume; (*chèque*) to endorse.

endroit [ãdrwa] *nm* **1** place, spot; (*de film, livre*) part, place. **2** (*de tissu*) right side; **à l'e.** (*vêtement*) right side out, the right way round.

enduire* [ãdɥir] *vt* to smear, coat (**de** with). ◆**enduit** *nm* coating; (*de mur*) plaster.

endurant [ãdyrã] *a* hardy, tough. ◆**endurance** *nf* endurance.

endurc/ir [ãdyrsir] *vt* to harden; **s'e. à** (*personne*) to become hardened to (*pain etc*). ◆—**i** *a* hardened; (*célibataire*) confirmed. ◆—**issement** *nm* hardening.

endurer [ãdyre] *vt* to endure, bear.

énergie [enerʒi] *nf* energy; **avec é.** (*protester*

etc) forcefully. ◆**énergétique** *a* (*ressources etc*) energy-. ◆**énergique** *a* (*dynamique*) energetic; (*remède*) powerful; (*mesure, ton*) forceful. ◆**énergiquement** *adv* (*protester etc*) energetically.

énergumène [energymen] *nmf Péj* rowdy character.

énerv/er [enerve] *vt* **é. qn** (*irriter*) to get on s.o.'s nerves; (*rendre énervé*) to make s.o. nervous; — **s'é.** *vpr* to get worked up. ◆—**é** *a* on edge, irritated. ◆—**ement** *nm* irritation, nervousness.

enfant [ãfã] *nmf* child (*pl* children); **e. en bas âge** infant; **un e. de** (*originaire*) a native of; **attendre un e.** to expect a baby *ou* a child; **e. trouvé** foundling; **e. de chœur** Rel altar boy; **e. prodige** child prodigy; **e. prodigue** prodigal son; **bon e.** (*caractère*) good natured. ◆**enfance** *nf* childhood; **première e.** infancy, early childhood; **dans son e.** (*science etc*) in its infancy. ◆**enfanter** *vt* to give birth to; — *vi* to give birth. ◆**enfantillage** *nm* childishness. ◆**enfantin** *a* (*voix, joie*) childlike; (*langage, jeu*) children's; (*puéril*) childish; (*simple*) easy.

enfer [ãfer] *nm* hell; **d'e.** (*vision, bruit*) infernal; **feu d'e.** roaring fire; **à un train d'e.** at breakneck speed.

enfermer [ãferme] *vt* (*personne etc*) to shut up, lock up; (*objet précieux*) to lock up, shut away; (*jardin*) to enclose; **s'e. dans** (*chambre etc*) to shut *ou* lock oneself (up) in; (*attitude etc*) Fig to maintain stubbornly.

enferrer (s') [sãfere] *vpr* **s'e. dans** to get caught up in.

enfiévré [ãfjevre] *a* (*surexcité*) feverish.

enfiler [ãfile] *vt* (*aiguille*) to thread; (*perles etc*) to string; (*vêtement*) Fam to slip on, pull on; (*rue, couloir*) to take; **s'e. dans** (*rue etc*) to take. ◆**enfilade** *nf* (*série*) row, string.

enfin [ãfɛ̃] *adv* (*à la fin*) finally, at last; (*en dernier lieu*) lastly; (*en somme*) in a word; (*conclusion résignée*) well; **e. bref** (*en somme*) Fam in a word; **il est grand, e. pas trop petit** he's tall – well, not too short anyhow; **mais e.** but; (**mais**) **e.!** for heaven's sake!

enflamm/er [ãflame] *vt* to set fire to, ignite; (*allumette*) to light; (*irriter*) Méd to inflame; (*imagination, colère*) to excite, inflame; — **s'e.** *vpr* to catch fire, ignite; **s'e. de colère** to flare up. ◆—**é** *a* (*discours*) fiery.

enfler [ɑ̃fle] vt to swell; (voix) to raise; — vi Méd to swell (up). ◆**enflure** nf swelling.

enfonc/er [ɑ̃fɔ̃se] vt (clou etc) to knock in, drive in; (chapeau) to push ou force down; (porte, voiture) to smash in; **e. dans** (couteau, mains etc) to plunge into; — vi, — **s'e.** vpr (s'enliser) to sink (**dans** into); **s'e. dans** (pénétrer) to plunge into, disappear (deep) into. ◆**—é** a (yeux) sunken.

enfouir [ɑ̃fwir] vt to bury.

enfourcher [ɑ̃furʃe] vt (cheval etc) to mount, bestride.

enfourner [ɑ̃furne] vt to put in the oven.

enfreindre* [ɑ̃frɛ̃dr] vt to infringe.

enfuir* (s') [sɑ̃fɥir] vpr to run away ou off, flee (de from).

enfumer [ɑ̃fyme] vt (pièce) to fill with smoke; (personne) to smoke out.

engag/er [ɑ̃gaʒe] vt (bijou etc) to pawn; (parole) to pledge; (discussion, combat) to start; (clef etc) to insert (**dans** into); (capitaux) to tie up, invest; **e. la bataille avec** to join battle with; **e. qn** (lier) to bind s.o., commit s.o.; (embaucher) to hire s.o., engage s.o.; **e. qn dans** (affaire etc) to involve s.o. in; **e. qn à faire** (exhorter) to urge s.o. to do; — **s'e.** vpr (s'inscrire) Mil to enlist; Sp to enter; (au service d'une cause) to commit oneself; (action) to start; **s'e. à faire** to commit oneself to doing, undertake to do; **s'e. dans** (voie) to enter; (affaire etc) to get involved in. ◆**—eant** a engaging, inviting. ◆**—é** a (écrivain etc) committed. ◆**—ement** nm (promesse) commitment; (commencement) start; (de recrues) Mil enlistment; (inscription) Sp entry; (combat) Mil engagement; **prendre l'e. de** to undertake to.

engelure [ɑ̃ʒlyr] nf chilblain.

engendrer [ɑ̃ʒɑ̃dre] vt (procréer) to beget; (causer) to generate, engender.

engin [ɑ̃ʒɛ̃] nm machine, device; (projectile) missile; **e. explosif** explosive device.

englober [ɑ̃glɔbe] vt to include, embrace.

engloutir [ɑ̃glutir] vt (avaler) to wolf (down), gobble (up); (faire sombrer ou disparaître) to engulf.

engorger [ɑ̃gɔrʒe] vt to block up, clog.

engouement [ɑ̃gumɑ̃] nm craze.

engouffrer [ɑ̃gufre] vt (avaler) to wolf (down); (fortune) to consume; **s'e. dans** to sweep ou rush into.

engourd/ir [ɑ̃gurdir] vt (membre) to numb; (esprit) to dull; — **s'e.** vpr to go numb; to become dull. ◆**—issement** nm numbness; dullness.

engrais [ɑ̃grɛ] nm (naturel) manure; (chimique) fertilizer.

engraisser [ɑ̃grese] vt (animal) to fatten (up); — vi, — **s'e.** vpr to get fat, put on weight.

engrenage [ɑ̃grənaʒ] nm Tech gears; Fig mesh, chain, web.

engueuler [ɑ̃gœle] vt **e. qn** Fam to swear at s.o., give s.o. hell. ◆**engueulade** nf Fam (réprimande) dressing-down, severe talking-to; (dispute) slanging match, row.

enhardir [ɑ̃ardir] vt to make bolder; **s'e. à faire** to make bold to do.

énième [ɛnjɛm] a Fam umpteenth, nth.

énigme [enigm] nf enigma, riddle. ◆**énigmatique** a enigmatic.

enivrer [ɑ̃nivre] vt (soûler, troubler) to intoxicate; — **s'e.** vpr to get drunk (de on).

enjamber [ɑ̃ʒɑ̃be] vt to step over; (pont etc) to span (river etc). ◆**enjambée** nf stride.

enjeu, -x [ɑ̃ʒø] nm (mise) stake(s).

enjoindre [ɑ̃ʒwɛ̃dr] vt **e. à qn de faire** Litt to order s.o. to do.

enjôler [ɑ̃ʒole] vt to wheedle, coax.

enjoliv/er [ɑ̃ʒolive] vt to embellish. ◆**—eur** nm Aut hubcap.

enjoué [ɑ̃ʒwe] a playful. ◆**enjouement** nm playfulness.

enlacer [ɑ̃lase] vt to entwine; (serrer dans ses bras) to clasp.

enlaidir [ɑ̃ledir] vt to make ugly; — vi to grow ugly.

enlev/er [ɑ̃lve] vt to take away ou off, remove (à qn from s.o.); (ordures) to collect; (vêtement) to take off, remove; (tache) to take out, lift, remove; (enfant etc) to kidnap, abduct; — **s'e.** vpr (tache) to come out; (vernis) to come off. ◆**—é** a (scène, danse etc) well-rendered. ◆**enlèvement** nm kidnapping, abduction; (d'un objet) removal; (des ordures) collection.

enliser (s') [sɑ̃lize] vpr (véhicule) & Fig to get bogged down (**dans** in).

enneigé [ɑ̃neʒe] a snow-covered. ◆**enneigement** nm snow coverage; **bulletin d'e.** snow report.

ennemi, -ie [ɛnmi] nmf enemy; — a (personne) hostile (de to); (pays etc) enemy-.

ennui [ɑ̃nɥi] nm boredom; (mélancolie) weariness; **un e.** (tracas) (some) trouble ou bother; **des ennuis** trouble(s), bother; **l'e., c'est que . . .** the annoying thing is that . . .

ennuy/er [ɑ̃nɥije] vt (agacer) to annoy, bother; (préoccuper) to bother; (fatiguer) to bore; — **s'e.** vpr to get bored. ◆**—é**

a (*air*) bored; **je suis e.** that annoys *ou* bothers me. ◆**ennuyeux, -euse** *a* (*fastidieux*) boring; (*contrariant*) annoying.

énonc/er [enɔ̃se] *vt* to state, express. ◆**—é** *nm* (*de texte*) wording, terms; (*phrase*) *Ling* utterance.

enorgueillir [ɑ̃nɔrɡœjir] *vt* to make proud; **s'e. de** to pride oneself on.

énorme [enɔrm] *a* enormous, huge, tremendous. ◆**énormément** *adv* enormously, tremendously; **e. de** an enormous *ou* tremendous amount of. ◆**énormité** *nf* (*dimension*) enormity; (*faute*) (enormous) blunder.

enquérir (s') [sɑ̃kerir] *vpr* **s'e. de** to inquire about.

enquête [ɑ̃kɛt] *nf* (*de police etc*) investigation; (*judiciaire, administrative*) inquiry; (*sondage*) survey. ◆**enquêter** *vi* (*police etc*) to investigate; **e. sur** (*crime*) to investigate. ◆**enquêteur, -euse** *nmf* investigator.

enquiquiner [ɑ̃kikine] *vt Fam* to annoy, bug.

enraciner (s') [sɑ̃rasine] *vpr* to take root; **enraciné dans** (*personne, souvenir*) rooted in; **bien enraciné** (*préjugé etc*) deep-rooted.

enrag/er [ɑ̃raʒe] *vi* **e. de faire** to be furious about doing; **faire e. qn** to get on s.o.'s nerves. ◆**—eant** *a* infuriating. ◆**—é** *a* (*chien*) rabid, mad; (*joueur etc*) *Fam* fanatical (**de** about); **rendre/devenir e.** (*furieux*) to make/become furious.

enrayer [ɑ̃reje] *vt* (*maladie etc*) to check; **— s'e.** *vpr* (*fusil*) to jam.

enregistr/er [ɑ̃rʒistre] *vt* **1** (*inscrire*) to record; (*sur registre*) to register; (*constater*) to note, register; **(faire) e.** (*bagages*) to register, *Am* check. **2** (*musique, émission etc*) to record. ◆**—ement** *nm* (*des bagages*) registration, *Am* checking; (*d'un acte*) registration; (*sur bande etc*) recording. ◆**—eur, -euse** *a* (*appareil*) recording-; **caisse enregistreuse** cash register.

enrhumer [ɑ̃ryme] *vt* **e. qn** to give s.o. a cold; **être enrhumé** to have a cold; **— s'e.** *vpr* to catch a cold.

enrich/ir [ɑ̃riʃir] *vt* to enrich (**de** with); **— s'e.** *vpr* (*personne*) to get rich. ◆**—issement** *nm* enrichment.

enrober [ɑ̃rɔbe] *vt* to coat (**de** in); **enrobé de chocolat** chocolate-coated.

enrôl/er [ɑ̃role] *vt*, **— s'e.** *vpr* to enlist. ◆**—ement** *nm* enlistment.

enrou/er (s') [sɑ̃rwe] *vpr* to get hoarse. ◆**—é** *a* hoarse. ◆**—ement** [ɑ̃rumɑ̃] *nm* hoarseness.

enrouler [ɑ̃rule] *vt* (*fil etc*) to wind; (*tapis, cordage*) to roll up; **s'e. dans** (*couvertures*) to roll *ou* wrap oneself up in; **s'e. sur** *ou* **autour de qch** to wind round sth.

ensabler [ɑ̃sable] *vt*, **— s'e.** *vpr* (*port*) to silt up.

ensanglanté [ɑ̃sɑ̃ɡlɑ̃te] *a* bloodstained.

enseigne [ɑ̃sɛɲ] **1** *nf* (*de magasin etc*) sign; **e. lumineuse** neon sign; **logés à la même e.** *Fig* in the same boat. **2** *nm* **e. de vaisseau** lieutenant, *Am* ensign.

enseign/er [ɑ̃sɛɲe] *vt* to teach; **e. qch à qn** to teach s.o. sth; **— vi** to teach. ◆**—ant, -ante** [-ɛɲɑ̃, -ɑ̃t] *a* (*corps*) teaching-; **— *nmf*** teacher. ◆**—ement** [-ɛɲmɑ̃] *nm* education; (*action, métier*) teaching.

ensemble [ɑ̃sɑ̃bl] **1** *adv* together. **2** *nm* (*d'objets*) group, set; *Math* set; *Mus* ensemble; (*mobilier*) suite; (*vêtement féminin*) outfit; (*harmonie*) unity; **l'e. du personnel** (*totalité*) the whole (of the) staff; **l'e. des enseignants** all (of) the teachers; **dans l'e.** on the whole; **d'e.** (*vue etc*) general; **grand e.** (*quartier*) housing complex *ou Am* development; (*ville*) = new town; = *Am* planned community. ◆**ensemblier** *nm* (interior) decorator.

ensemencer [ɑ̃səmɑ̃se] *vt* (*terre*) to sow.

ensevelir [ɑ̃səvlir] *vt* to bury.

ensoleillé [ɑ̃sɔleje] *a* (*endroit, journée*) sunny.

ensommeillé [ɑ̃sɔmeje] *a* sleepy.

ensorceler [ɑ̃sɔrsəle] *vt* (*envoûter, séduire*) to bewitch. ◆**ensorcellement** *nm* (*séduction*) spell.

ensuite [ɑ̃sɥit] *adv* (*puis*) next, then; (*plus tard*) afterwards.

ensuivre* (s') [sɑ̃sɥivr] *vpr* to follow, ensue; **— *v imp* il s'ensuit que** it follows that.

entacher [ɑ̃taʃe] *vt* (*honneur etc*) to sully, taint.

entaille [ɑ̃taj] *nf* (*fente*) notch; (*blessure*) gash, slash. ◆**entailler** *vt* to notch; to gash, slash.

entame [ɑ̃tam] *nf* first slice.

entamer [ɑ̃tame] *vt* (*pain, peau etc*) to cut (into), (*bouteille, boîte etc*) to start (on); (*négociations etc*) to enter into, start; (*sujet*) to broach; (*capital*) to break *ou* eat into; (*métal, plastique*) to damage; (*résolution, réputation*) to shake.

entass/er [ɑ̃tase] *vt*, **— s'e.** *vpr* (*objets*) to pile up, heap up; **(s')e. dans** (*passagers etc*) to crowd *ou* pack *ou* pile into; **ils s'entassaient sur la plage** they were crowded *ou* packed (together) on the beach.

◆**—ement** *nm* (*tas*) pile, heap; (*de gens*) crowding.

entend/re [ātādr] *vt* to hear; (*comprendre*) to understand; (*vouloir*) to intend, mean; **e. parler de** to hear of; **e. dire que** to hear (it said) that; **e. raison** to listen to reason; **laisser e. à qn que** to give s.o. to understand that; **— s'e.** *vpr* (*être entendu*) to be heard; (*être compris*) to be understood; **s'e.** (**sur**) (*être d'accord*) to agree (on); **s'e.** (**avec qn**) (*s'accorder*) to get on (with s.o.); **on ne s'entend plus!** (*à cause du bruit etc*) we can't hear ourselves speak!; **il s'y entend** (*est expert*) he knows all about that. ◆**—u** *a* (*convenu*) agreed; (*compris*) understood; (*sourire, air*) knowing; **e.!** all right!; **bien e.** of course. ◆**—ement** *nm* (*faculté*) understanding. ◆**entente** *nf* (*accord*) agreement, understanding; (**bonne**) **e.** (*amitié*) good relationship, harmony.

entériner [āterine] *vt* to ratify.

enterrer [ātere] *vt* (*mettre en ou sous terre*) to bury; (*projet*) Fig to scrap. ◆**enterrement** *nm*: burial; (*funérailles*) funeral.

entêtant [ātetā] *a* (*enivrant*) heady.

en-tête [ātet] *nm* (*de papier*) heading; **papier à en-tête** headed paper.

entêt/er (s') [sātete] *vpr* to persist (à faire in doing). ◆**—é** *a* (*têtu*) stubborn; (*persévérant*) persistent. ◆**—ement** [ātetmā] *nm* stubbornness; (*à faire qch*) persistence.

enthousiasme [ātuzjasm] *nm* enthusiasm. ◆**enthousiasmer** *vt* to fill with enthusiasm, enthuse; **s'e. pour** to be *ou* get enthusiastic over, enthuse over. ◆**enthousiaste** *a* enthusiastic.

enticher (s') [sātife] *vpr* **s'e. de** to become infatuated with.

entier, -ière [ātje, -jɛr] **1** *a* (*total*) whole, entire; (*absolu*) absolute, complete, entire; (*intact*) intact; **payer place entière** to pay full price; **le pays tout e.** the whole *ou* entire country; **–** *nm* (*unité*) whole; **en e.**, **dans son e.** in its entirety, completely. **2** *a* (*caractère, personne*) unyielding. ◆**entièrement** *adv* entirely.

entité [ātite] *nf* entity.

entonner [ātɔne] *vt* (*air*) to start singing.

entonnoir [ātɔnwar] *nm* (*ustensile*) funnel.

entorse [ātɔrs] *nf* Méd sprain; **e. à** (*règlement*) infringement of.

entortill/er [ātɔrtije] *vt* **e. qch autour de qch** (*papier etc*) to wrap sth around sth; **e. qn** Fam to dupe s.o., get round s.o.; **— s'e.** *vpr* (*lierre etc*) to wind, twist. ◆**—é** *a* (*phrase etc*) convoluted.

entour/er [āture] *vt* to surround (**de** with);

(*envelopper*) to wrap (**de** in); **e. qn de ses bras** to put one's arms round s.o.; **s'e. de** to surround oneself with. ◆**—age** *nm* (*proches*) circle of family and friends.

entourloupette [āturlupet] *nf* Fam nasty trick.

entracte [ātrakt] *nm* Th interval, Am intermission.

entraide [ātrɛd] *nf* mutual aid. ◆**s'entraider** [sātrede] *vpr* to help each other.

entrailles [ātraj] *nfpl* entrails.

entrain [ātrɛ̃] *nm* spirit, liveliness; **plein d'e.** lively.

entraîn/er [ātrene] **1** *vt* (*charrier*) to sweep *ou* carry away; (*roue*) Tech to drive; (*causer*) to bring about; (*impliquer*) to entail, involve; **e. qn** (*emmener*) to lead *ou* draw s.o. (away); (*de force*) to drag s.o. (away); (*attirer*) Péj to lure s.o.; (*charmer*) to carry s.o. away; **e. qn à faire** (*amener*) to lead s.o. to do. **2** *vt* (*athlète, cheval etc*) to train (à for); **— s'e.** *vpr* to train oneself; Sp to train. ◆**—ant** [-ɛnā] *a* (*musique*) captivating. ◆**—ement** [-ɛnmā] *nm* **1** Sp training. **2** Tech drive; (*élan*) impulse. ◆**—eur** [-ɛnœr] *nm* (*instructeur*) Sp trainer, coach; (*de cheval*) trainer.

entrave [ātrav] *nf* (*obstacle*) Fig hindrance (à to). ◆**entraver** *vt* to hinder, hamper.

entre [ātr(ə)] *prép* between; (*parmi*) among(st); **l'un d'e. vous** one of you; (**soit dit**) **e. nous** between you and me; **se dévorer e. eux** (*réciprocité*) to devour each other; **e. deux âges** middle-aged; **e. autres** among other things; **e. les mains de** in the hands of.

entrebâill/er [ātrəbaje] *vt* (*porte*) to open slightly. ◆**—é** *a* ajar, slightly open. ◆**—eur** *nm* **e. de porte** door chain.

entrechoquer (s') [sātrəfɔke] *vpr* (*bouteilles etc*) to knock against each other, chink.

entrecôte [ātrəkot] *nf* (*boned*) rib steak.

entrecouper [ātrəkupe] *vt* (*entremêler*) to punctuate (**de** with), intersperse (**de** with).

entrecroiser [ātrəkrwaze] *vt*, **— s'e.** *vpr* (*fils*) to interlace; (*routes*) to intersect.

entre-deux-guerres [ātrədøgɛr] *nm inv* inter-war period.

entrée [ātre] *nf* (*action*) entry, entrance; (*porte*) entrance; (*accès*) entry, admission (**dc** to); (*vestibule*) entrance hall, entry; (*billet*) ticket (of admission); Culin first course, entrée; (*mot dans un dictionnaire etc*) entry; (*processus informatique*) input; **à son e.** as he *ou* she came in; **'e. interdite'** 'no entry', 'no admittance'; **'e. libre'** 'admission free'; **e. en matière** (*d'un discours*) opening.

entrefaites (sur ces) [syrsezɑ̃trəfɛt] *adv* at that moment.

entrefilet [ɑ̃trəfilɛ] *nm Journ* (news) item.

entrejambes [ɑ̃trəʒɑ̃b] *nm inv* (*de pantalon*) crutch, crotch.

entrelacer [ɑ̃trəlase] *vt*, **— s'e.** *vpr* to intertwine.

entremêler [ɑ̃trəmele] *vt*, **— s'e.** *vpr* to intermingle.

entremets [ɑ̃trəmɛ] *nm* (*plat*) sweet, dessert.

entremetteur, -euse [ɑ̃trəmɛtœr, -øz] *nmf Péj* go-between.

entremise [ɑ̃trəmiz] *nf* intervention; **par l'e. de qn** through s.o.

entreposer [ɑ̃trəpoze] *vt* to store; *Jur* to bond. ◆**entrepôt** *nm* warehouse; (*de la douane*) *Jur* bonded warehouse.

entreprendre* [ɑ̃trəprɑ̃dr] *vt* (*travail, voyage etc*) to start on, undertake; **e. de faire** to undertake to do. ◆**entreprenant** *a* enterprising; (*galant*) brash, forward. ◆**entrepreneur** *nm* (*en bâtiment*) (building) contractor. ◆**entreprise** *nf* **1** (*opération*) undertaking. **2** (*firme*) company, firm.

entrer [ɑ̃tre] *vi* (*aux être*) (*aller*) to go in, enter; (*venir*) to come in, enter; **e. dans** to go into; (*carrière*) to enter, go into; (*club*) to join, enter; (*détail, question*) to go *ou* enter into; (*pièce*) to come *ou* go into, enter; (*arbre etc*) *Aut* to crash into; **e. en action** to go *ou* get into action; **e. en ébullition** to start boiling; **entrez!** come in!; **faire/laisser e. qn** to show/let s.o. in.

entresol [ɑ̃trəsɔl] *nm* mezzanine (floor).

entre-temps [ɑ̃trətɑ̃] *adv* meanwhile.

entretenir* [ɑ̃trətnir] *vt* **1** (*voiture, maison etc*) to maintain; (*relations, souvenir etc*) to keep up; (*famille*) to keep, maintain; (*sentiment*) to entertain; **e. sa forme/sa santé** to keep fit/healthy. **e. qn de** to talk to s.o. about; **s'e. de** to talk about (**avec** with). ◆**—u** *a* (*femme*) kept. ◆**entretien** *nm* **1** (*de route, maison etc*) maintenance, upkeep; (*subsistance*) keep. **2** (*dialogue*) conversation; (*entrevue*) interview.

entre-tuer (s') [sɑ̃trətɥe] *vpr* to kill each other.

entrevoir* [ɑ̃trəvwar] *vt* (*rapidement*) to catch a glimpse of; (*pressentir*) to (fore)see.

entrevue [ɑ̃trəvy] *nf* interview.

entrouvrir* [ɑ̃truvrir] *vt*, **— s'e.** *vpr* to half-open. ◆**entrouvert** *a* (*porte, fenêtre*) ajar, half-open.

énumérer [enymere] *vt* to enumerate, list. ◆**énumération** *nf* enumeration.

envah/ir [ɑ̃vair] *vt* to invade; (*herbe etc*) to overrun; **e. qn** (*doute, peur etc*) to overcome s.o. ◆**—issant** *a* (*voisin etc*) intrusive. ◆**—issement** *nm* invasion. ◆**—isseur** *nm* invader.

enveloppe [ɑ̃vlɔp] *nf* (*pli*) envelope; (*de colis*) wrapping; (*de pneu*) casing; (*d'oreiller*) cover; (*apparence*) *Fig* exterior; **mettre sous e.** to put into an envelope. ◆**envelopp/er** *vt* to wrap (up); **e. la ville** (*brouillard etc*) to envelop the town; **enveloppé de mystère** shrouded *ou* enveloped in mystery; **— s'e.** *vpr* to wrap oneself (up) (**dans** in). ◆**—ant** *a* (*séduisant*) captivating.

envenimer [ɑ̃vnime] *vt* (*plaie*) to make septic; (*querelle*) *Fig* to envenom; **— s'e.** *vpr* to turn septic; *Fig* to become envenomed.

envergure [ɑ̃vɛrgyr] *nf* **1** (*d'avion, d'oiseau*) wingspan. **2** (*de personne*) calibre; (*ampleur*) scope, importance; **de grande e.** wide-ranging, far-reaching.

envers [ɑ̃vɛr] **1** *prép* towards, *Am* toward(s). **2** *nm* (*de tissu*) wrong side; (*de médaille*) reverse side; **à l'e.** (*chaussette*) inside out; (*pantalon*) back to front; (*à contresens, de travers*) the wrong way; (*en désordre*) upside down.

envie [ɑ̃vi] *nf* **1** (*jalousie*) envy; (*désir*) longing, desire; **avoir e. de qch** to want sth; **j'ai e. de faire** I feel like doing, I would like to do; **elle meurt d'e.** she's dying *ou* longing to do. **2** (*peau autour des ongles*) hangnail. ◆**envier** *vt* to envy (**qch à qn** s.o. sth). ◆**envieux, -euse** *a & nmf* envious (person); **faire des envieux** to cause envy.

environ [ɑ̃virɔ̃] *adv* (*à peu près*) about; **—** *nmpl* outskirts, surroundings; **aux environs de** (*Paris, Noël, dix francs etc*) around, in the vicinity of. ◆**environn/er** *vt* to surround. ◆**—ant** *a* surrounding. ◆**—ement** *nm* environment.

envisag/er [ɑ̃vizaʒe] *vt* to consider; (*imaginer comme possible*) to envisage, *Am* envision, consider; **e. de faire** to consider *ou* contemplate doing. ◆**—eable** *a* thinkable.

envoi [ɑ̃vwa] *nm* (*action*) dispatch, sending; (*paquet*) consignment; **coup d'e.** *Fb* kickoff.

envol [ɑ̃vɔl] *nm* (*d'oiseau*) taking flight; (*d'avion*) take-off; **piste d'e.** *Av* runway. ◆**s'envol/er** *vpr* (*oiseau*) to fly away; (*avion*) to take off; (*emporté par le vent*) to blow away; (*espoir*) *Fig* to vanish. ◆**—ée** *nf* (*élan*) *Fig* flight.

envoût/er [ɑ̃vute] *vt* to bewitch. ◆**—ement** *nm* bewitchment.

envoy/er* [ɑ̃vwaje] *vt* to send; (*pierre*) to throw; (*gifle*) to give; **e. chercher qn** to send for s.o.; **— s'e.** *vpr Fam* (*travail etc*) to take on, do; (*repas etc*) to put *ou* stash away. ◆**—é, -ée** *nmf* envoy; *Journ* correspondent. ◆**—eur** *nm* sender.

épagneul, -eule [epaɲœl] *nmf* spaniel.

épais, -aisse [epɛ, -ɛs] *a* thick; (*personne*) thick-set; (*esprit*) dull. ◆**épaisseur** *nf* thickness; (*dimension*) depth. ◆**épaissir** *vt* to thicken; — *vi*, **— s'é.** *vpr* to thicken; (*grossir*) to fill out; **le mystère s'épaissit** the mystery is deepening.

épanch/er [epɑ̃ʃe] *vt* (*cœur*) *Fig* to pour out; **— s'é.** *vpr* (*parler*) to pour out one's heart, unbosom oneself. ◆**—ement** *nm* (*aveu*) outpouring; *Méd* effusion.

épanou/ir (s') [epanwir] *vpr* (*fleur*) to open out; (*personne*) *Fig* to fulfil oneself, blossom (out); (*visage*) to beam. ◆**—i** *a* (*fleur, personne*) in full bloom; (*visage*) beaming. ◆**—issement** *nm* (*éclat*) full bloom; (*de la personnalité*) fulfilment.

épargne [eparɲ] *nf* saving (**de** of); (*qualité, vertu*) thrift; (*sommes d'argent*) savings. ◆**épargn/er** *vt* (*ennemi etc*) to spare; (*denrée rare etc*) to be sparing with; (*argent, temps*) to save; **e. qch à qn** (*ennuis, chagrin etc*) to spare s.o. sth. ◆**—ant, -ante** *nmf* saver.

éparpiller [eparpije] *vt*, **— s'é.** *vpr* to scatter; (*efforts*) to dissipate. ◆**épars** *a* scattered.

épaté [epate] *a* (*nez*) flat. ◆**épatement** *nm* flatness.

épat/er [epate] *vt Fam* to stun, astound. ◆**—ant** *a Fam* stunning, marvellous.

épaule [epol] *nf* shoulder. ◆**épauler** *vt* (*fusil*) to raise (to one's shoulder); **é. qn** (*aider*) to back s.o. up.

épave [epav] *nf* (*bateau, personne*) wreck; *pl* (*débris*) *Nau* (pieces of) wreckage.

épée [epe] *nf* sword; **un coup d'é.** a sword thrust.

épeler [eple] *vt* (*mot*) to spell.

éperdu [eperdy] *a* frantic, wild (**de** with); (*regard*) distraught. ◆**—ment** *adv* (*aimer*) madly; **elle s'en moque e.** she couldn't care less.

éperon [eprɔ̃] *nm* (*de cavalier, coq*) spur. ◆**éperonner** (*cheval, personne*) to spur (on).

épervier [epɛrvje] *nm* sparrowhawk.

éphémère [efemɛr] *a* short-lived, ephemeral, transient.

épi [epi] *nm* (*de blé etc*) ear; (*mèche de cheveux*) tuft of hair.

épice [epis] *nf Culin* spice. ◆**épic/er** *vt* to spice. ◆**—é** *a* (*plat, récit etc*) spicy.

épicier, -ière [episje, -jɛr] *nmf* grocer. ◆**épicerie** *nf* (*magasin*) grocer's (shop); (*produits*) groceries.

épidémie [epidemi] *nf* epidemic. ◆**épidémique** *a* epidemic.

épiderme [epidɛrm] *nm Anat* skin.

épier [epje] *vt* (*observer*) to watch closely; (*occasion*) to watch out for; **é. qn** to spy on s.o.

épilepsie [epilɛpsi] *nf* epilepsy. ◆**épileptique** *a* & *nmf* epileptic.

épiler [epile] *vt* (*jambe*) to remove unwanted hair from; (*sourcil*) to pluck.

épilogue [epilɔg] *nm* epilogue.

épinard [epinar] *nm* (*plante*) spinach; *pl* (*feuilles*) *Culin* spinach.

épine [epin] *nf* **1** (*de buisson*) thorn; (*d'animal*) spine, prickle. **2 é. dorsale** *Anat* spine. ◆**épineux, -euse** *a* (*tige, question*) thorny.

épingle [epɛ̃gl] *nf* pin; **é. de nourrice, é. de sûreté** safety pin; **é. à linge** clothes peg, *Am* clothes pin; **virage en é. à cheveux** hairpin bend; **tiré à quatre épingles** very spruce. ◆**épingler** *vt* to pin; **é. qn** (*arrêter*) *Fam* to nab s.o.

épique [epik] *a* epic.

épiscopal, -aux [episkɔpal, -o] *a* episcopal.

épisode [epizɔd] *nm* episode; **film à épisodes** serial. ◆**épisodique** *a* occasional, episodic; (*accessoire*) minor.

épitaphe [epitaf] *nf* epitaph.

épithète [epitɛt] *nf* epithet; *Gram* attribute.

épître [epitr] *nf* epistle.

éploré [eplɔre] *a* (*personne, air*) tearful.

éplucher [eplyʃe] *vt* (*pommes de terre*) to peel; (*salade*) to clean, pare; (*texte*) *Fig* to dissect. ◆**épluchure** *nf* peeling.

éponge [epɔ̃ʒ] *nf* sponge. ◆**éponger** *vt* (*liquide*) to sponge up, mop up; (*carrelage*) to sponge (down), mop; (*dette etc*) *Fin* to absorb; **s'é. le front** to mop one's brow.

épopée [epɔpe] *nf* epic.

époque [epɔk] *nf* (*date*) time, period; (*historique*) age; **meubles d'é.** period furniture; **à l'é.** at the *ou* that time.

épouse [epuz] *nf* wife, *Jur* spouse.

épouser [epuze] *vt* **1 é. qn** to marry s.o. **2** (*opinion etc*) to espouse; (*forme*) to assume, adopt.

épousseter [epuste] *vt* to dust.

époustoufler [epustufle] vt Fam to astound.
épouvantail [epuvãtaj] nm (à oiseaux) scarecrow.
épouvante [epuvãt] nf (peur) terror; (appréhension) dread; **d'é.** (film etc) horror-. ◆**épouvant/er** vt to terrify. ◆**-able** a terrifying; (très mauvais) appalling.
époux [epu] nm husband, Jur spouse; pl husband and wife.
éprendre* (s') [seprãdr] vpr **s'é. de qn** to fall in love with s.o. ◆**épris** a in love (de with).
épreuve [eprœv] nf (essai, examen) test; Sp event, heat; Phot print; Typ proof; (malheur) ordeal, trial; **mettre à l'é.** to put to the test. ◆**éprouv/er** vt to test, try; (sentiment etc) to experience, feel; **é. qn** (mettre à l'épreuve) to put s.o. to the test; (faire souffrir) to distress s.o. ◆**-ant** a (pénible) trying. ◆**-é** a (sûr) well-tried.
éprouvette [epruvɛt] nf test tube; **bébé é.** test tube baby.
épuis/er [epɥize] vt (personne, provisions, sujet) to exhaust; — **s'é.** vpr (réserves, patience) to run out; **s'é. à faire** to exhaust oneself doing. ◆**-ant** a exhausting. ◆**-é** a exhausted; (édition) out of print; (marchandise) out of stock. ◆**-ement** nm exhaustion.
épuisette [epɥizɛt] nf fishing net (on pole).
épurer [epyre] vt to purify; (personnel etc) to purge; (goût) to refine. ◆**épuration** nf purification; purging; refining.
équateur [ekwatœr] nm equator; **sous l'é.** at ou on the equator. ◆**équatorial, -aux** a equatorial.
équation [ekwasjõ] nf Math equation.
équerre [ekɛr] nf **é.** (à dessiner) setsquare, Am triangle; **d'é.** straight, square.
équestre [ekɛstr] a (figure etc) equestrian; (exercices etc) horseriding-.
équilibre [ekilibr] nm balance; **tenir ou mettre en é.** to balance (sur on); **se tenir en é.** to (keep one's) balance; **perdre l'é.** to lose one's balance. ◆**équilibrer** vt (charge, budget etc) to balance; — **s'é.** vpr (équipes etc) to (counter)balance each other; (comptes) to balance.
équinoxe [ekinɔks] nm equinox.
équipage [ekipaʒ] nm Nau Av crew.
équipe [ekip] nf team; (d'ouvriers) gang; **é. de nuit** night shift; **é. de secours** search party; **faire é. avec** to team up with. ◆**équipier, -ière** nmf team member.
équipée [ekipe] nf escapade.
équip/er [ekipe] vt to equip (de with); — **s'é.** vpr to equip oneself. ◆**-ement** nm

equipment; (de camping, ski etc) gear, equipment.
équitation [ekitasjõ] nf (horse) riding.
équité [ekite] nf fairness. ◆**équitable** a fair, equitable. ◆**équitablement** adv fairly.
équivalent [ekivalã] a & nm equivalent. ◆**équivalence** nf equivalence. ◆**équivaloir** vi **é. à** to be equivalent to.
équivoque [ekivɔk] a (ambigu) equivocal; (douteux) dubious; — nf ambiguity.
érable [erabl] nm (arbre, bois) maple.
érafler [erafle] vt to graze, scratch. ◆**éraflure** nf graze, scratch.
éraillée [eraje] af (voix) rasping.
ère [ɛr] nf era.
érection [erɛksjõ] nf (de monument etc) erection.
éreinter [erɛ̃te] vt (fatiguer) to exhaust; (critiquer) to tear to pieces, slate, slam.
ergot [ɛrgo] nm (de coq) spur.
ergoter [ɛrgote] vi to quibble, cavil.
ériger [eriʒe] vt to erect; **s'é. en** to set oneself up as.
ermite [ɛrmit] nm hermit.
érosion [erozjõ] nf erosion. ◆**éroder** vt to erode.
érotique [erɔtik] a erotic. ◆**érotisme** nm eroticism.
err/er [ɛre] vi to wander, roam. ◆**-ant** a wandering, roving; (animal) stray.
erreur [ɛrœr] nf (faute) error, mistake; (action blâmable, opinion fausse) error; **par e.** by mistake, in error; **dans l'e.** mistaken. ◆**erroné** a erroneous.
ersatz [ɛrzats] nm substitute.
éructer [erykte] vi Litt to belch.
érudit, -ite [erydi, -it] a scholarly, erudite; — nmf scholar. ◆**érudition** nf scholarship, erudition.
éruption [erypsjõ] nf (de volcan, colère) eruption (de of); Méd rash.
es voir **être.**
ès [ɛs] prép of; **licencié/docteur ès lettres =** BA/PhD.
escabeau, -x [ɛskabo] nm stepladder, (pair of) steps; (tabouret) stool.
escadre [ɛskadr] nf Nau Av fleet, squadron. ◆**escadrille** nf (unité) Av flight. ◆**escadron** nm squadron.
escalade [ɛskalad] nf climbing; (de prix) & Mil escalation. ◆**escalader** vt to climb, scale.
escale [ɛskal] nf Av stop(over); Nau port of call; **faire e. à** Av to stop (over) at; Nau to put in at; **vol sans e.** non-stop flight.
escalier [ɛskalje] nm staircase, stairs; **e. mé-**

canique *ou* **roulant** escalator; **e. de secours** fire escape.

escalope [ɛskalɔp] *nf* Culin escalope.

escamot/er [ɛskamɔte] *vt* (*faire disparaître*) to make vanish; (*esquiver*) to dodge. ◆**—able** *a* Av Tech retractable.

escapade [ɛskapad] *nf* (*excursion*) jaunt; **faire une e.** to run off.

escargot [ɛskargo] *nm* snail.

escarmouche [ɛskarmuʃ] *nf* skirmish.

escarpé [ɛskarpe] *a* steep. ◆**escarpement** *nm* (*côte*) steep slope.

escarpin [ɛskarpɛ̃] *nm* (*soulier*) pump, court shoe.

escient [ɛsjɑ̃] *nm* **à bon e.** discerningly, wisely.

esclaffer (s') [sɛsklafe] *vpr* to roar with laughter.

esclandre [ɛsklɑ̃dr] *nm* (noisy) scene.

esclave [ɛsklav] *nmf* slave; **être l'e. de** to be a slave to. ◆**esclavage** *nm* slavery.

escompte [ɛskɔ̃t] *nm* discount; **taux d'e.** bank rate. ◆**escompter** *vt* 1 (*espérer*) to anticipate (**faire doing**), expect (**faire** to do). 2 *Com* to discount.

escorte [ɛskɔrt] *nf* Mil Nau etc escort. ◆**escorter** *vt* to escort.

escouade [ɛskwad] *nf* (*petite troupe*) squad.

escrime [ɛskrim] *nf* Sp fencing. ◆**escrimeur, -euse** *nmf* fencer.

escrimer (s') [sɛskrime] *vpr* to slave away (**à faire** at doing).

escroc [ɛskro] *nm* swindler, crook. ◆**escroquer** *vt* **e. qn** to swindle s.o.; **e. qch à qn** to swindle s.o. out of sth. ◆**escroquerie** *nf* swindling; **une e.** a swindle.

espace [ɛspas] *nm* space; **e. vert** garden, park. ◆**espacer** *vt* to space out; **espacés d'un mètre** (spaced out) one metre apart; **— s'e.** (*maisons, visites etc*) to become less frequent.

espadon [ɛspadɔ̃] *nm* swordfish.

espadrille [ɛspadrij] *nf* rope-soled sandal.

Espagne [ɛspaɲ] *nf* Spain. ◆**espagnol, -ole** *a* Spanish; **—** *nmf* Spaniard; **—** *nm* (*langue*) Spanish.

espèce [ɛspɛs] 1 *nf* (*race*) species; (*genre*) kind, sort; **c'est une e. d'idiot** he's a silly fool; **e. d'idiot!/de maladroit!/etc** (you) silly fool!/oaf!/etc. 2 *nfpl* (*argent*) **en espèces** in cash.

espérance [ɛsperɑ̃s] *nf* hope; **avoir des espérances** to have expectations; **e. de vie** life expectancy. ◆**espérer** *vt* to hope for; **e. que** to hope that; **e. faire** to hope to do; **—** *vi* to hope; **e. en qn/qch** to trust in s.o./sth.

espiègle [ɛspjɛgl] *a* mischievous. ◆**es-**

pièglerie *nf* mischievousness; (*farce*) mischievous trick.

espion, -onne [ɛspjɔ̃, -ɔn] *nmf* spy. ◆**espionnage** *nm* espionage, spying. ◆**espionner** *vt* to spy on; **—** *vi* to spy.

esplanade [ɛsplanad] *nf* esplanade.

espoir [ɛspwar] *nm* hope; **avoir de l'e.** to have hope(s); **sans e.** (*cas etc*) hopeless.

esprit [ɛspri] *nm* (*attitude, fantôme*) spirit; (*intellect*) mind; (*humour*) wit; (*être humain*) person; **avoir de l'e.** to be witty; **cette idée m'est venue à l'e.** this idea crossed my mind.

esquimau, -aude, -aux [ɛskimo, -od, -o] 1 *a* & *nmf* Eskimo. 2 *nm* (*glace*) choc-ice (*on a stick*).

esquinter [ɛskɛ̃te] *vt* Fam (*voiture etc*) to damage, bash; (*critiquer*) to slam, pan (*author, film etc*); **s'e. la santé** to damage one's health; **s'e. à faire** (*se fatiguer*) to wear oneself out doing.

esquisse [ɛskis] *nf* (*croquis, plan*) sketch. ◆**esquisser** *vt* to sketch; **e. un geste** to make a (slight) gesture.

esquive [ɛskiv] *nf* Boxe dodge; **e. de** (*question*) dodging of, evasion of. ◆**esquiver** *vt* (*coup, problème*) to dodge; **— s'e.** *vpr* to slip away.

essai [ɛse] *nm* (*épreuve*) test, trial; (*tentative*) try, attempt; Rugby try; Littér essay; **à l'e.** (*objet*) Com on trial, on approval; **pilote d'e.** test pilot; **période d'e.** trial period.

essaim [ɛsɛ̃] *nm* swarm (*of bees etc*).

essayer [eseje] *vt* to try (**de faire** to do); (*vêtement*) to try on; (*méthode*) to try (out); **s'e. à qch/à faire** to try one's hand at sth/at doing. ◆**essayage** *nm* (*de costume*) fitting.

essence [esɑ̃s] *nf* 1 (*extrait*) Ch Culin essence; Aut petrol, Am gas; **poste d'e.** filling station. 2 Phil essence. 3 (*d'arbres*) species. ◆**essentiel, -ielle** *a* essential (**à, pour** for); **—** *nm* **l'e.** the main thing *ou* point; (*quantité*) the main part (**de** of). ◆**essentiellement** *adv* essentially.

essieu, -x [esjø] *nm* axle.

essor [esɔr] *nm* (*de pays, d'entreprise etc*) development, rise, expansion; **en plein e.** (*industrie etc*) booming.

essor/er [esɔre] *vt* (*linge*) to wring; (*dans une essoreuse*) to spin-dry; (*dans une machine à laver*) to spin. ◆**—euse** *nf* (*à main*) wringer; (*électrique*) spin dryer.

essouffler [esufle] *vt* to make (s.o.) out of breath; **— s'e.** *vpr* to get out of breath.

essuyer [esɥije] 1 *vt* to wipe; **— s'e.** *vpr* to wipe oneself. 2 *vt* (*subir*) to suffer. ◆**es-**

suie-glace *nm inv* windscreen wiper, *Am* windshield wiper. ◆**essuie-mains** *nm inv* (hand) towel.

est¹ [ɛ] *voir* être.

est² [ɛst] *nm* east; − *a inv* (*côte*) east(ern); **d'e.** (*vent*) east(erly); **de l'e.** eastern; **Allemagne de l'E.** East Germany. ◆**e.-allemand, -ande** *a* & *nmf* East German.

estafilade [ɛstafilad] *nf* gash, slash.

estampe [ɛstɑ̃p] *nf* (*gravure*) print.

estamper [ɛstɑ̃pe] *vt* (*rouler*) *Fam* to swindle.

estampille [ɛstɑ̃pij] *nf* mark, stamp.

esthète [ɛstɛt] *nmf* aesthete, *Am* esthete. ◆**esthétique** *a* aesthetic, *Am* esthetic.

esthéticienne [ɛstetisjɛn] *nf* beautician.

estime [ɛstim] *nf* esteem, regard. ◆**estim/er** *vt* (*objet*) to value; (*juger*) to consider (**que** that); (*calculer*) to estimate; (*apprécier*) to appreciate; **e. qn** to have high regard for s.o., esteem s.o.; **s'e. heureux**/*etc* to consider oneself happy/*etc*. ◆**−able** *a* respectable. ◆**estimation** *nf* (*de mobilier etc*) valuation; (*calcul*) estimation.

estival, -aux [ɛstival, -o] *a* (*période etc*) summer-. ◆**estivant, -ante** *nmf* holidaymaker, *Am* vacationer.

estomac [ɛstɔma] *nm* stomach.

estomaquer [ɛstɔmake] *vt* *Fam* to flabbergast.

estomper [ɛstɔ̃pe] *vt* (*rendre flou*) to blur; − **s'e.** *vpr* to become blurred.

estrade [ɛstrad] *nf* (*tribune*) platform.

estropi/er [ɛstrɔpje] *vt* to cripple, maim. ◆**−é, -ée** *nmf* cripple.

estuaire [ɛstɥɛr] *nm* estuary.

esturgeon [ɛstyrʒɔ̃] *nm* (*poisson*) sturgeon.

et [e] *conj* and; **vingt et un**/*etc* twenty-one/*etc*.

étable [etabl] *nf* cowshed.

établi [etabli] *nm* *Menuis* (work)bench.

établ/ir [etablir] *vt* to establish; (*installer*) to set up; (*plan, chèque, liste*) to draw up; − **s'é.** *vpr* (*habiter*) to settle; (*épicier etc*) to set up shop as, set (oneself) up as. ◆**−issement** *nm* (*action, bâtiment, institution*) establishment; *Com* firm, establishment; **é. scolaire** school.

étage [etaʒ] *nm* (*d'immeuble*) floor, storey, *Am* story; (*de fusée etc*) stage; **à l'é.** upstairs; **au premier é.** on the first *ou Am* second floor. ◆**étager** *vt*, − **s'é.** *vpr* (*rochers, maisons*) to range above one another.

étagère [etaʒɛr] *nf* shelf; (*meuble*) shelving unit.

étai [etɛ] *nm* *Tech* prop, stay.

étain [etɛ̃] *nm* (*métal*) tin; (*de gobelet etc*) pewter.

était [etɛ] *voir* être.

étal, *pl* **étals** [etal] *nm* (*au marché*) stall.

étalage [etalaʒ] *nm* display; (*vitrine*) display window; **faire é. de** to make a show *ou* display of. ◆**étalagiste** *nmf* window dresser.

étaler [etale] *vt* (*disposer*) to lay out; (*luxe etc*) & *Com* to display; (*crème, beurre etc*) to spread; (*vacances*) to stagger; − **s'é.** *vpr* (*s'affaler*) to sprawl; (*tomber*) *Fam* to fall flat; **s'é. sur** (*congés, paiements etc*) to be spread over.

étalon [etalɔ̃] *nm* **1** (*cheval*) stallion. **2** (*modèle*) standard.

étanche [etɑ̃ʃ] *a* watertight; (*montre*) waterproof.

étancher [etɑ̃ʃe] *vt* (*sang*) to stop the flow of; (*soif*) to quench, slake.

étang [etɑ̃] *nm* pond.

étant [etɑ̃] *voir* être.

étape [etap] *nf* (*de voyage etc*) stage; (*lieu*) stop(over); **faire é. à** to stop off *ou* over at.

état [eta] *nm* **1** (*condition, manière d'être*) state; (*registre, liste*) statement, list; **en bon é.** in good condition; **en é. de faire** in a position to do; **é. d'esprit** state *ou* frame of mind; **é. d'âme** mood; **é. civil** civil status (*birth, marriage, death etc*); **é. de choses** situation, state of affairs; **à l'é. brut** in a raw state; **de son é.** (*métier*) by trade; **faire é. de** (*mention*) to mention, put forward. **2** É. (*nation*) State; **homme d'É.** statesman. ◆**étatisé** *a* state-controlled, state-owned.

état-major [etamaʒɔr] *nm* (*pl* **états-majors**) (*d'un parti etc*) senior staff.

États-Unis [etazyni] *nmpl* É.-Unis (**d'Amérique**) United States (of America).

étau, -x [eto] *nm* *Tech* vice, *Am* vise.

étayer [eteje] *vt* to prop up, support.

été¹ [ete] *nm* summer.

été² [ete] *voir* être.

éteindre* [etɛ̃dr] *vt* (*feu, cigarette etc*) to put out, extinguish; (*lampe etc*) to turn *ou* switch off; (*dette, espoir*) to extinguish; − *vi* to switch off; − **s'é.** *vpr* (*feu*) to go out; (*personne*) to pass away; (*race*) to die out. ◆**éteint** *a* (*feu*) out; (*volcan, race, amour*) extinct; (*voix*) faint.

étendard [etɑ̃dar] *nm* (*drapeau*) standard.

étend/re [etɑ̃dr] *vt* (*nappe*) to spread (out); (*beurre*) to spread; (*linge*) to hang out; (*agrandir*) to extend; **é. le bras**/*etc* to stretch out one's arm/*etc*; **é. qn** to stretch s.o. out; − **s'é.** *vpr* (*personne*) to stretch (oneself) out; (*plaine etc*) to stretch; (*feu*) to spread; (*pouvoir*) to extend; **s'é. sur** (*sujet*) to dwell on. ◆—**u** *a* (*forêt, vocabulaire etc*) extensive; (*personne*) stretched out. ◆—**ue** *nf* (*importance*) extent; (*surface*) area; (*d'eau*) expanse, stretch.

éternel, -elle [etɛrnɛl] *a* eternal. ◆**éternellement** *adv* eternally, for ever. ◆**éterniser** *vt* to perpetuate; — **s'é.** *vpr* (*débat etc*) to drag on endlessly; (*visiteur etc*) to stay for ever. ◆**éternité** *nf* eternity.

éternu/er [etɛrnɥe] *vi* to sneeze. ◆—**ement** [-ymɑ̃] *nm* sneeze.

êtes [ɛt] *voir* **être**.

éther [etɛr] *nm* ether.

Éthiopie [etjɔpi] *nf* Ethiopia. ◆**éthiopien, -ienne** *a & nmf* Ethiopian.

éthique [etik] *a* ethical; — *nf Phil* ethics; **l'é. puritaine**/*etc* the Puritan/*etc* ethic.

ethnie [etni] *nf* ethnic group. ◆**ethnique** *a* ethnic.

étinceler [etɛ̃sle] *vi* to sparkle. ◆**étincelle** *nf* spark. ◆**étincellement** *nm* sparkle.

étioler (s') [setjɔle] *vpr* to wilt, wither.

étiqueter [etikte] *vt* to label. ◆**étiquette** *nf* **1** (*marque*) label. **2** (*protocole*) diplomatic *ou* court) etiquette.

étirer [etire] *vt* to stretch; — **s'é.** *vpr* to stretch (oneself).

étoffe [etɔf] *nf* material, cloth, fabric; (*de héros etc*) *Fig* stuff (**de** of).

étoffer [etɔfe] *vt*, — **s'é.** *vpr* to fill out.

étoile [etwal] *nf* **1** star; **à la belle é.** in the open. **2** é. **de mer** starfish. ◆**étoilé** *a* (*ciel, nuit*) starry; (*vitre*) cracked (*star-shaped*); **é. de** (*rubis etc*) studded with; **la bannière étoilée** *Am* the Star-Spangled Banner.

étonn/er [etɔne] *vt* to surprise, astonish; — **s'é.** *vpr* to be surprised *ou* astonished (**de qch** at sth, **que** (+ *sub*) that). ◆—**ant** *a* (*ahurissant*) surprising; (*remarquable*) amazing. ◆—**ement** *nm* surprise, astonishment.

étouff/er [etufe] *vt* (*tuer*) to suffocate, smother; (*bruit*) to muffle; (*feu*) to smother; (*révolte, sentiment*) to stifle; (*scandale*) to hush up; **é. qn** (*chaleur*) to stifle s.o.; (*aliment, colère*) to choke s.o.; — *vi* to suffocate; **on étouffe!** it's stifling!; **é. de colère** to choke with anger. — **s'é.** *vpr* (*en mangeant*) to choke, gag (**sur, avec** on); (*mourir*) to suffocate. ◆—**ant** *a* (*air*) stifling. ◆—**ement** *nm Méd* suffocation.

étourd/i, -ie [eturdi] *a* thoughtless; — *nmf* scatterbrain. ◆**étourderie** *nf* thoughtlessness; **une é.** (*faute*) a thoughtless blunder. **étourd/ir** [eturdir] *vt* to stun, daze; (*vertige,*

vin) to make dizzy; (*abrutir*) to deafen. ◆—**issant** *a* (*bruit*) deafening; (*remarquable*) stunning. ◆—**issement** *nm* dizziness; (*syncope*) dizzy spell.

étourneau, -x [eturno] *nm* starling.

étrange [etrɑ̃ʒ] *a* strange, odd. ◆—**ment** *adv* strangely, oddly. ◆**étrangeté** *nf* strangeness, oddness.

étranger, -ère [etrɑ̃ʒe, -ɛr] *a* (*d'un autre pays*) foreign; (*non familier*) strange (**à** to); **il m'est é.** he's unknown to me; — *nmf* foreigner; (*inconnu*) stranger; **à l'é.** abroad; **de l'é.** from abroad.

étrangl/er [etrɑ̃gle] *vt* **é. qn** (*tuer*) to strangle s.o.; (*col, aliment*) to choke s.o.; — **s'é.** *vpr* (*de colère, en mangeant etc*) to choke. ◆—**é** *a* (*voix*) choking; (*passage*) constricted. ◆—**ement** *nm* (*d'une victime*) strangulation. ◆—**eur, -euse** *nmf* strangler.

être* [etr] **1** *vi* to be; **il est tailleur** he's a tailor; **est-ce qu'elle vient?** is she coming?; **il vient, n'est-ce pas?** he's coming, isn't he?; **est-ce qu'il aime le thé?** does he like tea?; **nous sommes dix** there are ten of us; **nous sommes le dix** today is the tenth (of the month); **où en es-tu?** how far have you got?; **il a été à Paris** (*est allé*) he's been to Paris; **elle est de Paris** she's from Paris; **elle est de la famille** she's one of the family; **c'est à faire tout de suite** it must be done straight away; **c'est à lui** it's his; **cela étant** that being so. **2** *v aux* (*avec venir, partir etc*) to have; **elle est déjà arrivée** she has already arrived. **3** *nm* (*personne*) being; **ê. humain** human being; **les êtres chers** the loved ones.

étreindre [etrɛ̃dr] *vt* to grip; (*ami*) to embrace. ◆**étreinte** *nf* grip; (*amoureuse etc*) embrace.

étrenner [etrene] *vt* to use *ou* wear for the first time.

étrennes [etren] *nfpl* New Year gift; (*gratification*) = Christmas box *ou* tip.

étrier [etrije] *nm* stirrup.

étriper (s') [setripe] *vpr Fam* to fight (each other) to the kill.

étriqué [etrike] *a* (*vêtement*) tight, skimpy; (*esprit, vie*) narrow.

étroit [etrwa] *a* narrow; (*vêtement*) tight; (*parenté, collaboration etc*) close; (*discipline*) strict; **être à l'é.** to be cramped. ◆**étroitement** *adv* (*surveiller etc*) closely. ◆**étroitesse** *nf* narrowness; closeness; **é. d'esprit** narrow-mindedness.

étude [etyd] *nf* **1** (*action, ouvrage*) study; (*salle*) *Scol* study room; **à l'é.** (*projet*) under consideration; **faire des études de** (*médecine etc*) to study. **2** (*de notaire etc*) office. ◆**étudiant, -ante** *nmf* & *a* student. ◆**étudier** *vti* to study.

étui [etɥi] *nm* (*à lunettes, à cigarettes etc*) case; (*de revolver*) holster.

étymologie [etimɔlɔʒi] *nf* etymology.

eu, eue [y] *voir* avoir.

eucalyptus [økaliptys] *nm* (*arbre*) eucalyptus.

Eucharistie [økaristi] *nf* Rel Eucharist.

euh! [ø] *int* hem!, er!, well!

euphémisme [øfemism] *nm* euphemism.

euphorie [øfɔri] *nf* euphoria.

eurent [yr] *voir* avoir.

euro- [øro] *préf* Euro-.

Europe [ørɔp] *nf* Europe. ◆**européen, -enne** *a* & *nmf* European.

eut [y] *voir* avoir.

euthanasie [øtanazi] *nf* euthanasia.

eux [ø] *pron* (*sujet*) they; (*complément*) them; (*réfléchi, emphase*) themselves. ◆**eux-mêmes** *pron* themselves.

évacuer [evakɥe] *vt* to evacuate; (*liquide*) to drain off. ◆**évacuation** *nf* evacuation.

évad/er (s') [sevade] *vpr* to escape (**de** from). ◆—**é, -ée** *nmf* escaped prisoner.

évaluer [evalɥe] *vt* (*chiffre, foule etc*) to estimate; (*meuble etc*) to value. ◆**évaluation** *nf* estimation; valuation.

évangile [evɑ̃ʒil] *nm* gospel; É. Gospel. ◆**évangélique** *a* evangelical.

évanou/ir (s') [sevanwir] *vpr Méd* to black out, faint; (*espoir, crainte etc*) to vanish. ◆—**i** *a Méd* unconscious. ◆—**issement** *nm* (*syncope*) blackout, fainting fit; (*disparition*) vanishing.

évaporer (s') [sevapɔre] *vpr Ch* to evaporate; (*disparaître*) *Fam* to vanish into thin air. ◆**évaporation** *nf* evaporation.

évasif, -ive [evazif, -iv] *a* evasive.

évasion [evazjɔ̃] *nf* escape (**d'un lieu** from a place, **devant un danger/etc** from a danger/etc); (*hors de la réalité*) escapism; **é. fiscale** tax evasion.

évêché [eveʃe] *nm* (*territoire*) bishopric, see.

éveil [evɛj] *nm* awakening; **en é.** on the alert; **donner l'é. à** to alert.

éveill/er [eveje] *vt* (*susciter*) to arouse; **é. qn** to awake(n) s.o.; **— s'é.** *vpr* to awake(n) (à to); (*sentiment, idée*) to be aroused. ◆—**é** *a* awake; (*vif*) lively, alert.

événement [evenmɑ̃] *nm* event.

éventail [evɑ̃taj] *nm* **1** (*instrument portatif*) fan; **en é.** (*orteils*) spread out. **2** (*choix*) range.

évent/er [evɑ̃te] *vt* **1** (*secret*) to discover. **2**

é. qn to fan s.o. **3 s'é.** *vpr* (*bière, vin etc*) to turn stale. ◆—**é** *a* (*bière, vin etc*) stale.

éventrer [evɑ̃tre] *vt* (*animal etc*) to disembowel; (*sac*) to rip open.

éventuel, -elle [evɑ̃tɥɛl] *a* possible. ◆**éventuellement** *adv* possibly. ◆**éventualité** *nf* possibility; **dans l'é. de** in the event of.

évêque [evɛk] *nm* bishop.

évertuer (s') [severtɥe] *vpr* **s'é. à faire** to do one's utmost to do, struggle to do.

éviction [eviksjɔ̃] *nf* (*de concurrent etc*) & *Pol* ousting.

évident [evidɑ̃] *a* obvious, evident (**que** that). ◆**évidemment** [-amɑ̃] *adv* certainly, obviously. ◆**évidence** *nf* obviousness; **une é.** an obvious fact; **nier l'é.** to deny the obvious; **être en é.** to be conspicuous *ou* in evidence; **mettre en é.** (*fait*) to underline.

évider [evide] *vt* to hollow out.

évier [evje] *nm* (kitchen) sink.

évincer [evɛ̃se] *vt* (*concurrent etc*) & *Pol* to oust.

éviter [evite] *vt* to avoid (**de faire** doing); **é. qch à qn** to spare *ou* save s.o. sth.

évolu/er [evɔlɥe] *vi* **1** (*changer*) to develop, change; (*société, idée, situation*) to evolve. **2** (*se déplacer*) to move; *Mil* to manœuvre, *Am* maneuver. ◆—**é** *a* (*pays*) advanced; (*personne*) enlightened. ◆**évolution** *nf* **1** (*changement*) development; evolution. **2** (*d'un danseur etc*) & *Mil* movement.

évoquer [evɔke] *vt* to evoke, call to mind. ◆**évocateur, -trice** *a* evocative. ◆**évocation** *nf* evocation, recalling.

ex [eks] *nmf* (*mari, femme*) *Fam* ex.

ex- [eks] *préf* ex-; **ex-mari** ex-husband.

exacerber [egzaserbe] *vt* (*douleur etc*) to exacerbate.

exact [egzakt] *a* (*précis*) exact, accurate; (*juste, vrai*) correct, exact, right; (*ponctuel*) punctual. ◆**exactement** *adv* exactly. ◆**exactitude** *nf* exactness; accuracy; correctness; punctuality.

exaction [egzaksjɔ̃] *nf* exaction.

ex aequo [egzeko] *adv* **être classés ex ae.** *Sp* to tie, be equally placed.

exagér/er [egzaʒere] *vt* to exaggerate; **— vi** (*parler*) to exaggerate; (*agir*) to overdo it, go too far. ◆—**é** *a* excessive. ◆—**ément** *adv* excessively. ◆**exagération** *nf* exaggeration; (*excès*) excessiveness.

exalt/er [egzalte] *vt* (*glorifier*) to exalt; (*animer*) to fire, stir. ◆—**ant** *a* stirring. ◆—**é, -ée** *a* (*sentiment*) impassioned,

wild; – *nmf Péj* fanatic. ◆**exaltation** *nf*
(*délire*) elation, excitement.

examen [εgzamɛ̃] *nm* examination; *Scol* ex-
am(ination); **e. blanc** *Scol* mock ex-
am(ination). ◆**examinateur, -trice** *nmf*
Scol examiner. ◆**examiner** *vt* (*considérer,
regarder*) to examine.

exaspérer [εgzaspere] *vt* (*énerver*) to aggravate, exasperate. ◆**exaspération** *nf* exasperation, aggravation.

exaucer [εgzose] *vt* (*désir*) to grant; **e. qn** to
grant s.o.'s wish(es).

excavation [εkskavasjɔ̃] *nf* (*trou*) hollow.

excéder [εksede] *vt* **1** (*dépasser*) to exceed. **2**
é. qn (*fatiguer, énerver*) to exasperate s.o.
◆**excédent** *nm* surplus, excess; **e. de**
bagages excess luggage *ou Am* baggage.
◆**excédentaire** *a* (*poids etc*) excess-.

excellent [εksɛlɑ̃] *a* excellent. ◆**excellence** *nf* **1** excellence; **par e.** above all else
ou all others. **2 E.** (*titre*) Excellency.
◆**exceller** *vi* to excel (**en qch** in sth, **à faire**
in doing).

excentrique [εksɑ̃trik] **1** *a & nmf* (*original*)
eccentric. **2** *a* (*quartier*) remote. ◆**excentricité** *nf* (*bizarrerie*) eccentricity.

excepté [εksɛpte] *prép* except. ◆**excepter**
vt to except. ◆**exception** *nf* exception; **à**
l'e. de except (for), with the exception of;
faire e. to be an exception. ◆**exceptionnel, -elle** *a* exceptional. ◆**exceptionnellement** *adv* exceptionally.

excès [εksɛ] *nm* excess; (*de table*)
over-eating; **e. de vitesse** *Aut* speeding.
◆**excessif, -ive** *a* excessive. ◆**excessivement** *adv* excessively.

excit/er [εksite] *vt* (*faire naître*) to excite,
rouse, stir; **e. qn** (*mettre en colère*) to provoke s.o.; (*agacer*) to annoy s.o.; (*enthousiasmer*) to thrill s.o., excite s.o.; **e. qn à**
faire to incite s.o. to do; – **s'e.** *vpr*
(*nerveux, enthousiaste*) to get excited.
◆**—ant** *a* exciting; – *nm* stimulant. ◆**—é**
a excited. ◆**—able** *a* excitable. ◆**excitation** *nf* (*agitation*) excitement; **e. à** (*haine
etc*) incitement to.

exclamer (s') [εksklame] *vpr* to exclaim.
◆**exclamatif, -ive** *a* exclamatory. ◆**exclamation** *nf* exclamation.

excl/ure* [εksklyr] *vt* (*écarter*) to exclude
(**de** from); (*chasser*) to expel (**de** from); **e.**
qch (*rendre impossible*) to preclude sth.
◆**—u** *a* (*solution etc*) out of the question;
(*avec une date*) exclusive. ◆**exclusif, -ive**
a (*droit, modèle, préoccupation*) exclusive.
◆**exclusion** *nf* exclusion. ◆**exclusivement** *adv* exclusively. ◆**exclusivité** *nf*

Com exclusive rights; **en e.** (*film*) having an
exclusive showing (**à** at).

excommunier [εkskɔmynje] *vt* to excommunicate. ◆**excommunication** *nf* excommunication.

excrément(s) [εkskremɑ̃] *nm(pl)* excrement.

excroissance [εkskrwasɑ̃s] *nf* (out)growth.

excursion [εkskyrsjɔ̃] *nf* outing, excursion,
tour; (*à pied*) hike.

excuse [εkskyz] *nf* (*prétexte*) excuse; *pl* (*regrets*) apology; **des excuses** an apology;
faire des excuses to apologize (**à** to); **toutes**
mes excuses (my) sincere apologies.
◆**excuser** *vt* (*justifier, pardonner*) to excuse (**qn d'avoir fait, qn de faire** s.o. for doing); – **s'e.** *vpr* to apologize (**de** for, **auprès**
de to); **excusez-moi!, je m'excuse!** excuse
me!

exécrer [εgzekre] *vt* to loathe. ◆**exécrable**
a atrocious.

exécut/er [εgzekyte] *vt* **1** (*projet, tâche etc*)
to carry out, execute; (*statue, broderie etc*)
to produce; (*jouer*) *Mus* to perform. **2 e. qn**
(*tuer*) to execute s.o. **3 s'e.** *vpr* to comply.
◆**—ant, -ante** *nmf Mus* performer.
◆**—able** *a* practicable. ◆**exécutif** *am*
(*pouvoir*) executive; – *nm* **l'e.** *Pol* the executive. ◆**exécution** *nf* **1** carrying out, execution; production; performance. **2** (*mise
à mort*) execution.

exemple [εgzɑ̃pl] *nm* example; **par e.** for example, for instance; (**ça**) **par e.!** *Fam* good
heavens!; **donner l'e.** to set an example (**à**
to). ◆**exemplaire 1** *a* exemplary. **2** *nm*
(*livre etc*) copy.

exempt [εgzɑ̃] *a* **e. de** (*dispensé de*) exempt
from; (*sans*) free from. ◆**exempter** *vt* to
exempt (**de** from). ◆**exemption** *nf* exemption.

exercer [εgzεrse] *vt* (*muscles, droits*) to exercise; (*autorité, influence*) to exert (**sur** over);
(*métier*) to carry on, work at; (*profession*)
to practise; **e. qn à** (*couture etc*) to train s.o.
in; **e. qn à faire** to train s.o. to do; – *vi*
(*médecin*) to practise; – **s'e.** *vpr* (*influence
etc*) to be exerted; **s'e.** (**à qch**) (*sportif etc*) to
practise (sth); **s'e. à faire** to practise doing.
◆**exercice** *nm* (*physique etc*) & *Scol* exercise; *Mil* drill, exercise; (*de métier*) practice; **l'e. de** (*pouvoir etc*) the exercise of; **en**
e. (*fonctionnaire*) in office; (*médecin*) in
practice; **faire de l'e., prendre de l'e.** to
(take) exercise.

exhaler [εgzale] *vt* (*odeur etc*) to give off.

exhaustif, -ive [εgzostif, -iv] *a* exhaustive.

exhiber [εgzibe] *vt* to exhibit, show.

◆**exhibition** *nf* exhibition. ◆**exhibitionniste** *nmf* exhibitionist.

exhorter [ɛgzɔrte] *vt* to urge, exhort (**à faire** to do).

exhumer [ɛgzyme] *vt* (*cadavre*) to exhume; (*vestiges*) to dig up.

exiger [ɛgziʒe] *vt* to demand, require (**de** from, **que** (+ *sub*) that). ◆**exigeant** *a* demanding, exacting. ◆**exigence** *nf* demand, requirement; **d'une grande e.** very demanding.

exigu, -uë [ɛgzigy] *a* (*appartement etc*) cramped, tiny. ◆**exiguïté** *nf* crampedness.

exil [ɛgzil] *nm* (*expulsion*) exile. ◆**exil/er** *vt* to exile; **— s'e.** *vpr* to go into exile. ◆**—é, -ée** *nmf* (*personne*) exile.

existence [ɛgzistɑ̃s] *nf* existence. ◆**existentialisme** *nm* existentialism. ◆**exist/er** *vi* to exist; **— *v imp* il existe** ... (*sing*) there is ... ; (*pl*) there are .... ◆**—ant** *a* existing.

exode [ɛgzɔd] *nm* exodus.

exonérer [ɛgzɔnere] *vt* to exempt (**de** from). ◆**exonération** *nf* exemption.

exorbitant [ɛgzɔrbitɑ̃] *a* exorbitant.

exorciser [ɛgzɔrsize] *vt* to exorcize. ◆**exorcisme** *nm* exorcism.

exotique [ɛgzɔtik] *a* exotic. ◆**exotisme** *nm* exoticism.

expansif, -ive [ɛkspɑ̃sif, -iv] *a* expansive, effusive.

expansion [ɛkspɑ̃sjɔ̃] *nf Com Phys Pol* expansion; **en (pleine) e.** (fast *ou* rapidly) expanding.

expatri/er (s') [sɛkspatrije] *vpr* to leave one's country. ◆**—é, -ée** *a* & *nmf* expatriate.

expectative [ɛkspɛktativ] *nf* **être dans l'e.** to be waiting to see what happens.

expédient [ɛkspedjɑ̃] *nm* (*moyen*) expedient.

expédier [ɛkspedje] *vt* **1** (*envoyer*) to send off. **2** (*affaires, client*) to dispose of quickly, dispatch. ◆**expéditeur, -trice** *nmf* sender. ◆**expéditif, -ive** *a* expeditious, quick. ◆**expédition** *nf* **1** (*envoi*) dispatch. **2** (*voyage*) expedition.

expérience [ɛksperjɑ̃s] *nf* (*pratique, connaissance*) experience; (*scientifique*) experiment; **faire l'e. de qch** to experience sth. ◆**expérimental, -aux** *a* experimental. ◆**expérimentation** *nf* experimentation. ◆**expériment/er** *vt Phys Ch* to try out, experiment with; **—** *vi* to experiment. ◆**—é** *a* experienced.

expert [ɛkspɛr] *a* expert, skilled (**en** in); **—** *nm* expert; (*d'assurances*) valuer. ◆**e.-comptable** *nm* (*pl* **experts-comptables**) = chartered accountant, = *Am* certified public accountant. ◆**expertise** *nf* (*évaluation*) (expert) appraisal; (*compétence*) expertise.

expier [ɛkspje] *vt* (*péchés, crime*) to expiate, atone for. ◆**expiation** *nf* expiation (**de** of).

expir/er [ɛkspire] **1** *vti* to breathe out. **2** *vi* (*mourir*) to pass away; (*finir, cesser*) to expire. ◆**—ant** *a* dying. ◆**expiration** *nf* (*échéance*) expiry, *Am* expiration.

explicite [ɛksplisit] *a* explicit. ◆**—ment** *adv* explicitly.

expliquer [ɛksplike] *vt* to explain (**à** to); **— s'e.** *vpr* to explain oneself; (*discuter*) to talk things over, have it out (**avec** with); **s'e. qch** (*comprendre*) to understand sth; **ça s'explique** that is understandable. ◆**explicable** *a* understandable. ◆**explicatif, -ive** *a* explanatory. ◆**explication** *nf* explanation; (*mise au point*) discussion.

exploit [ɛksplwa] *nm* exploit, feat.

exploit/er [ɛksplwate] *vt* **1** (*champs*) to farm; (*ferme, entreprise*) to run; (*mine*) to work; (*situation*) Fig to exploit. **2** (*abuser de*) Péj to exploit (s.o.). ◆**—ant, -ante** *nmf* farmer. ◆**exploitation** *nf* **1** Péj exploitation. **2** farming; running; working; (*entreprise*) concern; (*agricole*) farm.

explorer [ɛksplɔre] *vt* to explore. ◆**explorateur, -trice** *nmf* explorer. ◆**exploration** *nf* exploration.

exploser [ɛksploze] *vi* (*gaz etc*) to explode; (*bombe*) to blow up, explode; **e. (de colère)** *Fam* to explode, blow up; **faire e.** (*bombe*) to explode. ◆**explosif, -ive** *a* & *nm* explosive. ◆**explosion** *nf* explosion; (*de colère, joie*) outburst.

exporter [ɛkspɔrte] *vt* to export (**vers** to, **de** from). ◆**exportateur, -trice** *nmf* exporter; **—** *a* exporting. ◆**exportation** *nf* (*produit*) export; (*action*) export(ation), exporting.

expos/er [ɛkspoze] *vt* (*présenter, soumettre*) & *Phot* to expose (**à** to); (*marchandises*) to display; (*tableau etc*) to exhibit; (*idée, théorie*) to set out; (*vie, réputation*) to risk, endanger; **s'e. à** to expose oneself to. ◆**—ant, -ante** *nmf* exhibitor. ◆**—é 1 bien e.** (*édifice*) having a good exposure; **e. au sud** facing south. **2** *nm* (*compte rendu*) account (**de** of); (*discours*) talk; *Scol* paper. ◆**exposition** *nf* (*de marchandises etc*) display; (*salon*) exhibition; (*au danger etc*) &

Phot exposure (à to); (*de maison etc*) aspect.

exprès[1] [ɛksprɛ] *adv* on purpose, intentionally; (*spécialement*) specially.

exprès[2], **-esse** [ɛkspres] **1** *a* (*ordre, condition*) express. **2** *a inv* **lettre/colis e.** express letter/parcel. ◆**expressément** *adv* expressly.

express [ɛkspres] *a & nm inv* (*train*) express; (*café*) espresso.

expressif, -ive [ɛkspresif, -iv] *a* expressive. ◆**expression** *nf* (*phrase, mine etc*) expression. ◆**exprimer** *vt* to express; **— s'e.** *vpr* to express oneself.

exproprier [ɛksprɔprije] *vt* to seize the property of by compulsory purchase.

expulser [ɛkspylse] *vt* to expel (**de** from); (*joueur*) *Sp* to send off; (*locataire*) to evict. ◆**expulsion** *nf* expulsion; eviction; sending off.

expurger [ɛkspyrʒe] *vt* to expurgate.

exquis [ɛkski] *a* exquisite.

extase [ɛkstaz] *nf* ecstasy, rapture. ◆**s'extasi/er** *vpr* to be in raptures (**sur** over, about). ◆**—é** *a* ecstatic.

extensible [ɛkstɑ̃sibl] *a* expandable. ◆**extension** *nf* extension; (*essor*) expansion.

exténuer [ɛkstenɥe] *vt* (*fatiguer*) to exhaust. ◆**exténuation** *nf* exhaustion.

extérieur [ɛksterjœr] *a* (*monde etc*) outside; (*surface*) outer; (*signe*) outward, external; (*politique*) foreign; **e. à** external to; **—** *nm* outside, exterior; **à l'e. (de)** outside; **à l'e.** (*match*) away; **en e.** *Cin* on location. ◆**—ement** *adv* externally; (*en apparence*) outwardly. ◆**extérioriser** *vt* to express.

exterminer [ɛkstɛrmine] *vt* to exterminate,

wipe out. ◆**extermination** *nf* extermination.

externe [ɛkstɛrn] **1** *a* external. **2** *nmf Scol* day pupil; *Méd* non-resident hospital doctor, *Am* extern.

extincteur [ɛkstɛ̃ktœr] *nm* fire extinguisher. ◆**extinction** *nf* (*de feu*) extinguishing; (*de voix*) loss; (*de race*) extinction.

extirper [ɛkstirpe] *vt* to eradicate.

extorquer [ɛkstɔrke] *vt* to extort (**à** from). ◆**extorsion** *nf* extortion.

extra [ɛkstra] **1** *a inv* (*très bon*) *Fam* top-quality. **2** *nm inv Culin* (extra-special) treat; (*serviteur*) extra hand *ou* help.

extra- [ɛkstra] *préf* extra-. ◆**e.-fin** *a* extra-fine. ◆**e.-fort** *a* extra-strong.

extradition [ɛkstradisjɔ̃] *nf* extradition. ◆**extrader** *vt* to extradite.

extraire* [ɛkstrɛr] *vt* to extract (**de** from); (*charbon*) to mine. ◆**extraction** *nf* extraction. ◆**extrait** *nm* extract; **un e. de naissance** a (copy of one's) birth certificate.

extraordinaire [ɛkstraɔrdinɛr] *a* extraordinary. ◆**—ment** *adv* exceptionally; (*très, bizarrement*) extraordinarily.

extravagant [ɛkstravagɑ̃] *a* extravagant. ◆**extravagance** *nf* extravagance.

extrême [ɛkstrɛm] *a* extreme; **—** *nm* extreme; **pousser à l'e.** to take *ou* carry to extremes. ◆**—ment** *adv* extremely. ◆**extrémiste** *a & nmf* extremist. ◆**extrémité** *nf* (*bout*) extremity, end; *pl* (*excès*) extremes.

exubérant [ɛgzyberɑ̃] *a* exuberant. ◆**exubérance** *nf* exuberance.

exulter [ɛgzylte] *vi* to exult, rejoice. ◆**exultation** *nf* exultation.

F

F, f [ɛf] *nm* F, f.
F *abrév* franc(s).
fable [fɑbl] *nf* fable.
fabrique [fabrik] *nf* factory; **marque de f.** trade mark.
fabriquer [fabrike] *vt* (*objet*) to make; (*industriellement*) to manufacture; (*récit*) *Péj* to fabricate, make up; **qu'est-ce qu'il fabrique?** *Fam* what's he up to? ◆**fabricant, -ante** *nmf* manufacturer. ◆**fabrication** *nf* manufacture; (*artisanale*) making; **de f. française** of French make.

fabuleux, -euse [fabylø, -øz] *a* (*légendaire, incroyable*) fabulous.
fac [fak] *nf Univ Fam* = **faculté 2.**
façade [fasad] *nf* (*de bâtiment*) front, façade; (*apparence*) *Fig* pretence, façade; **de f.** (*luxe etc*) sham.
face [fas] *nf* face; (*de cube etc*) side; (*de monnaie*) head; **de f.** (*photo*) full-face; (*vue*) front; **faire f. à** (*situation etc*) to face, face up to; **en f.** opposite; **en f. de** opposite, facing; (*en présence de*) in front of; **en f. d'un problème, f. à un problème** in the face of a

problem, faced with a problem; **f. à
(vis-à-vis de)** facing; **regarder qn en f.** to
look s.o. in the face; **f. à f.** face to face; **un f.
à f.** TV a face to face encounter;
sauver/perdre la f. to save/lose face.

facétie [fasesi] *nf* joke, jest. ◆**facétieux,
-euse** [-esjø, -øz] *a (personne)* facetious.

facette [faset] *nf (de diamant, problème etc)*
facet.

fâch/er [faʃe] *vt* to anger; **— se f.** *vpr* to get
angry *ou* annoyed **(contre** with); **se f. avec
qn** *(se brouiller)* to fall out with s.o. ◆**—é** *a
(air)* angry; *(amis)* on bad terms; **c'est f. à
contre qn** angry *ou* annoyed with s.o.; **f. de
qch** sorry about sth. ◆**fâcherie** *nf* quarrel.
◆**fâcheux, -euse** *a (nouvelle etc)* unfortunate.

facho [faʃo] *a & nmf Fam* fascist.

facile [fasil] *a* easy; *(caractère, humeur)*
easygoing; *(banal) Péj* facile; **c'est f. à faire**
it's easy to do; **il est f. de faire ça** it's easy to
do that; **f. à vivre** easy to get along with,
easygoing. ◆**—ment** *adv* easily. ◆**facilité**
nf (simplicité) easiness; *(aisance)* ease;
facilités de paiement *Com* easy terms; **avoir
de la f.** to be gifted; **avoir toutes facilités
pour** to have every facility *ou* opportunity
to. ◆**faciliter** *vt* to facilitate, make easier.

façon [fasɔ̃] *nf* **1** way; **la f. dont elle parle** the
way (in which) she talks; **f. (d'agir)** behaviour; **je n'aime pas ses façons** I don't like
his *ou* her manners *ou* ways; **une f. de parler**
a manner of speaking; **à la f. de** in the fashion of; **de toute f.** anyway, anyhow; **de f. à**
so as to; **de f. générale** generally speaking;
à ma f. my way, (in) my own way; **faire des
façons** to make a fuss; **table f. chêne** imitation oak table. **2** *(coupe de vêtement)* cut,
style. ◆**façonner** *vt (travailler, former)* to
fashion, shape; *(fabriquer)* to manufacture.

facteur [faktœr] *nm* **1** postman, *Am* mailman. **2** *(élément)* factor. ◆**factrice** *nf Fam*
postwoman.

factice [faktis] *a* false, artificial; *(diamant)*
imitation-.

faction [faksjɔ̃] *nf* **1** *(groupe) Pol* faction. **2**
de f. *Mil* on guard (duty), on sentry duty.

facture [faktyr] *nf Com* invoice, bill. ◆**facturer** *vt* to invoice, to bill.

facultatif, -ive [fakyltatif, -iv] *a* optional;
arrêt f. request stop.

faculté [fakylte] *nf* **1** *(aptitude)* faculty;
(possibilité) freedom **(de faire** to do); **une f.
de travail** a capacity for work. **2** *Univ*
faculty; **à la f.** *Fam* at university, *Am* at
school.

fadaises [fadɛz] *nfpl* twaddle, nonsense.

fade [fad] *a* insipid. ◆**fadasse** *a Fam*
wishy-washy.

fagot [fago] *nm* bundle (of firewood).

fagoter [fagɔte] *vt Péj* to dress, rig out.

faible [fɛbl] *a* weak, feeble; *(bruit, voix)*
faint; *(vent, quantité, chances)* slight;
(revenus) small; **f. en anglais/etc** poor at
English/etc; **— nm** *(personne)* weakling; **les
faibles** the weak; **avoir un f. pour** to have a
weakness *ou* a soft spot for. ◆**faiblement**
adv weakly; *(légèrement)* slightly; *(éclairer,
parler)* faintly. ◆**faiblesse** *nf* weakness,
feebleness; faintness; slightness; smallness; *(défaut, syncope)* weakness. ◆**faiblir**
vi (forces) to weaken; *(courage, vue)* to fail;
(vent) to slacken.

faïence [fajɑ̃s] *nf (matière)* earthenware; *pl
(objets)* crockery, earthenware.

faille [faj] *nf Géol* fault; *Fig* flaw.

faillible [fajibl] *a* fallible.

faillir* [fajir] *vi* **1** **il a failli tomber** he almost
ou nearly fell. **2** **f. à** *(devoir)* to fail in.

faillite [fajit] *nf Com* bankruptcy; *Fig* failure; **faire f.** to go bankrupt.

faim [fɛ̃] *nf* hunger; **avoir f.** to be hungry;
donner f. à qn to make s.o. hungry; **manger
à sa f.** to eat one's fill; **mourir de f.** to die of
starvation; *(avoir très faim) Fig* to be starving.

fainéant, -ante [feneɑ̃, -ɑ̃t] *a* idle; **— nmf**
idler. ◆**fainéanter** *vi* to idle. ◆**fainéan-
tise** *nf* idleness.

faire* [fɛr] **1** *vt (bruit, pain, faute etc)* to
make; *(devoir, dégâts, ménage etc)* to do;
(rêve, chute) to have; *(sourire, grognement)*
to give; *(promenade, sieste)* to have, take;
(guerre) to wage, make; **ça fait dix mètres
de large** *(mesure)* it's ten metres wide; **2 et 2
font 4** 2 and 2 are 4; **ça fait dix francs** that is
ou comes to ten francs; **qu'a-t-il fait (de)?**
what's he done (with)?; **que f.?** what's to be
done?; **f. du tennis/du piano/etc** to play
tennis/the piano/etc; **f. l'idiot** to act *ou*
play the fool; **ça ne fait rien** that doesn't
matter; **comment as-tu fait pour . . . ?** how
did you manage to . . . ?; **il ne fait que
travailler** he does nothing but work, he
keeps on working; **je ne fais que d'arriver**
I've just arrived; **oui, fit-elle** yes, she said. **2**
vi (agir) to do; *(paraître)* to look; **il fait
vieux** he looks old; **il fera un bon médecin**
he'll be *ou* make a good doctor; **elle ferait
bien de partir** she'd do well to leave. **3** *v imp*
il fait beau/froid/etc it's fine/cold/etc; **quel
temps fait-il?** what's the weather like?; **ça
fait deux ans que je ne l'ai pas vu** I haven't

seen him for two years, it's (been) two years since I saw him. **4** *v aux* (+ *inf*); **f. construire une maison** to have *ou* get a house built (**à qn, par qn** by s.o.); **f. crier/souffrir**/*etc* **qn** to make s.o. shout/suffer/*etc*; **se f. couper les cheveux** to have one's hair cut; **se f. craindre/obéir**/*etc* to make oneself feared/obeyed/*etc*; **se f. tuer/renverser**/*etc* to get *ou* be killed/knocked down/*etc*. **5 se f.** *vpr* (*fabrication*) to be made; (*activité*) to be done; **se f. des illusions** to have illusions; **se f. des amis** to make friends; **se f. vieux**/*etc* (*devenir*) to get old/*etc*; **il se fait tard** it's getting late; **comment se fait-il que?** how is it that?; **se f. à** to get used to, adjust to; **ne t'en fais pas!** don't worry!

faire-part [fɛrpar] *nm inv* (*de mariage etc*) announcement.

faisable [fəzabl] *a* feasible.

faisan [fəzɑ̃] *nm* (*oiseau*) pheasant.

faisandé [fəzɑ̃de] *a* (*gibier*) high.

faisceau, -x [fɛso] *nm* (*lumineux*) beam; (*de tiges etc*) bundle.

fait [fɛ] **1** *voir* **faire**; – *a* (*fromage*) ripe; (*homme*) grown; (*yeux*) made up; (*ongles*) polished; **tout f.** ready made; **bien f.** (*jambes, corps etc*) shapely; **c'est bien f.!** it serves you right! **2** *nm* event, occurrence; (*donnée, réalité*) fact; **prendre sur le f.** Jur to catch in the act; **du f. de** on account of; **f. divers** Journ (miscellaneous) news item; **au f.** (*à propos*) by the way; **aller au f.** to get to the point; **faits et gestes** actions; **en f.** in fact; **en f. de** in the matter of.

faîte [fɛt] *nm* (*haut*) top; (*apogée*) Fig height.

faites [fɛt] *voir* **faire**.

faitout [fɛtu] *nm* stewing pot, casserole.

falaise [falɛz] *nf* cliff.

falloir* [falwar] **1** *v imp* **il faut qch/qn** I, you, we *etc* need sth/s.o.; **il lui faut un stylo** he *ou* she needs a pen; **il faut partir**/*etc* I, you, we *etc* have to go/*etc*; **il faut que je parte** I have to go; **il faudrait qu'elle reste** she ought to stay; **il faut un jour** it takes a day (**pour faire** to do); **comme il faut** proper(ly); **s'il le faut** if need be. **2 s'en f.** *v imp* **peu s'en est fallu qu'il ne pleure** he almost cried; **tant s'en faut** far from it.

falsifier [falsifje] *vt* (*texte etc*) to falsify. ◆**falsification** *nf* falsification.

famé (mal) [malfame] *a* of ill repute.

famélique [famelik] *a* ill-fed, starving.

fameux, -euse [famø, -øz] *a* (*excellent*) Fam first-class; **pas f.** Fam not much good.

familial, -aux [familjal, -o] *a* family-.

familier, -ière [familje, -jɛr] *a* (*bien connu*) familiar (**à** to); (*amical*) friendly, informal; (*locution*) colloquial, familiar; **f. avec qn** (over)familiar with s.o.; – *nm* (*de club etc*) regular visitor. ◆**familiariser** *vt* to familiarize (**avec** with); – **se f.** *vpr* to familiarize oneself (**avec** with). ◆**familiarité** *nf* familiarity; *pl* Péj liberties. ◆**familièrement** *adv* familiarly; (*parler*) informally.

famille [famij] *nf* family; **en f.** (*dîner etc*) with one's family; **un père de f.** a family man.

famine [famin] *nf* famine.

fan [fɑ̃] *nm* (*admirateur*) Fam fan.

fana [fana] *nmf* Fam fan; **être f. de** to be crazy about.

fanal, -aux [fanal, -o] *nm* lantern, light.

fanatique [fanatik] *a* fanatical; – *nmf* fanatic. ◆**fanatisme** *nm* fanaticism.

fan/er (se) [səfane] *vpr* (*fleur, beauté*) to fade. ◆**-é** *a* faded.

fanfare [fɑ̃far] *nf* (*orchestre*) brass band; (*air, musique*) fanfare.

fanfaron, -onne [fɑ̃farɔ̃, -ɔn] *a* boastful; – *nmf* braggart.

fange [fɑ̃ʒ] *nf* Litt mud, mire.

fanion [fanjɔ̃] *nm* (*drapeau*) pennant.

fantaisie [fɑ̃tezi] *nf* (*caprice*) fancy, whim; (*imagination*) imagination, fantasy; **(de) f.** (*bouton etc*) fancy. ◆**fantaisiste** *a* (*pas sérieux*) fanciful; (*irrégulier*) unorthodox.

fantasme [fɑ̃tasm] *nm* Psy fantasy. ◆**fantasmer** *vi* to fantasize (**sur** about).

fantasque [fɑ̃task] *a* whimsical.

fantassin [fɑ̃tasɛ̃] *nm* Mil infantryman.

fantastique [fɑ̃tastik] *a* (*imaginaire, excellent*) fantastic.

fantoche [fɑ̃tɔʃ] *nm & a* puppet.

fantôme [fɑ̃tom] *nm* ghost, phantom; – *a* (*ville, train*) ghost-; (*firme*) bogus.

faon [fɑ̃] *nm* (*animal*) fawn.

faramineux, -euse [faraminø, -øz] *a* Fam fantastic.

farce¹ [fars] *nf* practical joke, prank; Th farce; **magasin de farces et attrapes** joke shop. ◆**farceur, -euse** *nmf* (*blagueur*) wag, joker.

farce² [fars] *nf* Culin stuffing. ◆**farcir** *vt* **1** Culin to stuff. **2 se f. qn/qch** Fam to put up with s.o./sth.

fard [far] *nm* make-up. ◆**farder** *vt* (*vérité*) to camouflage; – **se f.** *vpr* (*se maquiller*) to make up.

fardeau, -x [fardo] *nm* burden, load.

farfelu, -ue [farfəly] *a* Fam crazy, bizarre; – *nmf* Fam weirdo.

farine [farin] *nf* (*de blé*) flour; **f. d'avoine**

oatmeal. ◆**farineux, -euse** a Péj floury, powdery.

farouche [faruʃ] a **1** (timide) shy, unsociable; (animal) easily scared. **2** (violent, acharné) fierce. ◆**—ment** adv fiercely.

fart [far(t)] nm (ski) wax. ◆**farter** vt (skis) to wax.

fascicule [fasikyl] nm volume.

fasciner [fasine] vt to fascinate. ◆**fascination** nf fascination.

fascisme [faʃism] nm fascism. ◆**fasciste** a & nmf fascist.

fasse(nt) [fas] voir faire.

faste [fast] nm ostentation, display.

fastidieux, -euse [fastidjø, -øz] a tedious, dull.

fatal, mpl **-als** [fatal] a (mortel) fatal; (inévitable) inevitable; (moment, ton) fateful; **c'était f.!** it was bound to happen! ◆**—ement** adv inevitably. ◆**fataliste** a fatalistic; – nmf fatalist. ◆**fatalité** nf (destin) fate. ◆**fatidique** a (jour, date) fateful.

fatigue [fatig] nf tiredness, fatigue, weariness. ◆**fatigant** a (épuisant) tiring; (ennuyeux) tiresome. ◆**fatigu/er** vt to tire, fatigue; (yeux) to strain; (importuner) to annoy; (raser) to bore; – vi (moteur) to strain; – **se f.** vpr (se lasser) to get tired, tire (de of); (travailler) to tire oneself out (à faire doing). ◆**—é** a tired, weary (de of).

fatras [fatra] nm jumble, muddle.

faubourg [fobur] nm suburb. ◆**faubourien, -ienne** a (accent etc) suburban, common.

fauché [foʃe] a (sans argent) Fam broke.

fauch/er [foʃe] vt **1** (herbe) to mow; (blé) to reap; (abattre, renverser) Fig to mow down. **2** (voler) Fam to snatch, pinch. ◆**—euse** nf (machine) reaper.

faucille [fosij] nf (instrument) sickle.

faucon [fokɔ̃] nm (oiseau) falcon, hawk; (personne) Fig hawk.

faudra, faudrait [fodra, fodrɛ] voir falloir.

faufiler (se) [səfofile] vpr to edge ou inch one's way (dans through, into; entre between).

faune [fon] nf wildlife, fauna; (gens) Péj set.

faussaire [fosɛr] nm (faux-monnayeur) forger.

fausse [fos] voir faux¹. ◆**faussement** adv falsely.

fausser [fose] vt (sens, réalité etc) to distort; (clé etc) to buckle; **f. compagnie à qn** to give s.o. the slip.

fausseté [foste] nf (d'un raisonnement etc) falseness; (hypocrisie) duplicity.

faut [fo] voir falloir.

faute [fot] nf (erreur) mistake; (responsabilité) fault; (délit) offence; (péché) sin; Fb foul; **c'est ta f.** it's your fault, you're to blame; **f. de temps/etc** for lack of time/etc; **f. de mieux** for want of anything better; **en f.** at fault; **sans f.** without fail. ◆**fautif, -ive** a (personne) at fault; (erroné) faulty.

fauteuil [fotœj] nm armchair; (de président) chair; **f. d'orchestre** Th seat in the stalls; **f. roulant** wheelchair; **f. pivotant** swivel chair.

fauteur [fotœr] nm **f. de troubles** troublemaker.

fauve [fov] **1** a & nm (couleur) fawn. **2** nm wild beast; **chasse aux fauves** big game hunting.

faux¹, fausse [fo, fos] a (inauthentique) false; (pas vrai) untrue, false; (pas exact) wrong; (monnaie) counterfeit, forged; (bijou, marbre) imitation-, fake; (voix) out of tune; (col) detachable; – adv (chanter) out of tune; – nm (contrefaçon) forgery; **le f.** the false, the untrue. ◆**f.-filet** nm Culin sirloin. ◆**f.-fuyant** nm subterfuge. ◆**f.-monnayeur** nm counterfeiter.

faux² [fo] nf (instrument) scythe.

faveur [favœr] nf favour; **en f. de** (au profit de) in favour of; **de f.** (billet) complimentary; (traitement, régime) preferential. ◆**favorable** a favourable (à to). ◆**favori, -ite** a & nmf favourite. ◆**favoriser** vt to favour. ◆**favoritisme** nm favouritism.

favoris [favori] nmpl sideburns, side whiskers.

fébrile [febril] a feverish. ◆**fébrilité** nf feverishness.

fécond [fekɔ̃] a (femme, idée etc) fertile. ◆**féconder** vt to fertilize. ◆**fécondité** nf fertility.

fécule [fekyl] nf starch. ◆**féculents** nmpl (aliments) carbohydrates.

fédéral, -aux [federal, -o] a federal. ◆**fédération** nf federation. ◆**fédérer** vt to federate.

fée [fe] nf fairy. ◆**féerie** nf Th fantasy extravaganza; Fig fairy-like spectacle. ◆**féerique** a fairy(-like), magical.

feindre* [fɛ̃dr] vt to feign, sham; **f. de faire** to pretend to do. ◆**feint** a feigned, sham. ◆**feinte** nf sham, pretence; Boxe Mil feint.

fêler [fele] vt, – **se f.** vpr (tasse) to crack. ◆**fêlure** nf crack.

félicité [felisite] nf bliss, felicity.

féliciter [felisite] vt to congratulate (**qn de** ou **sur** s.o. on); **se f. de** to congratulate oneself on. **◆félicitations** *nfpl* congratulations (**pour** on).

félin [felɛ̃] *a* & *nm* feline.

femelle [fəmɛl] *a* & *nf* (*animal*) female.

féminin [feminɛ̃] *a* (*prénom, hormone etc*) female; (*trait, intuition etc*) & *Gram* feminine; (*mode, revue, équipe etc*) women's. **◆féministe** *a* & *nmf* feminist. **◆féminité** *nf* femininity.

femme [fam] *nf* woman; (*épouse*) wife; **f. médecin** woman doctor; **f. de chambre** (chamber)maid; **f. de ménage** cleaning lady, maid; **bonne f.** *Fam* woman.

fémur [femyr] *nm* thighbone, femur.

fendiller (se) [səfɑ̃dije] *vpr* to crack.

fendre [fɑ̃dr] *vt* (*bois etc*) to split; (*foule*) to force one's way through; (*onde, air*) to cleave; (*cœur*) *Fig* to break, rend; **— se f.** *vpr* (*se fissurer*) to crack.

fenêtre [f(ə)nɛtr] *nf* window.

fenouil [fənuj] *nm Bot Culin* fennel.

fente [fɑ̃t] *nf* (*de tirelire, palissade, jupe etc*) slit; (*de rocher*) split, crack.

féodal, -aux [feɔdal, -o] *a* feudal.

fer [fɛr] *nm* iron; (*partie métallique de qch*) metal (part); **de f., en f.** (*outil etc*) iron-; **fil de f.** wire; **f. à cheval** horseshoe; **f.** (**à repasser**) iron; **f. à friser** curling tongs; **f. de lance** *Fig* spearhead; **de f.** (*santé*) *Fig* cast-iron; (*main, volonté*) *Fig* iron-. **◆fer-blanc** *nm* (*pl* **fers-blancs**) tin(-plate).

fera, ferait [fəra, fərɛ] *voir* **faire**.

férié [ferje] *a* **jour f.** (public) holiday.

ferme¹ [fɛrm] *nf* farm; (*maison*) farm(house).

ferme² [fɛrm] *a* (*beurre, décision etc*) firm; (*autoritaire*) firm (**avec** with); (*pas, voix*) steady; (*pâte*) stiff; **— adv** (*travailler, boire*) hard; (*discuter*) keenly; **tenir f.** to stand firm *ou* fast. **◆—ment** [-əmɑ̃] *adv* firmly.

ferment [fɛrmɑ̃] *nm* ferment. **◆fermentation** *nf* fermentation. **◆fermenter** *vi* to ferment.

ferm/er [fɛrme] *vt* to close, shut; (*gaz, radio etc*) to turn *ou* switch off; (*passage*) to block; (*vêtement*) to do up; **f. (à clef)** to lock; **f. la marche** to bring up the rear; **— vi,** **— se f.** *vpr* to close, shut. **◆—é** *a* (*porte, magasin etc*) closed, shut; (*route, circuit etc*) closed; (*gaz etc*) off. **◆fermeture** *nf* closing, closure; (*heure*) closing time; (*mécanisme*) catch; **f. éclair®** zip (fastener), *Am* zipper. **◆fermoir** *nm* clasp, (snap) fastener.

fermeté [fɛrməte] *nf* firmness; (*de geste, voix*) steadiness.

fermier, -ière [fɛrmje, -jɛr] *nmf* farmer; **— a** (*poulet, produit*) farm-.

féroce [ferɔs] *a* fierce, ferocious. **◆férocité** *nf* ferocity, fierceness.

ferraille [fɛraj] *nf* scrap-iron; **mettre à la f.** to scrap. **◆ferrailleur** *nm* scrap-iron merchant.

ferré [fɛre] *a* **1** (*canne*) metal-tipped; **voie ferrée** railway, *Am* railroad; (*rails*) track. **2** (*calé*) *Fam* well up (**en** in, **sur** on).

ferrer [fɛre] *vt* (*cheval*) to shoe.

ferronnerie [fɛrɔnri] *nf* ironwork.

ferroviaire [fɛrɔvjɛr] *a* (*compagnie etc*) railway-, *Am* railroad-.

ferry-boat [feribot] *nm* ferry.

fertile [fɛrtil] *a* (*terre, imagination*) fertile; **f. en incidents** eventful. **◆fertiliser** *vt* to fertilize. **◆fertilité** *nf* fertility.

fervent, -ente [fɛrvɑ̃, -ɑ̃t] *a* fervent; **— nmf** devotee (**de** of). **◆ferveur** *nf* fervour.

fesse [fɛs] *nf* buttock; **les fesses** one's behind. **◆fessée** *nf* spanking.

festin [fɛstɛ̃] *nm* (*banquet*) feast.

festival, pl -als [fɛstival] *nm Mus Cin* festival.

festivités [fɛstivite] *nfpl* festivities.

festoyer [fɛstwaje] *vi* to feast, carouse.

fête [fɛt] *nf* (*civile*) holiday; *Rel* festival, feast; (*entre amis*) party; **f. du village** village fair *ou* fête; **f. de famille** family celebration; **c'est sa f.** it's his *ou* her saint's day; **f. des Mères** Mother's Day; **jour de f.** (public) holiday; **faire la f.** to make merry, revel; **air de f.** festive air. **◆fêter** *vt* (*évènement*) to celebrate.

fétiche [fetiʃ] *nm* (*objet de culte*) fetish; (*mascotte*) *Fig* mascot.

fétide [fetid] *a* fetid, stinking.

feu¹, -x [fø] *nm* fire; (*lumière*) *Aut Nau Av* light; (*de réchaud*) burner; (*de dispute*) *Fig* heat; *pl* (*de signalisation*) traffic lights; **feux de position** *Aut* parking lights; **feux de croisement** *Aut* dipped headlights, *Am* low beams; **f. rouge** *Aut* (*lumière*) red light; (*objet*) traffic lights; **tous feux éteints** *Aut* without lights; **mettre le f. à** to set fire to; **en f.** on fire, ablaze; **avez-vous du f.?** have you got a light?; **donner le f. vert** to give the go-ahead (**à** to); **ne pas faire long f.** not to last very long; **à f. doux** *Culin* on a low light; **au f.!** (there's a fire!; **f.!** *Mil* fire!; **coup de f.** (*bruit*) gunshot; **feux croisés** *Mil* crossfire.

feu² [fø] *a inv* late; **f. ma tante** my late aunt.

feuille [fœj] *nf* leaf; (*de papier etc*) sheet; (*de température*) chart; *Journ* newssheet; **f. d'impôt** tax form *ou* return; **f. de paye** pay slip. ◆**feuillage** *nm* foliage. ◆**feuillet** *nm* (*de livre*) leaf. ◆**feuilleter** *vt* (*livre*) to flip *ou* leaf through; **pâte feuilletée** puff *ou* flaky pastry. ◆**feuilleton** *nm* (*roman, film etc*) serial. ◆**feuillu** *a* leafy.

feutre [føtr] *nm* felt; (*chapeau*) felt hat; **crayon f.** felt-tip(ped) pen. ◆**feutré** *a* (*bruit*) muffled; **à pas feutrés** silently.

fève [fɛv] *nf* bean.

février [fevrije] *nm* February.

fiable [fjabl] *a* reliable. ◆**fiabilité** *nf* reliability.

fiacre [fjakr] *nm* Hist hackney carriage.

fianc/er (se) [səfjɑ̃se] *vpr* to become engaged (**avec** to). ◆—**é** *nm* fiancé; *pl* engaged couple. ◆—**ée** *nf* fiancée. ◆**fiançailles** *nfpl* engagement.

fiasco [fjasko] *nm* fiasco; **faire f.** to be a fiasco.

fibre [fibr] *nf* fibre; **f. (alimentaire)** roughage, (*dietary*) fibre; **f. de verre** fibreglass.

ficelle [fisɛl] *nf* **1** string; **connaître les ficelles** (*d'un métier etc*) to known the ropes. **2** (*pain*) long thin loaf. ◆**ficeler** *vt* to tie up.

fiche [fiʃ] *nf* **1** (*carte*) index *ou* record card; (*papier*) slip, form; **f. technique** data record. **2** *Él* (*broche*) pin; (*prise*) plug. ◆**fichier** *nm* card index, file.

fiche(r) [fiʃ(e)] *vt* (*pp* **fichu**) *Fam* (*faire*) to do; (*donner*) to give; (*jeter*) to throw; (*mettre*) to put; **f. le camp** to shove off; **fiche-moi la paix!** leave me alone!; **se f. de qn** to make fun of s.o.; **je m'en fiche!** I don't give a damn!

ficher [fiʃe] *vt* **1** (*enfoncer*) to drive in. **2** (*renseignement, personne*) to put on file.

fichu [fiʃy] *a* **1** *Fam* (*mauvais*) lousy, rotten; (*capable*) able (**de faire** to do); **il est f.** he's had it, he's done for; **mal f.** (*malade*) not well. **2** *nm* (head) scarf.

fictif, -ive [fiktif, -iv] *a* fictitious. ◆**fiction** *nf* fiction.

fidèle [fidɛl] *a* faithful (**à** to); − *nmf* faithful supporter; (*client*) regular (customer); **les fidèles** (*croyants*) the faithful; (*à l'église*) the congregation. ◆—**ment** *adv* faithfully. ◆**fidélité** *nf* fidelity, faithfulness.

fief [fjɛf] *nm* (*spécialité, chasse gardée*) domain.

fiel [fjɛl] *nm* gall.

fier (se) [səfje] *vpr* **se f. à** to trust.

fier, fière [fjɛr] *a* proud (**de** of); **un f. culot** *Péj* a rare cheek. ◆**fièrement** *adv* proudly. ◆**fierté** *nf* pride.

fièvre [fjɛvr] *nf* (*maladie*) fever; (*agitation*) frenzy; **avoir de la f.** to have a temperature *ou* a fever. ◆**fiévreux, -euse** *a* feverish.

fig/er [fiʒe] *vt* (*sang, sauce etc*) to congeal; **f. qn** (*paralyser*) *Fig* to freeze s.o.; − *vi* (*liquide*) to congeal; − **se f.** *vpr* (*liquide*) to congeal; (*sourire, personne*) *Fig* to freeze. ◆—**é** *a* (*locution*) set, fixed; (*regard*) frozen; (*société*) petrified.

fignol/er [fiɲɔle] *vt* *Fam* to round off meticulously, refine. ◆—**é** *a* *Fam* meticulous.

figue [fig] *nf* fig; **mi-f., mi-raisin** (*accueil etc*) neither good nor bad, mixed. ◆**figuier** *nm* fig tree.

figurant, -ante [figyrɑ̃, -ɑ̃t] *nmf* *Cin* *Th* extra.

figure [figyr] *nf* **1** (*visage*) face. **2** (*personnage*) & *Géom* figure; (*de livre*) figure, illustration; **faire f. de riche/d'imbécile/***etc* to look rich/a fool/*etc.* ◆**figurine** *nf* statuette.

figur/er [figyre] *vt* to represent; − *vi* to appear, figure; − **se f.** *vpr* to imagine; **figurez-vous que . . . ?** would you believe that . . . ? ◆—**é** *a* (*sens*) figurative; − *nm* **au f.** figuratively.

fil [fil] *nm* **1** (*de coton, pensée etc*) thread; (*lin*) linen; **f. dentaire** dental floss; **de f. en aiguille** bit by bit. **2** (*métallique*) wire; **f. de fer** wire; **f. à plomb** plumbline; **au bout du f.** *Tél* on the line; **passer un coup de f. à qn** *Tél* to give s.o. a ring *ou* a call. **3** (*de couteau*) edge. **4** **au f. de l'eau/des jours** with the current/the passing of time.

filament [filamɑ̃] *nm* *Él* filament.

filandreux, -euse [filɑ̃drø, -øz] *a* (*phrase*) long-winded.

filante [filɑ̃t] *af* **étoile f.** shooting star.

file [fil] *nf* line; (*couloir*) *Aut* lane; **f. d'attente** queue, *Am* line; **en f. (indienne)** in single file; **chef de f.** leader; **(se) mettre en f.** to line up.

filer [file] **1** *vt* (*coton etc*) to spin. **2** *vt* **f. qn** (*suivre*) to shadow s.o., tail s.o. **3** *vt* *Fam* **f. qch à qn** (*objet*) to slip s.o. sth; **f. un coup de pied/***etc* **à qn** to give s.o. a kick/*etc.* **4** *vi* (*partir*) to shoot off, bolt; (*aller vite*) to speed along; (*temps*) to fly; (*bas, collant*) to ladder, run; (*liquide*) to trickle, run; **filez!** hop it!; **f. entre les doigts de qn** to slip through s.o.'s fingers; **f. doux** to be obedient. ◆**filature** *nf* **1** (*usine*) textile mill. **2** (*de policiers etc*) shadowing; **prendre en f.** to shadow.

filet [filɛ] *nm* **1** (*de pêche*) & *Sp* net; (*à bagages*) *Rail* (luggage) rack; **f. (à provisions)** string *ou* net bag (*for shopping*). **2** (*d'eau*) trickle. **3** (*de poisson, viande*) fillet.

filial, -aux [filjal, -o] *a* filial.

filiale [filjal] *nf* subsidiary (company).

filiation [filjɑsjɔ̃] *nf* relationship.

filière [filjɛr] *nf* (*de drogue*) network; **suivre la f.** (*pour obtenir qch*) to go through the official channels; (*employé*) to work one's way up.

filigrane [filigran] *nm* (*de papier*) watermark.

filin [filɛ̃] *nm* Nau rope.

fille [fij] *nf* **1** girl; **petite f.** (little *ou* young) girl; **jeune f.** girl, young lady; **vieille f.** Péj old maid; **f. (publique)** Péj prostitute. **2** (*parenté*) daughter, girl. ◆**f.-mère** *nf* (*pl* **filles-mères**) Péj unmarried mother. ◆**fillette** *nf* little girl.

filleul [fijœl] *nm* godson. ◆**filleule** *nf* goddaughter.

film [film] *nm* film, movie; (*pellicule*) film; **f. muet/parlant** silent/talking film *ou* movie; **le f. des événements** the sequence of events. ◆**filmer** *vt* (*personne, scène*) to film.

filon [filɔ̃] *nm* Géol seam; **trouver le (bon) f.** to strike it lucky.

filou [filu] *nm* rogue, crook.

fils [fis] *nm* son; **Dupont f.** Dupont junior.

filtre [filtr] *nm* filter; **(à bout) f.** (*cigarette*) (filter-)tipped; **(bout) f.** filter tip. ◆**filtrer** *vt* to filter; (*personne, nouvelles*) to scrutinize; – *vi* to filter (through).

fin [fɛ̃] **1** *nf* end; (*but*) end, aim; **mettre f. à** to put an end *ou* a stop to; **prendre f.** to come to an end; **tirer à sa f.** to draw to an end *ou* a close; **sans f.** endless; **à la f.** in the end; **arrêtez, à la f.!** stop, for heaven's sake!; **f. de semaine** weekend; **f. mai** at the end of May; **à cette f.** to this end. **2** *a* (*pointe, travail, tissu etc*) fine; (*taille, tranche*) thin; (*plat*) delicate, choice; (*esprit, oreille*) sharp; (*observation*) sharp, fine; (*gourmet*) discerning; (*rusé*) shrewd; (*intelligent*) clever; **au f. fond de** in the depths of; – *adv* (*couper, moudre*) finely; (*écrire*) small.

final, -aux *ou* **-als** [final, -o] *a* final; – *nm* Mus finale. ◆**finale** *nf* Sp final; Gram final syllable; – *nm* Mus finale. ◆**finalement** *adv* finally; (*en somme*) after all. ◆**finaliste** *nmf* Sp finalist.

finance [finɑ̃s] *nf* finance. ◆**financ/er** *vt* to finance. ◆**—ement** *nm* financing. ◆**financier, -ière** *a* financial; – *nm* financier. ◆**financièrement** *adv* financially.

fine [fin] *nf* liqueur brandy.

finement [finmɑ̃] *adv* (*broder, couper etc*) finely; (*agir*) cleverly.

finesse [fincs] *nf* (*de pointe etc*) fineness; (*de taille etc*) thinness; (*de plat*) delicacy; (*d'esprit, de goût*) finesse; *pl* (*de langue*) niceties.

fin/ir [finir] *vt* to finish; (*discours, vie*) to end, finish; – *vi* to finish, end; **f. de faire** to finish doing; (*cesser*) to stop doing; **f. par faire** to end up *ou* finish up doing; **f. par qch** to finish (up) *ou* end (up) with sth; **en f. avec** to put an end to, finish with; **elle n'en finit pas** there's no end to it, she goes on and on. ◆**—i** *a* (*produit*) finished; (*univers etc*) & Math finite; **c'est f.** it's over *ou* finished; **il est f.** (*fichu*) he's done for *ou* finished; – *nm* (*poli*) finish. ◆**—issant** *a* (*siècle*) declining. ◆**finish** *nm* Sp finish. ◆**finition** *nf* (*action*) Tech finishing; (*résultat*) finish.

Finlande [fɛ̃lɑ̃d] *nf* Finland. ◆**finlandais, -aise** *a* – *nmf* Finn. ◆**finnois, -oise** *a* Finnish; – *nmf* Finn; – *nm* (*langue*) Finnish.

fiole [fjɔl] *nf* phial, flask.

firme [firm] *nf* (*entreprise*) Com firm.

fisc [fisk] *nm* tax authorities, = Inland Revenue, = Am Internal Revenue. ◆**fiscal, -aux** *a* fiscal, tax-. ◆**fiscalité** *nf* tax system; (*charges*) taxation.

fission [fisjɔ̃] *nf* Phys fission.

fissure [fisyr] *nf* split, crack, fissure. ◆**se fissurer** *vpr* to split, crack.

fiston [fistɔ̃] *nm* Fam son, sonny.

fixe [fiks] *a* fixed; (*prix, heure*) set, fixed; **idée f.** obsession; **regard f.** stare; **être au beau f.** Mét to be set fair; – *nm* (*paie*) fixed salary. ◆**—ment** [-əmɑ̃] *adv* **regarder f.** to stare at. ◆**fixer** *vt* (*attacher*) to fix (à to); (*choix*) to settle; (*règle, date etc*) to decide, fix; **f. (du regard)** to stare at; **f. qn sur** to inform s.o. clearly about; **être fixé** (*décidé*) to be decided; **comme ça on est fixé!** (*renseigné*) we've got the picture!; **– se f.** *vpr* (*regard*) to become fixed; (*s'établir*) to settle. ◆**fixateur** *nm* Phot fixer; (*pour cheveux*) setting lotion. ◆**fixation** *nf* (*action*) fixing; (*dispositif*) fastening, binding; Psy fixation.

flacon [flakɔ̃] *nm* bottle, flask.

flageoler [flaʒɔle] *vi* to shake, tremble.

flageolet [flaʒɔlc] *nm* Bot Culin (dwarf) kidney bean.

flagrant [flagrɑ̃] *a* (*injustice etc*) flagrant, glaring; **pris en f. délit** caught in the act *ou* red-handed.

flair [flɛr] *nm* **1** (*d'un chien etc*) (sense of) smell, scent. **2** (*clairvoyance*) intuition, flair. ◆**flairer** *vt* to sniff at, smell; (*discerner*) Fig to smell, sense.

flamand, -ande [flamɑ̃, -ɑ̃d] *a* Flemish; – *nmf* Fleming; – *nm* (*langue*) Flemish.

flamant [flamɑ̃] *nm* (*oiseau*) flamingo.

flambant [flãbã] *adv* **f. neuf** brand new.

flambeau, -x [flãbo] *nm* torch.

flamb/er [flãbe] **1** *vi* to burn, blaze; – *vt* (*aiguille*) Méd to sterilize; (*poulet*) to singe. **2** *vi* (*jouer*) Fam to gamble for big money. ◆**—é** *a* (*ruiné*) Fam done for. ◆**—ée** *nf* blaze; (*de colère, des prix etc*) Fig surge; (*de violence*) flare-up, eruption. ◆**—eur** *nm* Fam big gambler. ◆**flamboyer** *vi* to blaze, flame.

flamme [flam] *nf* flame; (*ardeur*) Fig fire; **en flammes** on fire. ◆**flammèche** *nf* spark.

flan [flã] *nm* **1** Culin custard tart *ou* pie. **2 au f.** Fam on the off chance, on the spur of the moment.

flanc [flã] *nm* side; (*d'une armée, d'un animal*) flank; **tirer au f.** Arg to shirk, idle.

flancher [flãʃe] *vi* Fam to give in, weaken.

Flandre(s) [flãdr] *nf(pl)* Flanders.

flanelle [flanel] *nf* (*tissu*) flannel.

flâner [flãne] *vi* to stroll, dawdle. ◆**flânerie** *nf* (*action*) strolling; (*promenade*) stroll.

flanquer [flãke] *vt* **1** to flank (**de** with). **2** Fam (*jeter*) to chuck; (*donner*) to give; **f. qn à la porte** to throw s.o. out.

flaque [flak] *nf* puddle, pool.

flash, *pl* **flashes** [flaʃ] *nm* **1** Phot (*éclair*) flashlight; (*dispositif*) flash(gun). **2** TV Rad (news)flash.

flasque [flask] *a* flabby, floppy.

flatt/er [flate] *vt* to flatter; **se f. d'être malin/de réussir** to flatter oneself on being smart/on being able to succeed. ◆**—é** *a* flattered (**de qch** by sth, **de faire** to do, **que** that). ◆**flatterie** *nf* flattery. ◆**flatteur, -euse** *nmf* flatterer; – *a* flattering.

fléau, -x [fleo] *nm* **1** (*calamité*) scourge; (*personne, chose*) bane, plague. **2** Agr flail.

flèche [flɛʃ] *nf* arrow; (*d'église*) spire; **monter en f.** (*prix*) to (sky)rocket, shoot ahead. ◆**flécher** [fleʃe] *vt* to signpost (with arrows). ◆**fléchette** *nf* dart; *pl* (*jeu*) darts.

fléchir [fleʃir] *vt* (*membre*) to flex, bend; **f. qn** Fig to move s.o., persuade s.o.; – *vi* (*membre*) to bend; (*poutre*) to sag; (*faiblir*) to give way; (*baisser*) to fall off.

flegme [flɛgm] *nm* composure. ◆**flegmatique** *a* phlegmatic, stolid.

flemme [flɛm] *nf* Fam laziness; **il a la f.** he can't be bothered, he's just too lazy. ◆**flemmard, -arde** *a* Fam lazy; – *nmf* Fam lazybones.

flétrir [fletrir] **1** *vt*, — **se f.** *vpr* to wither. **2** *vt* (*blâmer*) to stigmatize, brand.

fleur [flœr] *nf* flower; (*d'arbre, d'arbuste*) blossom; **en f.** in flower, in bloom; in blos-

som; **à** *ou* **dans la f. de l'âge** in the prime of life; **à f. d'eau** just above the water; **à fleurs** (*tissu*) floral. ◆**fleur/ir** *vi* to flower, bloom; (*arbre etc*) to blossom; (*art, commerce etc*) Fig to flourish; – *vt* (*table etc*) to decorate with flowers. ◆**—i** *a* (*fleur, jardin*) in bloom; (*tissu*) flowered, floral; (*teint*) florid; (*style*) flowery, florid. ◆**fleuriste** *nmf* florist.

fleuve [flœv] *nm* river.

flexible [flɛksibl] *a* flexible, pliable. ◆**flexibilité** *nf* flexibility.

flexion [flɛksjɔ̃] *nf* **1** Anat flexion, flexing. **2** Gram inflexion.

flic [flik] *nm* Fam cop, policeman.

flinguer [flɛ̃ge] *vt* **f. qn** Arg to shoot s.o.

flipper [flipœr] *nm* (*jeu*) pinball.

flirt [flœrt] *nm* (*rapports*) flirtation; (*personne*) flirt. ◆**flirter** *vi* to flirt (**avec** with). ◆**flirteur, -euse** *a* flirtatious; – *nmf* flirt.

flocon [flɔkɔ̃] *nm* (*de neige*) flake; (*de laine*) flock; **flocons d'avoine** Culin porridge oats. ◆**floconneux, -euse** *a* fluffy.

floraison [flɔrɛzɔ̃] *nf* flowering; **en pleine f.** in full bloom. ◆**floral, -aux** *a* floral. ◆**floralies** *nfpl* flower show.

flore [flɔr] *nf* flora.

florissant [flɔrisã] *a* flourishing.

flot [flo] *nm* (*de souvenirs, larmes*) flood, stream; (*marée*) floodtide; *pl* (*de mer*) waves; (*de lac*) waters; **à flots** in abundance; **à f.** (*bateau, personne*) afloat; **mettre à f.** (*bateau, firme*) to launch; **remettre qn à f.** to restore s.o.'s fortunes.

flotte [flɔt] *nf* **1** Nau Av fleet. **2** Fam (*pluie*) rain; (*eau*) water. ◆**flottille** *nf* Nau flotilla.

flott/er [flɔte] *vi* to float; (*drapeau*) to fly; (*cheveux*) to flow; (*pensées*) to drift; (*pleuvoir*) Fam to rain. ◆**—ant** *a* **1** (*bois, dette etc*) floating; (*vêtement*) flowing, loose. **2** (*esprit*) indecisive. ◆**—ement** *nm* (*hésitation*) indecision. ◆**—eur** *nm* Pêche *etc* float.

flou [flu] *a* (*photo*) fuzzy, blurred; (*idée*) hazy, fuzzy; – *nm* fuzziness.

fluctuant [flyktɥã] *a* (*prix, opinions*) fluctuating. ◆**fluctuations** *nfpl* fluctuation(s) (**de** in).

fluet, -ette [flɥɛ, -ɛt] *a* thin, slender.

fluide [flɥid] *a* (*liquide*) & Fig fluid; – *nm* (*liquide*) fluid. ◆**fluidité** *nf* fluidity.

fluorescent [flyɔresã] *a* fluorescent.

flûte [flyt] *nf* **1** Mus flute. **2** *nf* (*verre*) champagne glass. **3** *int* heck!, darn!, dash it! ◆**flûté** *a* (*voix*) piping. ◆**flûtiste** *nmf* flautist, Am flutist.

fluvial, -aux [flyvjal, -o] *a* **a** river-, fluvial.

flux [fly] *nm* (*abondance*) flow; **f. et reflux** ebb and flow.

focal, -aux [fɔkal, -o] *a* focal. ◆**focaliser** *vt* (*intérêt etc*) to focus.

fœtus [fetys] *nm* foetus, *Am* fetus.

foi [fwa] *nf* faith; **sur la f.** de on the strength of; **agir de bonne/mauvaise f.** to act in good/bad faith; **ma f., oui!** yes, indeed!

foie [fwa] *nm* liver.

foin [fwɛ̃] *nm* hay; **faire du f.** (*scandale*) *Fam* to make a stink.

foire [fwar] *nf* fair; **faire la f.** *Fam* to go on a binge, have a ball.

fois [fwa] *nf* time; **une f.** once; **deux f.** twice, two times; **chaque f. que** each time (that), whenever; **une f. qu'il sera arrivé** (*dès que*) once he has arrived; **à la f.** at the same time, at once; **à la f. riche et heureux** both rich and happy; **une autre f.** (*elle fera attention etc*) next time; **des f.** *Fam* sometimes; **non mais des f.!** *Fam* you must be joking!; **une f. pour toutes, une bonne f.** once and for all.

foison [fwazɔ̃] *nf* **à f.** in plenty. ◆**foisonn/er** *vi* to abound (**de, en** in). ◆**—ement** *nm* abundance.

fol [fɔl] *voir* **fou**.

folâtre [fɔlatr] *a* playful. ◆**folâtrer** *vi* to romp, frolic.

folichon, -onne [fɔliʃɔ̃, -ɔn] *a* **pas f.** not very funny, not much fun.

folie [fɔli] *nf* madness, insanity; **faire une f.** to do a foolish thing; (*dépense*) to be wildly extravagant; **aimer qn à la f.** to be madly in love with s.o..

folklore [fɔlklɔr] *nm* folklore. ◆**folklorique** *a* (*danse etc*) folk-; (*pas sérieux*) *Fam* lightweight, trivial, silly.

folle [fɔl] *voir* **fou**. ◆**follement** *adv* madly.

fomenter [fɔmɑ̃te] *vt* (*révolte etc*) to foment.

foncé [fɔ̃se] *a* (*couleur*) dark.

foncer [fɔ̃se] **1** *vi* (*aller vite*) to tear *ou* charge along; **f. sur qn** to charge into *ou* at s.o. **2** *vti* (*couleur*) to darken.

foncier, -ière [fɔ̃sje, -jɛr] *a* **1** fundamental, basic. **2** (*propriété*) landed. ◆**foncièrement** *adv* fundamentally.

fonction [fɔ̃ksjɔ̃] *nf* (*rôle*) & *Math* function; (*emploi*) office, function, duty; **f. publique** civil service; **faire f. de** (*personne*) to act as; (*objet*) to serve *ou* act as; **en f. de** according to. ◆**fonctionnaire** *nmf* civil servant. ◆**fonctionnel, -elle** *a* functional. ◆**fonctionn/er** *vi* (*machine etc*) to work, operate, function; (*organisation*) to function; **faire f.** to operate, work. ◆**—ement** *nm* working.

fond [fɔ̃] *nm* (*de boîte, jardin, vallée etc*) bottom; (*de salle, armoire etc*) back; (*de culotte*) seat; (*de problème, débat etc*) essence; (*arrière-plan*) background; (*contenu*) content; (*du désespoir*) *Fig* depths; **au f. de** at the bottom of; at the back of; **fonds de verre** dregs; **f. de teint** foundation cream; **f. sonore** background music; **un f. de bon sens** a stock of good sense; **au f.** basically, in essence; **à f.** (*connaître etc*) thoroughly; **de f. en comble** from top to bottom; **de f.** (*course*) long-distance; (*bruit*) background-.

fondamental, -aux [fɔ̃damɑ̃tal, -o] *a* fundamental, basic.

fond/er [fɔ̃de] *vt* (*ville etc*) to found; (*commerce*) to set up; (*famille*) to start; (**se) f. sur** to base (oneself) on; **être fondé à croire/etc** to be justified in thinking/etc; **bien fondé** well-founded. ◆**—ement** *nm* foundation. ◆**fondateur, -trice** *nmf* founder; – *a* (*membre*) founding, founder-. ◆**fondation** *nf* (*création, œuvre*) foundation (**de** of).

fond/re [fɔ̃dr] *vt* to melt; (*métal*) to smelt; (*cloche*) to cast; (*amalgamer*) *Fig* to fuse (**avec** with); **faire f.** (*dissoudre*) to dissolve; – *vi* to melt; (*se dissoudre*) to dissolve; **f. en larmes** to burst into tears; **f. sur** to swoop on; – **se f.** *vpr* to merge, fuse. ◆**—ant** *a* (*fruit*) which melts in the mouth. ◆**—u** *nm* **f. enchaîné** *Cin* dissolve. ◆**—ue** *nf* *Culin* fondue. ◆**fonderie** *nf* (*usine*) smelting works, foundry.

fonds [fɔ̃] **1** *nm* **un f.** (*de commerce*) a business. **2** *nmpl* (*argent*) funds. **3** *nm* (*culturel etc*) *Fig* fund.

font [fɔ̃] *voir* **faire**.

fontaine [fɔ̃tɛn] *nf* (*construction*) fountain; (*source*) spring.

fonte [fɔ̃t] *nf* **1** (*des neiges*) melting; (*d'acier*) smelting. **2** (*fer*) cast iron; **en f.** (*poêle etc*) cast-iron.

fonts [fɔ̃] *nmpl* **f. baptismaux** *Rel* font.

football [futbol] *nm* football, soccer. ◆**footballeur, -euse** *nmf* footballer.

footing [futiŋ] *nm* *Sp* jogging, jog-trotting.

forage [fɔraʒ] *nm* drilling, boring.

forain [fɔrɛ̃] *a* (*marchand*) itinerant; **fête foraine** (fun)fair.

forçat [fɔrsa] *nm* (*prisonnier*) convict.

force [fɔrs] *nf* force; (*physique, morale*) strength; (*atomique etc*) power; **de toutes ses forces** with all one's strength; **les forces armées** the armed forces; **de f.** by force, forcibly; **en f.** (*attaquer, venir*) in force; **cas de f. majeure** circumstances beyond one's control; **dans la f. de l'âge** in the prime of life; **à f. de** through sheer force of, by dint of. ◆**forc/er** vt (*porte, fruits etc*) to force; (*attention*) to force, compel; (*voix*) to strain; (*sens*) to stretch; **f. qn à faire** to force *ou* compel s.o. to do; − vi (*y aller trop fort*) to overdo it; − **se f.** vpr to force oneself (**à faire** to do). ◆−**é** a forced (**de faire** to do); **un sourire f.** a forced smile; **c'est f.** *Fam* it's inevitable *ou* obvious. ◆−**ément** adv inevitably, obviously; **pas f.** not necessarily.

forcené, -ée [fɔrsəne] a frantic, frenzied; − nmf madman, madwoman.

forceps [fɔrsεps] nm forceps.

forcir [fɔrsir] vi (*grossir*) to fill out.

forer [fɔre] vt to drill, bore. ◆**foret** nm drill.

forêt [fɔrε] nf forest. ◆**forestier, -ière** a forest-; − nm (*garde*) f. forester, *Am* (forest) ranger.

forfait [fɔrfε] nm 1 (*prix*) all-inclusive price; **travailler à f.** to work for a lump sum. 2 **déclarer f.** *Sp* to withdraw from the game. 3 (*crime*) *Litt* heinous crime. ◆**forfaitaire** a **prix f.** all-inclusive price.

forge [fɔrʒ] nf forge. ◆**forg/er** vt (*métal, liens etc*) to forge; (*inventer*) to make up. ◆−**é** a **fer f.** wrought iron. ◆**forgeron** nm (black)smith.

formaliser (se) [səfɔrmalize] vpr to take offence (**de** at).

formalité [fɔrmalite] nf formality.

format [fɔrma] nm format, size.

forme [fɔrm] nf (*contour*) shape, form; (*manière, genre*) form; pl (*de femme, d'homme*) figure; **en f. de** in the form of; **en f. d'aiguille/de poire**/*etc* needle-/pear-/*etc* shaped; **dans les formes** in due form; **en (pleine) f.** in good shape *ou* form, on form; **prendre f.** to take shape. ◆**formateur, -trice** a formative. ◆**formation** nf formation; (*éducation*) education, training. ◆**formel, -elle** a (*structure, logique etc*) formal; (*démenti*) categorical, formal; (*preuve*) positive, formal. ◆**formellement** adv (*interdire*) strictly. ◆**form/er** vt (*groupe, caractère etc*) to form; (*apprenti etc*) to train; − **se f.** vpr (*apparaître*) to form; (*institution*) to be formed. ◆−**é** a (*personne*) fully-formed.

formidable [fɔrmidabl] a tremendous.

formule [fɔrmyl] nf 1 formula; (*phrase*) (set) expression; (*méthode*) method; **f. de politesse** polite expression. 2 (*feuille*) form. ◆**formulaire** nm (*feuille*) form. ◆**formulation** nf formulation. ◆**formuler** vt to formulate.

fort¹ [fɔr] a strong; (*pluie, mer*) heavy; (*voix*) loud; (*fièvre*) high; (*femme, homme*) large; (*élève*) bright; (*pente*) steep; (*ville*) fortified; (*chances*) good; **f. en** (*maths etc*) good at; **c'est plus f. qu'elle** she can't help it; **c'est un peu f.** *Fam* that's a bit much; **à plus forte raison** all the more reason; − adv 1 (*frapper*) hard; (*pleuvoir*) hard, heavily; (*parler*) loud; (*serrer*) tight; **sentir f.** to have a strong smell. 2 (*très*) *Vieilli* very; (*beaucoup*) *Litt* very much; − nm **son f.** one's strong point; **les forts** the strong; **au plus f. de** in the thick of. ◆**fortement** adv greatly; (*frapper*) hard.

fort² [fɔr] nm *Hist Mil* fort. ◆**forteresse** nf fortress.

fortifi/er [fɔrtifje] vt to strengthen, fortify; − **se f.** vpr (*malade*) to fortify oneself. ◆−**ant** nm *Méd* tonic. ◆−**é** a (*ville, camp*) fortified. ◆**fortification** nf fortification.

fortuit [fɔrtɥi] a (*rencontre etc*) chance-, fortuitous. ◆**fortuitement** adv by chance.

fortune [fɔrtyn] nf (*argent, hasard*) fortune; **avoir de la f.** to have (private) means; **faire f.** to make one's fortune; **de f.** (*moyens etc*) makeshift; **dîner à la f. du pot** to take pot luck. ◆**fortuné** a (*riche*) well-to-do.

forum [fɔrɔm] nm forum.

fosse [fos] nf (*trou*) pit; (*tombe*) grave; **f. d'aisances** cesspool.

fossé [fose] nm ditch; (*douve*) moat; (*dissentiment*) *Fig* gulf, gap.

fossette [fosεt] nf dimple.

fossile [fɔsil] nm & a fossil.

fossoyeur [foswajœr] nm gravedigger.

fou (*or* **fol** *before vowel or mute* h), **folle** [fu, fɔl] a (*personne, projet etc*) mad, insane, crazy; (*envie*) wild, mad; (*espoir*) foolish; (*rire*) uncontrollable; (*cheval, camion*) runaway; (*succès, temps*) tremendous; **f. à lier** raving mad; **f. de** (*musique, personne etc*) mad *ou* wild *ou* crazy about; **f. de joie** wild with joy; − nmf madman, madwoman; − nm (*bouffon*) jester; *Échecs* bishop; **faire le f.** to play the fool.

foudre [fudr] nf **la f.** lightning; **coup de f.** *Fig* love at first sight. ◆**foudroy/er** vt to strike by lightning; *Él* to electrocute; (*malheur etc*) *Fig* to strike (s.o.) down. ◆−**ant** a (*succès, vitesse etc*) staggering. ◆−**é** a (*stupéfait*) thunderstruck.

fouet [fwε] nm whip; *Culin* (egg) whisk. ◆**fouetter** vt to whip; (*œufs*) to whisk; (*pluie etc*) to lash (*face, windows etc*); **crème fouettée** whipped cream.

fougère [fuʒεr] nf fern.

fougue [fug] *nf* fire, ardour. **◆fougueux, -euse** *a* fiery, ardent.

fouille [fuj] *nf* **1** (*archéologique*) excavation, dig. **2** (*de personne, bagages etc*) search. **◆fouiller 1** *vti* (*creuser*) to dig. **2** *vt* (*personne, maison etc*) to search; – *vi* **f. dans** (*tiroir etc*) to rummage *ou* search through.

fouillis [fuji] *nm* jumble.

fouine [fwin] *nf* (*animal*) stone marten.

fouin/er [fwine] *vi Fam* to nose about. **◆—eur, -euse** *a Fam* nosy; – *nmf Fam* nosy parker.

foulard [fular] *nm* (*head*) scarf.

foule [ful] *nf* crowd; **en f.** in mass; **une f. de** (*objets etc*) a mass of; **un bain de f.** a walkabout.

foulée [fule] *nf Sp* stride; **dans la f.** *Fam* at one and the same time.

fouler [fule] *vt* to press; (*sol*) to tread; **f. aux pieds** to trample on; **se f. la cheville**/*etc* to sprain one's ankle/*etc*; **il ne se foule pas (la rate)** *Fam* he doesn't exactly exert himself. **◆foulure** *nf* sprain.

four [fur] *nm* **1** oven; (*de potier etc*) kiln. **2** **petit f.** (*gâteau*) (small) fancy cake. **3** *Th Cin* flop; **faire un f.** to flop.

fourbe [furb] *a* deceitful; – *nmf* cheat. **◆fourberie** *nf* deceit.

fourbi [furbi] *nm* (*choses*) *Fam* stuff, gear, rubbish.

fourbu [furby] *a* (*fatigué*) dead beat.

fourche [furʃ] *nf* fork; **f. à foin** pitchfork. **◆fourchette** *nf* **1** *Culin* fork. **2** (*de salaires etc*) *Écon* bracket. **◆fourchu** *a* forked.

fourgon [furgɔ̃] *nm* (*camion*) van; (*mortuaire*) hearse; *Rail* luggage van, *Am* baggage car. **◆fourgonnette** *nf* (*small*) van.

fourmi [furmi] *nf* **1** (*insecte*) ant. **2 avoir des fourmis** *Méd* to have pins and needles (**dans** in). **◆fourmilière** *nf* anthill. **◆fourmiller** *vi* **1** to teem, swarm (**de** with). **2** *Méd* to tingle.

fournaise [furnez] *nf* (*chambre etc*) *Fig* furnace.

fourneau, -x [furno] *nm* (*poêle*) stove; (*four*) furnace; **haut f.** blast furnace.

fournée [furne] *nf* (*de pain, gens*) batch.

fourn/ir [furnir] *vt* to supply, provide; (*effort*) to make; **f. qch à qn** to supply s.o. with sth; – *vi* **f. à** (*besoin etc*) to provide for; – **se f.** *vpr* to get one's supplies (**chez** from), shop (**chez** at). **◆—i** *a* (*barbe*) bushy; **bien f.** (*boutique*) well-stocked. **◆fournisseur** *nm* (*commerçant*) supplier. **◆fourniture** *nf* (*action*) supply(ing) (**de** of); *pl* (*objets*) supplies.

fourrage [furaʒ] *nm* fodder.

fourrager [furaʒe] *vi Fam* to rummage (**dans** in, through).

fourreau, -x [furo] *nm* (*gaine*) sheath.

fourr/er [fure] **1** *vt Culin* to fill, stuff; (*vêtement*) to fur-line. **2** *vt Fam* (*mettre*) to stick; (*flanquer*) to chuck; **f. qch dans la tête de qn** to knock sth into s.o.'s head; **f. son nez dans** to poke one's nose into; – **se f.** *vpr* to put *ou* stick oneself (**dans** in). **◆—é 1** *a* (*gant etc*) fur-lined; (*gâteau*) jam- *ou* cream-filled; **coup f.** (*traîtrise*) stab in the back. **2** *nm Bot* thicket. **◆—eur** *nm* furrier. **◆fourrure** *nf* (*pour vêtement etc, de chat etc*) fur.

fourre-tout [furtu] *nm inv* (*pièce*) junk room; (*sac*) holdall, *Am* carryall.

fourrière [furjer] *nf* (*lieu*) pound.

fourvoyer (se) [səfurvwaje] *vpr* to go astray.

foutre* [futr] *vt Arg* = **fiche(r)**. **◆foutu** *a Arg* = **fichu 1**. **◆foutaise** *nf Arg* rubbish, rot.

foyer [fwaje] *nm* (*domicile*) home; (*d'étudiants etc*) hostel; (*âtre*) hearth; (*lieu de réunion*) club; *Th* foyer; *Géom Phys* focus; **f. de** (*maladie etc*) seat of; (*énergie, lumière*) source of; **fonder un f.** to start a family.

fracas [fraka] *nm* din; (*d'un objet qui tombe*) crash. **◆fracass/er** *vt*, – **se f.** *vpr* to smash. **◆—ant** *a* (*nouvelle, film etc*) sensational.

fraction [fraksjɔ̃] *nf* fraction. **◆fractionner** *vt*, – **se f.** *vpr* to split (up).

fracture [fraktyr] *nf* fracture; **se faire une f. au bras**/*etc* to fracture one's arm/*etc*. **◆fracturer** *vt* (*porte etc*) to break (open); **se f. la jambe**/*etc* to fracture one's leg/*etc*.

fragile [fraʒil] *a* (*verre, santé etc*) fragile; (*enfant etc*) frail; (*équilibre*) shaky. **◆fragilité** *nf* fragility; (*d'un enfant etc*) frailty.

fragment [fragmã] *nm* fragment. **◆fragmentaire** *a* fragmentary, fragmented. **◆fragmentation** *nf* fragmentation. **◆fragmenter** *vt* to fragment, divide.

frais¹, fraîche [frɛ, frɛʃ] *a* (*poisson, souvenir etc*) fresh; (*temps*) cool, fresh, (*plutôt désagréable*) chilly; (*œufs*) new-laid, fresh; (*boisson*) cold, cool; (*peinture*) wet; (*date*) recent; **boire f.** to drink something cold *ou* cool; **servir f.** (*vin etc*) to serve chilled; – *nm* **prendre le f.** to get some fresh air; **il fait f.** it's cool; (*froid*) it's chilly; **mettre au f.** to put in a cool place. **◆fraîchement** *adv* **1** (*récemment*) freshly. **2** (*accueillir etc*) coolly. **◆fraîcheur** *nf* freshness; coolness;

chilliness. ◆**fraîchir** vi (temps) to get cooler ou chillier, freshen.

frais² [frɛ] nmpl expenses; (droits) fees; à mes f. at my expense; faire des f. to go to some expense; faire les f. to bear the cost (de of); j'en ai été pour mes f. I wasted my time and effort; faux f. incidental expenses; f. généraux running expenses, overheads.

fraise [frɛz] nf 1 (fruit) strawberry. 2 (de dentiste) drill. ◆**fraisier** nm (plante) strawberry plant.

framboise [frãbwaz] nf raspberry. ◆**framboisier** nm raspberry cane.

franc¹, franche [frã, frãʃ] a 1 (personne, réponse etc) frank; (visage, gaieté) open; (net) clear; (cassure, coupe) clean; (vrai) Péj downright. 2 (zone) free; coup f. Fb free kick; f. de port carriage paid. ◆**franchement** adv (honnêtement) frankly; (sans ambiguïté) clearly; (vraiment) really. ◆**franchise** nf 1 frankness; openness; en toute f. quite frankly. 2 (exemption) Com exemption; en f. (produit) duty-free; 'f. postale' 'official paid'. 3 (permis de vendre) Com franchise.

franc² [frã] nm (monnaie) franc.

France [frãs] nf France. ◆**français, -aise** a French; — nmf Frenchman, Frenchwoman; les F. the French; — nm (langue) French.

franch/ir [frãʃir] vt (fossé) to jump (over), clear; (frontière, seuil etc) to cross; (porte) to go through; (distance) to cover; (limites) to exceed; (mur du son) to break (through), go through. ◆**—issable** a (rivière, col) passable.

franc-maçon [frãmasɔ̃] nm (pl francs-maçons) Freemason. ◆**franc-maçonnerie** nf Freemasonry.

franco [frãko] adv carriage paid.

franco- [frãko] préf Franco-.

francophile [frãkɔfil] a & nmf francophile. ◆**francophone** a French-speaking; — nmf French speaker. ◆**francophonie** nf la f. the French-speaking community.

frange [frãʒ] nf (de vêtement etc) fringe; (de cheveux) fringe, Am bangs.

frangin [frãʒɛ̃] nm Fam brother. ◆**frangine** nf Fam sister.

franquette (à la bonne) [alabɔnfrãkɛt] adv without ceremony.

frappe [frap] nf 1 (dactylographie) typing; (de dactylo etc) touch; faute de f. typing error. 2 force de f. Mil strike force. ◆**frapp/er** vt (battre) to strike, hit; (monnaie) to mint; f. qn (surprendre, affecter) to

strike s.o.; (impôt, mesure etc) to hit s.o.; frappé de (horreur etc) stricken with; frappé de panique panic-stricken; — vi (à la porte etc) to knock, bang (à at); f. du pied to stamp (one's foot); — se f. vpr (se tracasser) to worry. ◆**—ant** a striking. ◆**—é** a (vin) chilled.

frasque [frask] nf prank, escapade.

fraternel, -elle [fratɛrnɛl] a fraternal, brotherly. ◆**fraterniser** vi to fraternize (avec with). ◆**fraternité** nf fraternity, brotherhood.

fraude [frod] nf Jur fraud; (à un examen) cheating; passer qch en f. to smuggle sth; prendre qn en f. to catch s.o. cheating. ◆**fraud/er** vt to defraud; — vi Jur to commit fraud; (à un examen) to cheat (à in); f. sur (poids etc) to cheat on ou over. ◆**—eur, -euse** nmf Jur defrauder. ◆**frauduleux, -euse** a fraudulent.

frayer [freje] vt (voie etc) to clear; se f. un passage to clear a way, force one's way (à travers, dans through).

frayeur [frejœr] nf fear, fright.

fredaine [frɔdɛn] nf prank, escapade.

fredonner [frɔdɔne] vt to hum.

freezer [frizœr] nm (de réfrigérateur) freezer.

frégate [fregat] nf (navire) frigate.

frein [frɛ̃] nm brake; donner un coup de f. to brake; mettre un f. à Fig to put a curb on. ◆**frein/er** vi Aut to brake; — vt (gêner) Fig to check, curb. ◆**—age** nm Aut braking.

frelaté [frɔlate] a (vin etc) & Fig adulterated.

frêle [frɛl] a frail, fragile.

frelon [frɔlɔ̃] nm (guêpe) hornet.

frémir [fremir] vi to shake, shudder (de with); (feuille) to quiver; (eau chaude) to simmer.

frêne [frɛn] nm (arbre, bois) ash.

frénésie [frenezi] nf frenzy. ◆**frénétique** a frenzied, frantic.

fréquent [frekã] a frequent. ◆**fréquemment** [-amã] adv frequently. ◆**fréquence** nf frequency.

fréquent/er [frekãte] vt (lieu) to visit, frequent; (école, église) to attend; f. qn to see ou visit s.o.; — se f. vpr (fille et garçon) to see each other, go out together; (voisins) to see each other socially. ◆**—é** a très f. (lieu) very busy. ◆**fréquentable** a peu f. (personne, endroit) not very commendable. ◆**fréquentation** nf visiting; pl (personnes) company.

frère [frɛr] nm brother.

fresque [frɛsk] nf (œuvre peinte) fresco.

fret [frɛ] nm freight.

frétiller [fretije] vi (*poisson*) to wriggle; **f. de** (*impatience*) to quiver with; **f. de joie** to tingle with excitement.

fretin [frətɛ̃] nm **menu f.** small fry.

friable [frijabl] a crumbly.

friand [frijã] a **f. de** fond of, partial to. ◆**friandises** nfpl sweet stuff, sweets, *Am* candies.

fric [frik] nm (*argent*) *Fam* cash, dough.

fric-frac [frikfrak] nm (*cambriolage*) *Fam* break-in.

friche (en) [ɑ̃friʃ] adv fallow.

friction [friksjɔ̃] nf **1** massage, rub(-down); (*de cheveux*) friction. **2** (*désaccord*) friction. ◆**frictionner** vt to rub (down).

frigidaire® [friʒidɛr] nm fridge. ◆**frigo** nm *Fam* fridge. ◆**frigorifié** a (*personne*) *Fam* very cold. ◆**frigorifique** a (*vitrine*) refrigerated; (*wagon*) refrigerator-.

frigide [friʒid] a frigid. ◆**frigidité** nf frigidity.

frileux, -euse [frilø, -øz] a sensitive to cold, chilly.

frime [frim] nf *Fam* sham, show.

frimousse [frimus] nf *Fam* little face.

fringale [frɛ̃gal] nf *Fam* raging appetite.

fringant [frɛ̃gã] a (*allure etc*) dashing.

fringues [frɛ̃g] nfpl (*vêtements*) *Fam* togs, clothes.

frip/er [fripe] vt to crumple; **— se f.** vpr to get crumpled. ◆**—é** a (*visage*) crumpled, wrinkled.

fripier, -ière [fripje, -jɛr] nmf secondhand clothes dealer.

fripon, -onne [fripɔ̃, -ɔn] nmf rascal; — a rascally.

fripouille [fripuj] nf rogue, scoundrel.

frire* [frir] vti to fry; **faire f.** to fry.

frise [friz] nf *Archit* frieze.

fris/er [frize] **1** vti (*cheveux*) to curl, wave; **f. qn** to curl ou wave s.o.'s hair. **2** vt (*effleurer*) to skim; (*accident etc*) to be within an ace of; **f. la trentaine** to be close on thirty. ◆**—é** a curly. ◆**frisette** nf ringlet, little curl.

frisquet [friskɛ] am chilly, coldish.

frisson [frisɔ̃] nm shiver; shudder; **donner le f. à qn** to give s.o. the creeps ou shivers. ◆**frissonner** vi (*de froid*) to shiver; (*de peur etc*) to shudder (**de** with).

frit [fri] voir **frire**; — a (*poisson etc*) fried. ◆**frites** nfpl chips, *Am* French fries. ◆**friteuse** nf (deep) fryer. ◆**friture** nf (*matière*) (frying) oil ou fat; (*aliment*) fried fish; (*bruit*) *Rad Tél* crackling.

frivole [frivɔl] a frivolous. ◆**frivolité** nf frivolity.

froid [frwa] a cold; **garder la tête froide** to keep a cool head; — nm cold; **avoir/ prendre f.** to be/catch cold; **il fait f.** it's cold; **coup de f.** *Méd* chill; **jeter un f.** to cast a chill (**dans** over); **démarrer à f.** *Aut* to start (from) cold; **être en f.** to be on bad terms (**avec** with). ◆**froidement** adv coldly. ◆**froideur** nf (*de sentiment, personne etc*) coldness.

froisser [frwase] **1** vt, **— se f.** vpr (*tissu etc*) to crumple, rumple; **se f. un muscle** to strain a muscle. **2** vt **f. qn** to offend s.o.; **se f.** to take offence (**de** at).

frôler [frole] vt (*toucher*) to brush against, touch lightly; (*raser*) to skim; (*la mort etc*) to come within an ace of.

fromage [frɔmaʒ] nm cheese; **f. blanc** soft white cheese. ◆**fromager, -ère** a (*industrie*) cheese-; — nm (*fabricant*) cheesemaker. ◆**fromagerie** nf cheese dairy.

froment [frɔmã] nm wheat.

fronce [frɔ̃s] nf (*pli dans un tissu*) gather, fold. ◆**fronc/er** vt **1** (*étoffe*) to gather. **2 f. les sourcils** to frown. ◆**—ement** nm **f. de sourcils** frown.

fronde [frɔ̃d] nf **1** (*arme*) sling. **2** (*sédition*) revolt.

front [frɔ̃] nm forehead, brow; *Mil Pol* front; **de f.** (*heurter*) head-on; (*côte à côte*) abreast; (*à la fois*) (all) at once; **faire f. à** to face.

frontière [frɔ̃tjɛr] nf border, frontier; — a inv **ville/etc f.** border town/etc. ◆**frontalier, -ière** a border-, frontier-.

fronton [frɔ̃tɔ̃] nm *Archit* pediment.

frott/er [frɔte] vt to rub; (*astiquer*) to rub (up), shine; (*plancher*) to scrub; (*allumette*) to strike; **se f. à qn** (*défier*) to meddle with s.o., provoke s.o.; — vi to rub; (*nettoyer, laver*) to scrub. ◆**—ement** nm rubbing; *Tech* friction.

froufrou(s) [frufru] nm(pl) (*bruit*) rustling.

frousse [frus] nf *Fam* funk, fear; **avoir la f.** to be scared. ◆**froussard, -arde** nmf *Fam* coward.

fructifier [fryktifje] vi (*arbre, capital*) to bear fruit. ◆**fructueux, -euse** a (*profitable*) fruitful.

frugal, -aux [frygal, -o] a frugal. ◆**frugalité** nf frugality.

fruit [frɥi] nm fruit; **des fruits, les fruits** fruit; **porter f.** to bear fruit; **fruits de mer** seafood; **avec f.** fruitfully. ◆**frulté** a fruity. ◆**fruitier, -ière** a (*arbre*) fruit-; — nmf fruiterer.

frusques [frysk] nfpl (*vêtements*) *Fam* togs, clothes.

fruste [fryst] *a* (*personne*) rough.

frustr/er [frystre] *vt* f. qn to frustrate s.o.; f. qn de to deprive s.o. of. ◆—é *a* frustrated. ◆**frustration** *nf* frustration.

fuel [fjul] *nm* (fuel) oil.

fugace [fygas] *a* fleeting.

fugitif, -ive [fyʒitif, -iv] **1** *nmf* runaway, fugitive. **2** *a* (*passager*) fleeting.

fugue [fyg] *nf* **1** *Mus* fugue. **2** (*absence*) flight; **faire une f.** to run away.

fuir* [fɥir] *vi* to flee, run away; (*temps*) to fly; (*gaz, robinet, stylo etc*) to leak; − *vt* (*éviter*) to shun, avoid. ◆**fuite** *nf* (*évasion*) flight (de from); (*de gaz etc*) leak(age); (*de documents*) leak; **en f.** on the run; **prendre la f.** to take flight; **f. des cerveaux** brain drain; **délit de f.** *Aut* hit-and-run offence.

fulgurant [fylgyrɑ̃] *a* (*regard*) flashing; (*vitesse*) lightning-; (*idée*) spectacular, striking.

fulminer [fylmine] *vi* (*personne*) to thunder forth (contre against).

fumée [fyme] *nf* smoke; (*vapeur*) steam, fumes; *pl* (*de vin*) fumes. ◆**fum/er** *vi* to smoke; (*liquide brûlant*) to steam; (*rager*) *Fam* to fume; − *vt* to smoke. ◆—é *a* (*poisson, verre etc*) smoked. ◆—**eur, -euse** *nmf* smoker; **compartiment fumeurs** *Rail* smoking compartment. ◆**fume-cigarette** *nm inv* cigarette holder.

fumet [fymɛ] *nm* aroma, smell.

fumeux, -euse [fymø, -øz] *a* (*idée etc*) hazy, woolly.

fumier [fymje] *nm* manure, dung; (*tas*) dunghill.

fumigation [fymigasjɔ̃] *nf* fumigation.

fumigène [fymiʒɛn] *a* (*bombe, grenade etc*) smoke-.

fumiste [fymist] *nmf* (*étudiant etc*) time-waster, good-for-nothing. ◆**fumisterie** *nf Fam* farce, con.

funambule [fynɑ̃byl] *nmf* tightrope walker.

funèbre [fynɛbr] *a* (*service, marche etc*) funeral-; (*lugubre*) gloomy. ◆**funérailles** *nfpl* funeral. ◆**funéraire** *a* (*frais, salon etc*) funeral-.

funeste [fynɛst] *a* (*désastreux*) catastrophic.

funiculaire [fynikyler] *nm* funicular.

fur et à mesure (au) [ofyreamzyr] *adv* as one goes along, progressively; **au f. et à m. que** as.

furent [fyr] *voir* être.

furet [fyrɛ] *nm* (*animal*) ferret. ◆**furet/er** *vi* to pry *ou* ferret about. ◆—**eur, -euse** *a* inquisitive, prying; −− *nmf* inquisitive person.

fureur [fyrœr] *nf* (*violence*) fury; (*colère*) rage, fury; (*passion*) passion (de for); **en f.** furious; **faire f.** (*mode etc*) to be all the rage. ◆**furibond** *a* furious. ◆**furie** *nf* (*colère, mégère*) fury. ◆**furieux, -euse** *a* (*violent, en colère*) furious (contre with, at); (*vent*) raging; (*coup*) *Fig* tremendous.

furoncle [fyrɔ̃kl] *nm Méd* boil.

furtif, -ive [fyrtif, -iv] *a* furtive, stealthy.

fusain [fyzɛ̃] *nm* **1** (*crayon, dessin*) charcoal. **2** *Bot* spindle tree.

fuseau, -x [fyzo] *nm* **1** *Tex* spindle; **en f.** (*jambes*) spindly. **2** **f. horaire** time zone. **3** (*pantalon*) ski pants. ◆**fuselé** *a* slender.

fusée [fyze] *nf* rocket; (*d'obus*) fuse; **f. éclairante** flare.

fuselage [fyzlaʒ] *nm Av* fuselage.

fuser [fyze] *vi* (*rires etc*) to burst forth.

fusible [fyzibl] *nm Él* fuse.

fusil [fyzi] *nm* rifle, gun; (*de chasse*) shotgun; **coup de f.** gunshot, report; **un bon f.** (*personne*) a good shot. ◆**fusillade** *nf* (*tirs*) gunfire; (*exécution*) shooting. ◆**fusiller** *vt* (*exécuter*) to shoot; **f. qn du regard** to glare at s.o.

fusion [fyzjɔ̃] *nf* **1** melting; *Phys Biol* fusion; **point de f.** melting point; **en f.** (*métal*) molten. **2** (*union*) fusion; *Com* merger. ◆**fusionner** *vti Com* to merge.

fut [fy] *voir* être.

fût [fy] *nm* **1** (*tonneau*) barrel, cask. **2** (*d'arbre*) trunk. ◆**futaie** *nf* timber forest.

futé [fyte] *a* cunning, smart.

futile [fytil] *a* (*propos, prétexte etc*) frivolous, futile; (*personne*) frivolous; (*tentative, action*) futile. ◆**futilité** *nf* futility; *pl* (*bagatelles*) trifles.

futur, -ure [fytyr] *a* future; **future mère** mother-to-be; − *nmf* **f. (mari)** husband-to-be; **future (épouse)** wife-to-be; − *nm* future.

fuyant [fɥijɑ̃] *voir* fuir; −− *a* (*front, ligne*) receding; (*personne*) evasive. ◆**fuyard** *nm* (*soldat*) runaway, deserter.

G

G, g [ʒe] *nm* G, g.

gabardine [gabardin] *nf* (*tissu, imperméable*) gabardine.

gabarit [gabari] *nm* (*de véhicule etc*) size, dimension.

gâcher [gɑʃe] *vt* **1** (*gâter*) to spoil; (*occasion, argent*) to waste; (*vie, travail*) to mess up. **2** (*plâtre*) to mix. ◆**gâchis** *nm* (*désordre*) mess; (*gaspillage*) waste.

gâchette [gɑʃɛt] *nf* (*d'arme à feu*) trigger; **une fine g.** (*personne*) *Fig* a marksman.

gadget [gadʒɛt] *nm* gadget.

gadoue [gadu] *nf* (*boue*) dirt, sludge; (*neige*) slush.

gaffe [gaf] *nf* (*bévue*) *Fam* blunder, gaffe. ◆**gaff/er** *vi* to blunder. ◆**—eur, -euse** *nmf* blunderer.

gag [gag] *nm* (*effet comique*) *Cin Th* (sight) gag.

gaga [gaga] *a Fam* senile, gaga.

gage [gaʒ] **1** *nm* (*promesse*) pledge; (*témoignage*) proof; (*caution*) security; **mettre en g.** to pawn. **2** *nmpl* (*salaire*) pay; **tueur à gages** hired killer, hitman.

gager [gaʒe] *vt* **g. que** *Litt* to wager that. ◆**gageure** [gaʒyr] *nf Litt* (impossible) wager.

gagn/er [gaɲe] **1** *vt* (*par le travail*) to earn; (*mériter*) *Fig* to earn. **2** *vt* (*par le jeu*) to win; (*réputation, estime etc*) *Fig* to win, gain; **g. qn** to win s.o. over (**à** to); **g. une heure/etc** (*économiser*) to save an hour/etc; **g. du temps** (*temporiser*) to gain time; **g. du terrain/du poids** to gain ground/weight; — *vi* (*être vainqueur*) to win; **g. à être connu** to be well worth getting to know. **3** *vt* (*atteindre*) to reach; **g. qn** (*sommeil, faim etc*) to overcome s.o.; — *vi* (*incendie etc*) to spread, gain. ◆**—ant, -ante** *a* (*billet, cheval*) winning; — *nmf* winner. ◆**gagne-pain** *nm inv* (*emploi*) job, livelihood.

gai [ge] *a* (*personne, air etc*) cheerful, gay, jolly; (*ivre*) merry, tipsy; (*couleur, pièce*) bright, cheerful. ◆**gaiement** *adv* cheerfully, gaily. ◆**gaieté** *nf* (*de personne etc*) gaiety, cheerfulness, jollity.

gaillard [gajar] *a* vigorous; (*grivois*) coarse; — *nm* (*robuste*) strapping fellow; (*type*) *Fam* fellow. ◆**gaillarde** *nf Péj* brazen wench.

gain [gɛ̃] *nm* (*profit*) gain, profit; (*avantage*) *Fig* advantage; *pl* (*salaire*) earnings; (*au jeu*) winnings; **un g. de temps** a saving of time.

gaine [gɛn] *nf* **1** (*sous-vêtement*) girdle. **2** (*étui*) sheath.

gala [gala] *nm* official reception, gala.

galant [galɑ̃] *a* (*homme*) gallant; (*ton, propos*) *Hum* amorous; — *nm* suitor. ◆**galanterie** *nf* (*courtoisie*) gallantry.

galaxie [galaksi] *nf* galaxy.

galbe [galb] *nm* curve, contour. ◆**galbé** *a* (*jambes*) shapely.

gale [gal] *nf* **la g.** *Méd* the itch, scabies; (*d'un chien*) mange; **une (mauvaise) g.** (*personne*) *Fam* a pest.

galère [galɛr] *nf* (*navire*) *Hist* galley. ◆**galérien** *nm Hist & Fig* galley slave.

galerie [galri] *nf* **1** (*passage, magasin etc*) gallery; *Th* balcony. **2** *Aut* roof rack.

galet [galɛ] *nm* pebble, stone; *pl* shingle, pebbles.

galette [galɛt] *nf* **1** round, flat, flaky cake; (*crêpe*) pancake. **2** (*argent*) *Fam* dough, money.

galeux, -euse [galø, -øz] *a* (*chien*) mangy.

galimatias [galimatja] *nm* gibberish.

Galles [gal] *nfpl* **pays de G.** Wales. ◆**gallois, -oise** *a* Welsh; — *nm* (*langue*) Welsh; — *nmf* Welshman, Welshwoman.

gallicisme [galisism] *nm* (*mot etc*) gallicism.

galon [galɔ̃] *nm* (*ruban*) braid; (*signe*) *Mil* stripe; **prendre du g.** *Mil & Fig* to get promoted.

galop [galo] *nm* gallop; **aller au g.** to gallop; **g. d'essai** *Fig* trial run. ◆**galopade** *nf* (*ruée*) stampede. ◆**galop/er** *vi* (*cheval*) to gallop; (*personne*) to rush. ◆**—ant** *a* (*inflation etc*) *Fig* galloping.

galopin [galopɛ̃] *nm* urchin, rascal.

galvaniser [galvanize] *vt* (*métal*) *& Fig* to galvanize.

galvauder [galvode] *vt* (*talent, avantage etc*) to debase, misuse.

gambade [gɑ̃bad] *nf* leap, caper. ◆**gambader** *vi* to leap *ou* frisk about.

gambas [gɑ̃bas] *nfpl* scampi.

gamelle [gamɛl] *nf* (*de soldat*) mess tin; (*de campeur*) billy(can).

gamin, -ine [gamɛ̃, -in] *nmf* (*enfant*) *Fam*

kid; – a playful, naughty. ◆**gaminerie** nf
playfulness; (acte) naughty prank.
gamme [gam] nf Mus scale; (série) range.
gammée [game] af **croix g.** swastika.
gang [gɑ̃g] nm (de malfaiteurs) gang.
◆**gangster** nm gangster.
gangrène [gɑ̃grɛn] nf gangrene. ◆**se gan-
grener** [səgɑ̃grəne] vpr Méd to become
gangrenous.
gangue [gɑ̃g] nf (enveloppe) Fig Péj outer
crust.
gant [gɑ̃] nm glove; **g. de toilette** face cloth,
cloth glove (for washing); **jeter/relever le
g.** Fig to throw down/take up the gauntlet;
boîte à gants glove compartment. ◆**ganté**
a (main) gloved; (personne) wearing gloves.
garage [garaʒ] nm Aut garage; **voie de g.**
Rail siding; Fig dead end. ◆**garagiste**
nmf garage owner.
garant, -ante [garɑ̃, -ɑ̃t] nmf (personne) Jur
guarantor; **se porter g. de** to guarantee,
vouch for; – nm (garantie) guarantee.
◆**garantie** nf guarantee; (caution) security; (protection) Fig safeguard; **garantie(s)**
(de police d'assurance) cover. ◆**garantir** vt
to guarantee (**contre** against); **g. (à qn) que**
to guarantee (s.o.) that; **g. de** (protéger) to
protect from.
garce [gars] nf Péj Fam bitch.
garçon [garsɔ̃] nm boy, lad; (jeune homme)
young man; (célibataire) bachelor; **g. (de
café)** waiter; **g. d'honneur** (d'un mariage)
best man; **g. manqué** tomboy; **de g.** (comportement) boyish. ◆**garçonnet** nm little
boy. ◆**garçonnière** nf bachelor flat ou
Am apartment.
garde [gard] **1** nm (gardien) guard; Mil
guardsman; **g. champêtre** rural policeman;
g. du corps bodyguard; **G. des Sceaux** Justice Minister. **2** nf (d'enfants, de bagages
etc) care, custody (**de**); **avoir la g. de** to
be in charge of; **faire bonne g.** to keep a
close watch; **prendre g.** to pay attention (**à
qch** to sth), be careful (**à qch** of sth); **prendre g. de ne pas faire** to be careful not to
do; **mettre en g.** to warn (**contre** against);
mise en g. warning; **de g.** on duty; (soldat)
on guard duty; **monter la g.** to stand ou
mount guard; **sur ses gardes** on one's
guard; **g. à vue** (police) custody; **chien de g.**
watchdog. **3** nf (escorte, soldats) guard.
garde-à-vous [gardavu] nm inv Mil (position of) attention. ◆**g.-boue** nm inv mudguard, Am fender. ◆**g.-chasse** nm (pl
gardes-chasses) gamekeeper. ◆**g.-côte**
nm (personne) coastguard. ◆**g.-fou** nm
railing(s), parapet. ◆**g.-malade** nmf (pl

gardes-malades) nurse. ◆**g.-manger** nm
inv (armoire) food safe; (pièce) larder.
◆**g.-robe** nf (habits, armoire) wardrobe.
garder [garde] vt (maintenir, conserver, mettre de côté) to keep; (vêtement) to keep on;
(surveiller) to watch (over); (défendre) to
guard; (enfant) to look after, watch; (habitude) to keep up; **g. qn** (retenir) to keep s.o.;
g. la chambre to keep to one's room; **g. le lit**
to stay in bed; – **se g.** vpr (aliment) to
keep; **se g. de qch** (éviter) to beware of sth;
se g. de faire to take care not to do.
◆**garderie** nf day nursery. ◆**gardeuse**
nf **g. d'enfants** babysitter.
gardien, -ienne [gardjɛ̃, -jɛn] nmf (d'immeuble, d'hôtel) caretaker; (de prison)
(prison) guard, warder; (de zoo, parc) keeper; (de musée) attendant; **g. de but** Fb goalkeeper; **gardienne d'enfants** child minder;
g. de nuit night watchman; **g. de la paix**
policeman; **g. de** (libertés etc) Fig guardian
of; – am **ange g.** guardian angel.
gare [gar] **1** nf Rail station; **g. routière** bus
ou coach station. **2** int **g. à** to watch ou look
out for; **g. à toi!** watch ou look out!; **sans
crier g.** without warning.
garer [gare] vt (voiture etc) to park; (au garage) to garage; – **se g.** vpr (se protéger) to
get out of the way (**de** of); Aut to park.
gargariser (se) [səgargarize] vpr to gargle.
◆**gargarisme** nm gargle.
gargote [gargɔt] nf cheap eating house.
gargouille [garguj] nf Archit gargoyle.
gargouiller [garguje] vi (fontaine, eau) to
gurgle; (ventre) to rumble. ◆**gargouillis**
nm gurgling; rumbling.
garnement [garnəmɑ̃] nm rascal, urchin.
garn/ir [garnir] vt (équiper) to furnish, fit
out (**de** with); (magasin) to stock; (tissu) to
line; (orner) to adorn (**de** with); (enjoliver)
to trim (**de** with); (couvrir) to cover; Culin
to garnish; – **se g.** vpr (lieu) to fill (up) (**de**
with). ◆**-i** a (plat) served with vegetables; bien g. (portefeuille) Fig well-lined.
◆**garniture** nf Culin garnish, trimmings;
pl Aut fittings, upholstery; **g. de lit** bed
linen.
garnison [garnizɔ̃] nf Mil garrison.
gars [gɑ] nm Fam fellow, guy.
gas-oil [gazwal] nm diesel (oil).
gaspill/er [gaspije] vt to waste. ◆**-age** nm
waste.
gastrique [gastrik] a gastric. ◆**gastro-
nome** nmf gourmet. ◆**gastronomie** nf
gastronomy.
gâteau, -x [gɑto] nm cake; **g. de riz** rice
pudding; **g. sec** (sweet) biscuit, Am cookie;

c'était du g. (*facile*) *Fam* it was a piece of cake.

gât/er [gɑte] *vt* to spoil; (*plaisir, vue*) to mar, spoil; **— se g.** *vpr* (*aliment, dent*) to go bad; (*temps, situation*) to get worse; (*relations*) to turn sour. ◆**—é** *a* (*dent, fruit etc*) bad. ◆**gâteries** *nfpl* (*cadeaux*) treats.

gâteux, -euse [gɑtø, -øz] *a* senile, soft in the head.

gauche¹ [goʃ] *a* (*côté, main etc*) left; **— nf la g.** (*côté*) the left (side); *Pol* the left (wing); **à g.** (*tourner etc*) (to the) left; (*marcher, se tenir*) on the left(-hand) side; **de g.** (*fenêtre etc*) left-hand; (*parti, politique etc*) left-wing; **à g. de** on *ou* to the left of. ◆**gaucher, -ère** *a & nmf* left-handed (person). ◆**gauchisant** *a Pol* leftist. ◆**gauchiste** *a & nmf Pol* (extreme) leftist.

gauche² [goʃ] *a* (*maladroit*) awkward. ◆**—ment** *adv* awkwardly. ◆**gaucherie** *nf* awkwardness; (*acte*) blunder.

gauchir [goʃir] *vti* to warp.

gaufre [gofr] *nf Culin* waffle. ◆**gaufrette** *nf* wafer (biscuit).

gaule [gol] *nf* long pole; *Pêche* fishing rod.

Gaule [gol] *nf* (*pays*) *Hist* Gaul. ◆**gaulois** *a* Gallic; (*propos etc*) *Fig* broad, earthy; **— nmpl les G.** *Hist* the Gauls. ◆**gauloiserie** *nf* broad joke.

gausser (se) [sogose] *vpr Litt* to poke fun (de at).

gaver [gave] *vt* (*animal*) to force-feed; (*personne*) *Fig* to cram (with); **— se g.** *vpr* to gorge *ou* stuff oneself (de with).

gaz [gɑz] *nm inv* gas; **usine à g.** gasworks; **chambre/réchaud à g.** gas chamber/stove; **avoir des g.** to have wind *ou* flatulence.

gaze [gɑz] *nf* (*tissu*) gauze.

gazelle [gɑzɛl] *nf* (*animal*) gazelle.

gazer [gɑze] **1** *vi Aut Fam* to whizz along; **ça gaze!** everything's just fine! **2** *vt Mil* to gas.

gazette [gazɛt] *nf Journ* newspaper.

gazeux, -euse [gɑzø, -øz] *a* (*état*) gaseous; (*boisson, eau*) fizzy. ◆**gazomètre** *nm* gasometer.

gazinière [gazinjɛr] *nf* gas cooker *ou Am* stove.

gazole [gɑzɔl] *nm* diesel (oil).

gazon [gɑzɔ̃] *nm* grass, lawn.

gazouiller [gazuje] *vi* (*oiseau*) to chirp; (*bébé, ruisseau*) to babble. ◆**gazouillis** *nm* chirping; babbling.

geai [ʒɛ] *nm* (*oiseau*) jay.

géant, -ante [ʒeã, -ãt] *a & nmf* giant.

Geiger [ʒeʒɛr] *nm* **compteur G.** Geiger counter.

geindre [ʒɛ̃dr] *vi* to whine, whimper.

gel [ʒɛl] *nm* **1** (*temps, glace*) frost; (*de crédits*) *Écon* freezing. **2** (*substance*) gel. ◆**gel/er** *vti* to freeze; **on gèle ici** it's freezing here; **– v imp il gèle** it's freezing. ◆**—é** *a* frozen; (*doigts*) *Méd* frostbitten. ◆**—ée** *nf* frost; *Culin* jelly, *Am* jello; **g. blanche** ground frost.

gélatine [ʒelatin] *nf* gelatin(e).

gélule [ʒelyl] *nf* (*médicament*) capsule.

Gémeaux [ʒemo] *nmpl* **les G.** (*signe*) Gemini.

gém/ir [ʒemir] *vi* to groan, moan. ◆**—issement** *nm* groan, moan.

gencive [ʒãsiv] *nf Anat* gum.

gendarme [ʒãdarm] *nm* gendarme, policeman (*soldier performing police duties*). ◆**gendarmerie** *nf* police force; (*local*) police headquarters.

gendre [ʒãdr] *nm* son-in-law.

gène [ʒɛn] *nm Biol* gene.

gène [ʒɛn] *nf* (*trouble physique*) discomfort; (*confusion*) embarrassment; (*dérangement*) bother, trouble; **dans la g.** *Fin* in financial difficulties. ◆**gên/er** *vt* (*déranger, irriter*) to bother, annoy; (*troubler*) to embarrass; (*mouvement, action*) to hamper, hinder; (*circulation*) *Aut* to hold up, block; **g. qn** (*vêtement*) to be uncomfortable on s.o.; (*par sa présence*) to be in s.o.'s way; **ça ne me gêne pas** I don't mind (si if); **— se g.** *vpr* (*se déranger*) to put oneself out; **ne te gêne pas pour moi!** don't mind me! ◆**—ant** *a* (*objet*) cumbersome; (*présence, situation*) awkward; (*personne*) annoying. ◆**—é** *a* (*intimidé*) embarrassed; (*mal à l'aise*) uneasy, awkward; (*silence, sourire*) awkward; (*sans argent*) short of money.

généalogie [ʒenealɔʒi] *nf* genealogy. ◆**généalogique** *a* genealogical; **arbre g.** family tree.

général, -aux [ʒeneral, -o] **1** *a* (*global, commun*) general; **en g.** in general. **2** *nm* (*officier*) *Mil* general. ◆**générale** *nf Th* dress rehearsal. ◆**généralement** *adv* generally; **g. parlant** broadly *ou* generally speaking. ◆**généralisation** *nf* generalization. ◆**généraliser** *vti* to generalize; **— se g.** *vpr* to become general *ou* widespread. ◆**généraliste** *nmf Méd* general practitioner, GP. ◆**généralité** *nf* generality; **la g. de** the majority of.

générateur [ʒeneratœr] *nm*, ◆**génératrice** *nf Él* generator.

génération [ʒenerasjɔ̃] *nf* generation.

généreux, -euse [ʒenerø, -øz] *a* generous (de with). ◆**généreusement** *adv* generously. ◆**générosité** *nf* generosity.

générique [ʒenerik] *nm Cin* credits.

genèse [ʒɔnɛz] *nf* genesis.

genêt [ʒɔnɛ] *nm (arbrisseau)* broom.

génétique [ʒenetik] *nf* genetics; – *a* genetic.

Genève [ʒɔnɛv] *nm ou f* Geneva.

génie [ʒeni] *nm* **1** *(aptitude, personne)* genius; **avoir le g. pour faire/de qch** to have a genius for doing/for sth. **2** *(lutin)* genie, spirit. **3** **g. civil** civil engineering; **g. militaire** engineering corps. ◆**génial, -aux** *a (personne, invention)* brilliant; *(formidable) Fam* fantastic.

génisse [ʒenis] *nf (vache)* heifer.

génital, -aux [ʒenital, -o] *a* genital; **organes génitaux** genitals.

génocide [ʒenɔsid] *nm* genocide.

genou, -x [ʒ(ə)nu] *nm* knee; **être à genoux** to be kneeling (down); **se mettre à genoux** to kneel (down); **prendre qn sur ses genoux** to take s.o. on one's lap *ou* knee. ◆**genouillère** *nf Fb etc* knee pad.

genre [ʒɑ̃r] *nm* **1** *(espèce)* kind, sort; *(attitude)* manner, way; **g. humain** mankind; **g. de vie** way of life. **2** *Littér Cin* genre; *Gram* gender; *Biol* genus.

gens [ʒɑ̃] *nmpl ou nfpl* people; **jeunes g.** young people; *(hommes)* young men.

gentil, -ille [ʒɑ̃ti, -ij] *a (agréable)* nice, pleasant; *(aimable)* kind, nice; *(mignon)* pretty; **g. avec qn** nice *ou* kind to s.o.; **sois g.** *(sage)* be good. ◆**gentillesse** *nf* kindness; **avoir la g. de faire** to be kind enough to do. ◆**gentiment** *adv (aimablement)* kindly; *(sagement)* nicely.

gentilhomme, *pl* **gentilshommes** [ʒɑ̃tijɔm, ʒɑ̃tizɔm] *nm (noble) Hist* gentleman.

géographie [ʒeɔgrafi] *nf* geography. ◆**géographique** *a* geographical.

geôlier, -ière [ʒolje, -jɛr] *nmf* jailer, gaoler.

géologie [ʒeɔlɔʒi] *nf* geology. ◆**géologique** *a* geological. ◆**géologue** *nmf* geologist.

géomètre [ʒeɔmɛtr] *nm (arpenteur)* surveyor.

géométrie [ʒeɔmetri] *nf* geometry. ◆**géométrique** *a* geometric(al).

géranium [ʒeranjɔm] *nm Bot* geranium.

gérant, -ante [ʒerɑ̃, -ɑ̃t] *nmf* manager, manageress; **g. d'immeubles** landlord's agent. ◆**gérance** *nf (gestion)* management.

gerbe [ʒɛrb] *nf (de blé)* sheaf; *(de fleurs)* bunch; *(d'eau)* spray; *(d'étincelles)* shower.

gercer [ʒɛrse] *vti,* **— se g.** *vpr (peau, lèvres)* to chap, crack. ◆**gerçure** *nf* chap, crack.

gérer [ʒere] *vt (fonds, commerce etc)* to manage.

germain [ʒɛrmɛ̃] *a* **cousin g.** first cousin.

germanique [ʒɛrmanik] *a* Germanic.

germe [ʒɛrm] *nm Méd Biol* germ; *Bot* shoot; *(d'une idée) Fig* seed, germ. ◆**germer** *vi Bot & Fig* to germinate.

gésir [ʒezir] *vi (être étendu) Litt* to be lying; **il gît/gisait** he is/was lying; **ci-gît** here lies.

gestation [ʒɛstasjɔ̃] *nf* gestation.

geste [ʒɛst] *nm* gesture; **ne pas faire un g.** *(ne pas bouger)* not to make a move. ◆**gesticuler** *vi* to gesticulate.

gestion [ʒɛstjɔ̃] *nf (action)* management, administration. ◆**gestionnaire** *nmf* administrator.

geyser [ʒɛzɛr] *nm Géol* geyser.

ghetto [geto] *nm* ghetto.

gibecière [ʒibsjɛr] *nf* shoulder bag.

gibier [ʒibje] *nm (animaux, oiseaux)* game.

giboulée [ʒibule] *nf* shower, downpour.

gicler [ʒikle] *vi (liquide)* to spurt, squirt; *(boue)* to splash; **faire g.** to spurt, squirt. ◆**—ée** *nf* jet, spurt. ◆**—eur** *nm (de carburateur) Aut* jet.

gifle [ʒifl] *nf* slap (in the face). ◆**gifler** *vt* **g. qn** to slap s.o., slap s.o.'s face.

gigantesque [ʒigɑ̃tɛsk] *a* gigantic.

gigogne [ʒigɔɲ] *a* **table g.** nest of tables.

gigot [ʒigo] *nm* leg of mutton *ou* lamb.

gigoter [ʒigɔte] *vi Fam* to kick, wriggle.

gilet [ʒilɛ] *nm* waistcoat, *Am* vest; *(cardigan)* cardigan; **g. (de corps)** vest, *Am* undershirt; **g. pare-balles** bulletproof jacket *ou Am* vest; **g. de sauvetage** life jacket.

gin [dʒin] *nm (eau-de-vie)* gin.

gingembre [ʒɛ̃ʒɑ̃br] *nm Bot Culin* ginger.

girafe [ʒiraf] *nf* giraffe.

giratoire [ʒiratwar] *a* **sens g.** *Aut* roundabout, *Am* traffic circle.

girl [gœrl] *nf (danseuse)* chorus girl.

girofle [ʒirɔfl] *nm* **clou de g.** *Bot* clove.

giroflée [ʒirɔfle] *nf Bot* wall flower.

girouette [ʒirwɛt] *nf* weathercock, weather vane.

gisement [ʒizmɑ̃] *nm (de minerai, pétrole) Géol* deposit.

gitan, -ane [ʒitɑ̃, -an] *nmf (Spanish)* gipsy.

gîte [ʒit] *nm (abri)* resting place.

gîter [ʒite] *vi (navire)* to list.

givre [ʒivr] *nm (hoar)frost.* ◆**se givrer** *vpr (pare-brise etc)* to ice up, frost up. ◆**givré** *a* frost-covered.

glabre [glabr] *a (visage)* smooth.

glace [glas] *nf* **1** *(eau gelée)* ice; *(crème glacée)* ice cream. **2** *(vitre)* window; *(miroir)* mirror; *(verre)* plate glass.

glacer [glase] **1** *vt* (*sang*) *Fig* to chill; **g. qn** (*transir, paralyser*) to chill s.o.; **— se g.** *vpr* (*eau*) to freeze. **2** *vt* (*gâteau*) to ice, (*au jus*) to glaze; (*papier*) to glaze. ◆**glaçant** *a* (*attitude etc*) chilling, icy. ◆**glacé** *a* **1** (*eau, main, pièce*) ice-cold, icy; (*vent*) freezing, icy; (*accueil*) *Fig* icy, chilly. **2** (*thé*) iced; (*fruit, marron*) candied; (*papier*) glazed. ◆**glaçage** *nm* (*de gâteau etc*) icing. ◆**glacial, -aux** *a* icy. ◆**glacier** *nm* **1** *Géol* glacier. **2** (*vendeur*) ice-cream man. ◆**glacière** *nf* (*boîte, endroit*) icebox. ◆**glaçon** *nm* *Culin* ice cube; *Géol* block of ice; (*sur le toit*) icicle.

glaïeul [glajœl] *nm Bot* gladiolus.

glaires [glɛr] *nfpl Méd* phlegm.

glaise [glɛz] *nf* clay.

gland [glɑ̃] *nm* **1** *Bot* acorn. **2** (*pompon*) *Tex* tassel.

glande [glɑ̃d] *nf* gland.

glander [glɑ̃de] *vi Arg* to fritter away one's time.

glaner [glane] *vt* (*blé, renseignement etc*) to glean.

glapir [glapir] *vi* to yelp, yap.

glas [glɑ] *nm* (*de cloche*) knell.

glauque [glok] *a* sea-green.

gliss/er [glise] *vi* (*involontairement*) to slip; (*patiner, coulisser*) to slide; (*sur l'eau*) to glide; **g. sur** (*sujet*) to slide *ou* gloss over; **ça glisse** it's slippery; **—** *vt* (*introduire*) to slip (**dans** into); (*murmurer*) to whisper; **se g. dans/sous** to slip into/under. ◆**—ant** *a* slippery. ◆**glissade** *nf* (*involontaire*) slip; (*volontaire*) slide. ◆**glissement** *nm* (*de sens*) *Ling* shift; **g. à gauche** *Pol* swing *ou* shift to the left; **g. de terrain** *Géol* landslide. ◆**glissière** *nf* groove; **porte à g.** sliding door; **fermeture à g.** zip (fastener), *Am* zipper.

global, -aux [glɔbal, -o] *a* total, global; **somme globale** lump sum. ◆**—ement** *adv* collectively, as a whole.

globe [glɔb] *nm* globe; **g. de l'œil** eyeball.

globule [glɔbyl] *nm* (*du sang*) corpuscle.

gloire [glwar] *nf* (*renommée, louange, mérite*) glory; (*personne célèbre*) celebrity; **se faire g. de** to glory in; **à la g. de** in praise of. ◆**glorieux, -euse** *a* (*plein de gloire*) glorious. ◆**glorifier** *vt* to glorify; **se g.** to glory in.

glossaire [glɔsɛr] *nm* glossary.

glouglou [gluglu] *nm* (*de liquide*) gurgle. ◆**glouglouter** *vi* to gurgle.

glouss/er [gluse] *vi* (*poule*) to cluck; (*personne*) to chuckle. ◆**—ement** *nm* cluck; chuckle.

glouton, -onne [glutɔ̃, -ɔn] *a* greedy, gluttonous; **—** *nmf* glutton. ◆**gloutonnerie** *nf* gluttony.

gluant [glyɑ̃] *a* sticky.

glucose [glykoz] *nm* glucose.

glycérine [gliserin] *nf* glycerin(e).

glycine [glisin] *nf Bot* wisteria.

gnome [gnom] *nm* (*nain*) gnome.

gnon [ɲɔ̃] *nm Arg* blow, punch.

goal [gol] *nm Fb* goalkeeper.

gobelet [gɔblɛ] *nm* tumbler; (*de plastique, papier*) cup.

gober [gɔbe] *vt* (*œuf, mouche etc*) to swallow (whole); (*propos*) *Fig* to swallow.

godasse [gɔdas] *nf Fam* shoe.

godet [gɔdɛ] *nm* (*récipient*) pot; (*verre*) *Arg* drink.

goéland [gɔelɑ̃] *nm* (sea)gull.

gogo [gogo] *nm* (*homme naïf*) *Fam* sucker.

gogo (à) [gogo] *adv Fam* galore.

goguenard [gɔgnar] *a* mocking.

goguette (en) [ɑ̃gɔgɛt] *adv Fam* on the spree.

goinfre [gwɛ̃fr] *nm* (*glouton*) *Fam* pig, guzzler. ◆**se goinfrer** *vpr Fam* to stuff oneself (**de** with).

golf [gɔlf] *nm* golf; (*terrain*) golf course. ◆**golfeur, -euse** *nmf* golfer.

golfe [gɔlf] *nm* gulf, bay.

gomme [gɔm] *nf* **1** (*substance*) gum. **2** (*à effacer*) rubber, *Am* eraser. ◆**gommé** *a* (*papier*) gummed. ◆**gommer** *vt* (*effacer*) to rub out, erase.

gomme (à la) [alagɔm] *adv Fam* useless.

gond [gɔ̃] *nm* (*de porte etc*) hinge.

gondole [gɔ̃dɔl] *nf* (*bateau*) gondola. ◆**gondolier** *nm* gondolier.

gondoler [gɔ̃dɔle] **1** *vi*, **— se g.** *vpr* (*planche*) to warp. **2 se g.** *vpr* (*rire*) *Fam* to split one's sides.

gonfl/er [gɔ̃fle] *vt* to swell; (*pneu*) to inflate, pump up; (*en soufflant*) to blow up; (*poitrine*) to swell out; (*grossir*) *Fig* to inflate; **—** *vi*, **— se g.** *vpr* to swell; **se g. de** (*orgueil, émotion*) to swell with. ◆**—é** *a* swollen; **être g.** *Fam* (*courageux*) to have plenty of pluck; (*insolent*) to have plenty of nerve. ◆**—able** *a* inflatable. ◆**—ement** *nm* swelling. ◆**—eur** *nm* (air) pump.

gong [gɔ̃g] *nm* gong.

gorge [gɔrʒ] *nf* **1** throat; (*seins*) *Litt* bust. **2** *Géog* gorge. ◆**gorg/er** *vt* (*remplir*) to stuff (**de** with); **se g. de** to stuff *ou* gorge oneself with. ◆**—é** *a* **g. de** (*saturé*) gorged with. ◆**—ée** *nf* mouthful; **petite g.** sip; **d'une seule g.** in *ou* at one gulp.

gorille [gɔrij] nm **1** (*animal*) gorilla. **2** (*garde du corps*) *Fam* bodyguard.

gosier [gozje] nm throat, windpipe.

gosse [gɔs] nmf (*enfant*) *Fam* kid, young-ster.

gothique [gɔtik] a & nm Gothic.

gouache [gwaʃ] nf (*peinture*) gouache.

goudron [gudrɔ̃] nm tar. ◆**goudronner** vt to tar.

gouffre [gufr] nm gulf, chasm.

goujat [guʒa] nm churl, lout.

goulasch [gulaʃ] nf *Culin* goulash.

goulot [gulo] nm (*de bouteille*) neck; **boire au g.** to drink from the bottle.

goulu, -ue [guly] a greedy; – nmf glutton. ◆**goulûment** adv greedily.

goupille [gupij] nf (*cheville*) pin.

goupiller [gupije] vt (*arranger*) *Fam* to work out, arrange.

gourde [gurd] nf **1** (*à eau*) water bottle, flask. **2** (*personne*) *Péj Fam* chump, oaf.

gourdin [gurdɛ̃] nm club, cudgel.

gourer (se) [səgure] vpr *Fam* to make a mis-take.

gourmand, -ande [gurmɑ̃, -ɑ̃d] a fond of eating, *Péj* greedy; **g. de** fond of; **être g. (de sucreries)** to have a sweet tooth; – nmf hearty eater, *Péj* glutton. ◆**gourmandise** nf good eating, *Péj* gluttony; pl (*mets*) deli-cacies.

gourmet [gurmɛ] nm gourmet, epicure.

gourmette [gurmɛt] nf chain ou identity bracelet.

gousse [gus] nf **g. d'ail** clove of garlic.

goût [gu] nm taste; **de bon g.** in good taste; **prendre g. à qch** to take a liking to sth; **par g.** from ou by choice; **sans g.** tasteless. ◆**goûter** vt (*aliment*) to taste; (*apprécier*) to relish, enjoy; **g. à qch** to taste (a little of) sth; **g. de** (*pour la première fois*) to try out, taste; – vi to have a snack, have tea; – nm snack, tea.

goutte [gut] nf **1** drop. **couler g. à g.** to drip. **2** (*maladie*) gout. ◆**g.-à-goutte** nm inv *Méd* drip. ◆**gouttelette** nf droplet. ◆**goutter** vi (*eau, robinet, nez*) to drip (**de** from).

gouttière [gutjɛr] nf (*d'un toit*) gutter.

gouvernail [guvernaj] nm (*pale*) rudder; (*barre*) helm.

gouvernante [guvernɑ̃t] nf governess.

gouvernement [guvernəmɑ̃] nm govern-ment. ◆**gouvernemental, -aux** a (*parti, politique etc*) government-.

gouvern/er [guverne] vti *Pol & Fig* to gov-ern, rule. ◆**—ants** nmpl rulers. ◆**—eur** nm governor.

grabuge [grabyʒ] nm **du g.** (*querelle*) *Fam* a rumpus.

grâce [grɑs] **1** nf (*charme*) & *Rel* grace; (*avantage*) favour; (*miséricorde*) mercy; **crier g.** to cry for mercy; **de bonne/mauvaise g.** with good/bad grace; **donner le coup de g. à** to finish off; **faire g. de qch à qn** to spare s.o. sth. **2** prép **g. à** thanks to. ◆**gracier** vt (*condamné*) to pardon.

gracieux, -euse [grasjø, -øz] a **1** (*élégant*) graceful; (*aimable*) gracious. **2** (*gratuit*) gratuitous; **à titre g.** free (of charge). ◆**gracieusement** adv gracefully; gra-ciously; free (of charge).

gracile [grasil] a *Litt* slender.

gradation [gradɑsjɔ̃] nf gradation.

grade [grad] nm *Mil* rank; **monter en g.** to be promoted. ◆**gradé** nm *Mil* non-commissioned officer.

gradin [gradɛ̃] nm *Th etc* row of seats, tier.

graduel, -elle [graduɛl] a gradual.

graduer [gradue] vt (*règle*) to graduate; (*ex-ercices*) to grade, make gradually more dif-ficult.

graffiti [grafiti] nmpl graffiti.

grain [grɛ̃] nm **1** (*de blé etc*) & *Fig* grain; (*de café*) bean; (*de chapelet*) bead; (*de poussière*) speck; pl (*céréales*) grain; **le g.** (*de cuir, papier*) the grain; **g. de beauté** mole; (*sur le visage*) beauty spot; **g. de rai-sin** grape. **2** *Mét* shower.

graine [grɛn] nf seed; **mauvaise g.** (*enfant*) *Péj* bad lot, rotten egg.

graisse [grɛs] nf fat; (*lubrifiant*) grease. ◆**graissage** nm *Aut* lubrication. ◆**graisser** vt to grease. ◆**graisseux, -euse** a (*vêtement etc*) greasy, oily; (*bour-relets, tissu*) fatty.

grammaire [gramɛr] nf grammar. ◆**gram-matical, -aux** a grammatical.

gramme [gram] nm gram(me).

grand, grande [grɑ̃, grɑ̃d] a big, large; (*en hauteur*) tall; (*mérite, âge, chaleur, ami etc*) great; (*bruit*) loud, great; (*différence*) wide, great, big; (*adulte, mûr, plus âgé*) grown up, big; (*officier, maître*) grand; (*âme*) noble; **g. frère/etc** (*plus âgé*) big brother/etc; **le g. air** the open air; **il est g. temps** it's high time (**que** that); – adv **g. ouvert** (*yeux, fenêtre*) wide-open; **ouvrir g.** to open wide; **en g.** on a grand ou large scale; – nmf *Scol* senior; (*adulte*) grown-up; **les quatre Grands** *Pol* the Big Four. ◆**grandement** adv (*beaucoup*) greatly; (*généreusement*) grandly; **avoir g. de quoi vivre** to have plen-ty to live on. ◆**grandeur** nf (*importance, gloire*) greatness; (*dimension*) size, magnitude; (*majesté, splendeur*) grandeur; **g. nature** life-size; **g. d'âme** generosity.

grand-chose [grɑ̃ʃoz] *pron* **pas g.-chose** not much. ◆**g.-mère** *nf* (*pl* **grands-mères**) grandmother. ◆**grands-parents** *nmpl* grandparents. ◆**g.-père** *nm* (*pl* **grands-pères**) grandfather.

Grande-Bretagne [grɑ̃dbrətaɲ] *nf* Great Britain.

grandiose [grɑ̃djoz] *a* grandiose, grand.

grandir [grɑ̃dir] *vi* to grow; (*bruit*) to grow louder; − *vt* (*grossir*) to magnify; **g. qn** (*faire paraître plus grand*) to make s.o. seem taller.

grange [grɑ̃ʒ] *nf* barn.

granit(e) [granit] *nm* granite.

graphique [grafik] *a* (*signe, art*) graphic; − *nm* graph.

grappe [grap] *nf* (*de fruits etc*) cluster; **g. de raisin** bunch of grapes.

grappin [grapɛ̃] *nm* **mettre le g. sur** *Fam* to grab hold of.

gras, grasse [grɑ, grɑs] *a* (*personne, ventre etc*) fat; (*aliment*) fatty; (*graisseux*) greasy, oily; (*caractère*) bold, heavy; (*plante, contour*) thick; (*rire*) throaty, deep; (*toux*) loose, phlegmy; (*récompense*) rich; **matières grasses** fat; **foie g.** *Culin* foie gras, fatted goose liver; − *nm* (*de viande*) fat. ◆**grassement** *adv* (*abondamment*) handsomely. ◆**grassouillet, -ette** *a* plump.

gratifier [gratifje] *vt* **g. qn de** to present *ou* favour s.o. with. ◆**gratification** *nf* (*prime*) bonus.

gratin [gratɛ̃] *nm* **1 au g.** *Culin* baked with breadcrumbs and grated cheese. **2** (*élite*) *Fam* upper crust.

gratis [gratis] *adv* *Fam* free (of charge), gratis.

gratitude [gratityd] *nf* gratitude.

gratte-ciel [gratsjɛl] *nm inv* skyscraper.

gratte-papier [gratpapje] *nm* (*employé*) *Péj* pen-pusher.

gratter [grate] *vt* (*avec un outil etc*) to scrape; (*avec les ongles, les griffes etc*) to scratch; (*boue*) to scrape off; (*effacer*) to scratch out; **ça me gratte** *Fam* it itches, I have an itch; − *vi* (*à la porte etc*) to scratch; (*tissu*) to be scratchy; **− se g.** *vpr* to scratch oneself. ◆**grattoir** *nm* scraper.

gratuit [gratɥi] *a* (*billet etc*) free; (*hypothèse, acte*) gratuitous. ◆**gratuité** *nf* **la g. de l'enseignement**/*etc* free education/*etc*. ◆**gratuitement** *adv* free (of charge); gratuitously.

gravats [grava] *nmpl* rubble, debris.

grave [grav] *a* serious; (*juge, visage*) grave,

solemn; (*voix*) deep, low; (*accent*) *Gram* grave; **ce n'est pas g.!** it's not important! ◆**−ment** *adv* (*malade, menacé*) seriously; (*dignement*) gravely.

grav/er [grave] *vt* (*sur métal etc*) to engrave; (*sur bois*) to carve; (*disque*) to cut; (*dans sa mémoire*) to imprint, engrave. ◆**−eur** *nm* engraver.

gravier [gravje] *nm* gravel. ◆**gravillon** *nm* gravel; *pl* gravel, (loose) chippings.

gravir [gravir] *vt* to climb (*with effort*).

gravité [gravite] *nf* **1** (*de situation etc*) seriousness; (*solennité*) gravity. **2** *Phys* gravity.

graviter [gravite] *vi* to revolve (**autour de** around). ◆**gravitation** *nf* gravitation.

gravure [gravyr] *nf* (*action, art*) engraving; (*à l'eau forte*) etching; (*estampe*) print; (*de disque*) recording; **g. sur bois** (*objet*) woodcut.

gré [gre] *nm* **à son g.** (*goût*) to his *ou* her taste; (*désir*) as he *ou* she pleases; **de bon g.** willingly; **contre le g. de** against the will of; **bon g. mal g.** willy-nilly; **au g. de** (*vent etc*) at the mercy of.

Grèce [grɛs] *nf* Greece. ◆**grec, grecque** *a* & *nmf* Greek; − *nm* (*langue*) Greek.

greffe [grɛf] **1** *nf* (*de peau*) & *Bot* graft; (*d'organe*) transplant. **2** *nm* *Jur* record office. ◆**greffer** *vt* (*peau etc*) & *Bot* to graft (**à** on to); (*organe*) to transplant. ◆**greffier** *nm* clerk (of the court). ◆**greffon** *nm* (*de peau*) & *Bot* graft.

grégaire [greger] *a* (*instinct*) gregarious.

grêle [grɛl] **1** *nf* *Mét* & *Fig* hail. **2** *a* (*fin*) spindly, (very) slender *ou* thin. ◆**grêler** *v imp* to hail. ◆**grêlon** *nm* hailstone.

grêlé [grele] *a* (*visage*) pockmarked.

grelot [grəlo] *nm* (small round) bell.

grelotter [grələte] *vi* to shiver (**de** with).

grenade [grənad] *nf* **1** *Bot* pomegranate. **2** (*projectile*) *Mil* grenade. ◆**grenadine** *nf* pomegranate syrup, grenadine.

grenat [grəna] *a inv* (*couleur*) dark red.

grenier [grənje] *nm* attic; *Agr* granary.

grenouille [grənuj] *nf* frog.

grès [grɛ] *nm* (*roche*) sandstone; (*poterie*) stoneware.

grésiller [grezije] *vi* *Culin* to sizzle; *Rad* to crackle.

grève [grɛv] *nf* **1** strike; **g. de la faim** hunger strike; **g. du zèle** work-to-rule, *Am* rule-book slow-down; **g. perlée** go-slow, *Am* slow-down (strike); **g. sauvage/sur le tas** wildcat/sit-down strike; **g. tournante** strike by rota. **2** (*de mer*) shore; (*de rivière*) bank. ◆**gréviste** *nmf* striker.

gribouiller [gribuje] *vti* to scribble.
◆**gribouillis** *nm* scribble.

grief [grijɛf] *nm* (*plainte*) grievance.

grièvement [grijɛvmɑ̃] *adv* g. blessé seriously *ou* badly injured.

griffe [grif] *nf* 1 (*ongle*) claw; sous la g. de qn (*pouvoir*) in s.o.'s clutches. 2 (*de couturier*) (designer) label; (*tampon*) printed signature; (*d'auteur*) *Fig* mark, stamp. ◆**griffé** *a* (*vêtement*) designer-. ◆**griffer** *vt* to scratch, claw.

griffonn/er [grifɔne] *vt* to scrawl, scribble. ◆**—age** *nm* scrawl, scribble.

grignoter [grijɔte] *vti* to nibble.

gril [gril] *nm* *Culin* grill, grid(iron). ◆**grillade** [grijad] *nf* (*viande*) grill. ◆**grille-pain** *nm inv* toaster. ◆**griller** *vt* (*viande*) to grill, broil; (*pain*) to toast; (*café*) to roast; (*ampoule*) *El* to blow; (*brûler*) to scorch; (*cigarette*) *Fam* to smoke; g. un feu rouge *Aut Fam* to drive through *ou* jump a red light; – *vi* mettre à g. to put on the grill; on grille ici *Fam* it's scorching; g. de faire to be itching to do.

grille [grij] *nf* (*clôture*) railings; (*porte*) (iron) gate; (*de fourneau, foyer*) grate; (*de radiateur*) *Aut* grid, grille; (*des salaires*) *Fig* scale; *pl* (*de fenêtre*) bars, grating; g. (des horaires) schedule. ◆**grillage** *nm* wire netting.

grillon [grijɔ̃] *nm* (*insecte*) cricket.

grimace [grimas] *nf* (*pour faire rire*) (funny) face, grimace; (*de dégoût, douleur*) grimace. ◆**grimacer** *vi* to grimace (de with).

grimer [grime] *vt*, – se g. *vpr* (*acteur*) to make up.

grimp/er [grɛ̃pe] *vi* to climb (à qch up sth); (*prix*) *Fam* to rocket; – *vt* to climb. ◆**—ant** *a* (*plante*) climbing.

grinc/er [grɛ̃se] *vi* to grate, creak; g. des dents to grind *ou* gnash one's teeth. ◆**—ement** *nm* grating; grinding.

grincheux, -euse [grɛ̃ʃø, -øz] *a* grumpy, peevish.

gringalet [grɛ̃galɛ] *nm* (*homme*) *Péj* puny runt, weakling.

grippe [grip] *nf* 1 (*maladie*) flu, influenza. 2 prendre qch/qn en g. to take a strong dislike to sth/s.o. ◆**grippé** *a* être g. to have (the) flu.

gripper [gripe] *vi*, – se g. *vpr* (*moteur*) to seize up.

grippe-sou [gripsu] *nm* skinflint, miser.

gris [gri] *a* grey, *Am* gray; (*temps*) dull, grey; (*ivre*) tipsy; – *nm* grey. ◆**grisaille** *nf* (*de vie*) dullness, greyness, *Am* grayness. ◆**grisâtre** *a* greyish, *Am* grayish.

griser *vt* (*vin etc*) to make (s.o.) tipsy, intoxicate (s.o.); (*air vif, succès*) to exhilarate (s.o.). ◆**griserie** *nf* intoxication; exhilaration. ◆**grisonn/er** *vi* (*cheveux, personne*) to go grey. ◆**—ant** *a* greying.

grisou [grizu] *nm* (*gaz*) firedamp.

grive [griv] *nf* (*oiseau*) thrush.

grivois [grivwa] *a* bawdy. ◆**grivoiserie** *nf* (*propos*) bawdy talk.

Groenland [grɔɛnlɑ̃d] *nm* Greenland.

grog [grɔg] *nm* (*boisson*) grog, toddy.

grogn/er [grɔɲe] *vi* to growl, grumble (contre at); (*cochon*) to grunt. ◆**—ement** *nm* growl, grumble; grunt. ◆**grognon, -onne** *a* grumpy, peevish.

grommeler [grɔmle] *vti* to grumble, mutter.

gronder [grɔ̃de] *vi* (*chien*) to growl; (*tonnerre*) to rumble; – *vt* (*réprimander*) to scold. ◆**grondement** *nm* growl, rumble. ◆**gronderie** *nf* scolding.

gros, grosse [gro, gros] *a* big; (*gras*) fat; (*épais*) thick; (*effort, progrès*) great; (*fortune, somme*) large; (*bruit*) loud; (*averse, mer, rhume*) heavy; (*faute*) serious, gross; (*traits, laine, fil*) coarse; g. mot swear word; – *adv* gagner g. to earn big money; risquer g. to take a big risk; en g. (*globalement*) roughly; (*écrire*) in big letters; (*vendre*) in bulk, wholesale; – *nmf* (*personne*) fat man, fat woman; – *nm* le g. de the bulk of; de g. (*maison, prix*) wholesale.

groseille [grozɛj] *nf* (white *ou* red) currant; g. à maquereau gooseberry.

grossesse [grosɛs] *nf* pregnancy.

grosseur [grosœr] *nf* 1 (*volume*) size; (*obésité*) weight. 2 (*tumeur*) *Méd* lump.

grossier, -ière [grosje, -jɛr] *a* (*matière, tissu, traits*) coarse, rough; (*idée, solution*) rough, crude; (*instrument*) crude; (*erreur*) gross; (*personne, manières*) coarse, uncouth, rude; être g. envers (*insolent*) to be rude to. ◆**grossièrement** *adv* (*calculer*) roughly; (*se tromper*) grossly; (*répondre*) coarsely, rudely. ◆**grossièreté** *nf* coarseness; roughness; (*insolence*) rudeness; (*mot*) rude word.

gross/ir [grosir] *vi* (*personne*) to put on weight; (*fleuve*) to swell; (*nombre, bosse, foule*) to swell, get bigger; (*bruit*) to get louder; – *vt* to swell; (*exagérer*) *Fig* to magnify; – *vti* (*verre, loupe etc*) to magnify; verre **grossissant** magnifying glass. ◆**—issement** *nm* increase in weight; swelling, increase in size; (*de microscope etc*) magnification.

grossiste [grosist] *nmf Com* wholesaler.

grosso modo [grosomodo] *adv* (*en gros*) roughly.

grotesque [grotɛsk] *a* (*risible*) ludicrous, grotesque.

grotte [grot] *nf* grotto.

grouill/er [gruje] **1** *vi* (*rue, fourmis, foule etc*) to be swarming (**de** with). **2 se g.** *vpr* (*se hâter*) *Arg* to step on it. **◆—ant** *a* swarming (**de** with).

groupe [grup] *nm* group; **g. scolaire** (*bâtiments*) school block. **◆groupement** *nm* (*action*) grouping; (*groupe*) group. **◆grouper** *vt* to group (together); **— se g.** *vpr* to band together, group (together).

grue [gry] *nf* (*machine, oiseau*) crane.

grumeau, -x [grymo] *nm* (*dans une sauce etc*) lump. **◆grumeleux, -euse** *a* lumpy.

gruyère [gryjɛr] *nm* gruyère (cheese).

gué [ge] *nm* ford; **passer à g.** to ford.

guenilles [gənij] *nfpl* rags (and tatters).

guenon [gənɔ̃] *nf* female monkey.

guépard [gepar] *nm* cheetah.

guêpe [gɛp] *nf* wasp. **◆guêpier** *nm* (*nid*) wasp's nest; (*piège*) *Fig* trap.

guère [gɛr] *adv* (**ne**) . . . **g.** hardly, scarcely; **il ne sort g.** he hardly *ou* scarcely goes out.

guéridon [geridɔ̃] *nm* pedestal table.

guérilla [gerija] *nf* guerrilla warfare. **◆guérillero** *nm* guerrilla.

guér/ir [gerir] *vt* (*personne, maladie*) to cure (**de** of); (*blessure*) to heal; **—** *vi* to recover; (*blessure*) to heal; (*rhume*) to get better; **g. de** (*fièvre etc*) to get over, recover from. **◆—i** *a* cured, better, well. **◆guérison** *nf* (*de personne*) recovery; (*de maladie*) cure; (*de blessure*) healing. **◆guérisseur, -euse** *nmf* faith healer.

guérite [gerit] *nf* *Mil* sentry box.

guerre [gɛr] *nf* war; (*chimique etc*) warfare; **en g. at** war (**avec** with); **faire la g.** to wage *ou* make war (**à** on, against); **g. d'usure** war of attrition; **conseil de g.** court-martial. **◆guerrier, -ière** *a* (*chant, danse*) war-; (*nation*) war-like; **—** *nmf* warrior. **◆guerroyer** *vi* *Litt* to war.

guet [gɛ] *nm* **faire le g.** to be on the look-out. **◆guett/er** *vt* to be on the look-out for,

watch (out) for; (*gibier*) to lie in wait for. **◆—eur** *nm* (*soldat*) look-out.

guet-apens [gɛtapɑ̃] *nm inv* ambush.

guêtre [gɛtr] *nf* gaiter.

gueule [gœl] *nf* (*d'animal, de canon*) mouth; (*de personne*) *Fam* mouth; (*figure*) *Fam* face; **avoir la g. de bois** *Fam* to have a hangover; **faire la g.** *Fam* to sulk. **◆gueuler** *vti* to bawl (out). **◆gueuleton** *nm* (*repas*) *Fam* blow-out, feast.

gui [gi] *nm* *Bot* mistletoe.

guichet [giʃɛ] *nm* (*de gare, cinéma etc*) ticket office; (*de banque etc*) window; *Th* box office, ticket office; **à guichets fermés** *Th Sp* with all tickets sold in advance. **◆guichetier, -ière** *nmf* (*à la poste etc*) counter clerk; (*à la gare*) ticket office clerk.

guide [gid] **1** *nm* (*personne, livre etc*) guide. **2** *nf* (*éclaireuse*) (girl) guide. **3** *nfpl* (*rênes*) reins. **◆guider** *vt* to guide; **se g. sur** to guide oneself by.

guidon [gidɔ̃] *nm* (*de bicyclette etc*) handlebar(s).

guigne [giɲ] *nf* (*malchance*) *Fam* bad luck.

guignol [giɲɔl] *nm* (*spectacle*) = Punch and Judy show.

guillemets [gijmɛ] *nmpl* *Typ* inverted commas, quotation marks.

guilleret, -ette [gijrɛ, -ɛt] *a* lively, perky.

guillotine [gijɔtin] *nf* guillotine.

guimauve [gimov] *nf* *Bot Culin* marshmallow.

guimbarde [gɛ̃bard] *nf* (*voiture*) *Fam* old banger, *Am* (old) wreck.

guindé [gɛ̃de] *a* (*affecté*) stiff, stilted, stuck-up.

guingois (de) [dəgɛ̃gwa] *adv* askew.

guirlande [girlɑ̃d] *nf* garland, wreath.

guise [giz] *nf* **n'en faire qu'à sa g.** to do as one pleases; **en g. de** by way of.

guitare [gitar] *nf* guitar. **◆guitariste** *nmf* guitarist.

guttural, -aux [gytyral, -o] *a* guttural.

gymnase [ʒimnaz] *nm* gymnasium. **◆gymnaste** *nmf* gymnast. **◆gymnastique** *nf* gymnastics.

gynécologie [ʒinekɔlɔʒi] *nf* gynaecology, *Am* gynecology. **◆gynécologue** *nmf* gynaecologist, *Am* gynecologist.

H

H, h [aʃ] *nm* H, h; **l'heure H** zero hour; **bombe H** H-bomb.

ha! [ʼɑ] *int* ah!, oh!; **ha, ha!** (*rire*) ha-ha!

habile [abil] *a* clever, skilful (**à qch** at sth, **à faire** at doing). ◆**habilement** *adv* cleverly, skilfully. ◆**habileté** *nf* skill, ability.

habill/er [abije] *vt* to dress (**de** in); (*fournir en vêtements*) to clothe; (*couvrir*) to cover (**de** with); **h. qn en soldat**/*etc* (*déguiser*) to dress s.o. up as a soldier/*etc*; — **s'h.** *vpr* to dress (oneself), get dressed; (*avec élégance, se déguiser*) to dress up. ◆**—é** *a* dressed (**de** in); (*costume, robe*) smart, dressy. ◆**—ement** *nm* (*vêtements*) clothing, clothes.

habit [abi] *nm* costume, outfit; (*tenue de soirée*) evening dress, tails; *pl* (*vêtements*) clothes.

habit/er [abite] *vi* to live (**à, en, dans** in); — *vt* (*maison, région*) to live in; (*planète*) to inhabit. ◆**—ant, -ante** *nmf* (*de pays etc*) inhabitant; (*de maison*) resident, occupant. ◆**—é** *a* (*région*) inhabited; (*maison*) occupied. ◆**—able** *a* (in)habitable. ◆**habitat** *nm* (*d'animal, de plante*) habitat; (*conditions*) housing, living conditions. ◆**habitation** *nf* house, dwelling, (*action de résider*) living.

habitude [abityd] *nf* habit; **avoir l'h. de qch** to be used to sth; **avoir l'h. de faire** to be used to doing, be in the habit of doing; **prendre l'h. de faire** to get into the habit of doing; **d'h.** usually; **comme d'h.** as usual. ◆**habituel, -elle** *a* usual, customary. ◆**habituellement** *adv* usually. ◆**habitu/er** *vt* **h. qn à** to accustom s.o. to; **être habitué à** to be used *ou* accustomed to; — **s'h.** *vpr* to get accustomed (**à** to). ◆**—é, -ée** *nmf* regular (customer *ou* visitor).

hache [ʼaʃ] *nf* axe, *Am* ax. ◆**hachette** *nf* hatchet.

hach/er [ʼaʃe] *vt* (*au couteau*) to chop (up); (*avec un appareil*) to mince, *Am* grind; (*déchiqueter*) to cut to pieces. ◆**—é** *a* **1** (*viande*) minced, *Am* ground; chopped. **2** (*style*) staccato, broken. ◆**hachis** *nm* (*viande*) mince, minced *ou Am* ground meat. ◆**hachoir** *nm* (*couteau*) chopper; (*appareil*) mincer, *Am* grinder.

hagard [ʼagar] *a* wild-looking, frantic.

haie [ʼɛ] *nf* (*clôture*) *Bot* hedge; (*rangée*) row; (*de coureur*) *Sp* hurdle; (*de chevaux*) *Sp* fence, hurdle; **course de haies** (*coureurs*) hurdle race; (*chevaux*) steeplechase.

haillons [ʼajɔ̃] *nmpl* rags (and tatters).

haine [ʼɛn] *nf* hatred, hate. ◆**haineux, -euse** *a* full of hatred.

haïr* [ʼair] *vt* to hate. ◆**haïssable** *a* hateful, detestable.

hâle [ʼɑl] *nm* suntan. ◆**hâlé** *a* (*par le soleil*) suntanned; (*par l'air*) weather-beaten.

haleine [alɛn] *nf* breath; **hors d'h.** out of breath; **perdre h.** to get out of breath; **reprendre h.** to get one's breath back, catch one's breath; **de longue h.** (*travail*) long-term; **tenir en h.** to hold in suspense.

hal/er [ʼale] *vt Nau* to tow. ◆**—age** *nm* towing; **chemin de h.** towpath.

halet/er [ʼalte] *vi* to pant, gasp. ◆**—ant** *a* panting, gasping.

hall [ʼol] *nm* (*de gare*) main hall, concourse; (*d'hôtel*) lobby, hall; (*de maison*) hall(way).

halle [ʼal] *nf* (*couvered*) market; **les halles** the central food market.

hallucination [alysinasjɔ̃] *nf* hallucination. ◆**hallucinant** *a* extraordinary.

halo [ʼalo] *nm* (*auréole*) halo.

halte [ʼalt] *nf* (*arrêt*) stop, *Mil* halt; (*lieu*) stopping place, *Mil* halting place; **faire h.** to stop; — *int* stop!, *Mil* halt!

haltère [alter] *nm* (*poids*) *Sp* dumbbell. ◆**haltérophilie** *nf* weight lifting.

hamac [ʼamɑk] *nm* hammock.

hameau, -x [ʼamo] *nm* hamlet.

hameçon [amsɔ̃] *nm* (fish) hook; **mordre à l'h.** *Pêche & Fig* to rise to *ou* swallow the bait.

hamster [ʼamster] *nm* hamster.

hanche [ʼɑ̃ʃ] *nf Anat* hip.

hand(-)ball [ʼadbal] *nm Sp* handball.

handicap [ʼadikap] *nm* (*désavantage*) & *Sp* handicap. ◆**handicap/er** *vt* to handicap. ◆**—é, -ée** *a* & *nmf* handicapped (person); **h. moteur** spastic.

hangar [ʼãgar] *nm* (*entrepôt*) shed; (*pour avions*) hangar.

hanneton [ʼantɔ̃] *nm* (*insecte*) cockchafer.

hanter [ʼɑ̃te] *vt* to haunt.

hantise [ʼɑ̃tiz] *nf* **la h. de** an obsession with.

happer ['ape] *vt* (*saisir*) to catch, snatch; (*par la gueule*) to snap up.

haras ['aʀɑ] *nm* stud farm.

harasser ['aʀase] *vt* to exhaust.

harceler ['aʀsəle] *vt* to harass, torment (**de** with). ◆**harcèlement** *nm* harassment.

hardi ['aʀdi] *a* bold, daring. ◆**—ment** *adv* boldly. ◆**hardiesse** *nf* boldness, daring; **une h.** (*action*) *Litt* an audacity.

harem ['aʀɛm] *nm* harem.

hareng ['aʀɑ̃] *nm* herring.

hargne ['aʀɲ] *nf* aggressive bad temper. ◆**hargneux, -euse** *a* bad-tempered, aggressive.

haricot ['aʀiko] *nm* (*blanc*) (haricot) bean; (*vert*) French bean, green bean.

harmonica [aʀmɔnika] *nm* harmonica, mouthorgan.

harmonie [aʀmɔni] *nf* harmony. ◆**harmonieux, -euse** *a* harmonious. ◆**harmonique** *a & nm Mus* harmonic. ◆**harmoniser** *vt*, — **s'h.** *vpr* to harmonize. ◆**harmonium** *nm Mus* harmonium.

harnacher ['aʀnaʃe] *vt* (*cheval etc*) to harness. ◆**harnais** *nm* (*de cheval, bébé*) harness.

harpe ['aʀp] *nf* harp. ◆**harpiste** *nmf* harpist.

harpon ['aʀpɔ̃] *nm* harpoon. ◆**harponner** *vt* (*baleine*) to harpoon; **h. qn** (*arrêter*) *Fam* to waylay s.o.

hasard ['azaʀ] *nm* **le h.** chance; **un h.** (*coïncidence*) a coincidence; **un heureux h.** a stroke of luck; **un malheureux h.** a rotten piece of luck; **par h.** by chance; **si par h.** if by any chance; **au h.** at random, haphazardly; **à tout h.** just in case; **les hasards de** (*risques*) the hazards of. ◆**hasard/er** *vt* (*remarque, démarche*) to venture, hazard; (*vie, réputation*) to risk; **se h. dans** to venture into; **se h. à faire** to risk doing, venture to do. ◆**—é** *a*, ◆**hasardeux, -euse** *a* risky, hazardous.

haschisch ['aʃiʃ] *nm* hashish.

hâte ['ɑt] *nf* haste, speed; (*impatience*) eagerness; **en h., à la h.** hurriedly, in a hurry, in haste; **avoir h. de faire** (*désireux*) to be eager to do, be in a hurry to do. ◆**hâter** *vt* (*pas, départ etc*) to hasten; — **se h.** *vpr* to hurry, make haste (**de faire** to do). ◆**hâtif, -ive** *a* hasty, hurried; (*développement*) precocious; (*fruit*) early.

hausse ['os] *nf* rise (**de** in); **en h.** rising. ◆**hausser** *vt* (*prix, voix etc*) to raise; (*épaules*) to shrug; **se h. sur la pointe des pieds** to stand on tip-toe.

haut ['o] *a* high; (*de taille*) tall; (*classes*) up-per, higher; (*fonctionnaire etc*) high-ranking; **le h. Rhin** the upper Rhine; **la haute couture** high fashion; **à haute voix** aloud, in a loud voice; **h. de 5 mètres** 5 metres high *ou* tall; — *adv* (*voler, viser etc*) high (up); (*estimer*) highly; (*parler*) loud, loudly; **tout h.** (*lire, penser*) aloud, out loud; **être placé** (*personne*) in a high position; **plus h.** (*dans un texte*) above, further back; — *nm* (*partie haute*) top; **en h. de** at the top of; **en h.** (*loger*) upstairs; (*regarder*) up; (*mettre*) on (the) top; **d'en h.** (*de la partie haute, du ciel etc*) from high up, from up above; **avoir 5 mètres de h.** to be 5 metres high *ou* tall; **des hauts et des bas** *Fig* ups and downs.

hautain ['otɛ̃] *a* haughty.

hautbois ['obwa] *nm Mus* oboe.

haut-de-forme ['odfɔʀm] *nm* (*pl* **hauts-de-forme**) top hat.

hautement ['otmɑ̃] *adv* (*tout à fait, très*) highly. ◆**hauteur** *nf* height; *Géog* hill; (*orgueil*) *Péj* haughtiness; *Mus* pitch; **à la h. de** (*objet*) level with; (*rue*) opposite; (*situation*) *Fig* equal to; **il n'est pas à la h.** he isn't up to it; **saut en h.** *Sp* high jump.

haut-le-cœur ['olkœʀ] *nm inv* **avoir des h.-le-cœur** to retch, gag.

haut-le-corps ['olkɔʀ] *nm inv* (*sursaut*) sudden start, jump.

haut-parleur ['oparlœʀ] *nm* loudspeaker.

hâve ['av] *a* gaunt, emaciated.

havre ['avʀ] *nm* (*refuge*) *Litt* haven.

Haye (La) [la'ɛ] *nf* The Hague.

hayon ['ɛjɔ̃] *nm* (*porte*) *Aut* tailgate, hatchback.

hé! [e] *int* **hé** (**là**) (*appel*) hey!; **hé! hé!** well, well!

hebdomadaire [ɛbdɔmadɛʀ] *a* weekly; — *nm* (*publication*) weekly.

héberg/er [ebɛʀʒe] *vt* to put up, accommodate. ◆**—ement** *nm* accommodation; **centre d'h.** shelter.

hébété [ebete] *a* dazed, stupefied.

hébreu, -x [ebrø] *am* Hebrew; — *nm* (*langue*) Hebrew. ◆**hébraïque** *a* Hebrew.

hécatombe [ekatɔ̃b] *nf* (great) slaughter.

hectare [ɛktaʀ] *nm* hectare (= 2.47 acres).

hégémonie [eʒemɔni] *nf* hegemony, supremacy.

hein! [ɛ̃] *int* (*surprise, interrogation etc*) eh!

hélas! ['elas] *int* alas!, unfortunately.

héler ['ele] *vt* (*taxi etc*) to hail.

hélice [elis] *nf Av Nau* propeller.

hélicoptère [elikɔptɛʀ] *nm* helicopter. ◆**héliport** *nm* heliport.

hellénique [elenik] *a* Hellenic, Greek.

helvétique [ɛlvetik] *a* Swiss.

hem! ['ɛm] *int* (a)hem!, hm!

hémicycle [emisikl] *nm* semicircle; *Pol Fig* French National Assembly.

hémisphère [emisfɛr] *nm* hemisphere.

hémorragie [emɔraʒi] *nf Méd* h(a)emorrhage; (*de capitaux*) *Com* outflow, drain.

hémorroïdes [emɔrɔid] *nfpl* piles, h(a)emorrhoids.

henn/ir ['enir] *vi* (*cheval*) to neigh. ◆**—issement** *nm* neigh.

hep! ['ɛp] *int* hey!, hey there!

hépatite [epatit] *nf* hepatitis.

herbe [ɛrb] *nf* grass; (*médicinale etc*) herb; **mauvaise h.** weed; **fines herbes** *Culin* herbs; **en h.** (*blés*) green; (*poète etc*) *Fig* budding. ◆**herbage** *nm* grassland. ◆**herbeux, -euse** *a* grassy. ◆**herbicide** *nm* weed killer. ◆**herbivore** *a* grass-eating, herbivorous. ◆**herbu** *a* grassy.

hercule [ɛrkyl] *nm* Hercules, strong man. ◆**herculéen, -enne** *a* herculean.

hérédité [eredite] *nf* heredity. ◆**héréditaire** *a* hereditary.

hérésie [erezi] *nf* heresy. ◆**hérétique** *a* heretical; — *nmf* heretic.

hériss/er ['erise] *vt* (*poils*) to bristle (up); **h. qn** (*irriter*) to ruffle s.o., ruffle s.o.'s feathers; — **se h.** *vpr* to bristle (up); to get ruffled. ◆**—é** *a* (*cheveux*) bristly; (*cactus*) prickly; **h. de** bristling with.

hérisson ['erisɔ̃] *nm* (*animal*) hedgehog.

hérit/er [erite] *vti* to inherit (**qch de qn** sth from s.o.); **h. de qch** to inherit sth. ◆**—age** *nm* (*biens*) inheritance; (*culturel, politique etc*) *Fig* heritage. ◆**héritier** *nm* heir. ◆**héritière** *nf* heiress.

hermétique [ermetik] *a* hermetically sealed, airtight; (*obscur*) *Fig* impenetrable. ◆**—ment** *adv* hermetically.

hermine [ermin] *nf* (*animal, fourrure*) ermine.

hernie ['erni] *nf Méd* hernia, rupture; (*de pneu*) swelling.

héron ['erɔ̃] *nm* (*oiseau*) heron.

héros ['ero] *nm* hero. ◆**héroïne** [erɔin] *nf* **1** (*femme*) heroine. **2** (*stupéfiant*) heroin. ◆**héroïque** [erɔik] *a* heroic. ◆**héroïsme** [erɔism] *nm* heroism.

hésit/er [ezite] *vi* to hesitate (**sur** over, about; **à faire** to do); (*en parlant*) to falter, hesitate. ◆**—ant** *a* (*personne*) hesitant; (*pas, voix*) faltering, unsteady, wavering. ◆**hésitation** *nf* hesitation; **avec h.** hesitantly.

hétéroclite [eterɔklit] *a* (*disparate*) motley.

hétérogène [eterɔʒɛn] *a* heterogeneous.

hêtre ['ɛtr] *nm* (*arbre, bois*) beech.

heu! ['ø] *int* (*hésitation*) er!

heure [œr] *nf* (*mesure*) hour; (*moment*) time; **quelle h. est-il?** what time is it?; **il est six heures** it's six (o'clock); **six heures moins cinq** five to six; **six heures cinq** five past *ou Am* after six; **à l'h.** (*arriver*) on time; (*être payé*) by the hour; **dix kilomètres à l'h.** ten kilometres an hour; **à l'h. qu'il est** (by) now; **de dernière h.** (*nouvelle*) last minute; **de bonne h.** early; **à une h. avancée** at a late hour, late at night; **tout à l'h.** (*futur*) in a few moments, later; (*passé*) a moment ago; **à toute h.** (*continuellement*) at all hours; **faire des heures supplémentaires** to work *ou* do overtime; **heures creuses** off-peak *ou* slack periods; **l'h. d'affluence, l'h. de pointe** (*circulation etc*) rush hour; (*dans les magasins*) peak period; **l'h. de pointe** (*électricité etc*) peak period.

heureux, -euse [œrø, -øz] *a* happy; (*chanceux*) lucky, fortunate; (*issue, changement*) successful; (*expression, choix*) apt; **h. de qch/de voir qn** (*satisfait*) happy *ou* pleased *ou* glad about sth/to see s.o.; — *adv* (*vivre, mourir*) happily. ◆**heureusement** *adv* (*par chance*) fortunately, luckily, happily (**pour** for); (*avec succès*) successfully; (*exprimer*) aptly.

heurt ['œr] *nm* bump, knock; (*d'opinions etc*) *Fig* clash; **sans heurts** smoothly. ◆**heurt/er** *vt* (*cogner*) to knock, bump, hit (**contre** against); (*mur, piéton*) to bump into, hit; **h. qn** (*choquer*) to offend s.o., upset s.o.; **se h. à** to bump into, hit; (*difficultés*) *Fig* to come up against. ◆**—é** *a* (*couleurs, tons*) clashing; (*style, rythme*) jerky. ◆**heurtoir** *nm* (*door*) knocker.

hexagone [ɛgzagɔn] *nm* hexagon; **l'H.** *Fig* France. ◆**hexagonal, -aux** *a* hexagonal; *Fig Fam* French.

hiatus [jatys] *nm Fig* hiatus, gap.

hiberner [iberne] *vi* to hibernate. ◆**hibernation** *nf* hibernation.

hibou, -x ['ibu] *nm* owl.

hic ['ik] *nm* **voilà le h.** *Fam* that's the snag.

hideux, -euse ['idø, -øz] *a* hideous.

hier [(i)jɛr] *adv* & *nm* yesterday; **h. soir** last *ou* yesterday night, yesterday evening; **elle n'est pas née d'h.** *Fig* she wasn't born yesterday.

hiérarchie ['jerarʃi] *nf* hierarchy. ◆**hiérarchique** *a* (*ordre*) hierarchical; **par la voie h.** through (the) official channels. ◆**hiérarchiser** *vt* (*emploi, valeurs*) to grade.

hi-fi ['ifi] *a inv* & *nf inv Fam* hi-fi.

hilare [ilar] *a* merry. ◆**hilarant** *a* (*drôle*) hilarious. ◆**hilarité** *nf* (sudden) laughter.
hindou, -oue [ɛ̃du] *a* & *nmf* Hindu.
hippie [`ipi] *nmf* hippie.
hippique [ipik] *a* **un concours h.** a horse show, a show-jumping event. ◆**hippodrome** *nm* racecourse, racetrack (*for horses*).
hippopotame [ipɔpɔtam] *nm* hippopotamus.
hirondelle [irɔ̃dɛl] *nf* (*oiseau*) swallow.
hirsute [irsyt] *a* (*personne, barbe*) unkempt, shaggy.
hispanique [ispanik] *a* Spanish, Hispanic.
hisser [`ise] *vt* (*voile, fardeau etc*) to hoist, raise; — **se h.** *vpr* to raise oneself (up).
histoire [istwar] *nf* (*science, événements*) history; (*récit, mensonge*) story; (*affaire*) *Fam* business, matter; *pl* (*ennuis*) trouble; (*façons, chichis*) fuss; **toute une h.** (*problème*) quite a lot of trouble; (*chichis*) quite a lot of fuss; **h. de voir/etc** (so as) to see/*etc*; **h. de rire** for (the sake of) a laugh; **sans histoires** (*voyage etc*) uneventful. ◆**historien, -ienne** *nmf* historian. ◆**historique** *a* historical; (*lieu, événement*) historic; — *nm* **faire l'h. de** to give an historical account of.
hiver [iver] *nm* winter. ◆**hivernal, -aux** *a* (*froid etc*) winter-.
HLM [`aʃɛlɛm] *nm ou f abrév* (*habitation à loyer modéré*) = council flats, *Am* = low-rent apartment building (*sponsored by government*).
hoch/er [`ɔʃe] *vt* **h. la tête** (*pour dire oui*) to nod one's head; (*pour dire non*) to shake one's head. ◆**—ement** *nm* **h. de tête** nod; shake of the head.
hochet [`ɔʃɛ] *nm* (*jouet*) rattle.
hockey [`ɔkɛ] *nm* hockey; **h. sur glace** ice hockey.
holà! [`ɔla] *int* (*arrêtez*) hold on!, stop!; (*pour appeler*) hallo!; — *nm inv* **mettre le h.** à to put a stop to.
hold-up [`ɔldœp] *nm inv* (*attaque*) holdup, stick-up.
Hollande [`ɔlɑ̃d] *nf* Holland. ◆**hollandais, -aise** *a* Dutch; — *nmf* Dutchman, Dutchwoman; — *nm* (*langue*) Dutch.
holocauste [ɔlɔkost] *nm* (*massacre*) holocaust.
homard [`ɔmar] *nm* lobster.
homélie [ɔmeli] *nf* homily.
homéopathie [ɔmeɔpati] *nf* hom(o)eopathy.
homicide [ɔmisid] *nm* murder, homicide; **h. involontaire** manslaughter.

hommage [ɔmaʒ] *nm* tribute, homage (à to); *pl* (*civilités*) respects; **rendre h. à** to pay (a) tribute to, pay homage to.
homme [ɔm] *nm* man; **l'h.** (*espèce*) man(kind); **des vêtements d'h.** men's clothes; **d'h. à h.** man to man; **l'h. de la rue** *Fig* the man in the street; **h. d'affaires** businessman. ◆**h.-grenouille** *nm* (*pl* **hommes-grenouilles**) frogman.
homogène [ɔmɔʒɛn] *a* homogeneous. ◆**homogénéité** *nf* homogeneity.
homologue [ɔmɔlɔg] *a* equivalent (**de** to); — *nmf* counterpart, opposite number.
homologuer [ɔmɔlɔge] *vt* to approve *ou* recognize officially, validate.
homonyme [ɔmɔnim] *nm* (*personne, lieu*) namesake.
homosexuel, -elle [ɔmɔsɛksyɛl] *a* & *nmf* homosexual. ◆**homosexualité** *nf* homosexuality.
Hongrie [`ɔ̃gri] *nf* Hungary. ◆**hongrois, -oise** *a* & *nmf* Hungarian; — *nm* (*langue*) Hungarian.
honnête [ɔnɛt] *a* (*intègre*) honest; (*satisfaisant, passable*) decent, fair. ◆**honnêtement** *adv* honestly; decently. ◆**honnêteté** *nf* honesty.
honneur [ɔnœr] *nm* (*dignité, faveur*) honour; (*mérite*) credit; **en l'h. de** in honour of; **faire h. à** (*sa famille etc*) to be a credit to; (*par sa présence*) to do honour to; (*promesse etc*) to honour; (*repas etc*) to do justice to; **en h.** (*roman etc*) in vogue; **invité d'h.** guest of honour; **membre d'h.** honorary member; **avoir la place d'h.** to have pride of place *ou* the place of honour. ◆**honorabilité** *nf* respectability. ◆**honorable** *a* honourable; (*résultat, salaire etc*) *Fig* respectable. ◆**honoraire 1** *a* (*membre*) honorary. **2** *nmpl* (*d'avocat etc*) fees. ◆**honorer** *vt* to honour (**de** with); **h. qn** (*conduite etc*) to do credit to s.o.; **s'h. d'être** to pride oneself *ou* itself on being. ◆**honorifique** *a* (*titre*) honorary.
honte [`ɔ̃t] *nf* shame; **avoir h.** to be *ou* feel ashamed (**de qch/de faire** of sth/to do, of doing); **faire h. à** to put to shame; **fausse h.** self-consciousness. ◆**honteux, -euse** *a* (*déshonorant*) shameful; (*penaud*) ashamed, shamefaced; **être h. de** to be ashamed of. ◆**honteusement** *adv* shamefully.
hop! [`ɔp] *int* **allez, h.!** jump!, move!
hôpital, -aux [ɔpital, -o] *nm* hospital; **à l'h.** in hospital, *Am* in the hospital.
hoquet [`ɔkɛ] *nm* hiccup; **le h.** (the) hiccups. ◆**hoqueter** *vi* to hiccup.

horaire [ɔrɛr] a (salaire etc) hourly; (vitesse) per hour; – nm timetable, schedule.

horde [ɔrd] nf (troupe) Péj horde.

horizon [ɔrizɔ̃] nm horizon; (vue, paysage) view; à l'h. on the horizon.

horizontal, -aux [ɔrizɔ̃tal, -o] a horizontal. ◆–ement adv horizontally.

horloge [ɔrlɔʒ] nf clock. ◆horloger, -ère nmf watchmaker. ◆horlogerie nf (magasin) watchmaker's (shop); (industrie) watchmaking.

hormis ['ɔrmi] prép Litt save, except (for).

hormone [ɔrmɔn] nf hormone. ◆hormonal, -aux a (traitement etc) hormone-.

horoscope [ɔrɔskɔp] nm horoscope.

horreur [ɔrœr] nf horror; pl (propos) horrible things; faire h. à to disgust; avoir h. de to hate, loathe. ◆horrible a horrible, awful. ◆horriblement adv horribly. ◆horrifiant a horrifying, horrific. ◆horrifié a horrified.

horripiler [ɔripile] vt to exasperate.

hors ['ɔr] prép h. de (maison, boîte etc) outside, out of; (danger, haleine etc) Fig out of; h. de doute beyond doubt; h. de soi (furieux) beside oneself; être h. jeu Fb to be offside. ◆h.-bord nm inv speedboat; moteur h.-bord outboard motor. ◆h.-concours a inv non-competing. ◆h.-d'œuvre nm inv Culin starter, hors-d'œuvre. ◆h.-jeu nm inv Fb offside. ◆h.-la-loi nm inv outlaw. ◆h.-taxe a inv (magasin, objet) duty-free.

hortensia [ɔrtɑ̃sja] nm (arbrisseau) hydrangea.

horticole [ɔrtikɔl] a horticultural. ◆horticulteur, -trice nmf horticulturalist. ◆horticulture nf horticulture.

hospice [ɔspis] nm (pour vieillards) geriatric hospital.

hospitalier, -ière [ɔspitalje, -jɛr] a 1 (accueillant) hospitable. 2 (personnel etc) Méd hospital-. ◆hospitaliser vt to hospitalize. ◆hospitalité nf hospitality.

hostie [ɔsti] nf (pain) Rel host.

hostile [ɔstil] a hostile (à to, towards). ◆hostilité nf hostility (envers to, towards); pl Mil hostilities.

hôte [ot] 1 nm (maître) host. 2 nmf (invité) guest. ◆hôtesse nf hostess; h. (de l'air) (air) hostess.

hôtel [otɛl] nm hotel; h. particulier mansion, town house; h. de ville town hall; h. des ventes auction rooms. ◆hôtelier, -ière nmf hotel-keeper, hotelier; – a (industrie etc) hotel-. ◆hôtellerie nf 1 (auberge) inn, hostelry. 2 (métier) hotel trade.

hotte ['ɔt] nf 1 (panier) basket (carried on back). 2 (de cheminée etc) hood.

houblon ['ublɔ̃] nm le h. Bot hops.

houille ['uj] nf coal; h. blanche hydroelectric power. ◆houiller, -ère a (bassin, industrie) coal-; – nf coalmine, colliery.

houle ['ul] nf (de mer) swell, surge. ◆houleux, -euse a (mer) rough; (réunion etc) Fig stormy.

houppette [upɛt] nf powder puff.

hourra ['ura] nm & int hurray, hurrah.

houspiller ['uspije] vt to scold, upbraid.

housse ['us] nf (protective) cover.

houx ['u] nm holly.

hublot ['yblo] nm Nau Av porthole.

huche ['yʃ] nf h. à pain bread box ou chest.

hue! ['y] int gee up! (to horse).

huer ['ɥe] vt to boo. ◆huées nfpl boos.

huile [ɥil] nf 1 oil; peinture à l'h. oil painting. 2 (personnage) Fam big shot. ◆huiler vt to oil. ◆huileux, -euse a oily.

huis [ɥi] nm à h. clos Jur in camera.

huissier [ɥisje] nm (introducteur) usher; (officier) Jur bailiff.

huit ['ɥit] a (['ɥi] before consonant) eight; h. jours a week; – nm eight. ◆huitaine nf (about) eight; (semaine) week. ◆huitième a & nmf eighth; un h. an eighth.

huître [ɥitr] nf oyster.

hululer ['ylyle] vi (hibou) to hoot.

humain [ymɛ̃] a human; (compatissant) humane; – nmpl humans. ◆humainement adv (possible etc) humanly; (avec humanité) humanely. ◆humaniser vt (prison, ville etc) to humanize, make more humane. ◆humanitaire a humanitarian. ◆humanité nf (genre humain, sentiment) humanity.

humble [œbl] a humble. ◆humblement adv humbly.

humecter [ymɛkte] vt to moisten, damp(en).

humer ['yme] vt (respirer) to breathe in; (sentir) to smell.

humeur [ymœr] nf (caprice) mood, humour; (caractère) temperament; (irritation) bad temper; bonne h. (gaieté) good humour; de bonne/mauvaise h. in a good/bad mood ou humour; égalité d'h. evenness of temper.

humide [ymid] a damp, wet; (saison, route) wet; (main, yeux) moist; climat/temps h. (chaud) humid climate/weather; (froid, pluvieux) damp ou wet climate/weather. ◆humidifier vt to humidify. ◆humidité nf humidity; (plutôt froide) damp(ness); (vapeur) moisture.

humili/er [ymilje] vt to humiliate, humble.

◆—**ant** *a* humiliating. ◆**humiliation** *nf* humiliation. ◆**humilité** *nf* humility.

humour [ymur] *nm* humour; **avoir de l'h. ou beaucoup d'h. ou le sens de l'h.** to have a sense of humour. ◆**humoriste** *nmf* humorist. ◆**humoristique** *a* (*livre, ton etc*) humorous.

huppé ['ype] *a* (*riche*) *Fam* high-class, posh.

hurl/er ['yrle] *vi* (*loup, vent*) to howl; (*personne*) to scream, yell; − *vt* (*slogans, injures etc*) to scream. ◆—**ement** *nm* howl; scream, yell.

hurluberlu [yrlyberly] *nm* (*personne*) scatterbrain.

hutte ['yt] *nf* hut.

hybride [ibrid] *a* & *nm* hybrid.

hydrater [idrate] *vt* (*peau*) to moisturize; **crème hydratante** moisturizing cream.

hydraulique [idrolik] *a* hydraulic.

hydravion [idravjɔ̃] *nm* seaplane.

hydro-électrique [idroelɛktrik] *a* hydroelectric.

hydrogène [idrɔʒɛn] *nm Ch* hydrogen.

hydrophile [idrɔfil] *a* **coton h.** cotton wool, *Am* (absorbent) cotton.

hyène [jɛn] *nf* (*animal*) hyena.

hygiaphone [iʒjafɔn] *nm* (hygienic) grill.

hygiène [iʒjɛn] *nf* hygiene. ◆**hygiénique** *a* hygienic; (*promenade*) healthy: (*serviette, conditions*) sanitary; **papier h.** toilet paper.

hymne [imn] *nm Rel Littér* hymn; **h. national** national anthem.

hyper- [iper] *préf* hyper-.

hypermarché [ipermarʃe] *nm* hypermarket.

hypertension [ipɛrtɑ̃sjɔ̃] *nf* high blood pressure.

hypnose [ipnoz] *nf* hypnosis. ◆**hypnotique** *a* hypnotic. ◆**hypnotiser** *vt* to hypnotize. ◆**hypnotiseur** *nm* hypnotist. ◆**hypnotisme** *nm* hypnotism.

hypocrisie [ipɔkrizi] *nf* hypocrisy. ◆**hypocrite** *a* hypocritical; − *nmf* hypocrite.

hypodermique [ipɔdɛrmik] *a* hypodermic.

hypothèque [ipɔtɛk] *nf* mortgage. ◆**hypothéquer** (*maison, avenir*) to mortgage.

hypothèse [ipɔtɛz] *nf* assumption; (*en sciences*) hypothesis; **dans l'h. où . . .** supposing (that) . . . . ◆**hypothétique** *a* hypothetical.

hystérie [isteri] *nf* hysteria. ◆**hystérique** *a* hysterical.

I

I, i [i] *nm* I, i.

iceberg [isberg] *nm* iceberg.

ici [isi] *adv* here; **par i.** (*passer*) this way; (*habiter*) around here, hereabouts; **jusqu'i.** (*temps*) up to now; (*lieu*) as far as this *ou* here; **d'i. à mardi** by Tuesday, between now and Tuesday; **d'i. à une semaine** within a week; **d'i. peu** before long; **i. Dupont** *Tél* this is Dupont, Dupont here; **je ne suis pas d'i.** I'm a stranger around here; **les gens d'i.** the people (from) around here, the locals. ◆**i.-bas** *adv* on earth.

icône [ikon] *nf Rel* icon.

idéal, -aux [ideal, -o] *a* & *nm* ideal; **l'i.** (*valeurs spirituelles*) ideals; **c'est l'i.** *Fam* that's the ideal thing. ◆**idéalement** *adv* ideally. ◆**idéaliser** *vt* to idealize. ◆**idéalisme** *nm* idealism. ◆**idéaliste** *a* idealistic; − *nmf* idealist.

idée [ide] *nf* idea (de of, que that); **changer d'i.** to change one's mind; **il m'est venu à l'i. que** it occurred to me that; **se faire une i. de** (*rêve*) to imagine; (*concept*) to get *ou* have

an idea of; **avoir dans l'i. de faire** to have it in mind to do; **i. fixe** obsession.

idem [idɛm] *adv* ditto.

identifier [idɑ̃tifje] *vt* to identify (**à, avec** with). ◆**identification** *nf* identification. ◆**identique** *a* identical (**à** to, with). ◆**identité** *nf* identity; **carte d'i** identity card.

idéologie [ideɔlɔʒi] *nf* ideology. ◆**idéologique** *a* ideological.

idiome [idjom] *nm* (*langue*) idiom. ◆**idiomatique** *a* idiomatic.

idiot, -ote [idjo, -ɔt] *a* idiotic, silly; − *nmf* idiot. ◆**idiotement** *adv* idiotically. ◆**idiotie** [-ɔsi] *nf* (*état*) idiocy; **une i.** an idiotic *ou* silly thing.

idole [idɔl] *nm* idol. ◆**idolâtrer** *vt* to idolize.

idylle [idil] *nf* (*amourette*) romance.

idyllique [idilik] *a* (*merveilleux*) idyllic.

if [if] *nm* yew (tree).

igloo [iglu] *nm* igloo.

ignare [iɲar] *a Péj* ignorant; − *nmf* ignoramus.

ignifugé [iɲifyʒe] *a* fireproof(ed).

ignoble [iɲɔbl] *a* vile, revolting.

ignorant [iɲɔrɑ̃] *a* ignorant (**de** of). ◆**ignorance** *nf* ignorance. ◆**ignor/er** *vt* not to know, be ignorant of; **j'ignore si** l don't know if; **i. qn** (*être indifférent à*) to ignore s.o., cold-shoulder s.o. ◆**—é** *a* (*inconnu*) unknown.

il [il] *pron* (*personne*) he; (*chose, animal*) it; **il est** he is; it is; **il pleut** it's raining; **il est vrai que** it's true that; **il y a** there is; *pl* there are; **il y a six ans** (*temps écoulé*) six years ago; **il y a une heure qu'il travaille** (*durée*) he's been working for an hour; **qu'est-ce qu'il y a?** what's the matter?, what's wrong?; **il n'y a pas de quoi!** don't mention it!; **il doit/peut y avoir** there must/may be.

île [il] *nf* island; **les îles Britanniques** the British Isles.

illégal, -aux [ilegal, -o] *a* illegal. ◆**illégalité** *nf* illegality.

illégitime [ileʒitim] *a* (*enfant, revendication*) illegitimate; (*non fondé*) unfounded.

illettré, -ée [iletre] *a* & *nmf* illiterate.

illicite [ilisit] *a* unlawful, illicit.

illico [iliko] *adv* **i. (presto)** *Fam* straightaway.

illimité [ilimite] *a* unlimited.

illisible [ilizibl] *a* (*écriture*) illegible; (*livre*) unreadable.

illogique [ilɔʒik] *a* illogical.

illumin/er [ilymine] *vt* to light up, illuminate; **— s'i.** *vpr* (*visage, personne, ciel*) to light up. ◆**—é** *a* (*monument*) floodlit, lit up. ◆**illumination** *nf* (*action, lumière*) illumination.

illusion [ilyzjɔ̃] *nf* illusion (**sur** about); **se faire des illusions** to delude oneself. ◆**s'illusionner** *vpr* to delude oneself (**sur** about). ◆**illusionniste** *nmf* conjurer. ◆**illusoire** *a* illusory, illusive.

illustre [ilystr] *a* famous, illustrious.

illustr/er [ilystre] *vt* (*d'images, par des exemples*) to illustrate (**de** with); **— s'i.** *vpr* to become famous. ◆**—é** *a* (*livre, magazine*) illustrated; **— nm** (*périodique*) comic. ◆**illustration** *nf* illustration.

îlot [ilo] *nm* **1** (*île*) small island. **2** (*maisons*) block.

ils [il] *pron* they; **ils sont** they are.

image [imaʒ] *nf* picture; (*ressemblance, symbole*) image; (*dans une glace*) reflection; **i. de marque** (*de firme etc*) (public) image. ◆**imagé** *a* (*style*) colourful, full of imagery.

imagination [imaʒinɑsjɔ̃] *nf* imagination; *pl* (*chimères*) imaginings.

imaginer [imaʒine] *vt* (*envisager, supposer*) to imagine; (*inventer*) to devise; **— s'i.** (*se figurer*) to imagine (**que** that); (*se voir*) to imagine oneself. ◆**imaginable** *a* imaginable. ◆**imaginaire** *a* imaginary. ◆**imaginatif, -ive** *a* imaginative.

imbattable [ɛ̃batabl] *a* unbeatable.

imbécile [ɛ̃besil] *a* idiotic; **— nmf** imbecile, idiot. ◆**imbécillité** *nf* (*état*) imbecility; **une i.** (*action, parole*) an idiotic thing.

imbiber [ɛ̃bibe] *vt* to soak (**de** with, in); **— s'i.** *vpr* to become soaked.

imbriquer (s') [ɛ̃brike] *vpr* (*questions etc*) to overlap, be bound up with each other.

imbroglio [ɛ̃brɔljo] *nm* muddle, foul-up.

imbu [ɛ̃by] *a* **i. de** imbued with.

imbuvable [ɛ̃byvabl] *a* undrinkable; (*personne*) *Fig* insufferable.

imiter [imite] *vt* to imitate; (*contrefaire*) to forge; **i. qn** (*pour rire*) to mimic s.o., take s.o. off; (*faire comme*) to do the same as s.o., follow suit. ◆**imitateur, -trice** *nmf* imitator; (*artiste*) *Th* impersonator, mimic. ◆**imitatif, -ive** *a* imitative. ◆**imitation** *nf* imitation.

immaculé [imakyle] *a* (*sans tache, sans péché*) immaculate.

immangeable [ɛ̃mɑ̃ʒabl] *a* inedible.

immanquable [ɛ̃mɑ̃kabl] *a* inevitable.

immatriculer [imatrikyle] *vt* to register; **se faire i.** to register. ◆**immatriculation** *nf* registration.

immédiat [imedja] *a* immediate; **— nm dans l'i.** for the time being. ◆**immédiatement** *adv* immediately.

immense [imɑ̃s] *a* immense, vast. ◆**immensément** *adv* immensely. ◆**immensité** *nf* immensity, vastness.

immerger [imerʒe] *vt* to immerse, put under water; **— s'i.** *vpr* (*sous-marin*) to submerge. ◆**immersion** *nf* immersion; submersion.

immettable [ɛ̃metabl] *a* (*vêtement*) unfit to be worn.

immeuble [imœbl] *nm* building; (*d'habitation*) block of flats, *Am* apartment building; (*de bureaux*) office block.

immigr/er [imigre] *vi* to immigrate. ◆**—ant, -ante** *nmf* immigrant. ◆**—é, -ée** *a* & *nmf* immigrant. ◆**immigration** *nf* immigration.

imminent [iminɑ̃] *a* imminent. ◆**imminence** *nf* imminence.

immiscer (s') [simise] *vpr* to interfere (**dans** in).

immobile [imɔbil] *a* still, motionless. ◆**immobiliser** *vt* to immobilize; (*arrêter*) to stop; — **s'i.** *vpr* to stop, come to a stand-still. ◆**immobilité** *nf* stillness; (*inactivité*) immobility.

immobilier, -ière [imɔbilje, -jɛr] *a* (*vente*) property-; (*société*) construction-; **agent i.** estate agent, *Am* real estate agent.

immodéré [imɔdere] *a* immoderate.

immonde [imɔ̃d] *a* filthy. ◆**immondices** *nfpl* refuse, rubbish.

immoral, -aux [imɔral, -o] *a* immoral. ◆**immoralité** *nf* immorality.

immortel, -elle [imɔrtɛl] *a* immortal. ◆**immortaliser** *vt* to immortalize. ◆**immortalité** *nf* immortality.

immuable [imɥabl] *a* immutable, unchanging.

immuniser [imynize] *vt* to immunize (**contre** against); **immunisé contre** (*à l'abri de*) *Méd & Fig* immune to *ou* from. ◆**immunitaire** *a* (*déficience etc*) *Méd* immune. ◆**immunité** *nf* immunity.

impact [ɛ̃pakt] *nm* impact (**sur** on).

impair [ɛ̃pɛr] **1** *a* (*nombre*) odd, uneven. **2** *nm* (*gaffe*) blunder.

imparable [ɛ̃parabl] *a* (*coup etc*) unavoidable.

impardonnable [ɛ̃pardɔnabl] *a* unforgivable.

imparfait [ɛ̃parfɛ] **1** *a* (*connaissance etc*) imperfect. **2** *nm* (*temps*) *Gram* imperfect.

impartial, -aux [ɛ̃parsjal, -o] *a* impartial, unbiased. ◆**impartialité** *nf* impartiality.

impartir [ɛ̃partir] *vt* to grant (**à** to).

impasse [ɛ̃pas] *nf* (*rue*) dead end, blind alley; (*situation*) *Fig* impasse; **dans l'i.** (*négociations*) in deadlock.

impassible [ɛ̃pasibl] *a* impassive, unmoved. ◆**impassibilité** *nf* impassiveness.

impatient [ɛ̃pasjɑ̃] *a* impatient; **i. de faire** eager *ou* impatient to do. ◆**impatiemment** [-amɑ̃] *adv* impatiently. ◆**impatience** *nf* impatience. ◆**impatienter** *vt* to annoy, make impatient; — **s'i.** *vpr* to get impatient.

impayable [ɛ̃pɛjabl] *a* (*comique*) *Fam* hilarious, priceless.

impayé [ɛ̃peje] *a* unpaid.

impeccable [ɛ̃pekabl] *a* impeccable, immaculate. ◆**—ment** [-əmɑ̃] *adv* impeccably, immaculately.

impénétrable [ɛ̃penetrabl] *a* (*forêt; mystère etc*) impenetrable.

impénitent [ɛ̃penitɑ̃] *a* unrepentant.

impensable [ɛ̃pɑ̃sabl] *a* unthinkable.

imper [ɛ̃pɛr] *nm Fam* raincoat, mac.

impératif, -ive [ɛ̃peratif, -iv] *a* (*consigne, ton*) imperative; – *nm* (*mode*) *Gram* imperative.

impératrice [ɛ̃peratris] *nf* empress.

imperceptible [ɛ̃persɛptibl] *a* imperceptible (**à** to).

imperfection [ɛ̃pɛrfɛksjɔ̃] *nf* imperfection.

impérial, -aux [ɛ̃perjal, -o] *a* imperial. ◆**impérialisme** *nm* imperialism.

impériale [ɛ̃perjal] *nf* (*d'autobus*) top deck.

impérieux, -euse [ɛ̃perjø, -øz] *a* (*autoritaire*) imperious; (*besoin*) pressing, imperative.

imperméable [ɛ̃pɛrmeabl] **1** *a* impervious (**à** to); (*manteau, tissu*) waterproof. **2** *nm* raincoat, mackintosh. ◆**imperméabilisé** *a* waterproof.

impersonnel, -elle [ɛ̃pɛrsɔnɛl] *a* impersonal.

impertinent [ɛ̃pɛrtinɑ̃] *a* impertinent (**envers** to). ◆**impertinence** *nf* impertinence.

imperturbable [ɛ̃pɛrtyrbabl] *a* unruffled, imperturbable.

impétueux, -euse [ɛ̃petɥø, -øz] *a* impetuous. ◆**impétuosité** *nf* impetuosity.

impitoyable [ɛ̃pitwajabl] *a* ruthless, pitiless, merciless.

implacable [ɛ̃plakabl] *a* implacable, relentless.

implanter [ɛ̃plɑ̃te] *vt* (*industrie, mode etc*) to establish; — **s'i.** *vpr* to become established. ◆**implantation** *nf* establishment.

implicite [ɛ̃plisit] *a* implicit. ◆**—ment** *adv* implicitly.

impliquer [ɛ̃plike] *vt* (*entraîner*) to imply; **i. que** (*supposer*) to imply that; **i. qn** (*engager*) to implicate s.o. (**dans** in). ◆**implication** *nf* (*conséquence, participation*) implication.

implorer [ɛ̃plɔre] *vt* to implore (**qn de faire** s.o. to do).

impoli [ɛ̃pɔli] *a* impolite, rude. ◆**impolitesse** *nf* impoliteness, rudeness; **une i.** an act of rudeness.

impopulaire [ɛ̃pɔpylɛr] *a* unpopular.

important [ɛ̃pɔrtɑ̃] *a* (*personnage, événement etc*) important; (*quantité, somme etc*) considerable, big, great; – *nm* **l'i., c'est de . . .** the important thing is to . . . . ◆**importance** *nf* importance, significance; (*taille*) size; (*de dégâts*) extent; **ça n'a pas d'i.** it doesn't matter.

importer [ɛ̃pɔrte] **1** *v imp* to matter, be important (**à** to); **il importe de faire** it's important to do; **peu importe, n'importe** it doesn't matter; **n'importe qui/quoi/ où/quand/comment** anyone/anything/ anywhere/any time/anyhow. **2** *vt* (*marchandises etc*) to import (**de** from). ◆**im-**

portateur, -trice *nmf* importer; — *a* importing. ◆importation *nf* (*objet*) import; (*action*) import(ing), importation; d'i. (*article*) imported.

importun, -une [ɛ̃pɔrtœ̃, -yn] *a* troublesome, intrusive; — *nmf* nuisance, intruder. ◆importuner *vt* to inconvenience, trouble.

impos/er [ɛ̃poze] 1 *vt* to impose, enforce (à on); (*exiger*) to demand; (*respect*) to command; — *vi* en i. à qn to impress s.o., command respect from s.o.; — s'i. *vpr* (*chez qn*) *Péj* to impose; (*s'affirmer*) to assert oneself, compel recognition; (*aller de soi*) to stand out; (*être nécessaire*) to be essential. 2 *vt* Fin to tax. ◆—ant *a* imposing. ◆—able *a* Fin taxable. ◆imposition *nf* Fin taxation.

impossible [ɛ̃pɔsibl] *a* impossible (à faire to do); il (nous) est i. de faire it is impossible (for us) to do; il est i. que (+ *sub*) it is impossible that; ça m'est i. I cannot possibly; — *nm* faire l'i. to do the impossible. ◆impossibilité *nf* impossibility.

imposteur [ɛ̃pɔstœr] *nm* impostor. ◆imposture *nf* deception.

impôt [ɛ̃po] *nm* tax; *pl* (*contributions*) (income) tax, taxes; i. sur le revenu income tax.

impotent, -ente [ɛ̃pɔtɑ̃, -ɑ̃t] *a* crippled, disabled; — *nmf* cripple, invalid.

impraticable [ɛ̃pratikabl] *a* (*projet etc*) impracticable; (*chemin etc*) impassable.

imprécis [ɛ̃presi] *a* imprecise. ◆imprécision *nf* lack of precision.

imprégner [ɛ̃preɲe] *vt* to saturate, impregnate (de with); — s'i. *vpr* to become saturated *ou* impregnated (de with); imprégné de (*idées*) imbued *ou* infused with. ◆imprégnation *nf* saturation.

imprenable [ɛ̃prənabl] *a* Mil impregnable.

impresario [ɛ̃presarjo] *nm* (business) manager, impresario.

impression [ɛ̃presjɔ̃] *nf* 1 impression; avoir l'i. que to have the feeling *ou* impression that; be under the impression that; faire une bonne i. à qn to make a good impression on s.o. 2 Typ printing.

impressionn/er [ɛ̃presjɔne] *vt* (*influencer*) to impress; (*émouvoir, troubler*) to make a strong impression on. ◆—ant *a* impressive. ◆—able *a* impressionable.

imprévisible [ɛ̃previzibl] *a* unforeseeable. ◆imprévoyance *nf* lack of foresight. ◆imprévoyant *a* shortsighted. ◆imprévu *a* unexpected, unforeseen; — *nm* en cas d'i. in case of anything unexpected.

imprim/er [ɛ̃prime] *vt* 1 (*livre etc*) to print;

(*trace*) to impress (dans in); (*cachet*) to stamp. 2 (*communiquer*) Tech to impart (à to). ◆—ante *nf* (*d'ordinateur*) printer. ◆—é *nm* (*formulaire*) printed form; — *nm(pl)* (*par la poste*) printed matter. ◆imprimerie *nf* (*technique*) printing; (*lieu*) printing works. ◆imprimeur *nm* printer.

improbable [ɛ̃prɔbabl] *a* improbable, unlikely. ◆improbabilité *nf* improbability, unlikelihood.

impromptu [ɛ̃prɔ̃pty] *a* & *adv* impromptu.

impropre [ɛ̃prɔpr] *a* inappropriate; i. à qch unfit for sth. ◆impropriété *nf* (*incorrection*) Ling impropriety.

improviser [ɛ̃prɔvize] *vti* to improvise. ◆improvisation *nf* improvisation.

improviste (à l') [aleprɔvist] *adv* unexpectedly; une visite à l'i. an unexpected visit; prendre qn à l'i. to catch s.o. unawares.

imprudent [ɛ̃prydɑ̃] *a* (*personne, action*) careless, rash; il est i. de it is unwise to. ◆imprudemment [-amɑ̃] *adv* carelessly. ◆imprudence *nf* carelessness; une i. an act of carelessness.

impudent [ɛ̃pydɑ̃] *a* impudent ◆impudence *nf* impudence.

impudique [ɛ̃pydik] *a* lewd.

impuissant [ɛ̃pɥisɑ̃] *a* helpless; *Méd* impotent; i. à faire powerless to do. ◆impuissance *nf* helplessness; *Méd* impotence.

impulsif, -ive [ɛ̃pylsif, -iv] *a* impulsive. ◆impulsion *nf* impulse; donner une i. à (*élan*) Fig to give an impetus *ou* impulse to.

impunément [ɛ̃pynemɑ̃] *adv* with impunity. ◆impuni *a* unpunished.

impur [ɛ̃pyr] *a* impure. ◆impureté *nf* impurity.

imputer [ɛ̃pyte] *vt* to attribute, impute (à to); (*affecter*) Fin to charge (à to). ◆imputable *a* attributable (à to). ◆imputation *nf* Jur accusation.

inabordable [inabɔrdabl] *a* (*lieu*) inaccessible; (*personne*) unapproachable; (*prix*) prohibitive.

inacceptable [inaksɛptabl] *a* unacceptable.

inaccessible [inaksesibl] *a* inaccessible.

inaccoutumé [inakutyme] *a* unusual, unaccustomed.

inachevé [inaʃve] *a* unfinished.

inactif, -ive [inaktif, -iv] *a* inactive. ◆inaction *nf* inactivity, inaction. ◆inactivité *nf* inactivity.

inadapté, -ée [inadapte] *a* & *nmf* maladjusted (person). ◆inadaptation *nf* maladjustment.

inadmissible [inadmisibl] *a* unacceptable, inadmissible.
inadvertance (par) [parinadvɛrtɑ̃s] *adv* inadvertently.
inaltérable [inalterabl] *a* (*couleur*) fast; (*sentiment*) unchanging.
inamical, -aux [inamikal, -o] *a* unfriendly.
inanimé [inanime] *a* (*mort*) lifeless; (*évanoui*) unconscious; (*matière*) inanimate.
inanité [inanite] *nf* (*vanité*) futility.
inanition [inanisjɔ̃] *nf* **mourir d'i.** to die of starvation.
inaperçu [inapɛrsy] *a* **passer i.** to go unnoticed.
inapplicable [inaplikabl] *a* inapplicable (à to).
inappliqué [inaplike] *a* (*élève etc*) inattentive.
inappréciable [inapresjabl] *a* invaluable.
inapte [inapt] *a* unsuited (à qch to sth), inept (à qch at sth); *Mil* unfit ◆**inaptitude** *nf* ineptitude, incapacity.
inarticulé [inartikyle] *a* (*son*) inarticulate.
inattaquable [inatakabl] *a* unassailable.
inattendu [inatɑ̃dy] *a* unexpected.
inattentif, -ive [inatɑ̃tif, -iv] *a* inattentive, careless; **i.** à (*soucis, danger etc*) heedless of. ◆**inattention** *nf* lack of attention; **dans un moment d'i.** in a moment of distraction.
inaudible [inodibl] *a* inaudible.
inaugurer [inogyre] *vt* (*politique, édifice*) to inaugurate; (*école, congrès*) to open, inaugurate; (*statue*) to unveil. ◆**inaugural, -aux** *a* inaugural. ◆**inauguration** *nf* inauguration; opening; unveiling.
inauthentique [inotɑ̃tik] *a* not authentic.
inavouable [inavwabl] *a* shameful.
incalculable [ɛ̃kalkylabl] *a* incalculable.
incandescent [ɛ̃kɑ̃desɑ̃] *a* incandescent.
incapable [ɛ̃kapabl] *a* incapable; **i. de faire** unable to do, incapable of doing; – *nmf* (*personne*) incompetent. ◆**incapacité** *nf* incapacity, inability (**de faire** to do); *Méd* disability, incapacity.
incarcérer [ɛ̃karsere] *vt* to incarcerate. ◆**incarcération** *nf* incarceration.
incarné [ɛ̃karne] *a* (*ongle*) ingrown.
incarner [ɛ̃karne] *vt* to embody, incarnate. ◆**incarnation** *nf* embodiment, incarnation.
incartade [ɛ̃kartad] *nf* indiscretion, prank.
incassable [ɛ̃kasabl] *a* unbreakable.
incendie [ɛ̃sɑ̃di] *nm* fire; (*guerre*) *Fig* conflagration. ◆**incendiaire** *nmf* arsonist; – *a* (*bombe*) incendiary; (*discours*) inflammatory. ◆**incendier** *vt* to set fire to, set on fire.

incertain [ɛ̃sɛrtɛ̃] *a* uncertain; (*temps*) unsettled; (*entreprise*) chancy; (*contour*) indistinct. ◆**incertitude** *nf* uncertainty.
incessamment [ɛ̃sesamɑ̃] *adv* without delay, shortly.
incessant [ɛ̃sesɑ̃] *a* incessant.
inceste [ɛ̃sɛst] *nm* incest. ◆**incestueux, -euse** *a* incestuous.
inchangé [ɛ̃ʃɑ̃ʒe] *a* unchanged.
incidence [ɛ̃sidɑ̃s] *nf* (*influence*) effect.
incident [ɛ̃sidɑ̃] *nm* incident; (*accroc*) hitch.
incinérer [ɛ̃sinere] *vt* (*ordures*) to incinerate; (*cadavre*) to cremate. ◆**incinération** *nf* incineration; cremation.
inciser [ɛ̃size] *vt* to make an incision in. ◆**incision** *nf* (*entaille*) incision.
incisif, -ive[1] [ɛ̃sizif, -iv] *a* incisive, sharp.
incisive[2] [ɛ̃siziv] *nf* (*dent*) incisor.
inciter [ɛ̃site] *vt* to urge, incite (à faire to do). ◆**incitation** *nf* incitement (à to).
incliner [ɛ̃kline] *vt* (*courber*) to bend; (*pencher*) to tilt, incline; **i. la tête** (*approuver*) to nod one's head; (*révérence*) to bow (one's head); **i. qn à faire** to make s.o. inclined to do, incline s.o. to do; – *vi* **i.** to be inclined towards; – **s'i.** *vpr* (*se courber*) to bow (down); (*s'avouer vaincu*) to admit defeat; (*chemin*) to slope down. ◆**inclinaison** *nf* incline, slope. ◆**inclination** *nf* (*goût*) inclination; (*de tête*) nod, (*révérence*) bow.
incl/ure[*] [ɛ̃klyr] *vt* to include; (*enfermer*) to enclose. ◆**—us** *a* inclusive; **du quatre jusqu'au dix mai i.** from the fourth to the tenth of May inclusive; **jusqu'à lundi i.** up to and including (next) Monday. ◆**inclusion** *nf* inclusion. ◆**inclusivement** *adv* inclusively.
incognito [ɛ̃kɔɲito] *adv* incognito.
incohérent [ɛ̃kɔerɑ̃] *a* incoherent. ◆**incohérence** *nf* incoherence.
incollable [ɛ̃kɔlabl] *a Fam* infallible, unable to be caught out.
incolore [ɛ̃kɔlɔr] *a* colourless; (*verre, vernis*) clear.
incomber [ɛ̃kɔ̃be] *vi* **i. à qn** (*devoir*) to fall to s.o.; **il lui incombe de faire** it's his *ou* her duty *ou* responsiblity to do.
incommode [ɛ̃kɔmɔd] *a* awkward. ◆**incommodité** *nf* awkwardness.
incommod/er [ɛ̃kɔmɔde] *vt* to bother, annoy. ◆**—ant** *a* annoying.
incomparable [ɛ̃kɔ̃parabl] *a* incomparable.
incompatible [ɛ̃kɔ̃patibl] *a* incompatible, inconsistent (**avec** with). ◆**incompatibilité** *nf* incompatibility, inconsistency.

incompétent [ɛ̃kɔ̃petɑ̃] *a* incompetent. ◆**incompétence** *nf* incompetence.

incomplet, -ète [ɛ̃kɔ̃plɛ, -ɛt] *a* incomplete; (*fragmentaire*) scrappy, sketchy.

incompréhensible [ɛ̃kɔ̃preɑ̃sibl] *a* incomprehensible. ◆**incompréhensif, -ive** *a* uncomprehending, lacking understanding. ◆**incompréhension** *nf* lack of understanding. ◆**incompris** *a* misunderstood.

inconcevable [ɛ̃kɔ̃svabl] *a* inconceivable.

inconciliable [ɛ̃kɔ̃siljabl] *a* irreconcilable.

inconditionnel, -elle [ɛ̃kɔ̃disjɔnɛl] *a* unconditional.

inconfort [ɛ̃kɔ̃fɔr] *nm* lack of comfort. ◆**inconfortable** *a* uncomfortable.

incongru [ɛ̃kɔ̃gry] *a* unseemly, incongruous.

inconnu, -ue [ɛ̃kɔny] *a* unknown (à to); — *nmf* (*étranger*) stranger; (*auteur*) unknown; — *nm* **l'i.** the unknown; — *nf Math* unknown (quantity).

inconscient [ɛ̃kɔ̃sjɑ̃] *a* unconscious (**de** of); (*irréfléchi*) thoughtless, senseless; — *nm* **l'i.** *Psy* the unconscious. ◆**inconsciemment** [-amɑ̃] *adv* unconsciously. ◆**inconscience** *nf* (*physique*) unconsciousness; (*irréflexion*) utter thoughtlessness.

inconséquence [ɛ̃kɔ̃sekɑ̃s] *nf* inconsistency.

inconsidéré [ɛ̃kɔ̃sidere] *a* thoughtless.

inconsolable [ɛ̃kɔ̃sɔlabl] *a* inconsolable.

inconstant [ɛ̃kɔ̃stɑ̃] *a* fickle. ◆**inconstance** *nf* fickleness.

incontestable [ɛ̃kɔ̃tɛstabl] *a* undeniable, indisputable. ◆**incontesté** *a* undisputed.

incontinent [ɛ̃kɔ̃tinɑ̃] *a* incontinent.

incontrôlé [ɛ̃kɔ̃trole] *a* unchecked. ◆**incontrôlable** *a* unverifiable.

inconvenant [ɛ̃kɔ̃vnɑ̃] *a* improper. ◆**inconvenance** *nf* impropriety.

inconvénient [ɛ̃kɔ̃venjɑ̃] *nm* (*désavantage*) drawback; (*risque*) risk; (*objection*) objection.

incorporer [ɛ̃kɔrpɔre] *vt* (*introduire, admettre*) to incorporate (**dans** into); (*ingrédient*) to blend (**à** with); *Mil* to enrol. ◆**incorporation** *nf* incorporation (**de** of); *Mil* enrolment.

incorrect [ɛ̃kɔrɛkt] *a* (*inexact*) incorrect; (*inconvenant*) improper; (*grossier*) impolite. ◆**incorrection** *nf* (*faute*) impropriety, error; (*inconvenance*) impropriety; **une i.** (*grossièreté*) an impolite word *ou* act.

incorrigible [ɛ̃kɔriʒibl] *a* incorrigible.

incorruptible [ɛ̃kɔryptibl] *a* incorruptible.

incrédule [ɛ̃kredyl] *a* incredulous. ◆**incrédulité** *nf* disbelief, incredulity.

increvable [ɛ̃krəvabl] *a* (*robuste*) *Fam* tireless.

incriminer [ɛ̃krimine] *vt* to incriminate.

incroyable [ɛ̃krwajabl] *a* incredible, unbelievable. ◆**incroyablement** *adv* incredibly. ◆**incroyant, -ante** *a* unbelieving; — *nmf* unbeliever.

incrusté [ɛ̃kryste] *a* (*de tartre*) encrusted; **i. de** (*orné*) inlaid with. ◆**incrustation** *nf* (*ornement*) inlay; (*action*) inlaying.

incruster (s') [sɛ̃kryste] *vpr* (*chez qn*) *Fig* to dig oneself in, be difficult to get rid of.

incubation [ɛ̃kybasjɔ̃] *nf* incubation.

inculp/er [ɛ̃kylpe] *vt Jur* to charge (**de** with), indict (**de** for). ◆**-é, -ée** *nmf* **l'i.** the accused. ◆**inculpation** *nf* charge, indictment.

inculquer [ɛ̃kylke] *vt* to instil (**à** into).

inculte [ɛ̃kylt] *a* (*terre*) uncultivated; (*personne*) uneducated.

incurable [ɛ̃kyrabl] *a* incurable.

incursion [ɛ̃kyrsjɔ̃] *nf* incursion, inroad (**dans** into).

incurver [ɛ̃kyrve] *vt* to curve.

Inde [ɛ̃d] *nf* India.

indécent [ɛ̃desɑ̃] *a* indecent. ◆**indécemment** [-amɑ̃] *adv* indecently. ◆**indécence** *nf* indecency.

indéchiffrable [ɛ̃deʃifrabl] *a* undecipherable.

indécis [ɛ̃desi] *a* (*victoire, résultat*) undecided; (*indistinct*) vague; **être i.** (*hésiter*) to be undecided; (*de tempérament*) to be indecisive *ou* irresolute. ◆**indécision** *nf* indecisiveness, indecision.

indéfectible [ɛ̃defɛktibl] *a* unfailing.

indéfendable [ɛ̃defɑ̃dabl] *a* indefensible.

indéfini [ɛ̃defini] *a* (*indéterminé*) indefinite; (*imprécis*) undefined. ◆**indéfiniment** *adv* indefinitely. ◆**indéfinissable** *a* indefinable.

indéformable [ɛ̃defɔrmabl] *a* (*vêtement*) which keeps its shape.

indélébile [ɛ̃delebil] *a* (*encre, souvenir*) indelible.

indélicat [ɛ̃delika] *a* (*grossier*) indelicate; (*malhonnête*) unscrupulous.

indemne [ɛ̃dɛmn] *a* unhurt, unscathed.

indemniser [ɛ̃dɛmnize] *vt* to indemnify, compensate (**de** for). ◆**indemnisation** *nf* compensation. ◆**indemnité** *nf* (*dédommagement*) indemnity; (*allocation*) allowance.

indémontable [ɛ̃demɔ̃tabl] *a* that cannot be taken apart.

indéniable [ɛ̃denjabl] *a* undeniable.

indépendant [ɛ̃depɑ̃dɑ̃] *a* independent (**de**

of); (*chambre*) self-contained; (*journaliste*) freelance. ◆**indépendamment** *adv* independently (**de** of); **i. de** (*sans aucun égard à*) apart from. ◆**indépendance** *nf* independence.

indescriptible [ɛ̃dɛskriptibl] *a* indescribable.

indésirable [ɛ̃dezirabl] *a & nmf* undesirable.

indestructible [ɛ̃dɛstryktibl] *a* indestructible.

indéterminé [ɛ̃detɛrmine] *a* indeterminate. ◆**indétermination** *nf* (*doute*) indecision.

index [ɛ̃dɛks] *nm* (*liste*) index; *Anat* forefinger, index finger.

indexer [ɛ̃dɛkse] *vt* Écon to index-link, tie (**sur** to).

indicateur, -trice [ɛ̃dikatœr, -tris] **1** *nmf* (*espion*) (*police*) informer. **2** *nm* Rail guide, timetable; Tech indicator, gauge. **3** *a* **poteau i.** signpost. ◆**indicatif, -ive 1** *a* indicative (**de** of); – *nm* Mus signature tune; Tél dialling code, *Am* area code. **2** *nm* (*mode*) Gram indicative. ◆**indication** *nf* indication (**de** of); (*renseignement*) (piece of) information; (*directive*) instruction.

indice [ɛ̃dis] *nm* (*indication*) sign; (*dans une enquête*) Jur clue; (*des prix*) index; (*de salaire*) grade; **i. d'écoute** TV Rad rating.

indien, -ienne [ɛ̃djɛ̃, -jɛn] *a & nmf* Indian.

indifférent [ɛ̃diferã] *a* indifferent (**à** to); **ça m'est i.** that's all the same to me. ◆**indifféremment** [-amã] *adv* indifferently. ◆**indifférence** *nf* indifference (**à** to).

indigène [ɛ̃diʒɛn] *a & nmf* native.

indigent [ɛ̃diʒã] *a* (very) poor. ◆**indigence** *nf* poverty.

indigeste [ɛ̃diʒɛst] *a* indigestible. ◆**indigestion** *nf* (attack of) indigestion.

indigne [ɛ̃diɲ] *a* (*personne*) unworthy; (*chose*) shameful; **i. de qn/qch** unworthy of s.o./sth. ◆**indignité** *nf* unworthiness; **une i.** (*honte*) an indignity.

indigner [ɛ̃diɲe] *vt* **i. qn** to make s.o. indignant; — **s'i.** *vpr* to be *ou* become indignant (**de** at). ◆**indignation** *nf* indignation.

indigo [ɛ̃digo] *nm & a inv* (*couleur*) indigo.

indiqu/er [ɛ̃dike] *vt* (*montrer*) to show, indicate; (*dire*) to point out, tell; (*recommander*) to recommend; **i. du doigt** to point to *ou* at. ◆**—é** *a* (*heure*) appointed; (*conseillé*) recommended; (*adéquat*) appropriate.

indirect [ɛ̃dirɛkt] *a* indirect. ◆**—ement** *adv* indirectly.

indiscipline [ɛ̃disiplin] *nf* lack of discipline. ◆**indiscipliné** *a* unruly.

indiscret, -ète [ɛ̃diskrɛ, -ɛt] *a* (*indélicat*) indiscreet, tactless; (*curieux*) Péj inquisitive, prying. ◆**indiscrétion** *nf* indiscretion.

indiscutable [ɛ̃diskytabl] *a* indisputable.

indispensable [ɛ̃dispãsabl] *a* indispensable, essential.

indispos/er [ɛ̃dispoze] *vt* (*incommoder*) to make unwell, upset; **i. qn** (**contre soi**) (*mécontenter*) to antagonize s.o. ◆**—é** *a* (*malade*) indisposed, unwell. ◆**indisposition** *nf* indisposition.

indissoluble [ɛ̃disɔlybl] *a* (*liens etc*) solid, indissoluble.

indistinct, -incte [ɛ̃distɛ̃(kt), -ɛ̃kt] *a* indistinct. ◆**—ement** [-ɛ̃ktəmã] *adv* indistinctly; (*également*) without distinction.

individu [ɛ̃dividy] *nm* individual. ◆**individualiser** *vt* to individualize. ◆**individualiste** *a* individualistic; – *nmf* individualist. ◆**individualité** *nf* (*originalité*) individuality. ◆**individuel, -elle** *a* individual. ◆**individuellement** *adv* individually.

indivisible [ɛ̃divizibl] *a* indivisible.

Indochine [ɛ̃dɔʃin] *nf* Indo-China.

indolent [ɛ̃dɔlã] *a* indolent. ◆**indolence** *nf* indolence.

indolore [ɛ̃dɔlɔr] *a* painless.

indomptable [ɛ̃dɔ̃tabl] *a* (*énergie, volonté*) indomitable. ◆**indompté** *a* (*animal*) untamed.

Indonésie [ɛ̃dɔnezi] *nf* Indonesia.

indubitable [ɛ̃dybitabl] *a* beyond doubt.

indue [ɛ̃dy] *af* **à une heure i.** at an ungodly hour.

induire* [ɛ̃dɥir] *vt* **i. qn en erreur** to lead s.o. astray.

indulgent [ɛ̃dylʒã] *a* indulgent (**envers** to, **avec** with). ◆**indulgence** *nf* indulgence.

industrie [ɛ̃dystri] *nf* industry. ◆**industrialisé** *a* industrialized. ◆**industriel, -elle** *a* industrial; – *nmf* industrialist.

inébranlable [inebrãlabl] *a* (*certitude, personne*) unshakeable, unwavering.

inédit [inedi] *a* (*texte*) unpublished; (*nouveau*) Fig original.

ineffable [inefabl] *a* Litt inexpressible, ineffable.

inefficace [inefikas] *a* (*mesure, effort etc*) ineffective, ineffectual; (*personne*) inefficient. ◆**inefficacité** *nf* ineffectiveness; inefficiency.

inégal, -aux [inegal, -o] *a* unequal; (*sol, humeur*) uneven. ◆**inégalable** *a* incomparable. ◆**inégalé** *a* unequalled. ◆**inégalité** *nf* (*morale*) inequality; (*physique*)

difference; (*irrégularité*) unevenness; *pl*
(*bosses*) bumps.

inélégant [inelegɑ̃] *a* coarse, inelegant.

inéligible [ineliʒibl] *a* (*candidat*) ineligible.

inéluctable [inelyktabl] *a* inescapable.

inepte [inɛpt] *a* absurd, inept. ◆**ineptie**
[-si] *nf* absurdity, ineptitude.

inépuisable [inepɥizabl] *a* inexhaustible.

inerte [inɛrt] *a* inert; (*corps*) lifeless. ◆**inertie** [-si] *nf* inertia.

inespéré [inespere] *a* unhoped-for.

inestimable [inɛstimabl] *a* priceless.

inévitable [inevitabl] *a* inevitable, unavoidable.

inexact [inɛgzakt] *a* (*erroné*) inaccurate, inexact; **c'est i.!** it's incorrect! ◆**inexactitude** *nf* inaccuracy, inexactitude; (*manque
de ponctualité*) lack of punctuality.

inexcusable [inɛkskyzabl] *a* inexcusable.

inexistant [inɛgzistɑ̃] *a* non-existent.

inexorable [inɛgzɔrabl] *a* inexorable.

inexpérience [inɛksperjɑ̃s] *nf* inexperience.
◆**inexpérimenté** *a* (*personne*) inexperienced; (*machine, arme*) untested.

inexplicable [inɛksplikabl] *a* inexplicable.
◆**inexpliqué** *a* unexplained.

inexploré [inɛksplɔre] *a* unexplored.

inexpressif, -ive [inɛkspresif, -iv] *a* expressionless.

inexprimable [inɛksprimabl] *a* inexpressible.

inextricable [inɛkstrikabl] *a* inextricable.

infaillible [ɛ̃fajibl] *a* infallible. ◆**infaillibilité** *nf* infallibility.

infaisable [ɛ̃fəzabl] *a* (*travail etc*) that cannot be done.

infamant [ɛ̃famɑ̃] *a* ignominious.

infâme [ɛ̃fɑm] *a* (*odieux*) vile, infamous;
(*taudis*) squalid. ◆**infamie** *nf* infamy.

infanterie [ɛ̃fɑ̃tri] *nf* infantry.

infantile [ɛ̃fɑ̃til] *a* (*maladie, réaction*) infantile.

infarctus [ɛ̃farktys] *nm* **un i.** *Méd* a coronary.

infatigable [ɛ̃fatigabl] *a* tireless, indefatiga-
ble.

infect [ɛ̃fɛkt] *a* (*puant*) foul; (*mauvais*)
lousy, vile.

infecter [ɛ̃fɛkte] **1** *vt* (*air*) to contaminate,
foul. **2** *vt Méd* to infect; — **s'i.** *vpr* to get
infected. ◆**infectieux, -euse** *a* infectious.
◆**infection** *nf* **1** *Méd* infection. **2** (*odeur*)
stench.

inférer [ɛ̃fere] *vt* (*conclure*) to infer (**de** from,
que that).

inférieur, -eure [ɛ̃ferjœr] *a* (*partie*) lower;
(*qualité, personne*) inferior; **à l'étage i.** on

the floor below; **i. à** inferior to; (*plus petit
que*) smaller than; — *nmf* (*personne*) *Péj* inferior. ◆**infériorité** *nf* inferiority.

infernal, -aux [ɛ̃fɛrnal, -o] *a* infernal.

infester [ɛ̃fɛste] *vt* to infest, overrun (**de**
with). ◆**—é à i. de requins/de fourmis/etc**
shark-/ant-/etc infested.

infidèle [ɛ̃fidɛl] *a* unfaithful (**à** to).
◆**infidélité** *nf* unfaithfulness; **une i.** (*acte*)
an infidelity.

infiltrer (s') [sɛ̃filtre] *vpr* (*liquide*) to seep *ou*
percolate (through) (**dans** into); (*lumière*)
to filter (through) (**dans** into); **s'i. dans**
(*groupe, esprit*) *Fig* to infiltrate. ◆**infiltration** *nf* (*de personne, idée, liquide*) infiltration.

infime [ɛ̃fim] *a* (*très petit*) tiny; (*personne*)
Péj lowly.

infini [ɛ̃fini] *a* infinite; — *nm Math Phot* infinity; *Phil* infinite; **à l'i.** (*beaucoup*) ad infinitum, endlessly; *Math* to infinity.
◆**infiniment** *adv* infinitely; (*regretter,
remercier*) very much. ◆**infinité** *nf* **une i.
de** an infinite amount of.

infinitif [ɛ̃finitif] *nm Gram* infinitive.

infirme [ɛ̃firm] *a* disabled, crippled; — *nmf*
disabled person. ◆**infirmité** *nf* disability.

infirmer [ɛ̃firme] *vt* to invalidate.

infirmerie [ɛ̃firməri] *nf* infirmary, sickbay.
◆**infirmier** *nm* male nurse. ◆**infirmière**
nf nurse.

inflammable [ɛ̃flamabl] *a* (in)flammable.

inflammation [ɛ̃flamasjɔ̃] *nf Méd* inflammation.

inflation [ɛ̃flasjɔ̃] *nf Écon* inflation. ◆**inflationniste** *a Écon* inflationary.

infléchir [ɛ̃fleʃir] *vt* (*courber*) to inflect,
bend; (*modifier*) to shift. ◆**inflexion** *nf*
bend; (*de voix*) tone, inflexion; **une i. de la
tête** a nod.

inflexible [ɛ̃flɛksibl] *a* inflexible.

infliger [ɛ̃fliʒe] *vt* to inflict (**à** on); (*amende*)
to impose (**à** on).

influence [ɛ̃flyɑ̃s] *nf* influence. ◆**influencer** *vt* to influence. ◆**influençable** *a*
easily influenced. ◆**influent** *a* influential.
◆**influer** *vi* **i. sur** to influence.

information [ɛ̃fɔrmasjɔ̃] *nf* information;
(*nouvelle*) piece of news; (*enquête*) *Jur* inquiry; *pl* information; *Journ Rad TV* news.

informatique [ɛ̃fɔrmatik] *nf* (*science*) computer science; (*technique*) data processing. ◆**informaticien, -ienne** *nmf*
computer scientist. ◆**informatiser** *vt* to
computerize.

informe [ɛ̃fɔrm] *a* shapeless.

informer [ɛ̃fɔrme] *vt* to inform (**de** of, about;

que that); — **s'i.** *vpr* to inquire (**de** about; **si** if, whether). ◆**informateur, -trice** *nmf* informant.

infortune [ɛ̃fɔrtyn] *nf* misfortune. ◆**infortuné** *a* ill-fated, hapless.

infraction [ɛ̃fraksjɔ̃] *nf* (*délit*) offence; **i. à** breach of, infringement of.

infranchissable [ɛ̃frɑ̃ʃisabl] *a* (*mur, fleuve*) impassable; (*difficulté*) *Fig* insuperable.

infrarouge [ɛ̃fraruʒ] *a* infrared.

infroissable [ɛ̃frwasabl] *a* crease-resistant.

infructueux, -euse [ɛ̃fryktɥø, -øz] *a* fruitless.

infuser [ɛ̃fyze] *vt* (**faire**) **i.** (*thé*) to infuse. ◆**infusion** *nf* (*tisane*) (herb *ou* herbal) tea, infusion.

ingénier (s') [sɛ̃ʒenje] *vpr* to exercise one's wits (**à faire** in order to do).

ingénieur [ɛ̃ʒenjœr] *nm* engineer. ◆**ingénierie** [-iri] *nf* engineering.

ingénieux, -euse [ɛ̃ʒenjø, -øz] *a* ingenious. ◆**ingéniosité** *nf* ingenuity.

ingénu [ɛ̃ʒeny] *a* artless, naïve.

ingérer (s') [sɛ̃ʒere] *vpr* to interfere (**dans** in). ◆**ingérence** *nf* interference.

ingrat [ɛ̃gra] *a* (*personne*) ungrateful (**envers** to); (*sol*) barren; (*tâche*) thankless; (*visage, physique*) unattractive; (*âge*) awkward. ◆**ingratitude** *nf* ingratitude.

ingrédient [ɛ̃gredjɑ̃] *nm* ingredient.

inguérissable [ɛ̃gerisabl] *a* incurable.

ingurgiter [ɛ̃gyrʒite] *vt* to gulp down.

inhabitable [inabitabl] *a* uninhabitable. ◆**inhabité** *a* uninhabited.

inhabituel, -elle [inabitɥel] *a* unusual.

inhalateur [inalatœr] *nm Méd* inhaler. ◆**inhalation** *nf* inhalation; **faire des inhalations** to inhale.

inhérent [inerɑ̃] *a* inherent (**à** in).

inhibé [inibe] *a* inhibited. ◆**inhibition** *nf* inhibition.

inhospitalier, -ière [inɔspitalje, -jɛr] *a* inhospitable.

inhumain [inymɛ̃] *a* (*cruel, terrible*) inhuman.

inhumer [inyme] *vt* to bury, inter. ◆**inhumation** *nf* burial.

inimaginable [inimaʒinabl] *a* unimaginable.

inimitable [inimitabl] *a* inimitable.

inimitié [inimitje] *nf* enmity.

ininflammable [inɛ̃flamabl] *a* (*tissu etc*) non-flammable.

inintelligent [inɛ̃teliʒɑ̃] *a* unintelligent.

inintelligible [inɛ̃teliʒibl] *a* unintelligible.

inintéressant [inɛ̃teresɑ̃] *a* uninteresting.

ininterrompu [inɛ̃terɔ̃py] *a* uninterrupted, continuous.

inique [inik] *a* iniquitous. ◆**iniquité** *nf* iniquity.

initial, -aux [inisjal, -o] *a* initial. ◆**initiale** *nf* (*lettre*) initial. ◆**initialement** *adv* initially.

initiative [inisjativ] *nf* **1** initiative. **2** **syndicat d'i.** tourist office.

initi/er [inisje] *vt* to initiate (**à** into); **s'i. à** (*art, science*) to become acquainted with *ou* initiated into. ◆**—é, -ée** *nmf* initiate; **les initiés** the initiated. ◆**initiateur, -trice** *nmf* initiator. ◆**initiation** *nf* initiation.

injecter [ɛ̃ʒɛkte] *vt* to inject; **injecté de sang** bloodshot. ◆**injection** *nf* injection.

injonction [ɛ̃ʒɔ̃ksjɔ̃] *nf* order, injunction.

injure [ɛ̃ʒyr] *nf* insult; *pl* abuse, insults. ◆**injurier** *vt* to abuse, insult, swear at. ◆**injurieux, -euse** *a* abusive, insulting (**pour** to).

injuste [ɛ̃ʒyst] *a* (*contraire à la justice*) unjust; (*partial*) unfair. ◆**injustice** *nf* injustice.

injustifiable [ɛ̃ʒystifjabl] *a* unjustifiable. ◆**injustifié** *a* unjustified.

inlassable [ɛ̃lɑsabl] *a* untiring.

inné [ine] *a* innate, inborn.

innocent, -ente [inɔsɑ̃, -ɑ̃t] *a* innocent (**de** of); — *nmf Jur* innocent person; (*idiot*) simpleton. ◆**innocemment** [-amɑ̃] *adv* innocently. ◆**innocence** *nf* innocence. ◆**innocenter** *vt* **i. qn** to clear s.o. (**de** of).

innombrable [inɔ̃brabl] *a* innumerable.

innommable [inɔmabl] *a* (*dégoûtant*) unspeakable, foul.

innover [inɔve] *vi* to innovate. ◆**innovateur, -trice** *nmf* innovator. ◆**innovation** *nf* innovation.

inoccupé [inɔkype] *a* unoccupied.

inoculer [inɔkyle] *vt* **i. qch à qn** to infect *ou* inoculate s.o. with sth. ◆**inoculation** *nf* (*vaccination*) inoculation.

inodore [inɔdɔr] *a* odourless.

inoffensif, -ive [inɔfɑ̃sif, -iv] *a* harmless, inoffensive.

inonder [inɔ̃de] *vt* to flood, inundate; (*mouiller*) to soak; **inondé de** (*envahi*) inundated with; **inondé de soleil** bathed in sunlight. ◆**inondable** *a* (*chaussée etc*) liable to flooding. ◆**inondation** *nf* flood; (*action*) flooding (**de** of).

inopérant [inɔperɑ̃] *a* inoperative.

inopiné [inɔpine] *a* unexpected.

inopportun [inɔpɔrtœ̃] *a* inopportune.

inoubliable [inublijabl] *a* unforgettable.

inouï [inwi] *a* incredible, extraordinary.

inox [inɔks] *nm* stainless steel; **en i.** (*couteau etc*) stainless-steel. ◆**inoxydable** *a* (*couteau etc*) stainless-steel; **acier i.** stainless steel.

inqualifiable [ɛ̃kalifjabl] *a* (*indigne*) unspeakable.

inquiet, -ète [ɛ̃kjɛ, -jɛt] *a* anxious, worried (**de** about). ◆**inquiét/er** *vt* (*préoccuper*) to worry; (*police*) to bother, harass (*suspect etc*); **— s'i.** *vpr* to worry (**de** about). ◆**—ant** *a* worrying. ◆**inquiétude** *nf* anxiety, concern, worry.

inquisiteur, -trice [ɛ̃kizitœr, -tris] *a* (*regard*) *Péj* inquisitive. ◆**inquisition** *nf* inquisition.

insaisissable [ɛ̃sezizabl] *a* elusive.

insalubre [ɛ̃salybr] *a* unhealthy, insalubrious.

insanités [ɛ̃sanite] *nfpl* (*idioties*) absurdities.

insatiable [ɛ̃sasjabl] *a* insatiable.

insatisfait [ɛ̃satisfɛ] *a* unsatisfied, dissatisfied.

inscrire* [ɛ̃skrir] *vt* to write *ou* put down; (*sur un registre*) to register; (*graver*) to inscribe; **i. qn** to enrol s.o.; **— s'i.** *vpr* to enrol (**à** at); **s'i. à** (*parti, club*) to join, enrol in; (*examen*) to enter *ou* enrol *ou* register for; **s'i. dans (le cadre de)** to be part of; **s'i. en faux contre** to deny absolutely. ◆**inscription** *nf* writing down; enrolment; registration; (*de médaille, sur écriteau etc*) inscription; **frais d'i.** *Univ* tuition fees.

insecte [ɛ̃sɛkt] *nm* insect. ◆**insecticide** *nm* insecticide.

insécurité [ɛ̃sekyrite] *nf* insecurity.

insémination [ɛ̃seminasjɔ̃] *nf Méd* insemination.

insensé [ɛ̃sɑ̃se] *a* senseless, absurd.

insensible [ɛ̃sɑ̃sibl] *a* (*indifférent*) insensitive (**à** to); (*graduel*) imperceptible, very slight. ◆**insensiblement** *adv* imperceptibly. ◆**insensibilité** *nf* insensitivity.

inséparable [ɛ̃separabl] *a* inseparable (**de** from).

insérer [ɛ̃sere] *vt* to insert (**dans** into, in); **s'i. dans** (*programme etc*) to be part of. ◆**insertion** *nf* insertion.

insidieux, -euse [ɛ̃sidjø, -øz] *a* insidious.

insigne [ɛ̃sin] *nm* badge, emblem; *pl* (*de maire etc*) insignia.

insignifiant [ɛ̃sinifjɑ̃] *a* insignificant, unimportant. ◆**insignifiance** *nf* insignificance.

insinuer [ɛ̃sinɥe] *vt Péj* to insinuate (**que** that); **— s'i.** *vpr* to insinuate oneself (**dans** into). ◆**insinuation** *nf* insinuation.

insipide [ɛ̃sipid] *a* insipid.

insist/er [ɛ̃siste] *vi* to insist (**pour faire** on doing); (*continuer*) *Fam* to persevere; **i. sur** (*détail, syllabe etc*) to stress; **i. pour que** (+ *sub*) to insist that. ◆**—ant** *a* insistent, persistent. ◆**insistance** *nf* insistence, persistence.

insolation [ɛ̃sɔlasjɔ̃] *nf Méd* sunstroke.

insolent [ɛ̃sɔlɑ̃] *a* (*impoli*) insolent; (*luxe*) indecent. ◆**insolence** *nf* insolence.

insolite [ɛ̃sɔlit] *a* unusual, strange.

insoluble [ɛ̃sɔlybl] *a* insoluble.

insolvable [ɛ̃sɔlvabl] *a Fin* insolvent.

insomnie [ɛ̃sɔmni] *nf* insomnia; *pl* (periods of) insomnia; **nuit d'i.** sleepless night. ◆**insomniaque** *nmf* insomniac.

insondable [ɛ̃sɔ̃dabl] *a* unfathomable.

insonoriser [ɛ̃sɔnɔrize] *vt* to soundproof, insulate. ◆**insonorisation** *nf* soundproofing, insulation.

insouciant [ɛ̃susjɑ̃] *a* carefree; **i. de** unconcerned about. ◆**insouciance** *nf* carefree attitude, lack of concern.

insoumis [ɛ̃sumi] *a* rebellious. ◆**insoumission** *nf* rebelliousness.

insoupçonnable [ɛ̃supsɔnabl] *a* beyond suspicion. ◆**insoupçonné** *a* unsuspected.

insoutenable [ɛ̃sutnabl] *a* unbearable; (*théorie*) untenable.

inspecter [ɛ̃spɛkte] *vt* to inspect. ◆**inspecteur, -trice** *nmf* inspector. ◆**inspection** *nf* inspection.

inspir/er [ɛ̃spire] **1** *vt* to inspire; **i. qch à qn** to inspire s.o. with sth; **s'i. de** to take one's inspiration from. **2** *vi Méd* to breathe in. ◆**—é** *a* inspired; **être bien i. de faire** to have the good idea to do. ◆**inspiration** *nf* **1** inspiration. **2** *Méd* breathing in.

instable [ɛ̃stabl] *a* (*meuble*) unsteady, shaky; (*temps*) unsettled; (*caractère, situation*) unstable. ◆**instabilité** *nf* unsteadiness; instability.

installer [ɛ̃stale] *vt* (*équiper*) to fit out, fix up; (*appareil, meuble etc*) to install, put in; (*étagère*) to put up; **i. qn** (*dans une fonction, un logement*) to install s.o. (**dans** in); **— s'i.** *vpr* (*s'asseoir, s'établir*) to settle (down); (*médecin etc*) to set oneself up; **s'i. dans** (*maison, hôtel*) to move into. ◆**installateur** *nm* fitter. ◆**installation** *nf* fitting out; installation; putting in; moving in; *pl* (*appareils*) fittings; (*bâtiments*) facilities.

instance [ɛ̃stɑ̃s] **1** *nf* (*juridiction, autorité*) authority; **tribunal de première i.** = magistrates' court; **en i. de** (*divorce, départ*) in the process of. **2** *nfpl* (*prières*) insistence, entreaties.

instant [ɛ̃stɑ̃] *nm* moment, instant; **à l'i.** a moment ago; **pour l'i.** for the moment. ◆**instantané** *a* instantaneous; **café i.** instant coffee; -- *nm Phot* snapshot.

instaurer [ɛ̃stɔre] *vt* to found, set up.

instigateur, -trice [ɛ̃stigatœr, -tris] *nmf* instigator. ◆**instigation** *nf* instigation.

instinct [ɛ̃stɛ̃] *nm* instinct; **d'i.** instinctively, by instinct. ◆**instinctif, -ive** *a* instinctive.

instituer [ɛ̃stitɥe] *vt* (*règle, régime*) to establish, institute.

institut [ɛ̃stity] *nm* institute; **i. de beauté** beauty salon *ou* parlour; **i. universitaire de technologie** polytechnic, technical college.

instituteur, -trice [ɛ̃stitytœr, -tris] *nmf* primary school teacher.

institution [ɛ̃stitysjɔ̃] *nf* (*règle, organisation, structure etc*) institution; *Scol* private school. ◆**institutionnel, -elle** *a* institutional.

instructif, -ive [ɛ̃stryktif, -iv] *a* instructive.

instruction [ɛ̃stryksjɔ̃] *nf* education, schooling; *Mil* training; *Jur* investigation; (*document*) directive; *pl* (*ordres*) instructions. ◆**instructeur** *nm* (*moniteur*) & *Mil* instructor.

instruire* [ɛ̃strɥir] *vt* to teach, educate; *Mil* to train; *Jur* to investigate; **i. qn de** to inform *ou* instruct s.o. of; -- **s'i.** *vpr* to educate oneself; **s'i. de** to inquire about. ◆**instruit** *a* educated.

instrument [ɛ̃strymɑ̃] *nm* instrument; (*outil*) implement, tool. ◆**instrumental, -aux** *a Mus* instrumental. ◆**instrumentiste** *nmf Mus* instrumentalist.

insu de (à l') [alɛ̃syd(ə)] *prép* without the knowledge of.

insuccès [ɛ̃syksɛ] *nm* failure.

insuffisant [ɛ̃syfizɑ̃] *a* (*en qualité*) inadequate; (*en quantité*) insufficient, inadequate. ◆**insuffisance** *nf* inadequacy.

insulaire [ɛ̃sylɛr] *a* insular; -- *nmf* islander.

insuline [ɛ̃sylin] *nf Méd* insulin.

insulte [ɛ̃sylt] *nf* insult (à to). ◆**insulter** *vt* to insult.

insupportable [ɛ̃sypɔrtabl] *a* unbearable.

insurg/er (s') [sɛ̃syrʒe] *vpr* to rise (up), rebel (**contre** against). ◆**-é, -ée** *nmf a* insurgent, rebel. ◆**insurrection** *nf* insurrection, uprising.

insurmontable [ɛ̃syrmɔ̃tabl] *a* insurmountable, insuperable.

intact [ɛ̃takt] *a* intact.

intangible [ɛ̃tɑ̃ʒibl] *a* intangible.

intarissable [ɛ̃tarisabl] *a* inexhaustible.

intégral, -aux [ɛ̃tegral, -o] *a* full, complete; (*édition*) unabridged. ◆**intégralement** *adv* in full, fully. ◆**intégralité** *nf* whole (**de** of); **dans son i.** in full.

intègre [ɛ̃tɛgr] *a* upright, honest. ◆**intégrité** *nf* integrity.

intégr/er [ɛ̃tegre] *vt* to integrate (**dans** in); -- **s'i.** *vpr* to become integrated, adapt. ◆**-ante** *af* faire partie i. de to be part and parcel of. ◆**intégration** *nf* integration.

intellectuel, -elle [ɛ̃telɛktɥel] *a* & *nmf* intellectual.

intelligent [ɛ̃teliʒɑ̃] *a* intelligent, clever. ◆**intelligemment** [-amɑ̃] *adv* intelligently. ◆**intelligence** *nf* (*faculté*) intelligence; *pl Mil Pol* secret relations; **avoir l'i. de qch** (*compréhension*) to have an understanding of sth; **d'i. avec qn** in complicity with s.o. ◆**intelligentsia** [-dʒentsja] *nf* intelligentsia.

intelligible [ɛ̃teliʒibl] *a* intelligible. ◆**intelligibilité** *nf* intelligibility.

intempérance [ɛ̃tɑ̃perɑ̃s] *nf* intemperance.

intempéries [ɛ̃tɑ̃peri] *nfpl* les i. the elements, bad weather.

intempestif, -ive [ɛ̃tɑ̃pestif, -iv] *a* untimely.

intenable [ɛ̃tnabl] *a* (*position*) untenable; (*enfant*) unruly, uncontrollable.

intendant, -ante [ɛ̃tɑ̃dɑ̃, -ɑ̃t] *nmf Scol* bursar. ◆**intendance** *nf Scol* bursar's office.

intense [ɛ̃tɑ̃s] *a* intense; (*circulation, trafic*) heavy. ◆**intensément** *adv* intensely. ◆**intensif, -ive** *a* intensive. ◆**intensifier** *vt*, -- **s'i.** *vpr* to intensify. ◆**intensité** *nf* intensity.

intenter [ɛ̃tɑ̃te] *vt* **i. un procès à** *Jur* to institute proceedings against.

intention [ɛ̃tɑ̃sjɔ̃] *nf* intention; *Jur* intent; **avoir l'i. de faire** to intend to do; **à l'i. de qn** for s.o.; **à votre i.** for you. ◆**intentionné** *a* **bien i.** well-intentioned. ◆**intentionnel, -elle** *a* intentional, wilful. ◆**intentionnellement** *adv* intentionally.

inter- [ɛ̃ter] *préf* inter-.

interaction [ɛ̃teraksjɔ̃] *nf* interaction.

intercaler [ɛ̃terkale] *vt* to insert.

intercéder [ɛ̃tersede] *vt* to intercede (**auprès de** with).

intercepter [ɛ̃tersepte] *vt* to intercept. ◆**interception** *nf* interception.

interchangeable [ɛ̃terʃɑ̃ʒabl] *a* interchangeable.

interclasse [ɛ̃terklɑs] *nm Scol* break (between classes).

intercontinental, -aux [ɛ̃terkɔ̃tinɑtal, -o] *a* intercontinental.

interdépendant [ɛ̃tɛrdepɑ̃dɑ̃] *a* interdependent.

interd/ire* [ɛ̃tɛrdir] *vt* to forbid, not to allow (**qch à qn** s.o. sth); (*meeting, film etc*) to ban; **i. à qn de faire** (*médecin, père etc*) not to allow s.o. to do, forbid s.o. to do; (*attitude, santé etc*) to prevent s.o. from doing, not allow s.o. to do. ◆**—it a 1** forbidden, not allowed; **il est i. de** it is forbidden to; **'stationnement i.'** 'no parking'. **2** (*étonné*) nonplussed. ◆**interdiction** *nf* ban (**de** on); **'i. de fumer'** 'no smoking'.

intéress/er [ɛ̃terese] *vt* to interest; (*concerner*) to concern; **s'i. à** to take an interest in, be interested in. ◆**—ant** *a* (*captivant*) interesting; (*affaire, prix etc*) attractive, worthwhile. ◆**—é, -ée** *a* (*avide*) self-interested; (*motif*) selfish; (*concerné*) concerned; **–** *nmf* **l'i.** the interested party.

intérêt [ɛ̃terɛ] *nm* interest; *Péj* self-interest; *pl Fin* interest; **tu as i. à faire** it would pay you to do, you'd do well to do; **des intérêts dans** *Com* an interest *ou* stake in.

interface [ɛ̃tɛrfas] *nf Tech* interface.

intérieur [ɛ̃terjœr] *a* (*cour, paroi*) inner, interior; (*poche*) inside; (*vie, sentiment*) inner, inward; (*mer*) inland; (*politique, vol*) internal, domestic; **–** *nm* (*de boîte etc*) inside (**de** of); (*de maison*) interior, inside; (*de pays*) interior; **à l'i.** (**de**) inside; **d'i.** (*vêtement, jeux*) indoor; **femme d'i.** home-loving woman; **ministère de l'I.** Home Office, *Am* Department of the Interior. ◆**—ement** *adv* (*dans le cœur*) inwardly.

intérim [ɛ̃terim] *nm* **pendant l'i.** in the interim; **assurer l'i.** to deputize (**de** for); **ministre/etc par i.** acting minister/*etc.* ◆**intérimaire** *a* temporary, interim; **–** *nmf* (*fonctionnaire*) deputy; (*secrétaire*) temporary.

interligne [ɛ̃tɛrliɲ] *nm Typ* space (between the lines).

interlocuteur, -trice [ɛ̃tɛrlɔkytœr, -tris] *nmf Pol* negotiator; **mon i.** the person I am, was *etc* speaking to.

interloqué [ɛ̃tɛrlɔke] *a* dumbfounded.

interlude [ɛ̃tɛrlyd] *nm Mus TV* interlude.

intermède [ɛ̃tɛrmɛd] *nm* (*interruption*) & *Th* interlude.

intermédiaire [ɛ̃tɛrmedjɛr] *a* intermediate; **–** *nmf* intermediary; **par l'i. de** through (the medium of).

interminable [ɛ̃tɛrminabl] *a* endless, interminable.

intermittent [ɛ̃tɛrmitɑ̃] *a* intermittent. ◆**intermittence** *nf* **par i.** intermittently.

international, -aux [ɛ̃tɛrnasjɔnal, -o] *a* international; **–** *nm* (*joueur*) *Sp* international.

interne [ɛ̃tɛrn] **1** *a* (*douleur etc*) internal; (*oreille*) inner. **2** *nmf Scol* boarder; **i.** (**des hôpitaux**) houseman, *Am* intern. ◆**internat** *nm* (*école*) boarding school.

intern/er [ɛ̃tɛrne] *vt* (*réfugié*) to intern; (*aliéné*) to confine. ◆**—ement** *nm* internment; confinement.

interpeller [ɛ̃tɛrpele] *vt* to shout at, address sharply; (*dans une réunion*) to question, (*interrompre*) to heckle; (*arrêter*) *Jur* to take in for questioning. ◆**interpellation** *nf* sharp address; questioning; heckling; (*de police*) arrest.

interphone [ɛ̃tɛrfɔn] *nm* intercom.

interplanétaire [ɛ̃tɛrplanetɛr] *a* interplanetary.

interpoler [ɛ̃tɛrpɔle] *vt* to interpolate.

interposer (s') [sɛ̃tɛrpoze] *vpr* (*dans une dispute etc*) to intervene (**dans** in); **s'i. entre** to come between.

interprète [ɛ̃tɛrprɛt] *nmf Ling* interpreter; (*chanteur*) singer; *Th Mus* performer; (*porte-parole*) spokesman, spokeswoman; **faire l'i.** *Ling* to interpret. ◆**interprétariat** *nm* (*métier*) *Ling* interpreting. ◆**interprétation** *nf* interpretation; *Th Mus* performance. ◆**interpréter** *vt* (*expliquer*) to interpret; (*chanter*) to sing; (*jouer*) *Th* to play, perform; (*exécuter*) *Mus* to perform.

interroger [ɛ̃tɛrɔʒe] *vt* to question; *Jur* to interrogate; (*faits*) to examine. ◆**interrogateur, -trice** *a* (*air*) questioning; **–** *nmf Scol* examiner. ◆**interrogatif, -ive** *a* & *nm Gram* interrogative. ◆**interrogation** *nf* question; (*action*) questioning; (*épreuve*) *Scol* test. ◆**interrogatoire** *nm Jur* interrogation.

interrompre* [ɛ̃tɛrɔ̃pr] *vt* to interrupt, break off; **i. qn** to interrupt s.o.; **– s'i.** *vpr* (*personne*) to break off, stop. ◆**interrupteur** *nm* (*bouton*) *Él* switch. ◆**interruption** *nf* interruption; (*des hostilités, du courant*) break (**de** in).

intersection [ɛ̃tɛrseksjɔ̃] *nf* intersection.

interstice [ɛ̃tɛrstis] *nm* crack, chink.

interurbain [ɛ̃tɛryrbɛ̃] *a* & *nm* (**téléphone**) **i.** long-distance telephone service.

intervalle [ɛ̃tɛrval] *nm* (*écart*) space, gap; (*temps*) interval; **dans l'i.** (*entretemps*) in the meantime.

intervenir* [ɛ̃tɛrvənir] *vi* (*s'interposer, agir*) to intervene; (*survenir*) to occur; (*opérer*) *Méd* to operate; **être intervenu** (*accord*) to be reached. ◆**intervention** *nf* intervention; **i.** (**chirurgicale**) operation.

intervertir [ɛ̃tɛrvɛrtir] *vt* to invert. ◆**interversion** *nf* inversion.

interview [ɛ̃tɛrvju] *nf Journ TV* interview. ◆**interviewer** [-vjuve] *vt* to interview.

intestin [ɛ̃tɛstɛ̃] *nm* intestine, bowel. ◆**intestinal, -aux** *a* intestinal, bowel-.

intime [ɛ̃tim] *a* intimate; (*ami*) close, intimate; (*vie, fête, journal*) private; (*pièce, coin*) cosy; (*cérémonie*) quiet; — *nmf* close *ou* intimate friend. ◆—**ment** *adv* intimately. ◆**intimité** *nf* intimacy; privacy; cosiness; **dans l'i.** (*mariage etc*) in private.

intimider [ɛ̃timide] *vt* to intimidate, frighten. ◆**intimidation** *nf* intimidation.

intituler [ɛ̃tityle] *vt* to entitle; — **s'i.** *vpr* to be entitled.

intolérable [ɛ̃tɔlerabl] *a* intolerable (**que** that). ◆**intolérance** *nf* intolerance. ◆**intolérant** *a* intolerant (**de** of).

intonation [ɛ̃tɔnasjɔ̃] *nf Ling* intonation; (*ton*) tone.

intoxiqu/er [ɛ̃tɔksike] *vt* (*empoisonner*) to poison; *Psy Pol* to brainwash; — **s'i.** *vpr* to be *ou* become poisoned. ◆—**é, -ée** *nmf* addict. ◆**intoxication** *nf* poisoning; *Psy Pol* brainwashing.

intra- [ɛ̃tra] *préf* intra-.

intraduisible [ɛ̃tradɥizibl] *a* untranslatable.

intraitable [ɛ̃trɛtabl] *a* uncompromising.

intransigeant [ɛ̃trɑ̃ziʒɑ̃] *a* intransigent. ◆**intransigeance** *nf* intransigence.

intransitif, -ive [ɛ̃trɑ̃zitif, -iv] *a & nm Gram* intransitive.

intraveineux, -euse [ɛ̃travɛnø, -øz] *a Méd* intravenous.

intrépide [ɛ̃trepid] *a* (*courageux*) fearless, intrepid; (*obstiné*) headstrong. ◆**intrépidité** *nf* fearlessness.

intrigue [ɛ̃trig] *nf* intrigue; *Th Cin Littér* plot. ◆**intrigant, -ante** *nmf* schemer. ◆**intriguer 1** *vi* to scheme, intrigue. **2** *vt* **i. qn** (*intéresser*) to intrigue s.o., puzzle s.o.

intrinsèque [ɛ̃trɛ̃sɛk] *a* intrinsic. ◆—**ment** *adv* intrinsically.

introduire* [ɛ̃trɔdɥir] *vt* (*présenter*) to introduce, bring in; (*insérer*) to insert (**dans** into), put in (**dans** to); (*faire entrer*) to show (*s.o.*) in; **s'i. dans** to get into. ◆**introduction** *nf* (*texte, action*) introduction.

introspectif, -ive [ɛ̃trɔspɛktif, -iv] *a* introspective. ◆**introspection** *nf* introspection.

introuvable [ɛ̃truvabl] *a* that cannot be found anywhere.

introverti, -ie [ɛ̃trɔvɛrti] *nmf* introvert.

intrus, -use [ɛ̃try, -yz] *nmf* intruder. ◆**intrusion** *nf* intrusion (**dans** into).

intuition [ɛ̃tɥisjɔ̃] *nf* intuition. ◆**intuitif, -ive** *a* intuitive.

inusable [inyzabl] *a Fam* hard-wearing.

inusité [inyzite] *a Gram* unused.

inutile [inytil] *a* unnecessary, useless; **c'est i. de crier** it's pointless *ou* useless to shout. ◆**inutilement** *adv* (*vainement*) needlessly. ◆**inutilité** *nf* uselessness.

inutilisable [inytilizabl] *a* unusable. ◆**inutilisé** *a* unused.

invalider [ɛ̃valide] *vt* to invalidate.

invariable [ɛ̃varjabl] *a* invariable. ◆—**ment** [-əmɑ̃] *adv* invariably.

invasion [ɛ̃vasjɔ̃] *nf* invasion.

invective [ɛ̃vɛktiv] *nf* invective. ◆**invectiver** *vt* to abuse; — *vi* **i. contre** to inveigh against.

invendable [ɛ̃vɑ̃dabl] *a* unsaleable. ◆**invendu** *a* unsold.

inventaire [ɛ̃vɑ̃tɛr] *nm* (*liste*) *Com* inventory; (*étude*) *Fig* survey; **faire l'i.** *Com* to do the stocktaking (**de** of).

inventer [ɛ̃vɑ̃te] *vt* (*découvrir*) to invent; (*imaginer*) to make up. ◆**inventeur, -trice** *nmf* inventor. ◆**inventif, -ive** *a* inventive. ◆**invention** *nf* invention.

inverse [ɛ̃vɛrs] *a* (*sens*) opposite; (*ordre*) reverse; *Math* inverse; — *nm* **l'i.** the reverse, the opposite. ◆**inversement** *adv* conversely. ◆**inverser** *vt* (*ordre*) to reverse. ◆**inversion** *nf Gram Anat etc* inversion.

investigation [ɛ̃vɛstigasjɔ̃] *nf* investigation.

invest/ir [ɛ̃vɛstir] **1** *vti Com* to invest (**dans** in). **2** *vt* **i. qn de** (*fonction etc*) to invest s.o. with. ◆—**issement** *nm Com* investment. ◆**investiture** *nf Pol* nomination.

invétéré [ɛ̃vetere] *a* inveterate.

invincible [ɛ̃vɛ̃sibl] *a* invincible.

invisible [ɛ̃vizibl] *a* invisible.

invit/er [ɛ̃vite] *vt* to invite; **i. qn à faire** to invite *ou* ask s.o. to do; (*inciter*) to tempt s.o. to do. ◆—**é, -ée** *nmf* guest. ◆**invitation** *nf* invitation.

invivable [ɛ̃vivabl] *a* unbearable.

involontaire [ɛ̃vɔlɔ̃tɛr] *a* involuntary. ◆—**ment** *adv* accidentally, involuntarily.

invoquer [ɛ̃vɔke] *vt* (*argument etc*) to put forward; (*appeler*) to invoke, call upon. ◆**invocation** *nf* invocation (**à** to).

invraisemblable [ɛ̃vrɛsɑ̃blabl] *a* incredible; (*improbable*) improbable. ◆**invraisemblance** *nf* improbability.

invulnérable [ɛ̃vylnerabl] *a* invulnerable.

iode [jɔd] *nm* **teinture d'i.** *Méd* iodine.

ira, irait [ira, irɛ] *voir* **aller 1**.

Irak [irak] *nm* Iraq. ◆**irakien, -ienne** *a & nmf* Iraqi.

Iran [irã] *nm* Iran. ◆**Iranien, -ienne** *a* & *nmf* Iranian.
irascible [irasibl] *a* irascible.
iris [iris] *nm* *Anat Bot* iris.
Irlande [irlãd] *nf* Ireland. ◆**irlandais, -aise** *a* Irish; − *nmf* Irishman, Irishwoman; − *nm* (*langue*) Irish.
ironie [ironi] *nf* irony. ◆**ironique** *a* ironic(al).
irradier [iradje] *vt* to irradiate.
irraisonné [irezɔne] *a* irrational.
irréconciliable [irekɔ̃siljabl] *a* irreconciliable.
irrécusable [irekyzabl] *a* irrefutable.
irréel, -elle [ireɛl] *a* unreal.
irréfléchi [irefleʃi] *a* thoughtless, unthinking.
irréfutable [irefytabl] *a* irrefutable.
irrégulier, -ière [iregylje, -jɛr] *a* irregular. ◆**irrégularité** *nf* irregularity.
irrémédiable [iremedjabl] *a* irreparable.
irremplaçable [irãplasabl] *a* irreplaceable.
irréparable [ireparabl] *a* (*véhicule etc*) beyond repair; (*tort, perte*) irreparable.
irrépressible [irepresibl] *a* (*rires etc*) irrepressible.
irréprochable [ireprɔʃabl] *a* beyond reproach, irreproachable.
irrésistible [irezistibl] *a* (*personne, charme etc*) irresistible.
irrésolu [irezɔly] *a* irresolute.
irrespirable [irespirabl] *a* unbreathable; *Fig* stifling.
irresponsable [irɛspɔ̃sabl] *a* (*personne*) irresponsible.
irrévérencieux, -euse [ireverãsjø, -øz] *a* irreverent.
irréversible [ireversibl] *a* irreversible.
irrévocable [irevɔkabl] *a* irrevocable.
irriguer [irige] *vt* to irrigate. ◆**irrigation** *nf* irrigation.

irriter [irite] *vt* to irritate; − **s'i.** *vpr* to get angry (**de, contre** at). ◆**-ant** *a* irritating; − *nm* irritant. ◆**irritable** *a* irritable. ◆**irritation** *nf* (*colère*) & *Méd* irritation.
irruption [irypsjɔ̃] *nf* **faire i. dans** to burst into.
islam [islam] *nm* Islam. ◆**islamique** *a* Islamic.
Islande [islãd] *nf* Iceland. ◆**islandais, -aise** *a* Icelandic.
isoler [izɔle] *vt* to isolate (**de** from); (*contre le froid etc*) & *Él* to insulate; − **s'i.** *vpr* to cut oneself off, isolate oneself. ◆**-ant** *a* insulating; − *nm* insulating material. ◆**-é** *a* isolated; (*écarté*) remote, isolated; **i. de** cut off *ou* isolated from. ◆**isolation** *nf* insulation. ◆**isolement** *nm* isolation. ◆**isolément** *adv* in isolation, singly. ◆**isoloir** *nm* polling booth.
isorel® [izɔrel] *nm* hardboard.
Israël [israɛl] *nm* Israel. ◆**israélien, -ienne** *a* & *nmf* Israeli. ◆**israélite** *a* Jewish; − *nm* Jew; − *nf* Jewess.
issu [isy] *a* **être i. de** to come from.
issue [isy] *nf* (*sortie*) exit, way out; (*solution*) *Fig* way out; (*résultat*) outcome; **à l'i. de** at the close of; **rue** *etc* **sans i.** dead end; **situation** *etc* **sans i.** *Fig* dead end.
isthme [ism] *nm* *Géog* isthmus.
Italie [itali] *nf* Italy. ◆**italien, -ienne** *a* & *nmf* Italian; − *nm* (*langue*) Italian.
italique [italik] *a* *Typ* italic; − *nm* italics.
itinéraire [itinerɛr] *nm* itinerary, route.
itinérant [itinerã] *a* itinerant.
IVG [iveʒe] *nf* *abrév* (*interruption volontaire de grossesse*) (voluntary) abortion.
ivoire [ivwar] *nm* ivory.
ivre [ivr] *a* drunk (**de** with). ◆**ivresse** *nf* drunkenness; **en état d'i.** under the influence of drink. ◆**ivrogne** *nmf* drunk(ard).

J

J, j [ʒi] *nm* J, j; **le jour J.** D-day.
j' [ʒ] *voir* **je.**
jacasser [ʒakase] *vi* (*personne, pie*) to chatter.
jachère (en) [ãʒaʃer] *adv* (*champ etc*) fallow.
jacinthe [ʒasɛ̃t] *nf* hyacinth.
jacousi [ʒakuzi] *nm* (*baignoire, piscine*) jacuzzi.

jade [ʒad] *nm* (*pierre*) jade.
jadis [ʒadis] *adv* at one time, once.
jaguar [ʒagwar] *nm* (*animal*) jaguar.
jaillir [ʒajir] *vi* (*liquide*) to spurt (out), gush (out); (*lumière*) to flash, stream; (*cri*) to burst out; (*vérité*) to burst forth; (*étincelle*) to fly out. ◆**-issement** *nm* (*de liquide*) gush.
jais [ʒɛ] *nm* (*noir*) **de j.** jet-black.

jalon [ʒalɔ̃] *nm* (*piquet*) marker; **poser les jalons** *Fig* to prepare the way (**de** for). ◆**jalonner** *vt* to mark (out); (*border*) to line.

jaloux, -ouse [ʒalu, -uz] *a* jealous (**de** of). ◆**jalouser** *vt* to envy. ◆**jalousie** *nf* 1 jealousy. 2 (*persienne*) venetian blind.

Jamaïque [ʒamaik] *nf* Jamaica.

jamais [ʒamɛ] *adv* 1 (*négatif*) never; **sans j. sortir** without ever going out; **elle ne sort j.** she never goes out. 2 (*positif*) ever; **à (tout) j.** for ever; **si j.** if ever.

jambe [ʒɑ̃b] *nf* leg; **à toutes jambes** as fast as one can; **prendre ses jambes à son cou** to take to one's heels.

jambon [ʒɑ̃bɔ̃] *nm Culin* ham. ◆**jambonneau, -x** *nm* knuckle of ham.

jante [ʒɑ̃t] *nf* (*de roue*) rim.

janvier [ʒɑ̃vje] *nm* January.

Japon [ʒapɔ̃] *nm* Japan. ◆**japonais, -aise** *a & nmf* Japanese; — & *nm* (*langue*) Japanese.

japp/er [ʒape] *vi* (*chien etc*) to yap, yelp. ◆**-ement** *nm* yap, yelp.

jaquette [ʒakɛt] *nf* (*d'homme*) tailcoat, morning coat; (*de femme, livre*) jacket.

jardin [ʒardɛ̃] *nm* garden; **j. d'enfants** kindergarten, playschool; **j. public** park; (*plus petit*) gardens. ◆**jardinage** *nm* gardening. ◆**jardiner** *vi* to do the garden, be gardening. ◆**jardinerie** *nf* garden centre. ◆**jardinier** *nm* gardener. ◆**jardinière** *nf* (*personne*) gardener; (*caisse à fleurs*) window box; **j. (de légumes)** *Culin* mixed vegetable dish; **j. d'enfants** kindergarten teacher.

jargon [ʒargɔ̃] *nm* jargon.

jarret [ʒarɛ] *nm Anat* back of the knee.

jarretelle [ʒartɛl] *nf* (*de gaine*) suspender, *Am* garter. ◆**jarretière** *nf* (*autour de la jambe*) garter.

jaser [ʒaze] *vi* (*bavarder*) to jabber.

jasmin [ʒasmɛ̃] *nm Bot* jasmine.

jatte [ʒat] *nf* (*bol*) bowl.

jauge [ʒoʒ] *nf* 1 (*instrument*) gauge. 2 (*capacité*) capacity; *Nau* tonnage. ◆**jauger** *vt* (*personne*) *Litt* to size up.

jaune [ʒon] 1 *a* yellow; — *nm* (*couleur*) yellow; **j. d'œuf** (egg) yolk. 2 *nm* (*ouvrier*) *Péj* blackleg, scab. ◆**jaunâtre** *a* yellowish. ◆**jaunir** *vti* to (turn) yellow. ◆**jaunisse** *nf Méd* jaundice.

Javel (eau de) [odʒavɛl] *nf* bleach. ◆**javeliser** *vt* to chlorinate.

javelot [ʒavlo] *nm* javelin.

jazz [dʒaz] *nm* jazz.

je [ʒ(ə)] *pron* (**j'** *before vowel or mute h*) I; **je suis** I am.

jean [dʒin] *nm* (pair of) jeans.

jeep [dʒip] *nf* jeep.

je-m'en-fichisme [ʒmɑ̃fiʃism] *nm inv Fam* couldn't-care-less attitude.

jérémiades [ʒeremjad] *nfpl Fam* lamentations.

jerrycan [(d)ʒerikan] *nm* jerry can.

jersey [ʒɛrzɛ] *nm* (*tissu*) jersey.

Jersey [ʒɛrzɛ] *nf* Jersey.

jésuite [ʒezɥit] *nm* Jesuit.

Jésus [ʒezy] *nm* Jesus; **J.-Christ** Jesus Christ.

jet [ʒɛ] *nm* throw; (*de vapeur*) burst, gush; (*de lumière*) flash; **j. d'eau** fountain; **premier j.** (*ébauche*) first draft; **d'un seul j.** in one go.

jetée [ʒ(ə)te] *nf* pier, jetty.

jeter [ʒ(ə)te] *vt* to throw (**à** to, **dans** into); (*mettre à la poubelle*) to throw away; (*ancre, regard, sort*) to cast; (*bases*) to lay; (*cri, son*) to let out, utter; (*éclat, lueur*) to throw out, give out; (*noter*) to jot down; **j. un coup d'œil sur** *ou* **à** to have a look at; (*rapidement*) to glance at; **— se j.** *vpr* to throw oneself; **se j. sur** to fall on, pounce on; **se j. contre** (*véhicule*) to crash into; **se j. dans** (*fleuve*) to flow into. ◆**jetable** *a* (*rasoir etc*) disposable.

jeton [ʒ(ə)tɔ̃] *nm* (*pièce*) token; (*pour compter*) counter; (*à la roulette*) chip.

jeu, -x [ʒø] *nm* 1 game; (*amusement*) play; (*d'argent*) gambling; *Th* acting; *Mus* playing; **j. de mots** play on words, pun; **jeux de société** parlour *ou* party games; **j. télévisé** television quiz; **maison de jeux** gambling club; **en j.** (*en cause*) at stake; (*forces etc*) at work; **entrer en j.** to come into play. 2 (*série complète*) set; (*de cartes*) pack, deck, *Am* deck; (*cartes en main*) hand; **j. d'échecs** (*boîte, pièces*) chess set. 3 (*de ressort, verrou*) *Tech* play.

jeudi [ʒødi] *nm* Thursday.

jeun (à) [aʒœ̃] *adv* on an empty stomach; **être à j.** to have eaten no food.

jeune [ʒœn] *a* young; (*inexpérimenté*) inexperienced; **Dupont j.** Dupont junior; **d'allure j.** young-looking; **jeunes gens** young people; — *nmf* young person; **les jeunes** young people. ◆**jeunesse** *nf* youth; (*apparence*) youthfulness; **la j.** (*jeunes*) the young, the youth.

jeûne [ʒøn] *nm* fast; (*action*) fasting. ◆**jeûner** *vi* to fast.

joaillier, -ière [ʒɔaje, -jɛr] *nmf* jeweller.

◆**joaillerie** *nf* jewellery; (*magasin*) jewellery shop.

jockey [ʒɔkɛ] *nm* jockey.

jogging [dʒɔgiŋ] *nm Sp* jogging; (*chaussure*) running *ou* jogging shoe; **faire du j.** to jog.

joie [ʒwa] *nf* joy, delight; **feu de j.** bonfire.

joindre* [ʒwɛ̃dr] *vt* (*mettre ensemble, relier*) to join; (*efforts*) to combine; (*insérer dans une enveloppe*) to enclose (**à** with); (*ajouter*) to add (**à** to); **j. qn** (*contacter*) to get in touch with s.o.; **j. les deux bouts** *Fig* to make ends meet; **se j. à** (*se mettre avec, participer à*) to join. ◆**joint** *a* (*efforts*) joint, combined; **à pieds joints** with feet together; — *nm Tech* joint; (*de robinet*) washer. ◆**jointure** *nf Anat* joint.

joker [ʒɔkɛr] *nm Cartes* joker.

joli [ʒɔli] *a* nice, lovely; (*femme, enfant*) pretty. ◆**—ment** *adv* nicely; (*très, beaucoup*) awfully.

jonc [ʒ̃ɔ] *nm Bot* (bul)rush.

joncher [ʒ̃ɔʃe] *vt* to litter (**de** with); **jonché de** strewn *ou* littered with.

jonction [ʒ̃ɔksjɔ̃] *nf* (*de tubes, routes etc*) junction.

jongl/er [ʒ̃ɔgle] *vi* to juggle. ◆**—eur, -euse** *nmf* juggler.

jonquille [ʒ̃ɔkij] *nf* daffodil.

Jordanie [ʒɔrdani] *nf* Jordan.

joue [ʒu] *nf Anat* cheek; **coucher qn en j.** to aim (a gun) at s.o.

jouer [ʒwe] *vi* to play; *Th* to act; (*au tiercé etc*) to gamble, bet; (*à la Bourse*) to gamble; (*entrer en jeu*) to come into play; (*être important*) to count; (*fonctionner*) to work; **j. au tennis/aux cartes/etc** to play tennis/cards/etc; **j. du piano/du violon/etc** to play the piano/violin/etc; **j. des coudes** to use one's elbows; — *vt* (*musique, tour, jeu*) to play; (*risquer*) to gamble, bet (**sur** on); (*cheval*) to bet on; (*personnage, rôle*) *Th* to play; (*pièce*) *Th* to perform, put on; (*film*) to show, put on; **j. gros jeu** to play for high stakes; **se j. de** to scoff at; (*difficultés*) to make light of. ◆**jouet** *nm* toy; **le j. de qn** *Fig* s.o.'s plaything. ◆**joueur, -euse** *nmf* player; (*au tiercé etc*) gambler; **beau j., bon j.,** good loser.

joufflu [ʒufly] *a* (*visage*) chubby; (*enfant*) chubby-cheeked.

joug [ʒu] *nm Agr* & *Fig* yoke.

jouir [ʒwir] *vi* **1 j. de** (*savourer, avoir*) to enjoy. **2** (*éprouver le plaisir sexuel*) to come. ◆**jouissance** *nf* enjoyment; (*usage*) *Jur* use.

joujou, -x [ʒuʒu] *nm Fam* toy.

jour [ʒur] *nm* day; (*lumière*) (day)light;

(*ouverture*) gap, opening; (*aspect*) *Fig* light; **il fait j.** it's (day)light; **grand j., plein j.** broad daylight; **de nos jours** nowadays, these days; **au j. le j.** from day to day; **du j. au lendemain** overnight; **mettre à j.** to bring up to date; **mettre au j.** to bring into the open; **se faire j.** to come to light; **donner le j. à** to give birth to; **le j. de l'An** New Year's day. ◆**journalier, -ière** *a* daily. ◆**journée** *nf* day; **pendant la j.** during the day(time); **toute la j.** all day (long). ◆**journellement** *adv* daily.

journal, -aux [ʒurnal, -o] *nm* (news)paper; (*spécialisé*) journal; (*intime*) diary; **j.** (*parlé*) *Rad* news bulletin; **j. de bord** *Nau* logbook. ◆**journalisme** *nm* journalism. ◆**journaliste** *nmf* journalist. ◆**journalistique** *a* (*style etc*) journalistic.

jovial, -aux [ʒɔvjal, -o] *a* jovial, jolly. ◆**jovialité** *nf* jollity.

joyau, -aux [ʒwajo] *nm* jewel.

joyeux, -euse [ʒwajø, -øz] *a* merry, happy, joyful; **j. anniversaire!** happy birthday!; **j. Noël!** merry *ou* happy Christmas!

jubilé [ʒybile] *nm* (golden) jubilee.

jubiler [ʒybile] *vi* to be jubilant. ◆**jubilation** *nf* jubilation.

jucher [ʒyʃe] *vt*, **— se j.** *vpr* to perch (**sur** on).

judaïque [ʒydaik] *a* Jewish. ◆**judaïsme** *nm* Judaism.

judas [ʒyda] *nm* (*de porte*) peephole, spy hole.

judiciaire [ʒydisjɛr] *a* judicial, legal.

judicieux, -euse [ʒydisjø, -øz] *a* sensible, judicious.

judo [ʒydo] *nm* judo. ◆**judoka** *nmf* judo expert.

juge [ʒyʒ] *nm* judge; *Sp* referee, umpire; **j. d'instruction** examining magistrate; **j. de paix** Justice of the Peace; **j. de touche** *Fb* linesman. ◆**juger** *vt* (*personne, question etc*) to judge; (*affaire*) *Jur* to try; (*estimer*) to consider (**que** that); **j. qn** *Jur* to try s.o.; — *vi* **j. de** to judge; **jugez de ma surprise/etc** imagine my surprise/etc. ◆**jugement** *nm* judg(e)ment; (*verdict*) *Jur* sentence; **passer en j.** *Jur* to stand trial. ◆**jugeote** *nf Fam* commonsense.

jugé (au) [oʒyʒe] *adv* by guesswork.

juguler [ʒygyle] *vt* to check, suppress.

juif, juive [ʒɥif, ʒɥiv] *a* Jewish; — *nm* Jew; — *nf* Jew(ess).

juillet [ʒɥijɛ] *nm* July.

juin [ʒɥɛ̃] *nm* June.

jumeau, -elle, *pl* **-eaux, -elles** [ʒymo, -ɛl] **1** *a* (*frères, lits etc*) twin; — *nmf* twin. **2** *nfpl* (*longue-vue*) binoculars; **jumelles de théâ-tre** opera glasses. ◆**jumel/er** *vt* (*villes*) to twin. ◆**—age** *nm* twinning.

jument [ʒymɑ̃] *nf* (*cheval*) mare.

jungle [ʒɑ̃gl] *nf* jungle.

junior [ʒynjɔr] *nm* & *a* (*inv au sing*) *Sp* junior.

junte [ʒɛ̃t] *nf Pol* junta.

jupe [ʒyp] *nf* skirt. ◆**jupon** *nm* petticoat.

jurer [ʒyre] **1** *vi* (*blasphémer*) to swear. **2** *vt* (*promettre*) to swear (**que** that, **de faire** to do); — *vi* **j. de qch** to swear to sth. **3** *vi* (*contraster*) to clash (**avec** with). ◆**juré** *a* (*ennemi*) sworn; — *nm Jur* juror. ◆**juron** *nm* swearword, oath.

juridiction [ʒyridiksjɔ̃] *nf* jurisdiction.

juridique [ʒyridik] *a* legal. ◆**juriste** *nmf* legal expert, jurist.

jury [ʒyri] *nm Jur* jury; (*de concours*) panel (of judges), jury.

jus [ʒy] *nm* (*des fruits etc*) juice; (*de viande*) gravy; (*café*) *Fam* coffee; (*électricité*) *Fam* power.

jusque [ʒysk] *prép* **jusqu'à** (*espace*) as far as, (right) up to; (*temps*) until, (up) till, to; (*même*) even; **jusqu'à dix francs**/*etc* (*limite*) up to ten francs/*etc*; **jusqu'en mai**/*etc* until May/*etc*; **jusqu'où?** how far?; **j. dans/sous**/*etc* right into/under/*etc*; **j. chez moi** as far as my place; **jusqu'ici** as far as this; (*temps*) up till now; **en avoir j.-là** *Fam* to be fed up; — *conj* **jusqu'à ce qu'il vienne** until he comes.

juste [ʒyst] *a* (*équitable*) fair, just; (*légitime*) just; (*calcul, heure, réponse*) correct, right, accurate; (*remarque*) sound; (*oreille*) good; (*voix*) *Mus* true; (*vêtement*) tight; **un peu j.** (*quantité, repas etc*) barely enough; **très j.!** quite so *ou* right!; **à 3 heures j.** on the stroke of 3; — *adv* (*deviner, compter*) correctly, right, accurately; (*chanter*) in tune; (*exactement, seulement*) just; **au j.** exactly; **tout j.** (*à peine, seulement*) only just; **c'était j.!** (*il était temps*) it was a near thing!; **un peu j.** (*mesurer, compter*) a bit on the short side; — *nm* (*homme*) just man. ◆**justement** *adv* precisely, exactly, just; (*avec justesse ou justice*) justly. ◆**justesse** *nf* (*exactitude*) accuracy; **de j.** (*éviter, gagner etc*) just.

justice [ʒystis] *nf* justice; (*organisation, autorités*) law; **en toute j.** in all fairness; **rendre j. à** to do justice to. ◆**justicier, -ière** *nmf* dispenser of justice.

justifier [ʒystifje] *vt* to justify; — *vi* **j. de** to prove; — **se j.** *vpr Jur* to clear oneself (**de** of); (*attitude etc*) to be justified. ◆**justifiable** *a* justifiable. ◆**justificatif, -ive** *a* **document j.** supporting document, proof. ◆**justification** *nf* justification; (*preuve*) proof.

jute [ʒyt] *nm* (*fibre*) jute.

juteux, -euse [ʒytø, -øz] *a* juicy.

juvénile [ʒyvenil] *a* youthful.

juxtaposer [ʒykstapoze] *vt* to juxtapose. ◆**juxtaposition** *nf* juxtaposition.

K

K, k [kɑ] *nm* K, k.

kaki [kaki] *a inv* & *nm* khaki.

kaléidoscope [kaleidɔskɔp] *nm* kaleidoscope.

kangourou [kɑ̃guru] *nm* **1** (*animal*) kangaroo. **2**® (*porte-bébé*) baby sling.

karaté [karate] *nm Sp* karate.

kart [kart] *nm Sp* (go-)kart, go-cart. ◆**karting** [-iŋ] *nm Sp* (go-)karting.

kascher [kaʃɛr] *a inv Rel* kosher.

kayac [kajak] *nm* (*bateau*) *Sp* canoe.

képi [kepi] *nm* (*coiffure*) *Mil* kepi.

kermesse [kɛrmɛs] *nf* charity fête; (*en Belgique etc*) village fair.

kérosène [kerozɛn] *nm* kerosene, aviation fuel.

kibboutz [kibuts] *nm* kibbutz.

kidnapp/er [kidnape] *vt* to kidnap. ◆**—eur, -euse** *nmf* kidnapper.

kilo(gramme) [kilo, kilɔgram] *nm* kilo(gramme).

kilomètre [kilɔmetr] *nm* kilometre. ◆**kilométrage** *nm Aut* = mileage. ◆**kilométrique** *a* **borne k.** = milestone.

kilowatt [kilɔwat] *nm* kilowatt.

kimono [kimɔno] *nm* (*tunique*) kimono.

kinésithérapie [kineziterapi] *nf* physiotherapy. ◆**kinésithérapeute** *nmf* physiotherapist.

kiosque [kjɔsk] *nm* (*à journaux*) kiosk, stall; **k. à musique** bandstand.

kit [kit] *nm* (*meuble etc prêt à monter*) kit; **en k.** in kit form, ready to assemble.

klaxon® [klaksɔn] *nm Aut* horn. ◆**klaxon-ner** *vi* to hoot, *Am* honk.

km *abrév (kilomètre)* km.

k.-o. [kao] *a inv* **mettre k.-o.** *Boxe* to knock out.

kyrielle [kirjɛl] *nf* **une k. de** a long string of.

kyste [kist] *nm Méd* cyst.

L

L, l [ɛl] *nm* L, l.

l', la [l, la] *voir* **le.**

là [la] **1** *adv* there; *(chez soi)* in, home; **je reste là** I'll stay here; **c'est là que** *ou* **où** that's where; **c'est là ton erreur** that's *ou* there's your mistake; **là où il est** where he is; **à cinq mètres de là** five metres away; **de là son échec** *(cause)* hence his *ou* her failure; **jusque-là** *(lieu)* as far as that; **passe par là** go that way. **2** *adv* (*temps*) then; **jusque-là** up till then. **3** *int* **là, là!** *(pour rassurer)* there, there!; **alors là!** well!; **oh là là!** oh dear! **4** *voir* **ce², celui.**

là-bas [labɑ] *adv* over there.

label [label] *nm Com* label, mark *(of quality, origin etc).*

labeur [labœr] *nm Litt* toil.

labo [labo] *nm Fam* lab. ◆**laboratoire** *nm* laboratory; **l. de langues** language laboratory.

laborieux, -euse [labɔrjø, -øz] *a (pénible)* laborious; *(personne)* industrious; **les classes laborieuses** the working classes.

labour [labur] *nm* ploughing, *Am* plowing; digging over. ◆**labour/er** *vt (avec charrue)* to plough. *Am* plow; *(avec bêche)* to dig over; *(visage etc) Fig* to furrow. ◆**-eur** *nm* ploughman, *Am* plowman.

labyrinthe [labirɛ̃t] *nm* maze, labyrinth.

lac [lak] *nm* lake.

lacer [lase] *vt* to lace (up). ◆**lacet** *nm* **1** *(shoe- ou boot-)lace.* **2** *(de route)* twist, zig-zag; **route en l.** winding *ou* zigzag road.

lacérer [lasere] *vt (papier etc)* to tear; *(visage etc)* to lacerate.

lâche [lɑʃ] **1** *a* cowardly; – *nmf* coward. **2** *a (détendu)* loose, slack. ◆**lâchement** *adv* in a cowardly manner. ◆**lâcheté** *nf* cowardice; **une l.** *(action)* a cowardly act.

lâch/er [lɑʃe] *vt (main, objet etc)* to let go of; *(bombe, pigeon)* to release; *(place, études)* to give up; *(juron)* to utter, let slip; *(secret)* to let out; **l. qn** *(laisser tranquille)* to leave s.o. (alone); *(abandonner) Fam* to drop s.o.; **l. prise** to let go; – *vi (corde)* to give way; – *nm* release. ◆**-eur, -euse** *nmf Fam* deserter.

laconique [lakɔnik] *a* laconic.

lacrymogène [lakrimɔʒɛn] *a* **gaz l.** tear gas.

lacté [lakte] *a (régime)* milk-; **la Voie lactée** the Milky Way.

lacune [lakyn] *nf* gap, deficiency.

lad [lad] *nm* stable boy, groom.

là-dedans [lad(ə)dɑ̃] *adv (lieu)* in there, in-side. ◆**là-dessous** *adv* underneath. ◆**là-dessus** *adv* on it; on that; *(monter)* on top; *(alors)* thereupon. ◆**là-haut** *adv* up there; *(à l'étage)* upstairs.

lagon [lagɔ̃] *nm (small)* lagoon. ◆**lagune** *nf* lagoon.

laid [lɛ] *a* ugly; *(ignoble)* wretched. ◆**laideur** *nf* ugliness.

laine [lɛn] *nf* wool; **de l., en l.** woollen. ◆**lainage** *nm (vêtement)* woollen garment, woolly; *(étoffe)* woollen material; *pl (vêtements, objets fabriqués)* woollens. ◆**laineux, -euse** *a* woolly.

laïque [laik] *a (vie)* secular; *(habit, tribunal)* lay; – *nmf (non-prêtre)* layman, laywoman.

laisse [lɛs] *nf* lead, leash; **en l.** on a lead *ou* leash.

laisser [lese] *vt* to leave; **l. qn partir/entrer/etc** *(permettre)* to let s.o. go/come in/etc; **l. qch à qn** *(confier, donner)* to let s.o. have sth, leave sth with s.o.; *(vendre)* to let s.o. have sth; **laissez-moi le temps de le faire** give me *ou* leave me time to do it; **se l. aller/faire** to let oneself go/be pushed around. ◆**laissé(e)-pour-compte** *nmf (personne)* misfit, reject. ◆**laisser-aller** *nm inv* carelessness, slovenliness; ◆**laissez-passer** *nm inv (sauf-conduit)* pass.

lait [lɛ] *nm* milk; **frère/sœur de l.** fos-ter-brother/-sister; **dent de l.** milk tooth. ◆**laitage** *nm* milk product *ou* food. ◆**laiterie** *nf* dairy. ◆**laiteux, -euse** *a* milky. ◆**laitier, -ière** *a (produits)* dairy-; – *nm (livreur)* milkman; *(vendeur)* dairy-man; – *nf* dairywoman.

laiton [lɛtɔ̃] *nm* brass.

laitue [lety] *nf* lettuce.

laïus [lajys] *nm Fam* speech.

lama [lama] *nm* (*animal*) llama.

lambeau, -x [lɑ̃bo] *nm* shred, bit; **mettre en lambeaux** to tear to shreds; **tomber en lambeaux** to fall to bits.

lambin, -ine [lɑ̃bɛ̃, -in] *nmf* dawdler. ◆**lambiner** *vi* to dawdle.

lambris [lɑ̃bri] *nm* panelling. ◆**lambrisser** *vt* to panel.

lame [lam] *nf* **1** (*de couteau, rasoir etc*) blade; (*de métal*) strip, plate; **l. de parquet** floorboard. **2** (*vague*) wave; **l. de fond** ground swell.

lamelle [lamɛl] *nf* thin strip; **l. de verre** (*pour microscope*) slide.

lamenter (se) [səlamɑ̃te] *vpr* to moan, lament; **se l. sur** to lament (over). ◆**lamentable** *a* (*mauvais*) deplorable; (*voix, cri*) mournful. ◆**lamentation** *nf* lament(ation).

laminé [lamine] *a* (*métal*) laminated.

lampadaire [lɑ̃pader] *nm* standard lamp; (*de rue*) street lamp.

lampe [lɑ̃p] *nf* lamp; (*au néon*) light; (*de vieille radio*) valve, *Am* (vacuum) tube; **l. de poche** torch, *Am* flashlight.

lampée [lɑ̃pe] *nf Fam* gulp.

lampion [lɑ̃pjɔ̃] *nm* Chinese lantern.

lance [lɑ̃s] *nf* spear; (*de tournoi*) *Hist* lance; (*extrémité de tuyau*) nozzle; **l. d'incendie** fire hose.

lance-flammes [lɑ̃sflam] *nm inv* flame thrower. ◆**l.-pierres** *nm inv* catapult. ◆**l.-roquettes** *nm inv* rocket launcher.

lanc/er [lɑ̃se] *vt* (*jeter*) to throw (à to); (*avec force*) to hurl; (*navire, mode, acteur, idée*) to launch; (*regard*) to cast (à at); (*moteur*) to start; (*ultimatum*) to issue; (*bombe*) to drop; (*gifle*) to give; (*cri*) to utter; **— se l.** *vpr* (*se précipiter*) to rush; **se l. dans** (*aventure, discussion*) to launch into; **— nm un l.** a throw; **le l. de** the throwing of. ◆**—ée** *nf* momentum. ◆**—ement** *nm Sp* throwing; (*de fusée, navire etc*) launch(ing).

lancinant [lɑ̃sinɑ̃] *a* (*douleur*) shooting; (*obsédant*) haunting.

landau [lɑ̃do] *nm* (*pl* -s) pram, *Am* baby carriage.

lande [lɑ̃d] *nf* moor, heath.

langage [lɑ̃gaʒ] *nm* (*système, faculté d'expression*) language; **l. machine** computer language.

lange [lɑ̃ʒ] *nm* (baby) blanket. ◆**langer** *vt* (*bébé*) to change.

langouste [lɑ̃gust] *nf* (spiny) lobster.

◆**langoustine** *nf* (Dublin) prawn, Norway lobster.

langue [lɑ̃g] *nf Anat* tongue; *Ling* language; **de l. anglaise/française** English-/French-speaking; **l. maternelle** mother tongue; **mauvaise l.** (*personne*) gossip. ◆**languette** *nf* (*patte*) tongue.

langueur [lɑ̃gœr] *nf* languor. ◆**langu/ir** *vi* to languish (**après** for, after); (*conversation*) to flag. ◆**—issant** *a* languid; (*conversation*) flagging.

lanière [lanjer] *nf* strap; (*d'étoffe*) strip.

lanterne [lɑ̃tern] *nf* lantern; (*électrique*) lamp; *pl Aut* sidelights.

lanterner [lɑ̃terne] *vi* to loiter.

lapalissade [lapalisad] *nf* statement of the obvious, truism.

laper [lape] *vt* (*boire*) to lap up; *— vi* to lap.

lapider [lapide] *vt* to stone.

lapin [lapɛ̃] *nm* rabbit; **mon (petit) l.!** my dear!; **poser un l. à qn** *Fam* to stand s.o. up.

laps [laps] *nm* **un l. de temps** a lapse of time.

lapsus [lapsys] *nm* slip (of the tongue).

laquais [lakɛ] *nm Hist & Fig* lackey.

laque [lak] *nf* lacquer; **l. à cheveux** hair spray, (hair) lacquer. ◆**laquer** *vt* to lacquer.

laquelle [lakɛl] *voir* **lequel**.

larbin [larbɛ̃] *nm Fam* flunkey.

lard [lar] *nm* (*fumé*) bacon; (*gras*) (pig's) fat. ◆**lardon** *nm Culin* strip of bacon *ou* fat.

large [larʒ] *a* wide, broad; (*vêtement*) loose; (*idées, esprit*) broad; (*grand*) large; (*généreux*) liberal; **l. d'esprit** broad-minded; **l. de six mètres** six metres wide; *— adv* (*calculer*) liberally, broadly; *— nm* breadth, width; **avoir six mètres de l.** to be six metres wide; **le l.** (*mer*) the open sea; **au l. de Cherbourg** *Nau* off Cherbourg; **être au l.** to have lots of room. ◆**—ment** *adv* widely; (*ouvrir*) wide; (*servir, payer*) liberally; (*au moins*) easily; **avoir l. le temps** to have plenty of time, have ample time. ◆**largesse** *nf* liberality. ◆**largeur** *nf* width, breadth; (*d'esprit*) breadth.

larguer [large] *vt* (*bombe, parachutiste*) to drop; **l. qn** (*se débarrasser de*) to drop s.o.; **l. les amarres** *Nau* to cast off.

larme [larm] *nf* tear; (*goutte*) *Fam* drop; **en larmes** in tears; **rire aux larmes** to laugh till one cries. ◆**larmoyer** *vi* (*yeux*) to water.

larve [larv] *nf* (*d'insecte*) larva, grub.

larvé [larve] *a* latent, underlying.

larynx [larɛ̃ks] *nm Anat* larynx. ◆**laryngite** *nf Méd* laryngitis.

las, lasse [lɑ, lɑs] *a* tired, weary (**de** of).

◆**lasser** vt to tire, weary; **se l. de** to tire of.
◆**lassitude** nf tiredness, weariness.
lascar [laskar] nm Fam (clever) fellow.
lascif, -ive [lasif, -iv] a lascivious.
laser [lazɛr] nm laser.
lasso [laso] nm lasso.
latent [latã] a latent.
latéral, -aux [lateral, -o] a lateral, side-.
latin, -ine [latɛ̃, -in] a & nmf Latin; — nm (langue) Latin.
latitude [latityd] nf Géog & Fig latitude.
latrines [latrin] nfpl latrines.
latte [lat] nf slat, lath; (de plancher) board.
lauréat, -ate [lɔrea, -at] nmf (prize)winner; — a prize-winning.
laurier [lɔrje] nm Bot laurel, bay; **du l.** Culin bay leaves.
lavabo [lavabo] nm washbasin, sink; pl (cabinet) toilet(s), Am washroom.
lavande [lavãd] nf lavender.
lave [lav] nf Géol lava.
lave-auto [lavoto] nm car wash. ◆**l.-glace** nm windscreen ou Am windshield washer. ◆**l.-linge** nm washing machine. ◆**l.-vaisselle** nm dishwasher.
laver [lave] vt to wash; **l. qn de** (soupçon etc) to clear s.o. of; — **se l.** vpr to wash (oneself), Am wash up; **se l. les mains** to wash one's hands (Fig de of). ◆**lavable** a washable. ◆**lavage** nm washing; **l. de cerveau** Psy brainwashing. ◆**laverie** nf (automatique) launderette, Am laundromat. ◆**lavette** nf dish cloth; (homme) Péj drip. ◆**laveur** nm **l. de carreaux** window cleaner ou Am washer. ◆**lavoir** nm (bâtiment) washhouse.
laxatif, -ive [laksatif, -iv] nm & a Méd laxative.
laxisme [laksism] nm permissiveness, laxity. ◆**laxiste** a permissive, lax.
layette [lɛjɛt] nf baby clothes, layette.
le, la, pl **les** [l(ə), la, le] (le & la become l' before a vowel or mute h) **1** art déf (à + le = au, à + les = aux; de + le = du, de + les = des) the; **le garçon** the boy; **la fille** the girl; **venez, les enfants!** come children!; **les petits/rouges/etc** the little ones/red ones/etc; **mon ami le plus intime** my closest friend. **2** (généralisation, abstraction) **la beauté** beauty; **la France** France; **les Français** the French; **les hommes** men; **aimer le café** to like coffee. **3** (possession) **il ouvrit la bouche** he opened his mouth; **se blesser au pied** to hurt one's foot; **avoir les cheveux blonds** to have blond hair. **4** (mesure) **dix francs le kilo** ten francs a kilo. **5** (temps) **elle vient le lundi** she comes on Monday(s);

elle passe le soir she comes over in the evening(s); **l'an prochain** next year; **une fois l'an** once a year. **6** pron (homme) him; (femme) her; (chose, animal) it; pl them; **je la vois** I see her; I see it; **je le vois** I see him; I see it; **je les vois** I see them; **es-tu fatigué? — je le suis** are you tired? — I am; **je le crois** I think so.
leader [lidœr] nm Pol leader.
lécher [leʃe] vt to lick; **se l. les doigts** to lick one's fingers. ◆**lèche-vitrines** nm **faire du l.-vitrines** to go window-shopping.
leçon [ləsɔ̃] nf lesson; **faire la l. à qn** to lecture s.o.
lecteur, -trice [lɛktœr, -tris] nmf reader; Univ (foreign language) assistant; **l. de cassettes** cassette player. ◆**lecture** nf reading; pl (livres) books; **faire de la l. à qn** to read to s.o.; **de la l.** some reading matter.
légal, -aux [legal, -o] a legal; (médecine) forensic. ◆**légalement** adv legally. ◆**légaliser** vt to legalize. ◆**légalité** nf legality (de of); **respecter la l.** to respect the law.
légation [legasjɔ̃] nf Pol legation.
légende [leʒɑ̃d] nf **1** (histoire, fable) legend. **2** (de plan, carte) key, legend; (de photo) caption. ◆**légendaire** a legendary.
léger, -ère [leʒe, -ɛr] a light; (bruit, faute, fièvre etc) slight; (café, thé, argument) weak; (bière, tabac) mild; (frivole) frivolous; (irréfléchi) careless; **à la légère** (agir) rashly. ◆**légèrement** adv lightly; (un peu) slightly; (à la légère) rashly. ◆**légèreté** nf lightness; frivolity.
légiférer [leʒifere] vi to legislate.
légion [leʒjɔ̃] nf Mil & Fig legion. ◆**légionnaire** nm (de la Légion étrangère) legionnaire.
législatif, -ive [leʒislatif, -iv] a legislative; (élections) parliamentary. ◆**législation** nf legislation. ◆**législature** nf (période) Pol term of office.
légitime [leʒitim] a (action, enfant etc) legitimate; **en état de l. défense** acting in self-defence. ◆**légitimité** nf legitimacy.
legs [lɛg] nm Jur legacy, bequest; (héritage) Fig legacy. ◆**léguer** vt to bequeath (à to).
légume [legym] **1** nf vegetable. **2** nf **grosse l.** (personne) Fam bigwig.
lendemain [lɑ̃dmɛ̃] nm **le l.** the next day; (avenir) Fig the future; **le l. de** the day after; **le l. matin** the next morning.
lent [lɑ̃] a slow. ◆**lentement** adv slowly. ◆**lenteur** nf slowness.
lentille [lɑ̃tij] nf **1** Bot Culin lentil. **2** (verre) lens.
léopard [leɔpar] nm leopard.

lèpre [lɛpr] *nf* leprosy. ◆**lépreux, -euse** *a* leprous; – *nmf* leper.

lequel, laquelle, *pl* **lesquels, lesquelles** [ləkɛl, lakɛl, lekɛl] (+ à = **auquel,** à laquelle, **auxquel(le)s**; + de = **duquel,** de laquelle, **desquel(le)s**) *pron* (*chose, animal*) which; (*personne*) who, (*indirect*) whom; (*interrogatif*) which (one); **dans l.** in which; **parmi lesquels** (*choses, animaux*) among which; (*personnes*) among whom; **l. préférez-vous?** which (one) do you prefer?

les [le] *voir* **le.**

lesbienne [lɛsbjɛn] *nf* & *af* lesbian.

léser [leze] *vt* (*personne*) *Jur* to wrong.

lésiner [lezine] *vi* to be stingy (**sur** with).

lésion [lezjɔ̃] *nf* *Méd* lesion.

lessive [lesiv] *nf* (*produit*) washing powder; (*linge*) washing; **faire la l.** to do the wash(ing). ◆**lessiv/er** *vt* to scrub, wash. ◆**-é** *a* *Fam* (*fatigué*) washed-out; (*ruiné*) washed-up. ◆**-euse** *nf* (*laundry*) boiler.

lest [lɛst] *nm* ballast. ◆**lester** *vt* to ballast, weight down; (*remplir*) *Fam* to overload.

leste [lɛst] *a* (*agile*) nimble; (*grivois*) coarse.

léthargie [letarʒi] *nf* lethargy. ◆**léthargique** *a* lethargic.

lettre [lɛtr] *nf* (*missive, caractère*) letter; **en toutes lettres** (*mot*) in full; (*nombre*) in words; **les lettres** (*discipline*) *Univ* arts; **homme de lettres** man of letters. ◆**lettré, -ée** *a* well-read; – *nmf* scholar.

leucémie [løsemi] *nf* leuk(a)emia.

leur [lœr] **1** *a poss* their; **l. chat** their cat; **leurs voitures** their cars; – *pron poss* **le l., la l., les leurs** theirs. **2** *pron inv* (*indirect*) (to) them; **il l. est facile de...** it's easy for them to ....

leurre [lœr] *nm* illusion; (*tromperie*) trickery. ◆**leurrer** *vt* to delude.

lev/er [l(ə)ve] *vt* to lift (up), raise; (*blocus, interdiction*) to lift; (*séance*) to close; (*camp*) to strike; (*plan*) to draw up; (*impôts, armée*) to levy; **l. les yeux** to look up; – *vi* (*pâte*) to rise; (*blé*) to come up; – **se l.** *vpr* to get up; (*soleil, rideau*) to rise; (*jour*) to break; (*brume*) to clear, lift; – *nm* **le l. du soleil** sunrise; **le l. du rideau** *Th* the curtain. ◆**-ant** *a* (*soleil*) rising; – *nm* **le l. l'est.** ◆**-é** *a* **être l.** (*debout*) to be up. ◆**-ée** *nf* (*d'interdiction*) lifting; (*d'impôts*) levying; (*du courrier*) collection; **l. de boucliers** public outcry.

levier [ləvje] *nm* lever; (*pour soulever*) crowbar.

lèvre [lɛvr] *nf* lip; **du bout des lèvres** half-heartedly, grudgingly.

lévrier [levrije] *nm* greyhound.

levure [ləvyr] *nf* yeast.

lexique [lɛksik] *nm* vocabulary, glossary.

lézard [lezar] *nm* lizard.

lézarde [lezard] *nf* crack, split. ◆**lézarder 1** *vi* *Fam* to bask in the sun. **2 se l.** *vpr* to crack, split.

liaison [ljɛzɔ̃] *nf* (*rapport*) connection; (*routière etc*) link; *Gram Mil* liaison; **l. (amoureuse)** love affair; **en l. avec qn** in contact with s.o.

liane [ljan] *nf* *Bot* jungle vine.

liant [ljɑ̃] *a* sociable.

liasse [ljas] *nf* bundle.

Liban [libɑ̃] *nm* Lebanon. ◆**libanais, -aise** *a* & *nmf* Lebanese.

libell/er [libele] *vt* (*contrat etc*) to word, draw up; (*chèque*) to make out. ◆**-é** *nm* wording.

libellule [libelyl] *nf* dragonfly.

libéral, -ale, -aux [liberal, -o] *a* & *nmf* liberal. ◆**libéraliser** *vt* to liberalize. ◆**libéralisme** *nm* liberalism. ◆**libéralité** *nf* liberality; (*don*) liberal gift.

libérer [libere] *vt* (*prisonnier etc*) to (set) free, release; (*pays, esprit*) to liberate (**de** from); **l. qn de** to free s.o. of *ou* from; – **se l.** *vpr* to get free, free oneself (**de** of, from). ◆**libérateur, -trice** *a* (*sentiment etc*) liberating; – *nmf* liberator. ◆**libération** *nf* freeing, release; liberation; **l. conditionnelle** *Jur* parole. ◆**liberté** *nf* freedom, liberty; **en l. provisoire** *Jur* on bail; **mettre en l.** to free, release; **mise en l.** release.

libraire [librɛr] *nmf* bookseller. ◆**librairie** *nf* (*magasin*) bookshop.

libre [libr] *a* free (**de qch** from sth, **de faire** to do); (*voie, route*) clear; (*place*) vacant, free; (*école*) private (and religious); **l. penseur** freethinker. ◆**l.-échange** *nm* *Écon* free trade. ◆**l.-service** *nm* (*pl* **libres-services**) (*système, magasin etc*) self-service. ◆**librement** *adv* freely.

Libye [libi] *nf* Libya. ◆**libyen, -enne** *a* & *nmf* Libyan.

licence [lisɑ̃s] *nf* *Sp Com Littér* licence; *Univ* (*bachelor's*) degree; **l. ès lettres/sciences** arts/science degree; = BA/BSc, = *Am* BA/BS. ◆**licencié, -ée** *a* & *nmf* graduate; **l. ès lettres/sciences** bachelor of arts/science, = BA/BSc, = *Am* BA/BS.

licencier [lisɑ̃sje] *vt* (*ouvrier*) to lay off, dismiss. ◆**licenciement** *nm* dismissal.

licite [lisit] *a* licit, lawful.

licorne [likɔrn] *nf* unicorn.

lie [li] *nf* dregs.

liège [ljɛʒ] *nm* (*matériau*) cork.

lien [ljɛ̃] *nm* (*rapport*) link, connection; (*de*

parenté) tie, bond; (attache, ficelle) tie.
◆lier vt (attacher) to tie (up), bind; (relier)
to link (up), connect; (conversation, amitié)
to strike up; l. qn (unir, engager) to bind
s.o.; — se l. vpr (idées etc) to connect, link
together; se l. avec qn to make friends with
s.o.; amis très liés very close friends.

lierre [ljɛr] nm ivy.

lieu, -x [ljø] nm place; (d'un accident) scene;
les lieux (locaux) the premises; sur les lieux
on the spot; avoir l. to take place, be held;
au l. de instead of; avoir l. de faire (des
raisons) to have good reason to do; en premier l. in the first place, firstly; en dernier l.
lastly; l. commun commonplace. ◆l.-dit
nm (pl lieux-dits) Géog locality.

lieue [ljø] nf (mesure) Hist league.

lieutenant [ljøtnɑ̃] nm lieutenant.

lièvre [ljɛvr] nm hare.

ligament [ligamɑ̃] nm ligament.

ligne [liɲ] nf (trait, règle, contour, transport)
line; (belle silhouette de femme etc) figure;
(rangée) row, line; (se) mettre en l. to line
up; en l. Tél connected, through; entrer en
l. de compte to be of consequence, count;
faire entrer en l. de compte to take into account; grande l. Rail main line; les grandes
lignes Fig the broad outline; pilote de l. airline pilot; à la l. Gram new paragraph.

lignée [liɲe] nf line, ancestry.

ligoter [ligɔte] vt to tie up.

ligue [lig] nf (alliance) league. ◆se liguer
vpr to join together, gang up (contre
against).

lilas [lila] nm lilac; — a inv (couleur) lilac.

limace [limas] nf (mollusque) slug.

limaille [limaj] nf filings.

limande [limɑ̃d] nf (poisson) dab.

lime [lim] nf (outil) file. ◆limer vt to file.

limier [limje] nm (chien) bloodhound.

limite [limit] nf limit; (de propriété, jardin
etc) boundary; pl Fb boundary lines;
dépasser la l. to go beyond the bounds; — a
(cas) extreme; (vitesse, prix, âge etc) maximum; date l. latest date, deadline; date l.
de vente Com sell-by date. ◆limitatif, -ive
a restrictive. ◆limitation nf limitation;
(de vitesse) limit. ◆limiter vt to limit, restrict; (délimiter) to border; se l. à faire to
limit ou restrict oneself to doing.

limoger [limɔʒe] vt (destituer) to dismiss.

limonade [limɔnad] nf (fizzy) lemonade.

limpide [lɛ̃pid] a (eau, explication) (crystal)
clear. ◆limpidité nf clearness.

lin [lɛ̃] nm Bot flax; (tissu) linen; huile de l.
linseed oil.

linceul [lɛ̃sœl] nm shroud.

linéaire [lineɛr] a linear.

linge [lɛ̃ʒ] nm (pièces de tissu) linen; (à
laver) washing, linen; (torchon) cloth; l. (de
corps) underwear. ◆lingerie nf (de femmes) underwear; (local) linen room.

lingot [lɛ̃go] nm ingot.

linguiste [lɛ̃gɥist] nmf linguist. ◆linguis-
tique a linguistic; — nf linguistics.

lino [lino] nm lino. ◆linoléum nm linoleum.

linotte [linɔt] nf (oiseau) linnet; tête de l. Fig
scatterbrain.

lion [ljɔ̃] nm lion. ◆lionceau, -x nm lion
cub. ◆lionne nf lioness.

liquéfier [likefje] vt, — se l. vpr to liquefy.

liqueur [likœr] nf liqueur.

liquide [likid] a liquid; argent l. ready cash;
— nm liquid; du l. (argent) ready cash.

liquider [likide] vt (dette, stock etc) to liquidate; (affaire, travail) to wind up, finish
off; l. qn (tuer) Fam to liquidate s.o. ◆li-
quidation nf liquidation; winding up;
(vente) (clearance) sale.

lire¹ [lir] vti to read.

lire² [lir] nf (monnaie) lira.

lis¹ [lis] nm (plante, fleur) lily.

lis², lisent [li, liz] voir lire¹.

liseron [lizrɔ̃] nm Bot convolvulus.

lisible [lizibl] a (écriture) legible; (livre)
readable. ◆lisiblement adv legibly.

lisière [lizjɛr] nf edge, border.

lisse [lis] a smooth. ◆lisser vt to smooth;
(plumes) to preen.

liste [list] nf list; l. électorale register of electors, electoral roll; sur la l. rouge Tél
ex-directory, Am unlisted.

lit¹ [li] nm bed; l. d'enfant cot, Am crib; lits
superposés bunk beds; garder le l. to stay
in bed. ◆literie nf bedding, bed clothes.

lit² [li] voir lire¹.

litanie [litani] 1 nf (énumération) long list
(de of). 2 nfpl (prière) Rel litany.

litière [litjɛr] nf (couche de paille) litter.

litige [litiʒ] nm dispute; Jur litigation. ◆li-
tigieux, -euse a contentious.

litre [litr] nm litre.

littéraire [literɛr] a literary. ◆littérature nf
literature.

littéral, -aux [literal, -o] a literal.
◆—ement adv literally.

littoral, -aux [litɔral, -o] a coastal; — nm
coast(line).

liturgie [lityrʒi] nf liturgy. ◆liturgique a
liturgical.

livide [livid] a (bleuâtre) livid; (pâle) (ghastly) pale, pallid.

livre [livr] 1 nm book; l. de bord Nau log-

book; **l. de poche** paperback (book); **le l.,
l'industrie du l.** the book industry. **2** *nf*
(*monnaie, poids*) pound. ◆**livresque** *a*
(*savoir*) *Péj* bookish. ◆**livret** *nm* (*registre*)
book; *Mus* libretto; **l. scolaire** school report book; **l. de famille** family registration
book; **l. de caisse d'épargne** bankbook,
passbook.

livrée [livre] *nf* (*uniforme*) livery.

livrer [livre] *vt* (*marchandises*) to deliver (**à**
to); (*secret*) to give away; **l. qn à** (*la police
etc*) to give s.o. up *ou* over to; **l. bataille**
to do *ou* join battle; **— se l.** *vpr* (*se rendre*) to
give oneself up (**à** to); (*se confier*) to confide
(**à** in); **se l. à** (*habitude, excès etc*) to indulge
in; (*tâche*) to devote oneself to; (*désespoir,
destin*) to abandon oneself to. ◆**livraison**
nf delivery. ◆**livreur, -euse** *nmf* delivery
man, delivery woman.

lobe [lɔb] *nm Anat* lobe.

local, -aux [lɔkal, -o] **1** *a* local. **2** *nm & nmpl*
(*pièce, bâtiment*) premises. ◆**localement**
adv locally. ◆**localiser** *vt* (*déterminer*) to
locate; (*limiter*) to localize. ◆**localité** *nf*
locality.

locataire [lɔkatɛr] *nmf* tenant; (*hôte payant*)
lodger.

location [lɔkasjɔ̃] *nf* (*de maison etc*) renting;
(*à bail*) leasing; (*de voiture*) hiring; (*réservation*) booking; (*par propriétaire*) renting
(out), letting; leasing (out); hiring (out);
(*loyer*) rental; (*bail*) lease; **bureau de l.**
booking office; **en l.** on hire.

lock-out [lɔkawt] *nm inv* (*industriel*) lock-
out.

locomotion [lɔkɔmosjɔ̃] *nf* locomotion.
◆**locomotive** *nf* locomotive, engine.

locuteur [lɔkytœr] *nm Ling* speaker.
◆**locution** *nf* phrase, idiom; *Gram*
phrase.

logarithme [lɔgaritm] *nm* logarithm.

loge [lɔʒ] *nf* (*de concierge*) lodge; (*d'acteur*)
dressing-room; (*de spectateur*) *Th* box.

log/er [lɔʒe] *vt* (*recevoir, mettre*) to accommodate, house; (*héberger*) to put up; **être
logé et nourri** to have board and lodging; **—
vi** (*à l'hôtel etc*) to put up, lodge; (*habiter*)
to live; (*trouver à*) **se l.** to find somewhere
to live; (*temporairement*) to find somewhere to stay; **se l. dans** (*balle*) to lodge
(itself) in. ◆**—eable** *a* habitable.
◆**—ement** *nm* accommodation, lodging;
(*habitat*) housing; (*appartement*) lodgings,
flat, *Am* apartment; (*maison*) dwelling.
◆**—eur, -euse** *nmf* landlord, landlady.

logiciel [lɔʒisjɛl] *nm* (*d'un ordinateur*) software *inv*.

logique [lɔʒik] *a* logical; **—** *nf* logic.
◆**—ment** *adv* logically.

logistique [lɔʒistik] *nf* logistics.

logo [lɔgo] *nm* logo.

loi [lwa] *nf* law; *Pol* act; **projet de l.** *Pol* bill;
faire la l. to lay down the law (**à** to).

loin [lwɛ̃] *adv* far (away *ou* off); **Boston est l.
(de Paris)** Boston is a long way away (from
Paris); **plus l.** further, farther; (*ci-après*)
further on; **l. de là** *Fig* far from it; **au l.** in
the distance, far away; **de l.** from a distance; (*de beaucoup*) by far; **de l. en l.** every
so often. ◆**lointain** *a* distant, far-off; **—**
nm **dans le l.** in the distance.

loir [lwar] *nm* (*animal*) dormouse.

loisir [lwazir] *nm* **le l. de faire** the time to do;
moment de l. moment of leisure; **loisirs**
(*temps libre*) spare time, leisure (time); (*dis-
tractions*) spare-time *ou* leisure activities.

Londres [lɔ̃dr] *nm ou f* London.
◆**londonien, -ienne** *a* London-; **—** *nmf*
Londoner.

long, longue [lɔ̃, lɔ̃g] *a* long; **être l. (à faire)**
to be a long time *ou* slow (in doing); **l. de
deux mètres** two metres long; **—** *nm* **avoir
deux mètres de l.** to be two metres long;
tomber de tout son l. to fall flat; **(tout) le l.
de** (*espace*) (all) along; **tout le l. de** (*temps*)
throughout; **de l. en large** (*marcher etc*) up
and down; **en l. et en large** thoroughly; **en
l.** lengthwise; **à la longue** in the long run.
◆**l.-courrier** *nm Av* long-distance airliner.
◆**longue-vue** *nf* (*pl* **longues-vues**) telescope.

longer [lɔ̃ʒe] *vt* to pass *ou* go along; (*forêt,
mer*) to skirt; (*mur*) to hug.

longévité [lɔ̃ʒevite] *nf* longevity.

longitude [lɔ̃ʒityd] *nf* longitude.

longtemps [lɔ̃tɑ̃] *adv* (for) a long time;
trop/avant l. too/before long; **aussi l. que**
as long as.

longue [lɔ̃g] *voir* **long.** ◆**longuement** *adv*
at length. ◆**longuet, -ette** *a Fam* (fairly)
lengthy. ◆**longueur** *nf* length; *pl* (*de
texte, film*) over-long passages; **saut en l.** *Sp*
long jump; **à l. de journée** all day long; **l.
d'onde** *Rad & Fig* wavelength.

lopin [lɔpɛ̃] *nm* **l. de terre** plot *ou* patch of
land.

loquace [lɔkas] *a* loquacious.

loque [lɔk] **1** *nfpl* rags. **2** *nf* **l. (humaine)**
(*personne*) human wreck.

loquet [lɔkɛ] *nm* latch.

lorgner [lɔrɲe] *vt* (*regarder, convoiter*) to
eye.

lors [lɔr] *adv* **l. de** at the time of; **depuis l.,**

dès l. from then on; **dès l. que** (*puisque*) since.

losange [lɔzɑ̃ʒ] *nm Géom* diamond, lozenge.

lot [lo] *nm* **1** (*de loterie*) prize; **gros l.** top prize, jackpot. **2** (*portion, destin*) lot. ◆**loterie** *nf* lottery, raffle. ◆**lotir** *vt* (*terrain*) to divide into lots; **bien loti** *Fig* favoured by fortune. ◆**lotissement** *nm* (*terrain*) building plot; (*habitations*) housing estate *ou* development.

lotion [losjɔ̃] *nf* lotion.

loto [lɔto] *nm* (*jeu*) lotto.

louche [luʃ] **1** *a* (*suspect*) shady, fishy. **2** *nf Culin* ladle.

loucher [luʃe] *vi* to squint; **l. sur** *Fam* to eye.

louer [lwe] *vt* **1** (*prendre en location*) to rent (*house, flat etc*); (*à bail*) to lease; (*voiture*) to hire, rent; (*réserver*) to book; (*donner en location*) to rent (out), let; to lease (out); to hire (out); **maison/chambre à l.** house/room to let. **2** (*exalter*) to praise (**de** for); **se l. de** to be highly satisfied with. ◆**louable** *a* praiseworthy, laudable. ◆**louange** *nf* praise; **à la l. de** in praise of.

loufoque [lufɔk] *a* (*fou*) *Fam* nutty, crazy.

loukoum [lukum] *nm* Turkish delight.

loup [lu] *nm* wolf; **avoir une faim de l.** to be ravenous. ◆**l.-garou** *nm* (*pl* **loups-garous**) werewolf.

loupe [lup] *nf* magnifying glass.

louper [lupe] *vt Fam* (*train etc*) to miss; (*examen*) to fail; (*travail*) to mess up.

lourd [lur] *a* heavy (*Fig* **de** with); (*temps, chaleur*) close, sultry; (*faute*) gross; (*tâche*) arduous; (*esprit*) dull; – *adv* **peser l.** (*malle etc*) to be heavy. ◆**lourdaud, -aude** *a* loutish, oafish; – *nmf* lout, oaf. ◆**lourdement** *adv* heavily. ◆**lourdeur** *nf* heaviness; (*de temps*) closeness; (*d'esprit*) dullness.

loutre [lutr] *nf* otter.

louve [luv] *nf* she-wolf. ◆**louveteau, -x** *nm* (*scout*) cub (scout).

louvoyer [luvwaje] *vi* (*tergiverser*) to hedge, be evasive.

loyal, -aux [lwajal, -o] *a* (*fidèle*) loyal (**envers** to); (*honnête*) honest, fair (**envers** to). ◆**loyalement** *adv* loyally; fairly. ◆**loyauté** *nf* loyalty; honesty, fairness.

loyer [lwaje] *nm* rent.

lu [ly] *voir* **lire**[1].

lubie [lybi] *nf* whim.

lubrifi/er [lybrifje] *vt* to lubricate. ◆**—ant** *nm* lubricant.

lubrique [lybrik] *a* lewd, lustful.

lucarne [lykarn] *nf* (*ouverture*) skylight; (*fenêtre*) dormer window.

lucide [lysid] *a* lucid. ◆**lucidité** *nf* lucidity.

lucratif, -ive [lykratif, -iv] *a* lucrative.

lueur [lɥœr] *nf* (*lumière*) & *Fig* glimmer.

luge [lyʒ] *nf* toboggan, sledge.

lugubre [lygybr] *a* gloomy, lugubrious.

lui [lɥi] **1** *pron mf* (*complément indirect*) (to) him; (*femme*) (to) her; (*chose, animal*) (to) it; **je le lui ai montré** I showed it to him *ou* to her, I showed him it *ou* her it; **il lui est facile de . . .** it's easy for him *ou* her to . . . . **2** *pron m* (*complément direct*) him; (*chose, animal*) it; (*sujet emphatique*) he; **pour lui** for him; **plus grand que lui** taller than him; **il ne pense qu'à lui** he only thinks of himself. ◆**lui-même** *pron* himself; (*chose, animal*) itself.

luire* [lɥir] *vi* to shine, gleam. ◆**luisant** *a* (*métal etc*) shiny.

lumbago [lɔ̃bago] *nm* lumbago.

lumière [lymjɛr] *nf* light; **à la l. de** by the light of; (*grâce à*) *Fig* in the light of; **faire toute la l. sur** *Fig* to clear up; **mettre en l.** to bring to light. ◆**luminaire** *nm* (*appareil*) lighting appliance. ◆**lumineux, -euse** *a* (*idée, ciel etc*) bright, brilliant; (*ondes, source etc*) light-; (*cadran, corps etc*) *Tech* luminous.

lunaire [lynɛr] *a* lunar; **clarté l.** light *ou* brightness of of the moon.

lunatique [lynatik] *a* temperamental.

lunch [lœʃ, lœntʃ] *nm* buffet lunch, snack.

lundi [lœdi] *nm* Monday.

lune [lyn] *nf* moon; **l. de miel** honeymoon.

lunette [lynɛt] *nf* **1** **lunettes** glasses, spectacles; (*de protection, de plongée*) goggles; **lunettes de soleil** sunglasses. **2** (*astronomique*) telescope; **l. arrière** *Aut* rear window.

lurette [lyrɛt] *nf* **il y a belle l.** a long time ago.

luron [lyrɔ̃] *nm* **gai l.** gay fellow.

lustre [lystr] *nm* (*éclairage*) chandelier; (*éclat*) lustre. ◆**lustré** *a* (*par l'usure*) shiny.

luth [lyt] *nm Mus* lute.

lutin [lytɛ̃] *nm* elf, imp, goblin.

lutte [lyt] *nf* fight, struggle; *Sp* wrestling; **l. des classes** class warfare *ou* struggle. ◆**lutter** *vi* to fight, struggle; *Sp* to wrestle. ◆**lutteur, -euse** *nmf* fighter; *Sp* wrestler.

luxe [lyks] *nm* luxury; **un l. de** a wealth of; **de l.** (*article*) luxury-; (*modèle*) de luxe. ◆**luxueux, -euse** *a* luxurious.

Luxembourg [lyksɑ̃bur] *nm* Luxembourg.

luxure [lyksyr] *nf* lewdness, lust.

luxuriant [lyksyrjɑ̃] *a* luxuriant.

luzerne [lyzɛrn] *nf Bot* lucerne, *Am* alfalfa.
lycée [lise] *nm* (secondary) school, *Am* high school. ◆**lycéen, -enne** *nmf* pupil (*at lycée*).
lymphatique [lɛ̃fatik] *a* (*apathique*) sluggish.

lynch/er [lɛ̃ʃe] *vt* to lynch. ◆**—age** *nm* lynching.
lynx [lɛ̃ks] *nm* (*animal*) lynx.
lyre [lir] *nf Mus Hist* lyre.
lyrique [lirik] *a* (*poème etc*) lyric; (*passionné*) *Fig* lyrical. ◆**lyrisme** *nm* lyricism.
lys [lis] *nm* (*plante, fleur*) lily.

M

M, m [ɛm] *nm* M, m.
m *abrév* (*mètre*) metre.
M [məsjø] *abrév* = **Monsieur**.
m' [m] *voir* me.
ma [ma] *voir* mon.
macabre [makɑbr] *a* macabre, gruesome.
macadam [makadam] *nm* (*goudron*) tarmac.
macaron [makarɔ̃] *nm* (*gâteau*) macaroon; (*insigne*) (round) badge.
macaroni(s) [makarɔni] *nm(pl)* macaroni.
macédoine [masedwan] *nf* **m. (de légumes)** mixed vegetables; **m. (de fruits)** fruit salad.
macérer [masere] *vti Culin* to soak. ◆**macération** *nf* soaking.
mâcher [mɑʃe] *vt* to chew; **il ne mâche pas ses mots**, he doesn't mince matters *ou* his words.
machiavélique [makjavelik] *a* Machiavellian.
machin [maʃɛ̃] *nm Fam* (*chose*) thing, what's-it; (*personne*) what's-his-name.
machinal, -aux [maʃinal, -o] *a* (*involontaire*) unconscious, mechanical. ◆**—ement** *adv* unconsciously, mechanically.
machination [maʃinasjɔ̃] *nf* machination.
machine [maʃin] *nf* (*appareil, avion, système etc*) machine; (*locomotive, moteur*) engine; *pl Tech* machines, (heavy) machinery; **m. à coudre** sewing machine; **m. à écrire** typewriter; **m. à laver** washing machine. ◆**machinerie** *nf Nau* engine room. ◆**machiniste** *nm Th* stage-hand.
macho [matʃo] *nm* macho *m*; — *a* (*f inv*) (*attitude etc*) macho.
mâchoire [mɑʃwar] *nf* jaw.
mâchonner [mɑʃɔne] *vt* to chew, munch.
maçon [masɔ̃] *nm* builder; bricklayer; mason. ◆**maçonnerie** *nf* (*travaux*) building work; (*ouvrage de briques*) brickwork; (*de pierres*) masonry, stonework.
maculer [makyle] *vt* to stain (**de** with).

Madagascar [madagaskar] *nf* Madagascar.
madame, pl mesdames [madam, medam] *nf* madam; **oui m.** yes (madam); **bonjour mesdames** good morning (ladies); **Madame ou Mme Legras** Mrs Legras; **Madame** (*sur une lettre*) *Com* Dear Madam.
madeleine [madlɛn] *nf* (small) sponge cake.
mademoiselle, pl mesdemoiselles [madmwazɛl, medmwazɛl] *nf* miss; **oui m.** yes (miss); **bonjour mesdemoiselles** good morning (ladies); **Mademoiselle ou Mlle Legras** Miss Legras; **Mademoiselle** (*sur une lettre*) *Com* Dear Madam.
madère [madɛr] *nm* (*vin*) Madeira.
madone [madɔn] *nf Rel* madonna.
madrier [madrije] *nm* (*poutre*) beam.
maestro [maɛstro] *nm Mus* maestro.
maf(f)ia [mafja] *nf* Mafia.
magasin [magazɛ̃] *nm* shop, *Am* store; (*entrepôt*) warehouse; (*d'arme*) & *Phot* magazine; **grand m.** department store. ◆**magasinier** *nm* warehouseman.
magazine [magazin] *nm* (*revue*) magazine.
magie [maʒi] *nf* magic. ◆**magicien, -ienne** *nmf* magician. ◆**magique** *a* (*baguette, mot*) magic; (*mystérieux, enchanteur*) magical.
magistral, -aux [maʒistral, -o] *a* masterly, magnificent. ◆**—ement** *adv* magnificently.
magistrat [maʒistra] *nm* magistrate. ◆**magistrature** *nf* judiciary, magistracy.
magnanime [maɲanim] *a* magnanimous.
magnat [magna] *nm* tycoon, magnate.
magner (se) [səmaɲe] *vpr Fam* to hurry up.
magnésium [maɲezjɔm] *nm* magnesium.
magnétique [maɲetik] *a* magnetic. ◆**magnétiser** *vt* to magnetize. ◆**magnétisme** *nm* magnetism.
magnétophone [maɲetɔfɔn] *nm* (*Fam* **magnéto**) tape recorder; **m. à cassettes** cassette recorder. ◆**magnétoscope** *nm* video (cassette) recorder.

magnifique [maɲifik] *a* magnificent. ◆**magnificence** *nf* magnificence. ◆**magnifiquement** *adv* magnificently.

magnolia [maɲɔlja] *nm* (*arbre*) magnolia.

magot [mago] *nm* (*économies*) nest egg, hoard.

magouille(s) [maguj] *nf(pl)* Pol Fam fiddling, graft.

mai [mɛ] *nm* May.

maigre [mɛgr] *a* thin, lean; (*viande*) lean; (*fromage, yaourt*) low-fat; (*repas, salaire, espoir*) meagre; **faire m.** to abstain from meat ◆**maigrement** *adv* (*chichement*) meagrely. ◆**maigreur** *nf* thinness; (*de viande*) leanness; (*médiocrité*) Fig meagreness. ◆**maigrichon, -onne** *a* & *nmf* skinny (person). ◆**maigrir** *vi* to get thin(ner); – *vt* to make thin(ner).

maille [mɑj] *nf* (*de tricot*) stitch; (*de filet*) mesh; **m. filée** (*de bas*) run, ladder. ◆**maillon** *nm* (*de chaîne*) link.

maillet [majɛ] *nm* (*outil*) mallet.

maillot [majo] *nm* (*de sportif*) jersey; (*de danseur*) leotard, tights; **m. (de corps)** vest, *Am* undershirt; **m. (de bain)** (*de femme*) swimsuit; (*d'homme*) (swimming) trunks.

main [mɛ̃] *nf* hand; **tenir à la m.** to hold in one's hand; **à la m.** (*livrer, faire etc*) by hand; **la m. dans la m.** hand in hand; **haut les mains!** hands up!; **donner un coup de m. à qn** to lend s.o. a (helping) hand; **coup de m.** (*habileté*) knack; **sous la m.** at hand, handy; **en venir aux mains** to come to blows; **avoir la m. heureuse** to be lucky, have a lucky streak; **mettre la dernière m. à** to put the finishing touches to; **en m. propre** (*remettre qch*) in person; **attaque/vol à m. armée** armed attack/robbery; **homme de m.** henchman, hired man; **m. courante** handrail; **prêter m.-forte à** to lend assistance to. ◆**m.-d'œuvre** *nf* (*pl* **mains-d'œuvre**) (*travail*) manpower, labour; (*salariés*) labour *ou* work force.

maint [mɛ̃] *a* Litt many a; **maintes fois, à maintes reprises** many a time.

maintenant [mɛ̃tnɑ̃] *adv* now; (*de nos jours*) nowadays; **m. que** now that; **dès m.** from now on.

maintenir* [mɛ̃tnir] *vt* (*conserver*) to keep, maintain; (*retenir*) to hold, keep; (*affirmer*) to maintain (**que** that); **— se m.** *vpr* (*durer*) to be maintained; (*rester*) to keep; (*malade, vieillard*) to hold one's own. ◆**maintien** *nm* (*action*) maintenance (**de** of); (*allure*) bearing.

maire [mɛr] *nm* mayor. ◆**mairie** *nf* town hall; (*administration*) town council.

mais [mɛ] *conj* but; **m. oui, m. si** yes of course; **m. non** definitely not.

maïs [mais] *nm* (*céréale*) maize, *Am* corn; **farine de m.** cornflour, *Am* cornstarch.

maison [mɛzɔ̃] *nf* (*bâtiment*) house; (*immeuble*) building; (*chez-soi, asile*) home; *Com* firm; (*famille*) household; **à la m.** (*être*) at home; (*rentrer, aller*) home; – *a inv* (*pâté, tartes etc*) homemade; **m. de la culture** arts *ou* cultural centre; **m. d'étudiants** student hostel; **m. des jeunes** youth club; **m. de repos** rest home; **m. de retraite** old people's home. ◆**maisonnée** *nf* household. ◆**maisonnette** *nf* small house.

maître [mɛtr] *nm* master; **se rendre m. de** (*incendie*) to master, control; (*pays*) to conquer; **être m. de** (*situation etc*) to be in control of, be master of; **m. de soi** in control of oneself; **m. d'école** teacher; **m. d'hôtel** (*restaurant*) head waiter; **m. de maison** host; **m. chanteur** blackmailer; **m. nageur** (*sauveteur*) swimming instructor (and lifeguard). ◆**maîtresse** *nf* mistress; **m. d'école** teacher; **m. de maison** hostess; (*ménagère*) housewife; **être m. de** (*situation etc*) to be in control of; – *af* (*idée, poutre*) main; (*carte*) master.

maîtrise [mɛtriz] *nf* (*habileté, contrôle*) mastery (**de** of); (*grade*) *Univ* master's degree (**de** in); **m. (de soi)** self-control. ◆**maîtriser** *vt* (*émotion*) to master, control; (*sujet*) to master; (*incendie*) to (bring under) control; **m. qn** to subdue s.o.; **— se m.** *vpr* to control oneself.

majesté [maʒɛste] *nf* majesty; **Votre M.** (*titre*) Your Majesty. ◆**majestueux, -euse** *a* majestic, stately.

majeur [maʒœr] **1** *a* (*primordial*) & *Mus* major; **être m.** *Jur* to be of age; **la majeure partie de** most of; **en majeure partie** for the most part. **2** *nm* (*doigt*) middle finger.

majorer [maʒɔre] *vt* to raise, increase. ◆**majoration** *nf* (*hausse*) increase (**de** in).

majorette [maʒɔrɛt] *nf* (drum) majorette.

majorité [maʒɔrite] *nf* majority (**de** of); (*âge*) *Jur* coming of age, majority; (*gouvernement*) party in office, government; **en m.** in the *ou* a majority; (*pour la plupart*) in the main. ◆**majoritaire** *a* (*vote etc*) majority-; **être m.** to be in the *ou* a majority; **être m. aux élections** to win the elections.

Majorque [maʒɔrk] *nf* Majorca.

majuscule [maʒyskyl] *a* capital; – *nf* capital letter.

mal, maux [mal, mo] **1** *nm* Phil Rel evil;

(*dommage*) harm; (*douleur*) pain; (*maladie*) illness; (*malheur*) misfortune; **dire du m. de** to speak ill of; **m. de dents** toothache; **m. de gorge** sore throat; **m. de tête** headache; **m. de ventre** stomachache; **m. de mer** seasickness; **m. du pays** homesickness; **avoir le m. du pays**/*etc* to be homesick/*etc*; **avoir m. à la tête/à la gorge**/*etc* to have a headache/sore throat/*etc*; **ça (me) fait m., j'ai m.** it hurts (me); **faire du m. à** to harm, hurt; **avoir du m. à faire** to have trouble (in) doing; **se donner du m. pour faire** to go to a lot of trouble to do. **2** *adv* (*travailler etc*) badly; (*entendre, comprendre*) not too well; **aller m.** (*projet etc*) to be going badly; (*personne*) *Méd* to be bad *or* ill; **m. (à l'aise)** uncomfortable; **se trouver m.** to (feel) faint; **(ce n'est) pas m.** (*mauvais*) (that's) not bad; **pas m.** (*beaucoup*) *Fam* quite a lot (**de** of); **c'est m. de jurer**/*etc* (*moralement*) it's wrong to swear/*etc*; **de m. en pis** from bad to worse; **m. renseigner/interpréter/** *etc* to misinform/misinterpret/*etc.*

malade [malad] *a* ill, sick; (*arbre, dent*) diseased; (*estomac, jambe*) bad; **être m. du foie/cœur** to have a bad liver/heart; *– nmf* sick person; (*à l'hôpital, d'un médecin*) patient; **les malades** the sick. ◆**maladie** *nf* illness, sickness, disease. ◆**maladif, -ive** *a* (*personne*) sickly; (*morbide*) morbid.

maladroit [maladrwa] *a* (*malhabile*) clumsy, awkward; (*indélicat*) tactless. ◆**maladresse** *nf* clumsiness, awkwardness; tactlessness; (*bévue*) blunder.

malaise [malɛz] *nm* (*angoisse*) uneasiness, malaise; (*indisposition*) faintness, dizziness; **avoir un m.** to feel faint *ou* dizzy.

malaisé [maleze] *a* difficult.

Malaisie [malɛzi] *nf* Malaysia.

malaria [malarja] *nf* malaria.

malavisé [malavize] *a* ill-advised (**de faire** to do).

malax/er [malakse] *vt* (*pétrir*) to knead; (*mélanger*) to mix. ◆**–eur** *nm Tech* mixer.

malchance [malʃɑ̃s] *nf* bad luck; **une m.** (*mésaventure*) a mishap. ◆**malchanceux, -euse** *a* unlucky.

malcommode [malkɔmɔd] *a* awkward.

mâle [mal] *a* male; (*viril*) manly; *– nm* male.

malédiction [malediksjɔ̃] *nf* curse.

maléfice [malefis] *nm* evil spell. ◆**maléfique** *a* baleful, evil.

malencontreux, -euse [malɑ̃kɔ̃trø, -øz] *a* unfortunate.

malentendant, -ante [malɑ̃tɑ̃dɑ̃, -ɑ̃t] *nmf* person who is hard of hearing.

malentendu [malɑ̃tɑ̃dy] *nm* misunderstanding.

malfaçon [malfasɔ̃] *nf* defect.

malfaisant [malfəzɑ̃] *a* evil, harmful.

malfaiteur [malfɛtœr] *nm* criminal.

malformation [malfɔrmasjɔ̃] *nf* malformation.

malgré [malgre] *prép* in spite of; **m. tout** for all that, after all; **m. soi** (*à contrecœur*) reluctantly.

malhabile [malabil] *a* clumsy.

malheur [malœr] *nm* (*événement*) misfortune; (*accident*) mishap; (*malchance*) bad luck, misfortune; **par m.** unfortunately. ◆**malheureusement** *adv* unfortunately. ◆**malheureux, -euse** *a* (*misérable, insignifiant*) wretched, miserable; (*fâcheux*) unfortunate; (*malchanceux*) unlucky, unfortunate; *– nmf* (*infortuné*) (poor) wretch; (*indigent*) needy person.

malhonnête [malɔnɛt] *a* dishonest. ◆**malhonnêteté** *nf* dishonesty; **une m.** (*action*) a dishonest act.

malice [malis] *nf* mischievousness. ◆**malicieux, -euse** *a* mischievous.

malin, -igne [malɛ̃, -iɲ] *a* (*astucieux*) smart, clever; (*plaisir*) malicious; (*tumeur*) *Méd* malignant. ◆**malignité** *nf* (*méchanceté*) malignity; *Méd* malignancy.

malingre [malɛ̃gr] *a* puny, sickly.

malintentionné [malɛ̃tɑ̃sjɔne] *a* ill-intentioned (**à l'égard de** towards).

malle [mal] *nf* (*coffre*) trunk; (*de véhicule*) boot, *Am* trunk. ◆**mallette** *nf* small suitcase; (*pour documents*) attaché case.

malléable [maleabl] *a* malleable.

malmener [malməne] *vt* to manhandle, treat badly.

malodorant [malɔdɔrɑ̃] *a* smelly.

malotru, -ue [malɔtry] *nmf* boor, lout.

malpoli [malpɔli] *a* impolite.

malpropre [malprɔpr] *a* (*sale*) dirty. ◆**malpropreté** *nf* dirtiness.

malsain [malsɛ̃] *a* unhealthy, unwholesome.

malséant [malseɑ̃] *a* unseemly.

malt [malt] *nm* malt.

Malte [malt] *nf* Malta. ◆**maltais, -aise** *a nmf* Maltese.

maltraiter [maltrete] *vt* to ill-treat.

malveillant [malvɛjɑ̃] *a* malevolent. ◆**malveillance** *nf* malevolence, ill will.

malvenu [malvəny] *a* (*déplacé*) uncalled-for.

maman [mamɑ̃] *nf* mum(my), *Am* mom(my).

mamelle [mamɛl] *nf* (*d'animal*) teat; (*de*

vache) udder. ◆**mamelon** *nm* **1** (*de femme*) nipple. **2** (*colline*) hillock.

mamie [mami] *nf Fam* granny, grandma.

mammifère [mamifɛr] *nm* mammal.

manche [mɑ̃ʃ] **1** *nf* (*de vêtement*) sleeve; *Sp Cartes* round; **la M.** *Géog* the Channel. **2** *nm* (*d'outil etc*) handle; **m. à balai** broomstick; (*d'avion, d'ordinateur*) joystick. ◆**manchette** *nf* **1** (*de chemise etc*) cuff. **2** *Journ* headline. ◆**manchon** *nm* (*fourrure*) muff.

manchot, -ote [mɑ̃ʃo, -ɔt] **1** *a* & *nmf* one-armed *ou* one-handed (person). **2** *nm* (*oiseau*) penguin.

mandarin [mɑ̃darɛ̃] *nm* (*lettré influent*) *Univ Péj* mandarin.

mandarine [mɑ̃darin] *nf* (*fruit*) tangerine, mandarin (orange).

mandat [mɑ̃da] *nm* **1** (*postal*) money order. **2** *Pol* mandate; *Jur* power of attorney; **m. d'arrêt** warrant (**contre qn** for s.o.'s arrest). ◆**mandataire** *nmf* (*délégué*) representative, proxy. ◆**mandater** *vt* to delegate; *Pol* to give a mandate to.

manège [manɛʒ] *nm* **1** (*à la foire*) merry-go-round, roundabout; (*lieu*) riding-school; (*piste*) ring, manège; (*exercice*) horsemanship. **2** (*intrigue*) wiles, trickery.

manette [manɛt] *nf* lever, handle.

manger [mɑ̃ʒe] *vt* to eat; (*essence, électricité*) *Fig* to guzzle; (*fortune*) to eat up; (*corroder*) to eat into; **donner à m. à** to feed; — *vi* to eat; **on mange bien ici** the food is good here; **m. à sa faim** to have enough to eat; — *nm* food. ◆**mangeable** *a* eatable. ◆**mangeaille** *nf Péj* (bad) food. ◆**mangeoire** *nf* (feeding) trough. ◆**mangeur, -euse** *nmf* eater.

mangue [mɑ̃g] *nf* (*fruit*) mango.

manie [mani] *nf* mania, craze (**de** for). ◆**maniaque** *a* finicky, fussy; — *nmf* fusspot, *Am* fussbudget; **un m. de la propreté**/*etc* a maniac for cleanliness/*etc.*

manier [manje] *vt* to handle; **se m. bien** (*véhicule etc*) to handle well. ◆**maniabilité** *nf* (*de véhicule etc*) manoeuvrability. ◆**maniable** *a* easy to handle. ◆**maniement** *nm* handling; **m. d'armes** *Mil* drill.

manière [manjɛr] *nf* way, manner; *pl* (*politesse*) manners; **de toute m.** anyway, anyhow; **de m. à faire** so as to do; **à ma m.** my way, (in) my own way; **de cette m.** (in) this way; **la m. dont elle parle** the way (in which) she talks; **d'une m. générale** generally speaking; **faire des manières** (*chichis*) to make a fuss; (*être affecté*) to put on airs. ◆**maniéré** *a* affected; (*style*) mannered.

manif [manif] *nf Fam* demo.

manifeste [manifɛst] **1** *a* (*évident*) manifest, obvious. **2** *nm Pol* manifesto.

manifester [manifɛste] **1** *vt* to show, manifest; — **se m.** *vpr* (*apparaître*) to appear; (*sentiment, maladie etc*) to show *ou* manifest itself. **2** *vi Pol* to demonstrate. ◆**manifestant, -ante** *nmf* demonstrator. ◆**manifestation** *nf* **1** (*expression*) expression, manifestation; (*apparition*) appearance. **2** *Pol* demonstration; (*réunion, fête*) event.

manigance [manigɑ̃s] *nf* little scheme. ◆**manigancer** *vt* to plot.

manipuler [manipyle] *vt* (*manier*) to handle; (*faits, électeurs*) *Péj* to manipulate. ◆**manipulation** *nf* handling; *Péj* manipulation (**de** of); *pl Pol Péj* manipulation.

manivelle [manivɛl] *nf Aut* crank.

mannequin [mankɛ̃] *nm* (*femme, homme*) (fashion) model; (*statue*) dummy.

manœuvre [manœvr] **1** *nm* (*ouvrier*) labourer. **2** *nf* (*opération*) & *Mil* manoeuvre, *Am* maneuver; (*action*) manoeuvring; (*intrigue*) scheme. ◆**manœuvrer** *vt* (*véhicule, personne etc*) to manoeuvre, *Am* maneuver; (*machine*) to operate; — *vi* to manoeuvre, *Am* maneuver.

manoir [manwar] *nm* manor house.

manque [mɑ̃k] *nm* lack (**de** of); (*lacune*) gap; *pl* (*défauts*) shortcomings; **m. à gagner** loss of profit. ◆**manqu/er** *vt* (*chance, cible etc*) to miss; (*ne pas réussir*) to make a mess of, fail; (*examen*) to fail; — *vi* (*faire défaut*) to be short *ou* lacking; (*être absent*) to be absent (**à** from); (*être en moins*) to be missing *ou* short; (*défaillir, échouer*) to fail; **m. de** (*pain, argent etc*) to be short of; (*attention, cohérence*) to lack; **ça manque de sel**/*etc* it lacks salt/*etc*, there isn't any salt/*etc*; **m. à** (*son devoir*) to fail in; (*sa parole*) to break; **le temps lui manque** he's short of time, he has no time; **elle**/**cela lui manque** he misses her/that; **je ne manquerai pas de venir** I won't fail to come; **ne manquez pas de venir** don't forget to come; **elle a manqué (de) tomber** (*faillir*) she nearly fell; — *v imp* **il manque**/**il nous manque dix tasses** there are/we are ten cups short. ◆—**ant** *a* missing. ◆—**é** *a* (*médecin, pilote etc*) failed; (*livre*) unsuccessful. ◆—**ement** *nm* breach (**à** of).

mansarde [mɑ̃sard] *nf* attic.

manteau, -x [mɑ̃to] *nm* coat.

manucure [manykyr] *nmf* manicurist. ◆**manucurer** *vt Fam* to manicure.

manuel, -elle [manɥɛl] **1** a (travail etc) manual. **2** nm (livre) handbook, manual.

manufacture [manyfaktyr] nf factory. ◆**manufacturé** a (produit) manufactured.

manuscrit [manyskri] nm manuscript; (tapé à la machine) typescript.

manutention [manytɑ̃sjɔ̃] nf Com handling (of stores). ◆**manutentionnaire** nmf packer.

mappemonde [mapmɔ̃d] nf map of the world; (sphère) Fam globe.

maquereau, -x [makro] nm (poisson) mackerel.

maquette [makɛt] nf (scale) model.

maquill/er [makije] vt (visage) to make up; (voiture etc) Péj to tamper with; (vérité etc) Péj to fake; **— se m.** to make (oneself) up. ◆**—age** nm (fard) make-up.

maquis [maki] nm Bot scrub, bush; Mil Hist maquis.

maraîcher, -ère [mareʃe, -ɛʃɛr] nmf market gardener, Am truck farmer.

marais [marɛ] nm marsh, bog; **m. salant** saltworks, saltern.

marasme [marasm] nm Écon stagnation.

marathon [maratɔ̃] nm marathon.

maraudeur, -euse [marodœr, -øz] nmf petty thief.

marbre [marbr] nm marble. ◆**marbrier** nm (funéraire) monumental mason.

marc [mar] nm (eau-de-vie) marc, brandy; **m. (de café)** coffee grounds.

marchand, -ande [marʃɑ̃, -ɑ̃d] nmf trader, shopkeeper; (de vins, charbon) merchant; (de cycles, meubles) dealer; **m. de bonbons** confectioner; **m. de couleurs** hardware merchant ou dealer; **m. de journaux** (dans la rue) newsvendor; (dans un magasin) newsagent, Am news dealer; **m. de légumes** greengrocer; **m. de poissons** fishmonger; — a (valeur) market; (prix) trade-. ◆**marchandise(s)** nf(pl) goods, merchandise.

marchand/er [marʃɑ̃de] vi to haggle, bargain; — vt (objet) to haggle over. ◆**—age** nm haggling, bargaining.

marche [marʃ] nf **1** (d'escalier) step, stair. **2** (démarche, trajet) walk; Mil Mus march; (pas) pace; (de train, véhicule) movement; (de maladie, d'événement) progress, course; **la m.** (action) Sp walking; **faire m. arrière** Aut to reverse; **la bonne m.** (opération, machine) the smooth running of; **un train/véhicule en m.** a moving train/vehicle; **mettre qch en m.** to start sth (up). ◆**marcher** vi (à pied) to walk; Mil to

march; (poser le pied) to tread, step; (train, véhicule etc) to run, go, move; (fonctionner) to go, work, run; (prospérer) to go well; **faire m.** (machine) to work; (entreprise) to run; (personne) Fam to kid; **ça marche?** Fam how's it going?; **elle va m.** (accepter) Fam she'll go along (with it). ◆**marcheur, -euse** nmf walker.

marché [marʃe] nm (lieu) market; (contrat) deal; **faire son** ou **le m.** to do one's shopping (in the market); **être bon m.** to be cheap; **voiture(s)/etc bon m.** cheap car(s)/etc; **vendre (à) bon m.** to sell cheap(ly); **c'est meilleur m.** it's cheaper; **par-dessus le m.** Fig into the bargain; **au m. noir** on the black market; **le M. commun** the Common Market.

marchepied [marʃəpje] nm (de train, bus) step(s); (de voiture) running board.

mardi [mardi] nm Tuesday; **M. gras** Shrove Tuesday.

mare [mar] nf (flaque) pool; (étang) pond.

marécage [marekaʒ] nm swamp, marsh. ◆**marécageux, -euse** a marshy, swampy.

maréchal, -aux [mareʃal, -o] nm Fr Mil marshal. ◆**m.-ferrant** nm (pl maréchaux-ferrants) blacksmith.

marée [mare] nf tide; (poissons) fresh (sea) fish; **m. noire** oil slick.

marelle [marɛl] nf (jeu) hopscotch.

margarine [margarin] nf margarine.

marge [marʒ] nf margin; **en m. de** (en dehors de) on the periphery of, on the fringe(s) of; **m. de sécurité** safety margin. ◆**marginal, -ale, -aux** a (secondaire, asocial) marginal; — nmf misfit, dropout; (bizarre) weirdo.

marguerite [margərit] nf (fleur) marguerite, daisy.

mari [mari] nm husband.

mariage [marjaʒ] nm marriage; (cérémonie) wedding; (mélange) Fig blend, marriage; **demande en m.** proposal (of marriage). ◆**mari/er** vt (couleurs) to blend; **m. qn** (maire, prêtre etc) to marry s.o.; **m. qn avec** to marry s.o. (off) to; **— se m.** vpr to get married, marry; **se m. avec qn** to marry s.o., get married to s.o. ◆**—é** a married; — nm (bride)groom; **les mariés** the bride and (bride)groom; **les jeunes mariés** the newly-weds. ◆**—ée** nf bride.

marijuana [mariʒɥana] nf marijuana.

marin [marɛ̃] a (air, sel etc) sea-; (flore) marine; (mille) nautical; (costume) sailor-; — nm seaman, sailor. ◆**marine** nf m. (de guerre) navy; **m. marchande** merchant navy; **(bleu) m.** (couleur) navy (blue).

marina [marina] *nf* marina.

mariner [marine] *vti Culin* to marinate.

marionnette [marjɔnɛt] *nf* puppet; (*à fils*) marionette.

maritalement [maritalmɑ̃] *adv* **vivre m.** to live together (as husband and wife).

maritime [maritim] *a* (*droit, province, climat etc*) maritime; (*port*) sea-; (*gare*) harbour-; (*chantier*) naval; (*agent*) shipping-.

marjolaine [marʒɔlɛn] *nf* (*aromate*) marjoram.

mark [mark] *nm* (*monnaie*) mark.

marmaille [marmɑj] *nf* (*enfants*) *Fam* kids.

marmelade [marməlad] *nf* **m.** (**de fruits**) stewed fruit; **en m.** *Culin Fig* in a mush.

marmite [marmit] *nf* (*cooking*) pot.

marmonner [marmɔne] *vti* to mutter.

marmot [marmo] *nm* (*enfant*) *Fam* kid.

marmotter [marmɔte] *vti* to mumble.

Maroc [marɔk] *nm* Morocco. ◆**marocain, -aine** *a* & *nmf* Moroccan.

maroquinerie [marɔkinri] *nf* (*magasin*) leather goods shop. ◆**maroquinier** *nm* leather dealer.

marotte [marɔt] *nf* (*dada*) *Fam* fad, craze.

marque [mark] *nf* (*trace, signe*) mark; (*de fabricant*) make, brand; (*points*) *Sp* score; **m. de fabrique** trademark; **m. déposée** registered trademark; **la m. de** (*preuve*) the stamp of; **de m.** (*hôte, visiteur*) distinguished; (*produit*) of quality. ◆**marqu/er** *vt* (*par une marque etc*) to mark; (*écrire*) to note down; (*indiquer*) to show, mark; (*point, but*) *Sp* to score; **m. qn** *Sp* to mark s.o.; **m. les points** *Sp* to keep (the) score; **m. le coup** to mark the event; — *vi* (*trace*) to leave a mark; (*date, événement*) to stand out; *Sp* to score. ◆—**ant** *a* (*remarquable*) outstanding. ◆—**é** *a* (*différence, accent etc*) marked, pronounced. ◆—**eur** *nm* (*crayon*) marker.

marquis [marki] *nm* marquis. ◆**marquise** *nf* **1** marchioness. **2** (*auvent*) glass canopy.

marraine [marɛn] *nf* godmother.

marre [mar] *nf* **en avoir m.** *Fam* to be fed up (de with).

marr/er (se) [səmare] *vpr Fam* to have a good laugh. ◆—**ant** *a Fam* hilarious, funny.

marron¹ [marɔ̃] **1** *nm* chestnut; (*couleur*) (chestnut) brown; **m.** (**d'Inde**) horse chestnut; — *a inv* (*couleur*) (chestnut) brown. **2** *nm* (*coup*) *Fam* punch, clout. ◆**marronnier** *nm* (horse) chestnut tree.

marron², -onne [marɔ̃, -ɔn] *a* (*médecin etc*) bogus.

mars [mars] *nm* March.

marsouin [marswɛ̃] *nm* porpoise.

marteau, -x [marto] *nm* hammer; (*de porte*) (door)knocker; **m. piqueur, m. pneumatique** pneumatic drill. ◆**marteler** *vt* to hammer. ◆**martèlement** *nm* hammering.

martial, -aux [marsjal, -o] *a* martial; **cour martiale** court-martial; **loi martiale** martial law.

martien, -ienne [marsjɛ̃, -jɛn] *nmf* & *a* Martian.

martinet [martinɛ] *nm* (*fouet*) (small) whip.

martin-pêcheur [martɛ̃pɛʃœr] *nm* (*pl* martins-pêcheurs) (*oiseau*) kingfisher.

martyr, -yre¹ [martir] *nmf* (*personne*) martyr; **enfant m.** battered child. ◆**martyre²** *nm* (*souffrance*) martyrdom. ◆**martyriser** *vt* to torture; (*enfant*) to batter.

marxisme [marksism] *nm* Marxism. ◆**marxiste** *a* & *nmf* Marxist.

mascara [maskara] *nm* mascara.

mascarade [maskarad] *nf* masquerade.

mascotte [maskɔt] *nf* mascot.

masculin [maskylɛ̃] *a* male; (*viril*) masculine, manly; *Gram* masculine; (*vêtement, équipe*) men's; — *nm Gram* masculine. ◆**masculinité** *nf* masculinity.

masochisme [mazɔʃism] *nm* masochism. ◆**masochiste** *nmf* masochist; — *a* masochistic.

masque [mask] *nm* mask. ◆**masquer** *vt* (*dissimuler*) to mask (à from); (*cacher à la vue*) to block off.

massacre [masakr] *nm* massacre, slaughter. ◆**massacr/er** *vt* to massacre, slaughter; (*abîmer*) *Fam* to ruin. ◆—**ant** *a* (*humeur*) excruciating.

massage [masaʒ] *nm* massage.

masse [mas] *nf* **1** (*volume*) mass; (*gros morceau, majorité*) bulk (de of); **en m.** (*venir, vendre*) in large numbers; **départ en m.** mass *ou* wholesale departure; **manifestation de m.** mass demonstration; **la m.** (*foule*) the masses; **les masses** (*peuple*) the masses; **une m. de** (*tas*) a mass of; **des masses de** *Fam* masses of. **2** (*outil*) sledgehammer. **3** *El* earth, *Am* ground. ◆**mass/er 1** *vt*, — **se m.** *vpr* (*gens*) to mass. **2** *vt* (*frotter*) to massage. ◆—**eur** *nm* masseur. ◆—**euse** *nf* masseuse.

massif, -ive [masif, -iv] *a* (*argent, colonne etc*) massive; (*départs etc*) mass-; (*or, chêne etc*) solid. **2** *nm* (*d'arbres, de fleurs*) clump; *Géog* massif. ◆**massivement** *adv* (*en masse*) in large numbers.

massue [masy] *nf* (*bâton*) club.

mastic [mastik] *nm* (*pour vitres*) putty; (*pour bois*) filler; **m.** (**silicone**) mastic.

◆**mastiquer** vt (vitre) to putty; (porte) to mastic; (bois) to fill. **2** (mâcher) to chew, masticate.

mastoc [mastɔk] a inv Péj Fam massive.

mastodonte [mastɔdɔ̃t] nm (personne) Péj monster; (véhicule) juggernaut.

masturber (se) [səmastyrbe] vpr to masturbate. ◆**masturbation** nf masturbation.

masure [mazyr] nf tumbledown house.

mat [mat] **1** a (papier, couleur) mat(t); (bruit) dull. **2** a inv & nm Échecs (check)mate; **faire** ou **mettre m.** to (check)mate.

mât [mɑ] nm (de navire) mast; (poteau) pole.

match [matʃ] nm Sp match, Am game; **m. nul** le draw.

matelas [matla] nm mattress; **m. pneumatique** air bed. ◆**matelassé** a (meuble) padded; (tissu) quilted.

matelot [matlo] nm sailor, seaman.

mater [mate] vt (enfant, passion etc) to subdue.

matérialiser [materjalize] vt, **— se m.** vpr to materialize. ◆**matérialisation** nf materialization.

matérialisme [materjalism] nm materialism. ◆**matérialiste** a materialistic; – nmf materialist.

matériaux [materjo] nmpl (building) materials; (de roman, enquête etc) material.

matériel, -ielle [materjɛl] **1** a material; (personne) Péj materialistic; (financier) financial; (pratique) practical. **2** nm equipment, material(s); (d'un ordinateur) hardware inv. ◆**matériellement** adv materially; **m. impossible** physically impossible.

maternel, -elle [matɛrnɛl] a motherly, maternal; (parenté, réprimande) maternal; – nf (école) **maternelle** nursery school. ◆**materner** vt to mother. ◆**maternité** nf (état) motherhood, maternity; (hôpital) maternity hospital ou unit; (grossesse) pregnancy; **de m.** (congé, allocation) maternity-.

mathématique [matematik] a mathematical; – nfpl mathematics. ◆**mathématicien, -ienne** nmf mathematician. ◆**maths** [mat] nfpl Fam maths, Am math.

matière [matjɛr] nf (sujet) & Scol subject; (de livre) subject matter; **une m., la m., des matières** (substance(s)) matter; **m. première** raw material; **en m. d'art**/etc as regards art/etc, in art/etc; **s'y connaître en m. de** to be experienced in.

matin [matɛ̃] nm morning; **de grand m., de bon m., au petit m.** very early (in the morn-

ing); **le m.** (chaque matin) in the morning; **à sept heures du m.** at seven in the morning; **tous les mardis m.** every Tuesday morning. ◆**matinal, -aux** a (personne) early; (fleur, soleil etc) morning-. ◆**matinée** nf morning; Th matinée; **faire la grasse m.** to sleep late, lie in.

matou [matu] nm tomcat.

matraque [matrak] nf (de policier) truncheon, Am billy (club); (de malfaiteur) cosh, club. ◆**matraqu/er** vt (frapper) to club; (publicité etc) to plug (away) at. ◆**—age** nm **m. (publicitaire)** plugging, publicity build-up.

matrice [matris] nf **1** Anat womb. **2** Tech matrix.

matricule [matrikyl] nm (registration) number; – a (livret, numéro) registration-.

matrimonial, -aux [matrimɔnjal, -o] a matrimonial.

mâture [mɑtyr] nf Nau masts.

maturité [matyrite] nf maturity. ◆**maturation** nf maturing.

maudire* [modir] vt to curse. ◆**maudit** a (sacré) (ac)cursed, damned.

maugréer [mogree] vi to growl, grumble (contre at).

mausolée [mozɔle] nm mausoleum.

maussade [mosad] a (personne etc) glum, sullen; (temps) gloomy.

mauvais [move] a bad; (méchant, malveillant) evil, wicked; (mal choisi) wrong; (mer) rough; **plus m.** worse; **le plus m.** the worst; **il fait m.** the weather's bad; **ça sent m.** it smells bad; **être m. en** (anglais etc) to be bad at; **mauvaise santé** ill ou bad ou poor health; – nm **le bon et le m.** the good and the bad.

mauve [mov] a & nm (couleur) mauve.

mauviette [movjɛt] nf personne) Péj weakling.

maux [mo] voir **mal**.

maxime [maksim] nf maxim.

maximum [maksimɔm] nm maximum; **le m. de** (force etc) the maximum (amount of); **au m.** as much as possible; (tout au plus) at most; – a maximum; **la température m.** maximum temperature. ◆**maximal, -aux** a maximum.

mayonnaise [majɔnɛz] nf mayonnaise.

mazout [mazut] nm (fuel) oil.

me [m(ə)] (**m'** before vowel or mute h) pron **1** (complément direct) me; **il me voit** he sees me. **2** (indirect) (to) me; **elle me parle** she speaks to me; **tu me l'as dit** you told me. **3** (réfléchi) myself; **je me lave** I wash myself.

méandres [meɑ̃dr] nmpl meander(ing)s.

mec [mɛk] *nm* (*individu*) *Arg* guy, bloke.

mécanique [mekanik] *a* mechanical; (*jouet*) clockwork-; – *nf* (*science*) mechanics; (*mécanisme*) mechanism. ◆**mécanicien** *nm* mechanic; *Rail* train driver. ◆**mécanisme** *nm* mechanism.

mécaniser [mekanize] *vt* to mechanize. ◆**mécanisation** *nf* mechanization.

mécène [mesɛn] *nm* patron (of the arts).

méchant [meʃɑ̃] *a* (*cruel*) malicious, wicked, evil; (*désagréable*) nasty; (*enfant*) naughty; (*chien*) vicious; **ce n'est pas m.** (*grave*) *Fam* it's nothing much. ◆**méchamment** *adv* (*cruellement*) maliciously; (*très*) *Fam* terribly. ◆**méchanceté** *nf* malice, wickedness; **une m.** (*acte*) a malicious act; (*parole*) a malicious word.

mèche [mɛʃ] *nf* **1** (*de cheveux*) lock; *pl* (*reflets*) highlights. **2** (*de bougie*) wick; (*de pétard*) fuse; (*de perceuse*) drill, bit. **3 de m. avec qn** (*complicité*) *Fam* in collusion *ou* cahoots with s.o.

méconn/aître* [mekɔnɛtr] *vt* to ignore; (*méjuger*) to fail to appreciate. ◆**–u** *a* unrecognized. ◆**–aissable** *a* unrecognizable.

mécontent [mekɔ̃tɑ̃] *a* dissatisfied, discontented (**de** with). ◆**mécontent/er** *vt* to displease, dissatisfy. ◆**–ement** *nm* dissatisfaction, discontent.

médaille [medaj] *nf* (*décoration*) *Sp* medal; (*pieuse*) medallion; (*pour chien*) name tag; **être m. d'or/d'argent** *Sp* to be a gold/silver medallist. ◆**médaillé, -ée** *nmf* medal holder. ◆**médaillon** *nm* (*bijou*) locket, medallion; (*ornement*) *Archit* medallion.

médecin [medsɛ̃] *nm* doctor, physician. ◆**médecine** *nf* medicine; **étudiant en m.** medical student. ◆**médical, -aux** *a* medical. ◆**médicament** *nm* medicine. ◆**médicinal, -aux** *a* medicinal. ◆**médico-légal, -aux** *a* (*laboratoire*) forensic.

médias [medja] *nmpl* (mass) media. ◆**médiatique** *a* media-.

médiateur, -trice [medjatœr, -tris] *nmf* mediator; – *a* mediating. ◆**médiation** *nf* mediation.

médiéval, -aux [medjeval, -o] *a* medi(a)eval.

médiocre [medjɔkr] *a* mediocre, second-rate. ◆**médiocrement** *adv* (*pas très*) not very; (*pas très bien*) not very well. ◆**médiocrité** *nf* mediocrity.

médire* [medir] *vi* **m. de** to speak ill of, slander. ◆**médisance(s)** *nf*(*pl*) malicious gossip, slander; **une m.** a piece of malicious gossip.

méditer [medite] *vt* (*conseil etc*) to meditate on; **m. de faire** to consider doing; – *vi* to meditate (**sur** on). ◆**méditatif, -ive** *a* meditative. ◆**méditation** *nf* meditation.

Méditerranée [mediterane] *nf* **la M.** the Mediterranean. ◆**méditerranéen, -enne** *a* Mediterranean.

médium [medjɔm] *nm* (*spirite*) medium.

méduse [medyz] *nf* jellyfish.

méduser [medyze] *vt* to stun, dumbfound.

meeting [mitiŋ] *nm* *Pol Sp* meeting, rally.

méfait [mefɛ] *nm Jur* misdeed; *pl* (*dégâts*) ravages.

méfi/er (se) [səmefje] *vpr* **se m. de** to distrust, mistrust; (*faire attention à*) to watch out for, beware of; **méfie-toi!** watch out!, beware!; **je me méfie** I'm distrustful *ou* suspicious. ◆**–ant** *a* distrustful, suspicious. ◆**méfiance** *nf* distrust, mistrust.

mégalomane [megaloman] *nmf* megalomaniac. ◆**mégalomanie** *nf* megalomania.

mégaphone [megafon] *nm* loudhailer.

mégarde (par) [parmegard] *adv* inadvertently, by mistake.

mégère [meʒɛr] *nf* (*femme*) *Péj* shrew.

mégot [mego] *nm Fam* cigarette end *ou* butt.

meilleur, -eure [mɛjœr] *a* better (**que** than); **le m. moment/résultat/etc** the best moment/result/etc; – *nmf* **le m., la meilleure** the best (one).

mélancolie [melɑ̃kɔli] *nf* melancholy, gloom. ◆**mélancolique** *a* melancholy, gloomy.

mélange [melɑ̃ʒ] *nm* mixture, blend; (*opération*) mixing. ◆**mélanger** *vt* (*mêler*) to mix; (*brouiller*) to mix (up), muddle; – **se m.** *vpr* to mix; (*idées etc*) to get mixed (up) *ou* muddled.

mélasse [melas] *nf* treacle, *Am* molasses.

mêl/er [mele] *vt* to mix, mingle (**à** with); (*qualités, thèmes*) to combine; (*brouiller*) to mix (up), muddle; **m. qn à** (*impliquer*) to involve s.o. in; – **se m.** *vpr* to mix, mingle (**à** with); **se m. à** (*la foule etc*) to join; **se m. de** (*s'ingérer dans*) to meddle in; **mêle-toi de ce qui te regarde!** mind your own business! ◆**–é** *a* mixed (**de** with). ◆**–ée** *nf* (*bataille*) rough-and-tumble; *Rugby* scrum(mage).

méli-mélo [melimelo] *nm* (*pl* **mélis-mélos**) *Fam* muddle.

mélodie [melɔdi] *nf* melody. ◆**mélodieux, -euse** *a* melodious. ◆**mélodique** *a Mus* melodic. ◆**mélomane** *nmf* music lover.

mélodrame [melɔdram] *nm* melodrama.
◆**mélodramatique** *a* melodramatic.
melon [m(ə)lɔ̃] *nm* **1** (*fruit*) melon. **2** (*chapeau*) m. bowler (hat).
membrane [mãbran] *nf* membrane.
membre [mãbr] *nm* **1** *Anat* limb. **2** (*d'un groupe*) member.
même [mɛm] **1** *a* (*identique*) same; **en m. temps** at the same time (**que** as); **ce livre/ etc m.** (*exact*) this very book/*etc*; **il est la bonté m.** he is kindness itself; **lui-m./vous-m./***etc* himself/yourself/*etc*; − *pron* **le m., la m.** the same (one); **j'ai les mêmes** I have the same (ones). **2** *adv* (*y compris, aussi*) even; **m. si** even if; **tout de m., quand m.** all the same; **de m.** likewise; **de m. que** just as; **ici m.** in this very place; **à m. de** in a position to; **à m. le sol** on the ground; **à m. la bouteille** from the bottle.
mémento [memɛto] *nm* (*aide-mémoire*) handbook; (*agenda*) notebook.
mémoire [memwar] **1** *nf* memory; **de m. d'homme** in living memory; **à la m. de** in memory of. **2** *nm* (*requête*) petition; *Univ* memoir; *pl Littér* memoirs.
◆**mémorable** *a* memorable. ◆**mémorandum** [memɔrãdɔm] *nm Pol Com* memorandum. ◆**mémorial, -aux** *nm* (*monument*) memorial.
menace [mənas] *nf* threat, menace.
◆**mena/cer** *vt* to threaten (**de faire** to do). ◆**−çant** *a* threatening.
ménage [menaʒ] *nm* (*entretien*) housekeeping; (*couple*) couple, household; **faire le m.** to do the housework; **faire bon m. avec** to get on happily with. ◆**ménager¹, -ère** *a* (*appareil*) domestic, household-; **travaux ménagers** housework; − *nf* (*femme*) housewife.
ménag/er² [menaʒe] *vt* (*arranger*) to prepare *ou* arrange (carefully); (*épargner*) to use sparingly, be careful with; (*fenêtre, escalier etc*) to build; **m. qn** to treat *ou* handle s.o. gently *ou* carefully; (*soin*) care. ◆**−ement** *nm* (*soin*) care.
ménagerie [menaʒri] *nf* menagerie.
mendier [mãdje] *vi* to beg; − *vt* to beg for.
◆**mendiant, -ante** *nmf* beggar.
◆**mendicité** *nf* begging.
menées [məne] *nfpl* schemings, intrigues.
men/er [məne] *vt* (*personne, vie etc*) to lead; (*lutte, enquête, tâche etc*) to carry out; (*affaires*) to run; (*bateau*) to command; **m. qn à** (*accompagner, transporter*) to take s.o. to; **m. à bien** *Fig* to carry through; − *vi Sp* to lead. ◆**−eur, -euse** *nmf* (*de révolte*) (ring)leader.

méningite [menɛ̃ʒit] *nf Méd* meningitis.
ménopause [menɔpoz] *nf* menopause.
menottes [mənɔt] *nfpl* handcuffs.
mensonge [mãsɔ̃ʒ] *nm* lie; (*action*) lying.
◆**mensonger, -ère** *a* untrue, false.
menstruation [mãstryɑsjɔ̃] *nf* menstruation.
mensuel, -elle [mãsɥel] *a* monthly; − *nm* (*revue*) monthly. ◆**mensualité** *nf* monthly payment. ◆**mensuellement** *adv* monthly.
mensurations [mãsyrɑsjɔ̃] *nfpl* measurements.
mental, -aux [mãtal, -o] *a* mental.
◆**mentalité** *nf* mentality.
menthe [mãt] *nf* mint.
mention [mãsjɔ̃] *nf* mention, reference; (*annotation*) comment; **m. bien** *Scol Univ* distinction; **faire m. de** to mention. ◆**mentionner** *vt* to mention.
ment/ir* [mãtir] *vi* to lie, tell lies *ou* a lie (**à** to). ◆**−eur, -euse** *nmf* liar; − *a* lying.
menton [mãtɔ̃] *nm* chin.
menu [məny] **1** *a* (*petit*) tiny; (*mince*) slender, fine; (*peu important*) minor, petty; − *adv* (*hacher*) small, finely; − *nm* **par le m.** in detail. **2** *nm* (*carte*) *Culin* menu.
menuisier [mənɥizje] *nm* carpenter, joiner.
◆**menuiserie** *nf* carpentry, joinery; (*ouvrage*) woodwork.
méprendre (se) [səmeprãdr] *vpr* **se m. sur** to be mistaken about. ◆**méprise** *nf* mistake.
mépris [mepri] *nm* contempt (**de** of, for), scorn (**de** for); **au m. de** without regard to.
◆**mépris/er** *vt* to despise, scorn. ◆**−ant** *a* scornful, contemptuous. ◆**−able** *a* despicable.
mer [mɛr] *nf* sea; (*marée*) tide; **en m.** at sea; **par m.** by sea; **aller à la m.** to go to the seaside; **un homme à la m.!** man overboard!
mercantile [mɛrkãtil] *a Péj* money-grabbing.
mercenaire [mɛrsəner] *a & nm* mercenary.
mercerie [mɛrsəri] *nf* (*magasin*) haberdasher's, *Am* notions store. ◆**mercier, -ière** *nmf* haberdasher, *Am* notions merchant.
merci [mɛrsi] **1** *int & nm* thank you, thanks (**de, pour** for); **(non) m.!** no, thank you! **2** *nf* **à la m. de** at the mercy of.
mercredi [mɛrkrədi] *nm* Wednesday.
mercure [mɛrkyr] *nm* mercury.
merde! [mɛrd] *int Fam* (bloody) hell!
mère [mɛr] *nf* mother; **la m. de famille** mother (of a family); **la m. Dubois** *Fam* old Mrs Dubois; **maison m.** *Com* parent firm.
méridien [meridjɛ̃] *nm* meridian.

méridional, -ale, -aux [meridjɔnal, -o] *a* southern; − *nmf* southerner.

meringue [mərɛ̃g] *nf* (*gâteau*) meringue.

merisier [mərizje] *nm* (*bois*) cherry.

mérite [merit] *nm* merit; **homme de m.** (*valeur*) man of worth. ◆**mérit/er** *vt* (*être digne de*) to deserve; (*valoir*) to be worth; **m. de réussir**/*etc* to deserve to succeed/*etc*. ◆−**ant** *a* deserving. ◆**méritoire** *a* commendable.

merlan [mɛrlɑ̃] *nm* (*poisson*) whiting.

merle [mɛrl] *nm* blackbird.

merveille [mɛrvɛj] *nf* wonder, marvel; **à m.** wonderfully (well). ◆**merveilleusement** *adv* wonderfully. ◆**merveilleux, -euse** *a* wonderful, marvellous; − *nm* **le m.** (*surnaturel*) the supernatural.

mes [me] *voir* **mon.**

mésange [mezɑ̃ʒ] *nf* (*oiseau*) tit.

mésaventure [mezavɑ̃tyr] *nf* misfortune, misadventure.

mesdames [medam] *voir* **madame.**

mesdemoiselles [medmwazɛl] *voir* **mademoiselle.**

mésentente [mezɑ̃tɑ̃t] *nf* misunderstanding.

mesquin [mɛskɛ̃] *a* mean, petty. ◆**mesquinerie** *nf* meanness, pettiness; **une m.** an act of meanness.

mess [mɛs] *nm inv Mil* mess.

message [mesaʒ] *nm* message. ◆**messager, -ère** *nmf* messenger.

messageries [mesaʒri] *nfpl Com* courier service.

messe [mɛs] *nf Rel* mass.

Messie [mesi] *nm* Messiah.

messieurs [mesjø] *voir* **monsieur.**

mesure [məzyr] *nf* (*évaluation, dimension*) measurement; (*quantité, disposition*) measure; (*retenue*) moderation; (*cadence*) *Mus* time, beat; **fait sur m.** made to measure; **à m. que** as, as soon *ou* as fast as; **dans la m. où** in so far as; **dans une certaine m.** to a certain extent; **en m.** able to, in a position to; **dépasser la m.** to exceed the bounds. ◆**mesur/er** *vt* to measure; (*juger, estimer*) to calculate, assess, measure; (*argent, temps*) to ration (out); **m. 1 mètre 83** (*personne*) to be six feet tall; (*objet*) to measure six feet; **se m. à** *ou* **avec qn** *Fig* to pit oneself against s.o. ◆−**é** *a* (*pas, ton*) measured; (*personne*) moderate.

met [mɛ] *voir* **mettre.**

métal, -aux [metal, -o] *nm* metal. ◆**métallique** *a* (*objet*) metal-; (*éclat, reflet, couleur*) metallic. ◆**métallisé** *a* (*peinture*) metallic.

métallo [metalo] *nm Fam* steelworker. ◆**métallurgie** *nf* (*industrie*) steel industry; (*science*) metallurgy. ◆**métallurgique** *a* **usine m.** steelworks. ◆**métallurgiste** *a &* *nm* (*ouvrier*) m. steelworker.

métamorphose [metamɔrfoz] *nf* metamorphosis. ◆**métamorphoser** *vt*, − **se m.** *vpr* to transform (**en** into).

métaphore [metafɔr] *nf* metaphor. ◆**métaphorique** *a* metaphorical.

métaphysique [metafizik] *a* metaphysical.

météo [meteo] *nf* (*bulletin*) weather forecast.

météore [meteɔr] *nm* meteor. ◆**météorite** *nm* meteorite.

météorologie [meteɔrɔlɔʒi] *nf* (*science*) meteorology; (*service*) weather bureau. ◆**météorologique** *a* meteorological; ·(*bulletin, station, carte*) weather-.

méthode [metɔd] *nf* method; (*livre*) course. ◆**méthodique** *a* methodical.

méticuleux, -euse [metikylø, -øz] *a* meticulous.

métier [metje] *nm* **1** (*travail*) job; (*manuel*) trade; (*intellectuel*) profession; (*habileté*) professional skill; **homme de m.** specialist. **2 m.** (**à tisser**) loom.

métis, -isse [metis] *a &* *nmf* half-caste.

mètre [mɛtr] *nm* (*mesure*) metre; (*règle*) (metre) rule; **m.** (**à ruban**) tape measure. ◆**métr/er** *vt* (*terrain*) to survey. ◆−**age** *nm* **1** surveying. **2** (*tissu*) length; (*de film*) footage; **long m.** (*film*) full length film; **court m.** (*film*) short (film). ◆−**eur** *nm* quantity surveyor. ◆**métrique** *a* metric.

métro [metro] *nm* underground, *Am* subway.

métropole [metrɔpɔl] *nf* (*ville*) metropolis; (*pays*) mother country. ◆**métropolitain** *a* metropolitan.

mets [mɛ] *nm* (*aliment*) dish.

mett/re* [mɛtr] **1** *vt* to put; (*table*) to lay; (*vêtement, lunettes*) to put on, wear; (*chauffage, radio etc*) to put on, switch on; (*réveil*) to set (**à** for); (*dépenser*) to spend (**pour une robe**/*etc* on a dress/*etc*); **m. dix heures**/*etc* **à venir** (*consacrer*) to take ten hours/*etc* coming *ou* to come; **m. à l'aise** (*rassurer*) to put *ou* set at ease; (*dans un fauteuil etc*) to make comfortable; **m. en colère** to make angry; **m. en liberté** to free; **m. en bouteille(s)** to bottle; **m. du soin à faire** to take care to do; **mettons que** (+ *sub*) let's suppose that; − **se m.** *vpr* (*se placer*) to put oneself; (*debout*) to stand; (*assis*) to sit; (*objet*) to be put, go; **se m. en short/pyjama**/*etc* to get into one's shorts/pyjamas/*etc*; **se m. en rapport avec** to get in touch with; **se m. à** (*endroit*) to go to; (*travail*) to set oneself to, start; **se m. à faire** to start doing; **se m. à table** to sit (down) at the table; **se m. à l'aise** to make oneself comfortable; **se m. au beau/froid** (*temps*) to turn fine/cold. ◆—**able** *a* wearable. ◆—**eur** *nm* **m. en scène** *Th* producer; *Cin* director.

meuble [mœbl] *nm* piece of furniture; *pl* furniture. ◆**meubl/er** *vt* to furnish; (*remplir*) *Fig* to fill. ◆—**é** *nm* furnished flat *ou* *Am* apartment.

meugl/er [møgle] *vi* to moo, low. ◆—**ement(s)** *nm*(*pl*) mooing.

meule [møl] *nf* **1** (*de foin*) haystack. **2** (*pour moudre*) millstone.

meunier, -ière [mønje, -jɛr] *nmf* miller.

meurt [mœr] *voir* **mourir**.

meurtre [mœrtr] *nm* murder. ◆**meurtrier, -ière** *nmf* murderer; – *a* deadly, murderous.

meurtrir [mœrtrir] *vt* to bruise. ◆**meurtrissure** *nf* bruise.

meute [møt] *nf* (*de chiens, de créanciers etc*) pack.

Mexique [mɛksik] *nm* Mexico. ◆**mexicain, -aine** *a* & *nmf* Mexican.

mi- [mi] *préf* **la mi-mars**/*etc* mid March/*etc*; **à mi-distance** mid-distance, midway.

miaou [mjau] *int* (*cri du chat*) miaow. ◆**miaul/er** [mjole] *vi* to miaow, mew. ◆—**ement(s)** *nm*(*pl*) miaowing, mewing.

mi-bas [miba] *nm inv* knee sock.

miche [miʃ] *nf* round loaf.

mi-chemin (à) [amiʃmɛ̃] *adv* halfway.

mi-clos [miklo] *a* half-closed.

micmac [mikmak] *nm* (*manigance*) *Fam* intrigue.

mi-corps (à) [amikɔr] *adv* (up) to the waist.

mi-côte (à) [amikot] *adv* halfway up *ou* down (the hill).

micro [mikro] *nm* microphone, mike. ◆**microphone** *nm* microphone.

micro- [mikro] *préf* micro-.

microbe [mikrɔb] *nm* germ, microbe.

microcosme [mikrɔkɔsm] *nm* microcosm.

microfilm [mikrɔfilm] *nm* microfilm.

micro-onde [mikrɔ̃d] *nf* microwave; **four à micro-ondes** microwave oven.

microscope [mikrɔskɔp] *nm* microscope. ◆**microscopique** *a* microscopic.

midi [midi] *nm* **1** (*heure*) midday, noon, twelve o'clock; (*heure du déjeuner*) lunchtime. **2** (*sud*) south; **le M.** the south of France.

mie [mi] *nf* soft bread, crumb.

miel [mjɛl] *nm* honey. ◆**mielleux, -euse** *a* (*parole, personne*) unctuous.

mien, mienne [mjɛ̃, mjɛn] *pron poss* **le m., la mienne** mine, my one; **les miens, les miennes** mine, my ones; **les deux miens** my two; – *nmpl* **les miens** (*amis etc*) my (own) people.

miette [mjɛt] *nf* (*de pain, de bon sens etc*) crumb; **réduire en miettes** to smash to pieces.

mieux [mjø] *adv* & *a inv* better (**que** than); (*plus à l'aise*) more comfortable; (*plus beau*) better-looking; **le m., la m., les m.** (*convenir, être etc*) the best; (*de deux*) the better; **le m. serait de . . .** the best thing would be to . . . ; **de m. en m.** better and better; **tu ferais m. de partir** you had better leave; **je ne demande pas m.** there's nothing I'd like better (**que de faire** than to do); – *nm* (*amélioration*) improvement; **faire de son m.** to do one's best.

mièvre [mjɛvr] *a* (*doucereux*) *Péj* mannered, wishy-washy.

mignon, -onne [miɲ̃ɔ̃, -ɔn] *a* (*charmant*) cute; (*agréable*) nice.

migraine [migrɛn] *nf* headache; *Méd* migraine.

migration [migrasjɔ̃] *nf* migration. ◆**migrant, -ante** *a* & *nmf* (**travailleur**) **m. migrant** worker, migrant.

mijoter [miʒɔte] *vt* *Culin* to cook (lovingly); (*lentement*) to simmer; (*complot*) *Fig Fam* to brew; – *vi* to simmer.

mil [mil] *nm inv* (*dans les dates*) a *ou* one thousand; **l'an deux m.** the year two thousand.

milice [milis] *nf* militia. ◆**milicien** *nm* militiaman.

milieu, -x [miljø] *nm* (*centre*) middle; (*cadre, groupe social*) environment; (*entre extrêmes*) middle course; (*espace*) *Phys* medium; *pl* (*groupes, littéraires etc*) circles; **au m. de** in the middle of; **au m. du danger** in the midst of danger; **le juste m.** the happy medium; **le m.** (*de malfaiteurs*) the underworld.

militaire [militɛr] *a* military; – *nm* serviceman; (*dans l'armée de terre*) soldier.

milit/er [milite] *vi* (*personne*) to be a militant; (*arguments etc*) to militate (**pour** in favour of). ◆—**ant, -ante** *a* & *nmf* militant.

mille [mil] **1** *a* & *nm inv* thousand; **m. hommes**/*etc* a *ou* one thousand men/*etc*; **deux m.** two thousand; **mettre dans le m.** to hit the bull's-eye. **2** *nm* (*mesure*) mile. ◆**m.-pattes** *nm inv* (*insecte*) centipede.

◆**millième** a & nmf thousandth; **un m.** a thousandth. ◆**millier** nm thousand; **un m. (de)** a thousand or so.

millefeuille [milfœj] nm (*gâteau*) cream slice.

millénaire [milener] nm millennium.

millésime [milezim] nm date (*on coins, wine etc*).

millet [mijɛ] nm Bot millet.

milli- [mili] préf milli-.

milliard [miljar] nm thousand million, Am billion. ◆**milliardaire** a & nmf multimillionaire.

millimètre [milimetr] nm millimetre.

million [miljɔ̃] nm million; **un m. de livres**/*etc* a million pounds/*etc*; **deux millions** two million. ◆**millionième** a & nmf millionth. ◆**millionnaire** nmf millionaire.

mime [mim] nmf (*acteur*) mime; **le m.** (*art*) mime. ◆**mimer** vti to mime. ◆**mimique** nf (*mine*) (funny) face; (*gestes*) signs, sign language.

mimosa [mimoza] nm (*arbre, fleur*) mimosa.

minable [minabl] a (*médiocre*) pathetic; (*lieu, personne*) shabby.

minaret [minare] nm (*de mosquée*) minaret.

minauder [minode] vi to simper, make a show of affectation.

mince [mɛ̃s] 1 a (*thin*); (*élancé*) slim; (*insignifiant*) slim, paltry. 2 int **m. (alors)!** oh heck!, blast (it)! ◆**minceur** nf thinness; slimness. ◆**mincir** vi to grow slim.

mine [min] nf 1 appearance; (*physionomie*) look; **avoir bonne/mauvaise m.** (*santé*) to look well/ill; **faire m. de faire** to appear to do, make as if to do. 2 (*d'or, de charbon etc*) & Fig mine; **m. de charbon** coalmine. 3 (*de crayon*) lead. 4 (*engin explosif*) mine. ◆**miner** vt 1 (*saper*) to undermine. 2 (*garnir d'explosifs*) to mine.

minerai [minrɛ] nm ore.

minéral, -aux [mineral, -o] a & nm mineral.

minéralogique [mineralɔʒik] a **numéro m.** Aut registration ou Am license number.

minet, -ette [minɛ, -ɛt] nmf 1 (*chat*) puss. 2 (*personne*) Fam fashion-conscious young man ou woman.

mineur, -eure [minœr] 1 nm (*ouvrier*) miner. 2 a (*jeune, secondaire*) & Mus minor; – nmf Jur minor. ◆**minier, -ière** a (*industrie*) mining-.

mini- [mini] préf mini-.

miniature [minjatyr] nf miniature; – a inv (*train etc*) miniature-.

minibus [minibys] nm minibus.

minime [minim] a trifling, minor, minimal. ◆**minimiser** vt to minimize.

minimum [minimɔm] nm minimum; **le m. de** (*force etc*) the minimum (amount of); **au (grand) m.** at the very least; **la température m.** the minimum temperature. ◆**minimal, -aux** a minimum, minimal.

ministre [ministr] nm Pol Rel minister; **m. de l'Intérieur** = Home Secretary, Am Secretary of the Interior. ◆**ministère** nm ministry; (*gouvernement*) cabinet; **m. de l'Intérieur** = Home Office, Am Department of the Interior. ◆**ministériel, -ielle** a ministerial; (*crise, remaniement*) cabinet-.

minorer [minɔre] vt to reduce.

minorité [minɔrite] nf minority; **en m.** in the ou a minority. ◆**minoritaire** a (*parti etc*) minority-; **être m.** to be in the ou a minority.

Minorque [minɔrk] nf Minorca.

minuit [minɥi] nm midnight, twelve o'clock.

minus [minys] nm (*individu*) Péj Fam moron.

minuscule [minyskyl] 1 a (*petit*) tiny, minute. 2 a & nf (*lettre*) m. small letter.

minute [minyt] nf minute; **à la m.** (*tout de suite*) this (very) minute; **d'une m. à l'autre** any minute (now); – a inv **aliments** ou **plats m.** convenience food(s). ◆**minuter** vt to time. ◆**minuterie** nf time switch.

minutie [minysi] nf meticulousness. ◆**minutieux, -euse** a meticulous.

mioche [mjɔʃ] nmf (*enfant*) Fam kid, youngster.

miracle [mirakl] nm miracle; **par m.** miraculously. ◆**miraculeux, -euse** a miraculous.

mirador [miradɔr] nm Mil watchtower.

mirage [miraʒ] nm mirage.

mirifique [mirifik] a Hum fabulous.

mirobolant [mirɔbɔlɑ̃] a Fam fantastic.

miroir [mirwar] nm mirror. ◆**miroiter** vi to gleam, shimmer.

mis [mi] voir **mettre**; – a **bien m.** (*vêtu*) well dressed.

misanthrope [mizɑ̃trɔp] nmf misanthropist; – a misanthropic.

mise [miz] nf 1 (*action de mettre*) putting; **m. en service** putting into service; **m. en marche** starting up; **m. à la retraite** pensioning off; **m. à feu** (*de fusée*) blast-off; **m. en scène** Th production; Cin direction. 2 (*argent*) stake. 3 (*tenue*) attire. ◆**miser** vt (*argent*) to stake (sur on); – vi **m. sur** (*cheval*) to back; (*compter sur*) to bank on.

misère [mizɛr] nf (grinding) poverty; (*malheur*) misery; (*bagatelle*) trifle. ◆**mi-**

sérable *a* miserable, wretched; *(indigent)* poor, destitute; *(logement, quartier)* seedy, slummy; − *nmf* (poor) wretch; *(indigent)* pauper. ◆**miséreux, -euse** *a* destitute; − *nmf* pauper.

miséricorde [mizerikɔrd] *nf* mercy. ◆**miséricordieux, -euse** *a* merciful.

misogyne [mizɔʒin] *nmf* misogynist.

missile [misil] *nm (fusée)* missile.

mission [misjɔ̃] *nf* mission; *(tâche)* task. ◆**missionnaire** *nm & a* missionary.

missive [misiv] *nf (lettre)* missive.

mistral [mistral] *nm inv (vent)* mistral.

mite [mit] *nf* (clothes) moth; *(du fromage etc)* mite. ◆**mité** *a* a moth-eaten.

mi-temps [mitɑ̃] *nf (pause) Sp* half-time; *(période) Sp* half; **à mi-t.** *(travailler etc)* part-time.

miteux, -euse [mitø, -øz] *a* shabby.

mitigé [mitiʒe] *a (zèle etc)* moderate, lukewarm; *(mêlé) Fam* mixed.

mitraille [mitrɑj] *nf* gunfire. ◆**mitrailler** *vt* to machinegun; *(photographier) Fam* to click *ou* snap away at. ◆**mitraillette** *nf* submachine gun. ◆**mitrailleur** *a* **fusil m.** machinegun. ◆**mitrailleuse** *nf* machinegun.

mi-voix (à) [amivwa] *adv* in an undertone.

mixe(u)r [miksœr] *nm (pour mélanger)* (food) mixer.

mixte [mikst] *a* mixed; *(école)* co-educational, mixed; *(tribunal)* joint.

mixture [mikstyr] *nf (boisson) Péj* mixture.

Mlle [madmwazɛl] *abrév* = **Mademoiselle.**

MM [mesjø] *abrév* = **Messieurs.**

mm *abrév (millimètre)* mm.

Mme [madam] *abrév* = **Madame.**

mobile [mɔbil] **1** *a (pièce etc)* moving; *(personne)* mobile; *(feuillets)* detachable, loose; *(reflets)* changing; **échelle m.** sliding scale; **fête m.** mov(e)able feast; − *nm (œuvre d'art)* mobile. **2** *nm (motif)* motive (**de** for). ◆**mobilité** *nf* mobility.

mobilier [mɔbilje] *nm* furniture.

mobiliser [mɔbilize] *vti* to mobilize. ◆**mobilisation** *nf* mobilization.

mobylette [mɔbilɛt] *nf* moped.

mocassin [mɔkasɛ̃] *nm (chaussure)* moccasin.

moche [mɔʃ] *a Fam (laid)* ugly; *(mauvais, peu gentil)* lousy, rotten.

modalité [mɔdalite] *nf* method (**de** of).

mode [mɔd] **1** *nf* fashion; *(industrie)* fashion trade; **à la m.** in fashion, fashionable; **passé de m.** out of fashion; **à la m. de** in the manner of. **2** *nm* mode, method; **m. d'emploi**

directions (for use); **m. de vie** way of life. **3** *nm Gram* mood.

modèle [mɔdɛl] *nm (schéma, exemple, personne)* model; **m. (réduit)** (scale) model; − *a (élève etc)* model-. ◆**model/er** *vt* to model *(sur* on); **se m. sur** to model oneself on. ◆**-age** *nm (de statue etc)* modelling. ◆**modéliste** *nmf Tex* stylist, designer.

modéré [mɔdere] *a* moderate. ◆**-ment** *adv* moderately.

modérer [mɔdere] *vt* to moderate, restrain; *(vitesse, allure)* to reduce; − **se m.** *vpr* to restrain oneself. ◆**modérateur, -trice** *a* moderating; − *nmf* moderator. ◆**modération** *nf* moderation, restraint; reduction; **avec m.** in moderation.

moderne [mɔdɛrn] *a* modern; − *nm* **le m.** *(mobilier)* modern furniture. ◆**modernisation** *nf* modernization. ◆**moderniser** *vt*, − **se m.** *vpr* to modernize. ◆**modernisme** *nm* modernism.

modeste [mɔdɛst] *a* modest. ◆**modestement** *adv* modestly. ◆**modestie** *nf* modesty.

modifier [mɔdifje] *vt* to modify, alter; − **se m.** *vpr* to alter. ◆**modification** *nf* modification, alteration.

modique [mɔdik] *a (salaire, prix)* modest. ◆**modicité** *nf* modesty.

module [mɔdyl] *nm* module.

moduler [mɔdyle] *vt* to modulate. ◆**modulation** *nf* modulation.

moelle [mwal] *nf Anat* marrow; **m. épinière** spinal cord.

moelleux, -euse [mwalø, -øz] *a* soft; *(voix, vin)* mellow.

mœurs [mœr(s)] *nfpl (morale)* morals; *(habitudes)* habits, customs.

mohair [mɔɛr] *nm* mohair.

moi [mwa] *pron* **1** *(complément direct)* me; **laissez-moi** leave me; **pour moi** for me. **2** *(indirect)* (to) me; **montrez-le-moi** show it to me, show me it. **3** *(sujet)* I; **moi, je veux** *I* want. **4** *nm inv Psy* self, ego. ◆**moi-même** *pron* myself.

moignon [mwaɲɔ̃] *nm* stump.

moindre [mwɛ̃dr] *a* **être m.** *(moins grand)* to be less; **le m. doute/etc** the slightest *ou* least doubt/etc; **le m.** *(de mes problèmes etc)* the least *(de* of); *(de deux problèmes etc)* the lesser *(de* of).

moine [mwan] *nm* monk, friar.

moineau, -x [mwano] *nm* sparrow.

moins [mwɛ̃] **1** *adv* ([mwɛz] *before vowel)* less *(que* than); **m. de** *(temps, zèle etc)* less *(que* than), not so much *(que* as); *(gens, livres etc)* fewer *(que* than), not so many

(que as); (*cent francs etc*) less than; **m. froid/grand**/*etc* not as cold/big/*etc* (**que** as); **de m. en m.** less and less; **le m., la m., les m.** (*travailler etc*) the least; **le m. grand** the smallest; **au m., du m.** at least; **de m., en m.** (*qui manque*) missing; **dix ans**/*etc* de m. ten years/*etc* less; **en m.** (*personne, objet*) less; (*personnes, objets*) fewer; **les m. de vingt ans** those under twenty, the under-twenties; **à m. que** (+ *sub*) unless. **2** *prép Math* minus; **deux heures m. cinq** five to two; **il fait m. dix (degrés)** it's minus ten (degrees).

mois [mwa] *nm* month; **au m. de juin**/*etc* in (the month of) June/*etc*.

mois/ir [mwazir] *vi* to go mouldy; (*attendre*) *Fig* to hang about. ◆—**i** *a* mouldy; — *nm* mould, mildew; **sentir le m.** to smell musty. ◆**moisissure** *nf* mould, mildew.

moisson [mwasɔ̃] *nf* harvest. ◆**moisson-ner** *vt* to harvest. ◆**moissonneuse-batteuse** *nf* (*pl* moissonneuses-batteuses) combine-harvester.

moite [mwat] *a* sticky, moist. ◆**moiteur** *nf* stickiness, moistness.

moitié [mwatje] *nf* half; **la m. de la pomme**/*etc* half (of) the apple/*etc*; **à m.** (*remplir etc*) halfway; **à m. fermé/cru**/*etc* half closed/raw/*etc*; **à m. prix** (for *ou* at) half-price; **de m.** by half; **m.-moitié** *Fam* so-so; **partager m.-moitié** *Fam* to split fifty-fifty.

moka [mɔka] *nm* (*café*) mocha.

mol [mɔl] *voir* mou.

molaire [mɔlɛr] *nf* (*dent*) molar.

molécule [mɔlekyl] *nf* molecule.

moleskine [mɔlɛskin] *nf* imitation leather.

molester [mɔlɛste] *vt* to manhandle.

molette [mɔlɛt] *nf* **clé à m.** adjustable wrench *ou* spanner.

mollasse [mɔlas] *a Péj* flabby.

molle [mɔl] *voir* mou. ◆**mollement** *adv* feebly; (*paresseusement*) lazily. ◆**mol-lesse** *nf* softness; (*faiblesse*) feebleness. ◆**mollir** *vi* to go soft; (*courage*) to flag.

mollet [mɔlɛ] **1** *a* **œuf m.** soft-boiled egg. **2** *nm* (*de jambe*) calf.

mollusque [mɔlysk] *nm* mollusc.

môme [mom] *nmf* (*enfant*) *Fam* kid.

moment [mɔmɑ̃] *nm* (*instant*) moment; (*période*) time; **en ce m.** at the moment; **par moments** at times; **au m. de partir** when just about to leave; **au m. où** when, just as; **du m. que** (*puisque*) seeing that. ◆**mo-mentané** *a* momentary. ◆**momentané-ment** *adv* temporarily, for the moment.

momie [mɔmi] *nf* (*cadavre*) mummy.

mon, ma, *pl* **mes** [mɔ̃, ma, me] (**ma** *becomes* **mon** [mɔ̃n] *before a vowel or mute h*) *a poss* my; **mon père** my father; **ma mère** my mother; **mon ami(e)** my friend.

Monaco [mɔnako] *nf* Monaco.

monarque [mɔnark] *nm* monarch. ◆**mo-narchie** *nf* monarchy. ◆**monarchique** *a* monarchic.

monastère [mɔnastɛr] *nm* monastery.

monceau, -x [mɔ̃so] *nm* heap, pile.

monde [mɔ̃d] *nm* world; (*milieu social*) set; **du m.** (*gens*) people; (*beaucoup*) a lot of people; **un m. fou** a tremendous crowd; **le (grand) m.** (high) society; **le m. entier** the whole world; **tout le m.** everybody; **mettre au m.** to give birth to; **pas le moins du m.!** not in the least *ou* slightest! ◆**mondain, -aine** *a* (*vie, réunion etc*) society-. ◆**mondanités** *nfpl* (*évènements*) social events. ◆**mondial, -aux** *a* (*renommée etc*) world-; (*crise*) worldwide. ◆**mondiale-ment** *adv* the (whole) world over.

monégasque [mɔnegask] *a & nmf* Mone-gasque.

monétaire [mɔnetɛr] *a* monetary.

mongolien, -ienne [mɔ̃gɔljɛ̃, -jɛn] *a & nmf Méd* mongol.

moniteur, -trice [mɔnitœr, -tris] *nmf* **1** in-structor; (*de colonie de vacances*) assistant, *Am* camp counselor. **2** (*écran*) *Tech* moni-tor.

monnaie [mɔnɛ] *nf* (*devise*) currency, mon-ey; (*appoint, pièces*) change; **pièce de m.** coin; (*petite*) **m.** (small) change; **faire de la m.** to get change; **faire de la m. à qn** to give s.o. change (**sur un billet** for a note); **c'est m. courante** it's very frequent; **Hôtel de la M.** mint. ◆**monnayer** *vt* (*talent etc*) to cash in on; (*bien, titre*) *Com* to convert into cash.

mono [mɔno] *a inv* (*disque etc*) mono.

mono- [mɔno] *préf* mono-.

monocle [mɔnɔkl] *nm* monocle.

monologue [mɔnɔlɔg] *nm* monologue.

monoplace [mɔnɔplas] *a & nmf* (*avion, voi-ture*) single-seater.

monopole [mɔnɔpɔl] *nm* monopoly. ◆**monopoliser** *vt* to monopolize.

monosyllabe [mɔnɔsilab] *nm* monosylla-ble. ◆**monosyllabique** *a* monosyllabic.

monotone [mɔnɔtɔn] *a* monotonous. ◆**monotonie** *nf* monotony.

monseigneur [mɔ̃sɛɲœr] *nm* (*évêque*) His *ou* Your Grace; (*prince*) His *ou* Your High-ness.

monsieur, *pl* **messieurs** [məsjø, mesjø] *nm* gentleman; **oui m.** yes; (*avec déférence*) yes sir; **oui messieurs** yes (gentlemen); **M. Legras** Mr Legras; **Messieurs** *ou* **MM Legras** Messrs Legras; **tu vois ce m.?** do you see that man *ou* gentleman?; **Monsieur** (*sur une lettre*) Com Dear Sir.

monstre [mɔ̃str] *nm* monster; – *a* (*énorme*) *Fam* colossal. ◆**monstrueux, -euse** *a* (*abominable, énorme*) monstrous. ◆**monstruosité** *nf* (*horreur*) monstrosity.

mont [mɔ̃] *nm* (*montagne*) mount.

montagne [mɔ̃taɲ] *nf* mountain; **la m.** (*zone*) the mountains; **montagnes russes** *Fig* roller coaster. ◆**montagnard, -arde** *nmf* mountain dweller; – *a* (*peuple*) mountain-. ◆**montagneux, -euse** *a* mountainous.

mont-de-piété [mɔ̃dpjete] *nm* (*pl* **monts-de-piété**) pawnshop.

monte-charge [mɔ̃tʃarʒ] *nm inv* service lift *ou Am* elevator.

mont/er [mɔ̃te] *vi* (*aux être*) (*personne*) to go *ou* come up; (*s'élever*) to go up; (*grimper*) to climb (up) (**sur** onto); (*prix*) to go up, rise; (*marée*) to come in; (*avion*) to climb; **m. dans un véhicule** to get in(to) a vehicle; **m. dans un train** to get on(to) a train; **m. sur** (*échelle etc*) to climb up; (*trône*) to ascend; **en courant/etc** to run/*etc* up; **m. (à cheval)** *Sp* to ride (a horse); **m. en graine** (*salade etc*) to go to seed; – *vt* (*aux avoir*) (*côte etc*) to climb (up); (*objets*) to bring *ou* take up; (*cheval*) to ride; (*tente, affaire*) to set up; (*machine*) to assemble; (*bijou*) to set, mount; (*complot, démonstration*) to mount; (*pièce*) *Th* to stage, mount; **m. l'escalier** to go *ou* come upstairs *ou* up the stairs; **faire m.** (*visiteur etc*) to show up; **m. qn contre qn** to set s.o. against s.o.; – **se m.** *vpr* (*s'irriter*) *Fam* to get angry; **se m. à** (*frais*) to amount to. ◆**—ant 1** *a* (*chemin*) uphill; (*mouvement*) upward; (*marée*) rising; (*col*) stand-up; (*robe*) high-necked; **chaussure montante** boot. **2** *nm* (*somme*) amount. **3** *nm* (*de barrière*) post; (*d'échelle*) upright. ◆**—é** *a* (*police*) mounted. ◆**—ée** *nf* ascent, climb; (*de prix, des eaux*) rise; (*chemin*) slope. ◆**—age** *nm Tech* assembling, assembly; *Cin* editing. ◆**—eur, -euse** *nmf Tech* fitter; *Cin* editor.

montre [mɔ̃tr] *nf* **1** watch; **course contre la m.** race against time. **2 faire m. de** to show. ◆**m.-bracelet** *nf* (*pl* **montres-bracelets**) wristwatch.

Montréal [mɔ̃real] *nm ou f* Montreal.

montrer [mɔ̃tre] *vt* to show (**à** to); **m. du doigt** to point to; **m. à qn à faire qch** to

show s.o. how to do sth; – **se m.** *vpr* to show oneself, appear; (*s'avérer*) to turn out to be; **se m. courageux/etc** (*être*) to be courageous/*etc*.

monture [mɔ̃tyr] *nf* **1** (*cheval*) mount. **2** (*de lunettes*) frame; (*de bijou*) setting.

monument [mɔnymɑ̃] *nm* monument; **m. aux morts** war memorial. ◆**monumental, -aux** *a* (*imposant, énorme etc*) monumental.

moquer (se) [səmɔke] *vpr* **se m. de** (*allure etc*) to make fun of; (*personne*) to make a fool of, make fun of; **je m'en moque!** *Fam* I couldn't care less! ◆**moquerie** *nf* mockery. ◆**moqueur, -euse** *a* mocking.

moquette [mɔkɛt] *nf* fitted carpet(s), wall-to-wall carpeting.

moral, -aux [mɔral, -o] *a* moral; – *nm* **le m.** spirits, morale. ◆**morale** *nf* (*principes*) morals; (*code*) moral code; (*d'histoire etc*) moral; **faire la m. à qn** to lecture s.o. ◆**moralement** *adv* morally. ◆**moraliser** *vi* to moralize. ◆**moraliste** *nmf* moralist. ◆**moralité** *nf* (*mœurs*) morality; (*de fable, récit etc*) moral.

moratoire [mɔratwar] *nm* moratorium.

morbide [mɔrbid] *a* morbid.

morceau, -x [mɔrso] *nm* piece, bit; (*de sucre*) lump; (*de viande*) *Culin* cut; (*extrait*) *Littér* extract. ◆**morceler** *vt* (*terrain*) to divide up.

mordiller [mɔrdije] *vt* to nibble.

mord/re [mɔrdr] *vti* to bite; **ça mord** *Pêche* I have a bite. ◆**—ant 1** *a* (*voix, manière*) scathing; (*froid*) biting; (*personne, ironie*) caustic. **2** *nm* (*énergie*) punch. ◆**—u, -ue** *nmf* **un m. du jazz/etc** *Fam* a jazz/*etc* fan.

morfondre (se) [səmɔrfɔ̃dr] *vpr* to get bored (waiting), mope (about).

morgue [mɔrg] *nf* (*lieu*) mortuary, morgue.

moribond, -onde [mɔribɔ̃, -ɔ̃d] *a* & *nmf* dying *ou* moribund (person).

morne [mɔrn] *a* dismal, gloomy, dull.

morose [mɔroz] *a* morose, sullen.

morphine [mɔrfin] *nf* morphine.

mors [mɔr] *nm* (*de harnais*) bit.

morse [mɔrs] *nm* **1** Morse (code). **2** (*animal*) walrus.

morsure [mɔrsyr] *nf* bite.

mort¹ [mɔr] *nf* death; **mettre à m.** to put to death; **silence de m.** dead silence. ◆**mortalité** *nf* death rate, mortality. ◆**mortel, -elle** *a* (*hommes, ennemi, danger etc*) mortal; (*accident*) fatal; (*chaleur*) deadly; (*pâleur*) deathly; – *nmf* mortal. ◆**mortellement** *adv* (*blessé*) fatally.

mort², morte [mɔr, mɔrt] *a* (*personne, plante, ville etc*) dead; **m. de fatigue** dead tired; **m. de froid** numb with cold; **m. de peur** frightened to death; – *nmf* dead man, dead woman; **les morts** the dead; **de nombreux morts** (*victimes*) many deaths *ou* casualties; **le jour** *ou* **la fête des Morts** All Souls' Day. ◆**morte-saison** *nf* off season. ◆**mort-né** *a* (*enfant*) & *Fig* stillborn.

mortier [mɔrtje] *nm* mortar.

mortifier [mɔrtifje] *vt* to mortify.

mortuaire [mɔrtɥɛr] *a* (*avis, rites etc*) death-, funeral.

morue [mɔry] *nf* cod.

morve [mɔrv] *nf* (nasal) mucus. ◆**morveux, -euse** *a* (*enfant*) snotty (-nosed).

mosaïque [mozaik] *nf* mosaic.

Moscou [mɔsku] *nm ou f* Moscow.

mosquée [mɔske] *nf* mosque.

mot [mo] *nm* word; **envoyer un m. à** to drop a line to; **m. à** *ou* **pour m.** word for word; **bon m.** witticism; **mots croisés** crossword (puzzle); **m. d'ordre** *Pol* resolution, order; (*slogan*) watchword; **m. de passe** password.

motard [mɔtar] *nm Fam* motorcyclist.

motel [mɔtɛl] *nm* motel.

moteur[1] [mɔtœr] *nm* (*de véhicule etc*) engine, motor; *Él* motor.

moteur[2]**, -trice** [mɔtœr, -tris] *a* (*force*) driving-; (*nerf, muscle*) motor.

motif [mɔtif] *nm* **1** reason, motive. **2** (*dessin*) pattern.

motion [mosjɔ̃] *nf Pol* motion; **on a voté une m. de censure** a vote of no confidence was given.

motiver [mɔtive] *vt* (*inciter, causer*) to motivate; (*justifier*) to justify. ◆**motivation** *nf* motivation.

moto [mɔto] *nf* motorcycle, motorbike. ◆**motocycliste** *nmf* motorcyclist.

motorisé [mɔtɔrize] *a* motorized.

motte [mɔt] *nf* (*de terre*) clod, lump; (*de beurre*) block.

mou (*or* **mol** *before vowel or mute h*), **molle** [mu, mɔl] *a* soft; (*faible, sans énergie*) feeble; – *nm* **avoir du m.** (*cordage*) to be slack.

mouchard, -arde [muʃar, -ard] *nmf Péj* informer. ◆**moucharder** *vt* **m. qn** *Fam* to inform on s.o.

mouche [muʃ] *nf* (*insecte*) fly; **prendre la m.** (*se fâcher*) to go into a huff; **faire m.** to hit the bull's-eye. ◆**moucheron** *nm* (*insecte*) midge.

moucher [muʃe] *vt* **m. qn** to wipe s.o.'s nose; **se m.** to blow one's nose.

moucheté [muʃte] *a* speckled, spotted.

mouchoir [muʃwar] *nm* handkerchief; (*en papier*) tissue.

moudre* [mudr] *vt* (*café, blé*) to grind.

moue [mu] *nf* long face, pout; **faire la m.** to pout, pull a (long) face.

mouette [mwɛt] *nf* (sea)gull.

moufle [mufl] *nf* (*gant*) mitt(en).

mouill/er [muje] **1** *vt* to wet, make wet; **se faire m.** to get wet; – **se m.** *vpr* to get (oneself) wet; (*se compromettre*) *Fam* to get involved (*by taking risks*). **2** *vt* **m. l'ancre** *Nau* to (drop) anchor; – *vi* to anchor. ◆**—é** *a* wet (**de** with). ◆**—age** *nm* (*action*) *Nau* anchoring; (*lieu*) anchorage.

moule[1] [mul] *nm* mould, *Am* mold; **m. à gâteaux** cake tin. ◆**moul/er** *vt* to mould, *Am* mold; (*statue*) to cast; **m. qn** (*vêtement*) to fit s.o. tightly. ◆**—ant** *a* (*vêtement*) tight-fitting. ◆**—age** *nm* moulding; casting; (*objet*) cast. ◆**moulure** *nf Archit* moulding.

moule[2] [mul] *nf* (*mollusque*) mussel.

moulin [mulɛ̃] *nm* mill; (*moteur*) *Fam* engine; **m. à vent** windmill; **m. à café** coffee-grinder.

moulinet [mulinɛ] *nm* **1** (*de canne à pêche*) reel. **2** (*de bâton*) twirl.

moulu [muly] *voir* **moudre**; – *a* (*café*) ground; (*éreinté*) *Fam* dead tired.

mour/ir* [murir] *vi* (*aux* **être**) to die (**de** of, from); **m. de froid** to die of exposure; **m. d'ennui** *ou* **de fatigue** *Fig* to be dead bored/tired; **m. de peur** *Fig* to be frightened to death; **s'ennuyer à m.** to be bored to death; – **se m.** *vpr* to be dying. ◆**—ant, -ante** *a* dying; (*voix*) faint; – *nmf* dying person.

mousquetaire [muskətɛr] *nm Mil Hist* musketeer.

mousse [mus] **1** *nf Bot* moss. **2** *nf* (*écume*) froth, foam; (*de bière*) froth; (*de savon*) lather; **m. à raser** shaving foam. **3** *nf Culin* mousse. **4** *nm Nau* ship's boy. ◆**mousser** *vi* (*bière etc*) to froth; (*savon*) to lather; (*eau savonneuse*) to foam. ◆**mousseux, -euse** *a* frothy; (*vin*) sparkling; – *nm* sparkling wine. ◆**moussu** *a* mossy.

mousseline [muslin] *nf* (*coton*) muslin.

mousson [musɔ̃] *nf* (*vent*) monsoon.

moustache [mustaʃ] *nf* moustache, *Am* mustache; *pl* (*de chat etc*) whiskers. ◆**moustachu** *a* wearing a moustache.

moustique [mustik] *nm* mosquito. ◆**moustiquaire** *nf* mosquito net; (*en métal*) screen.

moutard [mutar] *nm* (*enfant*) *Arg* kid.

moutarde [mutard] *nf* mustard.

mouton [mutɔ̃] *nm* sheep; (*viande*) mutton;

pl (*sur la mer*) white horses; (*poussière*) bits of dust; **peau de m.** sheepskin.

mouvement [muvmɑ̃] *nm* (*geste, déplacement, groupe etc*) & *Mus* movement; (*de colère*) outburst; (*impulsion*) impulse; **en m.** in motion. ◆**mouvementé** *a* (*animé*) lively, exciting; (*séance, vie etc*) eventful.

mouv/oir* [muvwar] *vi,* — **se m.** *vpr* to move; **mû par** (*mécanisme*) driven by. ◆—**ant** *a* (*changeant*) changing; **sables mouvants** quicksands.

moyen¹, -enne [mwajɛ̃, -ɛn] *a* average; (*format, entreprise etc*) medium(-sized); (*solution*) intermediate, middle; — *nf* average; (*dans un examen*) pass mark; (*dans un devoir*) half marks; **la moyenne d'âge** the average age; **en moyenne** on average. ◆**moyennement** *adv* averagely, moderately.

moyen² [mwajɛ̃] *nm* (*procédé, façon*) means, way (**de faire** of doing, to do); *pl* (*capacités*) ability, powers; (*argent, resources*) means; **au m. de** by means of; **il n'y a pas m. de faire** it's not possible to do; **je n'ai pas les moyens** (*argent*) I can't afford it; **par mes propres moyens** under my own steam.

moyennant [mwajɛnɑ̃] *prép* (*pour*) (in return) for; (*avec*) with.

moyeu, -x [mwajø] *nm* (*de roue*) hub.

mucosités [mykozite] *nfpl* mucus.

mue [my] *nf* moulting; breaking of the voice. ◆**muer** [mɥe] *vi* (*animal*) to moult; (*voix*) to break; **se m. en** to become transformed into.

muet, -ette [mɥɛ, -ɛt] *a* (*infirme*) dumb; (*de surprise etc*) speechless; (*film, reproche etc*) silent; *Gram* mute; — *nmf* dumb person.

mufle [myfl] *nm* **1** (*d'animal*) nose, muzzle. **2** (*individu*) Péj lout.

mug/ir [myʒir] *vi* (*vache*) to moo; (*bœuf*) to bellow; (*vent*) *Fig* to roar. ◆—**issement(s)** *nm*(*pl*) moo(ing); bellow(ing); roar(ing).

muguet [mygɛ] *nm* lily of the valley.

mule [myl] *nf* **1** (*pantoufle*) mule. **2** (*animal*) (she-)mule. ◆**mulet¹** *nm* (he-)mule.

mulet² [mylɛ] *nm* (*poisson*) mullet.

multi- [mylti] *préf* multi-.

multicolore [myltikɔlɔr] *a* multicoloured.

multinationale [myltinasjɔnal] *nf* multinational.

multiple [myltipl] *a* (*nombreux*) numerous; (*ayant des formes variées*) multiple; — *nm Math* multiple. ◆**multiplication** *nf* multiplication; (*augmentation*) increase. ◆**multiplicité** *nf* multiplicity. ◆**multiplier** *vt* to

multiply; — **se m.** *vpr* to increase; (*se reproduire*) to multiply.

multitude [myltityd] *nf* multitude.

municipal, -aux [mynisipal, -o] *a* municipal; **conseil m.** town council. ◆**municipalité** *nf* (*corps*) town council; (*commune*) municipality.

munir [mynir] *vt* **m. de** to provide *ou* equip with; **se m. de** to provide oneself with; **muni de** (*papiers, arme etc*) in possession of.

munitions [mynisjɔ̃] *nfpl* ammunition.

muqueuse [mykøz] *nf* mucous membrane.

mur [myr] *nm* wall; **m. du son** sound barrier; **au pied du m.** *Fig* with one's back to the wall. ◆**muraille** *nf* (high) wall. ◆**mural, -aux** *a* (*carte etc*) wall-; **peinture murale** mural (painting). ◆**murer** *vt* (*porte*) to wall up; **m. qn** to wall s.o. in.

mûr [myr] *a* (*fruit, projet etc*) ripe; (*âge, homme*) mature. ◆**mûrement** *adv* (*réfléchir*) carefully. ◆**mûrir** *vti* (*fruit*) to ripen; (*personne, projet*) to mature.

muret [myrɛ] *nm* low wall.

murmure [myrmyr] *nm* murmur. ◆**murmurer** *vti* to murmur.

musc [mysk] *nm* (*parfum*) musk.

muscade [myskad] *nf* nutmeg.

muscle [myskl] *nm* muscle. ◆**musclé** *a* (*bras*) brawny, muscular. ◆**musculaire** *a* (*tissu, système etc*) muscular. ◆**musculature** *nf* muscles.

museau, -x [myzo] *nm* (*de chien etc*) muzzle; (*de porc*) snout. ◆**museler** *vt* (*animal, presse etc*) to muzzle. ◆**muselière** *nf* (*appareil*) muzzle.

musée [myze] *nm* museum; **m. de peinture** (public) art gallery. ◆**muséum** *nm* (natural history) museum.

musette [myzɛt] *nf* (*d'ouvrier*) duffel bag, kit bag.

music-hall [myzikol] *nm* variety theatre.

musique [myzik] *nf* music; (*fanfare*) *Mil* band. ◆**musical, -aux** *a* musical. ◆**musicien, -ienne** *nmf* musician; — *a* **être très/assez m.** to be very/quite musical.

musulman, -ane [myzylmɑ̃, -an] *a* & *nmf* Moslem, Muslim.

muter [myte] *vt* (*employé*) to transfer. ◆**mutation** *nf* **1** transfer. **2** *Biol* mutation.

mutil/er [mytile] *vt* to mutilate, maim; **être mutilé** to be disabled. ◆—**é, -ée** *nmf* **m. de guerre/du travail** disabled ex-serviceman/ worker. ◆**mutilation** *nf* mutilation.

mutin [mytɛ̃] **1** *a* (*espiègle*) saucy. **2** *nm* (*rebelle*) mutineer. ◆**se mutin/er** *vpr* to mutiny. ◆—**é** *a* mutinous. ◆**mutinerie** *nf* mutiny.

mutisme [mytism] *nm* (stubborn) silence.
mutualité [mytɥalite] *nf* mutual insurance. ◆**mutualiste** *nmf* member of a friendly *ou* Am benefit society. ◆**mutuelle**[1] *nf* friendly society, Am benefit society.
mutuel, -elle[2] [mytɥɛl] *a* (*réciproque*) mutual. ◆**mutuellement** *adv* (*l'un l'autre*) each other (mutually).
myope [mjɔp] *a* & *nmf* shortsighted (person). ◆**myopie** *nf* shortsightedness.
myosotis [mjozɔtis] *nm* Bot forget-me-not.
myrtille [mirtij] *nf* Bot bilberry.

mystère [mistɛr] *nm* mystery. ◆**mystérieux, -euse** *a* mysterious.
mystifier [mistifje] *vt* to fool, deceive, hoax. ◆**mystification** *nf* hoax.
mystique [mistik] *a* mystic(al); – *nmf* (*personne*) mystic; – *nf* mystique (**de** of). ◆**mysticisme** *nm* mysticism.
mythe [mit] *nm* myth. ◆**mythique** *a* mythical. ◆**mythologie** *nf* mythology. ◆**mythologique** *a* mythological.
mythomane [mitɔman] *nmf* compulsive liar.

N

N, n [ɛn] *nm* N, n.
n' [n] *voir* ne.
nabot [nabo] *nm* Péj midget.
nacelle [nasɛl] *nf* (*de ballon*) car, gondola; (*de landau*) carriage, carrycot.
nacre [nakr] *nf* mother-of-pearl. ◆**nacré** *a* pearly.
nage [naʒ] *nf* (swimming) stroke; **n. libre** freestyle; **traverser à la n.** to swim across; **en n.** Fig sweating. ◆**nager** *vi* to swim; (*flotter*) to float; **je nage dans le bonheur** my happiness knows no bounds; **je nage complètement** (*je suis perdu*) Fam I'm all at sea; – *vt* (*crawl etc*) to swim. ◆**nageur, -euse** *nmf* swimmer.
nageoire [naʒwar] *nf* (*de poisson*) fin; (*de phoque*) flipper.
naguère [nagɛr] *adv* Litt not long ago.
naïf, -ïve [naif, -iv] *a* simple, naïve; – *nmf* (*jobard*) simpleton.
nain, naine [nɛ̃, nɛn] *nmf* dwarf; – *a* (*arbre, haricot*) dwarf-.
naissance [nɛsɑ̃s] *nf* birth; (*de bras, cou*) base; **donner n. à** Fig to give rise to; **de n.** from birth.
naître* [nɛtr] *vi* to be born; (*jour*) to dawn; (*sentiment, difficulté*) to arise (**de** from); **faire n.** (*soupçon, industrie etc*) to give rise to, create. ◆**naissant** *a* (*amitié etc*) incipient.
naïveté [naivte] *nf* simplicity, naïveté.
nant/ir [nɑ̃tir] *vt* **n. de** to provide with. ◆**—i** *a* & *nmpl* (*riche*) affluent.
naphtaline [naftalin] *nf* mothballs.
nappe [nap] *nf* **1** table cloth. **2** (*d'eau*) sheet; (*de gaz, pétrole*) layer; (*de brouillard*) blanket. ◆**napperon** *nm* (soft) table mat; (*pour vase etc*) (soft) mat, cloth.

narcotique [narkɔtik] *a* & *nm* narcotic.
narguer [narge] *vt* to flout, mock.
narine [narin] *nf* nostril.
narquois [narkwa] *a* sneering.
narration [narasjɔ̃] *nf* (*récit, acte, art*) narration. ◆**narrateur, -trice** *nmf* narrator.
nasal, -aux [nazal, -o] *a* nasal.
naseau, -x [nazo] *nm* (*de cheval*) nostril.
nasiller [nazije] *vi* (*personne*) to speak with a twang; (*micro, radio*) to crackle. ◆**nasillard** *a* (*voix*) nasal; (*micro etc*) crackling.
natal, *mpl* -als [natal] *a* (*pays etc*) native; **sa maison natale** the house where he *ou* she was born. ◆**natalité** *nf* birthrate.
natation [natasjɔ̃] *nf* swimming.
natif, -ive [natif, -iv] *a* & *nmf* native; **être n. de** to be a native of.
nation [nasjɔ̃] *nf* nation; **les Nations Unies** the United Nations. ◆**national, -aux** *a* national; ◆**nationale** *nf* (*route*) trunk road, Am highway. ◆**nationaliser** *vt* to nationalize. ◆**nationaliste** *a* Péj nationalistic; – *nmf* nationalist. ◆**nationalité** *nf* nationality.
nativité [nativite] *nf* Rel nativity.
natte [nat] *nf* **1** (*de cheveux*) plait, Am braid. **2** (*tapis*) mat, (piece of) matting. ◆**natt/er** *vt* to plait, Am braid. ◆**—age** *n* (*matière*) matting.
naturaliser [natyralize] *vt* (*personne*) Pol to naturalize. ◆**naturalisation** *nf* naturalization.
nature [natyr] *nf* (*monde naturel, caractère*) nature; **de toute n.** of every kind; **être de n. à** to be likely to; **payer en n.** Fin to pay in kind; **n. morte** (*tableau*) still life; **plus grand que n.** larger than life; – *a inv* (*omelette, yaourt etc*) plain; (*café*) black. ◆**natura-**

liste *nmf* naturalist. ◆**naturiste** *nmf* nudist, naturist.

naturel, -elle [natyrɛl] *a* natural; **mort naturelle** death from natural causes; – *nm* (*caractère*) nature; (*simplicité*) naturalness. ◆**naturellement** *adv* naturally.

naufrage [nofraʒ] *nm* (ship)wreck; (*ruine*) *Litt Fig* ruin; **faire n.** to be (ship)wrecked. ◆**naufragé, -ée** *a* & *nmf* shipwrecked (person).

nausée [noze] *nf* nausea, sickness. ◆**nauséabond** *a* nauseating, sickening.

nautique [notik] *a* nautical; (*sports, ski*) water-.

naval, mpl -als [naval] *a* naval; **constructions navales** shipbuilding.

navet [navɛ] *nm* **1** *Bot Culin* turnip. **2** (*film etc*) *Péj* flop, dud.

navette [navɛt] *nf* (*transport*) shuttle (service); **faire la n.** (*véhicule, personne etc*) to shuttle back and forth (**entre** between); **n. spatiale** space shuttle.

naviguer [navige] *vi* (*bateau*) to sail; (*piloter, voler*) to navigate. ◆**navigabilité** *nf* (*de bateau*) seaworthiness; (*d'avion*) air-worthiness. ◆**navigable** *a* (*fleuve*) navigable. ◆**navigant** *a* **personnel n.** *Av Nau* crew. ◆**navigateur** *nm* *Av* navigator. ◆**navigation** *nf* (*pilotage*) navigation; (*trafic*) *Nau* shipping.

navire [navir] *nm* ship.

navr/er [navr] *vt* to upset (greatly), grieve. ◆**-ant** *a* upsetting. ◆**-é** *a* (*air*) grieved; **je suis n.** I'm (terribly) sorry (**de faire** to do).

nazi, -ie [nazi] *a* & *nmf* *Pol Hist* Nazi.

ne [n(ə)] (**n'** before vowel or mute h; used to form negative verb with **pas, jamais, que** etc) *adv* **1** (+ **pas**) not; **elle ne boit pas** she does not *ou* doesn't drink; **il n'ose** (pas) he doesn't dare; **n'importe** it doesn't matter. **2** (with **craindre, avoir peur** etc) **je crains qu'il ne parte** I'm afraid he'll leave.

né [ne] *a* born; **il est né** he was born; **née Dupont** née Dupont.

néanmoins [neãmwɛ] *adv* nevertheless, nonetheless.

néant [neã] *nm* nothingness, void; (*sur un formulaire*) = none.

nébuleux, -euse [nebylø, -øz] *a* hazy, nebulous.

nécessaire [nesesɛr] *a* necessary; (*inéluctable*) inevitable; – *nm* **le n.** (*biens*) the necessities; **le strict n.** the bare necessities; **n. de couture** sewing box, workbox; **n. de toilette** sponge bag, dressing case; **faire le n.** to do what's necessary *ou* the necessary. ◆**né-**

cessairement *adv* necessarily; (*échouer etc*) inevitably. ◆**nécessité** *nf* necessity. ◆**nécessiter** *vt* to necessitate, require. ◆**nécessiteux, -euse** *a* needy.

nécrologie [nekrɔlɔʒi] *nf* obituary.

nectarine [nektarin] *nf* (*fruit*) nectarine.

néerlandais, -aise [neɛrlɑ̃dɛ, -ɛz] *a* Dutch; – *nmf* Dutchman, Dutchwoman; – *nm* (*langue*) Dutch.

nef [nɛf] *nf* (*d'église*) nave.

néfaste [nefast] *a* (*influence etc*) harmful (**à** to).

négatif, -ive [negatif, -iv] *a* negative; – *nm* *Phot* negative; – *nf* **répondre par la négative** to answer in the negative. ◆**négation** *nf* negation, denial (**de** of); *Gram* negation; (*mot*) negative.

négligeable [negliʒabl] *a* negligible.

négligent [negliʒã] *a* negligent, careless. ◆**négligemment** [-amã] *adv* negligently, carelessly. ◆**négligence** *nf* negligence, carelessness; (*faute*) (careless) error.

néglig/er [neglige] *vt* (*personne, conseil, travail etc*) to neglect; **n. de faire** to neglect to do; – **se n.** *vpr* (*négliger sa tenue ou sa santé*) to neglect oneself. ◆**-é** *a* (*tenue*) untidy, neglected; (*travail*) careless; – *nm* (*de tenue*) untidiness; (*vêtement*) negligee.

négoci/er [negɔsje] *vti* *Fin Pol* to negotiate. ◆**-ant, -ante** *nmf* merchant, trader. ◆**-able** *a* *Fin* negotiable. ◆**négociateur, -trice** *nmf* negotiator. ◆**négociation** *nf* negotiation.

nègre [nɛgr] **1** *a* (*art, sculpture etc*) Negro. **2** *nm* (*écrivain*) ghost writer.

neige [nɛʒ] *nf* snow; **n. fondue** sleet; **n. carbonique** dry ice. ◆**neiger** *v imp* to snow. ◆**neigeux, -euse** *a* snowy.

nénuphar [nenyfar] *nm* water lily.

néo [neo] *préf* neo-.

néon [neõ] *nm* (*gaz*) neon; **au n.** (*éclairage etc*) neon-.

néophyte [neɔfit] *nmf* novice.

néo-zélandais, -aise [neɔzelɑ̃dɛ, -ɛz] *a* (*peuple etc*) New Zealand-; – *nmf* New Zealander.

nerf [nɛr] *nm* *Anat* nerve; **avoir du n.** (*vigueur*) *Fam* to have guts; **du n.!, un peu de n.!** buck up!; **ça me porte** *ou* **me tape sur les nerfs** it gets on my nerves; **être sur les nerfs** *Fig* to be keyed up *ou* het up. ◆**nerveux, -euse** *a* nervous; (*centre, cellule*) nerve-. ◆**nervosité** *nf* nervousness.

nervure [nɛrvyr] *nf* (*de feuille*) vein.

nescafé [nɛskafe] *nm* instant coffee.

n'est-ce pas? [nɛspɑ] *adv* isn't he?, don't

you? *etc*; **il fait beau, n'est-ce pas?** the weather's fine, isn't it?

net, nette [nɛt] **1** *a* (*conscience, idée, image, refus*) clear; (*coupure, linge*) clean; (*soigné*) neat; (*copie*) fair; – *adv* (*s'arrêter*) short, dead; (*tuer*) outright; (*parler*) plainly; (*refuser*) flat(ly); (*casser, couper*) clean. **2** *a* (*poids, prix etc*) *Com* net(t). ◆**nettement** *adv* clearly, plainly; (*sensiblement*) markedly. ◆**netteté** *nf* clearness; (*de travail*) neatness.

nettoyer [nɛtwaje] *vt* to clean (up); (*plaie*) to cleanse, clean (up); (*vider, ruiner*) *Fam* to clean out. ◆**nettoiement** *nm* cleaning; **service du n.** refuse *ou Am* garbage collection. ◆**nettoyage** *nm* cleaning; **n. à sec** dry cleaning.

neuf¹, neuve [nœf, nœv] *a* new; **quoi de n.?** what's new(s)?; – *nm* **il y a du n.** there's been something new; **remettre à n.** to make as good as new.

neuf² [nœf] *a* & *nm* ([nœv] before **heures** & **ans**) nine. ◆**neuvième** *a* & *nmf* ninth.

neurasthénique [nørastenik] *a* depressed.

neutre [nøtr] **1** *a* (*pays, personne etc*) neutral; – *nm* *Él* neutral. **2** *a* & *nm* *Gram* neuter. ◆**neutraliser** *vt* to neutralize. ◆**neutralité** *nf* neutrality.

neveu, -x [nəvø] *nm* nephew.

névralgie [nevralʒi] *nf* headache; *Méd* neuralgia. ◆**névralgique** *a* **centre n.** *Fig* nerve centre.

névrose [nevroz] *nf* neurosis. ◆**névrosé, -ée** *a* & *nmf* neurotic.

nez [ne] *nm* nose; **n. à n.** face to face (**avec** with); **au n. de qn** (*rire etc*) in s.o.'s face; **mettre le n. dehors** *Fam* to stick one's nose outside.

ni [ni] *conj* **ni . . . ni** (+ *ne*) neither . . . nor; **il n'a ni faim ni soif** he's neither hungry nor thirsty; **sans manger ni boire** without eating or drinking; **ni l'un(e) ni l'autre** neither (of them).

niais, -aise [njɛ, -ɛz] *a* silly, simple; – *nmf* simpleton. ◆**niaiserie** *nf* silliness; *pl* (*paroles*) nonsense.

niche [niʃ] *nf* (*de chien*) kennel; (*cavité*) niche, recess.

nich/er [niʃe] *vi* (*oiseau*) to nest; (*loger*) *Fam* to hang out; – **se n.** *vpr* (*oiseau*) to nest; (*se cacher*) to hide oneself. ◆**—ée** *nf* (*oiseaux, enfants*) brood; (*chiens*) litter.

nickel [nikɛl] *nm* (*métal*) nickel.

nicotine [nikɔtin] *nf* nicotine.

nid [ni] *nm* nest; **n. de poules** *Aut* pothole.

nièce [njɛs] *nf* niece.

nième [ɛnjɛm] *a* nth.

nier [nje] *vt* to deny (**que that**); – *vi* *Jur* to deny the charge.

nigaud, -aude [nigo, -od] *a* silly; – *nmf* silly fool.

Nigéria [niʒerja] *nm ou f* Nigeria.

n'importe [nɛ̃pɔrt] *voir* **importer 1.**

nippon, -one *ou* **-onne** [nipɔ̃, -ɔn] *a* Japanese.

niveau, -x [nivo] *nm* (*hauteur*) level; (*degré, compétence*) standard, level; **n. de vie** standard of living; **n. à bulle (d'air)** spirit level; **au n. de qn** (*élève etc*) up to s.o.'s standard. ◆**niveler** *vt* (*surface*) to level; (*fortunes etc*) to even (up).

noble [nɔbl] *a* noble; – *nmf* nobleman, noblewoman. ◆**noblement** *adv* nobly. ◆**noblesse** *nf* (*caractère, classe*) nobility.

noce(s) [nɔs] *nf*(*pl*) wedding; **faire la noce** *Fam* to have a good time, make merry; **noces d'argent/d'or** silver/golden wedding. ◆**noceur, -euse** *nmf* *Fam* fast liver, reveller.

nocif, -ive [nɔsif, -iv] *a* harmful. ◆**nocivité** *nf* harmfulness.

noctambule [nɔktɑ̃byl] *nmf* (*personne*) night bird *ou* prowler. ◆**nocturne** *a* nocturnal; night; – *nm* (*de magasins etc*) late night opening; (**match en**) **n.** *Sp* floodlit match, *Am* night game.

Noël [nɔɛl] *nm* Christmas; **le père N.** Father Christmas, Santa Claus.

nœud [nø] *nm* **1** knot; (*ruban*) bow; **le n. du problème/etc** the crux of the problem/*etc*; **n. coulant** noose, slipknot; **n. papillon** bow tie. **2** (*mesure*) *Nau* knot.

noir, noire [nwar] *a* black; (*nuit, lunettes etc*) dark; (*idées*) gloomy; (*âme, crime*) vile; (*misère*) dire; **roman n.** thriller; **film n.** film noir; **il fait n.** it's dark; – *nm* (*couleur*) black; (*obscurité*) dark; **N.** (*homme*) black; **vendre au n.** to sell on the black market; – *nf* *Mus* crotchet, *Am* quarter note; **Noire** (*femme*) black. ◆**noirceur** *nf* blackness; (*d'une action etc*) vileness. ◆**noircir** *vt* to blacken; – *vi*, – **se n.** *vpr* to turn black.

noisette [nwazɛt] *nf* hazelnut. ◆**noisetier** *nm* hazel (tree).

noix [nwa] *nf* (*du noyer*) walnut; **n. de coco** coconut; **n. du Brésil** Brazil nut; **n. de beurre** knob of butter; **à la n.** *Fam* trashy, awful.

nom [nɔ̃] *nm* name; *Gram* noun; **n. de famille** surname; **n. de jeune fille** maiden name; **n. propre** *Gram* proper noun; **au n. de qn** on s.o.'s behalf; **sans n.** (*anonyme*) nameless; (*vil*) vile; **n. d'un chien!** *Fam* oh hell!

nomade [nɔmad] *a* nomadic; – *nmf* nomad.

nombre [nɔ̃br] *nm* number; **ils sont au** *ou* **du n. de** (*parmi*) they're among; **ils sont au n. de dix** there are ten of them; **elle est au n. de** she's one of; **le plus grand n. de** the majority of. ◆**nombreux, -euse** *a* (*amis, livres etc*) numerous; (*famille, collection etc*) large; **peu n.** few; **venir n.** to come in large numbers.

nombril [nɔ̃bri] *nm* navel.

nominal, -aux [nɔminal, -o] *a* nominal. ◆**nomination** *nf* appointment, nomination.

nommer [nɔme] *vt* (*appeler*) to name; **n. qn** (*désigner*) to appoint s.o. (**à un poste**/*etc* to a post/*etc*); **n. qn président/lauréat** to nominate s.o. chairman/prizewinner; **— se n.** *vpr* (*s'appeler*) to be called. ◆**nommément** *adv* by name.

non [nɔ̃] *adv & nm inv* no; **n.!** no!; **tu viens ou n.?** are you coming or not?; **n. seulement** not only; **n. (pas) que** (+ *sub*) . . . not that . . . ; **c'est bien, n.?** *Fam* it's all right, isn't it?; **je crois que n.** I don't think so; **(ni) moi n. plus** neither do, am, can *etc* I; **une place n. réservée** an unreserved seat.

non- [nɔ̃] *préf* non-.

nonante [nɔnɑ̃t] *a* (*en Belgique, en Suisse*) ninety.

nonchalant [nɔ̃ʃalɑ̃] *a* nonchalant, apathetic. ◆**nonchalance** *nf* nonchalance, apathy.

non-conformiste [nɔ̃kɔ̃fɔrmist] *a & nmf* nonconformist.

non-fumeur, -euse [nɔ̃fymœr, -øz] *nmf* non-smoker.

non-sens [nɔ̃sɑ̃s] *nm inv* absurdity.

nord [nɔr] *nm* north; **au n. de** north of; **du n.** (*vent, direction*) northerly; (*ville*) northern; (*gens*) from *ou* in the north; **Amérique/Afrique du N.** North America/Africa; **l'Europe du N.** Northern Europe; – *a inv* (*côte*) north(ern). ◆**n.-africain, -aine** *a & nmf* North African. ◆**n.-américain, -aine** *a & nmf* North American. ◆**n.-est** *nm & a inv* north-east. ◆**n.-ouest** *nm & a inv* north-west.

nordique [nɔrdik] *a & nmf* Scandinavian.

normal, -aux [nɔrmal, -o] *a* normal. ◆**normale** *nf* norm, normality; **au-dessus de la n.** above normal. ◆**normalement** *adv* normally. ◆**normaliser** *vt* (*uniformiser*) to standardize; (*relations etc*) to normalize.

normand, -ande [nɔrmɑ̃, -ɑ̃d] *a & nmf* Norman. ◆**Normandie** *nf* Normandy.

norme [nɔrm] *nf* norm.

Norvège [nɔrveʒ] *nf* Norway. ◆**norvégien, -ienne** *a & nmf* Norwegian; – *nm* (*langue*) Norwegian.

nos [no] *voir* **notre.**

nostalgie [nɔstalʒi] *nf* nostalgia. ◆**nostalgique** *a* nostalgic.

notable [nɔtabl] *a* (*fait etc*) notable; – *nm* (*personne*) notable. ◆**—ment** [-əmɑ̃] *adv* (*sensiblement*) notably.

notaire [nɔtɛr] *nm* solicitor, notary.

notamment [nɔtamɑ̃] *adv* notably.

note [nɔt] *nf* (*remarque etc*) & *Mus* note; (*chiffrée*) *Scol* mark, *Am* grade; (*compte, facture*) bill, *Am* check; **prendre n. de** to make a note of. ◆**notation** *nf* notation; *Scol* marking. ◆**noter** *vt* (*prendre note de*) to note; (*remarquer*) to note, notice; (*écrire*) to note down; (*devoir etc*) *Scol* to mark, *Am* grade; **être bien noté** (*personne*) to be highly rated.

notice [nɔtis] *nf* (*résumé, préface*) note; (*mode d'emploi*) instructions.

notifier [nɔtifje] *vt* **n. qch à qn** to notify s.o. of sth.

notion [nɔsjɔ̃] *nf* notion, idea; *pl* (*éléments*) rudiments.

notoire [nɔtwar] *a* (*criminel, bêtise*) notorious; (*fait*) well-known. ◆**notoriété** *nf* (*renom*) fame; (*de fait*) general recognition.

notre, pl nos [nɔtr, no] *a poss* our. ◆**nôtre** *pron poss* **le** *ou* **la n., les nôtres** ours; – *nmpl* **les nôtres** (*parents etc*) our (own) people.

nouer [nwe] *vt* to tie, knot; (*amitié, conversation*) to strike up; **avoir la gorge nouée** to have a lump in one's throat. ◆**noueux, -euse** *a* (*bois*) knotty; (*doigts*) gnarled.

nougat [nuga] *nm* nougat.

nouille [nuj] *nf* (*idiot*) *Fam* drip.

nouilles [nuj] *nfpl* noodles.

nounours [nunurs] *nm* teddy bear.

nourrice [nuris] *nf* (*assistante maternelle*) child minder, nurse; (*qui allaite*) wet nurse; **mettre en n.** to put out to nurse.

nourr/ir [nurir] *vt* (*alimenter, faire vivre*) to feed; (*espoir etc*) *Fig* to nourish; (*esprit*) to enrich; **se n. de** to feed on; – *vi* (*aliment*) to be nourishing. ◆**—issant** *a* nourishing. ◆**nourriture** *nf* food.

nourrisson [nurisɔ̃] *nm* infant.

nous [nu] *pron* **1** (*sujet*) we; **n. sommes** we are. **2** (*complément direct*) us; **il n. connaît** he knows us. **3** (*indirect*) (to) us; **il n. l'a donné** he gave it to us, he gave us it. **4** (*réfléchi*) ourselves; **n. n. lavons** we wash ourselves. **5** (*réciproque*) each other;

n. n. détestons we hate each other. ◆**n.-mêmes** *pron* ourselves.

nouveau (*or* **nouvel** *before vowel or mute h*), **nouvelle**[1], *pl* **nouveaux, nouvelles** [nuvo, nuvɛl] *a* new; – *nmf Scol* new boy, new girl; – *nm* **du n.** something new; **de n., à n.** again. ◆**n.-né, -ée** *a* & *nmf* new-born (baby). ◆**n.-venu** *nm*, ◆**nouvelle-venue** *nf* newcomer. ◆**nouveauté** *nf* newness, novelty; *pl* (*livres*) new books; (*disques*) new releases; (*vêtements*) new fashions; **une n.** (*objet*) a novelty.

nouvelle[2] [nuvɛl] *nf* **1 nouvelle(s)** news; **une n.** a piece of news. **2** *Littér* short story.

Nouvelle-Zélande [nuvɛlzelɑ̃d] *nf* New Zealand.

novateur, -trice [nɔvatœr, -tris] *nmf* innovator.

novembre [nɔvɑ̃br] *nm* November.

novice [nɔvis] *nmf* novice; – *a* inexperienced.

noyau, -x [nwajo] *nm* (*de fruit*) stone, *Am* pit; (*d'atome, de cellule*) nucleus; (*groupe*) group; **un n. d'opposants** a hard core of opponents.

noyaut/er [nwajote] *vt Pol* to infiltrate. ◆**—age** *nm* infiltration.

noy/er[1] [nwaje] *vt* (*personne etc*) to drown; (*terres*) to flood; – **se n.** *vpr* to drown; (*se suicider*) to drown oneself; **se n. dans le détail** to get bogged down in details. ◆**—é, -ée** *nmf* (*mort*) drowned person; – *a* **être n.** (*perdu*) *Fig* to be out of one's depth. ◆**noyade** *nf* drowning.

noyer[2] [nwaje] *nm* (*arbre*) walnut tree.

nu [ny] *a* (*personne, vérité*) naked; (*mains, chambre*) bare; **tout nu** (*stark*) naked, (*in the*) nude; **voir à l'œil nu** to see with the naked eye; **mettre à nu** (*exposer*) to lay bare; **se mettre nu** to strip off; **tête nue, nu-tête** bare-headed; – *nm* (*femme, homme, œuvre*) nude.

nuage [nɥaʒ] *nm* cloud; **un n. de lait** *Fig* a dash of milk. ◆**nuageux, -euse** *a* (*ciel*) cloudy.

nuance [nɥɑ̃s] *nf* (*de sens*) nuance; (*de couleurs*) shade, nuance; (*de regret*) tinge, nuance. ◆**nuanc/er** *vt* (*teintes*) to blend,

shade; (*pensée*) to qualify. ◆**—é** *a* (*jugement*) qualified.

nucléaire [nykleɛr] *a* nuclear.

nudisme [nydism] *nm* nudism. ◆**nudiste** *nmf* nudist. ◆**nudité** *nf* nudity, nakedness; (*de mur etc*) bareness.

nuée [nɥe] *nf* **une n. de** (*foule*) a host of; (*groupe compact*) a cloud of.

nues [ny] *nfpl* **porter qn aux n.** to praise s.o. to the skies.

nuire* [nɥir] *vi* **n. à** (*personne, intérêts etc*) to harm. ◆**nuisible** *a* harmful.

nuit [nɥi] *nf* night; (*obscurité*) dark(ness); **il fait n.** it's dark; **avant la n.** before nightfall; **la n.** (*se promener etc*) at night; **cette n.** (*aujourd'hui*) tonight; (*hier*) last night. ◆**nuitée** *nf* overnight stay (*in hotel etc*).

nul, nulle [nyl] **1** *a* (*risque etc*) non-existent, nil; (*médiocre*) useless, hopeless; (*non valable*) *Jur* null (and void); **faire match n.** *Sp* to tie, draw. **2** *a* (*aucun*) no; **de nulle importance** of no importance; **sans n. doute** without any doubt; **nulle part** nowhere; – *pron m* (*aucun*) no one. ◆**nullard, -arde** *nmf Fam* useless person. ◆**nullement** *adv* not at all. ◆**nullité** *nf* (*d'un élève etc*) uselessness; (*personne*) useless person.

numéraire [nymerɛr] *nm* cash, currency.

numéral, -aux [nymeral, -o] *a* & *nm* numeral. ◆**numérique** *a* numerical; (*montre etc*) digital.

numéro [nymero] *nm* number; (*de journal*) issue, number; (*au cirque*) act; **un n. de danse/de chant** a dance/song number; **quel n.!** (*personne*) *Fam* what a character!; **n. vert** *Tél* = Freefone®, = *Am* tollfree number. ◆**numérot/er** *vt* (*pages, sièges*) to number. ◆**—age** *nm* numbering.

nu-pieds [nypje] *nmpl* open sandals.

nuptial, -aux [nypsjal, -o] *a* (*chambre*) bridal; (*anneau, cérémonie*) wedding-.

nuque [nyk] *nf* back *ou* nape of the neck.

nurse [nœrs] *nf* nanny, (children's) nurse.

nutritif, -ive [nytritif, -iv] *a* nutritious, nutritive. ◆**nutrition** *nf* nutrition.

nylon [nilɔ̃] *nm* (*fibre*) nylon.

nymphe [nɛ̃f] *nf* nymph. ◆**nymphomane** *nf Péj* nymphomaniac.

O

O, o [o] *nm* O, o.

oasis [ɔazis] *nf* oasis.

obédience [ɔbedjɑ̃s] *nf Pol* allegiance.

obé/ir [ɔbeir] *vi* to obey; **o. à qn/qch** to obey s.o./sth; **être obéi** to be obeyed. ◆**—issant** *a* obedient. ◆**obéissance** *nf* obedience (à to).

obélisque [ɔbelisk] *nm* (*monument*) obelisk.

obèse [ɔbez] *a* & *nmf* obese (person). ◆**obésité** *nf* obesity.

objecter [ɔbʒɛkte] *vt* (*prétexte*) to put forward, plead; **o. que** to object that; **on lui objecta son jeune âge** they objected that he *ou* she was too young. ◆**objecteur** *nm* **o. de conscience** conscientious objector. ◆**objection** *nf* objection.

objectif, -ive [ɔbʒɛktif, -iv] **1** *a* (*opinion etc*) objective. **2** *nm* (*but*) objective; *Phot* lens. ◆**objectivement** *adv* objectively. ◆**objectivité** *nf* objectivity.

objet [ɔbʒɛ] *nm* (*chose, sujet, but*) object; (*de toilette*) article; **faire l'o. de** (*étude, critiques etc*) to be the subject of; (*soins, surveillance*) to be given, receive; **objets trouvés** (*bureau*) lost property, *Am* lost and found.

obligation [ɔbligasjɔ̃] *nf* (*devoir, lieu, nécessité*) obligation; *Fin* bond. ◆**obligatoire** *a* compulsory, obligatory; (*inévitable*) *Fam* inevitable. ◆**obligatoirement** *adv* (*fatalement*) inevitably; **tu dois o. le faire** you have to do it.

oblig/er [ɔbliʒe] *vt* **1** (*contraindre*) to compel, oblige (à faire to do); (*engager*) to bind; **être obligé de faire** to have to do, be compelled *ou* obliged to do. **2** (*rendre service à*) to oblige; **être obligé à qn de qch** to be obliged to s.o. for sth. ◆**—eant** *a* obliging, kind. ◆**—é** *a* (*obligatoire*) necessary; (*fatal*) *Fam* inevitable. ◆**obligeamment** [-amɑ̃] *adv* obligingly. ◆**obligeance** *nf* kindness.

oblique [ɔblik] *a* oblique; **regard o.** sidelong glance; **en o.** at an (oblique) angle. ◆**obliquer** *vi* (*véhicule etc*) to turn off.

oblitérer [ɔblitere] *vt* (*timbre*) to cancel; (*billet, carte*) to stamp; **timbre oblitéré** (*non neuf*) used stamp. ◆**oblitération** *nf* cancellation; stamping.

oblong, -ongue [ɔblɔ̃, -ɔ̃g] *a* oblong.

obnubilé [ɔbnybile] *a* (*obsédé*) obsessed (par with).

obscène [ɔpsɛn] *a* obscene. ◆**obscénité** *nf* obscenity.

obscur [ɔpskyr] *a* (*noir*) dark; (*peu clair, inconnu, humble*) obscure. ◆**obscurcir** *vt* (*chambre etc*) to darken; (*rendre peu intelligible*) to obscure (*text, ideas etc*); **— s'o.** *vpr* (*ciel*) to cloud over, darken; (*vue*) to become dim. ◆**obscurément** *adv* obscurely. ◆**obscurité** *nf* dark(ness); (*de texte, d'acteur etc*) obscurity.

obséd/er [ɔpsede] *vt* to obsess, haunt. ◆**—ant** *a* haunting, obsessive. ◆**—é, -ée** *nmf* maniac (de for); **o. sexuel** sex maniac.

obsèques [ɔpsɛk] *nfpl* funeral.

obséquieux, -euse [ɔpsekjø, -øz] *a* obsequious.

observer [ɔpsɛrve] *vt* (*regarder*) to observe, watch; (*remarquer, respecter*) to observe; **faire o. qch à qn** (*signaler*) to point sth out to s.o. ◆**observateur, -trice** *a* observant; **— *nmf*** observer. ◆**observation** *nf* (*examen, remarque*) observation; (*reproche*) (critical) remark, rebuke; (*de règle etc*) observance; **en o.** (*malade*) under observation. ◆**observatoire** *nm* observatory; (*colline etc*) *Fig* & *Mil* observation post.

obsession [ɔpsesjɔ̃] *nf* obsession. ◆**obsessif, -ive** *a* (*peur etc*) obsessive. ◆**obsessionnel, -elle** *a Psy* obsessive.

obstacle [ɔpstakl] *nm* obstacle; **faire o. à** to stand in the way of.

obstétrique [ɔpstetrik] *nf Méd* obstetrics.

obstin/er (s') [sɔpstine] *vpr* to be obstinate *ou* persistent; **s'o. à faire** to persist in doing. ◆**—é** *a* stubborn, obstinate, persistent. ◆**obstination** *nf* stubbornness, obstinacy, persistence.

obstruction [ɔpstryksjɔ̃] *nf Méd Pol Sp* obstruction; **faire de l'o.** *Pol Sp* to be obstructive. ◆**obstruer** *vt* to obstruct.

obtempérer [ɔptɑ̃pere] *vi* to obey an injunction; **o. à** to obey.

obtenir* [ɔptənir] *vt* to get, obtain, secure. ◆**obtention** *nf* obtaining, getting.

obturer [ɔptyre] *vt* (*trou etc*) to stop *ou* close up. ◆**obturateur** *nm Phot* shutter; *Tech* valve.

obtus [ɔpty] *a* (*angle, esprit*) obtuse.

obus [ɔby] *nm Mil* shell.

occasion [ɔkazjɔ̃] *nf* **1** (*chance*) opportunity, chance (**de faire** to do); (*circonstance*) occasion; **à l'o.** on occasion, when the occasion arises; **à l'o. de** on the occasion of. **2** *Com* (*marché avantageux*) bargain; (*objet non neuf*) second-hand buy; **d'o.** second-hand, used. ◆**occasionner** *vt* to cause; **o. qch à qn** to cause s.o. sth.

occident [ɔksidã] *nm* **l'O.** *Pol* the West. ◆**occidental, -aux** *a Géog Pol* western; — *nmpl* **les occidentaux** *Pol* Westerners. ◆**occidentalisé** *a Pol* Westernized.

occulte [ɔkylt] *a* occult.

occup/er [ɔkype] *vt* (*maison, pays, usine etc*) to occupy; (*place, temps*) to take up, occupy; (*poste*) to hold, occupy; **o. qn** (*absorber*) to occupy s.o., keep s.o. busy; (*ouvrier etc*) to employ s.o.; — **s'o.** *vpr* to keep (oneself) busy (**à faire** doing); **s'o. de** (*affaire, problème etc*) to deal with; (*politique*) to be engaged in; **s'o. de qn** (*malade etc*) to take care of s.o.; (*client*) to see to s.o., deal with s.o.; **ne t'en occupe pas!** (*ne t'en fais pas*) don't worry!; (*ne t'en mêle pas*) mind your own business! ◆**-ant, -ante** *a* (*armée*) occupying; — *nmf* (*habitant*) occupant; — *nm Mil* forces of occupation, occupier. ◆**-é** *a* busy (**à faire** doing); (*place, maison etc*) occupied; (*ligne*) *Tél* engaged, *Am* busy; (*taxi*) hired. ◆**occupation** *nf* (*activité, travail etc*) occupation; **l'o. de** (*action*) the occupation of.

occurrence [ɔkyrãs] *nf Ling* occurrence; **en l'o.** in the circumstances, as it happens *ou* happened.

océan [ɔseã] *nm* ocean. ◆**océanique** *a* oceanic.

ocre [ɔkr] *nm & a inv* (*couleur*) ochre.

octave [ɔktav] *nf Mus* octave.

octobre [ɔktɔbr] *nm* October.

octogénaire [ɔktɔʒenɛr] *nmf* octogenarian.

octogone [ɔktɔgɔn] *nm* octagon. ◆**octogonal, -aux** *a* octagonal.

octroi [ɔktrwa] *nm Litt* granting. ◆**octroyer** *vt Litt* to grant (**à** to).

oculaire [ɔkylɛr] *a* **témoin o.** eyewitness; **globe o.** eyeball. ◆**oculiste** *nmf* eye specialist.

ode [ɔd] *nf* (*poème*) ode.

odeur [ɔdœr] *nf* smell, odour; (*de fleur*) scent. ◆**odorant** *a* sweet-smelling. ◆**odorat** *nm* sense of smell.

odieux, -euse [ɔdjø, -øz] *a* odious, obnoxious.

œcuménique [ekymenik] *a Rel* (o)ecumenical.

œil, *pl* **yeux** [œj, jø] *nm* eye; **sous mes yeux** before my very eyes; **lever/baisser les yeux** to look up/down; **fermer l'o.** (*dormir*) to shut one's eyes; **fermer les yeux sur** to turn a blind eye to; **ouvre l'o.!** keep your eyes open!; **coup d'o.** (*regard*) glance, look; **jeter un coup d'o. sur** to (have a) look *ou* glance at; **à vue d'o.** visibly; **faire les gros yeux à** to scowl at; **avoir à l'o.** (*surveiller*) to keep an eye on; **à l'o.** (*gratuitement*) *Fam* free; **faire de l'o. à** *Fam* to make eyes at; **o. au beurre noir** *Fig* black eye; **mon o.!** *Fam* (*incrédulité*) my foot!; (*refus*) no way!, no chance!

œillade [œjad] *nf* (*clin d'œil*) wink.

œillères [œjɛr] *nfpl* (*de cheval*) & *Fig* blinkers, *Am* blinders.

œillet [œjɛ] *nm* **1** *Bot* carnation. **2** (*trou de ceinture etc*) eyelet.

œuf, *pl* **œufs** [œf, ø] *nm* egg; *pl* (*de poisson*) (hard) roe; **o. sur le plat** fried egg; **étouffer qch dans l'o.** *Fig* to nip *ou* stifle sth in the bud.

œuvre [œvr] *nf* (*travail, acte, livre etc*) work; **o. (de charité)** (*organisation*) charity; **l'o. de** (*production artistique etc*) the works of; **mettre en o.** (*employer*) to make use of; **mettre tout en o.** to do everything possible (**pour faire** to do). ◆**œuvrer** *vi Litt* to work.

offense [ɔfãs] *nf* insult; *Rel* transgression. ◆**offens/er** *vt* to offend; **s'o.** **de** to take offence at. ◆**-ant** *a* offensive.

offensif, -ive [ɔfãsif, -iv] *a* offensive; — *nf* (*attaque*) offensive; (*du froid*) onslaught.

offert [ɔfɛr] *voir* **offrir**.

office [ɔfis] **1** *nm* (*fonction*) office; (*bureau*) office, bureau; **d'o.** (*être promu etc*) automatically; **faire o. de** to serve as; **ses bons offices** (*service*) one's good offices. **2** *nm Rel* service. **3** *nm ou f* (*pièce pour provisions*) pantry.

officiel, -ielle [ɔfisjɛl] *a* (*acte etc*) official; — *nm* (*personnage*) official. ◆**officiellement** *adv* officially. ◆**officieux, -euse** *a* unofficial.

officier [ɔfisje] **1** *vi Rel* to officiate. **2** *nm* (*dans l'armée etc*) officer.

offre [ɔfr] *nf* offer; (*aux enchères*) bid; **l'o. et la demande** *Écon* supply and demand; **offres d'emploi** *Journ* situations vacant. ◆**offrande** *nf* offering.

offr/ir* [ɔfrir] *vt* (*proposer, présenter*) to offer (**de faire** to do); (*donner en cadeau*) to give; (*démission*) to tender, offer; **je lui ai offert de le loger** I offered to put him up; — **s'o.** *vpr* (*cadeau etc*) to treat oneself to; (*se* *proposer*) to offer oneself (**comme** as); **s'o. à faire** to offer *ou* volunteer to do; **s'o. (aux yeux)** (*vue etc*) to present itself. ◆—**ant** *nm* **au plus o.** to the highest bidder.

offusquer [ɔfyske] *vt* to offend, shock; **s'o. de** to take offence at.

ogive [ɔʒiv] *nf* (*de fusée*) nose cone; **o. nucléaire** nuclear warhead.

ogre [ɔgr] *nm* ogre.

oh! [o] *int* oh!, o!

ohé! [ɔe] *int* hey (there)!

oie [wa] *nf* goose.

oignon [ɔɲɔ̃] *nm* (*légume*) onion; (*de tulipe, lis etc*) bulb; **occupe-toi de tes oignons!** *Fam* mind your own business!

oiseau, -x [wazo] *nm* bird; **à vol d'o.** as the crow flies; **drôle d'o.** (*individu*) *Péj* odd fish, *Am* oddball; **o. rare** (*personne étonnante*) *Iron* rare bird, perfect gem.

oiseux, -euse [wazø, -øz] *a* (*futile*) idle, vain.

oisif, -ive [wazif, -iv] *a* (*inactif*) idle; – *nmf* idler. ◆**oisiveté** *nf* idleness.

oléoduc [ɔleɔdyk] *nm* oil pipeline.

olive [ɔliv] *nf* (*fruit*) olive; **huile d'o.** olive oil; – *a inv* (*couleur*) (**vert**) **o.** olive (green). ◆**olivier** *nm* (*arbre*) olive tree.

olympique [ɔlɛ̃pik] *a* (*jeux, record etc*) Olympic.

ombilical, -aux [ɔ̃bilikal, -o] *a* (*cordon*) umbilical.

ombrage [ɔ̃braʒ] *nm* **1** (*ombre*) shade. **2 prendre o. de** (*jalousie, dépit*) to take umbrage at. ◆**ombrag/er** *vt* to give shade to. ◆—**é** *a* shady. ◆**ombrageux, -euse** *a* (*caractère, personne*) touchy.

ombre [ɔ̃br] *nf* (*d'arbre etc*) shade; (*de personne, objet*) shadow; **l'o. d'un doute** *Fig* the shadow of a doubt; **l'o. de** (*remords, reproche etc*) the trace of; **30° à l'o.** 30° in the shade; **dans l'o.** (*comploter, travailler etc*) in secret.

ombrelle [ɔ̃brɛl] *nf* sunshade, parasol.

omelette [ɔmlɛt] *nf* omelet(te); **o. au fromage/etc** cheese/etc omelet(te).

omettre* [ɔmɛtr] *vt* to omit (**de faire** to do). ◆**omission** *nf* omission.

omni- [ɔmni] *préf* omni-. ◆**omnipotent** *a* omnipotent.

omnibus [ɔmnibys] *a & nm* (**train**) **o.** slow train (*stopping at all stations*).

omoplate [ɔmɔplat] *nf* shoulder blade.

on [ɔ̃] (*sometimes* **l'on** [lɔ̃]) *pron* (*les gens*) they, people; (*nous*) we, one; (*vous*) you, one; **on dit** they say, people say, it is said; **on frappe** (*quelqu'un*) someone's knocking;

on me l'a donné it was given to me, I was given it.

once [ɔ̃s] *nf* (*mesure*) & *Fig* ounce.

oncle [ɔ̃kl] *nm* uncle.

onctueux, -euse [ɔ̃ktɥø, -øz] *a* (*liquide, crème*) creamy; (*manières, paroles*) *Fig* smooth.

onde [ɔ̃d] *nf Phys Rad* wave; **grandes ondes** long wave; **ondes courtes/moyennes** short/medium wave; **sur les ondes** (*sur l'antenne*) on the radio.

ondée [ɔ̃de] *nf* (*pluie*) (sudden) shower.

on-dit [ɔ̃di] *nm inv* rumour, hearsay.

ondoyer [ɔ̃dwaje] *vi* to undulate. ◆**ondulation** *nf* undulation; (*de cheveux*) wave. ◆**ondul/er** *vi* to undulate; (*cheveux*) to be wavy. ◆—**é** *a* wavy.

onéreux, -euse [ɔnerø, -øz] *a* costly.

ongle [ɔ̃gl] *nm* (finger) nail.

onglet [ɔ̃glɛ] *nm* (*entaille de canif etc*) (nail) groove.

ont [ɔ̃] *voir* avoir.

ONU [ɔny] *nf abrév* (*Organisation des nations unies*) UN.

onyx [ɔniks] *nm* (*pierre précieuse*) onyx.

onze [ɔ̃z] *a & nm* eleven. ◆**onzième** *a & nmf* eleventh.

opale [ɔpal] *nf* (*pierre*) opal.

opaque [ɔpak] *a* opaque. ◆**opacité** *nf* opacity.

opéra [ɔpera] *nm* (*ouvrage, art*) opera; (*édifice*) opera house. ◆**opérette** *nf* operetta.

opér/er [ɔpere] **1** *vt* (*exécuter*) to carry out; (*choix*) to make; – *vi* (*agir*) to work, act; (*procéder*) to proceed; – **s'o.** *vpr* (*se produire*) to take place. **2** *vt* (*personne, organe*) *Méd* to operate on (**de** for); (*tumeur*) to remove; **cela peut s'o.** this can be removed; **se faire o.** to have an operation; – *vi* (*chirurgien*) to operate. ◆—**ant** *a* (*efficace*) operative. ◆—**é, -ée** *nmf Méd* patient (*operated on*). ◆**opérateur, -trice** *nmf* (*de prise de vues*) *Cin* cameraman; (*sur machine*) operator. ◆**opération** *nf* (*acte*) & *Méd Mil Math etc* operation; *Fin* deal. ◆**opérationnel, -elle** *a* operational. ◆**opératoire** *a Méd* operative; **bloc o.** operating *ou* surgical wing.

opiner [ɔpine] *vi* **o. (de la tête** *ou* **du chef)** to nod assent.

opiniâtre [ɔpinjɑtr] *a* stubborn, obstinate. ◆**opiniâtreté** *nf* stubbornness, obstinacy.

opinion [ɔpinjɔ̃] *nf* opinion (**sur** about, on).

opium [ɔpjɔm] *nm* opium.

opportun [ɔpɔrtœ̃] *a* opportune, timely. ◆**opportunément** *adv* opportunely.

◆**opportunisme** nm opportunism. ◆**op-portunité** nf timeliness.

oppos/er [ɔpoze] vt (argument, résistance) to put up (à against); (équipes, rivaux) to bring together, set against each other; (objets) to place opposite each other; (couleurs) to contrast; **o. qch à qch** (objet) to place sth opposite sth; **o. qn à qn** to set s.o. against s.o.; **match qui oppose . . .** match between . . . ; **– s'o.** vpr (couleurs) to contrast; (équipes) to confront each other; **s'o. à** (mesure, personne etc) to oppose, be opposed to; **je m'y oppose** I'm opposed to it, I oppose. ◆**–ant, -ante** a opposing; **– nmf** opponent. ◆**–é** a (direction etc) opposite; (intérêts, équipe) opposing; (opinions) opposite, opposing; (couleurs) contrasting; **être o. à** to be opposed to; **– nm l'o.** the opposite (de of); **à l'o.** (côté) on the opposite side (de from, to); **à l'o. de** (contrairement à) contrary to. ◆**opposition** nf opposition; **faire o. à** to oppose; **par o. à** as opposed to.

oppress/er [ɔprese] vt (gêner) to oppress. ◆**–ant** a oppressive. ◆**–eur** nm Pol oppressor. ◆**oppressif, -ive** a (loi etc) oppressive. ◆**oppression** nf oppression. ◆**opprim/er** vt (tyranniser) to oppress. ◆**–és** nmpl les o. the oppressed.

opter [ɔpte] vi o. pour to opt for.

opticien, -ienne [ɔptisjɛ̃, -jɛn] nmf optician.

optimisme [ɔptimism] nm optimism. ◆**optimiste** a optimistic; **– nmf** optimist.

optimum [ɔptimɔm] nm & a optimum; **la température o.** the optimum temperature. ◆**optimal, -aux** a optimal.

option [ɔpsjɔ̃] nf (choix) option; (chose) optional extra.

optique [ɔptik] a (verre) optical; **– nf** optics; (aspect) Fig perspective; **d'o.** (illusion, instrument etc) optical.

opulent [ɔpylɑ̃] a opulent. ◆**opulence** nf opulence.

or [ɔr] **1** nm gold; **en or** (chaîne etc) gold-; **d'or** (cheveux, âge, règle) golden; (cœur) of gold; **mine d'or** Géol goldmine; (fortune) Fig goldmine; **affaire en or** (achat) bargain; (commerce) Fig goldmine; **or noir** (pétrole) Fig black gold. **2** conj (alors, cependant) now, well.

oracle [ɔrakl] nm oracle.

orage [ɔraʒ] nm (thunder)storm. ◆**orageux, -euse** a stormy.

oraison [ɔrezɔ̃] nf prayer; **o. funèbre** funeral oration.

oral, -aux [ɔral, -o] a oral; **– nm** (examen) Scol oral.

orange [ɔrɑ̃ʒ] nf (fruit) orange; **o. pressée** (fresh) orange juice; **– a & nm inv** (couleur) orange. ◆**orangé** a & nm (couleur) orange. ◆**orangeade** nf orangeade. ◆**oranger** nm orange tree.

orang-outan(g) [ɔrɑ̃utɑ̃] nm (pl orangs-outan(g)s) orang-outang.

orateur [ɔratœr] nm speaker, orator.

orbite [ɔrbit] nf (d'astre etc) & Fig orbit; (d'œil) socket; **mettre sur o.** (fusée etc) to put into orbit.

orchestre [ɔrkɛstr] nm (classique) orchestra; (moderne) band; (places) Th stalls, Am orchestra. ◆**orchestrer** vt (organiser) & Mus to orchestrate.

orchidée [ɔrkide] nf orchid.

ordinaire [ɔrdinɛr] a (habituel, normal) ordinary; (médiocre) ordinary, average; **d'o., à l'o.** usually; **comme d'o., comme à l'o.** as usual; **de l'essence o.** two-star (petrol), Am regular. ◆**–ment** adv usually.

ordinal, -aux [ɔrdinal, -o] a (nombre) ordinal.

ordinateur [ɔrdinatœr] nm computer.

ordination [ɔrdinasjɔ̃] nf Rel ordination.

ordonnance [ɔrdɔnɑ̃s] nf **1** (de médecin) prescription. **2** (décret) Jur order, ruling. **3** (disposition) arrangement. **4** (soldat) orderly.

ordonn/er [ɔrdɔne] vt **1** (enjoindre) to order (que (+ sub) that); **o. à qn de faire** to order s.o. to do. **2** (agencer) to arrange, order. **3** (médicament etc) to prescribe. **4** (prêtre) to ordain. ◆**–é** a (personne, maison etc) orderly.

ordre [ɔrdr] nm (commandement, structure, association etc) order; (absence de désordre) tidiness (of room, person etc); **en o.** (chambre etc) tidy; **mettre en o., mettre de l'o. dans** to tidy (up); **de premier o.** first-rate; **o. (public)** (law and) order; **par o. d'âge** in order of age; **à l'o. du jour** (au programme) on the agenda; (d'actualité) of topical interest; **les forces de l'o.** the police; **jusqu'à nouvel o.** until further notice; **de l'o. de** (environ) of the order of.

ordure [ɔrdyr] nf filth, muck; **pl** (débris) refuse, rubbish, Am garbage. ◆**ordurier, -ière** a (plaisanterie etc) lewd.

oreille [ɔrɛj] nf ear; **être tout oreilles** to be all ears; **faire la sourde o.** to turn a deaf ear; **casser les oreilles à qn** to deafen s.o.

oreiller [ɔreje] nm pillow.

oreillons [ɔrejɔ̃] nmpl Méd mumps.

ores (d') [dɔr] adv d'ores et déjà [dɔrzedeʒa] henceforth.

orfèvre [ɔrfɛvr] *nm* goldsmith, silversmith. ◆**orfèvrerie** *nf* (*magasin*) goldsmith's *ou* silversmith's shop; (*objets*) gold *ou* silver plate.

organe [ɔrgan] *nm Anat & Fig* organ; (*porte-parole*) mouthpiece. ◆**organique** *a* organic. ◆**organisme** *nm* **1** (*corps*) body; *Anat Biol* organism. **2** (*bureaux etc*) organization.

organisation [ɔrganizasjɔ̃] *nf* (*arrangement, association*) organization.

organis/er [ɔrganize] *vt* to organize; — **s'o.** *vpr* to organize oneself, get organized. ◆**—é** *a* (*esprit, groupe etc*) organized. ◆**organisateur, -trice** *nmf* organizer.

organiste [ɔrganist] *nmf Mus* organist.

orgasme [ɔrgasm] *nm* orgasm.

orge [ɔrʒ] *nf* barley.

orgie [ɔrʒi] *nf* orgy.

orgue [ɔrg] *nm Mus* organ; **o. de Barbarie** barrel organ; — *nfpl* organ; **grandes orgues** great organ.

orgueil [ɔrgœj] *nm* pride. ◆**orgueilleux, -euse** *a* proud.

orient [ɔrjɑ̃] *nm* **l'O.** the Orient, the East; **Moyen-O., Proche-O.** Middle East; **Extrême-O.** Far East. ◆**oriental, -ale, -aux** *a* eastern; (*de l'Orient*) oriental; — *nmf* oriental.

orient/er [ɔrjɑ̃te] *vt* (*lampe, antenne etc*) to position, direct; (*voyageur, élève etc*) to direct; (*maison*) to orientate, *Am* orient; — **s'o.** *vpr* to find one's bearings *ou* direction; **s'o. vers** (*carrière etc*) to move towards. ◆**—é** *a* (*ouvrage, film etc*) slanted. ◆**orientable** *a* (*lampe etc*) adjustable, flexible; (*bras de machine*) movable. ◆**orientation** *nf* direction; (*action*) positioning, directing; (*de maison*) aspect, orientation; (*tendance*) *Pol Littér etc* trend; **o. professionnelle** vocational guidance.

orifice [ɔrifis] *nm* opening, orifice.

originaire [ɔriʒinɛr] *a* **être o. de** (*natif*) to be a native of.

original, -ale, -aux [ɔriʒinal, -o] **1** *a* (*idée, artiste, version etc*) original; — *nm* (*modèle*) original. **2** *a & nmf* (*bizarre*) eccentric. ◆**originalité** *nf* originality; eccentricity.

origine [ɔriʒin] *nf* origin; **à l'o.** originally; **d'o.** (*pneu etc*) original; **pays d'o.** country of origin. ◆**originel, -elle** *a* (*sens, péché, habitant etc*) original.

orme [ɔrm] *nm* (*arbre, bois*) elm.

ornement [ɔrnəmɑ̃] *nm* ornament. ◆**ornemental, -aux** *a* ornamental. ◆**ornementation** *nf* ornamentation. ◆**ornementé** *a* adorned, ornamented (**de** with). ◆**orn/er** *vt* to decorate, adorn (**de** with). ◆**—é** *a* (*syle etc*) ornate.

ornière [ɔrnjɛr] *nf* (*sillon*) & *Fig* rut.

orphelin, -ine [ɔrfəlɛ̃, -in] *nmf* orphan; — *a* orphaned. ◆**orphelinat** *nm* orphanage.

orteil [ɔrtɛj] *nm* toe; **gros o.** big toe.

orthodoxe [ɔrtɔdɔks] *a* orthodox; — *nmpl* **les orthodoxes** the orthodox. ◆**orthodoxie** *nf* orthodoxy.

orthographe [ɔrtɔgraf] *nf* spelling. ◆**orthographier** *vt* (*mot*) to spell.

orthopédie [ɔrtɔpedi] *nf* orthop(a)edics.

ortie [ɔrti] *nf* nettle.

os [ɔs, *pl o ou* ɔs] *nm* bone; **trempé jusqu'aux os** soaked to the skin; **tomber sur un os** (*difficulté*) *Fam* to hit a snag.

OS [ɔɛs] *abrév* = **ouvrier spécialisé.**

oscar [ɔskar] *nm Cin* Oscar.

osciller [ɔsile] *vi Tech* to oscillate; (*se balancer*) to swing, sway; (*hésiter*) to waver; (*varier*) to fluctuate; (*flamme*) to flicker. ◆**oscillation** *nf Tech* oscillation; (*de l'opinion*) fluctuation.

oseille [ozɛj] *nf* **1** *Bot Culin* sorrel. **2** (*argent*) *Arg* dough.

os/er [oze] *vti* to dare; **o. faire** to dare (to) do. ◆**—é** *a* bold, daring.

osier [ozje] *nm* (*branches*) wicker.

ossature [ɔsatyr] *nf* (*du corps*) frame; (*de bâtiment*) & *Fig* framework. ◆**osselets** *nmpl* (*jeu*) jacks, knucklebones. ◆**ossements** *nmpl* (*de cadavres*) bones. ◆**osseux, -euse** *a* (*tissu*) bone-; (*maigre*) bony.

ostensible [ɔstɑ̃sibl] *a* conspicuous.

ostentation [ɔstɑ̃tasjɔ̃] *nf* ostentation.

otage [ɔtaʒ] *nm* hostage; **prendre qn en o.** to take s.o. hostage.

OTAN [ɔtɑ̃] *nf abrév* (*Organisation du traité de l'Atlantique Nord*) NATO.

otarie [ɔtari] *nf* (*animal*) sea lion.

ôter [ote] *vt* to remove, take away (**à qn** from s.o.); (*vêtement*) to take off, remove; (*déduire*) to take (away); **ôte-toi de là!** *Fam* get out of the way!

otite [ɔtit] *nf* ear infection.

oto-rhino [ɔtorino] *nmf Méd Fam* ear, nose and throat specialist.

ou [u] *conj* or; **ou bien** or else; **ou elle ou moi** either her or me.

où [u] *adv & pron* where; **le jour où** the day when, the day on which; **la table où** the table on which; **l'état où** the condition in which; **par où?** which way?; **d'où?** where from?; **d'où ma surprise**/*etc* (*conséquence*) hence my surprise/*etc*; **le pays d'où** the country from which; **où qu'il soit** wherever he may be.

ouate [wat] *nf Méd* cotton wool, *Am* absorbent cotton.

oubli [ubli] *nm* (*défaut*) forgetfulness; **l'o. de qch** forgetting sth; **un o.** a lapse of memory; (*omission*) an oversight; **tomber dans l'o.** to fall into oblivion. ◆**oublier** *vt* to forget (**de faire** to do); (*faute, problème*) to overlook; — **s'o.** *vpr* (*traditions etc*) to be forgotten; (*personne*) *Fig* to forget oneself. ◆**oublieux, -euse** *a* forgetful (**de** of).

oubliettes [ublijɛt] *nfpl* (*de château*) dungeon.

ouest [wɛst] *nm* west; **à l'o. de** west of; **d'o.** (*vent*) west(erly); **de l'o.** western; **Allemagne de l'O.** West Germany; **l'Europe de l'O.** Western Europe; — *a inv* (*côte*) west(ern). ◆**o.-allemand, -ande** *a & nmf* West German.

ouf! [uf] *int* (*soulagement*) ah!, phew!

oui [wi] *adv & nm inv* yes; **o.!** yes; **les o.** (*votes*) the ayes; **tu viens, o.?** come on, will you?; **je crois que o.** I think so; **si o.** if so.

ouï-dire [widir] *nm inv* hearsay.

ouïe[1] [wi] *nf* hearing; **être tout o.** *Fam* to be all ears.

ouïe[2]**!** [uj] *int* ouch!

ouïes [wi] *nfpl* (*de poisson*) gills.

ouille! [uj] *int* ouch!

ouragan [uragã] *nm* hurricane.

ourler [urle] *vt* to hem. ◆**ourlet** *nm* hem.

ours [urs] *nm* bear; **o. blanc/gris** polar/grizzly bear.

oursin [ursɛ̃] *nm* (*animal*) sea urchin.

ouste! [ust] *int Fam* scram!

outil [uti] *nm* tool. ◆**outill/er** *vt* to equip. ◆**—age** *nm* tools; (*d'une usine*) equipment.

outrage [utraʒ] *nm* insult (**à** to). ◆**outrag/er** *vt* to insult, offend. ◆**—eant** *a* insulting, offensive.

outrance [utrãs] *nf* (*excès*) excess; **à o.** (*travailler etc*) to excess; **guerre à o.** all-out war. ◆**outrancier, -ière** *a* excessive.

outre [utr] *prép* besides; — *adv* **en o.** besides, moreover; **o. mesure** inordinately; **passer o.** to take no notice (**à** of). ◆**o.-Manche**

adv across the Channel. ◆**o.-mer** *adv* overseas; **d'o.-mer** (*peuple*) overseas.

outrepasser [utrəpase] *vt* (*limite etc*) to go beyond, exceed.

outr/er [utre] *vt* to exaggerate, overdo; **o. qn** (*indigner*) to outrage s.o. ◆**—é** *a* (*excessif*) exaggerated; (*révolté*) outraged.

outsider [awtsajdœr] *nm Sp* outsider.

ouvert [uvɛr] *voir* **ouvrir**; — *a* open; (*robinet, gaz etc*) on; **à bras ouverts** with open arms. ◆**ouvertement** *adv* openly. ◆**ouverture** *nf* opening; (*trou*) hole; (*avance*) & *Mus* overture; (*d'objectif*) *Phot* aperture; **o. d'esprit** open-mindedness.

ouvrable [uvrabl] *a* **jour o.** working day.

ouvrage [uvraʒ] *nm* (*travail, objet, livre*) work; (*couture*) (needle)work; **un o.** (*travail*) a piece of work. ◆**ouvragé** *a* (*bijou etc*) finely worked.

ouvreuse [uvrøz] *nf Cin* usherette.

ouvrier, -ière [uvrije, -jɛr] *nmf* worker; **o. agricole** farm labourer; **o. qualifié/spécialisé** skilled/unskilled worker; — *a* (*législation etc*) industrial; (*quartier, éducation*) working-class; **classe ouvrière** working class.

ouvrir* [uvrir] *vt* to open (up); (*gaz, radio etc*) to turn on, switch on; (*inaugurer*) to open; (*hostilités*) to begin; (*appétit*) to whet; (*liste, procession*) to head; — *vi* to open; (*ouvrir la porte*) to open (up); — **s'o.** *vpr* (*porte, boîte etc*) to open (up); **s'o. la jambe** to cut one's leg open; **s'o. à qn** *Fig* to open one's heart to s.o. (**de qch** about sth). ◆**ouvre-boîtes** *nm inv* tin opener, *Am* can-opener. ◆**ouvre-bouteilles** *nm inv* bottle opener.

ovaire [ovɛr] *nm Anat* ovary.

ovale [ɔval] *a & nm* oval.

ovation [ɔvɑsjɔ̃] *nf* (standing) ovation.

OVNI [ɔvni] *nm abrév* (*objet volant non identifié*) UFO.

oxyde [ɔksid] *nm Ch* oxide; **o. de carbone** carbon monoxide. ◆**oxyder** *vt*, — **s'o.** *vpr* to oxidize.

oxygène [ɔksiʒɛn] *nm* oxygen; **à o.** (*masque, tente*) oxygen-. ◆**oxygén/er** *vt* (*cheveux*) to bleach; — **s'o.** *vpr Fam* to breathe *ou* get some fresh air. ◆**—ée** *af* **eau o.** (hydrogen) peroxide.

P

P, p [pe] *nm* P, p.

pachyderme [paʃidɛrm] *nm* elephant.

pacifier [pasifje] *vt* to pacify. ◆**pacification** *nf* pacification. ◆**pacifique 1** *a* (*non violent, non militaire*) peaceful; (*personne, peuple*) peace-loving. **2** *a* (*côte etc*) Pacific: **Océan P.** Pacific Ocean; – *nm* **le P.** the Pacific. ◆**pacifiste** *a* & *nmf* pacifist.

pack [pak] *nm* (*de lait etc*) carton.

pacotille [pakɔtij] *nf* (*camelote*) trash.

pacte [pakt] *nm* pact. ◆**pactiser** *vi* p. **avec qn** *Péj* to be in league with s.o.

paf! [paf] **1** *int* bang!, wallop! **2** *a inv* (*ivre*) *Fam* sozzled, plastered.

pagaie [pagɛ] *nf* paddle. ◆**pagayer** *vi* (*ramer*) to paddle.

pagaïe, pagaille [pagaj] *nf* (*désordre*) *Fam* mess, shambles; **en p.** *Fam* in a mess; **avoir des livres/etc en p.** *Fam* to have loads of books/etc.

paganisme [paganism] *nm* paganism.

page [paʒ] **1** *nf* (*de livre etc*) page; **à la p.** (*personne*) *Fig* up-to-date. **2** *nm* (*à la cour*) *Hist* page (boy).

pagne [paɲ] *nm* loincloth.

pagode [pagɔd] *nf* pagoda.

paie [pɛ] *nf* pay, wages. ◆**paiement** *nm* payment.

païen, -enne [pajɛ̃, -ɛn] *a* & *nmf* pagan, heathen.

paillasson [pajasɔ̃] *nm* (door)mat.

paille [paj] *nf* straw; (*pour boire*) (drinking) straw; **homme de p.** *Fig* stooge, man of straw; **tirer à la courte p.** to draw lots; **sur la p.** *Fig* penniless; **feu de p.** *Fig* flash in the pan. ◆**paillasse** *nf* **1** (*matelas*) straw mattress. **2** (*d'un évier*) draining-board.

paillette [pajɛt] ·*nf* (*d'habit*) sequin; *pl* (*de lessive, savon*) flakes; (*d'or*) *Géol* gold dust.

pain [pɛ̃] *nm* bread; **un p.** a loaf (of bread); **p. grillé** toast; **p. complet** wholemeal bread; **p. d'épice** gingerbread; **petit p.** roll; **p. de savon/de cire** bar of soap/wax; **avoir du p. sur la planche** (*travail*) *Fig* to have a lot on one's plate.

pair [pɛr] **1** *a* (*numéro*) even. **2** *nm* (*personne*) peer; **hors (de) p.** unrivalled, without equal; **aller de p.** to go hand in hand (**avec** with); **au p.** (*étudiante etc*) au pair; **travailler au p.** to work as an au pair.

paire [pɛr] *nf* pair (**de** of).

paisible [pezibl] *a* (*vie etc*) peaceful; (*caractère, personne*) peaceable.

paître* [pɛtr] *vi* to graze; **envoyer p.** *Fig* to send packing.

paix [pɛ] *nf* peace; (*traité*) *Pol* peace treaty; **en p.** in peace; (*avec sa conscience*) at peace (**avec** with); **avoir la p.** to have (some) peace and quiet.

Pakistan [pakistɑ̃] *nm* Pakistan. ◆**pakistanais, -aise** *a* & *nmf* Pakistani.

palabres [palabr] *nmpl* palaver.

palace [palas] *nm* luxury hotel.

palais [palɛ] *nm* **1** (*château*) palace; **P. de justice** law courts; **p. des sports** sports stadium *ou* centre. **2** *Anat* palate.

palan [palɑ̃] *nm* (*de navire etc*) hoist.

pâle [pal] *a* pale.

palet [palɛ] *nm* (*hockey sur glace*) puck.

paletot [palto] *nm* (knitted) cardigan.

palette [palɛt] *nf* **1** (*de peintre*) palette. **2** (*support pour marchandises*) pallet.

pâleur [palœr] *nf* paleness, pallor. ◆**pâlir** *vi* to go *ou* turn pale (**de** with).

palier [palje] *nm* **1** (*d'escalier*) landing; **être voisins de p.** to live on the same floor. **2** (*niveau*) level; (*phase de stabilité*) plateau; **par paliers** (*étapes*) in stages.

palissade [palisad] *nf* fence (of stakes).

pallier [palje] *vt* (*difficultés etc*) to alleviate. ◆**palliatif** *nm* palliative.

palmarès [palmarɛs] *nm* prize list; (*des chansons*) hit-parade.

palme [palm] *nf* **1** palm (leaf); (*symbole*) *Fig* palm. **2** (*de nageur*) flipper. ◆**palmier** *nm* palm (tree).

palmé [palme] *a* (*patte, pied*) webbed.

palombe [palɔ̃b] *nf* wood pigeon.

pâlot, -otte [palo, -ɔt] *a* pale.

palourde [palurd] *nf* (*mollusque*) clam.

palp/er [palpe] *vt* to feel, finger. ◆—**able** *a* tangible.

palpit/er [palpite] *vi* (*frémir*) to quiver; (*cœur*) to palpitate, throb. ◆—**ant** *a* (*film etc*) thrilling. ◆**palpitations** *nfpl* quivering; palpitations.

pâmer (se) [səpɑme] *vpr* **se p. de** (*joie etc*) to be paralysed *ou* ecstatic with.

pamphlet [pɑ̃flɛ] *nm* lampoon.

pamplemousse [pɑ̃pləmus] *nm* grapefruit.

pan [pɑ̃] **1** *nm* (*de chemise*) tail; (*de ciel*) patch; **p. de mur** section of wall. **2** *int* bang!

pan- [pɑ̃, pan] *préf* Pan-.

panacée [panase] *nf* panacea.

panache [panaʃ] *nm* (*plumet*) plume; **avoir du p.** (*fière allure*) to have panache; **un p. de fumée** a plume of smoke.

panaché [panaʃe] **1** *a* (*bigarré, hétéroclite*) motley. **2** *a & nm* (**demi**) **p.** shandy; **bière panachée** shandy.

pancarte [pɑ̃kart] *nf* sign, notice; (*de manifestant*) placard.

pancréas [pɑ̃kreɑs] *nm Anat* pancreas.

panda [pɑ̃da] *nm* (*animal*) panda.

pané [pane] *a Culin* breaded.

panier [panje] *nm* (*ustensile, contenu*) basket; **p. à salade** salad basket; (*voiture*) *Fam* police van, prison van. ◆**p.-repas** *nm* (*pl* **paniers-repas**) packed lunch.

panique [panik] *nf* panic; **pris de p.** panic-stricken; **– a peur p.** panic fear. ◆**paniqu/er** *vi* to panic. ◆**–é a** panic-stricken.

panne [pan] *nf* breakdown; **tomber en p.** to break down; **être en p.** to have broken down; **p. d'électricité** power cut, blackout; **avoir une p. sèche** to run out of petrol *ou Am* gas.

panneau, -x [pano] *nm* **1** (*écriteau*) sign, notice, board; **p. de signalisation** traffic *ou* road sign; **p.** (**d'affichage**) (*publicité*) hoarding, *Am* billboard. **2** (*de porte etc*) panel. ◆**panonceau, -x** *nm* (*enseigne*) sign.

panoplie [panɔpli] *nf* **1** (*jouet*) outfit. **2** (*gamme, arsenal*) (wide) range. assortment.

panorama [panɔrama] *nm* panorama. ◆**panoramique** *a* panoramic.

panse [pɑ̃s] *nf Fam* paunch, belly. ◆**pansu** *a* potbellied.

pans/er [pɑ̃se] *vt* (*plaie, main etc*) to dress, bandage; (*personne*) to dress the wound(s) of, bandage (up); (*cheval*) to groom. ◆**–ement** *nm* (*bande*) bandage, dressing; **p. adhésif** sticking plaster, *Am* Band-Aid®.

pantalon [pɑ̃talɔ̃] *nm* (pair of) trousers *ou Am* pants; **deux pantalons** two pairs of trousers *ou Am* pants; **en p.** in trousers, *Am* in pants.

pantelant [pɑ̃tlɑ̃] *a* gasping.

panthère [pɑ̃tɛr] *nf* (*animal*) panther.

pantin [pɑ̃tɛ̃] *nm* (*jouet*) jumping jack; (*personne*) *Péj* puppet.

pantois [pɑ̃twa] *a* flabbergasted.

pantoufle [pɑ̃tufl] *nf* slipper. ◆**pantou-**

flard, -arde *nmf Fam* stay-at-home, *Am* homebody.

paon [pɑ̃] *nm* peacock.

papa [papa] *nm* dad(dy); **de p.** (*désuet*) *Péj* outdated; **fils à p.** *Péj* rich man's son, daddy's boy.

pape [pap] *nm* pope. ◆**papauté** *nf* papacy.

paperasse(s) [papras] *nf*(*pl*) *Péj* (official) papers. ◆**paperasserie** *nf Péj* (official) papers; (*procédure*) red tape.

papeterie [papetri] *nf* (*magasin*) stationer's shop; (*articles*) stationery; (*fabrique*) paper mill. ◆**papetier, -ière** *nmf* stationer.

papi [papi] *nm Fam* grand(d)ad.

papier [papje] *nm* (*matière*) paper; **un p.** (*feuille*) a piece *ou* sheet of paper; (*formulaire*) a form; *Journ* an article; **en p.** (*sac etc*) paper-; **papiers** (**d'identité**) (identity) papers; **p. à lettres** writing paper; **du p. journal** (some) newspaper; **p. peint** wallpaper; **p. de verre** sandpaper.

papillon [papijɔ̃] *nm* **1** (*insecte*) butterfly; (*écrou*) butterfly nut, *Am* wing nut; **p.** (**de nuit**) moth. **2** (*contravention*) (parking) ticket.

papot/er [papɔte] *vi* to prattle. ◆**–age(s)** *nm*(*pl*) prattle.

paprika [paprika] *nm* (*poudre*) *Culin* paprika.

papy [papi] *nm Fam* grand(d)ad.

Pâque [pɑk] *nf* **la P.** *Rel* Passover.

paquebot [pakbo] *nm Nau* liner.

pâquerette [pɑkrɛt] *nf* daisy.

Pâques [pɑk] *nm & nfpl* Easter.

paquet [pakɛ] *nm* (*de sucre, bonbons etc*) packet; (*colis*) package; (*de cigarettes*) pack(et); (*de cartes*) pack.

par [par] *prép* **1** (*agent, manière, moyen*) by; **choisi/frappé/etc p.** chosen/hit/etc by; **p. erreur** by mistake; **p. mer** by sea; **p. le train** by train; **p. la force/le travail/etc** by *ou* through force/work/etc; **apprendre p. un voisin** to learn from *ou* through a neighbour; **commencer/s'ouvrir p. qch** (*récit etc*) to begin/open with sth; **p. malchance** unfortunately. **2** (*lieu*) through; **p. la porte/le tunnel/etc** through *ou* by the door/tunnel/etc; **regarder/jeter p. la fenêtre** to look/throw out (of) the window; **p. les rues** through the streets; **p. ici/là** (*aller*) this/that way; (*habiter*) around here/there. **3** (*motif*) out of, from; **p. respect/pitié/etc** out of *ou* from respect/pity/etc. **4** (*temps*) on; **p. un jour d'hiver/etc** on a winter's day/etc; **p. le passé** in the past; **p. ce froid** in this cold. **5** (*distributif*) **dix fois p. an** ten times a *ou* per year; **deux p. deux** two by two; **p. deux fois** twice. **6** (*trop*) **p. trop aimable**/*etc* far too kind/*etc*.

para [para] *nm Mil Fam* para(trooper).

para- [para] *préf* para-.

parabole [parabɔl] *nf* **1** (*récit*) parable. **2** *Math* parabola.

parachever [paraʃve] *vt* to perfect.

parachute [paraʃyt] *nf* parachute. ◆**parachuter** *vt* to parachute; (*nommer*) *Fam* to pitchfork (**à un poste** into a job). ◆**parachutisme** *nm* parachute jumping. ◆**parachutiste** *nmf* parachutist; *Mil* paratrooper.

parade [parad] *nf* **1** (*étalage*) show, parade; (*spectacle*) & *Mil* parade. **2** *Boxe Escrime* parry; (*riposte*) *Fig* reply. ◆**parader** *vi* to parade, show off.

paradis [paradi] *nm* paradise, heaven. ◆**paradisiaque** *a* (*endroit etc*) *Fig* heavenly.

paradoxe [paradɔks] *nm* paradox. ◆**paradoxalement** *adv* paradoxically.

parafe [paraf] *voir* **paraphe**. ◆**parafer** *voir* **parapher**.

paraffine [parafin] *nf* paraffin (wax).

parages [paraʒ] *nmpl* region, area (**de** of); **dans ces p.** in these parts.

paragraphe [paragraf] *nm* paragraph.

paraître* [parɛtr] **1** *vi* (*se montrer*) to appear; (*sembler*) to seem, look, appear; – *v imp* **il paraît qu'il va partir** it appears *ou* seems (that) he's leaving. **2** *vi* (*livre*) to be published, come out; **faire p.** to bring out.

parallèle [paralɛl] **1** *a* (*comparable*) & *Math* parallel (**à** with, to); (*marché*) *Com* unofficial. **2** *nm* (*comparaison*) & *Géog* parallel. ◆—**ment** *adv* **p. à** parallel to.

paralyser [paralize] *vt* to paralyse, *Am* paralyze. ◆**paralysie** *nf* paralysis. ◆**paralytique** *a* & *nmf* paralytic.

paramètre [parametr] *nm* parameter.

paranoïa [paranɔja] *nf* paranoia. ◆**paranoïaque** *a* & *nmf* paranoid.

parapet [parapɛ] *nm* parapet.

paraphe [paraf] *nm* initials, signature; (*traits*) flourish. ◆**parapher** *vt* to initial, sign.

paraphrase [parafraz] *nf* paraphrase. ◆**paraphraser** *vt* to paraphrase.

parapluie [paraplɥi] *nm* umbrella.

parasite [parazit] *nm* (*personne, organisme*) parasite; *pl Rad* interference; – *a* parasitic(al).

parasol [parasɔl] *nm* parasol, sunshade.

paratonnerre [paratɔnɛr] *nm* lightning conductor *ou Am* rod.

paravent [paravɑ̃] *nm* (folding) screen.

parc [park] *nm* **1** park; (*de château*) grounds. **2** (*de bébé*) (play) pen; (*à moutons, à bétail*) pen; **p. (de stationnement)** car park, *Am* parking lot; **p. à huîtres** oyster bed.

parcelle [parsɛl] *nf* fragment, particle; (*terrain*) plot; (*de vérité*) *Fig* grain.

parce que [parsk(ə)] *conj* because.

parchemin [parʃəmɛ̃] *nm* parchment.

parcimonie [parsimɔni] *nf* **avec p.** parsimoniously. ◆**parcimonieux, -euse** *a* parsimonious.

parcmètre [parkmetr] *nm* parking meter.

parcourir* [parkurir] *vt* (*région*) to travel through, tour, scour; (*distance*) to cover; (*texte*) to glance through. ◆**parcours** *nm* (*itinéraire*) route; (*de fleuve*) & *Sp* course; (*voyage*) trip, journey.

par-delà [pard(ə)la] *voir* **delà**.

par-derrière [pardɛrjɛr] *voir* **derrière**.

par-dessous [pard(ə)su] *prép* & *adv* under(neath).

pardessus [pard(ə)sy] *nm* overcoat.

par-dessus [pard(ə)sy] *prép* & *adv* over (the top of); **p.-dessus tout** above all.

par-devant [pard(ə)vɑ̃] *voir* **devant**.

pardon [pardɔ̃] *nm* forgiveness, pardon; **p.?** (*pour demander*) excuse me?, *Am* pardon me?; **p.!** (*je le regrette*) sorry!; **demander p.** to apologize (**à** to). ◆**pardonn/er** *vt* to forgive; **p. qch à qn/à qn d'avoir fait qch** to forgive s.o. for sth/for doing sth. ◆—**able** *a* forgivable.

pare-balles [parbal] *a inv* **gilet p.-balles** bulletproof jacket *ou Am* vest.

pare-brise [parbriz] *nm inv Aut* windscreen, *Am* windshield.

pare-chocs [parʃɔk] *nm inv Aut* bumper.

pareil, -eille [parɛj] *a* similar; **p. à** the same as, similar to; **être pareils** to be the same, be similar *ou* alike; **un p. désordre**/*etc* such a mess/*etc*; **en p. cas** in such a case; – *nmf* (*personne*) equal; **rendre la pareille à qn** to treat s.o. the same way; **sans p.** unparalleled, unique; – *adv Fam* in the same way; (*aussi*) likewise. ◆**pareillement** *adv* in the same way; (*aussi*) likewise.

parement [parmɑ̃] *nm* (*de pierre, de vêtement*) facing.

parent, -ente [parɑ̃, -ɑ̃t] *nmf* relation, relative; – *nmpl* (*père et mère*) parents; – *a* related (**de** to). ◆**parenté** *nf* (*rapport*) relationship, kinship.

parenthèse [parɑ̃tɛz] *nf* (*signe*) bracket, parenthesis; (*digression*) digression.

parer [pare] **1** *vt* (*coup*) to parry, ward off; −
vi **p. à** to be prepared for. **2** *vt* (*orner*) to
adorn (**de** with).

paresse [parɛs] *nf* laziness, idleness.
◆**paresser** *vi* to laze (about). ◆**paresseux, -euse** *a* lazy, idle; − *nmf* lazybones.

parfaire [parfɛr] *vt* to perfect. ◆**parfait** *a*
perfect; **p.!** excellent!; − *nm Gram* perfect
(tense). ◆**parfaitement** *adv* perfectly;
(*certainement*) certainly.

parfois [parfwa] *adv* sometimes.

parfum [parfœ̃] *nm* (*odeur*) fragrance, scent;
(*goût*) flavour; (*liquide*) perfume, scent.
◆**parfum/er** *vt* to perfume, scent; (*glace,
crème etc*) to flavour (**à** with); − **se p.** *vpr*
to put on perfume; (*habituellement*) to
wear perfume. ◆**−é** *a* (*savon, mouchoir*)
scented; **p. au café**/*etc* coffee-/*etc*
flavoured. ◆**parfumerie** *nf* (*magasin*) perfume shop.

pari [pari] *nm* bet, wager; *pl Sp* betting,
bets; **p. mutuel urbain** = the tote, *Am*
pari-mutuel. ◆**parier** *vti* to bet (**sur on,
que** that). ◆**parieur, -euse** *nmf Sp* better,
punter.

Paris [pari] *nm ou f* Paris. ◆**parisien,
-ienne** *a* (*accent etc*) Parisian, Paris-; −
nmf Parisian.

parité [parite] *nf* parity.

parjure [parʒyr] *nm* perjury; − *nmf* perjurer. ◆**se parjurer** *vpr* to perjure oneself.

parka [parka] *nm* parka.

parking [parkiŋ] *nm* (*lieu*) car park, *Am*
parking lot.

par-là [parla] *adv voir* **par-ci**.

parlement [parləmɑ̃] *nm* parliament.
◆**parlementaire** *a* parliamentary; − *nmf*
member of parliament.

parlementer [parləmɑ̃te] *vi* to parley, negotiate.

parl/er [parle] *vi* to talk, speak (**de** about,
of; **à** to); **tu parles!** *Fam* you must be joking!; **sans p. de** . . . not to mention . . . ; −
vt (*langue*) to speak; **p. affaires**/*etc* to talk
business/*etc*; − **se p.** *vpr* (*langue*) to be
spoken; − *nm* speech; (*régional*) dialect.
◆**−ant** *a* (*film*) talking; (*regard etc*) eloquent. ◆**−é** *a* (*langue*) spoken.

parloir [parlwar] *nm* (*de couvent, prison*) visiting room.

parmi [parmi] *prép* among(st).

parodie [parɔdi] *nf* parody. ◆**parodier** *vt*
to parody.

paroi [parwa] *nf* wall; (*de maison*) inside
wall; (*de rocher*) (rock) face.

paroisse [parwas] *nf* parish. ◆**paroissial,**

-aux *a* (*registre, activité etc*) parish-.
◆**paroissien, -ienne** *nmf* parishioner.

parole [parɔl] *nf* (*mot, promesse*) word;
(*faculté, langage*) speech; **adresser la p. à** to
speak to; **prendre la p.** to speak, make a
speech; **demander la p.** to ask to speak; **perdre la p.** to lose one's tongue.

paroxysme [parɔksism] *nm* (*de douleur etc*)
height.

parpaing [parpɛ̃] *nm* concrete block,
breezeblock.

parquer [parke] *vt* (*bœufs*) to pen; (*gens*) to
herd together, confine; (*véhicule*) to park;
− **se p.** *vpr Aut* to park.

parquet [parkɛ] *nm* **1** (parquet) floor(ing). **2**
Jur Public Prosecutor's office.

parrain [parɛ̃] *nm Rel* godfather; (*répondant*) sponsor. ◆**parrain/er** *vt* to
sponsor. ◆**−age** *nm* sponsorship.

pars, part [par] *voir* **partir**.

parsemer [parsəme] *vt* to strew, dot (**de**
with).

part [par] *nf* (*portion*) share, part; **prendre
p. à** (*activité*) to take part in; (*la joie etc de
qn*) to share; **de toutes parts** from *ou* on all
sides; **de p. et d'autre** on both sides; **d'une
p.,** . . . **d'autre p.** on the one hand, . . . on
the other hand; **d'autre p.** (*d'ailleurs*) moreover; **pour ma p.** as far as I'm concerned;
de la p. de (*provenance*) from; **c'est de la p.
de qui?** *Tél* who's speaking?; **faire p. de qch
à qn** to inform s.o. of sth; **quelque p.** somewhere; **nulle p.** nowhere; **autre p.** somewhere else; **à p.** (*séparément*) apart; (*mettre,
prendre*) aside; (*excepté*) apart from; **un
cas/une place**/*etc* **à p.** a separate *ou* special
case/place/*etc*; **membre à p. entière** full
member.

partage [partaʒ] *nm* dividing (up), division;
(*participation*) sharing; (*distribution*) sharing out; (*sort*) *Fig* lot. ◆**partag/er** *vt*
(*repas, frais, joie etc*) to share (**avec** with);
(*diviser*) to divide (up); (*distribuer*) to share
out; − **se p.** *vpr* (*bénéfices etc*) to share
(between themselves *etc*); **se p. entre** to divide one's time between. ◆**−é** *a* (*avis etc*)
divided; **p. entre** (*sentiments*) torn between.

partance (en) [ɑ̃partɑ̃s] *adv* (*train etc*)
about to depart (**pour** for).

partant [partɑ̃] *nm* (*coureur, cheval*) *Sp*
starter.

partenaire [partənɛr] *nmf* (*époux etc*) & *Sp
Pol* partner.

parterre [partɛr] *nm* **1** (*de jardin etc*) flower
bed. **2** *Th* stalls, *Am* orchestra.

parti [parti] *nm Pol* party; (*époux*) match;
prendre un p. to make a decision, follow a

course; **prendre p. pour** to side with; **tirer p. de** to turn to (good) account; **p. pris** (*préjugé*) prejudiced; **être de p. pris** to be prejudiced (**contre** against).

partial, -aux [parsjal, -o] *a* biased. **◆partialité** *nf* bias.

participe [partisip] *nm Gram* participle.

particip/er [partisipe] *vi* **p. à** (*activité, jeu etc*) to take part in, participate in; (*frais, joie etc*) to share (in). **◆—ant, -ante** *nmf* participant. **◆participation** *nf* participation; sharing; (*d'un acteur*) appearance, collaboration; **p. (aux frais)** (*contribution*) share (in the expenses).

particule [partikyl] *nf* particle.

particulier, -ière [partikylje, -jɛr] *a* (*spécial, spécifique*) particular; (*privé*) private; (*bizarre*) peculiar; **p. à** peculiar to; **en p.** (*surtout*) in particular; (*à part*) in private; – *nm* private individual *ou* citizen. **◆particularité** *nf* peculiarity. **◆particulièrement** *adv* particularly; **tout p.** especially.

partie [parti] *nf* part; (*de cartes, de tennis etc*) game; (*de chasse, de plaisir*) & *Jur* party; (*métier*) line, field; **en p.** partly, in part; **en grande p.** mainly; **faire p. de** to be a part of; (*adhérer à*) to belong to; (*comité*) to be on. **◆partiel, -ielle** *a* partial; – *nm* (*examen*) **p.** *Univ* term exam. **◆partiellement** *adv* partially.

part/ir [partir] *vi* (*aux être*) (*aller, disparaître*) to go; (*s'en aller*) to go (off); (*se mettre en route*) to set off; (*s'éloigner*) to go (away); (*moteur*) to start; (*fusil, coup de feu*) to go off; (*flèche*) to shoot off; (*bouton*) to come off; (*tache*) to come out; **p. de** (*commencer par*) to start (off) with; **ça part du cœur** it comes from the heart; **p. bien** to get off to a good start; **à p. de** (*date, prix*) from. **◆—i** *a* **bien p.** off to a good start.

partisan [partizɑ̃] *nm* follower, supporter; *Mil* partisan; – *a* (*esprit*) *Péj* partisan; **être p. de qch/de faire** to be in favour of sth/of doing.

partition [partisjɔ̃] *nf Mus* score.

partout [partu] *adv* everywhere; **p. où tu vas** *ou* **iras** everywhere *ou* wherever you go; **p. sur la table**/*etc* all over the table/*etc*.

paru [pary] *voir* **paraître**. **◆parution** *nf* (*de livre etc*) publication.

parure [paryr] *nf* (*toilette*) finery; (*bijoux*) jewellery.

parven/ir* [parvənir] *vi* (*aux être*) **p. à** (*lieu*) to reach; (*fortune, ses fins*) to achieve; **p. à faire** to manage to do. **◆—u, -ue** *nmf Péj* upstart.

parvis [parvi] *nm* square (*in front of church etc*).

pas¹ [pɑ] *adv* (*négatif*) not; **(ne) . . . p.** not; **je ne sais p.** I do not *ou* don't know; **p. de pain/de café**/*etc* no bread/coffee/*etc*; **p. encore** not yet; **p. du tout** not at all.

pas² [pɑ] *nm* **1** step, pace; (*allure*) pace; (*bruit*) footstep; (*trace*) footprint; **à deux p. (de)** close by; **revenir sur ses p.** to go back on one's tracks; **au p.** at a walking pace; **rouler au p.** (*véhicule*) to go dead slow(ly); **au p. (cadencé)** in step; **faire les cent p.** to walk up and down; **faux p.** stumble; (*faute*) *Fig* blunder; **le p. de la porte** the doorstep. **2** (*de vis*) thread. **3** *Géog* straits; **le p. de Calais** the Straits of Dover.

pascal [paskal] *a* (*semaine, messe etc*) Easter-.

passable [pɑsabl] *a* acceptable, tolerable; **mention p.** *Scol Univ* pass. **◆—ment** [-əmɑ̃] *adv* acceptably; (*beaucoup*) quite a lot.

passage [pɑsaʒ] *nm* (*action*) passing, passage; (*traversée*) *Nau* crossing, passage; (*extrait*) passage; (*couloir*) passage(way); (*droit*) right of way; (*venue*) arrival; (*chemin*) path; **p. clouté** *ou* **pour piétons** (pedestrian) crossing; **obstruer le p.** to block the way; **p. souterrain** subway, *Am* underpass; **p. à niveau** level crossing, *Am* grade crossing; **'p. interdit'** 'no thoroughfare'; **'cédez le p.'** *Aut* 'give way', *Am* 'yield'; **être de p.** to be passing through (**à Paris**/*etc* Paris/*etc*); **hôte de p.** passing guest. **◆passager, -ère** *nmf* passenger; **p. clandestin** stowaway. **2** *a* (*de courte durée*) passing, temporary. **◆passagèrement** *adv* temporarily.

passant, -ante [pɑsɑ̃, -ɑ̃t] **1** *a* (*rue*) busy; – *nmf* passer-by. **2** *nm* (*de ceinture etc*) loop.

passe [pɑs] *nf Sp* pass; **mot de p.** password; **en p. de faire** on the road to doing; **une mauvaise p.** *Fig* a bad patch.

passe-montagne [pɑsmɔ̃taɲ] *nm* balaclava.

passe-partout [pɑspartu] *nm inv* (*clé*) master key; – *a inv* (*compliment, phrase*) all-purpose.

passe-passe [pɑspas] *nm inv* **tour de p.-passe** conjuring trick.

passe-plat [pɑspla] *nm* service hatch.

passeport [pɑspɔr] *nm* passport.

passer [pɑse] *vi* (*aux être ou avoir*) (*aller, venir*) to pass (**à** to); (*facteur, laitier*) to come; (*temps*) to pass (by), go by; (*courant*) to flow; (*film, programme*) to be shown, be on; (*loi*) to be passed; (*douleur, mode*) pass; (*couleur*) to fade; **p. devant** (*maison etc*) to go past *ou* by, pass (by); **p. à** *ou* **par Paris** to pass through Paris; **p. à la radio** to come *ou* go on the radio; **p. à l'ennemi/à la caisse** to go over to the enemy/the cash desk; **laisser p.** (*personne, lumière*) to let in *ou* through; (*occasion*) to let slip; **p. prendre** to pick up, fetch; **p. voir qn** to drop in on s.o.; **p. pour** (*riche etc*) to be taken for; **faire p. qn pour** to pass s.o. off as; **p. sur** (*détail etc*) to overlook, pass over; **p. capitaine/etc** to be promoted captain/*etc*; **p. en** (*seconde etc*) *Scol* to pass up into; *Aut* to change up to; **ça passe** (*c'est passable*) that'll do; **en passant** (*dire qch*) in passing; – *vt* (*aux avoir*) (*frontière etc*) to pass, cross; (*maison etc*) to pass, go past; (*donner*) to pass, hand (**à** to): (*mettre*) to put; (*omettre*) to overlook; (*temps*) to spend, pass (**à faire** doing); (*disque*) to play, put on; (*film, programme*) to show, put on; (*loi, motion*) to pass; (*chemise*) to slip on; (*examen*) to take, sit (for); (*thé*) to strain; (*café*) to filter; (*commande*) to place; (*accord*) to conclude; (*colère*) to vent (**sur** on); (*limites*) to go beyond; (*visite médicale*) to go through; **p.** (**son tour**) to pass; **p. qch à qn** (*caprice etc*) to grant s.o. sth; (*pardonner*) to excuse s.o. sth; **je vous passe . . .** *Tél* I'm putting you through to . . . ; **p. un coup d'éponge/etc à qch** to go over sth with a sponge/*etc*; **— se p.** *vpr* (*se produire*) to take place, happen; (*douleur*) to pass, go (away); **se p. de** to do *ou* go without; **se p. de commentaires** to need no comment; **ça s'est bien passé** it went off all right. ◆**passé 1** *a* (*temps etc*) past; (*couleur*) faded; **la semaine passée** last week; **dix heures passées** after *ou* gone ten (o'clock); **être passé** (*personne*) to have been (and gone); (*orage*) to be over; **avoir vingt ans passés** to be over twenty; – *nm* (*temps, vie passée*) past; *Gram* past (tense). **2** *prép* after; **p. huit heures** after eight (o'clock).

passerelle [pasrɛl] *nf* (*pont*) footbridge; (*voie d'accès*) *Nau Av* gangway.

passe-temps [pastã] *nm inv* pastime.

passeur, -euse [pasœr, -øz] *nmf* **1** *Nau* ferryman, ferrywoman. **2** (*contrebandier*) smuggler.

passible [pasibl] *a* **p. de** (*peine*) *Jur* liable to.

passif, -ive [pasif, -iv] **1** *a* (*rôle, personne*) passive; – *nm Gram* passive. **2** *nm Com* liabilities. ◆**passivité** *nf* passiveness, passivity.

passion [pasjɔ̃] *nf* passion; **avoir la p. des**

voitures/d'écrire/*etc* to have a passion *ou* a great love for cars/writing/*etc*. ◆**passionnel, -elle** *a* (*crime*) of passion. ◆**passionner** *vt* to thrill, fascinate; **se p. pour** to have a passion for. ◆**—ant** *a* thrilling. ◆**—é, -ée** *a* passionate; **p. de qch** passionately fond of sth; – *nmf* fan (**de** of). ◆**—ément** *adv* passionately.

passoire [paswar] *nf* (*pour liquides*) sieve; (*à thé*) strainer; (*à légumes*) colander.

pastel [pastɛl] *nm* pastel; **au p.** (*dessin*) pastel-; – *a inv* (*ton*) pastel.

pastèque [pastɛk] *nf* watermelon.

pasteur [pastœr] *nm Rel* pastor.

pasteurisé [pastørize] *a* (*lait, beurre etc*) pasteurized.

pastiche [pastiʃ] *nm* pastiche.

pastille [pastij] *nf* pastille, lozenge.

pastis [pastis] *nm* aniseed liqueur, pastis.

pastoral, -aux [pastoral, -o] *a* pastoral.

patate [patat] *nf Fam* spud, potato.

patatras! [patatra] *int* crash!

pataud [pato] *a* clumsy, lumpish.

patauger [patoʒe] *vi* (*marcher*) to wade (**in** the mud *etc*); (*barboter*) to splash about; (*s'empêtrer*) *Fig* to flounder. ◆**pataugeoire** *nf* paddling pool.

patchwork [patʃwœrk] *nm* patchwork.

pâte [pat] *nf* (*substance*) paste; (*à pain, à gâteau*) dough; (*à tarte*) pastry; **pâtes (alimentaires)** pasta; **p. à modeler** plasticine®, modelling clay; **p. à frire** batter; **p. dentifrice** toothpaste.

pâté [pate] *nm* **1** (*charcuterie*) pâté; **p. (en croûte)** meat pie. **2** **p. (de sable)** sand castle; **p. de maisons** block of houses. **3** (*tache d'encre*) (ink) blot.

pâtée [pate] *nf* (*pour chien, volaille etc*) mash.

patelin [patlɛ̃] *nm Fam* village.

patent [patã] *a* patent, obvious.

patère [pater] *nf* (coat) peg.

paternel, -elle [paternɛl] *a* (*amour etc*) fatherly, paternal; (*parenté, réprimande*) paternal. ◆**paternité** *nf* (*état*) paternity, fatherhood; (*de livre*) authorship.

pâteux, -euse [patø, -øz] *a* (*substance*) doughy, pasty; (*style*) woolly; **avoir la bouche** *ou* **la langue pâteuse** (*après s'être enivré*) to have a mouth full of cotton wool *ou Am* cotton.

pathétique [patetik] *a* moving; – *nm* pathos.

pathologie [patɔlɔʒi] *nf* pathology. ◆**pathologique** *a* pathological.

patient, -ente [pasjã, -ãt] **1** *a* patient. **2** *nmf Méd* patient. ◆**patiemment** [-amã] *adv* patiently. ◆**patience** *nf* patience; **prendre p.** to have patience; **perdre p.** to lose patience. ◆**patienter** *vi* to wait (patiently).

patin [patɛ̃] *nm* skate; (*pour le parquet*) cloth pad (*used for walking*); **p. à glace/à roulettes** ice/roller skate. ◆**patin/er** *vi Sp* to skate; (*véhicule, embrayage*) to slip. ◆**—age** *nm Sp* skating; **p. artistique** figure skating. ◆**—eur, -euse** *nmf Sp* skater. ◆**patinoire** *nf* (*piste*) & *Fig* skating rink, ice rink.

patine [patin] *nf* patina.

patio [patjo] *nm* patio.

pâtir [pɑtir] *vi* **p. de** to suffer from.

pâtisserie [pɑtisri] *nf* pastry, cake; (*magasin*) cake shop; (*art*) cake *ou* pastry making. ◆**pâtissier, -ière** *nmf* pastrycook and cake shop owner.

patois [patwa] *nm Ling* patois.

patraque [patrak] *a* (*malade*) *Fam* under the weather.

patriarche [patrijarʃ] *nm* patriarch.

patrie [patri] *nf* (*native*) country; (*ville*) birth place. ◆**patriote** *nmf* patriot; — *a* (*personne*) patriotic. ◆**patriotique** *a* (*chant etc*) patriotic. ◆**patriotisme** *nm* patriotism.

patrimoine [patrimwan] *nm* (*biens*) & *Fig* heritage.

patron, -onne [patrɔ̃, -ɔn] **1** *nmf* (*chef*) employer, boss; (*propriétaire*) owner (**de** of); (*gérant*) manager, manageress; (*de bar*) landlord, landlady. **2** *nmf Rel* patron saint. **3** *nm* (*modèle de papier*) *Tex* pattern. ◆**patronage** *nm* **1** (*protection*) patronage. **2** (*centre*) youth club. ◆**patronal, -aux** *a* (*syndicat etc*) employers'. ◆**patronat** *nm* employers. ◆**patronner** *vt* to sponsor.

patrouille [patruj] *nf* patrol. ◆**patrouill/er** *vi* to patrol. ◆**—eur** *nm* (*navire*) patrol boat.

patte [pat] *nf* **1** (*membre*) leg; (*de chat, chien*) paw; (*main*) *Fam* hand; **à quatre pattes** on all fours. **2** (*de poche*) flap; (*languette*) tongue.

pattes [pat] *nfpl* (*favoris*) sideboards, *Am* sideburns.

pâture [pɑtyr] *nf* (*nourriture*) food; (*intellectuelle*) *Fig* fodder. ◆**pâturage** *nm* pasture.

paume [pom] *nf* (*de main*) palm.

paum/er [pome] *vt Fam* to lose; **un coin** *ou* **trou paumé** (*sans attrait*) a dump. ◆**—é, -ée** *nmf* (*malheureux*) *Fam* down-and-out, loser.

paupière [popjɛr] *nf* eyelid.

pause [poz] *nf* (*arrêt*) break; (*dans le discours etc*) pause.

pauvre [povr] *a* poor; (*terre*) impoverished, poor; **p. en** (*calories etc*) low in; (*ressources etc*) low on; — *nmf* (*indigent, malheureux*) poor man, poor woman; **les pauvres** the poor. ◆**pauvrement** *adv* poorly. ◆**pauvreté** *nf* (*besoin*) poverty; (*insuffisance*) poorness.

pavaner (se) [səpavane] *vpr* to strut (about).

pav/er [pave] *vt* to pave. ◆**—é** *nm* **un p. a** paving stone; (*rond, de vieille chaussée*) a cobblestone; **sur le p.** *Fig* on the streets. ◆**—age** *nm* (*travail, revêtement*) paving.

pavillon [pavijɔ̃] *nm* **1** (*maison*) house; (*de chasse*) lodge; (*d'hôpital*) ward; (*d'exposition*) pavilion. **2** (*drapeau*) flag.

pavoiser [pavwaze] *vt* to deck out with flags; — *vi* (*exulter*) *Fig* to rejoice.

pavot [pavo] *nm* (*cultivé*) poppy.

pay/er [peje] *vt* (*personne, somme*) to pay; (*service, objet, faute*) to pay for; (*récompenser*) to repay; **p. qch à qn** (*offrir en cadeau*) *Fam* to treat s.o. to sth; **p. qn pour faire** to pay s.o. to do *ou* for doing; — *vi* (*personne, métier, crime*) to pay; **se p. qch** (*s'acheter*) *Fam* to treat oneself to sth; **se p. la tête de qn** *Fam* to make fun of s.o. ◆**—ant** *a* (*hôte, spectateur*) who pays, paying; (*place, entrée*) that one has to pay for; (*rentable*) worthwhile. ◆**payable** *a* payable. ◆**paye** *nf* pay, wages. ◆**payement** *nm* payment.

pays [pei] *nm* country; (*région*) region; (*village*) village; **p. des rêves/du soleil** land of dreams/sun; **du p.** (*vin, gens etc*) local.

paysage [peizaʒ] *nm* landscape, scenery.

paysan, -anne [peizɑ̃, -an] *nmf* (*small*) farmer; (*rustre*) *Péj* peasant; — *a* country-; (*monde*) farming.

Pays-Bas [peibɑ] *nmpl* **les P.-Bas** the Netherlands.

PCV [peseve] *abrév* (*paiement contre vérification*) **téléphoner en PCV** to reverse the charges, *Am* call collect =

PDG [pedeʒe] *abrév* = **président directeur général.**

péage [peaʒ] *nm* (*droit*) toll; (*lieu*) tollgate.

peau, -x [po] *nf* skin; (*de fruit*) peel, skin; (*cuir*) hide, skin; (*fourrure*) pelt; **dans la p. de qn** *Fig* in s.o.'s shoes; **faire p. neuve** *Fig* to turn over a new leaf. ◆**P.-Rouge** *nmf* (*pl* **Peaux-Rouges**) (Red) Indian.

pêche¹ [pɛʃ] *nf* (*activité*) fishing; (*poissons*) catch; **p. (à la ligne)** angling; **aller à la p.** to go fishing. ◆**pêcher**¹ *vi* to fish; — *vt* (*chercher à prendre*) to fish for; (*attraper*) to catch; (*dénicher*) *Fam* to dig up. ◆**pêcheur** *nm* fisherman; angler.

pêche² [pɛʃ] *nf* (*fruit*) peach. ◆**pêcher²** *nm* (*arbre*) peach tree.

péché [peʃe] *nm* sin. ◆**péch/er** *vi* to sin; **p. par orgueil/etc** to be too proud/*etc*. ◆**—eur, -eresse** *nmf* sinner.

pectoraux [pɛktɔro] *nmpl* (*muscles*) chest muscles.

pécule [pekyl] *nm* **un p.** (*économies*) (some) savings, a nest egg.

pécuniaire [pekynjɛr] *a* monetary.

pédagogie [pedagɔʒi] *nf* (*science*) education, teaching methods. ◆**pédagogique** *a* educational. ◆**pédagogue** *nmf* teacher.

pédale [pedal] *nf* **1** pedal; **p. de frein** footbrake (pedal). **2** (*homosexuel*) *Péj Fam* pansy, queer. ◆**pédaler** *vi* to pedal.

pédalo [pedalo] *nm* pedal boat, pedalo.

pédant, -ante [pedã, -ãt] *nmf* pedant; – *a* pedantic. ◆**pédantisme** *nm* pedantry.

pédé [pede] *nm* (*homosexuel*) *Péj Fam* queer.

pédiatre [pedjatr] *nmf Méd* p(a)ediatrician.

pédicure [pedikyr] *nmf* chiropodist.

pedigree [pedigre] *nm* (*de chien, cheval etc*) pedigree.

pègre [pɛgr] *nf* **la p.** the (criminal) underworld.

peigne [pɛɲ] *nm* comb; **passer au p. fin** *Fig* to go through with a fine toothcomb; **un coup de p.** (*action*) a comb. ◆**peigner** *vt* (*cheveux*) to comb; **p. qn** to comb s.o.'s hair; **— se p.** *vpr* to comb one's hair.

peignoir [pɛɲwar] *nm* dressing gown, *Am* bathrobe; **p.** (**de bain**) bathrobe.

peinard [penar] *a Arg* quiet (and easy).

peindre* [pɛdr] *vt* to paint; (*décrire*) *Fig* to depict, paint; **p. en bleu/etc** to paint blue/*etc*; – *vi* to paint.

peine [pen] *nf* **1** (*châtiment*) punishment; **p. de mort** death penalty *ou* sentence; **p. de prison** prison sentence; **'défense d'entrer sous p. d'amende'** 'trespassers will be fined'. **2** (*chagrin*) sorrow, grief; **avoir de la p.** to be upset *ou* sad; **faire de la p. à** to upset, cause pain *ou* sorrow to. **3** (*effort, difficulté*) trouble; **se donner de la p.** *ou* **beaucoup de p.** to go to a lot of trouble (**pour faire** to do); **avec p.** with difficulty; **ça vaut la p. d'attendre/etc** it's worth (while) waiting/*etc*; **ce n'est pas** *ou* **ça ne vaut pas la p.** it's not worth while *ou* worth it *ou* worth bothering. ◆**peiner 1** *vt* to upset, grieve. **2** *vi* to labour, struggle.

peine (à) [apen] *adv* hardly, scarcely.

peintre [pɛtr] *nm* painter; **p.** (**en bâtiment**) (house) painter, (painter and) decorator. ◆**peinture** *nf* (*tableau, activité*) painting; (*couleur*) paint; **'p. fraîche'** 'wet paint'. ◆**peinturlurer** *vt Fam* to daub with colour; **se p.** (**le visage**) to paint one's face.

péjoratif, -ive [peʒɔratif, -iv] *a* pejorative, derogatory.

pékinois [pekinwa] *nm* (*chien*) pekin(g)ese.

pelage [pəlaʒ] *nm* (*d'animal*) coat, fur.

pelé [pəle] *a* bare.

pêle-mêle [pɛlmɛl] *adv* in disorder.

peler [pəle] *vt* (*fruit*) to peel; **se p. facilement** (*fruit*) to peel easily; – *vi* (*peau bronzée*) to peel.

pèlerin [pɛlrɛ] *nm* pilgrim. ◆**pèlerinage** *nm* pilgrimage.

pèlerine [pɛlrin] *nf* (*manteau*) cape.

pélican [pelikã] *nm* (*oiseau*) pelican.

pelisse [pəlis] *nf* fur-lined coat.

pelle [pɛl] *nf* shovel; (*d'enfant*) spade; **p. à poussière** dustpan; **ramasser** *ou* **prendre une p.** (*tomber*) *Fam* to come a cropper, *Am* take a spill; **à la p.** (*argent etc*) *Fam* galore. ◆**pelletée** *nf* shovelful. ◆**pelleteuse** *nf Tech* mechanical shovel, excavator.

pellicule [pelikyl] *nf Phot* film; (*couche*) film, layer; *pl Méd* dandruff.

pelote [pəlɔt] *nf* (*de laine*) ball; (à *épingles*) pincushion; **p.** (**basque**) *Sp* pelota.

peloter [pəlɔte] *vt* (*palper*) *Péj Fam* to paw.

peloton [pəlɔtõ] *nm* **1** (*coureurs*) *Sp* pack, main body. **2** *Mil* squad; **p. d'exécution** firing squad. **3** (*de ficelle*) ball.

pelotonner (se) [səplɔtɔne] *vpr* to curl up (into a ball).

pelouse [pluz] *nf* lawn; *Sp* enclosure.

peluche [plyʃ] *nf* (*tissu*) plush; *pl* (*flocons*) fluff, lint; **une p.** (*flocon*) a bit of fluff *ou* lint; **jouet en p.** soft toy; **chien/etc en p.** (*jouet*) furry dog/*etc*; **ours en p.** teddy bear. ◆**pelucher** *vi* to get fluffy *ou* linty. ◆**pelucheux, -euse** *a* fluffy, linty.

pelure [plyr] *nf* (*épluchure*) peeling; **une p.** a (piece of) peeling.

pénal, -aux [penal, -o] *a* (*droit, code etc*) penal. ◆**pénalisation** *nf Sp* penalty. ◆**pénaliser** *vt Sp Jur* to penalize (**pour** for). ◆**pénalité** *nf Jur Rugby* penalty.

penalty, *pl* **-ties** [penalti, -iz] *nm Fb* penalty.

penaud [pəno] *a* sheepish.

penchant [pãʃã] *nm* (*goût*) liking (**pour** for); (*tendance*) inclination (**à qch** towards sth).

pench/er [pãʃe] *vt* (*objet*) to tilt; (*tête*) to lean; – *vi* (*arbre etc*) to lean (over); **p. pour** *Fig* to be inclined towards; **— se p.** *vpr* to lean (forward); **se p. par** (*fenêtre*) to lean out of; **se p. sur** (*problème etc*) to examine. ◆**—é** *a* leaning.

pendaison [pɑ̃dɛzɔ̃] *nf* hanging.

pendant[1] [pɑ̃dɑ̃] *prép* (*au cours de*) during; **p. la nuit** during the night; **p. deux mois** (*pour une période de*) for two months; **p. que** while, whilst.

pendentif [pɑ̃dɑ̃tif] *nm* (*collier*) pendant.

penderie [pɑ̃dri] *nf* wardrobe.

pend/re [pɑ̃dr] *vti* to hang (à from); **— se p.** *vpr* (*se tuer*) to hang oneself; (*se suspendre*) to hang (à from). ◆**—ant**[2] **1** *a* hanging; (*langue*) hanging out; (*joues*) sagging; (*question*) *Fig* pending. **2** *nm* **p. (d'oreille)** drop earring. **3** *nm* **le p. de** the companion piece to. ◆**—u, -ue** *a* (*objet*) hanging (à from); *— nmf* hanged man, hanged woman.

pendule [pɑ̃dyl] **1** *nf* clock. **2** *nm* (*balancier*) & *Fig* pendulum. ◆**pendulette** *nf* small clock.

pénétr/er [penetre] *vi* **p. dans** to enter; (*profondément*) to penetrate (into); *— vt* (*substance, mystère etc*) to penetrate; **se p. de** (*idée*) to become convinced of. ◆**—ant** *a* (*esprit, froid etc*) penetrating, keen. ◆**pénétration** *nf* penetration.

pénible [penibl] *a* (*difficile*) difficult; (*douloureux*) painful, distressing; (*ennuyeux*) tiresome; (*agaçant*) annoying. ◆**—ment** [-əmɑ̃] *adv* with difficulty; (*avec douleur*) painfully.

péniche [peniʃ] *nf* barge; **p. de débarquement** *Mil* landing craft.

pénicilline [penisilin] *nf* penicillin.

péninsule [penɛ̃syl] *nf* peninsula. ◆**péninsulaire** *a* peninsular.

pénis [penis] *nm* penis.

pénitence [penitɑ̃s] *nf* (*punition*) punishment; (*peine*) *Rel* penance; (*regret*) penitence. ◆**pénitent, -ente** *nmf Rel* penitent.

pénitencier [penitɑ̃sje] *nm* prison. ◆**pénitentiaire** *a* (*régime etc*) prison-.

pénombre [penɔ̃br] *nf* half-light, darkness.

pensée [pɑ̃se] *nf* **1** thought. **2** (*fleur*) pansy. ◆**pens/er** *vi* to think (à of, about); **p. à qch/à faire qch** (*ne pas oublier*) to remember sth/to do sth; **p. à tout** (*prévoir*) to think of everything; **penses-tu!** you must be joking!, not at all!; *— vt* (*penser que*) to think that; (*concevoir*) to think out; (*imaginer*) to imagine (que that); **je pensais rester** (*intention*) I was thinking of staying, I thought I'd stay; **je pense réussir** (*espoir*) I hope to succeed; **que pensez-vous de . . . ?** what do you think of *ou* about . . . ?; **p. du bien de** to think highly of. ◆**—ant** *a* **bien p.** *Péj* or-

thodox. ◆**—eur** *nm* thinker. ◆**pensif, -ive** *a* thoughtful, pensive.

pension [pɑ̃sjɔ̃] *nf* **1** boarding school; (*somme, repas*) board; **être en p.** to board, be a boarder (**chez** with); **p. (de famille)** guesthouse, boarding house; **p. complète** full board. **2** (*allocation*) pension; **p. alimentaire** maintenance allowance. ◆**pensionnaire** *nmf* (*élève*) boarder; (*d'hôtel*) resident; (*de famille*) lodger. ◆**pensionnat** *nm* boarding school; (*élèves*) boarders. ◆**pensionné, -ée** *nmf* pensioner.

pentagone [pɛ̃tagɔn] *nm* **le P.** *Am Pol* the Pentagon.

pentathlon [pɛ̃tatlɔ̃] *nm Sp* pentathlon.

pente [pɑ̃t] *nf* slope; **être en p.** to slope, be sloping.

Pentecôte [pɑ̃tkot] *nf* Whitsun, *Am* Pentecost.

pénurie [penyri] *nf* scarcity, shortage (**de** of).

pépère [pepɛr] **1** *nm Fam* grand(d)ad. **2** *a* (*tranquille*) *Fam* quiet (and easy).

pépier [pepje] *vi* (*oiseau*) to cheep, chirp.

pépin [pepɛ̃] *nm* **1** (*de fruit*) pip, *Am* pit. **2** (*ennui*) *Fam* hitch, bother. **3** (*parapluie*) *Fam* brolly.

pépinière [pepinjɛr] *nf Bot* nursery.

pépite [pepit] *nf* (gold) nugget.

péquenaud, -aude [pɛkno, -od] *nmf Péj Arg* peasant, bumpkin.

perçant [pɛrsɑ̃] *a* (*cri, froid*) piercing; (*yeux*) sharp, keen.

percée [pɛrse] *nf* (*dans une forêt*) opening; (*avance technologique, attaque militaire*) breakthrough.

perce-neige [pɛrsənɛʒ] *nm ou f inv Bot* snowdrop.

perce-oreille [pɛrsɔrɛj] *nm* (*insecte*) earwig.

percepteur [pɛrsɛptœr] *nm* tax collector. ◆**perceptible** *a* perceptible (à to), noticeable. ◆**perception** *nf* **1** (*bureau*) tax office; (*d'impôt*) collection. **2** (*sensation*) perception.

perc/er [pɛrse] *vt* (*trouer*) to pierce; (*avec perceuse*) to drill (a hole in); (*trou, ouverture*) to make, drill; (*mystère etc*) to uncover; **p. une dent** (*bébé*) to cut a tooth; *— vi* (*soleil, ennemi, sentiment*) to break *ou* come through; (*abcès*) to burst. ◆**—euse** *nf* drill.

percevoir* [pɛrsəvwar] *vt* **1** (*sensation*) to perceive; (*son*) to hear. **2** (*impôt*) to collect.

perche [pɛrʃ] *nf* **1** (*bâton*) pole; **saut à la p.** pole-vaulting. **2** (*poisson*) perch.

perch/er [pɛrʃe] *vi* (*oiseau*) to perch; (*volailles*) to roost; (*loger*) *Fam* to hang out; *—*

vt (*placer*) *Fam* to perch; **— se p.** *vpr* (*oiseau, personne*) to perch. **◆—é** *a* perched. **◆perchoir** *nm* perch; (*de volailles*) roost.

percolateur [pɛrkɔlatœr] *nm* (*de restaurant*) percolator.

percussion [pɛrkysjɔ̃] *nf Mus* percussion.

percutant [pɛrkytɑ̃] *a Fig* powerful.

percuter [pɛrkyte] *vt* (*véhicule*) to crash into; – *vi* **p. contre** to crash into.

perd/re [pɛrdr] *vt* to lose; (*gaspiller*) to waste; (*ruiner*) to ruin; (*habitude*) to get out of; **p. de vue** to lose sight of; – *vi* to lose; (*récipient, tuyau*) to leak; **j'y perds** I lose out, I lose on the deal; **— se p.** *vpr* (*s'égarer*) to get lost; (*dans les détails*) to lose oneself; (*disparaître*) to disappear; **je m'y perds** I'm lost *ou* confused. **◆—ant, -ante** *a* (*billet*) losing; – *nmf* loser. **◆—u** *a* lost; wasted; (*malade*) finished; (*lieu*) isolated, in the middle of nowhere; **à ses moments perdus** in one's spare time; **une balle perdue** a stray bullet; **c'est du temps p.** it's a waste of time. **◆perdition (en)** *adv* (*navire*) in distress.

perdrix [pɛrdri] *nf* partridge. **◆perdreau, -x** *nm* young partridge.

père [pɛr] *nm* father; **Dupont p.** Dupont senior; **le p. Jean** *Fam* old John.

péremptoire [perɑ̃ptwar] *a* peremptory.

perfection [pɛrfɛksjɔ̃] *nf* perfection. **◆perfectionn/er** *vt* to improve, perfect; **se p. en anglais/***etc* to improve one's English/*etc*. **◆—é** *a* (*machine etc*) advanced. **◆—ement** *nm* improvement (**de** in, **par rapport à** on); **cours de p.** advanced *ou* refresher course. **◆perfectionniste** *nmf* perfectionist.

perfide [pɛrfid] *a Litt* treacherous, perfidious. **◆perfidie** *nf Litt* treachery.

perforer [pɛrfɔre] *vt* (*pneu, intestin etc*) to perforate; (*billet, carte*) to punch; **carte perforée** punch card. **◆perforateur** *nm* (*appareil*) drill. **◆perforation** *nf* perforation; (*trou*) punched hole. **◆perforatrice** *nf* (*pour cartes*) *Tech* (card) punch. **◆perforeuse** *nf* (paper) punch.

performance [pɛrfɔrmɑ̃s] *nf* (*d'athlète, de machine etc*) performance. **◆performant** *a* (highly) efficient.

péricliter [periklite] *vi* to go to rack and ruin.

péril [peril] *nm* peril; **à tes risques et périls** at your own risk. **◆périlleux, -euse** *a* perilous; **saut p.** somersault (*in mid air*).

périm/er [perime] *vi*, **— se p.** *vpr* laisser (**se**) **p.** (*billet*) to allow to expire. **◆—é** *a* expired; (*désuet*) outdated.

périmètre [perimɛtr] *nm* perimeter.

période [perjɔd] *nf* period. **◆périodique** *a* periodic; – *nm* (*revue*) periodical.

péripétie [peripesi] *nf* (unexpected) event.

périphérie [periferi] *nf* (*limite*) periphery; (*banlieue*) outskirts. **◆périphérique** *a* (*quartier*) outlying, peripheral; – *nm* (**boulevard**) **p.** (motorway) ring road, *Am* beltway.

périphrase [perifrɑz] *nf* circumlocution.

périple [peripl] *nm* trip, tour.

pér/ir [perir] *vi* to perish, die. **◆—issable** *a* (*denrée*) perishable.

périscope [periskɔp] *nm* periscope.

perle [pɛrl] *nf* (*bijou*) pearl; (*de bois, verre etc*) bead; (*personne*) *Fig* gem, pearl; (*erreur*) *Iron* howler, gem. **◆perler** *vi* (*sueur*) to form beads; **grève perlée** go-slow, *Am* slow-down strike.

permanent, -ente [pɛrmanɑ̃, -ɑ̃t] **1** *a* a permanent; (*spectacle*) *Cin* continuous; (*comité*) standing. **2** *nf* (*coiffure*) perm. **◆permanence** *nf* permanence; (*service, bureau*) duty office; (*salle*) *Scol* study room; **être de p.** to be on duty; **en p.** permanently.

perméable [pɛrmeabl] *a* permeable.

permettre* [pɛrmɛtr] *vt* to allow, permit; **p. à qn de faire** (*permission, possibilité*) to allow *ou* permit s.o. to do; **permettez!** excuse me!; **vous permettez?** may I?; **se p. de faire** to allow oneself to do, take the liberty to do; **se p. qch** (*se payer*) to afford sth. **◆permis** *a* allowed, permitted; – *nm* (*autorisation*) permit, licence; **p. de conduire** (*carte*) driving licence, *Am* driver's license; **p. de travail** work permit. **◆permission** *nf* permission; (*congé*) *Mil* leave; **demander la p.** to ask (for) permission (**de faire** to do).

permuter [pɛrmyte] *vt* to change round *ou* over, permutate. **◆permutation** *nf* permutation.

pernicieux, -euse [pɛrnisjø, -øz] *a* (*nocif*) & *Méd* pernicious.

pérorer [perɔre] *vi Péj* to speechify.

Pérou [peru] *nm* Peru.

perpendiculaire [pɛrpɑ̃dikylɛr] *a* & *nf* perpendicular (**à** to).

perpétrer [pɛrpetre] *vt* (*crime*) to perpetrate.

perpétuel, -elle [pɛrpetɥɛl] *a* perpetual; (*fonction, rente*) for life. **◆perpétuelle-ment** *adv* perpetually. **◆perpétuer** *vt* to perpetuate. ◆**perpétuité (à)** adv in perpetuity; (condamné) for life.

perplexe [pɛrplɛks] a perplexed, puzzled. ◆**perplexité** nf perplexity.

perquisition [pɛrkizisjɔ̃] nf (house) search (by police). ◆**perquisitionner** vti to search.

perron [pɛrɔ̃] nm (front) steps.

perroquet [pɛrɔke] nm parrot.

perruche [peryʃ] nf budgerigar, Am parakeet.

perruque [peryk] nf wig.

persan [pɛrsɑ̃] a (langue, tapis, chat) Persian; – nm (langue) Persian.

persécuter [pɛrsekyte] vt (tourmenter) to persecute; (importuner) to harass. ◆**persécuteur, -trice** nmf persecutor. ◆**persécution** nf persecution.

persévér/er [pɛrsevere] vi to persevere (dans in). ◆**—ant** a persevering. ◆**persévérance** nf perseverance.

persienne [pɛrsjɛn] nf (outside) shutter.

persil [pɛrsi] nm parsley.

persist/er [pɛrsiste] vi to persist (à faire in doing). ◆**—ant** a persistent; à feuilles persistantes (arbre etc) evergreen. ◆**persistance** nf persistence.

personnage [pɛrsɔnaʒ] nm (célébrité) (important) person; Th Littér character.

personnaliser [pɛrsɔnalize] vt to personalize; (voiture) to customize.

personnalité [pɛrsɔnalite] nf (individualité, personnage) personality.

personne [pɛrsɔn] 1 nf person; pl people; grande p. grown-up, adult; jolie p. pretty girl ou woman; en p. in person. 2 pron (négatif) nobody, no one; ne . . . p. nobody, no one; je ne vois p. I don't see anybody ou anyone; mieux que p. better than anybody ou anyone.

personnel, -elle [pɛrsɔnɛl] 1 a personal; (joueur, jeu) individualistic. 2 nm staff, personnel. ◆**personnellement** adv personally.

personnifier [pɛrsɔnifje] vt to personify. ◆**personnification** nf personification.

perspective [pɛrspɛktiv] nf (art) perspective; (point de vue) Fig viewpoint, perspective; (de paysage etc) view; (possibilité, espérance) prospect; en p. Fig in view, in prospect.

perspicace [pɛrspikas] a shrewd. ◆**perspicacité** nf shrewdness.

persuader [pɛrsɥade] vt to persuade (qn de faire s.o. to do); se p. que to be convinced that. ◆**persuasif, -ive** a persuasive.

◆**persuasion** nf persuasion; (croyance) conviction.

perte [pɛrt] nf loss; (gaspillage) waste (de temps/d'argent of time/money); (ruine) ruin; à p. de vue as far as the eye can see; vendre à p. to sell at a loss.

pertinent [pɛrtinɑ̃] a relevant, pertinent. ◆**pertinence** nf relevance.

perturb/er [pɛrtyrbe] vt (trafic, cérémonie etc) to disrupt; (ordre public, personne) to disturb. ◆**—é** a (troublé) Fam perturbed. ◆**perturbateur, -trice** a (élément) disruptive; – nmf trouble-maker. ◆**perturbation** nf disruption; (crise) upheaval.

péruvien, -ienne [peryvjɛ̃, -jɛn] a & nmf Peruvian.

pervenche [pɛrvɑ̃ʃ] nf Bot periwinkle.

pervers [pɛrvɛr] a wicked, perverse; (dépravé) perverted. ◆**perversion** nf perversion. ◆**perversité** nf perversity. ◆**pervert/ir** vt to pervert. ◆**—i, -ie** nmf pervert.

pesant [pəzɑ̃] a heavy, weighty; – nm valoir son p. d'or to be worth one's weight in gold. ◆**pesamment** adv heavily. ◆**pesanteur** nf heaviness; (force) Phys gravity.

pes/er [pəze] vt to weigh; – vi to weigh; p. lourd to be heavy; (argument etc) Fig to carry (a lot of) weight; p. sur (appuyer) to bear down upon; (influer) to bear upon; p. sur qn (menace) to hang over s.o.; p. sur l'estomac to lie (heavily) on the stomach. ◆**—ée** nf weighing; Boxe weigh-in; (effort) pressure. ◆**—age** nm weighing. ◆**pèse-bébé** nm (baby) scales. ◆**pèse-personne** nm (bathroom) scales.

pessimisme [pesimism] nm pessimism. ◆**pessimiste** a pessimistic; – nmf pessimist.

peste [pɛst] nf Méd plague; (personne, enfant) Fig pest.

pester [pɛste] vi to curse; p. contre qch/qn to curse sth/s.o.

pestilentiel, -ielle [pɛstilɑ̃sjɛl] a fetid, stinking.

pétale [petal] nm petal.

pétanque [petɑ̃k] nf (jeu) bowls.

pétarades [petarad] nfpl (de moto etc) backfiring. ◆**pétarader** vi to backfire.

pétard [petar] nm (explosif) firecracker, banger.

péter [pete] vi Fam (éclater) to go bang ou pop; (se rompre) to snap.

pétill/er [petije] vi (eau, champagne) to sparkle, fizz; (bois, feu) to crackle; (yeux) to sparkle. ◆**—ant** a (eau, vin, regard) sparkling.

petit, -ite [p(ə)ti, -it] *a* small, little; (*de taille*) short; (*bruit, espoir, coup*) slight; (*jeune*) young, small; (*mesquin, insignifiant*) petty; **tout p.** tiny; **un bon p. travail** a nice little job; **un p. Français** a (little) French boy; — *nmf* (little) boy, (little) girl; (*personne*) small person; *Scol* junior; *pl* (*d'animal*) young; (*de chien*) pups, young; (*de chat*) kittens, young; — *adv* **p. à p.** little by little. ◆**p.-bourgeois** *a Péj* middle-class. ◆**p.-suisse** *nm* soft cheese (*for dessert*). ◆**petitement** *adv* (*chichement*) shabbily, poorly. ◆**petitesse** *nf* (*de taille*) smallness; (*mesquinerie*) pettiness.

petit-fils [p(ə)tifis] *nm* (*pl* petits-fils) grandson, grandchild. ◆**petite-fille** *nf* (*pl* petites-filles) granddaughter, grandchild. ◆**petits-enfants** *nmpl* grandchildren.

pétition [petisjɔ̃] *nf* petition.

pétrifier [petrifje] *vt* (*de peur, d'émoi etc*) to petrify.

pétrin [petrɛ̃] *nm* (*situation*) *Fam* fix; **dans le p.** in a fix.

pétrir [petrir] *vt* to knead.

pétrole [petrɔl] *nm* oil, petroleum; **p.** (*lampant*) paraffin, *Am* kerosene; **nappe de p.** (*sur la mer*) oil slick. ◆**pétrolier, -ière** *a* (*industrie*) oil-; — *nm* (*navire*) oil tanker. ◆**pétrolifère** *a* **gisement p.** oil field.

pétulant [petylɑ̃] *a* exuberant.

pétunia [petynja] *nm Bot* petunia.

peu [pø] *adv* (*lire, manger etc*) not much, little; **elle mange p.** she doesn't eat much, she eats little; **un p.** (*lire, surpris etc*) a little, a bit; **p. de sel/de temps/etc** not much salt/time/etc, little salt/time/etc; **un p. de fromage/etc** a little cheese/etc, a bit of cheese/etc; **le p. de fromage que j'ai** the little cheese I have; **p. de gens/de livres/etc** few people/books/etc, not many people/books/etc; **p. sont...** few are...; **un (tout) petit p.** a (tiny) little bit; **p. intéressant/souvent/etc** not very interesting/often/etc; **p. de chose** not much; **p. à p.** gradually, little by little; **à p. près** more or less; **p. après/avant** shortly after/before.

peuplade [pœplad] *nf* tribe.

peuple [pœpl] *nm* (*nation, masse*) people; **les gens du p.** the common people. ◆**peupl/er** *vt* to populate, people. ◆**-é** *a* (*quartier etc*) populated (**de** with).

peuplier [pøplije] *nm* (*arbre, bois*) poplar.

peur [pœr] *nf* fear; **avoir p.** to be afraid *ou* frightened *ou* scared (**de** of); **faire p. à** to frighten, scare; **de p. que** (+ *sub*) for fear that; **de p. de faire** for fear of doing.

◆**peureux, -euse** *a* fearful, easily frightened.

peut, peux [pø] *voir* **pouvoir 1.**

peut-être [pøtetr] *adv* perhaps, maybe; **p.-être qu'il viendra** perhaps *ou* maybe he'll come.

phallique [falik] *a* phallic. ◆**phallocrate** *nm Péj* male chauvinist.

phare [far] *nm Nau* lighthouse; *Aut* headlight, headlamp; **rouler pleins phares** *Aut* to drive on full headlights; **faire un appel de phares** *Aut* to flash one's lights.

pharmacie [farmasi] *nf* chemist's shop, *Am* drugstore; (*science*) pharmacy; (*armoire*) medicine cabinet. ◆**pharmaceutique** *a* pharmaceutical. ◆**pharmacien, -ienne** *nmf* chemist, pharmacist, *Am* druggist.

pharynx [farɛ̃ks] *nm Anat* pharynx.

phase [faz] *nf* phase.

phénomène [fenɔmɛn] *nm* phenomenon; (*personne*) *Fam* eccentric. ◆**phénoménal, -aux** *a* phenomenal.

philanthrope [filɑ̃trɔp] *nmf* philanthropist. ◆**philanthropique** *a* philanthropic.

philatélie [filateli] *nf* philately, stamp collecting. ◆**philatélique** *a* philatelic. ◆**philatéliste** *nmf* philatelist, stamp collector.

philharmonique [filarmɔnik] *a* philharmonic.

Philippines [filipin] *nfpl* **les P.** the Philippines.

philosophe [filɔzɔf] *nmf* philosopher; — *a* (*sage, résigné*) philosophical. ◆**philosopher** *vi* to philosophize (**sur** about). ◆**philosophie** *nf* philosophy. ◆**philosophique** *a* philosophical.

phobie [fɔbi] *nf* phobia.

phonétique [fɔnetik] *a* phonetic; — *nf* phonetics.

phonographe [fɔnɔgraf] *nm* gramophone, *Am* phonograph.

phoque [fɔk] *nm* (*animal marin*) seal.

phosphate [fɔsfat] *nm Ch* phosphate.

phosphore [fɔsfɔr] *nm Ch* phosphorus.

photo [fɔto] *nf* photo; (*art*) photography; **prendre une p. de, prendre en p.** to take a photo of; — *a inv* **appareil p.** camera. ◆**photocopie** *nf* photocopy. ◆**photocopier** *vt* to photocopy. ◆**photocopieur** *nm*, ◆**photocopieuse** *nf* (*machine*) photocopier. ◆**photogénique** *a* photogenic. ◆**photographe** *nmf* photographer. ◆**photographie** *nf* (*art*) photography; (*image*) photograph. ◆**photographier** *vt* to photograph. ◆**photographique** *a* photographic. ◆**photomaton**® *nm* (*appareil*) photo booth.

phrase [fraz] *nf* (*mots*) sentence.

physicien, -ienne [fizisjɛ̃, -jɛn] *nmf* physicist.

physiologie [fizjɔlɔʒi] *nf* physiology. ◆**physiologique** *a* physiological.

physionomie [fizjɔnɔmi] *nf* face.

physique [fizik] **1** *a* physical; − *nm* (*corps, aspect*) physique; **au p.** physically. **2** *nf* (*science*) physics. ◆**—ment** *adv* physically.

piaffer [pjafe] *vi* (*cheval*) to stamp; **p. d'impatience** *Fig* to fidget impatiently.

piailler [pjɑje] *vi* (*oiseau*) to cheep; (*enfant*) *Fam* to squeal.

piano [pjano] *nm* piano; **p. droit/à queue** upright/grand piano. ◆**pianiste** *nmf* pianist.

piaule [pjol] *nf* (*chambre*) *Arg* room, pad.

pic [pik] *nm* **1** (*cime*) peak. **2** (*outil*) pick(axe); **p. à glace** ice pick. **3** (*oiseau*) woodpecker.

pic (à) [apik] *adv* (*verticalement*) sheer; **couler à p.** to sink to the bottom; **arriver à p.** *Fig* to arrive in the nick of time.

pichet [piʃɛ] *nm* jug, pitcher.

pickpocket [pikpɔkɛt] *nm* pickpocket.

pick-up [pikœp] *nm inv* (*camionnette*) pick-up truck.

picorer [pikɔre] *vti* to peck.

picoter [pikɔte] *vt* (*yeux*) to make smart; (*jambes*) to make tingle; **les yeux me picotent** my eyes are smarting.

pie [pi] **1** *nf* (*oiseau*) magpie. **2** *a inv* (*couleur*) piebald.

pièce [pjɛs] *nf* **1** (*de maison etc*) room. **2** (*morceau, objet etc*) piece; (*de pantalon*) patch; (*écrit*) & *Jur* document; **p. (de monnaie)** coin; **p. (de théâtre)** play; **p. (d'artillerie)** gun; **p. d'identité** proof of identity, identity card; **p. d'eau** pool, pond; **pièces détachées** *ou* **de rechange** (*de véhicule etc*) spare parts; **cinq dollars/etc (la) p.** five dollars/*etc* each; **travailler à la p.** to do piecework.

pied [pje] *nm* foot; (*de meuble*) leg; (*de verre, lampe*) base; *Phot* stand; **un p. de salade** a head of lettuce; **à p.** on foot; **aller à p.** to walk, go on foot; **au p.** de at the foot *ou* bottom of; **au p. de la lettre** *Fig* literally; **avoir p.** (*nageur*) to have a footing, touch the bottom; **coup de p.** kick; **donner un coup de p.** to kick (**à qn** s.o.); **sur p.** (*debout, levé*) up and about; **sur ses pieds** (*malade guéri*) up and about; **sur un p. d'égalité** on an equal footing; **comme un p.** (*mal*) *Fam* dreadfully; **faire un p. de nez** to thumb

one's nose (**à** at); **mettre sur p.** (*projet*) to set up. ◆**p.-noir** *nmf* (*pl* **pieds-noirs**) Algerian Frenchman *ou* Frenchwoman.

piédestal, -aux [pjedɛstal, -o] *nm* pedestal.

piège [pjɛʒ] *nm* (*pour animal*) & *Fig* trap. ◆**piéger** *vt* (*animal*) to trap; (*voiture etc*) to booby-trap; **engin piégé** booby trap; **lettre/colis/voiture piégé(e)** letter/parcel/car bomb.

pierre [pjɛr] *nf* stone; (*précieuse*) gem, stone; **p. à briquet** flint; **geler à p. fendre** to freeze (rock) hard. ◆**pierreries** *nfpl* gems, precious stones. ◆**pierreux, -euse** *a* stony.

piété [pjete] *nf* piety.

piétiner [pjetine] *vt* (*fouler aux pieds*) to trample (on); − *vi* to stamp (one's feet); (*marcher sur place*) to mark time; (*ne pas avancer*) *Fig* to make no headway.

piéton¹ [pjetɔ̃] *nm* pedestrian. ◆**piéton², -onne** *a*, ◆**piétonnier, -ière** *a* (*rue etc*) pedestrian-.

piètre [pjɛtr] *a* wretched, poor.

pieu, -x [pjø] *nm* **1** (*piquet*) post, stake. **2** (*lit*) *Fam* bed.

pieuvre [pjœvr] *nf* octopus.

pieux, -euse [pjø, -øz] *a* pious.

pif [pif] *nm* (*nez*) *Fam* nose. ◆**pifomètre (au)** *adv* (*sans calcul*) *Fam* at a rough guess.

pigeon [piʒɔ̃] *nm* pigeon; (*personne*) *Fam* dupe; **p. voyageur** carrier pigeon. ◆**pigeonner** *vt* (*voler*) *Fam* to rip off.

piger [piʒe] *vti Fam* to understand.

pigment [pigmɑ̃] *nm* pigment.

pignon [piɲɔ̃] *nm* (*de maison etc*) gable.

pile [pil] **1** *nf* *Él* battery; (*atomique*) pile; **radio à piles** battery radio. **2** *nf* (*tas*) pile; **en p.** in a pile. **3** *nf* (*de pont*) pier. **4** *nf* **p. (ou face)?** heads (or tails)?; **jouer à p. ou face** to toss up. **5** *adv* **s'arrêter p.** to stop short *ou* dead; **à deux heures p.** on the dot of two.

piler [pile] **1** *vt* (*amandes*) to grind; (*ail*) to crush. **2** *vi* (*en voiture*) to stop dead. ◆**pilonner** *vt Mil* to bombard, shell.

pilier [pilje] *nm* pillar.

pilon [pilɔ̃] *nm* (*de poulet*) drumstick.

piller [pije] *vti* to loot, pillage. ◆**pillage** *nm* looting, pillage. ◆**pillard, -arde** *nmf* looter.

pilori [pilɔri] *nm* **mettre au p.** *Fig* to pillory.

pilote [pilɔt] *nm Av Nau* pilot; (*de voiture, char*) driver; (*guide*) *Fig* guide; − *a* **usine(-)/projet(-)p.** pilot factory/plan. ◆**pilot/er** *vt Av* to fly, pilot; *Nau* to pilot; **p. qn** to show s.o. around. ◆**—age** *nm* piloting; **école de p.** flying school; **poste de p.** cockpit.

pilotis [piloti] *nm* (*pieux*) *Archit* piles.

pilule [pilyl] *nf* pill; **prendre la p.** (*femme*) to be on the pill; **se mettre à/arrêter la p.** to go on/off the pill.

piment [pimã] *nm* pimento, pepper. ◆**pimenté** *a Culin & Fig* spicy.

pimpant [pɛ̃pɑ̃] *a* pretty, spruce.

pin [pɛ̃] *nm* (*bois, arbre*) pine; **pomme de p.** pine cone.

pinailler [pinaje] *vi Fam* to quibble, split hairs.

pinard [pinar] *nm* (*vin*) *Fam* wine.

pince [pɛ̃s] *nf* (*outil*) pliers; *Méd* forceps; (*de cycliste*) clip; (*levier*) crowbar; *pl* (*de crabe*) pincers; **p. (à linge)** (clothes) peg *ou Am* pin; **p. (à épiler)** tweezers; **p. (à sucre)** sugar tongs; **p. à cheveux** hairgrip. ◆**pinc/er** *vt* to pinch; (*corde*) *Mus* to pluck; **p. qn** (*arrêter*) *Jur* to nab s.o., pinch s.o.; **se p. le doigt** to get one's finger caught (**dans** in). ◆**—é** *a* (*air*) stiff, constrained. ◆**—ée** *nf* (*de sel etc*) pinch (**de** of). ◆**pincettes** *nfpl* (*fire*) tongs; (*d'horloger*) tweezers. ◆**pinçon** *nm* pinch (mark).

pinceau, -x [pɛ̃so] *nm* (paint)brush.

pince-sans-rire [pɛ̃sɑ̃rir] *nm inv* person of dry humour.

pinède [pined] *nf* pine forest.

pingouin [pɛ̃gwɛ̃] *nm* auk, penguin.

ping-pong [piŋpɔ̃g] *nm* ping-pong.

pingre [pɛ̃gr] *a* stingy; – *nmf* skinflint.

pinson [pɛ̃sɔ̃] *nm* (*oiseau*) chaffinch.

pintade [pɛ̃tad] *nf* guinea fowl.

pin-up [pinœp] *nf inv* (*fille*) pinup.

pioche [pjɔʃ] *nf* pick(axe). ◆**piocher** *vti* (*creuser*) to dig (with a pick).

pion [pjɔ̃] *nm* **1** (*au jeu de dames*) piece; *Échecs & Fig* pawn. **2** *Scol* master (in charge of discipline).

pionnier [pjɔnje] *nm* pioneer.

pipe [pip] *nf* (*de fumeur*) pipe; **fumer la p.** to smoke a pipe.

pipeau, -x [pipo] *nm* (*flûte*) pipe.

pipe-line [piplin] *nm* pipeline.

pipi [pipi] *nm* **faire p.** *Fam* to go for a pee.

pique [pik] **1** *nm* (*couleur*) *Cartes* spades. **2** *nf* (*arme*) pike. **3** *nf* (*allusion*) cutting remark.

pique-assiette [pikasjɛt] *nmf inv* scrounger.

pique-nique [piknik] *nm* picnic. ◆**pique-niquer** *vi* to picnic.

piqu/er [pike] *vt* (*entamer, percer*) to prick; (*langue, yeux*) to sting; (*curiosité*) to rouse; (*coudre*) to (machine-)stitch; (*édredon, couvre-lit*) to quilt; (*crise de nerfs*) to have;

(*maladie*) to get; **p. qn** (*abeille*) to sting s.o.; (*serpent*) to bite s.o.; *Méd* to give s.o. an injection; **p. qch dans** (*enfoncer*) to stick sth into; **p. qn** (*arrêter*) *Jur Fam* to nab s.o., pinch s.o.; **p. qch** (*voler*) *Fam* to pinch sth; **p. une colère** to fly into a rage; **p. une tête** to plunge headlong; – *vi* (*avion*) to dive; (*moutarde etc*) to be hot; – **se p.** *vpr* to prick oneself; **se p. de faire qch** to pride oneself on being able to do sth. ◆**—ant** *a* (*épine*) prickly; (*froid*) biting; (*sauce, goût*) pungent, piquant; (*mot*) cutting; (*détail*) spicy; – *nm Bot* prickle, thorn; (*d'animal*) spine, prickle. ◆**—é** *a* (*meuble*) worm-eaten; (*fou*) *Fam* crazy; – *nm Av* (nose)dive; **descente en p.** *Av* nosedive. ◆**—eur, -euse** *nmf* (*sur machine à coudre*) machinist. ◆**piqûre** *nf* (*d'épingle*) prick; (*d'abeille*) sting; (*de serpent*) bite; (*trou*) hole; *Méd* injection; (*point*) stitch.

piquet [pikɛ] *nm* **1** (*pieu*) stake, picket; (*tente*) peg. **2 p. (de grève)** picket (line), strike picket. **3 au p.** *Scol* in the corner.

piqueté [pikte] *a* **p. de** dotted with.

pirate [pirat] *nm* pirate; **p. de l'air** hijacker; – *a* (*radio, bateau*) pirate-. ◆**piraterie** *nf* piracy; (*acte*) act of piracy; **p. (aérienne)** hijacking.

pire [pir] *a* worse (**que** than); **le p. moment/résultat/etc** the worst moment/result/etc; – *nmf* **le** *ou* **la p.** the worst (one); **le p. de tout** the worst (thing) of all; **au p.** at (the very) worst; **s'attendre au p.** to expect the (very) worst.

pirogue [pirɔg] *nf* canoe, dugout.

pis [pi] **1** *nm* (*de vache*) udder. **2** *a inv & adv Litt* worse; **de mal en p.** from bad to worse; – *nm* **le p.** *Litt* the worst.

pis-aller [pizale] *nm inv* (*personne, solution*) stopgap.

piscine [pisin] *nf* swimming pool.

pissenlit [pisɑ̃li] *nm* dandelion.

pistache [pistaʃ] *nf* (*fruit, parfum*) pistachio.

piste [pist] *nf* (*trace de personne ou d'animal*) track, trail; *Sp* track, racetrack; (*de magnétophone*) track; *Av* runway; (*de cirque*) ring; (*de patinage*) rink; (*pour chevaux*) racecourse, racetrack; **p. cyclable** cycle track, *Am* bicycle path; **p. de danse** dance floor; **p. de ski** ski run; **tour de p.** *Sp* lap.

pistolet [pistɔlɛ] *nm* gun, pistol; (*de peintre*) spray gun.

piston [pistɔ̃] *nm* **1** *Aut* piston. **2 avoir du p.** (*appui*) to have connections. ◆**pistonner** *vt* (*appuyer*) to pull strings for.

pitié [pitje] *nf* pity; **j'ai p. de lui, il me fait p.** I pity him, I feel sorry for him. ◆**piteux, -euse** *a Iron* pitiful. ◆**pitoyable** *a* pitiful.

piton [pitɔ̃] *nm* **1** (*à crochet*) hook. **2** *Géog* peak.

pitre [pitr] *nm* clown. ◆**pitrerie(s)** *nf(pl)* clowning.

pittoresque [pitɔresk] *a* picturesque.

pivert [piver] *nm* (*oiseau*) woodpecker.

pivoine [pivwan] *nf Bot* peony.

pivot [pivo] *nm* pivot; (*personne*) *Fig* linchpin, mainspring. ◆**pivoter** *vi* (*personne*) to swing round; (*fauteuil*) to swivel; (*porte*) to revolve.

pizza [pidza] *nf* pizza. ◆**pizzeria** *nf* pizza parlour.

placage [plakaʒ] *nm* (*revêtement*) facing; (*en bois*) veneer.

placard [plakar] *nm* **1** (*armoire*) cupboard, *Am* closet. **2** (*pancarte*) poster. ◆**placarder** *vt* (*affiche*) to post (up); (*mur*) to cover with posters.

place [plas] *nf* (*endroit, rang*) & *Sp* place; (*occupée par qn ou qch*) room; (*lieu public*) square; (*siège*) seat, place; (*prix d'un trajet*) *Aut* fare; (*emploi*) job, position; **p. (forte)** *Mil* fortress; **p. (de parking)** (parking) space; **p. (financière)** (money) market; **à la p.** (*échange*) instead (**de** of); **à votre p.** in your place; **sur p.** on the spot; **en p.** (*objet*) in place; **ne pas tenir en p.** to be unable to keep still; **mettre en p.** to install, set up; **faire p. à** to give way to; **changer qch de p.** to move sth.

plac/er [plase] *vt* (*mettre*) to put, place; (*situer*) to place, position; (*invité, spectateur*) to seat; (*argent*) to invest, place (**dans** in); (*vendre*) to place, sell; **p. un mot** to get a word in edgeways *ou Am* edgewise; **— se p.** *vpr* (*personne*) to take up a position, place oneself; (*objet*) to be put *ou* placed; (*cheval, coureur*) to be placed; **se p. troisième/etc** *Sp* to come *ou* be third/*etc*. ◆**—é** *a* (*objet*) & *Sp* placed; **bien/mal p. pour faire** in a good/bad position to do; **les gens haut placés** people in high places. ◆**—ement** *nm* (*d'argent*) investment.

placide [plasid] *a* placid.

plafond [plafɔ̃] *nm* ceiling. ◆**plafonnier** *nm Aut* roof light.

plage [plaʒ] *nf* **1** beach; (*ville*) (seaside) resort. **2** (*sur disque*) track. **3 p. arrière** *Aut* parcel shelf.

plagiat [plaʒja] *nm* plagiarism. ◆**plagier** *vt* to plagiarize.

plaid [plɛd] *nm* travelling rug.

plaider [plede] *vti Jur* to plead. ◆**plaideur,**

-euse *nmf* litigant. ◆**plaidoirie** *nf Jur* speech (for the defence). ◆**plaidoyer** *nm* plea.

plaie [plɛ] *nf* (*blessure*) wound; (*coupure*) cut; (*corvée, personne*) *Fig* nuisance.

plaignant, -ante [plɛɲɑ̃, -ɑ̃t] *nmf Jur* plaintiff.

plaindre* [plɛ̃dr] **1** *vt* to feel sorry for, pity. **2 se p.** *vpr* (*protester*) to complain (**de** about, **que** that); **se p. de** (*maux de tête etc*) to complain of *ou* about. ◆**plainte** *nf* complaint; (*cri*) moan, groan. ◆**plaintif, -ive** *a* sorrowful, plaintive.

plaine [plɛn] *nf Géog* plain.

plaire* [plɛr] *vi* & *v imp* **p. à** to please; **elle lui plaît** he likes her, she pleases him; **ça me plaît** I like it; **il me plaît de faire** I like doing; **s'il vous** *ou* **te plaît** please; **— se p.** (*à Paris etc*) to like *ou* enjoy it; (*l'un l'autre*) to like each other.

plaisance [plɛzɑ̃s] *nf* **bateau de p.** pleasure boat; **navigation de p.** yachting.

plaisant [plɛzɑ̃] *a* (*drôle*) amusing; (*agréable*) pleasing; **— nm mauvais p.** *Péj* joker. ◆**plaisanter** *vi* to joke, jest; **p. avec qch** to trifle with sth; **— vt** to tease. ◆**plaisanterie** *nf* joke, jest; (*bagatelle*) trifle; **par p.** for a joke. ◆**plaisantin** *nm Péj* joker.

plaisir [plezir] *nm* pleasure; **faire p. à** to please; **faites-moi le p. de . . .** would you be good enough to . . . ; **pour le p.** for fun, for the fun of it; **au p. (de vous revoir)** see you again sometime.

plan [plɑ̃] **1** *nm* (*projet, dessin*) plan; (*ville*) plan, map; (*niveau*) *Géom* plane; **au premier p.** in the foreground; **gros p.** *Phot Cin* close-up; **sur le p. politique/etc** from the political/*etc* viewpoint, politically/*etc*; **de premier p.** (*question etc*) major; **p. d'eau** stretch of water; **laisser en p.** (*abandonner*) to ditch. **2** *a* (*plat*) even, flat.

planche [plɑ̃ʃ] *nf* **1** board, plank; **p. à repasser/à dessin** ironing/drawing board; **p. (à roulettes)** skateboard; **p. (de surf)** surfboard; **p. (à voile)** sailboard; **faire de la p. (à voile)** to go windsurfing; **faire la p.** to float on one's back. **2** (*illustration*) plate. **3** (*de légumes*) bed, plot.

plancher [plɑ̃ʃe] *nm* floor.

plan/er [plane] *vi* (*oiseau*) to glide, hover; (*avion*) to glide; **p. sur qn** (*mystère, danger*) to hang over s.o.; **vol plané** glide. ◆**—eur** *nm* (*avion*) glider.

planète [planɛt] *nf* planet. ◆**planétaire** *a* planetary. ◆**planétarium** *nm* planetarium.

planifier [planifje] *vt Écon* to plan. ◆**pla-**

nification nf Écon planning. ◆**planning** nm (industriel, commercial) planning; **p familial** family planning.

planque [plɑ̃k] nf **1** (travail) Fam cushy job. **2** (lieu) Fam hideout. ◆**planquer** vt, — **se p.** vpr Fam to hide.

plant [plɑ̃] nm (plante) seedling; (de légumes etc) bed.

plante [plɑ̃t] nf **1** Bot plant; **p. d'appartement** house plant; **jardin des plantes** botanical gardens. **2 p. des pieds** sole (of the foot). ◆**plant/er** vt (arbre, plante etc) to plant; (clou, couteau) to drive in; (tente, drapeau, échelle) to put up; (mettre) to put (sur on, contre against); (regard) to fix (sur on); **p. là qn** to leave s.o. standing; **se p. devant** to plant oneself in front of. ◆—**é** a (immobile) standing; **bien p.** (personne) sturdy. ◆**plantation** nf (action) planting; (terrain) bed; (de café, d'arbres etc) plantation. ◆**planteur** nm plantation owner.

planton [plɑ̃tɔ̃] nm Mil orderly.

plantureux, -euse [plɑ̃tyrø, -øz] a (repas etc) abundant.

plaque [plak] nf plate; (de verre, métal) sheet, plate; (de verglas) sheet; (de marbre) slab; (de chocolat) bar; (commémorative) plaque; (tache) Méd blotch; **p. chauffante** Culin hotplate; **p. tournante** (carrefour) Fig centre; **p. minéralogique, p. d'immatriculation** Aut number ou Am license plate; **p. dentaire** (dental) plaque.

plaqu/er [plake] vt (métal, bijou) to plate; (bois) to veneer; (cheveux) to plaster (down); Rugby to tackle; (aplatir) to flatten (contre against); (abandonner) Fam to give (sth) up; **p. qn** Fam to ditch s.o.; **se p. contre** to flatten oneself against. ◆—**é** a (bijou) plated; **p. or** gold-plated; — nm **p. or** gold plate. ◆—**age** nm Rugby tackle.

plasma [plasma] nm Méd plasma.

plastic [plastik] nm plastic explosive. ◆**plastiquer** vt to blow up.

plastique [plastik] a (art, substance) plastic; **matière p.** plastic; — nm (matière) plastic; **en p.** (bouteille etc) plastic.

plastron [plastrɔ̃] nm shirtfront.

plat [pla] **1** a flat; (mer) calm, smooth; (fade) flat, dull; **à fond p.** flat-bottomed; **à p. ventre** flat on one's face; **à p.** (pneu, batterie) flat; (déprimé, épuisé) Fam low; **poser à p.** to put ou lay (down) flat; **tomber à p.** to fall down flat; **assiette plate** dinner plate; **calme p.** dead calm; — nm (de la main) flat. **2** nm (récipient, mets) dish; (partie du repas) course; '**p. du jour**' (au restaurant) 'today's special'.

platane [platan] nm plane tree.

plateau, -x [plato] nm (pour servir) tray; (de balance) pan; (de tourne-disque) turntable; (plate-forme) Cin TV set; Th stage; Géog plateau; **p. à fromages** cheeseboard.

plate-bande [platbɑ̃d] nf (pl **plates-bandes**) flower bed.

plate-forme [platform] nf (pl **plates-formes**) platform; **p.-forme pétrolière** oil rig.

platine [platin] **1** nm (métal) platinum. **2** nf (d'électrophone) deck. ◆**platiné** a (cheveux) platinum, platinum-blond(e).

platitude [platityd] nf platitude.

plâtre [plɑtr] nm (matière) plaster; **un p.** Méd a plaster cast; **dans le p.** Méd in plaster; **les plâtres** (d'une maison etc) the plasterwork; **p. à mouler** plaster of Paris. ◆**plâtr/er** vt (mur) to plaster; (membre) to put in plaster. ◆—**age** nm plastering. ◆**plâtrier** nm plasterer.

plausible [plozibl] a plausible.

plébiscite [plebisit] nm plebiscite.

plein [plɛ̃] a (rempli, complet) full; (paroi) solid; (ivre) Fam tight; **p. de** full of; **en pleine mer** on the open sea; **en p. visage**/etc right in the middle of the face/etc; **en p. jour** in broad daylight; — prép & adv **des billes p. les poches** pockets full of marbles; **du chocolat p. la figure** chocolate all over one's face; **p. de lettres/d'argent**/etc (beaucoup de) Fam lots of letters/money/etc; **à p.** (travailler) to full capacity; — nm **faire le p.** Aut to fill up (the tank); **battre son p.** (fête) to be in full swing. ◆**pleinement** adv fully.

pléonasme [pleonasm] nm (expression) redundancy.

pléthore [pletor] nf plethora.

pleurer [plœre] vi to cry, weep (sur over); — vt (regretter) to mourn (for). ◆**pleureur** a **saule p.** weeping willow. ◆**pleurnicher** vi to snivel, grizzle. ◆**pleurs (en)** adv in tears.

pleurésie [plœrezi] nf Méd pleurisy.

pleuvoir* [pløvwar] v imp to rain; **il pleut** it's raining; — vi (coups etc) to rain down (sur on).

pli [pli] nm **1** (de papier etc) fold; (de jupe, robe) pleat; (de pantalon, de bouche) crease; (de bras) bend; (faux) p. crease; **mise en plis** (coiffure) set. **2** (enveloppe) Com envelope, letter; **sous p. séparé** under separate cover. **3** Cartes trick. **4** (habitude) habit; **prendre le p. de faire** to get into the habit of doing. ◆**pli/er** vt to fold; (courber) to bend; **p. qn à** to submit s.o. to; — vi (branche) to bend; — **se p.** vpr (lit, chaise *etc*) to fold (up); **se p. à** to submit to, give in to. **◆—ant** *a* (*chaise etc*) folding; (*parapluie*) telescopic; — *nm* folding stool. **◆—able** *a* pliable. **◆—age** *nm* (*manière*) fold; (*action*) folding.

plinthe [plɛ̃t] *nf* skirting board, *Am* base-board.

pliss/er [plise] *vt* (*jupe, robe*) to pleat; (*froisser*) to crease; (*lèvres*) to pucker; (*front*) to wrinkle, crease; (*yeux*) to screw up. **◆—é** *nm* pleating, pleats.

plomb [plɔ̃] *nm* (*métal*) lead; (*fusible*) *Él* fuse; (*poids pour rideau etc*) lead weight; *pl* (*de chasse*) lead shot, buckshot; **de p.** (*tuyau etc*) lead-; (*sommeil*) *Fig* heavy; (*soleil*) blazing; (*ciel*) leaden. **◆plomb/er** *vt* (*dent*) to fill; (*colis*) to seal (with lead). **◆—é** *a* (*teint*) leaden. **◆—age** *nm* (*de dent*) filling.

plombier [plɔ̃bje] *nm* plumber. **◆plomberie** *nf* (*métier, installations*) plumbing.

plong/er [plɔ̃ʒe] *vi* (*personne, avion etc*) to dive, plunge; (*route, regard*) *Fig* to plunge; — *vt* (*mettre, enfoncer*) to plunge, thrust (**dans** into); **se p. dans** (*lecture etc*) to immerse oneself in. **◆—eant** *a* (*décolleté*) plunging; (*vue*) bird's eye-. **◆—é** *a p. dans* (*lecture etc*) immersed *ou* deep in. **◆—ée** *nf* diving; (*de sous-marin*) submersion; **en p.** (*sous-marin*) submerged. **◆plongeoir** *nm* diving board. **◆plongeon** *nm* dive. **◆plongeur, -euse** *nmf* diver; (*employé de restaurant*) dishwasher.

plouf [pluf] *nm & int* splash.

ployer [plwaje] *vti* to bend.

plu [ply] *voir* **plaire, pleuvoir**.

pluie [plɥi] *nf* rain; **une p.** (*averse*) & *Fig* a shower; **sous la p.** in the rain.

plume [plym] *nf* **1** (*d'oiseau*) feather. **2** (*pour écrire*) *Hist* quill (pen); (*pointe en acier*) (pen) nib; **stylo à p.** (fountain) pen; **vivre de sa p.** *Fig* to live by one's pen. **◆plumage** *nm* plumage. **◆plumeau, -x** *nm* feather duster. **◆plumer** *vt* (*volaille*) to pluck; **p. qn** (*voler*) *Fig* to fleece s.o. **◆plumet** *nm* plume. **◆plumier** *nm* pencil box, pen box.

plupart (la) [laplypar] *nf* most; **la p. des cas**/*etc* most cases/*etc*; **la p. du temps** most of the time; **la p. d'entre eux** most of them; **pour la p.** mostly.

pluriel, -ielle [plyrjɛl] *a & nm* *Gram* plural; **au p.** (*nom*) plural, in the plural.

plus¹ [ply] ([plys] *before vowel*, [plys] *in end position*) **1** *adv comparatif* (*travailler etc*) more (**que** than); **p. d'un kilo/de dix**/*etc* (*quantité, nombre*) more than a kilo/ten/

etc; **p. de thé**/*etc* (*davantage*) more tea/*etc*; **p. beau/rapidement**/*etc* more beautiful/rapidly/*etc* (**que** than); **p. tard** later; **p. petit** smaller; **de p. en p.** more and more; **de p. en p. vite** quicker and quicker; **p. il crie p. il s'enroue** the more he shouts the more hoarse he gets; **p. ou moins** more or less; **en p.** in addition (**de** to); **de p.** more (**que** than); (*en outre*) moreover; **les enfants (âgés) de p. de dix ans** children over ten; **j'ai dix ans de p. qu'elle** I'm ten years older than she is; **il est p. de cinq heures** it's after five (o'clock). **2** *adv superlatif* **le p.** (*travailler etc*) (the) most; **le p. beau**/*etc* the most beautiful/*etc*; (*de deux*) the more beautiful/*etc*; **le p. grand**/*etc* the biggest/*etc*; (*de deux*) the bigger/*etc*; **j'ai le p. de livres** I have (the) most books; **j'en ai le p.** I have (the) most; (**tout**) *au* **p. at** (the very) most.

plus² [ply] *adv de négation* **p. de** (*pain, argent etc*) no more; **il n'a p. de pain** he has no more bread, he doesn't have any more bread; **tu n'es p. jeune** you're no longer young, you're not young any more *ou* any longer; **elle ne le fait p.** she no longer does it, she doesn't do it any more *ou* any longer; **je ne la reverrai p.** I won't see her again.

plus³ [plys] *prép* plus; **deux p. deux font quatre** two plus two are four; **il fait p. deux (degrés)** it's two degrees above freezing; — *nm* **le signe p.** the plus sign.

plusieurs [plyzjœr] *a & pron* several.

plus-value [plyvaly] *nf* (*bénéfice*) profit.

plutonium [plytɔnjɔm] *nm* plutonium.

plutôt [plyto] *adv* rather (**que** than).

pluvieux, -euse [plyvjø, -øz] *a* rainy, wet.

PMU [peemy] *abrév* = **pari mutuel urbain**.

pneu [pnø] *nm* (*pl* **-s**) **1** (*de roue*) tyre, *Am* tire. **2** (*lettre*) express letter. **◆pneumatique 1** *a* (*matelas etc*) inflatable; **marteau p.** pneumatic drill. **2** *nm* = **pneu.**

pneumonie [pnømɔni] *nf* pneumonia.

poche [pɔʃ] *nf* pocket; (*de kangourou etc*) pouch; (*sac en papier·etc*) bag; *pl* (*sous les yeux*) bags; **livre de p.** paperback; **faire des poches** (*pantalon*) to be baggy; **j'ai un franc en p.** I have one franc on me. **◆pochette** *nf* (*sac*) bag, envelope; (*d'allumettes*) book; (*de disque*) sleeve, jacket; (*mouchoir*) pocket handkerchief; (*sac à main*) (clutch) bag.

poch/er [pɔʃe] *vt* **1 p. l'œil à qn** to give s.o. a black eye. **2** (*œufs*) to poach. **◆—é** *a* **œil p.** black eye.

podium [pɔdjɔm] *nm* *Sp* rostrum, podium.

poêle [pwal] **1** *nm* stove. **2** *nf* **p.** (**à frire**) frying pan.

poème [pɔɛm] *nm* poem. **◆poésie** *nf* poetry; **une p.** (*poème*) a piece of poetry. ◆**poète** *nm* poet; – *a* **femme p.** poetess. ◆**poétique** *a* poetic.

pognon [pɔɲɔ̃] *nm* (*argent*) *Fam* dough.

poids [pwa] *nm* weight; **au p.** by weight; **de p.** (*influent*) influential; **p. lourd** (*heavy*) lorry *ou Am* truck; **lancer le p.** *Sp* to put *ou* hurl the shot.

poignant [pwaɲɑ̃] *a* (*souvenir etc*) poignant.

poignard [pwaɲar] *nm* dagger; **coup de p.** stab. ◆**poignarder** *vt* to stab.

poigne [pwaɲ] *nf* (*étreinte*) grip.

poignée [pwaɲe] *nf* (*quantité*) handful (**de** of); (*de porte, casserole etc*) handle; (*d'épée*) hilt; **p. de main** handshake; **donner une p. de main à** to shake hands with.

poignet [pwaɲɛ] *nm* wrist; (*de chemise*) cuff.

poil [pwal] *nm* hair; (*pelage*) coat, fur; (*de brosse*) bristle; *pl* (*de tapis*) pile; (*d'étoffe*) nap; **à p.** (*nu*) *Arg* (stark) naked; **au p.** (*travail etc*) *Arg* top-rate; **de bon/mauvais p.** *Fam* in a good/bad mood; **de tout p.** *Fam* of all kinds. ◆**poilu** *a* hairy.

poinçon [pwɛ̃sɔ̃] *nm* (*outil*) awl, bradawl; (*marque de bijou etc*) hallmark. ◆**poinçonner** *vt* (*bijou*) to hallmark; (*billet*) to punch. ◆**poinçonneuse** *nf* (*machine*) punch.

poindre [pwɛ̃dr] *vi* (*jour*) *Litt* to dawn.

poing [pwɛ̃] *nm* fist; **coup de p.** punch.

point¹ [pwɛ̃] *nm* (*lieu, question, degré, score etc*) point; (*sur i, à l'horizon etc*) dot; (*tache*) spot; (*note*) *Scol* mark; (*de couture*) stitch; **sur le p. de faire** about to do, on the point of doing; **p. (final)** full stop, period; **p. d'exclamation** exclamation mark *ou Am* point; **p. d'interrogation** question mark; **p. de vue** point of view, viewpoint; (*endroit*) viewing point; **à p. (nommé)** (*arriver etc*) at the right moment; **à p.** (*rôti etc*) medium (cooked); (*steak*) medium rare; **mal en p.** in bad shape; **mettre au p.** *Phot* to focus; *Aut* to tune; (*technique etc*) to elaborate, perfect; (*éclaircir*) *Fig* to clarify, clear up; **mise au p.** focusing; tuning, tune-up; elaboration; *Fig* clarification; **faire le p.** *Fig* to take stock, sum up; **p. mort** *Aut* neutral; **au p. mort** *Fig* at a standstill; **p. noir** *Aut* (accident) black spot; **p. du jour** daybreak; **p. de côté** (*douleur*) stitch (in one's side). ◆**p.-virgule** *nm* (*pl* **points-virgules**) semicolon.

point² [pwɛ̃] *adv Litt* = **pas¹**.

pointe [pwɛ̃t] *nf* (*extrémité*) point, tip; (*pour grille*) spike; (*clou*) nail; *Géog* headland; (*maximum*) *Fig* peak; **une p. de** (*soupçon, nuance*) a touch of; **sur la p. des pieds** on

tiptoe; **en p.** pointed; **de p.** (*technique etc*) latest, most advanced; **à la p. de** (*progrès, etc*) *Fig* in *ou* at the forefront of.

point/er [pwɛ̃te] **1** *vt* (*cocher*) to tick (off), *Am* check (off). **2** *vt* (*braquer, diriger*) to point (**sur, vers** at). **3** *vti* (*employé*) to clock in, (*à la sortie*) to clock out; – **se p.** *vpr* (*arriver*) *Fam* to show up. **4** *vi* (*bourgeon etc*) to appear; **p. vers** to point upwards towards. ◆**—age** *nm* (*de personnel*) clocking in; clocking out.

pointillé [pwɛ̃tije] *nm* dotted line; – *a* dotted.

pointilleux, -euse [pwɛ̃tijø, -øz] *a* fussy, particular.

pointu [pwɛ̃ty] *a* (*en pointe*) pointed; (*voix*) shrill.

pointure [pwɛ̃tyr] *nf* (*de chaussure, gant*) size.

poire [pwar] *nf* **1** (*fruit*) pear. **2** (*figure*) *Fam* mug. **3** (*personne*) *Fam* sucker. ◆**poirier** *nm* pear tree.

poireau, -x [pwaro] *nm* leek.

poireauter [pwarote] *vi* (*attendre*) *Fam* to kick one's heels.

pois [pwa] *nm* (*légume*) pea; (*dessin*) (polka) dot; **petits p.** (garden) peas; **p. chiche** chickpea; **à p.** (*vêtement*) spotted, dotted.

poison [pwazɔ̃] *nm* (*substance*) poison.

poisse [pwas] *nf Fam* bad luck.

poisseux, -euse [pwasø, -øz] *a* sticky.

poisson [pwasɔ̃] *nm* fish; **p. rouge** goldfish; **les Poissons** (*signe*) Pisces. ◆**poissonnerie** *nf* fish shop. ◆**poissonnier, -ière** *nmf* fishmonger.

poitrine [pwatrin] *nf Anat* chest; (*seins*) breast, bosom; (*de veau, mouton*) *Culin* breast.

poivre [pwavr] *nm* pepper. ◆**poivr/er** *vt* to pepper. ◆**—é** *a Culin* peppery; (*plaisanterie*) *Fig* spicy. ◆**poivrier** *nm Bot* pepper plant; (*ustensile*) pepperpot. ◆**poivrière** *nf* pepperpot.

poivron [pwavrɔ̃] *nm* pepper, capsicum.

poivrot, -ote [pwavro, -ɔt] *nmf Fam* drunk(ard).

poker [pɔkɛr] *nm Cartes* poker.

polar [pɔlar] *nm* (*roman*) *Fam* whodunit.

polariser [pɔlarize] *vt* to polarize.

pôle [pol] *nm Géog* pole; **p. Nord/Sud** North/South Pole. ◆**polaire** *a* polar.

polémique [pɔlemik] *a* controversial, polemical; – *nf* controversy, polemic.

poli [pɔli] **1** *a* (*courtois*) polite (**avec** to, with). **2** *a* (*lisse, brillant*) polished; – *nm* (*aspect*) polish. ◆**—ment** *adv* politely.

police [pɔlis] *nf* **1** police; **faire** *ou* **assurer la**

p. to maintain order (**dans** in); **p. secours** emergency services; **p. mondaine** *ou* **des mœurs** = vice squad. **2 p. (d'assurance)** (insurance) policy. ◆**policier** *a* (*enquête, état*) police-; **roman p.** detective novel; – *nm* policeman, detective.

polichinelle [pɔliʃinɛl] *nf* **secret de p.** open secret.

polio [pɔljo] *nf* (*maladie*) polio; – *nmf* (*personne*) polio victim. ◆**poliomyélite** *nf* poliomyelitis.

polir [pɔlir] *vt* (*substance dure, style*) to polish.

polisson, -onne [pɔlisɔ̃, -ɔn] *a* naughty; – *nmf* rascal.

politesse [pɔlites] *nf* politeness; **une p.** (*parole*) a polite word; (*action*) an act of politeness.

politique [pɔlitik] *a* political; **homme p.** politician; – *nf* (*science, activité*) politics; (*mesures, manières de gouverner*) *Pol* policies; **une p.** (*tactique*) a policy. ◆**politicien, -ienne** *nmf Péj* politician. ◆**politiser** *vt* to politicize.

pollen [pɔlɛn] *nm* pollen.

polluer [pɔlɥe] *vt* to pollute. ◆**polluant** *nm* pollutant. ◆**pollution** *nf* pollution.

polo [pɔlo] *nm* **1** (*chemise*) sweat shirt. **2** *Sp* polo.

polochon [pɔlɔʃɔ̃] *nm* (*traversin*) *Fam* bolster.

Pologne [pɔlɔɲ] *nf* Poland. ◆**polonais, -aise** *a* Polish; – *nmf* Pole; – *nm* (*langue*) Polish.

poltron, -onne [pɔltrɔ̃, -ɔn] *a* cowardly; – *nmf* coward.

polycopi/er [pɔlikɔpje] *vt* to mimeograph, duplicate. ◆**-é** *nm Univ* mimeographed copy (*of lecture etc*).

polyester [pɔliɛstɛr] *nm* polyester.

Polynésie [pɔlinezi] *nf* Polynesia.

polyvalent [pɔlivalɑ̃] *a* (*rôle*) multi-purpose, varied; (*professeur, ouvrier*) all-round; **école polyvalente, lycée p.** comprehensive school.

pommade [pɔmad] *nf* ointment.

pomme [pɔm] *nf* **1** apple; **p. d'Adam** *Anat* Adam's apple. **2** (*d'arrosoir*) rose. **3 p. de terre** potato; **pommes vapeur** steamed potatoes; **pommes frites** chips, *Am* French fries; **pommes chips** potato crisps *ou Am* chips. ◆**pommier** *nm* apple tree.

pommette [pɔmɛt] *nf* cheekbone.

pompe [pɔ̃p] *nf* **1** pump; **p. à essence** petrol *ou Am* gas station; **p. à incendie** fire engine; **coup de p.** *Fam* tired feeling. **2** *nf* (*chaussure*) *Fam* shoe. **3** *nf* (*en gymnastique*)

press-up, *Am* push-up. **4** *nfpl* **pompes funèbres** undertaker's; **entrepreneur de pompes funèbres** undertaker. **5** *nf* **p. anti-sèche** *Scol* crib. **6** *nf* (*splendeur*) pomp. ◆**pomper** *vt* to pump; (*évacuer*) to pump out (**de** of); (*absorber*) to soak up; (*épuiser*) *Fam* to tire out; – *vi* to pump. ◆**pompeux, -euse** *a* pompous. ◆**pompier** **1** *nm* fireman; **voiture des pompiers** fire engine. **2** *a* (*emphatique*) pompous. ◆**pompiste** *nmf Aut* pump attendant.

pompon [pɔ̃pɔ̃] *nm* (*ornement*) pompon.

pomponner [pɔ̃pɔne] *vt* to doll up.

ponce [pɔ̃s] *nf* (*pierre*) **p.** pumice (stone). ◆**poncer** *vt* to rub down, sand. ◆**ponceuse** *nf* (*machine*) sander.

ponctuation [pɔ̃ktɥasjɔ̃] *nf* punctuation. ◆**ponctuer** *vt* to punctuate (**de** with).

ponctuel, -elle [pɔ̃ktɥɛl] *a* (*à l'heure*) punctual; (*unique*) *Fig* one-off, *Am* one-of-a-kind. ◆**ponctualité** *nf* punctuality.

pondéré [pɔ̃dere] *a* level-headed. ◆**pondération** *nf* level-headedness.

pondre [pɔ̃dr] *vt* (*œuf*) to lay; (*livre, discours*) *Péj Fam* to produce; – *vi* (*poule*) to lay.

poney [pɔnɛ] *nm* pony.

pont [pɔ̃] *nm* bridge; (*de bateau*) deck; **p. (de graissage)** *Aut* ramp; **faire le p.** *Fig* to take the intervening day(s) off (*between two holidays*); **p. aérien** airlift. ◆**p.-levis** *nm* (*pl* **ponts-levis**) drawbridge.

ponte [pɔ̃t] **1** *nf* (*d'œufs*) laying. **2** *nm* (*personne*) *Fam* bigwig.

pontife [pɔ̃tif] *nm* **1** (*souverain*) **p.** pope. **2** (*ponte*) *Fam* bigshot. ◆**pontifical, -aux** *a* papal, pontifical.

pop [pɔp] *nm & a inv Mus* pop.

popote [pɔpɔt] *nf* (*cuisine*) *Fam* cooking.

populace [pɔpylas] *nf Péj* rabble.

populaire [pɔpylɛr] *a* (*personne, tradition, gouvernement etc*) popular; (*quartier, milieu*) lower-class; (*expression*) colloquial; (*art*) folk-. ◆**populariser** *vt* to popularize. ◆**popularité** *nf* popularity (**auprès de** with).

population [pɔpylasjɔ̃] *nf* population. ◆**populeux, -euse** *a* populous, crowded.

porc [pɔr] *nm* pig; (*viande*) pork; (*personne*) *Péj* swine.

porcelaine [pɔrsəlɛn] *nf* china, porcelain.

porc-épic [pɔrkepik] *nm* (*pl* **porcs-épics**) (*animal*) porcupine.

porche [pɔrʃ] *nm* porch.

porcherie [pɔrʃəri] *nf* pigsty.

pore [pɔr] *nm* pore. ◆**poreux, -euse** *a* porous.

pornographie [pɔrnɔgrafi] *nf* pornography. ◆**pornographique** *a* (*Fam* **porno**) pornographic.

port [pɔr] *nm* **1** port, harbour; **arriver à bon p.** to arrive safely. **2** (*d'armes*) carrying; (*de barbe*) wearing; (*prix*) carriage, postage; (*attitude*) bearing.

portable [pɔrtabl] *a* (*robe etc*) wearable; (*portatif*) portable.

portail [pɔrtaj] *nm* (*de cathédrale etc*) portal.

portant [pɔrtɑ̃] *a* **bien p.** in good health.

portatif, -ive [pɔrtatif, -iv] *a* portable.

porte [pɔrt] *nf* door, (*passage*) doorway; (*de jardin*) gate, (*passage*) gateway; (*de ville*) entrance, *Hist* gate; **p. (d'embarquement)** *Av* (departure) gate; **Alger, p. de . . .** Algiers, gateway to . . . ; **p. d'entrée** front door; **mettre à la p.** (*jeter dehors*) to throw out; (*renvoyer*) to sack. ◆**p.-fenêtre** *nf* (*pl* **portes-fenêtres**) French window.

porte-à-faux [pɔrtafo] *nm inv* **en p.-à-faux** (*en déséquilibre*) unstable.

porte-avions [pɔrtavjɔ̃] *nm inv* aircraft carrier. ◆**p.-bagages** *nm inv* luggage rack. ◆**p.-bébé** *nm* (*nacelle*) carrycot, *Am* baby basket; (*kangourou*®) baby sling. ◆**p.-bonheur** *nm inv* (*fétiche*) (lucky) charm. ◆**p.-cartes** *nm inv* card holder *ou* case. ◆**p.-clés** *nm inv* key ring. ◆**p.-documents** *nm inv* briefcase. ◆**p.-drapeau, -x** *nm Mil* standard bearer. ◆**p.-jarretelles** *nm inv* suspender *ou Am* garter belt. ◆**p.-monnaie** *nm inv* purse. ◆**p.-parapluie** *nm inv* umbrella stand. ◆**p.-plume** *nm inv* pen (*for dipping in ink*). ◆**p.-revues** *nm inv* newspaper rack. ◆**p.-savon** *nm* soapdish. ◆**p.-serviettes** *nm inv* towel rail. ◆**p.-voix** *nm inv* megaphone.

portée [pɔrte] *nf* **1** (*de fusil etc*) range; **à la p. de qn** within reach of s.o.; (*richesse, plaisir etc*) *Fig* within s.o.'s grasp; **à p. de la main** within (easy) reach; **à p. de voix** within earshot; **hors de p.** out of reach. **2** (*animaux*) litter. **3** (*importance, effet*) significance, import. **4** *Mus* stave.

portefeuille [pɔrtəfœj] *nm* wallet; *Pol Com* portfolio.

portemanteau, -x [pɔrtmɑ̃to] *nm* (*sur pied*) hatstand; (*barre*) hat *ou* coat peg.

porte-parole [pɔrtparɔl] *nm inv* (*homme*) spokesman; (*femme*) spokeswoman (**de** for, of).

port/er [pɔrte] *vt* to carry; (*vêtement, lunettes, barbe etc*) to wear; (*trace, responsabilité, fruits etc*) to bear; (*regard*) to cast; (*attaque*) to make (**contre** against); (*coup*) to strike; (*sentiment*) to have (**à** for); (*inscrire*) to enter, write down; **p. qch à** (*amener*) to bring *ou* take sth to; **p. qn à faire** (*pousser*) to lead *ou* prompt s.o. to do; **p. bonheur/malheur** to bring good/bad luck; **se faire p. malade** to report sick; – *vi* (*voix*) to carry; (*canon*) to fire; (*vue*) to extend; **p. (juste)** (*coup*) to hit the mark; (*mot, reproche*) to hit home; **p. sur** (*reposer sur*) to rest on; (*concerner*) to bear on; (*accent*) to fall on; (*heurter*) to strike; — **se p.** *vpr* (*vêtement*) to be worn; **se p. bien/mal** to be well/ill; **comment te portes-tu?** how are you?; **se p. candidat** to stand as a candidate. ◆**—ant** *a* **bien p.** in good health. ◆**—é à** *a* **p. à croire**/*etc* inclined to believe/*etc*; **p. sur qch** fond of sth. ◆**—eur, -euse** *nm Rail* porter; – *nmf Méd* carrier; (*de nouvelles, chèque*) bearer; **mère porteuse** surrogate mother.

portier [pɔrtje] *nm* doorkeeper, porter. ◆**portière** *nf* (*de véhicule, train*) door. ◆**portillon** *nm* gate.

portion [pɔrsjɔ̃] *nf* (*part, partie*) portion; (*de nourriture*) helping, portion.

portique [pɔrtik] *nm* **1** *Archit* portico. **2** (*de balançoire etc*) crossbar, frame.

porto [pɔrto] *nm* (*vin*) port.

portrait [pɔrtre] *nm* portrait; **être le p. de** (*son père etc*) to be the image of; **faire un p.** to paint *ou* draw a portrait (**de** of); **p. en pied** full-length portrait. ◆**p.-robot** *nm* (*pl* **portraits-robots**) identikit (picture), photofit.

portuaire [pɔrtɥer] *a* (*installations etc*) harbour-.

Portugal [pɔrtygal] *nm* Portugal. ◆**portugais, -aise** *a & nmf* Portuguese; – *nm* (*langue*) Portuguese.

pose [poz] *nf* **1** (*installation*) putting up; putting in; laying. **2** (*attitude de modèle, affectation*) pose; (*temps*) *Phot* exposure. ◆**pos/er** *vt* to put (down); (*papier peint, rideaux*) to put up; (*sonnette, chauffage*) to put in; (*mine, moquette, fondations*) to lay; (*question*) to ask (**à qn** s.o.); (*principe, conditions*) to lay down; **se porter candidate** to apply, put in one's application (**à** for); **ça pose la question de . . .** it poses the question of . . . ; – *vi* (*modèle etc*) to pose (**pour** for); — **se p.** *vpr* (*oiseau, avion*) to land; (*problème, question*) to arise; **se p. sur** (*yeux*) to fix on; **se p. en chef**/*etc* to set oneself up as *ou* pose as a leader/*etc*; **la question se pose!** this question should be asked! ◆**—é** *a* (*calme*) calm, staid.

◆**—ément** adv calmly. ◆**—eur, -euse** nmf Péj poseur.

positif, -ive [pozitif, -iv] a positive. ◆**positivement** adv positively.

position [pozisjɔ̃] nf (attitude, emplacement, opinion etc) position; **prendre p.** Fig to take a stand (**contre** against); **prise de p.** stand.

posologie [pozɔlɔʒi] nf (de médicament) dosage.

posséder [posede] vt to possess; (maison etc) to own, possess; (bien connaître) to master. ◆**possesseur** nm possessor; owner. ◆**possessif, -ive** a (personne, adjectif etc) possessive; – nm Gram possessive. ◆**possession** nf possession; **en p. de** in possession of; **prendre p. de** to take possession of.

possible [posibl] a possible (à faire to do); **il (nous) est p. de le faire** it is possible (for us) to do it; **il est p. que** (+ sub) it is possible that; **si p.** if possible; **le plus tôt/etc p.** as soon/etc as possible; **autant que p.** as much ou as many as possible; – nm **faire son p.** to do one's utmost (**pour faire** to do); **dans la mesure du p.** as far as possible. ◆**possibilité** nf possibility.

post- [pɔst] préf post-.

postdater [pɔstdate] vt to postdate.

poste [pɔst] **1** nf (service) post, mail; (local) post office; **bureau de p.** post office; **Postes (et Télécommunications)** (administration) Post Office; **par la p.** by post, by mail; **p. aérienne** airmail; **mettre à la p.** to post, mail. **2** nm (lieu, emploi) post; **p. de secours** first aid post; **p. de police** police station; **p. d'essence** petrol ou Am gas station; **p. d'incendie** fire hydrant; **p. d'aiguillage** signal box ou Am tower. **3** nm (appareil) Rad TV set; Tél extension (number). ◆**postal, -aux** a postal; **boîte postale** PO Box; **code p.** postcode, Am zip code. ◆**poster 1** vt **p. qn** (placer) Mil to post s.o. **2** vt (lettre) to post, mail. **3** [pɔstɛr] nm poster.

postérieur [pɔsterjœr] **1** a (document etc) later; **p. à** after. **2** nm (derrière) Fam posterior.

postérité [pɔsterite] nf posterity.

posthume [pɔstym] a posthumous; **à titre p.** posthumously.

postiche [pɔstiʃ] a (barbe etc) false.

postier, -ière [pɔstje, -jɛr] nmf postal worker.

postillonner [pɔstijɔne] vi to sputter.

post-scriptum [pɔstskriptɔm] nm inv postscript.

postul/er [pɔstyle] vt **1** (emploi) to apply for. **2** (poser) Math to postulate. ◆**—ant, -ante** nmf applicant.

posture [pɔstyr] nf posture.

pot [po] nm **1** pot; (à confiture) jar, pot; (à lait) jug; (à bière) mug; (de crème, yaourt) carton; **p. de chambre** chamber pot; **p. de fleurs** flower pot; **prendre un p.** (verre) Fam to have a drink. **2** (chance) Fam luck; **avoir du p.** to be lucky.

potable [pɔtabl] a drinkable; (passable) Fam tolerable; **'eau p.'** 'drinking water'.

potage [pɔtaʒ] nm soup.

potager, -ère [pɔtaʒe, -ɛr] a (jardin) vegetable-; **plante potagère** vegetable; – nm vegetable garden.

potasser [pɔtase] vt (examen) to cram for; – vi to cram.

pot-au-feu [pɔtofø] nm inv (plat) beef stew.

pot-de-vin [pɔdvɛ̃] nm (pl **pots-de-vin**) bribe.

pote [pɔt] nm (ami) Fam pal, buddy.

poteau, -x [pɔto] nm post; (télégraphique) pole; **p. d'arrivée** Sp winning post.

potelé [pɔtle] a plump, chubby.

potence [pɔtɑ̃s] nf (gibet) gallows.

potentiel, -ielle [pɔtɑ̃sjɛl] a & nm potential.

poterie [pɔtri] nf (art) pottery; **une p.** a piece of pottery; **des poteries** (objets) pottery. ◆**potier** nm potter.

potin [pɔtɛ̃] **1** nmpl (cancans) gossip. **2** nm (bruit) Fam row.

potion [pɔsjɔ̃] nf potion.

potiron [pɔtirɔ̃] nm pumpkin.

pot-pourri [popuri] nm (pl **pots-pourris**) Mus medley.

pou, -x [pu] nm louse; **poux** lice.

poubelle [pubɛl] nf dustbin, Am garbage can.

pouce [pus] nm **1** thumb; **un coup de p.** Fam a helping hand. **2** (mesure) Hist & Fig inch.

poudre [pudr] nf powder; **p. (à canon)** (explosif) gunpowder; **en p.** (lait) powdered; (chocolat) drinking; **sucre en p.** castor ou caster sugar. ◆**poudrer** vt to powder; – **se p.** vpr (femme) to powder one's nose. ◆**poudreux, -euse** a powdery, dusty. ◆**poudrier** nm (powder) compact. ◆**poudrière** nf powder magazine; (région) Fig powder keg.

pouf [puf] **1** int thump! **2** nm (siège) pouf(fe).

pouffer [pufe] vi **p. (de rire)** to burst out laughing, guffaw.

pouilleux, -euse [pujø, -øz] a (sordide) miserable; (mendiant) lousy.

poulain [pulɛ̃] nm (cheval) foal; **le p. de qn** Fig s.o.'s protégé.

poule [pul] *nf* **1** hen, *Culin* fowl; **être p. mouillée** (*lâche*) to be chicken; **oui, ma p.!** *Fam* yes, my pet! **2** (*femme*) *Péj* tart. ◆**poulailler** *nm* **1** (hen) coop. **2 le p.** *Th Fam* the gods, the gallery. ◆**poulet** *nm* **1** (*poule, coq*) *Culin* chicken. **2** (*policier*) *Fam* cop.

pouliche [pulif] *nf* (*jument*) filly.

poulie [puli] *nf* pulley.

poulpe [pulp] *nm* octopus.

pouls [pu] *nm* *Méd* pulse.

poumon [pumɔ̃] *nm* lung; **à pleins poumons** (*respirer*) deeply; (*crier*) loudly; **p. d'acier** iron lung.

poupe [pup] *nf* *Nau* stern, poop.

poupée [pupe] *nf* doll.

poupin [pupɛ̃] *a* **visage p.** baby face.

poupon [pupɔ̃] *nm* (*bébé*) baby; (*poupée*) doll.

pour [pur] **1** *prép* for; **p. toi/moi**/*etc* for you/me/*etc*; **faites-le p. lui** do it for him, do it for his sake; **partir p.** (*Paris etc*) to leave for; **elle va partir p. cinq ans** she's leaving for five years; **p. femme/base**/*etc* as a wife/basis/*etc*; **p. moi, p. ma part** (*quant à moi*) as for me; **dix p. cent** ten per cent; **gentil p.** kind to; **elle est p.** she's in favour; **p. faire** (in order) to do, so as to do; **p. que tu saches** so (that) you may know; **p. quoi faire?** what for?; **trop petit/poli**/*etc* **p.** too small/polite/*etc* to do; **assez grand**/*etc* **p. faire** big/*etc* enough to do; **p. cela** for that reason; **jour p. jour/heure p. heure** to the day/hour; **p. intelligent**/*etc* **qu'il soit** however clever/*etc* he may be; **ce n'est pas p. me plaire** it doesn't exactly please me; **acheter p. cinq francs de bonbons** to buy five francs' worth of sweets. **2** *nm* **le p. et le contre** the pros and cons.

pourboire [purbwar] *nm* (*argent*) tip.

pourcentage [pursɑ̃taʒ] *nm* percentage.

pourchasser [purfase] *vt* to pursue.

pourparlers [purparle] *nmpl* negotiations, talks.

pourpre [purpr] *a & nm* purple.

pourquoi [purkwa] *adv & conj* why; **p. pas?** why not?; – *nm inv* reason (**de** for); **le p. et le comment** the whys and wherefores.

pourra, pourrait [pura, pure] *voir* **pouvoir 1.**

pourrir [purir] *vi*, – **se p.** *vpr* to rot; – *vt* to rot; **p. qn** to corrupt s.o. ◆**pourri** *a* (*fruit, temps, personne etc*) rotten. ◆**pourriture** *nf* rot, rottenness; (*personne*) *Péj* swine.

poursuite [pursɥit] **1** *nf* chase, pursuit; (*du bonheur, de créancier*) pursuit (**de** of); (*continuation*) continuation; **se mettre à la p. de** to go in pursuit of. **2** *nfpl* *Jur* legal proceed-

ings (**contre** against). ◆**poursuiv/re*** **1** *vt* (*courir après*) to chase, pursue; (*harceler, relancer*) to hound, pursue; (*obséder*) to haunt; (*but, idéal etc*) to pursue. **2** *vt* **p. qn** *Jur* (*au criminel*) to prosecute s.o.; (*au civil*) to sue s.o. **3** *vt* (*lecture, voyage etc*) to continue (with), carry on (with), pursue; – *vi*, – **se p.** *vpr* to continue, go on. ◆**-ant, -ante** *nmf* pursuer.

pourtant [purtɑ̃] *adv* yet, nevertheless.

pourtour [purtur] *nm* perimeter.

pourvoir* [purvwar] *vt* to provide (**de** with); **être pourvu de** to have, be provided with; – *vi* **p. à** (*besoins etc*) to provide for. ◆**pourvoyeur, -euse** *nmf* supplier.

pourvu que [purvyk(ə)] *conj* (*condition*) provided *ou* providing (that); **p. qu'elle soit là** (*souhait*) I only hope (that) she's there.

pousse [pus] *nf* **1** (*bourgeon*) shoot, sprout. **2** (*croissance*) growth.

pousse-café [puskafe] *nm inv* after-dinner liqueur.

pouss/er [puse] **1** *vt* to push; (*du coude*) to nudge, poke; (*véhicule, machine*) to drive hard; (*recherches*) to pursue; (*cri*) to utter; (*soupir*) to heave; **p. qn à faire** to urge s.o. to do; **p. qn à bout** to push s.o. to his limits; **p. trop loin** (*gentillesse etc*) to carry too far; **p. à la perfection** to bring to perfection; – *vi* to push; **p. jusqu'à Paris**/*etc* to push on as far as Paris/*etc*; – **se p.** *vpr* (*se déplacer*) to move up *ou* over. **2** *vi* (*croître*) to grow; **faire p.** (*plante, barbe etc*) to grow. ◆**-é a** (*travail, études*) advanced. ◆**-ée** *nf* (*pression*) pressure; (*coup*) push; (*d'ennemi*) thrust, push; (*de fièvre etc*) outbreak; (*de l'inflation*) upsurge. ◆**poussette** *nf* pushchair, *Am* stroller; **p. canne** (baby) buggy, *Am* (collapsible) stroller; **p. de marché** shopping trolley *ou* *Am* cart. ◆**poussoir** *nm* (push) button.

poussière [pusjɛr] *nf* dust; **dix francs et des poussières** *Fam* a bit over ten francs. ◆**poussiéreux, -euse** *a* dusty.

poussif, -ive [pusif, -iv] *a* short-winded, puffing.

poussin [pusɛ̃] *nm* (*poulet*) chick.

poutre [putr] *nf* (*en bois*) beam; (*en acier*) girder. ◆**poutrelle** *nf* girder.

pouvoir* [puvwar] **1** *v aux* (*capacité*) to be able, can; (*permission, éventualité*) may, can; **je peux deviner** I can guess, I'm able to guess; **tu peux entrer** you may *ou* can come in; **il peut être malade** he may *ou* might be ill; **elle pourrait/pouvait venir** she might/could come; **j'ai pu l'obtenir** I managed to get it; **j'aurais pu l'obtenir** I could have got it *ou Am* gotten it; **je n'en peux plus** I'm utterly exhausted; – *v imp* **il peut neiger** it may snow; **— se p.** *vpr* **il se peut qu'elle parte** (it's possible that) she might leave. **2** *nm* (*capacité, autorité*) power; (*procuration*) power of attorney; **les pouvoirs publics** the authorities; **au p.** *Pol* in power; **en son p.** in one's power (**de faire** to do).

poux [pu] *voir* **pou.**

pragmatique [pragmatik] *a* pragmatic.

praire [prɛr] *nf* (*mollusque*) clam.

prairie [preri] *nf* meadow.

praline [pralin] *nf* sugared almond. ◆**praliné** *a* (*glace*) praline-flavoured.

praticable [pratikabl] *a* (*projet, chemin*) practicable.

praticien, -ienne [pratisjɛ̃, -jɛn] *nmf* practitioner.

pratique [pratik] **1** *a* (*connaissance, personne, instrument etc*) practical. **2** *nf* (*exercice, procédé*) practice; (*expérience*) practical experience; **la p. de la natation/du golf/etc** swimming/golfing/*etc*; **mettre en p.** to put into practice; **en p.** (*en réalité*) in practice. ◆**pratiqu/er** *vt* (*art etc*) to practise; (*football*) to play, practise; (*trou, route*) to make; (*opération*) to carry out; **p. la natation** to go swimming; – *vi* to practise. ◆**—ant, -ante** *a Rel* practising; – *nmf* churchgoer.

pratiquement [pratikmɑ̃] *adv* (*presque*) practically; (*en réalité*) in practice.

pré [pre] *nm* meadow.

pré- [pre] *préf* pre-.

préalable [prealabl] *a* previous, preliminary; **p. à** prior to; – *nm* precondition, prerequisite; **au p.** beforehand. ◆**—ment** [-əmɑ̃] *adv* beforehand.

préambule [preɑ̃byl] *nm* (*de loi*) preamble; *Fig* prelude (**à** to).

préau, -x [preo] *nm Scol* covered playground.

préavis [preavi] *nm* (*de congé etc*) (advance) notice (**de** of).

précaire [prekɛr] *a* precarious.

précaution [prekosjɔ̃] *nf* (*mesure*) precaution; (*prudence*) caution; **par p.** as a precaution. ◆**précautionneux, -euse** *a* cautious.

précédent, -ente [presedɑ̃, -ɑ̃t] **1** *a* previous, preceding, earlier; – *nmf* previous one. **2** *nm* **un p.** (*fait, exemple*) a precedent; **sans p.** unprecedented. ◆**précédemment** [-amɑ̃] *adv* previously. ◆**précéder** *vti* to precede; **faire p. qch de qch** to precede sth by sth.

précepte [presɛpt] *nm* precept.

précepteur, -trice [preseptœr, -tris] *nmf* (private) tutor.

prêcher [preʃe] *vti* to preach; **p. qn** *Rel & Fig* to preach to s.o.

précieux, -euse [presjø, -øz] *a* precious.

précipice [presipis] *nm* abyss, chasm.

précipit/er [presipite] *vt* (*jeter*) to throw, hurl; (*plonger*) to plunge (**dans** into); (*hâter*) to hasten; **— se p.** *vpr* (*se jeter*) to throw *ou* hurl oneself; (*foncer*) to rush (**à, sur** on to); (*s'accélérer*) to speed up. ◆**—é a** hasty. ◆**précipitamment** *adv* hastily. ◆**précipitation 1** *nf* haste. **2** *nfpl* (*pluie*) precipitation.

précis [presi] **1** *a* precise; (*idée, mécanisme*) accurate, precise; **à deux heures précises** at two o'clock sharp *ou* precisely. **2** *nm* (*résumé*) summary; (*manuel*) handbook. ◆**précisément** *adv* precisely. ◆**préciser** *vt* to specify (**que** that); **— se p.** *vpr* to become clear(er). ◆**précision** *nf* precision; accuracy; (*détail*) detail; (*explication*) explanation.

précoce [prekɔs] *a* (*fruit, mariage, mort etc*) early; (*personne*) precocious. ◆**précocité** *nf* precociousness; earliness.

préconçu [prekɔ̃sy] *a* preconceived.

préconiser [prekɔnize] *vt* to advocate (**que** that).

précurseur [prekyrsœr] *nm* forerunner, precursor; – *a* **un signe p. de qch** a sign heralding sth.

prédécesseur [predesesœr] *nm* predecessor.

prédestiné [predestine] *a* fated, predestined (**à faire** to do).

prédicateur [predikatœr] *nm* preacher.

prédilection [predilɛksjɔ̃] *nf* (special) liking; **de p.** favourite.

prédire* [predir] *vt* to predict (**que** that). ◆**prédiction** *nf* prediction.

prédisposer [predispoze] *vt* to predispose (**à qch** to sth, **à faire** to do). ◆**prédisposition** *nf* predisposition.

prédomin/er [predomine] *vi* to predominate. ◆**—ant** *a* predominant. ◆**prédominance** *nf* predominance.

préfabriqué [prefabrike] *a* prefabricated.

préface [prefas] *nf* preface. ◆**préfacer** *vt* to preface.

préfér/er [prefere] *vt* to prefer (**à** to); **p. faire** to prefer to do. ◆**—é, -ée** *a & nmf* favourite. ◆**—able** *a* preferable (**à** to). ◆**préférence** *nf* preference; **de p.** preferably; **de p. à** in preference to. ◆**préférentiel, -ielle** *a* preferential.

préfet [prefɛ] *nm* prefect, *chief administrator in a department*; **p. de police** prefect of police, *Paris chief of police*. ◆**préfecture** *nf* prefecture; **p. de police** Paris police headquarters.

préfixe [prefiks] *nm* prefix.

préhistoire [preistwar] *nf* prehistory. ◆**préhistorique** *a* prehistoric.

préjudice [preʒydis] *nm Jur* prejudice, harm; **porter p. à** to prejudice, harm. ◆**préjudiciable** *a* prejudicial (à to).

préjugé [preʒyʒe] *nm* (*parti pris*) prejudice; **avoir un p.** *ou* **des préjugés** to be prejudiced (**contre** against).

prélasser (se) [səprelase] *vpr* to loll (about), lounge (about).

prélat [prela] *nm Rel* prelate.

prélever [prelve] *vt* (*échantillon*) to take (**sur** from); (*somme*) to deduct (**sur** from). ◆**prélèvement** *nm* taking; deduction; **p. de sang** blood sample; **p. automatique** *Fin* standing order.

préliminaire [preliminer] *a* preliminary; − *nmpl* preliminaries.

prélude [prelyd] *nm* prelude (à to).

prématuré [prematyre] *a* premature; − *nm* (*bébé*) premature baby. ◆**−ment** *adv* prematurely, too soon.

préméditer [premedite] *vt* to premeditate. ◆**préméditation** *nf Jur* premeditation.

premier, -ière [prəmje, -jɛr] *a* first; (*enfance*) early; (*page*) *Journ* front, first; (*qualité, nécessité, importance*) prime; (*état*) original; (*notion, cause*) basic; (*danseuse, rôle*) leading; (*inférieur*) bottom; (*supérieur*) top; **nombre p.** *Math* prime number; **le p. rang** the front *ou* first row; **à la première occasion** at the earliest opportunity; **P. ministre** Prime Minister, Premier; − *nmf* first (one); **arriver le p.** *ou* **en p.** to arrive first; **être le p. de la classe** to be (at the) top of the class; − *nm* (*date*) first; (*étage*) first *ou Am* second floor; **le p. de l'an** New Year's Day; − *nf Th Cin* première; *Rail* first class; *Scol* = sixth form, *Am* = twelfth grade; *Aut* first (gear); (*événement historique*) first. ◆**premier-né** *nm*, ◆**première-née** *nf* first-born (child). ◆**premièrement** *adv* firstly.

prémisse [premis] *nf* premiss.

prémonition [premɔnisjɔ̃] *nf* premonition.

prémunir [premynir] *vt* to safeguard (**contre** against).

prénatal, mpl -als [prenatal] *a* antenatal, *Am* prenatal.

prendre* [prɑ̃dr] *vt* to take (**à qn** from s.o.); (*attraper*) to catch, get; (*voyager par*) to take, travel by; (*acheter*) to get; (*douche, bain*) to take, have; (*repas*) to have; (*nouvelles*) to get; (*temps, heure*) to take (up); (*pensionnaire*) to take (in); (*ton, air*) to put on; (*engager*) to take (*s.o.*) (on); (*chercher*) to pick up, get; **p. qn pour** (*un autre*) to (mis)take s.o. for; (*considérer*) to take s.o. for; **p. qn** (*doute etc*) to seize s.o.; **p. feu** to catch fire; **p. de la place** to take up room; **p. du poids/de la vitesse** to put on weight/speed; **à tout p.** on the whole; **qu'est-ce qui te prend?** what's got *ou Am* gotten into you?; − *vi* (*feu*) to catch; (*gelée, ciment*) to set; (*greffe, vaccin*) to take; (*mode*) to catch on; − **se p.** *vpr* (*objet*) to be taken; (*s'accrocher*) to get caught; (*eau*) to freeze; **se p. pour un génie/etc** to think one is a genius/etc; **s'y p.** to go *ou* set about it; **s'en p. à** (*critiquer, attaquer*) to attack; (*accuser*) to blame; **se p. à faire** to begin to do. ◆**prenant** *a* (*travail, film etc*) engrossing; (*voix*) engaging. ◆**preneur, -euse** *nmf* taker, buyer.

prénom [prenɔ̃] *nm* first name. ◆**prénommer** *vt* to name; **il se prénomme Louis** his first name is Louis.

préoccuper [preɔkype] *vt* (*inquiéter*) to worry; (*absorber*) to preoccupy; **se p. de** to be worried about; to be preoccupied about. ◆**−ant** *a* worrying. ◆**−é** *a* worried. ◆**préoccupation** *nf* worry; (*idée, problème*) preoccupation.

préparer [prepare] *vt* to prepare; (*repas etc*) to get ready, prepare; (*examen*) to study for, prepare (for); **p. qch à qn** to prepare sth for s.o.; **p. qn à** (*examen*) to prepare *ou* coach s.o. for; − **se p.** *vpr* to get (oneself) ready, prepare oneself (à qch for sth); (*orage*) to brew, threaten. ◆**préparatifs** *nmpl* preparations (de for). ◆**préparation** *nf* preparation. ◆**préparatoire** *a* preparatory.

prépondérant [prepɔ̃derɑ̃] *a* dominant. ◆**prépondérance** *nf* dominance.

préposer [prepoze] *vt* **p. qn à** to put s.o. in charge of. ◆**−é, -ée** *nmf* employee; (*facteur*) postman, postwoman.

préposition [prepozisjɔ̃] *nf* preposition.

préretraite [prerətrɛt] *nf* early retirement.

prérogative [prerɔgativ] *nf* prerogative.

près [prɛ] *adv* **p. de** (*qn, qch*) near (to), close to; **p. de deux ans/etc** (*presque*) nearly two years/etc; **p. de partir/etc** about to leave/etc; **tout p.** nearby (**de qn/qch** s.o./sth), close by (**de qn/qch** s.o./sth); **de p.** (*lire, examiner, suivre*) closely; **à peu de chose p.** almost; **à cela p.** except for that; **voici le**

chiffre à un franc p. here is the figure give or take a franc; **calculer au franc p.** to calculate to the nearest franc.

présage [preza3] *nm* omen, foreboding. ◆**présager** *vt* to forebode.

presbyte [presbit] *a* & *nmf* long-sighted (person). ◆**presbytie** [-bisi] *nf* long-sightedness.

presbytère [presbiter] *nm Rel* presbytery.

préscolaire [preskɔler] *a* (*âge etc*) pre-school.

prescrire* [preskrir] *vt* to prescribe. ◆**prescription** *nf* (*instruction*) & *Jur* prescription.

préséance [preseɑ̃s] *nf* precedence (**sur** over).

présent¹ [prezɑ̃] **1** *a* (*non absent*) present; **les personnes présentes** those present. **2** *a* (*actuel*) present; − *nm* (*temps*) present; *Gram* present (tense); **à p.** now, at present; **dès à p.** as from now. ◆**présence** *nf* presence; (*à l'école, au bureau etc*) attendance (**à** at); **feuille de p.** attendance sheet; **faire acte de p.** to put in an appearance; **en p.** (*personnes*) face to face; **en p. de** in the presence of; **p. d'esprit** presence of mind.

présent² [prezɑ̃] *nm* (*cadeau*) present.

présent/er [prezɑ̃te] *vt* (*offrir, exposer, animer etc*) to present; (*montrer*) to show, present; **p. qn à qn** to introduce *ou* present s.o. to s.o.; − **se p.** *vpr* to introduce *ou* present oneself (**à** to); (*chez qn*) to show up; (*occasion etc*) to arise; **se p. à** (*examen*) to sit for; (*élections*) to stand in *ou* at, run in; (*emploi*) to apply for; (*autorités*) to report to; **ça se présente bien** it looks promising. ◆**−able** *a* presentable. ◆**présentateur, -trice** *nmf TV* announcer, presenter. ◆**présentation** *nf* presentation; introduction. ◆**présentoir** *nm* (*étagère*) (display) stand.

préserver [prezɛrve] *vt* to protect, preserve (**de** from). ◆**préservatif** *nm* sheath, condom. ◆**préservation** *nf* protection, preservation.

présidence [prezidɑ̃s] *nf* (*de nation*) presidency; (*de firme etc*) chairmanship. ◆**président, -ente** *nmf* (*de nation*) president; (*de réunion, firme*) chairman, chairwoman; **p. directeur général** chairman and managing director, *Am* chief executive officer. ◆**présidentiel, -ielle** *a* presidential.

présider [prezide] *vt* (*réunion*) to preside at *ou* over, chair; − *vi* to preside.

présomption [prezɔ̃psjɔ̃] *nf* (*conjecture, suffisance*) presumption.

présomptueux, -euse [prezɔ̃ptɥø, -øz] *a* presumptuous.

presque [prɛsk(ə)] *adv* almost, nearly; **p. jamais/rien** hardly ever/anything.

presqu'île [prɛskil] *nf* peninsula.

presse [prɛs] *nf* (*journaux, appareil*) press; *Typ* (printing) press; **de p.** (*conférence, agence*) press-.

presse-citron [prɛsitrɔ̃] *nm inv* lemon squeezer. ◆**p.-papiers** *nm inv* paperweight. ◆**p.-purée** *nm inv* (potato) masher.

pressentir* [presɑ̃tir] *vt* (*deviner*) to sense (**que** that). ◆**pressentiment** *nm* foreboding, presentiment.

press/er [prese] *vt* (*serrer*) to squeeze, press; (*bouton*) to press; (*fruit*) to squeeze; (*départ etc*) to hasten; **p. qn** to hurry s.o. (**de faire** to do); (*assaillir*) to harass s.o. (**de questions** with questions); **p. le pas** to speed up; − *vi* (*temps*) to press; (*affaire*) to be pressing *ou* urgent; **rien ne presse** there's no hurry; − **se p.** *vpr* (*se grouper*) to crowd, swarm; (*se serrer*) to squeeze (together); (*se hâter*) to hurry (**de faire** to do); **presse-toi** (**de partir**) hurry up (and go). ◆**−ant** *a* pressing, urgent. ◆**−é** *a* (*personne*) in a hurry; (*air*) hurried; (*travail*) pressing, urgent. ◆**pressing** [-iŋ] *nm* (*magasin*) dry cleaner's. ◆**pressoir** *nm* (*wine*) press.

pression [presjɔ̃] *nf* pressure; **faire p. sur qn** to put pressure on s.o., pressurize s.o.; **bière (à la) p.** draught beer; − *nm* (*bouton-*)p. press-stud, *Am* snap.

pressuriser [presyrize] *vt Av* to pressurize.

prestance [prestɑ̃s] *nf* (*imposing*) presence.

prestation [prestasjɔ̃] *nf* **1** (*allocation*) allowance, benefit. **2** (*performance*) performance.

prestidigitateur, -trice [prestidiʒitatœr, -tris] *nmf* conjurer. ◆**prestidigitation** *nf* conjuring.

prestige [prestiʒ] *nm* prestige. ◆**prestigieux, -euse** *a* prestigious.

presto [presto] *Fam voir* **illico.**

présumer [prezyme] *vt* to presume (**que** that).

présupposer [presypoze] *vt* to presuppose (**que** that).

prêt¹ [prɛ] *a* (*préparé, disposé*) ready (**à faire** to do, **à qch** for sth). ◆**p.-à-porter** [prɛtapɔrte] *nm inv* ready-to-wear clothes.

prêt² [prɛ] *nm* (*emprunt*) loan. ◆**p.-logement** *nm* (*pl* prêts-logement) mortgage.

prétend/re [pretɑ̃dr] *vt* to claim (**que** that); (*vouloir*) to intend (**faire** to do); **p.**

être/savoir to claim to be/to know; **elle se prétend riche** she claims to be rich; – *vi* p. à (*titre etc*) to lay claim to. ◆—**ant** *nm* (*amoureux*) suitor. ◆—**u** *a* so-called. ◆—**ument** *adv* supposedly.

prétentieux, -euse [pretɑ̃sjø, -øz] *a & nmf* pretentious (person). ◆**prétention** *nf* (*vanité*) pretension; (*revendication, ambition*) claim.

prêt/er [prete] *vt* (*argent, objet*) to lend (à to); (*aide, concours*) to give (à to); (*attribuer*) to attribute (à to); **p. attention** to pay attention (à to); **p. serment** to take an oath; – *vi* p. à (*phrase etc*) to lend itself to; **se p. à** (*consentir à*) to agree to; (*sujet etc*) to lend itself to. ◆—**eur, -euse** *nmf* (*d'argent*) lender; **p. sur gages** pawnbroker.

prétexte [pretɛkst] *nm* pretext, excuse; **sous p. de/que** on the pretext of/that. ◆**prétexter** *vt* to plead (**que** that).

prêtre [prɛtr] *nm* priest; **grand p.** high priest.

preuve [prœv] *nf* proof, evidence; **faire p. de** to show; **faire ses preuves** (*personne*) to prove oneself; (*méthode*) to prove itself.

prévaloir [prevalwar] *vi* to prevail (**contre** against, **sur** over).

prévenant [prevnɑ̃] *a* considerate. ◆**prévenance(s)** *nf*(*pl*) (*gentillesse*) consideration.

préven/ir* [prevnir] *vt* **1** (*avertir*) to warn (**que** that); (*aviser*) to tell, inform (**que** that). **2** (*désir, question*) to anticipate; (*malheur*) to avert. ◆—**u, -ue 1** *nmf Jur* defendant, accused. **2** *a* prejudiced (**contre** against). ◆**préventif, -ive** *a* preventive. ◆**prévention** *nf* **1** prevention; **p. routière** road safety. **2** (*opinion*) prejudice.

prév/oir* [prevwar] *vt* (*anticiper*) to foresee (**que** that); (*prédire*) forecast (**que** that); (*temps*) *Mét* to forecast; (*projeter, organiser*) to plan (for); (*réserver, préparer*) to allow, provide. ◆—**u** *a* (*conditions*) laid down; **un repas est p.** a meal is provided; **au moment p.** at the appointed time; **comme p.** as planned, as expected; **p. pour** (*véhicule, appareil etc*) designed for. ◆**prévisible** *a* foreseeable. ◆**prévision** *nf* (*opinion*) & *Mét* forecast; **en p. de** in expectation of.

prévoyant [prevwajɑ̃] *a* (*personne*) provident. ◆**prévoyance** *nf* foresight; **société de p.** provident society.

prier [prije] **1** *vi Rel* to pray; – *vt* **p. Dieu pour qu'il nous accorde qch** to pray (to God) for sth. **2** *vt* **p. qn de faire** to ask *ou* request s.o. to do; (*implorer*) to beg s.o. to do; **je vous en prie** (*faites donc, allez-y*)

please; (*en réponse à 'merci'*) don't mention it; **je vous prie** please; **se faire p.** to wait to be asked. ◆**prière** *nf Rel* prayer; (*demande*) request; **p. de répondre**/*etc* please answer/*etc*.

primaire [primɛr] *a* primary.

prime [prim] **1** *nf* (*d'employé*) bonus; (*d'État*) subsidy; (*cadeau*) *Com* free gift; **p. (d'assurance)** (insurance) premium. **2** *a* **de p. abord** at the very first glance.

primé [prime] *a* (*animal*) prize-winning.

primer [prime] *vi* to excel, prevail; – *vt* to prevail over.

primeurs [primœr] *nfpl* early fruit and vegetables.

primevère [primvɛr] *nf* (*à fleurs jaunes*) primrose.

primitif, -ive [primitif, -iv] *a* (*art, société etc*) primitive; (*état, sens*) original; – *nm* (*artiste*) primitive. ◆**primitivement** *adv* originally.

primo [primo] *adv* first(ly).

primordial, -aux [primɔrdjal, -o] *a* vital (**de faire** to do).

prince [prɛ̃s] *nm* prince. ◆**princesse** *nf* princess. ◆**princier, -ière** *a* princely. ◆**principauté** *nf* principality.

principal, -aux [prɛ̃sipal, -o] *a* main, chief, principal; – *nm* (*de collège*) *Scol* principal; **le p.** (*essentiel*) the main *ou* chief thing. ◆—**ement** *adv* mainly.

principe [prɛ̃sip] *nm* principle; **par p.** on principle; **en p.** theoretically, in principle; (*normalement*) as a rule.

printemps [prɛ̃tɑ̃] *nm* (*saison*) spring. ◆**printanier, -ière** *a* (*temps etc*) spring-, spring-like.

priorité [priɔrite] *nf* priority; **la p.** *Aut* the right of way; **la p. à droite** *Aut* right of way to traffic coming from the right; **'cédez la p.'** *Aut* 'give way', *Am* 'yield'; **en p.** as a matter of priority. ◆**prioritaire** *a* (*industrie etc*) priority-; **être p.** to have priority; *Aut* to have the right of way.

pris [pri] *voir* **prendre**; – *a* (*place*) taken; (*crème, ciment*) set; (*eau*) frozen; (*gorge*) infected; (*nez*) congested; **être (très) p.** (*occupé*) to be (very) busy; **p. de** (*peur, panique*) stricken with.

prise [priz] *voir* **prendre**; – *nf* taking; (*manière d'empoigner*) grip, hold; (*de ville*) capture, taking; (*objet saisi*) catch; (*de tabac*) pinch; **p. (de courant)** *Él* (*mâle*) plug; (*femelle*) socket; **p. multiple** *Él* adaptor; **p. d'air** air vent; **p. de conscience** awareness; **p. de contact** first meeting; **p. de position** *Fig* stand; **p. de sang** blood test; **p.**

de son (sound) recording; **p. de vue(s)** *Cin Phot* (action) shooting; (*résultat*) shot; **aux prises avec** at grips with.

priser [prize] **1** *vt tabac* **à p.** snuff; – *vi* to take snuff. **2** *vt* (*estimer*) to prize.

prisme [prism] *nm* prism.

prison [prizɔ̃] *nf* prison, jail, gaol; (*réclusion*) imprisonment; **mettre en p.** to imprison, put in prison. **◆prisonnier, -ière** *nmf* prisoner; **faire qn p.** to take s.o. prisoner.

privé [prive] *a* private; **en p.** (*seul à seul*) in private; – *nm* **dans le p.** in private life; *Com Fam* in the private sector.

priver [prive] *vt* to deprive (**de** of); **se p. de** to deprive oneself of, do without. **◆privation** *nf* deprivation (**de** of); *pl* (*sacrifices*) hardships.

privilège [privileʒ] *nm* privilege. **◆privilégié, -ée** *a & nmf* privileged (person).

prix [pri] *nm* **1** (*d'un objet, du succès etc*) price; **à tout p.** at all costs; **à aucun p.** on no account; **hors (de) p.** exorbitant; **attacher du p. à** to attach importance to; **menu à p. fixe** set price menu. **2** (*récompense*) prize.

pro- [pro] *préf* pro-.

probable [prɔbabl] *a* probable, likely; **peu p.** unlikely. **◆probabilité** *nf* probability, likelihood; **selon toute p.** in all probability. **◆probablement** *adv* probably.

probant [prɔbɑ̃] *a* conclusive.

probité [prɔbite] *nf* (*honnêteté*) integrity.

problème [prɔblɛm] *nm* problem. **◆problématique** *a* doubtful, problematic.

procéd/er [prɔsede] *vi* (*agir*) to proceed; (*se conduire*) to behave; **p. à** (*enquête etc*) to carry out. **◆—é** *nm* process; (*conduite*) behaviour. **◆procédure** *nf* procedure; *Jur* proceedings.

procès [prɔsɛ] *nm* (*criminel*) trial; (*civil*) lawsuit; **faire un p. à** to take to court.

processeur [prɔsesœr] *nm* (*d'ordinateur*) processor.

procession [prɔsesjɔ̃] *nf* procession.

processus [prɔsesys] *nm* process.

procès-verbal, -aux [prɔsɛvɛrbal, -o] *nm* (*de réunion*) minutes; (*constat*) *Jur* report; (*contravention*) fine, ticket.

prochain, -aine [prɔʃɛ̃, -ɛn] **1** *a* next; (*avenir*) near; (*parent*) close; (*mort, arrivée*) impending; (*mariage*) forthcoming; **un jour p.** one day soon; – *nf* **à la prochaine!** *Fam* see you soon!; **à la prochaine (station)** at the next stop. **2** *nm* (*semblable*) fellow (man). **◆prochainement** *adv* shortly, soon.

proche [prɔʃ] *a* (*espace*) near, close; (*temps*)

close (at hand); (*parent, ami*) close; (*avenir*) near; **p. de** near (to), close to; **une maison/etc p.** a house/etc nearby *ou* close by; – *nmpl* close relations.

proclamer [prɔklame] *vt* to proclaim, declare (**que** that); **p. roi** to proclaim king. **◆proclamation** *nf* proclamation, declaration.

procréer [prɔkree] *vt* to procreate. **◆procréation** *nf* procreation.

procuration [prɔkyrasjɔ̃] *nf* power of attorney; **par p.** (*voter*) by proxy.

procurer [prɔkyre] *vt* **p. qch à qn** (*personne*) to obtain sth for s.o.; (*occasion etc*) to afford s.o. sth; **se p. qch** to obtain sth.

procureur [prɔkyrœr] *nm* = *Br* public prosecutor, = *Am* district attorney.

prodige [prɔdiʒ] *nm* (*miracle*) wonder; (*personne*) prodigy. **◆prodigieux, -euse** *a* prodigious, extraordinary.

prodigue [prɔdig] *a* (*dépensier*) wasteful, prodigal. **◆prodiguer** *vt* to lavish (**à qn** on s.o.).

production [prɔdyksjɔ̃] *nf* production; (*de la terre*) yield. **◆producteur, -trice** *nmf Com Cin* producer; – *a* producing; **pays p. de pétrole** oil-producing country. **◆productif, -ive** *a* (*terre, réunion etc*) productive. **◆productivité** *nf* productivity.

produire* [prɔduir] **1** *vt* (*fabriquer, présenter etc*) to produce; (*causer*) to bring about, produce. **2 se p.** *vpr* (*événement etc*) to happen, occur. **◆produit** *nm* (*article etc*) product; (*pour la vaisselle*) liquid; (*d'une vente, d'une collecte*) proceeds; *pl* (*de la terre*) produce; **p. (chimique)** chemical; **p. de beauté** cosmetic.

proéminent [prɔeminɑ̃] *a* prominent.

prof [prɔf] *nm Fam* = **professeur.**

profane [prɔfan] **1** *nmf* lay person. **2** *a* (*art etc*) secular.

profaner [prɔfane] *vt* to profane, desecrate. **◆profanation** *nf* profanation, desecration.

proférer [prɔfere] *vt* to utter.

professer [prɔfese] *vt* to profess (**que** that).

professeur [prɔfesœr] *nm* teacher; *Univ* lecturer, *Am* professor; (*titulaire d'une chaire*) *Univ* professor.

profession [prɔfesjɔ̃] *nf* **1** occupation, vocation; (*libérale*) profession; (*manuelle*) trade; **de p.** (*chanteur etc*) professional, by profession. **2 p. de foi** *Fig* declaration of principles. **◆professionnel, -elle** *a* professional; (*école*) vocational, trade-; – *nmf* (*non amateur*) professional.

profil [prɔfil] *nm* (*de personne, objet*) profile;

de p. in profile. ◆**profiler** *vt* to outline, profile; **— se p.** *vpr* to be outlined *ou* profiled (*sur* against).

profit [prɔfi] *nm* profit; (*avantage*) advantage, profit; **vendre à p.** to sell at a profit; **tirer p. de** to benefit by, profit by; **au p. de** for the benefit of. ◆**profitable** *a* profitable (**à** to). ◆**profiter** *vi* **p. de** to take advantage of; **p. à qn** to profit s.o.; **p. (bien)** (*enfant*) *Fam* to thrive. ◆**profiteur, -euse** *nmf Péj* profiteer.

profond [prɔfɔ̃] *a* deep; (*esprit, joie, erreur etc*) profound, great; (*cause*) underlying; **p. de deux mètres** two metres deep; *— adv* (*pénétrer etc*) deep; *— nm* **au plus p. de** in the depths of. ◆**profondément** *adv* deeply; (*dormir*) soundly; (*triste, souhaiter*) profoundly; (*extrêmement*) thoroughly. ◆**profondeur** *nf* depth; profoundness; *pl* depths (**de** of); **en p.** (*étudier etc*) in depth; **à six mètres de p.** at a depth of six metres.

profusion [prɔfyzjɔ̃] *nf* profusion; **à p.** in profusion.

progéniture [prɔʒenityr] *nf Hum* offspring.

progiciel [prɔʒisjɛl] *nm* (*pour ordinateur*) (software) package.

programme [prɔgram] *nm* programme, *Am* program; (*d'une matière*) *Scol* syllabus; (*d'ordinateur*) program; **p. (d'études)** (*d'une école*) curriculum. ◆**programmation** *nf* programming. ◆**programmer** *vt Cin Rad TV* to programme, *Am* program; (*ordinateur*) to program. ◆**programmeur, -euse** *nmf* (computer) programmer.

progrès [prɔgrɛ] *nm & nmpl* progress; **faire des p.** to make (good) progress. ◆**progresser** *vi* to progress. ◆**progressif, -ive** *a* progressive. ◆**progression** *nf* progression. ◆**progressiste** *a & nmf Pol* progressive. ◆**progressivement** *adv* progressively, gradually.

prohiber [prɔibe] *vt* to prohibit, forbid. ◆**prohibitif, -ive** *a* prohibitive. ◆**prohibition** *nf* prohibition.

proie [prwa] *nf* prey; **être en p. à** to be (a) prey to, be tortured by.

projecteur [prɔʒɛktœr] *nm* (*de monument*) floodlight; (*de prison*) & *Mil* searchlight; *Th* spot(light); *Cin* projector.

projectile [prɔʒɛktil] *nm* missile.

projet [prɔʒɛ] *nm* plan; (*ébauche*) draft; (*entreprise, étude*) project.

projeter [prɔʒte] *vt* **1** (*lancer*) to hurl, project. **2** (*film, ombre*) to project; (*lumière*) to flash. **3** (*voyage, fête etc*) to plan; **p. de faire** to plan to do. ◆**projection** *nf* (*lancement*)

hurling, projection; (*de film, d'ombre*) projection; (*séance*) showing.

prolétaire [prɔleter] *nmf* proletarian. ◆**prolétariat** *nm* proletariat. ◆**prolétarien, -ienne** *a* proletarian.

proliférer [prɔlifere] *vi* to proliferate. ◆**prolifération** *nf* proliferation.

prolifique [prɔlifik] *a* prolific.

prolixe [prɔliks] *a* verbose, wordy.

prologue [prɔlɔg] *nm* prologue (**de, à** to).

prolonger [prɔlɔ̃ʒe] *vt* to prolong, extend; **— se p.** *vpr* (*séance, rue, effet*) to continue. ◆**prolongateur** *nm* (*rallonge*) *Él* extension cord. ◆**prolongation** *nf* extension; *pl Fb* extra time. ◆**prolongement** *nm* extension.

promenade [prɔmnad] *nf* (*à pied*) walk; (*en voiture*) ride, drive; (*en vélo, à cheval*) ride; (*action*) *Sp* walking; (*lieu*) walk, promenade; **faire une p.** = **se promener**. ◆**promener** *vt* to take for a walk *ou* ride; (*visiteur*) to take *ou* show around; **p. qch sur qch** (*main, regard*) to run sth over sth; **envoyer p.** *Fam* to send packing; **— se p.** *vpr* (*à pied*) to (go for a) walk; (*en voiture*) to (go for a) ride *ou* drive. ◆**promeneur, -euse** *nmf* walker, stroller.

promesse [prɔmɛs] *nf* promise. ◆**promett/re*** *vt* to promise (**qch à qn** s.o. sth); **p. de faire** to promise to do; **c'est promis** it's a promise; *— vi* **p. (beaucoup)** *Fig* to be promising; **se p. qch** to promise oneself sth; **se p. de faire** to resolve to do. ◆**—eur, -euse** *a* promising.

promontoire [prɔmɔ̃twar] *nm Géog* headland.

promoteur [prɔmɔtœr] *nm* **p. (immobilier)** property developer.

promotion [prɔmosjɔ̃] *nf* **1** promotion; **en p.** *Com* on (special) offer. **2** (*candidats*) *Univ* year. ◆**promouvoir*** *vt* (*personne, produit etc*) to promote; **être promu** (*employé*) to be promoted (**à** to).

prompt [prɔ̃] *a* swift, prompt, quick. ◆**promptitude** *nf* swiftness, promptness.

promulguer [prɔmylge] *vt* to promulgate.

prôner [prone] *vt* (*vanter*) to extol; (*préconiser*) to advocate.

pronom [prɔnɔ̃] *nm Gram* pronoun. ◆**pronominal, -aux** *a* pronominal.

prononc/er [prɔnɔ̃se] *vt* (*articuler*) to pronounce; (*dire*) to utter; (*discours*) to deliver; (*jugement*) *Jur* to pronounce, pass; *— vi Jur Ling* to pronounce; **— se p.** *vpr* (*mot*) to be pronounced; (*personne*) to reach a decision (*sur* about, on); **se p. pour** to come out in favour of. ◆**—é** *a* (*visible*) pronounced, marked. ◆**prononciation** *nf* pronunciation.

pronostic [prɔnɔstik] *nm* (*prévision*) & *Sp* forecast. ◆**pronostiquer** *vt* to forecast.

propagande [prɔpagɑ̃d] *nf* propaganda. ◆**propagandiste** *nmf* propagandist.

propager [prɔpaʒe] *vt*, **— se p.** *vpr* to spread. ◆**propagation** *nf* spread(ing).

propension [prɔpɑ̃sjɔ̃] *nf* propensity (**à qch** for sth, **à faire** to do).

prophète [prɔfɛt] *nm* prophet. ◆**prophétie** [-fesi] *nf* prophecy. ◆**prophétique** *a* prophetic. ◆**prophétiser** *vti* to prophesy.

propice [prɔpis] *a* favourable (**à** to).

proportion [prɔpɔrsjɔ̃] *nf* proportion; *Math* ratio; **en p. de** in proportion to; **hors de p.** out of proportion (**avec** to). ◆**proportionnel, -elle** *a* proportional (**à** to). ◆**proportionn/er** *vt* to proportion (**à** to). ◆**-é** *a* proportionate (**à** to); **bien p.** well *ou* nicely proportioned.

propos [prɔpo] **1** *nmpl* (*paroles*) remarks, utterances. **2** *nm* (*intention*) purpose. **3** *nm* (*sujet*) subject; **à p. de** about; **à p. de rien** for no reason; **à tout p.** for no reason, at every turn. **4** *adv* **à p.** (*arriver etc*) at the right time; **à p.!** by the way!; **juger à p. de faire** to consider it fit to do.

proposer [prɔpoze] *vt* (*suggérer*) to suggest, propose (**qch à qn** sth to s.o., **que** (+ *sub*) that); (*offrir*) to offer (**qch à qn** s.o. sth, **de faire** to do); (*candidat*) to put forward, propose; **je te propose de rester** I suggest (that) you stay; **se p. pour faire** to offer to do; **se p. de faire** to propose *ou* mean to do. ◆**proposition** *nf* suggestion, proposal; (*de paix*) proposal, (*affirmation*) proposition; *Gram* clause.

propre[1] [prɔpr] *a* clean; (*soigné*) neat; (*honnête*) decent; — *nm* **mettre qch au p.** to make a fair copy of sth. ◆**proprement**[1] *adv* (*avec propreté*) cleanly; (*avec netteté*) neatly; (*comme il faut*) decently. ◆**propreté** *nf* cleanliness; (*netteté*) neatness.

propre[2] [prɔpr] **1** *a* (*à soi*) own; **mon p. argent** my own money; **ses propres mots** his very *ou* his own words. **2** *a* (*qui convient*) right, proper; **p. à** (*attribut, coutume etc*) peculiar to; (*approprié*) well-suited to; **p. à faire** likely to do; **sens p.** literal meaning; **nom p.** proper noun; — *nm* **le p. de** (*qualité*) the distinctive quality of; **au p.** (*au sens propre*) literally. ◆**proprement**[2] *adv* (*strictement*) strictly; **à p. parler** strictly speaking; **le village/etc p. dit** the village/etc proper *ou* itself.

propriété [prɔprijete] *nf* **1** (*bien*) property;

(*droit*) ownership, property. **2** (*qualité*) property. **3** (*de mot*) suitability. ◆**propriétaire** *nmf* owner; (*d'hôtel*) proprietor, owner; (*qui loue*) landlord, landlady; **p. foncier** landowner.

propulser [prɔpylse] *vt* (*faire avancer, projeter*) to propel. ◆**propulsion** *nf* propulsion.

prosaïque [prɔzaik] *a* prosaic, pedestrian.

proscrire* [prɔskrir] *vt* to proscribe, banish. ◆**proscrit, -ite** *nmf* (*personne*) exile. ◆**proscription** *nf* banishment.

prose [proz] *nf* prose.

prospecter [prɔspɛkte] *vt* (*sol*) to prospect; (*pétrole*) to prospect for; (*région*) *Com* to canvass. ◆**prospecteur, -trice** *nmf* prospector. ◆**prospection** *nf* prospecting; *Com* canvassing.

prospectus [prɔspɛktys] *nm* leaflet, prospectus.

prospère [prɔspɛr] *a* (*florissant*) thriving, prosperous; (*riche*) prosperous. ◆**prospérer** *vi* to thrive, flourish, prosper. ◆**prospérité** *nf* prosperity.

prostate [prɔstat] *nf* *Anat* prostate (gland).

prostern/er (se) [səprɔstɛrne] *vpr* to prostrate oneself (**devant** before). ◆**-é** *a* prostrate. ◆**-ement** *nm* prostration.

prostituer [prɔstitɥe] *vt* to prostitute; **— se p.** *vpr* to prostitute oneself. ◆**prostituée** *nf* prostitute. ◆**prostitution** *nf* prostitution.

prostré [prɔstre] *a* (*accablé*) prostrate. ◆**prostration** *nf* prostration.

protagoniste [prɔtagɔnist] *nmf* protagonist.

protecteur, -trice [prɔtɛktœr, -tris] *nmf* protector; (*mécène*) patron; — *a* (*geste etc*) & *Écon* protective; (*ton, air*) *Péj* patronizing. ◆**protection** *nf* protection; (*mécénat*) patronage; **de p.** (*écran etc*) protective. ◆**protectionnisme** *nm* *Écon* protectionism.

protég/er [prɔteʒe] *vt* to protect (**de** from, **contre** against); (*appuyer*) *Fig* to patronize; **— se p.** *vpr* to protect oneself. ◆**-é** *nm* protégé. ◆**-ée** *nf* protégée. ◆**protège-cahier** *nm* exercise book cover.

protéine [prɔtein] *nf* protein.

protestant, -ante [prɔtɛstɑ̃, -ɑ̃t] *a* & *nmf* Protestant. ◆**protestantisme** *nm* Protestantism.

protester [prɔteste] *vi* to protest (**contre** against); **p. de** (*son innocence etc*) to protest; — *vt* to protest (**que** that). ◆**protestation** *nf* protest (**contre** against); *pl* (*d'amitié*) protestations (**de** of).

prothèse [prɔtɛz] *nf* **(appareil de) p.** (*membre*) artificial limb; (*dents*) false teeth.

protocole [prɔtɔkɔl] *nm* protocol.

prototype [prɔtɔtip] *nm* prototype.

protubérance [prɔtyberɑ̃s] *nf* protuberance. ◆**protubérant** *a* (*yeux*) bulging; (*menton*) protruding.

proue [pru] *nf* Nau prow, bow(s).

prouesse [pruɛs] *nf* feat, exploit.

prouver [pruve] *vt* to prove (**que** that).

Provence [prɔvɑ̃s] *nf* Provence. ◆**provençal, -ale, -aux** *a & nmf* Provençal.

provenir* [prɔvnir] *vi* **p. de** to come from. ◆**provenance** *nf* origin; **en p. de** from.

proverbe [prɔvɛrb] *nm* proverb. ◆**proverbial, -aux** *a* proverbial.

providence [prɔvidɑ̃s] *nf* providence. ◆**providentiel, -ielle** *a* providential.

province [prɔvɛ̃s] *nf* province; **la p.** the provinces; **en p.** in the provinces; **de p.** (*ville etc*) provincial. ◆**provincial, -ale, -aux** *a & nmf* provincial.

proviseur [prɔvizœr] *nm* (*de lycée*) headmaster.

provision [prɔvizjɔ̃] *nf* **1** (*réserve*) supply, stock; *pl* (*achats*) shopping; (*vivres*) provisions: **panier/sac à provisions** shopping basket/bag. **2** (*acompte*) advance payment; **chèque sans p.** dud cheque.

provisoire [prɔvizwar] *a* temporary, provisional. ◆**—ment** *adv* temporarily, provisionally.

provoquer [prɔvɔke] *vt* **1** (*causer*) to bring about, provoke; (*désir*) to arouse. **2** (*défier*) to provoke (*s.o.*). ◆**provocant** *a* provocative. ◆**provocateur** *nm* troublemaker. ◆**provocation** *nf* provocation.

proxénète [prɔksenɛt] *nm* pimp.

proximité [prɔksimite] *nf* closeness, proximity; **à p.** close by; **à p. de** close to.

prude [pryd] *a* prudish; − *nf* prude.

prudent [prydɑ̃] *a* (*circonspect*) cautious, careful; (*sage*) sensible. ◆**prudemment** [-amɑ̃] *adv* cautiously, carefully; (*sagement*) sensibly. ◆**prudence** *nf* caution, care, prudence; (*sagesse*) wisdom; **par p.** as a precaution.

prune [pryn] *nf* (*fruit*) plum. ◆**pruneau, -x** *nm* prune. ◆**prunelle** *nf* **1** (*fruit*) sloe. **2** (*de l'œil*) pupil. ◆**prunier** *nm* plum tree.

P.-S. [pɛɛs] *abrév* (*post-scriptum*) PS.

psaume [psom] *nm* psalm.

pseudo- [psødo] *préf* pseudo-.

pseudonyme [psødɔnim] *nm* pseudonym.

psychanalyse [psikanaliz] *nf* psychoanalysis. ◆**psychanalyste** *nmf* psychoanalyst.

psychiatre [psikjatr] *nmf* psychiatrist. ◆**psychiatrie** *nf* psychiatry. ◆**psychiatrique** *a* psychiatric.

psychique [psiʃik] *a* mental, psychic.

psycho [psiko] *préf* psycho-.

psychologie [psikɔlɔʒi] *nf* psychology. ◆**psychologique** *a* psychological. ◆**psychologue** *nmf* psychologist.

psychose [psikoz] *nf* psychosis.

PTT [petete] *nfpl* (*Postes, Télégraphes, Téléphones*) Post Office, = GPO.

pu [py] *voir* **pouvoir 1.**

puant [pɥɑ̃] *a* stinking. ◆**puanteur** *nf* stink, stench.

pub [pyb] *nf* Fam (*réclame*) advertising; (*annonce*) ad.

puberté [pybɛrte] *nf* puberty.

public, -ique [pyblik] *a* public; **dette publique** national debt; − *nm* public; (*de spectacle*) audience; **le grand p.** the general public; **en p.** in public. ◆**publiquement** *adv* publicly.

publication [pyblikasjɔ̃] *nf* (*action, livre etc*) publication. ◆**publier** *vt* to publish.

publicité [pyblisite] *nf* publicity (**pour** for); (*réclame*) advertising, publicity; (*annonce*) advertisement; Rad TV commercial. ◆**publicitaire** *a* (*agence, film*) publicity-, advertising-.

puce [pys] *nf* **1** flea; **le marché aux puces, les puces** the flea market. **2** (*d'un ordinateur*) chip, microchip.

puceron [pysrɔ̃] *nm* greenfly.

pudeur [pydœr] *nf* (sense of) modesty; **attentat à la p.** Jur indecency. ◆**pudibond** *a* prudish. ◆**pudique** *a* modest.

puer [pɥe] *vi* to stink; − *vt* to stink of.

puériculture [pɥerikyltyr] *nf* infant care, child care. ◆**puéricultrice** *nf* children's nurse.

puéril [pɥeril] *a* puerile. ◆**puérilité** *nf* puerility.

puis [pɥi] *adv* then; **et p. quoi?** and so what?

puiser [pɥize] *vt* to draw, take (**dans** from); − *vi* **p. dans** to dip into.

puisque [pɥisk(ə)] *conj* since, as.

puissant [pɥisɑ̃] *a* powerful. ◆**puissamment** *adv* powerfully. ◆**puissance** *nf* (*force, nation*) & Math Tech power; **en p.** (*talent, danger etc*) potential.

puits [pɥi] *nm* well; (*de mine*) shaft.

pull(-over) [pyl(ɔvɛr)] *nm* pullover, sweater.

pulluler [pylyle] *vi* Péj to swarm.

pulmonaire [pylmɔnɛr] *a* (*congestion, maladie*) of the lungs, lung-.

pulpe [pylp] *nf* (*de fruits*) pulp.
pulsation [pylsɑsjɔ̃] *nf* (heart)beat.
pulvériser [pylverize] *vt* (*broyer*) & *Fig* to pulverize; (*liquide*) to spray. ◆**pulvérisateur** *nm* spray, atomizer. ◆**pulvérisation** *nf* (*de liquide*) spraying.
punaise [pynɛz] *nf* 1 (*insecte*) bug. 2 (*clou*) drawing pin, *Am* thumbtack. ◆**punaiser** *vt* (*fixer*) to pin (up).
punch [pɔ̃ʃ] *nm* 1 (*boisson*) punch. 2 [pœnʃ] (*énergie*) punch.
punir [pynir] *vt* to punish. ◆**punissable** *a* punishable (de by). ◆**punition** *nf* punishment.
pupille [pypij] *nf* 1 (*de l'œil*) pupil. 2 *nmf* (*enfant sous tutelle*) ward.
pupitre [pypitr] *nm* (*d'écolier*) desk; (*d'orateur*) lectern; **p. à musique** music stand.
pur [pyr] *a* pure; (*alcool*) neat, straight. ◆**purement** *adv* purely. ◆**pureté** *nf* purity.
purée [pyre] *nf* purée; **p.** (**de pommes de terre**) mashed potatoes, mash.
purgatoire [pyrgatwar] *nm* purgatory.
purge [pyrʒ] *nf* *Pol Méd* purge.
purger [pyrʒe] *vt* 1 (*conduite*) *Tech* to drain, clear. 2 (*peine*) *Jur* to serve.

purifier [pyrifje] *vt* to purify. ◆**purification** *nf* purification.
purin [pyrɛ̃] *nm* liquid manure.
puriste [pyrist] *nmf Gram* purist.
puritain, -aine [pyritɛ̃, -ɛn] *a* & *nmf* puritan.
pur-sang [pyrsɑ̃] *nm inv* (*cheval*) thoroughbred.
pus [py] *nm* (*liquide*) pus, matter.
pus², put [py] *voir* **pouvoir 1.**
putain [pytɛ̃] *nf Péj Fam* whore.
putois [pytwa] *nm* (*animal*) polecat.
putréfier [pytrefje] *vt*, **— se p.** *vpr* to putrefy. ◆**putréfaction** *nf* putrefaction.
puzzle [pœzl] *nm* (jigsaw) puzzle, jigsaw.
p.-v. [peve] *nm inv* (*procès-verbal*) (traffic) fine.
PVC [pevese] *nm* (*plastique*) PVC.
pygmée [pigme] *nm* pygmy.
pyjama [piʒama] *nm* pyjamas, *Am* pajamas; **un p.** a pair of pyjamas *ou Am* pajamas; **de p.** (*veste, pantalon*) pyjama-, *Am* pajama-.
pylône [pilon] *nm* pylon.
pyramide [piramid] *nf* pyramid.
Pyrénées [pirene] *nfpl* **les P.** the Pyrenees.
pyromane [pirɔman] *nmf* arsonist, firebug.
python [pitɔ̃] *nm* (*serpent*) python.

Q

Q, q [ky] *nm* Q, q.
QI [kyi] *nm inv abrév* (*quotient intellectuel*) IQ.
qu' [k] *voir* **que.**
quadrill/er [kadrije] *vt* (*troupes, police*) to be positioned throughout, comb, cover (*town etc*). ◆**—é** *a* (*papier*) squared. ◆**—age** *nm* (*lignes*) squares.
quadrupède [k(w)adrypɛd] *nm* quadruped.
quadruple [k(w)adrypl] *a* **q. de** fourfold; — *nm* **le q.** de four times as much as. ◆**quadrupl/er** *vti* to quadruple. ◆**—és, -ées** *nmfpl* (*enfants*) quadruplets, quads.
quai [ke] *nm Nau* quay; (*pour marchandises*) wharf; (*de fleuve*) embankment, bank; *Rail* platform.
qualification [kalifikasjɔ̃] *nf* 1 description. 2 (*action*) *Sp* qualifying, qualification. ◆**qualificatif** *nm* (*mot*) term. ◆**qualifi/er** 1 *vt* (*décrire*) to describe (de as); **se faire q. de menteur**/*etc* to be called a liar/*etc*. 2 *vt* (*rendre apte*) & *Sp* to qualify

(**pour qch** for sth, **pour faire** to do); **— se q.** *vpr Sp* to qualify (**pour** for). 3 *vt Gram* to qualify. ◆**—é** *a* qualified (**pour faire** to do); (*ouvrier, main-d'œuvre*) skilled.
qualité [kalite] *nf* quality; (*condition sociale etc*) occupation, status; **produit**/*etc* **de q.** high-quality product/*etc*; **en sa q. de** in one's capacity as. ◆**qualitatif, -ive** *a* qualitative.
quand [kɑ̃] *conj* & *adv* when; **q. je viendrai** when I come; **c'est pour q.?** (*réunion, mariage*) when is it?; **q. bien même vous le feriez** even if you did it; **q. même** all the same.
quant (à) [kɑ̃ta] *prép* as for.
quantité [kɑ̃tite] *nf* quantity; **une q., des quantités** (*beaucoup*) a lot (**de** of); **en q.** (*abondamment*) in plenty. ◆**quantifier** *vt* to quantify. ◆**quantitatif, -ive** *a* quantitative.
quarante [karɑ̃t] *a* & *nm* forty. ◆**quarantaine** *nf* 1 **une q.** (**de**) (*nombre*)

(about) forty; **avoir la q.** (*âge*) to be about forty. **2** *Méd* quarantine; **mettre en q.** *Méd* to quarantine; *Fig* to send to Coventry, *Am* give the silent treatment to. ◆**quarantième** *a* & *nmf* fortieth.

quart [kar] *nm* **1** quarter; **q. (de litre)** quarter litre, quarter of a litre; **q. d'heure** quarter of an hour; **un mauvais q. d'heure** *Fig* a trying time; **une heure et q.** an hour and a quarter; **il est une heure et q.** it's a quarter past *ou Am* after one; **une heure moins le q.** a quarter to one. **2** *Nau* watch; **de q.** on watch.

quartette [kwartɛt] *nm* (jazz) quartet(te).

quartier [kartje] *nm* **1** neighbourhood, district; (*chinois etc*) quarter; **de q.** (*cinéma etc*) local; **les gens du q.** the local people. **2** *nm* (*de pomme, lune*) quarter; (*d'orange*) segment. **3** *nm*(*pl*) **quartier(s)** *Mil* quarters; **q. général** headquarters.

quartz [kwarts] *nm* quartz; **montre**/*etc* **à q.** quartz watch/*etc*.

quasi [kazi] *adv* almost. ◆**quasi-** *préf* near; **q.-obscurité** near darkness. ◆**quasiment** *adv* almost.

quatorze [katɔrz] *a* & *nm* fourteen. ◆**quatorzième** *a* & *nmf* fourteenth.

quatre [katr] *a* & *nm* four; **se mettre en q.** to go out of one's way (**pour faire** to do); **son q. heures** (*goûter*) one's afternoon snack; **un de ces q.** *Fam* some day soon. ◆**quatrième** *a* & *nmf* fourth. ◆**quatrièmement** *adv* fourthly.

quatre-vingt(s) [katrəvɛ̃] *a* & *nm* eighty; **q.-vingts ans** eighty years; **q.-vingt-un** eighty-one. ◆**q.-vingt-dix** *a* & *nm* ninety.

quatuor [kwatɥɔr] *nm Mus* quartet(te).

que [k(ə)] (**qu'** *before a vowel or mute h*) **1** *conj* that; **je pense qu'elle restera** I think (that) she'll stay; **qu'elle vienne ou non** whether she comes or not; **qu'il s'en aille!** let him leave!; **ça fait un an q. je suis là** I've been here for a year; **ça fait un an q. je suis parti** I left a year ago. **2** (**ne**) . . . **q.** only; **tu n'as qu'un franc** you only have one franc. **3** (*comparaison*) than; (*avec aussi, même, tel, autant*) as; **plus/moins âgé q.** lui older/younger than him; **aussi sage**/*etc* **q.** as wise/*etc* as; **le même q.** the same as. **4** *adv* (**ce) qu'il est bête!** (*comme*) how silly he is!; **q. de gens!** (*combien*) what a lot of people! **5** *pron rel* (*chose*) that, which; (*personne*) that, whom; (*temps*) when; **le livre q. j'ai** the book (that *ou* which) I have; **l'ami q. j'ai** the friend (that *ou* whom) I have; **un jour/mois**/*etc* **q.** one day/month/*etc* when. **6** *pron interrogatif* what; **q. fait-il?**,

qu'est-ce qu'il fait? what is he doing?; **qu'est-ce qui est dans ta poche?** what's in your pocket?; **q. préférez-vous?** which do you prefer?

Québec [kebɛk] *nm* **le Q.** Quebec.

quel, quelle [kɛl] **1** *a interrogatif* what, which; (*qui*) who; **q. livre/acteur?** what *ou* which book/actor?; **q. livre/acteur préférez-vous?** which *ou* what book/actor do you prefer?; **q. est cet homme?** who is that man?; **je sais q. est ton but** I know what your aim is; **q. qu'il soit** (*chose*) whatever it may be; (*personne*) whoever it *ou* he may be; — *pron interrogatif* which (one); **q. est le meilleur?** which (one) is the best? **2** *a exclamatif* **q. idiot!** what a fool!; **q. joli bébé!** what a pretty baby!

quelconque [kɛlkɔ̃k] *a* **1** any, some (or other); **une raison q.** any reason (whatever *ou* at all), some reason (or other). **2** (*banal*) ordinary.

quelque [kɛlk(ə)] **1** *a* some; **q. jour** some day; **quelques femmes** a few women, some women; **les quelques amies qu'elle a** the few friends she has. **2** *adv* (*environ*) about, some; **q.** *Fam* and a bit; **q. grand qu'il soit** however tall he may be; **q. numéro qu'elle choisisse** whichever number she chooses; **q. peu** somewhat. **3** *pron* **q. chose** something; (*interrogation*) anything, something; **il a q. chose** *Fig* there's something the matter with him; **q. chose d'autre** something else; **q. chose de grand**/*etc* something big/*etc*. **4** *adv* **q. part** somewhere; (*interrogation*) anywhere, somewhere.

quelquefois [kɛlkəfwa] *adv* sometimes.

quelques-uns, -unes [kɛlkəzœ̃, -yn] *pron pl* some.

quelqu'un [kɛlkœ̃] *pron* someone, somebody; (*interrogation*) anyone, anybody, someone, somebody; **q. d'intelligent**/*etc* someone clever/*etc*.

quémander [kemɑ̃de] *vt* to beg for.

qu'en-dira-t-on [kɑ̃diratɔ̃] *nm inv* (*propos*) gossip.

quenelle [kənɛl] *nf Culin* quenelle, fish *ou* meat roll.

querelle [kərɛl] *nf* quarrel, dispute. ◆**se quereller** *vpr* to quarrel. ◆**querelleur, -euse** *a* quarrelsome.

question [kɛstjɔ̃] *nf* question; (*affaire, problème*) matter, issue, question; **il est q. de** it's a matter *ou* question of (**faire** doing); (*on projette de*) there's some question of (**faire** doing); **il n'en est pas q.** there's no question of it, it's out of the question; **en q.** in question; **hors de q.** out of the question;

(re)mettre en q. to (call in) question.
◆**questionner** vt to question (**sur** about).

quête [kɛt] nf 1 (collecte) collection. 2 (recherche) quest (**de** for); **en q. de** in quest ou search of. ◆**quêter** vt to seek, beg for; – vi to collect money.

queue [kø] nf 1 (d'animal) tail; (de fleur) stalk, stem; (de fruit) stalk; (de poêle) handle; (de comète) trail; (de robe) train; (de cortège, train) rear; **q. de cheval** (coiffure) ponytail; **faire une q. de poisson** Aut to cut in (**à qn** in front of s.o.); **à la q.** at the bottom of; **à la q. leu leu** (marcher) in single file. 2 (file) queue, Am line; **faire la q.** to queue up, Am line up. 3 (de billard) cue. ◆**q.-de-pie** nf (pl queues-de-pie) (habit) tails.

qui [ki] pron (personne) who, that; (interrogatif) who; (après prép) whom; (chose) which, that; **l'homme q.** the man who ou that; **la maison q.** the house which ou that; **q.? who?; q. (est-ce q.) est là?** who's there?; **q. désirez-vous voir?, q. est-ce que vous désirez voir?** who(m) do you want to see?; **sans q.** without whom; **la femme de q. je parle** the woman I'm talking about ou about whom I'm talking; **l'ami sur l'aide de q. je compte** the friend on whose help I rely; **q. que vous soyez** whoever you are, whoever you may be; **q. que ce soit** anyone (at all); **à q. est ce livre?** whose book is this?

quiche [kiʃ] nf (tarte) quiche.

quiconque [kikɔ̃k] pron (celui qui) whoever; (n'importe qui) anyone.

quignon [kiɲɔ̃] nm chunk (of bread).

quille [kij] nf 1 (de navire) keel. 2 (de jeu) skittle; pl (jeu) skittles, ninepins. 3 (jambe) Fam leg.

quincaillier, -ière [kɛ̃kaje, -jɛr] nmf hardware dealer, ironmonger. ◆**quincaillerie** nf hardware; (magasin) hardware shop.

quinine [kinin] nf Méd quinine.

quinquennal, -aux [kɛ̃kenal, -o] a (plan) five-year.

quinte [kɛ̃t] nf Méd coughing fit.

quintessence [kɛ̃tesɑ̃s] nf quintessence.

quintette [kɛ̃tɛt] nm Mus quintet(te).

quintuple [kɛ̃typl] a **q. de** fivefold; – nm **le q. de** five times as much as. ◆**quintupler** vti to increase fivefold. ◆**-és, -ées** nmfpl (enfants) quintuplets, quins.

quinze [kɛ̃z] a & nm fifteen; **q. jours** two weeks, fortnight. ◆**quinzaine** nf **une q. (de)** (nombre) about fifteen; **q. (de jours)** two weeks, fortnight. ◆**quinzième** a & nmf fifteenth.

quiproquo [kiproko] nm misunderstanding.

quittance [kitɑ̃s] nf receipt.

quitte [kit] a quits, even (**envers** with); **q. à faire** even if it means doing; **en être q. pour une amende/etc** to be (lucky enough to) get off with a fine/etc.

quitter [kite] vt to leave; (ôter) to take off; – vi **ne quittez pas!** Tél hold the line!, hold on!; – **se q.** vpr (se séparer) to part.

qui-vive (sur le) [syrləkiviv] adv on the alert.

quoi [kwa] pron what; (après prép) which; **à q. penses-tu?** what are you thinking about?; **après q.** after which; **ce à q. je m'attendais** what I was expecting; **de q. manger/etc** (assez) enough to eat/etc; **de q. couper/écrire/etc** (instrument) something to cut/write/etc with; **q. que je dise** whatever I say; **q. que ce soit** anything (at all); **q. qu'il en soit** be that as it may; **il n'y a pas de q.!** (en réponse à 'merci') don't mention it!; **q.? what?; c'est un idiot, q.!** (non traduit) Fam he's a fool!

quoique [kwak(ə)] conj (+ sub) (al)though.

quolibet [kɔlibɛ] nm Litt gibe.

quorum [k(w)ɔrɔm] nm quorum.

quota [k(w)ɔta] nm quota.

quote-part [kɔtpar] nf (pl quotes-parts) share.

quotidien, -ienne [kɔtidjɛ̃, -jɛn] a (journalier) daily; (banal) everyday; – nm daily (paper). ◆**quotidiennement** adv daily.

quotient [kɔsjɑ̃] nm quotient.

R

R, r [ɛr] nm R, r.

rabâcher [rabaʃe] vt to repeat endlessly; – vi to repeat oneself ◆**-age** nm endless repetition.

rabais [rabɛ] nm (price) reduction, discount; **au r.** (acheter) cheap, at a reduction.

rabaisser [rabese] vt (dénigrer) to belittle, humble; **r. à** (ravaler) to reduce to.

rabat-joie [rabaʒwa] nm inv killjoy.

rabattre* [rabatr] vt (baisser) to put ou pull down; (refermer) to close (down); (replier) to fold down ou over; (déduire) to take off; **en r.** (prétentieux) Fig to climb down (from one's high horse); **— se r.** vpr (se refermer) to close; (après avoir doublé) Aut to cut in (**devant** in front of); **se r. sur** Fig to fall back on.

rabbin [rabɛ̃] nm rabbi; **grand r.** chief rabbi.

rabibocher [rabibɔʃe] vt (réconcilier) Fam to patch it up between; **— se r.** vpr Fam to patch it up.

rabiot [rabjo] nm (surplus) Fam extra (helping); **faire du r.** Fam to work extra time.

râblé [rɑble] a stocky, thickset.

rabot [rabo] nm (outil) plane. ◆**raboter** vt to plane.

raboteux, -euse [rabɔtø, -øz] a uneven, rough.

rabougri [rabugri] a (personne, plante) stunted.

rabrouer [rabrue] vt to snub, rebuff.

racaille [rakɑj] nf rabble, riffraff.

raccommod/er [rakɔmɔde] 1 vt to mend; (chaussette) to darn. 2 vt (réconcilier) Fam to reconcile; **— se r.** vpr Fam to make it up (avec with). ◆**—age** nm mending; darning.

raccompagner [rakɔ̃paɲe] vt to see ou take back (home); **r. à la porte** to see to the door, see out.

raccord [rakɔr] nm (dispositif) connection; (de papier peint) join; **r.** (de peinture) touch-up. ◆**raccord/er** vt, **— se r.** vpr to connect (up), join (up) (à with, to). ◆**—ement** nm (action, résultat) connection.

raccourc/ir [rakursir] vt to shorten; **— vi** to get shorter; (au lavage) to shrink. ◆**—i** nm 1 (chemin) short cut. 2 **en r.** (histoire etc) in a nutshell.

raccroc (par) [parrakro] adv by (a lucky) chance.

raccrocher [rakrɔʃe] vt to hang back up; (récepteur) Tél to put down; (relier) to connect (à with, to); (client) to accost; **se r. à** to hold on to, cling to; (se rapporter à) to link (up) with; **— vi** Tél to hang up, ring off.

race [ras] nf (groupe ethnique) race; (animale) breed; (famille) stock; (engeance) Péj breed; **de r.** (chien) pedigree-; (cheval) thoroughbred. ◆**racé** a (chien) pedigree-; (cheval) thoroughbred; (personne) distinguished. ◆**racial, -aux** a racial. ◆**racisme** nm racism, racialism. ◆**raciste** a & nmf racist, racialist.

rachat [raʃa] nm Com repurchase; (de firme)

take-over; Rel redemption. ◆**racheter** vt to buy back; (objet d'occasion) to buy; (nouvel article) to buy another; (firme) to take over, buy out; (pécheur, dette) to redeem; (compenser) to make up for; **r. des chaussettes/du pain/etc** to buy (some) more socks/bread/etc; **— se r.** vpr to make amends, redeem oneself.

racine [rasin] nf (de plante, personne etc) & Math root; **prendre r.** (plante) & Fig to take root.

racket [rakɛt] nm (association) racket; (activité) racketeering.

raclée [rɑkle] nf Fam hiding, thrashing.

racler [rɑkle] vt to scrape; (enlever) to scrape off; **se r. la gorge** to clear one's throat. ◆**raclette** nf scraper; (à vitres) squeegee. ◆**racloir** nm scraper. ◆**raclures** nfpl (déchets) scrapings.

racol/er [rakɔle] vt (prostituée) to solicit (s.o.); (vendeur etc) to tout for (s.o.), solicit (s.o.). ◆**—age** nm soliciting; touting. ◆**—eur, -euse** nmf tout.

raconter [rakɔ̃te] vt (histoire) to tell, relate; (décrire) to describe; **r. qch à qn** (vacances etc) to tell s.o. about sth; **r. à qn que** to tell s.o. that, say to s.o. that. ◆**racontars** nmpl gossip, stories.

racornir [rakɔrnir] vt to harden; **— se r.** vpr to get hard.

radar [radar] nm radar; **contrôle r.** (pour véhicules etc) radar control. ◆**radariste** nmf radar operator.

rade [rad] nf 1 Nau (natural) harbour. 2 **laisser en r.** to leave stranded, abandon; **rester en r.** to be left behind.

radeau, -x [rado] nm raft.

radiateur [radjatœr] nm (à eau) & Aut radiator; (électrique, à gaz) heater.

radiation [radjɑsjɔ̃] nf 1 Phys radiation. 2 (suppression) removal (de from).

radical, -ale, -aux [radikal, -o] a radical; **—** nm Ling stem; **— nmf** Pol radical.

radier [radje] vt to strike ou cross off (de from).

radieux, -euse [radjø, -øz] a (personne, visage) radiant, beaming; (soleil) brilliant; (temps) glorious.

radin, -ine [radɛ̃, -in] a Fam stingy; **— nmf** Fam skinflint.

radio [radjo] 1 nf radio; (poste) radio (set); **à la r.** on the radio. 2 nf (photo) Méd X-ray; **passer ou faire une r.** to be X-rayed, have an X-ray. 3 nm (opérateur) radio operator. ◆**radioactif, -ive** a radioactive. ◆**radioactivité** nf radioactivity. ◆**radiodiffuser** vt to broadcast (on the radio). ◆**radio-**

diffusion *nf* broadcasting. ◆**radiographie** *nf* (*photo*) X-ray; (*technique*) radiography. ◆**radiographier** *vt* to X-ray. ◆**radiologie** *nf* *Méd* radiology. ◆**radiologue** *nmf* (*technicien*) radiographer; (*médecin*) radiologist. ◆**radiophonique** *a* (*programme*) radio-. ◆**radiotélévisé** *a* broadcast on radio and television.

radis [radi] *nm* radish; **r. noir** horseradish.

radot/er [radɔte] *vi* to drivel (on), ramble (on). ◆**—age** *nm* (*propos*) drivel.

radouc/ir (se) [sǝradusir] *vpr* to calm down; (*temps*) to become milder. ◆**—issement** *nm* **r.** (**du temps**) milder weather.

rafale [rafal] *nf* (*vent*) gust, squall; (*de mitrailleuse*) burst; (*de balles*) hail.

raffermir [rafɛrmir] *vt* to strengthen; (*muscles etc*) to tone up; — **se r.** *vpr* to become stronger.

raffin/er [rafine] *vt* (*pétrole, sucre, manières*) to refine. ◆**—é** *a* refined. ◆**—age** *nm* (*du pétrole, sucre*) refining. ◆**—ement** *nm* (*de personne*) refinement. ◆**raffinerie** *nf* refinery.

raffoler [rafɔle] *vi* **r. de** (*aimer*) to be very fond of, be mad ou wild about.

raffut [rafy] *nm* Fam din, row.

rafiot [rafjo] *nm* (*bateau*) Péj (old) tub.

rafistoler [rafistɔle] *vt* Fam to patch up.

rafle [rafl] *nf* (*police*) raid.

rafler [rafle] *vt* (*enlever*) Fam to swipe, make off with.

rafraîch/ir [rafreʃir] *vt* to cool (down); (*remettre à neuf*) to brighten up; (*mémoire, personne*) to refresh; — *vi* **mettre à r.** Culin to chill; — **se r.** *vpr* (*boire*) to refresh oneself; (*se laver*) to freshen (oneself) up; (*temps*) to get cooler. ◆**—issant** *a* refreshing. ◆**—issement** *nm* **1** (*de température*) cooling. **2** (*boisson*) cold drink; *pl* (*fruits, glaces etc*) refreshments.

ragaillardir [ragajardir] *vt* to buck up.

rage [raʒ] *nf* **1** (*colère*) rage; **r. de dents** violent toothache; **faire r.** (*incendie, tempête*) to rage. **2** (*maladie*) rabies. ◆**rager** *vi* (*personne*) Fam to rage, fume. ◆**rageant** *a* Fam infuriating. ◆**rageur, -euse** *a* bad-tempered, furious.

ragots [rago] *nmpl* Fam gossip.

ragoût [ragu] *nm* Culin stew.

ragoûtant [ragutɑ̃] *a* **peu r.** (*mets, personne*) unsavoury.

raid [rɛd] *nm* (*incursion, attaque*) Mil Av raid.

raide [rɛd] *a* (*rigide, guindé*) stiff; (*côte*) steep; (*cheveux*) straight; (*corde etc*) tight; **c'est r.!** (*exagéré*) Fam it's a bit stiff ou much!; — *adv* (*grimper*) steeply; **tomber r. mort** to drop dead. ◆**raideur** *nf* stiffness; steepness. ◆**raidillon** *nm* (*pente*) short steep rise. ◆**raidir** *vt*, — **se r.** *vpr* to stiffen; (*corde*) to tighten; (*position*) to harden; **se r. contre** Fig to steel oneself against.

raie [rɛ] *nf* **1** (*trait*) line; (*de tissu, zèbre*) stripe; (*de cheveux*) parting, Am part. **2** (*poisson*) skate, ray.

rail [raj] *nm* (*barre*) rail; **le r.** (*transport*) rail.

railler [raje] *vt* to mock, make fun of. ◆**raillerie** *nf* gibe, mocking remark. ◆**railleur, -euse** *a* mocking.

rainure [renyr] *nf* groove.

raisin [rezɛ̃] *nm* **raisin(s)** grapes; **grain de r.** grape; **manger du r.** ou **des raisins** to eat grapes; **r. sec** raisin.

raison [rezɔ̃] *nf* **1** (*faculté, motif*) reason; **entendre r.** to listen to reason; **la r. pour laquelle je . . .** the reason (why ou that) I . . . ; **pour raisons de famille/de santé/etc** for family/health/etc reasons; **en r. de** (*cause*) on account of; **à r. de** (*proportion*) at the rate of; **avoir r. de qn/de qch** to get the better of s.o./sth; **mariage de r.** marriage of convenience; **à plus forte r.** all the more so; **r. de plus** all the more reason (**pour faire** to do, for doing). **2** **avoir r.** to be right (**de faire** to do, in doing); **donner r. à qn** to agree with s.o.; (*événement etc*) to prove s.o. right; **avec r.** rightly. ◆**raisonnable** *a* reasonable. ◆**raisonnablement** *adv* reasonably.

raisonn/er [rezɔne] *vi* (*penser*) to reason; (*discuter*) to argue; — *vt* **r. qn** to reason with s.o. ◆**—é** *a* (*projet*) well-thought-out. ◆**—ement** *nm* (*faculté, activité*) reasoning; (*propositions*) argument. ◆**—eur, -euse** *a* Péj argumentative; — *nmf* Péj arguer.

rajeun/ir [raʒœnir] *vt* to make (feel ou look) younger; (*personnel*) to infuse new blood into; (*moderniser*) to modernize, update; (*personne âgée*) Méd to rejuvenate; — *vi* to get ou feel ou look younger. ◆**—issant** *a* Méd rejuvenating. ◆**—issement** *nm* Méd rejuvenation; **le r. de la population** the population getting younger.

rajout [raʒu] *nm* addition. ◆**rajouter** *vt* to add (à to); **en r.** Fig to overdo it.

rajuster [raʒyste] *vt* (*mécanisme*) to readjust; (*lunettes, vêtements*) to straighten, adjust; (*cheveux*) to rearrange; — **se r.** *vpr* to straighten ou tidy oneself up.

râle [rɑl] *nm* (*de blessé*) groan; (*de mourant*) death rattle. ◆**râler** *vi* (*blessé*) to groan; (*mourant*) to give the death rattle; (*protes-*

er) Fam to grouse, moan. ◆**râleur, -euse** *nmf Fam* grouser, moaner.

ralent/ir [ralɑ̃tir] *vti,* — **se r.** *vpr* to slow down. ◆—**i** *nm Cin TV* slow motion; **au r.** (*filmer, travailler*) in slow motion; (*vivre*) at a slower pace; **tourner au r.** (*moteur, usine*) to idle, tick over, *Am* turn over.

rallier [ralje] *vt* (*rassembler*) to rally; (*rejoindre*) to rejoin; **r. qn à** (*convertir*) to win s.o. over to; — **se r.** *vpr* (*se regrouper*) to rally; **se r. à** (*point de vue*) to come over *ou* round to.

rallonge [ralɔ̃ʒ] *nf* (*de table*) extension; (*fil électrique*) extension (lead); **une r. (de)** (*supplément*) *Fam* (some) extra. ◆**rallonger** *vti* to lengthen.

rallumer [ralyme] *vt* to light again, relight; (*lampe*) to switch on again; (*conflit, haine*) to rekindle; — **se r.** *vpr* (*guerre, incendie*) to flare up again.

rallye [rali] *nm Sp Aut* rally.

ramage [ramaʒ] **1** *nm* (*d'oiseaux*) song, warbling. **2** *nmpl* (*dessin*) foliage.

ramass/er [ramase] **1** *vt* (*prendre par terre, réunir*) to pick up; (*ordures, copies*) to collect, pick up; (*fruits, coquillages*) to gather; (*rhume, amende*) *Fam* to pick up, get; **r. une bûche** *ou* **une pelle** *Fam* to come a cropper, *Am* take a spill. **2 se r.** *vpr* (*se pelotonner*) to curl up. ◆—**é** *a* (*trapu*) squat, stocky; (*recroquevillé*) huddled; (*concis*) compact. ◆—**age** *nm* picking up; collection; gathering; **r. scolaire** school bus service.

ramassis [ramasi] *nm* **r. de** (*voyous etc*) *Péj* bunch of.

rambarde [rɑ̃bard] *nf* guardrail.

rame [ram] *nf* **1** (*aviron*) oar. **2** (*de métro*) train. **3** (*de papier*) ream. ◆**ramer** *vi* to row. ◆**rameur, -euse** *nmf* rower.

rameau, -x [ramo] *nm* branch; **les Rameaux** *Rel* Palm Sunday.

ramener [ramne] *vt* to bring *ou* take back; (*paix, calme, ordre etc*) to restore, bring back; (*remettre en place*) to put back; **r. à** (*réduire à*) to reduce to; **r. à la vie** to bring back to life; — **se r.** *vpr* (*arriver*) *Fam* to turn up; **se r. à** (*problème etc*) to boil down to.

ramier [ramje] *nm* (**pigeon**) **r.** wood pigeon.

ramification [ramifikasjɔ̃] *nf* ramification.

ramoll/ir [ramɔlir] *vt,* — **se r.** *vpr* to soften. ◆—**i** *a* soft; (*personne*) soft-headed.

ramon/er [ramɔne] *vt* (*cheminée*) to sweep. ◆—**age** *nm* (chimney) sweeping. ◆—**eur** *nm* (chimney)sweep.

rampe [rɑ̃p] *nf* **1** (*pente*) ramp, slope; **r. de lancement** (*de fusées etc*) launch(ing) pad. **2**

(*d'escalier*) banister(s). **3** (*projecteurs*) *Th* footlights.

ramper [rɑ̃pe] *vi* to crawl; (*plante*) to creep; **r. devant** *Fig* to cringe *ou* crawl to.

rancard [rɑ̃kar] *nm Fam* (*rendez-vous*) date; (*renseignement*) tip.

rancart [rɑ̃kar] *nm* **mettre au r.** *Fam* to throw out, scrap.

rance [rɑ̃s] *a* rancid. ◆**rancir** *vi* to turn rancid.

ranch [rɑ̃tʃ] *nm* ranch.

rancœur [rɑ̃kœr] *nf* rancour, resentment.

rançon [rɑ̃sɔ̃] *nf* ransom; **la r. de** (*inconvénient*) the price of (*success, fame etc*). ◆**rançonner** *vt* to hold to ransom.

rancune [rɑ̃kyn] *nf* grudge; **garder r. à qn** to bear s.o. a grudge; **sans r.!** no hard feelings! ◆**rancunier, -ière** *a* vindictive, resentful.

randonnée [rɑ̃dɔne] *nf* (*à pied*) walk, hike; (*en voiture*) drive, ride; (*en vélo*) ride.

rang [rɑ̃] *nm* (*rangée*) row, line; (*condition, grade, classement*) rank; **les rangs** (*hommes*) *Mil* the ranks (**de** of); **les rangs de ses ennemis** (*nombre*) *Fig* the ranks of his enemies; **se mettre en rang(s)** to line up (*par trois/etc* in threes/*etc*); **par r. de** in order of. ◆**rangée** *nf* row, line.

rang/er [rɑ̃ʒe] *vt* (*papiers, vaisselle etc*) to put away; (*chambre etc*) to tidy (up); (*chiffres, mots*) to arrange; (*voiture*) to park; **r. parmi** (*auteur etc*) to rank among; — **se r.** *vpr* (*élèves etc*) to line up; (*s'écarter*) to stand aside; (*voiture*) to pull over; (*s'assagir*) to settle down; **se r. à** (*avis de qn*) to fall in with. ◆—**é** *a* (*chambre etc*) tidy; (*personne*) steady; (*bataille*) pitched. ◆—**ement** *nm* putting away; (*de chambre etc*) tidying (up); (*espace*) storage space.

ranimer [ranime] *vt* (*réanimer, revigorer*) to revive; (*encourager*) to spur on; (*feu, querelle*) to rekindle.

rapace [rapas] **1** *a* (*avide*) grasping. **2** *nm* (*oiseau*) bird of prey.

rapatrier [rapatrije] *vt* to repatriate. ◆**rapatriement** *nm* repatriation.

râpe [rɑp] *nf Culin* grater; shredder; (*lime*) rasp. ◆**râp/er** *vt* (*fromage*) to grate; (*carottes etc*) to shred, (*finement*) to grate; (*bois*) to rasp. ◆—**é** **1** *a* (*fromage*) grated; — *nm* grated cheese. **2** *a* (*vêtement*) threadbare.

rapetisser [raptise] *vt* to make (look) smaller; (*vêtement*) to shorten; — *vi* to get smaller; (*au lavage*) to shrink; (*jours*) to get shorter.

râpeux, -euse [rɑpø, -øz] *a* rough.

raphia [rafja] *nm* raffia.

rapide [rapid] *a* fast, quick, rapid; (*pente*) steep; — *nm* (*train*) express (train); (*de fleuve*) rapid. ◆—**ment** *adv* fast, quickly, rapidly. ◆**rapidité** *nf* speed, rapidity.

rapiécer [rapjese] *vt* to patch (up).

rappel [rapεl] *nm* (*de diplomate etc*) recall; (*évocation, souvenir*) reminder; (*paiement*) back pay; *pl Th* curtain calls; (**vaccination de**) **r.** *Méd* booster; **r. à l'ordre** call to order. ◆**rappeler** *vt* (*pour faire revenir*) & *Tél* to call back; (*diplomate, souvenir*) to recall; **r. qch à qn** (*redire*) to remind s.o. of sth; — *vi Tél* to call back; — **se r.** *vpr* (*histoire, personne etc*) to remember, recall, recollect.

rappliquer [raplike] *vi* (*arriver*) *Fam* to show up.

rapport [rapɔr] *nm* **1** (*lien*) connection, link; *pl* (*entre personnes*) relations; **rapports** (**sexuels**) (sexual) intercourse; **par r. à** compared to *ou* with; (*envers*) towards; **se mettre en r. avec qn** to get in touch with s.o.; **en r. avec** in keeping with; **sous le r. de** from the point of view of. **2** (*revenu*) *Com* return, yield. **3** (*récit*) report. ◆**rapporter 1** *vt* (*ramener*) to bring *ou* take back; (*ajouter*) to add; — *vi* (*chien*) to retrieve. **2** *vt* (*récit*) to report; (*mot célèbre*) to repeat; — *vi* (*moucharder*) *Fam* to tell tales. **3** *vt* (*profit*) *Com* to bring in, yield; — *vi* (*investissement*) *Com* to bring in a good return. **4** *vt* **r. qch à** (*rattacher*) to relate sth to; **se r. à** to relate to, be connected with; **s'en r. à** to rely on. ◆**rapporteur, -euse 1** *nmf* (*mouchard*) telltale. **2** *nm Jur* reporter. **3** *nm Géom* protractor.

rapproch/er [raprɔʃe] *vt* to bring closer (**de** to); (*chaise*) to pull up (**de** to); (*réconcilier*) to bring together; (*réunir*) to join; (*comparer*) to compare; — **se r.** *vpr* to come *ou* get closer (**de** to); (*se réconcilier*) to come together, be reconciled; (*ressembler*) to be close (**de** to). ◆—**é** *a* close, near; (*yeux*) close-set; (*fréquent*) frequent. ◆—**ement** *nm* (*réconciliation*) reconciliation; (*rapport*) connection; (*comparaison*) comparison.

rapt [rapt] *nm* (*d'enfant*) abduction.

raquette [rakεt] *nf* (*de tennis*) racket; (*de ping-pong*) bat.

rare [rar] *a* rare; (*argent, main-d'œuvre etc*) scarce; (*barbe, herbe*) sparse; **il est r. que** (+ *sub*) it's seldom *ou* rare that. ◆**se raréfier** *vpr* (*denrées etc*) to get scarce. ◆**rarement** *adv* rarely, seldom. ◆**rareté** *nf* rarity; scarcity; **une r.** (*objet*) a rarity.

ras [rɑ] *a* (*cheveux*) close-cropped; (*herbe, poil*) short; (*mesure*) full; **en rase campagne** in (the) open country; **à r. de** very close to; **à r. bord** (*remplir*) to the brim; **en avoir r. le bol** *Fam* to be fed up (**de** with); **pull** (**au**) **r. du cou** *ou* **à col r.** crew-neck(ed) pullover; — *adv* short.

ras/er [rɑze] **1** *vt* (*menton, personne*) to shave; (*barbe, moustache*) to shave off; — **se r.** *vpr* to (have a) shave. **2** *vt* (*démolir*) to raze, knock down. **3** *vt* (*frôler*) to skim, brush. **4** *vt* (*ennuyer*) *Fam* to bore. ◆—**ant** *a Fam* boring. ◆—**é** *a* **bien r.** clean-shaven; **mal r.** unshaven. ◆—**age** *nm* shaving. ◆—**eur, -euse** *nmf Fam* bore. ◆**rasoir 1** *nm* shaver. **2** *a inv Fam* boring.

rassasier [rasazje] *vti* to satisfy; **être rassasié** to have had enough (**de** of).

rassembler [rasãble] *vt* to gather (together), assemble; (*courage*) to summon up, muster; — **se r.** *vpr* to gather, assemble. ◆**rassemblement** *nm* (*action, gens*) gathering.

rasseoir* (**se**) [səraswar] *vpr* to sit down again.

rassis, *f* rassie [rasi] *a* (*pain, brioche etc*) stale. ◆**rassir** *vti* to turn stale.

rassur/er [rasyre] *vt* to reassure; **rassure-toi** set your mind at rest, don't worry. ◆—**ant** *a* (*nouvelle*) reassuring, comforting.

rat [ra] *nm* rat; **r. de bibliothèque** *Fig* bookworm.

ratatiner (se) [sərətatine] *vpr* to shrivel (up); (*vieillard*) to become wizened.

rate [rat] *nf Anat* spleen.

râteau, -x [rɑto] *nm* rake.

râtelier [rɑtəlje] *nm* **1** (*support pour outils, armes etc*) rack. **2** (*dentier*) *Fam* set of false teeth.

rat/er [rate] *vt* (*bus, cible, occasion etc*) to miss; (*gâcher*) to spoil, ruin; (*vie*) to waste; (*examen*) to fail; — *vi* (*projet etc*) to fail; (*pistolet*) to misfire. ◆—**é, -ée 1** *nmf* (*personne*) failure. **2** *nmpl* **avoir des ratés** *Aut* to backfire. ◆—**age** *nm* (*échec*) *Fam* failure.

ratifier [ratifje] *vt* to ratify. ◆**ratification** *nf* ratification.

ration [rɑsjɔ̃] *nf* ration; **r. de** *Fig* share of. ◆**rationn/er** *vt* (*vivres, personne*) to ration. ◆—**ement** *nm* rationing.

rationaliser [rasjɔnalize] *vt* to rationalize. ◆**rationalisation** *nf* rationalization.

rationnel, -elle [rasjɔnεl] *a* (*pensée, méthode*) rational.

ratisser [ratise] *vt* **1** (*allée etc*) to rake; (*feuilles etc*) to rake up. **2** (*fouiller*) to comb. **3 r. qn** (*au jeu*) *Fam* to clean s.o. out.

raton [ratɔ̃] *nm* **r. laveur** rac(c)oon.

rattach/er [rataʃe] *vt* to tie up again; (*in-*

corporer, joindre) to join (à to); (*idée, question*) to link (à to); **r. qn à** (*son pays etc*) to bind s.o. to; **se r. à** to be linked to. ◆**—ement** nm (*annexion*) joining (à to).

rattrap/er [ratrape] vt to catch; (*prisonnier etc*) to recapture; (*erreur, temps perdu*) to make up for; **r. qn** (*rejoindre*) to catch up with s.o., catch s.o. up; **— se r.** vpr to catch up; (*se dédommager, prendre une compensation*) to make up for it; **se r. à** (*branche etc*) to catch hold of. ◆**—age** nm **cours de r.** Scol remedial classes; **r. des prix/salaires** adjustment of prices/wages (*to the cost of living*).

rature [ratyr] nf deletion. ◆**raturer** vt to delete, cross out.

rauque [rok] a (*voix*) hoarse, raucous.

ravages [ravaʒ] nmpl devastation; (*de la maladie, du temps*) ravages; **faire des r.** to wreak havoc. ◆**ravager** vt to devastate, ravage.

raval/er [ravale] vt **1** (*façade etc*) to clean (and restore). **2** (*salive, sanglots*) to swallow. **3** (*avilir*) Litt to lower. ◆**—ement** nm (*de façade etc*) cleaning (and restoration).

ravi [ravi] a delighted (**de** with, **de faire** to do).

ravier [ravje] nm hors-d'œuvre dish.

ravigoter [ravigɔte] vt Fam to buck up.

ravin [ravɛ̃] nm ravine, gully.

ravioli [ravjɔli] nmpl ravioli.

rav/ir [ravir] vt **1** (*enchanter*) to delight; **à r.** (*chanter etc*) delightfully. **2** (*emporter*) to snatch (à from). ◆**—issant** a delightful, lovely. ◆**ravisseur, -euse** nmf kidnapper.

raviser (se) [səravize] vpr to change one's mind.

ravitaill/er [ravitaje] vt to provide with supplies, supply; (*avion*) to refuel; **— se r.** vpr to stock up (with supplies). ◆**—ement** nm supplying; refuelling; (*denrées*) supplies; **aller au r.** (*faire des courses*) Fam to stock up, get stocks in.

raviver [ravive] vt (*feu, sentiment*) to revive; (*couleurs*) to brighten up.

ray/er [reje] vt (*érafler*) to scratch; (*mot etc*) to cross out; **r. qn de** (*liste*) to cross ou strike s.o. off. ◆**—é** a scratched; (*tissu*) striped; (*papier*) lined, ruled. ◆**rayure** nf scratch; (*bande*) stripe; **à rayures** striped.

rayon [rejɔ̃] nm **1** (*de lumière, soleil etc*) Phys ray; (*de cercle*) radius; (*de roue*) spoke; (*d'espoir*) Fig ray; **r. X** X-ray; **r. d'action** range; **dans un r. de** within a radius of. **2** (*planche*) shelf; (*de magasin*) department. **3** (*de ruche*) honeycomb. ◆**rayonnage** nm shelving, shelves.

rayonn/er [rejɔne] vi to radiate; (*dans une région*) to travel around (*from a central base*); **r. de joie** to beam with joy. ◆**—ant** a (*visage etc*) radiant, beaming (**de** with). ◆**—ement** nm (*éclat*) radiance; (*influence*) influence; (*radiation*) radiation.

raz-de-marée [radmare] nm inv tidal wave; (*bouleversement*) Fig upheaval; **r.-de-marée électoral** landslide.

razzia [ra(d)zja] nf **faire une r. sur** (*tout enlever sur*) Fam to raid.

re- [r(ə)] préf re-.

ré- [re] préf re-.

réabonn/er (se) [səreabɔne] vpr to renew one's subscription (à to). ◆**—ement** nm renewal of subscription.

réacteur [reaktœr] nm (*d'avion*) jet engine; (*nucléaire*) reactor.

réaction [reaksjɔ̃] nf reaction; **r. en chaîne** chain reaction; **avion à r.** jet (aircraft); **moteur à r.** jet engine. ◆**réactionnaire** a & nmf reactionary.

réadapter [readapte] vt, **— se r.** vpr to readjust (à to). ◆**réadaptation** nf readjustment.

réaffirmer [reafirme] vt to reaffirm.

réagir [reaʒir] vi to react (**contre** against, **à** to); (*se secouer*) Fig to shake oneself out of it.

réalis/er [realize] vt (*projet etc*) to carry out, realize; (*ambition, rêve*) to fulfil; (*achat, bénéfice, vente*) to make; (*film*) to direct; (*capital*) Com to realize; (*se rendre compte*) to realize (**que** that); **— se r.** vpr (*vœu*) to come true; (*projet*) to be carried out; (*personne*) to fulfil oneself. ◆**—able** a (*plan*) workable; (*rêve*) attainable. ◆**réalisateur, -trice** nmf Cin TV director. ◆**réalisation** nf realization; (*de rêve*) fulfilment; Cin TV direction; (*œuvre*) achievement.

réalisme [realism] nm realism. ◆**réaliste** a realistic; **— nmf** realist.

réalité [realite] nf reality; **en r.** in (actual) fact, in reality.

réanimer [reanime] vt Méd to resuscitate. ◆**réanimation** nf resuscitation; (**service de**) **r.** intensive care unit.

réapparaître [reaparɛtr] vi to reappear. ◆**réapparition** nf reappearance.

réarmer [rearme] vt (*fusil etc*) to reload; — vi, **— se r.** vpr (*pays*) to rearm. ◆**réarmement** nm rearmament.

rébarbatif, -ive [rebarbatif, -iv] a forbidding, off-putting.

rebâtir [r(ə)batir] vt to rebuild.

rebattu [r(ə)baty] a (*sujet*) hackneyed.

rebelle [rəbɛl] *a* rebellious; (*troupes*) rebel-; (*fièvre*) stubborn; (*mèche*) unruly; **r. à** resistant to; – *nmf* rebel. ◆**se rebeller** *vpr* to rebel (**contre** against). ◆**rébellion** *nf* rebellion.

rebiffer (se) [sər(ə)bife] *vpr Fam* to rebel.

rebond [r(ə)bɔ̃] *nm* bounce; (*par ricochet*) rebound. ◆**rebondir** *vi* to bounce; to rebound; (*faire*) **r.** (*affaire, discussion etc*) to get going again. ◆**rebondissement** *nm* new development (**de** in).

rebondi [r(ə)bɔ̃di] *a* chubby, rounded.

rebord [r(ə)bɔr] *nm* edge; (*de plat etc*) rim; (*de vêtement*) hem; **r. de (la) fenêtre** windowsill, window ledge.

reboucher [r(ə)buʃe] *vt* (*flacon*) to put the top back on.

rebours (à) [ar(ə)bur] *adv* the wrong way.

rebrousse-poil (à) [arbruspwal] *adv* **prendre qn à r.-poil** *Fig* to rub s.o. up the wrong way.

rebrousser [r(ə)bruse] *vt* **r. chemin** to turn back.

rebuffade [rəbyfad] *nf Litt* rebuff.

rébus [rebys] *nm inv* (*jeu*) rebus.

rebut [rəby] *nm* **mettre au r.** to throw out, scrap; **le r. de la société** *Péj* the dregs of society.

rebut/er [r(ə)byte] *vt* (*décourager*) to put off; (*choquer*) to repel. ◆**—ant** *a* offputting; (*choquant*) repellent.

récalcitrant [rekalsitrã] *a* recalcitrant.

recaler [r(ə)kale] *vt* **r. qn** *Scol Fam* to fail s.o., flunk s.o.; **être recalé, se faire r.** *Scol Fam* to fail, flunk.

récapituler [rekapityle] *vti* to recapitulate. ◆**récapitulation** *nf* recapitulation.

recel [rəsɛl] *nm* receiving stolen goods, fencing; harbouring. ◆**receler** *vt* (*mystère, secret etc*) to contain; (*objet volé*) to receive; (*malfaiteur*) to harbour. ◆**receleur, -euse** *nmf* receiver (*of stolen goods*), fence.

recens/er [r(ə)sãse] *vt* (*population*) to take a census of; (*inventorier*) to make an inventory of. ◆**—ement** *nm* census; inventory.

récent [resã] *a* recent. ◆**récemment** [-amã] *adv* recently.

récépissé [resepise] *nm* (*reçu*) receipt.

récepteur [reseptœr] *nm Tél Rad* receiver. ◆**réceptif, -ive** *a* receptive (**à** to). ◆**réception** *nf* (*accueil, soirée*) & *Rad* reception; (*de lettre etc*) *Com* receipt; (*d'hôtel etc*) reception (desk). ◆**réceptionniste** *nmf* receptionist.

récession [resesjɔ̃] *nf Écon* recession.

recette [r(ə)sɛt] *nf* **1** *Culin* & *Fig* recipe. **2** (*argent, bénéfice*) takings; (*bureau*) tax office; **recettes** (*rentrées*) *Com* receipts; **faire r.** *Fig* to be a success.

recev/oir* [rəsəvwar] *vt* to receive; (*obtenir*) to get, receive; (*accueillir*) to welcome; (*accepter*) to accept; **être reçu (à)** (*examen*) to pass; **être reçu premier** to come first; – *vi* to receive guests *ou* visitors *ou* *Méd* patients. ◆**—able** *a* (*excuse etc*) admissible. ◆**—eur, -euse** *nmf* (*d'autobus*) (bus) conductor, (bus) conductress; (*des impôts*) tax collector; (*des postes*) postmaster, postmistress.

rechange (de) [dər(ə)ʃãʒ] *a* (*pièce, outil etc*) spare; (*solution etc*) alternative; **vêtements/chaussures de r.** a change of clothes/shoes.

rechapé [r(ə)ʃape] *a* **pneu r.** retread.

réchapper [reʃape] *vi* **r. de** *ou* **à** (*accident etc*) to come through.

recharge [r(ə)ʃarʒ] *nf* (*de stylo etc*) refill. ◆**recharger** *vt* (*camion, fusil*) to reload; (*briquet, stylo etc*) to refill; (*batterie*) to recharge.

réchaud [reʃo] *nm* (portable) stove.

réchauff/er [reʃofe] *vt* (*personne, aliment etc*) to warm up; – **se r.** *vpr* to warm oneself up; (*temps*) to get warmer. ◆**—é** *nm* **du r.** *Fig Péj* old hat. ◆**—ement** *nm* (*de température*) rise (**de** in).

rèche [rɛʃ] *a* rough, harsh.

recherche [r(ə)ʃɛrʃ] *nf* **1** search, quest (**de** for); **à la r. de** in search of. **2** **la r., des recherches** (*scientifique etc*) research (**sur** on, into); **faire des recherches** to research; (*enquête*) to make investigations. **3** (*raffinement*) studied elegance; *Péj* affectation. ◆**recherch/er** *vt* to search *ou* hunt for; (*cause, faveur, perfection*) to seek. ◆**—é a 1** (*très demandé*) in great demand; (*rare*) much sought-after; **r. pour meurtre** wanted for murder. **2** (*élégant*) elegant; *Péj* affected.

rechigner [r(ə)ʃine] *vi* (*renâcler*) to jib (**à qch** at sth, **à faire** at doing).

rechute [r(ə)ʃyt] *nf Méd* relapse. ◆**rechuter** *vi Méd* to (have a) relapse.

récidive [residiv] *nf Jur* further offence; *Méd* recurrence (**de** of). ◆**récidiver** *vi Jur* to commit a further offence; (*maladie*) to recur. ◆**récidiviste** *nmf Jur* further offender.

récif [resif] *nm* reef.

récipient [resipjã] *nm* container, receptacle.

réciproque [resiprɔk] *a* mutual, reciprocal; – *nf* (*inverse*) opposite; **rendre la r. à qn** to get even with s.o. ◆**réciprocité** *nf* reciprocity. ◆**réciproquement** adv (l'un l'autre) each other; **et r.** and vice versa.

récit [resi] nm (compte rendu) account; (histoire) story.

récital, pl -**als** [resital] nm Mus recital.

réciter [resite] vt to recite. ◆**récitation** nf recitation.

réclame [reklam] nf advertising; (annonce) advertisement; **en r.** Com on (special) offer; – **a** inv **prix r.** (special) offer price; **vente r.** (bargain) sale.

réclamer [reklame] vt (demander, nécessiter) to demand, call for; (revendiquer) to claim; – vi to complain; **se r. de qn** to invoke s.o.'s authority. ◆**réclamation** nf complaint; pl (bureau) complaints department.

reclasser [r(ə)klase] vt (fiches etc) to reclassify.

reclus, -use [rəkly, -yz] a (vie) cloistered; – nmf recluse.

réclusion [reklyzjɔ̃] nf imprisonment (with hard labour); **r. à perpétuité** life imprisonment.

recoiffer (se) [sər(ə)kwafe] vpr (se peigner) to do ou comb one's hair.

recoin [rəkwɛ̃] nm nook, recess.

recoller [r(ə)kɔle] vt (objet cassé) to stick together again; (enveloppe) to stick back down.

récolte [rekɔlt] nf (action) harvest; (produits) crop, harvest; (collection) Fig crop. ◆**récolter** vt to harvest, gather (in); (recueillir) Fig to collect, gather; (coups) Fam to get.

recommand/er [r(ə)kɔmɑ̃de] 1 vt (appuyer, conseiller) to recommend; **r. à qn de faire** to recommend s.o. to do. 2 vt (lettre etc) to register. 3 vt **r. à** (âme) to commend to. 4 **se r.** vpr **se r. de qn** to invoke s.o.'s authority. ◆—**é** nm **en r.** (envoyer) by registered post. ◆—**able** a peu r. not very commendable. ◆**recommandation** nf 1 (appui, conseil, louange) recommendation. 2 (de lettre etc) registration.

recommenc/er [r(ə)kɔmɑ̃se] vti to start ou begin again. ◆—**ement** nm (reprise) renewal (**de** of).

récompense [rekɔ̃pɑ̃s] nf reward (**de** for); (prix) award; **en r. de** in return for. ◆**récompenser** vt to reward (**de, pour** for).

réconcilier [rekɔ̃silje] vt to reconcile; — **se r.** vpr to become reconciled, make it up (**avec** with). ◆**réconciliation** nf reconciliation.

reconduire* [r(ə)kɔ̃dɥir] vt 1 **r. qn** to see ou

take s.o. back; (à la porte) to show s.o. out. 2 (mesures etc) to renew. ◆**reconduction** nf renewal.

réconfort [rekɔ̃fɔr] nm comfort. ◆**réconfort/er** vt to comfort; (revigorer) to fortify. ◆—**ant** a comforting; (boisson etc) fortifying.

reconnaissant [r(ə)kɔnɛsɑ̃] a grateful, thankful (**à qn de qch** to s.o. for sth). ◆**reconnaissance¹** nf (gratitude) gratitude.

reconnaître* [r(ə)kɔnɛtr] vt to recognize (**à qch** by sth); (admettre) to acknowledge, admit (**que** that); (terrain) Mil to reconnoitre; **être reconnu coupable** to be found guilty; — **se r.** (s'orienter) to find one's bearings; **se r. coupable** to admit one's guilt. ◆**reconnu** a (chef, fait) acknowledged, recognized. ◆**reconnaissable** a recognizable (**à qch** by sth). ◆**reconnaissance²** nf recognition; (aveu) acknowledgement; Mil reconnaissance; **r. de dette** IOU.

reconsidérer [r(ə)kɔ̃sidere] vt to reconsider.

reconstituant [r(ə)kɔ̃stitɥɑ̃] adj (aliment, régime) restorative.

reconstituer [r(ə)kɔ̃stitɥe] vt (armée, parti) to reconstitute; (crime, quartier) to reconstruct; (faits) to piece together; (fortune) to build up again. ◆**reconstitution** nf reconstitution; reconstruction.

reconstruire* [r(ə)kɔ̃strɥir] vt (ville, fortune) to rebuild. ◆**reconstruction** nf rebuilding.

reconvertir [r(ə)kɔ̃vertir] 1 vt (bâtiment etc) to reconvert. 2 **se r.** vpr to take up a new form of employment. ◆**reconversion** nf reconversion.

recopier [r(ə)kɔpje] vt to copy out.

record [r(ə)kɔr] nm & a inv Sp record.

recoucher (se) [sər(ə)kuʃe] vpr to go back to bed.

recoudre* [r(ə)kudr] vt (bouton) to sew back on.

recoup/er [r(ə)kupe] vt (témoignage etc) to tally with, confirm; — **se r.** vpr to tally, match ou tie up. ◆—**ement** nm crosscheck(ing).

recourbé [r(ə)kurbe] a curved; (nez) hooked.

recours [r(ə)kur] nm recourse (**à** to); Jur appeal; **avoir r. à** to resort to; (personne) to turn to; **notre dernier r.** our last resort. ◆**recourir*** vi **r. à** to resort to; (personne) to turn to.

recouvrer [r(ə)kuvre] vt (argent, santé) to recover.

recouvrir* [r(ə)kuvrir] vt (livre, meuble, sol etc) to cover; (de nouveau) to recover; (cacher) Fig to conceal, mask.

récréation [rekreasjɔ̃] nf recreation; (temps) Scol break, playtime.

récriminer [rekrimine] vi to complain bitterly (contre about). ◆**récrimination** nf (bitter) complaint.

récrire [rekrir] vt (lettre etc) to rewrite.

recroqueviller (se) [sər(ə)krɔkvije] vpr (papier, personne etc) to curl up.

recrudescence [rəkrydesɑ̃s] nf new outbreak (de of).

recrue [rəkry] nf recruit. ◆**recrut/er** vt to recruit. ◆**—ement** nm recruitment.

rectangle [rɛktɑ̃gl] nm rectangle. ◆**rectangulaire** a rectangular.

rectifier [rɛktifje] vt (erreur etc) to correct, rectify; (ajuster) to adjust. ◆**rectificatif** nm (document) amendment, correction. ◆**rectification** nf correction, rectification.

recto [rɛkto] nm front (of the page).

reçu [r(ə)sy] voir **recevoir**; — a (usages etc) accepted; (idée) conventional, received; (candidat) successful; — nm (écrit) Com receipt.

recueil [r(ə)kœj] nm (ouvrage) collection (de of).

recueill/ir* [r(ə)kœjir] 1 vt to collect, gather; (suffrages) to win, get; (prendre chez soi) to take in. 2 se r. vpr to meditate; (devant un monument) to stand in silence. ◆**—i** a (air) meditative. ◆**—ement** nm meditation.

recul [r(ə)kyl] nm (d'armée, de négociateur, de maladie) retreat; (éloignement) distance; (déclin) decline; (mouvement de) r. (de véhicule) backward movement; (personne) to recoil; **phare de r.** Aut reversing light. ◆**reculade** nf Péj retreat. ◆**recul/er** vi to move ou step back; Aut to reverse; (armée) to retreat; (épidémie, glacier) to recede, retreat; (renoncer) to back down, retreat; (diminuer) to decline; **r. devant** Fig to recoil ou shrink from; — vt to move ou push back; (différer) to postpone. ◆**—é** a (endroit, temps) remote.

reculons (à) [arkylɔ̃] adv backwards.

récupérer [rekypere] vt to recover, get back; (ferraille etc) to salvage; (heures) to make up; (mouvement, personne etc) Pol Péj to take over, convert; — vi to recuper-

ate, recover. ◆**récupération** nf recovery; salvage; recuperation.

récurer [rekyre] vt (casserole etc) to scour; **poudre à r.** scouring powder.

récuser [rekyze] vt to challenge; — **se r.** vpr to decline to give an opinion.

recycl/er [r(ə)sikle] vt (reconvertir) to retrain (s.o.); (matériaux) to recycle; — **se r.** vpr to retrain. ◆**—age** nm retraining; recycling.

rédacteur, -trice [redaktœr, -tris] nmf writer; (de chronique) Journ editor; (de dictionnaire etc) compiler; **r. en chef** Journ editor(-in-chief). ◆**rédaction** nf (action) writing; (de contrat) drawing up; (devoir) Scol essay, composition; (rédacteurs) Journ editorial staff; (bureaux) Journ editorial offices.

reddition [redisjɔ̃] nf surrender.

redemander [rədmɑ̃de] vt (pain etc) to ask for more; **r. qch à qn** to ask s.o. for sth back.

rédemption [redɑ̃psjɔ̃] nf Rel redemption.

redescendre [r(ə)desɑ̃dr] vi (aux être) to come ou go back down; — vt (aux avoir) (objet) to bring ou take back down.

redevable [rədvabl] a **être r. de qch à qn** (argent) to owe s.o. sth; Fig to be indebted to s.o. for sth.

redevance [rədvɑ̃s] nf (taxe) TV licence fee; Tél rental charge.

redevenir* [rədvənir] vi (aux être) to become again.

rédiger [rediʒe] vt to write; (contrat) to draw up; (dictionnaire etc) to compile.

redire* [r(ə)dir] 1 vt to repeat. 2 vi **avoir** ou **trouver à r. à qch** to find fault with sth. ◆**redite** nf (pointless) repetition.

redondant [r(ə)dɔ̃dɑ̃] a (style) redundant.

•**redonner** [r(ə)dɔne] vt to give back; (de nouveau) to give more.

redoubl/er [r(ə)duble] vti 1 to increase; **r. de patience/etc** to be much more patient/etc; **à coups redoublés** (frapper) harder and harder. 2 **r. (une classe)** Scol to repeat a year ou Am a grade. ◆**—ant, -ante** nmf pupil repeating a year ou Am a grade. ◆**—ement** nm increase (de in); repeating a year ou Am a grade.

redout/er [r(ə)dute] vt to dread (de faire doing). ◆**—able** a formidable, fearsome.

redress/er [r(ə)drese] vt to straighten (out); (économie, mât, situation, tort) to right; — **se r.** vpr (se mettre assis) to sit up; (debout) to stand up; (pays, situation etc) to right itself. ◆**—ement** [-ɛsmɑ̃] nm (essor) recovery.

réduction [redyksjɔ̃] *nf* reduction (**de** in); **en r.** (*copie, modèle etc*) small-scale.

réduire* [redɥir] *vt* to reduce (**à** to, **de** by); **r. qn à** (*contraindre à*) to reduce s.o. to (*silence, inaction etc*); **se r. à** (*se ramener à*) to come down to, amount to; **se r. en cendres/etc** to be reduced to ashes/*etc*; – *vi* (**faire**) **r.** (*sauce*) to reduce, boil down. ◆**réduit 1** *a* (*prix, vitesse*) reduced; (*moyens*) limited; (*à petite échelle*) small-scale. **2** *nm* (*pièce*) *Péj* cubbyhole; (*recoin*) recess.

réécrire [reekrir] *vt* (*texte*) to rewrite.

rééduquer [reedyke] *vt* (*membre*) *Méd* to re-educate; **r. qn** to rehabilitate s.o., re-educate s.o. ◆**rééducation** *nf* re-education; rehabilitation.

réel, -elle [reɛl] *a* real; **le r.** reality. ◆**réellement** *adv* really.

réélire [reelir] *vt* to re-elect.

réexpédier [reekspedje] *vt* (*lettre etc*) to forward; (*à l'envoyeur*) to return.

refaire* [r(ə)fer] *vt* to do again, redo; (*erreur, voyage*) to make again; (*réparer*) to do up, redo; (*duper*) *Fam* to take in. ◆**réfection** *nf* repair(ing).

réfectoire [refɛktwar] *nm* refectory.

référendum [referɑ̃dɔm] *nm* referendum.

référer [refere] *vi* **en r. à** to refer the matter to; – **se r.** *vpr* **se r. à** to refer to. ◆**référence** *nf* reference.

refermer [r(ə)fɛrme] *vt*, – **se r.** *vpr* to close *ou* shut (again).

refiler [r(ə)file] *vt* (*donner*) *Fam* to palm off (**à** on).

réfléch/ir [reflefir] **1** *vt* (*image*) to reflect; – **se r.** *vpr* to be reflected. **2** *vi* (*penser*) to think (**à, sur** about); – *vt* **r. que** to realize that. ◆**–i** *a* (*personne*) thoughtful, reflective; (*action, décision*) carefully thought-out; (*verbe*) *Gram* reflexive. ◆**réflecteur** *nm* reflector. ◆**réflexion** *nf* **1** (*de lumière etc*) reflection. **2** (*méditation*) thought, reflection; (*remarque*) remark; **à la r., r. faite** on second thoughts *ou Am* thought,on reflection.

reflet [r(ə)flɛ] *nm* (*image*) & *Fig* reflection; (*lumière*) glint; (*couleur*) tint. ◆**refléter** *vt* (*image, sentiment etc*) to reflect; – **se r.** *vpr* to be reflected.

réflexe [reflɛks] *nm & a* reflex.

refluer [r(ə)flye] *vi* (*eaux*) to ebb, flow back; (*foule*) to surge back. ◆**reflux** *nm* ebb; backward surge.

réforme *nf* **1** (*changement*) reform. **2** (*de soldat*) discharge. ◆**réformateur, -trice** *nmf* reformer. ◆**réformer 1** *vt* to reform;

– **se r.** *vpr* to mend one's ways. **2** *vt* (*soldat*) to invalid out, discharge.

refoul/er [r(ə)fule] *vt* to force *ou* drive back; (*sentiment*) to repress; (*larmes*) to hold back. ◆**–é a** (*personne*) *Psy* repressed. ◆**–ement** *nm Psy* repression.

réfractaire [refraktɛr] *a* **r. à** resistant to.

refrain [r(ə)frɛ̃] *nm* (*de chanson*) refrain, chorus; (*rengaine*) *Fig* tune.

réfréner [r(ə)frene] *vt* to curb, check.

réfrigér/er [refriʒere] *vt* to refrigerate. ◆**–ant** *a* (*accueil, air*) *Fam* icy. ◆**réfrigérateur** *nm* refrigerator. ◆**réfrigération** *nf* refrigeration.

refroid/ir [r(ə)frwadir] *vt* to cool (down); (*décourager*) *Fig* to put off; (*ardeur*) to dampen, cool; – *vi* to get cold, cool down; – **se r.** *vpr Méd* to catch cold; (*temps*) to get cold; (*ardeur*) to cool (off). ◆**–isse-ment** *nm* cooling; (*rhume*) chill; **r. de la température** fall in the temperature.

refuge [r(ə)fyʒ] *nm* refuge; (*pour piétons*) (traffic) island; (*de montagne*) (mountain) hut. ◆**se réfugi/er** *vpr* to take refuge. ◆**–é, -ée** *nmf* refugee.

refus [r(ə)fy] *nm* refusal; **ce n'est pas de r.** *Fam* I won't say no. ◆**refuser** *vt* to refuse (**qch à qn** s.o. sth, **de faire** to do); (*offre, invitation*) to turn down, refuse; (*client*) to turn away, refuse; (*candidat*) to fail; – **se r.** *vpr* (*plaisir etc*) to deny oneself; **se r. à** (*évidence etc*) to refuse to accept, reject; **se r. à croire** *etc* to refuse to believe/*etc.*

réfuter [refyte] *vt* to refute.

regagner [r(ə)ɡaɲe] *vt* (*récupérer*) to regain; (*revenir à*) to get back to. ◆**regain** *nm* **r. de** (*retour*) renewal of.

régal, pl -als [reɡal] *nm* treat. ◆**régaler** *vt* to treat to a delicious meal; **r. de** to treat to; – **se r.** *vpr* to have a delicious meal.

regard *nm* **1** (*coup d'œil, expression*) look; (*fixe*) stare, gaze; **chercher du r.** to look (a)round for; **attirer les regards** to attract attention; **jeter un r. sur** to glance at. **2 au r. de** in regard to; **en r. de** compared with. ◆**regard/er 1** *vt* to look at; (*fixement*) to stare at, gaze at; (*observer*) to watch; (*considérer*) to consider, regard (**comme** as); **r. qn faire** to watch s.o. do; – *vi* to look; to stare, gaze; to watch; **r. à** (*dépense, qualité etc*) to pay attention to; **r. vers** (*maison etc*) to face; – **se r.** *vpr* (*personnes*) to look at each other. **2** *vt* (*concerner*) to concern. ◆**–ant** *a* (*économe*) careful (with money).

régates [reɡat] *nfpl* regatta.

régence [reʒɑ̃s] *nf* regency.

régénérer [reʒenere] *vt* to regenerate.

régenter [reʒɑ̃te] *vt* to rule over.

régie [reʒi] *nf* (*entreprise*) state-owned company; *Th* stage management; *Cin* TV production department.

regimber [r(ə)ʒɛ̃be] *vi* to balk (**contre** at).

régime [reʒim] *nm* **1** system; *Pol* régime. **2** *Méd* diet; **se mettre au r.** to go on a diet; **suivre un r.** to be on a diet. **3** (*de moteur*) speed; **à ce r.** *Fig* at this rate. **4** (*de bananes, dattes*) bunch.

régiment [reʒimɑ̃] *nm Mil* regiment; **un r. de** (*quantité*) *Fig* a host of.

région [reʒjɔ̃] *nf* region, area. ◆**régional, -aux** *a* regional.

régir [reʒir] *vt* (*déterminer*) to govern.

régisseur [reʒisœr] *nm* (*de propriété*) steward; *Th* stage manager; *Cin* assistant director.

registre [rəʒistr] *nm* register.

règle [rɛgl] **1** *nf* (*principe*) rule; **en r.** (*papiers d'identité etc*) in order; **être/se mettre en r. avec qn** to be/put oneself right with s.o.; **en r. générale** as a (general) rule. **2** *nf* (*instrument*) ruler; **r. à calcul** slide rule. **3** *nfpl* (*menstruation*) period.

règlement [rɛgləmɑ̃] *nm* **1** (*arrêté*) regulation; (*règles*) regulations. **2** (*de conflit, problème etc*) settling; (*paiement*) payment; **r. de comptes** *Fig* (violent) settling of scores. ◆**réglementaire** *a* in accordance with the regulations; (*tenue*) *Mil* regulation-. ◆**réglementation** *nf* **1** (*action*) regulation. **2** (*règles*) regulations. ◆**réglementer** *vt* to regulate.

régler [regle] **1** *vt* (*conflit, problème etc*) to settle; (*mécanisme*) to regulate, adjust; (*moteur*) to tune; (*papier*) to rule; **se r. sur** to model oneself on. **2** *vti* (*payer*) to pay; **r. qn** to settle up with s.o.; **r. son compte à** *Fig* to settle old scores with. ◆**réglé** *a* (*vie*) ordered; (*papier*) ruled. ◆**réglable** *a* (*siège etc*) adjustable. ◆**réglage** *nm* adjustment; (*de moteur*) tuning.

réglisse [reglis] *nf* liquorice, *Am* licorice.

règne [rɛɲ] *nm* reign; (*animal, minéral, végétal*) kingdom. ◆**régner** *vi* to reign; (*prédominer*) to prevail; **faire r. l'ordre** to maintain (law and) order.

regorger [r(ə)gɔrʒe] *vi* **r. de** to be overflowing with.

régresser [regrese] *vi* to regress. ◆**régression** *nf* regression; **en r.** on the decline.

regret [r(ə)grɛ] *nm* regret; **à r.** with regret; **avoir le r.** *ou* **être au r. de faire** to be sorry to do. ◆**regrett/er** *vt* to regret; **r. qn** to miss s.o.; **je regrette** I'm sorry; **r. que** (+ *sub*) to

be sorry that, regret that. ◆**—able** *a* regrettable.

regrouper [r(ə)grupe] *vt*, **— se r.** *vpr* to gather together.

régulariser [regylarize] *vt* (*situation*) to regularize.

régulation [regylasjɔ̃] *nf* (*action*) regulation.

régulier, -ière [regylje, -jɛr] *a* regular; (*progrès, vie, vitesse*) steady; (*légal*) legal; (*honnête*) honest. ◆**régularité** *nf* regularity; steadiness; legality. ◆**régulièrement** *adv* regularly; (*normalement*) normally.

réhabiliter [reabilite] *vt* (*dans l'estime publique*) to rehabilitate.

réhabituer (se) [səreabitɥe] *vpr* **se r. à qch/à faire qch** to get used to sth/to doing sth again.

rehausser [rəose] *vt* to raise; (*faire valoir*) to enhance.

réimpression [reɛ̃presjɔ̃] *nf* (*livre*) reprint.

rein [rɛ̃] *nm* kidney; *pl* (*dos*) (small of the) back; **r. artificiel** *Méd* kidney machine.

reine [rɛn] *nf* queen.

reine-claude [rɛnklod] *nf* greengage.

réintégrer [reɛ̃tegre] *vt* **1** (*fonctionnaire etc*) to reinstate. **2** (*lieu*) to return to. ◆**réintégration** *nf* reinstatement.

réitérer [reitere] *vt* to repeat.

rejaillir [r(ə)ʒajir] *vi* to spurt (up *ou* out); **r. sur** *Fig* to rebound on.

rejet [r(ə)ʒɛ] *nm* **1** (*refus*) & *Méd* rejection. **2** *Bot* shoot. ◆**rejeter** *vt* to throw back; (*épave*) to cast up; (*vomir*) to bring up; (*refuser*) & *Méd* to reject; **r. une erreur/etc sur qn** to put the blame for a mistake/etc on s.o.

rejeton [rəʒtɔ̃] *nm* (*enfant*) *Fam* kid.

rejoindre* [r(ə)ʒwɛ̃dr] *vt* (*famille, régiment*) to rejoin, get *ou* go back to; (*lieu*) to get back to; (*route, rue*) to join; **r. qn** to join *ou* meet s.o.; (*rattraper*) to catch up with s.o.; **— se r.** *vpr* (*personnes*) to meet; (*routes, rues*) to join, meet.

réjou/ir [reʒwir] *vt* to delight; **— se r.** *vpr* to be delighted (**de** at, about; **de faire** to do). ◆**—i** *a* (*air*) joyful. ◆**—issant** *a* cheering. ◆**réjouissance** *nf* rejoicing; *pl* festivities, rejoicings.

relâche [r(ə)lɑʃ] *nf Th Cin* (temporary) closure; **faire r.** (*théâtre, cinéma*) to close; (*bateau*) to put in (**dans un port** at a port); **sans r.** without a break.

relâch/er [r(ə)lɑʃe] **1** *vt* to slacken; (*discipline, étreinte*) to relax; **r. qn** to release s.o.; **— se r.** *vpr* to slacken; (*discipline*) to get lax. **2** *vi* (*bateau*) to put in. ◆**—é** *a* lax.

◆—**ement** nm (de corde etc) slackness; (de discipline) slackening.

relais [r(ə)lɛ] nm Él Rad TV relay; (**course de**) **r.** Sp relay (race); **r. routier** transport café, Am truck stop (café); **prendre le r.** to take over (de from).

relance [r(ə)lãs] nf (reprise) revival. ◆**relancer** vt to throw back; (moteur) to restart; (industrie etc) to put back on its feet; **r. qn** (solliciter) to pester s.o.

relater [r(ə)late] vt to relate (que that).

relatif, -ive [r(ə)latif, -iv] a relative (à to). ◆**relativement** adv relatively; **r. à** compared to, relative to.

relation [r(ə)lasjɔ̃] nf (rapport) relation(ship); (ami) acquaintance; **avoir des relations** (amis influents) to have connections; **entrer/être en relations avec** to come into/be in contact with; **relations internationales/etc** international/etc relations.

relax(e) [rəlaks] a Fam relaxed, informal.

relaxer (se) [sər(ə)lakse] vpr to relax. ◆**relaxation** nf relaxation.

relayer [r(ə)leje] vt to relieve, take over from; (émission) to relay; — **se r.** vpr to take (it in) turns (**pour faire** to do); Sp to take over from one another.

reléguer [r(ə)lege] vt to relegate (à to).

relent [rəlã] nm stench, smell.

relève [r(ə)lɛv] nf (remplacement) relief; **prendre la r.** to take over (de from).

relev/er [rəlve] vt to raise; (ramasser) to pick up; (chaise etc) to put up straight; (personne tombée) to help up; (col) to turn up; (manches) to roll up; (copier) to note down; (traces) to find; (relayer) to relieve; (rehausser) to enhance; (sauce) to season; (faute) to pick ou point out; (compteur) to read; (défi) to accept; (économie, pays) to put back on its feet; (mur) to rebuild; **r. qn de** (fonctions) to relieve s.o. of; — vi **r. de** (dépendre de) to come under; (maladie) to get over; — **se r.** vpr (personne) to get up; **se r. de** (malheur) to recover from; (ruines) to rise from. ◆—**é** nm list; (de dépenses) statement; (de compteur) reading; **r. de compte** (bank) statement. ◆**relèvement** nm (d'économie, de pays) recovery.

relief [rəljɛf] 1 nm (forme, ouvrage) relief; **en r.** (cinéma) three-D; (livre) pop-up; **mettre en r.** Fig to highlight. 2 nmpl (de repas) remains.

relier [rəlje] vt to link, connect (à to); (ensemble) to link (together); (livre) to bind.

religion [r(ə)liȝjɔ̃] nf religion; (foi) faith. ◆**religieux, -euse 1** a religious; **mariage r.** church wedding; — nm monk; — nf nun. **2** nf Culin cream bun.

reliquat [r(ə)lika] nm (de dette etc) remainder.

relique [r(ə)lik] nf relic.

relire* [r(ə)lir] vt to reread.

reliure [rəljyr] nf (couverture de livre) binding; (art) bookbinding.

reluire [r(ə)lɥir] vi to shine, gleam; **faire r.** (polir) to shine (up). ◆**reluisant** a shiny; **peu r.** Fig far from brilliant.

reluquer [r(ə)lyke] vt Fig to eye (up).

remâcher [r(ə)maʃe] vt Fig to brood over.

remanier [r(ə)manje] vt (texte) to revise; (ministère) to reshuffle. ◆**remaniement** nm revision; reshuffle.

remarier (se) [sər(ə)marje] vpr to remarry.

remarque [r(ə)mark] nf remark; (annotation) note; **je lui en ai fait la r.** I remarked on it to him ou her. ◆**remarquable** a remarkable (par for). ◆**remarquablement** adv remarkably. ◆**remarquer** vt **1** (apercevoir) to notice (que that); **faire r.** to point out (à to, que that); **se faire r.** to attract attention; **remarque!** mind (you)! **2** (dire) to remark (que that).

rembarrer [rãbare] vt to rebuff, snub.

remblai [rãblɛ] nm (terres) embankment. ◆**remblayer** vt (route) to bank up; (trou) to fill in.

rembourr/er [rãbure] vt (matelas etc) to stuff, pad; (vêtement) to pad. ◆—**age** nm (action, matière) stuffing; padding.

rembourser [rãburse] vt to pay back, repay; (billet) to refund. ◆**remboursement** nm repayment; refund; **envoi contre r.** cash on delivery.

remède [r(ə)mɛd] nm remedy, cure; (médicament) medicine. ◆**remédier** vi **r. à** to remedy.

remémorer (se) [sər(ə)memɔre] vpr (histoire etc) to recollect, recall.

remercier [r(ə)mɛrsje] vt **1** to thank (de qch, pour qch, for sth); **je vous remercie d'être venu** thank you for coming; **je vous remercie** (non merci) no thank you. **2** (congédier) to dismiss. ◆**remerciements** nmpl thanks.

remettre* [r(ə)mɛtr] vt to put back, replace; (vêtement) to put back on; (donner) to hand over (à to); (restituer) to give back (à to); (démission, devoir) to hand in; (différer) to postpone (à until); (ajouter) to add more ou another; (peine) Jur to remit; (guérir) to restore to health; (reconnaître) to place, remember; **r. en cause** ou **question** to call into question; **r. en état** to repair; **r. ça** Fam to

start again; **se r. à** (*activité*) to go back to;
se r. à faire to start to do again; **se r. de**
(*chagrin, maladie*) to recover from, get
over; **s'en r. à** to rely on. ◆**remise** *nf* **1** (*de
lettre etc*) delivery; (*de peine*) *Jur* remission; (*ajournement*) postponement; **r. en
cause** *ou* **question** calling into question; **r.
en état** repair(ing). **2** (*rabais*) discount. **3**
(*local*) shed; *Aut* garage. ◆**remiser** *vt* to
put away.

réminiscences [reminisɑ̃s] *nfpl* (vague)
recollections, reminiscences.

rémission [remisjɔ̃] *nf Jur Rel Méd* remission; **sans r.** (*travailler etc*) relentlessly.

remmener [rɑ̃mne] *vt* to take back.

remonte-pente [r(ə)mɔ̃tpɑ̃t] *nm* ski lift.

remont/er [r(ə)mɔ̃te] *vi* (*aux être*) to come
ou go back up; (*niveau, prix*) to rise again,
go back up; (*dans le temps*) to go back (à
to); **r. dans** (*voiture*) to go *ou* get back
in(to); (*bus, train*) to go *ou* get back on(to);
r. sur (*cheval, vélo*) to remount; – *vt* (*aux
avoir*) (*escalier, pente*) to come *ou* go back
up; (*porter*) to bring *ou* take back up;
(*montre*) to wind up; (*relever*) to raise; (*col*)
to turn up; (*objet démonté*) to reassemble;
(*garde-robe etc*) to restock; **r. qn** (*ragaillardir*) to buck s.o. up; **r. le moral à qn** to
cheer s.o. up. ◆**—ant** *a* (*boisson*) fortifying; – *nm Méd* tonic. ◆**—ée** *nf* **1** (*de pente
etc*) ascent; (*d'eau, de prix*) rise. **2 r. mécanique** ski lift. ◆**remontoir** *nm* (*de mécanisme, montre*) winder.

remontrance [r(ə)mɔ̃trɑ̃s] *nf* reprimand;
faire des remontrances à to reprimand, remonstrate with.

remontrer [r(ə)mɔ̃tre] *vi* **en r. à qn** to prove
one's superiority over s.o.

remords [r(ə)mɔr] *nm* & *nmpl* remorse;
avoir des r. to feel remorse.

remorque [r(ə)mɔrk] *nf Aut* trailer; (**câble
de**) **r.** towrope; **prendre en r.** to tow; **en r.**
on tow. ◆**remorquer** *vt* (*voiture, bateau*)
to tow. ◆**remorqueur** *nm* tug(boat).

remous [r(ə)mu] *nm* eddy; (*de foule*) bustle;
(*agitation*) *Fig* turmoil.

rempart [rɑ̃par] *nm* rampart.

remplacer [rɑ̃plase] *vt* to replace (**par** with,
by); (*succéder à*) to take over from;
(*temporairement*) to stand in for. ◆**remplaçant, -ante** *nmf* (*personne*) replacement; (*enseignant*) supply teacher; *Sp* reserve. ◆**remplacement** *nm* (*action*)
replacement; **assurer le r. de qn** to stand in
for s.o.; **en r. de** in place of.

rempl/ir [rɑ̃plir] *vt* to fill (up) (**de** with);
(*fiche etc*) to fill in *ou* out; (*condition, de-*

voir, tâche) to fulfil; (*fonctions*) to perform;
– se r. *vpr* to fill (up). ◆**—i** *a* full (**de** of).
◆**remplissage** *nm* filling; (*verbiage*) *Péj*
padding.

remporter [rɑ̃porte] *vt* **1** (*objet*) to take
back. **2** (*prix, victoire*) to win; (*succès*) to
achieve.

remu/er [r(ə)mɥe] *vt* (*déplacer, émouvoir*) to
move; (*café etc*) to stir; (*terre*) to turn over;
(*salade*) to toss; – *vi* to move; (*gigoter*) to
fidget; (*se rebeller*) to stir; **— se r.** *vpr* to
move; (*se démener*) to exert oneself.
◆**—ant** *a* (*enfant*) restless, fidgety.
◆**remue-ménage** *nm inv* commotion.

rémunérer [remynere] *vt* (*personne*) to pay;
(*travail*) to pay for. ◆**rémunérateur,
-trice** *a* remunerative. ◆**rémunération** *nf*
payment (**de** for).

renâcler [r(ə)nɑkle] *vi* **1** (*cheval*) to snort. **2
r. à** to jib at, balk at.

renaître* [r(ə)nɛtr] *vi* (*fleur*) to grow again;
(*espoir, industrie*) to revive. ◆**renaissance** *nf* rebirth, renaissance.

renard [r(ə)nar] *nm* fox.

renchérir [rɑ̃ʃerir] *vi* **r. sur qn** *ou* **sur ce que
qn dit** /*etc* to go further than s.o. in what
one says/*etc*.

rencontre [rɑ̃kɔ̃tr] *nf* meeting; (*inattendue*)
& *Mil* encounter; *Sp* match, *Am* game; (*de
routes*) junction; **aller à la r. de** to go to
meet. ◆**rencontrer** *vt* to meet; (*difficultés*)
to come up against, encounter; (*trouver*) to
come across, find; (*heurter*) to hit; (*équipe*)
Sp to play; **— se r.** *vpr* to meet.

rendez-vous [rɑ̃devu] *nm inv* appointment;
(*d'amoureux*) date; (*lieu*) meeting place;
donner r.-vous à qn, prendre r.-vous avec qn
to make an appointment with s.o.

rendormir* (se) [sərɑ̃dɔrmir] *vpr* to go
back to sleep.

rend/re [rɑ̃dr] *vt* (*restituer*) to give back, return; (*hommage*) to pay; (*invitation*) to return; (*santé*) to restore; (*monnaie, son*) to
give; (*justice*) to dispense; (*jugement*) to
pronounce, give; (*armes*) to surrender; (*exprimer, traduire*) to render; (*vomir*) to bring
up; **r. célèbre/plus grand/possible**/*etc* to
make famous/bigger/possible/*etc*; – *vi*
(*arbre, terre*) to yield; (*vomir*) to be sick; **—
se r.** *vpr* (*capituler*) to surrender (à to); (*aller*) to go (à to); **se r. à** (*évidence, ordres*) to
submit to; **se r. malade/utile**/*etc* to make
oneself ill/useful/*etc*. ◆**—u** *a* (*fatigué*) exhausted; **être r.** (*arrivé*) to have arrived.
◆**rendement** *nm Agr Fin* yield; (*de personne, machine*) output.

renégat, -ate [rənega, -at] *nmf* renegade.

rènes [rɛn] *nfpl* reins.

renferm/er [rɑ̃fɛrme] *vt* to contain; — **se r.** *vpr* **se r. (en soi-même)** to withdraw into oneself. ◆**—é 1** *a* (*personne*) withdrawn. **2** *nm* **sentir le r.** (*chambre etc*) to smell stuffy.

renflé [rɑ̃fle] *a* bulging. ◆**renflement** *nm* bulge.

renflouer [rɑ̃flue] *vt* (*navire*) & *Com* to refloat.

renfoncement [rɑ̃fɔ̃səmɑ̃] *nm* recess; **dans le r. d'une porte** in a doorway.

renforcer [rɑ̃fɔrse] *vt* to reinforce, strengthen. ◆**renforcement** *nm* reinforcement, strengthening. ◆**renfort** *nm* **des renforts** *Mil* reinforcements; **de r.** (*armée, personnel*) back-up; **à grand r. de** *Fig* with a great deal of.

renfrogn/er (se) [sərɑ̃frɔɲe] *vpr* to scowl. ◆**—é** *a* scowling, sullen.

rengaine [rɑ̃gɛn] *nf* **la même r.** *Fig Péj* the same old song *ou* story.

rengorger (se) [sərɑ̃gɔrʒe] *vpr* to give oneself airs.

renier [rənje] *vt* (*ami, pays etc*) to disown; (*foi, opinion*) to renounce. ◆**reniement** *nm* disowning; renunciation.

renifler [r(ə)nifle] *vti* to sniff. ◆**reniflement** *nm* sniff.

renne [rɛn] *nm* reindeer.

renom [rənɔ̃] *nm* renown; (*réputation*) reputation (**de for**). ◆**renommé** *a* famous, renowned (**pour for**). ◆**renommée** *nf* fame, renown; (*réputation*) reputation.

renoncer [r(ə)nɔ̃se] *vi* **r. à** to give up, abandon; **r. à faire** to give up (the idea of) doing. ◆**renoncement** *nm*, ◆**renonciation** *nf* renunciation (**à** of).

renouer [rənwe] **1** *vt* (*lacet etc*) to retie. **2** *vt* (*reprendre*) to renew; — *vi* **r. avec qch** (*mode, tradition etc*) to revive sth; **r. avec qn** to take up with s.o. again.

renouveau, -x [r(ə)nuvo] *nm* revival.

renouveler [r(ə)nuvle] *vt* to renew; (*action, erreur, question*) to repeat; — **se r.** *vpr* (*incident*) to recur, happen again; (*cellules, sang*) to be renewed. ◆**renouvelable** *a* renewable. ◆**renouvellement** *nm* renewal.

rénover [renɔve] *vt* (*institution, méthode*) to reform; (*édifice, meuble etc*) to renovate. ◆**rénovation** *nf* reform; renovation.

renseign/er [rɑ̃sɛɲe] *vt* to inform, give information to (**sur** about); — **se r.** *vpr* to inquire, make inquiries, find out (**sur** about). ◆**—ement** *nm* (piece of) information; *pl* information; *Tél* directory inquiries, *Am* information; *Mil* intelligence;

prendre *ou* **demander des reseignements** to make inquiries.

rentable [rɑ̃tabl] *a* profitable. ◆**rentabilité** *nf* profitability.

rente [rɑ̃t] *nf* (private) income; (*pension*) pension; **avoir des rentes** to have private means. ◆**rentier, -ière** *nmf* person of private means.

rentr/er [rɑ̃tre] *vi* (*aux* **être**) to go *ou* come back, return; (*chez soi*) to go *ou* come (back) home; (*entrer*) to go *ou* come in; (*entrer de nouveau*) to go *ou* come back in; (*école*) to start again; (*argent*) to come in; **r. dans** (*entrer dans*) to go *ou* come into; (*entrer de nouveau dans*) to go *ou* come back into; (*famille, pays*) to return to; (*ses frais*) to get back; (*catégorie*) to come under; (*heurter*) to crash into; (*s'emboîter dans*) to fit into; **r. (en classe)** to start (school) again; **je lui suis rentré dedans** (*frapper*) *Fam* I laid into him *ou* her; — *vt* (*aux* **avoir**) to bring *ou* take in; (*voiture*) to put away; (*chemise*) to tuck in; (*griffes*) to draw in. ◆**—é** *a* (*colère*) suppressed; (*yeux*) sunken. ◆**—ée** *nf* **1** (*retour*) return; (*de parlement*) reassembly; (*d'acteur*) comeback; **r. (des classes)** beginning of term *ou* of the school year. **2** (*des foins etc*) bringing in; (*d'impôt*) collection; *pl* (*argent*) receipts.

renverse (à la) [alɑrɑ̃vɛrs] *adv* (*tomber*) backwards, on one's back.

renvers/er [rɑ̃vɛrse] *vt* (*mettre à l'envers*) to turn upside down; (*faire tomber*) to knock over *ou* down; (*piéton*) to knock down, run over; (*liquide*) to spill, knock over; (*courant, ordre*) to reverse; (*gouvernement*) to overturn, overthrow; (*projet*) to upset; (*tête*) to tip back; — **se r.** *vpr* (*en arrière*) to lean back; (*bouteille, vase etc*) to fall over. ◆**—ant** *a* (*nouvelle etc*) astounding. ◆**—ement** *nm* (*d'ordre, de situation*) reversal; (*de gouvernement*) overthrow.

renvoi [rɑ̃vwa] *nm* **1** return; dismissal; expulsion; postponement; (*dans un livre*) reference. **2** (*rot*) belch, burp. ◆**renvoyer*** *vt* to send back, return; (*importun*) to send away; (*employé*) to dismiss; (*élève*) to expel; (*balle etc*) to throw back; (*ajourner*) to postpone (**à** until); (*lumière, image etc*) to reflect; **r. qn à** (*adresser à*) to refer s.o. to.

réorganiser [reɔrganize] *vt* to reorganize.

réouverture [reuvɛrtyr] *nf* reopening.

repaire [r(ə)pɛr] *nm* den.

repaître (se) [sərəpɛtr] *vpr* **se r. de** (*sang*) *Fig* to wallow in.

répand/re [repɑ̃dr] *vt* (*liquide*) to spill;

(*idées, joie, nouvelle*) to spread; (*fumée, odeur*) to give off; (*chargement, lumière, larmes, sang*) to shed; (*gravillons etc*) to scatter; (*dons*) to lavish; **— se r.** *vpr* (*nouvelle, peur etc*) to spread; (*liquide*) to spill; **se r. dans** (*fumée, odeur*) to spread through; **se r. en louanges**/*etc* to pour forth praise/*etc*. **◆—u** *a* (*opinion, usage*) widespread; (*épars*) scattered.

reparaître [r(ə)parɛtr] *vi* to reappear.

réparer [repare] *vt* to repair, mend; (*forces, santé*) to restore; (*faute*) to make amends for; (*perte*) to make good; (*erreur*) to put right. **◆réparable** *a* (*montre etc*) repairable. **◆réparateur, -trice** *nmf* repairer; *— a* (*sommeil*) refreshing. **◆réparation** *nf* repair(ing); (*compensation*) amends, compensation (**de** for); *pl Mil Hist* reparations; **en r.** under repair.

reparler [r(ə)parle] *vi* **r. de** to talk about again.

repartie [reparti] *nf* (*réponse vive*) repartee.

repartir* [r(ə)partir] *vi* (*aux être*) to set off again; (*s'en retourner*) to go back; (*reprendre*) to start again; **r. à** *ou* **de zéro** to go back to square one.

répartir [repartir] *vt* to distribute; (*partager*) to share out; (*classer*) to divide (up); (*étaler dans le temps*) to spread (out) (**sur** over). **◆répartition** *nf* distribution; sharing; division.

repas [r(ə)pɑ] *nm* meal; **prendre un r.** to have *ou* eat a meal.

repass/er [r(ə)pase] **1** *vi* to come *ou* go back; *— vt* (*traverser*) to go back over; (*examen*) to resit; (*leçon, rôle*) to go over; (*film*) to show again; (*maladie, travail*) to pass on (**à** to). **2** *vt* (*linge*) to iron. **3** *vt* (*couteau*) to sharpen. **◆—age** *nm* ironing.

repêcher [r(ə)peʃe] *vt* to fish out; (*candidat*) *Fam* to allow to pass.

repenser [r(ə)pɑ̃se] *vt* to rethink.

repentir [r(ə)pɑ̃tir] *nm* repentance. **◆se repentir*** *vpr Rel* to repent (**de** of); **se r. de** (*regretter*) to regret, be sorry for. **◆repentant** *a*, **◆repenti** *a* repentant.

répercuter [reperkyte] *vt* (*son*) to echo; **— se r.** *vpr* to echo, reverberate; **se r. sur** *Fig* to have repercussions on. **◆répercussion** *nf* repercussion.

repère [r(ə)pɛr] *nm* (guide) mark; (*jalon*) marker; **point de r.** (*espace, temps*) landmark, point of reference. **◆repérer** *vt* to locate; (*personne*) *Fam* to spot; **— se r.** *vpr* to get one's bearings.

répertoire [repɛrtwar] *nm* **1** index; (*carnet*) indexed notebook; **r. d'adresses** address

book. **2** *Th* repertoire. **◆répertorier** *vt* to index.

répéter [repete] *vti* to repeat; *Th* to rehearse; **— se r.** *vpr* (*radoter*) to repeat oneself; (*se reproduire*) to repeat itself. **◆répétitif, -ive** *a* repetitive. **◆répétition** *nf* repetition; *Th* rehearsal; **r. générale** *Th* (final) dress rehearsal.

repiquer [r(ə)pike] *vt* **1** (*plante*) to plant out. **2** (*disque*) to tape, record (on tape).

répit [repi] *nm* rest, respite; **sans r.** ceaselessly.

replacer [r(ə)plase] *vt* to replace, put back.

repli [r(ə)pli] *nm* fold; withdrawal; *pl* (*de l'âme*) recesses. **◆replier 1** *vt* to fold (up); (*siège*) to fold up; (*couteau, couverture*) to fold back; (*ailes, jambes*) to tuck in; **— se r.** *vpr* (*siège*) to fold up; (*couteau, couverture*) to fold back. **2** *vt*, **— se r.** *vpr Mil* to withdraw; **se r. sur soi-même** to withdraw into oneself.

réplique [replik] *nf* **1** (*réponse*) reply; (*riposte*) retort; *Th* lines; **pas de r.!** no answering back!; **sans r.** (*argument*) irrefutable. **2** (*copie*) replica. **◆répliquer** *vt* to reply (**que** that); (*riposter*) to retort (**que** that); *— vi* (*être impertinent*) to answer back.

répond/re [repɔ̃dr] *vi* to answer, reply; (*être impertinent*) to answer back; (*réagir*) to respond (**à** to); **r. à qn** to answer s.o., reply to s.o.; (*avec impertinence*) to answer s.o. back; *— vt* (*lettre, objection, question*) to answer, reply to; (*salut*) to return; (*besoin*) to meet, answer; (*correspondre à*) to correspond to; **r. de** (*garantir*) to answer for (*s.o., sth*); *— vt* (*remarque etc*) to answer *ou* reply with; **r. que** to answer *ou* reply that. **◆—ant, -ante 1** *nmf* guarantor. **2** *nm* **avoir du r.** to have money behind one. **◆—eur** *nm Tél* answering machine. **◆réponse** *nf* answer, reply; (*réaction*) response (**à** to); **en r. à** in answer *ou* reply *ou* response to.

reporter¹ [r(ə)pɔrte] *vt* to take back; (*différer*) to postpone, put off (**à** until); (*transcrire, transférer*) to transfer (**sur** to); (*somme*) *Com* to carry forward (**sur** to); **se r. à** (*texte etc*) to refer to; (*en esprit*) to go *ou* think back to. **◆report** *nm* postponement; transfer; *Com* carrying forward. **◆reportage** *nm* (news) report, article; (*en direct*) commentary; (*métier*) reporting.

reporter² [r(ə)pɔrter] *nm* reporter.

repos [r(ə)po] *nm* rest; (*tranquillité*) peace (and quiet); (*de l'esprit*) peace of mind; **r.!** *Mil* at ease!; **jour de r.** day off; **de tout r.** (*situation etc*) safe. **◆repos/er 1** *vt* (*objet*) to put back down; (*problème, question*) to raise again. **2** *vt* (*délasser*) to rest, relax; **r. sa tête sur** (*appuyer*) to rest one's head on; – *vi* (*être enterré ou étendu*) to rest, lie; **r. sur** (*bâtiment*) to be built on; (*théorie etc*) to be based on, rest on; **laisser r.** (*vin*) to allow to settle; **— se r.** *vpr* to rest; **se r. sur qn** to rely on s.o. ◆**—ant** a relaxing, restful. ◆**—é** a rested, fresh.

repouss/er [r(ə)puse] **1** *vt* to push back; (*écarter*) to push away; (*attaque, ennemi*) to repulse; (*importun etc*) to turn away, repulse; (*dégoûter*) to repel; (*décliner*) to reject; (*différer*) to put off, postpone. **2** *vi* (*cheveux, feuilles*) to grow again. ◆**—ant** a repulsive, repellent.

répréhensible [repreãsibl] a reprehensible, blameworthy.

reprendre* [r(ə)prãdr] *vt* (*objet*) to take back; (*évadé, ville*) to recapture; (*passer prendre*) to pick up again; (*souffle*) to get back; (*activité*) to resume, take up again; (*texte*) to go back over; (*vêtement*) to alter; (*histoire, refrain*) to take up; (*pièce*) *Th* to put on again; (*blâmer*) to admonish; (*corriger*) to correct; **r. de la viande/un œuf** *etc* to take (some) more meat/another egg/*etc*; **r. ses esprits** to come round; **r. des forces** to recover one's strength; – *vi* (*plante*) to take again; (*recommencer*) to resume, start (up) again; (*affaires*) to pick up; (*dire*) to go on, continue; **— se r.** *vpr* (*se ressaisir*) to take a hold on oneself; (*se corriger*) to correct oneself; **s'y r. à deux/plusieurs fois** to have another go/several goes (at it).

représailles [r(ə)prezaj] *nfpl* reprisals, retaliation.

représent/er [r(ə)prezãte] *vt* to represent; (*jouer*) *Th* to perform; **— se r.** *vpr* (*s'imaginer*) to imagine. ◆**—ant, -ante** *nmf* representative; **r. de commerce** (travelling) salesman *ou* saleswoman, sales representative. ◆**représentatif, -ive** a representative (de of). ◆**représentation** *nf* representation; *Th* performance.

répression [represjõ] *nf* suppression, repression; (*mesures de contrôle*) *Pol* repression. ◆**répressif, -ive** a repressive. ◆**réprimer** *vt* (*sentiment, révolte etc*) to suppress, repress.

réprimande [reprimãd] *nf* reprimand. ◆**réprimander** *vt* to reprimand.

repris [r(ə)pri] *nm* **r. de justice** hardened criminal.

reprise [r(ə)priz] *nf* (*de ville*) *Mil* recapture; (*recommencement*) resumption; (*de pièce de théâtre, de coutume*) revival; *Rad TV* repeat; (*de tissu*) mend, repair; *Boxe* round;

(*essor*) *Com* recovery, revival; (*d'un locataire*) money for fittings; (*de marchandise*) taking back; (*pour nouvel achat*) part exchange, trade-in; *pl Aut* acceleration; **à plusieurs reprises** on several occasions. ◆**repriser** *vt* (*chaussette etc*) to mend, darn.

réprobation [reprobasjõ] *nf* disapproval. ◆**réprobateur, -trice** a disapproving.

reproche [r(ə)prɔʃ] *nm* reproach; **faire des reproches à qn** to reproach s.o.; **sans r.** beyond reproach. ◆**reprocher** *vt* **r. qch à qn** to reproach *ou* blame s.o. for sth; **r. qch à qch** to have sth against sth; **n'avoir rien à se r.** to have nothing to reproach *ou* blame oneself for.

reproduire* [r(ə)prɔdɥir] **1** *vt* (*son, modèle etc*) to reproduce; **— se r.** *vpr Biol Bot* to reproduce. **2 se r.** *vpr* (*incident etc*) to happen again, recur. ◆**reproducteur, -trice** a reproductive. ◆**reproduction** *nf* (*de son etc*) & *Biol Bot* reproduction.

réprouver [repruve] *vt* to disapprove of, condemn.

reptile [reptil] *nm* reptile.

repu [rapy] a (*rassasié*) satiated.

république [repyblik] *nf* republic. ◆**républicain, -aine** a & *nmf* republican.

répudier [repydje] *vt* to repudiate.

répugnant [repynã] a repugnant, loathsome. ◆**répugnance** *nf* repugnance, loathing (pour for); (*manque d'enthousiasme*) reluctance. ◆**répugner** *vi* **r. à qn** to be repugnant to s.o.; **r. à faire** to be loath to do.

répulsion [repylsjõ] *nf* repulsion.

réputation [repytasjõ] *nf* reputation; **avoir la r. d'être franc** to have a reputation for frankness *ou* for being frank. ◆**réputé** a (*célèbre*) renowned (pour for); **r. pour être** (*considéré comme*) reputed to be.

requérir [rəkerir] *vt* (*nécessiter*) to demand, require; (*peine*) *Jur* to call for. ◆**requête** *nf* request; *Jur* petition. ◆**requis** a required, requisite.

requiem [rekɥijem] *nm inv* requiem.

requin [r(ə)kẽ] *nm* (*poisson*) & *Fig* shark.

réquisition [rekizisjõ] *nf* requisition. ◆**réquisitionner** *vt* to requisition, commandeer.

réquisitoire [rekizitwar] *nm* (*critique*) indictment (contre of).

rescapé, -ée [rɛskape] a surviving; – *nmf* survivor.

rescousse (à la) [alarɛskus] *adv* to the rescue.

réseau, -x [rezo] *nm* network; r. d'espionnage spy ring *ou* network.

réserve [rezɛrv] *nf* 1 (*restriction, doute*) reservation; (*réticence*) reserve; **sans r.** (*admiration etc*) unqualified; **sous r. de** subject to; **sous toutes réserves** without guarantee. 2 (*provision*) reserve; (*entrepôt*) storeroom; (*de bibliothèque*) stacks; **la r.** *Mil* the reserve; **les réserves** (*soldats*) the reserves; **en r.** in reserve. 3 (*de chasse, pêche*) preserve; (*indienne*) reservation; **r. naturelle** nature reserve.

réserv/er [rezɛrve] *vt* to reserve; (*garder*) to keep, save; (*marchandises*) to put aside (à for); (*place, table*) to book, reserve; (*sort, surprise etc*) to hold in store (à for); **se r. pour** to save oneself for; **se r. de faire** to reserve the right to do. ◆—**é** *a* (*personne, place*) reserved; (*prudent*) guarded. ◆**réservation** *nf* reservation, booking. ◆**réservoir** *nm* (*lac*) reservoir; (*citerne, cuve*) tank; **r. d'essence** *Aut* petrol *ou Am* gas tank.

résidence [rezidãs] *nf* residence; **r. secondaire** second home; **r. universitaire** hall of residence. ◆**résident, -ente** *nmf* (foreign) resident. ◆**résidentiel, -ielle** *a* (*quartier*) residential. ◆**résider** *vi* to reside, be resident (à, en, dans in); **r. dans** (*consister dans*) to lie in.

résidu [rezidy] *nm* residue.

résigner (se) [sərezine] *vpr* to resign oneself (à qch to sth, à faire to doing). ◆**résignation** *nf* resignation.

résilier [rezilje] *vt* (*contrat*) to terminate. ◆**résiliation** *nf* termination.

résille [rezij] *nf* (*pour cheveux*) hairnet.

résine [rezin] *nf* resin.

résistance [rezistãs] *nf* resistance (à to); (*conducteur*) *Él* (heating) element; **plat de r.** main dish. ◆**résist/er** *vi* **r. à** to resist; (*chaleur, fatigue, souffrance*) to withstand; (*examen*) to stand up to. ◆—**ant, -ante** *a* tough, strong; **r. à la chaleur** heat-resistant; **r. au choc** shockproof; — *nmf Mil Hist* Resistance fighter.

résolu [rezɔly] *voir* **résoudre**; — *a* resolute, determined; **r. à faire** resolved *ou* determined to do. ◆—**ment** *adv* resolutely. ◆**résolution** *nf* (*décision*) resolution; (*fermeté*) determination.

résonance [rezɔnãs] *nf* resonance.

résonner [rezɔne] *vi* to resound (**de** with); (*salle, voix*) to echo.

résorber [rezɔrbe] *vt* (*chômage*) to reduce; (*excédent*) to absorb; — **se r.** *vpr* to be re-

duced; to be absorbed. ◆**résorption** *nf* reduction; absorption.

résoudre* [rezudr] *vt* (*problème*) to solve; (*difficulté*) to resolve; **r. de faire** to decide *ou* resolve to do; **se r. à faire** to decide *ou* resolve to do; (*se résigner*) to bring oneself to do.

respect [rɛspɛ] *nm* respect (**pour, de** for); **mes respects à** my regards *ou* respects to; **tenir qn en r.** to hold s.o. in check. ◆**respectabilité** *nf* respectability. ◆**respectable** *a* (*honorable, important*) respectable. ◆**respecter** *vt* to respect; **qui se respecte** self-respecting. ◆**respectueux, -euse** *a* respectful (**envers** to, **de** of).

respectif, -ive [rɛspɛktif, -iv] *a* respective. ◆**respectivement** *adv* respectively.

respirer [rɛspire] *vi* to breathe; (*reprendre haleine*) to get one's breath (back); (*être soulagé*) to breathe again; — *vt* to breathe (in); (*exprimer*) *Fig* to exude. ◆**respiration** *nf* breathing; (*haleine*) breath; **r. artificielle** *Méd* artificial respiration. ◆**respiratoire** *a* breathing-, respiratory.

resplend/ir [rɛsplãdir] *vi* to shine; (*visage*) to glow (**de** with). ◆—**issant** *a* radiant.

responsable [rɛspɔsabl] *a* responsible (**de qch** for sth, **devant qn** to s.o.); — *nmf* (*chef*) person in charge; (*dans une organisation*) official; (*coupable*) person responsible (**de** for). ◆**responsabilité** *nf* responsibility; (*légale*) liability.

resquiller [rɛskije] *vi* (*au cinéma, dans le métro etc*) to avoid paying; (*sans attendre*) to jump the queue, *Am* cut in (line).

ressaisir (se) [sər(ə)sezir] *vpr* to pull oneself together.

ressasser [r(ə)sase] *vt* (*ruminer*) to keep going over; (*répéter*) to keep trotting out.

ressemblance [r(ə)sãblãs] *nf* resemblance, likeness. ◆**ressembl/er** *vi* **à** to resemble, look *ou* be like; **cela ne lui ressemble pas** (*ce n'est pas son genre*) that's not like him *ou* her; — **se r.** *vpr* to look *ou* be alike. ◆—**ant** *a* portrait **r.** good likeness.

ressentiment [r(ə)sãtimã] *nm* resentment.

ressentir* [r(ə)sãtir] *vt* to feel; **se r. de** to feel *ou* show the effects of.

resserre [r(ə)sɛr] *nf* storeroom; (*remise*) shed.

resserrer [r(ə)sere] *vt* (*nœud, boulon etc*) to tighten; (*contracter*) to close (up), contract; (*liens*) *Fig* to strengthen; — **se r.** *vpr* to tighten; (*amitié*) to become closer; (*se contracter*) to close (up), contract; (*route etc*) to narrow.

resservir [r(ə)sɛrvir] 1 *vi* (*outil etc*) to come

in useful (again). **2 se r.** *vpr* **se r. de** (*plat etc*) to have another helping of.

ressort [r(ə)sɔr] *nm* **1** *Tech* spring. **2** (*énergie*) spirit. **3 du r. de** within the competence of; **en dernier r.** (*décider etc*) in the last resort, as a last resort.

ressortir¹* [r(ə)sɔrtir] *vi* (*aux être*) **1** to go *ou* come back out. **2** (*se voir*) to stand out; **faire r.** to bring out; **il ressort de** (*résulte*) it emerges from.

ressortir² [r(ə)sɔrtir] *vi* (*conjugated like* **finir**) **r. à** to fall within the scope of.

ressortissant, -ante [r(ə)sɔrtisã, -ãt] *nmf* (*citoyen*) national.

ressource [r(ə)surs] **1** *nfpl* (*moyens*) resources; (*argent*) means, resources. **2** *nf* (*recours*) recourse; (*possibilité*) possibility (**de faire** of doing); **dernière r.** last resort.

ressusciter [resysite] *vi* to rise from the dead; (*malade, pays*) to recover, revive; − *vt* (*mort*) to raise; (*malade, mode*) to revive.

restaurant [rɛstɔrã] *nm* restaurant.

restaurer [rɛstɔre] **1** *vt* (*réparer, rétablir*) to restore. **2 se r.** *vpr* to (have sth to) eat. ◆**restaurateur, -trice** *nmf* **1** (*de tableaux*) restorer. **2** (*hôtelier, hôtelière*) restaurant owner. ◆**restauration** *nf* **1** restoration. **2** (*hôtellerie*) catering.

reste [rɛst] *nm* rest, remainder (**de** of); *Math* remainder; *pl* remains (**de** of); (*de repas*) leftovers; **un r. de fromage**/*etc* some left-over cheese/*etc*; **au r., du r.** moreover, besides.

rester [rɛste] *vi* (*aux être*) to stay, remain; (*calme, jeune etc*) to keep, stay, remain; (*subsister*) to remain, be left; **il reste du pain**/*etc* there's some bread/*etc* left (over); **il me reste une minute**/*etc* I have one minute/*etc* left; **l'argent qui lui reste** the money he *ou* she has left; **reste à savoir** it remains to be seen; **il me reste deux choses à faire** I still have two things to do; **il me reste à vous remercier** it remains for me to thank you; **en r. à** to stop at; **restons-en là** let's leave it at that. ◆**restant** *a* remaining; **poste restante** poste restante, *Am* general delivery; −*nm* **le r.** the rest, the remainder; **un r. de viande**/*etc* some left-over meat/*etc*.

restituer [rɛstitɥe] *vt* **1** (*rendre*) to return, restore (**à** to). **2** (*son*) to reproduce; (*énergie*) to release. ◆**restitution** *nf* return.

restreindre* [rɛstrɛ̃dr] *vt* to restrict, limit (**à** to). − **se r.** *vpr* to decrease; (*faire des économies*) to cut back *ou* down. ◆**restreint** *a* limited, restricted (**à** to). ◆**restrictif, -ive**

a restrictive. ◆**restriction** *nf* restriction; **sans r.** unreservedly.

résultat [rezylta] *nm* result; (*conséquence*) outcome, result; **avoir qch pour r.** to result in sth. ◆**résulter** *vi* **r. de** to result from.

résum/er [rezyme] *vt* to summarize; (*récapituler*) to sum up; − **se r.** *vpr* (*orateur etc*) to sum up; **se r. à** (*se réduire à*) to boil down to. ◆**−é** *nm* summary; **en r.** in short; (*en récapitulant*) to sum up.

résurrection [rezyrɛksjɔ̃] *nf* resurrection.

rétabl/ir [retablir] *vt* to restore; (*fait, vérité*) to re-establish; (*malade*) to restore to health; (*employé*) to reinstate; − **se r.** *vpr* to be restored; (*malade*) to recover. ◆**−issement** *nm* restoring; re-establishment; *Méd* recovery.

retaper [r(ə)tape] *vt* (*maison, voiture etc*) to do up; (*lit*) to straighten; (*malade*) *Fam* to buck up.

retard [r(ə)tar] *nm* lateness; (*sur un programme etc*) delay; (*infériorité*) backwardness; **en r.** late; (*retardé*) backward; **en r. dans qch** behind in sth; **en r. sur qn/qch** behind s.o./sth; **rattraper** *ou* **combler son r.** to catch up; **avoir du r.** to be late; (*sur un programme*) to be behind (schedule); (*montre*) to be slow; **avoir une heure de r.** to be an hour late; **prendre du r.** (*montre*) to lose (time); **sans r.** without delay. ◆**retardataire** *a* (*arrivant*) late; **enfant r.** *Méd* slow learner; − *nmf* latecomer. ◆**retardement** *nm* **à r.** delayed-action-; **bombe à r.** time bomb.

retard/er [r(ə)tarde] *vt* to delay; (*date, départ, montre*) to put back; **r. qn** (*dans une activité*) to put s.o. behind; − *vi* (*montre*) to be slow; **r. de cinq minutes** to be five minutes slow; **r. sur son temps** (*personne*) to be behind the times. ◆**−é, -ée** *a* (*enfant*) backward; − *nmf* backward child.

retenir* [rətnir] *vt* (*empêcher d'agir, contenir*) to hold back; (*attention, souffle*) to hold; (*réserver*) to book; (*se souvenir de*) to remember; (*fixer*) to hold (in place), secure; (*déduire*) to take off; (*candidature, proposition*) to accept; (*chiffre*) *Math* to carry; (*chaleur, odeur*) to retain; (*invité, suspect etc*) to detain, keep; **r. qn prisonnier** to keep *ou* hold s.o. prisoner; **r. qn de faire** to stop s.o. (from) doing; − **se r.** *vpr* (*se contenir*) to restrain oneself; **se r. de faire** to stop oneself (from) doing; **se r. à** to cling to. ◆**retenue** *nf* **1** (*modération*) restraint. **2** (*de salaire*) deduction, stoppage; (*chiffre*) *Math* figure carried over. **3** *Scol* detention; **en r.** in detention.

retent/ir [r(ə)tãtir] *vi* to ring (out) (**de** with). **◆—issant** *a* resounding; (*scandale*) major. **◆—issement** *nm* (*effet*) effect; **avoir un grand r.** (*film etc*) to create a stir.

réticent [retisã] *a* (*réservé*) reticent; (*hésitant*) reluctant. **◆réticence** *nf* reticence; reluctance.

rétine [retin] *nf Anat* retina.

retir/er [r(ə)tire] *vt* to take out; (*sortir*) to take out; (*ôter*) to take off; (*éloigner*) to take away; (*reprendre*) to pick up; (*offre, plainte*) to take back, withdraw; **r. qch à qn** (*permis etc*) to take sth away from s.o.; **r. qch de** (*gagner*) to derive sth from; **— se r.** *vpr* to withdraw, retire (**de** from); (*mer*) to ebb. **◆—é** *a* (*lieu, vie*) secluded.

retomber [r(ə)tɔ̃be] *vi* to fall; (*de nouveau*) to fall again; (*pendre*) to hang (down); (*après un saut etc*) to land; (*intérêt*) to slacken; **r. dans** (*erreur, situation*) to fall *ou* sink back into; **r. sur qn** (*frais, responsabilité*) to fall on s.o. **◆retombées** *nfpl* (*radioactives*) fallout.

rétorquer [retorke] *vt* **r. que** to retort that.

retors [rɔtɔr] *a* wily, crafty.

rétorsion [retɔrsjɔ̃] *nf Pol* retaliation; **mesure de r.** reprisal.

retouche [r(ə)tuʃ] *nf* touching up; alteration. **◆retoucher** *vt* (*photo, tableau*) to touch up, retouch; (*texte, vêtement*) to alter.

retour [r(ə)tur] *nm* return; (*de fortune*) reversal; **être de r.** to be back (**de** from); **en r.** (*en échange*) in return; **par r.** (**du courrier**) by return (of post); *Am* by return mail; **à mon retour** when I get *ou* got back (**de** from); **r. en arrière** flashback; **r. de flamme** *Fig* backlash; **match r.** return match *ou* *Am* game.

retourner [r(ə)turne] *vt* (*aux avoir*) (*tableau etc*) to turn round; (*matelas, steak etc*) to turn over; (*foin, terre etc*) to turn; (*vêtement, sac etc*) to turn inside out; (*maison*) to turn upside down; (*compliment, lettre*) to return; **r. qn** (*bouleverser*) *Fam* to upset s.o., shake s.o.; **r. contre qn** (*argument*) to turn against s.o.; (*arme*) to turn on s.o.; **de quoi il retourne** what it's about; **— vi** (*aux être*) to go back, return; **— se r.** *vpr* (*pour regarder*) to turn round, look back; (*sur le dos*) to turn over *ou* round; (*dans son lit*) to toss and turn; (*voiture*) to overturn; **s'en r.** to go back; **se r. contre** *Fig* to turn against.

retracer [r(ə)trase] *vt* (*histoire etc*) to retrace.

rétracter [retrakte] *vt*, **— se r.** *vpr* to retract. **◆rétractation** *nf* (*désaveu*) retraction.

retrait [r(ə)trɛ] *nm* withdrawal; (*de bagages, billets*) collection; (*de mer*) ebb(ing); **en r.** (*maison etc*) set back.

retraite [r(ə)trɛt] *nf* **1** (*d'employé*) retirement; (*pension*) (retirement) pension; (*refuge*) retreat, refuge; **r. anticipée** early retirement; **prendre sa r.** to retire; **à la r.** retired; **mettre à la r.** to pension off. **2** *Mil* retreat; **r. aux flambeaux** torchlight tattoo. **◆retraité, -ée** *a* retired; **—** *nmf* senior citizen, (old age) pensioner.

retrancher [r(ə)trãʃe] *vt* **1** (*mot, passage etc*) to cut (**de** from); (*argent, quantité*) to deduct (**de** from). **2 se r.** *vpr* (*soldat, gangster etc*) to entrench oneself; **se r. dans/derrière** *Fig* to take refuge in/behind.

retransmettre [r(ə)trãsmɛtr] *vt* to broadcast. **◆retransmission** *nf* broadcast.

rétréc/ir [retresir] *vt* to narrow; (*vêtement*) to take in; **— vi, — se r.** *vpr* (*au lavage*) to shrink; (*rue etc*) to narrow. **◆—i** *a* (*esprit, rue*) narrow.

rétribuer [retribɥe] *vt* to pay, remunerate; (*travail*) to pay for. **◆rétribution** *nf* payment, remuneration.

rétro [retro] *a inv* (*mode etc*) which harks back to the past, retro.

rétro- [retro] *préf* retro-. **◆rétroactif, -ive** *a* retroactive.

rétrograde [retrograd] *a* retrograde. **◆rétrograder** *vi* (*reculer*) to move back; (*civilisation etc*) to go backwards; *Aut* to change down; **—** *vt* (*fonctionnaire, officier*) to demote.

rétrospectif, -ive [retrospektif, -iv] *a* (*sentiment etc*) retrospective; **—** *nf* (*de films, tableaux*) retrospective. **◆rétrospectivement** *adv* in retrospect.

retrouss/er [r(ə)truse] *vt* (*jupe etc*) to hitch *ou* tuck up; (*manches*) to roll up **◆—é** *a* (*nez*) snub, turned-up.

retrouver [r(ə)truve] *vt* to find (again); (*rejoindre*) to meet (again); (*forces, santé*) to regain; (*découvrir*) to rediscover; (*se rappeler*) to recall; **— se r.** *vpr* (*chose*) to be found (again); (*se trouver*) to find oneself (back); (*se rencontrer*) to meet (again); **s'y r.** (*s'orienter*) to find one's bearings *ou* way. **◆retrouvailles** *nfpl* reunion.

rétroviseur [retrovizœr] *nm Aut* (rear-view) mirror.

réunion [reynjɔ̃] *nf* (*séance*) meeting; (*d'objets*) collection, gathering; (*d'éléments divers*) combination; (*jonction*) joining. **◆réunir** *vt* to collect, gather; (*relier*) to join; (*convoquer*) to call together, assemble; (*rapprocher*) to bring together; (*qua-*

lités, tendances) to combine. ◆**réunis** *apl*
(*éléments*) combined.

réuss/ir [reysir] *vi* to succeed, be successful
(**à faire** in doing); (*plante*) to thrive; **r. à**
(*examen*) to pass; **r. à qn** to work (out) well
for s.o.; (*aliment, climat*) to agree with s.o.;
– *vt* to make a success of. ◆**—i** *a* successful. ◆**réussite** *nf* **1** success. **2 faire des
réussites** *Cartes* to play patience.

revaloir [r(ə)valwar] *vt* **je vous le revaudrai**
(*en bien ou en mal*) I'll pay you back.

revaloriser [r(ə)valɔrize] *vt* (*salaire*) to
raise. ◆**revalorisation** *nf* raising.

revanche [r(ə)vɑ̃ʃ] *nf* revenge; *Sp* return
game; **en r.** on the other hand.

rêve [rɛv] *nm* dream; **faire un r.** to have a
dream; **maison/voiture/***etc* **de r.** dream
house/car/*etc*. ◆**rêvasser** *vi* to daydream.

revêche [rəvɛʃ] *a* bad-tempered, surly.

réveil [revɛj] *nm* waking (up); *Fig* awakening; (*pendule*) alarm (clock). ◆**réveill/er**
vt (*personne*) to wake (up); (*sentiment, souvenir*) *Fig* to revive, awaken; — **se r.** *vpr* to
wake (up); *Fig* to revive, awaken. ◆**—é** *a*
awake. ◆**réveille-matin** *nm inv* alarm
(clock).

réveillon [revɛjɔ̃] *nm* (*repas*) midnight supper (*on Christmas Eve or New Year's Eve*).
◆**réveillonner** *vi* to take part in a *réveillon*.

révéler [revele] *vt* to reveal (**que** that); — **se
r.** to be revealed; **se r. facile/***etc* to turn out
to be easy/*etc*. ◆**révélateur, -trice** *a* re-
vealing; **r. de** indicative of. ◆**révélation**
nf revelation.

revenant [rəvnɑ̃] *nm* ghost.

revendiquer [r(ə)vɑ̃dike] *vt* to claim; (*exiger*) to demand. ◆**revendicatif, -ive** *a*
(*mouvement etc*) protest-. ◆**revendication** *nf* claim; demand; (*action*) claiming;
demanding.

revendre [r(ə)vɑ̃dr] *vt* to resell; **avoir (de)
qch à r.** to have sth to spare. ◆**revendeur,
-euse** *nmf* retailer; (*d'occasion*) second-
hand dealer; **r. (de drogue)** drug pusher; **r.
de billets** ticket tout. ◆**revente** *nf* resale.

revenir* [rəvnir] *vi* (*aux être*) to come back,
return; (*date*) to come round again; (*mot*)
to come *ou* crop up; (*coûter*) to cost (**à qn**
s.o.); **r. à** (*activité, sujet*) to go back to, return to; (*se résumer à*) to boil down to; **r. à
qn** (*forces, mémoire*) to come back to s.o.,
return to s.o.; (*honneur*) to fall to s.o.; **r. à
soi** to come to *ou* round; **r. de** (*maladie,
surprise*) to get over; **r. sur** (*décision,
promesse*) to go back on; (*passé, question*)

to go back over; **r. sur ses pas** to retrace
one's steps; **faire r.** (*aliment*) to brown.

revenu [rəvny] *nm* income (**de** from); (*d'un
État*) revenue (**de** from); **déclaration de
revenus** tax return.

rêv/er [reve] *vi* to dream (**de** of, **de faire** of
doing); – *vt* to dream (**que** that); (*désirer*)
to dream of. ◆**—é** *a* ideal.

réverbération [reverberasjɔ̃] *nf* (*de lumière*)
reflection; (*de son*) reverberation.

révérence [reverɑ̃s] *nf* reverence; (*salut
d'homme*) bow; (*salut de femme*) curts(e)y;
faire une r. to bow; to curts(e)y. ◆**révérer**
vt to revere.

révérend, -ende [reverɑ̃, -ɑ̃d] *a & nm Rel*
reverend.

rêverie [revri] *nf* daydream; (*activité*)
daydreaming.

revers [r(ə)ver] *nm* (*côté*) reverse; *Tennis*
backhand; (*de veste*) lapel; (*de pantalon*)
turn-up, *Am* cuff; (*d'étoffe*) wrong side;
(*coup du sort*) setback, reverse; **r. de main**
(*coup*) backhander; **le r. de la médaille** *Fig*
the other side of the coin.

réversible [reversibl] *a* reversible.

revêtir* [r(ə)vetir] *vt* to cover (**de** with);
(*habit*) to put on; (*caractère, forme*) to assume; (*route*) to surface; **r. qn** (*habiller*) to
dress s.o. (**de** in); **r. de** (*signature*) to provide with. ◆**revêtement** *nm* (*surface*) covering; (*de route*) surface.

rêveur, -euse [rɛvœr, -øz] *a* dreamy; – *nmf*
dreamer.

revient [rəvjɛ̃] *nm* **prix de r.** cost price.

revigorer [r(ə)vigɔre] *vt* (*personne*) to revive.

revirement [r(ə)virmɑ̃] *nm* (*changement*)
about-turn, *Am* about-face; (*de situation,
d'opinion, de politique*) reversal.

réviser [revize] *vt* (*notes, texte*) to revise;
(*jugement, règlement etc*) to review; (*machine, voiture*) to overhaul, service. ◆**révision** *nf* revision; review; overhaul, service.

revivre* [r(ə)vivr] *vi* to live again; **faire r.** to
revive; – *vt* (*incident etc*) to relive.

révocation [revɔkasjɔ̃] *nf* **1** (*de contrat etc*)
revocation. **2** (*de fonctionnaire*) dismissal.

revoici [r(ə)vwasi] *prép* **me r.** here I am
again.

revoilà [r(ə)vwala] *prép* **la r.** there she is
again.

revoir* [r(ə)vwar] *vt* to see (again); (*texte*)
to revise; **au r.** goodbye.

révolte [revɔlt] *nf* revolt. ◆**révolt/er 1** *vt* to
revolt, incense. **2 se r.** *vpr* to revolt, rebel
(**contre** against). ◆**—ant** *a* (*honteux*) revolting. ◆**—é, -ée** *nmf* rebel.

révolu [revɔly] a (*époque*) past; **avoir trente ans révolus** to be over thirty (years of age).

révolution [revɔlysjɔ̃] nf (*changement, rotation*) revolution. ◆**révolutionnaire** a & nmf revolutionary. ◆**révolutionner** vt to revolutionize; (*émouvoir*) *Fig* to shake up.

revolver [revɔlvɛr] nm revolver, gun.

révoquer [revɔke] vt 1 (*contrat etc*) to revoke. 2 (*fonctionnaire*) to dismiss.

revue [r(ə)vy] nf 1 (*examen*) & *Mil* review; **passer en r.** to review. 2 (*de music-hall*) variety show. 3 (*magazine*) magazine; (*spécialisée*) journal.

rez-de-chaussée [redʃose] nm inv ground floor, *Am* first floor.

rhabiller (se) [sərabije] vpr to get dressed again.

rhapsodie [rapsɔdi] nf rhapsody.

rhétorique [retɔrik] nf rhetoric.

Rhin [rɛ̃] nm le R. the Rhine.

rhinocéros [rinɔserɔs] nm rhinoceros.

rhododendron [rɔdɔdɛ̃drɔ̃] nm rhododendron.

rhubarbe [rybarb] nf rhubarb.

rhum [rɔm] nm rum.

rhumatisme [rymatism] nm *Méd* rheumatism; **avoir des rhumatismes** to have rheumatism. ◆**rhumatisant, -ante** a & nmf rheumatic. ◆**rhumatismal, -aux** a (*douleur*) rheumatic.

rhume [rym] nm cold; **r. de cerveau** head cold; **r. des foins** hay fever.

riant [rjɑ̃] a cheerful, smiling.

ricaner [rikane] vi (*sarcastiquement*) to snigger; (*bêtement*) to giggle.

riche [riʃ] a rich; (*personne, pays*) rich, wealthy; **r. en** (*minérai, vitamines etc*) rich in; – nmf rich ou wealthy person; **les riches** the rich. ◆**—ment** a (*vêtu, illustré etc*) richly. ◆**richesse** nf wealth; (*d'étoffe, de sol, vocabulaire*) richness; pl (*trésor*) riches; (*ressources*) wealth.

ricin [risɛ̃] nm **huile de r.** castor oil.

ricocher [rikɔʃe] vi to ricochet, rebound. ◆**ricochet** nm ricochet, rebound; **par r.** *Fig* as an indirect result.

rictus [riktys] nm grin, grimace.

ride [rid] nf wrinkle; ripple. ◆**rider** vt (*visage*) to wrinkle; (*eau*) to ripple; – **se r.** vpr to wrinkle.

rideau, -x [rido] nm curtain; (*métallique*) shutter; (*écran*) *Fig* screen (de of); **le r. de fer** *Pol* the Iron Curtain.

ridicule [ridikyl] a ridiculous, ludicrous; – nm (*moquerie*) ridicule; (*défaut*) absurdity; (*de situation etc*) ridiculousness; **tourner en r.** to ridicule. ◆**ridiculiser** vt to ridicule.

rien [rjɛ̃] pron nothing; **il ne sait r.** he knows nothing, he doesn't know anything; **r. du tout** nothing at all; **r. d'autre/de bon/etc** nothing else/good/etc; **r. de tel** nothing like it; **de r.!** (*je vous en prie*) don't mention it!; **ça ne fait r.** it doesn't matter; **en moins de r.** (*vite*) in no time; **trois fois r.** (*chose insignifiante*) next to nothing; **pour r.** (*à bas prix*) for next to nothing; **il n'en est r.** (*ce n'est pas vrai*) nothing of the kind; **r. que** only, just; – nm trifle, (mere) nothing; **un r. de** a hint ou touch of; **en un r. de temps** (*vite*) in no time; **un r. trop petit/etc** just a bit too small/etc.

rieur, -euse [rjœr, -øz] a cheerful.

riflard [riflar] nm *Fam* brolly, umbrella.

rigide [riʒid] a rigid; (*carton, muscle*) stiff; (*personne*) *Fig* inflexible; (*éducation*) strict. ◆**rigidité** nf rigidity; stiffness; inflexibility; strictness.

rigole [rigɔl] nf (*conduit*) channel; (*filet d'eau*) rivulet.

rigoler [rigɔle] vi *Fam* to laugh; (*s'amuser*) to have fun ou a laugh; (*plaisanter*) to joke (avec about). ◆**rigolade** nf *Fam* fun; (*chose ridicule*) joke, farce; **prendre qch à la r.** to make a joke out of sth. ◆**rigolo, -ote** a *Fam* funny; – nmf *Fam* joker.

rigueur [rigœr] nf rigour; harshness; strictness; (*précision*) precision; **être de r.** to be the rule; **à la r.** if absolutely necessary, at ou *Am* in a pinch; **tenir r. à qn de qch** *Fig* to hold sth against s.o. ◆**rigoureux, -euse** a rigorous; (*climat, punition*) harsh; (*personne, morale, sens*) strict.

rillettes [rijet] nfpl potted minced pork.

rime [rim] nf rhyme. ◆**rimer** vi to rhyme (avec with); **ça ne rime à rien** it makes no sense.

rincer [rɛ̃se] vt to rinse (out). ◆**rinçage** nm rinsing; (*opération*) rinse.

ring [riŋ] nm (boxing) ring.

ringard [rɛ̃gar] a (*démodé*) *Fam* unfashionable, fuddy-duddy.

ripaille [ripaj] nf *Fam* feast.

riposte [ripɔst] nf (*réponse*) retort; (*attaque*) counter(attack). ◆**riposter** vi to retort; **r. à** (*attaque*) to counter; (*insulte*) to reply to; – vt **r. que** to retort that.

rire* [rir] vi to laugh (de at); (*s'amuser*) to have a good time; (*plaisanter*) to joke; **faire qch pour r.** to do sth for a laugh ou a joke; **se r. de qch** to laugh sth off; – nm laugh; pl laughter; **le r.** (*activité*) laughter. ◆**risée** nf mockery; **être la r. de** to be the laughing stock of. ◆**risible** a laughable.

ris [ri] nm **r. de veau** *Culin* (calf) sweetbread.

risque [risk] *nm* risk; **r. du métier** occupational hazard; **au r. de qch/de faire** at the risk of sth/of doing; **à vos risques et périls** at your own risk; **assurance tous risques** comprehensive insurance. ◆**risquer** *vt* to risk; (*question, regard*) to venture, hazard; **r. de faire** to stand a good chance of doing; **se r. à faire** to dare to do; **se r. dans** to venture into. ◆**risqué** *a* risky; (*plaisanterie*) daring, risqué.

ristourne [risturn] *nf* discount.

rite [rit] *nm* rite; (*habitude*) *Fig* ritual. ◆**rituel, -elle** *a & nm* ritual.

rivage [rivaʒ] *nm* shore.

rival, -ale, -aux [rival, -o] *a & nmf* rival. ◆**rivaliser** *vi* to compete (**avec** with, **de** in). ◆**rivalité** *nf* rivalry.

rive [riv] *nf* (*de fleuve*) bank; (*de lac*) shore.

rivé [rive] *a* **r. à** (*chaise etc*) *Fig* riveted to; **r. sur** *Fig* riveted on. ◆**rivet** *nm* (*tige*) rivet. ◆**riveter** *vt* to rivet (together).

riverain, -aine [rivrɛ̃, -ɛn] *a* riverside; lakeside; – *nmf* riverside resident; (*de lac*) lakeside resident; (*de rue*) resident.

rivière [rivjɛr] *nf* river.

rixe [riks] *nf* brawl, scuffle.

riz [ri] *nm* rice; **r. au lait** rice pudding. ◆**rizière** *nf* paddy (field), ricefield.

RN *abrév* = route nationale.

robe [rɔb] *nf* (*de femme*) dress; (*d'ecclésiastique, de juge*) robe; (*de professeur*) gown; (*pelage*) coat; **r. de soirée** *ou* **du soir** evening dress *ou* gown; **r. de grossesse/de mariée** maternity/wedding dress; **r. de chambre** dressing gown; **r. chasuble** pinafore (dress).

robinet [rɔbinɛ] *nm* tap, *Am* faucet; **eau du r.** tap water.

robot [rɔbo] *nm* robot; **r. ménager** food processor, liquidizer.

robuste [rɔbyst] *a* robust. ◆**robustesse** *nf* robustness.

roc [rɔk] *nm* rock.

rocaille [rɔkaj] *nf* (*terrain*) rocky ground; (*de jardin*) rockery. ◆**rocailleux, -euse** *a* rocky, stony; (*voix*) harsh.

rocambolesque [rɔkɑ̃bɔlɛsk] *a* (*aventure etc*) fantastic.

roche [rɔʃ] *nf*, rocher [rɔʃe] *nm* (*bloc, substance*) rock. ◆**rocheux, -euse** *a* rocky.

rock [rɔk] *nm* (*musique*) rock; – *a inv* (*chanteur etc*) rock.

rod/er [rɔde] *vt* (*moteur, voiture*) to run in, *Am* break in; **être rodé** (*personne*) *Fig* to have got *ou Am* gotten the hang of things. ◆—**age** *nm* running in, *Am* breaking in.

rôd/er [rɔde] *vi* to roam (about); (*suspect*) to prowl (about). ◆—**eur, -euse** *nmf* prowler.

rogne [rɔɲ] *nf Fam* anger; **en r.** in a temper.

rogner [rɔɲe] *vt* to trim, clip; (*réduire*) to cut; – *vi* **r. sur** (*réduire*) to cut down on. ◆**rognures** *nfpl* clippings, trimmings.

rognon [rɔɲɔ̃] *nm Culin* kidney.

roi [rwa] *nm* king; **fête** *ou* **jour des rois** Twelfth Night.

roitelet [rwatlɛ] *nm* (*oiseau*) wren.

rôle [rol] *nm* role, part; **à tour de r.** in turn.

romain, -aine [rɔmɛ̃, -ɛn] **1** *a & nmf* Roman. **2** *nf* (*laitue*) cos (lettuce), *Am* romaine.

roman [rɔmɑ̃] **1** *nm* novel; (*histoire*) *Fig* story; **r.-fleuve** saga. **2** *a* (*langue*) Romance; *Archit* Romanesque. ◆**romancé** *a* (*histoire*) fictional. ◆**romancier, -ière** *nmf* novelist.

romanesque [rɔmanɛsk] *a* romantic; (*incroyable*) fantastic.

romanichel, -elle [rɔmaniʃɛl] *nmf* gipsy.

romantique [rɔmɑ̃tik] *a* romantic. ◆**romantisme** *nm* romanticism.

romarin [rɔmarɛ̃] *nm Bot Culin* rosemary.

romp/re* [rɔ̃pr] *vt* to break; (*pourparlers, relations*) to break off; (*digue*) to burst; – *vi* to break (*Fig* **avec** with); to burst; (*fiancés*) to break it off; – **se r.** *vpr* to break; to burst. ◆—**u** *a* **1** (*fatigué*) exhausted. **2 r. à** (*expérimenté*) experienced in.

romsteck [rɔmstɛk] *nm* rump steak.

ronces [rɔ̃s] *nfpl* (*branches*) brambles.

ronchonner [rɔ̃ʃɔne] *vi Fam* to grouse, grumble.

rond [rɔ̃] *a* round; (*gras*) plump; (*honnête*) straight; (*ivre*) *Fam* tight; **dix francs tout r.** ten francs exactly; – *adv* **tourner r.** (*machine etc*) to run smoothly; – *nm* (*objet*) ring; (*cercle*) circle; (*tranche*) slice; *pl* (*argent*) *Fam* money; **r. de serviette** napkin ring; **en r.** (*s'asseoir etc*) in a ring *ou* circle; **tourner en r.** (*toupie etc*) & *Fig* to go round and round. ◆**r.-de-cuir** *nm* (*pl ronds-de-cuir*) *Péj* pen pusher. ◆**r.-point** *nm* (*pl ronds-points*) *Aut* roundabout, *Am* traffic circle. ◆**ronde** *nf* (*tour de surveillance*) round; (*de policier*) beat; (*danse*) round (dance); (*note*) *Mus* semibreve, *Am* whole note; **à la r.** around; (*boire*) in turn. ◆**rondelet, -ette** *a* chubby; (*somme*) *Fig* tidy. ◆**rondelle** *nf* (*tranche*) slice; *Tech* washer. ◆**rondement** *adv* (*efficacement*) briskly; (*franchement*) straight. ◆**rondeur** *nf* roundness; (*du corps*) plumpness. ◆**rondin** *nm* log.

ronéotyper [rɔneɔtipe] *vt* to duplicate, roneo.

ronflant [rɔ̃flɑ̃] *a* (*langage etc*) *Péj* high-flown; (*feu*) roaring.

ronfler [rɔ̃fle] *vi* to snore; (*moteur*) to hum. ◆**ronflement** *nm* snore, snoring; hum(ming).

rong/er [rɔ̃ʒe] *vt* to gnaw (at); (*ver, mer, rouille*) to eat into (*sth*); **r. qn** (*chagrin, maladie*) to consume s.o.; **se r. les ongles** to bite one's nails; **se r. les sangs** (*s'inquiéter*) to worry oneself sick. ◆**—eur** *nm* (*animal*) rodent.

ronron [rɔ̃rɔ̃] *nm*, **ronronnement** [rɔ̃rɔnmɑ̃] *nm* purr(ing). ◆**ronronner** *vi* to purr.

roquette [rɔkɛt] *nf Mil* rocket.

rosbif [rɔsbif] *nm* **du r.** (*rôti*) roast beef; (*à rôtir*) roasting beef; **un r.** a joint of roast *ou* roasting beef.

rose [roz] **1** *nf* (*fleur*) rose. **2** *a* (*couleur*) pink; (*situation, teint*) rosy; – *nm* pink. ◆**rosé** *a* pinkish; & – *a* & *nm* (*vin*) rosé. ◆**rosette** *nf* (*d'un officier*) rosette; (*nœud*) bow. ◆**rosier** *nm* rose bush.

roseau, -x [rozo] *nm* (*plante*) reed.

rosée [roze] *nf* dew.

rosse [rɔs] *a* & *nf Fam* nasty (person).

ross/er [rɔse] *vt Fam* to thrash. ◆**—ée** *nf Fam* thrashing.

rossignol [rɔsiɲɔl] *nm* **1** (*oiseau*) nightingale. **2** (*crochet*) picklock.

rot [ro] *nm Fam* burp, belch. ◆**roter** *vi Fam* to burp, belch.

rotation [rɔtasjɔ̃] *nf* rotation; (*de stock*) turnover. ◆**rotatif, -ive** *a* rotary; – *nf* rotary press.

rotin [rɔtɛ̃] *nm* rattan, cane.

rôt/ir [rotir] *vti*, – **se r.** *vpr* to roast; **faire r.** to roast. ◆**—i** *nm* **du r.** roasting meat; (*cuit*) roast meat; **un r.** a joint; **r. de bœuf/de porc** (joint of) roast beef/pork. ◆**rôtissoire** *nf* (roasting) spit.

rotule [rɔtyl] *nf* kneecap.

roturier, -ière [rɔtyrje, -jɛr] *nmf* commoner.

rouage [rwaʒ] *nm* (*de montre etc*) (working) part; (*d'organisation etc*) Fig cog.

roublard [rublar] *a* wily, foxy.

rouble [rubl] *nm* (*monnaie*) r(o)uble.

roucouler [rukule] *vi* (*oiseau, amoureux*) to coo.

roue [ru] *nf* wheel; **r. (dentée)** cog(wheel); **faire la r.** (*paon*) to spread its tail; (*se pavaner*) *Fig* to strut; **faire r. libre** *Aut* to freewheel.

roué, -ée [rwe] *a* & *nmf* sly *ou* calculating (person).

rouer [rwe] *vt* **r. qn de coups** to beat s.o. black and blue.

rouet [rwɛ] *nm* spinning wheel.

rouge [ruʒ] *a* red; (*fer*) red-hot; – *nm* (*couleur*) red; (*vin*) *Fam* red wine; **r. (à lèvres)** lipstick; **r. (à joues)** rouge; **le feu est au r.** *Aut* the (traffic) lights are red; – *nmf* (*personne*) *Pol* Red. ◆**r.-gorge** *nm* (*pl* **rouges-gorges**) robin. ◆**rougeâtre** *a* reddish. ◆**rougeaud** *a* red-faced. ◆**rougeoyer** *vi* to glow (red). ◆**rougeur** *nf* redness; (*due à la gêne ou à la honte*) blush(ing); *pl Méd* red spots *ou* blotches. ◆**rougir** *vti* to redden, turn red; – *vi* (*de gêne, de honte*) to blush (**de** with); (*de colère, de joie*) to flush (**de** with).

rougeole [ruʒɔl] *nf* measles.

rouget [ruʒɛ] *nm* (*poisson*) mullet.

rouille [ruj] *nf* rust; – *a inv* (*couleur*) rust(-coloured). ◆**rouill/er** *vi* to rust; – **se r.** *vpr* to rust; (*esprit, sportif etc*) *Fig* to get rusty. ◆**—é** *a* rusty.

roul/er [rule] *vt* to roll; (*brouette, meuble*) to wheel, push; (*crêpe, ficelle, manches etc*) to roll up; **r. qn** (*duper*) *Fam* to cheat s.o.; – *vi* to roll; (*train, voiture*) to go, travel; (*conducteur*) to drive; **r. sur** (*conversation*) to turn on; **ça roule!** *Fam* everything's fine!; – **se r.** *vpr* to roll; **se r. dans** (*couverture etc*) to roll oneself (up) in. ◆**—ant** *a* (*escalier, trottoir*) moving; (*meuble*) on wheels. ◆**—é** *nm* (*gâteau*) Swiss roll. ◆**rouleau, -x** *nm* (*outil, vague*) roller; (*de papier, pellicule etc*) roll; **r. à pâtisserie** rolling pin; **r. compresseur** steamroller. ◆**roulement** *nm* (*bruit*) rumbling, rumble; (*de tambour, de tonnerre, d'yeux*) roll; (*ordre*) rotation; **par r.** in rotation; **r. à billes** *Tech* ball bearing. ◆**roulette** *nf* (*de meuble*) castor; (*de dentiste*) drill; (*jeu*) roulette. ◆**roulis** *nm* (*de navire*) roll(ing).

roulotte [rulɔt] *nf* (*de gitan*) caravan.

Roumanie [rumani] *nf* Romania. ◆**roumain, -aine** *a* & *nmf* Romanian; – *nm* (*langue*) Romanian.

round [rawnd, rund] *nm Boxe* round.

roupiller [rupije] *vi Fam* to kip, sleep.

rouquin, -ine [rukɛ̃, -in] *a Fam* red-haired; – *nmf Fam* redhead.

rouspét/er [ruspete] *vi Fam* to grumble, complain. ◆**—eur, -euse** *nmf* grumbler.

rousse [rus] *voir* **roux.**

rousseur [rusœr] *nf* redness; **tache de r.** freckle. ◆**roussir** *vt* (*brûler*) to singe, scorch; – *vi* (*feuilles*) to turn brown; **faire r.** *Culin* to brown.

route [rut] *nf* road (**de** to); (*itinéraire*) way,

route; (*aérienne*, *maritime*) route; (*chemin*) *Fig* path, way; **r. nationale/départementale** main/secondary road; **grande r., grand-r.** main road; **code de la r.** Highway Code; **en r.** on the way, en route; **en r.!** let's go!; **par la r.** by road; **sur la bonne r.** *Fig* on the right track; **mettre en r.** (*voiture etc*) to start (up); **se mettre en r.** to set out (**pour** for); **une heure de r.** *Aut* an hour's drive; **bonne r.!** *Aut* have a good trip! ◆**routier, -ière** *a* (*carte etc*) road-; – *nm* (*camionneur*) (long distance) lorry *ou Am* truck driver; (*restaurant*) transport café, *Am* truck stop.

routine [rutin] *nf* routine; **de r.** (*contrôle etc*) routine-. ◆**routinier, -ière** *a* (*travail etc*) routine-; (*personne*) addicted to routine.

rouvrir* [ruvrir] *vti*, – **se r.** *vpr* to reopen.

roux, rousse [ru, rus] *a* (*cheveux*) red, ginger; (*personne*) red-haired; – *nmf* redhead.

royal, -aux [rwajal, -o] *a* royal; (*cadeau, festin etc*) fit for a king; (*salaire*) princely. ◆**royalement** *adv* (*traiter*) royally. ◆**royaliste** *a & nmf* royalist. ◆**royaume** *nm* kingdom. ◆**Royaume-Uni** *nm* United Kingdom. ◆**royauté** *nf* (*monarchie*) monarchy.

ruade [rɥad] *nf* (*d'âne etc*) kick.

ruban [rybã] *nm* ribbon; (*d'acier, de chapeau*) band; **r. adhésif** adhesive *ou* sticky tape.

rubéole [rybeɔl] *nf* German measles, rubella.

rubis [rybi] *nm* (*pierre*) ruby; (*de montre*) jewel.

rubrique [rybrik] *nf* (*article*) *Journ* column; (*catégorie, titre*) heading.

ruche [ryʃ] *nf* (bee)hive.

rude [ryd] *a* (*grossier*) crude; (*rêche*) rough; (*pénible*) tough; (*hiver, voix*) harsh; (*remarquable*) *Fam* tremendous. ◆**—ment** *adv* (*parler, traiter*) harshly; (*frapper, pousser*) hard; (*très*) *Fam* awfully. ◆**rudesse** *nf* harshness. ◆**rudoyer** *vt* to treat harshly.

rudiments [rydimã] *nmpl* rudiments. ◆**rudimentaire** *a* rudimentary.

rue [ry] *nf* street; **être à la r.** (*sans domicile*) to be on the streets. ◆**ruelle** *nf* alley(way).

ruer [rɥe] **1** *vi* (*cheval*) to kick (out). **2 se r.** *vpr* (*foncer*) to rush, fling oneself (**sur** at). ◆**ruée** *nf* rush.

rugby [rygbi] *nm* rugby. ◆**rugbyman,** *pl* **-men** [rygbiman, -mɛn] *nm* rugby player.

rug/ir [ryʒir] *vi* to roar. ◆**—issement** *nm* roar.

rugueux, -euse [rygø, -øz] *a* rough. ◆**rugosité** *nf* roughness; *pl* (*aspérités*) roughness.

ruine [rɥin] *nf* (*décombres*) & *Fig* ruin; **en r.** (*édifice*) in ruins; **tomber en r.** to fall into ruin. ◆**ruiner** *vt* to ruin; – **se r.** *vpr* (*en dépensant*) to ruin oneself. ◆**ruineux, -euse** *a* (*goûts, projet*) ruinously expensive; (*dépense*) ruinous.

ruisseau, -x [rɥiso] *nm* stream; (*caniveau*) gutter. ◆**ruisseler** *vi* to stream (**de** with).

rumeur [rymœr] *nf* (*protestation*) clamour; (*murmure*) murmur; (*nouvelle*) rumour.

ruminer [rymine] *vt* (*méditer*) to ponder on, ruminate over.

rumsteak [rɔmstɛk] *nm* rump steak.

rupture [ryptyr] *nf* break(ing); (*de fiançailles, relations*) breaking off; (*de pourparlers*) breakdown (**de** in); (*brouille*) break (up), split; (*de contrat*) breach; (*d'organe*) *Méd* rupture.

rural, -aux [ryral, -o] *a* rural, country-; – *nmpl* country people.

ruse [ryz] *nf* (*subterfuge*) trick; **la r.** (*habileté*) cunning; (*fourberie*) trickery. ◆**rusé, -ée** *a & nmf* crafty *ou* cunning (person). ◆**ruser** *vi* to resort to trickery.

Russie [rysi] *nf* Russia. ◆**russe** *a & nmf* Russian; – *nm* (*langue*) Russian.

rustique [rystik] *a* (*meuble*) rustic.

rustre [rystr] *nm* lout, churl.

rutabaga [rytabaga] *nm* (*racine*) swede, *Am* rutabaga.

rutilant [rytilã] *a* gleaming, glittering.

rythme [ritm] *nm* rhythm; (*de travail*) rate, tempo; (*de la vie*) pace; **au r. de trois par jour** at a *ou* the rate of three a day. ◆**rythmé** *a,* ◆**rythmique** *a* rhythmic(al).

S

S, s [ɛs] *nm* S, s.
s' [s] *voir* se, si.
sa [sa] *voir* son².

SA *abrév* (*société anonyme*) *Com* plc, *Am* Inc.
sabbat [saba] *nm* (Jewish) Sabbath.

◆**sabbatique** a (*année etc*) *Univ* sabbatical.

sable [sɑbl] nm sand; **sables mouvants** quicksand(s). ◆**sabler** vt (*route*) to sand. ◆**sableux, -euse** a (*eau*) sandy. ◆**sablier** nm hourglass; *Culin* egg timer. ◆**sablière** nf (*carrière*) sandpit. ◆**sablonneux, -euse** a (*terrain*) sandy.

sablé [sɑble] nm shortbread biscuit *ou Am* cookie.

saborder [sabɔrde] vt (*navire*) to scuttle; (*entreprise*) *Fig* to shut down.

sabot [sabo] nm 1 (*de cheval etc*) hoof. 2 (*chaussure*) clog. 3 (*de frein*) *Aut* shoe; **s. (de Denver)** *Aut* (wheel) clamp.

sabot/er [sabɔte] vt to sabotage; (*bâcler*) to botch. ◆**—age** nm sabotage; **un s.** an act of sabotage. ◆**—eur, -euse** nmf saboteur.

sabre [sɑbr] nm sabre, sword.

sabrer [sɑbre] vt (*élève, candidat*) *Fam* to give a thoroughly bad mark to.

sac [sak] nm 1 bag; (*grand et en toile*) sack; **s. (à main)** handbag; **s. à dos** rucksack. 2 **mettre à s.** (*ville*) *Mil* to sack.

saccade [sakad] nf jerk, jolt; **par saccades** jerkily, in fits and starts. ◆**saccadé** a (*geste, style*) jerky.

saccager [sakaʒe] vt (*ville, région*) *Mil* to sack; (*bouleverser*) *Fig* to turn upside down.

saccharine [sakarin] nf saccharin.

sacerdoce [saserdɔs] nm (*fonction*) *Rel* priesthood; *Fig* vocation.

sachet [saʃɛ] nm (small) bag; (*de lavande etc*) sachet; **s. de thé** teabag.

sacoche [sakɔʃ] nf bag; (*de vélo, moto*) saddlebag; *Scol* satchel.

sacquer [sake] vt *Fam* (*renvoyer*) to sack; (*élève*) to give a thoroughly bad mark to.

sacre [sakr] nm (*d'évêque*) consecration; (*de roi*) coronation. ◆**sacrer** vt (*évêque*) to consecrate; (*roi*) to crown.

sacré [sakre] a (*saint*) sacred; (*maudit*) *Fam* damned. ◆**—ment** adv *Fam* (*très*) damn(ed); (*beaucoup*) a hell of a lot.

sacrement [sakrəmã] nm *Rel* sacrament.

sacrifice [sakrifis] nm sacrifice. ◆**sacrifier** vt to sacrifice (à to, pour for); – vi **s. à** (*mode etc*) to pander to; – **se s.** vpr to sacrifice oneself (à to, pour for).

sacrilège [sakrilɛʒ] nm sacrilege; – a sacrilegious.

sacristie [sakristi] nf vestry.

sacro-saint [sakrosɛ̃] a *Iron* sacrosanct.

sadisme [sadism] nm sadism. ◆**sadique** a sadistic; – nmf sadist.

safari [safari] nm safari; **faire un s.** to be *ou* go on safari.

safran [safrã] nm saffron.

sagace [sagas] a shrewd, sagacious.

sage [saʒ] a wise; (*enfant*) well-behaved, good; (*modéré*) moderate; – nm wise man, sage. ◆**sagement** adv wisely; (*avec calme*) quietly. ◆**sagesse** nf wisdom; good behaviour; moderation.

sage-femme [saʒfam] nf (*pl* sages-femmes) midwife.

Sagittaire [saʒiter] nm **le S.** (*signe*) Sagittarius.

Sahara [saara] nm **le S.** the Sahara (desert).

saign/er [seɲe] vti to bleed. ◆**—ant** a (*viande*) *Culin* rare, underdone. ◆**—ée** nf 1 *Méd* bleeding, blood-letting; (*perte*) *Fig* heavy loss. 2 **la s. du bras** *Anat* the bend of the arm. ◆**saignement** nm bleeding; **s. de nez** nosebleed.

saillant [sajã] a projecting, jutting out; (*trait etc*) *Fig* salient. ◆**saillie** nf projection; **en s., faisant s.** projecting.

sain [sɛ̃] a healthy; (*moralement*) sane; (*jugement*) sound; (*nourriture*) wholesome, healthy; **s. et sauf** safe and sound, unhurt. ◆**sainement** adv (*vivre*) healthily; (*raisonner*) sanely.

saindoux [sɛ̃du] nm lard.

saint, sainte [sɛ̃, sɛ̃t] a holy; (*personne*) saintly; **s. Jean** Saint John; **sainte nitouche** *Iron* little innocent; **la Sainte Vierge** the Blessed Virgin; – nmf saint. ◆**S.-bernard** nm (*chien*) St Bernard. ◆**S.-Esprit** nm Holy Spirit. ◆**S.-Siège** nm Holy See. ◆**S.-Sylvestre** nf New Year's Eve.

sais [sɛ] voir **savoir.**

saisie [sezi] nf *Jur* seizure; **s. de données** data capture *ou* entry.

sais/ir [sezir] 1 vt to grab (hold of), seize; (*occasion*) & *Jur* to seize; (*comprendre*) to understand, grasp; (*frapper*) *Fig* to strike; **se s. de** to grab (hold of), seize. 2 vt (*viande*) *Culin* to fry briskly. ◆**—i a s. de** (*joie, peur etc*) overcome by. ◆**—issant** a (*film etc*) gripping; (*contraste, ressemblance*) striking. ◆**—issement** nm (*émotion*) shock.

saison [sezõ] nf season; **en/hors s.** in/out of season; **en pleine** *ou* **haute s.** in (the) high season; **en basse s.** in the low season. ◆**saisonnier, -ière** a seasonal.

salt [sɛ] voir **savoir.**

salade [salad] nf 1 (*laitue*) lettuce; **s. (verte)** (green) salad; **s. de fruits/de tomates/etc** fruit/tomato/etc salad. 2 nf (*désordre*) *Fam* mess. 3 nfpl (*mensonges*) *Fam* stories, nonsense. ◆**saladier** nm salad bowl.

salaire [salɛr] *nm* wage(s), salary.

salaison [salɛzɔ̃] *nf Culin* salting; *pl* (*denrées*) salt(ed) meat *ou* fish.

salamandre [salamɑ̃dr] *nf* (*animal*) salamander.

salami [salami] *nm Culin* salami.

salarial, -aux [salarjal, -o] *a* (*accord etc*) wage-. **◆salarié, -ée** *a* wage-earning; — *nmf* wage earner.

salaud [salo] *nm Arg Péj* bastard, swine.

sale [sal] *a* dirty; (*dégoûtant*) filthy; (*mauvais*) nasty; (*couleur*) dingy. **◆salement** *adv* (*se conduire, manger*) disgustingly. **◆saleté** *nf* dirtiness; filthiness; (*crasse*) dirt, filth; (*action*) dirty trick; (*camelote*) *Fam* rubbish, junk; *pl* (*détritus*) mess, dirt; (*obscénités*) filth. **◆salir** *vt* to (make) dirty; (*réputation*) *Fig* to sully, tarnish; — **se s.** *vpr* to get dirty. **◆salissant** *a* (*métier*) dirty, messy; (*étoffe*) easily dirtied. **◆salissure** *nf* (*tache*) dirty mark.

sal/er [sale] *vt Culin* to salt. **◆—é** *a* **1** (*eau*) salt-; (*saveur*) salty; (*denrées*) salted; (*grivois*) *Fig* spicy. **2** (*excessif*) *Fam* steep. **◆salière** *nf* saltcellar.

salive [saliv] *nf* saliva. **◆saliver** *vi* to salivate.

salle [sal] *nf* room; (*très grande, publique*) hall; *Th* auditorium; (*d'hôpital*) ward; (*public*) *Th* house, audience; **s. à manger** dining room; **s. d'eau** washroom, shower room; **s. d'exposition** *Com* showroom; **s. de jeux** (*pour enfants*) games room; (*avec machines à sous*) amusement arcade; **s. d'opération** *Méd* operating theatre.

salon [salɔ̃] *nm* sitting room, lounge; (*exposition*) show; **s. de beauté/de coiffure** beauty/hairdressing salon; **s. de thé** tearoom(s).

salope [salɔp] *nf* (*femme*) *Arg Péj* bitch, cow. **◆saloperie** *nf Arg* (*action*) dirty trick; (*camelote*) rubbish, junk; **des saloperies** (*propos*) filth.

salopette [salɔpɛt] *nf* dungarees; (*d'ouvrier*) overalls.

salsifis [salsifi] *nf Bot Culin* salsify.

saltimbanque [saltɛ̃bɑ̃k] *nmf* (*travelling*) acrobat.

salubre [salybr] *a* healthy, salubrious. **◆salubrité** *nf* healthiness; **s. publique** public health.

saluer [salɥe] *vt* to greet; (*en partant*) to take one's leave; (*de la main*) to wave to; (*de la tête*) to nod to; *Mil* to salute; **s. qn comme** *Fig* to hail s.o. as. **◆salut 1** *nm* greeting; wave; nod; *Mil* salute; — *int Fam* hello!, hi!; (*au revoir*) bye! **2** *nm* (*de peuple etc*) salvation; (*sauvegarde*) safety. **◆salutation** *nf* greeting.

salutaire [salytɛr] *a* salutary.

salve [salv] *nf* salvo.

samedi [samdi] *nm* Saturday.

SAMU [samy] *nm abrév* (*service d'assistance médicale d'urgence*) emergency medical service.

sanatorium [sanatɔrjɔm] *nm* sanatorium.

sanctifier [sɑ̃ktifje] *vt* to sanctify.

sanction [sɑ̃ksjɔ̃] *nf* (*approbation, peine*) sanction. **◆sanctionner** *vt* (*confirmer, approuver*) to sanction; (*punir*) to punish.

sanctuaire [sɑ̃ktɥɛr] *nm Rel* sanctuary.

sandale [sɑ̃dal] *nf* sandal.

sandwich [sɑ̃dwitʃ] *nm* sandwich.

sang [sɑ̃] *nm* blood; **coup de s.** *Méd* stroke. **◆sanglant** *a* bloody; (*critique, reproche*) scathing. **◆sanguin, -ine 1** *a* (*vaisseau etc*) blood-; (*tempérament*) full-blooded. **2** *nf* (*fruit*) blood orange. **◆sanguinaire** *a* blood-thirsty.

sang-froid [sɑ̃frwa] *nm* self-control, calm; **avec s.-froid** calmly; **de s.-froid** (*tuer*) in cold blood.

sangle [sɑ̃gl] *nf* (*de selle, parachute*) strap.

sanglier [sɑ̃glije] *nm* wild boar.

sanglot [sɑ̃glo] *nm* sob. **◆sangloter** *vi* to sob.

sangsue [sɑ̃sy] *nf* leech.

sanitaire [sanitɛr] *a* health-; (*conditions*) sanitary; (*personnel*) medical; (*appareils etc*) bathroom-, sanitary.

sans [sɑ̃] ([sɑ̃z] *before vowel and mute h*) *prép* without; **s. faire** without doing; **ça va s. dire** that goes without saying; **s. qu'il le sache** without him *ou* his knowing; **s. cela, s. quoi** otherwise; **s. plus** (*but*) no more than that; **s. exception/faute** without exception/fail; **s. importance/travail** unimportant/unemployed; **s. argent/manches** penniless/sleeveless. **◆s.-abri** *nmf inv* homeless person; **les s.-abri** the homeless. **◆s.-gêne** *a inv* inconsiderate; — *nm inv* inconsiderateness. **◆s.-travail** *nmf inv* unemployed person.

santé [sɑ̃te] *nf* health; **en bonne/mauvaise s.** in good/bad health, well/not well; **(à votre) s.!** (*en trinquant*) your health!, cheers!; **maison de s.** nursing home.

saoul [su] = **soûl**.

saper [sape] *vt* to undermine.

sapeur-pompier [sapœrpɔ̃pje] *nm* (*pl* sapeurs-pompiers) fireman.

saphir [safir] *nm* (*pierre*) sapphire; (*d'électrophone*) sapphire, stylus.

sapin [sapɛ̃] nm (*arbre, bois*) fir; **s. de Noël** Christmas tree.

sarbacane [sarbakan] nf (*jouet*) pea-shooter.

sarcasme [sarkasm] nm sarcasm; **un s. a** piece of sarcasm. ◆**sarcastique** a sarcastic.

sarcler [sarkle] vt (*jardin etc*) to weed.

Sardaigne [sardɛɲ] nf Sardinia.

sardine [sardin] nf sardine.

sardonique [sardɔnik] a sardonic.

SARL abrév (*société à responsabilité limitée*) Ltd, *Am* Inc.

sarment [sarmɑ̃] nm vine shoot.

sarrasin [sarazɛ̃] nm buckwheat.

sas [sɑ(s)] nm (*pièce étanche*) Nau Av air-lock.

Satan [satɑ̃] nm Satan. ◆**satané** a (*maudit*) blasted. ◆**satanique** a satanic.

satellite [satelit] nm satellite; **pays s.** Pol satellite (country).

satiété [sasjete] nf à s. (*boire, manger*) one's fill; (*répéter*) ad nauseam.

satin [satɛ̃] nm satin. ◆**satiné** a satiny, silky.

satire [satir] nf satire (**contre** on). ◆**satirique** a satiric(al).

satisfaction [satisfaksjɔ̃] nf satisfaction. ◆**satisfaire*** vt to satisfy; – vi s. à (*conditions, engagement etc*) to fulfil. ◆**satisfaisant** a (*acceptable*) satisfactory. ◆**satisfait** a satisfied, content (**de** with).

saturateur [satyratœr] nm (*de radiateur*) humidifier.

saturer [satyre] vt to saturate (**de** with).

satyre [satir] nm Fam sex fiend.

sauce [sos] nf sauce; (*jus de viande*) gravy; **s. tomate** tomato sauce. ◆**saucière** nf sauce boat; gravy boat.

saucisse [sosis] nf sausage. ◆**saucisson** nm (cold) sausage.

sauf¹ [sof] prép except (**que** that); **s. avis contraire** unless you hear otherwise; **s. erreur** barring error.

sauf², **sauve** [sof, sov] a (*honneur*) intact, saved; **avoir la vie sauve** to be unharmed. ◆**sauf-conduit** nm (*document*) safe-conduct.

sauge [soʒ] nf Bot Culin sage.

saugrenu [sogrəny] a preposterous.

saule [sol] nm willow; **s. pleureur** weeping willow.

saumâtre [somɑtr] a (*eau*) briny, brackish.

saumon [somɔ̃] nm salmon; – a inv (*couleur*) salmon (pink).

saumure [somyr] nf (pickling) brine.

sauna [sona] nm sauna.

saupoudrer [sopudre] vt (*couvrir*) to sprinkle (**de** with).

saur [sɔr] am hareng s. smoked herring, kipper.

saut [so] nm jump, leap; **faire un s.** to jump, leap; **faire un s. chez qn** (*visite*) to pop round to s.o.; **au s. du lit** on getting out of bed; **s. à la corde** skipping, *Am* jumping rope. ◆**sauter** vi to jump, leap; (*bombe*) to go off, explode; (*poudrière etc*) to go up, blow up; (*fusible*) to blow; (*se détacher*) to come off; **faire s.** (*détruire*) to blow up; (*arracher*) to tear off; (*casser*) to break; (*renvoyer*) Fam to get rid of, fire; (*fusible*) to blow; Culin to sauté; **s. à la corde** to skip, *Am* jump rope; **ça saute aux yeux** it's obvious; – vt (*franchir*) to jump (over); (*mot, classe, repas*) to skip. ◆**saute-mouton** nm (*jeu*) leapfrog. ◆**sautiller** vi to hop. ◆**sautoir** nm Sp jumping area.

sauté [sote] a & nm Culin sauté. ◆**sauteuse** nf (shallow) pan.

sauterelle [sotrɛl] nf grasshopper.

sautes [sot] nfpl (*d'humeur, de température*) sudden changes (**de** in).

sauvage [sovaʒ] a wild; (*primitif, cruel*) savage; (*farouche*) unsociable, shy; (*illégal*) unauthorized; – nmf unsociable person; (*brute*) savage. ◆**sauvagerie** nf unsociability; (*cruauté*) savagery.

sauve [sov] a voir sauf².

sauvegarde [sovgard] nf safeguard (**contre** against). ◆**sauvegarder** vt to safeguard.

sauver [sove] 1 vt to save; (*d'un danger*) to rescue (**de** from); (*matériel*) to salvage; **s. la vie à qn** to save s.o.'s life. 2 **se s.** vpr (*s'enfuir*) to run away ou off; (*partir*) Fam to get off, go. ◆**sauve-qui-peut** nm inv stampede. ◆**sauvetage** nm rescue; **canot de s.** lifeboat; **ceinture de s.** life belt; **radeau de s.** life raft. ◆**sauveteur** nm rescuer. ◆**sauveur** nm saviour.

sauvette (à la) [alasovɛt] adv vendre à la s. to hawk illicitly (on the streets).

savant [savɑ̃] a learned, scholarly; (*manœuvre etc*) masterly, clever; – nm scientist. ◆**savamment** adv learnedly; (*avec habileté*) cleverly, skilfully.

savate [savat] nf old shoe ou slipper.

saveur [savœr] nf (*goût*) flavour; (*piment*) Fig savour.

savoir* [savwar] vt to know; (*nouvelle*) to know, have heard; **j'ai su la nouvelle** I heard ou got to know the news; **s. lire/nager/etc** (*pouvoir*) to know how to read/swim/etc; **faire s. à qn que** to inform ou tell s.o. that; **à s.** (*c'est-à-dire*) that is, namely; **je ne saurais pas** I could not, I cannot; **(pas) que je sache** (not) as far as I know; **je n'en sais rien** I have no idea, I don't know; **en s. long sur** to know a lot about; **un je ne sais quoi** a something or other; − *nm* (*culture*) learning, knowledge. ◆**s.-faire** *nm inv* know-how, ability. ◆**s.-vivre** *nm inv* good manners.

savon [savɔ̃] *nm* **1** soap; (*morceau*) bar of soap. **2 passer un s. à qn** (*réprimander*) *Fam* to give s.o. a dressing-down *ou* a talking-to. ◆**savonner** *vt* to soap. ◆**savonnette** *nf* bar of soap. ◆**savonneux, -euse** *a* soapy.

savourer [savure] *vt* to savour, relish. ◆**savoureux, -euse** *a* tasty; (*histoire etc*) *Fig* juicy.

saxophone [saksɔfɔn] *nm* saxophone.

sbire [sbir] *nm* (*homme de main*) *Péj* henchman.

scabreux, -euse [skabrø, -øz] *a* obscene.

scalpel [skalpɛl] *nm* scalpel.

scandale [skɑ̃dal] *nm* scandal; (*tapage*) uproar; **faire s.** (*livre etc*) to scandalize people; **faire un s.** to make a scene. ◆**scandaleux, -euse** *a* scandalous, outrageous. ◆**scandaleusement** *adv* outrageously. ◆**scandaliser** *vt* to scandalize, shock; − **se s.** *vpr* to be shocked *ou* scandalized (**de** by, **que** (+ *sub*) that).

scander [skɑ̃de] *vt* (*vers*) to scan; (*slogan*) to chant.

Scandinavie [skɑ̃dinavi] *nf* Scandinavia. ◆**scandinave** *a & nmf* Scandinavian.

scanner [skanɛr] *nm* (*appareil*) *Méd* scanner.

scaphandre [skafɑ̃dr] *nm* (*de plongeur*) diving suit; (*de cosmonaute*) spacesuit; **s. autonome** aqualung. ◆**scaphandrier** *nm* diver.

scarabée [skarabe] *nm* beetle.

scarlatine [skarlatin] *nf* scarlet fever.

scarole [skarɔl] *nf* endive.

sceau, -x [so] *nm* (*cachet, cire*) seal. ◆**scell/er** *vt* **1** (*document etc*) to seal. **2** (*fixer*) *Tech* to cement. ◆**−és** *nmpl* (*cachets de cire*) seals.

scélérat, -ate [selera, -at] *nmf* scoundrel.

scel-o-frais® [selɔfrɛ] *nm* clingfilm, *Am* plastic wrap.

scénario [senarjo] *nm* (*déroulement*) *Fig* scenario; (*esquisse*) *Cin* scenario; (*dialogues etc*) screenplay. ◆**scénariste** *nmf* *Cin* scriptwriter.

scène [sɛn] *nf* **1** *Th* scene; (*estrade, art*) stage; (*action*) action; **mettre en s.** (*pièce, film*) to direct. **2** (*dispute*) scene; **faire une s.** (**à qn**) to make *ou* create a scene; **s. de ménage** domestic quarrel.

scepticisme [sɛptisism] *nm* scepticism, *Am* skepticism. ◆**sceptique** *a* sceptical, *Am* skeptical; − *nmf* sceptic, *Am* skeptic.

scheik [ʃɛk] *nm* sheikh.

schéma [ʃema] *nm* diagram; *Fig* outline. ◆**schématique** *a* diagrammatic; (*succinct*) *Péj* sketchy. ◆**schématiser** *vt* to represent diagrammatically; (*simplifier*) *Péj* to oversimplify.

schizophrène [skizɔfrɛn] *a & nmf* schizophrenic.

sciatique [sjatik] *nf* *Méd* sciatica.

scie [si] *nf* (*outil*) saw. ◆**scier** *vt* to saw. ◆**scierie** *nf* sawmill.

sciemment [sjamɑ̃] *adv* knowingly.

science [sjɑ̃s] *nf* science; (*savoir*) knowledge; (*habileté*) skill; **sciences humaines** social science(s); **étudier les sciences** to study science. ◆**s.-fiction** *nf* science fiction. ◆**scientifique** *a* scientific; − *nmf* scientist.

scinder [sɛ̃de] *vt*, − **se s.** *vpr* to divide, split.

scintill/er [sɛ̃tije] *vi* to sparkle, glitter; (*étoiles*) to twinkle. ◆**−ement** *nm* sparkling; twinkling.

scission [sisjɔ̃] *nf* (*de parti etc*) split (**de** in).

sciure [sjyr] *nf* sawdust.

sclérose [skleroz] *nf* *Méd* sclerosis; *Fig* ossification; **s. en plaques** multiple sclerosis. ◆**sclérosé** *a* (*société etc*) *Fig* ossified.

scolaire [skɔlɛr] *a* school-. ◆**scolariser** *vt* (*pays*) to provide with schools; (*enfant*) to send to school, put in school. ◆**scolarité** *nf* schooling.

scooter [skuter] *nm* (motor) scooter.

score [skɔr] *nm Sp* score.

scories [skɔri] *nfpl* (*résidu*) slag.

scorpion [skɔrpjɔ̃] *nm* scorpion; **le S.** (*signe*) Scorpio.

scotch [skɔtʃ] *nm* **1** (*boisson*) Scotch, whisky. **2**® (*ruban adhésif*) sellotape®, *Am* scotch (tape)®. ◆**scotcher** *vt* to sellotape, *Am* to tape.

scout [skut] *a & nm* scout. ◆**scoutisme** *nm* scout movement, scouting.

script [skript] *nm* (*écriture*) printing.

scrupule [skrypyl] *nm* scruple; **sans scrupules** unscrupulous; (*agir*) unscrupulously. ◆**scrupuleux, -euse** *a* scrupulous. ◆**scrupuleusement** *adv* scrupulously.

scruter [skryte] *vt* to examine, scrutinize.

scrutin [skrytɛ̃] *nm* (*vote*) ballot; (*opérations électorales*) poll(ing).

sculpter [skylte] *vt* to sculpt(ure), carve.

◆**sculpteur** *nm* sculptor. ◆**sculptural, -aux** *a* (*beauté*) statuesque. ◆**sculpture** *nf* (*art, œuvre*) sculpture; **s. sur bois** wood-carving.

se [s(ǝ)] (**s'** *before vowel or mute h*) *pron* **1** (*complément direct*) himself; (*sujet femelle*) herself; (*non humain*) itself; (*indéfini*) one-self; *pl* themselves; **il se lave** he washes himself. **2** (*indirect*) to himself; to herself; to itself; to oneself; **se dire** to say to one-self; **elle se dit** she says to herself. **3** (*réciproque*) (to) each other, (to) one anoth-er; **ils s'aiment** they love each other *ou* one another; **ils** *ou* **elles se parlent** they speak to each other *ou* one another. **4** (*passif*) **ça se fait** that is done; **ça se vend bien** it sells well. **5** (*possessif*) **il se lave les mains** he washes his hands.

séance [seɑ̃s] *nf* **1** (*d'assemblée etc*) session, sitting; (*de travail etc*) session; **s.** (*de pose*) (*chez un peintre*) sitting. **2** *Cin Th* show, performance. **3 s. tenante** at once.

séant [seɑ̃] **1** *a* (*convenable*) seemly, proper. **2** *nm* **se mettre sur son s.** to sit up.

seau, -x [so] *nm* bucket, pail.

sec, sèche [sɛk, sɛʃ] *a* dry; (*fruits, légumes*) dried; (*ton*) curt, harsh; (*maigre*) spare; (*cœur*) *Fig* hard; **coup s.** sharp blow, tap; **bruit s.** (*rupture*) snap; – *adv* (*frapper, pleuvoir*) hard; (*boire*) neat, *Am* straight; – *nm* **à s.** dried up, dry; (*sans argent*) *Fam* broke; **au s.** in a dry place. ◆**séch/er 1** *vti* to dry; – **se s.** *vpr* to dry oneself. **2** *vt* (*cours*) *Scol Fam* to skip; – *vi* (*ignorer*) *Scol Fam* to be stumped. ◆**—age** *nm* drying. ◆**sécheresse** *nf* dryness; (*de ton*) curt-ness; *Mét* drought. ◆**séchoir** *nm* (*ap-pareil*) drier; **s. à linge** clotheshorse.

sécateur [sekatœr] *nm* pruning shears, se-cateurs.

sécession [sesesjɔ̃] *nf* secession; **faire s.** to secede.

sèche [sɛʃ] *voir* **sec**. ◆**sèche-cheveux** *nm inv* hair drier. ◆**sèche-linge** *nm inv* tum-ble drier.

second, -onde¹ [sgɔ̃, -ɔ̃d] *a & nmf* second; **de seconde main** second-hand; – *nm* (*ad-joint*) second in command; (*étage*) second floor, *Am* third floor; – *nf Rail* second class; *Scol* = fifth form, *Am* = eleventh grade; (*vitesse*) *Aut* second (gear). ◆**secondaire** *a* secondary.

seconde² [sgɔ̃d] *nf* (*instant*) second.

seconder [sgɔ̃de] *vt* to assist.

secouer [s(ǝ)kwe] *vt* to shake; (*paresse, poussière*) to shake off; **s. qn** (*maladie, nou-velle etc*) to shake s.o. up; **s. qch de qch**

(*enlever*) to shake sth out of sth; – **se s.** *vpr* (*faire un effort*) *Fam* to shake oneself out of it.

secour/ir [skurir] *vt* to assist, help. ◆**—able** *a* (*personne*) helpful. ◆**secou-risme** *nm* first aid. ◆**secouriste** *nmf* first-aid worker.

secours [s(ǝ)kur] *nm* assistance, help; (*aux indigents*) aid, relief; **le s., les s.** *Mil* relief; **(premiers) s.** *Méd* first aid; **au s.!** help!; **porter s. à qn** to give s.o. assistance *ou* help; **de s.** (*sortie*) emergency-; (*équipe*) rescue-; (*roue*) spare.

secousse [s(ǝ)kus] *nf* jolt, jerk; (*psycho-logique*) shock; *Géol* tremor.

secret, -ète [sǝkrɛ, -ɛt] *a* secret; (*cachottier*) secretive; – *nm* (*discrétion*) secrecy; **en s.** in secret, secretly; **dans le s.** (*au cou-rant*) in on the secret.

secrétaire [sǝkretɛr] **1** *nmf* secretary; **s. d'État** Secretary of State; **s. de mairie** town clerk; **s. de rédaction** subeditor. **2** *nm* (*meuble*) writing desk. ◆**secrétariat** *nm* (*bureau*) secretary's office; (*d'organisation internationale*) secretariat; (*métier*) secreta-rial work; **de s.** (*école, travail*) secretarial.

sécréter [sekrete] *vt* *Méd Biol* to secrete. ◆**sécrétion** *nf* secretion.

secte [sɛkt] *nf* sect. ◆**sectaire** *a &* *nmf Péj* sectarian.

secteur [sɛktœr] *nm* *Mil Com* sector; (*de ville*) district; (*domaine*) *Fig* area; (*de réseau*) *Él* supply area; (*ligne*) *Él* mains.

section [sɛksjɔ̃] *nf* section; (*de ligne d'autobus*) fare stage; *Mil* platoon. ◆**sec-tionner** *vt* to divide (into sections); (*artère, doigt*) to sever.

séculaire [sekylɛr] *a* (*tradition etc*) age-old.

secundo [s(ǝ)gɔ̃do] *adv* secondly.

sécurité [sekyrite] *nf* (*tranquillité*) security; (*matérielle*) safety; **s. routière** road safety; **s. sociale** = social services *ou* security; **de s.** (*dispositif, ceinture, marge etc*) safety-; **en s.** secure; safe. ◆**sécuriser** *vt* to reassure, make feel (emotionally) secure.

sédatif [sedatif] *nm* sedative.

sédentaire [sedɑ̃tɛr] *a* sedentary.

sédiment [sedimɑ̃] *nm* sediment.

séditieux, -euse [sedisjø, -øz] *a* seditious. ◆**sédition** *nf* sedition.

séduire* [sedɥir] *vt* to charm, attract; (*plaire à*) to appeal to; (*abuser de*) to se-duce. ◆**séduisant** *a* attractive. ◆**sé-ducteur, -trice** *a* seductive; – *nmf* seduc-er. ◆**séduction** *nf* attraction.

segment [sɛgmɑ̃] *nm* segment.

ségrégation [segregasjɔ̃] *nf* segregation.

seiche [sɛʃ] *nf* cuttlefish.

seigle [sɛgl] *nm* rye.

seigneur [sɛɲœr] *nm Hist* lord; **S.** *Rel* Lord.

sein [sɛ̃] *nm* (*mamelle, poitrine*) breast; *Fig* bosom; **bout de s.** nipple; **au s. de** (*parti etc*) within; (*bonheur etc*) in the midst of.

Seine [sɛn] *nf* **la S.** the Seine.

séisme [seism] *nm* earthquake.

seize [sɛz] *a & nm* sixteen. ◆**seizième** *a & nmf* sixteenth.

séjour [seʒur] *nm* stay; (**salle de**) **s.** living room. ◆**séjourner** *vi* to stay.

sel [sɛl] *nm* salt; (*piquant*) *Fig* spice; (*humour*) wit; *pl Méd* (smelling) salts; **sels de bain** bath salts.

sélect [selɛkt] *a Fam* select.

sélectif, -ive [selɛktif, -iv] *a* selective. ◆**sélection** *nf* selection. ◆**sélectionner** *vt* to select.

self(-service) [sɛlf(sɛrvis)] *nm* self-service restaurant *ou* shop.

selle [sɛl] **1** *nf* (*de cheval*) saddle. **2** *nfpl* **les selles** *Méd* bowel movements, stools. ◆**seller** *vt* (*cheval*) to saddle.

sellette [sɛlɛt] *nf* **sur la s.** (*personne*) under examination, in the hot seat.

selon [s(ə)lɔ̃] *prép* according to (**que** whether); **c'est s.** *Fam* it (all) depends.

Seltz (eau de) [odsɛls] *nf* soda (water).

semailles [s(ə)maj] *nfpl* (*travail*) sowing; (*période*) seedtime.

semaine [s(ə)mɛn] *nf* week; **en s.** (*opposé à week-end*) in the week.

sémantique [semɑ̃tik] *a* semantic; – *nf* semantics.

sémaphore [semafɔr] *nm* (*appareil*) *Rail Nau* semaphore.

semblable [sɑ̃blabl] *a* similar (**à** to); **être semblables** to be alike *ou* similar; **de semblables propos**/*etc* (*tels*) such remarks/*etc*; – *nm* fellow (creature); **toi et tes semblables** you and your kind.

semblant [sɑ̃blɑ̃] *nm* **faire s.** to pretend (**de faire** to do); **un s. de** a semblance of.

sembler [sɑ̃ble] *vi* to seem (**à** to); **il (me) semble vieux** he seems *ou* looks old (to me); **s. être/faire** to seem to be/to do; – *v imp* **il semble que** (+ *sub ou indic*) it seems that, it looks as if; **il me semble que** it seems to me that, I think that.

semelle [s(ə)mɛl] *nf* (*de chaussure*) sole; (*intérieure*) insole.

semer [s(ə)me] *vt* **1** (*graines*) to sow; (*jeter*) *Fig* to strew; (*répandre*) to spread; **semé de** *Fig* strewn with, dotted with. **2** (*concurrent, poursuivant*) to shake off. ◆**semence** *nf*

seed; (*clou*) tack. ◆**semeur, -euse** *nmf* sower (**de** of).

semestre [s(ə)mɛstr] *nm* half-year; *Univ* semester. ◆**semestriel, -ielle** *a* half-yearly.

semi- [səmi] *préf* semi-.

séminaire [seminɛr] *nm* **1** *Univ* seminar. **2** *Rel* seminary.

semi-remorque [səmirəmɔrk] *nm* (*camion*) articulated lorry, *Am* semi(trailer).

semis [s(ə)mi] *nm* sowing; (*terrain*) seedbed; (*plant*) seedling.

sémite [semit] *a* Semitic; – *nmf* Semite. ◆**sémitique** *a* (*langue*) Semitic.

semonce [səmɔ̃s] *nf* reprimand; **coup de s.** *Nau* warning shot.

semoule [s(ə)mul] *nf* semolina.

sempiternel, -elle [sɑ̃pitɛrnɛl] *a* endless, ceaseless.

sénat [sena] *nm Pol* senate. ◆**sénateur** *nm Pol* senator.

sénile [senil] *a* senile. ◆**sénilité** *nf* senility.

sens [sɑ̃s] *nm* **1** (*faculté, raison*) sense; (*signification*) meaning, sense; **à mon s.** to my mind; **s. commun** commonsense; **s. de l'humour** sense of humour; **ça n'a pas de s.** that doesn't make sense. **2** (*direction*) direction; **s. giratoire** *Aut* roundabout, *Am* traffic circle, rotary; **s. interdit** *ou* **unique** (*rue*) one-way street; **'s. interdit'** 'no entry'; **à s. unique** (*rue*) one-way; **s. dessus dessous** [sɑ̃dsydsu] upside down; **dans le s./le s. inverse des aiguilles d'une montre** clockwise/anticlockwise, *Am* counterclockwise.

sensation [sɑ̃sasjɔ̃] *nf* sensation, feeling; **faire s.** to cause *ou* create a sensation; **à s.** (*film etc*) *Péj* sensational. ◆**sensationnel, -elle** *a Fig* sensational.

sensé [sɑ̃se] *a* sensible.

sensible [sɑ̃sibl] *a* sensitive (**à** to); (*douloureux*) tender, sore; (*perceptible*) perceptible; (*progrès etc*) appreciable. ◆**sensiblement** *adv* (*notablement*) appreciably; (*à peu près*) more or less. ◆**sensibiliser** *vt* **s. qn à** (*problème etc*) to make s.o. alive to *ou* aware of. ◆**sensibilité** *nf* sensitivity.

sensoriel, -ielle [sɑ̃sɔrjɛl] *a* sensory.

sensuel, -elle [sɑ̃sɥɛl] *a* (*sexuel*) sensual; (*musique, couleur etc*) sensuous. ◆**sensualité** *nf* sensuality; sensuousness.

sentence [sɑ̃tɑ̃s] *nf* **1** *Jur* sentence. **2** (*maxime*) maxim.

senteur [sɑ̃tœr] *nf* (*odeur*) scent.

sentier [sɑ̃tje] *nm* path.

sentiment [sɑ̃timɑ̃] *nm* feeling; **avoir le s. de** (*apprécier*) to be aware of; **faire du s.** to be sentimental. ◆**sentimental, -aux** *a* senti-

mental; (*amoureux*) love-. ◆**sentimentalité** *nf* sentimentality.
sentinelle [sɑ̃tinɛl] *nf* sentry.
sentir* [sɑ̃tir] *vt* to feel; (*odeur*) to smell;
(*goût*) to taste; (*racisme etc*) to smack of;
(*connaître*) to sense, be conscious of; **s. le
moisi/le parfum**/*etc* to smell musty/of per-
fume/*etc*; **s. le poisson**/*etc* (*avoir le goût de*)
to taste of fish/*etc*; **je ne peux pas le s.** (*supporter*) *Fam* I can't bear *ou* stand him; **se
faire s.** (*effet etc*) to make itself felt; **se s.
fatigué/humilié**/*etc* to feel tired/humil-
iated/*etc*; − *vi* to smell.
séparation [separɑsjɔ̃] *nf* separation; (*en
deux*) division, split; (*départ*) parting.
◆**séparer** *vt* to separate (**de** from);
(*diviser en deux*) to divide, split (up);
(*cheveux*) to part; − **se s.** *vpr* (*se quitter*) to
part; (*adversaires, époux*) to separate; (*assemblée, cortège*) to disperse, break up; (*se
détacher*) to split off; **se s. de** (*objet aimé,
chien etc*) to part with. ◆**séparé** *a* (*distinct*) separate; (*époux*) separated (**de**
from). ◆**séparément** *adv* separately.
sept [sɛt] *a* & *nm* seven. ◆**septième** *a* &
nmf seventh; **un s.** a seventh.
septante [sɛptɑ̃t] *a* & *nm* (*en Belgique,
Suisse*) seventy.
septembre [sɛptɑ̃br] *nm* September.
septennat [sɛptena] *nm Pol* seven-year
term (of office).
septentrional, -aux [sɛptɑ̃trijɔnal, -o] *a*
northern.
sépulcre [sepylkr] *nm Rel* sepulchre.
sépulture [sepyltyr] *nf* burial; (*lieu*) burial
place.
séquelles [sekɛl] *nfpl* (*de maladie etc*) aftereffects; (*de guerre*) aftermath.
séquence [sekɑ̃s] *nf Mus Cartes Cin* sequence.
séquestrer [sekɛstre] *vt* to confine (illegal-
ly), lock up.
sera, serait [s(ə)ra, s(ə)rɛ] *voir* être.
serein [sɔrɛ̃] *a* serene. ◆**sérénité** *nf* serenity.
sérénade [serenad] *nf* serenade.
sergent [sɛrʒɑ̃] *nm Mil* sergeant.
série [seri] *nf* series; (*ensemble*) set; **s. noire**
Fig string *ou* series of disasters; **de s.** (*article etc*) standard; **fabrication en s.** mass
production; **fins de s.** *Com* oddments; **hors
s.** *Fig* outstanding.
sérieux, -euse [serjø, -øz] *a* (*personne,
maladie, doute etc*) serious; (*de bonne foi*)
genuine, serious; (*digne de foi, fiable*) reliable; (*bénéfices*) substantial; **de sérieuses
chances de . . .** a good chance of . . . ; −

nm seriousness; (*fiabilité*) reliability; **prendre au s.** to take seriously; **garder son s.** to
keep a straight face; **manquer de s.** (*travailleur*) to lack application. ◆**sérieusement**
adv seriously; (*travailler*) conscientiously.
serin [s(ə)rɛ̃] *nm* canary.
seriner [s(ə)rine] *vt* **s. qch à qn** to repeat sth
to s.o. over and over again.
seringue [s(ə)rɛ̃g] *nf* syringe.
serment [sɛrmɑ̃] *nm* (*affirmation solennelle*)
oath; (*promesse*) pledge; **prêter s.** to take
an oath; **faire le s. de faire** to swear to do;
sous s. *Jur ou* on *ou* under oath.
sermon [sɛrmɔ̃] *nm Rel* sermon; (*discours*)
Péj lecture. ◆**sermonner** *vt* (*faire la morale à*) to lecture.
serpe [sɛrp] *nf* bill(hook).
serpent [sɛrpɑ̃] *nm* snake; **s. à sonnette** rattlesnake.
serpenter [sɛrpɑ̃te] *vi* (*sentier etc*) to meander.
serpentin [sɛrpɑ̃tɛ̃] *nm* (*ruban*) streamer.
serpillière [sɛrpijɛr] *nf* floor cloth.
serre [sɛr] **1** *nf* greenhouse. **2** *nfpl* (*d'oiseau*)
claws, talons.
serre-livres [sɛrlivr] *nm inv* bookend.
◆**s.-tête** *nm inv* (*bandeau*) headband.
serr/er [sere] *vt* (*saisir, tenir*) to grip, clasp;
(*presser*) to squeeze, press; (*corde, nœud,
vis*) to tighten; (*poing*) to clench; (*taille*) to
hug; (*pieds*) to pinch; (*frein*) to apply, put
on; (*rapprocher*) to close up; (*rangs*) *Mil* to
close; **s. la main à** to shake hands with; **s.
les dents** *Fig* to grit one's teeth; **s. qn** (*embrasser*) to hug s.o.; (*vêtement*) to be too
tight for s.o.; **s. qn de près** (*talonner*) to be
close behind s.o.; − *vi* **s. à droite** *Aut* to
keep (to the) right; − **se s.** *vpr* (*se rapprocher*) to squeeze up *ou* together; **se s.
contre** to squeeze up against. ◆**-é** *a*
(*budget, nœud, vêtement*) tight; (*gens*)
packed (together); (*mailles, lutte*) close;
(*rangs*) serried; (*dense*) dense, thick; (*cœur*)
Fig heavy; **avoir la gorge serrée** *Fig* to have
a lump in one's throat.
serrure [seryr] *nf* lock. ◆**serrurier** *nm*
locksmith.
sertir [sɛrtir] *vt* (*diamant etc*) to set.
sérum [serɔm] *nm* serum.
servante [sɛrvɑ̃t] *nf* (*maid*)servant.
serveur, -euse [sɛrvœr, -øz] *nmf* waiter,
waitress; (*au bar*) barman, barmaid.
serviable [sɛrvjabl] *a* helpful, obliging.
◆**serviabilité** *nf* helpfulness.
service [sɛrvis] *nm* service; (*fonction, travail*) duty; (*pourboire*) service (charge);
(*département*) *Com* department; *Tennis*

serve, service; **un s.** (*aide*) a favour; **rendre s.** to be of service (**à qn** to s.o.), help (**à qn** s.o.); **rendre un mauvais s. à qn** to do s.o. a disservice; **ça pourrait rendre s.** *Fam* that might come in useful; **s. (non) compris** service (not) included; **s. après-vente** *Com* aftersales (service); **s. d'ordre** (*policiers*) police; **être de s.** to be on duty; **s. à café/à thé** coffee/tea service *ou* set; **à votre s.!** at your service!

serviette [sɛrvjɛt] *nf* **1** towel; **s. de bain/de toilette** bath/hand towel; **s. hygiénique** sanitary towel; **s. (de table)** serviette, napkin. **2** (*sac*) briefcase.

servile [sɛrvil] *a* servile; (*imitation*) slavish. ◆**servilité** *nf* servility; slavishness.

servir* [sɛrvir] **1** *vt* to serve (**qch à qn** s.o. with sth, sth to s.o.); (*convive*) to wait on; − *vi* to serve; − **se s.** *vpr* (*à table*) to help oneself (**de to**). **2** *vi* (*être utile*) to be useful, serve; **s. à qch/à faire** (*objet*) to be used for sth/to do *ou* for doing; **ça ne sert à rien** it's useless, it's no good *ou* use (**de faire** doing); **à quoi ça sert de protester/***etc* what's the use *ou* good of protesting/*etc*; **s. de qch** (*objet*) to be used for sth, serve as sth; **ça me sert à faire/de qch** I use it to do *ou* for doing/as sth; **s. à qn de guide/***etc* to act as a guide/*etc* to s.o. **3 se s.** *vpr* **se s. de** (*utiliser*) to use.

serviteur [sɛrvitœr] *nm* servant. ◆**servitude** *nf* (*esclavage*) servitude; (*contrainte*) *Fig* constraint.

ses [se] *voir* **son²**.

session [sesjɔ̃] *nf* session.

set [sɛt] *nm* **1** *Tennis* set. **2 s. (de table)** (*napperon*) place mat.

seuil [sœj] *nm* doorstep; (*entrée*) doorway; (*limite*) *Fig* threshold; **au s. de** *Fig* on the threshold of.

seul, seule [sœl] **1** *a* (*sans compagnie*) alone; **tout s.** all alone, by oneself, on one's own; **se sentir s.** to feel lonely *ou* alone; − *adv* (*tout*) **s.** (*agir, vivre*) by oneself, alone, on one's own; (*parler*) to oneself; **s. à s.** (*parler*) in private. **2** *a* (*unique*) only; **la seule femme/***etc* the only *ou* sole woman/*etc*; **un s. chat/***etc* only one cat/*etc*; **une seule fois** only once; **pas un s. livre/***etc* not a single book/*etc*; **seuls les garçons . . . , les garçons seuls . . .** only the boys . . . ; − *nmf* **le s., la seule** the only one; **un s., une seule** only one, one only; **pas un s.** not (a single) one. ◆**seulement** *adv* only; **non s. . . . mais . . .** not only . . . but (also) . . . ; **pas s.** (*même*) not even; **sans s. faire** without even doing.

sève [sɛv] *nf* *Bot* & *Fig* sap.

sévère [sever] *a* severe; (*parents, professeur*) strict. ◆**−ment** *adv* severely; (*élever*) strictly. ◆**sévérité** *nf* severity; strictness.

sévices [sevis] *nmpl* brutality.

sévir [sevir] *vi* (*fléau*) *Fig* to rage; **s. contre** to deal severely with.

sevrer [səvre] *vt* (*enfant*) to wean; **s. de** (*priver*) *Fig* to deprive of.

sexe [sɛks] *nm* (*catégorie, sexualité*) sex; (*organes*) genitals; **l'autre s.** the opposite sex. ◆**sexiste** *a* & *nmf* sexist. ◆**sexualité** *nf* sexuality. ◆**sexuel, -elle** *a* sexual; (*éducation, acte etc*) sex-.

sextuor [sɛkstɥɔr] *nm* sextet.

seyant [sɛjɑ̃] *a* (*vêtement*) becoming.

shampooing [ʃɑ̃pwɛ̃] *nm* shampoo; **s. colorant** rinse; **faire un s. à qn** to shampoo s.o.'s hair.

shérif [ʃerif] *nm* *Am* sheriff.

shooter [ʃute] *vti* *Fb* to shoot.

short [ʃɔrt] *nm* (pair of) shorts.

si [si] **1** (= **s'** [s] *before* **il, ils**) *conj* if; **s'il vient** if he comes; **si j'étais roi** if I were *ou* was king; **je me demande si** I wonder whether *ou* if; **si on restait?** (*suggestion*) what if we stayed?; **si je dis ça, c'est que . . .** I say this because . . . ; **si ce n'est** (*sinon*) if not; **si oui** if so. **2** *adv* (*tellement*) so; **pas si riche que toi/que tu crois** not as rich as you/as you think; **un si bon dîner** such a good dinner; **si grand qu'il soit** however big he may be; **si bien que** with the result that. **3** *adv* (*après négative*) yes; **tu ne viens pas? − si!** you're not coming? − yes (I am!)

siamois [sjamwa] *a* Siamese; **frères s., sœurs siamoises** Siamese twins.

Sicile [sisil] *nf* Sicily.

SIDA [sida] *nm* *Méd* AIDS. ◆**sidéen, -enne** *nmf* AIDS sufferer.

sidérer [sidere] *vt* *Fam* to flabbergast.

sidérurgie [sideryrʒi] *nf* iron and steel industry.

siècle [sjɛkl] *nm* century; (*époque*) age.

siège [sjɛʒ] *nm* **1** (*meuble, centre*) & *Pol* seat; (*d'autorité, de parti etc*) headquarters; **s. (social)** (*d'entreprise*) head office. **2** *Mil* siege; **mettre le s. devant** to lay siege to. ◆**siéger** *vi* *Pol* to sit.

sien, sienne [sjɛ̃, sjɛn] *pron poss* **le s., la sienne,** les siens **his; (de femme) hers;** (*de chose*) its; **les deux siens** his *ou* her two; − *nmpl* **les siens** (*amis etc*) one's (own) people.

sieste [sjɛst] *nf* siesta; **faire la s.** to have *ou* take a nap.

siffler [sifle] *vi* to whistle; (*avec un sifflet*) to

blow one's whistle; (gaz, serpent) to hiss; (en respirant) to wheeze; − vt (chanson) to whistle; (chien) to whistle to; (faute, fin de match) Sp to blow one's whistle for; (acteur, pièce) to boo; (boisson) Fam to knock back. ◆**sifflement** nm whistling, whistle; hiss(ing). ◆**sifflet** nm (instrument) whistle; pl Th booing, boos; (**coup de**) **s.** (son) whistle. ◆**siffloter** vti to whistle.

sigle [sigl] nm (initiales) abbreviation; (prononcé comme un mot) acronym.

signal, -aux [siɲal, -o] nm signal; **s. d'alarme** Rail communication cord; **signaux routiers** road signs. ◆**signal/er 1** vt (faire remarquer) to point out (à qn to s.o., **que** that); (annoncer, indiquer) to indicate, signal; (dénoncer à la police etc) to report (à to). **2 se s.** vpr se s. **par** to distinguish oneself by. ◆**—ement** nm (de personne) description, particulars. ◆**signalisation** nf signalling; Aut signposting; **s. (routière)** (signaux) road signs.

signature [siɲatyr] nf signature; (action) signing. ◆**signataire** nmf signatory. ◆**signer 1** vt to sign. **2 se s.** vpr Rel to cross oneself.

signe [siɲ] nm (indice) sign, indication; **s. particulier/de ponctuation** distinguishing/ punctuation mark; **faire s. à qn** (geste) to motion to ou beckon s.o. (**de faire** to do); (contacter) to get in touch with s.o.; **faire s. que oui** to nod (one's head); **faire s. que non** to shake one's head.

signet [siɲɛ] nm bookmark.

signification [siɲifikasjɔ̃] nf meaning. ◆**significatif, -ive** a significant, meaningful; **s. de** indicative of. ◆**signifier** vt to mean, signify (**que** that); **s. qch à qn** (faire connaître) to make sth known to s.o., signify sth to s.o.

silence [silɑ̃s] nm silence; Mus rest; **en s.** in silence; **garder le s.** to keep quiet ou silent (**sur** about). ◆**silencieux, -euse 1** a silent. **2** nm Aut silencer, Am muffler; (d'arme) silencer. ◆**silencieusement** adv silently.

silex [silɛks] nm (roche) flint.

silhouette [silwɛt] nf outline; (en noir) silhouette; (ligne du corps) figure.

silicium [silisjɔm] nm silicon. ◆**silicone** nf silicone.

sillage [sijaʒ] nm (de bateau) wake; **dans le s. de** Fig in the wake of.

sillon [sijɔ̃] nm furrow; (de disque) groove.

sillonner [sijɔne] vt (traverser) to cross; (en tous sens) to criss-cross.

silo [silo] nm silo.

simagrées [simagre] nfpl airs (and graces); (cérémonies) fuss.

similaire [similɛr] a similar. ◆**similitude** nf similarity.

similicuir [similikɥir] nm imitation leather.

simple [sɛ̃pl] a simple; (non multiple) single; (employé, particulier) ordinary; − nmf **s. d'esprit** simpleton; − nm Tennis singles. ◆**simplement** adv simply. ◆**simplet, -ette** a (personne) a bit simple. ◆**simplicité** nf simplicity. ◆**simplification** nf simplification. ◆**simplifier** vt to simplify. ◆**simpliste** a simplistic.

simulacre [simylakr] nm un **s. de** Péj a pretence of.

simuler [simyle] vt to simulate; (feindre) to feign. ◆**simulateur, -trice 1** nmf (hypocrite) shammer; (tire-au-flanc) & Mil malingerer. **2** nm (appareil) simulator. ◆**simulation** nf simulation; feigning.

simultané [simyltane] a simultaneous. ◆**—ment** adv simultaneously.

sincère [sɛ̃sɛr] a sincere. ◆**sincèrement** adv sincerely. ◆**sincérité** nf sincerity.

sinécure [sinekyr] nf sinecure.

singe [sɛ̃ʒ] nm monkey, ape. ◆**singer** vt (imiter) to ape, mimic. ◆**singeries** nfpl antics, clowning.

singulariser (se) [səsɛ̃gylarize] vpr to draw attention to oneself.

singulier, -ière [sɛ̃gylje, -jɛr] **1** a peculiar, odd. **2** a & nm Gram singular. ◆**singularité** nf peculiarity. ◆**singulièrement** adv (notamment) particularly; (beaucoup) extremely.

sinistre [sinistr] **1** a (effrayant) sinister. **2** nm disaster; (incendie) fire; (dommage) Jur damage. ◆**sinistré, -ée** a (population, région) disaster-stricken; − nmf disaster victim.

sinon [sinɔ̃] conj (autrement) otherwise, or else; (sauf) except (**que** that); (si ce n'est) if not.

sinueux, -euse [sinɥø, -øz] a winding. ◆**sinuosités** nfpl twists (and turns).

sinus [sinys] nm inv Anat sinus.

siphon [sifɔ̃] nm siphon; (d'évier) trap, U-bend.

sirène [sirɛn] nf **1** (d'usine etc) siren. **2** (femme) mermaid.

sirop [siro] nm syrup; (à diluer, boisson) (fruit) cordial; **s. contre la toux** cough mixture ou syrup.

siroter [sirɔte] vt Fam to sip (at).

sis [si] a Jur situated.

sismique [sismik] *a* seismic; **secousse s.** earth tremor.

site [sit] *nm* (*endroit*) site; (*environnement*) setting; (*pittoresque*) beauty spot; **s. (touristique)** (*monument etc*) place of interest.

sitôt [sito] *adv* **s. que** as soon as; **s. levée, elle partit** as soon as she was up, she left; **s. après** immediately after; **pas de s.** not for some time.

situation [sityasjɔ̃] *nf* situation, position; (*emploi*) position; **s. de famille** marital status. ◆**situ/er** *vt* to situate, locate; **— se s.** *vpr* (*se trouver*) to be situated. ◆**—é** *a* (*maison etc*) situated.

six [sis] ([si] *before consonant*, [siz] *before vowel*) *a* & *nm* six. ◆**sixième** *a* & *nmf* sixth; **un s.** a sixth.

sketch [skɛtʃ] *nm* (*pl* **sketches**) *Th* sketch.

ski [ski] *nm* (*objet*) ski; (*sport*) skiing; **faire du s.** to ski; **s. nautique** water skiing. ◆**ski/er** *vi* to ski. ◆**—eur, -euse** *nmf* skier.

slalom [slalom] *nm Sp* slalom.

slave [slav] *a* Slav; (*langue*) Slavonic; *— nmf* Slav.

slip [slip] *nm* (*d'homme*) briefs, (under)pants; (*de femme*) panties, pants, knickers; **s. de bain** (*swimming*) trunks; (*d'un bikini*) briefs.

slogan [slɔgã] *nm* slogan.

SMIC [smik] *nm abrév* (*salaire minimum interprofessionnel de croissance*) minimum wage.

smoking [smokiŋ] *nm* (*veston, costume*) dinner jacket, *Am* tuxedo.

snack(-bar) [snak(bar)] *nm* snack bar.

SNCF [ɛsɛnseɛf] *nf abrév* (*Société nationale des Chemins de fer français*) French railways.

snob [snɔb] *nmf* snob; *— a* snobbish. ◆**snober** *vt* **s. qn** to snub s.o. ◆**snobisme** *nm* snobbery.

sobre [sɔbr] *a* sober. ◆**sobriété** *nf* sobriety.

sobriquet [sɔbrikɛ] *nm* nickname.

sociable [sɔsjabl] *a* sociable. ◆**sociabilité** *nf* sociability.

social, -aux [sɔsjal, -o] *a* social. ◆**socialisme** *nm* socialism. ◆**socialiste** *a* & *nmf* socialist.

société [sɔsjete] *nf* society; (*compagnie*) & *Com* company; **s. anonyme** *Com* (public) limited company, *Am* incorporated company. ◆**sociétaire** *nmf* (*d'une association*) member.

sociologie [sɔsjɔlɔʒi] *nf* sociology.

◆**sociologique** *a* sociological. ◆**sociologue** *nmf* sociologist.

socle [sɔkl] *nm* (*de statue, colonne*) plinth, pedestal; (*de lampe*) base.

socquette [sɔkɛt] *nf* ankle sock.

soda [sɔda] *nm* (*à l'orange etc*) fizzy drink, *Am* soda (pop).

sœur [sœr] *nf* sister; *Rel* nun, sister.

sofa [sɔfa] *nm* sofa, settee.

soi [swa] *pron* oneself; **chacun pour s.** every man for himself; **en s.** in itself; **cela va de s.** it's self-evident (**que** that); **amour/conscience de s.** self-love/-awareness. ◆**s.-même** *pron* oneself.

soi-disant [swadizã] *a inv* so-called; *— adv* supposedly.

soie [swa] *nf* **1** silk. **2** (*de porc etc*) bristle. ◆**soierie** *nf* (*tissu*) silk.

soif [swaf] *nf* thirst (*Fig* **de** for); **avoir s.** to be thirsty; **donner s. à qn** to make s.o. thirsty.

soign/er [swaɲe] *vt* to look after, take care of; (*malade*) to tend, nurse; (*maladie*) to treat; (*détails, présentation, travail*) to take care over; **— se s.** *vpr* to take care of oneself, look after oneself. ◆**—é** *a* (*personne*) well-groomed; (*vêtement*) neat, tidy; (*travail*) careful. ◆**soigneux, -euse** *a* careful (**de** with); (*propre*) tidy, neat. ◆**soigneusement** *adv* carefully.

soin [swɛ̃] *nm* care; (*ordre*) tidiness, neatness; *pl* care; *Méd* treatment; **avoir** *ou* **prendre s. de qch/de faire** to take care of sth/to do; **les premiers soins** first aid; **soins de beauté** beauty care *ou* treatment; **aux bons soins de** (*sur lettre*) care of, c/o; **avec s.** carefully, with care.

soir [swar] *nm* evening; **le s.** (*chaque soir*) in the evening; **à neuf heures du s.** at nine in the evening; **du s.** (*repas, robe etc*) evening-. ◆**soirée** *nf* evening; (*réunion*) party; **s. dansante** dance.

soit 1 [swa] *voir* **être. 2** [swa] *conj* (*à savoir*) that is (to say); **s. . . . . s. . . . .** either . . . or . . . . **3** [swat] *adv* (*oui*) very well.

soixante [swasãt] *a* & *nm* sixty. ◆**soixantaine** *nf* **une s. (de)** (*nombre*) (about) sixty; **avoir la s.** (*âge*) to be about sixty. ◆**soixante-dix** *a* & *nm* seventy. ◆**soixante-dixième** *a* & *nmf* seventieth. ◆**soixantième** *a* & *nmf* sixtieth.

soja [sɔʒa] *nm* (*plante*) soya; **graine de s.** soya bean; **germes** *ou* **pousses de s.** beansprouts.

sol [sɔl] *nm* ground; (*plancher*) floor; (*matière, territoire*) soil.

solaire [sɔlɛr] *a* solar; (*chaleur, rayons*) sun's; (*crème, filtre*) sun-; (*lotion, huile*) suntan-.

soldat [sɔlda] *nm* soldier; **simple s.** private.

solde [sɔld] **1** *nm* (*de compte, à payer*) balance. **2** *nm* **en s.** (*acheter*) at sale price, *Am* on ▸ sale; *pl* (*marchandises*) sale goods; (*vente*) (clearance) sale(s). **3** *nf Mil* pay; **à la s. de** *Fig Péj* in s.o.'s pay. ◆**sold/er** *vt* (*articles*) to sell off, clear. **2** *vt* (*compte*) to pay the balance of. **3 se s.** *vpr* **se s. par** (*un échec, une défaite etc*) to end in. ◆**—é** *a* (*article etc*) reduced. ◆**solderie** *nf* discount *ou* reject shop.

sole [sɔl] *nf* (*poisson*) sole.

soleil [sɔlɛj] *nm* sun; (*chaleur, lumière*) sunshine; (*fleur*) sunflower; **au s.** in the sun; **il fait (du) s.** it's sunny, the sun's shining; **prendre un bain de s.** to sunbathe; **coup de s.** *Méd* sunburn.

solennel, -elle [sɔlanɛl] *a* solemn. ◆**solennellement** *adv* solemnly. ◆**solennité** [-anite] *nf* solemnity.

solex® [sɔlɛks] *nm* moped.

solfège [sɔlfɛʒ] *nm* rudiments of music.

solidaire [sɔlidɛr] *a* **être s.** (*ouvriers etc*) to be as one, show solidarity (**de** with); (*pièce de machine*) to be interdependent (**de** with). ◆**solidairement** *adv* jointly. ◆**se solidariser** *vpr* to show solidarity (**avec** with). ◆**solidarité** *nf* solidarity; (*d'éléments*) interdependence.

solide [sɔlid] *a* (*voiture, nourriture, caractère etc*) & *Ch* solid; (*argument, qualité, raison*) sound; (*vigoureux*) robust; — *nm Ch* solid. ◆**solidement** *adv* solidly. ◆**se solidifier** *vpr* to solidify. ◆**solidité** *nf* solidity; (*d'argument etc*) soundness.

soliste [sɔlist] *nmf Mus* soloist.

solitaire [sɔlitɛr] *a* solitary; — *nmf* loner; (*ermite*) recluse, hermit; **en s.** on one's own. ◆**solitude** *nf* solitude.

solive [sɔliv] *nf* joist, beam.

solliciter [sɔlisite] *vt* (*audience, emploi etc*) to seek; (*tenter*) to tempt, entice; **s. qn** (*faire appel à*) to appeal to s.o. (**de faire** to do); **être (très) sollicité** (*personne*) to be in (great) demand. ◆**sollicitation** *nf* (*demande*) appeal; (*tentation*) temptation.

sollicitude [sɔlisityd] *nf* solicitude, concern.

solo [sɔlo] *a inv* & *nm Mus* solo.

solstice [sɔlstis] *nm* solstice.

soluble [sɔlybl] *a* (*substance, problème*) soluble; **café s.** instant coffee. ◆**solution** *nf* (*d'un problème etc*) & *Ch* solution (**de** to).

solvable [sɔlvabl] *a Fin* solvent. ◆**solvabilité** *nf Fin* solvency.

solvant [sɔlvã] *nm Ch* solvent.

sombre [sɔbr] *a* dark; (*triste*) sombre, gloomy; **il fait s.** it's dark.

sombrer [sɔbre] *vi* (*bateau*) to sink, founder; **s. dans** (*folie, sommeil etc*) to sink into.

sommaire [sɔmɛr] *a* summary; (*repas, tenue*) scant; — *nm* summary, synopsis.

sommation [sɔmasjɔ] *nf Jur* summons; (*de sentinelle etc*) warning.

somme [sɔm] **1** *nf* sum; **faire la s. de** to add up; **en s., s. toute** in short. **2** *nm* (*sommeil*) nap; **faire un s.** to have *ou* take a nap.

sommeil [sɔmɛj] *nm* sleep; (*envie de dormir*) sleepiness, drowsiness; **avoir s.** to be *ou* feel sleepy *ou* drowsy. ◆**sommeiller** *vi* to doze; (*faculté, qualité*) *Fig* to slumber.

sommelier [sɔmalje] *nm* wine waiter.

sommer [sɔme] *vt* **s. qn de faire** (*enjoindre*) & *Jur* to summon s.o. to do.

sommes [sɔm] *voir* être.

sommet [sɔmɛ] *nm* top; (*de montagne*) summit, top; (*de la gloire etc*) *Fig* height, summit; **conférence au s.** summit (conference).

sommier [sɔmje] *nm* (*de lit*) base; **s. à ressorts** spring base.

sommité [sɔmite] *nf* leading light, top person (**de** in).

somnambule [sɔmnãbyl] *nmf* sleepwalker; **être s.** to sleepwalk. ◆**somnambulisme** *nm* sleepwalking.

somnifère [sɔmnifɛr] *nm* sleeping pill.

somnolence [sɔmnɔlãs] *nf* drowsiness, sleepiness. ◆**somnolent** *a* drowsy, sleepy. ◆**somnoler** *vi* to doze, drowse.

somptueux, -euse [sɔptɥø, -øz] *a* sumptuous, magnificent. ◆**somptuosité** *nf* sumptuousness, magnificence.

son¹ [sɔ] *nm* **1** (*bruit*) sound. **2** (*de grains*) bran.

son², sa, *pl* **ses** [sɔ, sa, se] (*sa becomes son* [sɔn] *before a vowel or mute h*) *a poss* his; (*de femme*) her; (*de chose*) its; (*indéfini*) one's; **son père** his *ou* her *ou* one's father; **sa durée** its duration.

sonate [sɔnat] *nf Mus* sonata.

sonde [sɔd] *nf Géol* drill; *Nau* sounding line; *Méd* probe; (*pour l'alimentation*) (feeding) tube; **s. spatiale** *Av* space probe. ◆**sondage** *nm* sounding; drilling; probing; **s. (d'opinion)** opinion poll. ◆**sonder** *vt* (*rivière etc*) to sound; (*terrain*) to drill; *Av* & *Méd* to probe; (*personne, l'opinion*) *Fig* to sound out.

songe [sɔʒ] *nm* dream.

song/er [sɔʒe] *vi* **s. à qch/à faire** to think of sth/of doing; — *vt* **s. que** to consider *ou* think that. ◆—**eur, -euse** a thoughtful, pensive.

sonner [sɔne] *vi* to ring; (*cor, cloches etc*) to sound; **midi a sonné** it has struck twelve; − *vt* to ring; (*domestique*) to ring for; (*cor etc*) to sound; (*l'heure*) to strike; (*assommer*) to knock out. ◆**sonnantes** *afpl* **à cinq/etc heures s.** on the stroke of five/*etc.* ◆**sonné** a **1** **trois/etc heures sonnées** gone *ou* past three/*etc* o'clock. **2** (*fou*) crazy. ◆**sonnerie** *nf* (*son*) ring(ing); (*de cor etc*) sound; (*appareil*) bell. ◆**sonnette** *nf* bell; **s. d'alarme** alarm (bell); **coup de s.** ring.

sonnet [sɔne] *nm* (*poème*) sonnet.

sonore [sɔnɔr] a (*rire*) loud; (*salle, voix*) resonant; (*effet, film, ondes etc*) sound-. ◆**sonorisation** *nf* (*matériel*) sound equipment *ou* system. ◆**sonoriser** *vt* (*film*) to add sound to; (*salle*) to wire for sound. ◆**sonorité** *nf* (*de salle*) acoustics, resonance; (*de violon etc*) tone.

sont [sɔ̃] *voir* **être**.

sophistiqué [sɔfistike] a sophisticated.

soporifique [sɔpɔrifik] a (*médicament, discours etc*) soporific.

soprano [sɔprano] *nmf* (*personne*) Mus soprano; − *nm* (*voix*) soprano.

sorbet [sɔrbe] *nm* Culin water ice, sorbet.

sorcellerie [sɔrselri] *nf* witchcraft, sorcery. ◆**sorcier** *nm* sorcerer. ◆**sorcière** *nf* witch; **chasse aux sorcières** Pol witch-hunt.

sordide [sɔrdid] a (*acte, affaire etc*) sordid; (*maison etc*) squalid.

sornettes [sɔrnet] *nfpl* (*propos*) Péj twaddle.

sort [sɔr] *nm* **1** (*destin, hasard*) fate; (*condition*) lot. **2** (*maléfice*) spell.

sorte [sɔrt] *nf* sort, kind (**de** of); **en quelque s.** as it were, in a way; **de (telle) s. que** so that, in such a way that; **de la s.** (*de cette façon*) in that way; **faire en s. que** (+ *sub*) to see to it that.

sortie [sɔrti] *nf* **1** departure, exit; (*de scène*) exit; (*promenade*) walk; (*porte*) exit, way out; (*de livre, modèle*) Com appearance; (*de disque, film*) release; (*d'ordinateur*) output; *pl* (*argent*) outgoings; **à la s. de l'école** (*moment*) when school comes out; **l'heure de la s. de qn** the time at which s.o. leaves; **première s.** (*de convalescent etc*) first time out. **2 s. de bain** (*peignoir*) bathrobe.

sortilège [sɔrtilɛʒ] *nm* (magic) spell.

sortir [sɔrtir] *vi* (*aux* **être**) to go out, leave; (*venir*) to come out; (*pour s'amuser*) to go out; (*film, modèle, bourgeon etc*) to come out; (*numéro gagnant*) to come up; **s. de** (*endroit*) to leave; (*sujet*) to stray from;

(*université*) to be a graduate of; (*famille, milieu*) to come from; (*légalité, limites*) to go beyond; (*compétence*) to be outside; (*gonds, rails*) to come off; **s. de l'ordinaire** to be out of the ordinary; **s. de table** to leave the table; **s. de terre** (*plante, fondations*) to come up; **s. indemne** to escape unhurt (**de** from); − *vt* (*aux* **avoir**) to take out (**de** of); (*film, modèle, livre etc*) Com to bring out; (*dire*) Fam to come out with; (*expulser*) Fam to throw out; **s'en s., se s. d'affaire** to pull *ou* come through, get out of trouble. ◆—**ant** a (*numéro*) winning; (*député etc*) Pol outgoing. ◆—**able** a (*personne*) presentable.

sosie [sozi] *nm* (*de personne*) double.

sot, sotte [so, sɔt] a foolish; − *nmf* fool. ◆**sottement** *adv* foolishly. ◆**sottise** *nf* foolishness; (*action, parole*) foolish thing; *pl* (*injures*) Fam insults; **faire des sottises** (*enfant*) to be naughty, misbehave.

sou [su] *nm* **sous** (*argent*) money; **elle n'a pas un *ou* le s.** she doesn't have a penny, she's penniless; **pas un s. de** (*bon sens etc*) not an ounce of; **machine à sous** fruit machine, one-armed bandit.

soubresaut [subrəso] *nm* (*sursaut*) (sudden) start.

souche [suʃ] *nf* (*d'arbre*) stump; (*de carnet*) stub, counterfoil; (*famille, de vigne*) stock.

souci [susi] *nm* (*inquiétude*) worry, concern; (*préoccupation*) concern; **se faire du s.** to be worried, worry; **ça lui donne du s.** it worries him *ou* her. ◆**se soucier** *vpr* **se s. de** to be concerned *ou* worried about. ◆**soucieux, -euse** a concerned, worried (**de qch** about sth); **s. de plaire/etc** anxious to please/*etc.*

soucoupe [sukup] *nf* saucer; **s. volante** flying saucer.

soudain [sudɛ̃] a sudden; − *adv* suddenly. ◆**soudainement** *adv* suddenly. ◆**soudaineté** *nf* suddenness.

Soudan [sudɑ̃] *nm* Sudan.

soude [sud] *nf* Ch soda; **cristaux de s.** washing soda.

souder [sude] *vt* to solder; (*par soudure autogène*) to weld; (*groupes etc*) Fig to unite (closely); − **se s.** *vpr* (*os*) to knit (together). ◆**soudure** *nf* soldering; (*métal*) solder; **s.** (**autogène**) welding.

soudoyer [sudwaje] *vt* to bribe.

souffle [sufl] *nm* puff, blow; (*haleine*) breath; (*respiration*) breathing; (*de bombe etc*) blast; (*inspiration*) Fig inspiration; **s. (d'air)** breath of air. ◆**souffler** *vi* to blow; (*haleter*) to puff; **laisser s. qn** (*reprendre haleine*) to let s.o. get his breath back; − *vt* (*bougie*) to blow out; (*fumée, poussière, verre*) to blow; (*par une explosion*) to blow down, blast; (*chuchoter*) to whisper; (*voler*) *Fam* to pinch (**à** from); (*étonner*) *Fam* to stagger; **s. son rôle à qn** *Th* to prompt s.o.; **ne pas s. mot** not to breathe a word. ◆**soufflet** *nm* **1** (*instrument*) bellows. **2** (*gifle*) *Litt* slap. ◆**souffleur, -euse** *nmf Th* prompter.

soufflé [sufle] *nm Culin* soufflé.

souffrance [sufrɑ̃s] *nf* **1** suffering. **2 en s.** (*colis etc*) unclaimed; (*affaire*) in abeyance.

souffreteux, -euse [sufrətø, -øz] *a* sickly.

souffr/ir* [sufrir] **1** *vi* to suffer; **s. de** to suffer from; (*gorge, pieds etc*) to have trouble with; **faire s. qn** (*physiquement*) to hurt s.o.; (*moralement*) to make s.o. suffer, hurt s.o. **2** *vt* (*endurer*) **je ne peux pas le s.** I can't bear him. **3** *vt* (*exception*) to admit of. ◆**—ant** *a* unwell.

soufre [sufr] *nm* sulphur, *Am* sulfur.

souhait [swɛ] *nm* wish; **à vos souhaits!** (*après un éternuement*) bless you!; **à s.** perfectly. ◆**souhait/er** *vt* (*bonheur etc*) to wish for; **s. qch à qn** to wish s.o. sth; **s. faire** to hope to do; **s. que** (+ *sub*) to hope that. ◆**—able** *a* desirable.

souiller [suje] *vt* to soil, dirty; (*déshonorer*) *Fig* to sully.

soûl [su] **1** *a* drunk. **2** *nm* **tout son s.** (*boire etc*) to one's heart's content. ◆**soûler** *vt* to make drunk; **— se s.** *vpr* to get drunk.

soulager [sulaʒe] *vt* to relieve (**de** of). ◆**soulagement** *nm* relief.

soulever [sulve] *vt* to raise, lift (up); (*l'opinion, le peuple*) to stir up; (*poussière, question*) to raise; (*sentiment*) to arouse; **cela me soulève le cœur** it makes me feel sick, it turns my stomach; **— se s.** *vpr* (*malade etc*) to lift oneself (up); (*se révolter*) to rise (up). ◆**soulèvement** *nm* (*révolte*) (up)rising.

soulier [sulje] *nm* shoe.

souligner [suliɲe] *vt* (*d'un trait*) to underline; (*accentuer, faire remarquer*) to emphasize, underline; **s. que** to emphasize that.

soumettre* [sumɛtr] **1** *vt* (*pays, rebelles*) to subjugate, subdue; **s. à** (*assujettir*) to subject to; **— se s.** *vpr* to submit (**à** to). **2** *vt* (*présenter*) to submit (**à** to). ◆**soumis** *a* (*docile*) submissive; **s. à** subject to. ◆**soumission** *nf* **1** submission; (*docilité*) submissiveness. **2** (*offre*) *Com* tender.

soupape [supap] *nf* valve.

soupçon [supsɔ̃] *nm* suspicion; **un s. de** (*quantité*) *Fig* a hint *ou* touch of. ◆**soupçonner** *vt* to suspect (**de** of, **d'avoir fait** of

doing, **que** that). ◆**soupçonneux, -euse** *a* suspicious.

soupe [sup] *nf* soup. ◆**soupière** *nf* (soup) tureen.

soupente [supɑ̃t] *nf* (*sous le toit*) loft.

souper [supe] *nm* supper; **—** *vi* to have supper.

soupeser [supəze] *vt* (*objet dans la main*) to feel the weight of; (*arguments etc*) *Fig* to weigh up.

soupir [supir] *nm* sigh. ◆**soupir/er** *vi* to sigh; **s. après** to yearn for. ◆**—ant** *nm* (*amoureux*) suitor.

soupirail, -aux [supiraj, -o] *nm* basement window.

souple [supl] *a* (*personne, esprit, règlement*) flexible; (*cuir, membre, corps*) supple. ◆**souplesse** *nf* flexibility; suppleness.

source [surs] *nf* **1** (*point d'eau*) spring; **eau de s.** spring water; **prendre sa s.** (*rivière*) to rise (**à** at, **dans** in). **2** (*origine*) source; **de s. sûre** on good authority.

sourcil [sursi] *nm* eyebrow. ◆**sourciller** *vi* **ne pas s.** *Fig* not to bat an eyelid.

sourd, sourde [sur, surd] **1** *a* deaf (*Fig* **à** to); **—** *nmf* deaf person. **2** *a* (*bruit, douleur*) dull; (*caché*) secret. ◆**s.-muet** (*pl* **sourds-muets**), ◆**sourde-muette** (*pl* **sourdes-muettes**) *a* deaf and dumb; **—** *nmf* deaf mute.

sourdine [surdin] *nf* (*dispositif*) *Mus* mute; **en s.** *Fig* quietly, secretly.

souricière [surisjɛr] *nf* mousetrap; *Fig* trap.

sourire* [surir] *vi* to smile (**à** at); **s. à qn** (*fortune*) to smile on s.o.; **—** *nm* smile; **faire un s. à qn** to give s.o. a smile.

souris [suri] *nf* mouse.

sournois [surnwa] *a* sly, underhand. ◆**sournoisement** *adv* slyly. ◆**sournoiserie** *nf* slyness.

sous [su] *prép* (*position*) under(neath), beneath; (*rang*) under; **s. la pluie** in the rain; **s. cet angle** from that angle *ou* point of view; **s. le nom de** under the name of; **s. Charles X** under Charles X; **s. peu** (*bientôt*) shortly.

sous- [su] *préf* (*subordination, subdivision*) sub-; (*insuffisance*) under-.

sous-alimenté [suzalimɑ̃te] *a* undernourished. ◆**sous-alimentation** *nf* undernourishment.

sous-bois [subwa] *nm* undergrowth.

sous-chef [suʃɛf] *nmf* second-in-command.

souscrire* [suskrir] *vi* **s. à** (*payer, approuver*) to subscribe to. ◆**souscription** *nf* subscription.

sous-développé [sudevlɔpe] a (*pays*) underdeveloped.

sous-directeur, -trice [sudirɛktœr, -tris] nmf assistant manager, assistant manageress.

sous-entend/re [suzɑ̃tɑ̃dr] vt to imply. ◆**-u** nm insinuation.

sous-estimer [suzɛstime] vt to underestimate.

sous-jacent [suʒasɑ̃] a underlying.

sous-louer [sulwe] vt (*appartement*) to sublet.

sous-main [sumɛ̃] nm inv desk pad.

sous-marin [sumarɛ̃] a underwater; plongée sous-marine skin diving; – nm submarine.

sous-officier [suzɔfisje] nm noncommissioned officer.

sous-payer [supeje] vt (*ouvrier etc*) to underpay.

sous-produit [suprɔdɥi] nm by-product.

soussigné, -ée [susiɲe] a & nmf undersigned; je s. I the undersigned.

sous-sol [susɔl] nm basement; Géol subsoil.

sous-titre [sutitr] nm subtitle. ◆**sous-titrer** vt (*film*) to subtitle.

soustraire* [sustrer] vt to remove; Math to subtract, take away (de from); s. qn à (*danger etc*) to shield ou protect s.o. from; se s. à to escape from; (*devoir, obligation*) to avoid. ◆**soustraction** nf Math subtraction.

sous-trait/er [sutrete] vi Com to subcontract. ◆**-ant** nm subcontractor.

sous-verre [suvɛr] nm inv (*encadrement*) (frameless) glass mount.

sous-vêtement [suvɛtmɑ̃] nm undergarment; pl underwear.

soutane [sutan] nf (*de prêtre*) cassock.

soute [sut] nf (*magasin*) Nau hold.

souten/ir* [sutnir] vt to support, hold up; (*droits, opinion*) to uphold, maintain; (*candidat etc*) to back, support; (*malade*) to sustain; (*effort, intérêt*) to sustain, keep up; (*thèse*) to defend; (*résister à*) to withstand; s. que to maintain that; — se s. vpr (*blessé etc*) to hold oneself up; (*se maintenir, durer*) to be sustained. ◆**-u** a (*attention, effort*) sustained; (*style*) lofty. ◆**soutien** nm support; (*personne*) supporter; s. de famille breadwinner. ◆**soutien-gorge** nm (pl soutiens-gorge) bra.

souterrain [sutrɛ̃] a underground; – nm underground passage.

soutirer [sutire] vt s. qch à qn to extract ou get sth from s.o.

souvenir [suvnir] nm memory, recollection;

(*objet*) memento; (*cadeau*) keepsake; (*pour touristes*) souvenir; en s. de in memory of; mon bon s. à (give) my regards to. ◆**se souvenir*** vpr se s. de to remember, recall; se s. que to remember ou recall that.

souvent [suvɑ̃] adv often; peu s. seldom; le plus s. more often than not, most often.

souverain, -aine [suvrɛ̃, -ɛn] a sovereign; (*extrême*) Péj supreme; – nmf sovereign. ◆**souveraineté** nf sovereignty.

soviétique [sɔvjetik] a Soviet; l'Union s. the Soviet Union; – nmf Soviet citizen.

soyeux, -euse [swajø, -øz] a silky.

spacieux, -euse [spasjø, -øz] a spacious, roomy.

spaghetti(s) [spageti] nmpl spaghetti.

sparadrap [sparadra] nm Méd sticking plaster, Am adhesive tape.

spasme [spasm] nm spasm. ◆**spasmodique** a spasmodic.

spatial, -aux [spasjal, -o] a (*vol etc*) space-; engin s. spaceship, spacecraft.

spatule [spatyl] nf spatula.

speaker [spikœr] nm, **speakerine** [spikrin] nf Rad TV announcer.

spécial, -aux [spesjal, -o] a special; (*bizarre*) peculiar. ◆**spécialement** adv especially, particularly; (*exprès*) specially.

spécialiser (se) [səspesjalize] vpr to specialize (dans in). ◆**spécialisation** nf specialization. ◆**spécialiste** nmf specialist. ◆**spécialité** nf speciality, Am specialty.

spécifier [spesifje] vt to specify (que that).

spécifique [spesifik] a Phys Ch specific.

spécimen [spesimɛn] nm specimen; (*livre etc*) specimen copy.

spectacle [spɛktakl] nm 1 (*vue*) spectacle, sight; se donner en s. Péj to make an exhibition of oneself. 2 (*représentation*) show; le s. (*industrie*) show business. ◆**spectateur, -trice** nmf Sp spectator; (*témoin*) onlooker, witness; pl Th Cin audience.

spectaculaire [spɛktakyler] a spectacular.

spectre [spɛktr] nm 1 (*fantôme*) spectre, ghost. 2 (*solaire*) spectrum.

spéculer [spekyle] vi Fin Phil to speculate; s. sur (*tabler sur*) to bank ou rely on. ◆**spéculateur, -trice** nmf speculator. ◆**spéculatif, -ive** a Fin Phil speculative. ◆**spéculation** nf Fin Phil speculation.

spéléologie [speleɔlɔʒi] nf (*activité*) potholing, caving, Am spelunking. ◆**spéléologue** nmf potholer, Am spelunker.

sperme [spɛrm] nm sperm, semen.

sphère [sfɛr] nf (*boule, domaine*) sphere. ◆**sphérique** a spherical.

sphinx [sfɛ̃ks] nm sphinx.

spirale [spiral] nf spiral.

spirite [spirit] nmf spiritualist. ◆**spiritisme** nm spiritualism.

spirituel, -elle [spirituɛl] a 1 (amusant) witty. 2 (pouvoir, vie etc) spiritual.

spiritueux [spirituø] nmpl (boissons) spirits.

splendide [splɑ̃did] a (merveilleux, riche, beau) splendid. ◆**splendeur** nf splendour.

spongieux, -euse [spɔ̃ʒjø, -øz] a spongy.

spontané [spɔ̃tane] a spontaneous. ◆**spontanéité** nf spontaneity. ◆**spontanément** adv spontaneously.

sporadique [spɔradik] a sporadic.

sport [spɔr] nm sport; **faire du s.** to play sport ou Am sports; **(de) s.** (chaussures, vêtements) casual, sports; **voiture/veste de s.** sports car/jacket. ◆**sportif, -ive** a (attitude, personne) sporting; (association, journal, résultats) sports, sporting; (allure) athletic; − nmf sportsman, sportswoman. ◆**sportivité** nf (esprit) sportsmanship.

spot [spɔt] nm 1 (lampe) spot(light). 2 **s.** **(publicitaire)** Rad TV commercial.

sprint [sprint] nm Sp sprint. ◆**sprint/er** vi to sprint; − nm [-œr] sprinter. ◆**—euse** nf sprinter.

square [skwar] nm public garden.

squelette [skəlɛt] nm skeleton. ◆**squelettique** a (personne, maigreur) skeleton-like; (exposé) sketchy.

stable [stabl] a stable. ◆**stabilisateur** nm stabilizer. ◆**stabiliser** vt to stabilize; − **se s.** vpr to stabilize. ◆**stabilité** nf stability.

stade [stad] nm 1 Sp stadium. 2 (phase) stage.

stage [staʒ] nm training period; (cours) (training) course. ◆**stagiaire** a & nmf trainee.

stagner [stagne] vi to stagnate. ◆**stagnant** a stagnant. ◆**stagnation** nf stagnation.

stalle [stal] nf (box) & Rel stall.

stand [stɑ̃d] nm (d'exposition etc) stand, stall; **s. de ravitaillement** Sp pit; **s. de tir** (de foire) shooting range; Mil firing range.

standard [stɑ̃dar] nm 1 Tél switchboard. 2 a inv (modèle etc) standard. ◆**standardiser** vt to standardize. ◆**standardiste** nmf (switchboard) operator.

standing [stɑ̃diŋ] nm standing, status; **de (grand) s.** (immeuble) luxury-.

starter [startɛr] nm 1 Aut choke. 2 Sp starter.

station [stasjɔ̃] nf (de métro, d'observation etc) & Rad station; (de ski etc) resort; (d'autobus) stop; **s. de taxis** taxi rank, Am

taxi stand; **s. debout** standing (position); **s. (thermale)** spa. ◆**s.-service** nf (pl stations-service) Aut service station.

stationnaire [stasjɔnɛr] vi a stationary.

stationn/er [stasjɔne] vi (se garer) to park; (être garé) to be parked. ◆**—ement** nm parking.

statique [statik] a static.

statistique [statistik] nf (donnée) statistic; **la s.** (techniques) statistics; − a statistical.

statue [staty] nf statue. ◆**statuette** nf statuette.

statuer [statɥe] vi **s. sur** Jur to rule on.

statu quo [statykwo] nm inv status quo.

stature [statyr] nf stature.

statut [staty] nm 1 (position) status. 2 pl (règles) statutes. ◆**statutaire** a statutory.

steak [stɛk] nm steak.

stencil [stɛnsil] nm stencil.

sténo [steno] nf (personne) stenographer; (sténographie) shorthand, stenography; **prendre en s.** to take down in shorthand. ◆**sténodactylo** nf shorthand typist, Am stenographer. ◆**sténographie** nf shorthand, stenography.

stéréo [stereo] nf stereo; − a inv (disque etc) stereo. ◆**stéréophonique** a stereophonic.

stéréotype [stereotip] nm stereotype. ◆**stéréotypé** a stereotyped.

stérile [steril] a sterile; (terre) barren. ◆**stérilisation** nf sterilization. ◆**stériliser** vt to sterilize. ◆**stérilité** nf sterility; (de terre) barrenness.

stérilet [sterilɛ] nm IUD, coil.

stéthoscope [stetɔskɔp] nm stethoscope.

steward [stiwart] nm Av Nau steward.

stigmate [stigmat] nm Fig mark, stigma (de of). ◆**stigmatiser** vt (dénoncer) to stigmatize.

stimul/er [stimyle] vt to stimulate. ◆**—ant** nm Fig stimulus; Méd stimulant. ◆**stimulateur** nm **s. cardiaque** pacemaker. ◆**stimulation** nf stimulation.

stimulus [stimylys] nm (pl stimuli [-li]) (physiologique) stimulus.

stipuler [stipyle] vt to stipulate (**que** that). ◆**stipulation** nf stipulation.

stock [stɔk] nm Com & Fig stock (**de** of). ◆**stock/er** vt to (keep in) stock. ◆**—age** nm stocking.

stoïque [stɔik] a stoic(al). ◆**stoïcisme** nm stoicism.

stop [stɔp] 1 int stop; − nm (panneau) Aut stop sign; (feu arrière) Aut brake light. 2 nm **faire du s.** Fam to hitchhike. ◆**stopp/er** 1 vti to stop. 2 vt (vêtement) to mend (invisibly). ◆—age nm (invisible) mending.

store [stɔr] nm blind, Am (window) shade; (de magasin) awning.

strabisme [strabism] nm squint.

strapontin [strapɔ̃tɛ̃] nm tip-up seat.

stratagème [strataʒɛm] nm stratagem, ploy.

stratège [strateʒ] nm strategist. ◆stratégie nf strategy. ◆stratégique a strategic.

stress [strɛs] nm inv Méd Psy stress. ◆stressant a stressful. ◆stressé a under stress.

strict [strikt] a strict; (langue, tenue, vérité) plain; (droit) basic; le s. minimum/nécessaire the bare minimum/necessities. ◆strictement adv strictly; (vêtu) plainly.

strident [stridɑ̃] a strident, shrill.

strie [stri] nf streak; (sillon) groove. ◆strier vt to streak.

strip-tease [striptiz] nm striptease. ◆strip-teaseuse nf stripper.

strophe [strɔf] nf stanza, verse.

structure [stryktyr] nf structure. ◆structural, -aux a structural. ◆structurer vt to structure.

stuc [styk] nm stucco.

studieux, -euse [stydjø, -øz] a studious; (vacances etc) devoted to study.

studio [stydjo] nm (de peintre) & Cin TV studio; (logement) studio flat ou Am apartment.

stupéfait [stypefɛ] a amazed, astounded (de at, by). ◆stupéfaction nf amazement. ◆stupéfi/er vt to amaze, astound. ◆—ant 1 a amazing, astounding. 2 nm drug, narcotic. ◆stupeur nf 1 (étonnement) amazement. 2 (inertie) stupor.

stupide [stypid] a stupid. ◆stupidement adv stupidly. ◆stupidité nf stupidity; (action, parole) stupid thing.

style [stil] nm style; de s. (meuble) period-. ◆stylisé a stylized. ◆styliste nmf (de mode etc) designer. ◆stylistique a stylistic.

stylé [stile] a well-trained.

stylo [stilo] nm pen; s. à bille ballpoint (pen), biro®; s. à encre fountain pen.

su [sy] voir savoir.

suave [sчav] a (odeur, voix) sweet.

subalterne [sybaltern] a & nmf subordinate.

subconscient [sypkɔ̃sjɑ̃] a & nm subconscious.

subdiviser [sybdivize] vt to subdivide (en into). ◆subdivision nf subdivision.

subir [sybir] vt to undergo; (conséquences, défaite, perte, tortures) to suffer; (influence) to be under; s. qn (supporter) Fam to put up with s.o.

subit [sybi] a sudden. ◆subitement adv suddenly.

subjectif, -ive [sybʒɛktif, -iv] a subjective. ◆subjectivement adv subjectively. ◆subjectivité nf subjectivity.

subjonctif [sybʒɔ̃ktif] nm Gram subjunctive.

subjuguer [sybʒyge] vt to subjugate; (envoûter) to captivate.

sublime [syblim] a & nm sublime.

sublimer [syblime] vt Psy to sublimate.

submerger [sybmɛrʒe] vt to submerge; (envahir) Fig to overwhelm; submergé de (travail etc) overwhelmed with; submergé par (ennemi, foule) swamped by. ◆submersible nm submarine.

subordonn/er [sybordone] vt to subordinate (à to). ◆—é, -ée a subordinate (à to); être s. à (dépendre de) to depend on; — nmf subordinate. ◆subordination nf subordination.

subreptice [sybreptis] a surreptitious.

subside [sypsid] nm grant, subsidy.

subsidiaire [sybsidjer] a subsidiary; question s. (de concours) deciding question.

subsister [sybziste] vi (rester) to remain; (vivre) to get by, subsist; (doutes, souvenirs etc) to linger (on), subsist. ◆subsistance nf subsistence.

substance [sypstɑ̃s] nf substance; en s. Fig in essence. ◆substantiel, -ielle a substantial.

substantif [sypstɑ̃tif] nm Gram noun, substantive.

substituer [sypstitɥe] vt to substitute (à for); se s. à qn to take the place of s.o., substitute for s.o.; (représenter) to substitute for s.o. ◆substitution nf substitution.

subterfuge [sypterfyʒ] nm subterfuge.

subtil [syptil] a subtle. ◆subtilité nf subtlety.

subtiliser [syptilize] vt (dérober) Fam to make off with.

subvenir* [sybvənir] vi s. à (besoins, frais) to meet.

subvention [sybvɑ̃sjɔ̃] nf subsidy. ◆subventionner vt to subsidize.

subversif, -ive [sybversif, -iv] a subversive. ◆subversion nf subversion.

suc [syk] nm (gastrique, de fruit) juice; (de plante) sap.

succédané [syksedane] *nm* substitute (de for).

succéder [syksede] *vi* s. à qn to succeed s.o.; s. à qch to follow sth, come after sth; **— se s.** *vpr* to succeed one another; to follow one another. ◆**successeur** *nm* successor. ◆**successif, -ive** *a* successive. ◆**successivement** *adv* successively. ◆**succession** *nf* 1 succession (de of, à to); **prendre la s. de qn** to succeed s.o. 2 (*patrimoine*) *Jur* inheritance, estate.

succès [sykse] *nm* success; s. de librairie (*livre*) best-seller; **avoir du s.** to be successful, be a success; à s. (*auteur, film etc*) successful; **avec s.** successfully.

succinct [syksɛ̃] *a* succinct, brief.

succion [sy(k)sjɔ̃] *nf* suction.

succomber [sykɔ̃be] *vi* 1 (*mourir*) to die. 2 s. à (*céder à*) to succumb to, give in to.

succulent [sykylɑ̃] *a* succulent.

succursale [sykyrsal] *nf* *Com* branch; magasin à succursales multiples chain *ou* multiple store.

sucer [syse] *vt* to suck. ◆**sucette** *nf* lollipop; (*tétine*) dummy, comforter, *Am* pacifier.

sucre [sykr] *nm* sugar; (*morceau*) sugar lump; s. cristallisé granulated sugar; s. en morceaux lump sugar; s. en poudre, s. semoule caster sugar, *Am* finely ground sugar; s. d'orge barley sugar. ◆**sucr/er** *vt* to sugar, sweeten. ◆**—é** *a* sweet, sugary; (*artificiellement*) sweetened; (*douceureux*) *Fig* sugary, syrupy. ◆**sucrerie 1** *nf* (*usine*) sugar refinery. 2 *nfpl* (*bonbons*) sweets, *Am* candy. ◆**sucrier, -ière** *a* (*industrie*) sugar-; *— nm* (*récipient*) sugar bowl.

sud [syd] *nm* south; **au s. de** south of; **du s.** (*vent, direction*) southerly; (*ville*) southern; (*gens*) from *ou* in the south; **Amérique/Afrique du S.** South America/Africa; **l'Europe du S.** Southern Europe; *— a inv* (*côte*) south(ern). ◆**s.-africain, -aine** *a* & *nmf* South African. ◆**s.-américain, -aine** *a* & *nmf* South American. ◆**s.-est** *nm* & *a inv* south-east. ◆**s.-ouest** *nm* & *a inv* south-west.

Suède [syɛd] *nf* Sweden. ◆**suédois, -oise** *a* Swedish; *— nmf* Swede; *— nm* (*langue*) Swedish.

suer [sye] *vi* (*personne, mur etc*) to sweat; faire s. qn *Fam* to get on s.o.'s nerves; se faire s. *Fam* to be bored stiff; *— vt* (*sang etc*) to sweat. ◆**sueur** *nf* sweat; (**tout**) **en s.** sweating.

suffire* [syfir] *vi* to be enough *ou* sufficient, suffice (à for); **ça suffit!** that's enough!; il suffit de faire one only has to do; **il suffit d'une goutte/etc pour faire** a drop/*etc* is enough to do; **il ne me suffit pas de faire** I'm not satisfied with doing; *— se s.* *vpr* se s. (à soi-même) to be self-sufficient. ◆**suffisant** *a* 1 sufficient, adequate. 2 (*vaniteux*) conceited. ◆**suffisamment** *adv* sufficiently; s. de sufficient, enough. ◆**suffisance** *nf* (*vanité*) conceit.

suffixe [syfiks] *nm* *Gram* suffix.

suffoquer [syfɔke] *vti* to choke, suffocate. ◆**suffocant** *a* stifling, suffocating. ◆**suffocation** *nf* suffocation; (*sensation*) feeling of suffocation.

suffrage [syfraʒ] *nm* *Pol* (*voix*) vote; (*droit*) suffrage.

suggérer [syɡʒere] *vt* (*proposer*) to suggest (de faire doing, que (+ sub) that); (*évoquer*) to suggest. ◆**suggestif, -ive** *a* suggestive. ◆**suggestion** *nf* suggestion.

suicide [sɥisid] *nm* suicide. ◆**suicidaire** *a* suicidal. ◆**se suicid/er** *vpr* to commit suicide. ◆**—é, -ée** *nmf* suicide (victim).

suie [sɥi] *nf* soot.

suif [sɥif] *nm* tallow.

suinter [sɥɛ̃te] *vi* to ooze, seep. ◆**suintement** *nm* oozing, seeping.

suis [sɥi] *voir* être, suivre.·

Suisse [sɥis] *nf* Switzerland. ◆**suisse** *a* & *nmf* Swiss. ◆**Suissesse** *nf* Swiss (woman *ou* girl).

suite [sɥit] *nf* (*reste*) rest; (*continuation*) continuation; (*de film, roman*) sequel; (*série*) series, sequence; (*appartement, escorte*) & *Mus* suite; (*cohérence*) order; *pl* (*résultats*) consequences; (*séquelles*) effects; **attendre la s.** to wait and see what happens next; **donner s. à** (*demande etc*) to follow up; **faire s. (à)** to follow; **prendre la s. de qn** to take over from s.o.; **par la s.** afterwards; **par s. de** as a result of; **à la s.** one after another; **à la s. de** (*derrière*) behind; (*événement, maladie etc*) as a result of; **de s.** in succession.

suiv/re* [sɥivr] *vt* to follow; (*accompagner*) to go with, accompany; (*classe*) *Scol* to attend, go to; (*malade*) to treat; s. (des yeux *ou* du regard) to watch; s. son chemin to go on one's way; se s. to follow each other; *— vi* to follow; faire s. (*courrier*) to forward; 'à s.' 'to be continued'; **comme suit** as follows. ◆**—ant¹, -ante** *a* next, following; (*ci-après*) following; *— nmf* next (one); au s.! next!, the next person! ◆**—ant²** *prép* (*selon*) according to. ◆**—i** *a* (*régulier*) regular, steady; (*cohérent*) coherent; (*article*)

Com regularly on sale; **peu/très s.** (*cours*) poorly/well attended.

sujet[1], **-ette** [syʒɛ, -ɛt] *a* s. à (*maladie etc*) subject *ou* liable to; – *nmf* (*personne*) *Pol* subject.

sujet[2] [syʒɛ] *nm* **1** (*question*) & *Gram* subject; (*d'examen*) question; **au s. de** about; **à quel s.?** about what? **2** (*raison*) cause; **avoir s. de faire** to have (good) cause *ou* (good) reason to do. **3** *nm* (*individu*) subject; **un mauvais s.** (*garçon*) a rotten egg.

sulfurique [sylfyrik] *a* (*acide*) sulphuric, *Am* sulfuric.

sultan [syltɑ̃] *nm* sultan.

summum [sɔmɔm] *nm* (*comble*) *Fig* height.

super [sypɛr] **1** *a* (*bon*) *Fam* great. **2** *nm* (*supercarburant*) *Fam* four-star (petrol), *Am* premium *ou* hi-test gas.

superbe [sypɛrb] *a* superb.

supercarburant [sypɛrkarbyrɑ̃]   *nm* high-octane petrol *ou* *Am* gasoline.

supercherie [sypɛrʃəri] *nf* deception.

superficie [sypɛrfisi] *nf* surface; (*dimensions*) area. ◆**superficiel, -ielle** *a* superficial. ◆**superficiellement** *adv* superficially.

superflu [sypɛrfly] *a* superfluous.

super-grand [sypɛrgrɑ̃] *nm* *Pol Fam* superpower.

supérieur, -eure [sypɛrjœr] *a* (*étages, partie etc*) upper; (*qualité, air, ton*) superior; (*études*) higher; **à l'étage s.** on the floor above; **s. à** (*meilleur que*) superior to, better than; (*plus grand que*) above, greater than; – *nmf* superior. ◆**supériorité** *nf* superiority.

superlatif, -ive [sypɛrlatif, -iv] *a* & *nm* *Gram* superlative.

supermarché [sypɛrmarʃe] *nm* supermarket.

superposer [sypɛrpoze] *vt* (*objets*) to put on top of each other; (*images etc*) to superimpose.

superproduction   [sypɛrprɔdyksjɔ̃]   *nf* (*film*) blockbuster.

superpuissance [sypɛrpɥisɑ̃s] *nf* *Pol* superpower.

supersonique [sypɛrsonik] *a* supersonic.

superstitieux, -euse [sypɛrstisjø, -øz] *a* superstitious. ◆**superstition** *nf* superstition.

superviser [sypɛrvize] *vt* to supervise.

supplanter [syplɑ̃te] *vt* to take the place of.

suppl/er [syplee] *vt* (*remplacer*) to replace; (*compenser*) to make up for; – *vi* **s. à** (*compenser*) to make up for. ◆**—ant, -ante**

a & *nmf* (*personne*) substitute, replacement; (*professeur*) *s.* supply teacher.

supplément [syplemɑ̃] *nm* (*argent*) extra charge, supplement; (*de livre, revue*) supplement; **en s.** extra; **un s. de** (*information, travail etc*) extra, additional. ◆**supplémentaire** *a* extra, additional.

supplice [syplis] *nm* torture; **au s.** *Fig* on the rack. ◆**supplicier** *vt* to torture.

suppli/er [syplije] *vt* **s. qn de faire** to beg *ou* implore s.o. to do; **je vous en supplie!** I beg *ou* implore you! ◆**—ant, -ante** *a* (*regard etc*) imploring. ◆**supplication** *nf* plea, entreaty.

support [sypɔr] *nm* **1** support; (*d'instrument etc*) stand. **2** (*moyen*) *Fig* medium; **s. audio-visuel** audio-visual aid.

support/er[1] [sypɔrte] *vt* to bear, endure; (*frais*) to bear; (*affront etc*) to suffer; (*résister à*) to withstand; (*soutenir*) to support. ◆**—able** *a* bearable; (*excusable, passable*) tolerable.

supporter[2] [sypɔrtɛr] *nm* *Sp* supporter.

supposer [sypoze] *vt* to suppose, assume (**que** that); (*impliquer*) to imply (**que** that); **à s.** *ou* **en supposant que** (+ *sub*) supposing (that). ◆**supposition** *nf* supposition, assumption.

suppositoire [sypozitwar] *nm* *Méd* suppository.

supprimer [syprime] *vt* to remove, get rid of; (*institution, loi*) to abolish; (*journal etc*) to suppress; (*mot, passage*) to cut, delete; (*train etc*) to cancel; (*tuer*) to do away with; **s. qch à qn** to take sth away from s.o. ◆**suppression** *nf* removal; abolition; suppression; cutting; cancellation.

suprématie [sypremasi] *nf* supremacy. ◆**suprême** *a* supreme.

sur [syr] *prép* on, upon; (*par-dessus*) over; (*au sujet de*) on, about; **s. les trois heures** at about three o'clock; **six s. dix** six out of ten; **un jour s. deux** every other day; **coup s. coup** blow after *ou* upon blow; **six mètres s. dix** six metres by ten; **mettre/monter/***etc* **s.** to put/climb/*etc* on (to); **aller/tourner/***etc* **s.** to go/turn/*etc* towards; **s. ce** after which, and then; (*maintenant*) and now.

sur- [syr] *préf* over-.

sûr [syr] *a* sure, certain (**de** of, **que** that); (*digne de confiance*) reliable; (*avenir*) secure; (*lieu*) safe; (*main*) steady; (*goût*) unerring; (*jugement*) sound; **s. de soi** self-assured; **bien s.!** of course!

surabondant [syrabɔ̃dɑ̃] *a* over-abundant.

suranné [syrane] *a* outmoded.

surboum [syrbum] *nf* *Fam* party.

surcharge [syrʃarʒ] *nf* **1** overloading; (*poids*) extra load; **s. de travail** extra work; **en s.** (*passagers etc*) extra. **2** (*correction de texte etc*) alteration; (*de timbre-poste*) surcharge. ◆**surcharger** *vt* (*voiture, personne etc*) to overload (**de** with).

surchauffer [syrʃofe] *vt* to overheat.

surchoix [syrʃwa] *a inv Com* top-quality.

surclasser [syrklase] *vt* to outclass.

surcroît [syrkrwa] *nm* increase (**de** in); **de s., par s.** in addition.

surdité [syrdite] *nf* deafness.

surdoué, -ée [syrdwe] *nmf* child who has a genius-level IQ.

surélever [syrelve] *vt* to raise (the height of).

sûrement [syrmã] *adv* certainly; (*sans danger*) safely.

surenchère [syrãʃɛr] *nf Com* higher bid; **s. électorale** *Fig* bidding for votes. ◆**surenchérir** *vi* to bid higher (**sur** than).

surestimer [syrɛstime] *vt* to overestimate; (*peinture etc*) to overvalue.

sûreté [syrte] *nf* safety; (*de l'état*) security; (*garantie*) surety; (*de geste*) sureness; (*de jugement*) soundness; **être en s.** to be safe; **mettre en s.** to put in a safe place; **de s.** (*épingle, soupape etc*) safety-.

surexcité [syrɛksite] *a* overexcited.

surf [sœrf] *nm Sp* surfing; **faire du s.** to surf, go surfing.

surface [syrfas] *nf* surface; (*dimensions*) (surface) area; **faire s.** (*sous-marin etc*) to surface; (**magasin à**) **grande s.** hypermarket.

surfait [syrfɛ] *a* overrated.

surgelé [syrʒəle] *a* (deep-)frozen; – *nmpl* (deep-)frozen foods.

surgir [syrʒir] *vi* to appear suddenly (**de** from); (*conflit, problème*) to arise.

surhomme [syrɔm] *nm* superman. ◆**surhumain** *a* superhuman.

sur-le-champ [syrləʃã] *adv* immediately.

surlendemain [syrlãdmɛ̃] *nm* **le s.** two days later; **le s. de** two days after.

surmen/er [syrməne] *vt*, **— se s.** *vpr* to overwork. ◆**—age** *nm* overwork.

surmonter [syrmɔ̃te] *vt* **1** (*obstacle, peur etc*) to overcome, get over. **2** (*être placé sur*) to be on top of, top.

surnager [syrnaʒe] *vi* to float.

surnaturel, -elle [syrnatyrɛl] *a* & *nm* supernatural.

surnom [syrnɔ̃] *nm* nickname. ◆**surnommer** *vt* to nickname.

surnombre [syrnɔ̃br] *nm* **en s.** too many; **je suis en s.** I am one too many.

surpasser [syrpase] *vt* to surpass (**en** in); **— se s.** *vpr* to surpass oneself.

surpeuplé [syrpœple] *a* overpopulated.

surplomb [syrplɔ̃] *nm* **en s.** overhanging. ◆**surplomber** *vti* to overhang.

surplus [syrply] *nm* surplus; *pl Com* surplus (stock).

surprendre* [syrprãdr] *vt* (*étonner, prendre sur le fait*) to surprise; (*secret*) to discover; (*conversation*) to overhear; **se s. à faire** to find oneself doing. ◆**surprenant** *a* surprising. ◆**surpris** *a* surprised (**de** at, **que** (+ *sub*) that). ◆**surprise** *nf* surprise. ◆**surprise-partie** *nf* (*pl* **surprises-parties**) party.

surréaliste [syrealist] *a* (*bizarre*) *Fam* surrealistic.

sursaut [syrso] *nm* (sudden) start *ou* jump; **en s.** with a start; **s. de** (*énergie etc*) burst of. ◆**sursauter** *vi* to start, jump.

sursis [syrsi] *nm Mil* deferment; (*répit*) *Fig* reprieve; **un an (de prison) avec s.** a one-year suspended sentence.

surtaxe [syrtaks] *nf* surcharge.

surtout [syrtu] *adv* especially; (*avant tout*) above all; **s. pas** certainly not; **s. que** especially as *ou* since.

surveill/er [syrveje] *vt* (*garder*) to watch, keep an eye on; (*épier*) to watch; (*contrôler*) to supervise; **s. son langage/sa santé** *Fig* to watch one's language/health; **— se s.** *vpr* to watch oneself. ◆**—ant, -ante** *nmf* (*de lycée*) supervisor (in charge of discipline); (*de prison*) warder; (*de chantier*) supervisor; **s. de plage** lifeguard. ◆**surveillance** *nf* watch (**sur** over); (*de travaux, d'ouvriers*) supervision; (*de la police*) surveillance, observation.

survenir* [syrvənir] *vi* to occur; (*personne*) to turn up.

survêtement [syrvɛtmã] *nm Sp* tracksuit.

survie [syrvi] *nf* survival. ◆**surviv/re*** *vi* to survive (**à qch** sth); **s. à qn** to outlive s.o., survive s.o. ◆**—ant, -ante** *nmf* survivor. ◆**survivance** *nf* (*chose*) survival, relic.

survol [syrvɔl] *nm* **le s. de** flying over; (*question*) *Fig* the overview of. ◆**survoler** *vt* (*en avion*) to fly over; (*question*) *Fig* to go over (quickly).

survolté [syrvɔlte] *a* (*surexcité*) worked up.

susceptible [sysɛptibl] *a* **1** (*ombrageux*) touchy, sensitive. **2 s. de** (*interprétations etc*) open to; **s. de faire** likely *ou* liable to do; (*capable*) able to do. ◆**susceptibilité** *nf* touchiness, sensitiveness.

susciter [sysite] *vt* (*sentiment*) to arouse; (*ennuis, obstacles etc*) to create.

suspect, -ecte [syspɛ(kt), -ɛkt] *a* suspicious, suspect; **s. de** suspected of; − *nmf* suspect. ◆**suspecter** *vt* to suspect (**de qch** of sth, **de faire** of doing); (*bonne foi etc*) to question, suspect, doubt.

suspend/re [syspɑ̃dr] *vt* **1** (*destituer, différer, interrompre*) to suspend. **2** (*fixer*) to hang (up) (**à** on); **se s. à** to hang from. ◆**−u** *a* s. **à** hanging from; **pont s.** suspension bridge. ◆**suspension** *nf* **1** (*d'hostilités, d'employé etc*) & *Aut* suspension; **points de s.** *Gram* dots, suspension points. **2** (*lustre*) hanging lamp.

suspens (en) [ɑ̃syspɑ̃] *adv* **1** (*affaire, travail*) in abeyance. **2** (*dans l'incertitude*) in suspense.

suspense [syspɛns] *nm* suspense; **film à s.** thriller, suspense film.

suspicion [syspisjɔ̃] *nf* suspicion.

susurrer [sysyre] *vti* to murmur.

suture [sytyr] *nf Méd* stitching; **point de s.** stitch. ◆**suturer** *vt* to stitch up.

svelte [svɛlt] *a* slender. ◆**sveltesse** *nf* slenderness.

SVP *abrév* (*s'il vous plaît*) please.

syllabe [silab] *nf* syllable.

symbole [sɛ̃bɔl] *nm* symbol. ◆**symbolique** *a* symbolic; (*salaire*) nominal. ◆**symboliser** *vt* to symbolize. ◆**symbolisme** *nm* symbolism.

symétrie [simetri] *nf* symmetry. ◆**symétrique** *a* symmetrical.

sympa [sɛ̃pa] *a inv Fam* = sympathique.

sympathie [sɛ̃pati] *nf* liking, affection; (*affinité*) affinity; (*condoléances*) sympathy; **avoir de la s. pour qn** to be fond of s.o. ◆**sympathique** *a* nice, pleasant; (*accueil, geste*) friendly. ◆**sympathis/er** *vi* to get

on well (**avec** with). ◆**−ant, -ante** *nmf Pol* sympathizer.

symphonie [sɛ̃fɔni] *nf* symphony. ◆**symphonique** *a* symphonic; (*orchestre*) symphony-.

symposium [sɛ̃pozjɔm] *nm* symposium.

symptôme [sɛ̃ptom] *nm* symptom. ◆**symptomatique** *a* symptomatic (**de** of).

synagogue [sinagɔg] *nf* synagogue.

synchroniser [sɛ̃krɔnize] *vt* to synchronize.

syncope [sɛ̃kɔp] *nf Méd* blackout; **tomber en s.** to black out.

syndicat [sɛ̃dika] *nm* **1** (*d'employés, d'ouvriers*) (trade) union; (*de patrons etc*) association. **2 s. d'initiative** tourist (information) office. ◆**syndical, -aux** *a* (*réunion etc*) (trade) union-. ◆**syndicalisme** *nm* trade unionism. ◆**syndicaliste** *nmf* trade unionist; − *a* (trade) union-. ◆**syndiqu/er** *vt* to unionize; − **se s.** *vpr* (*adhérer*) to join a (trade) union. ◆**−é, -ée** *nmf* (trade) union member.

syndrome [sɛ̃drom] *nm Méd* & *Fig* syndrome.

synode [sinɔd] *nm Rel* synod.

synonyme [sinɔnim] *a* synonymous (**de** with); − *nm* synonym.

syntaxe [sɛ̃taks] *nf Gram* syntax.

synthèse [sɛ̃tɛz] *nf* synthesis. ◆**synthétique** *a* synthetic.

syphilis [sifilis] *nf* syphilis.

Syrie [siri] *nf* Syria. ◆**syrien, -ienne** *a* & *nmf* Syrian.

système [sistɛm] *nm* (*structure, réseau etc*) & *Anat* system; **le s. D** *Fam* resourcefulness. ◆**systématique** *a* systematic; (*soutien*) unconditional. ◆**systématiquement** *adv* systematically.

T

T, t [te] *nm* T, t.

t' [t] *voir* te.

ta [ta] *voir* ton¹.

tabac [taba] **1** *nm* tobacco; (*magasin*) tobacconist's (shop), *Am* tobacco store; **t. (à priser)** snuff. **2** *nm* **passer à t.** to beat up; **passage à t.** beating up. **3** *a inv* (*couleur*) buff. ◆**tabatière** *nf* (*boîte*) snuffbox.

tabasser [tabase] *vt Fam* to beat up.

table [tabl] *nf* **1** (*meuble*) table; (*nourriture*) fare; **t. de jeu/de nuit/d'opération** card/bedside/operating table; **t. basse** coffee

table; **t. à repasser** ironing board; **t. roulante** (tea) trolley, *Am* (serving) cart; **mettre/débarrasser la t.** to lay *ou* set/clear the table; **être à t.** to be sitting at the table; **à t.!** (*food's*) ready!; **faire t. rase** *Fig* to make a clean sweep (**de** of); **mettre sur t. d'écoute** (*téléphone*) to tap. **2** (*liste*) table; **t. des matières** table of contents.

tableau, -x [tablo] *nm* **1** (*peinture*) picture, painting; (*image, description*) picture; *Th* scene; **t. de maître** (*peinture*) old master. **2** (*panneau*) board; *Rail* train-indicator;

(*liste*) list; (*graphique*) chart; **t. (noir)** (b[ack)board; **t. d'affichage** notice board, *Am* bulletin board; **t. de bord** *Aut* dashboard; **t. de contrôle** *Tech* control panel.

tabler [table] *vi* **t. sur** to count *ou* rely on.

tablette [tablɛt] *nf* (*d'armoire, de lavabo*) shelf; (*de cheminée*) mantelpiece; (*de chocolat*) bar, slab.

tablier [tablije] *nm* **1** (*vêtement*) apron; (*d'écolier*) smock; **rendre son t.** (*démissionner*) to give notice. **2** (*de pont*) roadway.

tabou [tabu] *a* & *nm* taboo.

tabouret [taburɛ] *nm* stool.

tabulateur [tabylatœr] *nm* (*de machine à écrire etc*) tabulator.

tac [tak] *nm* **répondre du t. au t.** to give tit for tat.

tache [taʃ] *nf* spot, mark; (*salissure*) stain; **faire t.** (*détonner*) *Péj* to jar, stand out; **faire t. d'huile** *Fig* to spread. **◆tacher** *vt*, **— se t.** *vpr* (*tissu etc*) to stain; — *vi* (*vin etc*) to stain. **◆tacheté** *a* speckled, spotted.

tâche [taʃ] *nf* task, job; **travailler à la t.** to do piecework.

tâcher [taʃe] *vi* **t. de faire** to try *ou* endeavour to do.

tâcheron [taʃrɔ̃] *nm* drudge.

tacite [tasit] *a* tacit. **◆—ment** *adv* tacitly.

taciturne [tasityrn] *a* taciturn.

tacot [tako] *nm* (*voiture*) *Fam* (old) wreck, banger.

tact [takt] *nm* tact.

tactile [taktil] *a* tactile.

tactique [taktik] *a* tactical; — *nf* **la t.** tactics; **une t.** a tactic.

Tahiti [taiti] *nm* Tahiti. **◆tahitien, -ienne** [taisjɛ̃, -jɛn] *a* *nmf* Tahitian.

taie [tɛ] *nf* **t. d'oreiller** pillowcase, pillowslip.

taillade [tajad] *nf* gash, slash. **◆taillader** *vt* to gash, slash.

taille¹ [taj] *nf* **1** (*stature*) height; (*dimension, mesure commerciale*) size; **de haute t.** (*personne*) tall; **de petite t.** short; **de t. moyenne** (*objet, personne*) medium-sized; **être de t. à faire** *Fig* to be capable of doing; **de t.** (*erreur, objet*) *Fam* enormous. **2** *Anat* waist; **tour de t.** waist measurement.

taille² [taj] *nf* cutting; cutting out; trimming; pruning; (*forme*) cut. **◆taill/er 1** *vt* to cut; (*vêtement*) to cut out; (*haie, barbe*) to trim; (*arbre*) to prune; (*crayon*) to sharpen. **2 se t.** *vpr* (*partir*) *Arg* to clear off. **◆—é** *a* **t. en athlète**/*etc* built like an athlete/*etc*; **t. pour faire** *Fig* cut out for doing.

taille-crayon(s) [tajkrɛjɔ̃] *nm inv* pencil-sharpener. **◆t.-haies** *nm inv* (garden) shears; (*électrique*) hedge trimmer.

tailleur [tajœr] *nm* **1** (*personne*) tailor. **2** (*costume féminin*) suit.

taillis [taji] *nm* copse, coppice.

tain [tɛ̃] *nm* (*de glace*) silvering; **glace sans t.** two-way mirror.

taire* [tɛr] *vt* to say nothing about; — *vi* **faire t. qn** to silence s.o. **— se t.** *vpr* (*rester silencieux*) to keep quiet (**sur qch** about sth); (*cesser de parler*) to fall silent, shut up; **tais-toi!** be *ou* keep quiet!, shut up!

talc [talk] *nm* talcum powder.

talent [talɑ̃] *nm* talent; **avoir du t. pour** to have a talent for. **◆talentueux, -euse** *a* talented.

taler [tale] *vt* (*fruit*) to bruise.

talion [taljɔ̃] *nm* **la loi du t.** (*vengeance*) an eye for an eye.

talisman [talismɑ̃] *nm* talisman.

talkie-walkie [talkiwalki] *nm* (*poste*) walkie-talkie.

taloche [talɔʃ] *nf* (*gifle*) *Fam* clout, smack.

talon [talɔ̃] *nm* **1** heel; (**chaussures à) talons hauts** high heels, high-heeled shoes. **2** (*de chèque, carnet*) stub, counterfoil; (*bout de pain*) crust; (*de jambon*) heel. **◆talonner** *vt* (*fugitif etc*) to follow on the heels of; (*ballon*) *Rugby* to heel; (*harceler*) *Fig* to hound, dog.

talus [taly] *nm* slope, embankment.

tambour [tɑ̃bur] *nm* **1** (*de machine etc*) & *Mus* drum; (*personne*) drummer. **2** (*porte*) revolving door. **◆tambourin** *nm* tambourine. **◆tambouriner** *vi* (*avec les doigts etc*) to drum (**sur** on).

tamis [tami] *nm* sieve. **◆tamiser** *vt* to sift; (*lumière*) to filter, subdue.

Tamise [tamiz] *nf* **la T.** the Thames.

tampon [tɑ̃pɔ̃] *nm* **1** (*bouchon*) plug, stopper; (*d'ouate*) wad, pad; *Méd* swab; **t. hygiénique** *ou* **périodique** tampon; **t. à récurer** scouring pad. **2** (*de train etc*) & *Fig* buffer; **état t.** buffer state. **3** (*marque, instrument*) stamp; **t. buvard** blotter; **t. encreur** ink(ing) pad. **◆tamponn/er 1** *vt* (*visage etc*) to dab; (*plaie*) to swab. **2** *vt* (*train, voiture*) to crash into; **— se t.** *vpr* to crash into each other. **3** *vt* (*lettre, document*) to stamp. **◆—euses** *afpl* **autos t.** dodgems, bumper cars.

tam-tam [tamtam] *nm* (*tambour*) tom-tom.

tandem [tɑ̃dɛm] *nm* **1** (*bicyclette*) tandem. **2** (*duo*) *Fig* duo, pair; **en t.** (*travailler etc*) in tandem.

tandis que [tɑ̃dik(ə)] *conj* (*pendant que*) while; (*contraste*) whereas, while.

tangent [tɑ̃ʒɑ̃] *a* **1** *Géom* tangential (**à** to).

2 (*juste*) *Fam* touch and go, close. ◆**tangente** *nf Géom* tangent.

tangible [tãʒibl] *a* tangible.

tango [tãgo] *nm* tango.

tang/uer [tãge] *vi* (*bateau, avion*) to pitch. ◆**—age** *nm* pitching.

tanière [tanjɛr] *nf* den, lair.

tank [tãk] *nm Mil* tank.

tanker [tãkɛr] *nm* (*navire*) tanker.

tann/er [tane] *vt* (*cuir*) to tan. ◆**—é** *a* (*visage*) weather-beaten, tanned.

tant [tã] *adv* so much (*que* that); **t. de** (*pain, temps etc*) so much (*que* that); (*gens, choses etc*) so many (*que* that); **t. de fois** so often, so many times; **t. que** (*autant que*) as much as; (*aussi fort que*) as hard as; (*aussi longtemps que*) as long as; **en t. que** (*considéré comme*) as; **t. mieux!** good!, I'm glad!; **t. pis!** too bad!, pity!; **t. soit peu** (even) remotely *ou* slightly; **un t. soit peu** somewhat; **t. s'en faut** far from it; **t. bien que mal** more or less, so-so.

tante [tãt] *nf* aunt.

tantinet [tãtinɛ] *nm & adv* **un t.** a tiny bit (**de** of).

tantôt [tãto] *adv* **1** **t. . . . t.** sometimes . . . sometimes, now . . . now. **2** (*cet après-midi*) this afternoon.

taon [tã] *nm* horsefly, gadfly.

tapage [tapaʒ] *nm* din, uproar. ◆**tapageur, -euse** *a* **1** (*bruyant*) rowdy. **2** (*criard*) flashy.

tape [tap] *nf* slap. ◆**tap/er** **1** *vt* (*enfant, cuisse*) to slap; (*table*) to bang; **t. qn** (*emprunter de l'argent à qn*) *Fam* to touch s.o., tap s.o. (**de** for); **—** *vi* (*soleil*) to beat down; **t. sur qch** to bang on sth; **t. à la porte** to bang on the door; **t. sur qn** (*critiquer*) *Fam* to run s.o. down, knock s.o.; **t. sur les nerfs de qn** *Fam* to get on s.o.'s nerves; **t. dans** (*provisions etc*) to dig into; **t. du pied** to stamp one's foot; **t. dans l'œil à qn** *Fam* to take s.o.'s fancy; **— se t.** *vpr* (*travail*) *Fam* to do, take on; (*repas, vin*) *Fam* to put away. **2** *vti* (*écrire à la machine*) to type. ◆**—ant** *a* **à midi t.** at twelve sharp; **à huit heures tapant(es)** at eight sharp. ◆**—eur, -euse** *nmf Fam* person who borrows money.

tape-à-l'œil [tapalœj] *a inv* flashy, gaudy.

tapée [tape] *nf* **une t. de** *Fam* a load of.

tapioca [tapjɔka] *nm* tapioca.

tapir (se) [sətapir] *vpr* to crouch (down). ◆**tapi** *a* crouching, crouched.

tapis [tapi] *nm* carpet; **t. de bain** bathmat; **t. roulant** (*pour marchandises*) conveyor belt; (*pour personnes*) moving pavement *ou Am* sidewalk; **t. de sol** groundsheet; **t. de table** table cover; **envoyer qn au t.** (*abattre*) to floor s.o.; **mettre sur le t.** (*sujet*) to bring up for discussion. ◆**t.-brosse** *nm* doormat.

tapisser [tapise] *vt* (*mur*) to (wall)paper; to hang with tapestry; (*recouvrir*) *Fig* to cover. ◆**tapisserie** *nf* (*tenture*) tapestry; (*papier peint*) wallpaper. ◆**tapissier, -ière** *nmf* (*qui pose des tissus etc*) upholsterer; **t.(-décorateur)** interior decorator.

tapoter [tapɔte] *vt* to tap; (*joue*) to pat; **—** *vi* **t. sur** to tap (on).

taquin, -ine [takɛ̃, -in] *a* (*fond of*) teasing; **—** *nmf* tease(r). ◆**taquiner** *vt* to tease; (*inquiéter, agacer*) to bother. ◆**taquinerie(s)** *nf(pl)* teasing.

tarabiscoté [tarabiskɔte] *a* over-elaborate.

tarabuster [tarabyste] *vt* (*idée etc*) to trouble (*s.o.*).

tard [tar] *adv* late; **plus t.** later (on); **au plus t.** at the latest; **sur le t.** late in life. ◆**tarder** *vi* (*lettre, saison*) to be a long time coming; **il a fait** to take one's time doing; (*différer*) to delay (in) doing; **ne tardez pas** (*agissez tout de suite*) don't delay; **elle ne va pas t.** she won't be long; **sans t.** without delay; **il me tarde de faire** I long to do. ◆**tardif, -ive** *a* late; (*regrets*) belated. ◆**tardivement** *adv* late.

tare [tar] *nf* **1** (*poids*) tare. **2** (*défaut*) *Fig* defect. ◆**taré** *a* (*corrompu*) corrupt; *Méd* defective; (*fou*) *Fam* mad, idiotic.

targuer (se) [sətarge] *vpr* **se t. de qch/de faire** to boast about sth/about doing.

tarif [tarif] *nm* (*prix*) rate; *Aut Rail* fare; (*tableau*) price list, tariff. ◆**tarification** *nf* (*price*) fixing.

tarir [tarir] *vti*, **— se t.** *vpr* (*fleuve etc*) & *Fig* to dry up; **ne pas t. d'éloges sur qn** to rave about s.o.

tartare [tartar] *a* **sauce t.** tartar sauce.

tarte [tart] **1** *nf* tart, flan, *Am* (*open*) pie. **2** *a inv Fam* (*sot*) silly; (*laid*) ugly. ◆**tartelette** *nf* (*small*) tart.

tartine [tartin] *nf* slice of bread; **t. (de beurre/de confiture)** slice of bread and butter/jam. ◆**tartiner** *vt* (*beurre*) to spread; **fromage à t.** cheese spread.

tartre [tartr] *nm* (*de bouilloire*) scale, fur; (*de dents*) tartar.

tas [tɑ] *nm* pile, heap; **un** *ou* **des t. de** (*beaucoup*) *Fam* lots of; **mettre en t.** to pile *ou* heap up; **former qn sur le t.** (*au travail*) to train s.o. on the job.

tasse [tas] *nf* cup; **t. à café** coffee cup; **t. à thé** teacup; **boire la t.** *Fam* to swallow a mouthful (*when swimming*).

tasser [tɑse] vt to pack, squeeze (**dans** into); (*terre*) to pack down; **un café**/*etc* **bien tassé** (*fort*) a good strong coffee/*etc*; — **se t.** vpr (*se voûter*) to become bowed; (*se serrer*) to squeeze up; (*sol*) to sink, collapse; **ça va se t.** (*s'arranger*) *Fam* things will pan out (all right).

tâter [tate] vt to feel; (*sonder*) *Fig* to sound out; — vi **t. de** (*métier, prison*) to have a taste of, experience; — **se t.** vpr (*hésiter*) to be in *ou* of two minds. ◆**tâtonn/er** vi to grope about, feel one's way. ◆—**ement** *nm* **par t.** (*procéder*) by trial and error. ◆**tâtons (à)** adv **avancer à t.** to feel one's way (along); **chercher à t.** to grope for.

tatillon, -onne [tatijɔ̃, -ɔn] a finicky.

tatou/er [tatwe] vt (*corps, dessin*) to tattoo. ◆—**age** *nm* (*dessin*) tattoo; (*action*) tattooing.

taudis [todi] *nm* slum, hovel.

taule [tol] *nf* (*prison*) *Fam* nick, jug, *Am* can.

taupe [top] *nf* (*animal, espion*) mole. ◆**taupinière** *nf* molehill.

taureau, -x [tɔro] *nm* bull; **le T.** (*signe*) Taurus. ◆**tauromachie** *nf* bull-fighting.

taux [to] *nm* rate; **t. d'alcool/de cholestérol**/*etc* alcohol/cholesterol/*etc* level.

taverne [tavɛrn] *nf* tavern.

taxe [taks] *nf* (*prix*) official price; (*impôt*) tax; (*douanière*) duty; **t. de séjour** tourist tax; **t. à la valeur ajoutée** value-added tax. ◆**taxation** *nf* fixing of the price (**de** of); taxation (**de** of). ◆**taxer** vt **1** (*produit*) to fix the price of; (*objet de luxe etc*) to tax. **2 t. qn de** to accuse s.o. of.

taxi [taksi] *nm* taxi.

taxiphone [taksifon] *nm* pay phone.

Tchécoslovaquie [tʃekɔslɔvaki] *nf* Czechoslovakia. ◆**tchèque** a & *nmf* Czech; — *nm* (*langue*) Czech.

te [t(ə)] (**t'** *before vowel or mute h*) *pron* **1** (*complément direct*) you; **je te vois** I see you. **2** (*indirect*) (to) you; **il te parle** he speaks to you; **elle te l'a dit** she told you. **3** (*réfléchi*) yourself; **tu te laves** you wash yourself.

technicien, -ienne [tɛknisjɛ̃, -jɛn] *nmf* technician. ◆**technique** a technical; — *nf* technique. ◆**techniquement** adv technically. ◆**technocrate** *nm* technocrat. ◆**technologie** *nf* technology. ◆**technologique** a technological.

teck [tɛk] *nm* (*bois*) teak.

teckel [tekɛl] *nm* (*chien*) dachshund.

tee-shirt [tiʃœrt] *nm* tee-shirt.

teindre* [tɛ̃dr] vt to dye; — **se t.** vpr to dye

one's hair. ◆**teinture** *nf* dyeing; (*produit*) dye. ◆**teinturerie** *nf* (*boutique*) (dry) cleaner's. ◆**teinturier, -ière** *nmf* dry cleaner.

teint [tɛ̃] *nm* **1** (*de visage*) complexion. **2 bon** *ou* **grand t.** (*tissu*) colourfast; **bon t.** (*catholique etc*) *Fig* staunch.

teinte [tɛ̃t] *nf* shade, tint; **une t. de** (*dose*) *Fig* a tinge of. ◆**teinter** vt to tint; (*bois*) to stain; **se t. de** (*remarque, ciel*) *Fig* to be tinged with.

tel, telle [tɛl] a such; **un t. homme/livre**/*etc* such a man/book/*etc*; **un t. intérêt**/*etc* such interest/*etc*; **de tels mots**/*etc* such words/*etc*; **t. que** such as, like; **t. que je l'ai laissé** just as I left it; **laissez-le t. quel** leave it just as it is; **en tant que t., comme t.** as such; **t. ou t.** such and such; **rien de t. que . . .** (there's) nothing like . . . ; **rien de t.** nothing like it; **Monsieur Un t.** Mr So-and-so; **t. père t. fils** like father like son.

télé [tele] *nf* (*téléviseur*) *Fam* TV, telly; **à la t.** on TV, on the telly; **regarder la t.** to watch TV *ou* the telly.

télé- [tele] *préf* tele-.

télébenne [teleben] *nf*, **télécabine** [telekabin] *nf* (*cabine, système*) cable car.

télécommande [telekɔmɑ̃d] *nf* remote control. ◆**télécommander** vt to operate by remote control.

télécommunications [telekɔmynikɑsjɔ̃] *nfpl* telecommunications.

téléfilm [telefilm] *nm* TV film.

télégramme [telegram] *nm* telegram.

télégraphe [telegraf] *nm* telegraph. ◆**télégraphie** *nf* telegraphy. ◆**télégraphier** vt (*message*) to wire, cable (que that). ◆**télégraphique** a (*fil, poteau*) telegraph-; (*style*) *Fig* telegraphic. ◆**télégraphiste** *nm* (*messager*) telegraph boy.

téléguid/er [telegide] vt to radio-control. ◆—**age** *nm* radio-control.

télématique [telematik] *nf* telematics, computer communications.

télépathie [telepati] *nf* telepathy.

téléphérique [teleferik] *nm* (*système*) cable car, cableway.

téléphone [telefon] *nm* (tele)phone; **coup de t.** (phone) call; **passer un coup de t. à qn** to give s.o. a call *ou* a ring; **au t.** on the (tele)phone; **avoir le t.** to be on the (tele)phone; **par le t. arabe** *Fig* on the grapevine. ◆**téléphoner** vt (*nouvelle etc*) to (tele)phone (**à** to); — vi to (tele)phone; **t. à qn** to (tele)phone s.o., call s.o. (up). ◆**téléphonique** a (*appel etc*) (tele)phone-. ◆**téléphoniste** *nmf* operator, telephonist.

télescope [telɛskɔp] *nm* telescope. ◆**télescopique** *a* telescopic.

télescop/er [telɛskɔpe] *vt Aut Rail* to smash into; **se t.** to smash into each other. ◆**—age** *nm* smash.

téléscripteur [teleskriptœr] *nm* (*appareil*) teleprinter.

télésiège [telesjɛʒ] *nm* chair lift.

téléski [teleski] *nm* ski tow.

téléspectateur, -trice [telespɛktatœr, -tris] *nmf* (television) viewer.

téléviser [televize] *vt* to televise; **journal télévisé** television news. ◆**téléviseur** *nm* television (set). ◆**télévision** *nf* television; **à la t.** on (the) television; **regarder la t.** to watch (the) television; **de t.** (*programme etc*) television-.

télex [telɛks] *nm* (*service, message*) telex.

telle [tɛl] *voir* **tel**.

tellement [tɛlmɑ̃] *adv* (*si*) so; (*tant*) so much; **t. grand/etc que** so big/etc that; **crier/etc t. que** to shout/etc so much that; **t. de** (*travail etc*) so much; (*soucis etc*) so many; **personne ne peut le supporter, t. il est bavard** nobody can stand him, he's so talkative; **tu aimes ça? - pas t.** do you like it? - not much *ou* a lot.

téméraire [temerɛr] *a* rash, reckless. ◆**témérité** *nf* rashness, recklessness.

témoign/er [temwaɲe] **1** *vi Jur* to testify (**contre** against); **t. de qch** (*personne, attitude etc*) to testify to sth; **—** *vt* **t. que** *Jur* to testify that. **2** *vt* (*gratitude etc*) to show (**à qn** (to) s.o.). ◆**—age** *nm* **1** testimony, evidence; (*récit*) account; **faux t.** (*délit*) *Jur* perjury. **2** (*d'affection etc*) *Fig* token, sign (**de** of); **en t. de** as a token *ou* sign of.

témoin [temwɛ̃] **1** *nm* witness; **t. oculaire** eyewitness; **être t. de** (*accident etc*) to witness; **—** *a* **appartement t.** show flat *ou* *Am* apartment. **2** *nm Sp* baton.

tempe [tɑ̃p] *nf Anat* temple.

tempérament [tɑ̃peramɑ̃] *nm* **1** (*caractère*) temperament; (*physique*) constitution. **2** **acheter à t.** to buy on hire purchase *ou* *Am* on the installment plan.

tempérance [tɑ̃perɑ̃s] *nf* temperance.

température [tɑ̃peratyr] *nf* temperature; **avoir** *ou* **faire de la t.** *Méd* to have a temperature.

tempér/er [tɑ̃pere] *vt Litt* to temper. ◆**—é** *a* (*climat, zone*) temperate.

tempête [tɑ̃pɛt] *nf* storm; **t. de neige** snowstorm, blizzard.

tempêter [tɑ̃pete] *vi* (*crier*) to storm, rage (**contre** against).

temple [tɑ̃pl] *nm Rel* temple; (*protestant*) church.

tempo [tɛmpo] *nm* tempo.

temporaire [tɑ̃pɔrɛr] *a* temporary. ◆**—ment** *adv* temporarily.

temporel, -elle [tɑ̃pɔrɛl] *a* temporal.

temporiser [tɑ̃pɔrize] *vi* to procrastinate, play for time.

temps [tɑ̃] *nm* (*durée, période, moment*) time; *Gram* tense; (*étape*) stage; **t. d'arrêt** pause, break; **en t. de guerre** in time of war, in wartime; **avoir/trouver le t.** to have/find (the) time (**de faire** to do); **il est t.** it is time (**de faire** to do); **il était t.!** it was about time (too)!; **pendant un t.** for a while *ou* time; **ces derniers t.** lately; **de t. en t.** [dətɑ̃zɑ̃tɑ̃], **de t. à autre** [dətɑ̃zaotr] from time to time, now and again; **en t. utile** [ɑ̃tɑ̃zytil] in good *ou* due time; **en même t.** at the same time (**que** as); **à t.** (*arriver*) in time; **à plein t.** (*travailler etc*) full-time; **à t. partiel** (*travailler etc*) part-time; **dans le t.** (*autrefois*) once, at one time; **avec le t.** (*à la longue*) in time; **tout le t.** all the time; **du t. de** in the time of; **de mon t.** in my time; **à quatre t.** (*moteur*) four-stroke.

temps [tɑ̃] *nm* (*atmosphérique*) weather; **il fait beau/mauvais t.** the weather's fine/bad; **quel t. fait-il?** what's the weather like?

tenable [tənabl] *a* bearable.

tenace [tənas] *a* stubborn, tenacious. ◆**ténacité** *nf* stubbornness, tenacity.

tenailler [tənaje] *vt* (*faim, remords*) to rack, torture (*s.o.*).

tenailles [tənaj] *nfpl* (*outil*) pincers.

tenancier, -ière [tənɑ̃sje, -jɛr] *nmf* (*d'hôtel etc*) manager, manageress.

tenant, -ante [tənɑ̃, -ɑ̃t] *nmf* (*de titre*) *Sp* holder. **2** *nm* (*partisan*) supporter (**de**).

tenants [tənɑ̃] *nmpl* **les t. et les aboutissants** (*d'une question etc*) the ins and outs (**de** of).

tendance [tɑ̃dɑ̃s] *nf* (*penchant*) tendency; (*évolution*) trend (**à** towards); **avoir t. à faire** to have a tendency to do, tend to do.

tendancieux, -euse [tɑ̃dɑ̃sjø, -øz] *a Péj* tendentious.

tendeur [tɑ̃dœr] *nm* (*pour arrimer des bagages*) elastic strap.

tendon [tɑ̃dɔ̃] *nm Anat* tendon, sinew.

tend/re [tɑ̃dr] **1** *vt* to stretch; (*main*) to hold out (**à qn** to s.o.); (*bras, jambe*) to stretch out; (*cou*) to strain, crane; (*muscle*) to tense, flex; (*arc*) to bend; (*piège*) to lay, set; (*filet*) to spread; (*tapisserie*) to hang; **t. qch à qn** to hold out sth to s.o.; **t. l'oreille** *Fig* to prick up one's ears; **— se t.** *vpr* (*rap-*

ports) to become strained. **2** *vi* **t. à qch/à faire** to tend towards sth/to do. **◆—u** *a* (*corde*) tight, taut; (*personne, situation*) tense; (*rapports*) strained; (*main*) outstretched.

tendre [tɑ̃dr] *a* **1** (*viande*) tender; (*peau*) delicate, tender; (*bois, couleur*) soft. **2** (*affectueux*) loving, tender. **◆—ment** [-əmɑ̃] *adv* lovingly, tenderly. **◆tendresse** *nf* (*affection*) affection, tenderness. **◆tendreté** *nf* (*de viande*) tenderness.

ténèbres [tenɛbr] *nfpl* darkness, gloom. **◆ténébreux, -euse** *a* dark, gloomy; (*mystérieux*) mysterious.

teneur [tənœr] *nf* (*de lettre etc*) content; **t. en alcool**/*etc* alcohol/*etc* content (of).

tenir* [tənir] *vt* (*à la main etc*) to hold; (*pari, promesse*) to keep; (*hôtel*) to run, keep; (*comptes*) Com to keep; (*propos*) to utter; (*rôle*) to play; **t. propre/chaud**/*etc* to keep clean/hot/*etc*; **je le tiens!** (*je l'ai attrapé*) I've got him!; **je le tiens de** (*fait etc*) I got it from; (*caractère héréditaire*) I get it from; **pour** to regard as; **t. sa droite** *Aut* to keep to the right; **t. la route** (*voiture*) to hold the road; **–** *vi* (*nœud etc*) to hold; (*coiffure, neige*) to last, hold; (*offre*) to stand; (*résister*) to hold out; **t. à** (*personne, jouet etc*) to be attached to, be fond of; (*la vie*) to value; (*provenir*) to stem from; **t. à faire** to be anxious to do; **t. dans qch** (*être contenu*) to fit into sth; **t. de qn** to take after s.o.; **tenez!** (*prenez*) here (you are)!; **tiens!** (*surprise*) hey!, well!; **–** *v imp* **il ne tient qu'à vous** it's up to you (**de faire** to do); **— se t.** *vpr* (*rester*) to keep, remain; (*avoir lieu*) to be held; **se t.** (**debout**) to stand (up); **se t. droit** to stand up *ou* sit up straight; **se t. par la main** to hold hands; **se t. à** to hold on to; **se t. bien** to behave oneself; **tout se tient** *Fig* it all hangs together; **s'en t. à** (*se limiter à*) to stick to; **savoir à quoi s'en t.** to know what's what.

tennis [tenis] *nm* tennis; (*terrain*) (tennis) court; **t. de table** table tennis; **–** *nfpl* (*chaussures*) plimsolls, pumps, *Am* sneakers.

ténor [tenor] *nm* Mus tenor.

tension [tɑ̃sjɔ̃] *nf* tension; **t.** (**artérielle**) blood pressure; **t. d'esprit** concentration; **avoir de la t.** *Méd* to have high blood pressure.

tentacule [tɑ̃takyl] *nm* tentacle.

tente [tɑ̃t] *nf* tent.

tenter¹ [tɑ̃te] *vt* (*essayer*) to try; **t. de faire** to try *ou* attempt to do. **◆tentative** *nf* attempt; **t. de suicide** suicide attempt.

tent/er² [tɑ̃te] *vt* (*allécher*) to tempt; **tenté de faire** tempted to do. **◆—ant** *a* tempting. **◆tentation** *nf* temptation.

tenture [tɑ̃tyr] *nf* (wall) hanging; (*de porte*) drape, curtain.

tenu [təny] *voir* **tenir**; **–** *a* **t. de faire** obliged to do; **bien/mal t.** (*maison etc*) well/badly kept.

ténu [teny] *a* (*fil etc*) fine; (*soupçon, différence*) tenuous; (*voix*) thin.

tenue [təny] *nf* **1** (*vêtements*) clothes, outfit; (*aspect*) appearance; **t. de combat** *Mil* combat dress; **t. de soirée** (*smoking*) evening dress. **2** (*conduite*) (good) behaviour; (*maintien*) posture; **manquer de t.** to lack (good) manners. **3** (*de maison, hôtel*) running; (*de comptes*) Com keeping. **4 t. de route** *Aut* road-holding.

ter [tɛr] *a* **4 t.** (*numéro*) 4B.

térébenthine [terebɑ̃tin] *nf* turpentine.

tergal® [tɛrgal] *nm* Terylene®, *Am* Dacron®.

tergiverser [tɛrʒiverse] *vi* to procrastinate.

terme [tɛrm] *nm* **1** (*mot*) term. **2** (*loyer*) rent; (*jour*) rent day; (*période*) rental period. **3** (*date limite*) time (limit), date; (*fin*) end; **mettre un t. à** to put an end to; **à court/long t.** (*projet etc*) short-/long-term; **être né avant/à t.** to be born prematurely/at (full) term. **4 moyen t.** (*solution*) middle course. **5 en bons/mauvais termes** on good/bad terms (**avec qn** with s.o.).

terminer [tɛrmine] *vt* (*achever*) to finish, complete; (*lettre, phrase, débat, soirée*) to end; **— se t.** *vpr* to end (**par** with, **en** in). **◆terminaison** *nf* Gram ending. **◆terminal, -aux 1** *a* final; (*phase*) Méd terminal; **–** *a & nf* (*classe*) **terminale** Scol = sixth form, *Am* = twelfth grade. **2** *nm* (*d'ordinateur, pétrolier*) terminal.

terminologie [tɛrminɔlɔʒi] *nf* terminology.

terminus [tɛrminys] *nm* terminus.

termite [tɛrmit] *nm* (*insecte*) termite.

terne [tɛrn] *a* (*couleur, journée etc*) dull, drab; (*personne*) dull. **◆ternir** *vt* (*métal, réputation*) to tarnish; (*miroir, meuble*) to dull; **— se t.** *vpr* (*métal*) to tarnish.

terrain [tɛrɛ̃] *nm* (*sol*) & *Fig* ground; (*étendue*) land; *Mil Géol* terrain; (*à bâtir*) plot, site; **un t. a** piece of land; **t. d'aviation** airfield; **t. de camping** campsite; **t. de football/rugby** football/rugby pitch; **t. de golf** golf course; **t. de jeu** playground; **t. de sport** sports ground, playing field; **t. vague** waste ground, *Am* vacant lot; **céder/ gagner/perdre du t.** *Mil & Fig* to give/

lose ground; **tout t., tous terrains** (*véhicule*) all-purpose.

terrasse [tɛras] *nf* **1** terrace; (*toit*) terrace (roof). **2** (*de café*) pavement *ou Am* sidewalk area; **à la t.** outside.

terrassement [tɛrasmɑ̃] *nm* (*travail*) excavation.

terrasser [tɛrase] *vt* (*adversaire*) to floor, knock down; (*accabler*) *Fig* to overcome.

terrassier [tɛrasje] *nm* labourer, navvy.

terre [tɛr] *nf* (*matière*) earth; (*sol*) ground; (*opposé à mer, étendue*) land; *pl* (*domaine*) land, estate; *El* earth, *Am* ground; **la t.** (*le monde*) the earth; **la T.** (*planète*) Earth; **à ou par t.** (*poser, tomber*) to the ground; **par t.** (*assis, couché*) on the ground; **aller à t.** *Nau* to go ashore; **sous t.** underground; **t. cuite** (baked) clay, earthenware; **en t. cuite** (*poterie*) clay-. ◆**t.-à-terre** *a inv* downto-earth. ◆**t.-plein** *nm* (earth) platform; (*au milieu de la route*) central reservation, *Am* median strip. ◆**terrestre** *a* (*vie, joies*) earthly; (*animaux, transport*) land-; **la surface t.** the earth's surface; **globe t.** (terrestrial) globe. ◆**terreux, -euse** *a* (*goût*) earthy; (*sale*) grubby; (*couleur*) dull; (*teint*) ashen. ◆**terrien, -ienne** *a* land-owning; **propriétaire t.** landowner; − *nmf* (*habitant de la terre*) earth dweller, earthling.

terreau [tɛro] *nm* compost.

terrer (se) [sətɛre] *vpr* (*fugitif, animal*) to hide, go to ground *ou* earth.

terreur [tɛrœr] *nf* terror; **t. de** fear of. ◆**terrible** *a* terrible; (*formidable*) *Fam* terrific. ◆**terriblement** *adv* (*extrêmement*) terribly. ◆**terrifier** *vt* to terrify; ◆**−ant** *a* terrifying; (*extraordinaire*) incredible.

terrier [tɛrje] *nm* **1** (*de lapin etc*) burrow. **2** (*chien*) terrier.

terrine [tɛrin] *nf* (*récipient*) *Culin* terrine; (*pâté*) pâté.

territoire [tɛritwar] *nm* territory. ◆**territorial, -aux** *a* territorial.

terroir [tɛrwar] *nm* (*sol*) soil; (*région*) region; **du t.** (*accent etc*) rural.

terroriser [tɛrorize] *vt* to terrorize. ◆**terrorisme** *nm* terrorism. ◆**terroriste** *a & nmf* terrorist.

tertiaire [tɛrsjɛr] *a* tertiary.

tertre [tɛrtr] *nm* hillock, mound.

tes [te] *voir* **ton** [1].

tesson [tɛsɔ̃] *nm* **t. de bouteille** piece of broken bottle.

test [tɛst] *nm* test. ◆**tester** *vt* (*élève, produit*) to test.

testament [tɛstamɑ̃] *nm* **1** *Jur* will; (*œuvre*)

Fig testament. **2 Ancien/Nouveau T.** *Rel* Old/New Testament.

testicule [tɛstikyl] *nm Anat* testicle.

tétanos [tetanos] *nm Méd* tetanus.

têtard [tɛtar] *nm* tadpole.

tête [tɛt] *nf* head; (*figure*) face; (*cheveux*) (head of) hair; (*cerveau*) brain; (*cime*) top; (*de clou, cortège, lit*) head; (*de page, liste*) top, head; (*coup*) *Fb* header; **t. nucléaire** nuclear warhead; **tenir t. à** (*s'opposer à*) to stand up to; **t. nue** bare-headed; **tu n'as pas de t.!** you're a scatterbrain!; **faire la t.** (*bouder*) to sulk; **faire une t.** *Fb* to head the ball; **avoir/faire une drôle de t.** to have/give a funny look; **perdre la t.** *Fig* to lose one's head; **tomber la t. la première** to fall headlong *ou* head first; **calculer qch de t.** to work sth out in one's head; **se mettre dans la t. de faire** to get it into one's head to do; **à t. reposée** at one's leisure; **à la t. de** (*entreprise, parti*) at the head of; (*classe*) *Scol* at the top of; **de la t. aux pieds** from head *ou* top to toe; **en t.** *Sp* in the lead; **en t. à t.** head to toe to. ◆**t.-à-queue** *nm inv* **faire un t.-à-queue** *Aut* to spin right round. ◆**t.-à-tête** *adv* (**en**) **t.-à-tête** (*seul*) in private, alone together; − *nm inv* tête-à-tête. ◆**t.-bêche** *adv* head to tail.

téter [tete] *vt* (*lait, biberon etc*) to suck; **t. sa mère** (*bébé*) to suck, feed; − *vi* **donner à t.** à to feed, suckle. ◆**−ée** *nf* (*de bébé*) feed. ◆**tétine** *nf* **1** (*de biberon*) teat, *Am* nipple; (*sucette*) dummy, *Am* pacifier. **2** (*de vache*) udder. ◆**téton** *nm Fam* breast.

têtu [tɛty] *a* stubborn, obstinate.

texte [tɛkst] *nm* text; *Th* lines, text; (*de devoir*) *Scol* subject; (*morceau choisi*) *Littér* passage. ◆**textuel, -elle** *a* (*traduction*) literal.

textile [tɛkstil] *a & nm* textile.

texture [tɛkstyr] *nf* texture.

TGV [teʒeve] *abrév* = **train à grande vitesse.**

Thaïlande [tailɑ̃d] *nf* Thailand. ◆**thaïlandais, -aise** *a & nmf* Thai.

thé [te] *nm* (*boisson, réunion*) tea. ◆**théière** *nf* teapot.

théâtre [teatr] *nm* (*art, lieu*) theatre; (*œuvres*) drama; (*d'un crime*) *Fig* scene; (*des opérations*) *Mil* theatre; **faire du t.** to act. ◆**théâtral, -aux** *a* theatrical.

thème [tɛm] *nm* theme; (*traduction*) *Scol* translation, prose.

théologie [teɔlɔʒi] *nf* theology. ◆**théologien** *nm* theologian. ◆**théologique** *a* theological.

théorème [teɔrɛm] *nm* theorem.

théorie [teɔri] *nf* theory; **en t.** in theory.

◆**théoricien, -ienne** *nmf* theorist, theoretician. ◆**théorique** *a* theoretical. ◆**théoriquement** *adv* theoretically.

thérapeutique [terapøtik] *a* therapeutic; – *nf* (*traitement*) therapy. ◆**thérapie** *nf Psy* therapy.

thermal, -aux [tɛrmal, -o] *a* **station thermale** spa; **eaux thermales** hot springs.

thermique [tɛrmik] *a* (*énergie, unité*) thermal.

thermomètre [tɛrmɔmɛtr] *nm* thermometer.

thermonucléaire [tɛrmɔnyklɛɛr] *a* thermonuclear.

thermos® [tɛrmɔs] *nm ou f* Thermos (flask)®, vacuum flask.

thermostat [tɛrmɔsta] *nm* thermostat.

thèse [tɛz] *nf* (*proposition, ouvrage*) thesis.

thon [tɔ̃] *nm* tuna (fish).

thorax [tɔraks] *nm Anat* thorax.

thym [tɛ̃] *nm Bot Culin* thyme.

thyroïde [tirɔid] *a & nf Anat* thyroid.

tibia [tibja] *nm* shin bone, tibia.

tic [tik] *nm* (*contraction*) tic, twitch; (*manie*) *Fig* mannerism.

ticket [tikɛ] *nm* ticket; **t. de quai** *Rail* platform ticket.

tic(-)tac [tiktak] *int & nm inv* tick-tock.

tiède [tjɛd] *a* (*luke*)warm, tepid; (*climat, vent*) mild; (*accueil, partisan*) half-hearted. ◆**tiédeur** *nf* (*luke*)warmness, tepidness; mildness; half-heartedness. ◆**tiédir** *vt* to cool (down); (*chauffer*) to warm (up); – *vi* to cool (down); to warm up.

tien, tienne [tjɛ̃, tjɛn] *pron poss* **le t., la tienne, les tien(ne)s** yours; **les deux tiens** your two; – *nmpl* **les tiens** (*amis etc*) your (own) people.

tiens, tient [tjɛ̃] *voir* tenir.

tiercé [tjɛrse] *nm* (*pari*) place betting (*on horses*); **gagner au t.** to win on the races.

tiers, tierce [tjɛr, tjɛrs] *a* third; – *nm* (*fraction*) third; (*personne*) third party; **assurance au t.** third-party insurance. ◆**T.-Monde** *nm* Third World.

tige [tiʒ] *nf* (*de plante*) stem, stalk; (*de botte*) leg; (*barre*) rod.

tignasse [tiɲas] *nf* mop (of hair).

tigre [tigr] *nm* tiger. ◆**tigresse** *nf* tigress.

tigré [tigre] *a* (*tacheté*) spotted; (*rayé*) striped.

tilleul [tijœl] *nm* lime (tree), linden (tree); (*infusion*) lime (blossom) tea.

timbale [tɛ̃bal] *nf* **1** (*gobelet*) (metal) tumbler. **2** *Mus* kettledrum.

timbre [tɛ̃br] *nm* **1** (*marque, tampon, vignette*) stamp; (*cachet de la poste*) postmark. **2** (*sonnette*) bell. **3** (*d'instrument, de voix*) tone (quality). ◆**t.-poste** *nm* (*pl* timbres-poste*) (postage) stamp. ◆**timbr/er** *vt* (*affranchir*) to stamp (letter); (*marquer*) to stamp (document). ◆**—é** *a* **1** (*voix*) sonorous. **2** (*fou*) *Fam* crazy.

timide [timid] *a* (*gêné*) shy, timid; (*timoré*) timid. ◆**—ment** *adv* shyly; timidly. ◆**timidité** *nf* shyness; timidity.

timonier [timɔnje] *nm Nau* helmsman.

timoré [timɔre] *a* timorous, fearful.

tintamarre [tɛ̃tamar] *nm* din, racket.

tint/er [tɛ̃te] *vi* (*cloche*) to ring, toll; (*clés, monnaie*) to jingle; (*verres*) to chink. ◆**—ement(s)** *nm(pl)* ringing; jingling; chinking.

tique [tik] *nf* (*insecte*) tick.

tiquer [tike] *vi* (*personne*) to wince.

tir [tir] *nm* (*sport*) shooting; (*action*) firing, shooting; (*feu, rafale*) fire; *Fb* shot; **t. (forain), (stand de) t.** shooting *ou* rifle range; **t. à l'arc** archery; **ligne de t.** line of fire.

tirade [tirad] *nf Th & Fig* monologue.

tirail/er [tiraje] **1** *vt* to pull (away) at; (*harceler*) *Fig* to pester, plague; **tiraillé entre** (*possibilités etc*) torn between. **2** *vi* (*au fusil*) to shoot wildly. ◆**—ement** *nm* **1** (*conflit*) conflict (**entre** between). **2** (*crampe*) *Méd* cramp.

tire [tir] *nf* **vol à la t.** *Fam* pickpocketing.

tire-au-flanc [tiroflɑ̃] *nm inv* (*paresseux*) shirker. ◆**t.-bouchon** *nm* corkscrew. ◆**t.-d'aile (à)** *adv* swiftly.

tirelire [tirlir] *nf* moneybox, *Am* coin bank.

tir/er [tire] *vt* to pull; (*langue*) to stick out; (*trait, conclusion, rideaux*) to draw; (*chapeau*) to raise; (*balle, canon*) to fire, shoot; (*gibier*) to shoot; *Typ Phot* to print; **t. de** (*sortir*) to take *ou* pull *ou* draw out of; (*obtenir*) to get from; (*nom, origine*) to derive from; (*produit*) to extract from; **t. qn de** (*danger, lit*) to get s.o. out of; – *vi* to pull (sur on, at); (*faire feu*) to fire, shoot (sur at); *Fb* to shoot; (*cheminée*) to draw; **t. sur** (*couleur*) to verge on; **t. au sort** to draw lots; **t. à sa fin** to draw to a close; – **se t.** *vpr* (*partir*) *Fam* to beat it; **se t. de** (*problème, travail*) to cope with; (*danger, situation*) to get out of; **se t. d'affaire** to get out of trouble; **s'en t.** *Fam* (*en réchapper*) to come *ou* pull through; (*réussir*) to get along. ◆**—é** *a* (*traits, visage*) drawn; **t. par les cheveux** *Fig* far-fetched. ◆**—age** *nm* **1** (*action*) *Typ Phot* printing; (*édition*) edition; (*quantité*) (print) run; (*de journal*) circulation. **2** (*de loterie*) draw; **t. au sort**

drawing of lots. **3** (*de cheminée*) draught.
◆**—eur** *nm* gunman; t. **d'élite** marksman;
un **bon/mauvais** t. a good/bad shot.
◆**—euse** *nf* t. de cartes fortune-teller.

tiret [tirɛ] *nm* (*trait*) dash.

tiroir [tirwar] *nm* (*de commode etc*) drawer.
◆**t.-caisse** *nm* (*pl* tiroirs-caisses) (cash)
till.

tisane [tizan] *nf* herb(al) tea.

tison [tizɔ̃] *nm* (fire)brand, ember. ◆**tisonner** *vt* (*feu*) to poke. ◆**tisonnier** *nm*
poker.

tiss/er [tise] *vt* to weave. ◆**—age** *nm* (*action*) weaving. ◆**tisserand, -ande** *nmf*
weaver.

tissu [tisy] *nm* fabric, material, cloth; *Biol*
tissue; un t. de (*mensonges etc*) a web of; le
t. **social** the fabric of society, the social
fabric; du t.-éponge (terry) towelling.

titre [titr] *nm* (*nom, qualité*) title; *Com* bond;
(*diplôme*) qualification; *pl* (*droits*) claims (à
to); (*gros*) t. *Journ* headline; t. de propriété
title deed; t. de transport ticket; à quel t.?
(*pour quelle raison*) on what grounds?; à ce
t. (*en cette qualité*) as such; (*pour cette
raison*) therefore; à aucun t. on no account;
au même t. in the same way (que as); à t.
d'exemple/d'ami as an example/friend; à t.
exceptionnel exceptionally; à t. privé in
a private capacity; à juste t. rightly.
◆**titr/er** *vt* (*film*) to title; *Journ* to run as a
headline. ◆**—é** *a* (*personne*) titled. ◆**titulaire** *a* (*professeur*) staff-, full; être t. de
(*permis etc*) to be the holder of; (*poste*) to
hold; – *nmf* (*de permis, poste*) holder (**de**
of). ◆**titulariser** *vt* (*fonctionnaire*) to give
tenure to.

tituber [titybe] *vi* to reel, stagger.

toast [tost] *nm* **1** (*pain grillé*) piece *ou* slice
of toast. **2** (*allocution*) toast; **porter un** t. à
to drink (a toast) to.

toboggan [tɔbɔgɑ̃] *nm* **1** (*pente*) slide;
(*traîneau*) toboggan. **2** *Aut* flyover, *Am*
overpass.

toc [tɔk] **1** *int* t. t.! knock knock! **2** *nm* du t.
(*camelote*) rubbish, trash; **en** t. (*bijou*) imi-
tation-.

tocsin [tɔksɛ̃] *nm* alarm (bell).

tohu-bohu [tɔybɔy] *nm* (*bruit*) hubbub,
commotion; (*confusion*) hurly-burly.

toi [twa] *pron* **1** (*complément*) you; **c'est** t.
it's you; **avec** t. with you. **2** (*sujet*) you; t., **tu
peux** you may. **3** (*réfléchi*) **assieds-t.** sit
(yourself) down; **dépêche-t.** hurry up.
◆**t.-même** *pron* yourself.

toile [twal] *nf* **1** cloth; (*à voile*) canvas; (*à
draps*) linen; **une** t. a piece of cloth *ou* can-

vas *ou* linen; t. de jute hessian; **drap de** t.
linen sheet; t. de fond *Th* & *Fig* backcloth.
2 (*tableau*) canvas, painting. **3** t. **d'araignée**
cobweb, (spider's) web.

toilette [twalɛt] *nf* (*action*) wash(ing); (*vêtements*) outfit, clothes; **articles de** t. toiletr-
ries; **cabinet de** t. washroom; **eau/savon/
trousse de** t. toilet water/soap/bag; **table
de** t. dressing table; **faire sa** t. to wash (and
dress); **les toilettes** (*W-C*) the toilet(s);
aller aux toilettes to go to the toilet.

toiser [twaze] *vt* to eye scornfully.

toison [twazɔ̃] *nf* (*de mouton*) fleece.

toit [twa] *nm* roof; t. **ouvrant** *Aut* sunroof.
◆**toiture** *nf* roof(ing).

tôle [tol] *nf* la t. sheet metal; **une** t. a steel *ou*
metal sheet; t. **ondulée** corrugated iron.

tolér/er [tɔlere] *vt* (*permettre*) to tolerate,
allow; (*supporter*) to tolerate, bear; (*à la
douane*) to allow. ◆**—ant** *a* tolerant (**à
l'égard de** of). ◆**—able** *a* tolerable.
◆**tolérance** *nf* tolerance; (*à la douane*) allowance.

tollé [tɔle] *nm* outcry.

tomate [tɔmat] *nf* tomato; **sauce** t. tomato
sauce.

tombe [tɔ̃b] *nf* grave; (*avec monument*)
tomb. ◆**tombale** *af* pierre t. gravestone,
tombstone. ◆**tombeau, -x** *nm* tomb.

tomb/er [tɔ̃be] *vi* (*aux être*) to fall; (*température*) to drop, fall; (*vent*) to drop (off);
(*cheveux, robe*) to hang down; t. **malade** to
fall ill; t. (**par terre**) to fall (down); **faire** t.
(*personne*) to knock over; (*gouvernement,
prix*) to bring down; **laisser** t. (*objet*) to
drop; (*personne, projet etc*) *Fig* to drop,
give up; **tu m'as laissé** t. **hier** *Fig* you let me
down yesterday; **se laisser** t. **dans un fauteuil** to drop into an armchair; **tu tombes
bien/mal** *Fig* you've come at the right/
wrong time; t. **de fatigue** *ou* **de sommeil** to
be ready to drop; t. **un lundi** to fall on a
Monday; t. **sur** (*trouver*) to come across.
◆**—ée** *nf* t. de la nuit nightfall.

tombereau, -x [tɔ̃bro] *nm* (*charrette*) tip
cart.

tombola [tɔ̃bɔla] *nf* raffle.

tome [tɔm] *nm* (*livre*) volume.

ton¹, ta, *pl* **tes** [tɔ̃, ta, te] (ta *becomes* ton
[tɔ̃n] *before a vowel or mute h*) *a poss* your; t.
père your father; ta mère your mother; ton
ami(e) your friend.

ton² [tɔ̃] *nm* tone; (*de couleur*) shade, tone;
(*gamme*) *Mus* key; (*hauteur de son*) & *Ling*
pitch; de bon t. (*goût*) in good taste; **donner
le** t. *Fig* to set the tone. ◆**tonalité** *nf* (*de*

radio etc) tone; *Tél* dialling tone, *Am* dial tone.

tond/re [tɔ̃dr] *vt* **1** (*mouton*) to shear; (*cheveux*) to clip, crop; (*gazon*) to mow. **2 t. qn** (*escroquer*) *Fam* to fleece s.o. ◆**—euse** *nf* shears; (*à cheveux*) clippers; **t. (à gazon)** (lawn)mower.

tonifi/er [tɔnifje] *vt* (*muscles, peau*) to tone up; (*esprit, personne*) to invigorate. ◆**—ant** *a* (*activité, climat etc*) invigorating.

tonique [tɔnik] **1** *a* (*accent*) *Ling* tonic. **2** *a* (*froid, effet, vin*) tonic, invigorating; – *nm* *Méd* tonic.

tonitruant [tɔnitryɑ̃] *a* (*voix*) *Fam* booming.

tonnage [tɔnaʒ] *nm* *Nau* tonnage.

tonne [tɔn] *nf* (*poids*) metric ton, tonne; **des tonnes de** (*beaucoup*) *Fam* tons of.

tonneau, -x [tɔno] *nm* **1** (*récipient*) barrel, cask. **2** (*manœuvre*) *Av* roll; **faire un t.** *Aut* to roll over. **3** (*poids*) *Nau* ton. ◆**tonnelet** *nm* keg.

tonnelle [tɔnɛl] *nf* arbour, bower.

tonner [tɔne] *vi* (*canons*) to thunder; (*crier*) *Fig* to thunder, rage (**contre** against); – *v imp* **il tonne** it's thundering. ◆**tonnerre** *nm* thunder; **coup de t.** thunderclap; *Fig* bombshell, thunderbolt; **du t.** (*excellent*) *Fam* terrific.

tonte [tɔ̃t] *nf* (*de moutons*) shearing; (*de gazon*) mowing.

tonton [tɔ̃tɔ̃] *nm* *Fam* uncle.

tonus [tɔnys] *nm* (*énergie*) energy, vitality.

top [tɔp] *nm* (*signal sonore*) *Rad* stroke.

topaze [tɔpaz] *nf* (*pierre*) topaz.

topinambour [tɔpinɑ̃bur] *nm* Jerusalem artichoke.

topo [tɔpo] *nm* (*exposé*) *Fam* talk, speech.

topographie [tɔpɔgrafi] *nf* topography.

toque [tɔk] *nf* (*de fourrure*) fur hat; (*de juge, jockey*) cap; (*de cuisinier*) hat.

toqu/er (se) [sətɔke] *vpr* **se t. de qn** *Fam* to become infatuated with s.o. ◆**—é** *a* (*fou*) *Fam* crazy. ◆**toquade** *nf* *Fam* (*pour qch*) craze (**pour** for); (*pour qn*) infatuation (**pour** with).

torche [tɔrʃ] *nf* (*flambeau*) torch; **t. électrique** torch, *Am* flashlight.

torcher [tɔrʃe] *vt* **1** (*travail*) to skimp. **2** (*essuyer*) *Fam* to wipe.

torchon [tɔrʃɔ̃] *nm* (*à vaisselle*) tea towel, *Am* dish towel; (*de ménage*) duster, cloth.

tord/re [tɔrdr] *vt* to twist; (*linge, cou*) to wring; (*barre*) to bend; **se t. la cheville/le pied/le dos** to twist *ou* sprain one's ankle/foot/back; **— se t.** *vpr* to twist; (*barre*) to bend; **se t. de douleur** to writhe with pain; **se t. (de rire)** to split one's sides

(laughing). ◆**—ant** *a* (*drôle*) *Fam* hilarious. ◆**—u** *a* twisted; (*esprit*) warped.

tornade [tɔrnad] *nf* tornado.

torpeur [tɔrpœr] *nf* lethargy, torpor.

torpille [tɔrpij] *nf* torpedo. ◆**torpill/er** *vt* *Mil & Fig* to torpedo. ◆**—eur** *nm* torpedo boat.

torréfier [tɔrefje] *vt* (*café*) to roast.

torrent [tɔrɑ̃] *nm* (*ruisseau*) torrent; **un t. de** (*injures, larmes*) a flood of; **il pleut à torrents** it's pouring (down). ◆**torrentiel, -ielle** *a* (*pluie*) torrential.

torride [tɔrid] *a* (*chaleur etc*) torrid, scorching.

torsade [tɔrsad] *nf* (*de cheveux*) twist, coil. ◆**torsader** *vt* to twist (together).

torse [tɔrs] *nm* *Anat* chest; (*statue*) torso.

torsion [tɔrsjɔ̃] *nf* twisting; *Phys Tech* torsion.

tort [tɔr] *nm* (*dommage*) wrong; (*défaut*) fault; **avoir t.** to be wrong (**de faire** to do, in doing); **tu as t. de fumer!** you shouldn't smoke!; **être dans son t.** *ou* **en t.** to be in the wrong; **donner t. à qn** (*accuser*) to blame s.o.; (*faits etc*) to prove s.o. wrong; **faire du t. à qn** to harm *ou* wrong s.o.; **à t.** wrongly; **à t. et à travers** wildly, indiscriminately; **à t. ou à raison** rightly or wrongly.

torticolis [tɔrtikɔli] *nm* stiff neck.

tortill/er [tɔrtije] *vt* to twist, twirl; (*moustache*) to twirl; (*tripoter*) to twiddle with; **— se t.** *vpr* (*ver, personne*) to wriggle; (*en dansant, des hanches*) to wiggle. ◆**—ement** *nm* wriggling, wiggling.

tortionnaire [tɔrsjɔnɛr] *nm* torturer.

tortue [tɔrty] *nf* tortoise; (*marine*) turtle; **quelle t.!** *Fig* what a slowcoach *ou* *Am* slowpoke!

torture [tɔrtyr] *nf* torture. ◆**torturer** *vt* to torture; **se t. les méninges** to rack one's brains.

tôt [to] *adv* early; **au plus t.** at the earliest; **le plus t. possible** as soon as possible; **t. ou tard** sooner or later; **je n'étais pas plus t. sorti que . . .** no sooner had I gone out than . . . .

total, -aux [tɔtal, -o] *a & nm* total; **au t.** all in all, in total; (*somme toute*) all in all. ◆**totalement** *adv* totally, completely. ◆**totaliser** *vt* to total. ◆**totalité** *nf* entirety; **la t. de** all of; **en t.** entirely, totally.

totalitaire [tɔtalitɛr] *a* *Pol* totalitarian.

toubib [tubib] *nm* (*médecin*) *Fam* doctor.

touche [tuʃ] *nf* (*de peintre*) touch; *Pêche* bite; (*clavier*) key; **une t. de** (*un peu de*) a touch *ou* hint of; **(ligne de)** t. *Fb Rugby* touchline.

touche-à-tout [tuʃatu] **1** *a* & *nmf inv* (*qui touche*) meddlesome (person). **2** *nmf inv* (*qui se disperse*) dabbler.

touch/er [tuʃe] *vt* to touch; (*paie*) to draw; (*chèque*) to cash; (*cible*) to hit; (*émouvoir*) to touch, move; (*concerner*) to affect; **t. qn** (*contacter*) to get in touch with s.o., reach s.o.; − *vi* **t. à** to touch; (*sujet*) to touch on; (*but, fin*) to approach; − **se t.** *vpr* (*lignes etc*) to touch; − *nm* (*sens*) touch; **au t.** to the touch. ◆**—ant** *a* (*émouvant*) touching, moving.

touffe [tuf] *nf* (*de cheveux, d'herbe*) tuft; (*de plantes*) cluster. ◆**touffu** *a* (*barbe, haie*) thick, bushy; (*livre*) *Fig* heavy.

toujours [tuʒur] *adv* always; (*encore*) still; **pour t.** for ever; **essaie t.!** (*quand même*) try anyhow!; **t. est-il que . . .** the fact remains that . . . .

toupet [tupε] *nm* (*audace*) *Fam* cheek, nerve.

toupie [tupi] *nf* (spinning) top.

tour[1] [tur] *nf* **1** *Archit* tower; (*immeuble*) tower block, high-rise. **2** *Échecs* rook, castle.

tour[2] [tur] *nm* **1** (*mouvement, ordre, tournure*) turn; (*artifice*) trick; (*excursion*) trip, outing; (*à pied*) stroll, walk; (*en voiture*) drive; **t. (de phrase)** turn of phrase; **t. (de piste)** *Sp* lap; **t. de cartes** card trick; **t. d'horizon** survey; **t. de poitrine/***etc* chest/*etc* measurement *ou* size; **de dix mètres de t.** ten metres round; **faire le t. de** to go round; (*question, situation*) to review; **faire un t.** (*à pied*) to go for a stroll *ou* walk; (*en voiture*) to go for a drive; (*voyage*) to go on a trip; **faire** *ou* **jouer un t. à qn** to play a trick on s.o.; **c'est mon t.** it's my turn; **à qui le tour?** whose turn (is it)?; **à son t.** in (one's) turn; **à t. de rôle** in turn; **t. à t.** in turn, by turns. **2** *Tech* lathe; (*de potier*) wheel.

tourbe [turb] *nf* peat. ◆**tourbière** *nf* peat bog.

tourbillon [turbijɔ̃] *nm* (*de vent*) whirlwind; (*d'eau*) whirlpool; (*de neige, sable*) eddy; (*tournoiement*) *Fig* whirl, swirl. ◆**tourbillonner** *vi* to whirl, swirl; to eddy.

tourelle [turεl] *nf* turret.

tourisme [turism] *nm* tourism; **faire du t.** to do some sightseeing *ou* touring; **agence/office de t.** tourist agency/office. ◆**touriste** *nmf* tourist. ◆**touristique** *a* (*guide, menu etc*) tourist-; **route t., circuit t.** scenic route.

tourment [turmɑ̃] *nm* torment. ◆**tour-**

ment/er *vt* to torment; − **se t.** *vpr* to worry (oneself). ◆**—é** *a* (*mer, vie*) turbulent, stormy; (*sol*) rough, uneven; (*expression, visage*) anguished.

tourmente [turmɑ̃t] *nf* (*troubles*) turmoil.

tourne-disque [turnədisk] *nm* record player.

tournée [turne] *nf* **1** (*de livreur etc*) round; (*théâtrale*) tour; **faire la t. de** (*magasins etc*) to make the rounds of, go round. **2** (*de boissons*) round.

tourn/er [turne] *vt* to turn; (*film*) to shoot, make; (*difficulté*) to get round; **t. en ridicule** to ridicule; − *vi* to turn; (*tête, toupie*) to spin; (*Terre*) to revolve, turn; (*moteur*) to run, go; (*usine*) to run; (*lait, viande*) to go off; *Cin* to shoot; **t. autour de** (*objet*) to go round; (*maison, personne*) to hang around; (*question*) to centre on; **t. bien/mal** (*évoluer*) to turn out well/badly; **t. au froid** (*temps*) to turn cold; **t. à l'aigre** (*ton, conversation etc*) to turn nasty *ou* sour; **t. de l'œil** *Fam* to faint; − **se t.** *vpr* to turn (**vers** to, towards). ◆**—ant 1** *a* **pont t.** swing bridge. **2** *nm* (*virage*) bend, turning; (*moment*) *Fig* turning point. ◆**—age** *nm Cin* shooting, filming. ◆**—eur** *nm* (*ouvrier*) turner. ◆**tournoyer** *vi* to spin (round), whirl. ◆**tournure** *nf* (*expression*) turn of phrase; **t. d'esprit** way of thinking; **t. des événements** turn of events; **prendre t.** (*forme*) to take shape.

tournesol [turnəsɔl] *nm* sunflower.

tournevis [turnəvis] *nm* screwdriver.

tourniquet [turnikε] *nm* **1** (*barrière*) turnstile. **2** (*pour arroser*) sprinkler.

tournoi [turnwa] *nm Sp & Hist* tournament.

tourte [turt] *nf* pie.

tourterelle [turtərεl] *nf* turtledove.

Toussaint [tusε̃] *nf* All Saints' Day.

tousser [tuse] *vi* to cough.

tout, toute, *pl* **tous, toutes** [tu, tut, tu, tut] **1** *a* all; **tous les livres/***etc* all the books/*etc*; **t. l'argent/le village/***etc* the whole of the money/village/*etc*; **toute la nuit** all night, the whole (of the) night; **tous (les) deux both; tous (les) trois** all three; **t. un problème** quite a problem. **2** *a* (*chaque*) every, each; (*n'importe quel*) any; **tous les ans/jours/***etc* every *ou* each year/day/*etc*; **tous les deux/trois mois/***etc* every second/third month/*etc*; **tous les cinq mètres** every five metres; **t. homme** [tutɔm] every *ou* any man; **à toute heure** at any time. **3** *pron pl* (**tous =** [tus]) all; **ils sont tous là, tous sont là** they're all there. **4** *pron m sing* **tout** everything;

dépenser t. to spend everything, spend it all; t. ce que everything that, all that; en t. (au total) in all. 5 adv (tout à fait) quite; (très) very; t. petit very small; t. neuf brand new; t. simplement quite simply; t. seul all alone; t. droit straight ahead; t. autour all around, right round; t. au début right at the beginning; le t. premier the very first; t. au moins/plus the very least/most; t. en chantant/etc while singing/etc; t. rusé qu'il est however sly he may be; t. à coup suddenly, all of a sudden; t. à fait completely, quite; t. de même all the same; (indignation) really!; t. de suite at once. 6 nm le t. everything, the lot; un t. a whole; le t. est (l'important) the main thing is (que that, de faire to do); pas du t. not at all; rien du t. nothing at all; du t. au t. (changer) entirely, completely. ◆t.-puissant, toute-puissante a all-powerful.

tout-à-l'égout [tutalegu] nm inv mains drainage.

toutefois [tutfwa] adv nevertheless, however.

toutou [tutu] nm (chien) Fam doggie.

toux [tu] nf cough.

toxicomane [tɔksikɔman] nmf drug addict. ◆toxicomanie nf drug addiction. ◆toxine nf toxin. ◆toxique a toxic.

trac [trak] nm le t. (peur) the jitters; (de candidat) exam nerves; Th stage fright.

tracas [traka] nm worry. ◆tracasser vt, — se t. vpr to worry. ◆tracasseries nfpl annoyances. ◆tracassier, -ière a irksome.

trace [tras] nf (quantité, tache, vestige) trace; (marque) mark; (de fugitif etc) trail; pl (de bête, de pneus) tracks; traces de pas footprints; suivre les traces de qn Fig to follow in s.o.'s footsteps.

trac/er [trase] vt (dessiner) to draw; (écrire) to trace; t. une route to mark out a route; (frayer) to open up a route. ◆—é nm (plan) layout; (ligne) line.

trachée [traʃe] nf Anat windpipe.

tract [trakt] nm leaflet.

tractations [traktasjɔ̃] nfpl Péj dealings.

tracter [trakte] vt (caravane etc) to tow. ◆tracteur nm (véhicule) tractor.

traction [traksjɔ̃] nf Tech traction; Sp pull-up; t. arrière/avant Aut rear-/front-wheel drive.

tradition [tradisjɔ̃] nf tradition. ◆traditionnel, -elle a traditional.

traduire* [traduir] vt 1 to translate (de from, en into); (exprimer) Fig to express. 2 t. qn en justice to bring s.o. before the

courts. ◆traducteur, -trice nmf translator. ◆traduction nf translation. ◆traduisible a translatable.

trafic [trafik] nm 1 Aut Rail etc traffic. 2 Com Péj traffic, trade; faire du t. to traffic, trade; faire le t. de to traffic in, trade in. ◆trafiqu/er 1 vi to traffic, trade. 2 vt (produit) Fam to tamper with. ◆—ant, -ante nmf trafficker, dealer; t. d'armes/de drogue arms/drug trafficker ou dealer.

tragédie [traʒedi] nf Th & Fig tragedy. ◆tragique a tragic. ◆tragiquement adv tragically.

trahir [trair] vt to betray; (secret etc) to betray, give away; (forces) to fail (s.o.); — se t. vpr to give oneself away, betray oneself. ◆trahison nf betrayal; (crime) Pol treason.

train [trɛ̃] nm 1 (locomotive, transport, jouet) train; t. à grande vitesse high-speed train; t. couchettes sleeper; t. auto-couchettes (car) sleeper. 2 en t. (forme) on form; se mettre en t. to get (oneself) into shape. 3 être en t. de faire to be busy doing; mettre qch en t. to get sth going, start sth off. 4 (allure) pace; t. de vie life style. 5 (de pneus) set; (de péniches, véhicules) string. 6 t. d'atterrissage Av undercarriage.

traîne [trɛn] nf 1 (de robe) train. 2 à la t. (en arrière) lagging behind.

traîneau, -x [trɛno] nm sledge, sleigh, Am sled.

traînée [trɛne] nf 1 (de substance) trail, streak; (bande) streak; se répandre comme une t. de poudre (vite) to spread like wildfire. 2 (prostituée) Arg tart.

traîner [trɛne] vt to drag; (mots) to drawl; (faire) t. en longueur (faire durer) to drag out; — vi (jouets, papiers etc) to lie around; (subsister) to linger on; (s'attarder) to lag behind, dawdle; (errer) to hang around; t. (par terre) (robe etc) to trail (on the ground); t. (en longueur) (durer) to drag on; — se t. vpr (avancer) to drag oneself (along); (par terre) to crawl; (durer) to drag on. ◆traînant a (voix) drawling. ◆traînailler vi Fam = traînasser. ◆traînard, -arde nmf slowcoach, Am slowpoke. ◆traînasser vi Fam to dawdle; (errer) to hang around.

train-train [trɛ̃trɛ̃] nm routine.

traire* [trɛr] vt (vache) to milk.

trait [trɛ] nm 1 line; (en dessinant) stroke; (caractéristique) feature, trait; pl (du visage) features; t. d'union hyphen; (intermédiaire) Fig link; d'un t. (boire) in one gulp, in one go; **à grands traits** in outline; **t. de** (*esprit, génie*) flash of; (*bravoure*) act of; **avoir t. à** (*se rapporter à*) to relate to. **2 cheval de t.** draught horse.

traite [trɛt] *nf* **1** (*de vache*) milking. **2** *Com* bill, draft. **3 d'une (seule) t.** (*sans interruption*) in one go. **4 t. des Noirs** slave trade; **t. des blanches** white slave trade.

traité [trete] *nm* **1** *Pol* treaty. **2** (*ouvrage*) treatise (**sur** on).

trait/er [trete] *vt* (*se comporter envers*) & *Méd* to treat; (*problème, sujet*) to deal with; (*marché*) *Com* to negotiate; (*matériau, produit*) to treat, process; **t. qn de lâche**/*etc* to call s.o. a coward/*etc*; — *vi* to negotiate, deal (**avec** with); **t. de** (*sujet*) to deal with. ◆—**ant** [-ɛtã] *a* **médecin t.** regular doctor. ◆—**ement** [-ɛtmã] *nm* **1** treatment; **mauvais traitements** rough treatment; **t. de données/de texte** data/word processing; **machine de t. de texte** word processor. **2** (*gains*) salary.

traiteur [trɛtœr] *nm* (*fournisseur*) caterer; **chez le t.** (*magasin*) at the delicatessen.

traître [trɛtr] *nm* traitor; **en t.** treacherously; — *a* (*dangereux*) treacherous; **être t. à** to be a traitor to. ◆**traîtrise** *nf* treachery.

trajectoire [traʒɛktwar] *nf* path, trajectory.

trajet [traʒɛ] *nm* journey, trip; (*distance*) distance; (*itinéraire*) route.

trame [tram] *nf* **1** (*de récit etc*) framework. **2** (*de tissu*) weft.

tramer [trame] *vt* (*évasion etc*) to plot; (*complot*) to hatch.

trampoline [trãpɔlin] *nm* trampoline.

tram(way) [tram(wɛ)] *nm* tram, *Am*. streetcar.

tranche [trãʃ] *nf* (*morceau coupé*) slice; (*bord*) edge; (*partie*) portion; (*de salaire, impôts*) bracket; **t. d'âge** age bracket.

tranchée [trãʃe] *nf* trench.

tranch/er [trãʃe] **1** *vt* to cut. **2** *vt* (*difficulté, question*) to settle; — *vi* (*décider*) to decide. **3** *vi* (*contraster*) to contrast (**avec, sur** with). ◆—**ant 1** *a* (*couteau*) sharp; — *nm* (*cutting*) edge. **2** *a* (*péremptoire*) trenchant, cutting. ◆—**é** *a* (*couleurs*) distinct; (*opinion*) clear-cut.

tranquille [trãkil] *a* quiet; (*mer*) calm, still; (*conscience*) clear; (*certain*) *Fam* confident; **je suis t.** (*rassuré*) my mind is at rest; **soyez t.** don't worry; **laisser t.** to leave be *ou* alone. ◆**tranquillement** *adv* calmly. ◆**tranquillis/er** *vt* to reassure; **tranquillisez-vous** set your mind at rest. ◆—**ant** *nm Méd* tranquillizer. ◆**tranquil-**

lité *nf* (peace and) quiet; (*d'esprit*) peace of mind.

trans- [trãz, trãs] *préf* trans-.

transaction [trãzaksjõ] *nf* **1** (*compromis*) compromise. **2** *Com* transaction.

transatlantique [trãzatlãtik] *a* transatlantic; — *nm* (*paquebot*) transatlantic liner; (*chaise*) deckchair.

transcend/er [trãsãde] *vt* to transcend. ◆—**ant** *a* transcendent.

transcrire* [trãskrir] *vt* to transcribe. ◆**transcription** *nf* transcription; (*document*) transcript.

transe [trãs] *nf* **en t.** (*mystique*) in a trance; (*excité*) very exited.

transférer [trãsfere] *vt* to transfer (**à** to). ◆**transfert** *nm* transfer.

transfigurer [trãsfigyre] *vt* to transform, transfigure.

transformer [trãsfɔrme] *vt* to transform, change; (*maison, matière première*) to convert; (*robe etc*) to alter; (*essai*) *Rugby* to convert; **t. en** to turn into; — **se t.** *vpr* to change, be transformed (**en** into). ◆**transformateur** *nm Él* transformer. ◆**transformation** *nf* transformation, change; conversion.

transfuge [trãsfyʒ] *nm Mil* renegade; — *nmf Pol* renegade.

transfusion [trãsfyzjõ] *nf* **t. (sanguine)** (blood) transfusion.

transgresser [trãsgrese] *vt* (*loi, ordre*) to disobey.

transi [trãzi] *a* (*personne*) numb with cold; **t. de peur** paralysed by fear.

transiger [trãziʒe] *vi* to compromise.

transistor [trãzistɔr] *nm* (*dispositif, poste*) transistor. ◆**transistorisé** *a* (*téléviseur etc*) transistorized.

transit [trãzit] *nm* transit; **en t.** in transit. ◆**transiter** *vt* (**faire**) **t.** to send in transit; — *vi* to be in transit.

transitif, -ive [trãzitif, -iv] *a Gram* transitive.

transition [trãzisjõ] *nf* transition. ◆**transitoire** *a* (*qui passe*) transient; (*provisoire*) transitional.

transmettre* [trãsmetr] *vt* (*héritage, message etc*) to pass on (**à** to); *Phys Tech* to transmit; *Rad TV* to broadcast, transmit. ◆**transmetteur** *nm* (*appareil*) transmitter, transmitting device. ◆**transmission** *nf* transmission; passing on.

transparaître* [trãsparɛtr] *vi* to show (through).

transparent [trãsparã] *a* transparent. ◆**transparence** *nf* transparency.

transpercer [trɑ̃spɛrse] *vt* to pierce, go through.

transpirer [trɑ̃spire] *vi* (*suer*) to perspire; (*information*) *Fig* to leak out. ◆**transpiration** *nf* perspiration.

transplanter [trɑ̃splɑ̃te] *vt* (*organe, plante etc*) to transplant. ◆**transplantation** *nf* transplantation; (*greffe*) *Méd* transplant.

transport [trɑ̃spɔr] *nm* 1 (*action*) transport, transportation (**de** of); *pl* (*moyens*) transport; **moyen de t.** means of transport; **transports en commun** public transport. 2 (*émotion*) *Litt* rapture. ◆**transporter** 1 *vt* (*véhicule, train*) to transport, convey; (*à la main*) to carry, take; **t. d'urgence à l'hôpital** to rush to hospital; — **se t.** *vpr* (*aller*) to take oneself (à to). 2 *vt* *Litt* to enrapture. ◆**transporteur** *nm* **t.** (*routier*) haulier, *Am* trucker.

transposer [trɑ̃spoze] *vt* to transpose. ◆**transposition** *nf* transposition.

transvaser [trɑ̃svaze] *vt* (*vin*) to decant.

transversal, -aux [trɑ̃svɛrsal, -o] *a* (*barre, rue etc*) cross-, transverse.

trapèze [trapɛz] *nm* (*au cirque*) trapeze. ◆**trapéziste** *nmf* trapeze artist.

trappe [trap] *nf* (*dans le plancher*) trap door.

trappeur [trapœr] *nm* (*chasseur*) trapper.

trapu [trapy] *a* 1 (*personne*) stocky, thickset. 2 (*problème etc*) *Fam* tough.

traquenard [traknar] *nm* trap.

traquer [trake] *vt* to track *ou* hunt (down).

traumatis/er [tromatize] *vt* to traumatize. ◆**—ant** *a* traumatic. ◆**traumatisme** *nm* (*choc*) trauma.

travail, -aux [travaj, -o] *nm* (*activité, lieu*) work; (*emploi, tâche*) job; (*façonnage*) working (**de** of); (*ouvrage, étude*) work, publication; *Écon Méd* labour; *pl* work; (*dans la rue*) roadworks; (*aménagement*) alterations; **travaux forcés** hard labour; **travaux ménagers** housework; **travaux pratiques** *Scol Univ* practical work; **travaux publics** public works; **t. au noir** moonlighting; **en t.** (*femme*) *Méd* in labour.

travaill/er [travaje] 1 *vi* to work (à qch at *ou* on sth); — *vt* (*discipline, rôle, style*) to work on; (*façonner*) to work; (*inquiéter*) to worry; **t. la terre** to work the land. 2 *vi* (*bois*) to warp. ◆**—é** *a* (*style*) elaborate. ◆**—eur, -euse** *a* hard-working; — *nmf* worker. ◆**travailliste** *a* *Pol* Labour-; — *nmf* *Pol* member of the Labour party.

travers [travɛr] 1 *prép & adv* **à t.** through; **en t.** (**de**) across. 2 *adv* **de t.** (*chapeau, nez etc*) crooked; (*comprendre*) badly; (*regarder*) askance; **aller de t.** *Fig* to go

wrong; **j'ai avalé de t.** it went down the wrong way. 3 *nm* (*défaut*) failing.

traverse [travɛrs] *nf* 1 *Rail* sleeper, *Am* tie. 2 **chemin de t.** short cut.

travers/er [travɛrse] *vt* to cross, go across; (*foule, période, mur*) to go through. ◆**—ée** *nf* (*action, trajet*) crossing.

traversin [travɛrsɛ̃] *nm* (*coussin*) bolster.

travest/ir [travɛstir] *vt* to disguise; (*pensée, vérité*) to misrepresent. ◆**—i** *nm* *Th* female impersonator; (*homosexuel*) transvestite. ◆**—issement** *nm* disguise; misrepresentation.

trébucher [trebyʃe] *vi* to stumble (**sur** over); **faire t.** to trip (up).

trèfle [trɛfl] *nm* 1 (*plante*) clover. 2 (*couleur*) *Cartes* clubs.

treille [trɛj] *nf* climbing vine.

treillis [treji] *nm* 1 lattice(work); (*en métal*) wire mesh. 2 (*tenue militaire*) combat uniform.

treize [trɛz] *a & nm inv* thirteen. ◆**treizième** *a & nmf* thirteenth.

tréma [trema] *nm* *Gram* di(a)eresis.

trembl/er [trɑ̃ble] *vi* to tremble, shake; (*de froid, peur*) to tremble (**de** with); (*flamme, lumière*) to flicker; (*voix*) to tremble, quaver; (*avoir peur*) to be afraid (**que** (+ *sub*) that, **de faire** to do); **t. pour qn** to fear for s.o. ◆**—ement** *nm* (*action, frisson*) trembling; **t. de terre** earthquake. ◆**trembloter** *vi* to quiver.

trémousser (se) [sɔtremuse] *vpr* to wriggle (about).

trempe [trɑ̃p] *nf* (*caractère*) stamp; **un homme de sa t.** a man of his stamp.

tremper [trɑ̃pe] 1 *vt* to soak, drench; (*plonger*) to dip (**dans** in); — *vi* to soak; **faire t.** to soak; — **se t.** *vpr* (*se baigner*) to take a dip. 2 *vt* (*acier*) to temper. 3 *vi* **t. dans** (*participer*) *Péj* to be mixed up in. ◆**trempette** *nf* **faire t.** (*se baigner*) to take a dip.

tremplin [trɑ̃plɛ̃] *nm* *Natation & Fig* springboard.

trente [trɑ̃t] *a & nm* thirty; **un t.-trois tours** (*disque*) an LP. ◆**trentaine** *nf* **une t.** (**de**) (*nombre*) (about) thirty; **avoir la t.** (*âge*) to be about thirty. ◆**trentième** *a & nmf* thirtieth.

trépidant [trepidɑ̃] *a* (*vie etc*) hectic.

trépied [trepje] *nm* tripod.

trépigner [trepiɲe] *vi* to stamp (one's feet).

très [trɛ] *adv* ([trɛz] *before vowel or mute h*) very; **t. aimé/critiqué/etc** much liked/criticized/etc.

trésor [trezɔr] *nm* treasure; **le T.** (*public*)

(*service*) public revenue (department); (*finances*) public funds; **des trésors de** *Fig* a treasure house of. ◆**trésorerie** *nf* (*bureaux d'un club etc*) accounts department; (*capitaux*) funds; (*gestion*) accounting. ◆**trésorier, -ière** *nmf* treasurer.

tressaill/ir* [tresajir] *vi* (*sursauter*) to jump, start; (*frémir*) to shake, quiver; (*de joie, peur*) to tremble (**de** with). ◆**—ement** *nm* start; quiver; trembling.

tressauter [tresote] *vi* (*sursauter*) to start, jump.

tresse [trɛs] *nf* (*cordon*) braid; (*cheveux*) plait, *Am* braid. ◆**tresser** *vt* to braid; to plait.

tréteau, -x [treto] *nm* trestle.

treuil [trœj] *nm* winch, windlass.

trêve [trɛv] *nf Mil* truce; (*répit*) *Fig* respite.

tri [tri] *nm* sorting (out); **faire le t. de** to sort (out); (**centre de**) **t.** (*des postes*) sorting office. ◆**triage** *nm* sorting (out).

triangle [trijɑ̃gl] *nm* triangle. ◆**triangulaire** *a* triangular.

tribord [tribɔr] *nm Nau Av* starboard.

tribu [triby] *nf* tribe. ◆**tribal, -aux** *a* tribal.

tribulations [tribylɑsjɔ̃] *nfpl* tribulations.

tribunal, -aux [tribynal, -o] *nm Jur* court; (*militaire*) tribunal.

tribune [tribyn] *nf* **1** (*de salle publique etc*) gallery; (*de stade*) (grand)stand; (*d'orateur*) rostrum. **2 t. libre** (*dans un journal*) open forum.

tribut [triby] *nm* tribute (**à** to).

tributaire [tribytɛr] *a* **t. de** *Fig* dependent on.

tricher [triʃe] *vi* to cheat. ◆**tricherie** *nf* cheating, trickery; **une t.** a piece of trickery. ◆**tricheur, -euse** *nmf* cheat, *Am* cheater.

tricolore [trikɔlɔr] *a* **1** (*cocarde etc*) red, white and blue; **le drapeau/l'équipe t.** the French flag/team. **2 feu t.** traffic lights.

tricot [triko] *nm* (*activité, ouvrage*) knitting; (*chandail*) jumper, sweater; **un t.** (*ouvrage*) a piece of knitting; **en t.** knitted; **t. de corps** vest, *Am* undershirt. ◆**tricoter** *vti* to knit.

tricycle [trisikl] *nm* tricycle.

trier [trije] *vt* (*séparer*) to sort (out); (*choisir*) to pick *ou* sort out.

trilogie [trilɔʒi] *nf* trilogy.

trimbal(l)er [trɛ̃bale] *vt Fam* to cart about, drag around; **— se t.** *vpr Fam* to trail around.

trimer [trime] *vi Fam* to slave (away), toil.

trimestre [trimɛstr] *nm* (*période*) *Com* quarter; *Scol* term. ◆**trimestriel, -ielle** *a* (*revue*) quarterly; (*bulletin*) *Scol* end-of-term.

tringle [trɛ̃gl] *nf* rail, rod; **t. à rideaux** curtain rail *ou* rod.

Trinité [trinite] *nf* **la T.** (*fête*) Trinity; (*dogme*) the Trinity.

trinquer [trɛ̃ke] *vi* to chink glasses; **t. à** to drink to.

trio [trijo] *nm* (*groupe*) & *Mus* trio.

triomphe [trijɔ̃f] *nm* triumph (**sur** over); **porter qn en t.** to carry s.o. shoulder-high. ◆**triomphal, -aux** *a* triumphal. ◆**triomph/er** *vi* to triumph (**de** over); (*jubiler*) to be jubilant. ◆**—ant** *a* triumphant.

tripes [trip] *nfpl* (*intestins*) *Fam* guts; *Culin* tripe. ◆**tripier, -ière** *nmf* tripe butcher.

triple [tripl] *a* treble, triple; **— nm le t.** three times as much (**de** as). ◆**tripl/er** *vti* to treble, triple. ◆**—és, -ées** *nmfpl* (*enfants*) triplets.

tripot [tripo] *nm* (*café etc*) *Péj* gambling den.

tripoter [tripɔte] *vt* to fiddle about *ou* mess about with; **— vi** to fiddle *ou* mess about.

trique [trik] *nf* cudgel, stick.

triste [trist] *a* sad; (*couleur, temps, rue*) gloomy, dreary; (*lamentable*) unfortunate, sorry. ◆**tristement** *adv* sadly. ◆**tristesse** *nf* sadness; gloom, dreariness.

triturer [trityre] *vt* (*manipuler*) to manipulate.

trivial, -aux [trivjal, -o] *a* coarse, vulgar. ◆**trivialité** *nf* coarseness, vulgarity.

troc [trɔk] *nm* exchange, barter.

troène [trɔɛn] *nm* (*arbuste*) privet.

trognon [trɔɲɔ̃] *nm* (*de pomme, poire*) core; (*de chou*) stump.

trois [trwa] *a* & *nm* three. ◆**troisième** *a* & *nmf* third. ◆**troisièmement** *adv* thirdly.

trolley(bus) [trɔlɛ(bys)] *nm* trolley(bus).

trombe [trɔ̃b] *nf* **t. d'eau** (*pluie*) rainstorm, downpour; **en t.** (*entrer etc*) *Fig* like a whirlwind.

trombone [trɔ̃bɔn] *nm* **1** *Mus* trombone. **2** (*agrafe*) paper clip.

trompe [trɔ̃p] *nf* **1** (*d'éléphant*) trunk; (*d'insecte*) proboscis. **2** *Mus* horn.

tromper [trɔ̃pe] *vt* to deceive, mislead; (*escroquer*) to cheat; (*échapper à*) to elude; (*être infidèle à*) to be unfaithful to; **— se t.** *vpr* to be mistaken, make a mistake; **se t. de route/de train/etc** to take the wrong road/train/etc; **se t. de date/de jour/etc** to get the date/day/etc wrong. ◆**tromperie** *nf* deceit, deception. ◆**trompeur, -euse** *a* (*apparences etc*) deceptive, misleading; (*personne*) deceitful.

trompette [trɔ̃pɛt] *nf* trumpet. ◆**trompettiste** *nmf* trumpet player.

tronc [trɔ̃] *nm* **1** *Bot Anat* trunk. **2** *Rel* collection box.

tronçon [trɔ̃sɔ̃] *nm* section. ◆**tronçonn/er** *vt* to cut (into sections). ◆**—euse** *nf* chain saw.

trône [tron] *nm* throne. ◆**trôner** *vi* (*vase, personne etc*) *Fig* to occupy the place of honour.

tronquer [trɔ̃ke] *vt* to truncate; (*texte etc*) to curtail.

trop [tro] *adv* too; too much; **t. dur/loin/**etc too hard/far/etc; **t. fatigué** too tired, overtired; **boire/lire/**etc **t.** to drink/read/etc too much; **t. de sel/**etc (*quantité*) too much salt/etc; **t. de gens/**etc (*nombre*) too many people/etc; **du fromage/**etc **de** ou **en t.** (*quantité*) too much cheese/etc; **des œufs/**etc **de** ou **en t.** (*nombre*) too many eggs/etc; **un franc/verre/**etc **de t.** ou **en t.** one franc/glass/etc too many; **se sentir de t.** *Fig* to feel in the way.

trophée [trɔfe] *nm* trophy.

tropique [trɔpik] *nm* tropic. ◆**tropical, -aux** *a* tropical.

trop-plein [trɔplɛ̃] *nm* (*dispositif, liquide*) overflow; (*surabondance*) *Fig* excess.

troquer [trɔke] *vt* to exchange (**contre** for).

trot [tro] *nm* trot; **aller au t.** to trot; **au t.** (*sans traîner*) *Fam* at the double. ◆**trott/er** [trɔte] *vi* (*cheval*) to trot; (*personne*) *Fig* to scurry (along).

trotteuse [trɔtøz] *nf* (*de montre*) second hand.

trottiner [trɔtine] *vi* (*personne*) to patter (along).

trottinette [trɔtinɛt] *nf* (*jouet*) scooter.

trottoir [trɔtwar] *nm* pavement, *Am* sidewalk; **t. roulant** moving walkway, travolator.

trou [tru] *nm* hole; (*d'aiguille*) eye; (*manque*) *Fig* gap (**dans** in); (*village*) *Péj* hole, dump; **t. d'homme** (*ouverture*) manhole; **t. de** (**la**) **serrure** keyhole; **t. (de mémoire)** *Fig* lapse (of memory).

trouble [trubl] **1** *a* (*liquide*) cloudy; (*image*) blurred; (*affaire*) shady; **voir t.** to see blurred. **2** *nm* (*émoi, émotion*) agitation; (*désarroi*) distress; (*désordre*) confusion; *pl Méd* trouble; (*révolte*) disturbances, troubles. ◆**troubl/er** *vt* to disturb; (*liquide*) to make cloudy; (*projet*) to upset; (*esprit*) to unsettle; (*vue*) to blur; (*inquiéter*) to trouble; **— se t.** *vpr* (*liquide*) to become cloudy; (*candidat etc*) to become flustered. ◆**—ant** *a* (*détail etc*) disquieting. ◆**trouble-fête** *nmf inv* killjoy, spoilsport.

trou/er [true] *vt* to make a hole ou holes in; (*silence, ténèbres*) to cut through. ◆**—ée** *nf* gap; (*brèche*) *Mil* breach.

trouille [truj] *nf* **avoir la t.** *Fam* to have the jitters, be scared. ◆**trouillard** *a* (*poltron*) *Fam* chicken.

troupe [trup] *nf Mil* troop; (*groupe*) group; *Th* company, troupe; **la t., les troupes** (*armée*) the troops.

troupeau, -x [trupo] *nm* (*de vaches*) & *Fig Péj* herd; (*de moutons, d'oies*) flock.

trousse [trus] **1** *nf* (*étui*) case, kit; (*d'écolier*) pencil case; **t. à outils** toolkit; **t. à pharmacie** first-aid kit. **2** *nfpl* **aux trousses de qn** *Fig* on s.o.'s heels.

trousseau, -x [truso] *nm* **1** (*de clés*) bunch. **2** (*de mariée*) trousseau.

trouver [truve] *vt* to find; **aller/venir t. qn** to go/come and see s.o.; **je trouve que** (*je pense que*) I think that; **comment la trouvez-vous?** what do you think of her?; **— se t.** *vpr* to be; (*être situé*) to be situated; (*se sentir*) to feel; (*dans une situation*) to find oneself; **se t. mal** (*s'évanouir*) to faint; **il se trouve que** it happens that. ◆**trouvaille** *nf* (*lucky*) find.

truand [tryɑ̃] *nm* crook.

truc [tryk] *nm* **1** (*astuce*) trick; (*moyen*) way; **avoir/trouver le t.** to have/get the knack (**pour faire** of doing). **2** (*chose*) *Fam* thing. ◆**—age** *nm* = **truquage**.

truchement [tryʃmɑ̃] *nm* **par le t. de qn** through (the intermediary of) s.o.

truculent [trykylɑ̃] *a* (*langage, personnage*) colourful.

truelle [tryɛl] *nf* trowel.

truffe [tryf] *nf* **1** (*champignon*) truffle. **2** (*de chien*) nose.

truff/er [tryfe] *vt* (*remplir*) to stuff (**de** with). ◆**—é** *a* (*pâté etc*) *Culin* with truffles.

truie [trɥi] *nf* (*animal*) sow.

truite [trɥit] *nf* trout.

truqu/er [tryke] *vt* (*photo etc*) to fake; (*élections, match*) to rig, fix. ◆**—é** *a* (*photo etc*) fake-; (*élections, match*) rigged, fixed; (*scène*) *Cin* trick-. ◆**—age** *nm Cin* (special) effect; (*action*) faking; rigging.

trust [trœst] *nm Com* (*cartel*) trust; (*entreprise*) corporation.

tsar [dzar] *nm* tsar, czar.

TSF [teɛsɛf] *nf abrév* (*télégraphie sans fil*) wireless, radio.

tsigane [tsigan] *a* & *nmf* (Hungarian) gipsy.

TSVP [teɛsvepe] *abrév* (*tournez s'il vous plaît*) PTO.

TTC [tetese] *abrév* (*toutes taxes comprises*) inclusive of tax.

tu [ty] *pron* you (*familiar form of address*).

tu² [ty] *voir* taire.

tuba [tyba] *nm* **1** *Mus* tuba. **2** *Sp* snorkel.

tube [tyb] *nm* **1** tube; (*de canalisation*) pipe. **2** (*chanson, disque*) *Fam* hit. ◆**tubulaire** *a* tubular.

tuberculeux, -euse [tybɛrkylø, -øz] *a* tubercular; **être t.** to have tuberculosis *ou* TB. ◆**tuberculose** *nf* tuberculosis, TB.

tue-mouches [tymuʃ] *a inv* **papier t.-mouches** flypaper. ◆**t.-tête (à)** *adv* at the top of one's voice.

tu/er [tɥe] *vt* to kill; (*d'un coup de feu*) to shoot (dead), kill; (*épuiser*) *Fig* to wear out; **— se t.** *vpr* to kill oneself; to shoot oneself; (*dans un accident*) to be killed; **se t. à faire** *Fig* to wear oneself out doing. ◆**—ant** *a* (*fatigant*) exhausting. ◆**tuerie** *nf* slaughter. ◆**tueur, -euse** *nmf* killer.

tuile [tɥil] *nf* **1** tile. **2** (*malchance*) *Fam* (stroke of) bad luck.

tulipe [tylip] *nf* tulip.

tuméfié [tymefje] *a* swollen.

tumeur [tymœr] *nf* tumour, growth.

tumulte [tymylt] *nm* commotion; (*désordre*) turmoil. ◆**tumultueux, -euse** *a* turbulent.

tunique [tynik] *nf* tunic.

Tunisie [tynizi] *nf* Tunisia. ◆**tunisien, -ienne** *a & nmf* Tunisian.

tunnel [tynɛl] *nm* tunnel.

turban [tyrbɑ̃] *nm* turban.

turbine [tyrbin] *nf* turbine.

turbulences [tyrbylɑ̃s] *nfpl Phys Av* turbulence.

turbulent [tyrbylɑ̃] *a* (*enfant etc*) boisterous, turbulent.

turfiste [tyrfist] *nmf* racegoer, punter.

Turquie [tyrki] *nf* Turkey. ◆**turc, turque** *a* Turkish; **—** *nmf* Turk; **—** *nm* (*langue*) Turkish.

turquoise [tyrkwaz] *a inv* turquoise.

tuteur, -trice [tytœr, -tris] **1** *nmf Jur* guardian. **2** *nm* (*bâton*) stake, prop. ◆**tutelle** *nf Jur* guardianship; *Fig* protection.

tutoyer [tytwaje] *vt* to address familiarly (*using tu*). ◆**tutoiement** *nm* familiar address, use of *tu*.

tutu [tyty] *nm* ballet skirt, tutu.

tuyau, -x [tɥijo] *nm* **1** pipe; **t. d'arrosage** hose(pipe); **t. de cheminée** flue; **t. d'échappement** *Aut* exhaust (pipe). **2** (*renseignement*) *Fam* tip. ◆**tuyauter** *vt* **t. qn** (*conseiller*) *Fam* to give s.o. a tip. ◆**tuyauterie** *nf* (*tuyaux*) piping.

TVA [tevea] *nf abrév* (*taxe à la valeur ajoutée*) VAT.

tympan [tɛ̃pɑ̃] *nm* eardrum.

type [tip] *nm* (*modèle*) type; (*traits*) features; (*individu*) *Fam* fellow, guy, bloke; **le t. même de** *Fig* the very model of; **—** *a inv* (*professeur etc*) typical. ◆**typique** *a* typical (**de** of). ◆**typiquement** *adv* typically.

typhoïde [tifɔid] *nf Méd* typhoid (fever).

typhon [tifɔ̃] *nm Mét* typhoon.

typographe [tipɔgraf] *nmf* typographer. ◆**typographie** *nf* typography, printing. ◆**typographique** *a* typographical, printing-.

tyran [tirɑ̃] *nm* tyrant. ◆**tyrannie** *nf* tyranny. ◆**tyrannique** *a* tyrannical. ◆**tyranniser** *vt* to tyrannize.

tzigane [dzigan] *a & nmf* (Hungarian) gipsy.

U

U, u [y] *nm* U, u.

ulcère [ylsɛr] *nm* ulcer, sore.

ulcérer [ylsere] *vt* (*blesser, irriter*) to embitter.

ultérieur [ylterjœr] *a* later. ◆**—ement** *adv* later.

ultimatum [yltimatɔm] *nm* ultimatum.

ultime [yltim] *a* final, last.

ultra- [yltra] *préf* ultra-. ◆**u.-secret, -ète** *a* (*document*) top-secret.

ultramoderne [yltramɔdɛrn] *a* ultramodern.

ultraviolet, -ette [yltravjɔlɛ, -ɛt] *a* ultraviolet.

un, une [œ̃, yn] **1** *art indéf* a, (*devant voyelle*) an; **une page** a page; **un ange** [œ̃nɑ̃ʒ] an angel. **2** *a* one; **la page un** page one; **un kilo** one kilo; **un type** (*un quelconque*) some *ou* a fellow. **3** *pron & nmf* one; **l'un** one; **les uns** some; **le numéro un** number one; **j'en ai un** I have one; **l'un d'eux** one of them; **la une** *Journ* page one.

unanime [ynanim] *a* unanimous. ◆**unanimité** *nf* unanimity; **à l'u.** unanimously.

uni [yni] *a* united; (*famille etc*) close; (*surface*) smooth; (*couleur, étoffe*) plain.

unième [ynjɛm] *a* (*après un numéral*) (-)first; **trente et u.** thirty-first; **cent u.** hundred and first.

unifier [ynifje] *vt* to unify. ◆**unification** *nf* unification.

uniforme [ynifɔrm] **1** *a* (*régulier*) uniform. **2** *nm* (*vêtement*) uniform. ◆**uniformément** *adv* uniformly. ◆**uniformiser** *vt* to standardize. ◆**uniformité** *nf* uniformity.

unijambiste [yniʒãbist] *a & nmf* one-legged (man *ou* woman).

unilatéral, -aux [ynilateral, -o] *a* unilateral; (*stationnement*) on one side of the road only.

union [ynjɔ̃] *nf* union; (*association*) association; (*entente*) unity. ◆**unir** *vt* to unite, join (together); **u. la force au courage/***etc* to combine strength with courage/*etc* **;** — **s'u.** *vpr* to unite; (*se marier*) to be joined together; (*se joindre*) to join (together).

unique [ynik] *a* **1** (*fille, fils*) only; (*espoir, souci etc*) only, sole; (*prix, salaire, voie*) single, one; **son seul et u. souci** his *ou* her one and only worry. **2** (*incomparable*) unique. ◆**uniquement** *adv* only, solely.

unisexe [ynisɛks] *a inv* (*vêtements etc*) unisex.

unisson (à l') [alynisɔ̃] *adv* in unison (de with).

unité [ynite] *nf* (*élément, grandeur*) & *Mil* unit; (*cohésion, harmonie*) unity. ◆**unitaire** *a* (*prix*) per unit.

univers [yniver] *nm* universe.

universel, -elle [yniversɛl] *a* universal. ◆**universellement** *adv* universally. ◆**universalité** *nf* universality.

université [yniversite] *nf* university; **à l'u.** at university. ◆**universitaire** *a* university-; — *nmf* academic.

uranium [yranjɔm] *nm* uranium.

urbain [yrbɛ̃] *a* urban, town-, city-. ◆**urbaniser** *vt* to urbanize, build up. ◆**urbanisme** *nm* town planning, *Am* city planning. ◆**urbaniste** *nmf* town planner, *Am* city planner.

urgent [yrʒã] *a* urgent, pressing. ◆**urgence** *nf* (*cas*) emergency; (*de décision, tâche etc*) urgency; **d'u.** (*mesures etc*) emergency-; **état d'u.** *Pol* state of emergency; **faire qch d'u.** to do sth urgently.

urine [yrin] *nf* urine. ◆**uriner** *vi* to urinate. ◆**urinoir** *nm* (public) urinal.

urne [yrn] *nf* **1** (*électorale*) ballot box; **aller aux urnes** to go to the polls. **2** (*vase*) urn.

URSS [yrs] *nf abrév* (*Union des Républiques Socialistes Soviétiques*) USSR.

usage [yzaʒ] *nm* use; *Ling* usage; (*habitude*) custom; **faire u. de** to make use of; **faire de l'u.** (*vêtement etc*) to wear well; **d'u.** (*habituel*) customary; **à l'u. de** for (the use of); **hors d'u.** no longer usable. ◆**usagé** *a* worn, (*d'occasion*) used. ◆**usager** *nm* user. ◆**us/er** *vt* (*vêtement, personne*) to wear out; (*consommer*) to use (up); (*santé*) to ruin; — *vi* **u. de** to use; — **s'u.** *vpr* (*tissu, machine*) to wear out; (*personne*) to wear oneself out. ◆**-é** *a* (*tissu etc*) worn (out); (*sujet etc*) well-worn; (*personne*) worn out.

usine [yzin] *nf* factory; (*à gaz, de métallurgie*) works.

usiner [yzine] *vt* (*pièce*) *Tech* to machine.

usité [yzite] *a* commonly used.

ustensile [ystãsil] *nm* utensil.

usuel, -elle [yzyɛl] *a* everyday, ordinary; — *nmpl* (*livres*) reference books.

usure [yzyr] *nf* (*détérioration*) wear (and tear); **avoir qn à l'u.** *Fig* to wear s.o. down (in the end).

usurier, -ière [yzyrje, -jɛr] *nmf* usurer.

usurper [yzyrpe] *vt* to usurp.

utérus [yterys] *nm Anat* womb, uterus.

utile [ytil] *a* useful (à to). ◆**utilement** *adv* usefully.

utiliser [ytilize] *vt* to use, utilize. ◆**utilisable** *a* usable. ◆**utilisateur, -trice** *nmf* user. ◆**utilisation** *nf* use. ◆**utilité** *nf* use(fulness); **d'une grande u.** very useful.

utilitaire [ytiliter] *a* utilitarian; (*véhicule*) utility-.

utopie [ytɔpi] *nf* (*idéal*) utopia; (*projet, idée*) utopian plan *ou* idea. ◆**utopique** *a* utopian.

V

V, v [ve] *nm* V, v.
va [va] *voir* **aller 1.**
vacances [vakãs] *nfpl* holiday(s), *Am* vaca-

tion; **en v.** on holiday, *Am* on vacation; **prendre ses v.** to take one's holiday(s) *ou Am* vacation; **les grandes v.** the summer

holidays *ou Am* vacation. ◆**vacancier, -ière** *nmf* holidaymaker, *Am* vacationer.
vacant [vakɑ̃] *a* vacant. ◆**vacance** *nf* (*poste*) vacancy.

vacarme [vakarm] *nm* din, uproar.

vaccin [vaksɛ̃] *nm* vaccine; **faire un v.** à to vaccinate. ◆**vaccination** *nf* vaccination. ◆**vacciner** *vt* to vaccinate.

vache [vaʃ] **1** *nf* cow; **v. laitière** dairy cow. **2** *nf* (**peau de**) **v.** (*personne*) *Fam* swine; – *a* (*méchant*) *Fam* nasty. ◆**vachement** *adv Fam* (*très*) damned; (*beaucoup*) a hell of a lot. ◆**vacherie** *nf Fam* (*action, parole*) nasty thing; (*caractère*) nastiness.

vacill/er [vasije] *vi* to sway, wobble; (*flamme, lumière*) to flicker; (*jugement, mémoire etc*) to falter, waver. ◆**—ant** *a* (*démarche, mémoire*) shaky; (*lumière etc*) flickering.

vadrouille [vadruj] *nf* **en v.** *Fam* roaming *ou* wandering about. ◆**vadrouiller** *vi Fam* to roam *ou* wander about.

va-et-vient [vaevjɛ̃] *nm inv* (*mouvement*) movement to and fro; (*de personnes*) comings and goings.

vagabond, -onde [vagabɔ̃, -ɔ̃d] *a* wandering; – *nmf* (*clochard*) vagrant, tramp. ◆**vagabond/er** *vi* to roam *ou* wander about; (*pensée*) to wander. ◆**—age** *nm* wandering; *Jur* vagrancy.

vagin [vaʒɛ̃] *nm* vagina.

vagir [vaʒir] *vi* (*bébé*) to cry, wail.

vague [vag] **1** *a* vague; (*regard*) vacant; (*souvenir*) dim, vague; – *nm* vagueness; **regarder dans le v.** to gaze into space, gaze vacantly; **rester dans le v.** (*être évasif*) to keep it vague. **2** *nf* (*de mer*) & *Fig* wave; **v. de chaleur** heat wave; **v. de froid** cold snap *ou* spell; **v. de fond** (*dans l'opinion*) *Fig* tidal wave. ◆**vaguement** *adv* vaguely.

vaillant [vajɑ̃] *a* brave, valiant; (*vigoureux*) healthy. ◆**vaillamment** *adv* bravely, valiantly. ◆**vaillance** *nf* bravery.

vain [vɛ̃] *a* **1** (*futile*) vain, futile; (*mots, promesse*) empty; **en v.** in vain, vainly. **2** (*vaniteux*) vain. ◆**vainement** *adv* in vain, vainly.

vainc/re* [vɛ̃kr] *vt* to defeat, beat; (*surmonter*) to overcome. ◆**—u, -ue** *nmf* defeated man *ou* woman; *Sp* loser. ◆**vainqueur** *nm* victor; *Sp* winner; – *am* victorious.

vaisseau, -x [vɛso] *nm* **1** *Anat Bot* vessel. **2** (*bateau*) ship, vessel; **v. spatial** spaceship.

vaisselle [vɛsɛl] *nf* crockery; (*à laver*) washing up; **faire la v.** to do the washing up, do *ou* wash the dishes.

val, *pl* **vals** *ou* **vaux** [val, vo] *nm* valley.

valable [valabl] *a* (*billet, motif etc*) valid; (*remarquable, rentable*) *Fam* worthwhile.

valet [valɛ] *nm* **1** *Cartes* jack. **2** **v.** (**de chambre**) valet, manservant; **v. de ferme** farmhand.

valeur [valœr] *nf* value; (*mérite*) worth; (*poids*) importance, weight; *pl* (*titres*) *Com* stocks and shares; **la v. de** (*quantité*) the equivalent of; **avoir de la v.** to be valuable; **mettre en v.** (*faire ressortir*) to highlight; **de v.** (*personne*) of merit, able; **objets de v.** valuables.

valide [valid] *a* **1** (*personne*) fit, ablebodied; (*population*) able-bodied. **2** (*billet etc*) valid. ◆**valider** *vt* to validate. ◆**validité** *nf* validity.

valise [valiz] *nf* (*suit*)case; **v. diplomatique** diplomatic bag *ou Am* pouch; **faire ses valises** to pack (one's bags).

vallée [vale] *nf* valley. ◆**vallon** *nm* (small) valley. ◆**vallonné** *a* (*région etc*) undulating.

valoir* [valwar] *vi* to be worth; (*s'appliquer*) to apply (**pour** to); **v. mille francs/cher/etc** to be worth a thousand francs/a lot/etc; **un vélo vaut bien une auto** a bicycle is as good as a car; **il vaut mieux rester** it's better to stay; **il vaut mieux que j'attende** I'd better wait; **ça ne vaut rien** it's worthless, it's no good; **ça vaut le coup** *Fam ou* **la peine** it's worthwhile (**de faire** doing); **faire v.** (*faire ressortir*) to highlight, set off; (*argument*) to put forward; (*droit*) to assert; – *vt* **v.** **qch à qn** to bring *ou* get s.o. sth; – **se v.** *vpr* (*objets, personnes*) to be as good as each other; **ça se vaut** *Fam* it's all the same.

valse [vals] *nf* waltz. ◆**valser** *vi* to waltz.

valve [valv] *nf* (*clapet*) valve. ◆**valvule** *nf* (*du cœur*) valve.

vampire [vɑ̃pir] *nm* vampire.

vandale [vɑ̃dal] *nmf* vandal. ◆**vandalisme** *nm* vandalism.

vanille [vanij] *nf* vanilla; **glace/etc à la v.** vanilla ice cream/etc. ◆**vanillé** *a* vanilla-flavoured.

vanité [vanite] *nf* vanity. ◆**vaniteux, -euse** *a* vain, conceited.

vanne [van] *nf* **1** (*d'écluse*) sluice (gate), floodgate. **2** (*remarque*) *Fam* dig, jibe.

vanné [vane] *a* (*fatigué*) *Fam* dead beat.

vannerie [vanri] *nf* (*fabrication, objets*) basketwork, basketry.

vantail, -aux [vɑ̃taj, -o] *nm* (*de porte*) leaf.

vanter [vɑ̃te] *vt* to praise; – **se v.** *vpr* to boast, brag (**de** about, of). ◆**vantard, -arde** *a* boastful; – *nmf* boaster, braggart.

◆**vantardise** *nf* boastfulness; (*propos*) boast.

va-nu-pieds [vanypje] *nmf inv* tramp, beggar.

vapeur [vapœr] *nf* (*brume*, *émanation*) vapour; *v.* (**d'eau**) steam; **cuire à la v.** to steam; **bateau à v.** steamship. ◆**vaporeux, -euse** *a* hazy, misty; (*tissu*) translucent, diaphanous.

vaporiser [vapɔrize] *vt* to spray. ◆**vaporisateur** *nm* (*appareil*) spray.

vaquer [vake] *vi* **v. à** to attend to.

varappe [varap] *nf* rock-climbing.

varech [varɛk] *nm* wrack, seaweed.

vareuse [varøz] *nf* (*d'uniforme*) tunic.

varicelle [varisɛl] *nf* chicken pox.

varices [varis] *nfpl* varicose veins.

vari/er [varje] *vti* to vary (**de** from). ◆**—é** *a* (*diversifié*) varied; (*divers*) various. ◆**—able** *a* variable; (*humeur*, *temps*) changeable. ◆**variante** *nf* variant. ◆**variation** *nf* variation. ◆**variété** *nf* variety; **spectacle de variétés** *Th* variety show.

variole [varjɔl] *nf* smallpox.

vas [va] *voir* **aller 1.**

vase [vaz] **1** *nm* vase. **2** *nf* (*boue*) silt, mud.

vaseline [vazlin] *nf* Vaseline®.

vaseux, -euse [vazø, -øz] *a* **1** (*boueux*) silty, muddy. **2** (*fatigué*) off colour. **3** (*idées etc*) woolly, hazy.

vasistas [vazistas] *nm* (*dans une porte ou une fenêtre*) hinged panel.

vaste [vast] *a* vast, huge.

Vatican [vatikã] *nm* Vatican.

va-tout [vatu] *nm inv* **jouer son v.-tout** to stake one's all.

vaudeville [vodvil] *nm Th* light comedy.

vau-l'eau (à) [avolo] *adv* **aller à v.-l'eau** to go to rack and ruin.

vaurien, -ienne [vorjɛ̃, -jɛn] *nmf* good-for-nothing.

vautour [votur] *nm* vulture.

vautrer (se) [səvotre] *vpr* to sprawl; **se v. dans** (*boue*, *vice*) to wallow in.

va-vite (à la) [alavavit] *adv Fam* in a hurry.

veau, -x [vo] *nm* (*animal*) calf; (*viande*) veal; (*cuir*) calf(skin).

vécu [veky] *voir* **vivre**; — *a* (*histoire etc*) real(-life), true.

vedette [vədɛt] *nf* **1** *Cin Th* star; **avoir la v.** (*artiste*) to head the bill; **en v.** (*personne*) in the limelight; (*objet*) in a prominent position. **2** (*canot*) motor boat, launch.

végétal, -aux [veʒetal, -o] *a* (*huile*, *règne*) vegetable-; — *nm* plant. ◆**végétarien,**

-ienne *a* & *nmf* vegetarian. ◆**végétation 1** *nf* vegetation. **2** *nfpl Méd* adenoids.

végéter [veʒete] *vi* (*personne*) *Péj* to vegetate.

véhément [veemã] *a* vehement. ◆**véhémence** *nf* vehemence.

véhicule [veikyl] *nm* vehicle. ◆**véhiculer** *vt* to convey.

veille [vɛj] *nf* **1 la v. (de)** (*jour précédent*) the day before; **à la v. de** (*événement*) on the eve of; **la v. de Noël** Christmas Eve. **2** (*état*) wakefulness; *pl* vigils.

veill/er [veje] *vi* to stay up *ou* awake; (*sentinelle etc*) to be on watch; **v. à qch** to attend to sth, see to sth; **v. à ce que** (+ *sub*) to make sure that; **v. sur qn** to watch over s.o.; — *vt* (*malade*) to sit with, watch over. ◆**—ée** *nf* (*soirée*) evening; (*réunion*) evening get-together; (*mortuaire*) vigil. ◆**—eur** *nm* **v. de nuit** night watchman. ◆**—euse** *nf* (*lampe*) night light; (*de voiture*) sidelight; (*de réchaud*) pilot light.

veine [vɛn] *nf* **1** *Anat Bot Géol* vein. **2** (*chance*) *Fam* luck; **avoir de la v.** to be lucky; **une v.** a piece *ou* stroke of luck. ◆**veinard, -arde** *nmf Fam* lucky devil; — *a Fam* lucky.

vêler [vele] *vi* (*vache*) to calve.

vélin [velɛ̃] *nm* (*papier*, *peau*) vellum.

velléité [veleite] *nf* vague desire.

vélo [velo] *nm* bike, bicycle; (*activité*) cycling; **faire du v.** to cycle, go cycling. ◆**vélodrome** *nm Sp* velodrome, cycle track. ◆**vélomoteur** *nm* (lightweight) motorcycle.

velours [v(ə)lur] *nm* velvet; **v. côtelé** corduroy, cord. ◆**velouté** *a* soft, velvety; (*goût*) mellow, smooth; — *nm* smoothness; **v. d'asperges**/*etc* (*potage*) cream of asparagus/*etc* soup.

velu [vəly] *a* hairy.

venaison [vənɛzɔ̃] *nf* venison.

vénal, -aux [venal, -o] *a* mercenary, venal.

vendange(s) [vãdãʒ] *nf(pl)* grape harvest, vintage. ◆**vendanger** *vi* to pick the grapes. ◆**vendangeur, -euse** *nmf* grape-picker.

vendetta [vãdeta] *nf* vendetta.

vend/re [vãdr] *vt* to sell; **v. qch à qn** to sell s.o. sth, sell sth to s.o.; **v. qn** (*trahir*) to sell s.o. out; **à v.** (*maison etc*) for sale; — **se v.** *vpr* to be sold; **ça se vend bien** it sells well. ◆**—eur, -euse** *nmf* (*de magasin*) sales *ou* shop assistant, *Am* sales clerk; (*marchand*) salesman, saleswoman; *Jur* vendor, seller.

vendredi [vãdrədi] *nm* Friday; **V. saint** Good Friday.

vénéneux, -euse [venenø, -øz] a poisonous.

vénérable [venerabl] a venerable. ◆**vénérer** vt to venerate.

vénérien, -ienne [venerjɛ̃, -jɛn] a Méd venereal.

venger [vãʒe] vt to avenge; **— se v.** vpr to take (one's) revenge, avenge oneself (**de qn** on s.o., **de qch** for sth). ◆**vengeance** nf revenge, vengeance. ◆**vengeur, -eresse** a vengeful; — nmf avenger.

venin [vənɛ̃] nm (substance) & Fig venom. ◆**venimeux, -euse** a poisonous, venomous; (haineux) Fig venomous.

venir* [v(ə)nir] vi (aux être) to come (**de** from); **v. faire** to come to do; **viens me voir** come and ou to see me; **je viens/venais d'arriver** I've/I'd just arrived; **en v. à** (conclusion etc) to come to; **où veux-tu en v.?** what are you driving ou getting at?; **d'où vient que...?** how is it that...?; **s'il venait à faire** (éventualité) if he happened to do; **les jours/etc qui viennent** the coming days/etc; **une idée m'est venue** an idea occurred to me; **faire v.** to send for, get.

vent [vã] nm wind; **il fait** ou **il y a du v.** it's windy; **coup de v.** gust of wind; **avoir v. de** (connaissance de) to get wind of; **dans le v.** (à la mode) Fam trendy, with it.

vente [vãt] nf sale; **v. (aux enchères)** auction (sale); **v. de charité** bazaar, charity sale; **en v.** (disponible) on sale; **point de v.** sales ou retail outlet; **prix de v.** selling price; **salle des ventes** auction room.

ventilateur [vãtilatœr] nm (électrique) & Aut fan; (dans un mur) ventilator. ◆**ventilation** nf ventilation. ◆**ventiler** vt to ventilate.

ventouse [vãtuz] nf (pour fixer) suction grip; **à v.** (crochet, fléchette etc) suction-.

ventre [vãtr] nm belly, stomach; (utérus) womb; (de cruche etc) bulge; **avoir/prendre du v.** to have/get a paunch; **à plat v.** flat on one's face. ◆**ventru** a (personne) pot-bellied; (objet) bulging.

ventriloque [vãtrilɔk] nmf ventriloquist.

venu, -ue¹ [v(ə)ny] voir venir; — nmf **nouveau v., nouvelle venue** newcomer; **premier v.** anyone; — a **bien v.** (à propos) timely; **mal v.** untimely; **être bien/mal v. de faire** to have good grounds/no grounds for doing.

venue² [v(ə)ny] nf (arrivée) coming.

vêpres [vɛpr] nfpl Rel vespers.

ver [vɛr] nm worm; (larve) grub; (de fruits, fromage etc) maggot; **v. luisant** glow-worm;

v. **à soie** silkworm; v. **solitaire** tapeworm; v. **de terre** earthworm.

véracité [verasite] nf truthfulness, veracity.

véranda [verãda] nf veranda(h).

verbe [vɛrb] nm Gram verb. ◆**verbal, -aux** a (promesse, expression etc) verbal. ◆**verbeux, -euse** [vɛrbø, -øz] a verbose. ◆**verbiage** nm verbiage.

verdâtre [vɛrdɑtr] a greenish.

verdeur [vɛrdœr] nf (de fruit, vin) tartness; (de vieillard) sprightliness; (de langage) crudeness.

verdict [vɛrdikt] nm verdict.

verdir [vɛrdir] vti to turn green. ◆**verdoyant** a green, verdant. ◆**verdure** nf (arbres etc) greenery.

véreux, -euse [verø, -øz] a (fruit etc) wormy, maggoty; (malhonnête) Fig dubious, shady.

verge [vɛrʒ] nf Anat penis.

verger [vɛrʒe] nm orchard.

vergetures [vɛrʒətyr] nfpl stretch marks.

verglas [vɛrgla] nm (black) ice, Am sleet. ◆**verglacé** a (route) icy.

vergogne (sans) [sãvɛrgɔɲ] a shameless; — adv shamelessly.

véridique [veridik] a truthful.

vérifier [verifje] vt to check, verify; (confirmer) to confirm; (comptes) to audit. ◆**vérifiable** a verifiable. ◆**vérification** nf verification, confirmation; audit(ing).

vérité [verite] nf truth; (de personnage, tableau etc) trueness to life; (sincérité) sincerity; **en v.** in fact. ◆**véritable** a true, real; (non imité) real, genuine; (exactement nommé) veritable, real. ◆**véritablement** adv really.

vermeil, -eille [vɛrmɛj] a bright red, vermilion.

vermicelle(s) [vɛrmisɛl] nm(pl) Culin vermicelli.

vermine [vɛrmin] nf (insectes, racaille) vermine.

vermoulu [vɛrmuly] a worm-eaten.

vermouth [vɛrmut] nm vermouth.

verni [vɛrni] a (chanceux) Fam lucky.

vernir [vɛrnir] vt to varnish; (poterie) to glaze. ◆**vernis** nm varnish; glaze; (apparence) Fig veneer; **v. à ongles** nail polish ou varnish. ◆**vernissage** nm (d'exposition de peinture) first day. ◆**vernisser** vt (poterie) to glaze.

verra, verrait [vɛra, vɛrɛ] voir voir.

verre [vɛr] nm (substance, récipient) glass; **boire** ou **prendre un v.** to have a drink; v. **à bière/à vin** beer/wine glass; v. **de contact**

contact lens. **◆verrerie** *nf* (*objets*) glass-ware. **◆verrière** *nf* (*toit*) glass roof.
verrou [vɛru] *nm* bolt; **fermer au v.** to bolt; **sous les verrous** behind bars. **◆verrouiller** *vt* to bolt.
verrue [vɛry] *nf* wart.
vers¹ [vɛr] *prép* (*direction*) towards, toward; (*approximation*) around, about.
vers² [vɛr] *nm* (*d'un poème*) line; *pl* (*poésie*) verse.
versant [vɛrsɑ̃] *nm* slope, side.
versatile [vɛrsatil] *a* fickle, volatile.
verse (à) [avɛrs] *adv* in torrents; **pleuvoir à v.** to pour (down).
versé [vɛrse] *a* **v. dans** (well-)versed in.
Verseau [vɛrso] *nm* **le V.** (*signe*) Aquarius.
vers/er [vɛrse] **1** *vt* to pour; (*larmes, sang*) to shed. **2** *vt* (*argent*) to pay. **3** *vti* (*basculer*) to overturn. **◆—ement** *nm* payment. **◆—eur** *a* bec **v.** spout.
verset [vɛrsɛ] *nm* Rel verse.
version [vɛrsjɔ̃] *nf* version; (*traduction*) Scol translation, unseen.
verso [vɛrso] *nm* back (of the page); **'voir au v.'** 'see overleaf.'
vert [vɛr] *a* green; (*pas mûr*) unripe; (*vin*) young; (*vieillard*) Fig sprightly; – *nm* green.
vert-de-gris [vɛrdəgri] *nm inv* verdigris.
vertèbre [vɛrtɛbr] *nf* vertebra.
vertement [vɛrtəmɑ̃] *adv* (*réprimander etc*) sharply.
vertical, -ale, -aux [vɛrtikal, -o] *a* & *nf* vertical; **à la verticale** vertically. **◆verticalement** *adv* vertically.
vertige [vɛrtiʒ] *nm* (feeling of) dizziness *ou* giddiness; (*peur de tomber dans le vide*) vertigo; *pl* dizzy spells; **avoir le v.** to feel dizzy *ou* giddy. **◆vertigineux, -euse** *a* (*hauteur*) giddy, dizzy; (*très grand*) Fig staggering.
vertu [vɛrty] *nf* virtue; **en v. de** in accordance with. **◆vertueux, -euse** *a* virtuous.
verve [vɛrv] *nf* (*d'orateur etc*) brilliance.
verveine [vɛrvɛn] *nf* (*plante*) verbena.
vésicule [vezikyl] *nf* **v. biliaire** gall bladder.
vessie [vesi] *nf* bladder.
veste [vɛst] *nf* jacket, coat.
vestiaire [vɛstjɛr] *nm* cloakroom, *Am* locker room; (*meuble métallique*) locker.
vestibule [vɛstibyl] *nm* (entrance) hall.
vestiges [vɛstiʒ] *nmpl* (*restes, ruines*) remains; (*traces*) traces, vestiges.
vestimentaire [vɛstimɑ̃tɛr] *a* (*dépense*) clothing-; (*détail*) of dress.
veston [vɛstɔ̃] *nm* (suit) jacket.
vêtement [vɛtmɑ̃] *nm* garment, article of

clothing; *pl* clothes; **du v.** (*industrie, commerce*) clothing-; **vêtements de sport** sportswear.
vétéran [veterɑ̃] *nm* veteran.
vétérinaire [veterinɛr] *a* veterinary; – *nmf* vet, veterinary surgeon, *Am* veterinarian.
vétille [vetij] *nf* trifle, triviality.
vêt/ir* [vetir] *vt*, **– se v.** *vpr* to dress. **◆—u** *a* dressed (**de** in).
veto [veto] *nm inv* veto; **mettre** *ou* **opposer son v.** à to veto.
vétuste [vetyst] *a* dilapidated.
veuf, veuve [vœf, vœv] *a* widowed; – *nm* widower; – *nf* widow.
veuille [vœj] *voir* **vouloir.**
veule [vøl] *a* feeble. **◆veulerie** *nf* feeble-ness.
veut, veux [vø] *voir* **vouloir.**
vex/er [vɛkse] *vt* to upset, hurt; **– se v.** *vpr* to be *ou* get upset (**de** at). **◆—ant** *a* hurt-ful; (*contrariant*) annoying. **◆vexation** *nf* humiliation.
viable [vjabl] *a* (*enfant, entreprise etc*) via-ble. **◆viabilité** *nf* viability.
viaduc [vjadyk] *nm* viaduct.
viager, -ère [vjaʒe, -ɛr] *a* **rente viagère** life annuity; – *nm* life annuity.
viande [vjɑ̃d] *nf* meat.
vibrer [vibre] *vi* to vibrate; (*être ému*) to thrill (**de** with); **faire v.** (*auditoire etc*) to thrill. **◆vibrant** *a* (*émouvant*) emotional; (*voix, son*) resonant, vibrant. **◆vibration** *nf* vibration. **◆vibromasseur** *nm* (*appareil*) vibrator.
vicaire [vikɛr] *nm* curate.
vice [vis] *nm* vice; (*défectuosité*) defect.
vice- [vis] *préf* vice-.
vice versa [vis(e)vɛrsa] *adv* vice versa.
vicier [visje] *vt* to taint, pollute.
vicieux, -euse [visjø, -øz] **1** *a* depraved; – *nmf* pervert. **2** *a* **cercle v.** vicious circle.
vicinal, -aux [visinal, -o] *a* **chemin v.** by-road, minor road.
vicissitudes [visisityd] *nfpl* vicissitudes.
vicomte [vikɔ̃t] *nm* viscount. **◆vicom-tesse** *nf* viscountess.
victime [viktim] *nf* victim; (*d'un accident*) casualty; **être v. de** to be the victim of.
victoire [viktwar] *nf* victory; Sp win. **◆victorieux, -euse** *a* victorious; (*équipe*) winning.
victuailles [viktyaj] *nfpl* provisions.
vidange [vidɑ̃ʒ] *nf* emptying, draining; Aut oil change; (*dispositif*) waste outlet. **◆vidanger** *vt* to empty, drain.
vide [vid] *a* empty; – *nm* emptiness, void; (*absence d'air*) vacuum; (*gouffre etc*) drop;

(*trou, manque*) gap; **regarder dans le v.** to stare into space; **emballé sous v.** vacuum-packed; **à v.** empty.

vidéo [video] *a inv* video. ◆**vidéocassette** *nf* video (cassette).

vide-ordures [vidɔrdyr] *nm inv* (refuse) chute. ◆**vide-poches** *nm inv Aut* glove compartment.

vid/er [vide] *vt* to empty; (*lieu*) to vacate; (*poisson, volaille*) Culin to gut; (*querelle*) to settle; **v. qn** Fam (*chasser*) to throw s.o. out; (*épuiser*) to tire s.o. out; **— se v.** *vpr* to empty. ◆**—é** *a* (*fatigué*) Fam exhausted. ◆**—eur** *nm* (*de boîte de nuit*) bouncer.

vie [vi] *nf* life; (*durée*) lifetime; **coût de la v.** cost of living; **gagner sa v.** to earn one's living *ou* livelihood; **en v.** living; **à v., pour la v.** for life; **donner la v. à** to give birth to; **avoir la v. dure** (*préjugés etc*) to die hard; **jamais de la v.!** not on your life!, never!

vieill/ir [vjejir] *vi* to grow old; (*changer*) to age; (*théorie, mot*) to become old-fashioned; **— v. qn** (*vêtement etc*) to age s.o. ◆**—i** *a* (*démodé*) old-fashioned. ◆**—issant** *a* ageing. ◆**—issement** *nm* ageing.

viens, vient [vjɛ̃] *voir* **venir**.

vierge [vjɛrʒ] *nf* virgin; **la V.** (*signe*) Virgo; **— a** (*femme, neige etc*) virgin; (*feuille de papier, film*) blank; **être v.** (*femme, homme*) to be a virgin.

Viêt-nam [vjɛtnam] *nm* Vietnam. ◆**vietnamien, -ienne** *a & nmf* Vietnamese.

vieux (*or* **vieil** *before vowel or mute h*), **vieille**, *pl* **vieux, vieilles** [vjø, vjɛj] *a* old; **être v. jeu** (*a inv*) to be old-fashioned; **v. garçon** bachelor; **vieille fille** Péj old maid; **— nm** old man; *pl* old people; **mon v.** (*mon cher*) Fam old boy, old man; **— nf** old woman; **ma vieille** (*ma chère*) Fam old girl. ◆**vieillard** *nm* old man; *pl* old people. ◆**vieillerie** *nf* (*objet*) old thing; (*idée*) old idea. ◆**vieillesse** *nf* old age. ◆**vieillot** *a* antiquated.

vif, vive [vif, viv] *a* (*enfant, mouvement*) lively; (*alerte*) quick, sharp; (*intelligence, intérêt, vent*) keen; (*couleur, lumière*) bright; (*froid*) biting; (*pas*) quick, brisk; (*impression, imagination, style*) vivid; (*parole*) sharp; (*regret, satisfaction, succès etc*) great; (*coléreux*) quick-tempered; **brûler/enterrer qn v.** to burn/bury s.o. alive; **— nm le v. du sujet** the heart of the matter; **à v.** (*plaie*) open; **piqué au v.** (*vexé*) cut to the quick.

vigie [viʒi] *nf* (*matelot*) lookout; (*poste*) lookout post.

vigilant [viʒilã] *a* vigilant. ◆**vigilance** *nf* vigilance.

vigile [viʒil] *nm* (*gardien*) watchman; (*de nuit*) night watchman.

vigne [viɲ] *nf* (*plante*) vine; (*plantation*) vineyard. ◆**vigneron, -onne** *nmf* wine grower. ◆**vignoble** *nm* vineyard; (*région*) vineyards.

vignette [viɲɛt] *nf Aut* road tax sticker; (*de médicament*) price label (*for reimbursement by Social Security*).

vigueur [vigœr] *nf* vigour; **entrer/être en v.** (*loi*) to come into/be in force. ◆**vigoureux, -euse** *a* (*personne, style etc*) vigorous; (*bras*) sturdy.

vilain [vilɛ̃] *a* (*laid*) ugly; (*mauvais*) nasty; (*enfant*) naughty.

villa [villa] *nf* (detached) house.

village [vilaʒ] *nm* village. ◆**villageois, -oise** *a* village-; **— nmf** villager.

ville [vil] *nf* town; (*grande*) city; **aller/être en v.** to go into/be in town; **v. d'eaux** spa (town).

villégiature [vileʒjatyr] *nf* **lieu de v.** (holiday) resort.

vin [vɛ̃] *nm* wine; **v. ordinaire** *ou* **de table** table wine; **v. d'honneur** reception (*in honour of s.o.*). ◆**vinicole** *a* (*région*) wine-growing; (*industrie*) wine-.

vinaigre [vinegr] *nm* vinegar. ◆**vinaigré** *a* seasoned with vinegar. ◆**vinaigrette** *nf* (*sauce*) vinaigrette, French dressing, Am Italian dressing.

vindicatif, -ive [vɛ̃dikatif, -iv] *a* vindictive.

vingt [vɛ̃] ([vɛ̃t] *before vowel or mute h and in numbers 22–29*) *a & nm* twenty; **v. et un** twenty-one. ◆**vingtaine** *nf* **une v. (de)** (*nombre*) about twenty; **avoir la v.** (*âge*) to be about twenty. ◆**vingtième** *a & nmf* twentieth.

vinyle [vinil] *nm* vinyl.

viol [vjɔl] *nm* rape; (*de loi, lieu*) violation. ◆**violation** *nf* violation. ◆**violenter** *vt* to rape. ◆**violer** *vt* (*femme*) to rape; (*loi, lieu*) to violate. ◆**violeur** *nm* rapist.

violent [vjɔlã] *a* violent; (*remède*) drastic. ◆**violemment** [-amã] *adv* violently. ◆**violence** *nf* violence; (*acte*) act of violence.

violet, -ette [vjɔlɛ, -ɛt] **1** *a & nm* (*couleur*) purple, violet. **2** *nf* (*fleur*) violet. ◆**violacé** *a* purplish.

violon [vjɔlɔ̃] *nm* violin. ◆**violoncelle** *nm* cello. ◆**violoncelliste** *nmf* cellist. ◆**violoniste** *nmf* violinist.

vipère [viper] *nf* viper, adder.

virage [viraʒ] *nm* (*de route*) bend; (*de véhicule*) turn; (*revirement*) Fig change of

virée 303 vivre

course. ◆vir/er 1 *vi* to turn, veer; (*sur soi*)
to turn round; v. au bleu/*etc* to turn
blue/*etc*. 2 *vt* (*expulser*) *Fam* to throw out.
3 *vt* (*somme*) *Fin* to transfer (à to).
◆—ement *nm Fin* (bank *ou* credit) transfer.

virée [vire] *nf Fam* trip, outing.
virevolter [virvɔlte] *vi* to spin round.
virginité [virʒinite] *nf* virginity.
virgule [virgyl] *nf Gram* comma; *Math* (decimal) point; 2 v. 5 2 point 5.
viril [viril] *a* virile, manly; (*attribut, force*)
male. ◆virilité *nf* virility, manliness.
virtuel, -elle [virtɥɛl] *a* potential.
virtuose [virtɥoz] *nmf* virtuoso. ◆vir-
tuosité *nf* virtuosity.
virulent [virylɑ̃] *a* virulent. ◆virulence *nf*
virulence.
virus [virys] *nm* virus.
vis¹ [vi] *voir* vivre, voir.
vis² [vis] *nf* screw.
visa [viza] *nm* (*timbre*) stamp, stamped signature; (*de passeport*) visa; v. de censure
(*d'un film*) certificate.
visage [vizaʒ] *nm* face.
vis-à-vis [vizavi] *prép* v.-à-vis de opposite;
(*à l'égard de*) with respect to; (*envers*) towards; (*comparé à*) compared to; − *nm inv*
(*personne*) person opposite; (*bois, maison
etc*) opposite view.
viscères [viser] *nmpl* intestines. ◆viscé-
ral, -aux *a* (*haine etc*) *Fig* deeply felt.
viscosité [viskozite] *nf* viscosity.
viser [vize] 1 *vi* to aim (à at); v. à faire to aim
to do; − *vt* (*cible*) to aim at; (*concerner*) to
be aimed at. 2 *vt* (*passeport, document*) to
stamp. ◆visées *nfpl* (*desseins*) *Fig* aims;
avoir des visées sur to have designs on.
◆viseur *nm Phot* viewfinder; (*d'arme*)
sight.
visible [vizibl] *a* visible. ◆visiblement *adv*
visibly. ◆visibilité *nf* visibility.
visière [vizjer] *nf* (*de casquette*) peak; (*en
plastique etc*) eyeshade; (*de casque*) visor.
vision [vizjɔ̃] *nf* (*conception, image*) vision;
(*sens*) (eye)sight, vision; avoir des visions
Fam to be seeing things. ◆visionnaire *a*
& *nmf* visionary. ◆visionner *vt Cin* to
view. ◆visionneuse *nf* (*pour diapositives*)
viewer.
visite [vizit] *nf* visit; (*personne*) visitor; (*examen*) inspection; rendre v. à, faire une v. à
to visit; v. (à domicile) *Méd* call, visit; v.
(médicale) medical examination; v. guidée
guided tour; de v. (*carte, heures*) visiting-.
◆visiter *vt* to visit; (*examiner*) to inspect.
◆visiteur, -euse *nmf* visitor.

vison [vizɔ̃] *nm* mink.
visqueux, -euse [viskø, -øz] *a* viscous; (*surface*) sticky; (*répugnant*) *Fig* slimy.
visser [vise] *vt* to screw on.
visuel, -elle [vizɥɛl] *a* visual.
vit [vi] *voir* vivre, voir.
vital, -aux [vital, -o] *a* vital. ◆vitalité *nf*
vitality.
vitamine [vitamin] *nf* vitamin. ◆vitaminé
a (*biscuits etc*) vitamin-enriched.
vite [vit] *adv* quickly, fast; (*tôt*) soon; v.!
quick(ly)! ◆vitesse *nf* speed; (*régime*)
Aut gear; boîte de vitesses gearbox; à toute
v. at top *ou* full speed; v. de pointe top
speed; en v. quickly.
viticole [vitikɔl] *a* (*région*) wine-growing;
(*industrie*) wine-. ◆viticulteur *nm* wine
grower. ◆viticulture *nf* wine growing.
vitre [vitr] *nf* (window)pane; (*de véhicule*)
window. ◆vitrage *nm* (*vitres*) windows.
◆vitrail, -aux *nm* stained-glass window.
◆vitré *a* glass-, glazed. ◆vitreux, -euse
a (*regard, yeux*) *Fig* glassy. ◆vitrier *nm*
glazier.
vitrine [vitrin] *nf* (*de magasin*) (shop) window; (*meuble*) showcase, display cabinet.
vitriol [vitrijɔl] *nm Ch* & *Fig* vitriol.
vivable [vivabl] *a* (*personne*) easy to live
with; (*endroit*) fit to live in.
vivace [vivas] *a* (*plante*) perennial; (*haine*)
Fig inveterate.
vivacité [vivasite] *nf* liveliness; (*de l'air,
d'émotion*) keenness; (*agilité*) quickness;
(*de couleur, d'impression, de style*) vivid-
ness; (*emportement*) petulance; v. d'esprit
quick-wittedness.
vivant [vivɑ̃] *a* (*en vie*) alive, living; (*être,
matière, preuve*) living; (*conversation, enfant, récit, rue*) lively; langue vivante modern language; − *nm* de son v. in one's lifetime; bon v. jovial fellow; les vivants the
living.
vive¹ [viv] *voir* vif.
vive² [viv] *int* v. le roi/*etc*! long live the
king/*etc*!; v. les vacances! hurray for the
holidays!
vivement [vivmɑ̃] *adv* quickly, briskly;
(*répliquer*) sharply; (*sentir*) keenly; (*regretter*) deeply; v. demain! roll on tomorrow!, I
can hardly wait for tomorrow!; v. que (+
sub) I'll be glad when.
vivier [vivje] *nm* fish pond.
vivifier [vivifje] *vt* to invigorate.
vivisection [vivisɛksjɔ̃] *nf* vivisection.
vivre* [vivr] 1 *vi* to live; elle vit encore she's
still alive *ou* living; faire v. (*famille etc*) to

support; **v. vieux** to live to be old; **difficile/facile à v.** hard/easy to get on with; **manière de v.** way of life; **v. de** (*fruits etc*) to live on; (*travail etc*) to live by; **avoir de quoi v.** to have enough to live on; **vivent les vacances!** hurray for the holidays!; – *vt* (*vie*) to live; (*aventure, époque*) to live through; (*éprouver*) to experience. **2** *nmpl* food, supplies. ◆**vivoter** *vi* to jog along, get by.

vlan! [vlɑ̃] *int* bang!, wham!

vocable [vɔkabl] *nm* term, word.

vocabulaire [vɔkabylɛr] *nm* vocabulary.

vocal, -aux [vɔkal, -o] *a* (*cordes, musique*) vocal.

vocation [vɔkasjɔ̃] *nf* vocation, calling.

vociférer [vɔsifere] *vti* to shout angrily. ◆**vocifération** *nf* angry shout.

vodka [vɔdka] *nf* vodka.

vœu, -x [vø] *nm* (*souhait*) wish; (*promesse*) vow; **faire le v. de faire** to (make a) vow to do; **tous mes vœux!** (my) best wishes!

vogue [vɔg] *nf* fashion, vogue; **en v.** in fashion, in vogue.

voici [vwasi] *prép* here is, this is; *pl* here are, these are; **me v.** here I am; **me v. triste** I'm sad now; **v. dix ans**/*etc* ten years/*etc* ago; **v. dix ans que** it's ten years since.

voie [vwa] *nf* (*route*) road; (*rails*) track, line; (*partie de route*) lane; (*chemin*) way; (*moyen*) means, way; (*de communication*) line; (*diplomatique*) channels; (*quai*) *Rail* platform; **en v. de** in the process of; **en v. de développement** (*pays*) developing; **v. publique** public highway; **v. navigable** waterway; **v. sans issue** cul-de-sac, dead end; **préparer la v.** *Fig* to pave the way; **sur la (bonne) v.** on the right track.

voilà [vwala] *prép* there is, that is; *pl* there are, those are; **les v.** there they are; **v., j'arrive!** all right, I'm coming!; **le v. parti** he has left now; **v. dix ans**/*etc* ten years/*etc* ago; **v. dix ans que** it's ten years since.

voile¹ [vwal] *nm* (*étoffe qui cache, coiffure etc*) & *Fig* veil. ◆**voilage** *nm* net curtain. ◆**voil/er¹** *vt* (*visage, vérité etc*) to veil; – **se v.** *vpr* (*personne*) to wear a veil; (*ciel, regard*) to cloud over. ◆**—é** *a* (*femme, allusion*) veiled; (*terne*) dull; (*photo*) hazy.

voile² [vwal] *nf* (*de bateau*) sail; (*activité*) sailing; **bateau à voiles** sailing boat, *Am* sailboat; **faire de la v.** to sail, go sailing. ◆**voilier** *nm* sailing ship; (*de plaisance*) sailing boat, *Am* sailboat. ◆**voilure** *nf* *Nau* sails.

voiler² [vwale] *vt*, – **se v.** *vpr* (*roue*) to buckle.

voir* [vwar] *vti* to see; **faire** *ou* **laisser v. qch** to show sth; **fais v.** let me see, show me; **v. qn faire** to see s.o. do *ou* doing; **voyons!** (*sois raisonnable*) come on!; **y v. clair** (*comprendre*) to see clearly; **je ne peux pas la v.** (*supporter*) *Fam* I can't stand (the sight of) her; **v. venir** (*attendre*) to wait and see; **on verra bien** (*attendons*) we'll see; **ça n'a rien à v. avec** that's got nothing to do with; – **se v.** *vpr* to see oneself; (*se fréquenter*) to see each other; (*objet, attitude etc*) to be seen; (*reprise, tache*) to show; **ça se voit** that's obvious.

voire [vwar] *adv* indeed.

voirie [vwari] *nf* (*enlèvement des ordures*) refuse collection; (*routes*) public highways.

voisin, -ine [vwazɛ̃, -in] *a* (*pays, village etc*) neighbouring; (*maison, pièce*) next (**de** to); (*idée, état etc*) similar (**de** to); – *nmf* neighbour. ◆**voisinage** *nm* (*quartier, voisins*) neighbourhood; (*proximité*) proximity. ◆**voisiner** *vi* **v. avec** to be side by side with.

voiture [vwatyr] *nf* *Aut* car; *Rail* carriage, coach, *Am* car; (*charrette*) cart; **v. (à cheval)** (horse-drawn) carriage; **v. de course/de tourisme** racing/private car; **v. d'enfant** pram, *Am* baby carriage; **en v.!** *Rail* all aboard!

voix [vwa] *nf* voice; (*suffrage*) vote; **à v. basse** in a whisper; **à portée de v.** within earshot; **avoir v. au chapitre** *Fig* to have a say.

vol [vɔl] *nm* **1** (*d'avion, d'oiseau*) flight; (*groupe d'oiseaux*) flock, flight; **v. libre** hang gliding; **v. à voile** gliding. **2** (*délit*) theft; (*hold-up*) robbery; **v. à l'étalage** shoplifting; **c'est du v.!** (*trop cher*) it's daylight robbery!

volage [vɔlaʒ] *a* flighty, fickle.

volaille [vɔlaj] *nf* **la v.** (*oiseaux*) poultry; **une v.** (*oiseau*) a fowl. ◆**volailler** *nm* poulterer.

volatile [vɔlatil] *nm* (*oiseau domestique*) fowl.

volatiliser (se) [səvɔlatilize] *vpr* (*disparaître*) to vanish (into thin air).

vol-au-vent [vɔlovɑ̃] *nm inv* *Culin* vol-au-vent.

volcan [vɔlkɑ̃] *nm* volcano. ◆**volcanique** *a* volcanic.

voler [vɔle] **1** *vi* (*oiseau, avion etc*) to fly; (*courir*) *Fig* to rush. **2** *vt* (*dérober*) to steal (**à** from); **v. qn** to rob s.o.; – *vi* to steal. ◆**volant 1** *a* (*tapis etc*) flying; **feuille volante** loose sheet. **2** *nm* *Aut* (steering) wheel; (*objet*) *Sp* shuttlecock; (*de jupe*) flounce. ◆**volée** *nf* flight; (*groupe d'oiseaux*) flock, flight; (*de coups, flèches etc*) volley; (*suite de* *coups*) thrashing; **lancer à toute v.** to throw as hard as one can; **sonner à toute v.** to peal *ou* ring out. ◆**voleter** *vi* to flutter. ◆**voleur, -euse** *nmf* thief; **au v.!** stop thief!; – *a* thieving.

volet [vɔlɛ] *nm* **1** (*de fenêtre*) shutter. **2** (*de programme, reportage etc*) section, part.

volière [vɔljɛr] *nf* aviary.

volley(-ball) [vɔlɛ(bol)] *nm* volleyball. ◆**volleyeur, -euse** *nmf* volleyball player.

volonté [vɔlɔ̃te] *nf* (*faculté, intention*) will; (*désir*) wish; *Phil Psy* free will; **elle a de la v.** she has willpower; **bonne v.** goodwill; **mauvaise v.** ill will; **à v.** at will; (*quantité*) as much as desired. ◆**volontaire** *a* (*délibéré, qui agit librement*) voluntary; (*opiniâtre*) wilful, *Am* willful; – *nmf* volunteer. ◆**volontairement** *adv* voluntarily; (*exprès*) deliberately. ◆**volontiers** [-ɔ̃tje] *adv* willingly, gladly; (*habituellement*) readily; **v.!** (*oui*) I'd love to!

volt [vɔlt] *nm* *Él* volt. ◆**voltage** *nm* voltage.

volte-face [vɔltəfas] *nf inv* about turn, *Am* about face; **faire v.-face** to turn round.

voltige [vɔltiʒ] *nf* acrobatics.

voltiger [vɔltiʒe] *vi* to flutter.

volubile [vɔlybil] *a* (*bavard*) loquacious, voluble.

volume [vɔlym] *nm* (*capacité, intensité, tome*) volume. ◆**volumineux, -euse** *a* bulky, voluminous.

volupté [vɔlypte] *nf* sensual pleasure. ◆**voluptueux, -euse** *a* voluptuous.

vom/ir [vɔmir] *vt* to vomit, bring up; (*exécrer*) *Fig* to loathe; – *vi* to vomit, be sick. ◆**—i** *nm Fam* vomit. ◆**—issement** *nm* (*action*) vomiting. ◆**vomitif, -ive** *a Fam* nauseating.

vont [vɔ̃] *voir* **aller 1**.

vorace [vɔras] *a* (*appétit, lecteur etc*) voracious.

vos [vo] *voir* **votre**.

vote [vɔt] *nm* (*action*) vote, voting; (*suffrage*) vote; (*de loi*) passing; **bureau de v.** polling station. ◆**voter** *vi* to vote; – *vt* (*loi*) to pass; (*crédits*) to vote. ◆**votant, -ante** *nmf* voter.

votre, *pl* **vos** [vɔtr, vo] *a poss* your. ◆**vôtre** *pron poss* **le** *ou* **la v.,** **les vôtres** yours; **à la v.!** (*toast*) cheers!; – *nmpl* **les vôtres** (*parents etc*) your (own) people.

vouer [vwe] *vt* (*promettre*) to vow (à to); (*consacrer*) to dedicate (à to); (*condamner*) to doom (à to); **se v. à** to dedicate oneself to.

vouloir* [vulwar] *vt* to want (**faire** to do); **je veux qu'il parte** I want him to go; **v. dire** to

mean (**que** that); **je voudrais rester** I'd like to stay; **je voudrais un pain** I'd like a loaf of bread; **voulez-vous me suivre** will you follow me; **si tu veux** if you like *ou* wish; **en v. à qn d'avoir fait qch** to hold it against s.o. for doing sth; **l'usage veut que . . .** (+ *sub*) custom requires that . . . ; **v. du bien à qn** to wish s.o. well; **je veux bien** I don't mind (**faire** doing); **que voulez-vous!** (*résignation*) what can you expect!; **sans le v.** unintentionally; **ça ne veut pas bouger** it won't move; **ne pas v. de qch/de qn** not to want sth/s.o.; **veuillez attendre** kindly wait. ◆**voulu** *a* (*requis*) required; (*délibéré*) deliberate, intentional.

vous [vu] *pron* **1** (*sujet, complément direct*) you; **v. êtes** you are; **il v. connaît** he knows you. **2** (*complément indirect*) (to) you; **il v. l'a donné** he gave it to you, he gave you it. **3** (*réfléchi*) yourself, *pl* yourselves; **v. v. lavez** you wash yourself; you wash yourselves. **4** (*réciproque*) each other; **v. v. aimez** you love each other. ◆**v.-même** *pron* yourself. ◆**v.-mêmes** *pron* *pl* yourselves.

voûte [vut] *nf* (*plafond*) vault; (*porche*) arch(way). ◆**voûté** *a* (*personne*) bent, stooped.

vouvoyer [vuvwaje] *vt* to address formally (*using vous*).

voyage [vwajaʒ] *nm* trip, journey; (*par mer*) voyage; **aimer les voyages** to like travelling; **faire un v., partir en v.** to go on a trip; **être en v.** to be (away) travelling; **de v.** (*compagnon etc*) travelling; **bon v.!** have a pleasant trip!; **v. de noces** honeymoon; **v. organisé** (package) tour. ◆**voyager** *vi* to travel. ◆**voyageur, -euse** *nmf* traveller; (*passager*) passenger; **v. de commerce** commercial traveller. ◆**voyagiste** *nm* tour operator.

voyant [vwajɑ̃] **1** *a* gaudy, loud. **2** *nm* (*signal*) (warning) light; (*d'appareil électrique*) pilot light.

voyante [vwajɑ̃t] *nf* clairvoyant.

voyelle [vwajɛl] *nf* vowel.

voyeur, -euse [vwajœr, -øz] *nmf* peeping Tom, voyeur.

voyou [vwaju] *nm* hooligan, hoodlum.

vrac (en) [ɑ̃vrak] *adv* (*en désordre*) haphazardly; (*au poids*) loose, unpackaged.

vrai [vrɛ] *a* true; (*réel*) real; (*authentique*) genuine; – *adv* **dire v.** to be right (in what one says); – *nm* (*vérité*) truth. ◆**—ment** *adv* really.

vraisemblable [vrɛsɑ̃blabl] *a* (*probable*) likely, probable; (*plausible*) plausible. ◆**vraisemblablement** *adv* probably.

◆**vraisemblance** *nf* likelihood; plausibility.

vrille [vrij] *nf* **1** (*outil*) gimlet. **2** *Av* (tail)spin.

vromb/ir [vrɔ̃bir] *vi* to hum. ◆**—issement** *nm* hum(ming).

vu [vy] **1** *voir* **voir;** *− a* **bien vu** well thought of; **mal vu** frowned upon. **2** *prép* in view of; **vu que** seeing that.

vue [vy] *nf* (*spectacle*) sight; (*sens*) (eye)sight; (*panorama, photo, idée*) view; **en v.** (*proche*) in sight; (*en évidence*) on view; (*personne*) *Fig* in the public eye; **avoir en v.** to have in mind; **à v.** (*tirer*) on sight; (*payable*) at sight; **à première v.** at first sight; **de v.** (*connaître*) by sight; **en v. de faire** with a view to doing.

vulgaire [vylgɛr] *a* (*grossier*) vulgar, coarse; (*ordinaire*) common. ◆**—ment** *adv* vulgarly, coarsely; (*appeler*) commonly. ◆**vulgariser** *vt* to popularize. ◆**vulgarité** *nf* vulgarity, coarseness.

vulnérable [vylnerabl] *a* vulnerable. ◆**vulnérabilité** *nf* vulnerability.

W

W, w [dublave] *nm* W, w.

wagon [vagɔ̃] *nm* *Rail* (*de voyageurs*) carriage, coach, *Am* car; (*de marchandises*) wag(g)on, truck, *Am* freight car. ◆**w.-lit** *nm* (*pl* **wagons-lits**) sleeping car, sleeper. ◆**w.-restaurant** *nm* (*pl* **wagons-restaurants**) dining car, diner. ◆**wagonnet** *nm* (small) wagon *ou* truck.

wallon, -onne [walɔ̃, -ɔn] *a & nmf* Walloon.

waters [water] *nmpl* toilet.

watt [wat] *nm* *Él* watt.

w-c [(dubla)vese] *nmpl* toilet.

week-end [wikɛnd] *nm* weekend.

western [wɛstɛrn] *nm* *Cin* western.

whisky, *pl* **-ies** [wiski] *nm* whisky, *Am* whiskey.

X

X, x [iks] *nm* X, x; **rayon X** X-ray.

xénophobe [ksenɔfɔb] *a* xenophobic; *−* *nmf* xenophobe. ◆**xénophobie** *nf* xenophobia.

xérès [gzeres] *nm* sherry.

xylophone [ksilɔfɔn] *nm* xylophone.

Y

Y, y¹ [igrɛk] *nm* Y, y.

y² [i] **1** *adv* there; (*dedans*) in it; *pl* in them; (*dessus*) on it; *pl* on them; **elle y vivra** she'll live there; **j'y entrai** I entered (it); **allons-y** let's go; **j'y suis!** (*je comprends*) now I get it!; **je n'y suis pour rien** I have nothing to do with it, that's nothing to do with me. **2** *pron* (= *à cela*) **j'y pense** I think of it; **je m'y attendais** I was expecting it; **ça y est!** that's it!

yacht [jɔt] *nm* yacht.

yaourt [jaur(t)] *nm* yog(h)urt.

yeux [jø] *voir* **œil.**

yiddish [(j)idiʃ] *nm & a* Yiddish.

yoga [jɔga] *nm* yoga.

yog(h)ourt [jɔgur(t)] *voir* **yaourt.**

Yougoslavie [jugɔslavi] *nf* Yugoslavia. ◆**yougoslave** *a & nmf* Yugoslav(ian).

yo-yo [jojo] *nm inv* yoyo.

Z

Z, z [zɛd] *nm* Z, z.

zèbre [zɛbr] *nm* zebra. ◆**zébré** *a* striped, streaked (**de** with).

zèle [zɛl] *nm* zeal; **faire du z.** to overdo it. ◆**zélé** *a* zealous.

zénith [zenit] *nm* zenith.

zéro [zero] *nm* (*chiffre*) nought, zero; (*dans un numéro*) 0 [əu]; (*température*) zero; (*rien*) nothing; (*personne*) *Fig* nobody, nonentity; **deux buts à z.** *Fb* two nil, *Am* two zero; **partir de z.** to start from scratch.

zeste [zɛst] *nm* **un z. de citron** (a piece of) lemon peel.

zézayer [zezeje] *vi* to lisp.

zibeline [ziblin] *nf* (*animal*) sable.

zigzag [zigzag] *nm* zigzag; **en z.** (*route etc*) zigzag(ging). ◆**zigzaguer** *vi* to zigzag.

zinc [zɛ̃g] *nm* (*métal*) zinc; (*comptoir*) *Fam* bar.

zizanie [zizani] *nf* discord.

zodiaque [zɔdjak] *nm* zodiac.

zona [zona] *nm* *Méd* shingles.

zone [zon] *nf* zone, area; (*domaine*) *Fig* sphere; (*faubourgs misérables*) shanty town; **z. bleue** restricted parking zone; **z. industrielle** trading estate, *Am* industrial park.

zoo [zo(o)] *nm* zoo. ◆**zoologie** [zɔɔlɔʒi] *nf* zoology. ◆**zoologique** *a* zoological; **jardin** *ou* **parc z.** zoo.

zoom [zum] *nm* (*objectif*) zoom lens.

zut! [zyt] *int* *Fam* bother!, heck!

PART 2
English-French

A

A, a [eɪ] *n* A, a *m*; **5A** (*number*) 5 bis; **A1** (*dinner etc*) *Fam* super, superbe; **to go from A to B** aller du point A au point B.

a [ə, *stressed* eɪ] (*before vowel or mute h* **an** [ən, *stressed* æn]) *indef art* **1** un, une; **a man** un homme; **an apple** une pomme. **2** (= *def art in Fr*) **six pence a kilo** six pence le kilo; **50 km an hour** 50 km à l'heure; **I have a broken arm** j'ai le bras cassé. **3** (*art omitted in Fr*) **he's a doctor** il est médecin; **Caen, a town in Normandy** Caen, ville de Normandie; **what a man!** quel homme! **4** (*a certain*) **a Mr Smith** un certain M. Smith. **5** (*time*) **twice a month** deux fois par mois. **6** (*some*) **to make a noise/a fuss** faire du bruit/des histoires.

aback [əˈbæk] *adv* **taken a.** déconcerté.

abandon [əˈbændən] **1** *vt* abandonner. **2** *n* (*freedom of manner*) laisser-aller *m*, abandon *m*. ◆**—ment** *n* abandon *m*.

abase [əˈbeɪs] *vt* **to a. oneself** s'humilier, s'abaisser.

abashed [əˈbæʃt] *a* confus, gêné.

abate [əˈbeɪt] *vi* (*of storm, pain*) se calmer; (*of flood*) baisser; – *vt* diminuer, réduire. ◆**—ment** *n* diminution *f*, réduction *f*.

abbey [ˈæbɪ] *n* abbaye *f*.

abbot [ˈæbət] *n* abbé *m*. ◆**abbess** *n* abbesse *f*.

abbreviate [əˈbriːvɪeɪt] *vt* abréger. ◆**abbreviˈation** *n* abréviation *f*.

abdicate [ˈæbdɪkeɪt] *vti* abdiquer. ◆**abdiˈcation** *n* abdication *f*.

abdomen [ˈæbdəmən] *n* abdomen *m*. ◆**abˈdominal** *a* abdominal.

abduct [æbˈdʌkt] *vt Jur* enlever. ◆**abduction** *n* enlèvement *m*, rapt *m*.

aberration [æbəˈreɪʃ(ə)n] *n* (*folly, lapse*) aberration *f*.

abet [əˈbet] *vt* (**-tt-**) **to aid and a. s.o.** *Jur* être le complice de qn.

abeyance [əˈbeɪəns] *n* **in a.** (*matter*) en suspens.

abhor [əbˈhɔːr] *vt* (**-rr-**) avoir horreur de, exécrer. ◆**abhorrent** *a* exécrable. ◆**abhorrence** *n* horreur *f*.

abide [əˈbaɪd] **1** *vi* **to a. by** (*promise etc*) rester fidèle à. **2** *vt* supporter; **I can't a. him** je ne peux pas le supporter.

ability [əˈbɪlətɪ] *n* capacité *f* (**to do** pour faire), aptitude *f* (**to do** à faire); **to the best of my a.** de mon mieux.

abject [ˈæbdʒekt] *a* abject; **a. poverty** la misère.

ablaze [əˈbleɪz] *a* en feu; **a. with** (*light*) resplendissant de; (*anger*) enflammé de.

able [ˈeɪb(ə)l] *a* (**-er, -est**) capable, compétent; **to be a. to do** être capable de faire, pouvoir faire; **to be a. to swim/drive** savoir nager/conduire. ◆**a.-ˈbodied** *a* robuste. ◆**ably** *adv* habilement.

ablutions [əˈbluːʃ(ə)nz] *npl* ablutions *fpl*.

abnormal [æbˈnɔːm(ə)l] *a* anormal. ◆**abnorˈmality** *n* anomalie *f*; (*of body*) difformité *f*. ◆**abnormally** *adv Fig* exceptionnellement.

aboard [əˈbɔːd] *adv Nau* à bord; **all a.** *Rail* en voiture; – *prep* **a. the ship** à bord du navire; **a. the train** dans le train.

abode [əˈbəʊd] *n* (*house*) *Lit* demeure *f*; *Jur* domicile *m*.

abolish [əˈbɒlɪʃ] *vt* supprimer, abolir. ◆**aboˈlition** *n* suppression *f*, abolition *f*.

abominable [əˈbɒmɪnəb(ə)l] *a* abominable. ◆**abomiˈnation** *n* abomination *f*.

aboriginal [æbəˈrɪdʒən(ə)l] *a* & *n* aborigène (*m*). ◆**aborigines** *npl* aborigènes *mpl*.

abort [əˈbɔːt] *vt Med* faire avorter; (*space flight, computer program*) abandonner; – *vi Med* & *Fig* avorter. ◆**abortion** *n* avortement *m*; **to have an a.** se faire avorter. ◆**abortive** *a* (*plan etc*) manqué, avorté.

abound [əˈbaʊnd] *vi* abonder (**in, with** en).

about [əˈbaʊt] *adv* **1** (*approximately*) à peu près, environ; (**at**) **a. two o'clock** vers deux heures. **2** (*here and there*) çà et là, ici et là; (*ideas, flu*) *Fig* dans l'air; (*rumour*) en circulation; **to look a.** regarder autour; **to follow a.** suivre partout; **to bustle a.** s'affairer; **there are lots a.** il en existe beaucoup; (**out and**) **a.** (*after illness*) sur pied, guéri; (**up and**) **a.** (*out of bed*) levé, debout; **a. turn, a. face** *Mil* demi-tour *m*; *Fig* volte-face *f inv*; – *prep* **1** (*around*) **a. the garden** autour du jardin; **a. the streets** par *or* dans les rues. **2** (*near to*) **a. here** par ici. **3** (*concerning*) au sujet de; **to talk a.** parler de; **a book a.** un livre sur; **what's it (all) a.?** de quoi s'agit-il?; **while you're a.** it pendant que

vous y êtes; **what** or **how a. me?** et moi
alors?; **what** or **how a. a drink?** que dirais-tu
de prendre un verre? **4** (+ *inf*) **a. to do** sur
le point de faire; **I was a. to say** j'étais sur le
point de dire, j'allais dire.

above [ə'bʌv] *adv* au-dessus; (*in book*)
ci-dessus; **from a.** d'en haut; **floor a.** étage
m supérieur or du dessus; – *prep* au-dessus
de; **a.** all par-dessus tout, surtout; **a. the
bridge** (*on river*) en amont du pont; **he's a.
me** (*in rank*) c'est mon supérieur; **a. lying**
incapable de mentir; **a. asking** trop fier
pour demander. ◆**a.-'mentioned** *a*
susmentionné. ◆**aboveboard** *a* ouvert,
honnête; – *adv* sans tricherie, cartes sur
table.

abrasion [ə'breɪʒ(ə)n] *n* frottement *m*; *Med*
écorchure *f.* ◆**abrasive** *a* (*substance*)
abrasif; (*rough*) *Fig* rude, dur; (*irritating*)
agaçant; – *n* abrasif *m.*

abreast [ə'brest] *adv* côte à côte, de front;
four a. par rangs de quatre; **to keep a. of** or
with se tenir au courant de.

abridge [ə'brɪdʒ] *vt* (*book etc*) abréger.
◆**abridg(e)ment** *n* abrégement *m* (**of** de);
(*abridged version*) abrégé *m.*

abroad [ə'brɔːd] *adv* **1** (*in or to a foreign
country*) à l'étranger; **from a.** de l'étranger.
2 (*over a wide area*) de tous côtés; **rumour
a.** bruit *m* qui court.

abrogate ['æbrəgeɪt] *vt* abroger.

abrupt [ə'brʌpt] *a* (*sudden*) brusque;
(*person*) brusque, abrupt; (*slope, style*)
abrupt. ◆**—ly** *adv* (*suddenly*) brusquement; (*rudely*) avec brusquerie.

abscess ['æbses] *n* abcès *m.*

abscond [əb'skɒnd] *vi* *Jur* s'enfuir.

absence ['æbsəns] *n* absence *f*; **in the a. of
sth** à défaut de qch, faute de qch; **a. of mind**
distraction *f.*

absent ['æbsənt] *a* absent (**from** de); (*look*)
distrait; – [æb'sent] *vt* **to a. oneself**
s'absenter. ◆**a.-'minded** *a* distrait.
◆**a.-'mindedness** *n* distraction *f.*
◆**absen'tee** *n* absent, -ente *mf.*
◆**absen'teeism** *n* absentéisme *m.*

absolute ['æbsəluːt] *a* absolu; (*proof etc*)
indiscutable; (*coward etc*) parfait, véritable. ◆**—ly** *adv* absolument; (*forbidden*)
formellement.

absolve [əb'zɒlv] *vt* *Rel Jur* absoudre; **to a.
from** (*vow*) libérer de. ◆**absolution**
[æbsə'luːʃ(ə)n] *n* absolution *f.*

absorb [əb'zɔːb] *vt* absorber; (*shock*) amortir; **to become absorbed in** (*work*)
s'absorber dans. ◆**—ing** *a* (*work*)

absorbant; (*book, film*) prenant.
◆**absorbent** *a* & *n* absorbant (*m*); **a.
cotton** *Am* coton *m* hydrophile.
◆**absorber** *n* **shock a.** *Aut* amortisseur *m.*
◆**absorption** *n* absorption *f.*

abstain [əb'steɪn] *vi* s'abstenir (**from** de).
◆**abstemious** *a* sobre, frugal. ◆**abstention** *n* abstention *f.* ◆**'abstinence** *n*
abstinence *f.*

abstract ['æbstrækt] **1** *a* & *n* abstrait (*m*). **2**
n (*summary*) résumé *m.* **3** [əb'strækt] *vt*
(*remove*) retirer; (*notion*) abstraire.
◆**ab'straction** *n* (*idea*) abstraction *f*;
(*absent-mindedness*) distraction *f.*

abstruse [əb'struːs] *a* obscur.

absurd [əb'sɜːd] *a* absurde, ridicule.
◆**absurdity** *n* absurdité *f.* ◆**absurdly**
adv absurdement.

abundant [ə'bʌndənt] *a* abondant.
◆**abundance** *n* abondance *f.* ◆**abundantly** *adv* **a. clear** tout à fait clair.

abuse [ə'bjuːs] *n* (*abusing*) abus *m* (**of** de);
(*curses*) injures *fpl*; – [ə'bjuːz] *vt* (*misuse*)
abuser de; (*malign*) dire du mal de; (*insult*)
injurier. ◆**abusive** [ə'bjuːsɪv] *a* injurieux.

abysmal [ə'bɪzm(ə)l] *a* (*bad*) *Fam* désastreux, exécrable.

abyss [ə'bɪs] *n* abîme *m.*

acacia [ə'keɪʃə] *n* (*tree*) acacia *m.*

academic [ækə'demɪk] *a* universitaire;
(*scholarly*) érudit, intellectuel; (*issue etc*)
Pej théorique; (*style, art*) académique; – *n*
(*teacher*) *Univ* universitaire *mf.*

academy [ə'kædəmɪ] *n* (*society*) académie *f*;
Mil Mus école *f.* ◆**acade'mician** *n*
académicien, -ienne *mf.*

accede [ək'siːd] *vi* **to a. to** (*request, throne,
position*) accéder à.

accelerate [ək'seləreɪt] *vt* accélérer; – *vi*
s'accélérer; *Aut* accélérer. ◆**accele-
'ration** *n* accélération *f.* ◆**accelerator** *n*
Aut accélérateur *m.*

accent ['æksənt] *n* accent *m*; – [æk'sent] *vt*
accentuer. ◆**accentuate** [æk'sentʃueɪt] *vt*
accentuer.

accept [ək'sept] *vt* accepter. ◆**—ed** *a* (*opinion etc*) reçu, admis. ◆**acceptable** *a*
(*worth accepting, tolerable*) acceptable.
◆**acceptance** *n* acceptation *f*; (*approval,
favour*) accueil *m* favorable.

access ['ækses] *n* accès *m* (**to sth** à qch, **to
s.o.** auprès de qn). ◆**ac'cessible** *a* accessible.

accession [æk'seʃ(ə)n] *n* accession *f* (**to** à);
(*increase*) augmentation *f*; (*sth added*)
nouvelle acquisition *f.*

accessory [ək'sesərɪ] **1** n (*person*) Jur complice mf. **2** npl (*objects*) accessoires mpl.

accident ['æksɪdənt] n accident m; **by a.** (*by chance*) par accident; (*unintentionally*) accidentellement, sans le vouloir. ◆**a.-prone** a prédisposé aux accidents. ◆**acci'dental** a accidentel, fortuit. ◆**acci'dentally** adv accidentellement, par mégarde; (*by chance*) par accident.

acclaim [ə'kleɪm] vt acclamer; **to a. king** proclamer roi. ◆**accla'mation** n acclamation(s) f(pl), louange(s) f(pl).

acclimate ['æklɪmeɪt] vti Am = **acclimatize**. ◆**a'cclimatize** vt acclimater; – vi s'acclimater. ◆**accli'mation** n Am, ◆**acclimati'zation** n acclimatisation f.

accolade ['ækəleɪd] n (*praise*) Fig louange f.

accommodat/e [ə'kɒmədeɪt] vt (*of house*) loger, recevoir; (*have room for*) avoir dela place pour (mettre); (*adapt*) adapter (to à); (*supply*) fournir (s.o. with sth qch à qn); (*oblige*) rendre service à; (*reconcile*) concilier; **to a. oneself to** s'accomoder à. ◆**—ing** a accommodant, obligeant. ◆**accommo'dation** n **1** (*lodging*) logement m; (*rented room or rooms*) chambre(s) f(pl); pl (*in hotel*) Am chambre(s) f(pl). **2** (*compromise*) compromis m, accommodement m.

accompany [ə'kʌmpənɪ] vt accompagner. ◆**accompaniment** n accompagnement m. ◆**accompanist** n Mus accompagnateur, -trice mf.

accomplice [ə'kʌmplɪs] n complice mf.

accomplish [ə'kʌmplɪʃ] vt (*task, duty*) accomplir; (*aim*) réaliser. ◆**—ed** a accompli. ◆**—ment** n accomplissement m; (*of aim*) réalisation f; (*thing achieved*) réalisation f; pl (*skills*) talents mpl.

accord [ə'kɔːd] **1** n accord m; **of my own a.** volontairement, de mon plein gré; – vi concorder. **2** vt (*grant*) accorder. ◆**accordance** n in a. with conformément à.

according to [ə'kɔːdɪŋtuː] prep selon, d'après, suivant. ◆**accordingly** adv en conséquence.

accordion [ə'kɔːdɪən] n accordéon m.

accost [ə'kɒst] vt accoster, aborder.

account [ə'kaʊnt] **1** n Com compte m; pl comptabilité f, comptes mpl; **accounts department** comptabilité f; **to take into a.** tenir compte de; **ten pounds on a.** un acompte de dix livres; **of some a.** d'une certaine importance; **on a. of** à cause de; **on**

no a. en aucun cas. **2** n (*report*) compte rendu m, récit m; (*explanation*) explication f; **by all accounts** au dire de tous; **to give a good a. of oneself** s'en tirer à son avantage; – vi **to a. for** (*explain*) expliquer; (*give reckoning of*) rendre compte de. **3** vt **to a. oneself lucky/etc** (*consider*) se considérer heureux/etc. ◆**accountable** a responsable (**for de, to** devant); (*explainable*) explicable.

accountant [ə'kaʊntənt] n comptable mf. ◆**accountancy** n comptabilité f.

accoutrements [ə'kuːtrəmənts] (*Am* accouterments [ə'kuːtəmənts]) npl équipement m.

accredit [ə'kredɪt] vt (*ambassador*) accréditer; **to a. s.o. with sth** attribuer qch à qn.

accrue [ə'kruː] vi (*of interest*) Fin s'accumuler; **to a. to** (*of advantage etc*) revenir à.

accumulate [ə'kjuːmjʊleɪt] vt accumuler, amasser; – vi s'accumuler. ◆**accumu-'lation** n accumulation f; (*mass*) amas m. ◆**accumulator** n El accumulateur m.

accurate ['ækjʊrət] a exact, précis. ◆**accuracy** n exactitude f, précision f. ◆**accurately** adv avec précision.

accursed [ə'kɜːsɪd] a maudit, exécrable.

accus/e [ə'kjuːz] vt accuser (**of** de). ◆**—ed** n the a. Jur l'inculpé, -ée mf, l'accusé, -ée mf. ◆**—ing** a accusateur. ◆**accu'sation** n accusation f.

accustom [ə'kʌstəm] vt habituer, accoutumer. ◆**—ed** a habitué (**to sth** à qch, **to doing** à faire); **to get a. to** s'habituer à, s'accoutumer à.

ace [eɪs] n (*card, person*) as m.

acetate ['æsɪteɪt] n acétate m.

acetic [ə'siːtɪk] a acétique.

ache [eɪk] n douleur f, mal m; **to have an a. in one's arm** avoir mal au bras; – vi faire mal; **my head aches** ma tête me fait mal; **it makes my heart a.** cela me serre le cœur; **to be aching to do** brûler de faire. ◆**aching** a douloureux.

achieve [ə'tʃiːv] vt accomplir, réaliser; (*success, aim*) atteindre; (*victory*) remporter. ◆**—ment** n accomplissement m, réalisation f (**of** de); (*feat*) réalisation f, exploit m.

acid ['æsɪd] a & n acide (m). ◆**a'cidity** n acidité f.

acknowledge [ək'nɒlɪdʒ] vt reconnaître (**as** pour); (*greeting*) répondre à; **to a. (receipt of)** accuser réception de; **to a. defeat** s'avouer vaincu. ◆**—ment** n reconnaissance f; (*of letter*) accusé m de réception; (*receipt*) reçu m, récépissé m.

acme ['ækmɪ] *n* sommet *m*, comble *m*.
acne ['æknɪ] *n* acné *f*.
acorn ['eɪkɔːn] *n Bot* gland *m*.
acoustic [ə'kuːstɪk] *a* acoustique; – *npl* acoustique *f*.
acquaint [ə'kweɪnt] *vt* **to a. s.o. with sth** informer qn de qch; **to be acquainted with** (*person*) connaître; (*fact*) savoir; **we are acquainted** on se connaît. ◆**acquaintance** *n* (*person, knowledge*) connaissance *f*.
acquiesce [ækwɪ'es] *vi* acquiescer (**in** à). ◆**acquiescence** *n* acquiescement *m*.
acquire [ə'kwaɪər] *vt* acquérir; (*taste*) prendre (**for** à); (*friends*) se faire; **aquired taste** goût *m* qui s'acquiert. ◆**acqui'sition** *n* acquisition *f*. ◆**acquisitive** *a* avide, cupide.
acquit [ə'kwɪt] *vt* (-tt-) **to a. s.o. (of a crime)** acquitter qn. ◆**acquittal** *n* acquittement *m*.
acre ['eɪkər] *n* acre *f* (= 0,4 hectare). ◆**acreage** *n* superficie *f*.
acrid ['ækrɪd] *a* (*smell, manner etc*) âcre.
acrimonious [ækrɪ'məʊnɪəs] *a* acerbe.
acrobat ['ækrəbæt] *n* acrobate *mf*. ◆**acro'batic** *a* acrobatique; – *npl* acrobatie(s) *f*(*pl*).
acronym ['ækrənɪm] *n* sigle *m*.
across [ə'krɒs] *adv & prep* (*from side to side (of)*) d'un côté à l'autre (de); (*on the other side (of)*) de l'autre côté (de); (*crossways*) en travers (de); **to be a kilometre/**etc **a.** (*wide*) avoir un kilomètre/etc de large; **to walk** *or* **go a.** (*street etc*) traverser; **to come a.** (*person*) rencontrer (par hasard), tomber sur; (*thing*) trouver (par hasard); **to get sth a. to s.o.** faire comprendre qch à qn.
acrostic [ə'krɒstɪk] *n* acrostiche *m*.
acrylic [ə'krɪlɪk] *a* & *n* acrylique (*m*).
act [ækt] **1** *n* (*deed*) acte *m*; **a.** (*of parliament*) loi *f*; **caught in the a.** pris sur le fait; **a. of walking** action *f* de marcher; **an a. of folly** une folie. **2** *n* (*of play*) Th acte *m*; (*turn*) Th numéro *m*; **in on the a.** *Fam* dans le coup; **to put on an a.** *Fam* jouer la comédie; – *vt* (*part*) Th jouer; **to a. the fool** faire l'idiot; – *vi* Th Cin jouer; (*pretend*) jouer la comédie. **3** *vi* (*do sth, behave*) agir; (*function*) fonctionner; **to a. as** (*secretary etc*) faire office de; (*of object*) servir de; **to a.** (**up)on** (*affect*) agir sur; (*advice*) suivre; **to a. on behalf of** représenter; **to a. up** (*of person, machine*) *Fam* faire des siennes. ◆**—ing 1** *a* (*manager etc*) intérimaire, provisoire. **2** *n* (*of play*) représentation *f*; (*actor's art*) jeu *m*; (*career*) théâtre *m*.

action ['ækʃ(ə)n] *n* action *f*; *Mil* combat *m*; *Jur* procès *m*, action *f*; **to take a.** prendre des mesures; **to put into a.** (*plan*) exécuter; **out of a.** hors d'usage, hors (de) service; (*person*) hors de combat; **killed in a.** mort au champ d'honneur; **to take industrial a.** se mettre en grève.
active ['æktɪv] *a* actif; (*interest*) vif; (*volcano*) en activité. ◆**activate** *vt Ch* activer; (*mechanism*) actionner. ◆**activist** *n* activiste *mf*. ◆**ac'tivity** *n* activité *f*; (*in street*) mouvement *m*.
actor ['æktər] *n* acteur *m*. ◆**actress** *n* actrice *f*.
actual ['æktʃuəl] *a* réel, véritable; (*example*) concret; **the a. book** le livre même; **in a. fact** en réalité, effectivement. ◆**—ly** *adv* (*truly*) réellement; (*in fact*) en réalité, en fait.
actuary ['æktʃuərɪ] *n* actuaire *mf*.
actuate ['æktʃueɪt] *vt* (*person*) animer; (*machine*) actionner.
acumen ['ækjumen, *Am* ə'kjuːmən] *n* perspicacité *f*, finesse *f*.
acupuncture ['ækjupʌŋktʃər] *n* acupuncture *f*.
acute [ə'kjuːt] *a* aigu; (*anxiety, emotion*) vif, profond; (*observer*) perspicace; (*shortage*) grave. ◆**—ly** *adv* (*to suffer, feel*) vivement, profondément. ◆**—ness** *n* acuité *f*; perspicacité *f*.
ad [æd] *n Fam* pub *f*; (*private, in newspaper*) annonce *f*; **small ad** petite annonce.
AD [eɪ'diː] *abbr* (*anno Domini*) après Jésus-Christ.
adage ['ædɪdʒ] *n* adage *m*.
Adam ['ædəm] *n* **A.'s apple** pomme *f* d'Adam.
adamant ['ædəmənt] *a* inflexible.
adapt [ə'dæpt] *vt* adapter (**to** à); **to a.** (**oneself**) s'adapter. ◆**adaptable** *a* (*person*) capable de s'adapter, adaptable. ◆**adaptor** *n* (*device*) adaptateur *m*; (*plug*) prise *f* multiple. ◆**adap'tation** *n* adaptation *f*.
add [æd] *vt* ajouter (**to** à, **that** que); **to a.** (**up** *or* **together**) (*total*) additionner; **to a. in** inclure; – *vi* **to a. to** (*increase*) augmenter; **to a. up to** (*total*) s'élever à; (*mean*) signifier; **it all adds up** *Fam* ça s'explique. ◆**a'ddendum**, *pl* **-da** *n* supplément *m*. ◆**adding machine** *n* machine *f* à calculer. ◆**a'ddition** *n* addition *f*; augmentation *f*; **in a.** de plus; **in a. to** en plus de. ◆**a'dditional** *a* supplémentaire. ◆**a'dditionally** *adv* de plus. ◆**additive** *n* additif *m*.
adder ['ædər] *n* vipère *f*.

addict ['ædɪkt] *n* intoxiqué, -ée *mf*; **jazz/sport a.** fanatique *mf* du jazz/du sport; **drug a.** drogué, -ée *mf*. ◆**a'ddicted** *a* **to be a. to** (*study, drink*) s'adonner à; (*music*) se passionner pour; (*to have the habit of*) avoir la manie de; **a. to cigarettes** drogué par la cigarette. ◆**a'ddiction** *n* (*habit*) manie *f*; (*dependency*) *Med* dépendance *f*; **drug a.** toxicomanie *f*. ◆**a'ddictive** *a* qui crée une dépendance.

address [ə'dres, *Am* 'ædres] *n* (*on letter etc*) adresse *f*; (*speech*) allocution *f*; **form of a.** formule *f* de politesse; – [ə'dres] *vt* (*person*) s'adresser à; (*audience*) parler devant; (*words, speech*) adresser (**to** à); (*letter*) mettre l'adresse sur; **a. to s.o.** (*send, intend for*) adresser à qn. ◆**addressee** [ædre'siː] *n* destinataire *mf*.

adenoids ['ædɪnɔɪdz] *npl* végétations *fpl* (adénoïdes).

adept ['ædept, *Am* ə'dept] *a* expert (**in, at** à).

adequate ['ædɪkwət] *a* (*quantity*) suffisant; (*acceptable*) convenable; (*person, performance*) compétent. ◆**adequacy** *n* (*of person*) compétence *f*; **to doubt the a. of sth** douter que qch soit suffisant. ◆**adequately** *adv* suffisamment; convenablement.

adhere [əd'hɪər] *vi* **to a. to** adhérer à; (*decision*) s'en tenir à; (*rule*) respecter. ◆**adherence** *n*, ◆**adhesion** *n* (*grip*) adhérence *f*; (*support*) *Fig* adhésion *f*. ◆**adhesive** *a & n* adhésif (*m*).

ad infinitum [ædɪnfɪ'naɪtəm] *adv* à l'infini.

adjacent [ə'dʒeɪsənt] *a* (*house, angle etc*) adjacent (**to** à).

adjective ['ædʒɪktɪv] *n* adjectif *m*.

adjoin [ə'dʒɔɪn] *vt* avoisiner. ◆**—ing** *a* avoisinant, voisin.

adjourn [ə'dʒɜːn] *vt* (*postpone*) adjourner; (*session*) lever, suspendre; – *vi* lever la séance; **to a. to** (*go*) passer à. ◆**—ment** *n* ajournement *m*; suspension *f* (de séance), levée *f* de séance.

adjudicate [ə'dʒuːdɪkeɪt] *vti* juger. ◆**adjudi'cation** *n* jugement *m*. ◆**adjudicator** *n* juge *m*, arbitre *m*.

adjust [ə'dʒʌst] *vt Tech* régler, ajuster; (*prices*) (r)ajuster; (*arrange*) arranger; **to a.** (**oneself**) **to** s'adapter à. ◆**—able** *a* réglable. ◆**—ment** *n Tech* réglage *m*; (*of person*) adaptation *f*; (*of prices*) (r)ajustement *m*.

ad-lib [æd'lɪb] *vi* (**-bb-**) improviser; – *a* (*joke etc*) improvisé.

administer [əd'mɪnɪstər] **1** *vt* (*manage, dispense*) administrer (**to** à). **2** *vi* **to a. to**

pourvoir à. ◆**admini'stration** *n* administration *f*; (*ministry*) gouvernement *m*. ◆**administrative** *a* administratif. ◆**administrator** *n* administrateur, -trice *mf*.

admiral ['ædmərəl] *n* amiral *m*.

admir/e [əd'maɪər] *vt* admirer. ◆**—ing** *a* admiratif. ◆**—er** *n* admirateur, -trice *mf*. ◆'**admirable** *a* admirable. ◆**admi'ration** *n* admiration *f*.

admit [əd'mɪt] *vt* (**-tt-**) (*let in*) laisser entrer; (*accept*) admettre; (*acknowledge*) reconnaître, avouer; – *vi* **to a. to sth** (*confess*) avouer qch; **to a. of** permettre. ◆**admittedly** *adv* c'est vrai (que). ◆**admissible** *a* admissible. ◆**admission** *n* (*entry to theatre etc*) entrée *f* (**to** à, de); (*to club, school*) admission *f*; (*acknowledgement*) aveu *m*; **a. (charge)** (prix *m* d')entrée *f*. ◆**admittance** *n* entrée *f*; '**no a.**' 'entrée interdite'.

admonish [əd'mɒnɪʃ] *vt* (*reprove*) réprimander; (*warn*) avertir.

ado [ə'duː] *n* **without further a.** sans (faire) plus de façons.

adolescent [ædə'lesənt] *n* adolescent, -ente *mf*. ◆**adolescence** *n* adolescence *f*.

adopt [ə'dɒpt] *vt* (*child, method, attitude etc*) adopter; (*candidate*) *Pol* choisir. ◆**—ed** *a* (*child*) adoptif; (*country*) d'adoption. ◆**adoption** *n* adoption *f*. ◆**adoptive** *a* (*parent*) adoptif.

adore [ə'dɔːr] *vt* adorer; **he adores being flattered** il adore qu'on le flatte. ◆**adorable** *a* adorable. ◆**ado'ration** *n* adoration *f*.

adorn [ə'dɔːn] *vt* (*room, book*) orner; (*person, dress*) parer. ◆**—ment** *n* ornement *m*; parure *f*.

adrenalin(e) [ə'drenəlɪn] *n* adrénaline *f*.

Adriatic [eɪdrɪ'ætɪk] *n* **the A.** l'Adriatique *f*.

adrift [ə'drɪft] *a & adv Nau* à la dérive; **to come a.** (*of rope, collar etc*) se détacher; **to turn s.o. a.** *Fig* abandonner qn à son sort.

adroit [ə'drɔɪt] *a* adroit, habile.

adulation [ædjuː'leɪʃ(ə)n] *n* adulation *f*.

adult ['ædʌlt] *a & n* adulte (*mf*). ◆**adulthood** *n* âge *m* adulte.

adulterate [ə'dʌltəreɪt] *vt* (*food*) altérer.

adultery [ə'dʌltərɪ] *n* adultère *m*. ◆**adulterous** *a* adultère.

advanc/e [əd'vɑːns] *n* (*movement, money*) avance *f*; (*of science*) progrès *mpl*; *pl* (*of friendship, love*) avances *fpl*; **in a.** à l'avance, d'avance; (*to arrive*) en avance; **in a. of s.o.** avant qn; – *a* (*payment*) anticipé; **a. booking** réservation *f*; **a. guard** avant-garde *f*; – *vt* (*put forward, lend*) avancer; (*science, work*) faire avancer; – *vi* (*go forward, progress*) avancer; (*towards s.o.*) s'avancer, avancer. ◆**—ed** a avancé; (*studies*) supérieur; **a. in years** âgé. ◆**—ement** n (*progress, promotion*) avancement m.

advantage [əd'vɑːntɪdʒ] n avantage m (**over** sur); **to take a.** of profiter de; (*person*) tromper, exploiter; (*woman*) séduire; **to show (off) to a.** faire valoir. ◆**advan-'tageous** a avantageux (**to**, pour), profitable.

advent ['ædvent] n arrivée f, avènement m; **A.** *Rel* l'Avent m.

adventure [əd'ventʃər] n aventure f; – a (*film etc*) d'aventures. ◆**adventurer** n aventurier, -ière mf. ◆**adventurous** a aventureux.

adverb ['ædvɜːb] n adverbe m.

adversary ['ædvəsəri] n adversaire mf.

adverse ['ædvɜːs] a hostile, défavorable. ◆**ad'versity** n adversité f.

advert ['ædvɜːt] n *Fam* pub f; (*private, in newspaper*) annonce f.

advertis/e ['ædvətaɪz] vt (*goods*) faire de la publicité pour; (*make known*) annoncer; – vi faire de la publicité; **to a. (for s.o.)** mettre une annonce (pour chercher qn). ◆**—er** n annonceur m. ◆**—ement** [əd'vɜːtɪsmənt, *Am* ædvə'taɪzmənt] n publicité f; (*private or classified in newspaper*) annonce f; (*poster*) affiche f; **classified a.** petite annonce; **the advertisements** *TV* la publicité.

advice [əd'vaɪs] n conseil(s) m(pl); *Com* avis m; **a piece of a.** un conseil.

advis/e [əd'vaɪz] vt (*counsel*) conseiller; (*recommend*) recommander; (*notify*) informer; **to a. s.o. to do** conseiller à qn de faire; **to a. against** déconseiller. ◆**—ed** a **well-a.** (*action*) prudent. ◆**—able** a (*wise*) prudent (**to do** de faire); (*act*) à conseiller. ◆**—edly** [-ɪdlɪ] adv après réflexion. ◆**—er** n conseiller, -ère mf. ◆**advisory** a consultatif.

advocate 1 ['ædvəkət] n (*of cause*) défenseur m, avocat, -ate mf; *Jur* avocat m. **2** ['ædvəkeɪt] vt préconiser, recommander.

aegis ['iːdʒɪs] n **under the a. of** sous l'égide de.

aeon ['iːɒn] n éternité f.

aerial ['eərɪəl] n antenne f; – a aérien.

aerobatics [eərə'bætɪks] npl acrobatie f aérienne. ◆**ae'robics** npl aérobic f. ◆**'aerodrome** n aérodrome m. ◆**aero-'dynamic** a aérodynamique. ◆**aero'-nautics** npl aéronautique f. ◆**'aeroplane**

n avion m. ◆**'aerosol** n aérosol m. ◆**'aerospace** a (*industry*) aérospatial.

aesthetic [iːs'θetɪk, *Am* es'θetɪk] a esthétique.

afar [ə'fɑːr] adv **from a.** de loin.

affable ['æfəb(ə)l] a affable, aimable.

affair [ə'feər] n (*matter, concern*) affaire f; (*love*) **a.** liaison f; **state of affairs** état m de choses.

affect [ə'fekt] vt (*move, feign*) affecter; (*concern*) toucher, affecter; (*harm*) nuire à; (*be fond of*) affectionner. ◆**—ed** a (*manner*) affecté; (*by disease*) atteint. ◆**affec'tation** n affectation f.

affection [ə'fekʃ(ə)n] n affection f (**for** pour). ◆**affectionate** a affectueux, aimant. ◆**affectionately** adv affectueusement.

affiliate [ə'fɪlɪeɪt] vt affilier; **to be affiliated** s'affilier (**to** à); **affiliated company** filiale f. ◆**affili'ation** n affiliation f; pl (*political*) attaches fpl.

affinity [ə'fɪnɪtɪ] n affinité f.

affirm [ə'fɜːm] vt affirmer. ◆**affir'mation** n affirmation f. ◆**affirmative** a affirmatif; – n affirmative f.

affix [ə'fɪks] vt apposer.

afflict [ə'flɪkt] vt affliger (**with** de). ◆**afflic-tion** n (*misery*) affliction f; (*disorder*) infirmité f.

affluent ['æfluənt] a riche; **a. society** société f d'abondance. ◆**affluence** n richesse f.

afford [ə'fɔːd] vt **1** (*pay for*) avoir les moyens d'acheter, pouvoir se payer; (*time*) pouvoir trouver; **I can a. to wait** je peux me permettre d'attendre. **2** (*provide*) fournir, donner; **to a. s.o. sth** fournir qch à qn.

affray [ə'freɪ] n *Jur* rixe f, bagarre f.

affront [ə'frʌnt] n affront m; – vt faire un affront à.

Afghanistan [æf'gænɪstɑːn] n Afghanistan m. ◆**'Afghan** a & n afghan, -ane (mf).

afield [ə'fiːld] adv **further a.** plus loin; **too far a.** trop loin.

afloat [ə'fləʊt] adv (*ship, swimmer, business*) à flot; (*awash*) submergé; **life a.** la vie sur l'eau.

afoot [ə'fʊt] adv **there's sth a.** il se trame qch; **there's a plan a. to** on prépare un projet pour.

aforementioned [ə'fɔːmenʃ(ə)nd] a susmentionné.

afraid [ə'freɪd] a **to be a.** avoir peur (**of**, **to** de; **that** que); **to make s.o. afraid** faire peur à qn; **he's a. (that) she may be ill** il a peur qu'elle (ne) soit malade; **I'm a. he's out** (*I regret to say*) je regrette, il est sorti.

afresh [əˈfreʃ] *adv* de nouveau.

Africa [ˈæfrɪkə] *n* Afrique *f.* ◆**African** *a* & *n* africain, -aine (*mf*).

after [ˈɑːftər] *adv* après; **the month a.** le mois suivant, le mois d'après; – *prep* après; **a. all** après tout; **a. eating** après avoir mangé; **day a. day** jour après jour; **page a. page** page sur page; **time a. time** bien des fois; **a. you!** je vous en prie!; **ten a. four** *Am* quatre heures dix; **to be a. sth/s.o.** (*seek*) chercher qch/qn; – *conj* après que; **a. he saw you** après qu'il t'a vu. ◆**aftercare** *n Med* soins *mpl* postopératoires; *Jur* surveillance *f.* ◆**aftereffects** *npl* suites *fpl*, séquelles *fpl.* ◆**afterlife** *n* vie *f* future. ◆**aftermath** [-mɑːθ] *n* suites *fpl.* ◆**after'noon** *n* après-midi *m* or *f inv*; **in the a.** l'après-midi; **good a.!** (*hello*) bonjour!; (*goodbye*) au revoir! ◆**after'noons** *adv Am* l'après-midi. ◆**aftersales** (**service**) *n* service *m* après-vente. ◆**aftershave** (**lotion**) *n* lotion *f* après-rasage. ◆**aftertaste** *n* arrière-goût *m.* ◆**afterthought** *n* réflexion *f* après coup. ◆**afterward(s)** *adv* après, plus tard.

afters [ˈɑːftəz] *npl Fam* dessert *m.*

again [əˈgen, əˈgeɪn] *adv* de nouveau, encore une fois; (*furthermore*) en outre; **to do a.** refaire; **to go down/up a.** redescendre/remonter; **never a.** plus jamais; **half as much a.** moitié plus; **a. and a.,** time and (time) a. maintes fois; **what's his name a.?** comment s'appelle-t-il déjà?

against [əˈgenst, əˈgeɪnst] *prep* contre; **to go or be a.** s'opposer à; **a law a.** drinking une loi qui interdit de boire; **his age is a. him** son âge lui est défavorable; **a. a background of** sur (un) fond de; **a. the light** à contre-jour; **a. the law** illégal; **a. the rules** interdit, contraire aux règlements.

age [eɪdʒ] *n* (*lifespan, period*) âge *m*; (*old*) a. vieillesse *f*; **the Middle Ages** le moyen âge; **what a. are you?, what's your a.?** quel âge as-tu?; **five years of a.** âgé de cinq ans; **to be of a.** être majeur; **under a.** trop jeune, mineur; **to wait** (**for**) **ages** *Fam* attendre une éternité; **a. group** tranche *f* d'âge; – *vti* (*pres p* ag(e)ing) vieillir. ◆**a.-old** *a* séculaire. ◆**aged** *a* [eɪdʒd] **a. ten** âgé de dix ans; [ˈeɪdʒɪd] vieux, âgé; **the a.** les personnes *fpl* âgées. ◆**ageless** *a* toujours jeune.

agenda [əˈdʒendə] *n* ordre *m* du jour.

agent [ˈeɪdʒənt] *n* agent *m*; (*dealer*) *Com* concessionnaire *mf.* ◆**agency** *n* 1 (*office*) agence *f.* 2 **through the a. of s.o.** par l'intermédiaire de qn.

agglomeration [əglɒməˈreɪʃ(ə)n] *n* agglomération *f.*

aggravate [ˈægrəveɪt] *vt* (*make worse*) aggraver; **to a. s.o.** *Fam* exaspérer qn. ◆**aggra'vation** *n* aggravation *f*; *Fam* exaspération *f*; (*bother*) *Fam* ennui(s) *m(pl)*.

aggregate [ˈægrɪgət] *a* global; – *n* (*total*) ensemble *m.*

aggression [əˈgreʃ(ə)n] *n* agression *f.* ◆**aggressive** *a* agressif. ◆**aggressiveness** *n* agressivité *f.* ◆**aggressor** *n* agresseur *m.*

aggrieved [əˈgriːvd] *a* (*offended*) blessé, froissé; (*tone*) peiné.

aghast [əˈgɑːst] *a* consterné, horrifié.

agile [ˈædʒaɪl, *Am* ˈædʒ(ə)l] *a* agile. ◆**a'gility** *n* agilité *f.*

agitate [ˈædʒɪteɪt] *vt* (*worry, shake*) agiter; – *vi* **to a. for** *Pol* faire campagne pour. ◆**agi'tation** *n* (*anxiety, unrest*) agitation *f.* ◆**agitator** *n* agitateur, -trice *mf.*

aglow [əˈgləʊ] *a* **to be a.** briller (**with** de).

agnostic [ægˈnɒstɪk] *a* & *n* agnostique (*mf*).

ago [əˈgəʊ] *adv* **a year a.** il y a un an; **how long a.?** il y a combien de temps (de cela)?; **as long a. as 1800** (déjà) en 1800.

agog [əˈgɒg] *a* (*excited*) en émoi; (*eager*) impatient.

agony [ˈægənɪ] *n* (*pain*) douleur *f* atroce; (*anguish*) angoisse *f*; **to be in a.** souffrir horriblement; **a. column** *Journ* courrier *m* du cœur. ◆**agonize** *vi* se faire beaucoup de souci. ◆**agonized** *a* (*look*) angoissé; (*cry*) de douleur. ◆**agonizing** *a* (*pain*) atroce; (*situation*) angoissant.

agree [əˈgriː] *vi* (*come to terms*) se mettre d'accord, s'accorder; (*be in agreement*) être d'accord, s'accorder (**with** avec); (*of facts, dates etc*) concorder; *Gram* s'accorder; **to a. upon** (*decide*) convenir de; **to a. to sth/to doing** consentir à qch/à faire; **it doesn't a. with me** (*food, climate*) ça ne me réussit pas; – *vt* (*figures*) faire concorder; (*accounts*) *Com* approuver; **to a. to do** accepter de faire; **to a. that** (*admit*) admettre que. ◆**agreed** *a* (*time, place*) convenu; **we are a.** nous sommes d'accord; **a.!** entendu! ◆**agreeable** *a* **1** (*pleasant*) agréable. **2 to be a.** (*agree*) être d'accord; **to be a. to sth** consentir à qch. ◆**agreement** *n* accord *m*; *Pol Com* convention *f*, accord *m*; **in a. with** d'accord avec.

agriculture [ˈægrɪkʌltʃər] *n* agriculture *f.* ◆**agri'cultural** *a* agricole.

aground [əˈgraʊnd] *adv* **to run a.** *Nau* (s')échouer.

ah! [ɑː] *int* ah!

ahead [əˈhed] *adv* (*in space*) en avant; (*leading*) en tête; (*in the future*) dans l'avenir; **a. (of time or of schedule)** en avance (sur l'horaire); **one hour/etc a.** une heure/*etc* d'avance (**of** sur); **a. of** (*space*) devant; (*time, progress*) en avance sur; **to go a.** (*advance*) avancer; (*continue*) continuer; (*start*) commencer; **go a.!** allez-y!; **to go a. with** (*task*) poursuivre; **to get a.** prendre de l'avance; (*succeed*) réussir; **to think a.** penser à l'avenir; **straight a.** tout droit.

aid [eɪd] *n* (*help*) aide *f*; (*apparatus*) support *m*, moyen *m*; **with the a. of** (*a stick etc*) à l'aide de; **in a. of** (*charity etc*) au profit de; **what's this in a. of?** *Fam* quel est le but de tout ça?, ça sert à quoi?; – *vt* aider (**to do** à faire).

aide [eɪd] *n Pol* aide *mf*.

AIDS [eɪdz] *n Med* SIDA *m*.

ail [eɪl] *vt* **what ails you?** de quoi souffrez-vous? ◆**—ing** *a* souffrant, malade. ◆**—ment** *n* maladie *f*.

aim [eɪm] *n* but *m*; **to take a.** viser; **with the a. of** dans le but de; – *vt* (*gun*) braquer, diriger (**at** sur); (*lamp*) diriger (**at** vers); (*stone*) lancer (**at** à, vers); (*blow, remark*) décocher (**at** à); – *vi* viser; **to a. at s.o.** viser qn; **to a. to do or at doing** avoir l'intention de faire. ◆**—less** *a*, ◆**—lessly** *adv* sans but.

air [eər] **1** *n* air *m*; **in the open a.** en plein air; **by a.** (*to travel*) en *or* par avion; (*letter, freight*) par avion; **to be or go on the a.** (*person*) passer à l'antenne; (*programme*) être diffusé; **(up) in the a.** (*to throw*) en l'air; (*plan*) incertain, en l'air; **there's sth in the a.** *Fig* il se prépare qch; – *a* (*raid, base etc*) aérien; **a. force/hostess** armée *f*/hôtesse *f* de l'air; **a. terminal** aérogare *f*; – *vt* (*room*) aérer; (*views*) exposer; **airing cupboard** armoire *f* sèche-linge. **2** *n* (*appearance, tune*) air *m*; **to put on airs** se donner des airs; **with an a. of sadness/etc** d'un air triste/*etc*.

airborne [ˈeəbɔːn] *a* en (cours de) vol; (*troops*) aéroporté; **to become a.** (*of aircraft*) décoller. ◆**airbridge** *n* pont *m* aérien. ◆**air-conditioned** *a* climatisé. ◆**air-conditioner** *n* climatiseur *m*. ◆**aircraft** *n inv* avion(s) *m(pl)*; **a. carrier** porte-avions *m inv*. ◆**aircrew** *n Av* équipage *m*. ◆**airfield** *n* terrain *m* d'aviation. ◆**airgun** *n* carabine *f* à air comprimé. ◆**airletter** *n* aérogramme *m*. ◆**airlift** *n* pont *m* aérien; – *vt* transporter par avion. ◆**airline** *n* ligne *f* aérienne. ◆**airliner** *n*

avion *m* de ligne. ◆**airlock** *n* (*chamber*) *Nau Av* sas *m*; (*in pipe*) bouchon *m*. ◆**airmail** *n* poste *f* aérienne; **by a.** par avion. ◆**airman** *n* (*pl* **-men**) aviateur *m*. ◆**airplane** *n Am* avion *m*. ◆**airpocket** *n* trou *m* d'air. ◆**airship** *n* dirigeable *m*. ◆**airsickness** *n* mal *m* de l'air. ◆**airstrip** *n* terrain *m* d'atterrissage. ◆**airtight** *a* hermétique. ◆**airway** *n* (*route*) couloir *m* aérien. ◆**airworthy** *a* en état de navigation.

airy [ˈeərɪ] *a* (**-ier, -iest**) (*room*) bien aéré; (*promise*) vain; (*step*) léger. ◆**a.-fairy** *a Fam* farfelu. ◆**airily** *adv* (*not seriously*) d'un ton léger.

aisle [aɪl] *n* couloir *m*; (*of church*) nef *f* latérale.

aitch [eɪtʃ] *n* (*letter*) h *m*.

ajar [əˈdʒɑːr] *a & adv* (*door*) entrouvert.

akin [əˈkɪn] *a a.* (**to**) apparenté (à).

alabaster [ˈæləbɑːstər] *n* albâtre *m*.

alacrity [əˈlækrɪtɪ] *n* empressement *m*.

à la mode [ælæˈməʊd] *a Culin Am* avec de la crème glacée.

alarm [əˈlɑːm] *n* (*warning, fear*) alarme *f*; (*apparatus*) sonnerie *f* (d'alarme); **false a.** fausse alerte *f*; **a.** (*clock*) réveil *m*, réveille-matin *m inv*; – *vt* (*frighten*) alarmer. ◆**alarmist** *n* alarmiste *mf*.

alas! [əˈlæs] *int* hélas!

albatross [ˈælbətrɒs] *n* albatros *m*.

albeit [ɔːlˈbiːɪt] *conj Lit* quoique.

albino [ælˈbiːnəʊ, *Am* ælˈbaɪnəʊ] *n* (*pl* **-os**) albinos *mf*.

album [ˈælbəm] *n* (*book, record*) album *m*.

alchemy [ˈælkəmɪ] *n* alchimie *f*. ◆**alchemist** *n* alchimiste *m*.

alcohol [ˈælkəhɒl] *n* alcool *m*. ◆**alco'holic** *a* (*person*) alcoolique; (*drink*) alcoolisé; – *n* (*person*) alcoolique *mf*. ◆**alcoholism** *n* alcoolisme *m*.

alcove [ˈælkəʊv] *n* alcôve *f*.

alderman [ˈɔːldəmən] *n* (*pl* **-men**) conseiller, -ère *mf* municipal(e).

ale [eɪl] *n* bière *f*.

alert [əˈlɜːt] *a* (*watchful*) vigilant; (*sharp, awake*) éveillé; – *n* alerte *f*; **on the a.** sur le qui-vive; – *vt* alerter. ◆**—ness** *n* vigilance *f*.

alfalfa [ælˈfælfə] *n Am* luzerne *f*.

algebra [ˈældʒɪbrə] *n* algèbre *f*. ◆**alge'braic** *a* algébrique.

Algeria [ælˈdʒɪərɪə] *n* Algérie *f*. ◆**Algerian** *a & n* algérien, -ienne (*mf*).

alias [ˈeɪlɪəs] *adv* alias; – *n* nom *m* d'emprunt.

alibi [ˈælɪbaɪ] *n* alibi *m*.

alien ['eɪlɪən] *a* étranger (**to** à); − *n* étranger, -ère *mf*. ◆**alienate** *vt* aliéner; **to a. s.o.** (*make unfriendly*) s'aliéner qn.

alight [ə'laɪt] **1** *a* (*fire*) allumé; (*building*) en feu; (*face*) éclairé; **to set a.** mettre le feu à. **2** *vi* descendre (**from** de); (*of bird*) se poser.

align [ə'laɪn] *vt* aligner. ◆**—ment** *n* alignement *m*.

alike [ə'laɪk] **1** *a* (*people, things*) semblables, pareils; **to look** *or* **be a.** se ressembler. **2** *adv* de la même manière; **summer and winter a.** été comme hiver.

alimony ['ælɪmənɪ, *Am* 'ælɪməʊnɪ] *n Jur* pension *f* alimentaire.

alive [ə'laɪv] *a* vivant, en vie; **a.** conscient de; **a. with** (*crawling with*) grouillant de; (*burnt*) brûlé vif; **anyone a.** n'importe qui; **to keep a.** (*custom, memory*) entretenir, perpétuer; **a. and kicking** *Fam* plein de vie; **look a.!** *Fam* active-toi!

all [ɔːl] *a* tout, toute, *pl* tous, toutes; **a. day** toute la journée; **a. (the) men** tous les hommes; **with a. speed** à toute vitesse; **for a. her wealth** malgré toute sa fortune; − *pron* tous *mpl*, toutes *fpl*; (*everything*) tout; **a. will die** tous mourront; **my sisters are a. here** toutes mes sœurs sont ici; **he ate a. of it** il a tout mangé; **a. (that) he has** tout ce qu'il a; **a. in a.** à tout prendre; **in a., a.** told en tout; **a. but impossible**/*etc* presque impossible/*etc*; **anything at a.** quoi que ce soit; **if he comes at a.** s'il vient effectivement; **if there's any wind at a.** s'il y a le moindre vent; **not at a.** pas du tout; (*after 'thank you'*) il n'y a pas de quoi; **a. of us** nous tous; **take a. of it** prends (le) tout; − *adv* tout seul; **a. alone** tout seul; **a. bad** entièrement mauvais; **a. over** (*everywhere*) partout; (*finished*) fini; **a. right** (très) bien; **he's a. right** (*not harmed*) il est sain et sauf; (*healthy*) il va bien; **a. too soon** bien trop tôt; **six a.** *Fb* six buts partout; **a. there** *Fam* éveillé, intelligent; **not a. there** *Fam* simple d'esprit; **a. in** *Fam* épuisé; **a.-in price** prix global; − *n* **my a.** tout ce que j'ai. ◆**a.-'clear** *n Mil* fin *f* d'alerte. ◆**a.-night** *a* (*party*) qui dure toute la nuit; (*shop*) ouvert toute la nuit. ◆**a.-out** *a* (*effort*) violent; (*war, strike*) tous azimuts. ◆**a.-'powerful** *a* tout-puissant. ◆**a.-purpose** *a* (*tool*) universel. ◆**a.-round** *a* complet. ◆**a.-'rounder** *n* personne *f* qui fait de tout. ◆**a.-time** *a* (*record*) jamais atteint; **to reach an a.-time low/high** arriver au point le plus bas/le plus haut.

allay [ə'leɪ] *vt* calmer, apaiser.

alleg/e [ə'ledʒ] *vt* prétendre. ◆**—ed** *a*

(*so-called*) prétendu; (*author, culprit*) présumé; **he is a. to be** on prétend qu'il est. ◆**—edly** [-ɪdlɪ] *adv* d'après ce qu'on dit. ◆**alle'gation** *n* allégation *f*.

allegiance [ə'liːdʒəns] *n* fidélité *f* (**to** à).

allegory ['ælɪgərɪ, *Am* 'æləgɔːrɪ] *n* allégorie *f*. ◆**alle'gorical** *a* allégorique.

allergy ['ælədʒɪ] *n* allergie *f*. ◆**a'llergic** *a* allergique (**to** à).

alleviate [ə'liːvɪeɪt] *vt* alléger.

alley ['ælɪ] *n* ruelle *f*; (*in park*) allée *f*; **blind a.** impasse *f*; **that's up my a.** *Fam* c'est mon truc. ◆**alleyway** *n* ruelle *f*.

alliance [ə'laɪəns] *n* alliance *f*.

allied ['ælaɪd] *a* (*country*) allié; (*matters*) connexe.

alligator ['ælɪgeɪtər] *n* alligator *m*.

allocate ['æləkeɪt] *vt* (*assign*) attribuer, allouer (**to** à); (*distribute*) répartir. ◆**allo-'cation** *n* attribution *f*.

allot [ə'lɒt] *vt* (**-tt-**) (*assign*) attribuer; (*distribute*) répartir. ◆**—ment** *n* attribution *f*; (*share*) partage *m*; (*land*) lopin *m* de terre (*loué pour la culture*).

allow [ə'laʊ] **1** *vt* permettre; (*grant*) accorder; (*a request*) accéder à; (*deduct*) *Com* déduire; (*add*) *Com* ajouter; **to a. s.o. to do** permettre à qn de faire, autoriser qn à faire; **a. me!** permettez(-moi)!; **not allowed** interdit; **you're not allowed to go** on vous interdit de partir. **2** *vi* **to a. for** tenir compte de. ◆**—able** *a* (*acceptable*) admissible; (*expense*) déductible.

allowance [ə'laʊəns] *n* allocation *f*; (*for travel, housing, food*) indemnité *f*; (*for duty-free goods*) tolérance *f*; (*tax-free amount*) abattement *m*; **to make allowance(s) for** (*person*) être indulgent envers; (*thing*) tenir compte de.

alloy ['ælɔɪ] *n* alliage *m*.

allude [ə'luːd] *vi* **to a. to** faire allusion à. ◆**allusion** *n* allusion *f*.

allure [ə'lʊər] *vt* attirer.

ally ['ælaɪ] *n* allié, -ée *mf*; − [ə'laɪ] *vt* (*country, person*) allier.

almanac ['ɔːlmənæk] *n* almanach *m*.

almighty [ɔːl'maɪtɪ] **1** *a* tout-puissant; **the A.** le Tout-Puissant. **2** *a* (*great*) *Fam* terrible, formidable.

almond ['ɑːmənd] *n* amande *f*.

almost ['ɔːlməʊst] *adv* presque; **he a. fell**/*etc* il a failli tomber/*etc*.

alms [ɑːmz] *npl* aumône *f*.

alone [ə'ləʊn] *a & adv* seul; **an expert a. can . . .** seul un expert peut . . . ; **I did it (all) a.** je l'ai fait à moi (tout) seul, je l'ai fait (tout) seul; **to leave** or **let a.** (*person*) laisser tranquille or en paix; (*thing*) ne pas toucher à. ◆**—ness** n réserve f.

along [ə'lɒŋ] *prep* (**all**) **a.** (tout) le long de; **to go** or **walk a.** (*street*) passer par; **a. here** per ici; **a. with** avec; – *adv* **all a.** d'un bout à l'autre; (*time*) dès le début; **come a.!** venez!; **move a.!** avancez!

alongside [əlɒŋ'saɪd] *prep & adv* à côté (de); **to come a.** *Nau* accoster; **a. the kerb** le long du trottoir.

aloof [ə'luːf] *a* distant; – *adv* à distance; **to keep a.** garder ses distances (**from** par rapport à). ◆**—ness** n réserve f.

aloud [ə'laʊd] *adv* à haute voix.

alphabet ['ælfəbet] *n* alphabet *m*. ◆**alpha'betical** *a* alphabétique.

Alps [ælps] *npl* **the A.** les Alpes *fpl*. ◆**alpine** *a* (*club, range etc*) alpin; (*scenery*) alpestre.

already [ɔːl'redɪ] *adv* déjà.

alright [ɔːl'raɪt] *adv Fam* = **all right**.

Alsatian [æl'seɪʃ(ə)n] *n* (*dog*) berger *m* allemand, chien-loup *m*.

also ['ɔːlsəʊ] *adv* aussi, également. ◆**a.-ran** *n* (*person*) *Fig* perdant, -ante *mf*.

altar ['ɔːltər] *n* autel *m*.

alter ['ɔːltər] *vt* changer, modifier; (*clothing*) retoucher; – *vi* changer. ◆**alte'ration** *n* changement *m*, modification *f*; retouche *f*.

altercation [ɔːltə'keɪʃ(ə)n] *n* altercation *f*.

alternat/e [ɔːl'tɜːnɪt] *a* alterné; **on a. days** tous les deux jours; **a. laughter and tears** des rires et des larmes qui se succèdent; – [ˈɔːltəneɪt] *vi* alterner (**with** avec); – *vt* faire alterner. ◆**—ing** *a* (*current*) *El* alternatif. ◆**—ely** *adv* alternativement. ◆**alter'nation** *n* alternance *f*.

alternative [ɔːl'tɜːnətɪv] *a* **an a. way**/*etc* une autre façon/*etc*; **a. answers**/*etc* d'autres réponses/*etc* (différentes); – *n* (*choice*) alternative *f*. ◆**—ly** *adv* comme alternative; **or a.** (*or else*) ou bien.

although [ɔːl'ðəʊ] *adv* bien que, quoique (+ *sub*).

altitude ['æltɪtjuːd] *n* altitude *f*.

altogether [ɔːltə'geðər] *adv* (*completely*) tout à fait; (*on the whole*) somme toute; **how much a.?** combien en tout?

aluminium [ælju'mɪnjəm] (*Am* **aluminum** [ə'luːmɪnəm]) *n* aluminium *m*.

alumnus, *pl* **-ni** [ə'lʌmnəs, -naɪ] *n Am* ancien(ne) élève *mf*, ancien(ne) étudiant, -ante *mf*.

always ['ɔːlweɪz] *adv* toujours; **he's a. criticizing** il est toujours à critiquer.

am [æm, *unstressed* əm] *see* **be**.

a.m. [eɪ'em] *adv* du matin.

amalgam [ə'mælgəm] *n* amalgame *m*. ◆**a'malgamate** *vt* amalgamer; (*society*) *Com* fusionner; – *vi* s'amalgamer; fusionner.

amass [ə'mæs] *vt* (*riches*) amasser.

amateur ['æmətər] *n* amateur *m*; – *a* (*interest, sports*) d'amateur; **a. painter**/*etc* peintre/*etc* amateur. ◆**amateurish** *a* (*work*) *Pej* d'amateur; (*person*) *Pej* maladroit, malhabile. ◆**amateurism** *n* amateurisme *m*.

amaz/e [ə'meɪz] *vt* stupéfier, étonner. ◆**—ed** *a* stupéfait (**at sth** de qch), étonné (**at sth** par or de qch); **a. at seeing**/*etc* stupéfait or étonné de voir/*etc*. ◆**—ing** *a* stupéfiant; *Fam* extraordinaire. ◆**—ingly** *adv* extraordinairement; (*miraculously*) par miracle. ◆**amazement** *n* stupéfaction *f*.

ambassador [æm'bæsədər] *n* ambassadeur *m*; (*woman*) ambassadrice *f*.

amber ['æmbər] *n* ambre *m*; **a. (light)** *Aut* (feu *m*) orange *m*.

ambidextrous [æmbɪ'dekstrəs] *a* ambidextre.

ambiguous [æm'bɪgjʊəs] *a* ambigu. ◆**ambi'guity** *n* ambiguïté *f*.

ambition [æm'bɪʃ(ə)n] *n* ambition *f*. ◆**ambitious** *a* ambitieux.

ambivalent [æm'bɪvələnt] *a* ambigu, équivoque.

amble ['æmb(ə)l] *vi* marcher d'un pas tranquille.

ambulance ['æmbjʊlɒns] *n* ambulance *f*; **a. man** ambulancier *m*.

ambush ['æmbʊʃ] *n* guet-apens *m*, embuscade *f*; – *vt* prendre en embuscade.

amen [ɑː'men, eɪ'men] *int* amen.

amenable [ə'miːnəb(ə)l] *a* docile; **a.** to (*responsive to*) sensible à; **a. to reason** raisonnable.

amend [ə'mend] *vt* (*text*) modifier; (*conduct*) corriger; *Pol* amender. ◆**—ment** *n Pol* amendement *m*.

amends [ə'mendz] *npl* **to make a. for** réparer; **to make a.** réparer son erreur.

amenities [ə'miːnɪtɪz, *Am* ə'menɪtɪz] *npl* (*pleasant things*) agréments *mpl*; (*of sports club etc*) équipement *m*; (*of town*) aménagements *mpl*.

America [ə'merɪkə] *n* Amérique *f*; **North/South A.** Amérique du Nord/du Sud. ◆**American** *a & n* américain, -aine (*mf*). ◆**Americanism** *n* américanisme *m*.

amethyst ['æmɪθɪst] *n* améthyste *f*.

amiable ['eɪmɪəb(ə)l] *a* aimable.

amicab/le ['æmɪkəb(ə)l] *a* amical. ◆**—ly** *adv* amicalement; *Jur* à l'amiable.

amid(st) [əˈmɪd(st)] *prep* au milieu de. parmi.

amiss [əˈmɪs] *adv* & *a* mal (à propos); **sth is a.** (*wrong*) qch ne va pas; **that wouldn't come a.** ça ne ferait pas de mal; **to take a.** prendre en mauvaise part.

ammonia [əˈməunjə] *n* (*gas*) ammoniac *m*; (*liquid*) ammoniaque *f*.

ammunition [æmjuˈnɪʃ(ə)n] *n* munitions *fpl*.

amnesia [æmˈniːzjə] *n* amnésie *f*.

amnesty [ˈæmnəstɪ] *n* amnistie *f*.

amok [əˈmɒk] *adv* **to run a.** se déchaîner, s'emballer.

among(st) [əˈmʌŋ(st)] *prep* parmi, entre; **a. themselves/friends** entre eux/amis; **a. the French**/*etc* (*group*) chez les Français/*etc*; **a. the crowd** dans *or* parmi la foule.

amoral [eɪˈmɒrəl] *a* amoral.

amorous [ˈæmərəs] *a* amoureux.

amount [əˈmaunt] **1** *n* quantité *f*; (*sum of money*) somme *f*; (*total of bill etc*) montant *m*; (*scope, size*) importance *f*. **2** *vi* **to a. to** s'élever à; (*mean*) *Fig* signifier; **it amounts to the same thing** ça revient au même.

amp(ere) [ˈæmp(eər)] *n El* ampère *m*.

amphibian [æmˈfɪbɪən] *n* & *a* amphibie (*m*). ◆**amphibious** *a* amphibie.

amphitheatre [ˈæmfɪθɪətər] *n* amphithéâtre *m*.

ample [ˈæmp(ə)l] *a* (*roomy*) ample; (*enough*) largement assez de; (*reasons, means*) solides; **you have a. time** tu as largement le temps. ◆**amply** *adv* largement, amplement.

amplify [ˈæmplɪfaɪ] *vt* amplifier. ◆**amplifier** *n El* amplificateur *m*.

amputate [ˈæmpjuteɪt] *vt* amputer. ◆**ampu'tation** *n* amputation *f*.

amuck [əˈmʌk] *adv see* **amok.**

amulet [ˈæmjulət] *n* amulette *f*.

amus/e [əˈmjuːz] *vt* amuser, divertir; **to keep s.o. amused** amuser qn. ◆**—ing** *a* amusant. ◆**—ement** *n* amusement *m*, divertissement *m*; (*pastime*) distraction *f*; **a. arcade** salle *f* de jeux.

an [æn, *unstressed* ən] *see* **a.**

anachronism [əˈnækrənɪz(ə)m] *n* anachronisme *m*.

an(a)emia [əˈniːmɪə] *n* anémie *f*. ◆**an(a)emic** *a* anémique.

an(a)esthesia [ænɪsˈθiːzɪə] *n* anesthésie *f*. ◆**an(a)esthetic** [ænɪsˈθetɪk] *n* (*substance*) anesthésique *m*; **under the a.** sous anesthésie; **general/local a.** anesthésie *f* générale/locale. ◆**an(a)esthetize** [əˈniːsθɪtaɪz] *vt* anesthésier.

anagram [ˈænəgræm] *n* anagramme *f*.

analogy [əˈnælədʒɪ] *n* analogie *f*. ◆**analogous** *a* analogue (**to** à).

analyse [ˈænəlaɪz] *vt* analyser. ◆**analysis**, *pl* **-yses** [əˈnæləsɪs, -ɪsiːz] *n* analyse *f*. ◆**analyst** *n* analyste *mf*. ◆**ana'lytical** *a* analytique.

anarchy [ˈænəkɪ] *n* anarchie *f*. ◆**a'narchic** *a* anarchique. ◆**anarchist** *n* anarchiste *mf*.

anathema [əˈnæθəmə] *n Rel* anathème *m*; **it is (an) a. to me** j'ai une sainte horreur de cela.

anatomy [əˈnætəmɪ] *n* anatomie *f*. ◆**ana-'tomical** *a* anatomique.

ancestor [ˈænsestər] *n* ancêtre *m*. ◆**an'cestral** *a* ancestral. ◆**ancestry** *n* (*lineage*) ascendance *f*; (*ancestors*) ancêtres *mpl*.

anchor [ˈæŋkər] *n* ancre *f*; **to weigh a.** lever l'ancre; – *vt* (*ship*) mettre à l'ancre; – *vi* jeter l'ancre, mouiller. ◆**—ed** *a* à l'ancre. ◆**—age** *n* mouillage *m*.

anchovy [ˈæntʃəvɪ, *Am* ænˈtʃəuvɪ] *n* anchois *m*.

ancient [ˈeɪnʃənt] *a* ancien; (*pre-medieval*) antique; (*person*) *Hum* vétuste.

ancillary [ænˈsɪlərɪ] *a* auxiliaire.

and [ænd, *unstressed* ən(d)] *conj* et; **a knife a. fork** un couteau et une fourchette; **two hundred a. two** deux cent deux; **better a. better** de mieux en mieux; **go a. see** va voir.

anecdote [ˈænɪkdəut] *n* anecdote *f*.

anemone [əˈnemənɪ] *n* anémone *f*.

anew [əˈnjuː] *adv* *Lit* de *or* à nouveau.

angel [ˈeɪndʒəl] *n* ange *m*. ◆**an'gelic** *a* angélique.

anger [ˈæŋgər] *n* colère *f*; **in a., out of a.** sous le coup de la colère; – *vt* mettre en colère, fâcher.

angl/e [ˈæŋg(ə)l] **1** *n* angle *m*; **at an a.** en biais. **2** *vi* (*to fish*) pêcher à la ligne; **to a. for** *Fig* quêter. ◆**—er** *n* pêcheur, -euse *mf* à la ligne. ◆**—ing** *n* pêche *f* à la ligne.

Anglican [ˈæŋglɪkən] *a* & *n* anglican, -ane (*mf*).

anglicism [ˈæŋglɪsɪz(ə)m] *n* anglicisme *m*.

Anglo- [ˈæŋgləu] *pref* anglo-. ◆**Anglo-'Saxon** *a* & *n* anglo-saxon, -onne (*mf*).

angora [æŋˈgɔːrə] *n* (*wool*) angora *m*.

angry [ˈæŋgrɪ] *a* (**-ier, -iest**) (*person, look*) fâché; (*letter*) indigné; **to get a.** se fâcher, se mettre en colère (**with** contre). ◆**angrily** *adv* en colère; (*to speak*) avec colère.

anguish [ˈæŋgwɪʃ] *n* angoisse *f*. ◆**—ed** *a* angoissé.

angular [ˈæŋgjulər] *a* (*face*) anguleux.

animal ['ænɪməl] *a* animal; – *n* animal *m*, bête *f*.

animate ['ænɪmeɪt] *vt* animer; **to become animated** s'animer; – ['ænɪmət] *a* (*alive*) animé. ◆**ani'mation** *n* animation *f*.

animosity [ænɪ'mɒsɪtɪ] *n* animosité *f*.

aniseed ['ænɪsiːd] *n* Culin anis *m*.

ankle ['æŋk(ə)l] *n* cheville *f*; **a. sock** socquette *f*.

annals ['æn(ə)lz] *npl* annales *fpl*.

annex [ə'neks] *vt* annexer.

annex(e) ['æneks] *n* (*building*) annexe *f*. ◆**annex'ation** *n* annexion *f*.

annihilate [ə'naɪəleɪt] *vt* anéantir, annihiler. ◆**annihi'lation** *n* anéantissement *m*.

anniversary [ænɪ'vɜːsərɪ] *n* (*of event*) anniversaire *m*, commémoration *f*.

annotate ['ænəteɪt] *vt* annoter. ◆**anno'tation** *n* annotation *f*.

announc/e [ə'naʊns] *vt* annoncer; (*birth, marriage*) faire part de. ◆**—ement** *n* annonce *f*; (*of birth, marriage*) avis *m*; (*private letter*) faire-part *m inv*. ◆**—er** *n* TV speaker *m*, speakerine *f*.

annoy [ə'nɔɪ] *vt* (*inconvenience*) ennuyer, gêner; (*irritate*) agacer, contrarier. ◆**—ed** *a* contrarié, fâché; **to get a.** se fâcher (**with** contre). ◆**—ing** *a* ennuyeux, contrariant. ◆**annoyance** *n* contrariété *f*, ennui *m*.

annual ['ænjʊəl] *a* annuel; – *n* (*book*) annuaire *m*. ◆**—ly** *adv* annuellement.

annuity [ə'njuːɪtɪ] *n* (*of retired person*) pension *f* viagère.

annul [ə'nʌl] *vt* (-ll-) annuler. ◆**—ment** *n* annulation *f*.

anoint [ə'nɔɪnt] *vt* oindre (**with** de). ◆**—ed** *a* oint.

anomalous [ə'nɒmələs] *a* anormal. ◆**anomaly** *n* anomalie *f*.

anon [ə'nɒn] *adv Hum* tout à l'heure.

anonymous [ə'nɒnɪməs] *a* anonyme; **to remain a.** garder l'anonymat. ◆**ano'nymity** *n* anonymat *m*.

anorak ['ænəræk] *n* anorak *m*.

anorexia [ænə'reksɪə] *n* anorexie *f*.

another [ə'nʌðər] *a* & *pron* un(e) autre; **a. man** un autre homme; **a. month** (*additional*) encore un mois, un autre mois; **a. ten** encore dix; **one a.** l'un(e) l'autre, *pl* les un(e)s les autres; **they love one a.** ils s'aiment (l'un l'autre).

answer ['ɑːnsər] *n* réponse *f*; (*to problem*) solution *f* (**to** de); (*reason*) explication *f*; – *vt* (*person, question, phone etc*) répondre à; (*word*) répondre; (*problem*) résoudre; (*prayer, wish*) exaucer; **to a. the bell** *or* **the door** ouvrir la porte; – *vi* répondre; **to a.**

back répliquer, répondre; **to a. for** (*s.o., sth*) répondre de. ◆**—able** *a* responsable (**for** sth de qch, **to s.o.** devant qn).

ant [ænt] *n* fourmi *f*. ◆**anthill** *n* fourmilière *f*.

antagonism [æn'tægənɪz(ə)m] *n* antagonisme *m*; (*hostility*) hostilité *f*. ◆**antagonist** *n* antagoniste *mf*. ◆**antago'nistic** *a* antagoniste; (*hostile*) hostile. ◆**antagonize** *vt* provoquer (l'hostilité de).

antarctic [æn'tɑːktɪk] *a* antarctique; – *n* **the A.** l'Antarctique *m*.

antecedent [æntɪ'siːd(ə)nt] *n* antécédent *m*.

antechamber ['æntɪtʃeɪmbər] *n* antichambre *f*.

antedate ['æntɪdeɪt] *vt* (*letter*) antidater.

antelope ['æntɪləʊp] *n* antilope *f*.

antenatal [æntɪ'neɪt(ə)l] *a* prénatal.

antenna[1], *pl* **-ae** [æn'tenə, -iː] *n* (*of insect etc*) antenne *f*.

antenna[2] [æn'tenə] *n* (*pl* -**as**) (*aerial*) *Am* antenne *f*.

anteroom ['æntɪrʊm] *n* antichambre *f*.

anthem ['ænθəm] *n* **national a.** hymne *m* national.

anthology [æn'θɒlədʒɪ] *n* anthologie *f*.

anthropology [ænθrə'pɒlədʒɪ] *n* anthropologie *f*.

anti- [æntɪ, *Am* 'æntaɪ] *pref* anti-; **to be a. sth** *Fam* être contre qch. ◆**anti'aircraft** *a* antiaérien. ◆**antibi'otic** *a* & *n* antibiotique (*m*). ◆**antibody** *n* anticorps *m*. ◆**anti'climax** *n* chute *f* dans l'ordinaire; (*let-down*) déception *f*. ◆**anti'clockwise** *adv* dans le sens inverse des aiguilles d'une montre. ◆**anti'cyclone** *n* anticyclone *m*. ◆**antidote** *n* antidote *m*. ◆**antifreeze** *n* *Aut* antigel *m*. ◆**anti'histamine** *n* *Med* antihistaminique *m*. ◆**anti'perspirant** *n* antisudoral *m*. ◆**anti-Se'mitic** *a* antisémite. ◆**anti-'Semitism** *n* antisémitisme *m*. ◆**anti'septic** *a* & *n* antiseptique (*m*). ◆**anti'social** *a* (*misfit*) asocial; (*measure, principles*) antisocial; (*unsociable*) insociable.

anticipate [æn'tɪsɪpeɪt] *vt* (*foresee*) prévoir; (*forestall*) devancer; (*expect*) s'attendre à; (*the future*) anticiper sur. ◆**antici'pation** *n* prévision *f*; (*expectation*) attente *f*; **in a. of** en prévision de, dans l'attente de; **in a.** (*to thank s.o., pay etc*) d'avance.

antics ['æntɪks] *npl* bouffonneries *fpl*.

antipathy [æn'tɪpəθɪ] *n* antipathie *f*.

antipodes [æn'tɪpədiːz] *npl* antipodes *mpl*.

antiquarian [æntɪ'kweərɪən] *a* **a. bookseller**

libraire *mf* spécialisé(e) dans le livre ancien.

antiquated ['æntɪkweɪtɪd] *a* vieilli; (*person*) vieux jeu *inv*.

antique [æn'tiːk] *a* (*furniture etc*) ancien; (*of Greek etc antiquity*) antique; **a. dealer** antiquaire *mf*; **a. shop** magasin *m* d'antiquités; – *n* objet *m* ancien *or* d'époque, antiquité *f*. ◆**antiquity** *n* (*period etc*) antiquité *f*.

antithesis, *pl* **-eses** [æn'tɪθəsɪs, -ɪsiːz] *n* antithèse *f*.

antler ['æntlər] *n* (*tine*) andouiller *m*; *pl* bois *mpl*.

antonym ['æntənɪm] *n* antonyme *m*.

Antwerp ['æntwɜːp] *n* Anvers *m or f*.

anus ['eɪnəs] *n* anus *m*.

anvil ['ænvɪl] *n* enclume *f*.

anxiety [æŋ'zaɪətɪ] *n* (*worry*) inquiétude *f* (**about** au sujet de); (*fear*) anxiété *f*; (*eagerness*) impatience *f* (**for** de).

anxious ['æŋkʃəs] *a* (*worried*) inquiet (**about** de, pour); (*troubled*) anxieux; (*causing worry*) inquiétant; (*eager*) impatient (**to do** de faire); **I'm a. (that) he should go** je tiens beaucoup à ce qu'il parte. ◆**—ly** *adv* avec inquiétude; (*to wait etc*) impatiemment.

any ['enɪ] *a* **1** (*interrogative*) du, de la, des; **have you a. milk/tickets?** avez-vous du lait/des billets?; **is there a. man (at all) who ...?** y a-t-il un homme (quelconque) qui ...? **2** (*negative*) de; (*not any at all*) aucun; **he hasn't a. milk/tickets** il n'a pas de lait/de billets; **there isn't a. proof** il n'y a aucune preuve. **3** (*no matter which*) n'importe quel. **4** (*every*) tout; **at a. hour** à toute heure; **in a. case, at a. rate** de toute façon; – *pron* **1** (*no matter which one*) n'importe lequel; (*somebody*) quelqu'un; **if a. of you** si l'un d'entre vous, si quelqu'un parmi vous; **more than a.** plus qu'aucun. **2** (*quantity*) en; **have you a.?** en as-tu?; **I don't see a.** je n'en vois pas; – *adv* (*usually not translated*) (not) **a. further/happier/etc** (pas) plus loin/plus heureux/*etc*; **I don't see her a. more** je ne la vois plus; **a. more tea?** (*a little*) encore du thé?, encore un peu de thé?; **a. better?** (un peu) mieux?

anybody ['enɪbɒdɪ] *pron* **1** (*somebody*) quelqu'un; **do you see a.?** vois-tu quelqu'un?; **more than a.** plus qu'aucun. **2** (*negative*) personne; **he doesn't know a.** il ne connaît personne. **3** (*no matter who*) n'importe qui; **a. would think that ...** on croirait que ....

anyhow ['enɪhaʊ] *adv* (*at any rate*) de toute façon; (*badly*) n'importe comment; **to**

leave sth a. (*in confusion*) laisser qch sens dessus dessous.

anyone ['enɪwʌn] *pron* = **anybody**.

anyplace ['enɪpleɪs] *adv Am* = **anywhere**.

anything ['enɪθɪŋ] *pron* **1** (*something*) quelque chose; **can you see a.?** voyez-vous quelque chose? **2** (*negative*) rien; **he doesn't do a.** il ne fait rien; **without a.** sans rien. **3** (*everything*) tout; **a. you like** (tout) ce que tu veux; **like a.** (*to work etc*) *Fam* comme un fou. **4** (*no matter what*) **a. (at all)** n'importe quoi.

anyway ['enɪweɪ] *adv* (*at any rate*) de toute façon.

anywhere ['enɪweər] *adv* **1** (*no matter where*) n'importe où. **2** (*everywhere*) partout; **a. you go** partout où vous allez, où que vous alliez; **a. you like** là où tu veux. **3** (*somewhere*) quelque part; **is he going a.?** va-t-il quelque part? **4** (*negative*) nulle part; **he doesn't go a.** il ne va nulle part; **without a. to put it** sans un endroit où le mettre.

apace [ə'peɪs] *adv* rapidement.

apart [ə'pɑːt] *adv* (*to or at one side*) à part; **to tear a.** (*to pieces*) mettre en pièces; **we kept them a.** (*separate*) on les tenait séparés; **with legs (wide) a.** les jambes écartées; **they are a metre a.** ils se trouvent à un mètre l'un de l'autre; **a. from** (*except for*) à part; **to take a.** démonter; **to come a.** (*of two objects*) se séparer; (*of knot etc*) se défaire; **to tell a.** distinguer entre; **worlds a.** (*very different*) diamétralement opposé.

apartheid [ə'pɑːteɪt] *n* apartheid *m*.

apartment [ə'pɑːtmənt] *n* (*flat*) *Am* appartement *m*; (*room*) chambre *f*; **a. house** *Am* immeuble *m* (*d'habitation*).

apathy ['æpəθɪ] *n* apathie *f*. ◆**apa'thetic** *a* apathique.

ape [eɪp] *n* singe; – *vt* (*imitate*) singer.

aperitif [ə'perɪtiːf] *n* apéritif *m*.

aperture ['æpətʃʊər] *n* ouverture *f*.

apex ['eɪpeks] *n Geom & Fig* sommet *m*.

aphorism ['æfərɪz(ə)m] *n* aphorisme *m*.

aphrodisiac [æfrə'dɪzɪæk] *a & n* aphrodisiaque (*m*).

apiece [ə'piːs] *adv* chacun; **a pound a.** une livre (la) pièce *or* chacun.

apish ['eɪpɪʃ] *a* simiesque; (*imitative*) imitateur.

apocalypse [ə'pɒkəlɪps] *n* apocalypse *f*. ◆**apoca'lyptic** *a* apocalyptique.

apocryphal [ə'pɒkrɪfəl] *a* apocryphe.

apogee ['æpədʒiː] *n* apogée *m*.

apologetic [əpɒlə'dʒetɪk] *a* (*letter*) plein d'excuses; **to be a. about** s'excuser de. ◆**apologetically** *adv* en s'excusant.

apology [ə'pɒlədʒɪ] n excuses fpl; **an a. for a dinner** Fam Pej un dîner minable. ◆**apologist** n apologiste mf. ◆**apologize** vi s'excuser **(for** de); **to a. to s.o.** faire ses excuses à qn **(for** pour).

apoplexy ['æpəpleksɪ] n apoplexie f. ◆**apo'plectic** a & n apoplectique (mf).

apostle [ə'pɒs(ə)l] n apôtre m.

apostrophe [ə'pɒstrəfɪ] n apostrophe f.

appal [ə'pɔːl] (Am **appall**) vt (-ll-) épouvanter. ◆**appalling** a épouvantable.

apparatus [æpə'reɪtəs, Am -'rætəs] n (equipment, organization) appareil m; (in gym) agrès mpl.

apparel [ə'pærəl] n habit m, habillement m.

apparent [ə'pærənt] a (obvious, seeming) apparent; **it's a. that** il est évident que. ◆**—ly** adv apparemment.

apparition [æpə'rɪʃ(ə)n] n apparition f.

appeal [ə'piːl] n (call) appel m; (entreaty) supplication f; (charm) attrait m; (interest) intérêt m; Jur appel m; – vt **to a. to** (s.o., s.o.'s kindness) faire appel à; **to a. to s.o.** (attract) plaire à qn, séduire qn; (interest) intéresser qn; **to a. to s.o. for sth** demander qch à qn; **to a. to s.o. to do** supplier qn de faire; – vi Jur faire appel. ◆**—ing** a (begging) suppliant; (attractive) séduisant.

appear [ə'pɪər] vi (become visible) apparaître; (present oneself) se présenter; (seem, be published) paraître; (act) Th jouer; Jur comparaître; **it appears that** (it seems) il semble que (+ sub or indic); (it is rumoured) il paraîtrait que (+ indic). ◆**appearance** n (act) apparition f; (look) apparence f, aspect m; (of book) parution f; **to put in an a.** faire acte de présence.

appease [ə'piːz] vt apaiser; (curiosity) satisfaire.

append [ə'pend] vt joindre, ajouter **(to** à). ◆**—age** n Anat appendice m.

appendix, pl **-ixes** or **-ices** [ə'pendɪks, -ɪksɪz, -ɪsiːz] n (of book) & Anat appendice m. ◆**appendicitis** [əpendɪ'saɪtɪs] n appendicite f.

appertain [æpə'teɪn] vi **to a. to** se rapporter à.

appetite ['æpɪtaɪt] n appétit m; **to take away s.o.'s a.** couper l'appétit à qn. ◆**appetizer** n (drink) apéritif m; (food) amuse-gueule m inv. ◆**appetizing** a appétissant.

applaud [ə'plɔːd] vt (clap) applaudir; (approve of) approuver, applaudir à; – vi applaudir. ◆**applause** n applaudissements mpl.

apple ['æp(ə)l] n pomme f; **stewed apples, a. sauce** compote f de pommes; **eating/**

cooking a. pomme f à couteau/à cuire; **a. pie** tarte f aux pommes; **a. core** trognon m de pomme; **a. tree** pommier m.

appliance [ə'plaɪəns] n appareil m.

apply [ə'plaɪ] **1** vt (put, carry out etc) appliquer; (brake) Aut appuyer sur; **to a. oneself to** s'appliquer à. **2** vi (be relevant) s'appliquer **(to** à); **to a. for** (job) poser sa candidature à, postuler; **to a. to s.o.** (ask) s'adresser à qn **(for** pour). ◆**applied** a (maths etc) appliqué. ◆**applicable** a applicable **(to** à). ◆**'applicant** n candidat, -ate nf **(for** à). ◆**appli'cation** n application f; (request) demande f; (for job) candidature f; (for membership) demande f d'adhésion or d'inscription; **a. (form)** (job) formulaire m de candidature; (club) formulaire m d'inscription or d'adhésion.

appoint [ə'pɔɪnt] vt (person) nommer **(to sth** à qch, **to do** pour faire); (time etc) désigner, fixer; **at the appointed time** à l'heure dite; **well-appointed** bien équipé. ◆**—ment** n nomination f; (meeting) rendez-vous m inv; (post) place f, situation f.

apportion [ə'pɔːʃ(ə)n] vt répartir.

apposite ['æpəzɪt] a juste, à propos.

appraise [ə'preɪz] vt évaluer. ◆**appraisal** n évaluation f.

appreciate [ə'priːʃɪeɪt] **1** vt (enjoy, value, assess) apprécier; (understand) comprendre; (be grateful for) être reconnaissant de. **2** vi prendre de la valeur. ◆**appreciable** a appréciable, sensible. ◆**appreci'ation** n **1** (judgement) appréciation f; (gratitude) reconnaissance f. **2** (rise in value) plus-value f. ◆**appreciative** a (grateful) reconnaissant **(of** de); (laudatory) élogieux; **to be a. of** (enjoy) apprécier.

apprehend [æprɪ'hend] vt (seize, arrest) appréhender. ◆**apprehension** n (fear) appréhension f. ◆**apprehensive** a inquiet **(about** de, au sujet de); **to be a. of** redouter.

apprentice [ə'prentɪs] n apprenti, -ie mf; – vt mettre en apprentissage **(to** chez). ◆**apprenticeship** n apprentissage m.

approach [ə'prəʊtʃ] vt (draw near to) s'approcher de (qn, feu, porte etc); (age, result, town) approcher de; (subject) aborder; (accost) aborder (qn); **to a. s.o. about** parler à qn de; – vi (of person, vehicle) s'approcher; (of date etc) approcher; – n approche f; (method) façon f de s'y prendre; (path) (voie f d')accès m; **a. to** (question) manière f d'aborder; **to make approaches to** faire des avances à.

◆—able a (place) accessible; (person) abordable.

appropriate 1 [əˈprəʊprɪət] a (place, tools, clothes etc) approprié, adéquat; (remark, time) opportun; **a. to** or **for** propre à, approprié à. **2** [əˈprəʊprɪeɪt] vt (set aside) affecter; (steal) s'approprier. **◆—ly** adv convenablement.

approv/e [əˈpruːv] vt approuver; **to a. of** sth approuver qch; **I don't a. of him** il ne me plaît pas, je ne l'apprécie pas; **I a. of his going** je trouve bon qu'il y aille; **I a. of her having accepted** j'approuve d'avoir accepté. **◆—ing** a approbateur. **◆approval** n approbation f; **on a.** (goods) Com à l'essai.

approximate [əˈprɒksɪmət] a approximatif; — [əˈprɒksɪmeɪt] vi **to a. to** se rapprocher de. **◆—ly** adv à peu près, approximativement. **◆approxiˈmation** n approximation f.

apricot [ˈeɪprɪkɒt] n abricot m.

April [ˈeɪprəl] n avril m; **to make an A. fool of** faire un poisson d'avril à.

apron [ˈeɪprən] n (garment) tablier m.

apse [æps] n (of church) abside f.

apt [æpt] a (suitable) convenable; (remark, reply) juste; (word, name) bien choisi; (student) doué, intelligent; **to be a. to** avoir tendance à; **a. at sth** habile à qch. **◆aptitude** n aptitude f (for à, pour). **◆aptly** adv convenablement; **a. named** qui porte bien son nom.

aqualung [ˈækwəlʌŋ] n scaphandre m autonome.

aquarium [əˈkweərɪəm] n aquarium m.

Aquarius [əˈkweərɪəs] n (sign) le Verseau.

aquatic [əˈkwætɪk] a (plant etc) aquatique; (sport) nautique.

aqueduct [ˈækwɪdʌkt] n aqueduc m.

aquiline [ˈækwɪlaɪn] a (nose, profile) aquilin.

Arab [ˈærəb] a & n arabe (mf). **◆Arabian** [əˈreɪbɪən] a arabe. **◆Arabic** a & n (language) arabe (m); **A. numerals** chiffres mpl arabes.

arabesque [ærəˈbesk] n (decoration) arabesque f.

arable [ˈærəb(ə)l] a (land) arable.

arbiter [ˈɑːbɪtər] n arbitre m. **◆arbitrate** vti arbitrer. **◆arbiˈtration** n arbitrage m; **to go to a.** soumettre la question à l'arbitrage. **◆arbitrator** n (in dispute) médiateur, -trice mf.

arbitrary [ˈɑːbɪtrəri] a arbitraire.

arbour [ˈɑːbər] n tonnelle f, charmille f.

arc [ɑːk] n (of circle) arc m.

arcade [ɑːˈkeɪd] n (market) passage m couvert.

arch [ɑːtʃ] n (of bridge) arche f; Archit voûte f, arc m; (of foot) cambrure f; — vt (one's back etc) arquer, courber. **◆archway** n passage m voûté, voûte f.

arch- [ɑːtʃ] pref (villain etc) achevé; **a. enemy** ennemi m numéro un.

arch(a)eology [ɑːkɪˈɒlədʒɪ] n archéologie f. **◆arch(a)eologist** n archéologue mf.

archaic [ɑːˈkeɪɪk] a archaïque.

archangel [ˈɑːkeɪndʒəl] n archange m.

archbishop [ɑːtʃˈbɪʃəp] n archevêque m.

archer [ˈɑːtʃər] n archer m. **◆archery** n tir m à l'arc.

archetype [ˈɑːkɪtaɪp] n archétype m.

archipelago [ɑːkɪˈpeləgəʊ] n (pl -oes or -os) archipel m.

architect [ˈɑːkɪtekt] n architecte m. **◆architecture** n architecture f.

archives [ˈɑːkaɪvz] npl archives fpl. **◆archivist** n archiviste mf.

arctic [ˈɑːktɪk] a arctique; (weather) polaire, glacial; — n **the A.** l'Arctique m.

ardent [ˈɑːdənt] a ardent. **◆—ly** adv ardemment. **◆ardour** n ardeur f.

arduous [ˈɑːdjʊəs] a ardu.

are [ɑːr] see be.

area [ˈeərɪə] n Math superficie f; Geog région f; (of town) quartier m; Mil zone f; (domain) Fig domaine m, secteur m, terrain m; **built-up a.** agglomération f; **parking a.** aire f de stationnement; **a. code** Tel Am indicatif m.

arena [əˈriːnə] n Hist & Fig arène f.

Argentina [ɑːdʒənˈtiːnə] n Argentine f. **◆Argentine** [ˈɑːdʒəntaɪn] a & n, **◆Argentinian** a & n argentin, -ine (mf).

argu/e [ˈɑːgjuː] vi (quarrel) se disputer (**with** avec, **about** au sujet de); (reason) raisonner (**with** avec, **about** sur); **to a. in favour of** plaider pour; — vt (matter) discuter; **to a. that** (maintain) soutenir que. **◆—able** [ˈɑːgjuəb(ə)l] a discutable. **◆—ably** adv on pourrait soutenir que. **◆—ment** n (quarrel) dispute f; (reasoning) argument m; (debate) discussion f; **to have an a.** se disputer. **◆arguˈmentative** a raisonneur.

aria [ˈɑːrɪə] n Mus air m (d'opéra).

arid [ˈærɪd] a aride.

Aries [ˈeəriːz] n (sign) le Bélier.

arise [əˈraɪz] vi (pt arose, pp arisen) (of problem, opportunity etc) se présenter; (of cry, objection) s'élever; (result) résulter (**from** de); (get up) Lit se lever.

aristocracy [ærɪˈstɒkrəsɪ] n aristocratie f. **◆aristocrat** [ˈærɪstəkræt, Am əˈrɪstəkræt] *n* aristocrate *mf*. ◆**aristo'cratic** *a* aristocratique.

arithmetic [əˈrɪθmətɪk] *n* arithmétique *f*.

ark [ɑːk] *n* Noah's a. l'arche *f* de Noé.

arm [ɑːm] **1** *n* bras *m*; a. in a. bras dessus bras dessous; **with open arms** à bras ouverts. **2** *n* (*weapon*) arme *f*; **arms race** course *f* aux armements; − *vt* armer (**with** de). ◆**armament** *n* armement *m*. ◆**armband** *n* brassard *m*. ◆**armchair** *n* fauteuil *m*. ◆**armful** *n* brassée *f*. ◆**armhole** *n* emmanchure *f*. ◆**armpit** *n* aisselle *f*. ◆**armrest** *n* accoudoir *m*.

armadillo [ɑːməˈdɪləʊ] *n* (*pl* -os) tatou *m*.

armistice [ˈɑːmɪstɪs] *n* armistice *m*.

armour [ˈɑːmər] *n* (*of knight etc*) armure *f*; (*of tank etc*) blindage *m*. ◆**armoured** *a*, ◆**armour-plated** *a* blindé. ◆**armoury** *n* arsenal *m*.

army [ˈɑːmɪ] *n* armée *f*; − *a* (*uniform etc*) militaire; **to join the** a. s'engager; **regular a.** armée *f* active.

aroma [əˈrəʊmə] *n* arôme *m*. ◆**aro'matic** *a* aromatique.

arose [əˈrəʊz] *see* **arise**.

around [əˈraʊnd] *prep* autour de; (*approximately*) environ, autour de; **to go a. the world** faire le tour du monde; − *adv* autour; **all a.** tout autour; **to follow a.** suivre partout; **to rush a.** courir çà et là; **a. here** par ici; **he's still a.** il est encore là; **there's a lot of flu a.** il y a pas mal de grippes dans l'air; **up and a.** (*after illness*) *Am* sur pied, guéri.

arouse [əˈraʊz] *vt* éveiller, susciter; (*sexually*) exciter; **to a. from sleep** tirer du sommeil.

arrange [əˈreɪndʒ] *vt* arranger; (*time, meeting*) fixer; **it was arranged that** il était convenu que; **to a. to do** s'arranger pour faire. ◆**−ment** *n* (*layout, agreement*) arrangement *m*; *pl* (*preparations*) préparatifs *mpl*; (*plans*) projets *mpl*; **to make arrangements to** s'arranger pour.

array [əˈreɪ] *n* (*display*) étalage *m*. ◆**arrayed** *a* (*dressed*) *Lit* (re)vêtu (**in** de).

arrears [əˈrɪəz] *npl* (*payment*) arriéré *m*; **to be in a.** avoir des arriérés.

arrest [əˈrest] *vt* arrêter; − *n Jur* arrestation *f*; **under a.** en état d'arrestation; **cardiac a.** arrêt *m* du cœur. ◆**−ing** *a* (*striking*) *Fig* frappant.

arrive [əˈraɪv] *vi* arriver. ◆**arrival** *n* arrivée *f*; **new a.** nouveau venu *m*, nouvelle venue *f*; (*baby*) nouveau-né, -ée *mf*.

arrogant [ˈærəgənt] *a* arrogant. ◆**arro-**

gance *n* arrogance *f*. ◆**arrogantly** *adv* avec arrogance.

arrow [ˈærəʊ] *n* flèche *f*.

arsenal [ˈɑːsən(ə)l] *n* arsenal *m*.

arsenic [ˈɑːsnɪk] *n* arsenic *m*.

arson [ˈɑːs(ə)n] *n* incendie *m* volontaire. ◆**arsonist** *n* incendiaire *mf*.

art [ɑːt] *n* art *m*; (*cunning*) artifice *m*; **work of a.** œuvre *f* d'art; **fine arts** beaux-arts *mpl*; **faculty of arts** *Univ* faculté *f* des lettres; **school** école *f* des beaux-arts.

artefact [ˈɑːtɪfækt] *n* objet *m* fabriqué.

artery [ˈɑːtərɪ] *n Anat Aut* artère *f*. ◆**ar'terial** *a Anat* artériel; **a. road** route *f* principale.

artful [ˈɑːtfəl] *a* rusé, astucieux. ◆**−ly** *adv* astucieusement.

arthritis [ɑːˈθraɪtɪs] *n* arthrite *f*.

artichoke [ˈɑːtɪtʃəʊk] *n* (*globe*) a. artichaut *m*; **Jerusalem a.** topinambour *m*.

article [ˈɑːtɪk(ə)l] *n* (*object, clause*) & *Journ Gram* article *m*; **a. of clothing** vêtement *m*; **articles of value** objets *mpl* de valeur; **leading a.** *Journ* éditorial *m*.

articulate [ɑːˈtɪkjʊlət] *a* (*sound*) net, distinct; (*person*) qui s'exprime clairement; − [ɑːˈtɪkjʊleɪt] *vti* (*speak*) articuler. ◆**−ed** *a* **a. lorry** semi-remorque *m*. ◆**articu-'lation** *n* articulation *f*.

artifact [ˈɑːtɪfækt] *n* objet *m* fabriqué.

artifice [ˈɑːtɪfɪs] *n* artifice *m*.

artificial [ɑːtɪˈfɪʃ(ə)l] *a* artificiel. ◆**artifici-'ality** *n* caractère *m* artificiel. ◆**artificially** *adv* artificiellement.

artillery [ɑːˈtɪlərɪ] *n* artillerie *f*.

artisan [ˈɑːtɪzæn] *n* artisan *m*.

artist [ˈɑːtɪst] *n* (*actor, painter etc*) artiste *mf*. ◆**artiste** [ɑːˈtiːst] *n Th Mus* artiste *m*. ◆**ar'tistic** *a* (*sense, treasure etc*) artistique; (*person*) artiste. ◆**artistry** *n* art *m*.

artless [ˈɑːtləs] *a* naturel, naïf.

arty [ˈɑːtɪ] *a Pej* du genre artiste.

as [æz, *unstressed* əz] *adv* & *conj* **1** (*manner etc*) comme; **as you like** comme tu veux; **such as** comme, tel que; **as much** *or* **as hard as I can** (au)tant que je peux; **as it is** (*this being the case*) les choses étant ainsi; (*to leave sth*) comme ça, tel quel; **it's late as it is** il est déjà tard; **as if, as though** comme si. **2** (*comparison*) **as tall as you** aussi grand que vous; **is he as tall as you?** est-il aussi *or* si grand que vous?; **as white as a sheet** blanc comme un linge; **as much** *or* **as hard as you** autant que vous; **as the same as** le même que; **twice as big as** deux fois plus grand que. **3** (*concessive*) **(as) clever as he is** si *or* aussi intelligent qu'il soit. **4** (*capacity*) **as a**

teacher comme professeur, en tant que *or* en qualité de professeur; **to act as a father** agir en père. **5** (*reason*) puisque, comme; **as it's late** puisqu'il est tard, comme il est tard. **6** (*time*) **as I left** comme je partais; **as one grows older** à mesure que l'on vieillit; **as he slept** pendant qu'il dormait; **one day as . . .** un jour que . . . ; **as from, as of** (*time*) à partir de. **7** (*concerning*) **as for that, as to that** quant à cela. **8** (*+ inf*) **so as to de** manière à; **so stupid as to** assez bête pour.

asbestos [æs'bestəs] *n* amiante *f*.

ascend [ə'send] *vi* monter; *– vt* (*throne*) monter sur; (*stairs*) monter; (*mountain*) faire l'ascension de. ◆**ascent** *n* ascension *f* (**of** de); (*slope*) côte *f*.

ascertain [æsə'tein] *vt* (*discover*) découvrir; (*check*) s'assurer de.

ascetic [ə'setik] *a* ascétique; *– n* ascète *mf*.

ascribe [ə'skraib] *vt* attribuer (**to** à).

ash [æʃ] *n* **1** (*of cigarette etc*) cendre *f*; A. **Wednesday** mercredi *m* des Cendres. **2** (*tree*) frêne *m*. ◆**ashen** *a* (*pale grey*) cendré; (*face*) pâle. ◆**ashcan** *n Am* poubelle *f*. ◆**ashtray** *n* cendrier *m*.

ashamed [ə'ʃeimd] *a* honteux; **to be a. of** avoir honte de; **to be a. (of oneself)** avoir honte.

ashore [ə'ʃɔːr] *adv* **to go a.** débarquer; **to put s.o. a.** débarquer qn.

Asia ['eiʃə] *n* Asie *f*. ◆**Asian** *a* asiatique; *– n* Asiatique *mf*, Asiate *mf*.

aside [ə'said] **1** *adv* de côté; **to draw a.** (*curtain*) écarter; **to take** *or* **draw s.o. a.** prendre qn à part; **to step a.** s'écarter; **a. from** en dehors de. **2** *n Th* aparté *m*.

asinine ['æsinain] *a* stupide, idiot.

ask [ɑːsk] *vt* demander; (*a question*) poser; (*invite*) inviter; **to a. s.o. (for) sth** demander qch à qn; **to a. s.o. to do** demander à qn de faire; *– vi* demander; **to a. for sth/s.o.** demander qch/qn; **to a. for sth back** redemander qch; **to a. about sth** se renseigner sur qch; **to a. after** *or* **about s.o.** demander des nouvelles de qn; **to a. s.o. about** interroger qn sur; **asking price** prix *m* demandé.

askance [ə'skɑːns] *adv* **to look a. at** regarder avec méfiance.

askew [ə'skjuː] *adv* de biais, de travers.

aslant [ə'slɑːnt] *adv* de travers.

asleep [ə'sliːp] *a* endormi; (*arm, leg*) engourdi; **to be a.** dormir; **to fall a.** s'endormir.

asp [æsp] *n* (*snake*) aspic *m*.

asparagus [ə'spærəgəs] *n* (*plant*) asperge *f*; (*shoots*) *Culin* asperges *fpl*.

aspect ['æspekt] *n* aspect *m*; (*of house*) orientation *f*.

aspersions [ə'spɜːʃ(ə)nz] *npl* **to cast a. on** dénigrer.

asphalt ['æsfælt, *Am* 'æsfɔːlt] *n* asphalte *m*; *– vt* asphalter.

asphyxia [əs'fiksiə] *n* asphyxie *f*. ◆**asphyxiate** *vt* asphyxier. ◆**asphyxi-'ation** *n* asphyxie *f*.

aspire [ə'spaiər] *vi* **to a. to** aspirer à. ◆**aspi-'ration** *n* aspiration *f*.

aspirin ['æsprin] *n* aspirine *f*.

ass [æs] *n* (*animal*) âne *m*; (*person*) *Fam* imbécile *mf*, âne *m*; **she-a.** ânesse *f*.

assail [ə'seil] *vt* assaillir (**with** de). ◆**assailant** *n* agresseur *m*.

assassin [ə'sæsin] *n Pol* assassin *m*. ◆**assassinate** *vt Pol* assassiner. ◆**assassi'nation** *n Pol* assassinat *m*.

assault [ə'sɔːlt] *n Mil* assaut *m*; *Jur* agression *f*; *– vt Jur* agresser; (*woman*) violenter.

assemble [ə'semb(ə)l] *vt* (*objects, ideas*) assembler; (*people*) rassembler; (*machine*) monter; *– vi* se rassembler. ◆**assembly** *n* (*meeting*) assemblée *f*; *Tech* montage *m*, assemblage *m*; *Sch* rassemblement *m*; **a. line** (*in factory*) chaîne *f* de montage.

assent [ə'sent] *n* assentiment *m*; *– vi* consentir (**to** à).

assert [ə'sɜːt] *vt* affirmer (**that** que); (*rights*) revendiquer; **to a. oneself** s'affirmer. ◆**assertion** *n* affirmation *f*; revendication *f*. ◆**assertive** *a* affirmatif; *Pej* autoritaire.

assess [ə'ses] *vt* (*estimate, evaluate*) évaluer; (*decide amount of*) fixer le montant de; (*person*) juger. ◆**—ment** *n* évaluation *f*; jugement *m*. ◆**assessor** *n* (*valuer*) expert *m*.

asset ['æset] *n* atout *m*, avantage *m*; *pl Com* biens *mpl*, avoir *m*.

assiduous [ə'sidjuəs] *a* assidu.

assign [ə'sain] *vt* (*allocate*) assigner; (*day etc*) fixer; (*appoint*) nommer (**to** à). ◆**—ment** *n* (*task*) mission *f*; *Sch* devoirs *mpl*.

assimilate [ə'simileit] *vt* assimiler; *– vi* s'assimiler. ◆**assimi'lation** *n* assimilation *f*.

assist [ə'sist] *vti* aider (**in doing, to do** à faire). ◆**assistance** *n* aide *f*; **to be of a. to s.o.** aider qn. ◆**assistant** *n* assistant, -ante *mf*; (*in shop*) vendeur, -euse *mf*; *– a* adjoint.

assizes [ə'saiziz] *npl Jur* assises *fpl*.

associate [ə'səʊʃieit] *vt* associer (**with** à, avec); *– vi* **to a. with s.o.** fréquenter qn; **to**

a. (oneself) with (*in business venture*) s'associer à *or* avec; – [ə'səʊʃɪət] *n* & *a* associé, -ée (*mf*). ◆**associ'ation** *n* association *f*; *pl* (*memories*) souvenirs *mpl*.

assort/ed [ə'sɔːtɪd] *a* (*different*) variés; (*foods*) assortis; **well-a.** bien assorti. ◆**—ment** *n* assortiment *m*.

assuage [ə'sweɪdʒ] *vt* apaiser, adoucir.

assum/e [ə'sjuːm] *vt* **1** (*take on*) prendre; (*responsibility, role*) assumer; (*attitude, name*) adopter. **2** (*suppose*) présumer (*that* que). ◆**—ed** *a* (*feigned*) faux; **a. name** nom *m* d'emprunt. ◆**assumption** *n* (*supposition*) supposition *f*.

assur/e [ə'ʃʊər] *vt* assurer. ◆**—edly** [-ɪdlɪ] *adv* assurément. ◆**assurance** *n* assurance *f*.

asterisk ['æstərɪsk] *n* astérisque *m*.

astern [ə'stɜːn] *adv* Nau à l'arrière.

asthma ['æsmə] *n* asthme *m*. ◆**asth'matic** *a* & *n* asthmatique (*mf*).

astir [ə'stɜːr] *a* (*excited*) en émoi; (*out of bed*) debout.

astonish [ə'stɒnɪʃ] *vt* étonner; **to be astonished** s'étonner (**at sth** de qch). ◆**—ing** *a* étonnant. ◆**—ingly** *adv* étonnamment. ◆**—ment** *n* étonnement *m*.

astound [ə'staʊnd] *vt* stupéfier, étonner. ◆**—ing** *a* stupéfiant.

astray [ə'streɪ] *adv* **to go a.** s'égarer; **to lead a.** égarer.

astride [ə'straɪd] *adv* à califourchon; – *prep* à cheval sur.

astringent [ə'strɪndʒənt] *a* (*harsh*) sévère.

astrology [ə'strɒlədʒɪ] *n* astrologie *f*. ◆**astrologer** *n* astrologue *mf*.

astronaut ['æstrənɔːt] *n* astronaute *mf*.

astronomy [ə'strɒnəmɪ] *n* astronomie *f*. ◆**astronomer** *n* astronome *m*. ◆**astro-'nomical** *a* astronomique.

astute [ə'stjuːt] *a* (*crafty*) rusé; (*clever*) astucieux.

asunder [ə'sʌndər] *adv* (*to pieces*) en pièces; (*in two*) en deux.

asylum [ə'saɪləm] *n* asile *m*; **lunatic a.** Pej maison *f* de fous, asile *m* d'aliénés.

at [æt, *unstressed* ət] *prep* **1** à; **at the end** à la fin; **at work** au travail; **at six (o'clock)** à six heures. **2** chez; **at the doctor's** chez le médecin; **at home** chez soi, à la maison. ◆**at-home** *n* réception *f*. **3** en; **at sea** en mer; **at war** en guerre; **good at** (*geography etc*) fort en. **4** contre; **angry at** fâché contre. **5** sur; **to shoot at** tirer sur; **at my request** sur ma demande. **6** de; **to laugh at** rire de; **surprised at** surpris de. **7** (au)près de; **at the window** (au)près de la fenêtre. **8** par; **to**

come in at the door entrer par la porte; **six at a time** six par six. **9 at night** la nuit; **to look at** regarder; **not at all** pas du tout; (*after 'thank you'*) pas de quoi!; **nothing at all** rien du tout; **to be (hard) at it** être très occupé, travailler dur; **he's always (on) at me** Fam il est toujours après moi.

ate [et, *Am* eɪt] *see* eat.

atheism ['eɪθɪz(ə)m] *n* athéisme *m*. ◆**atheist** *n* athée *mf*.

Athens ['æθɪnz] *n* Athènes *m or f*.

athlete ['æθliːt] *n* athlète *mf*; **a.'s foot** Med mycose *f*. ◆**ath'letic** *a* athlétique; **a. meeting** réunion *f* sportive. ◆**ath'letics** *npl* athlétisme *m*.

atishoo! [ə'tɪʃuː] (*Am* **atchoo** [ə'tʃuː]) *int* atchoum!

Atlantic [ət'læntɪk] *a* atlantique; – *n* **the A.** l'Atlantique *m*.

atlas ['ætləs] *n* atlas *m*.

atmosphere ['ætməsfɪər] *n* atmosphère *f*. ◆**atmos'pheric** *a* atmosphérique.

atom ['ætəm] *n* atome *m*; **a. bomb** bombe *f* atomique. ◆**a'tomic** *a* atomique. ◆**atomizer** *n* atomiseur *m*.

atone [ə'təʊn] *vi* **to a. for** expier. ◆**—ment** *n* expiation *f* (for de).

atrocious [ə'trəʊʃəs] *a* atroce. ◆**atrocity** *n* atrocité *f*.

atrophy ['ætrəfɪ] *vi* s'atrophier.

attach [ə'tætʃ] *vt* attacher (**to** à); (*document*) joindre (**to** à); **attached to** (*fond of*) attaché à. ◆**—ment** *n* (*affection*) attachement *m*; (*fastener*) attache *f*; (*tool*) accessoire *m*.

attaché [ə'tæʃeɪ] *n* **1** Pol attaché, -ée *mf*. **2 a. case** attaché-case *m*.

attack [ə'tæk] *n* Mil Med & Fig attaque *f*; (*of fever*) accès *m*; (*on s.o.'s life*) attentat *m*; **heart a.** crise *f* cardiaque; – *vt* attaquer; (*problem, plan*) s'attaquer à; – *vi* attaquer. ◆**—er** *n* agresseur *m*.

attain [ə'teɪn] *vt* parvenir à, atteindre, réaliser. ◆**—able** *a* accessible. ◆**—ment** *n* (*of ambition, aim etc*) réalisation *f* (of de); *pl* (*skills*) talents *mpl*.

attempt [ə'tempt] *n* tentative *f*; **to make an a. to** essayer *or* tenter de; **a. on** (*record*) tentative pour battre; **a. on s.o.'s life** attentat *m* contre qn; – *vt* tenter; (*task*) entreprendre; **to a. to do** essayer *or* tenter de faire; **attempted murder** tentative de meurtre.

attend [ə'tend] *vt* (*match etc*) assister à; (*course*) suivre; (*school, church*) aller à; (*wait on, serve*) servir; (*escort*) accompagner; (*patient*) soigner; – *vi* assister; **to a. to** (*pay attention to*) prêter attention à;

(*take care of*) s'occuper de. ◆—**ed** *a*
well-a. (*course*) très suivi; (*meeting*) où il y a
du monde. ◆**attendance** *n* présence *f* (**at**
à); (*people*) assistance *f*; **school a.** scolarité
f; **in a.** de service. ◆**attendant 1** *n*
employé, -ée *mf*; (*in museum*) gardien,
-ienne *mf*; *pl* (*of prince, king etc*) suite *f*. **2** *a*
(*fact*) concomitant.

attention [ə'tenʃ(ə)n] *n* attention *f*; **to pay a.**
prêter *or* faire attention (**to** à); **a.!** *Mil*
garde-à-vous!; **to stand at a.** *Mil* être au
garde-à-vous; **a. to detail** minutie *f*.
◆**attentive** *a* (*heedful*) attentif (**to** à);
(*thoughtful*) attentionné (**to** pour).
◆**attentively** *adv* avec attention, attentivement.

attenuate [ə'tenjʊeɪt] *vt* atténuer.

attest [ə'test] *vti* **to a. (to)** témoigner de.

attic ['ætɪk] *n* grenier *m*.

attire [ə'taɪər] *n* *Lit* vêtements *mpl*.

attitude ['ætɪtjuːd] *n* attitude *f*.

attorney [ə'tɜːnɪ] *n* (*lawyer*) *Am* avocat *m*;
district a. *Am* = procureur *m* (de la République).

attract [ə'trækt] *vt* attirer. ◆**attraction** *n*
attraction *f*; (*charm, appeal*) attrait *m*.
◆**attractive** *a* (*price etc*) intéressant; (*girl*)
belle, jolie; (*boy*) beau; (*manners*)
attrayant.

attribut/e 1 ['ætrɪbjuːt] *n* (*quality*) attribut
m. **2** [ə'trɪbjuːt] *vt* (*ascribe*) attribuer (**to** à).
◆—**able** *a* attribuable (**to** à).

attrition [ə'trɪʃ(ə)n] *n* **war of a.** guerre *f*
d'usure.

attuned [ə'tjuːnd] *a* **a. to** (*of ideas, trends etc*)
en accord avec; (*used to*) habitué à.

atypical [eɪ'tɪpɪk(ə)l] *a* peu typique.

aubergine ['əʊbəʒiːn] *n* aubergine *f*.

auburn ['ɔːbən] *a* (*hair*) châtain roux.

auction ['ɔːkʃən] *n* vente *f* (aux enchères); —
vt **to a. (off)** vendre (aux enchères).
◆**auctio'neer** *n* commissaire-priseur *m*,
adjudicateur, -trice *mf*.

audacious [ɔː'deɪʃəs] *a* audacieux.
◆**audacity** *n* audace *f*.

audib/le ['ɔːdɪb(ə)l] *a* perceptible, audible.
◆—**ly** *adv* distinctement.

audience ['ɔːdɪəns] *n* assistance *f*, public *m*;
(*of speaker, musician*) auditoire *m*; *Th Cin*
spectateurs *mpl*; *Rad* auditeurs *mpl*; (*interview*) audience *f*.

audio ['ɔːdɪəʊ] *a* (*cassette, system etc*) audio
inv. ◆**audiotypist** *n* dactylo *f* au
magnétophone, audiotypiste *mf*.
◆**audio-'visual** *a* audio-visuel.

audit ['ɔːdɪt] *vt* (*accounts*) vérifier; — *n* vérifi-

cation *f* (des comptes). ◆**auditor** *n*
commissaire *m* aux comptes.

audition [ɔː'dɪʃ(ə)n] *n* audition *f*; — *vti* auditionner.

auditorium [ɔːdɪ'tɔːrɪəm] *n* salle *f* (*de spectacle, concert etc*).

augment [ɔːg'ment] *vt* augmenter (**with, by**
de).

augur ['ɔːgər] *vt* présager; — *vi* **to a. well** être
de bon augure.

august [ɔː'gʌst] *a* auguste.

August ['ɔːgəst] *n* août *m*.

aunt [ɑːnt] *n* tante *f*. ◆**auntie** *or* **aunty** *n*
Fam tata *f*.

au pair [əʊ'peər] *adv* au pair; — *n* **au p. (girl)**
jeune fille *f* au pair.

aura ['ɔːrə] *n* émanation *f*, aura *f*; (*of place*)
atmosphère *f*.

auspices ['ɔːspɪsɪz] *npl* auspices *mpl*.

auspicious [ɔː'spɪʃəs] *a* favorable.

austere [ɔː'stɪər] *a* austère. ◆**austerity** *n*
austérité *f*.

Australia [ɒ'streɪlɪə] *n* Australie *f*. ◆**Australian** *a* & *n* australien, -ienne (*mf*).

Austria ['ɒstrɪə] *n* Autriche *f*. ◆**Austrian** *a*
& *n* autrichien, -ienne (*mf*).

authentic [ɔː'θentɪk] *a* authentique.
◆**authenticate** *vt* authentifier.
◆**authen'ticity** *n* authenticité *f*.

author ['ɔːθər] *n* auteur *m*. ◆**authoress** *n*
femme *f* auteur. ◆**authorship** *n* (*of book
etc*) paternité *f*.

authority [ɔː'θɒrɪtɪ] *n* autorité *f*; (*permission*)
autorisation *f* (**to do** de faire); **to be in a.** (*in
charge*) être responsable. ◆**authori-
'tarian** *a* & *n* autoritaire (*mf*).
◆**authoritative** *a* (*report*) autorisé; (*tone,
person*) autoritaire.

authorize ['ɔːθəraɪz] *vt* autoriser (**to do** à
faire). ◆**authori'zation** *n* autorisation *f*.

autistic [ɔː'tɪstɪk] *a* autiste, autistique.

autobiography [ɔːtəʊbaɪ'ɒgrəfɪ] *n* autobiographie *f*.

autocrat ['ɔːtəkræt] *n* autocrate *m*. ◆**auto-
'cratic** *a* autocratique.

autograph ['ɔːtəgrɑːf] *n* autographe *m*; — *vt*
dédicacer (**for** à).

automat ['ɔːtəmæt] *n* *Am* cafétéria *f* à
distributeurs automatiques.

automate ['ɔːtəmeɪt] *vt* automatiser.
◆**auto'mation** *n* automatisation *f*, automation *f*.

automatic [ɔːtə'mætɪk] *a* automatique.
◆**automatically** *adv* automatiquement.

automaton [ɔː'tɒmətən] *n* automate *m*.

automobile ['ɔːtəməbiːl] *n* *Am* auto(mobile)
f.

autonomous [ɔː'tɒnəməs] *a* autonome. ◆**autonomy** *n* autonomie *f*.

autopsy ['ɔːtɒpsɪ] *n* autopsie *f*.

autumn ['ɔːtəm] *n* automne *m*. ◆**autumnal** [ɔː'tʌmnəl] *a* automnal.

auxiliary [ɔːg'zɪljərɪ] *a & n* auxiliaire (*mf*); a. (**verb**) (verbe *m*) auxiliaire *m*.

avail [ə'veɪl] **1** *vt* to a. oneself of profiter de, tirer parti de. **2** *n* to no a. en vain; of no a. inutile.

available [ə'veɪləb(ə)l] *a* (*thing, means etc*) disponible; (*person*) libre, disponible; (*valid*) valable; **a. to all** (*goal etc*) accessible à tous. ◆**availa'bility** *n* disponibilité *f*; validité *f*; accessibilité *f*.

avalanche ['ævəlɑːnʃ] *n* avalanche *f*.

avarice ['ævərɪs] *n* avarice *f*. ◆**ava'ricious** *a* avare.

avenge [ə'vendʒ] *vt* venger; **to a. oneself** se venger (**on** de).

avenue ['ævənjuː] *n* avenue *f*; (*way to a result*) *Fig* voie *f*.

average ['ævərɪdʒ] *n* moyenne *f*; **on a.** en moyenne; – *a* moyen; – *vt* (*do*) faire en moyenne; (*reach*) atteindre la moyenne de; (*figures*) faire la moyenne de.

averse [ə'vɜːs] *a* to be a. to doing répugner à faire. ◆**aversion** *n* (*dislike*) aversion *f*, répugnance *f*.

avert [ə'vɜːt] *vt* (*prevent*) éviter; (*turn away*) détourner (**from** de).

aviary ['eɪvɪərɪ] *n* volière *f*.

aviation [eɪvɪ'eɪʃ(ə)n] *n* aviation *f*. ◆'**aviator** *n* aviateur, -trice *mf*.

avid ['ævɪd] *a* avide (**for** de).

avocado [ævə'kɑːdəʊ] *n* (*pl* -os) a. (**pear**) avocat *m*.

avoid [ə'vɔɪd] *vt* éviter; **to a. doing** éviter de faire. ◆—**able** *a* évitable. ◆**avoidance** *n* his a. of (*danger etc*) son désir *m* d'éviter; **tax a.** évasion *f* fiscale.

avowed [ə'vaʊd] *a* (*enemy*) déclaré, avoué.

await [ə'weɪt] *vt* attendre.

awake [ə'weɪk] *vi* (*pt* awoke, *pp* awoken) s'éveiller; – *vt* (*person, hope etc*) éveiller; – *a* réveillé, éveillé; (**wide-**)a. éveillé; **to keep s.o. a.** empêcher qn de dormir, tenir qn éveillé; **he's (still) a.** il ne dort pas (encore); **a. to** (*conscious of*) conscient de. ◆**awaken** *vti* = awake. **2** *vt* **to a. s.o. to sth** faire prendre conscience de qch à qn. ◆**awakening** *n* réveil *m*.

award [ə'wɔːd] *vt* (*money*) attribuer; (*prize*) décerner, attribuer; (*damages*) accorder; – *n* (*prize*) prix *m*, récompense *f*; (*scholarship*) bourse *f*.

aware [ə'weər] *a* avisé, informé; **a. of** (*conscious*) conscient de; (*informed*) au courant de; **to become a. of** prendre conscience de. ◆—**ness** *n* conscience *f*.

awash [ə'wɒʃ] *a* inondé (**with** de).

away [ə'weɪ] *adv* **1** (*distant*) loin; (**far**) a. au loin, très loin; **5 km a.** à 5 km (de distance). **2** (*absent*) parti, absent; **a. with you!** va-t-en!; **to drive a.** partir (en voiture); **to look a.** détourner les yeux; **to work/talk/** *etc* **a.** travailler/parler/*etc* sans relâche; **to fade/melt a.** disparaître/fondre complètement. **3 to play a.** *Sp* jouer à l'extérieur.

awe [ɔː] *n* crainte *f* (*mêlée de respect*); **to be in a. of s.o.** éprouver de la crainte envers qn. ◆**a.-inspiring** *a*, ◆**awesome** *a* (*impressive*) imposant; (*frightening*) effrayant.

awful ['ɔːfəl] *a* affreux; (*terrifying*) épouvantable; (*ill*) malade; **an a. lot of** *Fam* un nombre incroyable de; **I feel a.** (**about it**) j'ai vraiment honte. ◆—**ly** *adv* affreusement; (*very*) *Fam* terriblement; **thanks a.** merci infiniment.

awhile [ə'waɪl] *adv* quelque temps; (*to stay, wait*) un peu.

awkward ['ɔːkwəd] *a* **1** (*clumsy*) maladroit; (*age*) ingrat. **2** (*difficult*) difficile; (*cumbersome*) gênant; (*tool*) peu commode; (*time*) inopportun; (*silence*) gêné. ◆—**ly** *adv* maladroitement; (*speak*) d'un ton gêné; (*placed*) à un endroit difficile. ◆—**ness** *n* maladresse *f*; difficulté *f*; (*discomfort*) gêne *f*.

awning ['ɔːnɪŋ] *n* auvent *m*; (*over shop*) store *m*; (*glass canopy*) marquise *f*.

awoke(n) [ə'wəʊk(ən)] *see* awake.

awry [ə'raɪ] *adv* to go a. (*of plan etc*) mal tourner.

axe [æks] (*Am* ax) *n* hache *f*; (*reduction*) *Fig* coupe *f* sombre; – *vt* réduire; (*eliminate*) supprimer.

axiom ['æksɪəm] *n* axiome *m*.

axis, pl axes ['æksɪs, 'æksiːz] *n* axe *m*.

axle ['æks(ə)l] *n* essieu *m*.

ay(e) [aɪ] **1** *adv* oui. **2** *n* the ayes (*votes*) les voix *fpl* pour.

azalea [ə'zeɪlɪə] *n* (*plant*) azalée *f*.

B

B, b [biː] *n* B, b *m*; **2B** (*number*) 2 ter.
BA *abbr* = **Bachelor of Arts.**
babble ['bæb(ə)l] *vi* (*of baby, stream*) gazouiller; (*mumble*) bredouiller; – *vt* **to b. (out)** bredouiller; – *n inv* gazouillement *m*, gazouillis *m*; (*of voices*) rumeur *f*.
babe [beɪb] *n* **1** petit(e) enfant *mf*, bébé *m*. **2** (*girl*) *Sl* pépée *f*.
baboon [bə'buːn] *n* babouin *m*.
baby ['beɪbɪ] **1** *n* bébé *m*; – *a* (*clothes etc*) de bébé; **b. boy** petit garçon *m*; **b. girl** petite fille *f*; **b. carriage** *Am* voiture *f* d'enfant; **b. sling** kangourou® *m*, porte-bébé *m*; **b. tiger/***etc* bébé-tigre/*etc m*; **b. face** visage *m* poupin. **2** *n Sl* (*girl*) pépée *f*; (*girlfriend*) copine *f*. **3** *vt Fam* dorloter. ◆**b.-batterer** *n* bourreau *m* d'enfants. ◆**b.-minder** *n* gardien, -ienne *mf* d'enfants. ◆**b.-sit** *vi* (*pt & pp* **-sat,** *pres p* **-sitting**) garder les enfants, faire du baby-sitting. ◆**b.-sitter** *n* baby-sitter *mf*. ◆**b.-snatching** *n* rapt *m* d'enfant. ◆**b.-walker** *n* trotteur *m*, youpala® *m*.
babyish ['beɪbɪɪʃ] *a Pej* de bébé; (*puerile*) enfantin.
bachelor ['bætʃələr] *n* **1** célibataire *m*; **b. flat** garçonnière *f*. **2 B. of Arts/of Science** licencié -ée *mf* ès lettres/ès sciences.
back [bæk] *n* (*of person, animal*) dos *m*; (*of chair*) dossier *m*; (*of hand*) revers *m*; (*of house*) derrière *m*, arrière *m*; (*of room*) fond *m*; (*of page*) verso *m*,(*of fabric*) envers *m*; *Fb* arrière *m*; **at the b. of** (*book*) à la fin de; (*car*) à l'arrière de; **at the b. of one's mind** derrière la tête; **b. to front** devant derrière, à l'envers; **to get s.o.'s b. up** *Fam* irriter qn; **in b. of** *Am* derrière; – *a* arrière *inv*, de derrière; (*taxes*) arriéré; **b. door** porte *f* de derrière; **b. room** pièce *f* du fond; **b. end** (*of bus*) arrière *m*; **b. street** rue *f* écartée; **b. number** vieux numéro *m*; **b. pay** rappel *m* de salaire; **b. tooth** molaire *f*; – *adv* en arrière; **far b.** loin derrière; **far b. in the past** à une époque reculée; **to stand b.** (*of house*) être en retrait (**from** par rapport à); **to go b. and forth** aller et venir; **to come b.** revenir; **he's b.** il est de retour, il est rentré *or* revenu; **a month b.** il y a un mois; **the trip there and b.** le voyage aller et retour; – *vt Com* financer; (*horse etc*) parier sur, jouer; (*car*) faire reculer; (*wall*) renforcer; **to b. s.o (up)** (*support*) appuyer qn; – *vi* (*move backwards*) reculer; **to b. down** se dégonfler; **to b. out** (*withdraw*) se retirer; *Aut* sortir en marche arrière; **to b. on to** (*of window etc*) donner par derrière sur; **to b. up** *Aut* faire marche arrière. ◆**—ing** *n* (*aid*) soutien *m*; (*material*) support *m*, renfort *m*. ◆**—er** *n* (*supporter*) partisan *m*; *Sp* parieur, -euse *mf*; *Fin* bailleur *m* de fonds.
backache ['bækeɪk] *n* mal *m* aux reins. ◆**back'bencher** *n Pol* membre *m* sans portefeuille. ◆**backbiting** *n* médisance *f*. ◆**backbreaking** *a* éreintant. ◆**backcloth** *n* toile *f* de fond. ◆**backchat** *n* impertinence *f*. ◆**back'date** *vt* (*cheque*) antidater. ◆**back'handed** *a* (*compliment*) équivoque. ◆**backhander** *n* revers *m*; (*bribe*) *Fam* pot-de-vin *m*. ◆**backrest** *n* dossier *m*. ◆**backside** *n* (*buttocks*) *Fam* derrière *m*. ◆**back'stage** *adv* dans les coulisses. ◆**backstroke** *n Sp* dos *m* crawlé. ◆**backtrack** *vi* rebrousser chemin. ◆**backup** *n* appui *m*; (*tailback*) *Am* embouteillage *m*; **b. lights** *Aut* feux *mpl* de recul. ◆**backwater** *n* (*place*) trou *m* perdu. ◆**backwoods** *npl* forêts *f* vierges. ◆**back'yard** *n* arrière-cour *f*; *Am* jardin *m* (*à l'arrière d'une maison*).
backbone ['bækbəʊn] *n* colonne *f* vertébrale; (*of fish*) grande arête *f*; (*main support*) pivot *m*.
backfire [bæk'faɪər] *vi Aut* pétarader; (*of plot etc*) *Fig* échouer.
backgammon ['bækgæmən] *n* trictrac *m*.
background ['bækgraʊnd] *n* fond *m*, arrière-plan *m*; (*events*) *Fig* antécédents *mpl*; (*education*) formation *f*; (*environment*) milieu *m*; (*conditions*) *Pol* climat *m*, contexte *m*; **to keep s.o. in the b.** tenir qn à l'écart; **b. music** musique *f* de fond.
backlash ['bæklæʃ] *n* choc *m* en retour, retour *m* de flamme.
backlog ['bæklɒg] *n* (*of work*) arriéré *m*.
backward ['bækwəd] *a* (*glance etc*) en arrière; (*retarded*) arriéré; **b. in doing** lent à faire; – *adv* = **backwards.** ◆**—ness** *n* (*of country etc*) retard *m*. ◆**backwards** *adv* en arrière; (*to walk*) à reculons; (*to fall*) à la

renverse; **to move b.** reculer; **to go b. and
forwards** aller et venir.

bacon ['beɪkən] n lard m; (in rashers) bacon
m; **b. and eggs** œufs mpl au jambon.

bacteria [bæk'tɪərɪə] npl bactéries fpl.

bad [bæd] a (**worse, worst**) mauvais;
(wicked) méchant; (sad) triste; (accident,
wound etc) grave; (tooth) carié; (arm, leg)
malade; (pain) violent; (air) vicié; **b.
language** gros mots mpl; **it's b. to think that
. . .** ce n'est pas bien de penser que . . . ; **to
feel b.** Med se sentir mal; **I feel b. about it**
ça m'a chagriné; **things are b.** ça va mal;
she's not b.! elle n'est pas mal!; **to go b.** se
gâter; (of milk) tourner; **in a b. way** mal en
point; (ill) très mal; (in trouble) dans le
pétrin; **too b.!** tant pis! ◆**b.-'mannered** a
mal élevé. ◆**b.-'tempered** a grincheux.
◆**badly** adv mal; (hurt) grièvement; **b.
affected/shaken** très touché/bouleversé; **to
be b. mistaken** se tromper lourdement; **to be
off** dans la gêne; **to be b. off for** manquer
de; **to want b.** avoir grande envie de.

badge [bædʒ] n insigne m; (of postman etc)
plaque f; (bearing slogan or joke) badge m.

badger ['bædʒər] **1** n (animal) blaireau m. **2**
vt importuner.

badminton ['bædmɪntən] n badminton m.

baffle ['bæf(ə)l] vt (person) déconcerter,
dérouter.

bag [bæg] **1** n sac m; pl (luggage) valises fpl,
bagages mpl; (under the eyes) poches fpl;
bags of Fam (lots of) beaucoup de; **an old b.**
une vieille taupe; **in the b.** Fam dans la
poche. **2** vt (-gg-) (take, steal) Fam piquer,
s'adjuger; (animal) Sp tuer.

baggage ['bægɪdʒ] n bagages mpl; Mil
équipement m; **b. car** Am fourgon m; **b.
room** Am consigne f.

baggy ['bægɪ] a (-ier, -iest) (clothing) trop
ample; (trousers) faisant des poches.

bagpipes ['bægpaɪps] npl cornemuse f.

Bahamas [bə'hɑːməz] npl the B. les Bahamas fpl.

bail [beɪl] **1** n Jur caution f; **on b.** en liberté
provisoire; – vt **to b. (out)** fournir une
caution pour; **to b. out** (ship) écoper;
(person, company) Fig tirer d'embarras. **2**
vi **to b. out** Am Av sauter (en parachute).

bailiff ['beɪlɪf] n Jur huissier m; (of landowner) régisseur m.

bait [beɪt] **1** n amorce f, appât m; – vt (fishing hook) amorcer. **2** vt (annoy) asticoter,
tourmenter.

baize [beɪz] n green b. (on card table etc)
tapis m vert.

bak/e [beɪk] vt (faire) cuire (au four); – vi

(of cook) faire de la pâtisserie or du pain;
(of cake etc) cuire (au four); **we're** or **it's
baking (hot)** Fam on cuit. ◆**-ed** a (potatoes) au four; **b. beans** haricots mpl blancs
(à la tomate). ◆**-ing** n cuisson f; **b.
powder** levure f (chimique). ◆**-er** n
boulanger, -ère mf. ◆**bakery** n boulangerie f.

balaclava [bælə'klɑːvə] n b. (helmet)
passe-montagne m.

balance ['bæləns] n (scales) & Econ Pol
Com balance f; (equilibrium) équilibre m;
(of account) Com solde m; (remainder) reste
m; **to strike a b.** trouver le juste milieu;
sense of b. sens m de la mesure; **in the b.**
incertain; **on b.** à tout prendre; **b. sheet**
bilan m; – vt tenir or mettre en équilibre
(on sur); (budget, account) équilibrer;
(compare) mettre en balance, peser; **to b.
(out)** (compensate for) compenser; **to b.
(oneself)** se tenir en équilibre; – vi (of
accounts) être en équilibre, s'équilibrer.

balcony ['bælkənɪ] n balcon m.

bald [bɔːld] a (-er, -est) chauve; (statement)
brutal; (tyre) lisse; **b. patch** or **spot** tonsure
f. ◆**b.-'headed** a chauve. ◆**balding** a to
be b. perdre ses cheveux. ◆**baldness** n
calvitie f.

balderdash ['bɔːldədæʃ] n balivernes fpl.

bale [beɪl] **1** n (of cotton etc) balle f. **2** vi **to b.
out** Av sauter (en parachute).

baleful ['beɪlfʊl] a sinistre, funeste.

balk [bɔːk] vi reculer (at devant), regimber
(at contre).

ball[1] [bɔːl] n balle f; (inflated) Fb Rugby etc
ballon m; Billiards bille f; (of string, wool)
pelote f; (sphere) boule f; (of meat or fish)
Culin boulette f; **on the b.** (alert) Fam
éveillé; **he's on the b.** (efficient, knowledgeable) Fam il connaît son affaire, il est au
point; **b. bearing** roulement m à billes; **b.
game** Am partie f de baseball; **it's a whole
new b. game** or **a different b. game** Am Fig
c'est une tout autre affaire. ◆**ballcock** n
robinet m à flotteur. ◆**ballpoint** n stylo m
à bille.

ball[2] [bɔːl] n (dance) bal m. ◆**ballroom** n
salle f de danse.

ballad ['bæləd] n Liter ballade f; Mus
romance f.

ballast ['bæləst] n lest m; – vt lester.

ballet ['bæleɪ] n ballet m. ◆**balle'rina** n
ballerine f.

ballistic [bə'lɪstɪk] a b. missile engin m balistique.

balloon [bə'luːn] n ballon m; Met
ballon-sonde m.

ballot ['bælət] *n* (*voting*) scrutin *m*; **b. (paper)** bulletin *m* de vote; **b. box** urne *f*; – *vt* (*members*) consulter (par un scrutin).

ballyhoo [bælɪ'huː] *n* *Fam* battage *m* (publicitaire).

balm [bɑːm] *n* (*liquid, comfort*) baume *m*. ◆**balmy** *a* (-ier, -iest) **1** (*air*) *Lit* embaumé. **2** (*crazy*) *Fam* dingue, timbré.

baloney [bə'ləʊnɪ] *n* *Sl* foutaises *fpl*.

Baltic ['bɔːltɪk] *n* the B. la Baltique.

balustrade ['bæləstreɪd] *n* balustrade *f*.

bamboo [bæm'buː] *n* bambou *m*.

bamboozle [bæm'buːz(ə)l] *vt* (*cheat*) *Fam* embobiner.

ban [bæn] *n* interdiction *f*; – *vt* (-nn-) interdire; **to b. from** (*club etc*) exclure de; **to ban s.o. from doing** interdire à qn de faire.

banal [bə'nɑːl, *Am* 'beɪn(ə)l] *a* banal. ◆**ba'nality** *n* banalité *f*.

banana [bə'nɑːnə] *n* banane *f*.

band [bænd] **1** *n* (*strip*) bande *f*; (*of hat*) ruban *m*; **rubber** *or* **elastic b.** élastique *m*. **2** *n* (*group*) bande *f*; *Mus* (petit) orchestre *m*; *Mil* fanfare *f*; – *vi* **to b. together** former une bande, se grouper. ◆**bandstand** *n* kiosque *m* à musique. ◆**bandwagon** *n* **to jump on the b.** *Fig* suivre le mouvement.

bandage ['bændɪdʒ] *n* (*strip*) bande *f*; (*for wound*) pansement *m*; (*for holding in place*) bandage *m*; – *vt* **to b. (up)** (*arm, leg*) bander; (*wound*) mettre un pansement sur.

Band-Aid® ['bændeɪd] *n* pansement *m* adhésif.

bandit ['bændɪt] *n* bandit *m*. ◆**banditry** *n* banditisme *m*.

bandy ['bændɪ] **1** *a* (-ier, -iest) (*person*) bancal; (*legs*) arqué. ◆**b.-'legged** *a* bancal. **2** *vt* **to b. about** (*story etc*) faire circuler, propager.

bane [beɪn] *n* *Lit* fléau *m*. ◆**baneful** *a* funeste.

bang [bæŋ] **1** *n* (*hit, noise*) coup *m* (violent); (*of gun etc*) détonation *f*; (*of door*) claquement *m*; – *vt* cogner, frapper; (*door*) (faire) claquer; **to b. one's head** se cogner la tête; – *vi* cogner, frapper; (*of door*) claquer; (*of gun*) détoner; (*of firework*) éclater; **to b. down** (*lid*) rabattre (violemment); **to b. into** sth heurter qch; – *int* vlan!, pan!; **to go (off) b.** éclater. **2** *adv* (*exactly*) *Fam* exactement; **b. in the middle** en plein milieu; **b. on six** à six heures tapantes.

banger [bæŋər] *n* **1** *Culin* *Fam* saucisse *f*. **2** (*firecracker*) pétard *m*. **3** **old b.** (*car*) *Fam* tacot *m*, guimbarde *f*.

bangle ['bæŋg(ə)l] *n* bracelet *m* (rigide).

bangs [bæŋz] *npl* (*of hair*) *Am* frange *f*.

banish ['bænɪʃ] *vt* bannir.

banister ['bænɪstər] *n* banister(s) rampe *f* (d'escalier).

banjo ['bændʒəʊ] *n* (*pl* -os *or* -oes) banjo *m*.

bank [bæŋk] **1** *n* (*of river*) bord *m*, rive *f*; (*raised*) berge *f*; (*of earth*) talus *m*; (*of sand*) banc *m*; **the Left B.** (*in Paris*) la Rive gauche; – *vt* **to b. (up)** (*earth etc*) amonceler; (*fire*) couvrir. **2** *n* *Com* banque *f*; **b. account** compte *m* en banque; **b. card** carte *f* d'identité bancaire; **b. holiday** jour *m* férié; **b. note** billet *m* de banque; **b. rate** taux *m* d'escompte; – *vt* (*money*) *Com* mettre en banque; – *vi* avoir un compte en banque (**with à**). **3** *vi* *Av* virer. **4** *vi* **to b. on s.o./sth** (*rely on*) compter sur qn/qch. ◆**—ing** *a* bancaire; – *n* (*activity, profession*) la banque. ◆**—er** *n* banquier *m*.

bankrupt ['bæŋkrʌpt] *a* **to go b.** faire faillite; **b. of** (*ideas*) *Fig* dénué de; – *vt* mettre en faillite. ◆**bankruptcy** *n* faillite *f*.

banner ['bænər] *n* (*at rallies etc*) banderole *f*; (*flag*) & *Fig* bannière *f*.

banns [bænz] *npl* bans *mpl*.

banquet ['bæŋkwɪt] *n* banquet *m*.

banter ['bæntər] *vti* plaisanter; – *n* plaisanterie *f*. ◆**—ing** *a* (*tone, air*) plaisantin.

baptism ['bæptɪzəm] *n* baptême *m*. ◆**bap-'tize** *vt* baptiser.

bar [bɑːr] **1** *n* barre *f*; (*of gold*) lingot *m*; (*of chocolate*) tablette *f*; (*on window*) & *Jur* barreau *m*; **b. of soap** savonnette *f*; **behind bars** *Jur* sous les verrous; **to be a b. to** *Fig* faire obstacle à. **2** *n* (*pub*) bar *m*; (*counter*) comptoir *m*. **3** *n* (*group of notes*) *Mus* mesure *f*. **4** *vt* (-rr-) (*way etc*) bloquer, barrer; (*window*) griller. **5** *vt* (*prohibit*) interdire (**s.o. from doing** à qn de faire); (*exclude*) exclure (**from à**). **6** *prep* sauf. ◆**barmaid** *n* serveuse *f* de bar. ◆**barman** *n*, ◆**bartender** *n* barman *m*.

Barbados [bɑː'beɪdɒs] *n* Barbade *f*.

barbarian [bɑː'beərɪən] *n* barbare *mf*. ◆**barbaric** *a* barbare. ◆**barbarity** *n* barbarie *f*.

barbecue ['bɑːbɪkjuː] *n* barbecue *m*; – *vt* griller (au barbecue).

barbed [bɑːbd] *a* **b. wire** fil *m* de fer barbelé; (*fence*) barbelés *mpl*.

barber ['bɑːbər] *n* coiffeur *m* (*pour hommes*).

barbiturate [bɑː'bɪtjʊrət] *n* barbiturique *m*.

bare [beər] *a* (-er, -est) nu; (*tree, hill etc*) dénudé; (*cupboard*) vide; (*mere*) simple; **the b. necessities** le strict nécessaire; **with his b. hands** à mains nues; – *vt* mettre à nu.

◆**—ness** n (of person) nudité f.
◆**bareback** adv **to ride b.** monter à cru.
◆**barefaced** a (lie) éhonté. ◆**barefoot** adv nu-pieds; – a aux pieds nus. ◆**bare-'headed** a & adv nu-tête inv.

barely ['beəlɪ] adv (scarcely) à peine, tout juste.

bargain ['baɪgɪn] n (deal) marché m, affaire f; **a (good) b.** (cheap buy) une occasion, une bonne affaire; **it's a b.!** (agreed) c'est entendu!; **into the b.** par-dessus le marché; **b. price** prix m exceptionnel; **b. counter** rayon m des soldes; – vi (negotiate) négocier; (haggle) marchander; **to b. for** or **on sth** Fig s'attendre à qch. ◆**—ing** n négociations fpl; marchandage m.

barge [baɪdʒ] **1** n chaland m, péniche f. **2** vi **to b. in** (enter a room) faire irruption; (interrupt) interrompre; **to b. into** (hit) se cogner contre.

baritone ['bærɪtəʊn] n (voice, singer) baryton m.

bark [baɪk] **1** n (of tree) écorce f. **2** vi (of dog etc) aboyer; – n aboiement m. ◆**—ing** n aboiements mpl.

barley ['baɪlɪ] n orge f; **b. sugar** sucre m d'orge.

barmy [baɪmɪ] a (-ier, -iest) Fam dingue, timbré.

barn [baɪn] n (for crops etc) grange f; (for horses) écurie f; (for cattle) étable f. ◆**barnyard** n basse-cour f.

barometer [bəˈrɒmɪtər] n baromètre m.

baron ['bærən] n baron m; (industrialist) Fig magnat m. ◆**baroness** n baronne f.

baroque [bəˈrɒk, Am bəˈrəʊk] a & n Archit Mus etc baroque (m).

barracks ['bærəks] npl caserne f.

barrage ['bæraɪʒ, Am bəˈraɪʒ] n (barrier) barrage m; **a b. of** (questions etc) un feu roulant de.

barrel ['bærəl] n **1** (cask) tonneau m; (of oil) baril m. **2** (of gun) canon m. **3** **b. organ** orgue m de Barbarie.

barren ['bærən] a stérile; (style) Fig aride.

barrette [bəˈret] n (hair slide) Am barrette f.

barricade ['bærɪkeɪd] n barricade f; – vt barricader; **to b. oneself (in)** se barricader.

barrier ['bærɪər] n barrière f; Fig obstacle m, barrière f; (ticket) b. Rail portillon m; **sound b.** mur m du son.

barring ['baɪrɪŋ] prep sauf, excepté.

barrister ['bærɪstər] n avocat m.

barrow ['bærəʊ] n charrette f or voiture f à bras; (wheelbarrow) brouette f.

barter ['baɪtər] vt troquer, échanger (**for** contre); – n troc m, échange m.

base [beɪs] **1** n (bottom, main ingredient) base f; (of tree, lamp) pied m. **2** n Mil base f. **3** vt baser, fonder (**on** sur); **based in** or **on London** basé à Londres. **4** a (dishonourable) bas, ignoble; (metal) vil. ◆**—less** a sans fondement. ◆**—ness** n bassesse f. ◆**baseball** n base-ball m. ◆**baseboard** n Am plinthe f.

basement ['beɪsmənt] n sous-sol m.

bash [bæʃ] n Fam (bang) coup m; **to have a b.** (try) essayer un coup; – vt Fam (hit) cogner; **to b.** (about) (ill-treat) malmener; **to b. s.o. up** tabasser qn; **to b. in** or **down** (door etc) défoncer. ◆**—ing** n (thrashing) Fam raclée f.

bashful ['bæʃfəl] a timide.

basic ['beɪsɪk] a fondamental; (pay etc) de base; – n **the basics** Fam l'essentiel m. ◆**—ally** [-klɪ] adv au fond.

basil ['bæz(ə)l] n Bot Culin basilic m.

basilica [bəˈzɪlɪkə] n basilique f.

basin ['beɪs(ə)n] n bassin m, bassine f; (for soup, food) bol m; (of river) bassin m; (portable washbasin) cuvette f; (sink) lavabo m.

basis ['beɪsɪs, pl -siːz] n base f; **on the b. of** d'après; **on that b.** dans ces conditions; **on a weekly/etc b.** chaque semaine/etc.

bask [baɪsk] vi se chauffer.

basket ['baɪskɪt] n panier m; (for bread, laundry, litter) corbeille f. ◆**basketball** n basket(-ball) m.

Basque [bæsk] a & n basque (mf).

bass¹ [beɪs] n Mus basse f; – a (note, voice) bas.

bass² [bæs] n (sea fish) bar m; (fresh-water) perche f.

bassinet [bæsɪˈnet] n (cradle) Am couffin m.

bastard ['baɪstəd] **1** n & a bâtard, -arde (mf). **2** n Pej Sl salaud m, salope f.

baste [beɪst] vt **1** (fabric) bâtir. **2** Culin arroser.

bastion ['bæstɪən] n bastion m.

bat [bæt] **1** n (animal) chauve-souris f. **2** n Cricket batte f; Table Tennis raquette f; **off my own b.** de ma propre initiative; – vt (-tt-) (ball) frapper. **3** vt **she didn't b. an eyelid** elle n'a pas sourcillé.

batch [bætʃ] n (of people) groupe m; (of letters) paquet m; (of books) lot m; (of loaves) fournée f; (of papers) liasse f.

bated ['beɪtɪd] a **with b. breath** en retenant son souffle.

bath [baɪθ] n (pl -s [baɪðz]) bain m; (tub) baignoire f; **swimming baths** piscine f; – vt baigner; – vi prendre un bain.

◆**bathrobe** n peignoir m (de bain); Am robe f de chambre. ◆**bathroom** n salle f de bain(s); (toilet) Am toilettes fpl. ◆**bathtub** n baignoire f.

bath/e [beɪð] vt baigner; (wound) laver; – vi se baigner; Am prendre un bain; – n bain m (de mer), baignade f. ◆**—ing** n baignade(s) f(pl); **b. costume** or **suit** maillot m de bain.

baton ['bætən, Am bə'tɒn] n Mus Mil bâton m; (truncheon) matraque f.

battalion [bə'tæljən] n bataillon m.

batter ['bætər] 1 n pâte f à frire. 2 vt battre, frapper; (baby) martyriser; Mil pilonner; **to b. down** (door) défoncer. ◆**—ed** a (car, hat) cabossé; (house) délabré; (face) meurtri; (wife) battu. ◆**—ing** n **to take a b.** Fig souffrir beaucoup.

battery ['bætərɪ] n Mil Aut Agr batterie f; (in radio etc) pile f.

battle ['bæt(ə)l] n bataille f; (struggle) Fig lutte f; **that's half the b.** Fam c'est ça le secret de la victoire; **b. dress** tenue f de campagne; – vi se battre, lutter. ◆**battlefield** n champ m de bataille. ◆**battleship** n cuirassé m.

battlements ['bæt(ə)lmənts] npl (indentations) créneaux mpl; (wall) remparts mpl.

batty ['bætɪ] a (-ier, -iest) Sl dingue, toqué.

baulk [bɔːk] vi reculer (at devant), regimber (at contre).

bawdy ['bɔːdɪ] a (-ier, -iest) paillard, grossier.

bawl [bɔːl] vti **to b. (out)** beugler, brailler; **to b. s.o. out** Am Sl engueuler qn.

bay [beɪ] 1 n Geog Archit baie f. 2 n Bot laurier m. 3 n (for loading etc) aire f. 4 n (of dog) aboiement m; **at b.** aux abois; **to hold at b.** tenir à distance; – vi aboyer. 5 a (horse) bai.

bayonet ['beɪənɪt] n baïonnette f.

bazaar [bə'zɑːr] n (market, shop) bazar m; (charity sale) vente f de charité.

bazooka [bə'zuːkə] n bazooka m.

BC [biː'siː] abbr (before Christ) avant Jésus-Christ.

be [biː] vi (pres t am, are, is; pt was, were; pp been; pres p being) 1 être; **it is green/small** c'est vert/petit; **she's a doctor** elle est médecin; **he's an Englishman** c'est un Anglais; **it's 3 (o'clock)** il est trois heures; **it's the sixth of May** c'est or nous sommes le six mai. 2 avoir; **to be hot/right/lucky** avoir chaud/raison/de la chance; **my feet are cold** j'ai froid aux pieds; **he's 20** (age) il a 20 ans; **to be 2 metres high** avoir 2 mètres de haut; **to be 6 feet tall** mesurer 1,80 m. 3

(health) aller; **how are you?** comment vas-tu? 4 (place, situation) se trouver, être; **she's in York** elle se trouve or elle est à York. 5 (exist) être; **the best painter there is** le meilleur peintre qui soit; **leave me be** laissez-moi (tranquille); **that may be** cela se peut. 6 (go, come) **I've been to see her** je suis allé or j'ai été la voir; **he's (already) been** il est (déjà) venu. 7 (weather) & Math faire; **it's fine** il fait beau; **2 and 2 are 4** 2 et 2 font 4. 8 (cost) coûter, faire; **it's 20 pence** ça coûte 20 pence; **how much is it?** ça fait combien?, c'est combien? 9 (auxiliary) **I am/was doing** je fais/faisais; **I'm listening to the radio** (in the process of) je suis en train d'écouter la radio; **she's been there some time** elle est là depuis longtemps; **he was killed** il a été tué, on l'a tué; **I've been waiting (for) two hours** j'attends depuis deux heures; **it is said** on dit; **to be pitied** à plaindre; **isn't it?, aren't you?** etc n'est-ce pas?, non?; **I am!, he is!** etc oui! 10 (+ inf) **he is to come** (must) il doit venir; **he's shortly to go** (intends to) il va bientôt partir. 11 **there is** or **are** il y a; (pointing) voilà; **here is** or **are** voici.

beach [biːtʃ] n plage f. ◆**beachcomber** n (person) ramasseur, -euse mf d'épaves.

beacon ['biːkən] n Nau Av balise f; (lighthouse) phare m.

bead [biːd] n (small sphere, drop of liquid) perle f; (of rosary) grain m; (of sweat) goutte f; (string of) **beads** collier m.

beak [biːk] n bec m.

beaker ['biːkər] n gobelet m.

beam [biːm] 1 n (of wood) poutre f. 2 n (of light) rayon m; (of headlight, torch) faisceau m (lumineux); – vi rayonner; (of person) Fig sourire largement. 3 vt Rad diffuser. ◆**—ing** a (radiant) radieux.

bean [biːn] n haricot m; (of coffee) grain m; (broad) **b.** fève f; **to be full of beans** Fam déborder d'entrain. ◆**beanshoots** npl, ◆**beansprouts** npl germes mpl de soja.

bear[1] [beər] n (animal) ours m.

bear[2] [beər] vt (pt bore, pp borne) (carry, show) porter; (endure) supporter; (resemblance) offrir; (comparison) soutenir; (responsibility) assumer; (child) donner naissance à; **to b. in mind** tenir compte de; **to b. out** corroborer; – vi **to b. left/etc** (turn) tourner à gauche/etc; **to b. north/etc** (go) aller en direction du nord/etc; **to b. (up)on** (relate to) se rapporter à; **to b. heavily on** (of burden) Fig peser sur; **to b. with** être indulgent envers, être patient avec; **to bring to b.** (one's energies) consacrer (on à);

(*pressure*) exercer (**on** sur); **to b. up** ne pas se décourager, tenir le coup; **b. up!** du courage! ◆**—ing** n (*posture, conduct*) maintien m; (*relationship, relevance*) relation f (**on** avec); Nau Av position f; **to get one's bearings** s'orienter. ◆**—able** a supportable. ◆**—er** n porteur, -euse mf.

beard [biəd] n barbe f. ◆**bearded** a barbu.

beast [biːst] n bête f, animal m; (*person*) Pej brute f. ◆**beastly** a Fam (*bad*) vilain, infect; (*spiteful*) méchant; – adv Fam terriblement.

beat [biːt] n (*of heart, drum*) battement m; (*of policeman*) ronde f; Mus mesure f, rythme m; – vt (pt **beat**, pp **beaten**) battre; (*defeat*) vaincre, battre; **to b. a drum** battre du tambour; **that beats me** Fam ça me dépasse; **to b. s.o. to it** devancer qn; **b. it!** Sl fichez le camp!; **to b. back** or **off** repousser; **to b. down** (*price*) faire baisser; **to b. in** or **down** (*door*) défoncer; **to b. out** (*rhythm*) marquer; (*tune*) jouer; **to b. s.o. up** tabasser qn; – vi battre; (*at door*) frapper (**at** à); **to b. about** or **around the bush** Fam tourner autour du pot; **to b. down** (*of rain*) tomber à verse; (*of sun*) taper. ◆**—ing** n (*blows, defeat*) raclée f. ◆**—er** n (*for eggs*) batteur m.

beauty ['bjuːtɪ] n (*quality, woman*) beauté f; **it's a b.!** c'est une merveille!; **the b. of it is** ... le plus beau, c'est que ... ; **b. parlour** institut m de beauté; **b. spot** (*on skin*) grain m de beauté; (*in countryside*) site m pittoresque. ◆**beau'tician** n esthéticienne f. ◆**beautiful** a (*très*) beau; (*superb*) merveilleux. ◆**beautifully** adv merveilleusement.

beaver ['biːvər] n castor m; – vi **to b. away** travailler dur (**at sth** à qch).

because [bɪ'kɒz] conj parce que; **b. of** à cause de.

beck [bek] n **at s.o.'s b. and call** aux ordres de qn.

beckon ['bekən] vti **to b. (to) s.o.** faire signe à qn (**to do** de faire).

becom/e [bɪ'kʌm] 1 vi (pt **became**, pp **become**) devenir; **to b. a painter** devenir peintre; **to b. thin** maigrir; **to b. worried** commencer à s'inquiéter; **what has b. of her?** qu'est-elle devenue? 2 vt **that hat becomes her** ce chapeau lui sied or lui va. ◆**—ing** a (*clothes*) seyant; (*modesty*) bienséant.

bed [bed] n lit m; Geol couche f; (*of vegetables*) carré m; (*of sea*) fond m; (*flower bed*) parterre m; **to go to b.** (aller) se coucher; **in b.** couché; **to get out of b.** se lever; **b. and**

breakfast (*in hotel etc*) chambre f avec petit déjeuner; **b. settee** (canapé m) convertible m; **air b.** matelas m pneumatique; – vt (-dd-) **to b. (out)** (*plant*) repiquer; – vi **to b. down** se coucher. ◆**bedding** n literie f. ◆**bedbug** n punaise f. ◆**bedclothes** npl couvertures fpl et draps mpl. ◆**bedridden** a alité. ◆**bedroom** n chambre f à coucher. ◆**bedside** n chevet m; – a (*lamp, book, table*) de chevet. ◆**bed'sitter** n, Fam ◆**bedsit** n chambre f meublée. ◆**bedspread** n dessus-de-lit m inv. ◆**bedtime** n heure f du coucher.

bedeck [bɪ'dek] vt orner (**with** de).

bedevil [bɪ'dev(ə)l] vt (-ll-, Am -l-) (*plague*) tourmenter; (*confuse*) embrouiller; **bedevilled by** (*problems etc*) perturbé par, empoisonné par.

bedlam ['bedləm] n (*noise*) Fam chahut m.

bedraggled [bɪ'dræg(ə)ld] a (*clothes, person*) débraillé.

bee [biː] n abeille f. ◆**beehive** n ruche f. ◆**beekeeping** n apiculture f. ◆**beeline** n **to make a b. for** aller droit vers.

beech [biːtʃ] n (*tree, wood*) hêtre m.

beef [biːf] 1 n bœuf m. 2 vi (*complain*) Sl rouspéter. ◆**beefburger** n hamburger m. ◆**beefy** a (-ier, -iest) Fam musclé, costaud.

beer [bɪər] n bière f; **b. glass** chope f. ◆**beery** a (*room, person*) qui sent la bière.

beet [biːt] n betterave f (à sucre); Am = beetroot. ◆**beetroot** n betterave f (potagère).

beetle ['biːt(ə)l] 1 n cafard m, scarabée m. 2 vi **to b. off** Fam se sauver.

befall [bɪ'fɔːl] vt (pt **befell**, pp **befallen**) arriver à.

befit [bɪ'fɪt] vt (-tt-) convenir à.

before [bɪ'fɔːr] adv avant; (*already*) déjà; (*in front*) devant; **the month b.** le mois d'avant or précédent; **the day b.** la veille; **I've never done it b.** je ne l'ai jamais (encore) fait; – prep (*time*) avant; (*place*) devant; **the year b. last** il y a deux ans; – conj avant que (+ ne + sub), avant de (+ inf); **b. he goes** avant qu'il (ne) parte; **b. going** avant de partir. ◆**beforehand** adv à l'avance, avant.

befriend [bɪ'frend] vt offrir son amitié à, aider.

befuddled [bɪ'fʌd(ə)ld] a (*drunk*) ivre.

beg [beg] vt (-gg-) **to b. (for)** solliciter, demander; (*bread, money*) mendier; **to b. s.o. to do** prier or supplier qn de faire; **I b. to** je me permets de; **to b. the question** esquiver la question; – vi mendier;

(*entreat*) supplier; **to go begging** (*of food, articles*) ne pas trouver d'amateurs. ◆**beggar** *n* mendiant, -ante *mf*; (*person*) *Sl* individu *m*; **lucky b.** veinard, -arde *mf*. ◆**beggarly** *a* misérable.

beget [bɪ'get] *vt* (*pt* begot, *pp* begotten, *pres p* begetting) engendrer.

begin [bɪ'gɪn] *vt* (*pt* began, *pp* begun, *pres p* beginning) commencer; (*fashion, campaign*) lancer; (*bottle, sandwich*) entamer; (*conversation*) engager; **to b. doing** *or* **to do** commencer *or* se mettre à faire; – *vi* commencer (**with** par, **by doing** par faire); **to b. on sth** commencer qch; **beginning from** à partir de; **to b. with** (*first*) d'abord. ◆—**ning** *n* commencement *m*, début *m*. ◆—**ner** *n* débutant, -ante *mf*.

begrudge [bɪ'grʌdʒ] *vt* (*give unwillingly*) donner à contrecœur; (*envy*) envier (**s.o. sth** qch à qn); (*reproach*) reprocher (**s.o. sth** qch à qn); **to b. doing** faire à contrecœur.

behalf [bɪ'hɑːf] *n* **on b. of** pour, au nom de, de la part de; (*in the interest of*) en faveur de, pour.

behave [bɪ'heɪv] *vi* se conduire; (*of machine*) fonctionner; **to b.** (**oneself**) se tenir bien; (*of child*) être sage. ◆**behaviour** *n* conduite *f*, comportement *m*; **to be on one's best b.** se conduire de son mieux.

behead [bɪ'hed] *vt* décapiter.

behest [bɪ'hest] *n Lit* ordre *m*.

behind [bɪ'haɪnd] **1** *prep* derrière; (*more backward than, late according to*) en retard sur; – *adv* derrière; (*late*) en retard (**with**, in dans). **2** *n* (*buttocks*) *Fam* derrière *m*. ◆**behindhand** *adv* en retard.

beholden [bɪ'həʊldən] *a* redevable (**to** à, **for** de).

beige [beɪʒ] *a* & *n* beige (*m*).

being [bɪːɪŋ] *n* (*person, life*) être *m*; **to come into b.** naître, être créé.

belated [bɪ'leɪtɪd] *a* tardif.

belch [beltʃ] **1** *vi* (*of person*) faire un renvoi, éructer; – *n* renvoi *m*. **2** *vt* **to b.** (**out**) (*smoke*) vomir.

beleaguered [bɪ'liːgəd] *a* (*besieged*) assiégé.

belfry ['belfrɪ] *n* beffroi *m*, clocher *m*.

Belgium ['beldʒəm] *n* Belgique *f*. ◆**Belgian** [beldʒən] *a* & *n* belge (*mf*).

belie [bɪ'laɪ] *vt* démentir.

belief [bɪ'liːf] *n* (*believing, thing believed*) croyance *f* (**in s.o.** en qn, **in sth** à *or* en qch); (*trust*) confiance *f*, foi *f*; (*faith*) *Rel* foi *f* (**in** en).

believ/e [bɪ'liːv] *vti* croire (**in sth** à qch, **in God/s.o.** en Dieu/qn); **I b. so** je crois que oui; **I b. I'm right** je crois avoir raison; **to b.**

in doing croire qu'il faut faire; **he doesn't b. in smoking** il désapprouve que l'on fume. ◆—**able** *a* croyable. ◆—**er** *n Rel* croyant, -ante *mf*; **b. in** (*supporter*) partisan, -ane *mf* de.

belittle [bɪ'lɪt(ə)l] *vt* déprécier.

bell [bel] *n* cloche *f*; (*small*) clochette *f*; (*in phone*) sonnerie *f*; (*on door, bicycle*) sonnette *f*; (*on dog*) grelot *m*. ◆**bellboy** *n*, ◆**bellhop** *n Am* groom *m*.

belle [bel] *n* (*woman*) beauté *f*, belle *f*.

belligerent [bɪ'lɪdʒərənt] *a* & *n* belligérant, -ante (*mf*).

bellow ['beləʊ] *vi* beugler, mugir.

bellows ['beləʊz] *npl* (**pair of**) **b.** soufflet *m*.

belly ['belɪ] *n* ventre *m*; **b. button** *Sl* nombril *m*. ◆**bellyache** *n* mal *m* au ventre; – *vi* rouspéter. ◆**bellyful** *n* **to have a b.** *Sl* en avoir plein le dos.

belong [bɪ'lɒŋ] *vi* appartenir (**to** à); **to b. to** (*club*) être membre de; **the cup belongs here** la tasse se range ici. ◆—**ings** *npl* affaires *fpl*.

beloved [bɪ'lʌvɪd] *a* & *n* bien-aimé, -ée (*mf*).

below [bɪ'ləʊ] *prep* (*lower than*) au-dessous de; (*under*) sous, au-dessous de; (*unworthy of*) *Fig* indigne de; – *adv* en dessous; **see b.** (*in book etc*) voir ci-dessous.

belt [belt] **1** *n* ceinture *f*; (*area*) zone *f*, région *f*; *Tech* courroie *f*. **2** *vt* (*hit*) *Sl* rosser. **3** *vi* **to b.** (**along**) (*rush*) *Sl* filer à toute allure; **b. up!** (*shut up*) *Sl* boucle-la!

bemoan [bɪ'məʊn] *vt* déplorer.

bench [bentʃ] *n* (*seat*) banc *m*; (*work table*) établi *m*, banc *m*; **the B.** *Jur* la magistrature (assise); (*court*) le tribunal.

bend [bend] *n* courbe *f*; (*in river, pipe*) coude *m*; (*in road*) *Aut* virage *m*; (*of arm, knee*) pli *m*; **round the b.** (*mad*) *Sl* tordu; – *vt* (*pt* & *pp* bent) courber; (*leg, arm*) plier; (*direct*) diriger; **to b. the rules** faire une entorse au règlement; – *vi* (*of branch*) plier, être courbé; (*of road*) tourner; **to b.** (**down**) se courber; **to b.** (**over** *or* **forward**) se pencher; **to b. to** (*s.o.'s will*) se soumettre à.

beneath [bɪ'niːθ] *prep* au-dessous de, sous; (*unworthy of*) indigne de; – *adv* (au-)dessous.

benediction [benɪ'dɪkʃ(ə)n] *n* bénédiction *f*.

benefactor ['benɪfæktər] *n* bienfaiteur *m*. ◆**benefactress** *n* bienfaitrice *f*.

beneficial [benɪ'fɪʃəl] *a* bénéfique.

beneficiary [benɪ'fɪʃərɪ] *n* bénéficiaire *mf*.

benefit ['benɪfɪt] *n* (*advantage*) avantage *m*; (*money*) allocation *f*; *pl* (*of science, education etc*) bienfaits *mpl*; **to s.o.'s b.** dans l'intérêt de qn; **for your** (**own**) **b.** pour vous, pour votre bien; **to be of b.** faire du bien (to à); **to give s.o. the b. of the doubt** accorder à qn le bénéfice du doute; **b. concert**/*etc* concert/*etc* m de bienfaisance; – *vt* faire du bien à; (*be useful to*) profiter à; – *vi* gagner (**from doing** à faire); **you'll b. from** *or* **by the rest** le repos vous fera du bien.

Benelux ['benɪlʌks] *n* Bénélux *m*.

benevolent [bɪ'nevələnt] *a* bienveillant. ◆**benevolence** *n* bienveillance *f*.

benign [bɪ'naɪn] *a* bienveillant, bénin; (*climate*) doux; (*tumour*) bénin.

bent [bent] **1** *a* (*nail, mind*) tordu; (*dishonest*) *Sl* corrompu; **b. on doing** résolu à faire. **2** *n* (*talent*) aptitude *f* (**for** pour); (*inclination, liking*) penchant *m*, goût *m* (**for** pour).

bequeath [bɪ'kwiːð] *vt* léguer (**to** à). ◆**bequest** *n* legs *m*.

bereaved [bɪ'riːvd] *a* endeuillé; – *n* **the b.** la famille, la femme *etc* du disparu. ◆**bereavement** *n* deuil *m*.

bereft [bɪ'reft] *a* **b. of** dénué de.

beret ['bereɪ, *Am* bə'reɪ] *n* béret *m*.

berk [bɜːk] *n* *Sl* imbécile *mf*.

Bermuda [bə'mjuːdə] *n* Bermudes *fpl*.

berry ['berɪ] *n* baie *f*.

berserk [bə'zɜːk] *a* **to go b.** devenir fou, se déchaîner.

berth [bɜːθ] *n* (*in ship, train*) couchette *f*; (*anchorage*) mouillage *m*; – *vi* (*of ship*) mouiller.

beseech [bɪ'siːtʃ] *vt* (*pt & pp* besought *or* beseeched) *Lit* implorer (**to do** de faire).

beset [bɪ'set] *vt* (*pt & pp* beset, *pres p* besetting) assaillir (*qn*); **b. with obstacles**/*etc* semé *or* hérissé d'obstacles/*etc*.

beside [bɪ'saɪd] *prep* à côté de; **that's b. the point** ça n'a rien à voir; **b. oneself** (*angry, excited*) hors de soi.

besides [bɪ'saɪdz] *prep* (*in addition to*) en plus de; (*except*) excepté; **there are ten of us b.** Paul nous sommes dix sans compter Paul; – *adv* (*in addition*) de plus; (*moreover*) d'ailleurs.

besiege [bɪ'siːdʒ] *vt* (*of soldiers, crowd*) assiéger; (*annoy*) *Fig* assaillir (**with** de).

besotted [bɪ'sɒtɪd] *a* (*drunk*) abruti; **b. with** (*infatuated*) entiché de.

bespatter [bɪ'spætər] *vt* éclabousser (**with** de).

bespectacled [bɪ'spektɪk(ə)ld] *a* à lunettes.

bespoke [bɪ'spəʊk] *a* (*tailor*) à façon.

best [best] *a* meilleur; **the b. page in the book** la meilleure page du livre; **the b. part of** (*most*) la plus grande partie de; **the b. thing** le mieux; **b. man** (*at wedding*) témoin *m*, garçon *m* d'honneur; – *n* **the b. (one)** le

meilleur, la meilleure; **it's for the b.** c'est pour le mieux; **at b.** au mieux; **to do one's b.** faire de son mieux; **to look one's b., be at one's b.** être à son avantage; **to the b. of my knowledge** autant que je sache; **to make the b. of** (*accept*) s'accommoder de; **to get the b. of it** avoir le dessus; **in one's Sunday b.** endimanché; **all the b.!** portez-vous bien!; (*in letter*) amicalement; – *adv* (**the**) **b.** (*to play etc*) le mieux; **the b. loved** le plus aimé; **to think it b. to** juger prudent de ◆**b.-'seller** *n* (*book*) best-seller *m*.

bestow [bɪ'stəʊ] *vt* accorder, conférer (**on** à).

bet [bet] *n* pari *m*; – *vti* (*pt & pp* bet *or* betted, *pres p* betting) parier (**on** sur, **that** que); **you b.!** *Fam* (*of course*) tu parles! ◆**betting** *n* pari(s) *m*(*pl*); **b. shop** *or* **office** bureau *m* du pari mutuel.

betoken [bɪ'təʊkən] *vt* *Lit* annoncer.

betray [bɪ'treɪ] *vt* trahir; **to b. to s.o.** (*give away to*) livrer à qn. ◆**betrayal** *n* (*disloyalty*) trahison *f*; (*disclosure*) révélation *f*.

better ['betər] *a* meilleur (**than** que); **she's (much) b.** *Med* elle va (bien) mieux; **he's b. than** (*at games*) il joue mieux que; (*at maths etc*) il est plus fort que; **that's b.** c'est mieux; **to get b.** (*recover*) se remettre; (*improve*) s'améliorer; **it's b. to go** il vaut mieux partir; **the b. part of** (*most*) la grande partie de; – *adv* mieux; **I had b. go** il vaut mieux que je parte; **so much the b., all the b.** tant mieux (**for** pour); – *n* **to get the b. of s.o.** l'emporter sur qn; **change for the b.** amélioration *f*; **one's betters** ses supérieurs *mpl*; – *vt* (*improve*) améliorer; (*outdo*) dépasser; **to b. oneself** améliorer sa condition. ◆—**ment** *n* amélioration *f*.

between [bɪ'twiːn] *prep* entre; **we did it b. (the two of) us** nous l'avons fait à nous deux; **b. you and me** entre nous; **in b.** entre; – *adv* **in b.** (*space*) au milieu, entre les deux; (*time*) dans l'intervalle.

bevel ['bevəl] *n* (*edge*) biseau *m*.

beverage ['bevərɪdʒ] *n* boisson *f*.

bevy ['bevɪ] *n* (*of girls*) essaim *m*, bande *f*.

beware [bɪ'weər] *vi* **to b. of** (*s.o., sth*) se méfier de, prendre garde à; **b.!** méfiez-vous!, prenez garde!; **b. of falling**/*etc* prenez garde de (ne pas) tomber/*etc*; **'b. of the trains'** 'attention aux trains'.

bewilder [bɪ'wɪldər] *vt* dérouter, rendre perplexe. ◆—**ment** *n* confusion *f*.

bewitch [bɪ'wɪtʃ] *vt* enchanter. ◆—**ing** *a* enchanteur.

beyond [bɪ'jɒnd] *prep* (*further than*) au-delà

de; (*reach, doubt*) hors de; (*except*) sauf; **b. a year**/*etc* (*longer than*) plus d'un an/*etc*; **b. belief** incroyable; **b. his** *or* **her means** au-dessus de ses moyens; **it's b. me** ça me dépasse; – *adv* (*further*) au-delà.

bias ['baɪəs] **1** *n* penchant *m* (**towards** pour); (*prejudice*) préjugé *m*, parti pris *m*; – *vt* (-**ss**- *or* -**s**-) influencer. **2** *n* cut on the **b**. (*fabric*) coupé dans le biais. ◆**bias(s)ed** *a* partial; **to be b. against** avoir des préjugés contre.

bib [bɪb] *n* (*baby's*) bavoir *m*.

bible ['baɪb(ə)l] *n* bible *f*; **the B.** la Bible. ◆**biblical** ['bɪblɪk(ə)l] *a* biblique.

bibliography [bɪblɪ'ɒɡrəfɪ] *n* bibliographie *f*.

bicarbonate [baɪ'kɑːbənət] *n* bicarbonate *m*.

bicentenary [baɪsen'tiːnərɪ] *n*, ◆**bicentennial** *n* bicentenaire *m*.

biceps ['baɪseps] *n* *Anat* biceps *m*.

bicker ['bɪkər] *vi* se chamailler. ◆**—ing** *n* chamailleries *fpl*.

bicycle ['baɪsɪk(ə)l] *n* bicyclette *f*; – *vi* faire de la bicyclette.

bid [bɪd] *vt* (*pt & pp* **bid**, *pres p* **bidding**) offrir, faire une offre de; – *vi* faire une offre (**for** pour); **to b. for** *Fig* tenter d'obtenir; – *n* (*at auction*) offre *f*, enchère *f*; (*tender*) *Com* soumission *f*; (*attempt*) tentative *f*. ◆**—ding** *n* enchères *fpl*. ◆**—der** *n* enchérisseur *m*; soumissionnaire *mf*; **to the highest b.** au plus offrant.

bid[2] [bɪd] *vt* (*pt* **bade** [bæd], *pp* **bidden** *or* **bid**, *pres p* **bidding**) (*command*) commander (**s.o. to do** à qn de faire); (*say*) dire. ◆**—ding**[2] *n* ordre(s) *m*(*pl*).

bide [baɪd] *vt* **to b. one's time** attendre le bon moment.

bier [bɪər] *n* (*for coffin*) brancards *mpl*.

bifocals [baɪ'fəʊkəlz] *npl* verres *mpl* à double foyer.

big [bɪɡ] *a* (**bigger, biggest**) grand, gros; (*in age, generous*) grand; (*in bulk, amount*) gros; **b. deal!** *Am Fam* (bon) et alors!; **b. mouth** *Fam* grande gueule *f*; **b. toe** gros orteil *m*; – *adv* **to do things b.** *Fam* faire grand; **to talk b.** fanfaronner. ◆**bighead** *n*, ◆**big'headed** *a* *Fam* prétentieux, crâne (*mf*). ◆**big-'hearted** *a* généreux. ◆**big-shot** *n*, ◆**bigwig** *n* *Fam* gros bonnet *m*. ◆**big-time** *a* *Fam* important.

bigamy ['bɪɡəmɪ] *n* bigamie *f*. ◆**bigamist** *n* bigame *mf*. ◆**bigamous** *a* bigame.

bigot ['bɪɡət] *n* fanatique *mf*; *Rel* bigot, -ote *mf*. ◆**bigoted** *a* fanatique; *Rel* bigot.

bike [baɪk] *n* *Fam* vélo *m*; – *vi* *Fam* aller à vélo.

bikini [bɪ'kiːnɪ] *n* bikini *m*.

bilberry ['bɪlbərɪ] *n* myrtille *f*.

bile [baɪl] *n* bile *f*. ◆**bilious** ['bɪlɪəs] *a* bilieux.

bilge [bɪldʒ] *n* (*nonsense*) *Sl* foutaises *fpl*.

bilingual [baɪ'lɪŋɡwəl] *a* bilingue.

bill [bɪl] **1** *n* (*of bird*) bec *m*. **2** *n* (*invoice*) facture *f*, note *f*; (*in restaurant*) addition *f*; (*in hotel*) note *f*; (*draft*) *Com* effet *m*; (*of sale*) acte *m*; (*banknote*) *Am* billet *m*; (*law*) *Pol* projet *m* de loi; (*poster*) affiche *f*; **b. of fare** menu *m*; **b. of rights** déclaration *f* des droits; – *vt* *Th* mettre à l'affiche, annoncer; **to b. s.o.** *Com* envoyer la facture à qn. ◆**billboard** *n* panneau *m* d'affichage. ◆**billfold** *n* *Am* portefeuille *m*.

billet ['bɪlɪt] *vt* *Mil* cantonner; – *n* cantonnement *m*.

billiard ['bɪljəd] *a* (*table etc*) de billard. ◆**billiards** *npl* (jeu *m* de) billard *m*.

billion ['bɪljən] *n* billion *m*; *Am* milliard *m*.

billow ['bɪləʊ] *n* flot *m*; – *vi* (*of sea*) se soulever; (*of smoke*) tourbillonner.

billy-goat ['bɪlɪɡəʊt] *n* bouc *m*.

bimonthly [baɪ'mʌnθlɪ] *a* (*fortnightly*) bimensuel; (*every two months*) bimestriel.

bin [bɪn] *n* boîte *f*; (*for bread*) coffre *m*, huche *f*; (*for litter*) boîte *f* à ordures, poubelle *f*.

binary ['baɪnərɪ] *a* binaire.

bind [baɪnd] **1** *vt* (*pt & pp* **bound**) lier; (*fasten*) attacher, lier; (*book*) relier; (*fabric, hem*) border; **to b. s.o. to do** *Jur* obliger *or* astreindre qn à faire. **2** *n* (*bore*) *Fam* plaie *f*. ◆**—ing** *n* (*contract*) irrévocable; **to be b. on s.o.** *Jur* lier qn. **2** *n* (*of book*) reliure *f*. ◆**—er** *n* (*for papers*) classeur *m*.

binge [bɪndʒ] *n* **to go on a b.** *Sl* faire la bringue.

bingo ['bɪŋɡəʊ] *n* loto *m*.

binoculars [bɪ'nɒkjʊləz] *npl* jumelles *fpl*.

biochemistry [baɪəʊ'kemɪstrɪ] *n* biochimie *f*.

biodegradable [baɪəʊdɪ'ɡreɪdəb(ə)l] *a* biodégradable.

biography [baɪ'ɒɡrəfɪ] *n* biographie *f*. ◆**biographer** *n* biographe *mf*.

biology [baɪ'ɒlədʒɪ] *n* biologie *f*. ◆**bio'logical** *a* biologique.

biped ['baɪped] *n* bipède *m*.

birch [bɜːtʃ] *n* **1** (*tree*) bouleau *m*. **2** (*whip*) verge *f*; – *vt* fouetter.

bird [bɜːd] *n* oiseau *m*; (*fowl*) *Culin* volaille *f*; (*girl*) *Sl* poulette *f*, nana *f*; **b.'s-eye view**

perspective *f* à vol d'oiseau; *Fig* vue *f*
d'ensemble. ◆**birdseed** *n* grains *mpl* de
millet.
biro® ['baɪərəʊ] *n* (*pl* -os) stylo *m* à bille,
bic® *m*.
birth [bɜːθ] *n* naissance *f*; **to give b. to**
donner naissance à; **b. certificate** acte *m* de
naissance; **b. control** limitation *f* des naissances. ◆**birthday** *n* anniversaire *m*;
happy b.! bon anniversaire! ◆**birthplace**
n lieu *m* de naissance; (*house*) maison *f*
natale. ◆**birthrate** *n* (taux *m* de) natalité *f*.
◆**birthright** *n* droit *m* (*qu'on a dès sa naissance*), patrimoine *m*.
biscuit ['bɪskɪt] *n* biscuit *m*, gâteau *m* sec;
Am petit pain *m* au lait.
bishop ['bɪʃəp] *n* évêque *m*; (*in chess*) fou *m*.
bison ['baɪs(ə)n] *n inv* bison *m*.
bit¹ [bɪt] *n* **1** morceau *m*; (*of string, time*)
bout *m*; **a b.** (*a little*) un peu; **a tiny b.** un
tout petit peu; **quite a b.** (*very*) très; (*much*)
beaucoup; **not a b.** pas du tout; **a b. of luck**
une chance; **b. by b.** petit à petit; **in bits
(and pieces)** en morceaux; **to come to bits**
se démonter. **2** (*coin*) pièce *f*. **3** (*of horse*)
mors *m*. **4** (*of drill*) mèche *f*. **5** (*computer
information*) bit *m*.
bit² [bɪt] *see* bite.
bitch [bɪtʃ] **1** *n* chienne *f*; (*woman*) *Pej Fam*
garce *f*. **2** *vi* (*complain*) *Fam* râler. ◆**bitchy**
a (-ier, -iest) *Fam* vache.
bit/e [baɪt] *n* (*wound*) morsure *f*; (*from
insect*) piqûre *f*; *Fishing* touche *f*; (*mouthful*) bouchée *f*; (*of style etc*) *Fig* mordant
m; **a b. to eat** un morceau à manger; – *vti*
(*pt* bit, *pp* bitten) mordre; (*of insect*)
piquer, mordre; **to b. one's nails** se ronger
les ongles; **to b. on sth** mordre qch; **to b. sth
off** arracher qch d'un coup de dent(s).
◆**—ing** *a* mordant; (*wind*) cinglant.
bitter ['bɪtər] **1** *a* (*person, taste, irony etc*)
amer; (*cold, wind*) glacial, âpre; (*criticism*)
acerbe; (*shock, fate*) cruel; (*conflict*)
violent. **2** *n* bière *f* (pression). ◆**—ness** *n*
amertume *f*; âpreté *f*; violence *f*. ◆**bitter-
'sweet** *a* aigre-doux.
bivouac ['bɪvuæk] *n Mil* bivouac *m*; – *vi*
(-ck-) bivouaquer.
bizarre [bɪ'zɑːr] *a* bizarre.
blab [blæb] *vi* (-bb-) jaser. ◆**blabber** *vi*
jaser. ◆**blabbermouth** *n* jaseur, -euse *mf*.
black [blæk] *a* (-er, -est) noir; **b. eye** œil *m*
au beurre noir; **to give s.o. a b. eye** pocher
l'œil à qn; **b. and blue** (*bruised*) couvert de
bleus; **b. sheep** *Fig* brebis *f* galeuse; **b. ice**
verglas *m*; **b. pudding** boudin *m*; – *n*
(*colour*) noir *m*; (*Negro*) Noir, -e *mf*; – *vt*

noircir; (*refuse to deal with*) boycotter; – *vi*
to b. out (*faint*) s'évanouir. ◆**blacken** *vti*
noircir. ◆**blackish** *a* noirâtre. ◆**blackness** *n* noirceur *f*; (*of night*) obscurité *f*.
blackberry ['blækbərɪ] *n* mûre *f*.
◆**blackbird** *n* merle *m*. ◆**blackboard** *n*
tableau *m* (noir). ◆**black'currant** *n* cassis
m. ◆**blackleg** *n* (*strike breaker*) jaune *m*.
◆**blacklist** *n* liste *f* noire; – *vt* mettre sur
la liste noire. ◆**blackmail** *n* chantage *m*;
– *vt* faire chanter. ◆**blackmailer** *n* maître
chanteur *m*. ◆**blackout** *n* panne *f*
d'électricité; (*during war*) *Mil* black-out *m*;
Med syncope *f*; (**news**) **b.** black-out *m*.
◆**blacksmith** *n* forgeron *m*.
blackguard ['blægɑːd, -gəd] *n* canaille *f*.
bladder ['blædər] *n* vessie *f*.
blade [bleɪd] *n* lame *f*; (*of grass*) brin *m*; (*of
windscreen wiper*) caoutchouc *m*.
blame [bleɪm] *vt* accuser; (*censure*) blâmer;
to b. sth on s.o. or **s.o. for sth** rejeter la
responsabilité de qch sur qn; **to b. s.o. for
sth** (*reproach*) reprocher qch à qn; **you're to
b.** c'est ta faute; – *n* faute *f*; (*censure*)
blâme *m*. ◆**—less** *a* irréprochable.
blanch [blɑːntʃ] *vt* (*vegetables*) blanchir; –
vi (*turn pale with fear etc*) blêmir.
blancmange [blə'mɒnʒ] *n* blanc-manger *m*.
bland [blænd] *a* (-er, -est) doux; (*food*)
fade.
blank [blæŋk] *a* (*paper, page*) blanc, vierge;
(*cheque*) en blanc; (*look, mind*) vide;
(*puzzled*) ébahi; (*refusal*) absolu; – *a* & *n*
b. (space) blanc *m*; **b. (cartridge)** cartouche
f à blanc; **my mind's a b.** j'ai la tête vide.
◆**blankly** *adv* sans expression.
blanket ['blæŋkɪt] **1** *n* couverture *f*; (*of snow
etc*) *Fig* couche *f*; – *vt* (*cover*) *Fig* recouvrir.
2 *a* (*term etc*) général. ◆**—ing** *n* (*blankets*)
couvertures *fpl*.
blare [bleər] *n* (*noise*) beuglement *m*; (*of
trumpet*) sonnerie *f*; – *vi* **to b.** (**out**) (*of
radio*) beugler; (*of music, car horn*) retentir.
blarney ['blɑːnɪ] *n Fam* boniment(s) *m(pl)*.
blasé ['blɑːzeɪ] *a* blasé.
blaspheme [blæs'fiːm] *vti* blasphémer.
◆**'blasphemous** *a* blasphématoire;
(*person*) blasphémateur. ◆**'blasphemy** *n*
blasphème *m*.
blast [blɑːst] **1** *n* explosion *f*; (*air from
explosion*) souffle *m*; (*of wind*) rafale *f*,
coup *m*; (*of trumpet*) sonnerie *f*; (**at**) **full b.**
(*loud*) à plein volume; (*fast*) à pleine
vitesse; **b. furnace** haut fourneau *m*; – *vt*
(*blow up*) faire sauter; (*hopes*) *Fig* détruire;
to b. s.o. *Fam* réprimander qn. **2** *int* zut!,

merde! ◆—ed *a Fam* fichu. ◆blast-off *n*
(*of spacecraft*) mise *f* à feu.

blatant ['bleɪtənt] *a* (*obvious*) flagrant,
criant; (*shameless*) éhonté.

blaz/e [bleɪz] **1** *n* (*fire*) flamme *f*, feu *m*;
(*conflagration*) incendie *m*; (*splendour*) *Fig*
éclat *m*; **b. of light** torrent *m* de lumière; −
vi (*of fire*) flamber; (*of sun, colour, eyes*)
flamboyer. **2** *vt* **to b. a trail** marquer la voie.
◆—ing *a* (*burning*) en feu; (*sun*) brûlant;
(*argument*) *Fig* violent.

blazer ['bleɪzər] *n* blazer *m*.

bleach [bliːtʃ] *n* décolorant *m*; (*household
detergent*) eau *f* de Javel; − *vt* (*hair*)
décolorer, oxygéner; (*linen*) blanchir.

bleak [bliːk] *a* (*-er, -est*) (*appearance, future
etc*) morne; (*countryside*) désolé.

bleary ['blɪərɪ] *a* (*eyes*) troubles, voilés.

bleat [bliːt] *vi* bêler.

bleed [bliːd] *vti* (*pt & pp* bled) saigner; **to b.
to death** perdre tout son sang. ◆—ing *a*
(*wound*) saignant; (*bloody*) *Sl* fichu.

bleep [bliːp] *n* signal *m*, bip *m*; − *vt* appeler
au bip-bip. ◆bleeper *n* bip-bip *m*.

blemish ['blemɪʃ] *n* (*fault*) défaut *m*; (*on
fruit, reputation*) tache *f*; − *vt* (*reputation*)
ternir.

blend [blend] *n* mélange *m*; − *vt* mélanger;
− *vi* se mélanger; (*go together*) se marier
(**with** avec). ◆—er *n* *Culin* mixer *m*.

bless [bles] *vt* bénir; **to be blessed with** avoir
le bonheur de posséder; **b. you!** (*sneezing*) à
vos souhaits! ◆—ed [-ɪd] *a* saint, béni;
(*happy*) *Rel* bienheureux; (*blasted*) *Fam*
fichu, sacré. ◆—ing *n* bénédiction *f*;
(*divine favour*) grâce *f*; (*benefit*) bienfait *m*;
what a b. that . . . quelle chance que . . . .

blew [bluː] *see* blow[1].

blight [blaɪt] *n* (*on plants*) rouille *f*; (*scourge*)
Fig fléau *m*; **to be** *or* **cast a b. on** avoir une
influence néfaste sur; **urban b.** (*area*)
quartier *m* délabré; (*condition*) délabrement *m* (de quartier). ◆blighter *n* *Pej
Fam* type *m*.

blimey! ['blaɪmɪ] *int Fam* zut!, mince!

blimp [blɪmp] *n* dirigeable *m*.

blind [blaɪnd] **1** *a* aveugle; **b. person** aveugle
mf; **b. in one eye** borgne; **he's b. to** (*fault*) il
ne voit pas; **to turn a b. eye to** fermer les
yeux sur; **b. alley** impasse *f*; − *n* **the b.** les
aveugles *mpl*; − *vt* aveugler. **2** *n* (*on
window*) store *m*; (*deception*) feinte *f*.
◆—ly *adv* aveuglément. ◆—ness *n* cécité
f; *Fig* aveuglement *m*. ◆blinders *npl Am*
œillères *fpl*. ◆blindfold *n* bandeau *m*; −
vt bander les yeux à; − *adv* les yeux bandés.

blink [blɪŋk] *vi* cligner des yeux; (*of eyes*)

cligner; (*of light*) clignoter; − *vt* **to b. one's
eyes** cligner des yeux; − *n* clignement *m*;
on the b. (*machine*) *Fam* détraqué. ◆—ing
a (*bloody*) *Fam* sacré. ◆blinkers *npl* (*for
horse*) œillères *fpl*; (*indicators*) *Aut* cligno-
tants *mpl*.

bliss [blɪs] *n* félicité *f*. ◆blissful *a* (*happy*)
très joyeux; (*wonderful*) merveilleux.
◆blissfully *adv* (*happy, unaware*) parfaitement.

blister ['blɪstər] *n* (*on skin*) ampoule *f*; − *vi*
se couvrir d'ampoules.

blithe [blaɪð] *a* joyeux.

blitz [blɪts] *n* (*attack*) *Av* raid *m* éclair;
(*bombing*) bombardement *m* aérien; *Fig
Fam* offensive *f*; − *vt* bombarder.

blizzard ['blɪzəd] *n* tempête *f* de neige.

bloat [bləʊt] *vt* gonfler.

bloater ['bləʊtər] *n* hareng *m* saur.

blob [blɒb] *n* (*of water*) (grosse) goutte *f*; (*of
ink, colour*) tache *f*.

bloc [blɒk] *n* *Pol* bloc *m*.

block [blɒk] **1** *n* (*of stone etc*) bloc *m*; (*of
buildings*) pâté *m* (de maisons); (*in pipe*)
obstruction *f*; (*mental*) blocage *m*; **b. of
flats** immeuble *m*; **a b. away** *Am* une rue
plus loin; **school b.** groupe *m* scolaire; **b.
capitals** *or* **letters** majuscules *fpl*. **2** *vt*
(*obstruct*) bloquer; (*pipe*) boucher;
(*one's view*) boucher; **to b. off** (*road*) barrer; (*light*) intercepter; **to b. up**
(*pipe, hole*) bloquer. ◆blo'ckade *n*
blocus *m*; − *vt* bloquer. ◆blockage *n*
obstruction *f*. ◆blockbuster *n* *Cin* superproduction *f*, film *m* à grand spectacle.
◆blockhead *n* imbécile *mf*.

bloke [bləʊk] *n* *Fam* type *m*.

blond [blɒnd] *a* & *n* blond (*m*). ◆blonde *a*
& *n* blonde (*f*).

blood [blʌd] *n* sang *m*; − *a* (*group, orange
etc*) sanguin; (*donor, bath etc*) de sang;
(*poisoning etc*) du sang; **b. pressure** tension
f (artérielle); **high b. pressure** (hyper)ten-
sion *f*. ◆bloodcurdling *a* à vous tourner
le sang. ◆bloodhound *n* (*dog, detective*)
limier *m*. ◆bloodletting *n* saignée *f*.
◆bloodshed *n* effusion *f* de sang.
◆bloodshot *a* (*eye*) injecté de sang.
◆bloodsucker *n* (*insect, person*) sangsue
f. ◆bloodthirsty *a* sanguinaire.

bloody ['blʌdɪ] **1** *a* (*-ier, -iest*) sanglant. **2** *a*
(*blasted*) *Fam* sacré; − *adv Fam* vache-
ment. ◆b.-'minded *a* hargneux, pas
commode.

bloom [bluːm] *n* fleur *f*; **in b.** en fleur(s); − *vi*
fleurir; (*of person*) *Fig* s'épanouir. ◆—ing

a 1 (*in bloom*) en fleur(s); (*thriving*) florissant. 2 (*blinking*) *Fam* fichu.

bloomer ['bluːmər] *n Fam* (*mistake*) gaffe *f*.

blossom ['blɒsəm] *n* fleur(s) *f*(*pl*); – *vi* fleurir; **to b. (out)** (*of person*) s'épanouir; **to b. (out) into** devenir.

blot [blɒt] *n* tache *f*; – *vt* (-tt-) tacher; (*dry*) sécher; **to b. out** (*word*) rayer; (*memory*) effacer. ◆**blotting** *a* **b. paper** (papier *m*) buvard *m*. ◆**blotter** *n* buvard *m*.

blotch [blɒtʃ] *n* tache *f*. ◆**blotchy** *a* (-ier, -iest) couvert de taches; (*face*) marbré.

blouse [blauz, *Am* blaus] *n* chemisier *m*.

blow [bləu] *vt* (*pt* **blew**, *pp* **blown**) (*of wind*) pousser (*un navire etc*), chasser (*la pluie etc*); (*smoke, glass*) souffler; (*bubbles*) faire; (*trumpet*) souffler dans; (*fuse*) faire sauter; (*kiss*) envoyer (**to** à); (*money*) *Fam* claquer; **to b. one's nose** se moucher; **to b. a whistle** siffler; **to b. away** (*of wind*) emporter; **to b. down** (*chimney etc*) faire tomber; **to b. off** (*hat etc*) emporter; (*arm*) arracher; **to b. out** (*candle*) souffler; (*cheeks*) gonfler; **to b. up** (*building etc*) faire sauter; (*tyre*) gonfler; (*photo*) agrandir; – *vi* (*of wind, person*) souffler; (*of fuse*) sauter; (*of papers etc*) s'éparpiller; **b.! Fam** zut!; **to b. down** (*fall*) tomber; **to b. off** *or* **away** s'envoler; **to b. out** (*of light*) s'éteindre; **to b. over** (*pass*) passer; **to b. up** (*explode*) exploser. ◆**—er** *n* (*telephone*) *Fam* bigophone *m*. ◆**blow-dry** *n* brushing *m*. ◆**blowlamp** *n* chalumeau *m*. ◆**blowout** *n* (*of tyre*) éclatement *m*; (*meal*) *Sl* gueuleton *m*. ◆**blowtorch** *n Am* chalumeau *m*. ◆**blow-up** *n Phot* agrandissement *m*.

blow² [bləu] *n* coup *m*; **to come to blows** en venir aux mains.

blowy ['bləuɪ] *a* **it's b.** *Fam* il y a du vent.

blowzy ['blauzɪ] *a* **b. woman** (*slovenly*) *Fam* femme *f* débraillée.

blubber ['blʌbər] *n* graisse *f* (de baleine).

bludgeon ['blʌdʒən] *n* gourdin *m*; – *vt* matraquer.

blue [bluː] *a* (**bluer, bluest**) bleu; **to feel b.** *Fam* avoir le cafard; **b. film** *Fam* film *m* porno; – *n* bleu *m*; **the blues** (*depression*) *Fam* le cafard; *Mus* le blues. ◆**bluebell** *n* jacinthe *f* des bois. ◆**blueberry** *n* airelle *f*. ◆**bluebottle** *n* mouche *f* à viande. ◆**blueprint** *n Fig* plan *m* (de travail).

bluff [blʌf] 1 *a* (*person*) brusque, direct. 2 *vti* bluffer; – *n* bluff *m*.

blunder ['blʌndər] 1 *n* (*mistake*) bévue *f*, gaffe *f*; – *vi* faire une bévue. 2 *vi* (*move awkwardly*) avancer à tâtons. ◆**—ing** *a* maladroit; – *n* maladresse *f*.

blunt [blʌnt] *a* (-er, -est) (*edge*) émoussé; (*pencil*) épointé; (*person*) brusque; (*speech*) franc; – *vt* émousser; épointer. ◆**—ly** *adv* carrément. ◆**—ness** *n Fig* brusquerie *f*; (*of speech*) franchise *f*.

blur [blɜːr] *n* tache *f* floue, contour *m* imprécis; – *vt* (-rr-) estomper, rendre flou; (*judgment*) *Fig* troubler. ◆**blurred** *a* (*image*) flou, estompé.

blurb [blɜːb] *n Fam* résumé *m* publicitaire, laïus *m*.

blurt [blɜːt] *vt* **to b. (out)** laisser échapper, lâcher.

blush [blʌʃ] *vi* rougir (**at, with** de); – *n* rougeur *f*; **with a b.** en rougissant.

bluster ['blʌstər] *vi* (*of person*) tempêter; (*of wind*) faire rage. ◆**blustery** *a* (*weather*) de grand vent, à bourrasques.

boa ['bəuə] *n* (*snake*) boa *m*.

boar [bɔːr] *n* (*wild*) **b.** sanglier *m*.

board¹ [bɔːd] 1 *n* (*piece of wood*) planche *f*; (*for notices, games etc*) tableau *m*; (*cardboard*) carton *m*; (*committee*) conseil *m*, commission *f*; **b. (of directors)** conseil *m* d'administration; **on b.** *Nau Av* à bord (de); **B. of Trade** *Br Pol* ministère *m* du Commerce; **across the b.** (*pay rise*) général; **to go by the b.** (*of plan*) être abandonné. 2 *vt Nau Av* monter à bord de; (*bus, train*) monter dans; **to b. up** (*door*) boucher. ◆**—ing** *n Nau Av* embarquement *m*. ◆**boardwalk** *n Am* promenade *f*.

board² [bɔːd] *n* (*food*) pension *f*; **b. and lodging, bed and b.** (chambre *f* avec) pension *f*; (*in lodge*) être en pension (**with** chez); **boarding house** pension *f* (de famille); **boarding school** pensionnat *m*. ◆**—er** *n* pensionnaire *mf*.

boast [bəust] *vi* se vanter (**about, of** de); – *vt* se glorifier de; **to b. that one can do . . .** se vanter de (pouvoir) faire . . . ; – *n* vantardise *f*. ◆**—ing** *n* vantardise *f*. ◆**boastful** *a* vantard. ◆**boastfully** *adv* en se vantant.

boat [bəut] *n* bateau *m*; (*small*) barque *f*, canot *m*; (*liner*) paquebot *m*; **in the same b.** *Fig* logé à la même enseigne; **b. race** course *f* d'aviron. ◆**—ing** *n* canotage *m*; **b. trip** excursion *f* en bateau.

boatswain ['bəus(ə)n] *n* maître *m* d'équipage.

bob [bɒb] *vi* (-bb-) **to b. (up and down)** (*on water*) danser sur l'eau.

bobbin ['bɒbɪn] *n* bobine *f*.

bobby ['bɒbɪ] *n* 1 (*policeman*) *Fam* flic *m*, agent *m*. 2 **b. pin** *Am* pince *f* à cheveux.

bode [bəʊd] *vi* **to b. well/ill** être de bon/mauvais augure.

bodice ['bɒdɪs] *n* corsage *m*.

body ['bɒdɪ] *n* corps *m*; (*of vehicle*) carrosserie *f*; (*quantity*) masse *f*; (*institution*) organisme *m*; **the main b. of** le gros de; **b. building** culturisme *m*. ◆**bodily** *a* physique; (*need*) matériel; – *adv* physiquement; (*as a whole*) tout entier. ◆**bodyguard** *n* garde *m* du corps, gorille *m*. ◆**bodywork** *n* carrosserie *f*.

boffin ['bɒfɪn] *n Fam* chercheur, -euse *mf* scientifique.

bog [bɒg] *n* marécage *m*; – *vt* **to get bogged down** s'enliser. ◆**boggy** *a* (-ier, -iest) marécageux.

bogey ['bəʊgɪ] *n* spectre *m*; **b. man** croque-mitaine *m*.

boggle ['bɒg(ə)l] *vi* **the mind boggles** cela confond l'imagination.

bogus ['bəʊgəs] *a* faux.

bohemian [bəʊ'hiːmɪən] *a & n* (*artist etc*) bohème (*mf*).

boil [bɔɪl] **1** *n Med* furoncle *m*, clou *m*. **2** *vi* bouillir; **to b. away** (*until dry*) s'évaporer; (*on and on*) bouillir sans arrêt; **to b. down to** *Fig* se ramener à; **to b. over** (*of milk, emotions etc*) déborder; – *vt* **to b. (up)** faire bouillir; – *n* **to be on the b.**, **come to the b.** bouillir; **to bring to the b.** amener à ébullition. ◆**—ed** *a* (*beef*) bouilli; (*potato*) (cuit) à l'eau; **b. egg** œuf *m* à la coque. ◆**—ing** *n* ébullition *f*; **at b. point** à ébullition; – *a & adv* **b. (hot)** bouillant; **it's b. (hot)** (*weather*) il fait une chaleur infernale. ◆**—er** *n* chaudière *f*; **b. suit** bleu *m* de travail).

boisterous ['bɔɪstərəs] *a* (*noisy*) tapageur; (*child*) turbulent; (*meeting*) houleux.

bold [bəʊld] *a* (-er, -est) hardi; **b. type** caractères *mpl* gras. ◆**—ness** *n* hardiesse *f*.

Bolivia [bə'lɪvɪə] *n* Bolivie *f*. ◆**Bolivian** *a & n* bolivien, -ienne (*mf*).

bollard ['bɒləd, 'bɒlɑːd] *n Aut* borne *f*.

boloney [bə'ləʊnɪ] *n Sl* foutaises *fpl*.

bolster ['bəʊlstər] **1** *n* (*pillow*) traversin *m*, polochon *m*. **2** *vt* **to b. (up)** (*support*) soutenir.

bolt [bəʊlt] **1** *n* (*on door etc*) verrou *m*; (*for nut*) boulon *m*; – *vt* (*door*) verrouiller. **2** *n* (*dash*) fuite *f*, ruée *f*; – *vi* (*dash*) se précipiter; (*flee*) détaler; (*of horse*) s'emballer. **3** *n* **b. (of lightning)** éclair *m*. **4** *vt* (*food*) engloutir. **5** *adv* **b. upright** tout droit.

bomb [bɒm] *n* bombe *f*; **letter b.** lettre *f* piégée; **b. disposal** désamorçage *m*; – *vt* bombarder. ◆**—ing** *n* bombardement *m*.

◆**—er** *n* (*aircraft*) bombardier *m*; (*terrorist*) plastiqueur *m*. ◆**bombshell** *n* **to come as a b.** tomber comme une bombe. ◆**bombsite** *n* terrain *m* vague, lieu *m* bombardé.

bombard [bɒm'bɑːd] *vt* bombarder (**with** de). ◆**—ment** *n* bombardement *m*.

bona fide [bəʊnə'faɪdɪ, *Am* -'faɪd] *a* sérieux, de bonne foi.

bonanza [bə'nænzə] *n Fig* mine *f* d'or.

bond [bɒnd] **1** *n* (*agreement, promise*) engagement *m*; (*link*) lien *m*; *Com* bon *m*, obligation *f*; (*adhesion*) adhérence *f*. **2** *vt* (*goods*) entreposer.

bondage ['bɒndɪdʒ] *n* esclavage *m*.

bone [bəʊn] **1** *n* os *m*; (*of fish*) arête *f*; **b. of contention** pomme *f* de discorde; **b. china** porcelaine *f* tendre; – *vt* (*meat etc*) désosser. **2** *vi* **to b. up on** (*subject*) *Am Fam* bûcher. ◆**bony** *a* (-ier, -iest) (*thin*) osseux, maigre; (*fish*) plein d'arêtes.

bone-dry [bəʊn'draɪ] *a* tout à fait sec. ◆**b.-idle** *a* paresseux comme une couleuvre.

bonfire ['bɒnfaɪər] *n* (*for celebration*) feu *m* de joie; (*for dead leaves*) feu *m* de jardin.

bonkers ['bɒŋkəz] *a* (*crazy*) *Fam* dingue.

bonnet ['bɒnɪt] *n* (*hat*) bonnet *m*; *Aut* capot *m*.

bonus ['bəʊnəs] *n* prime *f*; **no claims b.** *Aut* bonus *m*.

boo [buː] **1** *int* hou! **2** *vti* huer; – *npl* huées *fpl*.

boob [buːb] *n* (*mistake*) gaffe *f*; – *vi Sl* gaffer.

booby-trap ['buːbɪtræp] *n* engin *m* piégé; – *vt* (-pp-) piéger.

book [bʊk] **1** *n* livre *m*; (*of tickets*) carnet *m*; (*record*) registre *m*; *pl* (*accounts*) comptes *mpl*; (*excercise*) **b.** cahier *m*. **2** *vt* **to b. (up)** (*seat etc*) réserver, retenir; **to b. s.o.** *Jur* donner un procès-verbal à qn; **to b. (down)** inscrire; (**fully**) **booked (up)** (*hotel, concert*) complet; (*person*) pris; – *vi* **to b. (up)** réserver des places; **to b. in** (*in hotel*) signer le registre. ◆**—ing** *n* réservation *f*; **b. clerk** guichetier, -ière *mf*; **b. office** bureau *m* de location, guichet *m*. ◆**—able** *a* (*seat*) qu'on peut réserver. ◆**bookish** *a* (*word, theory*) livresque; (*person*) studieux.

bookbinding ['bʊkbaɪndɪŋ] *n* reliure *f*. ◆**bookcase** *n* bibliothèque *f*. ◆**bookend** *n* serre-livres *m inv*. ◆**bookkeeper** *n* comptable *mf*. ◆**bookkeeping** *n* comptabilité *f*. ◆**booklet** *n* brochure *f*. ◆**book-lover** *n* bibliophile *mf*. ◆**bookmaker** *n* bookmaker *m*. ◆**bookmark** *n*

marque *f*. ◆**bookseller** *n* libraire *mf*.
◆**bookshelf** *n* rayon *m*. ◆**bookshop** *n*,
Am ◆**bookstore** *n* librairie *f*. ◆**book-**
stall *n* kiosque *m* (à journaux). ◆**book-**
worm *n* rat *m* de bibliothèque.

boom [buːm] **1** *vi* (*of thunder, gun etc*)
gronder; – *n* grondement *m*; **sonic b.** bang
m **2** *n Econ* expansion *f*, essor *m*, boom *m*.

boomerang ['buːməræŋ] *n* boomerang *m*.

boon [buːn] *n* aubaine *f*, avantage *m*.

boor [buər] *n* rustre *m*. ◆**boorish** *a* rustre.

boost [buːst] *vt* (*push*) donner une poussée
à; (*increase*) augmenter; (*product*) faire de
la réclame pour; (*economy*) stimuler;
(*morale*) remonter; – *n* **to give a b. to** = to
boost. ◆**—er** *n* **b. (injection)** piqûre *f* de
rappel.

boot [buːt] **1** *n* (*shoe*) botte *f*; (*ankle*) **b.**
bottillon *m*; (*knee*) **b.** bottine *f*; **to get the b.**
Fam être mis à la porte; **b. polish** cirage *m*;
– *vt* (*kick*) donner un coup *or* des coups de
pied à; **to b. out** mettre à la porte. **2** *n Aut*
coffre *m*. **3** *n* **to b.** en plus. ◆**bootblack** *n*
cireur *m*. ◆**boo'tee** *n* (*of baby*) chausson
m.

booth [buːð, buːθ] *n Tel* cabine *f*; (*at fair*)
baraque *f*.

booty ['buːtɪ] *n* (*stolen goods*) butin *m*.

booz/e [buːz] *n Fam* alcool *m*, boisson(s)
f(pl); (*drinking bout*) beuverie *f*; – *vi Fam*
boire (beaucoup). ◆**—er** *n Fam* (*person*)
buveur, -euse *mf*; (*place*) bistrot *m*.

border ['bɔːdər] *n* (*of country*) & *Fig*
frontière *f*; (*edge*) bord *m*; (*of garden etc*)
bordure *f*; – *a* (*town*) frontière *inv*; (*inci-*
dent) de frontière; – *vt* (*street*) border; **to b.**
(**on**) (*country*) toucher à; **to b. (up)on**
(*resemble*) être voisin de. ◆**borderland** *n*
pays *m* frontière. ◆**borderline** *n* frontière
f; **b. case** cas *m* limite.

bor/e [bɔːr] **1** *vt* (*weary*) ennuyer; **to be**
bored s'ennuyer; – *n* (*person*) raseur, -euse
mf; (*thing*) ennui *m*. **2** *vt Tech* forer,
creuser; (*hole*) percer; – *vi* forer. **3** *n* (*of*
gun) calibre *m*. ◆**—ing** *a* ennuyeux.
◆**boredom** *n* ennui *m*.

bore² [bɔːr] *see* bear².

born [bɔːn] *a* né; **to be b.** naître; **he was b.** il
est né.

borne [bɔːn] *see* bear².

borough ['bʌrə] *n* (*town*) municipalité *f*;
(*part of town*) arrondissement *m*.

borrow ['bɒrəʊ] *vt* emprunter (**from** à).
◆**—ing** *n* emprunt *m*.

Borstal ['bɔːst(ə)l] *n* maison *f* d'éducation
surveillée.

bosom ['buzəm] *n* (*chest*) & *Fig* sein *m*; **b.**
friend ami, -ie *mf* intime.

boss [bɒs] *n Fam* patron, -onne *mf*, chef *m*;
– *vt Fam* diriger; **to b. s.o. around** *or* **about**
régenter qn. ◆**bossy** *a* (**-ier, -iest**) *Fam*
autoritaire.

boss-eyed ['bɒsaɪd] *a* **to be b.-eyed** loucher.

bosun ['bəʊs(ə)n] *n* maître *m* d'équipage.

botany ['bɒtənɪ] *n* botanique *f*. ◆**bo'tan-**
ical *a* botanique. ◆**botanist** *n* botaniste
mf.

botch [bɒtʃ] *vt* **to b. (up)** (*spoil*) bâcler;
(*repair*) rafistoler.

both [bəʊθ] *a* les deux, l'un(e) et l'autre; –
pron tous *or* toutes (les) deux, l'un(e) et
l'autre; **b. of us** nous deux; – *adv* (*at the*
same time) à la fois; **b. you and I** vous et
moi.

bother ['bɒðər] *vt* (*annoy, worry*) ennuyer;
(*disturb*) déranger; (*pester*) importuner; **I**
can't be bothered! je n'en ai pas envie!; ça
m'embête!; – *vi* **to b. about** (*worry about*) se
préoccuper de; (*deal with*) s'occuper de; **to**
b. doing *or* **to do** se donner la peine de faire;
– *n* (*trouble*) ennui *m*; (*effort*) peine *f*;
(*inconvenience*) dérangement *m*; (**oh**) **b.!**
zut alors!

bottle ['bɒt(ə)l] *n* bouteille *f*; (*small*) flacon
m; (*wide-mouthed*) bocal *m*; (*for baby*)
biberon *m*; (*hot-water*) **b.** bouillotte *f*; **b.**
opener ouvre-bouteilles *m inv*; – *vt* mettre
en bouteille; **to b. up** (*feeling*) contenir.
◆**b.-feed** *vt* (*pt & pp* **-fed**) nourrir au
biberon. ◆**bottleneck** *n* (*in road*) goulot
m d'étranglement; (*traffic holdup*) bouchon
m.

bottom ['bɒtəm] *n* (*of sea, box, etc*) fond *m*;
(*of page, hill etc*) bas *m*; (*buttocks*) *Fam*
derrière *m*; (*of table*) bout *m*; **to be (at the)**
b. of the class être le dernier de la classe; –
a (*part, shelf*) inférieur, du bas; **b. floor**
rez-de-chaussée *m*; **b. gear** première vitesse
f. ◆**—less** *a* insondable.

bough [baʊ] *n Lit* rameau *m*.

bought [bɔːt] *see* buy.

boulder ['bəʊldər] *n* rocher *m*.

boulevard ['buːləvɑːd] *n* boulevard *m*.

bounc/e [baʊns] **1** *vi* (*of ball*) rebondir; (*of*
person) faire des bonds; **to b. into** bondir
dans; – *vt* (*ball*) faire rebondir. – *n* (re)bond *m*.
2 *vi* (*of cheque*) *Fam* être sans provision,
être en bois. ◆**—ing** *a* (*baby*) robuste.
◆**—er** *n* (*at club etc*) *Fam* videur *m*.

bound¹ [baʊnd] **1** *a* **b. to do** (*obliged*) obligé
de faire; (*certain*) sûr de faire; **it's b. to**
happen ça arrivera sûrement; **to be b. for**

être en route pour. **2** *n* (*leap*) bond *m*; – *vi* bondir.

bound² [baʊnd] *see* **bind 1**; – *a* **b. up with** (*connected*) lié à.

bounds [baʊndz] *npl* limites *fpl*; **out of b.** (*place*) interdit. ◆**boundary** *n* limite *f*. ◆**bounded** *a* **b. by** limité par. ◆**boundless** *a* sans bornes.

bountiful ['baʊntɪfʊl] *a* généreux.

bounty ['baʊntɪ] *n* (*reward*) prime *f*.

bouquet [bəʊ'keɪ] *n* (*of flowers, wine*) bouquet *m*.

bourbon ['bɜːbən] *n* (*whisky*) *Am* bourbon *m*.

bout [baʊt] *n* période *f*; *Med* accès *m*, crise *f*; *Boxing* combat *m*; (*session*) séance *f*.

boutique [buː'tiːk] *n* boutique *f* (de mode).

bow¹ [bəʊ] *n* (*weapon*) arc *m*; *Mus* archet *m*; (*knot*) nœud *m*; **b. tie** nœud *m* papillon. ◆**b.-'legged** *a* aux jambes arquées.

bow² [baʊ] **1** *n* révérence *f*; (*nod*) salut *m*; – *vt* courber, incliner; – *vi* s'incliner (**to** devant); (*nod*) incliner la tête; **to b. down** (*submit*) s'incliner. **2** *n Nau* proue *f*.

bowels ['baʊəlz] *npl* intestins *mpl*; (*of earth*) *Fig* entrailles *fpl*.

bowl [bəʊl] **1** *n* (*for food*) bol *m*; (*basin*) & *Geog* cuvette *f*; (*for sugar*) sucrier *m*; (*for salad*) saladier *m*; (*for fruit*) coupe *f*; **2** *npl Sp* boules *fpl*. **3** *vi Cricket* lancer la balle; **to b. along** *Aut* rouler vite; – *vt* (*ball*) *Cricket* servir; **to b. s.o. over** (*knock down*) renverser qn; (*astound*) bouleverser qn. ◆**—ing** *n* (tenpin) **b.** bowling *m*; **b. alley** bowling *m*. ◆**—er¹** *n Cricket* lanceur, -euse *mf*.

bowler² ['bəʊlər] *n* **b. (hat)** (*chapeau m*) melon *m*.

box [bɒks] **1** *n* boîte *f*; (*large*) caisse *f*; (*of cardboard*) carton *m*; *Th* loge *f*; *Jur* barre *f*, banc *m*; (*for horse*) box *m*; *TV Fam* télé *f*; **b. office** bureau *m* de location, guichet *m*; **b. room** (*lumber room*) débarras *m*; (*bedroom*) petite chambre *f* (carrée); – *vt* to **b. (up)** mettre en boîte; **to b. in** (*enclose*) enfermer. **2** *vti Boxing* boxer; **to b. s.o.'s ears** gifler qn. ◆**—ing** *n* **1** boxe *f*; **b. ring** ring *m*. **2 B. Day** le lendemain de Noël. ◆**—er** *n* boxeur *m*. ◆**boxcar** *n Rail Am* wagon *m* couvert. ◆**boxwood** *n* buis *m*.

boy [bɔɪ] *n* garçon *m*; **English b.** jeune Anglais *m*; **old b.** *Sch* ancien élève *m*; **yes, old b.!** oui, mon vieux!; **the boys** (*pals*) *Fam* les copains *mpl*; **my dear b.** mon cher ami; **oh b.!** *Am* mon Dieu! ◆**boyfriend** *n* petit ami *m*. ◆**boyhood** *n* enfance *f*. ◆**boyish** *a* de garçon; *Pej* puéril.

boycott ['bɔɪkɒt] *vt* boycotter; – *n* boycottage *m*.

bra [brɑː] *n* soutien-gorge *m*.

brac/e [breɪs] *n* (*for fastening*) attache *f*; (*dental*) appareil *m*; – *pl* (*trouser straps*) bretelles *fpl*; – *vt* (*fix*) attacher; (*press*) appuyer; **to b. oneself for** (*news, shock*) se préparer à. ◆**—ing** *a* (*air etc*) fortifiant.

bracelet ['breɪslɪt] *n* bracelet *m*.

bracken ['brækən] *n* fougère *f*.

bracket ['brækɪt] *n Tech* support *m*, tasseau *m*; (*round sign*) *Typ* parenthèse *f*; (*square*) *Typ* crochet *m*; *Fig* groupe *m*, tranche *f*; – *vt* mettre entre parenthèses *or* crochets; **to b. together** *Fig* mettre dans le même groupe.

bradawl ['brædɔːl] *n* poinçon *m*.

brag [bræg] *vi* (**-gg-**) se vanter (**about, of** de). ◆**—ging** *n* vantardise *f*. ◆**braggart** *n* vantard, -arde *mf*.

braid [breɪd] *vt* (*hair*) tresser; (*trim*) galonner; – *n* tresse *f*; galon *m*.

Braille [breɪl] *n* braille *m*.

brain [breɪn] *n* cerveau *m*; (*of bird etc*) & *Pej* cervelle *f*; – *a* (*operation, death*) cérébral; – *vt Fam* assommer; **to have brains** (*sense*) avoir de l'intelligence; **b. drain** fuite *f* des cerveaux. ◆**brainchild** *n* invention *f* personnelle. ◆**brainstorm** *n Psy Fig* aberration *f*; *Am* idée *f* géniale. ◆**brainwash** *vt* faire un lavage de cerveau à. ◆**brainwave** *n* idée *f* géniale.

brainy ['breɪnɪ] *a* (**-ier, -iest**) *Fam* intelligent.

braise [breɪz] *vt Culin* braiser.

brak/e [breɪk] *vi* freiner; – *n* frein *m*; **b. light** *Aut* stop *m*. ◆**—ing** *n* freinage *m*.

bramble ['bræmb(ə)l] *n* ronce *f*.

bran [bræn] *n Bot* son *m*.

branch [brɑːntʃ] *n* branche *f*; (*of road*) embranchement *m*; (*of store etc*) succursale *f*; **b. office** succursale *f*; – *vi* **to b. off** (*of road*) bifurquer; **to b. out** (*of family, tree*) se ramifier; *Fig* étendre ses activités.

brand [brænd] *n* (*trademark, stigma & on cattle*) marque *f*; – *vt* (*mark*) marquer; (*stigmatize*) flétrir; **to be branded as** avoir la réputation de.

brandish ['brændɪʃ] *vt* brandir.

brand-new [brænd'njuː] *a* tout neuf, flambant neuf.

brandy ['brændɪ] *n* cognac *m*; (*made with pears etc*) eau-de-vie *f*.

brash [bræʃ] *a* effronté, fougueux.

brass [brɑːs] *n* cuivre *m*; (*instruments*) *Mus* cuivres *mpl*; **the top b.** (*officers, executives*) *Fam* les huiles *fpl*; **b. band** fanfare *f*.

brassiere ['bræzɪər, *Am* brə'zɪər] *n*
soutien-gorge *m*.

brat [bræt] *n Pej* môme *mf*, gosse *mf*; (*badly behaved*) galopin *m*.

bravado [brə'vɑːdəʊ] *n* bravade *f*.

brave [breɪv] *a* (-er, -est) courageux, brave; − *n* (*Red Indian*) guerrier *m* (indien), brave *m*; − *vt* braver. ◆**bravery** *n* courage *m*.

bravo! ['brɑːvəʊ] *int* bravo!

brawl [brɔːl] *n* (*fight*) bagarre *f*; − *vi* se bagarrer. ◆**—ing** *a* bagarreur.

brawn [brɔːn] *n* muscles *mpl*. ◆**brawny** *a* (-ier, -iest) musclé.

bray [breɪ] *vi* (*of ass*) braire.

brazen ['breɪz(ə)n] *a* (*shameless*) effronté; − *vt* to b. it out payer d'audace, faire front.

Brazil [brə'zɪl] *n* Brésil *m*. ◆**Brazilian** *a* & *n* brésilien, -ienne (*mf*).

breach [briːtʃ] **1** *n* violation *f*, infraction *f*; (*of contract*) rupture *f*; (*of trust*) abus *m*; − *vt* (*law, code*) violer. **2** *n* (*gap*) brèche *f*; − *vt* (*wall etc*) ouvrir une brèche dans.

bread [bred] *n inv* pain *m*; (*money*) *Sl* blé *m*, fric *m*; **loaf of b.** pain *m*; (*slice or piece of*) b. and butter tartine *f*; b. and butter (*job*) *Fig* gagne-pain *m*. ◆**breadbin** *n*, *Am* ◆**breadbox** *n* coffre *m* à pain. ◆**breadboard** *n* planche *f* à pain. ◆**breadcrumb** *n* miette *f* (de pain); *pl Culin* chapelure *f*. ◆**breadline** *n* on the b. indigent. ◆**breadwinner** *n* soutien *m* de famille.

breadth [bretθ] *n* largeur *f*.

break [breɪk] *vt* (*pt* **broke**, *pp* **broken**) casser; (*into pieces*) briser; (*silence, vow etc*) rompre; (*strike, heart, ice etc*) briser; (*record*) *Sp* battre; (*law*) violer; (*one's word*) manquer à; (*journey*) interrompre; (*sound barrier*) franchir; (*a fall*) amortir; (*news*) révéler (to à); to b. (*oneself of*) (*habit*) se débarrasser de; to b. open (*safe*) percer; to b. new ground innover; − *vi* (se) casser; se briser; se rompre; (*of voice*) s'altérer; (*of boy's voice*) muer; (*of weather*) se gâter; (*of news*) éclater; (*of day*) se lever; (*of wave*) déferler; to b. free se libérer; to b. loose s'échapper; to b. with s.o. rompre avec qn; − *n* cassure *f*; (*in relationship, continuity etc*) rupture *f*; (*in journey*) interruption *f*; (*rest*) repos *m*; (*for tea*) pause *f*; *Sch* récréation *f*; (*change*) *Met* changement *m*; a lucky b. *Fam* une chance. ◆**—ing** *a* b. point *Tech* point *m* de rupture; at b. point (*patience*) à bout; (*person*) sur le point de craquer, à bout. ◆**—able** *a* cassable. ◆**—age** *n* casse *f*; *pl* (*things broken*) la casse. ◆**—er** *n* (*wave*) brisant *m*; (*dealer*)

Aut casseur *m*. ■ to b. away *vi* se détacher; − *vt* détacher. ◆**breakaway** *a* (*group*) dissident; to b. down *vt* (*door*) enfoncer; (*resistance*) briser; (*analyse*) analyser; − *vi Aut Tech* tomber en panne; (*of negotiations etc*) échouer; (*collapse*) s'effondrer. ◆**breakdown** *n* panne *f*; analyse *f*; (*in talks*) rupture *f*; (*nervous*) dépression *f*; − *a* (*service*) *Aut* de dépannage; b. lorry dépanneuse *f*; to b. in *vi* interrompre; (*of burglar*) entrer par effraction; − *vt* (*door*) enfoncer; (*horse*) dresser; (*vehicle*) *Am* roder. ◆**break-in** *n* cambriolage *m*; to b. into *vt* (*safe*) forcer; (*start*) entamer; to b. off *vt* détacher; (*relations*) rompre; − *vi* se détacher; (*stop*) s'arrêter; to b. off with rompre avec; to b. out *vi* éclater; (*escape*) s'échapper; to b. out in (*pimples*) avoir une poussée de; to b. through *vi* (*of sun*) & *Mil* percer; − *vt* (*defences*) percer. ◆**breakthrough** *n Fig* percée *f*, découverte *f*; to b. up *vt* mettre en morceaux; (*marriage*) briser; (*fight*) mettre fin à; − *vi* (*end*) prendre fin; (*of group*) se disperser; (*of marriage*) se briser; *Sch* partir en vacances. ◆**breakup** *n* fin *f*; (*in friendship, marriage*) rupture *f*.

breakfast ['brekfəst] *n* petit déjeuner *m*.

breakwater ['breɪkwɔːtər] *n* brise-lames *m inv*.

breast [brest] *n* sein *m*; (*chest*) poitrine *f*. ◆**b.-feed** *vt* (*pt & pp* **-fed**) allaiter. ◆**breaststroke** *n* (*swimming*) brasse *f*.

breath [breθ] *n* haleine *f*, souffle *m*; (*of air*) souffle *m*; **under one's b.** tout bas; **one's last b.** son dernier soupir; **out of b.** à bout de souffle; to get a b. of air prendre l'air; to take a deep b. respirer profondément. ◆**breathalyser®** *n* alcootest® *m*. ◆**breathless** *a* haletant. ◆**breathtaking** *a* sensationnel.

breath/e [briːð] *vti* respirer; to b. in aspirer; to b. out expirer; to b. air into sth souffler dans qch; − *vt* (*a sigh*) pousser; (*a word*) dire. ◆**—ing** *n* respiration *f*; b. space moment *m* de repos. ◆**—er** *n Fam* moment *m* de repos; to go for a b. sortir prendre l'air.

bred [bred] *see* **breed 1**; − *a* well-b. bien élevé.

breeches ['brɪtʃɪz] *npl* culotte *f*.

breed [briːd] **1** *vt* (*pt & pp* **bred**) (*animals*) élever; (*cause*) *Fig* engendrer; − *vi* (*of animals*) se reproduire. **2** *n* race *f*, espèce *f*. ◆**—ing** *n* élevage *m*; reproduction *f*; *Fig* éducation *f*. ◆**—er** *n* éleveur, -euse *mf*.

breeze [briːz] *n* brise *f*. ◆**breezy** *a* (-ier,

-iest) 1 (*weather, day*) frais, venteux. **2** (*cheerful*) jovial; (*relaxed*) décontracté.

breezeblock ['briːzblɒk] *n* parpaing *m*, briquette *f*.

brevity ['brevɪtɪ] *n* brièveté *f*.

brew [bruː] *vt* (*beer*) brasser; (*trouble, plot*) préparer; **to b. tea** préparer du thé; (*infuse*) (faire) infuser du thé; – *vi* (*of beer*) fermenter; (*of tea*) infuser; (*of storm, trouble*) se préparer; – *n* (*drink*) breuvage *m*; (*of tea*) infusion *f*. ◆**—er** *n* brasseur *m*. ◆**brewery** *n* brasserie *f*.

bribe [braɪb] *n* pot-de-vin *m*; – *vt* soudoyer, corrompre. ◆**bribery** *n* corruption *f*.

brick [brɪk] *n* brique *f*; (*child's*) cube *m*; **to drop a b.** *Fam* faire une gaffe; – *vt* **to b. up** (*gap, door*) murer. ◆**bricklayer** *n* maçon *m*. ◆**brickwork** *n* ouvrage *m* en briques; (*bricks*) briques *fpl*.

bridal ['braɪd(ə)l] *a* (*ceremony*) nuptial; **b. gown** robe *f* de mariée.

bride [braɪd] *n* mariée *f*; **the b. and groom** les mariés *mpl*. ◆**bridegroom** *n* marié *m*. ◆**bridesmaid** *n* demoiselle *f* d'honneur.

bridge [brɪdʒ] **1** *n* pont *m*; (*on ship*) passerelle *f*; (*of nose*) arête *f*; (*false tooth*) bridge *m*; – *vt* **to b. a gap** combler une lacune. **2** *n* *Cards* bridge *m*.

bridle ['braɪd(ə)l] *n* (*for horse*) bride *f*; – *vt* (*horse, instinct etc*) brider; **b. path** allée *f* cavalière.

brief [briːf] **1** *a* (**-er, -est**) bref; **in b.** en résumé. **2** *n* *Jur* dossier *m*; (*instructions*) *Mil Pol* instructions *fpl*; *Fig* tâche *f*, fonctions *fpl*; – *vt* donner des instructions à; (*inform*) mettre au courant (**on** de). **3** *npl* (*underpants*) slip *m*. ◆**—ing** *n* *Mil Pol* instructions *fpl*; *Av* briefing *m*. ◆**—ly** *adv* (*quickly*) en vitesse; (*to say*) brièvement.

brigade [brɪˈɡeɪd] *n* brigade *f*. ◆**brigadier** *n* général *m* de brigade.

bright [braɪt] *a* (**-er, -est**) brillant, vif; (*weather, room*) clair; (*clever*) intelligent; (*happy*) joyeux; (*future*) brillant, prometteur; (*idea*) génial; **b. interval** *Met* éclaircie *f*; – *adv* **b. and early** (*to get up*) de bonne heure. ◆**—ly** *adv* brillamment. ◆**—ness** *n* éclat *m*; (*of person*) intelligence *f*. ◆**brighten** *vt* **to b. (up)** (*person, room*) égayer; – *vi* **to b. (up)** (*of weather*) s'éclaircir; (*of face*) s'éclaircir.

brilliant ['brɪljənt] *a* (*light*) éclatant; (*very clever*) brillant. ◆**brilliance** *n* éclat *m*; (*of person*) grande intelligence *f*.

brim [brɪm] *n* bord *m*; – *vi* (**-mm-**) **to b. over** déborder (**with** de).

brine [braɪn] *n* *Culin* saumure *f*.

bring [brɪŋ] *vt* (*pt & pp* **brought**) (*person, vehicle etc*) amener; (*thing*) apporter; (*to cause*) amener; (*action*) *Jur* intenter; **to b. along** *or* **over** *or* **round** amener; apporter; **to b. back** ramener; rapporter; (*memories*) rappeler; **to b. sth up/down** monter/descendre qch; **to b. sth in/out** rentrer/sortir qch; **to b. sth to** (*perfection, a peak etc*) porter qch à; **to b. to an end** mettre fin à; **to b. to mind** rappeler; **to b. sth on oneself** s'attirer qch; **to b. oneself to do** se résoudre à faire; **to b. about** provoquer, amener; **to b. down** (*overthrow*) faire tomber; (*reduce*) réduire; (*shoot down*) abattre; **to b. forward** (*in time or space*) avancer; (*witness*) produire; **to b. in** (*person*) faire entrer *or* venir; (*introduce*) introduire; (*income*) *Com* rapporter; **to b. off** (*task*) mener à bien; **to b. out** (*person*) faire sortir; (*meaning*) faire ressortir; (*book*) publier; (*product*) lancer; **to b. over to** (*convert to*) convertir à; **to b. round** *Med* ranimer; (*convert*) convertir (**to** à); **to b. s.o. to** *Med* ranimer qn; **to b. together** mettre en contact; (*reconcile*) réconcilier; **to b. up** (*child etc*) élever; (*question*) soulever; (*subject*) mentionner; (*vomit*) vomir.

brink [brɪŋk] *n* bord *m*.

brisk [brɪsk] *a* (**-er, -est**) vif; (*trade*) actif; **at a b. pace** d'un bon pas. ◆**—ly** *adv* vivement; (*to walk*) d'un bon pas. ◆**—ness** *n* vivacité *f*.

bristl/e ['brɪs(ə)l] *n* poil *m*; – *vi* se hérisser. ◆**—ing** *a* **b. with** (*difficulties*) hérissé de.

Britain ['brɪt(ə)n] *n* Grande-Bretagne *f*. ◆**British** *a* britannique; – *n* **the B.** les Britanniques *mpl*. ◆**Briton** *n* Britannique *mf*.

Brittany ['brɪtənɪ] *n* Bretagne *f*.

brittle ['brɪt(ə)l] *a* cassant, fragile.

broach [brəʊtʃ] *vt* (*topic*) entamer.

broad [brɔːd] *a* (**-er, -est**) (*wide*) large; (*outline*) grand, général; (*accent*) prononcé; **in b. daylight** au grand jour; **b. bean** fève *f*; **b. jump** *Sp Am* saut *m* en longueur. ◆**b.-'minded** *a* à l'esprit large. ◆**b.-'shouldered** *a* large d'épaules. ◆**broaden** *vt* élargir; – *vi* s'élargir. ◆**broadly** *adv* **b. (speaking)** en gros, grosso modo.

broad² [brɔːd] *n* (*woman*) *Am Sl* nana *f*.

broadcast ['brɔːdkɑːst] *vt* (*pt & pp* **broadcast**) *Rad & Fig* diffuser; *TV* téléviser; – *vi* (*of station*) émettre; (*of person*) parler à la radio *or* à la télévision; – *a* (radio)diffusé; télévisé; – *n* émission *f*. ◆**—ing** *n* radiodiffusion *f*; télévision *f*.

broccoli ['brɒkəlɪ] *n inv* brocoli *m.*
brochure ['brəʊʃər] *n* brochure *f*, dépliant *m.*
brogue [brəʊg] *n Ling* accent *m* irlandais.
broil [brɔɪl] *vti* griller. ◆**—er** *n* poulet *m* (à rôtir); (*apparatus*) gril *m.*
broke [brəʊk] **1** *see* **break. 2** *a* (*penniless*) fauché. ◆**broken** *see* **break;** – *a* (*ground*) accidenté; (*spirit*) abattu; (*man, voice, line*) brisé; **b. English** mauvais anglais *m*; **b. home** foyer *m* brisé. ◆**broken-'down** *a* (*machine etc*) (tout) déglingué, détraqué.
brolly ['brɒlɪ] *n* (*umbrella*) *Fam* pépin *m.*
bronchitis [brɒŋ'kaɪtɪs] *n* bronchite *f.*
bronze [brɒnz] *n* bronze *m*; – *a* (*statue etc*) en bronze.
brooch [brəʊtʃ] *n* (*ornament*) broche *f.*
brood [bruːd] **1** *n* couvée *f*, nichée *f*; – *vi* (*of bird*) couver. **2** *vi* méditer tristement (**over, on** sur); **to b. over** (*a plan*) ruminer. ◆**broody** *a* (**-ier, -iest**) (*person*) maussade, rêveur; (*woman*) *Fam* qui a envie d'avoir un enfant.
brook [brʊk] **1** *n* ruisseau *m.* **2** *vt* souffrir, tolérer.
broom [bruːm] *n* **1** (*for sweeping*) balai *m.* **2** *Bot* genêt *m.* ◆**broomstick** *n* manche *m* à balai.
Bros *abbr* (*Brothers*) Frères *mpl.*
broth [brɒθ] *n* bouillon *m.*
brothel ['brɒθ(ə)l] *n* maison *f* close, bordel *m.*
brother ['brʌðər] *n* frère *m.* ◆**b.-in-law** *n* (*pl* **brothers-in-law**) beau-frère *m.* ◆**brotherhood** *n* fraternité *f.* ◆**brotherly** *a* fraternel.
brow [braʊ] *n* (*forehead*) front *m*; (*of hill*) sommet *m.*
browbeat ['braʊbiːt] *vt* (*pt* **-beat**, *pp* **-beaten**) intimider.
brown [braʊn] *a* (**-er, -est**) brun; (*reddish*) marron; (*hair*) châtain; (*tanned*) bronzé; – *n* brun *m*; marron *m*; – *vt* brunir; *Culin* faire dorer; **to be browned off** *Fam* en avoir marre. ◆**brownish** *a* brunâtre.
Brownie ['braʊnɪ] *n* **1** (*girl scout*) jeannette *f.* **2 b.** *Culin Am* petit gâteau *m* au chocolat.
browse [braʊz] *vi* (*in shop*) regarder; (*in bookshop*) feuilleter des livres; (*of animal*) brouter; **to b. through** (*book*) feuilleter.
bruis/e [bruːz] *vt* contusionner, meurtrir; (*fruit, heart*) meurtrir; – *n* bleu *m*, contusion *f.* ◆**—ed** *a* couvert de bleus.
brunch [brʌntʃ] *n* repas *m* mixte (*petit déjeuner pris comme déjeuner*).
brunette [bruː'net] *n* brunette *f.*

brunt [brʌnt] *n* **to bear the b. of** (*attack etc*) subir le plus gros de.
brush [brʌʃ] *n* brosse *f*; (*for shaving*) blaireau *m*; (*little broom*) balayette *f*; (*action*) coup *m* de brosse; (*fight*) accrochage *m*; – *vt* (*teeth, hair etc*) brosser; (*clothes*) donner un coup de brosse à; **to b. aside** écarter; **to b. away** *or* **off** enlever; **to b. up (on)** (*language*) se remettre à; – *vi* **to b. against** effleurer. ◆**b.-off** *n Fam* **to give s.o. the b.-off** envoyer promener qn. ◆**b.-up** *n* coup *m* de brosse. ◆**brushwood** *n* broussailles *fpl.*
brusque [bruːsk] *a* brusque.
Brussels ['brʌs(ə)lz] *n* Bruxelles *m or f*; **B. sprouts** choux *mpl* de Bruxelles.
brutal ['bruːt(ə)l] *a* brutal. ◆**bru'tality** *n* brutalité *f.*
brute [bruːt] *n* (*animal, person*) brute *f*; – *a* **by b. force** par la force.
BSc, *Am* **BS** *abbr* = **Bachelor of Science.**
bubble ['bʌb(ə)l] *n* (*of air, soap etc*) bulle *f*; (*in boiling liquid*) bouillon *m*; **b. and squeak** *Fam* friture *f* de purée et de viande réchauffées; **b. bath** bain *m* moussant; **b. gum** chewing-gum *m*; – *vi* bouillonner; **to b. over** déborder (**with** de). ◆**bubbly** *n Hum Fam* champagne *m.*
buck [bʌk] **1** *n Am Fam* dollar *m.* **2** *n* (*animal*) mâle *m.* **3** *vt* **to b. up** remonter le moral à; – *vi* **to b. up** prendre courage; (*hurry*) se grouiller. ◆**buckshot** *n inv* du gros plomb *m.* ◆**buck'tooth** *n* (*pl* **-teeth**) dent *f* saillante.
bucket ['bʌkɪt] *n* seau *m.*
buckle ['bʌk(ə)l] **1** *n* boucle *f*; – *vt* boucler. **2** *vti* (*warp*) voiler, gauchir. **3** *vi* **to b. down to** (*task*) s'atteler à.
bud [bʌd] *n* (*of tree*) bourgeon *m*; (*of flower*) bouton *m*; – *vi* (**-dd-**) bourgeonner; pousser des boutons. ◆**budding** *a* (*talent*) naissant; (*doctor etc*) en herbe.
Buddhist ['bʊdɪst] *a* & *n* bouddhiste (*mf*).
buddy ['bʌdɪ] *n Am Fam* copain *m*, pote *m.*
budge [bʌdʒ] *vi* bouger; – *vt* faire bouger.
budgerigar ['bʌdʒərɪgɑːr] *n* perruche *f.*
budget ['bʌdʒɪt] *n* budget *m*; – *vi* dresser un budget; **to b. for** inscrire au budget. ◆**budgetary** *a* budgétaire.
budgie ['bʌdʒɪ] *n Fam* perruche *f.*
buff [bʌf] **1** *a* **b.(-coloured)** chamois *inv.* **2** *n jazz/etc* **b.** *Fam* fana(tique) *mf* du jazz/*etc.* **3** *n* **in the b.** *Fam* tout nu.
buffalo ['bʌfələʊ] *n* (*pl* **-oes** *or* **-o**) buffle *m*; (*American*) **b.** bison *m.*
buffer ['bʌfər] *n* (*on train*) tampon *m*; (*at end of track*) butoir *m*; **b. state** état *m* tampon.

buffet 1 ['bʌfɪt] vt frapper; (of waves) battre; (of wind, rain) cingler (qn). **2** ['bufeɪ] n (table, meal, café) buffet m; **cold b.** viandes fpl froides.

buffoon [bə'fuːn] n bouffon m.

bug¹ [bʌg] 1 n punaise f; (any insect) Fam bestiole f; Med Fam microbe m, virus m; **the travel b.** (urge) le désir de voyager. **2** n Fam (in machine) défaut m; (in computer program) erreur f. **3** n (apparatus) Fam micro m; – vt (-gg-) (room) Fam installer des micros dans.

bug² [bʌg] vt (-gg-) (annoy) Am Fam embêter.

bugbear ['bʌgbeər] n (worry) cauchemar m.

buggy ['bʌgɪ] n **(baby) b.** (pushchair) poussette f; (folding) poussette-canne f; (pram) Am landau m.

bugle ['bjuːg(ə)l] n clairon m. ◆**bugler** n (person) clairon m.

build [bɪld] 1 n (of person) carrure f. 2 vt (pt & pp built) construire; (house, town) construire, bâtir; **to b. in** (cupboard etc) encastrer; – vi bâtir, construire. ◆**built-in** a (cupboard etc) encastré; (element of machine etc) incorporé; (innate) Fig inné. 3 **to b. up** vt (reputation) bâtir; (increase) augmenter; (accumulate) accumuler; (business) monter; (speed, one's strength) prendre; – vi augmenter, monter; s'accumuler. ◆**build-up** n montée f; accumulation f; Mil concentration f; Journ publicité f. ◆**built-up** a urbanisé; **b.-up area** agglomération f.

builder ['bɪldər] n maçon m; (contractor) entrepreneur m; (of cars etc) constructeur m; (labourer) ouvrier m.

building ['bɪldɪŋ] n bâtiment m; (flats, offices) immeuble m; (action) construction f; **b. society** caisse f d'épargne-logement, = société f de crédit immobilier.

bulb [bʌlb] n Bot bulbe m, oignon m; El ampoule f. ◆**bulbous** a bulbeux.

Bulgaria [bʌl'geərɪə] n Bulgarie f. ◆**Bulgarian** a & n bulgare (mf).

bulg/e [bʌldʒ] vi **to b. (out)** se renfler, bomber; (of eyes) sortir de la tête; – n renflement m; (increase) Fam augmentation f. ◆**—ing** a renflé, bombé; (eyes) protubérant; (bag) gonflé (with de).

bulk [bʌlk] n inv grosseur f, volume m; **the b. of** (most) la majeure partie de; **in b.** (to buy, sell) en gros. ◆**bulky** a (-ier, -iest) gros, volumineux.

bull [bul] n 1 taureau m. 2 (nonsense) Fam foutaises fpl. ◆**bullfight** n corrida f.

◆**bullfighter** n matador m. ◆**bullring** n arène f.

bulldog ['buldɒg] n bouledogue m; **b. clip** pince f (à dessin).

bulldoz/e ['buldəuz] vt passer au bulldozer. ◆**—er** n bulldozer m, bouteur m.

bullet ['bulɪt] n balle f. ◆**bulletproof** a (jacket, Am vest) pare-balles inv; (car) blindé.

bulletin ['bulɪtɪn] n bulletin m.

bullion ['buljən] n or m or argent m en lingots.

bullock ['bulək] n bœuf m.

bull's-eye ['bulzaɪ] n (of target) centre m; **to hit the b.-eye** faire mouche.

bully ['bulɪ] n (grosse) brute f, tyran m; – vt brutaliser; (persecute) tyranniser; **to b. into doing** forcer à faire.

bulwark ['bulwək] n rempart m.

bum [bʌm] **1** n (loafer) Am Fam clochard m; – vi (-mm-) **to b. (around)** se balader. **2** vt (-mm-) **to b. sth off s.o.** (cadge) Am Fam taper qn de qch. **3** n (buttocks) Fam derrière m.

bumblebee ['bʌmb(ə)lbiː] n bourdon m.

bumf [bʌmf] n Pej Sl paperasses fpl.

bump [bʌmp] vt (of car etc) heurter; **to b. one's head/knee** se cogner la tête/le genou; **to b. into** se cogner contre; (of car) rentrer dans; (meet) Fam tomber sur; **to b. off** (kill) Sl liquider; **to b. up** Fam augmenter; – vi **to b. along** (on rough road) Aut cahoter; – n (impact) choc m; (jerk) cahot m; (on road, body) bosse f. ◆**—er** n (of car etc) pare-chocs m inv; – a (crop etc) exceptionnel; **b. cars** autos fpl tamponneuses. ◆**bumpy** a (-ier, -iest) (road, ride) cahoteux.

bumpkin ['bʌmpkɪn] n rustre m.

bumptious ['bʌmpʃəs] a prétentieux.

bun [bʌn] n **1** Culin petit pain m au lait. **2** (of hair) chignon m.

bunch [bʌntʃ] n (of flowers) bouquet m; (of keys) trousseau m; (of bananas) régime m; (of people) bande f; **b. of grapes** grappe f de raisin; **a b. of** (mass) Fam un tas de.

bundle ['bʌnd(ə)l] 1 n paquet m; (of papers) liasse f; (of firewood) fagot m. 2 vt (put) fourrer; (push) pousser (into dans); **to b. (up)** mettre en paquet; **to b. s.o. off** expédier qn; – vi **to b. (oneself) up** se couvrir (bien).

bung [bʌŋ] **1** n (stopper) bonde f; – vt **to b. up** (stop up) boucher. **2** vt (toss) Fam balancer, jeter.

bungalow ['bʌŋgələu] n bungalow m.

bungl/e ['bʌŋg(ə)l] vt gâcher; – vi travailler

mal. ◆**—ing** n gâchis m; − a (clumsy) maladroit.

bunion ['bʌnjən] n (on toe) oignon m.

bunk [bʌŋk] n **1** Rail Nau couchette f; **b. beds** lits mpl superposés. **2** Sl = bunkum. ◆**bunkum** n Sl foutaises fpl.

bunker ['bʌŋkər] n Mil Golf bunker m; (coalstore in garden) coffre m.

bunny ['bʌnɪ] n Fam Jeannot m lapin.

buoy [bɔɪ] n bouée f; − vt to **b. up** (support) Fig soutenir.

buoyant ['bɔɪənt] a Fig gai, optimiste; (market) Fin ferme.

burden ['bɜːd(ə)n] n fardeau m; (of tax) poids m; − vt charger, accabler (with de).

bureau, pl **-eaux** ['bjʊərəu, -əuz] n (office) bureau m; (desk) secrétaire m. ◆**bureaucracy** [bjʊəˈrɒkrəsɪ] n bureaucratie f. ◆**bureaucrat** ['bjʊərəkræt] n bureaucrate mf.

burger ['bɜːgər] n Fam hamburger m.

burglar ['bɜːglər] n cambrioleur, -euse mf; **b. alarm** sonnerie f d'alarme. ◆**burglarize** vt Am cambrioler. ◆**burglary** n cambriolage m. ◆**burgle** vt cambrioler.

burial ['berɪəl] n enterrement m; − a (service) funèbre; **b. ground** cimetière m.

burlap ['bɜːlæp] n (sacking) Am toile f à sac.

burlesque [bɜːˈlesk] n parodie f; Th Am revue f.

burly ['bɜːlɪ] a (-ier, -iest) costaud.

Burma ['bɜːmə] n Birmanie f. ◆**Bur'mese** a & n birman, -ane (mf).

burn [bɜːn] n brûlure f; − vt (pt & pp burned or burnt) brûler; to **b. down** or **off** or **up** brûler; **burnt alive** brûlé vif; − vi brûler; to **b. down** (of house) brûler (complètement), être réduit en cendres; to **b. out** (of fire) s'éteindre; (of fuse) sauter. ◆**—ing** a en feu; (fire) allumé; (topic, fever etc) Fig brûlant; − n smell of **b.** odeur f de brûlé. ◆**—er** n (of stove) brûleur m.

burp [bɜːp] n Fam rot m; − vi Fam roter.

burrow ['bʌrəu] n (hole) terrier m; − vti creuser.

bursar ['bɜːsər] n (in school) intendant, -ante mf.

bursary ['bɜːsərɪ] n (grant) bourse f.

burst [bɜːst] n éclatement m, explosion f; (of laughter) éclat m; (of applause) salve f; (of thunder) coup m; (surge) élan m; (fit) accès m; (burst water pipe) Fam tuyau m crevé; − vi (pt & pp burst) (of bomb etc) éclater; (of bubble, tyre, cloud etc) crever; to **b. into** (room) faire irruption dans; to **b. into tears** fondre en larmes; to **b. into flames** prendre feu, s'embraser; to **b. open** s'ouvrir avec

force; to **b. out laughing** éclater de rire; − vt crever, faire éclater; (rupture) rompre; to **b. open** ouvrir avec force. ◆**—ing** a (full) plein à craquer (with de); **b. with** (joy) débordant de; to be **b.** to do mourir d'envie de faire.

bury ['berɪ] vt (dead person) enterrer; (hide) enfouir; (plunge, absorb) plonger.

bus [bʌs] n (auto)bus m; (long-distance) (auto)car m; − a (driver, ticket etc) d'autobus; d'autocar; **b. shelter** abribus m; **b. station** gare f routière; **b. stop** arrêt m d'autobus; − vt (-ss-) (children) transporter (en bus) à l'école. ◆**bussing** n Sch ramassage m scolaire.

bush [bʊʃ] n buisson m; (of hair) tignasse f; the **b.** (land) la brousse. ◆**bushy** a (-ier, -iest) (hair, tail etc) broussailleux.

bushed [bʊʃt] a (tired) Fam crevé.

business ['bɪznɪs] n affaires fpl, commerce m; (shop) commerce m; (task, concern, matter) affaire f; the **textile b.** le textile; **big b.** Fam les grosses entreprises fpl commerciales; **on b.** (to travel) pour affaires; **it's your b. to . . .** c'est à vous de . . . ; **you have no b. to . . .** vous n'avez pas le droit de . . . ; **that's none of your b.!** ça ne vous regarde pas!; to **mean b.** Fam ne pas plaisanter; − a commercial; (meeting, trip) d'affaires; **b. hours** (office) heures fpl de travail; (shop) heures fpl d'ouverture. ◆**businesslike** a sérieux, pratique. ◆**businessman** n (pl -men) homme m d'affaires. ◆**businesswoman** n (pl -women) femme f d'affaires.

busker ['bʌskər] n musicien, -ienne mf des rues.

bust [bʌst] n **1** (sculpture) buste m; (woman's breasts) poitrine f. **2** a (broken) Fam fichu; to go **b.** (bankrupt) faire faillite; − vti (pt & pp bust or busted) Fam = to burst & to break. ◆**b.-up** n Fam (quarrel) engueulade f; (breakup) rupture f.

bustl/e ['bʌs(ə)l] vi to **b. (about)** s'affairer; − n activité f, branle-bas m. ◆**—ing** a (street) bruyant.

bus/y ['bɪzɪ] a (-ier, -iest) occupé (doing à faire); (active) actif; (day) chargé; (street) animé; (line) Tel Am occupé; to be **b.** doing (in the process of) être en train de faire; − vt to **b.** oneself s'occuper (with à qch, doing à faire). ◆**—ily** adv activement. ◆**busybody** n to be a **b.** faire la mouche du coche.

but [bʌt, unstressed bət] **1** conj mais. **2** prep (except) sauf; **b. for that** sans cela; **b. for him** sans lui; **no one b. you** personne d'autre que toi. **3** *adv* (*only*) ne ... que, seulement.

butane ['bjuːteɪn] *n* (*gas*) butane *m*.

butcher ['bʊtʃər] *n* boucher *m*; **b.'s shop** boucherie *f*; − *vt* (*people*) massacrer; (*animal*) abattre. ◆**butchery** *n* massacre *m* (**of** de).

butler ['bʌtlər] *n* maître *m* d'hôtel.

butt [bʌt] **1** *n* (*of cigarette*) mégot *m*; (*of gun*) crosse *f*; (*buttocks*) *Am Fam* derrière *m*; **b. for ridicule** objet *m* de risée. **2** *vi* **to b. in** interrompre, intervenir.

butter ['bʌtər] *n* beurre *m*; **b. bean** haricot *m* blanc; **b. dish** beurrier *m*; − *vt* beurrer; **to b. s.o. up** *Fam* flatter qn. ◆**buttercup** *n* bouton-d'or *m*. ◆**buttermilk** *n* lait *m* de beurre.

butterfly ['bʌtəflaɪ] *n* papillon *m*; **to have butterflies** *Fam* avoir le trac; **b. stroke** *Swimming* brasse *f* papillon.

buttock ['bʌtək] *n* fesse *f*.

button ['bʌtən] *n* bouton *m*; − *vt* **to b. (up)** boutonner; − *vi* **to b. up** (*of garment*) se boutonner. ◆**buttonhole 1** *n* boutonnière *f*; (*flower*) fleur *f*. **2** *vt* (*person*) *Fam* accrocher.

buttress ['bʌtrɪs] *n Archit* contrefort *m*; *Fig* soutien *m*; **flying b.** arc-boutant *m*; − *vt* (*support*) *Archit & Fig* soutenir.

buxom ['bʌksəm] *a* (*woman*) bien en chair.

buy [baɪ] *vt* (*pt & pp* **bought**) acheter (**from s.o.** à qn, **for s.o.** à *or* pour qn); (*story etc*) *Am Fam* avaler, croire; **to b. back** racheter; **to b. over** (*bribe*) corrompre; **to b. up** acheter en bloc; − *n* **a good b.** une bonne affaire. ◆−**er** *n* acheteur, -euse *mf*.

buzz [bʌz] **1** *vi* bourdonner; **to b. off** *Fam* décamper; − *n* bourdonnement *m*. **2** *vt* (*building etc*) *Av* raser. **3** *vt* **to b. s.o.** *Tel* appeler qn; − *n Tel Fam* coup *m* de fil. ◆−**er** *n* interphone *m*; (*of bell, clock*) sonnerie *f*; (*hooter*) sirène *f*.

by [baɪ] *prep* **1** (*agent, manner*) par; **hit/chosen/etc by** frappé/choisi/*etc* par; **surrounded/followed/etc by** entouré/suivi/*etc* de; **by doing** en faisant; **by sea** par mer; **by mistake** par erreur; **by car** en voiture; **by bicycle** à bicyclette; **by moonlight** au clair de lune; **one by one** un à un; **day by day** de jour en jour; **by sight/day/far** de vue/jour/loin; **by the door** (*through*) par la porte; (**all**) **by oneself** tout seul. **2** (*next to*) à côté de; (*near*) près de; **by the lake/sea** au bord du lac/de la mer; **to pass by the bank** passer devant la banque. **3** (*before in time*) avant; **by Monday** avant lundi, d'ici lundi; **by now** à cette heure-ci, déjà; **by yesterday** (dès) hier. **4** (*amount, measurement*) à; **by the kilo** au kilo; **taller by a metre** plus grand d'un mètre; **paid by the hour** payé à l'heure. **5** (*according to*) d'après; − *adv* **close by** tout près; **to go by, pass by** passer; **to put by** mettre de côté; **by and by** bientôt; **by and large** en gros. ◆**by-election** *n* élection *f* partielle. ◆**by-law** *n* arrêté *m*; (*of organization*) *Am* statut *m*. ◆**by-product** *n* sous-produit *m*. ◆**by-road** *n* chemin *m* de traverse.

bye(-bye)! [baɪ('baɪ)] *int Fam* salut!, au revoir!

bygone ['baɪgɒn] *a* **in b. days** jadis.

bypass ['baɪpɑːs] *n* déviation *f* (routière), dérivation *f*; − *vt* contourner; (*ignore*) *Fig* éviter de passer par.

bystander ['baɪstændər] *n* spectateur, -trice *mf*; (*in street*) badaud, -aude *mf*.

byword ['baɪwɜːd] *n* **a b. for** *Pej* un synonyme de.

C

C, c [siː] *n* C, c *m*.

c *abbr* = cent.

cab [kæb] *n* taxi *m*; (*horse-drawn*) *Hist* fiacre *m*; (*of train driver etc*) cabine *f*. ◆**cabby** *n Fam* (*chauffeur m de*) taxi *m*; *Hist* cocher *m*.

cabaret ['kæbəreɪ] *n* (*show*) spectacle *m*; (*place*) cabaret *m*.

cabbage ['kæbɪdʒ] *n* chou *m*.

cabin ['kæbɪn] *n Nau Rail* cabine *f*; (*hut*) cabane *f*, case *f*; **c. boy** mousse *m*.

cabinet ['kæbɪnɪt] **1** *n* (*cupboard*) armoire *f*; (*for display*) vitrine *f*; (*filing*) **c.** classeur *m* (de bureau). **2** *n Pol* cabinet *m*; − *a* ministériel; **c. minister** ministre *m*. ◆**c.-maker** *n* ébéniste *m*.

cable ['keɪb(ə)l] *n* câble *m*; **c. car** (*with overhead cable*) téléphérique *m*; *Rail* funiculaire *m*; **c. television** la télévision par câble; **to have c.** *Fam* avoir le câble; − *vt* (*message etc*) câbler (**to** à).

caboose [kə'buːs] n Rail Am fourgon m (de queue).

cache [kæʃ] n (place) cachette f; **an arms' c.** des armes cachées, une cache d'armes.

cachet ['kæʃeɪ] n (mark, character etc) cachet m.

cackle ['kæk(ə)l] vi (of hen) caqueter; (laugh) glousser; – n caquet m; gloussement m.

cacophony [kə'kɒfənɪ] n cacophonie f.

cactus, pl -ti or -tuses ['kæktəs, -taɪ, -təsɪz] n cactus m.

cad [kæd] n Old-fashioned Pej goujat m.

cadaverous [kə'dævərəs] a cadavérique.

caddie ['kædɪ] n Golf caddie m.

caddy ['kædɪ] n (tea) c. boîte f à thé.

cadence ['keɪdəns] n Mus cadence f.

cadet [kə'det] n Mil élève m officier.

cadge [kædʒ] vi (beg) Pej quémander; – vt (meal) se faire payer (off s.o. par qn); **to c. money from** or **off s.o.** taper qn.

Caesarean [sɪ'zeərɪən] n c. (section) Med césarienne f.

café ['kæfeɪ] n café(-restaurant) m. ◆**cafeteria** [kæfɪ'tɪərɪə] n cafétéria f.

caffeine ['kæfiːn] n caféine f.

cage [keɪdʒ] n cage f; – vt **to c. (up)** mettre en cage.

cagey ['keɪdʒɪ] a Fam peu communicatif (about à l'égard de).

cahoots [kə'huːts] n **in c.** Sl de mèche, en cheville (with avec).

cajole [kə'dʒəʊl] vt amadouer, enjôler.

cak/e [keɪk] **1** n gâteau m; (small) pâtisserie f; c. **of soap** savonnette f. **2** vi (harden) durcir; – vt (cover) couvrir (with de). ◆**—ed** a (mud) séché.

calamine ['kæləmaɪn] n c. (lotion) lotion f apaisante (à la calamine).

calamity [kə'læmɪtɪ] n calamité f. ◆**calamitous** a désastreux.

calcium ['kælsɪəm] n calcium m.

calculat/e ['kælkjʊleɪt] vti calculer; **to c. that** Fam supposer que; **to c. on** compter sur. ◆**—ing** a (shrewd) calculateur. ◆**calcu'lation** n calcul m. ◆**calculator** n (desk computer) calculatrice f; (pocket) c. calculatrice (de poche). ◆**calculus** n Math Med calcul m.

calendar ['kælɪndər] n calendrier m; (directory) annuaire m.

calf [kɑːf] n (pl calves) **1** (animal) veau m. **2** Anat mollet m.

calibre ['kælɪbər] n calibre m. ◆**calibrate** vt calibrer.

calico ['kælɪkəʊ] n (pl -oes or -os) (fabric) calicot m; (printed) Am indienne f.

call [kɔːl] n appel m; (shout) cri m; (vocation) vocation f; (visit) visite f; (telephone) c. communication f, appel m téléphonique; **to make a c.** Tel téléphoner (to à); **on c.** de garde; **no c. to do** aucune raison de faire; **there's no c. for that article** Com cet article n'est pas très demandé; c. **box** cabine f (téléphonique); – vt appeler; (wake up) réveiller; (person to meeting) convoquer (to à); (attention) attirer (to sur); (truce) demander; (consider) considérer; **he's called David** il s'appelle David; **to c. a meeting** convoquer une assemblée; **to c. s.o. a liar/etc** qualifier or traiter qn de menteur/etc; **to c. into question** mettre en question; **let's c. it a day** Fam on va s'arrêter là, ça suffit; **to c. sth (out)** (shout) crier qch; – vi appeler; **to c. (out)** (cry out) crier; **to c. (in** or **round** or **by** or **over)** (visit) passer. ■ **to c. back** vti appeler; **to c. for** vt (require) demander; (summon) appeler; (collect) passer prendre; **to c. in** vt faire venir or entrer; (police) appeler; (recall) rappeler, faire rentrer; – vi **to c. in on s.o.** passer chez qn. ◆**call-in** a (programme) Rad à ligne ouverte; **to c. off** vt (cancel) annuler; (dog) rappeler; **to c. out** vt (doctor) appeler; (workers) donner une consigne de grève à; – vi **to c. out for** demander à haute voix; **to c. up** vt Mil Tel appeler; (memories) évoquer. ◆**call-up** n Mil appel m, mobilisation f; **to c. (up)on** vi (visit) passer voir, passer chez; (invoke) invoquer; **to c. (up)on s.o. to do** inviter qn à faire; (urge) sommer qn de faire. ◆**calling** n vocation f; c. **card** Am carte f de visite. ◆**caller** n visiteur, -euse mf; Tel correspondant, -ante mf.

calligraphy [kə'lɪgrəfɪ] n calligraphie f.

callous ['kæləs] a **1** cruel, insensible. **2** (skin) calleux. ◆**callus** n durillon m, cal m.

callow ['kæləʊ] a inexpérimenté.

calm [kɑːm] a (-er, -est) calme, tranquille; **keep c.!** (don't panic) du calme!; – n calme m; – vt **to c. (down)** calmer; – vi **to c. down** se calmer. ◆**—ly** adv calmement. ◆**—ness** n calme m.

calorie ['kælərɪ] n calorie f.

calumny ['kæləmnɪ] n calomnie f.

calvary ['kælvərɪ] n Rel calvaire m.

calve [kɑːv] vi (of cow) vêler.

camber ['kæmbər] n (in road) bombement m.

came [keɪm] see come.

camel ['kæməl] n chameau m.

camellia [kə'miːlɪə] n Bot camélia m.

cameo ['kæmɪəʊ] n camée m.

camera ['kæmrə] n appareil(-photo) m; TV Cin caméra f. ◆cameraman n (pl -men) caméraman m.

camomile ['kæməmaɪl] n Bot camomille f.

camouflage ['kæmʊflɑːʒ] n camouflage m; – vt camoufler.

camp¹ [kæmp] n camp m, campement m; c. bed lit m de camp; – vi to c. (out) camper. ◆—ing n Sp camping m; c. site (terrain m de) camping m. ◆—er n (person) campeur, -euse mf; (vehicle) camping-car m. ◆campfire n feu m de camp. ◆campsite n camping m.

camp² [kæmp] a (affected) affecté, exagéré (de façon à provoquer le rire).

campaign [kæm'peɪn] n Pol Mil Journ etc campagne f; – vi faire campagne. ◆—er n militant, -ante mf (for pour).

campus ['kæmpəs] n Univ campus m.

can¹ [kən, unstressed kən] v aux (pres t can; pt could) (be able to) pouvoir; (know how to) savoir; if I c. si je peux; she c. swim elle sait nager; if I could swim si je savais nager; he could do it tomorrow il pourrait le faire demain; he couldn't help me il ne pouvait pas m'aider; he could have done it il aurait pu le faire; you could be wrong (possibility) tu as peut-être tort; he can't be old (probability) il ne doit pas être vieux; c. I come in? (permission) puis-je entrer?; you can't or c. not come tu ne peux pas venir; I c. see je vois.

can² [kæn] n (for water etc) bidon m; (tin for food) boîte f; – vt (-nn-) mettre en boîte. ◆canned a en boîte, en conserve; c. food conserves fpl. ◆can-opener n ouvre-boîtes m inv.

Canada ['kænədə] n Canada m. ◆Canadian [kə'neɪdɪən] a & n canadien, -ienne (mf).

canal [kə'næl] n canal m.

canary [kə'neərɪ] n canari m, serin m.

cancan ['kænkæn] n french-cancan m.

cancel ['kænsəl] vt (-ll-, Am -l-) annuler; (goods, taxi, appointment) décommander; (word, paragraph etc) biffer; (train) supprimer; (stamp) oblitérer; to c. a ticket (with date) composter un billet; (punch) poinçonner un billet; to c. each other out s'annuler. ◆cance'llation n annulation f; suppression f; oblitération f.

cancer ['kænsər] n cancer m; C. (sign) le Cancer; c. patient cancéreux, -euse mf. ◆cancerous a cancéreux.

candelabra [kændɪ'lɑːbrə] n candélabre m.

candid ['kændɪd] a franc, sincère. ◆candour n franchise f, sincérité f.

candidate ['kændɪdeɪt] n candidat, -ate mf. ◆candidacy n, ◆candidature n candidature f.

candle ['kænd(ə)l] n bougie f; (tallow) chandelle f; Rel cierge m; c. grease suif m. ◆candlelight n by c. à la (lueur d'une) bougie; to have dinner by c. dîner aux chandelles. ◆candlestick n bougeoir m; (tall) chandelier m.

candy ['kændɪ] n Am bonbon(s) m(pl); (sugar) c. sucre m candi; c. store Am confiserie f. ◆candied a (fruit) confit, glacé. ◆candyfloss n barbe f à papa.

cane [keɪn] n canne f; (for basket) rotin m; Sch baguette f; – vt (punish) Sch fouetter.

canine ['keɪnaɪn] 1 a canin. 2 n (tooth) canine f.

canister ['kænɪstər] n boîte f (en métal).

canker ['kæŋkər] n (in disease) & Fig chancre m.

cannabis ['kænəbɪs] n (plant) chanvre m indien; (drug) haschisch m.

cannibal ['kænɪbəl] n & a cannibale (mf).

cannon ['kænən] n (pl -s or inv) canon m. ◆cannonball n boulet m (de canon).

cannot ['kænɒt] = can not.

canny ['kænɪ] a (-ier, -iest) rusé, malin.

canoe [kə'nuː] n canoë m, kayak m; – vi faire du canoë or du kayak. ◆—ing n to go c. Sp faire du canoë or du kayak. ◆canoeist n canoéiste mf.

canon ['kænən] n (law) canon m; (clergyman) chanoine m. ◆canonize vt Rel canoniser.

canopy ['kænəpɪ] n (over bed, altar etc) dais m; (hood of pram) capote f; (awning) auvent m; (made of glass) marquise f; (of sky) Fig voûte f.

cant [kænt] n (jargon) jargon m.

can't [kɑːnt] = can not.

cantaloup(e) ['kæntəluːp, Am -ləʊp] n (melon) cantaloup m.

cantankerous [kæn'tæŋkərəs] a grincheux, acariâtre.

cantata [kæn'tɑːtə] n Mus cantate f.

canteen [kæn'tiːn] n (place) cantine f; (flask) gourde f; c. of cutlery ménagère f.

canter ['kæntər] n petit galop m; – vi aller au petit galop.

cantor ['kæntər] n Rel chantre m, maître m de chapelle.

canvas ['kænvəs] n (grosse) toile f; (for embroidery) canevas m.

canvass ['kænvəs] vt (an area) faire du démarchage dans; (opinions) sonder; to c.

s.o. *Pol* solliciter des voix de qn; *Com* solliciter des commandes de qn. ◆**—ing** n *Com* démarchage m, prospection f; *Pol* démarchage m (électoral). ◆**—er** n *Pol* agent m électoral; *Com* démarcheur, -euse mf.

canyon ['kænjən] n cañon m, canyon m.

cap¹ [kæp] n 1 (*hat*) casquette f; (*for shower etc*) & *Nau* bonnet m; *Mil* képi m. 2 (*of bottle, tube, valve*) bouchon m; (*of milk or beer bottle*) capsule f; (*of pen*) capuchon m. 3 (*of child's gun*) amorce f, capsule f. 4 (*Dutch*) diaphragme m.

cap² [kæp] vt (-pp-) (*outdo*) surpasser; **to c. it all** pour comble; **capped with** (*covered*) coiffé de.

capable ['keɪpəb(ə)l] a (*person*) capable (**of** sth de qch, **of doing** de faire), compétent; **c. of** (*thing*) susceptible de. ◆**capa'bility** n capacité f. ◆**capably** adv avec compétence.

capacity [kə'pæsətɪ] n (*of container*) capacité f, contenance f; (*ability*) aptitude f, capacité f; (*output*) rendement m; **in my c. as** en ma qualité de; **in an advisory/etc c.** à titre consultatif/etc; **filled to c.** absolument plein, comble; **c. audience** salle f comble.

cape [keɪp] n 1 (*cloak*) cape f; (*of cyclist*) pèlerine f. 2 *Geog* cap m; **C. Town** Le Cap.

caper ['keɪpər] 1 vi (*jump about*) gambader. 2 n (*activity*) *Sl* affaire f; (*prank*) *Fam* farce f; (*trip*) *Fam* virée f. 3 n *Bot Culin* câpre f.

capital ['kæpɪtl] 1 a (*punishment, letter, importance*) capital; — n c. (*city*) capitale f; **c. (letter)** majuscule f, capitale f. 2 n (*money*) capital m, capitaux mpl. ◆**capitalism** n capitalisme m. ◆**capitalist** a & n capitaliste (mf). ◆**capitalize** vi **to c. on** tirer parti de.

capitulate [kə'pɪtʃʊleɪt] vi capituler. ◆**capitu'lation** n capitulation f.

caprice [kə'priːs] n caprice m. ◆**capricious** [kə'prɪʃəs] a capricieux.

Capricorn ['kæprɪkɔːn] n (*sign*) le Capricorne.

capsize [kæp'saɪz] vi *Nau* chavirer; — vt (faire) chavirer.

capsule ['kæpsəl, 'kæpsjuːl] n (*medicine, of spaceship etc*) capsule f.

captain ['kæptɪn] n capitaine m; — vt *Nau* commander; *Sp* être le capitaine de.

caption ['kæpʃ(ə)n] n *Cin Journ* sous-titre m; (*under illustration*) légende f.

captivate ['kæptɪveɪt] vt captiver.

captive ['kæptɪv] n captif, -ive mf, prisonnier, -ière mf. ◆**cap'tivity** n captivité f.

capture ['kæptʃər] n capture f; — vt (*person, animal*) prendre, capturer; (*town*) prendre; (*attention*) capter; (*represent in words, on film etc*) rendre, reproduire.

car [kɑːr] n voiture f, auto(mobile) f; *Rail* wagon m; — a (*industry*) automobile; **c. ferry** ferry-boat m; **c. park** parking m; **c. radio** autoradio m; **c. wash** (*action*) lavage m automatique; (*machine*) lave-auto m. ◆**carfare** n *Am* frais mpl de voyage. ◆**carport** n auvent m (pour voiture). ◆**carsick** a **to be c.** être malade en voiture.

carafe [kə'ræf] n carafe f.

caramel ['kærəməl] n (*flavouring, toffee*) caramel m.

carat ['kærət] n carat m.

caravan ['kærəvæn] n (*in desert*) & *Aut* caravane f; (*horse-drawn*) roulotte f; **c. site** camping m pour caravanes.

caraway ['kærəweɪ] n *Bot Culin* cumin m, carvi m.

carbohydrates [kɑːbəʊ'haɪdreɪts] npl (*in diet*) féculents mpl.

carbon ['kɑːbən] n carbone m; **c. copy** double m (au carbone); *Fig* réplique f, double m; **c. paper** (papier m) carbone m.

carbuncle ['kɑːbʌŋk(ə)l] n *Med* furoncle m, clou m.

carburettor [kɑːbjʊ'retər] (*Am* **carburetor** ['kɑːbəreɪtər]) n carburateur m.

carcass ['kɑːkəs] n (*body, framework*) carcasse f.

carcinogenic [kɑːsɪnə'dʒenɪk] a cancérigène.

card [kɑːd] n carte f; (*cardboard*) carton m; (*index*) fiche f; **c. index** fichier m; **c. table** table f de jeu; **to play cards** jouer aux cartes; **on** or *Am* **in the cards** *Fam* très vraisemblable; **to get one's cards** (*be dismissed*) *Fam* être renvoyé. ◆**cardboard** n carton m. ◆**cardsharp** n tricheur, -euse mf.

cardiac ['kɑːdɪæk] a cardiaque.

cardigan ['kɑːdɪgən] n cardigan m, gilet m.

cardinal ['kɑːdɪn(ə)l] 1 a (*number etc*) cardinal. 2 n (*priest*) cardinal m.

care [keər] 1 vi **to c. about** (*feel concern about*) se soucier de, s'intéresser à; **I don't c.** ça m'est égal; **I couldn't c. less** *Fam* je m'en fiche; **who cares?** qu'est-ce que ça fait? 2 vi (*like*) aimer, vouloir; **would you c. to try?** voulez-vous essayer?, aimeriez-vous essayer?; **I don't c. for it** (*music etc*) je n'aime pas tellement ça; **to c. for** (*a drink, a change etc*) avoir envie de; **to c. about** or **for s.o.** avoir de la sympathie pour qn; **to c. for**

(*look after*) s'occuper de; (*sick person*) soigner. **3** *n* (*application, heed*) soin(s) *m*(*pl*), attention *f*; (*charge, protection*) garde *f*, soin *m*; (*anxiety*) souci *m*; **to take c. not to do** faire attention à ne pas faire; **take c. to put everything back** veillez à tout ranger; **to take c. of** s'occuper de; **to take c. of itself** (*of matter*) s'arranger; **to take c. of oneself** (*manage*) se débrouiller; (*keep healthy*) faire attention à sa santé. ◆**carefree** *a* insouciant. ◆**caretaker** *n* gardien, -ienne *mf*, concierge *mf*.

career [kə'rɪər] **1** *n* carrière *f*; – *a* (*diplomat etc*) de carrière. **2** *vi* **to c. along** aller à toute vitesse.

careful ['keəf(ə)l] *a* (*diligent*) soigneux (*about, of* de); (*cautious*) prudent; **c. (with money)** regardant; **to be c. of** *or* **with** (*heed*) faire attention à. ◆**—ly** *adv* avec soin; prudemment. ◆**careless** *a* négligent; (*thoughtless*) irréfléchi; (*inattentive*) inattentif (*of* à). ◆**carelessness** *n* négligence *f*, manque *m* de soin.

caress [kə'res] *n* caresse *f*; – *vt* (*stroke*) caresser; (*kiss*) embrasser.

cargo ['kɑːɡəʊ] *n* (*pl* **-oes,** *Am* **-os**) cargaison *f*; **c. boat** cargo *m*.

Caribbean [kærɪ'biːən, *Am* kə'rɪbɪən] *a* caraïbe; – *n* **the C. (Islands)** les Antilles *fpl*.

caricature ['kærɪkətʃʊər] *n* caricature *f*; – *vt* caricaturer.

caring ['keərɪŋ] *a* (*loving*) aimant; (*understanding*) compréhensif; – *n* affection *f*.

carnage ['kɑːnɪdʒ] *n* carnage *m*.

carnal ['kɑːnəl] *a* charnel, sexuel.

carnation [kɑː'neɪʃən] *n* œillet *m*.

carnival ['kɑːnɪvəl] *n* carnaval *m*.

carnivore ['kɑːnɪvɔːr] *n* carnivore *m*. ◆**carnivorous** *a* carnivore.

carol ['kærəl] *n* chant *m* (de Noël).

carouse [kə'raʊz] *vi* faire la fête.

carp [kɑːp] **1** *n* (*fish*) carpe *f*. **2** *vi* critiquer; **to c. at** critiquer.

carpenter ['kɑːpɪntər] *n* (*for house building*) charpentier *m*; (*light woodwork*) menuisier *m*. ◆**carpentry** *n* charpenterie *f*; menuiserie *f*.

carpet ['kɑːpɪt] *n* tapis *m*; (*fitted*) moquette *f*; **c. sweeper** balai *m* mécanique; – *vt* recouvrir d'un tapis *or* d'une moquette; (*of snow etc*) *Fig* tapisser. ◆**—ing** *n* (*carpets*) tapis *mpl*; moquette *f*.

carriage ['kærɪdʒ] *n* (*horse-drawn*) voiture *f*, équipage *m*; *Rail* voiture *f*; *Com* transport *m*; (*bearing of person*) port *m*; (*of typewriter*) chariot *m*; **c. paid** port payé. ◆**carriageway** *n* (*of road*) chaussée *f*.

carrier ['kærɪər] *n Com* entreprise *f* de transports; *Med* porteur, -euse *mf*; **c. (bag)** sac *m* (en plastique); **c. pigeon** pigeon *m* voyageur.

carrion ['kærɪən] *n* charogne *f*.

carrot ['kærət] *n* carotte *f*.

carry ['kærɪ] *vt* porter; (*goods*) transporter; (*by wind*) emporter; (*involve*) comporter; (*interest*) *Com* produire; (*extend*) faire passer; (*win*) remporter; (*authority*) avoir; (*child*) *Med* attendre; (*motion*) *Pol* faire passer, voter; (*sell*) stocker; *Math* retenir; **to c. too far** pousser trop loin; **to c. oneself** se comporter; – *vi* (*of sound*) porter. ■ **to c. away** *vt* emporter; *Fig* transporter; **to be** *or* **get carried away** (*excited*) s'emballer; **to c. back** *vt* (*thing*) rapporter; (*person*) ramener; (*in thought*) reporter; **to c. off** *vt* emporter; (*kidnap*) enlever; (*prize*) remporter; **to c. it off** réussir; **to c. on** *vt* continuer; (*conduct*) diriger, mener; (*sustain*) soutenir; – *vi* continuer (**doing** faire); (*behave*) *Pej* se conduire (mal); (*complain*) se plaindre; **to c. on with sth** continuer qch; **to c. on about** (*talk*) causer de. ◆**carryings-'on** *npl Pej* activités *fpl*; (*behaviour*) *Pej* façons *fpl*; **to c. out** *vt* (*plan etc*) exécuter, réaliser; (*repair etc*) effectuer; (*duty*) accomplir; (*meal*) *Am* emporter; **to c. through** *vt* (*plan etc*) mener à bonne fin.

carryall ['kærɪɔːl] *n Am* fourre-tout *m inv*. ◆**carrycot** *n* (nacelle *f*) porte-bébé *m*.

cart [kɑːt] **1** *n* charrette *f*; (*handcart*) voiture *f* à bras. **2** *vt* (*goods, people*) transporter; **to c. (around)** *Fam* trimbal(l)er; **to c. away** emporter. ◆**carthorse** *n* cheval *m* de trait.

cartel [kɑː'tel] *n Econ Pol* cartel *m*.

cartilage ['kɑːtɪlɪdʒ] *n* cartilage *m*.

carton ['kɑːtən] *n* (*box*) carton *m*; (*of milk, fruit juice etc*) brick *m*, pack *m*; (*of cigarettes*) cartouche *f*; (*of cream*) pot *m*.

cartoon [kɑː'tuːn] *n Journ* dessin *m* (humoristique); *Cin* dessin *m* animé; (*strip*) **c.** bande *f* dessinée. ◆**cartoonist** *n Journ* dessinateur, -trice *mf* (humoristique).

cartridge ['kɑːtrɪdʒ] *n* (*of firearm, pen, camera, tape deck*) cartouche *f*, (*of record player*) cellule *f*; **c. belt** cartouchière *f*.

carv/e [kɑːv] *vt* (*cut*) tailler (**out of** dans); (*sculpt*) sculpter; (*initials etc*) graver; **to c. (up)** (*meat*) découper; **to c. up** (*country*) dépecer, morceler; **to c. out sth for oneself** (*career etc*) se tailler qch. ◆**—ing** *n* (**wood**) **c.** sculpture *f* (sur bois).

cascade [kæs'keɪd] *n* (*of rocks*) chute *f*; (*of*

blows) déluge *m*; (*of lace*) flot *m*; — *vi* tomber: (*hang*) pendre.

case [keɪs] *n* **1** (*instance*) & *Med* cas *m*; *Jur* affaire *f*; *Phil* arguments *mpl*; **in any c.** en tout cas; **in c. it rains** au cas où il pleuvrait; **in c. of** en cas de; (*just*) **in c.** à tout hasard. **2** (*bag*) valise *f*; (*crate*) caisse *f*; (*for pen, glasses, camera, violin, cigarettes*) étui *m*; (*for jewels*) coffret *m*. ◆**casing** *n* (*covering*) enveloppe *f*.

cash [kæʃ] *n* argent *m*; **to pay (in) c.** (*not by cheque*) payer en espèces *or* en liquide; **to pay c. (down)** payer comptant; **c. price** *prix m* (au) comptant; **c. box** caisse *f*; **c. desk** caisse *f*; **c. register** caisse *f* enregistreuse; — *vt* (*banknote*) changer; **to c. a cheque** (*of person*) encaisser un chèque; (*of bank*) payer un chèque; **to c. in on** *Fam* profiter de. ◆**ca'shier 1** *n* caissier, -ière *mf*. **2** *vt* (*dismiss*) *Mil* casser.

cashew [kæʃuː] *n* (*nut*) cajou *m*.

cashmere [kæʃmɪər] *n* cachemire *m*.

casino [kəsiːnəʊ] *n* (*pl* -os) casino *m*.

cask [kɑːsk] *n* fût *m*, tonneau *m*. ◆**casket** *n* (*box*) coffret *m*; (*coffin*) cercueil *m*.

casserole [kæsərəʊl] *n* (*covered dish*) cocotte *f*; (*stew*) ragoût *m* en cocotte.

cassette [kəset] *n* cassette *f*; *Phot* cartouche *f*; **c. player** lecteur *m* de cassettes; **c. recorder** magnétophone *m* à cassettes.

cassock [kæsək] *n* soutane *f*.

cast [kɑːst] **1** *n* *Th* acteurs *mpl*; (*list*) *Th* distribution *f*; (*mould*) moulage *m*; (*of dice*) coup *m*; *Med* plâtre *m*; (*squint*) léger strabisme *m*; **c. of mind** tournure *f* d'esprit. **2** *vt* (*pt & pp* cast) (*throw*) jeter; (*light, shadow*) projeter; (*blame*) rejeter; (*glance*) jeter; (*doubt*) exprimer; (*lose*) perdre; (*metal*) couler; (*role*) *Th* distribuer; (*actor*) donner un rôle à; **to c. one's mind back** se reporter en arrière; **to c. a vote** voter; **to c. aside** rejeter; **to c. off** (*chains etc*) se libérer de; (*shed, lose*) se dépouiller de; *Fig* abandonner. **3** *vi* **to c. off** *Nau* appareiller. **4** *n* **c. iron** fonte *f*. ◆**c.-'iron** *a* (*pan etc*) en fonte; (*will etc*) *Fig* de fer, solide.

castaway [kɑːstəweɪ] *n* naufragé, -ée *mf*.

caste [kɑːst] *n* caste *f*.

caster [kɑːstər] *n* (*wheel*) roulette *f*; **c. sugar** sucre *m* en poudre.

castle [kɑːs(ə)l] *n* château *m*; (*in chess*) tour *f*.

castoffs [kɑːstɒfs] *npl* vieux vêtements *mpl*.

castor [kɑːstər] *n* (*wheel*) roulette *f*; **c. oil** huile *f* de ricin; **c. sugar** sucre *m* en poudre.

castrate [kæstreɪt] *vt* châtrer. ◆**castration** *n* castration *f*.

casual [kæʒjʊəl] *a* (*meeting*) fortuit; (*remark*) fait en passant; (*stroll*) sans but; (*offhand*) désinvolte, insouciant; (*worker*) temporaire; (*work*) irrégulier; **c. clothes** vêtements *mpl* sport; **a c. acquaintance** quelqu'un que l'on connaît un peu. ◆**—ly** *adv* par hasard; (*informally*) avec désinvolture; (*to remark*) en passant.

casualty [kæʒjʊltɪ] *n* (*dead*) mort *m*, morte *f*; (*wounded*) blessé, -ée *mf*; (*accident victim*) accidenté, -ée *mf*; **casualties** morts et blessés *mpl*; *Mil* pertes *fpl*; **c. department** *Med* service *m* des accidentés.

cat [kæt] *n* chat *m*, chatte *f*; **c. burglar** monte-en-l'air *m inv*; **c.'s eyes®** cataphotes® *mpl*, clous *mpl*. ◆**catcall** *n* sifflet *m*, huée *f*.

cataclysm [kætəklɪzəm] *n* cataclysme *m*.

catalogue [kætəlɒg] (*Am* catalog) *n* catalogue *m*; — *vt* cataloguer.

catalyst [kætəlɪst] *n* *Ch* & *Fig* catalyseur *m*.

catapult [kætəpʌlt] *n* lance-pierres *m inv*; *Hist Av* catapulte *f*; — *vt* catapulter.

cataract [kætərækt] *n* (*waterfall*) & *Med* cataracte *f*.

catarrh [kətɑːr] *n* catarrhe *m*, rhume *m*.

catastrophe [kətæstrəfɪ] *n* catastrophe *f*. ◆**cata'strophic** *a* catastrophique.

catch [kætʃ] *vt* (*pt & pp* caught) (*ball, thief, illness etc*) attraper; (*grab*) prendre, saisir; (*surprise*) (sur)prendre; (*understand*) saisir; (*train etc*) attraper, (réussir à) prendre; (*attention*) attirer; (*of nail etc*) accrocher; (*finger etc*) se prendre (in dans); **to c. sight of** apercevoir; **to c. fire** prendre feu; **to c. s.o. (in)** *Fam* trouver qn (chez soi); **to c. one's breath** (*rest a while*) reprendre haleine; (*stop breathing*) retenir son souffle; **I didn't c. the train/etc** j'ai manqué le train/etc; **to c. s.o. out** prendre qn en défaut; **to c. s.o. up** rattraper qn; — *vi* (*of fire*) prendre; **her skirt (got) caught in the door** sa jupe s'est prise *or* coincée dans la porte; **to c. on** prendre, devenir populaire; (*understand*) saisir; **to c. up** se rattraper; **to c. up with s.o.** rattraper qn; — *n* capture *f*, prise *f*; (*trick, snare*) piège *m*; (*on door*) loquet *m*. ◆**—ing** *a* contagieux. ◆**catchphrase** *n*, ◆**catchword** *n* slogan *m*.

catchy [kætʃɪ] *a* (-ier, -iest) (*tune*) *Fam* facile à retenir.

catechism [kætɪkɪzəm] *n* *Rel* catéchisme *m*.

category [kætɪgərɪ] *n* catégorie *f*. ◆**cate-**

'gorical *a* catégorique. ◆**categorize** *vt* classer (par catégories).

cater ['keɪtər] *vi* s'occuper de la nourriture; to c. for *or* to (*need, taste*) satisfaire; (*readership*) *Journ* s'adresser à. ◆**—ing** *n* restauration *f.* ◆**—er** *n* traiteur *m.*

caterpillar ['kætəpɪlər] *n* chenille *f.*

catgut ['kætɡʌt] *n* (*cord*) boyau *m.*

cathedral [kə'θiːdrəl] *n* cathédrale *f.*

catholic ['kæθlɪk] **1** *a* & *n* C. catholique (*mf*). **2** *a* (*taste*) universel; (*view*) libéral. ◆**Ca'tholicism** *n* catholicisme *m.*

cattle ['kæt(ə)l] *npl* bétail *m*, bestiaux *mpl.*

catty ['kætɪ] *a* (-ier, -iest) *Fam* rosse, méchant.

caucus ['kɔːkəs] *n Pol Am* comité *m* électoral.

caught [kɔːt] *see* **catch.**

cauldron ['kɔːldrən] *n* chaudron *m.*

cauliflower ['kɒlɪflaʊər] *n* chou-fleur *m.*

cause [kɔːz] *n* cause *f;* (*reason*) raison *f;* c. for complaint sujet *m* de plainte; *− vt* causer, occasionner; (*trouble*) créer, causer (for à); to c. sth to move/*etc* faire bouger/*etc* qch.

causeway ['kɔːzweɪ] *n* chaussée *f.*

caustic ['kɔːstɪk] *a* (*remark, substance*) caustique.

cauterize ['kɔːtəraɪz] *vt Med* cautériser.

caution ['kɔːʃ(ə)n] *n* (*care*) prudence *f*, précaution *f;* (*warning*) avertissement *m; − vt* (*warn*) avertir; to c. s.o. against sth mettre qn en garde contre qch. ◆**cautionary** *a* (*tale*) moral. ◆**cautious** *a* prudent, circonspect. ◆**cautiously** *adv* prudemment.

cavalcade ['kævəlkeɪd] *n* (*procession*) cavalcade *f.*

cavalier [kævə'lɪər] **1** *a* (*selfish*) cavalier. **2** *n* (*horseman, knight*) *Hist* cavalier *m.*

cavalry ['kævəlrɪ] *n* cavalerie *f.*

cave [keɪv] **1** *n* caverne *f*, grotte *f.* **2** *vi* to c. in (*fall in*) s'effondrer. ◆**caveman** *n* (*pl* -men) homme *m* des cavernes. ◆**cavern** ['kævər.] *n* caverne *f.*

caviar(e) ['kævɪɑːr] *n* caviar *m.*

cavity ['kævɪtɪ] *n* cavité *f.*

cavort [kə'vɔːt] *vi Fam* cabrioler; to c. naked/*etc* se balader tout nu/*etc.*

cease [siːs] *vti* cesser (doing de faire). ◆**c.-fire** *n* cessez-le-feu *m inv.* ◆**ceaseless** *a* incessant. ◆**ceaselessly** *adv* sans cesse.

cedar ['siːdər] *n* (*tree, wood*) cèdre *m.*

cedilla [sɪ'dɪlə] *n Gram* cédille *f.*

ceiling ['siːlɪŋ] *n* (*of room, on wages etc*) plafond *m.*

celebrat/e ['selɪbreɪt] *vt* (*event*) fêter; (*mass, s.o.'s merits etc*) célébrer; *− vi* faire la fête; we should c. (that)! il faut fêter ça! ◆**—ed** *a* célèbre. ◆**cele'bration** *n* fête *f;* the c. of (*marriage etc*) la célébration de. ◆**ce'lebrity** *n* (*person*) célébrité *f.*

celery ['selərɪ] *n* céleri *m.*

celibate ['selɪbət] *a* (*abstaining from sex*) célibataire; (*monk etc*) abstinent. ◆**celibacy** *n* (*of young person etc*) célibat *m;* (*of monk etc*) abstinence *f.*

cell [sel] *n* cellule *f;* El élément *m.* ◆**cellular** *a* cellulaire; c. blanket couverture *f* en cellulaire.

cellar ['selər] *n* cave *f.*

cello ['tʃeləʊ] *n* (*pl* -os) violoncelle *m.* ◆**cellist** *n* violoncelliste *mf.*

cellophane® ['seləfeɪn] *n* cellophane® *f.*

celluloid ['seljʊlɔɪd] *n* celluloïd *m.*

cellulose ['seljʊləʊs] *n* cellulose *f.*

Celsius ['selsɪəs] *a* Celsius *inv.*

Celt [kelt] *n* Celte *mf.* ◆**Celtic** *a* celtique, celte.

cement [sɪ'ment] *n* ciment *m;* c. mixer bétonnière *f; − vt* cimenter.

cemetery ['semətrɪ, *Am* 'seməterɪ] *n* cimetière *m.*

cenotaph ['senətɑːf] *n* cénotaphe *m.*

censor ['sensər] *n* censeur *m; − vt* (*film etc*) censurer. ◆**censorship** *n* censure *f.*

censure ['senʃər] *vt* blâmer; *Pol* censurer; *− n* blâme *m;* c. motion, vote of c. motion *f* de censure.

census ['sensəs] *n* recensement *m.*

cent [sent] *n* (*coin*) cent *m;* per c. pour cent.

centenary [sen'tiːnərɪ, *Am* sen'tenərɪ] *n* centenaire *m.*

centigrade ['sentɪɡreɪd] *a* centigrade.

centimetre ['sentɪmiːtər] *n* centimètre *m.*

centipede ['sentɪpiːd] *n* mille-pattes *m inv.*

centre ['sentər] *n* centre *m;* c. forward *Fb* avant-centre *m; − vt* centrer; *− vi* to c. on (*of thoughts etc*) se concentrer sur; (*of question*) tourner autour de. ◆**central** *a* central. ◆**centralize** *vt* centraliser. ◆**centrifugal** [sen'trɪfjʊɡəl] *a* centrifuge.

century ['sentʃərɪ] *n* siècle *m;* (*score*) *Sp* cent points *mpl.*

ceramic [sə'ræmɪk] *a* (*tile etc*) de *or* en céramique; *− npl* (*objects*) céramiques *fpl;* (*art*) céramique *f.*

cereal ['sɪərɪəl] *n* céréale *f.*

cerebral ['serɪbrəl, *Am* sə'riːbrəl] *a* cérébral.

ceremony ['serɪmənɪ] *n* (*event*) cérémonie *f;* to stand on c. faire des cérémonies *or* des façons. ◆**cere'monial** *a* de cérémonie; −

n cérémonial *m*. ◆**cere'monious** *a* cérémonieux.

certain ['sɜːtən] *a* (*particular, some*) certain; (*sure*) sûr, certain; **she's c. to come, she'll come for c.** c'est certain *or* sûr qu'elle viendra; **I'm not c. what to do** je ne sais pas très bien ce qu'il faut faire; **to be c. of sth/that** être certain de qch/que; **for c.** (*to say, know*) avec certitude; **be c. to go!** vas-y sans faute!; **to make c. of** (*fact*) s'assurer de; (*seat etc*) s'assurer. ◆**—ly** *adv* certainement; (*yes*) bien sûr; (*without fail*) sans faute; (*without any doubt*) sans aucun doute. ◆**certainty** *n* certitude *f*.

certificate [sə'tɪfɪkɪt] *n* certificat *m*; *Univ* diplôme *m*.

certify ['sɜːtɪfaɪ] *vt* certifier; **to c. (insane)** déclarer dément; **–** *vi* **to c. to sth** attester qch.

cervix ['sɜːvɪks] *n* col *m* de l'utérus.

cesspool ['sespuːl] *n* fosse *f* d'aisances; *Fig* cloaque *f*.

chafe [tʃeɪf] *vt* (*skin*) *Lit* frotter.

chaff [tʃæf] *vt* (*tease*) taquiner.

chaffinch ['tʃæfɪntʃ] *n* (*bird*) pinson *m*.

chagrin ['ʃægrɪn, *Am* ʃə'grɪn] *n* contrariété *f*; **–** *vt* contrarier.

chain [tʃeɪn] *n* (*of rings, mountains*) chaîne *f*; (*of ideas, events*) enchaînement *m*, suite *f*; (*of lavatory*) chasse *f* d'eau; **c. reaction** réaction *f* en chaîne; **to be a c.-smoker, to c.-smoke** fumer cigarette sur cigarette, fumer comme un pompier; **c. saw** tronçonneuse *f*; **c. store** magasin *m* à succursales multiples; **–** *vt* **to c. (down)** enchaîner; **to c. (up)** (*dog*) mettre à l'attache.

chair [tʃeər] *n* chaise *f*; (*armchair*) fauteuil *m*; *Univ* chaire *f*; **the c.** (*office*) la présidence; **c. lift** télésiège *m*; **–** *vt* (*meeting*) présider. ◆**chairman** *n* (*pl* -men) président, -ente *mf*. ◆**chairmanship** *n* présidence *f*.

chalet ['ʃæleɪ] *n* chalet *m*.

chalk [tʃɔːk] *n* craie *f*; **not by a long c.** loin de là, tant s'en faut; **–** *vt* marquer *or* écrire à la craie; **to c. up** (*success*) *Fig* remporter. ◆**chalky** *a* (-**ier, -iest**) crayeux.

challenge ['tʃælɪndʒ] *n* défi *m*; (*task*) gageure *f*; *Mil* sommation *f*; **c. for** (*bid*) tentative *f* d'obtenir; **–** *vt* défier (**s.o. to do** qn de faire); (*dispute*) contester; **to c. s.o. to a game** inviter qn à jouer; **to c. s.o. to a duel** provoquer qn en duel. ◆**—ing** *a* (*job*) exigeant; (*book*) stimulant. ◆**—er** *n Sp* challenger *m*.

chamber ['tʃeɪmbər] *n* chambre *f*; (*of judge*) cabinet *m*; **–** *a* (*music, orchestra*) de chambre; **c. pot** pot *m* de chambre. ◆**chambermaid** *n* femme *f* de chambre.

chameleon [kə'miːliən] *n* (*reptile*) caméléon *m*.

chamois ['ʃæmɪ] *n* **c. (leather)** peau *f* de chamois.

champagne [ʃæm'peɪn] *n* champagne *m*.

champion ['tʃæmpiən] *n* champion, -onne *mf*; **c. skier** champion, -onne du ski; **–** *vt* (*support*) se faire le champion de. ◆**championship** *n Sp* championnat *m*.

chance [tʃɑːns] *n* (*luck*) hasard *m*; (*possibility*) chances *fpl*, possibilité *f*; (*opportunity*) occasion *f*; (*risk*) risque *m*; **by c.** par hasard; **by any c.** (*possibly*) par hasard; **on the off c. (that)** you could help me au cas où tu pourrais m'aider; **–** *a* (*remark*) fait au hasard; (*occurrence*) accidentel; **–** *vt* **to c. doing** prendre le risque de faire; **to c. to find**/*etc* trouver/*etc* par hasard; **to c. it** risquer le coup; **–** *v imp* **it chanced that** (*happened*) il s'est trouvé que.

chancel ['tʃɑːnsəl] *n* (*in church*) chœur *m*.

chancellor ['tʃɑːnsələr] *n Pol Jur* chancelier *m*. ◆**chancellery** *n* chancellerie *f*.

chandelier [ʃændə'lɪər] *n* lustre *m*.

change [tʃeɪndʒ] *n* changement *m*; (*money*) monnaie *f*; **for a c.** pour changer; **it makes a c. from** ça change de; **to have a c. of heart** changer d'avis; **a c. of clothes** des vêtements de rechange; **–** *vt* (*modify*) changer; (*exchange*) échanger (**for** contre); (*money*) changer; (*transform*) transformer (**into** en); **to c. trains/one's skirt**/*etc* changer de train/de jupe/*etc*; **to c. gear** *Aut* changer de vitesse; **to c. the subject** changer de sujet; **–** *vi* (*alter*) changer; (*change clothes*) se changer; **to c. over** passer. ◆**—ing** *n* (*of guard*) relève *f*; **c. room** vestiaire *m*. ◆**changeable** *a* (*weather, mood etc*) changeant, variable. ◆**changeless** *a* immuable. ◆**changeover** *n* passage *m* (**from** de, **to** à).

channel ['tʃæn(ə)l] *n* (*navigable*) chenal *m*; *TV* chaîne *f*, canal *m*; (*groove*) rainure *f*; *Fig* direction *f*; **through the c. of** par le canal de; **the C.** *Geog* la Manche; **the C. Islands** les îles anglo-normandes; **–** *vt* (**-ll-,** *Am* **-l-**) (*energies, crowd etc*) canaliser (**into** vers).

chant [tʃɑːnt] *n* (*of demonstrators*) chant *m* scandé; *Rel* psalmodie *f*; **–** *vt* (*slogan*) scander; **–** *vi* scander les slogans.

chaos ['keɪɒs] *n* chaos *m*. ◆**cha'otic** *a* chaotique.

chap [tʃæp] **1** *n* (*fellow*) *Fam* type *m*; **old c.!**

mon vieux! **2** *n* (*on skin*) gerçure *f*; − *vi*
(**-pp-**) se gercer; − *vt* gercer.

chapel ['tʃæp(ə)l] *n* chapelle *f*; (*non-conformist church*) temple *m*.

chaperon(e) ['ʃæpərəʊn] *n* chaperon *m*; − *vt* chaperonner.

chaplain ['tʃæplɪn] *n* aumônier *m*.

chapter ['tʃæptər] *n* chapitre *m*.

char [tʃɑːr] **1** *vt* (**-rr-**) (*convert to carbon*) carboniser; (*scorch*) brûler légèrement. **2** *n Fam* femme *f* de ménage; − *vi* to go char-ring *Fam* faire des ménages. **3** *n* (*tea*) *Sl* thé *m*.

character ['kærɪktər] *n* (*of person, place etc*) & *Typ* caractère *m*; (*in book, film*) person-nage *m*; (*strange person*) numéro *m*; **c. actor** acteur *m* de genre. ◆**characte-'ristic** *a* & *n* caractéristique (*f*). ◆**characte'ristically** *adv* typiquement. ◆**characterize** *vt* caractériser.

charade [ʃəˈrɑːd] *n* (*game*) charade *f* (mimée); (*travesty*) parodie *f*, comédie *f*.

charcoal ['tʃɑːkəʊl] *n* charbon *m* (de bois); (*crayon*) fusain *m*, charbon *m*.

charge [tʃɑːdʒ] *n* (*in battle*) *Mil* charge *f*; *Jur* accusation *f*; (*cost*) prix *m*; (*responsibil-ity*) responsabilité *f*, charge *f*; (*care*) garde *f*; *pl* (*expenses*) frais *mpl*; **there's a c.** (for it) c'est payant; **free of c.** gratuit; **extra c.** supplément *m*; **to take c. of** prendre en charge; **to be in c. of** (*child etc*) avoir la garde de; (*office etc*) être responsable de; **the person in c.** le *or* la responsable; **who's in c. here?** qui commande ici?; − *vt Mil El* charger; *Jur* accuser, inculper; (*price*) *Com* faire payer qn; **to c. (up) to** *Com* mettre sur le compte de; **how much do you c.?** combien demandez-vous?; − *vi* (*rush*) se précipiter; **to c.!** *Mil* chargez! ◆**—able** *a* **c. to** aux frais de. ◆**charger** *n* (*for battery*) chargeur *m*.

chariot ['tʃærɪət] *n Mil* char *m*.

charisma [kəˈrɪzmə] *n* magnétisme *m*.

charity ['tʃærɪtɪ] *n* (*kindness, alms*) charité *f*; (*society*) fondation *f or* œuvre *f* charitable; **to give to c.** faire la charité. ◆**charitable** *a* charitable.

charlady ['tʃɑːleɪdɪ] *n* femme *f* de ménage.

charlatan ['ʃɑːlətən] *n* charlatan *m*.

charm [tʃɑːm] *n* (*attractiveness, spell*) charme *m*; (*trinket*) amulette *f*; − *vt* charmer. ◆**—ing** *a* charmant. ◆**—ingly** *adv* d'une façon charmante.

chart [tʃɑːt] *n* (*map*) carte *f*; (*graph*) graphique *m*, tableau *m*; (**pop**) **charts** hit-parade *m*; **flow c.** organigramme *m*; −

vt (*route*) porter sur la carte; (*figures*) faire le graphique de; (*of graph*) montrer.

charter ['tʃɑːtər] *n* (*document*) charte *f*; (*aircraft*) charter *m*; **the c. of** (*hiring*) l'affrètement *m* de; **c. flight** charter *m*; − *vt* (*aircraft etc*) affréter. ◆**—ed** *a* **c. accoun-tant** expert-comptable *m*.

charwoman ['tʃɑːwʊmən] *n* (*pl* **-women**) femme *f* de ménage.

chary ['tʃeərɪ] *a* (**-ier, -iest**) (*cautious*) pru-dent.

chase [tʃeɪs] *n* poursuite *f*, chasse *f*; **to give c.** se lancer à la poursuite (**to** de); − *vt* poursuivre; **to c. away** *or* **off** chasser; **to c. sth up** *Fam* essayer d'obtenir qch, rechercher qch; − *vi* **to c. after** courir après.

chasm ['kæzəm] *n* abîme *m*, gouffre *m*.

chassis ['ʃæsɪ, *Am* 'tʃæsɪ] *n Aut* châssis *m*.

chaste [tʃeɪst] *a* chaste. ◆**chastity** *n* chas-teté *f*.

chasten ['tʃeɪs(ə)n] *vt* (*punish*) châtier; (*cause to improve*) faire se corriger, assagir. ◆**—ing** *a* (*experience*) instructif.

chastise [tʃæˈstaɪz] *vt* punir.

chat [tʃæt] *n* causette *f*; **to have a c.** bavarder; − *vi* (**-tt-**) causer, bavarder; − *vt* **to c. up** *Fam* baratiner, draguer. ◆**chatty** *a* (**-ier, -iest**) (*person*) bavard; (*style*) familier; (*text*) plein de bavardages.

chatter ['tʃætər] *vi* bavarder; (*of birds, monkeys*) jacasser; **his teeth are chattering** il claque des dents; − *n* bavardage *m*; jacassement *m*. ◆**chatterbox** *n* bavard, -arde *mf*.

chauffeur ['ʃəʊfər] *n* chauffeur *m* (de maître).

chauvinist ['ʃəʊvɪnɪst] *n* & *a* chauvin, -ine (*mf*); **male c.** *Pej* phallocrate *m*.

cheap [tʃiːp] *a* (**-er, -est**) bon marché *inv*, pas cher; (*rate etc*) réduit; (*worthless*) sans valeur; (*superficial*) facile; (*mean, petty*) mesquin; **cheaper** moins cher, meilleur marché; − *adv* (*to buy*) (à) bon marché, au rabais; (*to feel*) humilié. ◆**cheapen** *vt Fig* déprécier. ◆**cheaply** *adv* (à) bon marché. ◆**cheapness** *n* bas prix *m*; *Fig* mesquinerie *f*.

cheat [tʃiːt] *vt* (*deceive*) tromper; (*defraud*) frauder; **to c. s.o. out of sth** escroquer qch à qn; **to c. on** (*wife, husband*) faire une infidé-lité *or* des infidélités à; − *vi* tricher; (*defraud*) frauder; − *n* (*at games etc*) tricheur, -euse *mf*; (*crook*) escroc *m*. ◆**—ing** *n* (*deceit*) tromperie *f*; (*trickery*) tricherie *f*. ◆**—er** *n Am* = **cheat**.

check [tʃek] *vt* (*examine*) vérifier; (*inspect*) contrôler; (*tick*) cocher, pointer; (*stop*) arrêter, enrayer; (*restrain*) contenir, maîtriser; (*rebuke*) réprimander; (*baggage*) *Am* mettre à la consigne; **to c. in** (*luggage*) *Av* enregistrer; **to c. sth out** confirmer qch; – *vi* vérifier; **to c. in** (*at hotel etc*) signer le registre; (*arrive at hotel*) arriver; (*at airport*) se présenter (à l'enregistrement), enregistrer ses bagages; **to c. on sth** vérifier qch; **to c. out** (*at hotel etc*) régler sa note; **to c. up** vérifier, se renseigner; – *n* vérification *f*; contrôle *m*; (*halt*) arrêt *m*; *Chess* échec *m*; (*curb*) frein *m*; (*tick*) = croix *f*; (*receipt*) *Am* reçu *m*; (*bill in restaurant etc*) *Am* addition *f*; (*cheque*) *Am* chèque *m*. ◆**c.-in** *n Av* enregistrement *m* (des bagages). ◆**checking account** *n Am* compte *m* courant. ◆**checkmate** *n Chess* échec et mat *m*. ◆**checkout** *n* (*in supermarket*) caisse *f*. ◆**checkpoint** *n* contrôle *m*. ◆**checkroom** *n Am* vestiaire *m*; (*left-luggage office*) *Am* consigne *f*. ◆**checkup** *n* bilan *m* de santé.

check [tʃek] *n* (*pattern*) carreaux *mpl*; – *a* à carreaux. ◆**checked** *a* à carreaux.

checkered ['tʃekəd] *a Am* = **chequered**.

checkers ['tʃekəz] *npl Am* jeu *m* de dames.

cheddar ['tʃedər] *n* (*cheese*) cheddar *m*.

cheek [tʃiːk] *n* joue *f*; (*impudence*) *Fig* culot *m*. ◆**cheekbone** *n* pommette *f*. ◆**cheeky** *a* (-ier, -iest) (*person, reply etc*) effronté.

cheep [tʃiːp] *vi* (*of bird*) piauler.

cheer¹ [tʃiər] *n* **cheers** (*shouts*) acclamations *fpl*; **cheers!** *Fam* à votre santé! – *vt* (*applaud*) acclamer; **to c. on** encourager; **to c. (up)** donner du courage à; (*amuse*) égayer; – *vi* applaudir; **to c. up** prendre courage; s'égayer; **c. up!** (du) courage! ◆**—ing** *n* (*shouts*) acclamations *fpl*; – *a* (*encouraging*) réjouissant.

cheer² [tʃiər] *n* (*gaiety*) joie *f*; **good c.** (*food*) la bonne chère. ◆**cheerful** *a* gai. ◆**cheerfully** *adv* gaiement. ◆**cheerless** *a* morne.

cheerio! [tʃiəri'əu] *int* salut!, au revoir!

cheese [tʃiːz] *n* fromage *m*. ◆**cheeseburger** *n* cheeseburger *m*. ◆**cheesecake** *n* tarte *f* au fromage blanc. ◆**cheesed** *a* **to be c. (off)** *Fam* en avoir marre (**with** de). ◆**cheesy** *a* (-ier, -iest) (*shabby, bad*) *Am Fam* miteux.

cheetah ['tʃiːtə] *n* guépard *m*.

chef [ʃef] *n Culin* chef *m*.

chemistry ['kemistri] *n* chimie *f*. ◆**chemical** *a* chimique; – *n* produit *m* chimique. ◆**chemist** *n* (*dispensing*) pharmacien,

-ienne *mf*; (*scientist*) chimiste *mf*; **chemist('s)** (*shop*) pharmacie *f*.

cheque [tʃek] *n* chèque *m*. ◆**chequebook** *n* carnet *m* de chèques.

chequered ['tʃekəd] *a* (*pattern*) à carreaux; (*career etc*) qui connaît des hauts et des bas.

cherish ['tʃeriʃ] *vt* (*person*) chérir; (*hope*) nourrir, caresser.

cherry ['tʃeri] *n* cerise *f*; – *a* cerise *inv*. **brandy** cherry *m*.

chess [tʃes] *n* échecs *mpl*. ◆**chessboard** *n* échiquier *m*.

chest [tʃest] *n* **1** *Anat* poitrine *f*. **2** (*box*) coffre *m*; **c. of drawers** commode *f*.

chestnut ['tʃesnʌt] *n* châtaigne *f*, marron *m*; – *a* (*hair*) châtain; **c. tree** châtaignier *m*.

chew [tʃuː] *vt* **to c. (up)** mâcher; **to c. over** *Fig* ruminer; – *vi* mastiquer; **chewing gum** chewing-gum *m*.

chick [tʃik] *n* poussin *m*; (*girl*) *Fam* nana *f*. ◆**chicken 1** *n* poulet *m*; *pl* (*poultry*) volaille *f*; **it's c. feed** *Fam* c'est deux fois rien, c'est une bagatelle. **2** *a Fam* froussard; – *vi* **to c. out** *Fam* se dégonfler. ◆**chickenpox** *n* varicelle *f*.

chickpea ['tʃikpiː] *n* pois *m* chiche.

chicory ['tʃikəri] *n* (*in coffee etc*) chicorée *f*; (*for salad*) endive *f*.

chide [tʃaid] *vt* gronder.

chief [tʃiːf] *n* chef *m*; (*boss*) *Fam* patron *m*, chef *m*; **in c.** (*commander, editor*) en chef; – *a* (*main, highest in rank*) principal. ◆**—ly** *adv* principalement, surtout. ◆**chieftain** *n* (*of clan etc*) chef *m*.

chilblain ['tʃilblein] *n* engelure *f*.

child, *pl* **children** ['tʃaild, 'tʃildrən] *n* enfant *mf*; **c. care** *or* **welfare** protection *f* de l'enfance; **child's play** *Fig* jeu *m* d'enfant; **c. minder** gardien, -ienne *mf* d'enfants. ◆**childbearing** *n* (*act*) accouchement *m*; (*motherhood*) maternité *f*. ◆**childbirth** *n* accouchement *m*, couches *fpl*. ◆**childhood** *n* enfance *f*. ◆**childish** *a* puéril, enfantin. ◆**childishness** *n* puérilité *f*. ◆**childlike** *a* naïf, innocent.

chill [tʃil] *n* froid *m*; (*coldness in feelings*) froideur *f*; *Med* refroidissement *m*; **to catch a c.** prendre froid; – *vt* (*wine, melon*) faire rafraîchir; (*meat, food*) réfrigérer; **to c. s.o.** (*with fear, cold etc*) faire frissonner qn (**with** de); **to be chilled to the bone** être transi. ◆**—ed** *a* (*wine*) frais. ◆**chilly** *a* (-ier, -iest) froid; (*sensitive to cold*) frileux; **it's c.** il fait (un peu) froid.

chilli ['tʃili] *n* (*pl* -ies) piment *m* (de Cayenne).

chime [tʃaɪm] *vi* (*of bell*) carillonner; (*of clock*) sonner; **to c. in** (*interrupt*) interrompre; – *n* carillon *m*; sonnerie *f*.

chimney ['tʃɪmnɪ] *n* cheminée *f*. ◆**chimneypot** *n* tuyau *m* de cheminée. ◆**chimneysweep** *n* ramoneur *m*.

chimpanzee [tʃɪmpæn'zɪː] *n* chimpanzé *m*.

chin [tʃɪn] *n* menton *m*.

china ['tʃaɪnə] *n inv* porcelaine *f*; – *a* en porcelaine. ◆**chinaware** *n* (*objects*) porcelaine *f*.

China ['tʃaɪnə] *n* Chine *f*. ◆**Chi'nese** *a & n* chinois, -oise (*mf*); – *n* (*language*) chinois *m*.

chink [tʃɪŋk] **1** *n* (*slit*) fente *f*. **2** *vi* tinter; – *vt* faire tinter; – *n* tintement *m*.

chip [tʃɪp] *vt* (-pp-) (*cup etc*) ébrécher; (*table etc*) écorner; (*paint*) écailler; (*cut*) tailler; – *vi* **to c. in** *Fam* contribuer; – *n* (*splinter*) éclat *m*; (*break*) ébréchure *f*; écornure *f*; (*microchip*) puce *f*; (*counter*) jeton *m*; *pl* (*French fries*) frites *fpl*; (*crisps*) *Am* chips *mpl*. ◆**chipboard** *n* (bois *m*) aggloméré *m*. ◆**chippings** *npl* **road** *or* **loose c.** gravillons *mpl*.

chiropodist [kɪ'rɒpədɪst] *n* pédicure *mf*.

chirp [tʃɜːp] *vi* (*of bird*) pépier; – *n* pépiement *m*.

chirpy ['tʃɜːpɪ] *a* (-ier, -iest) gai, plein d'entrain.

chisel ['tʃɪz(ə)l] *n* ciseau *m*; – *vt* (-ll-, *Am* -l-) ciseler.

chit [tʃɪt] *n* (*paper*) note *f*, billet *m*.

chitchat ['tʃɪttʃæt] *n* bavardage *m*.

chivalry ['ʃɪvəlrɪ] *n* (*practices etc*) chevalerie *f*; (*courtesy*) galanterie *f*. ◆**chivalrous** *a* (*man*) galant.

chives [tʃaɪvz] *npl* ciboulette *f*.

chloride ['klɔːraɪd] *n* chlorure *m*. ◆**chlorine** *n* chlore *m*. ◆**chloroform** *n* chloroforme *m*.

choc-ice ['tʃɒkaɪs] *n* (*ice cream*) esquimau *m*.

chock [tʃɒk] *n* (*wedge*) cale *f*; – *vt* caler.

chock-a-block [tʃɒkə'blɒk] *a*, ◆**c.-'full** *a* *Fam* archiplein.

chocolate ['tʃɒklɪt] *n* chocolat *m*; **milk c.** chocolat au lait; **plain** *or Am* **bittersweet c.** chocolat à croquer; – *a* (*cake*) au chocolat; (*colour*) chocolat *inv*.

choice [tʃɔɪs] *n* choix *m*; **from c., out of c.** de son propre choix; – *a* (*goods*) de choix.

choir ['kwaɪər] *n* chœur *m*. ◆**choirboy** *n* jeune choriste *m*.

chok/e [tʃəʊk] **1** *vt* (*person*) étrangler, étouffer; (*clog*) boucher, engorger; **to c. back** (*sobs etc*) étouffer; – *vi* s'étrangler,

étouffer; **to c. on** (*fish bone etc*) s'étrangler avec. **2** *n Aut* starter *m*. ◆**—er** *n* (*scarf*) foulard *m*; (*necklace*) collier *m* (de chien).

cholera ['kɒlərə] *n* choléra *m*.

cholesterol [kə'lestərɒl] *n* cholestérol *m*.

choose [tʃuːz] *vt* (*pt* **chose**, *pp* **chosen**) choisir (**to do** de faire); (*decide*) juger bon de faire; – *vi* choisir; **as I/you/etc c.** comme il me/vous/*etc* plaît. ◆**choos(e)y** *a* (-sier, -siest) difficile (**about** sur).

chop [tʃɒp] **1** *n* (*of lamb, pork*) côtelette *f*; **to lick one's chops** *Fig* s'en lécher les babines; **to get the c.** *Sl* être flanqué à la porte. **2** *vt* (-pp-) couper (à la hache); (*food*) hacher; **to c. down** (*tree*) abattre; **to c. off** trancher; **to c. up** hacher. **3** *vti* (-pp-) **to c. and change** changer constamment d'idées, de projets *etc*. ◆**chopper** *n* hachoir *m*; *Sl* hélicoptère *m*. ◆**choppy** *a* (*sea*) agité.

chopsticks ['tʃɒpstɪks] *npl* *Culin* baguettes *fpl*.

choral ['kɔːrəl] *a* choral; **c. society** chorale *f*. ◆**chorister** ['kɒrɪstər] *n* choriste *mf*.

chord [kɔːd] *n* *Mus* accord *m*.

chore [tʃɔːr] *n* travail *m* (routinier); (*unpleasant*) corvée *f*; *pl* (*domestic*) travaux *mpl* du ménage.

choreographer [kɒrɪ'ɒɡrəfər] *n* chorégraphe *mf*.

chortle ['tʃɔːt(ə)l] *vi* glousser; – *n* gloussement *m*.

chorus ['kɔːrəs] *n* chœur *m*; (*dancers*) *Th* troupe *f*; (*of song*) refrain *m*; **c. girl** girl *f*.

chose, chosen [tʃəʊz, 'tʃəʊz(ə)n] *see* **choose**.

chowder ['tʃaʊdər] *n Am* soupe *f* aux poissons.

Christ [kraɪst] *n* Christ *m*. ◆**Christian** ['krɪstʃən] *a & n* chrétien, -ienne (*mf*); **C. name** prénom *m*. ◆**Christi'anity** *n* christianisme *m*.

christen ['krɪs(ə)n] *vt* (*name*) & *Rel* baptiser. ◆**—ing** *n* baptême *m*.

Christmas ['krɪsməs] *n* Noël *m*; **at C.** (*time*) à (la) Noël; **Merry C.** Joyeux Noël; **Father C.** le père Noël; – *a* (*tree, card, day, party etc*) de Noël; **C. box** étrennes *fpl*.

chrome [krəʊm] *n*, ◆**chromium** *n* chrome *m*.

chromosome ['krəʊməsəʊm] *n* chromosome *m*.

chronic ['krɒnɪk] *a* (*disease, state etc*) chronique; (*bad*) *Sl* atroce.

chronicle ['krɒnɪk(ə)l] *n* chronique *f*; – *vt* faire la chronique de.

chronology [krə'nɒlədʒɪ] n chronologie f. ◆**chrono'logical** a chronologique.

chronometer [krə'nɒmɪtər] n chronomètre m.

chrysanthemum [krɪ'sænθəməm] n chrysanthème m.

chubby ['tʃʌbɪ] a (-ier, -iest) (body) dodu; (cheeks) rebondi. ◆**c.-'cheeked** a joufflu.

chuck [tʃʌk] vt Fam jeter, lancer; **to c. (in)** or **(up)** (give up) Fam laisser tomber; **to c. away** Fam balancer; (money) gaspiller; **to c. out** Fam balancer.

chuckle ['tʃʌk(ə)l] vi glousser, rire; – n gloussement m.

chuffed [tʃʌft] a Sl bien content; (displeased) Iron Sl pas heureux.

chug [tʃʌg] vi (-gg-) **to c. along** (of vehicle) avancer lentement (en faisant teuf-teuf).

chum [tʃʌm] n Fam copain m. ◆**chummy** a (-ier, -iest) Fam amical; **c. with** copain avec.

chump [tʃʌmp] n (fool) crétin, -ine mf.

chunk [tʃʌŋk] n (gros) morceau m. ◆**chunky** a (-ier, -iest) (person) Fam trapu; (coat, material etc) de grosse laine.

church [tʃɜːtʃ] n église f; (service) office m; (Catholic) messe f; **c. hall** salle f paroissiale. ◆**churchgoer** n pratiquant, -ante mf. ◆**churchyard** n cimetière m.

churlish ['tʃɜːlɪʃ] a (rude) grossier; (bad-tempered) hargneux.

churn [tʃɜːn] 1 n (for making butter) baratte f; (milk can) bidon m. 2 vt **to c. out** Pej produire (en série).

chute [ʃuːt] n glissière f; (in playground, pool) toboggan m; (for refuse) vide-ordures m inv.

chutney ['tʃʌtnɪ] n condiment m épicé (à base de fruits).

cider ['saɪdər] n cidre m.

cigar [sɪ'gɑːr] n cigare m. ◆**ciga'rette** n cigarette f; **c. end** mégot m; **c. holder** fume-cigarette m inv; **c. lighter** briquet m.

cinch [sɪntʃ] n **it's a c.** Fam (easy) c'est facile; (sure) c'est (sûr et) certain.

cinder ['sɪndər] n cendre f; **c. track** Sp cendrée f.

Cinderella [sɪndə'relə] n Liter Cendrillon f; Fig parent m pauvre.

cine-camera ['sɪnɪkæmrə] n caméra f.

cinema ['sɪnəmə] n cinéma m. ◆**cinemagoer** n cinéphile mf. ◆**cinemascope** n cinémascope m.

cinnamon ['sɪnəmən] n Bot Culin cannelle f.

cipher ['saɪfər] n (code, number) chiffre m; (zero, person) Fig zéro m.

circle ['sɜːk(ə)l] n (shape, group, range etc)

cercle m; (around eyes) cerne m; Th balcon m; pl (milieux) milieux mpl; – vt (move round) faire le tour de; (word etc) entourer d'un cercle; – vi (of aircraft, bird) décrire des cercles. ◆**circular** a circulaire; – n (letter) circulaire f; (advertisement) prospectus m. ◆**circulate** vi circuler; – vt faire circuler. ◆**circu'lation** n circulation f; Journ tirage m; **in c.** (person) Fam dans le circuit.

circuit ['sɜːkɪt] n circuit m; Jur Th tournée f; **c. breaker** El disjoncteur m. ◆**circuitous** [sɜː'kjuːɪtəs] a (route, means) indirect. ◆**circuitry** n El circuits mpl.

circumcised ['sɜːkəmsaɪzd] a circoncis. ◆**circum'cision** n circoncision f.

circumference [sɜː'kʌmfərəns] n circonférence f.

circumflex ['sɜːkəmfleks] n circonflexe m.

circumscribe ['sɜːkəmskraɪb] vt circonscrire.

circumspect ['sɜːkəmspekt] a circonspect.

circumstance ['sɜːkəmstæns] n circonstance f; pl Com situation f financière; **in** or **under no circumstances** en aucun cas. ◆**circum'stantial** a (evidence) Jur indirect.

circus ['sɜːkəs] n Th Hist cirque m.

cirrhosis [sɪ'rəʊsɪs] n Med cirrhose f.

cistern ['sɪstən] n (in house) réservoir m (d'eau).

citadel ['sɪtəd(ə)l] n citadelle f.

cite [saɪt] vt citer. ◆**citation** [saɪ'teɪʃ(ə)n] n citation f.

citizen ['sɪtɪz(ə)n] n Pol Jur citoyen, -enne mf; (of town) habitant, -ante mf; Citizens' Band Rad la CB. ◆**citizenship** n citoyenneté f.

citrus ['sɪtrəs] a **c. fruit(s)** agrumes mpl.

city ['sɪtɪ] n (grande) ville f, cité f; **c. dweller** citadin, -ine mf; **c. centre** centre-ville m inv; **c. hall** Am hôtel m de ville; **c. page** Journ rubrique f financière.

civic ['sɪvɪk] a (duty) civique; (centre) administratif; (authorities) municipal; – npl (social science) instruction f civique.

civil ['sɪv(ə)l] a **1** (rights, war, marriage etc) civil; **c. defence** défense f passive; **c. servant** fonctionnaire mf; **c. service** fonction f publique. **2** (polite) civil. ◆**ci'vilian** a & n civil, -ile (mf). ◆**ci'vility** n civilité f.

civilize ['sɪvɪlaɪz] vt civiliser. ◆**civili'zation** n civilisation f.

civvies ['sɪvɪz] npl **in c.** Sl (habillé) en civil.

clad [klæd] a vêtu (**in** de).

claim [kleɪm] vt (one's due etc) revendiquer, réclamer; (require) réclamer; **to c. that**

(*assert*) prétendre que; – *n* (*demand*) prétention *f*, revendication *f*; (*statement*) affirmation *f*; (*complaint*) réclamation *f*; (*right*) droit *m*; (*land*) concession *f*; (**insurance**) c. demande *f* d'indemnité; **to lay c. to** prétendre à. ◆**claimant** *n* allocataire *mf*.

clairvoyant [kleə'vɔɪənt] *n* voyant, -ante *mf*.

clam [klæm] *n* (*shellfish*) praire *f*.

clamber ['klæmbər] *vi* **to c. (up)** grimper; **to c. up** (*stairs*) grimper; (*mountain*) gravir.

clammy ['klæmɪ] *a* (*hands etc*) moite (et froid).

clamour ['klæmər] *n* clameur *f*; – *vi* vociférer (**against** contre); **to c. for** demander à grands cris.

clamp [klæmp] *n* crampon *m*; *Carp* serre-joint(s) *m*; (**wheel**) c. *Aut* sabot *m* (de Denver); – *vt* serrer; – *vi* **to c. down** *Fam* sévir (**on** contre). ◆**clampdown** *n* (*limitation*) *Fam* coup *m* d'arrêt, restriction *f*.

clan [klæn] *n* clan *m*.

clandestine [klæn'destɪn] *a* clandestin.

clang [klæŋ] *n* son *m* métallique. ◆**clanger** *n* *Sl* gaffe *f*; **to drop a c.** faire une gaffe.

clap [klæp] **1** *vti* (**-pp-**) (*applaud*) applaudir; **to c. (one's hands)** battre des mains; – *n* battement *m* (des mains); (*on back*) tape *f*; (*of thunder*) coup *m*. **2** *vt* (**-pp-**) (*put*) *Fam* fourrer. ◆**clapped-'out** *a* (*car, person*) *Sl* crevé. ◆**clapping** *n* applaudissements *mpl*. ◆**claptrap** *n* (*nonsense*) *Fam* boniment *m*.

claret ['klærət] *n* (*wine*) bordeaux *m* rouge.

clarify ['klærɪfaɪ] *vt* clarifier. ◆**clarifi-'cation** *n* clarification *f*.

clarinet [klærɪ'net] *n* clarinette *f*.

clarity ['klærɪtɪ] *n* (*of water, expression etc*) clarté *f*.

clash [klæʃ] *vi* (*of plates, pans*) s'entrechoquer; (*of interests, armies*) se heurter; (*of colours*) jurer (**with** avec); (*of people*) se bagarrer; (*coincide*) tomber en même temps (**with** que); – *n* (*noise, of armies*) choc *m*, heurt *m*; (*of interests*) conflit *m*; (*of events*) coïncidence *f*.

clasp [klɑːsp] *vt* (*hold*) serrer; **to c. one's hands** joindre les mains; – *n* (*fastener*) fermoir *m*; (*of belt*) boucle *f*.

class [klɑːs] *n* classe *f*; (*lesson*) cours *m*; (*grade*) *Univ* mention *f*; **the c. of 1987** *Am* la promotion de 1987; – *vt* classer. ◆**classmate** *n* camarade *mf* de classe. ◆**classroom** *n* (salle *f* de) classe *f*.

classic ['klæsɪk] *a* classique; – *n* (*writer, work etc*) classique *m*; **to study classics** étudier les humanités *fpl*. ◆**classical** *a* classique. ◆**classicism** *n* classicisme *m*.

classif/y ['klæsɪfaɪ] *vt* classer, classifier. ◆**–ied** *a* (*information*) secret. ◆**classifi-'cation** *n* classification *f*.

classy ['klɑːsɪ] *a* (**-ier, -iest**) *Fam* chic *inv*.

clatter ['klætər] *n* bruit *m*, fracas *m*.

clause [klɔːz] *n* *Jur* clause *f*; *Gram* proposition *f*.

claustrophobia [klɔːstrə'fəʊbɪə] *n* claustrophobie *f*. ◆**claustrophobic** *a* claustrophobe.

claw [klɔː] *n* (*of cat, sparrow etc*) griffe *f*; (*of eagle*) serre *f*; (*of lobster*) pince *f*; – *vt* (*scratch*) griffer; **to c. back** (*money etc*) *Pej Fam* repiquer, récupérer.

clay [kleɪ] *n* argile *f*.

clean [kliːn] *a* (**-er, -est**) propre; (*clear-cut*) net; (*fair*) *Sp* loyal; (*joke*) non paillard; (*record*) *Jur* vierge; **c. living** vie *f* saine; **to make a c. breast of it** tout avouer; – *adv* (*utterly*) complètement, carrément; **to break c.** se casser net; **to cut c.** couper net; – *n* **to give sth a c.** nettoyer qch; – *vt* nettoyer; (*wash*) laver; (*wipe*) essuyer; **to c. one's teeth** se brosser *or* se laver les dents; **to c. out** nettoyer; (*empty*) *Fig* vider; **to c. up** nettoyer; (*reform*) *Fig* épurer; – *vi* **to c. (up)** faire le nettoyage. ◆**–ing** *n* nettoyage *m*; (*housework*) ménage *m*; **c. woman** femme *f* de ménage. ◆**–er** *n* (*woman*) femme *f* de ménage; (**dry**) c. teinturier, -ière *mf*. ◆**–ly** *adv* (*to break, cut*) net. ◆**–ness** *n* propreté *f*. ◆**clean-'cut** *a* net. ◆**clean-'living** *a* honnête, chaste. ◆**clean-'shaven** *a* rasé (de près). ◆**clean-up** *n* *Fig* épuration *f*.

cleanliness ['klenlɪnɪs] *n* propreté *f*.

cleans/e [klenz] *vt* nettoyer; (*soul, person etc*) *Fig* purifier. ◆**–ing** *a* **c. cream** crème *f* démaquillante. ◆**–er** *n* (*cream, lotion*) démaquillant *m*.

clear [klɪər] *a* (**-er, -est**) (*water, sound etc*) clair; (*glass*) transparent; (*outline, photo*) net, clair; (*mind*) lucide; (*road*) libre, dégagé; (*profit*) net; (*obvious*) évident, clair; (*certain*) certain; (*complete*) entier; **to be c. of** (*free of*) être libre de; (*out of*) être hors de; **to make oneself c.** se faire comprendre; **c. conscience** conscience *f* nette *or* tranquille; – *adv* (*quite*) complètement; **c. of** (*away from*) à l'écart de; **to keep** *or* **steer c. of** se tenir à l'écart de; **to get c. of** (*away from*) s'éloigner de; – *vt* (*path, place, table*) débarrasser, dégager; (*land*) défricher; (*fence*) franchir (sans toucher); (*obstacle*) éviter; (*person*) *Jur* disculper;

(*cheque*) compenser; (*goods, debts*) liquider; (*through customs*) dédouaner; (*for security etc*) autoriser; **to c. s.o. of** (*suspicion*) laver qn de; **to c. one's throat** s'éclaircir la gorge; – *vi* **to c. (up)** (*of weather*) s'éclaircir; (*of fog*) se dissiper. ■ **to c. away** *vt* (*remove*) enlever; – *vi* (*of fog*) se dissiper; **to c. off** *vi* (*leave*) *Fam* filer; – *vt* (*table*) débarrasser; **to c. out** *vt* (*empty*) vider; (*clean*) nettoyer; (*remove*) enlever; **to c. up** *vt* (*mystery etc*) éclaircir; – *vti* (*tidy*) ranger. ◆**–ing** *n* (*in woods*) clairière *f*. ◆**–ly** *adv* clairement; (*to understand*) bien, clairement; (*obviously*) évidemment. ◆**–ness** *n* (*of sound*) clarté *f*, netteté *f*; (*of mind*) lucidité *f*. ◆**clearance** *n* (*sale*) soldes *mpl*; (*space*) dégagement *m*; (*permission*) autorisation *f*; (*of cheque*) compensation *f*. ◆**clear-'cut** *a* net. ◆**clear-'headed** *a* lucide.

clearway ['klɪəweɪ] *n* route *f* à stationnement interdit.

cleavage ['kliːvɪdʒ] *n* (*split*) clivage *m*; (*of woman*) *Fam* naissance *f* des seins.

cleft [kleft] *a* (*palate*) fendu; (*stick*) fourchu; – *n* fissure *f*.

clement ['klemənt] *a* clément. ◆**clemency** *n* clémence *f*.

clementine ['kleməntaɪn] *n* clémentine *f*.

clench [klentʃ] *vt* (*press*) serrer.

clergy ['klɜːdʒɪ] *n* clergé *m*. ◆**clergyman** *n* (*pl* **-men**) ecclésiastique *m*.

cleric ['klerɪk] *n* *Rel* clerc *m*. ◆**clerical** *a* (*job*) d'employé; (*work*) de bureau; (*error*) d'écriture; *Rel* clérical.

clerk [klɑːk, *Am* klɜːk] *n* employé, -ée *mf* (de bureau); *Jur* clerc *m*; (*in store*) *Am* vendeur, -euse *mf*; **c. of the court** *Jur* greffier *m*.

clever ['klevər] *a* (**-er, -est**) intelligent; (*smart, shrewd*) astucieux; (*skilful*) habile (**at sth** à qch, **at doing** à faire); (*ingenious*) ingénieux; (*gifted*) doué; **c. at** (*English etc*) fort en; **c. with one's hands** habile *or* adroit de ses mains. ◆**–ly** *adv* intelligemment; astucieusement; habilement. ◆**–ness** *n* intelligence *f*; astuce *f*; habileté *f*.

cliché ['kliːʃeɪ] *n* (*idea*) cliché *m*.

click [klɪk] **1** *n* déclic *m*, bruit *m* sec; – *vi* faire un déclic; (*of lovers etc*) *Fam* se plaire du premier coup; **it clicked** (*I realized*) *Fam* j'ai compris tout à coup. **2** *vt* **to c. one's heels** *Mil* claquer des talons.

client ['klaɪənt] *n* client, -ente *mf*. ◆**clientele** [kliːɑːn'tel] *n* clientèle *f*.

cliff [klɪf] *n* falaise *f*.

climate ['klaɪmɪt] *n* *Met* & *Fig* climat *m*; **c.**

of opinion opinion *f* générale. ◆**cli'matic** *a* climatique.

climax ['klaɪmæks] *n* point *m* culminant; (*sexual*) orgasme *m*; – *vi* atteindre son point culminant.

climb [klaɪm] *vt* **to c. (up)** (*steps*) monter, gravir; (*hill, mountain*) gravir, faire l'ascension de; (*tree, ladder*) monter à, grimper à; **to c. (over)** (*wall*) escalader; **to c. down (from)** descendre de; – *vi* **to c. (up)** monter; (*of plant*) grimper; **to c. down** descendre; (*back down*) *Fig* en rabattre; – *n* montée *f*. ◆**–ing** *n* montée *f*; (*mountain*) **c.** alpinisme *m*. ◆**–er** *n* grimpeur, -euse *mf*; *Sp* alpiniste *mf*; *Bot* plante *f* grimpante; **social c.** arriviste *mf*.

clinch [klɪntʃ] *vt* (*deal, bargain*) conclure; (*argument*) consolider.

cling [klɪŋ] *vt* (*pt* & *pp* **clung**) se cramponner, s'accrocher (**to** à); (*stick*) adhérer (**to** à). ◆**–ing** *a* (*clothes*) collant. ◆**clingfilm** *n* scel-o-frais®*m*, film *m* étirable.

clinic ['klɪnɪk] *n* (*private*) clinique *f*; (*health centre*) centre *m* médical. ◆**clinical** *a* *Med* clinique; *Fig* scientifique, objectif.

clink [klɪŋk] *vi* tinter; – *vt* faire tinter; – *n* tintement *m*.

clip [klɪp] **1** *vt* (**-pp-**) (*cut*) couper; (*sheep*) tondre; (*hedge*) tailler; (*ticket*) poinçonner; **to c. sth out of** (*newspaper etc*) découper qch dans. **2** *n* (*for paper*) attache *f*, trombone *m*; (*of brooch, of cyclist, for hair*) pince *f*; – *vt* (**-pp-**) **to c. (on)** attacher. **3** *n* (*of film*) extrait *m*; (*blow*) *Fam* taloche *f*. ◆**clipping** *n* *Journ* coupure *f*. ◆**clippers** *npl* (*for hair*) tondeuse *f*; (*for nails*) pince *f* à ongles; (*pocket-sized, for finger nails*) coupe-ongles *m inv*.

clique [kliːk] *n* *Pej* clique *f*. ◆**cliquey** *a* *Pej* exclusif.

cloak [kləʊk] *n* (grande) cape *f*; *Fig* manteau *m*; **c. and dagger** (*film etc*) d'espionnage. ◆**cloakroom** *n* vestiaire *m*; (*for luggage*) *Rail* consigne *f*; (*lavatory*) toilettes *fpl*.

clobber ['klɒbər] **1** *vt* (*hit*) *Sl* rosser. **2** *n* (*clothes*) *Sl* affaires *fpl*.

clock [klɒk] *n* (*large*) horloge *f*; (*small*) pendule *f*; *Aut* compteur *m*; **against the c.** *Fig* contre la montre; **round the c.** *Fig* vingt-quatre heures sur vingt-quatre; **c. tower** clocher *m*; – *vt* *Sp* chronométrer; **to c. up** (*miles*) *Aut* *Fam* faire; – *vi* **to c. in** *or* **out** (*of worker*) pointer. ◆**clockwise** *adv* dans le sens des aiguilles d'une montre. ◆**clockwork** *a* mécanique; *Fig* régulier;

— *n* **to go like c.** aller comme sur des roulettes.

clod [klɒd] *n* **1** (*of earth*) motte *f.* **2** (*oaf*) *Fam* balourd, -ourde *mf.*

clog [klɒg] **1** *n* (*shoe*) sabot *m.* **2** *vt* (-gg-) **to c. (up)** (*obstruct*) boucher.

cloister ['klɔɪstər] *n* cloître *m*; -- *vt* cloîtrer.

close¹ [kləʊs] *a* (-er, -est) (*place, relative etc*) proche (**to** de); (*collaboration, resemblance, connection*) étroit; (*friend etc*) intime; (*order, contest*) serré; (*study*) rigoureux; (*atmosphere*) Met lourd; (*vowel*) fermé; **c. to** (*near*) près de, proche de; **c. to tears** au bord des larmes; **to have a c. shave** *or* **call** l'échapper belle; — *adv* **c. (by), (at hand)** (tout) près; **c. to** *or* près de; **c. behind** juste derrière; **c. on** (*almost*) *Fam* pas loin de; **c. together** (*to stand*) serrés; **to follow c.** suivre de près; — *n* (*enclosed area*) enceinte *f.* ◆**c.-'cropped** *a* (*hair*) (coupé) ras. ◆**c.-'knit** *a* très uni. ◆**c.-up** *n* gros plan *m.*

close² [kləʊz] *n* fin *f*, conclusion *f*; **to bring to a c.** mettre fin à; **to draw to a c.** tirer à sa fin; — *vt* fermer; (*discussion*) terminer, clore; (*opening*) boucher; (*road*) barrer; (*gap*) réduire; (*deal*) conclure; **to c. the meeting** lever la séance; **to c. ranks** serrer les rangs; **to c. in** (*enclose*) enfermer; **to c. up** fermer; — *vi* se fermer; (*end*) se terminer; **to c. (up)** (*of shop*) fermer; (*of wound*) se refermer; **to c. in** (*approach*) approcher; **to c. in on s.o.** se rapprocher de qn. ■ **to c. down** *vti* (*close for good*) fermer (définitivement); — *vi* TV terminer les émissions. ◆**c.-down** *n* fermeture *f* (définitive); TV fin *f* (des émissions). ◆**closing** *n* fermeture *f*; (*of session*) clôture *f*; — *a* final; **c. time** heure *f* de fermeture. ◆**closure** ['kləʊʒər] *n* fermeture *f.*

closely ['kləʊslɪ] *adv* (*to link, guard*) étroitement; (*to follow*) de près; (*to listen*) attentivement; **c. contested** très disputé; **to hold s.o. c.** tenir qn contre soi. ◆**closeness** *n* proximité *f*; (*of collaboration etc*) étroitesse *f*; (*of friendship*) intimité *f*; (*of weather*) lourdeur *f.*

closet ['klɒzɪt] *n* (*cupboard*) *Am* placard *m*; (*wardrobe*) *Am* penderie *f.*

clot [klɒt] **1** *n* (*of blood*) caillot *m*; — *vt* (-tt-) (*blood*) coaguler; — *vi* (*of blood*) se coaguler. **2** *n* (*person*) *Fam* imbécile *mf.*

cloth [klɒθ] *n* tissu *m,* étoffe *f*; (*of linen*) toile *f*; (*of wool*) drap *m*; (*for dusting*) chiffon *m*; (*for dishes*) torchon *m*; (*tablecloth*) nappe *f.*

cloth/e [kləʊð] *vt* habiller, vêtir (**in** de).

◆**—ing** *n* habillement *m*; (*clothes*) vêtements *mpl*; **an article of c.** un vêtement.

clothes [kləʊðz] *npl* vêtements *mpl*; **to put one's c. on** s'habiller; **c. brush** brosse *f* à habits; **c. shop** magasin *m* d'habillement; **c. peg,** *Am* **c. pin** pince *f* à linge; **c. line** corde *f* à linge.

cloud [klaʊd] *n* nuage *m*; (*of arrows, insects*) *Fig* nuée *f*; — *vt* (*mind, issue*) obscurcir; (*window*) embuer; — *vi* **to c. (over)** (*of sky*) se couvrir. ◆**cloudburst** *n* averse *f.* ◆**cloudy** *a* (-ier, -iest) (*weather*) couvert, nuageux; (*liquid*) trouble.

clout [klaʊt] **1** *n* (*blow*) *Fam* taloche *f*; — *vt* *Fam* flanquer une taloche à, talocher. **2** *n* *Pol* *Fam* influence *f*, pouvoir *m.*

clove [kləʊv] *n* clou *m* de girofle; **c. of garlic** gousse *f* d'ail.

clover ['kləʊvər] *n* trèfle *m.*

clown [klaʊn] *n* clown *m*; — *vi* **to c. (around)** faire le clown.

cloying ['klɔɪɪŋ] *a* écœurant.

club [klʌb] **1** *n* (*weapon*) matraque *f*, massue *f*; (*golf*) **c.** (*stick*) club *m*; — *vt* (-bb-) matraquer. **2** *n* (*society*) club *m*, cercle *m*; — *vi* (-bb-) **to c. together** se cotiser (**to buy** pour acheter). **3** *n* & *npl* Cards trèfle *m.* ◆**clubhouse** *n* pavillon *m.*

clubfoot ['klʌbfʊt] *n* pied *m* bot. ◆**club-'footed** *a* pied bot *inv.*

cluck [klʌk] *vi* (*of hen*) glousser.

clue [kluː] *n* indice *m*; (*of crossword*) définition *f*; (*to mystery*) clef *f*; **I don't have a c.** *Fam* je n'en ai pas la moindre idée. ◆**clueless** *a* *Fam* stupide.

clump [klʌmp] *n* (*of flowers, trees*) massif *m.*

clumsy ['klʌmzɪ] *a* (-ier, -iest) maladroit; (*shape*) lourd; (*tool*) peu commode. ◆**clumsily** *adv* maladroitement. ◆**clumsiness** *n* maladresse *f.*

clung [klʌŋ] *see* cling.

cluster ['klʌstər] *n* groupe *m*; (*of flowers*) grappe *f*; (*of stars*) amas *m*; — *vi* se grouper.

clutch [klʌtʃ] **1** *vt* (*hold tight*) serrer, étreindre; (*cling to*) se cramponner à; (*grasp*) saisir; — *vi* **to c.** at essayer de saisir; — *n* étreinte *f.* **2** *n* (*apparatus*) Aut embrayage *m*; (*pedal*) pédale *f* d'embrayage. **3** *npl* **s.o.'s clutches** (*power*) les griffes *fpl* de qn.

clutter ['klʌtər] *n* (*objects*) fouillis *m,* désordre *m*; — *vt* **to c. (up)** encombrer (**with** de).

cm *abbr* (*centimetre*) cm.

co- [kəʊ] *prep* co-.

Co *abbr* (*company*) Cie.

coach [kəʊtʃ] **1** *n* (*horse-drawn*) carrosse *m*; Rail voiture *f,* wagon *m*; Aut autocar *m.* **2** *n* (*person*) Sch répétiteur, -trice *mf*; Sp entraîneur m; − vt (*pupil*) donner des leçons (particulières) à; (*sportsman etc*) entraîner; **to c. s.o. for** (*exam*) préparer qn à. ◆**coachman** n (pl **-men**) cocher m.

coagulate [kəʊˈægjuleɪt] vi (*of blood*) se coaguler; − vt coaguler.

coal [kəʊl] n charbon m; Geol houille f; − a (*basin etc*) houiller; (*merchant, fire*) de charbon; (*cellar, bucket*) à charbon. ◆**coalfield** n bassin m houiller. ◆**coalmine** n mine f de charbon.

coalition [kəʊəˈlɪʃ(ə)n] n coalition f.

coarse [kɔːs] a (-er, -est) (*person, manners*) grossier, vulgaire; (*surface*) rude; (*fabric*) grossier; (*salt*) gros; (*accent*) commun, vulgaire. ◆**−ness** n grossièreté f; vulgarité f.

coast [kəʊst] **1** n côte f. **2** vi **to c.** (**down** or **along**) (*of vehicle etc*) descendre en roue libre. ◆**coastal** a côtier. ◆**coaster** n (*ship*) caboteur m; (*for glass etc*) dessous m de verre, rond. m. ◆**coastguard** n (*person*) garde m maritime, garde-côte m. ◆**coastline** n littoral m.

coat [kəʊt] n manteau m; (*overcoat*) pardessus m; (*jacket*) veste f; (*of animal*) pelage m; (*of paint*) couche f; **c. of arms** blason m, armoiries fpl; **c. hanger** cintre m; − vt couvrir, enduire (**with** de); (*with chocolate*) enrober (**with** de). ◆**−ed** a **c. tongue** langue f chargée. ◆**−ing** n couche f.

coax [kəʊks] vt amadouer, cajoler; **to c. s.o. to do** or **into doing** amadouer qn pour qu'il fasse. ◆**−ing** n cajoleries fpl.

cob [kɒb] n **corn on the c.** épi m de maïs.

cobble [ˈkɒb(ə)l] n pavé m; − vt **to c. together** (*text etc*) Fam bricoler. ◆**cobbled** a pavé. ◆**cobblestone** n pavé m.

cobbler [ˈkɒblər] n cordonnier m.

cobra [ˈkəʊbrə] n (*snake*) cobra m.

cobweb [ˈkɒbweb] n toile f d'araignée.

cocaine [kəʊˈkeɪn] n cocaïne f.

cock [kɒk] **1** n (*rooster*) coq m; (*male bird*) (*oiseau m*) mâle m. **2** vt (*gun*) armer; **to c.** (**up**) (*ears*) dresser. ◆**c.-a-doodle-'doo** & int cocorico (*m*). ◆**c.-and-'bull story** n histoire f à dormir debout.

cockatoo [kɒkəˈtuː] n (*bird*) cacatoès m.

cocker [ˈkɒkər] n **c. (spaniel)** cocker m.

cockerel [ˈkɒkərəl] n jeune coq m, coquelet m.

cock-eyed [kɒkˈaɪd] a Fam **1** (*cross-eyed*) bigleux. **2** (*crooked*) de travers. **3** (*crazy*) absurde, stupide.

cockle [ˈkɒk(ə)l] n (*shellfish*) coque f.

cockney [ˈkɒknɪ] a & n cockney (*mf*).

cockpit [ˈkɒkpɪt] n Av poste m de pilotage.

cockroach [ˈkɒkrəʊtʃ] n (*beetle*) cafard m.

cocksure [kɒkˈʃʊər] a Fam trop sûr de soi.

cocktail [ˈkɒkteɪl] n (*drink*) cocktail m; (**fruit**) **c.** macédoine f (de fruits); **c. party** cocktail m; **prawn c.** crevettes fpl à la mayonnaise.

cocky [ˈkɒkɪ] a (-ier, -iest) Fam trop sûr de soi, arrogant.

cocoa [ˈkəʊkəʊ] n cacao m.

coconut [ˈkəʊkənʌt] n noix f de coco; **c. palm** cocotier m.

cocoon [kəˈkuːn] n cocon m.

cod [kɒd] n morue f; (*bought fresh*) cabillaud m. ◆**c.-liver 'oil** n huile f de foie de morue.

COD [siːəʊˈdiː] abbr (*cash on delivery*) livraison f contre remboursement.

coddle [ˈkɒd(ə)l] vt dorloter.

cod/e [kəʊd] n code m; − vt coder. ◆**−ing** n codage m. ◆**codify** vt codifier.

co-educational [kəʊedjʊˈkeɪʃən(ə)l] a (*school, teaching*) mixte.

coefficient [kəʊɪˈfɪʃənt] n Math coefficient m.

coerce [kəʊˈɜːs] vt contraindre. ◆**coercion** n contrainte f.

coexist [kəʊɪɡˈzɪst] vi coexister. ◆**coexistence** n coexistence f.

coffee [ˈkɒfɪ] n café m; **white c.** café m au lait; (*ordered in restaurant etc*) (*café m*) crème m; **black c.** café m noir, café nature; **c. bar, c. house** café m, cafétéria f; **c. break** pause-café f; **c. table** table f basse. ◆**coffeepot** n cafetière f.

coffers [ˈkɒfəz] npl (*funds*) coffres mpl.

coffin [ˈkɒfɪn] n cercueil m.

cog [kɒɡ] n Tech dent f; (*person*) Fig rouage m.

cogent [ˈkəʊdʒənt] a (*reason, argument*) puissant, convaincant.

cogitate [ˈkɒdʒɪteɪt] vi Iron cogiter.

cognac [ˈkɒnjæk] n cognac m.

cohabit [kəʊˈhæbɪt] vi (*of unmarried people*) vivre en concubinage.

coherent [kəʊˈhɪərənt] a cohérent; (*speech*) compréhensible. ◆**cohesion** n cohésion f. ◆**cohesive** a cohésif.

cohort [ˈkəʊhɔːt] n (*group*) cohorte f.

coil [kɔɪl] n (*of wire etc*) rouleau m; El bobine f; (*contraceptive*) stérilet m; − vt (*rope, hair*) enrouler; − vi (*of snake etc*) s'enrouler.

coin [kɔɪn] n pièce f (de monnaie); (*currency*) monnaie f; − vt (*money*) frapper; (*word*) Fig inventer, forger; **to c. a phrase** pour ainsi dire. ◆**c.-operated** a automatique. ◆**coinage** *n* (*coins*) monnaie *f*; *Fig* invention *f*.

coincide [kəʊɪn'saɪd] *vi* coïncider (**with** avec). ◆**co'incidence** *n* coïncidence *f*. ◆**coinci'dental** *a* fortuit; **it's c.** c'est une coïncidence.

coke [kəʊk] *n* **1** (*fuel*) coke *m*. **2** (*Coca-Cola®*) coca *m*.

colander ['kʌləndər] *n* (*for vegetables etc*) passoire *f*.

cold [kəʊld] *n* froid *m*; *Med* rhume *m*; **to catch c.** prendre froid; **out in the c.** *Fig* abandonné, en carafe; – *a* (*-er, -est*) froid; **to be** *or* **feel c.** (*of person*) avoir froid; **my hands are c.** j'ai les mains froides; **it's c.** (*of weather*) il fait froid; **to get c.** (*of weather*) se refroidir; (*of food*) refroidir; **to get c. feet** *Fam* se dégonfler; **in c. blood** de sang-froid; **c. cream** crème *f* de beauté; **c. meats**, *Am* **c. cuts** *Culin* assiette *f* anglaise. ◆**c.-'blooded** *a* (*person*) cruel, insensible; (*act*) de sang-froid. ◆**c.-'shoulder** *vt* snober. ◆**coldly** *adv* avec froideur. ◆**coldness** *n* froideur *f*.

coleslaw ['kəʊlslɔː] *n* salade *f* de chou cru.

colic ['kɒlɪk] *n* *Med* coliques *fpl*.

collaborate [kə'læbəreɪt] *vi* collaborer (**on** à). ◆**collabo'ration** *n* collaboration *f*. ◆**collaborator** *n* collaborateur, -trice *mf*.

collage ['kɒlɑːʒ] *n* (*picture*) collage *m*.

collapse [kə'læps] *vi* (*fall*) s'effondrer, s'écrouler; (*of government*) tomber; (*faint*) *Med* se trouver mal; – *n* effondrement *m*, écroulement *m*; (*of government*) chute *f*. ◆**collapsible** *a* (*chair etc*) pliant.

collar ['kɒlər] *n* (*on garment*) col *m*; (*of dog*) collier *m*; **to seize by the c.** saisir au collet; – *vt* *Fam* saisir (*qn*) au collet; *Fig Fam* retenir (*qn*); (*take, steal*) *Sl* piquer. ◆**collarbone** *n* clavicule *f*.

collate [kə'leɪt] *vt* collationner, comparer (**with** avec).

colleague ['kɒliːg] *n* collègue *mf*, confrère *m*.

collect [kə'lekt] *vt* (*pick up*) ramasser; (*gather*) rassembler, recueillir; (*taxes*) percevoir; (*rent, money*) encaisser; (*stamps etc as hobby*) collectionner; (*fetch, call for*) (*passer*) prendre; – *vi* (*of dust*) s'accumuler; (*of people*) se rassembler; **to c. for** (*in street, church*) quêter pour; – *adv* **to call** *or* **phone c.** *Am* téléphoner en PCV. ◆**collection** [kə'lekʃ(ə)n] *n* ramassage *m*; (*of taxes*) perception *f*; (*of objects*) collection *f*; (*of poems etc*) recueil *m*; (*of money in church etc*) quête *f*; (*of mail*) levée *f*. ◆**collective** *a* collectif. ◆**collectively** *adv*

collectivement. ◆**collector** *n* (*of stamps etc*) collectionneur, -euse *mf*.

college ['kɒlɪdʒ] *n* *Pol Rel Sch* collège *m*; (*university*) université *f*; *Mus* conservatoire *m*; **teachers' training c.** école *f* normale; **art c.** école *f* des beaux-arts; **agricultural c.** institut *m* d'agronomie, lycée *m* agricole.

collide [kə'laɪd] *vi* entrer en collision (**with** avec), se heurter (**with** à). ◆**collision** *n* collision *f*; *Fig* conflit *m*, collision *f*.

colliery ['kɒlɪəri] *n* houillère *f*.

colloquial [kə'ləʊkwɪəl] *a* (*word etc*) familier. ◆**colloquialism** *n* expression *f* familière.

collusion [kə'luːʒ(ə)n] *n* collusion *f*.

collywobbles ['kɒliwɒb(ə)lz] *npl* **to have the c.** (*feel nervous*) *Fam* avoir la frousse.

cologne [kə'ləʊn] *n* eau *f* de Cologne.

colon ['kəʊlən] *n* **1** *Gram* deux-points *m inv*. **2** *Anat* côlon *m*.

colonel ['kɜːn(ə)l] *n* colonel *m*.

colony ['kɒləni] *n* colonie *f*. ◆**colonial** [kə'ləʊnɪəl] *a* colonial. ◆**coloni'zation** *n* colonisation *f*. ◆**colonize** *vt* coloniser.

colossal [kə'lɒs(ə)l] *a* colossal.

colour ['kʌlər] *n* couleur *f*; – *a* (*photo, television*) en couleurs; (*television set*) couleur *inv*; (*problem*) racial; **c. supplement** *Journ* supplément *m* illustré; **off c.** (*not well*) mal fichu; (*improper*) scabreux; – *vt* colorer; **to c. (in)** (*drawing*) colorier. ◆**—ed** *a* (*person, pencil*) de couleur; (*glass, water*) coloré. ◆**—ing** *n* coloration *f*; (*with crayons*) coloriage *m*; (*hue, effect*) coloris *m*; (*matter*) colorant *m*. ◆**colour-blind** *a* daltonien. ◆**colourful** *a* (*crowd, story*) coloré; (*person*) pittoresque.

colt [kəʊlt] *n* (*horse*) poulain *m*.

column ['kɒləm] *n* colonne *f*. ◆**columnist** *n* *Journ* chroniqueur *m*; **gossip c.** échotier, -ière *mf*.

coma ['kəʊmə] *n* coma *m*; **in a c.** dans le coma.

comb [kəʊm] *n* peigne *m*; – *vt* peigner; (*search*) *Fig* ratisser; **to c. one's hair** se peigner; **to c. out** (*hair*) démêler.

combat ['kɒmbæt] *n* combat *m*; – *vti* combattre (**for** pour). ◆**'combatant** *n* combattant, -ante *mf*.

combine¹ [kəm'baɪn] *vt* unir, joindre (**with** à); (*elements, sounds*) combiner; (*qualities, efforts*) allier, joindre; – *vi* s'unir; **everything combined to** ... tout s'est ligué pour .... ◆**—ed** *a* (*effort*) conjugué; **c. wealth/etc** (*put together*) richesses/*etc fpl* réunies; **c. forces** *Mil* forces *fpl* alliées. ◆**combi'nation** *n* combinaison *f*; (*of* *qualities*) réunion *f*; (*of events*) concours *m*; **in c. with** en association avec.

combine² ['kɒmbaɪn] *n Com* cartel *m*; **c. harvester** *Agr* moissonneuse-batteuse *f*.

combustion [kəm'bʌstʃ(ə)n] *n* combustion *f*.

come [kʌm] *vi* (*pt* came, *pp* come) venir (**from** de, **to** à); (*arrive*) arriver, venir; (*happen*) arriver; **c. and see me** viens me voir; **I've just c. from** j'arrive de; **to c. for** venir chercher; **to c. home** rentrer; **coming!** j'arrive!; **c. now!** voyons!; **to c. as a surprise (to)** surprendre; **to c. near** or **close to doing** faillir faire; **to c. on page 2** se trouver à la page 2; **nothing came of it** ça n'a abouti à rien; **to c. to** (*understand etc*) en venir à; (*a decision*) parvenir à; **to c. to an end** toucher à sa fin; **to c. true** se réaliser; **c. May**/*etc Fam* en mai/*etc*; **the life to c.** la vie future; **how c. that ...?** *Fam* comment se fait-il que ...? ■ **to c. about** *vi* (*happen*) se faire, arriver; **to c. across** *vi* (*of speech*) faire de l'effet; (*of feelings*) se montrer; – *vt* (*thing, person*) tomber sur; **to c. along** *vi* venir (**with** avec); (*progress*) avancer; **c. along!** allons!; **to c. at** *vt* (*attack*) attaquer; **to c. away** *vi* (*leave, come off*) partir; **to c. back** *vi* revenir; (*return home*) rentrer. ◆**comeback** *n* retour *m*; *Th Pol* rentrée *f*; (*retort*) réplique *f*; **to c. by** *vt* (*obtain*) obtenir; (*find*) trouver; **to c. down** *vi* descendre; (*of rain, price*) tomber. ◆**comedown** *n Fam* humiliation *f*; **to c. forward** *vi* (*make oneself known, volunteer*) se présenter; **to c. forward with** offrir, suggérer; **to c. in** *vi* entrer; (*of tide*) monter; (*of train, athlete*) arriver; *Pol* arriver au pouvoir; (*of clothes*) devenir la mode, se faire beaucoup; (*of money*) rentrer; **to c. in for** recevoir; **to c. into** (*money*) hériter de; **to c. off** *vi* se détacher, partir; (*succeed*) réussir; (*happen*) avoir lieu; (*fare, manage*) s'en tirer; – *vt* (*fall from*) tomber de; (*get down from*) descendre de; **to c. on** *vi* (*follow*) suivre; (*progress*) avancer; (*start*) commencer; (*arrive*) arriver; (*of play*) être joué; **c. on!** allez!; **to c. out** *vi* sortir; (*of sun, book*) paraître; (*of stain*) s'enlever, partir; (*of secret*) être révélé; (*of photo*) réussir; **to c. out** (**on strike**) se mettre en grève; **to c. over** *vi* (*visit*) venir, passer; **to c. over funny** or **peculiar** se trouver mal; – *vt* (*take hold of*) saisir (*qn*), prendre (*qn*); **to c. round** *vi* (*visit*) venir, passer; (*recur*) revenir; (*regain consciousness*) revenir à soi; **to c. through** *vi* (*survive*) s'en tirer; – *vt* se tirer indemne de; **to c. to** *vi* (*regain consciousness*) revenir

à soi; (*amount to*) *Com* revenir à, faire; **to c. under** *vi* être classé sous; (*s.o.'s influence*) tomber sous; **to c. up** *vi* (*rise*) monter; (*of plant*) sortir; (*of question, job*) se présenter; **to c. up against** (*wall, problem*) se heurter à; **to c. up to** (*reach*) arriver jusqu'à; (*one's hopes*) répondre à; **to c. up with** (*idea, money*) trouver; **to c. upon** *vt* (*book, reference etc*) tomber sur. ◆**coming** *a* (*future*) à venir; – *n Rel* avènement *m*; **comings and goings** allées *fpl* et venues.

comedy ['kɒmɪdɪ] *n* comédie *f*. ◆**co'median** *n* (*acteur m*) comique *m*, actrice *f* comique.

comet ['kɒmɪt] *n* comète *f*.

comeuppance [kʌm'ʌpəns] *n* **he got his c.** *Pej Fam* il n'a eu que ce qu'il mérite.

comfort ['kʌmfət] *n* confort *m*; (*consolation*) réconfort *m*, consolation *f*; (*peace of mind*) tranquillité *f* d'esprit; **to like one's comforts** aimer ses aises *fpl*; **c. station** *Am* toilettes *fpl*; – *vt* consoler; (*cheer*) réconforter. ◆**-able** *a* (*chair, house etc*) confortable; (*rich*) aisé; **he's c.** (*in chair etc*) il est à l'aise, il est bien; **make yourself c.** mets-toi à l'aise. ◆**-ably** *adv* **c. off** (*rich*) à l'aise. ◆**-er** *n* (*baby's dummy*) sucette *f*; (*quilt*) *Am* édredon *m*. ◆**comfy** *a* (-ier, -iest) (*chair etc*) *Fam* confortable; **I'm c.** je suis bien.

comic ['kɒmɪk] *a* comique; – *n* (*actor*) comique *m*; (*actress*) actrice *f* comique; (*magazine*) illustré *m*; **c. strip** bande *f* dessinée. ◆**comical** *a* comique, drôle.

comma ['kɒmə] *n Gram* virgule *f*.

command [kə'mɑːnd] *vt* (*order*) commander (**s.o. to do** à qn de faire); (*control, dominate*) commander (*régiment, vallée etc*); (*be able to use*) disposer de; (*respect*) imposer (**from** à); (*require*) exiger; – *vi* commander; – *n* ordre *m*; (*power*) commandement *m*; (*troops*) troupes *fpl*; (*mastery*) maîtrise *f* (**of** de); **at one's c.** (*disposal*) à sa disposition; **to be in c.** (**of**) (*ship, army etc*) commander; (*situation*) être maître (de). ◆**-ing** *a* (*authoritative*) imposant; (*position*) dominant; **c. officer** commandant *m*. ◆**-er** *n* chef *m*; *Mil* commandant *m*. ◆**-ment** *n Rel* commandement *m*.

commandant ['kɒmənkænt] *n Mil* commandant *m* (*d'un camp etc*). ◆**comman'deer** *vt* réquisitionner.

commando [kə'mɑːndəʊ] *n* (*pl* -os *or* -oes) *Mil* commando *m*.

commemorate [kə'meməreɪt] *vt* commémorer. ◆**commemo'ration** *n* commémoration f. ◆**commemorative** a commémoratif.

commence [kə'mens] vti commencer (**doing** à faire). ◆**—ment** n commencement m; Univ Am remise f des diplômes.

commend [kə'mend] vt (praise) louer; (recommend) recommander; (entrust) confier (**to** à). ◆**—able** a louable. ◆**commen'dation** n éloge m.

commensurate [kə'menʃərət] a proportionné (**to, with** à).

comment [kɒment] n commentaire m, remarque f; – vi faire des commentaires or des remarques (**on** sur); **to c. on** (text, event, news item) commenter; **to c. that** remarquer que. ◆**commentary** n commentaire m; (live) c. TV Rad reportage m. ◆**commentate** vi TV Rad faire un reportage (**on** sur). ◆**commentator** n TV Rad reporter m, commentateur, -trice mf.

commerce [kɒmɜːs] n commerce m. ◆**co'mmercial** 1 a commercial; (street) commerçant; (traveller) de commerce. 2 n (advertisement) TV publicité f; **the commercials** TV la publicité. ◆**co'mmercialize** vt (event) Pej transformer en une affaire de gros sous.

commiserate [kə'mɪzəreɪt] vi **to c. with** s.o. s'apitoyer sur (le sort de) qn. ◆**commise'ration** n commisération f.

commission [kə'mɪʃ(ə)n] n (fee, group) commission f; (order for work) commande f; **out of c.** hors service; **to get one's c.** Mil être nommé officier; – vt (artist) passer une commande à; (book) commander; Mil nommer (qn) officier; **to c. to do** charger de faire. ◆**commissio'naire** n (in hotel etc) commissionnaire m. ◆**commissioner** n Pol commissaire m; (police) c. préfet m (de police).

commit [kə'mɪt] vt (-tt-) (crime) commettre; (entrust) confier (**to** à); **to c. suicide** se suicider; **to c. to memory** apprendre par cœur; **to c. to prison** incarcérer; **to c. oneself** s'engager (**to** à); (compromise oneself) se compromettre. ◆**—ment** n obligation f; (promise) engagement m.

committee [kə'mɪtɪ] n comité m.

commodity [kə'mɒdɪtɪ] n produit m, article m.

common [kɒmən] 1 a (-er, -est) (shared, vulgar) commun; (frequent) courant, fréquent, commun; **the c. man** l'homme m du commun; **in c.** (shared) en commun (**with** avec); **to have nothing in c.** n'avoir rien de commun (**with** avec); **in c. with** (like) comme; **c. law** droit m coutumier; C.

Market Marché m commun; **c. room** salle f commune; **c. or garden** ordinaire. 2 n (land) terrain m communal; **House of Commons** Pol Chambre f des Communes; **the Commons** Pol les Communes fpl. ◆**—er** n roturier, -ière mf. ◆**—ly** adv (generally) communément; (vulgarly) d'une façon commune. ◆**—ness** n fréquence f; (vulgarity) vulgarité f. ◆**commonplace** a banal; – n banalité f. ◆**common'sense** n sens m commun; – a sensé.

Commonwealth [kɒmənwelθ] n **the C.** le Commonwealth.

commotion [kə'məʊʃ(ə)n] n agitation f.

communal [kə'mjuːn(ə)l] a (of the community) communautaire; (shared) commun. ◆**—ly** adv en commun; (to live) en communauté.

commune 1 [kɒmjuːn] n (district) commune f; (group) communauté f. 2 [kə'mjuːn] vi Rel & Fig communier (**with** avec). ◆**co'mmunion** n communion f; (Holy) C. communion f.

communicate [kə'mjuːnɪkeɪt] vt communiquer; (illness) transmettre; – vi (of person, rooms etc) communiquer. ◆**communi'cation** n communication f; **c. cord** Rail signal m d'alarme. ◆**communicative** a communicatif. ◆**communiqué** n Pol communiqué m.

communism [kɒmjunɪz(ə)m] n communisme m. ◆**communist** a & n communiste (mf).

community [kə'mjuːnɪtɪ] n communauté f; – a (rights, life etc) communautaire; **the student c.** les étudiants mpl; **c. centre** centre m socio-culturel; **c. worker** animateur, -trice mf socio-culturel(le).

commut/e [kə'mjuːt] 1 vt Jur commuer (**to** en). 2 vi (travel) faire la navette (**to work** pour se rendre à son travail). ◆**—ing** n trajets mpl journaliers. ◆**—er** n banlieusard, -arde mf; **c. train** train m de banlieue.

compact 1 [kəm'pækt] a (car, crowd, substance) compact; (style) condensé; **c. disc** [kɒmpækt] disque m compact. 2 [kɒmpækt] n (for face powder) poudrier m.

companion [kəm'pænjən] n (person) compagnon m, compagne f; (handbook) manuel m. ◆**companionship** n camaraderie f.

company [kʌmpənɪ] n (fellowship, firm) compagnie f; (guests) invités, -ées mfpl; **to keep s.o. c.** tenir compagnie à qn; **to keep good c.** avoir de bonnes fréquentations; **he's good c.** c'est un bon compagnon.

compar/e [kəm'peər] *vt* comparer; **compared to** *or* **with** en comparaison de; – *vi* être comparable, se comparer (**with** à). **◆—able** ['kɒmpərəb(ə)l] *a* comparable. **◆comparative** *a* comparatif; (*relative*) relatif. **◆comparatively** *adv* relativement. **◆comparison** *n* comparaison *f* (**between** entre; **with** à, avec).

compartment [kəm'pɑːtmənt] *n* compartiment *m*. **◆compart'mentalize** *vt* compartimenter.

compass ['kʌmpəs] *n* **1** (*for navigation*) boussole *f*; *Nau* compas *m*; (*range*) *Fig* portée *f*. **2** (*for measuring etc*) *Am* compas *m*; (**pair of**) **compasses** compas *m*.

compassion [kəm'pæʃ(ə)n] *n* compassion *f*. **◆compassionate** *a* compatissant; **on c. grounds** pour raisons de famille.

compatible [kəm'pætɪb(ə)l] *a* compatible. **◆compati'bility** *n* compatibilité *f*.

compatriot [kəm'pætrɪət, kəm'peɪtrɪət] *n* compatriote *mf*.

compel [kəm'pel] *vt* (-ll-) contraindre (**to do** à faire); (*respect etc*) imposer (**from** à); **compelled to do** contraint de faire. **◆compelling** *a* irrésistible.

compendium [kəm'pendɪəm] *n* abrégé *m*.

compensate ['kɒmpənseɪt] *vt* to **c. s.o.** (*with payment, recompense*) dédommager qn (**for** de); to **c. for sth** (*make up for*) compenser qch; – *vi* compenser. **◆compen'sation** *n* (*financial*) dédommagement *m*; (*consolation*) compensation *f*, dédommagement *m*; **in c. for** en compensation de.

compère ['kɒmpeər] *n* *TV Rad* animateur, -trice *mf*, présentateur, -trice *mf*; – *vt* (*a show*) animer, présenter.

compete [kəm'piːt] *vi* prendre part (**in** à), concourir (**in** à); (*vie*) rivaliser (**with** avec); *Com* faire concurrence (**with** à); to **c. for** (*prize etc*) concourir pour; **to c. in a rally** courir dans un rallye.

competent ['kɒmpɪtənt] *a* (*capable*) compétent (**to do** pour faire); (*sufficient*) suffisant. **◆—ly** *adv* avec compétence. **◆competence** *n* compétence *f*.

competition [kɒmpə'tɪʃ(ə)n] *n* (*rivalry*) compétition *f*, concurrence *f*; **a c.** (*contest*) un concours; *Sp* une compétition. **◆competitive** *a* (*price, market*) compétitif; (*selection*) par concours; (*person*) aimant la compétition; **c. exam(ination)** concours *m*. **◆com'petitor** *n* concurrent, -ente *mf*.

compil/e [kəm'paɪl] *vt* (*dictionary*) rédiger; (*list*) dresser; (*documents*) compiler. **◆—er** *n* rédacteur, -trice *mf*.

complacent [kəm'pleɪsənt] *a* content de

soi. **◆complacence** *n*, **◆complacency** *n* autosatisfaction *f*, contentement *m* de soi.

complain [kəm'pleɪn] *vi* se plaindre (**of, about** de; **that** que). **◆complaint** *n* plainte *f*; *Com* réclamation *f*; *Med* maladie *f*; (**cause for**) **c.** sujet *m* de plainte.

complement ['kɒmplɪmənt] *n* complément *m*; – ['kɒmplɪment] *vt* compléter. **◆comple'mentary** *a* complémentaire.

complete [kəm'pliːt] *a* (*total*) complet; (*finished*) achevé; (*downright*) *Pej* parfait; – *vt* (*add sth missing*) compléter; (*finish*) achever; (*a form*) remplir. **◆—ly** *adv* complètement. **◆completion** *n* achèvement *m*, réalisation *f*.

complex ['kɒmpleks] **1** *a* complexe. **2** *n* (*feeling, buildings*) complexe *m*; **housing c.** grand ensemble *m*. **◆com'plexity** *n* complexité *f*.

complexion [kəm'plekʃ(ə)n] *n* (*of the face*) teint *m*; *Fig* caractère *m*.

compliance [kəm'plaɪəns] *n* (*agreement*) conformité *f* (**with** avec).

complicat/e ['kɒmplɪkeɪt] *vt* compliquer. **◆—ed** *a* compliqué. **◆compli'cation** *n* complication *f*.

complicity [kəm'plɪsɪtɪ] *n* complicité *f*.

compliment ['kɒmplɪmənt] *n* compliment *m*; *pl* (*of author*) hommages *mpl*; **compliments of the season** meilleurs vœux pour Noël et la nouvelle année; – ['kɒmplɪment] *vt* complimenter. **◆compli'mentary** *a* **1** (*flattering*) flatteur. **2** (*free*) à titre gracieux; (*ticket*) de faveur.

comply [kəm'plaɪ] *vi* obéir (**with** à); (*request*) accéder à.

component [kəm'pəʊnənt] *a* (*part*) constituant; – *n* (*chemical, electronic*) composant *m*; *Tech* pièce *f*; (*element*) *Fig* composante *f*.

compos/e [kəm'pəʊz] *vt* composer; **to c. oneself** se calmer. **◆—ed** *a* calme. **◆—er** *n* *Mus* compositeur, -trice *mf*. **◆compo- 'sition** *n* *Mus Liter Ch* composition *f*; *Sch* rédaction *f*. **◆composure** *n* calme *m*, sang-froid *m*.

compost ['kɒmpɒst, *Am* 'kɒmpəʊst] *n* compost *m*.

compound **1** ['kɒmpaʊnd] *n* (*substance, word*) composé *m*; (*area*) enclos *m*; – *a* *Ch* composé; (*sentence, number*) complexe. **2** [kəm'paʊnd] *vt* *Ch* composer; (*increase*) *Fig* aggraver.

comprehend [kɒmprɪ'hend] *vt* comprendre. **◆comprehensible** *a* compréhensible. **◆comprehension** *n* compréhension *f.* ◆**comprehensive** *a* complet; (*knowledge*) étendu; (*view, measure*) d'ensemble; (*insurance*) tous-risques *inv*; − *a* & *n* c. (**school**) = collège *m* d'enseignement secondaire.

compress [kəm'pres] *vt* comprimer; (*ideas etc*) *Fig* condenser. ◆**compression** *n* compression *f*; condensation *f*.

comprise [kəm'praɪz] *vt* comprendre, englober.

compromise ['kɒmprəmaɪz] *vi* compromettre; − *vi* accepter un compromis; − *n* compromis *m*; − *a* (*solution*) de compromis.

compulsion [kəm'pʌlʃ(ə)n] *n* contrainte *f*. ◆**compulsive** *a* (*behaviour*) *Psy* compulsif; (*smoker, gambler*) invétéré; **c. liar** mythomane *mf*.

compulsory [kəm'pʌlsəri] *a* obligatoire.

compunction [kəm'pʌŋkʃ(ə)n] *n* scrupule *m*.

comput/e [kəm'pjuːt] *vt* calculer. ◆**−ing** *n* informatique *f*. ◆**computer** *n* ordinateur *m*; − *a* (*system*) informatique; (*course*) d'informatique; **c. operator** opérateur, -trice *mf* sur ordinateur; **c. science** informatique *f*; **c. scientist** informaticien, -ienne *mf*. ◆**computerize** *vt* informatiser.

comrade ['kɒmreɪd] *n* camarade *mf*. ◆**comradeship** *n* camaraderie *f*.

con [kɒn] *vt* (**-nn-**) *Sl* rouler, escroquer; **to be conned** se faire avoir *or* rouler; − *n Sl* escroquerie *f*; **c. man** escroc *m*.

concave ['kɒnkeɪv] *a* concave.

conceal [kən'siːl] *vt* (*hide*) dissimuler (**from s.o.** à qn); (*plan etc*) tenir secret. ◆**−ment** *n* dissimulation *f*.

concede [kən'siːd] *vt* concéder (**to** à, **that** que); − *vi* céder.

conceit [kən'siːt] *n* vanité *f*. ◆**conceited** *a* vaniteux. ◆**conceitedly** *adv* avec vanité.

conceiv/e [kən'siːv] *vt* (*idea, child etc*) concevoir; − *vi* (*of woman*) concevoir; **to c. of** concevoir. ◆**−able** *a* concevable, envisageable. ◆**−ably** *adv* yes, c. oui, c'est concevable.

concentrate ['kɒnsəntreɪt] *vt* concentrer; − *vi* se concentrer (**on** sur); **to c. on doing** s'appliquer à faire. ◆**concen'tration** *n* concentration *f*; **c. camp** camp *m* de concentration.

concentric [kən'sentrɪk] *a* concentrique.

concept ['kɒnsept] *n* concept *m*. ◆**con-'ception** *n* (*idea*) & *Med* conception *f*.

concern [kən'sɜːn] *vt* concerner; **to c. oneself with, be concerned with** s'occuper de; **to be concerned about** s'inquiéter de; −

n (*matter*) affaire *f*; (*anxiety*) inquiétude *f*; (*share*) *Com* intérêt(s) *m*(*pl*) (**in** dans); (**business**) c. entreprise *f*. ◆**−ed** *a* (*anxious*) inquiet; **the department c.** le service compétent; **the main person c.** le principal intéressé. ◆**−ing** *prep* en ce qui concerne.

concert ['kɒnsət] *n* concert *m*; **in c.** (*together*) de concert (**with** avec). ◆**c.-goer** *n* habitué, -ée *mf* des concerts. ◆**con'certed** *a* (*effort*) concerté.

concertina [kɒnsə'tiːnə] *n* concertina *m*; **c. crash** *Aut* carambolage *m*.

concession [kən'seʃ(ə)n] *n* concession *f* (**to** à).

conciliate [kən'sɪlɪeɪt] *vt* **to c. s.o.** (*win over*) se concilier qn; (*soothe*) apaiser qn. ◆**concili'ation** *n* conciliation *f*; apaisement *m*. ◆**conciliatory** [kən'sɪlɪətərɪ, *Am* -tɔːrɪ] *a* conciliant.

concise [kən'saɪs] *a* concis. ◆**−ly** *adv* avec concision. ◆**−ness** *n*, ◆**concision** *n* concision *f*.

conclud/e [kən'kluːd] *vt* (*end, settle*) conclure; **to c. that** (*infer*) conclure que; − *vi* (*of event etc*) se terminer (**with** par); (*of speaker*) conclure. ◆**−ing** *a* final. ◆**conclusion** *n* conclusion *f*; **in c.** pour conclure. ◆**conclusive** *a* concluant. ◆**conclusively** *adv* de manière concluante.

concoct [kən'kɒkt] *vt* *Culin Pej* concocter, confectionner; (*scheme*) *Fig* combiner. ◆**concoction** *n* (*substance*) *Pej* mixture *f*; (*act*) confection *f*; *Fig* combinaison *f*.

concord ['kɒnkɔːd] *n* concorde *f*.

concourse ['kɒnkɔːs] *n* (*hall*) *Am* hall *m*; *Rail* hall *m*, salle *f* des pas perdus.

concrete ['kɒnkriːt] **1** *a* (*real, positive*) concret. **2** *n* béton *m*; − *a* en béton; **c. mixer** bétonnière *f*, bétonneuse *f*.

concur [kən'kɜːr] *vi* (**-rr-**) **1** (*agree*) être d'accord (**with** avec). **2** **to c. to** (*contribute*) concourir à.

concurrent [kən'kʌrənt] *a* simultané. ◆**−ly** *adv* simultanément.

concussion [kən'kʌʃ(ə)n] *n* *Med* commotion *f* (cérébrale).

condemn [kən'dem] *vt* condamner; (*building*) déclarer inhabitable. ◆**condem-'nation** *n* condamnation *f*.

condense [kən'dens] *vt* condenser; − *vi* se condenser. ◆**conden'sation** *n* condensation *f* (**of** de); (*mist*) buée *f*.

condescend [kɒndɪ'send] *vi* condescendre (**to do** à faire). ◆**condescension** *n* condescendance *f*.

condiment ['kɒndɪmənt] *n* condiment *m*.

condition ['kəndɪʃ(ə)n] **1** n (*stipulation, circumstance, rank*) condition f; (*state*) état m, condition f; **on c. that one does** à condition de faire, à condition que l'on fasse; **in/out of c.** en bonne/mauvaise forme. **2** vt (*action etc*) déterminer, conditionner; **to c. s.o.** Psy conditionner qn (**into doing** à faire). ◆**conditional** a conditionnel; **to be c. upon** dépendre de. ◆**conditioner** n (**hair**) c. après-shampooing m.

condo ['kɒndəʊ] n abbr (pl -os) Am = **condominium**.

condolences [kən'dəʊlənsɪz] npl condoléances fpl.

condom ['kɒndəm] n préservatif m, capote f (anglaise).

condominium [kɒndə'mɪnɪəm] n Am (*building*) (immeuble m en) copropriété f; (*apartment*) appartement m dans une copropriété.

condone [kən'dəʊn] vt (*forgive*) pardonner; (*overlook*) fermer les yeux sur.

conducive [kən'dju:sɪv] a **c. to** favorable à.

conduct ['kɒndʌkt] n (*behaviour, directing*) conduite f; – [kən'dʌkt] vt (*lead*) conduire, mener; (*orchestra*) diriger; (*electricity etc*) conduire; **to c. oneself** se conduire. ◆—**ed** a (*visit*) guidé; **c. tour** excursion f accompagnée. ◆**conductor** n Mus chef m d'orchestre; (*on bus*) receveur m; Rail Am chef m de train; (*metal, cable etc*) conducteur m. ◆**conductress** n (*on bus*) receveuse f.

cone [kəʊn] n cône m; (*of ice cream*) cornet m; (**paper**) c. cornet m (de papier); **traffic c.** cône m de chantier.

confectioner [kən'fekʃənər] n (*of sweets*) confiseur, -euse mf; (*of cakes*) pâtissier, -ière mf. ◆**confectionery** n (*sweets*) confiserie f; (*cakes*) pâtisserie f.

confederate [kən'fedərət] a confédéré; – n (*accomplice*) complice mf, acolyte m. ◆**confederacy** n, ◆**confede'ration** n confédération f.

confer [kən'fɜːr] **1** vt (-rr-) (*grant*) conférer (**on** à); (*degree*) Univ remettre. **2** vi (-rr-) (*talk together*) conférer, se consulter.

conference ['kɒnfərəns] n conférence f; (*scientific etc*) congrès m.

confess [kən'fes] **1** vt avouer, confesser (**that** que, **to** à); – vi avouer; **to c. to** (*crime etc*) avouer, confesser. **2** vt Rel confesser; – vi se confesser. ◆**confession** n aveu m, confession f; Rel confession f. ◆**confessional** n Rel confessionnal m.

confetti [kən'fetɪ] n confettis mpl.

confide [kən'faɪd] vt confier (**to** à, **that** que);

– vi **to c. in** (*talk to*) se confier à. ◆'**confidant, -ante** [-ænt] n confident, -ente mf. ◆'**confidence** n (*trust*) confiance f; (*secret*) confidence f; (*self-*)c. confiance f en soi; **in c.** en confidence; **motion of no c.** Pol motion f de censure; **c. trick** escroquerie f; **c. trickster** escroc m. ◆'**confident** a sûr, assuré; (*self-*)c. sûr de soi. ◆**confi'dential** a confidentiel; (*secretary*) particulier. ◆**confi'dentially** adv en confidence. ◆'**confidently** adv avec confiance.

configuration [kənfɪgjʊ'reɪʃ(ə)n] n configuration f.

confin/e [kən'faɪn] vt enfermer, confiner (**to, in** dans); (*limit*) limiter (**to** à); **to c. oneself to doing** se limiter à faire. ◆—**ed** a (*atmosphere*) confiné; (*space*) réduit; **c. to bed** obligé de garder le lit. ◆—**ement** n Med couches fpl; Jur emprisonnement m. ◆'**confines** npl limites fpl, confins mpl.

confirm [kən'fɜːm] vt confirmer (**that** que); (*strengthen*) raffermir. ◆—**ed** a (*bachelor*) endurci; (*smoker, habit*) invétéré. ◆**confir'mation** n confirmation f; raffermissement m.

confiscate ['kɒnfɪskeɪt] vt confisquer (**from s.o.** à qn). ◆**confis'cation** n confiscation f.

conflagration [kɒnflə'greɪʃ(ə)n] n (grand) incendie m, brasier m.

conflict ['kɒnflɪkt] n conflit m; – [kən'flɪkt] vi être en contradiction, être incompatible (**with** avec); (*of dates, events, TV programmes*) tomber en même temps (**with** que). ◆—**ing** a (*views, theories etc*) contradictoires; (*dates*) incompatibles.

confluence ['kɒnflʊəns] n (*of rivers*) confluent m.

conform [kən'fɔːm] vi se conformer (**to, with** à); (*of ideas etc*) être en conformité. ◆**conformist** a & n conformiste (mf). ◆**conformity** n (*likeness*) conformité f; Pej conformisme m.

confound [kən'faʊnd] vt confondre; **c. him!** que le diable l'emporte! ◆—**ed** a (*damned*) Fam sacré.

confront [kən'frʌnt] vt (*danger*) affronter; (*problems*) faire face à; **to c. s.o.** (*be face to face with*) se trouver en face de qn; (*oppose*) s'opposer à qn; **to c. s.o. with** (*person*) confronter qn avec; (*thing*) mettre qn en présence de. ◆**confron'tation** n confrontation f.

confus/e [kən'fjuːz] vt (*perplex*) confondre; (*muddle*) embrouiller; **to c. with** (*mistake for*) confondre avec. ◆—**ed** a (*situation,* *noises etc*) confus; **to be c.** (*of person*) s'y perdre; **to get c.** s'embrouiller. ◆**—ing** *a* difficile à comprendre, déroutant. ◆**confusion** *n* confusion *f*; **in c.** en désordre.

congeal [kən'dʒiːl] *vt* figer; – *vi* (se) figer.

congenial [kən'dʒiːnɪəl] *a* sympathique.

congenital [kən'dʒenɪtl] *a* congénital.

congested [kən'dʒestɪd] *a* (*street*) encombré; (*town*) surpeuplé; *Med* congestionné. ◆**congestion** *n* (*traffic*) encombrement(s) *m*(*pl*); (*overcrowding*) surpeuplement *m*; *Med* congestion *f*.

Congo ['kɒŋɡəʊ] *n* Congo *m*.

congratulate [kən'ɡrætʃʊleɪt] *vt* féliciter (**s.o. on sth** qn de qch). ◆**congratu-'lations** *npl* félicitations *fpl* (**on** pour). ◆**congratu'latory** *a* (*telegram etc*) de félicitations.

congregate ['kɒŋɡrɪɡeɪt] *vi* se rassembler. ◆**congre'gation** *n* (*worshippers*) assemblée *f*, fidèles *mfpl*.

congress ['kɒŋɡres] *n* congrès *m*; **C. Pol** *Am* le Congrès. ◆**Congressman** *n* (*pl* -men) *Am* membre *m* du Congrès. ◆**Con-'gressional** *a* *Am* du Congrès.

conic(al) ['kɒnɪk(ə)l] *a* conique.

conifer ['kɒnɪfər] *n* (*tree*) conifère *m*.

conjecture [kən'dʒektʃər] *n* conjecture *f*; – *vt* conjecturer; – *vi* faire des conjectures. ◆**conjectural** *a* conjectural.

conjugal ['kɒndʒʊɡəl] *a* conjugal.

conjugate ['kɒndʒʊɡeɪt] *vt* (*verb*) conjuguer. ◆**conju'gation** *n* *Gram* conjugaison *f*.

conjunction [kən'dʒʌŋkʃ(ə)n] *n* *Gram* conjonction *f*; **in c. with** conjointement avec.

conjur/e ['kʌndʒər] *vt* **to c. (up)** (*by magic*) faire apparaître; **to c. up** (*memories etc*) *Fig* évoquer. ◆**—ing** *n* prestidigitation *f*. ◆**—er** *n* prestidigitateur, -trice *mf*.

conk [kɒŋk] **1** *n* (*nose*) *Sl* pif *m*. **2** *vi* **to c. out** (*break down*) *Fam* claquer, tomber en panne.

conker ['kɒŋkər] *n* (*horse-chestnut fruit*) *Fam* marron *m* (d'Inde).

connect [kə'nekt] *vt* relier (**with, to** à); (*telephone, stove etc*) brancher; **to c. with** *Tel* mettre en communication avec; (*in memory*) associer avec; – *vi* (*be connected*) être relié; **to c. with** (*of train, bus*) assurer la correspondance avec. ◆**—ed** *a* (*facts etc*) lié, connexe; (*speech*) suivi; **to be c. with** (*have dealings with*) être lié à; (*have to do with, relate to*) avoir rapport à; (*by marriage*) être allié à. ◆**connection** *n* (*link*) rapport *m*, relation *f* (**with** avec);

(*train, bus etc*) correspondance *f*; (*phone call*) communication *f*; (*between pipes etc*) *Tech* raccord *m*; *pl* (*contacts*) relations *fpl*; **in c. with** à propos de.

connive [kə'naɪv] *vi* **to c. at** fermer les yeux sur; **to c. to do** se mettre de connivence pour faire (**with** avec); **to c. together** agir en complicité. ◆**connivance** *n* connivence *f*.

connoisseur [kɒnə'sɜːr] *n* connaisseur *m*.

connotation [kɒnə'teɪʃ(ə)n] *n* connotation *f*.

conquer ['kɒŋkər] *vt* (*country, freedom etc*) conquérir; (*enemy, habit*) vaincre. ◆**—ing** *a* victorieux. ◆**conqueror** *n* conquérant, -ante *mf*, vainqueur *m*. ◆**conquest** *n* conquête *f*.

cons [kɒnz] *npl* **the pros and (the) c.** le pour et le contre.

conscience ['kɒnʃəns] *n* conscience *f*. ◆**c.-stricken** *a* pris de remords.

conscientious [kɒnʃɪ'enʃəs] *a* consciencieux; **c. objector** objecteur *m* de conscience. ◆**—ness** *n* application *f*, sérieux *m*.

conscious ['kɒnʃəs] *a* conscient (**of sth** de qch); (*intentional*) délibéré; *Med* conscient; **to be c. of doing** avoir conscience de faire. ◆**—ly** *adv* (*knowingly*) consciemment. ◆**—ness** *n* conscience *f* (**of** de); *Med* connaissance *f*.

conscript ['kɒnskrɪpt] *n* *Mil* conscrit *m*; – [kən'skrɪpt] *vt* enrôler (par conscription). ◆**con'scription** *n* conscription *f*.

consecrate ['kɒnsɪkreɪt] *vt* (*church etc*) *Rel* consacrer. ◆**conse'cration** *n* consécration *f*.

consecutive [kən'sekjʊtɪv] *a* consécutif. ◆**—ly** *adv* consécutivement.

consensus [kən'sensəs] *n* consensus *m*, accord *m* (général).

consent [kən'sent] *vi* consentir (**to** à); – *n* consentement *m*; **by common c.** de l'aveu de tous; **by mutual c.** d'un commun accord.

consequence ['kɒnsɪkwəns] *n* (*result*) conséquence *f*; (*importance*) importance *f*, conséquence *f*. ◆**consequently** *adv* par conséquent.

conservative [kən'sɜːvətɪv] **1** *a* (*estimate*) modeste; (*view*) traditionnel. **2** *a & n* **C. Pol** conservateur, -trice (*mf*). ◆**conservatism** *n* (*in behaviour*) & *Pol Rel* conservatisme *m*.

conservatoire [kən'sɜːvətwɑːr] *n* *Mus* conservatoire *m*.

conservatory [kən'sɜːvətrɪ] *n* (*greenhouse*) serre *f*.

conserve [kən'sɜːv] *vt* préserver, conserver;

(*one's strength*) ménager; **to c. energy** faire des économies d'énergie. ◆**conser'vation** *n* (*energy-saving*) économies *fpl* d'énergie; (*of nature*) protection *f* de l'environnement; *Phys* conservation *f*.

consider [kən'sɪdər] *vt* considérer; (*take into account*) tenir compte de; **I'll c. it** j'y réfléchirai; **to c. doing** envisager de faire; **to c. that** estimer *or* considérer que; **he's** *or* **she's being considered (for the job)** sa candidature est à l'étude; **all things considered** en fin de compte. ◆—**ing** *prep* étant donné, vu. ◆—**able** *a* (*large*) considérable; (*much*) beaucoup de. ◆—**ably** *adv* beaucoup, considérablement. ◆**conside'ration** *n* (*thought, thoughtfulness, reason*) considération *f*; **under c.** à l'étude; **out of c. for** par égard pour; **to take into c.** prendre en considération.

considerate [kən'sɪdərət] *a* plein d'égards (**to** pour), attentionné (**to** à l'égard de).

consign [kən'saɪn] *vt* (*send*) expédier; (*entrust*) confier (**to** à). ◆—**ment** *n* (*act*) expédition *f*; (*goods*) arrivage *m*.

consist [kən'sɪst] *vi* consister (**of** en, **in** dans, **in doing** à faire).

consistent [kən'sɪstənt] *a* logique, conséquent; (*coherent*) cohérent; (*friend*) fidèle; **c. with** compatible avec, conforme à. ◆—**ly** *adv* (*logically*) avec logique; (*always*) constamment. ◆**consistency** *n* **1** logique *f*; cohérence *f*. **2** (*of liquid etc*) consistance *f*.

console[1] [kən'səʊl] *vt* consoler. ◆**conso'lation** *n* consolation *f*; **c. prize** prix *m* de consolation.

console[2] ['kɒnsəʊl] *n* (*control desk*) *Tech* console *f*.

consolidate [kən'sɒlɪdeɪt] *vt* consolider; — *vi* se consolider. ◆**consoli'dation** *n* consolidation *f*.

consonant ['kɒnsənənt] *n* consonne *f*.

consort **1** ['kɒnsɔːt] *n* époux *m*, épouse *f*; **prince c.** prince *m* consort. **2** [kən'sɔːt] *vi* **to c. with** *Pej* fréquenter.

consortium [kən'sɔːtɪəm] *n* *Com* consortium *m*.

conspicuous [kən'spɪkjʊəs] *a* visible, en évidence; (*striking*) remarquable, manifeste; (*showy*) voyant; **to be c. by one's absence** briller par son absence; **to make oneself c.** se faire remarquer. ◆—**ly** *adv* visiblement.

conspire [kən'spaɪər] **1** *vi* (*plot*) conspirer (**against** contre); **to c. to do** comploter de faire. **2** *vt* **to c. to do** (*of events*) conspirer à faire. ◆**conspiracy** *n* conspiration *f*.

constable ['kʌnstəb(ə)l] *n* (**police**) **c.** agent *m* (de police). ◆**con'stabulary** *n* la police.

constant ['kɒnstənt] *a* (*frequent*) incessant; (*unchanging*) constant; (*faithful*) fidèle. ◆**constancy** *n* constance *f*. ◆**constantly** *adv* constamment, sans cesse.

constellation [kɒnstə'leɪʃ(ə)n] *n* constellation *f*.

consternation [kɒnstə'neɪʃ(ə)n] *n* consternation *f*.

constipate ['kɒnstɪpeɪt] *vt* constiper. ◆**consti'pation** *n* constipation *f*.

constituent [kən'stɪtjʊənt] **1** *a* (*element etc*) constituant, constitutif. **2** *n* *Pol* électeur, -trice *mf*. ◆**constituency** *n* circonscription *f* électorale; (*voters*) électeurs *mpl*.

constitute ['kɒnstɪtjuːt] *vt* constituer. ◆**consti'tution** *n* (*of person etc*) & *Pol* constitution *f*. ◆**consti'tutional** *a* *Pol* constitutionnel.

constrain [kən'streɪn] *vt* contraindre.

constrict [kən'strɪkt] *vt* (*tighten, narrow*) resserrer; (*movement*) gêner. ◆**con'striction** *n* resserrement *m*.

construct [kən'strʌkt] *vt* construire. ◆**construction** *n* construction *f*; **under c.** en construction. ◆**constructive** *a* constructif.

construe [kən'struː] *vt* interpréter, comprendre.

consul ['kɒnsəl] *n* consul *m*. ◆**consular** *a* consulaire. ◆**consulate** *n* consulat *m*.

consult [kən'sʌlt] *vt* consulter; — *vi* **to c. with** discuter avec, conférer avec. ◆—**ing** *a* (*room*) *Med* de consultation; (*physician*) consultant. ◆**consultancy** *n* **c.** (**firm**) *Com* cabinet *m* d'experts-conseils; **c. fee** honoraires *mpl* de conseils. ◆**consultant** *n* conseiller, -ère *mf*; *Med* spécialiste *mf*; (*financial, legal*) conseil *m*, expert-conseil *m*; — *a* (*engineer etc*) consultant. ◆**consul'tation** *n* consultation *f*. ◆**consultative** *a* consultatif.

consum/e [kən'sjuːm] *vt* (*food, supplies etc*) consommer; (*of fire, grief, hate*) consumer. ◆—**ing** *a* (*ambition*) brûlant. ◆—**er** *n* consommateur, -trice *mf*; **c. goods/society** biens *mpl*/société *f* de consommation. ◆**con'sumption** *n* consommation *f* (**of** de).

consummate ['kɒnsəmət] *a* (*perfect*) consommé.

contact ['kɒntækt] *n* contact *m*; (*person*) relation *f*; **in c. with** en contact avec; **c. lenses** lentilles *fpl* *or* verres *mpl* de contact; — *vt* se mettre en contact avec, contacter.

contagious [kən'teɪdʒəs] *a* contagieux.
contain [kən'teɪn] *vt* (*enclose, hold back*) contenir; **to c. oneself** se contenir. ◆**—er** *n* récipient *m*; (*for transporting freight*) conteneur *m*, container *m*.
contaminate [kən'tæmɪneɪt] *vt* contaminer. ◆**contami'nation** *n* contamination *f*.
contemplate ['kɒntəmpleɪt] *vt* (*look at*) contempler; (*consider*) envisager (**doing de** faire). ◆**contem'plation** *n* contemplation *f*; **in c. of** en prévision de.
contemporary [kən'tempərərɪ] *a* contemporain (**with** de); − *n* (*person*) contemporain, -aine *mf*.
contempt [kən'tempt] *n* mépris *m*; **to hold in c.** mépriser. ◆**contemptible** *a* méprisable. ◆**contemptuous** *a* dédaigneux (**of** de).
contend [kən'tend] **1** *vi* **to c. with** (*problem*) faire face à; (*person*) avoir affaire à; (*compete*) rivaliser avec; (*struggle*) se battre avec. **2** *vt* **to c. that** (*claim*) soutenir que. ◆**—er** *n* concurrent, -ente *mf*. ◆**contention** *n* **1** (*argument*) dispute *f*. **2** (*claim*) affirmation *f*. ◆**contentious** *a* (*issue*) litigieux.
content¹ [kən'tent] *a* satisfait (**with** de); **he's c. to do** il ne demande pas mieux que de faire. ◆**—ed** *a* satisfait. ◆**—ment** *n* contentement *m*.
content² ['kɒntent] *n* (*of text, film etc*) contenu *m*; *pl* (*of container*) contenu *m*; (**table of**) **contents** (*of book*) table *f* des matières; **alcoholic/iron/etc c.** teneur *f* en alcool/fer/*etc*.
contest [kən'test] *vt* (*dispute*) contester; (*fight for*) disputer; − ['kɒntest] *n* (*competition*) concours *m*; (*fight*) lutte *f*; *Boxing* combat *m*. ◆**con'testant** *n* concurrent, -ente *mf*; (*in fight*) adversaire *mf*.
context ['kɒntekst] *n* contexte *m*.
continent ['kɒntɪnənt] *n* continent *m*; **the C.** l'Europe *f* (continentale). ◆**conti'nental** *a* continental; européen; **c. breakfast** petit déjeuner *m* à la française.
contingent [kən'tɪndʒənt] **1** *a* (*accidental*) contingent; **to be c. upon** dépendre de. **2** *nm Mil* contingent *m*. ◆**contingency** *n* éventualité *f*; **c. plan** plan *m* d'urgence.
continu/e [kən'tɪnjuː] *vt* continuer (**to do** *or* **doing** à *or* de faire); (*resume*) reprendre; **to c. (with)** (*work, speech etc*) poursuivre, continuer; − *vi* continuer; (*resume*) reprendre; **to c. in** (*job*) garder. ◆**—ed** *a* (*interest, attention etc*) soutenu, assidu; (*presence*) continu(el); **to be c.** (*of story*) à suivre. ◆**continual** *a* continuel. ◆**continually**

adv continuellement. ◆**continuance** *n* continuation *f*. ◆**continu'ation** *n* continuation *f*; (*resumption*) reprise *f*; (*new episode*) suite *f*. ◆**continuity** [kɒntɪ'njuːɪtɪ] *n* continuité *f*. ◆**continuous** *a* continu; **c. performance** *Cin* spectacle *m* permanent. ◆**continuously** *adv* sans interruption.
contort [kən'tɔːt] *vt* (*twist*) tordre; **to c. oneself** se contorsionner. ◆**contortion** *n* contorsion *f*. ◆**contortionist** *n* (*acrobat*) contorsionniste *mf*.
contour ['kɒntuər] *n* contour *m*.
contraband ['kɒntrəbænd] *n* contrebande *f*.
contraception [kɒntrə'sepʃ(ə)n] *n* contraception *f*. ◆**contraceptive** *a* & *n* contraceptif (*m*).
contract 1 ['kɒntrækt] *n* contrat *m*; **c. work** travail *m* en sous-traitance; − *vi* **to c. out of** (*agreement etc*) se dégager de. **2** [kən'trækt] *vt* (*habit, debt, muscle etc*) contracter; − *vi* (*of heart etc*) se contracter. ◆**con'traction** *n* (*of muscle, word*) contraction *f*. ◆**con'tractor** *n* entrepreneur *m*.
contradict [kɒntrə'dɪkt] *vt* contredire; (*belie*) démentir. ◆**contradiction** *n* contradiction *f*. ◆**contradictory** *a* contradictoire.
contralto [kən'træltəu] *n* (*pl* -os) contralto *m*.
contraption [kən'træpʃ(ə)n] *n Fam* machin *m*, engin *m*.
contrary 1 ['kɒntrərɪ] *a* contraire (**to** à); − *adv* **c. to** contrairement à; − *n* contraire *m*; **on the c.** au contraire; **unless you, I** *etc* **hear to the c.** sauf avis contraire; **she said nothing to the c.** elle n'a rien dit contre. **2** [kən'treərɪ] *a* (*obstinate*) entêté, difficile.
contrast 1 ['kɒntrɑːst] *n* contraste *m*; **in c. to** par opposition à. **2** [kən'trɑːst] *vi* contraster (**with** avec); − *vt* faire contraster, mettre en contraste. ◆**—ing** *a* (*colours etc*) opposés.
contravene [kɒntrə'viːn] *vt* (*law*) enfreindre. ◆**contravention** *n* **in c. of** en contravention de.
contribute [kən'trɪbjuːt] *vt* donner, fournir (**to** à); (*article*) écrire (**to** pour); **to c. money to** contribuer à, verser de l'argent à; − *vi* **to c. to** contribuer à; (*publication*) collaborer à. ◆**contri'bution** *n* contribution *f*; (*to pension fund etc*) cotisation(s) *f*(*pl*); *Journ* article *m*. ◆**contributor** *n Journ* collaborateur, -trice *mf*; (*of money*) donateur, -trice *mf*. ◆**contributory** *a* **c. factor** un facteur qui a contribué (**in** à).
contrite [kən'traɪt] *a* contrit. ◆**contrition** *n* contrition *f*.
contriv/e [kən'traɪv] *vt* inventer; **to c. to do**

trouver moyen de faire. ◆**—ed** *a* artificiel. ◆**contrivance** *n* (*device*) dispositif *m*; (*scheme*) invention *f*.

control [kənˈtrəʊl] *vt* (**-ll-**) (*business, organization*) diriger; (*traffic*) régler; (*prices, quality*) contrôler; (*emotion, reaction*) maîtriser, contrôler; (*disease*) enrayer; (*situation*) être maître de; **to c. oneself** se contrôler; – *n* (*authority*) autorité *f* (**over** sur); (*of traffic*) réglementation *f*; (*of prices etc*) contrôle *m*; (*of emotion etc*) maîtrise *f*, *pl* (*of train etc*) commandes *fpl*; (*knobs*) TV Rad boutons *mpl*; **the c. of** (*fires etc*) la lutte contre; (**self-**)**c.** le contrôle de soi-même; **to keep s.o. under c.** tenir qn; **everything is under c.** tout est en ordre; **in c. of** maître de; **to lose c. of** (*situation, vehicle*) perdre le contrôle de; **out of c.** (*situation, crowd*) difficilement maîtrisable; **c. tower** *Av* tour *f* de contrôle. ◆**controller** *n* **air traffic c.** aiguilleur *m* du ciel.

controversy [ˈkɒntrəvɜːsɪ] *n* controverse *f*. ◆**contro'versial** *a* (*book, author*) contesté, discuté; (*doubtful*) discutable.

conundrum [kəˈnʌndrəm] *n* devinette *f*, énigme *f*; (*mystery*) énigme *f*.

conurbation [kɒnɜːˈbeɪʃ(ə)n] *n* agglomération *f*, conurbation *f*.

convalesce [kɒnvəˈles] *vi* être en convalescence. ◆**convalescence** *n* convalescence *f*. ◆**convalescent** *n* convalescent, -ente *mf*; **c. home** maison *f* de convalescence.

convector [kənˈvektər] *n* radiateur *m* à convection.

convene [kənˈviːn] *vt* convoquer; – *vi* se réunir.

convenient [kənˈviːnɪənt] *a* commode, pratique; (*well-situated*) bien situé (**for the shops**/etc par rapport aux magasins/etc); (*moment*) convenable, opportun; **to be c.** (**for**) (*suit*) convenir (à). ◆**—ly** *adv* (*to arrive*) à propos; **c. situated** bien situé. ◆**convenience** *n* commodité *f*; (*comfort*) confort *m*; (*advantage*) avantage *m*; **to** *or* **at one's c.** à sa convenance; **c. food(s)** plats *mpl* *or* aliments *mpl* minute; (**public**) **conveniences** toilettes *fpl*.

convent [ˈkɒnvənt] *n* couvent *m*.

convention [kənˈvenʃ(ə)n] *n* (*agreement*) & *Am Pol* convention *f*; (*custom*) usage *m*, convention *f*; (*meeting*) Pol assemblée *f*. ◆**conventional** *a* conventionnel.

converg/e [kənˈvɜːdʒ] *vi* converger. ◆**—ing** *a* convergent. ◆**convergence** *n* convergence *f*.

conversant [kənˈvɜːsənt] *a* **to be c. with**

(*custom etc*) connaître; (*fact*) savoir; (*cars etc*) s'y connaître en.

conversation [kɒnvəˈseɪʃ(ə)n] *n* conversation *f*. ◆**conversational** *a* (*tone*) de la conversation; (*person*) loquace. ◆**conversationalist** *n* causeur, -euse *mf*.

converse 1 [kənˈvɜːs] *vi* s'entretenir (**with** avec). **2** [ˈkɒnvɜːs] *a* & *n* inverse (*m*). ◆**con'versely** *adv* inversement.

convert [kənˈvɜːt] *vt* (*change*) convertir (**into** en); (*building*) aménager (**into** en); **to c. s.o.** convertir qn (**to** à); – [ˈkɒnvɜːt] *n* converti, -ie *mf*. ◆**con'version** *n* conversion *f*; aménagement *m*. ◆**con'vertible** *a* convertible; – *n* (*car*) (voiture *f*) décapotable *f*.

convex [ˈkɒnveks] *a* convexe.

convey [kənˈveɪ] *vt* (*goods, people*) transporter; (*sound, message, order*) transmettre; (*idea*) communiquer; (*evoke*) évoquer; (*water etc through pipes*) amener. ◆**conveyance** *n* transport *m*; *Aut* véhicule *m*. ◆**conveyor** *a* **c. belt** tapis *m* roulant.

convict [ˈkɒnvɪkt] *n* forçat *m*; – [kənˈvɪkt] *vt* déclarer coupable, condamner. ◆**con'viction** *n* Jur condamnation *f*; (*belief*) conviction *f*; **to carry c.** (*of argument etc*) être convaincant.

convinc/e [kənˈvɪns] *vt* convaincre, persuader. ◆**—ing** *a* convaincant. ◆**—ingly** *adv* de façon convaincante.

convivial [kənˈvɪvɪəl] *a* joyeux, gai; (*person*) bon vivant.

convoke [kənˈvəʊk] *vt* (*meeting etc*) convoquer.

convoluted [kɒnvəˈluːtɪd] *a* (*argument, style*) compliqué, tarabiscoté.

convoy [ˈkɒnvɔɪ] *n* (*ships, cars, people*) convoi *m*.

convulse [kənˈvʌls] *vt* bouleverser, ébranler; (*face*) convulser. ◆**convulsion** *n* convulsion *f*. ◆**convulsive** *a* convulsif.

coo [kuː] *vi* (*of dove*) roucouler.

cook [kʊk] *vt* (faire) cuire; (*accounts*) Fam truquer; **to c. up** Fam inventer; – *vi* (*of food*) cuire; (*of person*) faire la cuisine; **what's cooking?** Fam qu'est-ce qui se passe?; – *n* (*person*) cuisinier, -ière *mf*. ◆**—ing** *n* cuisine *f*; **c. apple** pomme *f* à cuire. ◆**—er** *n* (*stove*) cuisinière *f*; (*apple*) pomme *f* à cuire. ◆**cookbook** *n* livre *m* de cuisine. ◆**cookery** *n* cuisine *f*; **c. book** livre *m* de cuisine.

cookie [ˈkʊkɪ] *n Am* biscuit *m*, gâteau *m* sec.

cool [kuːl] *a* (**-er, -est**) (*weather, place etc*) frais; (*manner, person*) calme; (*reception etc*) froid; (*impertinent*) Fam effronté; **I feel**

c. j'ai (un peu) froid; **a c. drink** une boisson fraîche; **a c. £50** la coquette somme de 50 livres; − *n* (*of evening*) fraîcheur *f*; **to keep (in the) c.** tenir au frais; **to keep/lose one's c.** garder/perdre son sang-froid; − *vt* **to c. (down)** refroidir, rafraîchir; − *vi* **to c. (down** *or* **off)** (*of enthusiasm*) se refroidir; (*of anger, angry person*) se calmer; (*of hot liquid*) refroidir; **to c. off** (*refresh oneself by drinking, bathing etc*) se rafraîchir; **to c. off towards s.o.** se refroidir envers qn. ◆**—ing** *n* (*of air, passion etc*) refroidissement *m*. ◆**—er** *n* (*for food*) glacière *f*. ◆**—ly** *adv* calmement; (*to welcome*) froidement; (*boldly*) effrontément. ◆**—ness** *n* fraîcheur *f*; (*unfriendliness*) froideur *f*. ◆**cool-'headed** *a* calme.

coop [kuːp] **1** *n* (*for chickens*) poulailler *m*. **2** *vt* **to c. up** (*person*) enfermer.

co-op ['kəʊɒp] *n Am* appartement *m* en copropriété.

co-operate [kəʊ'ɒpəreɪt] *vi* coopérer (**in** à, **with** avec). ◆**co-ope'ration** *n* coopération *f*. ◆**co-operative** *a* coopératif; − *n* coopérative *f*.

co-opt [kəʊ'ɒpt] *vt* coopter.

co-ordinate [kəʊ'ɔːdɪneɪt] *vt* coordonner. ◆**co-ordinates** [kəʊ'ɔːdɪnəts] *npl Math* coordonnées *fpl*; (*clothes*) coordonnés *mpl*. ◆**co-ordi'nation** *n* coordination *f*.

cop [kɒp] **1** *n* (*policeman*) *Fam* flic *m*. **2** *vt* (**-pp-**) (*catch*) *Sl* piquer. **3** *vi* (**-pp-**) **to c. out** *Sl* se défiler, éviter ses responsabilités.

cope [kəʊp] *vi* **to c. with** s'occuper de; (*problem*) faire face à; (**to be able) to c.** (savoir) se débrouiller.

co-pilot ['kəʊpaɪlət] *n* copilote *m*.

copious ['kəʊpɪəs] *a* copieux.

copper ['kɒpər] *n* **1** cuivre *m*; *pl* (*coins*) petite monnaie *f*. **2** (*policeman*) *Fam* flic *m*.

coppice ['kɒpɪs] *n*, ◆**copse** [kɒps] *n* taillis *m*.

copulate ['kɒpjʊleɪt] *vi* s'accoupler. ◆**copu'lation** *n* copulation *f*.

copy ['kɒpɪ] *n* copie *f*; (*of book etc*) exemplaire *m*; *Phot* épreuve *f*; − *vti* copier; − *vt* **to c. out** *or* **down** (re)copier. ◆**copyright** *n* copyright *m*.

coral ['kɒrəl] *n* corail *m*; **c. reef** récif *m* de corail.

cord [kɔːd] **1** *n* (*of curtain, pyjamas etc*) cordon *m*; *El* cordon *m* électrique; **vocal cords** cordes *fpl* vocales. **2** *npl Fam* velours *m*, pantalon *m* en velours (côtelé).

cordial ['kɔːdɪəl] **1** *a* (*friendly*) cordial. **2** *n* (fruit) **c.** sirop *m*.

cordon ['kɔːdən] *n* cordon *m*; − *vt* **to c. off** (*place*) boucler, interdire l'accès à.

corduroy ['kɔːdərɔɪ] *n* (*fabric*) velours *m* côtelé; *pl* pantalon *m* en velours (côtelé), velours *m*.

core [kɔːr] *n* (*of fruit*) trognon *m*; (*of problem*) cœur *m*; (*group of people*) & *Geol* El noyau *m*; − *vt* (*apple*) vider. ◆**corer** *n* vide-pomme *m*.

cork [kɔːk] *n* liège *m*; (*for bottle*) bouchon *m*; − *vt* **to c. (up)** (*bottle*) boucher. ◆**corkscrew** *n* tire-bouchon *m*.

corn [kɔːn] *n* **1** (*wheat*) blé *m*; (*maize*) *Am* maïs *m*; (*seed*) grain *m*; **c. on the cob** épi *m* de maïs. **2** (*hard skin*) cor *m*. ◆**corned** *a* **c. beef** corned-beef *m*, singe *m*. ◆**cornflakes** *npl* céréales *fpl*. ◆**cornflour** *n* farine *f* de maïs, maïzena® *f*. ◆**cornflower** *n* bleuet *m*. ◆**cornstarch** *n Am* = **cornflour.**

cornea ['kɔːnɪə] *n Anat* cornée *f*.

corner ['kɔːnər] **1** *n* coin *m*; (*of street, room*) coin *m*, angle *m*; (*bend in road*) virage *m*; *Fb* corner *m*; **in a (tight) c.** dans une situation difficile. **2** *vt* (*animal, enemy etc*) acculer; (*person in corridor etc*) *Fig* coincer, accrocher; (*market*) *Com* accaparer; − *vi Aut* prendre un virage. ◆**cornerstone** *n* pierre *f* angulaire.

cornet ['kɔːnɪt] *n* (*of ice cream etc*) & *Mus* cornet *m*.

Cornwall ['kɔːnwəl] *n* Cornouailles *fpl*. ◆**Cornish** *a* de Cornouailles.

corny ['kɔːnɪ] *a* (**-ier, -iest**) (*joke etc*) rebattu.

corollary [kə'rɒlərɪ, *Am* 'kɒrələrɪ] *n* corollaire *m*.

coronary ['kɒrənərɪ] *n Med* infarctus *m*.

coronation [kɒrə'neɪʃ(ə)n] *n* couronnement *m*, sacre *m*.

coroner ['kɒrənər] *n Jur* coroner *m*.

corporal ['kɔːpərəl] **1** *n Mil* caporal(-chef) *m*. **2** *a* **c. punishment** châtiment *m* corporel.

corporation [kɔːpə'reɪʃ(ə)n] *n* (*business*) société *f* commerciale; (*of town*) conseil *m* municipal. ◆**'corporate** *a* collectif; **c. body** corps *m* constitué.

corps [kɔːr, *pl* kɔːz] *n Mil Pol* corps *m*.

corpse [kɔːps] *n* cadavre *m*.

corpulent ['kɔːpjʊlənt] *a* corpulent. ◆**corpulence** *n* corpulence *f*.

corpus ['kɔːpəs] *n Ling* corpus *m*.

corpuscle ['kɔːpʌs(ə)l] *n Med* globule *m*.

corral [kə'ræl] *n Am* corral *m*.

correct [kə'rekt] *a* (*right, accurate*) exact, correct; (*proper*) correct; **he's c.** il a raison; − *vt* corriger. ◆**—ly** *adv* correctement.

◆—**ness** n (*accuracy, propriety*) correction f. ◆**correction** n correction f. ◆**corrective** a (*act, measure*) rectificatif.

correlate ['kɒrəleɪt] vi correspondre (**with** à); – vt faire correspondre. ◆**corre'lation** n corrélation f.

correspond [kɒrɪ'spɒnd] vi 1 (*agree, be similar*) correspondre (**to** à, **with** avec). 2 (*by letter*) correspondre (**with** avec). ◆—**ing** a (*matching*) correspondant; (*similar*) semblable. ◆**correspondence** n correspondance f; **c. course** cours m par correspondance. ◆**correspondent** n correspondant, -ante mf; *Journ* envoyé, -ée mf.

corridor ['kɒrɪdɔːr] n couloir m, corridor m.

corroborate [kə'rɒbəreɪt] vt corroborer.

corrode [kə'rəʊd] vt ronger, corroder; – vi se corroder. ◆**corrosion** n corrosion f. ◆**corrosive** a corrosif.

corrugated ['kɒrəgeɪtɪd] a (*cardboard*) ondulé; **c. iron** tôle f ondulée.

corrupt [kə'rʌpt] vt corrompre; – a corrompu. ◆**corruption** n corruption f.

corset ['kɔːsɪt] n (*boned*) corset m; (*elasticated*) gaine f.

Corsica ['kɔːsɪkə] n Corse f.

cos [kɒs] n c. (**lettuce**) (laitue f) romaine f.

cosh [kɒʃ] n matraque f; – vt matraquer.

cosiness ['kəʊzɪnəs] n intimité f, confort m.

cosmetic [kɒz'metɪk] n produit m de beauté; – a esthétique; *Fig* superficiel.

cosmopolitan [kɒzmə'pɒlɪtən] a & n cosmopolite (*mf*).

cosmos ['kɒzmɒs] n cosmos m. ◆**cosmic** a cosmique. ◆**cosmonaut** n cosmonaute mf.

Cossack ['kɒsæk] n cosaque m.

cosset ['kɒsɪt] vt choyer.

cost [kɒst] vti (*pt & pp* cost) coûter; **how much does it c.?** ça coûte *or* ça vaut combien?; **to c. the earth** *Fam* coûter les yeux de la tête; – n coût m, prix m; **at great c.** à grands frais; **to my c.** à mes dépens; **at any c., at all costs** à tout prix; **at c. price** au prix coûtant. ◆**costly** a (**-ier, -iest**) (*expensive*) coûteux; (*valuable*) précieux.

co-star ['kəʊstɑːr] n *Cin Th* partenaire mf.

costume ['kɒstjuːm] n costume m; (*woman's suit*) tailleur m; (**swimming**) **c.** maillot m (de bain); **c. jewellery** bijoux mpl de fantaisie.

cosy ['kəʊzɪ] 1 a (**-ier, -iest**) douillet, intime; **make yourself (nice and) c.** mets-toi à l'aise; **we're c.** on est bien ici. 2 n (**tea**) **c.** couvre-théière m.

cot [kɒt] n lit m d'enfant; (*camp bed*) *Am* lit m de camp.

cottage ['kɒtɪdʒ] n petite maison f de campagne; (**thatched**) **c.** chaumière f. **c. cheese** fromage m blanc (maigre); **c. industry** travail m à domicile (*activité artisanale*).

cotton ['kɒtən] 1 n coton m; (*yarn*) fil m (de coton); **absorbent c.** *Am, c.* **wool** coton m hydrophile, ouate f; **c. candy** *Am* barbe f à papa. 2 vi **to c. on (to)** *Sl* piger.

couch [kaʊtʃ] 1 n canapé m. 2 vt (*express*) formuler.

couchette [kuːʃet] n *Rail* couchette f.

cough [kɒf] 1 n toux f; **c. mixture** sirop m contre la toux; – vi tousser; – vt **to c. up** (*blood*) cracher. 2 vt **to c. up** (*money*) *Sl* cracher; – vi **to c. up** *Sl* payer, casquer.

could [kʊd, *unstressed* kəd] *see* can[1].

couldn't ['kʊd(ə)nt] = could not.

council ['kaʊns(ə)l] n conseil m; **c. flat/house** appartement m/maison f loué(e) à la municipalité, HLM m or f. ◆**councillor** n conseiller, -ère mf; (**town**) **c.** conseiller m municipal.

counsel ['kaʊnsəl] n (*advice*) conseil m; *Jur* avocat, -ate mf; – vt (**-ll-**, *Am* **-l-**) conseiller (**s.o. to do** à qn de faire). ◆**counsellor** n conseiller, -ère mf.

count[1] [kaʊnt] vt (*find number of, include*) compter; (*deem*) considérer; **not counting Paul** sans compter Paul; **to c. in** (*include*) inclure; **to c. out** exclure; (*money*) compter; – vi (*calculate, be important*) compter; **to c. against s.o.** être un désavantage pour qn, jouer contre qn; **to c. on s.o.** (*rely on*) compter sur qn; **to c. on doing** compter faire; – n compte m; *Jur* chef m (d'accusation); **he's lost c. of the books he has** il ne sait plus combien il a de livres. ◆**countdown** n compte m à rebours.

count[2] [kaʊnt] n (*title*) comte m.

countenance ['kaʊntɪnəns] 1 n (*face*) mine f, expression f. 2 vt (*allow*) tolérer; (*approve*) approuver.

counter ['kaʊntər] 1 n (*in shop, bar etc*) comptoir m; (*in bank etc*) guichet m; **under the c.** *Fig* clandestinement, au marché noir; **over the c.** (*to obtain medicine*) sans ordonnance. 2 n (*in games*) jeton m. 3 n *Tech* compteur m. 4 adv **c. to** à l'encontre de. 5 vt (*plan*) contrarier; (*insult*) riposter à; (*blow*) parer; – vi riposter (**with** par).

counter- ['kaʊntər] pref contre-.

counterattack ['kaʊntərətæk] n contre-attaque f; – vti contre-attaquer.

counterbalance ['kaʊntəbæləns] n contre-poids m; – vt contrebalancer.

counterclockwise [kaʊntə'klɒkwaɪz] *a* & *adv Am* dans le sens inverse des aiguilles d'une montre.

counterfeit ['kaʊntəfɪt] *a* faux; – *n* contrefaçon *f*, faux *m*; – *vt* contrefaire.

counterfoil ['kaʊntəfɔɪl] *n* souche *f*.

counterpart ['kaʊntəpɑːt] *n* (*thing*) équivalent *m*; (*person*) homologue *m*.

counterpoint ['kaʊntəpɔɪnt] *n Mus* contrepoint *m*.

counterproductive [kaʊntəprə'dʌktɪv] *a* (*action*) inefficace, qui produit l'effet contraire.

countersign ['kaʊntəsaɪn] *vt* contresigner.

countess ['kaʊntɪs] *n* comtesse *f*.

countless ['kaʊntləs] *a* innombrable.

countrified ['kʌntrɪfaɪd] *a* rustique.

country ['kʌntrɪ] *n* pays *m*; (*region*) région *f*, pays *m*; (*homeland*) patrie *f*; (*opposed to town*) campagne *f*; – *a* (*house etc*) de campagne; **c. dancing** la danse folklorique. ◆**countryman** *n* (*pl* -**men**) (*fellow*) **c.** compatriote *m*. ◆**countryside** *n* campagne *f*.

county ['kaʊntɪ] *n* comté *m*; **c. seat** *Am*, **c. town** chef-lieu *m*.

coup [kuː, *pl* kuːz] *n Pol* coup *m* d'État.

couple ['kʌp(ə)l] **1** *n* (*of people, animals*) couple *m*; **a c.** of deux ou trois; (*a few*) quelques. **2** *vt* (*connect*) accoupler. **3** *vi* (*mate*) s'accoupler.

coupon ['kuːpɒn] *n* (*voucher*) bon *m*; (*ticket*) coupon *m*.

courage ['kʌrɪdʒ] *n* courage *m*. ◆**courageous** [kə'reɪdʒəs] *a* courageux.

courgette [kʊə'ʒet] *n* courgette *f*.

courier ['kʊrɪər] *n* (*for tourists*) guide *m*; (*messenger*) messager *m*; **c. service** service *m* de messagerie.

course [kɔːs] **1** *n* (*duration, movement*) cours *m*; (*of ship*) route *f*; (*of river*) cours *m*; (*way*) *Fig* route *f*, chemin *m*; (*means*) moyen *m*; **c.** (**of action**) ligne *f* de conduite; (*option*) parti *m*; **your best c. is to . . .** le mieux c'est de . . . ; **as a matter of c.** normalement; **in (the) c. of time** avec le temps, à la longue; **in due c.** en temps utile. **2** *n Sch Univ* cours *m*; **c. of lectures** série *f* de conférences; (**of treatment**) *Med* traitement *m*. **3** *n Culin* plat *m*; **first c.** entrée *f*. **4** *n* (*racecourse*) champ *m* de courses; (*golf*) **c.** terrain *m* (de golf). **5** *adv* **of c.!** bien sûr!, mais oui!; **of c. not!** bien sûr que non!

court [kɔːt] **1** *n* (*of monarch*) cour *f*; *Jur* cour *f*, tribunal *m*; *Tennis* court *m*; **c. of enquiry** commission *f* d'enquête; **high c.** cour *f* suprême; **to take to c.** poursuivre en justice; **c. shoe** escarpin *m*. **2** *vt* (*woman*) faire la cour à; (*danger, support*) rechercher. ◆—**ing** *a* (*couple*) d'amoureux; **they are c.** ils sortent ensemble. ◆**courthouse** *n* palais *m* de justice. ◆**courtier** *n Hist* courtisan *m*. ◆**courtroom** *n* salle *f* du tribunal. ◆**courtship** *n* (*act, period of time*) cour *f*. ◆**courtyard** *n* cour *f*.

courteous ['kɜːtɪəs] *a* poli, courtois. ◆**courtesy** *n* politesse *f*, courtoisie *f*.

court-martial [kɔːt'mɑːʃəl] *n* conseil *m* de guerre; – *vt* (-**ll**-) faire passer en conseil de guerre.

cousin ['kʌz(ə)n] *n* cousin, -ine *mf*.

cove [kəʊv] *n* (*bay*) *Geog* anse *f*.

covenant ['kʌvənənt] *n Jur* convention *f*; *Rel* alliance *f*.

Coventry ['kɒvəntrɪ] *n* to send s.o. to C. *Fig* mettre qn en quarantaine.

cover ['kʌvər] *n* (*lid*) couvercle *m*; (*of book*) & *Fin* couverture *f*; (*for furniture, typewriter*) housse *f*; (*bedspread*) dessus-de-lit *m*; **the covers** (*blankets*) les couvertures *fpl*; **to take c.** se mettre à l'abri; **c. charge** (*in restaurant*) couvert *m*; **c. note** certificat *m* provisoire d'assurance; **under separate c.** (*letter*) sous pli séparé; – *vt* couvrir; (*protect*) protéger, couvrir; (*distance*) parcourir, couvrir; (*include*) englober, recouvrir; (*treat*) traiter; (*event*) *Journ TV Rad* couvrir, faire le reportage de; (*aim gun at*) tenir en joue; (*insure*) assurer; **to c. over** recouvrir; **to c. up** recouvrir; (*truth, tracks*) dissimuler; (*scandal*) étouffer, camoufler; – *vi* **to c. (oneself) up** se couvrir; **to c. up for s.o.** couvrir qn. ◆**c.-up** tentative *f* pour étouffer *or* camoufler une affaire. ◆**covering** *n* (*wrapping*) enveloppe *f*; (*layer*) couche *f*; **c. letter** lettre *f* jointe (*à un document*).

coveralls ['kʌvərɔːlz] *npl Am* bleus *mpl* de travail.

covert ['kəʊvət, 'kʌvət] *a* secret.

covet ['kʌvɪt] *vt* convoiter. ◆**covetous** *a* avide.

cow [kaʊ] **1** *n* vache *f*; (*of elephant etc*) femelle *f*; (*nasty woman*) *Fam* chameau *m*. **2** *vt* (*person*) intimider. ◆**cowboy** *n* cow-boy *m*. ◆**cowhand** *n* vacher, -ère *mf*. ◆**cowshed** *n* étable *f*.

coward ['kaʊəd] *n* lâche *mf*. ◆—**ly** *a* lâche. ◆**cowardice** *n* lâcheté *f*.

cower ['kaʊər] *vi* (*crouch*) se tapir; (*with fear*) *Fig* reculer (par peur).

cowslip ['kaʊslɪp] *n Bot* coucou *m*.

cox [kɒks] *vt Nau* barrer; – *n* barreur, -euse *mf.*

coy [kɔɪ] *a* (**-er, -est**) qui fait son *or* sa timide. ◆**coyness** *n* timidité *f* feinte.

coyote [kaɪ'əʊtɪ] *n* (*wolf*) *Am* coyote *m.*

cozy ['kəʊzɪ] *Am* = **cosy.**

crab [kræb] **1** *n* crabe *m.* **2** *n* c. **apple** pomme *f* sauvage. **3** *vi* (**-bb-**) (*complain*) *Fam* rouspéter. ◆**crabbed** *a* (*person*) grincheux.

crack¹ [kræk] *n* (*fissure*) fente *f*; (*in glass etc*) fêlure *f*; (*in skin*) crevasse *f*; (*snapping noise*) craquement *m*; (*of whip*) claquement *m*; (*blow*) coup *m*; (*joke*) *Fam* plaisanterie *f* (at aux dépens de); **to have a c. at doing** *Fam* essayer de faire; **at the c. of dawn** au point du jour; – *vt* (*glass, ice*) fêler; (*nut*) casser; (*ground, skin*) crevasser; (*whip*) faire claquer; (*joke*) lancer; (*problem*) résoudre; (*code*) déchiffrer; (*safe*) percer; **it's not as hard as it's cracked up to be** ce n'est pas aussi dur qu'on le dit; – *vi* se fêler; se crevasser; (*of branch, wood*) craquer; **to get cracking** (*get to work*) *Fam* s'y mettre; (*hurry*) *Fam* se grouiller; **to c. down on** sévir contre; **to c. up** (*mentally*) *Fam* craquer. ◆**c.-up** *n Fam* dépression *f* nerveuse; (*crash*) *Am Fam* accident *m.* ◆**cracked** *a* (*crazy*) *Fam* fou. ◆**cracker** *n* **1** (*cake*) biscuit *m* (salé). **2** (*firework*) pétard *m*; **Christmas c.** diablotin *m.* **3 she's a c.** *Fam* elle est sensationnelle. ◆**crackers** *a* (*mad*) *Sl* cinglé. ◆**crackpot** *a Fam* fou; – *n* fou *m*, folle *f.*

crack² [kræk] *a* (*first-rate*) de premier ordre; **c. shot** tireur *m* d'élite.

crackle ['kræk(ə)l] *vi* crépiter; (*of sth frying*) *Culin* grésiller; – *n* crépitement *m*; grésillement *m.*

cradle ['kreɪd(ə)l] *n* berceau *m*; – *vt* bercer.

craft [krɑːft] **1** *n* (*skill*) art *m*; (*job*) métier *m* (artisanal); – *vt* façonner. **2** *n* (*cunning*) ruse *f.* **3** *n inv* (*boat*) bateau *m.* ◆**craftsman** *n* (*pl* -men) artisan *m.* ◆**craftsmanship** *n* (*skill*) art *m*; **a piece of c.** un beau travail, une belle pièce. ◆**crafty** *a* (-ier, -iest) astucieux, *Pej* rusé.

crag [kræg] *n* rocher *m* à pic. ◆**craggy** *a* (*rock*) à pic; (*face*) rude.

cram [kræm] *vt* (**-mm-**) **to c. into** (*force*) fourrer dans; **to c. with** (*fill*) bourrer de; – *vi* **to c. into** (*of people*) s'entasser dans; **to c.** (**for an exam**) bachoter.

cramp [kræmp] *n Med* crampe *f* (**in** à). ◆**cramped** *a* (*in a room or one's clothes*) à l'étroit; **in c. conditions** à l'étroit.

cranberry ['krænbərɪ] *n Bot* canneberge *f.*

crane [kreɪn] **1** *n* (*bird*) & *Tech* grue *f.* **2** *vt* **to c. one's neck** tendre le cou.

crank [kræŋk] **1** *n* (*person*) *Fam* excentrique *mf*; (*fanatic*) fanatique *mf.* **2** *n* (*handle*) *Tech* manivelle *f*; – *vt* **to c.** (**up**) (*vehicle*) faire démarrer à la manivelle. ◆**cranky** *a* (-ier, -iest) excentrique; (*bad-tempered*) *Am* grincheux.

crannies ['krænɪz] *npl* **nooks and c.** coins et recoins *mpl.*

craps [kræps] *n* **to shoot c.** *Am* jouer aux dés.

crash [kræʃ] *n* accident *m*; (*of firm*) faillite *f*; (*noise*) fracas *m*; (*of thunder*) coup *m*; **c. course/diet** cours *m*/régime *m* intensif; **c. helmet** casque *m* (anti-choc); **c. landing** atterrissage *m* en catastrophe; – *int* (*of fallen object*) patatras!; – *vt* (*car*) avoir un accident avec; **to c. one's car into** faire rentrer sa voiture dans; – *vi Aut Av* s'écraser; **to c. into** rentrer dans; **the cars crashed** (**into each other**) les voitures se sont percutées *or* carambolées; **to c.** (**down**) tomber; (*break*) se casser; (*of roof*) s'effondrer. ◆**c.-land** *vi* atterrir en catastrophe.

crass [kræs] *a* grossier; (*stupidity*) crasse.

crate [kreɪt] *n* caisse *f*, cageot *m.*

crater ['kreɪtər] *n* cratère *m*; (**bomb**) c. entonnoir *m.*

cravat [krə'væt] *n* foulard *m* (*autour du cou*).

crav/e [kreɪv] *vt* **to c.** (**for**) éprouver un grand besoin de; (*mercy*) implorer. ◆**—ing** *n* désir *m*, grand besoin *m* (**for** de).

craven ['kreɪvən] *a Pej* lâche.

crawl [krɔːl] *vi* ramper; (*of child*) se traîner (à quatre pattes); *Aut* avancer au pas; **to be crawling with** grouiller de; – *n Swimming* crawl *m*; **to move at a c.** *Aut* avancer au pas.

crayfish ['kreɪfɪʃ] *n inv* écrevisse *f.*

crayon ['kreɪən] *n* crayon *m*, pastel *m.*

craze [kreɪz] *n* manie *f* (**for** de), engouement *m* (**for** pour). ◆**crazed** *a* affolé.

crazy ['kreɪzɪ] *a* (-ier, -iest) fou; **c. about sth** fana de qch; **c. about s.o.** fou de qn; **c. paving** dallage *m* irrégulier. ◆**craziness** *n* folie *f.*

creak [kriːk] *vi* (*of hinge*) grincer; (*of timber*) craquer. ◆**creaky** *a* grinçant; qui craque.

cream [kriːm] *n* crème *f*; (*élite*) *Fig* crème *f*, gratin *m*; – *a* (*cake*) à la crème; **c.(-coloured)** crème *inv*; **c. cheese** fromage *m* blanc; – *vt* (*milk*) écrémer; **to c. off** *Fig* écrémer. ◆**creamy** *a* (-ier, -iest) crémeux.

crease [kriːs] *vt* froisser, plisser; – *vi* se froisser; – *n* pli *m*; (*accidental*) (faux) pli *m.* ◆**c.-resistant** *a* infroissable.

create [kriː'eɪt] *vt* créer; (*impression, noise*) faire. ◆**creation** *n* création *f.* ◆**creative** *a* créateur, créatif. ◆**creativeness** *n* créativité *f.* ◆**crea'tivity** *n* créativité *f.* ◆**creator** *n* créateur, -trice *mf.*

creature ['kriːtʃər] *n* animal *m,* bête *f;* (*person*) créature *f;* **one's c. comforts** ses aises *fpl.*

crèche [kreʃ] *n* (*nursery*) crèche *f;* (*manger*) *Rel Am* crèche *f.*

credence ['kriːdəns] *n* **to give** *or* **lend c. to** ajouter foi à.

credentials [krɪ'denʃəlz] *npl* références *fpl;* (*identity*) pièces *fpl* d'identité; (*of diplomat*) lettres *fpl* de créance.

credible ['kredɪb(ə)l] *a* croyable; (*politician, information*) crédible. ◆**credi'bility** *n* crédibilité *f.*

credit ['kredɪt] *n* (*influence, belief*) & *Fin* crédit *m;* (*merit*) mérite *m; Univ* unité *f* de valeur; *pl Cin* générique *m;* **to give c. to** (*person*) *Fin* faire crédit à; *Fig* reconnaître le mérite de; (*statement*) ajouter foi à; **to be a c. to** faire honneur à; **on c.** à crédit; **in c.** (*account*) créditeur; **to one's c.** *Fig* à son actif; − *a* (*balance*) créditeur; **c. card** carte *f* de crédit; **c. facilities** facilités *fpl* de paiement; − *vt* (*believe*) croire; *Fin* créditer (**s.o. with sth** qn de qch); **to c. s.o. with** (*qualities*) attribuer à qn. ◆**creditable** *a* honorable. ◆**creditor** *n* créancier, -ière *mf.* ◆**creditworthy** *a* solvable.

credulous ['kredjʊləs] *a* crédule.

creed [kriːd] *n* credo *m.*

creek [kriːk] *n* (*bay*) crique *f;* (*stream*) *Am* ruisseau *m;* **up the c.** (*in trouble*) *Sl* dans le pétrin.

creep [kriːp] **1** *vi* (*pt & pp* **crept**) ramper; (*silently*) se glisser (furtivement); (*slowly*) avancer lentement; **it makes my flesh c.** ça me donne la chair de poule. **2** *n* (*person*) *Sl* salaud *m;* **it gives me the creeps** *Fam* ça me fait froid dans le dos. ◆**creepy** *a* (**-ier, -iest**) *Fam* terrifiant; (*nasty*) *Fam* vilain. ◆**creepy-'crawly** *n Fam, Am* ◆**creepy-'crawler** *n Fam* bestiole *f.*

cremate [krɪ'meɪt] *vt* incinérer. ◆**cremation** *n* crémation *f.* ◆**crema'torium** *n* crématorium *m.* ◆**'crematory** *n Am* crématorium *m.*

Creole ['kriːəʊl] *n* créole *mf; Ling* créole *m.*

crêpe [kreɪp] *n* (*fabric*) crêpe *m;* **c.** (**rubber**) crêpe *m;* **c. paper** papier *m* crêpon.

crept [krept] *see* **creep 1.**

crescendo [krɪ'ʃendəʊ] *n* (*pl* **-os**) crescendo *m inv.*

crescent ['kres(ə)nt] *n* croissant *m;* (*street*) *Fig* rue *f* (en demi-lune).

cress [kres] *n* cresson *m.*

crest [krest] *n* (*of bird, wave, mountain*) crête *f;* (*of hill*) sommet *m;* (*on seal, letters etc*) armoiries *fpl.*

Crete [kriːt] *n* Crète *f.*

cretin ['kretɪn, *Am* 'kriːt(ə)n] *n* crétin, -ine *mf.* ◆**cretinous** *a* crétin.

crevasse [krɪ'væs] *n* (*in ice*) *Geol* crevasse *f.*

crevice ['krevɪs] *n* (*crack*) crevasse *f,* fente *f.*

crew [kruː] *n Nau Av* équipage *m;* (*gang*) équipe *f;* **c. cut** (coupe *f* en) brosse *f.* ◆**c.-neck(ed)** *a* à col ras.

crib [krɪb] **1** *n* (*cradle*) berceau *m;* (*cot*) *Am* lit *m* d'enfant; *Rel* crèche *f.* **2** *n* (*copy*) plagiat *m;* *Sch* traduction *f;* (*list of answers*) *Sch* pompe *f* anti-sèche; − *vti* (**-bb-**) copier.

crick [krɪk] *n* **c. in the neck** torticolis *m;* **c. in the back** tour *m* de reins.

cricket ['krɪkɪt] *n* **1** (*game*) cricket *m.* **2** (*insect*) grillon *m.* ◆**cricketer** *n* joueur, -euse *mf* de cricket.

crikey! ['kraɪkɪ] *int Sl* zut (alors)!

crime [kraɪm] *n* crime *m;* (*not serious*) délit *m;* (*criminal practice*) criminalité *f.* ◆**criminal** *a & n* criminel, -elle (*mf*).

crimson ['krɪmz(ə)n] *a & n* cramoisi (*m*).

cring/e [krɪndʒ] *vi* reculer (**from** devant); *Fig* s'humilier (**to, before** devant). ◆**−ing** *a Fig* servile.

crinkle ['krɪŋk(ə)l] *vt* froisser; − *vi* se froisser; − *n* fronce *f.* ◆**crinkly** *a* froissé; (*hair*) frisé.

cripp/le ['krɪpəl] *n* (*lame*) estropié, -ée *mf;* (*disabled*) infirme *mf;* − *vt* estropier; (*disable*) rendre infirme; (*nation etc*) *Fig* paralyser. ◆**−ed** *a* estropié; infirme; (*ship*) désemparé; **c. with** (*rheumatism, pains*) perclus de. ◆**−ing** *a* (*tax*) écrasant.

crisis, *pl* **-ses** ['kraɪsɪs, -siːz] *n* crise *f.*

crisp [krɪsp] **1** *a* (**-er, -est**) (*biscuit*) croustillant; (*apple etc*) croquant; (*snow*) craquant; (*air, style*) vif. **2** *npl* (**potato**) **crisps** (pommes *fpl*) chips *mpl.* ◆**crispbread** *n* pain *m* suédois.

criss-cross ['krɪskrɒs] *a* (*lines*) entre-croisés; (*muddled*) enchevêtrés; − *vi* s'entrecroiser; − *vt* sillonner (en tous sens).

criterion, *pl* **-ia** [kraɪ'tɪərɪən, -ɪə] *n* critère *m.*

critic ['krɪtɪk] *n* critique *m.* ◆**critical** *a* critique. ◆**critically** *adv* (*to examine etc*) en critique; (*harshly*) sévèrement; (*ill*) gravement. ◆**criticism** *n* critique *f.* ◆**criticize** *vti* critiquer. ◆**cri'tique** *n* (*essay etc*) critique *f.*

croak [krəʊk] *vi* (*of frog*) croasser; − *n* croassement *m*.

crochet ['krəʊʃeɪ] *vt* faire au crochet; − *vi* faire du crochet; − *n* (*travail m au*) crochet *m*; **c. hook** crochet *m*.

crock [krɒk] *n* **a c., an** (*old*) **c.** *Fam* (*person*) un croulant; (*car*) un tacot.

crockery ['krɒkərɪ] *n* (*cups etc*) vaisselle *f*.

crocodile ['krɒkədaɪl] *n* crocodile *m*.

crocus ['krəʊkəs] *n* crocus *m*.

crony ['krəʊnɪ] *n Pej Fam* copain *m*, copine *f*.

crook [krʊk] *n* **1** (*thief*) escroc *m*. **2** (*shepherd's stick*) houlette *f*.

crooked ['krʊkɪd] *a* courbé; (*path*) tortueux; (*hat, picture*) de travers; (*deal, person*) malhonnête; − *adv* de travers. ◆**—ly** *adv* de travers.

croon [kruːn] *vti* chanter (à voix basse).

crop [krɒp] *n* **1** (*harvest*) récolte *f*; (*produce*) culture *f*; (*of questions etc*) *Fig* série *f*; (*of people*) groupe *m*. **2** *vt* (**-pp-**) (*hair*) couper (ras); − *n* **c. of hair** chevelure *f*. **3** *vi* (**-pp-**) **to c. up** se présenter, survenir. ◆**cropper** *n* **to come a c.** *Sl* (*fall*) ramasser une pelle; (*fail*) échouer.

croquet ['krəʊkeɪ] *n* (*game*) croquet *m*.

croquette [krəʊ'ket] *n Culin* croquette *f*.

cross¹ [krɒs] **1** *n* croix *f*; **a c. between** (*animal*) un croisement entre *or* de. **2** *vt* traverser; (*threshold, barrier*) franchir; (*legs, animals*) croiser; (*thwart*) contrecarrer; (*cheque*) barrer; **to c. off** *or* **out** rayer; **it never crossed my mind that . . .** il ne m'est pas venu à l'esprit que . . . ; **crossed lines** *Tel* lignes *fpl* embrouillées; − *vi* (*of paths*) se croiser; **to c.** (*over*) traverser. ◆**—ing** *n Nau* traversée *f*; (*pedestrian*) **c.** passage *m* clouté. ◆**cross-breed** *n* métis, -isse *mf*, hybride *m*. ◆**c.-'country** *a* à travers champs; **c.-country race** cross(-country) *m*. ◆**c.-exami'nation** *n* contre-interrogatoire *m*. ◆**c.-e'xamine** *vt* interroger. ◆**c.-eyed** *a* qui louche. ◆**c.-'legged** *a & adv* les jambes croisées. ◆**c.-'purposes** *npl* **to be at c.-purposes** se comprendre mal. ◆**c.-'reference** *n* renvoi *m*. ◆**c.-section** *n* coupe *f* transversale; *Fig* échantillon *m*.

cross² [krɒs] *a* (*angry*) fâché (**with** contre). ◆**—ly** *adv* d'un air fâché.

crossbow ['krɒsbəʊ] *n* arbalète *f*.

crosscheck [krɒs'tʃek] *n* contre-épreuve *f*; − *vt* vérifier.

crossfire ['krɒsfaɪər] *n* feux *mpl* croisés.

crossroads ['krɒsrəʊdz] *n* carrefour *m*.

crosswalk ['krɒswɔːk] *n Am* passage *m* clouté.

crossword ['krɒswɜːd] *n* **c.** (**puzzle**) mots *mpl* croisés.

crotch [krɒtʃ] *n* (*of garment*) entre-jambes *m inv*.

crotchet ['krɒtʃɪt] *n Mus* noire *f*.

crotchety ['krɒtʃɪtɪ] *a* grincheux.

crouch [kraʊtʃ] *vi* **to c.** (**down**) s'accroupir, se tapir. ◆**—ing** *a* accroupi, tapi.

croupier ['kruːpɪər] *n* (*in casino*) croupier *m*.

crow [krəʊ] **1** *n* corbeau *m*, corneille *f*; **as the c. flies** à vol d'oiseau; **c.'s nest** *Nau* nid *m* de pie. **2** *vi* (*of cock*) chanter; (*boast*) *Fig* se vanter (**about** de). ◆**crowbar** *n* levier *m*.

crowd [kraʊd] *n* foule *f*; (*particular group*) bande *f*; (*of things*) *Fam* masse *f*; **quite a c.** beaucoup de monde; − *vi* **to c. into** (*of people*) s'entasser dans; **to c. round s.o.** se presser autour de qn; **to c. together** se serrer; − *vt* (*fill*) remplir; **to c. into** (*press*) entasser dans; **don't c. me!** *Fam* ne me bouscule pas! ◆**—ed** *a* plein (**with** de); (*train etc*) bondé, plein; (*city*) encombré; **it's very c.!** il y a beaucoup de monde!

crown [kraʊn] *n* (*of king, tooth*) couronne *f*; (*of head, hill*) sommet *m*; **c. court** cour *f* d'assises; **C. jewels** joyaux *mpl* de la Couronne; − *vt* couronner. ◆**—ing** *a* (*glory etc*) suprême; · **c. achievement** couronnement *m*.

crucial ['kruːʃəl] *a* crucial.

crucify ['kruːsɪfaɪ] *vt* crucifier. ◆**crucifix** ['kruːsɪfɪks] *n* crucifix *m*. ◆**cruci'fixion** *n* crucifixion *f*.

crude [kruːd] *a* (**-er, -est**) (*oil, fact*) brut; (*manners, person*) grossier; (*language, light*) cru; (*painting, work*) rudimentaire. ◆**—ly** *adv* (*to say, order etc*) crûment. ◆**—ness** *n* grossièreté *f*; crudité *f*; état *m* rudimentaire.

cruel [krʊəl] *a* (**crueller, cruellest**) cruel. ◆**cruelty** *n* cruauté *f*; **an act of c.** une cruauté.

cruet ['kruːɪt] *n* **c.** (**stand**) salière *f*, poivrière *f* et huilier *m*.

cruis/e [kruːz] *vi Nau* croiser; *Aut* rouler; *Av* voler; (*of taxi*) marauder; (*of tourists*) faire une croisière; − *n* croisière *f*. ◆**—ing** *a* **c. speed** *Nau Av & Fig* vitesse *f* de croisière. ◆**—er** *n Nau* croiseur *m*.

crumb [krʌm] *n* miette *f*; (*of comfort*) *Fig* brin *m*; **crumbs!** *Hum Fam* zut!

crumble ['krʌmb(ə)l] *vt* (*bread*) émietter; − *vi* (*collapse*) s'effondrer; **to c.** (**away**) (*in small pieces*) & *Fig* s'effriter. ◆**crumbly** *a* friable.

crummy ['krʌmɪ] *a* (**-ier, -iest**) *Fam* moche, minable.

crumpet ['krʌmpɪt] n Culin petite crêpe f grillée (servie beurrée).

crumple ['krʌmp(ə)l] vt froisser; – vi se froisser.

crunch [krʌntʃ] 1 vt (food) croquer; – vi (of snow) craquer. 2 n the c. Fam le moment critique. ◆**crunchy** a (-ier, -iest) (apple etc) croquant.

crusade [kruː'seɪd] n Hist & Fig croisade f; – vi faire une croisade. ◆**crusader** n Hist croisé m; Fig militant, -ante mf.

crush [krʌʃ] 1 n (crowd) cohue f; (rush) bousculade f; to have a c. on s.o. Fam avoir le béguin pour qn. 2 vt écraser; (hope) détruire; (clothes) froisser; (cram) entasser (into dans). ◆**–ing** a (defeat) écrasant.

crust [krʌst] n croûte f. ◆**crusty** a (-ier, -iest) (bread) croustillant.

crutch [krʌtʃ] n 1 Med béquille f. 2 (crotch) entre-jambes m inv.

crux [krʌks] n the c. of (problem, matter) le nœud de.

cry [kraɪ] n (shout) cri m; to have a c. Fam pleurer; – vi (weep) pleurer; to c. (out) pousser un cri, crier; (exclaim) s'écrier; to c. (out) for demander (à grands cris); to be crying out for avoir grand besoin de; to c. off (withdraw) abandonner; to c. off (sth) se désintéresser (de qch); to c. over pleurer (sur); – vt (shout) crier. ◆**–ing** a (need etc) très grand; a c. shame une véritable honte; – n cris mpl; (weeping) pleurs mpl.

crypt [krɪpt] n crypte f.

cryptic ['krɪptɪk] a secret, énigmatique.

crystal ['krɪst(ə)l] n cristal m. ◆**c.-'clear** a (water, sound) cristallin; Fig clair comme le jour or l'eau de roche. ◆**crystallize** vt cristalliser; – vi (se) cristalliser.

cub [kʌb] n 1 (of animal) petit m. 2 (scout) louveteau m.

Cuba ['kjuːbə] n Cuba m. ◆**Cuban** a & n cubain, -aine (mf).

cubbyhole ['kʌbɪhəʊl] n cagibi m.

cube [kjuːb] n cube m; (of meat etc) dé m. ◆**cubic** a (shape) cubique; (metre etc) cube; c. capacity volume m; Aut cylindrée f.

cubicle ['kjuːbɪk(ə)l] n (for changing) cabine f; (in hospital) box m.

cuckoo ['kʊkuː] 1 n (bird) coucou m; c. clock coucou m. 2 a (stupid) Sl cinglé.

cucumber ['kjuːkʌmbər] n concombre m.

cuddle ['kʌd(ə)l] vt (hug) serrer (dans ses bras); (caress) câliner; – vi (of lovers) se serrer; to (kiss and) c. s'embrasser; to c. up to (huddle) se serrer or se blottir contre; – n

caresse f. ◆**cuddly** a (-ier, -iest) a câlin, caressant; (toy) doux, en peluche.

cudgel ['kʌdʒəl] n trique f, gourdin m.

cue [kjuː] n 1 Th réplique f; (signal) signal m. 2 (billiard) c. queue f (de billard).

cuff [kʌf] 1 n (of shirt etc) poignet m, manchette f; (of trousers) Am revers m; off the c. Fig impromptu; c. link bouton m de manchette. 2 vt (strike) gifler.

cul-de-sac ['kʌldəsæk] n impasse f, cul-de-sac m.

culinary ['kʌlɪnərɪ] a culinaire.

cull [kʌl] vt choisir; (animals) abattre sélectivement.

culminate ['kʌlmɪneɪt] vi to c. in finir par. ◆**culmi'nation** n point m culminant.

culprit ['kʌlprɪt] n coupable mf.

cult [kʌlt] n culte m.

cultivat/e ['kʌltɪveɪt] vt (land, mind etc) cultiver. ◆**–ed** a cultivé. ◆**culti'vation** n culture f; land or fields under c. cultures fpl.

culture ['kʌltʃər] n culture f. ◆**cultural** a culturel. ◆**cultured** a cultivé.

cumbersome ['kʌmbəsəm] a encombrant.

cumulative ['kjuːmjʊlətɪv] a cumulatif; c. effect (long-term) effet m or résultat m à long terme.

cunning ['kʌnɪŋ] a astucieux; Pej rusé; – n astuce f; ruse f. ◆**–ly** adv avec astuce; avec ruse.

cup [kʌp] n tasse f; (goblet, prize) coupe f; that's my c. of tea Fam c'est à mon goût; c. final Fb finale f de la coupe. ◆**c.-tie** n Fb match m éliminatoire. ◆**cupful** n tasse f.

cupboard ['kʌbəd] n armoire f; (built-in) placard m.

Cupid ['kjuːpɪd] n Cupidon m.

cupola ['kjuːpələ] n Archit coupole f.

cuppa ['kʌpə] n Fam tasse f de thé.

curate ['kjuərɪt] n vicaire m.

curator [kjuə'reɪtər] n (of museum) conservateur m.

curb [kɜːb] 1 n (kerb) Am bord m du trottoir. 2 vt (feelings) refréner, freiner; (ambitions) modérer; (expenses) limiter; – n frein m; to put a c. on mettre un frein à.

curdle ['kɜːd(ə)l] vt cailler; – vi se cailler; (of blood) Fig se figer.

curds [kɜːdz] npl lait m caillé. ◆**curd cheese** n fromage m blanc (maigre).

cure [kjuər] 1 vt guérir (of de); (poverty) Fig éliminer; – n remède m (for contre); (recovery) guérison f; rest c. cure f de repos. 2 vt Culin (smoke) fumer; (salt) saler; (dry) sécher. ◆**curable** a guérissable, curable. ◆**curative** a curatif.

curfew ['kɜːfjuː] n couvre-feu m.

curio ['kjuərɪəu] n (pl -os) bibelot m, curiosité f.

curious ['kjuərɪəs] a (odd) curieux; (inquisitive) curieux (about de); **c. to know** curieux de savoir. ◆—**ly** adv (oddly) curieusement. ◆**curi'osity** n curiosité f.

curl [kɜːl] 1 vti (hair) boucler, friser; — n boucle f; (of smoke) Fig spirale f. 2 vi **to c. up** (shrivel) se racornir; **to c. oneself up** (into a ball) se pelotonner. ◆—**er** n bigoudi m. ◆**curly** a (-ier, -iest) bouclé, frisé.

currant ['kʌrənt] n (fruit) groseille f; (dried grape) raisin m de Corinthe.

currency ['kʌrənsɪ] n (money) monnaie f; (acceptance) Fig cours m; **(foreign) c.** devises fpl (étrangères).

current ['kʌrənt] 1 a (fashion, trend etc) actuel; (opinion, use, phrase) courant; (year, month) en cours, courant; **c. affairs** questions fpl d'actualité; **c. events** actualité f; **the c. issue** (of magazine etc) le dernier numéro. 2 n (of river, air) & El courant m. ◆—**ly** adv actuellement, à présent.

curriculum, pl -**la** [kə'rɪkjʊləm, -lə] n programme m (scolaire); **c. (vitae)** curriculum (vitae) m inv.

curry ['kʌrɪ] 1 n Culin curry m, cari m. 2 vt **to c. favour with** s'insinuer dans les bonnes grâces de.

curs/e [kɜːs] n malédiction f; (swearword) juron m; (bane) Fig fléau m; — vt maudire; — vi (swear) jurer. ◆—**ed** [-ɪd] a Fam maudit.

cursor ['kɜːsər] n (on computer screen) curseur m.

cursory ['kɜːsərɪ] a (trop) rapide, superficiel.

curt [kɜːt] a brusque. ◆—**ly** adv d'un ton brusque. ◆—**ness** n brusquerie f.

curtail [kɜː'teɪl] vt écourter, raccourcir; (expenses) réduire. ◆—**ment** n raccourcissement m; réduction f.

curtain ['kɜːt(ə)n] n rideau m; **c. call** Th rappel m.

curts(e)y ['kɜːtsɪ] n révérence f; — vi faire une révérence.

curve [kɜːv] n courbe f; (in road) Am virage m; pl (of woman) Fam rondeurs fpl; — vt courber; — vi se courber; (of road) tourner, faire une courbe.

cushion ['kuʃən] n coussin m; — vt (shock) Fig amortir. ◆**cushioned** a (seat) rembourré; **c. against** Fig protégé contre.

cushy ['kuʃɪ] a (-ier, -iest) (job, life) Fam pépère, facile.

custard ['kʌstəd] n crème f anglaise; (when set) crème f renversée.

custodian [kʌ'stəudɪən] n gardien, -ienne mf.

custody ['kʌstədɪ] n (care) garde f; **to take into c.** Jur mettre en détention préventive. ◆**cu'stodial** a **c. sentence** peine f de prison.

custom ['kʌstəm] n coutume f; (patronage) Com clientèle f. ◆**customary** a habituel, coutumier; **it is c. to** il est d'usage de. ◆**custom-built,** ◆**customized** a (car etc) (fait) sur commande.

customer ['kʌstəmər] n client, -ente mf; Pej individu m.

customs ['kʌstəmz] n & npl **(the) c.** la douane; **c. (duties)** droits mpl de douane; **c. officer** douanier m; **c. union** union f douanière.

cut [kʌt] n coupure f; (stroke) coup m; (of clothes, hair) coupe f; (in salary) réduction f; (of meat) morceau m; — vt (pt & pp cut, pres p cutting) couper; (meat) découper; (glass, tree) tailler; (record) graver; (hay) faucher; (profits, prices etc) réduire; (tooth) percer; (corner) Aut prendre à la corde; **to c. open** ouvrir (au couteau etc); **to c. short** (visit) abréger; — vi (of person, scissors) couper; (of material) se couper; **to c. into** (cake) entamer. ■ **to c. away** vt (remove) enlever; **to c. back (on)** vti réduire. ◆**cutback** n réduction f; **to c. down** vt (tree) abattre, couper; **to c. down (on)** vti réduire; **to c. in** vi interrompre; Aut faire une queue de poisson (**on s.o.** à qn); **to c. off** vt couper; (isolate) isoler; **to c. out** vi (of engine) Aut caler; — vt (article) découper; (garment) tailler; (remove) enlever; (leave out, get rid of) Fam supprimer; **to c. out drinking** (stop) Fam s'arrêter de boire; **c. it out!** Fam ça suffit!; **c. out to be a doctor/etc** fait pour être médecin/etc. ◆**cutout** n (picture) découpage m; El coupe-circuit m inv; **to c. up** vt couper (en morceaux); (meat) découper; **c. up about** démoralisé par. ◆**cutting** n coupe f; (of diamond) taille f; (article) Journ coupure f; (plant) bouture f; Cin montage m; — a (wind, word) cinglant; **c. edge** tranchant m.

cute [kjuːt] a (-er, -est) Fam (pretty) mignon; (shrewd) astucieux.

cuticle ['kjuːtɪk(ə)l] n petites peaux fpl (de l'ongle).

cutlery ['kʌtlərɪ] n couverts mpl.

cutlet ['kʌtlɪt] n (of veal etc) côtelette f.

cut-price [kʌt'praɪs] a à prix réduit.

cutthroat ['kʌtθrəut] n assassin m; — a (competition) impitoyable.

cv [siː'viː] *n abbr* curriculum (vitae) *m inv.*
cyanide ['saɪənaɪd] *n* cyanure *m.*
cybernetics [saɪbə'netɪks] *n* cybernétique *f.*
cycle ['saɪk(ə)l] **1** *n* bicyclette *f*, vélo *m*; – *a* (*path, track*) cyclable; (*race*) cycliste; – *vi* aller à bicyclette (**to** à); *Sp* faire de la bicyclette. **2** *n* (*series, period*) cycle *m*. ◆**cycling** *n* cyclisme *m*; – *a* (*champion*) cycliste. ◆**cyclist** *n* cycliste *mf*. ◆**cyclic(al)** ['sɪklɪk(əl)] *a* cyclique.
cyclone ['saɪkləʊn] *n* cyclone *m.*
cylinder ['sɪlɪndər] *n* cylindre *m.* ◆**cy-'lindrical** *a* cylindrique.

cymbal ['sɪmbəl] *n* cymbale *f.*
cynic ['sɪnɪk] *n* cynique *mf.* ◆**cynical** *a* cynique. ◆**cynicism** *n* cynisme *m.*
cypress ['saɪprəs] *n* (*tree*) cyprès *m.*
Cyprus ['saɪprəs] *n* Chypre *f.* ◆**Cypriot** ['sɪprɪət] *a & n* cypriote (*mf*).
cyst [sɪst] *n Med* kyste *m.*
czar [zɑːr] *n* tsar *m.*
Czech [tʃek] *a & n* tchèque (*mf*). ◆**Czecho'slovak** *a & n* tchécoslovaque (*mf*). ◆**Czechoslo'vakia** *n* Tchécoslovaquie *f.* ◆**Czechoslo'vakian** *a & n* tchécoslovaque (*mf*).

D

D, d [diː] *n* D, d *m.* ◆**D.-day** *n* le jour J.
dab [dæb] *n a* **d. of** un petit peu de; – *vt* (-bb-) (*wound, brow etc*) tamponner; **to d. sth on sth** appliquer qch (à petits coups) sur qch.
dabble ['dæb(ə)l] *vi* **to d. in** s'occuper *or* se mêler un peu de.
dad [dæd] *n Fam* papa *m.* ◆**daddy** *n Fam* papa *m*; **d. longlegs** (*cranefly*) tipule *f*; (*spider*) *Am* faucheur *m.*
daffodil ['dæfədɪl] *n* jonquille *f.*
daft [dɑːft] *a* (-er, -est) *Fam* idiot, bête.
dagger ['dægər] *n* poignard *m*; **at daggers drawn** à couteaux tirés (**with** avec).
dahlia ['deɪljə, *Am* 'dæljə] *n* dahlia *m.*
daily ['deɪlɪ] *a* quotidien, journalier; (*wage*) journalier; – *adv* quotidiennement; – *n* **d.** (*paper*) quotidien *m*; **d.** (**help**) (*cleaning woman*) femme *f* de ménage.
dainty ['deɪntɪ] *a* (-ier, -iest) délicat; (*pretty*) mignon; (*tasteful*) élégant. ◆**daintily** *adv* délicatement; élégamment.
dairy ['deərɪ] *n* (*on farm*) laiterie *f*; (*shop*) crémerie *f*; – *a* (*produce, cow etc*) laitier. ◆**dairyman** *n* (*pl* -men) (*dealer*) laitier *m.* ◆**dairywoman** *n* (*pl* -women) laitière *f.*
daisy ['deɪzɪ] *n* pâquerette *f.*
dale [deɪl] *n Geog Lit* vallée *f.*
dally ['dælɪ] *vi* musarder, lanterner.
dam [dæm] *n* (*wall*) barrage *m*; – *vt* (-mm-) (*river*) barrer.
damag/e ['dæmɪdʒ] *n* dégâts *mpl*, dommages *mpl*; (*harm*) *Fig* préjudice *m*; *pl Jur* dommages-intérêts *mpl*; – *vt* (*spoil*) abîmer; (*material object*) endommager, abîmer; (*harm*) *Fig* nuire à. ◆—**ing** *a* préjudiciable (**to** à).

dame [deɪm] *n Lit* dame *f*; *Am Sl* nana *f*, fille *f.*
damn [dæm] *vt* (*condemn, doom*) condamner; *Rel* damner; (*curse*) maudire; **d. him!** *Fam* qu'il aille au diable!; – *int* **d. (it)!** *Fam* zut!, merde!; – *n* **he doesn't care a d.** *Fam* il s'en fiche pas mal; – *a Fam* fichu, sacré; – *adv Fam* sacrément; **d. all** rien du tout. ◆—**ed 1** *a* (*soul*) damné. **2** *Fam* = **damn** *a & adv.* ◆—**ing** *a* (*evidence etc*) accablant. ◆**dam'nation** *n* damnation *f.*
damp [dæmp] *a* (-er, -est) humide; (*skin*) moite; – *n* humidité *f.* ◆**damp(en)** *vt* humecter; **to d.** (**down**) (*zeal*) refroidir; (*ambition*) étouffer. ◆**damper** *n* **to put a d. on** jeter un froid sur. ◆**dampness** *n* humidité *f.*
damsel ['dæmzəl] *n Lit & Hum* demoiselle *f.*
damson ['dæmzən] *n* prune *f* de Damas.
danc/e [dɑːns] *n* danse *f*; (*social event*) bal *m*; **d. hall** dancing *m*; – *vi* danser; **to d. for joy** sauter de joie; – *vt* (*polka etc*) danser. ◆—**ing** *n* danse *f*; **d. partner** cavalier, -ière *mf.* ◆—**er** *n* danseur, -euse *mf.*
dandelion ['dændɪlaɪən] *n* pissenlit *m.*
dandruff ['dændrʌf] *n* pellicules *fpl.*
dandy ['dændɪ] **1** *n* dandy *m.* **2** *a* (*very good*) *Am Fam* formidable.
Dane [deɪn] *n* Danois, -oise *mf.*
danger ['deɪndʒər] *n* (*peril*) danger *m* (**to** pour); (*risk*) risque *m*; **in d.** en danger; **in d. of** (*threatened by*) menacé de; **to be in d. of falling**/*etc* risquer de tomber/*etc*; **on the d. list** *Med* dans un état critique; **d. signal** signal *m* d'alarme; **d. zone** zone *f* dangereuse. ◆**dangerous** *a* (*place, illness,*

person etc) dangereux (**to** pour). ◆**dangerously** *adv* dangereusement; (*ill*) gravement.

dangle ['dæŋg(ə)l] *vt* balancer; (*prospect*) *Fig* faire miroiter (**before s.o.** aux yeux de qn); – *vi* (*hang*) pendre; (*swing*) se balancer.

Danish ['deɪnɪʃ] *a* danois; – *n* (*language*) danois *m*.

dank [dæŋk] *a* (**-er, -est**) humide (et froid).

dapper ['dæpər] *a* pimpant, fringant.

dappled ['dæp(ə)ld] *a* pommelé, tacheté.

dar/e [deər] *vt* oser (**do** faire); **she d. not come** elle n'ose pas venir; **he doesn't d.** (**to**) **go** il n'ose pas y aller; **if you d.** (**to**) si tu l'oses, si tu oses le faire; **I d. say he tried** il a sans doute essayé, je suppose qu'il a essayé; **to d. s.o. to do** défier qn de faire. ◆**-ing** *a* audacieux; – *n* audace *f*. ◆**daredevil** *n* casse-cou *m inv*, risque-tout *m inv*.

dark [dɑːk] *a* (**-er, -est**) obscur, noir, sombre; (*colour*) foncé, sombre; (*skin*) brun, foncé; (*hair*) brun, noir, foncé; (*eyes*) foncé; (*gloomy*) sombre; **it's d.** il fait nuit *or* noir; **to keep sth d.** tenir qch secret; **d. glasses** lunettes *fpl* noires; – *n* noir *m*, obscurité *f*; **after d.** après la tombée de la nuit; **to keep s.o. in the d.** laisser qn dans l'ignorance (**about** de). ◆**d.-'haired** *a* aux cheveux bruns. ◆**d.-'skinned** *a* brun; (*race*) de couleur. ◆**darken** *vt* assombrir, obscurcir; (*colour*) foncer; – *vi* s'assombrir; (*of colour*) foncer. ◆**darkness** *n* obscurité *f*, noir *m*.

darkroom ['dɑːkruːm] *n Phot* chambre *f* noire.

darling ['dɑːlɪŋ] *n* (*favourite*) chouchou, -oute *mf*; (**my**) **d.** (mon) chéri, (ma) chérie; **he's a d.** c'est un amour; **be a d.!** sois un ange!; – *a* chéri; (*delightful*) *Fam* adorable.

darn [dɑːn] **1** *vt* (*socks*) repriser. **2** *int* **d. it!** bon sang! ◆**-ing** *n* reprise *f*; – *a* (*needle, wool*) à repriser.

dart [dɑːt] **1** *vi* se précipiter, s'élancer (**for** vers); – *n* **to make a d.** se précipiter (**for** vers). **2** *n Sp* fléchette *f*; *pl* (*game*) fléchettes *fpl*. ◆**dartboard** *n Sp* cible *f*.

dash [dæʃ] **1** *n* (*run, rush*) ruée *f*; **to make a d.** se précipiter (**for** vers); – *vi* se précipiter; (*of waves*) se briser (**against** contre); **to d. off** *or* **away** partir *or* filer en vitesse; – *vt* jeter (avec force); (*shatter*) briser; **d. (it)!** *Fam* zut!; **to d. off** (*letter*) faire en vitesse. **2** *n* **a d. of** un (petit) peu de; **a d. of milk** une goutte *or* un nuage de lait. **3** *n* (*stroke*) trait

m; *Typ* tiret *m*. ◆**-ing** *a* (*person*) sémillant.

dashboard ['dæʃbɔːd] *n Aut* tableau *m* de bord.

data ['deɪtə] *npl* données *fpl*. **d. processing** informatique *f*.

date¹ [deɪt] *n* date *f*; (*on coin*) millésime *m*; (*meeting*) *Fam* rendez-vous *m inv*; (*person*) *Fam* copain, -ine *mf* (avec qui on a un rendez-vous); **up to d.** moderne; (*information*) à jour; (*well-informed*) au courant (**on** de); **out of d.** (*old-fashioned*) démodé; (*expired*) périmé; **to d.** à ce jour, jusqu'ici; **d. stamp** (*object*) (tampon *m*) dateur *m*; (*mark*) cachet *m*; – *vt* (*letter etc*) dater; (*girl, boy*) *Fam* sortir avec; – *vi* (*become out of date*) dater; **to d. back to, d. from** dater de. ◆**dated** *a* démodé.

date² [deɪt] *n Bot* datte *f*.

datebook ['deɪtbʊk] *n Am* agenda *m*.

daub [dɔːb] *vt* barbouiller (**with** de).

daughter ['dɔːtər] *n* fille *f*. ◆**d.-in-law** *n* (*pl* **daughters-in-law**) belle-fille *f*, bru *f*.

daunt [dɔːnt] *vt* décourager, rebuter. ◆**-less** *a* intrépide.

dawdl/e ['dɔːd(ə)l] *vi* traîner, lambiner. ◆**-er** *n* traînard, -arde *mf*.

dawn [dɔːn] *n* aube *f*, aurore *f*; – *vi* (*of day*) poindre; (*of new era, idea*) naître, voir le jour; **it dawned upon him that** . . . il lui est venu à l'esprit que . . . . ◆**-ing** *a* naissant.

day [deɪ] *n* jour *m*; (*working period, whole day long*) journée *f*; *pl* (*period*) époque *f*, temps *mpl*; **all d.** (**long**) toute la journée; **what d. is it?** quel jour sommes-nous?; **the following** *or* **next d.** le lendemain; **the d. before** la veille; **the d. before yesterday** avant-hier; **the d. after tomorrow** après-demain; **to the d.** jour pour jour; **d. boarder** demi-pensionnaire *mf*; **d. nursery** crèche *f*; **d. return** *Rail* aller et retour *m* (*pour une journée*); **d. tripper** excursionniste *mf*. ◆**d.-to-'d.** *a* journalier; **on a d.-to-day basis** (*every day*) journellement. ◆**daybreak** *n* point *m* du jour. ◆**daydream** *n* rêverie *f*; – *vi* rêvasser. ◆**daylight** *n* (lumière *f* du) jour *m*; (*dawn*) point *m* du jour; **it's d.** il fait jour. ◆**daytime** *n* journée *f*.

daze [deɪz] *vt* (*with drugs etc*) hébéter; (*by blow*) étourdir; – *n* **in a d.** étourdi; hébété.

dazzle ['dæz(ə)l] *vt* éblouir; – *n* éblouissement *m*.

deacon ['diːkən] *n Rel* diacre *m*.

dead [ded] *a* mort; (*numb*) engourdi; (*party etc*) qui manque de vie, mortel; (*telephone*) sans tonalité; **in (the) d. centre** au beau milieu; **to be a d. loss** (*person*) *Fam* n'être bon à rien; **it's a d. loss** *Fam* ça ne vaut rien; **d. silence** un silence de mort; **a d. stop** un arrêt complet; **d. end** (*street*) & *Fig* impasse *f*; **a d.-end job** un travail sans avenir; − *adv* (*completely*) absolument; (*very*) très; **d. beat** *Fam* éreinté; **d. drunk** *Fam* ivre mort; **to stop d.** s'arrêter net; − *n* **the d.** les morts *mpl*; **in the d. of** (*night, winter*) au cœur de. ◆**—ly** *a* (-ier, -iest) (*enemy, silence, paleness*) mortel; (*weapon*) meurtrier; **d. sins** péchés *mpl* capitaux; − *adv* mortellement. ◆**deadbeat** *n Am Fam* parasite *m*. ◆**deadline** *n* date *f* limite; (*hour*) heure *f* limite. ◆**deadlock** *n Fig* impasse *f*. ◆**deadpan** *a* (*face*) figé, impassible.

deaden ['ded(ə)n] *vt* (*shock*) amortir; (*pain*) calmer; (*feeling*) émousser.

deaf [def] *a* sourd (**to** à); **d. and dumb** sourd-muet; **d. in one ear** sourd d'une oreille; − *n* **the d.** les sourds *mpl*. ◆**d.-aid** *n* audiophone *m*, prothèse *f* auditive. ◆**deafen** *vt* assourdir. ◆**deafness** *n* surdité *f*.

deal [di:l] **1** *n* **a good** or **great d.** beaucoup (**of** de). **2** *n Com* marché *m*, affaire *f*; *Cards* donne *f*; **fair d.** traitement *m or* arrangement *m* équitable; **it's a d.** d'accord; **big d.!** *Iron* la belle affaire! **3** *vt* (*pt & pp* **dealt** [delt]) (*blow*) porter; **to d.** (**out**) (*cards*) donner; (*money*) distribuer. **4** *vi* (*trade*) traiter (**with s.o.** avec qn); **to d. in** faire le commerce de; **to d. with** (*take care of*) s'occuper de; (*concern*) traiter de, parler de; **I can d. with him** (*handle*) je sais m'y prendre avec lui. ◆**—ings** *npl* relations *fpl* (**with** avec); *Com* transactions *fpl*. ◆**—er** *n* marchand, -ande *mf* (**in** de); (*agent*) dépositaire *mf*; (*for cars*) concessionnaire *mf*; (*in drugs*) *Sl* revendeur, -euse *mf* de drogues; *Cards* donneur, -euse *mf*.

deal² [di:l] *n* (*wood*) sapin *m*.

dean [di:n] *n Rel Univ* doyen *m*.

dear [diər] *a* (-er, -est) (*loved, precious, expensive*) cher; (*price*) élevé; **D. Sir** (*in letter*) *Com* Monsieur; **D. Uncle** (mon) cher oncle; **oh d.!** oh là là!, oh mon Dieu!; − *n* (my) **d.** (*darling*) (mon) chéri, (ma) chérie; (*friend*) mon cher, ma chère; **she's a d.** c'est un amour; **yes d.!** sois un ange!; − *adv* (*to cost, pay*) cher. ◆**—ly** *adv* tendrement; (*very much*) beaucoup; **to pay d. for sth** payer qch cher.

dearth [dɜ:θ] *n* manque *m*, pénurie *f*.

death [deθ] *n* mort *f*; **to put to d.** mettre à mort; **to be bored to d.** s'ennuyer à mourir;

to be burnt to d. mourir carbonisé; **to be sick to d.** en avoir vraiment marre; **many deaths** (*people killed*) de nombreux morts *mpl*; − *a* (*march*) funèbre; (*mask*) mortuaire; **d. certificate** acte *m* de décès; **d. duty penalty** droits *mpl* de succession; **d. penalty** or **sentence** peine *f* de mort; **d. rate** mortalité *f*; **it's a d. trap** il y a danger de mort. ◆**deathbed** *n* lit *m* de mort. ◆**deathblow** *n* coup *m* mortel. ◆**deathly** *a* mortel, de mort; − *adv* **d. pale** d'une pâleur mortelle.

debar [di'bɑ:r] *vt* (-rr-) exclure; **to d. from doing** interdire de faire.

debase [di'beis] *vt* (*person*) avilir; (*reputation, talents*) galvauder; (*coinage*) altérer.

debat/e [di'beit] *vti* discuter; **to d.** (**with oneself**) **whether to leave**/*etc* se demander si on doit partir/*etc*; − *n* débat *m*, discussion *f*. ◆**—able** *a* discutable, contestable.

debauch [di'bɔ:tʃ] *vt* corrompre, débaucher. ◆**debauchery** *n* débauche *f*.

debilitate [di'biliteit] *vt* débiliter. ◆**debility** *n* faiblesse *f*, débilité *f*.

debit ['debit] *n* débit *m*; **in d.** (*account*) débiteur; − *a* (*balance*) *Fin* débiteur; − *vt* débiter (**s.o. with sth** qn de qch).

debonair [debə'neər] *a* jovial; (*charming*) charmant; (*polite*) poli.

debris ['debri] *n* débris *mpl*.

debt [det] *n* dette *f*; **to be in d.** avoir des dettes; **to be £50 in d.** devoir 50 livres; **to run** or **get into d.** faire des dettes. ◆**debtor** *n* débiteur, -trice *mf*.

debunk [di'bʌŋk] *vt Fam* démystifier.

debut ['debju:] *n Th* début *m*.

decade ['dekeid] *n* décennie *f*.

decadent ['dekədənt] *a* décadent. ◆**decadence** *n* décadence *f*.

decaffeinated [di:'kæfineitid] *a* décaféiné.

decal ['di:kæl] *n Am* décalcomanie *f*.

decant [di'kænt] *vt* (*wine*) décanter. ◆**—er** *n* carafe *f*.

decapitate [di'kæpiteit] *vt* décapiter.

decathlon [di'kæθlɒn] *n Sp* décathlon *m*.

decay [di'kei] *vi* (*go bad*) se gâter; (*rot*) pourrir; (*of tooth*) se carier, se gâter; (*of building*) tomber en ruine; (*decline*) *Fig* décliner; − *n* pourriture *f*; *Archit* délabrement *m*; (*of tooth*) carie(s) *f*(*pl*); (*of building*) décadence *f*; **to fall into d.** (*of building*) tomber en ruine. ◆**—ing** *a* (*nation*) décadent; (*meat, fruit etc*) pourrissant.

deceased [di'si:st] *a* décédé, défunt; − *n* **the d.** le défunt, la défunte; *pl* les défunt(e)s.

deceit [di'si:t] *n* tromperie *f*. ◆**deceitful** *a*

trompeur. ◆**deceitfully** *adv* avec dupli-
cité.

deceive [dɪ'siːv] *vti* tromper; **to d. oneself** se
faire des illusions.

December [dɪ'sembər] *n* décembre *m*.

decent ['diːsənt] *a* (*respectable*) convenable,
décent; (*good*) *Fam* bon; (*kind*) *Fam*
gentil; **that was d. (of you)** c'était chic de ta
part. ◆**decency** *n* décence *f*; (*kindness*)
Fam gentillesse *f*. ◆**decently** *adv* décemment.

decentralize [diː'sentrəlaɪz] *vt* décentraliser. ◆**decentrali'zation** *n* décentralisation *f*.

deception [dɪ'sepʃ(ə)n] *n* tromperie *f*.
◆**deceptive** *a* trompeur.

decibel ['desɪbel] *n* décibel *m*.

decid/e [dɪ'saɪd] *vt* (*question etc*) régler,
décider; (*s.o.'s career, fate etc*) décider de;
to d. to do décider de faire; **to d.** that
décider que; **to d. s.o. to do** décider qn à
faire; – *vi* (*make decisions*) décider; (*make
up one's mind*) se décider (**on doing** à faire);
to d. on sth décider de qch, se décider à
qch; (*choose*) se décider pour qch. ◆**—ed** *a*
(*firm*) décidé, résolu; (*clear*) net. ◆**—edly**
adv résolument; nettement. ◆**—ing** *a*
(*factor etc*) décisif.

decimal ['desɪməl] *a* décimal; **d. point**
virgule *f*; – *n* décimale *f*. ◆**decimali-**
'zation *n* décimalisation *f*.

decimate ['desɪmeɪt] *vt* décimer.

decipher [dɪ'saɪfər] *vt* déchiffrer.

decision [dɪ'sɪʒ(ə)n] *n* décision *f*. ◆**deci-**
sive [dɪ'saɪsɪv] *a* (*defeat, tone etc*) décisif;
(*victory*) net, incontestable. ◆**decisively**
adv (*to state*) avec décision; (*to win*) nettement, incontestablement.

deck [dek] **1** *n* Nau pont *m*; **top d.** (*of bus*)
impériale *f*. **2** *n* **d. of cards** jeu *m* de cartes. **3**
n (*of record player*) platine *f*. **4** *vt* **to d. (out)**
(*adorn*) orner. ◆**deckchair** *n* chaise *f*
longue.

declare [dɪ'kleər] *vt* déclarer (**that** que);
(*verdict, result*) proclamer. ◆**decla'ration**
n déclaration *f*; proclamation *f*.

declin/e [dɪ'klaɪn] **1** *vi* (*deteriorate*)
décliner; (*of birthrate, price etc*) baisser; **to
d. in importance** perdre de l'importance; –
n déclin *m*; (*fall*) baisse *f*. **2** *vt* refuser,
décliner; **to d. to do** refuser de faire.
◆**—ing** *a* one's **d. years** ses dernières
années.

decode [diː'kəʊd] *vt* (*message*) décoder.

decompose [diːkəm'pəʊz] *vt* décomposer;
– *vi* se décomposer. ◆**decompo'sition** *n*
décomposition *f*.

decompression [diːkəm'preʃ(ə)n] *n*
décompression *f*.

decontaminate [diːkən'tæmɪneɪt] *vt* décontaminer.

decor ['deɪkɔːr] *n* décor *m*.

decorat/e ['dekəreɪt] *vt* (*cake, house,
soldier*) décorer (**with** de); (*paint etc*) peindre (et tapisser); (*hat, skirt etc*) orner (**with**
de). ◆**—ing** *n* **interior d.** décoration *f*
d'intérieurs. ◆**deco'ration** *n* décoration
f. ◆**decorative** *a* décoratif. ◆**decorator**
n (*house painter etc*) peintre *m* décorateur;
(*interior*) **d.** ensemblier *m*, décorateur,
-trice *mf*.

decorum [dɪ'kɔːrəm] *n* bienséances *fpl*.

decoy ['diːkɔɪ] *n* (*artificial bird*) appeau *m*;
(*police*) **d.** policier *m* en civil.

decreas/e [dɪ'kriːs] *vti* diminuer; –
['diːkriːs] *n* diminution *f* (**in** de). ◆**—ing** *a*
(*number etc*) décroissant. ◆**—ingly** *adv* de
moins en moins.

decree [dɪ'kriː] *n* Pol Rel décret *m*; Jur jugement *m*; (*municipal*) arrêté *m*; – *vt* (*pt &
pp* decreed) décréter.

decrepit [dɪ'krepɪt] *a* (*building*) en ruine;
(*person*) décrépit.

decry [dɪ'kraɪ] *vt* décrier.

dedicat/e ['dedɪkeɪt] *vt* (*devote*) consacrer
(**to** à); (*book*) dédier (**to** à); **to d. oneself to**
se consacrer à. ◆**dedi'cation** *n* (*in book*)
dédicace *f*; (*devotion*) dévouement *m*.

deduce [dɪ'djuːs] *vt* (*conclude*) déduire (**from**
de, **that** que).

deduct [dɪ'dʌkt] *vt* (*subtract*) déduire,
retrancher (**from** de); (*from wage, account*)
prélever (**from** sur). ◆**deductible** *a* à
déduire (**from** de); (*expenses*) déductible.
◆**deduction** *n* (*inference*) & Com déduction *f*.

deed [diːd] *n* action *f*, acte *m*; (*feat*) exploit
m; Jur acte *m* (notarié).

deem [diːm] *vt* juger, estimer.

deep [diːp] *a* (-er, -est) profond; (*snow*)
épais; (*voice*) grave; (*note*) Mus bas;
(*person*) insondable; **to be six metres/*etc* d.**
avoir six mètres/*etc* de profondeur; **d. in
thought** absorbé *or* plongé dans ses
pensées; **the d. end** (*in swimming pool*) le
grand bain; **d. red** rouge foncé; – *adv* (*to
breathe*) profondément; **d. into the night**
tard dans la nuit; – *n* **the d.** l'océan *m*.
◆**—ly** *adv* (*grateful, to regret etc*)
profondément. ◆**deep-'freeze** *vt* surgeler; – *n* congélateur *m*. ◆**d.-'fryer** *n*
friteuse *f*. ◆**d.-'rooted** *a*, ◆**d.-'seated** *a*
bien ancré, profond. ◆**d.-'set** *a* (*eyes*)
enfoncés.

deepen ['diːpən] *vt* approfondir; (*increase*) augmenter; − *vi* devenir plus profond; (*of mystery*) s'épaissir. **◆—ing** *a* grandissant.

deer [dɪər] *n inv* cerf *m*.

deface [dɪ'feɪs] *vt* (*damage*) dégrader; (*daub*) barbouiller.

defamation [defə'meɪʃ(ə)n] *n* diffamation *f*. **◆de'famatory** *a* diffamatoire.

default [dɪ'fɔːlt] *n* by d. *Jur* par défaut; to win by d. gagner par forfait; − *vi Jur* faire défaut; to d. on one's payments *Fin* être en rupture de paiement.

defeat [dɪ'fiːt] *vt* battre, vaincre; (*plan*) faire échouer; − *n* défaite *f*; (*of plan*) échec *m*. **◆defeatism** *n* défaitisme *m*.

defect 1 ['diːfekt] *n* défaut *m*. **2** [dɪ'fekt] *vi Pol* déserter, faire défection; to d. to (*the West, the enemy*) passer à. **◆de'fection** *n* défection *f*. **◆de'fective** *a* défectueux; *Med* déficient. **◆de'fector** *n* transfuge *mf*.

defence [dɪ'fens] (*Am* defense) *n* défense *f*; the body's defences la défense de l'organisme (against contre); in his d. *Jur* à sa décharge, pour le défendre. **◆defence-less** *a* sans défense. **◆defensible** *a* défendable. **◆defensive** *a* défensif; − *n* on the d. sur la défensive.

defend [dɪ'fend] *vt* défendre. **◆defendant** *n* (*accused*) *Jur* prévenu, -ue *mf*. **◆defender** *n* défenseur *m*; (*of title*) *Sp* détenteur, -trice *mf*.

defer [dɪ'fɜːr] **1** *vt* (-rr-) (*postpone*) différer, reporter. **2** *vi* (-rr-) to d. to (*yield*) déférer à. **◆—ment** *n* report *m*.

deference ['defərəns] *n* déférence *f*. **◆defe'rential** *a* déférent, plein de déférence.

defiant [dɪ'faɪənt] *a* (*tone etc*) de défi; (*person*) rebelle. **◆defiance** *n* (*resistance*) défi *m* (of à); in d. of (*contempt*) au mépris de. **◆defiantly** *adv* d'un air de défi.

deficient [dɪ'fɪʃənt] *a* insuffisant; *Med* déficient; to be d. in manquer de. **◆deficiency** *n* manque *m*; (*flaw*) défaut *m*; *Med* carence *f*; (*mental*) déficience *f*.

deficit ['defɪsɪt] *n* déficit *m*.

defile [dɪ'faɪl] *vt* souiller, salir.

define [dɪ'faɪn] *vt* définir. **◆defi'nition** *n* définition *f*.

definite ['defɪnɪt] *a* (*date, plan*) précis, déterminé; (*obvious*) net, évident; (*firm*) ferme; (*certain*) certain; d. article *Gram* article *m* défini. **◆—ly** *adv* certainement; (*appreciably*) nettement; (*to say*) catégoriquement.

definitive [dɪ'fɪnɪtɪv] *a* définitif.

deflate [dɪ'fleɪt] *vt* (*tyre*) dégonfler. **◆deflation** *n* dégonflement *m*; *Econ* déflation *f*.

deflect [dɪ'flekt] *vt* faire dévier; − *vi* dévier.

deform [dɪ'fɔːm] *vt* déformer. **◆—ed** *a* (*body*) difforme. **◆deformity** *n* difformité *f*.

defraud [dɪ'frɔːd] *vt* (*customs, State etc*) frauder; to d. s.o. of sth escroquer qch à qn.

defray [dɪ'freɪ] *vt* (*expenses*) payer.

defrost [diː'frɒst] *vt* (*fridge*) dégivrer; (*food*) décongeler.

deft [deft] *a* adroit (with de). **◆—ness** *n* adresse *f*.

defunct [dɪ'fʌŋkt] *a* défunt.

defuse [diː'fjuːz] *vt* (*bomb, conflict*) désamorcer.

defy [dɪ'faɪ] *vt* (*person, death etc*) défier; (*effort, description*) résister à; to d. s.o. to do défier qn de faire.

degenerate [dɪ'dʒenəreɪt] *vi* dégénérer (into en); − [dɪ'dʒenərət] *a & n* dégénéré, -ée (*mf*). **◆degene'ration** *n* dégénérescence *f*.

degrade [dɪ'greɪd] *vt* dégrader. **◆degradation** [degrə'deɪʃ(ə)n] *n Mil Ch* dégradation *f*; (*of person*) déchéance *f*.

degree [dɪ'griː] *n* **1** degré *m*; not in the slightest d. pas du tout; to such a d. à tel point (that que). **2** *Univ* diplôme *m*; (*Bachelor's*) licence *f*; (*Master's*) maîtrise *f*; (*PhD*) doctorat *m*.

dehumanize [diː'hjuːmənaɪz] *vt* déshumaniser.

dehydrate [diːhaɪ'dreɪt] *vt* déshydrater.

de-ice [diː'aɪs] *vt Av Aut* dégivrer.

deign [deɪn] *vt* daigner (to do faire).

deity ['diːɪtɪ] *n* dieu *m*.

dejected [dɪ'dʒektɪd] *a* abattu, découragé. **◆dejection** *n* abattement *m*.

dekko ['dekəʊ] *n Sl* coup *m* d'œil.

delay [dɪ'leɪ] *vt* retarder; (*payment*) différer; − *vi* (*be slow*) tarder (doing à faire); (*linger*) s'attarder; − *n* (*lateness*) retard *m*; (*waiting period*) délai *m*; without d. sans tarder. **◆delayed-'action** *a* (*bomb*) à retardement. **◆delaying** *a* d. tactics moyens *mpl* dilatoires.

delectable [dɪ'lektəb(ə)l] *a* délectable.

delegate 1 ['delɪgeɪt] *vt* déléguer (to à). **2** ['delɪgət] *n* délégué, -ée *mf*. **◆dele'gation** *n* délégation *f*.

delete [dɪ'liːt] *vt* rayer, supprimer. **◆deletion** *n* (*thing deleted*) rature *f*; (*act*) suppression *f*.

deleterious [delɪ'tɪərɪəs] *a* néfaste.

deliberate¹ [dɪ'lɪbəreɪt] *vi* délibérer; − *vt* délibérer sur.

deliberate² [dɪ'lɪbərət] *a* (*intentional*) délibéré; (*cautious*) réfléchi; (*slow*) mesuré.

◆**—ly** adv (intentionally) exprès, délibéré-ment; (to walk) avec mesure. ◆**delibe-'ration** n délibération f.

delicate ['delɪkət] a délicat. ◆**delicacy** n délicatesse f; Culin mets m délicat, gour-mandise f. ◆**delicately** adv délicatement. ◆**delica'tessen** n (shop) épicerie f fine, traiteur m.

delicious [dɪ'lɪʃəs] a délicieux.

delight [dɪ'laɪt] n délice m, grand plaisir m, joie f; pl (pleasures, things) délices fpl; **to be the d. of** faire les délices de; **to take d. in sth/in doing** se délecter de qch/à faire; – vt réjouir; – vi se délecter (**in doing** à faire). ◆**—ed** a ravi, enchanté (**with sth** de qch, **to do** de faire, **that** que). ◆**delightful** a charmant; (meal, perfume, sensation) délicieux. ◆**delightfully** adv avec beaucoup de charme; (wonderfully) merveilleusement.

delineate [dɪ'lɪnɪeɪt] vt (outline) esquisser; (portray) décrire.

delinquent [dɪ'lɪŋkwənt] a & n délinquant, -ante (mf). ◆**delinquency** n délinquance f.

delirious [dɪ'lɪərɪəs] a délirant; **to be d.** avoir le délire, délirer. ◆**delirium** n Med délire m.

deliver [dɪ'lɪvər] vt 1 (goods, milk etc) livrer; (letters) distribuer; (hand over) remettre (**to** à). 2 (rescue) délivrer (**from** de). 3 (give birth to) mettre au monde, accoucher de; **to d. a woman('s baby)** accoucher une femme. 4 (speech) prononcer; (ultimatum, warning) lancer; (blow) porter. ◆**deliverance** n délivrance f. ◆**delivery** n 1 livraison f; distribution f; remise f 2 Med accouche-ment m. 3 (speaking) débit m. ◆**deliver-yman** n (pl -men) livreur m.

delta ['deltə] n (of river) delta m.

delude [dɪ'luːd] vt tromper; **to d. oneself** se faire des illusions. ◆**delusion** n illusion f; Psy aberration f mentale.

deluge ['deljuːdʒ] n (of water, questions etc) déluge m; – vt inonder (**with** de).

de luxe [dɪ'lʌks] a de luxe.

delve [delv] vi **to d. into** (question, past) fouiller; (books) fouiller dans.

demagogue ['deməgɒg] n démagogue mf.

demand [dɪ'mɑːnd] vt exiger (**sth from s.o.** qch de qn), réclamer (**sth from s.o.** qch à qn); (rights, more pay) revendiquer; **to d. that** exiger que; **to d. to know** insister pour savoir; – n exigence f; (claim) revendica-tion f, réclamation f; (request) & Econ demande f; **in great d.** très demandé; **to make demands on s.o.** exiger beaucoup de qn. ◆**—ing** a exigeant.

demarcation [diːmɑːkeɪʃ(ə)n] n démarca-tion f.

demean [dɪ'miːn] vt **to d. oneself** s'abaisser, s'avilir.

demeanour [dɪ'miːnər] n (behaviour) comportement m.

demented [dɪ'mentɪd] a dément.

demerara [demə'reərə] n **d.** (**sugar**) cassonade f, sucre m roux.

demise [dɪ'maɪz] n (death) décès m; Fig disparition f.

demo ['deməʊ] n (pl -os) (demonstration) Fam manif f.

demobilize [diː'məʊbɪlaɪz] vt démobiliser.

democracy [dɪ'mɒkrəsɪ] n démocratie f. ◆**democrat** ['deməkræt] n démocrate mf. ◆**demo'cratic** a démocratique; (person) démocrate.

demography [dɪ'mɒgrəfɪ] n démographie f.

demolish [dɪ'mɒlɪʃ] vt démolir. ◆**demo-'lition** n démolition f.

demon ['diːmən] n démon m.

demonstrate ['demənstreɪt] vt démontrer; (machine) faire une démonstration de; – vi Pol manifester. ◆**demon'stration** n démonstration f; Pol manifestation f. ◆**de'monstrative** a démonstratif. ◆**demonstrator** n Pol manifestant, -ante mf; (in shop etc) démonstrateur, -trice mf.

demoralize [dɪ'mɒrəlaɪz] vt démoraliser.

demote [dɪ'məʊt] vt rétrograder.

demure [dɪ'mjʊər] a sage, réservé.

den [den] n antre m, tanière f.

denationalize [diː'næʃ(ə)nəlaɪz] vt déna-tionaliser.

denial [dɪ'naɪəl] n (of truth etc) dénégation f; (of rumour) démenti m; (of authority) rejet m; **to issue a d.** publier un démenti.

denigrate ['denɪgreɪt] vt dénigrer.

denim ['denɪm] n (toile f de) coton m; pl (jeans) (blue-)jean m.

denizen ['denɪz(ə)n] n habitant, -ante mf.

Denmark ['denmɑːk] n Danemark m.

denomination [dɪnɒmɪ'neɪʃ(ə)n] n confes-sion f, religion f; (sect) secte m; (of coin, banknote) valeur f; Math unité f. ◆**denominational** a (school) confession-nel.

denote [dɪ'nəʊt] vt dénoter.

denounce [dɪ'naʊns] vt (person, injustice etc) dénoncer (**to** à); **to d. s.o. as a spy/etc** accuser qn publiquement d'être un espion/etc. ◆**denunci'ation** n dénoncia-tion f; accusation f publique.

dense [dens] a (-er, -est) dense; (stupid)

Fam lourd, bête. ◆—**ly** *adv* **d. popu-lated**/*etc* très peuplé/*etc.* ◆**density** *n* densité *f.*

dent [dent] *n* (*in metal*) bosselure *f*; (*in car*) bosse *f*, gnon *m*; **full of dents** (*car*) cabossé; **to make a d. in one's savings** taper dans ses économies; − *vt* cabosser, bosseler.

dental ['dent(ə)l] *a* dentaire; **d. surgeon** chirurgien *m* dentiste. ◆**dentist** *n* dentiste *mf.* ◆**dentistry** *n* médecine *f* dentaire; **school of d.** école *f* dentaire. ◆**dentures** *npl* dentier *m.*

deny [dɪ'naɪ] *vt* nier (**doing** avoir fait, **that** que); (*rumour*) démentir; (*authority*) rejeter; (*disown*) renier; **to d. s.o. sth** refuser qch à qn.

deodorant [diː'əʊdərənt] *n* déodorant *m.*

depart [dɪ'pɑːt] *vi* partir; (*deviate*) s'écarter (**from** de); − *vt* **to d. this world** *Lit* quitter ce monde. ◆—**ed** *a* & *n* (*dead*) défunt, -unte (*mf*). ◆**departure** *n* départ *m*; **a d. from** (*custom, rule*) un écart par rapport à, une entorse à; **to be a new d. for** constituer une nouvelle voie pour.

department [dɪ'pɑːtmənt] *n* département *m*; (*in office*) service *m*; (*in shop*) rayon *m*; *Univ* section *f*, département *m*; **that's your d.** (*sphere*) c'est ton rayon; **d. store** grand magasin *m.* ◆**depart'mental** *a* **d. manager** (*office*) chef *m* de service; (*shop*) chef *m* de rayon.

depend [dɪ'pend] *vi* dépendre (**on, upon** de); **to d.** (**up)on** (*rely on*) compter sur (**for sth** pour qch); **you can d. on it!** tu peux en être sûr! ◆—**able** *a* (*person, information etc*) sûr; (*machine*) fiable, sûr. ◆**dependant** *n* personne *f* à charge. ◆**dependence** *n* dépendance *f.* ◆**dependency** *n* (*country*) dépendance *f.* ◆**dependent** *a* dépendant (**on, upon** de); (*relative*) à charge; **to be d. (up)on** dépendre de.

depict [dɪ'pɪkt] *vt* (*describe*) dépeindre; (*pictorially*) représenter. ◆**depiction** *n* peinture *f*; représentation *f.*

deplete [dɪ'pliːt] *vt* (*use up*) épuiser; (*reduce*) réduire. ◆**depletion** *n* épuisement *m*; réduction *f.*

deplor/e [dɪ'plɔːr] *vt* déplorer. ◆—**able** *a* déplorable.

deploy [dɪ'plɔɪ] *vt* (*troops etc*) déployer.

depopulate [diː'pɒpjʊleɪt] *vt* dépeupler. ◆**depopu'lation** *n* dépeuplement *m.*

deport [dɪ'pɔːt] *vt Pol Jur* expulser; (*to concentration camp etc*) *Hist* déporter. ◆**depor'tation** *n* expulsion *f*; déportation *f.*

deportment [dɪ'pɔːtmənt] *n* maintien *m.*

depose [dɪ'pəʊz] *vt* (*king etc*) déposer.

deposit [dɪ'pɒzɪt] *vt* (*object, money etc*) déposer; − *n* (*in bank, wine*) & *Ch* dépôt *m*; (*part payment*) acompte *m*; (*against damage*) caution *f*; (*on bottle*) consigne *f*; **d. account** *Fin* compte *m* d'épargne. ◆—**or** *n* déposant, -ante *mf*, épargnant, -ante *mf.*

depot ['depəʊ, *Am* 'diːpəʊ] *n* dépôt *m*; (*station*) *Rail Am* gare *f*; (**bus**) **d.** *Am* gare *f* routière.

deprave [dɪ'preɪv] *vt* dépraver. ◆**depravity** *n* dépravation *f.*

deprecate ['deprɪkeɪt] *vt* désapprouver.

depreciate [dɪ'priːʃɪeɪt] *vt* (*reduce in value*) déprécier; − *vi* se déprécier. ◆**depreci-'ation** *n* dépréciation *f.*

depress [dɪ'pres] *vt* (*discourage*) déprimer; (*push down*) appuyer sur. ◆—**ed** *a* déprimé; (*in decline*) en déclin; (*in crisis*) en crise; **to get d.** se décourager. ◆**depression** *n* dépression *f.*

depriv/e [dɪ'praɪv] *vt* priver (**of** de). ◆—**ed** *a* (*child etc*) déshérité. ◆**depri'vation** *n* privation *f*; (*loss*) perte *f.*

depth [depθ] *n* profondeur *f*; (*of snow*) épaisseur *f*; (*of interest*) intensité *f*; **in the depths of** (*forest, despair*) au plus profond de; (*winter*) au cœur de; **to get out of one's d.** *Fig* perdre pied, nager; **in d.** en profondeur.

deputize ['depjʊtaɪz] *vi* assurer l'intérim (**for** de); − *vt* députer (**s.o. to do** qn pour faire). ◆**depu'tation** *n* députation *f.* ◆**deputy** *n* (*replacement*) suppléant, -ante *mf*; (*assistant*) adjoint, -ointe *mf*; **d.** (**sher-iff**) *Am* shérif *m* adjoint; **d. chairman** vice-président, -ente *mf.*

derailed [dɪ'reɪld] *a* **to be d.** (*of train*) dérailler. ◆**derailment** *n* déraillement *m.*

deranged [dɪ'reɪndʒd] *a* (*person, mind*) dérangé.

derelict ['derɪlɪkt] *a* à l'abandon, aban-donné.

deride [dɪ'raɪd] *vt* tourner en dérision. ◆**derision** *n* dérision *f.* ◆**derisive** *a* (*laughter etc*) moqueur; (*amount*) dérisoire. ◆**derisory** *a* dérisoire.

derive [dɪ'raɪv] *vt* **to d. from** (*pleasure, profit etc*) tirer de; *Ling* dériver de; **to be derived from** dériver de, provenir de; − *vi* **to d. from** dériver de. ◆**deri'vation** *n Ling* dériva-tion *f.* ◆**derivative** *a* & *n Ling Ch* dérivé (*m*).

dermatology [dɜːmə'tɒlədʒɪ] *n* dermato-logie *f.*

derogatory [dɪ'rɒgət(ə)rɪ] *a* (*word*) péjora-tif; (*remark*) désobligeant (**to** pour).

derrick ['derɪk] n (over oil well) derrick m.
derv [dɜːv] n gazole m, gas-oil m.
descend [dɪ'send] vi descendre (**from** de); (of rain) tomber; **to d. upon** (attack) faire une descente sur, tomber sur; (of tourists) envahir; — vt (stairs) descendre; **to be descended from** descendre de. ◆—**ing** a (order) décroissant. ◆**descendant** n descendant, -ante mf. ◆**descent** n 1 descente f; (into crime) chute f. **2** (ancestry) souche f, origine f.
describe [dɪ'skraɪb] vt décrire. ◆**description** n description f; (on passport) signalement m; **of every d.** de toutes sortes. ◆**descriptive** a descriptif.
desecrate ['desɪkreɪt] vt profaner. ◆**dese-'cration** n profanation f.
desegregate [diː'segrɪgeɪt] vt supprimer la ségrégation raciale dans. ◆**desegre-'gation** n déségrégation f.
desert[1] ['dezət] n désert m; — a désertique; **d. island** île f déserte.
desert[2] [dɪ'zɜːt] vt déserter, abandonner; **to d. s.o.** (of luck etc) abandonner qn; — vi Mil déserter. ◆—**ed** a (place) désert. ◆—**er** n Mil déserteur m. ◆**desertion** n désertion f; (by spouse) abandon m (du domicile conjugal).
deserts [dɪ'zɜːts] n **one's just d.** ce qu'on mérite.
deserv/e [dɪ'zɜːv] vt mériter (**to do** de faire). ◆—**ing** a (person) méritant; (act, cause) louable, méritoire; **d. of** digne de. ◆—**edly** [-ɪdlɪ] adv à juste titre.
desiccated ['desɪkeɪtɪd] a (des)séché.
design [dɪ'zaɪn] vt (car, furniture etc) dessiner; (dress) créer, dessiner; (devise) concevoir (**for s.o.** pour qn, **to do** pour faire); **well designed** bien conçu; — n (aim) dessein m, intention f; (sketch) plan m, dessin m; (of dress, car) modèle m; (planning) conception f, création f; (pattern) motif m, dessin m; **industrial d.** dessin m industriel; **by d.** intentionnellement; **to have designs on** avoir des desseins sur. ◆—**er** n dessinateur, -trice mf; **d. clothes** vêtements mpl griffés.
designate ['dezɪgneɪt] vt désigner. ◆**desig-'nation** n désignation f.
desir/e [dɪ'zaɪər] n désir m; **I've no d.** to je n'ai aucune envie de; — vt désirer (**to do** faire). ◆—**able** a désirable; **d. property/etc** (in advertising) (très) belle propriété/etc.
desk [desk] n Sch pupitre m; (in office) bureau m; (in shop) caisse f; (reception) **d.** réception f; **the news d.** Journ le service des

informations; — a (job) de bureau; **d. clerk** (in hotel) Am réceptionniste mf.
desolate ['desələt] a (deserted) désolé; (in ruins) dévasté; (dreary, bleak) morne, triste. ◆**deso'lation** n (ruin) dévastation f; (emptiness) solitude f.
despair [dɪ'speər] n désespoir m; **to drive s.o. to d.** désespérer qn; **in d.** au désespoir; — vi désespérer (**of s.o.** de qn, **of doing** de faire). ◆—**ing** a désespéré. ◆'**desperate** a désespéré; (criminal) capable de tout; (serious) grave; **to be d. for** (money, love etc) avoir désespérément besoin de; (a cigarette, baby etc) mourir d'envie d'avoir. ◆'**desperately** adv (ill) gravement; (in love) éperdument. ◆**despe'ration** n désespoir m; **in d.** (as a last resort) en désespoir de cause.
despatch [dɪ'spætʃ] see dispatch.
desperado [despə'rɑːdəʊ] n (pl -oes or -os) criminel m.
despise [dɪ'spaɪz] vt mépriser. ◆**despicable** a ignoble, méprisable.
despite [dɪ'spaɪt] prep malgré.
despondent [dɪ'spɒndənt] a découragé. ◆**despondency** n découragement m.
despot ['despɒt] n despote m. ◆**despotism** n despotisme m.
dessert [dɪ'zɜːt] n dessert m. ◆**dessert-spoon** n cuiller f à dessert.
destabilize [diː'steɪbəlaɪz] vt déstabiliser.
destination [destɪ'neɪʃ(ə)n] n destination f.
destine ['destɪn] vt destiner (**for** à, **to do** à faire); **it was destined to happen** ça devait arriver. ◆**destiny** n destin m; (fate of individual) destinée f.
destitute ['destɪtjuːt] a (poor) indigent; **d. of** (lacking in) dénué de. ◆**desti'tution** n dénuement m.
destroy [dɪ'strɔɪ] vt détruire; (horse etc) abattre. ◆—**er** n (person) destructeur, -trice mf; (ship) contre-torpilleur m. ◆**destruct** vt Mil détruire. ◆**destruction** n destruction f. ◆**destructive** a (person, war) destructeur; (power) destructif.
detach [dɪ'tætʃ] vt détacher (**from** de). ◆—**ed** a (indifferent) détaché; (view) désintéressé; **d. house** maison f individuelle. ◆—**able** a (lining) amovible. ◆—**ment** n (attitude) & Mil détachement m; **the d. of** (action) la séparation de.
detail ['diːteɪl, Am dɪ'teɪl] **1** n détail m; **in d.** en détail; — vt raconter or exposer en détail or par le menu, détailler. **2** vt Mil détacher (**to do** pour faire); — n détachement m. ◆—**ed** a (account etc) détaillé.
detain [dɪ'teɪn] vt retenir; (imprison) détenir.

◆**detai'nee** n Pol Jur détenu, -ue mf. ◆**detention** n Jur détention f; Sch retenue f.

detect [dɪ'tekt] vt découvrir; (perceive) distinguer; (identify) identifier; (mine) détecter; (illness) dépister. ◆**detection** n découverte f; identification f; détection f; dépistage m. ◆**detector** n détecteur m.

detective [dɪ'tektɪv] n agent m de la Sûreté, policier m (en civil); (private) détective m; – a (film etc) policier; **d. story** roman m policier; **d. constable** = inspecteur m de police.

deter [dɪ'tɜːr] vt (-rr-) **to d. s.o.** dissuader or décourager qn (**from doing** de faire, **from sth** de qch).

detergent [dɪ'tɜːdʒənt] n détergent m.

deteriorate [dɪ'tɪərɪəreɪt] vi se détériorer; (of morals) dégénérer. ◆**deterio'ration** n détérioration f; dégénérescence f.

determin/e [dɪ'tɜːmɪn] vt déterminer; (price) fixer; **to d. s.o. to do** décider qn à faire; **to d. that** décider que; **to d. to do se** déterminer à faire. ◆**—ed** a (look, quantity) déterminé; **d. to do or on doing** décidé à faire; **I'm d. she'll succeed** je suis bien décidé à ce qu'elle réussisse.

deterrent [dɪ'terənt, Am dɪ'tɜːrənt] n Mil force f de dissuasion; **to be a d.** Fig être dissuasif.

detest [dɪ'test] vt détester (doing faire). ◆**—able** a détestable.

detonate ['detəneɪt] vt faire détoner or exploser; – vi détoner. ◆**deto'nation** n détonation f. ◆**detonator** n détonateur m.

detour ['diːtuər] n détour m.

detract [dɪ'trækt] vi **to d. from** (make less) diminuer. ◆**detractor** n détracteur, -trice mf.

detriment ['detrɪmənt] n détriment m. ◆**detri'mental** a préjudiciable (**to** à).

devalue [diː'væljuː] vt (money) & Fig dévaluer. ◆**devalu'ation** n dévaluation f.

devastat/e ['devəsteɪt] vt (lay waste) dévaster; (opponent) anéantir; (person) foudroyer. ◆**—ing** a (storm etc) dévastateur; (overwhelming) confondant, accablant; (charm) irrésistible.

develop [dɪ'veləp] vt développer; (area, land) mettre en valeur; (habit, illness) contracter; (talent) manifester; Phot développer; **to d. a liking for** prendre goût à; – vi se développer; (of event) se produire; **to d. into** devenir. ◆**—ing** a (country) en voie de développement; – n Phot développement m. ◆**—er** n (property) **d.** promoteur m (de construction).

◆**—ment** n développement m; (of land) mise f en valeur; (housing) **d.** lotissement m; (large) grand ensemble m; **a (new) d.** (in situation) un fait nouveau.

deviate ['diːvɪeɪt] vi dévier (**from** de); **to d. from the norm** s'écarter de la norme. ◆**deviant** a anormal. ◆**devi'ation** n déviation f.

device [dɪ'vaɪs] n dispositif m, engin m; (scheme) procédé m; **left to one's own devices** livré à soi-même.

devil ['dev(ə)l] n diable m; **a or the d. of a problem** Fam un problème épouvantable; **a or the d. of a noise** Fam un bruit infernal; **I had a or the d. of a job** Fam j'ai eu un mal fou (**doing, to do** à faire); **what/where/why the d.?** Fam que/où/pourquoi diable?; **like the d.** (to run etc) comme un fou. ◆**devilish** a diabolique. ◆**devilry** n (mischief) diablerie f.

devious ['diːvɪəs] a (mind, behaviour) tortueux; **he's d.** il a l'esprit tortueux. ◆**—ness** n (of person) esprit m tortueux.

devise [dɪ'vaɪz] vt (plan) combiner; (plot) tramer; (invent) inventer.

devitalize [diː'vaɪtəlaɪz] vt rendre exsangue, affaiblir.

devoid [dɪ'vɔɪd] a **d. of** dénué or dépourvu de; (guilt) exempt de.

devolution [diːvə'luːʃ(ə)n] n Pol décentralisation f; **the d. of** (power) la délégation de.

devolve [dɪ'vɒlv] vi **to d. upon** incomber à.

devot/e [dɪ'vəʊt] vt consacrer (**to** à). ◆**—ed** a dévoué; (admirer) fervent. ◆**—edly** adv avec dévouement. ◆**devo'tee** n Sp Mus passionné, -ée mf. ◆**devotion** n dévouement m; (religious) dévotion f; pl (prayers) dévotions fpl.

devour [dɪ'vaʊər] vt (eat, engulf, read etc) dévorer.

devout [dɪ'vaʊt] a dévot, pieux; (supporter, prayer) fervent.

dew [djuː] n rosée f. ◆**dewdrop** n goutte f de rosée.

dext(e)rous ['dekst(ə)rəs] a adroit, habile. ◆**dex'terity** n adresse f, dextérité f.

diabetes [daɪə'biːtiːz] n Med diabète m. ◆**diabetic** a & n diabétique (mf).

diabolical [daɪə'bɒlɪk(ə)l] a diabolique; (bad) épouvantable.

diadem ['daɪədem] n diadème m.

diagnosis, pl **-oses** [daɪəg'nəʊsɪs, -əʊsiːz] n diagnostic m. ◆**'diagnose** vt diagnostiquer.

diagonal [daɪ'ægən(ə)l] a diagonal; – n (line) diagonale f. ◆**—ly** adv en diagonale.

diagram ['daɪəgræm] n schéma m,

diagramme *m*; *Geom* figure *f*. ◆**dia-gra'mmatic** *a* schématique.

dial ['daɪəl] *n* cadran *m*; — *vt* (-**ll**-, *Am* -**l**-) (*number*) *Tel* faire, composer; (*person*) appeler; **to d. s.o. direct** appeler qn par l'automatique; **d. tone** *Am* tonalité *f*. ◆**dialling** *a* **d. code** indicatif *m*; **d. tone** tonalité *f*.

dialect ['daɪəlekt] *n* (*regional*) dialecte *m*; (*rural*) patois *m*.

dialogue ['daɪəlɒg] (*Am* **dialog**) *n* dialogue *m*.

dialysis, pl -yses [daɪ'ælɪsɪs, -ɪsiːz] *n Med* dialyse *f*.

diameter [daɪ'æmɪtər] *n* diamètre *m*. ◆**dia-'metrically** *adv* (*opposed*) diamétralement.

diamond ['daɪəmənd] **1** *n* (*stone*) diamant *m*; (*shape*) losange *m*; (**baseball**) **d.** *Am* terrain *m* (de baseball); **d. necklace/**etc rivière *f*/etc de diamants. **2** *n* & *npl* Cards carreau *m*.

diaper ['daɪəpər] *n* (*for baby*) *Am* couche *f*.

diaphragm ['daɪəfræm] *n* diaphragme *m*.

diarrh(o)ea [daɪə'riːə] *n* diarrhée *f*.

diary ['daɪərɪ] *n* (*calendar*) agenda *m*; (*private*) journal *m* (intime).

dice [daɪs] *n inv* dé *m* (à jouer); — *vt* Culin couper en dés.

dicey ['daɪsɪ] *a* (-**ier**, -**iest**) *Fam* risqué.

dichotomy [daɪ'kɒtəmɪ] *n* dichotomie *f*.

dickens ['dɪkɪnz] *n* **where/why/what the d.?** *Fam* où/pourquoi/que diable?

dictate [dɪk'teɪt] *vt* dicter (**to** à); — *vi* dicter; **to d. to s.o.** (*order around*) régenter qn. ◆**dictation** *n* dictée *f*. ◆'**dictaphone**® *n* dictaphone® *m*.

dictates ['dɪkteɪts] *npl* préceptes *mpl*; **the d. of conscience** la voix de la conscience.

dictator [dɪk'teɪtər] *n* dictateur *m*. ◆**dicta-'torial** *a* dictatorial. ◆**dictatorship** *n* dictature *f*.

diction ['dɪkʃ(ə)n] *n* langage *m*; (*way of speaking*) diction *f*.

dictionary ['dɪkʃənərɪ] *n* dictionnaire *m*.

dictum ['dɪktəm] *n* dicton *m*.

did [dɪd] *see* do.

diddle ['dɪd(ə)l] *vt Sl* rouler; **to d. s.o. out of sth** carotter qch à qn; **to get diddled out of sth** se faire refaire de qch.

die [daɪ] **1** *vi* (*pt* & *pp* **died**, *pres p* **dying**) mourir (**of**, **from** de); **to be dying to do** *Fam* mourir d'envie de faire; **to be dying for sth** *Fam* avoir une envie folle de qch; **to d. away** (*of noise*) mourir; **to d. down** (*of fire*) mourir; (*of storm*) se calmer; **to d. off** mourir (les uns après les autres); **to d. out** (*of custom*) mourir. **2** *n* (*in engraving*) coin

m; *Tech* matrice *f*; **the d. is cast** *Fig* les dés sont jetés.

diehard ['daɪhɑːd] *n* réactionnaire *mf*.

diesel ['diːzəl] *a* & *n* **d. (engine)** (moteur *m*) diesel *m*; **d. (oil)** gazole *m*.

diet ['daɪət] *n* (*for slimming*) régime *m*; (*usual food*) alimentation *f*; **to go on a d.** faire un régime; — *vi* suivre un régime. ◆**dietary** *a* diététique; **d. fibre** fibre(s) *f*(*pl*) alimentaire(s). ◆**die'tician** *n* diététicien, -ienne *mf*.

differ ['dɪfər] *vi* différer (**from** de); (*disagree*) ne pas être d'accord (avec). ◆**differ-ence** *n* différence *f* (**in** de); (*in age, weight etc*) écart *m*, différence *f*; **d. (of opinion)** différend *m*; **it makes no d.** ça n'a pas d'importance; **it makes no d. to me** ça m'est égal; **to make a d. in sth** changer qch. ◆**different** *a* différent (**from, to** de); (*another*) autre; (*various*) différents, divers. ◆**diffe-'rential** *a* différentiel; — *npl* Econ écarts *mpl* salariaux. ◆**diffe'rentiate** *vt* diffé-rencier (**from** de); **to d. (between)** faire la différence entre. ◆**differently** *adv* diffé-remment (**from, to** de), autrement (**from, to** que).

difficult ['dɪfɪkəlt] *a* difficile (**to do** à faire); **it's d. for us to . . .** il nous est difficile de . . . ; **the d. thing is to . . .** le plus difficile est de . . . . ◆**difficulty** *n* difficulté *f*; **to have d. doing** avoir du mal à faire; **to be in d.** avoir des difficultés; **d. with** des ennuis *mpl* avec.

diffident ['dɪfɪdənt] *a* (*person*) qui manque d'assurance; (*smile, tone*) mal assuré. ◆**diffidence** *n* manque *m* d'assurance.

diffuse [dɪ'fjuːz] *vt* (*spread*) diffuser; — [dɪ'fjuːs] *a* (*spread out, wordy*) diffus. ◆**diffusion** *n* diffusion *f*.

dig [dɪg] *vt* (*pt* & *pp* **dug**, *pres p* **digging**) (*ground*) bêcher; (*hole, grave etc*) creuser; (*understand*) *Sl* piger; (*appreciate*) *Sl* aimer; **to d. sth into** (*thrust*) enfoncer qch dans; **to d. out** (*animal, fact*) déterrer; (*accident victim*) dégager; (*find*) *Fam* dénicher; **to d. up** (*weed*) arracher; (*earth*) retourner; (*street*) piocher; — *vi* creuser; (*of pig*) fouiller; **to d. (oneself) in** *Mil* se retrancher; **to d. in** (*eat*) *Fam* manger; **to d. into** (*s.o.'s past*) fouiller dans; (*meal*) *Fam* attaquer; — *n* (*with spade*) coup *m* de bêche; (*push*) coup *m* de poing *or* de coude; (*remark*) *Fam* coup *m* de griffe. ◆**digger** *n* (*machine*) pelleteuse *f*.

digest [daɪ'dʒest] *vti* digérer; — ['daɪdʒest] *n* *Journ* condensé *m*. ◆**digestible** *a* digeste.

◆**digestion** n digestion f. ◆**digestive** a digestif.

digit ['dɪdʒɪt] n (number) chiffre m. ◆**digital** a (watch, keyboard etc) numérique.

dignified ['dɪgnɪfaɪd] a digne, qui a de la dignité. ◆**dignify** vt donner de la dignité à; **to d. with** the name of honorer du nom de. ◆**dignitary** n dignitaire m. ◆**dignity** n dignité f.

digress [daɪ'gres] vi faire une digression; **to d. from** s'écarter de. ◆**digression** n digression f.

digs [dɪgz] npl Fam chambre f (meublée), logement m.

dilapidated [dɪ'læpɪdeɪtɪd] a (house) délabré. ◆**dilapi'dation** n délabrement m.

dilate [daɪ'leɪt] vt dilater; – vi se dilater. ◆**dilation** n dilatation f.

dilemma [daɪ'lemə] n dilemme m.

dilettante [dɪlɪ'tæntɪ] n dilettante mf.

diligent ['dɪlɪdʒənt] a assidu, appliqué; **to be d. in doing sth** faire qch avec zèle. ◆**diligence** n zèle m, assiduité f.

dilly-dally [dɪlɪ'dælɪ] vi Fam (dawdle) lambiner, lanterner; (hesitate) tergiverser.

dilute [daɪ'luːt] vt diluer; – a dilué.

dim [dɪm] a (dimmer, dimmest) (feeble) faible; (colour) terne; (room) sombre; (memory, outline) vague; (person) stupide; – vt (-mm-) (light) baisser, réduire; (glory) ternir; (memory) estomper. ◆**—ly** adv faiblement; (vaguely) vaguement. ◆**—ness** n faiblesse f; (of memory etc) vague m; (of room) pénombre f. ◆**dimwit** n idiot, -ote mf. ◆**dim'witted** a idiot.

dime [daɪm] n (US & Can coin) (pièce f de) dix cents mpl; **a d. store** = un Prisunic®, un Monoprix®.

dimension [daɪ'menʃ(ə)n] n dimension f; (extent) Fig étendue f. ◆**dimensional** a **two-d.** à deux dimensions.

diminish [dɪ'mɪnɪʃ] vti diminuer. ◆**—ing** a qui diminue.

diminutive [dɪ'mɪnjʊtɪv] **1** a (tiny) minuscule. **2** a & n Gram diminutif (m).

dimple ['dɪmp(ə)l] n fossette f. ◆**dimpled** a (chin, cheek) à fossettes.

din [dɪn] n **1** (noise) vacarme m. **2** vt (-nn-) **to d. into s.o. that** rabâcher à qn que.

din/e [daɪn] vi dîner (off, on de); **to d. out** dîner en ville. ◆**—ing** a **d. car** Rail wagon-restaurant m; **d. room** salle f à manger. ◆**—er** n dîneur, -euse mf; Rail wagon-restaurant m; (short-order restaurant) Am petit restaurant m.

ding(dong)! ['dɪŋ(dɒŋ)] int (of bell) dring!, ding (dong)!

dinghy ['dɪŋgɪ] n petit canot m, youyou m; (rubber) **d.** canot m pneumatique.

dingy ['dɪndʒɪ] a (-ier, -iest) (dirty) malpropre; (colour) terne. ◆**dinginess** n malpropreté f.

dinner ['dɪnər] n (evening meal) dîner m; (lunch) déjeuner m; (for dog, cat) pâtée f; **to have d.** dîner; **to have s.o. to d.** avoir qn à dîner; **d. dance** dîner-dansant m; **d. jacket** smoking m; **d. party** dîner m (à la maison); **d. plate** grande assiette f; **d. service**, **d. set** service m de table.

dinosaur ['daɪnəsɔːr] n dinosaure m.

dint [dɪnt] n **by d. of** à force de.

diocese ['daɪəsɪs] n Rel diocèse m.

dip [dɪp] vt (-pp-) plonger; (into liquid) tremper, plonger; **to d. one's headlights** se mettre en code; – vi (of sun etc) baisser; (of road) plonger; **to d. into** (pocket, savings) puiser dans; (book) feuilleter; – n (in road) déclivité f; **to go for a d.** faire trempette.

diphtheria [dɪp'θɪərɪə] n diphtérie f.

diphthong ['dɪfθɒŋ] n Ling diphtongue f.

diploma [dɪ'pləʊmə] n diplôme m.

diplomacy [dɪ'pləʊməsɪ] n (tact) & Pol diplomatie f. ◆**diplomat** n diplomate mf. ◆**diplo'matic** a diplomatique; **to be d.** (tactful) Fig être diplomate.

dipper ['dɪpər] n **the big d.** (at fairground) les montagnes fpl russes.

dire ['daɪər] a affreux; (poverty, need) extrême.

direct [daɪ'rekt] **1** a (result, flight, person etc) direct; (danger) immédiat; – adv directement. **2** vt (work, one's steps, one's attention) diriger; (letter, remark) adresser (**to** à); (efforts) orienter (**to, towards** vers); (film) réaliser; (play) mettre en scène; **to d. s.o. to** (place) indiquer à qn le chemin de; **to d. s.o. to do** charger qn de faire. ◆**direction** n direction f, sens m; (management) direction f; (of film) réalisation f; (of play) mise f en scène; pl (orders) indications fpl; **directions (for use)** mode m d'emploi; **in the opposite d.** en sens inverse. ◆**directive** [dɪ'rektɪv] n directive f. ◆**directly** adv (without detour) directement; (at once) tout de suite; (to speak) franchement; – conj Fam aussitôt que. ◆**directness** n (of reply) franchise f. ◆**director** n directeur, -trice mf; (of film) réalisateur, -trice mf; (of play) metteur m en scène. ◆**directorship** n Com poste m de directeur.

directory [daɪ'rektərɪ] n Tel annuaire m; (of

streets) guide *m*; (*of addresses*) répertoire *m*; **d. enquiries** *Tel* renseignements *mpl*.

dirge [dɜːdʒ] *n* chant *m* funèbre.

dirt [dɜːt] *n* saleté *f*; (*filth*) ordure *f*; (*mud*) boue *f*; (*earth*) terre *f*; (*talk*) *Fig* obscénité(s) *f*(*pl*); **d. cheap** *Fam* très bon marché; **d. road** chemin *m* de terre; **d. track** *Sp* cendrée *f*. ◆**dirty** *a* (**-ier, -iest**) sale; (*job*) salissant; (*obscene, unpleasant*) sale; (*word*) grossier, obscène; **to get d.** se salir; **to get sth d.** salir qch; **a d. joke** une histoire cochonne; **a d. trick** un sale tour; **a d. old man** un vieux cochon; – *adv* (*to fight*) déloyalement; – *vt* salir; (*machine*) encrasser; – *vi* se salir.

disabl/e [dɪsˈeɪb(ə)l] *vt* rendre infirme; (*maim*) mutiler. ◆**-ed** *a* infirme, handicapé; (*maimed*) mutilé; – *n* **the d.** les infirmes *mpl*, les handicapés *mpl*. ◆**disa-'bility** *n* infirmité *f*; *Fig* désavantage *m*.

disadvantage [dɪsədˈvɑːntɪdʒ] *n* désavantage *m*; – *vt* désavantager.

disaffected [dɪsəˈfektɪd] *a* mécontent. ◆**disaffection** *n* désaffection *f* (**for** pour).

disagree [dɪsəˈɡriː] *vi* ne pas être d'accord, être en désaccord (**with** avec); (*of figures*) ne pas concorder; **to d. with** (*of food etc*) ne pas réussir à. ◆**-able** *a* désagréable. ◆**-ment** *n* désaccord *m*; (*quarrel*) différend *m*.

disallow [dɪsəˈlaʊ] *vt* rejeter.

disappear [dɪsəˈpɪər] *vi* disparaître. ◆**disappearance** *n* disparition *f*.

disappoint [dɪsəˈpɔɪnt] *vt* décevoir; **I'm disappointed with it** ça m'a déçu. ◆**-ing** *a* décevant. ◆**-ment** *n* déception *f*.

disapprov/e [dɪsəˈpruːv] *vi* **to d. of s.o./sth** désapprouver qn/qch; **I d.** je suis contre. ◆**-ing** *a* (*look etc*) désapprobateur. ◆**disapproval** *n* désapprobation *f*.

disarm [dɪsˈɑːm] *vti* désarmer. ◆**disarmament** *n* désarmement *m*.

disarray [dɪsəˈreɪ] *n* (*disorder*) désordre *m*; (*distress*) désarroi *m*.

disaster [dɪˈzɑːstər] *n* désastre *m*, catastrophe *f*; **d. area** région *f* sinistrée. ◆**d.-stricken** *a* sinistré. ◆**disastrous** *a* désastreux.

disband [dɪsˈbænd] *vt* disperser; – *vi* se disperser.

disbelief [dɪsbəˈliːf] *n* incrédulité *f*.

disc [dɪsk] (*Am* **disk**) *n* disque *m*; **identity d.** plaque *f* d'identité; **d. jockey** animateur, -trice *mf* (*de variétés etc*), disc-jockey *m*.

discard [dɪsˈkɑːd] *vt* (*get rid of*) se débarrasser de; (*plan, hope etc*) *Fig* abandonner.

discern [dɪˈsɜːn] *vt* discerner. ◆**-ing** *a*

(*person*) averti, sagace. ◆**-ible** *a* perceptible. ◆**-ment** *n* discernement *m*.

discharge [dɪsˈtʃɑːdʒ] *vt* (*gun, accused person*) décharger; (*liquid*) déverser; (*patient, employee*) renvoyer; (*soldier*) libérer; (*unfit soldier*) réformer; (*one's duty*) accomplir; – *vi* (*of wound*) suppurer; – [ˈdɪstʃɑːdʒ] *n* (*of gun*) & *El* décharge *f*; (*of liquid*) & *Med* écoulement *m*; (*dismissal*) renvoi *m*; (*freeing*) libération *f*; (*of unfit soldier*) réforme *f*.

disciple [dɪˈsaɪp(ə)l] *n* disciple *m*.

discipline [ˈdɪsɪplɪn] *n* (*behaviour, subject*) discipline *f*; – *vt* (*control*) discipliner; (*punish*) punir. ◆**disci'plinarian** *n* partisan, -ane *mf* de la discipline; **to be a (strict) d.** être très à cheval sur la discipline. ◆**disci'plinary** *a* disciplinaire.

disclaim [dɪsˈkleɪm] *vt* désavouer; (*responsibility*) (dé)nier.

disclose [dɪsˈkləʊz] *vt* révéler, divulguer. ◆**disclosure** *n* révélation *f*.

disco [ˈdɪskəʊ] *n* (*pl* **-os**) *Fam* disco(thèque) *f*.

discolour [dɪsˈkʌlər] *vt* décolorer; (*teeth*) jaunir; – *vi* se décolorer; jaunir. ◆**discolo(u)ration** *n* décoloration *f*; jaunissement *m*.

discomfort [dɪsˈkʌmfət] *n* (*physical, mental*) malaise *m*, gêne *f*; (*hardship*) inconvénient *m*.

disconcert [dɪskənˈsɜːt] *vt* déconcerter.

disconnect [dɪskəˈnekt] *vt* (*unfasten etc*) détacher; (*unplug*) débrancher; (*wires*) *El* déconnecter; (*gas, telephone etc*) couper. ◆**-ed** *a* (*speech*) décousu.

discontent [dɪskənˈtent] *n* mécontentement *m*. ◆**discontented** *a* mécontent.

discontinu/e [dɪskənˈtɪnjuː] *vt* cesser, interrompre. ◆**-ed** *a* (*article*) *Com* qui ne se fait plus.

discord [ˈdɪskɔːd] *n* discorde *f*; *Mus* dissonance *f*.

discotheque [ˈdɪskətek] *n* (*club*) discothèque *f*.

discount 1 [ˈdɪskaʊnt] *n* (*on article*) remise *f*; (*on account paid early*) escompte *m*; **at à d.** (*to buy, sell*) au rabais; **d. store** solderie *f*. **2** [dɪsˈkaʊnt] *vt* (*story etc*) ne pas tenir compte de.

discourage [dɪsˈkʌrɪdʒ] *vt* décourager; **to get discouraged** se décourager. ◆**-ment** *n* découragement *m*.

discourse [ˈdɪskɔːs] *n* discours *m*.

discourteous [dɪsˈkɜːtɪəs] *a* impoli, discourtois. ◆**discourtesy** *n* impolitesse *f*.

discover [dɪsˈkʌvər] *vt* découvrir. ◆**discovery** *n* découverte *f*.

discredit [dɪs'kredɪt] *vt* (*cast slur on*) discréditer; (*refuse to believe*) ne pas croire; − *n* discrédit *m*. ◆**—able** *a* indigne.

discreet [dɪ'skriːt] *a* (*careful*) prudent, avisé; (*unassuming, reserved etc*) discret. ◆**discretion** *n* prudence *f*; discrétion *f*; **I'll use my own d.** je ferai comme bon me semblera. ◆**discretionary** *a* discrétionnaire.

discrepancy [dɪ'skrepənsɪ] *n* divergence *f*, contradiction *f* (**between** entre).

discriminat/e [dɪ'skrɪmɪneɪt] *vi* **to d. between** distinguer entre; **to d. against** établir une discrimination contre; − *vt* **to d. sth/s.o. from** distinguer qch/qn de. ◆**—ing** *a* (*person*) averti, sagace; (*ear*) fin. ◆**discrimi'nation** *n* (*judgement*) discernement *m*; (*distinction*) distinction *f*; (*partiality*) discrimination *f*. ◆**discriminatory** [-ətərɪ] *a* discriminatoire.

discus ['dɪskəs] *n Sp* disque *m*.

discuss [dɪ'skʌs] *vt* (*talk about*) discuter de; (*examine in detail*) discuter. ◆**discussion** *n* discussion *f*; **under d.** (*matter etc*) en question, en discussion.

disdain [dɪs'deɪn] *vt* dédaigner; − *n* dédain *m*. ◆**disdainful** *a* dédaigneux; **to be d. of** dédaigner.

disease [dɪ'ziːz] *n* maladie *f*. ◆**diseased** *a* malade.

disembark [dɪsɪm'bɑːk] *vti* débarquer. ◆**disembar'kation** *n* débarquement *m*.

disembodied [dɪsɪm'bɒdɪd] *a* désincarné.

disembowel [dɪsɪm'bauəl] *vt* (**-ll-**, *Am* **-l-**) éventrer.

disenchant [dɪsɪn'tʃɑːnt] *vt* désenchanter. ◆**—ment** *n* désenchantement *m*.

disengage [dɪsɪn'geɪdʒ] *vt* (*object*) dégager; (*troops*) désengager.

disentangle [dɪsɪn'tæŋg(ə)l] *vt* démêler; **to d. oneself from** se dégager de.

disfavour [dɪs'feɪvər] *n* défaveur *f*.

disfigure [dɪs'fɪgər] *vt* défigurer. ◆**—ment** *n* défigurement *m*.

disgorge [dɪs'gɔːdʒ] *vt* (*food*) vomir.

disgrac/e [dɪs'greɪs] *n* (*shame*) honte *f* (**to** à); (*disfavour*) disgrâce *f*; − *vt* déshonorer, faire honte à. ◆**—ed** *a* (*politician etc*) disgracié. ◆**disgraceful** *a* honteux (**of s.o.** de la part de qn). ◆**disgracefully** *adv* honteusement.

disgruntled [dɪs'grʌnt(ə)ld] *a* mécontent.

disguise [dɪs'gaɪz] *vt* déguiser (**as en**); − *n* déguisement *m*; **in d.** déguisé.

disgust [dɪs'gʌst] *n* dégoût *m* (**for, at, with** de); **in d.** dégoûté; − *vt* dégoûter, écœurer. ◆**—ed** *a* dégoûté (**at, by, with** de); **to be d. with s.o.** (*annoyed*) être fâché contre qn; **d.**

to hear that . . . indigné d'apprendre que . . . . ◆**—ing** *a* dégoûtant, écœurant. ◆**—ingly** *adv* d'une façon dégoûtante.

dish [dɪʃ] **1** *n* (*container*) plat *m*; (*food*) mets *m*, plat *m*; **the dishes** la vaisselle; **she's a (real) d.** *Sl* c'est un beau brin de fille. **2** *vt* **to d. out** distribuer; **to d. out** *or* **up** (*food*) servir. ◆**dishcloth** *n* (*for washing*) lavette *f*; (*for drying*) torchon *m*. ◆**dishpan** *n Am* bassine *f* (à vaisselle). ◆**dishwasher** *n* lave-vaisselle *m inv*.

disharmony [dɪs'hɑːmənɪ] *n* désaccord *m*; *Mus* dissonance *f*.

dishearten [dɪs'hɑːt(ə)n] *vt* décourager.

dishevelled [dɪ'ʃevəld] *a* hirsute, échevelé.

dishonest [dɪs'ɒnɪst] *a* malhonnête; (*insincere*) de mauvaise foi. ◆**dishonesty** *n* malhonnêteté *f*; mauvaise foi *f*.

dishonour [dɪs'ɒnər] *n* déshonneur *m*; − *vt* déshonorer; (*cheque*) refuser d'honorer. ◆**—able** *a* peu honorable. ◆**—ably** *adv* avec déshonneur.

dishy ['dɪʃɪ] *a* (**-ier, -iest**) (*woman, man*) *Sl* beau, sexy, qui a du chien.

disillusion [dɪsɪ'luːʒ(ə)n] *vt* désillusionner; − *n* désillusion *f*. ◆**—ment** *n* désillusion *f*.

disincentive [dɪsɪn'sentɪv] *n* mesure *f* dissuasive; **to be a d. to s.o.** décourager qn; **it's a d. to work/invest/***etc* cela n'encourage pas à travailler/investir/*etc*.

disinclined [dɪsɪn'klaɪnd] *a* peu disposé (**to** à). ◆**disincli'nation** *n* répugnance *f*.

disinfect [dɪsɪn'fekt] *vt* désinfecter. ◆**disinfectant** *a* & *n* désinfectant (*m*). ◆**disinfection** *n* désinfection *f*.

disinherit [dɪsɪn'herɪt] *vt* déshériter.

disintegrate [dɪs'ɪntɪgreɪt] *vi* se désintégrer; − *vt* désintégrer. ◆**disinte'gration** *n* désintégration *f*.

disinterested [dɪs'ɪntrɪstɪd] *a* (*impartial*) désintéressé; (*uninterested*) *Fam* indifférent (**in** à).

disjointed [dɪs'dʒɔɪntɪd] *a* décousu.

disk [dɪsk] *n* **1** *Am* = **disc. 2** (**magnetic**) **d.** (*of computer*) disque *m* (magnétique).

dislike [dɪs'laɪk] *vt* ne pas aimer (**doing** faire); **he doesn't d. it** ça ne lui déplaît pas; − *n* aversion *f* (**for, of** pour); **to take a d. to** (*person, thing*) prendre en grippe; **our likes and dislikes** nos goûts et dégoûts *mpl*.

dislocate ['dɪsləkeɪt] *vt* (*limb*) disloquer; *Fig* désorganiser. ◆**dislo'cation** *n* dislocation *f*.

dislodge [dɪs'lɒdʒ] *vt* faire bouger, déplacer; (*enemy*) déloger.

disloyal [dɪs'lɔɪəl] *a* déloyal. ◆**disloyalty** *n* déloyauté *f*.

dismal ['dızməl] *a* morne, triste. **◆—ly** *adv* (*to fail, behave*) lamentablement.

dismantle [dıs'mænt(ə)l] *vt* (*machine etc*) démonter; (*organization*) démanteler.

dismay [dıs'meı] *vt* consterner; — *n* consternation *f*.

dismember [dıs'membər] *vt* (*country etc*) démembrer.

dismiss [dıs'mıs] *vt* congédier, renvoyer (**from** de); (*official*) destituer; (*appeal*) *Jur* rejeter; (*thought etc*) *Fig* écarter; **d.!** *Mil* rompez!; (*class*) **d.!** *Sch* vous pouvez partir. **◆dismissal** *n* renvoi *m*; destitution *f*.

dismount [dıs'maunt] *vi* descendre (**from** de); — *vt* (*rider*) démonter, désarçonner.

disobey [dısə'beı] *vt* désobéir à; — *vi* désobéir. **◆disobedience** *n* désobéissance *f*. **◆disobedient** *a* désobéissant.

disorder [dıs'ɔːdər] *n* (*confusion*) désordre *m*; (*riots*) désordres *mpl*; **disorder(s)** *Med* troubles *mpl*. **◆disorderly** *a* (*meeting etc*) désordonné.

disorganize [dıs'ɔːgənaız] *vt* désorganiser.

disorientate [dıs'ɔːrıənteıt] (*Am* **disorient** [dıs'ɔːrıənt]) *vt* désorienter.

disown [dıs'əun] *vt* désavouer, renier.

disparag/e [dıs'pærıdʒ] *vt* dénigrer. **◆—ing** *a* peu flatteur.

disparate ['dıspərət] *a* disparate. **◆dis'parity** *n* disparité *f* (**between** entre, de).

dispassionate [dıs'pæʃənət] *a* (*unemotional*) calme; (*not biased*) impartial.

dispatch [dıs'pætʃ] *vt* (*letter, work*) expédier; (*troops, messenger*) envoyer; — *n* expédition *f* (**of** de); *Journ Mil* dépêche *f*; **d. rider** *Mil etc* courrier *m*.

dispel [dıs'pel] *vt* (**-ll-**) dissiper.

dispensary [dıs'pensərı] *n* (*in hospital*) pharmacie *f*; (*in chemist's shop*) officine *f*.

dispense [dıs'pens] **1** *vt* (*give out*) distribuer; (*justice*) administrer; (*medicine*) préparer. **2** *vi* **to d. with** (*do without*) se passer de; **to d. with the need for** rendre superflu. **◆dispen'sation** *n* distribution *f*; **special d.** (*exemption*) dérogation *f*. **◆dispenser** *n* (*device*) distributeur *m*; **cash d.** distributeur *m* de billets.

disperse [dı'spɜːs] *vt* disperser; — *vi* se disperser. **◆dispersal** *n*, **◆dispersion** *n* dispersion *f*.

dispirited [dı'spırıtıd] *a* découragé.

displace [dıs'pleıs] *vt* (*bone, furniture, refugees*) déplacer; (*replace*) supplanter.

display [dı'spleı] *vt* montrer; (*notice, electronic data etc*) afficher; (*painting, goods*) exposer; (*courage etc*) faire preuve de; — *n*

(*in shop*) étalage *m*; (*of force*) déploiement *m*; (*of anger etc*) manifestation *f*; (*of paintings*) exposition *f*; (*of luxury*) étalage *m*; *Mil* parade *f*; (*of electronic data*) affichage *m*; **d. (unit)** (*of computer*) moniteur *m*; **on d.** exposé; **air d.** fête *f* aéronautique.

displeas/e [dıs'pliːz] *vt* déplaire à. **◆—ed** *a* mécontent (**with** de). **◆—ing** *a* désagréable. **◆displeasure** *n* mécontentement *m*.

dispos/e [dı'spəuz] *vt* disposer (**s.o. to do** qn à faire); — *vi* **to d. of** (*get rid of*) se débarrasser de; (*one's time, money*) disposer de; (*sell*) vendre; (*matter*) expédier, liquider; (*kill*) liquider. **◆—ed** *a* disposé (**to do** à faire); **well-d. towards** bien disposé envers. **◆—able** *a* (*plate etc*) à jeter, jetable; (*income*) disponible. **◆disposal** *n* (*sale*) vente *f*; (*of waste*) évacuation *f*; **at the d. of** à la disposition de. **◆dispo'sition** *n* (*placing*) disposition *f*; (*character*) naturel *m*; (*readiness*) inclination *f*.

dispossess [dıspə'zes] *vt* déposséder (**of** de).

disproportion [dısprə'pɔːʃ(ə)n] *n* disproportion *f*. **◆disproportionate** *a* disproportionné.

disprove [dıs'pruːv] *vt* réfuter.

dispute [dı'spjuːt] *n* discussion *f*; (*quarrel*) dispute *f*; *Pol* conflit *m*; *Jur* litige *m*; **beyond d.** incontestable; **in d.** (*matter*) en litige; (*territory*) contesté; — *vt* (*claim etc*) contester; (*discuss*) discuter.

disqualify [dıs'kwɒlıfaı] *vt* (*make unfit*) rendre inapte (**from** à); *Sp* disqualifier; **to d. from driving** retirer le permis à. **◆disqualifi'cation** *n* *Sp* disqualification *f*.

disquiet [dıs'kwaıət] *n* inquiétude *f*; — *vt* inquiéter.

disregard [dısrı'gaːd] *vt* ne tenir aucun compte de; — *n* indifférence *f* (**for** à); (*law*) désobéissance *f* (**for** à).

disrepair [dısrı'peər] *n* **in (a state of) d.** en mauvais état.

disreputable [dıs'repjutəb(ə)l] *a* peu recommandable; (*behaviour*) honteux.

disrepute [dısrı'pjuːt] *n* discrédit *m*; **to bring into d.** jeter le discrédit sur.

disrespect [dısrı'spekt] *n* manque *m* de respect. **◆disrespectful** *a* irrespectueux (**to** envers).

disrupt [dıs'rʌpt] *vt* perturber; (*communications*) interrompre; (*plan*) déranger. **◆disruption** *n* perturbation *f*; interruption *f*;

dérangement m. ◆**disruptive** a (element etc) perturbateur.

dissatisfied [dɪ'sætɪsfaɪd] a mécontent (with de). ◆**dissatis'faction** n mécontentement m.

dissect [daɪ'sekt] vt disséquer. ◆**dissection** n dissection f.

disseminate [dɪ'semɪneɪt] vt disséminer.

dissension [dɪ'senʃ(ə)n] n dissension f.

dissent [dɪ'sent] vi différer (d'opinion) (from sth à l'égard de qch); – n dissentiment m. ◆**—ing** a dissident.

dissertation [dɪsə'teɪʃ(ə)n] n Univ mémoire m.

dissident ['dɪsɪdənt] a & n dissident, -ente (mf). ◆**dissidence** n dissidence f.

dissimilar [dɪ'sɪmɪlər] a dissemblable (to à).

dissipate ['dɪsɪpeɪt] vt dissiper; (energy) gaspiller. ◆**dissi'pation** n dissipation f; gaspillage m.

dissociate [dɪ'səʊʃɪeɪt] vt dissocier (from de).

dissolute ['dɪsəluːt] a (life, person) dissolu.

dissolve [dɪ'zɒlv] vt dissoudre; – vi se dissoudre. ◆**disso'lution** n dissolution f.

dissuade [dɪ'sweɪd] vt dissuader (from doing de faire); to d. s.o. from sth détourner qn de qch. ◆**dissuasion** n dissuasion f.

distance ['dɪstəns] n distance f; in the d. au loin; from a d. de loin; at a d. à quelque distance; it's within walking d. on peut y aller à pied; to keep one's d. garder ses distances. ◆**distant** a éloigné, lointain; (relative) éloigné; (reserved) distant; 5 km d. from à (une distance de) 5 km de. ◆**distantly** adv we're d. related nous sommes parents éloignés.

distaste [dɪs'teɪst] n aversion f (for pour). ◆**distasteful** a désagréable, déplaisant.

distemper [dɪ'stempər] 1 n (paint) badigeon m; – vt badigeonner. 2 n (in dogs) maladie f.

distend [dɪ'stend] vt distendre; – vi se distendre.

distil [dɪ'stɪl] vt (-ll-) distiller. ◆**distil'lation** n distillation f. ◆**distillery** n distillerie f.

distinct [dɪ'stɪŋkt] a 1 (voice, light etc) distinct; (definite, marked) net, marqué; (promise) formel. 2 (different) distinct (from de). ◆**distinction** n distinction f; Univ mention f très bien; of d. (singer, writer etc) de marque. ◆**distinctive** a distinctif. ◆**distinctively** adv distinctement; (to stipulate, forbid) formellement; (noticeably) nettement, sensiblement; d. possible tout à fait possible.

distinguish [dɪ'stɪŋgwɪʃ] vti distinguer (from de, between entre); to d. oneself se distinguer (as en tant que). ◆**—ed** a distingué. ◆**—ing** a d. mark signe m particulier. ◆**—able** a qu'on peut distinguer; (discernible) visible.

distort [dɪ'stɔːt] vt déformer. ◆**—ed** a (false) faux. ◆**distortion** n El Med distorsion f; (of truth) déformation f.

distract [dɪ'strækt] vt distraire (from de). ◆**—ed** a (troubled) préoccupé; (mad with worry) éperdu. ◆**—ing** a (noise etc) gênant. ◆**distraction** n (lack of attention, amusement) distraction f; to drive to d. rendre fou.

distraught [dɪ'strɔːt] a éperdu, affolé.

distress [dɪ'stres] n (pain) douleur f; (anguish) chagrin m; (misfortune, danger) détresse f; in d. (ship, soul) en détresse; in (great) d. (poverty) dans la détresse; – vt affliger, peiner. ◆**—ing** a affligeant, pénible.

distribute [dɪ'strɪbjuːt] vt distribuer; (spread evenly) répartir. ◆**distri'bution** n distribution f; répartition f. ◆**distributor** n Aut Cin distributeur m; (of goods) Com concessionnaire mf.

district ['dɪstrɪkt] n région f; (of town) quartier m; (administrative) arrondissement m; d. attorney Am = procureur m (de la République); d. nurse infirmière f visiteuse.

distrust [dɪs'trʌst] vt se méfier de; – n méfiance f (of de). ◆**distrustful** a méfiant; to be d. of se méfier de.

disturb [dɪ'stɜːb] vt (sleep, water) troubler; (papers, belongings) déranger; to d. s.o. (bother) déranger qn; (alarm, worry) troubler qn. ◆**—ed** a (person etc) Psy troublé. ◆**—ing** a (worrying) inquiétant; (annoying, irksome) gênant. ◆**disturbance** n (noise) tapage m; pl Pol troubles mpl.

disunity [dɪs'juːnɪtɪ] n désunion f.

disuse [dɪs'juːs] n to fall into d. tomber en désuétude. ◆**disused** [-'juːzd] a désaffecté.

ditch [dɪtʃ] 1 n fossé m. 2 vt Fam se débarrasser de.

dither ['dɪðər] vi Fam hésiter, tergiverser; to d. (around) (waste time) tourner en rond.

ditto ['dɪtəʊ] adv idem.

divan [dɪ'væn] n divan m.

div/e [daɪv] 1 vi (pt dived, Am dove [dəʊv]) plonger; (rush) se précipiter, se jeter; to d. for (pearls) pêcher; – n plongeon m; (of submarine) plongée f; (of aircraft) piqué m. 2 n (bar, club) Pej boui-boui m. ◆**—ing** n (*underwater*) plongée *f* sous-marine; **d. suit** scaphandre *m*; **d. board** plongeoir *m*. **◆—er** *n* plongeur, -euse *mf*; (*in suit*) scaphandrier *m*.

diverge [daɪˈvɜːdʒ] *vi* diverger (**from** de). **◆divergence** *n* divergence *f*. **◆divergent** *a* divergent.

diverse [daɪˈvɜːs] *a* divers. **◆diversify** *vt* diversifier; – *vi Econ* se diversifier. **◆diversity** *n* diversité *f*.

divert [daɪˈvɜːt] *vt* détourner (**from** de); (*traffic*) dévier; (*aircraft*) dérouter; (*amuse*) divertir. **◆diversion** *n Aut* déviation *f*; (*amusement*) divertissement *m*; *Mil* diversion *f*.

divest [daɪˈvest] *vt* **to d. of** (*power, rights*) priver de.

divide [dɪˈvaɪd] *vt* diviser (**into** en); **to d. (off) from** séparer de; **to d. up** (*money*) partager; **to d. one's time between** partager son temps entre; – *vi* se diviser. **◆—ed** *a* (*opinion*) partagé. **◆—ing** *a* **d. line** ligne *f* de démarcation.

dividend [ˈdɪvɪdənd] *n Math Fin* dividende *m*.

divine [dɪˈvaɪn] *a* divin. **◆divinity** *n* (*quality, deity*) divinité *f*; (*study*) théologie *f*.

division [dɪˈvɪʒ(ə)n] *n* division *f*; (*dividing object*) séparation *f*. **◆divisible** *a* divisible. **◆divisive** [-ˈvaɪsɪv] *a* qui sème la zizanie.

divorce [dɪˈvɔːs] *n* divorce *m*; – *vt* (*spouse*) divorcer d'avec; *Fig* séparer; – *vi* divorcer. **◆—ed** *a* divorcé (**from** d'avec); **to get d.** divorcer. **◆divorcee** [dɪvɔːˈsiː, *Am* dɪvɔːˈseɪ] *n* divorcé, -ée *mf*.

divulge [dɪˈvʌldʒ] *vt* divulguer.

DIY [diːaɪˈwaɪ] *n abbr* (*do-it-yourself*) bricolage *m*.

dizzy [ˈdɪzɪ] *a* (-**ier**, -**iest**) (*heights*) vertigineux; **to feel d.** avoir le vertige; **to make s.o. (feel) d.** donner le vertige à qn. **◆dizziness** *n* vertige *m*.

DJ [diːˈdʒeɪ] *abbr* = **disc jockey**.

do [duː] **1** *v aux* (*3rd person sing pres t* **does**; *pt* **did**; *pp* **done**; *pres p* **doing**) **do you know?** savez-vous?, est-ce que vous savez?; **I do not** *or* **don't see** je ne vois pas; **he did say so** (*emphasis*) il l'a bien dit; **do stay** reste donc; **you know him, don't you?** tu le connais, n'est-ce pas?; **better than I do** mieux que je ne le fais; **neither do I** moi non plus; **so do I** moi aussi; **oh, does he?** (*surprise*) ah oui?; **don't!** non! **2** *vt* faire; **to do nothing but sleep** ne faire que dormir; **what does she do?** (*in general*), **what is she doing?** (*now*) qu'est-ce qu'elle fait?, que

fait-elle?; **what have you done (with)** . . . ? qu'as-tu fait (de) . . . ?; **well done** (*congratulations*) bravo!; *Culin* bien cuit; **it's over and done (with)** c'est fini; **that'll do me** (*suit*) ça fera mon affaire; **I've been done** (*cheated*) *Fam* je me suis fait avoir; **I'll do you!** *Fam* je t'aurai!; **to do s.o. out of sth** escroquer qch à qn; **he's hard done by** on le traite durement; **I'm done (in)** (*tired*) *Sl* je suis claqué *or* vanné; **he's done for** *Fam* il est fichu; **to do in** (*kill*) *Sl* supprimer; **to do out** (*clean*) nettoyer; **to do over** (*redecorate*) refaire; **to do up** (*coat, button*) boutonner; (*zip*) fermer; (*house*) refaire; (*goods*) emballer; **do yourself up (well)!** (*wrap up*) couvre-toi (bien)! **3** *vi* (*get along*) aller, marcher; (*suit*) faire l'affaire, convenir; (*be enough*) suffire; (*finish*) finir; **how do you do?** (*introduction*) enchanté; (*greeting*) bonjour; **he did well** *or* **right to leave** il a bien fait de partir; **do as I do** fais comme moi; **to make do** se débrouiller; **to do away with sth/s.o.** supprimer qch/qn; **I could do with** (*need, want*) j'aimerais bien (avoir *or* prendre); **to do without** sth/s.o. se passer de qch/qn; **to have to do with** (*relate to*) avoir à voir avec; (*concern*) concerner; **anything doing?** *Fam* est-ce qu'il se passe quelque chose? **4** *n* (*pl* **dos** *or* **do's**) (*party*) soirée *f*, fête *f*; **the do's and don'ts** ce qu'il faut faire ou ne pas faire.

docile [ˈdəʊsaɪl] *a* docile.

dock [dɒk] **1** *n Nau* dock *m*; – *vi* (*in port*) relâcher; (*at quayside*) se mettre à quai; (*of spacecraft*) s'arrimer. **2** *n Jur* banc *m* des accusés. **3** *vt* (*wages*) rogner; **to d. sth from** (*wages*) retenir qch sur. **◆—er** *n* docker *m*. **◆dockyard** *n* chantier *m* naval.

docket [ˈdɒkɪt] *n* fiche *f*, bordereau *m*.

doctor [ˈdɒktər] **1** *n Med* médecin *m*, docteur *m*; *Univ* docteur *m*. **2** *vt* (*text, food*) altérer; (*cat*) *Fam* châtrer. **◆doctorate** *n* doctorat *m* (**in** ès, en).

doctrine [ˈdɒktrɪn] *n* doctrine *f*. **◆doctrinaire** *a* & *n Pej* doctrinaire (*mf*).

document [ˈdɒkjʊmənt] *n* document *m*; – [ˈdɒkjʊment] *vt* (*inform*) documenter; (*report in detail*) *Journ* accorder une large place à. **◆documentary** *a* & *n* documentaire (*m*).

doddering [ˈdɒdərɪŋ] *a* (*senile*) gâteux; (*shaky*) branlant.

dodge [dɒdʒ] *vt* (*question, acquaintance etc*) esquiver; (*pursuer*) échapper à; (*tax*) éviter de payer; – *vi* faire un saut (de côté); **to d. out of sight** s'esquiver; **to d. through**

(*crowd*) se faufiler dans; − *n* mouvement *m* de côté; (*trick*) *Fig* truc *m*, tour *m*.

dodgems ['dɒdʒəmz] *npl* autos *fpl* tamponneuses.

dodgy ['dɒdʒı] *a* (**-ier, -iest**) *Fam* (*tricky*) délicat; (*dubious*) douteux; (*unreliable*) peu sûr.

doe [dəu] *n* (*deer*) biche *f*.

doer ['duːər] *n Fam* personne *f* dynamique.

does [dʌz] *see* do.

dog [dɒg] **1** *n* chien *m*; (*person*) *Pej* type *m*; **d. biscuit** biscuit *m* or croquette *f* pour chien; **d. collar** *Fam* col *m* de pasteur; **d. days** canicule *f*. **2** *vt* (**-gg-**) (*follow*) poursuivre. ◆**d.-eared** *a* (*page etc*) écorné. ◆**d.-'tired** *a Fam* claqué, crevé. ◆**doggy** *n Fam* toutou *m*; **d. bag** (*in restaurant*) *Am* petit sac *m* pour emporter les restes.

dogged ['dɒgıd] *a* obstiné. ◆**—ly** *adv* obstinément.

dogma ['dɒgmə] *n* dogme *m*. ◆**dog'matic** *a* dogmatique. ◆**dogmatism** *n* dogmatisme *m*.

dogsbody ['dɒgzbɒdı] *n Pej* factotum *m*, sous-fifre *m*.

doily ['dɔılı] *n* napperon *m*.

doing ['duːıŋ] *n* **that's your d.** c'est toi qui as fait ça; **doings** *Fam* activités *fpl*, occupations *fpl*.

do-it-yourself [duːıtjə'self] *n* bricolage *m*; − *a* (*store, book*) de bricolage.

doldrums ['dɒldrəmz] *npl* **to be in the d.** (*of person*) avoir le cafard; (*of business*) être en plein marasme.

dole [dəul] **1** *n* **d. (money)** allocation *f* de chômage; **to go on the d.** s'inscrire au chômage. **2** *vt* **to d. out** distribuer au compte-gouttes.

doleful ['dəulfʊl] *a* morne, triste.

doll [dɒl] **1** *n* poupée *f*; (*girl*) *Fam* nana *f*; **doll's house,** *Am* **dollhouse** maison *f* de poupée. **2** *vt* **to d. up** *Fam* bichonner.

dollar ['dɒlər] *n* dollar *m*.

dollop ['dɒləp] *n* (*of food*) *Pej* gros morceau *m*.

dolphin ['dɒlfın] *n* (*sea animal*) dauphin *m*.

domain [dəu'meın] *n* (*land, sphere*) domaine *m*.

dome [dəum] *n* dôme *m*, coupole *f*.

domestic [də'mestık] *a* familial, domestique; (*animal*) domestique; (*trade, flight*) intérieur; (*product*) national; **d. science** arts *mpl* ménagers; **d. servant** domestique *mf*. ◆**domesticated** *a* habitué à la vie du foyer; (*animal*) domestiqué.

domicile ['dɒmısaıl] *n* domicile *m*.

dominant ['dɒmınənt] *a* dominant;

(*person*) dominateur. ◆**dominance** *n* prédominance *f*. ◆**dominate** *vti* dominer. ◆**domi'nation** *n* domination *f*. ◆**domi-'neering** *a* dominateur.

dominion [də'mınjən] *n* domination *f*; (*land*) territoire *m*; *Br Pol* dominion *m*.

domino ['dɒmınəu] *n* (*pl* **-oes**) domino *m*; *pl* (*game*) dominos *mpl*.

don [dɒn] **1** *n Br Univ* professeur *m*. **2** *vt* (**-nn-**) revêtir.

donate [dəu'neıt] *vt* faire don de; (*blood*) donner; − *vi* donner. ◆**donation** *n* don *m*.

done [dʌn] *see* do.

donkey ['dɒŋkı] *n* âne *m*; **for d.'s years** *Fam* depuis belle lurette, depuis un siècle; **d. work** travail *m* ingrat.

donor ['dəunər] *n* (*of blood, organ*) donneur, -euse *mf*.

doodle ['duːd(ə)l] *vi* griffonner.

doom [duːm] *n* ruine *f*; (*fate*) destin *m*; (*gloom*) *Fam* tristesse *f*; − *vt* condamner, destiner (**to** à); **to be doomed (to failure)** être voué à l'échec.

door [dɔːr] *n* porte *f*; (*of vehicle, train*) portière *f*, porte *f*; **out of doors** dehors; **d.-to-door salesman** démarcheur *m*. ◆**doorbell** *n* sonnette *f*. ◆**doorknob** *n* poignée *f* de porte. ◆**doorknocker** *n* marteau *m*. ◆**doorman** *n* (*pl* **-men**) (*of hotel etc*) portier *m*, concierge *m*. ◆**doormat** *n* paillasson *m*. ◆**doorstep** *n* seuil *m*. ◆**doorstop(per)** *n* butoir *m* (de porte). ◆**doorway** *n* **in the d.** dans l'encadrement de la porte.

dope [dəup] **1** *n Fam* drogue *f*; (*for horse, athlete*) doping *m*; − *vt* doper. **2** *n* (*information*) *Fam* tuyaux *mpl*. **3** *n* (*idiot*) *Fam* imbécile *mf*. ◆**dopey** *a* (**-ier, -iest**) *Fam* (*stupid*) abruti; (*sleepy*) endormi; (*drugged*) drogué, camé.

dormant ['dɔːmənt] *a* (*a volcano, matter*) en sommeil; (*passion*) endormi.

dormer ['dɔːmər] *n* **d. (window)** lucarne *f*.

dormitory ['dɔːmıtrı, *Am* 'dɔːmıtɔːrı] *n* dortoir *m*; *Am* résidence *f* (universitaire).

dormouse, *pl* **-mice** ['dɔːmaus, -maıs] *n* loir *m*.

dos/e [dəus] *n* dose *f*; (*of hard work*) *Fig* période *f*; (*of illness*) attaque *f*; − *vt* **to d. oneself (up)** se bourrer de médicaments. ◆**—age** *n* (*amount*) dose *f*.

dosshouse ['dɒshaus] *n Sl* asile *m* (de nuit).

dossier ['dɒsıeı] *n* (*papers*) dossier *m*.

dot [dɒt] *n* point *m*; **polka d.** pois *m*; **on the d.** *Fam* à l'heure pile; − *vt* (**-tt-**) (*an i*) mettre un point sur. ◆**dotted** *a* **d. line** pointillé *m*; **d. with** parsemé de.

dot/e [dəʊt] *vt* **to d. on** être gaga de. ◆**—ing** *a* affectueux; **her d. husband/ father** son mari/père qui lui passe tout.

dotty ['dɒtɪ] *a* (**-ier, -iest**) *Fam* cinglé, toqué.

double ['dʌb(ə)l] *a* double; **a d. bed** un grand lit; **a d. room** une chambre pour deux personnes; **d. 's'** deux 's'; **d. six** deux fois six; **d. three four two** (*phone number*) trente-trois quarante-deux; – *adv* deux fois; (*to fold*) en deux; **he earns d. what I earn** il gagne le double de moi *or* deux fois plus que moi; **to see d.** voir double; – *n* double *m*; (*person*) double *m*, sosie *m*; (*stand-in*) *Cin* doublure *f*; **on** *or* **at the d.** au pas de course; – *vt* doubler; **to d. back** *or* **over** replier; – *vi* doubler; **to d. back** (*of person*) revenir en arrière; **to d. up** (*with pain, laughter*) être plié en deux. ◆**d.-'barrelled** *a* (*gun*) à deux canons; (*name*) à rallonges. ◆**d.-'bass** *n Mus* contrebasse *f*. ◆**d.-'breasted** *a* (*jacket*) croisé. ◆**d.-'cross** *vt* tromper. ◆**d.-'dealing** *n* double jeu *m*. ◆**d.-'decker (bus)** *n* autobus *m* à impériale. ◆**d.-'door** *n* porte *f* à deux battants. ◆**d.-'dutch** *n Fam* baragouin *m*. ◆**d.-'glazing** *n* (*window*) double vitrage *m*, double(s) fenêtre(s) *f(pl)*. ◆**d.-'parking** *n* stationnement *m* en double file. ◆**d.-'quick** *adv* en vitesse.

doubly ['dʌblɪ] *adv* doublement.

doubt [daʊt] *n* doute *m*; **to be in d. about** avoir des doutes sur; **I have no d. about it** je n'en doute pas; **no d.** (*probably*) sans doute; **in d.** (*result, career etc*) dans la balance; – *vt* douter de; **to d. whether** *or* **that** *or* **if** douter que (+ *sub*). ◆**doubtful** *a* douteux; **to be d. about sth** avoir des doutes sur qch; **it's d. whether** *or* **that** il est douteux que (+ *sub*). ◆**doubtless** *adv* sans doute.

dough [dəʊ] *n* pâte *f*; (*money*) *Fam* fric *m*, blé *m*. ◆**doughnut** *n* beignet *m* (rond).

dour ['dʊər] *a* austère.

douse [daʊs] *vt* arroser, tremper; (*light*) *Fam* éteindre.

dove[1] [dʌv] *n* colombe *f*. ◆**dovecote** [-kɒt] *n* colombier *m*.

dove[2] [dəʊv] *Am see* **dive 1.**

Dover ['dəʊvər] *n* Douvres *m or f*.

dovetail ['dʌvteɪl] **1** *n Carp* queue *f* d'aronde. **2** *vi* (*fit*) *Fig* concorder.

dowdy ['daʊdɪ] *a* (**-ier, -iest**) peu élégant, sans chic.

down[1] [daʊn] *adv* en bas; (*to the ground*) par terre, à terre; (*of sun*) couché; (*of blind,* *temperature*) baissé; (*out of bed*) descendu; (*of tyre*) dégonflé, (*worn*) usé; **d. (in writing)** inscrit; (*lie*) **d.!** (*to dog*) couché!; **to come** *or* **go d.** descendre; **to come d. from** (*place*) arriver de; **to fall d.** tomber (par terre); **d. there** *or* **here** en bas; **d. with traitors/etc!** à bas les traîtres/etc!; **d. with** (*the*) **flu** grippé; **to feel d.** (*depressed*) *Fam* avoir le cafard; **d. to** (*in series, numbers, dates etc*) jusqu'à; **d. payment** acompte *m*; **d. under** aux antipodes, en Australie; **d. at heel,** *Am* **d. at the heels** miteux; – *prep* (*at bottom of*) en bas de; (*from top to bottom of*) du haut en bas de; (*along*) le long de; **to go d.** (*hill etc*) descendre; **to live d. the street** habiter plus loin dans la rue; – *vt* (*shoot down*) abattre; (*knock down*) terrasser; **to d. a drink** vider un verre. ◆**down-and-'out** *a* sur le pavé; – *n* clochard, -arde *mf*. ◆**downbeat** *a* (*gloomy*) *Fam* pessimiste. ◆**downcast** *a* découragé. ◆**downfall** *n* chute *f*. ◆**downgrade** *vt* (*job etc*) déclasser; (*person*) rétrograder. ◆**down'hearted** *a* découragé. ◆**down'hill** *adv* en pente; **to go d.** descendre; *Fig* être sur le déclin. ◆**downmarket** *a Com* bas de gamme. ◆**downpour** *n* averse *f*, pluie *f* torrentielle. ◆**downright** *a* (*rogue etc*) véritable; (*refusal etc*) catégorique; **a d. nerve** *or* **cheek** un sacré culot; – *adv* (*rude etc*) franchement. ◆**'downstairs** *a* (*room, neighbours*) d'en bas; (*on the ground floor*) du rez-de-chaussée; – [daʊn'steəz] *adv* en bas; au rez-de-chaussée; **to come** *or* **go d.** descendre l'escalier. ◆**down'stream** *adv* en aval. ◆**down-to-'earth** *a* terre-à-terre *inv*. ◆**down'town** *adv* en ville; **d. Chicago/etc** le centre de Chicago/etc. ◆**downtrodden** *a* opprimé. ◆**downward** *a* vers le bas; (*path*) qui descend; (*trend*) à la baisse. ◆**downward(s)** *adv* vers le bas.

down[2] [daʊn] *n* (*on bird, person etc*) duvet *m*.

downs [daʊnz] *npl* collines *fpl*.

dowry ['daʊərɪ] *n* dot *f*.

doze [dəʊz] *n* petit somme *m*; – *vi* sommeiller; **to d. off** s'assoupir. ◆**dozy** *a* (**-ier, -iest**) assoupi; (*silly*) *Fam* bête, gourde.

dozen ['dʌz(ə)n] *n* douzaine *f*; **a d.** (*eggs, books etc*) une douzaine de; **dozens of** *Fig* des dizaines de.

Dr *abbr* (*Doctor*) Docteur.

drab [dræb] *a* terne; (*weather*) gris. ◆**—ness** *n* caractère *m* terne; (*of weather*) grisaille *f*.

draconian [drəˈkəʊnɪən] *a* draconien.

draft [drɑːft] **1** n (outline) ébauche f; (of letter etc) brouillon m; (bill) Com traite f; − vt **to d. (out)** (sketch out) faire le brouillon de; (write out) rédiger. **2** n Mil Am conscription f; (men) contingent m; − vt (conscript) appeler (sous les drapeaux). **3** n Am = **draught**.

draftsman ['drɑːftsmən] n = **draughtsman**.

drag [dræg] vt (-gg-) traîner, tirer; (river) draguer; **to d. sth from s.o.** (confession etc) arracher qch à qn; **to d. along** (en)traîner; **to d. s.o. away from** arracher qn à; **to d. s.o. into** entraîner qn dans; − vi traîner; **to d. on** or **out** (last a long time) se prolonger; − n Fam (tedium) corvée f; (person) raseur, -euse mf; (on cigarette) bouffée f (**on** de); **in d.** (clothing) en travesti.

dragon ['drægən] n dragon m. ◆**dragonfly** n libellule f.

drain [dreɪn] n (sewer) égout m; (pipe, channel) canal m; (outside house) puisard m; (in street) bouche f d'égout; **it's (gone) down the d.** (wasted) Fam c'est fichu; **to be a d. on** (resources, patience) épuiser; − vt (land) drainer; (glass, tank) vider; (vegetables) égoutter; (resources) épuiser; **to d. (off)** (liquid) faire écouler; **to d. of** (deprive of) priver de; − vi **to d. (off)** (of liquid) s'écouler; **to d. away** (of strength) s'épuiser; **draining board** paillasse f. ◆**—age** n (act) drainage m; (sewers) système m d'égouts. ◆**—er** n (board) paillasse f; (rack, basket) égouttoir m. ◆**drainboard** n Am paillasse f. ◆**drainpipe** n tuyau m d'évacuation.

drake [dreɪk] n canard m (mâle).

dram [dræm] n (drink) Fam goutte f.

drama ['drɑːmə] n (event) drame m; (dramatic art) théâtre m; **d. critic** critique m dramatique. ◆**dra'matic** a dramatique; (very great, striking) spectaculaire. ◆**dra-'matically** adv (to change, drop etc) de façon spectaculaire. ◆**dra'matics** n théâtre m. ◆**dramatist** ['dræmətɪst] n dramaturge m. ◆**dramatize** vt (exaggerate) dramatiser; (novel etc) adapter (pour la scène or l'écran).

drank [dræŋk] see **drink**.

drap/e [dreɪp] vt draper (**with** de); (wall) tapisser (de tentures); − npl tentures fpl; (heavy curtains) Am rideaux mpl. ◆**—er** n marchand, -ande mf de nouveautés.

drastic ['dræstɪk] a radical, sévère; (reduction) massif. ◆**drastically** adv radicalement.

draught [drɑːft] n courant m d'air; (for fire) tirage m; pl (game) dames fpl; − a (horse) de trait; (beer) (à la) pression; **d. excluder**

bourrelet m (de porte, de fenêtre). ◆**draughtboard** n damier m. ◆**draughty** a (-ier, -iest) (room) plein de courants d'air.

draughtsman ['drɑːftsmən] n (pl **-men**) dessinateur, -trice mf (industriel(le) or technique).

draw [drɔː] n (of lottery) tirage m au sort; Sp match m nul; (attraction) attraction f; − vt (pt **drew**, pp **drawn**) (pull) tirer; (pass) passer (**over** sur, **into** dans); (prize) gagner; (applause) provoquer; (money from bank) retirer (**from**, **out of** de); (salary) toucher; (attract) attirer; (well-water, comfort) puiser (**from** dans); **to d. a smile** faire sourire (**from s.o.** qn); **to d. a bath** faire couler un bain; **to d. sth to a close** mettre fin à qch; **to d. a match** Sp faire match nul; **to d. in** (claws) rentrer; **to d. out** (money) retirer; (meeting) prolonger; **to d. up** (chair) approcher; (contract, list, plan) dresser, rédiger; **to d. (up)on** (savings) puiser dans; − vi (enter) entrer (**into** dans); (arrive) arriver; **to d. near (to)** s'approcher (de); (of time) approcher (de); **to d. to a close** tirer à sa fin; **to d. aside** (step aside) s'écarter; **to d. away** (go away) s'éloigner; **to d. back** (recoil) reculer; **to d. in** (of days) diminuer; **to d. on** (of time) s'avancer; **to d. up** (of vehicle) s'arrêter. ◆**drawback** n inconvénient m. ◆**drawbridge** n pont-levis m.

draw [drɔː] vt (pt **drew**, pp **drawn**) (picture) dessiner; (circle) tracer; (parallel, distinction) Fig faire (**between** entre); − vi (as artist) dessiner. ◆**—ing** n dessin m; **d. board** planche f à dessin; **d. pin** punaise f; **d. room** salon m.

drawer [drɔːr] **1** n (in furniture) tiroir m. **2** npl (women's knickers) culotte f.

drawl [drɔːl] vi parler d'une voix traînante; − n voix f traînante.

drawn [drɔːn] see **draw** 1,2; − a (face) tiré, crispé; **d. match** or **game** match m nul.

dread [dred] vt redouter (**doing** de faire); − n crainte f, terreur f. ◆**dreadful** a épouvantable; (child) insupportable; (ill) malade; **I feel d. (about it)** j'ai vraiment honte. ◆**dreadfully** adv terriblement; **to be** or **feel d. sorry** regretter infiniment.

dream [driːm] vti (pt & pp **dreamed** or **dreamt** [dremt]) rêver; (imagine) songer (**of** à, **that** que); **I wouldn't d. of it!** (il n'en est pas question!; **to d. up** imaginer qch; − n rêve m; (wonderful thing or person) Fam merveille f; **to have a d.** faire un rêve (**about** de); **to have dreams of** rêver de; **a d. house/etc** une maison/etc de rêve; **a d.**

world un monde imaginaire. ◆—er n rêveur, -euse mf. ◆dreamy a (-ier, -iest) rêveur.

dreary ['drɪərɪ] a (-ier, -iest) (gloomy) morne; (monotonous) monotone; (boring) ennuyeux.

dredg/e [dredʒ] vt (river etc) draguer; – n drague f. ◆—er n 1 (ship) dragueur m. 2 Culin saupoudreuse f.

dregs [dregz] npl the d. (in liquid, of society) la lie.

drench [drentʃ] vt tremper; to get drenched se faire tremper (jusqu'aux os).

dress [dres] 1 n (woman's garment) robe f; (style of dressing) tenue f; d. circle Th (premier) balcon m; d. designer dessinateur, -trice mf de mode; (well-known) couturier m; d. rehearsal (répétition f) générale f; d. shirt chemise f de soirée. 2 vt (clothe) habiller; (adorn) orner; (salad) assaisonner; (wound) panser; (skins, chicken) préparer; to get dressed s'habiller; dressed for tennis/etc en tenue de tennis/etc; – vi s'habiller; to d. up (smartly) bien s'habiller; (in disguise) se déguiser (as en). ◆—ing n Med pansement m; (seasoning) Culin assaisonnement m; to give s.o. a d.-down passer un savon à qn; d. gown robe f de chambre; (of boxer) peignoir m; d. room Th loge f; d. table coiffeuse f. ◆—er n 1 (furniture) vaisselier m; Am coiffeuse f. 2 she's a good d. elle s'habille toujours bien. ◆dressmaker n couturière f. ◆dressmaking n couture f.

dressy ['dresɪ] a (-ier, -iest) (smart) chic inv; (too) d. trop habillé.

drew [druː] see draw [1,2].

dribble ['drɪb(ə)l] vi (of baby) baver; (of liquid) tomber goutte à goutte; Sp dribbler; – vt laisser tomber goutte à goutte; (ball) Sp dribbler.

dribs [drɪbz] npl in d. and drabs par petites quantités; (to arrive) par petits groupes.

dried [draɪd] a (fruit) sec; (milk) en poudre; (flowers) séché.

drier ['draɪər] n = dryer.

drift [drɪft] vi être emporté par le vent or le courant; (of ship) dériver; Fig aller à la dérive; (of snow) s'amonceler; to d. about (aimlessly) se promener sans but, traînailler; to d. apart (of husband and wife) devenir des étrangers l'un pour l'autre; to d. into/towards glisser dans/vers; – n mouvement m; (direction) sens m; (of events) cours m; (of snow) amoncellement m, congère f; (meaning) sens m général.

◆—er n (aimless person) paumé, -ée mf. ◆driftwood n bois m flotté.

drill [drɪl] 1 n (tool) perceuse f; (bit) mèche f; (for rock) foreuse f; (for tooth) fraise f; (pneumatic) marteau m pneumatique; – vt percer; (tooth) fraiser; (oil well) forer; – vi to d. for oil faire de la recherche pétrolière. 2 n Mil Sch exercice(s) m(pl); (procedure) Fig marche f à suivre; – vi faire l'exercice; – vt faire faire l'exercice à.

drink [drɪŋk] n boisson f; (glass of sth) verre m; to give s.o. a d. donner (quelque chose) à boire à qn; – vt (pt drank, pp drunk) boire; to d. oneself to death se tuer à force de boire; to d. down or up boire; – vi boire (out of dans); to d. up finir son verre; to d. to boire à la santé de. ◆—ing a (water) potable; (song) à boire; d. bout beuverie f; d. fountain fontaine f publique, borne-fontaine f; d. trough abreuvoir m. ◆—able a (fit for drinking) potable; (palatable) buvable. ◆—er n buveur, -euse mf.

drip [drɪp] vi (-pp-) dégouliner, dégoutter; (of washing, vegetables) s'égoutter; (of tap) fuir; – vt (paint etc) laisser couler; – n (drop) goutte f; (sound) bruit m (de goutte); (fool) Fam nouille f. ◆d.-dry a (shirt etc) sans repassage. ◆dripping n (Am drippings) Culin graisse f; – a & adv d. (wet) dégoulinant.

driv/e [draɪv] n promenade f en voiture; (energy) énergie f; Psy instinct m; Pol campagne f; (road to private house) allée f; an hour's d. une heure de voiture; left-hand d. Aut (véhicule m à) conduite f à gauche; front-wheel d. Aut traction f avant; – vt (pt drove, pp driven) (vehicle, train, passenger) conduire; (machine) actionner; to d. (away or out) (chase away) chasser; to d. s.o. to do pousser qn à faire; to d. to despair réduire au désespoir; to d. mad or crazy rendre fou; to d. the rain/smoke against (of wind) rabattre la pluie/fumée contre; to d. back (enemy etc) repousser; (passenger) Aut ramener qn en voiture; to d. in (thrust) enfoncer; to d. s.o. hard surmener qn; he drives a Ford il a une Ford; – vi (drive a car) conduire; to d. (along) (go, run) Aut rouler; to d. on the left rouler à gauche; to d. away or off Aut partir; to d. back Aut revenir; to d. on Aut continuer; to d. to Aut aller (en voiture) à; to d. up Aut arriver; what are you driving at? Fig où veux-tu en venir? ◆—ing 1 n conduite f; d. lesson leçon f de conduite; d. licence, d. test permis m de conduire; d. school auto-école *f*. **2** *a* (*forceful*) **d. force** force *f* agissante; **d. rain** pluie *f* battante. ◆**—er** *n* (*of car*) conducteur, -trice *mf*; (*of taxi, lorry*) chauffeur *m*, conducteur, -trice *mf*; (*train*) **d.** mécanicien *m*; **she's a good d.** elle conduit bien; **driver's license** *Am* permis *m* de conduire.

drivel ['drɪv(ə)l] *vi* (**-ll-**, *Am* **-l-**) radoter; — *n* radotage *m*.

drizzle ['drɪz(ə)l] *n* bruine *f*, crachin *m*; — *vi* bruiner. ◆**drizzly** *a* (*weather*) de bruine; **it's d.** il bruine.

droll [drəul] *a* drôle, comique.

dromedary ['drɒmədərɪ, *Am* 'drɒmɪderɪ] *n* dromadaire *m*.

drone [drəun] **1** *n* (*bee*) abeille *f* mâle. **2** *n* (*hum*) bourdonnement *m*; (*purr*) ronronnement *m*; *Fig* débit *m* monotone; — *vi* (*of bee*) bourdonner; (*of engine*) ronronner; **to d. (on)** *Fig* parler d'une voix monotone.

drool [druːl] *vi* (*slaver*) baver; *Fig* radoter; **to d. over** *Fig* s'extasier devant.

droop [druːp] *vi* (*of head*) pencher; (*of eyelid*) tomber; (*of flower*) se faner.

drop [drɒp] **1** *n* (*of liquid*) goutte *f*. **2** *n* (*fall*) baisse *f*, chute *f* (**in** de); (*slope*) descente *f*; (*distance of fall*) hauteur *f* (de chute); (*jump*) *Av* saut *m*; — *vt* (**-pp-**) laisser tomber; (*price, voice*) baisser; (*bomb*) larguer; (*passenger, goods*) *Aut* déposer; *Nau* débarquer; (*letter*) envoyer (**to** à); (*put*) mettre; (*omit*) omettre; (*remark*) laisser échapper; (*get rid of*) supprimer; (*habit*) abandonner; (*team member*) *Sp* écarter; **to d. s.o. off** *Aut* déposer qn; **to d. a line** écrire un petit mot (**to** à); **to d. a hint** faire une allusion; **to d. a hint that** laisser entendre que; **to d. one's h's** ne pas aspirer les h; **to d. a word in s.o.'s ear** glisser un mot à l'oreille de qn; — *vi* (*fall*) tomber; (*of person*) (se laisser) tomber; (*of price*) baisser; (*of conversation*) cesser; **he's ready to d.** *Fam* il tombe de fatigue; **let it d.!** *Fam* laisse tomber!; **to d. across** *or* **in** passer (chez qn); **to d. away** (*diminish*) diminuer; **to d. back** *or* **behind** rester en arrière, se laisser distancer; **to d. off** (*fall asleep*) s'endormir; (*fall off*) tomber; (*of interest, sales etc*) diminuer. ◆**d.-off** *n* (*decrease*) diminution *f* (**in** de); **to d. out** (*fall out*) tomber; (*withdraw*) se retirer; (*socially*) se mettre en marge de la société; *Sch Univ* laisser tomber ses études. ◆**d.-out** *n* marginal, -ale *mf*; *Univ* étudiant, -ante *mf* qui abandonne ses études. ◆**droppings** *npl* (*of animal*) crottes *fpl*; (*of bird*) fiente *f*.

dross [drɒs] *n* déchets *mpl*.

drought [draut] *n* sécheresse *f*.

drove [drəuv] *see* drive.

droves [drəuvz] *npl* (*of people*) foules *fpl*; **in d.** en foule.

drown [draun] *vi* se noyer; — *vt* noyer; **to d. oneself, be drowned** se noyer. ◆**—ing** *a* qui se noie; — *n* (*death*) noyade *f*.

drowse [drauz] *vi* somnoler. ◆**drows/y** *a* (**-ier, -iest**) somnolent; **to feel d.** avoir sommeil; **to make s.o. (feel) d.** assoupir qn. ◆**—ily** *adv* d'un air somnolent. ◆**—iness** *n* somnolence *f*.

drubbing ['drʌbɪŋ] *n* (*beating*) raclée *f*.

drudge [drʌdʒ] *n* bête *f* de somme, esclave *mf* du travail; — *vi* trimer. ◆**drudgery** *n* corvée(s) *f(pl)*, travail *m* ingrat.

drug [drʌg] *n* *Med* médicament *m*, drogue *f*; (*narcotic*) stupéfiant *m*, drogue *f*; *Fig* drogue *f*; **drugs** (*dope in general*) la drogue; **to be on drugs, take drugs** se droguer; **d. addict** drogué, -ée *mf*; **d. addiction** toxicomanie *f*; **d. taking** usage *m* de la drogue; — *vt* (**-gg-**) droguer; (*drink*) mêler un somnifère à. ◆**druggist** *n* *Am* pharmacien, -ienne *mf*, droguiste *mf*. ◆**drugstore** *n* *Am* drugstore *m*.

drum [drʌm] *n* *Mus* tambour *m*; (*for oil*) bidon *m*; **the big d.** *Mus* la grosse caisse; **the drums** *Mus* la batterie; — *vi* (**-mm-**) *Mil* battre du tambour; (*with fingers*) tambouriner; — *vt* **to d. sth into s.o.** *Fig* rabâcher qch à qn; **to d. up** (*support, interest*) susciter; **to d. up business** *or* **custom** attirer les clients. ◆**drummer** *n* (joueur, -euse *mf* de) tambour *m*; (*in pop or jazz group*) batteur *m*. ◆**drumstick** *n* *Mus* baguette *f* de tambour; (*of chicken*) pilon *m*, cuisse *f*.

drunk [drʌŋk] *see* drink; — *a* ivre; **d. with** *Fig* ivre de; **to get d.** s'enivrer; — *n* ivrogne *mf*, pochard, -arde *mf*. ◆**drunkard** *n* ivrogne *mf*. ◆**drunken** *a* (*quarrel*) d'ivrogne; (*person*) ivrogne; (*driver*) ivre; **d. driving** conduite *f* en état d'ivresse. ◆**drunkenness** *n* (*state*) ivresse *f*; (*habit*) ivrognerie *f*.

dry [draɪ] *a* (**drier, driest**) sec; (*well, river*) à sec; (*day*) sans pluie; (*toast*) sans beurre; (*wit*) caustique; (*subject, book*) aride; **on d. land** sur la terre ferme; **to keep sth d.** tenir qch au sec; **to wipe d.** essuyer; **to run d.** se tarir; **to feel** *or* **be d.** *Fam* avoir soif; **d. dock** cale *f* sèche. **d. goods store** *Am* magasin *m* de nouveautés; — *vt* sécher; (*dishes etc*) essuyer; **to d. off** *or* **up** sécher; — *vi* sécher; **to d. off** sécher; **to d. up** sécher; (*run dry*) tarir; **d. up!** *Fam* tais-toi! ◆**—ing** *n* séchage *m*; essuyage *m*. ◆**—er** *n* (*for hair,* *clothes*) séchoir *m*; (*helmet-style for hair*) casque *m*. ◆—ness *n* sécheresse *f*; (*of wit*) causticité *f*; (*of book etc*) aridité *f*. ◆dry-'clean *vt* nettoyer à sec. ◆dry-'cleaner *n* teinturier, -ière *mf*.

dual ['djuːəl] *a* double; d. carriageway route *f* à deux voies (séparées). ◆du'ality *n* dualité *f*.

dub [dʌb] *vt* (-bb-) 1 (*film*) doubler. 2 (*nick-name*) surnommer. ◆dubbing *n* Cin doublage *m*.

dubious ['djuːbɪəs] *a* (*offer, person etc*) douteux; I'm d. about going *or* whether to go je me demande si je dois y aller; to be d. about sth douter de qch.

duchess ['dʌtʃɪs] *n* duchesse *f*. ◆duchy *n* duché *m*.

duck [dʌk] 1 *n* canard *m*. 2 *vi* se baisser (vivement); – *vt* (*head*) baisser; to d. s.o. plonger qn dans l'eau. ◆—ing *n* bain *m* forcé. ◆duckling *n* caneton *m*.

duct [dʌkt] *n* Anat Tech conduit *m*.

dud [dʌd] *a* Fam (*bomb*) non éclaté; (*coin*) faux; (*cheque*) en bois; (*watch etc*) qui ne marche pas; – *n* (*person*) zéro *m*, type *m* nul.

dude [duːd] *n* Am Fam dandy *m*; d. ranch ranch(-hôtel) *m*.

due¹ [djuː] *a* (*money, sum*) dû (to à); (*rent, bill*) à payer; (*respect*) qu'on doit (to à); (*fitting*) qui convient; to fall d. échoir; she's d. for (*a rise etc*) elle doit *or* devrait recevoir; he's d. to (*to arrive*) (*is awaited*) il doit arriver, il est attendu; I'm d. there je dois être là-bas; in d. course (*at proper time*) en temps utile; (*finally*) à la longue; d. to (*attributable to*) dû à; (*because of*) à cause de; (*thanks to*) grâce à; – *n* dû *m*; *pl* (*of club*) cotisation *f*; (*official charges*) droits *mpl*; to give s.o. his d. admettre que qn a raison.

due² [djuː] *adv* (tout) droit; d. north/south plein nord/sud.

duel ['djuːəl] *n* duel *m*; – *vi* (-ll-, *Am* -l-) se battre en duel.

duet [djuː'et] *n* duo *m*.

duffel, duffle ['dʌf(ə)l] *a* d. bag sac *m* de marin; d. coat duffel-coat *m*.

dug [dʌg] *see* dig. ◆dugout *n* 1 Mil abri *m* souterrain. 2 (*canoe*) pirogue *f*.

duke [djuːk] *n* duc *m*.

dull [dʌl] *a* (-er, -est) (*boring*) ennuyeux; (*colour, character*) terne; (*weather*) maus-sade; (*mind*) lourd, borné; (*sound, ache*) sourd; (*edge, blade*) émoussé; (*hearing, sight*) faible; – *vt* (*senses*) émousser; (*sound, pain*) amortir; (*colour*) ternir;

(*mind*) engourdir. ◆—ness *n* (*of mind*) lourdeur *f* d'esprit; (*tedium*) monotonie *f*; (*of colour*) manque *m* d'éclat.

duly ['djuːlɪ] *adv* (*properly*) comme il convient (convenait *etc*); (*in fact*) en effet; (*in due time*) en temps utile.

dumb [dʌm] *a* (-er, -est) muet; (*stupid*) Fam idiot, bête. ◆—ness *n* mutisme *m*; bêtise *f*. ◆dumbbell *n* (*weight*) haltère *m*. ◆dumb'waiter *n* (*lift for food*) monte-plats *m inv*.

dumbfound [dʌm'faund] *vt* sidérer, ahurir.

dummy ['dʌmɪ] 1 *n* (*of baby*) sucette *f*; (*of dressmaker*) mannequin *m*; (*of book*) maquette *f*; (*of ventriloquist*) pantin *m*; (*fool*) Fam idiot, -ote *mf*. 2 *a* factice, faux; d. run (*on car etc*) essai *m*.

dump [dʌmp] *vt* (*rubbish*) déposer; to d. (down) déposer; to d. s.o. (*ditch*) Fam plaquer qn; – *n* (*for ammunition*) Mil dépôt *m*; (*dirty or dull town*) Fam trou *m*; (*house, slum*) Fam baraque *f*; (*rubbish*) d. tas *m* d'ordures; (*place*) dépôt *m* d'ordures, décharge *f*; to be (down) in the dumps Fam avoir le cafard; d. truck = dumper. ◆—er *n* d. (truck) camion *m* à benne basculante.

dumpling ['dʌmplɪŋ] *n* Culin boulette *f* (de pâte).

dumpy ['dʌmpɪ] *a* (-ier, -iest) (*person*) boulot, gros et court.

dunce [dʌns] *n* cancre *m*, âne *m*.

dune [djuːn] *n* dune *f*.

dung [dʌŋ] *n* crotte *f*; (*of cattle*) bouse *f*; (*manure*) fumier *m*.

dungarees [dʌŋgə'riːz] *npl* (*of child, work-man*) salopette *f*; (*jeans*) *Am* jean *m*.

dungeon ['dʌndʒən] *n* cachot *m*.

dunk [dʌŋk] *vt* (*bread, biscuit etc*) tremper.

dupe [djuːp] *vt* duper; – *n* dupe *f*.

duplex ['djuːpleks] *n* (*apartment*) *Am* duplex *m*.

duplicate ['djuːplɪkeɪt] *vt* (*key, map*) faire un double de; (*on machine*) polycopier; – ['djuːplɪkət] *n* double *m*; in d. en deux exemplaires; a d. copy/etc une copie/etc en double; a d. key un double de la clef. ◆dupli'cation *n* (*on machine*) polycopie *f*; (*of effort*) répétition *f*. ◆duplicator *n* duplicateur *m*.

duplicity [djuː'plɪsɪtɪ] *n* duplicité *f*.

durable ['djuːrəb(ə)l] *a* (*shoes etc*) résistant; (*friendship, love*) durable. ◆dura'bility *n* résistance *f*; durabilité *f*.

duration [djuː'reɪʃ(ə)n] *n* durée *f*.

duress [djuː'res] *n* under d. sous la contrainte.

during ['djuərɪŋ] *prep* pendant, durant.

dusk [dʌsk] n (twilight) crépuscule m.
dusky ['dʌskɪ] a (-ier, -iest) (complexion) foncé.
dust [dʌst] n poussière f; **d. cover** (for furniture) housse f; (for book) jaquette f; **d. jacket** jaquette f; − vt épousseter; (sprinkle) saupoudrer (**with** de). ◆**−er** n chiffon m. ◆**dustbin** n poubelle f. ◆**dustcart** n camion-benne m. ◆**dustman** n (pl **-men**) éboueur m, boueux m. ◆**dustpan** n petite pelle f (à poussière).
dusty ['dʌstɪ] a (-ier, -iest) poussiéreux.
Dutch [dʌtʃ] a néerlandais, hollandais; **D. cheese** hollande m; **to go D.** partager les frais (**with** avec); − n (language) hollandais m. ◆**Dutchman** n (pl **-men**) Hollandais m. ◆**Dutchwoman** n (pl **-women**) Hollandaise f.
duty ['djuːtɪ] n devoir m; (tax) droit m; pl (responsibilities) fonctions fpl; **on d.** Mil de service; (doctor etc) de garde; **Sch** de permanence; **off d.** libre. ◆**d.-'free** a (goods, shop) hors-taxe inv. ◆**dutiful** a respectueux, obéissant; (worker) consciencieux.
dwarf [dwɔːf] n nain m, naine f; − vt (of building, person etc) rapetisser, écraser.

dwell [dwel] vi (pt & pp **dwelt**) demeurer; **to d. (up)on** (think about) penser sans cesse à; (speak about) parler sans cesse de, s'étendre sur; (insist on) appuyer sur. ◆**−ing** n habitation f. ◆**−er** n habitant, -ante mf.
dwindl/e ['dwɪnd(ə)l] vt diminuer (peu à peu). ◆**−ing** a (interest etc) décroissant.
dye [daɪ] n teinture f; − vt teindre; **to d. green/etc** teindre en vert/etc. ◆**dyeing** n teinture f; (industry) teinturerie f. ◆**dyer** n teinturier, -ière mf.
dying ['daɪɪŋ] see **die 1**; − a mourant, moribond; (custom) qui se perd; (day, words) dernier; − n (death) mort f.
dyke [daɪk] n (wall) digue f; (ditch) fossé m.
dynamic [daɪ'næmɪk] a dynamique. ◆**'dynamism** n dynamisme m.
dynamite ['daɪnəmaɪt] n dynamite f; − vt dynamiter.
dynamo ['daɪnəməʊ] n (pl **-os**) dynamo f.
dynasty ['dɪnəstɪ, Am 'daɪnəstɪ] n dynastie f.
dysentery ['dɪsəntrɪ] n Med dysenterie f.
dyslexic [dɪs'leksɪk] a & n dyslexique (mf).

E

E, e [iː] n E, e m.
each [iːtʃ] a chaque; − pron chacun, -une; **e. one** chacun, -une; **e. other** l'un(e) l'autre, pl les un(e)s les autres; **to see e. other** se voir (l'un(e) l'autre); **e. of us** chacun, -une d'entre nous.
eager ['iːgər] a impatient (**to do** de faire); (enthusiastic) ardent, passionné; **to be e. for** désirer vivement; **e. for** (money) avide de; **e. to help** empressé (à aider); **to be e. to do** (want) avoir envie de faire. ◆**−ly** adv (to await) avec impatience; (to work, serve) avec empressement. ◆**−ness** n impatience f (**to do** de faire); (zeal) empressement m (**to do** à faire); (greed) avidité f.
eagle ['iːg(ə)l] n aigle m. ◆**e.-'eyed** a au regard d'aigle.
ear¹ [ɪər] n oreille f; **all ears** Fam tout ouïe; **up to one's ears in work** débordé de travail; **to play it by e.** Fam agir selon la situation; **thick e.** Fam gifle f. ◆**earache** n mal m d'oreille. ◆**eardrum** n tympan m. ◆**earmuffs** npl serre-tête m inv (pour

protéger les oreilles), protège-oreilles m inv. ◆**earphones** npl casque m. ◆**earpiece** n écouteur m. ◆**earplug** n (to keep out noise) boule f Quiès®. ◆**earring** n boucle f d'oreille. ◆**earshot** n **within e.** à portée de voix. ◆**ear-splitting** a assourdissant.
ear² [ɪər] n (of corn) épi m.
earl [ɜːl] n comte m.
early ['ɜːlɪ] a (-ier, -iest) (first) premier; (fruit, season) précoce; (death) prématuré; (age) jeune; (painting, work) de jeunesse; (reply) rapide; (return, retirement) anticipé; (ancient) ancien; **it's e.** (looking at time) il est tôt; (referring to appointment etc) c'est tôt; **it's too e. to get up/etc** il est trop tôt pour se lever/etc; **to be e.** (ahead of time) arriver de bonne heure ou tôt, être en avance; (in getting up) être matinal; **in e. times** jadis; **in e. summer** au début de l'été; **one's e. life** sa jeunesse; − adv tôt, de bonne heure; (ahead of time) en avance; (to die) prématurément; **as e. as possible** le plus tôt possible; **earlier (on)** plus tôt; **at**

the earliest au plus tôt; **as e. as yesterday** déjà hier. ◆**e.-'warning system** n dispositif m de première alerte.

earmark ['ɪəmɑːk] vt (funds) assigner (**for** à).

earn [ɜːn] vt gagner; (interest) Fin rapporter. ◆**—ings** npl (wages) rémunérations fpl; (profits) bénéfices mpl.

earnest ['ɜːnɪst] a sérieux; (sincere) sincère; – n **in e.** sérieusement; **it's raining in e.** il pleut pour de bon; **he's in e.** il est sérieux. ◆**—ness** n sérieux m; sincérité f.

earth [ɜːθ] n (world, ground) terre f; El terre f, masse f; **to fall to e.** tomber à or par terre; **nothing/nobody on e.** rien/personne au monde; **where/what on e.?** où/que diable? ◆**earthly** a (possessions etc) terrestre; **not an e. chance** Fam pas la moindre chance; **for no e. reason** Fam sans la moindre raison. ◆**earthy** a terreux; (person) Fig terre-à-terre inv. ◆**earthquake** n tremblement m de terre. ◆**earthworks** npl (excavations) terrassements mpl. ◆**earthworm** n ver m de terre.

earthenware ['ɜːθənweər] n faïence f; – a en faïence.

earwig ['ɪəwɪg] n (insect) perce-oreille m.

ease [iːz] **1** n (physical) bien-être m; (mental) tranquillité f; (facility) facilité f; (ill) **at e.** (in situation) (mal) à l'aise; **at e.** (of mind) tranquille; (stand) **at e.!** Mil repos!; **with e.** facilement. **2** vt (pain) soulager; (mind) calmer; (tension) diminuer; (loosen) relâcher; **to e. off/along** enlever/déplacer doucement; **to e. oneself through** se glisser par; – vi **to e. (off** or **up)** (of situation) se détendre; (of pressure) diminuer; (of demand) baisser; (of pain) se calmer; (not work so hard) se relâcher. ◆**easily** adv facilement; **e. the best/etc** de loin le meilleur/etc; **that could e. be** ça pourrait bien être. ◆**easiness** n aisance f.

easel ['iːz(ə)l] n chevalet m.

east [iːst] n est m; **Middle/Far E.** Moyen-/Extrême-Orient m; – a (coast) est inv; (wind) d'est; **E. Africa** Afrique f orientale; **E. Germany** Allemagne f de l'Est; – adv à l'est, vers l'est. ◆**eastbound** a (carriageway) est inv; (traffic) en direction de l'est. ◆**easterly** a (point) est inv; (direction) de l'est; (wind) d'est. ◆**eastern** a (coast) est inv; **E. France** l'Est m de la France; **E. Europe** Europe f de l'Est. ◆**easterner** n habitant, -ante mf de l'Est. ◆**eastward(s)** a & adv vers l'est.

Easter ['iːstər] n Pâques m sing or fpl; **E. week** semaine f pascale; **Happy E.!** joyeuses Pâques!

easy ['iːzɪ] a (-ier, -iest) facile; (manners) naturel; (life) tranquille; (pace) modéré; **to feel e. in one's mind** être tranquille; **to be an e. first** Sp être bon premier; **I'm e.** Fam ça m'est égal; **e. chair** fauteuil m (rembourré); – adv doucement; **go e. on** (sugar etc) vas-y doucement or mollo avec; (person) ne sois pas trop dur avec or envers; **take it e.** (rest) repose-toi; (work less) ne te fatigue pas; (calm down) calme-toi; (go slow) ne te presse pas. ◆**easy'going** a (carefree) insouciant; (easy to get on with) traitable.

eat [iːt] vt (pt **ate** [et, Am eɪt], pp **eaten** ['iːt(ə)n]) manger; (meal) prendre; (one's words) Fig ravaler; **to e. breakfast** or **lunch** déjeuner; **what's eating you?** Sl qu'est-ce qui te tracasse?; **to e. up** (finish) finir; **eaten up with** (envy) dévoré de; – vi manger; **to e. into** (of acid) ronger; **to e. out** (lunch) déjeuner dehors; (dinner) dîner dehors. ◆**—ing** a **e. apple** pomme f à couteau; **e. place** restaurant m. ◆**—able** a mangeable. ◆**—er** n **big e.** gros mangeur m, grosse mangeuse f.

eau de Cologne [əʊdəkə'ləʊn] n eau f de Cologne.

eaves [iːvz] npl avant-toit m. ◆**eavesdrop** vt (-pp-) **to e. (on)** écouter (de façon indiscrète). ◆**eavesdropper** n oreille f indiscrète.

ebb [eb] n reflux m; **and flow** le flux et le reflux; **e. tide** marée f descendante; **at a low e.** Fig très bas; – vi refluer; **to e. (away)** (of strength etc) Fig décliner.

ebony ['ebənɪ] n (wood) ébène f.

ebullient [ɪ'bʌlɪənt] a exubérant.

eccentric [ɪk'sentrɪk] a & n excentrique (mf). ◆**eccen'tricity** n excentricité f.

ecclesiastic [ɪkliːzɪ'æstɪk] a & n ecclésiastique (m). ◆**ecclesiastical** a ecclésiastique.

echelon ['eʃəlɒn] n (of organization) échelon m.

echo ['ekəʊ] n (pl -oes) écho m; – vt (sound) répercuter; (repeat) Fig répéter; – vi (of explosion/etc) echoed l'écho de l'explosion/etc se répercuta; **to e. with the sound of** résonner de l'écho de.

éclair [eɪ'kleər] n (cake) éclair m.

eclectic [ɪ'klektɪk] a éclectique.

eclipse [ɪ'klɪps] n (of sun etc) & Fig éclipse f; – vt éclipser.

ecology [ɪ'kɒlədʒɪ] n écologie f. ◆**eco'logical** a écologique.

economic [iːkə'nɒmɪk] a économique; (profitable) rentable. ◆**economical** a économique; (*thrifty*) économe. ◆**economically** *adv* économiquement. ◆**economics** *n* (science *f*) économique *f*; (*profitability*) aspect *m* financier.

economy [ɪ'kɒnəmɪ] *n* (*saving, system, thrift*) économie *f*; **e. class** *Av* classe *f* touriste. ◆**economist** *n* économiste *mf*. ◆**economize** *vti* économiser (on sur).

ecstasy ['ekstəsɪ] *n* extase *f*. ◆**ec'static** *a* extasié; **to be e. about** s'extasier sur. ◆**ec'statically** *adv* avec extase.

ecumenical [iːkjuː'menɪk(ə)l] *a* œcuménique.

eczema ['eksɪmə] *n Med* eczéma *m*.

eddy ['edɪ] *n* tourbillon *m*, remous *m*.

edg/e [edʒ] *n* bord *m*; (*of forest*) lisière *f*; (*of town*) abords *mpl*; (*of page*) marge *f*; (*of knife etc*) tranchant *m*, fil *m*; **on e.** (*person*) énervé; (*nerves*) tendu; **to set s.o.'s teeth on e.** (*irritate s.o.*) crisper qn, faire grincer les dents à qn; **to have the e.** *or* **a slight e.** *Fig* être légèrement supérieur (over, on à); — *vt* (*clothing etc*) border (with de); — *vti* **to e.** (*oneself*) **into** (*move*) se glisser dans; **to e.** (*oneself*) **forward** avancer doucement. ◆**—ing** *n* (*border*) bordure *f*. ◆**edgeways** *adv* de côté; **to get a word in e.** *Fam* placer un mot.

edgy ['edʒɪ] *a* (-ier, -iest) énervé. ◆**edginess** *n* nervosité *f*.

edible ['edɪb(ə)l] *a* (*mushroom, berry etc*) comestible; (*meal, food*) mangeable.

edict ['iːdɪkt] *n* décret *m*; *Hist* édit *m*.

edifice ['edɪfɪs] *n* (*building, organization*) édifice *m*.

edify ['edɪfaɪ] *vt* (*improve the mind of*) édifier.

Edinburgh ['edɪnb(ə)rə] *n* Édimbourg *m* or *f*.

edit ['edɪt] *vt* (*newspaper etc*) diriger; (*article etc*) mettre au point; (*film*) monter; (*annotate*) éditer; (*compile*) rédiger; **to e.** (**out**) (*cut out*) couper. ◆**editor** *n* (*of review*) directeur, -trice *mf*; (*compiler*) rédacteur, -trice *mf*; *TV Rad* réalisateur, -trice *mf*; *sports* e. *Journ* rédacteur *m* sportif, rédactrice *f* sportive; **the e.** (**in chief**) (*of newspaper*) le rédacteur *m* en chef. ◆**edi'torial** *a* de la rédaction; **e. staff** rédaction *f*; − *n* éditorial *m*.

edition [ɪ'dɪʃ(ə)n] *n* édition *f*.

educat/e ['edʒukeɪt] *vt* (*family, children*) éduquer; (*pupil*) instruire; (*mind*) former, éduquer; **to be educated at** faire ses études à. ◆**—ed** *a* (*voice*) cultivé; (**well-**)**e.** (*person*) instruit. ◆**edu'cation** *n* éducation *f*; (*teaching*) instruction *f*, enseigne-

ment *m*; (*training*) formation *f*; (*subject*) *Univ* pédagogie *f*. ◆**edu'cational** *a* (*establishment*) d'enseignement; (*method*) pédagogique; (*game*) éducatif; (*supplies*) scolaire. ◆**edu'cationally** *adv* du point de vue de l'éducation. ◆**educator** *n* éducateur, -trice *mf*.

EEC [iːiː'siː] *n abbr* (*European Economic Community*) CEE *f*.

eel [iːl] *n* anguille *f*.

eerie ['ɪərɪ] *a* (-ier, -iest) sinistre, étrange.

efface [ɪ'feɪs] *vt* effacer.

effect [ɪ'fekt] **1** *n* (*result, impression*) effet *m* (on sur); *pl* (*goods*) biens *mpl*; **to no e.** en vain; **in e.** en fait; **to put into e.** mettre en application, faire entrer en vigueur; **to come into e., take e.** entrer en vigueur; **to take e.** (*of drug etc*) agir; **to have an e.** (*of medicine etc*) faire de l'effet; **to have no e.** rester sans effet; **to this e.** (*in this meaning*) dans ce sens; **to the e. that** (*saying that*) comme quoi. **2** *vt* (*carry out*) effectuer, réaliser.

effective [ɪ'fektɪv] *a* (*efficient*) efficace; (*actual*) effectif; (*striking*) frappant; **to become e.** (*of law*) prendre effet. ◆**—ly** *adv* efficacement; (*in effect*) effectivement. ◆**—ness** *n* efficacité *f*; (*quality*) effet *m* frappant.

effeminate [ɪ'femɪnɪt] *a* efféminé.

effervescent [efə'ves(ə)nt] *a* (*mixture, youth*) effervescent; (*drink*) gazeux. ◆**effervesce** *vi* (*of drink*) pétiller. ◆**effervescence** *n* (*excitement*) & *Ch* effervescence *f*; pétillement *m*.

effete [ɪ'fiːt] *a* (*feeble*) mou, faible; (*decadent*) décadent.

efficient [ɪ'fɪʃ(ə)nt] *a* (*method*) efficace; (*person*) compétent, efficace; (*organization*) efficace, performant; (*machine*) performant, à haut rendement. ◆**efficiency** *n* efficacité *f*; compétence *f*; performances *fpl*. ◆**efficiently** *adv* efficacement; avec compétence; **to work e.** (*of machine*) bien fonctionner.

effigy ['efɪdʒɪ] *n* effigie *f*.

effort ['efət] *n* effort *m*; **to make an e.** faire un effort (to pour); **it isn't worth the e.** ça ne or n'en vaut pas la peine; **his** or **her latest e.** *Fam* ses dernières tentatives. ◆**—less** *a* (*victory etc*) facile. ◆**—lessly** *adv* facilement, sans effort.

effrontery [ɪ'frʌntərɪ] *n* effronterie *f*.

effusive [ɪ'fjuːsɪv] *a* (*person*) expansif; (*thanks, excuses*) sans fin. ◆**—ly** *adv* avec effusion.

e.g. [iːdʒiː] *abbr (exempli gratia)* par exemple.

egalitarian [ɪɡælɪˈteərɪən] *a (society etc)* égalitaire.

egg¹ [eg] *n* œuf *m*; **e. timer** sablier *m*; **e. whisk** fouet *m* (à œufs). ◆**eggcup** *n* coquetier *m*. ◆**egghead** *n Pej* intellectuel, -elle *mf*. ◆**eggplant** *n* aubergine *f*. ◆**eggshell** *n* coquille *f*.

egg² [eg] *vt* **to e. on** *(encourage)* inciter **(to do** à faire).

ego [ˈiːɡəʊ] *n (pl -os)* the **e.** *Psy* le moi. ◆**ego'centric** *a* égocentrique. ◆**egoism** *n* égoïsme *m*. ◆**egoist** *n* égoïste *mf*. ◆**ego'istic(al)** *a* égoïste. ◆**egotism** *n* égotisme *m*.

Egypt [ˈiːdʒɪpt] *n* Égypte *f*. ◆**E'gyptian** *a & n* égyptien, -ienne *(mf)*.

eh? [eɪ] *int Fam* hein?

eiderdown [ˈaɪdədaʊn] *n* édredon *m*.

eight [eɪt] *a & n* huit *(m)*. ◆**eigh'teen** *a & n* dix-huit *(m)*. ◆**eigh'teenth** *a & n* dix-huitième *(mf)*. ◆**eighth** *a & n* huitième *(mf)*; **an e.** un huitième. ◆**eightieth** *a & n* quatre-vingtième *(mf)*. ◆**eighty** *a & n* quatre-vingts *(m)*; **e.-one** quatre-vingt-un.

Eire [ˈeərə] *n* République *f* d'Irlande.

either [ˈaɪðər] **1** *a & pron (one or other)* l'un(e) ou l'autre; *(with negative)* ni l'un(e) ni l'autre; *(each)* chaque; **on e. side de** chaque côté, des deux côtés. **2** *adv* **she can't swim e.** elle ne sait pas nager non plus; **I don't e.** (ni) moi non plus; **not so far off e.** *(moreover)* pas si loin d'ailleurs. **3** *conj* **e. ... or** ou (bien) ... ou (bien), soit ... soit; *(with negative)* ni ... ni.

eject [ɪˈdʒekt] *vt* expulser; *Tech* éjecter. ◆**ejector** *a* **e. seat** *Av* siège *m* éjectable.

eke [iːk] *vt* **to e. out** *(income etc)* faire durer; **to e. out a living** gagner (difficilement) sa vie.

elaborate [ɪˈlæbərət] *a* compliqué, détaillé; *(preparation)* minutieux; *(style)* recherché; *(meal)* raffiné; — [ɪˈlæbəreɪt] *vt (theory etc)* élaborer; — *vi* entrer dans les détails **(on** de). ◆**—ly** *adv (to plan)* minutieusement; *(to decorate)* avec recherche. ◆**elabo-'ration** *n* élaboration *f*.

elapse [ɪˈlæps] *vi* s'écouler.

elastic [ɪˈlæstɪk] *a (object, character)* élastique; **e. band** élastique *m*; — *n (fabric)* élastique *m*. ◆**e'lasticity** *n* élasticité *f*.

elated [ɪˈleɪtɪd] *a* transporté de joie. ◆**ela-tion** *n* exaltation *f*.

elbow [ˈelbəʊ] *n* coude *m*; **e. grease** *Fam* huile *f* de coude; **to have enough e. room**

avoir assez de place; — *vt* **to e. one's way se frayer un chemin (à coups de coude) (through** à travers).

elder¹ [ˈeldər] *a & n (of two people)* aîné, -ée *(mf)*. ◆**elderly** *a* assez âgé, entre deux âges. ◆**eldest** *a & n* aîné, -ée *(mf)*; **his** *or* **her e. brother** l'aîné de ses frères.

elder² [ˈeldər] *n (tree)* sureau *m*.

elect [ɪˈlekt] *vt Pol* élire **(to** à); **to e. to do** choisir de faire; — *a* **the president/etc e.** le président/*etc* désigné. ◆**election** *n* élection *f*; **general e.** élections *fpl* législatives; — *a (campaign)* électoral; *(day, results)* du scrutin, des élections. ◆**electio'neering** *n* campagne *f* électorale. ◆**elective** *a (course) Am* facultatif. ◆**electoral** *a* électoral. ◆**electorate** *n* électorat *m*.

electric [ɪˈlektrɪk] *a* électrique; **e. blanket** couverture *f* chauffante; **e. shock** décharge *f* électrique; **e. shock treatment** électrochoc *m*. ◆**electrical** *a* électrique; **e. engineer** ingénieur *m* électricien. ◆**elec'trician** *n* électricien *m*. ◆**elec'tricity** *n* électricité *f*. ◆**electrify** *vt Rail* électrifier; *(excite) Fig* électriser. ◆**electrocute** *vt* électrocuter.

electrode [ɪˈlektrəʊd] *n El* électrode *f*.

electron [ɪˈlektrɒn] *n* électron *m*; — *a (microscope)* électronique. ◆**elec'tronic** *a* électronique. ◆**elec'tronics** *n* électronique *f*.

elegant [ˈelɪɡənt] *a* élégant. ◆**elegance** *n* élégance *f*. ◆**elegantly** *adv* avec élégance, élégamment.

elegy [ˈelədʒɪ] *n* élégie *f*.

element [ˈelɪmənt] *n (component, environment)* élément *m*; *(of heater)* résistance *f*; **an e. of truth** un grain *or* une part de vérité; **the human/chance e.** le facteur humain/chance; **in one's e.** dans son élément. ◆**ele'mental** *a* élémentaire. ◆**ele'mentary** *a* élémentaire; *(school) Am* primaire; **e. courtesy** la courtoisie la plus élémentaire.

elephant [ˈelɪfənt] *n* éléphant *m*. ◆**ele-phantine** [elɪˈfæntaɪn] *a (large)* éléphantesque; *(clumsy)* gauche.

elevate [ˈelɪveɪt] *vt* élever **(to** à). ◆**ele-'vation** *n* élévation *f* **(of** de); *(height)* altitude *f*. ◆**elevator** *n Am* ascenseur *m*.

eleven [ɪˈlev(ə)n] *a & n* onze *(m)*. ◆**elevenses** [ɪˈlev(ə)nzɪz] *n Fam* pause-café *f (vers onze heures du matin)*. ◆**eleventh** *a & n* onzième *(mf)*.

elf [elf] *n (pl elves)* lutin *m*.

elicit [ɪˈlɪsɪt] *vt* tirer, obtenir **(from** de).

elide [ɪˈlaɪd] *vt Ling* élider. ◆**elision** *n* élision *f*.

eligible ['elɪdʒəb(ə)l] *a* (*for post etc*) admissible (for à); (*for political office*) éligible (for à); **to be e. for** (*entitled to*) avoir droit à; **an e. young man** (*suitable as husband*) un beau parti. ◆**eligi'bility** *n* admissibilité *f*; *Pol* éligibilité *f*.

eliminate [ɪ'lɪmɪneɪt] *vt* éliminer (**from** de). ◆**elimi'nation** *n* élimination *f*.

elite [eɪ'liːt] *n* élite *f* (**of** de).

elk [elk] *n* (*animal*) élan *m*.

ellipse [ɪ'lɪps] *n* *Geom* ellipse *f*. ◆**elliptical** *a* elliptique.

elm [elm] *n* (*tree, wood*) orme *m*.

elocution [elə'kjuːʃ(ə)n] *n* élocution *f*.

elongate ['iːlɒŋɡeɪt] *vt* allonger. ◆**elon'gation** *n* allongement *m*.

elope [ɪ'ləʊp] *vi* (*of lovers*) s'enfuir (**with** avec). ◆**—ment** *n* fugue *f* (amoureuse).

eloquent ['eləkwənt] *a* éloquent. ◆**eloquence** *n* éloquence *f*.

else [els] *adv* d'autre; **someone e.** quelqu'un d'autre; **everybody e.** tout le monde à part moi, vous *etc*, tous les autres; **nobody/nothing e.** personne/rien d'autre; **something e.** autre chose; **something *or* anything e.?** encore quelque chose?; **somewhere e.** ailleurs, autre part; **who e.?** qui encore?, qui d'autre?; **how e.?** de quelle autre façon?; **or e.** ou bien, sinon. ◆**elsewhere** *adv* ailleurs; **e. in the town** dans une autre partie de la ville.

elucidate [ɪ'luːsɪdeɪt] *vt* élucider.

elude [ɪ'luːd] *vt* (*enemy*) échapper à; (*question*) éluder; (*obligation*) se dérober à; (*blow*) esquiver. ◆**elusive** *a* (*enemy, aims*) insaisissable; (*reply*) évasif.

emaciated [ɪ'meɪsɪeɪtɪd] *a* émacié.

emanate ['eməneɪt] *vi* émaner (**from** de).

emancipate [ɪ'mænsɪpeɪt] *vt* (*women*) émanciper. ◆**emanci'pation** *n* émancipation *f*.

embalm [ɪm'bɑːm] *vt* (*dead body*) embaumer.

embankment [ɪm'bæŋkmənt] *n* (*of path etc*) talus *m*; (*of river*) berge *f*.

embargo [ɪm'bɑːɡəʊ] *n* (*pl* -oes) embargo *m*.

embark [ɪm'bɑːk] *vt* embarquer; – *vi* (s')embarquer; **to e. on** (*start*) commencer, entamer; (*launch into*) se lancer dans, s'embarquer dans. ◆**embar'kation** *n* embarquement *m*.

embarrass [ɪm'bærəs] *vt* embarrasser, gêner. ◆**—ing** *a* (*question etc*) embarrassant. ◆**—ment** *n* embarras *m*, gêne *f*; (*financial*) embarras *mpl*.

embassy ['embəsɪ] *n* ambassade *f*.

embattled [ɪm'bæt(ə)ld] *a* (*political party, person etc*) assiégé de toutes parts; (*attitude*) belliqueux.

embedded [ɪm'bedɪd] *a* (*stick, bullet*) enfoncé; (*jewel*) & *Ling* enchâssé; (*in one's memory*) gravé; (*in stone*) scellé.

embellish [ɪm'belɪʃ] *vt* embellir. ◆**—ment** *n* embellissement *m*.

embers ['embəz] *npl* braise *f*, charbons *mpl* ardents.

embezzle [ɪm'bez(ə)l] *vt* (*money*) détourner. ◆**—ement** *n* détournement *m* de fonds. ◆**—er** *n* escroc *m*, voleur *m*.

embitter [ɪm'bɪtər] *vt* (*person*) aigrir; (*situation*) envenimer.

emblem ['embləm] *n* emblème *m*.

embody [ɪm'bɒdɪ] *vt* (*express*) exprimer; (*represent*) incarner; (*include*) réunir. ◆**embodiment** *n* incarnation *f* (**of** de).

emboss [ɪm'bɒs] *vt* (*metal*) emboutir; (*paper*) gaufrer, emboutir. ◆**—ed** *a* en relief.

embrace [ɪm'breɪs] *vt* étreindre, embrasser; (*include, adopt*) embrasser; – *vi* s'étreindre, s'embrasser; – *n* étreinte *f*.

embroider [ɪm'brɔɪdər] *vt* (*cloth*) broder; (*story, facts*) *Fig* enjoliver. ◆**embroidery** *n* broderie *f*.

embroil [ɪm'brɔɪl] *vt* **to e. s.o. in** mêler qn à.

embryo ['embrɪəʊ] *n* (*pl* -os) embryon *m*. ◆**embry'onic** *a* *Med* & *Fig* embryonnaire.

emcee [em'siː] *n* *Am* présentateur, -trice *mf*.

emend [ɪ'mend] *vt* (*text*) corriger.

emerald ['emərəld] *n* émeraude *f*.

emerge [ɪ'mɜːdʒ] *vi* apparaître (**from** de); (*from hole etc*) sortir; (*of truth, from water*) émerger; (*of nation*) naître; **it emerges that** il apparaît que. ◆**emergence** *n* apparition *f*.

emergency [ɪ'mɜːdʒənsɪ] *n* (*case*) urgence *f*; (*crisis*) crise *f*; (*contingency*) éventualité *f*; **in an e.** en cas d'urgence; – *a* (*measure etc*) d'urgence; (*exit, brake*) de secours; (*ward, services*) *Med* des urgences; **e. landing** atterrissage *m* forcé; **e. powers** *Pol* pouvoirs *mpl* extraordinaires.

emery ['emərɪ] *a* **e. cloth** toile *f* (d')émeri.

emigrant ['emɪɡrənt] *n* émigrant, -ante *mf*. ◆**emigrate** *vi* émigrer. ◆**emi'gration** *n* émigration *f*.

eminent ['emɪnənt] *a* éminent. ◆**eminence** *n* distinction *f*; **his E.** *Rel* son Éminence *f*. ◆**eminently** *adv* hautement, remarquablement.

emissary ['emɪsərɪ] *n* émissaire *m*.

emit [ɪ'mɪt] *vt* (-tt-) (*light, heat etc*) émettre;

(*smell*) dégager. ◆**emission** *n* émission *f*; dégagement *m*.

emotion [ɪ'məʊʃ(ə)n] *n* (*strength of feeling*) émotion *f*; (*joy, love etc*) sentiment *m*. ◆**emotional** *a* (*person, reaction*) émotif; (*story, speech*) émouvant; (*moment*) d'émotion intense; (*state*) *Psy* émotionnel. ◆**emotionally** *adv* (*to say*) avec émotion; **to be e. unstable** avoir des troubles émotifs. ◆**emotive** *a* (*person*) émotif; (*word*) affectif; **an e. issue** une question sensible.

emperor ['empərər] *n* empereur *m*.

emphasize ['emfəsaɪz] *vt* souligner (**that** que); (*word, fact*) appuyer *or* insister sur, souligner. ◆**emphasis** *n* *Ling* accent *m* (tonique); (*insistence*) insistance *f*; **to lay** *or* **put e. on** mettre l'accent sur. ◆**em'phatic** *a* (*person, refusal*) catégorique; (*forceful*) énergique; **to be e. about** insister sur. ◆**em'phatically** *adv* catégoriquement; énergiquement; **e. no!** absolument pas!

empire ['empaɪər] *n* empire *m*.

empirical [em'pɪrɪk(ə)l] *a* empirique. ◆**empiricism** *n* empirisme *m*.

employ [ɪm'plɔɪ] *vt* (*person, means*) employer; – *n* **in the e. of** employé par. ◆**employee** [ɪm'plɔɪiː, emplɔɪ'iː] *n* employé, -ée *mf*. ◆**employer** *n* patron, -onne *mf*. ◆**employment** *n* emploi *m*; **place of e.** lieu *m* de travail; **in the e. of** employé par; **e. agency** bureau *m* de placement.

empower [ɪm'paʊər] *vt* autoriser (**to do** à faire).

empress ['emprɪs] *n* impératrice *f*.

empt/y ['emptɪ] *a* (-ier, -iest) vide; (*threat, promise etc*) vain; (*stomach*) creux; **on an e. stomach** à jeun; **to return**/*etc* **e.-handed** revenir/*etc* les mains vides; – *npl* (*bottles*) bouteilles *fpl* vides; – *vt* **to e. (out)** (*box, pocket, liquid etc*) vider; (*vehicle*) décharger; (*objects in box etc*) sortir (**from, out of** de); – *vi* se vider; (*of river*) se jeter (**into** dans). ◆**-iness** *n* vide *m*.

emulate ['emjʊleɪt] *vt* imiter. ◆**emu'lation** *n* émulation *f*.

emulsion [ɪ'mʌlʃ(ə)n] *n* (*paint*) peinture *f* (mate); *Phot* émulsion *f*.

enable [ɪ'neɪb(ə)l] *vt* **to e. s.o. to do** permettre à qn de faire.

enact [ɪn'ækt] *vt* (*law*) promulguer; (*part of play*) jouer.

enamel [ɪ'næm(ə)l] *n* émail *m*; – *a* en émail; – *vt* (-ll-, *Am* -l-) émailler.

enamoured [ɪn'æməd] *a* **e. of** (*thing*) séduit par; (*person*) amoureux de.

encamp [ɪn'kæmp] *vi* camper. ◆**—ment** *n* campement *m*.

encapsulate [ɪn'kæpsjʊleɪt] *vt* *Fig* résumer.

encase [ɪn'keɪs] *vt* recouvrir (**in** de).

enchant [ɪn'tʃɑːnt] *vt* enchanter. ◆**—ing** *a* enchanteur. ◆**—ment** *n* enchantement *m*.

encircle [ɪn'sɜːk(ə)l] *vt* entourer; *Mil* encercler. ◆**—ment** *n* encerclement *m*.

enclave ['enkleɪv] *n* enclave *f*.

enclos/e [ɪn'kləʊz] *vt* (*send with letter*) joindre (**in, with** à); (*fence off*) clôturer; **to e. with** (*a fence, wall*) entourer de. ◆**—ed** *a* (*space*) clos; (*cheque etc*) ci-joint; (*market*) couvert. ◆**enclosure** *n* *Com* pièce *f* jointe; (*fence, place*) enceinte *f*.

encompass [ɪn'kʌmpəs] *vt* (*surround*) entourer; (*include*) inclure.

encore ['ɒŋkɔːr] *int* & *n* bis (*m*); – *vt* bisser.

encounter [ɪn'kaʊntər] *vt* rencontrer; – *n* rencontre *f*.

encourage [ɪn'kʌrɪdʒ] *vt* encourager (**to do** à faire). ◆**—ment** *n* encouragement *m*.

encroach [ɪn'krəʊtʃ] *vi* empiéter (**on, upon** sur); **to e. on the land** (*of sea*) gagner du terrain. ◆**—ment** *n* empiétement *m*.

encumber [ɪn'kʌmbər] *vt* encombrer (**with** de). ◆**encum'brance** *n* embarras *m*.

encyclical [ɪn'sɪklɪk(ə)l] *n* *Rel* encyclique *f*.

encyclop(a)edia [ɪnsaɪklə'piːdɪə] *n* encyclopédie *f*. ◆**encyclop(a)edic** *a* encyclopédique.

end [end] *n* (*of street, object etc*) bout *m*, extrémité *f*; (*of time, meeting, book etc*) fin *f*; (*purpose*) but *m*, fin *m*; **at an e.** (*discussion etc*) fini; (*period*) écoulé; (*patience*) à bout; **in the e.** à la fin; **to come to an e.** prendre fin; **to put an e. to, bring to an e.** mettre fin à; **there's no e. to it** ça n'en finit plus; **no e. of** *Fam* beaucoup de; **six days on e.** six jours d'affilée; **for days on e.** pendant des jours (et des jours); (**standing**) **on e.** (*box etc*) debout; (*hair*) hérissé; – *a* (*row, house*) dernier; **e. product** *Com* produit *m* fini; *Fig* résultat *m*; – *vt* finir, terminer, achever (**with** par); (*rumour, speculation*) mettre fin à; – *vi* finir, se terminer, s'achever; **to e. in failure** se solder par un échec; **to e. in a point** finir en pointe; **to e. up doing** finir par faire; **to e. up in** (*London etc*) se retrouver à; **he ended up in prison/a doctor** il a fini en prison/par devenir médecin.

endanger [ɪn'deɪndʒər] *vt* mettre en danger.

endear [ɪn'dɪər] *vt* faire aimer *or* apprécier (**to** de); **that's what endears him to me** c'est cela qui me plaît en lui. ◆**—ing** *a* attachant, sympathique. ◆**—ment** *n* parole f tendre; **term of e.** terme m d'affection.

endeavour [ɪn'devər] vi s'efforcer (**to do** de faire); − n effort m (**to do** pour faire).

ending ['endɪŋ] n fin f; (*outcome*) issue f; **Ling** terminaison f. ◆**endless** a (*speech, series etc*) interminable; (*patience*) infini; (*countless*) innombrable. ◆**endlessly** adv interminablement.

endive ['endɪv, Am 'endaɪv] n Bot Culin (*curly*) chicorée f; (*smooth*) endive f.

endorse [ɪn'dɔɪs] vt (*cheque etc*) endosser; (*action*) approuver; (*claim*) appuyer. ◆−**ment** n (*on driving licence*) contravention f.

endow [ɪn'daʊ] vt (*institution*) doter (**with** de); (*chair, hospital bed*) fonder; **endowed with** (*person*) Fig doté de. ◆−**ment** n dotation f; fondation f.

endur/e [ɪn'djʊər] 1 vt (*bear*) supporter (**doing** de faire). 2 vi (*last*) durer. ◆−**ing** a durable. ◆−**able** a supportable. ◆**endurance** n endurance f, résistance f.

enemy ['enəmɪ] n ennemi, -ie mf; − a (*army, tank etc*) ennemi.

energy ['enədʒɪ] n énergie f; − a (*crisis, resources etc*) énergétique. ◆**ener'getic** a énergique; **to feel e.** se sentir en pleine forme. ◆**ener'getically** adv énergiquement.

enforc/e [ɪn'fɔɪs] vt (*law*) faire respecter; (*discipline*) imposer (**on** à). ◆−**ed** a (*rest, silence etc*) forcé.

engag/e [ɪn'geɪdʒ] vt (*take on*) engager, prendre; **to e. s.o. in conversation** engager la conversation avec qn; **to e. the clutch** Aut embrayer; − vi **to e. in** (*launch into*) se lancer dans; (*be involved in*) être mêlé à. ◆−**ed** a 1 (*person, toilet*) & Tel occupé; **e. in doing** occupé à faire; **to be e. in business**/etc être dans les affaires/etc. 2 (*betrothed*) fiancé; **to get e.** se -fiancer. ◆−**ing** a (*smile*) engageant. ◆−**ement** n (*agreement to marry*) fiançailles fpl; (*meeting*) rendez-vous m inv; (*undertaking*) engagement m; **to have a prior e.** (*be busy*) être déjà pris, ne pas être libre; **e. ring** bague f de fiançailles.

engender [ɪn'dʒendər] vt (*produce*) engendrer.

engine ['endʒɪn] n Aut moteur m; Rail locomotive f; Nau machine f; **e. driver** mécanicien m.

engineer [endʒɪ'nɪər] 1 n ingénieur m; (*repairer*) dépanneur m; Rail Am mécanicien m; **civil e.** ingénieur m des travaux publics; **mechanical e.** ingénieur m

mécanicien. **2** vt (*arrange secretly*) machiner. ◆−**ing** n ingénierie f; (**civil**) **e.** génie m civil, travaux mpl publics; (**mechanical**) **e.** mécanique f; **e. factory** atelier m de construction mécanique.

England ['ɪŋglənd] n Angleterre f. ◆**English** a anglais; **the E. Channel** la Manche; **the E.** les Anglais mpl; − n (*language*) anglais m. ◆**Englishman** n (*pl* -men) Anglais m. ◆**English-speaking** a anglophone. ◆**Englishwoman** n (*pl* -women) Anglaise f.

engrav/e [ɪn'greɪv] vt graver. ◆−**ing** n gravure f. ◆−**er** n graveur m.

engrossed [ɪn'groʊst] a absorbé (**in** par).

engulf [ɪn'gʌlf] vt engloutir.

enhance [ɪn'hɑːns] vt (*beauty etc*) rehausser; (*value*) augmenter.

enigma [ɪ'nɪgmə] n énigme f. ◆**enig'matic** a énigmatique.

enjoy [ɪn'dʒɔɪ] vt aimer (**doing** faire); (*meal*) apprécier; (*income, standard of living etc*) jouir de; **to e. the evening** passer une bonne soirée; **to e. oneself** s'amuser; **to e. being in London**/etc se plaire à Londres/etc. ◆−**able** a agréable. ◆−**ably** adv agréablement. ◆−**ment** n plaisir m.

enlarge [ɪn'lɑːdʒ] vt agrandir; − vi s'agrandir; **to e. (up)on** (*say more about*) s'étendre sur. ◆−**ment** n agrandissement m.

enlighten [ɪn'laɪt(ə)n] vt éclairer (**s.o. on** or **about sth** qn sur qch). ◆−**ing** a instructif. ◆−**ment** n (*explanations*) éclaircissements mpl; **an age of e.** une époque éclairée.

enlist [ɪn'lɪst] vi (*in the army etc*) s'engager; − vt (*recruit*) engager; (*supporter*) recruter; (*support*) obtenir. ◆−**ment** n engagement m; recrutement m.

enliven [ɪn'laɪv(ə)n] vt (*meeting, people etc*) égayer, animer.

enmeshed [ɪn'meʃt] a empêtré (**in** dans).

enmity ['enmɪtɪ] n inimitié f (**between** entre).

enormous [ɪ'nɔɪməs] a énorme; (*explosion*) terrible; (*success*) fou. ◆**enormity** n (*vastness, extent*) énormité f; (*atrocity*) atrocité f. ◆**enormously** adv (*very much*) énormément; (*very*) extrêmement.

enough [ɪ'nʌf] a & n assez (de); **e. time**/**cups**/etc assez de temps/de tasses/etc; **to have e. to live on** avoir de quoi vivre; **to have e. to drink** avoir assez à boire; **to have had e. of** Pej en avoir assez de; **it's e. for me to see that** . . . il me suffit de voir que . . . ; **that's e.** ça suffit, c'est assez; − adv assez, suffisamment (**to** pour); **strangely e., he left** chose curieuse, il est parti.

enquire [ɪnˈkwaɪər] *vi* = **inquire.**

enquiry [ɪnˈkwaɪərɪ] *n* = **inquiry.**

enrage [ɪnˈreɪdʒ] *vt* mettre en rage.

enrapture [ɪnˈræptʃər] *vt* ravir.

enrich [ɪnˈrɪtʃ] *vt* enrichir; (*soil*) fertiliser. ◆**—ment** *n* enrichissement *m*.

enrol [ɪnˈrəʊl] (*Am* **enroll**) *vi* (**-ll-**) s'inscrire (**in, for** à); – *vt* inscrire. ◆**—ment** *n* inscription *f*; (*people enrolled*) effectif *m*.

ensconced [ɪnˈskɒnst] *a* bien installé (**in** dans).

ensemble [ɒnˈsɒmb(ə)l] *n* (*clothes*) & *Mus* ensemble *m*.

ensign [ˈensən] *n* (*flag*) pavillon *m*; (*rank*) *Am Nau* enseigne *m* de vaisseau.

enslave [ɪnˈsleɪv] *vt* asservir.

ensu/e [ɪnˈsjuː] *vi* s'ensuivre. ◆**—ing** *a* (*day, year etc*) suivant; (*event*) qui s'ensuit.

ensure [ɪnˈʃʊər] *vt* assurer; **to e. that** (*make sure*) s'assurer que.

entail [ɪnˈteɪl] *vt* (*imply, involve*) entraîner, impliquer.

entangle [ɪnˈtæŋg(ə)l] *vt* emmêler, enchevêtrer; **to get entangled** s'empêtrer. ◆**—ment** *n* enchevêtrement *m*; **an e. with** (*police*) des démêlés *mpl* avec.

enter [ˈentər] *vt* (*room, vehicle, army etc*) entrer dans; (*road*) s'engager dans; (*university*) s'inscrire à; (*write down*) inscrire (**in** dans, **on** sur); (*in ledger*) porter (**in** sur); **to e. s.o. for** (*exam*) présenter qn à; **to e. a painting**/*etc* **in** (*competition*) présenter un tableau/*etc* à; **it didn't e. my head** ça ne m'est pas venu à l'esprit (**that** que); – *vi* entrer; **to e. for** (*race, exam*) s'inscrire pour; **to e. into** (*plans*) entrer dans; (*conversation, relations*) entrer en; **you don't e. into it** tu n'y es pour rien; **to e. into** *or* **upon** (*career*) entrer dans; (*negotiations*) entamer; (*agreement*) conclure.

enterpris/e [ˈentəpraɪz] *n* (*undertaking, firm*) entreprise *f*; (*spirit*) *Fig* initiative *f*. ◆**—ing** *a* (*person*) plein d'initiative; (*attempt*) hardi.

entertain [entəˈteɪn] *vt* amuser, distraire; (*guest*) recevoir; (*idea, possibility*) envisager; (*hope*) chérir; **to e. s.o. to a meal** recevoir qn à dîner; – *vi* (*receive guests*) recevoir. ◆**—ing** *a* amusant. ◆**—er** *n* artiste *mf*. ◆**—ment** *n* amusement *m*, distraction *f*; (*show*) spectacle *m*.

enthral(l) [ɪnˈθrɔːl] *vt* (**-ll-**) (*delight*) captiver.

enthuse [ɪnˈθjuːz] *vi* **to e. over** *Fam* s'emballer pour. ◆**enthusiasm** *n* enthousiasme *m*. ◆**enthusiast** *n* enthousiaste

mf; **jazz**/*etc* **e.** passionné, -ée *mf* du jazz/*etc*. ◆**enthusi'astic** *a* enthousiaste; (*golfer etc*) passionné; **to be e. about** (*hobby*) être passionné de; **he was e. about** *or* **over** (*gift etc*) il a été emballé par; **to get e.** s'emballer (**about** pour). ◆**enthusi-'astically** *adv* avec enthousiasme.

entic/e [ɪnˈtaɪs] *vt* attirer (par la ruse); **to e. to do** entraîner (par la ruse) à faire. ◆**—ing** *a* séduisant, alléchant. ◆**—ement** *n* (*bait*) attrait *m*.

entire [ɪnˈtaɪər] *a* entier. ◆**—ly** *adv* tout à fait, entièrement. ◆**entirety** [ɪnˈtaɪərətɪ] *n* intégralité *f*; **in its e.** en entier.

entitl/e [ɪnˈtaɪt(ə)l] *vt* **to e. s.o. to do** donner à qn le droit de faire; **to e. s.o. to sth** donner à qn (le) droit à qch; **that entitles me to believe that . . .** ça m'autorise à croire que . . . . ◆**—ed** *a* (*book*) intitulé; **to be e. to do** avoir le droit de faire; **to be e. to sth** avoir droit à qch. ◆**—ement** *n* **one's e.** son dû.

entity [ˈentɪtɪ] *n* entité *f*.

entourage [ˈɒntʊrɑːʒ] *n* entourage *m*.

entrails [ˈentreɪlz] *npl* entrailles *fpl*.

entrance 1 [ˈentrəns] *n* entrée *f* (**to** de); (*to university etc*) admission *f* (**to** à); **e. examination** examen *m* d'entrée. **2** [ɪnˈtrɑːns] *vt Fig* transporter, ravir.

entrant [ˈentrənt] *n* (*in race*) concurrent, -ente *mf*; (*for exam*) candidat, -ate *mf*.

entreat [ɪnˈtriːt] *vt* supplier, implorer (**to do** de faire). ◆**entreaty** *n* supplication *f*.

entrée [ˈɒntreɪ] *n Culin* entrée *f*; (*main dish*) *Am* plat *m* principal.

entrench [ɪnˈtrentʃ] *vt* **to e. oneself** *Mil* & *Fig* se retrancher.

entrust [ɪnˈtrʌst] *vt* confier (**to** à); **to e. s.o. with sth** confier qch à qn.

entry [ˈentrɪ] *n* (*way in, action*) entrée *f*; (*in ledger*) écriture *f*; (*term in dictionary or logbook*) entrée *f*; (*competitor*) *Sp* concurrent, -ente *mf*; (*thing to be judged in competition*) objet *m* (*or* œuvre *f or* projet *m*) soumis à un jury; **e. form** feuille *f* d'inscription; **'no e.'** (*on door etc*) 'entrée interdite'; (*road sign*) 'sens interdit'.

entwine [ɪnˈtwaɪn] *vt* entrelacer.

enumerate [ɪˈnjuːmərcɪt] *vt* énumérer. ◆**enume'ration** *n* énumération *f*.

enunciate [ɪˈnʌnsɪeɪt] *vt* (*word*) articuler; (*theory*) énoncer. ◆**enunci'ation** *n* articulation *f*; énonciation *f*.

envelop [ɪnˈveləp] *vt* envelopper (**in fog/mystery**/*etc* de brouillard/mystère/*etc*).

envelope [ˈenvələʊp] *n* enveloppe *f*.

envious [ˈenvɪəs] *a* envieux (**of sth** de qch);

e. of s.o. jaloux de qn. ◆**enviable** *a* enviable. ◆**enviously** *adv* avec envie.

environment [ɪn'vaɪərənmənt] *n* milieu *m*; (*cultural, natural*) environnement *m*. ◆**environ'mental** *a* du milieu; de l'environnement. ◆**environ'mentalist** *n* écologiste *mf*.

envisage [ɪn'vɪzɪdʒ] *vt* (*imagine*) envisager; (*foresee*) prévoir.

envision [ɪn'vɪʒ(ə)n] *vt Am* = envisage.

envoy ['envɔɪ] *n Pol* envoyé, -ée *mf*.

envy ['envɪ] *n* envie *f*; – *vt* envier (s.o. sth qch à qn).

ephemeral [ɪ'femərəl] *a* éphémère.

epic ['epɪk] *a* épique; – *n* épopée *f*; (screen) e. film *m* à grand spectacle.

epidemic [epɪ'demɪk] *n* épidémie *f*; – *a* épidémique.

epilepsy ['epɪlepsɪ] *n* épilepsie *f*. ◆**epi'leptic** *a* & *n* épileptique (*mf*).

epilogue ['epɪlɒg] *n* épilogue *m*.

episode ['epɪsəʊd] *n* épisode *m*. ◆**epi'sodic** [epɪ'sɒdɪk] *a* épisodique.

epistle [ɪ'pɪs(ə)l] *n* épître *f*.

epitaph ['epɪtɑːf] *n* épitaphe *f*.

epithet ['epɪθet] *n* épithète *f*.

epitome [ɪ'pɪtəmɪ] *n* the e. of l'exemple même de, l'incarnation de. ◆**epitomize** *vt* incarner.

epoch ['iːpɒk] *n* époque *f*. ◆**e.-making** *a* (*event*) qui fait date.

equal ['iːkwəl] *a* égal (to à); with e. hostility avec la même hostilité; on an e. footing sur un pied d'égalité (with avec); to be e. to égaler; e. to (*task, situation*) *Fig* à la hauteur de; – *n* égal, -ale *mf*; to treat s.o. as an e. traiter qn en égal or d'égal à égal; he doesn't have his e. il n'a pas son pareil; – *vt* (-ll-, *Am* -l-) égaler (in beauty/*etc* en beauté/*etc*); equals sign *Math* signe *m* d'égalité. ◆**e'quality** *n* égalité *f*. ◆**equalize** *vt* égaliser; – *vi Sp* égaliser. ◆**equally** *adv* (*to an equal degree, also*) également; (*to divide*) en parts égales; he's e. stupid (*just as*) il est tout aussi bête.

equanimity [ekwə'nɪmɪtɪ] *n* égalité *f* d'humeur.

equate [ɪ'kweɪt] *vt* mettre sur le même pied (with que), assimiler (with à).

equation [ɪ'kweɪʒ(ə)n] *n Math* équation *f*.

equator [ɪ'kweɪtər] *n* équateur *m*; at or on the e. sous l'équateur. ◆**equatorial** [ekwə'tɔːrɪəl] *a* équatorial.

equestrian [ɪ'kwestrɪən] *a* équestre.

equilibrium [iːkwɪ'lɪbrɪəm] *n* équilibre *m*.

equinox ['iːkwɪnɒks] *n* équinoxe *m*.

equip [ɪ'kwɪp] *vt* (-pp-) équiper (with de);

(well-)equipped with pourvu de; (well-)equipped to do compétent pour faire. ◆**—ment** *n* équipement *m*, matériel *m*.

equity ['ekwɪtɪ] *n* (*fairness*) équité *f*; *pl Com* actions *fpl*. ◆**equitable** *a* équitable.

equivalent [ɪ'kwɪvələnt] *a* & *n* équivalent (*m*). ◆**equivalence** *n* équivalence *f*.

equivocal [ɪ'kwɪvək(ə)l] *a* équivoque.

era ['ɪərə, *Am* 'erə] *n* époque *f*; (*historical, geological*) ère *f*.

eradicate [ɪ'rædɪkeɪt] *vt* supprimer; (*evil, prejudice*) extirper.

erase [ɪ'reɪz, *Am* ɪ'reɪs] *vt* effacer. ◆**eraser** *n* (*rubber*) gomme *f*. ◆**erasure** *n* rature *f*.

erect [ɪ'rekt] **1** *a* (*upright*) (bien) droit. **2** *vt* (*build*) construire; (*statue, monument*) ériger; (*scaffolding*) monter; (*tent*) dresser. ◆**erection** *n* construction *f*; érection *f*; montage *m*; dressage *m*.

ermine ['ɜːmɪn] *n* (*animal, fur*) hermine *f*.

erode [ɪ'rəʊd] *vt* éroder; (*confidence etc*) *Fig* miner, ronger. ◆**erosion** *n* érosion *f*.

erotic [ɪ'rɒtɪk] *a* érotique. ◆**eroticism** *n* érotisme *m*.

err [ɜːr] *vi* (*be wrong*) se tromper; (*sin*) pécher.

errand ['erənd] *n* commission *f*, course *f*; e. boy garçon *m* de courses.

erratic [ɪ'rætɪk] *a* (*conduct etc*) irrégulier; (*person*) lunatique.

error ['erər] *n* (*mistake*) erreur *f*, faute *f*; (*wrongdoing*) erreur *f*; in e. par erreur. ◆**erroneous** [ɪ'rəʊnɪəs] *a* erroné.

erudite ['eruːdaɪt, *Am* 'erjʊdaɪt] *a* érudit, savant. ◆**eru'dition** *n* érudition *f*.

erupt [ɪ'rʌpt] *vi* (*of volcano*) entrer en éruption; (*of pimples*) apparaître; (*of war, violence*) éclater. ◆**eruption** *n* (*of volcano, pimples, anger*) éruption *f* (**of** de); (*of violence*) flambée *f*.

escalate ['eskəleɪt] *vi* (*of war, violence*) s'intensifier; (*of prices*) monter en flèche; – *vt* intensifier. ◆**esca'lation** *n* escalade *f*.

escalator ['eskəleɪtər] *n* escalier *m* roulant.

escapade ['eskəpeɪd] *n* (*prank*) frasque *f*.

escape [ɪ'skeɪp] *vi* (*of gas, animal etc*) s'échapper; (*of prisoner*) s'évader, s'échapper; to e. from (*person*) s'échapper de; (*place, object*) s'échapper de; escaped prisoner évadé, -ée *mf*; – *vt* (*death*) échapper à; (*punishment*) éviter; that name escapes me ce nom m'échappe; to e. notice passer inaperçu; – *n* (*of gas etc*) fuite *f*; (*of person*) évasion *f*, fuite *f*; to have a lucky or narrow e. l'échapper belle. ◆**escapism** *n* évasion *f* (hors de la réalité). ◆**escapist** *a* (*film etc*) d'évasion.

eschew [ɪˈstʃuɪ] *vt* éviter, fuir.

escort [ˈeskɔɪt] *n Mil Nau* escorte *f*; (*of woman*) cavalier *m*; − [ɪˈskɔɪt] *vt* escorter.

Eskimo [ˈeskɪməʊ] *n* (*pl* -os) Esquimau, -aude *mf*; − *a* esquimau.

esoteric [esəʊˈterɪk] *a* obscur, ésotérique.

especial [ɪˈspeʃəl] *a* particulier. ◆—ly *adv* (*in particular*) particulièrement; (*for particular purpose*) (tout) exprès; e. as d'autant plus que.

espionage [ˈespɪənɑːʒ] *n* espionnage *m*.

esplanade [ˈespləneɪd] *n* esplanade *f*.

espouse [ɪˈspaʊz] *vt* (*a cause*) épouser.

espresso [eˈspresəʊ] *n* (*pl* -os) (café *m*) express *m*.

Esq [ɪˈskwaɪər] *abbr* (*esquire*) J. Smith Esq (*on envelope*) Monsieur J. Smith.

essay [ˈeseɪ] *n* (*attempt*) & *Liter* essai *m*; *Sch* rédaction *f*; *Univ* dissertation *f*.

essence [ˈesəns] *n Phil Ch* essence *f*; *Culin* extrait *m*, essence *f*; (*main point*) essentiel *m* (of de); in e. essentiellement.

essential [ɪˈsenʃ(ə)l] *a* (*principal*) essentiel; (*necessary*) indispensable, essentiel; it's e. that il est indispensable que (+ *sub*); − *npl* the essentials l'essentiel *m* (of de); (*of grammar*) les éléments *mpl*. ◆—ly *adv* essentiellement.

establish [ɪˈstæblɪʃ] *vt* établir; (*state, society*) fonder. ◆—ed *a* (well-)e. (*firm*) solide; (*fact*) reconnu; (*reputation*) établi; she's (well-)e. elle a une réputation établie. ◆—ment *n* (*institution, firm*) établissement *m*; the e. of l'établissement de; la fondation de; the E. les classes *fpl* dirigeantes.

estate [ɪˈsteɪt] *n* (*land*) terre(s) *f(pl)*, propriété *f*; (*possessions*) *Jur* fortune *f*; (*of deceased person*) succession *f*; housing e. lotissement *m*; (*workers*) cité *f* (ouvrière); industrial e. complexe *m* industriel; e. agency agence *f* immobilière; e. agent agent *m* immobilier; e. car break *m*; e. tax *Am* droits *mpl* de succession.

esteem [ɪˈstiːm] *vt* estimer; highly esteemed très estimé; − *n* estime *f*.

esthetic [esˈθetɪk] *a Am* esthétique.

estimate [ˈestɪmeɪt] *vt* (*value*) estimer, évaluer; (*consider*) estimer (that que); − [ˈestɪmət] *n* (*assessment*) évaluation *f*, estimation *f*; (*judgement*) évaluation *f*; (*price for work to be done*) devis *m*; rough e. chiffre *m* approximatif. ◆esti'mation *n* jugement *m*; (*esteem*) estime *f*; in my e. à mon avis.

estranged [ɪˈstreɪndʒd] *a* to become e. (*of couple*) se séparer.

estuary [ˈestjʊərɪ] *n* estuaire *m*.

etc [etˈsetərə] *adv* etc.

etch [etʃ] *vti* graver à l'eau forte. ◆—ing *n* (*picture*) eau-forte *f*.

eternal [ɪˈtɜːn(ə)l] *a* éternel. ◆eternally *adv* éternellement. ◆eternity *n* éternité *f*.

ether [ˈiːθər] *n* éther *m*. ◆e'thereal *a* éthéré.

ethic [ˈeθɪk] *n* éthique *f*. ◆ethics *n* (*moral standards*) moralité *f*; (*study*) *Phil* éthique *f*. ◆ethical *a* moral, éthique.

Ethiopia [iːθɪˈəʊpɪə] *n* Éthiopie *f*. ◆Ethiopian *a* & *n* éthiopien, -ienne (*mf*).

ethnic [ˈeθnɪk] *a* ethnique.

ethos [ˈiːθɒs] *n* génie *m*.

etiquette [ˈetɪket] *n* (*rules*) bienséances *fpl*; (*diplomatic*) e. protocole *m*, étiquette *f*; professional e. déontologie *f*.

etymology [etɪˈmɒlədʒɪ] *n* étymologie *f*.

eucalyptus [juːkəˈlɪptəs] *n* (*tree*) eucalyptus *m*.

eulogy [ˈjuːlədʒɪ] *n* panégyrique *m*, éloge *m*.

euphemism [ˈjuːfɪmɪz(ə)m] *n* euphémisme *m*.

euphoria [juːˈfɔːrɪə] *n* euphorie *f*. ◆euphoric *a* euphorique.

Euro- [ˈjʊərəʊ] *pref* euro-.

Europe [ˈjʊərəp] *n* Europe *f*. ◆Euro'pean *a* & *n* européen, -éenne (*mf*).

euthanasia [juːθəˈneɪzɪə] *n* euthanasie *f*.

evacuate [ɪˈvækjʊeɪt] *vt* évacuer. ◆evacu-'ation *n* évacuation *f*.

evade [ɪˈveɪd] *vt* éviter, esquiver; (*pursuer, tax*) échapper à; (*law, question*) éluder.

evaluate [ɪˈvæljʊeɪt] *vt* évaluer (at à). ◆evalu'ation *n* évaluation *f*.

evangelical [iːvænˈdʒelɪk(ə)l] *a Rel* évangélique.

evaporat/e [ɪˈvæpəreɪt] *vi* s'évaporer; (*of hopes*) s'évanouir. ◆—ed *a* e. milk lait *m* concentré. ◆evapo'ration *n* évaporation *f*.

evasion [ɪˈveɪʒ(ə)n] *n* e. of (*pursuer etc*) fuite *f* devant; (*question*) esquive *f* de; tax e. évasion *f* fiscale. ◆evasive *a* évasif.

eve [iːv] *n* the e. of la veille de.

even [ˈiːv(ə)n] **1** *a* (*flat*) uni, égal, lisse; (*equal*) égal; (*regular*) régulier; (*number*) pair; to get e. with se venger de; I'll get e. with him (for that) je lui revaudrai ça; we're e. (*quits*) nous sommes quittes; (*in score*) nous sommes à égalité; to break e. *Fin* s'y retrouver; − *vt* to e. (out *or* up) égaliser. **2** *adv* même; e. better/more encore mieux/plus; e. if *or* though même si; e. so quand même. ◆—ly *adv* de manière égale; (*regularly*) régulièrement. ◆—ness *n* (of surface, temper) égalité f; (of movement etc) régularité f. ◆**even-'tempered** a de caractère égal.

evening ['iivnɪŋ] n soir m; (duration of evening, event) soirée f; **in the e.**, Am **evenings** le soir; **at seven in the e.** à sept heures du soir; **every Tuesday e.** tous les mardis soir; **all e. (long)** toute la soirée; – a (newspaper etc) du soir; **e. performance** Th soirée f; **e. dress** tenue f de soirée; (of woman) robe f du soir or de soirée.

event [ɪ'vent] n événement m; Sp épreuve f; **in the e. of death** en cas de décès; **in any e.** en tout cas; **after the e.** après coup. ◆**eventful** a (journey etc) mouvementé; (occasion) mémorable.

eventual [ɪ'ventʃuəl] a final, définitif. ◆**eventu'ality** n éventualité f. ◆**eventually** adv finalement, à la fin; (some day or other) un jour ou l'autre; (after all) en fin de compte.

ever ['evər] adv jamais; **has he e. seen it?** l'a-t-il jamais vu?; **more than e.** plus que jamais; **nothing e.** jamais rien; **hardly e.** presque jamais; **e. ready** toujours prêt; **the first e.** le tout premier; **e. since** (that event etc) depuis; **e. since then** depuis lors, dès lors; **for e.** (for always) pour toujours; (continually) sans cesse; **the best son e.** le meilleur fils du monde; **e. so sorry/happy/etc** Fam vraiment désolé/heureux/etc; **thank you e. so much** Fam merci mille fois; **it's e. such a pity** Fam c'est vraiment dommage; **why e. not?** pourquoi pas donc? ◆**evergreen** n arbre m à feuilles persistantes. ◆**ever'lasting** a éternel. ◆**ever'more** adv **for e.** à (tout) jamais.

every ['evrɪ] a chaque; **e. child** chaque enfant, tous les enfants; **e. time** chaque fois (that que); **e. one** chacun; **e. single one** tous (sans exception); **to have e. confidence in** avoir pleine confiance en; **e. second** or **other day** tous les deux jours; **her e. gesture** ses moindres gestes; **e. bit as big** tout aussi grand (as que); **e. so often**, **e. now and then** de temps en temps. ◆**everybody** pron tout le monde; **e. in turn** chacun à son tour. ◆**everyday** a (happening, life etc) de tous les jours; (banal) banal; **in e. use** d'usage courant. ◆**everyone** pron = everybody. ◆**everyplace** adv Am = everywhere. ◆**everything** pron tout; **e. I have** tout ce que j'ai. ◆**everywhere** adv partout; **e. she goes** où qu'elle aille, partout où elle va.

evict [ɪ'vɪkt] vt expulser (from de). ◆**eviction** n expulsion f.

evidence ['evɪdəns] n (proof) preuve(s)

f(pl); (testimony) témoignage m; (obviousness) évidence f; **to give e.** témoigner (against contre); **e. of** (wear etc) des signes mpl de; **in e.** (noticeable) (bien) en vue. ◆**evident** a évident (that que); **it is e. from ...** il apparaît de ... (that que). ◆**evidently** adv (obviously) évidemment; (apparently) apparemment.

evil ['iiv(ə)l] a (spell, influence, person) malfaisant; (deed, advice, system) mauvais; (consequence) funeste; – n mal m; **to speak e.** dire du mal (about, of de).

evince [ɪ'vɪns] vt manifester.

evoke [ɪ'vəʊk] vt (recall, conjure up) évoquer; (admiration) susciter. ◆**evocative** a évocateur.

evolution [iivə'luːʃ(ə)n] n évolution f. ◆**evolve** vi (of society, idea etc) évoluer; (of plan) se développer; – vt (system etc) développer.

ewe [juː] n brebis f.

ex [eks] n (former spouse) Fam ex mf.

ex- [eks] pref ex-; **ex-wife** ex-femme f.

exacerbate [ɪk'sæsəbeɪt] vt (pain) exacerber.

exact [ɪg'zækt] **1** a (accurate, precise etc) exact; **to be (more) e. about** préciser. **2** vt (demand) exiger (from de); (money) extorquer (from à). ◆**–ing** a exigeant. ◆**–ly** adv exactement; **it's e. 5 o'clock** il est 5 heures juste. ◆**–ness** n exactitude f.

exaggerate [ɪg'zædʒəreɪt] vt exagérer; (in one's own mind) s'exagérer; – vi exagérer. ◆**exagge'ration** n exagération f.

exalt [ɪg'zɔːlt] vt (praise) exalter. ◆**–ed** a (position, rank) élevé. ◆**exal'tation** n exaltation f.

exam [ɪg'zæm] n Univ Sch Fam examen m.

examine [ɪg'zæmɪn] vt examiner; (accounts, luggage) vérifier; (passport) contrôler; (orally) interroger (témoin, élève). ◆**exami'nation** n (inspection) & Univ Sch examen m; (of accounts etc) vérification f; (of passport) contrôle m; **class e.** Sch composition f. ◆**examiner** n Sch examinateur, -trice mf.

example [ɪg'zɑːmp(ə)l] n exemple m; **for e.** par exemple; **to set a good/bad e.** donner le bon/mauvais exemple (to à); **to make an e. of** punir pour l'exemple.

exasperate [ɪg'zɑːspəreɪt] vt exaspérer; **to get exasperated** s'exaspérer (at de). ◆**exaspe'ration** n exaspération f.

excavate ['ekskəveɪt] vt (dig) creuser; (for relics etc) fouiller; (uncover) déterrer. ◆**exca'vation** n Tech creusement m; (archeological) fouille f.

exceed [ɪk'siːd] vt dépasser, excéder. ◆—**ingly** adv extrêmement.

excel [ɪk'sel] vi (-ll-) exceller (**in sth** en qch, **in doing** à faire); − vt surpasser.

Excellency ['eksələnsɪ] n (title) Excellence f.

excellent ['eksələnt] a excellent. ◆**excellence** n excellence f. ◆**excellently** adv parfaitement, admirablement.

except [ɪk'sept] prep sauf, excepté; **e. for** à part; **e. that** à part le fait que, sauf que; **e. if** sauf si; **to do nothing e. wait** ne rien faire sinon attendre; − vt excepter. ◆**exception** n exception f; **with the e. of** à l'exception de; **to take e. to** (object to) désapprouver; (be hurt by) s'offenser de. ◆**exceptional** a exceptionnel. ◆**exceptionally** adv exceptionnellement.

excerpt ['eksɜːpt] n (from film, book etc) extrait m.

excess ['ekses] n excès m; (surplus) Com excédent m; **one's excesses** ses excès mpl; **to e.** à l'excès; **an e. of** (details) un luxe de; − a (weight etc) excédentaire, en trop; **e. fare** supplément m (de billet); **e. luggage** excédent m de bagages. ◆**ex'cessive** a excessif. ◆**ex'cessively** adv (too, too much) excessivement; (very) extrêmement.

exchange [ɪks'tʃeɪndʒ] vt (addresses, blows etc) échanger (**for** contre); − n échange m; Fin change m; (telephone) **e.** central m (téléphonique); **in e.** en échange (**for** de).

Exchequer [ɪks'tʃekər] n ◆**Chancellor of the E.** = ministre m des Finances.

excise ['eksaɪz] n taxe f (**on** sur).

excit/e [ɪk'saɪt] vt (agitate, provoke, stimulate) exciter; (enthuse) passionner, exciter. ◆—**ed** a excité; (laughter) énervé; **to get e.** (nervous, angry, enthusiastic) s'exciter; **to be e. about** (new car, news) se réjouir de; **to be e. about the holidays** être surexcité à l'idée de partir en vacances. ◆—**ing** a (book, adventure) passionnant. ◆—**able** a excitable. ◆—**edly** adv avec agitation; (to wait, jump about) dans un état de surexcitation. ◆—**ement** n agitation f, excitation f, fièvre f; (emotion) vive émotion f; (adventure) aventure f; **great e.** surexcitation f.

exclaim [ɪk'skleɪm] vti s'exclamer, s'écrier (**that** que). ◆**excla'mation** n exclamation f; **e. mark** or Am **point** point m d'exclamation.

exclude [ɪks'kluːd] vt exclure (**from** de); (name from list) écarter (**from** de). ◆**exclusion** n exclusion f. ◆**exclusive** a (right, interest, design) exclusif; (club, group) fermé; (interview) en exclusivité; **e.**

of wine/etc vin/etc non compris. ◆**exclusively** adv exclusivement.

excommunicate [ekskə'mjuːnɪkeɪt] vt excommunier.

excrement ['ekskrəmənt] n excrément(s) m(pl).

excruciating [ɪk'skruːʃɪeɪtɪŋ] a insupportable, atroce.

excursion [ɪk'skɜːʃ(ə)n] n excursion f.

excuse [ɪk'skjuːz] vt (justify, forgive) excuser (**s.o. for doing** qn d'avoir fait, qn de faire); (exempt) dispenser (**from** de); **e. me for asking** permettez-moi de demander; **e. me!** excusez-moi!, pardon!; **you're excused** tu peux t'en aller or sortir; − [ɪk'skjuːs] n excuse f; **it was an e. for** cela a servi de prétexte à.

ex-directory [eksdaɪ'rektərɪ] a Tel sur la liste rouge.

execute ['eksɪkjuːt] vt (criminal, order, plan etc) exécuter. ◆**exe'cution** n exécution f. ◆**exe'cutioner** n bourreau m.

executive [ɪg'zekjutɪv] a (power) exécutif; (ability) d'exécution; (job) de cadre; (car, plane) de direction; − n (person) cadre m; (board, committee) bureau m; **the e.** Pol l'exécutif m; (senior) **e.** cadre m supérieur; **junior e.** jeune cadre m; **business e.** directeur m commercial.

exemplary [ɪg'zemplərɪ] a exemplaire. ◆**exemplify** vt illustrer.

exempt [ɪg'zempt] a exempt (**from** de); − vt exempter (**from** de). ◆**exemption** n exemption f.

exercise ['eksəsaɪz] n (of power etc) & Sch Sp Mil exercice m; pl Univ Am cérémonies fpl; **e. book** cahier m; − vt exercer; (troops) faire faire l'exercice à; (dog, horse etc) promener; (tact, judgement etc) faire preuve de; (rights) faire valoir, exercer; − vi (take exercise) prendre de l'exercice.

exert [ɪg'zɜːt] vt exercer; (force) employer; **to e. oneself** (physically) se dépenser; **he never exerts himself** (takes the trouble) il ne se fatigue jamais; **to e. oneself to do** (try hard) s'efforcer de faire. ◆**exertion** n effort m; (of force) emploi m.

exhale [eks'heɪl] vt (breathe out) expirer; (give off) exhaler; − vi expirer.

exhaust [ɪg'zɔːst] **1** vt (use up, tire) épuiser; **to become exhausted** s'épuiser. **2** n **e. (pipe)** Aut pot m or tuyau m d'échappement. ◆—**ing** a épuisant. ◆**exhaustion** n épuisement m. ◆**exhaustive** a (study etc) complet; (research) approfondi.

exhibit [ɪg'zɪbɪt] vt (put on display) exposer; (ticket, courage etc) montrer; − n objet m exposé; *Jur* pièce *f* à conviction. ◆**exhi-'bition** *n* exposition *f*; **an e. of** (*display*) une démonstration de; **to make an e. of oneself** se donner en spectacle. ◆**exhi'bitionist** *n* exhibitionniste *mf*. ◆**exhibitor** *n* exposant, -ante *mf*.

exhilarate [ɪgˈzɪləreɪt] *vt* stimuler; (*of air*) vivifier; (*elate*) rendre fou de joie. ◆**exhila'ration** *n* liesse *f*, joie *f*.

exhort [ɪgˈzɔːt] *vt* exhorter (**to do** à faire, **to sth** à qch).

exhume [eksˈhjuːm] *vt* exhumer.

exile [ˈegzaɪl] *vt* exiler; − *n* (*absence*) exil *m*; (*person*) exilé, -ée *mf*.

exist [ɪgˈzɪst] *vi* exister; (*live*) vivre (**on** de); (**to continue**) **to e.** subsister; **the notion exists that . . .** il existe une notion selon laquelle . . . . ◆**−ing** *a* (*law*) existant; (*circumstances*) actuel. ◆**existence** *n* existence *f*; **to come into e.** être créé; **to be in e.** exister. ◆**exi'stentialism** *n* existentialisme *m*.

exit [ˈeksɪt, ˈegzɪt] *n* (*action*) sortie *f*; (*door, window*) sortie *f*, issue *f*; − *vi Th* sortir.

exodus [ˈeksədəs] *n inv* exode *m*.

exonerate [ɪgˈzɒnəreɪt] *vt* (*from blame*) disculper (**from** de).

exorbitant [ɪgˈzɔːbɪtənt] *a* exorbitant. ◆**−ly** *adv* démesurément.

exorcize [ˈeksɔːsaɪz] *vt* exorciser. ◆**exorcism** *n* exorcisme *m*.

exotic [ɪgˈzɒtɪk] *a* exotique.

expand [ɪkˈspænd] *vt* (*one's fortune, knowledge etc*) étendre; (*trade, ideas*) développer; (*production*) augmenter; (*gas, metal*) dilater; − *vi* s'étendre; se développer; augmenter; se dilater; **to e. on** développer ses idées sur; (**fast or rapidly**) **expanding sector**/*etc Com* secteur/*etc* en (pleine) expansion. ◆**expansion** *n Com Phys Pol* expansion *f*; développement *m*; augmentation *f*. ◆**expansionism** *n* expansionnisme *m*.

expanse [ɪkˈspæns] *n* étendue *f*.

expansive [ɪkˈspænsɪv] *a* expansif. ◆**−ly** *adv* avec effusion.

expatriate [eksˈpætrɪət, *Am* eksˈpeɪtrɪət] *a* & *n* expatrié, -ée (*mf*).

expect [ɪkˈspekt] *vt* (*anticipate*) s'attendre à, attendre, escompter; (*think*) penser (**that** que); (*suppose*) supposer (**that** que); (*await*) attendre; **to e. sth from s.o.**/**sth** attendre qch de qn/qch; **to e. to do** compter faire; **to e. that** (*anticipate*) s'attendre à ce que (+ *sub*); **I e. you to come** (*want*) je te demande de venir; **it was expected** c'était prévu (**that** que); **she's expecting a baby** elle attend un

bébé. ◆**expectancy** *n* attente *f*; **life e.** espérance *f* de vie. ◆**expectant** *a* (*crowd*) qui attend; **e. mother** future mère *f*. ◆**expec'tation** *n* attente *f*; **to come up to s.o.'s expectations** répondre à l'attente de qn.

expedient [ɪksˈpiːdɪənt] *a* avantageux; (*suitable*) opportun; − *n* (*resource*) expédient *m*.

expedite [ˈekspədaɪt] *vt* (*hasten*) accélérer; (*task*) expédier.

expedition [ekspɪˈdɪʃ(ə)n] *n* expédition *f*.

expel [ɪkˈspel] *vt* (**-ll-**) expulser (**from** de); (*from school*) renvoyer; (*enemy*) chasser.

expend [ɪkˈspend] *vt* (*energy, money*) dépenser; (*resources*) épuiser. ◆**−able** *a* (*object*) remplaçable; (*soldiers*) sacrifiable. ◆**expenditure** *n* (*money spent*) dépenses *fpl*; **an e. of** (*time, money*) une dépense de.

expense [ɪkˈspens] *n* frais *mpl*, dépense *f*; *pl Fin* frais *mpl*; **business**/**travelling expenses** frais *mpl* généraux/de déplacement; **to go to some e.** faire des frais; **at s.o.'s e.** aux dépens de qn; **an or one's e. account** une or sa note de frais (professionnels).

expensive [ɪkˈspensɪv] *a* (*goods etc*) cher, coûteux; (*hotel etc*) cher; (*tastes*) dispendieux; **to be e.** coûter cher; **an e. mistake** une faute qui coûte cher. ◆**−ly** *adv* à grands frais.

experienc/e [ɪkˈspɪərɪəns] *n* (*knowledge, skill, event*) expérience *f*; **from or by e.** par expérience; **he's had e. of** (*work etc*) il a déjà fait; (*grief etc*) il a déjà éprouvé; **I've had e. of driving** j'ai déjà conduit; **terrible experiences** de rudes épreuves *fpl*; **unforgettable e.** moment *m* inoubliable; − *vt* (*undergo*) connaître, subir; (*remorse, difficulty*) éprouver; (*joy*) ressentir. ◆**−ed** *a* (*person*) expérimenté; (*eye, ear*) exercé; **to be e. in** s'y connaître en (matière de).

experiment [ɪkˈsperɪmənt] *n* expérience *f*; − [ɪkˈsperɪment] *vi* faire une expérience or des expériences; **to e. with sth** *Phys Ch* expérimenter qch. ◆**experi'mental** *a* expérimental; **e. period** période *f* d'expérimentation.

expert [ˈekspɜːt] *n* expert *m* (**on, in** en), spécialiste *mf* (**on, in** de); − *a* expert (**in sth** en qch, **in** *or* **at doing** à faire); (*advice*) d'un expert, d'expert; (*eye*) connaisseur; **e. touch** doigté *m*, grande habileté *f*. ◆**exper'tise** *n* compétence *f* (**in** en). ◆**expertly** *adv* habilement.

expiate [ˈekspɪeɪt] *vt* (*sins*) expier.

expir/e [ɪkˈspaɪər] *vi* expirer. ◆**−ed** *a*

(*ticket, passport etc*) périmé. ◆**expi'ration** *n Am*, ◆**expiry** *n* expiration *f*.

explain [ɪk'spleɪn] *vt* expliquer (**to** à, **that** que); (*reasons*) exposer; (*mystery*) éclaircir; **e. yourself!** explique-toi!; **to e. away** justifier. ◆**-able** *a* explicable. ◆**expla-'nation** *n* explication *f*. ◆**explanatory** *a* explicatif.

expletive [ɪk'splirtɪv, *Am* 'eksplətɪv] *n* (*oath*) juron *m*.

explicit [ɪk'splɪsɪt] *a* explicite. ◆**-ly** *adv* explicitement.

explode [ɪk'spləud] *vi* exploser; **to e. with laughter** *Fig* éclater de rire; — *vt* faire exploser; (*theory*) *Fig* démythifier, discréditer.

exploit 1 [ɪk'splɔɪt] *vt* (*person, land etc*) exploiter. **2** ['eksplɔɪt] *n* (*feat*) exploit *m*. ◆**exploi'tation** *n* exploitation *f*.

explore [ɪk'splɔːr] *vt* explorer; (*possibilities*) examiner. ◆**explo'ration** *n* exploration *f*. ◆**exploratory** *a* d'exploration; (*talks, step etc*) préliminaire, exploratoire; **e. operation** *Med* sondage *m*. ◆**explorer** *n* explorateur, -trice *mf*.

explosion [ɪk'spləuʒ(ə)n] *n* explosion *f*. ◆**explosive** *a* (*weapon, question*) explosif; (*mixture, gas*) détonant; — *n* explosif *m*.

exponent [ɪk'spəunənt] *n* (*of opinion, theory etc*) interprète *m* (of de).

export ['ekspɔːt] *n* exportation *f*; — *a* (*goods etc*) d'exportation; — [ɪk'spɔːt] *vt* exporter (**to** vers, **from** de). ◆**expor'tation** *n* exportation *f*. ◆**ex'porter** *n* exportateur, -trice *mf*; (*country*) pays *m* exportateur.

expose [ɪk'spəuz] *vt* (*leave uncovered, describe*) & *Phot* exposer; (*wire*) dénuder; (*plot, scandal etc*) révéler, dévoiler; (*crook etc*) démasquer; **to e. to** (*subject to*) exposer à; **to e. oneself** *Jur* commettre un attentat à la pudeur. ◆**expo'sition** *n* exposition *f*. ◆**exposure** *n* exposition *f* (**to** à); (*of plot etc*) révélation *f*; (*of house etc*) exposition *f*; *Phot* pose *f*; **to die of e.** mourir de froid.

expound [ɪk'spaund] *vt* (*theory etc*) exposer.

express [ɪk'spres] **1** *vt* exprimer; (*proposition*) énoncer; **to e. oneself** s'exprimer. **2** *a* (*order*) exprès, formel; (*intention*) explicite; (*purpose*) seul; (*letter, delivery*) exprès *inv*; (*train*) rapide, express *inv*; — *adv* (*to send*) par exprès; — *n* (*train*) rapide *m*, express *m inv*. ◆**expression** *n* (*phrase, look etc*) expression *f*; **an e. of** (*gratitude, affection etc*) un témoignage de. ◆**expressive** *a* expressif. ◆**expressly** *adv* expressément. ◆**expressway** *n Am* autoroute *f*.

expulsion [ɪk'spʌlʃ(ə)n] *n* expulsion *f*; (*from school*) renvoi *m*.

expurgate ['ekspəgeɪt] *vt* expurger.

exquisite [ɪk'skwɪzɪt] *a* exquis. ◆**-ly** *adv* d'une façon exquise.

ex-serviceman [eks'sɜːvɪsmən] *n* (*pl* -men) ancien combattant *m*.

extant ['ekstənt, ek'stænt] *a* existant.

extend [ɪk'stend] *vt* (*arm, business*) étendre; (*line, visit, meeting*) prolonger (**by** de); (*hand*) tendre (**to s.o.** à qn); (*house*) agrandir; (*knowledge*) élargir; (*time limit*) reculer; (*help, thanks*) offrir (**to** à); **to e. an invitation to** faire une invitation à; — *vi* (*of wall, plain etc*) s'étendre (**to** jusqu'à); (*in time*) se prolonger; **to e. to s.o.** (*of joy etc*) gagner qn. ◆**extension** *n* (*in space*) prolongement *m*; (*in time*) prolongation *f*; (*of powers, measure, meaning, strike*) extension *f*; (*for table, wire*) rallonge *f*; (*to building*) agrandissement(s) *m(pl)*; (*of telephone*) appareil *m* supplémentaire; (*of office telephone*) poste *m*; **an e. (of time)** un délai. ◆**extensive** *a* étendu, vaste; (*repairs, damage*) important; (*use*) courant. ◆**extensively** *adv* (*very much*) beaucoup, considérablement; **e. used** largement répandu.

extent [ɪk'stent] *n* (*scope*) étendue *f*; (*size*) importance *f*; (*degree*) mesure *f*; **to a large/certain e.** dans une large/certaine mesure; **to such an e. that** à tel point que.

extenuating [ɪk'stenjʊeɪtɪŋ] *a* **e. circumstances** circonstances *fpl* atténuantes.

exterior [ɪks'tɪərɪər] *a* & *n* extérieur (*m*).

exterminate [ɪk'stɜːmɪneɪt] *vt* (*people etc*) exterminer; (*disease*) supprimer; (*evil*) extirper. ◆**extermi'nation** *n* extermination *f*; suppression *f*.

external [ek'stɜːn(ə)l] *a* (*influence, trade etc*) extérieur; **for e. use** (*medicine*) à usage externe; **e. affairs** *Pol* affaires *fpl* étrangères. ◆**-ly** *adv* extérieurement.

extinct [ɪk'stɪŋkt] *a* (*volcano, love*) éteint; (*species, animal*) disparu. ◆**extinction** *n* extinction *f*; disparition *f*.

extinguish [ɪk'stɪŋgwɪʃ] *vt* éteindre. ◆**-er** *n* (*fire*) **e.** extincteur *m*.

extol [ɪk'stəul] *vt* (-ll-) exalter, louer.

extort [ɪk'stɔːt] *vt* (*money*) extorquer (**from** à); (*consent*) arracher (**from** à). ◆**extortion** *Jur* extorsion *f* de fonds; **it's (sheer) e.!** c'est du vol! ◆**extortionate** *a* exorbitant.

extra ['ekstrə] *a* (*additional*) supplémentaire; **one e. glass** un verre de *or* en plus, encore un verre; (**any) e. bread?**

encore du pain?; **to be e.** (*spare*) être en
trop; (*cost more*) être en supplément; (*of
postage*) être en sus; **wine is 3 francs e.** il y a
un supplément de 3F pour le vin; **e. care**
un soin tout particulier; **e. charge** *or*
portion supplément *m*; **e. time** Fb prolongation *f*; − *adv* **e.** big/*etc* plus grand/*etc*
que d'habitude; − *n* (*perk*) à-côté *m*; Cin
Th figurant, -ante *mf*; *pl* (*expenses*) frais
mpl supplémentaires; **an optional e.** (*for
car etc*) un accessoire en option.

extra- ['ekstrə] *pref* extra-. ◆**e.-'dry** *a*
(*champagne*) brut. ◆**e.-'fine** *a* extra-fin.
◆**e.-'strong** *a* extra-fort.

extract [ɪk'strækt] *vt* extraire (**from** de);
(*tooth*) arracher, extraire; (*promise*)
arracher, soutirer (**from** à); (*money*)
soutirer (**from** à); − ['ekstrækt] *n* (*of book
etc*) & Culin Ch extrait *m*. ◆**ex'traction** *n*
extraction *f*; arrachement *m*; (*descent*)
origine *f*.

extra-curricular [ekstrəkə'rɪkjulər] *a* (*activities etc*) en dehors des heures de cours,
extrascolaire.

extradite ['ekstrədaɪt] *vt* extrader. ◆**extra-
'dition** *n* extradition *f*.

extramarital [ekstrə'mærɪt(ə)l] *a* en dehors
du mariage, extra-conjugal.

extramural [ekstrə'mjuərəl] *a* (*studies*) hors
faculté.

extraneous [ɪk'streɪnɪəs] *a* (*detail etc*) accessoire.

extraordinary [ɪk'strɔɪdən(ə)rɪ] *a* (*strange,
exceptional*) extraordinaire.

extra-special [ekstrə'speʃəl] *a* (*occasion*)
très spécial; (*care*) tout particulier.

extravagant [ɪk'strævəgənt] *a* (*behaviour,
idea etc*) extravagant; (*claim*) exagéré;
(*wasteful with money*) dépensier, prodigue.
◆**extravagance** *n* extravagance *f*; prodi-
galité *f*; (*thing bought*) folle dépense *f*.

extravaganza [ɪkstrævə'gænzə] *n* Mus Liter
& Fig fantaisie *f*.

extreme [ɪk'striːm] *a* (*exceptional, furthest*)
extrême; (*danger, poverty*) très grand;
(*praise*) outré; **at the e. end** à l'extrémité; **of**

e. importance de première importance; − *n*
(*furthest degree*) extrême *m*; **to carry** *or*
take to extremes pousser à l'extrême;
extremes of temperature températures *fpl*
extrêmes; **extremes of climate** excès *mpl* du
climat. ◆**extremely** *adv* extrêmement.
◆**extremist** *a* & *n* extrémiste (*mf*).
◆**extremity** [ɪk'stremɪtɪ] *n* extrémité *f*.

extricate ['ekstrɪkeɪt] *vt* dégager (**from** de);
to e. oneself from (*difficulty*) se tirer de.

extrovert ['ekstrəvɜɪt] *n* extraverti, -ie *mf*.

exuberant [ɪg'z(j)uɪbərənt] *a* exubérant.
◆**exuberance** *n* exubérance *f*.

exude [ɪg'zjuɪd] *vt* (*charm, honesty etc*) Fig
respirer.

exultation [egzʌl'teɪʃ(ə)n] *n* exultation *f*.

eye[1] [aɪ] *n* œil *m* (*pl* yeux); **before my very
eyes** sous mes yeux; **to be all eyes** être tout
yeux; **as far as the e. can see** à perte de vue;
up to one's eyes in debt endetté jusqu'au
cou; **up to one's eyes in work** débordé de
travail; **to have an e. on** (*house, car*) avoir
en vue; **to keep an e. on** surveiller; **to make
eyes at** Fam faire de l'œil à; **to lay** *or* **set
eyes on** voir, apercevoir; **to take one's eyes
off s.o./sth** quitter qn/qch des yeux; **to
catch the e.** attirer l'œil, accrocher le
regard; **keep an e. out!, keep your eyes
open!** ouvre l'œil!, sois vigilant!; **we don't
see e. to e.** nous n'avons pas le même point
de vue; **e. shadow** fard *m* à paupières; **to be
an e.-opener for s.o.** Fam être une révélation pour qn. ◆**eyeball** *n* globe *m*
oculaire. ◆**eyebrow** *n* sourcil *m*. ◆**eyecatching** *a* (*title etc*) accrocheur.
◆**eyeglass** *n* monocle *m*. ◆**eyeglasses**
npl (*spectacles*) Am lunettes *fpl*. ◆**eyelash**
n cil *m*. ◆**eyelid** *n* paupière *f*. ◆**eyeliner**
n eye-liner *m*. ◆**eyesight** *n* vue *f*.
◆**eyesore** *n* (*building etc*) horreur *f*.
◆**eyestrain** *n* **to have e.** avoir les yeux qui
tirent. ◆**eyewash** *n* (*nonsense*) Fam
sottises *fpl*. ◆**eyewitness** *n* témoin *m*
oculaire.

eye[2] [aɪ] *vt* reluquer, regarder.

F

F, f [ef] *n* F, f *m*.

fable ['feɪb(ə)l] *n* fable *f*.

fabric ['fæbrɪk] *n* (*cloth*) tissu *m*, étoffe *f*; (*of
building*) structure *f*; **the f. of society** le tissu

social.

fabricate ['fæbrɪkeɪt] *vt* (*invent, make*)
fabriquer. ◆**fabri'cation** *n* fabrication
f.

fabulous ['fæbjʊləs] *a* (*incredible, legendary*) fabuleux; (*wonderful*) *Fam* formidable.

façade [fə'sɑːd] *n Archit & Fig* façade *f*.

face [feɪs] *n* visage *m*, figure *f*; (*expression*) mine *f*; (*of clock*) cadran *m*; (*of building*) façade *f*; (*of cliff*) paroi *f*; (*of the earth*) surface *f*; **she laughed in my f.** elle m'a ri au nez; **to show one's f.** se montrer; **f. down(wards)** (*person*) face contre terre; (*thing*) tourné à l'envers; **f. to f.** face à face; **in the f. of** devant; (*despite*) en dépit de; **to save/lose f.** sauver/perdre la face; **to make** *or* **pull faces** faire des grimaces; **to tell s.o. sth to his f.** dire qch à qn tout cru; **f. powder** poudre *f* de riz; **f. value** (*of stamp etc*) valeur *f*; **to take sth at f. value** prendre qch au pied de la lettre; – *vt* (*danger, enemy etc*) faire face à; (*accept*) accepter; (*look in the face*) regarder (*qn*) bien en face; **to f., be facing** (*be opposite*) être en face de; (*window etc*) donner sur; **faced with** (*prospect, problem*) face à, devant; (*defeat*) menacé par; (*bill*) contraint à payer; **he can't f. leaving** il n'a pas le courage de partir; – *vi* (*of house*) être orienté (**north**/*etc* au nord/*etc*); (*of person*) se tourner (**towards** vers); **to f. up to** (*danger*) faire face à; (*fact*) accepter; **about f.!** *Am Mil* demi-tour! ◆**facecloth** *n* gant *m* de toilette. ◆**facelift** *n Med* lifting *m*; (*of building*) ravalement *m*.

faceless ['feɪsləs] *a* anonyme.

facet ['fæsɪt] *n* (*of problem, diamond etc*) facette *f*.

facetious [fə'siːʃəs] *a* (*person*) facétieux; (*remark*) plaisant.

facial ['feɪʃ(ə)l] *a* du visage; *Med* facial; – *n* soin *m* du visage.

facile ['fæsaɪl, *Am* 'fæs(ə)l] *a* facile, superficiel.

facilitate [fə'sɪlɪteɪt] *vt* faciliter. ◆**facility** *n* (*ease*) facilité *f*, *pl* (*possibilities*) facilités *fpl*; (*for sports*) équipements *mpl*; (*in harbour, airport etc*) installations *fpl*; (*means*) moyens *mpl*, ressources *fpl*; **special facilities** (*conditions*) conditions *fpl* spéciales (**for** pour).

facing ['feɪsɪŋ] *n* (*of dress etc*) parement *m*.

fact [fækt] *n* fait *m*; **as a matter of f., in f.** en fait; **the facts of life** les choses *fpl* de la vie; **is that a f.?** c'est vrai?; **f. and fiction** le réel et l'imaginaire.

faction ['fækʃ(ə)n] *n* (*group*) *Pol* faction *f*.

factor ['fæktər] *n* (*element*) facteur *m*.

factory ['fækt(ə)rɪ] *n* (*large*) usine *f*; (*small*) fabrique *f*; **arms/porcelain f.** manufacture *f* d'armes/de porcelaine.

factual ['fæktʃʊəl] *a* objectif, basé sur les faits, factuel; (*error*) de fait.

faculty ['fækəltɪ] *n* (*aptitude*) & *Univ* faculté *f*.

fad [fæd] *n* (*personal habit*) marotte *f*; (*fashion*) folie *f*, mode *f* (**for** de).

fade [feɪd] *vi* (*of flower*) se faner; (*of light*) baisser; (*of colour*) passer; (*of fabric*) se décolorer; **to f. (away)** (*of memory, smile*) s'effacer; (*of sound*) s'affaiblir; (*of person*) dépérir; – *vt* (*fabric*) décolorer.

fag [fæg] *n* **1** (*cigarette*) *Fam* clope *m*, tige *f*; **f. end** mégot *m*. **2** (*male homosexual*) *Am Sl* pédé *m*.

fagged [fægd] *a* **f. (out)** (*tired*) *Sl* claqué.

faggot ['fægət] *n* **1** *Culin* boulette *f* (de viande). **2** (*male homosexual*) *Am Sl* pédé *m*.

fail [feɪl] *vi* (*of person, plan etc*) échouer; (*of business*) faire faillite; (*of light, health, sight*) baisser; (*of memory, strength*) défaillir; (*of brakes*) *Aut* lâcher; (*run short*) manquer; (*of gas, electricity*) être coupé; (*of engine*) tomber en panne; **to f. in** (*one's duty*) manquer à; (*exam*) échouer à; – *vt* (*exam*) échouer à; (*candidate*) refuser, recaler; **to f. s.o.** (*let down*) laisser tomber qn, décevoir qn; (*of words*) manquer à qn, faire défaut à qn; **to f. to do** (*omit*) manquer de faire; (*not be able*) ne pas arriver à faire; **I f. to see** je ne vois pas; – *n* **without f.** à coup sûr, sans faute. ◆**—ed** *a* (*attempt, poet*) manqué. ◆**—ing** *n* (*fault*) défaut *m*; – *prep* à défaut de; **f. this, f. that** à défaut. ◆**failure** *n* échec *m*; (*of business*) faillite *f*; (*of engine, machine*) panne *f*; (*of gas etc*) coupure *f*, panne *f*; (*person*) raté, -ée *mf*; **f. to do** (*inability*) incapacité *f* de faire; **her f. to leave** le fait qu'elle n'est pas partie; **to end in f.** se solder par un échec; **heart f.** arrêt *m* du cœur.

faint [feɪnt] **1** *a* (**-er, -est**) léger; (*voice*) faible; (*colour*) pâle; (*idea*) vague; **I haven't the faintest idea** je n'en ai pas la moindre idée. **2** *a Med* défaillant (**with** de); **to feel f.** se trouver mal, défaillir; – *vi* s'évanouir (**from** de); **fainting fit** évanouissement *m*. ◆**—ly** *adv* (*weakly*) faiblement; (*slightly*) légèrement. ◆**—ness** *n* légèreté *f*; faiblesse *f*. ◆**faint-'hearted** *a* timoré, timide.

fair¹ [feər] *n* foire *f*; (*for charity*) fête *f*; (*funfair*) fête *f* foraine; (*larger*) parc *m* d'attractions. ◆**fairground** *n* champ *m* de foire.

fair² [feər] **1** *a* (-er, -est) (*equitable*) juste, équitable; (*game, fight*) loyal; **f. (and square)** honnête(ment); **f. play** fair-play *m inv*; **that's not f. play!** ce n'est pas du jeu!; **that's not f. to him** ce n'est pas juste pour lui; **f. enough!** très bien!; – *adv* (*to play*) loyalement. **2** *a* (*rather good*) passable, assez bon; (*amount, warning*) raisonnable; **a f. amount (of)** pas mal (de); **f. copy** copie *f* au propre. **3** *a* (*wind*) favorable; (*weather*) beau. ◆**—ly** *adv* **1** (*to treat*) équitablement; (*to get*) loyalement. **2** (*rather*) assez, plutôt; **f. sure** presque sûr. ◆**—ness¹** *n* justice *f*; (*of decision*) équité *f*; **in all f.** en toute justice. ◆**fair-'minded** *a* impartial. ◆**fair-'sized** *a* assez grand.

fair³ [feər] *a* (*hair, person*) blond; (*complexion, skin*) clair. ◆**—ness²** *n* (*of hair*) blond *m*; (*of skin*) blancheur *f*. ◆**fair-'haired** *a* blond. ◆**fair-'skinned** *a* à la peau claire.

fairy ['feəri] *n* fée *f*; **f. lights** guirlande *f* multicolore; **f. tale** conte *m* de fées.

faith [feiθ] *n* foi *f*; **to have f. in s.o.** avoir confiance en qn; **to put one's f. in** (*justice, medicine etc*) se fier à; **in good/bad f.** de bonne/mauvaise foi; **f. healer** guérisseur, -euse *mf*. ◆**faithful** *a* fidèle. ◆**faithfully** *adv* fidèlement; **yours f.** (*in letter*) *Com* veuillez agréer l'expression de mes salutations distinguées. ◆**faithfulness** *n* fidélité *f*. ◆**faithless** *a* déloyal, infidèle.

fake [feik] *n* (*painting, document etc*) faux *m*; (*person*) imposteur *m*; – *vt* (*document, signature etc*) falsifier, maquiller; (*election*) truquer; **to f. death** faire semblant d'être mort; – *vi* (*pretend*) faire semblant; – *a* faux; (*elections*) truqué.

falcon ['fɔːlkən] *n* faucon *m*.

fall [fɔːl] *n* chute *f*; (*in price, demand etc*) baisse *f*; *pl* (*waterfall*) chutes *fpl* (d'eau); **the f.** *Am* l'automne *m*; – *vi* (*pt* fell, *pp* fallen) tomber; (*of building*) s'effondrer; **her face fell** *Fig* son visage se rembrunit; **to f. into** tomber dans; (*habit*) *Fig* prendre; **to f. off a bicycle/etc** tomber d'une bicyclette/etc; **to f. off** *or* **down a ladder** tomber (en bas) d'une échelle; **to fall on s.o.** (*of onus*) retomber sur qn; **to f. on a Monday/etc** (*of event*) tomber un lundi/etc; **to f. over sth** tomber en butant contre qch; **to f. short of** (*expectation*) ne pas répondre à; **to f. short of being** être loin d'être; **to f. victim** devenir victime (to de); **to f. asleep** s'endormir; **to f. ill** tomber malade; **to f. due** échoir. ■ **to f. apart** (*of mechanism*) tomber en morceaux; *Fig* se désagréger; **to f. away** (*come off*) se

détacher, tomber; (*of numbers*) diminuer; **to f. back on** (*as last resort*) se rabattre sur; **to f. behind** rester en arrière; (*in work*) prendre du retard; **to f. down** tomber; (*of building*) s'effondrer; **to f. for** (*person*) tomber amoureux de; (*trick*) se laisser prendre à; **to f. in** (*collapse*) s'écrouler; **to f. in with** (*tally with*) cadrer avec; (*agree to*) accepter; **to f. off** (*come off*) se détacher, tomber; (*of numbers*) diminuer. ◆**falling-'off** *n* diminution *f*; **to f. out with** (*quarrel with*) se brouiller avec; **to f. over** tomber; (*of table, vase*) se renverser; **to f. through** (*of plan*) tomber à l'eau, échouer. ◆**fallen** *a* tombé; (*angel, woman*) déchu; **f. leaf** feuille *f* morte. ◆**fallout** *n* (*radioactive*) retombées *fpl*.

fallacious [fə'leiʃəs] *a* faux. ◆**fallacy** ['fæləsi] *n* erreur *f*; *Phil* faux raisonnement *m*.

fallible ['fæləb(ə)l] *a* faillible.

fallow ['fæləu] *a* (*land*) en jachère.

false [fɔːls] *a* faux; **a f. bottom** un double fond. ◆**falsehood** *n* mensonge *m*; **truth and f.** le vrai et le faux. ◆**falseness** *n* fausseté *f*. ◆**falsify** *vt* falsifier.

falter ['fɔːltər] *vi* (*of step, resolution*) chanceler; (*of voice, speaker*) hésiter; (*of courage*) vaciller.

fame [feim] *n* renommée *f*; (*glory*) gloire *f*. ◆**famed** *a* renommé.

familiar [fə'miljər] *a* (*task, atmosphere etc*) familier; (*event*) habituel; **f. with s.o.** (*too friendly*) familier avec qn; **to be f. with** (*know*) connaître; **I'm f. with her voice** je connais bien sa voix, sa voix m'est familière; **to make oneself f. with** se familiariser avec; **he looks f. (to me)** je l'ai déjà vu (quelque part). ◆**famili'arity** *n* familiarité *f* (with avec); (*of event, sight etc*) caractère *m* familier. ◆**familiarize** *vt* familiariser (with avec); **to f. oneself with** se familiariser avec.

family ['fæmili] *n* famille *f*; – *a* (*name, doctor etc*) de famille; (*planning, problem*) familial; (*tree*) généalogique; **f. man** père *m* de famille.

famine ['fæmin] *n* famine *f*.

famished ['fæmiʃt] *a* affamé.

famous ['feiməs] *a* célèbre (for par, pour). ◆**—ly** *adv* (*very well*) *Fam* rudement bien.

fan [fæn] **1** *n* (*hand-held*) éventail *m*; (*mechanical*) ventilateur *m*; **f. heater** radiateur *m* soufflant; – *vt* (-nn-) (*person etc*) éventer; (*fire, quarrel*) attiser. **2** *n* (*of person*) admirateur, -trice *mf*, fan *m*; *Sp* supporter *m*; **to be a jazz/sports f.** être passionné *or* mordu de jazz/de sport.

fanatic [fə'nætik] *n* fanatique *mf*. ◆**fanatical** *a* fanatique. ◆**fanaticism** *n* fanatisme *m.*

fancy ['fænsɪ] **1** *n* (*whim, imagination*) fantaisie *f*; (*liking*) goût *m*; **to take a f. to s.o.** se prendre d'affection pour qn; **I took a f. to it, it took my f.** j'en ai eu envie; **when the f. takes me** quand ça me chante; *– a* (*hat, button etc*) fantaisie *inv*; (*idea*) fantaisiste; (*price*) exorbitant; (*car*) de luxe; (*house, restaurant*) chic; **f. dress** (*costume*) travesti *m*; **f.-dress ball** bal *m* masqué. **2** *vt* (*imagine*) se figurer (**that** que); (*think*) croire (**that** que); (*want*) avoir envie de; (*like*) aimer; **f. that!** tiens (donc)!; **he fancies her** *Fam* elle lui plaît; **to f. oneself as** se prendre pour; **she fancies herself!** elle se prend pour qn! ◆**fancier** *n* **horse/***etc* **f.** amateur *m* de chevaux/*etc*. ◆**fanciful** *a* fantaisiste.

fanfare ['fænfeər] *n* (*of trumpets*) fanfare *f*.

fang [fæŋ] *n* (*of dog etc*) croc *m*; (*of snake*) crochet *m*.

fantastic [fæn'tæstɪk] *a* fantastique; **a f. idea** (*absurd*) une idée aberrante.

fantasy ['fæntəsɪ] *n* (*imagination*) fantaisie *f*; *Psy* fantasme *m*. ◆**fantasize** *vi* fantasmer (**about** sur).

far [fɑːr] *adv* (**farther** *or* **further, farthest** *or* **furthest**) (*distance*) loin; **f. bigger/more expensive/***etc* (*much*) beaucoup plus grand/plus cher/*etc* (**than** que); **f. more** beaucoup plus; **f. advanced** très avancé; **how f. is it to . . . ?** combien y a-t-il d'ici à . . . ?; **is it f. to . . . ?** sommes-nous, suis-je *etc* loin de . . . ?; **how f. are you going?** jusqu'où vas-tu?; **how f. has he got with?** (*plans, work etc*) où en est-il de?; **so f.** (*time*) jusqu'ici; (*place*) jusque-là; **as f. as** (*place*) jusqu'à; **as f.** *or* **so f. as I know** autant que je sache; **as f.** *or* **so f. as I'm concerned** en ce qui me concerne; **as f. back as 1820** dès 1820; **f. from doing** loin de faire; **f. from it!** loin de là!; **f. away** *or* **off** au loin; **to be (too) f. away** être (trop) loin (**from** de); **f. and wide** partout; **by f.** de loin; **f. into the night** très avant dans la nuit; *– a* (*side, end*) autre; **it's a f. cry from** on est loin de. ◆**faraway** *a* lointain; (*look*) distrait, dans le vague. ◆**far-'fetched** *a* forcé, exagéré. ◆**f.-'flung** *a* (*widespread*) vaste. ◆**f.-'off** *a* lointain. ◆**f.-'reaching** *a* de grande portée. ◆**f.-'sighted** *a* clairvoyant.

farce [fɑːs] *n* farce *f*. ◆**farcical** *a* grotesque, ridicule.

fare [feər] **1** *n* (*price*) prix *m* du billet; (*ticket*) billet *m*; (*taxi passenger*) client, -ente *mf*. **2** *n* (*food*) chère *f*, nourriture *f*; **prison f.** régime *m* de prison; **bill of f.** menu *m*. **3** *vi* (*manage*) se débrouiller; **how did she f.?** comment ça s'est passé (pour elle)?

farewell [feə'wel] *n & int* adieu (*m*); *– a* (*party etc*) d'adieu.

farm [fɑːm] *n* ferme *f*, *– a* (*worker, produce etc*) agricole; **f. land** terres *fpl* cultivées; *– vt* cultiver; *– vi* être agriculteur. ◆**—ing** *n* agriculture *f*; (*breeding*) élevage *m*; **dairy f.** industrie *f* laitière. ◆**—er** *n* fermier, -ière *mf*, agriculteur *m*. ◆**farmhand** *n* ouvrier, -ière *mf* agricole. ◆**farmhouse** *n* ferme *f*. ◆**farmyard** *n* basse-cour *f*.

farther ['fɑːðər] *adv* plus loin; **nothing is f. from** (*my mind, the truth etc*) rien n'est plus éloigné de; **f. forward** plus avancé; **to get f. away** s'éloigner; *– a* (*end*) autre. ◆**farthest** *a* le plus éloigné; *– adv* le plus loin.

fascinate ['fæsɪneɪt] *vt* fasciner. ◆**fasci-'nation** *n* fascination *f*.

fascism ['fæʃɪz(ə)m] *n* fascisme *m*. ◆**fascist** *a & n* fasciste (*mf*).

fashion ['fæʃ(ə)n] **1** *n* (*style in clothes etc*) mode *f*; **in f.** à la mode; **out of f.** démodé; **f. designer** (grand) couturier *m*; **f. house** maison *f* de couture; **f. show** présentation *f* de collections. **2** *n* (*manner*) façon *f*; (*custom*) habitude *f*; **after a f.** tant bien que mal, plus ou moins. **3** *vt* (*make*) façonner. ◆**—able** *a* à la mode; (*place*) chic *inv*; **it's f. to do** il est de bon ton de faire. ◆**—ably** *adv* (*dressed etc*) à la mode.

fast [fɑːst] **1** *a* (**-er, -est**) rapide; **to be f.** (*of clock*) avancer (**by** de); **f. colour** couleur *f* grand teint *inv*; **f. living** vie *f* dissolue; *– adv* (*quickly*) vite; (*firmly*) ferme, bien; **how f.?** à quelle vitesse?; **f. asleep** profondément endormi. **2** *vi* (*go without food*) jeûner; *– n* jeûne *m*.

fasten ['fɑːs(ə)n] *vt* attacher (**to** à); (*door, window*) fermer (**bien**); **to f. down** *or* **up** attacher; *– vi* (*of dress etc*) s'attacher; (*of door, window*) se fermer. ◆**—er** *n*, ◆**—ing** *n* (*clip*) attache *f*; (*of garment*) fermeture *f*; (*of bag*) fermoir *m*; (*hook*) agrafe *f*.

fastidious [fə'stɪdɪəs] *a* difficile (à contenter), exigeant.

fat [fæt] **1** *n* graisse *f*; (*on meat*) gras *m*; **vegetable f.** huile *f* végétale. **2** *a* (**fatter, fattest**) gras; (*cheek, salary, volume*) gros; **to get f.** grossir; **that's a f. lot of good** *or* **use!** *Iron*

Fam ça va vraiment servir (à quelque chose)! ◆**fathead** *n* imbécile *mf*.

fatal ['feɪt(ə)l] *a* mortel; (*error, blow etc*) *Fig* fatal. ◆**-ly** *adv* (*wounded*) mortellement.

fatality [fə'tælɪtɪ] *n* 1 (*person killed*) victime *f*. 2 (*of event*) fatalité *f*.

fate [feɪt] *n* destin *m*, sort *m*; one's f. son sort. ◆**fated** *a* f. to do destiné à faire; our meeting/his death/*etc* was f. notre rencontre/sa mort/*etc* devait arriver. ◆**fateful** *a* (*important*) fatal, décisif; (*prophetic*) fatidique; (*disastrous*) néfaste.

father ['fɑːðər] *n* père *m*; - *vt* engendrer; (*idea*) *Fig* inventer. ◆**f.-in-law** *n* (*pl* fathers-in-law) beau-père *m*. ◆**fatherhood** *n* paternité *f*. ◆**fatherland** *n* patrie *f*. ◆**fatherly** *a* paternel.

fathom ['fæðəm] 1 *n Nau* brasse *f* (= 1,8 m). 2 *vt* to f. (out) (*understand*) comprendre.

fatigue [fə'tiːg] 1 *n* fatigue *f*; - *vt* fatiguer. 2 *n* f. (duty) *Mil* corvée *f*.

fatness ['fætnɪs] *n* corpulence *f*. ◆**fatten** *vt* engraisser. ◆**fattening** *a* qui fait grossir. ◆**fatty** *a* (-ier, -iest) (*food*) gras; (*tissue*) *Med* adipeux; - *n* (*person*) *Fam* gros lard *m*.

fatuous ['fætʃuəs] *a* stupide.

faucet ['fɔːsɪt] *n* (*tap*) *Am* robinet *m*.

fault [fɔːlt] *n* (*blame*) faute *f*; (*failing, defect*) défaut *m*; (*mistake*) erreur *f*; *Geol* faille *f*; to find f. (with) critiquer; he's at f. c'est sa faute, il est fautif; his *or* her memory is at f. sa mémoire lui fait défaut; - *vt* to f. s.o./sth trouver des défauts chez qn/à qch. ◆**f.-finding** *a* critique, chicanier. ◆**faultless** *a* irréprochable. ◆**faulty** *a* (-ier, -iest) défectueux.

fauna ['fɔːnə] *n* (*animals*) faune *f*.

favour ['feɪvər] *n* (*approval, advantage*) faveur *f*; (*act of kindness*) service *m*; to do s.o. a f. rendre service à qn; in f. (*person*) bien vu; (*fashion*) en vogue; it's in her f. to do elle a intérêt à faire; in f. of (*for the sake of*) au profit de, en faveur de; to be in f. of (*support*) être pour, être partisan de; (*prefer*) préférer; - *vt* (*encourage*) favoriser; (*support*) être partisan de; (*prefer*) préférer; he favoured me with a visit il a eu la gentillesse de me rendre visite. ◆**-able** *a* favorable (to à). ◆**favourite** *a* favori, préféré; - *n* favori, -ite *mf*. ◆**favouritism** *n* favoritisme *m*.

fawn [fɔːn] 1 *n* (*deer*) faon *m*; - *a & n* (*colour*) fauve (*m*). 2 *vi* to f. (up)on flatter, flagorner.

fear [fɪər] *n* crainte *f*, peur *f*; for f. of de peur de; for f. that de peur que (+ ne + sub);

there's no f. of his going il ne risque pas d'y aller; there are fears (that) he might leave on craint qu'il ne parte; - *vt* craindre; I f. (that) he might leave je crains qu'il ne parte; to f. for (one's life etc) craindre pour. ◆**fearful** *a* (*frightful*) affreux; (*timid*) peureux. ◆**fearless** *a* intrépide. ◆**fearlessness** *n* intrépidité *f*. ◆**fearsome** *a* redoutable.

feasible ['fiːzəb(ə)l] *a* (*practicable*) faisable; (*theory, explanation etc*) plausible. ◆**feasibility** *n* possibilité *f* (*of doing* de faire); plausibilité *f*.

feast [fiːst] *n* festin *m*, banquet *m*; *Rel* fête *f*; - *vi* banqueter; to f. on (*cakes etc*) se régaler de.

feat [fiːt] *n* exploit *m*, tour *m* de force; f. of skill tour *m* d'adresse.

feather ['feðər] 1 *n* plume *f*; f. duster plumeau *m*. 2 *vt* to f. one's nest (*enrich oneself*) faire sa pelote.

feature ['fiːtʃər] 1 *n* (*of face, person*) trait *m*; (*of thing, place, machine*) caractéristique *f*; f. (article) article *m* de fond; f. (film) grand film *m*; to be a regular f. (*in newspaper*) paraître régulièrement. 2 *vt* représenter (*as* comme); *Journ Cin* présenter; a film featuring Chaplin un film avec Charlot en vedette; - *vi* (*appear*) figurer (in dans).

February ['februərɪ] *n* février *m*.

fed [fed] *see* feed; - *a* to be f. up *Fam* en avoir marre (with de).

federal ['fedərəl] *a* fédéral. ◆**federate** *vt* fédérer. ◆**federation** *n* fédération *f*.

fee [fiː] *n* (*price*) prix *m*; (*sum*) somme *f*; fee(s) (*professional*) honoraires *mpl*; (*of artist*) cachet *m*; (*for registration*) droits *mpl*; tuition fees frais *mpl* de scolarité; entrance f. droit *m* d'entrée; membership fee(s) cotisation *f*; f.-paying school école *f* privée.

feeble ['fiːb(ə)l] *a* (-er, -est) faible; (*excuse*) pauvre. ◆**f.-'minded** *a* imbécile.

feed [fiːd] *n* (*food*) nourriture *f*; (*baby's breast feed*) tétée *f*; (*baby's bottle feed*) biberon *m*; - *vt* (*pt & pp* fed) donner à manger à, nourrir; (*breast-feed*) allaiter (*un bébé*); (*bottle-feed*) nourrir le biberon à (*un bébé*); (*machine*) *Fig* alimenter; - *vi* (*eat*) manger; to f. on se nourrir de. ◆**-ing** *n* alimentation *f*. ◆**feedback** *n* réaction(s) *f(pl)*.

feel [fiːl] *n* (*touch*) toucher *m*; (*sensation*) sensation *f*; - *vt* (*pt & pp* felt) (*be aware of*) sentir; (*experience*) éprouver, ressentir; (*touch*) tâter, palper; (*think*) avoir l'impression (that que); to f. one's way avancer à tâtons; – *vi* (*tired, old etc*) se sentir; **to f. (about)** (*grope*) tâtonner; (*in pocket etc*) fouiller; **it feels hard** c'est dur (au toucher); **I f. sure** je suis sûr (**that** que); **I f. hot/sleepy/hungry** j'ai chaud/ sommeil/faim; **she feels better** elle va mieux; **to f. like** (*want*) avoir envie de; **to f. as if** avoir l'impression que; **it feels like cotton** on dirait du coton; **what do you f. about . . . ?** que pensez-vous de . . . ?; **I f. bad about it** ça m'ennuie, ça me fait de la peine; **what does it f. like?** quelle impression ça (te) fait?; **to f. for** (*look for*) chercher; (*pity*) éprouver de la pitié pour; **to f. up to doing** être (assez) en forme pour faire. ◆**—ing** *n* (*emotion, impression*) sentiment *m*; (*physical*) sensation *f*; **a f. for** (*person*) de la sympathie pour; (*music*) une appréciation de; **bad f.** animosité *f*. ◆**—er** *n* (*of snail etc*) antenne *f*; **to put out a f.** *Fig* lancer un ballon d'essai.

feet [fiːt] *see* **foot** [^1].

feign [feɪn] *vt* feindre, simuler.

feint [feɪnt] *n Mil Boxing* feinte *f*.

feisty [ˈfaɪstɪ] *a* (**-ier, -iest**) (*lively*) *Am Fam* plein d'entrain.

felicitous [fəˈlɪsɪtəs] *a* heureux.

feline [ˈfiːlaɪn] *a* félin.

fell [fel] **1** *see* **fall**. **2** *vt* (*tree etc*) abattre.

fellow [ˈfeləʊ] *n* **1** (*man, boy*) garçon *m*, type *m*; **an old f.** un vieux; **poor f.!** pauvre malheureux! **2** (*comrade*) compagnon *m*, compagne *f*; **f. being** *or* **man** semblable *m*; **f. countryman**, **f. countrywoman** compatriote *mf*; **f. passenger** compagnon *m* de voyage, compagne *f* de voyage. **3** (*of society*) membre *m*. ◆**fellowship** *n* camaraderie *f*; (*group*) association *f*; (*membership*) qualité *f* de membre; (*grant*) bourse *f* universitaire.

felony [ˈfelənɪ] *n* crime *m*.

felt [^1] [felt] *see* **feel**.

felt [^2] [felt] *n* feutre *m*; **f.-tip(ped) pen** crayon *m* feutre.

female [ˈfiːmeɪl] *a* (*animal etc*) femelle; (*quality, name, voice etc*) féminin; (*vote*) des femmes; **f. student** étudiante *f*; – *n* (*woman*) femme *f*; (*animal*) femelle *f*.

feminine [ˈfemɪnɪn] *a* féminin. ◆**femi'ninity** *n* féminité *f*. ◆**feminist** *a & n* féministe (*mf*).

fenc/e [fens] **1** *n* barrière *f*, clôture *f*; *Sp* obstacle *m*; – *vt* **to f. (in)** clôturer. **2** *vi* (*with sword*) *Sp* faire de l'escrime. **3** *n* (*criminal*) *Fam* receleur, -euse *mf*. ◆**—ing** *n Sp* escrime *f*.

fend [fend] **1** *vi* **to f. for oneself** se débrouil-

ler. **2** *vt* **to f. off** (*blow etc*) parer, éviter. ◆**—er** *n* **1** (*for fire*) garde-feu *m inv*. **2** (*on car*) *Am* aile *f*.

fennel [ˈfenəl] *n Bot Culin* fenouil *m*.

ferment [ˈfɜːment] *n* ferment *m*; *Fig* effervescence *f*; – [fəˈment] *vi* fermenter. ◆**fermen'tation** *n* fermentation *f*.

fern [fɜːn] *n* fougère *f*.

ferocious [fəˈrəʊʃəs] *a* féroce. ◆**ferocity** *n* férocité *f*.

ferret [ˈferɪt] *n* (*animal*) furet *m*; – *vi* **to f. about** (*pry*) fureter; – *vt* **to f. out** dénicher.

Ferris wheel [ˈferɪswiːl] *n* (*at funfair*) grande roue *f*.

ferry [ˈferɪ] *n* ferry-boat *m*; (*small, for river*) bac *m*; – *vt* transporter.

fertile [ˈfɜːtaɪl, *Am* ˈfɜːt(ə)l] *a* (*land, imagination*) fertile; (*person, creature*) fécond. ◆**fer'tility** *n* fertilité *f*; fécondité *f*. ◆**fertilize** *vt* (*land*) fertiliser; (*egg, animal etc*) féconder. ◆**fertilizer** *n* engrais *m*.

fervent [ˈfɜːv(ə)nt] *a* fervent. ◆**fervour** *n* ferveur *f*.

fester [ˈfestər] *vi* (*of wound*) suppurer; (*of anger etc*) *Fig* couver.

festival [ˈfestɪv(ə)l] *n Mus Cin* festival *m*; *Rel* fête *f*. ◆**festive** *a* (*atmosphere, clothes*) de fête; (*mood*) joyeux; **f. season** période *f* des fêtes. ◆**fe'stivities** *npl* réjouissances *fpl*, festivités *fpl*.

fetch [fetʃ] *vt* **1** (*person*) amener; (*object*) apporter; **to (go and) f.** aller chercher; **to f. in** rentrer; **to f. out** sortir. **2** (*be sold for*) rapporter; (**ten pounds**/*etc* dix livres/*etc*); (*price*) atteindre. ◆**—ing** *a* (*smile etc*) charmant, séduisant.

fête [feɪt] *n* fête *f*; – *vt* fêter.

fetid [ˈfetɪd] *a* fétide.

fetish [ˈfetɪʃ] *n* (*magical object*) fétiche *m*; **to make a f.** of *Fig* être obsédé par.

fetter [ˈfetər] *vt* (*hinder*) entraver.

fettle [ˈfet(ə)l] *n* **in fine f.** en pleine forme.

fetus [ˈfiːtəs] *n Am* fœtus *m*.

feud [fjuːd] *n* querelle *f*, dissension *f*.

feudal [ˈfjuːd(ə)l] *a* féodal.

fever [ˈfiːvər] *n* fièvre *f*; **to have a f.** (*temperature*) avoir de la fièvre. ◆**feverish** *a* (*person, activity*) fiévreux.

few [fjuː] *a & pron* peu (de); **f. towns**/*etc* peu de villes/*etc*; **a f. towns**/*etc* quelques villes/*etc*; **f. of them** peu d'entre eux; **a f.** quelques-un(e)s (**of** de); **a f. of us** quelques-uns d'entre nous; **one of the f. books** l'un des rares livres; **quite a f., a good f.** bon nombre (de); **a f. more books**/*etc* encore quelques livres/*etc*; **f. and far between** rares (et espacés); **f. came** peu sont venus; **to be f.** être peu nombreux; **every f. days** tous les trois ou quatre jours. ◆**fewer** *a & pron* moins (de) (**than** que); **to be f.** être moins nombreux (**than** que); **no f. than** pas moins de. ◆**fewest** *a & pron* le moins (de).

fiancé(e) [fɪˈɒnseɪ] *n* fiancé, -ée *mf*.

fiasco [fɪˈæskəʊ] *n* (*pl* -os, *Am* -oes) fiasco *m*.

fib [fɪb] *n Fam* blague *f*, bobard *m*; – *vi* (-bb-) *Fam* raconter des blagues. ◆**fibber** *n Fam* blagueur, -euse *mf*.

fibre [ˈfaɪbər] *n* fibre *f*; *Fig* caractère *m*. ◆**fibreglass** *n* fibre *f* de verre.

fickle [ˈfɪk(ə)l] *a* inconstant.

fiction [ˈfɪkʃ(ə)n] *n* fiction *f*; (**works of**) **f.** romans *mpl*. ◆**fictional** *a*, ◆**fic'titious** *a* fictif.

fiddl/e [ˈfɪd(ə)l] **1** *n* (*violin*) *Fam* violon *m*; – *vi Fam* jouer du violon. **2** *vi Fam* **to f. about** (*waste time*) traînailler, glandouiller; **to f. (about) with** (*watch, pen etc*) tripoter; (*cars etc*) bricoler. **3** *n* (*dishonesty*) *Fam* combine *f*, fraude *f*; – *vi* (*swindle*) *Fam* faire de la fraude; – *vt* (*accounts etc*) *Fam* falsifier. ◆**—ing** *a* (*petty*) insignifiant. ◆**—er** *n* **1** *Fam* joueur, -euse *mf* de violon. **2** (*swindler*) *Sl* combinard, -arde *mf*. ◆**fiddly** *a* (*task*) délicat.

fidelity [fɪˈdelɪtɪ] *n* fidélité *f* (**to** à).

fidget [ˈfɪdʒɪt] *vi* **to f. (about)** gigoter, se trémousser; **to f. (about) with** tripoter; – *n* personne *f* qui ne tient pas en place. ◆**fidgety** *a* agité, remuant.

field [fiːld] *n* champ *m*; *Sp* terrain *m*; (*sphere*) domaine *m*; **to have a f. day** (*a good day*) s'en donner à cœur joie; **f. glasses** jumelles *fpl*; **f. marshal** maréchal *m*.

fiend [fiːnd] *n* démon *m*; **a jazz/***etc* **f.** *Fam* un(e) passionné, -ée de jazz/*etc*; (*sex*) **f.** *Fam* satyre *m*. ◆**fiendish** *a* diabolique.

fierce [fɪəs] *a* (-er, -est) féroce; (*wind, attack*) furieux. ◆**—ness** *n* férocité *f*; fureur *f*.

fiery [ˈfaɪərɪ] *a* (-ier, -iest) (*person, speech*) fougueux; (*sun, eyes*) ardent.

fiesta [fɪˈestə] *n* fiesta *f*.

fifteen [fɪfˈtiːn] *a & n* quinze (*m*). ◆**fifteenth** *a & n* quinzième (*mf*). ◆**fifth** *a & n* cinquième (*mf*); **a f.** un cinquième. ◆**'fiftieth** *a & n* cinquantième (*mf*). ◆**'fifty** *a & n* cinquante (*m*).

fig [fɪg] *n* figue *f*; **f. tree** figuier *m*.

fight [faɪt] *n* bagarre *f*, rixe *f*; *Mil Boxing* combat *m*; (*struggle*) lutte *f*; (*quarrel*) dispute *f*; (*spirit*) combativité *f*; **to put up a (good) f.** bien se défendre; – *vi* (*pt & pp* fought) se battre (**against** contre); *Mil* se battre, combattre; (*struggle*) lutter; (*quarrel*) se disputer; **to f. back** se défendre; **to f. over sth** se disputer qch; – *vt* se battre avec (**s.o.** qn); (*evil*) lutter contre, combattre; **to f. a battle** livrer bataille; **to f. back** (*tears*) refouler; **to f. off** (*attacker, attack*) repousser; (*illness*) lutter contre; **to f. it out** se bagarrer. ◆**—ing** *n Mil* combat(s) *m(pl)*; – *a* (*person*) combatif; (*troops*) de combat. ◆**—er** *n* combattant, -ante *mf*; *Boxing* boxeur *m*; *Fig* battant *m*, lutteur, -euse *mf*; (*aircraft*) chasseur *m*.

figment [ˈfɪgmənt] *n* **a f. of one's imagination** une création de son esprit.

figurative [ˈfɪgjʊrətɪv] *a* (*meaning*) figuré; (*art*) figuratif. ◆**—ly** *adv* au figuré.

figure[1] [ˈfɪgər, *Am* ˈfɪgjər] *n* **1** (*numeral*) chiffre *m*; (*price*) prix *m*; *pl* (*arithmetic*) calcul *m*. **2** (*shape*) forme *f*; (*outlined shape*) silhouette *f*; (*of woman*) ligne *f*; **she has a nice f.** elle est bien faite. **3** (*diagram*) & *Liter* figure *f*; **a f. of speech** une figure de rhétorique; *Fig* une façon de parler; **f. of eight**, *Am* **f. eight** huit *m*; **f. skating** patinage *m* artistique. **4** (*important person*) figure *f*, personnage *m*. ◆**figurehead** *n Nau* figure *f* de proue; (*person*) *Fig* potiche *f*.

figure[2] [ˈfɪgər, *Am* ˈfɪgjər] **1** *vt* (*imagine*) (s')imaginer; (*guess*) penser (**that** que); **to f. out** arriver à comprendre; (*problem*) résoudre; – *vi* (*make sense*) s'expliquer; **to f. on doing** *Am* compter faire. **2** *vi* (*appear*) figurer (**on** sur).

filament [ˈfɪləmənt] *n* filament *m*.

filch [fɪltʃ] *vt* (*steal*) voler (**from** à).

fil/e [faɪl] **1** *n* (*tool*) lime *f*; – *vt* **to f. (down)** limer. **2** *n* (*folder, information*) dossier *m*; (*loose-leaf*) classeur *m*; (*for card index, computer data*) fichier *m*; – *vt* (*claim, application*) déposer; **to f. (away)** classer. **3** *n* **in single f.** en file; – *vi* **to f. in/out** entrer/sortir à la queue leu leu; **to f. past** (*coffin etc*) défiler devant. ◆**—ing 1** *a*. **clerk** documentaliste *mf*; **f. cabinet** classeur *m*. **2** *npl* (*particles*) limaille *f*.

fill [fɪl] *vt* remplir (**with** de); (*tooth*) plomber; (*sail*) gonfler; (*need*) répondre à; **to f. in** (*form*) remplir; (*hole*) combler; (*door*) condamner; **to f. s.o. in on** *Fam* mettre qn au courant de; **to f. up** (*glass etc*) remplir; **to f. up** *or* **out** (*form*) remplir; – *vi* **to f. (up)** se remplir; **to f. out** (*get fatter*) grossir, se remplumer; **to f. up** *Aut* faire le plein; – *n* **to eat one's f.** manger à sa faim; **to have had one's f. of** *Pej* en avoir assez de. ◆**—ing** *a* (*meal etc*) substantiel, nourrissant; – *n* (*in tooth*) plombage *m*; *Culin* garniture *f*; **f. station** poste *m* d'essence. ◆**–er** *n* (*for cracks in wood*) mastic *m*.

fillet ['filit, *Am* fi'leɪ] *n Culin* filet *m*; – *vt* (*pt & pp Am* [fi'leɪd]) (*fish*) découper en filets; (*meat*) désosser.

fillip ['filip] *n* (*stimulus*) coup *m* de fouet.

filly ['fili] *n* (*horse*) pouliche *f*.

film [film] *n* film *m*; (*layer*) & *Phot* pellicule *f*; – *a* (*festival*) du film; (*studio, technician, critic*) de cinéma. **f. fan** *or* **buff** cinéphile *mf*; **f. library** cinémathèque *f*; **f. star** vedette *f* (de cinéma); – *vt* filmer.

filter ['filtər] *n* filtre *m*; (*traffic sign*) flèche *f*; **f. lane** *Aut* couloir *m* (pour tourner); **f. tip** (bout *m*) filtre *m*; **f.-tipped cigarette** cigarette *f* (à bout) filtre; – *vt* filtrer; – *vi* filtrer (**through sth** à travers qch); **to f. through** filtrer.

filth [filθ] *n* saleté *f*; (*obscenities*) *Fig* saletés *fpl*. ◆**filthy** *a* (**-ier, -iest**) (*hands etc*) sale; (*language*) obscène; (*habit*) dégoûtant; **f. weather** un temps infect, un sale temps.

fin [fin] *n* (*of fish, seal*) nageoire *f*; (*of shark*) aileron *m*.

final ['faɪn(ə)l] *a* dernier; (*decision*) définitif; (*cause*) final; – *n Sp* finale *f*; *pl Univ* examens *mpl* de dernière année. ◆**finalist** *n Sp* finaliste *mf*. ◆**finalize** *vt* (*plan*) mettre au point; (*date*) fixer (définitivement). ◆**finally** *adv* (*lastly*) enfin, en dernier lieu; (*eventually*) finalement, enfin; (*once and for all*) définitivement.

finale [fi'nɑːlɪ] *n Mus* finale *m*.

finance ['faɪnæns] *n* finance *f*; – *a* (*company, page*) financier; – *vt* financer. ◆**fi'nancial** *a* financier; **f. year** année *f* budgétaire. ◆**fi'nancially** *adv* financièrement. ◆**fi'nancier** *n* (grand) financier *m*.

find [faɪnd] *n* (*discovery*) trouvaille *f*; – *vt* (*pt & pp* **found**) trouver; (*sth or s.o. lost*) retrouver; (*difficulty*) éprouver, trouver (**in doing** à faire); **I f. that** je trouve que; **£20 all found** 20 livres logé et nourri; **to f. s.o. guilty** *Jur* prononcer qn coupable; **to f. one's feet** (*settle in*) s'adapter; **to f. oneself** (*to be*) se trouver. ■ **to f. out** *vt* (*information etc*) découvrir; (*person*) démasquer; – *vi* (*enquire*) se renseigner (**about** sur); **to f. out about** (*discover*) découvrir. ◆**–ings** *npl* conclusions *fpl*.

fine[1] [faɪn] *n* (*money*) amende *f*; *Aut* contravention *f*; – *vt* **to f. s.o.** (**£10**/*etc*) infliger une amende (de dix livres/*etc*) à qn.

fine[2] [faɪn] **1** *a* (**-er, -est**) (*thin, small, not coarse*) fin; (*gold*) pur; (*feeling*) délicat;

(*distinction*) subtil; – *adv* (*to cut, write*) menu. **2** *a* (**-er, -est**) (*beautiful*) beau; (*good*) bon; (*excellent*) excellent; **to be f.** (*in good health*) aller bien; – *adv* (*well*) très bien. ◆**–ly** *adv* (*dressed*) magnifiquement; (*chopped*) menu; (*embroidered, ground*) finement.

finery ['faɪnərɪ] *n* (*clothes*) parure *f*, belle toilette *f*.

finesse [fi'nes] *n* (*skill, tact*) doigté *m*; (*refinement*) finesse *f*.

finger ['fiŋgər] *n* doigt *m*; **little f.** auriculaire *m*, petit doigt *m*; **middle f.** majeur *m*, **f. mark** trace *f* de doigt; – *vt* toucher (des doigts), palper. ◆**–ing** *n Mus* doigté *m*. ◆**fingernail** *n* ongle *m*. ◆**fingerprint** *n* empreinte *f* digitale. ◆**fingerstall** *n* doigtier *m*. ◆**fingertip** *n* bout *m* du doigt.

finicky ['finiki] *a* (*precise*) méticuleux; (*difficult*) difficile (**about** sur).

finish ['finiʃ] *n* (*end*) fin *f*; *Sp* arrivée *f*; (*of article, car etc*) finition *f*; **paint with a matt f.** peinture *f* mate; – *vt* **to f. sth** (**off** *or* **up**) finir, terminer; **to f. doing** finir de faire; **to f. s.o. off** (*kill*) achever qn; – *vi* (*of meeting etc*) finir, se terminer; (*of person*) finir, terminer; **to f. first** terminer premier; (*in race*) arriver premier; **to have finished with** (*object*) ne plus avoir besoin de; (*situation, person*) en avoir fini avec; **to f. off** *or* **up** (*of person*) finir, terminer; **to f. up in** (*end up in*) se retrouver à; **to f. up doing** finir par faire; **finishing school** institution *f* pour jeunes filles; **finishing touch** touche *f* finale. ◆**–ed** *a* (*ended, done for*) fini.

finite ['faɪnaɪt] *a* fini.

Finland ['finlənd] *n* Finlande *f*. ◆**Finn** *n* Finlandais, -aise *mf*, Finnois, -oise *mf*. ◆**Finnish** *a* finlandais, finnois; – *n* (*language*) finnois *m*.

fir [fɜːr] *n* (*tree, wood*) sapin *m*.

fire[1] ['faɪər] *n* feu *m*; (*accidental*) incendie *m*; (*electric*) radiateur *m*; **on f.** en feu; (**there's a**) **f.!** au feu!; **f.!** *Mil* feu!; **f. alarm** avertisseur *m* d'incendie; **f. brigade,** *Am* **f. department** pompiers *mpl*; **f. engine** (*vehicle*) voiture *f* de pompiers; (*machine*) pompe *f* à incendie; **f. escape** escalier *m* de secours; **f. station** caserne *f* de pompiers. ◆**firearm** *n* arme *f* à feu. ◆**firebug** *n* pyromane *mf*. ◆**firecracker** *n Am* pétard *m*. ◆**fireguard** *n* garde-feu *m inv*. ◆**fireman** *n* (*pl* **-men**) (sapeur-)pompier *m*. ◆**fireplace** *n* cheminée *f*. ◆**fireproof** *a* (*door*) ignifugé, anti-incendie. ◆**fireside** *n* coin *m* du feu; **f. chair** fauteuil *m*. ◆**firewood** *n* bois *m* de chauffage.

◆**firework** *n* feu *m* d'artifice; **a f. display**, **fireworks**, un feu d'artifice.

fire² ['faɪər] *vt* (*cannon*) tirer; (*pottery*) cuire; (*imagination*) enflammer; **to f. a gun** tirer un coup de fusil; **to f. questions at** bombarder de questions; **to f. s.o.** (*dismiss*) *Fam* renvoyer qn; – *vi* tirer (at sur); **f. away!** *Fam* vas-y, parle!; **firing squad** peloton *m* d'exécution; **in** *or Am* **on the firing line** en butte aux attaques.

firm [fɜːm] **1** *n Com* maison *f*, firme *f*. **2** *a* (**-er, -est**) (*earth, decision etc*) ferme; (*strict*) ferme (**with** avec); (*faith*) solide; (*character*) résolu. ◆**—ly** *adv* fermement; (*to speak*) d'une voix ferme. ◆**—ness** *n* fermeté *f*; (*of faith*) solidité *f*.

first [fɜːst] *a* premier; **I'll do it f. thing in the morning** je le ferai dès le matin, sans faute; **f. cousin** cousin, -ine *mf* germain(e); – *adv* d'abord, premièrement; (*for the first time*) pour la première fois; **f. of all** tout d'abord; **at f.** d'abord; **to come f.** (*in race*) arriver premier; (*in exam*) être le premier; – *n* premier, -ière *mf*; *Univ* = licence *f* avec mention très bien; **from the f.** dès le début; **f. aid** premiers soins *mpl* *or* secours *mpl*; **f. (gear)** *Aut* première *f*. ◆**f.-'class** *a* (*ticket etc*) de première (classe); (*mail*) ordinaire; – *adv* (*to travel*) en première. ◆**f.-'hand** *a* & *adv* de première main; **to have (had) f.-hand experience of** avoir fait l'expérience personnelle de. ◆**f.-'rate** *a* excellent. ◆**firstly** *adv* premièrement.

fiscal ['fɪsk(ə)l] *a* fiscal.

fish [fɪʃ] *n* (*pl inv or* **-es** [-ɪz]) poisson *m*; **f. market** marché *m* aux poissons; **f. bone** arête *f*; **f. bowl** bocal *m*; **f. fingers**, *Am* **f. sticks** *Culin* bâtonnets *mpl* de poisson; **f. shop** poissonnerie *f*; – *vi* pêcher; **to f. for** (*salmon etc*) pêcher; (*compliment etc*) *Fig* chercher; – *vt* **to f. out** (*from water*) repêcher; (*from pocket etc*) *Fig* sortir. ◆**—ing** *n* pêche *f*; **to go f.** aller à la pêche; **f. net** (*of fisherman*) filet *m* (de pêche); (*of angler*) épuisette *f*; **f. rod** canne *f* à pêche. ◆**fisherman** *n* (*pl* **-men**) pêcheur *m*. ◆**fishmonger** *n* poissonnier, -ière *mf*. ◆**fishy** *a* (**-ier, -iest**) (*smell*) de poisson; *Fig Pej* louche.

fission ['fɪʃ(ə)n] *n Phys* fission *f*.

fissure ['fɪʃər] *n* fissure *f*.

fist [fɪst] *n* poing *m*. ◆**fistful** *n* poignée *f*.

fit¹ [fɪt] **1** *a* (**fitter, fittest**) (*suited*) propre, bon (**for** à); (*fitting*) convenable; (*worthy*) digne (**for** de); (*able*) capable (**for** de, **to do** de faire); (*healthy*) en bonne santé; **f. to eat** bon à manger, mangeable; **to see f. to do**

juger à propos de faire; **as you see f.** comme bon vous semble; **f. to drop** *Fam* prêt à tomber; **to keep f.** se maintenir en forme. **2** *vt* (**-tt-**) (*of coat etc*) aller (bien) à (qn), être à la taille de (qn); (*match*) répondre à; (*equal*) égaler; **to f. sth on s.o.** (*garment*) ajuster qch à qn; **to f. sth (on) to sth** (*put*) poser qch sur qch; (*adjust*) adapter qch à qch; (*fix*) fixer qch à qch; **to f. (out or up) with** (*house, ship etc*) équiper de; **to f. (in)** (*window*) poser; **to f. in** (*object*) faire entrer; (*patient, customer*) prendre; **to f. (in) the lock** (*of key*) aller dans la serrure; – *vi* (*of clothes*) aller (bien) (à qn); **this shirt fits** (*fits me*) cette chemise me va (bien); **to f. (in)** (*go in*) entrer, aller; (*of facts, plans*) s'accorder, cadrer (**with** avec); **he doesn't f. in** il ne peut pas s'intégrer; – *n* **a good f.** (*dress etc*) à la bonne taille; **a close** *or* **tight f.** ajusté. ◆**fitted** *a* (*cupboard*) encastré; (*garment*) ajusté; **f. carpet** moquette *f*; **f. (kitchen) units** éléments *mpl* de cuisine. ◆**fitting 1** *a* (*suitable*) convenable. **2** *n* (*of clothes*) essayage *m*; **f. room** salon *m* d'essayage; (*booth*) cabine *f* d'essayage. **3** *npl* (*in house etc*) installations *fpl*. ◆**fitment** *n* (*furniture*) meuble *m* encastré; (*accessory*) *Tech* accessoire *m*. ◆**fitness** *n* (*of remark etc*) à-propos *m*; (*for job*) aptitudes *fpl* (**for** pour); *Med* santé *f*. ◆**fitter** *n* *Tech* monteur, -euse *mf*.

fit² [fɪt] *n Med & Fig* accès *m*, crise *f*; **in fits and starts** par à-coups. ◆**fitful** *a* (*sleep*) agité.

five [faɪv] *a* & *n* cinq (*m*). ◆**fiver** *n Fam* billet *m* de cinq livres.

fix [fɪks] **1** *vt* (*make firm, decide*) fixer; (*tie with rope*) attacher; (*mend*) réparer; (*deal with*) arranger; (*prepare, cook*) *Am* préparer, faire; (*in s.o.'s mind*) graver (**in** dans); (*conduct fraudulently*) *Fam* truquer; (*bribe*) *Fam* acheter; (*hopes, ambitions*) mettre (**on** en); **to f. s.o.** (*punish*) *Fam* régler son compte à qn; **to f. (on)** (*lid etc*) mettre en place; **to f. up** arranger; **to f. s.o. up with sth** (*job etc*) procurer qch à qn. **2** *n Av Nau* position *f*; (*injection*) *Sl* piqûre *f*; **in a f.** *Fam* dans le pétrin. ◆**—ed** *a* (*idea, price etc*) fixe; (*resolution*) inébranlable; **how's he f. for...?** *Fam* (*cash etc*) a-t-il assez de...?; (*tomorrow etc*) qu'est-ce qu'il fait pour...? ◆**fixings** *npl Culin* *Am* garniture *f*. ◆**fix'ation** *n* fixation *f*. ◆**fixer** *n* (*schemer*) *Fam* combinard, -arde *mf*. ◆**fixture 1** *n Sp* match *m* (prévu). **2** *npl* (*in house*) meubles *mpl* fixes, installations *fpl*.

fizz [fɪz] vi (of champagne) pétiller; (of gas) siffler. ◆**fizzy** a (-ier, -iest) pétillant.

fizzle ['fɪz(ə)l] vi (hiss) siffler; (of liquid) pétiller; **to f. out** (of fireworks) rater, faire long feu; (of plan) Fig tomber à l'eau; (of custom) disparaître.

flabbergasted ['flæbəɡɑːstɪd] a Fam sidéré.

flabby ['flæbɪ] a (-ier, -iest) (skin, character, person) mou, flasque.

flag [flæɡ] **1** n drapeau m; Nau pavillon m; (for charity) insigne m; **f. stop** Am arrêt m facultatif; – vt (-gg-) **to f. down** (taxi) faire signe à. **2** vi (-gg-) (of plant) dépérir; (of conversation) languir; (of worker) fléchir. ◆**flagpole** n mât m.

flagrant ['fleɪɡrənt] a flagrant.

flagstone ['flæɡstəʊn] n dalle f.

flair [fleər] n (intuition) flair m; **to have a f. for** (natural talent) avoir un don pour.

flake [fleɪk] n (of snow etc) flocon m; (of metal, soap) paillette f; – vi **to f. (off)** (of paint) s'écailler. ◆**flaky** a **f. pastry** pâte f feuilletée.

flamboyant [flæm'bɔɪənt] a (person, manner) extravagant.

flam/e [fleɪm] n flamme f; **to go up in flames** s'enflammer; – vi **to f. (up)** (of fire, house) flamber. ◆**—ing** a **1** (sun) flamboyant. **2** (damn) Fam fichu.

flamingo [flə'mɪŋɡəʊ] n (pl -os or -oes) (bird) flamant m.

flammable ['flæməb(ə)l] a inflammable.

flan [flæn] n tarte f.

flank [flæŋk] n flanc m; – vt flanquer (with de).

flannel ['flænəl] n (cloth) flanelle f; (face) f. gant m de toilette, carré-éponge m. ◆**flanne'lette** n pilou m, finette f.

flap [flæp] **1** vi (-pp-) (of wings, sail, shutter etc) battre; – vt **to f. its wings** (of bird) battre des ailes; – n battement m. **2** n (of pocket, envelope) rabat m; (of table) abattant m; (of door) battant m.

flare [fleər] n (light) éclat m; Mil fusée f éclairante; (for runway) balise f; – vi (blaze) flamber; (shine) briller; **to f. up** (of fire) s'enflammer; (of region) Fig s'embraser; (of war) éclater; (get angry) s'emporter. ◆**f.-up** n (of violence, fire) flambée f; (of region) embrasement m. ◆**flared** a (skirt) évasé; (trousers) à pattes d'éléphant.

flash [flæʃ] n (of light) éclat m; (of anger, genius) éclair m; Phot flash m; **f. of lightning** éclair m; **news f.** flash m; **in a f.** en un clin d'œil; – vi (shine) briller; (on and off) clignoter; **to f. past** (rush) Fig passer comme un éclair; – vt (aim) diriger (on, at sur); (a light) projeter; (a glance) jeter; **to f. (around)** (flaunt) étaler; **to f. one's head-lights** faire un appel de phares. ◆**flashback** n retour m en arrière. ◆**flashlight** n lampe f électrique or de poche; Phot flash m.

flashy ['flæʃɪ] a (-ier, -iest) a voyant, tape-à-l'œil inv.

flask [flɑːsk] n thermos® m or f inv; Ch flacon m; (phial) fiole f.

flat¹ [flæt] a (flatter, flattest) plat; (tyre, battery) à plat; (nose) aplati; (beer) éventé; (refusal) net; (rate, fare) fixe; (voice) Mus faux; (razed to the ground) rasé; **to put sth (down) f.** mettre qch à plat; **f. (on one's face)** à plat ventre; **to fall f.** Fig tomber à plat; **to be f.-footed** avoir les pieds plats; – adv (to say) carrément; (to sing) faux; **f. broke** Fam complètement fauché; **in two minutes f.** en deux minutes pile; **f. out** (to work) d'arrache-pied; (to run) à toute vitesse; – n (of hand) plat m; (puncture) Aut crevaison f; Mus bémol m. ◆**—ly** adv (to deny etc) catégoriquement. ◆**—ness** n (of surface) égalité f. ◆**flatten** vt (crops) coucher; (town) raser; **to f. (out)** (metal etc) aplatir.

flat² [flæt] n (rooms) appartement m.

flatter ['flætər] vt flatter; (of clothes) avantager (qn). ◆**—ing** a flatteur; (clothes) avantageux. ◆**—er** n flatteur, -euse mf. ◆**flattery** n flatterie f.

flatulence ['flætjʊləns] n **to have f.** avoir des gaz.

flaunt [flɔːnt] vt (show off) faire étalage de; (defy) Am narguer, défier.

flautist ['flɔːtɪst] n flûtiste mf.

flavour ['fleɪvər] n (taste) goût m, saveur f; (of ice cream, sweet etc) parfum m; – vt (food) assaisonner; (sauce) relever; (ice cream etc) parfumer (with à). ◆**—ing** n assaisonnement m; (in cake) parfum m.

flaw [flɔː] n défaut m. ◆**flawed** a imparfait. ◆**flawless** a parfait.

flax [flæks] n lin m. ◆**flaxen** a de lin.

flay [fleɪ] vt (animal) écorcher; (criticize) Fig éreinter.

flea [fliː] n puce f; **f. market** marché m aux puces. ◆**fleapit** n Fam cinéma m miteux.

fleck [flek] n (mark) petite tache f.

fledgling ['fledʒlɪŋ] n (novice) blanc-bec m.

flee [fliː] vi (pt & pp fled) fuir, s'enfuir, se sauver; – vt (place) s'enfuir de; (danger etc) fuir.

fleece [fliːs] **1** n (sheep's coat) toison f. **2** vt (rob) voler.

fleet [fliːt] n (of ships) flotte f; **a f. of cars** un parc automobile.

fleeting ['fliːtɪŋ] a (visit, moment) bref; (beauty) éphémère.

Flemish ['flemɪʃ] a flamand; − n (language) flamand m.

flesh [fleʃ] n chair f; **her (own) f. and blood** la chair de sa chair; **in the f.** en chair et en os; **f. wound** blessure f superficielle. ◆**fleshy** a (-ier, -iest) charnu.

flew [fluː] see **fly²**.

flex [fleks] **1** vt (limb) fléchir; (muscle) faire jouer, bander. **2** n (wire) fil m (souple); (for telephone) cordon m.

flexible ['fleksɪb(ə)l] a flexible, souple. ◆**flexi'bility** n flexibilité f.

flick [flɪk] vt donner un petit coup à; **to f. off** (remove) enlever (d'une chiquenaude); − vi **to f. over** or **through** (pages) feuilleter; − n petit coup m; (with finger) chiquenaude f; **f. knife** couteau m à cran d'arrêt.

flicker ['flɪkər] vi (of flame, light) vaciller; (of needle) osciller; − n vacillement m; **f. of light** lueur f.

flier ['flaɪər] n **1** (person) aviateur, -trice mf. **2** (handbill) Am prospectus m, Pol tract m.

flies [flaɪz] npl (on trousers) braguette f.

flight [flaɪt] n **1** (of bird, aircraft etc) vol m; (of bullet) trajectoire f; (of imagination) élan m; (floor, storey) étage m; **f. of stairs** escalier m; **f. deck** cabine f de pilotage. **2** (fleeing) fuite f (from de); **to take f.** prendre la fuite.

flighty ['flaɪtɪ] a (-ier, -iest) inconstant, volage.

flimsy ['flɪmzɪ] a (-ier, -iest) (cloth, structure etc) (trop) léger or mince; (excuse) mince, frivole.

flinch [flɪntʃ] vi (with pain) tressaillir; **to f. from** (duty etc) se dérober à; **without flinching** (complaining) sans broncher.

fling [flɪŋ] **1** vt (pt & pp flung) jeter, lancer; **to f. open** (door etc) ouvrir brutalement. **2** n **to have one's** or **a f.** (indulge oneself) s'en donner à cœur joie.

flint [flɪnt] n silex m; (for cigarette lighter) pierre f.

flip [flɪp] **1** vt (-pp-) (with finger) donner une chiquenaude à; − vi **to f. through** (book etc) feuilleter; − n chiquenaude f; **the f. side** (of record) la face deux. **2** a (cheeky) Am Fam effronté.

flip-flops ['flɪpflɒps] npl tongs fpl.

flippant ['flɪpənt] a irrévérencieux; (offhand) désinvolte.

flipper ['flɪpər] n (of seal) nageoire f; (of swimmer) palme f.

flipping ['flɪpɪŋ] a Fam sacré; − adv Fam sacrément, bougrement.

flirt [flɜːt] vi flirter (with avec); − n flirteur, -euse mf. ◆**flir'tation** n flirt m. ◆**flir-'tatious** a flirteur.

flit [flɪt] vi (-tt-) (fly) voltiger; **to f. in and out** (of person) Fig entrer et sortir (rapidement).

float [fləʊt] n Fishing flotteur m; (in parade) char m; − vi flotter (on sur); **to f. down the river** descendre la rivière; − vt (boat, currency) faire flotter; (loan) Com émettre. ◆**—ing** a (wood, debt etc) flottant; (population) instable; (voters) indécis.

flock [flɒk] n (of sheep etc) troupeau m; (of birds) volée f; Rel Hum ouailles fpl; (of tourists etc) foule f; − vi venir en foule; **to f. round s.o.** s'attrouper autour de qn.

floe [fləʊ] n (ice) f. banquise f.

flog [flɒg] vt (-gg-) **1** (beat) flageller. **2** (sell) Sl vendre. ◆**flogging** n flagellation f.

flood [flʌd] n inondation f; (of letters, tears etc) Fig flot m, déluge m, torrent m; − vt (field etc) inonder (with de); (river) faire déborder; **to f. (out)** (house) inonder; − vi (of building) être inondé; (of river) déborder; (of people, money) affluer; **to f. into** (of tourists etc) envahir. ◆**—ing** n inondation f. ◆**floodgate** n (in water) vanne f.

floodlight ['flʌdlaɪt] n projecteur m; − vt (pt & pp floodlit) illuminer; **floodlit match** Sp (match m en) nocturne m.

floor [flɔːr] **1** n (ground) sol m; (wooden etc in building) plancher m; (storey) étage m; (dance) f. piste f (de danse); **on the f.** par terre; **first f.** premier étage m; (ground floor) Am rez-de-chaussée m inv; **f. polish** encaustique f; **f. show** spectacle m (de cabaret). **2** vt (knock down) terrasser; (puzzle) stupéfier. ◆**floorboard** n planche f.

flop [flɒp] **1** vi (-pp-) **to f. down** (collapse) s'effondrer; **to f. about** s'agiter mollement. **2** vi (-pp-) Fam échouer; (of play, film etc) faire un four; − n Fam échec m, fiasco m; Th Cin four m.

floppy ['flɒpɪ] a (-ier, -iest) (soft) mou; (clothes) (trop) large; (ears) pendant; **f. disk** (of computer) disquette f.

flora ['flɔːrə] n (plants) flore f. ◆**floral** a floral; (material) à fleurs.

florid ['flɒrɪd] a (style) fleuri; (complexion) rougeaud, fleuri.

florist ['flɒrɪst] n fleuriste mf.

floss [flɒs] n (dental) f. fil m (de soie) dentaire.

flotilla [flə'tɪlə] n Nau flottille f.

flounce [flauns] *n* (*frill on dress etc*) volant *m*.

flounder ['flaundər] **1** *vi* (*in water etc*) patauger (avec effort), se débattre; (*in speech*) hésiter, patauger. **2** *n* (*fish*) carrelet *m*.

flour ['flauər] *n* farine *f*.

flourish ['flʌrɪʃ] **1** *vi* (*of person, business, plant etc*) prospérer; (*of the arts*) fleurir. **2** *vt* (*wave*) brandir. **3** *n* (*decoration*) fioriture *f*; *Mus* fanfare *f*. ◆—**ing** *a* prospère, florissant.

flout [flaut] *vt* narguer, braver.

flow [fləu] *vi* couler; (*of current*) *El* circuler; (*of hair, clothes*) flotter; (*of traffic*) s'écouler; **to f. in** (*of people, money*) affluer; **to f. back** refluer; **to f. into the sea** se jeter dans la mer; − *n* (*of river*) courant *m*; (*of tide*) flux *m*; (*of blood*) & *El* circulation *f*; (*of traffic, liquid*) écoulement *m*; (*of words*) *Fig* flot *m*. ◆—**ing** *a* (*movement*) gracieux; (*style*) coulant; (*beard*) flottant.

flower ['flauər] *n* fleur *f*; **f. bed** plate-bande *f*; **f. shop** (boutique *f* de) fleuriste *mf*; **f. show** floralies *fpl*; − *vi* fleurir. ◆—**ed** *a* (*dress*) à fleurs. ◆—**ing** *n* floraison *f*; − *a* (*in bloom*) en fleurs; (*with flowers*) à fleurs. ◆**flowery** *a* (*style etc*) fleuri; (*material*) à fleurs.

flown [fləun] *see* fly [2].

flu [flu:] *n* (*influenza*) *Fam* grippe *f*.

fluctuate ['flʌktʃueɪt] *vi* varier. ◆**fluctu-'ation(s)** *n(pl)* (*in prices etc*) fluctuations *fpl* (**in** de).

flue [flu:] *n* (*of chimney*) conduit *m*.

fluent ['flu:ənt] *a* (*style*) aisé; **to be f., be a f. speaker** s'exprimer avec facilité; **he's f. in Russian, his Russian is f.** il parle couramment le russe. ◆**fluency** *n* facilité *f*. ◆**fluently** *adv* avec facilité; (*to speak*) *Ling* couramment.

fluff [flʌf] **1** *n* (*down*) duvet *m*; (*of material*) peluche(s) *f(pl)*; (*on floor*) moutons *mpl*. **2** *vt* (*bungle*) *Fam* rater. ◆**fluffy** *a* (-ier, -iest) (*bird etc*) duveteux; (*material*) pelucheux; (*toy*) en peluche; (*hair*) bouffant.

fluid ['flu:ɪd] *a* fluide; (*plans*) flexible, non arrêté; − *n* fluide *m*, liquide *m*.

fluke [flu:k] *n* *Fam* coup *m* de chance; **by a f.** par raccroc.

flummox ['flʌməks] *vt* *Fam* désorienter, dérouter.

flung [flʌŋ] *see* fling 1.

flunk [flʌŋk] *vi* (*in exam*) *Am* *Fam* être collé; − *vt* *Am* *Fam* (*pupil*) coller; (*exam*) être collé à; (*school*) laisser tomber.

flunk(e)y ['flʌŋkɪ] *n* *Pej* larbin *m*.

fluorescent [fluə'res(ə)nt] *a* fluorescent.

fluoride ['fluəraɪd] *n* (*in water, toothpaste*) fluor *m*.

flurry ['flʌrɪ] *n* **1** (*of activity*) poussée *f*. **2** (*of snow*) rafale *f*.

flush [flʌʃ] **1** *n* (*of blood*) flux *m*; (*blush*) rougeur *f*; (*of youth, beauty*) éclat *m*; (*of victory*) ivresse *f*; − *vi* (*blush*) rougir. **2** *vt* **to f. (out)** (*clean*) nettoyer à grande eau; **to f. the pan** *or* **the toilet** tirer la chasse d'eau; **to f. s.o. out** (*chase away*) faire sortir qn (**from** de). **3** *a* (*level*) de niveau (**with** de); **f. (with money)** *Fam* bourré de fric. ◆—**ed** *a* (*cheeks etc*) rouge; **f. with** (*success*) ivre de.

fluster ['flʌstər] *vt* énerver; **to get flustered** s'énerver.

flute [flu:t] *n* flûte *f*. ◆**flutist** *n* *Am* flûtiste *mf*.

flutter ['flʌtər] **1** *vi* voltiger; (*of wing*) battre; (*of flag*) flotter (mollement); (*of heart*) palpiter; **to f. about** (*of person*) papillonner; − *vt* **to f. its wings** battre des ailes. **2** *n* **to have a f.** (*bet*) *Fam* parier.

flux [flʌks] *n* changement *m* continuel.

fly [1] [flaɪ] *n* (*insect*) mouche *f*; **f. swatter** (*instrument*) tapette *f*. ◆**flypaper** *n* papier *m* tue-mouches.

fly [2] [flaɪ] *vi* (*pt* flew, *pp* flown) (*of bird, aircraft etc*) voler; (*of passenger*) aller en avion; (*of time*) passer vite; (*of flag*) flotter; (*flee*) fuir; **to f. away** *or* **off** s'envoler; **to f. out** *Av* partir en avion; (*from room*) sortir à toute vitesse; **I must f.!** il faut que je file!; **to f. at s.o.** (*attack*) sauter sur qn; − *vt* (*aircraft*) piloter; (*passengers*) transporter (par avion); (*airline*) voyager par; (*flag*) arborer; (*kite*) faire voler; **to f. the French flag** battre pavillon français; **to f. across** *or* **over** survoler. ◆—**ing** *n* (*flight*) vol *m*; (*air travel*) aviation *f*; **to like f.** aimer l'avion; − *a* (*personnel, saucer etc*) volant; (*visit*) éclair *inv*; **with f. colours** (*to succeed*) haut la main; **a f. start** un très bon départ; **f. time** (*length*) *Av* durée *f* du vol; **ten hours**/*etc* **f. time** dix heures/*etc* de vol. ◆—**er** *n* = flier. ◆**flyby** *n* *Av* *Am* défilé *m* aérien. ◆**fly-by-night** *a* (*firm*) véreux. ◆**flyover** *n* (*bridge*) toboggan *m*. ◆**flypast** *n* *Av* défilé *m* aérien.

fly [3] [flaɪ] *n* (*on trousers*) braguette *f*.

foal [fəul] *n* poulain *m*.

foam [fəum] *n* (*on sea, mouth*) écume *f*; (*on beer*) mousse *f*; **f. rubber** caoutchouc *m* mousse; **f. (rubber) mattress**/*etc* matelas *m*/*etc* mousse; − *vi* (*of sea, mouth*) écumer; (*of beer, soap*) mousser.

fob [fɒb] *vt* (**-bb-**) **to f. sth off on s.o., f. s.o. off with sth,** refiler qch à qn.

focal ['fəʊk(ə)l] *a* focal; **f. point** point *m* central. ◆**focus** *n* foyer *m*; (*of attention, interest*) centre *m*; **in f.** au point; – *vt Phot* mettre au point; (*light*) faire converger; (*efforts, attention*) concentrer (**on** sur); – *vi* (*converge*) converger (**on** sur); **to f. (one's eyes) on** fixer les yeux sur; **to f. on** (*direct one's attention to*) se concentrer sur.

fodder ['fɒdər] *n* fourrage *m*.

foe [fəʊ] *n* ennemi, -ie *mf*.

foetus ['fiːtəs] *n* fœtus *m*.

fog [fɒg] *n* brouillard *m*, brume *f*; – *vt* (**-gg-**) (*issue*) *Fig* embrouiller. ◆**fogbound** *a* bloqué par le brouillard. ◆**foghorn** *n* corne *f* de brume; (*voice*) *Pej* voix *f* tonitruante. ◆**foglamp** *n* (phare *m*) anti-brouillard *m*. ◆**foggy** *a* (**-ier, -iest**) (*day*) de brouillard; **it's f.** il fait du brouillard; **f. weather** brouillard *m*; **she hasn't the foggiest (idea)** *Fam* elle n'en a pas la moindre idée.

fog(e)y ['fəʊgɪ] *n* **old f.** vieille baderne *f*.

foible ['fɔɪb(ə)l] *n* petit défaut *m*.

foil [fɔɪl] **1** *n* feuille *f* de métal; *Culin* papier *m* alu(minium). **2** *n* (*contrasting person*) repoussoir *m*. **3** *vt* (*plans etc*) déjouer.

foist [fɔɪst] *vt* **to f. sth on s.o.** (*fob off*) refiler qch à qn; **to f. oneself on s.o.** s'imposer à qn.

fold[1] [fəʊld] *n* pli *m*; – *vt* plier; (*wrap*) envelopper (**in** dans); **to f. away** *or* **down** *or* **up** plier; **to f. back** *or* **over** replier; **to f. one's arms** (se) croiser les bras; – *vi* (*of chair etc*) se plier; (*of business*) *Fam* s'écrouler; **to f. away** *or* **down** *or* **up** (*of chair etc*) se plier; **to f. back** *or* **over** (*of blanket etc*) se replier. ◆**—ing** *a* (*chair etc*) pliant. ◆**—er** *n* (*file holder*) chemise *f*; (*pamphlet*) dépliant *m*.

fold[2] [fəʊld] *n* (*for sheep*) parc *m* à moutons; *Rel Fig* bercail *m*.

-fold [fəʊld] *suffix* **tenfold** *a* par dix; – *adv* dix fois.

foliage ['fəʊlɪdʒ] *n* feuillage *m*.

folk [fəʊk] **1** *n* gens *mpl* *or* *fpl*; *pl* gens *mpl* *or* *fpl*; (*parents*) *Fam* parents *mpl*; **hello folks!** *Fam* salut tout le monde!; **old f.** **like** it les vieux l'apprécient. **2** *a* (*dance etc*) folklorique; **f. music** (*contemporary*) (musique *f*) folk *m*. ◆**folklore** *n* folklore *m*.

follow ['fɒləʊ] *vt* suivre; (*career*) poursuivre; **followed by** suivi de; **to f. suit** *Fig* en faire autant; **to f. s.o. around** suivre qn partout; **to f. through** (*idea etc*) poursuivre

jusqu'au bout; **to f. up** (*suggestion, case*) suivre; (*advantage*) exploiter; (*letter*) donner suite à; (*remark*) faire suivre (**with** de); – *vi* **to f. (on)** suivre; **it follows that** il s'ensuit que; **that doesn't f.** ce n'est pas logique. ◆**—ing 1** *a* suivant; – *prep* à la suite de. **2** *n* (*supporters*) partisans *mpl*; **to have a large f.** avoir de nombreux partisans; (*of serial, fashion*) être très suivi. ◆**—er** *n* partisan *m*. ◆**follow-up** *n* suite *f*; (*letter*) rappel *m*.

folly ['fɒlɪ] *n* folie *f*, sottise *f*.

foment [fəʊ'ment] *vt* (*revolt etc*) fomenter.

fond [fɒnd] *a* (**-er, -est**) (*loving*) tendre, affectueux; (*doting*) indulgent; (*wish, ambition*) naïf; **to be (very) f. of** aimer (beaucoup). ◆**—ly** *adv* tendrement. ◆**—ness** *n* (*for things*) prédilection *f* (**for** pour); (*for people*) affection *f* (**for** pour).

fondle ['fɒnd(ə)l] *vt* caresser.

food [fuːd] *n* nourriture *f*; (*particular substance*) aliment *m*; (*cooking*) cuisine *f*; (*for cats, pigs*) pâtée *f*; (*for plants*) engrais *m*; *pl* (*foodstuffs*) aliments *mpl*; – *a* (*needs etc*) alimentaire; **a fast f. shop** un fast-food; **f. poisoning** intoxication *f* alimentaire; **f. value** valeur *f* nutritive. ◆**foodstuffs** *npl* denrées *fpl* *or* produits *mpl* alimentaires.

fool [fuːl] *n* imbécile *mf*, idiot, -ote *mf*; (*you*) **silly f.!** espèce d'imbécile!; **to make a f. of** (*ridicule*) ridiculiser; (*trick*) duper; **to be f. enough to do** être assez stupide pour faire; **to play the f.** faire l'imbécile; – *vt* (*trick*) duper; – *vi* **to f. (about** *or* **around)** faire l'imbécile; (*waste time*) perdre son temps; **to f. around** (*make love*) *Am Fam* faire l'amour (**with** avec). ◆**foolish** *a* bête, idiot. ◆**foolishly** *adv* bêtement. ◆**foolishness** *n* bêtise *f*, sottise *f*. ◆**foolproof** *a* (*scheme etc*) infaillible.

foolhardy ['fuːlhɑːdɪ] *a* téméraire. ◆**foolhardiness** *n* témérité *f*.

foot[1], *pl* **feet** [fʊt, fiːt] *n* pied *m*; (*of animal*) patte *f*; (*measure*) pied *m* (= 30,48 cm); **at the f. of** (*page, stairs*) au bas de; (*table*) au bout de; **on f.** à pied; **on one's feet** (*standing*) debout; (*recovered*) *Med* sur pied; **f. brake** *Aut* frein *m* au plancher; **f.-and-mouth disease** fièvre *f* aphteuse. ◆**footbridge** *n* passerelle *f*. ◆**foothills** *npl* contreforts *mpl*. ◆**foothold** *n* prise *f* (de pied); *Fig* position *f*; **to gain a f.** prendre pied. ◆**footlights** *npl Th* rampe *f*. ◆**footloose** *a* libre de toute attache. ◆**footman** *n* (*pl* **-men**) valet *m* de pied. ◆**footmark** *n* empreinte *f* (de pied). ◆**footnote** *n* note *f* au bas de la page; *Fig* post-scriptum *m*. ◆**footpath** *n* sentier *m*; (*at roadside*) chemin *m* (piétonnier). ◆**footstep** *n* pas *m*; **to follow in s.o.'s footsteps** suivre les traces de qn. ◆**footwear** *n* chaussures *fpl*.

foot² [fut] *vt* (*bill*) payer.

football ['futbɔːl] *n* (*game*) football *m*; (*ball*) ballon *m*. ◆**footballer** *n* joueur, -euse *mf* de football.

footing ['futɪŋ] *n* prise *f* (de pied); *Fig* position *f*; **on a war f.** sur le pied de guerre; **on an equal f.** sur un pied d'égalité.

for [fɔr, *unstressed* fər] **1** *prep* pour; (*in exchange for*) contre; (*for a distance of*) pendant; (*in spite of*) malgré; **you/me/***etc* pour toi/moi/*etc*; **what f.?** pourquoi?; **what's it f.?** ça sert à quoi?; **f. example** par exemple; **f. love** par amour; **f. sale** à vendre; **to swim f.** (*towards*) nager vers; **a train f.** un train à destination de *or* en direction de; **the road f. London** la route (en direction) de Londres; **fit f. eating** bon à manger; **eager f.** avide de; **to look f.** chercher; **to come f. dinner** venir dîner; **to sell f. £7** vendre sept livres; **what's the Russian f. 'book'?** comment dit-on 'livre' en russe?; **but f. her** sans elle; **he was away f. a month** (*throughout*) il a été absent pendant un mois; **he won't be back f. a month** il ne sera pas de retour avant un mois; **he's been here f. a month** (*he's still here*) il est ici depuis un mois; **I haven't seen him f. ten years** voilà dix ans que je ne l'ai vu; **it's easy f. her to do it** il lui est facile de le faire; **it's f. you to say** c'est à toi de dire; **f. that to be done** pour que ça soit fait. **2** *conj* (*because*) car.

forage ['fɔrɪdʒ] *vi* **to f.** (**about**) fourrager (**for** pour trouver).

foray ['fɔreɪ] *n* incursion *f*.

forbearance [fɔː'beərəns] *n* patience *f*.

forbid [fə'bɪd] *vt* (*pt* forbad(**e**), *pp* forbidden, *pres p* forbidding) interdire, défendre (**s.o. to do** à qn de faire); **to f. s.o. sth** interdire *or* défendre qch à qn. ◆**forbidden** *a* (*fruit etc*) défendu; **she is f. to leave** il lui est interdit de partir. ◆**forbidding** *a* menaçant, sinistre.

force [fɔːs] *n* force *f*; **the (armed) forces** *Mil* les forces armées; **by (sheer) f.** de force; **in f.** (*rule*) en vigueur; (*in great numbers*) en grand nombre, en force; – *vt* contraindre, forcer (**to do** à faire); (*impose*) imposer (**on** à); (*push*) pousser; (*lock*) forcer; (*confession*) arracher (**from** à); **to f. back** (*enemy etc*) faire reculer; (*repress*) refouler; **to f. down** (*aircraft*) forcer à atterrir; **to f. out**

faire sortir de force. ◆**forced** *a* forcé (**to do** de faire); **a f. smile** un sourire forcé. ◆**force-feed** *vt* (*pt & pp* **f.-fed**) nourrir de force. ◆**forceful** *a* énergique, puissant. ◆**forcefully** *adv* avec force, énergiquement. ◆**forcible** *a* de force; (*forceful*) énergique. ◆**forcibly** *adv* (*by force*) de force.

forceps ['fɔːseps] *n* forceps *m*.

ford [fɔːd] *n* gué *m*; – *vt* (*river etc*) passer à gué.

fore [fɔːr] *n* **to come to the f.** se mettre en évidence.

forearm ['fɔːrɑːm] *n* avant-bras *m inv*.

forebod/e [fɔː'bəud] *vt* (*be a warning of*) présager. ◆—**ing** *n* (*feeling*) pressentiment *m*.

forecast ['fɔːkɑːst] *vt* (*pt & pp* **forecast**) prévoir; – *n* prévision *f*; *Met* prévisions *fpl*; *Sp* pronostic *m*.

forecourt ['fɔːkɔːt] *n* avant-cour *f*; (*of filling station*) aire *f* (de service), devant *m*.

forefathers ['fɔːfɑːðəz] *npl* aïeux *mpl*.

forefinger ['fɔːfɪŋgər] *n* index *m*.

forefront ['fɔːfrʌnt] *n* **in the f. of** au premier rang de.

forego [fɔː'gəu] *vt* (*pp* **foregone**) renoncer à. ◆**'foregone** *a* **it's a f. conclusion** c'est couru d'avance.

foregoing [fɔː'gəuɪŋ] *a* précédent.

foreground ['fɔːgraund] *n* premier plan *m*.

forehead ['fɔrɪd, 'fɔːhed] *n* (*brow*) front *m*.

foreign ['fɔrən] *a* étranger; (*trade*) extérieur; (*travel, correspondent*) à l'étranger; (*produce*) de l'étranger; **F. Minister** ministre *m* des Affaires étrangères. ◆**foreigner** *n* étranger, -ère *mf*.

foreman ['fɔːmən] *n* (*pl* -men) (*worker*) contremaître *m*; (*of jury*) président *m*.

foremost ['fɔːməust] **1** *a* principal. **2** *adv* **first and f.** tout d'abord.

forensic [fə'rensɪk] *a* (*medicine*) légal; (*laboratory*) médico-légal.

forerunner ['fɔːrʌnər] *n* précurseur *m*.

foresee [fɔː'siː] *vt* (*pt* **foresaw**, *pp* **foreseen**) prévoir. ◆—**able** *a* prévisible.

foreshadow [fɔː'ʃædəu] *vt* présager.

foresight ['fɔːsaɪt] *n* prévoyance *f*.

forest ['fɔrɪst] *n* forêt *f*. ◆**forester** *n* (garde *m*) forestier *m*.

forestall [fɔː'stɔːl] *vt* devancer.

foretaste ['fɔːteɪst] *n* avant-goût *m*.

foretell [fɔː'tel] *vt* (*pt & pp* **foretold**) prédire.

forethought ['fɔːθɔːt] *n* prévoyance *f*.

forever [fə'revər] *adv* (*for always*) pour toujours; (*continually*) sans cesse.

forewarn [fɔː'wɔːn] *vt* avertir.

foreword ['fɔːwɜːd] *n* avant-propos *m inv*.

forfeit ['fɔːfɪt] *vt* (*lose*) perdre; – *n* (*penalty*) peine *f*; (*in game*) gage *m*.

forg/e [fɔːdʒ] **1** *vt* (*signature, money*) contrefaire; (*document*) falsifier. **2** *vt* (*friendship, bond*) forger. **3** *vi* to f. ahead (*progress*) aller de l'avant. **4** *vt* (*metal*) forger; – *n* forge *f*. ◆**—er** *n* (*of banknotes etc*) faussaire *m*. ◆**forgery** *n* faux *m*, contrefaçon *f*.

forget [fə'get] *vt* (*pt* forgot, *pp* forgotten, *pres p* forgetting) oublier (to do de faire); **f. it!** *Fam* (*when thanked*) pas de quoi!; (*it doesn't matter*) peu importe!; to **f. oneself** s'oublier; – *vi* oublier; to **f. about** oublier. ◆**f.-me-not** *n* *Bot* myosotis *m*. ◆**forgetful** *a* to be **f.** (*of*) oublier, être oublieux (de). ◆**forgetfulness** *n* manque *m* de mémoire; (*carelessness*) négligence *f*; **in a moment of f.** dans un moment d'oubli.

forgiv/e [fə'gɪv] *vt* (*pt* forgave, *pp* forgiven) pardonner (**s.o. sth** qch à qn). ◆**—ing** *a* indulgent. ◆**forgiveness** *n* pardon *m*; (*compassion*) clémence *f*.

forgo [fɔː'gəʊ] *vt* (*pt* forgone) renoncer à.

fork [fɔːk] **1** *n* (*for eating*) fourchette *f*; (*for garden etc*) fourche *f*. **2** *vi* (*of road*) bifurquer; to **f. left** (*in vehicle*) prendre à gauche; – *n* bifurcation *f*, fourche *f*. **3** *vt* to **f. out** (*money*) *Fam* allonger; – *vi* to **f. out** (*pay*) *Fam* casquer. ◆**—ed** *a* fourchu. ◆**forklift truck** *n* chariot *m* élévateur.

forlorn [fə'lɔːn] *a* (*forsaken*) abandonné; (*unhappy*) triste, affligé.

form [fɔːm] **1** *n* (*shape, type, style*) forme *f*; (*document*) formulaire *m*; *Sch* classe *f*; **it's good f.** c'est ce qui se fait; **in the f. of** en forme de; **a f. of speech** une façon de parler; **on f., in good f.** en (pleine) forme; – *vt* (*group, character etc*) former; (*clay*) façonner; (*habit*) contracter; (*an opinion*) se former; (*constitute*) constituer, former; to **f. part of** faire partie de; – *vi* (*appear*) se former. ◆**for'mation** *n* formation *f*. ◆**formative** *a* formateur.

formal ['fɔːm(ə)l] *a* (*person, tone etc*) cérémonieux; (*stuffy*) *Pej* compassé; (*official*) officiel; (*in due form*) en bonne et due forme; (*denial, structure, logic*) formel; (*resemblance*) extérieur; **f. dress** tenue *f* or habit *m* de cérémonie; **f. education** éducation *f* scolaire. ◆**for'mality** *n* cérémonie *f*; (*requirement*) formalité *f*. ◆**formally** *adv* (*to declare etc*) officiellement; **f. dressed** en tenue de cérémonie.

format ['fɔːmæt] *n* format *m*.

former ['fɔːmər] **1** *a* (*previous*) ancien; (*situation*) antérieur; **her f. husband** son ex-mari *m*; **in f. days** autrefois. **2** *a* (*of two*) premier; – *pron* the **f.** celui-là, celle-là, le premier, la première. ◆**—ly** *adv* autrefois.

formidable ['fɔːmɪdəb(ə)l] *a* effroyable, terrible.

formula ['fɔːmjulə] *n* **1** (*pl* -as or -ae [-iː]) formule *f*. **2** (*pl* -as) (*baby's feed*) *Am* mélange *m* lacté. ◆**formulate** *vt* formuler. ◆**formu'lation** *n* formulation *f*.

forsake [fə'seɪk] *vt* (*pt* forsook, *pp* forsaken) abandonner.

fort [fɔːt] *n* *Hist Mil* fort *m*; to **hold the f.** (*in s.o.'s absence*) *Fam* prendre la relève.

forte ['fɔːteɪ, *Am* fɔːt] *n* (*strong point*) fort *m*.

forth [fɔːθ] *adv* en avant; **from this day f.** désormais; **and so f.** et ainsi de suite.

forthcoming [fɔːθ'kʌmɪŋ] *a* **1** (*event*) à venir; (*book, film*) qui va sortir; **my f. book** mon prochain livre. **2** (*available*) disponible. **3** (*open*) communicatif; (*helpful*) serviable.

forthright ['fɔːθraɪt] *a* direct, franc.

forthwith [fɔːθ'wɪθ] *adv* sur-le-champ.

fortieth ['fɔːtɪəθ] *a* & *n* quarantième (*mf*).

fortify ['fɔːtɪfaɪ] *vt* (*strengthen*) fortifier; to **f. s.o.** (*of food, drink*) réconforter qn, remonter qn. ◆**fortifi'cation** *n* fortification *f*.

fortitude ['fɔːtɪtjuːd] *n* courage *m* (moral).

fortnight ['fɔːtnaɪt] *n* quinze jours *mpl*, quinzaine *f*. ◆**—ly** *adv* bimensuel; – *adv* tous les quinze jours.

fortress ['fɔːtrɪs] *n* forteresse *f*.

fortuitous [fɔː'tjuːɪtəs] *a* fortuit.

fortunate ['fɔːtʃənɪt] *a* (*choice, event etc*) heureux; to **be f.** (*of person*) avoir de la chance; **it's f.** (*for her*) **that** c'est heureux (pour elle) que. ◆**—ly** *adv* heureusement.

fortune ['fɔːtʃuːn] *n* (*wealth*) fortune *f*; (*luck*) chance *f*; (*chance*) sort *m*, hasard *m*, fortune *f*; to **have the good f. to** avoir la chance or le bonheur de; to **tell s.o.'s f.** dire la bonne aventure à qn; to **make one's f.** faire fortune. ◆**f.-teller** *n* diseur, -euse *mf* de bonne aventure.

forty ['fɔːtɪ] *a* & *n* quarante (*m*).

forum ['fɔːrəm] *n* forum *m*.

forward ['fɔːwəd] *adv* forward(s) en avant; to **go f.** avancer; **from this time f.** désormais; – *a* (*movement*) en avant; (*gears*) *Aut* avant *inv*; (*child*) *Fig* précoce; (*pert*) effronté; – *n* *Fb* avant *m*; – *vt* (*letter*) faire suivre; (*goods*) expédier. ◆**—ness** *n* précocité *f*; effronterie *f*. ◆**forward-looking** *a* tourné vers l'avenir.

fossil ['fɒs(ə)l] *n* & *a* fossile (*m*).

foster ['fɒstər] **1** vt encourager; (hope) nourrir. **2** vt (child) élever; – a (child, family) adoptif.

fought [fɔːt] see fight.

foul [faul] **1** a (-er, -est) infect; (air) vicié; (breath) fétide; (language) grossier; (action, place) immonde; to be f.-mouthed avoir un langage grossier. **2** n Sp coup m irrégulier; Fb faute f; – a f. play Sp jeu m irrégulier; Jur acte m criminel. **3** vt to f. (up) salir; (air) vicier; (drain) encrasser; to f. up (life, plans) Fam gâcher. ◆f.-up n (in system) Fam raté m.

found [faund] see find.

found [faund] vt (town, opinion etc) fonder (on sur). ◆—er n fondateur, -trice mf. ◆foun'dation n fondation f; (basis) Fig base f, fondement m; without f. sans fondement; f. cream fond m de teint.

founder ['faundər] vi (of ship) sombrer.

foundry ['faundrɪ] n fonderie f.

fountain ['fauntɪn] n fontaine f; f. pen stylo(-plume) m.

four [fɔːr] a & n quatre (m); on all fours à quatre pattes; the Big F. Pol les quatre Grands; f.-letter word = mot m de cinq lettres. ◆fourfold a quadruple; – adv au quadruple. ◆foursome n deux couples mpl. ◆four'teen a & n quatorze (m). ◆fourth a & n quatrième (mf).

fowl [faul] n (hens) volaille f; a f. une volaille.

fox [fɒks] **1** n renard m. **2** vt (puzzle) mystifier; (trick) tromper. ◆foxy a (sly) rusé, futé.

foxglove ['fɒksglʌv] n Bot digitale f.

foyer ['fɔɪeɪ] n Th foyer m; (in hotel) hall m.

fraction ['frækʃ(ə)n] n fraction f. ◆fractionally adv un tout petit peu.

fractious ['frækʃəs] a grincheux.

fracture ['fræktʃər] n fracture f; – vt fracturer; to f. one's leg/etc se fracturer la jambe/etc; – vi se fracturer.

fragile ['frædʒaɪl, Am 'frædʒ(ə)l] a fragile. ◆fra'gility n fragilité f.

fragment ['frægmənt] n fragment m, morceau m. ◆frag'mented a, ◆fragmentary a fragmentaire.

fragrant ['freɪgrənt] a parfumé. ◆fragrance n parfum m.

frail [freɪl] a (-er, -est) (person) frêle, fragile; (hope, health) fragile. ◆frailty n fragilité f.

frame [freɪm] n **1** (of person, building) charpente f; (of picture, bicycle) cadre m; (of window, car) châssis m; (of spectacles) monture f; f. of mind humeur f; – vt (picture) encadrer; (proposals etc) Fig

formuler. **2** vt to f. s.o. Fam monter un coup contre qn. ◆f.-up n Fam coup m monté. ◆framework n structure f; (with)in the f. of (context) dans le cadre de.

franc [fræŋk] n franc m.

France [frɑːns] n France f.

franchise ['fræntʃaɪz] n **1** Pol droit m de vote. **2** (right to sell product) Com franchise f.

Franco- ['fræŋkəʊ] pref franco-.

frank [fræŋk] **1** a (-er, -est) (honest) franc. **2** vt (letter) affranchir. ◆—ly adv franchement. ◆—ness n franchise f.

frankfurter ['fræŋkfɜːtər] n saucisse f de Francfort.

frantic ['fræntɪk] a (activity, shout) frénétique; (rush, desire) effréné; (person) hors de soi; f. with joy fou de joie. ◆frantically adv comme un fou.

fraternal [frə'tɜːn(ə)l] a fraternel. ◆fraternity n (bond) fraternité f; (society) & Univ Am confrérie f. ◆fraternize ['frætənaɪz] vi fraterniser (with avec).

fraud [frɔːd] n **1** Jur fraude f. **2** (person) imposteur m. ◆fraudulent a frauduleux.

fraught [frɔːt] a f. with plein de, chargé de; to be f. (of situation) être tendu; (of person) Fam être contrarié.

fray [freɪ] **1** vt (garment) effilocher; (rope) user; – vi s'effilocher; s'user. **2** n (fight) rixe f. ◆—ed a (nerves) Fig tendu.

freak [friːk] n (person) phénomène m, monstre m; a jazz/etc f. Fam un(e) fana de jazz/etc; – a (result, weather etc) anormal. ◆freakish a anormal.

freckle ['frek(ə)l] n tache f de rousseur. ◆freckled a couvert de taches de rousseur.

free [friː] a (freer, freest) (at liberty, not occupied) libre; (gratis) gratuit; (lavish) généreux (with de); to get f. se libérer; f. to do libre de faire; to let s.o. go f. relâcher qn; f. of charge gratuit; f. of (without) sans; f. of s.o. (rid of) débarrassé de qn; to have a f. hand Fig avoir carte blanche (to do pour faire); f. and easy décontracté; f. trade libre-échange m; f. speech liberté f d'expression; f. kick Fb coup m franc; f.-range egg œuf m de ferme; – adv f. (of charge) gratuitement; – vt (pt & pp freed) (prisoner etc) libérer; (trapped person, road) dégager; (country) affranchir, libérer; (untie) détacher. ◆Freefone® Tel = numéro m vert. ◆free-for-'all n mêlée f générale. ◆freehold n propriété f foncière libre. ◆freelance a indépendant; – n collaborateur, -trice mf indépen-

dant(e). ◆**freeloader** n (*sponger*) Am
parasite m. ◆**Freemason** n franc-maçon
m. ◆**Freemasonry** n franc-maçonnerie f.
◆**freestyle** n Swimming nage f libre.
◆**free'thinker** n libre penseur, -euse mf.
◆**freeway** n Am autoroute f.
freedom ['friːdəm] n liberté f; f. from (*worry,
responsibility*) absence f de.
freely ['friːlɪ] adv (*to speak, circulate etc*)
librement; (*to give*) libéralement.
freez/e [friːz] vi (*pt froze, pp frozen*) geler;
(*of smile*) Fig se figer; Culin se congeler; to
f. to death mourir de froid; to f. up or over
geler; (*of windscreen*) se givrer; – vt Culin
congeler, surgeler; (*credits, river*) geler;
(*prices, wages*) bloquer; **frozen food**
surgelés mpl; – n Met gel m; (*of prices etc*)
blocage m. ◆**—ing** a (*weather etc*) glacial;
(*hands, person*) gelé; **it's f.** on gèle; – n
below f. au-dessous de zéro. ◆**—er** n
(*deep-freeze*) congélateur m; (*in fridge*)
freezer m.
freight [freɪt] n (*goods, price*) fret m; (*transport*) transport m; **f. train** Am train m de
marchandises; – vt (*ship*) affréter. ◆**—er** n
(*ship*) cargo m.
French [frentʃ] a français; (*teacher*) de français; (*embassy*) de France; **F. fries** Am
frites fpl; **the F.** les Français mpl; – n
(*language*) français m. ◆**Frenchman** n (*pl
-men*) Français m. ◆**French-speaking** a
francophone. ◆**Frenchwoman** n (*pl
-women*) Française f.
frenzy ['frenzɪ] n frénésie f. ◆**frenzied** a
(*shouts etc*) frénétique; (*person*) effréné;
(*attack*) violent.
frequent ['friːkwənt] a fréquent; **f. visitor**
habitué, -ée mf (**to** de); – [frɪ'kwent] vt
fréquenter. ◆**frequency** n fréquence f.
◆**frequently** adv fréquemment.
fresco ['freskəʊ] n (*pl -oes* or *-os*) fresque f.
fresh [freʃ] **1** a (**-er, -est**) frais; (*new*)
nouveau; (*impudent*) Fam culotté; **to get
some f. air** prendre le frais; **f. water** eau f
douce. **2** adv **f. from** fraîchement arrivé de;
f. out of, f. from (*university*) frais émoulu
de. ◆**freshen 1** vi (*of wind*) fraîchir. **2** vi to
f. up faire un brin de toilette; – vt to f. up
(*house etc*) retaper; **to f. s.o. up** (*of bath*)
rafraîchir qn. ◆**freshener** n **air f.**
désodorisant m. ◆**freshman** n (*pl -men*)
étudiant, -ante mf de première année.
◆**freshness** n fraîcheur f; (*cheek*) Fam
culot m.
fret [fret] vi (**-tt-**) (*worry*) se faire du souci,
s'en faire; (*of baby*) pleurer. ◆**fretful** a
(*baby etc*) grognon.

friar ['fraɪər] n frère m, moine m.
friction ['frɪkʃ(ə)n] n friction f.
Friday ['fraɪdɪ] n vendredi m.
fridge [frɪdʒ] n Fam frigo m.
fried [fraɪd] pt & pp of fry 1; – a (*fish etc*)
frit; **f. egg** œuf m sur le plat. ◆**frier** n (*pan*)
friteuse f.
friend [frend] n ami, -ie mf; (*from school,
work*) camarade mf; **to be friends with** être
ami avec; **to make friends** se lier (**with**
avec). ◆**friendly** a (**-ier, -iest**) amical;
(*child, animal*) gentil, affectueux; (*kind*)
gentil; **some f. advice** un conseil d'ami; **to
be f. with** être ami avec. ◆**friendship** n
amitié f.
frieze [friːz] n Archit frise f.
frigate ['frɪgət] n (*ship*) frégate f.
fright [fraɪt] n peur f; (*person, hat etc*) Fig
Fam horreur f; **to have a f.** avoir peur; **to
give s.o. a f.** faire peur à qn. ◆**frighten** vt
effrayer, faire peur à; **to f. away** or **off**
(*animal*) effaroucher; (*person*) chasser.
◆**frightened** a effrayé; **to be f.** avoir peur
(**of** de). ◆**frightening** a effrayant.
◆**frightful** a affreux. ◆**frightfully** adv
(*ugly, late*) affreusement; (*kind, glad*)
terriblement.
frigid ['frɪdʒɪd] a (*air, greeting etc*) froid; Psy
frigide.
frill [frɪl] n Tex volant m; pl (*fuss*) Fig
manières fpl, chichis mpl; (*useless embel-
lishments*) fioritures fpl, superflu m; **no
frills** (*spartan*) spartiate.
fringe [frɪndʒ] **1** n (*of hair, clothes etc*)
frange f. **2** n (*of forest*) lisière f; **on the
fringe(s) of society** en marge de la société;
– a (*group, theatre*) marginal; **f. benefits**
avantages mpl divers.
frisk [frɪsk] **1** vt (*search*) fouiller (au corps).
2 vi to f. (**about**) gambader. ◆**frisky** a (**-ier,
-iest**) a vif.
fritter ['frɪtər] **1** vt to f. away (*waste*) gaspiller. **2** n Culin beignet m.
frivolous ['frɪvələs] a frivole. ◆**fri'volity** n
frivolité f.
frizzy ['frɪzɪ] a (*hair*) crépu.
fro [frəʊ] adv to go to and f. aller et venir.
frock [frɒk] n (*dress*) robe f; (*of monk*) froc
m.
frog [frɒg] n grenouille f; **a f. in one's throat**
Fig un chat dans la gorge. ◆**frogman** n
(*pl -men*) homme-grenouille m.
frolic ['frɒlɪk] vi (*pt & pp frolicked*) to f.
(**about**) gambader; – npl (*capers*) ébats
mpl; (*pranks*) gamineries fpl.
from [frɒm, unstressed frəm] prep **1** de; **a
letter f.** une lettre de; **to suffer f.** souffrir de;

where are you f.? d'où êtes-vous?; a train f. un train en provenance de; to be ten metres (away) f. the house être à dix mètres de la maison. 2 (time onwards) à partir de, dès, depuis; f. today (on), as f. today à partir d'aujourd'hui, dès aujourd'hui; f. her child-hood dès or depuis son enfance. 3 (numbers, prices onwards) à partir de; f. five francs à partir de cinq francs. 4 (away from) à; to take/hide/borrow f. pren-dre/cacher/emprunter à. 5 (out of) dans; sur; to take f. (box) prendre dans; (table) prendre sur; to drink f. a cup/etc boire dans une tasse/etc; to drink (straight) f. the bottle boire à (même) la bouteille. 6 (according to) d'après; f. what I saw d'après ce que j'ai vu. 7 (cause) par; f. convic-tion/habit/etc par conviction/habitude/ etc. 8 (on the part of, on behalf of) de la part de; tell her f. me dis-lui de ma part.

front [frʌnt] n (of garment, building) devant m; (of boat, car) avant m; (of crowd) premier rang m; (of book) début m; Mil Pol Met front m; (beach) front m de mer; (appearance) Fig façade f; in f. (of) devant; in f. (ahead) en avant; Sp en tête; in the f. (of vehicle) à l'avant; (of house) devant; − a (tooth etc) de devant; (part, wheel, car seat) avant inv; (row, page) premier; (view) de face; f. door porte f d'entrée; f. line Mil front m; f. room (lounge) salon m; f. runner Fig favori, -ite mf; f.-wheel drive (on vehi-cle) traction f avant; − vi to f. on to (of windows etc) donner sur. ◆frontage n façade f. ◆frontal a (attack) de front.

frontier ['frʌntiər] n frontière f; − a (town, post) frontière inv.

frost [frɒst] n gel m, gelée f; (frozen drops on glass, grass etc) gelée f blanche, givre m; − vi to f. up (of windscreen etc) se givrer. ◆frostbite n gelure f. ◆frostbitten a gelé. ◆frosty a (-ier, -iest) glacial; (window) givré; it's f. il gèle.

frosted ['frɒstɪd] a (glass) dépoli.

frosting ['frɒstɪŋ] n (icing) Culin glaçage m.

froth [frɒθ] n mousse f; − vi mousser. ◆frothy a (-ier, -iest) (beer etc) mousseux.

frown [fraʊn] n froncement m de sourcils; − vi froncer les sourcils; to f. (up)on Fig désapprouver.

froze, frozen [frəʊz, 'frəʊz(ə)n] see freeze.

frugal ['fruːg(ə)l] a (meal) frugal; (thrifty) parcimonieux. ◆−ly adv parcimonieuse-ment.

fruit [fruːt] n fruit m; (some) f. (one item) un fruit; (more than one) des fruits; − a

(basket) à fruits; (drink) aux fruits; (salad) de fruits; f. tree arbre m fruitier. ◆fruit-cake n cake m. ◆fruiterer n fruitier, -ière mf. ◆fruitful a (meeting, career etc) fruc-tueux, fécond. ◆fruitless a stérile. ◆fruity a (-ier, -iest) a fruité, de fruit; (joke) Fig Fam corsé.

fruition [fruː'ɪʃ(ə)n] n to come to f. se réaliser.

frumpish ['frʌmpɪʃ] a, frumpy ['frʌmpɪ] a Fam (mal) fagoté.

frustrat/e [frʌ'streɪt] vt (person) frustrer; (plans) faire échouer. ◆−ed a (mentally, sexually) frustré; (effort) vain. ◆−ing a irritant. ◆fru'stration n frustration f; (disappointment) déception f.

fry [fraɪ] 1 vt (faire) frire; − vi frire. 2 n small f. menu fretin m. ◆−ing n friture f; f. pan poêle f (à frire). ◆−er n (pan) friteuse f.

ft abbr (measure) = foot, feet.

fuddled ['fʌd(ə)ld] a (drunk) gris; (confused) embrouillé.

fuddy-duddy ['fʌdɪdʌdɪ] n he's an old f.-duddy Fam il est vieux jeu.

fudge [fʌdʒ] 1 n (sweet) caramel m mou. 2 vt to f. the issue refuser d'aborder le problème.

fuel [fjuːəl] n combustible m; Aut carburant m; f. (oil) mazout m; − vt (-ll-, Am -l-) (stove) alimenter; (ship) ravitailler (en combustible); (s.o.'s anger etc) attiser.

fugitive ['fjuːdʒɪtɪv] n fugitif, -ive mf.

fugue [fjuːg] n Mus fugue f.

fulfil, Am fulfill [fʊl'fɪl] vt (-ll-) (ambition, dream) accomplir, réaliser; (condition, duty) remplir; (desire) satisfaire; to f. oneself s'épanouir. ◆fulfilling a satis-faisant. ◆fulfilment n, Am ◆fulfillment n accomplissement m, réalisation f; (feel-ing) satisfaction f.

full [fʊl] a (-er, -est) plein (of de); (bus, thea-tre, meal) complet; (life, day) (bien) rempli; (skirt) ample; (hour) entier; (member) à part entière; the f. price le prix fort; to pay (the) f. fare payer plein tarif; to be f. (up) (of person) Culin n'avoir plus faim; (of hotel) être complet; the f. facts tous les faits; at f. speed à toute vitesse; f. name (on form) nom et prénom; f. stop Gram point m; − adv to know f. well savoir fort bien; f. in the face (to hit etc) en pleine figure; − n in f. (text) intégral; (to publish, read) intégralement; (to write one's name) en toutes lettres; to the f. (completely) tout à fait. ◆fullness n (of details) abondance *f*; (*of dress*) ampleur *f*. ◆**fully** *adv* entièrement; (*at least*) au moins.

full-back ['fʊlbæk] *n Fb* arrière *m*. ◆**f.-'grown** *a* adulte; (*foetus*) arrivé à terme. ◆**f.-'length** *a* (*film*) de long métrage; (*portrait*) en pied; (*dress*) long. ◆**f.-'scale** *a* (*model etc*) grandeur nature *inv*; (*operation etc*) *Fig* de grande envergure. ◆**f.-'sized** *a* (*model*) grandeur nature *inv*. ◆**f.-'time** *a* & *adv* à plein temps.

fully-fledged, *Am* **full-fledged** [fʊl(ɪ)'fledʒd] *a* (*engineer etc*) diplômé; (*member*) à part entière. ◆**f.-formed** *a* (*baby etc*) formé. ◆**f.-grown** *a* = **full-grown.**

fulsome ['fʊlsəm] *a* (*praise etc*) excessif.

fumble ['fʌmb(ə)l] *vi* to f. (about) (*grope*) tâtonner; (*search*) fouiller (**for** pour trouver); to f. (about) with tripoter.

fume [fjuːm] *vi* (*give off fumes*) fumer; (*of person*) *Fig* rager; – *npl* émanations *fpl*; (*from car exhaust*) gaz *m inv.*

fumigate ['fjuːmɪɡeɪt] *vt* désinfecter (par fumigation).

fun [fʌn] *n* amusement *m*; to be (good) f. être très amusant; to have (some) f. s'amuser; to make f. of, poke f. at se moquer de; for f., for the f. of it pour le plaisir.

function ['fʌŋkʃ(ə)n] **1** *n* (*role, duty*) & *Math* fonction *f*; (*meeting*) réunion *f*; (*ceremony*) cérémonie *f* (publique). **2** *vi* (*work*) fonctionner. ◆**functional** *a* fonctionnel.

fund [fʌnd] *n* (*for pension, relief etc*) *Fin* caisse *f*; (*of knowledge etc*) *Fig* fond *m*; *pl* (*money resources*) fonds *mpl*; (*for special purpose*) crédits *mpl*; – *vt* (*with money*) fournir des fonds *or* des crédits à.

fundamental [fʌndə'ment(ə)l] *a* fondamental; – *npl* principes *mpl* essentiels.

funeral ['fjuːnərəl] *n* enterrement *m*; (*grandiose*) funérailles *fpl*; – *a* (*service, march*) funèbre; (*expenses, parlour*) funéraire.

funfair ['fʌnfeər] *n* fête *f* foraine; (*larger*) parc *m* d'attractions.

fungus, *pl* **-gi** ['fʌŋɡəs, -ɡaɪ] *n Bot* champignon *m*; (*mould*) moisissure *f*.

funicular [fjuː'nɪkjʊlər] *n* funiculaire *m*.

funk [fʌŋk] *n* to be in a f. (*afraid*) *Fam* avoir la frousse; (*depressed, sulking*) *Am Fam* faire la gueule.

funnel ['fʌn(ə)l] *n* **1** (*of ship*) cheminée *f*. **2** (*tube for pouring*) entonnoir *m*.

funny ['fʌnɪ] *a* (**-ier, -iest**) (*amusing*) drôle; (*strange*) bizarre; a f. idea une drôle d'idée; there's some f. business going on il y a quelque chose de louche; to feel f. ne pas se sentir très bien. ◆**funnily** *adv* drôlement; bizarrement; f. enough . . . chose bizarre . . . .

fur [fɜːr] **1** *n* (*of animal*) poil *m*, pelage *m*; (*for wearing etc*) fourrure *f*. **2** *n* (*in kettle*) dépôt *m* (de tartre); – *vi* (**-rr-**) to f. (up) s'entartrer.

furious ['fjʊərɪəs] *a* (*violent, angry*) furieux (**with, at** contre); (*pace, speed*) fou. ◆**—ly** *adv* furieusement; (*to drive, rush*) à une allure folle.

furnace ['fɜːnɪs] *n* (*forge*) fourneau *m*; (*room etc*) *Fig* fournaise *f*.

furnish ['fɜːnɪʃ] *vt* **1** (*room*) meubler. **2** (*supply*) fournir (**s.o. with sth** qch à qn). ◆**—ings** *npl* ameublement *m*.

furniture ['fɜːnɪtʃər] *n* meubles *mpl*; a piece of f. un meuble.

furrier ['fʌrɪər] *n* fourreur *m*.

furrow ['fʌrəʊ] *n* (*on brow*) & *Agr* sillon *m*.

furry ['fɜːrɪ] *a* (*animal*) à poil; (*toy*) en peluche.

further ['fɜːðər] **1** *adv* & *a* = **farther. 2** *adv* (*more*) davantage, plus; (*besides*) en outre; – *a* (*additional*) supplémentaire; (*education*) post-scolaire; f. details de plus amples détails; a f. case/*etc* (*another*) un autre cas/*etc*; without f. delay sans plus attendre. **3** *vt* (*cause, research etc*) promouvoir. ◆**furthermore** *adv* en outre. ◆**furthest** *a* & *adv* = **farthest.**

furtive ['fɜːtɪv] *a* furtif.

fury ['fjʊərɪ] *n* (*violence, anger*) fureur *f*.

fuse [fjuːz] **1** *vti* (*melt*) *Tech* fondre; *Fig* fusionner. **2** *vt* to f. the lights *etc* faire sauter les plombs; – *vi* the lights *etc* have fused les plombs ont sauté; – *n* (*wire*) *El* fusible *m*, plomb *m*. **3** *n* (*of bomb*) amorce *f*. ◆**fused** *a* (*plug*) *El* avec fusible incorporé. ◆**fusion** *n* (*union*) & *Phys Biol* fusion *f*.

fuselage ['fjuːzəlɑːʒ] *n Av* fuselage *m*.

fuss [fʌs] *n* façons *fpl*, histoires *fpl*, chichis *mpl*; (*noise*) agitation *f*; what a (lot of) f.! quelle histoire!; to kick up *or* make a f. faire des histoires; to make a f. of être aux petits soins pour; – *vi* faire des chichis; (*worry*) se tracasser (**about** pour); (*rush about*) s'agiter; to f. over s.o. être aux petits soins pour qn. ◆**fusspot** *n*, *Am* ◆**fussbudget** *n Fam* enquiquineur, -euse *mf*. ◆**fussy** *a* (**-ier, -iest**) méticuleux; (*difficult*) difficile (**about** sur).

fusty ['fʌstɪ] *a* (**-ier, -iest**) (*smell*) de renfermé.

futile ['fjuːtaɪl, *Am* 'fjuːt(ə)l] *a* futile, vain. ◆**fu'tility** *n* futilité *f*.

future ['fjuːtʃər] n avenir m; *Gram* futur m; **in f.** (*from now on*) à l'avenir; **in the f.** (*one day*) un jour (futur); − a futur, à venir; (*date*) ultérieur.

fuzz [fʌz] n **1** (*down*) *Fam* duvet m. **2 the f.** (*police*) *Sl* les flics mpl. ◆**fuzzy** a (*-ier, -iest*) (*hair*) crépu; (*picture, idea*) flou.

G

G, g [dʒiː] n G, g m. ◆**G.-string** n (*cloth*) cache-sexe m inv.

gab [gæb] n **to have the gift of the g.** *Fam* avoir du bagou(t).

gabardine [gæbəˈdiːn] n (*material, coat*) gabardine f.

gabble [ˈgæb(ə)l] vi (*chatter*) jacasser; (*indistinctly*) bredouiller; − n baragouin m.

gable [ˈgeɪb(ə)l] n *Archit* pignon m.

gad [gæd] vi (-dd-) **to g. about** se balader, vadrouiller.

gadget [ˈgædʒɪt] n gadget m.

Gaelic [ˈgeɪlɪk, ˈgælɪk] a & n gaélique (m).

gaffe [gæf] n (*blunder*) gaffe f, bévue f.

gag [gæg] **1** n (*over mouth*) bâillon m; − vt (-gg-) (*victim, press etc*) bâillonner. **2** n (*joke*) plaisanterie f; *Cin Th* gag m. **3** vi (-gg-) (*choke*) *Am* s'étouffer (**on** avec).

gaggle [ˈgæg(ə)l] n (*of geese*) troupeau m.

gaiety [ˈgeɪtɪ] n gaieté f; (*of colour*) éclat m. ◆**gaily** adv gaiement.

gain [geɪn] vt (*obtain, win*) gagner; (*objective*) atteindre; (*experience, reputation*) acquérir; (*popularity*) gagner en; **to g. speed/weight** prendre de la vitesse/du poids; − vi (*of watch*) avancer; **to g. in strength** gagner en force; **to g. on** (*catch up with*) rattraper; − n (*increase*) augmentation f (**in** de); (*profit*) *Com* bénéfice m, gain m; *Fig* avantage m. ◆**gainful** a profitable; (*employment*) rémunéré.

gainsay [geɪnˈseɪ] vt (pt & pp **gainsaid** [-sed]) (*person*) contredire; (*facts*) nier.

gait [geɪt] n (*walk*) démarche f.

gala [ˈgɑːlə, ˈgeɪlə] n gala m, fête f; **swimming g.** concours m de natation.

galaxy [ˈgæləksɪ] n galaxie f.

gale [geɪl] n grand vent m, rafale f (de vent).

gall [gɔːl] **1** n *Med* bile f; (*bitterness*) *Fig* fiel m; (*cheek*) *Fam* effronterie f; **g. bladder** vésicule f biliaire. **2** vt (*vex*) blesser, froisser.

gallant [ˈgælənt] a (*brave*) courageux; (*splendid*) magnifique; (*chivalrous*) galant. ◆**gallantry** n (*bravery*) courage m.

galleon [ˈgælɪən] n (*ship*) *Hist* galion m.

gallery [ˈgælərɪ] n (*room etc*) galerie f; (*for public, press*) tribune f; **art g.** (*private*) galerie f d'art; (*public*) musée m d'art.

galley [ˈgælɪ] n (*ship*) *Hist* galère f; (*kitchen*) *Nau Av* cuisine f.

Gallic [ˈgælɪk] a (*French*) français. ◆**gallicism** n (*word etc*) gallicisme m.

gallivant [ˈgælɪvænt] vi **to g. (about)** *Fam* courir, vadrouiller.

gallon [ˈgælən] n gallon m (*Br* = 4,5 litres, *Am* = 3,8 litres).

gallop [ˈgæləp] n galop m; − vi galoper; **to g. away** (*rush*) *Fig* partir au galop or en vitesse. ◆**-ing** a (*inflation etc*) *Fig* galopant.

gallows [ˈgæləʊz] npl potence f.

gallstone [ˈgɔːlstəʊn] n *Med* calcul m biliaire.

galore [gəˈlɔːr] adv à gogo, en abondance.

galoshes [gəˈlɒʃɪz] npl (*shoes*) caoutchoucs mpl.

galvanize [ˈgælvənaɪz] vt (*metal*) & *Fig* galvaniser.

gambit [ˈgæmbɪt] n **opening g.** *Fig* manœuvre f stratégique.

gambl/e [ˈgæmb(ə)l] vi jouer (**on** sur, **with** avec); **to g. on** (*count on*) miser sur; − vt (*wager*) jouer; **to g. (away)** (*lose*) perdre (au jeu); − n (*bet*) & *Fig* coup m risqué. ◆**-ing** n jeu m. ◆**-er** n joueur, -euse mf.

game [geɪm] **1** n jeu m; (*of football, cricket etc*) match m; (*of tennis, chess, cards*) partie f; **to have a g. of** jouer un match de; **games** une partie de; **games** *Sch* le sport; **games teacher** professeur m d'éducation physique. **2** n (*animals, birds*) gibier m; **to be fair g. for** *Fig* être une proie idéale pour. **3** a (*brave*) courageux; **g. for** (*willing*) prêt à. **4** a (*leg*) estropié; **to have a g. leg** être boiteux. ◆**gamekeeper** n garde-chasse m.

gammon [ˈgæmən] n (*ham*) jambon m fumé.

gammy [ˈgæmɪ] a *Fam* = **game 4**.

gamut [ˈgæmət] n *Mus* & *Fig* gamme f.

gang [gæŋ] n bande f; (*of workers*) équipe f; (*of crooks*) gang m; − vi **to g. up on** or

against se liguer contre. ◆**gangster** *n* gangster *m*.

gangling ['gæŋglɪŋ] *a* dégingandé.

gangrene ['gæŋgriːn] *n* gangrène *f*.

gangway ['gæŋweɪ] *n* passage *m*; (*in train*) couloir *m*; (*in bus, cinema, theatre*) allée *f*; (*footbridge*) *Av Nau* passerelle *f*; g.! dégagez!

gaol [dʒeɪl] *n* & *vt* = **jail**.

gap [gæp] *n* (*empty space*) trou *m*, vide *m*; (*breach*) trou *m*; (*in time*) intervalle *m*; (*in knowledge*) lacune *f*; **the g. between** (*divergence*) l'écart *m*.

gap/e [geɪp] *vi* (*stare*) rester *or* être bouche bée; **to g. at** regarder bouche bée. ◆**—ing** *a* (*chasm, wound*) béant.

garage ['gærɑː(dʒ, 'gærɪdʒ, *Am* gə'rɑːʒ] *n* garage *m*; — *vt* mettre au garage.

garb [gɑːb] *n* (*clothes*) costume *m*.

garbage ['gɑːbɪdʒ] *n* ordures *fpl*; g. can *Am* poubelle *f*; g. collector *or* man *Am* éboueur *m*; g. truck *Am* camion-benne *m*.

garble ['gɑːb(ə)l] *vt* (*words etc*) déformer, embrouiller.

garden ['gɑːd(ə)n] *n* jardin *m*; **the gardens** (*park*) le parc; g. centre (*store*) jardinerie *f*; (*nursery*) pépinière *f*; g. party garden-party *f*; g. produce produits *mpl* maraîchers; — *vi* to be gardening jardiner. ◆**—ing** *n* jardinage *m*. ◆**—er** *n* jardinier, -ière *mf*.

gargle ['gɑːg(ə)l] *vi* se gargariser; — *n* gargarisme *m*.

gargoyle ['gɑːgɔɪl] *n Archit* gargouille *f*.

garish ['geərɪʃ, *Am* 'gærɪʃ] *a* voyant, criard.

garland ['gɑːlənd] *n* guirlande *f*.

garlic ['gɑːlɪk] *n* ail *m*; g. sausage saucisson *m* à l'ail.

garment ['gɑːmənt] *n* vêtement *m*.

garnish ['gɑːnɪʃ] *vt* garnir (**with** de); — *n* garniture *f*.

garret ['gærət] *n* mansarde *f*.

garrison ['gærɪsən] *n Mil* garnison *f*.

garrulous ['gærələs] *a* (*talkative*) loquace.

garter ['gɑːtər] *n* (*round leg*) jarretière *f*; (*attached to belt*) *Am* jarretelle *f*; (*for men*) fixe-chaussette *m*.

gas [gæs] **1** *n* gaz *m inv*; (*gasoline*) *Am* essence *f*; *Med Fam* anesthésie *f* au masque; — *a* (*meter, mask, chamber*) à gaz; (*pipe*) de gaz; (*industry*) du gaz; (*heating*) au gaz; g. fire *or* heater appareil *m* de chauffage à gaz; g. station *Am* poste *m* d'essence; g. stove (*portable*) réchaud *m* à gaz; (*large*) cuisinière *f* à gaz; — *vt* (-ss-) (*poison*) asphyxier; *Mil* gazer. **2** *vi* (-ss-) (*talk*) *Fam* bavarder; — *n* **for a g.** (*fun*) *Am Fam* pour rire. ◆**gasbag** *n Fam* commère

f. ◆**gasman** *n* (*pl* -men) employé *m* du gaz. ◆**gasoline** *n Am* essence *f*. ◆**gasworks** *n* usine *f* à gaz.

gash [gæʃ] *n* entaille *f*; — *vt* entailler.

gasp [gɑːsp] **1** *vi* to g. (for breath) haleter; — *n* halètement *m*. **2** *vi* to g. with *or* in surprise/*etc* avoir le souffle coupé de surprise/*etc*; — *vt* (*say gasping*) hoqueter; — *n* a g. of surprise/*etc* un hoquet de surprise/*etc*.

gassy ['gæsɪ] *a* (-ier, -iest) (*drink*) gazeux.

gastric ['gæstrɪk] *a* (*juices, ulcer*) gastrique. ◆**ga'stronomy** *n* gastronomie *f*.

gate [geɪt] *n* (*of castle, airport etc*) porte *f*; (*at level crossing, field etc*) barrière *f*; (*metal*) grille *f*; (*in Paris Metro*) portillon *m*. ◆**gateway** *n* **the g. to success**/*etc* le chemin du succès/*etc*.

gâteau, *pl* **-eaux** ['gætəu, -əuz] *n Culin* gros gâteau *m* à la crème.

gatecrash ['geɪtkræʃ] *vti* to g. (a party) s'inviter de force (à une réception).

gather ['gæðər] *vt* (*people, objects*) rassembler; (*pick up*) ramasser; (*flowers*) cueillir; (*information*) recueillir; (*understand*) comprendre; (*skirt, material*) froncer; **I g. that ...** (*infer*) je crois comprendre que ...; **to g. speed** prendre de la vitesse; **to g. in** (*crops, harvest*) rentrer; (*essays, exam papers*) ramasser; **to g. up** (*strength*) rassembler; (*papers*) ramasser; — *vi* (*of people*) se rassembler, s'assembler, s'amasser; (*of clouds*) se former; (*of dust*) s'accumuler; **to g. round** s'approcher; **to g. round s.o.** entourer qn. ◆**—ing** *n* (*group*) réunion *f*.

gaudy ['gɔːdɪ] *a* (-ier, -iest) voyant, criard.

gauge [geɪdʒ] *n* (*instrument*) jauge *f*, indicateur *m*; *Rail* écartement *m*; **to be a g. of sth** *Fig* permettre de jauger qch; — *vt* (*measure*) mesurer; (*estimate*) évaluer, jauger.

gaunt [gɔːnt] *a* (*thin*) décharné.

gauntlet ['gɔːntlɪt] *n* gant *m*; **to run the g. of** *Fig* essuyer (le feu de).

gauze [gɔːz] *n* (*fabric*) gaze *f*.

gave [geɪv] *see* give.

gawk [gɔːk] *vi* to g. (at) regarder bouche bée.

gawp [gɔːp] *vi* = **gawk**.

gay [geɪ] *a* (-er, -est) **1** (*cheerful*) gai, joyeux; (*colour*) vif, gai. **2** *Fam* homo(sexuel), gay *inv*.

gaze [geɪz] *n* regard *m* (fixe); — *vi* regarder; **to g. at** regarder (fixement).

gazelle [gə'zel] *n* (*animal*) gazelle *f*.

gazette [gə'zet] *n* journal *m* officiel.

GB [dʒiːˈbiː] *abbr* (*Great Britain*) Grande-Bretagne *f*.

GCSE [dʒiːsiːesˈiː] *abbr* (*General Certificate of Secondary Education*) = baccalauréat *m*.

gear [gɪər] **1** *n* matériel *m*, équipement *m*; (*belongings*) affaires *fpl*; (*clothes*) *Fam* vêtements *mpl* (à la mode); (*toothed wheels*) *Tech* engrenage *m*; (*speed*) *Aut* vitesse *f*; **in g.** *Aut* en prise; **not in g.** *Aut* au point mort; **g. lever**, *Am* **g. shift** levier *m* de (changement de) vitesse. **2** *vt* (*adapt*) adapter (**to** à); **geared (up) to do** prêt à faire; **to g. oneself up for** se préparer pour. ◆**gearbox** *n* boîte *f* de vitesses.

gee! [dʒiː] *int Am Fam* ça alors!

geese [giːs] *see* **goose.**

geezer ['giːzər] *n Hum Sl* type *m*.

Geiger counter ['gaɪgəkauntər] *n* compteur *m* Geiger.

gel [dʒel] *n* (*substance*) gel *m*.

gelatin(e) ['dʒelətɪn, *Am* -tən] *n* gélatine *f*.

gelignite ['dʒelɪgnaɪt] *n* dynamite *f* (au nitrate de soude).

gem [dʒem] *n* pierre *f* précieuse; (*person or thing of value*) *Fig* perle *f*; (*error*) *Iron* perle *f*.

Gemini ['dʒemɪnaɪ] *n* (*sign*) les Gémeaux *mpl*.

gen [dʒen] *n* (*information*) *Sl* coordonnées *fpl*; — *vi* (**-nn-**) **to g. up on** *Sl* se rancarder sur.

gender ['dʒendər] *n Gram* genre *m*; (*of person*) sexe *m*.

gene [dʒiːn] *n Biol* gène *m*.

genealogy [dʒiːnɪˈælədʒɪ] *n* généalogie *f*.

general ['dʒenərəl] **1** *a* général; **in g.** en général; **the g. public** le (grand) public; **for g. use** à l'usage du public; **a g. favourite** aimé *or* apprécié de tous; **g. delivery** *Am* poste *f* restante; **to be g.** (*widespread*) être très répandu. **2** *n* (*officer*) *Mil* général *m*. ◆**gene'rality** *n* généralité *f*. ◆**generali-'zation** *n* généralisation *f*. ◆**generalize** *vti* généraliser. ◆**generally** *adv* généralement; **g. speaking** en général, généralement parlant.

generate ['dʒenəreɪt] *vt* (*heat*) produire; (*fear, hope etc*) & *Ling* engendrer. ◆**gene-'ration** *n* génération *f*; **the g. of** (*heat*) la production de; **g. gap** conflit *m* des générations. ◆**generator** *n El* groupe *m* électrogène, génératrice *f*.

generous ['dʒenərəs] *a* généreux (**with** de); (*helping, meal etc*) copieux. ◆**gene'rosity** *n* générosité *f*. ◆**generously** *adv* généreusement; (*to serve s.o.*) copieusement.

genesis ['dʒenəsɪs] *n* genèse *f*.

genetic [dʒɪˈnetɪk] *a* génétique. ◆**genetics** *n* génétique *f*.

Geneva [dʒɪˈniːvə] *n* Genève *m or f*.

genial ['dʒiːnɪəl] *a* (*kind*) affable; (*cheerful*) jovial.

genie ['dʒiːnɪ] *n* (*goblin*) génie *m*.

genital ['dʒenɪt(ə)l] *a* génital; — *npl* organes *mpl* génitaux.

genius ['dʒiːnɪəs] *n* (*ability, person*) génie *m*; **to have a g. for doing/for sth** avoir le génie pour faire/de qch.

genocide ['dʒenəsaɪd] *n* génocide *m*.

gent [dʒent] *n Fam* monsieur *m*; **gents' shoes** *Com* chaussures *fpl* pour hommes; **the gents** *Fam* les toilettes *fpl* (pour hommes).

genteel [dʒenˈtiːl] *a Iron* distingué.

gentle ['dʒent(ə)l] *a* (**-er, -est**) (*person, sound, slope etc*) doux; (*hint, reminder*) discret; (*touch*) léger; (*pace*) mesuré; (*exercise, progress*) modéré; (*birth*) noble. ◆**gentleman** *n* (*pl* **-men**) monsieur *m*; (*well-bred*) gentleman *m*, monsieur *m* bien élevé. ◆**gentlemanly** *a* distingué, bien élevé. ◆**gentleness** *n* douceur *f*. ◆**gently** *adv* doucement; (*to remind*) discrètement; (*smoothly*) en douceur.

genuine ['dʒenjuɪn] *a* (*authentic*) véritable, authentique; (*sincere*) sincère, vrai. ◆**-ly** *adv* authentiquement; sincèrement. ◆**-ness** *n* authenticité *f*; sincérité *f*.

geography [dʒɪˈɒgrəfɪ] *n* géographie *f*. ◆**geo'graphical** *a* géographique.

geology [dʒɪˈɒlədʒɪ] *n* géologie *f*. ◆**geo-'logical** *a* géologique. ◆**geologist** *n* géologue *mf*.

geometry [dʒɪˈɒmɪtrɪ] *n* géométrie *f*. ◆**geo'metric(al)** *a* géométrique.

geranium [dʒɪˈreɪnɪəm] *n Bot* géranium *m*.

geriatric [dʒerɪˈætrɪk] *a* (*hospital*) du troisième âge; **g. ward** service *m* de gériatrie.

germ [dʒɜːm] *n Biol & Fig* germe *m*; *Med* microbe *m*; **g. warfare** guerre *f* bactériologique.

German ['dʒɜːmən] *a & n* allemand, -ande (*mf*); **G. measles** *Med* rubéole *f*; **G. shepherd** (*dog*) *Am* berger *m* allemand; — *n* (*language*) allemand *m*. ◆**Ger'manic** *a* germanique.

Germany ['dʒɜːmənɪ] *n* Allemagne *f*; **West G.** Allemagne de l'Ouest.

germinate ['dʒɜːmɪneɪt] *vi Bot & Fig* germer.

gestation [dʒeˈsteɪʃ(ə)n] *n* gestation *f*.

gesture ['dʒestʃər] *n* geste *m*; — *vi* **to g. to**

s.o. to do faire signe à qn de faire.
◆**ge'sticulate** vi gesticuler.

get [get] 1 vt (pt & pp got, pp Am **gotten**, pres p **getting**) (obtain) obtenir, avoir; (find) trouver; (buy) acheter, prendre; (receive) recevoir, avoir; (catch) attraper, prendre; (seize) prendre, saisir; (fetch) aller chercher (qn, qch); (put) mettre; (derive) tirer (from de); (understand) comprendre, saisir; (prepare) préparer; (lead) mener; (target) atteindre, avoir; (reputation) se faire; (annoy) Fam ennuyer; **I have got,** Am **I have gotten** j'ai; to g. s.o. to do sth faire faire qch à qn; to g. sth built/etc faire construire/etc qch; to g. things going or started faire démarrer les choses. 2 vi (go) aller; (arrive) arriver (to à); (become) devenir, se faire; to g. caught/run over/etc se faire prendre/écraser/etc; to g. married se marier; to g. dressed/washed s'habiller/se laver; **where have you got** or Am **gotten to?** où en es-tu?; **you've got to stay** (must) tu dois rester; to g. to do (succeed in doing) parvenir à faire; to g. working se mettre à travailler. ■ to g. **about** or **(a)round** vi se déplacer; (of news) circuler; (of person) faire traverser; (message) communiquer; − vi traverser; (of speaker) se faire comprendre (to de); to g. **across to s.o. that** faire comprendre à qn que; to g. **along** vi (leave) se sauver; (manage) se débrouiller; (progress) avancer; (be on good terms) s'entendre (with avec); to g. **at** vt (reach) parvenir à, atteindre; (taunt) s'en prendre à; **what is he getting at?** où veut-il en venir?; to g. **away** vi (leave) partir, s'en aller; (escape) s'échapper; **there's no getting away from it** il faut le reconnaître, c'est comme ça. ◆**getaway** n (escape) fuite f; to g. **back** vt (recover) récupérer; (replace) remettre; − vi (return) revenir, retourner; to g. back at, g. one's own back at (punish) se venger de; g. back! (move back) reculez!; to g. **by** vi (pass) passer; (manage) se débrouiller; to g. **down** vi (go down) descendre (from de); − vt (write) noter; (depress) Fam déprimer; to g. **down to** (task, work) se mettre à; to g. **in** vt (bicycle, washing etc) rentrer; (buy) acheter; (summon) faire venir; to g. **in a car**/etc monter dans une voiture/etc; − vi (enter) entrer; (come home) rentrer; (enter vehicle or train) monter; (of plane, train) arriver; (of candidate) Pol être élu; to g. **into** vt entrer dans; (vehicle, train) monter dans;

(habit) prendre; to g. **into bed/a rage** se mettre au lit/en colère; to g. **into trouble** avoir des ennuis; to g. **off** vi (leave) partir; (from vehicle or train) descendre (from de); (escape) s'en tirer; (finish work) sortir; (be acquitted) Jur être acquitté; − vt (remove) enlever; (despatch) expédier; Jur faire acquitter (qn); to g. **off (from) a chair** se lever d'une chaise; to g. **off doing** Fam se dispenser de faire; to g. **on** vt (shoes, clothes) mettre; (bus, train) monter dans; − vi (progress) marcher, avancer; (continue) continuer; (succeed) réussir; (enter bus or train) monter; (be on good terms) s'entendre (with avec); **how are you getting on?** comment ça va?; to g. **on to s.o.** (telephone) toucher qn, contacter qn; to g. **on with** (task) continuer; to g. **out** vi sortir; (from vehicle or train) descendre (from de); to g. **out of** (obligation) échapper à; (trouble) se tirer de; (habit) perdre; − vt (remove) enlever; (bring out) sortir (qch), faire sortir (qn); to g. **over** vt (road) traverser; (obstacle) surmonter; (fence) franchir; (illness) se remettre de; (surprise) revenir de; (ideas) communiquer; **let's g. it over with** finissons-en; − vi (cross) traverser; to g. **round** vt (obstacle) contourner; (person) entortiller; − vi to g. **round to doing** en venir à faire; to g. **through** vi (pass) passer; (finish) finir; (pass exam) être reçu; to g. **through to s.o.** se faire comprendre de qn; (on the telephone) contacter qn; − vt (hole etc) passer par; (task, meal) venir à bout de; (exam) être reçu à; **g. me through to your boss** (on the telephone) passe-moi ton patron; to g. **together** vi (of people) se rassembler. ◆**g.-together** n réunion f; to g. **up** vi (rise) se lever (from de); to g. **up to** (in book) en arriver à; (mischief, trouble etc) faire; − vt (ladder, stairs etc) monter; (party, group) organiser; to g. **sth up** (bring up) monter qch. ◆**g.-up** n (clothes) Fam accoutrement m.

geyser ['giːzər] n 1 (water heater) chauffe-eau m inv. 2 Geol geyser m.

Ghana ['gɑːnə] n Ghana m.

ghastly ['gɑːstlɪ] a (-ier, -iest) (pale) blême, pâle; (horrible) affreux.

gherkin ['gɜːkɪn] n cornichon m.

ghetto ['getəʊ] n (pl -os) ghetto m.

ghost [gəʊst] n fantôme m; **not the g. of a chance** pas l'ombre d'une chance; − a (story) de fantômes; (ship) fantôme; (town) mort. ◆**-ly** a spectral.

ghoulish ['guːlɪʃ] a morbide.

giant ['dʒaɪənt] n géant m; – a géant, gigantesque; (steps) de géant; (packet etc) Com géant.

gibberish ['dʒɪbərɪʃ] n baragouin m.

gibe [dʒaɪb] vi railler; **to g. at** railler; – n raillerie f.

giblets ['dʒɪblɪts] npl (of fowl) abats mpl.

giddy ['gɪdɪ] a (-ier, -iest) (heights) vertigineux; **to feel g.** avoir le vertige; **to make g.** donner le vertige à. ◆**giddiness** n vertige m.

gift ['gɪft] n cadeau m; (talent) & Jur don m; **g. voucher** chèque-cadeau m. ◆**gifted** a doué (with de, for pour). ◆**giftwrapped** a en paquet-cadeau.

gig [gɪg] n Mus Fam engagement m, séance f.

gigantic [dʒaɪ'gæntɪk] a gigantesque.

giggle ['gɪg(ə)l] vi rire (sottement); – n petit rire m sot; **to have the giggles** avoir le fou rire.

gild [gɪld] vt dorer. ◆**gilt** a doré; – n dorure f.

gills [gɪlz] npl (of fish) ouïes fpl.

gimmick ['gɪmɪk] n (trick, object) truc m.

gin [dʒɪn] n (drink) gin m.

ginger ['dʒɪndʒər] 1 a (hair) roux. 2 n Bot Culin gingembre m; **g. beer** boisson f gazeuse au gingembre. ◆**gingerbread** n pain m d'épice.

gingerly ['dʒɪndʒəlɪ] adv avec précaution.

gipsy ['dʒɪpsɪ] n bohémien, -ienne mf; (Central European) Tsigane mf; – a (music) tsigane.

giraffe [dʒɪ'rɑːf, dʒɪ'ræf] n girafe f.

girder ['gɜːdər] n (metal beam) poutre f.

girdle ['gɜːd(ə)l] n (belt) ceinture f; (corset) gaine f.

girl ['gɜːl] n (jeune) fille f; (daughter) fille f; (servant) bonne f; (sweetheart) Fam petite amie f; **English g.** jeune Anglaise f; **g. guide** éclaireuse f. ◆**girlfriend** n amie f; (of boy) petite amie f. ◆**girlish** a de (jeune) fille.

girth [gɜːθ] n (measure) circonférence f; (of waist) tour m.

gist [dʒɪst] n **to get the g. of** comprendre l'essentiel de.

give [gɪv] vt (pt gave, pp given) donner (to à); (help, support) prêter; (gesture, pleasure) faire; (a sigh) pousser; (a look) jeter; (a blow) porter; **g. me York 234** passez-moi le 234 à York; **she doesn't g. a damn** Fam elle s'en fiche; **to g. way** (yield, break) céder (to à); (collapse) s'effondrer; Aut céder la priorité (to à); (in fabric etc) élasticité f. ■ **to g. away** vt (prize) distribuer; (money) donner; (facts) révéler; (betray) trahir (qn);

to g. back vt (return) rendre; **to g. in** vi (surrender) céder (to à); – vt (hand in) remettre; **to g. off** vt (smell, heat) dégager; **to g. out** vt distribuer; – vi (of supplies, patience) s'épuiser; (of engine) rendre l'âme; **to g. over** vt (devote) donner, consacrer (to à); **to g. oneself over to** s'adonner à; – vi **g. over!** (stop) Fam arrête!; **to g. up** vi abandonner, renoncer; – vt abandonner, renoncer à; (seat) céder (to à); (prisoner) livrer (to à); (patient) condamner; **to g. up smoking** cesser de fumer. ◆**given** a (fixed) donné; **to be g. to doing** (prone to do) avoir l'habitude de faire; **g. your age** (in view of) étant donné votre âge; **g. that** étant donné que. ◆**giver** n donateur, -trice mf.

glacier ['glæsɪər, Am 'gleɪʃər] n glacier m.

glad [glæd] a (person) content (of, about de). ◆**gladden** vt réjouir. ◆**gladly** adv (willingly) volontiers.

glade [gleɪd] n clairière f.

gladiolus, pl **-i** [glædɪ'əʊləs, -aɪ] n Bot glaïeul m.

glamour ['glæmər] n (charm) enchantement m; (splendour) éclat m. ◆**glamorize** vt montrer sous un jour séduisant. ◆**glamorous** a séduisant.

glance [glɑːns] 1 n coup m d'œil; – vi jeter un coup d'œil (at à, sur). 2 vt **to g. off sth** (of bullet) ricocher sur qch.

gland [glænd] n glande f. ◆**glandular** a **g. fever** Med mononucléose f infectieuse.

glar/e [gleər] 1 vi **to g. at s.o.** foudroyer qn (du regard); – n regard m furieux. 2 vi (of sun) briller d'un éclat aveuglant; – n éclat m aveuglant. ◆**—ing** a (sun) aveuglant; (eyes) furieux; (injustice) flagrant; **a g. mistake** une faute grossière.

glass [glɑːs] n verre m; (mirror) miroir m, glace f; pl (spectacles) lunettes fpl; **a pane of g.** une vitre, un carreau; – a (door) vitré; (industry) du verre. ◆**glassful** n (plein) verre m.

glaze [gleɪz] vt (door) vitrer; (pottery) vernisser; (paper) glacer; – n (on pottery) vernis m; (on paper) glacé m. ◆**glazier** n vitrier m.

gleam [gliːm] n lueur f; – vi (re)luire.

glean [gliːn] vt (grain, information etc) glaner.

glee [gliː] n joie f. ◆**gleeful** a joyeux.

glen [glen] n vallon m.

glib [glɪb] a (person) qui a la parole facile; (speech) facile, peu sincère. ◆**—ly** adv (to say) peu sincèrement.

glid/e [glaɪd] vi glisser; (of vehicle) avancer

silencieusement; (*of aircraft, bird*) planer. ◆**—ing** *n Av Sp* vol m à voile. ◆**—er** *n Av* planeur *m*.

glimmer ['glɪmər] *vi* luire (faiblement); *— n* (*light, of hope etc*) (faible) lueur *f*.

glimpse [glɪmps] *n* aperçu *m*; **to catch** *or* **get a g.** **of** entrevoir.

glint [glɪnt] *vi* (*shine with flashes*) briller; *— n* éclair *m*; (*in eye*) étincelle *f*.

glisten ['glɪs(ə)n] *vi* (*of wet surface*) briller; (*of water*) miroiter.

glitter ['glɪtər] *vi* scintiller, briller; *— n* scintillement *m*.

gloat [gləʊt] *vi* jubiler (**over** à la vue de).

globe [gləʊb] *n* globe *m*. ◆**global** *a* (*comprehensive*) global; (*universal*) universel, mondial.

gloom [gluːm] *n* (*darkness*) obscurité *f*; (*sadness*) *Fig* tristesse *f*. ◆**gloomy** *a* (**-ier, -iest**) (*dark, dismal*) sombre, triste; (*sad*) *Fig* triste; (*pessimistic*) pessimiste.

glory ['glɔːrɪ] *n* gloire *f*; **in all one's g.** *Fig* dans toute sa splendeur; **to be in one's g.** (*very happy*) *Fam* être à son affaire; *— vi* **to g. in** se glorifier de. ◆**glorify** *vt* (*praise*) glorifier; **it's a glorified barn**/*etc* ce n'est guère plus qu'une grange/*etc*. ◆**glorious** *a* (*full of glory*) glorieux; (*splendid, enjoyable*) magnifique.

gloss [glɒs] **1** *n* (*shine*) brillant *m*; **g. paint** peinture *f* brillante; **g. finish** brillant *m*. **2** *n* (*note*) glose *f*, commentaire *m*. **3** *vt* **to g. over** (*minimize*) glisser sur; (*conceal*) dissimuler. ◆**glossy** *a* (**-ier, -iest**) brillant; (*paper*) glacé; (*magazine*) de luxe.

glossary ['glɒsərɪ] *n* glossaire *m*.

glove [glʌv] *n* gant *m*; **g. compartment** *Aut* (*shelf*) vide-poches *m inv*; (*enclosed*) boîte *f* à gants. ◆**gloved** *a* **a g. hand** une main gantée.

glow [gləʊ] *vi* (*of sky, fire*) rougeoyer; (*of lamp*) luire; (*of eyes, person*) *Fig* rayonner (**with** de); *— n* rougeoiement *m*; (*of colour*) éclat *m*; (*of lamp*) lueur *f*. ◆**—ing** *a* (*account, terms etc*) très favorable, enthousiaste. ◆**glow-worm** *n* ver *m* luisant.

glucose ['gluːkəʊs] *n* glucose *m*.

glue [gluː] *n* colle *f*; *— vt* coller (**to, on** à). ◆**glued** *a* **g. to** (*eyes*) *Fam* fixés *or* rivés sur; **to be g. to** (*television*) *Fam* être cloué devant.

glum [glʌm] *a* (**glummer, glummest**) triste.

glut [glʌt] *vt* (**-tt-**) (*overfill*) rassasier; (*market*) *Com* surcharger (**with** de); *— n* (*of produce, oil etc*) *Com* surplus *m* (**of** de).

glutton ['glʌt(ə)n] *n* glouton, -onne *mf*; **g. for work** bourreau *m* de travail; **g. for**

punishment masochiste *mf*. ◆**gluttony** *n* gloutonnerie *f*.

glycerin(e) ['glɪsərɪn] *n* glycérine *f*.

GMT [dʒiːem'tiː] *abbr* (*Greenwich Mean Time*) GMT.

gnarled [nɑːld] *a* noueux.

gnash [næʃ] *vt* **to g. one's teeth** grincer des dents.

gnat [næt] *n* (*insect*) cousin *m*.

gnaw [nɔː] *vti* **to g. (at)** ronger.

gnome [nəʊm] *n* (*little man*) gnome *m*.

go [gəʊ] **1** *vi* (*3rd person sing pres t* **goes**; *pt* **went**; *pp* **gone**; *pres p* **going**) aller (**to** à, **from** de); (*depart*) partir, s'en aller; (*disappear*) disparaître; (*be sold*) se vendre; (*function*) marcher, fonctionner; (*progress*) aller, marcher; (*become*) devenir; (*be*) être; (*of time*) passer; (*of hearing, strength*) baisser; (*of rope*) céder; (*of fuse*) sauter; (*of material*) s'user; **to go well/badly** (*of event*) se passer bien/mal; **she's going to do** (*is about to, intends to*) elle va faire; **it's all gone** (*finished*) il n'y en a plus; **to go and get** (*fetch*) aller chercher; **to go and see** aller voir; **to go riding/sailing/on a trip**/*etc* faire du cheval/de la voile/un voyage/*etc*; **to let go of** lâcher; **to go to** (*doctor, lawyer etc*) aller voir; **to get things going** faire démarrer les choses; **is there any beer going?** (*available*) y a-t-il de la bière?; **it goes to show that . . .** ça sert à montrer que . . . ; **two hours**/*etc* **to go** (*still left*) encore deux heures/*etc*. **2** *n* (*pl* **goes**) (*energy*) dynamisme *m*; (*attempt*) coup *m*; **to have a go at** (*doing*) *sth* essayer (de faire) qch; **at one go** d'un seul coup; **on the go** en mouvement, actif; **to make a go of** (*make a success of*) réussir. ■ **to go about** *or* **(a)round** *vi* se déplacer; (*of news, rumour*) circuler; **to go about** *vt* (*one's duties etc*) s'occuper de; **to know how to go about it** savoir s'y prendre; **to go across** *vt* traverser; *— vi* (*cross*) traverser; (*go*) aller (**to** à); **to go across to s.o.('s)** faire un saut chez qn; **to go after** *vt* (*follow*) suivre; (*job*) viser; **to go against** *vt* (*of result*) être défavorable à; (*s.o.'s wishes*) aller contre; (*harm*) nuire à; **to go ahead** *vi* aller de l'avant; **to go ahead with** (*plan etc*) poursuivre; **go ahead!** allez-y! ◆**go-ahead** *a* dynamique; *— n* **to get the go-ahead** avoir le feu vert; **to go along** *vi* aller, avancer; **to go along with** (*agree*) être d'accord avec; **to go away** *vi* partir, s'en aller; **to go back** *vi* retourner, revenir; (*in time*) remonter; (*retreat, step back*) reculer; **to go back on** (*promise*) revenir sur; **to go by** *vi* passer; *— vt* (*act according to*) se fonder sur; (*judge from*) juger d'après; (*instruction*) suivre; **to go down** *vi* descendre; (*fall down*) tomber; (*of ship*) couler; (*of sun*) se coucher; (*of storm*) s'apaiser; (*of temperature, price etc*) baisser; (*of tyre*) se dégonfler; **to go down well** (*of speech etc*) être bien reçu; **to go down with** (*illness*) attraper; − *vt* **to go down the stairs/street** descendre l'escalier/la rue; **to go for** *vt* (*fetch*) aller chercher; (*attack*) attaquer; (*like*) *Fam* aimer beaucoup; **to go forward(s)** *vi* avancer; **to go in** *vi* (r)entrer; (*of sun*) se cacher; **to go in for** (*exam*) se présenter à; (*hobby, sport*) (*career*) entrer dans; (*like*) *Fam* aimer beaucoup; − *vt* **to go in a room/etc** entrer dans une pièce/*etc*; **to go into** *vt* (*room etc*) entrer dans; (*question*) examiner; **to go off** *vi* (*leave*) partir; (*go bad*) se gâter; (*of effect*) passer; (*of alarm*) se déclencher; (*of event*) se passer; − *vt* (*one's food*) perdre le goût de; **to go on** *vi* continuer (*doing* à faire); (*travel*) poursuivre sa route; (*happen*) se passer; (*last*) durer; (*of time*) passer; **to go on at** (*nag*) *Fam* s'en prendre à; **to go on about** *Fam* parler sans cesse de; **to go out** *vi* sortir; (*of light, fire*) s'éteindre; (*of tide*) descendre; (*of newspaper, product*) être distribué (**to** à); (*depart*) partir; **to go out to work** travailler (au dehors); **to go over** *vi* (*go*) aller (**to** à); (*cross over*) traverser; (*to enemy*) passer (**to** à); **to go over to s.o.('s)** faire un saut chez qn; − *vt* examiner; (*speech*) revoir; (*in one's mind*) repasser; (*touch up*) retoucher; (*overhaul*) réviser (*véhicule, montre*); **to go round** *vi* (*turn*) tourner; (*make a detour*) faire le tour; (*be sufficient*) suffire; **to go round to s.o.('s)** passer chez qn, faire un saut chez qn; **enough to go round** assez pour tout le monde; − *vt* **to go round a corner** tourner un coin; **to go through** *vi* passer; (*of deal*) être conclu; − *vt* (*undergo, endure*) subir; (*examine*) examiner; (*search*) fouiller; (*spend*) dépenser; (*wear out*) user; (*perform*) accomplir; **to go through with** (*carry out*) réaliser, aller jusqu'au bout de; **to go under** *vi* (*of ship, person, firm*) couler; **to go up** *vi* monter; (*explode*) sauter; − *vt* **to go up the stairs/street** monter l'escalier/la rue; **to go without** *vi* se passer de.

goad [gəʊd] *n* aiguillon *m*; − *vt* **to g. (on)** aiguillonner.

goal [gəʊl] *n* but *m*. ◆**goalkeeper** *n* Fb gardien *m* de but, goal *m*. ◆**goalpost** *n* Fb poteau *m* de but.

goat [gəʊt] *n* chèvre *f*; **to get s.o.'s g.** *Fam*

énerver qn. ◆**goa'tee** *n* (*beard*) barbiche *f*.

gobble [ˈgɒb(ə)l] *vt* **to g. (up)** engloutir, engouffrer.

go-between [ˈgəʊbɪtwiːn] *n* intermédiaire *mf*.

goblet [ˈgɒblɪt] *n* verre *m* à pied.

goblin [ˈgɒblɪn] *n* (*evil spirit*) lutin *m*.

god [gɒd] *n* dieu *m*; **G.** Dieu *m*; **the gods** *Th Fam* le poulailler. ◆**g.-fearing** *a* croyant. ◆**g.-forsaken** *a* (*place*) perdu, misérable. ◆**goddess** *n* déesse *f*. ◆**godly** *a* dévot.

godchild [ˈgɒdtʃaɪld] *n* (*pl* **-children**) filleul, -eule *mf*. ◆**goddaughter** *n* filleule *f*. ◆**godfather** *n* parrain *m*. ◆**godmother** *n* marraine *f*. ◆**godson** *n* filleul *m*.

goddam(n) [ˈgɒdæm] *a Am Fam* foutu.

godsend [ˈgɒdsend] *n* aubaine *f*.

goes [gəʊz] *see* **go 1.**

goggle [ˈgɒg(ə)l] **1** *vi* **to g. at** regarder en roulant de gros yeux. **2** *npl* (*spectacles*) lunettes *fpl* (protectrices). ◆**g.-'eyed** *a* aux yeux saillants.

going [ˈgəʊɪŋ] **1** *n* (*departure*) départ *m*; (*speed*) allure *f*; (*conditions*) conditions *fpl*; **it's hard g.** c'est difficile. **2** *a* **the g. price** prix pratiqué (**for** pour); **a g. concern** une entreprise qui marche bien. ◆**goings-'on** *npl Pej* activités *fpl*.

go-kart [ˈgəʊkɑːt] *n Sp* kart *m*.

gold [gəʊld] *n* or *m*; − *a* (*watch etc*) en or; (*coin, dust*) d'or. ◆**golden** *a* (*made of gold*) d'or; (*in colour*) doré, d'or; (*opportunity*) excellent. ◆**goldmine** *n* mine *f* d'or. ◆**gold-'plated** *a* plaqué or. ◆**goldsmith** *n* orfèvre *m*.

goldfinch [ˈgəʊldfɪntʃ] *n* (*bird*) chardonneret *m*.

goldfish [ˈgəʊldfɪʃ] *n* poisson *m* rouge.

golf [gɒlf] *n* golf *m*. ◆**golfer** *n* golfeur, -euse *mf*.

golly! [ˈgɒlɪ] *int* (**by**) **g.!** *Fam* mince (alors)!

gondola [ˈgɒndələ] *n* (*boat*) gondole *f*. ◆**gondo'lier** *n* gondolier *m*.

gone [gɒn] *see* **go 1;** − *a* **it's g. two** *Fam* il est plus de deux heures. ◆**goner** *n* **to be a g.** *Sl* être fichu.

gong [gɒŋ] *n* gong *m*.

good [gʊd] *a* (**better, best**) bon; (*kind*) gentil; (*weather*) beau; (*pleasant*) bon, agréable; (*well-behaved*) sage; **be g. enough to . . .** ayez la gentillesse de . . . ; **my g. friend** mon cher ami; **a g. chap** *or* **fellow** un brave type; **g. and strong** bien fort; **a g. (long) walk** une bonne promenade; **very g.!** (*all right*) très bien!; **that's g. of you** c'est gentil de ta part; **to feel g.** se sentir bien;

that isn't g. enough (*bad*) ça ne va pas; (*not sufficient*) ça ne suffit pas; **it's g. for us** ça nous fait du bien; **g. at** (*French etc*) *Sch* bon or fort en; **to be g. with** (*children*) savoir s'y prendre avec; **it's a g. thing (that)** . . . heureusement que . . . ; **a g. many, a g. deal (of)** beaucoup (de); **as g. as** (*almost*) pratiquement; **g. afternoon, g. morning** bonjour; (*on leaving someone*) au revoir; **g. evening** bonsoir; **g. night** bonsoir; (*before going to bed*) bonne nuit; **to make g.** *vi* (*succeed*) réussir; – *vt* (*loss*) compenser; (*damage*) réparer; **G. Friday** Vendredi *m* Saint; – *n* (*virtue*) bien *m*; **for her g.** pour son bien; **there's some g. in him** il a du bon; **it's no g. crying/shouting**/*etc* ça ne sert à rien de pleurer/crier/*etc*; **that's no g.** (*worthless*) ça ne vaut rien; (*bad*) ça ne va pas; **what's the g.?** à quoi bon?; **for g.** (*to leave, give up etc*) pour de bon. ◆**g.-for-nothing** *a & n* propre à rien (*mf*). ◆**g.-'humoured** *a* de bonne humeur. ◆**g.-'looking** *a* beau. ◆**goodness** *n* bonté *f*; **my g.!** mon Dieu! ◆**good'will** *n* bonne volonté *f*; (*zeal*) zèle *m*.

goodbye [gud'baɪ] *int & n* au revoir (*m inv*).

goodly ['gudlɪ] *a* (*size, number*) grand.

goods [gudz] *npl* marchandises *fpl*; (*articles for sale*) articles *mpl*.

gooey ['guːɪ] *a Fam* gluant, poisseux.

goof [guːf] *vi* **to g. (up)** (*blunder*) *Am* faire une gaffe.

goon [guːn] *n Fam* idiot, -ote *mf*.

goose, *pl* **geese** [guːs, giːs] *n* oie *f*; **g. pimples** *or* **bumps** chair *f* de poule. ◆**gooseflesh** *n* chair *f* de poule.

gooseberry ['guzbərɪ, *Am* 'guːsbərɪ] *n* groseille *f* à maquereau.

gorge [gɔːdʒ] **1** *n* (*ravine*) gorge *f*. **2** *vt* (*food*) engloutir; **to g. oneself** s'empiffrer (**on** de).

gorgeous ['gɔːdʒəs] *a* magnifique.

gorilla [gə'rɪlə] *n* gorille *m*.

gormless ['gɔːmləs] *a Fam* stupide.

gorse [gɔːs] *n inv* ajonc(s) *m*(*pl*).

gory ['gɔːrɪ] *a* (**-ier, -iest**) (*bloody*) sanglant; (*details*) *Fig* horrible.

gosh! [gɒʃ] *int Fam* mince (alors)!

go-slow [gəu'sləu] *n* (*strike*) grève *f* perlée.

gospel ['gɒspəl] *n* évangile *m*.

gossip ['gɒsɪp] *n* (*talk*) bavardage(s) *m*(*pl*); (*malicious*) cancan(s) *m*(*pl*); (*person*) commère *f*; **g. column** *Journ* échos *mpl*; – *vi* bavarder; (*maliciously*) cancaner. ◆**-ing** *a,* ◆**gossipy** *a* bavard, cancanier.

got, *Am* gotten [gɒt, 'gɒt(ə)n] *see* get.

Gothic ['gɒθɪk] *a & n* gothique (*m*).

gouge [gaudʒ] *vt* **to g. out** (*eye*) crever.

goulash ['guːlæʃ] *n Culin* goulasch *f*.

gourmet ['guəmeɪ] *n* gourmet *m*.

gout [gaut] *n Med* goutte *f*.

govern ['gʌvən] *vt* (*rule*) gouverner; (*city*) administrer; (*business*) gérer; (*emotion*) maîtriser, gouverner; (*influence*) déterminer; – *vi Pol* gouverner; **governing body** conseil *m* d'administration. ◆**governess** *n* gouvernante *f*. ◆**government** *n* gouvernement *m*; (*local*) administration *f*; – *a* (*department, policy etc*) gouvernemental; (*loan*) d'État. ◆**govern'mental** *a* gouvernemental. ◆**governor** *n* gouverneur *m*; (*of school*) administrateur, -trice *mf*; (*of prison*) directeur, -trice *mf*.

gown [gaun] *n* (*dress*) robe *f*; (*of judge, lecturer*) toge *f*.

GP [dʒiː'piː] *n abbr* (*general practitioner*) (médecin *m*) généraliste *m*.

GPO [dʒiːpiː'əu] *abbr* (*General Post Office*) = PTT *fpl*.

grab [græb] *vt* (**-bb-**) **to g. (hold of)** saisir, agripper; **to g. sth from s.o.** arracher qch à qn.

grace [greɪs] **1** *n* (*charm, goodwill etc*) *Rel* grâce *f*; (*extension of time*) délai *m* de grâce; **to say g.** dire le bénédicité. **2** *vt* (*adorn*) orner; (*honour*) honorer (**with** de). ◆**graceful** *a* gracieux. ◆**gracious** *a* (*kind*) aimable, gracieux (**to** envers); (*elegant*) élégant; **good g.!** *Fam* bonté divine!

gradation [grə'deɪʃ(ə)n, *Am* greɪ'deɪʃ(ə)n] *n* gradation *f*.

grade [greɪd] *n* catégorie *f*; *Mil Math* grade *m*; (*of milk*) qualité *f*; (*of eggs*) calibre *m*; (*level*) niveau *m*; (*mark*) *Sch Univ* note *f*; (*class*) *Am Sch* classe *f*; **g. school** *Am* école *f* primaire; **g. crossing** *Am* passage *m* à niveau; – *vt* (*classify*) classer; (*colours etc*) graduer; (*paper*) *Sch Univ* noter.

gradient ['greɪdɪənt] *n* (*slope*) inclinaison *f*.

gradual ['grædʒuəl] *a* progressif, graduel; (*slope*) doux. ◆**—ly** *adv* progressivement, peu à peu.

graduat/e ['grædʒueɪt] *vi Univ* obtenir son diplôme; *Am Sch* obtenir son baccalauréat; **to g. from** sortir de; – *vt* (*mark with degrees*) graduer; – ['grædʒuət] *n* diplômé, -ée *mf*, licencié, -ée *mf*. ◆**—ed** *a* (*tube etc*) gradué; **to be g.** *Am Sch Univ* = **to graduate** *vi*. ◆**gradu'ation** *n Univ* remise *f* des diplômes.

graffiti [grə'fiːtɪ] *npl* graffiti *mpl*.

graft [grɑːft] *n Med Bot* greffe *f*; – *vt* greffer (**on** to à).

grain [greɪn] *n* (*seed, particle*) grain *m*;

(seeds) grain(s) m (pl); (in cloth) fil m; (in wood) fibre f; (in leather, paper) grain m; (of truth) Fig once f.

gram(me) [græm] n gramme m.

grammar ['græmər] n grammaire f; **g. school** lycée m. ◆**gra'mmatical** a grammatical.

gramophone ['græməfəʊn] n phonographe m.

granary ['grænərɪ] n Agr grenier m; **g. loaf** pain m complet.

grand [grænd] **1** a (-er, -est) magnifique, grand; (style) grandiose; (concert, duke) grand; (piano) à queue; (wonderful) Fam magnifique. **2** n inv Am Sl mille dollars mpl; Br Sl mille livres fpl. ◆**grandeur** ['grændʒər] n magnificence f; (of person, country) grandeur f.

grandchild ['græntʃaɪld] n (pl -children) petit(e)-enfant mf. ◆**grand(d)ad** n Fam pépé m, papi m. ◆**granddaughter** n petite-fille f. ◆**grandfather** n grand-père m. ◆**grandmother** n grand-mère f. ◆**grandparents** npl grands-parents mpl. ◆**grandson** n petit-fils m.

grandstand ['grændstænd] n Sp tribune f.

grange [greɪndʒ] n (house) manoir m.

granite ['grænɪt] n granit(e) m.

granny ['grænɪ] n Fam mamie f.

grant [grɑːnt] **1** vt accorder (to à); (request) accéder à; (prayer) exaucer; (admit) admettre (that que); **to take for granted** (event) considérer comme allant de soi; (person) considérer comme faisant partie du décor; **I take (it) for granted that** . . . je présume que . . . . **2** n subvention f, allocation f; Univ bourse f.

granule ['grænjuːl] n granule m. ◆**granulated** a **g. sugar** sucre m cristallisé.

grape [greɪp] n grain m de raisin; pl le raisin, les raisins mpl; **to eat grapes** manger du raisin or des raisins; **g. harvest** vendange f. ◆**grapefruit** n pamplemousse m. ◆**grapevine** n **on the g.** Fig par le téléphone arabe.

graph [græf, grɑːf] n graphique m, courbe f; **g. paper** papier m millimétré.

graphic ['græfɪk] a graphique; (description) Fig explicite, vivant. ◆**graphically** adv (to describe) explicitement.

grapple ['græp(ə)l] vi **to g. with** (person, problem etc) se colleter avec.

grasp [grɑːsp] vt (seize, understand) saisir; – n (firm hold) prise f; (understanding) compréhension f; (knowledge) connaissance f; **to have a strong g.** (strength of hand) avoir de la poigne; **within s.o.'s g.**

(reach) à la portée de qn. ◆**—ing** a (greedy) rapace.

grass [grɑːs] n herbe f; (lawn) gazon m; **the g. roots** Pol la base. ◆**grasshopper** n sauterelle f. ◆**grassland** n prairie f. ◆**grassy** a herbeux.

grat/e [greɪt] **1** n (for fireplace) grille f de foyer. **2** vt Culin râper. **3** vi (of sound) grincer (on sur); **to g. on the ears** écorcher les oreilles; **to g. on s.o.'s nerves** taper sur les nerfs de qn. ◆**—ing 1** a (sound) grinçant; Fig irritant. **2** n (bars) grille f. ◆**—er** n Culin râpe f.

grateful ['greɪtfʊl] a reconnaissant (to à, for de); (words, letter) de remerciement; (friend, attitude) plein de reconnaissance; **I'm g. (to you) for your help** je vous suis reconnaissant de votre aide; **I'd be g. if you'd be quieter** j'aimerais bien que tu fasses moins de bruit; **g. thanks** mes sincères remerciements. ◆**—ly** adv avec reconnaissance.

gratif/y ['grætɪfaɪ] vt (whim) satisfaire; **to g. s.o.** faire plaisir à qn. ◆**—ied** a très content (with or at sth de qch, to do de faire). ◆**—ying** a très satisfaisant; **it's g. to** . . . ça fait plaisir de . . . . ◆**gratifi'cation** n satisfaction f.

gratis ['grætɪs, 'greɪtɪs] adv gratis.

gratitude ['grætɪtjuːd] n reconnaissance f, gratitude f (for de).

gratuitous [grə'tjuːɪtəs] a (act etc) gratuit.

gratuity [grə'tjuːɪtɪ] n (tip) pourboire m.

grave¹ [greɪv] n tombe f; **g. digger** fossoyeur m. ◆**gravestone** n pierre f tombale. ◆**graveyard** n cimetière m; **auto g.** Am Fam cimetière m de voitures.

grave² [greɪv] a (-er, -est) (serious) grave. ◆**—ly** adv gravement; (concerned, displeased) extrêmement.

gravel ['græv(ə)l] n gravier m.

gravitate ['grævɪteɪt] vi **to g. towards** (be drawn towards) être attiré vers; (move towards) se diriger vers. ◆**gravi'tation** n gravitation f.

gravity ['grævɪtɪ] n **1** (seriousness) gravité f. **2** Phys pesanteur f, gravité f.

gravy ['greɪvɪ] n jus m de viande.

gray [greɪ] Am = grey.

graze [greɪz] **1** vi (of cattle) paître. **2** vt (scrape) écorcher; (touch lightly) frôler, effleurer; – n (wound) écorchure f.

grease [griːs] n graisse f; – vt graisser. ◆**greaseproof** a & n **g. (paper)** papier m sulfurisé. ◆**greasy** a (-ier, -iest) graisseux; (hair) gras; (road) glissant.

great [greɪt] a (-er, -est) grand; (effort, heat,

parcel) gros, grand; (*excellent*) magnifique, merveilleux; **g. at** (*English, tennis etc*) doué pour; **a g. deal** *or* **number** (**of**), **a g. many** beaucoup (de); **a g. opinion** of une haute opinion de; **a very g. age** un âge très avancé; **the greatest team**/*etc* (*best*) la meilleure équipe/*etc*; **Greater London** le grand Londres. ◆**g.-'grandfather** *n* arrière-grand-père *m*. ◆**g.-'grandmother** *n* arrière-grand-mère *f*. ◆**greatly** *adv* (*much*) beaucoup; (*very*) très, bien; **I g. prefer** je préfère de beaucoup. ◆**greatness** *n* (*in size, importance*) grandeur *f*; (*in degree*) intensité *f*.

Great Britain [greɪt'brɪt(ə)n] *n* Grande-Bretagne *f*.

Greece [griːs] *n* Grèce *f*. ◆**Greek** *a* grec; – *n* Grec *m*, Greque *f*; (*language*) grec *m*.

greed [griːd] *n* avidité *f* (**for** de); (*for food*) gourmandise *f*. ◆**greed/y** *a* (**-ier, -iest**) avide (**for** de); (*for food*) glouton, gourmand. ◆**—ily** *adv* avidement; (*to eat*) gloutonnement. ◆**—iness** *n* = **greed**.

green [griːn] *a* (**-er, -est**) vert; (*pale*) blême, vert; (*immature*) *Fig* inexpérimenté, naïf; **to turn** *or* **go g.** verdir; **the g. belt** (*land*) la ceinture verte; **the g. light** *Fig* le (feu) vert; **to have g. fingers** *or Am* **a g. thumb** avoir la main verte; **g. with envy** *Fig* vert de jalousie; – *n* (*colour*) vert *m*; (*lawn*) pelouse *f*; (*village square*) place *f* gazonnée; *pl* (*food*) légumes *mpl* verts. ◆**greenery** *n* (*plants, leaves*) verdure *f*. ◆**greenfly** *n* puceron *m* (des plantes). ◆**greengrocer** *n* marchand, -ande *mf* de légumes. ◆**greenhouse** *n* serre *f*. ◆**greenish** *a* verdâtre. ◆**greenness** *n* (*colour*) vert *m*; (*greenery*) verdure *f*.

greengage ['griːngeɪdʒ] *n* (*plum*) reine-claude *f*.

Greenland ['griːnlənd] *n* Groenland *m*.

greet [griːt] *vt* saluer, accueillir; **to g. s.o.** (*of sight*) s'offrir aux regards de qn. ◆**—ing** *n* salutation *f*; (*welcome*) accueil *m*; *pl* (*for birthday, festival*) vœux *mpl*; **send my greetings to . . .** envoie mon bon souvenir à . . . ; **greetings card** carte *f* de vœux.

gregarious [grɪ'geərɪəs] *a* (*person*) sociable; (*instinct*) grégaire.

gremlin ['gremlɪn] *n* *Fam* petit diable *m*.

grenade [grə'neɪd] *n* (*bomb*) grenade *f*.

grew [gruː] *see* **grow**.

grey [greɪ] *a* (**-er, -est**) gris; (*outlook*) *Fig* sombre; **to be going g.** grisonner; – *vi* **to be greying** être grisonnant. ◆**g.-'haired** *a* aux cheveux gris. ◆**greyhound** *n* lévrier *m*. ◆**greyish** *a* grisâtre.

grid [grɪd] *n* (*grating*) grille *f*; (*system*) *El* réseau *m*; *Culin* gril *m*. ◆**gridiron** *n* *Culin* gril *m*.

griddle ['grɪd(ə)l] *n* (*on stove*) plaque *f* à griller.

grief [griːf] *n* chagrin *m*, douleur *f*; **to come to g.** avoir des ennuis; (*of driver, pilot etc*) avoir un accident; (*of plan*) échouer; **good g.!** ciel!, bon sang!

grieve [griːv] *vt* peiner, affliger; – *vi* s'affliger (**over** de); **to g. for s.o.** pleurer qn. ◆**grievance** *n* grief *m*; *pl* (*complaints*) doléances *fpl*.

grievous ['griːvəs] *a* (*serious*) très grave.

grill [grɪl] **1** *n* (*utensil*) gril *m*; (*dish*) grillade *f*; – *vti* griller. **2** *vt* (*question*) *Fam* cuisiner.

grille [grɪl] *n* (*metal bars*) grille *f*; (*radiator*) *g. Aut* calandre *f*.

grim [grɪm] *a* (**grimmer, grimmest**) sinistre; (*face*) sévère; (*truth*) brutal; (*bad*) *Fam* (plutôt) affreux; **a g. determination** une volonté inflexible. ◆**—ly** *adv* (*to look at*) sévèrement.

grimace ['grɪməs] *n* grimace *f*; – *vi* grimacer.

grime [graɪm] *n* saleté *f*. ◆**grimy** *a* (**-ier, -iest**) sale.

grin [grɪn] *vi* (**-nn-**) avoir un large sourire; (*with pain*) avoir un rictus; – *n* large sourire *m*; rictus *m*.

grind [graɪnd] **1** *vt* (*pt & pp* **ground**) moudre; (*blade, tool*) aiguiser; (*handle*) tourner; (*oppress*) *Fig* écraser; **to g. one's teeth** grincer des dents; – *vi* **to g. to a halt** s'arrêter (*progressivement*). **2** *n* *Fam* corvée *f*, travail *m* long et monotone. ◆**—ing** *a* **g. poverty** la misère noire. ◆**—er** *n* **coffee g.** moulin *m* à café.

grip [grɪp] *vt* (**-pp-**) (*seize*) saisir; (*hold*) serré; (*of story*) *Fig* empoigner (*qn*); **to g. the road** (*of tyres*) adhérer à la route; – *vi* (*of brakes*) mordre; – *n* (*hold*) prise *f*; (*hand clasp*) poigne *f*; **get a g. on yourself!** secoue-toi!; **to get to grips with** (*problem*) s'attaquer à; **in the g. of** en proie à. ◆**gripping** *a* (*book, film etc*) prenant.

gripe [graɪp] *vi* (*complain*) *Sl* rouspéter.

grisly ['grɪzlɪ] *a* (*gruesome*) horrible.

gristle ['grɪs(ə)l] *n* *Culin* cartilage *m*.

grit [grɪt] **1** *n* (*sand*) sable *m*; (*gravel*) gravillon *m*; – *vt* (**-tt-**) (*road*) sabler. **2** *n* (*pluck*) *Fam* cran *m*. **3** *vt* (**-tt-**) **to g. one's teeth** serrer les dents.

grizzle ['grɪz(ə)l] *vi* *Fam* pleurnicher. ◆**grizzly** *a* **1** (*child*) *Fam* pleurnicheur. **2** (*bear*) gris.

groan [grəʊn] *vi* (*with pain*) gémir;

(*complain*) grogner, gémir; − *n* gémissement *m*; grognement *m*.

grocer ['grəʊsər] *n* épicier, -ière *mf*; **grocer's (shop)** épicerie *f*. ◆**grocery** *n* (*shop*) épicerie *f*; *pl* (*food*) épicerie *f*.

grog [grɒg] *n* (*drink*) grog *m*.

groggy ['grɒgɪ] *a* (**-ier, -iest**) (*weak*) faible; (*shaky on one's feet*) pas solide sur les jambes.

groin [grɔɪn] *n Anat* aine *f*.

groom [gruːm] **1** *n* (*bridegroom*) marié *m*. **2** *n* (*for horses*) lad *m*; − *vt* (*horse*) panser; **to g. s.o. for** (*job*) *Fig* préparer qn pour; **well groomed** (*person*) très soigné.

groove [gruːv] *n* (*for sliding door etc*) rainure *f*; (*in record*) sillon *m*.

grope [grəʊp] *vi* **to g. (about)** tâtonner; **to g. for** chercher à tâtons.

gross [grəʊs] **1** *a* (**-er, -est**) (*coarse*) grossier; (*error*) gros, grossier; (*injustice*) flagrant. **2** *a* (*weight, income*) *Com* brut; − *vt* faire une recette brute de. **3** *n* (*number*) grosse *f*. ◆**-ly** *adv* grossièrement; (*very*) énormément, extrêmement.

grotesque [grəʊ'tesk] *a* (*ludicrous, strange*) grotesque; (*frightening*) monstrueux.

grotto ['grɒtəʊ] *n* (*pl* **-oes** *or* **-os**) grotte *f*.

grotty ['grɒtɪ] *a* (**-ier, -iest**) *Fam* affreux, moche.

ground[1] [graʊnd] **1** *n* terre *f*, sol *m*; (*area for camping, football etc*) & *Fig* terrain *m*; (*estate*) terres *fpl*; (*earth*) *El Am* terre *f*, masse *f*; (*background*) fond *m*; *pl* (*reasons*) raisons *fpl*, motifs *mpl*; (*gardens*) parc *m*; **on the g.** (*lying etc*) par terre; **to lose g.** perdre du terrain; **g. floor** rez-de-chaussée *m inv*; **g. frost** gelée *f* blanche. **2** *vt* (*aircraft*) bloquer *or* retenir au sol. ◆**-ing** *n* connaissances *fpl* (*de fond*) (**in** en). ◆**groundless** *a* sans fondement. ◆**groundnut** *n* arachide *f*. ◆**groundsheet** *n* tapis *m* de sol. ◆**groundswell** *n* lame *f* de fond. ◆**groundwork** *n* préparation *f*.

ground[2] [graʊnd] *see* **grind 1**; − *a* (*coffee*) moulu; − *npl* (**coffee**) **grounds** marc *m* (de café).

group [gruːp] *n* groupe *m*; − *vt* **to g. (together)** grouper; − *vi* se grouper. ◆**-ing** *n* (*group*) groupe *m*.

grouse [graʊs] **1** *n inv* (*bird*) coq *m* de bruyère. **2** *vi* (*complain*) *Fam* rouspéter.

grove [grəʊv] *n* bocage *m*.

grovel ['grɒv(ə)l] *vi* (**-ll-**, *Am* **-l-**) *Pej* ramper, s'aplatir (**to s.o.** devant qn).

grow [grəʊ] *vi* (*pt* **grew**, *pp* **grown**) (*of person*) grandir; (*of plant, hair*) pousser;

(*increase*) augmenter, grandir, croître; (*expand*) s'agrandir; **to g. fat(ter)** grossir; **to g. to like** finir par aimer; **to g. into** devenir; **to g. on s.o.** (*of book, music etc*) plaire progressivement à qn; **to g. out of** (*one's clothes*) devenir trop grand pour; (*a habit*) perdre; **to g. up** devenir adulte; **when I g. up** quand je serai grand; − *vt* (*plant, crops*) cultiver, faire pousser; (*beard, hair*) laisser pousser. ◆**-ing** *a* (*child*) qui grandit; (*number*) grandissant. ◆**grown** *a* (*full-grown*) adulte. ◆**grown-up** *n* grande personne *f*, adulte *mf*; − *a* (*ideas etc*) d'adulte. ◆**grower** *n* (*person*) cultivateur, -trice *mf*.

growl [graʊl] *vi* grogner (**at** contre); − *n* grognement *m*.

growth [grəʊθ] *n* croissance *f*; (*increase*) augmentation *f* (**in** de); (*of hair*) pousse *f*; (*beard*) barbe *f*; *Med* tumeur *f* (**on** à).

grub [grʌb] *n* (*food*) *Fam* bouffe *f*.

grubby ['grʌbɪ] *a* (**-ier, -iest**) sale.

grudg/e [grʌdʒ] **1** *vt* (*give*) donner à contrecœur; (*reproach*) reprocher (**s.o. sth** qch à qn); **to g. doing** faire à contrecœur. **2** *n* rancune *f*; **to have a g. against** en vouloir à. ◆**-ing** *a* peu généreux. ◆**-ingly** *adv* (*to give etc*) à contrecœur.

gruelling, *Am* **grueling** ['grʊəlɪŋ] *a* (*day, detail etc*) éprouvant, atroce.

gruesome ['gruːsəm] *a* horrible.

gruff [grʌf] *a* (**-er, -est**) (*voice, person*) bourru.

grumble ['grʌmb(ə)l] *vi* (*complain*) grogner (**about, at** contre), se plaindre (**about, at** de).

grumpy ['grʌmpɪ] *a* (**-ier, -iest**) grincheux.

grunt [grʌnt] *vti* grogner; − *n* grognement *m*.

guarantee [gærən'tiː] *n* garantie *f*; − *vt* garantir (**against** contre); (**vouch for**) se porter garant de; **to g. (s.o.) that** certifier *or* garantir (à qn) que. ◆**guarantor** *n* garant, -ante *mf*.

guard [gɑːd] *n* (*vigilance, group of soldiers etc*) garde *f*; (*individual person*) garde *m*; *Rail* chef *m* de train; **to keep a g. on** surveiller; **under g.** sous surveillance; **on one's g.** sur ses gardes; **to catch s.o. off his g.** prendre qn au dépourvu; **on g. (duty)** de garde; **to stand g.** monter la garde; − *vt* (*protect*) protéger (**against** contre); (*watch over*) surveiller, garder; − *vi* **to g. against** (*protect oneself*) se prémunir contre; (*prevent*) empêcher; **to g. against doing** se garder de faire. ◆**-ed** *a* (*cautious*) prudent.

◆**guardian** *n* gardien, -ienne *mf*; *(of child)* *Jur* tuteur, -trice *mf*.

guerrilla [gə'rɪlə] *n* *(person)* guérillero *m*; g. **warfare** guérilla *f*.

guess [ges] *n* conjecture *f*; *(intuition)* intuition *f*; *(estimate)* estimation *f*; **to make a g.** (essayer de) deviner; **an educated** *or* **informed g.** une conjecture fondée; **at a g.** au jugé, à vue de nez; – *vt* deviner **(that** que); *(estimate)* estimer; *(suppose)* *Am* supposer **(that** que); *(think)* *Am* croire **(that** que); – *vi* deviner; **I g. (so)** *Am* je suppose; je crois. ◆**guesswork** *n* hypothèse *f*; **by g.** au jugé.

guest [gest] *n* invité, -ée *mf*; *(in hotel)* client, -ente *mf*; *(at meal)* convive *mf*; – *a* *(speaker, singer etc)* invité. ◆**guesthouse** *n* pension *f* de famille. ◆**guestroom** *n* chambre *f* d'ami.

guffaw [gə'fɔː] *vi* rire bruyamment.

guidance ['gaɪdəns] *n* *(advice)* conseils *mpl*.

guid/e [gaɪd] *n* *(person, book etc)* guide *m*; *(indication)* indication *f*; **(girl) g.** éclaireuse *f*; **g. dog** chien *m* d'aveugle; **g. book** guide *m*; – *v* *(lead)* guider. ◆**—ed** *a* *(missile, rocket)* téléguidé; **g. tour** visite *f* guidée. ◆**—ing** *a* *(principle)* directeur. ◆**guidelines** *npl* lignes *fpl* directrices, indications *fpl* à suivre.

guild [gɪld] *n* association *f*; *Hist* corporation *f*.

guile [gaɪl] *n* *(deceit)* ruse *f*.

guillotine ['gɪlətiːn] *n* guillotine *f*; *(for paper)* massicot *m*.

guilt [gɪlt] *n* culpabilité *f*. ◆**guilty** *a* (-ier, -iest) coupable; **g. person** coupable *mf*; **to find s.o. g.** déclarer qn coupable.

guinea pig ['gɪnɪpɪg] *n* *(animal)* & *Fig* cobaye *m*.

guise [gaɪz] *n* **under the g. of** sous l'apparence de.

guitar [gɪ'tɑːr] *n* guitare *f*. ◆**guitarist** *n* guitariste *mf*.

gulf [gʌlf] *n* *(in sea)* golfe *m*; *(chasm)* gouffre *m*; **a g. between** *Fig* un abîme entre.

gull [gʌl] *n* *(bird)* mouette *f*.

gullet ['gʌlɪt] *n* gosier *m*.

gullible ['gʌlɪb(ə)l] *a* crédule.

gully ['gʌlɪ] *n* *(valley)* ravine *f*; *(drain)* rigole *f*.

gulp [gʌlp] **1** *vt* **to g. (down)** avaler (vite); – *n* *(of drink)* gorgée *f*, lampée *f*; **in** *or* **at one g. d'une seule gorgée. 2** *vi* *(with emotion)* avoir la gorge serrée; – *n* serrement *m* de gorge.

gum¹ [gʌm] *n* *Anat* gencive *f*. ◆**gumboil** *n* abcès *m* (dentaire).

gum² [gʌm] **1** *n* *(glue from tree)* gomme *f*; *(any glue)* colle *f*; – *vt* (-mm-) coller. **2** *n* *(for chewing)* chewing-gum *m*.

gumption ['gʌmpʃ(ə)n] *n* *Fam* *(courage)* initiative *f*; *(commonsense)* jugeote *f*.

gun [gʌn] *n* pistolet *m*, revolver *m*; *(cannon)* canon *m*; – *vt* (-nn-) **to g. down** abattre. ◆**gunfight** *n* échange *m* de coups de feu. ◆**gunfire** *n* coups *mpl* de feu; *Mil* tir *m* d'artillerie. ◆**gunman** *n* *(pl -men)* bandit *m* armé. ◆**gunner** *n* *Mil* artilleur *m*. ◆**gunpoint** *n* **at g.** sous la menace d'un pistolet *or* d'une arme. ◆**gunpowder** *n* poudre *f* à canon. ◆**gunshot** *n* coup *m* de feu; **g. wound** blessure *f* par balle.

gurgle ['gɜːg(ə)l] *vi* *(of water)* glouglouter; – *n* glouglou *m*.

guru ['gʊruː] *n* *(leader)* *Fam* gourou *m*.

gush [gʌʃ] *vi* jaillir **(out of** de); – *n* jaillissement *m*.

gust [gʌst] *n* *(of smoke)* bouffée *f*; **g. (of wind)** rafale *f* (de vent). ◆**gusty** *a* (-ier, -iest) *(weather)* venteux; *(day)* de vent.

gusto ['gʌstəʊ] *n* **with g.** avec entrain.

gut [gʌt] **1** *n* *Anat* intestin *m*; *(catgut)* boyau *m*; *pl* *Fam* *(innards)* ventre *m*, tripes *fpl*; *(pluck)* cran *m*, tripes *fpl*; **he hates your guts** *Fam* il ne peut pas te sentir. **2** *vt* (-tt-) *(of fire)* dévaster.

gutter ['gʌtər] *n* *(on roof)* gouttière *f*; *(in street)* caniveau *m*.

guttural ['gʌtərəl] *a* guttural.

guy [gaɪ] *n* *(fellow)* *Fam* type *m*.

guzzle ['gʌz(ə)l] *vi* *(eat)* bâfrer; – *vt* *(eat)* engloutir; *(drink)* siffler.

gym [dʒɪm] *n* gym(nastique) *f*; *(gymnasium)* gymnase *m*; **g. shoes** tennis *fpl*. ◆**gym-'nasium** *n* gymnase *m*. ◆**gymnast** *n* gymnaste *mf*. ◆**gym'nastics** *n* gymnastique *f*.

gynaecology, *Am* **gynecology** [gaɪn-ɪ'kɒlədʒɪ] *n* gynécologie *f*. ◆**gynae-cologist** *n*, *Am* ◆**gynecologist** *n* gynécologue *mf*.

gypsy ['dʒɪpsɪ] = **gipsy**.

gyrate [dʒaɪ'reɪt] *vi* tournoyer.

H

H, h [eɪtʃ] n H, h m; **H bomb** bombe f H.
haberdasher ['hæbədæʃər] n mercier, -ière
mf; (men's outfitter) Am chemisier m.
◆**haberdashery** n mercerie f; Am
chemiserie f.
habit ['hæbɪt] n 1 habitude f; **to be in/get**
into the h. of doing avoir/prendre
l'habitude de faire; **to make a h. of doing**
avoir pour habitude de faire. 2 (addiction)
Med accoutumance f; **a h.-forming drug**
une drogue qui crée une accoutumance. 3
(costume) Rel habit m. ◆**ha'bitual** a
habituel; (smoker, drinker etc) invétéré.
◆**ha'bitually** adv habituellement.
habitable ['hæbɪtəb(ə)l] a habitable.
◆**habitat** n (of animal, plant) habitat m.
◆**habi'tation** n habitation f; **fit for h.**
habitable.
hack [hæk] 1 vt (cut) tailler, hacher. 2 n (old
horse) rosse f; (hired) cheval m de louage;
h. (writer) Pej écrivaillon m.
hackney ['hæknɪ] a **h. carriage** Hist fiacre m.
hackneyed ['hæknɪd] a (saying) rebattu,
banal.
had [hæd] see have.
haddock ['hædək] n (fish) aiglefin m;
smoked h. haddock m.
haemorrhage ['hemərɪdʒ] n Med hémorragie f.
haemorrhoids ['hemərɔɪdz] npl hémorroïdes fpl.
hag [hæg] n (woman) Pej (vieille) sorcière f.
haggard ['hægəd] a (person, face) hâve,
émacié.
haggle ['hæg(ə)l] vi marchander; **to h. over**
(thing) marchander; (price) débattre,
discuter. ◆**—ing** n marchandage m.
Hague (The) [ðə'heɪg] n La Haye.
ha-ha! [hɑː'hɑː] int (laughter) ha, ha!
hail¹ [heɪl] n Met & Fig grêle f; – v imp Met
grêler; **it's hailing** il grêle. ◆**hailstone** n
grêlon m.
hail² [heɪl] 1 vt (greet) saluer; (taxi) héler. 2
vi **to h. from** (of person) être originaire de;
(of ship etc) être en provenance de.
hair [heər] n (on head) cheveux mpl; (on
body, of animal) poils mpl; **a h.** (on head)
un cheveu; (on body, of animal) un poil; **by**
a hair's breadth de justesse; **long-/red-/etc**
haired aux cheveux longs/roux/etc; **h.**

cream brillantine f; **h. dryer** sèche-cheveux
m inv; **h. spray** (bombe f de) laque f.
◆**hairbrush** n brosse f à cheveux.
◆**haircut** n coupe f de cheveux; **to have a**
h. se faire couper les cheveux. ◆**hairdo** n
(pl -dos) Fam coiffure f. ◆**hairdresser** n
coiffeur, -euse mf. ◆**hairgrip** n pince f à
cheveux. ◆**hairnet** n résille f.
◆**hairpiece** n postiche m. ◆**hairpin** n
épingle f à cheveux; **h. bend** Aut virage m
en épingle à cheveux. ◆**hair-raising** a à
faire dresser les cheveux sur la tête.
◆**hair-splitting** n ergotage m. ◆**hair-**
style n coiffure f.
hairy ['heərɪ] a (-ier, -iest) (person, animal,
body) poilu; (unpleasant, frightening) Fam
effroyable.
hake [heɪk] n (fish) colin m.
hale [heɪl] a **h. and hearty** vigoureux.
half [hɑːf] n (pl halves) moitié f, demi, -ie
mf; (of match) Sp mi-temps f; **h. (of) the**
apple/etc la moitié de la pomme/etc; **ten**
and a h. dix et demi; **ten and a h. weeks** dix
semaines et demie; **to cut in h.** couper en
deux; **to go halves with** partager les frais
avec; – a demi; **h. a day, a h.-day** une
demi-journée; **at h. price** à moitié prix; **h.**
man h. beast mi-homme mi-bête; **h. sleeves**
manches fpl mi-longues; – adv (dressed,
full etc) à demi, à moitié; (almost) presque;
h. asleep à moitié endormi; **h. past one** une
heure et demie; **he isn't h. lazy/etc** Fam il
est rudement paresseux/etc; **h. as much as**
moitié moins que; **h. as much again** moitié
plus.
half-back ['hɑːfbæk] n Fb demi m.
◆**h.-'baked** a (idea) Fam à la manque, à
la noix. ◆**h.-breed** n, ◆**h.-caste** n Pej
métis, -isse mf. ◆**h.-(a-)'dozen** n
demi-douzaine f. ◆**h.-'hearted** a (person,
manner) peu enthousiaste; (effort) timide.
◆**h.-'hour** n demi-heure f. ◆**h.-light** n
demi-jour m. ◆**h.-'mast** n **at h.-mast**
(flag) en berne. ◆**h.-'open** a entrouvert.
◆**h.-'term** n Sch petites vacances fpl,
congé m de demi-trimestre. ◆**h.-'time** n
Sp mi-temps f. ◆**half'way** adv (between
places) à mi-chemin (between entre); **to**
fill/etc h. remplir/etc à moitié; **h. through**

(*book*) à la moitié de. ◆**h.-wit** *n*,
◆**h.-'witted** *a* imbécile (*mf*).

halibut ['hælɪbət] *n* (*fish*) flétan *m*.

hall [hɔːl] *n* (*room*) salle *f*; (*house entrance*)
entrée *f*, vestibule *m*; (*of hotel*) hall *m*;
(*mansion*) manoir *m*; (*for meals*) *Univ*
réfectoire *m*; **h. of residence** *Univ* pavillon
m universitaire; **halls of residence** cité *f*
universitaire; **lecture h.** *Univ* amphithéâtre
m. ◆**hallmark** *n* (*on silver or gold*) poinçon *m*; *Fig* sceau *m*. ◆**hallstand** *n* portemanteau *m*. ◆**hallway** *n* entrée *f*, vestibule *m*.

hallelujah [hælɪ'luːjə] *n* & *int* alléluia (*m*).

hallo! [hə'ləu] *int* (*greeting*) bonjour!; *Tel*
allô!; (*surprise*) tiens!

hallow ['hæləu] *vt* sanctifier.

Hallowe'en [hæləu'iːn] *n* la veille de la
Toussaint.

hallucination [həluːsɪ'neɪʃ(ə)n] *n* hallucination *f*.

halo ['heɪləu] *n* (*pl* -oes *or* -os) auréole *f*,
halo *m*.

halt [hɔːlt] *n* halte *f*; **to call a h.** to mettre fin
à; **to come to a h.** s'arrêter; – *vi* faire halte;
– *int Mil* halte! ◆**—ing** *a* (*voice*) hésitant.

halve [hɑːv] *vt* (*time, expense*) réduire de
moitié; (*cake, number etc*) diviser en deux.

ham [hæm] *n* **1** jambon *m*; **h. and eggs** œufs
mpl au jambon. **2** (*actor*) *Th Pej* cabotin,
-ine *mf*. ◆**h.-'fisted** *a Fam* maladroit.

hamburger ['hæmbɜːgər] *n* hamburger *m*.

hamlet ['hæmlɪt] *n* hameau *m*.

hammer ['hæmər] *n* marteau *m*; – *vt* (*metal,
table*) marteler; (*nail*) enfoncer (**into** dans);
(*defeat*) *Fam* battre à plate(s) couture(s);
(*criticize*) *Fam* démolir; **to h. out** (*agreement*) mettre au point; – *vi* frapper (au
marteau). ◆**—ing** *n* (*defeat*) *Fam* raclée *f*,
défaite *f*.

hammock ['hæmək] *n* hamac *m*.

hamper ['hæmpər] **1** *vt* gêner. **2** *n* (*basket*)
panier *m*; (*laundry basket*) *Am* panier *m* à
linge.

hamster ['hæmstər] *n* hamster *m*.

hand [hænd] *n* **1** main *f*; **to hold in one's h.**
tenir à la main; **by h.** (*to deliver etc*) à la
main; **at** *or* **to h.** (*within reach*) sous la
main, à portée de la main; (*close*) **at h.**
(*person etc*) tout près; (*day etc*) proche; **in
h.** (*situation*) bien en main; (*matter*) en
question; (*money*) disponible; **on h.** (*ready
for use*) disponible; **to have s.o. on one's
hands** *Fig* avoir qn sur les bras; **on the right
h.** du côté droit (**of** de); **on the one h. . . . .**
d'une part . . . ; **on the other h. . . . .** d'autre
part . . . ; **hands up!** (*in attack*) haut les

mains!; *Sch* levez la main!; **hands off!** (*don't
touche!*, bas les pattes!; **my hands are full**
Fig je suis très occupé; **to give s.o. a** (*helping*) **h.** donner un coup de main à qn; **to get
out of h.** (*of person*) devenir impossible; (*of
situation*) devenir incontrôlable; **h. in h.**
main dans la main; **h. in h. with** (*together
with*) *Fig* de pair avec; **at first h.** de
première main; **to win hands down** gagner
haut la main; – *a* (*luggage etc*) à main. **2** *n*
(*worker*) ouvrier, -ière *mf*; (*of clock*)
aiguille *f*; *Cards* jeu *m*; (*writing*) écriture *f*.
◆**handbag** *n* sac *m* à main. ◆**handbook**
n (*manual*) manuel *m*; (*guide*) guide *m*.
◆**handbrake** *n* frein *m* à main. ◆**hand-
brush** *n* balayette *f*. ◆**handcuff** *vt* passer
les menottes à. ◆**handcuffs** *npl* menottes
fpl. ◆**hand'made** *a* fait à la main.
◆**hand'picked** *a Fig* trié sur le volet.
◆**handrail** *n* (*on stairs*) rampe *f*. ◆**handshake** *n* poignée *f* de main. ◆**handwriting** *n* écriture *f*. ◆**hand'written** *a* écrit à
la main.

hand [hænd] *vt* (*give*) donner (**to** à); **to h.
down** (*bring down*) descendre; (*knowledge,
heirloom*) transmettre (**to** à); **to h. in** remettre; **to h. out** distribuer; **to h. over** remettre;
(*power*) transmettre; **to h. round** (*cakes*)
passer. ◆**handout** *n* (*leaflet*) prospectus
m; (*money*) aumône *f*.

handful ['hændful] *n* (*bunch, group*) poignée
f; (*quite*) **a h.** (*difficult*) *Fig* difficile.

handicap ['hændɪkæp] *n* (*disadvantage*) &
Sp handicap *m*; – *vt* (-pp-) handicaper.
◆**handicapped** *a* (*disabled*) handicapé.

handicraft ['hændɪkrɑːft] *n* artisanat *m*
d'art. ◆**handiwork** *n* artisanat *m* d'art;
(*action*) *Fig* ouvrage *m*.

handkerchief ['hæŋkətʃɪf] *n* (*pl* -fs)
mouchoir *m*; (*for neck*) foulard *m*.

handle ['hænd(ə)l] **1** *n* (*of door*) poignée *f*;
(*of knife*) manche *m*; (*of bucket*) anse *f*; (*of
saucepan*) queue *f*; (*of pump*) bras *m*. **2** *vt*
(*manipulate*) manier; (*touch*) toucher à;
(*ship, vehicle*) manœuvrer; (*deal with*)
s'occuper de; (*difficult child etc*) s'y prendre
avec; – *vi* **to h. well** (*of machine*) être facile
à manier.

handlebars ['hænd(ə)lbɑːz] *npl* guidon *m*.

handsome ['hænsəm] *a* (*person, building
etc*) beau; (*gift*) généreux; (*profit, sum*)
considérable. ◆**—ly** *adv* (*generously*)
généreusement.

handy ['hændɪ] *a* (-ier, -iest) (*convenient,
practical*) commode, pratique; (*skilful*)
habile (**at doing** à faire); (*useful*) utile;
(*near*) proche, accessible; **to come in h.** se

révéler utile; **to keep h.** avoir sous la main.
◆**handyman** n (pl -men) (DIY enthusiast)
bricoleur m.

hang¹ [hæŋ] **1** vt (pt & pp hung) suspendre
(**on, from** à); (on hook) accrocher (**on, from**
à), suspendre; (wallpaper) poser; (let
dangle) laisser pendre (**from, out of** de); **to
h. with** (decorate with) orner de; **to h. out**
(washing) étendre; (flag) arborer; **to h. up**
(picture etc) accrocher; – vi (dangle)
pendre; (of threat) planer; (of fog, smoke)
flotter; **to h. about** (loiter) traîner, rôder;
(wait) Fam attendre; **to h. down** (dangle)
pendre; (of hair) tomber; **to h. on** (hold out)
résister; (wait) Fam attendre; **to h. on to**
(cling to) ne pas lâcher; (keep) garder; **to h.
out** (of tongue, shirt) pendre; (live) Sl
crécher; **to h. together** (of facts) se tenir; (of
plan) tenir debout; **to h. up** Tel raccrocher.
2 n **to get the h. of sth** Fam arriver à
comprendre qch; **to get the h. of doing** Fam
trouver le truc pour faire. ◆**—ing**¹ n
suspension f; – a suspendu (**from** à); (leg,
arm) pendant; **h. on** (wall) accroché à.
◆**hang-glider** n delta-plane® m.
◆**hang-gliding** n vol m libre. ◆**hangnail**
n petites peaux fpl. ◆**hangover** n Fam
gueule f de bois. ◆**hangup** n Fam
complexe m.

hang² [hæŋ] vt (pt & pp hanged) (criminal)
pendre (**for** pour); – vi (of criminal) être
pendu. ◆**—ing**² n Jur pendaison f.
◆**hangman** n (pl -men) bourreau m.

hangar ['hæŋər] n Av hangar m.

hanger ['hæŋər] n (coat) **h.** cintre m.
◆**hanger-'on** n (pl hangers-on) (person)
Pej parasite m.

hanker ['hæŋkər] vi **to h. after** or **for** avoir
envie de. ◆**—ing** n (forte) envie f, (vif)
désir m.

hankie, hanky ['hæŋkɪ] n Fam mouchoir m.

hanky-panky [hæŋkɪ'pæŋkɪ] n inv Fam
(deceit) manigances fpl, magouilles fpl;
(sexual behaviour) papouilles fpl, pelotage
m.

haphazard [hæp'hæzəd] a au hasard, au
petit bonheur; (selection, arrangement)
aléatoire. ◆**—ly** adv au hasard.

hapless ['hæplɪs] a Lit infortuné.

happen ['hæpən] vi arriver, se passer, se
produire; **to h. to s.o./sth** arriver à qn/qch;
it (so) happens that I know, I h. to know il se
trouve que je le sais; **do you h. to have . . . ?**
est-ce que par hasard vous avez . . . ?;
whatever happens quoi qu'il arrive.
◆**—ing** n événement m.

happy ['hæpɪ] a (-ier, -iest) heureux (**to do**

de faire, **about sth** de qch); **I'm not (too** or
very) h. about (doing) it ça ne me plaît pas
beaucoup (de le faire); **H. New Year!**
bonne année!; **H. Christmas!** joyeux Noël!.
◆**h.-go-'lucky** a insouciant. ◆**happily**
adv (contentedly) tranquillement; (joy-
ously) joyeusement; (fortunately) heureusement. ◆**happiness** n bonheur m.

harass ['hærəs, Am hə'ræs] vt harceler.
◆**—ment** n harcèlement m.

harbour ['hɑːbər] **1** n port m. **2** vt (shelter)
héberger; (criminal) cacher, abriter; (fear,
secret) nourrir.

hard [hɑːd] a (-er, -est) (not soft, severe) dur;
(difficult) difficile, dur; (study) assidu;
(fact) brutal; (drink) alcoolisé; (water)
calcaire; **h. drinker/worker** gros buveur
m/travailleur m; **a h. frost** une forte gelée;
to be h. on or **to s.o.** être dur avec qn; **to find
it h. to sleep**/etc avoir du mal à dormir/etc;
h. labour Jur travaux mpl forcés; **h. cash**
espèces fpl; **h. core** (group) noyau m; **h. of
hearing** malentendant; **h. up** (broke) Fam
fauché; **to be h. up for** manquer de; – adv
(-er, -est) (to work) dur; (to pull) fort; (to
hit, freeze) dur, fort; (to study) assidûment;
(to think) sérieusement; (to rain) à verse;
(badly) mal; **h. by** tout près; **h. done by**
traité injustement.

hard-and-fast [hɑːdən(d)'fɑːst] a (rule)
strict. ◆**'hardback** n livre m relié.
◆**'hardboard** n Isorel® m. ◆**hard-
'boiled** a (egg) dur. ◆**hard-'core** a
(rigid) Pej inflexible. ◆**hard'headed** a
réaliste. ◆**hard'wearing** a résistant.
◆**hard-'working** a travailleur.

harden ['hɑːd(ə)n] vti durcir; **to h. oneself to**
s'endurcir à. ◆**—ed** a (criminal) endurci.

hardly ['hɑːdlɪ] adv à peine; **he h. talks** il
parle à peine, il ne parle guère; **h. ever**
presque jamais.

hardness ['hɑːdnɪs] n dureté f.

hardship ['hɑːdʃɪp] n (ordeal) épreuve(s)
f(pl); (deprivation) privation(s) f(pl).

hardware ['hɑːdweər] n inv quincaillerie f;
(of computer) & Mil matériel m.

hardy ['hɑːdɪ] a (-ier, -iest) (person, plant)
résistant.

hare [heər] n lièvre m. ◆**h.-brained** a
(person) écervelé; (scheme) insensé.

harem ['hɑːriːm] n harem m.

hark [hɑːk] vi Lit écouter; **to h. back to**
(subject etc) Fam revenir sur.

harm [hɑːm] n (hurt) mal m; (prejudice) tort
m; **he means (us) no h.** il ne nous veut pas
de mal; **she'll come to no h.** il ne lui arrivera
rien; – vt (hurt) faire du mal à; (prejudice)

nuire à, faire du tort à; *(object)* endommager, abîmer. ◆**harmful** *a* nuisible. ◆**harmless** *a* (*person, treatment*) inoffensif; *(hobby, act)* innocent; *(gas, fumes etc)* qui n'est pas nuisible, inoffensif.

harmonica [hɑːˈmɒnɪkə] *n* harmonica *m*.

harmony [ˈhɑːmənɪ] *n* harmonie *f*. ◆**har'monic** *a* & *n Mus* harmonique *(m)*. ◆**har'monious** *a* harmonieux. ◆**har'monium** *n Mus* harmonium *m*. ◆**harmonize** *vt* harmoniser; — *vi* s'harmoniser.

harness [ˈhɑːnɪs] *n* (*for horse, baby*) harnais *m*; — *vt* (*horse*) harnacher; *(energy etc) Fig* exploiter.

harp [hɑːp] **1** *n Mus* harpe *f*. **2** *vt* to h. on (about) sth *Fam* rabâcher qch. ◆**harpist** *n* harpiste *mf*.

harpoon [hɑːˈpuːn] *n* harpon *m*; — *vt* (*whale*) harponner.

harpsichord [ˈhɑːpsɪkɔːd] *n Mus* clavecin *m*.

harrowing [ˈhærəʊɪŋ] *a* (*tale, memory*) poignant; *(cry, sight)* déchirant.

harsh [hɑːʃ] *a* (-er, -est) (*severe*) dur, sévère; *(sound, taste)* âpre; *(surface)* rugueux; *(fabric)* rêche. ◆**—ly** *adv* durement, sévèrement. ◆**—ness** *n* dureté *f*, sévérité *f*; âpreté *f*; rugosité *f*.

harvest [ˈhɑːvɪst] *n* moisson *f*, récolte *f*; *(of people, objects) Fig* ribambelle *f*; — *vt* moissonner, récolter.

has [hæz] *see* have. ◆**has-been** *n Fam* personne *f* finie.

hash [hæʃ] **1** *n Culin* hachis *m*; — *vt* to h. (up) hacher. **2** *n* (*mess*) *Fam* gâchis *m*. **3** *n* (*hashish*) *Sl* hasch *m*, H *m*.

hashish [ˈhæʃiːʃ] *n* haschisch *m*.

hassle [ˈhæs(ə)l] *n Fam* (*trouble*) histoires *fpl*; *(bother)* mal *m*, peine *f*.

haste [heɪst] *n* hâte *f*; in h. à la hâte; to make h. se hâter. ◆**hasten** *vi* se hâter (to do de faire); — *vt* hâter. ◆**hasty** *a* (-ier, -iest) (*sudden*) précipité; *(visit)* rapide; *(decision, work)* hâtif. ◆**hastily** *adv* (*quickly*) en hâte; *(too quickly)* hâtivement.

hat [hæt] *n* chapeau *m*; that's old h. *Fam* (*old-fashioned*) c'est vieux jeu; *(stale)* c'est vieux comme les rues; to score *or* get a h. trick *Sp* réussir trois coups consécutifs.

hatch [hætʃ] **1** *vi* (*of chick, egg*) éclore; — *vt* faire éclore; *(plot) Fig* tramer. **2** *n* (*in kitchen wall*) passe-plats *m inv*.

hatchback [ˈhætʃbæk] *n* (*door*) hayon *m*; *(car)* trois-portes *f inv*, cinq-portes *f inv*.

hatchet [ˈhætʃɪt] *n* hachette *f*.

hate [heɪt] *vt* détester, haïr; to h. doing *or* to

do détester faire; I h. to say it ça me gêne de le dire; — *n* haine *f*; pet h. *Fam* bête *f* noire. ◆**hateful** *a* haïssable. ◆**hatred** *n* haine *f*.

haughty [ˈhɔːtɪ] *a* (-ier, -iest) hautain. ◆**haughtily** *adv* avec hauteur.

haul [hɔːl] **1** *vt* (*pull*) tirer, traîner; *(goods)* camionner. **2** *n* (*fish*) prise *f*; *(of thief)* butin *m*; a long h. (*trip*) un long voyage. ◆**haulage** *n* camionnage *m*. ◆**hauler** *n Am*, ◆**haulier** *n* transporteur *m* routier.

haunt [hɔːnt] **1** *vt* hanter. **2** *n* endroit *m* favori; *(of criminal)* repaire *m*. ◆**—ing** *a* (*music, memory*) obsédant.

have [hæv] **1** (*3rd person sing pres t* has; *pt & pp* had; *pres p* having) *vt* avoir; *(get)* recevoir, avoir; *(meal, shower etc)* prendre; he has got, he has il a; to h. a walk/dream/*etc* faire une promenade/un rêve/*etc*; to h. a drink prendre *or* boire un verre; to h. a wash se laver; to h. a holiday *(spend)* passer des vacances; will you h. ... ? *(a cake, some tea etc)* est-ce que tu veux ... ?; to let s.o. h. sth donner qch à qn; to h. it from s.o. that tenir de qn que; he had me by the hair il me tenait par les cheveux; I won't h. this *(allow)* je ne tolérerai pas ça; you've had it! *Fam* tu es fichu!; to h. on *(clothes)* porter; to have sth on *(be busy)* être pris; to h. s.o. over inviter qn chez soi. **2** *v aux* avoir; *(with monter, sortir etc & pronominal verbs)* être; to h. decided/been avoir décidé/été; to h. gone être allé; to h. cut oneself s'être coupé; I've just done it je viens de le faire; I've to do *(must)* devoir faire; I've got to go, I h. to go je dois partir, je suis obligé de partir, il faut que je parte; I don't h. to go je ne suis pas obligé de partir; to h. sth done *(get sth done)* faire faire qch; he's had his suitcase brought up il a fait monter sa valise; I've had my car stolen on m'a volé mon auto; she's had her hair cut elle s'est fait couper les cheveux; I've been doing it for months je le fais depuis des mois; haven't I?, hasn't she? *etc* n'est-ce pas?; no I haven't! non!; yes I h.! si!; after he had eaten, he left après avoir mangé, il partit. **3** *npl* the haves and (the) have-nots les riches *mpl* et les pauvres *mpl*.

haven [ˈheɪv(ə)n] *n* refuge *m*, havre *m*.

haversack [ˈhævəsæk] *n* (*shoulder bag*) musette *f*.

havoc [ˈhævək] *n* ravages *mpl*.

hawk [hɔːk] **1** *n* (*bird*) & *Pol* faucon *m*. **2** *vt* (*goods*) colporter. ◆**—er** *n* colporteur, -euse *mf*.

hawthorn [ˈhɔːθɔːn] *n* aubépine *f*.

hay [heɪ] *n* foin *m*; **h. fever** rhume *m* des foins. ◆**haystack** *n* meule *f* de foin.

haywire ['heɪwaɪər] *a* **to go h.** (*of machine*) se détraquer; (*of scheme, plan*) mal tourner.

hazard ['hæzəd] *n* risque *m*; **health h.** risque *m* pour la santé; **it's a fire h.** ça risque de provoquer un incendie; – *vt* (*guess, remark etc*) hasarder, risquer. ◆**hazardous** *a* hasardeux.

haze [heɪz] *n* brume *f*; **in a h.** (*person*) *Fig* dans le brouillard. ◆**hazy** *a* (**-ier, -iest**) (*weather*) brumeux; (*sun*) voilé; (*photo, idea*) flou; **I'm h. about my plans** je ne suis pas sûr de mes projets.

hazel ['heɪz(ə)l] *n* (*bush*) noisetier *m*; – *a* (*eyes*) noisette *inv*. ◆**hazelnut** *n* noisette *f*.

he [hiː] *pron* il; (*stressed*) lui; **he wants it** il veut; **he's a happy man** c'est un homme heureux; **if I were he** si j'étais lui; **he and I** lui et moi; – *n* mâle *m*; **he-bear** ours *m* mâle.

head [hed] **1** *n* (*of person, hammer etc*) tête *f*; (*of page*) haut *m*; (*of bed*) chevet *m*, tête *f*; (*of arrow*) pointe *f*; (*of beer*) mousse *f*; (*leader*) chef *m*; (*subject heading*) rubrique *f*; **h. of hair** chevelure *f*; **h. cold** rhume *m* de cerveau; **it didn't enter my h.** ça ne m'est pas venu à l'esprit (**that que**); **to take it into one's h. to do** se mettre en tête de faire; **the h.** *Sch* = **the headmaster**; = **the headmistress**; **to shout one's h. off** *Fam* crier à tue-tête; **to have a good h. for business** avoir le sens des affaires; **at the h. of** (*in charge of*) à la tête de; **at the h. of the table** au haut bout de la table; **at the h. of the list** en tête de liste; **it's above my h.** ça me dépasse; **to keep one's h.** garder son sang-froid; **to go off one's h.** devenir fou; **it's coming to a h.** (*of situation*) ça devient critique; **heads or tails?** pile ou face?; **per h., a h.** (*each*) par personne. **2** *a* principal; (*gardener*) en chef; **h. waiter** maître *m* d'hôtel; **a h. start** une grosse avance. **3** *vt* (*group, firm*) être à la tête de; (*list, poll*) être en tête de; (*vehicle*) diriger (**towards** vers); **to h. the ball** *Fb* faire une tête; **to h. off** (*person*) détourner de son chemin; (*prevent*) empêcher; **to be headed for** *Am* = **to h. for**; – *vi* **to h. for, be heading for** (*place*) se diriger vers; (*ruin etc*) *Fig* aller à. ◆**—ed** *a* (*paper*) à en-tête. ◆**—ing** *n* (*of chapter, page etc*) titre *m*; (*of subject*) rubrique *f*; (*printed on letter etc*) en-tête *m*. ◆**—er** *n* *Fb* coup *m* de tête.

headache ['hedeɪk] *n* mal *m* de tête; (*difficulty, person*) *Fig* problème *m*. ◆**head-dress** *n* (*ornamental*) coiffe *f*.

◆**headlamp** *n*, ◆**headlight** *n* *Aut* phare *m*. ◆**headline** *n* (*of newspaper*) manchette *f*; *pl* (*gros*) titres *mpl*; *Rad TV* (**grands**) titres *mpl*. ◆**headlong** *adv* (*to fall*) la tête la première; (*to rush*) tête baissée. ◆**head-'master** *n* *Sch* directeur *m*; (*of lycée*) proviseur *m*. ◆**head'mistress** *n* *Sch* directrice *f*; (*of lycée*) proviseur *m*. ◆**head-'on** *adv* & *a* (*to collide, collision*) de plein fouet. ◆**headphones** *npl* casque *m* (à écouteurs). ◆**headquarters** *npl* *Com Pol* siège *m* (central); *Mil* quartier *m* général. ◆**headrest** *n* appuie-tête *m inv*. ◆**headscarf** *n* (*pl* **-scarves**) foulard *m*. ◆**headstrong** *a* têtu. ◆**headway** *n* progrès *mpl*.

heady ['hedɪ] *a* (**-ier, -iest**) (*wine etc*) capiteux; (*action, speech*) emporté.

heal [hiːl] *vi* **to h. (up)** (*of wound*) se cicatriser; – *vt* (*wound*) cicatriser, guérir; (*person, sorrow*) guérir. ◆**—er** *n* guérisseur, -euse *mf*.

health [helθ] *n* santé *f*; **h. food** aliment *m* naturel; **h. food shop** *or* *Am* store magasin *m* diététique; **h. resort** station *f* climatique; **the H. Service** = la Sécurité Sociale. ◆**healthful** *a* (*climate*) sain. ◆**healthy** *a* (**-ier, -iest**) (*person*) en bonne santé, sain; (*food, attitude etc*) sain; (*appetite*) bon, robuste.

heap [hiːp] *n* tas *m*; **heaps of** *Fam* des tas de; **to have heaps of time** *Fam* avoir largement le temps; – *vt* entasser, empiler; **to h. on** s.o. (*gifts, praise*) couvrir qn de; (*work*) accabler qn de. ◆**—ed** *a* **h. spoonful** grosse cuillerée *f*. ◆**—ing** *a* **h. spoonful** *Am* grosse cuillerée *f*.

hear [hɪər] *vt* (*pt* & *pp* **heard** [hɜːd]) entendre; (*listen to*) écouter; (*learn*) apprendre (**that que**); **I heard him coming** je l'ai entendu venir; **to h. it said that** entendre dire que; **have you heard the news?** connais-tu la nouvelle?; **I've heard that ...** on m'a dit que ..., j'ai appris que ...; **to h. out** écouter jusqu'au bout; **h., h.!** bravo!; – *vi* entendre; (*get news*) recevoir *or* avoir des nouvelles (**from** de); **I've heard of** *or* **about him** j'ai entendu parler de lui; **she wouldn't h. of it** elle ne voulait pas en entendre parler; **I wouldn't h. of it!** pas question! ◆**—ing** *n* (*sense*) ouïe *f*; *Jur* audition *f*; **h. aid** appareil *m* auditif. ◆**hearsay** *n* ouï-dire *m inv*.

hearse [hɜːs] *n* corbillard *m*.

heart [hɑːt] *n* cœur *m*; *pl* *Cards* cœur *m*; (**off**) **by h.** par cœur; **to lose h.** perdre courage; **to one's h.'s content** tout son

saoul *or* content; **at h.** au fond; **his h. is set
on it** il le veut à tout prix, il y tient; **his h. is
set on doing it** il veut le faire à tout prix, il
tient à le faire; **h. disease** maladie *f* de
cœur; **h. attack** crise *f* cardiaque.
◆**heartache** *n* chagrin *m.* ◆**heartbeat** *n*
battement *m* de cœur. ◆**heartbreaking** *a*
navrant. ◆**heartbroken** *a* navré, au cœur
brisé. ◆**heartburn** *n Med* brûlures *fpl*
d'estomac. ◆**heartthrob** *n* (*man*) *Fam*
idole *f.*

hearten ['hɑːt(ə)n] *vt* encourager. ◆**—ing** *a*
encourageant.

hearth [hɑːθ] *n* foyer *m.*

hearty ['hɑːtɪ] *a* (**-ier, -iest**) (*meal, appetite*)
gros. ◆**heartily** *adv* (*to eat*) avec appétit;
(*to laugh*) de tout son cœur; (*absolutely*)
absolument.

heat [hiːt] **1** *n* chaleur *f;* (*of oven*) température *f;* (*heating*) chauffage *m;* **in the h. of**
(*argument etc*) dans le feu de; (*the day*) au
plus chaud de; **at low h., on a low h.** *Culin* à
feu doux; **h. wave** vague *f* de chaleur; – *vti*
to h. (up) chauffer. **2** *n* (*in race, competition*)
éliminatoire *f;* **it was a dead h.** ils sont
arrivés ex aequo. ◆**—ed** *a* (*swimming
pool*) chauffé; (*argument*) passionné.
◆**—edly** *adv* avec passion. ◆**—ing** *n*
chauffage *m.* ◆**—er** *n* radiateur *m,* appareil
m de chauffage; **water h.** chauffe-eau *m inv.*

heath [hiːθ] *n* (*place, land*) lande *f.*

heathen ['hiːð(ə)n] *a & n* païen, -enne (*mf*).

heather ['heðər] *n* (*plant*) bruyère *f.*

heave [hiːv] *vt* (*lift*) soulever; (*pull*) tirer;
(*drag*) traîner; (*throw*) *Fam* lancer; (*a sigh*)
pousser; – *vi* (*of stomach, chest*) se
soulever; (*retch*) *Fam* avoir des
haut-le-cœur; – *n* (*effort*) effort *m* (*pour
soulever etc*).

heaven ['hev(ə)n] *n* ciel *m,* paradis *m;* **h.
knows when** *Fam* Dieu sait quand; **good
heavens!** *Fam* mon Dieu!; **it was h.** *Fam*
c'était divin. ◆**—ly** *a* céleste; (*pleasing*)
Fam divin.

heavy ['hevɪ] *a* (**-ier, -iest**) lourd; (*weight etc*)
lourd, pesant; (*work, cold etc*) gros; (*blow*)
violent; (*concentration, rain*) fort; (*traffic*)
dense; (*smoker, drinker*) grand; (*film, text*)
difficile; **a h. day** une journée chargée; **h.
casualties** de nombreuses victimes; **to be h.
on petrol** *or Am* **gas** *Aut* consommer
beaucoup; **it's h. going** c'est difficile.
◆**heavily** *adv* (*to walk, tax etc*) lourdement; (*to breathe*) péniblement; (*to smoke,
drink*) beaucoup; (*underlined*) fortement;
(*involved*) très; **to rain h.** pleuvoir à verse.
◆**heaviness** *n* pesanteur *f,* lourdeur *f.*

◆**heavyweight** *n Boxing* poids *m* lourd;
Fig personnage *m* important.

Hebrew ['hiːbruː] *a* hébreu (*m only*),
hébraïque; – *n* (*language*) hébreu *m.*

heck [hek] *int Fam* zut!; – *n* = **hell** *in
expressions.*

heckl/e ['hek(ə)l] *vt* interpeller, interrompre. ◆**—ing** *n* interpellations *fpl.* ◆**—er**
n interpellateur, -trice *mf.*

hectic ['hektɪk] *a* (*activity*) fiévreux;
(*period*) très agité; (*trip*) mouvementé; **h.
life** vie *f* trépidante.

hedge [hedʒ] **1** *n Bot* haie *f.* **2** *vi* (*answer
evasively*) ne pas se mouiller, éviter de se
compromettre. ◆**hedgerow** *n Bot* haie *f.*

hedgehog ['hedʒhɒg] *n* (*animal*) hérisson
m.

heed [hiːd] *vt* faire attention à; – *n* **to pay h.
to** faire attention à. ◆**—less** *a* **h. of**
(*danger etc*) inattentif à.

heel [hiːl] *n* **1** talon *m;* **down at h.,** *Am* **down
at the heels** (*shabby*) miteux; **h. bar** cordonnerie *f* express; (*on sign*) 'talon minute'. **2**
(*person*) *Am Fam* salaud *m.*

hefty ['heftɪ] *a* (**-ier, -iest**) (*large, heavy*) gros;
(*person*) costaud.

heifer ['hefər] *n* (*cow*) génisse *f.*

height [haɪt] *n* hauteur *f;* (*of person*) taille *f;*
(*of mountain*) altitude *f;* **the h. of** (*glory,
success, fame*) le sommet de, l'apogée *m* de;
(*folly, pain*) le comble de; **at the h. of**
(*summer, storm*) au cœur de. ◆**heighten**
vt (*raise*) rehausser; (*tension, interest*) *Fig*
augmenter.

heinous ['heɪnəs] *a* (*crime etc*) atroce.

heir [eər] *n* héritier *m.* ◆**heiress** *n* héritière
f. ◆**heirloom** *n* héritage *m,* bijou *m or*
meuble *m* de famille.

heist [haɪst] *n Am Sl* hold-up *m inv.*

held [held] *see* **hold.**

helicopter ['helɪkɒptər] *n* hélicoptère *m.*
◆**heliport** *n* héliport *m.*

hell [hel] *n* enfer *m;* **a h. of a lot** (*very much*)
Fam énormément, vachement; **a h. of a lot
of** (*very many, very much*) *Fam* énormément de; **a h. of a nice guy** *Fam* un type
super; **what the h. are you doing?** *Fam*
qu'est-ce que tu fous?; **to h. with him** *Fam*
qu'il aille se faire voir; **h.!** *Fam* zut!; **to be
h.-bent on** *Fam* être acharné à. ◆**hellish** *a*
diabolique.

hello! [hə'ləʊ] *int* = **hallo.**

helm [helm] *n Nau* barre *f.*

helmet ['helmɪt] *n* casque *m.*

help [help] *n* aide *f,* secours *m;* (*cleaning
woman*) femme *f* de ménage; (*office or shop
workers*) employés, -ées *mfpl;* **with the h. of**

(*stick etc*) à l'aide de; **to cry** *or* **shout for h.** crier au secours; **h.!** au secours!; – *vt* aider (**do, to do** à faire); **to h. s.o. to soup**/*etc* (*serve*) servir du potage/*etc* à qn; **to h. out** aider; **to h. up** aider à monter; **to h. oneself** se servir (**to** de); **I can't h. laughing**/*etc* je ne peux m'empêcher de rire/*etc*; **he can't h. being blind**/*etc* ce n'est pas sa faute s'il est aveugle/*etc*; **it can't be helped** on n'y peut rien; – *vi* **to h.** (**out**) aider. ◆**—ing** *n* (*serving*) portion *f*. ◆**—er** *n* assistant, -ante *mf*. ◆**helpful** *a* (*useful*) utile; (*obliging*) serviable. ◆**helpless** *a* (*powerless*) impuissant; (*baby*) désarmé; (*disabled*) impotent. ◆**helplessly** *adv* (*to struggle*) en vain.

helter-skelter [heltə'skeltər] **1** *adv* à la débandade. **2** *n* (*slide*) toboggan *m*.

hem [hem] *n* ourlet *m*; – *vt* (**-mm-**) (*garment*) ourler; **to h. in** *Fig* enfermer, cerner.

hemisphere ['hemisfiər] *n* hémisphère *m*.

hemorrhage ['hemərıdʒ] *n Med* hémorragie *f*.

hemorrhoids ['hemərɔıdz] *npl* hémorroïdes *fpl*.

hemp [hemp] *n* chanvre *m*.

hen [hen] *n* poule *f*; **h. bird** oiseau *m* femelle. ◆**henpecked** *a* (*husband*) harcelé *or* dominé par sa femme.

hence [hens] *adv* **1** (*therefore*) d'où. **2** (*from now*) **ten years**/*etc* **h.** d'ici dix ans/*etc*. ◆**henceforth** *adv* désormais.

henchman ['hentʃmən] *n* (*pl* **-men**) *Pej* acolyte *m*.

hepatitis [hepə'taıtıs] *n* hépatite *f*.

her [hɜːr] **1** *pron* la, l'; (*after prep etc*) elle; (**to**) **h.** (*indirect*) lui; **I see h.** je la vois; **I saw h.** je l'ai vue; **I'll give** (**to**) **h.** je lui donne; **with h.** avec elle. **2** *poss a* son, sa, *pl* ses.

herald ['herəld] *vt* annoncer.

heraldry ['herəldrı] *n* héraldique *f*.

herb [hɜːb, *Am* ɜːb] *n* herbe *f*; *pl Culin* fines herbes *fpl*. ◆**herbal** *a* **h. tea** infusion *f* (d'herbes).

Hercules ['hɜːkjʊliːz] *n* (*strong man*) hercule *m*.

herd [hɜːd] *n* troupeau *m*; – *vti* **to h. together** (se) rassembler (en troupeau).

here [hıər] **1** *adv* ici; (*then*) alors; **h. is, h. are** voici; **h. he is** le voici; **h. she is** la voici; **this man h.** cet homme-ci; **I won't be h. tomorrow** je ne serai pas là demain; **h. and there** çà et là; **h. you are!** (*take this*) tenez!; **h.'s to you!** (*toast*) à la tienne! **2** *int* (*calling s.o.'s attention*) holà!, écoutez!; (*giving s.o. sth*) tenez! ◆**herea'bouts** *adv* par ici. ◆**here-**

'after *adv* après; (*in book*) ci-après. ◆**here'by** *adv* (*to declare*) par le présent acte. ◆**here'with** *adv* (*with letter*) *Com* ci-joint.

heredity [hı'redıtı] *n* hérédité *f*. ◆**hereditary** *a* héréditaire.

heresy ['herəsı] *n* hérésie *f*. ◆**heretic** *n* hérétique *mf*. ◆**he'retical** *a* hérétique.

heritage ['herıtıdʒ] *n* héritage *m*.

hermetically [hɜː'metıklı] *adv* hermétiquement.

hermit ['hɜːmıt] *n* solitaire *mf*, ermite *m*.

hernia ['hɜːnıə] *n Med* hernie *f*.

hero ['hıərəʊ] *n* (*pl* **-oes**) héros *m*. ◆**he'roic** *a* héroïque. ◆**he'roics** *npl Pej* grandiloquence *f*. ◆**heroine** ['herəʊın] *n* héroïne *f*. ◆**heroism** ['herəʊız(ə)m] *n* héroïsme *m*.

heroin ['herəʊın] *n* (*drug*) héroïne *f*.

heron ['herən] *n* (*bird*) héron *m*.

herring ['herıŋ] *n* hareng *m*; **a red h.** *Fig* une diversion.

hers [hɜːz] *poss pron* le sien, la sienne, *pl* les sien(ne)s; **this hat is h.** ce chapeau est à elle *or* est le sien; **a friend of h.** une amie à elle. ◆**her'self** *pron* elle-même; (*reflexive*) se, s'; (*after prep*) elle; **she cut h.** elle s'est coupée; **she thinks of h.** elle pense à elle.

hesitate ['hezıteıt] *vi* hésiter (**over, about** sur; **to do** à faire). ◆**hesitant** *a* hésitant. ◆**hesitantly** *adv* avec hésitation. ◆**hesi'tation** *n* hésitation *f*.

hessian ['hesıən] *n* toile *f* de jute.

heterogeneous [het(ə)rəʊ'dʒiːnıəs] *a* hétérogène.

het up [het'ʌp] *a Fam* énervé.

hew [hjuː] *vt* (*pp* **hewn** *or* **hewed**) tailler.

hexagon ['heksəgən] *n* hexagone *m*. ◆**hex'agonal** *a* hexagonal.

hey! [heı] *int* hé!, holà!

heyday ['heıdeı] *n* (*of person*) apogée *m*, zénith *m*; (*of thing*) âge *m* d'or.

hi! [haı] *int Am Fam* salut!

hiatus [haı'eıtəs] *n* (*gap*) hiatus *m*.

hibernate ['haıbəneıt] *vi* hiberner. ◆**hiber-'nation** *n* hibernation *f*.

hiccough, hiccup ['hıkʌp] *n* hoquet *m*; (**the**) **hiccoughs,** (**the**) **hiccups** le hoquet; – *vi* hoqueter.

hick [hık] *n* (*peasant*) *Am Sl Pej* plouc *mf*.

hide¹ [haıd] *vt* (*pt* **hid**, *pp* **hidden**) cacher, dissimuler (**from** à); – *vi* **to h.** (**away** *or* **out**) se cacher (**from** de). ◆**h.-and-'seek** *n* cache-cache *m inv*. ◆**h.-out** *n* cachette *f*. ◆**hiding** *n* **1 to go into h.** se cacher; **h. place** cachette *f*. **2 a good h.** (*thrashing*) *Fam* une bonne volée *or* correction.

hide² [haɪd] n (skin) peau f.
hideous ['hɪdɪəs] a horrible; (person, sight, crime) hideux. ◆—**ly** adv (badly, very) horriblement.
hierarchy ['haɪərɑːkɪ] n hiérarchie f.
hi-fi ['haɪfaɪ] n hi-fi f inv; (system) chaîne f hi-fi; – a hi-fi inv.
high [haɪ] a (-er, -est) haut; (speed) grand; (price) élevé; (fever) fort, gros; (colour, complexion) vif; (idea, number) grand, élevé; (meat, game) faisandé; (on drugs) Fam défoncé; **to be five metres h.** être haut de cinq mètres, avoir cinq mètres de haut; **it is h. time that** il est grand temps que (+ sub); **h. jump** Sp saut m en hauteur; **h. noon** plein midi m; **h. priest** grand prêtre m; **h. school** Am = collège m d'enseignement secondaire; **h. spirits** entrain m; **h. spot** (of visit, day) point m culminant; (of show) clou m; **h. street** grand-rue f; **h. summer** le cœur de l'été; **h. table** table f d'honneur; **h. and mighty** arrogant; **to leave s.o. h. and dry** Fam laisser qn en plan; – adv h. (up) (to fly, throw etc) haut; **to aim h.** viser haut; – n on **h.** en haut; **a new h., an all-time h.** (peak) Fig un nouveau record. ◆—**er** a supérieur (than à). ◆—**ly** adv hautement, fortement; (interesting) très; (paid) très bien; (to recommend) chaudement; **to speak h. of** dire beaucoup de bien de; **h. strung** nerveux. ◆—**ness** n H. (title) Altesse f.
highbrow ['haɪbraʊ] a & n intellectuel, -elle (mf).
high-chair ['haɪtʃeər] n chaise f haute. ◆**h.-'class** a (service) de premier ordre; (building) de luxe; (person) raffiné. ◆**h.-'flown** a (language) ampoulé. ◆**h.-'handed** a tyrannique. ◆**h.-'minded** a à l'âme noble. ◆**h.-'pitched** a (sound) aigu. ◆**h.-'powered** a (person) très dynamique. ◆**h.-rise** a h.-rise flats tour f. ◆**h.-'speed** a ultra-rapide. ◆**h.-'strung** a Am nerveux. ◆**h.-'up** a (person) haut placé.
highlands ['haɪləndz] npl régions fpl montagneuses.
highlight ['haɪlaɪt] n (of visit, day) point m culminant; (of show) clou m; (in hair) reflet m; – vt souligner.
highroad ['haɪrəʊd] n grand-route f.
highway ['haɪweɪ] n grande route f; Am autoroute f; **public h.** voie f publique; **h. code** code m de la route.
hijack ['haɪdʒæk] vt (aircraft, vehicle) détourner; – n détournement m. ◆—**ing** n (air piracy) piraterie f aérienne; (hijack)

détournement m. ◆—**er** n Av pirate m de l'air.
hik/e [haɪk] **1** n excursion f à pied; – vi marcher à pied. **2** vt (price) Am Fam augmenter; – n Am Fam hausse f. ◆—**er** n excursionniste mf.
hilarious [hɪ'leərɪəs] a (funny) désopilant.
hill [hɪl] n colline f; (small) coteau m; (slope) pente f. ◆**hillbilly** n Am Fam péquenaud, -aude mf. ◆**hillside** n coteau m; **on the h.** à flanc de coteau. ◆**hilly** a (-ier, -iest) accidenté.
hilt [hɪlt] n (of sword) poignée f; **to the h.** Fig au maximum.
him [hɪm] pron le, l'; (after prep etc) lui; **(to) h.** (indirect) lui; **I see h.** je le vois; **I saw h.** je l'ai vu; **I give (to) h.** je lui donne; **with h.** avec lui. ◆**him'self** pron lui-même; (reflexive) se, s'; (after prep) lui; **he cut h.** il s'est coupé; **he thinks of h.** il pense à lui.
hind [haɪnd] a de derrière, postérieur. ◆**hindquarters** npl arrière-train m.
hinder ['hɪndər] vt (obstruct) gêner; (prevent) empêcher (from doing de faire). ◆**hindrance** n gêne f.
hindsight ['haɪndsaɪt] n with h. rétrospectivement.
Hindu ['hɪnduː] a & n hindou, -oue (mf).
hing/e [hɪndʒ] **1** n (of box, stamp) charnière f; (of door) gond m, charnière f. **2** vi **to h. on** (depend on) dépendre de. ◆—**ed** a à charnière(s).
hint [hɪnt] n indication f; (insinuation) allusion f; (trace) trace f; pl (advice) conseils mpl; **to drop a h.** faire une allusion; – vt laisser entendre (that que); – vi **to h.** at faire allusion à.
hip [hɪp] n Anat hanche f.
hippie ['hɪpɪ] n hippie mf.
hippopotamus [hɪpə'pɒtəməs] n hippopotame m.
hire ['haɪər] vt (vehicle etc) louer; (person) engager; **to h. out** donner en location, louer; – n location f; (of boat, horse) louage m; **for h.** à louer; **on h.** en location; **h. purchase** vente f à crédit, location-vente f; **on h. purchase** à crédit.
his [hɪz] **1** poss a son, sa, pl ses. **2** poss pron le sien, la sienne, pl les siens; **this hat is h.** ce chapeau est à lui or est le sien; **a friend of h.** un ami à lui.
Hispanic [hɪs'pænɪk] a & n Am hispano-américain, -aine (mf).
hiss [hɪs] vti siffler; – n sifflement m; pl Th sifflets mpl. ◆—**ing** n sifflement(s) m(pl).
history ['hɪstərɪ] n (study, events) histoire f; **it will make h.** or go down in h. ça va faire

date; **your medical h.** vos antécédents médicaux. ◆**hi'storian** *n* historien, -ienne *mf*. ◆**hi'storic(al)** *a* historique.

histrionic [hɪstrɪ'ɒnɪk] *a Pej* théâtral; – *npl* attitudes *fpl* théâtrales.

hit [hɪt] *vti* (*pt & pp* hit, *pres p* hitting) (*strike*) frapper; (*knock against*) & *Aut* heurter; (*reach*) atteindre; (*affect*) toucher, affecter; (*find*) trouver, rencontrer; **to h. the headlines** *Fam* faire les gros titres; **to h. back** rendre coup pour coup; (*verbally, militarily etc*) riposter; **to h. it off** *Fam* s'entendre bien (**with** avec); **to h. out** (**at**) *Fam* attaquer; **to h. (up)on** (*find*) tomber sur; – *n* (*blow*) coup *m*; (*success*) coup *m* réussi; *Th* succès *m*; **h.** (**song**) chanson *f* à succès; **to make a h. with** *Fam* avoir un succès avec; **h.-and-run driver** chauffard *m* (*qui prend la fuite*). ◆**h.-or-'miss** *a* (*chancy, random*) aléatoire.

hitch [hɪtʃ] **1** *n* (*snag*) anicroche *f*, os *m*, problème *m*. **2** *vt* (*fasten*) accrocher (**to** à). **3** *vti* **to h.** (**a lift** *or* **a ride**) *Fam* faire du stop (**to** jusqu'à). ◆**hitchhike** *vi* faire de l'auto-stop (**to** jusqu'à). ◆**hitchhiking** *n* auto-stop *m*. ◆**hitchhiker** *n* auto-stoppeur, -euse *mf*.

hitherto [hɪðə'tuː] *adv* jusqu'ici.

hive [haɪv] **1** *n* ruche *f*. **2** *vt* **to h. off** (*industry*) dénationaliser.

hoard [hɔːd] *n* réserve *f*; (*of money*) trésor *m*; – *vt* amasser. ◆**—ing** *n* (*fence*) panneau *m* d'affichage.

hoarfrost ['hɔːfrɒst] *n* givre *m*.

hoarse [hɔːs] *a* (-er, -est) (*person, voice*) enroué. ◆**—ness** *n* enrouement *m*.

hoax [həʊks] *n* canular *m*; – *vt* faire un canular à, mystifier.

hob [hɒb] *n* (*on stove*) plaque *f* chauffante.

hobble ['hɒb(ə)l] *vi* (*walk*) clopiner.

hobby ['hɒbɪ] *n* passe-temps *m inv*; **my h.** mon passe-temps favori. ◆**hobbyhorse** *n* (*favourite subject*) dada *m*.

hobnob ['hɒbnɒb] *vi* (-bb-) **to h. with** frayer avec.

hobo ['həʊbəʊ] *n* (*pl* -oes *or* -os) *Am* vagabond *m*.

hock [hɒk] *vt* (*pawn*) *Fam* mettre au clou; – *n* **in h.** *Fam* au clou.

hockey ['hɒkɪ] *n* hockey *m*; **ice h.** hockey sur glace.

hocus-pocus [həʊkəs'pəʊkəs] *n* (*talk*) charabia *m*; (*deception*) tromperie *f*.

hodgepodge ['hɒdʒpɒdʒ] *n* fatras *m*.

hoe [həʊ] *n* binette *f*, houe *f*; – *vt* biner.

hog [hɒg] **1** *n* (*pig*) cochon *m*, porc *m*; **road h.** *Fig* chauffard *m*. **2** *n* **to go the whole h.**

Fam aller jusqu'au bout. **3** *vt* (-gg-) *Fam* monopoliser, garder pour soi.

hoist [hɔɪst] *vt* hisser; – *n Tech* palan *m*.

hold [həʊld] *n* (*grip*) prise *f*; (*of ship*) cale *f*; (*of aircraft*) soute *f*; **to get h. of** (*grab*) saisir; (*contact*) joindre; (*find*) trouver; **to get a h. of oneself** se maîtriser; – *vt* (*pt & pp* held) tenir; (*breath, interest, heat, attention*) retenir; (*a post*) occuper; (*a record*) détenir; (*weight*) supporter; (*possess*) posséder; (*contain*) contenir; (*maintain, believe*) maintenir (**that** que); (*ceremony, mass*) célébrer; (*keep*) garder; **to h. hands** se tenir par la main; **to h. one's own** se débrouiller; (*of sick person*) se maintenir; **h. the line!** *Tel* ne quittez pas!; **h. it!** (*stay still*) ne bouge pas!; **to be held** (*of event*) avoir lieu; **to h. back** (*crowd, tears*) contenir; (*hide*) cacher (**from** à); **to h. down** (*job*) occuper, (*keep*) garder; (*person on ground*) maintenir au sol; **to h. in** (*stomach*) rentrer; **to h. off** (*enemy*) tenir à distance; **to h. on** (*keep in place*) tenir en place (*son chapeau etc*); **to h. out** (*offer*) offrir; (*arm*) étendre; **to h. over** (*postpone*) remettre; **to h. together** (*nation, group*) assurer l'union de; **to h. up** (*raise*) lever; (*support*) soutenir; (*delay*) retarder; (*bank*) attaquer (à main armée); – *vi* (*of nail, rope*) tenir; (*of weather*) se maintenir; **to h. (good)** (*of argument*) valoir (**for** pour); **to h. forth** (*talk*) *Pej* disserter; **if the rain holds off** s'il ne pleut pas; **to h. on** (*endure*) tenir bon; (*wait*) attendre; **h. on!** *Tel* ne quittez pas!; **to h. onto** (*cling to*) tenir bien; (*keep*) garder; **h. on** (*tight*)! tenez bon!; **to h. out** (*resist*) résister; (*last*) durer. ◆**holdall** *n* (*bag*) fourre-tout *m inv*. ◆**holdup** *n* (*attack*) hold-up *m inv*; (*traffic jam*) bouchon *m*; (*delay*) retard *m*.

holder ['həʊldər] *n* (*of post, passport*) titulaire *mf*; (*of record, card*) détenteur, -trice *mf*; (*container*) support *m*.

holdings ['həʊldɪŋz] *npl Fin* possessions *fpl*.

hole [həʊl] *n* trou *m*; (*town etc*) *Fam* bled *m*, trou *m*; (*room*) *Fam* baraque *f*; – *vt* trouer; – *vi* **to h. up** (*hide*) *Fam* se terrer.

holiday ['hɒlɪdeɪ] *n* (*rest*) vacances *fpl*; **holiday(s)** (*from work, school etc*) vacances *fpl*; **a h.** (*day off*) un congé; **a** (**public** *or* **bank**) **h.**, *Am* **a legal h.** un jour férié; **on h.** en vacances; **holidays with pay** congés *mpl* payés; – *a* (*camp, clothes etc*) de vacances; **in h. mood** d'humeur folâtre. ◆**holidaymaker** *n* vacancier, -ière *mf*.

holiness ['həʊlɪnəs] *n* sainteté *f*.

Holland ['hɒlənd] *n* Hollande *f*.

hollow ['hɒləʊ] *a* creux; (*victory*) faux; (*promise*) vain; – *n* creux *m*; – *vt* to h. out creuser.

holly ['hɒlɪ] *n* houx *m*.

holocaust ['hɒləkɔːst] *n* (*massacre*) holocauste *m*.

holster ['həʊlstər] *n* étui *m* de revolver.

holy ['həʊlɪ] *a* (-ier, -iest) saint; (*bread, water*) bénit; (*ground*) sacré.

homage ['hɒmɪdʒ] *n* hommage *m*.

home ¹ [həʊm] *n* maison *f*; (*country*) pays *m* (natal); (*for soldiers*) foyer *m*; (at) h. à la maison, chez soi; to feel at h. se sentir à l'aise; to play at h. *Fb* jouer à domicile; far from h. loin de chez soi; a broken h. un foyer désuni; a good h. une bonne famille; to make one's h. in s'installer à or en; my h. is here j'habite ici; – *adv* à la maison, chez soi; to go or come h. rentrer; to be h. être rentré; to drive h. ramener (qn) (en voiture); (*nail*) enfoncer; to bring sth h. to s.o. *Fig* faire voir qch à qn; – *a* (*life, pleasures etc*) de famille; *Pol* national; (*cooking, help*) familial; (*visit, match*) à domicile; h. economics économie *f* domestique; h. town (*birth place*) ville *f* natale; h. rule *Pol* autonomie *f*; H. Office = ministère *m* de l'Intérieur; H. Secretary = ministre *m* de l'Intérieur. ◆**homecoming** *n* retour *m* au foyer. ◆**home'grown** *a Bot* du jardin; *Pol* du pays. ◆**homeland** *n* patrie *f*. ◆**homeloving** *a* casanier. ◆**home'made** *a* (fait à la) maison *inv*. ◆**homework** *n Sch* devoir(s) *m*(*pl*).

home ² [həʊm] *vi* to h. in on se diriger automatiquement sur.

homeless ['həʊmlɪs] *a* sans abri; – *n* the h. les sans-abri *m inv*.

homely ['həʊmlɪ] *a* (-ier, -iest) (*simple*) simple; (*comfortable*) accueillant; (*ugly*) *Am* laid.

homesick ['həʊmsɪk] *a* nostalgique; to be h. avoir le mal du pays. ◆**–ness** *n* nostalgie *f*, mal *m* du pays.

homeward ['həʊmwəd] *a* (*trip*) de retour; – *adv* h. bound sur le chemin de retour.

homey ['həʊmɪ] *a* (-ier, -iest) *Am Fam* accueillant.

homicide ['hɒmɪsaɪd] *n* homicide *m*.

homily ['hɒmɪlɪ] *n* homélie *f*.

homogeneous [həʊmə'dʒiːnɪəs] *a* homogène.

homosexual [həʊmə'sekʃʊəl] *a & n* homosexuel, -elle (*mf*). ◆**homosexu-'ality** *n* homosexualité *f*.

honest ['ɒnɪst] *a* honnête; (*frank*) franc (with avec); (*profit, money*) honnêtement

gagné; the h. truth la pure vérité; to be (quite) h.... pour être franc.... ◆**honesty** *n* honnêteté *f*; franchise *f*; (*of report, text*) exactitude *f*.

honey ['hʌnɪ] *n* miel *m*; (*person*) *Fam* chéri, -ie *mf*. ◆**honeycomb** *n* rayon *m* de miel. ◆**honeymoon** *n* (*occasion*) lune *f* de miel; (*trip*) voyage *m* de noces. ◆**honeysuckle** *n Bot* chèvrefeuille *f*.

honk [hɒŋk] *vi Aut* klaxonner; – *n* coup *m* de klaxon®.

honour ['ɒnər] *n* honneur *m*; in h. of en l'honneur de; an honours degree *Univ* = une licence; – *vt* honorer (with de). ◆**honorary** *a* (*member*) honoraire; (*title*) honorifique. ◆**honourable** *a* honorable.

hood [hʊd] *n* **1** capuchon *m*; (*mask of robber*) cagoule *f*; (*soft car or pram roof*) capote *f*; (*bonnet*) *Aut Am* capot *m*; (*above stove*) hotte *f*. **2** (*hoodlum*) *Am Sl* gangster *m*. ◆**hooded** *a* (*person*) encapuchonné; (*coat*) à capuchon.

hoodlum ['huːdləm] *n Fam* (*hooligan*) voyou *m*; (*gangster*) gangster *m*.

hoodwink ['hʊdwɪŋk] *vt* tromper, duper.

hoof, *pl* **-fs, -ves** [huːf, -fs, -vz] (*Am* [huf, -fs, huvz]) *n* sabot *m*.

hoo-ha ['huːhɑː] *n Fam* tumulte *m*.

hook [hʊk] *n* crochet *m*; (*on clothes*) agrafe *f*; *Fishing* hameçon *m*; (*phone*) décroché; to let or get s.o. off the h. tirer qn d'affaire; – *vt* to h. (on or up) accrocher (to à). ◆**–ed** *a* (*nose, beak*) recourbé, crochu; (*end, object*) recourbé; h. on *Fam* (*chess etc*) enragé de; (*person*) entiché de; to be h. on drugs *Fam* ne plus pouvoir se passer de la drogue. ◆**–er** *n Am Sl* prostituée *f*.

hook(e)y ['hʊkɪ] *n* to play h. *Am Fam* faire l'école buissonnière.

hooligan ['huːlɪgən] *n* vandale *m*, voyou *m*. ◆**hooliganism** *n* vandalisme *m*.

hoop [huːp] *n* cerceau *m*; (*of barrel*) cercle *m*.

hoot [huːt] **1** *vi Aut* klaxonner; (*of train*) siffler; (*of owl*) hululer; – *n Aut* coup *m* de klaxon®. **2** *vti* (*jeer*) huer; – *n* huée *f*. ◆**–er** *n Aut* klaxon® *m*; (*of factory*) sirène *f*.

hoover® ['huːvər] *n* aspirateur *m*; – *vt Fam* passer à l'aspirateur.

hop [hɒp] *vi* (-pp-) (*of person*) sauter (à cloche-pied); (*of animal*) sauter; (*of bird*) sautiller; h. in! (*in car*) montez!; to h. on a bus monter dans un autobus; to h. on a plane attraper un vol; – *vt* h. it! *Fam* fiche le camp!; – *n* (*leap*) saut *m*; *Av* étape *f*.

hope [həʊp] *n* espoir *m*, espérance *f*; – *vi*

espérer; **to h. for** (*desire*) espérer; (*expect*) attendre; **I h. so/not** j'espère que oui/non; – *vt* espérer (**to do** faire, **that** que). ◆**hopeful** *a* (*person*) optimiste, plein d'espoir; (*promising*) prometteur; (*encouraging*) encourageant; **to be h. that** avoir bon espoir que. ◆**hopefully** *adv* avec optimisme; (*one hopes*) on espère (que). ◆**hopeless** *a* désespéré, sans espoir; (*useless, bad*) nul; (*liar*) invétéré. ◆**hopelessly** *adv* sans espoir; (*extremely*) complètement; (*in love*) éperdument.

hops [hɒps] *npl Bot* houblon *m*.

hopscotch ['hɒpskɒtʃ] *n* (*game*) marelle *f*.

horde [hɔːd] *n* horde *f*, foule *f*.

horizon [hə'raɪz(ə)n] *n* horizon *m*; **on the h.** à l'horizon.

horizontal [hɒrɪ'zɒnt(ə)l] *a* horizontal. ◆**—ly** *adv* horizontalement.

hormone ['hɔːməʊn] *n* hormone *f*.

horn [hɔːn] **1** *n* (*of animal*) corne *f*; *Mus* cor *m*; *Aut* klaxon® *m*. **2** *vi* **to h. in** *Am Fam* dire son mot, interrompre.

hornet ['hɔːnɪt] *n* (*insect*) frelon *m*.

horoscope ['hɒrəskəʊp] *n* horoscope *m*.

horror ['hɒrər] *n* horreur *f*; (*little*) **h.** (*child*) *Fam* petit monstre *m*; – *a* (*film etc*) d'épouvante, d'horreur. ◆**ho'rrendous** *a* horrible. ◆**horrible** *a* horrible, affreux. ◆**horribly** *adv* horriblement. ◆**horrid** *a* horrible; (*child*) épouvantable, méchant. ◆**ho'rrific** *a* horrible, horrifiant. ◆**horrify** *vt* horrifier.

hors-d'œuvre [ɔː'dɜːv] *n* hors-d'œuvre *m inv*.

horse [hɔːs] *n* **1** cheval *m*; **to go h. riding** faire du cheval; **h. show** concours *m* hippique. **2 h. chestnut** marron *m* (d'Inde). ◆**horseback** *n* **on h.** à cheval. ◆**horseman** *n* (*pl* **-men**) cavalier *m*. ◆**horseplay** *n* jeux *mpl* brutaux. ◆**horsepower** *n* cheval *m* (vapeur). ◆**horseracing** *n* courses *fpl*. ◆**horseradish** *n* radis *m* noir, raifort *m*. ◆**horseshoe** *n* fer *m* à cheval. ◆**horsewoman** *n* (*pl* **-women**) cavalière *f*.

horticulture ['hɔːtɪkʌltʃər] *n* horticulture *f*. ◆**horti'cultural** *a* horticole.

hose [həʊz] *n* (*tube*) tuyau *m*; – *vt* (*garden etc*) arroser. ◆**hosepipe** *n* tuyau *m*.

hosiery ['həʊzɪərɪ, *Am* 'həʊʒərɪ] *n* bonneterie *f*.

hospice ['hɒspɪs] *n* (*for dying people*) hospice *m* (pour incurables).

hospitable [hɒ'spɪtəb(ə)l] *a* hospitalier. ◆**hospitably** *adv* avec hospitalité. ◆**hospi'tality** *n* hospitalité *f*.

hospital ['hɒspɪt(ə)l] *n* hôpital *m*; **in h.,** *Am* **in the h.** à l'hôpital; – *a* (*bed etc*) d'hôpital; (*staff, services*) hospitalier. ◆**hospitalize** *vt* hospitaliser.

host [həʊst] *n* **1** (*man who receives guests*) hôte *m*. **2 a h. of** (*many*) une foule de. **3** *Rel* hostie *f*. ◆**hostess** *n* (*in house, aircraft, nightclub*) hôtesse *f*.

hostage ['hɒstɪdʒ] *n* otage *m*; **to take s.o. h.** prendre qn en otage.

hostel ['hɒst(ə)l] *n* foyer *m*; **youth h.** auberge *f* de jeunesse.

hostile ['hɒstaɪl, *Am* 'hɒst(ə)l] *a* hostile (**to, towards** à). ◆**ho'stility** *n* hostilité *f* (**to, towards** envers); *pl Mil* hostilités *fpl*.

hot¹ [hɒt] *a* (**hotter, hottest**) chaud; (*spice*) fort; (*temperament*) passionné; (*news*) *Fam* dernier; (*favourite*) *Sp* grand; **to be** *or* **feel h.** avoir chaud; **it's h.** il fait chaud; **not so h. at** (*good at*) *Fam* pas très calé en; **not so h.** (*bad*) *Fam* pas fameux; ◆**. dog** (*sausage*) hot-dog *m*. ◆**hotbed** *n Pej* foyer *m* (of de). ◆**hot-'blooded** *a* ardent. ◆**hothead** *n* tête *f* brûlée. ◆**hot-'headed** *a* impétueux. ◆**hothouse** *n* serre *f* (chaude). ◆**hotplate** *n* chauffe-plats *m inv*; (*on stove*) plaque *f* chauffante. ◆**hot-'tempered** *a* emporté. ◆**hot-'water bottle** *n* bouillotte *f*.

hot² [hɒt] *vi* (**-tt-**) **to h. up** (*increase*) s'intensifier; (*become dangerous or excited*) chauffer.

hotchpotch ['hɒtʃpɒtʃ] *n* fatras *m*.

hotel [həʊ'tel] *n* hôtel *m*; – *a* (*industry*) hôtelier. ◆**hotelier** [həʊ'telɪeɪ] *n* hôtelier, -ière *mf*.

hotly ['hɒtlɪ] *adv* passionnément.

hound [haʊnd] **1** *n* (*dog*) chien *m* courant. **2** *vt* (*pursue*) poursuivre avec acharnement; (*worry*) harceler.

hour ['aʊər] *n* heure *f*; **half an h., a half-h.** une demi-heure; **a quarter of an h.** un quart d'heure; **paid ten francs an h.** payé dix francs (de) l'heure; **ten miles an h.** dix miles à l'heure; **open all hours** ouvert à toute heure; **h. hand** (*of watch, clock*) petite aiguille *f*. ◆**—ly** *a* (*rate, pay*) horaire; **an h. bus/train/etc** un bus/train/etc toutes les heures; – *adv* toutes les heures; **h. paid, paid h.** payé à l'heure.

house¹, *pl* **-ses** [haʊs, -zɪz] *n* maison *f*; (*audience*) *Th* salle *f*, auditoire *m*; (*performance*) *Th* séance *f*; **the H.** *Pol* la Chambre; **the Houses of Parliament** le Parlement; **at** *or* **to my h.** chez moi; **on the h.** (*free of charge*) aux frais de la maison; **h. prices** prix *mpl* immobiliers. ◆**housebound** *a* confiné chez soi. ◆**house-**

breaking n Jur cambriolage m. ◆**house-broken** a (dog etc) Am propre. ◆**household** n ménage m, maison f, famille f; **h. duties** soins mpl du ménage; **a h. name** un nom très connu. ◆**house-holder** n (owner) propriétaire mf; (family head) chef m de famille. ◆**housekeeper** n (employee) gouvernante f; (housewife) ménagère f. ◆**housekeeping** n ménage m. ◆**houseman** n (pl -men) interne mf (des hôpitaux). ◆**houseproud** a qui s'occupe méticuleusement de sa maison. ◆**housetrained** a (dog etc) propre. ◆**housewarming** n & a **to have a h.-warming (party)** pendre la crémaillère. ◆**housewife** n (pl -wives) ménagère f. ◆**housework** n (travaux mpl de) ménage m.

hous/e² [hauz] vt loger; (of building) abriter; **it is housed in** (kept) on le garde dans. ◆**—ing** n logement m; (houses) logements mpl; – a (crisis etc) du logement.

hovel ['hɒv(ə)l] n (slum) taudis m.

hover ['hɒvər] vi (of bird, aircraft, danger etc) planer; (of person) rôder, traîner. ◆**hovercraft** n aéroglisseur m.

how [hau] adv comment; **h.'s that?, h. so?, h. come?** Fam comment ça?; **h. kind!** comme c'est gentil!; **h. do you do?** (greeting) bonjour; **h. long/high is . . . ?** quelle est la longueur/hauteur de . . . ?; **h. much?, h. many?** combien?; **h. much time/etc?** combien de temps/etc?; **h. many apples/etc?** combien de pommes/etc?; **h. about a walk?** si on faisait une promenade?; **h. about some coffee?** (si on prenait) du café?; **h. about me?** et moi?

howdy! [haudi] int Am Fam salut!

however [hau'evər] **1** adv **h. big he may be** quelque or si grand qu'il soit; **h. she may do it** de quelque manière qu'elle le fasse; **h. that may be** quoi qu'il en soit. **2** conj cependant.

howl [haul] vi hurler; (of baby) brailler; (of wind) mugir; – n hurlement m; braillement m; mugissement m; (of laughter) éclat m.

howler ['haulər] n (mistake) Fam gaffe f.

HP [eitʃ'piː] abbr = **hire purchase**.

hp abbr (horsepower) CV.

HQ [eitʃ'kjuː] abbr = **headquarters**.

hub [hʌb] n (of wheel) moyeu m; Fig centre m. ◆**hubcap** n Aut enjoliveur m.

hubbub ['hʌbʌb] n vacarme m.

huckleberry ['hʌk(ə)lbəri] n Bot Am myrtille f.

huddle ['hʌd(ə)l] vi **to h. (together)** se blottir (les uns contre les autres).

hue [hjuː] n (colour) teinte f.

huff [hʌf] n **in a h.** (offended) Fam fâché.

hug [hʌg] vt (-gg-) (person) serrer dans ses bras, étreindre; **to h. the kerb/coast** (stay near) serrer le trottoir/la côte; – n (embrace) étreinte f.

huge [hjuːdʒ] a énorme. ◆**—ly** adv énormément. ◆**—ness** n énormité f.

hulk [hʌlk] n (person) lourdaud, -aude mf.

hull [hʌl] n (of ship) coque f.

hullabaloo [hʌləbə'luː] n Fam (noise) vacarme m; (fuss) histoire(s) f(pl).

hullo! [hʌ'ləu] int = **hallo**.

hum [hʌm] vi (-mm-) (of insect) bourdonner; (of person) fredonner; (of top, radio) ronfler; (of engine) vrombir; – vt (tune) fredonner; – n (of insect) bourdonnement m.

human ['hjuːmən] a humain; **h. being** être m humain; – npl humains mpl. ◆**hu'mane** a (kind) humain. ◆**hu'manely** adv humainement. ◆**humani'tarian** a & n humanitaire (mf). ◆**hu'manity** n (human beings, kindness) humanité f. ◆**humanly** adv (possible etc) humainement.

humble ['hʌmb(ə)l] a humble; – vt humilier. ◆**humbly** adv humblement.

humbug ['hʌmbʌg] n (talk) fumisterie f; (person) fumiste mf.

humdrum ['hʌmdrʌm] a monotone.

humid ['hjuːmɪd] a humide. ◆**hu'midify** vt humidifier. ◆**hu'midity** n humidité f.

humiliate [hjuːˈmɪlɪeɪt] vt humilier. ◆**humili'ation** n humiliation f. ◆**humility** n humilité f.

humour ['hjuːmər] **1** n (fun) humour m; (temper) humeur f; **to have a sense of h.** avoir le sens de l'humour; **in a good h.** de bonne humeur. **2** vt **to h. s.o.** faire plaisir à qn, ménager qn. ◆**humorist** n humoriste mf. ◆**humorous** a (book etc) humoristique; (person) plein d'humour. ◆**humorously** adv avec humour.

hump [hʌmp] **1** n (lump, mound) bosse f; – vt (one's back) voûter. **2** n **to have the h.** Fam (depression) avoir le cafard; (bad temper) être en rogne. ◆**humpback** a **h. bridge** Aut pont m en dos d'âne.

hunch [hʌntʃ] **1** vt (one's shoulders) voûter. **2** n (idea) Fam intuition f, idée f. ◆**hunchback** n bossu, -ue mf.

hundred ['hʌndrəd] a & n cent (m); **a h. pages** cent pages; **two h. pages** deux cents pages; **hundreds of** des centaines de.

◆**hundredfold** a centuple; – adv au centuple. ◆**hundredth** a & n centième (mf). ◆**hundredweight** n 112 livres (= 50,8 kg); Am 100 livres (= 45,3 kg).

hung [hʌŋ] see hang¹.

Hungary ['hʌŋgərɪ] n Hongrie f. ◆**Hun'garian** a & n hongrois, -oise (mf); – n (language) hongrois m.

hunger ['hʌŋgər] n faim f. ◆**hungry** a (-ier, -iest) to be or feel h. avoir faim; to go h. souffrir de la faim; to make h. donner faim à; **h. for** (news etc) avide de. ◆**hungrily** adv avidement.

hunk [hʌŋk] n (gros) morceau m.

hunt [hʌnt] n Sp chasse f; (search) recherche f (**for** de); – vt Sp chasser; (pursue) poursuivre; (seek) chercher; **to h. down** (fugitive etc) traquer; **to h. out** (information etc) dénicher; – vi Sp chasser; **to h. for sth** (re)chercher qch. ◆**—ing** n Sp chasse f. ◆**—er** n (person) chasseur m.

hurdle ['hɜːd(ə)l] n (fence) Sp haie f; Fig obstacle m.

hurl [hɜːl] vt (throw) jeter, lancer; (abuse) lancer; **to h. oneself at s.o.** se ruer sur qn.

hurly-burly ['hɜːlɪbɜːlɪ] n tumulte m.

hurray! [hʊ'reɪ] int hourra!

hurricane ['hʌrɪkən, Am 'hʌrɪkeɪn] n ouragan m.

hurry ['hʌrɪ] n hâte f; **in a h.** à la hâte, en hâte; **to be in a h.** être pressé; **to be in a h. to do** avoir hâte de faire; **there's no h.** rien ne presse; – vi se dépêcher, se presser (**to do** de faire); **to h. out** sortir à la hâte; **to h. along** or **on** or **up** se dépêcher; – vt (person) bousculer, presser; (pace) presser; **to h. one's meal** manger à toute vitesse; **to h. s.o. out** faire sortir qn à la hâte. ◆**hurried** a (steps, decision etc) précipité; (travail) fait à la hâte; (visit) éclair inv; **to be h.** (in a hurry) être pressé.

hurt [hɜːt] vt (pt & pp hurt) (physically) faire du mal à, blesser; (emotionally) faire de la peine à; (offend) blesser; (prejudice, damage) nuire à; **to h. s.o.'s feelings** blesser qn; **his arm hurts (him)** son bras lui fait mal; – vi faire mal; – n mal m; – a (injured) blessé. ◆**hurtful** a (remark) blessant.

hurtle ['hɜːt(ə)l] vi **to h. along** aller à toute vitesse; **to h. down** dégringoler.

husband ['hʌzbənd] n mari m.

hush [hʌʃ] int chut!; – n silence m; – vt (person) faire taire; (baby) calmer; **to h. up** (scandal) Fig étouffer. ◆**—ed** a (voice)

étouffé; (silence) profond. ◆**hush-hush** a Fam ultra-secret.

husk [hʌsk] n (of rice, grain) enveloppe f.

husky ['hʌskɪ] a (-ier, -iest) (voice) enroué, voilé.

hussy ['hʌsɪ] n Pej fripone f, coquine f.

hustings ['hʌstɪŋz] npl campagne f électorale, élections fpl.

hustle ['hʌs(ə)l] 1 vt (shove, rush) bousculer (qn); – vi (work busily) Am se démener (**to get sth** pour avoir qch). 2 n **h. and bustle** agitation f, activité f, tourbillon m.

hut [hʌt] n cabane f, hutte f.

hutch [hʌtʃ] n (for rabbit) clapier m.

hyacinth ['haɪəsɪnθ] n jacinthe f.

hybrid ['haɪbrɪd] a & n hybride (m).

hydrangea [haɪ'dreɪndʒə] n (shrub) hortensia m.

hydrant ['haɪdrənt] n (fire) h. bouche f d'incendie.

hydraulic [haɪ'drɒlɪk] a hydraulique.

hydroelectric [haɪdrəʊɪ'lektrɪk] a hydroélectrique.

hydrogen ['haɪdrədʒən] n Ch hydrogène m.

hyena [haɪ'iːnə] n (animal) hyène f.

hygiene ['haɪdʒiːn] n hygiène f. ◆**hy'gienic** a hygiénique.

hymn [hɪm] n Rel cantique m, hymne m.

hyper- ['haɪpər] pref hyper-.

hypermarket ['haɪpəmɑːkɪt] n hypermarché m.

hyphen ['haɪf(ə)n] n trait m d'union. ◆**hyphenat/e** vt mettre un trait d'union à. ◆**—ed** a (word) à trait d'union.

hypnosis [hɪp'nəʊsɪs] n hypnose f. ◆**hypnotic** a hypnotique. ◆**'hypnotism** n hypnotisme m. ◆**'hypnotist** n hypnotiseur m. ◆**'hypnotize** vt hypnotiser.

hypochondriac [haɪpə'kɒndriæk] n malade mf imaginaire.

hypocrisy [hɪ'pɒkrɪsɪ] n hypocrisie f. ◆**'hypocrite** n hypocrite mf. ◆**hypo'critical** a hypocrite.

hypodermic [haɪpə'dɜːmɪk] a hypodermique.

hypothesis, pl **-eses** [haɪ'pɒθɪsɪs, -ɪsiːz] n hypothèse f. ◆**hypo'thetical** a hypothétique.

hysteria [hɪ'stɪərɪə] n hystérie f. ◆**hysterical** a hystérique; (funny) Fam désopilant; **to be** or **become h.** (wildly upset) avoir une crise de nerfs. ◆**hysterically** adv (to cry) sans pouvoir s'arrêter; **to laugh h.** rire aux larmes. ◆**hysterics** npl (tears etc) crise f de nerfs; (laughter) crise f de rire.

I

I, i [aɪ] n I, i m.

I [aɪ] pron je, j'; (stressed) moi; **I want** je veux; **she and I** elle et moi.

ice/e¹ [aɪs] n glace f; (on road) verglas m; **i. (cream)** glace f; **black i.** (on road) verglas m; **i. cube** glaçon m; – vi to **i. (over)** (of lake) geler; (of windscreen) givrer. **◆—ed** a (tea) glacé. **◆iceberg** n iceberg m **◆icebox** n (box) & Fig glacière f; Am réfrigérateur m. **◆ice-'cold** a glacial; (drink) glacé. **◆ice-skating** n patinage m (sur glace). **◆icicle** n glaçon m.

ice/e² [aɪs] vt (cake) glacer. **◆—ing** n (on cake etc) glaçage m.

Iceland ['aɪslənd] n Islande f. **◆Ice'landic** a islandais.

icon ['aɪkɒn] n Rel icône f.

icy ['aɪsɪ] a (-ier, -iest) (water, hands, room) glacé; (manner, weather) glacial; (road etc) verglacé.

idea [aɪ'dɪə] n idée f (of de); **I have an i. that** ... j'ai l'impression que ...; **that's my i. of rest** c'est ce que j'appelle du repos; **that's the i.!** Fam c'est ça!; **not the slightest or foggiest i.** pas la moindre idée.

ideal [aɪ'dɪəl] a idéal; – n (aspiration) idéal m; pl (spiritual etc) idéal m. **◆idealism** n idéalisme m. **◆idealist** n idéaliste mf. **◆idea'listic** a idéaliste. **◆idealize** vt idéaliser. **◆ideally** adv idéalement; **i. we should stay** l'idéal, ce serait de rester or que nous restions.

identical [aɪ'dentɪk(ə)l] a identique (**to, with** à). **◆identifi'cation** n identification f; **I have (some) i.** j'ai une pièce d'identité. **◆identify** vt identifier; **to i. (oneself) with** s'identifier avec. **◆identikit** n portrait-robot m. **◆identity** n identité f; **i. card** carte f d'identité.

ideology [aɪdɪ'ɒlədʒɪ] n idéologie f. **◆ideo-'logical** a idéologique.

idiom ['ɪdɪəm] n expression f idiomatique; (language) idiome m. **◆idio'matic** a idiomatique.

idiosyncrasy [ɪdɪə'sɪŋkrəsɪ] n particularité f.

idiot ['ɪdɪət] n idiot, -ote mf. **◆idiocy** n idiotie f. **◆idi'otic** a idiot, bête. **◆idi'otically** adv idiotement.

idle ['aɪd(ə)l] a (unoccupied) désœuvré, oisif;

(lazy) paresseux; (unemployed) en chômage; (moment) de loisir; (machine) au repos; (promise) vain; (pleasure, question) futile; (rumour) sans fondement; – vi (laze about) paresser; (of machine, engine) tourner au ralenti; – vt to **i. away** (time) gaspiller. **◆—ness** n oisiveté f; (laziness) paresse f. **◆idler** n paresseux, -euse mf. **◆idly** adv paresseusement; (to suggest, say) négligemment.

idol ['aɪd(ə)l] n idole f. **◆idolize** vt idolâtrer.

idyllic [aɪ'dɪlɪk] a idyllique.

i.e. [aɪ'iː] abbr (id est) c'est-à-dire.

if [ɪf] conj si; **if he comes** s'il vient; **even if** même si; **if so** dans ce cas, si c'est le cas; **if not for pleasure** sinon pour le plaisir; **if only I were rich** si seulement j'étais riche; **if only to look** ne serait-ce que pour regarder; **as if** comme si; **as if nothing had happened** comme si de rien n'était; **as if to say** comme pour dire; **if necessary** s'il le faut.

igloo ['ɪgluː] n igloo m.

ignite [ɪg'naɪt] vt mettre le feu à; – vi prendre feu. **◆ignition** n Aut allumage m; **to switch on the i.** mettre le contact.

ignominious [ɪgnə'mɪnɪəs] a déshonorant, ignominieux.

ignoramus [ɪgnə'reɪməs] n ignare mf.

ignorance ['ɪgnərəns] n ignorance f (of de). **◆ignorant** a ignorant (of de). **◆ignorantly** adv par ignorance.

ignore [ɪg'nɔːr] vt ne prêter aucune attention à, ne tenir aucun compte de; (duty) méconnaître; (pretend not to recognize) faire semblant de ne pas reconnaître.

ilk [ɪlk] n of that i. (kind) de cet acabit.

ill [ɪl] a (sick) malade; (bad) mauvais; **i. will** malveillance f; – npl (misfortunes) maux mpl, malheurs mpl; – adv mal; **to speak i. of** dire du mal de. **◆ill-ad'vised** a malavisé, peu judicieux. **◆ill-'fated** a malheureux. **◆ill-'gotten** a mal acquis. **◆ill-in'formed** a mal renseigné. **◆ill-'mannered** a mal élevé. **◆ill-'natured** a (mean, unkind) désagréable. **◆ill-'timed** a inopportun. **◆ill-'treat** vt maltraiter.

illegal [ɪ'liːg(ə)l] a illégal. **◆ille'gality** n illégalité f.

illegible [ɪ'ledʒəb(ə)l] a illisible.

illegitimate [ɪlɪˈdʒɪtɪmət] a (child, claim) illégitime. ◆**illegitimacy** n illégitimité f.

illicit [ɪˈlɪsɪt] a illicite.

illiterate [ɪˈlɪtərət] a & n illettré, -ée (mf), analphabète (mf). ◆**illiteracy** n analphabétisme m.

illness [ˈɪlnɪs] n maladie f.

illogical [ɪˈlɒdʒɪk(ə)l] a illogique.

illuminate [ɪˈluːmɪneɪt] vt (street, question etc) éclairer; (monument etc for special occasion) illuminer. ◆**illumiˈnation** n éclairage m; illumination f.

illusion [ɪˈluːʒ(ə)n] n illusion f (about sur); **I'm not under any i.** je ne me fais aucune illusion (about sur, quant à). ◆**illusive** a, ◆**illusory** a illusoire.

illustrate [ˈɪləstreɪt] vt (with pictures, examples) illustrer (with de). ◆**illuˈstration** n illustration f. ◆**iˈllustrative** a (example) explicatif.

illustrious [ɪˈlʌstrɪəs] a illustre.

image [ˈɪmɪdʒ] n image f; (public) i. (of firm etc) image f de marque; **he's the** (living or spitting or very) **i. of his brother** c'est (tout) le portrait de son frère. ◆**imagery** n images fpl.

imagin/e [ɪˈmædʒɪn] vt (picture to oneself) (s')imaginer, se figurer (that que); (suppose) imaginer (that que); **i. that ...** imaginez que ...; **you're imagining (things)!** tu te fais des illusions! ◆**—ings** npl (dreams) imaginations fpl. ◆**—able** a imaginable; **the worst thing i.** le pire que l'on puisse imaginer. ◆**imaginary** a imaginaire. ◆**imagiˈnation** n imagination f. ◆**imaginative** a plein d'imagination, imaginatif.

imbalance [ɪmˈbæləns] n déséquilibre m.

imbecile [ˈɪmbəsiːl, Am ˈɪmbəs(ə)l] a & n imbécile (mf). ◆**imbeˈcility** n imbécillité f.

imbibe [ɪmˈbaɪb] vt absorber.

imbued [ɪmˈbjuːd] a **i. with** (ideas) imprégné de; (feelings) pénétré de, imbu de.

imitate [ˈɪmɪteɪt] vt imiter. ◆**imiˈtation** n imitation f; – a (jewels) artificiel; **i. leather** imitation f cuir. ◆**imitative** a imitateur. ◆**imitator** n imitateur, -trice mf.

immaculate [ɪˈmækjʊlət] a (person, appearance, shirt etc) impeccable.

immaterial [ɪməˈtɪərɪəl] a peu important (to pour).

immature [ɪməˈtʃʊər] a (fruit) vert; (animal) jeune; (person) qui manque de maturité.

immeasurable [ɪˈmeʒərəb(ə)l] a incommensurable.

immediate [ɪˈmiːdɪət] a immédiat. ◆**immediacy** n caractère m immédiat. ◆**immediately** adv (at once) tout de suite, immédiatement; (to concern, affect) directement; – conj (as soon as) dès que.

immense [ɪˈmens] a immense. ◆**immensely** adv (rich etc) immensément; **to enjoy oneself i.** s'amuser énormément. ◆**immensity** n immensité f.

immerse [ɪˈmɜːs] vt plonger, immerger; **immersed in work** plongé dans le travail. ◆**immersion** n immersion f; **i. heater** chauffe-eau m inv électrique.

immigrate [ˈɪmɪgreɪt] vi immigrer. ◆**immigrant** n immigrant, -ante mf; (long-established) immigré, -ée mf; – a immigré. ◆**immiˈgration** n immigration f.

imminent [ˈɪmɪnənt] a imminent. ◆**imminence** n imminence f.

immobile [ɪˈməʊbaɪl, Am ɪˈməʊb(ə)l] a immobile. ◆**immoˈbility** n immobilité f. ◆**immobilize** vt immobiliser.

immoderate [ɪˈmɒdərət] a immodéré.

immodest [ɪˈmɒdɪst] a impudique.

immoral [ɪˈmɒrəl] a immoral. ◆**immoˈrality** n immoralité f.

immortal [ɪˈmɔːt(ə)l] a immortel. ◆**immorˈtality** n immortalité f. ◆**immortalize** vt immortaliser.

immune [ɪˈmjuːn] a Med & Fig immunisé (to, from contre). ◆**immunity** n immunité f. ◆**ˈimmunize** vt immuniser (against contre).

immutable [ɪˈmjuːtəb(ə)l] a immuable.

imp [ɪmp] n diablotin m, lutin m.

impact [ˈɪmpækt] n impact m (on sur).

impair [ɪmˈpeər] vt détériorer; (hearing, health) abîmer.

impale [ɪmˈpeɪl] vt empaler.

impart [ɪmˈpɑːt] vt communiquer (to à).

impartial [ɪmˈpɑːʃ(ə)l] a impartial. ◆**impartiˈality** n impartialité f.

impassable [ɪmˈpɑːsəb(ə)l] a (road) impraticable; (river) infranchissable.

impasse [ˈæmpɑːs, Am ˈɪmpæs] n (situation) impasse f.

impassioned [ɪmˈpæʃ(ə)nd] a (speech etc) enflammé, passionné.

impassive [ɪmˈpæsɪv] a impassible. ◆**—ness** n impassibilité f.

impatient [ɪmˈpeɪʃ(ə)nt] a impatient (to do de faire); **i. of or with** intolérant à l'égard de. ◆**impatience** n impatience f. ◆**impatiently** adv impatiemment.

impeccab/le [ɪmˈpekəb(ə)l] a impeccable. ◆**—ly** adv impeccablement.

impecunious [ɪmpɪ'kjuːnɪəs] a Hum sans le sou, impécunieux.

impede [ɪm'piːd] vt (hamper) gêner; **to i. s.o. from doing** (prevent) empêcher qn de faire.

impediment [ɪm'pedɪmənt] n obstacle m; (of speech) défaut m d'élocution.

impel [ɪm'pel] vt (-ll-) (drive) pousser; (force) obliger (**to do** à faire).

impending [ɪm'pendɪŋ] a imminent.

impenetrable [ɪm'penɪtrəb(ə)l] a (forest, mystery etc) impénétrable.

imperative [ɪm'perətɪv] a (need, tone) impérieux; (necessary) essentiel; **it is i. that you come** il faut absolument que or il est indispensable que tu viennes; – n Gram impératif m.

imperceptible [ɪmpə'septəb(ə)l] a imperceptible (**to** à).

imperfect [ɪm'pɜːfɪkt] **1** a imparfait; (goods) défectueux. **2** n (tense) Gram imparfait m. ◆**imper'fection** n imperfection f.

imperial [ɪm'pɪərɪəl] a impérial; (majestic) majestueux; (measure) Br légal. ◆**imperialism** n impérialisme m.

imperil [ɪm'perɪl] vt (-ll-, Am -l-) mettre en péril.

imperious [ɪm'pɪərɪəs] a impérieux.

impersonal [ɪm'pɜːsən(ə)l] a impersonnel.

impersonate [ɪm'pɜːsəneɪt] vt (mimic) imiter; (pretend to be) se faire passer pour. ◆**imperso'nation** n imitation f. ◆**impersonator** n imitateur, -trice mf.

impertinent [ɪm'pɜːtɪnənt] a impertinent (**to** envers). ◆**impertinence** n impertinence f. ◆**impertinently** adv avec impertinence.

impervious [ɪm'pɜːvɪəs] a imperméable (**to** à).

impetuous [ɪm'petjʊəs] a impétueux. ◆**impetu'osity** n impétuosité f.

impetus ['ɪmpɪtəs] n impulsion f.

impinge [ɪm'pɪndʒ] vi **to i. on** (affect) affecter; (encroach on) empiéter sur.

impish ['ɪmpɪʃ] a (naughty) espiègle.

implacable [ɪm'plækəb(ə)l] a implacable.

implant [ɪm'plɑːnt] vt (ideas) inculquer (**in** à).

implement¹ ['ɪmplɪmənt] n (tool) instrument m; (utensil) Culin ustensile m; pl Agr matériel m.

implement² ['ɪmplɪment] vt (carry out) mettre en œuvre, exécuter. ◆**implemen'tation** n mise f en œuvre, exécution f.

implicate ['ɪmplɪkeɪt] vt impliquer (**in** dans). ◆**impli'cation** n (consequence, involvement) implication f; (innuendo) insinuation f; (impact) portée f; **by i.** implicitement.

implicit [ɪm'plɪsɪt] a (implied) implicite;

(belief, obedience etc) absolu. ◆**—ly** adv implicitement.

implore [ɪm'plɔːr] vt implorer (**s.o. to do** qn de faire).

imply [ɪm'plaɪ] vt (assume) impliquer, supposer (**that** que); (suggest) laisser entendre (**that** que); (insinuate) Pej insinuer (**that** que). ◆**implied** a implicite.

impolite [ɪmpə'laɪt] a impoli. ◆**—ness** n impolitesse f.

import 1 [ɪm'pɔːt] vt (goods etc) importer (**from** de); – ['ɪmpɔːt] n (object, action) importation f. **2** ['ɪmpɔːt] n (meaning) sens m. ◆**im'porter** n importateur, -trice mf.

importance [ɪm'pɔːtəns] n importance f; **to be of i.** avoir de l'importance; **of no i.** sans importance. ◆**important** a (significant) important. ◆**importantly** adv **more i.** ce qui est plus important.

impose [ɪm'pəʊz] vt imposer (**on** à); (fine, punishment) infliger (**on** à); **to i. (oneself) on s.o.** s'imposer à qn; – vi s'imposer. ◆**impo'sition** n imposition f (**of** de); (inconvenience) dérangement m.

impossible [ɪm'pɒsəb(ə)l] a impossible (**to do** à faire); **it is i. (for us) to do** il (nous) est impossible de faire; **it is i.** that il est impossible que (+ sub); **to make it i. for s.o. to do** mettre qn dans l'impossibilité de faire; – n **to do the i.** faire l'impossible. ◆**impossi'bility** n impossibilité f. ◆**impossibly** adv (late, hard) incroyablement.

impostor [ɪm'pɒstər] n imposteur m.

impotent ['ɪmpətənt] a Med impuissant. ◆**impotence** n Med impuissance f.

impound [ɪm'paʊnd] vt (of police) saisir, confisquer; (vehicle) emmener à la fourrière.

impoverish [ɪm'pɒvərɪʃ] vt appauvrir.

impracticable [ɪm'præktɪkəb(ə)l] a irréalisable, impraticable.

impractical [ɪm'præktɪk(ə)l] a peu réaliste.

imprecise [ɪmprɪ'saɪs] a imprécis.

impregnable [ɪm'pregnəb(ə)l] a Mil imprenable; (argument) Fig inattaquable.

impregnate ['ɪmpregneɪt] vt (imbue) imprégner (**with** de); (fertilize) féconder.

impresario [ɪmprɪ'sɑːrɪəʊ] n (pl -os) impresario m.

impress [ɪm'pres] vt impressionner (qn); (mark) imprimer; **to i. sth on s.o.** faire comprendre qch à qn. ◆**impression** n impression f; **to be under** or **have the i.** that avoir l'impression que; **to make a good i. on s.o.** faire une bonne impression à qn. ◆**impressionable** a (person) impression-

nable; (*age*) où l'on est impressionnable.
◆**Impressive** *a* impressionnant.

imprint [ɪmˈprɪnt] *vt* imprimer; – [ˈɪmprɪnt] *n* empreinte *f*.

imprison [ɪmˈprɪz(ə)n] *vt* emprisonner. ◆**—ment** *n* emprisonnement *m*; **life i.** la prison à vie.

improbable [ɪmˈprɒbəb(ə)l] *a* improbable; (*story, excuse*) invraisemblable. ◆**improba'bility** *n* improbabilité *f*; invraisemblance *f*.

impromptu [ɪmˈprɒmptjuː] *a* & *adv* impromptu.

improper [ɪmˈprɒpər] *a* (*indecent*) inconvenant, indécent; (*wrong*) incorrect. ◆**impropriety** [ɪmprəˈpraɪətɪ] *n* inconvenance *f*; (*wrong use*) *Ling* impropriété *f*.

improve [ɪmˈpruːv] *vt* améliorer; (*mind*) cultiver, développer; **to i. one's English** se perfectionner en anglais; **to i. s.o.'s looks** embellir qn; **to i. oneself** se cultiver; – *vi* s'améliorer; (*of business*) aller de mieux en mieux, reprendre; **to i. on** (*do better than*) faire mieux que. ◆**—ment** *n* amélioration *f*; (*of mind*) développement *m*; (*progress*) progrès *m(pl)*; **there has been some** *or* **an i.** il y a du mieux.

improvise [ˈɪmprəvaɪz] *vti* improviser. ◆**improvi'sation** *n* improvisation *f*.

impudent [ˈɪmpjʊdənt] *a* impudent. ◆**impudence** *n* impudence *f*.

impulse [ˈɪmpʌls] *n* impulsion *f*; **on i.** sur un coup de tête. ◆**im'pulsive** *a* (*person, act*) impulsif, irréfléchi; (*remark*) irréfléchi. ◆**im'pulsively** *adv* de manière impulsive.

impunity [ɪmˈpjuːnɪtɪ] *n* **with i.** impunément.

impure [ɪmˈpjʊər] *a* impur. ◆**impurity** *n* impureté *f*.

in [ɪn] *prep* **1** dans; **in the box/the school/etc** dans la boîte/l'école/*etc*; **in an hour('s time)** dans une heure; **in so far as** dans la mesure où. **2** à; **in school** à l'école; **in the garden** dans le jardin, au jardin; **in Paris** à Paris; **in the USA** aux USA; **in Portugal** au Portugal; **in fashion** à la mode; **in pencil** au crayon; **in my opinion** à mon avis. **3** en; **in summer/secret/French** en été/secret/français; **in Spain** en Espagne; **in May** en mai, au mois de mai; **in season** en saison; **in an hour** (*during the period of an hour*) en une heure; **in doing en** faisant; **dressed in black** habillé en noir; **in all** en tout. **4** de; **in a soft voice** d'une voix douce; **the best in the class** le meilleur de la classe. **5** **in the rain** sous la pluie; **in the morning** le matin; **he hasn't done it in years** ça fait des années qu'il ne l'a pas fait; **in an hour** (*at the end of*

an hour) au bout d'une heure; **one in ten** un sur dix; **in thousands** par milliers; **in here** ici; **in there** là-dedans. **6** *adv* **to be in** (*home*) être là, être à la maison; (*of train*) être arrivé; (*in fashion*) être en vogue; (*in season*) être en saison; (*in power*) *Pol* être au pouvoir; **day in day out** jour après jour; **in on** (*a secret*) au courant de; **we're in for some rain/trouble/etc** on va avoir de la pluie/des ennuis/*etc*; **it's the in thing** *Fam* c'est dans le vent. **7** *npl* **the ins and outs of** les moindres détails de.

inability [ɪnəˈbɪlɪtɪ] *n* incapacité *f* (**to do** de faire).

inaccessible [ɪnəkˈsesəb(ə)l] *a* inaccessible.

inaccurate [ɪnˈækjʊrət] *a* inexact. ◆**inaccuracy** *n* inexactitude *f*.

inaction [ɪnˈækʃ(ə)n] *n* inaction *f*.

inactive [ɪnˈæktɪv] *a* inactif; (*mind*) inerte. ◆**inac'tivity** *n* inactivité *f*, inaction *f*.

inadequate [ɪnˈædɪkwət] *a* (*quantity*) insuffisant; (*person*) pas à la hauteur, insuffisant; (*work*) médiocre. ◆**inadequacy** *n* insuffisance *f*. ◆**inadequately** *adv* insuffisamment.

inadmissible [ɪnədˈmɪsəb(ə)l] *a* inadmissible.

inadvertently [ɪnədˈvɜːtəntlɪ] *adv* par inadvertance.

inadvisable [ɪnədˈvaɪzəb(ə)l] *a* (*action*) à déconseiller; **it is i. to** il est déconseillé de.

inane [ɪˈneɪn] *a* (*absurd*) inepte.

inanimate [ɪnˈænɪmət] *a* inanimé.

inappropriate [ɪnəˈprəʊprɪət] *a* (*unsuitable*) peu approprié, inadéquat; (*untimely*) inopportun.

inarticulate [ɪnɑːˈtɪkjʊlət] *a* (*person*) incapable de s'exprimer; (*sound*) inarticulé.

inasmuch as [ɪnəzˈmʌtʃəz] *adv* (*because*) vu que; (*to the extent that*) en ce sens que.

inattentive [ɪnəˈtentɪv] *a* inattentif (**to** à).

inaudible [ɪnˈɔːdɪb(ə)] *a* inaudible.

inaugural [ɪˈnɔːgjʊrəl] *a* inaugural. ◆**inaugurate** *vt* (*policy, building*) inaugurer; (*official*) installer (dans ses fonctions). ◆**inaugu'ration** *n* inauguration *f*, investiture *f*.

inauspicious [ɪnɔːˈspɪʃəs] *a* peu propice.

inborn [ɪnˈbɔːn] *a* inné.

inbred [ɪnˈbred] *a* (*quality etc*) inné.

Inc *abbr* (*Incorporated*) *Am Com* SA, SARL.

incalculable [ɪnˈkælkjʊləb(ə)l] *a* incalculable.

incandescent [ɪnkænˈdes(ə)nt] *a* incandescent.

incapable [ɪnˈkeɪpəb(ə)l] *a* incapable (**of**

doing de faire); **i. of** (*pity etc*) inaccessible à.

incapacitate [ɪnkə'pæsɪteɪt] *vt Med* rendre incapable (*de travailler etc*). ◆**incapacity** *n* (*inability*) *Med* incapacité *f*.

incarcerate [ɪn'kɑɪsəreɪt] *vt* incarcérer. ◆**incarce'ration** *n* incarcération *f*.

incarnate [ɪn'kɑɪnət] *a* incarné; — [ɪn'kɑɪneɪt] *vt* incarner. ◆**incar'nation** *n* incarnation *f*.

incendiary [ɪn'sendɪərɪ] *a* (*bomb*) incendiaire.

incense 1 [ɪn'sens] *vt* mettre en colère. **2** [ɪnsens] *n* (*substance*) encens *m*.

incentive [ɪn'sentɪv] *n* encouragement *m*, motivation *f*; **to give s.o. an i. to work**/*etc* encourager qn à travailler/*etc*.

inception [ɪn'sepʃ(ə)n] *n* début *m*.

incessant [ɪn'ses(ə)nt] *a* incessant. ◆**—ly** *adv* sans cesse.

incest [ɪnsest] *n* inceste *m*. ◆**in'cestuous** *a* incestueux.

inch [ɪntʃ] *n* pouce *m* (= 2,54 *cm*); (*loosely*) *Fig* centimètre *m*; **within an i. of** (*success*) à deux doigts de; **i. by i.** petit à petit; — *vti to* **i. (one's way) forward** avancer petit à petit.

incidence [ɪnsɪdəns] *n* fréquence *f*.

incident [ɪnsɪdənt] *n* incident *m*; (*in book, film etc*) épisode *m*.

incidental [ɪnsɪ'dent(ə)l] *a* accessoire, secondaire; (*music*) de fond; **i. expenses** frais *mpl* accessoires. ◆**—ly** *adv* accessoirement; (*by the way*) à propos.

incinerate [ɪn'sɪnəreɪt] *vt* (*refuse, leaves etc*) incinérer. ◆**incinerator** *n* incinérateur *m*.

incipient [ɪn'sɪpɪənt] *a* naissant.

incision [ɪn'sɪʒ(ə)n] *n* incision *f*.

incisive [ɪn'saɪsɪv] *a* incisif.

incisor [ɪn'saɪzər] *n* (*tooth*) incisive *f*.

incite [ɪn'saɪt] *vt* inciter (**to do** à faire). ◆**—ment** *n* incitation *f* (**to do** à faire).

incline 1 [ɪn'klaɪn] *vt* (*tilt, bend*) incliner; **to i. s.o. to do** incliner qn à faire; **to be inclined to do** (*feel a wish to*) être enclin à faire; (*tend to*) avoir tendance à faire; — *vi to* **i. or be inclined towards** (*indulgence etc*) incliner à. **2** [ɪnklaɪn] *n* (*slope*) inclinaison *f*. ◆**incli'nation** *n* inclination *f*; **to have no i. to do** n'avoir aucune envie de faire.

includ/e [ɪn'kluːd] *vt* (*contain*) comprendre, englober; (*refer to*) s'appliquer à; **my invitation includes you** mon invitation s'adresse aussi à vous; **to be included** être compris; (*on list*) être inclus. ◆**—ing** *prep* y compris; **i. service** service *m* compris. ◆**inclusion** *n* inclusion *f*. ◆**inclusive** *a* inclus; **from the fourth to the tenth of May**

i. du quatre jusqu'au dix mai inclus(ivement); **to be i. of** comprendre; **i. charge** prix *m* global.

incognito [ɪnkɒg'niːtəʊ] *adv* incognito.

incoherent [ɪnkəʊ'hɪərənt] *a* incohérent. ◆**—ly** *adv* sans cohérence.

income [ɪnkʌm] *n* revenu *m*; **private i.** rentes *fpl*; **i. tax** impôt *m* sur le revenu.

incoming [ɪnkʌmɪŋ] *a* (*tenant, president*) nouveau; **i. tide** marée *f* montante; **i. calls** *Tel* appels *mpl* de l'extérieur.

incommunicado [ɪnkəmjuːnɪ'kɑːdəʊ] *a* (*tenu*) au secret.

incomparable [ɪn'kɒmpərəb(ə)l] *a* incomparable.

incompatible [ɪnkəm'pætəb(ə)l] *a* incompatible (**with** avec). ◆**incompati'bility** *n* incompatibilité *f*.

incompetent [ɪn'kɒmpɪtənt] *a* incompétent. ◆**incompetence** *n* incompétence *f*.

incomplete [ɪnkəm'pliːt] *a* incomplet.

incomprehensible [ɪnkɒmprɪ'hensəb(ə)l] *a* incompréhensible.

inconceivable [ɪnkən'siːvəb(ə)l] *a* inconcevable.

inconclusive [ɪnkən'kluːsɪv] *a* peu concluant.

incongruous [ɪn'kɒŋgruəs] *a* (*building, colours*) qui jure(nt) (**with** avec); (*remark, attitude*) incongru; (*absurd*) absurde.

inconsequential [ɪnkɒnsɪ'kwenʃ(ə)l] *a* sans importance.

inconsiderate [ɪnkən'sɪdərət] *a* (*action, remark*) irréfléchi, inconsidéré; **to be i.** (*of person*) manquer d'égards (**towards** envers).

inconsistent [ɪnkən'sɪstənt] *a* inconséquent, incohérent; (*reports etc at variance*) contradictoire; **i. with** incompatible avec. ◆**inconsistency** *n* inconséquence *f*, incohérence *f*.

inconsolable [ɪnkən'səʊləb(ə)l] *a* inconsolable.

inconspicuous [ɪnkən'spɪkjʊəs] *a* peu en évidence, qui passe inaperçu. ◆**—ly** *adv* discrètement.

incontinent [ɪn'kɒntɪnənt] *a* incontinent.

inconvenient [ɪnkən'viːnɪənt] *a* (*room, situation*) incommode; (*time*) inopportun; **it's i. (for me) to** ... ça me dérange de ... ; **that's very i.** c'est très gênant. ◆**inconvenience** *n* (*bother*) dérangement *m*; (*disadvantage*) inconvénient *m*; — *vt* déranger, gêner.

incorporate [ɪn'kɔːpəreɪt] *vt* (*introduce*) incorporer (**into** dans); (*contain*) contenir;

incorporated society *Am* société *f* anonyme, société *f* à responsabilité limitée.

incorrect [ɪnkəˈrekt] *a* incorrect, inexact; **you're i.** vous avez tort.

incorrigible [ɪnˈkɒrɪdʒəb(ə)l] *a* incorrigible.

incorruptible [ɪnkəˈrʌptəb(ə)l] *a* incorruptible.

increas/e [ɪnˈkriːs] *vi* augmenter; (*of effort, noise*) s'intensifier; **to i. in weight** prendre du poids; − *vt* augmenter; intensifier; − [ˈɪnkriːs] *n* augmentation *f* (**in, of** de); intensification *f* (**in, of** de); **on the i.** en hausse. ◆**—ing** *a* (*amount etc*) croissant. ◆**—ingly** *adv* de plus en plus.

incredib/le [ɪnˈkredəb(ə)l] *a* incroyable. ◆**—ly** *adv* incroyablement.

incredulous [ɪnˈkredjʊləs] *a* incrédule. ◆**incre'dulity** *n* incrédulité *f*.

increment [ˈɪŋkrəmənt] *n* augmentation *f*.

incriminat/e [ɪnˈkrɪmɪneɪt] *vt* incriminer. ◆**—ing** *a* compromettant.

incubate [ˈɪŋkjʊbeɪt] *vt* (*eggs*) couver. ◆**incu'bation** *n* incubation *f*. ◆**incubator** *n* (*for baby, eggs*) couveuse *f*.

inculcate [ˈɪnkʌlkeɪt] *vt* inculquer (**in** à).

incumbent [ɪnˈkʌmbənt] *a* **it is i. upon him** *or* **her to** il lui incombe de; − *n Rel Pol* titulaire *mf*.

incur [ɪnˈkɜːr] *vt* (**-rr-**) (*debt*) contracter; (*expenses*) faire; (*criticism, danger*) s'attirer.

incurable [ɪnˈkjʊərəb(ə)l] *a* incurable.

incursion [ɪnˈkɜːʃ(ə)n] *n* incursion *f* (**into** dans).

indebted [ɪnˈdetɪd] *a* **i. to s.o. for sth/for doing sth** redevable à qn de qch/d'avoir fait qch. ◆**—ness** *n* dette *f*.

indecent [ɪnˈdiːs(ə)nt] *a* (*offensive*) indécent; (*unsuitable*) peu approprié. ◆**indecency** *n* indécence *f*; (*crime*) *Jur* outrage *m* à la pudeur. ◆**indecently** *adv* indécemment.

indecisive [ɪndɪˈsaɪsɪv] *a* (*person, answer*) indécis. ◆**indecision** *n*, ◆**indecisiveness** *n* indécision *f*.

indeed [ɪnˈdiːd] *adv* en effet; **very good/etc i.** vraiment très bon/*etc*; **yes i.!** bien sûr!; **thank you very much i.!** merci mille fois!

indefensible [ɪndɪˈfensəb(ə)l] *a* indéfendable.

indefinable [ɪndɪˈfaɪnəb(ə)l] *a* indéfinissable.

indefinite [ɪnˈdefɪnət] *a* (*feeling, duration etc*) indéfini; (*plan*) mal déterminé. ◆**—ly** *adv* indéfiniment.

indelible [ɪnˈdeləb(ə)l] *a* (*ink, memory*) indélébile; **i. pencil** crayon *m* à marquer.

indelicate [ɪnˈdelɪkət] *a* (*coarse*) indélicat.

indemnify [ɪnˈdemnɪfaɪ] *vt* indemniser (**for** de). ◆**indemnity** *n* indemnité *f*.

indented [ɪnˈdentɪd] *a* (*edge*) dentelé, découpé; (*line*) *Typ* renfoncé. ◆**inden'tation** *n* dentelure *f*, découpage *f*; *Typ* renfoncement *m*.

independent [ɪndɪˈpendənt] *a* indépendant (**of** de); (*opinions, reports*) de sources différentes. ◆**independence** *n* indépendance *f*. ◆**independently** *adv* de façon indépendante; **i. of** indépendamment de.

indescribable [ɪndɪˈskraɪbəb(ə)l] *a* indescriptible.

indestructible [ɪndɪˈstrʌktəb(ə)l] *a* indestructible.

indeterminate [ɪndɪˈtɜːmɪnət] *a* indéterminé.

index [ˈɪndeks] *n* (*in book etc*) index *m*; (*in library*) catalogue *m*; (*number, sign*) indice *m*; **i. card** fiche *f*; **i. finger** index *m*; − *vt* (*classify*) classer. ◆**i.-'linked** *a Econ* indexé (**to** sur).

India [ˈɪndɪə] *n* Inde *f*. ◆**Indian** *a* & *n* indien, -ienne (*mf*).

indicate [ˈɪndɪkeɪt] *vt* indiquer (**that** que); **I was indicating right** *Aut* j'avais mis mon clignotant droit. ◆**indi'cation** *n* (*sign*) indice *m*, indication *f*; (*idea*) idée *f*. ◆**in'dicative** *a* indicatif (**of** de); − *n* (*mood*) *Gram* indicatif *m*. ◆**indicator** *n* (*instrument*) indicateur *m*; (*sign*) indication *f* (**of** de); *Aut* clignotant *m*; (*display board*) tableau *m* (indicateur).

indict [ɪnˈdaɪt] *vt* inculper (**for** de). ◆**—ment** *n* inculpation *f*.

Indies [ˈɪndɪz] *npl* **the West I.** les Antilles *fpl*.

indifferent [ɪnˈdɪf(ə)rənt] *a* indifférent (**to** à); (*mediocre*) *Pej* médiocre. ◆**indifference** *n* indifférence *f* (**to** à). ◆**indifferently** *adv* indifféremment.

indigenous [ɪnˈdɪdʒɪnəs] *a* indigène.

indigestion [ɪndɪˈdʒestʃ(ə)n] *n* dyspepsie *f*; (**an attack of**) **i.** une indigestion, une crise de foie. ◆**indigestible** *a* indigeste.

indignant [ɪnˈdɪgnənt] *a* indigné (**at** de, **with** contre); **to become i.** s'indigner. ◆**indignantly** *adv* avec indignation. ◆**indig'nation** *n* indignation *f*.

indignity [ɪnˈdɪgnɪtɪ] *n* indignité *f*.

indigo [ˈɪndɪgəʊ] *n* & *a* (*colour*) indigo *m* & *inv*.

indirect [ɪndaɪˈrekt] *a* indirect. ◆**—ly** *adv* indirectement.

indiscreet [ɪndɪˈskriːt] *a* indiscret. ◆**indiscretion** *n* indiscrétion *f*.

indiscriminate [ɪndɪˈskrɪmɪnət] *a* (*person*)

qui manque de discernement; (*random*) fait, donné *etc* au hasard. ◆**—ly** *adv* (*at random*) au hasard; (*without discrimination*) sans discernement.

indispensable [ɪndɪ'spensəb(ə)l] *a* indispensable (**to** à).

indisposed [ɪndɪ'spəʊzd] *a* (*unwell*) indisposé. ◆**indispo'sition** *n* indisposition *f*.

indisputable [ɪndɪ'spjuːtəb(ə)l] *a* incontestable.

indistinct [ɪndɪ'stɪŋkt] *a* indistinct.

indistinguishable [ɪndɪ'stɪŋgwɪʃəb(ə)l] *a* indifférenciable (**from** de).

individual [ɪndɪ'vɪdʒʊəl] *a* individuel; (*unusual, striking*) singulier, particulier; — *n* (*person*) individu *m*. ◆**individualist** *n* individualiste *mf*. ◆**individua'listic** *a* individualiste. ◆**individu'ality** *n* (*distinctiveness*) individualité *f*. ◆**individually** *adv* (*separately*) individuellement; (*unusually*) de façon (très) personnelle.

indivisible [ɪndɪ'vɪzəb(ə)l] *a* indivisible.

Indo-China [ɪndəʊ'tʃaɪnə] *n* Indochine *f*.

indoctrinate [ɪn'dɒktrɪneɪt] *vt Pej* endoctriner. ◆**indoctri'nation** *n* endoctrinement *m*.

indolent ['ɪndələnt] *a* indolent. ◆**indolence** *n* indolence *f*.

indomitable [ɪn'dɒmɪtəb(ə)l] *a* (*will, energy*) indomptable.

Indonesia [ɪndəʊ'niːʒə] *n* Indonésie *f*.

indoor ['ɪndɔːr] *a* (*games, shoes etc*) d'intérieur; (*swimming pool etc*) couvert. ◆**in'doors** *adv* à l'intérieur; **to go** *or* **come i.** rentrer.

induce [ɪn'djuːs] *vt* (*persuade*) persuader (**to do** de faire); (*cause*) provoquer; **to i. labour** *Med* déclencher le travail. ◆**—ment** *n* encouragement *m* (**to do** à faire).

indulge [ɪn'dʌldʒ] *vt* (*s.o.'s desires*) satisfaire; (*child etc*) gâter, tout passer à; **to i. oneself** se gâter; — *vi* **to i. in** (*action*) s'adonner à; (*ice cream etc*) se permettre. ◆**indulgence** *n* indulgence *f*. ◆**indulgent** *a* indulgent (**to envers, with** avec).

industrial [ɪn'dʌstrɪəl] *a* industriel; (*conflict, legislation*) du travail; **i. action** action *f* revendicative; **i. park** *Am* complexe *m* industriel. ◆**industrialist** *n* industriel, -ielle *mf*. ◆**industrialized** *a* industrialisé.

industrious [ɪn'dʌstrɪəs] *a* travailleur.

industry ['ɪndəstrɪ] *n* industrie *f*; (*hard work*) application *f*.

inedible [ɪn'edəb(ə)l] *a* immangeable.

ineffective [ɪnɪ'fektɪv] *a* (*measure etc*) sans effet, inefficace; (*person*) incapable. ◆**—ness** *n* inefficacité *f*.

ineffectual [ɪnɪ'fektʃʊəl] *a* (*measure etc*) inefficace; (*person*) incompétent

inefficient [ɪnɪ'fɪʃ(ə)nt] *a* (*person, measure etc*) inefficace; (*machine*) peu performant. ◆**inefficiency** *n* inefficacité *f*.

ineligible [ɪn'elɪdʒəb(ə)l] *a* (*candidate*) inéligible; **to be i.** for ne pas avoir droit à.

inept [ɪ'nept] *a* (*foolish*) inepte; (*unskilled*) peu habile (**at sth** à qch); (*incompetent*) incapable, inapte. ◆**ineptitude** *n* (*incapacity*) inaptitude *f*.

inequality [ɪnɪ'kwɒlətɪ] *n* inégalité *f*.

inert [ɪ'nɜːt] *a* inerte. ◆**inertia** [ɪ'nɜːʃə] *n* inertie *f*.

inescapable [ɪnɪ'skeɪpəb(ə)l] *a* inéluctable.

inevitable [ɪn'evɪtəb(ə)l] *a* inévitable. ◆**inevitably** *adv* inévitablement.

inexcusable [ɪnɪk'skjuːzəb(ə)l] *a* inexcusable.

inexhaustible [ɪnɪg'zɔːstəb(ə)l] *a* inépuisable.

inexorable [ɪn'eksərəb(ə)l] *a* inexorable.

inexpensive [ɪnɪk'spensɪv] *a* bon marché *inv*.

inexperience [ɪnɪk'spɪərɪəns] *n* inexpérience *f*. ◆**inexperienced** *a* inexpérimenté.

inexplicable [ɪnɪk'splɪkəb(ə)l] *a* inexplicable.

inexpressible [ɪnɪk'spresəb(ə)l] *a* inexprimable.

inextricable [ɪnɪk'strɪkəb(ə)l] *a* inextricable.

infallible [ɪn'fæləb(ə)l] *a* infaillible. ◆**infalli'bility** *n* infaillibilité *f*.

infamous ['ɪnfəməs] *a* (*evil*) infâme. ◆**infamy** *n* infamie *f*.

infant ['ɪnfənt] *n* (*child*) petit(e) enfant *mf*; (*baby*) nourrisson *m*; **i. school** classes *fpl* préparatoires. ◆**infancy** *n* petite enfance *f*; **to be in its i.** (*of art, technique etc*) en être à ses premiers balbutiements. ◆**infantile** *a* (*illness, reaction etc*) infantile.

infantry ['ɪnfəntrɪ] *n* infanterie *f*.

infatuated [ɪn'fætʃʊeɪtɪd] *a* amoureux; **i. with** (*person*) amoureux de, engoué de; (*sport etc*) engoué de. ◆**infatu'ation** *n* engouement *m* (**for, with** pour).

infect [ɪn'fekt] *vt* (*contaminate*) *Med* infecter; **to become infected** s'infecter; **to i. s.o. with sth** communiquer qch à qn. ◆**infection** *n* infection *f*. ◆**infectious** *a* (*disease*) infectieux, contagieux; (*person, laughter etc*) contagieux.

infer [ɪn'fɜːr] *vt* (**-rr-**) déduire (**from** de, **that** que). ◆**'inference** *n* déduction *f*, conclusion *f*.

inferior [ɪnˈfɪərɪər] a inférieur (to à); (goods, work) de qualité inférieure; – n (person) Pej inférieur, -eure mf. ◆inferi'ority n infériorité f.

infernal [ɪnˈfɜːn(ə)l] a infernal. ◆—ly adv Fam épouvantablement.

inferno [ɪnˈfɜːnəʊ] n (pl -os) (blaze) brasier m, incendie m; (hell) enfer m.

infertile [ɪnˈfɜːtaɪl, Am ɪnˈfɜːt(ə)l] a (person, land) stérile.

infest [ɪnˈfest] vt infester (with de).

infidelity [ɪnfɪˈdelɪtɪ] n infidélité f.

infighting [ˈɪnfaɪtɪŋ] n (within group) luttes fpl intestines.

infiltrate [ˈɪnfɪltreɪt] vi s'infiltrer (into dans); – vt (group etc) s'infiltrer dans. ◆infil-'tration n infiltration f; Pol noyautage m.

infinite [ˈɪnfɪnɪt] a & n infini (m). ◆infin-itely adv infiniment. ◆in'finity n Math Phot infini m; to i. Math à l'infini.

infinitive [ɪnˈfɪnɪtɪv] n Gram infinitif m.

infirm [ɪnˈfɜːm] a infirme. ◆infirmary n (sickbay) infirmerie f; (hospital) hôpital m. ◆infirmity n (disability) infirmité f.

inflame [ɪnˈfleɪm] vt enflammer. ◆inflam-mable a inflammable. ◆infla'mmation n Med inflammation f. ◆inflammatory a (remark) incendiaire.

inflate [ɪnˈfleɪt] vt (tyre, prices etc) gonfler. ◆inflatable a gonflable. ◆inflation n Econ inflation f. ◆inflationary a Econ inflationniste.

inflection [ɪnˈflekʃ(ə)n] n Gram flexion f; (of voice) inflexion f.

inflexible [ɪnˈfleksəb(ə)l] a inflexible.

inflexion [ɪnˈflekʃ(ə)n] n = inflection.

inflict [ɪnˈflɪkt] vt infliger (on à); (wound) occasionner (on à).

influence [ˈɪnfluəns] n influence f; under the i. of (anger, drugs) sous l'effet de; under the i. of drink or alcohol Jur en état d'ébriété; – vt influencer. ◆influ'ential a influent.

influenza [ɪnfluˈenzə] n Med grippe f.

influx [ˈɪnflʌks] n flot m, afflux m.

info [ˈɪnfəʊ] n Sl tuyaux mpl, renseigne-ments mpl (on sur).

inform [ɪnˈfɔːm] vt informer (of de, that que); – vi to i. on dénoncer. ◆—ed a informé; to keep s.o. i. of tenir qn au courant de. ◆informant n informateur, -trice mf. ◆informative a instructif. ◆informer n (police) i. indicateur, -trice mf.

informal [ɪnˈfɔːm(ə)l] a (without fuss) simple, sans façon; (occasion) dénué de formalité; (tone, expression) familier; (announcement) officieux; (meeting) non-officiel. ◆infor-

'mality n simplicité f; (of tone etc) familiarité f. ◆informally adv (without fuss) sans cérémonie; (to meet) officieuse-ment; (to dress) simplement.

information [ɪnfəˈmeɪʃ(ə)n] n (facts) renseignements mpl (about, on sur); (knowledge) & Math information f; a piece of i. un renseignement, une information; to get some i. se renseigner.

infrared [ɪnfrəˈred] a infrarouge.

infrequent [ɪnˈfriːkwənt] a peu fréquent.

infringe [ɪnˈfrɪndʒ] vt (rule) contrevenir à; – vi to i. upon (encroach on) empiéter sur. ◆—ment n infraction f (of à).

infuriat/e [ɪnˈfjʊərɪeɪt] vt exaspérer. ◆—ing a exaspérant.

infuse [ɪnˈfjuːz] vt (tea) (faire) infuser. ◆infusion n infusion f.

ingenious [ɪnˈdʒiːnɪəs] a ingénieux. ◆inge'nuity n ingéniosité f.

ingot [ˈɪŋgət] n lingot m.

ingrained [ɪnˈgreɪnd] a (prejudice) enraciné; i. dirt crasse f.

ingratiat/e [ɪnˈgreɪʃɪeɪt] vt to i. oneself with s'insinuer dans les bonnes grâces de. ◆—ing a (person, smile) insinuant.

ingratitude [ɪnˈgrætɪtjuːd] n ingratitude f.

ingredient [ɪnˈgriːdɪənt] n ingrédient m.

ingrown [ɪnˈgrəʊn] a (nail) incarné.

inhabit [ɪnˈhæbɪt] vt habiter. ◆—able a habitable. ◆inhabitant n habitant, -ante mf.

inhale [ɪnˈheɪl] vt aspirer; to i. the smoke (of smoker) avaler la fumée. ◆inha'lation n inhalation f. ◆inhaler n Med inhalateur m.

inherent [ɪnˈhɪərənt] a inhérent (in à). ◆—ly adv intrinsèquement, en soi.

inherit [ɪnˈherɪt] vt hériter (de); (title) succéder à. ◆inheritance n héritage m; (process) Jur succession f; (cultural) patrimoine m.

inhibit [ɪnˈhɪbɪt] vt (hinder) gêner; (control) maîtriser; (prevent) empêcher (from de); to be inhibited être inhibé, avoir des inhibi-tions. ◆inhi'bition n inhibition f.

inhospitable [ɪnhɒˈspɪtəb(ə)l] a inhos-pitalier.

inhuman [ɪnˈhjuːmən] a (not human, cruel) inhumain. ◆inhu'mane a (not kind) inhumain. ◆inhu'manity n brutalité f, cruauté f.

inimitable [ɪˈnɪmɪtəb(ə)l] a inimitable.

iniquitous [ɪˈnɪkwɪtəs] a inique. ◆iniquity n iniquité f.

initial [ɪˈnɪʃ(ə)l] a initial, premier; – n (letter) initiale f; (signature) paraphe m; –

vt (-ll-, Am -l-) parapher. ◆—ly adv initialement, au début.

initiate [ɪˈnɪʃɪeɪt] vt (reforms) amorcer; (schemes) inaugurer; **to i. s.o. into** initier qn à; **the initiated** les initiés mpl. ◆**initiˈation** n amorce f; inauguration f; initiation f. ◆**initiator** n initiateur, -trice mf.

initiative [ɪˈnɪʃətɪv] n initiative f.

inject [ɪnˈdʒekt] vt injecter (**into** à); (new life etc) Fig insuffler (**into** à). ◆**injection** n Med injection f, piqûre f.

injunction [ɪnˈdʒʌŋkʃ(ə)n] n Jur ordonnance f.

injur/e [ˈɪndʒər] vt (physically) blesser; (prejudice, damage) nuire à; (one's chances) compromettre; **to i. one's foot/etc** se blesser au pied/etc. ◆**—ed** a blessé; – n **the i.** les blessés mpl. ◆**injury** n (to flesh) blessure f; (fracture) fracture f; (sprain) foulure f; (bruise) contusion f; (wrong) Fig préjudice m.

injurious [ɪnˈdʒʊərɪəs] a préjudiciable (**to** à).

injustice [ɪnˈdʒʌstɪs] n injustice f.

ink [ɪŋk] n encre f; **Indian i.** encre f de Chine. ◆**inkpot** n, ◆**inkwell** n encrier m. ◆**inky** a couvert d'encre.

inkling [ˈɪŋklɪŋ] n (petite) idée f; **to have some** or **an i. of sth** soupçonner qch, avoir une (petite) idée de qch.

inlaid [ɪnˈleɪd] a (marble etc) incrusté (**with** de); (wood) marqueté.

inland [ˈɪnlənd, ˈɪnlænd] a intérieur; **the I. Revenue** le fisc; – [ɪnˈlænd] adv à l'intérieur (des terres).

in-laws [ˈɪnlɔːz] npl belle-famille f.

inlet [ˈɪnlet] n (of sea) crique f; **i. pipe** tuyau m d'arrivée.

inmate [ˈɪnmeɪt] n résident, -ente mf; (of asylum) interné, -ée mf; (of prison) détenu, -ue mf.

inmost [ˈɪnməʊst] a le plus profond.

inn [ɪn] n auberge f. ◆**innkeeper** n aubergiste mf.

innards [ˈɪnədz] npl Fam entrailles fpl.

innate [ɪˈneɪt] a inné.

inner [ˈɪnər] a intérieur; (ear) interne; (feelings) intime, profond; **the i. city** le cœur de la ville; **an i. circle** (group of people) un cercle restreint; **the i. circle** le saint des saints; **i. tube** (of tyre) chambre f à air. ◆**innermost** a le plus profond.

inning [ˈɪnɪŋ] n Baseball tour m de batte. ◆**innings** n inv Cricket tour m de batte; **a good i.** Fig une vie longue.

innocent [ˈɪnəs(ə)nt] a innocent. ◆**inno-** cence n innocence f. ◆**innocently** adv innocemment.

innocuous [ɪˈnɒkjʊəs] a inoffensif.

innovate [ˈɪnəveɪt] vi innover. ◆**inno-** 'vation n innovation f. ◆**innovator** n innovateur, -trice mf.

innuendo [ɪnjuˈendəʊ] n (pl -oes or -os) insinuation f.

innumerable [ɪˈnjuːmərəb(ə)l] a innombrable.

inoculate [ɪˈnɒkjʊleɪt] vt vacciner (**against** contre). ◆**inocuˈlation** n inoculation f.

inoffensive [ɪnəˈfensɪv] a inoffensif.

inoperative [ɪnˈɒpərətɪv] a (without effect) inopérant.

inopportune [ɪnˈɒpətjuːn] a inopportun.

inordinate [ɪˈnɔːdɪnət] a excessif. ◆**—ly** adv excessivement.

in-patient [ˈɪnpeɪʃ(ə)nt] n malade mf hospitalisé(e).

input [ˈɪnpʊt] n (computer operation) entrée f; (data) données fpl; (current) El énergie f.

inquest [ˈɪnkwest] n enquête f.

inquir/e [ɪnˈkwaɪər] vi se renseigner (**about** sur); **to i. after** s'informer de; **to i. into** examiner, faire une enquête sur; – vt demander; **to i. how to** se demander le chemin de. ◆**—ing** a (mind, look) curieux. ◆**inquiry** n (question) question f; (request for information) demande f de renseignements; (information) renseignements mpl; Jur enquête f; **to make inquiries** demander des renseignements; (of police) enquêter.

inquisitive [ɪnˈkwɪzɪtɪv] a curieux. ◆**inquisitively** adv avec curiosité. ◆**inquiˈsition** n (inquiry) & Rel inquisition f.

inroads [ˈɪnrəʊdz] npl (attacks) incursions fpl (**into** dans); **to make i. into** (start on) Fig entamer.

insane [ɪnˈseɪn] a fou, dément. ◆**insanely** adv comme un fou. ◆**insanity** n folie f, démence f.

insanitary [ɪnˈsænɪt(ə)rɪ] a insalubre.

insatiable [ɪnˈseɪʃəb(ə)l] a insatiable.

inscribe [ɪnˈskraɪb] vt inscrire; (book) dédicacer (**to** à). ◆**inscription** n inscription f; dédicace f.

inscrutable [ɪnˈskruːtəb(ə)l] a impénétrable.

insect [ˈɪnsekt] n insecte m; – a (powder, spray) insecticide; **i. repellant** crème f anti-insecte. ◆**inˈsecticide** n insecticide m.

insecure [ɪnsɪˈkjʊər] a (not fixed) peu solide; (furniture, ladder) branlant, bancal; (window) mal fermé; (uncertain) incertain;

(*unsafe*) peu sûr; (*person*) qui manque d'assurance. ◆**insecurity** *n* (*of person, situation*) insécurité *f*.

insemination [ɪnsemɪ'neɪʃ(ə)n] *n Med* insémination *f*.

insensible [ɪn'sensəb(ə)l] *a Med* inconscient.

insensitive [ɪn'sensɪtɪv] *a* insensible (**to** à). ◆**insen'tivity** *n* insensibilité *f*.

inseparable [ɪn'sep(ə)rəb(ə)l] *a* inséparable (**from** de).

insert [ɪn'sɜːt] *vt* insérer (**in, into** dans). ◆**insertion** *n* insertion *f*.

inshore ['ɪnʃɔːr] *a* côtier.

inside [ɪn'saɪd] *adv* dedans, à l'intérieur; **come i.!** entrez!; − *prep* à l'intérieur de, dans; (*time*) en moins de; − *n* dedans *m*, intérieur *m*; *pl* (*stomach*) *Fam* ventre *m*; **on the i.** à l'intérieur (**of** de); **i. out** (*coat, socks etc*) à l'envers; (*to know, study etc*) à fond; **to turn everything i. out** *Fig* tout chambouler; − *a* intérieur; (*information*) obtenu à la source; **the i. lane** *Aut* la voie de gauche, *Am* la voie de droite.

insidious [ɪn'sɪdɪəs] *a* insidieux.

insight ['ɪnsaɪt] *n* perspicacité *f*; **to give an i. into** (*s.o.'s character*) permettre de comprendre, éclairer; (*question*) donner un aperçu de.

insignia [ɪn'sɪgnɪə] *npl* (*of important person*) insignes *mpl*.

insignificant [ɪnsɪg'nɪfɪkənt] *a* insignifiant. ◆**insignificance** *n* insignifiance *f*.

insincere [ɪnsɪn'sɪər] *a* peu sincère. ◆**insincerity** *n* manque *m* de sincérité.

insinuate [ɪn'sɪnjueɪt] *vt* **1** *Pej* insinuer (**that** que). **2 to i. oneself into** s'insinuer dans. ◆**insinu'ation** *n* insinuation *f*.

insipid [ɪn'sɪpɪd] *a* insipide.

insist [ɪn'sɪst] *vi* insister (**on doing** pour faire); **to i. on sth** (*demand*) exiger qch; (*assert*) affirmer qch; − *vt* insister (**that** pour que); (*declare firmly*) affirmer (**that** que); **I i. that you come** *or* **on your coming** j'insiste pour que tu viennes. ◆**insistence** *n* insistance *f*; **her i. on seeing me** l'insistance qu'elle mit à vouloir me voir. ◆**insistent** *a* insistant; **I was i.** (**about it**) j'ai été pressant. ◆**insistently** *adv* avec insistance.

insolent ['ɪnsələnt] *a* insolent. ◆**insolence** *n* insolence *f*. ◆**insolently** *adv* insolemment.

insoluble [ɪn'sɒljʊb(ə)l] *a* insoluble.

insolvent [ɪn'sɒlvənt] *a Fin* insolvable.

insomnia [ɪn'sɒmnɪə] *n* insomnie *f*. ◆**insomniac** *n* insomniaque *mf*.

insomuch as [ɪnsəʊ'mʌtʃəz] *adv* = **inasmuch as.**

inspect [ɪn'spekt] *vt* inspecter; (*tickets*) contrôler; (*troops*) passer en revue. ◆**inspection** *n* inspection *f*; contrôle *m*; revue *f*. ◆**inspector** *n* inspecteur, -trice *mf*; (*on bus*) contrôleur, -euse *mf*.

inspir/e [ɪn'spaɪər] *vt* inspirer (**s.o. with sth** qch à qn); **to be inspired to do** avoir l'inspiration de faire. ◆**−ed** *a* inspiré. ◆**−ing** *a* qui inspire. ◆**inspi'ration** *n* inspiration *f*; (*person*) source *f* d'inspiration.

instability [ɪnstə'bɪlɪtɪ] *n* instabilité *f*.

install [ɪn'stɔːl] *vt* installer. ◆**insta'llation** *n* installation *f*.

instalment [ɪn'stɔːlmənt] (*Am* **installment**) *n* (*of money*) acompte *m*, versement *m* (*partiel*); (*of serial*) épisode *m*; (*of publication*) fascicule *m*; **to buy on the i. plan** *Am* acheter à crédit.

instance ['ɪnstəns] *n* (*example*) exemple *m*; (*case*) cas *m*; (*occasion*) circonstance *f*; **for i.** par exemple; **in the first i.** en premier lieu.

instant ['ɪnstənt] *a* immédiat; **i. coffee** café *m* soluble *or* instantané, nescafé® *m*; **of the 3rd i.** (*in letter*) *Com* du 3 courant; − *n* (*moment*) instant *m*; **this (very) i.** (*at once*) à l'instant; **the i. that** (*as soon as*) dès que. ◆**instan'taneous** *a* instantané. ◆**instantly** *adv* immédiatement.

instead [ɪn'sted] *adv* (*as alternative*) au lieu de cela, plutôt; **i. of** au lieu de; **i. of s.o.** à la place de qn; **i. (of him** *or* **her)** à sa place.

instep ['ɪnstep] *n* (*of foot*) cou-de-pied *m*; (*of shoe*) cambrure *f*.

instigate ['ɪnstɪgeɪt] *vt* provoquer. ◆**insti'gation** *n* instigation *f*. ◆**instigator** *n* instigateur, -trice *mf*.

instil [ɪn'stɪl] *vt* (**-ll-**) (*idea*) inculquer (**into** à); (*courage*) insuffler (**into** à).

instinct ['ɪnstɪŋkt] *n* instinct *m*; **by i.** d'instinct. ◆**in'stinctive** *a* instinctif. ◆**in'stinctively** *adv* instinctivement.

institute ['ɪnstɪtjuːt] **1** *vt* (*rule, practice*) instituer; (*inquiry, proceedings*) *Jur* entamer, intenter. **2** *n* institut *m*. ◆**insti'tution** *n* (*custom, private or charitable organization etc*) institution *f*; (*school, hospital*) établissement *m*; (*home*) *Med* asile *m*. ◆**insti'tutional** *a* institutionnel.

instruct [ɪn'strʌkt] *vt* (*teach*) enseigner (**s.o. in sth** qch à qn); **to i. s.o. about sth** (*inform*) instruire qn de qch; **to i. s.o. to do** (*order*) charger qn de faire. ◆**instruction** *n* (*teaching*) instruction *f*; *pl* (*orders*) instructions *fpl*; **instructions (for use)** mode *m*

d'emploi. ◆**instructive** *a* instructif.
◆**instructor** *n* professeur *m*; *Sp* moniteur,
-trice *mf*; *Mil* instructeur *m*; *Univ Am*
maître-assistant, -ante *mf*; **driving i.**
moniteur, -trice *mf* de conduite.

instrument ['ɪnstrʊmənt] *n* instrument *m*.
◆**instru'mental** *a Mus* instrumental; **to
be i. in sth/in doing sth** contribuer à qch/à
faire qch. ◆**instru'mentalist** *n Mus*
instrumentaliste *mf*. ◆**instrumen'tation**
n Mus orchestration *f*.

insubordinate [ɪnsə'bɔːdɪnət] *a* indiscipliné. ◆**insubordi'nation** *n* indiscipline *f*.

insubstantial [ɪnsəb'stænʃ(ə)l] *a* (*argument,
evidence*) peu solide.

insufferable [ɪn'sʌf(ə)rəb(ə)l] *a* intolérable.

insufficient [ɪnsə'fɪʃənt] *a* insuffisant.
◆—**ly** *adv* insuffisamment.

insular ['ɪnsjʊlər] *a* (*climate*) insulaire;
(*views*) *Pej* étroit, borné.

insulate ['ɪnsjʊleɪt] *vt* (*against cold etc*) & *El*
isoler; (*against sound*) insonoriser; **to i. s.o.
from** *Fig* protéger qn de; **insulating tape**
chatterton *m*. ◆**insu'lation** *n* isolation *f*;
insonorisation *f*; (*material*) isolant *m*.

insulin ['ɪnsjʊlɪn] *n Med* insuline *f*.

insult [ɪn'sʌlt] *vt* insulter; − ['ɪnsʌlt] *n* insulte
f (**to** à).

insuperable [ɪn'suːpərəb(ə)l] *a* insurmontable.

insure [ɪn'ʃʊər] *vt* **1** (*protect against damage
etc*) assurer (**against** contre). **2** *Am* =
ensure. ◆**insurance** *n* assurance *f*; **i.
company** compagnie *f* d'assurances; **i.
policy** police *f* d'assurance.

insurgent [ɪn'sɜːdʒənt] *a & n* insurgé, -ée
(*mf*).

insurmountable [ɪnsə'maʊntəb(ə)l] *a*
insurmontable.

insurrection [ɪnsə'rekʃ(ə)n] *n* insurrection
f.

intact [ɪn'tækt] *a* intact.

intake ['ɪnteɪk] *n* (*of food*) consommation *f*;
Sch Univ admissions *fpl*; *Tech* admission *f*.

intangible [ɪn'tændʒəb(ə)l] *a* intangible.

integral ['ɪntɪɡrəl] *a* intégral; **to be an i. part
of** faire partie intégrante de.

integrate ['ɪntɪɡreɪt] *vt* intégrer (**into** dans);
− *vi* s'intégrer (**into** dans); (*racially*) **integrated** (*school etc*) *Am* où se pratique la
déségrégation raciale. ◆**integration** *n*
intégration *f*; (*racial*) **i.** déségrégation *f*
raciale.

integrity [ɪn'teɡrɪti] *n* intégrité *f*.

intellect ['ɪntɪlekt] *n* (*faculty*) intellect *m*,
intelligence *f*; (*cleverness, person*) intelli-

gence *f*. ◆**inte'llectual** *a & n* intellectuel,
-elle (*mf*).

intelligence [ɪn'telɪdʒəns] *n* intelligence *f*;
Mil renseignements *mpl*. ◆**intelligent** *a*
intelligent. ◆**intelligently** *adv* intelligemment. ◆**intelli'gentsia** *n* intelligentsia *f*.

intelligible [ɪn'telɪdʒəb(ə)l] *a* intelligible.
◆**intelligi'bility** *n* intelligibilité *f*.

intemperance [ɪn'tempərəns] *n* intempérance *f*.

intend [ɪn'tend] *vt* (*gift, remark etc*) destiner
(**for** à); **to i. to do** avoir l'intention de faire;
I i. you to stay mon intention est que vous
restiez. ◆—**ed** *a* (*deliberate*) intentionnel,
voulu; (*planned*) projeté; **i. to be** (*meant*)
destiné à être. ◆**intention** *n* intention *f* (**of
doing** de faire). ◆**intentional** *a* intentionnel; **it wasn't i.** ce n'était pas fait exprès.
◆**intentionally** *adv* intentionnellement,
exprès.

intense [ɪn'tens] *a* intense; (*interest*) vif;
(*person*) passionné. ◆**intensely** *adv* intensément; *Fig* extrêmement. ◆**intensifi-
'cation** *n* intensification *f*. ◆**intensify** *vt*
intensifier; − *vi* s'intensifier. ◆**intensity** *n*
intensité *f*. ◆**intensive** *a* intensif; **in i.
care** *Med* en réanimation.

intent [ɪn'tent] **1** *a* (*look*) attentif; **i. on** (*task*)
absorbé par; **i. on doing** résolu à faire. **2** *n*
intention *f*; **to all intents and purposes** en
fait, essentiellement.

inter [ɪn'tɜːr] *vt* (**-rr-**) enterrer.

inter- ['ɪntə(r)] *pref* inter-.

interact [ɪntə'rækt] *vi* (*of ideas etc*) être
interdépendants; (*of people*) agir conjointement; *Ch* interagir. ◆**interaction** *n*
interaction *f*.

intercede [ɪntə'siːd] *vi* intercéder (**with**
auprès de).

intercept [ɪntə'sept] *vt* intercepter. ◆**interception** *n* interception *f*.

interchange ['ɪntətʃeɪndʒ] *n Aut* échangeur
m. ◆**inter'changeable** *a* interchangeable.

intercom ['ɪntəkɒm] *n* interphone *m*.

interconnect/ed [ɪntəkə'nektɪd] *a* (*facts
etc*) liés. ◆—**ing** *a* **i. rooms** pièces *fpl*
communicantes.

intercontinental [ɪntəkɒntɪ'nent(ə)l] *a*
intercontinental.

intercourse ['ɪntəkɔːs] *n* (*sexual, social*)
rapports *mpl*.

interdependent [ɪntədɪ'pendənt] *a* interdépendant; (*parts of machine*) solidaire.

interest ['ɪnt(ə)rɪst, 'ɪntrəst] *n* intérêt *m*; *Fin*
intérêts *mpl*; **an i. in** (*stake*) *Com* des intérêts dans; **his** *or* **her i. is** (*hobby etc*) ce qui

l'intéresse c'est; **to take an i. in** s'intéresser
à; **to be of i. to s.o.** intéresser qn; − *vt* intéresser. ◆**—ed** *a* (*involved*) intéressé; (*look*)
d'intérêt; **to seem i.** sembler intéressé (**in**
par); **to be i. in** sth/s.o. s'intéresser à
qch/qn; **I'm i. in doing** ça m'intéresse de
faire; **are you i.?** ça vous intéresse? ◆**—ing**
a intéressant. ◆**—ingly** *adv* i. (**enough**),
she . . . curieusement, elle . . . .

interface ['ɪntəfeɪs] *n Tech* interface *f*.

interfer/e [ɪntə'fɪər] *vi* se mêler des affaires
d'autrui; **to i. in** s'ingérer dans; **to i. with**
(*upset*) déranger; (*touch*) toucher (à).
◆**—ing** *a* (*person*) importun. ◆**interference** *n* ingérence *f*; *Rad* parasites *mpl*.

interim ['ɪntərɪm] *n* intérim *m*; **in the i.**
pendant l'intérim; − *a* (*measure etc*)
provisoire; (*post*) intérimaire.

interior [ɪn'tɪərɪər] *a* intérieur; − *n* intérieur
m; **Department of the I.** *Am* ministère *m* de
l'Intérieur.

interjection [ɪntə'dʒekʃ(ə)n] *n* interjection *f*.

interlock [ɪntə'lɒk] *vi Tech* s'emboîter.

interloper ['ɪntələupər] *n* intrus, -use *mf*.

interlude ['ɪntəluːd] *n* intervalle *m*; *Th*
intermède *m*; *Mus TV* interlude *m*.

intermarry [ɪntə'mærɪ] *vi* se marier (**entre**
eux). ◆**intermarriage** *n* mariage *m* (*entre
personnes de races etc différentes*).

intermediary [ɪntə'miːdɪərɪ] *a* & *n*
intermédiare (*mf*).

intermediate [ɪntə'miːdɪət] *a* intermédiaire;
(*course*) *Sch* moyen.

interminable [ɪn'tɜːmɪnəb(ə)l] *a* interminable.

intermingle [ɪntə'mɪŋg(ə)l] *vi* se mélanger.

intermission [ɪntə'mɪʃ(ə)n] *n Cin Th*
entracte *m*.

intermittent [ɪntə'mɪtənt] *a* intermittent.
◆**—ly** *adv* par intermittence.

intern 1 [ɪn'tɜːn] *vt Pol* interner. **2** ['ɪntɜːn] *n
Med Am* interne *mf* (des hôpitaux).
◆**inter'nee** *n* interné, -ée *mf*.
◆**in'ternment** *n Pol* internement *m*.

internal [ɪn'tɜːn(ə)l] *a* interne; (*policy,
flight*) intérieur; **i. combustion engine**
moteur *m* à explosion; **the I. Revenue
Service** *Am* le fisc. ◆**—ly** *adv* intérieurement.

international [ɪntə'næʃ(ə)nəl] *a* international; (*fame, reputation*) mondial; − *n*
(*match*) rencontre *f* internationale;
(*player*) international *m*. ◆**—ly** *adv*
(*renowned etc*) mondialement.

interplanetary [ɪntə'plænɪt(ə)rɪ] *a* interplanétaire.

interplay ['ɪntəpleɪ] *n* interaction *f*, jeu *m*.

interpolate [ɪn'tɜːpəleɪt] *vt* interpoler.

interpret [ɪn'tɜːprɪt] *vt* interpréter; − *vi Ling*
faire l'interprète. ◆**interpre'tation** *n*
interprétation *f*. ◆**interpreter** *n* interprète
mf.

interrelated [ɪntərɪ'leɪtɪd] *a* en corrélation.
◆**interrelation** *n* corrélation *f*.

interrogate [ɪn'terəgeɪt] *vt* (*question closely*)
interroger. ◆**interro'gation** *n* interrogation *f*; *Jur* interrogatoire *m*. ◆**interro-
gator** *n* (*questioner*) interrogateur, -trice
mf.

interrogative [ɪntə'rɒgətɪv] *a* & *n Gram*
interrogatif (*m*).

interrupt [ɪntə'rʌpt] *vt* interrompre.
◆**interruption** *n* interruption *f*.

intersect [ɪntə'sekt] *vt* couper; − *vi*
s'entrecouper, se couper. ◆**intersection** *n*
(*crossroads*) croisement *m*; (*of lines etc*)
intersection *f*.

intersperse [ɪntə'spɜːs] *vt* parsemer (**with**
de).

intertwine [ɪntə'twaɪn] *vt* entrelacer.

interval ['ɪntəv(ə)l] *n* intervalle *m*; *Th*
entracte *m*; **at intervals** (*time*) de temps à
autre; (*space*) par intervalles; **bright intervals** *Met* éclaircies *fpl*.

intervene [ɪntə'viːn] *vi* intervenir; (*of event*)
survenir; **ten years intervened** dix années
s'écoulèrent; **if nothing intervenes** s'il
n'arrive rien entre-temps. ◆**intervention**
n intervention *f*.

interview ['ɪntəvjuː] *n* entrevue *f*, entretien
m (**with** avec); *Journ TV* interview *f*; **to call
for (an)** i. convoquer; − *vt* avoir une
entrevue avec; *Journ TV* interviewer.
◆**—er** *n Journ TV* interviewer *m*; *Com Pol*
enquêteur, -euse *mf*.

intestine [ɪn'testɪn] *n* intestin *m*.

intimate 1 ['ɪntɪmət] *a* intime; (*friendship*)
profond; (*knowledge, analysis*) approfondi.
◆**intimacy** *n* intimité *f*. ◆**intimately** *adv*
intimement.

intimate 2 ['ɪntɪmeɪt] *vt* (*hint*) suggérer (**that**
que). ◆**inti'mation** *n* (*announcement*)
annonce *f*; (*hint*) suggestion *f*; (*sign*) indication *f*.

intimidate [ɪn'tɪmɪdeɪt] *vt* intimider.
◆**intimi'dation** *n* intimidation *f*.

into ['ɪntuː, *unstressed* 'ɪntə] *prep* **1** dans; **to
put i.** mettre dans; **to go i.** (*room, detail*)
entrer dans. **2** **en**; **to translate i.** traduire
en; **to change i.** transformer *or* changer en;
to go i. town aller en ville; **i. pieces** (*to break
etc*) en morceaux. **3 to be i. yoga**/*etc Fam*
être à fond dans le yoga/*etc.*

intolerable [ɪn'tɒlərəb(ə)l] *a* intolérable

(that que (+ *sub*)). ◆**intolerably** *adv* insupportablement. ◆**intolerance** *n* intolérance *f*. ◆**Intolerant** *a* intolérant (**of** de). ◆**intolerantly** *adv* avec intolérance.

intonation [ɪntəˈneɪʃ(ə)n] *n Ling* intonation *f*.

intoxicate [ɪnˈtɒksɪkeɪt] *vt* enivrer. ◆**intoxicated** *a* ivre. ◆**intoxi'cation** *n* ivresse *f*.

intra- [ˈɪntrə] *pref* intra-.

intransigent [ɪnˈtrænsɪdʒənt] *a* intransigeant. ◆**intransigence** *n* intransigeance *f*.

intransitive [ɪnˈtrænsɪtɪv] *a & n Gram* intransitif (*m*).

intravenous [ɪntrəˈviːnəs] *a Med* intraveineux.

intrepid [ɪnˈtrepɪd] *a* intrépide.

intricate [ˈɪntrɪkət] *a* complexe, compliqué. ◆**intricacy** *n* complexité *f*. ◆**intricately** *adv* de façon complexe.

intrigu/e 1 [ɪnˈtriːg] *vt* (*interest*) intriguer; **I'm intrigued to know . . .** je suis curieux de savoir . . . . **2** [ˈɪntriːg] *n* (*plot*) intrigue *f*. ◆**—ing** *a* (*news etc*) curieux.

intrinsic [ɪnˈtrɪnsɪk] *a* intrinsèque. ◆**intrinsically** *adv* intrinsèquement.

introduce [ɪntrəˈdjuːs] *vt* (*insert, bring in*) introduire (**into** dans); (*programme, subject*) présenter; **to i. s.o. to s.o.** présenter qn à qn; **to i. s.o. to Dickens/geography/***etc* faire découvrir Dickens/la géographie/*etc* à qn. ◆**introduction** *n* introduction *f*; présentation *f*; (*book title*) initiation *f*; **her i.** (*life abroad etc*) son premier contact avec. ◆**introductory** *a* (*words*) d'introduction; (*speech*) de présentation; (*course*) d'initiation.

introspective [ɪntrəˈspektɪv] *a* introspectif. ◆**introspection** *n* introspection *f*.

introvert [ˈɪntrəvɜːt] *n* introverti, -ie *mf*.

intrude [ɪnˈtruːd] *vi* (*of person*) s'imposer (**on** s.o. à qn), déranger (**on** s.o. qn); **to i. on** (*s.o.'s time etc*) abuser de. ◆**intruder** *n* intrus, -use *mf*. ◆**intrusion** *n* intrusion *f* (**into** dans); **forgive my i.** pardonnez-moi de vous avoir dérangé.

intuition [ɪntjuːˈɪʃ(ə)n] *n* intuition *f*. ◆**in'tuitive** *a* intuitif.

inundate [ˈɪnʌndeɪt] *vt* inonder (**with** de); **inundated with work** submergé de travail. ◆**inun'dation** *n* inondation *f*.

invad/e [ɪnˈveɪd] *vt* envahir; (*privacy*) violer. ◆**—er** *n* envahisseur, -euse *mf*.

invalid¹ [ˈɪnvəlɪd] *a & n* malade (*mf*); (*through injury*) infirme (*mf*); **i. car** voiture *f* d'infirme.

invalid² [ɪnˈvælɪd] *a* non valable. ◆**invalidate** *vt* invalider, annuler.

invaluable [ɪnˈvæljʊəb(ə)l] *a* (*help etc*) inestimable.

invariab/le [ɪnˈveərɪəb(ə)l] *a* invariable. ◆**—ly** *adv* invariablement.

invasion [ɪnˈveɪʒ(ə)n] *n* invasion *f*; **i. of s.o.'s privacy** intrusion *f* dans la vie privée de qn.

invective [ɪnˈvektɪv] *n* invective *f*.

inveigh [ɪnˈveɪ] *vi* **to i. against** invectiver contre.

inveigle [ɪnˈveɪg(ə)l] *vt* **to i. s.o. into doing** amener qn à faire par la ruse.

invent [ɪnˈvent] *vt* inventer. ◆**invention** *n* invention *f*. ◆**inventive** *a* inventif. ◆**inventiveness** *n* esprit *m* d'invention. ◆**inventor** *n* inventeur, -trice *mf*.

inventory [ˈɪnvənt(ə)rɪ] *n* inventaire *m*.

inverse [ɪnˈvɜːs] *a & n Math* inverse (*m*).

invert [ɪnˈvɜːt] *vt* intervertir; **inverted commas** guillemets *mpl*. ◆**inversion** *n* interversion *f*; *Gram Anat etc* inversion *f*.

invest [ɪnˈvest] *vt* (*funds*) investir (**in** dans); (*money*) placer, investir; (*time, effort*) consacrer (**in** à); **to i. s.o. with** (*endow*) investir qn de; – *vi* **to i. in** (*project*) placer son argent dans; (*firm*) investir dans; (*house, radio etc*) *Fig* se payer. ◆**investiture** *n* (*of bishop etc*) investiture *f*. ◆**investment** *n* investissement *m*, placement *m*. ◆**investor** *n* (*shareholder*) actionnaire *mf*; (*saver*) épargnant, -ante *mf*.

investigate [ɪnˈvestɪgeɪt] *vt* (*examine*) examiner, étudier; (*crime*) enquêter sur. ◆**investi'gation** *n* examen *m*, étude *f*; (*by police*) enquête *f* (**of** sur); (*inquiry*) enquête *f*, investigation *f*. ◆**investigator** *n* (*detective*) enquêteur, -euse *mf*.

inveterate [ɪnˈvetərət] *a* invétéré.

invidious [ɪnˈvɪdɪəs] *a* qui suscite la jalousie; (*hurtful*) blessant; (*odious*) odieux.

invigilate [ɪnˈvɪdʒɪleɪt] *vi* être de surveillance (**à** un examen). ◆**invigilator** *n* surveillant, -ante *mf*.

invigorat/e [ɪnˈvɪgəreɪt] *vt* revigorer. ◆**—ing** *a* stimulant.

invincible [ɪnˈvɪnsəb(ə)l] *a* invincible.

invisible [ɪnˈvɪzəb(ə)l] *a* invisible; **i. ink** encre *f* sympathique.

invit/e [ɪnˈvaɪt] *vt* inviter (**to do** à faire); (*ask for*) demander; (*lead to, give occasion for*) appeler; (*trouble*) chercher; **to i. out** inviter (à sortir); **to i. over** inviter (à venir); – [ˈɪnvaɪt] *n Fam* invitation *f*. ◆**—ing** *a* engageant, invitant; (*food*) appétissant. ◆**invi'tation** *n* invitation *f*.

invoice [ˈɪnvɔɪs] *n* facture *f*; – *vt* facturer.

invoke [ɪnˈvəʊk] vt invoquer.

involuntar/y [ɪnˈvɒləntərɪ] a involontaire. ◆**—ily** adv involontairement.

involv/e [ɪnˈvɒlv] vt (include) mêler (qn) (in à), impliquer (qn) (in dans); (associate) associer (qn) (in à); (entail) entraîner; **to i. oneself, get involved** (commit oneself) s'engager (in dans); **to i. s.o. in expense** entraîner qn à des dépenses; **the job involves going abroad** le poste nécessite des déplacements à l'étranger. ◆**—ed** a (complicated) compliqué; **the factors/etc i.** (at stake) les facteurs/etc en jeu; **the person i.** la personne en question; **i. with s.o.** mêlé aux affaires de qn; **personally i.** concerné; **emotionally i.** with amoureux de; **to become i.** (of police) intervenir. ◆**—ement** n participation f (in à), implication f (in dans); (commitment) engagement m (in dans); (problem) difficulté f; **emotional i.** liaison f.

invulnerable [ɪnˈvʌln(ə)rəb(ə)l] a invulnérable.

inward [ˈɪnwəd] a & adv (movement, to move) vers l'intérieur; – a (inner) intérieur. ◆**i.-looking** a replié sur soi. ◆**inwardly** adv (inside) à l'intérieur; (to laugh, curse etc) intérieurement. ◆**inwards** adv vers l'intérieur.

iodine [ˈaɪədiːn, Am ˈaɪədaɪn] n Med teinture f d'iode.

iota [aɪˈəʊtə] n (of truth etc) grain m; (in text) iota m.

IOU [aɪəʊˈjuː] n abbr (I owe you) reconnaissance f de dette.

IQ [aɪˈkjuː] n abbr (intelligence quotient) QI m inv.

Iran [ɪˈrɑːn] n Iran m. ◆**Iranian** [ɪˈreɪnɪən] a & n iranien, -ienne (mf).

Iraq [ɪˈrɑːk] n Irak m. ◆**Iraqi** a & n irakien, -ienne (mf).

irascible [ɪˈræsəb(ə)l] a irascible.

ire [ˈaɪər] n Lit courroux m. ◆**i'rate** a furieux.

Ireland [ˈaɪələnd] n Irlande f. ◆**Irish** a irlandais; – n (language) irlandais m. ◆**Irishman** n (pl -men) Irlandais m. ◆**Irishwoman** n (pl -women) Irlandaise f.

iris [ˈaɪərɪs] n Anat Bot iris m.

irk [ɜːk] vt ennuyer. ◆**irksome** a ennuyeux.

iron [ˈaɪən] n fer m; (for clothes) fer m (à repasser); **old i., scrap i.** ferraille f; **i. and steel industry** sidérurgie f; **the I. Curtain** Pol le rideau de fer; – vt (clothes) repasser; **to i. out** (difficulties) Fig aplanir. ◆**—ing** n repassage m; **i. board** planche f à repasser. ◆**ironmonger** n quincailler m. ◆**iron-**

mongery n quincaillerie f. ◆**ironwork** n ferronnerie f.

irony [ˈaɪərənɪ] n ironie f. ◆**i'ronic(al)** a ironique.

irradiate [ɪˈreɪdɪeɪt] vt irradier.

irrational [ɪˈræʃən(ə)l] a (act) irrationnel; (fear) irraisonné; (person) peu rationnel, illogique.

irreconcilable [ɪrekənˈsaɪləb(ə)l] a irréconciliable, inconciliable; (views, laws etc) inconciliable.

irrefutable [ɪrɪˈfjuːtəb(ə)l] a irréfutable.

irregular [ɪˈregjʊlər] a irrégulier. ◆**irregu-'larity** n irrégularité f.

irrelevant [ɪˈreləvənt] a (remark) non pertinent; (course) peu utile; **i. to** sans rapport avec; **that's i.** ça n'a rien à voir. ◆**irrelevance** n manque m de rapport.

irreparable [ɪˈrep(ə)rəb(ə)l] a (harm, loss) irréparable.

irreplaceable [ɪrɪˈpleɪsəb(ə)l] a irremplaçable.

irrepressible [ɪrɪˈpresəb(ə)l] a (laughter etc) irrépressible.

irresistible [ɪrɪˈzɪstəb(ə)l] a (person, charm etc) irrésistible.

irresolute [ɪˈrezəluːt] a irrésolu, indécis.

irrespective of [ɪrɪˈspektɪvəv] prep sans tenir compte de.

irresponsible [ɪrɪˈspɒnsəb(ə)l] a (act) irréfléchi; (person) irresponsable.

irretrievable [ɪrɪˈtriːvəb(ə)l] a irréparable.

irreverent [ɪˈrevərənt] a irrévérencieux.

irreversible [ɪrɪˈvɜːsəb(ə)l] a (process) irréversible; (decision) irrévocable.

irrevocable [ɪˈrevəkəb(ə)l] a irrévocable.

irrigate [ˈɪrɪgeɪt] vt irriguer. ◆**irri'gation** n irrigation f.

irritat/e [ˈɪrɪteɪt] vt irriter. ◆**—ing** a irritant. ◆**irritable** a (easily annoyed) irritable. ◆**irritant** n irritant m. ◆**irri'tation** n (anger) & Med irritation f.

is [ɪz] see be.

Islam [ˈɪzlɑːm] n islam m. ◆**Islamic** [ɪzˈlæmɪk] a islamique.

island [ˈaɪlənd] n île f; **traffic i.** refuge m; – a insulaire. ◆**islander** n insulaire mf. ◆**isle** [aɪl] n île f; **the British Isles** les îles Britanniques.

isolate [ˈaɪsəleɪt] vt isoler (from de). ◆**isolated** a (remote, unique) isolé. ◆**iso'lation** n isolement m; **in i.** isolément.

Israel [ˈɪzreɪl] n Israël m. ◆**Is'raeli** a & n israélien, -ienne (mf).

issue [ˈɪʃuː] vt (book etc) publier; (an order) donner; (tickets) distribuer; (passport) délivrer; (stamps, banknotes) émettre;

(*warning*) lancer; (*supply*) fournir (**with** de, **to** à); – *vi* **to i. from** (*of smell*) se dégager de; (*stem from*) provenir de; – *n* (*matter*) question *f*; (*problem*) problème *m*; (*outcome*) résultat *m*; (*of text*) publication *f*; (*of stamps etc*) émission *f*; (*newspaper*) numéro *m*; **at i.** (*at stake*) en cause; **to make an i. of** faire toute une affaire de.

isthmus ['ɪsməs] *n Geog* isthme *m*.

it [ɪt] *pron* **1** (*subject*) il, elle; (*object*) le, la, l'; (**to**) **it** (*indirect object*) lui; **it bites** (*dog*) il mord; **I've done it** je l'ai fait. **2** (*impersonal*) il; **it's snowing** il neige; **it's hot** il fait chaud. **3** (*non specific*) ce, cela, ça; **it's good** c'est bon; **it was pleasant** c'était agréable; **who is it?** qui est-ce?; **that's it!** (*I agree*) c'est ça!; (*it's done*) ça y est!; **to consider it wise to do** juger prudent de faire; **it was Paul who . . .** c'est Paul qui . . . ; **she's got it in her to succeed** elle est capable de réussir; **to have it in for s.o.** en vouloir à qn. **4 of it, from it, about it** en; **in it, to it, at it** y; **on it** dessus; **under it** dessous.

italic [ɪ'tælɪk] *a Typ* italique; – *npl* italique *m*.

Italy ['ɪtəlɪ] *n* Italie *f*. ◆**I'talian** *a* & *n* italien, -ienne (*mf*); – *n* (*language*) italien *m*.

itch [ɪtʃ] *n* démangeaison(s) *f*(*pl*); **to have an i. to do** avoir une envie folle de faire; – *vi* démanger; **his arm itches** son bras le *or* lui démange; **I'm itching to do** *Fig* ça me démange de faire. ◆**—ing** *n* démangeaison(s) *f*(*pl*). ◆**itchy** *a* **an i. hand** une main qui me démange.

item ['aɪtəm] *n Com Journ* article *m*; (*matter*) question *f*; (*on entertainment programme*) numéro *m*; **a news i.** une information. ◆**itemize** *vt* détailler.

itinerant [aɪ'tɪnərənt] *a* (*musician, actor*) ambulant; (*judge, preacher*) itinérant.

itinerary [aɪ'tɪnərərɪ] *n* itinéraire *m*.

its [ɪts] *poss a* son, sa, *pl* ses. ◆**it'self** *pron* lui-même, elle-même; (*reflexive*) se, s'; **goodness i.** la bonté même; **by i.** tout seul.

IUD [ajju:'di:] *n abbr* (*intrauterine device*) stérilet *m*.

ivory ['aɪvərɪ] *n* ivoire *m*.

ivy ['aɪvɪ] *n* lierre *m*.

J

J, j [dʒeɪ] *n* J, j *m*.

jab [dʒæb] *vt* (**-bb-**) (*thrust*) enfoncer (**into** dans); (*prick*) piquer (*qn*) (**with sth** du bout de qch); – *n* coup *m* (sec); (*injection*) *Med Fam* piqûre *f*.

jabber ['dʒæbər] *vi* bavarder, jaser; – *vt* bredouiller. ◆**—ing** *n* bavardage *m*.

jack [dʒæk] **1** *n Aut* cric *m*; – *vt* **to j. up** soulever (*avec un cric*); (*price*) *Fig* augmenter. **2** *n Cards* valet *m*. **3** *vt* **to j. (in)** (*job etc*) *Fam* plaquer. **4** *n* **j. of all trades** homme *m* à tout faire. ◆**j.-in-the-box** *n* diable *m* (à ressort).

jackal ['dʒæk(ə)l] *n* (*animal*) chacal *m*.

jackass ['dʒækæs] *n* (*fool*) idiot, -ote *mf*.

jackdaw ['dʒækdɔ:] *n* (*bird*) choucas *m*.

jacket ['dʒækɪt] *n* (*short coat*) veste *f*; (*of man's suit*) veston *m*; (*of woman*) veste *f*, jaquette *f*; (*bulletproof*) gilet *m*; (*dust*) j. (*of book*) jaquette *f*; **in their jackets** (*potatoes*) en robe des champs.

jack-knife ['dʒæknaɪf] **1** *n* couteau *m* de poche. **2** *vi* (*of lorry, truck*) se mettre en travers de la route.

jackpot ['dʒækpɒt] *n* gros lot *m*.

jacks [dʒæks] *npl* (*jeu m d'*)osselets *mpl*.

jacuzzi [dʒə'ku:zɪ] *n* (*bath, pool*) jacousi *m*.

jade [dʒeɪd] *n* **1** (*stone*) jade *m*. **2** (*horse*) rosse *f*, canasson *m*.

jaded ['dʒeɪdɪd] *a* blasé.

jagged ['dʒægɪd] *a* déchiqueté.

jaguar ['dʒægjuər] *n* (*animal*) jaguar *m*.

jail [dʒeɪl] *n* prison *f*; – *vt* emprisonner (**for** theft/*etc* pour vol/*etc*); **to j. for life** condamner à perpétuité. ◆**jailbreak** *n* évasion *f* (de prison). ◆**jailer** *n* geôlier, -ière *mf*.

jalopy [dʒə'lɒpɪ] *n* (*car*) *Fam* vieux tacot *m*.

jam[1] [dʒæm] *n Culin* confiture *f*. ◆**jamjar** *n* pot *m*, à confiture.

jam[2] [dʒæm] **1** *n* (**traffic**) **j.** embouteillage *m*; **in a j.** (*trouble*) *Fig Fam* dans le pétrin. **2** *vt* (**-mm-**) (*squeeze, make stuck*) coincer, bloquer; (*gun*) enrayer; (*street, corridor etc*) encombrer; (*building*) envahir; *Rad* brouiller; **to j. sth into** (*pack, cram*) (en)tasser qch dans; (*thrust, put*) enfoncer *or* fourrer qch dans; **to j. on** (*brakes*) bloquer; – *vi* (*get stuck*) se coincer, se bloquer; (*of gun*) s'enrayer; **to j. into** (*of crowd*) s'entasser dans. ◆**jammed** a (machine etc) coincé, bloqué; (street etc) encombré. ◆**jam-'packed** a (hall etc) bourré de monde.

Jamaica [dʒə'meɪkə] n Jamaïque f.

jangl/e ['dʒæŋg(ə)l] vi cliqueter; – n cliquetis m. ◆—**ing** a (noise) discordant.

janitor ['dʒænɪtər] n concierge m.

January ['dʒænjʊərɪ] n janvier m.

Japan [dʒə'pæn] n Japon m. ◆**Japa'nese** a & n japonais, -aise (mf); – n (language) japonais m.

jar [dʒɑːr] **1** n (vessel) pot m; (large, glass) bocal m. **2** n (jolt) choc m; – vt (-rr-) (shake) ébranler. **3** vi (-rr-) (of noise) grincer; (of note) Mus détonner; (of colours, words) jurer (**with** avec); **to j. on** (s.o.'s nerves) porter sur; (s.o.'s ears) écorcher. ◆**jarring** a (note) discordant.

jargon ['dʒɑːɡən] n jargon m.

jasmine ['dʒæzmɪn] n Bot jasmin m.

jaundice ['dʒɔːndɪs] n Med jaunisse f. ◆**jaundiced** a (bitter) Fig aigri; **to take a j. view of** voir d'un mauvais œil.

jaunt [dʒɔːnt] n (journey) balade f.

jaunt/y ['dʒɔːntɪ] a (-ier, -iest) (carefree) insouciant; (cheerful, lively) allègre; (hat etc) coquet, chic. ◆—**ily** adv avec insouciance; allègrement.

javelin ['dʒævlɪn] n javelot m.

jaw [dʒɔː] **1** n Anat mâchoire f. **2** vi (talk) Pej Fam papoter; – n **to have a j.** Pej Fam tailler une bavette.

jay [dʒeɪ] n (bird) geai m.

jaywalker ['dʒeɪwɔːkər] n piéton m imprudent.

jazz [dʒæz] n jazz m; – vt **to j. up** Fam (music) jazzifier; (enliven) animer; (clothes, room) égayer.

jealous ['dʒeləs] a jaloux (**of** de). ◆**jealousy** n jalousie f.

jeans [dʒiːnz] npl (blue-)jean m.

jeep [dʒiːp] n jeep f.

jeer [dʒɪər] vti **to j.** (**at**) (mock) railler; (boo) huer; – n raillerie f; pl (boos) huées fpl. ◆—**ing** a railleur; – n railleries fpl; (of crowd) huées fpl.

jell [dʒel] vi (of ideas etc) Fam prendre tournure.

jello® ['dʒeləʊ] n inv Culin Am gelée f. ◆**jellied** a Culin en gelée. ◆**jelly** n Culin gelée f. ◆**jellyfish** n méduse f.

jeopardy ['dʒepədɪ] n danger m, péril m. ◆**jeopardize** vt mettre en danger or en péril.

jerk [dʒɜːk] **1** vt donner une secousse à (pour tirer, pousser etc); – n secousse f, saccade f. **2** n (person) Pej Fam pauvre type m;

(stupid) j. crétin, -ine mf. ◆**jerk/y** a (-ier, -iest) **1** saccadé. **2** (stupid) Am Fam stupide, bête. ◆—**ily** adv par saccades.

jersey ['dʒɜːzɪ] n (cloth) jersey m; (garment) & Fb maillot m.

Jersey ['dʒɜːzɪ] n Jersey f.

jest [dʒest] n plaisanterie f; **in j.** pour rire; – vi plaisanter. ◆—**er** n Hist bouffon m.

Jesus ['dʒiːzəs] n Jésus m; **J. Christ** Jésus-Christ m.

jet [dʒet] **1** n (of liquid, steam etc) jet m. **2** n Av (avion m à réaction); – a (engine) à réaction; **j. lag** fatigue f (due au décalage horaire). ◆**jet-lagged** a Fam qui souffre du décalage horaire.

jet-black [dʒet'blæk] a noir comme (du) jais, (noir) de jais.

jettison ['dʒetɪs(ə)n] vt Nau jeter à la mer; (fuel) Av larguer; Fig abandonner.

jetty ['dʒetɪ] n jetée f; (landing-place) embarcadère m.

Jew [dʒuː] n (man) Juif m; (woman) Juive f. ◆**Jewess** n Juive f. ◆**Jewish** a juif.

jewel ['dʒuːəl] n bijou m; (in watch) rubis m. ◆**jewelled** a orné de bijoux. ◆**jeweller** n bijoutier, -ière mf. ◆**jewellery** n, Am ◆**jewelry** n bijoux mpl.

jib [dʒɪb] vi (-bb-) regimber (**at** devant); **to j. at doing** se refuser à faire.

jibe [dʒaɪb] vi & n = **gibe**.

jiffy ['dʒɪfɪ] n Fam instant m.

jig [dʒɪɡ] n (dance, music) gigue f.

jigsaw ['dʒɪɡsɔː] n **j.** (**puzzle**) puzzle m.

jilt [dʒɪlt] vt (lover) laisser tomber.

jingle ['dʒɪŋɡ(ə)l] vi (of keys, bell etc) tinter; – vt faire tinter; – n tintement m.

jinx [dʒɪŋks] n (person, object) porte-malheur m inv; (spell, curse) (mauvais) sort m, poisse f.

jitters ['dʒɪtəz] npl **to have the j.** Fam avoir la frousse. ◆**jittery** a **to be j.** Fam avoir la frousse.

job [dʒɒb] n (task) travail m; (post) poste m, situation f; (crime) Fam coup m; **to have a j. doing** or **to do** (much trouble) avoir du mal à faire; **to have the j. of doing** (unpleasant task) être obligé de faire; (for a living etc) être chargé de faire; **it's a good j. (that)** Fam heureusement que; **that's just the j.** Fam c'est juste ce qu'il faut; **out of a j.** au chômage. ◆**jobcentre** n agence f nationale pour l'emploi. ◆**jobless** a au chômage.

jockey ['dʒɒkɪ] n jockey m; – vi **to j. for** (position, job) manœuvrer pour obtenir.

jocular ['dʒɒkjʊlər] a jovial, amusant.

jog [dʒɒɡ] **1** n (jolt) secousse f; (nudge) coup

m de coude; – *vt* (**-gg-**) (*shake*) secouer; (*elbow*) pousser; (*memory*) Fig rafraîchir. **2** *vi* (**-gg-**) **to j. along** (*of vehicle*) cahoter; (*of work*) aller tant bien que mal; (*of person*) faire son petit bonhomme de chemin. **3** *vi* (**-gg-**) Sp faire du jogging. ◆**jogging** *n* Sp jogging *m*.

john [dʒɒn] *n* (*toilet*) Am Sl cabinets *mpl*.

join [dʒɔɪn] **1** *vt* (*unite*) joindre, réunir; (*link*) relier; (*wires, pipes*) raccorder; **to j. s.o.** (*catch up with, meet*) rejoindre qn; (*associate oneself with, go with*) se joindre à qn (**in doing** pour faire); **to j. the sea** (*of river*) rejoindre la mer; **to j. hands** se donner la main; **to j. together** *or* **up** (*objects*) joindre; – *vi* (*of roads, rivers etc*) se rejoindre; **to j. (together** *or* **up**) (*of objects*) se joindre (**with** à); **to j. in** participer; **to j. in a game** prendre part à un jeu; – *n* raccord *m*, joint *m*. **2** *vt* (*become a member of*) s'inscrire à (*club, parti*); (*army*) s'engager dans; (*queue, line*) se mettre à; – *vi* (*become a member*) devenir membre; **to j. up** Mil s'engager.

joiner [ˈdʒɔɪnər] *n* menuisier *m*.

joint [dʒɔɪnt] **1** *n* Anat articulation *f*; Culin rôti *m*; Tech joint *m*; **out of j.** Med démis. **2** *n* (*nightclub etc*) Sl boîte *f*. **3** *a* (*account, statement etc*) commun; (*effort*) conjugué; **j. author** coauteur *m*. ◆**—ly** *adv* conjointement.

jok/e [dʒəʊk] *n* plaisanterie *f*; (*trick*) tour *m*; **it's no j.** (*it's unpleasant*) ce n'est pas drôle (**doing** de faire); – *vi* plaisanter (**about** sur). ◆**—er** *n* plaisantin *m*; (*fellow*) Fam type *m*; Cards joker *m*. ◆**—ingly** *adv* en plaisantant.

jolly [ˈdʒɒlɪ] **1** *a* (**-ier, -iest**) (*happy*) gai; (*drunk*) Fam éméché. **2** *adv* (*very*) Fam rudement. ◆**jollifi'cation** *n* (*merry-making*) réjouissances *fpl*. ◆**jollity** *n* jovialité *f*; (*merry-making*) réjouissances *fpl*.

jolt [dʒəʊlt] *vt* **to j. s.o.** (*of vehicle*) cahoter qn; (*shake*) Fig secouer qn; – *vi* **to j. (along)** (*of vehicle*) cahoter; – *n* cahot *m*, secousse *f*; (*shock*) Fig secousse *f*.

Jordan [ˈdʒɔːd(ə)n] *n* Jordanie *f*.

jostle [ˈdʒɒs(ə)l] *vt* (*push*) bousculer; – *vi* (*push each other*) se bousculer (**for** pour obtenir); **don't j.!** ne bousculez pas!

jot [dʒɒt] *vt* (**-tt-**) **to j. down** noter. ◆**jotter** *n* (*notepad*) bloc-notes *m*.

journal [ˈdʒɜːn(ə)l] *n* (*periodical*) revue *f*, journal *m*. ◆**journa'lese** *n* jargon *m* journalistique. ◆**journalism** *n* journalisme *m*. ◆**journalist** *n* journaliste *mf*.

journey [ˈdʒɜːnɪ] *n* (*trip*) voyage *m*;

(*distance*) trajet *m*; **to go on a j.** partir en voyage; – *vi* voyager.

jovial [ˈdʒəʊvɪəl] *a* jovial.

joy [dʒɔɪ] *n* joie *f*; *pl* (*of countryside, motherhood etc*) plaisirs *mpl* (**of** de). ◆**joyful** *a*, ◆**joyous** *a* joyeux. ◆**joyride** *n* virée *f* (*dans une voiture volée*).

joystick [ˈdʒɔɪstɪk] *n* (*of aircraft, computer*) manche *m* à balai.

JP [dʒeɪˈpiː] *abbr* = **Justice of the Peace.**

jubilant [ˈdʒuːbɪlənt] *a* **to be j.** jubiler. ◆**jubi'lation** *n* jubilation *f*.

jubilee [ˈdʒuːbɪliː] *n* (**golden**) **j.** jubilé *m*.

Judaism [ˈdʒuːdeɪɪz(ə)m] *n* judaïsme *m*.

judder [ˈdʒʌdər] *vi* (*shake*) vibrer; – *n* vibration *f*.

judg/e [dʒʌdʒ] *n* juge *m*; – *vti* juger; **judging by** à en juger par. ◆**—(e)ment** *n* jugement *m*.

judicial [dʒuːˈdɪʃ(ə)l] *a* judiciaire. ◆**judiciary** *n* magistrature *f*. ◆**judicious** *a* judicieux.

judo [ˈdʒuːdəʊ] *n* judo *m*.

jug [dʒʌg] *n* cruche *f*; (*for milk*) pot *m*.

juggernaut [ˈdʒʌgənɔːt] *n* (*truck*) poids *m* lourd, mastodonte *m*.

juggl/e [ˈdʒʌg(ə)l] *vi* jongler; – *vt* jongler avec. ◆**—er** *n* jongleur, -euse *mf*.

Jugoslavia [juːgəʊˈslɑːvɪə] *n* Yougoslavie *f*. ◆**Jugoslav** *a & n* yougoslave (*mf*).

juice [dʒuːs] *n* jus *m*; (*in stomach*) suc *m*. ◆**juicy** *a* (**-ier, -iest**) (*fruit*) juteux; (*meat*) succulent; (*story*) Fig savoureux.

jukebox [ˈdʒuːkbɒks] *n* juke-box *m*.

July [dʒuːˈlaɪ] *n* juillet *m*.

jumble [ˈdʒʌmb(ə)l] *vt* **to j. (up)** (*objects, facts etc*) brouiller, mélanger; – *n* fouillis *m*; **j. sale** (*used clothes etc*) vente *f* de charité.

jumbo [ˈdʒʌmbəʊ] *a* géant; – *a & n* (*pl* **-os**) **j. (jet)** jumbo-jet *m*, gros-porteur *m*.

jump [dʒʌmp] *n* (*leap*) saut *m*, bond *m*; (*start*) sursaut *m*; (*increase*) hausse *f*; – *vi* sauter (**at** sur); (*start*) sursauter; (*of price, heart*) faire un bond; **to j. about** sautiller; **to j. across sth** traverser qch d'un bond; **to j. to conclusions** tirer des conclusions hâtives; **j. in** *or* **on!** Aut montez!; **to j. on** (*bus*) sauter dans; **to j. off** *or* **out** sauter; **to j. off sth, j. out of sth** sauter de qch; **to j. out of the window** sauter par la fenêtre; **to j. up** se lever d'un bond; – *vt* sauter; **to j. the lights** Aut griller un feu rouge; **to j. the rails** (*of train*) dérailler; **to j. the queue** resquiller.

jumper [ˈdʒʌmpər] *n* pull-(over) *m*; (*dress*) Am robe *f* chasuble.

jumpy [ˈdʒʌmpɪ] *a* (**-ier, -iest**) nerveux.

junction ['dʒʌŋkʃ(ə)n] n (*joining*) jonction f; (*crossroads*) carrefour m.

juncture ['dʒʌŋktʃər] n **at this j.** (*critical point in time*) en ce moment même.

June [dʒuːn] n juin m.

jungle ['dʒʌŋg(ə)l] n jungle f.

junior ['dʒuːnɪər] a (*younger*) plus jeune; (*in rank, status etc*) subalterne; (*teacher, doctor*) jeune; **to be j. to s.o., be s.o.'s j.** être plus jeune que qn; (*in rank, status*) être au-dessous de qn; **Smith j.** Smith fils or junior; **j. school** école f primaire; **j. high school** *Am* = collège m d'enseignement secondaire; – n cadet, -ette mf; *Sch* petit, -ite mf, petit(e) élève mf; *Sp* junior mf, cadet, -ette mf.

junk [dʒʌŋk] **1** n (*objects*) bric-à-brac m inv; (*metal*) ferraille f; (*goods*) *Pej* camelote f; (*film, book etc*) *Pej* idiotie f; (*nonsense*) idioties fpl; **j. shop** (boutique f de) brocanteur m. **2** vt (*get rid of*) *Am Fam* balancer.

junkie ['dʒʌŋkɪ] n *Fam* drogué, -ée mf.

junta ['dʒʌntə] n *Pol* junte f.

jurisdiction [dʒuərɪs'dɪkʃ(ə)n] n juridiction f.

jury ['dʒuərɪ] n (*in competition*) & *Jur* jury m. ◆**juror** n *Jur* juré m.

just [dʒʌst] **1** adv (*exactly, slightly*) juste; (*only*) juste, seulement; (*simply*) (tout) simplement; **it's j. as I thought** c'est bien ce que je pensais; **j. at that time** à cet instant même; **she has/had j. left** elle vient/venait de partir; **I've j. come from** j'arrive de; **I'm j. coming!** j'arrive!; **he'll (only) j. catch the bus** il aura son bus de justesse; **he j. missed it** il l'a manqué de peu; **j. as big/light/***etc* tout aussi grand/léger/*etc* (as que); **j. listen!** écoute donc!; **j. a moment!** un instant!; **j. over ten** un peu plus de dix; **j. one** un(e) seul(e) (of de); **j. about** (*approximately*) à peu près; (*almost*) presque; **j. about to do** sur le point de faire. **2** a (*fair*) juste (to envers). ◆**—ly** adv avec justice. ◆**—ness** n (*of cause etc*) justice f.

justice ['dʒʌstɪs] n justice f; (*judge*) juge m; **to do j. to** (*meal*) faire honneur à; **it doesn't do you j.** (*hat, photo*) cela ne vous avantage pas; (*attitude*) cela ne vous fait pas honneur; **J. of the Peace** juge m de paix.

justify ['dʒʌstɪfaɪ] vt justifier; **to be justified in doing** (*have right*) être en droit de faire; (*have reason*) avoir toutes les bonnes raisons de faire. ◆**justi'fiable** a justifiable. ◆**justi'fiably** adv légitimement. ◆**justifi'cation** n justification f.

jut [dʒʌt] vi (-tt-) **to j. out** faire saillie; **to j. out over sth** (*overhang*) surplomber qch.

jute [dʒuːt] n (*fibre*) jute m.

juvenile ['dʒuːvənaɪl] n adolescent, -ente mf; – a (*court, book etc*) pour enfants; (*delinquent*) jeune; (*behaviour*) *Pej* puéril.

juxtapose [dʒʌkstə'pəuz] vt juxtaposer. ◆**juxtapo'sition** n juxtaposition f.

K

K, k [keɪ] n K, k m.

kaleidoscope [kə'laɪdəskəup] n kaléidoscope m.

kangaroo [kæŋgə'ruː] n kangourou m.

kaput [kə'put] a (*broken, ruined*) *Sl* fichu.

karate [kə'rɑːtɪ] n *Sp* karaté m.

keel [kiːl] n *Nau* quille f; – vi **to k. over** (*of boat*) chavirer.

keen [kiːn] a (*edge, appetite*) aiguisé; (*interest, feeling*) vif; (*mind*) pénétrant; (*wind*) coupant, piquant; (*enthusiastic*) enthousiaste; **a k. sportsman** un passionné de sport; **to be k. to do** or **on doing** tenir (beaucoup) à faire; **to be k. on** (*music, sport etc*) être passionné de; **he's k. on her/the idea** elle/l'idée lui plaît beaucoup. ◆**—ly** adv (*to work etc*) avec enthousiasme; (*to feel, interest*) vivement. ◆**—ness** n

enthousiasme m; (*of mind*) pénétration f; (*of interest*) intensité f; **k. to do** empressement m à faire.

keep[1] [kiːp] vt (pt & pp **kept**) garder; (*shop, car*) avoir; (*diary, promise*) tenir; (*family*) entretenir; (*rule*) observer, respecter; (*feast day*) célébrer; (*birthday*) fêter; (*detain, delay*) retenir; (*put*) mettre; **to k. (on) doing** (*continue*) continuer à faire; **to k. clean** tenir or garder propre; **to k. from** (*conceal*) cacher à; **to k. s.o. from doing** (*prevent*) empêcher qn de faire; **to k. s.o. waiting/working** faire attendre/travailler qn; **to k. sth going** (*engine, machine*) laisser qch en marche; **to k. s.o. in whisky/***etc* fournir qn en whisky/*etc*; **to k. an appointment** se rendre à un rendez-vous; **to k. back** (*withhold, delay*) retenir; (*conceal*) cacher (**from**

à); **to k. down** (*control*) maîtriser; (*restrict*) limiter; (*costs, price*) maintenir bas; **to k. in** empêcher de sortir; (*pupil*) *Sch* consigner; **to k. off** *or* **away** (*person*) éloigner (**from** de); **'k. off the grass'** 'ne pas marcher sur les pelouses'; **k. your hands off!** n'y touche(z) pas!; **to k. on** (*hat, employee*) garder; **to k. out** empêcher d'entrer; **to k. up** (*continue, maintain*) continuer (**doing sth** à faire qch); (*road, building*) entretenir; – *vi* (*continue*) continuer; (*remain*) rester; (*of food*) se garder, se conserver; (*wait*) attendre; **how is he keeping?** comment va-t-il?; **to k. still** rester *or* se tenir tranquille; **to k. from doing** (*refrain*) s'abstenir de faire; **to k. going** (*continue*) continuer; **to k. at it** (*keep doing it*) continuer à le faire; **to k. away** *or* **off** *or* **back** ne pas s'approcher (**from** de); **if the rain keeps off** s'il ne pleut pas; **to k. on at s.o.** harceler qn; **to k. out** rester en dehors (**of** de); **to k. to** (*subject, path*) ne pas s'écarter de; (*room*) garder; **to k. to the left** tenir la gauche; **to k. to oneself** se tenir à l'écart; **to k. up** (*continue*) continuer; (*follow*) suivre; **to k. up with s.o** (*follow*) suivre qn; (*in quality of work etc*) se maintenir à la hauteur de qn; – *n* (*food*) subsistance *f*; **to have one's k.** être logé et nourri; **for keeps** *Fam* pour toujours. ◆**—ing** *n* (*care*) garde *f*; **in k. with** rapport avec. ◆**—er** *n* gardien, -ienne *mf*.

keep² [kiːp] *n* (*tower*) *Hist* donjon *m*.

keepsake ['kiːpseɪk] *n* (*object*) souvenir *m*.

keg [keg] *n* tonnelet *m*.

kennel ['ken(ə)l] *n* niche *f*; (*for boarding*) chenil *m*.

Kenya ['kiːnjə, 'kenjə] *n* Kenya *m*.

kept [kept] *see* keep¹; – *a* **well** *or* **nicely k.** (*house etc*) bien tenu.

kerb [kɜːb] *n* bord *m* du trottoir.

kernel ['kɜːn(ə)l] *n* (*of nut*) amande *f*.

kerosene ['kerəsiːn] *n* (*aviation fuel*) kérosène *m*; (*paraffin*) *Am* pétrole *m* (lampant).

ketchup ['ketʃəp] *n* (*sauce*) ketchup *m*.

kettle ['ket(ə)l] *n* bouilloire *f*; **the k. is boiling** l'eau bout.

key [kiː] *n* clef *f*, clé *f*; (*of piano, typewriter, computer*) touche *f*; – *a* (*industry, post etc*) clef (*f inv*), clé (*f inv*); **k. man** pivot *m*; **k. ring** porte-clefs *m inv*. ◆**keyboard** *n* clavier *m*. ◆**keyhole** *n* trou *m* de (la) serrure. ◆**keynote** *n* (*of speech*) note *f* dominante. ◆**keystone** *n* (*of policy etc*) & *Archit* clef *f* de voûte.

keyed [kiːd] *a* **to be k. up** avoir les nerfs tendus.

khaki ['kɑːkɪ] *a & n* kaki *a inv & m*.

kibbutz [kɪˈbʊts] *n* kibboutz *m*.

kick [kɪk] *n* coup *m* de pied; (*of horse*) ruade *f*; **to get a k. out of doing** (*thrill*) *Fam* prendre un malin plaisir à faire; **for kicks** *Pej Fam* pour le plaisir; – *vt* donner un coup de pied à; (*of horse*) lancer une ruade à; **to k. back** (*ball*) renvoyer (*du pied*); **to k. down** *or* **in** démolir à coups de pied; **to k. out** (*eject*) *Fam* flanquer dehors; **to k. up** (*fuss, row*) *Fam* faire; – *vi* donner des coups de pied; (*of horse*) ruer; **to k. off** *Fb* donner le coup d'envoi; (*start*) *Fig* démarrer. ◆**k.-off** *n Fb* coup *m* d'envoi.

kid [kɪd] **1** *n* (*goat*) chevreau *m*. **2** *n* (*child*) *Fam* gosse *mf*; **his** *or* **her k.** brother *Am Fam* son petit frère. **3** *vti* (-**dd**-) (*joke, tease*) *Fam* blaguer; **to k. oneself** se faire des illusions.

kidnap ['kɪdnæp] *vt* (-**pp**-) kidnapper. ◆**kidnapping** *n* enlèvement *m*. ◆**kidnapper** *n* kidnappeur, -euse *mf*.

kidney ['kɪdnɪ] *n Anat* rein *m*; *Culin* rognon *m*; **on a k. machine** sous rein artificiel; **k. bean** haricot *m* rouge.

kill [kɪl] *vt* tuer; (*bill*) *Pol* repousser, faire échouer; (*chances*) détruire; (*rumour*) étouffer; (*story*) *Fam* supprimer; (*engine*) *Fam* arrêter; **my feet are killing me** *Fam* je ne sens plus mes pieds, j'ai les pieds en compote; **to k. off** (*person etc*) & *Fig* détruire; – *vi* tuer; – *n* mise *f* à mort; (*prey*) animaux *mpl* tués. ◆**—ing 1** *n* (*of person*) meurtre *m*; (*of group*) massacre *m*; (*of animal*) mise *f* à mort; **to make a k.** *Fin* réussir un beau coup. **2** *a* (*tiring*) *Fam* tuant. ◆**—er** *n* tueur, -euse *mf*. ◆**killjoy** *n* rabat-joie *m inv*.

kiln [kɪln] *n* (*for pottery*) four *m*.

kilo ['kiːləʊ] *n* (*pl* -**os**) kilo *m*. ◆**kilogramme** ['kɪləʊɡræm] *n* kilogramme *m*.

kilometre [kɪˈlɒmɪtər] *n* kilomètre *m*.

kilowatt ['kɪləʊwɒt] *n* kilowatt *m*.

kilt [kɪlt] *n* kilt *m*.

kimono [kɪˈməʊnəʊ] *n* (*pl* -**os**) kimono *m*.

kin [kɪn] *n* (*relatives*) parents *mpl*; **one's next of k.** son plus proche parent.

kind [kaɪnd] **1** *n* (*sort, type*) genre *m*; **a k. of** une sorte *or* une espèce de; **to pay in k.** payer en nature; **what k. of drink/etc is it?** qu'est-ce que c'est comme boisson/etc?; **that's the k. of man he is** il est comme ça; **nothing of the k.!** absolument pas!; **k. of worried/sad/etc** (*somewhat*) plutôt inquiet/triste/etc; **k. of fascinated** (*as if*) *Fam* comme fasciné; **in a k. of way** d'une certaine façon; **it's the only one of its k., it's one of a k.** c'est unique en son genre; **we are**

two of a k. nous nous ressemblons. **2** *a* (**-er,** **-est**) (*helpful, pleasant*) gentil (to avec, pour), bon (to pour); **that's k. of you** c'est gentil *or* aimable à vous. ◆**k.-'hearted** *a* qui a bon cœur. ◆**kindly** *adv* avec bonté; **k. wait/etc** ayez la bonté d'attendre/*etc*; **not to take k. to sth** ne pas apprécier qch; – *a* (*person*) bienveillant. ◆**kindness** *n* bonté *f*, gentillesse *f*.

kindergarten ['kɪndəgɑːt(ə)n] *n* jardin *m* d'enfants.

kindle ['kɪnd(ə)l] *vt* allumer; – *vi* s'allumer.

kindred ['kɪndrɪd] *n* (*relationship*) parenté *f*; (*relatives*) parents *mpl*; **k. spirit** semblable *mf*, âme *f* sœur.

king [kɪŋ] *n* roi *m*. ◆**k.-size(d)** *a* géant; (*cigarette*) long. ◆**kingdom** *n* royaume *m*; **animal/plant k.** règne *m* animal/végétal. ◆**kingly** *a* royal.

kingfisher ['kɪŋfɪʃər] *n* (*bird*) martin-pêcheur *m*.

kink [kɪŋk] *n* (*in rope*) entortillement *m*.

kinky ['kɪŋkɪ] *a* (**-ier, -iest**) (*person*) *Psy Pej* vicieux; (*clothes etc*) bizarre.

kinship ['kɪnʃɪp] *n* parenté *f*.

kiosk ['kiːɒsk] *n* kiosque *m*; (**telephone**) **k.** cabine *f* (téléphonique).

kip [kɪp] *vi* (**-pp-**) (*sleep*) *Sl* roupiller.

kipper ['kɪpər] *n* (*herring*) kipper *m*.

kiss [kɪs] *n* baiser *m*, bise *f*; **the k. of life** *Med* le bouche-à-bouche; – *vt* (*person*) embrasser; **to k. s.o.'s hand** baiser la main de qn; – *vi* s'embrasser.

kit [kɪt] *n* équipement *m*, matériel *m*; (*set of articles*) trousse *f*; **gym k.** (*belongings*) affaires *fpl* de gym; **tool k.** trousse *f* à outils; (**do-it-yourself**) **k.** kit *m*; **in k. form** en kit; **k. bag** sac *m* (*de soldat etc*); – *vt* (**-tt-**) **to k. out** équiper (**with** de).

kitchen ['kɪtʃɪn] *n* cuisine *f*; **k. cabinet** buffet *m* de cuisine; **k. garden** jardin *m* potager; **k. sink** évier *m*. ◆**kitche'nette** *n* kitchenette *f*, coin-cuisine *m*.

kite [kaɪt] *n* (*toy*) cerf-volant *m*.

kith [kɪθ] *n* **k. and kin** amis *mpl* et parents *mpl*.

kitten ['kɪt(ə)n] *n* chaton *m*, petit chat *m*.

kitty ['kɪtɪ] *n* (*fund*) cagnotte *f*.

km *abbr* (*kilometre*) km.

knack [næk] *n* (*skill*) coup *m* (de main), truc *m* (**of doing** pour faire); **to have a** *or* **the k. of doing** (*aptitude, tendency*) avoir le don de faire.

knackered ['nækəd] *a* (*tired*) *Sl* vanné.

knapsack ['næpsæk] *n* sac *m* à dos.

knead [niːd] *vt* (*dough*) pétrir.

knee [niː] *n* genou *m*; **to go down on one's**

knees se mettre à genoux; **k. pad** *Sp* genouillère *f*. ◆**kneecap** *n* *Anat* rotule *f*. ◆**knees-up** *n* *Sl* soirée *f* dansante, sauterie *f*.

kneel [niːl] *vi* (*pt & pp* knelt *or* kneeled) **to k. (down)** s'agenouiller; **to be kneeling (down)** être à genoux.

knell [nel] *n* glas *m*.

knew [njuː] *see* know.

knickers ['nɪkəz] *npl* (*woman's undergarment*) culotte *f*, slip *m*.

knick-knack ['nɪknæk] *n* babiole *f*.

knife [naɪf] *n* (*pl* knives) couteau *m*; (*penknife*) canif *m*; – *vt* poignarder.

knight [naɪt] *n* *Hist & Br Pol* chevalier *m*; *Chess* cavalier *m*; – *vt* (*of monarch*) *Br Pol* faire (qn) chevalier. ◆**knighthood** *n* titre *m* de chevalier.

knit [nɪt] *vt* (**-tt-**) tricoter; **to k. together** *Fig* souder; **to k. one's brow** froncer les sourcils; – *vi* tricoter; **to k. (together)** (*of bones*) se souder. ◆**knitting** *n* tricot *m*; **k. needle** aiguille *f* à tricoter. ◆**knitwear** *n* tricots *mpl*.

knob [nɒb] *n* (*on door etc*) bouton *m*; (*on stick*) pommeau *m*; (*of butter*) noix *f*.

knock [nɒk] *vt* (*strike*) frapper; (*collide with*) heurter; (*criticize*) *Fam* critiquer; **to k. one's head on** se cogner la tête contre; **to k. senseless** (*stun*) assommer; **to k. to the ground** jeter à terre; **to k. about** (*ill-treat*) malmener; **to k. back** (*drink, glass etc*) *Fam* s'envoyer (derrière la cravate), siffler; **to k. down** (*vase, pedestrian etc*) renverser; (*house, tree, wall etc*) abattre; (*price*) baisser, casser; **to k. in** (*nail*) enfoncer; **to k. off** (*person, object*) faire tomber (**from** de); (*do quickly*) *Fam* expédier; (*steal*) *Fam* piquer; **to k. £5 off (the price)** baisser le prix de cinq livres, faire cinq livres sur le prix; **to k. out** (*stun*) assommer; (*beat in competition*) éliminer; **to k. oneself out** (*tire*) *Fam* s'esquinter (**doing** à faire); **to k. over** (*pedestrian, vase etc*) renverser; **to k. up** (*meal*) *Fam* préparer à la hâte; – *vi* (*strike*) frapper; **to k. against** *or* **into** (*bump into*) heurter; **to k. about** (*travel*) *Fam* bourlinguer; (*lie around, stand around*) traîner; **to k. off** (*stop work*) *Fam* s'arrêter de travailler; – *n* (*blow*) coup *m*; (*collision*) heurt *m*; **there's a k. at the door** quelqu'un frappe; **I heard a k.** j'ai entendu frapper. ◆**knockdown** *a* **k. price** prix *m* imbattable. ◆**knock-'kneed** *a* cagneux. ◆**knock-out** *n* *Boxing* knock-out *m*; **to be a k.-out** (*of person, film etc*) *Fam* être formidable.

knocker ['nɒkər] n (for door) marteau m.
knot [nɒt] 1 n (in rope etc) nœud m; – vt (-tt-) nouer. 2 n (unit of speed) Nau nœud m. ◆**knotty** a (-ier, -iest) (wood etc) noueux; (problem) Fig épineux.
know [nəʊ] vt (pt knew, pp known) (facts, language etc) savoir; (person, place etc) connaître; (recognize) reconnaître (by à); to k. that savoir que; to k. how to do savoir faire; for all I k. (autant) que je sache; I'll let you k. je te le ferai savoir; I'll have you k. that . . . sachez que . . . ; to k. (a lot) about (person, event) en savoir long sur; (cars, sewing etc) s'y connaître en; I've never known him to complain je ne l'ai jamais vu se plaindre; to get to k. (about) sth apprendre qch; to get to k. s.o. (meet) faire la connaissance de qn; – vi savoir; I k. je (le) sais; I wouldn't k., I k. nothing about it je n'en sais rien; I k. about that je sais ça, je suis au courant; to k. of (have heard of) avoir entendu parler de; do you k. of? (a good tailor etc) connais-tu?; you (should) k. better than to do that tu es trop intelligent pour faire ça; you should have known better tu aurais dû réfléchir; – n in the k. Fam au courant. ◆—ing a (smile, look) entendu. ◆—ingly adv (consciously) sciemment. ◆known a connu; a k. expert un expert reconnu; well k. (bien) connu (that que); she is k. to be . . . on sait qu'elle est . . . . ◆know-all n, Am ◆know-it-all n je-sais-tout mf inv. ◆know-how n (skill) compétence f (to do pour faire), savoir-faire m inv.
knowledge ['nɒlɪdʒ] n connaissance f (of de); (learning) connaissances fpl, savoir m; to (the best of) my k. à ma connaissance; without the k. of à l'insu de; to have no k. of ignorer; general k. culture f générale. ◆**knowledgeable** a bien informé (about sur).
knuckle ['nʌk(ə)l] 1 n articulation f du doigt. 2 vi to k. down to (task) Fam s'atteler à; to k. under céder.
Koran [kə'rɑːn] n Rel Coran m.
kosher ['kəʊʃər] a Rel kascher inv.
kowtow [kaʊ'taʊ] vi se prosterner (to devant).
kudos ['kjuːdɒs] n (glory) gloire f.

L

L, l [el] L, l m.
lab [læb] n Fam labo m. ◆**laboratory** [lə'bɒrət(ə)rɪ, Am 'læbrətɔrɪ] n laboratoire m; language l. laboratoire m de langues.
label ['leɪb(ə)l] n étiquette f; – vt (-ll-, Am -l-) (goods, person) étiqueter (as comme).
laborious [lə'bɔːrɪəs] a laborieux.
labour ['leɪbər] n (work, childbirth) travail m; (workers) main-d'œuvre f; L. Br Pol les travaillistes mpl; in l. Med au travail; – a (market, situation) du travail; (conflict, dispute) ouvrier; (relations) ouvriers-patronat inv; l. force main-d'œuvre f; l. union Am syndicat m; – vi (toil) peiner; – vt to l. a point insister sur un point. ◆—ed a (style) laborieux. ◆—er n (on roads etc) manœuvre m; Agr ouvrier m agricole.
laburnum [lə'bɜːnəm] n Bot cytise f.
labyrinth ['læbɪrɪnθ] n labyrinthe m.
lace [leɪs] 1 n (cloth) dentelle f. 2 n (of shoe) lacet m; – vt to l. (up) (tie up) lacer. 3 vt (drink) additionner, arroser (with de).
lacerate ['læsəreɪt] vt (flesh etc) lacérer.
lack [læk] n manque m; for l. of à défaut de; – vt manquer de; – vi to be lacking manquer (in, for de).
lackey ['lækɪ] n Hist & Fig laquais m.
laconic [lə'kɒnɪk] a laconique.
lacquer ['lækər] n laque f; – vt laquer.
lad [læd] n gars m, garçon m; when I was a l. quand j'étais gosse.
ladder ['lædər] n échelle f; (in stocking) maille f filée; – vti (stocking) filer.
laden ['leɪd(ə)n] a chargé (with de).
ladle ['leɪd(ə)l] n louche f.
lady ['leɪdɪ] n dame f; a young l. une jeune fille; (married) une jeune femme; the l. of the house la maîtresse de maison; Ladies and Gentlemen! Mesdames, Mesdemoiselles, Messieurs!; l. doctor femme f médecin; l. friend amie f; ladies' room Fig toilettes fpl. ◆l.-in-'waiting n (pl ladies-in-waiting) dame f d'honneur. ◆**ladybird** n, Am ◆**ladybug** n coccinelle f. ◆**ladylike** a (manner) distingué; she's (very) l. elle est très grande dame.
lag [læg] 1 vi (-gg-) to l. behind (in progress, work) avoir du retard; (dawdle) traîner; to l. behind s.o. avoir du retard sur qn; – n

time l. (*between events*) décalage *m*; (*between countries*) décalage *m* horaire. **2** *vt* (-gg-) (*pipe*) calorifuger.

lager ['lɑːgər] *n* bière *f* blonde.

lagoon [lə'guːn] *n* lagune *f*; (*small, coral*) lagon *m*.

laid [leɪd] *see* lay². ◆l.-'back *a Fam* relax.

lain [leɪn] *see* lie¹.

lair [leər] *n* tanière *f*.

laity ['leɪtɪ] *n* the l. les laïcs *mpl*.

lake [leɪk] *n* lac *m*.

lamb [læm] *n* agneau *m*. ◆lambswool *n* laine *f* d'agneau.

lame [leɪm] *a* (-er, -est) (*person, argument*) boiteux; (*excuse*) piètre; to be l. boiter. ◆—ness *n Med* claudication *f*; (*of excuse*) *Fig* faiblesse *f*.

lament [lə'ment] *n* lamentation *f*; − *vt* to l. (over) se lamenter sur. ◆lamentable *a* lamentable. ◆lamen'tation *n* lamentation *f*.

laminated ['læmɪneɪtɪd] *a* (*metal*) laminé.

lamp [læmp] *n* lampe *f*; (*bulb*) ampoule *f*; *Aut* feu *m*. ◆lamppost *n* réverbère *m*. ◆lampshade *n* abat-jour *m inv*.

lance [lɑːns] **1** *n* (*weapon*) lance *f*. **2** *vt Med* inciser.

land [lænd] **1** *n* terre *f*; (*country*) pays *m*; (plot of) l. terrain *m*; on dry l. sur la terre ferme; no man's l. *Mil & Fig* no man's land *m inv*; − *a* (*flora, transport etc*) terrestre; (*reform, law*) agraire; (*owner, tax*) foncier. **2** *vi* (*of aircraft*) atterrir, se poser; (*of ship*) mouiller, relâcher; (*of passengers*) débarquer; (*of bomb etc*) (re)tomber; to l. up (*end up*) se retrouver; − *vt* (*passengers, cargo*) débarquer; (*aircraft*) poser; (*blow*) *Fig* flanquer (on à); (*job, prize etc*) *Fam* décrocher; to l. s.o. in trouble *Fam* mettre qn dans le pétrin; to be landed with *Fam* (*person*) avoir sur les bras; (*fine*) ramasser, écoper de. ◆—ed *a* (*owning land*) terrien. ◆—ing *n* **1** *Av* atterrissage *m*; *Nau* débarquement *m*; forced l. atterrissage *m* forcé; l. stage débarcadère *m*. **2** *n* (*at top of stairs*) palier *m*; (*floor*) étage *m*. ◆landlady *n* logeuse *f*, propriétaire *f*. ◆landlocked *a* sans accès à la mer. ◆landlord *n* propriétaire *m*; (*of pub*) patron *m*. ◆landmark *n* point *m* de repère. ◆landslide *n Geol* glissement *m* de terrain, éboulement *m*; *Pol* raz-de-marée *m inv* électoral.

landscape ['lændskeɪp] *n* paysage *m*.

lane [leɪn] *n* (*in country*) chemin *m*; (*in town*) ruelle *f*; (*division of road*) voie *f*; (*line of* traffic*) file *f*; *Av Nau Sp* couloir *m*; bus l. couloir *m* (réservé aux autobus).

language ['læŋgwɪdʒ] *n* (*faculty, style*) langage *m*; (*national tongue*) langue *f*; computer l. langage *m* machine; − *a* (*laboratory*) de langues; (*teacher, studies*) de langue(s).

languid ['læŋgwɪd] *a* languissant. ◆languish *vi* languir (for, after après).

lank [læŋk] *a* (*hair*) plat et terne.

lanky ['læŋkɪ] *a* (-ier, -iest) dégingandé.

lantern ['læntən] *n* lanterne *f*; Chinese l. lampion *m*.

lap [læp] **1** *n* (*of person*) genoux *mpl*; the l. of luxury le plus grand luxe. **2** *n Sp* tour *m* (de piste). **3** *vt* (-pp-) to l. up (*drink*) laper; (*like very much*) *Fam* adorer; (*believe*) *Fam* gober; − *vi* (*of waves*) clapoter. **4** *vt* (-pp-) to l. over (*overlap*) se chevaucher.

lapel [lə'pel] *n* (*of jacket etc*) revers *m*.

lapse [læps] **1** *n* (*fault*) faute *f*; (*weakness*) défaillance *f*; a l. of memory un trou de mémoire; a l. in behaviour un écart de conduite; − *vi* (*err*) commettre une faute; to l. into retomber dans. **2** *n* (*interval*) intervalle *m*; a l. of time un intervalle (between entre). **3** *vi* (*expire*) se périmer, expirer; (*of subscription*) prendre fin.

larceny ['lɑːsənɪ] *n* vol *m* simple.

lard [lɑːd] *n* saindoux *m*.

larder ['lɑːdər] *n* (*cupboard*) garde-manger *m inv*.

large [lɑːdʒ] *a* (-er, -est) (*in size or extent*) grand; (*in volume, bulkiness*) gros; (*quantity*) grand, important; to become *or* grow *or* get l. grossir, grandir; to a l. extent en grande mesure; at l. (*of prisoner, animal*) en liberté; (*as a whole*) en général; by and l. dans l'ensemble, généralement. ◆l.-scale *a* (*reform*) (fait) sur une grande échelle. ◆largely *adv* (*to a great extent*) en grande mesure. ◆largeness *n* grandeur *f*; grosseur *f*.

largesse [lɑː'ʒes] *n* largesse *f*.

lark [lɑːk] **1** *n* (*bird*) alouette *f*. **2** *n* (*joke*) *Fam* rigolade *f*, blague *f*; − *vi* to l. about *Fam* s'amuser.

larva, *pl* **-vae** ['lɑːvə, -viː] *n* (*of insect*) larve *f*.

larynx ['lærɪŋks] *n Anat* larynx *m*. ◆laryn'gitis *n Med* laryngite *f*.

lascivious [lə'sɪvɪəs] *a* lascif.

laser ['leɪzər] *n* laser *m*.

lash¹ [læʃ] *n* (*with whip*) coup *m* de fouet; − *vt* (*strike*) fouetter; (*tie*) attacher (to à); the dog lashed its tail le chien donna un coup de queue; − *vi* to l. out (*spend wildly*) *Fam* claquer son argent; to l. out at envoyer des

coups à; *(abuse)* *Fig* invectiver; *(criticize)* *Fig* fustiger. ◆**—ings** *npl* l. of *Culin Fam* des masses de, une montagne de.
lash² [læʃ] *n (eyelash)* cil *m*.
lass [læs] *n* jeune fille *f*.
lassitude ['læsɪtjuːd] *n* lassitude *f*.
lasso [læ'suː] *n (pl -os)* lasso *m*; *— vt* attraper au lasso.
last¹ [lɑːst] *a* dernier; **the l. ten lines** les dix dernières lignes; **l. but one** avant-dernier; **l. night** *(evening)* hier soir; *(during night)* cette nuit; **the day before l.** avant-hier; *— adv (lastly)* en dernier lieu, enfin; *(on the last occasion)* (pour) la dernière fois; **to leave l.** sortir le dernier *or* en dernier; *— n (person, object)* dernier, -ière *mf*; *(end)* fin *f*; **the l. of the beer/etc** *(remainder)* le reste de la bière/etc; **at (long) l.** enfin. ◆**l.-ditch** *a* désespéré. ◆**l.-minute** *a* de dernière minute. ◆**lastly** *adv* en dernier lieu, enfin.
last² [lɑːst] *vi* durer; **to l. (out)** *(endure, resist)* tenir; *(of money, supplies)* durer; **it lasted me ten years** ça m'a duré *or* fait dix ans. ◆**—ing** *a* durable.
latch [lætʃ] **1** *n* loquet *m*; **the door is on the l.** la porte n'est pas fermée à clef. **2** *vi* **to l. on to** *Fam (grab)* s'accrocher à; *(understand)* saisir.
late¹ [leɪt] *a (-er, -est) (not on time)* en retard (**for** à); *(former)* ancien; *(meal, fruit, season, hour)* tardif; *(stage)* avancé; *(edition)* dernier; **to be l.** *(of person, train etc)* être en retard, avoir du retard; **to be l. (in) coming** arriver en retard; **he's an hour l.** il a une heure de retard; **to make s.o. l.** mettre qn en retard; **it's l.** il est tard; **Easter/etc is l.** Pâques/etc est tard; **in l. June/etc** fin juin/etc; **a later edition/etc** *(more recent)* une édition/etc plus récente; **the latest edition/etc** *(last)* la dernière édition/etc; **in later life** plus tard dans la vie; **to take a later train** prendre un train plus tard; **at a later date** à une date ultérieure; **the latest date** la date limite; **at the latest** au plus tard; **of l.** dernièrement; *— adv (in the day, season etc)* tard; *(not on time)* en retard; **it's getting l.** il se fait tard; **later (on)** plus tard; **not** *or* **no later than** pas plus tard que. ◆**latecomer** *n* retardataire *mf*. ◆**lately** *adv* dernièrement. ◆**lateness** *n (of person, train etc)* retard *m*; **constant l.** des retards continuels; **the l. of the hour** l'heure tardive.
late² [leɪt] *a* **the l.** Mr Smith/*etc (deceased)* feu Monsieur Smith/*etc*; **our l. friend** notre regretté ami.
latent ['leɪtənt] *a* latent.

lateral ['lætərəl] *a* latéral.
lathe [leɪð] *n Tech* tour *m*.
lather ['lɑːðər] *n* mousse *f*; *— vt* savonner; *— vi* mousser.
Latin ['lætɪn] *a* latin; **L. America** Amérique *f* latine; **L. American** d'Amérique latine; *— n (person)* Latin, -ine *mf*; *(language)* latin *m*.
latitude ['lætɪtjuːd] *n Geog & Fig* latitude *f*.
latrines [lə'triːnz] *npl* latrines *fpl*.
latter ['lætər] *a (later, last-named)* dernier; *(second)* deuxième; *— n* dernier, -ière *mf*; second, -onde *mf*. ◆**—ly** *adv* dernièrement; *(late in life)* sur le tard.
lattice ['lætɪs] *n* treillis *m*.
laudable ['lɔːdəb(ə)l] *a* louable.
laugh [lɑːf] *n* rire *m*; **to have a good l.** bien rire; *— vi* rire (**at, about** de); **to l. to oneself** rire en soi-même; *— vt* **to l. off** tourner en plaisanterie. ◆**—ing** *a* riant; **it's no l. matter** il n'y a pas de quoi rire; **to be the l.-stock of** être la risée de. ◆**—able** *a* ridicule. ◆**laughter** *n* rire(s) *m(pl)*; **to roar with l.** rire aux éclats.
launch [lɔːntʃ] **1** *n (motor boat)* vedette *f*; *(pleasure boat)* bateau *m* de plaisance. **2** *vt (rocket, boat, fashion etc)* lancer; *— vi* **to l. (out) into** *(begin)* se lancer dans; *— n* lancement *m*. ◆**—ing** *n* lancement *m*.
launder ['lɔːndər] *vt (clothes)* blanchir; *(money from drugs etc)* *Fig* blanchir. ◆**—ing** *n* blanchissage *m*. ◆**launde'rette** *n*, *Am* ◆**laundromat** *n* laverie *f* automatique. ◆**laundry** *n (place)* blanchisserie *f*; *(clothes)* linge *m*.
laurel ['lɒrəl] *n Bot* laurier *m*.
lava ['lɑːvə] *n Geol* lave *f*.
lavatory ['lævətrɪ] *n* cabinets *mpl*.
lavender ['lævɪndər] *n* lavande *f*.
lavish ['lævɪʃ] *a* prodigue (**with** de); *(helping, meal)* généreux; *(decor, house etc)* somptueux; *(expenditure)* excessif; *— vt* prodiguer *(sth on s.o.* qch à qn). ◆**—ly** *adv (to give)* généreusement; *(to furnish)* somptueusement.
law [lɔː] *n (rule, rules)* loi *f*; *(study, profession, system)* droit *m*; **court of l.**, **l. court** cour *f* de justice; **l. and order** l'ordre public. ◆**l.-abiding** *a* respectueux des lois. ◆**lawful** *a (action)* légal; *(child, wife etc)* légitime. ◆**lawfully** *adv* légalement. ◆**lawless** *a (country)* anarchique. ◆**lawlessness** *n* anarchie *f*. ◆**lawsuit** *n* procès *m*.
lawn [lɔːn] *n* pelouse *f*, gazon *m*; **l. mower** tondeuse *f* (à gazon); **l. tennis** tennis *m* (sur gazon).
lawyer ['lɔːjər] *n (in court)* avocat *m*; *(author,*

legal expert) juriste *m*; (*for wills, sales*) notaire *m*.

lax [læks] *a* (*person*) négligent; (*discipline, behaviour*) relâché; **to be l. in doing** faire avec négligence. ◆**laxity** *n*, ◆**laxness** *n* négligence *f*; relâchement *m*.

laxative ['læksətɪv] *n & a Med* laxatif (*m*).

lay¹ [leɪ] *a* (*non-religious*) laïque; (*non-specialized*) d'un profane; **l. person** profane *mf*. ◆**layman** *n* (*pl* -**men**) (*non-specialist*) profane *mf*.

lay² [leɪ] (*pt & pp* **laid**) **1** *vt* (*put down, place*) poser; (*table*) mettre; (*blanket*) étendre (**over** sur); (*trap*) tendre; (*money*) miser (**on** sur); (*accusation*) porter; (*ghost*) exorciser; **to l. a bet** parier; **to l. bare** mettre à nu; **to l. waste** ravager; **to l. s.o. open to** exposer qn à; **to l. one's hands on** mettre la main sur; **to l. a hand** *or* **a finger on s.o.** lever la main sur qn; **to l. down** poser; (*arms*) déposer; (*condition*) (im)poser; **to l. down the law** faire la loi (**to** à); **to l. s.o. off** (*worker*) licencier qn; **to l. on** (*install*) mettre, installer; (*supply*) fournir; **to l. it on (thick)** *Fam* y aller un peu fort; **to l. out** (*garden*) dessiner; (*house*) concevoir; (*prepare*) préparer; (*display*) disposer; (*money*) *Fam* dépenser (**on** pour); **to be laid up** (*in bed*) *Med* être alité; – *vi* **to l. into** *Fam* attaquer; **to l. off** (*stop*) *Fam* arrêter; **l. off s.o.** (*leave alone*) *Fam* laisser qn tranquille; **l. off!** (*don't touch*) *Fam* pas touche!; **to l. out** *Fam* payer. **2** *vt* (*egg*) pondre; – *vi* (*of bird etc*) pondre. ◆**layabout** *n Fam* fainéant, -ante *mf*. ◆**lay-by** *n* (*pl* -**bys**) *Aut* aire *f* de stationnement *or* de repos. ◆**lay-off** *n* (*of worker*) licenciement *m*. **layout** *n* disposition *f*; *Typ* mise *f* en pages. ◆**lay-over** *n Am* halte *f*.

lay³ [leɪ] *see* **lie¹**.

layer ['leɪər] *n* couche *f*.

laze [leɪz] *vi* **to l.** (**about** *or* **around**) paresser. ◆**lazy** *a* (**-ier, -iest**) (*person etc*) paresseux; (*holiday*) passé à ne rien faire. ◆**lazybones** *n Fam* paresseux, -euse *mf*.

lb *abbr* (*libra*) = **pound** (*weight*).

lead¹ [liːd] *vt* (*pt & pp* **led**) (*conduct*) mener, conduire (**to** à); (*team, government etc*) diriger; (*regiment*) commander; (*life*) mener; **to l. s.o. in/out/etc** faire entrer/sortir/*etc* qn; **to l. s.o. to do** (*induce*) amener qn à faire; **to l. the way** montrer le chemin; **to l. the world** tenir le premier rang mondial; **easily led** influençable; **to l. away** *or* **off** emmener; **to l. back** ramener; **to l. on** (*tease*) faire marcher; – *vi* (*of street etc*) mener, conduire (**to** à); (*in match*) mener;

(*in race*) être en tête; (*go ahead*) aller devant; **to l. to** (*result in*) aboutir à; (*cause*) causer, amener; **to l. up to** (*of street*) conduire à, mener à; (*precede*) précéder; (*approach gradually*) en venir à; – *n* (*distance or time ahead*) *Sp* avance *f* (**over** sur); (*example*) exemple *m*; initiative *f*; (*clue*) piste *f*, indice *m*; (*star part*) *Th* rôle *m* principal; (*leash*) laisse *f*; (*wire*) *El* fil *m*; **to take the l.** *Sp* prendre la tête; **to be in the l.** (*in race*) être en tête; (*in match*) mener. ◆**leading** *a* (*main*) principal; (*important*) important; (*front*) de tête; **the l. author** l'auteur principal *or* le plus important; **a l. figure** un personnage marquant; **the l. lady** *Cin* la vedette féminine; **l. article** *Journ* éditorial *m*. ◆**leader** *n* chef *m*; *Pol* dirigeant, -ante *mf*; (*of strike, riot*) meneur, -euse *mf*; (*guide*) guide *m*; (*article*) *Journ* éditorial *m*. ◆**leadership** *n* direction *f*; (*qualities*) qualités *fpl* de chef; (*leaders*) *Pol* dirigeants *mpl*.

lead² [led] *n* (*metal*) plomb *m*; (*of pencil*) mine *f*; **l. pencil** crayon *m* à mine de plomb. ◆**leaden** *a* (*sky*) de plomb.

leaf [liːf] **1** *n* (*pl* **leaves**) *Bot* feuille *f*; (*of book*) feuillet *m*; (*of table*) rallonge *f*. **2** *vi* **to l. through** (*book*) feuilleter. ◆**leaflet** *n* prospectus *m*; (*containing instructions*) notice *f*. ◆**leafy** *a* (**-ier, -iest**) (*tree*) feuillu.

league [liːg] *n* **1** (*alliance*) ligue *f*; *Sp* championnat *m*; **in l. with** *Pej* de connivence avec. **2** (*measure*) *Hist* lieue *f*.

leak [liːk] *n* (*in pipe, information etc*) fuite *f*; (*in boat*) voie *f* d'eau; – *vi* (*of liquid, pipe, tap etc*) fuir; (*of ship*) faire eau; **to l. out** (*of information*) *Fig* être divulgué; – *vt* (*liquid*) répandre; (*information*) *Fig* divulguer. ◆—**age** *n* fuite *f*; (*amount lost*) perte *f*. ◆**leaky** *a* (**-ier, -iest**) *a* (*kettle etc*) qui fuit.

lean¹ [liːn] *a* (**-er, -est**) (*thin*) maigre; (*year*) difficile. ◆—**ness** *n* maigreur *f*.

lean² [liːn] *vi* (*pt & pp* **leaned** *or* **leant** [lent]) (*of object*) pencher; (*of person*) se pencher; **to l. against/on** (*of person*) s'appuyer contre/sur; **to l. back against** s'adosser à; **to l. on s.o.** (*influence*) *Fam* faire pression sur qn (**to do** pour faire); **to l. forward** *or* **over** (*of person*) se pencher (en avant); **to l. over** (*of object*) pencher; – *vt* appuyer (**against** contre); **to l. one's head on/out of** pencher la tête sur/par. ◆—**ing 1** *a* penché; **l. against** (*resting*) appuyé contre. **2** *npl* tendances *fpl* (**towards** à). ◆**lean-to** *n* (*pl* -**tos**) (*building*) appentis *m*.

leap [liːp] *n* (*jump*) bond *m*, saut *m*; (*change, increase etc*) *Fig* bond *m*; **l. year** année *f* bissextile; **in leaps and bounds** à pas de géant; − *vi* (*pt & pp* **leaped** *or* **leapt** [lept]) bondir, sauter; (*of flames*) jaillir; (*of profits*) faire un bond; **to l. to one's feet, l. up** se lever d'un bond. ◆**leapfrog** *n* saute-mouton *m inv.*

learn [lɜːn] *vt* (*pt & pp* **learned** *or* **learnt**) apprendre (**that** que); **to l. (how) to do** apprendre à faire; − *vi* apprendre; **to l. about** (*study*) étudier; (*hear about*) apprendre. ◆**—ed** [-ɪd] *a* savant. ◆**—ing** *n* érudition *f*, savoir *m*; (*of language*) apprentissage *m* (of de). ◆**—er** *n* débutant, -ante *mf.*

lease [liːs] *n Jur* bail *m*; **a new l. of life** *or Am* **on life** un regain de vie, une nouvelle vie; − *vt* (*house etc*) louer à bail. ◆**leasehold** *n* propriété *f* louée à bail.

leash [liːʃ] *n* laisse *f*; **on a l.** en laisse.

least [liːst] *a* (the l. (*smallest amount of*) le moins de; (*slightest*) le *or* la moindre; **he has (the) l. talent** il a le moins de talent (**of** all de tous); **the l. effort/noise/etc** le moindre effort/bruit/*etc*; − *n* **the l.** le moins; **at l.** (*with quantity*) au moins; **at l. that's what she says** du moins c'est ce qu'elle dit; **not in the l.** pas du tout; − *adv* (*to work, eat etc*) le moins; (*with adjective*) le *or* la moins; **l. of all** (*especially not*) surtout pas.

leather ['leðər] *n* cuir *m*; (**wash**) **l.** peau *f* de chamois.

leave [liːv] **1** *n* (*holiday*) congé *m*; (*consent*) & *Mil* permission *f*; **l. of absence** congé *m* exceptionnel; **to take (one's) l. of** prendre congé de. **2** *vt* (*pt & pp* **left**) (*allow to remain, forget*) laisser; (*depart from*) quitter; (*room*) sortir de, quitter; **to l. the table** sortir de table; **to l. s.o. in charge of s.o./sth** laisser à qn la garde de qn/qch; **to l. sth with s.o.** (*entrust, give*) laisser qch à qn; **to be left (over)** rester; **there's no hope/bread/etc left** il ne reste plus d'espoir/de pain/*etc*; **l. it to me!** laisse-moi faire!; **I'll l. it (up) to you** je m'en remets à toi; **to l. go (of)** (*release*) lâcher; **to l. behind** laisser; (*surpass*) dépasser; (*in race*) *Sp* distancer; **to l. off** (*lid*) ne pas (re)mettre; **to l. off doing** (*stop*) *Fam* arrêter de faire; **to l. on** (*hat, gloves*) garder; **to l. out** (*forget*) omettre; (*exclude*) exclure; − *vi* (*depart*) partir (**from** de, **for** pour); **to l. off** (*stop*) *Fam* s'arrêter. ◆**leavings** *npl* restes *mpl.*

Lebanon ['lebənən] *n* Liban *m*. ◆**Leba-'nese** *a & n* libanais, -aise (*mf*).

lecher ['letʃər] *n* débauché *m*. ◆**lecherous** *a* lubrique, luxurieux.

lectern ['lektən] *n* (*for giving speeches*) pupitre *m*; *Rel* lutrin *m*.

lecture ['lektʃər] **1** *n* (*public speech*) conférence *f*; (*as part of series*) *Univ* cours *m* (magistral); − *vi* faire une conférence *or* un cours; **I l. in chemistry** je suis professeur de chimie. **2** *vt* (*scold*) *Fig* faire la morale à, sermonner; − *n* (*scolding*) sermon *m*. ◆**lecturer** *n* conférencier, -ière *mf*; *Univ* enseignant, -ante *mf*. ◆**lectureship** *n* poste *m* à l'université.

led [led] *see* **lead**[1].

ledge [ledʒ] *n* rebord *m*; (*on mountain*) saillie *f.*

ledger ['ledʒər] *n Com* registre *m*, grand livre *m.*

leech [liːtʃ] *n* (*worm, person*) sangsue *f.*

leek [liːk] *n* poireau *m.*

leer [lɪər] *vi* **to l. (at)** lorgner; − *n* regard *m* sournois.

leeway ['liːweɪ] *n* (*freedom*) liberté *f* d'action; (*safety margin*) marge *f* de sécurité.

left[1] [left] *see* **leave 2**; − *a* **l. luggage office** consigne *f*. ◆**leftovers** *npl* restes *mpl.*

left[2] [left] *a* (*side, hand etc*) gauche; − *adv* à gauche; − *n* gauche *f*; **on** *or* **to the l.** à gauche (**of** de). ◆**l.-hand** *a* à *or* de gauche; **on the l.-hand side** à gauche (**of** de). ◆**l.-'handed** *a* (*person*) gaucher. ◆**l.-wing** *a Pol* de gauche. ◆**leftist** *n & a Pol* gauchiste (*mf*).

leg [leg] *n* jambe *f*; (*of bird, dog etc*) patte *f*; (*of lamb*) *Culin* gigot *m*; (*of chicken*) *Culin* cuisse *f*; (*of table*) pied *m*; (*of journey*) étape *f*; **to pull s.o.'s l.** (*make fun of*) mettre qn en boîte; **on its last legs** (*machine etc*) *Fam* prêt à claquer; **to be on one's last legs** *Fam* avoir un pied dans la tombe. ◆**l.-room** *n* place *f* pour les jambes. ◆**leggy** *a* (-ier, -iest) (*person*) aux longues jambes, tout en jambes.

legacy ['legəsɪ] *n Jur & Fig* legs *m.*

legal ['liːg(ə)l] *a* (*lawful*) légal; (*mind, affairs, adviser*) juridique; (*aid, error*) judiciaire; **l. expert** juriste *m*; **l. proceedings** procès *m*. ◆**le'gality** *n* légalité *f*. ◆**legalize** *vt* légaliser. ◆**legally** *adv* légalement.

legation [lɪ'geɪʃ(ə)n] *n Pol* légation *f.*

legend ['ledʒənd] *n* (*story, inscription etc*) légende *f*. ◆**legendary** *a* légendaire.

leggings ['legɪŋz] *npl* jambières *fpl.*

legible ['ledʒəb(ə)l] *a* lisible. ◆**legi'bility** *n* lisibilité *f*. ◆**legibly** *adv* lisiblement.

legion ['liːdʒən] *n Mil & Fig* légion *f.*

legislate ['ledʒɪsleɪt] *vi* légiférer. ◆**legis-**

'lation n (laws) législation f; (action) élaboration f des lois; **(piece of) l.** loi f. ◆**legislative** a législatif.

legitimate [lɪ'dʒɪtɪmət] a (reason, child etc) légitime. ◆**legitimacy** n légitimité f.

legless ['legləs] a (drunk) Fam (complètement) bourré.

leisure ['leʒər, Am 'liːʒər] n **l. (time)** loisirs mpl; **l. activities** loisirs mpl; **moment of l.** moment m de loisir; **at (one's) l.** à tête reposée. ◆**—ly** a (walk, occupation) peu fatigant; (meal, life) calme; **at a l. pace, in a l. way** sans se presser.

lemon ['lemən] n citron m; **l. drink, l. squash** citronnade f; **l. tea** thé m au citron. ◆**lemo'nade** n (fizzy) limonade f; (still) Am citronnade f.

lend [lend] vt (pt & pp lent) prêter (to à); (charm, colour etc) Fig donner (to à); **to l. credence to** ajouter foi à. ◆**—ing** n prêt m. ◆**—er** n prêteur, -euse mf.

length [leŋθ] n longueur f; (section of pipe etc) morceau m; (of road) tronçon m; (of cloth) métrage m; (of horse, swimming pool) Sp longueur f; (duration) durée f; **l. of time** temps m; **at l.** (at last) enfin; **at (great) l.** (in detail) dans le détail; (for a long time) longuement; **to go to great lengths** se donner beaucoup de mal (**to do** pour faire). ◆**lengthen** vt allonger; (in time) prolonger. ◆**lengthwise** adv dans le sens de la longueur. ◆**lengthy** a (-ier, -iest) long.

lenient ['liːnɪənt] a indulgent (**to** envers). ◆**leniency** n indulgence f. ◆**leniently** adv avec indulgence.

lens [lenz] n lentille f; (in spectacles) verre m; Phot objectif m.

Lent [lent] n Rel Carême m.

lentil ['lent(ə)l] n Bot Culin lentille f.

leopard ['lepəd] n léopard m.

leotard ['liːətɑːd] n collant m (de danse).

leper ['lepər] n lépreux, -euse mf. ◆**leprosy** n lèpre f.

lesbian ['lezbɪən] n & a lesbienne (f).

lesion ['liːʒ(ə)n] n Med lésion f.

less [les] a & n moins (de) (**than** que); **l. time/etc** moins de temps/etc; **she has l.** (than you) elle en a moins (que toi); **l. than a kilo/ten/etc** (with quantity, number) moins d'un kilo/de dix/etc; – adv (to sleep, know etc) moins (**than** que); **l. (often)** moins souvent; **l. and l.** de moins en moins; **one l.** un(e) de moins; – prep moins; **l. six francs** moins six francs. ◆**lessen** vti diminuer. ◆**lessening** n diminution f. ◆**lesser** a moindre; – n **the l. of** le or la moindre de.

-less [ləs] suffix sans; **childless** sans enfants.

lesson ['les(ə)n] n leçon f; **an English l.** une leçon or un cours d'anglais; **I have lessons now** j'ai cours maintenant.

lest [lest] conj Lit de peur que (+ ne + sub).

let¹ [let] **1** vt (pt & pp let, pres p letting) (allow) laisser (**s.o. do** qn faire); **to l. s.o. have sth** donner qch à qn; **to l. away** (allow to leave) laisser partir; **to l. down** (lower) baisser; (hair) dénouer; (dress) rallonger; (tyre) dégonfler; **to l. s.o. down** (disappoint) décevoir qn; **don't l. me down** je compte sur toi; **the car l. me down** la voiture est tombée en panne. ◆**letdown** n déception f; **to l. in** (person, dog) faire entrer; (noise, light) laisser entrer; **to l. in the clutch** Aut embrayer; **to l. s.o. in on** Fig mettre qn au courant de; **to l. oneself in for** (expense) se laisser entraîner à; (trouble) s'attirer; **to l. off** (bomb) faire éclater; (firework, gun) faire partir; **to l. s.o. off** laisser partir qn; (not punish) ne pas punir qn; (clear) Jur disculper qn; **to be l. off with** (a fine etc) s'en tirer avec; **to l. s.o. off doing** dispenser qn de faire; **to l. on that** Fam (admit) avouer que; (reveal) dire que; **to l. out** faire entrer or laisser sortir; (prisoner) relâcher; (cry, secret) laisser échapper; (skirt) élargir; **to l. s.o. out (of the house)** ouvrir la porte à qn; **to l. out the clutch** Aut débrayer; – vi **not to l. on** Fam ne rien dire, garder la bouche cousue; **to l. up** (of rain, person etc) s'arrêter. ◆**letup** n arrêt m, répit m. **2** v aux **l. us eat/go/etc, l.'s eat/go/etc** mangeons/partons/etc; **l.'s go for a stroll** allons nous promener; **l. him come** qu'il vienne.

let² [let] vt (pt & pp let, pres p letting) **to l. (off or out)** (house, room etc) louer. ◆**letting** n (renting) location f.

lethal ['liːθ(ə)l] a mortel; (weapon) meurtrier.

lethargy ['leθədʒɪ] n léthargie f. ◆**le'thargic** a léthargique.

letter ['letər] n (missive, character) lettre f; **man of letters** homme m de lettres; **l. bomb** lettre f piégée; **l. writer** correspondant, -ante mf. ◆**letterbox** n boîte f aux or à lettres. ◆**letterhead** n en-tête m. ◆**lettering** n (letters) lettres fpl; (on tomb) inscription f.

lettuce ['letɪs] n laitue f, salade f.

leuk(a)emia [luːˈkiːmɪə] n leucémie f.

level ['lev(ə)l] **1** n niveau m; **on the l.** (speed) en palier; – a (surface) plat, uni; (object on surface) horizontal; (spoonful) ras; (equal in score) à égalité (**with** avec); (in height) au même niveau, à la même hauteur (**with** que); **l. crossing** *Rail* passage *m* à niveau; – *vt* (**-ll-,** *Am* **-l-**) (*surface, differences*) niveler, aplanir; (*plane down*) raboter; (*building*) raser; (*gun*) braquer; (*accusation*) lancer (**at** contre); – *vi* **to l. off** *or* **out** (*stabilize*) *Fig* se stabiliser. **2** *n* **on the l.** *Fam* (*honest*) honnête, franc; (*frankly*) honnêtement, franchement; – *vi* (**-ll-,** *Am* **-l-**) **to l. with** *Fam* être franc avec. ◆**l.-'headed** *a* équilibré.

lever ['liːvər, *Am* 'levər] *n* levier *m*. ◆**leverage** *n* (*power*) influence *f*.

levity ['levɪtɪ] *n* légèreté *f*.

levy ['levɪ] *vt* (*tax, troops*) lever; – *n* (*tax*) impôt *m*.

lewd [luːd] *a* (**-er, -est**) obscène.

liable ['laɪəb(ə)l] *a* **l. to** (*dizziness etc*) sujet à; (*fine, tax*) passible de; **he's l. to do** il est susceptible de faire, il pourrait faire; **l. for** (*responsible*) responsable de. ◆**lia'bility** *n* responsabilité *f* (**for** de); (*disadvantage*) handicap *m*; *pl* (*debts*) dettes *fpl*.

liaise [lɪ'eɪz] *vi* travailler en liaison (**with** avec). ◆**liaison** *n* (*association*) & *Mil* liaison *f*.

liar ['laɪər] *n* menteur, -euse *mf*.

libel ['laɪb(ə)l] *vt* (**-ll-,** *Am* **-l-**) diffamer (par écrit); – *n* diffamation *f*.

liberal ['lɪbərəl] *a* (*open-minded*) & *Pol* libéral; (*generous*) généreux (**with** de); – *n* *Pol* libéral, -ale *mf*. ◆**liberalism** *n* libéralisme *m*.

liberate ['lɪbəreɪt] *vt* libérer. ◆**libe'ration** *n* libération *f*. ◆**liberator** *n* libérateur, -trice *mf*.

liberty ['lɪbətɪ] *n* liberté *f*; **at l. to do** libre de faire; **what a l.!** (*cheek*) *Fam* quel culot!; **to take liberties with s.o.** se permettre des familiarités avec qn.

Libra ['liːbrə] *n* (*sign*) la Balance.

library ['laɪbrərɪ] *n* bibliothèque *f*. ◆**li'brarian** *n* bibliothécaire *mf*.

libretto [lɪ'bretəʊ] *n* (*pl* **-os**) *Mus* livret *m*.

Libya ['lɪbjə] *n* Libye *f*. ◆**Libyan** *a* & *n* libyen, -enne (*mf*).

lice [laɪs] *see* **louse**.

licence, *Am* **license** ['laɪsəns] *n* **1** permis *m*, autorisation *f*; (*for driving*) permis *m*; *Com* licence *f*; **pilot's l.** brevet *m* de pilote; **l. fee** *Rad TV* redevance *f*; **l. plate/number** *Aut* plaque *f*/numéro *m* d'immatriculation. **2** (*freedom*) licence *f*.

license ['laɪsəns] *vt* accorder une licence à, autoriser; **licensed premises** établissement *m* qui a une licence de débit de boissons.

licit ['lɪsɪt] *a* licite.

lick [lɪk] *vt* lécher; (*defeat*) *Fam* écraser; (*beat physically*) *Fam* rosser; **to be licked** (*by problem etc*) *Fam* être dépassé; – *n* coup *m* de langue; **a l. of paint** un coup de peinture. ◆**—ing** *n Fam* (*defeat*) déculottée *f*; (*beating*) rossée *f*.

licorice ['lɪkərɪʃ, -rɪs] *n Am* réglisse *f*.

lid [lɪd] *n* **1** (*of box etc*) couvercle *m*. **2** (*of eye*) paupière *f*.

lido ['liːdəʊ] *n* (*pl* **-os**) piscine *f* (découverte).

lie[1] [laɪ] *vi* (*pt* **lay**, *pp* **lain**, *pres p* **lying**) (*in flat position*) s'allonger, s'étendre; (*remain*) rester; (*be*) être; (*in grave*) reposer; **to be lying** (*on the grass etc*) être allongé *or* étendu; **he lay asleep** il dormait; **here lies** (*on tomb*) ci-gît; **the problem lies in** le problème réside dans; **to l. heavy on** (*of meal etc*) & *Fig* peser sur; **to l. low** (*hide*) se cacher; (*be inconspicuous*) se faire tout petit; **to l. about** *or* **around** (*of objects, person*) traîner; **to l. down, to have a l.-down** s'allonger, se coucher; **lying down** (*resting*) allongé, couché; **to l. in, to have a l.-in** *Fam* faire la grasse matinée.

lie[2] [laɪ] *vi* (*pt* & *pp* **lied**, *pres p* **lying**) (*tell lies*) mentir; – *n* mensonge *m*; **to give the l. to** (*show as untrue*) démentir.

lieu [luː] *n* **in l. of** au lieu de.

lieutenant [lef'tenənt, *Am* luː'tenənt] *n* lieutenant *m*.

life [laɪf] *n* (*pl* **lives**) vie *f*; (*of battery, machine*) durée *f* (de vie); **to come to l.** (*of street, party etc*) s'animer; **at your time of l.** à ton âge; **loss of l.** perte *f* en vies humaines; **true to l.** conforme à la réalité; **to take one's (own) l.** se donner la mort; **bird l.** les oiseaux *mpl*; – *a* (*cycle, style*) de vie; (*belt, raft*) de sauvetage; (*force*) vital; **l. annuity** rente *f* viagère; **l. blood** *Fig* âme *f*; **l. insurance** assurance-vie *f*; **l. jacket** gilet *m* de sauvetage; **l. peer** pair *m* à vie. ◆**lifeboat** *n* canot *m* de sauvetage. ◆**lifebuoy** *n* bouée *f* de sauvetage. ◆**lifeguard** *n* maître-nageur *m* sauveteur. ◆**lifeless** *a* sans vie. ◆**lifelike** *a* qui semble vivant. ◆**lifelong** *a* de toute sa vie; (*friend*) de toujours. ◆**lifesaving** *n* sauvetage *m*. ◆**lifesize(d)** *a* grandeur nature *inv*. ◆**lifetime** *n* vie *f*; *Fig* éternité *f*; **in my l.** de mon vivant; **a once-in-a-l. experience**/*etc* l'expérience/*etc* de votre vie.

lift [lɪft] *vt* lever; (*sth heavy*) (sou)lever; (*ban, siege*) *Fam* lever; (*idea etc*) *Fig* voler, prendre (**from** à); **to l. down** *or* **off** (*take down*) descendre (**from** de); **to l. out** (*take out*) sortir; **to l. up** (*arm, eyes*) lever; (*object*) (sou)lever; − *vi* (*of fog*) se lever; **to l. off** (*of space vehicle*) décoller; − *n* (*elevator*) ascenseur *m*; **to give s.o. a l.** emmener *or* accompagner qn (en voiture) (**to** à). ◆**l.-off** *n Av* décollage *m*.

ligament ['lɪgəmənt] *n* ligament *m*.

light¹ [laɪt] **1** *n* lumière *f*; (*daylight*) jour *m*, lumière *f*; (*on vehicle*) feu *m*, (*headlight*) phare *m*; **by the l.** of à la lumière de; **in the l. of** (*considering*) à la lumière de; **in that l.** *Fig* sous ce jour *or* cet éclairage; **against the l.** à contre-jour; **to bring to l.** mettre en lumière; **to come to l.** être découvert; **to throw l. on** (*matter*) éclaircir; **do you have a l.?** (*for cigarette*) est-ce que vous avez du feu?; **to set l. to** mettre le feu à; **leading l.** (*person*) *Fig* phare *m*, sommité *f*, lumière *f*; **l. bulb** ampoule *f* (électrique); − *vt* (*pt & pp* **lit** *or* **lighted**) (*candle etc*) allumer; (*match*) gratter; **to l. (up)** (*room*) éclairer; − *vi* **to l. up** (*of window*) s'allumer. **2** *a* (*bright, not dark*) clair; **a l. green jacket** une veste vert clair. ◆**-ing** *n El* éclairage *m*; **the l. of** (*candle etc*) l'allumage *m* de. ◆**lighten¹** *vt* (*light up*) éclairer; (*colour, hair*) éclaircir. ◆**lighter** *n* (*for cigarettes etc*) briquet *m*; *Culin* allume-gaz *m inv*. ◆**lighthouse** *n* phare *m*. ◆**lightness¹** *n* clarté *f*.

light² [laɪt] *a* (*in weight, quantity, strength etc*) léger; (*task*) facile; **l. rain** pluie *f* fine; **to travel l.** voyager avec peu de bagages. ◆**l.-'fingered** *a* chapardeur. ◆**l.-'headed** *a* (*giddy, foolish*) étourdi. ◆**l.-'hearted** *a* gai. ◆**lighten²** *vt* (*a load*) alléger. ◆**lightly** *adv* légèrement. ◆**lightness²** *n* légèreté *f*.

light³ [laɪt] *vi* (*pt & pp* **lit** *or* **lighted**) **to l. upon** trouver par hasard.

lightning ['laɪtnɪŋ] *n Met* (*light*) éclair *m*; (*charge*) foudre *f*; (**flash of**) l. éclair *m*; − *a* (*speed*) foudroyant; (*visit*) éclair *inv*; **l. conductor** paratonnerre *m*.

lightweight ['laɪtweɪt] *a* (*cloth etc*) léger; (*not serious*) pas sérieux, léger.

like¹ [laɪk] *a* (*alike*) semblable, pareil; − *prep* comme; **l. this** comme ça; **what's he l.?** (*physically, as character*) comment est-il?; **to be** *or* **look l.** ressembler à; **what was the book l.?** comment as-tu trouvé le livre?; **I have one l. it** j'en ai un pareil; − *adv* **nothing l. as big/etc** loin d'être aussi grand/etc; − *conj* (*as*) *Fam* comme; **it's l. I say** c'est comme je vous le dis; − *n* . . . **and the l.** . . . et ainsi de suite; **the l. of which we shan't see again** comme on n'en reverra plus; **the likes of you** des gens de ton acabit.

like/e² [laɪk] *vt* aimer (bien) (**to do, doing** faire); **I l. him** je l'aime bien, il me plaît; **she likes it here** elle se plaît ici; **to l. best** préférer; **I'd l. to come** (*want*) je voudrais (bien) *or* j'aimerais (bien) venir; **I'd l. a kilo of apples** je voudrais un kilo de pommes; **would you l. a cigar?** voulez-vous un cigare?; **if you l.** si vous voulez; (**how**) **would you l. to come?** ça te plairait *or* te dirait de venir?; − *npl* **one's likes** nos goûts *mpl*. ◆**-ing** *n* **a l. for** (*person*) de la sympathie pour; (*thing*) du goût pour; **to my l.** à mon goût. ◆**likeable** *a* sympathique.

likely ['laɪklɪ] *a* (**-ier, -iest**) (*event, result etc*) probable; (*excuse*) vraisemblable; (*place*) propice; (*candidate*) prometteur; **a l. excuse!** *Iron* belle excuse!; **it's l. (that) she'll come** il est probable qu'elle viendra; **he's l. to come** il viendra probablement; **he's not l. to come** il ne risque pas de venir; − *adv* **very l.** très probablement; **not l.!** pas question! ◆**likelihood** *n* probabilité *f*; **there's little l. that** il y a peu de chances que (+ *sub*).

liken ['laɪkən] *vt* comparer (**to** à).

likeness ['laɪknɪs] *n* ressemblance *f*; **a family l.** un air de famille; **it's a good l.** c'est très ressemblant.

likewise ['laɪkwaɪz] *adv* (*similarly*) de même, pareillement.

lilac ['laɪlək] *n* lilas *m*; − *a* (*colour*) lilas *inv*.

Lilo® ['laɪləʊ] *n* (*pl* **-os**) matelas *m* pneumatique.

lilt [lɪlt] *n Mus* cadence *f*.

lily ['lɪlɪ] *n* lis *m*, lys *m*; **l. of the valley** muguet *m*.

limb [lɪm] *n Anat* membre *m*; **to be out on a l.** *Fig* être le seul de son opinion.

limber ['lɪmbər] *vi* **to l. up** faire des exercices d'assouplissement.

limbo (in) [ɪn'lɪmbəʊ] *adv* (*uncertain, waiting*) dans l'expectative.

lime [laɪm] *n* **1** (*tree*) tilleul *m*. **2** (*substance*) chaux *f*. **3** (*fruit*) lime *f*, citron *m* vert; **l. juice** jus *m* de citron vert.

limelight ['laɪmlaɪt] *n* **in the l.** (*glare of publicity*) en vedette.

limit ['lɪmɪt] *n* limite *f*; (*restriction*) limitation *f* (**of** de); **that's the l.!** *Fam* c'est le comble!; **within limits** dans une certaine limite; − *vt* limiter (**to** à); **to l. oneself to doing** se borner à faire. ◆**-ed** *a* (*restricted*) limité; (*mind*) borné; (*edition*) à tirage limité; **l. company** *Com* société *f* à responsabilité limitée; (**public**) **l. company** (*with shareholders*) société *f* anonyme; **to a**

l. degree jusqu'à un certain point. ◆**limi-'tation** *n* limitation *f*. ◆**limitless** *a* illimité.

limousine [lɪmə'ziːn] *n* (*car*) limousine *f*; (*airport etc shuttle*) *Am* voiture-navette *f*.

limp [lɪmp] **1** *vi* (*of person*) boiter; (*of vehicle etc*) *Fig* avancer tant bien que mal; – *n* **to have a l.** boiter. **2** *a* (-er, -est) (*soft*) mou; (*flabby*) flasque; (*person, hat*) avachi.

limpid ['lɪmpɪd] *a* (*liquid*) *Lit* limpide.

linchpin ['lɪntʃpɪn] *n* (*person*) pivot *m*.

linctus ['lɪŋktəs] *n Med* sirop *m* (contre la toux).

line [laɪn] *n* ligne *f*; (*stroke*) trait *m*, ligne *f*; (*of poem*) vers *m*; (*wrinkle*) ride *f*; (*track*) voie *f*; (*rope*) corde *f*; (*row*) rangée *f*, ligne *f*; (*of vehicles*) file *f*; (*queue*) *Am* file *f*, queue *f*; (*family*) lignée *f*; (*business*) métier *m*, rayon *m*; (*article*) *Com* article *m*; **one's lines** (*of actor*) son texte *m*; **on the l.** *Tel* (*speaking*) au téléphone; (*at other end of line*) au bout du fil; **to be on the l.** (*at risk*) être en danger; **hold the l.!** *Tel* ne quittez pas!; **the hot l.** *Tel* le téléphone rouge; **to stand in l.** *Am* faire la queue; **to step** *or* **get out of l.** *Fig* refuser de se conformer; (*misbehave*) faire une incartade; **out of l. with** (*ideas etc*) en désaccord avec; **in l. with** conforme à; **he's in l. for** (*promotion etc*) il doit recevoir; **to take a hard l.** adopter une attitude ferme; **along the same lines** (*to work, think*) de la même façon; **sth along those lines** qch dans ce genre-là; **to drop a l.** *Fam* envoyer un mot (**to** à); **where do we draw the l.?** où fixer les limites?; – *vt* (*paper*) régler; (*face*) rider; **to l. the street** (*of trees*) border la rue; (*of people*) faire la haie le long de la rue; **to l. up** (*children, objects*) aligner; (*arrange*) organiser; (*get ready*) préparer; **to have sth lined up** (*in mind*) avoir qch en vue; – *vi* **to l. up** s'aligner; (*queue*) *Am* faire la queue. ◆**l.-up** *n* (*row*) file *f*; *Pol* front *m*; *TV* programme(s) *m*(*pl*).

line [laɪn] *vt* (*clothes*) doubler; (*pockets*) *Fig* se remplir. ◆**lining** *n* (*of clothes*) doublure *f*; (*of brakes*) garniture *f*.

lineage ['lɪnɪɪdʒ] *n* lignée *f*.

linear ['lɪnɪər] *a* linéaire.

linen ['lɪnɪn] *n* (*sheets etc*) linge *m*; (*material*) (toile *f* de) lin *m*, fil *m*.

liner ['laɪnər] *n* **1** (*ship*) paquebot *m*. **2** (**dust**)**bin l.** sac *m* poubelle.

linesman ['laɪnzmən] *n* (*pl* -men) *Fb etc* juge *m* de touche.

linger ['lɪŋgər] *vi* **to l. (on)** (*of person*) s'attarder; (*of smell, memory*) persister; (*of doubt*) subsister. ◆**—ing** *a* (*death*) lent.

lingo ['lɪŋgəu] *n* (*pl* -os) *Hum Fam* jargon *m*.

linguist ['lɪŋgwɪst] *n* linguiste *mf*. ◆**lin-'guistic** *a* linguistique. ◆**lin'guistics** *n* linguistique *f*.

liniment ['lɪnɪmənt] *n* onguent *m*, pommade *f*.

link [lɪŋk] *vt* (*connect*) relier (**to** à); (*relate, associate*) lier (**to** à); **to l. up** *Tel* relier; – *vi* **to l. up** (*of roads*) se rejoindre; – *n* (*connection*) lien *m*; (*of chain*) maillon *m*; (*by road, rail*) liaison *f*. ◆**l.-up** *n TV Rad* liaison *f*; (*of spacecraft*) jonction *f*.

lino ['laɪnəu] *n* (*pl* -os) lino *m*. ◆**linoleum** [lɪ'nəulɪəm] *n* linoléum *m*.

linseed ['lɪnsiːd] *n* **l. oil** huile *f* de lin.

lint [lɪnt] *n Med* tissu *m* ouaté; (*fluff*) peluche(s) *f*(*pl*).

lion ['laɪən] *n* lion *m*; **l. cub** lionceau *m*. ◆**lioness** *n* lionne *f*.

lip [lɪp] *n Anat* lèvre *f*; (*rim*) bord *m*; (*cheek*) *Sl* culot *m*. ◆**l.-read** *vi* (*pt* & *pp* **-read** [red]) lire sur les lèvres. ◆**lipstick** *n* (*material*) rouge *m* à lèvres; (*stick*) tube *m* de rouge.

liqueur [lɪ'kjuər] *n* liqueur *f*.

liquid ['lɪkwɪd] *n* & *a* liquide (*m*). ◆**liquefy** *vt* liquéfier; – *vi* se liquéfier. ◆**liquidizer** *n Culin* (*for fruit juices*) centrifugeuse *f*; (*for purées etc*) robot *m*, moulinette® *f*.

liquidate ['lɪkwɪdeɪt] *vt* (*debt, person*) liquider. ◆**liqui'dation** *n* liquidation *f*.

liquor ['lɪkər] *n* alcool *m*, spiritueux *m*; **l. store** *Am* magasin *m* de vins et de spiritueux.

liquorice ['lɪkərɪs, -rɪs] *n* réglisse *f*.

lira, *pl* **lire** ['lɪərə, 'lɪəreɪ] *n* (*currency*) lire *f*.

lisp [lɪsp] *vi* zézayer; – *n* **to have a l.** zézayer.

list [lɪst] *n* **1** liste *f*; – *vt* (*one's possessions etc*) faire la liste de; (*names*) mettre sur la liste; (*enumerate*) énumérer; (*catalogue*) cataloguer. **2** *vi* (*of ship*) gîter. ◆**—ed** *a* (*monument etc*) classé.

listen ['lɪsən] *vi* écouter; **to l. to** écouter; **to l. (out) for** (*telephone, person etc*) tendre l'oreille pour, guetter; **to l. in** (*to*) *Rad* écouter. ◆**—ing** *n* écoute *f* (**to** de). ◆**—er** *n Rad* auditeur, -trice *mf*; **to be a good l.** (*pay attention*) savoir écouter.

listless ['lɪstləs] *a* apathique, indolent. ◆**—ness** *n* apathie *f*.

lit [lɪt] *see* **light**[1] **l.**

litany ['lɪtənɪ] *n Rel* litanies *fpl*.

literal ['lɪtərəl] *a* littéral; (*not exaggerated*) réel. ◆**—ly** *adv* littéralement; (*really*) réellement; **he took it l.** il l'a pris au pied de la lettre.

literate ['lɪtərət] *a* qui sait lire et écrire;

highly l. (*person*) très instruit. ◆**literacy** *n* capacité *f* de lire et d'écrire; (*of country*) degré *m* d'alphabétisation.

literature ['lɪt(ə)rɪtʃər] *n* littérature *f*; (*pamphlets etc*) documentation *f*. ◆**literary** *a* littéraire.

lithe [laɪð] *a* agile, souple.

litigation [lɪtɪ'geɪʃ(ə)n] *n* Jur litige *m*.

litre ['liːtər] *n* litre *m*.

litter ['lɪtər] **1** *n* (*rubbish*) détritus *m*; (*papers*) papiers *mpl*; (*bedding for animals*) litière *f*; (*confusion*) *Fig* fouillis *m*; **l. basket** *or* **bin** boîte *f* à ordures; **to l. (with papers** *or* **rubbish)** (*street etc*) laisser traîner des papiers *or* des détritus dans; **a street littered with** une rue jonchée de. **2** *n* (*young animals*) portée *f*.

little ['lɪt(ə)l] **1** *a* (*small*) petit; **the l. ones** les petits. **2** *a* & *n* (*not much*) peu (de); **l. time/money/etc** peu de temps/d'argent/*etc*; **I've l. left** il m'en reste peu; **she eats l.** elle mange peu; **to have l. to say** avoir peu de chose à dire; **as l. as possible** le moins possible; **a l. money/time/etc** (*some*) un peu d'argent/de temps/*etc*; **I have a l.** (*some*) j'en ai un peu; **the l. that I have** le peu que j'ai; *- adv* (*somewhat, rather*) peu; **a l. heavy/etc** un peu lourd/*etc*; **to work/etc a l.** travailler/*etc* un peu; **it's l. better** (*hardly*) ce n'est guère mieux; **l. by l.** peu à peu.

liturgy ['lɪtədʒɪ] *n* liturgie *f*.

live[1] [lɪv] *vi* vivre; (*reside*) habiter, vivre; **where do you l.?** où habitez-vous?; **to l. in Paris** habiter (à) Paris; **to l. off** *or* **on** (*eat*) vivre de; (*sponge on*) *Pej* vivre aux crochets *or* aux dépens de (*qn*); **to l. on** (*of memory etc*) survivre, se perpétuer; **to l. through** (*experience*) vivre; (*survive*) survivre à; **to l. up to** (*one's principles*) vivre selon; (*s.o.'s expectations*) se montrer à la hauteur de; *- vt* (*life*) vivre, mener; (*one's faith etc*) vivre pleinement; **to l. down** faire oublier (avec le temps); **to l. it up** *Fam* mener la grande vie.

live[2] [laɪv] **1** *a* (*alive, lively*) vivant; (*coal*) ardent; (*bomb*) non explosé; (*ammunition*) réel, de combat; (*wire*) *El* sous tension; (*switch*) *El* mal isolé; (*plugged in*) *El* branché; **a real l. king/etc** un roi/*etc* en chair et en os. **2** *a* & *adv* Rad TV en direct; **a l. broadcast** une émission en direct; **a l. audience** le *or* un public; **a l. recording** un enregistrement public.

livelihood ['laɪvlɪhʊd] *n* moyens *mpl* de subsistance; **my l.** mon gagne-pain; **to earn one's** *or* **a l.** gagner sa vie.

livel/y ['laɪvlɪ] *a* (**-ier, -iest**) (*person, style*) vif, vivant; (*street, story*) vivant; (*interest, mind, colour*) vif; (*day*) movementé; (*forceful*) vigoureux; (*conversation, discussion*) animé. ◆**—iness** *n* vivacité *f*.

liven ['laɪv(ə)n] *vt* **to l. up** (*person*) égayer; (*party*) animer; *- vi* **to l. up** (*of person, party*) s'animer.

liver ['lɪvər] *n* foie *m*.

livery ['lɪvərɪ] *n* (*uniform*) livrée *f*.

livestock ['laɪvstɒk] *n* bétail *m*.

livid ['lɪvɪd] *a* (*blue-grey*) livide; (*angry*) *Fig* furieux; **l. with cold** blême de froid.

living ['lɪvɪŋ] **1** *a* (*alive*) vivant; **not a l. soul** (*nobody*) personne, pas âme qui vive; **within l. memory** de mémoire d'homme; **l. or dead** mort ou vif; **the l.** les vivants *mpl*. **2** *n* (*livelihood*) vie *f*; **to make a** *or* **one's l.** gagner sa vie; **to work for a l.** travailler pour vivre; **the cost of l.** le coût de la vie; *- a* (*standard, conditions*) de vie; (*wage*) qui permet de vivre; **l. room** salle *f* de séjour.

lizard ['lɪzəd] *n* lézard *m*.

llama ['lɑːmə] *n* (*animal*) lama *m*.

load [ləʊd] *n* (*object carried, burden*) charge *f*; (*freight*) chargement *m*, charge *f*; (*strain, weight*) poids *m*; **a l. of, loads of** (*people, money etc*) *Fam* un tas de, énormément de; **to take a l. off s.o.'s mind** ôter un grand poids à qn; *- vt* charger; **to l. down** *or* **up** charger (**with** de); *- vi* **to l. (up)** charger la voiture, le navire *etc*. ◆**—ed** *a* (*gun, vehicle etc*) chargé; (*dice*) pipé; (*rich*) *Fam* plein aux as; **a l. question** une question piège; **l. (down) with** (*debts*) accablé de.

loaf [ləʊf] **1** *n* (*pl* loaves) pain *m*; **French l.** baguette *f*. **2** *vi* **to l. (about)** fainéanter. ◆**—er** *n* fainéant, -ante *mf*.

loam [ləʊm] *n* (*soil*) terreau *m*.

loan [ləʊn] *n* (*money lent*) prêt *m*; (*money borrowed*) emprunt *m*; **on l. from** prêté par; (**out) on l.** (*book*) sorti; **may I have the l. of** . . .? puis-je emprunter . . .?; *- vt* (*lend*) prêter (**to** à).

loath [ləʊθ] *a* **to do** *Lit* peu disposé à faire.

loath/e [ləʊð] *vt* détester (**doing** faire). ◆**—ing** *n* dégoût *m*. ◆**loathsome** *a* détestable.

lobby ['lɒbɪ] **1** *n* (*of hotel*) vestibule *m*, hall *m*; Th foyer *m*. **2** *n* Pol groupe *m* de pression, lobby *m*; *- vt* faire pression sur.

lobe [ləʊb] *n* Anat lobe *m*.

lobster ['lɒbstər] *n* homard *m*; (*spiny*) langouste *f*.

local ['ləʊk(ə)l] *a* local; (*of the neighbourhood*) du *or* de quartier; (*regional*) du pays; **are you l.?** êtes-vous du coin d'ici?; **the doctor is l.** le médecin est tout près d'ici; **a l. phone call** (*within town*) une communication urbaine; – *n* (*pub*) *Fam* bistrot *m* du coin, pub *m*; **she's a l.** elle est du coin; **the locals** (*people*) les gens du coin. ◆**lo'cality** *n* (*neighbourhood*) environs *mpl*; (*region*) région *f*; (*place*) lieu *m*; (*site*) emplacement *m*. ◆**localize** *vt* (*confine*) localiser. ◆**locally** *adv* dans les environs, dans le coin; (*around here*) par ici; (*in precise place*) localement.

locate [ləʊˈkeɪt] *vt* (*find*) repérer; (*pain, noise, leak*) localiser; (*situate*) situer; (*build*) construire. ◆**location** *n* (*site*) emplacement *m*; (*act*) repérage *m*; localisation *f*; **on l.** *Cin* en extérieur.

lock [lɒk] **1** *vt* to l. (up) fermer à clef; **to l. the wheels** *Aut* bloquer les roues; **to l. s.o. in** enfermer qn; **to l. s.o. in sth** enfermer qn dans qch; **to l. s.o. out** (*accidentally*) enfermer qn dehors; **to l. away** or **up** (*prisoner*) enfermer; (*jewels etc*) mettre sous clef, enfermer; – *vi* to l. (up) fermer à clef; – *n* (*on door, chest etc*) serrure *f*; (*of gun*) cran *m* de sûreté; (*turning circle*) *Aut* rayon *m* de braquage; (**anti-theft**) **l.** *Aut* antivol *m*; **under l. and key** sous clef. **2** *n* (*on canal*) écluse *f*. **3** *n* (*of hair*) mèche *f*. ◆**locker** *n* casier *m*; (*for luggage*) *Rail* casier *m* de consigne automatique; (*for clothes*) vestiaire *m* (métallique); **l. room** *Sp Am* vestiaire *m*. ◆**lockout** *n* (*industrial*) lock-out *m inv*. ◆**locksmith** *n* serrurier *m*.

locket [ˈlɒkɪt] *n* (*jewel*) médaillon *m*.

loco [ˈləʊkəʊ] *a Sl* cinglé, fou.

locomotion [ləʊkəˈməʊʃ(ə)n] *n* locomotion *f*. ◆**locomotive** *n* locomotive *f*.

locum [ˈləʊkəm] *n* (*doctor*) remplaçant, -ante *mf*.

locust [ˈləʊkəst] *n* criquet *m*, sauterelle *f*.

lodg/e [lɒdʒ] **1** *vt* (*person*) loger; (*valuables*) déposer (**with** chez); **to l. a complaint** porter plainte; – *vi* (*of bullet*) se loger (**in** dans); **to be lodging** (*accommodated*) être logé (**with** chez). **2** *n* (*house*) pavillon *m* de gardien or de chasse; (*of porter*) loge *f*. ◆**—ing** *n* (*accommodation*) logement *m*; – *pl* (*flat*) logement *m*; (*room*) chambre *f*; **in lodgings** en meublé. ◆**—er** *n* (*room and meals*) pensionnaire *mf*; (*room only*) locataire *mf*.

loft [lɒft] *n* (*attic*) grenier *m*.

loft/y [ˈlɒftɪ] *a* (*-ier, -iest*) (*high, noble*) élevé; (*haughty*) hautain. ◆**—iness** *n* hauteur *f*.

log [lɒg] **1** *n* (*tree trunk*) rondin *m*; (*for fire*) bûche *f*, rondin *m*; **l. fire** feu *m* de bois. **2** *vt* (*-gg-*) (*facts*) noter; **to l. (up)** (*distance*) faire, couvrir. ◆**logbook** *n* *Nau Av* journal *m* de bord.

logarithm [ˈlɒgərɪð(ə)m] *n* logarithme *m*.

loggerheads (at) [ætˈlɒgəhedz] *adv* en désaccord (**with** avec).

logic [ˈlɒdʒɪk] *n* logique *f*. ◆**logical** *a* logique. ◆**logically** *adv* logiquement.

logistics [ləˈdʒɪstɪks] *n* logistique *f*.

logo [ˈləʊgəʊ] *n* (*pl* -os) logo *m*.

loin [lɔɪn] *n* (*meat*) filet *m*.

loins [lɔɪnz] *npl* *Anat* reins *mpl*.

loiter [ˈlɔɪtər] *vi* traîner.

loll [lɒl] *vi* (*in armchair etc*) se prélasser.

lollipop [ˈlɒlɪpɒp] *n* (*sweet on stick*) sucette *f*; (*ice on stick*) esquimau *m*. ◆**lolly** *n Fam* sucette *f*; (*money*) *Sl* fric *m*; (**ice**) **l.** *Fam* esquimau *m*.

London [ˈlʌndən] *n* Londres *m* or *f*; – *a* (*taxi etc*) londonien. ◆**Londoner** *n* Londonien, -ienne *mf*.

lone [ləʊn] *a* solitaire; **l. wolf** *Fig* solitaire *mf*. ◆**loneliness** *n* solitude *f*. ◆**lonely** *a* (*-ier, -iest*) (*road, house, life etc*) solitaire; (*person*) seul, solitaire. ◆**loner** *n* solitaire *mf*. ◆**lonesome** *a* solitaire.

long¹ [lɒŋ] **1** *a* (*-er, -est*) long; **to be ten metres l.** être long de dix mètres, avoir dix mètres de long; **to be six weeks l.** durer six semaines; **how l. is ...** quelle est la longueur de ... ?; (*time*) quelle est la durée de ... ?; **a l. time** longtemps; **in the l. run** à la longue; **a l. face** une grimace; **a l. memory** une bonne mémoire; **l. jump** *Sp* saut *m* en longueur. **2** *adv* (*a long time*) longtemps; **l. before** longtemps avant; **has he been here?** il y a longtemps qu'il est ici?, il est ici depuis longtemps?; **how l. (ago)?** (il y a) combien de temps?; **not l. ago** il y a peu de temps; **before l.** sous or avant peu; **no longer** ne plus; **she no longer swims** elle ne nage plus; **a bit longer** (*to wait etc*) encore un peu; **I won't be l.** je n'en ai pas pour longtemps; **at the longest** (*tout*) au plus; **all summer l.** tout l'été; **l. live the queen**/*etc* vive la reine/*etc*; **as l. as, so l. as** (*provided that*) pourvu que (+ *sub*); **as l. as I live** tant que je vivrai.

long² [lɒŋ] *vi* **l. for sth** avoir très envie de qch; **to l. for s.o.** languir après qn; **to l. to do** avoir très envie de faire. ◆**—ing** *n* désir *m*, envie *f*.

long-distance [lɒŋˈdɪstəns] *a* (*race*) de fond; (*phone call*) interurbain; (*flight*) long-courrier. ◆**long-drawn-'out** *a* interminable. ◆**long'haired** *a* aux cheveux longs. ◆**'longhand** *n* écriture *f* normale. ◆**long-'playing** *a* **l.-playing record** 33 tours *m inv*. ◆**'long-range** *a* (*forecast*) à long terme. ◆**long'sighted** *a* *Med* presbyte. ◆**long'standing** a de longue date. ◆**long'suffering** a très patient. ◆**long-'term** a à long terme. ◆**long-'winded** a (speech, speaker) verbeux.

longevity [lɒnˈdʒevɪti] n longévité f.

longitude [ˈlɒndʒɪtjuːd] n longitude f.

longways [ˈlɒŋweɪz] adv en longueur.

loo [luː] n (toilet) Fam cabinets mpl.

look [lʊk] n regard m; (appearance) air m, allure f; (good) looks la beauté, un beau physique; **to have a l. (at)** jeter un coup d'œil (à), regarder; **to have a l. (for)** chercher; **to have a l. (a)round** regarder; (walk) faire un tour; **let me have a l.** fais voir; **I like the l. of him** il me fait bonne impression, il me plaît; – vti regarder; **to l. s.o. in the face** regarder qn dans les yeux; **to l. tired/happy/etc** (seem) sembler or avoir l'air fatigué/heureux/etc; **to l. pretty/ugly** (be) être joli/laid; **to l. one's age** faire son âge; **l. here!** dites donc!; **you l. like** or **as if you're tired** tu as l'air fatigué, on dirait que tu es fatigué; **it looks like** or **as if she won't leave** elle n'a pas l'air de vouloir partir; **it looks like it!** c'est probable; **to l. like a child** avoir l'air d'un enfant; **to l. like an apple** avoir l'air d'être une pomme; **you l. like my brother** (resemble) tu ressembles à mon frère; **it looks like rain (to me)** il me semble or on dirait qu'il va pleuvoir; **what does he l. like?** (describe him) comment est-il?; **to l. well** or **good** (of person) avoir bonne mine; **you l. good in that hat**/etc ce chapeau/etc te va très bien; **that looks bad** (action etc) ça fait mauvais effet. ■ **to l. after** vt (deal with) s'occuper de; (patient, hair) soigner; (keep safely) garder (for s.o. pour qn); **to l. after oneself** (keep healthy) faire bien attention à soi; **I can l. after myself** (cope) je suis assez grand pour me débrouiller; **to l. around** vt (visit) visiter; – vi (have a look) regarder; (walk round) faire un tour; **to l. at** vt regarder; (consider) considérer, voir; (check) vérifier; **to l. away** vi détourner les yeux; **to l. back** vi regarder derrière soi; (in time) regarder en arrière; **to l. down** vi baisser les yeux; (from height) regarder en bas; **to l. down on** (consider scornfully) mépriser, regarder de haut; **to l. for** (seek) chercher; **to l. forward to** vt (event) attendre avec impatience; **to l. in** vi regarder (à l'intérieur); **to l. in on s.o.** Fam passer voir qn; **to l. into** vt (examine) examiner; (find out about) se renseigner sur; **to l. on** vi regarder; – vt (consider) considérer; **to l. out** vi (be careful) faire attention (for à); **to l. out for** (seek)

chercher; (watch) guetter; **to l. (out) on to** (of window, house etc) donner sur; **to l. over** or **through** vt (examine fully) examiner, regarder de près; (briefly) parcourir; (region, town) parcourir, visiter; **to l. round** vt (visit) visiter; – vi (have a look) regarder; (walk round) faire un tour; (look back) se retourner; **to l. round for** (seek) chercher; **to l. up** vi (of person) lever les yeux; (into the air or sky) regarder en l'air; (improve) s'améliorer; **to l. up to s.o.** Fig respecter qn; – vt (word) chercher; **to l. s.o. up** (visit) passer voir qn. ◆**-looking** suffix **pleasant-/tired-/etc** à l'air agréable/fatigué/etc. ◆**looking-glass** n glace f, miroir m.

lookout [ˈlʊkaʊt] n (soldier) guetteur m; (sailor) vigie f; **l. (post)** poste m de guet; (on ship) vigie f; **to be on the l.** faire le guet; **to be on the l. for** guetter.

loom [luːm] **1** vi (up) (of mountain etc) apparaître indistinctement; Fig paraître imminent. **2** n Tex métier m à tisser.

loony [ˈluːni] n & a Sl imbécile (mf).

loop [luːp] n (in river etc) & Av boucle f; (contraceptive device) stérilet m; – vt **to l. the loop** Av boucler la boucle. ◆**loophole** n (in rules) point m faible, lacune f; (way out) échappatoire f.

loose [luːs] a (-er, -est) (screw, belt, knot) desserré; (tooth, stone) branlant; (page) détaché; (animal) libre, (set loose) lâché; (clothes) flottant; (hair) dénoué; (flesh) flasque; (wording, translation) approximatif, vague; (link) vague; (discipline) relâché; (articles) Com en vrac; (cheese, tea etc) Com au poids; (woman) Pej facile; **l. change** petite monnaie f; **l. covers** housses fpl; **l. living** vie f dissolue; **to l.** (of dog, page) se détacher; **to set** or **turn l.** (dog etc) libérer, lâcher; **he's at a l. end** or Am **at l. ends** il ne sait pas trop quoi faire; – n **on the l.** (prisoner etc) en liberté; – vt (animal) lâcher. ◆**loosely** adv (to hang) lâchement; (to hold, tie) sans serrer; (to translate) librement; (to link) vaguement. ◆**loosen** vt (knot, belt, screw) desserrer; (rope) détendre; (grip) relâcher; – vi **to l. up** Sp faire des exercices d'assouplissement. ◆**looseness** n (of screw, machine parts) jeu m.

loot [luːt] n butin m; (money) Sl fric m; – vt piller. ◆**-ing** n pillage m. ◆**-er** n pillard, -arde mf.

lop [lɒp] vt (-pp-) **to l. (off)** couper.

lop-sided [lɒpˈsaɪdɪd] a (crooked) de travers; **to walk l.-sided** (limp) se déhancher.

loquacious [ləʊˈkweɪʃəs] a loquace.

lord [lɔːd] n seigneur m; (title) Br lord m; **good L.!** Fam bon sang!; **oh L.!** Fam mince!; **the House of Lords** Pol la Chambre des Lords; − vt **to l. it over s.o.** Fam dominer qn. ◆**lordly** a digne d'un grand seigneur; (arrogant) hautain. ◆**lordship** n **Your L.** (to judge) Monsieur le juge.

lore [lɔːr] n traditions fpl.

lorry ['lɒrɪ] n camion m; (heavy) poids m lourd; **l. driver** camionneur m; **long-distance l. driver** routier m.

los/e [luːz] vt (pt & pp lost) perdre; **to get lost** (of person) se perdre; **the ticket/etc got lost** on a perdu le billet/etc; **get lost!** Fam fiche le camp!; **to l. s.o. sth** faire perdre qch à qn; **to l. interest in** se désintéresser de; **I've lost my bearings** je suis désorienté; **the clock loses six minutes a day** la pendule retarde de six minutes par jour; **to l. one's life** trouver la mort (in dans); − vi perdre; **to l. out** être perdant; **to l. to** Sp être battu par. ◆**—ing** a perdant; **a l. battle** Fig une bataille perdue d'avance. ◆**—er** n perdant, -ante mf; (failure in life) Fam paumé, -ée mf; **to be a good l.** être bon or beau joueur.

loss [lɒs] n perte f; **at a l.** (confused) perplexe; **to sell at a l.** Com vendre à perte; **at a l. to do** incapable de faire. ◆**lost** a perdu; **l. property**, Am **l. and found** objets mpl trouvés.

lot [lɒt] n (destiny) sort m; (batch, land) lot m; **to draw lots** tirer au sort; **parking l.** Am parking m; **a bad l.** (person) Fam un mauvais sujet. **2 the l.** (everything) (le) tout; **the l. of you** vous tous; **a l. of, lots of** beaucoup de; **a l.** beaucoup; **quite a l.** pas mal (of de); **such a l.** tellement (of de), tant (of de); **what a l. of flowers/water/etc!** que de fleurs/d'eau/etc!; **what a l.!** quelle quantité!; **what a l. of flowers/etc you have!** que vous avez (beaucoup) de fleurs/etc!

lotion ['ləʊʃ(ə)n] n lotion f.

lottery ['lɒtərɪ] n loterie f.

lotto ['lɒtəʊ] n (game) loto m.

loud [laʊd] a (-er, -est) bruyant, (voice, radio) fort; (noise, cry) grand; (gaudy) voyant; − adv (to shout etc) fort; **out l.** tout haut. ◆**-ly** adv (to speak, laugh etc) bruyamment, fort; (to shout) fort. ◆**—ness** n (of voice etc) force f; (noise) bruit m. ◆**loud'hailer** n mégaphone m. ◆**loudmouth** n (person) Fam grande gueule f. ◆**loud'speaker** n haut-parleur m; (of hi-fi unit) enceinte f.

lounge [laʊndʒ] 1 n salon m; **l. suit** complet

m veston. **2** vi (loll) se prélasser; **to l. about** (idle) paresser; (stroll) flâner.

louse, pl **lice** [laʊs, laɪs] 1 n (insect) pou m. **2** n (person) Pej Sl salaud m. **3** vt **to l. up** (mess up) Sl gâcher.

lousy ['laʊzɪ] a (-ier, -iest) (bad) Fam infect; **l. with** (crammed, loaded) Sl bourré de.

lout [laʊt] n rustre m. ◆**loutish** a (attitude) de rustre.

lov/e [lʌv] n amour m; Tennis zéro m; **in l.** amoureux (with de); **they're in l.** ils s'aiment; **art is his** or **her l.** l'art est sa passion; **yes, my l.** oui mon amour; − vt aimer; (like very much) adorer, aimer (beaucoup) (to do, doing faire); **give him** or **her my l.** (greeting) dis-lui bien des choses de ma part; **l. affair** liaison f (amoureuse). ◆**—ing** a affectueux, aimant. ◆**—able** a adorable. ◆**—er** n (man) amant m; (woman) maîtresse f; **a l. of** (art, music etc) un amateur de; **a nature l.** un amoureux de la nature. ◆**lovesick** a amoureux.

lovely ['lʌvlɪ] a (-ier, -iest) (pleasing) agréable, bon; (excellent) excellent; (pretty) joli; (charming) charmant; (kind) gentil; **the weather's l.** il fait beau; **l. to see you!** je suis ravi de te voir; **l. and hot/dry/etc** bien chaud/sec/etc.

low[1] [ləʊ] a (-er, -est) bas; (speed, income, intelligence) faible; (opinion, quality) mauvais; **she's l. on** (money etc) elle n'a plus beaucoup de; **to feel l.** (depressed) être déprimé; **in a l. voice** à voix basse; **lower** inférieur; − adv (-er, -est) bas; **to turn (down) l.** mettre plus bas; **to run l.** (of supplies) s'épuiser; − n Met dépression f; **to reach a new l.** or **an all-time l.** (of prices etc) atteindre leur niveau le plus bas. ◆**low-'calorie** a (diet) (à) basses calories. ◆**low_cost** a bon marché inv. ◆**low-cut** a décolleté. ◆**low-down** a méprisable. ◆**lowdown** n (facts) Fam tuyaux mpl. ◆**low-'fat** a (milk) écrémé; (cheese) de régime. ◆**low-'key** a (discreet) discret. ◆**lowland(s)** n plaine f. ◆**low-level** a bas. ◆**low-paid** a mal payé. ◆**low-'salt** a (food) à faible teneur en sel.

low[2] [ləʊ] vi (of cattle) meugler.

lower ['ləʊər] vt baisser; **to l. s.o./sth** (by rope) descendre qn/qch; **to l. oneself** Fig s'abaisser. ◆**—ing** n (drop) baisse f.

lowly ['ləʊlɪ] a (-ier, -iest) humble.

loyal ['lɔɪəl] a loyal (to envers), fidèle (to à). ◆**loyalty** n loyauté f, fidélité f.

lozenge ['lɒzɪndʒ] n (sweet) Med pastille f; (shape) Geom losange m.

LP [el'piː] abbr = long-playing record.

L-plates ['elpleɪts] *npl* Aut plaques *fpl* d'apprenti conducteur.

Ltd *abbr* (*Limited*) Com SARL.

lubricate ['luːbrɪkeɪt] *vt* lubrifier; Aut graisser. ◆**lubricant** *n* lubrifiant *m*. ◆**lubri'cation** *n* Aut graissage *m*.

lucid ['luːsɪd] *a* lucide. ◆**lu'cidity** *n* lucidité *f*.

luck [lʌk] *n* (*chance*) chance *f*; (*good fortune*) (bonne) chance *f*, bonheur *m*; (*fate*) hasard *m*, fortune *f*; **bad l.** malchance *f*, malheur *m*; **hard l.!**, **tough l.!** pas de chance!; **worse l.** (*unfortunately*) malheureusement. ◆**luckily** *adv* heureusement. ◆**lucky** *a* (-**ier, -iest**) (*person*) chanceux, heureux; (*guess, event*) heureux; **to be l.** (*of person*) avoir de la chance (**to do de** faire); **I've had a l. day** j'ai eu de la chance aujourd'hui; **l. charm** porte-bonheur *m inv*; **l. number**/*etc* chiffre *m*/*etc* porte-bonheur; **how l.!** quelle chance!

lucrative ['luːkrətɪv] *a* lucratif.

ludicrous ['luːdɪkrəs] *a* ridicule.

ludo ['luːdəʊ] *n* jeu *m* des petits chevaux.

lug [lʌg] *vt* (-**gg-**) (*pull*) traîner; **to l. around** trimbaler.

luggage ['lʌgɪdʒ] *n* bagages *mpl*.

lugubrious [luːˈguːbrɪəs] *a* lugubre.

lukewarm ['luːkwɔːm] *a* tiède.

lull [lʌl] **1** *n* arrêt *m*; (*in storm*) accalmie *f*. **2** *vt* (-**ll-**) apaiser; **to l. to sleep** endormir.

lullaby ['lʌləbaɪ] *n* berceuse *f*.

lumbago [lʌmˈbeɪgəʊ] *n* lumbago *m*.

lumber[1] ['lʌmbər] *n* (*timber*) bois *m* de charpente; (*junk*) bric-à-brac *m inv*. ◆**lumberjack** *n* Am Can bûcheron *m*. ◆**lumberjacket** *n* blouson *m*. ◆**lumber-room** *n* débarras *m*.

lumber[2] ['lʌmbər] *vt* **to l. s.o. with sth/s.o.** Fam coller qch/qn à qn; **he got lumbered with the chore** il s'est appuyé la corvée.

luminous ['luːmɪnəs] *a* (*dial etc*) lumineux.

lump [lʌmp] *n* morceau *m*; (*in soup*) grumeau *m*; (*bump*) bosse *f*; (*swelling*) Med grosseur *f*; **l. sum** somme *f* forfaitaire; — *vt* **to l. together** réunir; Fig Pej mettre dans le même sac. ◆**lumpy** *a* (-**ier, -iest**) (*soup etc*) grumeleux; (*surface*) bosselé.

lunar ['luːnər] *a* lunaire.

lunatic ['luːnətɪk] *a* fou, dément; — *n* fou *m*, folle *f*. ◆**lunacy** *n* folie *f*, démence *f*.

lunch [lʌntʃ] *n* déjeuner *m*; **to have l.** déjeuner; **l. break, l. hour, l. time** heure *f* du déjeuner; — *vi* déjeuner (**on, off** de). ◆**luncheon** *n* déjeuner *m*; **l. meat** mortadelle *f*, saucisson *m*; **l. voucher** chèque-déjeuner *m*.

lung [lʌŋ] *n* poumon *m*; **l. cancer** cancer *m* du poumon.

lunge [lʌndʒ] *n* coup *m* en avant; — *vi* **to l. at s.o.** se ruer sur qn.

lurch [lɜːtʃ] **1** *vi* (*of person*) tituber; (*of ship*) faire une embardée. **2** *n* **to leave s.o. in the l.** Fam laisser qn en plan, laisser tomber qn.

lure [lʊər] *vt* attirer (par la ruse) (**into** dans); — *n* (*attraction*) attrait *m*.

lurid ['lʊərɪd] *a* (*horrifying*) horrible, affreux; (*sensational*) à sensation; (*gaudy*) voyant; (*colour, sunset*) sanglant.

lurk [lɜːk] *vi* (*hide*) se cacher (**in** dans); (*prowl*) rôder; (*of suspicion, fear etc*) persister.

luscious ['lʌʃəs] *a* (*food etc*) appétissant.

lush [lʌʃ] **1** *a* (*vegetation*) luxuriant; (*wealthy*) Fam opulent. **2** *n* Am Sl ivrogne *mf*.

lust [lʌst] *n* (*for person, object*) convoitise *f* (**for** de); (*for power, knowledge*) soif *f* (**for** de); — *vi* **to l. after** (*object, person*) convoiter; (*power, knowledge*) avoir soif de.

lustre ['lʌstər] *n* (*gloss*) lustre *m*.

lusty ['lʌstɪ] *a* (-**ier, -iest**) vigoureux.

lute [luːt] *n* Mus luth *m*.

Luxembourg ['lʌksəmbɜːg] *n* Luxembourg *m*.

luxuriant [lʌgˈʒʊərɪənt] *a* luxuriant. ◆**luxuriate** *vi* (*laze about*) paresser (**in bed**/*etc* au lit/*etc*).

luxury ['lʌkʃərɪ] *n* luxe *m*; — *a* (*goods, flat etc*) de luxe. ◆**luxurious** [lʌgˈʒʊərɪəs] *a* luxueux.

lying ['laɪɪŋ] *see* **lie**[1,2]; — *n* le mensonge; — *a* (*account*) mensonger; (*person*) menteur.

lynch [lɪntʃ] *vt* lyncher. ◆**—ing** *n* lynchage *m*.

lynx [lɪŋks] *n* (*animal*) lynx *m*.

lyre ['laɪər] *n* Mus Hist lyre *f*.

lyric ['lɪrɪk] *a* lyrique; — *npl* (*of song*) paroles *fpl*. ◆**lyrical** *a* (*effusive*) lyrique. ◆**lyricism** *n* lyrisme *m*.

M

M, m [em] *n* M, m *m*.

m *abbr* **1** (*metre*) mètre *m*. **2** (*mile*) mile *m*.

MA *abbr* = **Master of Arts.**

ma'am [mæm] *n* madame *f*.

mac [mæk] *n* (*raincoat*) *Fam* imper *m*.

macabre [məˈkɑːbrə] *a* macabre.

macaroni [mækəˈrəʊnɪ] *n* macaroni(s) *m*(*pl*).

macaroon [mækəˈruːn] *n* (*cake*) macaron *m*.

mace [meɪs] *n* (*staff, rod*) masse *f*.

Machiavellian [mækɪəˈvelɪən] *a* machiavélique.

machination [mækɪˈneɪʃ(ə)n] *n* machination *f*.

machine [məˈʃiːn] *n* (*apparatus, car, system etc*) machine *f*. ◆**machinegun** *n* mitrailleuse *f*; – *vt* (**-nn-**) mitrailler. ◆**machinery** *n* (*machines*) machines *fpl*; (*works*) mécanisme *m*; *Fig* rouages *mpl*. ◆**machinist** *n* (*on sewing machine*) piqueur, -euse *mf*.

macho [ˈmætʃəʊ] *n* (*pl* **-os**) macho *m*; – *a* (*attitude etc*) macho (*f inv*).

mackerel [ˈmækrəl] *n inv* (*fish*) maquereau *m*.

mackintosh [ˈmækɪntɒʃ] *n* imperméable *m*.

mad [mæd] *a* (**madder, maddest**) fou; (*dog*) enragé; (*bull*) furieux; **m. (at)** (*angry*) *Fam* furieux (contre); **to be m. (keen) on** *Fam* (*person*) être fou de; (*films etc*) se passionner *or* s'emballer pour; **to drive m.** rendre fou; (*irritate*) énerver; **he drove me m. to go** *Fam* il m'a cassé les pieds pour que j'y aille; **like m.** comme un fou. ◆**maddening** *a* exaspérant. ◆**madhouse** *n Fam* maison *f* de fous. ◆**madly** *adv* (*in love, to spend money etc*) follement; (*desperately*) désespérément. ◆**madman** *n* (*pl* **-men**) fou *m*. ◆**madness** *n* folie *f*.

Madagascar [mædəˈgæskər] *n* Madagascar *f*.

madam [ˈmædəm] *n* (*married*) madame *f*; (*unmarried*) mademoiselle *f*.

made [meɪd] *see* **make.**

Madeira [məˈdɪərə] *n* (*wine*) madère *m*.

madonna [məˈdɒnə] *n Rel* madone *f*.

maestro [ˈmaɪstrəʊ] *n* (*pl* **-os**) *Mus* maestro *m*.

Mafia [ˈmæfɪə] *n* maf(f)ia *f*.

magazine [mægəˈziːn] *n* (*periodical*) magazine *m*, revue *f*; (*of gun, camera*) magasin *m*.

maggot [ˈmægət] *n* ver *m*, asticot *m*. ◆**maggoty** *a* véreux.

magic [ˈmædʒɪk] *n* magie *f*; – *a* (*word, wand*) magique. ◆**magical** *a* (*evening etc*) magique. ◆**ma'gician** *n* magicien, -ienne *mf*.

magistrate [ˈmædʒɪstreɪt] *n* magistrat *m*.

magnanimous [mægˈnænɪməs] *a* magnanime.

magnate [ˈmægneɪt] *n* (*tycoon*) magnat *m*.

magnesium [mægˈniːzɪəm] *n* magnésium *m*.

magnet [ˈmægnɪt] *n* aimant *m*. ◆**mag'netic** *a* magnétique. ◆**magnetism** *n* magnétisme *m*. ◆**magnetize** *vt* magnétiser.

magnificent [mægˈnɪfɪsənt] *a* magnifique. ◆**magnificence** *n* magnificence *f*. ◆**magnificently** *adv* magnifiquement.

magnify [ˈmægnɪfaɪ] *vt* (*image*) & *Fig* grossir; (*sound*) amplifier; **magnifying glass** loupe *f*. ◆**magnifi'cation** *n* grossissement *m*; amplification *f*. ◆**magnitude** *n* ampleur *f*.

magnolia [mægˈnəʊlɪə] *n* (*tree*) magnolia *m*.

magpie [ˈmægpaɪ] *n* (*bird*) pie *f*.

mahogany [məˈhɒgənɪ] *n* acajou *m*.

maid [meɪd] *n* (*servant*) bonne *f*; **old m.** *Pej* vieille fille *f*. ◆**maiden** *n Old-fashioned* jeune fille *f*; – *a* (*speech etc*) premier; (*flight*) inaugural; **m. name** nom *m* de jeune fille. ◆**maidenly** *a* virginal.

mail [meɪl] *n* (*system*) poste *f*; (*letters*) courrier *m*; – *a* (*van, bag etc*) postal; **m. order** vente *f* par correspondance; – *vt* mettre à la poste; **mailing list** liste *f* d'adresses. ◆**mailbox** *n Am* boîte *f* à *or* aux lettres. ◆**mailman** *n* (*pl* **-men**) *Am* facteur *m*.

maim [meɪm] *vt* mutiler, estropier.

main [meɪn] **1** *a* principal; **the m. thing is to ...** l'essentiel est de ... ; **m. line** *Rail* grande ligne *f*; **m. road** grande route *f*; **in the m.** (*mostly*) en gros, dans l'ensemble. **2** *n* **water/gas m.** conduite *f* d'eau/de gaz; **the mains** *El* le secteur; **a mains radio** une radio secteur. ◆**—ly** *adv* principalement, surtout. ◆**mainland** *n* continent *m*. ◆**main-**

stay *n* (*of family etc*) soutien *m*; (*of organization, policy*) pilier *m*. ◆**mainstream** *n* tendance *f* dominante.

maintain [meɪnˈteɪn] *vt* (*continue, assert*) maintenir (**that** que); (*vehicle, family etc*) entretenir; (*silence*) garder. ◆**maintenance** *n* (*of vehicle, road etc*) entretien *m*; (*of prices, order, position etc*) maintien *m*; (*alimony*) pension *f* alimentaire.

maisonette [meɪzəˈnet] *n* duplex *m*.

maize [meɪz] *n* (*cereal*) maïs *m*.

majesty [ˈmædʒəstɪ] *n* majesté *f*; **Your M.** (*title*) Votre Majesté. ◆**ma'jestic** *a* majestueux.

major [ˈmeɪdʒər] **1** *a* (*main, great*) & *Mus* majeur; **a m. road** une grande route. **2** *n Mil* commandant *m*. **3** *n* (*subject*) *Univ Am* dominante *f*; – *vi* **to m. in** se spécialiser en. ◆**majo'rette** *n* (**drum**) m. majorette *f*.

Majorca [məˈjɔːkə] *n* Majorque *f*.

majority [məˈdʒɒrɪtɪ] *n* majorité *f* (**of** de); **in the** *or* **a m.** en majorité, majoritaire; **the m. of people** la plupart des gens; – *a* (*vote etc*) majoritaire.

make [meɪk] *vt* (*pt* & *pp* **made**) faire; (*tool, vehicle etc*) fabriquer; (*decision*) prendre; (*friends, wage*) se faire; (*points*) *Sp* marquer; (*destination*) arriver à; **to m. happy/tired/***etc* rendre heureux/fatigué/*etc*; **he made ten francs on it** *Com* ça lui a rapporté dix francs; **she made the train** (*did not miss*) elle a eu le train; **to m. s.o. do sth** faire faire qch à qn, obliger qn à faire qch; **to m. oneself heard** se faire entendre; **to m. oneself at home** se mettre à l'aise; **to m. ready** préparer; **to m. yellow** jaunir; **she made him her husband** elle en a fait son mari; **to m. do** (*manage*) se débrouiller (**with** avec); **to m. do with** (*be satisfied with*) se contenter de; **to m. it** (*arrive*) arriver; (*succeed*) réussir; (*say*) dire; **I m. it five o'clock** j'ai cinq heures; **what do you m. of it?** qu'en penses-tu?; **I can't m. anything of it** je n'y comprends rien; **to m. a living** gagner sa vie; **you're made (for life)** ton avenir est assuré; **to m. believe** (*pretend*) faire semblant (**that one is** d'être); (*n*) **it's m.-believe** (*story etc*) c'est pure invention; **to live in a world of m.-believe** se bercer d'illusions; – *vi* **to m. as if to** (*appear to*) faire mine de; **to m. for** (*go towards*) aller vers; – *n* (*brand*) marque *f*; **of French/***etc* **m. de fabrication française/***etc*. ■ **to m. off** *vi* (*run away*) se sauver; **to m. out** *vt* (*see*) distinguer; (*understand*) comprendre; (*decipher*) déchiffrer; (*draw up*) faire (*chèque, liste*); (*claim*) prétendre (**that** que);

you made me out to be silly tu m'as fait passer pour un idiot; – *vi* (*manage*) *Fam* se débrouiller; **to m. over** *vt* (*transfer*) céder; (*change*) transformer (**into** en); **to m. up** *vt* (*story*) inventer; (*put together*) faire (*collection, liste, lit etc*); (*prepare*) préparer; (*form*) former, composer; (*loss*) compenser; (*quantity*) compléter; (*quarrel*) régler; (*one's face*) maquiller; – *vi* (*of friends*) se réconcilier; **to m. up for** (*loss, damage, fault*) compenser; (*lost time, mistake*) rattraper. ◆**m.-up** *n* (*of object etc*) constitution *f*; (*of person*) caractère *m*; (*for face*) maquillage *m*. ◆**making** *n* (*manufacture*) fabrication *f*; (*of dress*) confection *f*; **history in the m.** l'histoire en train de se faire; **the makings of** les éléments *mpl* (essentiels) de; **to have the makings of a pianist/***etc* avoir l'étoffe d'un pianiste/*etc*. ◆**maker** *n Com* fabricant *m*. ◆**makeshift** *n* expédient *m*; – *a* (*arrangement etc*) de fortune, provisoire.

maladjusted [mæləˈdʒʌstɪd] *a* inadapté.

malaise [mæˈleɪz] *n* malaise *m*.

malaria [məˈleərɪə] *n* malaria *f*.

Malaysia [məˈleɪzɪə] *n* Malaisie *f*.

male [meɪl] *a Biol Bot etc* mâle; (*clothes, sex*) masculin; – *n* (*man, animal*) mâle *m*.

malevolent [məˈlevələnt] *a* malveillant. ◆**malevolence** *n* malveillance *f*.

malfunction [mælˈfʌŋkʃ(ə)n] *n* mauvais fonctionnement *m*; – *vi* fonctionner mal.

malice [ˈmælɪs] *n* méchanceté *f*; **to bear s.o. m.** vouloir du mal à qn. ◆**ma'licious** *a* malveillant. ◆**ma'liciously** *adv* avec malveillance.

malign [məˈlaɪn] *vt* (*slander*) calomnier.

malignant [məˈlɪgnənt] *a* (*person etc*) malfaisant; **m. tumour** *Med* tumeur *f* maligne. ◆**malignancy** *n Med* malignité *f*.

malingerer [məˈlɪŋgərər] *n* (*pretending illness*) simulateur, -euse *mf*.

mall [mɔːl] *n* (**shopping**) **m.** (*covered*) galerie *f* marchande; (*street*) rue *f* piétonnière.

malleable [ˈmælɪəb(ə)l] *a* malléable.

mallet [ˈmælɪt] *n* (*tool*) maillet *m*.

malnutrition [mælnjuːˈtrɪʃ(ə)n] *n* malnutrition *f*, sous-alimentation *f*.

malpractice [mælˈpræktɪs] *n Med Jur* faute *f* professionnelle.

malt [mɔːlt] *n* malt *m*.

Malta [ˈmɔːltə] *n* Malte *f*. ◆**Mal'tese** *a* & *n* maltais, -aise (*mf*).

mammal [ˈmæm(ə)l] *n* mammifère *m*.

mammoth [ˈmæməθ] *a* (*large*) immense; – *n* (*extinct animal*) mammouth *m*.

man [mæn] *n* (*pl* **men** [men]) homme *m*; (*player*) *Sp* joueur *m*; (*chess piece*) pièce *f*; **a golf m.** (*enthusiast*) un amateur de golf; **he's a Bristol m.** (*by birth*) il est de Bristol; **to be m. and wife** être mari et femme; **my old m.** *Fam* (*father*) mon père; (*husband*) mon homme; **yes old m.!** *Fam* oui mon vieux!; **the m. in the street** l'homme de la rue; – *vt* (**-nn-**) (*ship*) pourvoir d'un équipage; (*fortress*) armer; (*guns*) servir; (*be on duty at*) être de service à; **manned spacecraft** engin *m* spatial habité. ◆**manhood** *n* (*period*) âge *m* d'homme. ◆**manhunt** *n* chasse *f* à l'homme. ◆**manlike** *a* (*quality*) d'homme viril. ◆**manly** *a* (**-ier, -iest**) viril. ◆**man-'made** *a* artificiel; (*fibre*) synthétique. ◆**manservant** *n* (*pl* **menservants**) domestique *m*. ◆**man-to-'man** *a* & *adv* d'homme à homme.

manacle ['mænɪk(ə)l] *n* menotte *f*.

manag/e ['mænɪdʒ] *vt* (*run*) diriger; (*affairs etc*) *Com* gérer; (*handle*) manier; (*take*) *Fam* prendre; (*eat*) *Fam* manger; (*contribute*) *Fam* donner; **to m. to do** (*succeed*) réussir *or* arriver à faire; (*contrive*) se débrouiller pour faire; **I'll m. it** j'y arriverai; – *vi* (*succeed*) y arriver; (*make do*) se débrouiller (**with** avec); **to m. without sth** se passer de qch. ◆**—ing** *a* **m. director** directeur *m* général; **the m. director** le PDG. ◆**—eable** *a* (*parcel, person etc*) maniable; (*feasible*) faisable. ◆**—ement** *n* direction *f*; (*of property etc*) gestion *f*; (*executive staff*) cadres *mpl*. ◆**—er** *n* directeur *m*; (*of shop, café*) gérant *m*; (*business*) **m.** (*of actor, boxer etc*) manager *m*. ◆**manage'ress** *n* directrice *f*, gérante *f*. ◆**managerial** [mænə'dʒɪərɪəl] *a* directorial; **the m. class** *or* **staff** les cadres *mpl*.

mandarin ['mændərɪn] **1** *n* (*high-ranking official*) haut fonctionnaire *m*; (*in political party*) bonze *m*; (*in university*) *Pej* mandarin *m*. **2** *a* & *n m.* (**orange**) mandarine *f*.

mandate ['mændeɪt] *n* mandat *m*. ◆**mandatory** *a* obligatoire.

mane [meɪn] *n* crinière *f*.

maneuver [mə'nuːvər] *n* & *vti Am* = manoeuvre.

mangle ['mæŋg(ə)l] **1** *n* (*for wringing*) essoreuse *f*; – *vt* (*clothes*) essorer. **2** *vt* (*damage*) mutiler.

mango ['mæŋgəʊ] *n* (*pl* **-oes** *or* **-os**) (*fruit*) mangue *f*.

mangy ['meɪndʒɪ] *a* (*animal*) galeux.

manhandle [mæn'hænd(ə)l] *vt* maltraiter.

manhole ['mænhəʊl] *n* trou *m* d'homme; **m. cover** plaque *f* d'égout.

mania ['meɪnɪə] *n* manie *f*. ◆**maniac** *n* fou *m*, folle *f*; *Psy Med* maniaque *mf*; **sex m.** obsédé *m* sexuel.

manicure ['mænɪkjʊər] *n* soin *m* des mains; – *vt* (*person*) manucurer; (*s.o.'s nails*) faire. ◆**manicurist** *n* manucure *mf*.

manifest ['mænɪfest] **1** *a* (*plain*) manifeste. **2** *vt* (*show*) manifester.

manifesto [mænɪ'festəʊ] *n* (*pl* **-os** *or* **-oes**) *Pol* manifeste *m*.

manifold ['mænɪfəʊld] *a* multiple.

manipulate [mə'nɪpjʊleɪt] *vt* manœuvrer; (*facts, electors etc*) *Pej* manipuler. ◆**manipu'lation** *n* manœuvre *f*; *Pej* manipulation *f* (**of** de).

mankind [mæn'kaɪnd] *n* (*humanity*) le genre humain.

manner ['mænər] *n* (*way*) manière *f*; (*behaviour*) attitude *f*, comportement *m*; *pl* (*social habits*) manières *fpl*; **in this m.** (*like this*) de cette manière; **all m. of** toutes sortes de. ◆**mannered** *a* (*affected*) maniéré; **well-/bad-m.** bien/mal élevé. ◆**mannerism** *n Pej* tic *m*.

manoeuvre [mə'nuːvər] *n* manœuvre *f*; – *vti* manœuvrer. ◆**manoeuvra'bility** *n* (*of vehicle etc*) maniabilité *f*.

manor ['mænər] *n* (*house*) manoir *m*.

manpower ['mænpaʊər] *n* (*labour*) main-d'œuvre *f*; *Mil* effectifs *mpl*; (*effort*) force *f*.

mansion ['mænʃ(ə)n] *n* hôtel *m* particulier; (*in country*) manoir *m*.

manslaughter ['mænslɔːtər] *n Jur* homicide *m* involontaire.

mantelpiece ['mænt(ə)lpiːs] *n* (*shelf*) cheminée *f*.

mantle ['mænt(ə)l] *n* (*cloak*) cape *f*.

manual ['mænjʊəl] **1** *a* (*work etc*) manuel. **2** *n* (*book*) manuel *m*.

manufactur/e [mænjʊ'fæktʃər] *vt* fabriquer; – *n* fabrication *f*. ◆**—er** *n* fabricant, -ante *mf*.

manure [mə'njʊər] *n* fumier *m*, engrais *m*.

manuscript ['mænjʊskrɪpt] *n* manuscrit *m*.

many ['menɪ] *a* & *n* beaucoup (**de**); **m. things** beaucoup de choses; **m. came** beaucoup sont venus; **very m., a good** *or* **great m.** un très grand nombre (de); (**a good** *or* **great**) **m. of** un (très) grand nombre de; **m. of them** un grand nombre d'entre eux; **m. times, m. a time** bien des fois; **m. kinds** toutes sortes (**of** de); **how m.?** combien (**de**)?; **too m.** trop (**de**); **one too m.** un de trop; **there are too m. of them** ils sont trop nombreux; **so m.** tant (**de**); **as m. books**/etc

as autant de livres/*etc* que; **as m. as** (*up to*) jusqu'à.

map [mæp] *n* (*of country etc*) carte *f*; (*plan*) plan *m*; – *vt* (**-pp-**) faire la carte *or* le plan de; **to m. out** (*road*) faire le tracé de; (*one's day etc*) *Fig* organiser.

maple ['meɪp(ə)l] *n* (*tree, wood*) érable *m*.

mar [mɑɪr] *vt* (**-rr-**) gâter.

marathon ['mærəθən] *n* marathon *m*.

maraud [mə'rɔɪd] *vi* piller. ◆—**ing** *a* pillard. ◆—**er** *n* pillard, -arde *mf*.

marble ['mɑɪb(ə)l] *n* (*substance*) marbre *m*; (*toy ball*) bille *f*.

march [mɑɪtʃ] *n Mil* marche *f*; – *vi Mil* marcher (au pas); **to m. in/out/etc** *Fig* entrer/sortir/*etc* d'un pas décidé; **to m. past** défiler; – *vt* **to m. s.o. off** *or* **away** emmener qn. ◆**m.-past** *n* défilé *m*.

March [mɑɪtʃ] *n* mars *m*.

mare [meər] *n* jument *f*.

margarine [mɑɪdʒə'riɪn] *n* margarine *f*.

margin ['mɑɪdʒɪn] *n* (*of page etc*) marge *f*; **by a narrow m.** (*to win*) de justesse. ◆**marginal** *a* marginal; **m. seat** *Pol* siège *m* disputé. ◆**marginally** *adv* très légèrement.

marguerite [mɑɪgə'riɪt] *n* (*daisy*) marguerite *f*.

marigold ['mærɪgəʊld] *n* (*flower*) souci *m*.

marijuana [mærɪ'wɑɪnə] *n* marijuana *f*.

marina [mə'riɪnə] *n* marina *f*.

marinate ['mærɪneɪt] *vti Culin* mariner.

marine [mə'riɪn] **1** *a* (*life, flora etc*) marin. **2** *n* (*soldier*) fusilier *m* marin, *Am* marine *m*.

marionette [mærɪə'net] *n* marionnette *f*.

marital ['mærɪt(ə)l] *a* matrimonial; (*relations*) conjugal; **m. status** situation *f* de famille.

maritime ['mærɪtaɪm] *a* (*province, climate etc*) maritime.

marjoram ['mɑɪdʒərəm] *n* (*spice*) marjolaine *f*.

mark[1] [mɑɪk] *n* (*symbol*) marque *f*; (*stain, trace*) trace *f*, tache *f*, marque *f*; (*token, sign*) *Fig* signe *m*; (*for exercise etc*) *Sch* note *f*; (*target*) but *m*; (*model*) *Tech* série *f*; **to make one's m.** *Fig* s'imposer; **up to the m.** (*person, work*) à la hauteur; – *vt* marquer; (*exam etc*) *Sch* corriger, noter; (*pay attention to*) faire attention à; **to m. time** *Mil* marquer le pas; *Fig* piétiner; **m. you . . . !** remarquez que . . . !; **to m. down** (*price*) baisser; **to m. off** (*separate*) séparer; (*on list*) cocher; **to m. out** (*area*) délimiter; **to m. s.o. out for** désigner qn pour; **to m. up** (*increase*) augmenter. ◆—**ed** *a* (*noticeable*) marqué. ◆—**edly** [-ɪdlɪ] *adv* visiblement.

◆—**ing(s)** *n*(*pl*) (*on animal etc*) marques *fpl*; (*on road*) signalisation *f* horizontale. ◆—**er** *n* (*flag etc*) marque *f*; (*pen*) feutre *m*, marqueur *m*.

mark[2] [mɑɪk] *n* (*currency*) mark *m*.

market ['mɑɪkɪt] *n* marché *m*; **on the open m.** en vente libre; **on the black m.** au marché noir; **the Common M.** le Marché commun; **m. value** valeur *f* marchande; **m. price** prix *m* courant; **m. gardener** maraîcher, -ère *mf*; – *vt* (*sell*) vendre; (*launch*) commercialiser. ◆—**ing** *n* marketing *m*, vente *f*. ◆—**able** *a* vendable.

marksman ['mɑɪksmən] *n* (*pl* -**men**) tireur *m* d'élite.

marmalade ['mɑɪməleɪd] *n* confiture *f* d'oranges.

maroon [mə'ruɪn] *a* (*colour*) bordeaux *inv*.

marooned [mə'ruɪnd] *a* abandonné; (*in snowstorm etc*) bloqué (by par).

marquee [mɑɪ'kiɪ] *n* (*for concerts, garden parties etc*) chapiteau *m*; (*awning*) *Am* marquise *f*.

marquis ['mɑɪkwɪs] *n* marquis *m*.

marrow ['mærəʊ] *n* **1** (*of bone*) moelle *f*. **2** (*vegetable*) courge *f*.

marr/y ['mærɪ] *vt* épouser, se marier avec; **to m. (off)** (*of priest etc*) marier; – *vi* se marier. ◆—**led** *a* marié; (*life, state*) conjugal; **m. name** nom *m* de femme mariée; **to get m.** se marier. ◆**marriage** *n* mariage *m*; **to be related by m. to** être parent par alliance de; – *a* (*bond*) conjugal; (*certificate*) de mariage; **m. bureau** agence *f* matrimoniale. ◆**marriageable** *a* en état de se marier.

marsh [mɑɪʃ] *n* marais *m*, marécage *m*. ◆**marshland** *n* marécages *mpl*. ◆**marsh-'mallow** *n Bot Culin* guimauve *f*.

marshal ['mɑɪʃ(ə)l] **1** *n* (*in army*) maréchal *m*; (*in airforce*) général *m*; (*at public event*) membre *m* du service d'ordre; *Jur Am* shérif *m*. **2** *vt* (**-ll-**, *Am* -**l-**) (*gather*) rassembler; (*lead*) mener cérémonieusement.

martial ['mɑɪʃ(ə)l] *a* martial; **m. law** loi *f* martiale.

Martian ['mɑɪʃ(ə)n] *n & a* martien, -ienne (*mf*).

martyr ['mɑɪtər] *n* martyr, -yre *mf*; – *vt Rel* martyriser. ◆**martyrdom** *n* martyre *m*.

marvel ['mɑɪv(ə)l] *n* (*wonder*) merveille *f*; (*miracle*) miracle *m*; – *vi* (**-ll-**, *Am* -**l-**) s'émerveiller (at de); – *vt* **to m. that** s'étonner de ce que (+ *sub or indic*). ◆**marvellous** *a* merveilleux.

Marxism ['mɑɪksɪz(ə)m] *n* marxisme *m*. ◆**Marxist** *a & n* marxiste (*mf*).

marzipan ['mɑːzɪpæn] *n* pâte *f* d'amandes.

mascara [mæˈskɑːrə] *n* mascara *m*.

mascot ['mæskɒt] *n* mascotte *f*.

masculine ['mæskjʊlɪn] *a* masculin. ◆**mascu'linity** *n* masculinité *f*.

mash [mæʃ] *n* (*for poultry etc*) pâtée *f*; (*potatoes*) Culin purée *f*; – *vt* to m. (up) (*potatoes*) Culin & Culin écraser; **mashed potatoes** purée *f* (de pommes de terre).

mask [mɑːsk] *n* masque *m*; – *vt* (*cover, hide*) masquer (**from** à).

masochism ['mæsəkɪz(ə)m] *n* masochisme *m*. ◆**masochist** *n* masochiste *mf*. ◆**maso'chistic** *a* masochiste.

mason ['meɪs(ə)n] *n* maçon *m*. ◆**masonry** *n* maçonnerie *f*.

masquerade [mɑːskəˈreɪd] *n* (*gathering, disguise*) mascarade *f*; – *vi* to m. as se faire passer pour.

mass¹ [mæs] *n* masse *f*; a m. of (*many*) une multitude de; (*pile*) un tas de, une masse de; to be a m. of bruises *Fam* être couvert de bleus; **masses of** *Fam* des masses de; the **masses** (*people*) les masses *fpl*; – *a* (*education*) des masses; (*culture, demonstration*) de masse; (*protests, departure*) en masse; (*production*) en série, en masse; (*hysteria*) collectif; m. grave fosse *f* commune; m. **media** mass media *mpl*; – *vi* (*of troops, people*) se masser. ◆**m.-pro'duce** *vt* fabriquer en série.

mass² [mæs] *n* Rel messe *f*.

massacre ['mæsəkər] *n* massacre *m*; – *vt* massacrer.

massage ['mæsɑːʒ] *n* massage *m*; – *vt* masser. ◆**ma'sseur** *n* masseur *m*. ◆**ma'sseuse** *n* masseuse *f*.

massive ['mæsɪv] *a* (*solid*) massif; (*huge*) énorme, considérable. ◆**—ly** *adv* (*to increase, reduce etc*) considérablement.

mast [mɑːst] *n* Nau mât *m*; Rad TV pylône *m*.

master ['mɑːstər] *n* maître *m*; (*in secondary school*) professeur *m*; a m.'s degree une maîtrise (**in** de); M. of Arts/Science (*person*) Univ Maître *m* ès lettres/sciences; m. of ceremonies (*presenter*) *Am* animateur, -trice *mf*; m. card carte *f* maîtresse; m. stroke coup *m* de maître; m. key passe-partout *m inv*; old m. (*painting*) tableau *m* de maître; **I'm my own m.** je ne dépends que de moi; – *vt* (*control*) maîtriser; (*subject, situation*) dominer; **she has mastered Latin** elle possède le latin. ◆**masterly** *a* magistral. ◆**mastery** *n* maîtrise *f* (**of** de).

mastermind ['mɑːstəmaɪnd] *n* (*person*) cerveau *m*; – *vt* organiser.

masterpiece ['mɑːstəpiːs] *n* chef-d'œuvre *m*.

mastic ['mæstɪk] *n* mastic *m* (silicone).

masturbate ['mæstəbeɪt] *vi* se masturber. ◆**mastur'bation** *n* masturbation *f*.

mat [mæt] **1** *n* tapis *m*, natte *f*; (*at door*) paillasson *m*; (**table**) m. (*of fabric*) napperon *m*; (*hard*) dessous-de-plat *m inv*; (**place**) m. set *m* (de table). **2** *a* (*paint, paper*) mat.

match¹ [mætʃ] *n* allumette *f*; **book of matches** pochette *f* d'allumettes. ◆**matchbox** *n* boîte *f* à allumettes. ◆**matchstick** *n* allumette *f*.

match² [mætʃ] **1** *n* (*game*) Sp match *m*; (*equal*) égal, -ale *mf*; (*marriage*) mariage *m*; **to be a good m.** (*of colours, people etc*) être bien assortis; **he's a good m.** (*man to marry*) c'est un bon parti; – *vt* (*of clothes*) aller (bien) avec; **to m.** (**up to**) (*equal*) égaler; **to m.** (**up**) (*plates etc*) assortir; **to be well-matched** (*of colours, people etc*) être (bien) assortis, aller (bien) ensemble; – *vi* (*go with each other*) être assortis, aller (bien) ensemble. ◆**—ing** *a* (*dress etc*) assorti.

mate [meɪt] **1** *n* (*friend*) camarade *mf*; (*of animal*) mâle *m*, femelle *f*; **builder's/electrician's/etc** m. aide-maçon/-électricien/*etc* m. **2** *vi* (*of animals*) s'accoupler (**with** avec). **3** *n* Chess mat *m*; – *vt* faire *or* mettre mat.

material [məˈtɪərɪəl] **1** *a* matériel; (*important*) important. **2** *n* (*substance*) matière *f*; (*cloth*) tissu *m*; (*for book*) matériaux *mpl*; **material(s)** (*equipment*) matériel *m*; **building material(s)** matériaux *mpl* de construction. ◆**materialism** *n* matérialisme *m*. ◆**materialist** *n* matérialiste *mf*. ◆**materia'listic** *a* matérialiste. ◆**materialize** *vi* se matérialiser. ◆**materially** *adv* matériellement; (*well-off etc*) sur le plan matériel.

maternal [məˈtɜːn(ə)l] *a* maternel. ◆**maternity** *n* maternité *f*; m. hospital, m. unit maternité *f*; – *a* (*clothes*) de grossesse; (*allowance, leave*) de maternité.

mathematical [mæθəˈmætɪk(ə)l] *a* mathématique; **to have a m. brain** être doué pour les maths. ◆**mathema'tician** *n* mathématicien, -ienne *mf*. ◆**mathematics** *n* mathématiques *fpl*. ◆**maths** *n*, *Am* ◆**math** *n* *Fam* maths *fpl*.

matinée ['mætɪneɪ] *n* Th matinée *f*.

matriculation [mətrɪkjuˈleɪʃ(ə)n] *n Univ* inscription *f.*

matrimony [ˈmætrɪmənɪ] *n* mariage *m.* ◆**matriˈmonial** *a* matrimonial.

matrix, *pl* **-ices** [ˈmeɪtrɪks, -ɪsiːz] *n Tech* matrice *f.*

matron [ˈmeɪtrən] *n Lit* mère *f* de famille, dame *f* âgée; (*nurse*) infirmière *f* (en) chef. ◆**matronly** *a* (*air etc*) de mère de famille; (*mature*) mûr; (*portly*) corpulent.

matt [mæt] *a* (*paint, paper*) mat.

matted [ˈmætɪd] *a* **m. hair** cheveux *mpl* emmêlés.

matter[1] [ˈmætər] *n* matière *f*; (*affair*) affaire *f*, question *f*; (*thing*) chose *f*; **no m.!** (*no importance*) peu importe!; **no m. what she does** quoi qu'elle fasse; **no m. where you go** où que tu ailles; **no m. who you are** qui que vous soyez; **no m. when** quel que soit le moment; **what's the m.?** qu'est-ce qu'il y a?; **what's the m. with you?** qu'est-ce que tu as?; **there's sth the m.** il y a qch qui ne va pas; **there's sth the m. with my leg** j'ai qch à la jambe; **there's nothing the m. with him** il n'a rien; – *vi* (*be important*) importer (**to** à); **it doesn't m. if/when/who/etc** peu importe si/quand/qui/*etc*; **it doesn't m.!** ça ne fait rien!, peu importe! ◆**m.-of-ˈfact** *a* (*person, manner*) terre à terre; (*voice*) neutre.

matter[2] [ˈmætər] *n* (*pus*) *Med* pus *m.*

matting [ˈmætɪŋ] *n* (*material*) nattage *m*; **a piece of m.**, **some m.** une natte.

mattress [ˈmætrəs] *n* matelas *m.*

mature [məˈtʃʊər] *a* mûr; (*cheese*) fait; – *vt* (*person, plan*) (faire) mûrir; – *vi* mûrir; (*of cheese*) se faire. ◆**maturity** *n* maturité *f.*

maul [mɔːl] *vt* (*of animal*) mutiler; (*of person*) *Fig* malmener.

mausoleum [mɔːsəˈlɪəm] *n* mausolée *m.*

mauve [məʊv] *a & n* (*colour*) mauve (*m*).

maverick [ˈmævərɪk] *n & a Pol* dissident, -ente (*mf*).

mawkish [ˈmɔːkɪʃ] *a* d'une sensiblerie excessive, mièvre.

maxim [ˈmæksɪm] *n* maxime *f.*

maximum [ˈmæksɪməm] *n* (*pl* **-ima** [-ɪmə] *or* **-imums**) maximum *m*; – *a* maximum (*f inv*), maximal. ◆**maximize** *vt* porter au maximum.

may [meɪ] *v aux* (*pt* **might**) **1** (*possibility*) **he m. come** il peut arriver; **he might come** il pourrait arriver; **I m. or might be wrong** il se peut que je me trompe, je me trompe peut-être; **you m. or might have** tu aurais pu; **I m. or might have forgotten** il se peut que je l'ai peut-être oublié; **we m. or might as well go**

nous ferions aussi bien de partir; **she fears I m. or might get lost** elle a peur que je ne me perde. **2** (*permission*) **m. I stay?** puis-je rester?; **m. I?** vous permettez?; **you m. go** tu peux partir. **3** (*wish*) **m. you be happy** (que tu) sois heureux. ◆**maybe** *adv* peut-être.

May [meɪ] *n* mai *m.*

mayhem [ˈmeɪhem] *n* (*chaos*) pagaïe *f*; (*havoc*) ravages *mpl.*

mayonnaise [meɪəˈneɪz] *n* mayonnaise *f.*

mayor [meər] *n* (*man, woman*) maire *m.* ◆**mayoress** *n* femme *f* du maire.

maze [meɪz] *n* labyrinthe *m.*

MC [emˈsiː] *abbr* = **master of ceremonies**.

me [miː] *pron* me, m'; (*after prep etc*) moi; **(to) me** (*indirect*) me, m'; **she knows me** elle me connaît; **he helps me** il m'aide; **he gives (to) me** il me donne; **with me** avec moi.

meadow [ˈmedəʊ] *n* pré *m*, prairie *f.*

meagre [ˈmiːgər] *a* maigre.

meal [miːl] *n* **1** (*food*) repas *m.* **2** (*flour*) farine *f.*

mealy-mouthed [miːlɪˈmaʊðd] *a* mielleux.

mean[1] [miːn] *vt* (*pt & pp* **meant** [ment]) (*signify*) vouloir dire, signifier; (*destine*) destiner (**for** à); (*entail*) entraîner; (*represent*) représenter; (*refer to*) faire allusion à; **to m. to do** (*intend*) avoir l'intention de faire, vouloir faire; **I m. it, I m. what I say** je suis sérieux; **to m. sth to s.o.** (*matter*) avoir de l'importance pour qn; **it means sth to me** (*name, face*) ça me dit qch; **I didn't m. to!** je ne l'ai pas fait exprès!; **you were meant to come** vous étiez censé venir. ◆**—ing** *n* sens *m*, signification *f.* ◆**meaningful** *a* significatif. ◆**meaningless** *a* qui n'a pas de sens; (*absurd*) *Fig* insensé.

mean[2] [miːn] *a* (**-er**, **-est**) (*stingy*) avare, mesquin; (*petty*) mesquin; (*nasty*) méchant; (*inferior*) misérable. ◆**—ness** *n* (*greed*) avarice *f*; (*nastiness*) méchanceté *f.*

mean[3] [miːn] *a* (*distance*) moyen; – *n* (*middle position*) milieu *m*; (*average*) *Math* moyenne *f*; **the happy m.** le juste milieu.

meander [mɪˈændər] *vi* (*of river*) faire des méandres.

means [miːnz] *n(pl)* (*method*) moyen(s) *m(pl)* (**to do, of doing** de faire); (*wealth*) moyens *mpl*; **by m. of** (*stick etc*) au moyen de; (*work, concentration*) à force de; **by all m.!** très certainement!; **by no m.** nullement; **independent** *or* **private m.** fortune *f* personnelle.

meant [ment] *see* **mean**[1].

meantime [ˈmiːntaɪm] *adv & n* **(in the) m.** entre-temps. ◆**meanwhile** *adv* entre-temps.

measles ['miːz(ə)lz] *n* rougeole *f*.

measly ['miːzlɪ] *a* (*contemptible*) *Fam* minable.

measur/e ['meʒər] *n* mesure *f*; (*ruler*) règle *f*; **made to m.** fait sur mesure; – *vt* mesurer; (*strength etc*) *Fig* estimer, mesurer; (*adjust, adapt*) adapter (**to** à); **to m. up** mesurer; – *vi* **to m. up** to être à la hauteur de. ◆**—ed** *a* (*careful*) mesuré. ◆**—ement** *n* (*of chest, waist etc*) tour *m*; *pl* (*dimensions*) mesures *fpl*; **your hip m.** ton tour de hanches.

meat [miːt] *n* viande *f*; (*of crab, lobster etc*) chair *f*; *Fig* substance *f*; **m. diet** régime *m* carné. ◆**meaty** *a* (**-ier, -iest**) (*fleshy*) charnu; (*flavour*) de viande; *Fig* substantiel.

mechanic [mɪˈkænɪk] *n* mécanicien, -ienne *mf*. ◆**mechanical** *a* mécanique; (*reply etc*) *Fig* machinal. ◆**mechanics** *n* (*science*) mécanique *f*; *pl* (*workings*) mécanisme *m*. ◆'**mechanism** *n* mécanisme *m*. ◆'**mechanize** *vt* mécaniser.

medal ['med(ə)l] *n* médaille *f*. ◆**me-'dallion** *n* (*ornament, jewel*) médaillon *m*. ◆**medallist** *n* médaillé, -ée *mf*; **to be a gold/silver m.** *Sp* être médaille d'or/ d'argent.

meddle ['med(ə)l] *vi* (*interfere*) se mêler (**in** de); (*tamper*) toucher (**with** à). ◆**meddlesome** *a* qui se mêle de tout.

media ['miːdɪə] *npl* **1** **the (mass) m.** les médias *mpl*. **2** *see* **medium 2**.

mediaeval [medɪˈiːv(ə)l] *a* médiéval.

median ['miːdɪən] *a* **m. strip** *Aut Am* bande *f* médiane.

mediate ['miːdɪeɪt] *vi* servir d'intermédiaire (**between** entre). ◆**medi'ation** *n* médiation *f*. ◆**mediator** *n* médiateur, -trice *mf*.

medical ['medɪk(ə)l] *a* médical; (*school, studies*) de médecine; (*student*) en médecine; – *n* (*in school, army*) visite *f* médicale; (*private*) examen *m* médical. ◆**medicated** *a* (*shampoo*) médical. ◆**medi'cation** *n* médicaments *mpl*. ◆**me'dicinal** *a* médicinal. ◆**medicine** *n* médecine *f*; (*substance*) médicament *m*; **m. cabinet, m. chest** pharmacie *f*.

medieval [medɪˈiːv(ə)l] *a* médiéval.

mediocre [miːdɪˈəʊkər] *a* médiocre. ◆**medi'ocrity** *n* médiocrité *f*.

meditate ['medɪteɪt] *vi* méditer (**on** sur). ◆**medi'tation** *n* méditation *f*. ◆**meditative** *a* méditatif.

Mediterranean [medɪtəˈreɪnɪən] *a* méditerranéen; – *n* **the M.** la Méditerranée.

medium ['miːdɪəm] **1** *a* (*average, middle*) moyen. **2** *n* (*pl* **media** ['miːdɪə]) *Phys* véhicule *m*; *Biol* milieu *m*; (*for conveying data or publicity*) support *m*; **through the m. of** par l'intermédiaire de; **the happy m.** le juste milieu. **3** *n* (*person*) médium *m*. ◆**m.-sized** *a* moyen, de taille moyenne.

medley ['medlɪ] *n* mélange *m*; *Mus* pot-pourri *m*.

meek [miːk] *a* (**-er, -est**) doux.

meet [miːt] *vt* (*pt & pp* **met**) (*encounter*) rencontrer; (*see again, join*) retrouver; (*pass in street, road etc*) croiser; (*fetch*) (aller ou venir) chercher; (*wait for*) attendre; (*debt, enemy, danger*) faire face à; (*need*) combler; (*be introduced to*) faire la connaissance de; **to arrange to m. s.o.** donner rendez-vous à qn; – *vi* (*of people, teams, rivers, looks*) se rencontrer; (*of people by arrangement*) se retrouver; (*be introduced*) se connaître; (*of society*) se réunir; (*of trains, vehicles*) se croiser; **to m. up with** rencontrer; (*by arrangement*) retrouver; **to m. up** se rencontrer; se retrouver; **to m. with** (*accident, problem*) avoir; (*loss, refusal*) essuyer; (*obstacle, difficulty*) rencontrer; **to m. with s.o.** *Am* rencontrer qn; retrouver qn; – *n* *Sp Am* réunion *f*; **to make a m. with** *Fam* donner rendez-vous à. ◆**—ing** *n* réunion *f*; (*large*) assemblée *f*; (*between two people*) rencontre *f*, (*prearranged*) rendez-vous *m inv*; **in a m.** en conférence.

megalomania [megələʊˈmeɪnɪə] *n* mégalomanie *f*. ◆**megalomaniac** *n* mégalomane *mf*.

megaphone ['megəfəʊn] *n* porte-voix *m inv*.

melancholy ['melənkəlɪ] *n* mélancolie *f*; – *a* mélancolique.

mellow ['meləʊ] *a* (**-er, -est**) (*fruit*) mûr; (*colour, voice, wine*) moelleux; (*character*) mûri par l'expérience; – *vi* (*of person*) s'adoucir.

melodrama ['melədrɑːmə] *n* mélodrame *m*. ◆**melodra'matic** *a* mélodramatique.

melody ['melədɪ] *n* mélodie *f*. ◆**me'lodic** *a* mélodique. ◆**me'lodious** *a* mélodieux.

melon ['melən] *n* (*fruit*) melon *m*.

melt [melt] *vi* fondre; **to m. into** (*merge*) *Fig* se fondre dans; – *vt* (faire) fondre; **to m. down** (*metal object*) fondre; **melting point** point *m* de fusion; **melting pot** *Fig* creuset *m*.

member ['membər] *n* membre *m*; **M. of Parliament** député *m*. ◆**membership** *n* adhésion *f* (**of** à); (*number*) nombre *m* de(s) membres; (*members*) membres *mpl*; **m. (fee)** cotisation *f*.

membrane ['membreɪn] n membrane f.

memento [mə'mentəʊ] n (pl -os or -oes) (object) souvenir m.

memo ['meməʊ] n (pl -os) note f; **m. pad** bloc-notes m. **◆memo'randum** n note f; Pol Com mémorandum m.

memoirs ['memwɑːz] npl (essays) mémoires mpl.

memory ['meməri] n mémoire f; (recollection) souvenir m; **to the** or **in m. of** à la mémoire de. **◆memorable** a mémorable. **◆me'morial** a (plaque etc) commémoratif; − n monument m, mémorial m. **◆memorize** vt apprendre par cœur.

men [men] see **man**. **◆menfolk** n Fam hommes mpl.

menac/e ['menɪs] n danger m; (nuisance) Fam plaie f; (threat) menace f; − vt menacer. **◆−ingly** adv (to say) d'un ton menaçant; (to do) d'une manière menaçante.

menagerie [mɪ'nædʒərɪ] n ménagerie f.

mend [mend] vt (repair) réparer; (clothes) raccommoder; **to m. one's ways** se corriger, s'amender; − n raccommodage m; **to be on the m.** (after illness) aller mieux.

menial ['miːnɪəl] a inférieur.

meningitis [menɪn'dʒaɪtɪs] n Med méningite f.

menopause ['menəpɔːz] n ménopause f.

menstruation [menstru'eɪʃ(ə)n] n menstruation f.

mental ['ment(ə)l] a mental; (hospital) psychiatrique; (mad) Sl fou; **m. strain** tension f nerveuse. **◆men'tality** n mentalité f. **◆mentally** adv mentalement; **he's m. handicapped** c'est un handicapé mental; **she's m. ill** c'est une malade mentale.

mention ['menʃ(ə)n] vt mentionner, faire mention de; **not to m.** . . . . sans parler de . . . , sans compter . . . ; **don't m. it!** il n'y a pas de quoi!; **no savings/etc worth mentioning** pratiquement pas d'économies/etc; − n mention f.

mentor ['mentɔː] n (adviser) mentor m.

menu ['menjuː] n menu m.

mercantile ['mɜːkəntaɪl] a (activity etc) commercial; (ship) marchand; (nation) commerçant.

mercenary ['mɜːsɪnərɪ] a mercenaire (m).

merchandise ['mɜːtʃəndaɪz] n (articles) marchandises fpl; (total stock) marchandise f.

merchant ['mɜːtʃ(ə)nt] n (trader) Fin négociant, -ante mf; (retail) m. commerçant m (en détail); **wine m.** négociant, -ante mf en vins; (shopkeeper) marchand m de vins; − a (vessel, navy) marchand; (seaman) de la marine marchande; **m. bank** banque f de commerce.

mercury ['mɜːkjʊrɪ] n mercure m.

mercy ['mɜːsɪ] n pitié f; Rel miséricorde f; **to beg for m.** demander grâce; **at the m. of** à la merci de; **it's a m. that . . .** (stroke of luck) c'est une chance que . . . . **◆merciful** a miséricordieux. **◆mercifully** adv (fortunately) Fam heureusement. **◆merciless** a impitoyable.

mere [mɪər] a simple; (only) ne . . . que; **she's a m. child** ce n'est qu'une enfant; **it's a m. kilometre** ça ne fait qu'un kilomètre; **by m. chance** par pur hasard; **the m. sight of her** or **him** sa seule vue. **◆−ly** adv (tout) simplement.

merg/e [mɜːdʒ] vi (blend) se mêler (with à); (of roads) se (re)joindre; (of firms) Com fusionner; − vt (unify) Pol unifier; Com fusionner. **◆−er** n Com fusion f.

meridian [mə'rɪdɪən] n méridien m.

meringue [mə'ræŋ] n (cake) meringue f.

merit ['merɪt] n mérite m; **on its merits** (to consider sth etc) objectivement; − vt mériter.

mermaid ['mɜːmeɪd] n (woman) sirène f.

merry ['merɪ] a (-ier, -iest) gai; (drunk) Fam éméché. **◆m.-go-round** n (at funfair etc) manège m. **◆m.-making** n réjouissances fpl. **◆merrily** adv gaiement. **◆merriment** n gaieté f, rires mpl.

mesh [meʃ] n (of net etc) maille f; (fabric) tissu m à mailles; (of intrigue etc) Fig réseau m; (of circumstances) Fig engrenage m; **wire m.** grillage m.

mesmerize ['mezməraɪz] vt hypnotiser.

mess¹ [mes] **1** n (confusion) désordre m, pagaïe f; (muddle) gâchis m; (dirt) saleté f; **in a m.** en désordre; (trouble) Fam dans le pétrin; (pitiful state) dans un triste état; **to make a m. of** (spoil) gâcher. **2** vt **to m. s.o. about** (bother, treat badly) Fam déranger qn, embêter qn; **to m. up** (spoil) gâcher; (dirty) salir; (room) mettre en désordre; − vi **to m. about** (have fun, idle) s'amuser; (play the fool) faire l'idiot; **to m. about with** (fiddle with) s'amuser avec. **◆m.-up** n (disorder) Fam gâchis m. **◆messy** a (-ier, -iest) (untidy) en désordre; (dirty) sale; (confused) Fig embrouillé, confus.

mess² [mes] n Mil mess m inv.

message ['mesɪdʒ] n message m. **◆messenger** n messager, -ère mf; (in office, hotel) coursier, -ière mf.

Messiah [mɪ'saɪə] n Messie m.

Messrs ['mesəz] *npl* **M. Brown** Messieurs *or* MM Brown.

met [met] *see* meet.

metal ['met(ə)l] *n* métal *m*. ◆**me'tallic** *a* métallique; (*paint*) métallisé. ◆**metalwork** *n* (*objects*) ferronnerie *f*; (*study, craft*) travail *m* des métaux.

metamorphosis, *pl* **-oses** [metə'mɔːfəsɪs, -əsiːz] *n* métamorphose *f*.

metaphor ['metəfər] *n* métaphore *f*. ◆**meta'phorical** *a* métaphorique.

metaphysical [metə'fɪzɪk(ə)l] *a* métaphysique.

mete [miːt] *vt* **to m. out** (*justice*) rendre; (*punishment*) infliger.

meteor ['miːtɪər] *n* météore *m*. ◆**mete'oric** *a* **m. rise** *Fig* ascension *f* fulgurante. ◆**meteorite** *n* météorite *m*.

meteorological [miːtɪərə'lɒdʒɪk(ə)l] *a* météorologique. ◆**meteo'rology** *n* météorologie *f*.

meter ['miːtər] *n* (*device*) compteur *m*; (*parking*) **m.** parcmètre *m*; **m. maid** *Aut Fam* contractuelle *f*.

method ['meθəd] *n* méthode *f*. ◆**me'thodical** *a* méthodique.

Methodist ['meθədɪst] *a* & *n Rel* méthodiste (*mf*).

methylated ['meθɪleɪtɪd] *a* **m. spirit(s)** alcool *m* à brûler. ◆**meths** *n Fam* = methylated spirits.

meticulous [mɪ'tɪkjʊləs] *a* méticuleux. ◆**-ness** *n* soin *m* méticuleux.

metre ['miːtər] *n* mètre *m*. ◆**metric** ['metrɪk] *a* métrique.

metropolis [mə'trɒpəlɪs] *n* (*chief city*) métropole *f*. ◆**metro'politan** *a* métropolitain.

mettle ['met(ə)l] *n* courage *m*, fougue *f*.

mew [mjuː] *vi* (*of cat*) miauler.

mews [mjuːz] *n* (*street*) ruelle *f*; **m. flat** appartement *m* chic (*aménagé dans une ancienne écurie*).

Mexico ['meksɪkəʊ] *n* Mexique *m*. ◆**Mexican** *a* & *n* mexicain, -aine (*mf*).

mezzanine ['mezəniːn] *n* **m. (floor)** entresol *m*.

miaow [miː'aʊ] *vi* (*of cat*) miauler; – *n* miaulement *m*; – *int* miaou.

mice [maɪs] *see* mouse.

mickey ['mɪkɪ] *n* **to take the m. out of s.o.** *Sl* charrier qn.

micro- ['maɪkrəʊ] *pref* micro-.

microbe ['maɪkrəʊb] *n* microbe *m*.

microchip ['maɪkrəʊtʃɪp] *n* puce *f*.

microcosm ['maɪkrəʊkɒz(ə)m] *n* microcosme *m*.

microfilm ['maɪkrəʊfɪlm] *n* microfilm *m*.

microphone ['maɪkrəfəʊn] *n* microphone *m*.

microscope ['maɪkrəskəʊp] *n* microscope *m*. ◆**micro'scopic** *a* microscopique.

microwave ['maɪkrəweɪv] *n* micro-onde *f*; **m. oven** four *m* à micro-ondes.

mid [mɪd] *a* **(in) m.-June** (à) la mi-juin; **(in) m. morning** au milieu de la matinée; **in m. air** en plein ciel; **to be in one's m.-twenties** avoir environ vingt-cinq ans.

midday [mɪd'deɪ] *n* midi *m*; – *a* de midi.

middle ['mɪd(ə)l] *n* milieu *m*; (*waist*) *Fam* taille *f*; (*right*) **in the m. of** au (beau) milieu de; **in the m. of work** en plein travail; **in the m. of saying/working/etc** en train de dire/travailler/*etc*; – *a* (*central*) du milieu; (*class, ear, quality*) moyen; (*name*) deuxième. ◆**m.-'aged** *a* d'un certain âge. ◆**m.-'class** *a* bourgeois. ◆**m.-of-the-'road** *a* (*politics, views*) modéré; (*music, tastes*) sage.

middling ['mɪdlɪŋ] *a* moyen, passable.

midge [mɪdʒ] *n* (*fly*) moucheron *m*.

midget ['mɪdʒɪt] *n* nain *m*, naine *f*; – *a* minuscule.

Midlands ['mɪdləndz] *npl* **the M.** les comtés *mpl* du centre de l'Angleterre.

midnight ['mɪdnaɪt] *n* minuit *f*.

midriff ['mɪdrɪf] *n Anat* diaphragme *m*; (*belly*) *Fam* ventre *m*.

midst [mɪdst] *n* **in the m. of** (*middle*) au milieu de; **in our/their m.** parmi nous/eux.

midsummer [mɪd'sʌmər] *n* milieu *m* de l'été; (*solstice*) solstice *m* d'été. ◆**midwinter** *n* milieu *m* de l'hiver; solstice *m* d'hiver.

midterm ['mɪdtɜːm] *a* **m. holidays** *Sch* petites vacances *fpl*.

midway [mɪd'weɪ] *a* & *adv* à mi-chemin.

midweek [mɪd'wiːk] *n* milieu *m* de la semaine.

midwife ['mɪdwaɪf] *n* (*pl* **-wives**) sage-femme *f*.

might [maɪt] **1** *see* may. **2** *n* (*strength*) force *f*. ◆**mighty** *a* (*-ier, -iest*) puissant; (*ocean*) vaste; (*very great*) *Fam* sacré; – *adv* (*very*) *Fam* rudement.

migraine ['miːgreɪn, 'maɪgreɪn] *n Med* migraine *f*.

migrate [maɪ'greɪt] *vi* émigrer. ◆**'migrant** *a* & *n* **m. (worker)** migrant, -ante (*mf*). ◆**migration** *n* migration *f*.

mike [maɪk] *n Fam* micro *m*.

mild [maɪld] *a* (*-er, -est*) (*person, weather, taste etc*) doux; (*beer, punishment*) léger; (*medicine, illness*) bénin. ◆**—ly** *adv* doucement; (*slightly*) légèrement; **to put it m.** pour ne pas dire plus. ◆**—ness** *n* douceur *f*; légèreté *f*; caractère *m* bénin.

mildew ['mɪldjuː] *n* (*on cheese etc*) moisissure *f*.

mile [maɪl] *n* mile *m*, mille *m* (= *1,6 km*); *pl* (*loosely*) = kilomètres *mpl*; **to walk for miles** marcher pendant des kilomètres; **miles better** (*much*) *Fam* bien mieux. ◆**mileage** *n* = kilométrage *m*; **m.** (**per gallon**) = consommation *f* aux cent kilomètres. ◆**milestone** *n* = borne *f* kilométrique; *Fig* jalon *m*.

militant ['mɪlɪtənt] *a & n* militant, -ante (*mf*). ◆**military** *a* militaire; – *n* **the m.** (*soldiers*) les militaires *mpl*; (*army*) l'armée *f*. ◆**militate** *vi* (*of arguments etc*) militer (**in favour of** pour).

militia [mə'lɪʃə] *n* milice *f*. ◆**militiaman** *n* (*pl* **-men**) milicien *m*.

milk [mɪlk] *n* lait *m*; **evaporated m.** lait *m* concentré; – *a* (*chocolate*) au lait; (*bottle*, *can*) à lait; (*diet*) lacté; (*produce*) laitier; **m. float** voiture *f* de laitier; **m. shake** milk-shake *m*; – *vt* (*cow*) traire; (*extract*) *Fig* soutirer (**s.o. of sth** qch à qn); (*exploit*) *Fig* jalon *m*. ◆**—ing** *n* traite *f*. ◆**milkman** *n* (*pl* **-men**) laitier *m*. ◆**milky** *a* (**-ier, -iest**) (*diet*) lacté; (*coffee*, *tea*) au lait; (*colour*) laiteux; **the M. Way** la Voie lactée.

mill [mɪl] **1** *n* moulin *m*; (*factory*) usine *f*; **cotton m.** filature *f* de coton; **paper m.** papeterie *f*; – *vt* (*grind*) moudre. **2** *vi* **to m. around** (*of crowd*) grouiller. ◆**miller** *n* meunier, -ière *mf*. ◆**millstone** *n* (*burden*) boulet *m* (**round one's neck** qu'on traîne).

millennium, *pl* **-nia** [mɪ'lenɪəm, -nɪə] *n* millénaire *m*.

millet ['mɪlɪt] *n Bot* millet *m*.

milli- [mɪlɪ] *pref* milli-.

millimetre ['mɪlɪmiːtər] *n* millimètre *m*.

million ['mɪljən] *n* million *m*; **a m. men/***etc* un million d'hommes/*etc*; **two m.** deux millions. ◆**millio'naire** *n* millionnaire *mf*. ◆**millionth** *a & n* millionième (*mf*).

mime [maɪm] *n* (*actor*) mime *mf*; (*art*) mime *m*; – *vti* mimer.

mimeograph® ['mɪmɪəɡræf] *vt* polycopier.

mimic ['mɪmɪk] *vt* (**-ck-**) imiter; – *n* imitateur, -trice *mf*. ◆**mimicking** *n*, ◆**mimicry** *n* imitation *f*.

mimosa [mɪ'məʊzə] *n Bot* mimosa *m*.

minaret [mɪnə'ret] *n* (*of mosque*) minaret *m*.

mince [mɪns] *n* (*meat*) hachis *m* (de viande); *Am* = **mincemeat**; – *vt* hacher; **not to m. matters** *or* **one's words** ne pas mâcher ses

mots. ◆**mincemeat** *n* (*dried fruit*) mélange *m* de fruits secs. ◆**mincer** *n* (*machine*) hachoir *m*.

mind [maɪnd] **1** *n* esprit *m*; (*sanity*) raison *f*; (*memory*) mémoire *f*; (*opinion*) avis *m*, idée *f*; (*thought*) pensée *f*; (*head*) tête *f*; **to change one's m.** changer d'avis; **to my m.** à mon avis; **in two minds** (*undecided*) irrésolu; **to make up one's m.** se décider; **to be on s.o.'s m.** (*worry*) préoccuper qn; **out of one's m.** (*mad*) fou; **to bring to m.** (*recall*) rappeler; **to bear** *or* **keep in m.** (*remember*) se souvenir de; **to have in m.** (*person*, *plan*) avoir en vue; **to have a good m. to do** avoir bien envie de faire. **2** *vti* (*heed*) faire attention à; (*look after*) garder, s'occuper de; (*noise*, *dirt etc*) être gêné par; (*one's language*) surveiller; **m. you don't fall** (*beware*) prends garde de ne pas tomber; **m. you do it** n'oublie pas de le faire; (*noise*, *dirt etc*) être gêné par; **m. you** . . . *ça* m'ennuie *or* me gêne que . . . ; **never m.!** (*it doesn't matter*) ça ne fait rien!, tant pis!; (*don't worry*) ne vous en faites pas!; **m. (out)!** (*watch out*) attention!; **m. you** . . . remarquez (que) . . . ; **m. your own business!, never you m.!** mêlez-vous de ce qui vous regarde! ◆**—ed** *suffix* **fair-m.** *a* impartial; **like-m.** *a* de même opinion. ◆**—er** *n* (*for children*) gardien, -ienne *mf*; (*nurse*) nourrice *f*; (*bodyguard*) *Fam* gorille *m*. ◆**mind-boggling** *a* stupéfiant, qui confond l'imagination. ◆**mindful** *a* **m. of sth/doing** attentif à qch/à faire. ◆**mindless** *a* stupide.

mine[1] [maɪn] *poss pron* le mien, la mienne, *pl* les mien(ne)s; **this hat is m.** ce chapeau est à moi *or* est le mien; **a friend of m.** un ami à moi.

min/e[2] [maɪn] **1** *n* (*for coal, gold etc*) & *Fig* mine *f*; – *vt* **to m. (for)** (*coal etc*) extraire. **2** *n* (*explosive*) mine *f*; – *vt* (*beach*, *bridge etc*) miner. ◆**—ing** *n* exploitation *f* minière; – *a* (*industry*) minier. ◆**—er** *n* mineur *m*.

mineral ['mɪnərəl] *a & n* minéral (*m*).

mingle ['mɪŋɡ(ə)l] *vi* se mêler (**with** à); **to m. with** (*socially*) fréquenter.

mingy ['mɪndʒɪ] *a* (**-ier, -iest**) (*mean*) *Fam* radin.

mini ['mɪnɪ] *pref* mini-.

miniature ['mɪnɪtʃər] *n* miniature *f*; – *a* (*train etc*) miniature *inv*; (*tiny*) minuscule.

minibus ['mɪnɪbʌs] *n* minibus *m*. ◆**mini-cab** *n* (radio-)taxi *m*.

minim ['mɪnɪm] *n Mus* blanche *f*.

minimum ['mɪnɪməm] *n* (*pl* -**ima** [-ɪmə] *or* -**imums**) minimum *m*; – *a* minimum (*f inv*), minimal. ◆**minimal** *a* minimal. ◆**minimize** *vt* minimiser.

minister ['mɪnɪstər] *n Pol Rel* ministre *m*. ◆**mini'sterial** *a* ministériel. ◆**ministry** *n* ministère *m*.

mink [mɪŋk] *n* (*animal, fur*) vison *m*.

minor ['maɪnər] *a* (*small*) *Jur Mus* mineur; (*detail, operation*) petit; – *n Jur* mineur, -eure *mf*.

Minorca [mɪ'nɔːkə] *n* Minorque *f*.

minority [maɪ'nɒrɪtɪ] *n* minorité *f*; **in the** *or* **a m.** en minorité, minoritaire; – *a* minoritaire.

mint [mɪnt] **1** *n* (*place*) Hôtel *m* de la Monnaie; **a m. (of money)** *Fig* une petite fortune; – *vt* (*money*) frapper; – *a* (*stamp*) neuf; **in m. condition** à l'état neuf. **2** *n Bot Culin* menthe *f*; (*sweet*) pastille *f* de menthe; – *a* à la menthe.

minus ['maɪnəs] *prep Math* moins; (*without*) *Fam* sans; **it's m. ten (degrees)** il fait moins dix (degrés); – *n* **m. (sign)** (signe *m*) moins *m*.

minute[1] ['mɪnɪt] **1** *n* minute *f*; **this (very) m.** (*now*) à la minute; **any m. (now)** d'une minute à l'autre; **m. hand** (*of clock*) grande aiguille *f*. **2** *npl* (*of meeting*) procès-verbal *m*.

minute[2] [maɪ'njuːt] *a* (*tiny*) minuscule; (*careful, exact*) minutieux.

minx [mɪŋks] *n* (*girl*) *Pej* diablesse *f*, chipie *f*.

miracle ['mɪrək(ə)l] *n* miracle *m*. ◆**mi'raculous** *a* miraculeux.

mirage ['mɪrɑːʒ] *n* mirage *m*.

mire [maɪər] *n Lit* fange *f*.

mirror ['mɪrər] *n* miroir *m*, glace *f*; *Fig* miroir *m*; (**rear view**) **m.** *Aut* rétroviseur *m*; – *vt* refléter.

mirth [mɜːθ] *n Lit* gaieté *f*, hilarité *f*.

misadventure [mɪsəd'ventʃər] *n* mésaventure *f*.

misanthropist [mɪ'zænθrəpɪst] *n* misanthrope *m*.

misapprehend [mɪsæprɪ'hend] *vt* mal comprendre. ◆**misapprehension** *n* malentendu *m*.

misappropriate [mɪsə'prəuprɪeɪt] *vt* (*money*) détourner.

misbehave [mɪsbɪ'heɪv] *vi* se conduire mal; (*of child*) faire des sottises.

miscalculate [mɪs'kælkjuleɪt] *vt* mal calculer; – *vi Fig* se tromper. ◆**miscalcu'lation** *n* erreur *f* de calcul.

miscarriage [mɪs'kærɪdʒ] *n* **to have a m.** *Med* faire une fausse couche; **m. of justice** erreur *f* judiciaire. ◆**miscarry** *vi Med* faire une fausse couche; (*of plan*) *Fig* échouer.

miscellaneous [mɪsɪ'leɪnɪəs] *a* divers.

mischief ['mɪstʃɪf] *n* espièglerie *f*; (*maliciousness*) méchanceté *f*; **to get into m.** faire des bêtises; **full of m. = mischievous; to make m. for** (*trouble*) créer des ennuis à; **to do s.o. a m.** (*harm*) faire mal à qn; **a little m.** (*child*) un petit démon. ◆**mischievous** *a* (*playful, naughty*) espiègle, malicieux; (*malicious*) méchant.

misconception [mɪskən'sepʃ(ə)n] *n* idée *f* fausse.

misconduct [mɪs'kɒndʌkt] *n* mauvaise conduite *f*; *Com* mauvaise gestion *f*.

misconstrue [mɪskən'struː] *vt* mal interpréter.

misdeed [mɪs'diːd] *n* méfait *m*.

misdemeanor [mɪsdɪ'miːnər] *n Jur* délit *m*.

misdirect [mɪsdɪ'rekt] *vt* (*letter*) mal adresser; (*energies*) mal diriger; (*person*) mal renseigner.

miser ['maɪzər] *n* avare *mf*. ◆**-ly** *a* avare.

misery ['mɪzərɪ] *n* (*suffering*) souffrances *fpl*; (*sadness*) tristesse *f*; (*sad person*) *Fam* grincheux, -euse *mf*; *pl* (*troubles*) misères *fpl*; **his life is a m.** il est malheureux. ◆**miserable** *a* (*wretched*) misérable; (*unhappy*) malheureux; (*awful*) affreux; (*derisory*) dérisoire. ◆**miserably** *adv* misérablement; (*to fail*) lamentablement.

misfire [mɪs'faɪər] *vi* (*of engine*) avoir des ratés; (*of plan*) *Fig* rater.

misfit ['mɪsfɪt] *n Pej* inadapté, -ée *mf*.

misfortune [mɪs'fɔːtʃuːn] *n* malheur *m*, infortune *f*.

misgivings [mɪs'gɪvɪŋz] *npl* (*doubts*) doutes *mpl*; (*fears*) craintes *fpl*.

misguided [mɪs'gaɪdɪd] *a* (*action etc*) imprudent; **to be m.** (*of person*) se tromper.

mishandle [mɪs'hænd(ə)l] *vt* (*affair, situation*) traiter avec maladresse; (*person*) s'y prendre mal avec.

mishap ['mɪshæp] *n* (*accident*) mésaventure *f*; (*hitch*) contretemps *m*.

misinform [mɪsɪn'fɔːm] *vt* mal renseigner.

misinterpret [mɪsɪn'tɜːprɪt] *vt* mal interpréter.

misjudge [mɪs'dʒʌdʒ] *vt* (*person, distance etc*) mal juger.

mislay [mɪs'leɪ] *vt* (*pt & pp* **mislaid**) égarer.

mislead [mɪs'liːd] *vt* (*pt & pp* **misled**) tromper. ◆**-ing** *a* trompeur.

mismanage [mɪs'mænɪdʒ] *vt* mal administrer. ◆—**ment** *n* mauvaise administration *f*.

misnomer [mɪs'nəʊmər] *n* (*name*) nom *m* or terme *m* impropre.

misogynist [mɪ'sɒdʒɪnɪst] *n* misogyne *mf*.

misplac/e [mɪs'pleɪs] *vt* (*trust etc*) mal placer; (*lose*) égarer. ◆—**ed** *a* (*remark etc*) déplacé.

misprint ['mɪsprɪnt] *n* faute *f* d'impression, coquille *f*.

mispronounce [mɪsprə'naʊns] *vt* mal prononcer.

misquote [mɪs'kwəʊt] *vt* citer inexactement.

misrepresent [mɪsreprɪ'zent] *vt* présenter sous un faux jour.

miss¹ [mɪs] *vt* (*train, target, opportunity etc*) manquer, rater; (*not see*) ne pas voir; (*not understand*) ne pas comprendre; (*one's youth, deceased person etc*) regretter; (*sth just lost*) remarquer l'absence de; **he misses Paris/her** Paris/elle lui manque; **I m. you** tu me manques; **don't m. seeing this play** (*don't fail to*) ne manque pas de voir cette pièce; **to m. out** (*omit*) sauter; – *vi* manquer, rater; **to m. out** (*lose a chance*) rater l'occasion; **to m. out on** (*opportunity etc*) rater, laisser passer; – *n* coup *m* manqué; **that was** or **we had a near m.** on l'a échappé belle; **I'll give it a m.** *Fam* (*not go*) je n'y irai pas; (*not take* or *drink* or *eat*) je n'en prendrai pas. ◆—**ing** *a* (*absent*) absent; (*in war, after disaster*) disparu; (*object*) manquant; **there are two cups/students m.** il manque deux tasses/deux étudiants.

miss² [mɪs] *n* mademoiselle *f*; **Miss Brown** Mademoiselle or Mlle Brown.

misshapen [mɪs'ʃeɪp(ə)n] *a* difforme.

missile ['mɪsaɪl, *Am* 'mɪs(ə)l] *n* (*rocket*) *Mil* missile *m*; (*object thrown*) projectile *m*.

mission ['mɪʃ(ə)n] *n* mission *f*. ◆**missionary** *n* missionnaire *m*.

missive ['mɪsɪv] *n* (*letter*) missive *f*.

misspell [mɪs'spel] *vt* (*pt & pp* -**ed** or **misspelt**) mal écrire.

mist [mɪst] *n* (*fog*) brume *f*; (*on glass*) buée *f*; – *vi* **to m. over** or **up** s'embuer.

mistake [mɪ'steɪk] *n* erreur *f*, faute *f*; **to make a m.** se tromper, faire (une) erreur; **by m.** par erreur; – *vt* (*pt* **mistook**, *pp* **mistaken**) (*meaning, intention etc*) se tromper sur; **to m. the date/place/**etc se tromper de date/de lieu/etc; **you can't m.**, **there's no mistaking** (*his face, my car etc*) il est impossible de ne pas reconnaître; **to m.**

s.o./sth **for** prendre qn/qch pour. ◆**mistaken** *a* (*idea etc*) erroné; **to be m.** se tromper. ◆**mistakenly** *adv* par erreur.

mister ['mɪstər] *n Fam* monsieur *m*.

mistletoe ['mɪs(ə)ltəʊ] *n Bot* gui *m*.

mistreat [mɪs'triːt] *vt* maltraiter.

mistress ['mɪstrɪs] *n* maîtresse *f*; (*in secondary school*) professeur *m*.

mistrust [mɪs'trʌst] *n* méfiance *f*; – *vt* se méfier de. ◆**mistrustful** *a* méfiant.

misty ['mɪstɪ] *a* (-**ier**, -**iest**) (*foggy*) brumeux; (*glass*) embué.

misunderstand [mɪsʌndə'stænd] *vt* (*pt & pp* -**stood**) mal comprendre. ◆**misunderstanding** *n* (*disagreement*) malentendu *m*; (*mistake*) erreur *f*. ◆**misunderstood** *a* (*person*) incompris.

misuse [mɪs'juːz] *vt* (*word, tool*) mal employer; (*power etc*) abuser de; – [mɪs'juːs] *n* (*of word*) emploi *m* abusif; (*of tool*) usage *m* abusif; (*of power etc*) abus *m*.

mite [maɪt] *n* **1** (*insect*) mite *f*. **2** (*poor*) m. (*child*) (pauvre) petit, -ite *mf*. **3 a m.** (*somewhat*) *Fam* un petit peu.

mitigate ['mɪtɪgeɪt] *vt* atténuer.

mitt(en) [mɪt, 'mɪt(ə)n] *n* (*glove*) moufle *f*.

mix [mɪks] *vt* mélanger, mêler; (*cement, cake*) préparer; (*salad*) remuer; **to m. up** mélanger; (*perplex*) embrouiller (qn); (*confuse, mistake*) confondre (**with** avec); **to be mixed up with s.o.** (*involved*) être mêlé aux affaires de qn; **to m. up in** (*involve*) mêler à; – *vi* se mêler; (*of colours*) s'allier; **to m. with** (*socially*) fréquenter; **she doesn't m. (in)** elle n'est pas sociable; – *n* (*mixture*) mélange *m*. ◆—**ed** *a* (*school, marriage*) mixte; (*society*) mêlé; (*feelings*) mitigés, mêlés; (*results*) divers; (*nuts, chocolates etc*) assortis; **to be (all) m. up** (*of person*) être désorienté; (*of facts, account etc*) être embrouillé. ◆—**ing** *n* mélange *m*. ◆—**er** *n Culin El* mixe(u)r *m*; (*for mortar*) *Tech* malaxeur *m*; **to be a good m.** (*of person*) être sociable. ◆**mixture** *n* mélange *m*; (*for cough*) sirop *m*. ◆**mix-up** *n Fam* confusion *f*.

mm *abbr* (*millimetre*) mm.

moan [məʊn] *vi* (*groan*) gémir; (*complain*) se plaindre (**to** à, **about** de, **that** que); – *n* gémissement *m*; plainte *f*.

moat [məʊt] *n* douve(s) *f(pl)*.

mob [mɒb] *n* (*crowd*) cohue *f*, foule *f*; (*gang*) bande *f*; **the m.** (*masses*) la populace; (*Mafia*) *Am Sl* la mafia; – *vt* (-**bb-**) assiéger. ◆**mobster** *n Am Sl* gangster *m*.

mobile ['məʊbaɪl, *Am* 'məʊb(ə)l] *a* mobile; (*having a car etc*) *Fam* motorisé; **m. home**

mobil-home *m*; **m. library** bibliobus *m*; – *n*
(*Am* ['məubiil]) (*ornament*) mobile *m*.
◆**mo'bility** *n* mobilité *f*. ◆**mobili'zation**
n mobilisation *f*. ◆**mobilize** *vti* mobiliser.

moccasin ['mɒkəsɪn] *n* (*shoe*) mocassin *m*.

mocha ['məukə] *n* (*coffee*) moka *m*.

mock [mɒk] **1** *vt* se moquer de; (*mimic*)
singer; – *vi* se moquer (**at de**). **2** *a* (*false*)
simulé; (*exam*) blanc. ◆**—ing** *n* moquerie
f; – *a* moqueur. ◆**mockery** *n* (*act*)
moquerie *f*; (*parody*) parodie *f*; **to make a
m. of** tourner en ridicule.

mock-up ['mɒkʌp] *n* (*model*) maquette *f*.

mod cons [mɒd'kɒnz] *abbr Fam* = **modern
conveniences.**

mode [məud] *n* (*manner, way*) mode *m*;
(*fashion, vogue*) mode *f*.

model ['mɒd(ə)l] *n* (*example, person etc*)
modèle *m*; (*fashion*) **m.** mannequin *m*;
(*scale*) **m.** modèle *m* (réduit); – *a* (*behaviour, factory etc*) modèle; (*car, plane*)
modèle réduit *inv*; **m. railway** train *n* miniature; – *vt* modeler (**on** sur); (*hats*)
présenter (les modèles de); – *vi* (*for fashion*) être mannequin; (*pose for artist*)
poser. ◆**modelling** *n* (*of statues etc*)
modelage *m*.

moderate[1] ['mɒdərət] *a* modéré; (*in speech*)
mesuré; (*result*) passable; – *n Pol* modéré,
-ée *mf*. ◆**—ly** *adv* (*in moderation*) modéré-
ment; (*averagely*) moyennement.

moderate[2] ['mɒdəreɪt] *vt* (*diminish, tone
down*) modérer. ◆**mode'ration** *n* modération *f*; **in m.** avec modération.

modern ['mɒd(ə)n] *a* moderne; **m.
languages** langues *fpl* vivantes; **m. conveniences** tout le confort moderne.
◆**modernism** *n* modernisme *m*. ◆**mod-
erni'zation** *n* modernisation *f*. ◆**modernize** *vt* moderniser.

modest ['mɒdɪst] *a* modeste. ◆**modesty** *n*
(*quality*) modestie *f*; (*moderation*) modération *f*; (*of salary etc*) modicité *f*.

modicum ['mɒdɪkəm] *n* **a m. of** un soupçon
de, un petit peu de.

modify ['mɒdɪfaɪ] *vt* (*alter*) modifier; (*tone
down*) modérer. ◆**modifi'cation** *n* modification *f*.

modulate ['mɒdjuleɪt] *vt* moduler. ◆**mod-
u'lation** *n* modulation *f*.

module ['mɒdjuil] *n* module *m*.

mogul ['məug(ə)l] *n* magnat *m*, manitou *m*.

mohair ['məuheər] *n* mohair *m*.

moist [mɔɪst] *a* (-er, -est) humide; (*clammy,
sticky*) moite. ◆**moisten** *vt* humecter.
◆**moisture** *n* humidité *f*; (*on glass*) buée *f*.

◆**moisturiz/e** *vt* (*skin*) hydrater. ◆**—er** *n*
(*cream*) crème *f* hydratante.

molar ['məulər] *n* (*tooth*) molaire *f*.

molasses [mə'læsɪz] *n* (*treacle*) *Am* mélasse
f.

mold [məuld] *Am* = **mould.**

mole [məul] *n* **1** (*on skin*) grain *m* de beauté.
2 (*animal, spy*) taupe *f*.

molecule ['mɒlɪkjuil] *n* molécule *f*.

molest [mə'lest] *vt* (*annoy*) importuner;
(*child, woman*) *Jur* attenter à la pudeur de.

mollusc ['mɒləsk] *n* mollusque *m*.

mollycoddle ['mɒlɪkɒd(ə)l] *vt* dorloter.

molt [məult] *Am* = **moult.**

molten ['məult(ə)n] *a* (*metal*) en fusion.

mom [mɒm] *n Am Fam* maman *f*.

moment ['məumənt] *n* moment *m*, instant
m; **this** (**very**) **m.** (*now*) à l'instant; **the m.
she leaves** dès qu'elle partira; **any m.** (**now**)
d'un moment *or* d'un instant à l'autre.
◆**momentarily** (*Am* [məumən'terɪlɪ]) *adv*
(*temporarily*) momentanément; (*soon*) *Am*
tout à l'heure. ◆**momentary** *a* momen-
tané.

momentous [məu'mentəs] *a* important.

momentum [məu'mentəm] *n* (*speed*) élan
m; **to gather** *or* **gain m.** (*of ideas etc*) *Fig*
gagner du terrain.

mommy ['mɒmɪ] *n Am Fam* maman *f*.

Monaco ['mɒnəkəu] *n* Monaco *f*.

monarch ['mɒnək] *n* monarque *m*. ◆**monarchy** *n* monarchie *f*.

monastery ['mɒnəst(ə)rɪ] *n* monastère *m*.

Monday ['mʌndɪ] *n* lundi *m*.

monetary ['mʌnɪt(ə)rɪ] *a* monétaire.

money ['mʌnɪ] *n* argent *m*; **paper m.**
papier-monnaie *m*, billets *mpl*; **to get one's
m.'s worth** en avoir pour son argent; **he
gets** *or* **earns good m.** il gagne bien (sa vie);
to be in the m. *Fam* rouler sur l'or; **m. order**
mandat *m*. ◆**moneybags** *n Pej Fam*
richard, -arde *mf*. ◆**moneybox** *n* tirelire *f*.
◆**moneychanger** *n* changeur *m*.
◆**moneylender** *n* prêteur, -euse *mf* sur
gages. ◆**moneymaking** *a* lucratif.
◆**money-spinner** *n* (*source of wealth*)
Fam mine *f* d'or.

mongol ['mɒŋg(ə)l] *n & a Med* mongolien,
-ienne (*mf*).

mongrel ['mʌŋgrəl] *n* (*dog*) bâtard *m*.

monitor ['mɒnɪtər] **1** *n* (*pupil*) chef *m* de
classe. **2** *n* (*screen*) *Tech* moniteur *m*. **3** *vt* (*a
broadcast*) *Rad* écouter; (*check*) *Fig* contrôler.

monk [mʌŋk] *n* moine *m*, religieux *m*.

monkey ['mʌŋkɪ] *n* singe *m*; **little m.** (*child*)
Fam polisson, -onne *mf*; **m. business** *Fam*

singeries *fpl*; – *vi* **to m. about** *Fam* faire l'idiot.

mono ['mɒnəʊ] *a* (*record etc*) mono *inv*.

mono- ['mɒnəʊ] *pref* mono-.

monocle ['mɒnək(ə)l] *n* monocle *m*.

monogram ['mɒnəgræm] *n* monogramme *m*.

monologue ['mɒnəlɒg] *n* monologue *m*.

monopoly [mə'nɒpəlɪ] *n* monopole *m*. ◆**monopolize** *vt* monopoliser.

monosyllable ['mɒnəsɪləb(ə)l] *n* monosyllabe *m*. ◆**monosy'llabic** *a* monosyllabique.

monotone ['mɒnətəʊn] *n* **in a m.** sur un ton monocorde.

monotony [mə'nɒtənɪ] *n* monotonie *f*. ◆**monotonous** *a* monotone.

monsoon [mɒn'suːn] *n* (*wind, rain*) mousson *f*.

monster ['mɒnstər] *n* monstre *m*. ◆**mon'strosity** *n* (*horror*) monstruosité *f*. ◆**monstrous** *a* (*abominable, enormous*) monstrueux.

month [mʌnθ] *n* mois *m*. ◆**monthly** *a* mensuel; **m. payment** mensualité *f*; – *n* (*periodical*) mensuel *m*; – *adv* (*every month*) mensuellement.

Montreal [mɒntrɪ'ɔːl] *n* Montréal *m or f*.

monument ['mɒnjʊmənt] *n* monument *m*. ◆**monu'mental** *a* monumental; **m. mason** marbrier *m*.

moo [muː] *vi* meugler; – *n* meuglement *m*.

mooch [muːtʃ] **1** *vi* **to m. around** *Fam* flâner. **2** *vt* **to m. sth off s.o.** (*cadge*) *Am Sl* taper qch à qn.

mood [muːd] *n* (*of person*) humeur *f*; (*of country*) état *m* d'esprit; *Gram* mode *m*; **in a good/bad m.** de bonne/mauvaise humeur; **to be in the m. to do** *or* **for doing** être d'humeur à faire, avoir envie de faire. ◆**moody** *a* (**-ier, -iest**) (*changeable*) d'humeur changeante; (*bad-tempered*) de mauvaise humeur.

moon [muːn] *n* lune *f*; **once in a blue m.** (*rarely*) tous les trente-six du mois; **over the m.** (*delighted*) *Fam* ravi (**about** de). ◆**moonlight 1** *n* clair *m* de lune. **2** *vi Fam* travailler au noir. ◆**moonshine** *n* (*talk*) *Fam* balivernes *fpl*.

moor [mʊər] **1** *vt Nau* amarrer; – *vi* mouiller. **2** *n* (*open land*) lande *f*. ◆**—ings** *npl Nau* (*ropes etc*) amarres *fpl*; (*place*) mouillage *m*.

moose [muːs] *n inv* (*animal*) orignac *m*, élan *m*.

moot [muːt] **1** *a* (*point*) discutable. **2** *vt* (*question*) soulever, suggérer.

mop [mɒp] **1** *n* balai *m* (à laver), balai *m* éponge; **dish m.** lavette *f*; **m. of hair** tignasse *f*. **2** *vt* (**-pp-**) **to m.** (**up**) (*wipe*) essuyer; **to m. one's brow** s'essuyer le front.

mope [məʊp] *vi* **to m.** (**about**) être déprimé, avoir le cafard.

moped ['məʊped] *n* cyclomoteur *m*, mobylette® *f*.

moral ['mɒrəl] *a* moral; – *n* (*of story etc*) morale *f*; *pl* (*standards*) moralité *f*, morale *f*. ◆**morale** [mə'rɑːl, *Am* mə'ræl] *n* moral *m*. ◆**moralist** *n* moraliste *mf*. ◆**mo'rality** *n* (*morals*) moralité *f*. ◆**moralize** *vi* moraliser. ◆**morally** *adv* moralement.

morass [mə'ræs] *n* (*land*) marais *m*; (*mess*) *Fig* bourbier *m*.

moratorium [mɒrə'tɔːrɪəm] *n* moratoire *m*.

morbid ['mɔːbɪd] *a* morbide.

more [mɔːr] *a & n* plus (de) (**than** que); (*other*) d'autres; **m. cars/etc** plus de voitures/*etc*; **he has m.** (**than you**) il en a plus (que toi); **a few m. months** encore quelques mois, quelques mois de plus; (*some*) **m. tea/etc** encore du thé/*etc*; (*some*) **m. details** d'autres détails; **m. than a kilo/ten/etc** (*with quantity, number*) plus d'un kilo/de dix/*etc*; – *adv* (*tired, rapidly etc*) plus (**than** que); **m. and m.** de plus en plus; **m. or less** plus ou moins; **the m. he shouts the m. hoarse** he gets plus il crie plus il s'enroue; **she hasn't any m.** elle n'en a plus. ◆**mo'reover** *adv* de plus, d'ailleurs.

moreish ['mɔːrɪʃ] *a Fam* qui a un goût de revenez-y.

mores ['mɔːreɪz] *npl* mœurs *fpl*.

morgue [mɔːg] *n* (*mortuary*) morgue *f*.

moribund ['mɒrɪbʌnd] *a* moribond.

morning ['mɔːnɪŋ] *n* matin *m*; (*duration of morning*) matinée *f*; **in the m.** (*every morning*) le matin; (*during the morning*) pendant la matinée; (*tomorrow*) demain matin; **at seven in the m.** à sept heures du matin; **every Tuesday m.** tous les mardis matin; **in the early m.** au petit matin; – *a* du matin, matinal. ◆**mornings** *adv Am* le matin.

Morocco [mə'rɒkəʊ] *n* Maroc *m*. ◆**Moroccan** *a & n* marocain, -aine (*mf*).

moron ['mɔːrɒn] *n* crétin, -ine *mf*.

morose [mə'rəʊs] *a* morose.

morphine ['mɔːfiːn] *n* morphine *f*.

Morse [mɔːs] *n & a* **M.** (**code**) morse *m*.

morsel ['mɔːs(ə)l] *n* (*of food*) petite bouchée *f*.

mortal ['mɔːt(ə)l] *a & n* mortel, -elle (*mf*). ◆**mor'tality** *n* (*death rate*) mortalité *f*.

mortar ['mɔːtər] *n* mortier *m*.

mortgage ['mɔːgɪdʒ] *n* prêt-logement *m*; – *vt* (*house, future*) hypothéquer.

mortician [mɔː'tɪʃ(ə)n] *n Am* entrepreneur *m* de pompes funèbres.

mortify ['mɔːtɪfaɪ] *vt* mortifier.

mortuary ['mɔːtʃʊərɪ] *n* morgue *f*.

mosaic [məʊ'zeɪɪk] *n* mosaïque *f*.

Moscow ['mɒskəʊ, *Am* 'mɒskaʊ] *n* Moscou *m or f*.

Moses ['məʊzɪz] *a* M. basket couffin *m*.

Moslem ['mɒzlɪm] *a* & *n* musulman, -ane (*mf*).

mosque [mɒsk] *n* mosquée *f*.

mosquito [mɒ'skiːtəʊ] *n* (*pl* -oes) moustique *m*; **m. net** moustiquaire *f*.

moss [mɒs] *n Bot* mousse *f*. ◆**mossy** *a* moussu.

most [məʊst] *a* & *n* the m. (*greatest in amount etc*) le plus (de); **I have (the) m. books** j'ai le plus de livres; **I have (the) m.** j'en ai le plus; **m. (of the) books/etc** la plupart des livres/*etc*; **m. of the cake/etc** la plus grande partie du gâteau/*etc*; **m. of them** la plupart d'entre eux; **m. of it** la plus grande partie; **at (the very) m.** tout au plus; **to make the m. of** profiter (au maximum) de; – *adv* (le) plus; (*very*) fort, très; **the m. beautiful** le plus beau, la plus belle (**in, of** de); **to talk (the) m.** parler le plus; **m. of all** (*especially*) surtout. ◆**—ly** *adv* surtout, pour la plupart.

motel [məʊ'tel] *n* motel *m*.

moth [mɒθ] *n* papillon *m* de nuit; (*clothes*) m. mite *f*. ◆**m.-eaten** *a* mité. ◆**mothball** *n* boule *f* de naphtaline.

mother ['mʌðər] *n* mère *f*; **M.'s Day** la fête des Mères; **m. tongue** langue *f* maternelle; – *vt* (*care for*) materner. ◆**motherhood** *n* maternité *f*. ◆**motherly** *a* maternel.

mother-in-law ['mʌðərɪnlɔː] *n* (*pl* **mothers-in-law**) belle-mère *f*. ◆**m.-of-pearl** *n* (*substance*) nacre *f*. ◆**m.-to-'be** *n* (*pl* **mothers-to-be**) future mère *f*.

motion ['məʊʃ(ə)n] *n* mouvement *m*; *Pol* motion *f*; **m. picture** film *m*; – *vti* **to m. (to) s.o. to do** faire signe à qn de faire. ◆**—less** *a* immobile.

motive ['məʊtɪv] *n* motif *m* (**for, of** de); *Jur* mobile *m* (**for** de). ◆**motivate** *vt* (*person, decision etc*) motiver. ◆**moti'vation** *n* motivation *f*; (*incentive*) encouragement *m*.

motley ['mɒtlɪ] *a* (*coloured*) bigarré; (*collection*) hétéroclite.

motor ['məʊtər] *n* (*engine*) moteur *m*; (*car*) *Fam* auto *f*; – *a* (*industry, vehicle etc*) automobile; (*accident*) d'auto; **m. boat** canot *m* automobile; **m. mechanic** mécanicien-auto

m; **m. mower** tondeuse *f* à moteur; – *vi* (*drive*) rouler en auto. ◆**—ing** *n' Sp* automobilisme *m*; **school of m.** auto-école *f*. ◆**motorbike** *n Fam* moto *f*. ◆**motorcade** *n* cortège *m* (officiel) (*de voitures*). ◆**motorcar** *n* automobile *f*. ◆**motorcycle** *n* moto *f*, motocyclette *f*. ◆**motorcyclist** *n* motocycliste *mf*. ◆**motorist** *n* automobiliste *mf*. ◆**motorized** *a* motorisé. ◆**motorway** *n* autoroute *f*.

mottled ['mɒt(ə)ld] *a* tacheté.

motto ['mɒtəʊ] *n* (*pl* -oes) devise *f*.

mould [məʊld] **1** *n* (*shape*) moule *m*; – *vt* (*clay etc*) mouler; (*statue, character*) modeler. **2** *n* (*growth, mildew*) moisissure *f*. ◆**mouldy** *a* (-ier, -iest) moisi; **to go m.** moisir.

moult [məʊlt] *vi* muer. ◆**—ing** *n* mue *f*.

mound [maʊnd] *n* (*of earth*) tertre *m*; (*pile*) *Fig* monceau *m*.

mount [maʊnt] **1** *n* (*mountain*) *Lit* mont *m*. **2** *n* (*horse*) monture *f*; (*frame for photo or slide*) cadre *m*; (*stamp hinge*) charnière *f*; – *vt* (*horse, hill, jewel, photo, demonstration etc*) monter; (*ladder, tree etc*) monter sur, grimper à; (*stamp*) coller (dans un album); – *vi* **to m. (up)** (*on horse*) se mettre en selle. **3** *vi* (*increase*) monter; **to m. up** (*add up*) chiffrer (**to** à); (*accumulate*) s'accumuler.

mountain ['maʊntɪn] *n* montagne *f*; – *a* (*people, life*) montagnard. ◆**mountai'neer** *n* alpiniste *mf*. ◆**mountai'neering** *n* alpinisme *m*. ◆**mountainous** *a* montagneux.

mourn [mɔːn] *vti* **to m. (for)** pleurer. ◆**—ing** *n* deuil *m*; **in m.** en deuil. ◆**—er** *n* parent, -ente *mf or* ami, -ie *mf* du défunt *or* de la défunte. ◆**mournful** *a* triste.

mouse, *pl* **mice** [maʊs, maɪs] *n* souris *f*. ◆**mousetrap** *n* souricière *f*.

mousse [muːs] *n Culin* mousse *f*.

moustache [mə'staːʃ, *Am* 'mʌstæʃ] *n* moustache *f*.

mousy ['maʊsɪ] *a* (-ier, -iest) (*hair*) *Pej* châtain terne; (*shy*) *Fig* timide.

mouth [maʊθ] *n* (*pl* -s [maʊðz]) bouche *f*; (*of dog, lion etc*) gueule *f*; (*of river*) embouchure *f*; (*of cave, harbour*) entrée *f*; – [maʊð] *vt Pej* dire. ◆**mouthful** *n* (*of food*) bouchée *f*; (*of liquid*) gorgée *f*. ◆**mouthorgan** *n* harmonica *m*. ◆**mouthpiece** *n Mus* embouchure *f*; (*spokesman*) *Fig* porte-parole *m inv*. ◆**mouthwash** *n* bain *m* de bouche. ◆**mouth-watering** *a* appétissant.

mov/e [muːv] *n* mouvement *m*; (*change of*

house etc) déménagement *m*; (*change of job*) changement *m* d'emploi; (*transfer of employee*) mutation *f*; (*in game*) coup *m*, (*one's turn*) tour *m*; (*act*) Fig démarche *f*; (*step*) pas *m*; (*attempt*) tentative *f*; **to make a m.** (*leave*) se préparer à partir; (*act*) Fig passer à l'action; **to get a m. on** *Fam* se dépêcher; **on the m.** en marche; – *vt* déplacer, remuer, bouger; (*arm, leg*) remuer; (*crowd*) faire partir; (*put*) mettre; (*transport*) transporter; (*piece in game*) jouer; (*propose*) *Pol* proposer; **to m. s.o.** (*incite*) pousser qn (*to do* à faire); (*emotionally*) émouvoir qn; (*transfer in job*) muter qn; **to m. house** déménager; **to m. sth back** reculer qch; **to m. sth down** descendre qch; **to m. sth forward** avancer qch; **to m. sth over** pousser qch; – *vi* bouger, remuer; (*go*) aller (**to** à); (*pass*) passer (**to** à); (*leave*) partir; (*change seats*) changer de place; (*progress*) avancer; (*act*) agir; (*play*) jouer; **to m. (out)** (*of house etc*) déménager; **to m. to** (*a new region etc*) aller habiter; **to m. about** se déplacer; (*fidget*) remuer; **to m. along** *or* **forward** *or* **on** avancer; **to m. away** *or* **off** (*go away*) s'éloigner; **to m. back** (*withdraw*) reculer; (*return*) retourner; **to m. in** (*to house*) emménager; **to m. into** (*house*) emménager dans; **m. on!** circulez!; **to m. over** *or* **up** se pousser. ◆**—ing** *a* en mouvement; (*part*) Tech mobile; (*stairs*) mécanique; (*touching*) émouvant. ◆**mov(e)able** *a* mobile. ◆**movement** *n* (*action, group etc*) & *Mus* mouvement *m*.

movie ['muːvɪ] *n Fam* film *m*; **the movies** (*cinema*) le cinéma; **m. camera** caméra *f*. ◆**moviegoer** *n* cinéphile *mf*.

mow [məʊ] *vt* (*pp* **mown** *or* **mowed**) (*field*) faucher; **to m. the lawn** tondre le gazon; **to m. down** (*kill etc*) Fig faucher. ◆**—er** *n* (lawn) m. tondeuse *f* (à gazon).

MP [em'piː] *n abbr* (*Member of Parliament*) député *m*.

Mrs ['mɪsɪz] *n* (*married woman*) **Mrs Brown** Madame *or* Mme Brown.

Ms [mɪz] *n* (*married or unmarried woman*) **Ms Brown** Madame *or* Mme Brown.

MSc, *Am* **MS** *abbr* = **Master of Science.**

much [mʌtʃ] *a & n* beaucoup (de); **not m. time/money/etc** pas beaucoup de temps/d'argent/*etc*; **not m.** pas beaucoup; **m. of** (*a good deal of*) une bonne partie de; **as m.** (*to do, know etc*) autant que; **as m. wine/etc as** autant de vin/*etc* que; **as m. as you like** autant que tu veux; **twice as m.** deux fois plus (de); **how m.?** combien (de)?; **too m.**

trop (de); **so m.** tant (de), tellement (de); **I know/I shall do this m.** je sais/je ferai ceci (du moins); **this m. wine** ça de vin; **it's not m. of a garden** ce n'est pas merveilleux comme jardin; **m. the same** presque le même; – *adv* **very m.** beaucoup; **not (very) m.** pas beaucoup; **she doesn't say very m.** elle ne dit pas grand-chose.

muck [mʌk] **1** *n* (*manure*) fumier *m*; (*filth*) Fig saleté *f*. **2** *vi* **to m. about** *Fam* (*have fun, idle*) s'amuser; (*play the fool*) faire l'idiot; **to m. about with** *Fam* (*fiddle with*) s'amuser avec; (*alter*) changer (*texte etc*); **to m. in** (*join in*) *Fam* participer, contribuer; – *vt* **to m. s.o. about** *Fam* embêter qn, déranger qn; **to m. up** (*spoil*) *Fam* gâcher, ruiner. ◆**m.-up** *n Fam* gâchis *m*. ◆**mucky** *a* (-ier, -iest) sale.

mucus ['mjuːkəs] *n* mucosités *fpl*.

mud [mʌd] *n* boue *f*. ◆**muddy** *a* (-ier, -iest) (*water*) boueux; (*hands etc*) couvert de boue. ◆**mudguard** *n* garde-boue *m inv*.

muddle ['mʌd(ə)l] *n* (*mess*) désordre *m*; (*mix-up*) confusion *f*; **in a m.** (*room etc*) sens dessus dessous, en désordre; (*person*) désorienté; (*mind, ideas*) embrouillé; – *vt* (*person, facts etc*) embrouiller; (*papers*) mélanger; – *vi* **to m. through** *Fam* se débrouiller tant bien que mal.

muff [mʌf] *n* (*for hands*) manchon *m*.

muffin ['mʌfɪn] *n* petit pain *m* brioché.

muffl/e ['mʌf(ə)l] *vt* (*noise*) assourdir. ◆**—ed** *a* (*noise*) sourd. ◆**—er** *n* (*scarf*) cache-col *m inv*; *Aut Am* silencieux *m*.

mug [mʌg] **1** *n* grande tasse *f*; (*of metal or plastic*) gobelet *m*; (*beer*) m. chope *f*. **2** *n* (*face*) *Sl* gueule *f*; **m. shot** *Pej* photo *f* (d'identité). **3** *n* (*fool*) *Fam* niais, -aise *mf*. **4** *vt* (-gg-) (*attack*) agresser. ◆**mugger** *n* agresseur *m*. ◆**mugging** *n* agression *f*.

muggy ['mʌgɪ] *a* (-ier, -iest) (*weather*) lourd.

mulberry ['mʌlbərɪ] *n* (*fruit*) mûre *f*.

mule [mjuːl] *n* (*male*) mulet *m*; (*female*) mule *f*.

mull [mʌl] **1** *vt* (*wine*) chauffer. **2** *vi* **to m. over** (*think over*) ruminer.

mullet ['mʌlɪt] *n* (*fish*) mulet *m*; (*red*) m. rouget *m*.

multi- ['mʌltɪ] *pref* multi-.

multicoloured ['mʌltɪkʌləd] *a* multicolore.

multifarious [mʌltɪ'feərɪəs] *a* divers.

multimillionaire [mʌltɪmɪljə'neər] *n* milliardaire *mf*.

multinational [mʌltɪ'naʃ(ə)nəl] *n* multinationale *f*.

multiple ['mʌltɪp(ə)l] *a* multiple; – *n Math* multiple *m.* ◆**multipli'cation** *n* multiplication *f.* ◆**multi'plicity** *n* multiplicité *f.* ◆**multiply** *vt* multiplier; – *vi* (*reproduce*) se multiplier.

multistorey [mʌltɪ'stɔːrɪ] (*Am* **multistoried**) *a* à étages.

multitude ['mʌltɪtjuːd] *n* multitude *f.*

mum [mʌm] **1** *n Fam* maman *f.* **2** *a* **to keep m.** garder le silence.

mumble ['mʌmb(ə)l] *vti* marmotter.

mumbo-jumbo [mʌmbəu'dʒʌmbəu] *n* (*words*) charabia *m.*

mummy ['mʌmɪ] *n* **1** *Fam* maman *f.* **2** (*body*) momie *f.*

mumps [mʌmps] *n* oreillons *mpl.*

munch [mʌntʃ] *vti* (*chew*) mastiquer; **to m.** (**on**) (*eat*) *Fam* bouffer.

mundane [mʌn'deɪn] *a* banal.

municipal [mjuː'nɪsɪp(ə)l] *a* municipal. ◆**munici'pality** *n* municipalité *f.*

munitions [mjuː'nɪʃ(ə)nz] *npl* munitions *fpl.*

mural ['mjuərəl] *a* mural; – *n* fresque *f,* peinture *f* murale.

murder ['mɜːdər] *n* meurtre *m,* assassinat *m*; **it's m.** (*dreadful*) *Fam* c'est affreux; – *vt* (*kill*) assassiner; (*spoil*) *Fig* massacrer. ◆**—er** *n* meurtrier, -ière *mf,* assassin *m.* ◆**murderous** *a* meurtrier.

murky ['mɜːkɪ] *a* (**-ier, -iest**) obscur; (*water, business, past*) trouble; (*weather*) nuageux.

murmur ['mɜːmər] *n* murmure *m*; (*of traffic*) bourdonnement *m*; – *vti* murmurer.

muscle ['mʌs(ə)l] *n* muscle *m*; – *vi* **to m. in on** (*group*) *Sl* s'introduire par la force à. ◆**muscular** *a* (*tissue etc*) musculaire; (*brawny*) musclé.

muse [mjuːz] *vi* méditer (**on** sur).

museum [mjuː'zɪəm] *n* musée *m.*

mush [mʌʃ] *n* (*soft mass*) bouillie *f*; *Fig* sentimentalité *f.* ◆**mushy** *a* (**-ier, -iest**) (*food etc*) en bouillie; *Fig* sentimental.

mushroom ['mʌʃrum] **1** *n* champignon *m.* **2** *vi* (*grow*) pousser comme des champignons; (*spread*) se multiplier.

music ['mjuːzɪk] *n* musique *f*; **m. centre** chaîne *f* stéréo compacte; **m. critic** critique *m* musical; **m. hall** music-hall *m*; **m. lover** mélomane *mf*; **canned m.** musique *f* (de fond) enregistrée. ◆**musical** *a* musical; (*instrument*) de musique; **to be (very) m.** être (très) musicien; – *n* (*film, play*)

comédie *f* musicale. ◆**mu'sician** *n* musicien, -ienne *mf.*

musk [mʌsk] *n* (*scent*) musc *m.*

Muslim ['muzlɪm] *a & n* musulman, -ane (*mf*).

muslin ['mʌzlɪn] *n* (*cotton*) mousseline *f.*

mussel ['mʌs(ə)l] *n* (*mollusc*) moule *f.*

must [mʌst] *v aux* **1** (*necessity*) **you m. obey** tu dois obéir, il faut que tu obéisses. **2** (*certainty*) **she m. be clever** elle doit être intelligente; **I m.** have seen it j'ai dû le voir; – *n* **this is a m.** ceci est (absolument) indispensable.

mustache ['mʌstæʃ] *n Am* moustache *f.*

mustard ['mʌstəd] *n* moutarde *f.*

muster ['mʌstər] *vt* (*gather*) rassembler; (*sum*) réunir; – *vi* se rassembler.

musty ['mʌstɪ] *a* (**-ier, -iest**) (*smell*) de moisi; **it smells m.,** it's m. ça sent le moisi.

mutation [mjuː'teɪʃ(ə)n] *n Biol* mutation *f.*

mut/e [mjuːt] *a* (*silent*) & *Gram* muet; – *vt* (*sound, colour*) assourdir. ◆**—ed** *a* (*criticism*) voilé.

mutilate ['mjuːtɪleɪt] *vt* mutiler. ◆**muti'lation** *n* mutilation *f.*

mutiny ['mjuːtɪnɪ] *n* mutinerie *f*; – *vi* se mutiner. ◆**mutinous** *a* (*troops*) mutiné.

mutter ['mʌtər] *vti* marmonner.

mutton ['mʌt(ə)n] *n* (*meat*) mouton *m.*

mutual ['mjuːtʃuəl] *a* (*help, love etc*) mutuel, réciproque; (*common, shared*) commun; **m. fund** *Fin Am* fonds *m* commun de placement. ◆**—ly** *adv* mutuellement.

muzzle ['mʌz(ə)l] *n* (*snout*) museau *m*; (*device*) muselière *f*; (*of gun*) gueule *f*; – *vt* (*animal, press etc*) museler.

my [maɪ] *poss a* mon, ma, *pl* mes. ◆**my'self** *pron* moi-même; (*reflexive*) me, m'; (*after prep*) moi; **I wash m.** je me lave; **I think of m.** je pense à moi.

mystery ['mɪstərɪ] *n* mystère *m.* ◆**my'sterious** *a* mystérieux.

mystic ['mɪstɪk] *a n* mystique (*mf*). ◆**mystical** *a* mystique. ◆**mysticism** *n* mysticisme *m.* ◆**my'stique** *n* (*mystery, power*) mystique *f* (of de).

mystify ['mɪstɪfaɪ] *vt* (*bewilder*) laisser perplexe; (*fool*) mystifier. ◆**mystifi'cation** *n* (*bewilderment*) perplexité *f.*

myth [mɪθ] *n* mythe *m.* ◆**mythical** *a* mythique. ◆**mytho'logical** *a* mythologique. ◆**my'thology** *n* mythologie *f.*

N

N, n [en] *n* N, n *m*; **the nth time** la énième fois.

nab [næb] *vt* (-bb-) (*catch, arrest*) *Fam* épingler.

nag [næg] *vti* (-gg-) (*criticize*) critiquer; **to n. (at) s.o.** (*pester*) harceler *or* embêter qn (**to do** pour qu'il fasse). ◆**nagging** *a* (*doubt, headache*) qui subsiste; – *n* critiques *fpl.*

nail [neɪl] **1** *n* (*of finger, toe*) ongle *m*; – *a* (*polish, file etc*) à ongles. **2** *n* (*metal*) clou *m*; – *vt* clouer; **to n. s.o.** (*nab*) *Fam* épingler qn; **to n. down** (*lid etc*) clouer.

naïve [nɑriːv] *a* naïf. ◆**naïveté** *n* naïveté *f*.

naked ['neɪkɪd] *a* (*person*) (tout) nu; (*eye, flame*) nu; **to see with the n. eye** voir à l'œil nu. ◆**—ness** *n* nudité *f*.

name [neɪm] *n* nom *m*; (*reputation*) *Fig* réputation *f*; **my n. is . . .** je m'appelle . . . ; **in the n. of** au nom de; **to put one's n. down for** (*school, course*) s'inscrire à; (*job, house*) demander, faire une demande pour avoir; **to call s.o. names** injurier qn; **first n., given n.** prénom *m*; **last n.** nom *m* de famille; **a good/bad n.** *Fig* une bonne/mauvaise réputation; **n. plate** plaque *f*; – *vt* nommer; (*ship, street*) baptiser; (*designate*) désigner, nommer; (*date, price*) fixer; **he was named after** *or Am* **for . . .** il a reçu le nom de . . . . ◆**—less** *a* sans nom, anonyme. ◆**—ly** *adv* (*that is*) à savoir. ◆**namesake** *n* (*person*) homonyme *m*.

nanny ['nænɪ] *n* nurse *f*, bonne *f* d'enfants; (*grandmother*) *Fam* mamie *f*.

nanny-goat ['nænɪɡəʊt] *n* chèvre *f*.

nap [næp] *n* (*sleep*) petit somme *m*; **to have** *or* **take a n.** faire un petit somme; (*after lunch*) faire la sieste; – *vi* (-pp-) **to be napping** sommeiller; **to catch napping** *Fig* prendre au dépourvu.

nape [neɪp] *n* **n. (of the neck)** nuque *f*.

napkin ['næpkɪn] *n* (*at table*) serviette *f*; (*for baby*) couche *f*. ◆**nappy** *n* (*for baby*) couche *f*. ◆**nappy-liner** *n* protège-couche *m*.

narcotic [nɑrˈkɒtɪk] *a & n* narcotique (*m*).

narrate [nəˈreɪt] *vt* raconter. ◆**narration** *n*, ◆'**narrative** (*story*) récit *m*, narration *f*; (*art, act*) narration *f*. ◆**narrator** *n* narrateur, -trice *mf*.

narrow ['nærəʊ] *a* (-er, -est) étroit; (*major-ity*) faible, petit; – *vi* (*of path*) se rétrécir; **to n. down** (*of choice etc*) se limiter (**to** à); – *vt* **to n. (down)** (*limit*) limiter. ◆**—ly** *adv* (*to miss etc*) de justesse; (*strictly*) strictement; **he n. escaped** *or* **missed being killed**/*etc* il a failli être tué/*etc*. ◆**—ness** *n* étroitesse *f*.

narow-minded [nærəʊˈmaɪndɪd] *a* borné. ◆**—ness** *n* étroitesse *f* d'esprit.

nasal ['neɪz(ə)l] *a* nasal; (*voice*) nasillard.

nasty ['nɑːstɪ] *a* (-ier, -iest) (*bad*) mauvais, vilain; (*spiteful*) méchant, désagréable (**to, towards** avec); **a n. mess** *or* **muddle** un gâchis. ◆**nastily** *adv* (*to act*) méchamment; (*to rain*) horriblement. ◆**nastiness** *n* (*malice*) méchanceté *f*; **the n. of the weather/taste**/*etc* le mauvais temps/goût/*etc.*

nation ['neɪʃ(ə)n] *n* nation *f*; **the United Nations** les Nations Unies. ◆**n.-wide** *a* & *adv* dans le pays (tout) entier. ◆**national** *a* national; **n. anthem** hymne *m* national; **N. Health Service** = Sécurité *f* Sociale; **n. insurance** = assurances *fpl* sociales; – *n* (*citizen*) ressortissant, -ante *mf*. ◆**nation-alist** *n* nationaliste *mf*. ◆**nationa'listic** *a Pej* nationaliste. ◆**natio'nality** *n* nationalité *f*. ◆**nationalize** *vt* nationaliser. ◆**nationally** *adv* (*to travel, be known etc*) dans le pays (tout) entier.

native ['neɪtɪv] *a* (*country*) natal; (*habits, costume*) du pays; (*tribe, plant*) indigène; (*charm, ability*) inné; **n. language** langue *f* maternelle; **to be an English n. speaker** parler l'anglais comme langue maternelle; – *n* (*person*) autochtone *mf*; (*non-European in colony*) indigène *mf*; **to be a n. of** être originaire *or* natif de.

nativity [nəˈtɪvɪtɪ] *n Rel* nativité *f*.

NATO ['neɪtəʊ] *n abbr* (*North Atlantic Treaty Organization*) OTAN *f*.

natter ['nætər] *vi Fam* bavarder; – *n Fam* **to have a n.** bavarder.

natural ['nætʃ(ə)rəl] *a* naturel; (*actor, gardener etc*) né; – *n* **to be a n. for** (*job etc*) *Fam* être celui qu'il faut pour, être fait pour. ◆**naturalist** *n* naturaliste *mf*. ◆**naturally** *adv* (*as normal, of course*) naturellement; (*by nature*) de nature; (*with naturalness*) avec naturel. ◆**naturalness** *n* naturel *m*.

naturalize ['nætʃ(ə)rəlaɪz] vt (person) Pol naturaliser. ◆**naturali'zation** n naturalisation f.

nature ['neɪtʃər] n (natural world, basic quality) nature f; (disposition) naturel m; **by n.** de nature; **n. study** sciences fpl naturelles.

naught [nɔːt] n **1** Math zéro m. **2** (nothing) Lit rien m.

naught/y ['nɔːtɪ] a (-ier, -iest) (child) vilain, malicieux; (joke, story) osé, grivois. ◆**—ily** adv (to behave) mal; (to say) avec malice. ◆**—iness** n mauvaise conduite f.

nausea ['nɔːzɪə] n nausée f. ◆**nauseate** vt écœurer. ◆**nauseous** a (smell etc) nauséabond; **to feel n.** Am (sick) avoir envie de vomir; (disgusted) Fig être écœuré.

nautical ['nɔːtɪk(ə)l] a nautique.

naval ['neɪv(ə)l] a naval; (power, hospital) maritime; (officer) de marine.

nave [neɪv] n (of church) nef f.

navel ['neɪv(ə)l] n Anat nombril m.

navigate ['nævɪgeɪt] vi naviguer; – vt (boat) diriger, piloter; (river) naviguer sur. ◆**navigable** a (river) navigable; (seaworthy) en état de naviguer. ◆**navi'gation** n navigation f. ◆**navigator** n Av navigateur m.

navvy ['nævɪ] n (labourer) terrassier m.

navy ['neɪvɪ] n marine f; – a n. (blue) bleu marine inv.

Nazi ['nɑːtsɪ] a & n Pol Hist nazi, -ie (mf).

near [nɪər] adv (-er, -est) près; **quite n., n. at hand** tout près; **to draw n.** (s')approcher (to de); (of date) approcher; **n. to** près de; **to come n. to being killed/etc** faillir être tué/etc; **n. enough** (more or less) Fam plus ou moins; – prep (-er, -est) n. (to) près de; **n. the bed** près du lit; **to be n. (to) victory/death** frôler la victoire/la mort; **n. the end** vers la fin; **to come n. s.o.** s'approcher de qn; – a (-er, -est) proche; (likeness) fidèle; **the nearest hospital** l'hôpital le plus proche; **the nearest way** la route la plus directe; **in the n. future** dans un avenir proche; **to the nearest franc** (to calculate) à un franc près; (to round up or down) au franc supérieur or inférieur; **n. side** Aut côté m gauche, Am côté m droit; – vt (approach) approcher de; **nearing completion** près d'être achevé. ◆**near'by** adv tout près; – ['nɪəbaɪ] a proche. ◆**nearness** n (in space, time) proximité f.

nearly ['nɪəlɪ] adv presque; **she (very) n. fell** elle a failli tomber; **not n. as clever/etc as** loin d'être aussi intelligent/etc que.

neat [niːt] a (-er, -est) (clothes, work) soigné,

propre, net; (room) ordonné, bien rangé; (style) élégant; (pretty) Fam joli, beau; (pleasant) Fam agréable; **to drink one's whisky/etc n.** prendre son whisky/etc sec. ◆**—ly** adv avec soin; (skilfully) habilement. ◆**—ness** n netteté f; (of room) ordre m.

necessary ['nesɪs(ə)rɪ] a nécessaire; **it's n. to do** il est nécessaire de faire, il faut faire; **to make it n. for s.o. to do** mettre qn dans la nécessité de faire; **to do what's n. or the n.** Fam faire le nécessaire (for pour); – npl **the necessaries** (food etc) l'indispensable m. ◆**nece'ssarily** adv nécessairement.

necessity [nɪ'sesɪtɪ] n (obligation, need) nécessité f; (poverty) indigence f; **there's no n. for you to do that** tu n'es pas obligé de faire cela; **of n.** nécessairement; **to be a n.** être indispensable; **the (bare) necessities** le (strict) nécessaire. ◆**necessitate** vt nécessiter.

neck¹ [nek] n Anat cou m; (of dress, horse) encolure f; (of bottle) col m; **low n.** (of dress) décolleté m; **n. and n.** Sp à égalité. ◆**necklace** n collier m. ◆**neckline** n encolure f. ◆**necktie** n cravate f.

neck² [nek] vi (kiss etc) Fam se peloter.

nectarine ['nektərɪn] n (fruit) nectarine f, brugnon m.

née [neɪ] adv **n. Dupont** née Dupont.

need [niːd] **1** n (necessity, want, poverty) besoin m; **in n.** dans le besoin; **to be in n. of** avoir besoin de; **there's no n. (for you) to do** tu n'as pas besoin de faire; **if n. be** si besoin est, s'il le faut; – vt avoir besoin de; **you n. it** tu en as besoin, il te le faut; **it needs an army to do, an army is needed to do** il faut une armée pour faire; **this sport needs patience** ce sport demande de la patience; **her hair needs cutting** il faut qu'elle se fasse couper les cheveux. **2** v aux **n. he wait?** est-il obligé d'attendre?, a-t-il besoin d'attendre?; **I needn't have rushed** ce n'était pas la peine de me presser; **I n. hardly say that . . .** je n'ai guère besoin de dire que . . . . ◆**needless** a inutile. ◆**needlessly** adv inutilement. ◆**needy** a (-ier, -iest) a nécessiteux.

needle ['niːd(ə)l] **1** n aiguille f; (of record player) saphir m. **2** vt (irritate) Fam agacer. ◆**needlework** n couture f, travaux mpl d'aiguille; (object) ouvrage m.

negate [nɪ'geɪt] vt (nullify) annuler; (deny) nier. ◆**negation** n (denial) & Gram négation f.

negative ['negətɪv] a négatif; – n Phot négatif m; (word) Gram négation f; (form)

Gram forme *f* négative; **to answer in the n.** répondre par la négative.

neglect [nɪˈglekt] *vt* (*person, health, work etc*) négliger; (*garden, car etc*) ne pas s'occuper de; (*duty*) manquer à; (*rule*) désobéir à, méconnaître; **to n. to do** négliger de faire; – *n* (*of person*) manque *m* de soins (**of** envers); (*of rule*) désobéissance *f* (**of** à); (*of duty*) manquement *m* (**of** à); (*carelessness*) négligence *f*; **in a state of n.** (*garden, house etc*) mal tenu. ◆**neglected** *a* (*appearance, person*) négligé; (*garden, house etc*) mal tenu; **to feel n.** sentir qu'on vous néglige. ◆**neglectful** *a* négligent; **to be n. of** négliger.

negligent [ˈneglɪdʒənt] *a* négligent. ◆**negligence** *n* négligence *f*. ◆**negligently** *adv* négligemment.

negligible [ˈneglɪdʒəb(ə)l] *a* négligeable.

negotiate [nɪˈgəʊʃɪeɪt] **1** *vti Fin Pol* négocier. **2** *vt* (*fence, obstacle*) franchir; (*bend*) *Aut* négocier. ◆**negotiable** *a Fin* négociable. ◆**negoti'ation** *n* négociation *f*; **in n. with** en pourparlers avec. ◆**negotiator** *n* négociateur, -trice *mf*.

Negro [ˈniːgrəʊ] *n* (*pl* -**oes**) (*man*) Noir *m*; (*woman*) Noire *f*; – *a* noir; (*art, sculpture etc*) nègre. ◆**Negress** *n* Noire *f*.

neigh [neɪ] *vi* (*of horse*) hennir; – *n* hennissement *m*.

neighbour [ˈneɪbər] *n* voisin, -ine *mf*. ◆**neighbourhood** *n* (*neighbours*) voisinage *m*; (*district*) quartier *m*, voisinage *m*; (*region*) région *f*; **in the n. of ten pounds** dans les dix livres. ◆**neighbouring** *a* avoisinant. ◆**neighbourly** *a* (*feeling etc*) de bon voisinage, amical; **they're n.** (*people*) ils sont bons voisins.

neither [ˈnaɪðər, *Am* ˈniːðər] *adv* ni; **n. . . . nor** ni . . . ni; **n. you nor me** ni toi ni moi; **he n. sings nor dances** il ne chante ni ne danse; – *conj* (*not either*) (ne) . . . non plus; **n. shall I go** je n'y irai pas non plus; **n. do I, n. can I** *etc* (ni) moi non plus; – *a* **n. boy** aucun des deux garçons (n'est venu); **on n. side** ni d'un côté ni de l'autre; – *pron* **n.** (**of them**) ni l'un(e) ni l'autre, aucun(e) (des deux).

neo- [ˈniːəʊ] *pref* néo-.

neon [ˈniːɒn] *n* (*gas*) néon *m*; – *a* (*lighting etc*) au néon.

nephew [ˈnevjuː, ˈnefjuː] *n* neveu *m*.

nepotism [ˈnepətɪz(ə)m] *n* népotisme *m*.

nerve [nɜːv] *n* nerf *m*; (*courage*) *Fig* courage *m* (**to do de** faire); (*confidence*) assurance *f*; (*calm*) sang-froid *m*; (*cheek*) *Fam* culot *m* (**to do de** faire); **you get on my nerves** *Fam*

tu me portes *or* me tapes sur les nerfs; **to have (an attack of) nerves** (*fear, anxiety*) avoir le trac; **a bundle** *or* **mass** *or* **bag of nerves** (*person*) *Fam* un paquet de nerfs; **to have bad nerves** être nerveux; – *a* (*cell, centre*) nerveux. ◆**n.-racking** *a* éprouvant pour les nerfs. ◆**nervous** *a* (*tense*) & *Anat* nerveux; (*worried*) inquiet (**about** de); **to be** *or* **feel n.** (*ill-at-ease*) se sentir mal à l'aise; (*before exam etc*) avoir le trac. ◆**nervously** *adv* nerveusement; (*worriedly*) avec inquiétude. ◆**nervousness** *n* nervosité *f*; (*fear*) trac *m*. ◆**nervy** *a* (-**ier**, -**iest**) *Fam* (*anxious*) nerveux; (*brash*) *Am* culotté.

nest [nest] *n* nid *m*; **n. egg** (*money saved*) pécule *m*; **n. of tables** table *f* gigogne; – *vi* (*of bird*) (se) nicher.

nestle [ˈnes(ə)l] *vi* se pelotonner (**up to** contre); **a village nestling in** (*forest, valley etc*) un village niché dans.

net [net] **1** *n* filet *m*; **n. curtain** voilage *m*; – *vt* (-**tt-**) (*fish*) prendre au filet. **2** *a* (*profit, weight etc*) net *inv*; – *vt* (-**tt-**) (*of person, firm etc*) gagner net; **this venture netted him** *or* **her . . .** cette entreprise lui a rapporté . . . . ◆**netting** *n* (*nets*) filets *mpl*; (*mesh*) mailles *fpl*; (*fabric*) voile *m*; (*wire*) **n.** treillis *m*.

Netherlands (the) [ˈðəˈneðələndz] *npl* les Pays-Bas *mpl*.

nettle [ˈnet(ə)l] *n Bot* ortie *f*.

network [ˈnetwɜːk] *n* réseau *m*.

neurosis, *pl* -**oses** [njʊəˈrəʊsɪs, -əʊsiːz] *n* névrose *f*. ◆**neurotic** *a* & *n* névrosé, -ée (*mf*).

neuter [ˈnjuːtər] **1** *a* & *n Gram* neutre (*m*). **2** *vt* (*cat etc*) châtrer.

neutral [ˈnjuːtrəl] *a* neutre; (*policy*) de neutralité; – *n El* neutre *m*; **in n. (gear)** *Aut* au point mort. ◆**neu'trality** *n* neutralité *f*. ◆**neutralize** *vt* neutraliser.

never [ˈnevər] *adv* **1** (*not ever*) (ne) . . . jamais; **she n. lies** elle ne ment jamais; **n. in (all) my life** jamais de ma vie; **n. again** plus jamais. **2** (*certainly not*) *Fam* **I n. did it** je ne l'ai pas fait. ◆**n.-'ending** *a* interminable.

nevertheless [nevəðəˈles] *adv* néanmoins, quand même.

new [njuː] *a* (-**er**, -**est**) nouveau; (*brand-new*) neuf; **to be n. to** (*job*) être nouveau dans; (*city*) être un nouveau-venu dans, être fraîchement installé dans; **a n. boy** *Sch* un nouveau; **what's n.?** *Fam* quoi de neuf?; **a n. glass/pen/**etc (*different*) un autre verre/stylo/*etc*; **to break n. ground** innover; **n. look** style *m* nouveau; **as good as**

n. comme neuf; **a n.-laid egg** un œuf du jour; **a n.-born baby** un nouveau-né, une nouveau-née. ◆**newcomer** *n* nouveau-venu *m*, nouvelle-venue *f*. ◆**new-'fangled** *a Pej* moderne. ◆**new-found** *a* nouveau. ◆**newly** *adv* (*recently*) nouvellement, fraîchement; **the n.-weds** les nouveaux mariés. ◆**newness** *n* (*condition*) état *m* neuf; (*novelty*) nouveauté *f*.

news [njuːz] *n* nouvelle(s) *f(pl)*; *Journ Rad TV* informations *fpl*, actualités *fpl*; **sports/etc n.** (*newspaper column*) chronique *f or* rubrique *f* sportive/*etc*; **a piece of n.**, **some n.** une nouvelle; *Journ Rad TV* une information; **n. headlines** titres *mpl* de l'actualité; **n. flash** flash *m*. ◆**newsagent** *n* marchand, -ande *mf* de journaux. ◆**newsboy** *n* vendeur *m* de journaux. ◆**newscaster** *n* présentateur, -trice *mf*. ◆**newsletter** *n* (*of club, group etc*) bulletin *m*. ◆**newspaper** *n* journal *m*. ◆**newsreader** *n* présentateur, -trice *mf*. ◆**newsreel** *n Cin* actualités *fpl*. ◆**newsworthy** *a* digne de faire l'objet d'un reportage. ◆**newsy** *a* (-ier, -iest) *Fam* plein de nouvelles.

newt [njuːt] *n* (*animal*) triton *m*.

New Zealand [njuːˈziːlənd] *n* Nouvelle-Zélande *f*; – *a* néo-zélandais. ◆**New Zealander** *n* Néo-Zélandais, -aise *mf*.

next [nekst] *a* prochain; (*room, house*) d'à-côté, voisin; (*following*) suivant; **n. month** (*in the future*) le mois prochain; **he returned the n. month** (*in the past*) il revint le mois suivant; **the n. day** le lendemain; **the n. morning** le lendemain matin; **within the n. ten days** d'ici (à) dix jours, dans un délai de dix jours; (**by**) **this time n. week** d'ici (à) la semaine prochaine; **from one year to the n.** d'une année à l'autre; **you're n.** c'est ton tour; **n. (please)!** (au) suivant!; **the n. thing to do is** . . . ce qu'il faut faire ensuite c'est . . . ; **the n. size (up)** la taille au-dessus; **to live/etc n. door** habiter/*etc* à côté (to de); **n.-door neighbour/room** voisin *m*/pièce *f* d'à-côté; – *n* (*in series etc*) suivant, -ante *mf*; – *adv* (*afterwards*) ensuite, après; (*now*) maintenant; **when you come n.** la prochaine fois que tu viendras; **the n. best solution** la seconde solution; – *prep* **n. to** (*beside*) à côté de; **n. to nothing** presque rien.

NHS [eneɪtʃˈes] *abbr* = National Health Service.

nib [nɪb] *n* (*of pen*) plume *f*, bec *m*.

nibble [ˈnɪb(ə)l] *vti* (*eat*) grignoter; (*bite*) mordiller.

nice [naɪs] *a* (-er, -est) (*pleasant*) agréable; (*charming*) charmant, gentil; (*good*) bon; (*fine*) beau; (*pretty*) joli; (*kind*) gentil (**to** avec); (*respectable*) bien *inv*; (*subtle*) délicat; **it's n. here** c'est bien ici; **n. and easy/warm/etc** (*very*) bien facile/chaud/*etc*. ◆**n.-'looking** *a* beau, joli. ◆**nicely** *adv* agréablement; (*kindly*) gentiment; (*well*) bien. ◆**niceties** [ˈnaɪsətiz] *npl* (*pleasant things*) agréments *mpl*; (*subtleties*) subtilités *fpl*.

niche [niːʃ, nɪtʃ] *n* **1** (*recess*) niche *f*. **2** (*job*) (bonne) situation *f*; (*direction*) voie *f*; **to make a n. for oneself** faire son trou.

nick [nɪk] **1** *n* (*on skin, wood*) entaille *f*; (*in blade, crockery*) brèche *f*. **2** *n* (*prison*) *Sl* taule *f*; – *vt* (*steal, arrest*) *Sl* piquer. **3** *n* **in the n. of time** juste à temps; **in good n.** *Sl* en bon état.

nickel [ˈnɪk(ə)l] *n* (*metal*) nickel *m*; (*coin*) *Am* pièce *f* de cinq cents.

nickname [ˈnɪkneɪm] *n* (*informal name*) surnom *m*; (*short form*) diminutif *m*; – *vt* surnommer.

nicotine [ˈnɪkətiːn] *n* nicotine *f*.

niece [niːs] *n* nièce *f*.

nifty [ˈnɪftɪ] *a* (-ier, -iest) (*stylish*) chic *inv*; (*skilful*) habile; (*fast*) rapide.

Nigeria [naɪˈdʒɪərɪə] *n* Nigéria *m or f*. ◆**Nigerian** *a & n* nigérian, -ane (*mf*).

niggardly [ˈnɪgədlɪ] *a* (*person*) avare; (*amount*) mesquin.

niggling [ˈnɪglɪŋ] *a* (*trifling*) insignifiant; (*irksome*) irritant; (*doubt*) persistant.

night [naɪt] *n* nuit *f*; (*evening*) soir *m*; *Th* soirée *f*; **last n.** (*evening*) hier soir; (*night*) la nuit dernière; **to have an early/late n.** se coucher tôt/tard; **to have a good n.** (*sleep well*) bien dormir; **first n.** *Th* première *f*; – *a* (*work etc*) de nuit; (*life*) nocturne; **n. school** cours *mpl* du soir; **n. watchman** veilleur *m* de nuit. ◆**nightcap** *n* (*drink*) boisson *f* (*alcoolisée ou chaude prise avant de se coucher*). ◆**nightclub** *n* boîte *f* de nuit. ◆**nightdress** *n*, ◆**nightgown** *n*, *Fam* ◆**nightie** *n* (*woman's*) chemise *f* de nuit. ◆**nightfall** *n* **at n.** à la tombée de la nuit. ◆**nightlight** *n* veilleuse *f*. ◆**nighttime** *n* nuit *f*.

nightingale [ˈnaɪtɪŋgeɪl] *n* rossignol *m*.

nightly [ˈnaɪtlɪ] *adv* chaque nuit *or* soir; – *a* de chaque nuit *or* soir.

nil [nɪl] *n* (*nothing*) & *Sp* zéro *m*; **the risk/result/etc is n.** le risque/résultat/*etc* est nul.

nimble [ˈnɪmb(ə)l] *a* (-er, -est) agile.

nincompoop ['nɪŋkəmpuːp] *n Fam* imbécile *mf*.

nine [naɪn] *a & n* neuf (*m*). ◆**nine'teen** *a & n* dix-neuf (*m*). ◆**nine'teenth** *a & n* dix-neuvième (*mf*). ◆**ninetieth** *a & n* quatre-vingt-dixième (*mf*). ◆**ninety** *a & n* quatre-vingt-dix (*m*). ◆**ninth** *a & n* neuvième (*mf*); **a n.** un neuvième.

nip [nɪp] **1** *vt* (-**pp**-) (*pinch, bite*) pincer; **to n. in the bud** *Fig* étouffer dans l'œuf; – *n* pinçon *m*; **there's a n. in the air** ça pince. **2** *vi* (-**pp**-) (*dash*) *Fam* **to n. round to s.o.** courir *or* faire un saut chez qn; **to n. in/out** entrer/sortir un instant.

nipper ['nɪpər] *n* (*child*) *Fam* gosse *mf*.

nipple ['nɪp(ə)l] *n* bout *m* de sein, mamelon *m*; (*teat on bottle*) *Am* tétine *f*.

nippy ['nɪpɪ] *a* **1** (-**ier**, -**iest**) (*chilly*) frais; **it's n.** (*weather*) ça pince. **2 to be n.** (*about it*) (*quick*) *Fam* faire vite.

nit [nɪt] *n* **1** (*fool*) *Fam* idiot, -ote *mf*. **2** (*of louse*) lente *f*. ◆**nitwit** *n* (*fool*) *Fam* idiot, -ote *mf*.

nitrogen ['naɪtrədʒən] *n* azote *m*.

nitty-gritty [nɪtɪ'grɪtɪ] *n* **to get down to the n.-gritty** *Fam* en venir au fond du problème.

no [nəʊ] *adv & n* non (*m inv*); **no!** non!; **no more than ten/a kilo/***etc* pas plus de dix/d'un kilo/*etc*; **no more time/***etc* plus de temps/*etc*; **I have no more time** je n'ai plus de temps; **no more than you** pas plus que vous; **you can do no better** tu ne peux pas faire mieux; **the noes** *Pol* les non; – *a* aucun(e); pas de; **I've (got)** *or* **I have no idea** je n'ai aucune idée; **no child came** aucun enfant n'est venu; **I've (got)** *or* **I have no time/***etc* je n'ai pas de temps/*etc*; **of no importance/value/***etc* sans importance/valeur/*etc*; **with no gloves/***etc* on sans gants/*etc*; **there's no knowing . . .** impossible de savoir . . . ; '**no smoking**' 'défense de fumer'; **no way!** *Am Fam* pas question!; **no one = nobody**.

noble ['nəʊb(ə)l] *a* (-**er**, -**est**) noble; (*building*) majestueux. ◆**nobleman** *n* (*pl* -**men**) noble *m*. ◆**noblewoman** *n* (*pl* -**women**) noble *f*. ◆**no'bility** *n* (*character, class*) noblesse *f*.

nobody ['nəʊbɒdɪ] *pron* (ne) . . . personne; **n. came** personne n'est venu; **he knows n.** il ne connaît personne; **n.!** personne!; – *n a* **n.** une nullité.

nocturnal [nɒk'tɜːn(ə)l] *a* nocturne.

nod [nɒd] **1** *vti* (-**dd**-) **to n.** (**one's head**) incliner la tête, faire un signe de tête; – *n*

inclination *f or* signe *m* de tête. **2** *vi* (-**dd**-) **to n. off** (*go to sleep*) s'assoupir.

noise [nɔɪz] *n* bruit *m*; (*of bell, drum*) son *m*; **to make a n.** faire du bruit. ◆**noisily** *adv* bruyamment. ◆**noisy** *a* (-**ier**, -**iest**) (*person, street etc*) bruyant.

nomad ['nəʊmæd] *n* nomade *mf*. ◆**no'madic** *a* nomade.

nominal ['nɒmɪn(ə)l] *a* (*value, fee etc*) nominal; (*head, ruler*) de nom.

nominate ['nɒmɪneɪt] *vt Pol* désigner, proposer (**for** comme candidat à); (*appoint*) désigner, nommer. ◆**nomi'nation** *n* désignation *f or* proposition *f* de candidat; (*appointment*) nomination *f*. ◆**nomi'nee** *n* (*candidate*) candidat *m*.

non- [nɒn] *pref* non-.

nonchalant ['nɒnʃələnt] *a* nonchalant.

noncommissioned [nɒnkə'mɪʃ(ə)nd] *a* **n. officer** *Mil* sous-officier *m*.

non-committal [nɒnkə'mɪt(ə)l] *a* (*answer, person*) évasif.

nonconformist [nɒnkən'fɔːmɪst] *a & n* non-conformiste (*mf*).

nondescript ['nɒndɪskrɪpt] *a* indéfinissable; *Pej* médiocre.

none [nʌn] *pron* aucun(e) *mf*; (*in filling a form*) néant; **n. of them** aucun d'eux; **she has n. (at all)** elle n'en a pas (du tout); **n. (at all) came** pas un(e) seul(e) n'est venu(e); **n. can tell** personne ne peut le dire; **n. of the cake/***etc* pas une seule partie du gâteau/*etc*; **n. of the trees/***etc* aucun arbre/*etc*, aucun des arbres/*etc*; **n. of it** *or* **this** rien (de ceci); – *adv* **n. too hot/***etc* pas tellement chaud/*etc*; **he's n. the happier/wiser/***etc* il n'en est pas plus heureux/sage/*etc*; **n. the less** néanmoins. ◆**nonethe'less** *adv* néanmoins.

nonentity [nɒ'nentɪtɪ] *n* (*person*) nullité *f*.

non-existent [nɒnɪg'zɪstənt] *a* inexistant.

non-fiction [nɒn'fɪkʃ(ə)n] *n* littérature *f* non-romanesque; (*in library*) ouvrages *mpl* généraux.

non-flammable [nɒn'flæməb(ə)l] *a* ininflammable.

nonplus [nɒn'plʌs] *vt* (-**ss**-) dérouter.

nonsense ['nɒnsəns] *n* absurdités *fpl*; **that's n.** c'est absurde. ◆**non'sensical** *a* absurde.

non-smoker [nɒn'sməʊkər] *n* (*person*) non-fumeur, -euse *mf*; (*compartment*) *Rail* compartiment *m* non-fumeurs.

non-stick [nɒn'stɪk] *a* (*pan*) anti-adhésif, qui n'attache pas.

non-stop [nɒn'stɒp] *a* sans arrêt; (*train,*

flight) direct; − *adv* (*to work etc*) sans arrêt; (*to fly*) sans escale.

noodles ['nuːd(ə)lz] *npl* nouilles *fpl*; (*in soup*) vermicelle(s) *m*(*pl*).

nook [nʊk] *n* coin *m*; **in every n. and cranny** dans tous les coins (et recoins).

noon [nuːn] *n* midi *m*; **at n.** à midi; − *a* (*sun etc*) de midi.

noose [nuːs] *n* (*loop*) nœud *m* coulant; (*of hangman*) corde *f*.

nor [nɔːr] *conj* ni; **neither you n. me** ni toi ni moi; **she neither drinks n. smokes** elle ne fume ni ne boit; **n. do I, n. can I** *etc* (ni) moi non plus; **n. will I (go)** je n'y irai pas non plus.

norm [nɔːm] *n* norme *f*.

normal ['nɔːm(ə)l] *a* normal; − *n* **above n.** au-dessus de la normale. ◆**nor'mality** *n* normalité *f*. ◆**normalize** *vt* normaliser. ◆**normally** *adv* normalement.

Norman ['nɔːmən] *a* normand.

north [nɔːθ] *n* nord *m*; − *a* (*coast*) nord *inv*; (*wind*) du nord; **to be n. of** être au nord de; **N. America/Africa** Amérique *f*/Afrique *f* du Nord; **N. American** *a* & *n* nord-américain, -aine (*mf*); − *adv* au nord, vers le nord. ◆**northbound** *a* (*carriageway*) nord *inv*; (*traffic*) en direction du nord. ◆**north-'east** *n* & *a* nord-est *m* & *a inv*. ◆**northerly** *a* (*point*) nord *inv*; (*direction, wind*) du nord. ◆**northern** *a* (*coast*) nord *inv*; (*town*) du nord; **N. France** le Nord de la France; **N. Europe** Europe *f* du Nord; **N. Ireland** Irlande *f* du Nord. ◆**northerner** *n* habitant, -ante *mf* du Nord. ◆**northward(s)** *a* & *adv* vers le nord. ◆**north-'west** *n* & *a* nord-ouest *m* & *a inv*.

Norway ['nɔːweɪ] *n* Norvège *f*. ◆**Nor'wegian** *a* & *n* norvégien, -ienne (*mf*); − *n* (*language*) norvégien *m*.

nose [nəʊz] *n* nez *m*; **her n. is bleeding** elle saigne du nez; **to turn one's n. up** *Fig* faire le dégoûté (**at** devant); − *vi* **to n. about** (*pry*) *Fam* fouiner. ◆**nosebleed** *n* saignement *m* de nez. ◆**nosedive** *n* *Av* piqué *m*; (*in prices*) chute *f*.

nos(e)y ['nəʊzɪ] *a* (**-ier, -iest**) fouineur, indiscret; **n. parker** fouineur, -euse *mf*.

nosh [nɒʃ] *vi* *Fam* (*eat heavily*) bouffer; (*nibble*) grignoter (entre les repas); − *n* (*food*) *Fam* bouffe *f*.

nostalgia [nɒ'stældʒɪə] *n* nostalgie *f*. ◆**nostalgic** *a* nostalgique.

nostril ['nɒstr(ə)l] *n* (*of person*) narine *f*; (*of horse*) naseau *m*.

not [nɒt] *adv* **1** (ne) . . . pas; **he's n. there, he** isn't there il n'est pas là; **n. yet** pas encore; **why n.?** pourquoi pas?; **n. one reply/***etc* pas une seule réponse/*etc*; **n. at all** pas du tout; (*after 'thank you'*) je vous en prie. **2** non; **I think/hope n.** je pense/j'espère que non; **n. guilty** non coupable; **isn't she?, don't you?** *etc* non?

notable ['nəʊtəb(ə)l] *a* (*remarkable*) notable; − *n* (*person*) notable *m*. ◆**notably** *adv* (*noticeably*) notablement; (*particularly*) notamment.

notary ['nəʊtərɪ] *n* notaire *m*.

notation [nəʊ'teɪʃ(ə)n] *n* notation *f*.

notch [nɒtʃ] **1** *n* (*in wood etc*) entaille *f*, encoche *f*; (*in belt, wheel*) cran *m*. **2** *vt* **to n. up** (*a score*) marquer; (*a victory*) enregistrer.

note [nəʊt] *n* (*written comment, tone etc*) & *Mus* note *f*; (*summary, preface*) notice *f*; (*banknote*) billet *m*; (*piano key*) touche *f*; (*message, letter*) petit mot *m*; **to take (a) n. of, make a n. of** prendre note de; **of n.** (*athlete, actor etc*) éminent; − *vt* (*take note of*) noter; (*notice*) remarquer, noter; **to n. down** noter. ◆**notebook** *n* carnet *m*; *Sch* cahier *m*; (*pad*) bloc-notes *m*. ◆**notepad** *n* bloc-notes *m*. ◆**notepaper** *n* papier *m* à lettres.

noted ['nəʊtɪd] *a* (*author etc*) éminent; **to be n. for** être connu pour.

noteworthy ['nəʊtwɜːðɪ] *a* notable.

nothing ['nʌθɪŋ] *pron* (ne) . . . rien; **he knows n.** il ne sait rien; **n. to do/eat/***etc* rien à faire/manger/*etc*; **n. big/***etc* rien de grand/*etc*; **n. much** pas grand-chose; **I've got n. to do with it** je n'y suis pour rien; **I can do n. (about it)** je n'y peux rien; **to come to n.** (*of effort etc*) ne rien donner; **there's n. like it** il n'y a rien de tel; **for n.** (*in vain, free of charge*) pour rien; − *adv* **to look n. like s.o.** ne ressembler nullement à qn; **n. like as large/***etc* loin d'être aussi grand/*etc*; − *n* **a (mere) n.** (*person*) une nullité; (*thing*) un rien. ◆**—ness** *n* (*void*) néant *m*.

notice ['nəʊtɪs] *n* (*notification*) avis *m*; *Journ* annonce *f*; (*sign*) pancarte *f*, écriteau *m*; (*poster*) affiche *f*; (*review of film etc*) critique *f*; (*attention*) attention *f*; (*knowledge*) connaissance *f*; **(advance) n.** (*of departure etc*) préavis *m*; **n. (to quit), n. (of dismissal)** congé *m*; **to give (in) one's n.** (*resignation*) donner sa démission; **to give s.o. n. of** (*inform of*) avertir qn de; **to take n.** faire attention (**of à**); **to bring sth to s.o.'s n.** porter qch à la connaissance de qn; **until further n.** jusqu'à nouvel ordre; **at short n.** à bref délai; **n. board** tableau *m* d'affichage; − *vt* (*perceive*) remarquer (qn); (*fact, trick, danger*) s'apercevoir de, remarquer; **I n. that** je m'aperçois que. ◆—**able** *a* visible, perceptible; **that's n.** ça se voit; **she's n.** elle se fait remarquer.

notify ['nəʊtɪfaɪ] *vt* (*inform*) aviser (**s.o. of sth** qn de qch); (*announce*) notifier (**to** à). ◆**notifi'cation** *n* annonce *f*, avis *m*.

notion ['nəʊʃ(ə)n] **1** *n* (*thought*) idée *f*; (*awareness*) notion *f*; **some n. of** (*knowledge*) quelques notions de. **2** *npl* (*sewing articles*) *Am* mercerie *f*.

notorious [nəʊ'tɔːrɪəs] *a* (*event, person etc*) tristement célèbre; (*stupidity, criminal*) notoire. ◆**notoriety** [-ə'raɪətɪ] *n* (triste) notoriété *f*.

notwithstanding [nɒtwɪð'stændɪŋ] *prep* malgré; − *adv* tout de même.

nougat ['nuːgɑː, 'nʌgət] *n* nougat *m*.

nought [nɔːt] *n Math* zéro *m*.

noun [naʊn] *n Gram* nom *m*.

nourish ['nʌrɪʃ] *vt* nourrir. ◆—**ing** *a* nourrissant. ◆—**ment** *n* nourriture *f*.

novel ['nɒv(ə)l] **1** *n Liter* roman *m*. **2** *a* (*new*) nouveau, original. ◆**novelist** *n* romancier, -ière *mf*. ◆**novelty** *n* (*newness, object, idea*) nouveauté *f*.

November [nəʊ'vembər] *n* novembre *m*.

novice ['nɒvɪs] *n* novice *mf* (**at** en).

now [naʊ] *adv* maintenant; **just n., right n.** en ce moment; **I saw her just n.** je l'ai vue à l'instant; **for n.** pour le moment; **even n.** encore maintenant; **from n. on** désormais, à partir de maintenant; **until n., up to n.** jusqu'ici; **before n.** avant; **n. and then** de temps à autre; **n. hot, n. cold** tantôt chaud, tantôt froid; **n. (then)!** bon!, alors!; (*telling s.o. off*) allons!; **n. it happened that . . .** or **il advint que . . .** ; − *conj* **n. (that)** maintenant que. ◆**nowadays** *adv* aujourd'hui, de nos jours.

noway ['nəʊweɪ] *adv Am* nullement.

nowhere ['nəʊweər] *adv* nulle part; **n. else** nulle part ailleurs; **it's n. I know** ce n'est pas un endroit que je connais; **n. near the house** loin de la maison; **n. near enough** loin d'être assez.

nozzle ['nɒz(ə)l] *n* (*of hose*) jet *m*, lance *f* (à eau); (*of syringe, tube*) embout *m*.

nth [enθ] *a* (*degree etc*) nième.

nuance ['njuːɑːns] *n* (*of meaning, colour etc*) nuance *f*.

nub [nʌb] *n* (*of problem*) cœur *m*.

nuclear ['njuːklɪər] *a* nucléaire; **n. scientist** spécialiste *mf* du nucléaire, atomiste *mf*.

nucleus, *pl* **-clei** ['njuːklɪəs, -klɪaɪ] *n* noyau *m*.

nude [njuːd] *a* nu; − *n* (*female or male figure*) nu *m*; **in the n.** (tout) nu. ◆**nudism** *n* nudisme *m*, naturisme *m*. ◆**nudist** *n* nudiste *mf*, naturiste *mf*; − *a* (*camp*) de nudistes, de naturistes. ◆**nudity** *n* nudité *f*.

nudge [nʌdʒ] *vt* pousser du coude; − *n* coup *m* de coude.

nugget ['nʌgɪt] *n* (*of gold etc*) pépite *f*.

nuisance ['njuːs(ə)ns] *n* (*annoyance*) embêtement *m*; (*person*) peste *f*; **that's a n.** c'est embêtant; **he's being a n., he's making a n. of himself** il nous embête, il m'embête *etc*.

null [nʌl] *a* **n. (and void)** nul (et non avenu). ◆**nullify** *vt* infirmer.

numb [nʌm] *a* (*stiff*) engourdi; *Fig* paralysé; − *vt* engourdir; *Fig* paralyser.

number ['nʌmbər] *n* nombre *m*; (*of page, house, newspaper etc*) numéro *m*; **a dance/song n.** un numéro de danse/de chant; **a/any n. of** un certain/grand nombre de; **n. plate** (*of vehicle*) plaque *f* d'immatriculation; − *vt* (*page etc*) numéroter; (*include, count*) compter; **they n. eight** ils sont au nombre de huit. ◆—**ing** *n* numérotage *m*.

numeral ['njuːm(ə)rəl] *n* chiffre *m*; − *a* numéral. ◆**nu'merical** *a* numérique. ◆**numerous** *a* nombreux.

numerate ['njuːm(ə)rət] *a* (*person*) qui sait compter.

nun [nʌn] *n* religieuse *f*.

nurs/e [nɜːs] **1** *n* infirmière *f*; (*nanny*) nurse *f*; (*male*) **n.** infirmier *m*. **2** *vt* (*look after*) soigner; (*cradle*) bercer; (*suckle*) nourrir; (*a grudge etc*) *Fig* nourrir; (*support, encourage*) *Fig* épauler (qn). ◆—**ing** *a* (*mother*) qui allaite; **the n. staff** le personnel infirmier; − *n* (*care*) soins *mpl*; (*job*) profession *f* d'infirmière or d'infirmier; **n. home** clinique *f*. ◆**nursemaid** *n* bonne *f* d'enfants.

nursery ['nɜːs(ə)rɪ] *n* (*room*) chambre *f* d'enfants; (*for plants, trees*) pépinière *f*; **(day) n.** (*school etc*) crèche *f*, garderie *f*; **n. rhyme** chanson *f* enfantine; **n. school** école *f* maternelle.

nurture ['nɜːtʃər] *vt* (*educate*) éduquer.

nut[1] [nʌt] *n* (*fruit*) fruit *m* à coque; (*walnut*) noix *f*; (*hazelnut*) noisette *f*; (*peanut*) cacah(o)uète *f*; **Brazil/cashew n.** noix *f* du Brésil/de cajou. ◆**nutcracker(s)** *n(pl)* casse-noix *m inv*. ◆**nutshell** *n* coquille *f* de noix; **in a n.** *Fig* en un mot.

nut[2] [nʌt] *n* **1** (*for bolt*) *Tech* écrou *m*. **2**

(*head*) *Sl* caboche *f.* **3** (*person*) *Sl* cinglé, -ée *mf*; **to be nuts** *Sl* être cinglé. ◆**nutcase** *n* cinglé, -ée *mf*. ◆**nutty** *a* (**-ier, -iest**) *Sl* cinglé.

nutmeg ['nʌtmeg] *n* muscade *f.*

nutritious [njuːˈtrɪʃəs] *a* nutritif. ◆'**nutri-**

ent *n* élément *m* nutritif. ◆**nutrition** *n* nutrition *f.*

nylon ['naɪlɒn] *n* nylon *m*; *pl* (*stockings*) bas *mpl* nylon.

nymph [nɪmf] *n* nymphe *f.* ◆**nympho-**'**maniac** *n Pej* nymphomane *f.*

O

O, o [əu] *n* O, o *m.*

oaf [əuf] *n* rustre *m.* ◆**oafish** *a* (*behaviour*) de rustre.

oak [əuk] *n* (*tree, wood*) chêne *m.*

OAP [əueɪ'piː] *n abbr* (*old age pensioner*) retraité, -ée *mf.*

oar [ɔːr] *n* aviron *m*, rame *f.*

oasis, pl oases [əu'eɪsɪs, əu'eɪsiːz] *n* oasis *f.*

oath [əuθ] *n* (*pl* -**s** [əuðz]) (*promise*) serment *m*; (*profanity*) juron *m*; **to take an o. to do** faire le serment de faire.

oats [əuts] *npl* avoine *f.* ◆**oatmeal** *n* flocons *mpl* d'avoine.

obedient [ə'biːdɪənt] *a* obéissant. ◆**obedience** *n* obéissance *f* (**to** à). ◆**obediently** *adv* docilement.

obelisk ['ɒbəlɪsk] *n* (*monument*) obélisque *m.*

obese [əu'biːs] *a* obèse. ◆**obesity** *n* obésité *f.*

obey [ə'beɪ] *vt* obéir à; **to be obeyed** être obéi; – *vi* obéir.

obituary [ə'bɪtʃuəri] *n* nécrologie *f.*

object¹ ['ɒbdʒɪkt] *n* (*thing*) objet *m*; (*aim*) but *m*, objet *m*; *Gram* complément *m* (d'objet); **with the o. of** dans le but de; **that's no o.** (*no problem*) ça ne pose pas de problème; **price no o.** prix *m* indifférent.

object² [ɒb'dʒekt] *vi* **to o. to sth/s.o.** désapprouver qch/qn; **I o. to you(r) doing that** ça me gêne que tu fasses ça; **I o.!** je proteste!; **she didn't o. when . . .** elle n'a fait aucune objection quand . . . ; – *vt* **to o. that** objecter que. ◆**objection** *n* objection *f*; **I've got no o.** ça ne me gêne pas, je n'y vois pas d'objection *or* d'inconvénient. ◆**objectionable** *a* très désagréable. ◆**objector** *n* opposant, -ante *mf* (**to** à); **conscientious o.** objecteur *m* de conscience.

objective [ɒb'dʒektɪv] **1** *a* (*opinion etc*) objectif. **2** *n* (*aim, target*) objectif *m.* ◆**objectively** *adv* objectivement. ◆**objec'tivity** *n* objectivité *f.*

obligate ['ɒblɪgeɪt] *vt* contraindre (**to do** à faire). ◆**obli'gation** *n* obligation *f*; (*debt*) dette *f*; **under an o. to do** dans l'obligation de faire; **under an o. to s.o.** redevable à qn (**for** de). ◆o'**bligatory** *a* (*compulsory*) obligatoire; (*imposed by custom*) de rigueur.

oblig/e [ə'blaɪdʒ] *vt* **1** (*compel*) obliger (**s.o. to do qn** à faire); **obliged to do** obligé de faire. **2** (*help*) rendre service à, faire plaisir à; **obliged to s.o.** reconnaissant à qn (**for** de); **much obliged!** merci infiniment! ◆—**ing** *a* (*kind*) obligeant. ◆—**ingly** *adv* obligeamment.

oblique [ə'bliːk] *a* oblique; (*reference*) *Fig* indirect.

obliterate [ə'blɪtəreɪt] *vt* effacer. ◆**oblite-**'**ration** *n* effacement *m.*

oblivion [ə'blɪvɪən] *n* oubli *m.* ◆**oblivious** *a* inconscient (**to, of** de).

oblong ['ɒblɒŋ] *a* (*elongated*) oblong; (*rectangular*) rectangulaire; – *n* rectangle *m.*

obnoxious [əb'nɒkʃəs] *a* odieux; (*smell*) nauséabond.

oboe ['əubəu] *n Mus* hautbois *m.*

obscene [əb'siːn] *a* obscène. ◆**obscenity** *n* obscénité *f.*

obscure [əb'skjuər] *a* (*reason, word, actor, life etc*) obscur; – *vt* (*hide*) cacher; (*confuse*) embrouiller, obscurcir. ◆**obscurely** *adv* obscurément. ◆**obscurity** *n* obscurité *f.*

obsequious [əb'siːkwɪəs] *a* obséquieux.

observe [əb'zɜːv] *vt* (*notice, watch, respect*) observer; (*say*) (faire) remarquer (**that** que); **to o. the speed limit** respecter la limitation de vitesse. ◆**observance** *n* (*of rule etc*) observation *f.* ◆**observant** *a* observateur. ◆**obser'vation** *n* (*observing, remark*) observation *f*; (*by police*) surveillance *f*; **under o.** (*hospital patient*) en obser-

vation. ◆**observatory** n observatoire m.
◆**observer** n observateur, -trice mf.

obsess [əb'ses] vt obséder. ◆**obsession** n obsession f; **to have an o. with** or **about** avoir l'obsession de. ◆**obsessive** a (memory, idea) obsédant; (fear) obsessif; (neurotic) Psy obsessionnel; **to be o. about** avoir l'obsession de.

obsolete ['ɒbsəliːt] a (out of date, superseded) désuet, dépassé; (ticket) périmé; (machinery) archaïque. ◆**obso'lescent** a quelque peu désuet; (word) vieilli.

obstacle ['ɒbstək(ə)l] n obstacle m.

obstetrics [əb'stetrɪks] n Med obstétrique f. ◆**obste'trician** n médecin m accoucheur.

obstinate ['ɒbstɪnət] a (person, resistance etc) obstiné, opiniâtre; (disease, pain) rebelle, opiniâtre. ◆**obstinacy** n obstination f. ◆**obstinately** adv obstinément.

obstreperous [əb'strepərəs] a turbulent.

obstruct [əb'strʌkt] vt (block) boucher; (hinder) entraver; (traffic) entraver, bloquer. ◆**obstruction** n (act, state) & Med Pol Sp obstruction f; (obstacle) obstacle m; (in pipe) bouchon m; (traffic jam) embouteillage m. ◆**obstructive** a **to be o.** faire de l'obstruction.

obtain [əb'teɪn] **1** vt obtenir. **2** vi (of practice etc) avoir cours. ◆**—able** a (available) disponible; (on sale) en vente.

obtrusive [əb'truːsɪv] a (person) importun; (building etc) trop en évidence.

obtuse [əb'tjuːs] a (angle, mind) obtus.

obviate ['ɒbvɪeɪt] vt (necessity) éviter.

obvious ['ɒbvɪəs] a évident; **he's the o. man to see** c'est évidemment l'homme qu'il faut voir. ◆**—ly** adv (evidently, of course) évidemment; (conspicuously) visiblement.

occasion [ə'keɪʒ(ə)n] **1** n (time, opportunity) occasion f; (event, ceremony) événement m; **on the o. of** à l'occasion de; **on o.** à l'occasion; **on several occasions** à plusieurs reprises or occasions. **2** n (cause) raison f, occasion f; – vt occasionner. ◆**occasional** a (event) qui a lieu de temps en temps; (rain, showers) intermittent; **she drinks the o. whisky** elle boit un whisky de temps en temps. ◆**occasionally** adv de temps en temps; **very o.** très peu souvent, rarement.

occult [ə'kʌlt] a occulte.

occupy ['ɒkjupaɪ] vt (house, time, space, post etc) occuper; **to keep oneself occupied** s'occuper (doing à faire). ◆**occupant** n (inhabitant) occupant, -ante mf. ◆**occu-'pation** n (activity) occupation f; (job) emploi m; (trade) métier m; (profession) profession f; **the o. of** (action) l'occupation f de; **fit for o.** (house) habitable. ◆**occu-'pational** a (hazard) du métier; (disease) du travail. ◆**occupier** n (of house) occupant, -ante mf; Mil occupant m.

occur [ə'kɜːr] vi (-rr-) (happen) avoir lieu; (be found) se rencontrer; (arise) se présenter; **it occurs to me that...** il me vient à l'esprit que...; **the idea occurred to her to...** l'idée lui est venue de.... ◆**occurrence** [ə'kʌrəns] n (event) événement m; (existence) existence f; (of word) Ling occurrence f.

ocean ['əʊʃ(ə)n] n océan m. ◆**oce'anic** a océanique.

o'clock [ə'klɒk] adv (**it's) three o'c.**/etc (il est) trois heures/etc.

octagon ['ɒktəgən] n octogone m. ◆**oc'tagonal** a octogonal.

octave ['ɒktɪv, 'ɒkteɪv] n Mus octave f.

October [ɒk'təʊbər] n octobre m.

octogenarian [ɒktəʊ'dʒɪneərɪən] n octogénaire mf.

octopus ['ɒktəpəs] n pieuvre f.

odd [ɒd] a **1** (strange) bizarre, curieux; **an o. size** une taille peu courante. **2** (number) impair. **3** (left over) **I have an o. penny** il me reste un penny; **a few o. stamps** quelques timbres (qui restent); **the o. man out,** the **o. one out** l'exception f; **sixty o.** soixante et quelques; **an o. glove/book**/etc un gant/livre/etc dépareillé. **4** (occasional) qu'on fait, voit etc de temps en temps; **to find the o. mistake** trouver de temps en temps une (petite) erreur; **at o. moments** de temps en temps; **o. jobs** (around house) menus travaux mpl; **o. job man** homme m à tout faire. ◆**oddity** n (person) personne f bizarre; (object) curiosité f; pl (of language, situation) bizarreries fpl. ◆**oddly** adv bizarrement; **o. (enough), he was...** chose curieuse, il était.... ◆**oddment** n Com fin f de série. ◆**oddness** n bizarrerie f.

odds [ɒdz] npl **1** (in betting) cote f; (chances) chances fpl; **we have heavy o. against us** nous avons très peu de chances de réussir. **2 it makes no o.** (no difference) Fam ça ne fait rien. **3 at o.** (in disagreement) en désaccord (with avec). **4 o. and ends** des petites choses.

ode [əʊd] n (poem) ode f.

odious ['əʊdɪəs] a détestable, odieux.

odour ['əʊdər] n odeur f. ◆**—less** a inodore.

oecumenical [iːkjuˈmenɪk(ə)l] a Rel œcuménique.

of [əv, stressed ɒv] prep de; **of the table** de la

table; **of the boy** du garçon; **of the boys** des garçons; **of a book** d'un livre; **of it, of them** en; **she has a lot of it** or **of them** elle en a beaucoup; **a friend of his** un ami à lui; **there are ten of us** nous sommes dix; **that's nice of you** c'est gentil de ta part; **of no value/interest/**etc sans valeur/intérêt/etc; **of late** ces derniers temps; **a man of fifty** un homme de cinquante ans; **the fifth of June** le cinq juin.

off [ɒf] **1** adv (absent) absent, parti; (light, gas, radio etc) éteint, fermé; (tap) fermé; (switched off at mains) coupé; (detached) détaché; (removed) enlevé; (cancelled) annulé; (not fit to eat or drink) mauvais; (milk, meat) tourné; **2 km o.** à 2 km (d'ici or de là), éloigné de 2 km; **to be** ou **go o.** (leave) partir; **where are you o. to?** où vas-tu?; **he has his hat o.** il a enlevé son chapeau; **with his, my** etc **gloves o.** sans gants; **a day o.** (holiday) un jour de congé; **I'm o. today, I have today o.** j'ai congé aujourd'hui; **the strike's o.** il n'y aura pas de grève, la grève est annulée; **5% o.** une réduction de 5%; **on and o., o. and on** (sometimes) de temps à autre; **to be better o.** (wealthier, in a better position) être mieux. **2** prep (from) de; (distant) éloigné de; **to fall/**etc **o. the wall/ladder/**etc tomber/etc du mur/de l'échelle/etc; **to get o. the bus/**etc descendre du bus/etc; **to take sth o. the table/**etc prendre qch sur la table/etc; **to eat o. a plate** manger dans une assiette; **to keep** or **stay o. the grass** ne pas marcher sur les pelouses; **she's o. her food** elle ne mange plus rien; **o. Dover/**etc Nau au large de Douvres/etc; **o. limits** interdit; **the o. side** Aut le côté droit, Am le côté gauche. ◆**off'beat** a excentrique. ◆**off-'colour** a (ill) patraque; (indecent) scabreux. ◆**off'hand** a désinvolte; – adv impromptu. ◆**off-'handedness** n désinvolture f. ◆**off-licence** n magasin m de vins et de spiritueux. ◆**off-'load** vt (vehicle etc) décharger; **to o.-load sth onto s.o.** (task etc) se décharger de qch sur qn. ◆**off-'peak** a (crowds, traffic) aux heures creuses; (rate, price) heures creuses inv; **o.-peak hours** heures fpl creuses. ◆**off-putting** a Fam rebutant. ◆**off'side** a **to be o.** Fb être hors jeu. ◆**off'stage** a & adv dans les coulisses. ◆**off-'white** a blanc cassé inv.

offal ['ɒf(ə)l] n Culin abats mpl.

offence [ə'fens] n Jur délit m; **to take o.** s'offenser (at de); **to give o.** offenser.

offend [ə'fend] vt froisser, offenser; (eye) Fig

choquer; **to be offended (at)** se froisser (de), s'offenser (de). ◆**-ing** a (object, remark) incriminé. ◆**offender** n Jur délinquant, -ante mf; (habitual) récidiviste mf.

offensive [ə'fensɪv] **1** a (unpleasant) choquant, repoussant; (insulting) insultant, offensant; (weapon) offensif. **2** n Mil offensive f.

offer ['ɒfər] n offre f; **on (special) o.** Com en promotion, en réclame; **o. of marriage** demande f en mariage; – vt offrir; (opinion, remark) proposer; **to o. to do** offrir or proposer de faire. ◆**-ing** n (gift) offrande f; (act) offre f; **peace o.** cadeau m de réconciliation.

office ['ɒfɪs] n **1** bureau m; (of doctor) Am cabinet m; (of lawyer) étude f; **head o.** siège m central; **o. block** immeuble m de bureaux; **o. worker** employé, -ée mf de bureau. **2** (post) fonction f; (duty) fonctions fpl; **to be in o.** (of party etc) Pol être au pouvoir. **3** one's good **offices** (help) ses bons offices mpl.

officer ['ɒfɪsər] n (in army, navy etc) officier m; (of company) Com directeur, -trice mf; (police) o. agent m (de police).

official [ə'fɪʃ(ə)l] a officiel; (uniform) réglementaire; – n (person of authority) officiel m; (civil servant) fonctionnaire m; (employee) employé, -ée mf. ◆**officialdom** n bureaucratie f. ◆**officially** adv officiellement. ◆**officiate** vi faire fonction d'officiel (at à); (preside) présider; Rel officier.

officious [ə'fɪʃəs] a Pej empressé.

offing ['ɒfɪŋ] n **in the o.** en perspective.

offset ['ɒfset, ɒf'set] vt (pt & pp offset, pres p offsetting) (compensate for) compenser; (s.o.'s beauty etc by contrast) faire ressortir.

offshoot ['ɒfʃuːt] n (of firm) ramification f; (consequence) conséquence f.

offspring ['ɒfsprɪŋ] n progéniture f.

often ['ɒf(t)ən] adv souvent; **how o.?** combien de fois?; **how o. do they run?** (trains, buses etc) il y en a tous les combien?; **once too o.** une fois de trop; **every so o.** de temps en temps.

ogle ['əʊg(ə)l] vt Pej reluquer.

ogre ['əʊgər] n ogre m.

oh! [əʊ] int ah!, ah!; (pain) aïe!; **oh yes?** ah oui?, ah bon?

oil [ɔɪl] n (for machine, in cooking etc) huile f; (mineral) pétrole m; (fuel oil) mazout m; **to paint in oils** faire de la peinture à l'huile; – a (industry, product) pétrolier; (painting, paints) à l'huile; **o. lamp** lampe f à pétrole or à huile; **o. change** Aut vidange f; – vt

graisser, huiler. ◆**oilcan** n burette f.
◆**oilfield** n gisement m pétrolifère. ◆**oil-fired** a au mazout. ◆**oilskin(s)** n(pl)
(garment) ciré m. ◆**oily** a (-ier, -iest)
(substance, skin) huileux; (hands) graisseux; (food) gras.

ointment ['ɔɪntmənt] n pommade f.

OK [əʊ'keɪ] int (approval, exasperation) ça
va!; (agreement) d'accord!, entendu!, OK!;
– a (satisfactory) bien inv; (unharmed) sain
et sauf; (undamaged) intact; (without
worries) tranquille; **it's OK now** (fixed) ça
marche maintenant; **I'm OK** (healthy) je
vais bien; – adv (to work etc) bien; – vt (pt
& pp OKed, pres p OKing) approuver.

okay [əʊ'keɪ] = OK.

old [əʊld] a (-er, -est) vieux; (former)
ancien; **how o. is he?** quel âge a-t-il?; **he's
ten years o.** il a dix ans, il est âgé de dix
ans; **he's older than** il est plus âgé que; **an
older son** un fils aîné; **the oldest son** le fils
aîné; **o. enough to do** assez grand pour
faire; **o. enough to marry/vote** en âge de se
marier/de voter; **an o. man** un vieillard, un
vieil homme; **an o. woman** une vieille
(femme); **to get** or **grow old(er)** vieillir; **o.
age** vieillesse f; **the O. Testament** l'Ancien
Testament; **the O. World** l'Ancien Monde;
any o. how Fam n'importe comment; – n
the o. (people) les vieux mpl. ◆**o.-
'fashioned** a (customs etc) d'autrefois;
(idea, attitude) Pej vieux jeu inv; (person)
de la vieille école, Pej vieux jeu inv.
◆**o.-'timer** n (old man) Fam vieillard m.

olden ['əʊld(ə)n] a in o. days jadis.

olive ['ɒlɪv] n (fruit) olive f; – a o. (green)
(vert) olive inv; **o. oil** huile f d'olive; **o. tree**
olivier m.

Olympic [ə'lɪmpɪk] a olympique.

ombudsman ['ɒmbʊdzmən] n (pl -men)
Pol médiateur m.

omelet(te) ['ɒmlɪt] n omelette f; **cheese/etc
o.** omelette au fromage/etc.

omen ['əʊmən] n augure m. ◆**ominous** a
de mauvais augure; (tone) menaçant;
(noise) sinistre.

omit [əʊ'mɪt] vt (-tt-) omettre (**to do** de
faire). ◆**omission** n omission f.

omni- ['ɒmnɪ] prep omni-. ◆**om'nipotent**
a omnipotent.

on [ɒn] prep **1** (position) sur; **on the chair** sur
la chaise; **to put on (to)** mettre sur; **to look
out on** donner sur. **2** (concerning, about)
sur; **an article on** un article sur; **to speak** or
talk on Dickens/etc parler sur Dickens/etc.
3 (manner, means) à; **on foot** à pied; **on the
blackboard** au tableau; **on the radio** à la
radio; **on the train/plane/etc** dans le
train/avion/etc; **on holiday**, Am **on vacation** en vacances; **to be on** (course) suivre;
(project) travailler à; (salary) toucher;
(team, committee) être membre de, faire
partie de; **to keep** or **stay on** (road, path etc)
suivre; **it's on me!** (I'll pay) Fam c'est moi
qui paie! **4** (time) **on Monday** lundi; **on
Mondays** le lundi; **on May 3rd** le 3 mai; **on
the evening of May 3rd** le 3 mai au soir; **on
my arrival** à mon arrivée. **5** (+ present
participle) en; **on learning that . . .** en
apprenant que . . . ; **on seeing this** en
voyant ceci. **6** adv (ahead) en avant; (in
progress) en cours; (started) commencé;
(lid, brake) mis; (light, radio) allumé; (gas,
tap) ouvert; (machine) en marche; **to (and
on)** sans cesse; **to play/etc on** continuer à
jouer/etc; **she has her hat on** elle a mis or
elle porte son chapeau; **he has sth/nothing
on** il est habillé/tout nu; **I've got sth on**
(I'm busy) je suis pris; **the strike's on** la
grève aura lieu; **what's on?** TV qu'y a-t-il à
la télé?; Cin Th qu'est-ce qu'on joue?;
there's a film on on passe un film; **to be on
at s.o.** (pester) Fam être après qn; **I've been
on to him** Tel je l'ai eu au bout du fil; **to be
on to s.o.** (of police etc) être sur la piste de
qn; **from then on** à partir de là.
◆**on-coming** a (vehicle) qui vient en sens
inverse. ◆**on-going** a (project) en cours.

once [wʌns] adv (on one occasion) une fois;
(formerly) autrefois; **o. a month/etc** une
fois par mois/etc; **o. again**, **o. more** encore
une fois; **at o.** (immediately) tout de suite;
all at o. (suddenly) tout à coup; (at the same
time) à la fois; **o. and for all** une fois pour
toutes; – conj une fois que. ◆**o.-over** n to
give sth the o.-over (quick look) Fam
regarder qch d'un coup d'œil.

one [wʌn] a **1** un, une; **o. man** un homme; **o.
woman** une femme; **twenty-o.** vingt-et-un.
2 (sole) seul; **my o. (and only) aim** mon seul
(et unique) but. **3** (same) même; **in the o.
bus** dans le même bus; – pron **1** un, une; **do
you want o.?** en veux-tu (un)?; **he's o. of us**
il est des nôtres; **o. of them** l'un d'eux, l'une
d'elles; **a big/small/etc o.** un grand/petit/
etc; **this book is o. that I've read** ce livre est
parmi ceux que j'ai lus; **she's o.** (a teacher,
gardener etc) elle l'est; **this o.** celui-ci,
celle-ci; **that o.** celui-là, celle-là; **the o. who**
or **which** celui or celle qui; **it's Paul's o.** Fam
c'est celui de Paul; **it's my o.** Fam c'est à
moi; **another o.** un(e) autre; **I for o.** pour
ma part. **2** (impersonal) on; **o. knows** on
sait; **it helps o.** ça nous or vous aide; **one's**

family sa famille. ◆**one-'armed** a (person) manchot. ◆**one-'eyed** a borgne. ◆**one-'off** a, Am **one-of-a-'kind** a Fam unique, exceptionnel. ◆**one-'sided** a (judgement etc) partial; (contest) inégal; (decision) unilatéral. ◆**one-time** a (former) ancien. ◆**one-'way** a (street) à sens unique; (traffic) en sens unique; (ticket) Am simple.

oneself [wʌn'self] pron soi-même; (reflexive) se, s'; **to cut o.** se couper.

onion ['ʌnjən] n oignon m.

onlooker ['ɒnlʊkər] n spectateur, -trice mf.

only ['əʊnlɪ] a seul; **the o. house/etc** la seule maison/etc; **the o. one** le seul, la seule; **an o. son** un fils unique; – adv seulement, ne ... que; **I o. have ten, I have ten o.** je n'en ai que dix, j'en ai dix seulement; **if o.** si seulement; **not o.** non seulement; **I have o. just seen it** je viens tout juste de le voir; **o. he knows** lui seul le sait; – conj (but) Fam seulement; **o. I can't** seulement je ne peux pas.

onset ['ɒnset] n (of disease) début m; (of old age) approche m.

onslaught ['ɒnslɔːt] n attaque f.

onto ['ɒntuː] prep = on to.

onus ['əʊnəs] n inv **the o. is on you/etc** c'est votre/etc responsabilité (**to do** de faire).

onward(s) ['ɒnwəd(z)] adv en avant; **from that time o.** à partir de là.

onyx ['ɒnɪks] n (precious stone) onyx m.

ooze [uːz] vi **to o. (out)** suinter; – vt (blood etc) laisser couler.

opal ['əʊp(ə)l] n (precious stone) opale f.

opaque [əʊ'peɪk] a opaque; (unclear) Fig obscur.

open ['əʊpən] a ouvert; (site, view, road) dégagé; (car) décapoté, découvert; (meeting) public; (competition) ouvert à tous; (post) vacant; (attempt, envy) manifeste; (question) nòn résolu; (result) indécis; (ticket) Av open inv; **wide o.** grand ouvert; **in the o. air** en plein air; **in the o.** country en rase campagne; **the o. spaces** les grands espaces; **it's o. to doubt** c'est douteux; **o. to** (criticism, attack) exposé à; (ideas, suggestions) ouvert à; **I've got an o. mind on it** je n'ai pas d'opinion arrêtée là-dessus; **to leave o.** (date) ne pas préciser; – n (out) **in the o.** (outside) en plein air; **to sleep (out) in the o.** dormir à la belle étoile; **to bring (out) into the o.** (reveal) divulguer; – vt ouvrir; (conversation) entamer; (legs) écarter; **to o. out or up** ouvrir; – vi (of flower, eyes etc) s'ouvrir; (of shop, office etc) ouvrir; (of play) débuter; (of film) sortir; **the door opens** (is

opened) la porte s'ouvre; (can open) la porte ouvre; **to o. on to** (of window etc) donner sur; **to o. out** or up s'ouvrir; **to o. out** (widen) s'élargir; **to o. up** (open a or the door) ouvrir. ◆**—ing** n ouverture f; (of flower) éclosion f; (career prospect, trade outlet) débouché m; – a (time, speech) d'ouverture; **o. night** Th première f. ◆**—ly** adv (not secretly, frankly) ouvertement; (publicly) publiquement. ◆**—ness** n (frankness) franchise f; **o. of mind** ouverture f d'esprit.

open-air [əʊpən'eər] a (pool etc) en plein air. ◆**o.-'heart** a (operation) Med à cœur ouvert. ◆**o.-'necked** a (shirt) sans cravate. ◆**o.-'plan** a Archit sans cloisons.

opera ['ɒprə] n opéra m; **o. glasses** jumelles fpl de théâtre. ◆**ope'ratic** a d'opéra. ◆**ope'retta** n opérette f.

operat/e ['ɒpəreɪt] **1** vi (of machine etc) fonctionner; (proceed) opérer; – vt faire fonctionner; (business) gérer. **2** vi (of surgeon) opérer (**on s.o.** qn, **for** de). ◆**—ing** a **o. costs** frais mpl d'exploitation; **o. theatre**, Am **o. room** Med salle f d'opération; **o. wing** Med bloc m opératoire. ◆**ope'ration** n (working) fonctionnement m; Med Mil Math etc opération f; **in o.** (machine) en service; (plan) Fig en vigueur. ◆**ope'rational** a opérationnel. ◆**operative** a Med opératoire; (law, measure etc) en vigueur; – n ouvrier, -ière mf. ◆**operator** n Tel standardiste mf; (on machine) opérateur, -trice mf; (criminal) escroc m; **tour o.** organisateur, -trice mf de voyages, voyagiste m.

opinion [ə'pɪnjən] n opinion f, avis m; **in my o.** à mon avis. ◆**opinionated** a dogmatique.

opium ['əʊpɪəm] n opium m.

opponent [ə'pəʊnənt] n adversaire mf.

opportune ['ɒpətjuːn] a opportun. ◆**oppor'tunism** n opportunisme m.

opportunity [ɒpə'tjuːnɪtɪ] n occasion f (**to do** de faire); pl (prospects) perspectives fpl; **equal opportunities** des chances fpl égales.

oppos/e [ə'pəʊz] vt (person, measure etc) s'opposer à; (law, motion) Pol faire opposition à. ◆**—ed** a opposé (**to** à); **as o. to** par opposition à. ◆**—ing** a (team, interests) opposé. ◆**oppo'sition** n opposition f (**to** à); **the o.** (rival camp) Fam l'adversaire m.

opposite ['ɒpəzɪt] a (side etc) opposé; (house) d'en face; **one's o. number** (counterpart) son homologue mf; – adv (to sit etc) en face; – prep **o. (to)** en face de; – n **the o.** le contraire, l'opposé m.

oppress [ə'pres] *vt* (*tyrannize*) opprimer; (*of heat, anguish*) oppresser; **the oppressed** les opprimés *mpl.* ◆**oppression** *n* oppression *f.* ◆**oppressive** *a* (*ruler etc*) oppressif; (*heat*) oppressant; (*régime*) tyrannique. ◆**oppressor** *n* oppresseur *m.*

opt [ɒpt] *vi* **to o. for** opter pour; **to o. to do** choisir de faire; **to o. out** *Fam* refuser de participer (of à). ◆**option** *n* option *f*; (*subject*) *Sch* matière *f* à option; **she has no o.** elle n'a pas le choix. ◆**optional** *a* facultatif; **o. extra** (*on car etc*) option *f*, accessoire *m* en option.

optical ['ɒptɪk(ə)l] *a* (*glass*) optique; (*illusion, instrument etc*) d'optique. ◆**op'tician** *n* opticien, -ienne *mf.*

optimism ['ɒptɪmɪz(ə)m] *n* optimisme *m.* ◆**optimist** *n* optimiste *mf.* ◆**opti'mistic** *a* optimiste. ◆**opti'mistically** *adv* avec optimisme.

optimum ['ɒptɪməm] *a & n* optimum (*m*); **the o. temperature** la température optimum. ◆**optimal** *a* optimal.

opulent ['ɒpjʊlənt] *a* opulent. ◆**opulence** *n* opulence *f.*

or [ɔːr] *conj* ou; **one or two** un ou deux; **he doesn't drink or smoke** il ne boit ni ne fume; **ten or so** environ dix.

oracle ['ɒrək(ə)l] *n* oracle *m.*

oral ['ɔːrəl] *a* oral; – *n* (*examination*) *Sch* oral *m.*

orange ['ɒrɪndʒ] **1** *n* (*fruit*) orange *f*; – *a* (*drink*) à l'orange; **o. tree** oranger *m.* **2** *a & n* (*colour*) orange *a & m inv.* ◆**orangeade** *n* orangeade *f.*

orang-outang [ɔːræŋuːˈtæŋ] *n* orang-ou-tan(g) *m.*

oration [ɔːˈreɪʃ(ə)n] *n* **funeral o.** oraison *f* funèbre.

oratory ['ɒrətərɪ] *n* (*words*) *Pej* rhétorique *f.*

orbit ['ɔːbɪt] *n* (*of planet etc*) & *Fig* orbite *f*; – *vt* (*sun etc*) graviter autour de.

orchard ['ɔːtʃəd] *n* verger *m.*

orchestra ['ɔːkɪstrə] *n* (*classical*) orchestre *m.* ◆**or'chestral** *a* (*music*) orchestral; (*concert*) symphonique. ◆**orchestrate** *vt* (*organize*) & *Mus* orchestrer.

orchid ['ɔːkɪd] *n* orchidée *f.*

ordain [ɔːˈdeɪn] *vt* (*priest*) ordonner; **to o. that** décréter que.

ordeal [ɔːˈdiːl] *n* épreuve *f*, supplice *m.*

order ['ɔːdər] *n* (*command, structure, association etc*) ordre *m*; (*purchase*) *Com* commande *f*; **in o.** (*drawer, room etc*) en ordre; (*passport etc*) en règle; **in** (**numerical**) **o.** dans l'ordre numérique; **in working o.** en état de marche; **in o. of age** par ordre

d'âge; **in o. to do** pour faire; **in o. that** que (+ *sub*); **it's in o. to smoke**/*etc* (*allowed*) il est permis de fumer/*etc*; **out of o.** (*machine*) en panne; (*telephone*) en dérangement; **to make** *or* **place an o.** *Com* passer une commande; **on o.** *Com* commandé; **money o.** mandat *m*; **postal o.** mandat *m* postal; – *vt* (*command*) ordonner (**s.o. to do** à qn de faire); (*meal, goods etc*) commander; (*taxi*) appeler; **to o. s.o. around** commander qn, régenter qn; – *vi* (*in café etc*) commander. ◆—**ly 1** *a* (*tidy*) ordonné; (*mind*) méthodique; (*crowd*) discipliné. **2** *n Mil* planton *m*; (*in hospital*) garçon *m* de salle.

ordinal ['ɔːdɪnəl] *a* (*number*) ordinal.

ordinary ['ɔːd(ə)nrɪ] *a* (*usual*) ordinaire; (*average*) moyen; (*mediocre*) médiocre, ordinaire; **an o. individual** un simple particulier; **an o. use** d'usage courant; **in the o. course of events** en temps normal; **in the o. way** normalement; **it's out of the o.** ça sort de l'ordinaire.

ordination [ɔːdɪˈneɪʃ(ə)n] *n Rel* ordination *f.*

ordnance ['ɔːdnəns] *n* (*guns*) *Mil* artillerie *f.*

ore [ɔːr] *n* minerai *m.*

organ ['ɔːgən] *n* **1** *Anat & Fig* organe *m.* **2** *Mus* orgue *m*, orgues *fpl*; **barrel o.** orgue *m* de Barbarie. ◆**organist** *n* organiste *mf.*

organic [ɔːˈgænɪk] *a* organique. ◆**'organism** *n* organisme *m.*

organization [ɔːgənaɪˈzeɪʃ(ə)n] *n* (*arrangement, association*) organisation *f.*

organiz/e ['ɔːgənaɪz] *vt* organiser. ◆—**ed** *a* (*mind, group etc*) organisé. ◆—**er** *n* organisateur, -trice *m.*

orgasm ['ɔːgæz(ə)m] *n* orgasme *m.*

orgy ['ɔːdʒɪ] *n* orgie *f.*

orient ['ɔːrɪənt] *vt Am =* **orientate.** ◆**orientate** *vt* orienter.

Orient ['ɔːrɪənt] *n* **the O.** l'Orient *m.* ◆**ori'ental** *a & n* oriental, -ale (*mf*).

orifice ['ɒrɪfɪs] *n* orifice *m.*

origin ['ɒrɪdʒɪn] *n* origine *f.*

original [əˈrɪdʒɪn(ə)l] *a* (*first*) premier, originel, primitif; (*novel, unusual*) original; (*sin*) originel; (*copy, version*) original; – *n* (*document etc*) original *m.* ◆**origi'nality** *n* originalité *f.* ◆**originally** *adv* (*at first*) à l'origine; (*in a novel way*) originalement; **she comes o. from** elle est originaire de. ◆**originate** *vi* (*begin*) prendre naissance (**in** dans); **to o. from** (*of idea etc*) émaner de; (*of person*) être originaire de; **to o.** *vt* être l'auteur de. ◆**originator** *n* auteur *m* (**of** de).

ornament ['ɔːnəmənt] *n* (*decoration*) orne-

ment *m*; *pl* (*vases etc*) bibelots *mpl*.
◆**orna'mental** *a* ornemental. ◆**orna-men'tation** *n* ornementation *f*. ◆**or'nate** *a* (*style etc*) (très) orné. ◆**or'nately** *adv* (*decorated etc*) de façon surchargée, à outrance.

orphan ['ɔːf(ə)n] *n* orphelin, -ine *mf*; – *a* orphelin. ◆**orphaned** *a* orphelin; **he was o. by the accident** l'accident l'a rendu orphelin. ◆**orphanage** *n* orphelinat *m*.

orthodox ['ɔːθədɒks] *a* orthodoxe. ◆**orthodoxy** *n* orthodoxie *f*.

orthop(a)edics [ɔːθə'piːdiks] *n* orthopédie *f*.

Oscar ['ɒskər] *n* Cin oscar *m*.

oscillate ['ɒsɪleɪt] *vi* osciller.

ostensibly [ɒ'stensɪblɪ] *adv* apparemment, en apparence.

ostentation [ɒsten'teɪʃ(ə)n] *n* ostentation *f*. ◆**ostentatious** *a* plein d'ostentation, prétentieux.

ostracism ['ɒstrəsɪz(ə)m] *n* ostracisme *m*. ◆**ostracize** *vt* proscrire, frapper d'ostracisme.

ostrich ['ɒstrɪtʃ] *n* autruche *f*.

other ['ʌðər] *a* autre; **o. people** d'autres; **the o. one** l'autre *mf*; **I have no o. gloves than these** je n'ai pas d'autres gants que ceux-ci; – *pron* autre; (*some*) **others** d'autres; **some do, others don't** les uns le font, les autres ne le font pas; **none o. than, no o. than** nul autre que; – *adv* **o. than** autrement que. ◆**otherwise** *adv* autrement; – *a* (*different*) (tout) autre.

otter ['ɒtər] *n* loutre *f*.

ouch! [aʊtʃ] *int* aïe!, ouille!

ought [ɔːt] *v aux* **1** (*obligation, desirability*) **you o. to leave** tu devrais partir; **I o. to have done it** j'aurais dû le faire; **he said he o. to stay** il a dit qu'il devait rester. **2** (*probability*) **it o. to be ready** ça devrait être prêt.

ounce [aʊns] *n* (*measure*) & *Fig* once *f* (= 28,35 *g*).

our [aʊər] *poss a* notre, *pl* nos. ◆**ours** *pron* le nôtre, la nôtre, *pl* les nôtres; **this book is o.** ce livre est à nous *or* est le nôtre; **a friend of o.** un ami à nous. ◆**our'selves** *pron* nous-mêmes; (*reflexive & after prep etc*) nous; **we wash o.** nous nous lavons.

oust [aʊst] *vt* évincer (**from** de).

out [aʊt] *adv* (*outside*) dehors; (*not at home etc*) sorti; (*light, fire*) éteint; (*news, secret*) connu, révélé; (*flower*) ouvert; (*book*) publié, sorti; (*finished*) fini; **to be** *or* **go o. a lot** sortir beaucoup; **he's o. in Italy** il est (parti) en Italie; **o. there** là-bas; **to have a**

day o. sortir pour la journée; **5 km o.** *Nau* à 5 km du rivage; **the sun's o.** il fait (du) soleil; **the tide's o.** la marée est basse; **you're o.** (*wrong*) tu t'es trompé; (*in game etc*) tu es éliminé (**of** de); **the trip** *or* **journey o.** l'aller *m*; **to be o. to win** être résolu à gagner; – *prep* **o. of** (*outside*) en dehors de; (*danger, breath, reach, water*) hors de; (*without*) sans; **o. of pity/love/etc** par pitié/amour/*etc*; **to look/jump/etc o. of** (*window etc*) regarder/sauter/*etc* par; **to drink/take/copy o. of** boire/prendre/copier dans; **made o. of** (*wood etc*) fait en; **to make sth o. of a box/rag/etc** faire qch avec une boîte/un chiffon/*etc*; **a page o. of** une page de; **she's o. of town** elle n'est pas en ville; **5 km o. of** (*away from*) à 5 km de; **four o. of five** quatre sur cinq; **o. of the blue** de manière inattendue; **to feel o. of it** *or* **of things** se sentir hors du coup. ◆**'out-and-out** *a* (*cheat, liar etc*) achevé; (*believer*) à tout crin. ◆**o.-of-'date** *a* (*expired*) périmé; (*old-fashioned*) démodé. ◆**o.-of-'doors** *adv* dehors. ◆**o.-of-the-'way** *a* (*place*) écarté.

outbid [aʊt'bɪd] *vt* (*pt & pp* outbid, *pres p* outbidding) **to o. s.o.** (sur)enchérir sur qn.

outboard ['aʊtbɔːd] *a* **o. motor** *Nau* moteur *m* hors-bord *inv*.

outbreak ['aʊtbreɪk] *n* (*of war*) début *m*; (*of violence, pimples*) éruption *f*; (*of fever*) accès *m*; (*of hostilities*) ouverture *f*.

outbuilding ['aʊtbɪldɪŋ] *n* (*of mansion, farm*) dépendance *f*.

outburst ['aʊtbɜːst] *n* (*of anger, joy*) explosion *f*; (*of violence*) flambée *f*; (*of laughter*) éclat *m*.

outcast ['aʊtkɑːst] *n* (**social**) **o.** paria *m*.

outcome ['aʊtkʌm] *n* résultat *m*, issue *f*.

outcry ['aʊtkraɪ] *n* tollé *m*.

outdated [aʊt'deɪtɪd] *a* démodé.

outdistance [aʊt'dɪstəns] *vt* distancer.

outdo [aʊt'duː] *vt* (*pt* outdid, *pp* outdone) surpasser (**o** en).

outdoor ['aʊtdɔːr] *a* (*game*) de plein air; (*pool, life*) en plein air; **o. clothes** tenue *f* pour sortir. ◆**out'doors** *adv* dehors.

outer ['aʊtər] *a* extérieur; **o. space** l'espace *m* (cosmique); **the o. suburbs** la grande banlieue.

outfit ['aʊtfɪt] *n* équipement *m*; (*kit*) trousse *f*; (*toy*) panoplie *f* (*de pompier, cow-boy etc*); (*clothes*) costume *m*; (*for woman*) toilette *f*; (*group, gang*) *Fam* bande *f*; (*firm*) *Fam* boîte *f*; **sports/ski o.** tenue *f* de sport/de ski. ◆**outfitter** *n* chemisier *m*.

outgoing ['aʊtgəʊɪŋ] **1** *a* (*minister etc*)

sortant; (*mail, ship*) en partance. **2** *a* (*sociable*) liant, ouvert. **3** *npl* (*expenses*) dépenses *fpl.*

outgrow [aʊt'grəʊ] *vt* (*pt* **outgrew**, *pp* **outgrown**) (*clothes*) devenir trop grand pour; (*habit*) perdre (en grandissant); **to o. s.o.** (*grow more than*) grandir plus vite que qn.

outhouse ['aʊthaʊs] *n* (*of mansion, farm*) dépendance *f*; (*lavatory*) *Am* cabinets *mpl* extérieurs.

outing ['aʊtɪŋ] *n* sortie *f*, excursion *f*.

outlandish [aʊt'lændɪʃ] *a* (*weird*) bizarre; (*barbaric*) barbare.

outlast [aʊt'lɑːst] *vt* durer plus longtemps que; (*survive*) survivre à.

outlaw ['aʊtlɔː] *n* hors-la-loi *m inv*; – *vt* (*ban*) proscrire.

outlay ['aʊtleɪ] *n* (*money*) dépense(s) *f(pl)*.

outlet ['aʊtlet] *n* (*for liquid, of tunnel etc*) sortie *f*; *El* prise *f* de courant; (*market for goods*) *Com* débouché *m*; (*for feelings, energy*) moyen *m* d'exprimer, exutoire *m*; **retail o.** *Com* point *m* de vente, magasin *m*.

outline ['aʊtlaɪn] *n* (*shape*) contour *m*, profil *m*; (*rough*) **o.** (*of article, plan etc*) esquisse *f*; **the broad** *or* **general** *or* **main outline(s)** (*chief features*) les grandes lignes; – *vt* (*plan, situation*) décrire à grands traits, esquisser; (*book, speech*) résumer; **to be outlined against** (*of tree etc*) se profiler sur.

outlive [aʊt'lɪv] *vt* survivre à.

outlook ['aʊtlʊk] *n inv* (*for future*) perspective(s) *f(pl)*; (*point of view*) perspective *f* (**on** sur), attitude *f* (**on** à l'égard de); *Met* prévisions *fpl*.

outlying ['aʊtlaɪɪŋ] *a* (*remote*) isolé; (*neighbourhood*) périphérique.

outmoded [aʊt'məʊdɪd] *a* démodé.

outnumber [aʊt'nʌmbər] *vt* être plus nombreux que.

outpatient ['aʊtpeɪʃ(ə)nt] *n* malade *mf* en consultation externe.

outpost ['aʊtpəʊst] *n* avant-poste *m*.

output ['aʊtpʊt] *n* rendement *m*, production *f*; (*computer process*) sortie *f*; (*computer data*) donnée(s) *f(pl)* de sortie.

outrage ['aʊtreɪdʒ] *n* atrocité *f*, crime *m*; (*indignity*) indignité *f*; (*scandal*) scandale *m*; (*indignation*) indignation *f*; **bomb o.** attentat *m* à la bombe; – *vt* (*morals*) outrager; **outraged by sth** indigné de qch. ◆**out'rageous** *a* (*atrocious*) atroce; (*shocking*) scandaleux; (*dress, hat etc*) grotesque.

outright [aʊt'raɪt] *adv* (*completely*) complètement; (*to say, tell*) franchement; (*to be* killed) sur le coup; **to buy o.** (*for cash*) acheter au comptant; – ['aʊtraɪt] *a* (*complete*) complet; (*lie, folly*) pur; (*refusal, rejection etc*) catégorique, net; (*winner*) incontesté.

outset ['aʊtset] *n* **at the o.** au début; **from the o.** dès le départ.

outside [aʊt'saɪd] *adv* (au) dehors, à l'extérieur; **to go o.** sortir; – *prep* à l'extérieur de, en dehors de; (*beyond*) *Fig* en dehors de; **o. my room** *or* **door** à la porte de ma chambre; – *n* extérieur *m*, dehors *m*; – ['aʊtsaɪd] *a* extérieur; (*bus or train seat etc*) côté couloir *inv*; (*maximum*) *Fig* maximum; **the o. lane** *Aut* la voie de droite, *Am* la voie de gauche; **an o. chance** une faible chance. ◆**out'sider** *n* (*stranger*) étranger, -ère *mf*; *Sp* outsider *m*.

outsize ['aʊtsaɪz] *a* (*clothes*) grande taille *inv*.

outskirts ['aʊtskɜːts] *npl* banlieue *f*.

outsmart [aʊt'smɑːt] *vt* être plus malin que.

outspoken [aʊt'spəʊk(ə)n] *a* (*frank*) franc.

outstanding [aʊt'stændɪŋ] *a* remarquable, exceptionnel; (*problem, business*) non réglé, en suspens; (*debt*) impayé; **work o.** travail *m* à faire.

outstay [aʊt'steɪ] *vt* **to o. one's welcome** abuser de l'hospitalité de son hôte, s'incruster.

outstretched [aʊt'stretʃt] *a* (*arm*) tendu.

outstrip [aʊt'strɪp] *vt* (**-pp-**) devancer.

outward ['aʊtwəd] *a* (*look, movement*) vers l'extérieur; (*sign, appearance*) extérieur; **o. journey** *or* **trip** aller *m*. ◆**outward(s)** *adv* vers l'extérieur.

outweigh [aʊt'weɪ] *vt* (*be more important than*) l'emporter sur.

outwit [aʊt'wɪt] *vt* (**-tt-**) être plus malin que.

oval ['əʊv(ə)l] *a* & *n* ovale (*m*).

ovary ['əʊvərɪ] *n Anat* ovaire *m*.

ovation [əʊ'veɪʃ(ə)n] *n* (*standing*) **o.** ovation *f*.

oven ['ʌv(ə)n] *n* four *m*; (*hot place*) *Fig* fournaise *f*; **o. glove** gant *m* isolant.

over ['əʊvər] *prep* (*on*) sur; (*above*) au-dessus de; (*on the other side of*) de l'autre côté de; **bridge o. the river** pont *m* sur le fleuve; **to jump/look/etc o. sth** sauter/regarder/etc par-dessus qch; **to fall o. the balcony/etc** tomber du balcon/etc; **she fell o. it** elle en est tombée; **o. it** (*on*) dessus; (*above*) au-dessus; (*to jump etc*) par-dessus; **to criticize/etc o. sth** (*about*) critiquer/etc à propos de qch; **an advantage o.** un avantage sur *or* par rapport à; **o. the radio** (*on*) à la radio; **o. the phone** au téléphone; **o. the holidays** (*during*) pendant les vacances; **o. ten days** (*more than*) plus de dix jours; **men o. sixty** les hommes de plus de soixante ans; **o. and above** en plus de; **he's o. his flu** (*recovered from*) il est remis de sa grippe; **all o. Spain** (*everywhere in*) dans toute l'Espagne, partout en Espagne; **all o. the carpet** (*everywhere on*) partout sur le tapis; – *adv* (*above*) (par-)dessus; (*finished*) fini; (*danger*) passé; (*again*) encore; (*too*) trop; **jump o.!** sautez par-dessus!; **o. here** ici; **o. there** là-bas; **to be** *or* **come** *or* **go o.** (*visit*) passer; **he's o. in Italy** il est (parti) en Italie; **she's o. from Paris** elle est venue de Paris; **all o.** (*everywhere*) partout; **wet all o.** tout mouillé; **it's (all) o.!** (*finished*) c'est fini!; **she's o.** (*fallen*) elle est tombée; **a kilo or o.** (*more*) un kilo ou plus; **I have ten o.** (*left*) il m'en reste dix; **there's some bread o.** il reste du pain; **o. and o.** (*again*) (*often*) à plusieurs reprises; **to start all o.** (*again*) recommencer à zéro; **o. pleased**/*etc* trop content/*etc*. ◆**o.-a'bundant** *a* surabondant. ◆**o.-de'veloped** *a* trop développé. ◆**o.-fa'miliar** *a* trop familier. ◆**o.-in'dulge** *vt* (*one's desires etc*) céder trop facilement à; (*person*) trop gâter. ◆**o.-sub'scribed** *a* (*course*) ayant trop d'inscrits.

overall 1 [əʊvər'ɔːl] *a* (*measurement, length, etc*) total; (*result, effort etc*) global; – *adv* globalement. **2** ['əʊvərɔːl] *n* blouse *f* (de travail); *pl* bleus *mpl* de travail.

overawe [əʊvər'ɔː] *vt* intimider.

overbalance [əʊvə'bæləns] *vi* basculer.

overbearing [əʊvə'beərɪŋ] *a* autoritaire.

overboard ['əʊvəbɔːd] *adv* à la mer.

overburden [əʊvə'bɜːd(ə)n] *vt* surcharger.

overcast [əʊvə'kɑːst] *a* (*sky*) couvert.

overcharge [əʊvə'tʃɑːdʒ] *vt* **to o. s.o. for sth** faire payer qch trop cher à qn.

overcoat ['əʊvəkəʊt] *n* pardessus *m*.

overcome [əʊvə'kʌm] *vt* (*pt* **overcame**, *pp* **overcome**) (*enemy, shyness etc*) vaincre; (*disgust, problem*) surmonter; **to be o. by** (*fatigue, grief*) être accablé par; (*fumes, temptation*) succomber à; **he was o. by emotion** l'émotion eut raison de lui.

overcrowded [əʊvə'kraʊdɪd] *a* (*house, country*) surpeuplé; (*bus, train*) bondé. ◆**overcrowding** *n* surpeuplement *m*.

overdo [əʊvə'duː] *vt* (*pt* **overdid**, *pp* **overdone**) exagérer; *Culin* cuire trop; **to o. it** (*exaggerate*) exagérer; (*work too much*) se surmener; *Iron* se fatiguer.

overdose ['əʊvədəʊs] *n* overdose *f*, dose *f* excessive (*de barbituriques etc*).

overdraft ['əʊvədrɑːft] *n* *Fin* découvert *m*. ◆**over'draw** *vt* (*pt* **overdrew**, *pp* **overdrawn**) (*account*) mettre à découvert.

overdress [əʊvə'dres] *vi* s'habiller avec trop de recherche.

overdue [əʊvə'djuː] *a* (*train etc*) en retard; (*debt*) arriéré; (*apology, thanks*) tardif.

overeat [əʊvər'iːt] *vi* manger trop.

overestimate [əʊvər'estɪmeɪt] *vt* surestimer.

overexcited [əʊvərɪk'saɪtɪd] *a* surexcité.

overfeed [əʊvə'fiːd] *vt* (*pt & pp* **overfed**) suralimenter.

overflow 1 ['əʊvəfləʊ] *n* (*outlet*) trop-plein *m*; (*of people, objects*) *Fig* excédent *m*. **2** [əʊvə'fləʊ] *vi* déborder (**with** de); **to be overflowing with** (*of town, shop, house etc*) regorger de (*visiteurs, livres etc*).

overgrown [əʊvə'grəʊn] *a* envahi par la végétation; **o. with** (*weeds etc*) envahi par; **you're an o. schoolgirl** *Fig Pej* tu as la mentalité d'une écolière.

overhang [əʊvə'hæŋ] *vi* (*pt & pp* **overhung**) faire saillie; – *vt* surplomber.

overhaul [əʊvə'hɔːl] *vt* (*vehicle, doctrine etc*) réviser; – ['əʊvəhɔːl] *n* révision *f*.

overhead [əʊvə'hed] *adv* au-dessus; – ['əʊvəhed] **1** *a* (*railway etc*) aérien. **2** *npl* (*expenses*) frais *mpl* généraux.

overhear [əʊvə'hɪər] *vt* (*pt & pp* **overheard**) surprendre, entendre.

overheat [əʊvə'hiːt] *vt* surchauffer; – *vi* (*of engine*) chauffer.

overjoyed [əʊvə'dʒɔɪd] *a* ravi, enchanté.

overland ['əʊvəlænd] *a & adv* par voie de terre.

overlap [əʊvə'læp] *vi* (**-pp-**) se chevaucher; – *vt* chevaucher; – ['əʊvəlæp] *n* chevauchement *m*.

overleaf [əʊvə'liːf] *adv* au verso.

overload [əʊvə'ləʊd] *vt* surcharger.

overlook [əʊvə'lʊk] *vt* **1** (*not notice*) ne pas remarquer; (*forget*) oublier; (*disregard, ignore*) passer sur. **2** (*of window, house etc*) donner sur; (*of tower, fort*) dominer.

overly ['əʊvəlɪ] *adv* excessivement.

overmuch [əʊvə'mʌtʃ] *adv* trop, excessivement.

overnight [əʊvə'naɪt] *adv* (*during the night*) (pendant) la nuit; (*all night*) toute la nuit; (*suddenly*) *Fig* du jour au lendemain; **to stay o.** passer la nuit; – ['əʊvənaɪt] *a* (*stay*) d'une nuit; (*clothes*) pour une nuit; (*trip*) de nuit.

overpass ['əʊvəpæs] *n* (*bridge*) *Am* toboggan *m*.

overpopulated [əuvə'pɒpuleɪtɪd] *a* sur-peuplé.

overpower [əuvə'pauər] *vt* (*physically*) maîtriser; (*defeat*) vaincre; *Fig* accabler. ◆—**ing** *a* (*charm etc*) irrésistible; (*heat etc*) accablant.

overrat/e [əuvə'reɪt] *vt* surestimer. ◆—**ed** *a* surfait.

overreach [əuvə'riːtʃ] *vt* **to o. oneself** trop entreprendre.

overreact [əuvərɪ'ækt] *vi* réagir excessivement.

overrid/e [əuvə'raɪd] *vt* (*pt* **overrode**, *pp* **overridden**) (*invalidate*) annuler; (*take no notice of*) passer outre à; (*be more important than*) l'emporter sur. ◆—**ing** *a* (*passion*) prédominant; (*importance*) primordial.

overrule [əuvə'ruːl] *vt* (*reject*) rejeter.

overrun [əuvə'rʌn] *vt* (*pt* **overran**, *pp* **overrun**, *pres p* **overrunning**) **1** (*invade*) envahir. **2** (*go beyond*) aller au-delà de.

overseas [əuvə'siːz] *adv* (*Africa etc*) outre-mer; (*abroad*) à l'étranger; — ['əuvəsiːz] *a* (*visitor, market etc*) d'outre-mer; étranger; (*trade*) extérieur.

overse/e [əuvə'siː] *vt* (*pt* **oversaw**, *pp* **overseen**) surveiller. ◆—**er** ['əuvəsiːər] *n* (*foreman*) contremaître *m*.

overshadow [əuvə'ʃædəu] *vt* (*make less important*) éclipser; (*make gloomy*) assombrir.

overshoot [əuvə'ʃuːt] *vt* (*pt & pp* **overshot**) (*of aircraft*) & *Fig* dépasser.

oversight ['əuvəsaɪt] *n* omission *f*, oubli *m*; (*mistake*) erreur *f*.

oversimplify [əuvə'sɪmplɪfaɪ] *vti* trop simplifier.

oversize(d) ['əuvəsaɪz(d)] *a* trop grand.

oversleep [əuvə'sliːp] *vi* (*pt & pp* **overslept**) dormir trop longtemps, oublier de se réveiller.

overspend [əuvə'spend] *vi* dépenser trop.

overstaffed [əuvə'stɑːft] *a* au personnel pléthorique.

overstay [əuvə'steɪ] *vt* **to o. one's welcome** abuser de l'hospitalité de son hôte, s'incruster.

overstep [əuvə'step] *vt* (**-pp-**) dépasser.

overt ['əuvɜːt] *a* manifeste.

overtake [əuvə'teɪk] *vt* (*pt* **overtook**, *pp* **overtaken**) dépasser; (*vehicle*) doubler, dépasser; **overtaken by** (*nightfall, storm*) surpris par; — *vi Aut* doubler, dépasser.

overtax [əuvə'tæks] *vt* **1** (*strength*) excéder; (*brain*) fatiguer. **2** (*taxpayer*) surimposer.

overthrow [əuvə'θrəu] *vt* (*pt* **overthrew**, *pp* **overthrown**) *Pol* renverser; — ['əuvəθrəu] *n* renversement *m*.

overtime ['əuvətaɪm] *n* heures *fpl* supplémentaires; — *adv* **to work o.** faire des heures supplémentaires.

overtones ['əuvətəunz] *npl Fig* note *f*, nuance *f* (**of** de).

overture ['əuvətjuər] *n Mus & Fig* ouverture *f*.

overturn [əuvə'tɜːn] *vt* (*chair, table etc*) renverser; (*car, boat*) retourner; (*decision etc*) *Fig* annuler; — *vi* (*of car, boat*) se retourner.

overweight [əuvə'weɪt] *a* **to be o.** (*of suitcase etc*) peser trop; (*of person*) avoir des kilos en trop.

overwhelm [əuvə'welm] *vt* (*of feelings, heat etc*) accabler; (*defeat*) écraser; (*amaze*) bouleverser. ◆—**ed** *a* (*overjoyed*) ravi (**by, with** de); **o. with** (*grief, work etc*) accablé de; (*offers*) submergé par; **o. by** (*kindness, gift etc*) vivement touché par. ◆—**ing** *a* (*heat, grief etc*) accablant; (*majority*) écrasant; (*desire*) irrésistible; (*impression*) dominant. ◆—**ingly** *adv* (*to vote, reject etc*) en masse; (*utterly*) carrément.

overwork [əuvə'wɜːk] *n* surmenage *m*; — *vi* se surmener; — *vt* surmener.

overwrought [əuvə'rɔːt] *a* (*tense*) tendu.

owe [əu] *vt* devoir (**to** à); **I'll o. it (to) you, I'll o. you (for) it** (*money*) je te le devrai; **to o. it to oneself to do** se devoir de faire. ◆**owing 1** *a* (*money etc*) dû, qu'on doit. **2** *prep* **o. to** à cause de.

owl [aul] *n* hibou *m*.

own [əun] **1** *a* propre; **my o. house** ma propre maison; — *pron* **it's my (very) o.** c'est à moi (tout seul); **a house of his o.** sa propre maison, sa maison à lui; **(all) on one's o.** (*alone*) tout seul; **to get one's o. back** prendre sa revanche (**on** sur, **for** de); **to come into one's o.** (*fulfil oneself*) s'épanouir. **2** *vt* (*possess*) posséder; **who owns this ball/etc?** à qui appartient cette balle/etc? **3** *vi* **to o. up** (*confess*) avouer; **to o. up to sth** avouer qch. ◆**owner** *n* propriétaire *mf*. ◆**ownership** *n* possession *f*; **home o.** accession *f* à la propriété; **public o.** *Econ* nationalisation *f*.

ox, *pl* **oxen** [ɒks, 'ɒks(ə)n] *n* bœuf *m*.

oxide ['ɒksaɪd] *n Ch* oxide *m*. ◆**oxidize** *vi* s'oxyder; — *vt* oxyder.

oxygen ['ɒksɪdʒ(ə)n] *n* oxygène *m*; — *a* (*mask, tent*) à oxygène.

oyster ['ɔɪstər] *n* huître *f*.

P

P, p [piː] *n* P, p *m*.

p [piː] *abbr* = **penny, pence.**

pa [pɑː] *n* (*father*) *Fam* papa *m*.

pace [peɪs] *n* (*speed*) pas *m*, allure *f*; (*measure*) pas *m*; **to keep p. with** (*follow*) suivre; (*in work, progress*) se maintenir à la hauteur de; – *vi* **to p. up and down** faire les cent pas; – *vt* (*room etc*) arpenter. ◆**pacemaker** *n* (*device*) stimulateur *m* cardiaque.

Pacific [pə'sɪfɪk] *a* (*coast etc*) pacifique; – *n* **the P.** le Pacifique.

pacify ['pæsɪfaɪ] *vt* (*country*) pacifier; (*calm, soothe*) apaiser. ◆**pacifier** *n* (*dummy*) *Am* sucette *f*, tétine *f*. ◆**pacifist** *n* & *a* pacifiste (*mf*).

pack [pæk] **1** *n* (*bundle, packet*) paquet *m*; (*bale*) balle *f*; (*of animal*) charge *f*; (*rucksack*) sac *m* (à dos); *Mil* paquetage *m*; (*of hounds, wolves*) meute *f*; (*of runners*) *Sp* peloton *m*; (*of thieves*) bande *f*; (*of cards*) jeu *m*; (*of lies*) tissu *m*. **2** *vt* (*fill*) remplir (**with** de); (*excessively*) bourrer; (*suitcase*) faire; (*object into box etc*) emballer; (*object into suitcase*) mettre dans sa valise; (*make into package*) empaqueter; **to p. into** (*cram*) entasser dans; (*put*) mettre dans; **to p. away** (*tidy away*) ranger; **to p. (down)** (*compress, crush*) tasser; **to p. off** (*person*) *Fam* expédier; **to p. up** (*put into box*) emballer; (*put into case*) mettre dans sa valise; (*give up*) *Fam* laisser tomber; – *vi* (*fill one's bags*) faire ses valises; **to p. into** (*of people*) s'entasser dans; **to p. in or up** (*of machine, vehicle*) *Fam* tomber en panne; **to p. up** (*stop*) *Fam* s'arrêter; (*leave*) plier bagage. ◆**—ed** *a* (*bus, cinema etc*) bourré; **p. lunch** panier-repas *m*; **p. out** (*crowded*) *Fam* bourré. ◆**—ing** *n* (*material, action*) emballage *m*; **p. case** caisse *f* d'emballage.

packag/e ['pækɪdʒ] *n* paquet *m*; (*computer programs*) progiciel *m*; **p. deal** *Com* contrat *m* global, train *m* de propositions; **p. tour** voyage *m* organisé; – *vt* emballer, empaqueter. ◆**—ing** *n* (*material, action*) emballage *m*.

packet ['pækɪt] *n* paquet *m*; (*of sweets*) sachet *m*, paquet *m*; **to make/cost a p.** *Fam* faire/coûter beaucoup d'argent.

pact [pækt] *n* pacte *m*.

pad [pæd] *n* (*wad, plug*) tampon *m*; (*for writing, notes etc*) bloc *m*; (*on leg*) *Sp* jambière *f*; (*on knee*) *Sp* genouillère *f*; (*room*) *Sl* piaule *f*; **launch(ing) p.** rampe *f* de lancement; **ink(ing) p.** tampon *m* encreur; – *vt* (**-dd-**) (*stuff*) rembourrer, matelasser; **to p. out** (*speech, text*) délayer. ◆**padding** *n* rembourrage *m*; (*of speech, text*) délayage *m*.

paddle ['pæd(ə)l] **1** *vi* (*splash about*) barboter; (*dip one's feet*) se mouiller les pieds; – *n* **to have a (little) p.** se mouiller les pieds. **2** *n* (*pole*) pagaie *f*; **p. boat, p. steamer** bateau *m* à roues; – *vt* **to p. a canoe** pagayer.

paddock ['pædək] *n* enclos *m*; (*at racecourse*) paddock *m*.

paddy ['pædɪ] *n* (*field*) rizière *f*.

padlock ['pædlɒk] *n* (*on door etc*) cadenas *m*; (*on bicycle, moped*) antivol *m*; – *vt* (*door etc*) cadenasser.

p(a)ediatrician [piːdɪə'trɪʃ(ə)n] *n Med* pédiatre *mf*.

pagan ['peɪgən] *a* & *n* païen, -enne (*mf*). ◆**paganism** *n* paganisme *m*.

page [peɪdʒ] **1** *n* (*of book etc*) page *f*. **2** *n* **p. (boy)** (*in hotel etc*) chasseur *m*; (*at court*) *Hist* page *m*; – *vt* **to p. s.o.** faire appeler qn.

pageant ['pædʒənt] *n* grand spectacle *m* historique. ◆**pageantry** *n* pompe *f*, apparat *m*.

pagoda [pə'gəudə] *n* pagode *f*.

paid [peɪd] *see* **pay**; – *a* (*assassin etc*) à gages; **to put p. to** (*hopes, plans*) anéantir; **to put p. to s.o.** (*ruin*) couler qn.

pail [peɪl] *n* seau *m*.

pain [peɪn] *n* (*physical*) douleur *f*; (*grief*) peine *f*; *pl* (*efforts*) efforts *mpl*; **to have a p. in one's arm** avoir mal *or* une douleur au bras; **to be in p.** souffrir; **to go to** *or* **take (great) pains to do** (*exert oneself*) se donner du mal à faire; **to go to** *or* **take (great) pains not to do** (*be careful*) prendre bien soin de ne pas faire; **to be a p. (in the neck)** (*of person*) *Fam* être casse-pieds; – *vt* (*grieve*) peiner. ◆**p.-killer** *n* analgésique *m*, calmant *m*. ◆**painful** *a* (*illness, operation*) douloureux; (*arm, leg*) qui fait mal, douloureux; (*distressing*) douloureux, pénible; (*difficult*) pénible; (*bad*) *Fam* affreux. ◆**painless** *a* sans douleur; (*illness, operation*) indolore; (*easy*) *Fam* facile. ◆**painstaking** *a* (*person*) soigneux; (*work*) soigné.

paint [peɪnt] *n* peinture *f*; *pl* (*in box, tube*) couleurs *fpl*; – *vt* (*colour, describe*) peindre; **to p. blue**/*etc* peindre en bleu/*etc*; – *vi* peindre. ◆**—ing** *n* (*activity*) peinture *f*; (*picture*) tableau *m*, peinture *f*. ◆**—er** *n* peintre *m*. ◆**paintbrush** *n* pinceau *m*. ◆**paintwork** *n* peinture(s) *f(pl)*.

pair [peər] *n* paire *f*; (*man and woman*) couple *m*; **a p. of shorts** un short; **the p. of you** *Fam* vous deux; – *vi* **to p. off** (*of people*) former un couple; – *vt* (*marry*) marier.

pajama(s) [pəˈdʒɑːmə(z)] *a & npl Am* = **pyjama(s).**

Pakistan [pɑːkɪˈstɑːn] *n* Pakistan *m*. ◆**Pakistani** *a & n* pakistanais, -aise (*mf*).

pal [pæl] *n Fam* copain *m*, copine *f*; – *vi* (**-ll-**) **to p. up** devenir copains; **to p. up with** devenir copain avec.

palace ['pælɪs] *n* (*building*) palais *m*. ◆**palatial** [pəˈleɪʃ(ə)l] *a* comme un palais.

palatable ['pælətəb(ə)l] *a* (*food*) agréable; (*fact, idea etc*) acceptable.

palate ['pælɪt] *n Anat* palais *m*.

palaver [pəˈlɑːvər] *n Fam* (*fuss*) histoire(s) *f(pl)*; (*talk*) palabres *mpl*.

pale [peɪl] *a* (**-er, -est**) (*face, colour etc*) pâle; **p. ale** bière *f* blonde; – *vi* pâlir. ◆**—ness** *n* pâleur *f*.

palette ['pælɪt] *n* (*of artist*) palette *f*.

paling ['peɪlɪŋ] *n* (*fence*) palissade *f*.

pall [pɔːl] **1** *vi* devenir insipide *or* ennuyeux (on **pour**). **2** *n* (*of smoke*) voile *m*.

pallbearer ['pɔːlbeərər] *n* personne *f* qui aide à porter un cercueil.

pallid ['pælɪd] *a* pâle. ◆**pallor** *n* pâleur *f*.

pally ['pælɪ] *a* (**-ier, -iest**) *Fam* copain *am*, copine *af* (**with** avec).

palm [pɑːm] **1** *n* (*of hand*) paume *f*. **2** *n* (*symbol*) palme *f*; **p.** (**tree**) palmier *m*; **p.** (**leaf**) palme *f*; **P. Sunday** les Rameaux *mpl*. **3** *vt Fam* **to p. sth off** (*pass off*) refiler qch (on à); **to p. s.o. off on s.o.** coller qn à qn.

palmist ['pɑːmɪst] *n* chiromancien, -ienne *mf*. ◆**palmistry** *n* chiromancie *f*.

palpable ['pælpəb(ə)l] *a* (*obvious*) manifeste.

palpitate ['pælpɪteɪt] *vi* (*of heart*) palpiter. ◆**palpi'tation** *n* palpitation *f*.

paltry ['pɔːltrɪ] *a* (**-ier, -iest**) misérable, dérisoire.

pamper ['pæmpər] *vt* dorloter.

pamphlet ['pæmflɪt] *n* brochure *f*.

pan [pæn] **1** *n* casserole *f*; (*for frying*) poêle *f* (à frire); (*of lavatory*) cuvette *f*. **2** *vt* (**-nn-**) (*criticize*) *Fam* éreinter. **3** *vi* (**-nn-**) **to p. out** (*succeed*) aboutir.

Pan- [pæn] *pref* pan-.

panacea [pænəˈsɪə] *n* panacée *f*.

panache [pəˈnæʃ] *n* (*showy manner*) panache *m*.

pancake ['pænkeɪk] *n* crêpe *f*.

pancreas ['pæŋkrɪəs] *n Anat* pancréas *m*.

panda ['pændə] *n* (*animal*) panda *m*; **P. car** = voiture *f* pie *inv* (de la police).

pandemonium [pændɪˈməʊnɪəm] *n* (*chaos*) chaos *m*; (*uproar*) tumulte *m*; (*place*) bazar *m*.

pander ['pændər] *vi* **to p. to** (*tastes, fashion etc*) sacrifier à; **to p. to s.o.** *or* **to s.o.'s desires** se plier aux désirs de qn.

pane [peɪn] *n* vitre *f*, carreau *m*.

panel ['pæn(ə)l] *n* **1** (*of door etc*) panneau *m*; (**control**) **p.** *Tech El* console *f*; (**instrument**) **p.** *Av Aut* tableau *m* de bord. **2** (*of judges*) jury *m*; (*of experts*) groupe *m*; (*of candidates*) équipe *f*; **a p. of guests** des invités; **a p. game** *TV Rad* un jeu par équipes. ◆**panelled** *a* (*room etc*) lambrissé. ◆**panelling** *n* lambris *m*. ◆**panellist** *n* *TV Rad* (*guest*) invité, -ée *mf*; (*expert*) expert *m*; (*candidate*) candidat, -ate *mf*.

pangs [pæŋz] *npl* **p. of conscience** remords *mpl* (de conscience); **p. of hunger**/**death** les affres *fpl* de la faim/de la mort.

panic ['pænɪk] *n* panique *f*; **to get into a p.** paniquer; – *vi* (**-ck-**) s'affoler, paniquer. ◆**p.-stricken** *a* affolé. ◆**panicky** (*person*) *a Fam* qui s'affole facilement; **to get p.** s'affoler.

panorama [pænəˈrɑːmə] *n* panorama *m*. ◆**panoramic** *a* panoramique.

pansy ['pænzɪ] *n Bot* pensée *f*.

pant [pænt] *vi* (*gasp*) haleter.

panther ['pænθər] *n* (*animal*) panthère *f*.

panties ['pæntɪz] *npl* (*female underwear*) slip *m*.

pantomime ['pæntəmaɪm] *n* (*show*) spectacle *m* de Noël.

pantry ['pæntrɪ] *n* (*larder*) garde-manger *m inv*; (*storeroom in hotel etc*) office *m or f*.

pants [pænts] *npl* (*male underwear*) slip *m*; (*loose, long*) caleçon *m*; (*female underwear*) slip *m*; (*trousers*) *Am* pantalon *m*.

pantyhose ['pæntɪhəʊz] *n* (*tights*) *Am* collant(s) *m(pl)*.

papacy ['peɪpəsɪ] *n* papauté *f*. ◆**papal** *a* papal.

paper ['peɪpər] *n* papier *m*; (*newspaper*) journal *m*; (*wallpaper*) papier *m* peint;

(*exam*) épreuve f (écrite); (*student's exercise*) *Sch* copie f; (*learned article*) exposé m, communication f; **brown p.** papier m d'emballage; **to put down on p.** mettre par écrit; – a (*bag etc*) en papier; (*cup, plate*) en carton; **p. clip** trombone m; **p. knife** coupe-papier m inv; **p. mill** papeterie f; **p. shop** marchand m de journaux; – vt (*room, wall*) tapisser. ◆**paperback** n (*book*) livre m de poche. ◆**paperboy** n livreur m de journaux. ◆**paperweight** n presse-papiers m inv. ◆**paperwork** n Com écritures fpl; (*red tape*) Pej paperasserie f.

paprika ['pæprɪkə] n paprika m.

par [paːr] n **on a p.** au même niveau (**with** que); **below p.** (*unwell*) Fam pas en forme.

para- ['pærə] pref para-.

parable ['pærəb(ə)l] n (*story*) parabole f.

parachute ['pærəʃuːt] n parachute f; **to drop by p.** (*men, supplies*) parachuter; – vi descendre en parachute; – vt parachuter. ◆**parachutist** n parachutiste mf.

parade [pəˈreɪd] **1** n Mil (*ceremony*) parade f; (*procession*) défilé m; **fashion p.** défilé m de mode or de mannequins; **p. ground** Mil terrain m de manœuvres; **to make a p. of** faire étalage de; – vi Mil défiler; **to p. about** (*walk about*) se balader; – vt faire étalage de. **2** n (*street*) avenue f.

paradise ['pærədaɪs] n paradis m.

paradox ['pærədɒks] n paradoxe m. ◆**para'doxically** adv paradoxalement.

paraffin ['pærəfɪn] n pétrole m (lampant); (*wax*) Am paraffine f; **p. lamp** lampe f à pétrole.

paragon ['pærəg(ə)n] n **p. of virtue** modèle m de vertu.

paragraph ['pærəgrɑːf] n paragraphe m; **'new p.'** 'à la ligne'.

parakeet ['pærəkiːt] n perruche f.

parallel ['pærəlel] a (*comparable*) & Math parallèle (**with, to** à); **to run p. to** or **with** être parallèle à; – n (*comparison*) & Geog parallèle m; (*line*) Math parallèle f; – vt être semblable à.

paralysis [pəˈrælɪsɪs] n paralysie f. ◆**'paralyse** vt (Am -**lyze**) paralyser. ◆**para'lytic** a & n paralytique (mf).

parameter [pəˈræmɪtər] n paramètre m.

paramount ['pærəmaunt] a **of p. importance** de la plus haute importance.

paranoia [pærəˈnɔɪə] n paranoïa f. ◆**'paranoid** a & n paranoïaque (mf).

parapet ['pærəpɪt] n parapet m.

paraphernalia [pærəfəˈneɪlɪə] n attirail m.

paraphrase ['pærəfreɪz] n paraphrase f; – vt paraphraser.

parasite ['pærəsaɪt] n (*person, organism*) parasite m.

parasol ['pærəsɒl] n (*over table, on beach*) parasol m; (*lady's*) ombrelle f.

paratrooper ['pærətruːpər] n Mil parachutiste m. ◆**paratroops** npl Mil parachutistes mpl.

parboil [paːˈbɔɪl] vt Culin faire bouillir à demi.

parcel ['paːs(ə)l] **1** n colis m, paquet m; **to be part and p. of** faire partie intégrante de. **2** vt (-ll-, Am -l-) **to p. out** (*divide*) partager; **to p. up** faire un paquet de.

parch [paːtʃ] vt dessécher; **to be parched** (*thirsty*) être assoiffé; **to make parched** (*thirsty*) donner très soif à.

parchment ['paːtʃmənt] n parchemin m.

pardon ['paːd(ə)n] n pardon m; Jur grâce f; **general p.** amnistie f; **I beg your p.** (*apologize*) je vous prie de m'excuser; (*not hearing*) vous dites?; **p.?** (*not hearing*) comment?; **p. (me)!** (*sorry*) pardon!; – vt pardonner (**s.o. for sth** qch à qn); **to p. s.o.** pardonner (à) qn; Jur gracier qn.

pare [peər] vt (*trim*) rogner; (*peel*) éplucher; **to p. down** Fig réduire, rogner.

parent ['peərənt] n père m, mère f; **one's parents** ses parent mpl, son père et sa mère; **p. firm, p. company** Com maison f mère. ◆**parentage** n (*origin*) origine f. ◆**pa'rental** a des parents, parental. ◆**parenthood** n paternité f, maternité f.

parenthesis, pl -**eses** [pəˈrenθəsɪs, -əsiːz] n parenthèse f.

Paris ['pærɪs] n Paris m or f. ◆**Parisian** [pəˈrɪzɪən, Am pəˈriːʒən] a & n parisien, -ienne (mf).

parish ['pærɪʃ] n Rel paroisse f; (*civil*) commune f; – a (*church, register*) paroissial; **p. council** conseil m municipal. ◆**pa'rishioner** n paroissien, -ienne mf.

parity ['pærɪtɪ] n parité f.

park [paːk] **1** n (*garden*) parc m. **2** vt (*vehicle*) garer; (*put*) Fam mettre, poser; – vi Aut se garer; (*remain parked*) stationner. ◆—**ing** n stationnement m; **'no p.'** 'défense de stationner'; **p. bay** aire f de stationnement; **p. lot** Am parking m; **p. meter** parcmètre m; **p. place** endroit m pour se garer; **p. ticket** contravention f.

parka ['paːkə] n (*coat*) parka m.

parkway ['paːkweɪ] n Am avenue f.

parliament ['paːləmənt] n parlement m; **P.** Br Parlement m. ◆**parliamen'tarian** n parlementaire mf (expérimenté(e)).

parlour ['paːlər] n (*in mansion*) (petit) salon

m; **ice-cream p.** *Am* salon de glaces; **p. game** jeu *m* de société.

parochial [pəˈrəʊkɪəl] *a* (*mentality, quarrel*) *Pej* de clocher; (*person*) *Pej* provincial, borné; *Rel* paroissial.

parody [ˈpærədɪ] *n* parodie *f*; – *vt* parodier.

parole [pəˈrəʊl] *n* **on p.** *Jur* en liberté conditionnelle.

parquet [ˈpaːkeɪ] *n* **p. (floor)** parquet *m*.

parrot [ˈpærət] *n* perroquet *m*; **p. fashion** *Pej* comme un perroquet.

parry [ˈpærɪ] *vt* (*blow*) parer; (*question*) éluder; – *n Sp* parade *f*.

parsimonious [paːsɪˈməʊnɪəs] *a* parcimonieux. ◆**—ly** *adv* avec parcimonie.

parsley [ˈpaːslɪ] *n* persil *m*.

parsnip [ˈpaːsnɪp] *n* panais *m*.

parson [ˈpaːs(ə)n] *n* pasteur *m*; **p.'s nose** (*of chicken*) croupion *m*.

part [paːt] **1** *n* partie *f*; (*of machine*) pièce *f*; (*of periodical*) livraison *f*; (*of serial*) épisode *m*; (*in play, film, activity*) rôle *m*; (*division*) *Culin* mesure *f*; (*in hair*) *Am* raie *f*; **to take p.** participer (**in** à); **to take s.o.'s p.** (*side*) prendre parti pour qn; **in p.** en partie; **for the most p.** dans l'ensemble; **to be a p. of** faire partie de; **on the p. of** (*on behalf of*) de la part de; **for my p.** pour ma part; **in these parts** dans ces parages; **p. exchange** reprise *f*; **to take in p. exchange** reprendre; **p. owner** copropriétaire *mf*; **p. payment** paiement *m* partiel; – *adv* en partie; **p. American** en partie américain. **2** *vt* (*separate*) séparer; (*crowd*) diviser; **to p. one's hair** se faire une raie; **to p. company with** (*leave*) quitter; – *vi* (*of friends etc*) se quitter; (*of married couple*) se séparer; **to p. with** (*get rid of*) se séparer de. ◆**—ing 1** *n* séparation *f*; – *a* (*gift, words*) d'adieu. **2** *n* (*in hair*) raie *f*.

partake [paːˈteɪk] *vi* (*pt* **partook**, *pp* **partaken**) **to p. in** participer à; **to p. of** (*meal, food*) prendre, manger.

partial [ˈpaːʃəl] *a* partiel; (*biased*) partial (**towards** envers); **to be p. to** (*fond of*) *Fam* avoir un faible pour. ◆**parti'ality** *n* (*bias*) partialité *f*; (*liking*) prédilection *f*.

participate [paːˈtɪsɪpeɪt] *vi* participer (**in** à). ◆**participant** *n* participant, -ante *mf*. ◆**partici'pation** *n* participation *f*.

participle [paːˈtɪsɪp(ə)l] *n* participe *m*.

particle [ˈpaːtɪk(ə)l] *n* (*of atom, dust, name*) particule *f*; (*of truth*) grain *m*.

particular [pəˈtɪkjʊlər] **1** *a* (*specific, special*) particulier; (*fastidious, fussy*) difficile (**about** sur); (*meticulous*) méticuleux; **this p. book** ce livre-ci en particulier; **in p. en**

particulier; **to be p. about** faire très attention à. **2** *n* (*detail*) détail *m*; **s.o.'s particulars** le nom et l'adresse de qn; (*description*) le signalement de qn. ◆**—ly** *adv* particulièrement.

partisan [paːtɪˈzæn, *Am* ˈpaːtɪz(ə)n] *n* partisan *m*.

partition [paːˈtɪʃ(ə)n] **1** *n* (*of room*) cloison *f*; – *vt* **to p. off** cloisonner. **2** *n* (*of country*) *Pol* partition *f*, partage *m*; – *vt Pol* partager.

partly [ˈpaːtlɪ] *adv* en partie; **p. English p. French** moitié anglais moitié français.

partner [ˈpaːtnər] *n Com* associé, -ée *mf*; (*lover, spouse*) & *Sp Pol* partenaire *mf*; (*of racing driver etc*) coéquipier, -ière *mf*; (*dancing*) **p.** cavalier, -ière *mf*. ◆**partnership** *n* association *f*; **to take into p.** prendre comme associé(e); **in p. with** en association avec.

partridge [ˈpaːtrɪdʒ] *n* perdrix *f*.

part-time [paːtˈtaɪm] *a & adv* à temps partiel; (*half-time*) à mi-temps.

party [ˈpaːtɪ] *n* **1** (*group*) groupe *m*; *Pol* parti *m*; (*in contract, lawsuit*) *Jur* partie *f*; *Mil* détachement *m*; *Tel* correspondant, -ante *mf*; **rescue p.** équipe *f* de sauveteurs *or* de secours; **third p.** *Jur* tiers *m*; **innocent p.** innocent, -ente *mf*; **to be (a) p. to** (*crime*) être complice de; **p. line** *Tel* ligne *f* partagée; *Pol* ligne *f* du parti; **p. ticket** billet *m* collectif. **2** (*gathering*) réception *f*; (*informal*) surprise-partie *f*; (*for birthday*) fête *f*; **cocktail p.** cocktail *m*; **dinner p.** dîner *m*; **tea p.** thé *m*.

pass [paːs] **1** *n* (*entry permit*) laissez-passer *m inv*; (*free ticket*) *Th* billet *m* de faveur; (*season ticket*) carte *f* d'abonnement; (*over mountains*) *Geog* col *m*; *Fb etc* passe *f*; (*in exam*) mention *f* passable (**in French**/*etc* en français/*etc*); **to make a p. at** faire des avances à; **p. mark** (*in exam*) moyenne *f*, barre *f* d'admissibilité; **p. key** passepartout *m inv*. **2** *vi* (*go, come, disappear*) passer (**to** à, **through** par); (*overtake*) *Aut* dépasser; (*in exam*) être reçu (**in French**/*etc* en français/*etc*); (*take place*) se passer; **that'll p.** (*be acceptable*) ça ira; **he can p. for thirty** on lui donnerait trente ans; **to p. along** *or* **through** passer; **to p. away** *or* **on** (*die*) mourir; **to p. by** passer (à côté); **to p. off** (*happen*) se passer; **to p. on to** (*move on to*) passer à; **to p. out** (*faint*) s'évanouir; – *vt* (*move, spend, give etc*) passer (**to** à); (*go past*) passer devant (*immeuble etc*); (*vehicle*) dépasser; (*exam*) être reçu à; (*candidate*) recevoir; (*judgement, opinion*) prononcer (**on** sur); (*remark*) faire; (*allow*) autoriser; (*bill, law*) *Pol* voter; **to p. (by) s.o.** (*in street*) croiser qn; **to p. by** (*building*) passer devant; **to p. oneself off as** se faire passer pour; **to p. sth off on** (*fob off on*) refiler qch à; **to p. on** (*message, title, illness etc*) transmettre (**to** à); **to p. out** *or* **round** (*hand out*) distribuer; **to p. over** (*ignore*) passer sur, oublier; **to p. round** (*cigarettes, sweets etc*) faire passer; **to p. up** (*chance etc*) laisser passer. ◆**—ing** *a* (*vehicle etc*) qui passe; (*beauty*) passager; − *n* (*of visitor, vehicle etc*) passage *m*; (*of time*) écoulement *m*; (*death*) disparition *f*.

passable ['pɑɪsəb(ə)l] *a* (*not bad*) passable; (*road*) praticable; (*river*) franchissable.

passage ['pæsɪdʒ] *n* (*passing, way through, of text, of speech etc*) passage *m*; (*of time*) écoulement *m*; (*corridor*) couloir *m*; *Nau* traversée *f*, passage *m*. ◆**passageway** *n* (*way through*) passage *m*; (*corridor*) couloir *m*.

passbook ['pɑɪsbʊk] *n* livret *m* de caisse d'épargne.

passenger ['pæsɪndʒər] *n* passager, -ère *mf*; *Rail* voyageur, -euse *mf*.

passer-by [pɑɪsə'baɪ] *n* (*pl* **passers-by**) passant, -ante *mf*.

passion ['pæʃ(ə)n] *n* passion *f*; **to have a p. for** (*cars etc*) avoir la passion de, adorer. ◆**passionate** *a* passionné. ◆**passionately** *adv* passionnément.

passive ['pæsɪv] *a* (*not active*) passif; − *n* *Gram* passif *m*. ◆**—ness** *n* passivité *f*.

Passover ['pɑɪsəʊvər] *n* *Rel* Pâque *f*.

passport ['pɑɪspɔːt] *n* passeport *m*.

password ['pɑɪswɜːd] *n* mot *m* de passe.

past [pɑɪst] **1** *n* (*time, history*) passé *m*; **in the p.** (*formerly*) dans le temps; **it's a thing of the p.** ça n'existe plus; − *a* (*gone by*) passé; (*former*) ancien; **these p. months** ces derniers mois; **that's all p.** c'est du passé; **in the p. tense** *Gram* au passé. **2** *prep* (*in front of*) devant; (*after*) après; (*further than*) plus loin que; (*too old for*) *Fig* trop vieux pour; **p. four o'clock** quatre heures passées, plus de quatre heures; **to be p. fifty** avoir cinquante ans passés; **it's p. belief** c'est incroyable; **I wouldn't put it p. him** ça ne m'étonnerait pas de lui, il en est bien capable; − *adv* devant; **to go p.** passer.

pasta ['pæstə] *n* *Culin* pâtes *fpl* (alimentaires).

paste [peɪst] **1** *n* (*of meat*) pâté *m*; (*of anchovy etc*) beurre *m*; (*dough*) pâte *f*. **2** *n* (*glue*) colle *f* (blanche); − *vt* coller; **to p. up** (*notice etc*) afficher.

pastel ['pæstəl, *Am* pæ'stel] *n* pastel *m*; − *a* (*shade*) pastel *inv*; (*drawing*) au pastel.

pasteurized ['pæstəraɪzd] *a* (*milk*) pasteurisé.

pastiche [pæ'stiːʃ] *n* pastiche *m*.

pastille ['pæstɪl, *Am* pæ'stiːl] *n* pastille *f*.

pastime ['pɑɪstaɪm] *n* passe-temps *m inv*.

pastor ['pɑɪstər] *n* *Rel* pasteur *m*. ◆**pastoral** *a* pastoral.

pastry ['peɪstrɪ] *n* (*dough*) pâte *f*; (*cake*) pâtisserie *f*; **puff p.** pâte *f* feuilletée. ◆**pastrycook** *n* pâtissier, -ière *mf*.

pasture ['pɑɪstʃər] *n* pâturage *m*.

pasty 1 ['peɪstɪ] *a* (**-ier, -iest**) (*complexion*) terreux. **2** ['pæstɪ] *n* *Culin* petit pâté *m* (en croûte).

pat [pæt] **1** *vt* (**-tt-**) (*cheek, table etc*) tapoter; (*animal*) caresser; − *n* petite tape; caresse *f*. **2** *adv* **to answer p.** avoir la réponse toute prête; **to know sth off p.** savoir qch sur le bout du doigt.

patch [pætʃ] *n* (*for clothes*) pièce *f*; (*over eye*) bandeau *m*; (*for bicycle tyre*) rustine® *f*; (*of colour*) tache *f*; (*of sky*) morceau *m*; (*of fog*) nappe *f*; (*of ice*) plaque *f*; **a cabbage/etc p.** un carré de choux/etc; **a bad p.** *Fig* une mauvaise passe; **not to be a p. on** (*not as good as*) *Fam* ne pas arriver à la cheville de; − *vt* **to p. up** (*clothing*) rapiécer; **to p. up** (*quarrel*) régler; (*marriage*) replâtrer. ◆**patchwork** *n* patchwork *m*. ◆**patchy** *a* (**-ier, -iest**) inégal.

patent 1 ['peɪtənt] *a* patent, manifeste; **p. leather** cuir *m* verni. **2** ['peɪtənt, 'pætənt] *n* brevet *m* (d'invention); − *vt* (*faire*) breveter. ◆**—ly** *adv* manifestement.

paternal [pə'tɜːn(ə)l] *a* paternel. ◆**paternity** *n* paternité *f*.

path [pɑːθ] *n* (*pl* **-s** [pɑːðz]) sentier *m*, chemin *m*; (*in park*) allée *f*; (*of river*) cours *m*; (*of bullet, planet*) trajectoire *f*. ◆**pathway** *n* sentier *m*, chemin *m*.

pathetic [pə'θetɪk] *a* pitoyable.

pathology [pə'θɒlədʒɪ] *n* pathologie *f*. ◆**patho'logical** *a* pathologique.

pathos ['peɪθɒs] *n* pathétique *m*.

patient ['peɪʃ(ə)nt] **1** *a* patient. **2** *n* (*in hospital*) malade *mf*, patient, -ente *mf*; (*on doctor's or dentist's list*) patient, -ente *mf*. ◆**patience** *n* patience *f*; **to have p.** prendre patience; **to lose p.** perdre patience; **I have no p. with him** il m'impatiente; **to play p.** *Cards* faire des réussites. ◆**patiently** *adv* patiemment.

patio ['pætɪəʊ] *n* (*pl* **-os**) patio *m*.

patriarch ['peɪtrɪɑːk] *n* patriarche *m*.

patriot ['pætrɪət, 'peɪtrɪət] n patriote mf. ◆**patri'otic** a (views, speech etc) patriotique; (person) patriote. ◆**patriotism** n patriotisme m.

patrol [pə'trəʊl] n patrouille f; **p. boat** patrouilleur m; **police p. car** voiture f de police; **p. wagon** Am fourgon m cellulaire; – vi (-ll-) patrouiller; – vt patrouiller dans. ◆**patrolman** n (pl -men) Am agent m de police; (repair man) Aut dépanneur m.

patron ['peɪtrən] n (of artist) protecteur, -trice mf; (customer) Com client, -ente mf; (of cinema, theatre) habitué, -ée mf; **p. saint** patron, -onne mf. ◆**patronage** n (support) patronage m; (of the arts) protection f; (custom) Com clientèle f. ◆**patroniz/e** ['pætrənaɪz, Am 'peɪtrənaɪz] vt **1** Com accorder sa clientèle à. **2** (person) Pej traiter avec condescendance. ◆**—ing** a condescendant.

patter ['pætər] **1** n (of footsteps) petit bruit m; (of rain, hail) crépitement m; – vi (of rain, hail) crépiter, tambouriner. **2** n (talk) baratin m.

pattern ['pæt(ə)n] n dessin m, motif m; (paper model for garment) patron m; (fabric sample) échantillon m; Fig modèle m; (plan) plan m; (method) formule f; (of a crime) scénario m. ◆**patterned** a (dress, cloth) à motifs.

paucity ['pɔːsɪtɪ] n pénurie f.

paunch [pɔːntʃ] n panse f, bedon m. ◆**paunchy** a (-ier, -iest) bedonnant.

pauper ['pɔːpər] n pauvre mf, indigent, -ente mf.

pause [pɔːz] n pause f; (in conversation) silence m; – vi (stop) faire une pause; (hesitate) hésiter.

pav/e [peɪv] vt paver; **to p. the way for** Fig ouvrir la voie à. ◆**—ing** n (surface) pavage m, dallage m; **p. stone** pavé m. ◆**pavement** n trottoir m; (roadway) Am chaussée f; (stone) pavé m.

pavilion [pə'vɪljən] n (building) pavillon m.

paw [pɔː] **1** n patte f; – vt (of animal) donner des coups de patte à. **2** vt (touch improperly) tripoter.

pawn [pɔːn] **1** n Chess pion m. **2** vt mettre en gage; – n in **p.** en gage. ◆**pawnbroker** n prêteur, -euse mf sur gages. ◆**pawnshop** n mont-de-piété m.

pay [peɪ] n salaire m; (of workman) paie f, salaire m; Mil solde f, paie f; **p. phone** téléphone m public; **p. day** jour m de paie; **p. slip** bulletin m or fiche f de paie; – vt (pt & pp **paid**) (person, sum) payer; (deposit) verser; (yield) Com rapporter; (compli-

ment, attention, visit) faire; **to p. s.o. to do** or **for doing** payer qn pour faire; **to p. s.o. for sth** payer qch à qn; **to p. money into one's account** or **the bank** verser de l'argent sur son compte; **it pays (one) to be cautious** on a intérêt à être prudent; **to p. homage** or **tribute to** rendre hommage à; **to p. back** (creditor, loan etc) rembourser; **I'll p. you back for this!** je te revaudrai ça!; **to p. in** (cheque) verser (**to one's account** sur son compte); **to p. off** (debt, creditor etc) rembourser; (in instalments) rembourser par acomptes; (staff, worker) licencier; **to p. off an old score** or **a grudge** Fig régler un vieux compte; **to p. out** (spend) dépenser; – vi payer; **to p. up** payer; **to p. for sth** payer qch; **to p. a lot (for)** payer cher; **to p. off** (be successful) être payant; **to p. up** payer. ◆**—ing** a (guest) payant; (profitable) rentable. ◆**—able** a (due) payable; **a cheque p. to** un chèque à l'ordre de. ◆**—ment** n paiement m; (of deposit) versement m; (reward) récompense f; **on p. of 20 francs** moyennant 20 francs. ◆**payoff** n Fam (reward) récompense f; (revenge) règlement m de comptes. ◆**payroll** n **to be on the p. of** (firm, factory) être employé par; **to have twenty workers on the p.** employer vingt ouvriers.

pea [piː] n pois m; **garden** or **green peas** petits pois mpl; **p. soup** soupe f aux pois.

peace [piːs] n paix f; **p. of mind** tranquillité f d'esprit; **in p.** en paix; **at p.** en paix (**with** avec); **to have (some) p. and quiet** avoir la paix; **to disturb the p.** troubler l'ordre public; **to hold one's p.** garder le silence. ◆**p.-keeping** a (force) de maintien de la paix; (measure) de pacification. ◆**p.-loving** a pacifique. ◆**peaceable** a paisible, pacifique. ◆**peaceful** a paisible, calme; (coexistence, purpose, demonstration) pacifique. ◆**peacefulness** n paix f.

peach [piːtʃ] n (fruit) pêche f; (tree) pêcher m; – a (colour) pêche inv.

peacock ['piːkɒk] n paon m.

peak [piːk] n (mountain top) sommet m; (mountain itself) pic m; (of cap) visière f; (of fame etc) Fig sommet m, apogée m; **the traffic has reached** or **is at its p.** la circulation est à son maximum; – a (hours, period) de pointe; (demand, production) maximum; – vi (of sales etc) atteindre son maximum. ◆**peaked** a **p. cap** casquette f.

peaky ['piːkɪ] a (-ier, -iest) Fam (ill) patraque; (pale) pâlot.

peal [piːl] **1** n (of laughter) éclat m; (of thun-

der) roulement *m*. **2** *n* **p. of bells** carillon *m*; – *vi* **to p. (out)** (*of bells*) carillonner.

peanut ['piːnʌt] *n* cacah(o)uète *f*; (*plant*) arachide *f*; **to earn/etc peanuts** (*little money*) *Fam* gagner/*etc* des clopinettes.

pear [peər] *n* poire *f*; **p. tree** poirier *m*.

pearl [pɜːl] *n* perle *f*; (*mother-of-pearl*) nacre *f*. ◆**pearly** *a* (**-ier, -iest**) (*colour*) nacré.

peasant ['pezənt] *n* & *a* paysan, -anne (*mf*).

peashooter ['piːʃuːtər] *n* sarbacane *f*.

peat [piːt] *n* tourbe *f*.

pebble ['peb(ə)l] *n* (*stone*) caillou *m*; (*on beach*) galet *m*. ◆**pebbly** *a* (*beach*) (couvert) de galets.

pecan ['piːkæn] *n* (*nut*) *Am* pacane *f*.

peck [pek] *vti* **to p. (at)** (*of bird*) picorer (*du pain etc*); (*person*) *Fig* donner un coup de bec à; **to p. at one's food** (*of person*) manger du bout des dents; – *n* coup *m* de bec; (*kiss*) *Fam* bécot *m*.

peckish ['pekiʃ] *a* **to be p.** (*hungry*) *Fam* avoir un petit creux.

peculiar [pɪ'kjuːliər] *a* (*strange*) bizarre; (*characteristic, special*) particulier (**to** à). ◆**peculi'arity** *n* (*feature*) particularité *f*; (*oddity*) bizarrerie *f*. ◆**peculiarly** *adv* bizarrement; (*specially*) particulièrement.

pedal ['ped(ə)l] *n* pédale *f*; **p. boat** pédalo *m*; – *vi* (**-ll-**, *Am* **-l-**) pédaler; – *vt* (*bicycle etc*) actionner les pédales de. ◆**pedalbin** *n* poubelle *f* à pédale.

pedant ['pedənt] *n* pédant, -ante *mf*. ◆**pe'dantic** *a* pédant. ◆**pedantry** *n* pédantisme *m*.

peddl/e ['ped(ə)l] *vt* colporter; (*drugs*) faire le trafic de; – *vi* faire du colportage. ◆**-er** *n* *Am* (*door-to-door*) colporteur, -euse *mf*; (*in street*) camelot *m*; **drug p.** revendeur, -euse *mf* de drogues.

pedestal ['pedist(ə)l] *n* *Archit* & *Fig* piédestal *m*.

pedestrian [pə'destriən] **1** *n* piéton *m*; **p. crossing** passage *m* pour piétons; **p. precinct** zone *f* piétonnière. **2** *a* (*speech, style*) prosaïque. ◆**pedestrianize** *vt* (*street etc*) rendre piétonnier.

pedigree ['pedigriː] *n* (*of dog, horse etc*) pedigree *m*; (*of person*) ascendance *f*; – *a* (*dog, horse etc*) de race.

pedlar ['pedlər] *n* (*door-to-door*) colporteur, -euse *mf*; (*in street*) camelot *m*.

pee [piː] *n* **to go for a p.** *Fam* faire pipi.

peek [piːk] *n* coup *m* d'œil (furtif); – *vi* jeter un coup d'œil (furtif) (**at** à).

peel [piːl] *n* (*of vegetable, fruit*) pelure(s) *f(pl)*, épluchure(s) *f(pl)*; (*of orange skin*) écorce *f*; (*in food, drink*) zeste *m*; **a piece of**

p. une pelure, une épluchure; – *vt* (*fruit, vegetable*) peler, éplucher; **to keep one's eyes peeled** *Fam* être vigilant; **to p. off** (*label etc*) décoller; – *vi* (*of sunburnt skin*) peler; (*of paint*) s'écailler; **to p. easily** (*of fruit*) se peler facilement. ◆**—ings** *npl* pelures *fpl*, épluchures *fpl*. ◆**—er** *n* (*knife etc*) éplucheur *m*.

peep [piːp] **1** *n* coup *m* d'œil (furtif); – *vi* **to p. (at)** regarder furtivement; **to p. out** se montrer; **peeping Tom** voyeur, -euse *mf*. **2** *vi* (*of bird*) pépier. ◆**peephole** *n* judas *m*.

peer [piər] **1** *n* (*equal*) pair *m*, égal, -ale *mf*; (*noble*) pair *m*. **2** *vi* **to p. (at)** regarder attentivement (*comme pour mieux voir*); **to p. into** (*darkness*) scruter. ◆**peerage** *n* (*rank*) pairie *f*.

peeved [piːvd] *a* *Fam* irrité.

peevish ['piːviʃ] *a* grincheux, irritable.

peg [peg] **1** *n* (*wooden*) *Tech* cheville *f*; (*metal*) *Tech* fiche *f*; (*for tent*) piquet *m*; (*for clothes*) pince *f* (à linge); (*for coat, hat etc*) patère *f*; **to buy off the p.** acheter en prêt-à-porter. **2** *vt* (**-gg-**) (*prices*) stabiliser.

pejorative [pɪ'dʒɒrətiv] *a* péjoratif.

pekin(g)ese [piːki'niːz] *n* (*dog*) pékinois *m*.

pelican ['pelik(ə)n] *n* (*bird*) pélican *m*.

pellet ['pelit] *n* (*of paper etc*) boulette *f*; (*for gun*) (grain *m* de) plomb *m*.

pelt [pelt] **1** *n* (*skin*) peau *f*; (*fur*) fourrure *f*. **2** *vt* **to p. s.o. with** (*stones etc*) bombarder qn de. **3** *vi* **it's pelting (down)** (*raining*) il pleut à verse. **4** *vi* **to p. along** (*run, dash*) *Fam* foncer, courir.

pelvis ['pelvis] *n* *Anat* bassin *m*.

pen [pen] **1** *n* (*dipped in ink*) porte-plume *m inv*; (*fountain pen*) stylo *m* (à encre *or* à plume); (*ballpoint*) stylo *m* à bille, stylo(-)bille *m*; **to live by one's p.** *Fig* vivre de sa plume; **p. friend, p. pal** correspondant, -ante *mf*; **p. name** pseudonyme *m*; **p. nib** (bec *m* de) plume *f*; **p. pusher** *Pej* gratte-papier *m inv*; – *vt* (**-nn-**) (*write*) écrire. **2** *n* (*enclosure for baby or sheep or cattle*) parc *m*.

penal ['piːn(ə)l] *a* (*law, code etc*) pénal; (*colony*) pénitentiaire. ◆**penalize** *vt* *Sp* *Jur* pénaliser (**for** pour); (*handicap*) désavantager.

penalty ['pen(ə)lti] *n* *Jur* peine *f*; (*fine*) amende *f*; *Sp* pénalisation *f*; *Fb* penalty *m*; *Rugby* pénalité *f*; **to pay the p.** *Fig* subir les conséquences.

penance ['penəns] *n* pénitence *f*.

pence [pens] *see* **penny**.

pencil ['pens(ə)l] *n* crayon *m*; **in p.** au crayon; **p. box** plumier *m*; **p. sharpener**

taille-crayon(s) *m inv*; – *vt* (-ll-, *Am* -l-) crayonner; **to p. in** *Fig* noter provisoirement.

pendant ['pendənt] *n* pendentif *m*; (*on earring, chandelier*) pendeloque *f*.

pending ['pendɪŋ] **1** *a* (*matter*) en suspens. **2** *prep* (*until*) en attendant.

pendulum ['pendjʊləm] *n* (*of clock*) balancier *m*, pendule *m*; *Fig* pendule *m*.

penetrat/e ['penɪtreɪt] *vt* (*substance, mystery etc*) percer; (*plan, secret etc*) découvrir; – *vti* **to p.** (**into**) (*forest, group etc*) pénétrer dans. ◆—**ing** *a* (*mind, cold etc*) pénétrant. ◆**pene'tration** *n* pénétration *f*.

penguin ['peŋgwɪn] *n* manchot *m*, pingouin *m*.

penicillin [penɪ'sɪlɪn] *n* pénicilline *f*.

peninsula [pə'nɪnsjʊlə] *n* presqu'île *f*, péninsule *f*. ◆**pen'insular** *a* péninsulaire.

penis ['piːnɪs] *n* pénis *m*.

penitent ['penɪtənt] *a* & *n* pénitent, -ente (*mf*). ◆**penitence** *n* pénitence *f*.

penitentiary [penɪ'tenʃərɪ] *n Am* prison *f* (centrale).

penknife ['pennaɪf] *n* (*pl* -knives) canif *m*.

pennant ['penənt] *n* (*flag*) flamme *f*, banderole *f*.

penny ['penɪ] *n* **1** (*pl* pennies) (*coin*) penny *m*; *Am Can* cent *m*; **I don't have a p.** *Fig* je n'ai pas le sou. **2** (*pl* pence [pens]) (*value, currency*) penny *m*. ◆**p.-pinching** *a* (*miserly*) *Fam* avare. ◆**penniless** *a* sans le sou.

pension ['penʃ(ə)n] *n* pension *f*; **retirement p.** (*pension f de*) retraite *f*; (*private*) retraite *f* complémentaire; – *vt* **to p. off** mettre à la retraite. ◆—**able** *a* (*age*) de la retraite; (*job*) qui donne droit à une retraite. ◆—**er** *n* pensionné, -ée *mf*; (**old age**) **p.** retraité, -ée *mf*.

pensive ['pensɪv] *a* pensif.

pentagon ['pentəgən] *n* **the P.** *Am Pol* le Pentagone.

pentathlon [pen'tæθlən] *n Sp* pentathlon *m*.

Pentecost ['pentɪkɒst] *n* (*Whitsun*) *Am* Pentecôte *f*.

penthouse ['penthaʊs] *n* appartement *m* de luxe (*construit sur le toit d'un immeuble*).

pent-up ['pentʌp] *a* (*feelings*) refoulé.

penultimate [pɪ'nʌltɪmət] *a* avant-dernier.

peony ['pɪənɪ] *n Bot* pivoine *f*.

people ['piːp(ə)l] *npl* (*in general*) gens *mpl or fpl*; (*specific persons*) personnes *fpl*; (*of region, town*) habitants *mpl*, gens *mpl or fpl*; **the p.** (*citizens*) *Pol* le peuple; **old p.** les personnes *fpl* âgées; **old people's home**

hospice *m* de vieillards; (*private*) maison *f* de retraite; **two p.** deux personnes; **English p.** les Anglais *mpl*, le peuple anglais; **a lot of p.** beaucoup de monde *or* de gens; **p. think that . . .** on pense que . . . ; – *n* (*nation*) peuple *m*; – *vt* (*populate*) peupler (**with** de).

pep [pep] *n* entrain *m*; **p. talk** *Fam* petit laïus d'encouragement; – *vt* (-pp-) **to p. up** (*perk up*) ragaillardir.

pepper ['pepər] *n* poivre *m*; (*vegetable*) poivron *m*; – *vt* poivrer. ◆**peppercorn** *n* grain *m* de poivre. ◆**peppermint** *n* (*plant*) menthe *f* poivrée; (*sweet*) pastille *f* de menthe. ◆**peppery** *a Culin* poivré.

per [pɜːr] *prep* par; **p. annum** par an; **p. head, p. person** par personne; **p. cent** pour cent; **50 pence p. kilo** 50 pence le kilo; **40 km p. hour** 40 km à l'heure. ◆**per'centage** *n* pourcentage *m*.

perceive [pə'siːv] *vt* (*see, hear*) percevoir; (*notice*) remarquer (**that** que). ◆**perceptible** *a* perceptible. ◆**perception** *n* perception *f* (**of** de); (*intuition*) intuition *f*. ◆**perceptive** *a* (*person*) perspicace; (*study, remark*) pénétrant.

perch [pɜːtʃ] **1** *n* perchoir *m*; – *vi* (*of bird*) (se) percher; (*of person*) *Fig* se percher, se jucher; – *vt* (*put*) percher. **2** *n* (*fish*) perche *f*.

percolate ['pɜːkəleɪt] *vi* (*of liquid*) filtrer, passer (**through** par); – *vt* (*coffee*) faire dans une cafetière; **percolated coffee** du vrai café. ◆**percolator** *n* cafetière *f*; (*in café or restaurant*) percolateur *m*.

percussion [pə'kʌʃ(ə)n] *n Mus* percussion *f*.

peremptory [pə'remptərɪ] *a* péremptoire.

perennial [pə'renɪəl] **1** *a* (*complaint, subject etc*) perpétuel. **2** *a* (*plant*) vivace; – *n* plante *f* vivace.

perfect ['pɜːfɪkt] *a* parfait; – *a* & *n* **p.** (**tense**) *Gram* parfait *m*; – [pə'fekt] *vt* (*book, piece of work etc*) parachever, parfaire; (*process, technique*) mettre au point; (*one's French etc*) parfaire ses connaissances en. ◆**per'fection** *n* perfection *f*; (*act*) parachèvement *m* (**of** de); **mise f au point** (**of** de); **to p. à la perfection**. ◆**per'fectionist** *n* perfectionniste *mf*. ◆**'perfectly** *adv* parfaitement.

perfidious [pə'fɪdɪəs] *a Lit* perfide.

perforate ['pɜːfəreɪt] *vt* perforer. ◆**perfo'ration** *n* perforation *f*.

perform [pə'fɔːm] *vt* (*task, miracle*) accomplir; (*a function, one's duty*) remplir; (*rite*) célébrer; (*operation*) *Med* pratiquer (**on**

sur); (*a play, symphony*) jouer; (*sonata*)
interpréter; – *vi* (*play*) jouer; (*sing*)
chanter; (*dance*) danser; (*of circus animal*)
faire un numéro; (*function*) fonctionner;
(*behave*) se comporter; **you performed very
well!** tu as très bien fait! ◆**—ing** *a*
(*animal*) savant. ◆**performance** *n* **1**
(*show*) *Th* représentation *f*, séance *f*; *Cin
Mus* séance *f*. **2** (*of athlete, machine etc*)
performance *f*; (*of actor, musician etc*)
interprétation *f*; (*circus act*) numéro *m*;
(*fuss*) *Fam* histoire(s) *f(pl)*; **the p. of one's
duties** l'exercice *m* de ses fonctions.
◆**performer** *n* interprète *mf* (**of** de);
(*entertainer*) artiste *mf*.

perfume ['pɜːfjuːm] *n* parfum *m*; –
[pə'fjuːm] *vt* parfumer.

perfunctory [pə'lʌŋktərɪ] *a* (*action*)
superficiel; (*smile etc*) de commande.

perhaps [pə'hæps] *adv* peut-être; **p. not**
peut-être que non.

peril ['perɪl] *n* péril *m*, danger *m*; **at your p.** à
vos risques et péril. ◆**perilous** *a* périlleux.

perimeter [pə'rɪmɪtər] *n* périmètre *m*.

period ['pɪərɪəd] **1** *n* (*length of time, moment
in time*) période *f*; (*historical*) époque *f*;
(*time limit*) délai *m*; (*lesson*) *Sch* leçon *f*;
(*full stop*) *Gram* point *m*; **in the p. of a
month** en l'espace d'un mois; **I refuse, p.!**
Am je refuse, un point c'est tout!; – *a*
(*furniture etc*) d'époque; (*costume*) de
l'époque. **2** *n* (*menstruation*) règles *fpl*.
◆**peri'odic** *a* périodique. ◆**peri'odical**
n (*magazine*) périodique *m*. ◆**peri-
'odically** *adv* périodiquement.

periphery [pə'rɪfərɪ] *n* périphérie *f*. ◆**peripheral** *a* (*question*) sans rapport direct (**to**
avec); (*interest*) accessoire; (*neighbourhood*) périphérique.

periscope ['perɪskəup] *n* périscope *m*.

perish ['perɪʃ] *vi* (*die*) périr; (*of food,
substance*) se détériorer; **to be perished** *or*
perishing (*of person*) *Fam* être frigorifié.
◆**—ing** *a* (*cold, weather*) *Fam* glacial.
◆**—able** *a* (*food*) périssable; – *npl*
denrées *fpl* périssables.

perjure ['pɜːdʒər] *vt* **to p. oneself** se parjurer.
◆**perjurer** *n* (*person*) parjure *mf*.
◆**perjury** *n* parjure *m*; **to commit p.** se
parjurer.

perk [pɜːk] **1** *vi* **to p. up** (*buck up*) se ragaillardir; – *vt* **to s.o. up** remonter qn, ragaillardir qn. **2** *n* (*advantage*) avantage *m*;
(*extra profit*) à-côté *m*. ◆**perky** *a* (**-ier,
-iest**) (*cheerful*) guilleret, plein d'entrain.

perm [pɜːm] *n* (*of hair*) permanente *f*; – *vt* **to**
have one's hair permed se faire faire une
permanente.

permanent ['pɜːmənənt] *a* permanent;
(*address*) fixe; **she's p. here** elle est ici à titre
permanent. ◆**permanence** *n* perma-
nence *f*. ◆**permanently** *adv* à titre permanent.

permeate ['pɜːmɪeɪt] *vt* (*of ideas etc*) se
répandre dans; **to p. (through)** (*of liquid
etc*) pénétrer. ◆**permeable** *a* perméable.

permit [pə'mɪt] *vt* (**-tt-**) permettre (**s.o. to do**
à qn de faire); **weather permitting** si le
temps le permet; – ['pɜːmɪt] *n* (*licence*)
permis *m*; (*entrance pass*) laissez-passer *m
inv*. ◆**per'missible** *a* permis. ◆**per-
'mission** *n* permission *f*, autorisation *f* (**to
do** de faire); **to ask (for)/give p.**
demander/donner la permission. ◆**per-
'missive** *a* (trop) tolérant, laxiste. ◆**per-
'missiveness** *n* laxisme *m*.

permutation [pɜːmjuː'teɪʃ(ə)n] *n* permutation *f*.

pernicious [pə'nɪʃəs] *a* (*harmful*) & *Med*
pernicieux.

pernickety [pə'nɪkətɪ] *a Fam* (*precise*) pointilleux; (*demanding*) difficile (**about** sur).

peroxide [pə'rɒksaɪd] *n* (*bleach*) eau *f*
oxygénée; – *a* (*hair, blond*) oxygéné.

perpendicular [pɜːpən'dɪkjʊlər] *a* & *n*
perpendiculaire (*f*).

perpetrate ['pɜːpɪtreɪt] *vt* (*crime*) perpétrer.
◆**perpetrator** *n* auteur *m*.

perpetual [pə'petʃʊəl] *a* perpétuel. ◆**perpetually** *adv* perpétuellement. ◆**perpetuate** *vt* perpétuer. ◆**perpetuity**
[pɜːpɪ'tjuːtɪ] *n* perpétuité *f*.

perplex [pə'pleks] *vt* rendre perplexe,
dérouter. ◆**—ed** *a* perplexe. ◆**—ing** *a*
déroutant. ◆**perplexity** *n* perplexité *f*;
(*complexity*) complexité *f*.

persecute ['pɜːsɪkjuːt] *vt* persécuter.
◆**perse'cution** *n* persécution *f*.

persever/e [pɜːsɪ'vɪər] *vi* persévérer (**in**
dans). ◆**—ing** *a* (*persistent*) persévérant.
◆**perseverance** *n* persévérance *f*.

Persian ['pɜːʃ(ə)n, 'pɜːʒ(ə)n] *a* (*language,
cat, carpet*) persan; – *n* (*language*) persan
m.

persist [pə'sɪst] *vi* persister (**in doing** à faire,
in sth dans qch). ◆**persistence** *n* persistance *f*. ◆**persistent** *a* (*fever, smell etc*)
persistant; (*person*) obstiné; (*attempts,
noise etc*) continuel. ◆**persistently** *adv*
(*stubbornly*) obstinément; (*continually*)
continuellement.

person ['pɜːs(ə)n] *n* personne *f*; **in p.** en
personne; **a p. to p. call** *Tel* une communi-

cation avec préavis. ◆**personable** *a* avenant, qui présente bien.

personal ['pɜːsən(ə)l] *a* personnel; (*application*) en personne; (*hygiene, friend*) intime; (*life*) privé; (*indiscreet*) indiscret; **p. assistant, p. secretary** secrétaire *m* particulier, secrétaire *f* particulière. ◆**perso'nality** *n* (*character, famous person*) personnalité *f*; **a television p.** une vedette de la télévision. ◆**personalize** *vt* personnaliser. ◆**personally** *adv* personnellement; (*in person*) en personne.

personify [pə'sɒnɪfaɪ] *vt* personnifier. ◆**personifi'cation** *n* personnification *f*.

personnel [pɜːsə'nel] *n* (*staff*) personnel *m*; (*department*) service *m* du personnel.

perspective [pə'spektɪv] *n* (*artistic & viewpoint*) perspective *f*; **in (its true) p.** *Fig* sous son vrai jour.

perspire [pə'spaɪər] *vi* transpirer. ◆**perspi'ration** *n* transpiration *f*, sueur *f*.

persuade [pə'sweɪd] *vt* persuader (**s.o. to do** qn de faire). ◆**persuasion** *n* persuasion *f*; *Rel* religion *f*. ◆**persuasive** *a* (*person, argument etc*) persuasif. ◆**persuasively** *adv* de façon persuasive.

pert [pɜːt] *a* (*impertinent*) impertinent; (*lively*) gai, plein d'entrain; (*hat etc*) coquet, chic. ◆**—ly** *adv* avec impertinence.

pertain [pə'teɪn] *vi* **to p. to** (*relate*) se rapporter à; (*belong*) appartenir à.

pertinent ['pɜːtɪnənt] *a* pertinent. ◆**—ly** *adv* pertinemment.

perturb [pə'tɜːb] *vt* troubler, perturber.

Peru [pə'ruː] *n* Pérou *m*. ◆**Peruvian** *a & n* péruvien, -ienne (*mf*).

peruse [pə'ruːz] *vt* lire (attentivement); (*skim through*) parcourir. ◆**perusal** *n* lecture *f*.

pervade [pə'veɪd] *vt* se répandre dans. ◆**pervasive** *a* qui se répand partout, envahissant.

perverse [pə'vɜːs] *a* (*awkward*) contrariant; (*obstinate*) entêté; (*wicked*) pervers. ◆**perversion** *n* perversion *f*; (*of justice, truth*) travestissement *m*. ◆**perversity** *n* esprit *m* de contradiction; (*obstinacy*) entêtement *m*; (*wickedness*) perversité *f*.

pervert [pə'vɜːt] *vt* pervertir; (*mind*) corrompre; (*justice, truth*) travestir; — ['pɜːvɜːt] *n* perverti, -ie *mf*.

pesky ['peskɪ] *a* (*-ier, -iest*) (*troublesome*) *Am Fam* embêtant.

pessimism ['pesɪmɪz(ə)m] *n* pessimisme *m*. ◆**pessimist** *n* pessimiste *mf*. ◆**pessi'mistic** *a* pessimiste. ◆**pessi'mistically** *adv* avec pessimisme.

pest [pest] *n* animal *m or* insecte *m* nuisible; (*person*) *Fam* casse-pieds *mf inv*, peste *f*. ◆**pesticide** *n* pesticide *m*.

pester ['pestər] *vt* (*harass*) harceler (**with questions** de questions); **to p. s.o. to do sth/for sth** harceler *or* tarabuster qn pour qu'il fasse qch/jusqu'à ce qu'il donne qch.

pet [pet] **1** *n* animal *m* (domestique); (*favourite person*) chouchou, -oute *mf*; **yes (my) p.** *Fam* oui mon chou; **to have** *or* **keep a p.** avoir un animal chez soi; — *a* (*dog etc*) domestique; (*tiger etc*) apprivoisé; (*favourite*) favori; **p. shop** magasin *m* d'animaux; **p. hate** bête *f* noire; **p. name** petit nom *m* (d'amitié); **p. subject** dada *m*. **2** *vt* (-tt-) (*fondle*) caresser; (*sexually*) *Fam* peloter; — *vi Fam* se peloter.

petal ['pet(ə)l] *n* pétale *m*.

peter ['piːtər] *vi* **to p. out** (*run out*) s'épuiser; (*dry up*) se tarir; (*die out*) mourir; (*disappear*) disparaître.

petite [pə'tiːt] *a* (*woman*) petite et mince, menue.

petition [pə'tɪʃ(ə)n] *n* (*signatures*) pétition *f*; (*request*) *Jur* requête *f*; **p. for divorce** demande *f* en divorce; — *vt* adresser une pétition *or* une requête à (**for sth** pour demander qch).

petrify ['petrɪfaɪ] *vt* (*frighten*) pétrifier de terreur.

petrol ['petrəl] *n* essence *f*; **I've run out of p.** je suis tombé en panne d'essence; **p. engine** moteur *m* à essence; **p. station** poste *m* d'essence, station-service *f*.

petroleum [pə'trəʊlɪəm] *n* pétrole *m*.

petticoat ['petɪkəʊt] *n* jupon *m*.

petty ['petɪ] *a* (*-ier, -iest*) (*small*) petit; (*trivial*) insignifiant, menu, petit; (*mean*) mesquin; **p. cash** *Com* petite caisse *f*, menue monnaie *f*. ◆**pettiness** *n* petitesse *f*; insignifiance *f*; mesquinerie *f*.

petulant ['petjʊlənt] *a* irritable. ◆**petulance** *n* irritabilité *f*.

petunia [pɪ'tjuːnɪə] *n Bot* pétunia *m*.

pew [pjuː] *n* banc *m* d'église; **take a p.!** *Hum* assieds-toi!

pewter ['pjuːtər] *n* étain *m*.

phallic ['fælɪk] *a* phallique.

phantom ['fæntəm] *n* fantôme *m*.

pharmacy ['fɑːməsɪ] *n* pharmacie *f*. ◆**pharmaceutical** [-'sjuːtɪk(ə)l] *a* pharmaceutique. ◆**pharmacist** *n* pharmacien, -ienne *mf*.

pharynx ['færɪŋks] *n Anat* pharynx *m*. ◆**pharyn'gitis** *n Med* pharyngite *f*.

phase [feɪz] *n* (*stage*) phase *f*; — *vt* **to p.**

in/out introduire/supprimer progressive-ment. ◆**phased** a (changes etc) progressif.
PhD [piːeitʃ'diː] n abbr (Doctor of Philosophy) (degree) Univ doctorat m.
pheasant ['fezənt] n (bird) faisan m.
phenomenon, pl -**ena** [fɪ'nɒmɪnən, -ɪnə] n phénomène m. ◆**phenomenal** a phéno-ménal.
phew! [fjuː] int (relief) ouf!
philanderer [fɪ'lændərər] n coureur m de jupons.
philanthropist [fɪ'lænθrəpɪst] n philan-thrope mf. ◆**philan'thropic** a philan-thropique.
philately [fɪ'lætəlɪ] n philatélie. ◆**phila-'telic** a philatélique. ◆**philatelist** n philatéliste mf.
philharmonic [fɪlə'mɒnɪk] a philharmo-nique.
Philippines ['fɪlɪpiːnz] npl the P. les Philip-pines fpl.
philistine ['fɪlɪstaɪn] n béotien, -ienne mf, philistin m.
philosophy [fɪ'lɒsəfɪ] n philosophie f. ◆**philosopher** n philosophe mf. ◆**philo-'sophical** a philosophique; (stoical, resigned) Fig philosophe. ◆**philo'soph-ically** adv (to say etc) avec philosophie. ◆**philosophize** vi philosopher.
phlegm [flem] n Med glaires fpl; (calmness) Fig flegme m. ◆**phleg'matic** a flegma-tique.
phobia ['fəʊbɪə] n phobie f.
phone [fəʊn] n téléphone m; on the p. (speaking here) au téléphone; (at other end) au bout du fil; to be on the p. (as subscriber) avoir le téléphone; p. call coup m de fil or de téléphone; to make a p. call téléphoner (to à); p. book annuaire m; p. box, p. booth cabine f téléphonique; p. number numéro m de téléphone; – vt (message) téléphoner (to à); to p. s.o. (up) téléphoner à qn; – vi to p. (up) téléphoner; to p. back rappeler. ◆**phonecard** n télécarte f.
phonetic [fə'netɪk] a phonétique. ◆**pho-netics** n (science) phonétique f.
phoney ['fəʊnɪ] a (-ier, -iest) Fam (jewels, writer etc) faux; (attack, firm) bidon inv; (attitude) fumiste; – n Fam (impostor) imposteur m; (joker, shirker) fumiste mf; it's a p. (jewel, coin etc) c'est du faux.
phonograph ['fəʊnəgræf] n Am élec-trophone m.
phosphate ['fɒsfeɪt] n Ch phosphate m.
phosphorus ['fɒsfərəs] n Ch phosphore m.
photo ['fəʊtəʊ] n (pl -os) photo f; to have one's p. taken se faire photographier.

◆**photocopier** n (machine) photocopieur m. ◆**photocopy** n photocopie f; – vt photocopier. ◆**photo'genic** a photogéni-que. ◆**photograph** n photographie f; – vt photographier; – vi to p. well être pho-togénique. ◆**photographer** [fə'tɒgrəfər] n photographe mf. ◆**photo'graphic** a photographique. ◆**photography** [fə'tɒ-grəfɪ] n (activity) photographie f. ◆**photo-stat**® = photocopy.
phras/e [freɪz] n (saying) expression f; (idiom) & Gram locution f; – vt (express) exprimer; (letter) rédiger. ◆—**ing** n (word-ing) termes mpl. ◆**phrasebook** n (for tourists) manuel m de conversation.
physical ['fɪzɪk(ə)l] a physique; (object, world) matériel; p. examination Med examen m médical; p. education, p. training éducation f physique. ◆**physically** adv physiquement; p. impossible matérielle-ment impossible.
physician [fɪ'zɪʃ(ə)n] n médecin m.
physics ['fɪzɪks] n (science) physique f. ◆**physicist** n physicien, -ienne mf.
physiology [fɪzɪ'ɒlədʒɪ] n physiologie f. ◆**physio'logical** a physiologique.
physiotherapy [fɪzɪəʊ'θerəpɪ] n kinésithé-rapie f. ◆**physiotherapist** n kinésithé-rapeute mf.
physique [fɪ'ziːk] n (appearance) physique m; (constitution) constitution f.
piano [pi'ænəʊ] n (pl -os) piano m. ◆**'pianist** n pianiste mf.
piazza [pi'ætsə] n (square) place f; (covered) passage m couvert.
picayune [pɪkə'juːn] a (petty) Am Fam mesquin.
pick [pɪk] n (choice) choix m; the p. of (best) le meilleur de; the p. of the bunch le dessus du panier; to take one's p. faire son choix, choisir; – vt (choose) choisir; (flower, fruit etc) cueillir; (hole) faire (in dans); (lock) crocheter; to p. one's nose se mettre les doigts dans le nez; to p. one's teeth se curer les dents; to p. a fight chercher la bagarre (with avec); to p. holes in Fig relever les défauts de; to p. (off) (remove) enlever; to p. out (choose) choisir; (identify) reconnaître, distinguer; to p. up (sth dropped) ramasser; (fallen person or chair) relever; (person into air, weight) soulever; (cold, money) Fig ramasser; (habit, accent, speed) prendre; (fetch, collect) (passer) prendre; (find) trouver; (baby) prendre dans ses bras; (programme etc) Rad capter; (survivor) recueillir; (arrest) arrêter, ramasser; (learn) apprendre; – vi to p. and choose choisir

avec soin; **to p. on** (*nag*) harceler; (*blame*) accuser; **why p. on me?** pourquoi moi?; **to p. up** (*improve*) s'améliorer; (*of business, trade*) reprendre; *Med* aller mieux; (*resume*) continuer. ◆**—ing 1** *n* (*choosing*) choix *m* (**of** de); (*of flower, fruit etc*) cueillette *f.* **2** *npl* (*leftovers*) restes *mpl*; *Com* profits *mpl.* ◆**pick-me-up** *n* (*drink*) *Fam* remontant *m.* ◆**pick-up** *n* (*of record player*) (bras *m* de) pick-up *m*; (*person*) *Pej Fam* partenaire *mf* de rencontre; **p.-up** (**truck**) pick-up *m.*

pick(axe) (*Am* (**-ax**)) ['pik(æks)] *n* (*tool*) pioche *f*; **ice pick** pic *m* à glace.

picket ['pikit] **1** *n* (*striker*) gréviste *mf*; **p. (line)** piquet *m* (de grève); — *vt* (*factory*) installer des piquets de grève aux portes de. **2** *n* (*stake*) piquet *m.*

pickle ['pik(ə)l] **1** *n* (*brine*) saumure *f*; (*vinegar*) vinaigre *m*; *pl* (*vegetables*) pickles *mpl*; *Am* concombres *mpl*, cornichons *mpl*; — *vt* mariner. **2** *n* **in a p.** (*trouble*) *Fam* dans le pétrin.

pickpocket ['pikpɒkit] *n* (*thief*) pickpocket *m.*

picky ['piki] *a* (**-ier, -iest**) (*choosey*) *Am* difficile.

picnic ['piknik] *n* pique-nique *m*; — *vi* (**-ck-**) pique-niquer.

pictorial [pik'tɔːriəl] *a* (*in pictures*) en images; (*periodical*) illustré.

picture ['piktʃər] **1** *n* image *f*; (*painting*) tableau *m*, peinture *f*; (*drawing*) dessin *m*; (*photo*) photo *f*; (*film*) film *m*; (*scene*) *Fig* tableau *m*; **the pictures** *Cin* le cinéma; **to put s.o. in the p.** *Fig* mettre qn au courant; **p. frame** cadre *m.* **2** *vt* (*imagine*) s'imaginer (**that** que); (*remember*) revoir; (*depict*) décrire.

picturesque [piktʃə'resk] *a* pittoresque.

piddling ['pidliŋ] *a Pej* dérisoire.

pidgin ['pidʒin] *n* **p.** (**English**) pidgin *m.*

pie [pai] *n* (*of meat, vegetable*) tourte *f*; (*of fruit*) tarte *f*, tourte *f*; (*compact filling*) pâté *m* en croûte; **cottage p.** hachis *m* Parmentier.

piebald ['paibɔːld] *a* pie *inv.*

piece [piːs] *n* morceau *m*; (*of bread, paper, chocolate, etc*) bout *m*, morceau *m*; (*of fabric, machine, game, artillery*) pièce *f*; (*coin*) pièce *f*; **bits and pieces** des petites choses; **in pieces** en morceaux, en pièces; **to smash to pieces** briser en morceaux; **to take to pieces** (*machine etc*) démonter; **to come to pieces** se démonter; **to go to pieces** (*of person*) *Fig* craquer; **a p. of luck/news/etc** une chance/nouvelle/*etc*; **in**

one p. (*object*) intact; (*person*) indemne; — *vt* **to p. together** (*facts*) reconstituer; (*one's life*) refaire. ◆**piecemeal** *adv* petit à petit; — *a* (*unsystematic*) peu méthodique. ◆**piecework** *n* travail *m* à la tâche *or* à la pièce.

pier [piər] *n* (*promenade*) jetée *f*; (*for landing*) appontement *m.*

pierc/e [piəs] *vt* percer; (*of cold, sword, bullet*) transpercer (*qn*). ◆**—ing** *a* (*voice, look etc*) perçant; (*wind etc*) glacial.

piety ['paiəti] *n* piété *f.*

piffling ['pifliŋ] *a Fam* insignifiant.

pig [pig] *n* cochon *m*, porc *m*; (*evil person*) *Pej* cochon *m*; (*glutton*) *Pej* goinfre *m.* ◆**piggish** *a Pej* (*dirty*) sale; (*greedy*) goinfre. ◆**piggy** *a* (*greedy*) *Fam* goinfre. ◆**piggybank** *n* tirelire *f* (*en forme de cochon*).

pigeon ['pidʒin] *n* pigeon *m.* ◆**pigeonhole** *n* casier *m*; — *vt* classer; (*shelve*) mettre en suspens.

piggyback ['pigibæk] *n* **to give s.o. a p.** porter qn sur le dos.

pigheaded [pig'hedid] *a* obstiné.

pigment ['pigmənt] *n* pigment *m.* ◆**pigmen'tation** *n* pigmentation *f.*

pigsty ['pigstai] *n* porcherie *f.*

pigtail ['pigteil] *n* (*hair*) natte *f.*

pike [paik] *n* **1** (*fish*) brochet *m.* **2** (*weapon*) pique *f.*

pilchard ['piltʃəd] *n* pilchard *m*, sardine *f.*

pile[1] [pail] *n* pile *f*; (*fortune*) *Fam* fortune *f*; **piles of, a p. of** *Fam* beaucoup de, un tas de; — *vt* **to p.** (**up**) (*stack up*) empiler; — *vi* **to p. into** (*of people*) s'entasser dans; **to p. up** (*accumulate*) s'accumuler, s'amonceler. ◆**p.-up** *n Aut* collision *f* en chaîne, carambolage *m.*

pile[2] [pail] *n* (*of carpet*) poils *mpl.*

piles [pailz] *npl Med* hémorroïdes *fpl.*

pilfer ['pilfər] *vt* (*steal*) chaparder (**from s.o.** à qn). ◆**—ing** *n*, ◆**—age** *n* chapardage *m.*

pilgrim ['pilgrim] *n* pèlerin *m.* ◆**pilgrimage** *n* pèlerinage *m.*

pill [pil] *n* pilule *f*; **to be on the p.** (*of woman*) prendre la pilule; **to go on/off the p.** se mettre à/arrêter la pilule.

pillage ['pilidʒ] *vti* piller; — *n* pillage *m.*

pillar ['pilər] *n* pilier *m*; (*of smoke*) *Fig* colonne *f.* **p.-box** *n* boîte *f* à *or* aux lettres (*située sur le trottoir*).

pillion ['piliən] *adv* **to ride p.** (*on motorbike*) monter derrière.

pillory ['piləri] *vt* (*ridicule, scorn*) mettre au pilori.

pillow ['piləʊ] n oreiller m. ◆**pillowcase** n, ◆**pillowslip** n taie f d'oreiller.

pilot ['paɪlət] **1** n (of aircraft, ship) pilote m; – vt piloter; – a **p. light** (on appliance) voyant m. **2** a (experimental) (-)pilote: **p. scheme** projet(-)pilote m.

pimento [pɪ'mentəʊ] n (pl -os) piment m.

pimp [pɪmp] n souteneur m.

pimple ['pɪmp(ə)l] n bouton m. ◆**pimply** a (-ier, iest) boutonneux.

pin [pɪn] n épingle f; (drawing pin) punaise f; Tech goupille f, fiche f; **to have pins and needles** Med Fam avoir des fourmis (**in** dans); **p. money** argent m de poche; – vt (-nn-) **to p. (on)** (attach) épingler (to sur, à); (to wall) punaiser (to, on à); **to p. one's hopes on** mettre tous ses espoirs dans; **to p. on (to) s.o.** (crime, action) accuser qn de; **to p. down** (immobilize) immobiliser; (fix) fixer; (enemy) clouer; **to p. s.o. down** Fig forcer qn à préciser ses idées; **to p. up** (notice) afficher. ◆**pincushion** n pelote f (à épingles). ◆**pinhead** n tête f d'épingle.

pinafore ['pɪnəfɔːr] n (apron) tablier m; (dress) robe f chasuble.

pinball ['pɪnbɔːl] a **p. machine** flipper m.

pincers ['pɪnsəz] npl tenailles fpl.

pinch [pɪntʃ] **1** n (mark) pinçon m; (of salt) pincée f; **to give s.o. a p.** pincer qn; **at a p.,** Am **in a p.** (if necessary) au besoin; **to feel the p.** Fig souffrir (du manque d'argent etc); – vt pincer; – vi (of shoes) faire mal. **2** vt Fam (steal) piquer (**from** à); (arrest) pincer.

pine [paɪn] **1** n (tree, wood) pin m; **p. forest** pinède f. **2** vi **to p. for** désirer vivement (retrouver), languir après; **to p. away** dépérir.

pineapple ['paɪnæp(ə)l] n ananas m.

ping [pɪŋ] n bruit m métallique. ◆**pinger** n (on appliance) signal m sonore.

ping-pong ['pɪŋpɒŋ] n ping-pong m.

pink [pɪŋk] a & n (colour) rose (m).

pinkie ['pɪŋkɪ] n Am petit doigt m.

pinnacle ['pɪnək(ə)l] n (highest point) Fig apogée m.

pinpoint ['pɪnpɔɪnt] vt (locate) repérer; (define) définir.

pinstripe ['pɪnstraɪp] a (suit) rayé.

pint [paɪnt] n pinte f (Br = 0,57 litre, Am = 0,47 litre); **a p. of beer** = un demi.

pinup ['pɪnʌp] n (girl) pin-up f inv.

pioneer [paɪə'nɪər] n pionnier, -ière mf; – vt (research, study) entreprendre pour la première fois.

pious ['paɪəs] a (person, deed) pieux.

pip [pɪp] **1** n (of fruit) pépin m. **2** n (on

uniform) Mil galon m, sardine f. **3** npl the **pips** (sound) Tel le bip-bip.

pip/e [paɪp] **1** n tuyau m; (of smoker) pipe f; (instrument) Mus pipeau m; **the pipes** (bagpipes) Mus la cornemuse; (peace) **p.** calumet m de la paix; **to smoke a p.** fumer la pipe; **p. cleaner** cure-pipe m; **p. dream** chimère f; – vt (water etc) transporter par tuyaux or par canalisation; **piped music** musique f (de fond) enregistrée. **2** vi **to p. down** (shut up) Fam la boucler, se taire. ◆**—ing** n (system of pipes) canalisations fpl, tuyaux mpl; **length of p.** tuyau m; – adv **it's p. hot** (soup etc) c'est très chaud. ◆**pipeline** n pipeline m; **it's in the p.** Fig c'est en route.

pirate ['paɪərət] n pirate m; – a (radio, ship) pirate. ◆**piracy** n piraterie f. ◆**pirated** a (book, record etc) pirate.

Pisces ['paɪsiːz] npl (sign) les Poissons mpl.

pistachio [pɪ'stæʃɪəʊ] n (pl -os) (fruit, flavour) pistache f.

pistol ['pɪstəl] n pistolet m.

piston ['pɪst(ə)n] n Aut piston m.

pit [pɪt] **1** n (hole) trou m; (mine) mine f; (quarry) carrière f; (of stomach) creux m; Th orchestre m; Sp Aut stand m de ravitaillement. **2** vt (-tt-) **to p. oneself** or **one's wits against** se mesurer à. **3** n (stone of fruit) Am noyau m. ◆**pitted** a **1** (face) grêlé; **p. with rust** piqué de rouille. **2** (fruit) Am dénoyauté.

pitch¹ [pɪtʃ] **1** n Sp terrain m; (in market) place f. **2** n (degree) degré m; (of voice) hauteur f; Mus ton m. **3** vt (ball) lancer; (camp) établir; (tent) dresser; **a pitched battle** Mil une bataille rangée; Fig une belle bagarre. **4** vi (of ship) tanguer. **5** vi **to p. in** (cooperate) Fam se mettre de la partie; **to p. into s.o.** attaquer qn.

pitch² [pɪtʃ] n (tar) poix f. ◆**p.-'black** a, ◆**p.-'dark** a noir comme dans un four.

pitcher ['pɪtʃər] n cruche f, broc m.

pitchfork ['pɪtʃfɔːk] n fourche f (à foin).

pitfall ['pɪtfɔːl] n (trap) piège m.

pith [pɪθ] n (of orange) peau f blanche; (essence) Fig moelle f. ◆**pithy** a (-ier, -iest) (remark etc) piquant et concis.

pitiful ['pɪtɪfəl] a pitoyable. ◆**pitiless** a impitoyable.

pittance ['pɪtəns] n (income) revenu m or salaire m misérable; (sum) somme f dérisoire.

pitter-patter ['pɪtəpætər] n = **patter 1.**

pity ['pɪtɪ] n pitié f; (what) **a p.!** (quel) dommage!; **it's a p.** c'est dommage (**that**

que (+ *sub*), **to do** de faire; **to have** *or* **take p. on** avoir pitié de; − *vt* plaindre.
pivot ['pɪvət] *n* pivot *m*; − *vi* pivoter.
pixie ['pɪksɪ] *n* (*fairy*) lutin *m*.
pizza ['pi:tsə] *n* pizza *f*.
placard ['plækɑːd] *n* (*notice*) affiche *f*.
placate [plə'keɪt, *Am* 'pleɪkeɪt] *vt* calmer.
place [pleɪs] *n* endroit *m*; (*specific*) lieu *m*; (*house*) maison *f*; (*premises*) locaux *mpl*; (*seat, position, rank*) place *f*; **in the first p.** (*firstly*) en premier lieu; **to take p.** (*happen*) avoir lieu; **p. of work** lieu *m* de travail; **market p.** (*square*) place *f* du marché; **at my p.,** to my p. *Fam* chez moi; **some p.** (*somewhere*) *Am* quelque part; **no p.** (*nowhere*) *Am* nulle part; **all over the p.** partout; **to lose one's p.** perdre sa place; (*in book etc*) perdre sa page; (*at the table*) mettre trois couverts; **to take the p. of** remplacer; **in p. of** à la place de; **out of p.** (*remark, object*) déplacé; (*person*) dépaysé; **p. mat** set *m* (de table); − *vt* (*put, situate, invest*) & *Sp* placer; (*an order*) *Com* passer (**with s.o.** à qn); (*remember*) se rappeler; (*identify*) reconnaître. ◆**placing** *n* (*of money*) placement *m*.
placid ['plæsɪd] *a* placide.
plagiarize ['pleɪdʒəraɪz] *vt* plagier. ◆**plagiarism** *n* plagiat *m*.
plague [pleɪg] **1** *n* (*disease*) peste *f*; (*nuisance*) *Fam* plaie *f*. **2** *vt* (*harass, pester*) harceler (**with** de).
plaice [pleɪs] *n* (*fish*) carrelet *m*, plie *f*.
plaid [plæd] *n* (*fabric*) tissu *m* écossais.
plain¹ [pleɪn] **1** *a* (-er, -est) (*clear, obvious*) clair; (*outspoken*) franc; (*simple*) simple; (*not patterned*) uni; (*woman, man*) sans beauté; (*sheer*) pur; **in p. clothes** en civil; **to make it p. to s.o.** that faire comprendre à qn que; **p. speaking** franc-parler *m*; − *adv* (*tired etc*) tout bonnement. ◆**−ly** *adv* clairement; franchement. ◆**−ness** *n* clarté *f*; simplicité *f*; manque *m* de beauté.
plain² [pleɪn] *n* *Geog* plaine *f*.
plaintiff ['pleɪntɪf] *n* *Jur* plaignant, -ante *mf*.
plait [plæt] *n* tresse *f*, natte *f*; − *vt* tresser, natter.
plan [plæn] *n* projet *m*; (*elaborate*) plan *m*; (*of house, book etc*) & *Pol Econ* plan *m*; **the best p. would be to . . .** le mieux serait de . . . ; **according to p.** comme prévu; **to have no plans** (*be free*) n'avoir rien de prévu; **to change one's plans** (*decide differently*) changer d'idée; **master p.** stratégie *f* d'ensemble; − *vt* (-nn-) (*envisage, decide on*) prévoir, projeter; (*organize*) organiser;

(*prepare*) préparer; (*design*) concevoir; *Econ* planifier; **to p. to do** (*intend*) avoir l'intention de faire; **as planned** comme prévu; − *vi* faire des projets; **to p. for** (*rain, disaster*) prévoir. ◆**planning** *n* *Econ* planification *f*; (*industrial, commercial*) planning *m*; **family p.** planning *m* familial; **town p.** urbanisme *m*. ◆**planner** *n* **town p.** urbaniste *mf*.
plane [pleɪn] *n* **1** (*aircraft*) avion *m*. **2** *Carp* rabot *m*. **3** (*tree*) platane *m*. **4** (*level*) & *Fig* plan *m*.
planet ['plænɪt] *n* planète *f*. ◆**plane-'tarium** *n* planétarium *m*. ◆**planetary** *a* planétaire.
plank [plæŋk] *n* planche *f*.
plant [plɑːnt] **1** *n* plante *f*; **house p.** plante d'appartement; − *vt* planter (**with** en, de); (*bomb*) *Fig* (dé)poser; **to p. sth on s.o.** (*hide*) cacher qch sur qn. **2** *n* (*machinery*) matériel *m*; (*fixtures*) installation *f*; (*factory*) usine *f*. ◆**plan'tation** *n* (*land, trees etc*) plantation *f*.
plaque [plæk] *n* **1** (*commemorative plate*) plaque *f*. **2** (*on teeth*) plaque *f* dentaire.
plasma ['plæzmə] *n* *Med* plasma *m*.
plaster ['plɑːstər] *n* (*substance*) plâtre *m*; (*sticking*) p. sparadrap *m*; **p. of Paris** plâtre *m* à mouler; **in p.** *Med* dans le plâtre; **p. cast** *Med* plâtre *m*; − *vt* plâtrer; **to p. down** (*hair*) plaquer; **to p. with** (*cover*) couvrir de. ◆**−er** *n* plâtrier *m*.
plastic ['plæstɪk] *a* (*substance, art*) plastique; (*object*) en plastique; **p. explosive** plastic *m*; **p. surgery** chirurgie *f* esthétique; − *n* plastique *m*, matière *f* plastique.
plasticine® ['plæstɪsiːn] *n* pâte *f* à modeler.
plate [pleɪt] *n* (*dish*) assiette *f*; (*metal sheet on door, on vehicle etc*) plaque *f*; (*book illustration*) gravure *f*; (*dental*) dentier *m*; **gold/silver p.** vaisselle *f* d'or/d'argent; **a lot on one's p.** (*work*) *Fig* du pain sur la planche; **p. glass** verre *m* à vitre; − *vt* (*jewellery, metal*) plaquer (**with** de). ◆**plateful** *n* assiettée *f*, assiette *f*.
plateau ['plætəʊ] *n* *Geog* (*pl* -**s** *or* -**x**) plateau *m*.
platform ['plætfɔːm] *n* estrade *f*; (*for speaker*) tribune *f*; (*on bus*) & *Pol Rail* quai *m*; **p. shoes** chaussures *fpl* à semelles compensées.
platinum ['plætɪnəm] *n* (*metal*) platine *m*; − *a* **p.** *or* **p.-blond(e) hair** cheveux *mpl* platinés.
platitude ['plætɪtjuːd] *n* platitude *f*.
platonic [plə'tɒnɪk] *a* (*love etc*) platonique.
platoon [plə'tuːn] *n* *Mil* section *f*.

platter ['plætər] n Culin plat m.

plaudits ['plɔːdɪts] npl applaudissements mpl.

plausible ['plɔːzəb(ə)l] a (argument etc) plausible; (speaker etc) convaincant.

play [pleɪ] n (amusement, looseness) jeu m; Th pièce f (de théâtre), spectacle m; **a p. on words** un jeu de mots; **to come into p.** entrer en jeu; **to call into p.** faire entrer en jeu; – vt (card, part, tune etc) jouer; (game) jouer à; (instrument) jouer de; (match) disputer (with avec); (team, opponent) jouer contre; (record) passer; (radio) faire marcher; **to p. ball with** Fig coopérer avec; **to p. the fool** faire l'idiot; **to p. a part in doing/in sth** contribuer a faire/à qch; **to p. it cool** Fam garder son sang-froid; **to p. back** (tape) réécouter; **to p. down** minimiser; **to p. s.o. up** Fam (of bad back etc) tracasser qn; (of child etc) faire enrager qn; **played out** Fam (tired) épuisé; (idea, method) périmé, vieux jeu inv; – vi jouer (with avec, at à); (of record player, tape recorder) marcher; **what are you playing at?** Fam qu'est-ce que tu fais?; **to p. about** or **around** jouer, s'amuser; **to p. on** (piano etc) jouer de; (s.o.'s emotions etc) jouer sur; **to p. up** (of child, machine etc) Fam faire des siennes; **to p. up to s.o.** faire de la lèche à qn. ◆—**ing** n jeu m; **p. card** carte f à jouer; **p. field** terrain m de jeu. ◆—**er** n Sp joueur, -euse mf; Th acteur m, actrice f; (of clarinette/etc) p. joueur, -euse mf de clarinette/etc; **cassette p.** lecteur m de cassettes.

play-act ['pleɪækt] vi jouer la comédie. ◆**playboy** n playboy m. ◆**playgoer** n amateur m de théâtre. ◆**playground** n Sch cour f de récréation. ◆**playgroup** n = playschool. ◆**playmate** n camarade mf. ◆**playpen** n parc m (pour enfants). ◆**playroom** n (in house) salle f de jeux. ◆**playschool** n garderie f (d'enfants). ◆**plaything** n (person) Fig jouet m. ◆**playtime** n Sch récréation f. ◆**playwright** n dramaturge mf.

playful ['pleɪfəl] a enjoué; (child) joueur. ◆—**ly** adv (to say) en badinant. ◆—**ness** n enjouement m.

plc [piːelˈsiː] abbr (public limited company) SA.

plea [pliː] n (request) appel m; (excuse) excuse f; **to make a p. of guilty** Jur plaider coupable. ◆**plead** vi Jur plaider; **to p. with s.o. to do** implorer qn de faire; **to p. for** (help etc) implorer; – vt Jur plaider; (as excuse) alléguer. ◆**pleading** n (requests) prières fpl.

pleasant ['plezənt] a agréable; (polite) aimable. ◆—**ly** adv agréablement. ◆—**ness** n (charm) charme m; (of person) amabilité f. ◆**pleasantries** npl (jokes) plaisanteries fpl; (polite remarks) civilités fpl.

pleas/e [pliːz] adv s'il vous plaît, s'il te plaît; **p. sit down** asseyez-vous, je vous prie; **p. do!** bien sûr!, je vous en prie! '**no smoking p.**' 'prière de ne pas fumer'; – vt plaire à; (satisfy) contenter; **hard to p.** difficile (à contenter), exigeant; **p. yourself!** comme tu veux!; – vi plaire; **do as you p.** fais comme tu veux; **as much or as many as you p.** autant qu'il vous plaira. ◆—**ed** a content (with de, that que (+ sub), to do faire); **p. to meet you!** enchanté!; **I'd be p. to!** avec plaisir! ◆—**ing** a agréable, plaisant.

pleasure ['pleʒər] n plaisir m; **p. boat** bateau m de plaisance. ◆**pleasurable** a très agréable.

pleat [pliːt] n (fold) pli m; – vt plisser.

plebiscite ['plebɪsɪt, -saɪt] n plébiscite m.

pledge [pledʒ] **1** n (promise) promesse f, engagement m (to do de faire); – vt promettre (to do de faire). **2** n (token, object) gage m; – vt (pawn) engager.

plenty ['plentɪ] n abondance f; **in p.** en abondance; **p. of** beaucoup de; **that's p.** (enough) c'est assez, ça suffit. ◆**plentiful** a abondant.

plethora ['pleθərə] n pléthore f.

pleurisy ['pluərɪsɪ] n Med pleurésie f.

pliable ['plaɪəb(ə)l] a souple.

pliers ['plaɪəz] npl (tool) pince(s) f(pl).

plight [plaɪt] n (crisis) situation f critique; **(sorry) p.** triste situation f.

plimsoll ['plɪmsəul] n chaussure f de tennis, tennis f.

plinth [plɪnθ] n socle m.

plod [plɒd] vi (-dd-) **to p. (along)** avancer or travailler laborieusement; **to p. through** (book) lire laborieusement. ◆**plodding** a (slow) lent; (step) pesant. ◆**plodder** n (steady worker) bûcheur, -euse mf.

plonk [plɒŋk] **1** int (splash) plouf! **2** vt **to p. (down)** (drop) Fam poser (bruyamment). **3** n (wine) Pej Sl pinard m.

plot [plɒt] **1** n (conspiracy) complot m (against contre); Cin Th Liter intrigue f; – vti (-tt-) comploter (**to do** de faire). **2** n **p.** (of land) terrain m; (patch in garden) carré m de terre; **building p.** terrain m à bâtir. **3** vt (-tt-) **p. (out)** déterminer; (graph, diagram) tracer; (one's position) relever. ◆**plotting** n (conspiracies) complots mpl.

plough [plau] n charrue f; – vt labourer; **to**

p. back into (*money*) *Fig* réinvestir dans; − *vi* labourer; **to p. into** (*crash into*) percuter; **to p. through** (*snow etc*) avancer péniblement dans; (*fence, wall*) défoncer. ◆**ploughman** *n* (*pl* **-men**) laboureur *m*; **p.'s lunch** *Culin* assiette *f* composée (*de crudités et fromage*).

plow [plau] *Am* = **plough**.

ploy [plɔɪ] *n* stratagème *m*.

pluck [plʌk] **1** *n* courage *m*; − *vt* **to p. up courage** s'armer de courage. **2** *vt* (*fowl*) plumer; (*eyebrows*) épiler; (*string*) *Mus* pincer; (*flower*) cueillir. ◆**plucky** *a* (**-ier, -iest**) courageux.

plug [plʌg] **1** *n* (*of cotton wool, wood etc*) tampon *m*, bouchon *m*; (*for sink etc drainage*) bonde *f*; − *vt* (**-gg-**) **to p. (up)** (*stop up*) boucher. **2** *n El* fiche *f*, prise *f* (*mâle*); − *vt* (**-gg-**) **to p. in** brancher. **3** *n Aut* bougie *f*. **4** *n* (*publicity*) *Fam* battage *m* publicitaire; − *vt* (**-gg-**) *Fam* faire du battage publicitaire pour. **5** *vi* (**-gg-**) **to p. away** (*work*) *Fam* bosser (**at** à). ◆**plughole** *n* trou *m* (*du lavabo etc*), vidange *f*.

plum [plʌm] *n* prune *f*; **a p. job** *Fam* un travail en or, un bon fromage.

plumage ['pluːmɪdʒ] *n* plumage *m*.

plumb [plʌm] **1** *vt* (*probe, understand*) sonder. **2** *adv* (*crazy etc*) *Am Fam* complètement; **p. in the middle** en plein milieu.

plumber ['plʌmər] *n* plombier *m*. ◆**plumbing** *n* plomberie *f*.

plume [pluːm] *n* (*feather*) plume *f*; (*on hat etc*) plumet *m*; **a p. of smoke** un panache de fumée.

plummet ['plʌmɪt] *vi* (*of aircraft etc*) plonger; (*of prices*) dégringoler.

plump [plʌmp] **1** *a* (**-er, -est**) (*person*) grassouillet; (*arm, chicken*) dodu; (*cushion, cheek*) rebondi. **2** *vi* **to p. for** (*choose*) se décider pour, choisir. ◆**—ness** *n* rondeur *f*.

plunder ['plʌndər] *vt* piller; − *n* (*act*) pillage *m*; (*goods*) butin *m*.

plung/e [plʌndʒ] *vt* (*thrust*) plonger (**into** dans); − *vi* (*dive*) plonger (**into** dans); (*fall*) tomber (**from** de); (*rush*) se lancer; − *n* (*dive*) plongeon *m*; (*fall*) chute *f*; **to take the p.** *Fig* se jeter à l'eau. ◆**—ing** *a* (*neckline*) plongeant. ◆**—er** *n* ventouse *f* (*pour déboucher un tuyau*), débouchoir *m*.

plural ['pluərəl] *a* (*form*) pluriel; (*noun*) au pluriel; − *n* pluriel *m*; **in the p.** au pluriel.

plus [plʌs] *prep* plus; − *a* (*factor etc*) & *El* positif; **twenty p.** vingt et quelques; − *n p.*

(*sign*) *Math* (signe *m*) plus *m*; **it's a p.** c'est un (avantage en) plus.

plush [plʌʃ] *a* (**-er, -est**) (*splendid*) somptueux.

plutonium [pluːˈtəʊnɪəm] *n* plutonium *m*.

ply [plaɪ] **1** *vt* (*trade*) exercer; (*oar, tool*) *Lit* manier. **2** *vi* **to p. between** (*travel*) faire la navette entre. **3** *vt* **to p. s.o. with** (*whisky etc*) faire boire continuellement à qn; (*questions*) bombarder qn de.

p.m. [piːˈem] *adv* (*afternoon*) de l'après-midi; (*evening*) du soir.

PM [piːˈem] *n abbr* (*Prime Minister*) Premier ministre *m*.

pneumatic [njuːˈmætɪk] *a* **p. drill** marteau-piqueur *m*, marteau *m* pneumatique.

pneumonia [njuːˈməʊnɪə] *n* pneumonie *f*.

poach [pəʊtʃ] **1** *vt* (*egg*) pocher. **2** *vi* (*hunt, steal*) braconner; − *vt* (*employee from rival firm*) débaucher, piquer. ◆**—ing** *n* braconnage *m* ◆**—er** *n* **1** (*person*) braconnier *m*. **2** (*egg*) p. pocheuse *f*.

PO Box [piːəʊˈbɒks] *abbr* (*Post Office Box*) BP.

pocket ['pɒkɪt] *n* poche *f*; (*area*) *Fig* petite zone *f*; (*of resistance*) poche *f*, îlot *m*; **I'm $5 out of p.** j'ai perdu 5 dollars; − *a* (*money, book etc*) de poche; − *vt* (*gain, steal*) empocher. ◆**pocketbook** *n* (*notebook*) carnet *m*; (*woman's handbag*) *Am* sac *m* à main. ◆**pocketful** *n* **a p. of** une pleine poche de.

pockmarked ['pɒkmɑːkt] *a* (*face*) grêlé.

pod [pɒd] *n* cosse *f*.

podgy ['pɒdʒɪ] *a* (**-ier, -iest**) (*arm etc*) dodu; (*person*) rondelet.

podium ['pəʊdɪəm] *n* podium *m*.

poem ['pəʊɪm] *n* poème *m*. ◆**poet** *n* poète *m*. ◆**po'etic** *a* poétique. ◆**poetry** *n* poésie *f*.

poignant ['pɔɪnjənt] *a* poignant.

point [pɔɪnt] **1** *n* (*of knife etc*) pointe *f*; *pl Rail* aiguillage *m*; (*power*) p. *El* prise *f* (de courant). **2** *n* (*dot, position, question, degree, score etc*) point *m*; (*decimal*) virgule *f*; (*meaning*) *Fig* sens *m*; (*importance*) intérêt *m*; (*remark*) remarque *f*; **p. of view** point *m* de vue; **at this p. in time** en ce moment; **on the p. of doing** sur le point de faire; **what's the p.?** à quoi bon? (*of waiting/etc* attendre/*etc*); **there's no p. (in) staying/etc** ça ne sert à rien de rester/*etc*; **that's not the p.** il ne s'agit pas de ça; **it's beside the p.** c'est à côté de la question; **to the p.** (*relevant*) pertinent; **get to the p.!** au fait!; **to make a p. of doing** prendre garde de faire; **his good**

points ses qualités *fpl*; **his bad points** ses défauts *mpl*. **3** *vt* (*aim*) pointer (**at** sur); (*vehicle*) tourner (**towards** vers); **to p. the way** indiquer le chemin (**to** à); *Fig* montrer la voie (**to** à); **to p. one's finger at** indiquer du doigt, pointer son doigt vers; **to p. out** (*show*) indiquer; (*mention*) signaler (**that** que); – *vi* **to p.** (**at** *or* **to s.o.**) indiquer (qn) du doigt; **to p. to, be pointing to** (*show*) indiquer; **to p. east** indiquer l'est; **to be pointing** (*of vehicle*) être tourné (**towards** vers); (*of gun*) être braqué (**at** sur). **◆—ed** *a* pointu; (*beard*) en pointe; (*remark, criticism*) *Fig* pertinent; (*incisive*) mordant. **◆—edly** *adv* (*to the point*) avec pertinence; (*incisively*) d'un ton mordant. **◆—er** *n* (*on dial etc*) index *m*; (*advice*) conseil *m*; (*clue*) indice *m*; **to be a p. to** (*possible solution etc*) laisser entrevoir. **◆—less** *a* inutile, futile. **◆—lessly** *adv* inutilement.

point-blank [pɔɪnt'blæŋk] *adv & a* (*to shoot, a shot*) à bout portant; (*to refuse, a refusal*) *Fig* (tout) net; (*to request, a request*) de but en blanc.

pois/e [pɔɪz] *n* (*balance*) équilibre *m*; (*of body*) port *m*; (*grace*) grâce *f*; (*confidence*) assurance *f*, calme *m*; – *vt* tenir en équilibre. **◆—ed** *a* en équilibre; (*hanging*) suspendu; (*composed*) calme; **p. to attack**/*etc* (*ready*) prêt à attaquer/*etc*.

poison ['pɔɪz(ə)n] *n* poison *m*; (*of snake*) venin *m*; **p. gas** gaz *m* toxique; – *vt* empoisonner; **to p. s.o.'s mind** corrompre qn. **◆poisoning** *n* empoisonnement *m*. **◆poisonous** *a* (*fumes, substance*) toxique; (*snake*) venimeux; (*plant*) vénéneux.

pok/e [pəʊk] *vt* (*push*) pousser (*avec un bâton etc*); (*touch*) toucher; (*fire*) tisonner; **to p. sth into** (*put, thrust*) fourrer *or* enfoncer qch dans; **to p. one's finger at** pointer son doigt vers; **to p. one's nose into** fourrer le nez dans; **to p. a hole in** faire un trou dans; **to p. one's head out of the window** passer la tête par la fenêtre; **to p. out s.o.'s eye** crever un œil à qn; – *vi* pousser; **to p. about** *or* **around in** fouiner dans; – *n* (*jab*) (petit) coup *m*; (*shove*) poussée *f*, coup *m*. **◆—er** *n* **1** (*for fire*) tisonnier *m*. **2** *Cards* poker *m*.

poky ['pəʊkɪ] *a* (**-ier, -iest**) (*small*) exigu et misérable, rikiki; (*slow*) *Am* lent.

Poland ['pəʊlənd] *n* Pologne *f*. **◆Pole** *n* Polonais, -aise *mf*.

polarize ['pəʊləraɪz] *vt* polariser.

pole [pəʊl] *n* **1** (*rod*) perche *f*; (*fixed*) poteau *m*; (*for flag*) mât *m*. **2** *Geog* pôle *m*;

North/South P. pôle Nord/Sud. **◆polar** *a* polaire; **p. bear** ours *m* blanc.

polemic [pə'lemɪk] *n* polémique *f*. **◆polemical** *a* polémique.

police [pə'liːs] *n* police *f*; **more** *or* **extra p.** des renforts *mpl* de police; – *a* (*inquiry etc*) de la police; (*state, dog*) policier; **p. cadet** agent *m* de police stagiaire; **p. car** voiture *f* de police; **p. force** police *f*; – *vt* (*city etc*) maintenir l'ordre *or* la paix dans; (*frontier*) contrôler. **◆policeman** *n* (*pl* -**men**) agent *m* de police. **◆policewoman** *n* (*pl* -**women**) femme-agent *f*.

policy ['pɒlɪsɪ] *n* **1** *Pol Econ etc* politique *f*; (*individual course of action*) règle *f*, façon *f* d'agir; *pl* (*ways of governing*) *Pol* politique *f*; **matter of p.** question *f* de principe. **2** (*insurance*) **p.** police *f* (d'assurance); **p. holder** assuré, -ée *mf*.

polio(myelitis) ['pəʊlɪəʊ(maɪə'laɪtɪs)] *n* polio(myélite) *f*; **p. victim** polio *mf*.

polish ['pɒlɪʃ] *vt* (*floor, table, shoes etc*) cirer; (*metal*) astiquer; (*rough surface*) polir; (*manners*) *Fig* raffiner; (*style*) *Fig* polir; **to p. off** (*food, work etc*) *Fam* liquider, finir (en vitesse); – *n* (*for shoes*) cirage *m*; (*for floor, furniture*) cire *f*; (*shine*) vernis *m*; *Fig* raffinement *m*; (**nail**) **p.** vernis *m* (à ongles); **to give sth a p.** faire briller qch.

Polish ['pəʊlɪʃ] *a* polonais; – *n* (*language*) polonais *m*.

polite [pə'laɪt] *a* (**-er, -est**) poli (**to, with** avec); **in p. society** dans la bonne société. **◆—ly** *adv* poliment. **◆—ness** *n* politesse *f*.

political [pə'lɪtɪk(ə)l] *a* politique. **◆politician** *n* homme *m* *or* femme *f* politique. **◆politicize** *vt* politiser. **◆politics** *n* politique *f*.

polka ['pɒlkə, *Am* 'pəʊlkə] *n* (*dance*) polka *f*; **p. dot** pois *m*.

poll [pəʊl] *n* (*voting*) scrutin *m*, élection *f*; (*vote*) vote *m*; (*turnout*) participation *f* électorale; (*list*) liste *f* électorale; **to go to the polls** aller aux urnes; (**opinion**) **p.** sondage *m* (d'opinion); **50% of the p.** 50% des votants; – *vt* (*votes*) obtenir; (*people*) sonder l'opinion de. **◆—ing** *n* (*election*) élections *fpl*; **p. booth** isoloir *m*; **p. station** bureau *m* de vote.

pollen ['pɒlən] *n* pollen *m*.

pollute [pə'luːt] *vt* polluer. **◆pollutant** *n* polluant *m*. **◆pollution** *n* pollution *f*.

polo ['pəʊləʊ] *n* *Sp* polo *m*; **p. neck** (*sweater, neckline*) col *m* roulé.

polyester [pɒlɪ'estər] *n* polyester *m*.

Polynesia [pɒlɪ'niːʒə] n Polynésie f.

polytechnic [pɒlɪ'teknɪk] n institut m universitaire de technologie.

polythene ['pɒlɪθiːn] n polyéthylène m; **p. bag** sac m en plastique.

pomegranate ['pɒmɪgrænɪt] n (fruit) grenade f.

pomp [pɒmp] n pompe f. ◆**pom'posity** n emphase f, solennité f. ◆**pompous** a pompeux.

pompon ['pɒmpɒn] n (ornament) pompon m.

pond [pɒnd] n étang m; (stagnant) mare f;(artificial) bassin m.

ponder ['pɒndər] vt **to p. (over)** réfléchir à; – vi réfléchir.

ponderous ['pɒndərəs] a (heavy, slow) pesant.

pong [pɒŋ] n Sl mauvaise odeur f; – vi (stink) Sl schlinguer.

pontificate [pɒn'tɪfɪkeɪt] vi (speak) Pej pontifier (**about** sur).

pony ['pəʊnɪ] n poney m. ◆**ponytail** n (hair) queue f de cheval.

poodle ['puːd(ə)l] n caniche m.

poof [puf] n (homosexual) Pej Sl pédé m.

pooh! [puː] int bah!; (bad smell) ça pue!

pooh-pooh [puːˈpuː] vt (scorn) dédaigner; (dismiss) se moquer de.

pool [puːl] **1** n (puddle) flaque f; (of blood) mare f; (pond) étang m; (for swimming) piscine f. **2** n (of experience, talent) réservoir m; (of advisers etc) équipe f; (of typists) Com pool m; (kitty) cagnotte f; (football) **pools** pronostics mpl (sur les matchs de football); – vt (share) mettre en commun; (combine) unir. **3** n Sp billard m américain.

pooped [puːpt] a (exhausted) Am Fam vanné, crevé.

poor [pʊər] a (-er, -est) (not rich, deserving pity) pauvre; (bad) mauvais; (inferior) médiocre; (meagre) maigre; (weak) faible; **p. thing!** le or la pauvre!; – n **the p.** les pauvres mpl. ◆**—ly 1** adv (badly) mal; (clothed, furnished) pauvrement. **2** a (ill) malade.

pop¹ [pɒp] **1** int pan! – n (noise) bruit m sec; **to go p.** faire pan; (of champagne bottle) faire pop; – vt (-pp-) (balloon etc) crever; (bottle top, button) faire sauter; – vi (burst) crever; (come off) sauter; (of ears) se déboucher. **2** vt (put) Fam mettre; – vi Fam **to p. in** (go in) entrer (en passant); **to p. off** (leave) partir; **to p. out** sortir (un instant); **to p. over** or **round** faire un saut (**to** chez); **to p. up** (of person) surgir, réapparaître; (of question etc) surgir.

◆**p.-'eyed** a aux yeux exorbités. ◆**p.-up book** n livre m en relief.

pop² [pɒp] **1** n (music) pop m; – a (concert, singer etc) pop inv. **2** n (father) Am Fam papa m. **3** n (soda) **p.** (drink) Am soda m.

popcorn ['pɒpkɔːn] n pop-corn m.

pope [pəʊp] n pape m; **p.'s nose** (of chicken) croupion m.

poplar ['pɒplər] n (tree, wood) peuplier m.

poppy ['pɒpɪ] n (cultivated) pavot m; (red, wild) coquelicot m.

poppycock ['pɒpɪkɒk] n Fam fadaises fpl.

popsicle® ['pɒpsɪk(ə)l] n (ice lolly) Am esquimau m.

popular ['pɒpjʊlər] a (person, song, vote, science etc) populaire; (fashionable) à la mode; **to be p. with** plaire beaucoup à. ◆**popu'larity** n popularité f (**with** auprès de). ◆**popularize** vt populariser; (science, knowledge) vulgariser. ◆**popularly** adv communément.

populat/e ['pɒpjʊleɪt] vt peupler. ◆**—ed** a peuplé (**with** de). ◆**popu'lation** n population f. ◆**populous** a (crowded) populeux.

porcelain ['pɔːsəlɪn] n porcelaine f.

porch [pɔːtʃ] n porche m; (veranda) Am véranda f.

porcupine ['pɔːkjʊpaɪn] n (animal) porc-épic m.

pore [pɔːr] **1** n (of skin) pore m. **2** vi **to p. over** (book, question etc) étudier de près. ◆**porous** a poreux.

pork [pɔːk] n (meat) porc m; **p. butcher** charcutier, -ière mf.

pornography [pɔːˈnɒgrəfɪ] n (Fam **porn**) pornographie f. ◆**porno'graphic** a pornographique, porno (f inv).

porpoise ['pɔːpəs] n (sea animal) marsouin m.

porridge ['pɒrɪdʒ] n porridge m; **p. oats** flocons mpl d'avoine.

port [pɔːt] **1** n (harbour) port m; **p. of call** escale f; – a (authorities, installations etc) portuaire. **2** n p. (side) (left) Nau Av bâbord m; – a de bâbord. **3** n (wine) porto m.

portable ['pɔːtəb(ə)l] a portatif, portable.

portal ['pɔːt(ə)l] n portail m.

porter ['pɔːtər] n (for luggage) porteur m; (doorman) portier m; (caretaker) concierge m, (of public building) gardien, -ienne mf.

portfolio [pɔːtˈfəʊlɪəʊ] n (pl -os) Com Pol portefeuille m.

porthole ['pɔːthəʊl] n Nau Av hublot m.

portico ['pɔːtɪkəʊ] n (pl -oes or -os) Archit portique m; (of house) porche m.

portion ['pɔːʃ(ə)n] n (share, helping) portion

f; (*of train, book etc*) partie *f*; – *vt* **to p. out** répartir.

portly ['pɔːtlɪ] *a* (**-ier, -iest**) corpulent.

portrait ['pɔːtrɪt, 'pɔːtreɪt] *n* portrait *m*; **p. painter** portraitiste *mf*.

portray [pɔː'treɪ] *vt* (*describe*) représenter. ◆**portrayal** *n* portrait *m*, représentation *f*.

Portugal ['pɔːtjʊg(ə)l] *n* Portugal *m*. ◆**Portu'guese** *a & n inv* portugais, -aise (*mf*); – *n* (*language*) portugais *m*.

pose [pəʊz] **1** *n* (*in art or photography*) & *Fig* pose *f*; – *vi* (*of model etc*) poser (**for** pour); **to p. as a lawyer/etc** se faire passer pour un avocat/etc. **2** *vt* (*question*) poser. ◆**poser** *n* **1** (*question*) *Fam* colle *f*. **2** = **poseur**. ◆**poseur** [-'zɜːr] *n Pej* poseur, -euse *mf*.

posh [pɒʃ] *a Pej Fam* (*smart*) chic *inv*; (*snobbish*) snob (*f inv*).

position [pə'zɪʃ(ə)n] *n* (*place, posture, opinion etc*) position *f*; (*of building, town*) emplacement *m*, position *f*; (*job, circumstances*) situation *f*; (*customer window in bank etc*) guichet *m*; **in a p. to do** en mesure *or* en position de faire; **in a good p. to do** bien placé pour faire; **in p.** en place, en position; – *vt* (*camera, machine etc*) mettre en position; (*put*) placer.

positive ['pɒzɪtɪv] *a* positif; (*order*) catégorique; (*progress, change*) réel; (*tone*) assuré; (*sure*) sûr, certain (**of** de, **that** que); **a p. genius** *Fam* un vrai génie. ◆**—ly** *adv* (*for certain*) & *El* positivement; (*undeniably*) indéniablement; (*completely*) complètement; (*categorically*) catégoriquement.

possess [pə'zes] *vt* posséder. ◆**possession** *n* possession *f*; **in p. of** en possession de; **to take p. of** prendre possession de. ◆**possessive** *a* (*adjective, person etc*) possessif; – *n Gram* possessif *m*. ◆**possessor** *n* possesseur *m*.

possible ['pɒsəb(ə)l] *a* possible (**to do** à faire); **it is p. (for us) to do it** il (nous) est possible de le faire; **it is p. that** il est possible que (+ *sub*); **as far as p.** dans la mesure du possible; **if p.** si possible; **as much** *or* **as many as p.** autant que possible; – *n* (*person, object*) *Fam* choix *m* possible. ◆**possi'bility** *n* possibilité *f*; **some p. of** quelques chances *fpl* de; **there's some p. that** il est (tout juste) possible que (+ *sub*); **she has possibilities** elle promet; **it's a distinct p.** c'est bien possible. ◆**possibly** *adv* **1** (*with can, could etc*) **if you p. can** si cela t'est possible; **to do all one p. can** faire tout son possible (**to do** pour faire); **he**

cannot p. stay il ne peut absolument pas rester. **2** (*perhaps*) peut-être.

post¹ [pəʊst] *n* (*postal system*) poste *f*; (*letters*) courrier *m*; **by p.** par la poste; **to catch/miss the p.** avoir/manquer la levée; – *a* (*bag, code etc*) postal; **p. office** (bureau *m* de) poste *f*; **P. Office** (*administration*) (service *m* des) postes *fpl*; – *vt* (*put in postbox*) poster, mettre à la poste; (*send*) envoyer; **to keep s.o. posted** *Fig* tenir qn au courant. ◆**postage** *n* tarif *m* (postal), tarifs *mpl* (postaux) (**to** pour); **p. stamp** timbre-poste *m*. ◆**postal** *a* (*district etc*) postal; (*inquiries*) par la poste; (*clerk*) des postes; (*vote*) par correspondance. ◆**postbox** *n* boîte *f* à *or* aux lettres. ◆**postcard** *n* carte *f* postale. ◆**postcode** *n* code *m* postal. ◆**post-'free** *adv*, ◆**post'paid** *adv* franco.

post² [pəʊst] *n* (*job, place*) & *Mil* poste *m*; – *vt* (*sentry, guard*) poster; (*employee*) affecter (**to** à). ◆**—ing** *n* (*appointment*) affectation *f*.

post³ [pəʊst] *n* (*pole*) poteau *m*; (*of bed, door*) montant *m*; **finishing** *or* **winning p.** *Sp* poteau *m* d'arrivée; – *vt* **to p. (up)** (*notice etc*) afficher.

post- [pəʊst] *pref* post-; **p.-1800** après 1800.

postdate [pəʊst'deɪt] *vt* postdater.

poster ['pəʊstər] *n* affiche *f*; (*for decoration*) poster *m*.

posterior [pɒ'stɪərɪər] *n* (*buttocks*) *Hum* postérieur *m*.

posterity [pɒ'sterɪtɪ] *n* postérité *f*.

postgraduate [pəʊst'grædʒʊət] *a* (*studies etc*) *Univ* de troisième cycle; – *n* étudiant, -ante *mf* de troisième cycle.

posthumous ['pɒstjʊməs] *a* posthume. ◆**—ly** *adv* à titre posthume.

postman ['pəʊstmən] *n* (*pl* -**men**) facteur *m*. ◆**postmark** *n* cachet *m* de la poste; – *vt* oblitérer. ◆**postmaster** *n* receveur *m* (des postes).

post-mortem [pəʊst'mɔːtəm] *n* **p.-mortem** (**examination**) autopsie *f* (**on** de).

postpone [pəʊ'spəʊn] *vt* remettre (**for** de), renvoyer (à plus tard). ◆**—ment** *n* remise *f*, renvoi *m*.

postscript ['pəʊstskrɪpt] *n* post-scriptum *m inv*.

postulate ['pɒstjʊleɪt] *vt* postuler.

posture ['pɒstʃər] *n* posture *f*; *Fig* attitude *f*; – *vi* (*for effect*) *Pej* poser.

postwar ['pəʊstwɔːr] *a* d'après-guerre.

posy ['pəʊzɪ] *n* petit bouquet *m* (de fleurs).

pot [pɒt] **1** *n* pot *m*; (*for cooking*) marmite *f*; **pots and pans** casseroles *fpl*; **jam p.** pot *m* à confiture; **to take p. luck** tenter sa chance; (*with food*) manger à la fortune du pot; **to go to p.** *Fam* aller à la ruine; **gone to p.** (*person, plans etc*) *Fam* fichu; – *vt* (-tt-) mettre en pot. **2** *n* (*marijuana*) *Sl* marie-jeanne *f*; (*hashish*) *Sl* haschisch *m*. ◆**potted** *a* **1** (*plant*) en pot; (*jam, meat*) en bocaux. **2** (*version etc*) abrégé, condensé.

potato [pəˈteɪtəʊ] *n* (*pl* **-oes**) pomme *f* de terre; **p. peeler** (*knife*) couteau *m* à éplucher, éplucheur *m*; **p. crisps**, *Am* **p. chips** pommes *fpl* chips.

potbelly [ˈpɒtbelɪ] *n* bedaine *f*. ◆**potbellied** *a* ventru.

potent [ˈpəʊtənt] *a* puissant; (*drink*) fort; (*man*) viril. ◆**potency** *n* puissance *f*; (*of man*) virilité *f*.

potential [pəˈtenʃ(ə)l] *a* (*danger, resources*) potentiel; (*client, sales*) éventuel; (*leader, hero etc*) en puissance; – *n* potentiel *m*; *Fig* (*perspectives fpl* d')avenir *m*; **to have p.** avoir de l'avenir. ◆**potenti'ality** *n* potentialité *f*; *pl Fig* (*perspectives fpl* d')avenir *m*. ◆**potentially** *adv* potentiellement.

pothole [ˈpɒthəʊl] *n* (*in road*) nid *m* de poules; (*in rock*) gouffre *m*; (*cave*) caverne *f*. ◆**potholing** *n* spéléologie *f*.

potion [ˈpəʊʃ(ə)n] *n* breuvage *m* magique; *Med* potion *f*.

potshot [ˈpɒtʃɒt] *n* **to take a p.** faire un carton (**at** sur).

potter [ˈpɒtər] **1** *n* (*person*) potier *m*. **2** *vi* **to p. (about)** bricoler. ◆**pottery** *n* (*art*) poterie *f*; (*objects*) poteries *fpl*; **a piece of p.** une poterie.

potty [ˈpɒtɪ] *a* **1** (-ier, -iest) (*mad*) *Fam* toqué. **2** *n* pot *m* (de bébé).

pouch [paʊtʃ] *n* petit sac *m*; (*of kangaroo, under eyes*) poche *f*; (*for tobacco*) blague *f*.

pouf(fe) [puːf] *n* (*seat*) pouf *m*.

poultice [ˈpəʊltɪs] *n Med* cataplasme *m*.

poultry [ˈpəʊltrɪ] *n* volaille *f*. ◆**poulterer** *n* volailler *m*.

pounce [paʊns] *vi* (*leap*) bondir, sauter (**on** sur); **to p. on** (*idea*) *Fig* sauter sur; – *n* bond *m*.

pound [paʊnd] **1** *n* (*weight*) livre *f* (= 453,6 grammes); **p. (sterling)** livre *f* (sterling). **2** *n* (*for cars, dogs*) fourrière *f*. **3** *vt* (*spices, nuts etc*) piler; (*meat*) attendrir; (*bombard*) *Mil* pilonner; **to p. (on)** (*thump*) *Fig* taper sur, marteler; (*of sea*) battre; – *vi* (*of heart*) battre à tout rompre; (*walk heavily*) marcher à pas pesants.

pour [pɔːr] *vt* (*liquid*) verser; (*wax*) couler; **to p. money into** investir beaucoup d'argent dans; **to p. away** *or* **off** (*empty*) vider; **to p. out** verser; (*empty*) vider; (*feelings*) épancher (**to** devant); – *vi* **to p. (out)** (*of liquid*) couler *or* sortir à flots; **to p. in** (*of liquid, sunshine*) entrer à flots; (*of people, money*) *Fig* affluer; **to p. out** (*of people*) sortir en masse (**from** de); (*of smoke*) s'échapper (**from** de); **it's pouring (down)** il pleut à verse; **pouring rain** pluie *f* torrentielle.

pout [paʊt] *vti* **to p. (one's lips)** faire la moue; – *n* moue *f*.

poverty [ˈpɒvətɪ] *n* pauvreté *f*; (*grinding or extreme*) **p.** misère *f*. ◆**p.-stricken** *a* (*person*) indigent; (*conditions*) misérable.

powder [ˈpaʊdər] *n* poudre *f*; **p. keg** (*place*) *Fig* poudrière *f*; **p. puff** houppette *f*; **p. room** toilettes *fpl* (*pour dames*); – *vt* (*hair, skin*) poudrer; **to p. one's face** *or* **nose** se poudrer. ◆**—ed** *a* (*milk, eggs*) en poudre. ◆**powdery** *a* (*snow*) poudreux; (*face*) couvert de poudre.

power [ˈpaʊər] *n* (*ability, authority*) pouvoir *m*; (*strength, nation*) & *Math Tech* puissance *f*; (*energy*) *Phys Tech* énergie *f*; (*current*) *El* courant *m*; **he's a p. within the firm** c'est un homme de poids au sein de l'entreprise; **in p.** *Pol* au pouvoir; **in one's p.** en son pouvoir; **the p. of speech** la faculté de la parole; **p. cut** coupure *f* de courant; **p. station**, *Am* **p. plant** *El* centrale *f* (électrique); – *vt* **to be powered by** être actionné *or* propulsé par; (*gas, oil etc*) fonctionnant à. ◆**powerful** *a* puissant. ◆**powerfully** *adv* puissamment. ◆**powerless** *a* impuissant (**to do** à faire).

practicable [ˈpræktɪkəb(ə)l] *a* (*project, road etc*) praticable.

practical [ˈpræktɪk(ə)l] *a* (*knowledge, person, tool etc*) pratique; **p. joke** farce *f*. ◆**practi'cality** *n* (*of scheme etc*) aspect *m* pratique; (*of person*) sens *m* pratique; (*detail*) détail *m* pratique.

practically [ˈpræktɪk(ə)lɪ] *adv* (*almost*) pratiquement.

practice [ˈpræktɪs] *n* (*exercise, proceeding*) pratique *f*; (*habit*) habitude *f*; *Sp* entraînement *m*; (*rehearsal*) répétition *f*; (*of profession*) exercice *m* (**of** de); (*clients*) clientèle *f*; **to put into p.** mettre en pratique; **in p.** (*in reality*) en pratique; **to be in p.** (*have skill etc*) être en forme; (*of doctor, lawyer*) exercer; **to be in general p.** (*of doctor*) faire de la médecine générale; **to be out of p.** avoir perdu la pratique. ◆**practis/e** *vt* (*put into practice*) pratiquer; (*medicine, law etc*) exercer; (*flute,* *piano etc*) s'exercer à; (*language*) (s'exercer à) parler (**on** avec); (*work at*) travailler; (*do*) faire; – *vi Mus Sp* s'exercer; (*of doctor, lawyer*) exercer; – *n Am* = **practice**. ◆**—ed** *a* (*experienced*) chevronné; (*ear, eye*) exercé. ◆**—ing** *a Rel* pratiquant; (*doctor, lawyer*) exerçant.

practitioner [præk'tɪʃ(ə)nər] *n* praticien, -ienne *mf*; **general p.** (médecin *m*) généraliste *m*.

pragmatic [præg'mætɪk] *a* pragmatique.

prairie(s) ['preərɪ(z)] *n(pl)* (*in North America*) Prairies *fpl*.

praise [preɪz] *vt* louer (**for** sth de qch); **to p. s.o. for doing** *or* **having done** louer qn d'avoir fait; – *n* louange(s) *f(pl)*, éloge(s) *m(pl)*; **in p. of** à la louange de. ◆**praiseworthy** *a* digne d'éloges.

pram [præm] *n* landau *m*, voiture *f* d'enfant.

prance [prɑːns] *vi* **to p. about** (*of dancer etc*) caracoler; (*strut*) se pavaner; (*go about*) *Fam* se balader.

prank [præŋk] *n* (*trick*) farce *f*, tour *m*; (*escape*) frasque *f*.

prattle ['præt(ə)l] *vi* jacasser.

prawn [prɔːn] *n* crevette *f* (rose), bouquet *m*.

pray [preɪ] *vt Lit* prier (**that** que (+ *sub*), **s.o. to do** qn de faire); – *vi Rel* prier; **to p.** (**to God**) **for** sth prier Dieu pour qu'il nous accorde qch. ◆**prayer** [preər] *n* prière *f*.

pre- [priː] *pref* **p.-1800** avant 1800.

preach [priːtʃ] *vti* prêcher; (*sermon*) faire; **to p. to s.o.** *Rel & Fig* prêcher qn. ◆**—ing** *n* prédication *f*. ◆**—er** *n* prédicateur *m*.

preamble [priː'æmb(ə)l] *n* préambule *m*.

prearrange [priːə'reɪndʒ] *vt* arranger à l'avance.

precarious [prɪ'keərɪəs] *a* précaire.

precaution [prɪ'kɔːʃ(ə)n] *n* précaution *f* (**of doing** de faire); **as a p.** par précaution.

preced/e [prɪ'siːd] *vti* précéder; **to p. sth by sth** faire précéder qch de qch. ◆**—ing** *a* précédent.

precedence ['presɪdəns] *n* (*in rank*) préséance *f*; (*importance*) priorité *f*; **to take p. over** avoir la préséance sur; avoir la priorité sur. ◆**precedent** *n* précédent *m*.

precept ['priːsept] *n* précepte *m*.

precinct ['priːsɪŋkt] *n* (*of convent etc*) enceinte *f*; (*boundary*) limite *f*; (*of town*) *Am Pol* circonscription *f*; (*for shopping*) zone *f* (piétonnière).

precious ['preʃəs] **1** *a* précieux; **her p. little bike** *Iron* son cher petit vélo. **2** *adv* **p. few**, **p. little** *Fam* très peu (de).

precipice ['presɪpɪs] *n* (*sheer face*) *Geog* à-pic *m inv*; (*chasm*) *Fig* précipice *m*.

precipitate [prɪ'sɪpɪteɪt] *vt* (*hasten, throw*) & *Ch* précipiter; (*trouble, reaction etc*) provoquer, déclencher. ◆**precipi'tation** *n* (*haste*) & *Ch* précipitation *f*; (*rainfall*) précipitations *fpl*.

précis ['preɪsiː, *pl* 'preɪsiːz] *n inv* précis *m*.

precise [prɪ'saɪs] *a* précis; (*person*) minutieux. ◆**—ly** *adv* (*accurately, exactly*) précisément; **at 3 o'clock p.** à 3 heures précises; **p. nothing** absolument rien. ◆**precision** *n* précision *f*.

preclude [prɪ'kluːd] *vt* (*prevent*) empêcher (**from doing** de faire); (*possibility*) exclure.

precocious [prɪ'kəʊʃəs] *a* (*child etc*) précoce. ◆**—ness** *n* précocité *f*.

preconceived [priːkən'siːvd] *a* préconçu. ◆**preconception** *n* préconception *f*.

precondition [priːkən'dɪʃ(ə)n] *n* préalable *m*.

precursor [priː'kɜːsər] *n* précurseur *m*.

predate [priː'deɪt] *vt* (*precede*) précéder; (*cheque etc*) antidater.

predator ['predətər] *n* (*animal*) prédateur *m*. ◆**predatory** *a* (*animal, person*) rapace.

predecessor ['priːdɪsesər] *n* prédécesseur *m*.

predicament [prɪ'dɪkəmənt] *n* situation *f* fâcheuse.

predict [prɪ'dɪkt] *vt* prédire. ◆**predictable** *a* prévisible. ◆**prediction** *n* prédiction *f*.

predispose [priːdɪ'spəʊz] *vt* prédisposer (**to do** à faire). ◆**predispo'sition** *n* prédisposition *f*.

predominant [prɪ'dɒmɪnənt] *a* prédominant. ◆**predominance** *n* prédominance *f*. ◆**predominantly** *adv* (*almost all*) pour la plupart, en majorité. ◆**predominate** *vi* prédominer (**over** sur).

preeminent [priː'emɪnənt] *a* prééminent.

preempt [priː'empt] *vt* (*decision, plans etc*) devancer.

preen [priːn] *vt* (*feathers*) lisser; **she's preening herself** *Fig* elle se bichonne.

prefab ['priːfæb] *n Fam* maison *f* préfabriquée. ◆**pre'fabricate** *vt* préfabriquer.

preface ['prefɪs] *n* préface *f*; – *vt* (*speech etc*) faire précéder (**with** de).

prefect ['priːfekt] *n Sch* élève *mf* chargé(e) de la discipline; (*French official*) préfet *m*.

prefer [prɪ'fɜːr] *vt* (**-rr-**) préférer (**to** à), aimer mieux (**to** que); **to p. to do** préférer faire, aimer mieux faire; **to p. charges** *Jur* porter plainte (**against** contre). ◆**'preferable** *a* préférable (**to** à). ◆**'preferably** *adv* de préférence. ◆**'preference** *n* préférence *f* (**for** pour); **in p. to** de préférence à. ◆**prefe'rential** *a* préférentiel.

prefix ['priːfiks] n préfixe m.

pregnant ['pregnant] a (woman) enceinte; (animal) pleine: **five months p.** enceinte de cinq mois. ◆**pregnancy** n (of woman) grossesse f.

prehistoric [priːhi'storik] a préhistorique.

prejudge [priː'dʒʌdʒ] vt (question) préjuger de; (person) juger d'avance.

prejudic/e ['predʒədis] n (bias) préjugé m, parti m pris; (attitude) préjugés mpl; Jur préjudice m; – vt (person) prévenir (against contre); (success, chances etc) porter préjudice à, nuire à. ◆—ed a (idea) partial; **she's p.** elle a des préjugés or un préjugé (against contre); (on an issue) elle est de parti pris. ◆**preju'dicial** a Jur préjudiciable.

preliminary [pri'liminəri] a (initial) initial; (speech, inquiry, exam) préliminaire; – npl préliminaires mpl.

prelude ['preljuːd] n prélude m; – vt préluder à.

premarital [priː'mærit(ə)l] a avant le mariage.

premature ['premətʃuər, Am priːmə'tʃuər] a prématuré. ◆—ly adv prématurément; (born) avant terme.

premeditate [priː'mediteit] vt préméditer. ◆**premedi'tation** n préméditation f.

premier ['premiər, Am pri'miər] n Premier ministre m.

première ['premieər, Am pri'mjeər] n Th Cin première f.

premise ['premis] n Phil prémisse f.

premises ['premisiz] npl locaux mpl; **on the p.** sur les lieux; **off the p.** hors des lieux.

premium ['priːmiəm] n Fin prime f; (insurance) p. prime f (d'assurance); **to be at a p.** (rare) être (une) denrée rare, faire prime; **p. bond** bon m à lots.

premonition [premə'niʃ(ə)n, Am priːmə'niʃ(ə)n] n prémonition f, pressentiment m.

prenatal [priː'neit(ə)l] a Am prénatal.

preoccupy [priː'ɒkjupai] vt (worry) préoccuper (with de). ◆**preoccu'pation** n préoccupation f; **a p. with** (money etc) une obsession de.

prep [prep] a **p. school** école f primaire privée; Am école f secondaire privée; – n (homework) Sch devoirs mpl.

prepaid [priː'peid] a (reply) payé.

prepar/e [pri'peər] vt préparer (sth for s.o. qch à qn, s.o. for sth qn à qch); **to p. to do** se préparer à faire; – vi **to p. for** (journey, occasion) faire des préparatifs pour; (get dressed up for) se préparer pour; (exam) préparer. ◆—ed a (ready) prêt, disposé (to

do à faire); **to be p. for** (expect) s'attendre à. ◆**prepa'ration** n préparation f; pl préparatifs mpl (for de). ◆**pre'paratory** a préparatoire; **p. school** = prep school.

preposition [prepə'ziʃ(ə)n] n préposition f.

prepossessing [priːpə'zesiŋ] a avenant, sympathique.

preposterous [pri'postərəs] a absurde.

prerecorded [priːri'kɔːdid] a (message etc) enregistré à l'avance; **p. broadcast** Rad TV émission f en différé.

prerequisite [priː'rekwizit] n (condition f) préalable m.

prerogative [pri'rɒgətiv] n prérogative f.

Presbyterian [prezbi'tiəriən] a & n Rel presbytérien, -ienne (mf).

preschool ['priːskuːl] a (age etc) préscolaire.

prescrib/e [pri'skraib] vt prescrire. ◆—ed a (textbook) (inscrit) au programme. ◆**prescription** n (order) prescription f; Med ordonnance f; **on p.** sur ordonnance.

presence ['prezəns] n présence f; **in the p. of** en présence de; **p. of mind** présence f d'esprit.

present¹ ['prezənt] **1** a (not absent) présent (at à, in dans); **those p.** les personnes présentes. **2** a (year, state etc) présent, actuel; (being considered) présent; (job, house etc) actuel; – n (time) présent m; **for the p.** pour le moment; **at p.** à présent. **3** n (gift) cadeau m. ◆—ly adv (soon) tout à l'heure; (now) à présent. ◆**present-'day** a actuel.

present² [pri'zent] vt (show, introduce, compere etc) présenter (to à); (concert etc) donner; (proof) fournir; **to p. s.o. with** (gift) offrir à qn; (prize) remettre à qn. ◆—able a présentable. ◆—er n présentateur, -trice mf. ◆**presen'tation** n présentation f; (of prize) remise f.

preserve [pri'zɜːv] **1** vt (keep, maintain) conserver; (fruit etc) Culin mettre en conserve; **to p. from** (protect) préserver de. **2** n (sphere) domaine m. **3** n & npl (fruit etc) Culin confiture f. ◆**preser'vation** n conservation f. ◆**preservative** n (in food) agent m de conservation. ◆**preserver** n life **p.** Am gilet m de sauvetage.

preside [pri'zaid] vi présider; **to p. over** or **at** (meeting) présider.

president ['prezidənt] n président, -ente mf. ◆**presidency** n présidence f. ◆**presi'dential** a présidentiel.

press¹ [pres] **1** n (newspapers) presse f; (printing firm) imprimerie f; (printing) p. presse f; – a (conference etc) de presse. **2** n *(machine for trousers, gluing etc)* presse *f*; *(for making wine)* pressoir *m*.

press² [pres] *vt (button, doorbell etc)* appuyer sur; *(tube, lemon, creditor)* presser; *(hand)* serrer; *(clothes)* repasser; *(demand, insist on)* insister sur; *(claim)* renouveler; **to p. s.o. to do** *(urge)* presser qn de faire; **to p. down** *(button etc)* appuyer sur; **to p. charges** *Jur* engager des poursuites **(against** contre); – *vi (with finger)* appuyer **(on** sur); *(of weight)* faire pression **(on** sur); *(of time)* presser; **to p. for sth** faire des démarches pour obtenir qch; *(insist)* insister pour obtenir qch; **to p. on** *(continue)* continuer **(with sth** qch); – *n* **to give sth a p.** *(trousers etc)* repasser qch. ◆**—ed** *a* **(hard)** p. *(busy)* débordé; **to be hard p.** *(in difficulties)* être en difficultés; **to be (hard) p. for** *(time, money)* être à court de. ◆**—ing 1** *a (urgent)* pressant. **2** *n (ironing)* repassage *m*.

pressgang ['presgæn] *vt* **to p. s.o.** faire pression sur qn **(into doing** pour qu'il fasse). ◆**press-stud** *n* (bouton-)pression *m*. ◆**press-up** *n Sp* pompe *f*.

pressure ['preʃər] *n* pression *f*; **the p. of work** le surmenage; **p. cooker** cocotte-minute *f*; **p. group** groupe *m* de pression; **under p.** *(duress)* sous la contrainte; *(hurriedly, forcibly)* sous pression; – *vt* **to p. s.o.** faire pression sur qn **(into doing** pour qu'il fasse). ◆**pressurize** *vt Av* pressuriser; **to p. s.o.** faire pression sur qn **(into doing** pour qu'il fasse).

prestige [pre'stiːʒ] *n* prestige *m*. ◆**prestigious** [pre'stɪdʒəs, *Am* -'stiːdʒəs] *a* prestigieux.

presume [prɪ'zjuːm] *vt (suppose)* présumer **(that** que); **to p. to do** se permettre de faire. ◆**presumably** *adv (you'll come etc)* je présume que. ◆**presumption** *n (supposition, bold attitude)* présomption *f*. ◆**presumptuous** *a* présomptueux.

presuppose [priːsə'pəuz] *vt* présupposer **(that** que).

pretence [prɪ'tens] *n* feinte *f*; *(claim, affectation)* prétention *f*; *(pretext)* prétexte *m*; **to make a p. of sth/of doing** feindre qch/de faire; **on** *or* **under false pretences** sous des prétextes fallacieux. ◆**pretend** *vt (make believe)* faire semblant **(to do** de faire, **that** que); *(claim, maintain)* prétendre **(to do** faire, **that** que); – *vi* faire semblant; **to p. to** *(throne, title)* prétendre à.

pretension [prɪ'tenʃ(ə)n] *n (claim, vanity)* prétention *f*. ◆**pre'tentious** *a* prétentieux.

pretext ['priːtekst] *n* prétexte *m*; **on the p. of/that** sous prétexte de/que.

pretty ['prɪtɪ] **1** *a* **(-ier, -iest)** joli. **2** *adv Fam (rather, quite)* assez; **p. well, p. much, p. nearly** *(almost)* pratiquement, à peu de chose près.

prevail [prɪ'veɪl] *vi (be prevalent)* prédominer; *(win)* prévaloir **(against** contre); **to p. (up)on s.o.** *(persuade)* persuader qn **(to do** de faire). ◆**—ing** *a (most common)* courant; *(most important)* prédominant; *(situation)* actuel; *(wind)* dominant.

prevalent ['prevələnt] *a* courant, répandu. ◆**prevalence** *n* fréquence *f*; *(predominance)* prédominance *f*.

prevaricate [prɪ'værɪkeɪt] *vi* user de faux-fuyants.

prevent [prɪ'vent] *vt* empêcher **(from doing** de faire). ◆**preventable** *a* évitable. ◆**prevention** *n* prévention *f*. ◆**preventive** *a* préventif.

preview ['priːvjuː] *n (of film, painting)* avant-première *f*; *(survey) Fig* aperçu *m*.

previous ['priːvɪəs] *a* précédent, antérieur; *(experience)* préalable; **she's had a p. job** elle a déjà eu un emploi; **p. to** avant. ◆**—ly** *adv* avant, précédemment.

prewar ['priːwɔːr] *a* d'avant-guerre.

prey [preɪ] *n* proie *f*; **to be (a) p. to** être en proie à; **bird of p.** rapace *m*, oiseau *m* de proie; – *vi* **to p. on** faire sa proie de; **to p. on s.o.** *or* **s.o.'s mind** *Fig* tracasser qn.

price [praɪs] *n (of object, success etc)* prix *m*; **to pay a high p. for sth** payer cher qch; *Fig* payer chèrement qch; **he wouldn't do it at any p.** il ne le ferait à aucun prix; – *a (control, war, rise etc)* des prix; **p. list** tarif *m*; – *vt* mettre un prix à; **it's priced at £5** ça coûte cinq livres. ◆**priceless** *a (jewel, help etc)* inestimable; *(amusing) Fam* impayable. ◆**pricey** *a* **(-ier, -iest)** *Fam* coûteux.

prick [prɪk] *vt* piquer **(with** avec); *(burst)* crever; **to p. up one's ears** dresser l'oreille; – *n (act, mark, pain)* piqûre *f*.

prickle ['prɪk(ə)l] *n (of animal)* piquant *m*; *(of plant)* épine *f*, piquant *m*. ◆**prickly** *a* **(-ier, -iest)** *(plant)* épineux; *(animal)* hérissé; *(subject) Fig* épineux; *(person) Fig* irritable.

pride [praɪd] *n (satisfaction)* fierté *f*; *(self-esteem)* amour-propre *m*, orgueil *m*; *(arrogance)* orgueil *m*; **to take p. in** *(person, work etc)* être fier de; *(look after)* prendre soin de; **to take p. in doing** mettre (toute) sa fierté à faire; **to be s.o.'s p. and joy** être la fierté de qn; **to have p. of place** avoir la

place d'honneur; − vt to p. oneself on
s'enorgueillir de.

priest [priːst] n prêtre m. ◆**priesthood** n
(function) sacerdoce m. ◆**priestly** a sacer-
dotal.

prig [prig] n hypocrite mf, pharisien, -ienne
mf. ◆**priggish** a hypocrite, suffisant.

prim [prim] a (primmer, primmest) p. (and
proper) (affected) guindé; (seemly) convenable; (neat) impeccable.

primacy ['praiməsi] n primauté f.

primary ['praiməri] a Sch Pol Geol etc
primaire; (main, basic) principal, premier;
of p. importance de première importance;
− n (election) Am primaire f. ◆**primarily**
[Am prai'merili] adv essentiellement.

prime [praim] 1 a (reason etc) principal;
(importance) primordial; (quality, number)
premier; (meat) de premier choix; (example, condition) excellent, parfait; P. Minister Premier ministre m. 2 n the p. of life la
force de l'âge. 3 vt (gun, pump) amorcer;
(surface) apprêter. ◆**primer** n 1 (book)
Sch premier livre m. 2 (paint) apprêt m.

primeval [prai'miːv(ə)l] a primitif.

primitive ['primitiv] a (art, society, conditions etc) primitif. ◆−**ly** adv (to live) dans
des conditions primitives.

primrose ['primrəuz] n Bot primevère f
(jaune).

prince [prins] n prince m. ◆**princely** a
princier. ◆**prin'cess** n princesse f.
◆**princi'pality** n principauté f.

principal ['prinsip(ə)l] 1 a (main) principal.
2 n (of school) directeur, -trice mf. ◆−**ly**
adv principalement.

principle ['prinsip(ə)l] n principe m; in p. en
principe; on p. par principe.

print [print] n (of finger, foot etc) empreinte
f; (letters) caractères mpl; (engraving)
estampe f, gravure f; (fabric, textile design)
imprimé m; Phot épreuve f; (ink) encre m;
in p. (book) disponible (en librairie); out of
p. (book) épuisé; − vt Typ imprimer; Phot
tirer; (write) écrire en caractères
d'imprimerie; to p. 100 copies of (book etc)
tirer à 100 exemplaires; to p. out (of
computer) imprimer. ◆−**ed** a imprimé; p.
matter or papers imprimés mpl; to have a
book p. publier un livre. ◆−**ing** n (action)
Typ impression f; (technique, art) Typ
imprimerie f; Phot tirage m; p. press Typ
presse f. ◆−**able** a not p. (word etc) Fig
obscène. ◆−**er** n (person) imprimeur m;
(of computer) imprimante f. ◆**print-out** n
(of computer) sortie f sur imprimante.

prior ['praiər] a précédent, antérieur; (expe-

rience) préalable; p. to sth/to doing avant
qch/de faire.

priority [prai'ɒriti] n priorité f (over sur).

priory ['praiəri] n Rel prieuré m.

prise [praiz] vt to p. open/off (box, lid)
ouvrir/enlever (en faisant levier).

prism ['priz(ə)m] n prisme m.

prison ['priz(ə)n] n prison f; in p. en prison;
− a (system, life etc) pénitentiaire; (camp)
de prisonniers; p. officer gardien, -ienne mf
de prison. ◆**prisoner** n prisonnier, -ière
mf; to take s.o. p. faire qn prisonnier.

prissy ['prisi] a (-ier, -iest) bégueule.

pristine ['pristiːn] a (condition) parfait;
(primitive) primitif.

privacy ['praivəsi, 'privəsi] n intimité f, solitude f; (quiet place) coin m retiré; (secrecy)
secret m; to give s.o. some p. laisser qn seul.
◆**private** 1 a privé; (lesson, car etc)
particulier; (confidential) confidentiel;
(personal) personnel; (wedding etc) intime;
a p. citizen un simple particulier; p. detective, p. investigator, Fam p. eye détective m
privé; p. parts parties fpl génitales; p. place
coin m retiré; p. tutor précepteur m; to be a
very p. person aimer la solitude; − n in p.
(not publicly) en privé; (ceremony) dans
l'intimité. 2 n Mil (simple) soldat m. ◆**pri-
vately** adv en privé; (inwardly) intérieurement; (personally) à titre personnel; (to
marry, dine etc) dans l'intimité; p. owned
appartenant à un particulier.

privet ['privit] n (bush) troène m.

privilege ['privilidʒ] n privilège m. ◆**privileged** a privilégié; to be p. to do avoir le
privilège de faire.

privy ['privi] a p. to (knowledge etc) au
courant de.

prize[1] [praiz] n prix m; (in lottery) lot m; the
first p. (in lottery) le gros lot; − a (essay,
animal etc) primé; a p. fool/etc Fig Hum un
parfait idiot/etc. ◆**p.-giving** n distribution f des prix. ◆**p.-winner** n lauréat, -ate
mf; (in lottery) gagnant, -ante mf.
◆**p.-winning** a (essay, animal etc) primé;
(ticket) gagnant.

prize[2] [praiz] vt (value) priser. ◆−**ed** a
(possession etc) précieux.

prize[3] [praiz] vt = prise.

pro [prəu] n (professional) Fam pro mf.

pro- [prəu] pref pro-.

probable ['prɒbəb(ə)l] a probable (that
que); (plausible) vraisemblable. ◆**proba-
'bility** n probabilité f; in all p. selon toute
probabilité. ◆**probably** adv probablement, vraisemblablement.

probation [prə'beiʃ(ə)n] n on p. Jur en

liberté surveillée, sous contrôle judiciaire; (*in job*) à l'essai; **p. officer** responsable *mf* des délinquants mis en liberté surveillée. ◆**probationary** *a* (*period*) d'essai, *Jur* de liberté surveillée.

prob/e ['prəub] *n* (*device*) sonde *f*; *Journ* enquête *f* (**into** dans); − *vt* (*investigate*) & *Med* sonder; (*examine*) examiner; − *vi* (*investigate*) faire des recherches; *Pej* fouiner; **to p. into** (*origins etc*) sonder. ◆**—ing** *a* (*question etc*) pénétrant.

problem ['prɒbləm] *n* problème *m*; **he's got a drug/a drink p.** c'est un drogué/un alcoolique; **you've got a smoking p.** tu fumes beaucoup trop; **no p.!** *Am Fam* pas de problème!; **to have a p. doing** avoir du mal à faire; − *a* (*child*) difficile, caractériel. ◆**proble'matic** *a* problématique; **it's p. whether** il est douteux que (+ *sub*).

procedure [prə'siːdʒər] *n* procédure *f*.

proceed [prə'siːd] *vi* (*go*) avancer, aller; (*act*) procéder; (*continue*) continuer; (*of debate*) se poursuivre; **to p. to** (*next question etc*) passer à; **to p. with** (*task etc*) continuer; **to p. to do** (*start*) se mettre à faire. ◆**—ing** *n* (*course of action*) procédé *m*; *pl* (*events*) évènements *mpl*; (*meeting*) séance *f*; (*discussions*) débats *mpl*; (*minutes*) actes *mpl*; **to take** (*legal*) **proceedings** intenter un procès (**against** contre).

proceeds ['prəusiːdz] *npl* (*profits*) produit *m*, bénéfices *mpl*.

process ['prəuses] **1** *n* (*operation, action*) processus *m*; (*method*) procédé *m* (**for** *or* **of doing** pour faire); **in p.** (*work etc*) en cours; **in the p. of doing** en train de faire. **2** *vt* (*food, data etc*) traiter; (*examine*) examiner; *Phot* développer; **processed cheese** fromage *m* fondu. ◆**—ing** *n* traitement *m*; *Phot* développement *m*; **data** *or* **information p.** informatique *f*. ◆**processor** *n* (*in computer*) processeur *m*; **food p.** robot *m* (*ménager*); **word p.** machine *f* de traitement de texte.

procession [prə'sef(ə)n] *n* cortège *m*, défilé *m*.

proclaim [prə'kleɪm] *vt* proclamer (**that** que); **to p. king** proclamer roi. ◆**procla-'mation** *n* proclamation *f*.

procrastinate [prə'kræstɪneɪt] *vi* temporiser, tergiverser.

procreate ['prəukrɪeɪt] *vt* procréer. ◆**procre'ation** *n* procréation *f*.

procure [prə'kjuər] *vt* obtenir; **to p. sth** (**for oneself**) se procurer qch; **to p. sth for s.o.** procurer qch à qn.

prod [prɒd] *vti* (**-dd-**) **to p.** (**at**) pousser (*du coude, avec un bâton etc*); **to p. s.o. into doing** *Fig* pousser qn à faire; − *n* (petit) coup *m*; (*shove*) poussée *f*.

prodigal ['prɒdɪg(ə)l] *a* (*son etc*) prodigue.

prodigious [prə'dɪdʒəs] *a* prodigieux.

prodigy ['prɒdɪdʒɪ] *n* prodige *m*; **infant p., child p.** enfant *mf* prodige.

produce [prə'djuːs] *vt* (*manufacture, yield etc*) produire; (*bring out, show*) sortir (*pistolet, mouchoir etc*); (*passport, proof*) présenter; (*profit*) rapporter; (*cause*) provoquer, produire; (*publish*) publier; (*play*) *Th TV* mettre en scène; (*film*) *Cin* produire; *Rad* réaliser; (*baby*) donner naissance à; **oil-producing country** pays *m* producteur de pétrole; − *vi* (*of factory etc*) produire; − ['prɒdjuːs] *n* (*agricultural etc*) produits *mpl*. ◆**pro'ducer** *n* (*of goods*) & *Cin* producteur, -trice *mf*; *Th TV* metteur *m* en scène; *Rad* réalisateur, -trice *mf*.

product ['prɒdʌkt] *n* produit *m*.

production [prə'dʌkʃ(ə)n] *n* production *f*; *Th TV* mise *f* en scène; *Rad* réalisation *f*; **to work on the p. line** travailler à la chaîne. ◆**productive** *a* (*land, meeting, efforts*) productif. ◆**produc'tivity** *n* productivité *f*.

profane [prə'feɪn] *a* (*sacrilegious*) sacrilège; (*secular*) profane; − *vt* (*dishonour*) profaner. ◆**profanities** *npl* (*oaths*) blasphèmes *mpl*.

profess [prə'fes] *vt* professer; **to p. to be** prétendre être. ◆**—ed** *a* (*anarchist etc*) déclaré.

profession [prə'fef(ə)n] *n* profession *f*; **by p.** de profession. ◆**professional** *a* professionnel; (*man, woman*) qui exerce une profession libérale; (*army*) de métier; (*diplomat*) de carrière; (*piece of work*) de professionnel; − *n* professionnel, -elle *mf*; (*executive, lawyer etc*) membre *m* des professions libérales. ◆**professionalism** *n* professionnalisme *m*. ◆**professionally** *adv* professionnellement; (*to perform, play*) en professionnel; (*to meet s.o.*) dans le cadre de son travail.

professor [prə'fesər] *n* *Univ* professeur *m* (titulaire d'une chaire). ◆**profe'ssorial** *a* professoral.

proffer ['prɒfər] *vt* offrir.

proficient [prə'fɪʃ(ə)nt] *a* compétent (**in** en). ◆**proficiency** *n* compétence *f*.

profile ['prəufaɪl] *n* (*of person, object*) profil *m*; **in p.** de profil; **to keep a low p.** *Fig* garder un profil bas. ◆**profiled** *a* **to be p. against** se profiler sur.

profit ['prɒfɪt] *n* profit *m*, bénéfice *m*; **to sell**

at a p. vendre à profit; **p. margin** marge *f* bénéficiaire; **p. motive** recherche *f* du profit; − *vi* to **p. by** *or* **from** tirer profit de. ◆**p.-making** *a* à but lucratif. ◆**profita-'bility** *n Com* rentabilité *f*. ◆**profitable** *a Com* rentable; (*worthwhile*) *Fig* rentable, profitable. ◆**profitably** *adv* avec profit. ◆**profi'teer** *n Pej* profiteur, -euse *mf*; − *vi Pej* faire des profits malhonnêtes.

profound [prə'faund] *a* (*silence, remark etc*) profond. ◆**profoundly** *adv* profondément. ◆**profundity** *n* profondeur *f*.

profuse [prə'fjuːs] *a* abondant; **p. in** (*praise etc*) prodigue de. ◆**profusely** *adv* (*to flow, grow*) à profusion; (*to bleed*) abondamment; (*to thank*) avec effusion; **to apologize p.** se répandre en excuses. ◆**profusion** *n* profusion *f*; **in p.** à profusion.

progeny ['prɒdʒɪnɪ] *n* progéniture *f*.

program¹ ['prəʊɡræm] *n* (*of computer*) programme *m*; − *vt* (**-mm-**) (*computer*) programmer. ◆**programming** *n* programmation *f*. ◆**programmer** *n* (**computer**) **p.** programmeur, -euse *mf*.

programme, *Am* **program²** ['prəʊɡræm] *n* programme *m*; (*broadcast*) emission *f*; − *vt* (*arrange*) programmer.

progress ['prəʊɡres] *n* progrès *m(pl)*; **to make (good) p.** faire des progrès; (*in walking, driving etc*) bien avancer; **in p.** en cours; − [prə'ɡres] *vi* (*advance, improve*) progresser; (*of story, meeting*) se dérouler. ◆**pro'gression** *n* progression *f*. ◆**pro-'gressive** *a* (*gradual*) progressif; (*party*) *Pol* progressiste; (*firm, ideas*) moderniste. ◆**pro'gressively** *adv* progressivement.

prohibit [prə'hɪbɪt] *vt* interdire (**s.o. from doing** à qn de faire); **we're prohibited from leaving**/*etc* nous est interdit de partir/*etc*. ◆**prohi'bition** *n* prohibition *f*. ◆**prohibitive** *a* (*price, measure etc*) prohibitif.

project¹ ['prɒdʒekt] *n* (*plan*) projet *m* (**for sth** pour qch; **to do, for doing** pour faire); (*undertaking*) entreprise *f*; (*study*) étude *f*; (*housing*) **p.** (*for workers*) *Am* cité *f* (ouvrière). **2** [prə'dʒekt] *vt* (*throw, show etc*) projeter; − *vi* (*jut out*) faire saillie. ◆**-ed** *a* (*planned*) prévu. ◆**pro'jection** *n* projection *f*; (*projecting object*) saillie *f*. ◆**pro'jectionist** *n Cin* projectionniste *mf*. ◆**pro'jector** *n Cin* projecteur *m*.

proletarian [prəʊlɪ'teərɪən] *n* prolétaire *mf*; − *a* (*class*) prolétarien; (*outlook*) de prolétaire. ◆**proletariat** *n* prolétariat *m*.

proliferate [prə'lɪfəreɪt] *vi* proliférer. ◆**prolife'ration** *n* prolifération *f*.

prolific [prə'lɪfɪk] *a* prolifique.

prologue ['prəʊlɒɡ] *n* prologue *m* (**to de, à**).

prolong [prə'lɒŋ] *vt* prolonger.

promenade [prɒmə'nɑːd] *n* (*place, walk*) promenade *f*; (*gallery*) *Th* promenoir *m*.

prominent ['prɒmɪnənt] *a* (*nose*) proéminent; (*chin, tooth*) saillant; (*striking*) *Fig* frappant, remarquable; (*role*) majeur; (*politician*) marquant; (*conspicuous*) (bien) en vue. ◆**prominence** *n* (*importance*) importance *f*. ◆**prominently** *adv* (*displayed, placed*) bien en vue.

promiscuous [prə'mɪskjʊəs] *a* (*person*) de mœurs faciles; (*behaviour*) immoral. ◆**promi'scuity** *n* liberté *f* de mœurs; immoralité *f*.

promis/e ['prɒmɪs] *n* promesse *f*; **to show great p., be full of p.** (*hope*) être très prometteur; − *vt* promettre (**s.o. sth, sth to s.o.** qch à qn; **to do** de faire; **that que**); − *vi* **I p.!** je te le promets!; **p.?** promis? ◆**-ing** *a* (*start etc*) prometteur; (*person*) qui promet; **that looks p.** ça s'annonce bien.

promote [prə'məʊt] *vt* (*product, research*) promouvoir; (*good health, awareness*) favoriser; **to p. s.o.** promouvoir qn (**to** à); **promoted (to) manager/general/***etc* promu directeur/général/*etc*. ◆**promoter** *n Sp* organisateur, -trice *mf*; (*instigator*) promoteur, -trice *mf*. ◆**promotion** *n* (*of person*) avancement *m*, promotion *f*; (*of sales, research etc*) promotion *f*.

prompt [prɒmpt] **1** *a* (*speedy*) rapide; (*punctual*) à l'heure, ponctuel; **p. to act** prompt à agir; − *adv* **at 8 o'clock p.** à 8 heures pile. **2** *vt* (*urge*) inciter, pousser (**to do** à faire); (*cause*) provoquer. **3** *vt* (*person*) *Th* souffler (son rôle) à. ◆**-ing** *n* (*urging*) incitation *f*. ◆**-er** *n Th* souffleur, -euse *mf*. ◆**-ness** *n* rapidité *f*; (*readiness to act*) promptitude *f*.

prone [prəʊn] *a* **1 p. to sth** (*liable*) prédisposé à qch; **to be p. to do** avoir tendance à faire. **2** (*lying flat*) sur le ventre.

prong [prɒŋ] *n* (*of fork*) dent *f*.

pronoun ['prəʊnaʊn] *n Gram* pronom *m*. ◆**pro'nominal** *a* pronominal.

pronounce [prə'naʊns] *vt* (*articulate, declare*) prononcer; − *vi* (*articulate*) prononcer; (*give judgment*) se prononcer (**on** sur). ◆**pronouncement** *n* déclaration *f*. ◆**pronunci'ation** *n* prononciation *f*.

pronto ['prɒntəʊ] *adv* (*at once*) *Fam* illico.

proof [pruːf] **1** *n* (*evidence*) preuve *f*; (*of book, photo*) épreuve *f*; (*of drink*) teneur *f* en alcool. **2** *a* **p. against** (*material*) à l'épreuve de *(feu, acide etc)*. ◆**proof-reader** *n Typ* correcteur, -trice *mf*.

prop [prɒp] **1** *n Archit* support *m*, étai *m*; *(for clothes line)* perche *f*; *(person) Fig* soutien *m*; – *vt* (**-pp-**) **to p. up** *(ladder etc)* appuyer (**against** contre); *(one's head)* caler; *(wall)* étayer; *(help) Fig* soutenir. **2** *n* **prop(s)** *Th* accessoire(s) *m(pl)*.

propaganda [prɒpə'gændə] *n* propagande *f*. ◆**propagandist** *n* propagandiste *mf*.

propagate ['prɒpəgeɪt] *vt* propager; – *vi* se propager.

propel [prə'pel] *vt* (**-ll-**) *(drive, hurl)* propulser. ◆**propeller** *n Av Nau* hélice *f*.

propensity [prə'pensɪtɪ] *n* propension *f* (**for** sth à qch, **to do** à faire).

proper ['prɒpər] *a (suitable, seemly)* convenable; *(correct)* correct; *(right)* bon; *(real, downright)* véritable; *(noun, meaning)* propre; **in the p. way** comme il faut; **the village**/*etc* **p.** le village/*etc* proprement dit. ◆**-ly** *adv* comme il faut, convenablement, correctement; *(completely) Fam* vraiment; **very p.** *(quite rightly)* à juste titre.

property ['prɒpətɪ] **1** *n (building etc)* propriété *f*; *(possessions)* biens *mpl*, propriété *f*; – *a (crisis, market etc)* immobilier; *(owner, tax)* foncier. **2** *n (of substance etc)* propriété *f*. ◆**propertied** *a* possédant.

prophecy ['prɒfɪsɪ] *n* prophétie *f*. ◆**prophesy** [-ɪsaɪ] *vti* prophétiser; **to p. that** prédire que.

prophet ['prɒfɪt] *n* prophète *m*. ◆**prophetic** *a* prophétique.

proponent [prə'pəʊnənt] *n (of cause etc)* défenseur *m*, partisan, -ane *f*.

proportion [prə'pɔːʃ(ə)n] *n (ratio)* proportion *f*; *(portion)* partie *f*; *(amount)* pourcentage *m*; *pl (size)* proportions *fpl*; **in p.** en proportion (**to** de); **out of p.** hors de proportion (**to** avec); – *vt* proportionner (**to** à); **well** *or* **nicely proportioned** bien proportionné. ◆**proportional** *a*, ◆**proportionate** *a* proportionnel (**to** à).

propose [prə'pəʊz] *vt (suggest)* proposer (**to** à, **that** que (+ *sub*)); **to p. to do, p. doing** *(intend)* se proposer de faire; – *vi* faire une demande (en mariage) (**to** à). ◆**proposal** *n* proposition *f*; *(of marriage)* demande *f* (en mariage). ◆**propo'sition** *n* proposition *f*; *(matter) Fig* affaire *f*.

propound [prə'paʊnd] *vt* proposer.

proprietor [prə'praɪətər] *n* propriétaire *mf*. ◆**proprietary** *a (article) Com* de marque déposée; **p. name** marque *f* déposée.

propriety [prə'praɪətɪ] *n (behaviour)* bienséance *f*; *(of conduct, remark)* justesse *f*.

propulsion [prə'pʌlʃ(ə)n] *n* propulsion *f*.

pros [prəʊz] *npl* **the p. and cons** le pour et le contre.

prosaic [prəʊ'zeɪɪk] *a* prosaïque.

proscribe [prəʊ'skraɪb] *vt* proscrire.

prose [prəʊz] *n* prose *f*; *(translation) Sch* thème *m*.

prosecute ['prɒsɪkjuːt] *vt* poursuivre (en justice) (**for stealing**/*etc* pour vol/*etc*). ◆**prose'cution** *n Jur* poursuites *fpl*; **the p.** *(lawyers)* = le ministère public. ◆**prosecutor** *n (public) Jur* procureur *m*.

prospect¹ ['prɒspekt] *n (idea, outlook)* perspective *f* (**of doing** de faire); *(possibility)* possibilité *f* (**of sth** de qch); *(future)* **prospects** perspectives *fpl* d'avenir; **it has prospects** c'est prometteur; **she has prospects** elle a de l'avenir. ◆**pro'spective** *a (possible)* éventuel; *(future)* futur.

prospect² [prə'spekt] *vt (land)* prospecter; – *vi* **to p. for** *(gold etc)* chercher. ◆**-ing** *n* prospection *f*. ◆**prospector** *n* prospecteur, -trice *mf*.

prospectus [prə'spektəs] *n (publicity leaflet)* prospectus *m*; *Univ* guide *m* (de l'étudiant).

prosper ['prɒspər] *vi* prospérer. ◆**pro'sperity** *n* prospérité *f*. ◆**prosperous** *a (thriving)* prospère; *(wealthy)* riche, prospère.

prostate ['prɒsteɪt] *n* **p. (gland)** *Anat* prostate *f*.

prostitute ['prɒstɪtjuːt] *n (woman)* prostituée *f*; – *vt* prostituer. ◆**prosti'tution** *n* prostitution *f*.

prostrate ['prɒstreɪt] *a (prone)* sur le ventre; *(worshipper)* prosterné; *(submissive)* soumis; *(exhausted)* prostré; – [prɒ'streɪt] *vt* **to p. oneself** se prosterner (**before** devant).

protagonist [prəʊ'tægənɪst] *n* protagoniste *mf*.

protect [prə'tekt] *vt* protéger (**from** de, **against** contre); *(interests)* sauvegarder. ◆**protection** *n* protection *f*. ◆**protective** *a (tone etc) & Econ* protecteur; *(screen, clothes etc)* de protection. ◆**protector** *n* protecteur, -trice *mf*.

protein ['prəʊtiːn] *n* protéine *f*.

protest ['prəʊtest] *n* protestation *f* (**against** contre); **under p.** contre son gré; – [prə'test] *vt* protester (**that** que); *(one's innocence)* protester de; – *vi* protester (**against** contre); *(in the streets etc) Pol* contester. ◆**-er** *n Pol* contestataire *mf*.

Protestant ['prɒtɪstənt] *a & n* protestant,

-ante (*mf*). ◆**Protestantism** *n* protestantisme *m*.

protocol ['prəʊtəkɒl] *n* protocole *m*.

prototype ['prəʊtəʊtaɪp] *n* prototype *m*.

protract [prə'trækt] *vt* prolonger.

protractor [prə'træktər] *n* (*instrument*) *Geom* rapporteur *m*.

protrud/e [prə'truːd] *vi* dépasser; (*of balcony, cliff etc*) faire saillie; (*of tooth*) avancer. ◆**—ing** *a* saillant; (*of tooth*) qui avance.

proud [praʊd] *a* (**-er, -est**) (*honoured, pleased*) fier (of de, to do de faire); (*arrogant*) orgueilleux. ◆**—ly** *adv* fièrement; orgueilleusement.

prove [pruːv] *vt* prouver (**that** que); **to p. oneself** faire ses preuves; − *vi* **to p. (to be) difficult/etc** s'avérer difficile/*etc*. ◆**proven** *a* (*method etc*) éprouvé.

proverb ['prɒvɜːb] *n* proverbe *m*. ◆**pro'verbial** *a* proverbial.

provid/e [prə'vaɪd] *vt* (*supply*) fournir (**s.o. with sth** qch à qn); (*give*) donner, offrir (to à); **to p. s.o. with** (*equip*) pourvoir qn de; **to p. that** *Jur* stipuler que; − *vi* **to p. for s.o.** (*s.o.'s needs*) pourvoir aux besoins de qn; (*s.o.'s future*) assurer l'avenir de qn; **to p. for sth** (*make allowance for*) prévoir qch. ◆**—ed** *conj* **p. (that)** pourvu que (+ *sub*). ◆**—ing** *conj* **p. (that)** pourvu que (+ *sub*).

providence ['prɒvɪdəns] *n* providence *f*.

provident ['prɒvɪdənt] *a* (*society*) de prévoyance; (*person*) prévoyant.

province ['prɒvɪns] *n* province *f*; *Fig* domaine *m*, compétence *f*; **the provinces** la province; **in the provinces** en province. ◆**pro'vincial** *a & n* provincial, -ale (*mf*).

provision [prə'vɪʒ(ə)n] *n* (*supply*) provision *f*; (*clause*) disposition *f*; **the p. of** (*supplying*) la fourniture de; **to make p. for** = **to provide for**.

provisional [prə'vɪʒən(ə)l] *a* provisoire. ◆**—ly** *adv* provisoirement.

proviso [prə'vaɪzəʊ] *n* (*pl* **-os**) stipulation *f*.

provok/e [prə'vəʊk] *vt* (*rouse, challenge*) provoquer (**to do, into doing** à faire); (*annoy*) agacer; (*cause*) provoquer (*accident, réaction etc*). ◆**—ing** *a* (*annoying*) agaçant. ◆**provo'cation** *n* provocation *f*. ◆**provocative** *a* (*person, remark etc*) provocant; (*thought-provoking*) qui donne à penser.

prow [praʊ] *n* *Nau* proue *f*.

prowess ['praʊɪs] *n* (*bravery*) courage *m*; (*skill*) talent *m*.

prowl [praʊl] *vi* **to p. (around)** rôder; − *n* **to**

be on the p. rôder. ◆**—er** *n* rôdeur, -euse *mf*.

proximity [prɒk'sɪmɪtɪ] *n* proximité *f*.

proxy ['prɒksɪ] *n* **by p.** par procuration.

prude [pruːd] *n* prude *f*. ◆**prudery** *n* pruderie *f*. ◆**prudish** *a* prude.

prudent ['pruːdənt] *a* prudent. ◆**prudence** *n* prudence *f*. ◆**prudently** *adv* prudemment.

prun/e [pruːn] **1** *n* (*dried plum*) pruneau *m*. **2** *vt* (*cut*) *Bot* tailler, élaguer; (*speech etc*) *Fig* élaguer. ◆**—ing** *n* *Bot* taille *f*.

pry [praɪ] **1** *vi* être indiscret; **to p. into** (*meddle*) se mêler de; (*s.o.'s reasons etc*) chercher à découvrir. **2** *vt* **to p. open** *Am* forcer (en faisant levier). ◆**—ing** *a* indiscret.

PS [piː'es] *abbr* (*postscript*) P.-S.

psalm [sɑːm] *n* psaume *m*.

pseud [sjuːd] *n* *Fam* bêcheur, -euse *mf*.

pseudo- ['sjuːdəʊ] *pref* pseudo-.

pseudonym ['sjuːdənɪm] *n* pseudonyme *m*.

psychiatry [saɪ'kaɪətrɪ] *n* psychiatrie *f*. ◆**psychi'atric** *a* psychiatrique. ◆**psychiatrist** *n* psychiatre *mf*.

psychic ['saɪkɪk] *a* (méta)psychique; **I'm not p.** *Fam* je ne suis pas devin; − *n* (*person*) médium *m*.

psycho- ['saɪkəʊ] *pref* psycho-. ◆**psychoa'nalysis** *n* psychanalyse *f*. ◆**psycho'analyst** *n* psychanalyste *mf*.

psychology [saɪ'kɒlədʒɪ] *n* psychologie *f*. ◆**psycho'logical** *a* psychologique. ◆**psychologist** *n* psychologue *mf*.

psychopath ['saɪkəʊpæθ] *n* psychopathe *mf*.

psychosis, *pl* **-oses** [saɪ'kəʊsɪs, -əʊsiːz] *n* psychose *f*.

PTO [piːtiː'əʊ] *abbr* (*please turn over*) TSVP.

pub [pʌb] *n* pub *m*.

puberty ['pjuːbətɪ] *n* puberté *f*.

public ['pʌblɪk] *a* public; (*baths, library*) municipal; **to make a p. protest** protester publiquement; **in the p. eye** très en vue; **p. building** édifice *m* public; **p. company** société *f* par actions; **p. corporation** société *f* nationalisée; **p. figure** personnalité *f* connue; **p. house** pub *m*; **p. life** les affaires *fpl* publiques; **to be p.-spirited** avoir le sens civique; − *n* public *m*; **in p.** en public; **a member of the p.** un simple particulier; **the sporting/etc p.** les amateurs *mpl* de sport/*etc*. ◆**—ly** *adv* publiquement; **p. owned** (*nationalized*) *Com* nationalisé.

publican ['pʌblɪk(ə)n] *n* patron, -onne *mf* d'un pub.

publication [pʌblɪ'keɪʃ(ə)n] n (*publishing, book etc*) publication f.

publicity [pʌb'lɪsɪtɪ] n publicité f. ◆'**publicize** vt rendre public; (*advertise*) Com faire de la publicité pour.

publish ['pʌblɪʃ] vt publier; (*book*) éditer, publier; **to p. s.o.** éditer qn; '**published weekly**' 'paraît toutes les semaines'. ◆—**ing** n publication f (*of* de); (*profession*) édition f. ◆—**er** n éditeur, -trice mf.

puck [pʌk] n (*in ice hockey*) palet m.

pucker ['pʌkər] vt **to p. (up)** (*brow, lips*) plisser; — vi **to p. (up)** se plisser.

pudding ['pʊdɪŋ] n dessert m, gâteau m; (*plum*) p. pudding m; **rice p.** riz m au lait.

puddle ['pʌd(ə)l] n flaque f (d'eau).

pudgy ['pʌdʒɪ] a (-ier, -iest) = podgy.

puerile ['pjʊəraɪl] a puérile.

puff [pʌf] n (*of smoke*) bouffée f; (*of wind, air*) bouffée f, souffle m; **to have run out of p.** Fam être à bout de souffle; — vi (*blow, pant*) souffler; **to p. at** (*cigar*) tirer sur; — vt (*smoke etc*) souffler (*into* dans); **to p. out** (*cheeks etc*) gonfler. ◆**puffy** a (-ier, -iest) (*swollen*) gonflé.

puke [pjuːk] vi (*vomit*) Sl dégueuler.

pukka ['pʌkə] a Fam authentique.

pull [pʊl] n (*attraction*) attraction f; (*force*) force f; (*influence*) influence f; **to give sth a p.** tirer qch; — vt (*draw, tug*) tirer; (*tooth*) arracher; (*stopper*) enlever; (*trigger*) appuyer sur; (*muscle*) se claquer; **to p. apart** or **to bits** or **to pieces** mettre en pièces; **to p. a face** faire la moue; **to (get s.o. to) p. strings** Fig se faire pistonner; — vi (*tug*) tirer; (*go, move*) aller; **to p. at** or **on** tirer (sur). ■ **to p. along** vt (*drag*) traîner (**to** jusqu'à); **to p. away** vt (*move*) éloigner; (*snatch*) arracher (**from** à); — vi Aut démarrer; **to p. away from** s'éloigner de; **to p. back** vi (*withdraw*) Mil se retirer; — vt retirer; (*curtains*) ouvrir; **to p. down** vt (*lower*) baisser; (*knock down*) faire tomber; (*demolish*) démolir, abattre; **to p. in** vt (*rope*) ramener; (*drag into room etc*) faire entrer; (*stomach*) rentrer; (*crowd*) attirer; — vi (*arrive*) Aut arriver; (*stop*) Aut se garer; **to p. into the station** (*of train*) entrer en gare; **to p. off** vt enlever; (*plan, deal*) mener à bien; **to p. it off** Fig réussir son coup; **to p. on** vt (*boots etc*) mettre; **to p. out** vt (*extract*) arracher (**from** à); (*remove*) enlever (**from** de); (*from pocket, bag etc*) tirer, sortir (**from** de); (*troops*) retirer; — vi (*depart*) Aut démarrer; (*move out*) Aut déboîter; **to p. out from** (*negotiations etc*) se retirer de; **to p. over** vt (*drag*) traîner (**to**

jusqu'à); (*knock down*) faire tomber; — vi Aut se ranger (sur le côté); **to p. round** vi Med se remettre; **to p. through** vi s'en tirer; **to p. oneself together** vt se ressaisir; **to p. up** vt (*socks, bucket etc*) remonter; (*haul up*) hisser; (*uproot*) arracher; (*stop*) arrêter; — vi Aut s'arrêter. ◆**p.-up** n Sp traction f.

pulley ['pʊlɪ] n poulie f.

pullout ['pʊlaʊt] n (*in newspaper etc*) supplément m détachable.

pullover ['pʊləʊvər] n pull(-over) m.

pulp [pʌlp] n (*of fruit etc*) pulpe f; (*for paper*) pâte f à papier; **in a p.** Fig en bouillie.

pulpit ['pʊlpɪt] n Rel chaire f.

pulsate [pʌl'seɪt] vi produire des pulsations, battre. ◆**pulsation** n (*heartbeat etc*) pulsation f.

pulse [pʌls] n Med pouls m.

pulverize ['pʌlvəraɪz] vt (*grind, defeat*) pulvériser.

pumice ['pʌmɪs] n p. (**stone**) pierre f ponce.

pump [pʌmp] **1** n pompe f; (*petrol*) **p. attendant** pompiste mf; — vt pomper; (*blood*) Med faire circuler; (*money*) Fig injecter (**into** dans); **to p. s.o. (for information)** tirer les vers du nez à qn; **to p. in** refouler (*à l'aide d'une pompe*); **to p. out** pomper (**of** de); **to p. air into, p. up** (*tyre*) gonfler; — vi (*pump, beat*) (*of heart*) battre. **2** n (*for dancing*) escarpin m; (*plimsoll*) tennis f.

pumpkin ['pʌmpkɪn] n potiron m.

pun [pʌn] n calembour m.

punch¹ [pʌntʃ] n (*blow*) coup m de poing; (*force*) Fig punch m; **to pack a p.** Boxing & Fig avoir du punch; **p. line** (*of joke*) astuce f finale; — vt (*person*) donner un coup de poing à; (*ball etc*) frapper d'un coup de poing. ◆**p.-up** n Fam bagarre f.

punch² [pʌntʃ] **1** n (*for tickets*) poinçonneuse f; (*for paper*) perforeuse f; **p. card** carte f perforée; — vt (*ticket*) poinçonner, (*with date*) composter; (*card, paper*) perforer; **to p. a hole in** faire un trou dans. **2** n (*drink*) punch m.

punctilious [pʌŋk'tɪlɪəs] a pointilleux.

punctual ['pʌŋktʃʊəl] a (*arriving on time*) à l'heure; (*regularly on time*) ponctuel, exact. ◆**punctu'ality** n ponctualité f, exactitude f. ◆**punctually** adv à l'heure; (*habitually*) ponctuellement.

punctuate ['pʌŋktʃʊeɪt] vt ponctuer (**with** de). ◆**punctu'ation** n ponctuation f; **p. mark** signe m de ponctuation.

puncture ['pʌŋktʃər] n (*in tyre*) crevaison f;

to have a p. crever; – *vt* (*burst*) crever; (*pierce*) piquer; – *vi* (*of tyre*) crever.
pundit ['pʌndɪt] *n* expert *m*, ponte *m*.
pungent ['pʌndʒənt] *a* âcre, piquant. ◆**pungency** *n* âcreté *f*.
punish ['pʌnɪʃ] *vt* punir (**for sth** de qch, **for doing** *or* **having done** pour avoir fait); (*treat roughly*) Fig malmener. ◆—**ing** *n* punition *f*; – *a* (*tiring*) éreintant. ◆—**able** *a* punissable (**by** de). ◆—**ment** *n* punition *f*, châtiment *m*; **capital p.** peine *f* capitale; **to take a (lot of) p.** (*damage*) Fig en encaisser.
punitive ['pjuːnɪtɪv] *a* (*measure etc*) punitif.
punk [pʌŋk] **1** *n* (*music*) punk *m*; (*fan*) punk *mf*; – *a* punk *inv*. **2** *n* (*hoodlum*) Am Fam voyou *m*.
punt [pʌnt] **1** *n* barque *f* (à fond plat). **2** *vi* (*bet*) Fam parier. ◆—**ing** *n* canotage *m*. ◆—**er** *n* **1** (*gambler*) parieur, -euse *mf*. **2** (*customer*) Sl client, -ente *mf*.
puny ['pjuːnɪ] *a* (**-ier, -iest**) (*sickly*) chétif; (*small*) petit; (*effort*) faible.
pup ['pʌp] *n* (*dog*) chiot *m*.
pupil ['pjuːp(ə)l] *n* **1** (*person*) élève *mf*. **2** (*of eye*) pupille *f*.
puppet ['pʌpɪt] *n* marionnette *f*; – *a* (*government, leader*) fantoche *m*.
puppy ['pʌpɪ] *n* (*dog*) chiot *m*.
purchas/e ['pɜːtʃɪs] *n* (*bought article, buying*) achat *m*; – *vt* acheter (**from s.o.** à qn, **for s.o.** à *or* pour qn). ◆—**er** *n* acheteur, -euse *mf*.
pure [pjʊər] *a* (**-er, -est**) pur. ◆**purely** *adv* purement. ◆**purifi'cation** *n* purification *f*. ◆**purify** *vt* purifier. ◆**purity** *n* pureté *f*.
purée ['pjʊəreɪ] *n* purée *f*.
purgatory ['pɜːgətrɪ] *n* purgatoire *m*.
purge [pɜːdʒ] *n* Pol Med purge *f*; – *vt* (*rid*) purger (**of** de); (*group*) Pol épurer.
purist ['pjʊərɪst] *n* puriste *mf*.
puritan ['pjʊərɪt(ə)n] *n* & *a* puritain, -aine (*mf*). ◆**puri'tanical** *a* puritain.
purl [pɜːl] *n* (*knitting stitch*) maille *f* à l'envers.
purple ['pɜːp(ə)l] *a* & *n* violet (*m*); **to go p.** (*with anger*) devenir pourpre; (*with shame*) devenir cramoisi.
purport [pɜːˈpɔːt] *vt* **to p. to be** (*claim*) prétendre être.
purpose ['pɜːpəs] *n* **1** (*aim*) but *m*; **for this p.** dans ce but; **on p.** exprès; **to no p.** inutilement; **to serve no p.** ne servir à rien; **for (the) purposes of** pour les besoins de. **2** (*determination, willpower*) résolution *f*; **to have a sense of p.** être résolu. ◆**p.-'built** *a* construit spécialement. ◆**purposeful** *a* (*determined*) résolu. ◆**purposefully** *adv*

dans un but précis; (*resolutely*) résolument. ◆**purposely** *adv* exprès.
purr [pɜːr] *vi* ronronner; – *n* ronron(nement) *m*.
purse [pɜːs] **1** *n* (*for coins*) porte-monnaie *m inv*; (*handbag*) Am sac *m* à main. **2** *vt* **to p. one's lips** pincer les lèvres.
purser ['pɜːsər] *n* Nau commissaire *m* du bord.
pursue [pəˈsjuː] *vt* (*chase, hound, seek, continue*) poursuivre; (*fame, pleasure*) rechercher; (*course of action*) suivre. ◆**pursuer** *n* poursuivant, -ante *mf*. ◆**pursuit** *n* (*of person, glory etc*) poursuite *f*; (*activity, pastime*) occupation *f*; **to go in p. of** se mettre à la poursuite de.
purveyor [pəˈveɪər] *n* Com fournisseur *m*.
pus [pʌs] *n* pus *m*.
push [pʊʃ] *n* (*shove*) poussée *f*; (*energy*) Fig dynamisme *m*; (*help*) coup *m* de pouce; (*campaign*) campagne *f*; **to give s.o./sth a p.** pousser qn/qch; **to give s.o. the p.** (*dismiss*) Fam flanquer qn à la porte; – *vt* pousser (**to, as far as** jusqu'à); (*product*) Com pousser la vente de; (*drugs*) Fam revendre; **to p. (down)** (*button*) appuyer sur; (*lever*) abaisser; **to p. (forward)** (*views etc*) mettre en avant; **to p. sth into/between** (*thrust*) enfoncer *or* fourrer qch dans/entre; **to p. s.o. into doing** (*urge*) pousser qn à faire; **to p. sth off the table** faire tomber qch de la table (en le poussant); **to p. s.o. off a cliff** pousser qn du haut d'une falaise; **to be pushing forty/etc** Fam friser la quarantaine/etc; – *vi* pousser; **to p. for** faire pression pour obtenir. ■ **to p. about** *or* **around** *vt* (*bully*) Fam marcher sur les pieds à; **to p. aside** *vt* (*person, objection etc*) écarter; **to p. away** *or* **back** *vt* repousser; (*curtains*) ouvrir; **to p. in** *vi* (*in queue*) Fam resquiller; **to p. off** *vi* (*leave*) Fam filer; **p. off!** Fam fiche le camp!; **to p. on** *vi* continuer (**with sth** qch); (*in journey*) poursuivre sa route; **to p. over** *vt* (*topple*) renverser; **to p. through** *vt* (*law*) faire adopter; – *vti* **to p. (one's way) through** se frayer un chemin (**a crowd**/etc à travers une foule/etc); **to p. up** *vt* (*lever etc*) relever; (*increase*) Fam augmenter, relever. ◆**pushed** *a* **to be p.** (*for time*) (*rushed, busy*) être très bousculé. ◆**pusher** *n* (*of drugs*) revendeur, -euse *mf* (de drogue).
pushbike ['pʊʃbaɪk] *n* Fam vélo *m*. ◆**push-button** *n* poussoir *m*; – *a* (*radio etc*) à poussoir. ◆**pushchair** *n* poussette *f* (pliante). ◆**pushover** *n* **to be a p.** (*easy*)

Fam être facile, être du gâteau. ◆**push-up** *n* Sp Am pompe *f*.

pushy ['puʃɪ] *a* (**-ier, -iest**) Pej entreprenant; (*in job*) arriviste.

puss(y) ['pus(ɪ)] *n* (*cat*) minet *m*, minou *m*.

put [put] *vt* (*pt* & *pp* **put**, *pres p* **putting**) mettre; (*savings, money*) placer (**into** dans); (*pressure, mark*) faire (**on** sur); (*problem, argument*) présenter (**to** à); (*question*) poser (**to** à); (*say*) dire; (*estimate*) évaluer (**at** à); **to p. it bluntly** pour parler franc. ■ **to p. across** *vt* (*idea etc*) communiquer (**to** à); **to p. away** *vt* (*in its place*) ranger (*livre, voiture etc*); **to p. s.o. away** (*criminal*) mettre qn en prison; (*insane person*) enfermer qn; **to p. back** *vt* remettre; (*receiver*) Tel raccrocher; (*progress, clock*) retarder; **to p. by** *vt* (*money*) mettre de côté; **to p. down** *vt* (*on floor, table etc*) poser; (*passenger*) déposer; (*deposit*) Fin verser; (*revolt*) réprimer; (*write down*) inscrire; (*assign*) attribuer (**to** à); (*kill*) faire piquer (*chien etc*); **to p. forward** *vt* (*argument, clock, meeting*) avancer; (*opinion*) exprimer; (*candidate*) proposer (**for** à); **to p. in** *vt* (*insert*) introduire; (*add*) ajouter; (*present*) présenter; (*request, application*) faire; (*enrol*) inscrire (**for** à); (*spend*) passer (*une heure etc*) (**doing** à faire); – *vi* **to p. in for** (*job etc*) faire une demande de; **to p. in at** (*of ship etc*) faire escale à; **to p. off** *vt* (*postpone*) renvoyer (à plus tard); (*passenger*) déposer; (*gas, radio*) fermer; (*dismay*) déconcerter; **to p. s.o. off** (*dissuade*) dissuader qn (**doing** de faire); **to p. s.o. off** (*disgust*) dégoûter qn (**sth de** qch); **to p. s.o. off doing** (*disgust*) ôter à qn l'envie de faire; **to p. on** *vt* (*clothes, shoe etc*) mettre; (*weight, accent*) prendre; (*film*) jouer; (*gas, radio*) mettre, allumer; (*record, cassette*) passer; (*clock*) avancer; **to p. s.o. on** (*tease*) Am faire marcher qn; **she p. me on to you elle m'a donné votre adresse; p. me on to him!** Tel passez-le-moi!; **to p. out** *vt* (*take

outside*) sortir; (*arm, leg*) étendre; (*hand*) tendre; (*tongue*) tirer; (*gas, light*) éteindre, fermer; (*inconvenience*) déranger; (*upset*) déconcerter; (*issue*) publier; (*dislocate*) démettre; **to p. through** *vt* Tel passer (**to** à); **to p. together** *vt* (*assemble*) assembler; (*compose*) composer; (*prepare*) préparer; (*collection*) faire; **to p. up** *vi* (*lodge*) descendre (**at a hotel** dans un hôtel); **to p. up with** (*tolerate*) supporter; – *vt* (*lift*) lever; (*window*) remonter; (*tent, statue, picture, ladder*) dresser; (*flag*) hisser; (*building*) construire; (*umbrella*) ouvrir; (*picture, poster*) mettre; (*price, sales, numbers*) augmenter; (*resistance, plea, suggestion*) offrir; (*candidate*) proposer (**for** à); (*guest*) loger; **p.-up job** *Fam* coup *m* monté. ◆**p.-you-up** *n* canapé-lit *m*, convertible *m*.

putrid ['pjuːtrɪd] *a* putride. ◆**putrify** *vi* se putréfier.

putt [pʌt] *n* Golf putt *m*. ◆**putting** *n* Golf putting *m*; **p. green** green *m*.

putter ['pʌtər] *vi* **to p. around** *Am* bricoler.

putty ['pʌtɪ] *n* (*pour fixer une vitre*) mastic *m*.

puzzl/e ['pʌz(ə)l] *n* mystère *m*, énigme *f*; (*game*) casse-tête *m inv*; (*jigsaw*) puzzle *m*; – *vt* laisser perplexe; **to p. out why/when/** *etc* essayer de comprendre pourquoi/quand/*etc*; – *vi* **to p. over** (*problem, event*) se creuser la tête sur. ◆**—ed** *a* perplexe. ◆**—ing** *a* mystérieux, surprenant.

PVC [piːviːˈsiː] *n* (*plastic*) PVC *m*.

pygmy ['pɪgmɪ] *n* pygmée *m*.

pyjama [pɪˈdʒɑːmə] *a* (*jacket etc*) de pyjama. ◆**pyjamas** *npl* pyjama *m*; **a pair of p.** un pyjama.

pylon ['paɪlən] *n* pylône *m*.

pyramid ['pɪrəmɪd] *n* pyramide *f*.

Pyrenees [pɪrəˈniːz] *npl* **the P.** les Pyrénées *fpl*.

python ['paɪθən] *n* (*snake*) python *m*.

Q

Q, q [kjuː] *n* Q, q *m*.

quack [kwæk] **1** *n* (*of duck*) coin-coin *m inv*. **2** *a* & *n* **q. (doctor)** charlatan *m*.

quad(rangle) ['kwɒd(ræŋg(ə)l)] *n* (*of college*) cour *f*.

quadruped ['kwɒdruped] *n* quadrupède *m*.

quadruple [kwɒˈdruːp(ə)l] *vt* quadrupler.

quadruplets [kwɒˈdruːplɪts] (*Fam* **quads** [kwɒdz]) *npl* quadruplés, -ées *mfpl*.

quaff [kwɒf] *vt* (*drink*) avaler.

quagmire ['kwægmaɪər] *n* bourbier *m*.

quail [kweɪl] *n* (*bird*) caille *f*.

quaint [kweɪnt] a (-er, -est) (*picturesque*) pittoresque; (*antiquated*) vieillot; (*odd*) bizarre. ◆**—ness** n pittoresque m; caractère m vieillot; bizarrerie f.

quake [kweɪk] vi trembler (**with** de); − n *Fam* tremblement m de terre.

Quaker ['kweɪkər] n quaker, -eresse mf.

qualification [kwɒlɪfɪ'keɪʃ(ə)n] n **1** (*competence*) compétence f (**for** pour, **to do** pour faire); (*diploma*) diplôme m; pl (*requirements*) conditions fpl requises. **2** (*reservation*) réserve f.

qualify ['kwɒlɪfaɪ] **1** vt (*make competent*) & *Sp* qualifier (**for sth** pour qch, **to do** pour faire); − vi obtenir son diplôme (**as a doctor**/*etc* de médecin/*etc*); *Sp* se qualifier (**for** pour); **to q. for** (*post*) remplir les conditions requises pour. **2** vt (*modify*) faire des réserves à; (*opinion*) nuancer; *Gram* qualifier. ◆**qualified** a (*able*) qualifié (**to do** pour faire); (*doctor etc*) diplômé; (*success*) limité; (*opinion*) nuancé; (*support*) conditionnel. ◆**qualifying** a (*exam*) d'entrée; **q. round** *Sp* (épreuve f) éliminatoire f.

quality ['kwɒlɪtɪ] n qualité f; − a (*product*) de qualité. ◆**qualitative** a qualitatif.

qualms [kwɑːmz] npl (*scruples*) scrupules mpl; (*anxieties*) inquiétudes fpl.

quandary ['kwɒndrɪ] n **in a q.** bien embarrassé; **to be in a q. about what to do** ne pas savoir quoi faire.

quantity ['kwɒntɪtɪ] n quantité f; **in q.** (*to purchase etc*) en grande(s) quantité(s). ◆**quantify** vt quantifier. ◆**quantitative** a quantitatif.

quarantine ['kwɒrəntiːn] n *Med* quarantaine f; − vt mettre en quarantaine.

quarrel ['kwɒrəl] n querelle f, dispute f; **to pick a q.** chercher querelle (**with s.o.** à qn); − vi (**-ll-**, *Am* **-l-**) se disputer, se quereller (**with** avec); **to q. with sth** trouver à redire à qch. ◆**quarrelling** n, *Am* ◆**quarreling** n (*quarrels*) querelles fpl. ◆**quarrelsome** a querelleur.

quarry ['kwɒrɪ] n **1** (*excavation*) carrière f. **2** (*prey*) proie f.

quart [kwɔːt] n litre m (*mesure approximative*) (*Br = 1,14 litres, Am = 0,95 litre*).

quarter ['kwɔːtər] n **1** n quart m; (*of year*) trimestre m; (*money*) *Am Can* quart m de dollar; (*of moon, fruit*) quartier m; **to divide into quarters** diviser en quatre; **q. (of a) pound** quart m de livre; **a q. past nine**, *Am* **a q. after nine** neuf heures et *or* un quart; **a q. to nine** neuf heures moins le quart; **from all quarters** de toutes parts. **2** n (*district*)

quartier m; pl (*circles*) milieux mpl; (*living*) **quarters** logement(s) m(pl); *Mil* quartier(s) m(pl); − vt (*troops*) *Mil* cantonner. ◆**—ly** a trimestriel; − adv trimestriellement; − n publication f trimestrielle.

quarterfinal [kwɔːtə'faɪn(ə)l] n *Sp* quart m de finale.

quartet(te) [kwɔː'tet] n *Mus* quatuor m; (**jazz**) q. quartette m.

quartz [kwɔːts] n quartz m; − a (*clock etc*) à quartz.

quash [kwɒʃ] vt (*rebellion etc*) réprimer; (*verdict*) *Jur* casser.

quaver ['kweɪvər] **1** vi chevroter; − n chevrotement m. **2** n *Mus* croche f.

quay [kiː] n *Nau* quai m. ◆**quayside** n **on the q.** sur les quais.

queas/y ['kwiːzɪ] a (-ier, -iest) **to feel** *or* **be q.** avoir mal au cœur. ◆**—iness** n mal m au cœur.

Quebec [kwɪ'bek] n le Québec.

queen [kwiːn] n reine f; *Chess Cards* dame f; **the q. mother** la reine mère.

queer ['kwɪər] a (-er, -est) (*odd*) bizarre; (*dubious*) louche; (*ill*) *Fam* patraque; − n (*homosexual*) *Pej Fam* pédé m.

quell [kwel] vt (*revolt etc*) réprimer.

quench [kwentʃ] vt (*fire*) éteindre; **to q. one's thirst** se désaltérer.

querulous ['kweruləs] a (*complaining*) grognon.

query ['kwɪərɪ] n question f; (*doubt*) doute m; − vt mettre en question.

quest [kwest] n quête f (**for** de); **in q. of** en quête de.

question ['kwestʃ(ə)n] n question f; **there's some q. of it** il en est question; **there's no q. of it**, **it's out of the q.** il n'en est pas question, c'est hors de question; **without q.** incontestable(ment); **in q.** en question, dont il s'agit; **q. mark** point m d'interrogation; **q. master** *TV Rad* animateur, -trice mf; − vt interroger (**about** sur); (*doubt*) mettre en question; **to q. whether** douter que (+ sub). ◆**—ing** a (*look etc*) interrogateur; − n interrogation f. ◆**—able** a douteux. ◆**questio'nnaire** n questionnaire m.

queue [kjuː] n (*of people*) queue f; (*of cars*) file f; **to stand in a q.**, **form a q.** faire la queue; − vi **to q. (up)** faire la queue.

quibbl/e ['kwɪb(ə)l] vi ergoter, discuter (**over** sur). ◆**—ing** n ergotage m.

quiche [kiːʃ] n (*tart*) quiche f.

quick [kwɪk] **1** a (-er, -est) rapide; **q. to react** prompt à réagir; **to be q.** faire vite; **to have a q. shave/meal**/*etc* se raser/manger/*etc* en vitesse; **to be a q. worker** travailler vite; − *adv* (*speak*) vite; **as q. as a flash** en un clin d'œil. **2** *n* **to cut to the q.** blesser au vif. ◆**q.-'tempered** *a* irascible. ◆**q.-'witted** *a* à l'esprit vif. ◆**quicken** *vt* accélérer; − *vi* s'accélérer. ◆**quickie** *n* (*drink*) *Fam* pot *m* (*pris en vitesse*). ◆**quickly** *adv* vite. ◆**quicksands** *npl* sables *mpl* mouvants.

quid [kwɪd] *n inv Fam* livre *f* (sterling).

quiet [kwaɪət] *a* (-er, -est) (*silent, still, peaceful*) tranquille, calme; (*machine, vehicle, temperament*) silencieux; (*gentle*) doux; (*voice*) bas, doux; (*sound*) léger, doux; (*private*) intime; (*colour*) discret; **to be** *or* **keep q.** (*shut up*) se taire; (*make no noise*) ne pas faire de bruit; **q.!** silence!; **to keep q. about sth, keep sth q.** ne pas parler de qch; **on the q.** (*secretly*) *Fam* en cachette; − *vt* = **quieten.** ◆**quieten** *vti* **to q.** (**down**) (*se*) calmer. ◆**quietly** *adv* tranquillement; (*gently, not loudly*) doucement; (*silently*) silencieusement; (*secretly*) en cachette; (*discreetly*) discrètement. ◆**quietness** *n* tranquillité *f*.

quill [kwɪl] *n* (*pen*) plume *f* (d'oie).

quilt [kwɪlt] *n* édredon *m*; (**continental**) **q.** couette *f*; − *vt* (*stitch*) piquer; (*pad*) matelasser.

quintessence [kwɪn'tesəns] *n* quintessence *f*.

quintet(te) [kwɪn'tet] *n* quintette *m*.

quintuplets [kwɪn'tjuɪplɪts] (*Fam* **quins** [kwɪnz]) *npl* quintuplés, -ées *mfpl*.

quip [kwɪp] *n* (*remark*) boutade *f*; − *vi* (-**pp**-) faire des boutades; − *vt* dire sur le ton de la boutade.

quirk [kwɜːk] *n* bizarrerie *f*; (*of fate*) caprice *m*.

quit [kwɪt] *vt* (*pt & pp* quit *or* quitted, *pres p* quitting) (*leave*) quitter; **to q. doing** arrêter de faire; − *vi* (*give up*) abandonner; (*resign*) démissionner.

quite [kwaɪt] *adv* (*entirely*) tout à fait; (*really*) vraiment; (*rather*) assez; **q. another matter** une tout autre affaire *or* question; **q. a genius** un véritable génie; **q. good** (*not bad*) pas mal (du tout); **q. (so)!** exactement!; **I q. understand** je comprends très bien; **q. a lot** pas mal (of de); **q. a (long) time ago** il y a pas mal de temps.

quits [kwɪts] *a* quitte (**with** envers); **to call it q.** en rester là.

quiver ['kwɪvər] *vi* frémir (**with** de); (*of voice*) trembler, frémir; (*of flame*) vaciller, trembler.

quiz [kwɪz] *n* (*pl* quizzes) (*riddle*) devinette *f*; (*test*) test *m*; **q.** (*programme*) TV Rad jeu(-concours) *m*; − *vt* (-**zz**-) questionner. ◆**quizmaster** *n* TV Rad animateur, -trice *mf.*

quizzical ['kwɪzɪk(ə)l] *a* (*mocking*) narquois; (*perplexed*) perplexe.

quorum ['kwɔːrəm] *n* quorum *m.*

quota ['kwəʊtə] *n* quota *m.*

quote [kwəʊt] *vt* citer; (*reference number*) *Com* rappeler; (*price*) indiquer; (*price on Stock Exchange*) coter; − *vi* **to q. from** (*author, book*) citer; − *n Fam* = **quotation;** **in quotes** entre guillemets. ◆**quo'tation** *n* citation *f*; (*estimate*) *Com* devis *m*; (*on Stock Exchange*) cote *f*; **q. marks** guillemets *mpl*; **in q. marks** entre guillemets.

quotient ['kwəʊʃ(ə)nt] *n* quotient *m.*

R

R, r [ɑːr] *n* R, r *m.*

rabbi ['ræbaɪ] *n* rabbin *m*; **chief r.** grand rabbin.

rabbit ['ræbɪt] *n* lapin *m.*

rabble ['ræb(ə)l] *n* (*crowd*) cohue *f*; **the r.** *Pej* la populace.

rabies ['reɪbiːz] *n Med* rage *f.* ◆**rabid** ['ræbɪd] *a* (*dog*) enragé; (*person*) *Fig* fanatique.

raccoon [rə'kuːn] *n* (*animal*) raton *m* laveur.

rac/e [reɪs] *n Sp & Fig* course *f*; − *vt* (*horse*) faire courir; (*engine*) emballer; **to r.** (**against** *or* **with**) **s.o.** faire une course avec qn; − *vi* (*run*) courir; (*of engine*) s'emballer; (*of pulse*) battre à tout rompre. ◆**—ing** *n* courses *fpl*; − *a* (*car, bicycle etc*) de course; **r. driver** coureur *m* automobile. ◆**racecourse** *n* champ *m* de courses. ◆**racegoer** *n* turfiste *mf.* ◆**racehorse** *n* cheval *m* de course. ◆**racetrack** *n* piste *f*; (*for horses*) *Am* champ *m* de courses.

race² [reɪs] *n* (*group*) race *f*; − *a* (*prejudice etc*) racial; **r. relations** rapports *mpl* entre les races. ◆**racial** a racial. ◆**racialism** n racisme m. ◆**racism** n racisme m. ◆**racist** a & n raciste (mf).

rack [ræk] **1** n (shelf) étagère f; (for bottles etc) casier m; (for drying dishes) égouttoir m; (luggage) r. (on bicycle) porte-bagages m inv; (on bus, train etc) filet m à bagages; (roof) r. (of car) galerie f. **2** vt to r. one's brains se creuser la cervelle. **3** n to go to r. and ruin (of person) aller à la ruine; (of building) tomber en ruine; (of health) se délabrer.

racket ['rækɪt] n **1** (for tennis etc) raquette f. **2** (din) vacarme m. **3** (crime) racket m; (scheme) combine f; the drug(s) r. le trafic m de (la) drogue. ◆**racke'teer** n racketteur m. ◆**racke'teering** n racket m.

racoon [rə'kuːn] n (animal) raton m laveur.

racy ['reɪsɪ] a (-ier, -iest) piquant; (suggestive) osé.

radar ['reɪdɑːr] n radar m; – a (control, trap etc) radar inv; r. operator radariste mf.

radiant ['reɪdɪənt] a (person) rayonnant (with de), radieux. ◆**radiance** n éclat m, rayonnement m. ◆**radiantly** adv (to shine) avec éclat; r. happy rayonnant de joie.

radiate ['reɪdɪeɪt] vt (emit) dégager; (joy) Fig rayonner de; – vi (of heat, lines) rayonner (from de). ◆**radia'tion** n (of heat etc) rayonnement m (of de); (radioactivity) Phys radiation f; (rays) irradiation f; r. sickness mal m des rayons.

radiator ['reɪdɪeɪtər] n radiateur m.

radical ['rædɪk(ə)l] a radical; – n (person) Pol radical, -ale mf.

radio ['reɪdɪəʊ] n (pl -os) radio f; on the r. à la radio; car r. autoradio m; r. set poste m (de) radio; r. operator radio m; r. wave onde f hertzienne; – vt (message) transmettre (par radio) (to à); to r. s.o. appeler qn par radio. ◆**r.-con'trolled** a radioguidé. ◆**radio'active** a radioactif. ◆**radioac'tivity** n radioactivité f.

radiographer [reɪdɪ'ɒɡrəfər] n (technician) radiologue mf. ◆**radiography** n radiographie f. ◆**radiologist** n (doctor) radiologue mf. ◆**radiology** n radiologie f.

radish ['rædɪʃ] n radis m.

radius, pl -**dii** ['reɪdɪəs, -dɪaɪ] n (of circle) rayon m; within a r. of dans un rayon de.

RAF [ɑːreɪ'ef] n abbr (Royal Air Force) armée f de l'air (britannique).

raffia ['ræfɪə] n raphia m.

raffle ['ræf(ə)l] n tombola f.

raft [rɑːft] n (boat) radeau m.

rafter ['rɑːftər] n (beam) chevron m.

rag [ræɡ] n **1** (old garment) loque f, haillon m; (for dusting etc) chiffon m; in rags (clothes) en loques; (person) en haillons; r.-and-bone man chiffonnier m. **2** (newspaper) torchon m. **3** (procession) Univ carnaval m (au profit d'œuvres de charité). ◆**ragged** ['ræɡɪd] a (clothes) en loques; (person) en haillons; (edge) irrégulier. ◆**ragman** n (pl -men) chiffonnier m.

ragamuffin ['ræɡəmʌfɪn] n va-nu-pieds m inv.

rag/e [reɪdʒ] n rage f; (of sea) furie f; to fly into a r. se mettre en rage; to be all the r. (of fashion etc) faire fureur; – vi (be angry) rager; (of storm, battle) faire rage. ◆**—ing** a (storm, fever) violent; a r. fire un grand incendie; in a r. temper furieux.

raid [reɪd] n Mil raid m; (by police) descente f; (by thieves) hold-up m; air r. raid m aérien, attaque f aérienne; – vt faire un raid or une descente or un hold-up dans; Av attaquer; (larder, fridge etc) Fam dévaliser. ◆**raider** n (criminal) malfaiteur m; pl Mil commando m.

rail [reɪl] **1** n (for train) rail m; by r. (to travel) par le train; (to send) par chemin de fer; to go off the rails (of train) dérailler; – a ferroviaire; (strike) des cheminots. **2** n (rod on balcony) balustrade f; (on stairs, for spotlight) rampe f; (for curtain) tringle f; (towel) r. porte-serviettes m inv. ◆**railing** n (of balcony) balustrade f; pl (fence) grille f. ◆**railroad** n Am = railway; r. track voie f ferrée. ◆**railway** n (system) chemin m de fer; (track) voie f ferrée; – a (ticket) de chemin de fer; (network) ferroviaire; r. line (route) ligne f de chemin de fer; (track) voie f ferrée; r. station gare f. ◆**railwayman** n (pl -men) cheminot m.

rain [reɪn] n pluie f; in the r. sous la pluie; I'll give you a r. check (for invitation) Am Fam j'accepterai volontiers à une date ultérieure; – vi pleuvoir; to r. (down) (of blows, bullets) pleuvoir; it's raining il pleut. ◆**rainbow** n arc-en-ciel m. ◆**raincoat** n imper(méable) m. ◆**raindrop** n goutte f de pluie. ◆**rainfall** n (shower) chute f de pluie; (amount) précipitations fpl. ◆**rainstorm** n trombe f d'eau. ◆**rainwater** n eau f de pluie. ◆**rainy** a (-ier, -iest) pluvieux; the r. season la saison des pluies.

raise [reɪz] vt (lift) lever; (sth heavy) (sou)lever; (child, animal, voice, statue) élever; (crops) cultiver; (salary, price) augmenter, relever; (temperature) faire monter; (question, protest) soulever; (taxes, blockade) lever; to r. a smile/a laugh (in others) faire sourire/rire; to r. s.o.'s hopes

faire naître les espérances de qn; **to r.
money** réunir des fonds; – *n* (*pay rise*) *Am*
augmentation *f* (de salaire).
raisin ['reɪz(ə)n] *n* raison *m* sec.

rake [reɪk] *n* râteau *m*; – *vt* (*garden*)
ratisser; (*search*) fouiller dans; **to r. (up)**
(*leaves*) ramasser (avec un râteau); **to r. in**
(*money*) *Fam* ramasser à la pelle; **to r. up**
(*the past*) remuer. ◆**r.-off** *n* *Fam*
pot-de-vin *m*, ristourne *f*.

rally ['rælɪ] *vt* (*unite, win over*) rallier (**to** à);
(*one's strength*) *Fig* reprendre; – *vi* se
rallier (**to** à); (*recover*) se remettre (**from**
de); **to r. round** (*help*) venir en aide (**s.o.** à
qn); – *n* *Mil* ralliement *m*; *Pol* rassemblement *m*; *Sp* *Aut* rallye *m*.

ram [ræm] **1** *n* (*animal*) bélier *m*. **2** *vt* (-**mm**-)
(*ship*) heurter; (*vehicle*) emboutir; **to r. sth
into** (*thrust*) enfoncer qch dans.

rambl/e ['ræmb(ə)l] **1** *n* (*hike*) randonnée *f*;
– *vi* faire une randonnée *or* des randon-
nées. **2** *vi* **to r. on** (*talk*) *Pej* discourir.
◆**-ing** **1** *a* (*house*) construit sans plan;
(*spread out*) vaste; (*rose etc*) grimpant. **2** *a*
(*speech*) décousu; – *npl* divagations *fpl*.
◆**-er** *n* promeneur, -euse *mf*.

ramification [ræmɪfɪ'keɪʃ(ə)n] *n* ramification *f*.

ramp [ræmp] *n* (*slope*) rampe *f*; (*in garage*)
Tech pont *m* (de graissage); *Av* passerelle *f*;
'r.' *Aut* 'dénivellation'.

rampage ['ræmpeɪdʒ] *n* **to go on the r.** (*of
crowd*) se déchaîner; (*loot*) se livrer au
pillage.

rampant ['ræmpənt] *a* **to be r.** (*of crime,
disease etc*) sévir.

rampart ['ræmpɑːt] *n* rempart *m*.

ramshackle ['ræmʃæk(ə)l] *a* délabré.

ran [ræn] *see* **run**.

ranch [ræntʃ] *n* *Am* ranch *m*; **r. house**
maison *f* genre bungalow (sur sous-sol).

rancid ['rænsɪd] *a* rance.

rancour ['ræŋkər] *n* rancœur *f*.

random ['rændəm] *n* **at r.** au hasard; – *a*
(*choice*) fait au hasard; (*sample*) prélevé au
hasard; (*pattern*) irrégulier.

randy ['rændɪ] *a* (-**ier**, -**iest**) *Fam* sensuel,
lascif.

rang [ræŋ] *see* **ring²**.

range [reɪndʒ] **1** *n* (*of gun, voice etc*) portée
f; (*of aircraft, ship*) rayon *m* d'action;
(*series*) gamme *f*; (*choice*) choix *m*; (*of
prices*) éventail *m*; (*of voice*) *Mus* étendue *f*;
(*of temperature*) variations *fpl*; (*sphere*) *Fig*
champ *m*, étendue *f*; – *vi* (*vary*) varier;
(*extend*) s'étendre; (*roam*) errer, rôder. **2** *n*
(*of mountains*) chaîne *f*; (*grassland*) *Am*

prairie *f*. **3** *n* (*stove*) *Am* cuisinière *f*. **4** *n*
(*shooting or* rifle) **r.** (*at funfair*) stand *m* de
tir; (*outdoors*) champ *m* de tir.

ranger ['reɪndʒər] *n* (**forest**) **r.** *Am* garde *m*
forestier.

rank [ræŋk] **1** *n* (*position, class*) rang *m*;
(*grade*) *Mil* grade *m*, rang *m*; **the r. and file**
(*workers etc*) *Pol* la base; **the ranks** (*men in
army, numbers*) les rangs *mpl* (of de); **taxi r.**
station *f* de taxi; – *vti* **to r. among** compter
parmi. **2** *a* (-**er**, -**est**) (*smell*) fétide; (*vegetation*) luxuriant; *Fig* absolu.

rankle ['ræŋk(ə)l] *vi* **it rankles (with me)** je
l'ai sur le cœur.

ransack ['rænsæk] *vt* (*search*) fouiller;
(*plunder*) saccager.

ransom ['ræns(ə)m] *n* rançon *f*; **to hold to r.**
rançonner; – *vt* (*redeem*) racheter.

rant [rænt] *vi* **to r. (and rave)** tempêter (**at**
contre).

rap [ræp] *n* petit coup *m* sec; – *vi* (-**pp**-)
frapper (**at** à); – *vt* **to r. s.o. over the knuck-
les** taper sur les doigts de qn.

rapacious [rə'peɪʃəs] *a* (*greedy*) rapace.

rape [reɪp] *vt* violer; – *n* viol *m*. ◆**rapist** *n*
violeur *m*.

rapid ['ræpɪd] **1** *a* rapide. **2** *n* & *npl* (*of river*)
rapide(s) *m(pl).* ◆**ra'pidity** *n* rapidité *f*.
◆**rapidly** *adv* rapidement.

rapport [ræ'pɔːr] *n* (*understanding*) rapport
m.

rapt [ræpt] *a* (*attention*) profond.

rapture ['ræptʃər] *n* extase *f*; **to go into
raptures** s'extasier (**about** sur). ◆**rap-
turous** *a* (*welcome, applause*) enthousiaste.

rare [reər] *a* (-**er**, -**est**) rare; (*meat*) *Culin*
saignant; (*first-rate*) *Fam* fameux; **it's r. for
her to do it** il est rare qu'elle le fasse. ◆**—ly**
adv rarement. ◆**—ness** *n* rareté *f*. ◆**rarity**
n (*quality, object*) rareté *f*.

rarefied ['reərɪfaɪd] *a* raréfié.

raring ['reərɪŋ] *a* **r. to start/***etc* impatient de
commencer/*etc*.

rascal ['rɑːsk(ə)l] *n* coquin, -ine *mf*. ◆**rascally** *a* (*child etc*) coquin; (*habit, trick etc*)
de coquin.

rash [ræʃ] **1** *n* *Med* éruption *f*. **2** *a* (-**er**, -**est**)
irréfléchi. ◆**—ly** *adv* sans réflexion.
◆**—ness** *n* irréflexion *f*.

rasher ['ræʃər] *n* tranche *f* de lard.

rasp [rɑːsp] *n* (*file*) râpe *f*.

raspberry ['rɑːzbərɪ] *n* (*fruit*) framboise *f*;
(*bush*) framboisier *m*.

rasping ['rɑːspɪŋ] *a* (*voice*) âpre.

rat [ræt] **1** *n* rat *m*; **r. poison** mort-aux-rats *f*;
the r. race *Fig* la course au bifteck, la
jungle. **2** *vi* (-**tt**-) **to r. on** (*desert*) lâcher;

(*denounce*) cafarder sur; (*promise etc*) manquer à.

rate [reɪt] **1** *n* (*percentage, level*) taux *m*; (*speed*) vitesse *f*; (*price*) tarif *m*; *pl* (*on housing*) impôts *mpl* locaux; **insurance rates** primes *fpl* d'assurance; **r. of flow** débit *m*; **postage** *or* **postal r.** tarif *m* postal; **at the r. of** à une vitesse de; (*amount*) à raison de; **at this r.** (*slow speed*) à ce train-là; **at any r.** en tout cas; **the success r.** (*chances*) les chances *fpl* de succès; (*candidates*) le pourcentage de reçus. **2** *vt* (*evaluate*) évaluer; (*regard*) considérer (**as** comme); (*deserve*) mériter; **to r. highly** apprécier (beaucoup); **to be highly rated** être très apprécié. ◆**rateable** *a* **r. value** valeur *f* locative nette. ◆**ratepayer** *n* contribuable *mf*.

rather ['rɑːðər] *adv* (*preferably, fairly*) plutôt; **I'd r. stay** j'aimerais mieux *or* je préférerais rester (**than** que); **I'd r. you came** je préférerais que vous veniez; **r. than leave**/*etc* plutôt que de partir/*etc*; **r. more tired**/*etc* un peu plus fatigué/*etc* (**than** que); **it's r. nice** c'est bien.

ratify ['rætɪfaɪ] *vt* ratifier. ◆**ratifi'cation** *n* ratification *f*.

rating ['reɪtɪŋ] *n* (*classification*) classement *m*; (*wage etc level*) indice *m*; **credit r.** *Fin* réputation *f* de solvabilité; **the ratings** *TV* l'indice *m* d'écoute.

ratio ['reɪʃɪəʊ] *n* (*pl* **-os**) proportion *f*.

ration ['ræʃ(ə)n, *Am* 'reɪʃ(ə)n] *n* ration *f*; *pl* (*food*) vivres *mpl*; − *vt* rationner; **I was rationed to ....** ma ration était ....

rational ['ræʃən(ə)l] *a* (*method, thought etc*) rationnel; (*person*) raisonnable. ◆**rationalize** *vt* (*organize*) rationaliser; (*explain*) justifier. ◆**rationally** *adv* raisonnablement.

rattle ['ræt(ə)l] **1** *n* (*baby's toy*) hochet *m*; (*of sports fan*) crécelle *f*. **2** *n* petit bruit *m* (sec); cliquetis *m*; crépitement *m*; − *vi* faire du bruit; (*of bottles*) cliqueter; (*of gunfire*) crépiter; (*of window*) trembler; − *vt* (*shake*) agiter; (*window*) faire trembler; (*keys*) faire cliqueter. **3** *vt* **to r. s.o.** (*make nervous*) *Fam* ébranler qn; **to r. off** (*poem etc*) *Fam* débiter (à toute vitesse). ◆**rattlesnake** *n* serpent *m* à sonnette.

ratty ['rætɪ] *a* (**-ier, -iest**) **1** (*shabby*) *Am Fam* minable. **2** **to get r.** (*annoyed*) *Fam* prendre la mouche.

raucous ['rɔːkəs] *a* rauque.

raunchy ['rɔːntʃɪ] *a* (**-ier, -iest**) (*joke etc*) *Am Fam* grivois.

ravage ['rævɪdʒ] *vt* ravager; − *npl* **ravages** *mpl.*

rav/e [reɪv] *vi* (*talk nonsense*) divaguer; (*rage*) tempêter (**at** contre); **to r. about** (*enthuse*) ne pas se tarir d'éloges sur; − **a r. review** *Fam* critique *f* dithyrambique. ◆**-ing** *a* **to be r. mad** être fou furieux; − *npl* (*wild talk*) divagations *fpl.*

raven ['reɪv(ə)n] *n* corbeau *m.*

ravenous ['rævənəs] *a* vorace; **I'm r.** *Fam* j'ai une faim de loup.

ravine [rə'viːn] *n* ravin *m.*

ravioli [rævɪ'əʊlɪ] *n* ravioli *mpl.*

ravish ['rævɪʃ] *vt* (*rape*) *Lit* violenter. ◆**-ing** *a* (*beautiful*) ravissant. ◆**-ingly** *adv* **r. beautiful** d'une beauté ravissante.

raw [rɔː] *a* (**-er, -est**) (*vegetable etc*) cru; (*sugar*) brut; (*immature*) inexpérimenté; (*wound*) à vif; (*skin*) écorché; (*weather*) rigoureux; **r. edge** bord *m* coupé; **r. material** matière *f* première; **to get a r. deal** *Fam* être mal traité.

Rawlplug® ['rɔːlplʌg] *n* cheville *f*, tampon *m.*

ray [reɪ] *n* (*of light, sun etc*) & *Phys* rayon *m*; (*of hope*) *Fig* lueur *f.*

raze [reɪz] *vt* **to r.** (**to the ground**) (*destroy*) raser.

razor ['reɪzər] *n* rasoir *m.*

re [riː] *prep Com* en référence à.

re- [riː] *pref* ré-, re-, r-.

reach [riːtʃ] *vt* (*place, aim etc*) atteindre, arriver à; (*gain access to*) accéder à; (*of letter*) parvenir à (qn); (*contact*) joindre (qn); **to r. s.o.** (**over**) **sth** (*hand over*) passer qch à qn; **to r. out** (*one's arm*) (é)tendre; − *vi* (*extend*) s'étendre (**to** à); (*of voice*) porter; **to r.** (**out**) (é)tendre le bras (**for** pour prendre); − *n* portée *f*; *Boxing* allonge *f*; **within r. of** à portée de; (*near*) à proximité de; **within easy r.** (*object*) à portée de main; (*shops*) facilement accessible.

react [rɪ'ækt] *vi* réagir. ◆**reaction** *n* réaction *f.* ◆**reactionary** *a* & *n* réactionnaire (*mf*).

reactor [rɪ'æktər] *n* réacteur *m.*

read [riːd] *vt* (*pt & pp* **read** [red]) lire; (*study*) *Univ* faire des études de; (*meter*) relever; (*of instrument*) indiquer; **to r. back** *or* **over** relire; **to r. out** lire (à haute voix); **to r. through** (*skim*) parcourir; **to r. up** (**on**) (*study*) étudier; − *vi* lire; **to r. well** (*of text*) se lire bien; **to r. to s.o.** faire la lecture à qn; **to r. about** (*s.o., sth*) lire qch sur; **to r. for** (*degree*) *Univ* préparer; − *n* **to have a r.** *Fam* faire un peu de lecture; **this book's a**

good r. *Fam* ce livre est agréable à lire.
◆**—ing** *n* lecture *f*; (*of meter*) relevé *m*; (*by instrument*) indication *f*; (*variant*) variante *f*; *– a* (*room*) de lecture; **r. matter** choses *fpl* à lire; **r. lamp** lampe *f* de bureau *or* de chevet. ◆**—able** *a* lisible. ◆**—er** *n* lecteur, -trice *mf*; (*book*) livre *m* de lecture.
◆**readership** *n* lecteurs *mpl*, public *m*.

readdress [riːə'dres] *vt* (*letter*) faire suivre.

readjust [riːə'dʒʌst] *vt* (*instrument*) régler; (*salary*) réajuster; *– vi* se réadapter (**to** à). ◆**—ment** *n* réglage *m*; réajustement *m*; réadaptation *f*.

readily ['redɪlɪ] *adv* (*willingly*) volontiers; (*easily*) facilement. ◆**readiness** *n* empressement *m* (**to do** à faire); **in r. for** prêt pour.

ready ['redɪ] *a* (-ier, -iest) prêt (**to do** à faire, **for sth** à *or* pour qch); (*quick*) *Fig* prompt (**to do** à faire); **to get sth r.** préparer qch; **to get r.** se préparer (**for sth** à qch, **to do** à faire); **r. cash, r. money** argent *m* liquide; *– n* **at the r.** tout prêt. ◆**r.-'cooked** *a* tout cuit. ◆**r.-'made** *a* tout fait; **r.-made clothes** prêt-à-porter *m inv*.

real [rɪəl] *a* vrai, véritable; (*life, world etc*) réel; **it's the r. thing** *Fam* c'est du vrai de vrai; **r. estate** *Am* immobilier *m*; *– adv Fam* vraiment; **r. stupid** vraiment bête; *– n* **for r.** *Fam* pour de vrai. ◆**realism** *n* réalisme *m*. ◆**realist** *n* réaliste *mf*. ◆**rea'listic** *a* réaliste. ◆**rea'listically** *adv* avec réalisme.

reality [rɪ'ælɪtɪ] *n* réalité *f*; **in r.** en réalité.

realize ['rɪəlaɪz] *vt* **1** (*know*) se rendre compte de, réaliser; (*understand*) comprendre (**that** que); **to r. that** (*know*) se rendre compte que. **2** (*carry out, convert into cash*) réaliser; (*price*) atteindre. ◆**reali'zation** *n* **1** (*carrying f de*) conscience *f*. **2** (*of aim, assets*) réalisation *f*.

really ['rɪəlɪ] *adv* vraiment; **is it r. true?** est-ce bien vrai?

realm [relm] *n* (*kingdom*) royaume *m*; (*of dreams etc*) *Fig* monde *m*.

realtor ['rɪəltər] *n Am* agent *m* immobilier.

reap [riːp] *vt* (*field, crop*) moissonner; *Fig* récolter.

reappear [riːə'pɪər] *vi* réapparaître.

reappraisal [riːə'preɪz(ə)l] *n* réévaluation *f*.

rear [rɪər] *n* **1** (*back part*) arrière *m*; (*of column*) queue *f*; **in** *or* **at the r.** à l'arrière (**of** de); **from the r.** par derrière; *– a* arrière *inv*, de derrière; **r.-view mirror** rétroviseur *m*. **2** *vt* (*family, animals etc*) élever; (*one's head*) relever. **3** *vi* **to r. (up)** (*of horse*) se cabrer. ◆**rearguard** *n* arrière-garde *f*.

rearrange [riːə'reɪndʒ] *vt* réarranger.

reason ['riːz(ə)n] *n* (*cause, sense*) raison *f*; **the r. for/why** *or* **that** . . . la raison de/pour laquelle . . . ; **for no r.** sans raison; **that stands to r.** cela va sans dire, c'est logique; **within r.** avec modération; **to do everything within r. to** . . . faire tout ce qu'il est raisonnable de faire pour . . . ; **to have every r. to believe/***etc* avoir tout lieu de croire/*etc*; *– vi* raisonner; **to r. with s.o.** raisonner qn; *– vt* **to r. that** calculer que. ◆**—ing** *n* raisonnement *m*. ◆**—able** *a* raisonnable. ◆**—ably** *adv* raisonnablement; (*fairly, rather*) assez; **r. fit** en assez bonne forme.

reassur/e [riːə'ʃʊər] *vt* rassurer. ◆**—ing** *a* rassurant. ◆**reassurance** *n* réconfort *m*.

reawaken [riːə'weɪk(ə)n] *vt* (*interest etc*) réveiller. ◆**—ing** *n* réveil *m*.

rebate ['riːbeɪt] *n* (*discount on purchase*) ristourne *f*; (*refund*) remboursement *m* (partiel).

rebel ['reb(ə)l] *a* & *n* rebelle (*mf*); *–* [rɪ'bel] *vi* (-ll-) se rebeller (**against** contre). ◆**re'bellion** *n* rébellion *f*. ◆**re'bellious** *a* rebelle.

rebirth ['riːbɜːθ] *n* renaissance *f*.

rebound [rɪ'baʊnd] *vi* (*of ball*) rebondir; (*of stone*) ricocher; (*of lies, action etc*) *Fig* retomber (**on sur**); *–* ['riːbaʊnd] *n* rebond *m*; ricochet *m*; **on the r.** (*to marry s.o. etc*) par dépit.

rebuff [rɪ'bʌf] *vt* repousser; *– n* rebuffade *f*.

rebuild [riː'bɪld] *vt* (*pt & pp* **rebuilt**) reconstruire.

rebuke [rɪ'bjuːk] *vt* réprimander; *– n* réprimande *f*.

rebuttal [rɪ'bʌt(ə)l] *n* réfutation *f*.

recalcitrant [rɪ'kælsɪtrənt] *a* récalcitrant.

recall [rɪ'kɔːl] *vt* (*call back*) rappeler; (*remember*) se rappeler (**that** que, **doing** avoir fait); **to r. sth to s.o.** rappeler qch à qn; *– n* rappel *m*; **beyond r.** irrévocable.

recant [rɪ'kænt] *vi* se rétracter.

recap [riː'kæp] *vti* (-pp-) récapituler; *– n* récapitulation *f*. ◆**reca'pitulate** *vti* récapituler. ◆**recapitu'lation** *n* récapitulation *f*.

recapture [riː'kæptʃər] *vt* (*prisoner etc*) reprendre; (*rediscover*) retrouver; (*recreate*) recréer; *– n* (*of prisoner*) arrestation *f*.

reced/e [rɪ'siːd] *vi* (*into the distance*) s'éloigner; (*of floods*) baisser. ◆**—ing** *a* (*forehead*) fuyant; **his hair(line) is r.** son front se dégarnit.

receipt [rɪ'siːt] *n* (*for payment*) reçu *m* (**for** de); (*for letter, parcel*) récépissé *m*, accusé *m* de réception; *pl* (*takings*) recettes *fpl*; **to acknowledge r.** accuser réception (**of** de); **on r. of** dès réception de.

receiv/e [rɪ'siːv] *vt* recevoir; (*stolen goods*) *Jur* receler. **◆—ing** *n* *Jur* recel *m*. **◆—er** *n* *Tel* combiné *m*; *Rad* récepteur *m*; (*of stolen goods*) *Jur* receleur, -euse *mf*; **to pick up** *or* **lift the r.** *Tel* décrocher.

recent ['riːsənt] *a* récent; **in r. months** ces mois-ci. **◆—ly** *adv* récemment; **as r. as** pas plus tard que.

receptacle [rɪ'septək(ə)l] *n* récipient *m*.

reception [rɪ'sepʃ(ə)n] *n* (*receiving, welcome, party etc*) & *Rad* réception *f*; **r. desk** réception *f*; **r. room** salle *f* de séjour. **◆receptionist** *n* réceptionniste *mf*. **◆receptive** *a* réceptif (**to an idea/etc** à une idée/*etc*); **r. to s.o.** compréhensif envers qn.

recess [rɪ'ses, 'riːses] *n* **1** (*holiday*) vacances *fpl*; *Sch Am* récréation *f*. **2** (*alcove*) renfoncement *m*; (*nook*) & *Fig* recoin *m*.

recession [rɪ'seʃ(ə)n] *n* *Econ* récession *f*.

recharge [riː'tʃɑːdʒ] *vt* (*battery*) recharger.

recipe ['resɪpɪ] *n* *Culin* & *Fig* recette *f* (**for** de).

recipient [rɪ'sɪpɪənt] *n* (*of award, honour*) récipiendaire *m*.

reciprocal [rɪ'sɪprək(ə)l] *a* réciproque. **◆reciprocate** *vt* (*compliment*) retourner; (*gesture*) faire à son tour; *– vi* (*do the same*) en faire autant.

recital [rɪ'saɪt(ə)l] *n* *Mus* récital *m*.

recite [rɪ'saɪt] *vt* (*poem etc*) réciter; (*list*) énumérer. **◆reci'tation** *n* récitation *f*.

reckless ['rekləs] *a* (*rash*) imprudent. **◆—ly** *adv* imprudemment.

reckon ['rek(ə)n] *vt* (*count*) compter; (*calculate*) calculer; (*consider*) considérer; (*think*) *Fam* penser (**that** que); *– vi* compter; calculer; **to r. with** (*take into account*) compter avec; (*deal with*) avoir affaire à; **to r. on/without** compter sur/sans; **to r. on doing** *Fam* compter *or* penser faire. **◆—ing** *n* calcul(s) *m*(*pl*).

reclaim [rɪ'kleɪm] *vt* **1** (*land*) mettre en valeur; (*from sea*) assécher. **2** (*ask for back*) réclamer; (*luggage at airport*) récupérer.

reclin/e [rɪ'klaɪn] *vi* (*of person*) être allongé; (*of head*) être appuyé; *– vt* (*head*) appuyer (**on** sur). **◆—ing** *a* (*seat*) à dossier inclinable *or* réglable.

recluse [rɪ'kluːs] *n* reclus, -use *mf*.

recognize ['rekəgnaɪz] *vt* reconnaître (**by** à, **that** que). **◆recog'nition** *n* reconnaissance *f*; **to change beyond** *or* **out of all r.** devenir méconnaissable; **to gain r.** être

reconnu. **◆recognizable** *a* reconnaissable.

recoil [rɪ'kɔɪl] *vi* reculer (**from doing** à l'idée de faire).

recollect [rekə'lekt] *vt* se souvenir de; **to r. that** se souvenir que; *– vi* se souvenir. **◆recollection** *n* souvenir *m*.

recommend [rekə'mend] *vt* (*praise, support, advise*) recommander (**to** à, **for** pour); **to r. s.o. to do** recommander à qn de faire. **◆recommen'dation** *n* recommandation *f*.

recompense ['rekəmpens] *vt* (*reward*) récompenser; *– n* récompense *f*.

reconcile ['rekənsaɪl] *vt* (*person*) réconcilier (**with, to** avec); (*opinion*) concilier (**with** avec); **to r. oneself to sth** se résigner à qch. **◆reconcili'ation** *n* réconciliation *f*.

reconditioned [riːkən'dɪʃ(ə)nd] *a* (*engine*) refait (à neuf).

reconnaissance [rɪ'kɒnɪsəns] *n* *Mil* reconnaissance *f*. **◆reconnoitre** [rekə'nɔɪtər] *vt* *Mil* reconnaître.

reconsider [riːkən'sɪdər] *vt* reconsidérer; *– vi* revenir sur sa décision.

reconstruct [riːkən'strʌkt] *vt* (*crime*) reconstituer.

record 1 ['rekɔːd] *n* (*disc*) disque *m*; **r. library** discothèque *f*; **r. player** électrophone *m*. **2** *n* *Sp* & *Fig* record *m*; *– a* (*attendance, time etc*) record *inv*. **3** *n* (*report*) rapport *m*; (*register*) registre *m*; (*recording on tape etc*) enregistrement *m*; (*mention*) mention *f*; (*note*) note *f*; (*background*) antécédents *mpl*; (*case history*) dossier *m*; (*police*) **r.** casier *m* judiciaire; (*public*) **records** archives *fpl*; **to make** *or* **keep a r. of** noter; **on r.** (*fact, event*) attesté; **off the r.** à titre confidentiel; **their safety r.** leurs résultats *mpl* en matière de sécurité. **4** [rɪ'kɔːd] *vt* (*on tape etc, in register etc*) enregistrer; (*in diary*) noter; (*relate*) rapporter (**that** que); *– vi* (*on tape etc*) enregistrer. **◆—ed** *a* enregistré; (*prerecorded*) *TV* en différé; (*fact*) attesté; **letter sent** (**by**) **r. delivery** = lettre *f* avec avis de réception. **◆—ing** *n* enregistrement *m*. **◆—er** *n* *Mus* flûte *f* à bec; (*tape*) **r.** magnétophone *m*.

recount 1 [rɪ'kaʊnt] *vt* (*relate*) raconter. **2** ['riːkaʊnt] *n* *Pol* nouveau dépouillement *m* du scrutin.

recoup [rɪ'kuːp] *vt* (*loss*) récupérer.

recourse ['riːkɔːs] *n* recours *m*; **to have r. to** avoir recours à.

recover [rɪ'kʌvər] **1** *vt* (*get back*) retrouver, récupérer. **2** *vi* (*from shock etc*) se remettre; (*get better*) *Med* se remettre (**from** de); (*of*

economy, *country*) se redresser; (*of currency*) remonter. ◆**recovery** *n* **1** *Econ* redressement *m*. **2 the r. of sth** (*getting back*) la récupération de qch.

recreate [riːkrɪˈeɪt] *vt* recréer.

recreation [rekrɪˈeɪʃ(ə)n] *n* récréation *f*. ◆**recreational** *a* (*activity etc*) de loisir.

recrimination [rɪkrɪmɪˈneɪʃ(ə)n] *n* *Jur* contre-accusation *f*.

recruit [rɪˈkruːt] *n* recrue *f*; – *vt* recruter; **to r. s.o. to do** (*persuade*) *Fig* embaucher qn pour faire. ◆**—ment** *n* recrutement *m*.

rectangle [ˈrektæŋg(ə)l] *n* rectangle *m*. ◆**rec'tangular** *a* rectangulaire.

rectify [ˈrektɪfaɪ] *vt* rectifier. ◆**rectifi-'cation** *n* rectification *f*.

rector [ˈrektər] *n* *Rel* curé *m*; *Univ* président *m*.

recuperate [rɪˈkuːpəreɪt] *vi* récupérer (ses forces); – *vt* récupérer.

recur [rɪˈkɜːr] *vi* (**-rr-**) (*of theme*) revenir; (*of event*) se reproduire; (*of illness*) réapparaître. ◆**recurrence** [rɪˈkʌrəns] *n* répétition *f*; (*of illness*) réapparition *f*. ◆**recurrent** *a* fréquent.

recycle [riːˈsaɪk(ə)l] *vt* (*material*) recycler.

red [red] *a* (**redder, reddest**) rouge; (*hair*) roux; **to turn** *or* **go r.** rougir; **r. light** (*traffic light*) feu *m* rouge; **R. Cross** Croix-Rouge *f*; **R. Indian** Peau-Rouge *mf*; **r. tape** bureaucratie *f*; – *n* (*colour*) rouge *m*; **R.** (*person*) *Pol* rouge *mf*; **in the r.** (*firm, account*) en déficit; (*person*) à découvert. ◆**r.-'faced** *a* *Fig* rouge de confusion. ◆**r.-'handed** *adv* **caught r.-handed** pris en flagrant délit. ◆**r.-'hot** *a* brûlant. ◆**redden** *vti* rougir. ◆**reddish** *a* rougeâtre; (*hair*) carotte. ◆**redness** *n* rougeur *f*; (*of hair*) rousseur *f*.

redcurrant [redˈkʌrənt] *n* groseille *f*.

redecorate [riːˈdekəreɪt] *vt* (*room etc*) refaire; – *vi* refaire la peinture et les papiers.

redeem [rɪˈdiːm] *vt* (*restore to favour, free, pay off*) racheter; (*convert into cash*) réaliser; **redeeming feature** point *m* favorable. ◆**redemption** *n* rachat *m*; réalisation *f*; *Rel* rédemption *f*.

redeploy [riːdɪˈplɔɪ] *vt* (*staff*) réorganiser; (*troops*) redéployer.

redhead [ˈredhed] *n* roux *m*, rousse *f*.

redirect [riːdaɪˈrekt] *vt* (*mail*) faire suivre.

redo [riːˈduː] *vt* (*pt* **redid,** *pp* **redone**) refaire.

redress [rɪˈdres] *n* **to seek r.** demander réparation (**for** de).

reduce [rɪˈdjuːs] *vt* réduire (**to** à, **by** de); (*temperature*) faire baisser; **at a reduced**

price (*ticket*) à prix réduit; (*goods*) au rabais. ◆**reduction** *n* réduction *f*; (*of temperature*) baisse *f*; (*discount*) rabais *m*.

redundant [rɪˈdʌndənt] *a* (*not needed*) superflu, de trop; **to make r.** (*workers*) mettre en chômage, licencier. ◆**redundancy** *n* (*of workers*) licenciement *m*; **r. pay(ment)** indemnité *f* de licenciement.

re-echo [riːˈekəʊ] *vi* résonner; – *vt* (*sound*) répercuter; *Fig* répéter.

reed [riːd] *n* **1** *Bot* roseau *m*. **2** *Mus* anche *f*; – *a* (*instrument*) à anche.

re-educate [riːˈedjʊkeɪt] *vt* (*criminal, limb*) rééduquer.

reef [riːf] *n* récif *m*, écueil *m*.

reek [riːk] *vi* puer; **to r. of** (*smell*) & *Fig* puer; – *n* puanteur *f*.

reel [riːl] **1** *n* (*of thread, film*) bobine *f*; (*film itself*) *Cin* bande *f*; (*of hose*) dévidoir *m*; (*for fishing line*) moulinet *m*. **2** *vi* (*stagger*) chanceler; (*of mind*) chavirer; (*of head*) tourner. **3** *vt* **to r. off** (*rattle off*) débiter (à toute vitesse).

re-elect [riːɪˈlekt] *vt* réélire.

re-entry [riːˈentrɪ] *n* (*of spacecraft*) rentrée *f*.

re-establish [riːɪˈstæblɪʃ] *vt* rétablir.

ref [ref] *n* *Sp Fam* arbitre *m*.

refectory [rɪˈfektərɪ] *n* réfectoire *m*.

refer [rɪˈfɜːr] *vi* (**-rr-**) **to r. to** (*allude to*) faire allusion à; (*speak of*) parler de; (*apply to*) s'appliquer à; (*consult*) se reporter à; – *vt* **to r. sth to** (*submit*) soumettre qch à; **to r. s.o. to** (*office, article etc*) renvoyer qn à. ◆**refe'ree** *n* *Sp* arbitre *m*; (*for job etc*) répondant, -ante *mf*; – *vt Sp* arbitrer. ◆**'reference** *n* (*in book, recommendation*) référence *f*; (*allusion*) allusion *f* (**to** à); (*mention*) mention *f* (**to** de); (*connection*) rapport *m* (**to** avec); **in** *or* **with r. to** concernant; *Com* suite à; **terms of r.** (*of person, investigating body*) compétence *f*; (*of law*) étendue *f*; **r. book** livre *m* de référence.

referendum [refəˈrendəm] *n* référendum *m*.

refill [riːˈfɪl] *vt* remplir (à nouveau); (*lighter, pen etc*) recharger; – [ˈriːfɪl] *n* recharge *f*; **a r.** (*drink*) *Fam* un autre verre.

refine [rɪˈfaɪn] *vt* (*oil, sugar, manners*) raffiner; (*metal, ore*) affiner; (*technique, machine*) perfectionner; – *vi* **to r. upon** raffiner sur. ◆**refinement** *n* (*of person*) raffinement *m*; (*of sugar, oil*) raffinage *m*; (*of technique*) perfectionnement *m*; *pl* (*improvements*) *Tech* améliorations *fpl*. ◆**refinery** *n* raffinerie *f*.

refit [riːˈfɪt] *vt* (**-tt-**) (*ship*) remettre en état.

reflate [riːˈfleɪt] *vt* (*economy*) relancer.

reflect [rɪ'flekt] **1** vt (light) & Fig refléter; (of mirror) réfléchir, refléter; **to r. sth on s.o.** (credit, honour) faire rejaillir qch sur qn; − vi **to r. on s.o., be reflected on s.o.** (rebound) rejaillir sur qn. **2** vi (think) réfléchir (on à); − vt **to r. that** penser que. ◆**reflection** n **1** (thought, criticism) réflexion (on sur); **on r.** tout bien réfléchi. **2** (image) & Fig reflet m; (reflecting) réflexion f (of de). ◆**reflector** n réflecteur m. ◆**reflexion** n = reflection. ◆**reflexive** a (verb) Gram réfléchi.

reflex ['riːfleks] n & a réflexe (m); **r. action** réflexe m.

refloat [riː'fləʊt] vt (ship) & Com renflouer.

reform [rɪ'fɔːm] n réforme f; − vt réformer; (person, conduct) corriger; − vi (of person) se réformer. ◆**−er** n réformateur, -trice mf.

refrain [rɪ'freɪn] **1** vi s'abstenir (**from doing** de faire). **2** n Mus & Fig refrain m.

refresh [rɪ'freʃ] vt (of bath, drink) rafraîchir; (of sleep, rest) délasser; **to r. oneself** (drink) se rafraîchir; **to r. one's memory** se rafraîchir la mémoire. ◆**−ing** a rafraîchissant; (sleep) réparateur; (pleasant) agréable; (original) nouveau. ◆**−er** a (course) de recyclage. ◆**−ments** npl (drinks) rafraîchissements mpl; (snacks) collation f.

refrigerate [rɪ'frɪdʒəreɪt] vt réfrigérer. ◆**refrigerator** n réfrigérateur m.

refuel [riː'fjʊəl] vi (-ll-, Am -l-) Av se ravitailler; − vt Av ravitailler.

refuge ['refjuːdʒ] n refuge m; **to take r.** se réfugier (**in** dans). ◆**refu'gee** n réfugié, -ée mf.

refund [rɪ'fʌnd] vt rembourser; − ['riːfʌnd] n remboursement m.

refurbish [riː'fɜːbɪʃ] vt remettre à neuf.

refuse[1] [rɪ'fjuːz] vt refuser (**s.o. sth** qch à qn, **to do** de faire); − vi refuser. ◆**refusal** n refus m.

refuse[2] ['refjuːs] n (rubbish) ordures fpl, détritus m; (waste materials) déchets mpl; **r. collector** éboueur m; **r. dump** dépôt m d'ordures.

refute [rɪ'fjuːt] vt réfuter.

regain [rɪ'geɪn] vt (favour, lost ground) regagner; (strength) récupérer, retrouver, reprendre; (health, sight) retrouver; (consciousness) reprendre.

regal ['riːg(ə)l] a royal, majestueux.

regalia [rɪ'geɪlɪə] npl insignes mpl (royaux).

regard [rɪ'gɑːd] vt (consider) considérer, regarder; (concern) regarder; **as regards** en ce qui concerne; − n considération f (for pour); **to have (a) great r. for** avoir de l'estime pour; **without r. to** sans égard

pour; **with r. to** en ce qui concerne; **to give or send one's regards to** (greetings) faire ses hommages à. ◆**−ing** prep en ce qui concerne. ◆**−less 1** a r. of sans tenir compte de. **2** adv (all the same) Fam quand même.

regatta [rɪ'gætə] n régates fpl.

regency ['riːdʒənsɪ] n régence f.

regenerate [rɪ'dʒenəreɪt] vt régénérer.

reggae ['regeɪ] n (music) reggae m; − a (group etc) reggae inv.

régime [reɪ'ʒiːm] n Pol régime m.

regiment ['redʒɪmənt] n régiment m. ◆**regi'mental** a régimentaire, du régiment. ◆**regimen'tation** n discipline f excessive.

region ['riːdʒ(ə)n] n région f; **in the r. of** (about) Fig environ; **in the r. of £500** dans les 500 livres. ◆**regional** a régional.

register ['redʒɪstər] n registre m; Sch cahier m d'appel; **electoral r.** liste f électorale; − vt (record, note) enregistrer; (birth, death) déclarer; (vehicle) immatriculer; (express) exprimer; (indicate) indiquer; (letter) recommander; (realize) Fam réaliser; − vi (enrol) s'inscrire; (in hotel) signer le registre; **it hasn't registered (with me)** Fam je n'ai pas encore réalisé ça. ◆**−ed** a (member) inscrit; (letter) recommandé; **r. trademark** marque f déposée. ◆**regi'strar** n officier m de l'état civil; Univ secrétaire m général. ◆**regi'stration** n enregistrement m; (enrolment) inscription f; **r. (number)** Aut numéro m d'immatriculation; **r. document** Aut = carte f grise. ◆**registry** a & n **r. (office)** bureau m de l'état civil.

regress [rɪ'gres] vi régresser.

regret [rɪ'gret] vt (-tt-) regretter (**doing, to do** de faire; **that** que (+ sub)); **I r. to hear that ...** je suis désolé d'apprendre que ...; − n regret m. ◆**regretfully** adv r., I ... à mon grand regret, je ... . ◆**regrettable** a regrettable (**that** que (+ sub)). ◆**regrettably** adv malheureusement; (poor, ill etc) fâcheusement.

regroup [riː'gruːp] vi se regrouper; − vt regrouper.

regular ['regjʊlər] a (steady, even) régulier; (surface) uni; (usual) habituel; (price, size) normal; (reader, listener) fidèle; (staff) permanent; (fool, slave etc) Fam vrai; **a r. guy** Am Fam un chic type; − n (in bar etc) habitué, -ée mf; Mil régulier m. ◆**regu'larity** n régularité f. ◆**regularly** adv régulièrement.

regulate ['regjʊleɪt] vt régler. ◆**regu-**

'lation 1 *n* (*rule*) règlement *m*; – *a* (*uniform etc*) réglementaire. **2** *n* (*regulating*) réglage *m*.

rehabilitate [riːhəˈbɪlɪteɪt] *vt* (*in public esteem*) réhabiliter; (*wounded soldier etc*) réadapter.

rehash [riːˈhæʃ] *vt* (*text*) *Pej* remanier; *Culin* réchauffer; – [ˈriːhæʃ] *n* a r. *Culin & Fig* du réchauffé.

rehearse [rɪˈhɜːs] *vt Th* répéter; (*prepare*) *Fig* préparer; – *vi Th* répéter. ◆**rehearsal** *n Th* répétition *f*.

reign [reɪn] *n* règne *m*; **in or during the r. of** sous le règne de; – *vi* régner (**over** sur).

reimburse [riːɪmˈbɜːs] *vt* rembourser (**for** de). ◆**—ment** *n* remboursement *m*.

rein [reɪn] *n* reins rênes *fpl*; **to give free r. to** *Fig* donner libre cours à.

reindeer [ˈreɪndɪər] *n inv* renne *m*.

reinforce [riːɪnˈfɔːs] *vt* renforcer (**with** de); **reinforced concrete** béton *m* armé. ◆**—ment** *n* renforcement *m* (**of** de); *pl Mil* renforts *mpl*.

reinstate [riːɪnˈsteɪt] *vt* réintégrer. ◆**—ment** *n* réintégration *f*.

reissue [riːˈɪʃuː] *vt* (*book*) rééditer.

reiterate [riːˈɪtəreɪt] *vt* (*say again*) réitérer.

reject [rɪˈdʒekt] *vt* (*refuse to accept*) rejeter; (*as useless*) refuser; – [ˈriːdʒekt] *n Com* article *m* de rebut; – *a* (*article*) de deuxième choix; **r. shop** solderie *f*. ◆**re'jection** *n* rejet *m*; (*of candidate etc*) refus *m*.

rejoic/e [rɪˈdʒɔɪs] *vi* se réjouir (**over** *or* **at** sth de qch, **in doing** de faire). ◆**—ing(s)** *n*(*pl*) réjouissance(s) *f*(*pl*).

rejoin [rɪˈdʒɔɪn] **1** *vt* (*join up with*) rejoindre. **2** *vi* (*retort*) répliquer.

rejuvenate [rɪˈdʒuːvəneɪt] *vt* rajeunir.

rekindle [riːˈkɪndl] *vt* rallumer.

relapse [rɪˈlæps] *n Med* rechute *f*; – *vi Med* rechuter; **to r. into** *Fig* retomber dans.

relat/e [rɪˈleɪt] **1** *vt* (*narrate*) raconter (**that** que); (*report*) rapporter (**that** que). **2** *vt* (*connect*) établir un rapport entre (*faits etc*); **to r. sth to** (*link*) rattacher qch à; – *vi* **to r. to** (*apply to*) se rapporter à; (*get on with*) communiquer *or* s'entendre avec. ◆**—ed** *a* (*linked*) lié (**to** à); (*languages, styles*) apparentés; **to be r. to** (*by family*) être parent de.

relation [rɪˈleɪʃ(ə)n] *n* (*relative*) parent, -ente *mf*; (*relationship*) rapport *m*, relation *f* (**between** entre, **with** avec); **what r. are you to him?** quel est ton lien de parenté avec lui?; **international**/*etc* **relations** relations *fpl* internationales/*etc*. ◆**relationship** *n* (*kinship*) lien(s) *m*(*pl*) de parenté; (*rela-*

tions) relations *fpl*, rapports *mpl*; (*connection*) rapport *m*; **in r. to** relativement à.

relative [ˈrelətɪv] *n* (*person*) parent, -ente *mf*; – *a* relatif (**to** à); (*respective*) respectif; **r. to** (*compared to*) relativement à; **to be r. to** (*depend on*) être fonction de. ◆**relatively** *adv* relativement.

relax [rɪˈlæks] **1** *vt* (*person, mind*) détendre; – *vi* se détendre; **r.!** (*calm down*) *Fam* du calme! **2** *vt* (*grip, pressure etc*) relâcher; (*restrictions, principles, control*) assouplir. ◆**—ed** *a* (*person, atmosphere*) décontracté, détendu. ◆**—ing** *a* (*bath etc*) délassant. ◆**rela'xation** *n* **1** (*rest, recreation*) détente *f*; (*of body*) décontraction *f*. **2** (*of grip etc*) relâchement *m*; (*of restrictions etc*) assouplissement *m*.

relay [ˈriːleɪ] *n* relais *m*; **r. race** course *f* de relais; – *vt* (*message etc*) *Rad* retransmettre, *Fig* transmettre (**to** à).

release [rɪˈliːs] *vt* (*free*) libérer (**from** de); (*bomb, s.o.'s hand*) lâcher; (*spring*) déclencher; (*brake*) desserrer; (*film, record*) sortir; (*news, facts*) publier; (*smoke, trapped person*) dégager; (*tension*) éliminer; – *n* libération *f*; (*of film, book*) sortie *f* (**of** de); (*record*) nouveau disque *m*; (*film*) nouveau film *m*; (*relief*) *Fig* délivrance *f*; *Psy* défoulement *m*; **press r.** communiqué *m* de presse; **to be on general r.** (*of film*) passer dans toutes les salles.

relegate [ˈrelɪgeɪt] *vt* reléguer (**to** à).

relent [rɪˈlent] *vi* (*be swayed*) se laisser fléchir; (*change one's mind*) revenir sur sa décision. ◆**—less** *a* implacable.

relevant [ˈreləvənt] *a* (*apt*) pertinent (**to** à); (*fitting*) approprié; (*useful*) utile; (*significant*) important; **that's not r.** ça n'a rien à voir. ◆**relevance** *n* pertinence *f* (**to** à); (*significance*) intérêt *m*; (*connection*) rapport *m* (**to** avec).

reliable [rɪˈlaɪəb(ə)l] *a* (*person, information, firm*) sérieux, sûr, fiable; (*machine*) fiable. ◆**relia'bility** *n* (*of person*) sérieux *m*, fiabilité *f*; (*of machine, information, firm*) fiabilité *f*. ◆**reliably** *adv* **to be r. informed that** apprendre de source sûre que.

reliance [rɪˈlaɪəns] *n* (*trust*) confiance *f* (**on** en); (*dependence*) dépendance *f* (**on** de). ◆**reliant** *a* **to be r. on** (*dependent*) dépendre de; (*trusting*) avoir confiance en.

relic [ˈrelɪk] *n* relique *f*; *pl* (*of the past*) vestiges *mpl*.

relief [rɪˈliːf] *n* (*from pain etc*) soulagement *m* (**from** à); (*help, supplies*) secours *m*; (*in art*) & *Geog* relief *m*; **tax r.** dégrèvement *m*; **to be on r.** *Am* recevoir l'aide sociale; – *a*

(*train etc*) supplémentaire; (*work etc*) de secours; **r. road** route *f* de délestage.
◆**relieve** *vt* (*pain etc*) soulager; (*boredom*) dissiper; (*situation*) remédier à; (*take over from*) relayer (*qn*); (*help*) secourir, soulager; **to r. s.o. of** (*rid*) débarrasser qn de; **to r. s.o. of his post** relever qn de ses fonctions; **to r. congestion in** *Aut* décongestionner; **to r. oneself** (*go to the lavatory*) *Hum Fam* se soulager.
religion [rɪ'lɪdʒ(ə)n] *n* religion *f*. ◆**religious** *a* religieux; (*war, book*) de religion. ◆**religiously** *adv* religieusement.
relinquish [rɪ'lɪŋkwɪʃ] *vt* (*give up*) abandonner; (*let go*) lâcher.
relish ['relɪʃ] *n* (*liking, taste*) goût *m* (**for** pour); (*pleasure*) plaisir *m*; (*seasoning*) assaisonnement *m*; **to eat with r.** manger de bon appétit; – *vt* (*food etc*) savourer; (*like*) aimer (**doing** faire).
relocate [riːləʊ'keɪt] *vi* (*move to new place*) déménager; **to r. in** or **to** s'installer à.
reluctant [rɪ'lʌktənt] *a* (*greeting, gift, promise*) accordé à contrecœur; **to be r. to do** être peu disposé à faire; **a r. teacher**/*etc* un professeur/*etc* malgré lui. ◆**reluctance** *n* répugnance *f* (**to do** à faire). ◆**reluctantly** *adv* à contrecœur.
rely [rɪ'laɪ] *vi* **to r. on** (*count on*) compter sur; (*be dependent upon*) dépendre de.
remain [rɪ'meɪn] **1** *vi* rester. **2** *npl* restes *mpl*; **mortal r.** dépouille *f* mortelle. ◆**—ing** *a* qui reste(nt). ◆**remainder** *n* **1** reste *m*; **the r.** (*remaining people*) les autres *mfpl*; **the r. of the girls** les autres filles. **2** (*book*) invendu *m* soldé.
remand [rɪ'maɪnd] *vt* **to r. (in custody)** *Jur* placer en détention préventive; – *n* **on r.** en détention préventive.
remark [rɪ'maɪk] *n* remarque *f*; – *vt* (faire) remarquer (**that** que); – *vi* **to r. on** faire des remarques sur. ◆**—able** *a* remarquable (**for** par). ◆**—ably** *adv* remarquablement.
remarry [riː'mærɪ] *vi* se remarier.
remedial [rɪ'miːdɪəl] *a* (*class*) *Sch* de rattrapage; (*measure*) de redressement; (*treatment*) *Med* thérapeutique.
remedy ['remɪdɪ] *vt* remédier à; – *n* remède *m* (**for** contre, à, de).
remember [rɪ'membər] *vt* se souvenir de, se rappeler; (*commemorate*) commémorer; **to r. that/doing** se rappeler que/d'avoir fait; **to r. to do** (*not forget to do*) penser à faire; **r. me to him** or **her!** rappelle-moi à son bon souvenir!; – *vi* se souvenir, se rappeler. ◆**remembrance** *n* (*memory*) souvenir *m*; **in r. of** en souvenir de.

remind [rɪ'maɪnd] *vt* rappeler (**s.o. of sth** qch à qn, **s.o. that** à qn que); **to r. s.o. to do** faire penser à qn à faire; **that** or **which reminds me!** à propos! ◆**—er** *n* (*of event & letter*) rappel *m*; (*note to do sth*) pense-bête *m*; **it's a r. (for him** or **her) that** ... c'est pour lui rappeler que. . . .
reminisce [remɪ'nɪs] *vi* raconter or se rappeler ses souvenirs (**about** de). ◆**reminiscences** *npl* réminiscences *fpl*. ◆**reminiscent** *a* **r. of** qui rappelle.
remiss [rɪ'mɪs] *a* négligent.
remit [rɪ'mɪt] *vt* (-tt-) (*money*) envoyer. ◆**remission** *n* *Jur* remise *f* (de peine); *Med Rel* rémission *f*. ◆**remittance** *n* (*sum*) paiement *m*.
remnant ['remnənt] *n* (*remaining part*) reste *m*; (*trace*) vestige *m*; (*of fabric*) coupon *m*; (*oddment*) fin *f* de série.
remodel [riː'mɒd(ə)l] *vt* (-ll-, *Am* -l-) remodeler.
remonstrate ['remənstreɪt] *vi* **to r. with s.o.** faire des remontrances à qn.
remorse [rɪ'mɔːs] *n* remords *m*(*pl*) (**for** pour); **without r.** sans pitié. ◆**—less** *a* implacable. ◆**—lessly** *adv* (*to hit etc*) implacablement.
remote [rɪ'məʊt] *a* (-er, -est) **1** (*far-off*) lointain, éloigné; (*isolated*) isolé; (*aloof*) distant; **r. from** loin de; **r. control** télécommande *f*. **2** (*slight*) petit, vague; **not the remotest idea** pas la moindre idée. ◆**—ly** *adv* (*slightly*) vaguement, un peu; (*situated*) au loin; **not r. aware**/*etc* nullement conscient/*etc*. ◆**—ness** *n* éloignement *m*; isolement *m*; *Fig* attitude *f* distante.
remould ['riːməʊld] *n* pneu *m* rechapé.
remove [rɪ'muːv] *vt* (*clothes, stain etc*) enlever (**from s.o.** à qn, **from sth** de qch); (*withdraw*) retirer; (*lead away*) emmener (**to** à); (*furniture*) déménager; (*obstacle, threat, word*) supprimer; (*fear, doubt*) dissiper; (*employee*) renvoyer; (**far**) **removed from** loin de. ◆**removable** *a* (*lining etc*) amovible. ◆**removal** *n* enlèvement *m*; déménagement *m*; suppression *f*; **r. man** déménageur *m*; **r. van** camion *m* de déménagement. ◆**remover** *n* (*for make-up*) démaquillant *m*; (*for nail polish*) dissolvant *m*; (*for paint*) décapant *m*; (*for stains*) détachant *m*.
remunerate [rɪ'mjuːnəreɪt] *vt* rémunérer. ◆**remune'ration** *n* rémunération *f*.
renaissance [rə'neɪsəns] *n* (*in art etc*) renaissance *f*.
rename [riː'neɪm] *vt* (*street etc*) rebaptiser.
render ['rendər] *vt* (*give, make*) rendre; *Mus*

interpréter; *(help)* prêter. ◆—**ing** *n Mus* interprétation *f*; *(translation)* traduction *f*.

rendez-vous ['rɒndɪvuː, *pl* -vuːz] *n inv* rendez-vous *m inv*.

renegade ['renɪgeɪd] *n* renégat, -ate *mf*.

reneg(u)e [rɪ'niːg] *vi* to r. on *(promise etc)* revenir sur.

renew [rɪ'njuː] *vt* renouveler; *(resume)* reprendre; *(library book)* renouveler le prêt de. ◆—**ed** *a (efforts)* renouvelés; *(attempt)* nouveau; with r. **vigour**/*etc* avec un regain de vigueur/*etc*. ◆**renewable** *a* renouvelable. ◆**renewal** *n* renouvellement *m*; *(resumption)* reprise *f*; *(of strength etc)* regain *m*.

renounce [rɪ'naʊns] *vt (give up)* renoncer à; *(disown)* renier.

renovate ['renəveɪt] *vt (house)* rénover, restaurer; *(painting)* restaurer. ◆**reno-'vation** *n* rénovation *f*; restauration *f*.

renown [rɪ'naʊn] *n* renommée *f*. ◆**renowned** *a* renommé (for pour).

rent [rent] *n* loyer *m*; *(of television)* (prix *m* de) location *f*; r. **collector** encaisseur *m* de loyers; – *vt* louer; **to r. out** louer; – *vi (of house etc)* se louer. ◆**r.-'free** *adv* sans payer de loyer; – *a* gratuit. ◆**rental** *n (of television)* (prix *m* de) location *f*; *(of telephone)* abonnement *m*.

renunciation [rɪnʌnsɪ'eɪʃ(ə)n] *n (giving up)* renonciation *f* (of à); *(disowning)* reniement *m* (of de).

reopen [riː'əʊpən] *vti* rouvrir. ◆—**ing** *n* réouverture *f*.

reorganize [riː'ɔːgənaɪz] *vt* réorganiser.

rep [rep] *n Fam* représentant, -ante *mf* de commerce.

repaid [riː'peɪd] *see* repay.

repair [rɪ'peər] *vt* réparer; – *n* réparation *f*; beyond r. irréparable; in good/bad r. en bon/mauvais état; 'road under r.' *Aut* 'travaux'; r. **man** réparateur *m*; r. **woman** réparatrice *f*.

reparation [repə'reɪʃ(ə)n] *n* réparation *f* (for de); *pl Mil Hist* réparations *fpl*.

repartee [repɑː'tiː] *n (sharp reply)* repartie *f*.

repatriate [riː'pætrɪeɪt] *vt* rapatrier.

repay [riː'peɪ] *vt (pt & pp* repaid) *(pay back)* rembourser; *(kindness)* payer de retour; *(reward)* récompenser (for de). ◆—**ment** *n* remboursement *m*; récompense *f*.

repeal [rɪ'piːl] *vt (law)* abroger; – *n* abrogation *f*.

repeat [rɪ'piːt] *vt* répéter (that que); *(promise, threat)* réitérer; *(class) Sch* redoubler; **to r. oneself** *or* itself se répéter; – *vi* répéter; **to r. on s.o.** *(of food) Fam* revenir à

qn; – *n TV Rad* rediffusion *f*; – *a (performance)* deuxième. ◆—**ed** *a* répété; *(efforts)* renouvelés. ◆—**edly** *adv* à maintes reprises.

repel [rɪ'pel] *vt* (-ll-) repousser. ◆**repellent** *a* repoussant; **insect r.** insectifuge *m*.

repent [rɪ'pent] *vi* se repentir (of de). ◆**repentance** *n* repentir *m*. ◆**repentant** *a* repentant.

repercussion [riːpə'kʌʃ(ə)n] *n* répercussion *f*.

repertoire ['repətwɑːr] *n Th & Fig* répertoire *m*. ◆**repertory** *n Th & Fig* répertoire *m*; r. **(theatre)** théâtre *m* de répertoire.

repetition [repɪ'tɪʃ(ə)n] *n* répétition *f*. ◆**repetitious** *a*, ◆**re'petitive** *a (speech etc)* répétitif.

replace [rɪ'pleɪs] *vt (take the place of)* remplacer (by, with par); *(put back)* remettre, replacer; *(receiver) Tel* raccrocher. ◆—**ment** *n* remplacement *m* (of de); *(person)* remplaçant, -ante *mf*; *(machine part)* pièce *f* de rechange.

replay ['riːpleɪ] *n Sp* match *m* rejoué; **(instant** *or* **action) r.** *TV* répétition *f* immédiate (au ralenti).

replenish [rɪ'plenɪʃ] *vt (refill)* remplir (de nouveau) (with de); *(renew)* renouveler.

replete [rɪ'pliːt] *a* r. **with** rempli de; r. **(with food)** rassasié.

replica ['replɪkə] *n* copie *f* exacte.

reply [rɪ'plaɪ] *vti* répondre; – *n* réponse *f*; **in r.** en réponse (to à).

report [rɪ'pɔːt] *n (account)* rapport *m*; *(meeting)* compte rendu *m*; *Journ TV Rad* reportage *m*; *Pol* enquête *f*; *Sch Met* bulletin *m*; *(rumour)* rumeur *f*; *(of gun)* détonation *f*; – *vt (give account of)* rapporter, rendre compte de; *(announce)* annoncer (that que); *(notify)* signaler (to à); *(denounce)* dénoncer (to à); *(event) Journ* faire un reportage sur; – *vi* faire un rapport *or Journ* un reportage (on sur); *(go)* se présenter (to à, to s.o. chez qn, for work au travail). ◆—**ed** *a (speech) Gram* indirect; **it is r. that** on dit que; r. **missing** porté disparu. ◆—**edly** *adv* à ce qu'on dit. ◆—**ing** *n Journ* reportage *m*. ◆—**er** *n* reporter *m*.

repose [rɪ'pəʊz] *n Lit* repos *m*.

repossess [riːpə'zes] *vt Jur* reprendre possession de.

reprehensible [reprɪ'hensəb(ə)l] *a* réprehensible.

represent [reprɪ'zent] *vt* représenter. ◆**represen'tation** *n* représentation *f*; *pl (complaints)* remontrances *fpl*. ◆**repre-**

sentative a représentatif (**of** de); – n représentant, -ante mf; Pol Am député m.

repress [rɪ'pres] vt réprimer; (feeling) refouler. ◆**repressive** a répressif.

reprieve [rɪ'priːv] n Jur sursis m; Fig répit m, sursis m; – vt accorder un sursis or Fig un répit à.

reprimand ['reprimɑːnd] n réprimande f; – vt réprimander.

reprint ['riːprɪnt] n (reissue) réimpression f; – vt réimprimer.

reprisal [rɪ'praɪz(ə)l] n reprisals représailles fpl; **in r. for** en représailles de.

reproach [rɪ'prəʊtʃ] n (blame) reproche m; (shame) honte f; **beyond r.** sans reproche; – vt reprocher (**s.o. for sth** qch à qn). ◆**reproachful** a réprobateur. ◆**reproachfully** adv d'un ton or d'un air réprobateur.

reproduce [riːprə'djuːs] vt reproduire; – vi Biol Bot se reproduire. ◆**reproduction** n (of sound etc) & Biol Bot reproduction f. ◆**reproductive** a reproducteur.

reptile ['reptaɪl] n reptile m.

republic [rɪ'pʌblɪk] n république f. ◆**republican** a & n républicain, -aine (mf).

repudiate [rɪ'pjuːdɪeɪt] vt (offer) repousser; (accusation) rejeter; (spouse, idea) répudier.

repugnant [rɪ'pʌgnənt] a répugnant; **he's r. to me** il me répugne. ◆**repugnance** n répugnance f (for pour).

repulse [rɪ'pʌls] vt repousser. ◆**repulsion** n répulsion f. ◆**repulsive** a repoussant.

reputable ['repjʊtəb(ə)l] a de bonne réputation. ◆**re'pute** n réputation f; **of r.** de bonne réputation. ◆**re'puted** a réputé (**to be** pour être). ◆**re'putedly** adv à ce qu'on dit.

reputation [repjʊ'teɪʃ(ə)n] n réputation f; **to have a r. for frankness/etc** avoir la réputation d'être franc/etc.

request [rɪ'kwest] n demande f (**for** de); **on r.** sur demande; **on s.o.'s r.** à la demande de qn; **by popular r.** à la demande générale; **r. stop** (for bus) arrêt m facultatif; – vt demander (**from or of s.o.** à qn, **s.o. to do** à qn de faire).

requiem ['rekwɪəm] n requiem m inv.

requir/e [rɪ'kwaɪər] vt (necessitate) demander; (demand) exiger; (of person) avoir besoin de (qch, qn); (staff) rechercher; **to r. sth of s.o.** (order) exiger qch de qn; **to r. s.o. to do** exiger de qn qu'il fasse; (ask) demander à qn de faire; **if required** s'il le faut. ◆**—ed** a requis, exigé. ◆**—ement** n

(need) exigence f; (condition) condition f (requise).

requisite ['rekwɪzɪt] 1 a nécessaire. 2 n (for travel etc) article m; **toilet requisites** articles mpl or nécessaire m de toilette.

requisition [rekwɪ'zɪʃ(ə)n] vt réquisitionner; – n réquisition f.

reroute [riː'ruːt] vt (aircraft etc) dérouter.

rerun ['riːrʌn] n Cin reprise f; TV rediffusion f.

resale ['riːseɪl] n revente f.

resat [riː'sæt] see resit.

rescind [rɪ'sɪnd] vt Jur annuler; (law) abroger.

rescu/e ['reskjuː] vt (save) sauver; (set free) délivrer (**from** de); – n (action) sauvetage m (of de); (help, troops etc) secours mpl; **to go/etc to s.o.'s r.** aller/etc au secours de qn; **to the r.** à la rescousse; – a (team, operation) de sauvetage. ◆**—er** n sauveteur m.

research [rɪ'sɜːtʃ] n recherches fpl (**on, into** sur); **some r.** de la recherche; **a piece of r.** (work) un travail de recherche; – vi faire des recherches (**on, into** sur). ◆**—er** n chercheur, -euse mf.

resemble [rɪ'zemb(ə)l] vt ressembler à. ◆**resemblance** n ressemblance f (**to** avec).

resent [rɪ'zent] vt (anger) s'indigner de, ne pas aimer; (bitterness) éprouver de l'amertume à l'égard de; **I r. that** ça m'indigne. ◆**resentful** a **to be r.** éprouver de l'amertume. ◆**resentment** n amertume f, ressentiment m.

reserv/e [rɪ'zɜːv] 1 vt (room, decision etc) réserver; (right) se réserver; (one's strength) ménager; – n (reticence) réserve f. 2 n (stock, land) réserve f; **r. (player)** Sp remplaçant, -ante mf; **the r.** Mil la réserve; **the reserves** (troops) Mil les réserves fpl; **nature r.** réserve f naturelle; **in r.** en réserve; **r. tank** Av Aut réservoir m de secours. ◆**—ed** a (person, room) réservé. ◆**reser'vation** n 1 (doubt etc) réserve f; (booking) réservation f. 2 (land) Am réserve f; **central r.** (on road) terre-plein m.

reservoir ['rezəvwɑːr] n réservoir m.

resettle [riː'set(ə)l] vt (refugees) implanter.

reshape [riː'ʃeɪp] vt (industry etc) réorganiser.

reshuffle [riː'ʃʌf(ə)l] n (cabinet) r. Pol remaniement m (ministériel); – vt Pol remanier.

reside [rɪ'zaɪd] vi résider. ◆**'residence** n (home) résidence f; (of students) foyer m; **in r.** (doctor) sur place; (students on campus) sur le campus, (in halls of residence) rentrés. ◆'**resident** n habitant, -ante mf; (of hotel) pensionnaire mf; (foreigner) résident, -ente mf; – a résidant, qui habite sur place; (population) fixe; (correspondent) permanent; **to be r. in London** résider à Londres. ◆**resi'dential** a (neighbourhood) résidentiel.

residue ['rezɪdjuː] n résidu m. ◆**re'sidual** a résiduel.

resign [rɪ'zaɪn] vt (right, claim) abandonner; **to r. (from) one's job** démissionner; **to r. oneself to sth/to doing** se résigner à qch/à faire; – vi démissionner (**from** de). ◆—**ed** a résigné. ◆**resig'nation** n (from job) démission f; (attitude) résignation f.

resilient [rɪ'zɪlɪənt] a élastique; (person) Fig résistant. ◆**resilience** n élasticité f; Fig résistance f.

resin ['rezɪn] n résine f.

resist [rɪ'zɪst] vt (attack etc) résister à; **to r. doing sth** s'empêcher de faire qch; **she can't r. cakes** elle ne peut pas résister devant les gâteaux; **he can't r. her** (indulgence) il ne peut rien lui refuser; (charm) il ne peut pas résister à son charme; – vi résister. ◆**resistance** n résistance f (**to** à). ◆**resistant** a résistant (**to** à); **r. to** Med rebelle à.

resit [riː'sɪt] vt (pt & pp resat, pres p resitting) (exam) repasser.

resolute ['rezəluːt] a résolu. ◆—**ly** adv résolument. ◆**reso'lution** n résolution f.

resolv/e [rɪ'zɒlv] vt résoudre (**to do** de faire, **that** que); – n résolution f. ◆—**ed** a résolu (**to do** à faire).

resonant ['rezənənt] a (voice) résonnant; **to be r. with** résonner de. ◆**resonance** n résonance f.

resort [rɪ'zɔːt] **1** n (recourse) recours m (**to** à); **as a last r.** en dernier ressort; – vi **to r. to s.o.** avoir recours à qn; **to r. to doing** en venir à faire; **to r. to drink** se rabattre sur la boisson. **2** n (holiday) r. station f de vacances; **seaside/ski r.** station f balnéaire/de ski.

resound [rɪ'zaʊnd] vi résonner (**with** de); Fig avoir du retentissement. ◆—**ing** a (success, noise) retentissant.

resource [rɪ'sɔːs, rɪ'zɔːs] n (expedient, recourse) ressource f; pl (wealth etc) ressources fpl. ◆**resourceful** a (person, scheme) ingénieux. ◆**resourcefulness** n ingéniosité f, ressource f.

respect [rɪ'spekt] n respect m (**for** pour, de); (aspect) égard m; **in r. of, with r. to** en ce qui concerne; **with all due r.** sans vouloir vous vexer; – vt respecter. ◆**respecta'bility** n

respectabilité f. ◆**respectable** a (honourable, sizeable) respectable; (satisfying) honnête; (clothes, behaviour) convenable. ◆**respectably** adv (to dress etc) convenablement; (rather well) passablement. ◆**respectful** a respectueux (**to** envers, **of** de). ◆**respectfully** adv respectueusement.

respective [rɪ'spektɪv] a respectif. ◆—**ly** adv respectivement.

respiration [respɪ'reɪʃ(ə)n] n respiration f.

respite ['respaɪt] n répit m.

respond [rɪ'spɒnd] vi répondre (**to** à); **to r. to treatment** Med réagir positivement au traitement. ◆**response** n réponse f; **in p. to** en réponse à.

responsible [rɪ'spɒnsəb(ə)l] a responsable (**for** de, **to s.o.** devant qn); (job) à responsabilités; **who's r. for ... ?** qui est (le) responsable de ... ? ◆**responsi'bility** n responsabilité f. ◆**responsibly** adv de façon responsable.

responsive [rɪ'spɒnsɪv] a (reacting) qui réagit bien; (alert) éveillé; (attentive) qui fait attention; **r. to** (kindness) sensible à; (suggestion) réceptif à. ◆—**ness** n (bonne) réaction f.

rest¹ [rest] n (repose) repos m; (support) support m; **to have** or **take a r.** se reposer; **to set** or **put s.o.'s mind at r.** tranquilliser qn; **to come to r.** (of ball etc) s'immobiliser; (of bird, eyes) se poser (**on** sur); **r. home** maison f de repos; **r. room** Am toilettes fpl; – vi (relax) se reposer; (be buried) reposer; **to r. on** (of roof, argument) reposer sur; **I won't r. till** je n'aurai de repos que (+ sub); **to be resting on** (of hand etc) être posé sur; **a resting place** un lieu de repos; – vt (eyes etc) reposer; (horse etc) laisser reposer; (lean) poser, appuyer (**on** sur); (base) fonder. ◆**restful** a reposant.

rest² [rest] n (remainder) reste m (**of** de); **the r.** (others) les autres mfpl; **the r. of the men/etc** les autres hommes/etc; – vi (remain) **it rests with you to do** il vous incombe de faire; **r. assured** soyez assuré (**that** que).

restaurant ['restərɒnt] n restaurant m.

restitution [restɪ'tjuːʃ(ə)n] n (for damage) Jur réparation f; **to make r.** of restituer.

restive ['restɪv] a (person, horse) rétif.

restless ['restləs] a agité. ◆—**ly** adv avec agitation. ◆—**ness** n agitation f.

restore [rɪ'stɔː] vt (give back) rendre (**to** à); (order, right) Jur rétablir; (building, painting) restaurer; (to life or power) ramener (qn) (**to** à).

restrain [rɪ'streɪn] *vt* (*person, emotions*) retenir, maîtriser; (*crowd*) contenir; (*limit*) limiter; **to r. s.o. from doing** retenir qn de faire; **to r. oneself** se maîtriser. ◆**—ed** *a* (*feelings*) contenu; (*tone*) mesuré. ◆**restraint** *n* (*moderation*) retenue *f*, mesure *f*; (*restriction*) contrainte *f*.

restrict [rɪ'strɪkt] *vt* limiter, restreindre (**to** à). ◆**—ed** *a* (*space, use*) restreint; (*sale*) contrôlé. ◆**restriction** *n* restriction *f*, limitation *f*. ◆**restrictive** *a* restrictif.

result [rɪ'zʌlt] *n* (*outcome, success*) résultat *m*; **as a r.** en conséquence; **as a r. of** par suite de; — *vi* résulter (**from** de); **to r. in** aboutir à.

resume [rɪ'zjuːm] *vti* (*begin or take again*) reprendre; **to r. doing** se remettre à faire. ◆**resumption** *n* reprise *f*.

résumé ['rezjumeɪ] *n* (*summary*) résumé *m*; *Am* curriculum vitae *m inv*.

resurface [riː'sɜːfɪs] *vt* (*road*) refaire le revêtement de.

resurgence [rɪ'sɜːdʒəns] *n* réapparition *f*.

resurrect [rezə'rekt] *vt* (*custom, hero*) *Pej* ressusciter. ◆**resurrection** *n* résurrection *f*.

resuscitate [rɪ'sʌsɪteɪt] *vt Med* réanimer.

retail ['riːteɪl] *n* (*vente f au*) détail *m*; — *a* (*price, shop etc*) de détail; — *vi* se vendre (au détail); — *vt* vendre (au détail), détailler; — *adv* (*to sell*) au détail. ◆**—er** *n* détaillant, -ante *mf*.

retain [rɪ'teɪn] *vt* (*hold back, remember*) retenir; (*freshness, hope etc*) conserver. ◆**retainer** *n* (*fee*) avance *f*, acompte *m*. ◆**retention** *n* (*memory*) mémoire *f*. ◆**retentive** *a* (*memory*) fidèle.

retaliate [rɪ'tælɪeɪt] *vi* riposter (**against s.o.** contre qn, **against an attack** à une attaque). ◆**retali'ation** *n* riposte *f*, représailles *fpl*; **in r. for** en représailles de.

retarded [rɪ'tɑːdɪd] *a* (*mentally*) r. arriéré.

retch [retʃ] *vi* avoir un *or* des haut-le-cœur.

rethink [riː'θɪŋk] *vt* (*pt & pp* rethought) repenser.

reticent ['retɪsənt] *a* réticent. ◆**reticence** *n* réticence *f*.

retina ['retɪnə] *n Anat* rétine *f*.

retir/e [rɪ'taɪər] **1** *vi* (*from work*) prendre sa retraite; — *vt* mettre à la retraite. **2** *vi* (*withdraw*) se retirer (**from** de, **to** à); (*go to bed*) aller se coucher. ◆**—ed** *a* (*having stopped working*) retraité. ◆**—ing** *a* **1** (*age*) de la retraite. **2** (*reserved*) réservé. ◆**retirement** *n* retraite *f*; **r. age** âge *m* de la retraite.

retort [rɪ'tɔːt] *vt* rétorquer; — *n* réplique *f*.

retrace [riː'treɪs] *vt* (*past event*) se remémorer, reconstituer; **to r. one's steps** revenir sur ses pas, rebrousser chemin.

retract [rɪ'trækt] *vt* (*statement etc*) rétracter; — *vi* (*of person*) se rétracter. ◆**retraction** *n* (*of statement*) rétractation *f*.

retrain [riː'treɪn] *vi* se recycler; — *vt* recycler. ◆**—ing** *n* recyclage *m*.

retread [riː'tred] *n* pneu *m* rechapé.

retreat [rɪ'triːt] *n* (*withdrawal*) retraite *f*; (*place*) refuge *m*; — *vi* se retirer (**from** de); *Mil* battre en retraite.

retrial [riː'traɪəl] *n Jur* nouveau procès *m*.

retribution [retrɪ'bjuːʃ(ə)n] *n* châtiment *m*.

retrieve [rɪ'triːv] *vt* (*recover*) récupérer; (*rescue*) sauver (**from** de); (*loss, error*) réparer; (*honour*) rétablir. ◆**retrieval** *n* récupération *f*; **information r.** recherche *f* documentaire. ◆**retriever** *n* (*dog*) chien *m* d'arrêt.

retro- ['retrəu] *pref* rétro-. ◆**retro'active** *a* rétroactif.

retrograde ['retrəgreɪd] *a* rétrograde.

retrospect ['retrəspekt] *n* **in r.** rétrospectivement. ◆**retro'spective 1** *a* (*law, effect*) rétroactif. **2** *n* (*of film director, artist*) rétrospective *f*.

return [rɪ'tɜːn] *vi* (*come back*) revenir; (*go back*) retourner; (*go back home*) rentrer; **to r. to** (*subject*) revenir à; — *vt* (*give back*) rendre; (*put back*) remettre; (*bring back*) & *Fin* rapporter; (*send back*) renvoyer; (*greeting*) répondre à; (*candidate*) *Pol* élire; — *n* retour *m*; (*yield*) *Fin* rapport *m*; *pl* (*profits*) *Fin* bénéfices *mpl*; **the r. to school** la rentrée (des classes); **r. (ticket)** (billet *m* d')aller et retour *m*; **tax r.** déclaration *f* de revenus; **many happy returns (of the day)!** bon anniversaire!; **in r.** (*exchange*) en échange (**for** de); — *a* (*trip, flight etc*) (de) retour; **r. match** match *m* retour. ◆**—able** *a* (*bottle*) consigné.

reunion [riː'juːnɪən] *n* réunion *f*. ◆**reu'nite** *vt* réunir.

rev [rev] *n Aut Fam* tour *m*; **r. counter** compte-tours *m inv*; — *vt* (-vv-) **to r. (up)** (*engine*) *Fam* faire ronfler.

revamp [riː'væmp] *vt* (*method, play etc*) *Fam* remanier.

reveal [rɪ'viːl] *vt* (*make known*) révéler (**that** que); (*make visible*) laisser voir. ◆**—ing** *a* (*sign etc*) révélateur.

revel ['rev(ə)l] *vi* (-ll-) faire la fête; **to r. in sth** se délecter de qch. ◆**revelling** *n*, ◆**revelry** *n* festivités *fpl*. ◆**reveller** *n* noceur, -euse *mf*.

revenge [rɪ'vendʒ] *n* vengeance *f*; *Sp* revanche *f*; **to have** *or* **get one's r.** se venger (on s.o. de qn, on s.o. for sth de qch sur qn); in r. pour se venger; – *vt* venger.

revenue ['revənjuː] *n* revenu *m*.

reverberate [rɪ'vɜːbəreɪt] *vi* (*of sound*) se répercuter.

revere [rɪ'vɪər] *vt* révérer. ◆**'reverence** *n* révérence *f*. ◆**'reverend** *a* (*father*) Rel révérend; – *n* R. Smith (*Anglican*) le révérend Smith; (*Catholic*) l'abbé *m* Smith; (*Jewish*) le rabbin Smith. ◆**'reverent** *a* respectueux.

reverse [rɪ'vɜːs] *a* contraire; (*order, image*) inverse; r. side (*of coin etc*) revers *m*; (*of paper*) verso *m*; – *n* contraire *m*; (*of coin, fabric etc*) revers *m*; (*of paper*) verso *m*; in r. (gear) Aut en marche arrière; – *vt* (*situation*) renverser; (*order, policy*) inverser; (*decision*) annuler; (*bucket etc*) retourner; to r. the charges Tel téléphoner en PCV; – *vti* to r. (the car) faire marche arrière; to r. in/out rentrer/sortir en marche arrière; reversing light phare *m* de recul. ◆**reversal** *n* renversement *m*; (*of policy, situation, opinion*) revirement *m*; (*of fortune*) revers *m*. ◆**reversible** *a* (*fabric etc*) réversible.

revert [rɪ'vɜːt] *vi* to r. to revenir à.

review [rɪ'vjuː] 1 *vt* (*troops, one's life*) passer en revue; (*situation*) réexaminer; (*book*) faire la critique de; – *n* revue *f*; (*of book*) critique *f*. 2 *n* (*magazine*) revue *f*. ◆**—er** *n* critique *m*.

revile [rɪ'vaɪl] *vt* injurier.

revise [rɪ'vaɪz] *vt* (*opinion, notes, text*) réviser; – *vi* (*for exam*) réviser (for pour). ◆**revision** *n* révision *f*.

revitalize [riː'vaɪt(ə)laɪz] *vt* revitaliser.

revive [rɪ'vaɪv] *vt* (*unconscious person, memory, conversation*) ranimer; (*dying person*) réanimer; (*custom, plan, fashion*) ressusciter; (*hope, interest*) faire renaître; – *vi* (*of unconscious person*) reprendre connaissance; (*of country, dying person*) ressusciter; (*of hope, interest*) renaître. ◆**revival** *n* (*of custom, business, play*) reprise *f*; (*of country*) essor *m*; (*of faith, fashion, theatre*) renouveau *m*.

revoke [rɪ'vəʊk] *vt* (*decision*) annuler; (*contract*) Jur révoquer.

revolt [rɪ'vəʊlt] *n* révolte *f*; – *vt* (*disgust*) révolter; – *vi* (*rebel*) se révolter (against contre). ◆**—ing** *a* dégoûtant; (*injustice*) révoltant.

revolution [revə'luːʃ(ə)n] *n* révolution *f*. ◆**revolutionary** *a & n* révolutionnaire (*mf*). ◆**revolutionize** *vt* révolutionner.

revolv/e [rɪ'vɒlv] *vi* tourner (around autour

de). ◆**—ing** *a* r. chair fauteuil *m* pivotant; r. door(s) (porte *f* à) tambour *m*.

revolver [rɪ'vɒlvər] *n* revolver *m*.

revue [rɪ'vjuː] *n* (*satirical*) Th revue *f*.

revulsion [rɪ'vʌlʃ(ə)n] *n* **1** (*disgust*) dégoût *m*. **2** (*change*) revirement *m*.

reward [rɪ'wɔːd] *n* récompense *f* (for de); – *vt* récompenser (s.o. for sth qn de *or* pour qch). ◆**—ing** *a* qui (en) vaut la peine; (*satisfying*) satisfaisant; (*financially*) rémunérateur.

rewind [riː'waɪnd] *vt* (*pt & pp* rewound) (*tape*) réembobiner.

rewire [riː'waɪər] *vt* (*house*) refaire l'installation électrique de.

rewrite [riː'raɪt] *vt* (*pt* rewrote, *pp* rewritten) récrire; (*edit*) réécrire.

rhapsody ['ræpsədɪ] *n* rhapsodie *f*.

rhetoric ['retərɪk] *n* rhétorique *f*. ◆**rhetorical** *a* (*question*) de pure forme.

rheumatism ['ruːmətɪz(ə)m] *n* Med rhumatisme *m*; to have r. avoir des rhumatismes. ◆**rheu'matic** *a* (*pain*) rhumatismal; (*person*) rhumatisant.

rhinoceros [raɪ'nɒsərəs] *n* rhinocéros *m*.

rhubarb ['ruːbɑːb] *n* rhubarbe *f*.

rhyme [raɪm] *n* rime *f*; (*poem*) vers *mpl*; – *vi* rimer.

rhythm ['rɪð(ə)m] *n* rythme *m*. ◆**rhythmic(al)** *a* rythmique.

rib [rɪb] *n* Anat côte *f*.

ribald ['rɪb(ə)ld] *a* Lit grivois.

ribbon ['rɪbən] *n* ruban *m*; to tear to ribbons mettre en lambeaux.

rice [raɪs] *n* riz *m*. ◆**ricefield** *n* rizière *f*.

rich [rɪtʃ] *a* (-er, -est) riche (in en); (*profits*) gros; – *n* the r. les riches *mpl*. ◆**riches** *npl* richesses *fpl*. ◆**richly** *adv* (*dressed, illustrated etc*) richement; (*deserved*) amplement. ◆**richness** *n* richesse *f*.

rick [rɪk] *vt* to r. one's back se tordre le dos.

rickety ['rɪkɪtɪ] *a* (*furniture*) branlant.

ricochet ['rɪkəʃeɪ] *vi* ricocher; – *n* ricochet *m*.

rid [rɪd] *vt* (*pt & pp* rid, *pres p* ridding) débarrasser (of de); to get r. of, r. oneself of se débarrasser de. ◆**riddance** *n* good r.! Fam bon débarras!

ridden ['rɪd(ə)n] *see* ride.

-ridden ['rɪd(ə)n] *suffix* debt-r. criblé de dettes; disease-r. en proie à la maladie.

riddle ['rɪd(ə)l] **1** *n* (*puzzle*) énigme *f*. **2** *vt* cribler (with de); riddled with (*bullets, holes, mistakes*) criblé de; (*criminals*) plein de; (*corruption*) en proie à.

rid/e [raɪd] *n* (*on bicycle, by car etc*) promenade *f*; (*distance*) trajet *m*; (*in taxi*) course *f*; (*on merry-go-round*) tour *m*; **to go for a (car) r.** faire une promenade (en voiture); **to give s.o. a r.** *Aut* emmener qn en voiture; **to have a r. on** (*bicycle*) monter sur; **to take s.o. for a r.** (*deceive*) *Fam* mener qn en bateau; — *vi* (*pt* **rode,** *pp* **ridden**) aller (à bicyclette, à moto, à cheval *etc*) (**to** à); (*on horse*) *Sp* monter (à cheval); **to be riding in a car** être en voiture; **to r. up** (*of skirt*) remonter; — *vt* (*a particular horse*) monter; (*distance*) faire à cheval *etc*); **to r. a horse or horses** (*go riding*) *Sp* monter à cheval; **I was riding (on) a bike/donkey** j'étais à bicyclette/à dos d'âne; **to know how to r. a bike** savoir faire de la bicyclette; **to r. a bike to** aller à bicyclette à; **may I r. your bike?** puis-je monter sur ta bicyclette?; **to r. s.o.** (*annoy*) *Am Fam* harceler qn. **◆—ing** *n* (*horse*) r. équitation *f*; **r. boots** bottes *fpl* de cheval. **◆—er** *n* **1** (*on horse*) cavalier, -ière *mf*; (*cyclist*) cycliste *mf*. **2** (*to document*) *Jur* annexe *f*.

ridge [rɪdʒ] *n* (*of roof, mountain*) arête *f*; crête *f*.

ridicule ['rɪdɪkjuːl] *n* ridicule *m*; **to hold up to r.** tourner en ridicule; **object of r.** objet *m* de risée; — *vt* tourner en ridicule, ridiculiser. **◆ri'diculous** *a* ridicule.

rife [raɪf] *a* (*widespread*) répandu.

riffraff ['rɪfræf] *n* racaille *f*.

rifle ['raɪf(ə)l] **1** *n* fusil *m*, carabine *f*. **2** *vt* (*drawers, pockets etc*) vider.

rift [rɪft] *n* (*crack*) fissure *f*; (*in party*) *Pol* scission *f*; (*disagreement*) désaccord *m*.

rig [rɪg] **1** *n* (*oil*) r. derrick *m*; (*at sea*) plate-forme *f* pétrolière. **2** *vt* (**-gg-**) (*result, election etc*) *Pej* truquer; **to r. up** (*equipment*) installer; (*meeting etc*) *Fam* arranger. **3** *vt* (**-gg-**) **to r. out** (*dress*) *Fam* habiller. **◆r.-out** *n Fam* tenue *f*.

right¹ [raɪt] **1** *a* (*correct*) bon, exact, juste; (*fair*) juste; (*angle*) droit; **to be r.** (*of person*) avoir raison (**to do** de faire); **it's the r. road** c'est la bonne route, c'est bien la route; **the r. time** l'heure exacte; **the clock's r. time** la pendule est à l'heure; **at the r. time** au bon moment; **he's the r. man** c'est l'homme qu'il faut; **the r. thing to do** la meilleure chose à faire; **it's not r. to steal** ce n'est pas bien de voler; **it doesn't look r.** ça ne va pas; **to put r.** (*error*) rectifier; (*fix*) arranger; **to put s.o. r.** (*inform*) éclairer qn, détromper qn; **r.!** bien!; **that's r.** c'est bien, c'est exact; — *adv* (*straight*) (tout) droit; (*completely*) tout à fait; (*correctly*) juste; (*well*) bien; **she did r.** elle a bien fait; **r. round** tout autour (**sth** de qch);

r. behind juste derrière; **r. here** ici même; **r. away, r. now** tout de suite; **R. Honourable** *Pol* Très Honorable; **— n to be in the r.** avoir raison; **r. and wrong** le bien et le mal; — *vt* (*error, wrong, car*) redresser. **2 all r.** *a* (*satisfactory*) bien *inv*; (*unharmed*) sain et sauf; (*undamaged*) intact; (*without worries*) tranquille; **it's all r.** ça va; **it's all r. now** (*fixed*) ça marche maintenant; **I'm all r.** (*healthy*) je vais bien, ça va; — *adv* (*well*) bien; **all r.!, r. you are!** (*yes*) d'accord!; **I got your letter all r.** j'ai bien reçu ta lettre. **◆rightly** *adv* bien, correctement; (*justifiably*) à juste titre; **r. or wrongly** à tort ou à raison.

right² [raɪt] *a* (*hand, side etc*) droit; — *adv* à droite; — *n* droite *f*; **on** *or* **to the r.** à droite (**of** de). **◆r.-hand** *a* à *or* de droite; **on the r.-hand side** à droite (**of** de); **r.-hand man** bras *m* droit. **◆r.-'handed** *a* (*person*) droitier. **◆r.-wing** *a Pol* de droite.

right³ [raɪt] *n* (*claim, entitlement*) droit *m* (**to do** de faire); **to have a r. to sth** avoir droit à qch; **he's famous in his own r.** il est lui-même célèbre; **r. of way** *Aut* priorité *f*; **human rights** les droits de l'homme.

righteous ['raɪtʃəs] *a* (*person*) vertueux; (*cause, indignation*) juste.

rightful ['raɪtfəl] *a* légitime. **◆—ly** *adv* légitimement.

rigid ['rɪdʒɪd] *a* rigide. **◆ri'gidity** *n* rigidité *f*. **◆rigidly** *adv* (*opposed*) rigoureusement (**to** à).

rigmarole ['rɪgmərəʊl] *n* (*process*) procédure *f* compliquée.

rigour ['rɪgər] *n* rigueur *f*. **◆rigorous** *a* rigoureux.

rile [raɪl] *vt* (*annoy*) *Fam* agacer.

rim [rɪm] *n* (*of cup etc*) bord *m*; (*of wheel*) jante *f*.

rind [raɪnd] *n* (*of cheese*) croûte *f*; (*of melon, lemon*) écorce *f*; (*of bacon*) couenne *f*.

ring¹ [rɪŋ] *n* anneau *m*; (*on finger*) anneau *m*, (*with stone*) bague *f*; (*of people, chairs*) cercle *m*; (*of smoke, for napkin*) rond *m*; (*gang*) bande *f*; (*at circus*) piste *f*; *Boxing* ring *m*; (*burner on stove*) brûleur *m*; **diamond r.** bague *f* de diamants; **to have rings under one's eyes** avoir les yeux cernés; **r. road** route *f* de ceinture; (*motorway*) périphérique *m*; — *vt* **to r.** (**round**) (*surround*) entourer (**with** de); (*item on list etc*) entourer d'un cercle. **◆ringleader** *n Pej* (*of gang*) chef *m* de bande; (*of rebellion etc*) meneur, -euse *mf*.

ring² [rɪŋ] *n* (*sound*) sonnerie *f*; **there's a r. on sonne**; **to give s.o. a r.** (*phone call*) passer un coup de fil à qn; **a r. of** (*truth*) *Fig* l'accent *m* de; − *vi* (*pt* rang, *pp* rung) (*of bell, person etc*) sonner; (*of sound, words*) retentir; **to r. (up)** *Tel* téléphoner; **to r. back** *Tel* rappeler; **to r. for s.o.** sonner qn; **to r. off** *Tel* raccrocher; **to r. out** (*of bell*) sonner; (*of sound*) retentir; − *vt* sonner; **to r. s.o. (up)** *Tel* téléphoner à qn; **to r. s.o. back** *Tel* rappeler qn; **to r. the bell** sonner; **to r. the doorbell** sonner à la porte; **that rings a bell** *Fam* ça me rappelle quelque chose; **to r. in** (*the New Year*) carillonner. ◆−**ing** *a* & **tone** *Tel* tonalité *f*; − *n* (*of bell*) sonnerie *f*; **a r. in one's ears** un bourdonnement dans les oreilles.

ringlet ['rɪŋlɪt] *n* (*curl*) anglaise *f*.

rink [rɪŋk] *n* (*ice-skating*) patinoire *f*; (*roller-skating*) skating *m*.

rinse [rɪns] *vt* rincer; **to r. one's hands** se passer les mains à l'eau; (*remove soap*) se rincer les mains; **to r. out** rincer; − *n* rinçage *m*; (*hair colouring*) shampooing *m* colorant; **to give sth a r.** rincer qch.

riot ['raɪət] *n* (*uprising*) émeute *f*; (*demonstration*) manifestation *f* violente; **a r. of colour** *Fig* une orgie de couleurs; **to run r.** (*of crowd*) se déchaîner; **the r. police** = les CRS *mpl*; − *vi* (*rise up*) faire une émeute; (*fight*) se bagarrer. ◆−**ing** *n* émeutes *fpl*; bagarres *fpl*. ◆−**er** *n* émeutier, -ière *mf*; (*demonstrator*) manifestant, -ante *mf* violent(e). ◆**riotous** *a* (*crowd etc*) tapageur; **r. living** vie *f* dissolue.

rip [rɪp] *vt* (-pp-) déchirer; **to r. off or out** arracher; **to r. off** *Fam* (*deceive*) rouler; (*steal*) *Am* voler; **to r. up** déchirer; − *vi* (*of fabric*) se déchirer; − *n* déchirure *f*; **it's a r.-off** *Fam* c'est du vol organisé.

ripe [raɪp] *a* (-er, -est) mûr; (*cheese*) fait. ◆**ripen** *vti* mûrir. ◆**ripeness** *n* maturité *f*.

ripple ['rɪp(ə)l] *n* (*on water*) ride *f*; (*of laughter*) *Fig* cascade *f*; − *vi* (*of water*) se rider.

ris/e [raɪz] *vi* (*pt* rose, *pp* risen) (*get up from chair or bed*) se lever; (*of temperature, balloon, price etc*) monter, s'élever; (*in society*) s'élever; (*of hope*) grandir; (*of sun, curtain, wind*) se lever; (*of dough*) lever; **to r. in price** augmenter de prix; **to r. to the surface** remonter à la surface; **the river rises in . . .** le fleuve prend sa source dans . . . ; **to r. (up)** (*rebel*) se soulever (**against** contre); **to r. to power** accéder au pouvoir; **to r. from the dead** ressusciter; − *n* (*of sun, curtain*) lever *m*; (*in pressure, price etc*) hausse *f* (**in** de); (*in river*) crue *f*; (*of leader*) *Fig* ascension *f*; (*of industry, technology*)

essor *m*; (*to power*) accession *f*; (*slope in ground*) éminence *f*; (**pay**) r. augmentation *f* (de salaire); **to give r. to** donner lieu à. ◆−**ing** *n* (*of curtain*) lever *m*; (*of river*) crue *f*; (*revolt*) soulèvement *m*; − *a* (*sun*) levant; (*number*) croissant; (*tide*) montant; (*artist etc*) d'avenir; **the r. generation** la nouvelle génération; **r. prices** la hausse des prix. ◆−**er** *n* **early r.** lève-tôt *mf inv*; **late r.** lève-tard *mf inv*.

risk [rɪsk] *n* risque *m* (**of doing** de faire); **at r.** (*person*) en danger; (*job*) menacé; **at your own r.** à tes risques et périls; − *vt* (*one's life, an accident etc*) risquer; **she won't r. leaving** (*take the risk*) elle ne se risquera pas à partir; **let's r. it** risquons le coup. ◆**riskiness** *n* risques *mpl*. ◆**risky** *a* (-ier, -iest) (*full of risk*) risqué.

rissole ['rɪsəʊl] *n* *Culin* croquette *f*.

rite [raɪt] *n* rite *m*; **the last rites** *Rel* les derniers sacrements *mpl*. ◆**ritual** *a* & *n* rituel (*m*).

ritzy ['rɪtsɪ] *a* (-ier, -iest) *Fam* luxueux, classe *inv*.

rival ['raɪv(ə)l] *a* (*firm etc*) rival; (*forces, claim etc*) opposé; − *n* rival, -ale *mf*; − *vt* (-ll-, *Am* -l-) (*compete with*) rivaliser avec (**in** de); (*equal*) égaler (**in** en). ◆**rivalry** *n* rivalité *f* (**between** entre).

river ['rɪvər] *n* (*small*) rivière *f*; (*major, flowing into sea*) & *Fig* fleuve *m*; **the R. Thames** la Tamise; − *a* (*port etc*) fluvial; **r. bank** rive *f*. ◆**riverside** *a* & *n* (**by the**) **r.** au bord de l'eau.

rivet ['rɪvɪt] *n* (*pin*) rivet *m*; − *vt* riveter; (*eyes*) *Fig* fixer. ◆−**ing** *a* (*story etc*) fascinant.

Riviera [rɪvɪ'eərə] *n* **the** (**French**) **R.** la Côte d'Azur.

road [rəʊd] *n* route *f* (**to** qui va à); (*small*) chemin *m*; (*in town*) rue *f*; (*roadway*) chaussée *f*; (*path*) *Fig* voie *f*, chemin *m*, route *f* (**to** de); **the Paris r.** la route de Paris; **across or over the r.** (*building etc*) en face; **by r.** par la route; **get out of the r.!** ne reste pas sur la chaussée!; − *a* (*map, safety*) routier; (*accident*) de la route; (*sense*) de la conduite; **r. hog** *Fam* chauffard *m*; **r. sign** panneau *m* (routier *or* de signalisation); **r. works** travaux *mpl*. ◆**roadblock** *n* barrage *m* routier. ◆**roadside** *a* & *n* (**by the**) **r.** au bord de la route. ◆**roadway** *n* chaussée *f*. ◆**roadworthy** *a* (*vehicle*) en état de marche.

roam [rəʊm] *vt* parcourir; − *vi* errer, rôder; **to r. (about) the streets** (*of child etc*) traîner dans les rues.

roar [rɔːr] *vi* hurler; (*of lion, wind, engine*) rugir; (*of thunder*) gronder; **to r. with laughter** éclater de rire; **to r. past** (*of truck etc*) passer dans un bruit de tonnerre; – *vt* **to r. (out)** hurler; – *n* hurlement *m*; rugissement *m*; grondement *m*. ◆**—ing** *n* = roar *n*; – *a* **a r. fire** une belle flambée; **a r. success** un succès fou; **to do a r. trade** vendre beaucoup (**in** de).

roast [rəʊst] *vt* rôtir; (*coffee*) griller; – *vi* (*of meat*) rôtir; **we're roasting here** *Fam* on rôtit ici; – *n* (*meat*) rôti *m*; – *a* (*chicken etc*) rôti; **r. beef** rosbif *m*.

rob [rɒb] *vt* (**-bb-**) (*person*) voler; (*bank, house*) dévaliser; **to r. s.o. of sth** voler qch à qn; (*deprive*) priver qn de qch. ◆**robber** *n* voleur, -euse *mf*. ◆**robbery** *n* vol *m*; **it's daylight r.!** c'est du vol organisé; **armed r.** vol *m* à main armée.

robe [rəʊb] *n* (*of priest, judge etc*) robe *f*; (*dressing gown*) peignoir *m*.

robin ['rɒbɪn] *n* (*bird*) rouge-gorge *m*.

robot ['rəʊbɒt] *n* robot *m*.

robust [rəʊ'bʌst] *a* robuste.

rock¹ [rɒk] **1** *vt* (*baby, boat*) bercer, balancer; (*cradle, branch*) balancer; (*violently*) secouer; – *vi* (*sway*) se balancer; (*of building, ground*) trembler. **2** *n Mus* rock *m*. ◆**—ing** *n* (*horse, chair*) à bascule. ◆**rocky¹** *a* (**-ier, -iest**) (*furniture etc*) branlant.

rock² [rɒk] *n* (*substance*) roche *f*; (*boulder, rock face*) rocher *m*; (*stone*) *Am* pierre *f*; **a stick of r.** (*sweet*) un bâton de sucre d'orge; **r. face** paroi *f* rocheuse; **on the rocks** (*whisky*) avec des glaçons; (*marriage*) en pleine débâcle. ◆**r.-'bottom** *n* point *m* le plus bas; – *a* (*prices*) les plus bas, très bas. ◆**r.-climbing** *n* varappe *f*. ◆**rockery** *n* (*in garden*) rocaille *f*. ◆**rocky²** *a* (**-ier, -iest**) (*road*) rocailleux; (*hill*) rocheux.

rocket ['rɒkɪt] *n* fusée *f*; – *vi* (*of prices*) *Fig* monter en flèche.

rod [rɒd] *n* (*wooden*) baguette *f*; (*metal*) tige *f*; (*of curtain*) tringle *f*; (*for fishing*) canne *f* à pêche.

rode [rəʊd] *see* ride.

rodent ['rəʊdənt] *n* (*animal*) rongeur *m*.

rodeo ['rəʊdɪəʊ] *n* (*pl* **-os**) *Am* rodéo *m*.

roe [rəʊ] *n* **1** (*eggs*) œufs *mpl* de poisson. **2 r.** (**deer**) chevreuil *m*.

rogue [rəʊg] *n* (*dishonest*) crapule *f*; (*mischievous*) coquin, -ine *mf*. ◆**roguish** *a* (*smile etc*) coquin.

role [rəʊl] *n* rôle *m*.

roll [rəʊl] *n* (*of paper, film etc*) rouleau *m*; (*of bread*) petit pain *m*; (*of fat, flesh*) bourrelet *m*; (*of drum, thunder*) roulement *m*; (*of ship*) roulis *m*; (*list*) liste *f*; **to have a r. call** faire l'appel; **r. neck** (*neckline, sweater*) col *m* roulé; – *vi* (*of ball, ship etc*) rouler; (*of person, animal*) se rouler; **to be rolling in money** *or* **in it** *Fam* rouler sur l'or; **r. on tonight!** *Fam* vivement ce soir!; **to r. in** *Fam* (*flow in*) affluer; (*of person*) s'amener; **to r. over** (*many times*) se rouler; (*once*) se retourner; **to r. up** (*arrive*) *Fam* s'amener; **to r. (up) into a ball** (*of animal*) se rouler en boule; – *vt* rouler; **to r. down** (*blind*) baisser; (*slope*) descendre (en roulant); **to r. on** (*paint, stocking*) mettre; **to r. out** (*dough*) étaler; **to r. up** (*map, cloth*) rouler; (*sleeve, trousers*) retrousser. ◆**—ing** *a* (*ground, gait*) onduleux; **r. pin** rouleau *m* à pâtisserie. ◆**—er** *n* (*for hair, painting etc*) rouleau *m*; **r. coaster** (*at funfair*) montagnes *fpl* russes. ◆**roller-skate** *n* patin *m* à roulettes; – *vi* faire du patin à roulettes.

rollicking ['rɒlɪkɪŋ] *a* joyeux (et bruyant).

roly-poly ['rəʊlɪ'pəʊlɪ] *a Fam* grassouillet.

Roman ['rəʊmən] **1** *a* & *n* romain, -aine *mf*. **2 R. Catholic** *a* & *n* catholique (*mf*).

romance [rəʊ'mæns] **1** *n* (*story*) histoire *f* or roman *m* d'amour; (*love*) amour *m*; (*affair*) aventure *f* amoureuse; (*charm*) poésie *f*. **2 a R. language** langue *f* romane. ◆**romantic** *a* (*of love, tenderness etc*) romantique; (*fanciful, imaginary*) romanesque; – *n* (*person*) romantique *mf*. ◆**romantically** *adv* (*to behave*) de façon romantique. ◆**romanticism** *n* romantisme *m*.

Romania [rəʊ'meɪnɪə] *n* Roumanie *f*. ◆**Romanian** *a* & *n* roumain, -aine *mf*; – *n* (*language*) roumain *m*.

romp [rɒmp] *vi* s'ébattre (bruyamment); **to r. through** (*exam*) *Fig* avoir les doigts dans le nez; – *n* ébats *mpl*.

rompers ['rɒmpəz] *npl* (*for baby*) barboteuse *f*.

roof [ruːf] *n* (*of building, vehicle*) toit *m*; (*of tunnel, cave*) plafond *m*; **r. of the mouth** voûte *f* du palais; **r. rack** (*of car*) galerie *f*. ◆**—ing** *n* toiture *f*. ◆**rooftop** *n* toit *m*.

rook [rʊk] *n* **1** (*bird*) corneille *f*. **2** *Chess* tour *f*.

rookie ['rʊkɪ] *n* (*new recruit*) *Mil Fam* bleu *m*.

room [ruːm, rʊm] *n* **1** (*in house etc*) pièce *f*; (*bedroom*) chambre *f*; (*large, public*) salle *f*; **one's rooms** son appartement *m*; **in rooms** en meublé; **men's r., ladies' r.** *Am* toilettes *fpl*. **2** (*space*) place *f* (**for** pour); (*some*) **r.** de la place; **there's r. for doubt** le doute est permis; **no r. for doubt** aucun doute possible. ◆**rooming house** n Am maison f de rapport. ◆**roommate** n camarade mf de chambre. ◆**roomy** a (-ier, -iest) spacieux; (clothes) ample.

roost [ruːst] vi (of bird) percher; – n perchoir m.

rooster ['ruːstər] n coq m.

root [ruːt] **1** n (of plant, person etc) & Math racine f; Fig cause f, origine f; **to pull up by the root(s)** déraciner; **to take r.** (of plant) & Fig prendre racine; **to put down (new) roots** Fig s'enraciner; **r. cause** cause f première; – vt **to r. out** (destroy) extirper. **2** vi (of plant cutting) s'enraciner; **to r. about for** fouiller pour trouver. **3** vi **to r. for** (cheer, support) Fam encourager. ◆**—ed** a **deeply r.** bien enraciné (in dans); **r. to the spot** (immobile) cloué sur place. ◆**—less** a sans racines.

rope [rəʊp] n corde f; Nau cordage m; **to know the ropes** Fam être au courant; – vt (tie) lier; **to r. s.o. in** (force to help) Fam embrigader qn (to do pour faire); **to r. off** séparer (par une corde).

rop(e)y ['rəʊpɪ] a (-ier, -iest) Fam (thing) minable; (person) patraque.

rosary ['rəʊzərɪ] n Rel chapelet m.

rose [rəʊz] n **1** (flower) rose f; (colour) rose m; **r. bush** rosier m. **2** (of watering can) pomme f. ◆**ro'sette** n Sp cocarde f; (rose-shaped) rosette f. ◆**rosy** a (-ier, -iest) (pink) rose; (future) Fig tout en rose.

rose² [rəʊz] see rise.

rosé ['rəʊzeɪ] n (wine) rosé m.

rosemary ['rəʊzmərɪ] n Bot Culin romarin m.

roster ['rɒstər] n (duty) r. liste f (de service).

rostrum ['rɒstrəm] n tribune f; Sp podium m.

rot [rɒt] n pourriture f; (nonsense) Fam inepties fpl; – vti (-tt-) **to r. (away)** pourrir.

rota ['rəʊtə] n liste f (de service).

rotate [rəʊ'teɪt] vi tourner; – vt faire tourner; (crops) alterner. ◆'**rotary** a rotatif; **r. airer** (washing line) séchoir m parapluie; – n (roundabout) Aut Am sens m giratoire. ◆**rotation** n rotation f; **in r.** à tour de rôle.

rote [rəʊt] n **by r.** machinalement.

rotten ['rɒt(ə)n] a (decayed, corrupt) pourri; (bad) Fam moche; (filthy) Fam sale; **to feel r.** (ill) être mal fichu. ◆**rottenness** n pourriture f. ◆**rotting** a (meat, fruit etc) qui pourrit.

rotund [rəʊ'tʌnd] a (round) rond; (plump) rondelet.

rouble ['ruːb(ə)l] n (currency) rouble m.

rouge [ruːʒ] n rouge m (à joues).

rough¹ [rʌf] a (-er, -est) (surface, task, manners) rude; (ground) inégal, accidenté; (rocky) rocailleux; (plank, bark) rugueux; (sound) âpre, rude; (coarse) grossier; (brutal) brutal; (weather, neighbourhood) mauvais; (sea) agité; (justice) sommaire; (diamond) brut; **a r. child** (unruly) un enfant dur; **to feel r.** (ill) Fam être mal fichu; **r. and ready** (conditions, solution) grossier (mais adéquat); – adv (to sleep, live) à la dure; (to play) brutalement; – n (violent man) Fam voyou m; – vt **to r. it** Fam vivre à la dure; **to r. up** (hair) ébouriffer; (person) Fam malmener. ◆**r.-and-'tumble** n (fight) mêlée f; (of s.o.'s life) remue-ménage m inv. ◆**roughen** vt rendre rude. ◆**roughly¹** adv (not gently) rudement; (coarsely) grossièrement; (brutally) brutalement. ◆**roughness** n rudesse f; inégalité f; grossièreté f; brutalité f.

rough² [rʌf] a (-er, -est) (calculation, figure, terms etc) approximatif; **r. copy, r. draft** brouillon m; **r. paper** du papier brouillon; **r. guess, r. estimate** approximation f; **a r. plan** l'ébauche f d'un projet; – vt **to r. out** (plan) ébaucher. ◆**—ly²** adv (approximately) à peu (de choses) près.

roughage ['rʌfɪdʒ] n (in food) fibres fpl (alimentaires).

roulette [ruː'let] n roulette f.

round [raʊnd] **1** adv autour; **all r., right r.** tout autour; **to go r. to s.o.** passer chez qn; **to ask r.** inviter chez soi; **he'll be r.** il passera; **r. here** par ici; **the long way r.** le chemin le plus long; – prep autour de; **r. about** (house etc) autour de; (approximately) environ; **r. (about) midday** vers midi; **to go r.** (world) faire le tour de; (corner) tourner. **2** a (-er, -est) rond; **a r. trip** Am un (voyage) aller et retour. **3** n (slice) Culin tranche f; Sp Pol manche f; (of golf) partie f; Boxing round m; (of talks) série f; (of drinks, visits) tournée f; **one's round(s)** (of milkman etc) sa tournée; (of doctor) ses visites fpl; (of policeman) sa ronde; **delivery r.** livraisons fpl, tournée f; **r. of applause** salve f d'applaudissements; **r. of ammunition** cartouche f, balle f; – vt **to r. a corner** (in car) prendre un virage; **to r. off** (finish) terminer; **to r. up** (gather) rassembler; (figure) arrondir au chiffre supérieur. ◆**r.-'shouldered** a voûté, aux épaules rondes. ◆**rounded** a arrondi. ◆**rounders** npl Sp sorte de baseball. ◆**roundness** n rondeur f. ◆**roundup** n (of criminals) rafle f.

roundabout ['raʊndəbaʊt] **1** a indirect, détourné. **2** n (at funfair) manège m; (junction) rond-point m (à sens giratoire).

rous/e [raʊz] vt éveiller; **roused (to anger)** en colère; **to r. to action** inciter à agir. ◆—**ing** a (welcome) enthousiaste; (speech) vibrant; (music) allègre.

rout [raʊt] n (defeat) déen déroute f; – vt mettre route.

route 1 [ruːt] n itinéraire m; (of aircraft) route f; **sea r.** route f maritime; **bus r.** ligne f d'autobus; – vt (train etc) fixer l'itinéraire de. **2** [raʊt] n (delivery round) Am tournée f.

routine [ruːˈtiːn] n routine f; **one's daily r.** (in office etc) son travail journalier; **the daily r.** (monotony) le train-train quotidien; – a (inquiry, work etc) de routine; Pej routinier.

rov/e [rəʊv] vi errer; – vt parcourir. ◆—**ing** a (life) nomade; (ambassador) itinérant.

row¹ [rəʊ] **1** n (line) rang m, rangée f; (of cars) file f; **two days in a r.** deux jours de suite or d'affilée. **2** vi (in boat) ramer; – vt (boat) faire aller à la rame; (person) transporter en canot; – n **to go for a r.** canoter; **r. boat** Am bateau m à rames. ◆—**ing** n canotage m; Sp aviron m; **r. boat** bateau m à rames.

row² [raʊ] n Fam (noise) vacarme m; (quarrel) querelle f; – vi Fam se quereller (**with** avec).

rowdy ['raʊdɪ] a (-ier, -iest) chahuteur (et brutal); – n (person) Fam voyou m.

royal ['rɔɪəl] a royal; – npl **the royals** Fam la famille royale. ◆**royalist** a & n royaliste (mf). ◆**royally** adv (to treat) royalement. ◆**royalty 1** n (persons) personnages mpl royaux. **2** npl (from book) droits mpl d'auteur; (on oil, from patent) royalties fpl.

rub [rʌb] vt (-bb-) frotter; (polish) astiquer; **to r. shoulders with** Fig coudoyer, côtoyer; **to r. away** (mark) effacer; (tears) essuyer; **to r. down** (person) frictionner; (wood, with sandpaper) poncer; **to r. in** (cream) Med faire pénétrer (en massant); **to r. it in** Pej Fam retourner le couteau dans la plaie; **to r. off or out** (mark) effacer; **rubbing alcohol** Am alcool m à 90°; – vi frotter; **to r. off** (of mark) partir; (of manners etc) déteindre (**on s.o.** sur qn); – n (massage) friction f; **to give sth a r.** frotter qch, (polish) astiquer qch.

rubber ['rʌbər] n (substance) caoutchouc m; (eraser) gomme f; (contraceptive) Am Sl capote f; **r. stamp** tampon m. ◆**r.-'stamp** vt Pej approuver (sans discuter). ◆**rubbery** a caoutchouteux.

rubbish ['rʌbɪʃ] **1** n (refuse) ordures fpl; détritus mpl; (waste) déchets mpl; (junk) saleté(s) f(pl); (nonsense) Fig absurdités fpl; **that's r.** (absurd) c'est absurde; (worthless) ça ne vaut rien; **r. bin** poubelle f; **r. dump** dépôt m d'ordures, décharge f (publique); (in garden) tas m d'ordures. **2** vt **to r. s.o./sth** (criticize) Fam dénigrer qn/qch. ◆**rubbishy** a (book etc) sans valeur; (goods) de mauvaise qualité.

rubble ['rʌb(ə)l] n décombres mpl.

ruble ['ruːb(ə)l] n (currency) rouble m.

ruby ['ruːbɪ] n (gem) rubis m.

rucksack ['rʌksæk] n sac m à dos.

ruckus ['rʌkəs] n (uproar) Fam chahut m.

rudder ['rʌdər] n gouvernail m.

ruddy ['rʌdɪ] a (-ier, -iest) **1** (complexion) coloré. **2** (bloody) Sl fichu.

rude [ruːd] a (-er, -est) (impolite) impoli (**to** envers); (coarse) grossier; (indecent) indécent, obscène; (shock) violent. ◆—**ly** adv impoliment; grossièrement. ◆—**ness** n impolitesse f; grossièreté f.

rudiments ['ruːdɪmənts] npl rudiments mpl. ◆**rudi'mentary** a rudimentaire.

ruffian ['rʌfɪən] n voyou m.

ruffle ['rʌf(ə)l] **1** vt (hair) ébouriffer; (water) troubler; **to r. s.o.** (offend) froisser qn. **2** n (frill) ruche f.

rug [rʌg] n carpette f, petit tapis m; (over knees) plaid m; (bedside) **r.** descente f de lit.

rugby ['rʌgbɪ] n **r. (football)** rugby m. ◆**rugger** n Fam rugby m.

rugged ['rʌgɪd] a (surface) rugueux, rude; (terrain, coast) accidenté; (person, features, manners) rude; (determination) Fig farouche.

ruin ['ruːɪn] n (destruction, rubble, building etc) ruine f; **in ruins** (building) en ruine; – vt (health, country, person etc) ruiner; (clothes) abîmer; (spoil) gâter. ◆—**ed** a (person, country etc) ruiné; (building) en ruine. ◆**ruinous** a ruineux.

rul/e [ruːl] **1** n (principle) règle f; (regulation) règlement m; (custom) coutume f; (authority) autorité f; Pol gouvernement m; **against the rules** contraire à la règle; **as a (general) r.** en règle générale; **it's the** or **a r. that** il est de règle que (+ sub); – vt (country) Pol gouverner; (decide) Jur Sp décider (**that** que); **to r. s.o.** (dominate) mener qn; **to r. out** (exclude) exclure; – vi (of monarch) régner (**over** sur); (of judge) statuer (**against** contre, **on** sur). **2** n (for measuring) règle f. ◆—**ed** a (paper) réglé, ligné. ◆—**ing** a (passion) dominant;

(*class*) dirigeant; (*party*) *Pol* au pouvoir; −
n Jur Sp décision *f*. ◆**ruler** *n* **1** (*of country*)
Pol dirigeant, -ante *mf*; (*sovereign*) souverain, -aine *mf*. **2** (*measure*) règle *f*.

rum [rʌm] *n* rhum *m*.

Rumania [ruːˈmeɪnɪə] *see* **Romania**.

rumble [ˈrʌmb(ə)l] *vi* (*of train, thunder, gun*)
gronder; (*of stomach*) gargouiller; − *n*
grondement *m*; gargouillement *m*.

ruminate [ˈruːmɪneɪt] *vi* to r. over (*scheme
etc*) ruminer.

rummage [ˈrʌmɪdʒ] *vi* to r. (about) farfouil-
ler; r. **sale** (*used clothes etc*) *Am* vente *f* de
charité.

rumour [ˈruːmər] *n* rumeur *f*, bruit *m*.
◆**rumoured** *a* it is r. that on dit que.

rump [rʌmp] *n* (*of horse*) croupe *f*; (*of fowl*)
croupion *m*; r. **steak** rumsteck *m*.

rumple [ˈrʌmp(ə)l] *vt* (*clothes*) chiffonner.

run [rʌn] *n* (*running*) course *f*; (*outing*) tour
m; (*journey*) parcours *m*, trajet *m*; (*series*)
série *f*; (*period*) période *f*; Cards suite *f*;
(*rush*) ruée *f* (on sur); (*trend*) tendance *f*;
(*for skiing*) piste *f*; (*in cricket*) point *m*; to
go for a r. courir, faire une course à pied;
on the r. (*prisoner etc*) en fuite; to have the
r. of (*house etc*) avoir à sa disposition; in
the long r. avec le temps, à la longue; the
runs *Med Fam* la diarrhée; − *vi* (*pt* ran, *pp*
run, *pres p* running) courir; (*flee*) fuir; (*of
curtain*) glisser; (*of river, nose, pen, tap*)
couler; (*of colour in washing*) déteindre; (*of
ink*) baver; (*melt*) fondre; (*of play, film*) se
jouer; (*of contract*) être valide; (*last*) durer;
(*pass*) passer; (*function*) marcher; (*tick
over*) *Aut* tourner; (*of stocking*) filer; to r.
down/in/etc descendre/entrer/etc en courant; to r. **for president** être candidat à la
présidence; to r. **with blood** ruisseler de
sang; to r. **between** (*of bus*) faire le service
entre; to go **running** *Sp* faire du jogging;
the **road runs to . . .** la route va à . . . ; the
river runs into the sea le fleuve se jette dans
la mer; it **runs into a hundred pounds** ça va
chercher dans les cent livres; it **runs in the
family** ça tient de famille; − *vt* (*race, risk*)
courir; (*horse*) faire courir; (*temperature,
errand*) faire; (*blockade*) forcer; (*machine*)
faire fonctionner; (*engine*) *Aut* faire
tourner; (*drive*) *Aut* conduire; (*furniture,
goods*) transporter (to à); (*business, country
etc*) diriger; (*courses, events*) organiser;
(*film, play*) présenter; (*house*) tenir; (*article*) publier (on sur); (*bath*) faire couler; to
r. **one's hand over** passer la main sur; to r.
one's eye over jeter un coup d'œil à *or* sur;
to r. **its course** (*of illness etc*) suivre son

cours; to r. **5 km** *Sp* faire 5 km de course à
pied; to r. **a car** avoir une voiture. ■ to r.
about *vi* courir çà et là; (*gallivant*) se
balader; to r. **across** *vt* (*meet*) tomber sur;
to r. **along** *vi* r. **along!** filez!; to r. **away** *vi*
(*flee*) s'enfuir, se sauver (**from** de); to r.
back *vt* (*person*) *Aut* ramener (to à); to r.
down *vt* (*pedestrian*) *Aut* renverser; (*belittle*) dénigrer; (*restrict*) limiter peu à peu.
◆**r.-'down** *a* (*weak, tired*) *Med* à plat;
(*district etc*) miteux; to r. **in** *vt* (*vehicle*)
roder; to r. **s.o. in** (*of police*) *Fam* arrêter
qn; to r. **into** *vt* (*meet*) tomber sur; (*crash
into*) *Aut* percuter; to r. **into debt**
s'endetter; to r. **off** *vt* (*print*) tirer; − *vi*
(*flee*) s'enfuir; to r. **out** *vi* (*of stocks*)
s'épuiser; (*of lease*) expirer; (*of time*)
manquer; to r. **out of** (*time, money*)
manquer de; we've r. **out of coffee** on n'a
plus de café; − *vt* to r. **s.o. out of** (*chase*)
chasser qn de; to r. **over** *vi* (*of liquid*)
déborder; − *vt* (*kill pedestrian*) *Aut* écraser;
(*knock down pedestrian*) *Aut* renverser;
(*notes, text*) revoir; to r. **round** *vt* (*surround*)
entourer; to r. **through** *vt* (*recap*) revoir; to
r. **up** *vt* (*bill, debts*) laisser s'accumuler.
◆**r.-up** *n* the r.**-up to** (*elections etc*) la
période qui précède. ◆**running** *n* course *f*;
(*of machine*) fonctionnement *m*; (*of firm,
country*) direction *f*; to be **in/out of the r.**
être/ne plus être dans la course; − *a*
(*commentary*) suivi; (*battle*) continuel; r.
water eau *f* courante; **six days/etc** r. six
jours/etc de suite; r. **costs** (*of factory*) frais
mpl d'exploitation; (*of car*) dépenses *fpl*
courantes. ◆**runner** *n Sp etc* coureur *m*; r.
bean haricot *m* (grimpant). ◆**runner-'up**
n Sp second, -onde *mf*. ◆**runny** *a* (-ier,
-iest) *a* (*nose*) qui coule.

runaway [ˈrʌnəweɪ] *n* fugitif, -ive *mf*; − *a*
(*car, horse*) emballé; (*lorry*) fou; (*wedding*)
clandestin; (*victory*) qu'on remporte haut
la main; (*inflation*) galopant.

rung¹ [rʌŋ] *n* (*of ladder*) barreau *m*.

rung² [rʌŋ] *see* **ring²**.

run-of-the-mill [rʌnəvðəˈmɪl] *a* ordinaire.

runway [ˈrʌnweɪ] *n Av* piste *f*.

rupture [ˈrʌptʃər] *n Med* hernie *f*; the r. of
(*breaking*) la rupture de; − *vt* rompre; to r.
oneself se donner une hernie.

rural [ˈrʊərəl] *a* rural.

ruse [ruːz] *n* (*trick*) ruse *f*.

rush¹ [rʌʃ] *vi* (*move fast, throw oneself*) se
précipiter, se ruer (**at** sur, **towards** vers); (*of
blood*) affluer (**to** à); (*hurry*) se dépêcher (**to
do** de faire); (*of vehicle*) foncer; to r. **out**
partir en vitesse; − *vt* (*attack*) *Mil* foncer

sur; **to r. s.o.** bousculer qn; **to r. s.o. to hospital** transporter qn d'urgence à l'hôpital; **to r. (through)** sth (*job, meal, order etc*) faire, manger, envoyer *etc* qch en vitesse; **to be rushed into** (*decision, answer etc*) être forcé à prendre, donner *etc*; – *n* ruée *f* (**for** vers, **on** sur); (*confusion*) bousculade *f*; (*hurry*) hâte *f*; (*of orders*) avalanche *f*; **to be in a r.** être pressé (**to do** de faire); **to leave/etc in a r.** partir/*etc* en vitesse; **the gold r.** la ruée vers l'or; **the r. hour** l'heure *f* d'affluence; **a r. job** un travail d'urgence.

rush² [rʌʃ] *n* (*plant*) jonc *m*.

rusk [rʌsk] *n* biscotte *f*.

russet ['rʌsɪt] *a* roux, roussâtre.

Russia ['rʌʃə] *n* Russie *f*. ◆**Russian** *a & n* russe (*mf*); – *n* (*language*) russe *m*.

rust [rʌst] *n* rouille *f*; – *vi* (se) rouiller. ◆**rustproof** *a* inoxydable. ◆**rusty** *a* (**-ier, -iest**) (*metal, athlete, memory etc*) rouillé.

rustic ['rʌstɪk] *a* rustique.

rustle ['rʌs(ə)l] **1** *vi* (*of leaves*) bruire; (*of skirt*) froufrouter; – *n* bruissement *m*; frou-frou *m*. **2** *vt* **to r. up** *Fam* (*prepare*) préparer; (*find*) trouver.

rut [rʌt] *n* ornière *f*; **to be in a r.** *Fig* être encroûté.

rutabaga [ruːtə'beɪɡə] *n* (*swede*) *Am* rutabaga *m*.

ruthless ['ruːθləs] *a* (*attack, person etc*) impitoyable, cruel; (*in taking decisions*) très ferme. ◆**—ness** *n* cruauté *f*.

rye [raɪ] *n* seigle *m*; **r. bread** pain *m* de

S

S, s [es] *n* S, s *m*.

Sabbath ['sæbəθ] *n* (*Jewish*) sabbat *m*; (*Christian*) dimanche *m*. ◆**sa'bbatical** *a* (*year etc*) *Univ* sabbatique.

sabotage ['sæbətɑːʒ] *n* sabotage *m*; – *vt* saboter. ◆**saboteur** [-'tɜːr] *n* saboteur, -euse *mf*.

sabre ['seɪbər] *n* (*sword*) sabre *m*.

saccharin ['sækərɪn] *n* saccharine *f*.

sachet ['sæʃeɪ] *n* (*of lavender etc*) sachet *m*; (*of shampoo*) dosette *f*.

sack [sæk] **1** *n* (*bag*) sac *m*. **2** *vt* (*dismiss*) *Fam* virer, renvoyer; – *n* *Fam* **to get the s.** se faire virer; **to give s.o. the s.** virer qn. **3** *vt* (*town etc*) saccager, mettre à sac. ◆**—ing** *n* **1** (*cloth*) toile *f* à sac. **2** (*dismissal*) *Fam* renvoi *m*.

sacrament ['sækrəmənt] *n* *Rel* sacrement *m*.

sacred ['seɪkrɪd] *a* (*holy*) sacré.

sacrifice ['sækrɪfaɪs] *n* sacrifice *m*; – *vt* sacrifier (**to** à, **for sth/s.o.** pour qch/qn).

sacrilege ['sækrɪlɪdʒ] *n* sacrilège *m*. ◆**sacri'legious** *a* sacrilège.

sacrosanct ['sækrəʊsæŋkt] *a* *Iron* sacro-saint.

sad [sæd] *a* (**sadder, saddest**) triste. ◆**sadden** *vt* attrister. ◆**sadly** *adv* tristement; (*unfortunately*) malheureusement; (*very*) très. ◆**sadness** *n* tristesse *f*.

saddle ['sæd(ə)l] *n* selle *f*; **to be in the s.** (*in* control*) *Fig* tenir les rênes; – *vt* (*horse*) seller; **to s. s.o. with** (*chore, person*) *Fam* coller à qn.

sadism ['seɪdɪz(ə)m] *n* sadisme *m*. ◆**sadist** *n* sadique *mf*. ◆**sa'distic** *a* sadique.

sae [eseɪiː] *abbr* = **stamped addressed envelope.**

safari [sə'fɑːrɪ] *n* safari *m*; **to be** *or* **go on s.** faire un safari.

safe¹ [seɪf] *a* (**-er, -est**) (*person*) en sécurité; (*equipment, toy, animal*) sans danger; (*place, investment, method*) sûr; (*bridge, ladder*) solide; (*prudent*) prudent; (*winner*) assuré, garanti; **s. (and sound)** sain et sauf; **it's s. to go out** on peut sortir sans danger; **the safest thing (to do) is . . .** le plus sûr est de . . . ; **s. from** à l'abri de; **to be on the s. side** pour plus de sûreté; **in s. hands** en mains sûres; **s. journey!** bon voyage! ◆**s.-'conduct** *n* sauf-conduit *m*. ◆**safe-'keeping** *n* **for s.** à garder en sécurité. ◆**safely** *adv* (*without mishap*) sans accident; (*securely*) en sûreté; (*without risk*) sans risque, sans danger. ◆**safety** *n* sécurité *f*; (*solidity*) solidité *f*; (*salvation*) salut *m*; – *a* (*belt, device, screen, margin*) de sécurité; (*pin, razor, chain, valve*) de sûreté; **s. precaution** mesure *f* de sécurité.

safe² [seɪf] *n* (*for money etc*) coffre-fort *m*.

safeguard ['seɪfɡɑːd] *n* sauvegarde *f* (**against** contre); – *vt* sauvegarder.

saffron ['sæfrən] *n* safran *m.*
sag [sæg] *vi* (-gg-) (*of roof, ground*) s'affaisser; (*of cheeks*) pendre; (*of prices, knees*) fléchir. ◆**sagging** *a* (*roof, breasts*) affaissé.
saga ['sɑːɡə] *n* Liter saga *f;* (*bad sequence of events*) Fig feuilleton *m.*
sage [seɪdʒ] *n* **1** Bot Culin sauge *f.* **2** (*wise man*) sage *m.*
Sagittarius [sædʒɪ'teərɪəs] *n* (*sign*) le Sagittaire.
sago ['seɪɡəʊ] *n* (*cereal*) sagou *m.*
Sahara [sə'hɑːrə] *n* the S. (*desert*) le Sahara.
said [sed] *see* **say.**
sail [seɪl] *vi* (*navigate*) naviguer; (*leave*) partir; Sp faire de la voile; (*glide*) Fig glisser; **to s. into port** entrer au port; **to s. round** (*world, island etc*) faire le tour de en bateau; **to s. through** (*exam etc*) Fig réussir haut la main; – *vt* (*boat*) piloter; (*seas*) parcourir; – *n* voile *f;* (*trip*) tour *m* en bateau; **to set s.** (*of boat*) partir (**for** à destination de). ◆**—ing** *n* navigation *f;* Sp voile *f;* (*departure*) départ *m;* (*crossing*) traversée *f;* **s. boat** voilier *m.* ◆**sailboard** *n* planche *f* (à voile). ◆**sailboat** *n* Am voilier *m.* ◆**sailor** *n* marin *m,* matelot *m.*
saint [seɪnt] *n* saint *m,* sainte *f;* **S. John** saint Jean; **s.'s day** Rel fête *f* (de saint). ◆**saintly** *a* (-ier, -iest) saint.
sake [seɪk] *n* **for my/your s.** pour moi/toi; **for your father's s.** pour (l'amour de) ton père; (**just**) **for the s. of eating**/*etc* simplement pour manger/*etc*; **for heaven's** *or* **God's s.** pour l'amour de Dieu.
salacious [sə'leɪʃəs] *a* obscène.
salad ['sæləd] *n* (*dish of vegetables, fruit etc*) salade *f;* **s. bowl** saladier *m;* **s. cream** mayonnaise *f;* **s. dressing** vinaigrette *f.*
salamander ['sæləmændər] *n* (*lizard*) salamandre *f.*
salami [sə'lɑːmɪ] *n* salami *m.*
salary ['sælərɪ] *n* (*professional*) traitement *m;* (*wage*) salaire *m.* ◆**salaried** *a* (*person*) qui perçoit un traitement.
sale [seɪl] *n* vente *f;* **sale(s)** (*at reduced prices*) Com soldes *mpl;* **in a** *or* **the s.,** Am **on s.** (*cheaply*) en solde; **on s.** (*available*) en vente; (**up**) **for s.** à vendre; **to put up for s.** mettre en vente; **s. price** Com prix *m* de solde; **sales check** *or* **slip** Am reçu *m.* ◆**saleable** *a* Com vendable. ◆**salesclerk** *n* Am vendeur, -euse *mf.* ◆**salesman** *n* (*pl* -men) (*in shop*) vendeur *m;* (*travelling*) s. représentant *m* (de commerce). ◆**saleswoman** *n* (*pl* -women) vendeuse *f,* représentante *f* (de commerce).

salient ['seɪlɪənt] *a* (*point, fact*) marquant.
saliva [sə'laɪvə] *n* salive *f.* ◆**salivate** *vi* saliver.
sallow ['sæləʊ] *a* (-er, -est) jaunâtre.
sally ['sælɪ] *n* Mil sortie *f;* – *vi* **to s. forth** Fig sortir allègrement.
salmon ['sæmən] *n* saumon *m.*
salmonella [sælmə'nelə] *n* (*poisoning*) salmonellose *f.*
salon ['sælɒn] *n* **beauty/hairdressing s.** salon *m* de beauté/de coiffure.
saloon [sə'luːn] *n* Nau salon *m;* (*car*) berline *f;* (*bar*) Am bar *m;* **s. bar** (*of pub*) salle *f* chic.
salt [sɔːlt] *n* sel *m;* **bath salts** sels *mpl* de bain; – *a* (*water, beef etc*) salé; (*mine*) de sel; **s. free** sans sel; – *vt* saler. ◆**saltcellar** *n,* Am ◆**saltshaker** *n* salière *f.* ◆**salty** *a* (-ier, -iest) *a* salé.
salubrious [sə'luːbrɪəs] *a* salubre.
salutary ['sæljʊtərɪ] *a* salutaire.
salute [sə'luːt] *n* Mil salut *m;* (*of guns*) salve *f;* – *vt* (*greet*) & Mil saluer; – *vi* Mil faire un salut.
salvage ['sælvɪdʒ] *n* sauvetage *m* (**of** de); récupération *f* (**of** de); (*saved goods*) objets *mpl* sauvés; – *vt* (*save*) sauver (**from** de); (*old iron etc to be used again*) récupérer.
salvation [sæl'veɪʃ(ə)n] *n* salut *m.*
same [seɪm] *a* même; **the** (**very**) **s. house as** (exactement) la même maison que; – *pron* **the s.** le même, la même; **the s.** (**thing**) la même chose; **it's all the s. to me** ça m'est égal; **all** *or* **just the s.** tout de même; **to do the s.** en faire autant. ◆**—ness** *n* identité *f;* Pej monotonie *f.*
sampl/e ['sɑːmp(ə)l] *n* échantillon *m;* (*of blood*) prélèvement *m;* – *vt* (*wine, cheese etc*) déguster, goûter; (*product, recipe etc*) essayer; (*army life etc*) goûter de. ◆**—ing** *n* (*of wine*) dégustation *f.*
sanatorium [sænə'tɔːrɪəm] *n* sanatorium *m.*
sanctify ['sæŋktɪfaɪ] *vt* sanctifier. ◆**sanctity** *n* sainteté *f.* ◆**sanctuary** *n* Rel sanctuaire *m;* (*refuge*) & Pol asile *m;* (*for animals*) réserve *f.*
sanctimonious [sæŋktɪ'məʊnɪəs] *a* (*person, manner*) tartuffe.
sanction ['sæŋkʃ(ə)n] *n* (*approval, punishment*) sanction *f;* – *vt* (*approve*) sanctionner.
sand [sænd] *n* sable *m;* **the sands** (*beach*) la plage; – *vt* (*road*) sabler; **to s.** (**down**) (*wood etc*) poncer. ◆**sandbag** *n* sac *m* de sable. ◆**sandcastle** *n* château *m* de sable. ◆**sander** *n* (*machine*) ponceuse *f.* ◆**sandpaper** *n* papier *m* de verre; – *vt*

poncer. ◆**sandstone** n (rock) grès m.
◆**sandy** a (-ier, -iest) (beach) de sable;
(road, ground) sablonneux; (water)
sableux. **2** (hair) blond roux inv.
sandal ['sænd(ə)l] n sandale f.
sandwich ['sænwɪdʒ] **1** n sandwich m;
cheese/etc s. sandwich au fromage/etc. **2** vt
to s. (in) (fit in) intercaler; **sandwiched in
between** (caught) coincé entre.
sane [seɪn] a (-er, -est) (person) sain
(d'esprit); (idea, attitude) raisonnable.
sang [sæŋ] see sing.
sanguine ['sæŋgwɪn] a (hopeful) optimiste.
sanitarium [sænɪ'teərɪəm] n Am sanatorium
m.
sanitary ['sænɪtərɪ] a (fittings, conditions)
sanitaire; (clean) hygiènique. ◆**sani-
'tation** n hygiène f (publique); (plumbing
etc) installations fpl sanitaires.
sanity ['sænɪtɪ] n santé f mentale; (reason)
raison f.
sank [sæŋk] see sink².
Santa Claus ['sæntəklɔːz] n le père Noël.
sap [sæp] **1** n Bot & Fig sève f. **2** vt (-pp-)
(weaken) miner (énergie etc).
sapphire ['sæfaɪər] n (jewel, needle) saphir
m.
sarcasm ['sɑːkæz(ə)m] n sarcasme m.
◆**sar'castic** a sarcastique.
sardine [sɑː'diːn] n sardine f.
Sardinia [sɑː'dɪnɪə] n Sardaigne f.
sardonic [sɑː'dɒnɪk] a sardonique.
sash [sæʃ] n **1** (on dress) ceinture f; (of
mayor etc) écharpe f. **2 s. window** fenêtre f à
guillotine.
sat [sæt] see sit.
Satan ['seɪt(ə)n] n Satan m. ◆**sa'tanic** a
satanique.
satchel ['sætʃ(ə)l] n cartable m.
satellite ['sætəlaɪt] n satellite m; **s. (country)**
Pol pays m satellite.
satiate ['seɪʃɪeɪt] vt rassasier.
satin ['sætɪn] n satin m.
satire ['sætaɪər] n satire f (on contre).
◆**sa'tirical** a satirique. ◆**satirist** n
écrivain m satirique. ◆**satirize** vt faire la
satire de.
satisfaction [sætɪs'fækʃ(ə)n] n satisfaction
f. ◆**satisfactory** a satisfaisant. ◆**'satisfy**
vt satisfaire; (persuade, convince)
persuader (that que); (demand, condition)
satisfaire à; **to s. oneself as to/that**
s'assurer de/que; **satisfied with** satisfait de;
– vi donner satisfaction. ◆**'satisfying** a
satisfaisant; (food, meal) substantiel.
satsuma [sæt'suːmə] n (fruit) mandarine f.
saturate ['sætʃəreɪt] vt (fill) saturer (with

de); (soak) tremper. ◆**satu'ration** n saturation f.
Saturday ['sætədɪ] n samedi m.
sauce [sɔːs] n **1** sauce f; **tomato s.** sauce
tomate; **s. boat** saucière f. **2** (cheek) Fam
toupet m. ◆**saucy** a (-ier, -iest) (cheeky)
impertinent; (smart) Fam coquet.
saucepan ['sɔːspən] n casserole f.
saucer ['sɔːsər] n soucoupe f.
Saudi Arabia [saudɪə'reɪbɪə, Am sɔːdɪə-
'reɪbɪə] n Arabie f Séoudite.
sauna ['sɔːnə] n sauna m.
saunter ['sɔːntər] vi flâner.
sausage ['sɒsɪdʒ] n (cooked, for cooking)
saucisse f; (precooked, dried) saucisson m.
sauté ['səʊteɪ] a Culin sauté.
savage ['sævɪdʒ] a (primitive) sauvage;
(fierce) féroce; (brutal, cruel) brutal, sauvage; – n (brute) sauvage mf; – vt (of
animal, critic etc) attaquer (férocement).
◆**savagery** n (cruelty) sauvagerie f.
sav/e [seɪv] **1** vt sauver (from de); (keep)
garder, réserver; (money, time) économiser,
épargner; (stamps) collectionner; (prevent)
empêcher (from de); (problems, trouble)
éviter; **that will s. him** or **her (the bother of)
going** ça lui évitera d'y aller; **to s. up**
(money) économiser; – vi **to s. (up)** faire
des économies (**for sth, to buy sth** pour
(s')acheter qch); – n Fb arrêt m. **2** prep
(except) sauf. ◆**—ing** n (of time, money)
économie f, épargne f (**of** de); (rescue)
sauvetage m; (thrifty habit) l'épargne f; pl
(money) économies fpl; **savings bank** caisse
f d'épargne. ◆**saviour** n sauveur m.
saveloy ['sævəlɔɪ] n cervelas m.
savour ['seɪvər] n (taste, interest) saveur f; –
vt savourer. ◆**savoury** a (tasty)
savoureux; (not sweet) Culin salé; **not very
s.** (neighbourhood) Fig peu recommandable.
saw¹ [sɔː] n scie f; – vt (pt sawed, pp sawn or
sawed) scier; **to s. off** scier; **a sawn-off** or
Am **sawed-off shotgun** un fusil à canon scié.
◆**sawdust** n sciure f. ◆**sawmill** n scierie
f.
saw² [sɔː] see see¹.
saxophone ['sæksəfəʊn] n saxophone m.
say [seɪ] vt (pt & pp said [sed]) dire (**to** à, **that**
que); (prayer) faire, dire; (of dial etc)
marquer; **to s. again** répéter; **it is said that**
... on dit que...; **what do you s. to a
walk?** que dirais-tu d'une promenade?;
(let's) **s. tomorrow** disons demain; **to s. the
least** c'est le moins que l'on puisse dire; **to
s. nothing of** ... sans parler de .... **that's
to s.** c'est-à-dire; – vi dire; **you don't s.!**

Fam sans blague!; **I s.!** dites donc!; **s.!** *Am Fam* dis donc!; − *n* **to have one's s.** dire ce que l'on a à dire, s'exprimer; **to have a lot of s.** avoir beaucoup d'influence; **to have no s.** ne pas avoir voix au chapitre (**in** pour). ◆**—ing** *n* proverbe *m.*

scab [skæb] *n* **1** *Med* croûte *f.* **2** (*blackleg*) *Fam* jaune *m.*

scaffold ['skæfəld] *n* échafaudage *m*; (*gallows*) échafaud *m.* ◆**—ing** *n* échafaudage *m.*

scald [skɔːld] *vt* (*burn, cleanse*) ébouillanter; (*sterilize*) stériliser; − *n* brûlure *f.*

scale [skeɪl] **1** *n* (*of map, wages etc*) échelle *f*; (*of numbers*) série *f*; *Mus* gamme *f*; **on a small/large s.** sur une petite/grande échelle; − *a* (*drawing*) à l'échelle; **s. model** modèle *m* réduit; − *vt* **to s. down** réduire (proportionnellement). **2** *n* (*on fish*) écaille *f*; (*dead skin*) *Med* squame *f*; (*on teeth*) tartre *m*; − *vt* (*teeth*) détartrer. **3** *vt* (*wall*) escalader.

scales [skeɪlz] *npl* (*for weighing*) balance *f*; (**bathroom**) **s.** pèse-personne *m*; (**baby**) **s.** pèse-bébé *m.*

scallion ['skæljən] *n* (*onion*) *Am* ciboule *f.*

scallop ['skɒləp] *n* coquille *f* Saint-Jacques.

scalp [skælp] *n Med* cuir *m* chevelu; − *vt* (*cut off too much hair from*) *Fig Hum* tondre (*qn*).

scalpel ['skælp(ə)l] *n* bistouri *m*, scalpel *m.*

scam [skæm] *n* (*swindle*) *Am Fam* escroquerie *f.*

scamp [skæmp] *n* coquin, -ine *mf.*

scamper ['skæmpər] *vi* **to s. off** *or* **away** détaler.

scampi ['skæmpɪ] *npl* gambas *fpl.*

scan [skæn] **1** *vt* (**-nn-**) (*look at briefly*) parcourir (des yeux); (*scrutinize*) scruter; (*poetry*) scander; (*of radar*) balayer. **2** *n* **to have a s.** (*of pregnant woman*) passer une échographie.

scandal ['skænd(ə)l] *n* (*disgrace*) scandale *m*; (*gossip*) médisances *fpl*; **to cause a s.** (*of film, book etc*) causer un scandale; (*of attitude, conduct*) faire (du) scandale. ◆**scandalize** *vt* scandaliser. ◆**scandalous** *a* scandaleux.

Scandinavia [skændɪ'neɪvɪə] *n* Scandinavie *f.* ◆**Scandinavian** *a* & *n* scandinave (*mf*).

scanner ['skænər] *n* (*device*) *Med* scanner *m.*

scant [skænt] *a* (*meal, amount*) insuffisant; **s. attention/regard** peu d'attention/de cas. ◆**scantily** *adv* insuffisamment; **s. dressed** à peine vêtu. ◆**scanty** *a* (**-ier, -iest**) insuffisant; (*bikini*) minuscule.

scapegoat ['skeɪpgəʊt] *n* bouc *m* émissaire.

scar [skɑːr] *n* cicatrice *f*; − *vt* (**-rr-**) marquer d'une cicatrice; *Fig* marquer.

scarce [skeəs] *a* (**-er, -est**) (*food, people, book etc*) rare; **to make oneself s.** se tenir à l'écart. ◆**scarcely** *adv* à peine. ◆**scarceness** *n*, ◆**scarcity** *n* (*shortage*) pénurie *f*; (*rarity*) rareté *f.*

scare [skeər] *n* peur *f*; **to give s.o. a s.** faire peur à qn; **bomb s.** alerte *f* à la bombe; − *vt* faire peur à; **to s. off** (*person*) faire fuir; (*animal*) effaroucher. ◆**scared** *a* effrayé; **to be s.** (**stiff**) avoir (très) peur. ◆**scarecrow** *n* épouvantail *m.* ◆**scaremonger** *n* alarmiste *mf.* ◆**scary** *a* (**-ier, -iest**) *Fam* qui fait peur.

scarf [skɑːf] *n* (*pl* **scarves**) (*long*) écharpe *f*; (*square, for women*) foulard *m.*

scarlet ['skɑːlət] *a* écarlate; **s. fever** scarlatine *f.*

scathing ['skeɪðɪŋ] *a* (*remark etc*) acerbe; **to be s. about** critiquer de façon acerbe.

scatter ['skætər] *vt* (*disperse*) disperser (*foule, nuages etc*); (*dot or throw about*) éparpiller; (*spread*) répandre; − *vi* (*of crowd*) se disperser. ◆**—ing** *n* **a s. of houses/etc** quelques maisons/etc dispersées. ◆**scatterbrain** *n* écervelé, -ée *mf.* ◆**scatty** *a* (**-ier, -iest**) *Fam* écervelé, farfelu.

scaveng/e ['skævɪndʒ] *vi* fouiller dans les ordures (**for** pour trouver). ◆**—er** *n Pej* clochard, -arde *mf* (qui fait les poubelles).

scenario [sɪ'nɑːrɪəʊ] *n* (*pl* **-os**) *Cin* & *Fig* scénario *m.*

scene [siːn] *n* (*setting, fuss*) & *Th* scène *f*; (*of crime, accident etc*) lieu *m*; (*situation*) situation *f*; (*incident*) incident *m*; (*view*) vue *f*; **behind the scenes** *Th* & *Fig* dans les coulisses; **on the s.** sur les lieux; **to make** *or* **create a s.** faire une scène (à qn). ◆**scenery** *n* paysage *m*, décor *m*; *Th* décor(s) *m*(*pl*). ◆**scenic** *a* (*beauty etc*) pittoresque.

scent [sent] *n* (*fragrance, perfume*) parfum *m*; (*animal's track*) & *Fig* piste *f*; − *vt* parfumer (**with** de); (*smell, sense*) flairer.

sceptic ['skeptɪk] *a n* sceptique (*mf*). ◆**sceptical** *a* sceptique. ◆**scepticism** *n* scepticisme *m.*

sceptre ['septər] *n* sceptre *m.*

schedul/e ['ʃedjuːl, *Am* 'skedjuːl] *n* (*of work etc*) programme *m*; (*timetable*) horaire *m*; (*list*) liste *f*; **to be behind s.** (*of person, train*) avoir du retard; **to be on s.** (*on time*) être à l'heure; (*up to date*) être à jour; **ahead of s.** en avance; **according to s.** comme prévu; −

scheme 588 scout

vt (*plan*) prévoir; (*event*) fixer le programme *or* l'horaire de. ◆**—ed** *a* (*planned*) prévu; (*service, flight*) régulier; **she's s. to leave at 8** elle doit partir à 8 h.

schem/e [skiːm] *n* plan *m* (**to do** pour faire); (*idea*) idée *f*; (*dishonest trick*) combine *f*, manœuvre *f*; (*arrangement*) arrangement *m*; – *vi* manœuvrer. ◆**—ing** *a* intrigant; – *npl Pej* machinations *fpl*. ◆**—er** *n* intrigant, -ante *mf*.

schizophrenic [skɪtsəʊ'frenɪk] *a* & *n* schizophrène (*mf*).

scholar ['skɒlər] *n* érudit, -ite *mf*; (*specialist*) spécialiste *mf*; (*grant holder*) boursier, -ière *mf*. ◆**scholarly** *a* érudit. ◆**scholarship** *n* érudition *f*; (*grant*) bourse *f* (d'études). ◆**scho'lastic** *a* scolaire.

school [skuːl] *n* école *f*; (*teaching, lessons*) classe *f*; *Univ Am* faculté *f*; (*within university*) institut *m*, département *m*; **in** *or* **at s.** à l'école; **secondary s.,** *Am* **high s.** collège *m*, lycée *m*; **public s.** école *f* privée; *Am* école publique; **s. of motoring** auto-école *f*; **summer s.** cours *mpl* d'été *or* de vacances; – *a* (*year, equipment etc*) scolaire; (*hours*) de classe; **s. fees** frais *mpl* de scolarité. ◆**—ing** *n* (*learning*) instruction *f*; (*attendance*) scolarité *f*. ◆**schoolboy** *n* écolier *m*. ◆**schooldays** *npl* années *fpl* d'école. ◆**schoolgirl** *n* écolière *f*. ◆**school-house** *n* école *f*. ◆**school-'leaver** *n* jeune *mf* qui a terminé ses études secondaires. ◆**schoolmaster** *n* (*primary*) instituteur *m*; (*secondary*) professeur *m*. ◆**schoolmate** *n* camarade *mf* de classe. ◆**schoolmistress** *n* institutrice *f*; professeur *m*. ◆**schoolteacher** *n* (*primary*) instituteur, -trice *mf*; (*secondary*) professeur *m*.

schooner ['skuːnər] *n Nau* goélette *f*.

science ['saɪəns] *n* science *f*; **to study s.** étudier les sciences; – *a* (*subject*) scientifique; (*teacher*) de sciences; **s. fiction** science-fiction *f*. ◆**scien'tific** *a* scientifique. ◆**scientist** *n* scientifique *mf*.

scintillating ['sɪntɪleɪtɪŋ] *a* (*conversation, wit*) brillant.

scissors ['sɪzəz] *npl* ciseaux *mpl*; **a pair of s.** une paire de ciseaux.

sclerosis [sklɪ'rəʊsɪs] *n Med* sclérose *f*; **multiple s.** sclérose en plaques.

scoff [skɒf] **1** *vi* **to s. at** se moquer de. **2** *vti* (*eat*) *Fam* bouffer.

scold [skəʊld] *vt* gronder, réprimander (**for doing** pour avoir fait). ◆**—ing** *n* réprimande *f*.

scone [skəʊn, skɒn] *n* petit pain *m* au lait.

scoop [skuːp] *n* (*shovel*) pelle *f* (à main);

(*spoon-shaped*) *Culin* cuiller *f*; *Journ* exclusivité *f*; **at one s.** d'un seul coup; – *vt* (*prizes*) rafler; **to s. out** (*hollow out*) (é)vider; **to s. up** ramasser (avec une pelle *or* une cuiller).

scoot [skuːt] *vi* (*rush, leave*) *Fam* filer.

scooter ['skuːtər] *n* (*child's*) trottinette *f*; (*motorcycle*) scooter *m*.

scope [skəʊp] *n* (*range*) étendue *f*; (*of mind*) envergure *f*; (*competence*) compétence(s) *f(pl)*; (*limits*) limites *fpl*; **s. for sth/for doing** (*opportunity*) des possibilités *fpl* de qch/de faire; **the s. of one's activity** le champ de ses activités.

scorch [skɔːtʃ] *vt* (*linen, grass etc*) roussir; – *n* **s.** (*mark*) brûlure *f* légère. ◆**—ing** *a* (*day*) torride; (*sun, sand*) brûlant. ◆**—er** *n Fam* journée *f* torride.

score¹ [skɔːr] *n Sp* score *m*; *Cards* marque *f*; *Mus* partition *f*; (*of film*) musique *f*; **a s. to settle** *Fig* un compte à régler; **on that s.** (*in that respect*) à cet égard; – *vt* (*point, goal*) marquer; (*exam mark*) avoir; (*success*) remporter; *Mus* orchestrer; – *vi* marquer un point *or* un but; (*keep score*) marquer les points. ◆**scoreboard** *n Sp* tableau *m* d'affichage. ◆**scorer** *n Sp* marqueur *m*.

score² [skɔːr] *n* (*twenty*) vingt; **a s. of** une vingtaine de; **scores of** *Fig* un grand nombre de.

score³ [skɔːr] *vt* (*cut*) rayer; (*paper*) marquer.

scorn [skɔːn] *vt* mépriser; – *n* mépris *m*. ◆**scornful** *a* méprisant; **to be s. of** mépriser. ◆**scornfully** *adv* avec mépris.

Scorpio ['skɔːpɪəʊ] *n* (*sign*) le Scorpion.

scorpion ['skɔːpɪən] *n* scorpion *m*.

Scot [skɒt] *n* Écossais, -aise *mf*. ◆**Scotland** *n* Écosse *f*. ◆**Scotsman** *n* (*pl* -men) Écossais *m*. ◆**Scotswoman** *n* (*pl* -women) Écossaise *f*. ◆**Scottish** *a* écossais.

scotch [skɒtʃ] **1** *a* **s. tape®** *Am* scotch® *m*. **2** *vt* (*rumour*) étouffer; (*attempt*) faire échouer.

Scotch [skɒtʃ] *n* (*whisky*) scotch *m*.

scot-free [skɒt'friː] *adv* sans être puni.

scoundrel ['skaʊndr(ə)l] *n* vaurien *m*.

scour ['skaʊər] *vt* (*pan*) récurer; (*streets etc*) *Fig* parcourir (**for** à la recherche de). ◆**—er** *n* tampon *m* à récurer.

scourge [skɜːdʒ] *n* fléau *m*.

scout [skaʊt] **1** *n* (*soldier*) éclaireur *m*; (*boy*) **s.** scout *m*, éclaireur *m*; **girl s.** *Am* éclaireuse *f*; **s. camp** camp *m* scout. **2** *vi* **to**

s. round for (*look for*) chercher. ◆**—ing** *n* scoutisme *m*.

scowl [skaul] *vi* se renfrogner; **to s. at s.o.** regarder qn d'un air mauvais. ◆**—ing** *a* renfrogné.

scraggy ['skrægɪ] *a* (**-ier, -iest**) (*bony*) osseux, maigrichon; (*unkempt*) débraillé.

scram [skræm] *vi* (**-mm-**) *Fam* filer.

scramble ['skræmb(ə)l] **1** *vi* **to s. for** se ruer vers; **to s. up** (*climb*) grimper; **to s. through** traverser avec difficulté; – *n* ruée *f* (**for** vers). **2** *vt* (*egg, message*) brouiller.

scrap [skræp] **1** *n* (*piece*) petit morceau *m* (**of** de); (*of information, news*) fragment *m*; *pl* (*food*) restes *mpl*; **not a s. of** (*truth etc*) pas un brin de; **s. paper** (papier *m*) brouillon *m*. **2** *n* (*metal*) ferraille *f*; **to sell for s.** vendre à la casse; – *a* (*yard, heap*) de ferraille; **s. dealer, s. merchant** marchand *m* de ferraille; **s. iron** ferraille *f*; **on the s. heap** *Fig* au rebut; – *vt* (**-pp-**) envoyer à la ferraille; (*unwanted object, idea, plan*) *Fig* mettre au rancart. **3** *n* (*fight*) *Fam* bagarre *f*. ◆**scrapbook** *n* album *m* (*pour collages etc*).

scrap/e [skreɪp] *vt* racler, gratter; (*skin*) *Med* érafler; **to s. away** *or* **off** (*mud etc*) racler; **to s. together** (*money, people*) réunir (difficilement); – *vi* **to s. against** frotter contre; **to s. along** *Fig* se débrouiller; **to s. through** (*in exam*) réussir de justesse; – *n* raclement *m*; éraflure *f*; **to get into a s.** *Fam* s'attirer des ennuis. ◆**—ings** *npl* raclures *fpl*. ◆**—er** *n* racloir *m*.

scratch [skrætʃ] *n* (*mark, injury*) éraflure *f*; (*on glass*) rayure *f*; **to have a s.** (*scratch oneself*) *Fam* se gratter; **to start from s.** (re)partir de zéro; **to be/come up to s.** être/se montrer à la hauteur; – *vt* (*to relieve an itch*) gratter; (*skin, wall etc*) érafler; (*glass*) rayer; (*with claw*) griffer; (*one's name*) graver (**on** sur); – *vi* (*relieve an itch*) se gratter; (*of cat etc*) griffer; (*of pen*) gratter, accrocher.

scrawl [skrɔːl] *vt* gribouiller; – *n* gribouillis *m*.

scrawny ['skrɔːnɪ] *a* (**-ier, -iest**) (*bony*) osseux, maigrichon.

scream [skriːm] *vti* crier, hurler; **to s. at s.o.** crier après qn; **to s. with pain/etc** hurler de douleur/etc; – *n* cri *m* (perçant).

screech [skriːtʃ] *vi* crier, hurler; (*of brakes*) hurler; – *n* cri *m*; hurlement *m*.

screen [skriːn] **1** *n* Fig masque *m*; (**folding**) **s.** paravent *m*. **2** *vt* (*hide*) cacher (**from s.o.** à qn); (*protect*) protéger (**from** de); (*a film*) projeter; (*visitors, documents*)

filtrer; (*for cancer etc*) *Med* faire subir un test de dépistage à (qn) (**for** pour). ◆**—ing** *n* (*of film*) projection *f*; (*selection*) tri *m*; (*medical examination*) (test *m* de) dépistage *m*. ◆**screenplay** *n* *Cin* scénario *m*.

screw [skruː] *n* vis *f*; – *vt* visser (**to** à); **to s. down** *or* **on** visser; **to s. off** dévisser; **to s. up** (*paper*) chiffonner; (*eyes*) plisser; (*mess up*) *Sl* gâcher; **to s. one's face up** grimacer. ◆**screwball** *n* & *a* *Am* *Fam* cinglé, -ée (*mf*). ◆**screwdriver** *n* tournevis *m*. ◆**screwy** *a* (**-ier, -iest**) (*idea, person etc*) farfelu.

scribble ['skrɪb(ə)l] *vti* griffonner; – *n* griffonnage *m*.

scribe [skraɪb] *n* scribe *m*.

scrimmage ['skrɪmɪdʒ] *n* *Fb* *Am* mêlée *f*.

script [skrɪpt] *n* (*of film*) scénario *m*; (*of play*) texte *m*; (*in exam*) copie *f*. ◆**scriptwriter** *n* *Cin* scénariste *mf*, dialoguiste *mf*; *TV Rad* dialoguiste *mf*.

Scripture ['skrɪptʃər] *n* *Rel* Écriture *f* (sainte).

scroll [skrəʊl] *n* rouleau *m* (de parchemin); (*book*) manuscrit *m*.

scrooge [skruːdʒ] *n* (*miser*) harpagon *m*.

scroung/e [skraʊndʒ] *vt* (*meal*) se faire payer (**off** *or* **from s.o.** par qn); (*steal*) piquer (**off** *or* **from s.o.** à qn); **to s. money off** *or* **from** taper; – *vi* vivre en parasite; (*beg*) quémander; **to s. around for** *Pej* chercher. ◆**—er** *n* parasite *m*.

scrub [skrʌb] **1** *vt* (**-bb-**) frotter, nettoyer (à la brosse); (*pan*) récurer; (*cancel*) *Fig* annuler; **to s. out** (*erase*) *Fig* effacer; – *vi* (*scrub floors*) frotter les planchers; **scrubbing brush** brosse *f* dure; – *n* **to give sth a s.** frotter qch; **s. brush** *Am* brosse *f* dure. **2** *n* (*land*) broussailles *fpl*.

scruff [skrʌf] *n* **1 by the s. of the neck** par la peau du cou. **2** (*person*) *Fam* individu *m* débraillé. ◆**scruffy** *a* (**-ier, -iest**) (*untidy*) négligé; (*dirty*) malpropre.

scrum [skrʌm] *n* *Rugby* mêlée *f*.

scrumptious ['skrʌmpʃəs] *a* *Fam* super bon, succulent.

scruple ['skruːp(ə)l] *n* scrupule *m*. ◆**scrupulous** *a* scrupuleux. ◆**scrupulously** *adv* (*conscientiously*) scrupuleusement; (*completely*) absolument.

scrutinize ['skruːtɪnaɪz] *vt* scruter. ◆**scrutiny** *n* examen *m* minutieux.

scuba ['skjuːbə, *Am* 'skuːbə] *n* scaphandre *m* autonome; **s. diving** la plongée sous-marine.

scuff [skʌf] *vt* **to s. (up)** (*scrape*) érafler.

scuffle ['skʌf(ə)l] *n* bagarre *f*.

scullery ['skʌlərɪ] n arrière-cuisine f.

sculpt [skʌlpt] vti sculpter. ◆**sculptor** n sculpteur m. ◆**sculpture** n (art, object) sculpture f; – vti sculpter.

scum [skʌm] n 1 (on liquid) écume f. 2 Pej (people) racaille f; (person) salaud m; **the s. of** (society etc) la lie de.

scupper ['skʌpər] vt (plan) Fam saboter.

scurf [skɜːf] n pellicules fpl.

scurrilous ['skʌrɪləs] a (criticism, attack) haineux, violent et grossier.

scurry ['skʌrɪ] vi (rush) se précipiter, courir; **to s. off** décamper.

scuttle ['skʌt(ə)l] 1 vt (ship) saborder. 2 vi to **s. off** filer.

scythe [saɪð] n faux f.

sea [siː] n mer f; (out) **at s.** en mer; **by s.** par mer; **by** or **beside the s.** au bord de la mer; **to be all at s.** Fig nager complètement; – a (level, breeze) de la mer; (water, fish) de mer; (air, salt) marin; (battle, power) naval; (route) maritime; **s. bed, s. floor** fond m de la mer; **s. lion** (animal) otarie f. ◆**seaboard** n littoral m. ◆**seafarer** n marin m. ◆**seafood** n fruits mpl de mer. ◆**seafront** n front m de mer. ◆**seagull** n mouette f. ◆**seaman** n (pl -men) marin m. ◆**seaplane** n hydravion m. ◆**seaport** n port m de mer. ◆**seashell** n coquillage m. ◆**seashore** n bord m de la mer. ◆**seasick** a to be **s.** avoir le mal de mer. ◆**seasickness** n mal m de mer. ◆**seaside** n bord m de la mer; – a (town, holiday) au bord de la mer; ◆**seaway** n route f maritime. ◆**seaweed** n algue(s) f(pl). ◆**seaworthy** a (ship) en état de naviguer.

seal [siːl] 1 n (animal) phoque m. 2 n (mark, design) sceau m; (on letter) cachet m (de cire); (putty for sealing) joint m; – vt (document, container) sceller; (with wax) cacheter; (stick down) coller; (with putty) boucher; (s.o.'s fate) Fig décider de; **to s. off** (room etc) interdire l'accès de; **to s. off a house/district** (of police, troops) boucler une maison/un quartier.

seam [siːm] n (in cloth etc) couture f; (of coal, quartz etc) veine f.

seamy ['siːmɪ] a (-ier, -iest) **the s. side** le côté peu reluisant (**of** de).

séance ['seɪɑːns] n séance f de spiritisme.

search [sɜːtʃ] n (quest) recherche f (**for** de); (of person, place) fouille f; **in s. of** à la recherche de; **s. party** équipe f de secours; – vt (person, place) fouiller (**for** pour trouver); (study) examiner (documents etc); **to s. (through)** one's papers/etc for sth chercher qch dans ses papiers/etc; – vi chercher; **to s. for sth** chercher qch. ◆**—ing** a (look) pénétrant; (examination) minutieux. ◆**searchlight** n projecteur m.

season ['siːz(ə)n] 1 n saison f; **the festive s.** la période des fêtes; **in the peak s., in the high s.** en pleine or haute saison; **in the low** or **off s.** en basse saison; **a Truffaut s.** Cin une rétrospective Truffaut; **s. ticket** carte f d'abonnement. 2 vt (food) assaisonner; **highly seasoned** (dish) relevé. ◆**—ed** a (worker) expérimenté; (soldier) aguerri. ◆**—ing** n Culin assaisonnement m. ◆**seasonable** a (weather) de saison. ◆**seasonal** a saisonnier.

seat [siːt] n (for sitting, centre) & Pol siège m; (on train, bus) banquette f; (place) place f; (of trousers) fond m; **to take** or **have a s.** s'asseoir; **in the hot s.** (in difficult position) Fam sur la sellette; **s. belt** ceinture f de sécurité; – vt (at table) placer (qn); (on one's lap) asseoir (qn); **the room seats 50** la salle a 50 places (assises); **be seated!** asseyez-vous! ◆**—ed** a (sitting) assis. ◆**—ing** n s. (room) (seats) places fpl assises; **the s. arrangements** la disposition des places; **s. capacity** nombre m de places assises. ◆**—er** a & n two-s. (car) voiture f à deux places.

secateurs [sekə'tɜːz] npl sécateur m.

secede [sɪ'siːd] vi faire sécession. ◆**secession** n sécession f.

secluded [sɪ'kluːdɪd] a (remote) isolé. ◆**seclusion** n solitude f.

second¹ ['sekənd] a deuxième, second; **every s. week** une semaine sur deux; **in s.** (gear) Aut en seconde; **s. to none** sans pareil; **s. in command** second m; Mil commandant m en second; – adv (to say) deuxièmement; **to come s.** Sp se classer deuxième; **the s. biggest** le deuxième en ordre de grandeur; **the s. richest country** le deuxième pays le plus riche; **my s. best** (choice) mon deuxième choix; – n (person, object) deuxième mf, second, -onde mf; **Louis the S.** Louis Deux; pl (goods) Com articles mpl de second choix; – vt (motion) appuyer. ◆**s.-'class** a (product) de qualité inférieure; (ticket) Rail de seconde (classe); (mail) non urgent. ◆**s.-'rate** a médiocre. ◆**secondly** adv deuxièmement.

second² ['sekənd] n (unit of time) seconde f; **s. hand** (of clock, watch) trotteuse f.

second³ [sɪ'kɒnd] vt (employee) détacher (**to** à). ◆**—ment** n détachement m; **on s.** en (position de) détachement (**to** à).

secondary ['sekəndərɪ] a secondaire.

secondhand [sekənd'hænd] 1 a & adv (not

new) d'occasion. **2** *a* (*report, news*) de seconde main.

secret ['siːkrɪt] *a* secret; – *n* secret *m*; **in s.** en secret; **an open s.** le secret de Polichinelle. ◆**secrecy** *n* (*discretion, silence*) secret *m*; **in s.** en secret. ◆**secretive** *a* (*person*) cachottier; (*organization*) qui a le goût du secret; **to be s. about** faire un mystère de; (*organization*) être très discret sur. ◆**secretively** *adv* en catimini.

secretary ['sekrət(ə)rɪ] *n* secrétaire *mf*; **Foreign S.,** *Am* **S. of State** = ministre *m* des Affaires étrangères. ◆**secre'tarial** *a* (*work*) de secrétaire, de secrétariat; (*school*) de secrétariat. ◆**secre'tariat** *n* (*in international organization*) secrétariat *m*.

secrete [sɪ'kriːt] *vt* *Med Biol* sécréter. ◆**sec'retion** *n* sécrétion *f*.

sect [sekt] *n* secte *f*. ◆**sec'tarian** *a & n* *Pej* sectaire (*mf*).

section ['sekʃ(ə)n] *n* (*of road, book, wood etc*) section *f*; (*of town, country*) partie *f*; (*of machine, furniture*) élément *m*; (*department*) section *f*; (*in store*) rayon *m*; **the sports/etc s.** (*of newspaper*) la page des sports/etc; – *vt* **to s. off** (*separate*) séparer.

sector ['sektər] *n* secteur *m*.

secular ['sekjʊlər] *a* (*teaching etc*) laïque; (*music, art*) profane.

secure [sɪ'kjʊər] **1** *a* (*person, valuables*) en sûreté, en sécurité; (*in one's mind*) tranquille; (*place*) sûr; (*solid, firm*) solide; (*door, window*) bien fermé; (*certain*) assuré; **s. from** à l'abri de; (*emotionally*) s. sécurisé; – *vt* (*fasten*) attacher; (*window etc*) bien fermer; (*success, future etc*) assurer; **to s. against** protéger de. **2** *vt* (*obtain*) procurer (*sth for s.o.* qch à qn); **to s. sth** (*for oneself*) se procurer qch. ◆**securely** *adv* (*firmly*) solidement; (*safely*) en sûreté. ◆**security** *n* sécurité *f*; (*for loan, bail*) caution *f*; **s. firm** société *f* de surveillance; **s. guard** agent *m* de sécurité; (*transferring money*) convoyeur *m* de fonds.

sedan [sɪ'dæn] *n* (*saloon*) *Aut Am* berline *f*.

sedate [sɪ'deɪt] **1** *a* calme. **2** *vt* mettre sous calmants. ◆**sedation** *n* **under s.** sous calmants. ◆**'sedative** *n* calmant *m*.

sedentary ['sedəntərɪ] *a* sédentaire.

sediment ['sedɪmənt] *n* sédiment *m*.

sedition [sə'dɪʃ(ə)n] *n* sédition *f*. ◆**seditious** *a* séditieux.

seduce [sɪ'djuːs] *vt* séduire. ◆**seducer** *n* séducteur, -trice *mf*. ◆**seduction** *n* séduc-

tion *f*. ◆**seductive** *a* (*person, offer*) séduisant.

see [siː] *vti* (*pt* saw, *pp* seen) voir; **we'll s. on** verra (bien); **I s.!** je vois!; **I can s.** (*clearly*) j'y vois clair; **I saw him run(ning)** je l'ai vu courir; **to s. reason** entendre raison; **to s. the joke** comprendre la plaisanterie; **s. who it is** va voir qui c'est; **s. you (later)!** à tout à l'heure!; **s. you (soon)!** à bientôt!; **to s. about** (*deal with*) s'occuper de; (*consider*) songer à; **to s. in the New Year** fêter la Nouvelle Année; **to s. s.o. off** accompagner qn (*à la gare etc*); **to s. s.o. out** raccompagner qn; **to s. through** (*task*) mener à bonne fin; **to s. s.o. through** (*be enough for*) suffire à qn; **to s. through s.o.** deviner le jeu de qn; **to s. to** (*deal with*) s'occuper de; (*mend*) réparer; **to s. (to it) that** (*attend*) veiller à ce que (+ *sub*); (*check*) s'assurer que; **to s. s.o. to** (*accompany*) raccompagner qn à. ◆**s.-through** *a* (*dress etc*) transparent.

see² [siː] *n* (*of bishop*) siège *m* (épiscopal).

seed [siːd] *n* *Agr* graine *f*; (*in grape*) pépin *m*; (*source*) *Fig* germe *m*; *Tennis* tête *f* de série; **seed(s)** (*for sowing*) *Agr* graines *fpl*; **to go to s.** (*of lettuce etc*) monter en graine. ◆**seedbed** *n* *Bot* semis *m*; (*of rebellion etc*) *Fig* foyer *m* (**of** de). ◆**seedling** *n* (*plant*) semis *m*.

seedy ['siːdɪ] *a* (**-ier, -iest**) miteux. ◆**seediness** *n* aspect *m* miteux.

seeing ['siːɪŋ] *conj* **s. (that)** vu que.

seek [siːk] *vt* (*pt & pp* sought) chercher (**to do** à faire); (*ask for*) demander (**from** à); **to s. (after)** rechercher; **to s. out** aller trouver.

seem [siːm] *vi* sembler (**to do** faire); **it seems that** . . . (*impression*) il semble que . . . (+ *sub or indic*); (*rumour*) il paraît que . . . ; **it seems to me that** . . . il me semble que . . . ; **we s. to know each other** il me semble qu'on se connaît; **I can't s. to do it** je n'arrive pas à le faire. ◆**-ing** *a* apparent. ◆**-ingly** *adv* apparemment.

seemly ['siːmlɪ] *a* convenable.

seen [siːn] *see* see¹.

seep [siːp] *vi* (*ooze*) suinter; **to s. into** s'infiltrer dans. ◆**-age** *n* suintement *m*; infiltration(s) *f(pl)* (**into** dans); (*leak*) fuite *f*.

seesaw ['siːsɔː] *n* (jeu *m* de) bascule *f*.

seethe [siːð] *vi* **to s. with anger** bouillir de colère; **to s. with people** grouiller de monde.

segment ['segmənt] *n* segment *m*; (*of orange*) quartier *m*.

segregate ['segrɪgeɪt] *vt* séparer; (**racially**)

segregated (*school*) où se pratique la ségrégation raciale. ◆**segre'gation** *n* ségrégation *f*.

seize [siːz] **1** *vt* saisir; (*power, land*) s'emparer de; – *vi* **to s. on** (*offer etc*) saisir. **2** *vi* **to s. up** (*of engine*) (se) gripper. ◆**seizure** [-ʒər] *n* (*of goods etc*) saisie *f*; Mil prise *f*; Med crise *f*.

seldom ['seldəm] *adv* rarement.

select [sɪ'lekt] *vt* choisir (**from** parmi); (*candidates, pupils etc*) & Sp sélectionner; – *a* (*chosen*) choisi; (*exclusive*) sélect, chic *inv*. ◆**selection** *n* sélection *f*. ◆**selective** *a* (*memory, recruitment etc*) sélectif; (*person*) qui opère un choix; (*choosey*) difficile.

self [self] *n* (*pl* **selves**) **the s.** Phil le moi; **he's back to his old s.** Fam il est redevenu lui-même. ◆**s.-a'ssurance** *n* assurance *f*. ◆**s.-a'ssured** *a* sûr de soi. ◆**s.-'catering** *a* où l'on fait la cuisine soi-même. ◆**s.-'centred** *a* égocentrique. ◆**s.-'cleaning** *a* (*oven*) autonettoyant. ◆**s.-con'fessed** *a* (*liar*) de son propre aveu. ◆**s.-'confident** *a* sûr de soi. ◆**s.-'conscious** *a* gêné. ◆**s.-'consciousness** *n* gêne *f*. ◆**s.-con'tained** *a* (*flat*) indépendant. ◆**s.-con'trol** *n* maîtrise *f* de soi. ◆**s.-de'feating** *a* qui a un effet contraire à celui qui est recherché. ◆**s.-de'fence** *n* Jur légitime défense *f*. ◆**s.-de'nial** *n* abnégation *f*. ◆**s.-determi'nation** *n* autodétermination *f*. ◆**s.-'discipline** *n* autodiscipline *f*. ◆**s.-em'ployed** *a* qui travaille à son compte. ◆**s.-es'teem** *n* amour-propre *m*. ◆**s.-'evident** *a* évident, qui va de soi. ◆**s.-ex'planatory** *a* qui tombe sous le sens, qui se passe d'explication. ◆**s.-'governing** *a* autonome. ◆**s.-im'portant** *a* suffisant. ◆**s.-in'dulgent** *a* qui ne se refuse rien. ◆**s.-'interest** *n* intérêt *m* (personnel). ◆**s.-o'pinionated** *a* entêté. ◆**s.-'pity** *n* **to feel s.-pity** s'apitoyer sur son propre sort. ◆**s.-'portrait** *n* autoportrait *m*. ◆**s.-po'ssessed** *a* assuré. ◆**s.-raising** or Am **s.-rising 'flour** *n* farine *f* à levure. ◆**s.-re'liant** *a* indépendant. ◆**s.-re'spect** *n* amour-propre *m*. ◆**s.-re'specting** *a* qui se respecte. ◆**s.-'righteous** *a* pharisaïque. ◆**s.-'sacrifice** *n* abnégation *f*. ◆**s.-'satisfied** *a* content de soi. ◆**s.-'service** *n* & *a* libre-service (*m inv*). ◆**s.-'styled** *a* soi-disant. ◆**s.-su'fficient** *a* indépendant, qui a son indépendance. ◆**s.-su'p-**porting *a* financièrement indépendant. ◆**s.-'taught** *a* autodidacte.

selfish ['selfɪʃ] *a* égoïste; (*motive*) intéressé. ◆**selfless** *a* désintéressé. ◆**selfishness** *n* égoïsme *m*.

selfsame ['selfseɪm] *a* même.

sell [sel] *vt* (*pt & pp* **sold**) vendre; (*idea etc*) Fig faire accepter; **she sold me it for twenty pounds** elle me l'a vendu vingt livres; **to s. back** revendre; **to s. off** liquider; **to have** or **be sold out of** (*cheese etc*) n'avoir plus de; **this book is sold out** ce livre est épuisé; – *vi* se vendre; (*of idea etc*) Fig être accepté; **to s. up** vendre sa maison; Com vendre son affaire; **selling price** prix *m* de vente. ◆**seller** *n* vendeur, -euse *mf*. ◆**sellout** *n* **1** (*betrayal*) trahison *f*. **2 it was a s.** Th Cin tous les billets ont été vendus.

sellotape® ['seləteɪp] *n* scotch® *m*; – *vt* scotcher.

semantic [sɪ'mæntɪk] *a* sémantique. ◆**semantics** *n* sémantique *f*.

semaphore ['seməfɔːr] *n* (*device*) Rail Nau sémaphore *m*; (*system*) signaux *mpl* à bras.

semblance ['sembləns] *n* semblant *m*.

semen ['siːmən] *n* sperme *m*.

semester [sɪ'mestər] *n* Univ semestre *m*.

semi- ['semɪ] *pref* demi-, semi-. ◆**semi-auto'matic** *a* semi-automatique. ◆**semi-breve** [-briːv] *n* Mus ronde *f*. ◆**semicircle** *n* demi-cercle *m*. ◆**semi'circular** *a* semi-circulaire. ◆**semi'colon** *n* point-virgule *m*. ◆**semi-'conscious** *a* à demi conscient. ◆**semide'tached** *a* **s. house** maison *f* jumelle. ◆**semi'final** *n* Sp demi-finale *f*.

seminar ['semɪnɑːr] *n* Univ séminaire *m*.

seminary ['semɪnərɪ] *n* Rel séminaire *m*.

Semite ['siːmaɪt, Am 'semaɪt] *n* Sémite *mf*. ◆**Se'mitic** *a* sémite; (*language*) sémitique.

semolina [semə'liːnə] *n* semoule *f*.

senate ['senɪt] *n* Pol sénat *m*. ◆**senator** *n* Pol sénateur *m*.

send [send] *vt* (*pt & pp* **sent**) envoyer (**to** à); **to s. s.o. for sth/s.o.** envoyer qn chercher qch/qn; **to s. s.o. crazy** or **mad** rendre qn fou; **to s. s.o. packing** Fam envoyer promener qn; **to s. away** or **off** envoyer (**to** à); (*dismiss*) renvoyer; **to s. back** renvoyer; **to s. in** (*form*) envoyer; (*person*) faire entrer; **to s. on** (*letter, luggage*) faire suivre; **to s. out** (*invitation etc*) envoyer; (*heat*) émettre; (*from room etc*) faire sortir (qn); **to s. up** (*balloon, rocket*) lancer; (*price, luggage*) faire monter; (*mock*) Fam parodier; – *vi* **to s. away** or **off for** commander (par courrier); **to s. for** (*doctor etc*) faire venir, envoyer chercher; **to s. (out) for** (*meal, groceries*) envoyer chercher. ◆**s.-off** *n* to give s.o. a s.-off *Fam* faire des adieux chaleureux à qn. ◆**s.-up** *n Fam* parodie *f.* ◆**sender** *n* expéditeur, -trice *mf.*

senile ['siːnail] *a* gâteux, sénile. ◆**se'nility** *n* gâtisme *m*, sénilité *f.*

senior ['siːniər] *a* (*older*) plus âgé; (*position, executive, rank*) supérieur; (*teacher, partner*) principal; **to be s. to s.o., be s.o.'s s.** être plus âgé que qn; (*in rank*) être au-dessus de qn; **Brown s.** Brown père; **s. citizen** personne *f* âgée; **s. year** *Sch Univ Am* dernière année *f;* — *n* aîné, -ée *mf; Sch* grand, -ande *mf; Sch Univ Am* étudiant, -ante *mf* de dernière année; *Sp* senior *mf.* ◆**seni'ority** *n* priorité *f* d'âge; (*in service*) ancienneté *f;* (*in rank*) supériorité *f.*

sensation [sen'seiʃ(ə)n] *n* sensation *f.* ◆**sensational** *a* (*event*) qui fait sensation; (*newspaper, film*) à sensation; (*terrific*) *Fam* sensationnel.

sense [sens] *n* (*faculty, awareness, meaning*) sens *m;* **a s. of hearing** (le sens de) l'ouïe *f;* **to have (good) s.** avoir du bon sens; **a s. of** (*physical*) une sensation de (*chaleur etc*); (*mental*) un sentiment de (*honte etc*); **a s. of humour/direction** le sens de l'humour/de l'orientation; **a s. of time** la notion de l'heure; **to bring s.o. to his senses** ramener qn à la raison; **to make s.** (*of story, action etc*) avoir du sens; **to make s. of** comprendre; — *vt* sentir (intuitivement) (**that** que); (*have a foreboding of*) pressentir. ◆**—less** *a* (*stupid, meaningless*) insensé; (*unconscious*) sans connaissance. ◆**—lessness** *n* stupidité *f.*

sensibility [sensi'biliti] *n* sensibilité *f; pl* (*touchiness*) susceptibilité *f.*

sensible ['sensəb(ə)l] *a* (*wise*) raisonnable, sensé; (*clothes*) pratique.

sensitive ['sensitiv] *a* (*responsive, painful*) sensible (**to** à); (*delicate*) délicat (*peau, question etc*); (*touchy*) susceptible (**about** à propos de). ◆**sensi'tivity** *n* sensibilité *f;* (*touchiness*) susceptibilité *f.*

sensory ['sensəri] *a* sensoriel.

sensual ['senʃuəl] *a* (*bodily, sexual*) sensuel. ◆**sensu'ality** *n* sensualité *f.* ◆**sensuous** *a* (*pleasing, refined*) sensuel. ◆**sensuously** *adv* avec sensualité. ◆**sensuousness** *n* sensualité *f.*

sent [sent] *see* **send.**

sentence ['sentəns] **1** *n Gram* phrase *f.* **2** *n Jur* condamnation *f;* (*punishment*) peine *f;*

to pass s. prononcer une condamnation (**on** s.o. contre qn); **to serve a s.** purger une peine; — *vt Jur* prononcer une condamnation contre; **to s. to** condamner à.

sentiment ['sentimənt] *n* sentiment *m.* ◆**senti'mental** *a* sentimental. ◆**senti-men'tality** *n* sentimentalité *f.*

sentry ['sentri] *n* sentinelle *f;* **s. box** guérite *f.*

separate ['sepərət] *a* (*distinct*) séparé; (*independent*) indépendant; (*different*) différent; (*individual*) particulier; — ['sepəreit] *vt* séparer (**from** de); — *vi* se séparer (**from** de). ◆**'separately** *adv* séparément. ◆**sepa-'ration** *n* séparation *f.*

separates ['sepərəts] *npl* (*garments*) coordonnés *mpl.*

September [sep'tembər] *n* septembre *m.*

septic ['septik] *a* (*wound*) infecté; **s. tank** fosse *f* septique.

sequel ['siːkw(ə)l] *n* suite *f.*

sequence ['siːkwəns] *n* (*order*) ordre *m;* (*series*) succession *f; Mus Cards* séquence *f;* **film s.** séquence de film; **in s.** dans l'ordre, successivement.

sequin ['siːkwin] *n* paillette *f.*

serenade [serə'neid] *n* sérénade *f;* — *vt* donner une *or* la sérénade à.

serene [sə'riːn] *a* serein. ◆**serenity** *n* sérénité *f.*

sergeant ['saːdʒənt] *n Mil* sergent *m;* (*in police force*) brigadier *m.*

serial ['siəriəl] *n* (*story, film*) feuilleton *m;* **s. number** (*of banknote, TV set etc*) numéro de série. ◆**serialize** *vt* publier en feuilleton; *TV Rad* adapter en feuilleton.

series ['siəriːz] *n inv* série *f;* (*book collection*) collection *f.*

serious ['siəriəs] *a* sérieux; (*illness, mistake, tone*) grave, sérieux; (*damage*) important. ◆**—ly** *adv* sérieusement; (*ill, damaged*) gravement; **to take s.** prendre au sérieux. ◆**—ness** *n* sérieux *m;* (*of illness etc*) gravité *f;* (*of damage*) importance *f;* **in all s.** sérieusement.

sermon ['səːmən] *n* sermon *m.*

serpent ['səːpənt] *n* serpent *m.*

serrated [sə'reitid] *a* (*knife*) à dents (de scie).

serum ['siərəm] *n* sérum *m.*

servant ['səːvənt] *n* (*in house etc*) domestique *mf;* (*person who serves*) serviteur *m;* **public s.** fonctionnaire *mf.*

serve [səːv] *vt* servir (**to** s.o. à qn, **s.o. with sth** qch à qn); (*of train, bus etc*) desservir (*un village, un quartier etc*); (*supply*) *El* alimenter; (*apprenticeship*) faire; (*summons*) *Jur* remettre (**on** à); **it serves its**

purpose ça fait l'affaire; **(it) serves you right!** *Fam* ça t'apprendra!; **to s. up** *or* **out** servir; – *vi* servir **(as de)**; **to s. on** (*jury, committee*) être membre de; **to s. to show**/*etc* servir à montrer/*etc*; – *n Tennis* service *m*.

servic/e ['sɜːvɪs] *n* (*serving*) & *Mil Rel Tennis* service *m*; (*machine or vehicle repair*) révision *f*; **to be of s.** être utile à, rendre service à; **the (armed) services** les forces *fpl* armées; **s. (charge)** (*tip*) service *m*; **s. department** (*workshop*) atelier *m*; **s. area** (*on motorway*) aire *f* de service; **s. station** station-service *f*; – *vt* (*machine, vehicle*) réviser. ◆**-ing** *n Tech Aut* révision *f*. ◆**serviceable** *a* (*usable*) utilisable; (*useful*) commode; (*durable*) solide. ◆**serviceman** *n* (*pl* **-men**) *n* militaire *m*.

serviette [sɜːvɪ'et] *n* serviette *f* (de table).

servile ['sɜːvaɪl] *a* servile.

session ['seʃ(ə)n] *n* séance *f*; *Jur Pol* session *f*, séance *f*; *Univ* année *f* or trimestre *m* universitaire; *Univ Am* semestre *m* universitaire.

set [set] **1** *n* (*of keys, needles, tools*) jeu *m*; (*of stamps, numbers*) série *f*; (*of people*) groupe *m*; (*of facts*) & *Math* ensemble *m*; (*of books*) collection *f*; (*of plates*) service *m*; (*of tyres*) train *m*; (*kit*) trousse *f*; (*stage*) *Th Cin* plateau *m*; (*scenery*) *Th Cin* décor *m*, scène *f*; (*hairstyle*) mise *f* en plis; *Tennis* set *m*; **television s.** téléviseur *m*; **radio s.** poste *m* de radio; **tea s.** service *m* à thé; **chess s.** (*box*) jeu *m* d'échecs; **a s. of teeth** une rangée de dents, une denture; **the skiing/racing s.** le monde du ski/des courses. **2** *a* (*time etc*) fixe; (*lunch*) à prix fixe; (*book etc*) *Sch* au programme; (*speech*) préparé à l'avance; (*in one's habits*) régulier; (*situated*) situé; **s. phrase** expression *f* consacrée; **a s. purpose** un but déterminé; **the s. menu** le plat du jour; **dead s. against** absolument opposé à; **s. on doing** résolu à faire; **to be s. on sth** vouloir qch à tout prix; **all s.** (*ready*) prêt (**to do** pour faire); **to be s. back from** (*of house etc*) être en retrait de (*route etc*). **3** *vt* (*pt & pp* **set**, *pres p.* **setting**) (*put*) mettre, poser; (*date, limit etc*) fixer; (*record*) *Sp* établir; (*adjust*) *Tech* régler; (*arm etc in plaster*) *Med* plâtrer; (*task*) donner (**for s.o.** à qn); (*problem*) poser; (*diamond*) monter; (*precedent*) créer; **to have one's hair s.** se faire faire une mise en plis; **to s. (loose)** (*dog*) lâcher (**on** contre); **to s. s.o. (off)** **crying**/*etc* faire pleurer/*etc* qn; **to s. back** (*in time*) retarder; (*cost*) *Fam* coûter; **to s.**

down déposer; **to s. off** (*bomb*) faire exploser; (*activity, mechanism*) déclencher; (*complexion, beauty*) rehausser; **to s. out** (*display, explain*) exposer (**to** à); (*arrange*) disposer; **to s. up** (*furniture*) installer; (*statue, tent*) dresser; (*school*) fonder; (*government*) établir; (*business*) créer; (*inquiry*) ouvrir; **to s. s.o. up in business** lancer qn dans les affaires; – *vi* (*of sun*) se coucher; (*of jelly*) prendre; (*of bone*) *Med* se ressouder; **to s. about** (*job*) se mettre à; **to s. about doing** se mettre à faire; **to s. in** (*start*) commencer; (*arise*) surgir; **to s. off** *or* **out** (*leave*) partir; **to s. out do do** entreprendre de faire; **to s. up in business** monter une affaire; **to s. upon** (*attack*) attaquer (*qn*). ◆**setting** *n* (*surroundings*) cadre *m*; (*of sun*) coucher *m*; (*of diamond*) monture *f*. ◆**setter** *n* chien *m* couchant.

setback ['setbæk] *n* revers *m*; *Med* rechute *f*.

setsquare ['setskweər] *n Math* équerre *f*.

settee [se'tiː] *n* canapé *m*.

settle ['set(ə)l] *vt* (*decide, arrange, pay*) régler; (*date*) fixer; (*place in position*) placer; (*person*) installer (*dans son lit etc*); (*nerves*) calmer; (*land*) coloniser; **let's s. things** arrangeons les choses; **that's (all) settled** (*decided*) c'est décidé; – *vi* (*live*) s'installer, s'établir; (*of dust*) se déposer; (*of bird*) se poser; (*of snow*) tenir; **to s. (down) into** (*armchair*) s'installer dans; (*job*) s'habituer à; **to s. (up) with s.o.** régler qn; **to s. for** se contenter de, accepter; **to s. down** (*in chair or house*) s'installer; (*of nerves*) se calmer; (*in one's lifestyle*) se ranger; (*marry*) se caser; **to s. down to** (*get used to*) s'habituer à; (*work, task*) se mettre à. ◆**settled** *a* (*weather, period*) stable; (*habits*) régulier. ◆**settlement** *n* (*of account etc*) règlement *m*; (*agreement*) accord *m*; (*colony*) colonie *f*. ◆**settler** *n* colon *m*.

set-to [set'tuː] *n* (*quarrel*) *Fam* prise *f* de bec.

setup ['setʌp] *n Fam* situation *f*.

seven ['sev(ə)n] *a & n* sept (*m*). ◆**seven'teen** *a & n* dix-sept (*m*). ◆**seven'teenth** *a & n* dix-septième (*mf*). ◆**seventh** *a & n* septième (*mf*). ◆**seventieth** *a & n* soixante-dixième (*mf*). ◆**seventy** *a & n* soixante-dix (*m*); **s.-one** soixante et onze.

sever ['sevər] *vt* sectionner, couper; (*relations*) *Fig* rompre. ◆**severing** *n*, ◆**severance** *n* (*of relations*) rupture *f*.

several ['sev(ə)rəl] *a & pron* plusieurs (**of** d'entre).

severe [sə'vɪər] a (judge, tone etc) sévère; (winter, training) rigoureux; (test) dur; (injury) grave; (blow, pain) violent; (cold, frost) intense; (overwork) excessif; **a s. cold** Med un gros rhume; **to s. to** or **with s.o.** sévère envers qn. ◆**severely** adv sévèrement; (wounded) gravement. ◆**se'verity** n sévérité f; rigueur f; gravité f; violence f.

sew [səu] vti (pt **sewed**, pp **sewn** [səun] or **sewed**) coudre; **to s. on** (button) (re)coudre; **to s. up** (tear) (re)coudre. ◆**—ing** n couture f; **s. machine** machine f à coudre.

sewage ['suɪdʒ] n eaux fpl usées or d'égout. ◆**sewer** n égout m.

sewn [səun] see sew.

sex [seks] n (gender, sexuality) sexe m; (activity) relations fpl sexuelles; **the opposite s.** l'autre sexe; **to have s. with** coucher avec; – a (education, act etc) sexuel; **s. maniac** obsédé, -ée mf sexuel(le). ◆**sexist** a & n sexiste (mf). ◆**sexual** a sexuel. ◆**sexu'ality** n sexualité f. ◆**sexy** a (-ier, -iest) (book, garment, person) sexy inv; (aroused) qui a envie (de faire l'amour).

sextet [sek'stet] n sextuor m.

sh! [ʃ] int chut!

shabby ['ʃæbɪ] a (-ier, -iest) (town, room etc) miteux; (person) pauvrement vêtu; (mean) Fig mesquin. ◆**shabbily** adv (dressed) pauvrement. ◆**shabbiness** n aspect m miteux; mesquinerie f.

shack [ʃæk] 1 n cabane f. 2 vi **to s. up with** Pej Fam se coller avec.

shackles ['ʃæk(ə)lz] npl chaînes fpl.

shade [ʃeɪd] n ombre f; (of colour) ton m, nuance f; (of opinion, meaning) nuance f; (of lamp) abat-jour m inv; (blind) store m; **in the s.** à l'ombre; **a s. faster/taller/etc** (slightly) un rien plus vite/plus grand/etc; – vt (of tree) ombrager; (protect) abriter (from de); **to s. in** (drawing) ombrer. ◆**shady** a (-ier, -iest) (place) ombragé; (person etc) Fig louche.

shadow ['ʃædəʊ] 1 n ombre f. 2 a (cabinet) Pol fantôme. 3 vt **to s. s.o.** (follow) filer qn. ◆**shadowy** a (-ier, -iest) (form etc) obscur, vague.

shaft [ʃɑːft] n 1 (of tool) manche m; (in machine) arbre m; **s. of light** trait m de lumière. 2 (of mine) puits m; (of lift) cage f.

shaggy ['ʃægɪ] a (-ier, -iest) (hair, beard) broussailleux; (dog etc) à longs poils.

shake [ʃeɪk] vt (pt **shook**, pp **shaken**) (move up and down) secouer; (bottle) agiter; (belief, resolution etc) Fig ébranler; (upset) bouleverser, secouer; **to s. the windows** (of shock) ébranler les vitres; **to s. one's head**

(say no) secouer la tête; **to s. hands with** serrer la main à; **we shook hands** nous nous sommes serré la main; **to s. off** (dust etc) secouer; (cough, infection, pursuer) Fig se débarrasser de; **to s. s.o. up** (disturb, rouse) secouer qn; **to s. sth out of sth** (remove) secouer qch de qch; **s. yourself out of it!** secoue-toi!; – vi trembler (with de); – n secousse f; **to give sth a s.** secouer qch; **with a s. of his** or **her head** en secouant la tête; **in two shakes** (soon) Fam dans une minute. ◆**s.-up** n Fig réorganisation f.

shaky ['ʃeɪkɪ] a (-ier, -iest) (trembling) tremblant; (ladder etc) branlant; (memory, health) chancelant; (on one's legs, in a language) mal assuré.

shall [ʃæl, unstressed ʃəl] v aux 1 (future) **I s. come, I'll come** je viendrai; **we s. not come, we shan't come** nous ne viendrons pas. 2 (question) **s. I leave?** veux-tu que je parte?; **s. we leave?** on part? 3 (order) **he s. do it if I order it** il devra le faire si je l'ordonne.

shallot [ʃə'lɒt] n (onion) échalote f.

shallow ['ʃæləʊ] a (-er, -est) peu profond; Fig Pej superficiel; – npl (of river) bas-fond m. ◆**—ness** n manque m de profondeur; Fig Pej caractère m superficiel.

sham [ʃæm] n (pretence) comédie f, feinte f; (person) imposteur m; (jewels) imitation f; – a (false) faux; (illness, emotion) feint; – vt (-mm-) feindre.

shambles ['ʃæmb(ə)lz] n désordre m, pagaïe f; **to be a s.** être en pagaïe; **to make a s. of** gâcher.

shame [ʃeɪm] n (feeling, disgrace) honte f; **it's a s.** c'est dommage (**to do** de faire); **it's a s. (that)** c'est dommage que (+ sub); **what a s.!** (quel) dommage!; **to put to s.** faire honte à; – vt (disgrace, make ashamed) faire honte à. ◆**shamefaced** a honteux; (bashful) timide. ◆**shameful** a honteux. ◆**shamefully** adv honteusement. ◆**shameless** a (brazen) effronté; (indecent) impudique.

shammy ['ʃæmɪ] n **s.** (leather) Fam peau f de chamois.

shampoo [ʃæm'puː] n shampooing m; – vt (carpet) shampooiner; **to s. s.o.'s hair** faire un shampooing à qn.

shandy ['ʃændɪ] n (beer) panaché m.

shan't [ʃɑːnt] = shall not.

shanty¹ ['ʃæntɪ] n (hut) baraque f. ◆**shantytown** n bidonville f.

shanty² ['ʃæntɪ] n **sea s.** chanson f de marins.

shap/e [ʃeɪp] n forme f; **in (good) s.** (fit) en forme; **to be in good/bad s.** (of vehicle, *house etc*) être en bon/mauvais état; (*of business*) marcher bien/mal; **to take s.** prendre forme; **in the s. of a pear** en forme de poire; – *vt* (*fashion*) façonner (**into** en); (*one's life*) *Fig* déterminer; – *vi* **to s. up** (*of plans*) prendre (bonne) tournure, s'annoncer bien; (*of pupil, wrongdoer*) s'y mettre, s'appliquer; (*of patient*) faire des progrès. ◆**—ed** *suffix* **pear-s.**/*etc* en forme de poire/*etc*. ◆**shapeless** *a* informe. ◆**shapely** *a* (**-ier, -iest**) (*woman, legs*) bien tourné.

share [ʃeər] *n* part *f* (**of, in** de); (*in company*) *Fin* action *f*; **one's (fair) s.** de sa part de; **to do one's (fair) s.** fournir sa part d'efforts; **stocks and shares** *Fin* valeurs *fpl* (boursières); – *vt* (*meal, joy, opinion etc*) partager (**with** avec); (*characteristic*) avoir en commun; **to s. out** (*distribute*) partager; – *vi* **to s. (in)** partager. ◆**shareholder** *n Fin* actionnaire *mf*.

shark [ʃɑːk] *n* (*fish*) & *Fig* requin *m*.

sharp [ʃɑːp] **1** *a* (**-er, -est**) (*knife, blade etc*) tranchant; (*pointed*) pointu; (*point, voice*) aigu; (*pace, mind*) vif; (*pain*) aigu, vif; (*change, bend*) brusque; (*taste*) piquant; (*words, wind, tone*) âpre; (*eyesight, ear*) perçant; (*distinct*) net; (*lawyer etc*) *Pej* peu scrupuleux; **s. practice** *Pej* procédé(s) *m*(*pl*) malhonnête(s); – *adv* (*to stop*) net; **five o'clock**/*etc* à cinq heures/*etc* pile; **s. right/left** tout de suite à droite/à gauche. **2** *n Mus* dièse *m*. ◆**sharpen** *vt* (*knife*) aiguiser; (*pencil*) tailler. ◆**sharpener** *n* (*for pencils*) taille-crayon(s) *m inv*; (*for blades*) aiguisoir *m*. ◆**sharply** *adv* (*suddenly*) brusquement; (*harshly*) vivement; (*clearly*) nettement. ◆**sharpness** *n* (*of blade*) tranchant *m*; (*of picture*) netteté *f*. ◆**sharpshooter** *n* tireur *m* d'élite.

shatter [ˈʃætər] *vt* (*smash*) fracasser; (*glass*) faire voler en éclats; (*career, health*) briser; (*person, hopes*) anéantir; – *vi* (*smash*) se fracasser; (*of glass*) voler en éclats. ◆**—ed** *a* (*exhausted*) anéanti. ◆**—ing** *a* (*defeat*) accablant; (*news, experience*) bouleversant.

shav/e [ʃeɪv] *vt* (*person, head*) raser; **to s. off one's beard**/*etc* se raser la barbe/*etc*; – *vi* se raser; – *n* **to have a s.** se raser, se faire la barbe; **to have a close s.** *Fig Fam* l'échapper belle. ◆**—ing** *n* rasage *m*; (*strip of wood*) copeau *m*; **s. brush** blaireau *m*; **s. cream, s. foam** crème *f* à raser. ◆**shaven** *a* rasé (de près). ◆**shaver** *n* rasoir *m* électrique.

shawl [ʃɔːl] *n* châle *m*.

she [ʃiː] *pron* elle; **s. wants** elle veut; **she's a**

happy woman c'est une femme heureuse; **if I were s.** si j'étais elle; – *n* femelle *f*; **s.-bear** ourse *f*.

sheaf [ʃiːf] *n* (*pl* **sheaves**) (*of corn*) gerbe *f*.

shear [ʃɪər] *vt* tondre; – *npl* cisaille(s) *f*(*pl*); **pruning shears** sécateur *m*. ◆**—ing** *n* tonte *f*.

sheath [ʃiːθ] *n* (*pl* **-s** [ʃiːðz]) (*container*) gaine *f*, fourreau *m*; (*contraceptive*) préservatif *m*.

shed [ʃed] **1** *n* (*in garden etc*) remise *f*; (*for goods or machines*) hangar *m*. **2** *vt* (*pt & pp* **shed**, *pres p* **shedding**) (*lose*) perdre; (*tears, warmth etc*) répandre; (*get rid of*) se défaire de; (*clothes*) enlever; **to s. light on** *Fig* éclairer.

sheen [ʃiːn] *n* lustre *m*.

sheep [ʃiːp] *n inv* mouton *m*. ◆**sheepdog** *n* chien *m* de berger. ◆**sheepskin** *n* peau *f* de mouton.

sheepish [ˈʃiːpɪʃ] *a* penaud. ◆**—ly** *adv* d'un air penaud.

sheer [ʃɪər] **1** *a* (*luck, madness etc*) pur; (*impossibility etc*) absolu; **it's s. hard work** ça demande du travail; **by s. determination/hard work** à force de détermination/de travail. **2** *a* (*cliff*) à pic; – *adv* (*to rise*) à pic. **3** *a* (*fabric*) très fin.

sheet [ʃiːt] *n* (*on bed*) drap *m*; (*of paper, wood etc*) feuille *f*; (*of glass, ice*) plaque *f*; (*dust cover*) housse *f*; (*canvas*) bâche *f*; **s. metal** tôle *f*.

sheikh [ʃeɪk] *n* scheik *m*, cheik *m*.

shelf [ʃelf] *n* (*pl* **shelves**) rayon *m*, étagère *f*; (*in shop*) rayon *m*; (*on cliff*) saillie *f*; **to be (left) on the s.** (*not married*) *Fam* être toujours célibataire.

shell [ʃel] **1** *n* coquille *f*; (*of tortoise*) carapace *f*; (*seashell*) coquillage *m*; (*of peas*) cosse *f*; (*of building*) carcasse *f*; – *vt* (*peas*) écosser; (*nut, shrimp*) décortiquer. **2** *n* (*explosive*) *Mil* obus *m*; – *vt* (*town etc*) *Mil* bombarder. ◆**—ing** *n Mil* bombardement *m*. ◆**shellfish** *n inv Culin* (*oysters etc*) fruits *mpl* de mer.

shelter [ˈʃeltər] *n* (*place, protection*) abri *m*; **to take s.** se mettre à l'abri (**from** de); **to seek s.** chercher un abri; – *vt* abriter (**from** de); (*criminal*) protéger; – *vi* s'abriter. ◆**—ed** *a* (*place*) abrité; (*life*) très protégé.

shelve [ʃelv] *vt* (*postpone*) laisser en suspens.

shelving [ˈʃelvɪŋ] *n* (*shelves*) rayonnage(s) *m*(*pl*); **s. unit** (*set of shelves*) étagère *f*.

shepherd [ˈʃepəd] **1** *n* berger *m*; **s.'s pie** hachis *m* Parmentier. **2** *vt* **to s. in** faire

entrer; **to s. s.o. around** piloter qn.
◆**shepherdess** n bergère f.

sherbet ['ʃɜːbət] n (*powder*) poudre f
acidulée; (*water ice*) Am sorbet m.

sheriff ['ʃerif] n Am shérif m.

sherry ['ʃeri] n xérès m, sherry m.

shh! [ʃ] int chut!

shield [ʃiːld] n bouclier m; (*on coat of arms*)
écu m; (*screen*) Tech écran m; – vt protéger
(**from** de).

shift [ʃift] n (*change*) changement m (**of, in**
de); (*period of work*) poste m; (*workers*)
équipe f; **gear s.** Aut Am levier m de vitesse;
s. work travail m en équipe; – vt (*move*)
déplacer, bouger; (*limb*) bouger;
(*employee*) muter (**to** à); (*scenery*) Th
changer; (*blame*) rejeter (**on to** sur); **to s.**
places changer de place; **to s. gear(s)** Aut
Am changer de vitesse; – vi bouger; (*of
heavy object*) se déplacer; (*of views*)
changer; (*pass*) passer (**to** à); (*go*) aller (**to**
à); **to s. to** (*new town*) déménager à; **to s.**
along avancer; **to s. over** *or* **up** se pousser.
◆**—ing** a (*views*) changeant.

shiftless ['ʃiftləs] a velléitaire, paresseux.

shifty ['ʃifti] a (**-ier, -iest**) (*sly*) sournois;
(*dubious*) louche.

shilling ['ʃiliŋ] n shilling m.

shilly-shally ['ʃiliʃæli] vi hésiter, tergiverser.

shimmer ['ʃimər] vi chatoyer, miroiter; – n
chatoiement m, miroitement m.

shin [ʃin] n tibia m; **s. pad** n Sp jambière f.

shindig ['ʃindig] n Fam réunion f bruyante.

shin/e [ʃain] vi (*pt & pp* **shone** [ʃɒn, Am
ʃəʊn]) briller; **to s. with** (*happiness etc*)
rayonner de; – vt (*polish*) faire briller; **to s.**
a light *or* **a torch** éclairer (**on** sth qch); – n
éclat m; (*on shoes, cloth*) brillant m.
◆**—ing** a (*bright, polished*) brillant; **a shin-**
ing example of un bel exemple de. ◆**shiny**
a (**-ier, -iest**) (*bright, polished*) brillant;
(*clothes, through wear*) lustré.

shingle ['ʃiŋg(ə)l] n (*on beach*) galets mpl;
(*on roof*) bardeau m.

shingles ['ʃiŋg(ə)lz] n Med zona m.

ship [ʃip] n navire m, bateau m; **by s.** en
bateau; **s. owner** armateur m; – vt (**-pp-**)
(*send*) expédier; (*transport*) transporter;
(*load up*) embarquer (**on to** sur). ◆**ship-**
ping n (*traffic*) navigation f; (*ships*) navires
mpl; – a (*agent*) maritime; **s. line** compagnie f de navigation. ◆**shipbuilding** n
construction f navale. ◆**shipmate** n
camarade m de bord. ◆**shipment** n
(*goods*) chargement m, cargaison f.
◆**shipshape** a & adv en ordre. ◆**ship-**
wreck n naufrage m. ◆**shipwrecked** a

naufragé; **to be s.** faire naufrage. ◆**ship-**
yard n chantier m naval.

shirk [ʃɜːk] vt (*duty*) se dérober à; (*work*)
éviter de faire; – vi tirer au flanc. ◆**—er** n
tire-au-flanc m inv.

shirt [ʃɜːt] n chemise f; (*of woman*) chemisier
m. ◆**shirtfront** n plastron m. ◆**shirt-**
sleeves npl **in** (one's) **s.** en bras de
chemise.

shiver ['ʃivər] vi frissonner (**with** de); – n
frisson m.

shoal [ʃəʊl] n (*of fish*) banc m.

shock [ʃɒk] n (*moral blow*) choc m; (*impact*)
& Med secousse f; (*of explosion*) secousse f;
(**electric**) **s.** décharge f (électrique) (**from**
sth en touchant qch); **a feeling of s.** un
sentiment d'horreur; **suffering from s.,**
in a state of s. en état de choc; **to come as**
a s. to s.o. stupéfier qn; – a (*tactics,
wave*) de choc; (*effect, image etc*) -choc
inv; **s. absorber** amortisseur m; – vt
(*offend*) choquer; (*surprise*) stupéfier; (*disgust*) dégoûter. ◆**—ing** a affreux; (*outrageous*) scandaleux; (*indecent*) choquant.
◆**—ingly** adv affreusement. ◆**—er** n **to be**
a s. Fam être affreux *or* horrible. ◆**shock-**
proof a résistant au choc.

shoddy ['ʃɒdi] a (**-ier, -iest**) (*goods etc*) de
mauvaise qualité. ◆**shoddily** adv (*made,
done*) mal.

shoe [ʃuː] n chaussure f, soulier m; (*for
horse*) fer m; Aut sabot m (de frein); **in your**
shoes Fig à ta place; **s. polish** cirage m; – vt
(*pt & pp* **shod**) (*horse*) ferrer. ◆**shoehorn**
n chausse-pied m. ◆**shoelace** n lacet m.
◆**shoemaker** n fabricant m de chaussures; (*cobbler*) cordonnier m. ◆**shoe-**
string n **on a s.** Fig avec peu d'argent (en
poche).

shone [ʃɒn, Am ʃəʊn] see **shine**.

shoo [ʃuː] vt **to s. (away)** chasser; – int
ouste!

shook [ʃʊk] see **shake**.

shoot¹ [ʃuːt] vt (*pt & pp* **shot**) (*kill*) tuer
(d'un coup de feu), abattre; (*wound*)
blesser (d'un coup de feu); (*execute*) fusiller; (*hunt*) chasser; (*gun*) tirer un coup de;
(*bullet*) tirer; (*missile, glance, questions*)
lancer (**at** à); (*film*) tourner; (*person*) Phot
prendre; **to s. down** (*aircraft*) abattre; – vi
(*with gun, bow etc*) tirer (**at** sur); **to s.**
ahead/off avancer/partir à toute vitesse; **to**
s. up (*grow*) pousser vite; (*rise, spurt*) jaillir;
(*of price*) monter en flèche. ◆**—ing** n
(*gunfire, execution*) fusillade f; (*shots*)
coups mpl de feu; (*murder*) meurtre m; (*of

film) tournage *m*; (*hunting*) chasse *f*.
◆**shoot-out** *n Fam* fusillade *f*.

shoot² [ʃuːt] *n* (*on plant*) pousse *f*.

shop [ʃɒp] **1** *n* magasin *m*; (*small*) boutique *f*; (*workshop*) atelier *m*; **at the baker's s.** à la boulangerie, chez le boulanger; **s. assistant** vendeur, -euse *mf*; **s. floor** (*workers*) ouvriers *mpl*; **s. steward** délégué, -ée *mf* syndical(e); **s. window** vitrine *f*; — *vi* (-**pp**-) faire ses courses; **to s. around** comparer les prix. **2** *vt* (-**pp**-) **to s. s.o.** *Fam* dénoncer qn (*à la police etc*). ◆**shopping** *n* (*goods*) achats *mpl*; **to go s.** faire des courses; **to do one's s.** faire ses courses; — *a* (*street, district*) commerçant; (*bag*) à provisions; **s. centre** centre *m* commercial. ◆**shopper** *n* (*buyer*) acheteur, -euse *mf*; (*customer*) client, -ente *mf*; (*bag*) sac *m* à provisions.

shopkeeper ['ʃɒpkiːpər] *n* commerçant, -ante *mf*. ◆**shoplifter** *n* voleur, -euse *mf* à l'étalage. ◆**shoplifting** *n* vol *m* à l'étalage. ◆**shopsoiled** *a*, *Am* ◆**shopworn** *a* abîmé.

shore [ʃɔːr] **1** *n* (*of sea, lake*) rivage *m*; (*coast*) côte *f*, bord *m* de (la) mer; (*beach*) plage *f*; **on s.** (*passenger*) *Nau* à terre. **2** *vt* **to s. up** (*prop up*) étayer.

shorn [ʃɔːn] *a* (*head*) tondu; **s. of** (*stripped of*) *Lit* dénué de.

short [ʃɔːt] *a* (-**er**, -**est**) court; (*person, distance*) petit; (*syllable*) bref; (*curt, impatient*) brusque; **a s. time** *or* **while ago** il y a peu de temps; **s. cut** raccourci *m*; **to be s. of money/time** être à court d'argent/de temps; **we're s. of ten men** il nous manque dix hommes; **money/time is s.** l'argent/le temps manque; **not far s. of** pas loin de; **s. of** (*except*) sauf; **to be s. for** (*of name*) être l'abréviation *or* le diminutif de; **in s.** bref; **s. circuit** *El* court-circuit *m*; **s. list** liste *f* de candidats choisis; — *adv* **to cut s.** (*visit etc*) abréger; (*person*) couper la parole à; **to go** *or* **get** *or* **run s. of** manquer de; **to get** *or* **run s.** manquer; **to stop s.** s'arrêter net; — *n El* court-circuit *m*; (**a pair of**) **shorts** un short. ◆**shorten** *vt* (*visit, line, dress etc*) raccourcir. ◆**shortly** *adv* (*soon*) bientôt; **s. after** peu après. ◆**shortness** *n* (*of person*) petitesse *f*; (*of hair, stick, legs*) manque *m* de longueur.

shortage ['ʃɔːtɪdʒ] *n* manque *m*, pénurie *f*; (*crisis*) crise *f*.

shortbread ['ʃɔːtbred] *n* sablé *m*. ◆**short-'change** *vt* (*buyer*) ne pas rendre juste à. ◆**short-'circuit** *vt El & Fig* court-circuiter. ◆**shortcoming** *n* défaut *m*.

◆**shortfall** *n* manque *m*. ◆**shorthand** *n* sténo *f*; **s. typist** sténodactylo *f*. ◆**short-'handed** *a* à court de personnel. ◆**short-'lived** *a* éphémère. ◆**short'sighted** *a* myope; *Fig* imprévoyant. ◆**short-'sightedness** *n* myopie *f*; imprévoyance *f*. ◆**short-'sleeved** *a* à manches courtes. ◆**short-'staffed** *a* à court de personnel. ◆**short-'term** *a* à court terme.

shortening ['ʃɔːt(ə)nɪŋ] *n Culin* matière *f* grasse.

shot [ʃɒt] *see* shoot¹; — *n* coup *m*; (*bullet*) balle *f*; *Cin Phot* prise *f* de vues; (*injection*) *Med* piqûre *f*; **a good s.** (*person*) un bon tireur; **to have a s. at (doing) sth** essayer de faire qch; **a long s.** (*attempt*) un coup à tenter; **big s.** *Fam* gros bonnet *m*; **like a s.** (*at once*) tout de suite; **to be s. of** (*rid of*) *Fam* être débarrassé de. ◆**shotgun** *n* fusil *m* de chasse.

should [ʃud, *unstressed* ʃəd] *v aux* **1** (= *ought to*) **you s. do it** vous devriez le faire; **I s. have stayed** j'aurais dû rester; **that s. be Pauline** ça doit être Pauline. **2** (= *would*) **I s. like to** j'aimerais bien; **it's strange she s. say no** il est étrange qu'elle dise non. **3** (*possibility*) **if he s. come** s'il vient; **s. I be free** si je suis libre.

shoulder ['ʃəuldər] **1** *n* épaule *f*; **to have round shoulders** avoir le dos voûté, être voûté; (**hard**) **s.** (*of motorway*) accotement *m* stabilisé; **s. bag** sac *m* à bandoulière; **s. blade** omoplate *f*; **s.-length hair** cheveux *mpl* mi-longs. **2** *vt* (*responsibility*) endosser, assumer.

shout [ʃaut] *n* cri *m*; **to give s.o. a s.** appeler qn; — *vi* **to s. (out)** crier; **to s. to** *or* **at s.o. to do** crier à qn de faire; **to s. at s.o.** (*scold*) crier après qn; — *vt* **to s. (out)** (*insult etc*) crier; **to s. down** (*speaker*) huer. ◆—**ing** *n* (*shouts*) cris *mpl*.

shove [ʃʌv] *n* poussée *f*; **to give a s. (to)** pousser; — *vt* pousser; (*put*) *Fam* fourrer; **to s. sth into** (*thrust*) enfoncer *or* fourrer qch dans; **to s. s.o. around** *Fam* régenter qn; — *vi* pousser; **to s. off** (*leave*) *Fam* ficher le camp, filer; **to s. over** (*move over*) *Fam* se pousser.

shovel ['ʃʌv(ə)l] *n* pelle *f*; — *vt* (-**ll**-, *Am* -**l**-) (*grain etc*) pelleter; **to s. up** *or* **away** (*remove*) enlever à la pelle; **to s. sth into** (*thrust*) *Fam* fourrer qch dans.

show [ʃəu] *n* (*of joy, force*) démonstration *f* (**of** de); (*semblance*) semblant *m* (**of** de); (*ostentation*) parade *f*; (*sight*) & *Th* spectacle *m*; (*performance*) *Cin* séance *f*; (*exhibition*) exposition *f*; **the Boat/Motor S.** le

Salon de la Navigation/de l'Automobile; **horse** s. concours *m* hippique; **to give a good** s. *Sp Mus Th* jouer bien; **good** s.! bravo!; **(just) for** s. pour l'effet; **on** s. (*painting etc*) exposé; s. **business** le monde du spectacle; s. **flat** appartement *m* témoin; − *vt* (*pt* **showed**, *pp* **shown**) montrer (**to** à, **that** que); (*exhibit*) exposer; (*film*) passer, donner; (*indicate*) montrer; **to** s. **s.o. to the door** reconduire qn; **it (just) goes to** s. **that** ... ça (dé)montre (bien) que ...; **I'll** s. **him** *or* **her!** *Fam* je lui apprendrai!; − *vi* (*be visible*) se voir; (*of film*) passer; 'now showing' *Cin* 'à l'affiche' (**at** à). ■ **to** s. **(a)round** *vt* faire visiter; **he** *or* **she was shown (a)round the house** on lui a fait visiter la maison; **to** s. **in** *vt* faire entrer; **to** s. **off** *vt Pej* étaler; (*highlight*) faire valoir; − *vi Pej* crâner. ◆s.-**off** *n Pej* crâneur, -euse *mf*; **to** s. **out** *vt* (*visitor*) reconduire; **to** s. **up** *vt* (*fault*) faire ressortir; (*humiliate*) faire honte à; − *vi* ressortir (**against** sur); (*of error*) être visible; (*of person*) *Fam* arriver, s'amener. ◆**showing** *n* (*of film*) projection *f* (**of** de); (*performance*) *Cin* séance *f*; (*of team*, *player*) performance *f*.

showcase ['ʃəʊkeɪs] *n* vitrine *f*. ◆**showdown** *n* confrontation *f*, conflit *m*. ◆**showgirl** *n* (*in chorus etc*) girl *f*. ◆**showjumping** *n Sp* jumping *m*. ◆**showmanship** *n* art *m* de la mise en scène. ◆**showpiece** *n* modèle *m* du genre. ◆**showroom** *n* (*for cars etc*) salle *f* d'exposition.

shower ['ʃaʊər] *n* (*of rain*) averse *f*; (*of blows*) déluge *m*; (*bath*) douche *f*; (*party*) *Am* réception *f* (*pour la remise de cadeaux*); − *vt* **to** s. **s.o. with** (*gifts*, *abuse*) couvrir qn de. ◆**showery** *a* pluvieux.

shown [ʃəʊn] *see* show.

showy ['ʃəʊɪ] *a* (**-ier**, **-iest**) (*colour*, *hat*) voyant; (*person*) prétentieux.

shrank [ʃræŋk] *see* shrink 1.

shrapnel ['ʃræpn(ə)l] *n* éclats *mpl* d'obus.

shred [ʃred] *n* lambeau *m*; (*of truth*) *Fig* grain *m*; **not a** s. **of evidence** pas la moindre preuve; − *vt* (**-dd-**) mettre en lambeaux; (*cabbage*, *carrots*) râper. ◆**shredder** *n* *Culin* râpe *f*.

shrew [ʃruː] *n* (*woman*) *Pej* mégère *f*.

shrewd [ʃruːd] *a* (**-er**, **-est**) (*person*, *plan*) astucieux. ◆−**ly** *adv* astucieusement. ◆−**ness** *n* astuce *f*.

shriek [ʃriːk] *n* cri *m* (aigu); − *vti* crier; **to** s. **with pain/laughter** hurler de douleur/de rire.

shrift [ʃrɪft] *n* **to get short** s. être traité sans ménagement.

shrill [ʃrɪl] *a* (**-er**, **-est**) aigu, strident.

shrimp [ʃrɪmp] *n* crevette *f*; (*person*) *Pej* nabot, -ote *mf*; (*child*) *Pej* puce *f*.

shrine [ʃraɪn] *n* lieu *m* saint; (*tomb*) châsse *f*.

shrink [ʃrɪŋk] **1** *vi* (*pt* **shrank**, *pp* **shrunk** *or* **shrunken**) (*of clothes*) rétrécir; (*of aging person*) se tasser; (*of amount*, *audience etc*) diminuer; **to** s. **from** reculer devant (**doing** l'idée de faire); − *vt* rétrécir. **2** *n* (*person*) *Am Hum* psy(chiatre) *m*. ◆−**age** *n* rétrécissement *m*; diminution *f*.

shrivel ['ʃrɪv(ə)l] *vi* (**-ll-**, *Am* **-l-**) **to** s. **(up)** se ratatiner; − *vt* **to** s. **(up)** ratatiner.

shroud [ʃraʊd] *n* linceul *m*; (*of mystery*) *Fig* voile *m*; − *vt* **shrouded in mist** enseveli *or* enveloppé sous la brume; **shrouded in mystery** enveloppé de mystère.

Shrove Tuesday [ʃrəʊv'tjuːzdɪ] *n* Mardi *m* gras.

shrub [ʃrʌb] *n* arbrisseau *m*.

shrug [ʃrʌg] *vt* (**-gg-**) **to** s. **one's shoulders** hausser les épaules; **to** s. **off** (*dismiss*) écarter (dédaigneusement); − *n* haussement *m* d'épaules.

shrunk(en) ['ʃrʌŋk(ən)] *see* shrink 1.

shudder ['ʃʌdər] *vi* frémir (**with** de); (*of machine etc*) vibrer; − *n* frémissement *m*; vibration *f*.

shuffle ['ʃʌf(ə)l] **1** *vti* **to** s. **(one's feet)** traîner les pieds. **2** *vt* (*cards*) battre.

shun [ʃʌn] *vt* (**-nn-**) fuir, éviter; **to** s. **doing** éviter de faire.

shunt [ʃʌnt] *vt* (*train*, *conversation*) aiguiller (**on** to sur); **we were shunted (to and fro)** *Fam* on nous a baladés (**from office to office**/*etc* de bureau en bureau/*etc*).

shush! [ʃʊʃ] *int* chut!

shut [ʃʌt] *vt* (*pt* & *pp* **shut**, *pp* **shutting**) fermer; **to** s. **one's finger in** (*door etc*) se prendre le doigt dans; **to** s. **away** *or* **in** (*lock away or in*) enfermer; **to** s. **down** fermer; **to** s. **off** fermer; (*engine*) arrêter; (*isolate*) isoler; **to** s. **out** (*light*) empêcher d'entrer; (*view*) boucher; (*exclude*) exclure (**of**, **from** de); **to** s. **s.o. out** (*lock out accidentally*) enfermer qn dehors; **to** s. **up** fermer; (*lock up*) enfermer (*personne*, *objet précieux etc*); (*silence*) *Fam* faire taire; − *vi* (*of door etc*) se fermer; (*of shop*, *museum etc*) fermer; **the door doesn't** s. la porte ne ferme pas; **to** s. **down** fermer (définitivement); **to** s. **up** (*be quiet*) *Fam* se taire. ◆**shutdown** *n* fermeture *f*.

shutter ['ʃʌtər] *n* volet *m*; (*of camera*) obturateur *m*.

shuttle ['ʃʌt(ə)l] *n* (*bus, spacecraft etc*) navette *f*; **s. service** navette; – *vi* faire la navette; – *vt* (*in vehicle etc*) transporter. ◆**shuttlecock** *n* (*in badminton*) volant *m*.

shy [ʃaɪ] *a* (-er, -est) timide; **to be s. of doing** avoir peur de faire; – *vi* **to s. away reculer** (**from s.o.** devant qn, **from doing** à l'idée de faire). ◆—**ness** *n* timidité *f*.

Siamese [saɪə'miːz] *a* siamois; **S. twins** frères *mpl* siamois, sœurs *fpl* siamoises.

sibling ['sɪblɪŋ] *n* frère *m*, sœur *f*.

Sicily ['sɪsɪlɪ] *n* Sicile *f*.

sick [sɪk] *a* (-er, -est) (*ill*) malade; (*mind*) malsain; (*humour*) noir; (*cruel*) sadique; **to be s.** (*vomit*) vomir; **to be off** *or* **away s., be on s. leave** être en congé de maladie; **to feel s.** avoir mal au cœur; **to be s. (and tired) of** *Fam* en avoir marre de; **he makes me s.** *Fam* il m'écœure; – *n* **the s.** les malades *mpl*; – *vi* (*vomit*) *Fam* vomir; – *vt* **to s. sth up** *Fam* vomir qch. ◆**sickbay** *n* infirmerie *f*. ◆**sickbed** *n* lit *m* de malade. ◆**sickly** *a* (-ier, -iest) maladif; (*pale, faint*) pâle; (*taste*) écœurant. ◆**sickness** *n* maladie *f*; (*vomiting*) vomissement(s) *m*(*pl*); **motion s.** *Aut* mal *m* de la route.

sicken ['sɪkən] **1** *vt* écœurer. **2** *vi* **to be sickening for** (*illness*) couver. ◆—**ing** *a* écœurant.

side [saɪd] *n* côté *m*; (*of hill, animal*) flanc *m*; (*of road, river*) bord *m*; (*of beef*) quartier *m*; (*of question*) aspect *m*; (*of character*) facette *f*, aspect *m*; *Sp* équipe *f*; *Pol* parti *m*; **the right s.** (*of fabric*) l'endroit *m*; **the wrong s.** (*of fabric*) l'envers *m*; **by the s. of** (*nearby*) à côté de; **at** *or* **by my s.** à côté de moi, à mes côtés; **s. by s.** l'un à côté de l'autre; **to move to one s.** s'écarter; **on this s.** de ce côté; **on the other s.** de l'autre côté; **the other s.** *TV Fam* l'autre chaîne *f*; **on the big**/*etc* **s.** *Fam* plutôt grand/*etc*; **to take sides with** se ranger du côté de; **on our s.** de notre côté, avec nous; **on the s.** *Fam* (*secretly*) en catimini; (*to make money*) en plus; – *a* (*lateral*) latéral; (*effect, issue*) secondaire; (*glance, view*) de côté; (*street*) transversal; – *vi* **to s. with** se ranger du côté de. ◆-**sided** *suffix* **ten-s.** à dix côtés. ◆**sideboard 1** *n* buffet *m*. **2** *npl* (*hair*) pattes *fpl*. ◆**sideburns** *npl* (*hair*) favoris *mpl*. ◆**sidecar** *n* side-car *m*. ◆**sidekick** *n* *Fam* associé, -ée *mf*. ◆**sidelight** *n* *Aut* feu *m* de position. ◆**sideline** *n* activité *f* secondaire. ◆**sidesaddle** *adv* (*to ride*) en amazone. ◆**sidestep** *vt* (-pp-) éviter. ◆**sidetrack** *vt* **to get sidetracked**

s'écarter du sujet. ◆**sidewalk** *n* *Am* trottoir *m*. ◆**sideways** *adv* & *a* de côté.

siding ['saɪdɪŋ] *n* *Rail* voie *f* de garage.

sidle ['saɪd(ə)l] *vi* **to s. up to s.o.** s'approcher furtivement de qn.

siege [siːdʒ] *n* *Mil* siège *m*.

siesta [sɪ'estə] *n* sieste *f*.

sieve [sɪv] *n* tamis *m*; (*for liquids*) *Culin* passoire *f*; – *vt* tamiser. ◆**sift** *vt* tamiser; **to s. out** (*truth*) Fig dégager; – *vi* **to s. through** (*papers etc*) examiner (à la loupe).

sigh [saɪ] *n* soupir *m*; – *vti* soupirer.

sight [saɪt] *n* vue *f*; (*spectacle*) spectacle *m*; (*on gun*) mire *f*; **to lose s. of** perdre de vue; **to catch s. of** apercevoir; **to come into s.** apparaître; **at first s.** à première vue; **by s.** de vue; **on** *or* **at s.** à vue; **in s.** (*target, end, date etc*) en vue; **keep out of s.!** ne te montre pas!; **he hates the s. of me** il ne peut pas me voir; **it's a lovely s.** c'est beau à voir; **the (tourist) sights** les attractions *fpl* touristiques; **to set one's sights on** (*job etc*) viser; **a s. longer**/*etc Fam* bien plus long/*etc*; – *vt* (*land*) apercevoir. ◆—**ed** *a* qui voit, clairvoyant. ◆—**ing** *n* **to make a s. of** voir. ◆**sightseer** *n* touriste *mf*. ◆**sightseeing** *n* tourisme *m*.

sightly ['saɪtlɪ] *a* **not very s.** laid.

sign [saɪn] **1** *n* signe *m*; (*notice*) panneau *m*; (*over shop, inn*) enseigne *f*; **no s. of** aucune trace de; **to use s. language** parler par signes. **2** *vt* (*put signature to*) signer; **to s. away** *or* **over** céder (**to** à); **to s. on** *or* **up** (*worker, soldier*) engager; – *vi* signer; **to s. for** (*letter*) signer le reçu de; **to s. in** signer le registre; **to s. off** dire au revoir; **to s. on** (*the dole*) s'inscrire au chômage; **to s. on** *or* **up** (*of soldier, worker*) s'engager; (*for course*) s'inscrire. ◆**signpost** *n* poteau *m* indicateur; – *vt* flécher.

signal ['sɪɡnəl] *n* signal *m*; **traffic signals** feux *mpl* de circulation; **s. box,** *Am* **s. tower** *Rail* poste *m* d'aiguillage; – *vt* (-ll-, *Am* -l-) (*message*) communiquer (**to** à); (*arrival etc*) signaler (**to** à); – *vi* faire des signaux; **to s. (to) s.o. to do** faire signe à qn de faire. ◆**signalman** *n* (*pl* -men) *Rail* aiguilleur *m*.

signature ['sɪɡnətʃər] *n* signature *f*; **s. tune** indicatif *m* (musical). ◆**signatory** *n* signataire *mf*.

signet ring ['sɪɡnɪtrɪŋ] *n* chevalière *f*.

significant [sɪɡ'nɪfɪkənt] *a* (*meaningful*) significatif; (*important, large*) important. ◆**significance** *n* (*meaning*) signification *f*; (*importance*) importance *f*. ◆**significantly** *adv* (*appreciably*) sensiblement; **s.,**

he'... fait significatif. il .... ◆'signify vt (mean) signifier (that que); (make known) indiquer, signifier (to à).

silence ['saıləns] n silence m; in s. en silence; – vt faire taire. ◆silencer n (on car, gun) silencieux m. ◆silent a silencieux; (film, anger) muet; to keep or be s. garder le silence (about sur). ◆silently adv silencieusement.

silhouette [sılu'et] n silhouette f. ◆silhouetted a to be s. against se profiler contre.

silicon ['sılıkən] n silicium m; s. chip puce f de silicium. ◆silicone ['sılıkən] n silicone f.

silk [sılk] n soie f. ◆silky a (-ier, -iest) soyeux.

sill [sıl] n (of window etc) rebord m.

silly ['sılı] a (-ier, -iest) idiot, bête; to do sth s. faire une bêtise; s. fool, Fam s. billy idiot, -ote mf; – adv (to act, behave) bêtement.

silo ['saıləu] n (pl -os) silo m.

silt [sılt] n vase f.

silver ['sılvər] n argent m; (silverware) argenterie f; £5 in s. 5 livres en pièces d'argent; – a (spoon etc) en argent, d'argent; (hair, colour) argenté; s. jubilee vingt-cinquième anniversaire m (d'un événement); s. paper papier m d'argent; s. plate argenterie f. ◆s.-'plated a plaqué argent. ◆silversmith n orfèvre m. ◆silverware n argenterie f. ◆silvery a (colour) argenté.

similar ['sımılər] a semblable (to à). ◆simi-'larity n ressemblance f (between entre, to avec). ◆similarly adv de la même façon; (likewise) de même.

simile ['sımılı] n Liter comparaison f.

simmer ['sımər] vi Culin mijoter, cuire à feu doux; (of water) frémir; (of revolt, hatred etc) couver; to s. with (rage) bouillir de; to s. down (calm down) Fam se calmer; – vt faire cuire à feu doux; (water) laisser frémir.

simper ['sımpər] vi minauder.

simple ['sımp(ə)l] a (-er, -est) (plain, uncom-plicated, basic etc) simple. ◆s.-'minded a simple d'esprit. ◆s.-'mindedness n simplicité f d'esprit. ◆simpleton n nigaud, -aude mf. ◆sim'plicity n simpli-cité f. ◆simplifi'cation n simplification f. ◆simplify vt simplifier. ◆sim'plistic a simpliste. ◆simply adv (plainly, merely) simplement; (absolutely) absolument.

simulate ['sımjuleɪt] vt simuler.

simultaneous [sıməl'teɪnɪəs, Am saıməl-'teɪnɪəs] a simultané. ◆—ly adv simultané-ment.

sin [sın] n péché m; – vi (-nn-) pécher.

since [sıns] 1 prep (in time) depuis; s. my departure depuis mon départ; – conj depuis que; s. she's been here depuis qu'elle est ici; it's a year s. I saw him ça fait un an que je ne l'ai pas vu; – adv (ever) s. depuis. 2 conj (because) puisque.

sincere [sın'sıər] a sincère. ◆sincerely adv sincèrement; yours s. (in letter) Com veuil-lez croire à mes sentiments dévoués. ◆sin'cerity n sincérité f.

sinew ['sınjuː] n Anat tendon m.

sinful ['sınfəl] a (guilt-provoking) coupable; (shocking) scandaleux; he's s. c'est un pécheur; that's s. c'est un péché.

sing [sıŋ] vti (pt sang, pp sung) chanter; to s. up chanter plus fort. ◆—ing n (of bird & musical technique) chant m; (way of sing-ing) façon f de chanter; – a (lesson, teacher) de chant. ◆—er n chanteur, -euse mf.

singe [sınʤ] vt (cloth) roussir; (hair) brûler; to s. s.o.'s hair (at hairdresser's) faire un brûlage à qn.

single ['sıŋg(ə)l] a (only one) seul; (room, bed) pour une personne; (unmarried) célibataire; s. ticket billet m simple; every s. day tous les jours sans exception; s. party Pol parti m unique; – n (ticket) aller m (simple); (record) 45 tours m inv; pl Tennis simples mpl; singles bar bar m pour célibataires; – vt to s. out (choose) choisir. ◆s.-'breasted a (jacket) droit. ◆s.-'decker n (bus) autobus m sans impériale. ◆s.-'handed a sans aide. ◆s.-'minded a (person) résolu, qui n'a qu'une idée en tête. ◆singly adv (one by one) un à un.

singlet ['sıŋglıt] n (garment) maillot m de corps.

singsong ['sıŋsɒŋ] n to get together for a s. se réunir pour chanter.

singular ['sıŋgjulər] 1 a (unusual) singulier. 2 a Gram (form) singulier; (noun) au singu-lier; – n Gram singulier m; in the s. au singulier.

sinister ['sınıstər] a sinistre.

sink¹ [sıŋk] n (in kitchen) évier m; (washba-sin) lavabo m.

sink² [sıŋk] vi (pt sank, pp sunk) (of ship, person etc) couler; (of sun, price, water level) baisser; (collapse, subside) s'affaisser; to s. (down) into (mud etc) s'enfoncer dans; (armchair etc) s'affaler dans; to s. in (of ink etc) pénétrer; (of fact etc) Fam rentrer (dans le crâne); **has that sunk in?** *Fam* as-tu compris ça?; – *vt* (*ship*) couler; (*well*) creuser; **to s. into** (*thrust*) enfoncer dans; (*money*) *Com* investir dans; **a sinking feeling** un serrement de cœur.

sinner ['sɪnər] *n* pécheur *m*, pécheresse *f*.

sinuous ['sɪnjʊəs] *a* sinueux.

sinus ['saɪnəs] *n* *Anat* sinus *m inv*.

sip [sɪp] *vi* (**-pp-**) boire à petites gorgées; – *n* (*mouthful*) petite gorgée *f*; (*drop*) goutte *f*.

siphon ['saɪfən] *n* siphon *m*; – *vt* **to s. off** (*petrol*) siphonner; (*money*) *Fig* détourner.

sir [sɜːr] *n* monsieur *m*; **S. Walter Raleigh** (*title*) sir Walter Raleigh.

siren ['saɪərən] *n* (*of factory etc*) sirène *f*.

sirloin ['sɜːlɔɪn] *n* (*steak*) faux-filet *m*; (*joint*) aloyau *m*.

sissy ['sɪsɪ] *n* (*boy, man*) *Fam* femmelette *f*.

sister ['sɪstər] *n* sœur *f*; (*nurse*) infirmière *f* en chef. ◆**s.-in-law** *n* (*pl* sisters-in-law) belle-sœur *f*. ◆**sisterly** *a* fraternel.

sit [sɪt] *vi* (*pp & pp* sat, *pres p* sitting) s'asseoir; (*for artist*) poser (for pour); (*remain*) rester; (*of assembly etc*) siéger, être en séance; **to be sitting** (*of person, cat etc*) être assis; (*of bird*) être perché; **she sat** *or* **was sitting reading** elle était assise à lire; **to s. around** (*do nothing*) ne rien faire; **to s. back** (*in chair*) se caler; (*rest*) se reposer; (*do nothing*) ne rien faire; **to s. down** s'asseoir; **s.-down strike** grève *f* sur le tas; **to s. in on** (*lecture etc*) assister à; **to s. on** (*jury etc*) être membre de; (*fact etc*) *Fam* garder pour soi; **to s. through** *or* **out** (*film etc*) rester jusqu'au bout de; **to s. up** (**straight**) s'asseoir (bien droit); **to s. up waiting for s.o.** (*at night*) ne pas se coucher en attendant qn; – *vt* **to s. s.o.** (**down**) asseoir qn; **to s. (for)** (*exam*) se présenter à; **to s. out** (*event, dance*) ne pas prendre part à. ◆**sitting** *n* séance *f*; (*for one's portrait*) séance *f* de pose; (*in restaurant*) service *m*; – *a* (*committee etc*) en séance; **s. duck** *Fam* victime *f* facile; **s. tenant** locataire *mf* en possession des lieux. ◆**sitting room** *n* salon *m*.

site [saɪt] *n* emplacement *m*; (*archaeological*) site *m*; (*building*) **s.** chantier *m*; **launching s.** aire *f* de lancement; – *vt* (*building*) placer.

sit-in ['sɪtɪn] *n Pol* sit-in *m inv*.

sitter ['sɪtər] *n* (*for child*) baby-sitter *mf*.

situate ['sɪtjʊeɪt] *vt* situer; **to be situated** être situé. ◆**situ'ation** *n* situation *f*.

six [sɪks] *a & n* six (*m*). ◆**six'teen** *a & n* seize (*m*). ◆**six'teenth** *a & n* seizième (*mf*). ◆**sixth** *a & n* sixième (*mf*); (**lower**) s.

form *Sch* = classe *f* de première; (**upper**) s. form *Sch* = classe *f* terminale; **a s.** (*fraction*) un sixième. ◆**sixtieth** *a & n* soixantième (*mf*). ◆**sixty** *a & n* soixante (*m*).

size [saɪz] **1** *n* (*of person, animal, garment etc*) taille *f*; (*measurements*) dimensions *fpl*; (*of egg, packet*) grosseur *f*; (*of book*) grandeur *f*, format *m*; (*of problem, town, damage*) importance *f*, étendue *f*; (*of sum*) montant *m*, importance *f*; (*of shoes, gloves*) pointure *f*; (*of shirt*) encolure *f*; **hip/chest s.** tour *m* de hanches/de poitrine; **it's the s. of** . . . c'est grand comme . . . . **2** *n* (*glue*) colle *f*. **3** *vt* **to s. up** (*person*) jauger; (*situation*) évaluer. ◆**sizeable** *a* assez grand *or* gros.

sizzl/e ['sɪz(ə)l] *vi* grésiller. ◆**—ing** *a* **s.** (**hot**) brûlant.

skat/e¹ [skeɪt] *n* patin *m*; – *vi* patiner. ◆**—ing** *n* patinage *m*; **to go s.** faire du patinage; **s. rink** (*ice*) patinoire *f*; (*roller*) skating *m*. ◆**skateboard** *n* skateboard *m*. ◆**skater** *n* patineur, -euse *mf*.

skate² [skeɪt] *n* (*fish*) raie *f*.

skedaddle [skɪˈdæd(ə)l] *vi Fam* déguerpir.

skein [skeɪn] *n* (*of yarn*) écheveau *m*.

skeleton ['skelɪt(ə)n] *n* squelette *m*; – *a* (*crew, staff*) (réduit au) minimum; **s. key** passe-partout *m inv*.

skeptic ['skeptɪk] *Am* = **sceptic**.

sketch [sketʃ] *n* (*drawing*) croquis *m*, esquisse *f*; *Th* sketch *m*; **a rough s. of** (*plan*) *Fig* une esquisse de; – *vt* **to s.** (**out**) (*view, idea etc*) esquisser; **to s. in** (*details*) ajouter; – *vi* faire un *or* des croquis. ◆**sketchy** *a* (**-ier, -iest**) incomplet, superficiel.

skew [skjuː] *n* **on the s.** de travers.

skewer ['skjʊər] *n* (*for meat etc*) broche *f*; (*for kebab*) brochette *f*.

ski [skiː] *n* (*pl* skis) ski *m*; **s. lift** télésiège *m*; **s. pants** fuseau *m*; **s. run** piste *f* de ski; **s. tow** téléski *m*; – *vi* (*pt* skied [skiːd], *pres p* **skiing**) faire du ski. ◆**—ing** *n Sp* ski *m*; – *a* (*school, clothes*) de ski. ◆**—er** *n* skieur, -euse *mf*.

skid [skɪd] **1** *vi* (**-dd-**) *Aut* déraper; **to s. into** déraper et heurter; – *n* dérapage *m*. **2** *a* **s. row** *Am* quartier *m* de clochards *or* de squats.

skill [skɪl] *n* habileté *f*, adresse *f* (**at** à); (*technique*) technique *f*; **one's skills** (*aptitudes*) ses compétences *fpl*. ◆**skilful**, *Am* ◆**skillful** *a* habile (**at doing** à faire, **at sth** à qch). ◆**skilled** *a* habile (**at doing** à faire, **at sth** à qch); (*worker*) qualifié; (*work*) de spécialiste, de professionnel.

skillet ['skɪlɪt] *n Am* poêle *f* (à frire).

skim [skɪm] **1** *vt* (**-mm-**) (*milk*) écrémer;

(*soup*) écumer. **2** *vti* (-mm-) **to s. (over)** (*surface*) effleurer; **to s. through** (*book*) parcourir.

skimp [skɪmp] *vi* (*on fabric, food etc*) lésiner (**on** sur). ◆**skimpy** *a* (-ier, -iest) (*clothes*) étriqué; (*meal*) insuffisant.

skin [skɪn] *n* peau *f*; **he has thick s.** *Fig* c'est un dur; **s. diving** plongée *f* sous-marine; **s. test** cuti(-réaction) *f*; – *vt* (-nn-) (*animal*) écorcher; (*fruit*) peler. ◆**s.-'deep** *a* superficiel. ◆**s.-'tight** *a* moulant, collant.

skinflint ['skɪnflɪnt] *n* avare *mf*.

skinhead ['skɪnhed] *n* skinhead *m*, jeune voyou *m*.

skinny ['skɪnɪ] *a* (-ier, -iest) maigre.

skint [skɪnt] *a* (*penniless*) *Fam* fauché.

skip[1] [skɪp] **1** *vi* (-pp-) (*jump*) sauter; (*hop about*) sautiller; (*with rope*) sauter à la corde; **to s. off** (*leave*) *Fam* filer; **skipping rope** corde *f* à sauter; – *n* petit saut *m*. **2** *vt* (-pp-) (*omit, miss*) sauter; **to s. classes** sécher les cours; **s. it!** (*forget it*) *Fam* laisse tomber!

skip[2] [skɪp] *n* (*container for debris*) benne *f*.

skipper ['skɪpər] *n* *Nau Sp* capitaine *m*.

skirmish ['skɜːmɪʃ] *n* accrochage *m*.

skirt [skɜːt] **1** *n* jupe *f*. **2** *vt* **to s. round** contourner; **skirting board** (*on wall*) plinthe *f*.

skit [skɪt] *n* *Th* pièce *f* satirique; **a s. on** une parodie de.

skittle ['skɪt(ə)l] *n* quille *f*; *pl* (*game*) jeu *m* de quilles.

skiv/e [skaɪv] *vi* (*skirk*) *Fam* tirer au flanc; **to s. off** (*slip away*) *Fam* se défiler. ◆**—er** *n* *Fam* tire-au-flanc *m* *inv*.

skivvy ['skɪvɪ] *n* *Pej Fam* bonne *f* à tout faire, bon(n)iche *f*.

skulk [skʌlk] *vi* rôder (furtivement).

skull [skʌl] *n* crâne *m*. ◆**skullcap** *n* calotte *f*.

skunk [skʌŋk] *n* (*animal*) mouffette *f*; (*person*) *Pej* salaud *m*.

sky [skaɪ] *n* ciel *m*. ◆**skydiving** *n* parachutisme *m* (en chute libre). ◆**sky-'high** *a* (*prices*) exorbitant. ◆**skylight** *n* lucarne *f*. ◆**skyline** *n* (*outline of buildings*) ligne *f* d'horizon. ◆**skyrocket** *vi* (*of prices*) *Fam* monter en flèche. ◆**skyscraper** *n* gratte-ciel *m* *inv*.

slab [slæb] *n* (*of concrete etc*) bloc *m*; (*thin, flat*) plaque *f*; (*of chocolate*) tablette *f*, plaque *f*; (*paving stone*) dalle *f*.

slack [slæk] *a* (-er, -est) (*knot, spring*) lâche; (*discipline, security*) relâché, lâche; (*trade, grip*) faible, mou; (*negligent*) négligent; (*worker, student*) peu sérieux; **s. periods**

(*weeks etc*) périodes *fpl* creuses; (*hours*) heures *fpl* creuses; **to be s.** (*of rope*) avoir du mou; – *vi* **to s. off** (*in effort*) se relâcher. ◆**slacken** *vi* **to s. (off)** (*in effort*) se relâcher; (*of production, speed, zeal*) diminuer; – *vt* **to s. (off)** (*rope*) relâcher; (*pace, effort*) ralentir. ◆**slacker** *n* (*person*) *Fam* flemmard, -arde *mf*. ◆**slackly** *adv* (*loosely*) lâchement. ◆**slackness** *n* négligence *f*; (*of discipline*) relâchement *m*; (*of rope*) mou *m*; *Com* stagnation *f*.

slacks [slæks] *npl* pantalon *m*.

slag [slæg] *n* (*immoral woman*) *Sl* salope *f*, traînée *f*.

slagheap ['slæghiːp] *n* terril *m*.

slake [sleɪk] *vt* (*thirst*) *Lit* étancher.

slalom ['slɑːləm] *n* *Sp* slalom *m*.

slam [slæm] **1** *vt* (-mm-) (*door, lid*) claquer; (*hit*) frapper violemment; **to s. (down)** (*put down*) poser violemment; **to s. on the brakes** écraser le frein, freiner à bloc; – *vi* (*of door*) claquer; – *n* claquement *m*. **2** *vt* (-mm-) (*criticize*) *Fam* critiquer (avec virulence).

slander ['slɑːndər] *n* diffamation *f*, calomnie *f*; – *vt* diffamer, calomnier.

slang [slæŋ] *n* argot *m*; – *a* (*word etc*) d'argot, argotique. ◆**slanging match** *n* *Fam* engueulade *f*.

slant [slɑːnt] *n* inclinaison *f*; (*point of view*) *Fig* angle *m* (**on** sur); (*bias*) *Fig* parti-pris *m*; **on a s.** penché; (*roof*) en pente; – *vi* (*of writing*) pencher; (*of roof*) être en pente; – *vt* (*writing*) faire pencher; (*news*) *Fig* présenter de façon partiale. ◆**—ed** *a*, ◆**—ing** *a* penché; (*roof*) en pente.

slap [slæp] **1** *n* tape *f*, claque *f*; (*on face*) gifle *f*; – *vt* (-pp-) donner une tape à; **to s. s.o.'s face** gifler qn; **to s. s.o.'s bottom** donner une fessée à qn. **2** *vt* (-pp-) (*put*) mettre, flanquer; **to s. on** (*apply*) appliquer à la va-vite; (*add*) ajouter. **3** *adv* **s. in the middle** *Fam* en plein milieu. ◆**slapdash** *a* (*person*) négligent; (*task*) fait à la va-vite; – *adv* à la va-vite. ◆**slaphappy** *a* *Fam* (*carefree*) insouciant; (*negligent*) négligent. ◆**slapstick** *a* & *n* **s. (comedy)** grosse farce *f*. ◆**slap-up 'meal** *n* *Fam* gueuleton *m*.

slash [slæʃ] **1** *vt* (*cut with blade etc*) entailler, taillader; (*sever*) trancher; – *n* entaille *f*, taillade *f*. **2** *vt* (*reduce*) réduire radicalement; (*prices*) *Com* écraser.

slat [slæt] *n* (*in blind*) lamelle *f*.

slate [sleɪt] **1** *n* ardoise *f*. **2** *vt* (*book etc*) *Fam* critiquer, démolir.

slaughter ['slɔːtər] *vt* (*people*) massacrer;

(*animal*) abattre; − *n* massacre *m*; abattage *m*. ◆**slaughterhouse** *n* abattoir *m*.

Slav [slɑːv] *a & n* slave (*mf*). ◆**Sla'vonic** *a* (*language*) slave.

slave [sleɪv] *n* esclave *mf*; **the s. trade** *Hist* la traite des noirs; **s. driver** *Fig Pej* négrier *m*; − *vi* **to s. (away)** se crever (au travail), bosser comme une bête; **to s. away doing** s'escrimer à faire. ◆**slavery** *n* esclavage *m*. ◆**slavish** *a* servile.

slaver ['slævər] *vi* (*dribble*) baver (**over** sur); − *n* bave *f*.

slay [sleɪ] *vt* (*pt* slew, *pp* slain) *Lit* tuer.

sleazy ['sliːzɪ] *a* (-ier, -iest) *Fam* sordide, immonde.

sledge [sledʒ] (*Am* **sled** [sled]) *n* luge *f*; (*horse-drawn*) traîneau *m*.

sledgehammer ['sledʒhæmər] *n* masse *f*.

sleek [sliːk] *a* (-er, -est) lisse, brillant; (*manner*) onctueux.

sleep [sliːp] *n* sommeil *m*; **to have a s., get some s.** dormir; **to send to s.** endormir; **to go or get to s.** s'endormir; **to go to s.** (*of arm, foot*) *Fam* s'engourdir; − *vi* (*pt & pp* slept) dormir; (*spend the night*) coucher; **s. tight or well!** dors bien!; **I'll s. on it** *Fig* je déciderai demain, la nuit portera conseil; − *vt* **this room sleeps six** on peut coucher *or* loger six personnes dans cette chambre; **to s. it off** *Fam*, **s. off a hangover** cuver son vin. ◆**—ing** *a* (*asleep*) endormi; **s. bag** sac *m* de couchage; **s. car** wagon-lit *m*; **s. pill** somnifère *m*; **s. quarters** chambre(s) *f(pl)*, dortoir *m*. ◆**sleeper** *n* **1** **to be a light/sound s.** avoir le sommeil léger/ lourd. **2** *Rail* (*on track*) traverse *f*; (*berth*) couchette *f*; (*train*) train *m* couchettes. ◆**sleepiness** *n* torpeur *f*. ◆**sleepless** *a* (*hours*) sans sommeil; (*night*) d'insomnie. ◆**sleepwalker** *n* somnambule *mf*. ◆**sleepwalking** *n* somnambulisme *n*. ◆**sleepy** *a* (-ier, -iest) (*town, voice*) endormi; **to be s.** (*of person*) avoir sommeil.

sleet [sliːt] *n* neige *f* fondue; (*sheet of ice*) *Am* verglas *m*; − *vi* **it's sleeting** il tombe de la neige fondue.

sleeve [sliːv] *n* (*of shirt etc*) manche *f*; (*of record*) pochette *f*; **up one's s.** (*surprise, idea etc*) *Fig* en réserve; **long-/short-sleeved** à manches longues/courtes.

sleigh [sleɪ] *n* traîneau *m*.

sleight [slaɪt] *n* **s. of hand** prestidigitation *f*.

slender ['slendər] *a* (*person*) mince, svelte; (*neck, hand*) fin; (*feeble, small*) *Fig* faible.

slept [slept] *see* sleep.

sleuth [sluːθ] *n* (*detective*) *Hum* (fin) limier *m*.

slew [sluː] *n* **a s. of** *Am Fam* un tas de, une tapée de.

slice [slaɪs] *n* tranche *f*; (*portion*) *Fig* partie *f*, part *f*; − *vt* **to s. (up)** couper (en tranches); **to s. off** (*cut off*) couper.

slick [slɪk] **1** *a* (-er, -est) (*glib*) qui a la parole facile; (*manner*) mielleux; (*cunning*) astucieux; (*smooth, slippery*) lisse. **2** *n* **oil s.** nappe *f* de pétrole; (*large*) marée *f* noire.

slid/e [slaɪd] *n* (*act*) (*glib*) glissade *f*; (*in value etc*) *Fig* (légère) baisse *f*; (*in playground*) toboggan *m*; (*on ice*) glissoire *f*; (*for hair*) barrette *f*; *Phot* diapositive *f*; (*of microscope*) lamelle *f*, lame *f*; **s. rule** règle *f* à calcul; − *vi* (*pt & pp* slid) glisser; **to s. into** (*room etc*) se glisser dans; − *vt* (*letter etc*) glisser (**into** dans); (*table etc*) faire glisser. ◆**—ing** *a* (*door, panel*) à glissière; (*roof*) ouvrant; **s. scale** *Com* échelle *f* mobile.

slight [slaɪt] **1** *a* (-er, -est) (*slim*) mince; (*frail*) frêle; (*intelligence*) faible; **the slightest thing** la moindre chose; **not in the slightest** pas le moins du monde. **2** *vt* (*offend*) offenser; (*ignore*) bouder; − *n* affront *m* (**on** à). ◆**—ly** *adv* légèrement, un peu; **s. built** fluet.

slim [slɪm] *a* (slimmer, slimmest) mince; − *vi* (-mm-) maigrir. ◆**slimming** *a* (*diet*) amaigrissant; (*food*) qui ne fait pas grossir. ◆**slimness** *n* minceur *f*.

slime [slaɪm] *n* boue *f* (visqueuse); (*of snail*) bave *f*. ◆**slimy** *a* (-ier, -iest) (*muddy*) boueux; (*sticky, smarmy*) visqueux.

sling [slɪŋ] **1** *n* (*weapon*) fronde *f*; (*toy*) lance-pierres *m inv*; (*for arm*) *Med* écharpe *f*; **in a s.** en écharpe. **2** *vt* (*pt & pp* slung) (*throw*) jeter, lancer; (*hang*) suspendre; **to s. away or out** (*throw out*) *Fam* balancer. ◆**slingshot** *n* *Am* lance-pierres *m inv*.

slip [slɪp] **1** *n* (*mistake*) erreur *f*; (*woman's undergarment*) combinaison *f*; (*of paper for filing*) fiche *f*; **a s. of paper** (*bit*) un bout de papier; **a s. (of the tongue)** un lapsus; **to give s.o. the s.** fausser compagnie à qn; **s. road** *Aut* bretelle *f*. **2** *vi* (-pp-) glisser; **to s. into** (*go, get*) se glisser dans; (*habit*) prendre; (*garment*) mettre; **to let s.** (*chance, oath, secret*) laisser échapper; **to s. through** (*crowd*) se faufiler parmi; **to s. along or over to** faire un saut chez; **to s. away** (*escape*) s'esquiver; **to s. back/in** retourner/entrer furtivement; **to s. out** sortir furtivement; (*of secret*) s'éventer; **to s. past** (*guards*) passer sans être vu de; **to s. up** (*make a* *mistake*) *Fam* gaffer; – *vt* (*slide*) glisser (**to à, into** dans); **it slipped his** *or* **her notice** ça lui a échappé; **it slipped his** *or* **her mind** ça lui est sorti de l'esprit; **to s. off** (*garment etc*) enlever; **to s. on** (*garment etc*) mettre. ◆**s.-up** *n Fam* gaffe *f*, erreur *f*.

slipcover ['slɪpkʌvər] *n Am* housse *f*.

slipper ['slɪpər] *n* pantoufle *f*.

slippery ['slɪpərɪ] *a* glissant.

slipshod ['slɪpʃɒd] *a* (*negligent*) négligent; (*slovenly*) négligé.

slit [slɪt] *n* (*opening*) fente *f*; (*cut*) coupure *f*; – *vt* (*pt & pp* **slit**, *pres p* **slitting**) (*cut*) couper; (*tear*) déchirer; **to s. open** (*sack*) éventrer.

slither ['slɪðər] *vi* glisser; (*of snake*) se couler.

sliver ['slɪvər] *n* (*of apple etc*) lichette *f*; (*of wood*) éclat *m*.

slob [slɒb] *n Fam* malotru *m*, goujat *m*.

slobber ['slɒbər] *vi* (*of dog etc*) baver (**over** sur); – *n* bave *f*.

slog [slɒg] **1** *n a* (**hard**) **s.** (*effort*) un gros effort; (*work*) un travail dur; – *vi* (**-gg-**) **to s. (away)** bosser, trimer. **2** *vt* (**-gg-**) (*hit*) donner un grand coup à.

slogan ['sləʊgən] *n* slogan *m*.

slop [slɒp] *n* **slops** eaux *fpl* sales; – *vi* (**-pp-**) **to s. (over)** (*spill*) se répandre; – *vt* répandre.

slop/e [sləʊp] *n* pente *f*; (*of mountain*) flanc *m*; (*slant*) inclinaison *f*; – *vi* être en pente; (*of handwriting*) pencher; **to s. down** descendre en pente. ◆**—ing** *a* en pente; (*handwriting*) penché.

sloppy ['slɒpɪ] *a* (**-ier, -iest**) (*work, appearance*) négligé; (*person*) négligent; (*mawkish*) sentimental; (*wet*) détrempé; (*watery*) liquide.

slosh [slɒʃ] *vt* (*pour*) *Fam* répandre. ◆**—ed** *a* (*drunk*) *Fam* bourré.

slot [slɒt] *n* (*slit*) fente *f*; (*groove*) rainure *f*; (*in programme*) *Rad TV* créneau *m*; **s. machine** (*vending*) distributeur *m* automatique; (*gambling*) machine *f* à sous; – *vt* (**-tt-**) (*insert*) insérer (**into** dans); – *vi* s'insérer (**into** dans).

sloth [sləʊθ] *n Lit* paresse *f*.

slouch [slaʊtʃ] **1** *vi* ne pas se tenir droit; (*have stoop*) avoir le dos voûté; (*in chair*) se vautrer (**in** dans); **slouching over** (*desk etc*) penché sur; – *n* mauvaise tenue *f*; **with a s.** (*to walk*) en se tenant mal; le dos voûté. **2** *n Fam* (*person*) lourdaud, -aude *mf*; (*lazy*) paresseux, -euse *mf*.

slovenly ['slʌvənlɪ] *a* négligé. ◆**slovenli-**

ness *n* (*of dress*) négligé *m*; (*carelessness*) négligence *f*.

slow [sləʊ] *a* (**-er, -est**) lent; (*business*) calme; (*party, event*) ennuyeux; **at (a) s. speed** à vitesse réduite; **to be a s. walker** marcher lentement; **to be s.** (*of clock, watch*) retarder; **to be five minutes s.** retarder de cinq minutes; **to be s. to act** *or* **in acting** être lent à agir; **in s. motion** au ralenti; – *adv* lentement; – *vt* **to s. down** *or* **up** ralentir; (*delay*) retarder; – *vi* **to s. down** *or* **up** ralentir. ◆**—ly** *adv* lentement; (*bit by bit*) peu à peu. ◆**—ness** *n* lenteur *f*.

slowcoach ['sləʊkəʊtʃ] *n Fam* lambin, -ine *mf*. ◆**slow-down** *n* ralentissement *m*; **s.-down** (*strike*) *Am* grève *f* perlée. ◆**slow-'moving** *a* (*vehicle etc*) lent. ◆**slowpoke** *n Am Fam* lambin, -ine *mf*.

sludge [slʌdʒ] *n* gadoue *f*.

slue [sluː] *n Am Fam* = **slew**.

slug [slʌg] **1** *n* (*mollusc*) limace *f*. **2** *n* (*bullet*) *Am Sl* pruneau *m*. **3** *vt* (**-gg-**) (*hit*) *Am Fam* frapper; – *n* coup *m*, marron *m*.

sluggish ['slʌgɪʃ] *a* lent, mou.

sluice [sluːs] *n* **s.** (**gate**) vanne *f*.

slum [slʌm] *n* (*house*) taudis *m*; **the slums** les quartiers *mpl* pauvres; – *a* (*district*) pauvre; – *vt* (**-mm-**) **to s. it** *Fam* manger de la vache enragée. ◆**slummy** *a* (**-ier, -iest**) sordide, pauvre.

slumber ['slʌmbər] *n Lit* sommeil *m*.

slump [slʌmp] *n* baisse *f* soudaine (**in** de); (*in prices*) effondrement *m*; *Econ* crise *f*; – *vi* (*decrease*) baisser; (*of prices*) s'effondrer; **to s. into** (*armchair etc*) s'affaisser dans.

slung [slʌŋ] *see* **sling 2**.

slur [slɜːr] **1** *vt* (**-rr-**) prononcer indistinctement; **to s. one's words** manger ses mots. **2** *n* **to cast a s. on** (*reputation etc*) porter atteinte à. ◆**slurred** *a* (*speech*) indistinct.

slush [slʌʃ] *n* (*snow*) neige *f* fondue; (*mud*) gadoue *f*. ◆**slushy** *a* (**-ier, -iest**) (*road*) couvert de neige fondue.

slut [slʌt] *n Pej* (*immoral*) salope *f*, traînée *f*; (*untidy*) souillon *f*.

sly [slaɪ] *a* (**-er, -est**) (*deceitful*) sournois; (*crafty*) rusé; – *n* **on the s.** en cachette. ◆**—ly** *adv* sournoisement; (*in secret*) en cachette.

smack [smæk] **1** *n* claque *f*; gifle *f*; fessée *f*; – *vt* donner une claque à; **to s. s.o.'s face** gifler qn; **to s. s.o.('s bottom)** donner une fessée à qn. **2** *adv* **s. in the middle** *Fam* en plein milieu. **3** *vi* (*Be suggestive of*) **to s. of** avoir des relents de. ◆**—ing** *n* fessée *f*.

small [smɔːl] *a* (**-er, -est**) petit; **in the s. hours** au petit matin; **s. talk** menus propos *mpl*; – *adv* (*to cut, chop*) menu; – *n* **the s. of the back** le creux *m* des reins. ◆**—ness** *n* petitesse *f*. ◆**smallholding** *n* petite ferme *f*. ◆**small-scale** *a Fig* peu important. ◆**small-time** *a* (*crook, dealer etc*) petit, sans grande envergure.

smallpox ['smɔːlpɒks] *n* petite vérole *f*.

smarmy ['smɑːmɪ] *a* (**-ier, -iest**) *Pej Fam* visqueux, obséquieux.

smart¹ [smɑːt] *a* (**-er, -est**) (*in appearance*) élégant; (*astute*) astucieux; (*clever*) intelligent; (*quick*) rapide; **s. aleck** *Fam* je-sais-tout *mf inv*. ◆**smarten** *vt* **to s. up** (*room etc*) embellir; – *vti* **to s.** (**oneself**) **up** (*make oneself spruce*) se faire beau, s'arranger. ◆**smartly** *adv* élégamment; (*quickly*) en vitesse; (*astutely*) astucieusement. ◆**smartness** *n* élégance *f*.

smart² [smɑːt] *vi* (*sting*) brûler, faire mal.

smash [smæʃ] *vt* (*break*) briser; (*shatter*) fracasser; (*enemy*) écraser; (*record*) pulvériser; **to s. s.o.'s face** (**in**) *Fam* casser la gueule à qn; **to s. down** *or* **in** (*door*) fracasser; **to s. up** (*car*) esquinter; (*room*) démolir; – *vi* se briser; **to s. into** (*of car*) se fracasser contre; – *n* (*noise*) fracas *m*; (*blow*) coup *m*; (*accident*) collision *f*; **s. hit** *Fam* succès *m* fou. ◆**s.-up** *n* collision *f*.

smashing ['smæʃɪŋ] *a* (*wonderful*) *Fam* formidable. ◆**smasher** *n* **to be a** (**real**) **s.** *Fam* être formidable.

smattering ['smætərɪŋ] *n* **a s. of** (*French etc*) quelques notions *fpl* de.

smear [smɪər] *vt* (*coat*) enduire (**with** de); (*stain*) tacher (**with** de); (*smudge*) faire une trace sur; – *n* (*mark*) trace *f*; (*stain*) tache *f*; *Med* frottis *m*; **a s. on** (*attack*) *Fig* une atteinte à; **s. campaign** campagne *f* de diffamation.

smell [smel] *n* odeur *f*; (**sense of**) **s.** odorat *m*; – *vt* (*pt & pp* **smelled** *or* **smelt**) sentir; (*of animal*) flairer; – *vi* (*stink*) sentir (mauvais); (*have smell*) avoir une odeur; **to s. of smoke/etc** sentir la fumée/*etc*; **smelling salts** sels *mpl*. ◆**smelly** *a* (**-ier, -iest**) **to be s.** sentir (mauvais).

smelt¹ [smelt] *see* **smell**.

smelt² [smelt] *vt* (*ore*) fondre; **smelting works** fonderie *f*.

smidgen ['smɪdʒən] *n* **a s.** (*a little*) *Am Fam* un brin (**of** de).

smil/e [smaɪl] *n* sourire *m*; – *vi* sourire (**at s.o.** à qn, **at sth** de qch). ◆**—ing** *a* souriant.

smirk [smɜːk] *n* (*smug*) sourire *m* suffisant; (*scornful*) sourire *m* goguenard.

smith [smɪθ] *n* (*blacksmith*) forgeron *m*.

smithereens [smɪðə'riːnz] *npl* **to smash to s.** briser en mille morceaux.

smitten ['smɪt(ə)n] *a* **s. with** *Hum* (*desire, remorse*) pris de; (*in love with*) épris de.

smock [smɒk] *n* blouse *f*.

smog [smɒg] *n* brouillard *m* épais, smog *m*.

smoke [sməʊk] *n* fumée *f*; **to have a s.** fumer une cigarette *etc*; – *vt* (*cigarette, salmon etc*) fumer; **to s. out** (*room etc*) enfumer; – *vi* fumer; **'no smoking'** 'défense de fumer'; **smoking compartment** *Rail* compartiment *m* fumeurs. ◆**smokeless** *a* **s. fuel** combustible *m* non polluant. ◆**smoker** *n* fumeur, -euse *mf*; *Rail* compartiment *m* fumeurs. ◆**smoky** *a* (**-ier, -iest**) (*air*) enfumé; (*wall*) noirci de fumée; **it's s. here** il y a de la fumée ici.

smooth [smuːð] *a* (**-er, -est**) (*surface, skin etc*) lisse; (*road*) à la surface égale; (*movement*) régulier, sans à-coups; (*flight*) agréable; (*cream, manners*) onctueux; (*person*) doucereux; (*sea*) calme; **the s. running** la bonne marche *f* de; – *vt* **to s. down** *or* **out** lisser; **to s. out** *or* **over** (*problems etc*) *Fig* aplanir. ◆**—ly** *adv* (*to land, pass off*) en douceur. ◆**—ness** *n* aspect *m* lisse; (*of road*) surface *f* égale.

smother ['smʌðər] *vt* (*stifle*) étouffer; **to s. with** (*kisses etc*) *Fig* couvrir de.

smoulder ['sməʊldər] *vi* (*of fire, passion etc*) couver.

smudge [smʌdʒ] *n* tache *f*, bavure *f*; – *vt* (*paper etc*) faire des taches sur, salir.

smug [smʌg] *a* (**smugger, smuggest**) (*smile etc*) béat; (*person*) content de soi, suffisant. ◆**—ly** *adv* avec suffisance.

smuggl/e ['smʌg(ə)l] *vt* passer (en fraude); **smuggled goods** contrebande *f*. ◆**—ing** *n* contrebande *f*. ◆**—er** *n* contrebandier, -ière *mf*.

smut [smʌt] *n inv* (*obscenity*) saleté(s) *f(pl)*. ◆**smutty** *a* (**-ier, -iest**) (*joke etc*) cochon.

snack [snæk] *n* casse-croûte *m inv*; **s. bar** snack(-bar) *m*.

snafu [snæ'fuː] *n Sl* embrouillamini *m*.

snag [snæg] *n* **1** (*hitch*) inconvénient *m*, os *m*. **2** (*in cloth*) accroc *m*.

snail [sneɪl] *n* escargot *m*; **at a s.'s pace** comme une tortue.

snake [sneɪk] *n* (*reptile*) serpent *m*; – *vi* (*of river*) serpenter.

snap [snæp] **1** *vt* (**-pp-**) casser (avec un bruit sec); (*fingers, whip*) faire claquer; **to s. up a bargain** sauter sur une occasion; – *vi* se casser net; (*of whip*) claquer; (*of person*) *Fig* parler sèchement (**at** à); **s. out of it!** *Fam* secoue-toi!; – *n* claquement *m*, bruit *m* sec; *Phot* photo *f*; (*fastener*) *Am* bouton-pression *m*; **cold s.** *Met* coup *m* de froid. **2** *a* soudain, brusque; **to make a s. decision** décider sans réfléchir. ◆**snapshot** *n* photo *f*, instantané *m*.

snappy ['snæpɪ] *a* (**-ier, -iest**) (*pace*) vif; **make it s.!** *Fam* dépêche-toi!

snare [sneər] *n* piège *m*.

snarl [snɑːl] *vi* gronder (en montrant les dents); – *n* grondement *m*. ◆**s.-up** *n Aut Fam* embouteillage *m*.

snatch [snætʃ] *vt* saisir (*d'un geste vif*); (*some rest etc*) *Fig* (réussir à) prendre; **to s. sth from s.o.** arracher qch à qn; – *n* (*theft*) vol *m* (à l'arraché).

snatches ['snætʃɪz] *npl* (*bits*) fragments *mpl* (of de).

snazzy ['snæzɪ] *a* (**-ier, -iest**) *Fam* (*flashy*) tapageur; (*smart*) élégant.

sneak [sniːk] **1** *vi* **to s. in/out** entrer/sortir furtivement; **to s. off** s'esquiver; – *a* (*attack, visit*) furtif. **2** *n* (*telltale*) *Sch Fam* rapporteur, -euse *mf*; – *vi* **to s. on** *Sch Fam* dénoncer. ◆**sneaking** *a* (*suspicion*) vague; (*desire*) secret. ◆**sneaky** *a* (**-ier, -iest**) (*sly*) *Fam* sournois.

sneaker ['sniːkər] *n* (*shoe*) tennis *f*.

sneer [snɪər] *n* ricanement *m*; – *vi* ricaner; **to s. at** se moquer de.

sneeze [sniːz] *n* éternuement *m*; – *vi* éternuer.

snicker ['snɪkər] *n & vi Am* = **snigger.**

snide [snaɪd] *a* (*remark etc*) sarcastique.

sniff [snɪf] *n* reniflement *m*; – *vt* renifler; (*of dog*) flairer, renifler; **to s. out** (*bargain*) *Fig* renifler; – *vi* **to s. (at)** renifler. ◆**sniffle** *vi* renifler; – *n* **a s., the sniffles** *Fam* un petit rhume.

snigger ['snɪgər] *n* (petit) ricanement *m*; – *vi* ricaner. ◆**—ing** *n* ricanement(s) *m(pl)*.

snip [snɪp] *n* (*piece*) petit bout *m* (coupé); (*bargain*) *Fam* bonne affaire *f*; **to make a s. couper**; – *vt* (**-pp-**) couper.

sniper ['snaɪpər] *n Mil* tireur *m* embusqué.

snippet ['snɪpɪt] *n* (*of conversation etc*) bribe *f*.

snivel ['snɪv(ə)l] *vi* (**-ll-**, *Am* **-l-**) pleurnicher. ◆**snivelling** *a* pleurnicheur.

snob [snɒb] *n* snob *mf*. ◆**snobbery** *n* snobisme *m*. ◆**snobbish** *a* snob *inv*.

snook [snuːk] *n* **to cock a s.** faire un pied de nez (**at** à).

snooker ['snuːkər] *n* snooker *m*, *sorte de jeu de billard*.

snoop [snuːp] *vi* fourrer son nez partout; **to s. on s.o.** (*spy on*) espionner qn.

snooty ['snuːtɪ] *a* (**-ier, -iest**) *Fam* snob *inv*.

snooze [snuːz] *n* petit somme *m*; – *vi* faire un petit somme.

snor/e [snɔːr] *vi* ronfler; – *n* ronflement *m*. ◆**—ing** *n* ronflements *mpl*.

snorkel ['snɔːk(ə)l] *n Sp Nau* tuba *m*.

snort [snɔːt] *vi* (*grunt*) grogner; (*sniff*) renifler; (*of horse*) renâcler; – *n* (*grunt*) grognement *m*.

snot [snɒt] *n Pej Fam* morve *f*. ◆**snotty** *a* (**-ier, -iest**) *Fam* (*nose*) qui coule; (*child*) morveux. ◆**snotty-nosed** *a Fam* morveux.

snout [snaʊt] *n* museau *m*.

snow [snəʊ] *n* neige *f*; – *vi* neiger; – *vt* **to be snowed in** être bloqué par la neige; **to be s. under with** (*work etc*) être submergé de. ◆**snowball** *n* boule *f* de neige; – *vi* (*increase*) faire boule de neige. ◆**snowbound** *a* bloqué par la neige. ◆**snow-capped** *a* (*mountain*) enneigé. ◆**snowdrift** *n* congère *f*. ◆**snowdrop** *n Bot* perce-neige *m or f inv*. ◆**snowfall** *n* chute *f* de neige. ◆**snowflake** *n* flocon *m* de neige. ◆**snowman** *n* (*pl* **-men**) bonhomme *m* de neige. ◆**snowmobile** *n* motoneige *f*. ◆**snowplough** *n*, *Am* ◆**snowplow** *n* chasse-neige *m inv*. ◆**snowstorm** *n* tempête *f* de neige. ◆**snowy** *a* (**-ier, -iest**) (*weather, hills, day etc*) neigeux.

snub [snʌb] **1** *n* rebuffade *f*; – *vt* (**-bb-**) (*offer etc*) rejeter; **to s.o.** snober qn. **2** *a* (*nose*) retroussé.

snuff [snʌf] **1** *n* tabac *m* à priser. **2** *vt* **to s. (out)** (*candle*) moucher. ◆**snuffbox** *n* tabatière *f*.

snuffle ['snʌf(ə)l] *vi & n* = **sniffle.**

snug [snʌg] *a* (**snugger, snuggest**) (*house etc*) confortable, douillet; (*garment*) bien ajusté; **we're s.** (*in chair etc*) on est bien; **s. in bed** bien au chaud dans son lit.

snuggle ['snʌg(ə)l] *vi* **to s. up to** se pelotonner contre.

so [səʊ] **1** *adv* (*to such a degree*) si, tellement (*that* que); (*thus*) ainsi, comme ça; **so that** (*purpose*) pour que (+ *sub*); (*result*) si bien que; **so as to do** pour faire; **I think so** je pense, je pense que oui; **do so!** faites-le!; **if so** si oui; **is that so?** c'est vrai?; **so am I, so do I** *etc* moi aussi; **so much** (*to work etc*) tant, tellement (*that* que); **so much courage/etc** tant *or* tellement de courage/*etc* (*that* que); **so many** tant, tellement; **so many books/etc** tant *or* tellement de livres/*etc* (*that* que); **so very fast/etc** vraiment si vite/*etc*; **ten or so** environ dix; **so long!** *Fam* au revoir!; **and so on** et ainsi de suite. **2** *conj* (*therefore*) donc; (*in that case*) alors; **so what?** et alors? ◆**So-and-so** *n* **Mr So-and-so** Monsieur Un tel. ◆**so-'called** *a* soi-disant *inv*. ◆**so-so** *a* *Fam* comme ci comme ça.

soak [səʊk] *vt* (*drench*) tremper; (*washing, food*) faire tremper; **to s. up** absorber; – *vi* (*of washing etc*) tremper; **to s. in** (*of liquid*) s'infiltrer; – *n* **to give sth a s.** faire tremper qch. ◆**—ed** *a* **s. (through)** trempé (jusqu'aux os). ◆**—ing** *a* & *adv* **s. (wet)** trempé; – *n* trempage *m*.

soap [səʊp] *n* savon *m*; **s. opera** téléroman *m*; **s. powder** lessive *f*; – *vt* savonner. ◆**soapflakes** *npl* savon *m* en paillettes. ◆**soapsuds** *npl* mousse *f* de savon. ◆**soapy** *a* (**-ier**, **-iest**) *a* savonneux.

soar [sɔːr] *vi* (*of bird etc*) s'élever; (*of price*) monter (en flèche); (*of hope*) *Fig* grandir.

sob [sɒb] *n* sanglot *m*; – *vi* (**-bb-**) sangloter. ◆**sobbing** *n* (*sobs*) sanglots *mpl*.

sober [ˈsəʊbər] **1** *a* **he's s.** (*not drunk*) il n'est pas ivre; – *vti* **to s. up** dessoûler. **2** *a* (*serious*) sérieux, sensé; (*meal, style*) sobre. ◆**—ly** *adv* sobrement.

soccer [ˈsɒkər] *n* football *m*.

sociable [ˈsəʊʃəb(ə)l] *a* (*person*) sociable; (*evening*) amical. ◆**sociably** *adv* (*to act, reply*) aimablement.

social [ˈsəʊʃəl] *a* social; (*life, gathering*) mondain; **s. club** foyer *m*; **s. science(s)** sciences *fpl* humaines; **s. security** (*aid*) aide *f* sociale; (*retirement pension*) *Am* pension *f* de retraite; **s. services** = sécurité *f* sociale; **s. worker** assistant *m* social; – *n* (*gathering*) réunion *f* (amicale). ◆**socialism** *n* socialisme *m*. ◆**socialist** *a* & *n* socialiste (*mf*). ◆**socialite** *n* mondain, -aine *mf*. ◆**socialize** *vi* (*mix*) se mêler aux autres; (*talk*) bavarder (**with** avec). ◆**socially** *adv* socialement; (*to meet s.o., behave*) en société.

society [səˈsaɪətɪ] *n* (*community, club, companionship etc*) société *f*; *Univ Sch* club *m*; – *a* (*wedding etc*) mondain.

sociology [səʊsɪˈɒlədʒɪ] *n* sociologie *f*. ◆**socio'logical** *a* sociologique. ◆**sociologist** *n* sociologue *mf*.

sock [sɒk] **1** *n* chaussette *f*. **2** *vt* (*hit*) *Sl* flanquer un marron à.

socket [ˈsɒkɪt] *n* (*of bone*) cavité *f*; (*of eye*) orbite *f*; (*power point*) *El* prise *f* de courant; (*of lamp*) douille *f*.

sod [sɒd] *n* (*turf*) *Am* gazon *m*.

soda [ˈsəʊdə] *n* **1** *Ch* soude *f*; **washing s.** cristaux *mpl* de soude. **2** (*water*) eau *f* de Seltz; **s. (pop)** *Am* soda *m*.

sodden [ˈsɒd(ə)n] *a* (*ground*) détrempé.

sodium [ˈsəʊdɪəm] *n* *Ch* sodium *m*.

sofa [ˈsəʊfə] *n* canapé *m*, divan *m*; **s. bed** canapé-lit *m*.

soft [sɒft] *a* (**-er**, **-est**) (*smooth, gentle, supple*) doux; (*butter, ground, snow*) mou; (*wood, heart, paste, colour*) tendre; (*flabby*) flasque, mou; (*easy*) facile; (*indulgent*) indulgent; (*cowardly*) *Fam* poltron; (*stupid*) *Fam* ramolli; **it's too s.** (*radio etc*) ce n'est pas assez fort; **s. drink** boisson *f* non alcoolisée. ◆**s.-'boiled** *a* (*egg*) à la coque. ◆**soften** [ˈsɒf(ə)n] *vt* (*object*) ramollir; (*voice, pain, colour*) adoucir; – *vi* se ramollir; s'adoucir. ◆**softie** *n* *Fam* sentimental, -âle *mf*; (*weakling*) mauviette *f*. ◆**softly** *adv* doucement. ◆**softness** *n* douceur *f*; (*of butter, ground, snow*) mollesse *f*.

software [ˈsɒftweər] *n* *inv* (*of computer*) logiciel *m*.

soggy [ˈsɒgɪ] *a* (**-ier**, **-iest**) (*ground*) détrempé; (*biscuit, bread*) ramolli.

soil [sɔɪl] **1** *n* (*earth*) sol *m*, terre *f*. **2** *vt* (*dirty*) salir; – *vi* se salir.

solar [ˈsəʊlər] *a* solaire.

sold [səʊld] *see* **sell**.

solder [ˈsɒldər, *Am* ˈsɒdər] *vt* souder; – *n* soudure *f*.

soldier [ˈsəʊldʒər] **1** *n* soldat *m*, militaire *m*. **2** *vi* **to s. on** persévérer.

sole [səʊl] **1** *n* (*of shoe*) semelle *f*; (*of foot*) plante *f*; – *vt* ressemeler. **2** *a* (*only*) seul, unique; (*rights, representative*) *Com* exclusif. **3** *n* (*fish*) sole *f*. ◆**—ly** *adv* uniquement; **you're s. to blame** tu es seul coupable.

solemn [ˈsɒləm] *a* (*formal*) solennel; (*serious*) grave. ◆**so'lemnity** *n* solennité *f*; gravité *f*. ◆**solemnly** *adv* (*to promise*) solennellement; (*to say*) gravement.

solicit [səˈlɪsɪt] *vt* (*seek*) solliciter; – *vi* (*of prostitute*) racoler. ◆**solicitor** *n* (*for wills etc*) notaire *m*.

solid [ˈsɒlɪd] *a* (*car, character, meal etc*) & *Ch* solide; (*wall, line, ball*) plein; (*gold, rock*) massif; (*crowd, mass*) compact; **frozen s.** entièrement gelé; **ten days s.** dix jours d'affilée; – *n* *Ch* solide *m*; *pl* *Culin* aliments *mpl* solides. ◆**so'lidify** *vi* se solidifier. ◆**so'lidity** *n* solidité *f*. ◆**solidly** *adv* (*built etc*) solidement; (*to support, vote*) en masse.

solidarity [sɒlɪˈdærətɪ] *n* solidarité *f* (**with** avec).

soliloquy [səˈlɪləkwɪ] *n* monologue *m*.

solitary [ˈsɒlɪtərɪ] *a* (*lonely, alone*) solitaire;

(*only*) seul; s. **confinement** *Jur* isolement *m* (cellulaire). ◆**solitude** *n* solitude *f*.

solo ['səʊləʊ] *n* (*pl* -os) *Mus* solo *m*; – *a* solo *inv*; – *adv Mus* en solo; (*to fly*) en solitaire. ◆**soloist** *n Mus* soliste *mf*.

solstice ['sɒlstɪs] *n* solstice *m*.

soluble ['sɒljʊb(ə)l] *a* (*substance, problem*) soluble.

solution [sə'luːʃ(ə)n] *n* (*to problem etc*) & *Ch* solution *f* (to de).

solv/e [sɒlv] *vt* (*problem etc*) résoudre. ◆**–able** *a* soluble.

solvent ['sɒlvənt] **1** *a* (*financially*) solvable. **2** *n Ch* (dis)solvant *m*. ◆**solvency** *n Fin* solvabilité *f*.

sombre ['sɒmbər] *a* sombre, triste.

some [sʌm] *a* **1** (*amount, number*) s. wine du vin; s. **glue** de la colle; s. **water** de l'eau; s. **dogs** des chiens; s. **pretty flowers** de jolies fleurs. **2** (*unspecified*) un, une; s. **man (or other)** un homme (quelconque); s. **charm** (*a certain amount of*) un certain charme; s. **other way** quelque autre *or* un autre moyen; **that's s. book!** *Fam* ça, c'est un livre! **3** (*a few*) quelques, certains; (*a little*) un peu de; – *pron* **1** (*number*) quelques-un(e)s, certain(e)s (of de, d'entre). **2** (*a certain quantity*) en; **I want s.** j'en veux; **do you have s.?** en as-tu?; s. **of it** is over il en reste un peu *or* une partie; – *adv* (*about*) quelque; s. **ten years** quelque dix ans.

somebody ['sʌmbɒdɪ] *pron* = **someone**. ◆**someday** *adv* un jour. ◆**somehow** *adv* (*in some way*) d'une manière ou d'une autre; (*for some reason*) on ne sait pourquoi. ◆**someone** *pron* quelqu'un; **at s.'s house** chez qn; s. **small/etc** quelqu'un de petit/*etc*. ◆**someplace** *adv Am* quelque part. ◆**something** *pron* quelque chose; s. **awful/etc** quelque chose d'affreux/*etc*; s. **of a liar/etc** un peu menteur/*etc*; – *adv* **she plays s. like . . .** elle joue un peu comme . . . ; **it was s. awful** c'était vraiment affreux. ◆**sometime 1** *adv* un jour; s. **in May/etc** au cours du mois de mai/*etc*; s. **before his departure** avant son départ. **2** *a* (*former*) ancien. ◆**sometimes** *adv* quelquefois, parfois. ◆**somewhat** *adv* quelque peu, assez. ◆**somewhere** *adv* quelque part; s. **about** fifteen (*approximately*) environ quinze.

somersault ['sʌməsɔːlt] *n* culbute *f*; (*in air*) saut *m* périlleux; – *vi* faire la *or* une culbute.

son [sʌn] *n* fils *m*. ◆**s.-in-law** *n* (*pl* **sons-in-law**) beau-fils *m*, gendre *m*.

sonar ['səʊnɑːr] *n* sonar *m*.

sonata [sə'nɑːtə] *n Mus* sonate *f*.

song [sɒŋ] *n* chanson *f*; (*of bird*) chant *m*. ◆**songbook** *n* recueil *m* de chansons.

sonic ['sɒnɪk] *a* s. **boom** bang *m* (supersonique).

sonnet ['sɒnɪt] *n* (*poem*) sonnet *m*.

soon [suːn] *adv* (-er, -est) (*in a short time*) bientôt; (*quickly*) vite; (*early*) tôt; s. **after** peu après; **as s. as she leaves** aussitôt qu'elle partira; **no sooner had he spoken than** à peine avait-il parlé que; **I'd sooner leave** je préférerais partir; **I'd just as s. leave** j'aimerais autant partir; **sooner or later** tôt ou tard.

soot [sʊt] *n* suie *f*. ◆**sooty** *a* (-ier, -iest) couvert de suie.

sooth/e [suːð] *vt* (*pain, nerves*) calmer; *Fig* rassurer. ◆**–ing** *a* (*ointment, words*) calmant.

sophisticated [sə'fɪstɪkeɪtɪd] *a* (*person, taste*) raffiné; (*machine, method, beauty*) sophistiqué.

sophomore ['sɒfəmɔːr] *n Am* étudiant, -ante *mf* de seconde année.

soporific [sɒpə'rɪfɪk] *a* (*substance, speech etc*) soporifique.

sopping ['sɒpɪŋ] *n* & *adv* s. **(wet)** trempé.

soppy ['sɒpɪ] *a* (-ier, -iest) *Fam* (*silly*) idiot, bête; (*sentimental*) sentimental.

soprano [sə'prɑːnəʊ] *n* (*pl* -os) *Mus* (*singer*) soprano *mf*; (*voice*) soprano *m*.

sorbet ['sɔːbeɪ] *n* (*water ice*) sorbet *m*.

sorcerer ['sɔːsərər] *n* sorcier *m*.

sordid ['sɔːdɪd] *a* (*act, street etc*) sordide.

sore [sɔːr] *a* (-er, -est) (*painful*) douloureux; (*angry*) *Am* fâché (at contre); **a s. point** *Fig* un sujet délicat; **she has a s. thumb** elle a mal au pouce; **he's still s.** *Med* il a encore mal; – *n Med* plaie *f*. ◆**–ly** *adv* (*tempted, regretted*) très; s. **needed** dont on a grand besoin. ◆**–ness** *n* (*pain*) douleur *f*.

sorrow ['sɒrəʊ] *n* chagrin *m*, peine *f*. ◆**sorrowful** *a* triste.

sorry ['sɒrɪ] *a* (-ier, -iest) (*sight, state etc*) triste; **to be s.** (*regret*) être désolé, regretter (to do de faire); **I'm s. she can't come** je regrette qu'elle ne puisse pas venir; **I'm s. about the delay** je m'excuse pour ce retard; **s.!** pardon!; **to say s.** demander pardon (to à); **to feel** *or* **be s. for** plaindre.

sort [sɔːt] **1** *n* genre *m*, espèce *f*, sorte *f*; **a s. of une sorte** *or* **espèce de; a good s.** (*person*) *Fam* **a brave type; s. of sad/etc** plutôt triste/*etc*. **2** *vt* (*letters*) trier; **to s.** (*classify, select*) trier; (*separate*) séparer (**from** de); (*arrange*) arranger; (*tidy*) ranger; (*problem*) régler; **to s. s.o. out** (*punish*) *Fam* faire voir à qn; − *vi* **to s. through** (*letters etc*) trier; **sorting office** centre *m* de tri. **◆−er** *n* (*person*) trieur, -euse *mf*.

soufflé ['su:fleɪ] *n Culin* soufflé *m*.

sought [sɔːt] *see* **seek**.

soul [səʊl] *n* âme *f*; **not a living s.** (*nobody*) personne, pas âme qui vive; **a good s.** *Fig* un brave type; **s. mate** âme *f* sœur. **◆s.-destroying** *a* abrutissant. **◆s.-searching** *n* examen *m* de conscience.

sound¹ [saʊnd] *n* son *m*; (*noise*) bruit *m*; **I don't like the s. of it** ça ne me plaît pas du tout; − *a* (*wave, film*) sonore; (*engineer*) du son; **s. archives** phonothèque *f*; **s. barrier** mur *m* du son; **s. effects** bruitage *m*; − *vt* (*bell, alarm etc*) sonner; (*bugle*) sonner de; (*letter*) *Gram* prononcer; **to s. one's horn** *Aut* klaxonner; − *vi* retentir, sonner; (*seem*) sembler; **to s. like** sembler être; (*resemble*) ressembler à; **it sounds like** *or* **as if it** semble que (+ *sub or indic*); **to s. off about** *Pej* (*boast*) se vanter de; (*complain*) rouspéter à propos de. **◆soundproof** *a* insonorisé; − *vt* insonoriser. **◆soundtrack** *n* (*of film etc*) bande *f* sonore.

sound² [saʊnd] *a* (**-er, -est**) (*healthy*) sain; (*sturdy, reliable*) solide; (*instinct*) sûr; (*advice*) sensé; (*beating, sense*) bon; − *adv* **s. asleep** profondément endormi. **◆−ly** *adv* (*asleep*) profondément; (*reasoned*) solidement; (*beaten*) . complètement. **◆−ness** *n* (*of mind*) santé *f*; (*of argument*) solidité *f*.

sound³ [saʊnd] *vt* (*test, measure*) sonder; **to s. s.o. out** sonder qn (**about** *sur*).

soup [suːp] *n* soupe *f*, potage *m*; **in the s.** (*in trouble*) *Fam* dans le pétrin.

sour ['saʊər] *a* (**-er, -est**) aigre; **to turn s.** (*of wine*) s'aigrir; (*of milk*) tourner; (*of friendship*) se détériorer; (*of conversation*) tourner au vinaigre; − *vi* (*of temper*) s'aigrir.

source [sɔːs] *n* (*origin*) source *f*; **s. of energy** source d'énergie.

south [saʊθ] *n* sud *m*; − *a* (*coast*) sud *inv*; (*wind*) du sud; **to be s. of** être au sud de; **S. America/Africa** Amérique *f*/Afrique *f* du Sud; **S. American** *a & n* sud-américain, -aine (*mf*); **S. African** *a & n* sud-africain, -aine (*mf*); − *adv* au sud, vers le sud. **◆southbound** *a* (*carriageway*) sud *inv*; (*traffic*) en direction du sud. **◆south-'east** *n & a* sud-est *m & a inv*. **◆southerly** ['sʌðəlɪ] *a* (*point*) sud *inv*; (*direction, wind*) du sud. **◆southern** ['sʌðən] *a* (*town*) du sud; (*coast*) sud *inv*; **S. Italy** le Sud de

l'Italie; **S. Africa** Afrique *f* australe. **◆southerner** ['sʌðənər] *n* habitant, -ante *mf* du Sud. **◆southward(s)** *a & adv* le sud. **◆south-'west** *n & a* sud-ouest *m & a inv*.

souvenir [suːvəˈnɪər] *n* (*object*) souvenir *m*.

sovereign ['sɒvrɪn] *n* souverain, -aine *mf*; − *a* (*State, authority*) souverain; (*rights*) de souveraineté. **◆sovereignty** *n* souveraineté *f*.

Soviet ['səʊvɪət] *a* soviétique; **the S. Union** l'Union *f* soviétique.

sow¹ [saʊ] *n* (*pig*) truie *f*.

sow² [səʊ] *vt* (*pt* **sowed**, *pp* **sowed** *or* **sown**) (*seeds, doubt etc*) semer; (*land*) ensemencer (**with** *de*).

soya ['sɔɪə] *n* **s. (bean)** graine *f* de soja. **◆soybean** *n Am* graine *f* de soja.

sozzled ['sɒz(ə)ld] *a* (*drunk*) *Sl* bourré.

spa [spaː] *n* (*town*) station *f* thermale; (*spring*) source *f* minérale.

space [speɪs] *n* (*gap, emptiness*) espace *m*; (*period*) période *f*; **blank s.** espace *m*, blanc *m*; (**outer**) **s.** l'espace (cosmique); **to take up s.** (*room*) prendre de la place; **in the s. of** en l'espace de; **s. heater** (*electric*) radiateur *m*; − *a* (*voyage etc*) spatial; − *vt* **to s. out** espacer; **double/single spacing** (*on typewriter*) double/simple interligne *m*. **◆spaceman** *n* (*pl* **-men**) astronaute *m*. **◆spaceship** *n*, **◆spacecraft** *n inv* engin *m* spatial. **◆spacesuit** *n* scaphandre *m* (de cosmonaute).

spacious ['speɪʃəs] *a* spacieux, grand. **◆−ness** *n* grandeur *f*.

spade [speɪd] *n* **1** (*for garden*) bêche *f*; (*of child*) pelle *f*. **2** *Cards* pique *m*. **◆spadework** *n Fig* travail *m* préparatoire; (*around problem or case*) débroussaillage *m*.

spaghetti [spəˈgetɪ] *n* spaghetti(s) *mpl*.

Spain [speɪn] *n* Espagne *f*.

span [spæn] *n* (*of arch*) portée *f*; (*of wings*) envergure *f*; (*of life*) *Fig* durée *f*; − *vt* (**-nn-**) (*of bridge etc*) enjamber (*rivière etc*); *Fig* couvrir, embrasser.

Spaniard ['spænjəd] *n* Espagnol, -ole *mf*. **◆Spanish** *a* espagnol; − *n* (*language*) espagnol *m*. **◆Spanish-A'merican** *a* hispano-américain.

spaniel ['spænjəl] *n* épagneul *m*.

spank [spæŋk] *vt* fesser, donner une fessée à; − *n* **to give s.o. a s.** fesser qn. **◆−ing** *n* fessée *f*.

spanner ['spænər] *n* (*tool*) clé *f* (à écrous); **adjustable s.** clé *f* à molette.

spar/e¹ [speər] **1** *a* (*extra, surplus*) de *or* en

trop; *(clothes, tyre)* de rechange; *(wheel)* de secours; *(available)* disponible; *(bed, room)* d'ami; **s. time** loisirs *mpl*; **– n s. (part)** *Tech Aut* pièce *f* détachée. **2** *vt (do without)* se passer de; *(s.o.'s life)* épargner; *(efforts, s.o.'s feelings)* ménager; **to s. s.o.** *(not kill)* épargner qn; *(grief, details etc)* épargner à qn; *(time)* accorder à qn; *(money)* donner à qn; **I can't s. the time** je n'ai pas le temps; **five to s.** cinq de trop. **◆—ing** *a (use)* modéré; **to be s. with** *(butter etc)* ménager.
spare² [speər] *a (lean)* maigre.
spark [spɑːk] **1** *n* étincelle *f*. **2** *vt* **to s. off** *(cause)* provoquer. **◆spark(ing) plug** *n* Aut bougie *f*.
sparkl/e [ˈspɑːk(ə)l] *vi* étinceler, scintiller; **– n** éclat *m*. **◆—ing** *a (wine, water)* pétillant.
sparrow [ˈspærəʊ] *n* moineau *m*.
sparse [spɑːs] *a* clairsemé. **◆—ly** *adv (populated etc)* peu.
spartan [ˈspɑːtən] *a* spartiate, austère.
spasm [ˈspæzəm] *n (of muscle)* spasme *m*; *(of coughing etc)* Fig accès *m*. **◆spasˈmodic** *a (pain etc)* spasmodique; Fig irrégulier.
spastic [ˈspæstɪk] *n* handicapé, -ée *mf* moteur.
spat [spæt] *see* **spit 1.**
spate [speɪt] *n* **s. of** *(orders etc)* une avalanche de.
spatter [ˈspætər] *vt (clothes, person etc)* éclabousser (with de); **– vi to s. over s.o.** *(of mud etc)* éclabousser qn.
spatula [ˈspætjʊlə] *n* spatule *f*.
spawn [spɔːn] *n (of fish etc)* frai *m*; **– vi** frayer; **– vt** pondre; Fig engendrer.
speak [spiːk] *vi (pt* **spoke**, *pp* **spoken)** parler; *(formally, in assembly)* prendre la parole; **so to s.** pour ainsi dire; **that speaks for itself** c'est évident; **nothing to s. of** pas grand-chose; **Bob speaking** Tel Bob à l'appareil; **that's spoken for** c'est pris *or* réservé; **to s. out** *or* **up** *(boldly)* parler (franchement); **to s. up** *(more loudly)* parler plus fort; **– vt** *(language)* parler; *(say)* dire; **to s. one's mind** dire ce que l'on pense. **◆—ing** *n* **public s.** art *m* oratoire; **– a to be on s. terms with** parler à; **English-/French-speaking** anglophone/francophone. **◆—er** *n (public)* orateur *m*; *(in dialogue)* interlocuteur, -trice *mf*; *(loudspeaker)* El haut-parleur *m*; *(of hi-fi)* enceinte *f*; **to be a Spanish/a bad/etc s.** parler espagnol/mal/etc.
spear [spɪər] *n* lance *f*. **◆spearhead** *vt*

(attack) être le fer de lance de; *(campaign)* mener.
spearmint [ˈspɪəmɪnt] *n Bot* menthe *f* (verte); **– a** à la menthe; *(chewing-gum)* mentholé.
spec [spek] *n* **on s.** *(as a gamble)* Fam à tout hasard.
special [ˈspeʃ(ə)l] *a* spécial; *(care, attention)* (tout) particulier; *(measures)* Pol extraordinaire; *(favourite)* préféré; **by s. delivery** *(letter etc)* par exprès; **– n today's s.** *(in restaurant)* le plat du jour. **◆specialist** *n* spécialiste *mf* (in de); **– a** *(dictionary, knowledge)* technique, spécialisé. **◆speciˈality** *n* spécialité *f*. **◆specialize** *vi* se spécialiser (in dans). **◆specialized** *a* spécialisé. **◆specially** *adv (specifically)* spécialement; *(on purpose)* (tout) spécialement. **◆specialty** *n Am* spécialité *f*.
species [ˈspiːʃiːz] *n inv* espèce *f*.
specific [spəˈsɪfɪk] *a* précis, explicite; *Phys Ch* spécifique. **◆specifically** *adv (expressly)* expressément; *(exactly)* précisément.
specify [ˈspesɪfaɪ] *vt* spécifier **(that** que). **◆specifiˈcation** *n* spécification*f*; *pl (of car, machine etc)* caractéristiques *fpl*.
specimen [ˈspesɪmɪn] *n (example, person)* spécimen *m*; *(of blood)* prélèvement *m*; *(of urine)* échantillon *m*; **s. signature** spécimen *m* de signature; **s. copy** *(of book etc)* spécimen *m*.
specious [ˈspiːʃəs] *a* spécieux.
speck [spek] *n (stain)* petite tache *f*; *(of dust)* grain *m*; *(dot)* point *m*.
speckled [ˈspek(ə)ld] *a* tacheté.
specs [speks] *npl Fam* lunettes *fpl*.
spectacle [ˈspektək(ə)l] **1** *n (sight)* spectacle *m*. **2** *npl (glasses)* lunettes *fpl*. **◆specˈtacular** *a* spectaculaire. **◆specˈtator** *n Sp etc* spectateur, -trice *mf*.
spectre [ˈspektər] *n (menacing image)* spectre *m* (of de).
spectrum, *pl* -tra [ˈspektrəm, -trə] *n Phys* spectre *m*; *(range)* Fig gamme *f*.
speculate [ˈspekjʊleɪt] *vi Fin Phil* spéculer; **to s. about** *(s.o.'s motives etc)* s'interroger sur; **– vt to s. that** *(guess)* conjecturer que. **◆specuˈlation** *n Fin Phil* spéculation *f*; *(guessing)* conjectures *fpl* **(about** sur). **◆speculator** *n* spéculateur, -trice *mf*. **◆speculative** *a Fin Phil* spéculatif; **that's s.** *(guesswork)* c'est (très) hypothétique.
sped [sped] *see* **speed 1.**
speech [spiːtʃ] *n (talk, address)* & *Gram* discours *m* **(on** sur); *(faculty)* parole *f*;

(*diction*) élocution *f*; (*of group*) langage *m*; **a short s.** une allocution *f*; **freedom of s.** liberté *f* d'expression; **part of s.** *Gram* catégorie *f* grammaticale. ◆**-less** *a* muet (**with de**).

speed [spiːd] **1** *n* (*rate of movement*) vitesse *f*; (*swiftness*) rapidité *f*; **s. limit** *Aut* limitation *f* de vitesse; – *vt* (*pt & pp* **sped**) **to s. up** accélérer; – *vi* **to s. up** (*of person*) aller plus vite; (*of pace*) s'accélérer; **to s. past** passer à toute vitesse (**sth devant qch**). **2** *vi* (*pt & pp* **speeded**) (*drive too fast*) aller trop vite. ◆**-ing** *n Jur* excès *m* de vitesse. ◆**speedboat** *n* vedette *f*. ◆**spee'dometer** *n Aut* compteur *m* (de vitesse). ◆**speedway** *n Sp* piste *f* de vitesse pour motos; *Sp Aut Am* autodrome *m*.

speed/y ['spiːdɪ] *a* (**-ier, -iest**) rapide. ◆**-ily** *adv* rapidement.

spell¹ [spel] *n* (*magic*) charme *m*, sortilège *m*; (*curse*) sort *m*; *Fig* charme *m*; **under a s.** envoûté. ◆**spellbound** *a* (*audience etc*) captivé.

spell² [spel] *n* (*period*) (courte) période *f*; (*moment, while*) moment *m*; **s. of duty** tour *m* de service.

spell³ [spel] *vt* (*pt & pp* **spelled** or **spelt**) (*write*) écrire; (*say aloud*) épeler; (*of letters*) former (*mot*); (*mean*) *Fig* signifier; **to be able to s.** savoir l'orthographe; **how is it spelt?** comment cela s'écrit-il?; **to s. out** (*aloud*) épeler; *Fig* expliquer très clairement. ◆**-ing** *n* orthographe *f*.

spend [spend] **1** *vt* (*pt & pp* **spent**) (*money*) dépenser (**on pour**); – *vi* dépenser. **2** *vt* (*pt & pp* **spent**) (*time, holiday etc*) passer (**on sth sur qch, doing à faire**); (*energy, care etc*) consacrer (**on sth à qch, doing à faire**). ◆**-ing** *n* dépenses *fpl*; – *a* (*money*) de poche. ◆**-er** *n* **to be a big s.** dépenser beaucoup. ◆**spendthrift** *n* **to be a s.** être dépensier.

spent [spent] *see* **spend**; – *a* (*used*) utilisé; (*energy*) épuisé.

sperm [spɜːm] *n* (*pl* **sperm** or **sperms**) sperme *m*.

spew [spjuː] *vt* vomir.

sphere [sfɪər] *n* (*of influence, action etc*) & *Geom Pol* sphère *f*; (*of music, poetry etc*) domaine *m*; **the social s.** le domaine social. ◆**spherical** ['sferɪk(ə)l] *a* sphérique.

sphinx [sfɪŋks] *n* sphinx *m*.

spice [spaɪs] *n Culin* épice *f*; (*interest etc*) *Fig* piment *m*; – *vt* épicer. ◆**spicy** *a* (**-ier, -iest**) épicé; (*story*) *Fig* pimenté.

spick-and-span [spɪkən'spæn] *a* (*clean*) impeccable.

spider ['spaɪdər] *n* araignée *f*.

spiel [ʃpiːl] *n Fam* baratin *m*.

spike [spaɪk] *n* (*of metal*) pointe *f*; – *vt* (*pierce*) transpercer. ◆**spiky** *a* (**-ier, -iest**) *a* garni de pointes.

spill [spɪl] *vt* (*pt & pp* **spilled** or **spilt**) (*liquid*) répandre, renverser (**on, over sur**); **to s. the beans** *Fam* vendre la mèche; – *vi* **to s. (out)** se répandre; **to s. over** déborder.

spin [spɪn] *n* (*motion*) tour *m*; (*car ride*) petit tour *m*; (*on washing machine*) essorage *m*; **s. dryer** essoreuse *f*; – *vt* (*pt & pp* **spun**, *pres p* **spinning**) (*web, yarn, wool etc*) filer (**into** en); (*wheel, top*) faire tourner; (*washing*) essorer; (*story*) *Fig* débiter; **to s. out** (*speech etc*) faire durer; – *vi* (*of spinner, spider*) filer; **to s. (round)** (*of dancer, top, planet etc*) tourner; (*of head, room*) *Fig* tourner; (*of vehicle*) faire un tête-à-queue. ◆**spinning** *n* (*by hand*) filage *m*; (*process*) *Tech* filature *f*; **s. top** toupie *f*; **s. wheel** rouet *m*. ◆**spin-'dry** *vt* essorer. ◆**spin-off** *n* avantage *m* inattendu; (*of process, book etc*) dérivé *m*.

spinach ['spɪnɪdʒ] *n* (*plant*) épinard *m*; (*leaves*) *Culin* épinards *mpl*.

spindle ['spɪnd(ə)l] *n Tex* fuseau *m*. ◆**spindly** *a* (**-ier, -iest**) (*legs, arms*) grêle.

spine [spaɪn] *n Anat* colonne *f* vertébrale; (*spike of animal or plant*) épine *f*. ◆**spinal** *a* (*column*) vertébral; **s. cord** moelle *f* épinière. ◆**spineless** *a Fig* mou, faible.

spinster ['spɪnstər] *n* célibataire *f*; *Pej* vieille fille *f*.

spiral ['spaɪərəl] **1** *n* spirale *f*; – *a* en spirale; (*staircase*) en colimaçon. **2** *vi* (**-ll-, *Am* -l-**) (*of prices*) monter en flèche.

spire ['spaɪər] *n* (*of church*) flèche *f*.

spirit ['spɪrɪt] **1** *n* (*soul, ghost etc*) esprit *m*; (*courage*) *Fig* courage *m*, vigueur *f*; *pl* (*drink*) alcool *m*, spiritueux *mpl*; **spirit(s)** (*morale*) moral *m*; *Ch* alcool *m*; **in good spirits** de bonne humeur; **the right s.** l'attitude *f* qu'il faut; – *a* (*lamp*) à alcool; **s. level** niveau *m* à bulle (d'air). **2** *vt* **to s. away** (*person*) faire disparaître mystérieusement; (*steal*) *Hum* subtiliser. ◆**-ed** *a* (*person, remark*) fougueux; (*campaign*) vigoureux.

spiritual ['spɪrɪtʃʊəl] *a Phil Rel* spirituel; – *n* (*Negro*) **s.** (negro-)spiritual *m*. ◆**spiritualism** *n* spiritisme *m*. ◆**spiritualist** *n* spirite *mf*.

spit [spɪt] **1** *n* crachat *m*; – *vi* (*pt & pp* **spat** or **spit**, *pres p* **spitting**) cracher; (*splutter*) *Fig* crépiter; – *vt* cracher; **to s. out** (re)cracher; **the spitting image of s.o.** le portrait (tout craché) de qn. **2** n (for meat) broche f.

spite [spaɪt] **1** n in s. of malgré; in s. of the fact that (although) bien que (+ sub). **2** n (dislike) rancune f; − vt (annoy) contrarier. ◆**spiteful** a méchant. ◆**spitefully** adv méchamment.

spittle ['spɪt(ə)l] n salive f, crachat(s) m (pl).

splash [splæʃ] vt (spatter) éclabousser (**with** de, **over** sur); (spill) répandre; − vi (of mud, ink etc) faire des éclaboussures; (of waves) clapoter, déferler; **to s. over sth/s.o.** éclabousser qch/qn; **to s. (about)** (in river, mud) patauger; (in bath) barboter; **to s. out** (spend money) Fam claquer de l'argent; − n (splashing) éclaboussement m; (of colour) Fig tache f; **s. (mark)** éclaboussure f; **s.!** plouf!

spleen [spliːn] n Anat rate f.

splendid ['splendɪd] a (wonderful, rich, beautiful) splendide. ◆**splendour** n splendeur f.

splint [splɪnt] n Med éclisse f.

splinter ['splɪntər] n (of wood etc) éclat m; (in finger) écharde f; **s. group** Pol groupe m dissident.

split [splɪt] n fente f; (tear) déchirure f; (of couple) Pol scission f; **to do the splits** (in gymnastics) faire le grand écart; **one's s.** (share) Fam sa part; − a **a s. second** une fraction de seconde; − vt (pt & pp **split**, pres p **splitting**) (break apart) fendre; (tear) déchirer; **to s. (up)** (group) diviser; (money, work) partager (**between** entre); **to s. one's head open** s'ouvrir la tête; **to s. one's sides (laughing)** se tordre (de rire); **to s. hairs** Fig couper les cheveux en quatre; **s.-level apartment** duplex m; − vi se fendre; (tear) se déchirer; **to s. (up)** (of group) éclater; (of couple) rompre, se séparer; **to s. off** (become loose) se détacher (**from** de); **to s. up** (of crowd) se disperser. ◆**splitting** a (headache) atroce. ◆**split-up** n (of couple) rupture f.

splodge [splɒdʒ] n, **splotch** [splɒtʃ] n (mark) tache f.

splurge [splɜːdʒ] vi (spend money) Fam claquer de l'argent.

splutter ['splʌtər] vi (of sparks, fat) crépiter; (stammer) bredouiller.

spoil [spɔɪl] vt (pt & pp **spoilt** or **spoiled**) (pamper, make unpleasant or less good) gâter; (damage, ruin) abîmer; (pleasure, life) gâcher, gâter. ◆**spoilsport** n rabat-joie m inv.

spoils [spɔɪlz] npl (rewards) butin m.

spoke[1] [spəʊk] n (of wheel) rayon m.

spoke[2] [spəʊk] see **speak**. ◆**spoken** see **speak**; − a (language etc) parlé; **softly s.** (person) à la voix douce. ◆**spokesman** n (pl -men) porte-parole m inv (**for**, of de).

sponge [spʌndʒ] **1** n éponge f; **s. bag** trousse f de toilette; **s. cake** gâteau m de Savoie; − vt **to s. down/off** laver/enlever à l'éponge. **2** vi **to s. off** or **on s.o.** Fam vivre aux crochets de qn; − vt **to s. sth off s.o.** Fam taper qn de qch. ◆**sponger** n Fam parasite m. ◆**spongy** a (-ier, -iest) spongieux.

sponsor ['spɒnsər] n (of appeal, advertiser etc) personne f assurant le patronage (**of** de); (for membership) parrain m, marraine f; Jur garant, -ante mf; Sp sponsor m; − vt (appeal etc) patronner; (member, firm) parrainer. ◆**sponsorship** n patronage m; parrainage m.

spontaneous [spɒnˈteɪnɪəs] a spontané. ◆**spontaneity** [spɒntəˈneɪɪtɪ] n spontanéité f. ◆**spontaneously** adv spontanément.

spoof [spuːf] n Fam parodie f (**on** de).

spooky ['spuːkɪ] a (-ier, -iest) Fam qui donne le frisson.

spool [spuːl] n bobine f.

spoon [spuːn] n cuiller f. ◆**spoonfeed** vt (pt & pp **spoonfed**) (help) Fig mâcher le travail à. ◆**spoonful** n cuillerée f.

sporadic [spəˈrædɪk] a sporadique; **s. fighting** échauffourées fpl. ◆**sporadically** adv sporadiquement.

sport [spɔːt] **1** n sport m; **a (good) s.** (person) Fam un chic type; **to play s.** or Am **sports** faire du sport; **sports club** club m sportif; **sports car/jacket** voiture f/veste f de sport; **sports results** résultats mpl sportifs. **2** vt (wear) arborer. ◆**-ing** a (conduct, attitude, person etc) sportif; **that's s. of you** Fig c'est chic de ta part. ◆**sportsman** n (pl -men) sportif m. ◆**sportsmanlike** a sportif. ◆**sportsmanship** n sportivité f. ◆**sportswear** n vêtements mpl de sport. ◆**sportswoman** n (pl -women) sportive f. ◆**sporty** a (-ier, -iest) sportif.

spot[1] [spɒt] n (stain, mark) tache f; (dot) point m; (polka dot) pois m; (pimple) bouton m; (place) endroit m, coin m; (act) Th numéro m; (drop) goutte f; **a s. of** (bit) Fam un peu de; **a soft s. for** un faible pour; **on the s.** sur place, sur les lieux; (at once) sur le coup; **in a (tight) s.** (difficulty) dans le pétrin; (accident) **black s.** Aut point m noir; **s. cash** argent m comptant; **s. check** contrôle m au hasard or ·l'improviste. ◆**spotless** a (clean) impeccable. ◆**spot-**

lessly *adv* s. **clean** impeccable. ◆**spot-light** *n* (*lamp*) Th projecteur *m*; (*for photography etc*) spot *m*; **in the s.** Th sous le feu des projecteurs. ◆**spot-'on** *a Fam* tout à fait exact. ◆**spotted** *a* (*fur*) tacheté; (*dress etc*) à pois; (*stained*) taché. ◆**spotty** *a* (**-ier, -iest**) **1** (*face etc*) boutonneux. **2** (*patchy*) *Am* inégal.

spot² [spɒt] *vt* (**-tt-**) (*notice*) apercevoir, remarquer.

spouse [spaʊs, spaʊz] *n* époux *m*, épouse *f*.

spout [spaʊt] **1** *n* (*of jug etc*) bec *m*; **up the s.** (*hope etc*) *Sl* fichu. **2** *vi* to s. (**out**) jaillir. **3** *vt* (*say*) *Pej* débiter.

sprain [spreɪn] *n* entorse *f*, foulure *f*; **to s. one's ankle/wrist** se fouler la cheville/le poignet.

sprang [spræŋ] *see* spring¹.

sprawl [sprɔːl] *vi* (*of town, person*) s'étaler; **to be sprawling** être étalé; – *n* **the urban s.** les banlieues *fpl* tentaculaires. ◆**—ing** *a* (*city*) tentaculaire.

spray [spreɪ] **1** *n* (*water drops*) (nuage *m* de) gouttelettes *fpl*; (*from sea*) embruns *mpl*; (*can, device*) bombe *f*, vaporisateur *m*; **hair s.** laque *f* à cheveux; – *vt* (*liquid, surface*) vaporiser; (*crops, plant*) arroser, traiter; (*car etc*) peindre à la bombe. **2** *n* (*of flowers*) petit bouquet *m*.

spread [spred] *vt* (*pt & pp* spread) (*stretch, open out*) étendre; (*legs, fingers*) écarter; (*strew*) répandre, étaler (**over** sur); (*paint, payment, cards, visits*) étaler; (*people*) disperser; (*fear, news*) répandre; (*illness*) propager; **to s. out** étendre; écarter; étaler; – *vi* (*of fire, town, fog*) s'étendre; (*of news, fear*) se répandre; **to s. out** (*of people*) se disperser; – *n* (*of fire, illness, ideas*) propagation *f*; (*of wealth*) répartition *f*; (*paste*) *Culin* pâte *f* (à tartiner); (*meal*) festin *m*; **cheese s.** fromage *m* à tartiner. ◆**s.-'eagled** *a* bras et jambes écartés.

spree [spriː] *n* **to go on a spending s.** faire des achats extravagants.

sprig [sprɪg] *n* (*branch of heather etc*) brin *m*; (*of parsley*) bouquet *m*.

sprightl/y [ˈspraɪtlɪ] *a* (**-ier, -iest**) alerte. ◆**—iness** *n* vivacité *f*.

spring¹ [sprɪŋ] *n* (*metal device*) ressort *m*; (*leap*) bond *m*; – *vi* (*pt* sprang, *pp* sprung) (*leap*) bondir; **to s. to mind** venir à l'esprit; **to s. into action** passer à l'action; **to s. from** (*stem from*) provenir de; **to s. up** (*appear*) surgir; – *vt* (*news*) annoncer brusquement (**on** à); (*surprise*) faire (**on** à); **to s. a leak** (*of boat*) commencer à faire eau. ◆**spring-**

board *n* tremplin *m*. ◆**springy** *a* (**-ier, -iest**) élastique.

spring² [sprɪŋ] *n* (*season*) printemps *m*; **in** (**the**) **s.** au printemps; **s. onion** ciboule *f*. ◆**s.-'cleaning** *n* nettoyage *m* de printemps. ◆**springlike** *a* printanier. ◆**springtime** *n* printemps *m*.

spring³ [sprɪŋ] *n* (*of water*) source *f*; **s. water** eau *f* de source.

sprinkl/e [ˈsprɪŋk(ə)l] *vt* (*sand etc*) répandre (**on, over** sur); **to s. with water, s. water on** asperger d'eau, arroser; **to s. with** (*sugar, salt, flour*) saupoudrer de. ◆**—ing** *n* a s. of (*a few*) quelques. ◆**—er** *n* (*in garden*) arroseur *m*.

sprint [sprɪnt] *n* Sp sprint *m*; – *vi* sprinter. ◆**—er** *n* sprinter *m*, sprinteuse *f*.

sprite [spraɪt] *n* (*fairy*) lutin *m*.

sprout [spraʊt] **1** *vi* (*of seed, bulb etc*) germer, pousser; **to s. up** (*grow*) pousser vite; (*appear*) surgir; – *vt* (*leaves*) pousser; (*beard*) *Fig* laisser pousser. **2** *n* (**Brussels**) **s.** chou *m* de Bruxelles.

spruce [spruːs] *a* (**-er, -est**) (*neat*) pimpant, net; – *vt* **to s. oneself up** se faire beau.

sprung [sprʌŋ] *see* spring¹; – *a* (*mattress, seat*) à ressorts.

spry [spraɪ] *a* (**spryer, spryest**) (*old person etc*) alerte.

spud [spʌd] *n* (*potato*) *Fam* patate *f*.

spun [spʌn] *see* spin.

spur [spɜːr] *n* (*of horse rider etc*) éperon *m*; (*stimulus*) *Fig* aiguillon *m*; **on the s. of the moment** sur un coup de tête; – *vt* (**-rr-**) **to s.** (**on**) (*urge on*) éperonner.

spurious [ˈspjʊərɪəs] *a* faux.

spurn [spɜːn] *vt* rejeter (avec mépris).

spurt [spɜːt] *vi* (*gush out*) jaillir; (*rush*) foncer; **to s. out** jaillir; – *n* jaillissement *m*; (*of energy*) sursaut *m*; **to put on a s.** (*rush*) foncer.

spy [spaɪ] *n* espion, -onne *mf*; – *a* (*story etc*) d'espionnage; **s. hole** (*peephole*) judas *m*; **s. ring** réseau *m* d'espionnage; – *vi* espionner; **to s. on s.o.** espionner qn; – *vt* (*notice*) *Lit* apercevoir. ◆**—ing** *n* espionnage *m*.

squabbl/e [ˈskwɒb(ə)l] *vi* se chamailler (**over** à propos de); – *n* chamaillerie *f*. ◆**—ing** *n* chamailleries *fpl*.

squad [skwɒd] *n* (*group*) & Mil escouade *f*; (*team*) Sp équipe *f*; **s. car** voiture *f* de police.

squadron [ˈskwɒdrən] *n* Mil escadron *m*; Nau Av escadrille *f*.

squalid [ˈskwɒlɪd] *a* sordide. ◆**squalor** *n* conditions *fpl* sordides.

squall [skwɔːl] *n* (*of wind*) rafale *f*.

squander ['skwɒndər] *vt* (*money, time etc*) gaspiller (**on** en).

square ['skweər] *n* carré *m*; (*on chessboard, graph paper*) case *f*; (*in town*) place *f*; (*drawing implement*) *Tech* équerre *f*; **to be back to s. one** repartir à zéro; – *a* carré; (*in order, settled*) *Fig* en ordre; (*honest*) honnête; (*meal*) solide; (**all**) **s.** (*quits*) quitte (**with** envers); – *vt* (*settle*) mettre en ordre, régler; (*arrange*) arranger; *Math* carrer; (*reconcile*) faire cadrer; – *vi* (*tally*) cadrer (**with** avec); **to s. up** faire face à. ◆**—ly** *adv* (*honestly*) honnêtement; (*exactly*) tout à fait; **s. in the face** bien en face.

squash [skwɒʃ] **1** *vt* (*crush*) écraser; (*squeeze*) serrer; – *n* **lemon/orange s.** (*concentrated*) sirop *m* de citron/d'orange; (*diluted*) citronnade *f*/orangeade *f*. **2** *n* (*game*) squash *m*. **3** *n* (*vegetable*) *Am* courge *f*. ◆**squashy** *a* (**-ier, -iest**) (*soft*) mou.

squat [skwɒt] **1** *a* (*short and thick*) trapu. **2** *vi* (**-tt-**) **to s.** (**down**) s'accroupir. **3** *n* (*house*) squat *m*. ◆**squatting** *a* accroupi. ◆**squatter** *n* squatter *m*.

squawk [skwɔːk] *vi* pousser des cris rauques; – *n* cri *m* rauque.

squeak [skwiːk] *vi* (*of door*) grincer; (*of shoe*) craquer; (*of mouse*) faire couic; – *n* grincement *m*; craquement *m*; couic *m*. ◆**squeaky** *a* (**-ier, -iest**) (*door*) grinçant; (*shoe*) qui craque.

squeal [skwiːl] *vi* pousser des cris aigus; (*of tyres*) crisser; – *n* cri *m* aigu; crissement *m*. **2** *vi* **to s. on s.o.** (*inform on*) *Fam* balancer qn.

squeamish ['skwiːmɪʃ] *a* bien délicat, facilement dégoûté.

squeegee ['skwiːdʒiː] *n* raclette *f* (à vitres).

squeez/e [skwiːz] *vt* (*press*) presser; (*hand, arm*) serrer; **to s. sth out of s.o.** (*information*) soutirer qch à qn; **to s. sth into** faire rentrer qch dans; **to s.** (**out**) (*extract*) exprimer (**from** de); – *vi* **to s. through/into/etc** (*force oneself*) se glisser par/dans/ *etc*; **to s. in** trouver un peu de place; – *n* pression *f*; **to give sth a s.** presser qch; **it's a tight s.** il y a peu de place; **credit s.** *Fin* restrictions *fpl* de crédit. ◆**—er** *n* **lemon s.** presse-citron *m inv*.

squelch [skweltʃ] **1** *vi* patauger (*en faisant floc-floc*). **2** *vt* (*silence*) *Fam* réduire au silence.

squid [skwɪd] *n* (*mollusc*) calmar *m*.

squiggle ['skwɪg(ə)l] *n* ligne *f* onduleuse, gribouillis *m*.

squint [skwɪnt] *n* *Med* strabisme *m*; **to have a s.** loucher; – *vi* loucher; (*in the sunlight etc*) plisser les yeux.

squire ['skwaɪər] *n* propriétaire *m* terrien.

squirm [skwɜːm] *vi* (*wriggle*) se tortiller; **to s. in pain** se tordre de douleur.

squirrel ['skwɪrəl, *Am* 'skwɜːrəl] *n* écureuil *m*.

squirt [skwɜːt] **1** *vt* (*liquid*) faire gicler; – *vi* gicler; – *n* giclée *f*, jet *m*. **2** *n* **little s.** (*person*) *Fam* petit morveux *m*.

stab [stæb] *vt* (**-bb-**) (*with knife etc*) poignarder; – *n* coup *m* (de couteau *or* de poignard). ◆**stabbing** *n* **there was a s.** quelqu'un a été poignardé; – *a* (*pain*) lancinant.

stable[1] ['steɪb(ə)l] *a* (**-er, -est**) stable; **mentally s.** (*person*) bien équilibré. ◆**sta-'bility** *n* stabilité *f*; **mental s.** équilibre *m*. ◆**stabilize** *vt* stabiliser; – *vi* se stabiliser. ◆**stabilizer** *n* stabilisateur *m*.

stable[2] ['steɪb(ə)l] *n* écurie *f*; **s. boy** lad *m*.

stack [stæk] **1** *n* (*heap*) tas *m*; **stacks of** (*lots of*) *Fam* un *or* des tas de; – *vt* **to s.** (**up**) entasser. **2** *npl* (*in library*) réserve *f*.

stadium ['steɪdɪəm] *n* *Sp* stade *m*.

staff [stɑːf] **1** *n* personnel *m*; *Sch* professeurs *mpl*; *Mil* état-major *m*; **s. meeting** *Sch Univ* conseil *m* des professeurs; **s. room** *Sch Univ* salle *f* des professeurs; – *vt* pourvoir en personnel. **2** *n* (*stick*) *Lit* bâton *m*.

stag [stæg] *n* cerf *m*; **s. party** réunion *f* entre hommes.

stage[1] [steɪdʒ] *n* (*platform*) *Th* scène *f*; **the s.** (*profession*) le théâtre; **on s.** sur (la) scène; **s. door** entrée *f* des artistes; **s. fright** le trac; – *vt* (*play*) *Th* monter; *Fig* organiser, effectuer; **it was staged** (*not real*) c'était un coup monté. ◆**s.-hand** *n* machiniste *m*. ◆**s.-manager** *n* régisseur *m*.

stage[2] [steɪdʒ] *n* (*phase*) stade *m*, étape *f*; (*of journey*) étape *f*; (*of track, road*) section *f*; **in (easy) stages** par étapes; **at an early s.** au début.

stagecoach ['steɪdʒkəʊtʃ] *n* *Hist* diligence *f*.

stagger ['stægər] **1** *vi* (*reel*) chanceler. **2** *vt* (*holidays etc*) étaler, échelonner. **3** *vt* **to s. s.o.** (*shock, amaze*) stupéfier qn. ◆**—ing** *a* stupéfiant.

stagnant ['stægnənt] *a* stagnant. ◆**stag-'nate** *vi* stagner. ◆**stag'nation** *n* stagnation *f*.

staid [steɪd] *a* posé, sérieux.

stain [steɪn] **1** *vt* (*mark, dirty*) tacher (**with**

de); – *n* tache *f*. **2** *vt* (*colour*) teinter (*du bois*); **stained glass window** vitrail *m*; – *n* (*colouring for wood*) teinture *f*. ◆**—less** *a* (*steel*) inoxydable; **s.-steel knife**/*etc* couteau *m*/*etc* inoxydable.

stair [steər] *n* **a s.** (*step*) une marche; **the stairs** (*staircase*) l'escalier *m*; – *a* (*carpet etc*) d'escalier. ◆**staircase** *n*, ◆**stairway** *n* escalier *m*.

stake [steɪk] **1** *n* (*post*) pieu *m*; (*for plant*) tuteur *m*; *Hist* bûcher *m*; – *vt* **to s.** (**out**) (*land*) jalonner, délimiter; **to s. one's claim to** revendiquer. **2** *n* (*betting*) enjeu *m*; (*investment*) *Fin* investissement *m*; (*interest*) *Fin* intérêts *mpl*; **at s.** en jeu; – *vt* (*bet*) jouer (**on** sur).

stale [steɪl] *a* (**-er**, **-est**) (*food*) pas frais; (*bread*) rassis; (*beer*) éventé; (*air*) vicié; (*smell*) de renfermé; (*news*) *Fig* vieux; (*joke*) usé, vieux; (*artist*) manquant d'invention. ◆**—ness** *n* (*of food*) manque *m* de fraîcheur.

stalemate ['steɪlmeɪt] *n* *Chess* pat *m*; *Fig* impasse *f*.

stalk [stɔːk] **1** *n* (*of plant*) tige *f*, queue *f*; (*of fruit*) queue *f*. **2** *vt* (*animal*, *criminal*) traquer. **3** *vi* **to s. out** (*walk*) partir avec raideur *or* en marchant à grands pas.

stall [stɔːl] **1** *n* (*in market*) étal *m*, éventaire *m*; (*for newspapers, flowers*) kiosque *m*; (*in stable*) stalle *f*; **the stalls** *Cin* l'orchestre *m*. **2** *vti* *Aut* caler. **3** *vi* **to s.** (**for time**) chercher à gagner du temps.

stallion ['stæljən] *n* (*horse*) étalon *m*.

stalwart ['stɔːlwət] *a* (*supporter*) brave, fidèle; – *n* (*follower*) fidèle *mf*.

stamina ['stæmɪnə] *n* vigueur *f*, résistance *f*.

stammer ['stæmər] *vti* bégayer; – *n* bégaiement *m*; **to have a s.** être bègue.

stamp [stæmp] **1** *n* (*for postage, implement*) timbre *m*; (*mark*) cachet *m*, timbre *m*; **the s. of** *Fig* la marque de; **men of your s.** les hommes de votre trempe; **s. collecting** philatélie *f*; – *vt* (*mark*) tamponner, timbrer; (*letter*) timbrer; (*metal*) estamper; **to s. sth on sth** (*affix*) apposer qch sur qch; **to s. out** (*rebellion, evil*) écraser; (*disease*) supprimer; **stamped addressed envelope** enveloppe *f* timbrée à votre adresse. **2** *vti* **to s.** (**one's feet**) taper *or* frapper des pieds; **stamping ground** *Fam* lieu *m* favori.

stampede [stæm'piːd] *n* fuite *f* précipitée; (*rush*) ruée *f*; – *vi* fuir en désordre; (*rush*) se ruer.

stance [stɑːns] *n* position *f*.

stand [stænd] *n* (*position*) position *f*; (*support*) support *m*; (*at exhibition*) stand *m*; (*for spectators*) *Sp* tribune *f*; (*witness*) *Jur Am* barre *f*; **to make a s., take one's s.** prendre position (**against** contre); **news/ flower s.** (*in street*) kiosque *m* à journaux/à fleurs; **hat s.** porte-chapeaux *m inv*; **music s.** pupitre *m* à musique; – *vt* (*pt & pp* **stood**) (*pain, journey, person etc*) supporter; **to s.** (**up**) (*put straight*) mettre (debout); **to s. s.o. sth** (*pay for*) payer qch à qn; **to s. a chance** avoir une chance; **to s. s.o. up** *Fam* poser un lapin à qn; – *vi* être *or* se tenir (debout); (*rise*) se lever; (*remain*) rester (debout); (*be situated*) se trouver; (*be*) être; (*of object, argument*) reposer (**on** sur); **to leave to s.** (*liquid*) laisser reposer; **to s. to lose** risquer de perdre; **to s. around** (*in street etc*) traîner; **to s. aside** s'écarter; **to s. back** reculer; **to s. by** (*do nothing*) rester là (sans rien faire); (*be ready*) être prêt (à partir *or* à intervenir); (*one's opinion etc*) s'en tenir à; (*friend etc*) rester fidèle à; **to s. down** (*withdraw*) se désister; **to s. for** (*represent*) représenter; *Pol* être candidat à; (*put up with*) supporter; **to s. in for** (*replace*) remplacer; **to s. out** (*be visible or conspicuous*) ressortir (**against** sur); **to s. over s.o.** (*watch closely*) surveiller qn; **to s. up** (*rise*) se lever; **to s. up for** (*defend*) défendre; **to s. up to** (*resist*) résister à. ◆**—ing** *a* debout *inv*; (*committee, offer, army*) permanent; **s. room** places *fpl* debout; **s. joke** plaisanterie *f* classique; – *n* (*reputation*) réputation *f*; (*social, professional*) rang *m*; (*financial*) situation *f*; **of six years' s.** (*duration*) qui dure depuis six ans; **of long s.** de longue date. ◆**standby** (*pl* **-bys**) **on s.** prêt à partir *or* à intervenir; – *a* (*battery etc*) de réserve; (*ticket*) *Av* sans garantie. ◆**stand-in** *n* remplaçant, -ante *mf* (**for** de); *Th* doublure *f* (**for** de).

standard ['stændəd] **1** *n* (*norm*) norme *f*, critère *m*; (*level*) niveau *m*; (*of weight, gold*) étalon *m*; *pl* (*morals*) principes *mpl*; **s. of living** niveau *m* de vie; **to be** *or* **come up to s.** (*of person*) être à la hauteur; (*of work etc*) être au niveau; – *a* (*average*) ordinaire, courant; (*model, size*) *Com* standard *inv*; (*weight*) étalon *inv*; (*dictionary, book*) classique; **s. lamp** lampadaire *m*. **2** *n* (*flag*) étendard *m*. ◆**standardize** *vt* standardiser.

stand-offish [stænd'ɒfɪʃ] *a* (*person*) distant, froid.

standpoint ['stændpɔɪnt] *n* point *m* de vue.

standstill ['stændstɪl] *n* **to bring to a s.** immobiliser; **to come to a s.** s'immobiliser;

at a s. immobile; (*industry, negotiations*) paralysé.

stank [stæŋk] *see* stink.

stanza ['stænzə] *n* strophe *f*.

stapl/e ['steɪp(ə)l] **1** *a* (*basic*) de base; s. food *or* diet nourriture *f* de base. **2** *n* (*for paper etc*) agrafe *f*; − *vt* agrafer. ◆**−er** *n* (*for paper etc*) agrafeuse *f*.

star [stɑːr] *n* étoile *f*; (*person*) *Cin* vedette *f*; shooting s. étoile *f* filante; s. part rôle *m* principal; the Stars and Stripes, the S.-Spangled Banner *Am* la bannière étoilée; two-s. (petrol) de l'ordinaire *m*; four-s. (petrol) du super; − *vi* (-rr-) (*of actor*) être la vedette (in de); − *vt* (*of film*) avoir pour vedette. ◆**stardom** *n* célébrité *f*. ◆**starfish** *n* étoile *f* de mer. ◆**starlit** *a* (*night*) étoilé.

starboard ['stɑːbəd] *n Nau Av* tribord *m*.

starch [stɑːtʃ] *n* (*for stiffening*) amidon *m*; *pl* (*foods*) féculents *mpl*; − *vt* amidonner. ◆**starchy** *a* (-ier, -iest) (*food*) féculent; (*formal*) *Fig* guindé.

stare [steər] *n* regard *m* (fixe); − *vi* to s. at fixer (du regard); − *vt* to s. s.o. in the face dévisager qn.

stark [stɑːk] *a* (-er, -est) (*place*) désolé; (*austere*) austère; (*fact, reality*) brutal; the s. truth la vérité toute nue; − *adv* s. naked complètement nu. ◆**starkers** *a* *Sl* complètement nu, à poil.

starling ['stɑːlɪŋ] *n* étourneau *m*.

starry ['stɑːrɪ] *a* (-ier, -iest) (*sky*) étoilé. ◆**s.-'eyed** *a* (*naïve*) ingénu, naïf.

start¹ [stɑːt] *n* commencement *m*, début *m*; (*of race*) départ *m*; (*lead*) *Sp* & *Fig* avance *f* (on sur); to make a s. commencer; for a s. pour commencer; from the s. dès le début; − *vt* commencer; (*bottle*) entamer, commencer; (*fashion*) lancer; to s. a war provoquer une guerre; to s. a fire (*in grate*) allumer un feu; (*accidentally*) provoquer un incendie; to s. s.o. (off) on (*career*) lancer qn dans; to s. (up) (*engine, vehicle*) mettre en marche; to s. doing *or* to do commencer *or* se mettre à faire; − *vi* commencer (with sth par qch, by doing par faire); to s. on sth commencer qch; to s. (up) commencer (*of vehicle*) démarrer; to s. (off or out) (*leave*) partir (for pour); (*in job*) débuter; to s. back (*return*) repartir; to s. with (*firstly*) pour commencer. ◆**−ing** *n* (*point, line*) de départ; s. post *Sp* ligne *f* de départ; s. from à partir de. ◆**−er** *n* (*runner*) partant *m*; (*official*) *Sp* starter *m*; (*device*) *Aut* démarreur *m*; *pl Culin* hors-d'œuvre *m inv*; for starters (*first*) pour commencer.

start² [stɑːt] *vi* (*be startled, jump*) sursauter; − *n* sursaut *m*; to give s.o. a s. faire sursauter qn.

startle ['stɑːt(ə)l] *vt* (*make jump*) faire sursauter; (*alarm*) *Fig* alarmer; (*surprise*) surprendre.

starve [stɑːv] *vi* (*die*) mourir de faim; (*suffer*) souffrir de la faim; I'm starving *Fig* je meurs de faim; − *vt* (*kill*) laisser mourir de faim; (*make suffer*) faire souffrir de la faim; (*deprive*) *Fig* priver (of de). ◆**star-**'vation *n* faim *f*; − *a* (*wage, ration*) de famine; on a s. diet à la diète.

stash [stæʃ] *vt* to s. away (*hide*) cacher; (*save up*) mettre de côté.

state¹ [steɪt] **1** *n* (*condition*) état *m*; (*pomp*) apparat *m*; not in a (fit) s. to, in no (fit) s. to hors d'état de; to lie in s. (*of body*) être exposé. **2** *n* S. (*nation etc*) État *m*; the States *Geog Fam* les États-Unis *mpl*; − *a* (*secret, document*) d'État; (*control, security*) de l'État; (*school, education*) public; s. visit voyage *m* officiel; S. Department *Pol Am* Département *m* d'État. ◆**stateless** *a* apatride; s. person apatride *mf*. ◆**state-**'owned *a* étatisé. ◆**statesman** *n* (*pl* -men) homme *m* d'État. ◆**statesman-ship** *n* diplomatie *f*.

state² [steɪt] *vt* déclarer (that que); (*opinion*) formuler; (*problem*) exposer; (*time, date*) fixer. ◆**statement** *n* déclaration *f*; *Jur* déposition *f*; bank s., s. of account *Fin* relevé *m* de compte.

stately ['steɪtlɪ] *a* (-ier, -iest) majestueux; s. home château *m*.

static ['stætɪk] *a* statique; − *n* (*noise*) *Rad* parasites *mpl*.

station ['steɪʃ(ə)n] *n Rail* gare *f*; (*underground*) station *f*; (*position*) & *Mil* poste *m*; (*social*) rang *m*; (*police*) s. commissariat *m* or poste *m* (de police); space/observation/radio/*etc* s. station *f* spatiale/d'observation/de radio/*etc*; bus *or* coach s. gare *f* routière; s. wagon *Aut Am* break *m*; − *vt* (*position*) placer, poster. ◆**stationmaster** *n Rail* chef *m* de gare.

stationary ['steɪʃ(ə)nərɪ] *a* (*motionless*) stationnaire; (*vehicle*) à l'arrêt.

stationer ['steɪʃ(ə)nər] *n* papetier, -ière *mf*; s.'s (shop) papeterie *f*. ◆**stationery** *n* (*paper*) papier *m*; (*articles*) papeterie *f*.

statistic [stə'tɪstɪk] *n* (*fact*) statistique *f*; *pl* (*science*) la statistique. ◆**statistical** *a* statistique.

statue ['stætʃur] n statue f. ◆**statu'esque** a (beauty etc) sculptural.

stature ['stætʃər] n stature f.

status ['steɪtəs] n (position) situation f; Jur statut m; (prestige) standing m, prestige m; **s. symbol** marque f de standing; **s. quo** statu quo m inv.

statute ['stætʃuːt] n (law) loi f; pl (of club, institution) statuts mpl. ◆**statutory** a (right etc) statutaire; **s. holiday** fête f légale.

staunch [stɔːntʃ] a (-er, -est) loyal, fidèle. ◆—**ly** adv loyalement.

stave [steɪv] 1 vt to s. off (danger, disaster) conjurer; (hunger) tromper. 2 n Mus portée f.

stay [steɪ] 1 n (visit) séjour m; – vi (remain) rester; (reside) loger; (visit) séjourner; **to s. put** ne pas bouger; **to s. with** (plan, idea) ne pas lâcher; **to s. away** (keep one's distance) ne pas s'approcher (**from** de); **to s. away from** (school, meeting etc) ne pas aller à; **to s. in** (at home) rester à la maison; (of nail, tooth etc) tenir; **to s. out** (outside) rester dehors; (not come home) ne pas rentrer; **to s. out of sth** (not interfere in) ne pas se mêler de qch; (avoid) éviter qch; **to s. up** (at night) ne pas se coucher; (of fence etc) tenir; **to s. up late** se coucher tard; **staying power** endurance f. 2 vt (hunger) tromper. ◆**s.-at-home** n & a Pej casanier, -ière (mf).

St Bernard [sənt'bɜːnəd, Am seɪntbə'nɑːd] n (dog) saint-bernard m.

stead [sted] n **to stand s.o. in good s.** être bien utile à qn; **in s.o.'s s.** à la place de qn.

steadfast ['stedfɑːst] a (intention etc) ferme.

steady ['stedɪ] a (-ier, -iest) (firm, stable) stable; (hand) sûr, assuré; (progress, speed, demand) régulier, constant; (nerves) solide; (staid) sérieux; **a s. boyfriend** un petit ami; **s. (on one's feet)** solide sur ses jambes; – adv **to go s. with** Fam sortir avec; – vt (chair etc) maintenir (en place); (hand) assurer; (nerves) calmer; (wedge, prop up) caler; **to s. oneself** (stop oneself falling) reprendre son aplomb. ◆**steadily** adv (to walk) d'un pas assuré; (regularly) régulièrement; (gradually) progressivement; (continuously) sans arrêt. ◆**steadiness** n stabilité f; régularité f.

steak [steɪk] n steak m, bifteck m. ◆**steakhouse** n grill(-room) m.

steal¹ [stiːl] vti (pt **stole**, pp **stolen**) voler (**from s.o.** à qn).

steal² [stiːl] vi (pt **stole**, pp **stolen**) **to s. in/out** entrer/sortir furtivement. ◆**stealth**

[stelθ] n **by s.** furtivement. ◆**stealthy** a (-ier, -iest) furtif.

steam [stiːm] n vapeur f; (on glass) buée f; **to let off s.** (unwind) Fam se défouler, décompresser; **s. engine/iron** locomotive f/fer m à vapeur; – vt Culin cuire à la vapeur; **to get steamed up** (of glass) se couvrir de buée; Fig Fam s'énerver; – vi (of kettle etc) fumer; **to s. up** (of glass) se couvrir de buée. ◆**steamer** n, ◆**steamship** n (bateau m à) vapeur m; (liner) paquebot m. ◆**steamroller** n rouleau m compresseur. ◆**steamy** a (-ier, -iest) humide; (window) embué; (love affair etc) brûlant.

steel [stiːl] 1 n acier m; **s. industry** sidérurgie f. 2 vt **to s. oneself** s'endurcir (**against** contre). ◆**steelworks** n aciérie f.

steep [stiːp] 1 a (-er, -est) (stairs, slope etc) raide; (hill) escarpé; (price) Fig excessif. 2 vt (soak) tremper (**in** dans); **steeped in** Fig imprégné de. ◆—**ly** adv (to rise) en pente raide, (of prices) Fig excessivement.

steeple ['stiːp(ə)l] n clocher m.

steeplechase ['stiːp(ə)ltʃeɪs] n (race) steeple(-chase) m.

steer [stɪər] vt (vehicle, person) diriger, piloter; (ship) diriger, gouverner; – vi (of person) Nau tenir le gouvernail, gouverner; **to s. towards** faire route vers; **to s. clear of** éviter. ◆—**ing** n Aut direction f; **s. wheel** volant m.

stem [stem] 1 n (of plant etc) tige f; (of glass) pied m. 2 vt (-mm-) **to s. (the flow of)** (stop) arrêter, contenir. 3 vi (-mm-) **to s. from** provenir de.

stench [stentʃ] n puanteur f.

stencil ['stens(ə)l] n (metal, plastic) pochoir m; (paper, for typing) stencil m; – vt (-ll-, Am -l-) (notes etc) polycopier.

stenographer [stə'nɒɡrəfər] n Am sténodactylo f.

step [step] n (movement, sound) pas m; (stair) marche f; (on train, bus) marchepied m; (doorstep) pas m de la porte; (action) Fig mesure f; **(flight of) steps** (indoors) escalier m; (outdoors) perron m; **(pair of) steps** (ladder) escabeau m; **s. by s.** pas à pas; **to keep in s.** marcher au pas; **in s. with** Fig en accord avec; – vi (-pp-) (walk) marcher (**on** sur); **s. this way!** (venez) par ici!; **to s. aside** s'écarter; **to s. back** reculer; **to s. down** descendre (**from** de); (withdraw) Fig se retirer; **to s. forward** faire un pas en avant; **to s. in** entrer; (intervene) Fig intervenir; **to s. into** (car etc) monter dans; **to s. off** (chair etc) descendre de; **to s. out of** (car etc) descende de; **to s. over** (*obstacle*) enjamber; – *vt* **to s. up** (*increase*) augmenter, intensifier; (*speed up*) activer. ◆**stepladder** *n* escabeau *m.* ◆**stepping-stone** *n* Fig tremplin *m* (**to** pour arriver à).

stepbrother ['stepbrʌðər] *n* demi-frère *m.* ◆**stepdaughter** *n* belle-fille *f.* ◆**stepfather** *n* beau-père *m.* ◆**stepmother** *n* belle-mère *f.* ◆**stepsister** *n* demi-sœur *f.* ◆**stepson** *n* beau-fils *m.*

stereo ['sterɪəʊ] *n* (*pl* -**os**) (*sound*) stéréo(phonie) *f;* (*record player*) chaîne *f* (stéréo *inv*); – *a* (*record etc*) stéréo *inv;* (*broadcast*) en stéréo. ◆**stereo'phonic** *a* stéréophonique.

stereotype ['sterɪətaɪp] *n* stéréotype *m.* ◆**stereotyped** *a* stéréotypé.

sterile ['steraɪl, *Am* 'sterəl] *a* stérile. ◆**ste'rility** *n* stérilité *f.* ◆**sterili'zation** *n* stérilisation *f.* ◆**sterilize** *vt* stériliser.

sterling ['stɜːlɪŋ] *n* (*currency*) livre(s) *f(pl)* sterling *inv;* – *a* (*pound*) sterling *inv;* (*silver*) fin; (*quality, person*) Fig sûr.

stern [stɜːn] **1** *a* (-**er**, -**est**) sévère. **2** *n* (*of ship*) arrière *m.*

stethoscope ['steθəskəʊp] *n* stéthoscope *m.*

stetson ['stetsən] *n Am* chapeau *m* à larges bords.

stevedore ['stiːvədɔːr] *n* docker *m.*

stew [stjuː] *n* ragoût *m;* **in a s.** Fig dans le pétrin; **s. pan, s. pot** cocotte *f;* – *vt* (*meat*) faire *or* cuire en ragoût; (*fruit*) faire cuire; **stewed fruit** compote *f;* – *vi* cuire. ◆—**ing** *a* (*pears etc*) à cuire.

steward ['stjuːəd] *n Av Nau* steward *m;* (*in college, club etc*) intendant *m* (*préposé au ravitaillement*); **shop s.** délégué, -ée *mf* syndical(e). ◆**stewar'dess** *n Av* hôtesse *f.*

stick¹ [stɪk] *n* (*piece of wood, chalk, dynamite*) bâton *m;* (*branch*) branche *f;* (*for walking*) canne *f;* **the sticks** Pej Fam la campagne, la cambrousse; **to give s.o. some s.** (*scold*) Fam engueuler qn.

stick² [stɪk] *vt* (*pt & pp* stuck) (*glue*) coller; (*put*) Fam mettre, planter; (*tolerate*) Fam supporter; **to s. sth into** (*thrust*) planter *or* enfoncer qch dans; **to s. down** (*envelope*) coller; (*put down*) Fam poser; **to s. on** (*stamp*) coller; (*hat etc*) mettre, planter; **to s. out** (*tongue*) tirer; (*head*) Fam sortir; **to s. it out** (*resist*) Fam tenir le coup; **to s. up** (*notice*) afficher; (*hand*) Fam lever; – *vi* coller, adhérer (**to** à); (*of food in pan*) attacher; (*remain*) Fam rester; (*of drawer etc*) être bloqué *or* coincé; **to s. by s.o.** rester fidèle à qn; **to s. to the facts** (*confine oneself to*) s'en tenir aux faits; **to s. around** Fam

rester dans les parages; **to s. out** (*of petticoat etc*) dépasser; (*of tooth*) avancer; **to s. up for** (*defend*) défendre; **sticking plaster** sparadrap *m.* ◆**sticker** *n* (*label*) autocollant *m.* ◆**stick-on** *a* (*label*) adhésif. ◆**stick-up** *n* Fam hold-up *m inv.*

stickler ['stɪklər] *n* **a s. for** (*rules, discipline, details*) intransigeant sur.

sticky ['stɪkɪ] *a* (-**ier**, -**iest**) collant, poisseux; (*label*) adhésif; (*problem*) Fig difficile.

stiff [stɪf] *a* (-**er**, -**est**) raide; (*joint, leg etc*) ankylosé; (*brush, paste*) dur; (*person*) Fig froid, guindé; (*difficult*) difficile; (*price*) élevé; (*whisky*) bien tassé; **to have a s. neck** avoir le torticolis; **to feel s.** être courbaturé; **to be bored s.** Fam s'ennuyer à mourir; **frozen s.** Fam complètement gelé. ◆**stiffen** *vt* raidir; – *vi* se raidir. ◆**stiffly** *adv* (*coldly*) Fig froidement. ◆**stiffness** *n* raideur *f;* (*hardness*) dureté *f.*

stifle ['staɪf(ə)l] *vt* (*feeling, person etc*) étouffer; – *vi* **it's stifling** on étouffe.

stigma ['stɪgmə] *n* (*moral stain*) flétrissure *f.* ◆**stigmatize** *vt* (*denounce*) stigmatiser.

stile [staɪl] *n* (*between fields etc*) échalier *m.*

stiletto [stɪ'letəʊ] *a* **s. heel** talon *m* aiguille.

still¹ [stɪl] *adv* encore, toujours; (*even*) encore; (*nevertheless*) tout de même; **better s., s. better** encore mieux.

still² [stɪl] *a* (-**er**, -**est**) (*motionless*) immobile; (*calm*) calme, tranquille; (*drink*) non gazeux; **to keep** *or* **lie** *or* **stand s.** rester tranquille; **s. life** nature *f* morte; – *n* (*of night*) silence *m;* Cin photo *f.* ◆**stillborn** *a* mort-né. ◆**stillness** *n* immobilité *f;* calme *m.*

still³ [stɪl] *n* (*for making alcohol*) alambic *m.*

stilt [stɪlt] *n* (*pole*) échasse *f.*

stilted ['stɪltɪd] *a* guindé.

stimulate ['stɪmjʊleɪt] *vt* stimuler. ◆**stimulant** *n* Med stimulant *m.* ◆**stimu'lation** *n* stimulation *f.* ◆**stimulus**, *pl* -**li** [-laɪ] *n* (*encouragement*) stimulant *m;* (*physiological*) stimulus *m.*

sting [stɪŋ] *vt* (*pt & pp* stung) (*of insect, ointment, wind etc*) piquer; (*of remark*) Fig blesser; – *vi* piquer; – *n* piqûre *f;* (*insect's organ*) dard *m.* ◆—**ing** *a* (*pain, remark*) cuisant.

sting/y ['stɪndʒɪ] *a* (-**ier**, -**iest**) avare, mesquin; **s. with** (*money, praise*) avare de; (*food, wine*) mesquin sur. ◆—**iness** *n* avarice *f.*

stink [stɪŋk] *n* puanteur *f;* **to cause** *or* **make a s.** (*trouble*) Fam faire du foin; – *vi* (*pt* stank *or* stunk, *pp* stunk) puer; (*of book, film etc*)

Fam être infect; **to s. of** smoke/*etc* empester la fumée/*etc*; – *vt* **to s. out** (*room etc*) empester. ◆**—ing** *a Fam* infect, sale. ◆**—er** *n Fam* (*person*) sale type *m*; (*question, task etc*) vacherie *f*.

stint [stɪnt] **1** *n* (*share*) part *f* de travail; (*period*) période *f* de travail. **2** *vi* **to s. on** lésiner sur.

stipend ['staɪpend] *n Rel* traitement *n*.

stipulate ['stɪpjʊleɪt] *vt* stipuler (**that** que). ◆**stipu'lation** *n* stipulation *f*.

stir [stɜːr] *n* agitation *f*; **to give sth a s.** remuer qch; **to cause a s.** *Fig* faire du bruit; – *vt* (**-rr-**) (*coffee, leaves etc*) remuer; (*excite*) *Fig* exciter; (*incite*) inciter (**to do** à faire); **to s. oneself** (*make an effort*) se secouer; **to s. up** (*trouble*) provoquer; (*memory*) réveiller; – *vi* remuer, bouger. ◆**stirring** *a* (*speech etc*) excitant, émouvant.

stirrup ['stɪrəp] *n* étrier *m*.

stitch [stɪtʃ] *n* point *m*; (*in knitting*) maille *f*; *Med* point *m* de suture; **a s. (in one's side)** (*pain*) un point de côté; **to be in stitches** *Fam* se tordre (de rire); – *vt* **to s. (up)** (*sew up*) coudre; *Med* suturer.

stoat [stəʊt] *n* (*animal*) hermine *f*.

stock [stɒk] *n* (*supply*) provision *f*, stock *m*, réserve *f*; (*of knowledge, jokes*) fonds *m*, mine *f*; *Fin* valeurs *fpl*, titres *mpl*; (*descent, family*) souche *f*; (*soup*) bouillon *m*; (*cattle*) bétail *m*; **the stocks** *Hist* le pilori; **in s.** (*goods*) en magasin, disponible; **out of s.** (*goods*) épuisé, non disponible; **to take s.** *Fig* faire le point (**of** de); **s. reply/size** réponse *f*/taille *f* courante; **s. phrase** expression *f* toute faite; **the S. Exchange** *or* **Market** la Bourse; – *vt* (*sell*) vendre; (*keep in store*) stocker; **to s. (up)** (*shop, larder*) approvisionner; **well-stocked** bien approvisionné; – *vi* **to s. up** s'approvisionner (**with** de, en). ◆**stockbroker** *n* agent *m* de change. ◆**stockcar** *n* stock-car *m*. ◆**stockholder** *n Fin* actionnaire *mf*. ◆**stockist** *n* dépositaire *mf*, stockiste *m*. ◆**stockpile** *vt* stocker, amasser. ◆**stockroom** *n* réserve *f*, magasin *m*. ◆**stocktaking** *n Com* inventaire *m*.

stocking ['stɒkɪŋ] *n* (*garment*) bas *m*.

stocky ['stɒkɪ] *a* (**-ier, -iest**) trapu.

stodge [stɒdʒ] *n* (*food*) *Fam* étouffe-chrétien *m inv*. ◆**stodgy** *a* (**-ier, -iest**) *Fam* lourd, indigeste; (*person, style*) compassé.

stoic ['stəʊɪk] *a* & *n* stoïque (*mf*). ◆**stoical** *a* stoïque. ◆**stoicism** *n* stoïcisme *m*.

stok/e [stəʊk] *vt* (*fire*) entretenir; (*engine*) chauffer. ◆**—er** *n Rail* chauffeur *m*.

stole[1] [stəʊl] *n* (*shawl*) étole *f*.

stole[2], **stolen** [stəʊl, 'stəʊl(ə)n] *see* **steal**[1,2].

stolid ['stɒlɪd] *a* (*manner, person*) impassible.

stomach ['stʌmək] **1** *n Anat* estomac *m*; (*abdomen*) ventre *m*; – *vt* (*put up with*) *Fig* supporter. ◆**stomachache** *n* mal *m* de ventre; **to have a s.** avoir mal au ventre.

stone [stəʊn] *n* pierre *f*; (*pebble*) caillou *m*; (*in fruit*) noyau *m*; (*in kidney*) *Med* calcul *m*; (*weight*) = 6,348 kg; **a stone's throw away** *Fig* à deux pas d'ici; – *vt* lancer des pierres sur, lapider; (*fruit*) dénoyauter. ◆**stonemason** *n* tailleur *m* de pierre, maçon *m*. ◆**stony** *a* **1** (**-ier, -iest**) (*path etc*) pierreux, caillouteux. **2 s. broke** (*penniless*) *Sl* fauché.

stone- [stəʊn] *pref* complètement. ◆**s.-'broke** *a Am Sl* fauché. ◆**s.-'cold** *a* complètement froid. ◆**s.-'dead** *a* raide mort. ◆**s.-'deaf** *a* sourd comme un pot.

stoned [stəʊnd] *a* (*high on drugs*) *Fam* camé.

stooge [stuːdʒ] *n* (*actor*) comparse *mf*; (*flunkey*) *Pej* larbin *m*; (*dupe*) *Pej* pigeon *m*.

stood [stʊd] *see* **stand**.

stool [stuːl] *n* tabouret *m*.

stoop [stuːp] **1** *n* **to have a s.** être voûté; – *vi* se baisser; **to s. to doing/to sth** *Fig* s'abaisser à faire/à qch. **2** *n* (*in front of house*) *Am* perron *m*.

stop [stɒp] *n* (*place, halt*) arrêt *m*, halte *f*; *Av Nau* escale *f*; *Gram* point *m*; **bus s.** arrêt *m* d'autobus; **to put a s. to** mettre fin à; **to bring to a s.** arrêter; **to come to a s.** s'arrêter; **without a s.** sans arrêt; **s. light** (*on vehicle*) stop *m*; **s. sign** (*road sign*) stop *m*; – *vt* (**-pp-**) arrêter; (*end*) mettre fin à; (*prevent*) empêcher (**from doing** de faire); (*cheque*) faire opposition à; **to s. up** (*sink, pipe, leak etc*) boucher; – *vi* s'arrêter; (*of pain, conversation etc*) cesser; (*stay*) rester; **to s. eating**/*etc* s'arrêter de manger/*etc*; **to s. snowing**/*etc* cesser de neiger/*etc*; **to s. by** passer (*s.o.'s* chez qn); **to s. off** *or* **over** (*on journey*) s'arrêter. ◆**stoppage** *n* arrêt *m*; (*in pay*) retenue *f*; (*in work*) arrêt *m* de travail; (*strike*) débrayage *m*; (*blockage*) obstruction *f*. ◆**stopper** *n* bouchon *m*.

stopcock ['stɒpkɒk] *n* robinet *m* d'arrêt. ◆**stopgap** *n* bouche-trou *m*; – *a* intérimaire. ◆**stopoff** *n*, ◆**stopover** *n* halte *f*. ◆**stopwatch** *n* chronomètre *m*.

store [stɔːr] n (supply) provision f; (of information, jokes etc) Fig fonds m; (depot, warehouse) entrepôt m; (shop) grand magasin m, Am magasin m; (computer memory) mémoire f; **to have sth in s. for s.o.** (surprise) réserver qch à qn; **to keep in s.** garder en réserve; **to set great s.** by attacher une grande importance à; – vt **to s. (up)** (in warehouse etc) emmagasiner; (for future use) mettre en réserve; **to s. (away)** (furniture) entreposer. ◆**storage** n emmagasinage m; (for future use) mise f en réserve; **s. space** or **room** espace m de rangement. ◆**storekeeper** n magasinier m; (shopkeeper) Am commerçant, -ante mf. ◆**storeroom** n réserve f.

storey ['stɔːrɪ] n étage m.

stork [stɔːk] n cigogne f.

storm [stɔːm] **1** n (weather) & Fig tempête f; (thunderstorm) orage m; **s. cloud** nuage m orageux. **2** vt (attack) Mil prendre d'assaut. **3** vi **to s. out** (angrily) sortir comme une furie. ◆**stormy** a (-ier, -iest) (weather, meeting etc) orageux; (wind) d'orage.

story ['stɔːrɪ] n **1** histoire f; (newspaper article) article m; **s. (line)** Cin Th intrigue f; **short s.** Liter nouvelle f, conte m; **fairy s.** conte m de fées. **2** (storey) Am étage m. ◆**storyteller** n conteur, -euse mf; (liar) Fam menteur, -euse mf.

stout [staut] **1** a (-er, -est) (person) gros, corpulent; (stick, volume) gros, épais; (shoes) solide. **2** n (beer) bière f brune. ◆**—ness** n corpulence f.

stove [stəuv] n (for cooking) cuisinière f; (solid fuel) fourneau m; (small) réchaud m; (for heating) poêle m.

stow [stəu] **1** vt (cargo) arrimer; **to s. away** (put away) ranger. **2** vi **to s. away** Nau voyager clandestinement. ◆**stowaway** n Nau passager, -ère mf clandestin f.

straddle ['stræd(ə)l] vt (chair, fence) se mettre or être à califourchon sur; (step over, span) enjamber; (line in road) Aut chevaucher.

straggl/e ['stræg(ə)l] vi (stretch) s'étendre (en désordre); (trail) traîner (en désordre); **to s. in** entrer par petits groupes. ◆**—er** n traînard, -arde mf.

straight [streɪt] a (-er, -est) droit; (hair) raide; (route) direct; (tidy) en ordre; (frank) franc; (refusal) net; (actor, role) sérieux; **I want to get this s.** comprenons-nous bien; **to keep a s. face** garder son sérieux; **to put** or **set s.** (tidy) ranger; – n **the s.** Sp la ligne droite; – adv (to walk etc) droit; (directly) tout droit, directe-

ment; (to drink gin, whisky etc) sec; **s. away** (at once) tout de suite; **s. out, s. off** sans hésiter; **s. opposite** juste en face; **s. ahead** or **on** (to walk etc) tout droit; **s. ahead** (to look) droit devant soi. ◆**straighta'way** adv tout de suite. ◆**straighten** vt **to s. (up)** redresser; (tie, room) arranger; **to s. things out** Fig arranger les choses. ◆**straight'forward** a (frank) franc; (easy) simple.

strain [streɪn] **1** n tension f; (tiredness) fatigue f; (stress) Med tension f nerveuse; (effort) effort m; – vt (rope, wire) tendre excessivement; (muscle) Med froisser; (ankle, wrist) fouler; (eyes) fatiguer; (voice) forcer; Fig mettre à l'épreuve; **to s. one's ears** (to hear) tendre l'oreille; **to s. oneself** (hurt oneself) se faire mal; (tire oneself) se fatiguer; – vi fournir un effort (**to do** pour faire). **2** vt (soup etc) passer; (vegetables) égoutter. **3** n (breed) lignée f; (of virus) souche f; (streak) tendance f. **4** npl Mus accents mpl (of de). ◆**—ed** a (relations) tendu; (laugh) forcé; (ankle, wrist) foulé. ◆**—er** n passoire f.

strait [streɪt] **1** n & npl Geog détroit m. **2** npl **in financial straits** dans l'embarras. ◆**straitjacket** n camisole f de force. ◆**strait'laced** a collet monté inv.

strand [strænd] n (of wool etc) brin m; (of hair) mèche f; (of story) Fig fil m.

stranded ['strændɪd] a (person, vehicle) en rade.

strange [streɪndʒ] a (-er, -est) (odd) étrange, bizarre; (unknown) inconnu; (new) nouveau; **to feel s.** (in a new place) se sentir dépaysé. ◆**strangely** adv étrangement; **s. (enough) she** ... chose étrange, elle ... . ◆**strangeness** n étrangeté f. ◆**stranger** n (unknown) inconnu, -ue mf; (outsider) étranger, -ère mf; **he's a s. here** il n'est pas d'ici; **she's a s. to me** elle m'est inconnue.

strangle ['stræŋg(ə)l] vt étrangler. ◆**strangler** n étrangleur, -euse mf. ◆**stranglehold** n emprise f totale (**on** sur).

strap [stræp] n courroie f, sangle f; (on dress) bretelle f; (on watch) bracelet m; (on sandal) lanière f; – vt (-pp-) **to s. (down** or **in)** attacher (avec une courroie).

strapping ['stræpɪŋ] a (well-built) robuste.

stratagem ['strætədʒəm] n stratagème m.

strategy ['strætədʒɪ] n stratégie f. ◆**stra'tegic** a stratégique.

stratum, pl **-ta** ['strɑːtəm, -tə] n couche f.

straw [strɔː] n paille f; **a (drinking) s.** une paille; **that's the last s.!** c'est le comble!

strawberry ['strɔːbərɪ] n fraise f; – a

(*flavour, ice cream*) à la fraise; (*jam*) de fraises; (*tart*) aux fraises.

stray [streɪ] *a* (*lost*) perdu; **a s. car**/*etc* une voiture/*etc* isolée; **a few s. cars**/*etc* quelques rares voitures/*etc*; − *n* animal *m* perdu; − *vi* s'égarer; **to s. from** (*subject, path*) s'écarter de.

streak [striːk] *n* (*line*) raie *f*; (*of light*) filet *m*; (*of colour*) strie *f*; (*trace*) *Fig* trace *f*; (*tendency*) tendance *f*; **grey**/*etc* **streaks** (*in hair*) mèches *fpl* grises/*etc*; **a mad s.** une tendance à la folie; **my literary s.** ma fibre littéraire. ◆**streaked** *a* (*marked*) strié, zébré; (*stained*) taché (**with** de). ◆**streaky** *a* (**-ier, -iest**) strié; (*bacon*) pas trop maigre.

stream [striːm] *n* (*brook*) ruisseau *m*; (*current*) courant *m*; (*flow*) & *Fig* flot *m*; *Sch* classe *f* (de niveau); − *vi* ruisseler (**with** de); **to s. in** (*of sunlight, people etc*) *Fig* entrer à flots.

streamer ['striːmər] *n* (*paper*) serpentin *m*; (*banner*) banderole *f*.

streamlin/e ['striːmlaɪn] *vt* (*work, method etc*) rationaliser. ◆**-ed** *a* (*shape*) aérodynamique.

street [striːt] *n* rue *f*; **s. door** porte *f* d'entrée; **s. lamp, s. light** réverbère *m*; **s. map, s. plan** plan *m* des rues; **up my s.** *Fig Fam* dans mes cordes; **streets ahead** *Fam* très en avance (**of** sur). ◆**streetcar** *n* (*tram*) *Am* tramway *m*.

strength [streŋθ] *n* force *f*; (*health, energy*) forces *fpl*; (*of wood, fabric*) solidité *f*; **on the s. of** *Fig* en vertu de; **in full s.** au (grand) complet. ◆**strengthen** *vt* (*building, position etc*) renforcer, consolider; (*body, soul, limb*) fortifier.

strenuous ['strenjuəs] *a* (*effort etc*) vigoureux, énergique; (*work*) ardu; (*active*) actif; (*tiring*) fatigant. ◆**-ly** *adv* énergiquement.

strep [strep] *a* **s. throat** *Med Am* angine *f*.

stress [stres] *n* (*pressure*) pression *f*; *Med Psy* tension *f* (nerveuse), stress *m*; (*emphasis*) & *Gram* accent *m*; *Tech* tension *f*; **under s.** *Med Psy* sous pression, stressé; − *vt* insister sur; (*word*) accentuer; **to s. that** souligner que. ◆**stressful** *a* stressant.

stretch [stretʃ] *vt* (*rope, neck*) tendre; (*shoe, rubber*) étirer; (*meaning*) *Fig* forcer; **to s. (out)** (*arm, leg*) étendre, allonger; **to s. (out) one's arm** (*reach out*) tendre le bras (**to take** pour prendre); **to s. one's legs** *Fig* se dégourdir les jambes; **to s. s.o.** *Fig* exiger un effort de qn; **to be (fully) stretched** (*of budget etc*) être tiré au maximum; **to s. out** (*visit*) prolonger; − *vi* (*of person, elastic*)

s'étirer; (*of influence etc*) s'étendre; **to s. (out)** (*of rope, plain*) s'étendre; − *n* (*area, duration*) étendue *f*; (*of road*) tronçon *m*, partie *f*; (*route, trip*) trajet *m*; **at a s.** d'une (seule) traite; **ten**/*etc* **hours at a s.** dix/*etc* heures d'affilée; **s. socks**/*etc* chaussettes *fpl*/*etc* extensibles; **s. nylon** nylon *m* stretch *inv*. ◆**stretchmarks** *npl* (*on body*) vergetures *fpl*.

stretcher ['stretʃər] *n* brancard *m*.

strew [struː] *vt* (*pt* **strewed**, *pp* **strewed** *or* **strewn**) (*scatter*) répandre; **strewn with** (*covered*) jonché de.

stricken ['strɪk(ə)n] *a* **s. with** (*illness*) atteint de; (*panic*) frappé de.

strict [strɪkt] *a* (**-er, -est**) (*severe, absolute*) strict. ◆**-ly** *adv* strictement; **s. forbidden** formellement interdit. ◆**-ness** *n* sévérité *f*.

stride [straɪd] *n* (grand) pas *m*, enjambée *f*; **to make great strides** *Fig* faire de grands progrès; − *vi* (*pt* **strode**) **s. across** *or* **over** enjamber; **to s. up and down a room** arpenter une pièce.

strident ['straɪdənt] *a* strident.

strife [straɪf] *n inv* conflit(s) *m*(*pl*).

strik/e [straɪk] **1** *n* (*attack*) *Mil* raid *m* (aérien); (*of oil etc*) découverte *f*; − *vt* (*pt & pp* **struck**) (*hit, impress*) frapper; (*collide with*) heurter; (*beat*) battre; (*a blow*) donner; (*a match*) frotter; (*gold, problem*) trouver; (*coin*) frapper; (*of clock*) sonner; **to s. a bargain** conclure un accord; **to s. a balance** trouver l'équilibre; **to s. (off)** (*from list*) rayer (**from** de); **to be struck off** (*of doctor*) être radié; **it strikes me as/that it** me semble être/que; **how did it s. you?** quelle impression ça t'a fait?; **to s. down** (*of illness etc*) terrasser (*qn*); **to s. up a friendship** lier amitié (**with** avec); − *vi* **to s. (at)** (*attack*) attaquer; **to s. back** (*retaliate*) riposter; **to s. out** donner des coups. **2** *n* (*of workers*) grève *f*; **to go (out) on s.** se mettre en grève (**for** pour obtenir, **against** pour protester contre); − *vi* (*pt & pp* **struck**) (*of workers*) faire grève. ◆**-ing** *a* (*impressive*) frappant. ◆**-ingly** *adv* (*beautiful etc*) extraordinairement. ◆**-er** *n* gréviste *mf*; *Fb* buteur *m*.

string [strɪŋ] *n* ficelle *f*; (*of anorak, apron*) cordon *m*; (*of violin, racket etc*) corde *f*; (*of pearls, beads*) rang *m*; (*of onions, insults*) chapelet *m*; (*of people, vehicles*) file *f*; (*of questions etc*) série *f*; **to pull strings** *Fig* faire jouer ses relations; − *a* (*instrument, quartet*) *Mus* à cordes; **s. bean** haricot *m* vert; − *vt* (*pt & pp* **strung**) (*beads*) enfiler; **to s. up**

(*hang up*) suspendre; − *vi* **to s. along (with)** *Fam* suivre. ◆**—ed** *a* (*instrument*) *Mus* à cordes. ◆**stringy** *a* (**-ier, -iest**) (*meat etc*) filandreux.

stringent ['strɪndʒ(ə)nt] *a* rigoureux. ◆**stringency** *n* rigueur *f*.

strip [strɪp] **1** *n* (*piece*) bande *f*; (*of water*) bras *m*; (**thin**) **s.** (*of metal etc*) lamelle *f*; **landing s.** piste *f or* terrain *m* d'atterrissage; **s. cartoon, comic s.** bande *f* dessinée. **2** *vt* (**-pp-**) (*undress*) déshabiller; (*bed*) défaire; (*deprive*) dépouiller (**of** de); **to s.** (**down**) (*machine*) démonter; **to s. off** (*remove*) enlever; − *vi* **to s.** (**off**) (*undress*) se déshabiller. ◆**stripper** *n* (*woman*) stripteaseuse *f*; (*paint*) décapant *m*. ◆**strip-'tease** *n* strip-tease *m*.

stripe [straɪp] *n* rayure *f*; *Mil* galon *m*. ◆**striped** *a* rayé (**with** de). ◆**stripy** *a* rayé.

strive [straɪv] *vi* (*pt* **strove**, *pp* **striven**) s'efforcer (**to do** de faire, **for** d'obtenir).

strode [strəʊd] *see* **stride**.

stroke [strəʊk] *n* (*movement*) coup *m*; (*of pen, genius*) trait *m*; (*of brush*) touche *f*; (*on clock*) coup *m*; (*caress*) caresse *f*; *Med* coup *m* de sang; (*swimming style*) nage *f*; **at a s.** d'un coup; **a s. of luck** un coup de chance; **you haven't done a s.** (*of work*) tu n'as rien fait; **heat s.** (*sunstroke*) insolation *f*; **four-s. engine** moteur *m* à quatre temps; − *vt* (*beard, cat etc*) caresser.

stroll [strəʊl] *n* promenade *f*; − *vi* se promener, flâner; **to s. in**/*etc* entrer/*etc* sans se presser. ◆**—ing** *a* (*musician etc*) ambulant.

stroller ['strəʊlər] *n* (*pushchair*) *Am* poussette *f*.

strong [strɒŋ] *a* (**-er, -est**) fort; (*shoes, nerves*) solide; (*interest*) vif; (*measures*) énergique; (*supporter*) ardent; **sixty s.** au nombre de soixante; − *adv* **to be going s.** aller toujours bien. ◆**—ly** *adv* (*to protest, defend*) énergiquement; (*to desire, advise, remind*) fortement; (*to feel*) profondément; **s. built** solide. ◆**strongarm** *a* brutal. ◆**strongbox** *n* coffre-fort *m*. ◆**stronghold** *n* bastion *m*. ◆**strong-'willed** *a* résolu.

strove [strəʊv] *see* **strive**.

struck [strʌk] *see* **strike** 1,2.

structure ['strʌktʃər] *n* structure *f*; (*of building*) armature *f*; (*building itself*) construction *f*. ◆**structural** *a* structural; (*fault*) *Archit* de construction.

struggle ['strʌg(ə)l] *n* (*fight*) lutte *f* (**to do** pour faire); (*effort*) effort *m*; **to put up a s.**

résister; **to have a s. doing** *or* **to do** avoir du mal à faire; − *vi* (*fight*) lutter, se battre (**with** avec); (*resist*) résister; (*thrash about wildly*) se débattre; **to s. to do** (*try hard*) s'efforcer de faire; **to s. out of** sortir péniblement de; **to s. along** *or* **on se** débrouiller; **a struggling lawyer**/*etc* un avocat/*etc* qui a du mal à débuter.

strum [strʌm] *vt* (**-mm-**) (*guitar etc*) gratter de.

strung [strʌŋ] *see* **string**; − *a* **s. out** (*things, people*) espacés; (*washing*) étendu.

strut [strʌt] **1** *vi* (**-tt-**) **to s.** (*about or around*) se pavaner. **2** *n* (*support*) *Tech* étai *m*.

stub [stʌb] **1** *n* (*of pencil, cigarette etc*) bout *m*; (*counterfoil of cheque etc*) talon *m*; − *vt* (**-bb-**) **to s. out** (*cigarette*) écraser. **2** *vt* (**-bb-**) **to s. one's toe** se cogner le doigt de pied (**on, against** contre).

stubble ['stʌb(ə)l] *n* barbe *f* de plusieurs jours.

stubborn ['stʌbən] *a* (*person*) entêté, opiniâtre; (*cough, efforts, manner etc*) opiniâtre. ◆**—ly** *adv* opiniâtrement. ◆**—ness** *n* entêtement *m*; opiniâtreté *f*.

stubby ['stʌbɪ] *a* (**-ier, -iest**) (*finger etc*) gros et court, épais; (*person*) trapu.

stuck [stʌk] *see* **stick**[2]; − *a* (*caught, jammed*) coincé; **s. in bed/indoors** cloué au lit/chez soi; **to be s.** (*unable to do sth*) ne pas savoir quoi faire; **I'm s.** (**for an answer**) je ne sais que répondre; **to be s. with sth/s.o.** se farcir qch/qn. ◆**s.-'up** *a* *Fam* prétentieux, snob *inv*.

stud [stʌd] *n* **1** (*nail*) clou *m* (à grosse tête); (*for collar*) bouton *m* de col. **2** (*farm*) haras *m*; (*horses*) écurie *f*; (*stallion*) étalon *m*; (*virile man*) *Sl* mâle *m*. ◆**studded** *a* (*boots, tyres*) clouté; **s. with** (*covered*) *Fig* constellé de, parsemé de.

student ['stjuːdənt] *n* *Univ* étudiant, -ante *mf*; *Sch* *Am* élève *mf*; **music**/*etc* **s.** étudiant, -ante en musique/*etc*; − *a* (*life, protest*) étudiant; (*restaurant, residence, grant*) universitaire.

studio ['stjuːdɪəʊ] *n* (*pl* **-os**) (*of painter etc*) & *Cin TV* studio *m*; **s. flat** *or* *Am* **apartment** studio *m*.

studious ['stjuːdɪəs] *a* (*person*) studieux. ◆**—ly** *adv* (*carefully*) avec soin. ◆**—ness** *n* application *f*.

study ['stʌdɪ] *n* étude *f*; (*office*) bureau *m*; − *vt* (*learn, observe*) étudier; − *vi* étudier; **to s. to be a doctor**/*etc* faire des études pour devenir médecin/*etc*; **to s. for** (*exam*) préparer. ◆**studied** *a* (*deliberate*) étudié.

stuff [stʌf] **1** *n* (*thing*) truc *m*, chose *f*;

(*substance*) substance *f*; (*things*) trucs *mpl*, choses *fpl*; (*possessions*) affaires *fpl*; (*nonsense*) sottises *fpl*; **this s.'s good, it's good s.** c'est bon (ça). **2** *vt* (*chair, cushion etc*) rembourrer (**with** avec); (*animal*) empailler; (*cram, fill*) bourrer (**with** de); (*put, thrust*) fourrer (**into** dans); (*chicken etc*) Culin farcir; **to s. (up)** (*hole etc*) colmater; **my nose is stuffed (up)** j'ai le nez bouché. ◆**—ing** *n* (*padding*) bourre *f*; *Culin* farce *f*.

stuffy ['stʌfɪ] *a* (**-ier, -iest**) (*room etc*) mal aéré; (*formal*) *Fig* compassé; (*old-fashioned*) vieux jeu *inv*; **it smells s.** ça sent le renfermé.

stumble ['stʌmb(ə)l] *vi* trébucher (**over** sur, **against** contre); **to s. across** *or* **on** (*find*) tomber sur; **stumbling block** pierre *f* d'achoppement.

stump [stʌmp] *n* (*of tree*) souche *f*; (*of limb*) moignon *m*; (*of pencil*) bout *m*; *Cricket* piquet *m*.

stumped ['stʌmpt] *a* **to be s. by sth** (*baffled*) ne pas savoir que penser de qch.

stun [stʌn] *vt* (**-nn-**) (*daze*) étourdir; (*animal*) assommer; (*amaze*) *Fig* stupéfier. ◆**stunned** *a Fig* stupéfait (**by** par). ◆**stunning** *a* (*blow*) étourdissant; (*news*) stupéfiant; (*terrific*) *Fam* sensationnel.

stung [stʌŋ] *see* sting.

stunk [stʌŋk] *see* stink.

stunt [stʌnt] **1** *n* (*feat*) tour *m* (de force); *Cin* cascade *f*; (*ruse, trick*) truc *m*; **s. man** *Cin* cascadeur *m*; **s. woman** *Cin* cascadeuse *f*. **2** *vt* (*growth*) retarder. ◆**—ed** *a* (*person*) rabougri.

stupefy ['stju:pɪfaɪ] *vt* (*of drink etc*) abrutir; (*amaze*) *Fig* stupéfier.

stupendous [stju:'pendəs] *a* prodigieux.

stupid ['stju:pɪd] *a* stupide, bête; **a s. thing** une sottise; **s. fool, s. idiot** idiot, -ote *mf*. ◆**stu'pidity** *n* stupidité *f*. ◆**stupidly** *adv* stupidement, bêtement.

stupor ['stju:pər] *n* (*daze*) stupeur *f*.

sturdy ['stɜ:dɪ] *a* (**-ier, -iest**) (*person, shoe etc*) robuste. ◆**sturdiness** *n* robustesse *f*.

sturgeon ['stɜ:dʒ(ə)n] *n* (*fish*) esturgeon *m*.

stutter ['stʌtər] *n* bégaiement *m*; **to have a s.** être bègue; – *vi* bégayer.

sty [staɪ] *n* (*pigsty*) porcherie *f*.

sty(e) [staɪ] *n* (*on eye*) orgelet *m*.

style [staɪl] *n* style *m*; (*fashion*) mode *f*; (*design of dress etc*) modèle *m*; (*of hair*) coiffure *f*; (*sort*) genre *m*; **to have s.** avoir de la classe; **s.** (*in superior manner*) de la meilleure façon possible; (*to live, travel*) dans le luxe; – *vt* (*design*) créer; **he styles**

himself . . . *Pej* il se fait appeler . . . ; **to s. s.o.'s hair** coiffer qn. ◆**styling** *n* (*cutting of hair*) coupe *f*. ◆**stylish** *a* chic, élégant. ◆**stylishly** *adv* élégamment. ◆**stylist** *n* (*hair*) **s.** coiffeur, -euse *mf*. ◆**sty'listic** *a* de style, stylistique. ◆**stylized** *a* stylisé.

stylus ['staɪləs] *n* (*of record player*) pointe *f* de lecture.

suave [swɑːv] *a* (**-er, -est**) (*urbane*) courtois; *Pej* doucereux.

sub- [sʌb] *pref* sous-, sub-.

subconscious [sʌb'kɒnʃəs] *a & n* subconscient (*m*). ◆**—ly** *adv* inconsciemment.

subcontract [sʌbkən'trækt] *vt* sous-traiter. ◆**subcontractor** *n* sous-traitant *m*.

subdivide [sʌbdɪ'vaɪd] *vt* subdiviser (**into** en). ◆**subdivision** *n* subdivision *f*.

subdu/e [səb'dju:] *vt* (*country*) asservir; (*feelings*) maîtriser. ◆**—ed** *a* (*light*) atténué; (*voice*) bas; (*reaction*) faible; (*person*) qui manque d'entrain.

subheading ['sʌbhedɪŋ] *n* sous-titre *m*.

subject¹ ['sʌbdʒɪkt] *n* **1** (*matter*) & *Gram* sujet *m*; *Sch Univ* matière *f*; **s. matter** (*topic*) sujet *m*; (*content*) contenu *m*. **2** (*citizen*) ressortissant, -ante *mf*; (*of monarch, monarchy*) sujet, -ette *mf*; (*person etc in experiment*) sujet *m*.

subject² ['sʌbdʒekt] *a* (*tribe etc*) soumis; **s. to** (*prone to*) sujet à (*maladie etc*); (*ruled by*) soumis à (*loi, règle etc*); (*conditional upon*) sous réserve de; **prices are s. to change** les prix peuvent être modifiés; – [səb'dʒekt] *vt* soumettre (**to** à); (*expose*) exposer (**to** à). ◆**sub'jection** *n* soumission *f* (**to** à).

subjective [səb'dʒektɪv] *a* subjectif. ◆**—ly** *adv* subjectivement. ◆**subjec'tivity** *n* subjectivité *f*.

subjugate ['sʌbdʒʊgeɪt] *vt* subjuguer.

subjunctive [səb'dʒʌŋktɪv] *n Gram* subjonctif *m*.

sublet [sʌb'let] *vt* (*pt & pp* sublet, *pres p* subletting) sous-louer.

sublimate ['sʌblɪmeɪt] *vt Psy* sublimer.

sublime [sə'blaɪm] *a* sublime; (*indifference, stupidity*) suprême; – *n* sublime *m*.

submachine-gun [sʌbmə'ʃiːngʌn] *n* mitraillette *f*.

submarine ['sʌbməriːn] *n* sous-marin *m*.

submerge [səb'mɜːdʒ] *vt* (*flood, overwhelm*) submerger; (*immerse*) immerger (**in** dans); – *vi* (*of submarine*) s'immerger.

submit [səb'mɪt] *vt* (**-tt-**) soumettre (**to** à); **to s. that** *Jur* suggérer que; – *vi* se soumettre (**to** à). ◆**submission** *n* soumission *f* (**to** à). ◆**submissive** *a* soumis. ◆**submissively** *adv* avec soumission.

subnormal [sʌb'nɔːm(ə)l] *a* au-dessous de la normale; (*mentally*) arriéré.

subordinate [sə'bɔːdɪnət] *a* subalterne; *Gram* subordonné; – *n* subordonné, -ée *mf*; – [sə'bɔːdɪneɪt] *vt* subordonner (**to** à). ◆**subordi'nation** *n* subordination *f* (**to** à).

subpoena [səb'piːnə] *vt Jur* citer; – *n Jur* citation *f*.

subscribe [səb'skraɪb] *vt* (*money*) donner (**to** à); – *vi* cotiser; **to s. to** (*take out subscription*) s'abonner à (*journal etc*); (*be a subscriber*) être abonné à (*journal etc*); (*fund, idea*) souscrire à. ◆**subscriber** *n Journ Tel* abonné, -ée *mf*. ◆**subscription** *n* (*to newspaper etc*) abonnement *m*; (*to fund, idea*) & *Fin* souscription *f*; (*to club etc*) cotisation *f*.

subsequent ['sʌbsɪkwənt] *a* postérieur (**to** à); **our s. problems** les problèmes que nous avons eus par la suite; **s. to** (*as a result of*) consécutif à. ◆**-ly** *adv* par la suite.

subservient [səb'sɜːvɪənt] *a* obséquieux; **to be s. to** (*a slave to*) être asservi à.

subside [səb'saɪd] *vi* (*of building, land*) s'affaisser; (*of wind, flood*) baisser. ◆**'subsidence** *n* affaissement *m*.

subsidiary [səb'sɪdɪərɪ] *a* accessoire; (*subject*) *Univ* secondaire; – *n* (*company*) *Com* filiale *f*.

subsidize ['sʌbsɪdaɪz] *vt* subventionner. ◆**subsidy** *n* subvention *f*.

subsist [səb'sɪst] *vi* (*of person, doubts etc*) subsister. ◆**subsistence** *n* subsistance *f*.

substance ['sʌbstəns] *n* substance *f*; (*firmness*) solidité *f*; **a man of s.** un homme riche. ◆**substantial** [səb'stænʃ(ə)l] *a* important, considérable; (*meal*) substantiel. ◆**substantially** *adv* considérablement, beaucoup; **s. true**/*etc* (*to a great extent*) en grande partie vrai/*etc*; **s. different** très différent.

substandard [sʌb'stændəd] *a* de qualité inférieure.

substantiate [səb'stænʃɪeɪt] *vt* prouver, justifier.

substitute ['sʌbstɪtjuːt] *n* (*thing*) produit *m* de remplacement; (*person*) remplaçant, -ante *mf* (**for** de); **there's no s. for . . .** rien ne peut remplacer . . . ; – *vt* substituer (**for** à); – *vi* **to s. for** remplacer; (*deputize for in job*) se substituer à. ◆**substi'tution** *n* substitution *f*.

subtitle ['sʌbtaɪt(ə)l] *n* sous-titre *m*; – *vt* sous-titrer.

subtle ['sʌt(ə)l] *a* (**-er**, **-est**) subtil. ◆**subtlety** *n* subtilité *f*. ◆**subtly** *adv* subtilement.

subtotal [sʌb'təʊt(ə)l] *n* total *m* partiel, sous-total *m*.

subtract [səb'trækt] *vt* soustraire (**from** de). ◆**subtraction** *n* soustraction *f*.

suburb ['sʌbɜːb] *n* banlieue *f*; **the suburbs** la banlieue; **in the suburbs** en banlieue. ◆**su'burban** *a* (*train*) de banlieue; (*accent*) de la banlieue. ◆**su'burbia** *n* la banlieue.

subversive [səb'vɜːsɪv] *a* subversif. ◆**subversion** *n* subversion *f*. ◆**subvert** *vt* (*system etc*) bouleverser; (*person*) corrompre.

subway ['sʌbweɪ] *n* passage *m* souterrain; *Rail Am* métro *m*.

succeed [sək'siːd] **1** *vi* réussir (**in doing** à faire, **in sth** dans qch). **2** *vt* **to s. s.o.** (*follow*) succéder à qn; – *vi* **to s. to the throne** succéder à la couronne. ◆**-ing** *a* (*in past*) suivant; (*in future*) futur; (*consecutive*) consécutif.

success [sək'ses] *n* succès *m*, réussite *f*; **to make a s. of sth** réussir qch; **he was a s.** il a eu du succès; **his** *or* **her s. in the exam** sa réussite à l'examen; **s. story** réussite *f* complète *or* exemplaire. ◆**successful** *a* (*venture etc*) couronné de succès, réussi; (*outcome*) heureux; (*firm*) prospère; (*candidate in exam*) admis, reçu; (*election*) élu; (*writer, film etc*) à succès; **to be s.** réussir (**in** dans, **in an exam** à un examen, **in doing** à faire). ◆**successfully** *adv* avec succès.

succession [sək'seʃ(ə)n] *n* succesion *f*; **in s.** successivement; **ten days in s.** dix jours consécutifs, **in rapid s.** coup sur coup. ◆**successive** *a* successif; **ten s. days** dix jours consécutifs. ◆**successor** *n* successeur *m* (**of, to** de).

succinct [sək'sɪŋkt] *a* succinct.

succulent ['sʌkjʊlənt] *a* succulent.

succumb [sə'kʌm] *vi* (*yield*) succomber (**to** à).

such [sʌtʃ] *a* tel; **s. a car**/*etc* une telle voiture/*etc*; **s. happiness**/*etc* (*so much*) tant *or* tellement de bonheur/*etc*; **there's no s. thing** ça n'existe pas; **I said no s. thing** je n'ai rien dit de tel; **s.** as comme, tel que; **s. and s.** tel ou tel; – *adv* (*so very*) si; (*in comparisons*) aussi; **s. a kind woman as you** une femme aussi gentille que vous; **s. long trips** de si longs voyages; **s. a large helping** une si grosse portion; – *pron* **happiness**/*etc* **as s.** le bonheur/*etc* en tant que tel; **s. was**

my idea telle était mon idée. ◆suchlike n ... and s. Fam ... et autres.

suck [sʌk] vt sucer; (of baby) téter (lait, biberon etc); to s. (up) (with straw, pump) aspirer; to s. up or in (absorb) absorber; — vi (of baby) téter; to s. at sucer. ◆—er n 1 (fool) Fam pigeon m, dupe f. 2 (pad) ventouse f.

suckle ['sʌk(ə)l] vt (of woman) allaiter; (of baby) téter.

suction ['sʌkʃ(ə)n] n succion f; s. disc, s. pad ventouse f.

Sudan [suː'dɑːn] n Soudan m.

sudden ['sʌd(ə)n] a soudain, subit; all of a s. tout à coup. ◆—ly adv subitement. ◆—ness n soudaineté f.

suds [sʌdz] npl mousse f de savon.

sue [suː] vt poursuivre (en justice); — vi engager des poursuites (judiciaires).

suede [sweɪd] n daim m; — a de daim.

suet ['suːɪt] n graisse f de rognon.

suffer ['sʌfər] vi souffrir (from de); to s. from pimples/the flu avoir des boutons/la grippe; your work/etc will s. ton travail/etc s'en ressentira; — vt (attack, loss etc) subir; (pain) ressentir; (tolerate) souffrir. ◆—ing n souffrance(s) f(pl). ◆—er n Med malade mf; (from misfortune) victime f.

suffice [sə'faɪs] vi suffire.

sufficient [sə'fɪʃ(ə)nt] a (quantity, number) suffisant; s. money/etc (enough) suffisamment d'argent/etc; to have s. en avoir suffisamment. ◆—ly adv suffisamment.

suffix ['sʌfɪks] n Gram suffixe m.

suffocate ['sʌfəkeɪt] vti étouffer, suffoquer. ◆suffo'cation n (of industry, mind etc) & Med étouffement m, asphyxie f.

suffrage ['sʌfrɪdʒ] n (right to vote) Pol suffrage m.

suffused [sə'fjuːzd] a s. with (light, tears) baigné de.

sugar ['ʃʊgər] n sucre m; — a (cane, tongs) à sucre; (industry) sucrier; s. bowl sucrier m; — vt sucrer. ◆sugary a (taste, tone) sucré.

suggest [sə'dʒest] vt (propose) suggérer, proposer (to à, that que (+ sub)); (evoke, imply) suggérer; (hint) Pej insinuer. ◆suggestion n suggestion f, proposition f; (evocation) suggestion f; Pej insinuation f. ◆suggestive a suggestif; to be s. of suggérer.

suicide ['suːɪsaɪd] n suicide m; to commit s. se suicider. ◆sui'cidal a suicidaire.

suit [suːt] n 1 (man's) complet m, costume m; (woman's) tailleur m; (of pilot, diver etc) combinaison f. 2 n (lawsuit) Jur procès m. 3 n Cards couleur f. 4 vt (satisfy, be appropri-

ate to) convenir à; (of dress, colour etc) aller (bien) à; (adapt) adapter (to à); it suits me to stay ça m'arrange de rester; s. yourself! comme tu voudras!; suited to (made for) fait pour; (appropriate to) approprié à; well suited (couple etc) bien assorti. ◆suita-'bility n (of remark etc) à-propos m; (of person) aptitudes fpl (for pour); I'm not sure of the s. of it (date etc) je ne sais pas si ça convient. ◆suitable a qui convient (for à); (dress, colour) qui va (bien); (example) approprié; (socially) convenable. ◆suitably adv convenablement.

suitcase ['suːtkeɪs] n valise f.

suite [swiːt] n (rooms) suite f; (furniture) mobilier m; bedroom s. (furniture) chambre f à coucher.

suitor ['suːtər] n soupirant m.

sulfur ['sʌlfər] n Am soufre m.

sulk [sʌlk] vi bouder. ◆sulky a (-ier, -iest) boudeur.

sullen ['sʌlən] a maussade. ◆—ly adv d'un air maussade.

sully ['sʌlɪ] vt Lit souiller.

sulphur ['sʌlfər] n soufre m.

sultan ['sʌltən] n sultan m.

sultana [sʌl'tɑːnə] n raisin m de Smyrne.

sultry ['sʌltrɪ] a (-ier, -iest) (heat) étouffant; Fig sensuel.

sum [sʌm] n 1 (amount, total) somme f; Math calcul m; pl (arithmetic) le calcul; s. total résultat m. 2 vt (-mm-) to s. up (facts etc) récapituler, résumer; (text) résumer; (situation) évaluer; (person) jauger; — vi to s. up récapituler. ◆summing-'up n (pl summings-up) résumé m.

summarize ['sʌməraɪz] vt résumer. ◆summary n résumé m; — a (brief) sommaire.

summer ['sʌmər] n été m; in (the) s. en été; Indian s. été indien or de la Saint-Martin; — a d'été; s. holidays grandes vacances fpl. ◆summerhouse n pavillon m (de gardien). ◆summertime n été m; in (the) s. en été. ◆summery a (weather etc) estival; (dress) d'été.

summit ['sʌmɪt] n (of mountain, power etc) sommet m; s. conference/meeting Pol conférence f/rencontre f au sommet.

summon ['sʌmən] vt (call) appeler; (meeting, s.o. to meeting) convoquer (to à); to s. s.o. to do sommer qn de faire; to s. up (courage, strength) rassembler.

summons ['sʌmənz] n Jur assignation f; — vt Jur assigner.

sumptuous ['sʌmptʃʊəs] a somptueux. ◆—ness n somptuosité f.

sun [sʌn] n soleil m; in the s. au soleil; the

sun's shining il fait (du) soleil; – *a* (*cream, filter etc*) solaire; **s. lounge** solarium *m*; – *vt* (**-nn-**) **to s. oneself** se chauffer au soleil. ◆**sunbaked** *a* brûlé par le soleil. ◆**sunbathe** *vi* prendre un bain de soleil. ◆**sunbeam** *n* rayon *m* de soleil. ◆**sunburn** *n* (*tan*) bronzage *m*; *Med* coup *m* de soleil. ◆**sunburnt** *a* bronzé; *Med* brûlé par le soleil. ◆**sundial** *n* cadran *m* solaire. ◆**sundown** *n* coucher *m* du soleil. ◆**sundrenched** *a* brûlé par le soleil. ◆**sunflower** *n* tournesol *m*. ◆**sunglasses** *npl* lunettes *fpl* de soleil. ◆**sunlamp** *f* lampe *f* à rayons ultraviolets. ◆**sunlight** *n* (lumière *f* du) soleil *m*. ◆**sunlit** *a* ensoleillé. ◆**sunrise** *n* lever *m* du soleil. ◆**sunroof** *n* *Aut* toit *m* ouvrant. ◆**sunset** *n* coucher *m* du soleil. ◆**sunshade** *n* (*on table*) parasol *m*; (*portable*) ombrelle *f*. ◆**sunshine** *n* soleil *m*. ◆**sunstroke** *n* insolation *f*. ◆**suntan** *n* bronzage *m*; – *a* (*lotion, oil*) solaire. ◆**suntanned** *a* bronzé. ◆**sunup** *n* *Am* lever *m* du soleil.

sundae ['sʌndeɪ] *n* glace *f* aux fruits.

Sunday ['sʌndɪ] *n* dimanche *m*.

sundry ['sʌndrɪ] *a* divers; **all and s.** tout le monde; – *npl Com* **articles** *mpl* divers.

sung [sʌŋ] *see* **sing**.

sunk [sʌŋk] *see* **sink²**; – *a* **I'm s.** *Fam* je suis fichu. ◆**sunken** *a* (*rock etc*) submergé; (*eyes*) cave.

sunny ['sʌnɪ] *a* (**-ier, -iest**) ensoleillé; **it's s.** il fait (du) soleil; **s. period** *Met* éclaircie *f*.

super ['suːpər] *a* *Fam* sensationnel.

super- ['suːpər] *pref* super-.

superannuation [suːpərænjuˈeɪʃ(ə)n] *n* (*amount*) cotisations *fpl* (pour la) retraite.

superb [suːˈpɜːb] *a* superbe.

supercilious [suːpəˈsɪlɪəs] *a* hautain.

superficial [suːpəˈfɪʃ(ə)l] *a* superficiel. ◆**—ly** *adv* superficiellement.

superfluous [suːˈpɜːflʊəs] *a* superflu.

superhuman [suːpəˈhjuːmən] *a* surhumain.

superimpose [suːpərɪmˈpəʊz] *vt* superposer (**on** à).

superintendent [suːpərɪnˈtendənt] *n* directeur, -trice *mf*; (**police**) **s.** commissaire *m* (de police).

superior [suːˈpɪərɪər] *a* supérieur (**to** à); (*goods*) de qualité supérieure; – *n* (*person*) supérieur, -eure *mf*. ◆**superiʹority** *n* supériorité *f*.

superlative [suːˈpɜːlətɪv] *a* sans pareil; – *a* & *n Gram* superlatif (*m*).

superman ['suːpəmæn] *n* (*pl* **-men**) surhomme *m*.

supermarket ['suːpəmɑːkɪt] *n* supermarché *m*.

supernatural [suːpəˈnætʃ(ə)rəl] *a* & *n* surnaturel (*m*).

superpower ['suːpəpaʊər] *n* *Pol* superpuissance *f*.

supersede [suːpəˈsiːd] *vt* remplacer, supplanter.

supersonic [suːpəˈsɒnɪk] *a* supersonique.

superstition [suːpəˈstɪʃ(ə)n] *n* superstition *f*. ◆**superstitious** *a* superstitieux.

supertanker ['suːpətæŋkər] *n* pétrolier *m* géant.

supervise ['suːpəvaɪz] *vt* (*person, work*) surveiller; (*office, research*) diriger. ◆**superʹvision** *n* surveillance *f*; direction *f*. ◆**supervisor** *n* surveillant, -ante *mf*; (*in office*) chef *m* de service; (*shop*) chef *m* de rayon. ◆**superʹvisory** *a* (*post*) de surveillant(e).

supper ['sʌpər] *n* dîner *m*; (*late-night*) souper *m*.

supple ['sʌp(ə)l] *a* souple. ◆**—ness** *n* souplesse *f*.

supplement ['sʌplɪmənt] *n* (*addition*) & *Journ* supplément *m* (**to** à); – ['sʌplɪment] *vt* compléter; **to s. one's income** arrondir ses fins de mois. ◆**suppleʹmentary** *a* supplémentaire.

supply [səˈplaɪ] *vt* (*provide*) fournir; (*feed*) alimenter (**with** en); (*equip*) équiper, pourvoir (**with** de); **to s. a need** subvenir à un besoin; **to s.o. with sth, s. sth to s.o.** (*facts etc*) fournir qch à qn; – *n* (*stock*) provision *f*, réserve *f*; (*equipment*) matériel *m*; **the s. of** (*act*) la fourniture de; **the s. of gas/electricity** to l'alimentation *f* en gaz/électricité de; (**food**) **supplies** vivres *mpl*; (**office**) **supplies** fournitures *fpl* (de bureau); **s. and demand** l'offre *f* et la demande; **to be in short s.** manquer; – *a* (*ship, train*) ravitailleur; **s. teacher** suppléant, -ante *mf*. ◆**—ing** *n* (*provision*) fourniture *f*; (*feeding*) alimentation *f*. ◆**supplier** *n* *Com* fournisseur *m*.

support [səˈpɔːt] *vt* (*bear weight of*) soutenir, supporter; (*help, encourage*) soutenir, appuyer; (*theory, idea*) appuyer; (*be in favour of*) être en faveur de; (*family, wife etc*) assurer la subsistance de; (*endure*) supporter; – *n* (*help, encouragement*) appui *m*, soutien *m*; *Tech* support *m*; **means of s.** moyens *mpl* de subsistance; **in s. of** en faveur de; (*evidence, theory*) à l'appui de. ◆**—ing** *a* (*role*) *Th Cin* secondaire; (*actor*) qui a un rôle secondaire. ◆**supporter** *n* partisan, -ane *mf*; *Fb* supporter *m*. ◆**supportive** *a* to be s. prêter son appui (**of**, **to** à).

suppos/e [sə'pəʊz] *vti* supposer (**that** que); **I'm supposed to work** *or* **be working** (*ought*) je suis censé travailler; **he's s. to be rich** on le dit riche; **I s.** (**so**) je pense; **I don't s. so**, **I s. not** je ne pense pas; **you're tired, I s.** vous êtes fatigué, je suppose; **s.** *or* **supposing we go** (*suggestion*) si nous partions; **s.** *or* **supposing** (**that**) **you're right** supposons que tu aies raison. ◆**—ed** *a* soi-disant. ◆**—edly** [-ɪdlɪ] *adv* soi-disant. ◆**supposition** *n* supposition *f*.

suppository [sə'pɒzɪtərɪ] *n Med* suppositoire *m*.

suppress [sə'pres] *vt* (*put an end to*) supprimer; (*feelings*) réprimer; (*scandal, yawn etc*) étouffer. ◆**suppression** *n* suppression *f*; répression *f*. ◆**suppressor** *n El* dispositif *m* antiparasite.

supreme [suː'priːm] *a* suprême. ◆**supremacy** *n* suprématie *f* (**over** sur).

supremo [suː'priːməʊ] *n* (*pl* -os) *Fam* grand chef *m*.

surcharge ['sɜːtʃɑːdʒ] *n* (*extra charge*) supplément *m*; (*on stamp*) surcharge *f*; (*tax*) surtaxe *f*.

sure [ʃʊər] *a* (-er, -est) sûr (**of** de, **that** que); **she's s. to accept** il est sûr qu'elle acceptera; **it's s. to snow** il va sûrement neiger; **to make s. of** s'assurer de; **for s.** à coup sûr, pour sûr; **s.!**, *Fam* **s. thing!** bien sûr!; **s. enough** (*in effect*) en effet; **it s. is cold** *Am* il fait vraiment froid; **be s. to do it!** ne manquez pas de le faire! ◆**surefire** *a* infaillible. ◆**surely** *adv* (*certainly*) sûrement; **s. he didn't refuse?** (*I think, I hope*) il n'a tout de même pas refusé.

surety ['ʃʊərətɪ] *n* caution *f*.

surf [sɜːf] *n* (*foam*) ressac *m*. ◆**surfboard** *n* planche *f* (de surf). ◆**surfing** *n Sp* surf *m*.

surface ['sɜːfɪs] *n* surface *f*; **s. area** superficie *f*; **s. mail** courrier *m* par voie(s) de surface; **on the s.** (*to all appearances*) *Fig* en apparence; – *vt* (*road*) revêtir; – *vi* (*of swimmer etc*) remonter à la surface; (*of ideas, person etc*) *Fam* apparaître.

surfeit ['sɜːfɪt] *n* (*excess*) excès *m* (**of** de).

surge [sɜːdʒ] *n* (*of sea, enthusiasm*) vague *f*; (*rise*) montée *f*; – *vi* (*of crowd, hatred*) déferler; (*rise*) monter; **to s. forward** se lancer en avant.

surgeon ['sɜːdʒ(ə)n] *n* chirurgien *m*. ◆**surgery** *n* (*science*) chirurgie *f*; (*doctor's office*) cabinet *m*; (*sitting, period*) consultation *f*; **to undergo s.** subir une intervention.

◆**surgical** *a* chirurgical; (*appliance*) orthopédique; **s. spirit** alcool *m* à 90°.

surly ['sɜːlɪ] *a* (-ier, -iest) bourru. ◆**surliness** *n* air *m* bourru.

surmise [sə'maɪz] *vt* conjecturer (**that** que).

surmount [sə'maʊnt] *vt* (*overcome, be on top of*) surmonter.

surname ['sɜːneɪm] *n* nom *m* de famille.

surpass [sə'pɑːs] *vt* surpasser (**in** en).

surplus ['sɜːpləs] *n* surplus *m*; – *a* (*goods*) en surplus; **some s. material**/*etc* (*left over*) un surplus de tissu/*etc*; **s. stock** surplus *mpl*.

surpris/e [sə'praɪz] *n* surprise *f*; **to give s.o. a s.** faire une surprise à qn; **to take s.o. by s.** prendre qn au dépourvu; – *a* (*visit, result etc*) inattendu; – *vt* (*astonish*) étonner, surprendre; (*come upon*) surprendre. ◆**—ed** *a* surpris (**that** que (+ *sub*), **at** sth de qch, **at seeing**/*etc* de voir/*etc*); **I'm s. at his** *or* **her stupidity** sa bêtise m'étonne *or* me surprend. ◆**—ing** *a* surprenant. ◆**—ingly** *adv* étonnamment; **s.** (**enough**) **he** . . . chose étonnante, il . . . .

surrealistic [sərɪə'lɪstɪk] *a* (*strange*) *Fig* surréaliste.

surrender [sə'rendər] **1** *vi* (*give oneself up*) se rendre (**to** à); **to s. to** (*police*) se livrer à; – *n Mil* reddition *f*, capitulation *f*. **2** *vt* (*hand over*) remettre, rendre (**to** à); (*right, claim*) renoncer à.

surreptitious [sʌrəp'tɪʃəs] *a* subreptice.

surrogate ['sʌrəgət] *n* substitut *m*; **s. mother** mère *f* porteuse.

surround [sə'raʊnd] *vt* entourer (**with** de); *Mil* encercler; **surrounded by** entouré de. ◆**—ing** *a* environnant. ◆**—ings** *npl* environs *mpl*; (*setting*) cadre *m*.

surveillance [sɜː'veɪləns] *n* (*of prisoner etc*) surveillance *f*.

survey [sə'veɪ] *vt* (*look at*) regarder; (*review*) passer en revue; (*house etc*) inspecter; (*land*) arpenter; – ['sɜːveɪ] *n* (*investigation*) enquête *f*; (*of house etc*) inspection *f*; (*of opinion*) sondage *m*; **a (general) s. of** une vue générale de. ◆**sur'veying** *n* arpentage *m*. ◆**sur'veyor** *n* (arpenteur *m*) géomètre *m*; (*of house etc*) expert *m*.

survive [sə'vaɪv] *vi* (*of person, custom etc*) survivre; – *vt* survivre à. ◆**survival** *n* (*act*) survie *f*; (*relic*) vestige *m*. ◆**survivor** *n* survivant, -ante *mf*.

susceptible [sə'septəb(ə)l] *a* (*sensitive*) sensible (**to** à); **s. to colds**/*etc* (*prone to*) prédisposé aux rhumes/*etc*. ◆**suscepti-'bility** *n* sensibilité *f*; prédisposition *f*; *pl* susceptibilité *f*.

suspect ['sʌspekt] *n & a* suspect, -ecte (*mf*); – [sə'spekt] *vt* soupçonner (**that que, of sth** de qch, **of doing** d'avoir fait); (*think questionable*) suspecter, douter de; **yes, I s.** oui, j'imagine.

suspend [sə'spend] *vt* **1** (*hang*) suspendre (**from** à). **2** (*stop, postpone, dismiss*) suspendre; (*passport etc*) retirer (provisoirement); (*pupil*) *Sch* renvoyer; **suspended sentence** *Jur* condamnation *f* avec sursis. ◆**suspender** *n* (*for stocking*) jarretelle *f*; *pl* (*braces*) *Am* bretelles *fpl*; **s. belt** porte-jarretelles *m inv.* ◆**suspension** *n* **1** (*stopping*) suspension *f*; (*of passport etc*) retrait *m* (provisoire). **2** (*of vehicle etc*) suspension *f*; **s. bridge** pont *m* suspendu.

suspense [sə'spens] *n* attente *f* (angoissée); (*in film, book etc*) suspense *m*; **in s.** (*person, matter*) en suspens.

suspicion [sə'spɪʃ(ə)n] *n* soupçon *m*; **to arouse s.** éveiller les soupçons; **with s.** (*distrust*) avec méfiance; **under s.** considéré comme suspect. ◆**suspicious** *a* (*a person*) soupçonneux, méfiant; (*behaviour*) suspect; **s.(-looking)** (*suspect*) suspect; **to be s. of** *or* **about** (*distrust*) se méfier de. ◆**suspiciously** *adv* (*to behave etc*) d'une manière suspecte; (*to consider etc*) avec méfiance.

sustain [sə'steɪn] *vt* (*effort, theory*) soutenir; (*weight*) supporter; (*with food*) nourrir; (*life*) maintenir; (*damage, attack*) subir; (*injury*) recevoir. ◆**sustenance** *n* (*food*) nourriture *f*; (*quality*) valeur *f* nutritive.

swab [swɒb] *n* (*pad*) *Med* tampon *m*; (*specimen*) *Med* prélèvement *m*.

swagger ['swægər] *vi* (*walk*) parader; – *n* démarche *f* fanfaronne.

swallow ['swɒləʊ] **1** *vt* avaler; **to s. down** *or* **up** avaler; **to s. up** *Fig* engloutir; – *vi* avaler. **2** *n* (*bird*) hirondelle *f*.

swam [swæm] *see* **swim**.

swamp [swɒmp] *n* marais *m*, marécage *m*; – *vt* (*flood, overwhelm*) submerger (**with** de). ◆**swampy** *a* (-ier, -iest) marécageux.

swan [swɒn] *n* cygne *m*.

swank [swæŋk] *vi* (*show off*) *Fam* crâner, fanfaronner.

swap [swɒp] *n* échange *m*; *pl* (*stamps etc*) doubles *mpl*; – *vt* (-pp-) échanger (**for** contre); **to s. seats** changer de place; – *vi* échanger.

swarm [swɔːm] *n* (*of bees, people etc*) essaim *m*; – *vi* (*of streets, insects, people etc*) fourmiller (**with** de); **to s. in** (*of people*) entrer en foule.

swarthy ['swɔːðɪ] *a* (-ier, -iest) (*dark*) basané.

swastika ['swɒstɪkə] *n* (*Nazi emblem*) croix *f* gammée.

swat [swɒt] *vt* (-tt-) (*fly etc*) écraser.

sway [sweɪ] *vi* se balancer, osciller; – *vt* balancer; *Fig* influencer; – *n* balancement *m*; *Fig* influence *f*.

swear ['sweər] *vt* (*pt* **swore,** *pp* **sworn**) jurer (**to do** de faire, **that** que); **to s. an oath** prêter serment; **to s. s.o. to secrecy** faire jurer le silence à qn; **sworn enemies** ennemis *mpl* jurés; – *vi* (*take an oath*) jurer (**to sth** de qch); (*curse*) jurer, pester (**at** contre); **she swears by this lotion** elle ne jure que par cette lotion. ◆**swearword** *n* gros mot *m*, juron *m*.

sweat [swet] *n* sueur *f*; **s. shirt** sweat-shirt *m*; – *vi* (*of person, wall etc*) suer (**with** de); – *vt* **to s. out** (*cold*) *Med* se débarrasser de (*en transpirant*). ◆**sweater** *n* (*garment*) pull *m*. ◆**sweaty** *a* (-ier, -iest) (*shirt etc*) plein de sueur; (*hand*) moite; (*person*) (*tout*) en sueur, (*tout*) en nage.

swede [swiːd] *n* (*vegetable*) rutabaga *m*.

Swede [swiːd] *n* Suédois, -oise *mf*. ◆**Sweden** *n* Suède *f*. ◆**Swedish** *a* suédois; – *n* (*language*) suédois *m*.

sweep [swiːp] *n* coup *m* de balai; (*movement*) *Fig* (*large*) mouvement *m*; (*curve*) courbe *f*; **to make a clean s.** (*removal*) faire table rase (**of** de); (*victory*) remporter une victoire totale; – *vt* (*pt & pp* **swept**) (*with broom*) balayer; (*chimney*) ramoner; (*river*) draguer; **to s. away** *or* **out** *or* **up** balayer; **to s. away** *or* **along** (*carry off*) emporter; **to s. aside** (*dismiss*) écarter; – *vi* **to s.** (**up**) balayer; **to s. in** (*of person*) *Fig* entrer rapidement *or* majestueusement; **to s. through** (*of fear etc*) saisir (*groupe etc*); (*of disease etc*) ravager (*pays etc*). ◆**—ing** *a* (*gesture*) large; (*change*) radical; (*statement*) trop général. ◆**sweepstake** *n* (*lottery*) sweepstake *m*.

sweet [swiːt] *a* (-er, -est) (*not sour*) doux; (*agreeable*) agréable, doux; (*tea, coffee etc*) sucré; (*person, house, kitchen*) mignon, gentil; **to have a s. tooth** aimer les sucreries; **to be s.-smelling** sentir bon; **s. corn** maïs *m*; **s. pea** *Bot* pois *m* de senteur; **s. potato** patate *f* douce; **s. shop** confiserie *f*; **s. talk** *Fam* cajoleries *fpl*, douceurs *fpl*; – *n* (*candy*) bonbon *m*; (*dessert*) dessert *m*; **my s.!** (*darling*) mon ange! ◆**sweeten** *vt* (*tea etc*) sucrer; *Fig* adoucir. ◆**sweetener** *n* saccharine *f*. ◆**sweetie** *n* (*darling*) *Fam* chéri, -ie *mf*. ◆**sweetly** *adv* (*kindly*) gentiment; (*softly*) doucement. ◆**sweetness** *n* douceur *f*; (*taste*) goût *m* sucré.

sweetbread ['swiːtbred] *n* ris *m* de veau *or* d'agneau.

sweetheart ['swiːthɑːt] *n* (*lover*) ami, -ie *mf*; **my s.!** (*darling*) mon ange!

swell [swel] **1** *n* (*of sea*) houle *f*. **2** *a* (*very good*) *Am Fam* formidable. **3** *vi* (*pt* swelled, *pp* swollen *or* swelled) se gonfler; (*of river, numbers*) grossir; **to s. (up)** *Med* enfler, gonfler; – *vt* (*river, numbers*) grossir. ◆**—ing** *n Med* enflure *f*.

swelter ['sweltər] *vi* étouffer. ◆**—ing** *a* étouffant; **it's s.** on étouffe.

swept [swept] *see* sweep.

swerve [swɜːv] *vi* (*while running etc*) faire un écart; (*of vehicle*) faire une embardée.

swift [swift] **1** *a* (-er, -est) rapide; **s. to act** prompt à agir. **2** *n* (*bird*) martinet *m*. ◆**—ly** *adv* rapidement. ◆**—ness** *n* rapidité *f*.

swig [swig] *n* (*of beer etc*) lampée *f*.

swill [swil] *vt* **to s. (out** *or* **down)** laver (à grande eau).

swim [swim] *n* baignade *f*; **to go for a s.** se baigner, nager; – *vi* (*pt* swam, *pp* swum, *pres p* swimming) nager; *Sp* faire de la natation; (*of head, room*) *Fig* tourner; **to go swimming** aller nager; **to s. away** se sauver (à la nage); – *vt* (*river*) traverser à la nage; (*length, crawl etc*) nager. ◆**swimming** *n* natation *f*; **s. costume** maillot *m* de bain; **s. pool, s. baths** piscine *f*; **s. trunks** slip *m* or caleçon *m* de bain. ◆**swimmer** *n* nageur, -euse *mf*. ◆**swimsuit** *n* maillot *m* de bain.

swindl/e ['swind(ə)l] *n* escroquerie *f*; – *vt* escroquer; **to s. s.o. out of money** escroquer de l'argent à qn. ◆**—er** *n* escroc *m*.

swine [swain] *n inv* (*person*) *Pej* salaud *m*.

swing [swiŋ] *n* (*seat*) balançoire *f*; (*movement*) balancement *m*; (*of pendulum*) oscillation *f*; (*in opinion*) revirement *m*; (*rhythm*) rythme *m*; **to be in full s.** battre son plein; **to be in the s. of things** *Fam* être dans le bain; **s. door** porte *f* de saloon; – *vi* (*pt & pp* swung) (*sway*) se balancer; (*of pendulum*) osciller; (*turn*) virer; **to s. round** (*turn suddenly*) virer, tourner; (*of person*) se retourner (vivement); (*of vehicle in collision etc*) faire un tête-à-queue; **to s. into action** passer à l'action; – *vt* (*arms etc*) balancer; (*axe*) brandir; (*influence*) *Fam* influencer; **to s. round** (*car etc*) faire tourner. ◆**—ing** *a* *Fam* (*trendy*) dans le vent; (*lively*) plein de vie; (*music*) entraînant.

swingeing ['swindʒiŋ] *a* **s. cuts** des réductions *fpl* draconiennes.

swipe [swaip] *vt Fam* (*hit*) frapper dur; (*steal*) piquer (**from s.o.** à qn); – *n Fam* grand coup *m*.

swirl [swɜːl] *n* tourbillon *m*; – *vi* tourbillonner.

swish [swiʃ] **1** *a* (*posh*) *Fam* rupin, chic. **2** *vi* (*of whip etc*) siffler; (*of fabric*) froufrouter; – *n* sifflement *m*; froufrou *m*.

Swiss [swis] *a* suisse; – *n inv* Suisse *m*, Suissesse *f*; **the S.** les Suisses *mpl*.

switch [switʃ] *n El* bouton *m* (électrique), interrupteur *m*; (*change*) changement *m* (in de); (*reversal*) revirement *m* (in de); – *vt* (*money, employee etc*) transférer (**to** à); (*affection, support*) reporter (**to** sur, **from** de); (*exchange*) échanger (**for** contre); **to s. buses**/*etc* changer de bus/*etc*; **to s. places** *or* **seats** changer de place; **to s. off** (*lamp, gas, radio etc*) éteindre; (*engine*) arrêter; **to s. itself off** (*of heating etc*) s'éteindre tout seul; **to s. on** (*lamp, gas, radio etc*) mettre, allumer; (*engine*) mettre en marche; – *vi* **to s. (over)** (*to* à) passer à; **to s. off** (*switch off light, radio etc*) éteindre; **to s. on** (*switch on light, radio etc*) allumer. ◆**switchback** *n* (*at funfair*) montagnes *fpl* russes. ◆**switchblade** *n Am* couteau *m* à cran d'arrêt. ◆**switchboard** *n Tel* standard *m*; **s. operator** standardiste *mf*.

Switzerland ['switsələnd] *n* Suisse *f*.

swivel ['swiv(ə)l] *vi* (-ll-, *Am* -l-) **to s. (round)** (*of chair etc*) pivoter; – *a* **s. chair** fauteuil *m* pivotant.

swollen ['swəul(ə)n] *see* swell 3; – *a* (*leg etc*) enflé.

swoon [swuːn] *vi Lit* se pâmer.

swoop [swuːp] **1** *vi* **to s. (down) on** (*of bird*) fondre sur. **2** *n* (*of police*) descente *f*; – *vi* faire une descente (**on** dans).

swop [swɒp] *n, vt & vi* = swap.

sword [sɔːd] *n* épée *f*. ◆**swordfish** *n* espadon *m*.

swore, sworn [swɔːr, swɔːn] *see* swear.

swot [swɒt] *vti* (-tt-) **to s. (up)** (*study*) *Fam* potasser; **to s. (up) for** (*exam*), **to s. up on** (*subject*) *Fam* potasser; – *n Pej Fam* bûcheur, -euse *mf*.

swum [swʌm] *see* swim.

swung [swʌŋ] *see* swing.

sycamore ['sikəmɔːr] *n* (*maple*) sycomore *m*; (*plane*) *Am* platane *m*.

sycophant ['sikəfænt] *n* flagorneur, -euse *mf*.

syllable ['siləb(ə)l] *n* syllabe *f*.

syllabus ['siləbəs] *n Sch Univ* programme *m*.

symbol ['simb(ə)l] *n* symbole *m*. ◆**sym-**

'**bolic** *a* symbolique. ◆**symbolism** *n* symbolisme *m*. ◆**symbolize** *vt* symboliser.

symmetry ['sɪmətrɪ] *n* symétrie *f*. ◆**sy'mmetrical** *a* symétrique.

sympathy ['sɪmpəθɪ] *n* (*pity*) compassion *f*; (*understanding*) compréhension *f*; (*condolences*) condoléances *fpl*; (*solidarity*) solidarité *f* (**for** avec); **to be in s. with** (*workers in dispute*) être du côté de; (*s.o.'s opinion etc*) comprendre, être en accord avec. ◆**sympa'thetic** *a* (*showing pity*) compatissant; (*understanding*) compréhensif; **s. to** (*favourable*) bien disposé à l'égard de. ◆**sympa'thetically** *adv* avec compassion; avec compréhension. ◆**sympathize** *vi* **I s.** (**with you**) (*pity*) je compatis (à votre sort); (*understanding*) je vous comprends. ◆**sympathizer** *n Pol* sympathisant, -ante *mf*.

symphony ['sɪmfənɪ] *n* symphonie *f*; − *a* (*orchestra, concert*) symphonique. ◆**sym'phonic** *a* symphonique.

symposium [sɪm'pəʊzɪəm] *n* symposium *m*.

symptom ['sɪmptəm] *n* symptôme *m*. ◆**sympto'matic** *a* symptomatique (**of** de).

synagogue ['sɪnəgɒg] *n* synagogue *f*.

synchronize ['sɪŋkrənaɪz] *vt* synchroniser.

syndicate ['sɪndɪkət] *n* (*of businessmen, criminals*) syndicat *m*.

syndrome ['sɪndrəʊɪn] *n Med & Fig* syndrome *m*.

synod ['sɪnəd] *n Rel* synode *m*.

synonym ['sɪnənɪm] *n* synonyme *m*. ◆**sy'nonymous** *a* synonyme (**with** de).

synopsis, *pl* **-opses** [sɪ'nɒpsɪs, -ɒpsiːz] *n* résumé *m*, synopsis *m*; (*of film*) synopsis *m*.

syntax ['sɪntæks] *n Gram* syntaxe *f*.

synthesis, *pl* **-theses** ['sɪnθəsɪs, -θəsiːz] *n* synthèse *f*.

synthetic [sɪn'θetɪk] *a* synthétique.

syphilis ['sɪfɪlɪs] *n* syphilis *f*.

Syria ['sɪrɪə] *n* Syrie *f*. ◆**Syrian** *a & n* syrien, -ienne (*mf*).

syringe [sɪ'rɪndʒ] *n* seringue *f*.

syrup ['sɪrəp] *n* sirop *m*; (**golden**) **s.** (*treacle*) mélasse *f* (raffinée). ◆**syrupy** *a* sirupeux.

system ['sɪstəm] *n* (*structure, plan, network etc*) & *Anat* système *m*; (*human body*) organisme *m*; (*order*) méthode *f*; **systems analyst** analyste-programmeur *mf*. ◆**syste'matic** *a* systématique. ◆**syste-'matically** *adv* systématiquement.

T

T, t [tiː] *n* T, t *m*. ◆**T-junction** *n Aut* intersection *f* en T. ◆**T-shirt** *n* tee-shirt *m*, T-shirt *m*.

ta! [tɑː] *int Sl* merci!

tab [tæb] *n* (*label*) étiquette *f*; (*tongue*) patte *f*; (*loop*) attache *f*; (*bill*) *Am* addition *f*; **to keep tabs on** *Fam* surveiller (de près).

tabby ['tæbɪ] *a* **t. cat** chat, chatte *mf* tigré(e).

table¹ ['teɪb(ə)l] *n* **1** (*furniture*) table *f*; **bedside/card/operating t.** table de nuit/de jeu/d'opération; **to lay** *or* **set/clear the t.** mettre/débarrasser la table; (**sitting**) **at the t.** à table; **t. top** dessus *m* de table. **2** (*list*) table *f*; **t. of contents** table des matières. ◆**tablecloth** *n* nappe *f*. ◆**tablemat** *n* (*of fabric*) napperon *m*; (*hard*) dessous-de-plat *m inv*. ◆**tablespoon** *n* = cuiller *f* à soupe. ◆**tablespoonful** *n* = cuillerée *f* à soupe.

table² ['teɪb(ə)l] *vt* (*motion etc*) *Pol* présenter; (*postpone*) *Am* ajourner.

tablet ['tæblɪt] *n* **1** (*pill*) *Med* comprimé *m*. **2** (*inscribed stone*) plaque *f*.

tabloid ['tæblɔɪd] *n* (*newspaper*) quotidien *m* populaire.

taboo [tə'buː] *a & n* tabou (*m*).

tabulator ['tæbjʊleɪtər] *n* (*of typewriter*) tabulateur *m*.

tacit ['tæsɪt] *a* tacite. ◆**—ly** *adv* tacitement.

taciturn ['tæsɪtɜːn] *a* taciturne.

tack [tæk] **1** *n* (*nail*) semence *f*; (*thumbtack*) *Am* punaise *f*; **to get down to brass tacks** *Fig* en venir aux faits; − *vt* **to t.** (**down**) clouer. **2** *n* (*stitch*) *Tex* point *m* de bâti; − *vt* **to t.** (**down** *or* **on**) bâtir; **to t. on** (*add*) *Fig* (r)ajouter. **3** *vi* (*of ship*) louvoyer. − *n* (*course of action*) *Fig* voie *f*.

tackle ['tæk(ə)l] **1** *n* (*gear*) matériel *m*, équipement *m*. **2** *vt* (*task, problem etc*) s'attaquer à; (*thief etc*) saisir; *Sp* plaquer; − *n Sp* plaquage *m*.

tacky ['tækɪ] *a* (**-ier, -iest**) **1** (*wet, sticky*) collant, pas sec. **2** (*clothes, attitude etc*) *Am Fam* moche.

tact [tækt] *n* tact *m*. ◆**tactful** *a* (*remark etc*) plein de tact, diplomatique; **she's t.** elle a du tact. ◆**tactfully** adv avec tact. ◆**tact-less** a qui manque de tact. ◆**tactlessly** adv sans tact.

tactic ['tæktɪk] n a t. une tactique; **tactics** la tactique. ◆**tactical** a tactique.

tactile ['tæktaɪl] a tactile.

tadpole ['tædpəʊl] n têtard m.

taffy ['tæfɪ] n (toffee) Am caramel m (dur).

tag [tæg] **1** n (label) étiquette f; (end piece) bout m; – vt (-gg-) **to t. on** (add) Fam rajouter (**to** à). **2** vi (-gg-) **to t. along** (follow) suivre.

Tahiti [tɑːˈhiːtɪ] n Tahiti m.

tail [teɪl] **1** n (of animal) queue f; (of shirt) pan m; pl (outfit) habit m, queue-de-pie f; **t. end** fin f, bout m; **heads or tails?** pile ou face? **2** vt (follow) suivre, filer. **3** vi **to t. off** (lessen) diminuer. ◆**tailback** n (of traffic) bouchon m. ◆**tailcoat** n queue-de-pie f. ◆**taillight** n Aut Am feu m arrière inv.

tailor ['teɪlər] n (person) tailleur m; – vt (garment) façonner; Fig adapter (**to, to suit** à). ◆**t.-'made** a fait sur mesure; **t.-made for** (specially designed) conçu pour; (suited) fait pour.

tainted ['teɪntɪd] a (air) pollué; (food) gâté; Fig souillé.

take [teɪk] vt (pt took, pp taken) prendre; (choice) faire; (prize) remporter; (exam) passer; (contain) contenir; Math soustraire (**from** de); (tolerate) supporter; (bring) apporter (qch) (**to** à), (person) amener (**to** à), (person by car) conduire (**to** à); (escort) accompagner (**to** à); (lead away) emmener; (of road) mener (qn); **to t. sth to s.o.** (ap)porter qch à qn; **to t. s.o. (out) to** (theatre etc) emmener qn à; **to t. sth with one** emporter qch; **to t. over** or **round** or **along** (object) apporter; (person) amener; **to t. s.o. home** (on foot, by car etc) ramener qn; **it takes an army/courage/etc** (requires) il faut une armée/du courage/etc (**to do** pour faire); **I took an hour to do it** or **over it** j'ai mis une heure à le faire, ça m'a pris une heure pour le faire; **I t. it that** je présume que; – n Cin prise f de vue(s); – vi (of fire) prendre. ■ **to t. after** vi (be like) ressembler à; **to t. apart** vt (machine) démonter; **to t. away** vt (thing) emporter; (person) emmener; (remove) enlever (**from** à); Math soustraire (**from** de). ◆**t.-away** a (meal) à emporter; – n café m or restaurant m qui fait des plats à emporter; (meal) plat m à emporter; **to t. back** vt reprendre; (return) rapporter; (statement) retirer; **to t. down** vt (object) descendre; (notes) prendre; **to t. in** vt (chair, car etc) rentrer; (orphan) recueil-

lir; (skirt) reprendre; (include) englober; (distance) couvrir; (understand) comprendre; (deceive) Fam rouler; **to t. off** vt (remove) enlever; (train, bus) supprimer; (lead away) emmener; (mimic) imiter; Math déduire (**from** de); – vi (of aircraft) décoller. ◆**takeoff** n (of aircraft) décollage m; **to t. on** vt (work, employee, passenger, shape) prendre; **to t. out** vt (from pocket etc) sortir; (stain) enlever; (tooth) arracher; (licence, insurance) prendre; **to t. it out on** Fam passer sa colère sur. ◆**t.-out** a & n Am = **t.-away**; **to t. over** vt (be responsible for the running of) prendre la direction de; (overrun) envahir; (buy out) Com racheter (compagnie) à; **to t. over s.o.'s job** remplacer qn; – vi Mil Pol prendre le pouvoir; (relieve) prendre la relève (**from** de); (succeed) prendre la succession (**from** de). ◆**t.-over** n Com rachat m; Pol prise f de pouvoir; **to t. round** vt (distribute) distribuer; (visitor) faire visiter; **to t. to vi to t. to doing** se mettre à qch; **I didn't t. to him/it** il/ça ne m'a pas plu; **to t. up** vt (carry up) monter; (hem) raccourcir; (continue) reprendre; (occupy) prendre; (hobby) se mettre à; – vi **to t. up with** se lier avec. ◆**taken** a (seat) pris; (impressed) impressionné (**with, by** par); **to be t. ill** tomber malade. ◆**taking** n (capture) Mil prise f; pl (money) Com recette f.

talcum ['tælkəm] a **t. powder** talc m.

tale [teɪl] n (story) conte m; (account, report) récit m; (lie) histoire f; **to tell tales** rapporter (**on** sur).

talent ['tælənt] n talent m; (talented people) talents mpl; **to have a t.** for avoir du talent pour. ◆**talented** a doué, talentueux.

talk [tɔːk] n (words) propos mpl; (gossip) bavardage(s) m(pl); (conversation) conversation f (**about** à propos de); (interview) entretien m; (lecture) exposé m (**on** sur); (informal) causerie f (**on** sur); pl (negotiations) pourparlers mpl; **to have a t. with** parler avec; **there's t. of** on parle de; – vi parler (**to** à; **with** avec; **about, of** de); (chat) bavarder; **to t. down to s.o.** parler à qn comme à un inférieur; – vt (nonsense) dire; **to t. politics** parler politique; **to t. s.o. into doing/out of doing** persuader qn de faire/de ne pas faire; **to t. over** discuter (de); **to t. s.o. round** persuader qn. ◆**—ing** a (film) parlant; **to give s.o. a talking-to** Fam passer un savon à qn. ◆**talkative** a bavard. ◆**talker** n causeur, -euse mf; **she's a good t.** elle parle bien.

tall [tɔːl] a (-er, -est) (person) grand; (tree,

house etc) haut; **how t. are you?** combien mesures-tu?; **a t. story** *Fig* une histoire invraisemblable *or* à dormir debout. ◆**tallboy** *n* grande commode *f*. ◆**tallness** *n* (*of person*) grande taille *f*; (*of building etc*) hauteur *f*.

tally ['tælɪ] *vi* correspondre (**with** à).

tambourine [tæmbə'riːn] *n* tambourin *m*.

tame [teɪm] *a* (**-er, -est**) (*animal, bird*) apprivoisé; (*person*) *Fig* docile; (*book, play*) fade. – *vt* (*animal, bird*) apprivoiser; (*lion, passion*) dompter.

tamper ['tæmpər] *vi* **to t. with** (*lock, car etc*) toucher à; (*text*) altérer.

tampon ['tæmpɒn] *n* tampon *m* hygiénique.

tan [tæn] **1** *n* (*suntan*) bronzage *m*; – *vti* (**-nn-**) bronzer **2** *a* (*colour*) marron clair *inv.* **3** *vt* (**-nn-**) (*hide*) tanner.

tandem ['tændəm] *n* **1** (*bicycle*) tandem *m*. **2** **in t.** (*to work etc*) en tandem.

tang [tæŋ] *n* (*taste*) saveur *f* piquante; (*smell*) odeur *f* piquante. ◆**tangy** *a* (**-ier, -iest**) piquant.

tangerine [tændʒə'riːn] *n* mandarine *f*.

tangible ['tændʒəb(ə)l] *a* tangible.

tangl/e ['tæŋg(ə)l] *n* enchevêtrement *m*; **to get into a t.** (*of rope*) s'enchevêtrer; (*of hair*) s'emmêler; (*of person*) *Fig* se mettre dans une situation pas possible. ◆**—ed** *a* enchevêtré; (*hair*) emmêlé; **to get t. = to get into a tangle**.

tank [tæŋk] *n* **1** (*for storage of water, fuel etc*) réservoir *m*; (*vat*) cuve *f*; (*fish*) **t.** aquarium *m.* **2** (*vehicle*) *Mil* char *m*, tank *m*.

tankard ['tæŋkəd] *n* (*beer mug*) chope *f*.

tanker ['tæŋkər] *n* (*truck*) *Aut* camion-citerne *m*; (*oil*) **t.** (*ship*) pétrolier *m*.

tantalizing ['tæntəlaɪzɪŋ] *a* (*irrésistiblement*) tentant. ◆**—ly** *adv* d'une manière tentante.

tantamount ['tæntəmaʊnt] *a* **it's t. to** cela équivaut à.

tantrum ['tæntrəm] *n* accès *m* de colère.

tap [tæp] **1** *n* (*for water*) robinet *m*; **on t.** *Fig* disponible. **2** *vti* (**-pp-**) frapper légèrement, tapoter; – *n* petit coup *m*; **t. dancing** claquettes *fpl.* **3** *vt* (**-pp-**) (*phone*) placer sur table d'écoute. **4** *vt* (**-pp-**) (*resources*) exploiter.

tape [teɪp] **1** *n* ruban *m*; (*sticky*) **t.** ruban adhésif; **t. measure** mètre *m* (à) ruban; – *vt* (*stick*) coller (*avec du ruban adhésif*). **2** *n* (*for sound recording*) bande *f* (*magnétique*); (*video*) **t.** bande (*vidéo*); **t. recorder** magnétophone *m*; – *vt* enregistrer.

taper ['teɪpər] **1** *vi* (*of fingers etc*) s'effiler; **to t. off** *Fig* diminuer. **2** *n* (*candle*) *Rel* cierge

m. ◆**—ed** *a*, ◆**—ing** *a* (*fingers*) fuselé; (*trousers*) à bas étroits.

tapestry ['tæpəstrɪ] *n* tapisserie *f*.

tapioca [tæpɪ'əʊkə] *n* tapioca *m*.

tar [tɑːr] *n* goudron *m*; – *vt* (**-rr-**) goudronner.

tardy ['tɑːdɪ] *a* (**-ier, -iest**) (*belated*) tardif; (*slow*) lent.

target ['tɑːgɪt] *n* cible *f*; *Fig* objectif *m*; **t. date** date *f* fixée; – *vt* (*aim*) *Fig* destiner (**at** à); (*aim at*) *Fig* viser.

tariff ['tærɪf] *n* (*tax*) tarif *m* douanier; (*prices*) tarif *m*.

tarmac ['tɑːmæk] *n* macadam *m* (*goudronné*); (*runway*) piste *f*.

tarnish ['tɑːnɪʃ] *vt* ternir.

tarpaulin [tɑː'pɔːlɪn] *n* bâche *f* (*goudronnée*).

tarragon ['tærəgən] *n* *Bot Culin* estragon *m*.

tarry ['tærɪ] *vi* (*remain*) *Lit* rester.

tart [tɑːt] **1** *n* (*pie*) tarte *f*. **2** *a* (**-er, -est**) (*taste, remark*) aigre. **3** *n* (*prostitute*) *Pej Fam* poule *f*. **4** *vt* **to t. up** *Pej Fam* (*decorate*) embellir; (*dress*) attifer. ◆**—ness** *n* aigreur *f*.

tartan ['tɑːt(ə)n] *n* tartan *m*; – *a* écossais.

tartar ['tɑːtər] *n* **1** (*on teeth*) tartre *m*. **2** **a t. sauce** sauce *f* tartare.

task [tɑːsk] *n* tâche *f*; **to take to t.** prendre à partie; **t. force** *Mil* détachement *m* spécial; *Pol* commission *f* spéciale.

tassel ['tæs(ə)l] *n* (*on clothes etc*) gland *m*.

taste [teɪst] *n* goût *m*; **to get a t. for** prendre goût à; **in good/bad t.** de bon/mauvais goût; **to have a t. of** goûter; goûter à; goûter de; – *vt* (*eat, enjoy*) goûter; (*try, sample*) goûter à; (*make out the taste of*) sentir (le goût de); (*experience*) goûter de; – *vi* **to t. of** *or* **like** avoir un goût de; **to t. delicious**/*etc* avoir un goût délicieux/*etc*; **how does it t.?** comment le trouves-tu?; – *a* **t. bud** papille *f* gustative. ◆**tasteful** *a* de bon goût. ◆**tastefully** *adv* avec goût. ◆**tasteless** *a* (*food etc*) sans goût; (*joke etc*) *Fig* de mauvais goût. ◆**tasty** *a* (**-ier, -iest**) savoureux.

tat [tæt] *see* **tit 2**.

ta-ta! [tæ'tɑː] *int* *Sl* au revoir!

tattered ['tætəd] *a* (*clothes*) en lambeaux; (*person*) déguenillé. ◆**tatters** *npl* **in t.** en lambeaux.

tattoo [tæ'tuː] **1** *n* (*pl* **-oos**) (*on body*) tatouage *m*; – *vt* tatouer. **2** *n* (*pl* **-oos**) *Mil* spectacle *m* militaire.

tatty ['tætɪ] *a* (**-ier, -iest**) (*clothes etc*) *Fam* miteux.

taught [tɔːt] *see* **teach**.

taunt [tɔːnt] *vt* railler; − *n* raillerie *f*.
◆—**ing** *a* railleur.

Taurus ['tɔːrəs] *n* (*sign*) le Taureau.

taut [tɔːt] *a* (*rope, person etc*) tendu.

tavern ['tævən] *n* taverne *f*.

tawdry ['tɔːdrɪ] *a* (-ier, -iest) *Pej* tape-à-l'œil *inv*.

tawny ['tɔːnɪ] *a* (*colour*) fauve; (*port*) ambré.

tax¹ [tæks] *n* taxe *f*, impôt *m*; (**income**) t. impôts *mpl* (sur le revenu); − *a* fiscal; **t. collector** percepteur *m*; **t. relief** dégrèvement *m* (d'impôt); − *vt* (*person, goods*) imposer. ◆**taxable** *a* imposable. ◆**tax-'ation** *n* (*act*) imposition *f*; (*taxes*) impôts *mpl*. ◆**tax-free** *a* exempt d'impôts. ◆**taxman** *n* (*pl* -**men**) *Fam* percepteur *m*. ◆**taxpayer** *n* contribuable *mf*.

tax² [tæks] *vt* (*patience etc*) mettre à l'épreuve; (*tire*) fatiguer. ◆—**ing** *a* (*journey etc*) éprouvant.

taxi ['tæksɪ] **1** *n* taxi *m*; **t. cab** taxi *m*; **t. rank**, *Am* **t. stand** station *f* de taxis. **2** *vi* (*of aircraft*) rouler au sol.

tea [tiː] *n* thé *m*; (*snack*) goûter *m*; **high t.** goûter *m* (dînatoire); **to have t.** prendre le thé; (*afternoon snack*) goûter; **t. break** pause-thé *f*; **t. chest** caisse *f* (à thé); **t. cloth** (*for drying dishes*) torchon *m*; **t. set** service *m* à thé; **t. towel** torchon *m*. ◆**teabag** *n* sachet *m* de thé. ◆**teacup** *n* tasse *f* à thé. ◆**tealeaf** *n* (*pl* -**leaves**) feuille *f* de thé. ◆**teapot** *n* théière *f*. ◆**tearoom** *n* salon *m* de thé. ◆**teaspoon** *n* petite cuiller *f*. ◆**teaspoonful** *n* cuillerée *f* à café. ◆**teatime** *n* l'heure *f* du thé.

teach [tiːtʃ] *vt* (*pt & pp* **taught**) apprendre (s.o. sth qch à qn; (*in school etc*) enseigner (s.o. sth qch à qn); **to t. s.o. (how) to do** apprendre à qn à faire; **to t. school** *Am* enseigner; **to t. oneself sth** apprendre qch tout seul; − *vi* enseigner. ◆—**ing** *n* enseignement *m*; − *a* (*staff*) enseignant; (*method, material*) pédagogique; **t. profession** enseignement *m*; (*teachers*) enseignants *mpl*; **t. qualification** diplôme *m* permettant d'enseigner. ◆—**er** *n* professeur *m*; (*in primary school*) instituteur, -trice *mf*.

teak [tiːk] *n* (*wood*) teck *m*.

team [tiːm] *n* *Sp* équipe *f*; (*of oxen*) attelage *m*; **t. mate** coéquipier, -ière *mf*; − *vi* **to t. up** faire équipe (**with** avec). ◆**teamster** *n* *Am* routier *m*. ◆**teamwork** *n* collaboration *f*.

tear¹ [teər] *n* déchirure *f*; − *vt* (*pt* **tore**, *pp* **torn**) (*rip*) déchirer; (*snatch*) arracher (**from** s.o. à qn); **torn between** *Fig* tiraillé entre; **to t. down** (*house etc*) démolir; **to t. away** *or* **off**

or **out** (*forcefully*) arracher; (*stub, receipt, stamp etc*) détacher; **to t. up** déchirer; − *vi* (*of cloth etc*) se déchirer. **2** *vi* (*pt* **tore**, *pp* **torn**) **to t. along** (*rush*) aller à toute vitesse.

tear² [tɪər] *n* larme *f*; **in tears** en larmes; **close to** *or* **near (to) tears** au bord des larmes. ◆**tearful** *a* (*eyes, voice*) larmoyant; (*person*) en larmes. ◆**tearfully** *adv* en pleurant. ◆**teargas** *n* gaz *m* lacrymogène.

tearaway ['teərəweɪ] *n* *Fam* petit voyou *m*.

teas/e [tiːz] *vt* taquiner; (*harshly*) tourmenter; − *n* (*person*) taquin, -ine *mf*. ◆—**ing** *a* (*remark etc*) taquin. ◆—**er** *n* **1** (*person*) taquin, -ine *mf*. **2** (*question*) *Fam* colle *f*.

teat [tiːt] *n* (*of bottle, animal*) tétine *f*.

technical ['teknɪk(ə)l] *a* technique. ◆**techni'cality** *n* (*detail*) détail *m* technique. ◆**technically** *adv* techniquement; *Fig* théoriquement. ◆**tech'nician** *n* technicien, -ienne *mf*. ◆**tech'nique** *n* technique *f*. ◆**technocrat** *n* technocrate *m*. ◆**techno'logical** *a* technologique. ◆**tech'nology** *n* technologie *f*.

teddy ['tedɪ] *n* **t. (bear)** ours *m* (en peluche).

tedious ['tiːdɪəs] *a* fastidieux. ◆**tediousness** *n*, ◆**tedium** *n* ennui *m*.

teem [tiːm] *vi* **1** (*swarm*) grouiller (**with** de). **2 to t. (with rain)** pleuvoir à torrents. ◆—**ing** *a* **1** (*crowd, street etc*) grouillant. **2 t. rain** pluie *f* torrentielle.

teenage ['tiːneɪdʒ] *a* (*person, behaviour*) adolescent; (*fashion*) pour adolescents. ◆**teenager** *n* adolescent, -ente *mf*. ◆**teens** *npl* **in one's t.** adolescent.

teeny (weeny) ['tiːnɪ('wiːnɪ)] *a* (*tiny*) *Fam* minuscule.

tee-shirt ['tiːʃɜːt] *n* tee-shirt *m*.

teeter ['tiːtər] *vi* chanceler.

teeth [tiːθ] *see* tooth. ◆**teeth/e** [tiːð] *vi* faire ses dents. ◆—**ing** *n* dentition *f*; **t. ring** anneau *m* de dentition; **t. troubles** *Fig* difficultés *fpl* de mise en route.

teetotal [tiːˈtəʊt(ə)l] *a*, ◆**teetotaller** *n* (*personne f*) qui ne boit pas d'alcool.

tele- ['telɪ] *pref* télé-.

telecommunications [telɪkəmjuːnɪˈkeɪʃ(ə)nz] *npl* télécommunications *fpl*.

telegram ['telɪgræm] *n* télégramme *m*.

telegraph ['telɪgrɑːf] *n* télégraphe *m*; − *a* (*wire etc*) télégraphique; **t. pole** poteau *m* télégraphique.

telepathy [təˈlepəθɪ] *n* télépathie *f*.

telephone ['telɪfəʊn] *n* téléphone *m*; **on the t.** (*speaking*) au téléphone; − *a* (*call, line etc*) téléphonique; (*directory*) du téléphone; (number) de téléphone; **t. booth, t. box** cabine f téléphonique; – vi téléphoner; – vt (message) téléphoner (to à); **to t. s.o.** téléphoner à qn. ◆**te'lephonist** n téléphoniste mf.

teleprinter ['telɪprɪntər] n téléscripteur m.

telescope ['telɪskəup] n télescope m. ◆**tele'scopic** a (pictures, aerial, umbrella) télescopique.

teletypewriter [telɪ'taɪpraɪtər] n Am téléscripteur m.

televise ['telɪvaɪz] vt téléviser. ◆**tele'vision** n télévision f; **on (the) t.** à la télévision; **to watch (the) t.** regarder la télévision; – a (programme etc) de télévision; (serial, report) télévisé.

telex ['teleks] n (service, message) télex m; – vt envoyer par télex.

tell [tel] vt (pt & pp told) dire (s.o. sth qch à qn, **that** que); (story) raconter; (future) prédire; (distinguish) distinguer (**from** de); (know) savoir; **to t. s.o. to do** dire à qn de faire; **to know how to t. the time** savoir lire l'heure; **to t. the difference** voir la différence (**between** entre); **to t. off** (scold) Fam gronder; – vi dire; (have an effect) avoir un effet; (know) savoir; **to t. of** or **about sth** parler de qch; **to t. on s.o.** Fam rapporter sur qn. ◆**—ing** a (smile etc) révélateur; (blow) efficace. ◆**telltale** n Fam rapporteur, -euse mf.

teller ['telər] n (bank) t. caissier, -ière mf.

telly ['telɪ] n Fam télé f.

temerity [tə'merɪtɪ] n témérité f.

temp [temp] n (secretary etc) Fam intérimaire mf.

temper ['tempər] 1 n (mood, nature) humeur f; (anger) colère f; **to lose one's t.** se mettre en colère; **in a bad t.** de mauvaise humeur; **to have a (bad** or **an awful) t.** avoir un caractère de cochon. 2 vt (steel) tremper; Fig tempérer.

temperament ['temp(ə)rəmənt] n tempérament m. ◆**tempera'mental** a (person, machine etc) capricieux; (inborn) inné.

temperance ['temp(ə)rəns] n (in drink) tempérance f.

temperate ['tempərət] a (climate etc) tempéré.

temperature ['temp(ə)rətʃər] n température f; **to have a t.** Med avoir or faire de la température.

tempest ['tempɪst] n Lit tempête f. ◆**tem'pestuous** a (meeting etc) orageux.

template ['templət] n (of plastic, metal etc) Tex patron m; Math trace-courbes m inv.

temple ['temp(ə)l] n 1 Rel temple m. 2 Anat tempe f.

tempo ['tempəu] n (pl -os) tempo m.

temporal ['temp(ə)rəl] a temporel.

temporary ['temp(ə)rərɪ] a provisoire; (job, worker) temporaire; (secretary) intérimaire.

tempt [tempt] vt tenter; **tempted to do** tenté de faire; **to t. s.o. to do** persuader qn de faire. ◆**—ing** a tentant. ◆**—ingly** adv d'une manière tentante. ◆**temp'tation** n tentation f.

ten [ten] a & n dix (m). ◆**tenfold** a t. increase augmentation f par dix; – adv to increase t. (se) multiplier par dix.

tenable ['tenəb(ə)l] a (argument) défendable; (post) qui peut etre occupé.

tenacious [tə'neɪʃəs] a tenace. ◆**tenacity** n ténacité f.

tenant ['tenənt] n locataire nmf. ◆**tenancy** n (lease) location f; (period) occupation f.

tend [tend] 1 vt (look after) s'occuper de. 2 vi **to t. to do** avoir tendance à faire; **to t. towards** incliner vers. ◆**tendency** n tendance f (to do à faire).

tendentious [ten'denʃəs] a Pej tendancieux.

tender[1] ['tendər] a (delicate, soft, loving) tendre; (painful, sore) sensible. ◆**—ly** adv tendrement. ◆**—ness** n tendresse f; (soreness) sensibilité f; (of meat) tendreté f.

tender[2] ['tendər] 1 vt (offer) offrir; **to t. one's resignation** donner sa démission. 2 n **to be legal t.** (of money) avoir cours. 3 n (for services etc) Com soumission f (**for** pour).

tendon ['tendən] n Anat tendon m.

tenement ['tenəmənt] n immeuble m (de rapport) (Am dans un quartier pauvre).

tenet ['tenɪt] n principe m.

tenner ['tenər] n Fam billet m de dix livres.

tennis ['tenɪs] n tennis m; **table t.** tennis de table; **t. court** court m (de tennis), tennis m.

tenor ['tenər] n 1 (sense, course) sens m général. 2 Mus ténor m.

tenpin ['tenpɪn] a **t. bowling** bowling m. ◆**tenpins** n Am bowling m.

tense [tens] 1 a (-er, -est) (person, muscle, situation) tendu; – vt tendre, crisper; – vi **to t. (up)** (of person, face) se crisper. 2 n Gram temps m. ◆**tenseness** n tension f. ◆**tension** n tension f.

tent [tent] n tente f.

tentacle ['tentək(ə)l] n tentacule m.

tentative ['tentətɪv] a (not definite) provisoire; (hesitant) timide. ◆**—ly** adv provisoirement; timidement.

tenterhooks ['tentəhuks] npl **on t.** (anxious) sur des charbons ardents.

tenth [tenθ] *a* & *n* dixième (*mf*); **a t.** un dixième.

tenuous ['tenjʊəs] *a* (*link, suspicion etc*) ténu.

tenure ['tenjər] *n* (*in job*) période *f* de jouissance; (*job security*) *Am* titularisation *f*.

tepid ['tepɪd] *a* (*liquid*) & *Fig* tiède.

term [tɜːm] *n* (*word, limit*) terme *m*; (*period*) période *f*; *Sch Univ* trimestre *m*; (*semester*) *Am* semestre *m*; *pl* (*conditions*) conditions *fpl*; (*prices*) Com prix *mpl*; **t. (of office)** *Pol* mandat *m*; **easy terms** *Fin* facilités *fpl* de paiement; **on good/bad terms** en bons/mauvais termes (**with s.o.** avec qn); **to be on close terms** être intime (**with** avec); **in terms of** (*speaking of*) sur le plan de; **in real terms** dans la pratique; **to come to terms with** (*person*) tomber d'accord avec; (*situation etc*) *Fig* faire face à; **in the long/short t.** à long/court terme; **at (full) t.** (*baby*) à terme; – *vt* (*name, call*) appeler.

terminal ['tɜːmɪn(ə)l] **1** *n* (*of computer*) terminal *m*; *El* borne *f*; (**air**) **t.** aérogare *f*; (**oil**) **t.** terminal *m* (pétrolier). **2** *a* (*patient, illness*) incurable; (*stage*) terminal. ◆**–ly** *adv* **t. ill** (*patient*) incurable.

terminate ['tɜːmɪneɪt] *vt* mettre fin à; (*contract*) résilier; (*pregnancy*) interrompre; – *vi* se terminer. ◆**termi'nation** *n* fin *f*; résiliation *f*; interruption *f*.

terminology [tɜːmɪ'nɒlədʒɪ] *n* terminologie *f*.

terminus ['tɜːmɪnəs] *n* terminus *m*.

termite ['tɜːmaɪt] *n* (*insect*) termite *m*.

terrace ['terɪs] *n* terrace *f*; (*houses*) maisons *fpl* en bande; **the terraces** *Sp* les gradins *mpl*. ◆**terraced t. house** maison *f* attenante aux maisons voisines.

terracota [terə'kɒtə] *n* terre *f* cuite.

terrain [tə'reɪn] *n Mil Geol* terrain *m*.

terrestrial [tə'restrɪəl] *a* terrestre.

terrible ['terəb(ə)l] *a* affreux, terrible. ◆**terribly** *adv* (*badly*) affreusement; (*very*) terriblement.

terrier ['terɪər] *n* (*dog*) terrier *m*.

terrific [tə'rɪfɪk] *a Fam* (*extreme*) terrible; (*excellent*) formidable, terrible. ◆**terrifically** *adv Fam* (*extremely*) terriblement; (*extremely well*) terriblement bien.

terrify ['terɪfaɪ] *vt* terrifier; **to be terrified of** avoir très peur de. ◆**–ing** *a* terrifiant. ◆**–ingly** *adv* épouvantablement.

territory ['terɪtərɪ] *n* territoire *m*. ◆**territorial** *a* territorial.

terror ['terər] *n* terreur *f*; (*child*) *Fam* polisson, -onne *mf*. ◆**terrorism** *n* terrorisme

m. ◆**terrorist** *n* & *a* terroriste (*mf*). ◆**terrorize** *vt* terroriser.

terry(cloth) ['terɪ(klɒθ)] *n* tissu-éponge *m*.

terse [tɜːs] *a* laconique.

tertiary ['tɜːʃərɪ] *a* tertiaire.

Terylene® ['terɪliːn] *n* tergal® *m*.

test [test] *vt* (*try*) essayer; (*examine*) examiner; (*analyse*) analyser; (*product, intelligence*) tester; (*pupil*) *Sch* faire subir une interrogation à; (*nerves, courage etc*) *Fig* éprouver; – *n* (*trial*) test *m*, essai *m*; examen *m*; analyse *f*; *Sch* interrogation *f*, test *m*; (*of courage etc*) *Fig* épreuve *f*; **driving t.** (examen *m* du) permis *m* de conduire; – *a* (*pilot, flight*) d'essai; **t. case** *Jur* affaire-test *f*; **t. match** *Sp* match *m* international; **t. tube** éprouvette *f*; **t. tube baby** bébé *m* éprouvette.

testament ['testəmənt] *n* testament *m*; (*proof, tribute*) témoignage *m*; **Old/New T.** *Rel* Ancien/Nouveau Testament.

testicle ['testɪk(ə)l] *n Anat* testicule *m*.

testify ['testɪfaɪ] *vi Jur* témoigner (**against** contre); **to t. to sth** (*of person, event etc*) témoigner de qch; – *vi* **to t. that** (*Jur témoigner que*). ◆**testi'monial** *n* références *fpl*, recommandation *f*. ◆**testimony** *n* témoignage *m*.

testy ['testɪ] *a* (-ier, -iest) irritable.

tetanus ['tetənəs] *n Med* tétanos *m*.

tête-à-tête [teɪtɑː'teɪt] *n* tête-à-tête *m inv*.

tether ['teðər] **1** *vt* (*fasten*) attacher. **2** *n* **at the end of one's t.** à bout de nerfs.

text [tekst] *n* texte *m*. ◆**textbook** *n* manuel *m*.

textile ['tekstaɪl] *a* & *n* textile (*m*).

texture ['tekstʃər] *n* (*of fabric, cake etc*) texture *f*; (*of paper, wood*) grain *m*.

Thames [temz] *n* the **T.** la Tamise *f*.

than [ðən, *stressed* ðæn] *conj* **1** que; **happier t.** plus heureux que; **he has more t. you** il en a plus que toi; **fewer oranges t. plums** moins d'oranges que de prunes. **2** (*with numbers*) de; **more t. six** plus de six.

thank [θæŋk] *vt* remercier (**for sth** de qch, **for doing** d'avoir fait); **t. you** merci (**for sth** pour *or* de qch, **for doing** d'avoir fait); **no, t. you** (non) merci; **t. God, t. heavens, t. goodness** Dieu merci; – *npl* remerciements *mpl*; **thanks to** (*because of*) grâce à; (**many**) **thanks!** merci (beaucoup)! ◆**thankful** *a* reconnaissant (**for** de); **t. that** bien heureux que (+ *sub*). ◆**thankfully** *adv* (*gratefully*) avec reconnaissance; (*happily*) heureusement. ◆**thankless** *a* ingrat. ◆**Thanksgiving** *n* **T. (day)** (*holiday*) *Am* jour *m* d'action de grâce(s).

that [ðət, *stressed* ðæt] **1** *conj* que; **to say t.** dire que. **2** *rel pron* (*subject*) qui; (*object*) que; **the boy t.** left le garçon qui est parti; **the book I. I read** le livre que j'ai lu; **the carpet t. I put it on** (*with prep*) le tapis sur lequel je l'ai mis; **the house t. she told me about** la maison dont elle m'a parlé; **the day/morning t. she arrived** le jour/matin où elle est arrivée. **3** *dem a* (*pl see* those) ce, cet (*before vowel or mute h*), cette; (*opposed to* 'this') ... + -là; **t. day** ce jour; ce jour-là; **t. man** cet homme; cet homme-là; **t. girl** cette fille; cette fille-là. **4** *dem pron* (*pl see* those) ça, cela; ce; **t.** (**one**) celui-là *m*, celle-là *f*; **give me t.** donne-moi ça *or* cela; **I prefer t.** (**one**) je préfère celui-là; **before t.** avant ça *or* cela; **t.'s right** c'est juste; **who's t.?** qui est-ce?; **t.'s the house** c'est la maison; (*pointing*) voilà la maison; **what do you mean by t.?** qu'entends-tu par là; **t. is** (**to say**) .... c'est-à-dire .... **5** *adv* (*so*) *Fam* si; **not t. good** pas si bon; **t. high** (*pointing*) haut comme ça; **t. much** (*to cost, earn etc*) autant que ça.

thatch [θætʃ] *n* chaume *m*. ◆**thatched** *a* (*roof*) de chaume; **t. cottage** chaumière *f*.

thaw [θɔː] *n* dégel *m*; – *vi* dégeler; (*of snow*) fondre; **it's thawing** *Met* ça dégèle; **to t.** (**out**) (*of person*) *Fig* se dégeler; – *vt* (*ice*) dégeler, faire fondre; (*food*) faire dégeler; (*snow*) faire fondre.

the [ðə, *before vowel* ði, *stressed* ðiː] *def art* le, l', la, *pl* les; **t. roof** le toit; **t. man** l'homme; **t. moon** la lune; **t. orange** l'orange; **t. boxes** les boîtes; **the smallest** le plus petit; **of t., from t.** du, de l', de la, *pl* des; **to t., at t.** au, à l', à la, *pl* aux; **Elizabeth t. Second** Élisabeth deux; **all t. better** d'autant mieux.

theatre ['θɪətər] *n* (*place, art*) & *Mil* théâtre *m*. ◆**theatregoer** *n* amateur *m* de théâtre. ◆**the'atrical** *a* théâtral; **t. company** troupe *f* de théâtre.

theft [θeft] *n* vol *m*.

their [ðeər] *poss a* leur, *pl* leurs; **t. house** leur maison *f*. ◆**theirs** [ðeəz] *poss pron* le leur, la leur, *pl* les leurs; **this book is t.** ce livre est à eux *or* est le leur; **a friend of t.** un ami à eux.

them [ðəm, *stressed* ðem] *pron* les; (*after prep etc*) eux *mpl*, elles *fpl*; (**to**) **t.** (*indirect*) leur; **I see t.** je les vois; **I give** (**to**) **t.** je leur donne; **with t.** avec eux, avec elles; **ten of t.** dix d'entre eux, dix d'entre elles; **all of t.** tous, toutes. ◆**them'selves** *pron* eux-mêmes *mpl*, elles-mêmes *fpl*; (*reflexive*) se, s'; (*after prep etc*) eux *mpl*, elles *fpl*;

they wash t. ils se lavent, elles se lavent; they think of t. ils pensent à eux, elles pensent à elles.

theme [θiːm] *n* thème *m*; **t. song** *or* **tune** *Cin TV* chanson *f* principale.

then [ðen] **1** *adv* (*at that time*) alors, à ce moment-là; (*next*) ensuite, puis; **from t. on** dès lors; **before t.** avant cela; **until t.** jusque-là, jusqu'alors; – **a the t. mayor/***etc* le maire/*etc* d'alors. **2** *conj* (*therefore*) donc, alors.

theology [θɪˈɒlədʒɪ] *n* théologie *f*. ◆**theo'logical** *a* théologique. ◆**theo'logian** *n* théologien *m*.

theorem ['θɪərəm] *n* théorème *m*.

theory ['θɪərɪ] *n* théorie *f*; **in t.** en théorie. ◆**theo'retical** *a* théorique. ◆**theo'retically** *adv* théoriquement. ◆**theorist** *n* théoricien, -ienne *mf*.

therapy ['θerəpɪ] *n* thérapeutique *f*. ◆**thera'peutic** *a* thérapeutique.

there [ðeər] *adv* là; (*down or over*) **t.** là-bas; **on t.** là-dessus; **she'll be t.** elle sera là, elle y sera; **t. is, t. are** il y a; (*pointing*) voilà; **t. he is** le voilà; **t. she is** la voilà; **t. they are** les voilà; **that man t.** cet homme-là; **t.** (**you are**)! (*take this*) tenez!; **t.,** (**t.,**) **don't cry!** allons, allons, ne pleure pas! ◆**therea'bout(s)** *adv* par là; (*in amount*) à peu près. ◆**there'after** *adv* après cela. ◆**thereby** *adv* de ce fait. ◆**therefore** *adv* donc. ◆**thereu'pon** *adv* sur ce.

thermal ['θɜːm(ə)l] *a* (*energy, unit*) thermique; (*springs*) thermal; (*underwear*) tribo-électrique, en thermolactyl®.

thermometer [θəˈmɒmɪtər] *n* thermomètre *m*.

thermonuclear [θɜːməʊˈnjuːklɪər] *a* thermonucléaire.

Thermos® ['θɜːməs] *n* **T.** (**flask**) thermos® *m or f*.

thermostat ['θɜːməstæt] *n* thermostat *m*.

thesaurus [θɪˈsɔːrəs] *n* dictionnaire *m* de synonymes.

these [ðiːz] **1** *dem a* (*sing see* this) ces; (*opposed to* 'those') ... + -ci; **t. men** ces hommes; ces hommes-ci. **2** *dem pron* (*sing see* this) **t.** (**ones**) ceux-ci *mpl*, celles-ci *fpl*; **t. are my friends** ce sont mes amis.

thesis, *pl* **theses** ['θiːsɪs, 'θiːsiːz] *n* thèse *f*.

they [ðeɪ] *pron* **1** ils *mpl*, elles *fpl*; (*stressed*) eux *mpl*, elles *fpl*; **t. go** ils vont, elles vont; **t. are doctors** ce sont des médecins. **2** (*people in general*) on; **t. say** on dit.

thick [θɪk] *a* (-er, -est) épais; (*stupid*) *Fam* lourd; **to be t.** (*of friends*) *Fam* être très liés; – *adv* (*to grow*) dru; (*to spread*) en couche épaisse; – *n* **in the t. of** (*battle etc*) au plus

gros de. ◆**thicken** vt épaissir; – vi
s'épaissir. ◆**thickly** adv (to grow, fall) dru;
(to spread) en couche épaisse; (populated,
wooded) très. ◆**thickness** n épaisseur f.
thicket ['θɪkɪt] n (trees) fourré m.
thickset [θɪk'set] a (person) trapu. ◆**thick-
skinned** a (person) dur, peu sensible.
thief [θiːf] n (pl **thieves**) voleur, -euse mf.
◆**thiev/e** vti voler. ◆**—ing** a voleur; – n
vol m.
thigh [θaɪ] n cuisse f. ◆**thighbone** n fémur
m.
thimble ['θɪmb(ə)l] n dé m (à coudre).
thin [θɪn] a (**thinner, thinnest**) (slice, paper
etc) mince; (person, leg) maigre, mince;
(soup) peu épais; (hair, audience) clairsemé; (powder) fin; (excuse, profit) Fig
maigre, mince; – adv (to spread) en couche
mince; – vt (-nn-) **to t. (down)** (paint etc)
délayer; – vi **to t. out** (of crowd, mist)
s'éclaircir. ◆**—ly** adv (to spread) en couche
mince; (populated, wooded) peu;
(disguised) à peine. ◆**—ness** n minceur f;
maigreur f.
thing [θɪŋ] n chose f; **one's things** (belongings, clothes) ses affaires fpl; **it's a funny t.**
c'est drôle; **poor little t.!** pauvre petit!;
that's (just) the t. voilà (exactement) ce
qu'il faut; **how are things?**, Fam **how's
things?** comment (ça) va?; **I'll think things
over** j'y réfléchirai; **for one t. . . . , and for
another t.** d'abord . . . et ensuite; **tea things**
(set) service m à thé; (dishes) vaisselle f.
◆**thingummy** n Fam truc m, machin m.
think [θɪŋk] vi (pt & pp **thought**) penser
(**about, of** à); **to t. (carefully)** réfléchir
(**about, of** à); **to t. of doing** penser or songer
à faire; **to t. highly of, t. a lot of** penser
beaucoup de bien de; **she doesn't t. much of
it** ça ne lui dit pas grand-chose; **to t. better
of it** se raviser; **I can't t. of it** je n'arrive pas
à m'en souvenir; – vt penser (**that** que); **I t.
so** je pense or crois que oui; **what do you t.
of him?** que penses-tu de lui?; **I thought it
difficult** je l'ai trouvé difficile; **to t. out** or
through (reply etc) réfléchir sérieusement à,
peser; **to t. over** réfléchir à; **to t. up** (invent)
inventer, avoir l'idée de; – n **to have a t.**
Fam réfléchir (**about** à); – a **t. tank** comité
m d'experts. ◆**—ing** a (person) intelligent;
– n (opinion) opinion f; **to my t.** à mon avis.
◆**—er** n penseur, -euse mf.
thin-skinned [θɪn'skɪnd] a (person) susceptible.
third [θɜːd] a troisième; **t. person** or **party**
tiers m; **t.-party insurance** assurance f au
tiers; **T. World** Tiers-Monde m; – n

troisième mf; **a t.** (fraction) un tiers; – adv
(in race) troisième. ◆**—ly** adv troisièmement.
third-class [θɜːd'klɑːs] a de troisième
classe. ◆**t.-rate** a (très) inférieur.
thirst [θɜːst] n soif f (**for** de). ◆**thirsty** a
(-ier, -iest) a **to be** or **feel t.** avoir soif; **to
make t.** donner soif à; **t. for** (power etc) Fig
assoiffé de.
thirteen [θɜː'tiːn] a & n treize (m).
◆**thirteenth** a & n treizième (mf).
◆'**thirtieth** a & n trentième (mf).
◆'**thirty** a & n trente (m).
this [ðɪs] **1** dem a (pl see **these**) ce, cet (before
vowel or mute h), cette; (opposed to 'that')
. . . + -ci; **t. book** ce livre; ce livre-ci; **t.
man** cet homme; cet homme-ci; **t. photo**
cette photo; cette photo-ci. **2** dem pron (pl
see **these**) ceci; ce; **t. (one)** celui-ci m,
celle-ci f; **give me t.** donne-moi ceci; **I
prefer t. (one)** je préfère celui-ci; **before t.**
avant ceci; **who's t.?** qui est-ce?; **t. is Paul**
c'est Paul; **t. is the house** voici la maison. **3**
adv (so) Fam si; **t. high** (pointing) haut
comme ceci; **t. far** (until now) jusqu'ici.
thistle ['θɪs(ə)l] n chardon m.
thorn [θɔːn] n épine f. ◆**thorny** a (-ier,
-iest) (bush, problem etc) épineux.
thorough ['θʌrə] a (painstaking, careful)
minutieux, consciencieux; (knowledge,
examination) approfondi; (rogue, liar)
fieffé; (disaster) complet; **to give sth a t.
washing** laver qch à fond. ◆**—ly** adv
(completely) tout à fait; (painstakingly)
avec minutie; (to know, clean, wash) à fond.
◆**—ness** n minutie f; (depth) profondeur
f.
thoroughbred ['θʌrəbred] n (horse)
pur-sang m inv.
thoroughfare ['θʌrəfeər] n (street) rue f; '**no
t.**' 'passage interdit'.
those [ðəʊz] **1** dem a (sing see **that**) ces;
(opposed to 'these') . . . + -là; **t. men** ces
hommes; ces hommes-là. **2** dem pron (sing
see **that**) **t. (ones)** ceux-là mpl, celles-là fpl;
t. are my friends ce sont mes amis.
though [ðəʊ] **1** conj (even) t. bien que (+
sub); **as t.** comme si; **strange t. it may seem**
si étrange que cela puisse paraître. **2** adv
(nevertheless) cependant, quand même.
thought [θɔːt] see **think**; – n pensée f; (idea)
idée f, pensée f; (careful) t. réflexion f; **without (a) t. for** sans penser à; **to have second
thoughts** changer d'avis; **on second
thoughts**, Am **on second t.** à la réflexion.
◆**thoughtful** a (pensive) pensif; (serious)
sérieux; (considerate, kind) gentil, préve-

nant. ◆**thoughtfully** *adv* (*considerately*) gentiment. ◆**thoughtfulness** *n* gentillesse *f*, prévenance *f*. ◆**thoughtless** *a* (*towards others*) désinvolte; (*careless*) étourdi. ◆**thoughtlessly** *adv* (*carelessly*) étourdiment; (*inconsiderately*) avec désinvolture.

thousand ['θauzənd] *a & n* mille *a & m inv*; **a t. pages** mille pages; **two t. pages** deux mille pages; **thousands of** des milliers de.

thrash [θræʃ] **1** *vt* **to t. s.o.** rouer qn de coups; (*defeat*) écraser qn; **to t. out** (*plan etc*) élaborer (à force de discussions). **2** *vi* **to t. about** (*struggle*) se débattre. ◆**—ing** *n* (*beating*) correction *f*.

thread [θred] *n* (*yarn*) & *Fig* fil *m*; (*of screw*) pas *m*; – *vt* (*needle, beads*) enfiler; **to t. one's way** *Fig* se faufiler (**through the crowd**/*etc* parmi la foule/*etc*). ◆**threadbare** *a* élimé, râpé.

threat [θret] *n* menace *f* (**to** à). ◆**threaten** *vi* menacer; – *vt* menacer (**to do** de faire, **with sth** de qch). ◆**threatening** *a* menaçant. ◆**threateningly** *adv* (*to say*) d'un ton menaçant.

three [θriː] *a & n* trois (*m*); **t.-piece suite** canapé *m* et deux fauteuils. ◆**threefold** *a* triple; – *adv* **to increase t.** tripler. ◆**three-'wheeler** *n* (*tricycle*) tricycle *m*; (*car*) voiture *f* à trois roues.

thresh [θreʃ] *vt* *Agr* battre.

threshold ['θreʃhəuld] *n* seuil *m*.

threw [θruː] *see* **throw**.

thrift [θrift] *n* (*virtue*) économie *f*. ◆**thrifty** (**-ier, -iest**) économe.

thrill [θril] *n* émotion *f*, frisson *m*; **to get a t. out of doing** prendre plaisir à faire; – *vt* (*delight*) réjouir; (*excite*) faire frissonner. ◆**—ed** *a* ravi (**with sth** de qch, **to do** de faire). ◆**—ing** *a* passionnant. ◆**—er** *n* film *m or* roman *m* à suspense.

thriv/e [θraɪv] *vi* (*of business, person, plant etc*) prospérer; **he** *or* **she thrives on hard work** le travail lui profite. ◆**—ing** *a* prospère, florissant.

throat [θrəut] *n* gorge *f*; **to have a sore t.** avoir mal à la gorge. ◆**throaty** *a* (*voice*) rauque; (*person*) à la voix rauque.

throb [θrɒb] *vi* (**-bb-**) (*of heart*) palpiter; (*of engine*) vrombir; *Fig* vibrer; **my finger is throbbing** mon doigt me fait des élancements; – *n* palpitation *f*; vrombissement *m*; élancement *m*.

throes [θrəuz] *npl* **in the t. of** au milieu de; (*illness, crisis*) en proie à; **in the t. of doing** en train de faire.

thrombosis [θrɒm'bəusɪs] *n* (*coronary*) *Med* infarctus *m*.

throne [θrəun] *n* trône *m*.

throng [θrɒŋ] *n* foule *f*; – *vi* (*rush*) affluer; – *vt* (*street, station etc*) se presser dans; **thronged with people** noir de monde.

throttle ['θrɒt(ə)l] **1** *n* *Aut* accélérateur *m*. **2** *vt* (*strangle*) étrangler.

through [θruː] *prep* (*place*) à travers; (*time*) pendant; (*means*) par; (*thanks to*) grâce à; **to go** *or* **get t.** (*forest etc*) traverser; (*hole etc*) passer par; **t. the window/door** par la fenêtre/porte; **to speak t. one's nose** parler du nez; **Tuesday t. Saturday** *Am* de mardi à samedi; – *adv* à travers; **to go t.** (*cross*) traverser; (*pass*) passer; **to let t.** laisser passer; **all** *or* **right t.** (*to the end*) jusqu'au bout; **French t. and t.** français jusqu'au bout des ongles; **to be t.** (*finished*) *Am Fam* avoir fini; **we're t.** *Am Fam* c'est fini entre nous; **I'm t. with the book** *Am Fam* je n'ai plus besoin du livre; **t. to** *or* **till** jusqu'à; **I'll put you t. (to him)** *Tel* je vous le passe; – *a* (*train, traffic, ticket*) direct; **'no t. road'** (*no exit*) 'voie sans issue'. ◆**through'out** *prep* **t. the neighbourhood**/*etc* dans tout le quartier/*etc*; **t. the day**/*etc* (*time*) pendant toute la journée/*etc*; – *adv* (*everywhere*) partout; (*all the time*) tout le temps. ◆**throughway** *n* *Am* autoroute *f*.

throw [θrəu] *n* (*of stone etc*) jet *m*; *Sp* lancer *m*; (*of dice*) coup *m*; (*turn*) tour *m*; – *vt* (*pt* **threw**, *pp* **thrown**) jeter (**to, at** à); (*stone, ball*) lancer, jeter; (*hurl*) projeter; (*of horse*) désarçonner (*qn*); (*party, reception*) donner; (*baffle*) *Fam* dérouter; **to t. away** (*discard*) jeter; (*ruin, waste*) *Fig* gâcher; **to t. back** (*ball*) renvoyer (**to** à); (*one's head*) rejeter en arrière; **to t. in** (*include as extra*) *Fam* donner en prime; **to t. off** (*get rid of*) se débarrasser de; **to t. out** (*discard*) jeter; (*suggestion*) repousser; (*expel*) mettre (*qn*) à la porte; (*distort*) fausser (*calcul etc*); **to t. over** abandonner; **to t. up** (*job*) *Fam* laisser tomber; – *vi* **to t. up** (*vomit*) *Sl* dégobiller. ◆**throwaway** *a* (*disposable*) à jeter, jetable.

thrush [θrʌʃ] *n* (*bird*) grive *f*.

thrust [θrʌst] *n* (*push*) poussée *f*; (*stab*) coup *m*; (*of argument*) poids *m*; (*dynamism*) allant *m*; – *vt* (*pt & pp* **thrust**) (*push*) pousser; (*put*) mettre (**into** dans); **to t. sth into sth** (*stick, knife, pin*) enfoncer qch dans qch; **to t. sth/s.o. upon s.o.** *Fig* imposer qch/qn à qn.

thud [θʌd] *n* bruit *m* sourd.

thug [θʌg] *n* voyou *m*.

thumb [θʌm] n pouce m; **with a t.** index (*book*) à onglets; − vt **to t. (through)** (*book etc*) feuilleter; **to t. a lift** or **a ride** Fam faire du stop. ◆**thumbtack** n Am punaise f.

thump [θʌmp] vt (*person*) frapper, cogner sur; (*table*) taper sur; **to t. one's head** (*on door etc*) se cogner la tête (**on** contre); − vi frapper, cogner (**on** sur); (*of heart*) battre à grands coups; − n (grand) coup m; (*noise*) bruit m sourd. ◆**—ing** a (*huge, great*) Fam énorme.

thunder ['θʌndər] n tonnerre m; − vi (*of weather, person, guns*) tonner; **it's thundering** Met il tonne; **to t. past** passer (vite) dans un bruit de tonnerre. ◆**thunderbolt** n (*event*) Fig coup m de tonnerre. ◆**thunderclap** n coup m de tonnerre. ◆**thunderstorm** n orage m. ◆**thunderstruck** a abasourdi.

Thursday ['θɜːzdɪ] n jeudi m.

thus [ðʌs] adv ainsi.

thwart [θwɔːt] vt (*plan, person*) contrecarrer.

thyme [taɪm] n Bot Culin thym m.

thyroid ['θaɪrɔɪd] a & n Anat thyroïde (f).

tiara [tɪ'ɑːrə] n (*of woman*) diadème m.

tic [tɪk] n (*in face, limbs*) tic m.

tick [tɪk] **1** n (*of clock*) tic-tac m; − vi faire tic-tac; **to t. over** (*of engine, factory, business*) tourner au ralenti. **2** n (*on list*) coche f, trait m; − vt **to t. (off)** cocher; **to t. off** (*reprimand*) Fam passer un savon à. **3** n (*moment*) Fam instant m. **4** n (*insect*) tique f. **5** adv **on t.** (*on credit*) Fam à crédit. ◆**—ing** n (*of clock*) tic-tac m; **to give s.o. a t.-off** Fam passer un savon à qn.

ticket ['tɪkɪt] n billet m; (*for tube, bus, cloak-room*) ticket m; (*for library*) carte f; (*fine*) Aut Fam contravention f, contredanse f; Pol Am liste f; (**price**) t. étiquette f; t. **collector** contrôleur, -euse mf; t. **holder** personne f munie d'un billet; t. **office** guichet m.

tickle ['tɪk(ə)l] vt chatouiller; (*amuse*) Fig amuser; − n chatouillement m. ◆**ticklish** a (*person*) chatouilleux; (*fabric*) qui chatouille; (*problem*) Fig délicat.

tidbit ['tɪdbɪt] n (*food*) Am bon morceau m.

tiddlywinks ['tɪdlɪwɪŋks] n jeu m de puce.

tide [taɪd] **1** n marée f; **against the t.** Nau & Fig à contre-courant; **the rising t. of discontent** le mécontentement grandissant. **2** vt **to t. s.o. over** (*help out*) dépanner qn. ◆**tidal** a (*river*) qui a une marée; **t. wave** raz-de-marée m inv; (*in public opinion etc*) Fig vague f de fond. ◆**tidemark** n Fig Hum ligne f de crasse.

tidings ['taɪdɪŋz] npl Lit nouvelles fpl.

tidy ['taɪdɪ] a (**-ier, -iest**) (*place, toys etc*) bien rangé; (*clothes, looks*) soigné; (*methodical*) ordonné; (*amount, sum*) Fam joli, bon; **to make t.** ranger; − vt **to t. (up** or **away)** ranger; **to t. oneself (up)** s'arranger; **to t. out** (*cupboard etc*) vider; − vi **to t. up** ranger. ◆**tidily** adv avec soin. ◆**tidiness** n (bon) ordre m; (*care*) soin m.

tie [taɪ] n (*string, strap etc*) & Fig lien m, attache f; (*necktie*) cravate f; (*sleeper*) Rail Am traverse f; Sp égalité f de points; (*match*) match m nul; − vt (*fasten*) attacher, lier (**to** à); (*a knot*) faire (**in** à); (*shoe*) lacer; (*link*) lier (**to** à); **to t. down** attacher; **to t. s.o. down to** (*date, place etc*) obliger qn à accepter; **to t. up** attacher; (*money*) Fig immobiliser; **to be tied up** (*linked*) être lié (**with** avec); (*busy*) Fam être occupé; − vi Sp finir à égalité de points; Fb faire match nul; (*in race*) être ex aequo; **to t. in with** (*tally with*) se rapporter à. ◆**t.-up** n (*link*) lien m; (*traffic jam*) Am Fam bouchon m.

tier [tɪər] n (*seats*) Sp Th gradin m; (*of cake*) étage m.

tiff [tɪf] n petite querelle f.

tiger ['taɪgər] n tigre m. ◆**tigress** n tigresse f.

tight [taɪt] a (**-er, -est**) (*rope etc*) raide; (*closely-fitting clothing*) ajusté, (*fitting too closely*) (trop) étroit, (trop) serré; (*drawer, lid*) dur; (*control*) strict; (*schedule, credit*) serré; (*drunk*) Fam gris; (*with money*) Fam avare; **a t. spot** or **corner** Fam une situation difficile; **it's a t. squeeze** il y a juste la place; − adv (*to hold, shut, sleep*) bien; (*to squeeze*) fort; **to sit t.** ne pas bouger. ◆**tighten** vt **to t. (up)** (*rope*) tendre; (*bolt etc*) (res)serrer; (*security*) Fig renforcer; − vi **to t. up on** se montrer plus strict à l'égard de. ◆**tightly** adv (*to hold*) bien; (*to squeeze*) fort; **t. knit** (*close*) très uni. ◆**tightness** n (*of garment*) étroitesse f; (*of control*) rigueur f; (*of rope*) tension f.

tight-fitting [taɪt'fɪtɪŋ] a (*garment*) ajusté. ◆**tightfisted** a avare. ◆**'tightrope** n corde f raide. ◆**'tightwad** n (*miser*) Am Fam grippe-sou m.

tights [taɪts] npl (*garment*) collant m; (*for dancer etc*) justaucorps m.

til/e [taɪl] n (*on roof*) tuile f; (*on wall or floor*) carreau m; − vt (*wall, floor*) carreler. ◆**—ed** a (*roof*) de tuiles; (*wall, floor*) carrelé.

till [tɪl] **1** prep & conj = **until**. **2** n (*for money*) caisse f (enregistreuse). **3** vt (*land*) Agr cultiver.

tilt [tɪlt] *vti* pencher; – *n* inclinaison *f*; **(at) full t.** à toute vitesse.

timber ['tɪmbər] *n* bois *m* (de construction); *(trees)* arbres *mpl*; – *a* de or en bois. ◆**timberyard** *n* entrepôt *m* de bois.

time [taɪm] *n* temps *m*; *(point in time)* moment *m*; *(epoch)* époque *f*; *(on clock)* heure *f*; *(occasion)* fois *f*; *Mus* mesure *f*; **in (the course of) t.,** **with (the passage of) t.** avec le temps; **some of the t.** *(not always)* une partie du temps; **most of the t.** la plupart du temps; **in a year's t.** dans un an; **a long t.** longtemps; **a short t.** peu de temps, un petit moment; **full-t.** à plein temps; **part-t.** à temps partiel; **to have a good or a nice t.** *(fun)* s'amuser (bien); **to have a hard t. doing** avoir du mal à faire; **t. off** du temps libre; **in no t. (at all)** en un rien de temps; **(just) in t.** *(to arrive)* à temps *(for sth* pour qch, **to do** pour faire); **in my t.** *(formerly)* de mon temps; **from t. to t.** de temps en temps; **what t. is it?** quelle heure est-il?; **the right** or **exact t.** l'heure *f* exacte; **on t.** à l'heure; **at the same t.** en même temps *(as* que); *(simultaneously)* à la fois; **for the t. being** pour le moment; **at the t.** à ce moment-là; **at the present t.** à l'heure actuelle; **at times** par moments, parfois; **at one t.** à un moment donné; **this t. tomorrow** demain à cette heure-ci; **(the) next t. you come** la prochaine fois que tu viendras; **(the) last t.** la dernière fois; **one at a t.** un à un; **t. and again** maintes fois; **ten times ten** dix fois dix; **t. bomb** bombe *f* à retardement; **t. lag** décalage *m*; **t. limit** délai *m*; **t. zone** fuseau *m* horaire; – *vt* *(sportsman, worker etc)* chronométrer; *(programme, operation)* minuter; *(choose the time of)* choisir le moment de; *(to plan)* prévoir. ◆**timing** *n* chronométrage *m*; minutage *m*; *(judgement of artist etc)* rythme *m*; **the t. of** *(time)* le moment choisi pour. ◆**time-consuming** *a* qui prend du temps. ◆**time-honoured** *a* consacré (par l'usage).

timeless ['taɪmləs] *a* éternel.

timely ['taɪmlɪ] *a* à propos. ◆**timeliness** *n* à-propos *m*.

timer ['taɪmər] *n* *Culin* minuteur *m*, compte-minutes *m inv*; *(sand-filled)* sablier *m*; *(on machine)* minuteur *m*; *(to control lighting)* minuterie *f*.

timetable ['taɪmteɪb(ə)l] *n* horaire *m*; *(in school)* emploi *m* du temps.

timid ['tɪmɪd] *a* *(shy)* timide; *(fearful)* timoré. ◆**—ly** *adv* timidement.

tin [tɪn] *n* étain *m*; *(tinplate)* fer-blanc *m*;

(can) boîte *f*; *(for baking)* moule *m*; **t. can** boîte *f* (en fer-blanc); **t. opener** ouvre-boîtes *m inv*; **t. soldier** soldat *m* de plomb. ◆**tinfoil** *n* papier *m* d'aluminium, papier alu. ◆**tinned** *a* en boîte. ◆**tinplate** *n* fer-blanc *m*.

tinge [tɪndʒ] *n* teinte *f*. ◆**tinged** *a* **t. with** *(pink etc)* teinté de; *(jealousy etc)* *Fig* empreint de.

tingle ['tɪŋg(ə)l] *vi* picoter; **it's tingling** ça me picote. ◆**tingly** *a* *(feeling)* de picotement.

tinker ['tɪŋkər] *vi* **to t. (about) with** bricoler.

tinkle ['tɪŋk(ə)l] *vi* tinter; – *n* tintement *m*; **to give s.o. a t.** *(phone s.o.)* *Fam* passer un coup de fil à qn.

tinny ['tɪnɪ] *a* (-ier, -iest) *(sound)* métallique; *(vehicle, machine)* de mauvaise qualité.

tinsel ['tɪns(ə)l] *n* clinquant *m*, guirlandes *fpl* de Noël.

tint [tɪnt] *n* teinte *f*; *(for hair)* shampooing *m* colorant; – *vt* *(paper, glass)* teinter.

tiny ['taɪnɪ] *a* (-ier, -iest) tout petit.

tip [tɪp] **1** *n* *(end)* bout *m*; *(pointed)* pointe *f*. **2** *n* *(money)* pourboire *m*; – *vt* (-pp-) donner un pourboire à. **3** *n* *(advice)* conseil *m*; *(information)* & *Sp* tuyau *m*; **to get a t.-off** se faire tuyauter; – *vt* (-pp-) **to t. a horse/**etc donner un cheval/etc gagnant; **to t. off** *(police)* prévenir. **4** *n* *(for rubbish)* décharge *f*; – *vt* (-pp-) **to t. (up** or **over)** *(tilt)* incliner, pencher; *(overturn)* faire basculer; **to t. (out)** *(liquid, load)* déverser *(into* dans); – *vi* **to t. (up** or **over)** *(tilt)* pencher; *(overturn)* basculer.

tipped [tɪpt] *a* **t. cigarette** cigarette *f* (à bout) filtre.

tipple ['tɪp(ə)l] *vi* *(drink)* *Fam* picoler.

tipsy ['tɪpsɪ] *a* (-ier, -iest) *(drunk)* gai, pompette.

tiptoe ['tɪptəʊ] *n* **on t.** sur la pointe des pieds; – *vi* marcher sur la pointe des pieds.

tiptop ['tɪptɒp] *a* *Fam* excellent.

tirade [taɪ'reɪd] *n* diatribe *f*.

tir/e [¹ ['taɪər] *vt* fatiguer; **to t. out** *(exhaust)* épuiser; – *vi* se fatiguer. ◆**—ed** *a* fatigué; **to be t. of sth/s.o./doing** en avoir assez de qch/de qn/de faire; **to get t. of doing** se lasser de faire. ◆**—ing** *a* fatigant. ◆**tiredness** *n* fatigue *f*. ◆**tireless** *a* infatigable. ◆**tiresome** *a* ennuyeux.

tire [²] ['taɪər] *n* *Am* pneu *m*.

tissue ['tɪʃuː] *n* *Biol* tissu *m*; *(handkerchief)* mouchoir *m* en papier, kleenex® *m*; **t. (paper)** papier *m* de soie.

tit [tɪt] *n* **1** *(bird)* mésange *f*. **2 to give t. for tat** rendre coup pour coup.

titbit ['tɪtbɪt] *n* *(food)* bon morceau *m*.

titillate ['tɪtɪleɪt] *vt* exciter.
titl/e ['taɪt(ə)l] *n* (*name, claim*) & *Sp* titre *m*; **t. deed** titre *m* de propriété; **t. role** *Th Cin* rôle *m* principal; – *vt* (*film*) intituler, titrer. ◆**—ed** *a* (*person*) titré.
titter ['tɪtər] *vi* rire bêtement.
tittle-tattle ['tɪt(ə)ltæt(ə)l] *n Fam* commérages *mpl*.
to [tə, *stressed* tuː] **1** *prep* à; (*towards*) vers; (*of feelings, attitude*) envers; (*right up to*) jusqu'à; (*of*) de; **give it to him** *or* **her** donne-le-lui; **to town** en ville; **to France** en France; **to Portugal** au Portugal; **to the butcher('s)**/*etc* chez le boucher/*etc*; **the road to** la route de; **the train to** le train pour; **well-disposed to** bien disposé envers; **kind to** gentil envers *or* avec *or* pour; **from bad to worse** de mal en pis; **ten to one** (*proportion*) dix contre un; **it's ten (minutes) to one** il est une heure moins dix; **one person to a room** une personne par chambre; **to say/to remember**/*etc* (*with inf*) dire/se souvenir/*etc*; **she tried to** elle a essayé; **wife**/*etc***-to-be** future femme *f*/*etc*. **2** *adv* **to push to** (*door*) fermer; **to go** *or* **walk to and fro** aller et venir. ◆**to-do** [tə'duː] *n* (*fuss*) *Fam* histoire *f*.
toad [təʊd] *n* crapaud *m*.
toadstool ['təʊdstuːl] *n* champignon *m* (vénéneux).
toast [təʊst] **1** *n Culin* pain *m* grillé, toast *m*; – *vt* (*bread*) (faire) griller. **2** *n* (*drink*) toast *m*; – *vt* (*person*) porter un toast à; (*success, event*) arroser. ◆**toaster** *n* grille-pain *m inv*.
tobacco [tə'bækəʊ] *n* (*pl* -os) tabac *m*. ◆**tobacconist** *n* buraliste *mf*; **t., tobacconist's (shop)** (*bureau m de*) tabac *m*.
toboggan [tə'bɒgən] *n* luge *f*, toboggan *m*.
today [tə'deɪ] *adv* & *n* aujourd'hui (*m*).
toddle ['tɒd(ə)l] *vi* **to t. off** (*leave*) *Hum Fam* se sauver.
toddler ['tɒdlər] *n* petit(e) enfant *mf*.
toddy ['tɒdɪ] *n* (*hot*) **t.** grog *m*.
toe [təʊ] **1** *n* orteil *m*; **on one's toes** *Fig* vigilant. **2** *vt* **to t. the line** se conformer; **to t. the party line** respecter la ligne du parti. ◆**toenail** *n* ongle *m* du pied.
toffee ['tɒfɪ] *n* (*sweet*) caramel *m* (*dur*); **t. apple** pomme *f* d'amour.
together [tə'geðər] *adv* ensemble; (*at the same time*) en même temps; **t. with** avec. ◆**—ness** *n* (*of group*) camaraderie *f*; (*of husband and wife*) intimité *f*.
togs [tɒgz] *npl* (*clothes*) *Sl* nippes *fpl*.
toil [tɔɪl] *n* labeur *m*; – *vi* travailler dur.
toilet ['tɔɪlɪt] *n* (*room*) toilettes *fpl*, cabinets

mpl; (*bowl, seat*) cuvette *f or* siège *m* des cabinets; **to go to the t.** aller aux toilettes; – *a* (*articles*) de toilette; **t. paper** papier *m* hygiénique; **t. roll** rouleau *m* de papier hygiénique; **t. water** (*perfume*) eau *f* de toilette. ◆**toiletries** *npl* articles *mpl* de toilette.
token ['təʊkən] *n* (*symbol, sign*) témoignage *m*; (*metal disc*) jeton *m*; (*voucher*) bon *m*; **gift t.** chèque-cadeau *m*; **book t.** chèque-livre *m*; **record t.** chèque-disque *m*; – *a* symbolique.
told [təʊld] *see* **tell**; – *adv* **all t.** (*taken together*) en tout.
tolerable ['tɒlərəb(ə)l] *a* (*bearable*) tolérable; (*fairly good*) passable. ◆**tolerably** *adv* (*fairly, fairly well*) passablement. ◆**tolerance** *n* tolérance *f*. ◆**tolerant** *a* tolérant (**of** à l'égard de). ◆**tolerantly** *adv* avec tolérance. ◆**tolerate** *vt* tolérer.
toll [təʊl] **1** *n* péage *m*; – *a* (*road*) à péage. **2** *n* **the death t.** le nombre de morts, le bilan en vies humaines; **to take a heavy t.** (*of accident etc*) faire beaucoup de victimes. **3** *vi* (*of bell*) sonner. ◆**tollfree** *a* **t. number** *Tel Am* numéro *m* vert.
tomato [tə'mɑːtəʊ, *Am* tə'meɪtəʊ] *n* (*pl* -oes) tomate *f*.
tomb [tuːm] *n* tombeau *m*. ◆**tombstone** *n* pierre *f* tombale.
tomboy ['tɒmbɔɪ] *n* (*girl*) garçon *m* manqué.
tomcat ['tɒmkæt] *n* matou *m*.
tome [təʊm] *n* (*book*) tome *m*.
tomfoolery [tɒm'fuːlərɪ] *n* niaiserie(s) *f(pl)*.
tomorrow [tə'mɒrəʊ] *adv* & *n* demain (*m*); **t. morning/evening** demain matin/soir; **the day after t.** après-demain.
ton [tʌn] *n* tonne *f* (*Br* = 1016 *kg, Am* = 907 *kg*); **metric t.** tonne *f* (= 1000 *kg*); **tons of** (*lots of*) *Fam* des tonnes de.
tone [təʊn] *n* ton *m*; (*of radio, telephone*) tonalité *f*; **in that t.** sur ce ton; **to set the t.** donner le ton; **she's t.-deaf** elle n'a pas d'oreille; – *vt* **to t. down** atténuer; **to t. up** (*muscles, skin*) tonifier; – *vi* **to t. in** s'harmoniser (**with** avec).
tongs [tɒŋz] *npl* pinces *fpl*; (*for sugar*) pince *f*; (*curling*) **t.** fer *m* à friser.
tongue [tʌŋ] *n* langue *f*; **t. in cheek** ironique(ment). ◆**t.-tied** *a* muet (*et gêné*).
tonic ['tɒnɪk] *a* & *n* tonique (*m*); **gin and t.** gin-tonic *m*.
tonight [tə'naɪt] *adv* & *n* (*this evening*) ce soir (*m*); (*during the night*) cette nuit (*f*).
tonne [tʌn] *n* (*metric*) tonne *f*. ◆**tonnage** *n* tonnage *m*.
tonsil ['tɒns(ə)l] *n* amygdale *f*. ◆**tonsi'l-**

lectomy *n* opération *f* des amygdales. ◆**tonsillitis** [tɒnsə'laɪtəs] *n* to have t. avoir une angine.

too [tuː] *adv* **1** (*excessively*) trop; **t. tired to play** trop fatigué pour jouer; **t. hard to solve** trop difficile à résoudre; **it's only t. true** ce n'est que trop vrai. **2** (*also*) aussi; (*moreover*) en plus.

took [tʊk] *see* take.

tool [tuːl] *n* outil *m*; **t. bag, t. kit** trousse *f* à outils.

toot [tuːt] *vti* to t. (the horn) *Aut* klaxonner.

tooth, *pl* **teeth** [tuːθ, tiːθ] *n* dent *f*; **front t.** dent de devant; **back t.** molaire *f*; **milk/wisdom t.** dent de lait/de sagesse; **t. decay** carie *f* dentaire; **to have a sweet t.** aimer les sucreries; **long in the t.** (*old*) *Hum* chenu, vieux. ◆**toothache** *n* mal *m* de dents. ◆**toothbrush** *n* brosse *f* à dents. ◆**toothcomb** *n* peigne *m* fin. ◆**toothpaste** *n* dentifrice *m*. ◆**toothpick** *n* cure-dent *m*.

top¹ [tɒp] *n* (*of mountain, tower, tree*) sommet *m*; (*of wall, dress, ladder, page*) haut *m*; (*of box, table, surface*) dessus *m*; (*of list*) tête *f* (*of water*) surface *f*; (*of car*) toit *m*; (*of bottle, tube*) bouchon *m*; (*bottle cap*) capsule *f*; (*of saucepan*) couvercle *m*; (*of pen*) capuchon *m*; **pyjama t.** veste *f* de pyjama; **(at the) t. of the class** le premier de la classe; **on t. of** sur; (*in addition to*) *Fig* en plus de; **on t.** (*in bus etc*) en haut; **from t. to bottom** de fond en comble; **the big t.** (*circus*) le chapiteau; – *a* (*drawer, shelf*) du haut, premier; (*step, layer, storey*) dernier; (*upper*) supérieur; (*in rank, exam*) premier; (*chief*) principal; (*best*) meilleur; (*great, distinguished*) éminent; (*maximum*) maximum; **in t. gear** *Aut* en quatrième vitesse; **at t. speed** à toute vitesse; **t. hat** (chapeau *m*) haut-de-forme *m*. ◆**t.-'flight** *a* *Fam* excellent. ◆**t.-'heavy** *a* trop lourd du haut. ◆**t.-level** *a* (*talks etc*) au sommet. ◆**t.-'notch** *a* *Fam* excellent. ◆**t.-'ranking** *a* (*official*) haut placé. ◆**t.-'secret** *a* ultra-secret.

top² [tɒp] *vt* (-pp-) (*exceed*) dépasser; **to t. up** (*glass etc*) remplir (de nouveau); (*coffee, oil etc*) rajouter; **and to t. it all . . .** et pour comble . . . ; **topped with** *Culin* nappé de.

top³ [tɒp] *n* (*toy*) toupie *f*.

topaz ['təʊpæz] *n* (*gem*) topaze *f*.

topic ['tɒpɪk] *n* sujet *m*. ◆**topical** *a* d'actualité. ◆**topi'cality** *n* actualité *f*.

topless ['tɒpləs] *a* (*woman*) aux seins nus.

topography [tə'pɒgrəfɪ] *n* topographie *f*.

topple ['tɒp(ə)l] *vi* to t. (over) tomber; – *vt* to t. (over) faire tomber.

topsy-turvy [tɒpsɪ'tɜːvɪ] *a* & *adv* sens dessus dessous.

torch [tɔːtʃ] *n* (*burning*) torche *f*, flambeau *m*; (*electric*) lampe *f* électrique. ◆**torchlight** *n* & *a* by t. à la lumière des flambeaux; **t. procession** retraite *f* aux flambeaux.

tore [tɔːr] *see* tear¹.

torment [tɔː'ment] *vt* (*make suffer*) tourmenter; (*annoy*) agacer; – ['tɔːment] *n* tourment *m*.

tornado [tɔː'neɪdəʊ] *n* (*pl* -oes) tornade *f*.

torpedo [tɔː'piːdəʊ] *n* (*pl* -oes) torpille *f*; **t. boat** torpilleur *m*; – *vt* torpiller.

torrent ['tɒrənt] *n* torrent *m*. ◆**torrential** [tə'renʃ(ə)l] *a* torrentiel.

torrid ['tɒrɪd] *a* (*love affair etc*) brûlant, passionné; (*climate, weather*) torride.

torso ['tɔːsəʊ] *n* (*pl* -os) torse *m*.

tortoise ['tɔːtəs] *n* tortue *f*. ◆**tortoiseshell** *a* (*comb etc*) en écaille; (*spectacles*) à monture d'écaille.

tortuous ['tɔːtjʊəs] *a* tortueux.

tortur/e ['tɔːtʃər] *n* torture *f*; – *vt* torturer. ◆**-er** *n* tortionnaire *m*.

Tory ['tɔːrɪ] *n* tory *m*; – *a* tory *inv*.

toss [tɒs] *vt* (*throw*) jeter, lancer (**to** à); **to t. s.o. (about)** (*of boat, vehicle*) ballotter qn, faire tressauter qn; **to t. a coin** jouer à pile ou à face; **to t. back** (*one's head*) rejeter en arrière; – *vi* to t. (about), t. and turn (*in one's sleep etc*) se tourner et se retourner; **we'll t. (up) for it, we'll t. up** on va jouer à pile ou à face; – *n* with a t. of the head d'un mouvement brusque de la tête. ◆**t.-up** *n* **it's a t.-up whether he leaves or stays** *Sl* il y a autant de chances pour qu'il parte ou pour qu'il reste.

tot [tɒt] **1** *n* (*tiny*) t. petit(e) enfant *mf*. **2** *vt* (-tt-) to t. up (*total*) *Fam* additionner.

total ['təʊt(ə)l] *a* total; **the t. sales** le total des ventes; – *n* total *m*; **in t.** au total; – *vt* (-ll-, *Am* -l-) (*of debt, invoice*) s'élever à; **to t. (up)** (*find the total of*) totaliser; **that totals $9** ça fait neuf dollars en tout. ◆**-ly** *adv* totalement.

totalitarian [təʊtælɪ'teərɪən] *a* *Pol* totalitaire.

tote [təʊt] **1** *n* *Sp* *Fam* pari *m* mutuel. **2** *vt* (*gun*) porter.

totter ['tɒtər] *vi* chanceler.

touch [tʌtʃ] *n* (*contact*) contact *m*, toucher *m*; (*sense*) toucher *m*; (*of painter*) & *Fb Rugby* touche *f*; **a t. of** (*small amount*) un petit peu de, un soupçon de; **the finishing**

touches la dernière touche; **in t. with** (*person*) en contact avec; (*events*) au courant de; **to be out of t. with** ne plus être en contact avec; (*events*) ne plus être au courant de; **to get in t.** se mettre en contact (**with** avec); **we lost t.** on s'est perdu de vue; – *vt* toucher; (*lay a finger on, tamper with, eat*) toucher à; (*move emotionally*) toucher; (*equal*) *Fig* égaler; **to t. up** retoucher; **I don't t. the stuff** (*beer etc*) je n'en bois jamais; – *vi* (*of lines, ends etc*) se toucher; **don't t.!** n'y or ne touche pas!; **he's always touching** c'est un touche-à-tout; **to t. down** (*of aircraft*) atterrir; **to t. on** (*subject*) toucher à. ◆**—ed** *a* (*emotionally*) touché (**by** de); (*crazy*) *Fam* cinglé. ◆**—ing** *a* (*story etc*) touchant. ◆**touch-and-'go** *a* (*uncertain*) *Fam* douteux. ◆**touchdown** *n Av* atterrissage *m*. ◆**touchline** *n Fb Rugby* (ligne *f* de) touche *f*.

touchy ['tʌtʃi] *a* (**-ier, -iest**) (*sensitive*) susceptible (**about** à propos de).

tough [tʌf] *a* (**-er, -est**) (*hard*) dur; (*meat, businessman*) coriace; (*sturdy*) solide; (*strong*) fort; (*relentless*) acharné; (*difficult*) difficile, dur; **t. guy** dur *m*; **t. luck!** *Fam* pas de chance!, quelle déveine!; – *n* (*tough guy*) *Fam* dur *m*. ◆**toughen** *vt* (*body, person*) endurcir; (*reinforce*) renforcer. ◆**toughness** *n* dureté *f*; solidité *f*; force *f*.

toupee ['tu:peɪ] *n* postiche *m*.

tour [tʊər] *n* (*journey*) voyage *m*; (*visit*) visite *f*; (*by artist, team etc*) tournée *f*; (*on bicycle, on foot*) randonnée *f*; **on t.** en voyage; en tournée; **a t. of** (*France*) un voyage en; une tournée en; une randonnée en; – *vt* visiter; (*of artist etc*) être en tournée en or dans *etc*. ◆**—ing** *n* tourisme *m*; **to go t.** faire du tourisme. ◆**tourism** *n* tourisme *m*. ◆**tourist** *n* touriste *mf*; – *a* touristique; (*class*) touriste *inv*; **t. office** syndicat *m* d'initiative. ◆**touristy** *a Pej Fam* (trop) touristique.

tournament ['tʊənəmənt] *n Sp & Hist* tournoi *m*.

tousled ['taʊz(ə)ld] *a* (*hair*) ébouriffé.

tout [taʊt] *vi* racoler; **to t. for** (*customers*) racoler; – *n* racoleur, -euse *mf*; **ticket t.** revendeur, -euse *mf* (en fraude) de billets.

tow [təʊ] *vt* (*car, boat*) remorquer; (*caravan, trailer*) tracter; **to t. away** (*vehicle*) *Jur* emmener à la fourrière; – *n* **'on t.'** 'en remorque'. ◆**t. truck** (*breakdown lorry*) *Am* dépanneuse *f*. ◆**towpath** *n* chemin *m* de halage. ◆**towrope** *n* (câble *m* de) remorque *f*.

toward(s) [tə'wɔːd(z), *Am* tɔːd(z)] *prep* vers;

(*of feelings*) envers; **money t.** de l'argent pour (acheter).

towel ['taʊəl] *n* serviette *f* (de toilette); (*for dishes*) torchon *m*; **t. rail** porte-serviettes *m inv*. ◆**towelling** *n, Am* ◆**toweling** *n* tissu-éponge *m*; (**kitchen**) **t.** *Am* essuie-tout *m inv*.

tower ['taʊər] *n* tour *f*; **t. block** tour *f*, immeuble *m*; **ivory t.** *Fig* tour *f* d'ivoire; – *vi* **to t. above** or **over** dominer. ◆**—ing** *a* très haut.

town [taʊn] *n* ville *f*; **in t.**, (**in)to t.** en ville; **out of t.** en province; **country t.** bourg *m*; **t. centre** centre-ville *m*; **t. clerk** secrétaire *mf* de mairie; **t. council** conseil *m* municipal; **t. hall** mairie *f*; **t. planner** urbaniste *mf*; **t. planning** urbanisme *m*. ◆**township** *n* (*in South Africa*) commune *f* (noire).

toxic ['tɒksɪk] *a* toxique. ◆**toxin** *n* toxine *f*.

toy [tɔɪ] *n* jouet *m*; **soft t.** (jouet *m* en) peluche *f*; – *a* (*gun*) d'enfant; (*house, car, train*) miniature; – *vi* **to t. with** jouer avec. ◆**toyshop** *n* magasin *m* de jouets.

trac/e [treɪs] *n* trace *f* (**of** de); **to vanish** or **disappear without** (**a) t.** disparaître sans laisser de traces; – *vt* (*draw*) tracer; (*with tracing paper*) (dé)calquer; (*locate*) retrouver (la trace de), dépister; (*follow*) suivre (la piste de) (**to** à); (*relate*) retracer; **to t.** (**back) to** (*one's family*) faire remonter jusqu'à. ◆**—ing** *n* (*drawing*) calque *m*; **t. paper** papier-calque *m inv*.

track [træk] *n* trace *f*; (*of bullet, rocket*) trajectoire *f*; (*of person, animal, tape recorder*) & *Sp* piste *f*; (*of record*) plage *f*; *Rail* voie *f*; (*path*) piste *f*, chemin *m*; *Sch Am* classe *f* (de niveau); **to keep t. of** suivre; **to lose t. of** (*friend*) perdre de vue; (*argument*) perdre le fil de; **to make tracks** *Fam* se sauver; **the right t.** la bonne voie or piste; **t. event** *Sp* épreuve *f* sur piste; **t. record** (*of person, firm etc*) *Fig* antécédents *mpl*; – *vt* **to t.** (**down**) (*locate*) retrouver, dépister; (*pursue*) traquer. ◆**—er** *a* **t. dog** chien *m* policier. ◆**tracksuit** *n Sp* survêtement *m*.

tract [trækt] *n* (*stretch of land*) étendue *f*.

traction ['trækʃ(ə)n] *n Tech* traction *f*.

tractor ['træktər] *n* tracteur *m*.

trade [treɪd] *n* commerce *m*; (*job*) métier *m*; (*exchange*) échange *m*; – *a* (*fair, balance, route*) commercial; (*price*) de (demi-)gros; (*secret*) de fabrication; (*barrier*) douanier; **t. union** syndicat *m*; **t. unionist** syndicaliste *mf*; – *vi* faire du commerce (**with** avec); **to t. in** (*sugar etc*) faire le commerce de; – *vt* (*exchange*) échanger (**for** contre); **to t. sth in** (*old article*) faire reprendre qch. ◆**t.-in** *n*

Com reprise *f*. ◆**t.-off** *n* échange *m*.
◆**trading** *n* commerce *m*; – *a* (*activity, port etc*) commercial; (*nation*) commerçant; **t. estate** zone *f* industrielle. ◆**trader** *n* commerçant, -ante *mf*; (**street**) **t.** vendeur, -euse *mf* de rue. ◆**tradesman** *n* (*pl* **-men**) commerçant *m*.

trademark ['treɪdmɑːk] *n* marque *f* de fabrique; (**registered**) **t.** marque déposée.

tradition [trə'dɪʃ(ə)n] *n* tradition *f*. ◆**tra-**
'**ditional** *a* traditionnel. ◆**traditionally** *adv* traditionnellement.

traffic ['træfɪk] **1** *n* (*on road*) circulation *f*; *Av Nau Rail* trafic *m*; **busy** *or* **heavy t.** beaucoup de circulation; **heavy t.** (*vehicles*) poids *mpl* lourds; **t. circle** *Am* rond-point *m*; **t. cone** cône *m* de chantier; **t. jam** embouteillage *m*; **t. lights** feux *mpl* de signalisation); (*when red*) feu *m* rouge; **t. sign** panneau *m* de signalisation. **2** *n* (*trade*) *Pej* trafic *m* (**in** de); – *vi* (**-ck-**) trafiquer (**in** de). ◆**trafficker** *n Pej* trafiquant, -ante *mf*.

tragedy ['trædʒədɪ] *n Th & Fig* tragédie *f*. ◆**tragic** *a* tragique. ◆**tragically** *adv* tragiquement.

trail [treɪl] *n* (*of powder, smoke, blood etc*) traînée *f*; (*track*) piste *f*, trace *f*; (*path*) sentier *m*; **in its t.** (*wake*) dans son sillage; – *vt* (*drag*) traîner; (*caravan*) tracter; (*follow*) suivre (la piste de); – *vi* (*on the ground etc*) traîner; (*of plant*) ramper; **to t. behind** (*lag behind*) traîner. ◆**-er** *n* **1** *Aut* remorque *f*; *Am* caravane *f*. **2** *Cin* bande *f* annonce.

train [treɪn] **1** *n* (*engine, transport, game*) train *m*; (*underground*) rame *f*; (*procession*) *Fig* file *f*; (*of events*) suite *f*; (*of dress*) traîne *f*; **my t. of thought** le fil de ma pensée; **t. set** train *m* électrique. **2** *vt* (*teach, develop*) former (**to do** à faire); *Sp* entraîner; (*animal, child*) dresser (**to do** à faire); (*ear*) exercer; **to t. oneself to do** s'entraîner à faire; **to t. sth on** (*aim*) braquer qch sur; – *vi* recevoir une formation (**as a doctor**/*etc* de médecin/*etc*); *Sp* s'entraîner. ◆**-ed** *a* (*having professional skill*) qualifié; (*nurse etc*) diplômé; (*animal*) dressé; (*ear*) exercé. ◆**-ing** *n* formation *f*; *Sp* entraînement *m*; (*of animal*) dressage *m*; **to be in t.** *Sp* s'entraîner; (**teachers'**) **t. college** école *f* normale. ◆**trai'nee** *n & a* stagiaire (*mf*). ◆**trainer** *n* (*of athlete, racehorse*) entraîneur *m*; (*of dog, lion etc*) dresseur *m*; (*running shoe*) jogging *m*, chaussure *f* de sport.

traipse [treɪps] *vi Fam* (*tiredly*) traîner les pieds; **to t.** (**about**) (*wander*) se balader.

trait [treɪt] *n* (*of character*) trait *m*.

traitor ['treɪtər] *n* traître *m*.

trajectory [trə'dʒektərɪ] *n* trajectoire *f*.

tram [træm] *n* tram(way) *m*.

tramp [træmp] **1** *n* (*vagrant*) clochard, -arde *mf*; (*woman*) *Pej* traînée *f*. **2** *vi* (*walk*) marcher d'un pas lourd; (*hike*) marcher à pied; – *vt* (*streets etc*) parcourir; – *n* (*sound*) pas lourds *mpl*; (*hike*) randonnée *f*.

trample ['træmp(ə)l] *vti* **to t. sth** (**underfoot**), **t. on sth** piétiner qch.

trampoline [træmpə'liːn] *n* trampoline *m*.

trance [trɑːns] *n* **in a t.** (*mystic*) en transe.

tranquil ['træŋkwɪl] *a* tranquille. ◆**tran-**
'**quillity** *n* tranquillité *f*. ◆**tranquillizer** *n Med* tranquillisant *m*.

trans- [træns, trænz] *pref* trans-.

transact [træn'zækt] *vt* (*business*) traiter. ◆**transaction** *n* (*in bank etc*) opération *f*; (*on Stock Market*) transaction *f*; **the t. of** (*business*) la conduite de.

transatlantic [trænzət'læntɪk] *a* transatlantique.

transcend [træn'send] *vt* transcender. ◆**transcendent** *a* transcendant.

transcribe [træn'skraɪb] *vt* transcrire. ◆'**transcript** *n* (*document*) transcription *f*. ◆**transcription** *n* transcription *f*.

transfer [træns'fɜːr] *vt* (**-rr-**) (*person, goods etc*) transférer (**to** à); (*power*) *Pol* faire passer (**to** à); **to t. the charges** téléphoner en PCV; – *vi* être transféré (**to** à); – ['trænsfɜːr] *n* transfert *m* (**to** à); (*of power*) *Pol* passation *f*; (*image*) décalcomanie *f*; **bank** *or* **credit t.** virement *m* (bancaire). ◆**trans'ferable** *a* **not t.** (*on ticket*) strictement personnel.

transform [træns'fɔːm] *vt* transformer (**into** en). ◆**transfor'mation** *n* transformation *f*. ◆**transformer** *n El* transformateur *m*.

transfusion [træns'fjuːʒ(ə)n] *n* (**blood**) **t.** transfusion *f* (sanguine).

transient ['trænzɪənt] *a* (*ephemeral*) transitoire.

transistor [træn'zɪstər] *n* (*device*) transistor *m*; **t.** (**radio**) transistor *m*.

transit ['trænzɪt] *n* transit *m*; **in t.** en transit.

transition [træn'zɪʃ(ə)n] *n* transition *f*. ◆**transitional** *a* de transition, transitoire.

transitive ['trænsɪtɪv] *a Gram* transitif.

transitory ['trænzɪtərɪ] *a* transitoire.

translate [træns'leɪt] *vt* traduire (**from** de, **into** en). ◆**translation** *n* traduction *f*; (*into mother tongue*) *Sch* version *f*; (*from mother tongue*) *Sch* thème *m*. ◆**translator** *n* traducteur, -trice *mf*.

transmit [trænz'mɪt] *vt* (**-tt-**) (*send, pass*)

transmettre; – *vti* (*broadcast*) émettre.
◆**transmission** *n* transmission *f*; (*broadcast*) émission *f*. ◆**transmitter** *n* Rad TV émetteur *m*.

transparent [træns'pærənt] *a* transparent. ◆**transparency** *n* transparence *f*; (*slide*) Phot diapositive *f*.

transpire [træn'spaɪər] *vi* (*of secret etc*) s'ébruiter; (*happen*) Fam arriver; **it transpired that** . . . il s'est avéré que . . . .

transplant [træns'plɑːnt] *vt* (*plant*) transplanter; (*organ*) Med greffer, transplanter; – ['trænsplɑːnt] *n* Med greffe *f*, transplantation *f*.

transport [træns'pɔːt] *vt* transporter; – ['trænspɔːt] *n* transport *m*; **public t.** les transports en commun; **do you have t.?** es-tu motorisé?; **t. café** routier *m*. ◆**transpor'tation** *n* transport *m*.

transpose [træns'pəʊz] *vt* transposer.

transvestite [trænz'vestaɪt] *n* travesti *m*.

trap [træp] *n* piège *m*; (*mouth*) Pej Sl gueule *f*; **t. door** trappe *f*; – *vt* (-pp-) (*snare*) prendre (au piège); (*jam, corner*) coincer, bloquer; (*cut off by snow etc*) bloquer (**by** par); **to t. one's finger** se coincer le doigt. ◆**trapper** *n* (*hunter*) trappeur *m*.

trapeze [trə'piːz] *n* (*in circus*) trapèze *m*; **t. artist** trapéziste *mf*.

trappings ['træpɪŋz] *npl* signes *mpl* extérieurs.

trash [træʃ] *n* (*nonsense*) sottises *fpl*; (*junk*) saleté(s) *f*(*pl*); (*waste*) Am ordures *fpl*; (*riffraff*) Am racaille *f*. ◆**trashcan** *n* Am poubelle *f*. ◆**trashy** *a* (-ier, -iest) (*book etc*) moche, sans valeur; (*goods*) de camelote.

trauma ['trɔːmə, 'traʊmə] *n* (*shock*) traumatisme *m*. ◆**trau'matic** *a* traumatisant. ◆**traumatize** *vt* traumatiser.

travel ['trævəl] *vi* (-ll-, Am -l-) voyager; (*move*) aller, se déplacer; – *vt* (*country, distance, road*) parcourir; – *n* & *npl* voyages *mpl*; **on one's travels** en voyage; – *a* (*agency, book*) de voyages; **t. brochure** dépliant *m* touristique. ◆**travelled** *a* **to be well** *or* **widely t.** avoir beaucoup voyagé. ◆**travelling** *n* voyages *mpl*; – *a* (*bag etc*) de voyage; (*expenses*) de déplacement; (*circus, musician*) ambulant. ◆**traveller** *n* voyageur, -euse *mf*; **traveller's cheque,** Am **traveler's check** chèque *m* de voyage. ◆**travelogue** *n*, Am ◆**travelog** *n* (*book*) récit *m* de voyages. ◆**travelsickness** *n* (*in car*) mal *m* de la route; (*in aircraft*) mal *m* de l'air.

travesty ['trævəstɪ] *n* parodie *f*.

travolator ['trævəleɪtər] *n* trottoir *m* roulant.

trawler ['trɔːlər] *n* (*ship*) chalutier *m*.

tray [treɪ] *n* plateau *m*; (*for office correspondence etc*) corbeille *f*.

treacherous ['tretʃ(ə)rəs] *a* (*person, action, road, journey etc*) traître. ◆**treacherously** *adv* traîtreusement; (*dangerously*) dangereusement. ◆**treachery** *n* traîtrise *f*.

treacle ['triːk(ə)l] *n* mélasse *f*.

tread [tred] *vi* (*pt* trod, *pp* trodden) (*walk*) marcher (**on** sur); (*proceed*) Fig avancer; – *vt* (*path*) parcourir; (*soil*) Fig fouler; **to t. sth into a carpet** étaler qch (avec les pieds) sur un tapis; – *n* (*step*) pas *m*; (*of tyre*) chape *f*. ◆**treadmill** *n* Pej Fig routine *f*.

treason ['triːz(ə)n] *n* trahison *f*.

treasure ['treʒər] *n* trésor *m*; **a real t.** (*person*) Fig une vraie perle; **t. hunt** chasse *f* au trésor; – *vt* (*value*) tenir à, priser; (*keep*) conserver (précieusement). ◆**treasurer** *n* trésorier, -ière *mf*. ◆**Treasury** *n* **the T.** Pol = le ministère des Finances.

treat [triːt] **1** *vt* (*person, product etc*) & Med traiter; (*consider*) considérer (**as** comme); **to t. with care** prendre soin de; **to t. s.o. to sth** offrir qch à qn. **2** *n* (*pleasure*) plaisir *m* (spécial); (*present*) cadeau-surprise *m*; (*meal*) régal *m*; **it was a t. (for me) to do it** ça m'a fait plaisir de le faire. ◆**treatment** *n* (*behaviour*) & Med traitement *m*; **his t. of her** la façon dont il la traite; **rough t.** mauvais traitements *mpl*.

treatise ['triːtɪz] *n* (*book*) traité *m* (**on** de).

treaty ['triːtɪ] *n* Pol traité *m*.

treble ['treb(ə)l] *a* triple; – *vti* tripler; – *n* le triple; **it's t. the price** c'est le triple du prix.

tree [triː] *n* arbre *m*; **Christmas t.** sapin *m* de Noël; **family t.** arbre *m* généalogique. ◆**t.-lined** *a* bordé d'arbres. ◆**t.-top** *n* cime *f* (d'un arbre). ◆**t.-trunk** *n* tronc *m* d'arbre.

trek [trek] *vi* (-kk-) cheminer *or* voyager (péniblement); Sp marcher à pied; (*go*) Fam trainer; – *n* voyage *m* (pénible); Sp randonnée *f*; (*distance*) Fam tirée *f*.

trellis ['trelɪs] *n* treillage *m*.

tremble ['tremb(ə)l] *vi* trembler (**with** de). ◆**tremor** *n* tremblement *m*; (**earth**) **t.** secousse *f* (sismique).

tremendous [trə'mendəs] *a* (*huge*) énorme; (*dreadful*) terrible; (*wonderful*) formidable, terrible. ◆**—ly** *adv* terriblement.

trench [trentʃ] *n* tranchée *f*.

trend [trend] *n* tendance *f* (**towards** à); **the t.** (*fashion*) la mode; **to set a** *or* **the t.** donner

le ton, lancer une *or* la mode. ◆**trendy** *a*
(**-ier, -iest**) (*person, clothes, topic etc*) *Fam* à
la mode, dans le vent.

trepidation [trepɪ'deɪʃ(ə)n] *n* inquiétude *f*.

trespass ['trespəs] *vi* s'introduire sans
autorisation (**on, upon** dans); '**no trespass-
ing**' 'entrée interdite'.

tresses ['tresɪz] *npl Lit* chevelure *f*.

trestle ['tres(ə)l] *n* tréteau *m*.

trial ['traɪəl] *n Jur* procès *m*; (*test*) essai *m*;
(*ordeal*) épreuve *f*; **t. of strength** épreuve de
force; **to go** *or* **be on t., stand t.** passer en
jugement; **to put s.o. on t.** juger qn; **by t.
and error** par tâtonnements; – *a* (*period,
flight etc*) d'essai; (*offer*) à l'essai; **t. run** (*of
new product etc*) période *f* d'essai.

triangle ['traɪæŋg(ə)l] *n* triangle *m*;
(*setsquare*) *Math Am* équerre *f*. ◆**tri-
'angular** *a* triangulaire.

tribe [traɪb] *n* tribu *f*. ◆**tribal** *a* tribal.

tribulations [trɪbju'leɪʃ(ə)nz] *npl* (**trials and**)
t. tribulations *fpl*.

tribunal [traɪ'bjuːn(ə)l] *n* commission *f*,
tribunal *m*; *Mil* tribunal *m*.

tributary ['trɪbjutərɪ] *n* affluent *m*.

tribute ['trɪbjuːt] *n* hommage *m*, tribut *m*; **to
pay t. to** rendre hommage à.

trick [trɪk] *n* (*joke, deception & of conjurer
etc*) tour *m*; (*ruse*) astuce *f*; (*habit*) manie *f*;
to play a t. on s.o. jouer un tour à qn; **card t.**
tour *m* de cartes; **that will do the t.** *Fam* ça
fera l'affaire; **t. photo** photo *f* truquée; **t.
question** question-piège *f*; – *vt* (*deceive*)
tromper, attraper; **to t. s.o. into doing sth**
amener qn à faire qch par la ruse. ◆**trick-
ery** *n* ruse *f*. ◆**tricky** *a* (**-ier, -iest**) (*problem etc*) difficile, délicat; (*person*) rusé.

trickle ['trɪk(ə)l] *n* (*of liquid*) filet *m*; **a t.** of
(*letters, people etc*) *Fig* un petit nombre de;
– *vi* (*flow*) dégouliner, couler (lentement); **
to t. in** (*of letters, people etc*) *Fig* arriver en
petit nombre.

tricycle ['traɪsɪk(ə)l] *n* tricycle *m*.

trier ['traɪər] *n* **to be a t.** être persévérant.

trifl/e ['traɪf(ə)l] *n* (*article, money*) bagatelle
f; (*dessert*) diplomate *m*; – *adv* **a t.
small/too much/etc** un tantinet petit/trop/
etc; – *vi* **to t. with** (*s.o.'s feelings*) jouer
avec; (*person*) plaisanter avec. ◆**—ing** *a*
insignifiant.

trigger ['trɪgər] *n* (*of gun*) gâchette *f*; – *vt* **to
t.** (**off**) (*start, cause*) déclencher.

trilogy ['trɪlədʒɪ] *n* trilogie *f*.

trim [trɪm] **1** *a* (**trimmer, trimmest**) (*neat*)
soigné, net; (*slim*) svelte; – *n* **in t.** (*fit*) en
(bonne) forme. **2** *n* (*cut*) légère coupe *f*;
(*haircut*) coupe *f* de rafraîchissement; **to

have a t.** se faire rafraîchir les cheveux; – *vt*
(**-mm-**) couper (légèrement); (*finger nail,
edge*) rogner; (*hair*) rafraîchir. **3** *n* (*on
garment*) garniture *f*; (*on car*) garnitures
fpl; – *vt* (**-mm-**) **to t. with** (*lace etc*) orner de.
◆**trimmings** *npl* garniture(s) *f*(*pl*);
(*extras*) *Fig* accessoires *mpl*.

Trinity ['trɪnɪtɪ] *n* **the T.** (*union*) *Rel* la Trinité.

trinket ['trɪŋkɪt] *n* colifichet *m*.

trio ['triːəʊ] *n* (*pl* **-os**) (*group*) & *Mus* trio *m*.

trip [trɪp] **1** *n* (*journey*) voyage *m*; (*outing*)
excursion *f*; **to take a t. to** (*cinema, shops
etc*) aller à. **2** *n* (*stumble*) faux pas *m*; – *vi*
(**-pp-**) **to t.** (**over** *or* **up**) trébucher; **to t. over
sth** trébucher contre qch; – *vt* **to t. s.o. up**
faire trébucher qn. **3** *vi* (**-pp-**) (*walk gently*)
marcher d'un pas léger. ◆**tripper** *n* **day t.**
excursionniste *mf*.

tripe [traɪp] *n Culin* tripes *fpl*; (*nonsense*)
Fam bêtises *fpl*.

triple ['trɪp(ə)l] *a* triple; – *vti* tripler.
◆**triplets** *npl* (*children*) triplés, -ées *mfpl*.

triplicate ['trɪplɪkət] *n* **in t.** en trois exemplaires.

tripod ['traɪpɒd] *n* trépied *m*.

trite [traɪt] *a* banal. ◆**—ness** *n* banalité *f*.

triumph ['traɪʌmf] *n* triomphe *m* (**over** sur);
– *vi* triompher (**over** de). ◆**tri'umphal** *a*
triomphal. ◆**tri'umphant** *a* (*team, army,
gesture*) triomphant; (*success, welcome,
return*) triomphal. ◆**tri'umphantly** *adv*
triomphalement.

trivia ['trɪvɪə] *npl* vétilles *fpl*. ◆**trivial** *a*
(*unimportant*) insignifiant; (*trite*) banal.
◆**trivi'ality** *n* insignifiance *f*; banalité *f*; *pl*
banalités *fpl*.

trod, trodden [trɒd, 'trɒd(ə)n] *see* **tread**.

trolley ['trɒlɪ] *n* (*for luggage*) chariot *m*; (*for
shopping*) poussette *f* (de marché); (*in
supermarket*) caddie® *m*; (*trolleybus*) trolley *m*; (*tea*) **t.** table *f* roulante; (*for tea urn*)
chariot *m*; **t.** (**car**) *Am* tramway *m*. ◆**trolleybus** *n* trolleybus *m*.

trombone [trɒm'bəʊn] *n Mus* trombone *m*.

troop [truːp] *n* bande *f*; *Mil* troupe *f*; **the
troops** (*army, soldiers*) les troupes, la
troupe; – *vi* **to t. in/out/etc** entrer/
sortir/*etc* en masse. ◆**—ing** *n* **t. the colour**
le salut du drapeau. ◆**—er** *n* (*state*) **t.** *Am*
membre *m* de la police montée.

trophy ['trəʊfɪ] *n* trophée *m*.

tropic ['trɒpɪk] *n* tropique *m*. ◆**tropical** *a*
tropical.

trot [trɒt] *n* (*of horse*) trot *m*; **on the t.** (*one
after another*) *Fam* de suite; – *vi* (**-tt-**) trot-

ter; **to t. off** *or* **along** (*leave*) *Hum Fam* se sauver; – *vt* **to t. out** (*say*) *Fam* débiter.

troubl/e ['trʌb(ə)l] *n* (*difficulty*) ennui(s) *m*(*pl*); (*bother, effort*) peine *f*, mal *m*; **trouble(s)** (*social unrest etc*) & *Med* troubles *mpl*; **to be in t.** avoir des ennuis; **to get into t.** s'attirer des ennuis (**with** avec); **the t.** (**with you**) **is** . . . l'ennui (avec toi) c'est que . . . ; **to go to the t. of doing, take the t. to do** se donner la peine *or* le mal de faire; **I didn't put her to any t.** je ne l'ai pas dérangée; **to find the t.** trouver le problème; **a spot of t.** un petit problème; **a t. spot** *Pol* un point chaud; – *vt* (*inconvenience*) déranger, ennuyer; (*worry, annoy*) ennuyer; (*hurt*) faire mal à; (*grieve*) peiner; **to t. to do** se donner la peine de faire; – *vi* **to t.** (**oneself**) se déranger. ◆**—ed** *a* (*worried*) inquiet; (*period*) agité. ◆**trouble-free** *a* (*machine, vehicle*) qui ne tombe jamais en panne, fiable. ◆**troublemaker** *n* fauteur *m* de troubles. ◆**troubleshooter** *n Tech* dépanneur *m*, expert *m*; *Pol* conciliateur, -trice *mf*.

troublesome ['trʌb(ə)ls(ə)m] *a* ennuyeux, gênant; (*leg etc*) qui fait mal.

trough [trɒf] *n* (*for drinking*) abreuvoir *m*; (*for feeding*) auge *f*; **t. of low pressure** *Met* dépression *f*.

trounce [traʊns] *vt* (*defeat*) écraser.

troupe [truːp] *n Th* troupe *f*.

trousers ['traʊzəz] *npl* pantalon *m*; **a pair of t., some t.** un pantalon; (**short**) **t.** culottes *fpl* courtes.

trousseau ['truːsəʊ] *n* (*of bride*) trousseau *m*.

trout [traʊt] *n* truite *f*.

trowel ['traʊəl] *n* (*for cement or plaster*) truelle *f*; (*for plants*) déplantoir *m*.

truant ['truːənt] *n* (*pupil, shirker*) absentéiste *mf*; **to play t.** faire l'école buissonnière. ◆**truancy** *n Sch* absentéisme *m* scolaire.

truce [truːs] *n Mil* trêve *f*.

truck [trʌk] *n* **1** (*lorry*) camion *m*; *Rail* wagon *m* plat; **t. driver** camionneur *m*; (*long-distance*) routier *m*; **t. stop** (*restaurant*) routier *m*. **2 t. farmer** *Am* maraîcher, -ère *mf*. ◆**trucker** *n Am* (*haulier*) transporteur *m* routier; (*driver*) camionneur *m*, routier *m*.

truculent ['trʌkjʊlənt] *a* agressif.

trudge [trʌdʒ] *vi* marcher d'un pas pesant.

true [truː] *a* (**-er, -est**) vrai; (*accurate*) exact; (*genuine*) vrai, véritable; **t. to** (*person, promise etc*) fidèle à; **t. to life** conforme à la réalité; **to come t.** se réaliser; **to hold t.** (*of argument etc*) valoir (**for** pour); **too t.!** *Fam*

ah, ça oui! ◆**truly** *adv* vraiment; (*faithfully*) fidèlement; **well and t.** bel et bien.

truffle ['trʌf(ə)l] *n* (*mushroom*) truffe *f*.

truism ['truːɪz(ə)m] *n* lapalissade *f*.

trump [trʌmp] **1** *n Cards* atout *m*; **t. card** (*advantage*) *Fig* atout *m*. **2** *vt* **to t. up** (*charge, reason*) inventer.

trumpet ['trʌmpɪt] *n* trompette *f*; **t. player** trompettiste *mf*.

truncate [trʌŋ'keɪt] *vt* tronquer.

truncheon ['trʌntʃ(ə)n] *n* matraque *f*.

trundle ['trʌnd(ə)l] *vti* **to t. along** rouler bruyamment.

trunk [trʌŋk] *n* (*of tree, body*) tronc *m*; (*of elephant*) trompe *f*; (*case*) malle *f*; (*of vehicle*) *Am* coffre *m*; *pl* (*for swimming*) slip *m or* caleçon *m* de bain; **t. call** *Tel* communication *f* interurbaine; **t. road** route *f* nationale.

truss [trʌs] *vt* **to t. (up)** (*prisoner*) ligoter.

trust [trʌst] *n* (*faith*) confiance *f* (**in** en); (*group*) *Fin* trust *m*; *Jur* fidéicommis *m*; **to take on t.** accepter de confiance; – *vt* (*person, judgement*) avoir confiance en, se fier à; (*instinct, promise*) se fier à; **to t. s.o. with sth, t. sth to s.o.** confier qch à qn; **to t. s.o. to do** (*rely on, expect*) compter sur qn pour faire; **I t. that** (*hope*) j'espère que; – *vi* **to t. in s.o.** se fier à qn; **to t. to luck** *or* **chance** se fier au hasard. ◆**—ed** *a* (*friend, method etc*) éprouvé. ◆**—ing** *a* confiant. ◆**trus'tee** *n* (*of school*) administrateur -trice *mf*. ◆**trustworthy** *a* sûr, digne de confiance.

truth [truːθ] *n* (*pl* **-s** [truːðz]) vérité *f*; **there's some t. in** . . . il y a du vrai dans . . . . ◆**truthful** *a* (*statement etc*) véridique, vrai; (*person*) sincère. ◆**truthfully** *adv* sincèrement.

try [traɪ] **1** *vt* essayer (**to do, doing** de faire); (*s.o.'s patience etc*) mettre à l'épreuve; **to t. one's hand at** s'essayer à; **to t. one's luck** tenter sa chance; **to t. (out)** (*car, method etc*) essayer; (*employee etc*) mettre à l'essai; **to t. on** (*clothes, shoes*) essayer; – *vi* essayer (**for sth** d'obtenir qch); **to t. hard** faire un gros effort; **t. and come!** essaie de venir!; – *n* (*attempt*) & *Rugby* essai *m*; **to have a t.** essayer; **at** (**the**) **first t.** du premier coup. **2** *vt* (*person*) *Jur* juger (**for theft**/*etc* pour vol/*etc*). ◆**—ing** *a* pénible, éprouvant.

tsar [zɑːr] *n* tsar *m*.

tub [tʌb] *n* (*for washing clothes etc*) baquet *m*; (*bath*) baignoire *f*; (*for ice cream etc*) pot *m*.

tuba ['tjuːbə] *n Mus* tuba *m*.

tubby ['tʌbɪ] *a* (**-ier, -iest**) *Fam* dodu.

tube [tjuːb] n tube m; Rail Fam métro m; (of tyre) chambre f à air. ◆**tubing** n (tubes) tubes mpl. ◆**tubular** a tubulaire.

tuberculosis [tjuːbɜːkjuˈləʊsɪs] n tuberculose f.

tuck [tʌk] 1 n (fold in garment) rempli m; – vt (put) mettre; **to t. away** ranger; (hide) cacher; **to t.** (shirt) rentrer; (person in bed, a blanket) border; **to t. up** (skirt) remonter. 2 vi **to t. in** (eat) Fam manger; **to t. into** (meal) Fam attaquer; – n t. **shop** Sch boutique f à provisions.

Tuesday [ˈtjuːzdɪ] n mardi m.

tuft [tʌft] n (of hair, grass) touffe f.

tug [tʌg] 1 vt (-gg-) (pull) tirer; – vi tirer (at, on sur); – n **to give sth a t.** tirer (sur) qch. 2 n (boat) remorqueur m.

tuition [tjuˈɪʃ(ə)n] n (teaching) enseignement m; (lessons) leçons fpl; (fee) frais mpl de scolarité.

tulip [ˈtjuːlɪp] n tulipe f.

tumble [ˈtʌmb(ə)l] vi **to t.** (over) (fall) dégringoler; (backwards) tomber à la renverse; **to t. to sth** (understand) Sl réaliser qch; – n (fall) dégringolade f; **t. drier** sèche-linge m inv.

tumbledown [ˈtʌmb(ə)ldaʊn] a délabré.

tumbler [ˈtʌmblər] n (drinking glass) gobelet m.

tummy [ˈtʌmɪ] n Fam ventre m.

tumour [ˈtjuːmər] n tumeur f.

tumult [ˈtjuːmʌlt] n tumulte m. ◆**tu'multuous** a tumultueux.

tuna [ˈtjuːnə] n t. (fish) thon m.

tun/e [tjuːn] n (melody) air m; **to be or sing in t./out of t.** chanter juste/faux; **in t.** (instrument) accordé; **out of t.** (instrument) désaccordé; **in t. with** (harmony) Fig en accord avec; **to the t. of £50** d'un montant de 50 livres, dans les 50 livres; – vt **to t.** (up) Mus accorder; Aut régler; – vi **to t. in** (to) Rad TV se mettre à l'écoute (de), écouter. ◆**—ing** n Aut réglage m; **t. fork** Mus diapason m. ◆**tuneful** a mélodieux.

tunic [ˈtjuːnɪk] n tunique f.

Tunisia [tjuˈnɪzɪə] n Tunisie f. ◆**Tunisian** a & n tunisien, -ienne (mf).

tunnel [ˈtʌn(ə)l] n tunnel m; (in mine) galerie f; – vi (-ll-, Am -l-) percer un tunnel (into dans).

turban [ˈtɜːbən] n turban m.

turbine [ˈtɜːbaɪn, Am ˈtɜːbɪn] n turbine f.

turbulence [ˈtɜːbjʊləns] n Phys Av turbulences fpl.

turbulent [ˈtɜːbjʊlənt] a (person etc) turbulent.

tureen [tjuˈriːm, təˈriːm] n (soup) t. soupière f.

turf [tɜːf] 1 n (grass) gazon m; **the t.** Sp le turf; **t. accountant** bookmaker m. 2 vt **to t. out** (get rid of) Fam jeter dehors.

turgid [ˈtɜːdʒɪd] a (style, language) boursouflé.

turkey [ˈtɜːkɪ] n dindon m, dinde f; (as food) dinde f.

Turkey [ˈtɜːkɪ] n Turquie f. ◆**Turk** n Turc m, Turque f. ◆**Turkish** a turc; **T. delight** (sweet) loukoum m; – n (language) turc m.

turmoil [ˈtɜːmɔɪl] n confusion f, trouble m; **in t.** en ébullition.

turn [tɜːn] n (movement, action & in game etc) tour m; (in road) tournant m; (of events, mind) tournure f; Med crise f; Psy choc m; (act) Th numéro m; **t. of phrase** tour m or tournure f (de phrase); **to take turns** se relayer; **in t.** à tour de rôle; **by turns** tour à tour; **in (one's) t.** à son tour; **it's your t. to play** c'est à toi de jouer; **to do s.o. a good t.** rendre service à qn; **the t. of the century** le début du siècle; – vt tourner; (mechanically) faire tourner; (mattress, pancake) retourner; **to turn s.o./sth into** (change) transformer qn/qch en; **to t. sth red/yellow** rougir/jaunir qch; **to t. sth on s.o.** (aim) braquer qch sur qn; **she's turned twenty** elle a vingt ans passés; **it's turned seven** il est sept heures passées; **it turns my stomach** cela me soulève le cœur; – vi (of wheel, driver etc) tourner; (turn head or body) se (re)tourner (towards vers); (become) devenir; **to t. to** (question, adviser etc) se tourner vers; **to t. against** se retourner contre; **to t. into** (change) se changer or se transformer en. ■ **to t. around** vi (of person) se retourner; **to t. away** vt (avert) détourner (**from** de); (refuse) renvoyer (qn); – vi (stop facing) détourner les yeux, se détourner; **to t. back** vt (bed sheet, corner of page) replier; (person) renvoyer; (clock) reculer (to jusqu'à); – vi (return) retourner (sur ses pas); **to t. down** vt (fold down) rabattre; (gas, radio etc) baisser; (refuse) refuser (qn, offre etc); **to t. in** vt (hand in) rendre (to à); (prisoner etc) Fam livrer (à la police); – vi (go to bed) Fam se coucher; **to t. off** vt (light, radio etc) éteindre; (tap) fermer; (machine) arrêter; – vi (in vehicle) tourner; **to t. on** vt (light, radio etc) mettre, allumer; (tap) ouvrir; (machine) mettre en marche; **to t. s.o. on** (sexually) Fam exciter qn; – vi **to t. on s.o.** (attack) attaquer qn; **to t. out** vt (light) éteindre; (contents of box etc) vider (**from** de); (produce) produire; – vi (of crowds) venir; (happen) se passer; **it turns out that** il s'avère que; **she turned out to be** ... elle s'est révélée être ... ; **to t. over** *vt* (*page*) tourner; – *vi* (*of vehicle, person etc*) se retourner; (*of car engine*) tourner au ralenti; **to t. round** *vt* (*head, object*) tourner; (*vehicle*) faire faire demi-tour à; – *vi* (*of person*) se retourner; **to t. up** *vt* (*radio, light etc*) mettre plus fort; (*collar*) remonter; (*unearth, find*) déterrer; **a turned-up nose** un nez retroussé; – *vi* (*arrive*) arriver; (*be found*) être (re)trouvé. ◆**turning** *n* (*street*) petite rue *f*; (*bend in road*) tournant *m*; **t. circle** *Aut* rayon *m* de braquage; **t. point** (*in time*) tournant *m*. ◆**turner** *n* (*workman*) tourneur *m*.

turncoat ['tɜːnkəʊt] *n* renégat, -ate *mf*. ◆**turn-off** *n* (*in road*) embranchement *m*. ◆**turnout** *n* (*people*) assistance *f*; (*at polls*) participation *f*. ◆**turnover** *n* (*money*) *Com* chiffre *m* d'affaires; (*of stock*) *Com* rotation *f*; **staff t.** (*starting and leaving*) la rotation du personnel; **apple t.** chausson *m* (aux pommes). ◆**turnup** *n* (*on trousers*) revers *m*.

turnip ['tɜːnɪp] *n* navet *m*.

turnpike ['tɜːnpaɪk] *n* *Am* autoroute *f* à péage.

turnstile ['tɜːnstaɪl] *n* (*gate*) tourniquet *m*.

turntable ['tɜːnteɪb(ə)l] *n* (*of record player*) platine *f*.

turpentine ['tɜːpəntaɪn] (*Fam* **turps** [tɜːps]) *n* térébenthine *f*.

turquoise ['tɜːkwɔɪz] *a* turquoise *inv*.

turret ['tʌrɪt] *n* tourelle *f*.

turtle ['tɜːt(ə)l] *n* tortue *f* de mer; *Am* tortue *f*. ◆**turtleneck** *a* (*sweater*) à col roulé; – *n* col *m* roulé.

tusk [tʌsk] *n* (*of elephant*) défense *f*.

tussle ['tʌs(ə)l] *n* bagarre *f*.

tutor ['tjuːtər] *n* précepteur, -trice *mf*; *Univ* directeur, -trice *mf* d'études; *Univ Am* assistant, -ante *mf*; – *vt* donner des cours particuliers à. ◆**tu'torial** *n* *Univ* travaux *mpl* dirigés.

tut-tut! [tʌt'tʌt] *int* allons donc!

tuxedo [tʌk'siːdəʊ] *n* (*pl* -os) *Am* smoking *m*.

TV [tiː'viː] *n* télé *f*.

twaddle ['twɒd(ə)l] *n* fadaises *fpl*.

twang [twæŋ] *n* son *m* vibrant; (*nasal*) **t.** nasillement *m*; – *vi* (*of wire etc*) vibrer.

twee [twiː] *a* (*fussy*) maniéré.

tweed [twiːd] *n* tweed *m*.

tweezers ['twiːzəz] *npl* pince *f* (à épiler).

twelve [twelv] *a & n* douze (*m*). ◆**twelfth** *a & n* douzième (*mf*).

twenty ['twentɪ] *a & n* vingt (*m*). ◆**twentieth** *a & n* vingtième (*mf*).

twerp [twɜːp] *n* *Sl* crétin, -ine *mf*.

twice [twaɪs] *adv* deux fois; **t. as heavy/etc** deux fois plus lourd/etc; **t. a month/etc**, **t. monthly/etc** deux fois par mois/etc.

twiddle ['twɪd(ə)l] *vti* **to t. (with) sth** (*pencil, knob etc*) tripoter qch; **to t. one's thumbs** se tourner les pouces.

twig [twɪg] **1** *n* (*of branch*) brindille *f*. **2** *vti* (-gg-) (*understand*) *Sl* piger.

twilight ['twaɪlaɪt] *n* crépuscule *m*; – *a* crépusculaire.

twin [twɪn] *n* jumeau *m*, jumelle *f*; **identical t.** vrai jumeau; **t. brother** frère *m* jumeau; **t. beds** lits *mpl* jumeaux; **t. town** ville *f* jumelée; – *vt* (-nn-) (*town*) jumeler. ◆**twinning** *n* jumelage *m*.

twine [twaɪn] **1** *n* (*string*) ficelle *f*. **2** *vi* (*twist*) s'enlacer (**round** autour de).

twinge [twɪndʒ] *n* **a t. (of pain)** un élancement; **a t. of remorse** un pincement de remords.

twinkle ['twɪŋk(ə)l] *vi* (*of star*) scintiller; (*of eye*) pétiller; – *n* scintillement *m*; pétillement *m*.

twirl [twɜːl] *vi* tournoyer; – *vt* faire tournoyer; (*moustache*) tortiller.

twist [twɪst] *vt* (*wine, arm etc*) tordre; (*roll round*) enrouler; (*weave together*) entortiller; (*knob*) tourner; (*truth etc*) *Fig* déformer; **to t. s.o.'s arm** *Fig* forcer la main à qn; – *vi* (*wind*) s'entortiller (**round sth** autour de qch); (*of road, river*) serpenter; – *n* torsion *f*; (*turn*) tour *m*; (*in rope*) entortillement *m*; (*bend in road*) tournant *m*; (*in story*) coup *m* de théâtre; (*in event*) tournure *f*; (*of lemon*) zeste *m*; **a road full of twists** une route qui fait des zigzags. ◆**—ed** *a* (*ankle, wire, mind*) tordu. ◆**—er** *n* **tongue t.** mot *m* or expression *f* imprononçable.

twit [twɪt] *n* *Fam* idiot, -ote *mf*.

twitch [twɪtʃ] **1** *n* (*nervous*) tic *m*; – *vi* (*of person*) avoir un tic; (*of muscle*) se convulser. **2** *n* (*jerk*) secousse *f*.

twitter ['twɪtər] *vi* (*of bird*) pépier.

two [tuː] *a & n* deux (*m*). ◆**t.-cycle** *n* *Am* = **t.-stroke**. ◆**t.-'faced** *a* *Fig* hypocrite. ◆**t.-'legged** *a* bipède. ◆**t.-piece** *n* (*garment*) deux-pièces *m inv*. ◆**t.-'seater** *n* *Aut* voiture *f* à deux places. ◆**t.-stroke** *n* **t.-stroke (engine)** deux-temps *m inv*. ◆**t.-way** *a* (*traffic*) dans les deux sens; **t.-way radio** émetteur-récepteur *m*.

twofold ['tuɪfəʊld] *a* double; – *adv* **to increase t.** doubler.
twosome ['tuɪsəm] *n* couple *m*.
tycoon [taɪ'kuɪn] *n* magnat *m*.
type[1] [taɪp] *n* **1** (*example, person*) type *m*; (*sort*) genre *m*, sorte *f*, type *m*; **blood t.** groupe *m* sanguin. **2** (*print*) Typ caractères *mpl*; **in large t.** en gros caractères. ◆**typesetter** *n* compositeur, trice *mf*.
typ/e[2] [taɪp] *vti* (*write*) taper (à la machine). ◆—**ing** *n* dactylo(graphie) *f*; **a page of t.** une page dactylographiée; **t. error** faute *f* de frappe. ◆**typewriter** *n* machine *f* à

écrire. ◆**typewritten** *a* dactylographié.
◆**typist** *n* dactylo *f*.
typhold ['taɪfɔɪd] *n* **t. (fever)** Med typhoïde *f*.
typhoon [taɪ'fuɪn] *n* Met typhon *m*.
typical ['tɪpɪk(ə)l] *a* typique (**of** de); (*customary*) habituel; **that's t. (of him)!** c'est bien lui! ◆**typically** *adv* typiquement; (*as usual*) comme d'habitude. ◆**typify** *vt* être typique de; (*symbolize*) représenter.
tyranny ['tɪrənɪ] *n* tyrannie *f*. ◆**ty'rannical** *a* tyrannique. ◆**tyrant** ['taɪərənt] *n* tyran *m*.
tyre ['taɪər] *n* pneu *m*.

U

U, u [juɪ] *n* U, u *m*. ◆**U-turn** *n* Aut demi-tour *m*; Fig Pej volte-face *f inv*.
ubiquitous [juɪ'bɪkwɪtəs] *a* omniprésent.
udder ['ʌdər] *n* (*of cow etc*) pis *m*.
ugh! [ɜɪ(h)] *int* pouah!
ugly ['ʌglɪ] *a* (**-ier, -iest**) laid, vilain. ◆**ugliness** *n* laideur *f*.
UK [juɪ'keɪ] *abbr* = **United Kingdom.**
ulcer ['ʌlsər] *n* ulcère *m*.
ulterior [ʌl'tɪərɪər] *a* **u. motive** arrière-pensée *f*.
ultimate ['ʌltɪmət] *a* (*final, last*) ultime; (*definitive*) définitif; (*basic*) fondamental; (*authority*) suprême. ◆—**ly** *adv* (*finally*) à la fin; (*fundamentally*) en fin de compte; (*subsequently*) à une date ultérieure.
ultimatum [ʌltɪ'meɪtəm] *n* ultimatum *m*.
ultra- ['ʌltrə] *pref* ultra-.
ultramodern [ʌltrə'mɒdən] *a* ultramoderne.
ultraviolet [ʌltrə'vaɪələt] *a* ultraviolet.
umbilical [ʌm'bɪlɪk(ə)l] *a* **u. cord** cordon *m* ombilical.
umbrage ['ʌmbrɪdʒ] *n* **to take u.** se froisser (**at** de).
umbrella [ʌm'brelə] *n* parapluie *m*; **u. stand** porte-parapluies *m inv*.
umpire ['ʌmpaɪər] *n* Sp arbitre *m*; – *vt* arbitrer.
umpteen [ʌmp'tiɪn] *a* (*many*) Fam je ne sais combien de. ◆**umpteenth** *a* Fam énième.
un- [ʌn] *pref* in-, peu, non, sans.
UN [juɪ'en] *abbr* = **United Nations.**
unabashed [ʌnə'bæʃt] *a* nullement déconcerté.
unabated [ʌnə'beɪtɪd] *a* aussi fort qu'avant.
unable [ʌn'eɪb(ə)l] *a* **to be u. to do** être inca-

pable de faire; **he's u. to swim** il ne sait pas nager.
unabridged [ʌnə'brɪdʒd] *a* intégral.
unacceptable [ʌnək'septəb(ə)l] *a* inacceptable.
unaccompanied [ʌnə'kʌmpənɪd] *a* (*person*) non accompagné; (*singing*) sans accompagnement.
unaccountable [ʌnə'kaʊntəb(ə)l] *a* inexplicable. ◆—**ly** *adv* inexplicablement.
unaccounted [ʌnə'kaʊntɪd] *a* **to be (still) u. for** rester introuvable.
unaccustomed [ʌnə'kʌstəmd] *a* inaccoutumé; **to be u. to sth/to doing** ne pas être habitué à qch/à faire.
unadulterated [ʌnə'dʌltəreɪtɪd] *a* pur.
unaided [ʌn'eɪdɪd] *a* sans aide.
unanimity [juɪnə'nɪmɪtɪ] *n* unanimité *f*. ◆**u'nanimous** *a* unanime. ◆**u'nanimously** *adv* à l'unanimité.
unappetizing [ʌn'æpɪtaɪzɪŋ] *a* peu appétissant.
unapproachable [ʌnə'prəʊtʃəb(ə)l] *a* (*person*) inabordable.
unarmed [ʌn'ɑɪmd] *a* (*person*) non armé; (*combat*) à mains nues.
unashamed [ʌnə'ʃeɪmd] *a* éhonté; **she's u. about it** elle n'en a pas honte. ◆—**ly** *-ɪdlɪ* *adv* sans vergogne.
unassailable [ʌnə'seɪləb(ə)l] *a* (*argument, reputation*) inattaquable.
unassuming [ʌnə'sjuɪmɪŋ] *a* modeste.
unattached [ʌnə'tætʃt] *a* (*independent, not married*) libre.
unattainable [ʌnə'teɪnəb(ə)l] *a* (*goal, aim*) inaccessible.

unattended [ʌnə'tendɪd] *a* sans surveillance.

unattractive [ʌnə'træktɪv] *a* (*idea, appearance etc*) peu attrayant; (*character*) peu sympathique; (*ugly*) laid.

unauthorized [ʌn'ɔːθəraɪzd] *a* non autorisé.

unavailable [ʌnə'veɪləb(ə)l] *a* (*person, funds*) indisponible; (*article* Com) épuisé.

unavoidab/le [ʌnə'vɔɪdəb(ə)l] *a* inévitable. ◆—**ly** *adv* inévitablement; (*delayed*) pour une raison indépendante de sa volonté.

unaware [ʌnə'weər] *a* to be u. of ignorer; to be u. that ignorer que. ◆**unawares** *adv* to catch s.o. u. prendre qn au dépourvu.

unbalanced [ʌn'bælənst] *a* (*mind, person*) déséquilibré.

unbearab/le [ʌn'beərəb(ə)l] *a* insupportable. ◆—**ly** *adv* insupportablement.

unbeatable [ʌn'biːtəb(ə)l] *a* imbattable. ◆**unbeaten** *a* (*player*) invaincu; (*record*) non battu.

unbeknown(st) [ʌnbɪ'nəʊn(st)] *a* u. to à l'insu de.

unbelievable [ʌnbɪ'liːvəb(ə)l] *a* incroyable. ◆**unbelieving** *a* incrédule.

unbend [ʌn'bend] *vi* (*pt & pp* unbent) (*relax*) se détendre. ◆—**ing** *a* inflexible.

unbias(s)ed [ʌn'baɪəst] *a* impartial.

unblock [ʌn'blɒk] *vt* (*sink etc*) déboucher.

unborn [ʌn'bɔːn] *a* (*child*) à naître.

unbounded [ʌn'baʊndɪd] *a* illimité.

unbreakable [ʌn'breɪkəb(ə)l] *a* incassable. ◆**unbroken** *a* (*continuous*) continu; (*intact*) intact; (*record*) non battu.

unbridled [ʌn'braɪd(ə)ld] *a* Fig débridé.

unburden [ʌn'bɜːd(ə)n] *vt* to u. oneself Fig s'épancher (to auprès de, avec).

unbutton [ʌn'bʌt(ə)n] *vt* déboutonner.

uncalled-for [ʌn'kɔːldfɔːr] *a* déplacé, injustifié.

uncanny [ʌn'kænɪ] *a* (-**ier**, -**iest**) étrange, mystérieux.

unceasing [ʌn'siːsɪŋ] *a* incessant. ◆—**ly** *adv* sans cesse.

unceremoniously [ʌnserɪ'məʊnɪəslɪ] *adv* (*to treat*) sans ménagement; (*to show out*) brusquement.

uncertain [ʌn'sɜːt(ə)n] *a* incertain (about, of de); it's or he's u. whether or that il n'est pas certain que (+ *sub*). ◆**uncertainty** *n* incertitude *f*.

unchanged [ʌn'tʃeɪndʒd] *a* inchangé. ◆**unchanging** *a* immuable.

uncharitable [ʌn'tʃærɪtəb(ə)l] *a* peu charitable.

unchecked [ʌn'tʃekt] *adv* sans opposition.

uncivil [ʌn'sɪv(ə)l] *a* impoli, incivil.

uncivilized [ʌn'sɪvɪlaɪzd] *a* barbare.

uncle ['ʌŋk(ə)l] *n* oncle *m*.

unclear [ʌn'klɪər] *a* (*meaning*) qui n'est pas clair; (*result*) incertain; it's u. whether . . . on ne sait pas très bien si . . . .

uncomfortable [ʌn'kʌmftəb(ə)l] *a* (*house, chair etc*) inconfortable; (*heat, experience*) désagréable; (*feeling*) troublant; she is or feels u. (*uneasy*) elle est mal à l'aise.

uncommon [ʌn'kɒmən] *a* rare. ◆—**ly** *adv* (*very*) extraordinairement; not u. (*fairly often*) assez souvent.

uncommunicative [ʌnkə'mjuːnɪkətɪv] *a* peu communicatif.

uncomplicated [ʌn'kɒmplɪkeɪtɪd] *a* simple.

uncompromising [ʌn'kɒmprəmaɪzɪŋ] *a* intransigeant.

unconcerned [ʌnkən'sɜːnd] *a* (*not anxious*) imperturbable; (*indifferent*) indifférent (by, with à).

unconditional [ʌnkən'dɪʃ(ə)nəl] *a* inconditionnel; (*surrender*) sans condition.

unconfirmed [ʌnkən'fɜːmd] *a* non confirmé.

uncongenial [ʌnkən'dʒiːnɪəl] *a* peu agréable; (*person*) antipathique.

unconnected [ʌnkə'nektɪd] *a* (*events, facts etc*) sans rapport (with avec).

unconscious [ʌn'kɒnʃəs] *a* Med sans connaissance; (*desire*) inconscient; u. of (*unaware of*) inconscient de; – *n* Psy inconscient *m*. ◆—**ly** *adv* inconsciemment.

uncontrollable [ʌnkən'trəʊləb(ə)l] *a* (*emotion, laughter*) irrépressible.

unconventional [ʌnkən'venʃ(ə)nəl] *a* peu conventionnel.

unconvinced [ʌnkən'vɪnst] *a* to be or remain u. ne pas être convaincu (of de). ◆**unconvincing** *a* peu convaincant.

uncooperative [ʌnkəʊ'ɒp(ə)rətɪv] *a* peu coopératif.

uncork [ʌn'kɔːk] *vt* (*bottle*) déboucher.

uncouple [ʌn'kʌp(ə)l] *vt* (*carriages*) Rail dételer.

uncouth [ʌn'kuːθ] *a* grossier.

uncover [ʌn'kʌvər] *vt* (*saucepan, conspiracy etc*) découvrir.

unctuous ['ʌŋktʃʊəs] *a* (*insincere*) onctueux.

uncut [ʌn'kʌt] *a* (*film, play*) intégral; (*diamond*) brut.

undamaged [ʌn'dæmɪdʒd] *a* (*goods*) en bon état.

undaunted [ʌn'dɔːntɪd] *a* nullement découragé.

undecided [ʌndɪ'saɪdɪd] *a* (*person*) indécis

(about sur); **I'm u. whether to do it or not** je n'ai pas décidé si je le ferai ou non.
undefeated [ʌndɪ'fiːtɪd] *a* invaincu.
undeniable [ʌndɪ'naɪəb(ə)l] *a* incontestable.
under ['ʌndər] *prep* sous; (*less than*) moins de; (*according to*) selon; **children u. nine** les enfants de moins de *or* enfants au-dessous de neuf ans; **u. the circumstances** dans les circonstances; **u. there** là-dessous; **u. it** dessous; **u. (the command of)** s.o. sous les ordres de qn; **u. age** mineur; **u. discussion/repair** en discussion/réparation; **u. way** (*in progress*) en cours; (*on the way*) en route; **to be u. the impression that** avoir l'impression que; – *adv* au-dessous.
under- ['ʌndər] *pref* sous-.
undercarriage ['ʌndəkærɪdʒ] *n* (*of aircraft*) train m d'atterrissage.
undercharge [ʌndə'tʃɑːdʒ] *vt* **I undercharged him (for it)** je ne (le) lui ai pas fait payer assez.
underclothes ['ʌndəkləʊðz] *npl* sous-vêtements *mpl*.
undercoat ['ʌndəkəʊt] *n* (*of paint*) couche *f* de fond.
undercooked [ʌndə'kʊkt] *a* pas assez cuit.
undercover [ʌndə'kʌvər] *a* (*agent, operation*) secret.
undercurrent ['ʌndəkʌrənt] *n* (*in sea*) courant m (sous-marin); **an u. of** *Fig* un courant profond de.
undercut [ʌndə'kʌt] *vt* (*pt & pp* undercut, *pres p* undercutting) *Com* vendre moins cher que.
underdeveloped [ʌndədɪ'veləpt] *a* (*country*) sous-développé.
underdog ['ʌndədɒg] *n* (*politically, socially*) opprimé, -ée *mf*; (*likely loser*) perdant, -ante *mf* probable.
underdone [ʌndə'dʌn] *a* *Culin* pas assez cuit; (*steak*) saignant.
underestimate [ʌndər'estɪmeɪt] *vt* sous-estimer.
underfed [ʌndə'fed] *a* sous-alimenté.
underfoot [ʌndə'fʊt] *adv* sous les pieds.
undergo [ʌndə'gəʊ] *vt* (*pt* underwent, *pp* undergone) subir.
undergraduate [ʌndə'grædjʊət] *n* étudiant, -ante *mf* (qui prépare la licence).
underground ['ʌndəgraʊnd] *a* souterrain; (*secret*) *Fig* clandestin; – *n* *Rail* métro m; (*organization*) *Pol* résistance *f*; – [ʌndə'graʊnd] *adv* sous terre; **to go u.** (*of fugitive etc*) *Fig* passer dans la clandestinité.
undergrowth ['ʌndəgrəʊθ] *n* sous-bois m inv.

underhand [ʌndə'hænd] *a* (*dishonest*) sournois.
underlie [ʌndə'laɪ] *vt* (*pt* underlay, *pp* underlain, *pres p* underlying) sous-tendre. ◆**underlying** *a* (*basic*) fondamental; (*hidden*) profond.
underline [ʌndə'laɪn] *vt* (*text, idea etc*) souligner.
undermanned [ʌndə'mænd] *a* (*office etc*) à court de personnel.
undermine [ʌndə'maɪn] *vt* (*building, strength, society etc*) miner, saper.
underneath [ʌndə'niːθ] *prep* sous; – *adv* (en) dessous; **the book u.** le livre d'en dessous; – *n* dessous m.
undernourished [ʌndə'nʌrɪʃt] *a* sous-alimenté.
underpants ['ʌndəpænts] *npl* (*male underwear*) slip m; (*loose, long*) caleçon m.
underpass ['ʌndəpɑːs] *n* (*for cars or pedestrians*) passage m souterrain.
underpay [ʌndə'peɪ] *vt* sous-payer. ◆**underpaid** *a* sous-payé.
underpriced [ʌndə'praɪst] *a* **it's u.** le prix est trop bas, c'est bradé.
underprivileged [ʌndə'prɪvɪlɪdʒd] *a* défavorisé.
underrate [ʌndə'reɪt] *vt* sous-estimer.
undershirt ['ʌndəʃɜːt] *n* *Am* tricot m or maillot m de corps.
underside ['ʌndəsaɪd] *n* dessous m.
undersigned ['ʌndəsaɪnd] *a* soussigné; **I the u.** je soussigné(e).
undersized [ʌndə'saɪzd] *a* trop petit.
underskirt ['ʌndəskɜːt] *n* jupon m.
understaffed [ʌndə'stɑːft] *a* à court de personnel.
understand [ʌndə'stænd] *vti* (*pt & pp* understood) comprendre; **I u. that** (*hear*) je crois comprendre que, il paraît que; **I've been given to u. that** on m'a fait comprendre que. ◆**—ing** *n* (*act, faculty*) compréhension *f*; (*agreement*) accord m, entente *f*; (*sympathy*) entente *f*; **on the u. that** à condition que (+ *sub*); – *a* (*person*) compréhensif. ◆**understood** *a* (*agreed*) entendu; (*implied*) sous-entendu. ◆**understandable** *a* compréhensible. ◆**understandably** *adv* naturellement.
understatement ['ʌndəsteɪtmənt] *n* euphémisme m.
understudy ['ʌndəstʌdɪ] *n* *Th* doublure *f*.
undertak/e [ʌndə'teɪk] *vt* (*pt* undertook, *pp* undertaken) (*task*) entreprendre; (*responsibility*) assumer; **to u. to do** se charger de faire. ◆**—ing** *n* (*task*) entreprise *f*; (*prom-*

ise) promesse *f*; **to give an u.** promettre (**that** que).

undertaker ['ʌndəteɪkər] *n* entrepreneur *m* de pompes funèbres.

undertone ['ʌndətəʊn] *n* **in an u.** à mi-voix; **an u. of** (*criticism, sadness etc*) *Fig* une note de.

undervalue [ʌndə'væljuː] *vt* sous-évaluer; **it's undervalued at ten pounds** ça vaut plus que dix livres.

underwater [ʌndə'wɔːtər] *a* sous-marin; – *adv* sous l'eau.

underwear ['ʌndəweər] *n* sous-vêtements *mpl*.

underweight [ʌndə'weɪt] *a* (*person*) qui ne pèse pas assez; (*goods*) d'un poids insuffisant.

underworld ['ʌndəwɜːld] *n* **the u.** (*criminals*) le milieu, la pègre.

undesirable [ʌndɪ'zaɪərəb(ə)l] *a* peu souhaitable (**that** que (+ *sub*)); (*person*) indésirable; – *n* (*person*) indésirable *mf*.

undetected [ʌndɪ'tektɪd] *a* non découvert; **to go u.** passer inaperçu.

undies ['ʌndɪz] *npl* (*female underwear*) *Fam* dessous *mpl*.

undignified [ʌn'dɪgnɪfaɪd] *a* qui manque de dignité.

undisciplined [ʌn'dɪsɪplɪnd] *a* indiscipliné.

undiscovered [ʌndɪ'skʌvəd] *a* **to remain u.** ne pas être découvert.

undisputed [ʌndɪ'spjuːtɪd] *a* incontesté.

undistinguished [ʌndɪ'stɪŋgwɪʃt] *a* médiocre.

undivided [ʌndɪ'vaɪdɪd] *a* **my u. attention** toute mon attention.

undo [ʌn'duː] *vt* (*pt* **undid**, *pp* **undone**) défaire; (*bad person, hands*) détacher, délier; (*a wrong*) réparer. ◆**—ing** *n* (*downfall*) perte *f*, ruine *f*. ◆**undone** *a* **to leave u.** (*work etc*) ne pas faire; **to come u.** (*of knot etc*) se défaire.

undoubted [ʌn'daʊtɪd] *a* indubitable. ◆**—ly** *adv* indubitablement.

undreamt-of [ʌn'dremtɒv] *a* insoupçonné.

undress [ʌn'dres] *vi* se déshabiller; – *vt* déshabiller; **to get undressed** se déshabiller.

undue [ʌn'djuː] *a* excessif. ◆**unduly** *adv* excessivement.

undulating ['ʌndjʊleɪtɪŋ] *a* (*movement*) onduleux; (*countryside*) vallonné.

undying [ʌn'daɪɪŋ] *a* éternel.

unearned [ʌn'ɜːnd] *a* **u. income** rentes *fpl*.

unearth [ʌn'ɜːθ] *vt* (*from ground*) déterrer; (*discover*) *Fig* dénicher, déterrer.

unearthly [ʌn'ɜːθlɪ] *a* sinistre, mystérieux; **u. hour** *Fam* heure *f* indue.

uneasy [ʌn'iːzɪ] *a* (*peace, situation*) précaire; (*silence*) gêné; **to be** or **feel u.** (*ill at ease*) être mal à l'aise, être gêné; (*worried*) être inquiet.

uneconomic(al) [ʌniːkə'nɒmɪk((ə)l)] *a* peu économique.

uneducated [ʌn'edʒʊkeɪtɪd] *a* (*person*) inculte; (*accent*) populaire.

unemployed [ʌnɪm'plɔɪd] *a* sans travail, en chômage; – *n* **the u.** les chômeurs *mpl*. ◆**unemployment** *n* chômage *m*.

unending [ʌn'endɪŋ] *a* interminable.

unenthusiastic [ʌnɪnθjuːzɪ'æstɪk] *a* peu enthousiaste.

unenviable [ʌn'envɪəb(ə)l] *a* peu enviable.

unequal [ʌn'iːkwəl] *a* inégal; **to be u. to** (*task*) ne pas être à la hauteur de. ◆**unequalled** *a* (*incomparable*) inégalé.

unequivocal [ʌnɪ'kwɪvək(ə)l] *a* sans équivoque.

unerring [ʌn'ɜːrɪŋ] *a* infaillible.

unethical [ʌn'eθɪk(ə)l] *a* immoral.

uneven [ʌn'iːv(ə)n] *a* inégal.

uneventful [ʌnɪ'ventfəl] *a* (*journey, life etc*) sans histoires.

unexceptionable [ʌnɪk'sepʃ(ə)nəb(ə)l] *a* irréprochable.

unexpected [ʌnɪk'spektɪd] *a* inattendu. ◆**—ly** *adv* à l'improviste; (*suddenly*) subitement; (*unusually*) exceptionnellement.

unexplained [ʌnɪk'spleɪnd] *a* inexpliqué.

unfailing [ʌn'feɪlɪŋ] *a* (*optimism, courage, support etc*) inébranlable; (*supply*) inépuisable.

unfair [ʌn'feər] *a* injuste (**to s.o.** envers qn); (*competition*) déloyal. ◆**—ly** *adv* injustement. ◆**—ness** *n* injustice *f*.

unfaithful [ʌn'feɪθfəl] *a* infidèle (**to** à).

unfamiliar [ʌnfə'mɪlɪər] *a* inconnu, peu familier; **to be u. with** ne pas connaître.

unfashionable [ʌn'fæʃ(ə)nəb(ə)l] *a* (*subject etc*) démodé; (*district etc*) peu chic *inv*, ringard; **it's u. to do** il n'est pas de bon ton de faire.

unfasten [ʌn'fɑːs(ə)n] *vt* défaire.

unfavourable [ʌn'feɪv(ə)rəb(ə)l] *a* défavorable.

unfeeling [ʌn'fiːlɪŋ] *a* insensible.

unfinished [ʌn'fɪnɪʃt] *a* inachevé; **to have some u. business** avoir une affaire à régler.

unfit [ʌn'fɪt] *a* (*unwell*) mal fichu; (*unsuited*) inapte (**for sth** à qch, **to do** à faire); (*unworthy*) indigne (**for sth** de qch, **to do** de faire);

to be u. to do (*incapable*) ne pas être en état de faire.

unflagging [ʌnˈflægɪŋ] *a* (*zeal*) inlassable; (*interest*) soutenu.

unflappable [ʌnˈflæpəb(ə)l] *a Fam* imperturbable.

unflattering [ʌnˈflæt(ə)rɪŋ] *a* peu flatteur.

unflinching [ʌnˈflɪntʃɪŋ] *a* (*fearless*) intrépide.

unfold [ʌnˈfəʊld] *vt* déplier; (*wings*) déployer; (*ideas, plan*) Fig exposer; – *vi* (*of story, view*) se dérouler.

unforeseeable [ʌnfɔːˈsiːəb(ə)l] *a* imprévisible. ◆**unforeseen** *a* imprévu.

unforgettable [ʌnfəˈgetəb(ə)l] *a* inoubliable.

unforgivable [ʌnfəˈgɪvəb(ə)l] *a* impardonnable.

unfortunate [ʌnˈfɔːtʃ(ə)nət] *a* malheureux; (*event*) fâcheux; **you were u.** tu n'as pas eu de chance. ◆**—ly** *adv* malheureusement.

unfounded [ʌnˈfaʊndɪd] *a* (*rumour etc*) sans fondement.

unfriendly [ʌnˈfrendlɪ] *a* peu amical, froid. ◆**unfriendliness** *n* froideur *f*.

unfulfilled [ʌnfʊlˈfɪld] *a* (*desire*) insatisfait; (*plan*) non réalisé; (*condition*) non rempli.

unfurl [ʌnˈfɜːl] *vt* (*flag etc*) déployer.

unfurnished [ʌnˈfɜːnɪʃt] *a* non meublé.

ungainly [ʌnˈgeɪnlɪ] *a* (*clumsy*) gauche.

ungodly [ʌnˈgɒdlɪ] *a* impie; **u. hour** *Fam* heure *f* indue.

ungrammatical [ʌngrəˈmætɪk(ə)l] *a* non grammatical.

ungrateful [ʌnˈgreɪtfəl] *a* ingrat.

unguarded [ʌnˈgɑːdɪd] *a* **in an u. moment** dans un moment d'inattention.

unhappy [ʌnˈhæpɪ] *a* (**-ier, -iest**) (*sad*) malheureux, triste; (*worried*) inquiet; **u. with** (*not pleased*) mécontent de; **he's u. about doing it** ça le dérange de le faire. ◆**unhappily** *adv* (*unfortunately*) malheureusement. ◆**unhappiness** *n* tristesse *f*.

unharmed [ʌnˈhɑːmd] *a* indemne, sain et sauf.

unhealthy [ʌnˈhelθɪ] *a* (**-ier, -iest**) (*person*) en mauvaise santé; (*climate, place, job*) malsain; (*lungs*) malade.

unheard-of [ʌnˈhɜːdɒv] *a* (*unprecedented*) inouï.

unheeded [ʌnˈhiːdɪd] *a* **it went u.** on n'en a pas tenu compte.

unhelpful [ʌnˈhelpfəl] *a* (*person*) peu obligeant *or* serviable; (*advice*) peu utile.

unhinge [ʌnˈhɪndʒ] *vt* (*person, mind*) déséquilibrer.

unholy [ʌnˈhəʊlɪ] *a* (**-ier, -iest**) impie; (*din*) Fam de tous les diables.

unhook [ʌnˈhʊk] *vt* (*picture, curtain*) décrocher; (*dress*) dégrafer.

unhoped-for [ʌnˈhəʊptfɔːr] *a* inespéré.

unhurried [ʌnˈhʌrɪd] *a* (*movement*) lent; (*stroll, journey*) fait sans hâte.

unhurt [ʌnˈhɜːt] *a* indemne, sain et sauf.

unhygienic [ʌnhaɪˈdʒiːnɪk] *a* pas très hygiénique.

unicorn [ˈjuːnɪkɔːn] *n* licorne *f*.

uniform [ˈjuːnɪfɔːm] **1** *n* uniforme *m*. **2** *a* (*regular*) uniforme; (*temperature*) constant. ◆**uniformed** *a* en uniforme. ◆**uni'formity** *n* uniformité *f*. ◆**uniformly** *adv* uniformément.

unify [ˈjuːnɪfaɪ] *vt* unifier. ◆**unifi'cation** *n* unification *f*.

unilateral [juːnɪˈlæt(ə)rəl] *a* unilatéral.

unimaginable [ʌnɪˈmædʒɪnəb(ə)l] *a* inimaginable. ◆**unimaginative** *a* (*person, plan etc*) qui manque d'imagination.

unimpaired [ʌnɪmˈpeəd] *a* intact.

unimportant [ʌnɪmˈpɔːtənt] *a* peu important.

uninhabitable [ʌnɪnˈhæbɪtəb(ə)l] *a* inhabitable. ◆**uninhabited** *a* inhabité.

uninhibited [ʌnɪnˈhɪbɪtɪd] *a* (*person*) sans complexes.

uninitiated [ʌnɪˈnɪʃɪeɪtɪd] *n* **the u.** les profanes *mpl*, les non-initiés.

uninjured [ʌnˈɪndʒəd] *a* indemne.

uninspiring [ʌnɪnˈspaɪərɪŋ] *a* (*subject etc*) pas très inspirant.

unintelligible [ʌnɪnˈtelɪdʒəb(ə)l] *a* inintelligible.

unintentional [ʌnɪnˈtenʃ(ə)nəl] *a* involontaire.

uninterested [ʌnˈɪntrɪstɪd] *a* indifférent (**in** à). ◆**uninteresting** *a* (*book etc*) inintéressant; (*person*) fastidieux.

uninterrupted [ʌnɪntəˈrʌptɪd] *a* ininterrompu.

uninvited [ʌnɪnˈvaɪtɪd] *a* (*to arrive*) sans invitation. ◆**uninviting** *a* peu attrayant.

union [ˈjuːnjən] *n* union *f*; (*trade union*) syndicat *m*; – *a* syndical; (**trade**) **u. member** syndiqué, -ée *mf*; **U. Jack** drapeau *m* britannique. ◆**unionist** *n* **trade u.** syndicaliste *mf*. ◆**unionize** *vt* syndiquer.

unique [juːˈniːk] *a* unique. ◆**—ly** *adv* exceptionnellement.

unisex [ˈjuːnɪseks] *a* (*clothes etc*) unisexe *inv*.

unison [ˈjuːnɪs(ə)n] *n* **in u.** à l'unisson (**with** de).

unit [ˈjuːnɪt] *n* unité *f*; (*of furniture etc*) élément *m*; (*system*) bloc *m*; (*group, team*) groupe *m*; **u. trust** *Fin* fonds *m* commun de placement.

unite [juːˈnaɪt] *vt* unir; (*country, party*) unifier; **United Kingdom** Royaume-Uni *m*; **United Nations** (Organisation *f* des) Nations unies *fpl*; **United States (of America)** États-Unis *mpl* (d'Amérique); − *vi* s'unir. **◆unity** *n* (*cohesion*) unité *f*; (*harmony*) *Fig* harmonie *f*.

universal [juːnɪˈvɜːs(ə)l] *a* universel. **◆−ly** *adv* universellement.

universe [ˈjuːnɪvɜːs] *n* univers *m*.

university [juːnɪˈvɜːsɪtɪ] *n* université *f*; **at u.** à l'université; − *a* universitaire; (*student, teacher*) d'université.

unjust [ʌnˈdʒʌst] *a* injuste.

unjustified [ʌnˈdʒʌstɪfaɪd] *a* injustifié.

unkempt [ʌnˈkempt] *a* (*appearance*) négligé; (*hair*) mal peigné.

unkind [ʌnˈkaɪnd] *a* peu aimable (**to s.o.** avec qn); (*nasty*) méchant (**to s.o.** avec qn). **◆−ly** *adv* méchamment.

unknowingly [ʌnˈnəʊɪŋlɪ] *adv* inconsciemment.

unknown [ʌnˈnəʊn] *a* inconnu; **u. to me**, **he'd left** il était parti, ce que j'ignorais; − *n* (*person*) inconnu, -ue *mf*; **the u.** *Phil* l'inconnu *m*; **u. (quantity)** *Math & Fig* inconnue *f*.

unlawful [ʌnˈlɔːfəl] *a* illégal.

unleaded [ʌnˈledɪd] *a* (*gasoline*) *Am* sans plomb.

unleash [ʌnˈliːʃ] *vt* (*force etc*) déchaîner.

unless [ʌnˈles] *conj* à moins que; **u. she comes** à moins qu'elle ne vienne; **u. you work harder, you'll fail** à moins de travailler plus dur, vous échouerez.

unlike [ʌnˈlaɪk] *a* différent; − *prep* **u. me, she . . .** à la différence de moi *or* contrairement à moi, elle . . . ; **he's very u. his father** il n'est pas du tout comme son père; **that's u. him** ça ne lui ressemble pas.

unlikely [ʌnˈlaɪklɪ] *a* improbable; (*implausible*) invraisemblable; **she's u. to win** il est peu probable qu'elle gagne. **◆unlike-lihood** *n* improbabilité *f*.

unlimited [ʌnˈlɪmɪtɪd] *a* illimité.

unlisted [ʌnˈlɪstɪd] *a* (*phone number*) *Am* qui ne figure pas à l'annuaire.

unload [ʌnˈləʊd] *vt* décharger.

unlock [ʌnˈlɒk] *vt* ouvrir (*avec une clef*).

unlucky [ʌnˈlʌkɪ] *a* (-ier, -iest) (*person*) malchanceux; (*colour, number etc*) qui porte malheur; **you're u.** tu n'as pas de chance. **◆unluckily** *adv* malheureusement.

unmade [ʌnˈmeɪd] *a* (*bed*) défait.

unmanageable [ʌnˈmænɪdʒəb(ə)l] *a* (*child*) difficile; (*hair*) difficile à coiffer; (*packet, size*) peu maniable.

unmanned [ʌnˈmænd] *a* (*ship*) sans équipage; (*spacecraft*) inhabité.

unmarked [ʌnˈmɑːkt] *a* (*not blemished*) sans marque; **u. police car** voiture *f* banalisée.

unmarried [ʌnˈmærɪd] *a* célibataire.

unmask [ʌnˈmɑːsk] *vt* démasquer.

unmentionable [ʌnˈmenʃ(ə)nəb(ə)l] *a* dont il ne faut pas parler; (*unpleasant*) innommable.

unmercifully [ʌnˈmɜːsɪf(ə)lɪ] *adv* sans pitié.

unmistakable [ʌnmɪˈsteɪkəb(ə)l] *a* (*obvious*) indubitable; (*face, voice etc*) facilement reconnaissable.

unmitigated [ʌnˈmɪtɪgeɪtɪd] *a* (*disaster*) absolu; (*folly*) pur.

unmoved [ʌnˈmuːvd] *a* **to be u.** (*feel no emotion*) ne pas être ému (**by** par); (*be unconcerned*) être indifférent (**by** à).

unnatural [ʌnˈnætʃ(ə)rəl] *a* (*not normal*) pas naturel; (*crime*) contre nature; (*affected*) qui manque de naturel. **◆−ly** *adv* **not u.** naturellement.

unnecessary [ʌnˈnesəs(ə)rɪ] *a* inutile; (*superfluous*) superflu.

unnerve [ʌnˈnɜːv] *vt* désarçonner, déconcerter.

unnoticed [ʌnˈnəʊtɪst] *a* inaperçu.

unobstructed [ʌnəbˈstrʌktɪd] *a* (*road, view*) dégagé.

unobtainable [ʌnəbˈteɪnəb(ə)l] *a* impossible à obtenir.

unobtrusive [ʌnəbˈtruːsɪv] *a* discret.

unoccupied [ʌnˈɒkjʊpaɪd] *a* (*person, house*) inoccupé; (*seat*) libre.

unofficial [ʌnəˈfɪʃ(ə)l] *a* officieux; (*visit*) privé; (*strike*) sauvage. **◆−ly** *adv* à titre officieux.

unorthodox [ʌnˈɔːθədɒks] *a* peu orthodoxe.

unpack [ʌnˈpæk] *vt* (*case*) défaire; (*goods, belongings, contents*) déballer; **to u. a comb/etc from** sortir un peigne/*etc* de; − *vi* défaire sa valise; (*take out goods*) déballer.

unpaid [ʌnˈpeɪd] *a* (*bill, sum*) impayé; (*work, worker*) bénévole; (*leave*) non payé.

unpalatable [ʌnˈpælətəb(ə)l] *a* désagréable, déplaisant.

unparalleled [ʌnˈpærəleld] *a* sans égal.

unperturbed [ʌnpəˈtɜːbd] *a* nullement déconcerté.

unplanned [ʌnˈplænd] *a* (*visit, baby etc*) imprévu.

unpleasant [ʌnˈplezənt] *a* désagréable (**to s.o.** avec qn). **◆−ness** *n* caractère *m* désagréable (**of** de); (*quarrel*) petite querelle *f*.

unplug [ʌn'plʌg] *vt* (**-gg-**) *El* débrancher; (*unblock*) déboucher.

unpopular [ʌn'pɒpjʊlər] *a* impopulaire; **to be u. with** ne pas plaire à.

unprecedented [ʌn'presidentid] *a* sans précédent.

unpredictable [ʌnprɪ'dɪktəb(ə)l] *a* imprévisible; (*weather*) indécis.

unprepared [ʌnprɪ'peəd] *a* non préparé; (*speech*) improvisé; **to be u. for** (*not expect*) ne pas s'attendre à.

unprepossessing [ʌnpriːpə'zesɪŋ] *a* peu avenant.

unpretentious [ʌnprɪ'tenʃəs] *a* sans prétention.

unprincipled [ʌn'prɪnsɪp(ə)ld] *a* sans scrupules.

unprofessional [ʌnprə'feʃ(ə)nəl] *a* (*unethical*) contraire aux règles de sa profession.

unpublished [ʌn'pʌblɪʃt] *a* (*text, writer*) inédit.

unpunished [ʌn'pʌnɪʃt] *a* **to go u.** rester impuni.

unqualified [ʌn'kwɒlɪfaɪd] *a* **1** (*teacher etc*) non diplômé; **he's u. to do it** il n'est pas qualifié pour faire. **2** (*support*) sans réserve; (*success, rogue*) parfait.

unquestionab/le [ʌn'kwestʃ(ə)nəb(ə)l] *a* incontestable. ◆**—ly** *adv* incontestablement.

unravel [ʌn'ræv(ə)l] *vt* (**-ll-**, *Am* **-l-**) (*threads etc*) démêler; (*mystery*) *Fig* éclaircir.

unreal [ʌn'rɪəl] *a* irréel. ◆**unrea'listic** *a* peu réaliste.

unreasonable [ʌn'riːz(ə)nəb(ə)l] *a* qui n'est pas raisonnable; (*price*) excessif.

unrecognizable [ʌnrekəg'naɪzəb(ə)l] *a* méconnaissable.

unrelated [ʌnrɪ'leɪtɪd] *a* (*facts etc*) sans rapport (**to** avec); **we're u.** il n'y a aucun lien de parenté entre nous.

unrelenting [ʌnrɪ'lentɪŋ] *a* (*person*) implacable; (*effort*) acharné.

unreliable [ʌnrɪ'laɪəb(ə)l] *a* (*person*) peu sérieux, peu sûr; (*machine*) peu fiable.

unrelieved [ʌnrɪ'liːvd] *a* (*constant*) constant; (*colour*) uniforme.

unremarkable [ʌnrɪ'mɑːkəb(ə)l] *a* médiocre.

unrepeatable [ʌnrɪ'piːtəb(ə)l] *a* (*offer*) unique.

unrepentant [ʌnrɪ'pentənt] *a* impénitent.

unreservedly [ʌnrɪ'zɜːvɪdlɪ] *adv* sans réserve.

unrest [ʌn'rest] *n* troubles *mpl*, agitation *f*.

unrestricted [ʌnrɪ'strɪktɪd] *a* illimité; (*access*) libre.

unrewarding [ʌnrɪ'wɔːdɪŋ] *a* ingrat; (*financially*) peu rémunérateur.

unripe [ʌn'raɪp] *a* (*fruit*) vert, pas mûr.

unroll [ʌn'rəʊl] *vt* dérouler; – *vi* se dérouler.

unruffled [ʌn'rʌf(ə)ld] *a* (*person*) calme.

unruly [ʌn'ruːlɪ] *a* (**-ier, -iest**) indiscipliné.

unsafe [ʌn'seɪf] *a* (*place, machine etc*) dangereux; (*person*) en danger.

unsaid [ʌn'sed] *a* **to leave sth u.** passer qch sous silence.

unsaleable [ʌn'seɪləb(ə)l] *a* invendable.

unsatisfactory [ʌnsætɪs'fæktə(r)ɪ] *a* peu satisfaisant. ◆**un'satisfied** *a* insatisfait; **u. with** peu satisfait de.

unsavoury [ʌn'seɪv(ə)rɪ] *a* (*person, place etc*) répugnant.

unscathed [ʌn'skeɪðd] *a* indemne.

unscrew [ʌn'skruː] *vt* dévisser.

unscrupulous [ʌn'skruːpjʊləs] *a* (*person, act*) peu scrupuleux.

unseemly [ʌn'siːmlɪ] *a* inconvenant.

unseen [ʌn'siːn] **1** *a* inaperçu. **2** *n* (*translation*) *Sch* version *f*.

unselfish [ʌn'selfɪʃ] *a* (*person, motive etc*) désintéressé.

unsettl/e [ʌn'set(ə)l] *vt* (*person*) troubler. ◆**—ed** *a* (*weather, situation*) instable; (*in one's mind*) troublé; (*in a job*) mal à l'aise.

unshakeable [ʌn'ʃeɪkəb(ə)l] *a* (*person, faith*) inébranlable.

unshaven [ʌn'ʃeɪv(ə)n] *a* pas rasé.

unsightly [ʌn'saɪtlɪ] *a* laid, disgracieux.

unskilled [ʌn'skɪld] *a* inexpert; (*work*) de manœuvre; **u. worker** manœuvre *m*, ouvrier, -ière *mf* non qualifié(e).

unsociable [ʌn'səʊʃəb(ə)l] *a* insociable.

unsocial [ʌn'səʊʃəl] *a* **to work u. hours** travailler en dehors des heures de bureau.

unsolved [ʌn'sɒlvd] *a* (*problem*) non résolu; (*mystery*) inexpliqué; (*crime*) dont l'auteur n'est pas connu.

unsophisticated [ʌnsə'fɪstɪkeɪtɪd] *a* simple.

unsound [ʌn'saʊnd] *a* (*construction etc*) peu solide; (*method*) peu sûr; (*decision*) peu judicieux; **he is of u. mind** il n'a pas toute sa raison.

unspeakable [ʌn'spiːkəb(ə)l] *a* (*horrible*) innommable.

unspecified [ʌn'spesifaɪd] *a* indéterminé.

unsporting [ʌn'spɔːtɪŋ] *a* déloyal.

unstable [ʌn'steɪb(ə)l] *a* instable.

unsteady [ʌn'stedɪ] *a* (*hand, voice, step etc*) mal assuré; (*table, ladder etc*) instable. ◆**unsteadily** *adv* (*to walk*) d'un pas mal assuré.

unstinting [ʌnˈstɪntɪŋ] a (generosity) sans bornes.

unstoppable [ʌnˈstɒpəb(ə)l] a qu'on ne peut (pas) arrêter.

unstuck [ʌnˈstʌk] a **to come u.** (of stamp etc) se décoller; (fail) Fam se planter.

unsuccessful [ʌnsəkˈsesfəl] a (attempt etc) infructueux; (outcome, candidate) malheureux; (application) non retenu; **to be u.** ne pas réussir (**in doing** à faire); (of book, artist) ne pas avoir de succès. ◆—**ly** adv en vain, sans succès.

unsuitable [ʌnˈsuːtəb(ə)l] a qui ne convient pas (**for** à); (example) peu approprié; (manners, clothes) peu convenable. ◆**unsuited** a **u. to** impropre à; **they're u.** ils ne sont pas compatibles.

unsure [ʌnˈʃʊər] a incertain (**of, about** de).

unsuspecting [ʌnsəˈspektɪŋ] a qui ne se doute de rien.

unswerving [ʌnˈswɜːvɪŋ] a (loyalty etc) inébranlable.

unsympathetic [ʌnsɪmpəˈθetɪk] a incompréhensif; **u. to** indifférent à.

untangle [ʌnˈtæŋg(ə)l] vt (rope etc) démêler.

untapped [ʌnˈtæpt] a inexploité.

untenable [ʌnˈtenəb(ə)l] a (position) intenable.

unthinkable [ʌnˈθɪŋkəb(ə)l] a impensable, inconcevable.

untidy [ʌnˈtaɪdɪ] a (-ier, -iest) (appearance, hair) peu soigné; (room) en désordre; (unmethodical) désordonné. ◆**untidily** adv sans soin.

untie [ʌnˈtaɪ] vt (person, hands) détacher; (knot, parcel) défaire.

until [ʌnˈtɪl] prep jusqu'à; **u. then** jusque-là; **not u. tomorrow/etc** (in the future) pas avant demain/etc; **I didn't come u. Monday** (in the past) je ne suis venu que lundi; — conj v. **she comes** jusqu'à ce qu'elle vienne, en attendant qu'elle vienne; **do nothing u. I come** (before) ne fais rien avant que j'arrive.

untimely [ʌnˈtaɪmlɪ] a inopportun; (death) prématuré.

untiring [ʌnˈtaɪ(ə)rɪŋ] a infatigable.

untold [ʌnˈtəʊld] a (quantity, wealth) incalculable.

untoward [ʌntəˈwɔːd] a malencontreux.

untranslatable [ʌntrænˈsleɪtəb(ə)l] a intraduisible.

untroubled [ʌnˈtrʌb(ə)ld] a (calm) calme.

untrue [ʌnˈtruː] a faux. ◆**untruth** n contre-vérité f. ◆**untruthful** a (person) menteur; (statement) mensonger.

unused 1 [ʌnˈjuːzd] a (new) neuf; (not in use) inutilisé. **2** [ʌnˈjuːst] a **u. to sth/to doing** peu habitué à qch/à faire.

unusual [ʌnˈjuːʒʊəl] a exceptionnel, rare; (strange) étrange. ◆—**ly** adv exceptionnellement.

unveil [ʌnˈveɪl] vt dévoiler. ◆—**ing** n (ceremony) inauguration f.

unwanted [ʌnˈwɒntɪd] a (useless) superflu, dont on n'a pas besoin; (child) non désiré.

unwarranted [ʌnˈwɒrəntɪd] a injustifié.

unwavering [ʌnˈweɪv(ə)rɪŋ] a (belief etc) inébranlable.

unwelcome [ʌnˈwelkəm] a (news, fact) fâcheux; (gift, visit) inopportun; (person) importun.

unwell [ʌnˈwel] a indisposé.

unwieldy [ʌnˈwiːldɪ] a (package etc) encombrant.

unwilling [ʌnˈwɪlɪŋ] a **he's u. to do** il ne neut pas faire, il est peu disposé à faire. ◆—**ly** adv à contrecœur.

unwind [ʌnˈwaɪnd] **1** vt (thread etc) dérouler; — vi se dérouler. **2** vi (relax) Fam décompresser.

unwise [ʌnˈwaɪz] a imprudent. ◆—**ly** adv imprudemment.

unwitting [ʌnˈwɪtɪŋ] a involontaire. ◆—**ly** adv involontairement.

unworkable [ʌnˈwɜːkəb(ə)l] a (idea etc) impraticable.

unworthy [ʌnˈwɜːðɪ] a indigne (**of** de).

unwrap [ʌnˈræp] vt (-pp-) ouvrir, défaire.

unwritten [ʌnˈrɪt(ə)n] a (agreement) verbal, tacite.

unyielding [ʌnˈjiːldɪŋ] a (person) inflexible.

unzip [ʌnˈzɪp] vt (-pp-) ouvrir (la fermeture éclair® de).

up [ʌp] adv en haut; (in the air) en l'air; (of sun, hand) levé; (out of bed) levé, debout; (of road) en travaux; (of building) construit; (finished) fini; **to come or go up** monter; **to be up** (of price, level etc) être monté (**by** de); **up there** là-haut; **up above** au-dessus; **up on** (roof etc) sur; **further or higher up** plus haut; **up to** (as far as) jusqu'à; (task) Fig à la hauteur de; **to be up to doing** (capable) être de taille à faire; (in a position to) être à même de faire; **it's up to you to do it** c'est à toi de le faire; **it's up to you** ça dépend de toi; **where are you up to?** (in book etc) où en es-tu?; **what are you up to?** Fam que fais-tu?; **what's up?** (what's the matter?) Fam qu'est-ce qu'il y a?; **time's up** c'est l'heure; **halfway up** (on hill etc) à mi-chemin; **to walk up and down** marcher de long en large; **to be well up in** (versed in) Fam s'y connaître en; **to be up against**

(*confront*) être confronté à; **up (with) the workers**/*etc*! *Fam* vive(nt) les travailleurs/*etc*!; − *prep* (*a hill*) en haut de; (*a tree*) dans; (*a ladder*) sur; **to go up** (*hill, stairs*) monter; **to live up the street** habiter plus loin dans la rue; − *npl* **to have ups and downs** avoir des hauts et des bas; − *vt* (**-pp-**) (*increase*) *Fam* augmenter.
◆**up-and-'coming** *a* plein d'avenir.
◆**upbeat** *a* (*cheerful*) *Am Fam* optimiste.
◆**upbringing** *n* éducation *f*. ◆**upcoming** *a Am* imminent. ◆**up'date** *vt* mettre à jour. ◆**up'grade** *vt* (*job*) revaloriser; (*person*) promouvoir. ◆**up'hill 1** *adv* **to go u.** monter. **2** ['ʌphɪl] *a* (*struggle, task*) pénible. ◆**up'hold** *vt* (*pt & pp* **upheld**) maintenir. ◆**upkeep** *n* entretien *m*. ◆**uplift** [ʌp'lɪft] *vt* élever; − ['ʌplɪft] *n* élévation *f* spirituelle. ◆**upmarket** *a Com* haut de gamme. ◆**upright 1** *a & adv* (*erect*) droit; − *n* (*post*) montant *m*. **2** *a* (*honest*) droit. ◆**uprising** *n* insurrection *f*. ◆**up'root** *vt* (*plant, person*) déraciner. ◆**upside 'down** *adv* à l'envers; **to turn u. down** (*room, plans etc*) *Fig* chambouler. ◆**up'stairs** *adv* en haut; **to go u. monter** (l'escalier); − ['ʌpsteəz] *a* (*people, room*) du dessus. ◆**up'stream** *adv* en amont. ◆**upsurge** *n* (*of interest*) recrudescence *f*; (*of anger*) accès *m*. ◆**uptake** *n* **to be quick on the u.** comprendre vite. ◆**up'tight** *a Fam* (*tense*) crispé; (*angry*) en colère. ◆**up-to-'date** *a* moderne; (*information*) à jour; (*well-informed*) au courant (on de). ◆**upturn** *n* (*improvement*) amélioration *f* (in de); (*rise*) hausse *f* (in de). ◆**up'turned** *a* (*nose*) retroussé. ◆**upward** *a* (*movement*) ascendant; (*path*) qui monte; (*trend*) à la hausse. ◆**upwards** *adv* vers le haut; **from five francs u.** à partir de cinq francs; **u. of fifty** cinquante et plus.

upheaval [ʌp'hiːv(ə)l] *n* bouleversement *m*.

upholster [ʌp'həulstər] *vt* (*pad*) rembourrer; (*cover*) recouvrir. ◆**upholsterer** *n* tapissier *m*. ◆**upholstery** *n* (*activity*) réfection *f* de sièges; (*in car*) sièges *mpl*.

upon [ə'pɒn] *prep* sur.

upper ['ʌpər] **1** *a* supérieur; **u. class** aristocratie *f*; **to have/get the u. hand** avoir/prendre le dessus. **2** *n* (*of shoe*) empeigne *f*, dessus *m*. ◆**u.-'class** *a* aristocratique. ◆**uppermost** *a* (*highest*) le plus haut; **to be u.** (*on top*) être en dessus.

uproar ['ʌprɔːr] *n* tumulte *m*.

upset [ʌp'set] *vt* (*pt & pp* **upset**, *pres p* **upsetting**) (*knock over*) renverser; (*plans, stomach, routine etc*) déranger; **to u. s.o.** (*grieve*)

peiner qn; (*offend*) vexer qn; (*annoy*) contrarier qh; − *a* vexé; contrarié; (*stomach*) dérangé; − ['ʌpset] *n* (*in plans etc*) dérangement *m* (in de); (*grief*) peine *f*; **to have a stomach u.** avoir l'estomac dérangé.

upshot ['ʌpʃɒt] *n* résultat *m*.

upstart ['ʌpstɑːt] *n Pej* parvenu, -ue *mf*.

uranium [jʊ'reɪnɪəm] *n* uranium *m*.

urban ['ɜːbən] *a* urbain.

urbane [ɜː'beɪn] *a* courtois, urbain.

urchin ['ɜːtʃɪn] *n* polisson, -onne *mf*.

urge [ɜːdʒ] *vt* **to u. s.o. to do** (*advise*) conseiller vivement à qn de faire; **to u. on** (*person, team*) encourager; − *n* forte envie *f*, besoin *m*.

urgency ['ɜːdʒənsɪ] *n* urgence *f*; (*of request, tone*) insistance *f*. ◆**urgent** *a* urgent, pressant; (*tone*) insistant; (*letter*) urgent. ◆**urgently** *adv* d'urgence; (*insistently*) avec insistance.

urinal [jʊ'raɪn(ə)l] *n* urinoir *m*.

urine [jʊ'(ə)rɪn] *n* urine *f*. ◆**urinate** *vi* uriner.

urn [ɜːn] *n* urne *f*; (*for coffee or tea*) fontaine *f*.

us [əs, *stressed* ʌs] *pron* nous; **(to) us** (*indirect*) nous; **she sees us** elle nous voit; **he gives (to) us** il nous donne; **with us** avec nous; **all of us** nous tous; **let's** *or* **let us eat!** mangeons!

US [juː'es] *abbr* = **United States.**

USA [juːes'eɪ] *abbr* = **United States of America.**

usage ['juːsɪdʒ] *n* (*custom*) & *Ling* usage *m*.

use [juːs] *n* usage *m*, emploi *m*; (*way of using*) emploi *m*; **to have the u. of** avoir l'usage de; **to make u. of** se servir de; **in u.** en usage; **out of u.** hors d'usage; **ready for u.** prêt à l'emploi; **to be of u.** servir, être utile; **it's no u. crying**/*etc* ça ne sert à rien de pleurer/*etc*; **what's the u. of worrying**/*etc*? à quoi bon s'inquiéter/*etc*?, à quoi ça sert de s'inquiéter/*etc*?; **I have no u. for it** je n'en ai pas l'usage, qu'est-ce que je ferais de ça?; **he's no u.** (*hopeless*) il est nul; − [juːz] *vt* se servir de, utiliser, employer (**as** comme; **to do, for doing** pour faire); **it's used to do** *or* **for doing** ça sert à faire; **it's used as** ça sert de; **I u. it to clean** je m'en sers pour nettoyer, ça me sert à nettoyer; **to u. (up)** (*fuel etc*) consommer; (*supplies*) épuiser; (*money*) dépenser. ◆**used 1** [juːzd] *a* (*second-hand*) d'occasion; (*stamp*) oblitéré. **2** [juːst] *v aux* **I u. to do** avant, je faisais; − *a* **u. to sth/to doing** (*accustomed*) habitué à qch/à faire; **to get u. to** s'habituer à. ◆**useful** ['juːsfəl] *a* utile; **to**

come in u. être utile; **to make oneself u.** se rendre utile. ◆**usefulness** n utilité f. ◆**useless** ['juːsləs] a inutile; (*unusable*) inutilisable; (*person*) nul, incompétent. ◆**user** ['juːzər] n (*of road, dictionary etc*) usager m; (*of machine*) utilisateur, -trice mf.

usher ['ʌʃər] n (*in church or theatre*) placeur m; (*in law court*) huissier m; — vt **to u. in** faire entrer; (*period etc*) Fig inaugurer. ◆**ushe'rette** n Cin ouvreuse f.

USSR [juːˈesesaːr] n abbr (*Union of Soviet Socialist Republics*) URSS f.

usual ['juːʒuəl] a habituel, normal; **as u.** comme d'habitude; **it's her u. practice** c'est son habitude; — n **the u.** (*food, excuse etc*) Fam la même chose que d'habitude. ◆**—ly** adv d'habitude.

usurer ['juːʒərər] n usurier, -ière mf.

usurp [juːˈzɜːp] vt usurper.

utensil [juːˈtens(ə)l] n ustensile m.

uterus ['juːt(ə)rəs] n Anat utérus m.

utilitarian [juːtɪlɪˈteərɪən] a utilitaire. ◆**u'tility** n (**public**) u. service m public; — a (*goods vehicle*) utilitaire.

utilize ['juːtɪlaɪz] vt utiliser. ◆**utili'zation** n utilisation f.

utmost ['ʌtməʊst] a **the u. ease**/etc (*greatest*) la plus grande facilité/etc; **the u. danger/limit**/etc (*extreme*) un danger/une limite/etc extrême; — n **to do one's u.** faire tout son possible (**to do** pour faire).

utopia [juːˈtəʊpɪə] n (*perfect state*) utopie f. ◆**utopian** a utopique.

utter ['ʌtər] **1** a complet, total; (*folly*) pur; (*idiot*) parfait; **it's u. nonsense** c'est complètement absurde. **2** vt (*say, express*) proférer; (*a cry, sigh*) pousser. ◆**utterance** n (*remark etc*) déclaration f; **to give u. to** exprimer. ◆**utterly** adv complètement.

V

V, v [viː] n V, v m. ◆**V.-neck(ed)** a (*pullover etc*) à col en V.

vacant ['veɪkənt] a (*post*) vacant; (*room, seat*) libre; (*look*) vague, dans le vide. ◆**vacancy** n (*post*) poste m vacant; (*room*) chambre f disponible; **'no vacancies'** (*in hotel*) 'complet'. ◆**vacantly** adv **to gaze v.** regarder dans le vide.

vacate [vəˈkeɪt, Am ˈveɪkeɪt] vt quitter.

vacation [veɪˈkeɪʃ(ə)n] n Am vacances fpl; **on v.** en vacances. ◆**—er** n Am vacancier, -ière mf.

vaccinate ['væksɪneɪt] vt vacciner. ◆**vacci'nation** n vaccination f. ◆**vaccine** [-iːn] n vaccin m.

vacillate ['væsɪleɪt] vi (*hesitate*) hésiter.

vacuum ['vækjʊ(ə)m] n vide m; **v. cleaner** aspirateur m; **v. flask** thermos® m or f; — vt (*carpet etc*) passer à l'aspirateur. ◆**v.-packed** a emballé sous vide.

vagabond ['væɡəbɒnd] n vagabond, -onde mf.

vagary ['veɪɡərɪ] n caprice m.

vagina [vəˈdʒaɪnə] n vagin m.

vagrant ['veɪɡrənt] n Jur vagabond, -onde mf.

vague [veɪɡ] a (-er, -est) vague; (*memory, outline, photo*) flou; **the vaguest idea** la moindre idée; **he was v. (about it)** il est resté vague. ◆**—ly** adv vaguement.

vain [veɪn] a (-er, -est) **1** (*attempt, hope*) vain; **in v.** en vain; **his or her efforts were in v.** ses efforts ont été inutiles. **2** (*conceited*) vaniteux. ◆**—ly** adv (*in vain*) vainement.

valentine ['væləntaɪn] n (*card*) carte f de la Saint-Valentin.

valet ['vælɪt, 'væleɪ] n valet m de chambre.

valiant ['vælɪənt] a courageux. ◆**valour** n bravoure f.

valid ['vælɪd] a (*ticket, motive etc*) valable. ◆**validate** vt valider. ◆**va'lidity** n validité f; (*of argument*) justesse f.

valley ['vælɪ] n vallée f.

valuable ['væljʊəb(ə)l] a (*object*) de (grande) valeur; (*help, time etc*) Fig précieux; — npl objets mpl de valeur.

value ['væljuː] n valeur f; **to be of great/little v.** (*of object*) valoir cher/peu (cher); **it's good v.** c'est très avantageux; **v. added tax** taxe f à la valeur ajoutée; — vt (*appraise*) évaluer; (*appreciate*) attacher de la valeur à. ◆**valu'ation** n évaluation f; (*by expert*) expertise f. ◆**valuer** n expert m.

valve [vælv] n (*of machine*) soupape f; (*in radio*) lampe f; (*of tyre*) valve f; (*of heart*) valvule f.

vampire ['væmpaɪər] n vampire m.

van [væn] n (*small*) camionnette f; (*large*) camion m; Rail fourgon m.

vandal ['vænd(ə)l] n vandale mf. ◆**vandal-**

ism n vandalisme m. ◆**vandalize** vt saccager, détériorer.

vanguard ['væŋgɑːd] n (of army, progress etc) avant-garde f.

vanilla [vəˈnɪlə] n vanille f; – a (ice cream) à la vanille.

vanish ['vænɪʃ] vi disparaître.

vanity ['vænɪtɪ] n vanité f; **v. case** vanity m inv.

vanquish ['væŋkwɪʃ] vt vaincre.

vantage point ['vɑːntɪdʒpɔɪnt] n (place, point of view) (bon) point m de vue.

vapour ['veɪpər] n vapeur f; (on glass) buée f.

variable ['veərɪəb(ə)l] a variable. ◆**variance** n at v. en désaccord (**with** avec). ◆**variant** a différent; – n variante f. ◆**vari'ation** n variation f.

varicose ['værɪkəʊs] a v. **veins** varices fpl.

variety [vəˈraɪətɪ] n 1 (diversity) variété f; **a v. of opinions/reasons**/etc (many) diverses opinions/raisons/etc; **a v. of** (articles) Com une gamme de. 2 Th variétés fpl; **v. show** spectacle m de variétés.

various ['veərɪəs] a divers. ◆**-ly** adv diversement.

varnish ['vɑːnɪʃ] vti vernir; – n vernis m.

vary ['veərɪ] vti varier (**from** de). ◆**varied** a varié. ◆**varying** a variable.

vase [vɑːz, Am veɪs] n vase m.

Vaseline® ['væsəliːn] n vaseline f.

vast [vɑːst] a vaste, immense. ◆**-ly** adv (very) infiniment, extrêmement. ◆**-ness** n immensité f.

vat [væt] n cuve f.

VAT [viːeɪˈtiː, væt] n abbr (value added tax) TVA f.

Vatican ['vætɪkən] n Vatican m.

vaudeville ['vɔːdəvɪl] n Th Am variétés fpl.

vault [vɔːlt] 1 n (cellar) cave f; (tomb) caveau m; (in bank) chambre f forte, coffres mpl; (roof) voûte f. 2 vti (jump) sauter.

veal [viːl] n (meat) veau m.

veer [vɪər] vi (of wind) tourner; (of car, road) virer; **to v. off the road** quitter la route.

vegan ['viːgən] n végétaliste mf.

vegetable ['vedʒtəb(ə)l] n légume m; – a (kingdom, oil) végétal; **v. garden** (jardin m) potager m. ◆**vege'tarian** a & n végétarien, -ienne (mf). ◆**vege'tation** n végétation f.

vegetate ['vedʒɪteɪt] vi (of person) Pej végéter.

vehement ['viːəmənt] a (feeling, speech) véhément; (attack) violent. ◆**-ly** adv avec véhémence; violemment.

vehicle ['viːɪk(ə)l] n véhicule m; **heavy goods v.** (lorry) poids m lourd.

veil [veɪl] n (covering) & Fig voile m; – vt (face, truth etc) voiler.

vein [veɪn] n (in body or rock) veine f; (in leaf) nervure f; (mood) Fig esprit m.

vellum ['veləm] n (paper, skin) vélin m.

velocity [vəˈlɒsɪtɪ] n vélocité f.

velvet ['velvɪt] n velours m; – a de velours. ◆**velvety** a velouté.

vendetta [venˈdetə] n vendetta f.

vending machine ['vendɪŋməʃiːn] n distributeur m automatique.

vendor ['vendər] n vendeur, -euse mf.

veneer [vəˈnɪər] n (wood) placage m; (appearance) Fig vernis m.

venerable ['ven(ə)rəb(ə)l] a vénérable. ◆**venerate** vt vénérer.

venereal [vəˈnɪərɪəl] a (disease etc) vénérien.

venetian [vəˈniːʃ(ə)n] a v. **blind** store m vénitien.

vengeance ['vendʒəns] n vengeance f; **with a v.** (to work, study etc) furieusement; (to rain, catch up etc) pour de bon.

venison ['venɪs(ə)n] n venaison f.

venom ['venəm] n (substance) & Fig venin m. ◆**venomous** a (speech, snake etc) venimeux.

vent [vent] 1 n (hole) orifice m; (for air) bouche f d'aération; (in jacket) fente f. 2 n **to give v. to** (feeling etc) donner libre cours à; – vt (anger) décharger (**on** sur).

ventilate ['ventɪleɪt] vt ventiler. ◆**venti-'lation** n ventilation f. ◆**ventilator** n (in wall etc) ventilateur m.

ventriloquist [venˈtrɪləkwɪst] n ventriloque mf.

venture ['ventʃər] n entreprise f (risquée); **my v. into** mon incursion f dans; – vt (opinion, fortune) hasarder; **to v. to do** (dare) oser faire; – vi s'aventurer, se risquer (**into** dans).

venue ['venjuː] n lieu m de rencontre or de rendez-vous.

veranda(h) [vəˈrændə] n véranda f.

verb [vɜːb] n verbe m. ◆**verbal** a (promise, skill etc) verbal. ◆**verbatim** [vɜːˈbeɪtɪm] a & adv mot pour mot.

verbose [vɜːˈbəʊs] a (wordy) verbeux.

verdict ['vɜːdɪkt] n verdict m.

verdigris ['vɜːdɪɡrɪs] n vert-de-gris m inv.

verge [vɜːdʒ] n (of road) accotement m, bord m; **on the v. of** Fig (ruin, tears etc) au bord de; (discovery) à la veille de; **on the v. of doing** sur le point de faire; – vi **to v. on** friser, frôler; (of colour) tirer sur.

verger ['vɜːdʒər] n Rel bedeau m.

verify ['verɪfaɪ] *vt* vérifier. ◆**verifi'cation** *n* vérification *f*.

veritable ['verɪtəb(ə)l] *a* véritable.

vermicelli [vɜːmɪ'selɪ] *n* Culin vermicelle(s) *m(pl)*.

vermin ['vɜːmɪn] *n* (*animals*) animaux *mpl* nuisibles; (*insects, people*) vermine *f*.

vermouth ['vɜːməθ] *n* vermouth *m*.

vernacular [və'nækjulər] *n* (*of region*) dialecte *m*.

versatile ['vɜːsətaɪl, *Am* 'vɜːsət(ə)l] *a* (*mind*) souple; (*material, tool, computer*) polyvalent; **he's v.** il a des talents variés, il est polyvalent. ◆**versa'tility** *n* souplesse *f*; **his v.** la variété de ses talents.

verse [vɜːs] *n* (*stanza*) strophe *f*; (*poetry*) vers *mpl*; (*of Bible*) verset *m*.

versed [vɜːst] *a* (**well**) **v. in** versé dans.

version ['vɜːʃ(ə)n] *n* version *f*.

versus ['vɜːsəs] *prep* contre.

vertebra, *pl* **-ae** ['vɜːtɪbrə, -iː] *n* vertèbre *f*.

vertical ['vɜːtɪk(ə)l] *a* vertical; – *n* verticale *f*. ◆**—ly** *adv* verticalement.

vertigo ['vɜːtɪgəʊ] *n* (*fear of falling*) vertige *m*.

verve [vɜːv] *n* fougue *f*.

very ['verɪ] **1** *adv* très; **I'm v. hot** j'ai très chaud; **v. much** beaucoup; **the v. first** le tout premier; **at the v. least/most** tout au moins/plus; **at the v. latest** au plus tard. **2** *a* (*actual*) même; **his** *or* **her v. brother** son frère même; **at the v. end** (*of play etc*) tout à la fin; **to the v. end** jusqu'au bout.

vespers ['vespəz] *npl* Rel vêpres *fpl*.

vessel ['ves(ə)l] *n* Anat Bot Nau vaisseau *m*; (*receptacle*) récipient *m*.

vest [vest] *n* tricot *m* or maillot *m* de corps; (*woman's*) chemise *f* (américaine); (*waistcoat*) *Am* gilet *m*.

vested ['vestɪd] *a* **v. interests** Com droits *mpl* acquis; **she's got a v. interest in** Fig elle est directement intéressée dans.

vestige ['vestɪdʒ] *n* vestige *m*; **not a v. of truth/good sense** pas un grain de vérité/de bon sens.

vestry ['vestrɪ] *n* sacristie *f*.

vet [vet] **1** *n* vétérinaire *mf*. **2** *vt* (**-tt-**) (*document*) examiner de près; (*candidate*) se renseigner à fond sur. ◆**veteri'narian** *n Am* vétérinaire *mf*. ◆**veterinary** *a* vétérinaire; **v. surgeon** vétérinaire *mf*.

veteran ['vet(ə)rən] *n* vétéran *m*; (**war**) **v.** ancien combattant *m*; – *a* **v. golfer/etc** golfeur/*etc* expérimenté.

veto ['viːtəʊ] *n* (*pl* **-oes**) (*refusal*) veto *m inv*; (*power*) droit *m* de veto; – *vt* mettre *or* opposer son veto à.

vex [veks] *vt* contrarier, fâcher; **vexed question** question *f* controversée.

via ['vaɪə] *prep* via, par.

viable ['vaɪəb(ə)l] *a* (*baby, firm, plan etc*) viable. ◆**via'bility** *n* viabilité *f*.

viaduct ['vaɪədʌkt] *n* viaduc *m*.

vibrate [vaɪ'breɪt] *vi* vibrer. ◆**'vibrant** *a* vibrant. ◆**vibration** *n* vibration *f*. ◆**vibrator** *n* vibromasseur *m*.

vicar ['vɪkər] *n* (*in Church of England*) pasteur *m*. ◆**vicarage** *n* presbytère *m*.

vicarious [vɪ'keərɪəs] *a* (*emotion*) ressenti indirectement. ◆**—ly** *adv* (*to experience*) indirectement.

vice [vaɪs] *n* **1** (*depravity*) vice *m*; (*fault*) défaut *m*; **v. squad** brigade *f* des mœurs. **2** (*tool*) étau *m*.

vice- [vaɪs] *pref* vice-. ◆**v.-'chancellor** *n Univ* président *m*.

vice versa [vaɪs(ɪ)'vɜːsə] *adv* vice versa.

vicinity [və'sɪnɪtɪ] *n* environs *mpl*; **in the v. of** (*place, amount*) aux environs de.

vicious ['vɪʃəs] *a* (*spiteful*) méchant; (*violent*) brutal; **v. circle** cercle *m* vicieux. ◆**—ly** *adv* méchamment; brutalement. ◆**—ness** *n* méchanceté *f*; brutalité *f*.

vicissitudes [vɪ'sɪsɪtjuːdz] *npl* vicissitudes *fpl*.

victim ['vɪktɪm] *n* victime *f*; **to be the v. of** être victime de. ◆**victimize** *vt* persécuter. ◆**victimi'zation** *n* persécution *f*.

Victorian [vɪk'tɔːrɪən] *a & n* victorien, -ienne (*mf*).

victory ['vɪktərɪ] *n* victoire *f*. ◆**victor** *n* vainqueur *m*. ◆**vic'torious** *a* victorieux.

video ['vɪdɪəʊ] *a* vidéo *inv*; – *n* **v.** (**cassette**) vidéocassette *f*; **v.** (**recorder**) magnétoscope *m*; **on v.** sur cassette; **to make a v. of** faire une cassette de; – *vt* (*programme etc*) enregistrer au magnétoscope. ◆**videotape** *n* bande *f* vidéo.

vie [vaɪ] *vi* (*pres p* **vying**) rivaliser (**with** avec).

Vietnam [vjet'næm, *Am* -'nɑːm] *n* Viêt-nam *m*. ◆**Vietna'mese** *a & n* vietnamien, -ienne (*mf*).

view [vjuː] *n* vue *f*; **to come into v.** apparaître; **in full v. of everyone** à la vue de tous; **in my v.** (*opinion*) à mon avis; **on v.** (*exhibit*) exposé; **in v. of** (*considering*) étant donné (**the fact that** que); **with a v. to doing** afin de faire; – *vt* (*regard*) considérer; (*house*) visiter. ◆**—er** *n* **1** TV téléspectateur, -trice *mf*. **2** (*for slides*) visionneuse *f*. ◆**viewfinder** *n* Phot viseur *m*. ◆**viewpoint** *n* point *m* de vue.

vigil ['vɪdʒɪl] n veille f; (over sick person or corpse) veillée f.

vigilant ['vɪdʒɪlənt] a vigilant. ◆**vigilance** n vigilance f.

vigilante [vɪdʒɪ'læntɪ] n Pej membre m d'une milice privée.

vigour ['vɪgər] n vigueur f. ◆**vigorous** a (person, speech etc) vigoureux.

vile [vaɪl] a (-er, -est) (base) infâme, vil; (unpleasant) abominable.

vilify ['vɪlɪfaɪ] vt diffamer.

villa ['vɪlə] n (in country) grande maison f de campagne.

village ['vɪlɪdʒ] n village m. ◆**villager** n villageois, -oise mf.

villain ['vɪlən] n scélérat, -ate mf; (in story or play) traître m. ◆**villainy** n infamie f.

vindicate ['vɪndɪkeɪt] vt justifier. ◆**vindi-'cation** n justification f.

vindictive [vɪn'dɪktɪv] a vindicatif, rancunier.

vine [vaɪn] n (grapevine) vigne f; v. **grower** viticulteur m. ◆**vineyard** ['vɪnjəd] n vignoble m.

vinegar ['vɪnɪgər] n vinaigre m.

vintage ['vɪntɪdʒ] **1** n (year) année f. **2** a (wine) de grand cru; (car) d'époque; (film) classique; (good) Fig bon; v. **Shaw**/etc du meilleur Shaw/etc.

vinyl ['vaɪn(ə)l] n vinyle m.

viola [vɪ'əʊlə] n (instrument) Mus alto m.

violate ['vaɪəleɪt] vt violer. ◆**vio'lation** n violation f.

violence ['vaɪələns] n violence f. ◆**violent** a violent; a v. **dislike** une aversion vive. ◆**violently** adv violemment; to be v. **sick** (vomit) vomir.

violet ['vaɪələt] **1** a & n (colour) violet (m). **2** n (plant) violette f.

violin [vaɪə'lɪn] n violon m; – a (concerto etc) pour violon. ◆**violinist** n violoniste mf.

VIP [vi:aɪ'pi:] n abbr (very important person) personnage m de marque.

viper ['vaɪpər] n vipère f.

virgin ['vɜ:dʒɪn] n vierge f; to be a v. (of woman, man) être vierge; – a (woman, snow etc) vierge. ◆**vir'ginity** n virginité f.

Virgo ['vɜ:gəʊ] n (sign) la Vierge.

virile ['vɪraɪl, Am 'vɪrəl] a viril. ◆**vi'rility** n virilité f.

virtual ['vɜ:tʃʊəl] a it was a v. **failure**/etc ce fut en fait un échec/etc. ◆**–ly** adv (in fact) en fait; (almost) pratiquement.

virtue ['vɜ:tʃu:] n **1** (goodness, chastity) vertu f; (advantage) mérite m, avantage m. **2** by or **in** v. **of** en raison de. ◆**virtuous** a vertueux.

virtuoso [vɜ:tʃʊ'əʊsəʊ, -si:] n virtuose mf. ◆**virtuosity** [-'ɒsɪtɪ] n virtuosité f.

virulent ['vɪrʊlənt] a virulent. ◆**virulence** n virulence f.

virus ['vaɪ(ə)rəs] n virus m.

visa ['vi:zə] n visa m.

vis-à-vis [vi:zə'vi:] prep vis-à-vis de.

viscount ['vaɪkaʊnt] n vicomte m. ◆**viscountess** n vicomtesse f.

viscous ['vɪskəs] a visqueux.

vise [vaɪs] n (tool) Am étau m.

visible ['vɪzəb(ə)l] a visible. ◆**visi'bility** n visibilité f. ◆**visibly** adv visiblement.

vision ['vɪʒ(ə)n] n vision f; a **man**/a **woman of** v. Fig un homme/une femme qui voit loin. ◆**visionary** a & n visionnaire (mf).

visit ['vɪzɪt] n (call, tour) visite f; (stay) séjour m; – vt (place) visiter; **to visit s.o.** (call on) rendre visite à qn; (stay with) faire un séjour chez qn; – vi être en visite (Am **with** chez). ◆**–ing** a (card, hours) de visite. ◆**visitor** n visiteur, -euse mf; (guest) invité, -ée mf; (in hotel) client, -ente mf.

visor ['vaɪzər] n (of helmet) visière f.

vista ['vɪstə] n (view of place etc) vue f; (of future) Fig perspective f.

visual ['vɪʒʊəl] a visuel; v. **aid** (in teaching) support m visuel. ◆**visualize** vt (imagine) se représenter; (foresee) envisager.

vital ['vaɪt(ə)l] a vital; **of** v. **importance** d'importance capitale; v. **statistics** (of woman) Fam mensurations fpl. ◆**–ly** adv extrêmement.

vitality [vaɪ'tælɪtɪ] n vitalité f.

vitamin ['vɪtəmɪn, Am 'vaɪtəmɪn] n vitamine f.

vitriol ['vɪtrɪəl] n Ch Fig vitriol m. ◆**vitri-'olic** a (attack, speech etc) au vitriol.

vivacious [vɪ'veɪʃəs] a plein d'entrain.

vivid ['vɪvɪd] a (imagination, recollection etc) vif; (description) vivant. ◆**–ly** adv (to describe) de façon vivante; **to remember sth** v. avoir un vif souvenir de qch.

vivisection [vɪvɪ'sekʃ(ə)n] n vivisection f.

vocabulary [və'kæbjʊlərɪ] n vocabulaire m.

vocal ['vəʊk(ə)l] a (cords, music) vocal; (outspoken, noisy, critical) qui se fait entendre. ◆**vocalist** n chanteur, -euse mf.

vocation [vəʊ'keɪʃ(ə)n] n vocation f. ◆**vocational** a professionnel.

vociferous [və'sɪf(ə)rəs] a bruyant.

vodka ['vɒdkə] n vodka f.

vogue [vəʊg] n vogue f; **in** v. en vogue.

voice [vɔɪs] n voix f; **at the top of one's** v. à

tue-tête; – *vt* (*feeling, opinion etc*) formuler, exprimer.

void [vɔɪd] **1** *n* vide *m*; – *a* **v. of** (*lacking in*) dépourvu de. **2** *a* (*not valid*) *Jur* nul.

volatile ['vɒlətaɪl, *Am* 'vɒlət(ə)l] *a* (*person*) versatile, changeant; (*situation*) explosif.

volcano [vɒl'keɪnəʊ] *n* (*pl* -**oes**) volcan *m*. ◆**volcanic** [-'kænɪk] *a* volcanique.

volition [və'lɪʃ(ə)n] *n* **of one's own v.** de son propre gré.

volley ['vɒlɪ] *n* (*of blows*) volée *f*; (*gunfire*) salve *f*; (*of insults*) *Fig* bordée *f*. ◆**volleyball** *n Sp* volley(-ball) *m*.

volt [vəʊlt] *n El* volt *m*. ◆**voltage** *n* voltage *m*.

volume ['vɒljuːm] *n* (*book, capacity, loudness*) volume *m*. ◆**voluminous** [və'luːmɪnəs] *a* volumineux.

voluntary ['vɒlənt(ə)rɪ] *a* volontaire; (*unpaid*) bénévole. ◆**voluntarily** [*Am* vɒlən'terɪlɪ] *adv* volontairement; bénévolement. ◆**volun'teer** *n* volontaire *mf*; – *vi* se proposer (**for sth** pour qch, **to do** pour faire); *Mil* s'engager comme volontaire (**for** dans); – *vt* offrir (spontanément).

voluptuous [və'lʌptʃʊəs] *a* voluptueux, sensuel.

vomit ['vɒmɪt] *vti* vomir; – *n* (*matter*) vomi *m*.

voracious [və'reɪʃəs] *a* (*appetite, reader etc*) vorace.

vot/e [vəʊt] *n* vote *m*; (*right to vote*) droit *m* de vote; **to win votes** gagner des voix; **v. of censure** *or* **no confidence** motion *f* de censure; **v. of thanks** discours *m* de remerciement; – *vt* (*bill, funds etc*) voter; (*person*) élire; – *vi* voter; **to v. Conservative** voter conservateur *or* pour les conservateurs. ◆**—ing** *n* vote *m* (**of** de); (*polling*) scrutin *m*. ◆**—er** *n Pol* électeur, -trice *mf*.

vouch [vaʊtʃ] *vi* **to v. for** répondre de.

voucher ['vaʊtʃər] *n* (*for meals etc*) bon *m*, chèque *m*.

vow [vaʊ] *n* vœu *m*; – *vt* (*obedience etc*) jurer (**to à**); **to v. to do** jurer de faire, faire le vœu de faire.

vowel ['vaʊəl] *n* voyelle *f*.

voyage ['vɔɪdʒ] *n* voyage *m* (par mer).

vulgar ['vʌlgər] *a* vulgaire. ◆**vul'garity** *n* vulgarité *f*.

vulnerable ['vʌln(ə)rəb(ə)l] *a* vulnérable. ◆**vulnera'bility** *n* vulnérabilité *f*.

vulture ['vʌltʃər] *n* vautour *m*.

W

W, w ['dʌb(ə)ljuː] *n* W, w *m*.

wacky ['wækɪ] *a* (-**ier**, -**iest**) *Am Fam* farfelu.

wad [wɒd] *n* (*of banknotes, papers etc*) liasse *f*; (*of cotton wool, cloth*) tampon *m*.

waddle ['wɒd(ə)l] *vi* se dandiner.

wade [weɪd] *vi* **to w. through** (*mud, water etc*) patauger dans; (*book etc*) *Fig* venir péniblement à bout de; **I'm wading through this book** j'avance péniblement dans ce livre.

wafer ['weɪfər] *n* (*biscuit*) gaufrette *f*; *Rel* hostie *f*.

waffle ['wɒf(ə)l] **1** *n* (*talk*) *Fam* verbiage *m*, blabla *m*; – *vi Fam* parler pour ne rien dire, blablater. **2** *n* (*cake*) gaufre *f*.

waft [wɒft] *vi* (*of smell etc*) flotter.

wag [wæg] **1** *vt* (-**gg**-) (*tail, finger*) agiter, remuer; – *vi* remuer; **tongues are wagging** *Pej* on en jase, les langues vont bon train. **2** *n* (*joker*) farceur, -euse *mf*.

wage [weɪdʒ] **1** *n* **wage(s)** salaire *m*, paie *f*; **w. claim** *or* **demand** revendication *f* salariale; **w. earner** salarié, -ée *mf*; (*breadwin-ner*) soutien *m* de famille; **w. freeze** blocage *m* des salaires; **w. increase** *or* **rise** augmentation *f* de salaire. **2** *vt* (*campaign*) mener; **to w. war** faire la guerre (**on** à).

wager ['weɪdʒər] *n* pari *m*; – *vt* parier (**that** que).

waggle ['wæg(ə)l] *vti* remuer.

wag(g)on ['wægən] *n* (*cart*) chariot *m*; *Rail* wagon *m* (de marchandises); **on the w.** (*abstinent*) *Fam* au régime sec.

waif [weɪf] *n* enfant *mf* abandonné(e).

wail [weɪl] *vi* (*cry out, complain*) gémir; (*of siren*) hurler; – *n* gémissement *m*; (*of siren*) hurlement *m*.

waist [weɪst] *n* taille *f*; **stripped to the w.** nu jusqu'à la ceinture. ◆**waistband** *n* (*part of garment*) ceinture *f*. ◆**waistcoat** ['weɪskəʊt] *n* gilet *m*. ◆**waistline** *n* taille *f*.

wait [weɪt] **1** *n* attente *f*; **to lie in w. (for)** guetter; – *vi* attendre; **to w. for** attendre; **w. until I've gone, w. for me to go** attends que je sois parti; **to keep s.o. waiting** faire attendre qn; **w. and see!** attends voir!; **I can't w.**

to do it j'ai hâte de le faire; **to w. about** (for) attendre; **to w. behind** rester; **to w. up** veiller; **to w. up for s.o.** attendre le retour de qn avant de se coucher. **2** vi (serve) **to w. at table** servir à table; **to w. on s.o.** servir qn. ◆**—ing** n attente f; **'no w.'** Aut 'arrêt interdit'; − a w. list/**room** liste f/salle f d'attente. ◆**waiter** n garçon m (de café), serveur m; w.! garçon! ◆**waitress** n serveuse f; w.! mademoiselle!

waive [weiv] vt renoncer à, abandonner.

wake¹ [weik] vi (pt **woke**, pp **woken**) **to w. (up)** se réveiller; **to w. up to** (fact etc) Fig prendre conscience de; − vt **to w. (up)** réveiller; **to spend one's waking hours working**/etc passer ses journées à travailler/etc. ◆**waken** vt éveiller, réveiller; − vi s'éveiller, se réveiller.

wake² [weik] n (of ship) & Fig sillage m; **in the w. of** Fig dans le sillage de, à la suite de.

Wales [weilz] n pays m de Galles.

walk [wɔ:k] n promenade f; (short) (petit) tour m; (gait) démarche f; (pace) marche f, pas m; (path) allée f, chemin m; **to go for a w.** faire une promenade, (shorter) faire un (petit) tour; **to take for a w.** (child etc) emmener se promener, (baby, dog) promener; **five minutes' w.** (away) à cinq minutes à pied; **walks of life** Fig conditions sociales fpl; − vi marcher; (stroll) se promener; (go on foot) aller à pied; w.! (don't run) ne cours pas!; **to w. away or off** s'éloigner, partir (**from** de); **to w. away or off with** (steal) Fam faucher; **to w. in** entrer; **to w. into** (tree etc) rentrer dans; (trap) tomber dans; **to w. out** (leave) partir; (of workers) se mettre en grève; **to w. out on s.o.** (desert) Fam laisser tomber qn; **to w. over** (go up to) s'approcher de; − vt (distance) faire à pied; (streets) (par)courir; (take for a walk) promener (bébé, chien); **to w. s.o. to** (station etc) accompagner qn à. ◆**—ing** n marche f (à pied); − a a w. **corpse/dictionary** (person) Fig un cadavre/dictionnaire ambulant; **at a w. pace** au pas; **w. stick** canne f. ◆**walker** n marcheur, -euse mf; (for pleasure) promeneur, -euse mf. ◆**walkout** n (strike) grève f surprise; (from meeting) départ m (en signe de protestation). ◆**walkover** n (in contest etc) victoire f facile. ◆**walkway** n moving w. trottoir m roulant.

walkie-talkie [wɔ:ki'tɔ:ki] n talkie-walkie m.

Walkman® ['wɔ:kmən] n (pl **Walkmans**) baladeur m.

wall [wɔ:l] n mur m; (of cabin, tunnel, stomach etc) paroi f; (of ice) Fig muraille f; (of

smoke) Fig rideau m; **to go to the w.** (of firm) Fig faire faillite; − a mural; − vt **to w. up** (door etc) murer; **walled city** ville f fortifiée. ◆**wallflower** n Bot giroflée f; **to be a w.** (at dance) faire tapisserie. ◆**wallpaper** n papier m peint; − vt tapisser. ◆**wall-to-wall 'carpet(ing)'** n moquette f.

wallet ['wɔlit] n portefeuille m.

wallop ['wɔləp] vt (hit) Fam taper sur; − n (blow) Fam grand coup m.

wallow ['wɔləu] vi **to w. in** (mud, vice etc) se vautrer dans.

wally ['wɔli] n (idiot) Fam andouille f, imbécile mf.

walnut ['wɔ:lnʌt] n (nut) noix f; (tree, wood) noyer m.

walrus ['wɔ:lrəs] n (animal) morse m.

waltz [wɔ:ls, Am wɔlts] n valse f; − vi valser.

wan [wɔn] a (pale) Lit pâle.

wand [wɔnd] n baguette f (magique).

wander ['wɔndər] vi (of thoughts) vagabonder; **to w. (about or around)** (roam) errer, vagabonder; (stroll) flâner; **to w. from or off** (path, subject) s'écarter de; **to w. off** (go away) s'éloigner; **my mind's wandering** je suis distrait; − vt **to w. the streets** errer dans les rues. ◆**—ing** a (life, tribe) vagabond, nomade; − npl vagabondages mpl. ◆**—er** n vagabond, -onde mf.

wane [wein] vi (of moon, fame, strength etc) décroître; − n to be on the w. décroître, être en déclin.

wangle ['wæŋg(ə)l] vt Fam (obtain) se débrouiller pour obtenir; (avoiding payment) carotter (**from** à).

want [wɔnt] vt vouloir (**to do** faire); (ask for) demander; (need) avoir besoin de; **I w. him to go** je veux qu'il parte; **you w. to try** (should) tu devrais essayer; **you're wanted on the phone** on vous demande au téléphone; − vi **not to w. for** (not lack) ne pas manquer de; − n (lack) manque m (**of** de); (poverty) besoin m; **for w. of** par manque de; **for w. of money/time** faute d'argent/de temps; **for w. of anything better** faute de mieux; **your wants** (needs) tes besoins mpl. ◆**—ed** a (man, criminal) recherché par la police; **to feel w.** sentir qu'on vous aime. ◆**—ing** a (inadequate) insuffisant; **to be w.** manquer (**in** de).

wanton ['wɔntən] a (gratuitous) gratuit; (immoral) impudique.

war [wɔ:] n guerre f; **at w.** en guerre (**with** avec); **to go to w.** entrer en guerre (**with** avec); **to declare w.** déclarer la guerre (**on** à); − a (wound, criminal etc) de guerre; w.

memorial monument *m* aux morts. ◆**warfare** *n* guerre *f.* ◆**warhead** *n* (*of missile*) ogive *f.* ◆**warlike** *a* guerrier. ◆**warmonger** *n* fauteur *m* de guerre. ◆**warpath** *n* to be on the w. (*angry*) *Fam* être d'humeur massacrante. ◆**warring** *a* (*countries etc*) en guerre; (*ideologies etc*) *Fig* en conflit. ◆**warship** *n* navire *m* de guerre. ◆**wartime** *n* in w. en temps de guerre.

warble ['wɔːb(ə)l] *vi* (*of bird*) gazouiller.

ward[1] [wɔːd] *n* **1** (*in hospital*) salle *f.* **2** (*child*) *Jur* pupille *mf.* **3** (*electoral division*) circonscription *f* électorale.

ward[2] [wɔːd] *vt* to w. off (*blow, anger*) détourner; (*danger*) éviter.

warden ['wɔːd(ə)n] *n* (*of institution, Am of prison*) directeur, -trice *mf*; (*of park*) gardien, -ienne *mf*; (**traffic**) w. contractuel, -elle *m*f.

warder ['wɔːdər] *n* gardien *m* (de prison).

wardrobe ['wɔːdrəʊb] *n* (*cupboard*) penderie *f*; (*clothes*) garde-robe *f.*

warehouse, *pl* -ses ['weəhaʊs, -zɪz] *n* entrepôt *m.*

wares [weəz] *npl* marchandises *fpl.*

warily ['weərɪlɪ] *adv* avec précaution.

warm [wɔːm] *a* (-er, -est) chaud; (*iron, oven*) moyen; (*welcome, thanks etc*) chaleureux; **to be** *or* **feel w.** avoir chaud; **it's (nice and) w.** (*of weather*) il fait (agréablement) chaud; **to get w.** (*of person, room etc*) se réchauffer; (*of food, water*) chauffer; − *vt* to **w. (up)** (*person, food etc*) réchauffer; − *vi* to **w. up** (*of person, room, engine*) se réchauffer; (*of food, water*) chauffer; (*of discussion*) s'échauffer; **to w. to s.o.** *Fig* se prendre de sympathie pour qn. ◆**warm-'hearted** *a* chaleureux. ◆**warmly** *adv* (*to wrap up*) chaudement; (*to welcome, thank etc*) chaleureusement. ◆**warmth** *n* chaleur *f.*

warn [wɔːn] *vt* avertir, prévenir (**that** que); **to w. s.o. against** *or* **off sth** mettre qn en garde contre qch; **to w. s.o. against doing** conseiller à qn de ne pas faire. ◆**—ing** *n* avertissement *m*; (*advance notice*) (pré)avis *m*; *Met* avis *m*; (*alarm*) alerte *f*; **without w.** sans prévenir; **a note** *or* **word of w.** une mise en garde; **w. light** (*on appliance etc*) voyant *m* lumineux; **hazard w. lights** *Aut* feux *mpl* de détresse.

warp [wɔːp] **1** *vt* (*wood etc*) voiler; (*judgment, person etc*) *Fig* pervertir; **a warped mind** un esprit tordu; **a warped account** un récit déformé; − *vi* se voiler. **2** *n Tex* chaîne *f.*

warrant ['wɒrənt] **1** *n Jur* mandat *m*; **a w. for**

your arrest un mandat d'arrêt contre vous. **2** *vt* (*justify*) justifier; **I w. you that . . .** (*declare confidently*) je t'assure que . . . . ◆**warranty** *n Com* garantie *f.*

warren ['wɒrən] *n* (**rabbit**) w. garenne *f.*

warrior ['wɒrɪər] *n* guerrier, -ière *mf.*

wart [wɔːt] *n* verrue *f.*

wary ['weərɪ] *a* (-ier, -iest) prudent; **to be w. of s.o./sth** se méfier de qn/qch; **to be w. of doing** hésiter beaucoup à faire.

was [wəz, *stressed* wɒz] *see* **be.**

wash [wɒʃ] *n* (*clothes*) lessive *f*; (*of ship*) sillage *m*; **to have a w.** se laver; **to give sth a w.** laver qch; **to do the w.** faire la lessive; **in the w.** à la lessive; − *vt* laver; (*flow over*) baigner; **to w. one's hands** se laver les mains (*Fig of* sth **de** qch); **to w. (away)** (*of sea etc*) emporter (qch, qn); **to w. away** *or* **off** *or* **out** (*stain*) faire partir (en lavant); **to w. down** (*vehicle, deck*) laver à grande eau; (*food*) arroser (**with** de); **to w. out** (*bowl etc*) laver; − *vi* se laver; (*do the dishes*) laver la vaisselle; **to w. away** *or* **off** *or* **out** (*of stain*) partir (au lavage); **to w. up** (*do the dishes*) faire la vaisselle; (*have a wash*) *Am* se laver. ◆**washed-'out** *a* (*tired*) lessivé. ◆**washed-'up** **a (all) w.-up** (*person, plan*) *Sl* fichu. ◆**washable** *a* lavable. ◆**washbasin** *n* lavabo *m.* ◆**washcloth** *n Am* gant *m* de toilette. ◆**washout** *n Sl* (*event etc*) fiasco *m*; (*person*) nullité *f.* ◆**washroom** *n Am* toilettes *fpl.*

washer ['wɒʃər] *n* (*ring*) rondelle *f*, joint *m.*

washing ['wɒʃɪŋ] *n* (*act*) lavage *m*; (*clothes*) lessive *f*, linge *m*; **to do the w.** faire la lessive; **w. line** corde *f* à linge; **w. machine** machine *f* à laver; **w. powder** lessive *f.* ◆**w.-'up** *n* vaisselle *f*; **to do the w.-up** faire la vaisselle; **w.-up liquid** produit *m* pour la vaisselle.

wasp [wɒsp] *n* guêpe *f.*

wast/e [weɪst] *n* gaspillage *m*; (*of time*) perte *f*; (*rubbish*) déchets *mpl*; *pl* (*land*) étendue *f* déserte; **w. disposal unit** broyeur *m* d'ordures; − *a* **w. material** *or* **products** déchets *mpl*; **w. land** (*uncultivated*) terres *fpl* incultes; (*in town*) terrain *m* vague; **w. paper** vieux papiers *mpl*; **w. pipe** tuyau *m* d'évacuation; − *vt* (*money, food etc*) gaspiller; (*time, opportunity*) perdre; **to w. one's time on frivolities/***etc* gaspiller son temps en frivolités/*etc*, perdre son temps à des frivolités/*etc*; **to w. one's life** gâcher sa vie; − *vi* **to w. away** dépérir. ◆**—ed** *a* (*effort*) inutile; (*body etc*) émacié. ◆**wastage** *n* gaspillage *m*; (*losses*) pertes *fpl*; **some w.** (*of goods, staff etc*) du déchet. ◆**wastebin** *n* (*in kitchen*) poubelle *f*. ◆**wastepaper basket** *n* corbeille *f* (à papier).

wasteful ['weɪstfəl] *a* (*person*) gaspilleur; (*process*) peu économique.

watch [wɒtʃ] **1** *n* (*small clock*) montre *f*. **2** *n* (*over suspect, baby etc*) surveillance *f*; *Nau* quart *m*; **to keep (a) w. on** *or* **over** surveiller; **to keep w.** faire le guet; **to be on the w.** (**for**) guetter; – *vt* regarder; (*observe*) observer; (*suspect, baby etc*) surveiller; (*be careful of*) faire attention à; – *vi* regarder; **to w.** (**out**) **for** (*be on the lookout for*) guetter; **to w. out** (*take care*) faire attention (**for** à); **w. out!** attention!; **to w. over** surveiller. ◆**watchdog** *n* chien *m* de garde. ◆**watchmaker** *n* horloger, -ère *mf*. ◆**watchman** *n* (*pl* **-men**) **night w.** veilleur *m* de nuit. ◆**watchstrap** *n* bracelet *m* de montre. ◆**watchtower** *n* tour *f* de guet.

watchful ['wɒtʃfəl] *a* vigilant.

water ['wɔːtər] *n* eau *f*; **by w.** en bateau; **under w.** (*road, field etc*) inondé; (*to swim*) sous l'eau; **at high w.** à marée haute; **it doesn't hold w.** (*of theory etc*) *Fig* ça ne tient pas debout; **in hot w.** *Fig* dans le pétrin; **w. cannon** lance *f* à eau; **w. ice** sorbet *m*; **w. lily** nénuphar *m*; **w. pistol** pistolet *m* à eau; **w. polo** *Sp* water-polo *m*; **w. power** énergie *f* hydraulique; **w. rates** taxes *fpl* sur l'eau; **w. skiing** ski *m* nautique; **w. tank** réservoir *m* d'eau; **w. tower** château *m* d'eau; – *vt* (*plant etc*) arroser; **to w. down** (*wine etc*) couper (d'eau); (*text etc*) édulcorer; – *vi* (*of eyes*) larmoyer; **it makes his** *or* **her mouth w.** ça lui fait venir l'eau à la bouche. ◆**—ing** *n* (*of plant etc*) arrosage *m*; **w. can** arrosoir *m*. ◆**watery** *a* (*colour*) délavé; (*soup*) *Pej* trop liquide; (*eyes*) larmoyant; **w. tea** *or* **coffee** de la lavasse.

watercolour ['wɔːtəkʌlər] *n* (*picture*) aquarelle *f*; (*paint*) couleur *f* pour aquarelle. ◆**watercress** *n* cresson *m* (de fontaine). ◆**waterfall** *n* chute *f* d'eau. ◆**waterhole** *n* (*in desert*) point *m* d'eau. ◆**waterline** *n* (*on ship*) ligne *f* de flottaison. ◆**waterlogged** *a* délavé. ◆**watermark** *n* (*in paper*) filigrane *m*. ◆**watermelon** *n* pastèque *f*. ◆**waterproof** *a* (*material*) imperméable. ◆**watershed** *n* (*turning point*) tournant *m* (décisif). ◆**watertight** *a* (*container etc*) étanche. ◆**waterway** *n* voie *f* navigable. ◆**waterworks** *n* (*place*) station *f* hydraulique.

watt [wɒt] *n El* watt *m*.

wave [weɪv] *n* (*of sea*) & *Fig* vague *f*; (*in hair*) ondulation *f*; *Rad* onde *f*; (*sign*) signe *m* (de la main); **long/medium/short w.** *Rad* ondes *fpl* longues/moyennes/ courtes; – *vi* (*with hand*) faire signe (de la main); (*of flag*) flotter; **to w. to** (*greet*) saluer de la main; – *vt* (*arm, flag etc*) agiter; (*hair*) onduler; **to w. s.o. on** faire signe à qn d'avancer; **to w. aside** (*objection etc*) écarter. ◆**waveband** *n Rad* bande *f* de fréquence. ◆**wavelength** *n Rad & Fig* longueur *f* d'ondes.

waver ['weɪvər] *vi* (*of flame, person etc*) vaciller.

wavy ['weɪvɪ] *a* (**-ier, -iest**) (*line*) onduleux; (*hair*) ondulé.

wax [wæks] **1** *n* cire *f*; (*for ski*) fart *m*; – *vt* cirer; (*ski*) farter; (*car*) lustrer; – *a* (*candle, doll etc*) de cire; **w. paper** *Culin Am* papier *m* paraffiné. **2** *vi* (*of moon*) croître. **3** *vi* **to w. lyrical/merry** (*become*) se faire lyrique/gai. ◆**waxworks** *npl* (*place*) musée *m* de cire; (*dummies*) figures *fpl* de cire.

way [weɪ] **1** *n* (*path, road*) chemin *m* (**to** de); (*direction*) sens *m*, direction *f*; (*distance*) distance *f*; **all the w., the whole w.** (*to talk etc*) pendant tout le chemin; **this w.** par ici; **that way** par là; **which w.?** par où?; **to lose one's w.** se perdre; **I'm on my w.** (*coming*) j'arrive; (*going*) je pars; **he made his w. out/home** il est sorti/rentré; **the w. there** l'aller *m*; **the w. back** le retour; **the w. in** l'entrée *f*; **the w. out** la sortie; **a w. out of** (*problem etc*) *Fig* une solution à; **the w. is clear** *Fig* la voie est libre; **across the w.** en face; **on the w.** en route (**to** pour); **by w. of** (*via*) par; (*as*) *Fig* comme; **out of the w.** (*isolated*) isolé; **to go out of one's w. to do** se donner du mal pour faire; **by the w .** . . . *Fig* à propos . . . ; **to be** *or* **stand in the w.** barrer le passage; **she's in my w.** (*hindrance*) *Fig* elle me gêne; **to get out of the w., make w.** s'écarter; **to give w.** céder; *Aut* céder le passage *or* la priorité; **a long w.** (**away** *or* **off**) très loin; **it's the wrong w. up** c'est dans le mauvais sens; **do it the other w. round** fais le contraire; **to get under w.** (*of campaign etc*) démarrer; – *adv* (*behind etc*) très loin; **w. ahead** très en avance (**of** sur). **2** *n* (*manner*) façon *f*; (*means*) moyen *m*; (*condition*) état *m*; (*habit*) habitude *f*; (*particular*) égard *m*; **one's ways** (*behaviour*) ses manières *fpl*; **to get one's own w.** obtenir ce qu'on veut; (**in**) **this w.** de cette façon; **in a way** (*to some extent*) dans un certain sens; **w. of life** façon *f* de vivre, mode *m* de vie; **no w.!** (*certainly not*) *Fam* pas question! ◆**wayfarer** *n* voyageur, -euse *mf*. ◆**way-'out** *a Fam* extraordinaire. ◆**wayside** n **by the w.** au bord de la route.

waylay [weɪˈleɪ] vt (pt & pp **-laid**) (attack) attaquer par surprise; (stop) Fig arrêter au passage.

wayward [ˈweɪwəd] a rebelle, capricieux.

WC [dʌb(ə)ljuːˈsiː] n w-c mpl, waters mpl.

we [wiː] pron nous; **we go** nous allons; **we teachers** nous autres professeurs; **we never know** (indefinite) on ne sait jamais.

weak [wiːk] a (-er, -est) faible; (tea, coffee) léger; (health, stomach) fragile. ◆**w.-'willed** a faible. ◆**weaken** vt affaiblir; − vi faiblir. ◆**weakling** n (in body) mauviette f; (in character) faible mf. ◆**weakly** adv faiblement. ◆**weakness** n faiblesse f; (of health, stomach) fragilité f; (fault) point m faible; **a w. for** (liking) un faible pour.

weal [wiːl] n (wound on skin) marque f, zébrure f.

wealth [welθ] n (money, natural resources) richesse(s) f(pl); **a w. of** (abundance) Fig une profusion de. ◆**wealthy** a (-ier, -iest) riche; − n **the w.** les riches mpl.

wean [wiːn] vt (baby) sevrer.

weapon [ˈwepən] n arme f. ◆**weaponry** n armements mpl.

wear [weər] **1** vt (pt **wore**, pp **worn**) (have on body) porter; (look, smile) avoir; (put on) mettre; **to have nothing to w.** n'avoir rien à se mettre; − n men's/sports w. vêtements mpl pour hommes/de sport; **evening w.** tenue f de soirée. **2** vt (pt **wore**, pp **worn**) **to w.** (**away** or **down** or **out**) (material, patience etc) user; **to w. s.o. out** (exhaust) épuiser qn; **to w. oneself out** s'épuiser (**doing** a faire); − vi (last) faire de l'usage, durer; **to w.** (**out**) (of clothes etc) s'user; **to w. off** (of colour, pain etc) passer, disparaître; **to w. on** (of time) passer; **to w. out** (of patience) s'épuiser; − n (use) usage m; **w.** (**and tear**) usure f. ◆**—ing** a (tiring) épuisant. ◆**—er** n **the w. of** (hat, glasses etc) la personne qui porte.

weary [ˈwɪərɪ] a (-ier, -iest) (tired) fatigué, las (**of doing** de faire); (tiring) fatigant; (look, smile) las; − vi **to w. of** se lasser de. ◆**wearily** adv avec lassitude. ◆**weariness** n lassitude f.

weasel [ˈwiːz(ə)l] n belette f.

weather [ˈweðər] n temps m; **what's the w. like?** quel temps fait-il?; **in (the) hot w.** par temps chaud; **under the w.** (not well) Fig patraque; − a (chart etc) météorologique; **w. forecast, w. report** prévisions fpl météorologiques, météo f; **w. vane** girouette f; −

vt (storm, hurricane) essuyer; (crisis) Fig surmonter. ◆**weather-beaten** a (face, person) tanné, hâlé. ◆**weathercock** n girouette f. ◆**weatherman** n (pl -men) TV Rad Fam monsieur m météo.

weav/e [wiːv] vt (pt **wove**, pp **woven**) (cloth, plot) tisser; (basket, garland) tresser; − vi Tex tisser; **to w. in and out of** (crowd, cars etc) Fig se faufiler entre; − n (style) tissage m. ◆**—ing** n tissage m. ◆**—er** n tisserand, -ande mf.

web [web] n (of spider) toile f; (of lies) Fig tissu m. ◆**webbed** a (foot) palmé. ◆**webbing** n (in chair) sangles fpl.

wed [wed] vt (-dd-) (marry) épouser; (qualities etc) Fig allier (**to** à); − vi se marier. ◆**wedded** a (bliss, life) conjugal. ◆**wedding** n mariage m; **golden/silver w.** noces fpl d'or/d'argent; − a (cake) de noces; (anniversary, present) de mariage; (dress) de mariée; **his** or **her w. day** le jour de son mariage; **w. ring**, Am **w. band** alliance f. ◆**wedlock** n **born out of w.** illégitime.

wedge [wedʒ] n (for splitting) coin m; (under wheel, table etc) cale f; **w. heel** (of shoe) semelle f compensée; − vt (wheel, table etc) caler; (push) enfoncer (**into** dans); **wedged (in) between** (caught, trapped) coincé entre.

Wednesday [ˈwenzdɪ] n mercredi m.

wee [wiː] a (tiny) Fam tout petit.

weed [wiːd] n (plant) mauvaise herbe f; (weak person) Fam mauviette f; **w. killer** désherbant m; − vti désherber; − vt **to w. out** Fig éliminer (**from** de). ◆**weedy** a (-ier, -iest) (person) Fam maigre et chétif.

week [wiːk] n semaine f; **the w. before last** pas la semaine dernière, celle d'avant; **the w. after next** pas la semaine prochaine, celle d'après; **tomorrow w., a w. tomorrow** demain en huit. ◆**weekday** n jour m de semaine. ◆**week'end** n week-end m; **at** or **on** or **over the w.** ce week-end, pendant le week-end. ◆**weekly** a hebdomadaire; − adv toutes les semaines; − n (magazine) hebdomadaire m.

weep [wiːp] vi (pt pp **wept**) pleurer; (of wound) suinter; **to w. for s.o.** pleurer qn; − vt (tears) pleurer; **weeping willow** saule m pleureur.

weft [weft] n Tex trame f.

weigh [weɪ] vt peser; **to w. down** (with load etc) surcharger (**with** de); (bend) faire plier; **to w. up** (goods, chances etc) peser; − vi peser; **it's weighing on my mind** ça me tracasse; **to w. down on s.o.** (of worries etc) accabler qn. ◆**weighing-machine** *n* balance *f*.

weight [weɪt] *n* poids *m*; **to put on w.** grossir; **to lose w.** maigrir; **to carry w.** (*of argument etc*) *Fig* avoir du poids (**with** pour); **to pull one's w.** (*do one's share*) *Fig* faire sa part du travail; **w. lifter** haltérophile *mf*; **w. lifting** haltérophilie *f*; – *vt* **to w.** (**down**) (*light object*) maintenir avec un poids; **to w. down with** (*overload*) surcharger de. ◆**weightlessness** *n* apesanteur *f*. ◆**weighty** *a* (-ier, -iest) lourd; (*argument, subject*) *Fig* de poids.

weighting ['weɪtɪŋ] *n* (*on salary*) indemnité *f* de résidence.

weir [wɪər] *n* (*across river*) barrage *m*.

weird [wɪəd] *a* (-er, -est) (*odd*) bizarre; (*eerie*) mystérieux.

welcome ['welkəm] *a* (*pleasant*) agréable; (*timely*) opportun; **to be w.** (*of person, people*) être le bienvenu *or* la bienvenue *or* les bienvenu(e)s; **w.!** soyez le bienvenu *or* la bienvenue *or* les bienvenu(e)s!; **to make s.o. (feel) w.** faire bon accueil à qn; **you're w.!** (*after 'thank you'*) il n'y a pas de quoi!; **w. to do** (*free*) libre de faire; **you're w. to (take *or* use) my bike** mon vélo est à ta disposition; **you're w. to it!** *Iron* grand bien vous fasse!; – *n* accueil *m*; **to extend a w. to** (*greet*) souhaiter la bienvenue à; – *vt* accueillir; (*warmly*) faire bon accueil à; (*be glad of*) se réjouir de; **I w. you!** je vous souhaite la bienvenue! ◆**welcoming** *a* (*smile etc*) accueillant; (*speech, words*) d'accueil.

weld [weld] *vt* **to w. (together)** souder; (*groups etc*) *Fig* unir; – *n* (*joint*) soudure *f*. ◆**—ing** *n* soudure *f*. ◆**—er** *n* soudeur *m*.

welfare ['welfeər] *n* (*physical, material*) bien-être *m*; (*spiritual*) santé *f*; (*public aid*) aide *f* sociale; **public w.** (*good*) le bien public; **the w. state** (*in Great Britain*) l'État-providence *m*; **w. work** assistance *f* sociale.

well¹ [wel] *n* (*for water*) puits *m*; (*of stairs, lift*) cage *f*; (*oil*) **w.** puits de pétrole. **2** *vi* **to w. up** (*rise*) monter.

well² [wel] *adv* (**better, best**) bien; **to do w.** (*succeed*) réussir; **you'd do w. to refuse** tu ferais bien de refuser; **w. done!** bravo!; **I, you, she** *etc* **might (just) as w. have left** it valait mieux partir, autant valait partir; **it's just as w. that** (*lucky*) heureusement que . . . ; **as w.** (*also*) aussi; **as w. as** aussi bien que; **as w. as two cats, he has** . . . en plus de deux chats, il a . . . ; – *a* bien *inv*; **she's w.** (*healthy*) elle va bien; **not a w. man** un

homme malade; **to get w.** se remettre; **that's all very w., but . . .** tout ça c'est très joli, mais . . . ; – *int* eh bien!; **w., w.!** (*surprise*) tiens, tiens!; **enormous, w., quite big** énorme, enfin, assez grand.

well-behaved [welbɪ'heɪvd] *a* sage. ◆**w.-'being** *n* bien-être *m*. ◆**w.-'built** *a* (*person, car*) solide. ◆**w.-'founded** *a* bien fondé. ◆**w.-'heeled** *a* (*rich*) *Fam* nanti. ◆**w.-in'formed** *a* (*person, newspaper*) bien informé. ◆**w.-'known** *a* (*a bien*) connu. ◆**w.-'meaning** *a* bien intentionné. ◆**'w.-nigh** *adv* presque. ◆**w.-'off** *a* aisé, riche. ◆**w.-'read** *a* instruit. ◆**w.-'spoken** *a* (*person*) qui a un accent cultivé, qui parle bien. ◆**w.-'thought-of** *a* hautement considéré. ◆**w.-'timed** *a* opportun. ◆**w.-to-'do** *a* aisé, riche. ◆**w.-'tried** *a* (*method*) éprouvé. ◆**w.-'trodden** *a* (*path*) battu. ◆**'w.-wishers** *npl* admirateurs, -trices *mfpl*. ◆**w.-'worn** *a* (*clothes, carpet*) usagé.

wellington ['welɪŋtən] *n* botte *f* de caoutchouc.

welsh [welʃ] *vi* **to w. on** (*debt, promise*) ne pas honorer.

Welsh [welʃ] *a* gallois; **W. rabbit** *Culin* toast *m* au fromage; – *n* (*language*) gallois *m*. ◆**Welshman** *n* (*pl* -**men**) Gallois *m*. ◆**Welshwoman** *n* (*pl* -**women**) Galloise *f*.

wench [wentʃ] *n* *Hum* jeune fille *f*.

wend [wend] *vt* **to w. one's way** s'acheminer (**to** vers).

went [went] *see* **go 1**.

wept [wept] *see* **weep**.

were [wər, *stressed* wɜːr] *see* **be**.

werewolf ['weəwʊlf] *n* (*pl* -**wolves**) loup-garou *m*.

west [west] *n* ouest *m*; – *a* (*coast*) ouest *inv*; (*wind*) d'ouest; **W. Africa** Afrique *f* occidentale; **W. Indian** *a* & *n* antillais, -aise (*mf*); **the W. Indies** les Antilles *fpl*; – *adv* à l'ouest, vers l'ouest. ◆**westbound** *a* (*carriageway*) ouest *inv*; (*traffic*) en direction de l'ouest. ◆**westerly** *a* (*point*) ouest *inv*; (*direction*) de l'ouest; (*wind*) d'ouest. ◆**western** *a* (*coast*) ouest *inv*; (*culture*) *Pol* occidental; **W. Europe** Europe *f* de l'Ouest; – *n* (*film*) western *m*. ◆**westerner** *n* habitant, -ante *mf* de l'Ouest; *Pol* occidental, -ale *mf*. ◆**westernize** *vt* occidentaliser. ◆**westward(s)** *a* & *adv* vers l'ouest.

wet [wet] *a* (**wetter, wettest**) mouillé; (*damp, rainy*) humide; (*day, month*) de pluie; **w. paint/ink** peinture *f*/encre *f* fraîche; **w. through** trempé; **to get w.** se mouiller; **it's w.** (*raining*) il pleut; **he's w.** (*weak-willed*)

Fam c'est une lavette; **w. blanket** *Fig* rabat-joie *m inv*; **w. nurse** nourrice *f*; **w. suit** combinaison *f* de plongée; – *n* the w. (*rain*) la pluie; (*damp*) l'humidité *f*; – *vt* (*-tt-*) mouiller. ◆**—ness** *n* humidité *f*.

whack [wæk] *n* (*blow*) grand coup *m*; – *vt* donner un grand coup à. ◆**—ed** *a* **w. (out)** (*tired*) *Fam* claqué. ◆**—ing** *a* (*big*) *Fam* énorme.

whale [weɪl] *n* baleine *f*. ◆**whaling** *n* pêche *f* à la baleine.

wham! [wæm] *int* vlan!

wharf [wɔːf] *n* (*pl* **wharfs** *or* **wharves**) (*for ships*) quai *m*.

what [wɒt] **1** *a* quel, quelle, *pl* quel(le)s; **w. book?** quel livre?; **w. one?** *Fam* lequel?, laquelle?; **w. a fool/***etc*! quel idiot/*etc*!; **I know w. book it is** je sais quel livre c'est; **w. (little) she has** le peu qu'elle a. **2** *pron* (*in questions*) qu'est-ce qui; (*object*) qu'est-ce que; (*after prep*) quoi; **w.'s happening?** qu'est-ce qui se passe?; **w. does he do?** qu'est-ce qu'il fait?, que fait-il?; **w. is it?** qu'est-ce que c'est?; **w.'s that book?** quel est ce livre?; **w.!** (*surprise*) quoi!, comment!; **w.'s it called?** comment ça s'appelle?; **w. for?** pourquoi?; **w. about me/***etc*? et moi/*etc*?; **w. about leaving/***etc*? si on partait/*etc*? **3** *pron* (*indirect, relative*) ce qui; (*object*) ce que; **I know w. will happen/w.** she'll do je sais ce qui arrivera/ce qu'elle fera; **w. happens is . . .** ce qui arrive c'est que . . . ; **w. I need** ce dont j'ai besoin. ◆**what'ever** *a* **w. (the) mistake/***etc* (*no matter what*) quelle que soit l'erreur/*etc*; **of w. size** de n'importe quelle taille; **no chance w.** pas la moindre chance; **nothing w.** rien du tout; – *pron* (*no matter what*) quoi que (+ *sub*); **w. happens** quoi qu'il arrive; **w. you do** quoi que tu fasses; **w. is important** tout ce qui est important; **w. you want** tout ce que tu veux. ◆**what's-it** *n* (*thing*) *Fam* machin *m*. ◆**whatso'ever** *a & pron* = **whatever**.

wheat [wiːt] *n* blé *m*, froment *m*. ◆**wheatgerm** *n* germes *mpl* de blé.

wheedle ['wiːd(ə)l] *vt* **to w. s.o.** enjôler qn (**into doing** pour qu'il fasse); **to w. sth out of s.o.** obtenir qch de qn par la flatterie.

wheel [wiːl] **1** *n* roue *f*; **at the w.** *Aut* au volant; *Nau* au gouvernail; – *vt* (*push*) pousser; – *vi* (*turn*) tourner. **2** *vi* **to w. and deal** *Fam* faire des combines. ◆**wheelbarrow** *n* brouette *f*. ◆**wheelchair** *n* fauteuil *m* roulant.

wheeze [wiːz] **1** *vi* respirer bruyamment. **2** *n*

(*scheme*) *Fam* combine *f*. ◆**wheezy** *a* (**-ier, -iest**) poussif.

whelk [welk] *n* (*mollusc*) buccin *m*.

when [wen] *adv* quand; – *conj* quand, lorsque; (*whereas*) alors que; **w. I finish, w. I've finished** quand j'aurai fini; **w. I saw him** *or* **w. I'd seen him,** I left après l'avoir vu, je suis parti; **the day/moment w.** le jour/moment où; **I talked about w. . . . .** j'ai parlé de l'époque où . . . . ◆**when'ever** *conj* (*at whatever time*) quand; (*each time that*) chaque fois que.

where [weər] *adv* où; **w. are you from?** d'où êtes-vous?; – *conj* où; (*whereas*) alors que; **that's w. you'll find it** c'est là que tu le trouveras; **I found it w.** she'd left it je l'ai trouvé là où elle l'avait laissé; **I went to w.** he was je suis allé à l'endroit où il était. ◆**whereabouts** *adv* où (donc); – *n* his w. l'endroit *m* où il est. ◆**where'as** *conj* alors que. ◆**where'by** *adv* par quoi. ◆**where'upon** *adv* sur quoi. ◆**wher-ever** *conj* **w. you go** (*everywhere*) partout où tu iras, où que tu ailles; **I'll go w. you like** (*anywhere*) j'irai (là) où vous voudrez.

whet [wet] *vt* (*-tt-*) (*appetite, desire etc*) aiguiser.

whether ['weðər] *conj* si; **I don't know w. to leave** je ne sais pas si je dois partir; **w. she does it or not** qu'elle le fasse ou non; **w. now or tomorrow** que ce soit maintenant ou demain; **it's doubtful w.** il est douteux que (+ *sub*).

which [wɪtʃ] **1** *a* (*in questions etc*) quel, quelle, *pl* quel(le)s; **w. hat?** quel chapeau?; **in w. case** auquel cas. **2** *rel pron* qui; (*object*) que; (*after prep*) lequel, laquelle, *pl* lesquel(le)s; **the house w. is . . .** la maison qui est . . . ; **the book w.** I like le livre que j'aime; **the film of w. . . . .** le film dont *or* duquel . . . ; **she's ill, w. is sad** elle est malade, ce qui est triste; **he lies, w.** I don't like il ment, ce que je n'aime pas; **after w.** (*whereupon*) après quoi. **3** *pron* **w. (one)** (*in questions*) lequel, laquelle, *pl* lesquel(le)s; **w. (one) of us?** lequel *or* laquelle d'entre nous?; **w. (ones) are the best of the books** quels sont les meilleurs de ces livres? **4** *pron* **w. (one)** (*the one that*) celui qui, celle qui, *pl* ceux qui, celles qui; (*object*) celui qui *or* celle qui; **show me w. (one) is red** montrez-moi celui *or* celle qui est rouge; **I know w. (ones) you want** je sais ceux *or* celles que vous désirez. ◆**which'ever** *a & pron* **w. book/***etc* **or** **w. of the books/***etc* **you buy** quel que soit le livre/*etc* que tu achètes; **take w. books** *or* **w. of the books interest you** prenez les livres qui vous intéressent; **take w. (one) you like** prends celui *or* celle que tu veux; **w. (ones) remain** ceux *or* celles qui restent.

whiff [wɪf] *n* (*puff*) bouffée *f*; (*smell*) odeur *f*.

while [waɪl] *conj* (*when*) pendant que; (*although*) bien que (+ *sub*); (*as long as*) tant que; (*whereas*) tandis que; **w. doing** (*in the course of*) en faisant; − *n* **a w.** un moment, quelque temps; **all the w.** tout le temps; − *vt* **to w. away** (*time*) passer. ◆**whilst** [waɪlst] *conj* = **while**.

whim [wɪm] *n* caprice *m*.

whimper [ˈwɪmpər] *vi* (*of dog, person*) gémir faiblement; (*snivel*) *Pej* pleurnicher; − *n* faible gémissement *m*; **without a w.** (*complaint*) *Fig* sans se plaindre.

whimsical [ˈwɪmzɪk(ə)l] *a* (*look, idea*) bizarre; (*person*) fantasque, capricieux.

whine [waɪn] *vi* gémir; (*complain*) *Fig* se plaindre; − *n* gémissement *m*; plainte *f*.

whip [wɪp] *n* fouet *m*; − *vt* (**-pp-**) (*person, cream etc*) fouetter; (*defeat*) *Fam* dérouiller; **to w. off** (*take off*) enlever brusquement; **to w. out** (*from pocket etc*) sortir brusquement (**from** de); **to w. up** (*interest*) susciter; (*meal*) *Fam* préparer rapidement; − *vi* (*move*) aller à toute vitesse; **to w. round to s.o.'s** faire un saut chez qn. ◆**whip-round** *n* *Fam* collecte *f*.

whirl [wɜːl] *vi* tourbillonner, tournoyer; − *vt* faire tourbillonner; − *n* tourbillon *m*. ◆**whirlpool** *n* tourbillon *m*; **w. bath** *Am* bain *m* à remous. ◆**whirlwind** *n* tourbillon *m* (de vent).

whirr [wɜːr] *vi* (*of engine*) vrombir; (*of top*) ronronner.

whisk [wɪsk] **1** *n* *Culin* fouet *m*; − *vt* fouetter. **2** *vt* **to w. away** *or* **off** (*tablecloth etc*) enlever rapidement; (*person*) emmener rapidement; (*chase away*) chasser.

whiskers [ˈwɪskəz] *npl* (*of animal*) moustaches *fpl*; (*beard*) barbe *f*; (*moustache*) moustache *f*; (**side**) **w.** favoris *mpl*.

whisky, *Am* **whiskey** [ˈwɪskɪ] *n* whisky *m*.

whisper [ˈwɪspər] *vti* chuchoter; **w. to me!** chuchote à mon oreille!; − *n* chuchotement *m*; (*rumour*) *Fig* rumeur *f*, bruit *m*.

whistle [ˈwɪs(ə)l] *n* sifflement *m*; (*object*) sifflet *m*; **to blow** *or* **give a w.** siffler; − *vti* siffler; **to w. at** (*girl*) siffler; **to w. for** (*dog, taxi*) siffler.

Whit [wɪt] *a* **W. Sunday** dimanche *m* de Pentecôte.

white [waɪt] *a* (**-er, -est**) blanc; **to go** *or* **turn w.** blanchir; **w. coffee** café *m* au lait; **w. elephant** *Fig* objet *m* *or* projet *m* *etc* inutile;

w. lie pieux mensonge *m*; **w. man** blanc *m*; **w. woman** blanche *f*; − *n* (*colour, of egg, of eye*) blanc *m*; (*person*) blanc *m*, blanche *f*. ◆**white-collar 'worker** *n* employé, -ée *mf* de bureau. ◆**whiten** *vti* blanchir. ◆**whiteness** *n* blancheur *f*. ◆**whitewash** *n* (*for walls etc*) blanc *m* de chaux; − *vt* blanchir à la chaux; (*person*) *Fig* blanchir; (*faults*) justifier.

whiting [ˈwaɪtɪŋ] *n* (*fish*) merlan *m*.

Whitsun [ˈwɪts(ə)n] *n* la Pentecôte.

whittle [ˈwɪt(ə)l] *vt* **to w. down** (*wood*) tailler; (*price etc*) *Fig* rogner.

whizz [wɪz] **1** *vi* (*rush*) aller à toute vitesse; **to w. past** passer à toute vitesse; **to w. through the air** fendre l'air. **2** *a* **w. kid** *Fam* petit prodige *m*.

who [huː] *pron* qui; **w. did it?** qui (est-ce qui) a fait ça?; **the woman w.** la femme qui; **w. did you see** tu as vu qui? ◆**who'ever** *pron* (*no matter who*) qui que ce soit qui; (*object*) qui que ce soit que; **w. has travelled** (*anyone who*) quiconque a *or* celui qui a voyagé; **w. you are** qui que vous soyez; **this man, w.** he is cet homme, quel qu'il soit; **w. did that?** qui donc a fait ça?

whodunit [huːˈdʌnɪt] *n* (*detective story*) *Fam* polar *m*.

whole [həʊl] *a* entier; (*intact*) intact; **the w. time** tout le temps; **the w. apple** toute la pomme, la pomme (tout) entière; **the w. truth** toute la vérité; **the w. world** le monde entier; **the w. lot** le tout; **to swallow sth w.** avaler qch tout rond; − *n* (*unit*) tout *m*; (*total*) totalité *f*; **the w. of the village** le village (tout) entier, tout le village; **the w. of the night** toute la nuit; **on the w., as a w.** dans l'ensemble. ◆**whole-'hearted** *a*, ◆**whole-'heartedly** *adv* sans réserve. ◆**wholemeal** *a*, *Am* ◆**wholewheat** *a* (*bread*) complet. ◆**wholly** *adv* entièrement.

wholesale [ˈhəʊlseɪl] *n* *Com* gros *m*; − *a* (*firm*) de gros; (*destruction etc*) *Fig* en masse; − *adv* (*in bulk*) en gros; (*to buy or sell one article*) au prix de gros; (*to destroy etc*) *Fig* en masse. ◆**wholesaler** *n* grossiste *mf*.

wholesome [ˈhəʊlsəm] *a* (*food, climate etc*) sain.

whom [huːm] *pron* (*object*) que; (*in questions and after prep*) qui; **w. did she see?** qui a-t-elle vu?; **the man w. you know** l'homme que tu connais; **with w.** avec qui; **of w.** dont.

whooping cough [ˈhuːpɪŋkɒf] *n* coqueluche *f*.

whoops! [wʊps] *int* (*apology etc*) oups!
whopping ['wɒpɪŋ] *a* (*big*) *Fam* énorme.
◆**whopper** *n Fam* chose *f* énorme.
whore [hɔːr] *n* (*prostitute*) putain *f*.
whose [huːz] *poss pron* & *a* à qui, de qui; w.
book is this?, w. is this book? à qui est ce
livre?; **w. daughter are you?** de qui es-tu la
fille?; **the woman w. book I have** la femme
dont *or* de qui j'ai le livre; **the man w.
mother I spoke to** l'homme à la mère de qui
j'ai parlé.
why [waɪ] 1 *adv* pourquoi; **w. not?** pourquoi
pas?; – *conj* **the reason w. they . . .** la
raison pour laquelle ils . . . ; – *npl* **the whys
and wherefores** le pourquoi et le comment.
2 *int* (*surprise*) eh bien!, tiens!
wick [wɪk] *n* (*of candle, lamp*) mèche *f*.
wicked ['wɪkɪd] *a* (*evil*) méchant, vilain;
(*mischievous*) malicieux. ◆**—ly** *adv*
méchamment; malicieusement. ◆**—ness**
n méchanceté *f*.
wicker ['wɪkər] *n* osier *m*; – *a* (*chair etc*) en
osier, d'osier. ◆**wickerwork** *n* (*objects*)
vannerie *f*.
wicket ['wɪkɪt] *n* (*cricket stumps*) guichet *m*.
wide [waɪd] *a* (**-er, -est**) large; (*desert, ocean*)
vaste; (*choice, knowledge, variety*) grand; **to
be three metres w.** avoir trois mètres de
large; – *adv* (*to fall, shoot*) loin du but; (*to
open*) tout grand. ◆**wide-'awake** *a* (*alert,
not sleeping*) éveillé. ◆**widely** *adv* (*to
broadcast, spread*) largement; (*to travel*)
beaucoup; **w. different** très différent; **it's w.
thought** *or* **believed that . . .** on pense
généralement que . . . . ◆**widen** *vt* élargir;
– *vi* s'élargir. ◆**wideness** *n* largeur *f*.
widespread ['waɪdspred] *a* (*très*) répandu.
widow ['wɪdəʊ] *n* veuve *f*. ◆**widowed** *a*
(*man*) veuf; (*woman*) veuve; **to be w.**
(*become a widower or widow*) devenir veuf
or veuve. ◆**widower** *n* veuf *m*.
width [wɪdθ] *n* largeur *f*.
wield [wiːld] *vt* (*handle*) manier; (*brandish*)
brandir; (*power*) *Fig* exercer.
wife [waɪf] *n* (*pl* **wives**) femme *f*, épouse *f*.
wig [wɪg] *n* perruque *f*.
wiggle ['wɪg(ə)l] *vt* agiter; **to w. one's hips**
tortiller des hanches; – *vi* (*of worm etc*) se
tortiller; (*of tail*) remuer.
wild [waɪld] *a* (**-er, -est**) (*animal, flower,
region etc*) sauvage; (*enthusiasm, sea*)
déchaîné; (*idea, life*) fou; (*look*) farouche;
(*angry*) furieux (**with** contre); **w. with** (*joy,
anger etc*) fou de; **I'm not w. about it** (*plan
etc*) *Fam* ça ne m'emballe pas; **to be w.
about s.o.** (*very fond of*) être dingue de qn;
to grow w. (*of plant*) pousser à l'état sau-

vage; **to run w.** (*of animals*) courir en
liberté; (*of crowd*) se déchaîner; **the W.
West** *Am* le Far West; – *npl* régions *fpl*
sauvages. ◆**wildcat 'strike** *n* grève *f* sauvage. ◆**wild-'goose chase** *n* fausse piste *f*.
◆**wildlife** *n* animaux *mpl* sauvages, faune
f.
wilderness ['wɪldənəs] *n* désert *m*.
wildly ['waɪldlɪ] *adv* (*madly*) follement;
(*violently*) violemment.
wile [waɪl] *n* ruse *f*, artifice *m*.
wilful ['wɪlfəl] *a* (*Am* **willful**) (*intentional,
obstinate*) volontaire. ◆**—ly** *adv* volontairement.
will¹ [wɪl] *v aux* **he will come, he'll come**
(*future tense*) il viendra (**won't he?** n'est-ce
pas?); **you will not come, you won't come** tu
ne viendras pas (**will you?** n'est-ce pas?); **w.
you have a tea?** veux-tu prendre un thé?; **w.
you be quiet!** veux-tu te taire!; **I w.!** (*yes*)
oui!; **it won't open** ça ne s'ouvre pas, ça ne
veut pas s'ouvrir.
will² [wɪl] 1 *vt* (*wish, intend*) vouloir (**that**
que (+ *sub*)); **to w. oneself to do** faire un
effort de volonté pour faire; – *n* volonté *f*;
against one's w. à contrecœur; **at w.** (*to
depart etc*) quand on veut; (*to choose*) à
volonté. 2 *n* (*legal document*) testament *m*.
◆**willpower** *n* volonté *f*.
willing ['wɪlɪŋ] *a* (*helper, worker*) de bonne
volonté; (*help etc*) spontané; **to be w. to do**
être disposé *or* prêt à faire, vouloir bien
faire; – *n* **to show w.** faire preuve de bonne
volonté. ◆**—ly** *adv* (*with pleasure*)
volontiers; (*voluntarily*) volontairement.
◆**—ness** *n* (*goodwill*) bonne volonté *f*; **his**
or **her w. to do** (*enthusiasm*) son empressement *m* à faire.
willow ['wɪləʊ] *n* (*tree, wood*) saule *m*.
◆**willowy** *a* (*person*) svelte.
willy-nilly [wɪlɪ'nɪlɪ] *adv* bon gré mal gré, de
gré ou de force.
wilt [wɪlt] *vi* (*of plant*) dépérir; (*of enthusiasm etc*) *Fig* décliner.
wily [waɪlɪ] *a* (**-ier, -iest**) rusé.
wimp [wɪmp] *n* (*weakling*) *Fam* mauviette *f*.
win [wɪn] *n* (*victory*) victoire *f*; – *vi* (*pt & pp*
won, *pres p* **winning**) gagner; – *vt* (*money,
race etc*) gagner; (*victory, prize*) remporter;
(*fame*) acquérir; (*friends*) se faire; **to w. s.o.
over** gagner qn (**to** à). ◆**winning** *a*
(*number, horse etc*) gagnant; (*team*) victorieux; (*goal*) décisif; (*smile*) engageant;
– *npl* gains *mpl*.
wince [wɪns] *vi* (*flinch*) tressaillir; (*pull a
face*) grimacer; **without wincing** sans
sourciller.

winch [wɪntʃ] n treuil m; − vt to w. (up) hisser au treuil.

wind¹ [wɪnd] n vent m; (breath) souffle m; to have w. Med avoir des gaz; to get w. of Fig avoir vent de; in the w. Fig dans l'air; w. instrument Mus instrument m à vent; − vt to w. s.o. (of blow etc) couper le souffle à qn. ◆**windbreak** n (fence, trees) brise-vent m inv. ◆**windcheater** n, Am ◆**windbreaker** n blouson m, coupe-vent m inv. ◆**windfall** n (piece of fruit) fruit m abattu par le vent; (unexpected money) Fig aubaine f. ◆**windmill** n moulin m à vent. ◆**windpipe** n Anat trachée f. ◆**windscreen** n, Am ◆**windshield** n Aut pare-brise m inv; w. wiper essuie-glace m inv. ◆**windsurfing** n to go w. faire de la planche à voile. ◆**windswept** a (street etc) balayé par les vents. ◆**windy** a (-ier, -iest) venteux, venté; it's w. (of weather) il y a du vent.

wind² [waɪnd] vt (pt & pp wound) (roll) enrouler; to w. (up) (clock) remonter; to w. up (meeting) terminer; (firm) liquider; − vi (of river, road) serpenter; to w. down (relax) se détendre; to w. up (end up) finir (doing par faire); to w. up with sth se retrouver avec qch. ◆**—ing** a (road etc) sinueux; (staircase) tournant. ◆**—er** n (of watch) remontoir m.

window ['wɪndəu] n fenêtre f; (pane) vitre f, carreau m; (in vehicle or train) vitre f; (in shop) vitrine f; (counter) guichet m; French w. porte-fenêtre f; w. box jardinière f; w. cleaner or Am washer laveur, -euse mf de carreaux; w. dresser étalagiste mf; w. ledge = windowsill; to go w. shopping faire du lèche-vitrines. ◆**windowpane** n vitre f, carreau m. ◆**windowsill** n (inside) appui m de (la) fenêtre; (outside) rebord m de (la) fenêtre.

wine [waɪn] n vin m; − a (bottle, cask) à vin; w. cellar cave f (à vin); w. grower viticulteur m; w. list carte f des vins; w. taster dégustateur, -trice mf de vins; w. tasting dégustation f de vins; w. waiter sommelier m; − vt to w. and dine s.o. offrir à dîner et à boire à qn. ◆**wineglass** n verre m à vin. ◆**wine-growing** a viticole.

wing [wɪŋ] n aile f; the wings Th les coulisses fpl; under one's w. Fig sous son aile. ◆**winged** a ailé. ◆**winger** n Sp ailier m. ◆**wingspan** n envergure f.

wink [wɪŋk] vi faire un clin d'œil (at, to à); (of light) clignoter; − n clin m d'œil.

winkle ['wɪŋk(ə)l] n (sea animal) bigorneau m.

winner ['wɪnər] n (of contest etc) gagnant, -ante mf; (of argument, fight) vainqueur m; that idea/etc is a w. Fam c'est une idée/etc en or.

winter ['wɪntər] n hiver m; − a d'hiver; in (the) w. en hiver. ◆**wintertime** n hiver m. ◆**wintry** a hivernal.

wip/e [waɪp] vt essuyer; to w. one's feet/hands s'essuyer les pieds/les mains; to w. away or off or up (liquid) essuyer; to w. out (clean) essuyer; (erase) effacer; (destroy) anéantir; − vi to w. up (dry the dishes) essuyer la vaisselle; − n coup m de torchon or d'éponge. ◆**—er** n Aut essuie-glace m inv.

wir/e ['waɪər] n fil m; (telegram) télégramme m; w. netting grillage m; − vt to w. (up) (house) El faire l'installation électrique de; to w. s.o. (telegraph) télégraphier à qn. ◆**—ing** n El installation f électrique. ◆**wirecutters** npl pince f coupante.

wireless ['waɪələs] n (set) TSF f, radio f; by w. (to send a message) par sans-fil.

wiry ['waɪərɪ] a (-ier, -iest) maigre et nerveux.

wisdom ['wɪzdəm] n sagesse f.

wise [waɪz] a (-er, -est) (prudent) sage, prudent; (learned) savant; to put s.o. w./be w. to Fam mettre qn/être au courant de; w. guy Fam gros malin m. ◆**wisecrack** n Fam (joke) astuce f; (sarcastic remark) sarcasme m. ◆**wisely** adv prudemment.

-wise [waɪz] suffix (with regard to) money/etc-wise question argent/etc.

wish [wɪʃ] vt souhaiter, vouloir (to do faire); I w. (that) you could help me/could have helped me je voudrais que/j'aurais voulu que vous m'aidiez; I w. I hadn't done that je regrette d'avoir fait ça; if you w. si tu veux; I w. you well or luck je vous souhaite bonne chance; I wished him or her (a) happy birthday je lui ai souhaité bon anniversaire; I w. I could si seulement je pouvais; − vi to w. for sth souhaiter qch; − n (specific) souhait m, vœu m; (general) désir m; the w. for sth/to do le désir de qch/de faire; best wishes (on greeting card) meilleurs vœux mpl; (in letter) amitiés fpl, bien amicalement; send him or her my best wishes fais-lui mes amitiés. ◆**wishbone** n bréchet m. ◆**wishful** a it's w. thinking (on your part) tu te fais des illusions, tu prends tes désirs pour la réalité.

wishy-washy ['wɪʃɪwɒʃɪ] a (taste, colour) fade.

wisp [wɪsp] n (of smoke) volute f; (of hair)

fine mèche *f*; **a (mere) w. of a girl** une fillette toute menue.

wisteria [wɪ'stɪərɪə] *n Bot* glycine *f*.

wistful ['wɪstfəl] *a* mélancolique et rêveur. ◆**—ly** *adv* avec mélancolie.

wit [wɪt] *n* **1** (*humour*) esprit *m*; (*person*) homme *m or* femme *f* d'esprit. **2 wit(s)** (*intelligence*) intelligence *f* (**to do** de faire); **to be at one's wits'** *or* **wit's end** ne plus savoir que faire.

witch [wɪtʃ] *n* sorcière *f*. ◆**witchcraft** *n* sorcellerie *f*. ◆**witch-hunt** *n Pol* chasse *f* aux sorcières.

with [wɪð] *prep* **1** avec; **come w. me** viens avec moi; **w. no hat** sans chapeau; **I'll be right w. you** je suis à vous dans une minute; **I'm w. you** (*I understand*) *Fam* je te suis; **w. it** (*up-to-date*) *Fam* dans le vent. **2** (*at the house, flat etc of*) chez; **she's staying w. me** elle loge chez moi; **it's a habit w. me** c'est une habitude chez moi. **3** (*cause*) de; **to jump w. joy** sauter de joie. **4** (*instrument, means*) avec, de; **to write w. a pen** écrire avec un stylo; **to fill w.** remplir de; **satisfied w.** satisfait de; **w. my own eyes** de mes propres yeux. **5** (*against*) à; **w. blue eyes** aux yeux bleus. **6** (*despite*) malgré.

withdraw [wɪð'drɔː] *vt* (*pt* withdrew, *pp* withdrawn) retirer (**from** de); – *vi* se retirer (**from** de). ◆**withdrawn** *a* (*person*) renfermé. ◆**withdrawal** *n* retrait *m*; **to suffer from w. symptoms** (*of drug addict etc*) être en manque.

wither ['wɪðər] *vi* (*of plant etc*) se flétrir; – *vt* flétrir. ◆**—ed** *a* (*limb*) atrophié. ◆**—ing** *a* (*look*) foudroyant; (*remark*) cinglant.

withhold [wɪð'həʊld] *vt* (*pt & pp* withheld) (*help, permission etc*) refuser (**from** à); (*decision*) différer; (*money*) retenir (**from** de); (*information etc*) cacher (**from** à).

within [wɪ'ðɪn] *adv* à l'intérieur; – *prep* (*place, container etc*) à l'intérieur de, dans; **w. a kilometre of** à moins d'un kilomètre de; **w. a month** (*to return etc*) avant un mois; (*to finish sth*) en moins d'un mois; (*to pay*) sous un mois; **w. my means** dans (les limites de) mes moyens; **w. sight** en vue.

without [wɪ'ðaʊt] *prep* sans; **w. a tie/etc** sans cravate/etc; **w. doing** sans faire.

withstand [wɪð'stænd] *vt* (*pt & pp* withstood) résister à.

witness ['wɪtnɪs] *n* (*person*) témoin *m*; (*evidence*) *Jur* témoignage *m*; **to bear w. to** témoigner de; – *vt* être (le) témoin de, voir; (*document*) signer (pour attester l'authenticité de).

witty ['wɪtɪ] *a* (-ier, -iest) spirituel. ◆**witti-**

cism *n* bon mot *m*, mot *m* d'esprit. ◆**wittiness** *n* esprit *m*.

wives [waɪvz] *see* wife.

wizard ['wɪzəd] *n* magicien *m*; (*genius*) *Fig* génie *m*, as *m*.

wizened ['wɪz(ə)nd] *a* ratatiné.

wobble ['wɒb(ə)l] *vi* (*of chair etc*) branler, boiter; (*of cyclist, pile etc*) osciller; (*of jelly, leg*) trembler; (*of wheel*) tourner de façon irrégulière. ◆**wobbly** *a* (*table etc*) bancal, boiteux; **to be w. = to wobble**.

woe [wəʊ] *n* malheur *m*. ◆**woeful** *a* triste.

woke, woken [wəʊk, 'wəʊk(ə)n] *see* wake 1.

wolf [wʊlf] **1** *n* (*pl* wolves) loup *m*; **w. whistle** sifflement *m* admiratif. **2** *vt* **to w. (down)** (*food*) engloutir.

woman, *pl* **women** ['wʊmən, 'wɪmɪn] *n* femme *f*; **she's a London w.** c'est une Londonienne; **w. doctor** femme *f* médecin; **women drivers** les femmes *fpl* au volant; **w. friend** amie *f*; **w. teacher** professeur *m* femme; **women's** (*attitudes, clothes etc*) féminin. ◆**womanhood** *n* (*quality*) féminité *f*; **to reach w.** devenir femme. ◆**womanizer** *n Pej* coureur *m* (de femmes *or* de jupons). ◆**womanly** *a* féminin.

womb [wuːm] *n* utérus *m*.

women ['wɪmɪn] *see* woman.

won [wʌn] *see* win.

wonder ['wʌndər] **1** *n* (*marvel*) merveille *f*, miracle *m*; (*sense, feeling*) émerveillement *m*; **in w.** (*to watch etc*) émerveillé; **(it's) no w.** ce n'est pas étonnant (**that** que (+ *sub*)); – *vi* (*marvel*) s'étonner (**at** de); – *vt* **I w. that** je *or* ça m'étonne que (+ *sub*). **2** *vt* (*ask oneself*) se demander (**if** si, **why** pourquoi); – *vi* (*reflect*) songer (**about** à). ◆**wonderful** *a* (*excellent, astonishing*) merveilleux. ◆**wonderfully** *adv* (*beautiful, hot etc*) merveilleusement; (*to do, work etc*) à merveille.

wonky ['wɒŋkɪ] *a* (-ier, -iest) *Fam* (*table etc*) bancal; (*hat, picture*) de travers.

won't [wəʊnt] = will not.

woo [wuː] *vt* (*woman*) faire la cour à, courtiser; (*try to please*) *Fig* chercher à plaire à.

wood [wʊd] *n* (*material, forest*) bois *m*. ◆**woodcut** *n* gravure *f* sur bois. ◆**wooded** *a* (*valley etc*) boisé. ◆**wooden** *a* de *or* en bois; (*manner, dancer etc*) *Fig* raide. ◆**woodland** *n* région *f* boisée. ◆**woodpecker** *n* (*bird*) pic *m*. ◆**woodwind** *n* (*instruments*) *Mus* bois *mpl*. ◆**woodwork** *n* (*craft, objects*) menuiserie *f*. ◆**woodworm** *n* (*larvae*) vers *mpl* (du bois); **it has w.** c'est vermoulu. ◆**woody** *a*

(**-ier, -iest**) (*hill etc*) boisé; (*stem etc*) ligneux.

wool [wʊl] *n* laine *f*; *– a* de laine; (*industry*) lainier. ◆**woollen** *a* de laine; (*industry*) lainier; *– npl* (*garments*) lainages *mpl.* ◆**woolly** *a* (**-ier, -iest**) laineux; (*unclear*) *Fig* nébuleux; *– n* (*garment*) *Fam* lainage *m.*

word [wɜːd] *n* mot *m*; (*spoken*) parole *f*, mot *m*; (*promise*) parole *f*; (*command*) ordre *m*; *pl* (*of song etc*) paroles *fpl*; **by w. of mouth** de vive voix; **to have a w. with s.o.** (*speak to*) parler à qn; (*advise, lecture*) avoir un mot avec qn; **in other words** autrement dit; **I have no w. from** (*news*) je suis sans nouvelles de; **to send w. that . . .** faire savoir que . . . ; **to leave w. that . . .** dire que . . . ; **the last w. in** (*latest development*) le dernier cri en matière de. ◆**w. processing** traitement *m* de texte; *– vt* (*express*) rédiger, formuler. ◆**wording** *n* termes *mpl.* ◆**wordy** *a* (**-ier, -iest**) verbeux.

wore [wɔːr] *see* **wear 1,2.**

work [wɜːk] *n* travail *m*; (*product*) & *Liter* œuvre *f*, ouvrage *m*; (*building or repair work*) travaux *mpl*; **to be at w.** travailler; **farm w.** travaux *mpl* agricoles; **out of w.** au *or* en chômage; **a day off w.** un jour de congé *or* de repos; **he's off w.** il n'est pas allé travailler; **the works** (*mechanism*) le mécanisme; **a gas works** (*factory*) une usine à gaz; **w. force** main-d'œuvre *f*; **a heavy w. load** beaucoup de travail; *– vi* travailler; (*of machine etc*) marcher, fonctionner; (*of drug*) agir; **to w. on** (*book etc*) travailler à; (*principle*) se baser sur; **to w. at** *or* **on sth** (*improve*) travailler qch; **to w. loose** (*of knot, screw*) se desserrer; (*of tooth*) se mettre à branler; **to w. towards** (*result, agreement, aim*) travailler à; **to w. out** (*succeed*) marcher; (*train*) *Sp* s'entraîner; **it works out at £5** ça fait cinq livres; **it works up to** (*climax*) ça tend vers; **to w. up to sth** (*in speech etc*) en venir à qch; *– vt* (*person*) faire travailler; (*machine*) faire marcher; (*mine*) exploiter; (*miracle*) faire; (*metal, wood etc*) travailler; **to get worked up** s'exciter; **to w. in** (*reference, bolt*) introduire; **to w. off** (*debt*) payer en travaillant; (*excess fat*) se débarrasser de (par l'exercice); (*anger*) passer, assouvir; **to w. out** (*solve*) résoudre; (*calculate*) calculer; (*scheme, plan*) élaborer; **to w. up an appetite** s'ouvrir l'appétit; **to w. up enthusiasm** s'enthousiasmer; **to w. one's way up** (*rise socially etc*) faire du chemin. ◆**working** *a* (*day, clothes etc*) de travail; (*population*) actif; **Monday's a w. day** on travaille le lundi, lundi est un jour ouvré; **w. class** *f* ouvrière; **in w. order** en état de marche; *– npl* (*mechanism*) mécanisme *m.* ◆**workable** *a* (*plan*) praticable. ◆**worker** *n* travailleur, -euse *mf*; (*manual*) ouvrier, -ière *mf*; (*employee, clerk*) employé, -ée *mf*; **blue-collar w.** col *m* bleu.

workaholic [wɜːkəˈhɒlɪk] *n Fam* bourreau *m* de travail. ◆**'workbench** *n* établi *m.* ◆**working-'class** *a* ouvrier. ◆**'workman** *n* (*pl* **-men**) ouvrier *m.* ◆**'workmanship** *n* maîtrise *f*, travail *m.* ◆**'workmate** *n* camarade *mf* de travail. ◆**'workout** *n Sp* (*séance f*) d'entraînement *m.* ◆**'workroom** *n* salle *f* de travail. ◆**'workshop** *n* atelier *m.* ◆**'work-shy** *a* peu enclin au travail. ◆**work-to-'rule** *n* grève *f* du zèle.

world [wɜːld] *n* monde *m*; **all over the w.** dans le monde entier; **the richest/etc in the world** le *or* la plus riche/*etc* du monde; **a w. of** (*a lot of*) énormément de; **to think the w. of** penser énormément de bien de; **why in the w. . . . ?** pourquoi diable . . . ?; **out of this w.** (*wonderful*) *Fam* formidable; *– a* (*war etc*) mondial; (*champion, cup, record*) du monde. ◆**world-'famous** *a* de renommée mondiale. ◆**worldly** *a* (*pleasures*) de ce monde; (*person*) qui a l'expérience du monde. ◆**world'wide** *a* universel.

worm [wɜːm] **1** *n* ver *m.* **2** *vt* **to w. one's way into** s'insinuer dans; **to w. sth out of s.o.** soutirer qch à qn. ◆**worm-eaten** *a* (*wood*) vermoulu; (*fruit*) véreux.

worn [wɔːn] *see* **wear 1,2;** *– a* (*tyre etc*) usé. ◆**worn-'out** *a* (*object*) complètement usé; (*person*) épuisé.

worry [ˈwʌrɪ] *n* souci *m*; *– vi* s'inquiéter (**about sth** de qch, **about s.o.** pour qn); *– vt* inquiéter; **to be worried** être inquiet; **to be worried sick** se ronger les sangs. ◆**—ing** *a* (*news etc*) inquiétant. ◆**worrier** *n* anxieux, -euse *mf.* ◆**worryguts** *n, Am* ◆**worrywart** *n Fam* anxieux, -euse *mf.*

worse [wɜːs] *a* pire, plus mauvais (**than que**); **to get w.** se détériorer; **he's getting w.** (*in health*) il va de plus en plus mal; (*in behaviour*) il se conduit de plus en plus mal; *– adv* plus mal (**than que**); **I could do w.** je pourrais faire pire; **to hate/etc w. than** détester/*etc* plus que; **to be w. off** (*financially*) aller moins bien financièrement; *– n* **there's w. (to come)** il y a pire encore; **a change for the w.** une détérioration. ◆**worsen** *vti* empirer.

worship [ˈwɜːʃɪp] *n* culte *m*; **his W. the Mayor** Monsieur le Maire; *– vt* (**-pp-**)

(*person*) & *Rel* adorer; (*money etc*) *Pej* avoir le culte de; − *vi Rel* faire ses dévotions (**at** à). ◆**worshipper** *n* adorateur, -trice *mf*; (*in church*) fidèle *mf*.

worst [wɜːst] *a* pire, plus mauvais; − *adv* (**the**) **w.** le plus mal; **to come off w.** (*in struggle etc*) avoir le dessous; − *n* **the w.** (*one*) (*object, person*) le *or* la pire, le *or* la plus mauvais(e); **the w. (thing) is that** . . . le pire c'est que . . . ; **at (the) w.** au pis aller; **at its w.** (*crisis*) à son plus mauvais point *or* moment; **to get the w. of it** (*in struggle etc*) avoir le dessous; **the w. is yet to come** on n'a pas encore vu le pire.

worsted ['wustɪd] *n* laine *f* peignée.

worth [wɜːθ] *n* valeur *f*; **to buy 50 pence w. of chocolates** acheter pour cinquante pence de chocolats; − *a* **to be w.** valoir; **how much** *or* **what is it w.?** ça vaut combien?; **the film's w. seeing** le film vaut la peine *or* le coup d'être vu; **it's w.** (*one's*) **while** ça (en) vaut la peine *or* le coup; **it's w. (while) waiting** ça vaut la peine d'attendre. ◆**worthless** *a* qui ne vaut rien. ◆**worth'while** *a* (*book, film etc*) qui vaut la peine d'être lu, vu *etc*; (*activity*) qui (en) vaut la peine; (*contribution, plan*) valable; (*cause*) louable; (*satisfying*) qui donne des satisfactions.

worthy ['wɜːðɪ] *a* (**-ier, -iest**) digne (**of** de); (*laudable*) louable; − *n* (*person*) notable *m*.

would [wud, *unstressed* wəd] *v aux* **I w. stay, I'd stay** (*conditional tense*) je resterais; **he w. have done it** il l'aurait fait; **w. you help me, please?** voulez-vous m'aider, s'il vous plaît?; **w. you like some tea?** voudriez-vous (prendre) du thé?; **I w. see her every day** (*used to*) je la voyais chaque jour. ◆**would-be** *a* (*musician etc*) soi-disant.

wound[1] [wuːnd] *vt* (*hurt*) blesser; **the wounded** les blessés *mpl*; − *n* blessure *f*.

wound[2] [waund] *see* **wind**[2].

wove, woven [wəuv, 'wəuv(ə)n] *see* **weave**.

wow! [wau] *int Fam* (c'est) formidable!

wrangle ['ræŋg(ə)l] *n* dispute *f*; − *vi* se disputer.

wrap [ræp] *vt* (**-pp-**) **to w. (up)** envelopper; **to w. (oneself) up** (*dress warmly*) se couvrir; **wrapped up in** (*engrossed*) *Fig* absorbé par; − *n* (*shawl*) châle *m*; (*cape*) pèlerine *f*; **plastic w.** *Am* scel-o-frais® *m*. ◆**wrapping** *n* (*action, material*) emballage *m*; **w. paper** papier *m* d'emballage. ◆**wrapper** *n* (*of sweet*) papier *m*; (*of book*) jaquette *f*.

wrath [rɒθ] *n Lit* courroux *m*.

wreak [riːk] *vt* **to w. vengeance on** se venger de; **to w. havoc on** ravager.

wreath [riːθ] *n* (*pl* **-s** [riːðz]) (*on head, for funeral*) couronne *f*.

wreck [rek] *n* (*ship*) épave *f*; (*sinking*) naufrage *m*; (*train etc*) train *m etc* accidenté; (*person*) épave *f* (humaine); **to be a nervous w.** être à bout de nerfs; − *vt* détruire; (*ship*) provoquer le naufrage de; (*career, hopes etc*) *Fig* briser, détruire. ◆**-age** *n* (*fragments*) débris *mpl*. ◆**-er** *n* (*breakdown truck*) *Am* dépanneuse *f*.

wren [ren] *n* (*bird*) roitelet *m*.

wrench [rentʃ] *vt* (*tug at*) tirer sur; (*twist*) tordre; **to w. sth from s.o.** arracher qch à qn; − *n* mouvement *m* de torsion; (*tool*) clé *f* (à écrous), *Am* clé *f* à mollette; (*distress*) *Fig* déchirement *m*.

wrest [rest] *vt* **to w. sth from s.o.** arracher qch à qn.

wrestl/e ['res(ə)l] *vi* lutter (**with s.o.** contre qn); **to w. with** (*problem etc*) *Fig* se débattre avec. ◆**-ing** *n Sp* lutte *f*; (**all-in**) **w.** catch *m*. ◆**-er** *n* lutteur, -euse *mf*; catcheur, -euse *mf*.

wretch [retʃ] *n* (*unfortunate person*) malheureux, -euse *mf*; (*rascal*) misérable *mf*. ◆**wretched** [-ɪd] *a* (*poor, pitiful*) misérable; (*dreadful*) affreux; (*annoying*) maudit.

wriggle ['rɪg(ə)l] *vi* **to w. (about)** se tortiller; (*of fish*) frétiller; **to w. out of** (*difficulty, task etc*) esquiver; − *vt* (*fingers, toes*) tortiller.

wring [rɪŋ] *vt* (*pt & pp* **wrung**) (*neck*) tordre; **to w. (out)** (*clothes*) essorer; (*water*) faire sortir; **to w. sth out of s.o.** *Fig* arracher qch à qn; **wringing wet** (trempé) à tordre.

wrinkle ['rɪŋk(ə)l] *n* (*on skin*) ride *f*; (*in cloth or paper*) pli *m*; − *vt* (*skin*) rider; (*cloth, paper*) plisser; − *vi* se rider; faire des plis.

wrist [rɪst] *n* poignet *m*. ◆**wristwatch** *n* montre-bracelet *f*.

writ [rɪt] *n* acte *m* judiciaire; **to issue a w. against s.o.** assigner qn (en justice).

write [raɪt] *vt* (*pt* **wrote**, *pp* **written**) écrire; **to w. down** noter; **to w. off** (*debt*) passer aux profits et pertes; **to w. out** écrire; (*copy*) recopier; **to w. up** (*from notes*) rédiger; (*diary, notes*) mettre à jour; − *vi* écrire; **to w. away** *or* **off** *or* **up for** (*details etc*) écrire pour demander; **to w. back** répondre; **to w. in** *Rad TV* écrire (**for information**/*etc* pour demander des renseignements/*etc*). ◆**w.-off** *n* **a** (**complete**) **w.-off** (*car*) une véritable épave. ◆**w.-up** *n* (*report*) *Journ* compte rendu *m*. ◆**writing** *n* (*handwriting*) écriture *f*; (*literature*) littérature *f*; **to put (down) in w.** mettre par écrit; **some w.** (*on page*) quelque chose d'écrit; **his** *or* **her**

writing(s) (*works*) ses écrits *mpl*; **w. desk** secrétaire *m*; **w. pad** bloc *m* de papier à lettres; **w. paper** papier *m* à lettres. ◆**writer** *n* auteur *m* (**of** de); (*literary*) écrivain *m*.

writhe [raɪð] *vi* (*in pain etc*) se tordre.

written ['rɪt(ə)n] *see* **write**.

wrong [rɒŋ] *a* (*sum, idea etc*) faux, erroné; (*direction, time etc*) mauvais; (*unfair*) injuste; **to be w.** (*of person*) avoir tort (**to do** de faire); (*mistaken*) se tromper; **it's w. to swear**/*etc* (*morally*) c'est mal de jurer/*etc*; **it's the w. road** ce n'est pas la bonne route; **you're the w. man** (*for job etc*) tu n'es pas l'homme qu'il faut; **the clock's w.** la pendule n'est pas à l'heure; **something's w.** quelque chose ne va pas; **something's w. with the phone** le téléphone ne marche pas bien; **something's w. with her arm** elle a quelque chose au bras; **nothing's w.** tout va bien; **what's w. with you?** qu'est-ce que tu as?; **the w. way round** *or* **up** à l'envers; – *adv* mal; **to go w.** (*err*) se tromper; (*of plan*) mal tourner; (*of vehicle, machine*) tomber en panne; – *n* (*injustice*) injustice *f*; (*evil*) mal *m*; **to be in the w.** avoir tort; **right and w.** le bien et le mal; – *vt* faire (du) tort à. ◆**wrongdoer** *n* (*criminal*) malfaiteur *m*. ◆**wrongful** *a* injustifié; (*arrest*) arbitraire. ◆**wrongfully** *adv* à tort. ◆**wrongly** *adv* incorrectement; (*to inform, translate*) mal; (*to suspect etc*) à tort.

wrote [rəʊt] *see* **write**.

wrought [rɔːt] *a* **w. iron** fer *m* forgé. ◆**w.-'iron** *a* en fer forgé.

wrung [rʌŋ] *see* **wring**.

wry [raɪ] *a* (**wryer, wryest**) (*comment*) ironique; (*smile*) forcé; **to pull a w. face** grimacer.

X

X, x [eks] *n* X, x *m*. ◆**X-ray** *n* (*beam*) rayon *m* X; (*photo*) radio(graphie) *f*; **to have an X-ray** passer une radio; **X-ray examination** examen *m* radioscopique; – *vt* radiographier.

xenophobia [zenə'fəʊbɪə] *n* xénophobie *f*.
Xerox® ['zɪərɒks] *n* photocopie *f*; – *vt* photocopier.
Xmas ['krɪsməs] *n Fam* Noël *m*.
xylophone ['zaɪləfəʊn] *n* xylophone *m*.

Y

Y, y [waɪ] *n* Y, y *m*.
yacht [jɒt] *n* yacht *m*. ◆**—ing** *n* yachting *m*.
yank [jæŋk] *vt Fam* tirer d'un coup sec; **to y. off** *or* **out** arracher; – *n* coup *m* sec.
Yank(ee) [jæŋk(ɪ)] *n Fam* Ricain, -aine *mf*, *Pej* Amerloque *mf*.
yap [jæp] *vi* (**-pp-**) (*of dog*) japper; (*jabber*) *Fam* jacasser.
yard [jɑːd] *n* **1** (*of house etc*) cour *f*; (*for storage*) dépôt *m*, chantier *m*; (*garden*) *Am* jardin *m* (*à l'arrière de la maison*); **builder's y.** chantier *m* de construction. **2** (*measure*) yard *m* (= 91,44 cm). ◆**yardstick** *n* (*criterion*) mesure *f*.
yarn [jɑːn] *n* **1** (*thread*) fil *m*. **2** (*tale*) *Fam* longue histoire *f*.
yawn [jɔːn] *vi* bâiller; – *n* bâillement *m*. ◆**—ing** *a* (*gulf etc*) béant.

yeah [jeə] *adv* (*yes*) *Fam* ouais.
year [jɪər] *n* an *m*, année *f*; (*of wine*) année *f*; **school/tax**/*etc* **y.** année *f* scolaire/fiscale/*etc*; **this y.** cette année; **in the y. 1990** en (l'an) 1990; **he's ten years old** il a dix ans; **New Y.** Nouvel An, Nouvelle Année; **New Year's Day** le jour de l'An; **New Year's Eve** la Saint-Sylvestre. ◆**yearbook** *n* annuaire *m*. ◆**yearly** *a* annuel; – *adv* annuellement.
yearn [jɜːn] *vi* **to y. for s.o.** languir après qn; **to y. for sth** avoir très envie de qch; **to y. to do** avoir très envie de faire. ◆**—ing** *n* grande envie *f* (**for** de, **to do** de faire); (*nostalgia*) nostalgie *f*.
yeast [jiːst] *n* levure *f*.
yell [jel] *vti* **to y.** (**out**) hurler; **to y. at s.o.** (*scold*) crier après qn; – *n* hurlement *m*.

yellow ['jeləʊ] **1** *a* & *n* (*colour*) jaune (*m*); – *vi* jaunir. **2** *a* (*cowardly*) *Fam* froussard. ◆**yellowish** *a* jaunâtre.

yelp [jelp] *vi* (*of dog*) japper; – *n* jappement *m*.

yen [jen] *n* (*desire*) grande envie *f* (for de, to do de faire).

yes [jes] *adv* oui; (*contradicting negative question*) si; – *n* oui *m inv*.

yesterday ['jestədɪ] *adv* & *n* hier (*m*); y. morning/evening hier matin/soir; the day before y. avant-hier.

yet [jet] **1** *adv* encore; (*already*) déjà; she hasn't come (as) y. elle n'est pas encore venue; has he come y.? est-il déjà arrivé?; the best y. le meilleur jusqu'ici; y. more complicated (*even more*) encore plus compliqué; not (just) y., not y. awhile pas pour l'instant. **2** *conj* (*nevertheless*) pourtant.

yew [juː] *n* (*tree, wood*) if *m*.

Yiddish ['jɪdɪʃ] *n* & *a* yiddish (*m*).

yield [jiːld] *n* rendement *m*; (*profit*) rapport *m*; – *vt* (*produce*) produire, rendre; (*profit*) rapporter; (*give up*) céder (to à); – *vi* (*surrender, give way*) céder (to à); (*of tree, land etc*) rendre; 'y.' (*road sign*) *Am* 'cédez la priorité'.

yob(bo) ['jɒb(əʊ)] *n* (*pl* yob(bo)s) *Sl* loubar(d) *m*.

yoga ['jəʊgə] *n* yoga *m*.

yog(h)urt ['jɒgət, *Am* 'jəʊgəɪt] *n* yaourt *m*.

yoke [jəʊk] *n* (*for oxen*) & *Fig* joug *m*.

yokel ['jəʊk(ə)l] *n Pej* plouc *m*.

yolk [jəʊk] *n* jaune *m* (d'œuf).

yonder ['jɒndər] *adv Lit* là-bas.

you [juː] *pron* **1** (*polite form singular*) vous; (*familiar form singular*) tu; (*polite and familar form plural*) vous; (*object*) vous; te, t'; *pl* vous; (*after prep & stressed*) vous; toi; *pl* vous; (to) y. (*indirect*) vous; te, t'; *pl*

vous; y. are vous êtes; tu es; I see y. je vous vois; je te vois; I give it to y. je vous le donne; je te le donne; with y. avec vous; avec toi; y. teachers vous autres professeurs; y. idiot! espèce d'imbécile! **2** (*indefinite*) on; (*object*) vous; te, t'; *pl* vous; y. never know on ne sait jamais.

young [jʌŋ] *a* (-er, -est) jeune; my young(er) brother mon (frère) cadet; his *or* her youngest brother le cadet de ses frères; the youngest son le cadet; – *n* (*of animals*) petits *mpl*; the y. (*people*) les jeunes *mpl*. ◆**young-looking** *a* qui a l'air jeune. ◆**youngster** *n* jeune *mf*.

your [jɔːr] *poss a* (*polite form singular, polite and familiar form plural*) votre, *pl* vos; (*familiar form singular*) ton, ta, *pl* tes; (*one's*) son, sa, *pl* ses. ◆**yours** *poss pron* le vôtre, la vôtre, *pl* les vôtres; (*familiar form singular*) le tien, la tienne, *pl* les tien(ne)s; this book is y. ce livre est à vous *or* est le vôtre; ce livre est à toi *or* est le tien; a friend of y. un ami à vous; un ami à toi. ◆**yourself** *pron* (*polite form*) vous-même; (*familiar form*) toi-même; (*reflexive*) vous; te, t'; (*after prep*) vous; toi; you wash y. vous vous lavez; tu te laves. ◆**yourselves** *pron pl* vous-mêmes; (*reflexive & after prep*) vous.

youth [juːθ] *n* (*pl* -s [juːðz]) (*age, young people*) jeunesse *f*; (*young man*) jeune *m*; y. club maison *f* des jeunes. ◆**youthful** *a* (*person*) jeune; (*quality, smile etc*) juvénile, jeune. ◆**youthfulness** *n* jeunesse *f*.

yoyo ['jəʊjəʊ] *n* (*pl* -os) yo-yo *m inv*.

yucky ['jʌkɪ] *a Sl* dégueulasse.

Yugoslav ['juːgəʊslɑːv] *a* & *n* yougoslave (*mf*). ◆**Yugo'slavia** *n* Yougoslavie *f*.

yummy ['jʌmɪ] *a* (-ier, -iest) *Sl* délicieux.

yuppie ['jʌpɪ] *n* jeune cadre *m* ambitieux, jeune loup *m*, NAP *mf*.

Z

Z, z [zed, *Am* ziː] *n* Z, z *m*.

zany ['zeɪnɪ] *a* (-ier, -iest) farfelu.

zeal [ziːl] *n* zèle *m*. ◆**zealous** ['zeləs] *a* zélé. ◆**zealously** *adv* avec zèle.

zebra ['ziːbrə, 'zebrə] *n* zèbre *m*; z. crossing passage *m* pour piétons.

zenith ['zenɪθ] *n* zénith *m*.

zero ['zɪərəʊ] *n* (*pl* -os) zéro *m*; z. hour *Mil* & *Fig* l'heure H.

zest [zest] *n* **1** (*gusto*) entrain *m*; (*spice*) *Fig* piquant *m*; z. for living appétit *m* de vivre. **2** (*of lemon, orange*) zeste *m*.

zigzag ['zɪgzæg] *n* zigzag *m*; – *a* & *adv* en zigzag; – *vi* (-gg-) zigzaguer.

zinc [zɪŋk] *n* (*metal*) zinc *m*.

zip [zɪp] **1** *n* z. (fastener) fermeture *f* éclair®; – *vt* (-pp-) to z. (up) fermer (avec une fermeture éclair®). **2** *n* (*vigour*) *Fam*

entrain *m*; – *vi* (**-pp-**) (*go quickly*) aller comme l'éclair. **3** *a* z. **code** *Am* code *m* postal. ◆**zipper** *n Am* fermeture *f* éclair®.
zit [zɪt] *n* (*pimple*) *Am Fam* bouton *m*.
zither ['zɪðər] *n* cithare *f*.
zodiac ['zəʊdɪæk] *n* zodiaque *m*.
zombie ['zɒmbɪ] *n* (*spiritless person*) *Fam* robot *m*, zombie *m*.
zone [zəʊn] *n* zone *f*; (*division of city*) secteur *m*.

zoo [zuː] *n* zoo *m*. ◆**zoological** [zuː-'lɒdʒɪk(ə)l] *a* zoologique. ◆**zoology** [zuː-'ɒlədʒɪ] *n* zoologie *f*.
zoom [zuːm] **1** *vi* (*rush*) se précipiter; **to z. past** passer comme un éclair. **2** *n* z. **lens** zoom *m*; – *vi* **to z. in** *Cin* faire un zoom, zoomer (**on** sur).
zucchini [zuː'kiːnɪ] *n* (*pl* **-ni** *or* **-nis**) *Am* courgette *f*.
zwieback ['zwiːbæk] *n* (*rusk*) *Am* biscotte *f*.

HARRAP'S

French Grammar

INTRODUCTION

This French grammar has been written to meet the new demands of
language teaching in school and colleges and is particularly suited for
study at GCSE level. The essential rules of the French language have
been explained in terms that are as accessible as possible to all users.
Where technical terms have been used then full explanations of these
terms have also been supplied. There is also a full glossary of
grammatical terminology on pages 5-9. While literary aspects of the
French language have not been ignored, the emphasis has been placed
squarely on modern spoken French. This grammar, with its wealth of
lively and typical illustrations of usage taken from the present-day
language, is the ideal study tool for all levels – from the beginner who
is starting to come to grips with the French language through to the
advanced user who requires a comprehensive and readily accessible
work of reference.

Abbreviations used in the text:

fem	feminine
masc	masculine
plur	plural
sing	singular

CONTENTS

1. GLOSSARY OF GRAMMATICAL TERMS

ADJECTIVE   A describing word, which adds information about a
                    noun, telling us what something is like (eg *a small
                    house*, *a red car*, *an interesting* pastime).

ADVERB   Adverbs are normally used with a verb to add extra
                    information by indicating **how** the action is done
                    (adverbs of manner), **when, where** and **with how much
                    intensity** the action is done (adverbs of time, place and
                    intensity), or **to what extent** the action is done (adverbs
                    of quantity). Adverbs may also be used with an
                    adjective or another adverb (eg *a very attractive girl,
                    very well*).

AGREEMENT   In French, words such as adjectives, articles and
                    pronouns are said to agree in number and gender with
                    the noun or pronoun they refer to. This means that
                    their spelling changes according to the **number** of the
                    noun (singular or plural) and according to its **gender**
                    (masculine or feminine).

ANTECEDENT   The antecedent of a relative pronoun is the word or
                    words to which the relative pronoun refers. The
                    antecedent is usually found directly before the relative
                    pronoun (eg in the sentence *I know the man who did
                    this*, *the man* is the antecedent of *who*).

APPOSITION   A word or a clause is said to be in apposition to
                    another when it is placed directly after it without any
                    joining word (eg *Mr Jones*, *our bank manager*, *rang
                    today*).

ARTICLE   See DEFINITE ARTICLE, INDEFINITE ARTICLE
                    and PARTITIVE ARTICLE.

AUXILIARY   The French auxiliary verbs, or 'helping' verbs, are
                    avoir (*to have*) and **être** (*to be*). They are used to make
                    up the first part of compound tenses, the second part
                    being a past participle (eg *I have eaten*).

CARDINAL   Cardinal numbers are numbers such as *one*, *two*, *ten*,
                    fourteen, as opposed to **ordinal** numbers (eg *first,
                    second*).

CLAUSE	A clause is a group of words which contains at least a subject and a verb: *he said* is a clause. A clause often contains more than this basic information, eg *he said this to her yesterday*. Sentences can be made up of several clauses, eg *he said/ he'd call me / if he were free*. See SENTENCE.
COMPARATIVE	The comparative forms of adjectives and adverbs allow us to compare two things, persons or actions. In English, *more ... than*, *...er than*, *less ... than* and *as ... as* are used for comparison.
COMPOUND	Compound tenses are verb tenses consisting of more than one element. In French, the compound tenses of a verb are formed by the **auxiliary** verb and the **past participle**: *j'ai visité, il est venu*.
CONDITIONAL	This mood is used to describe what someone would do, or something that would happen if a condition were fulfilled (eg *I would come if I were well; the chair would have broken if he had sat on it*).
CONJUGATION	The conjugation of a verb is the set of different forms taken in the particular tenses of that verb.
CONJUNCTION	Conjunctions are linking words. They may be coordinating or subordinating. Coordinating conjunctions are words like *and, but, or*; subordinating conjunctions are words like *because, after, although*.
DEFINITE ARTICLE	The definite article is *the* in English and *le, la* and *les* in French.
DEMONSTRATIVE	Demonstrative adjectives (eg *this, that, these*) and pronouns (eg *this one, that one*) are used to point out a particular person or object.
DIRECT OBJECT	A noun or a pronoun which in English follows a verb without any linking preposition, eg *I met a friend*.
ELISION	Elision consists in replacing the last letter of certain words (*le, la, je, me, te, se, de, que*) with an apostrophe (') before a word starting with a **vowel** or a **silent h** (eg *l'eau, l'homme, j'aime*).
ENDING	The ending of a verb is determined by the **person** (1st/2nd/3rd) and **number** (singular/plural) of its subject. In French, most tenses have six different endings. See PERSON and NUMBER.
EXCLAMATION	Words or sentences used to express surprise, wonder (eg *what!, how!, how lucky!, what a nice day!*).

FEMININE	See GENDER.
GENDER	The gender of a noun indicates whether the noun is **masculine** or **feminine** (all French nouns are either masculine or feminine).
IDIOMATIC	Idiomatic expressions (or idioms), are expressions which cannot normally be translated word for word. For example, *it's raining cats and dogs* is translated by *il pleut des cordes*.
IMPERATIVE	A mood used for giving orders (eg *eat!*, *don't go!*).
INDEFINITE	Indefinite pronouns and adjectives are words that do not refer to a definite person or object (eg *each*, *someone*, *every*).
INDEFINITE ARTICLE	The indefinite article is *a* in English and *un*, *une* and *des* in French.
INDICATIVE	The normal form of a verb as in *I like*, *he came*, *we are trying*. It is opposed to the subjunctive, conditional and imperative.
INDIRECT OBJECT	A pronoun or noun which follows a verb indirectly, with a linking preposition (usually **to**), eg *I spoke to **my friend**/**him***.
INFINITIVE	The infinitive is the basic form of the verb as found in dictionaries. Thus *to eat, to finish, to take* are infinitives. In French, the infinitive is recognized by its ending: *manger, finir, prendre*.
INTERROGATIVE	Interrogative words are used to ask a question. This may be a direct question (**when** *will you arrive?*) or an indirect question (*I don't know* **when** *he'll arrive*). See QUESTION.
MASCULINE	See GENDER.
MOOD	The name given to the four main areas within which a verb is conjugated. See INDICATIVE, SUBJUNCTIVE, CONDITIONAL, IMPERATIVE.
NOUN	A naming word, which can refer to living creatures, things, places or abstract ideas, eg *postman*, *cat*, *shop*, *passport*, *life*.
NUMBER	The number of a noun indicates whether the noun is **singular** or **plural**. A singular noun refers to one single thing or person (eg *boy*, *train*) and a plural noun to several (eg *boys*, *trains*).

ORDINAL

Ordinal numbers are *first, second, third, fourth* and all other numbers which end in **-th**. In French, all ordinal numbers, except for *premier* (first) and *second* (second), end in **-ième**.

PARTITIVE ARTICLE

The partitive articles are *some* and *any* in English and *du, de la* and *des* (as in *du pain, de la confiture, des bananes*) in French.

PASSIVE

A verb is used in the passive when the subject of the verb does not perform the action but is subjected to it. The passive is formed with the verb **to be** and the past participle of the verb, eg *he was rewarded*.

PAST PARTICIPLE

The past participle of a verb is the form which is used after **to have** in English, eg *I have **eaten**, I have **said**, you have **tried***.

PERSON

In any tense, there are three persons in the singular (1st: *I* ..., 2nd: *you* ..., 3rd: *he/she* ...), and three in the plural (1st: *we* ..., 2nd: *you* ..., 3rd: *they* ...). See also ENDING.

PERSONAL PRONOUNS

Personal pronouns stand for a noun. They usually accompany a verb and can be either the subject (*I, you, he/she/it, we, they*) or the object of the verb (*me, you, him/her/it, us, them*).

PLURAL

See NUMBER.

POSSESSIVE

Possessive adjectives and pronouns are used to indicate possession or ownership. They are words like *my/mine, your/yours, our/ours*.

PREPOSITION

Prepositions are words such as *with, in, to, at*. They are followed by a noun or a pronoun.

PRESENT PARTICIPLE

The present participle is the verb form which ends in **-ing** in English (**-ant** in French).

PRONOUN

A word which stands for a noun. The main categories of pronouns are:

★ **Relative pronouns** (eg *who, which, that*)
★ **Interrogative pronouns** (eg *who?, what?, which?*)
★ **Demonstrative pronouns** (eg *this, that, these*)
★ **Possessive pronouns** (eg *mine, yours, his*)
★ **Personal pronouns** (eg *you, him, us*)
★ **Reflexive pronouns** (eg *myself, himself*)
★ **Indefinite pronouns** (eg *something, all*)

QUESTION	There are two question forms: **direct** questions stand on their own and require a question mark at the end (eg *when will he come?*); **indirect** questions are introduced by a clause and require no question mark (eg *I wonder when he will come*).
REFLEXIVE	Reflexive verbs 'reflect' the action back onto the subject (eg *I dressed myself*). They are always found with a reflexive pronoun and are much more common in French than in English.
SENTENCE	A sentence is a group of words made up of one or more clauses (see CLAUSE). The end of a sentence is indicated by a punctuation mark (usually a full stop, a question mark or an exclamation mark).
SILENT H	The name 'silent **h**' is actually misleading since an **h** is never pronounced in French. The point is that, when a silent **h** occurs, any preceding vowel is not pronounced either. For example, the **h** in *j'habite* is silent (note the *j'*). The **h** in *je hurle* is not silent (note the **je**).
SIMPLE TENSE	Simple tenses are tenses in which the verb consists of one word only, eg *j'habite, Maurice partira*.
SINGULAR	See NUMBER
SUBJECT	The subject of a verb is the noun or pronoun which performs the action. In the sentences *the train left early* and *she bought a record*, *the train* and *she* are the subjects.
SUBJUNCTIVE	The subjunctive is a verb form which is rarely used in English (eg *if I were you, God save the Queen*), but common in French.
SUPERLATIVE	The form of an adjective or an adverb which, in English, is marked by *the most ..., the ...est* or *the least ....*
TENSE	Verbs are used in tenses, which tell us when an action takes place, eg in the present, the imperfect, the future.
VERB	A 'doing' word, which usually describes an action (eg *to sing, to work, to watch*). Some verbs describe a state (eg *to be, to have, to hope*).

2. ARTICLES

A. THE DEFINITE ARTICLE

1. Forms

In English, there is only one form of the definite article: **the**. In French, there are three forms, depending on the gender and number of the noun following the article:

– with a masculine singular noun: **le** ⎫
– with a feminine singular noun: **la** ⎬ the
– with a plural noun (masc or fem): **les** ⎭

MASC SING	FEM SING	PLURAL
le chauffeur	**la secrétaire**	**les étudiants**
the driver	the secretary	the students
le salon	**la cuisine**	**les chambres**
the lounge	the kitchen	the bedrooms

Note: **le** and **la** both change to **l'** before a vowel or a silent **h**:

	MASCULINE	FEMININE
BEFORE VOWEL	**l'avion**	**l'odeur**
	the plane	the smell
BEFORE SILENT H	**l'homme**	**l'hôtesse**
	the man	the hostess

Pronunciation: the **s** of **les** is pronounced **z** when the noun following it begins with a vowel or a silent **h**.

2. Forms with the prepositions 'à' and 'de'

When the definite article is used with **à** or **de**, the following spelling changes take place:

a) *with* **à** *(to, at)*

à + le	→	**au**
à + les	→	**aux**

à + la and **à + l'** do not change

au restaurant	**aux enfants**
at/to the restaurant	to the children
à la plage	**à l'aéroport**
at/to the beach	at/to the airport

Pronunciation: the **x** of **aux** is pronounced **z** when the noun following it begins with a vowel or a silent **h**.

b) *with **de** (of, from)*

  de + **le**   →   **du**
  de + **les**   →   **des**

  de + **la** and **de** + **l'** do not change

  du directeur   **des chômeurs**
  of/from the manager   of/from the unemployed

  de la région   **de l'usine**
  of/from the area   of/from the factory

Pronunciation: the **s** of **des** is pronounced **z** when the noun following it begins with a vowel or a silent **h**.

3. Use

As in English, the definite article is used when referring to a particular person or thing, or particular persons or things:

  les amis dont je t'ai parlé   **le café est prêt**
  the friends I told you about   the coffee is ready

However, the definite article is used far more frequently in French than in English. It is used in particular in the following cases where English uses no article:

a) *when the noun is used in a general sense*

  i)   to refer to all things of a kind:

       vous acceptez les chèques ?
       do you accept cheques?

       le sucre est mauvais pour les dents
       sugar is bad for the teeth

  ii) to refer to abstract things:

       le travail et les loisirs   **la musique classique**
       work and leisure   classical music

  iii) when stating likes and dislikes:

       j'aime la viande, mais je préfère le poisson
       I like meat, but I prefer fish

       je déteste les tomates
       I hate tomatoes

b) *with geographical names*

  i)   continents, countries and areas:

       le Canada   **la France**   **l'Europe**
       Canada   France   Europe

       la Bretagne   **l'Afrique**   **les Etats-Unis**
       Brittany   Africa   the United States

But: the article **la** is omitted with the prepositions **en** (to, in) and **de** (from):

       j'habite en France   **il vient d'Italie**
       I live in France   he comes from Italy

ii)   mountains, lakes and rivers:

    le mont Everest   **le lac de Genève**
    Mount Everest   Lake Geneva

c)   *with names of seasons*

    l'automne   autumn
    l'hiver   winter
    le printemps   spring
    l'été   summer

But: **en automne/ été/ hiver**
    in autumn/ summer/ winter

    au printemps   **un jour d'été**
    in spring   a summer's day

d)   *with names of languages*

    j'apprends le français
    I'm learning French

But: **ce film est en anglais**
    this film is in English

e)   *with parts of the body*

    j'ai les cheveux roux   **ouvrez la bouche**
    I've got red hair   open your mouth

    les mains en l'air !   **l'homme à la barbe noire**
    hands up!   the man with the black beard

f)   *with names following an adjective*

    le petit Pierre   **la pauvre Isabelle**
    little Peter   poor Isabelle

g)   *with titles*

    le docteur Coste   **le commandant Cousteau**
    Doctor Coste   Captain Cousteau

h)   *with days of the week to express regular occurrences*

    que fais-tu le samedi ?
    what do you do on Saturdays?

i)   *with names of subjects or leisure activities*

    les maths   **l'histoire et la géographie**
    maths   history and geography

    la natation, la lecture, le football
    swimming, reading, football

j)   *in expressions of price, quantity etc*

    c'est combien le kilo/ la douzaine/ la bouteille ?
    how much is it for a kilo/ dozen/ bottle?

B. THE INDEFINITE ARTICLE

1. Forms

In French, there are three forms of the indefinite article, depending on the number and gender of the noun it accompanies:

– with a masculine singular noun: **un**   a
– with a feminine singular noun: **une**   a
– with a plural noun (masc or fem):   **des**   some

Note: **des** is often not translated in English:

> **il y a des nuages dans le ciel**
> there are clouds in the sky

2. Use

a) On the whole, the French indefinite article is used in the same way as its English equivalent:

un homme	**une femme**	**des hommes/femmes**
a man	a woman	(some) men/women
un livre	**une tasse**	**des livres/ tasses**
a book	a cup	(some) books/ cups

b) However, the English indefinite article is not always translated in French:

   i)   when stating someone's profession or occupation:

> **mon père est architecte**
> my father is an architect

> **elle est médecin**
> she is a doctor

   But: the article is used after **c'est**, **c'était** etc:

> **c'est un acteur célèbre**
> he's a famous actor

> **ce sont des fraises**
> these are strawberries

   ii) with nouns in apposition:

> **Madame Leclerc, employée de bureau**
> Mrs Leclerc, an office worker

   iii) after **quel** in exclamations:

> **quel dommage !**   **quelle surprise !**
> what a pity!   what a surprise!

c) In negative sentences, **de** (or **d'**) is used instead of **un**, **une**, **des**:

> **je n'ai pas d'amis**   **je n'ai plus de voiture**
> I don't have any friends   I don't have a car any more

d) In French (but not in English), the indefinite article is used with abstract nouns followed by an adjective:

avec une patience remarquable
with remarkable patience

elle a fait des progrès étonnants
she's made amazing progress

But: the article is not used when there is no adjective:

avec plaisir　　　　　　**sans hésitation**
with pleasure　　　　　　without hesitation

C.   THE PARTITIVE ARTICLE

1.   Forms

There are three forms of the French partitive article, which corresponds to 'some'/ 'any' in English:

– with a masculine singular noun:　　**du**
– with a feminine singular noun:　　**de la**
– with plural nouns (masc or fem):　　**des**

du vin　　　　**de la bière**　　　　**des fruits**
some wine　　　some beer　　　some fruit

Note: **de l'** is used in front of masculine or feminine singular nouns beginning with a vowel or a silent **h**:

de l'argent　　　　**de l'eau**
some money　　　some water

2.   Use

a) On the whole, the French partitive article is used as in English. However, English tends to omit the partitive article where French does not:

achète du pain　　　　**vous avez du beurre ?**
buy (some) bread　　　do you have (any) butter?

je voudrais de la viande　　**tu veux de la soupe ?**
I'd like some meat　　　do you want (any) soup?

tu dois manger des légumes
you must eat (some) vegetables

as-tu acheté des poires ?
did you buy any pears?

b) The partitive article is replaced by **de** (or **d'**) in the following cases:

i) in negative expressions:

il n'y a plus de café　　**je n'ai pas de verres**
there isn't any coffee left　　I don't have any glasses

But:　**ce n'est pas du cuir, c'est du plastique**
it's not leather, it's plastic

je n'ai que de l'argent français
I have only French money

ii)   after expressions of quantity (see also pp 168-70):

il boit trop de café   **il gagne assez d'argent**
he drinks too much coffee   he earns enough money

iii)   after **avoir besoin de**:

j'ai besoin d'argent   **tu as besoin de timbres ?**
I need (some) money   do you need (any) stamps?

iv)   where an adjective is followed by a plural noun:

de grands enfants   **de petites villes**
(some) tall children   (some) small towns

But: if the adjective comes after the noun, **des** does not change:

des résultats encourageants
encouraging results

3.   Partitive or definite article?

When no article is used in English, be careful to use the right article in French: **le/ la/ les** or **du/ de la/ des**?

If **some/ any** can be inserted before the English noun, the French partitive article should be used. But if the noun is used in a general sense and inserting **some/ any** in front of the English noun does not make sense, the definite article must be used:

did you buy fish? (*ie any fish*)
tu as acheté *du* poisson ?

yes, I did; I like fish (*ie fish in general*)
oui ; j'aime *le* poisson

3. NOUNS

Nouns are naming words, which refer to persons, animals, things, places or abstract ideas.

A. GENDER

All French nouns are either masculine or feminine; there is no neuter as in English. Though no absolute rule can be stated, the gender can often be determined either by the meaning or the ending of the noun.

1. Masculine

a) *by meaning*

   i)   names of people and animals:

un homme	**le boucher**	**le tigre**
a man	the butcher	the tiger

   ii) names of common trees and shrubs:

le chêne	**le sapin**	**le laurier**
the oak	the fir tree	the laurel

But: | **une aubépine** | **la bruyère** |
|---|---|
| a hawthorn | the heather |

   iii) days, months, seasons:

lundi	**mars**	**le printemps**
Monday	March	spring

   iv) languages:

le français	**le polonais**	**le russe**
French	Polish	Russian

   v) rivers and countries not ending in a silent **e**:

le Nil	**le Portugal**	**le Danemark**
the Nile	Portugal	Denmark

But: | **le Danube** | **le Rhône** | **le Mexique** |
|---|---|---|
| the Danube | the Rhone | Mexico |

b) *by ending*

-acle	**le spectacle** (show) *But:* **une débâcle** (shambles)
-age	**le fromage** (cheese) *But:* **la cage** (cage), **une image** (picture), **la nage** (swimming), **la page** (page), **la plage** (beach), **la rage** (rage, rabies)
-é	**le marché** (market) *But:* nouns ending in **-té** and **-tié** (see p 18)

-eau	**le chapeau** (hat)
	But: **l'eau** (water), **la peau** (skin)
-ège	**le piège** (trap), **le collège** (secondary school)
-ème	**le thème** (theme, topic)
	But: **la crème** (the cream)
-isme, -asme	**le communisme** (communism), **le tourisme** (tourism), **l'enthousiasme** (enthusiasm)
-o	**le numéro** (the number)
	But: **la dynamo** (dynamo) and most abbreviated expressions: **une auto** (car), **la météo** (weather forecast), **la photo** (photograph), **la radio** (radio), **la sténo** (shorthand), **la stéréo** (stereo)

Nouns ending in a *consonant* are usually *masculine*.

Notable exceptions are:

i) most nouns ending in **-tion, -sion, -ation, -aison, -ison**

ii) most abstract nouns ending in **-eur** (see p 18)

iii) the following nouns ending in a consonant:

la clef (key)	**la nef** (nave)
la soif (thirst)	**la faim** (hunger)
la fin (end)	**la façon** (manner)
la leçon (lesson)	**la boisson** (drink)
la moisson (harvest)	**la rançon** (ransom)
la mer (sea)	**la cuiller** (spoon)
la chair (flesh)	**la basse-cour** (farmyard)
la cour (yard)	**la tour** (tower)
la brebis (ewe)	**une fois** (once)
la vis (screw)	**la souris** (mouse)
la part (share)	**la plupart** (majority, most)
la dent (tooth)	**la dot** (dowry)
la forêt (forest)	**la jument** (mare)
la mort (death)	**la nuit** (night)
la croix (cross)	**la noix** (nut)
la paix (peace)	**la perdrix** (partridge)
la toux (cough)	**la voix** (voice)

2. Feminine

a) *by meaning*

i) names of females (people and animals):

la mère	**la bonne**	**la génisse**
the mother	the maid	the heifer

ii) names of rivers and countries ending in a silent **e**:

la Seine	**la Russie**	**la Belgique**
the Seine	Russia	Belgium

iii)   saints days and festivals:

la Toussaint	**la Pentecôte**
All Saints' Day	Whitsun

But: **Noël** (Christmas) is masculine except with the definite article: **à la Noël** (at Christmas)

b)   *by ending*

-ace	**la place** (square, seat) *But:* **un espace** (space)
-ade	**la salade** (salad) *But:* **le grade** (degree, rank), **le stade** (stadium)
-ance, -anse	**la puissance** (power), **la danse** (dancing)
-ée	**la soirée** (evening) *But:* **le musée** (museum), **le lycée** (secondary school)
-ence, -ense	**une évidence** (evidence), **la défense** (defence) *But:* **le silence** (silence)
-ère	**la lumière** (light) *But:* **le mystère** (mystery), **le caractère** (character)
-eur	**la peur** (fear) *But:* **le bonheur** (happiness), **le chœur** (choir), **le cœur** (heart), **un honneur** (honour), **le labeur** (toil), **le malheur** (misfortune)
-ie	**la pluie** (rain) *But:* **le génie** (genius), **un incendie** (fire), **le parapluie** (umbrella)
-ière	**la bière** (beer) *But:* **le cimetière** (cemetery)
-oire	**la gloire** (glory) *But:* **le laboratoire** (laboratory), **le pourboire** (tip)
-tion, -sion, -ation, -aison, -ison	
	la fiction (fiction), **la nation** (nation), **la raison** (reason), **la prison** (prison)
-té	**la bonté** (goodness) *But:* **le côté** (side), **le comté** (county), **le traité** (treaty), **le pâté** (pâté)
-tié	**la moitié** (half), **la pitié** (pity)

Most nouns ending in a silent **e** following two consonants:

> **la botte** (boot), **la couronne** (crown), **la terre** (earth), **la masse** (mass), **la lutte** (struggle)

But: **le verre** (glass), **le parterre** (flower-bed), **le tonnerre** (thunder), **un intervalle** (interval), **le carosse** (carriage)

3. Difficulties

a) some nouns may have either gender depending on the sex of the person to whom they refer:

un artiste	**une artiste**
a (male) artist	a (female) artist
le Russe	**la Russe**
the Russian (man)	the Russian (woman)

similarly:

un aide/une aide	an assistant
un camarade/ une camarade	a friend
un domestique/une domestique	a servant
un enfant/une enfant	a child
un malade/une malade	a patient
un propriétaire/ une propriétaire	an owner

b) others have only one gender for both sexes:

un ange	**un amateur**	**un auteur**
an angel	an amateur	an author(ess)
une connaissance	**la dupe**	**un écrivain**
an acquaintance	the dupe	a writer
Sa Majesté	**le médecin**	**le peintre**
His/Her Majesty	the doctor	the painter
une personne	**le poète**	**le professeur**
a person	the poet(ess)	the teacher
la recrue	**le sculpteur**	**la sentinelle**
the recruit	the sculptor (sculptress)	the sentry
le témoin	**la victime**	**la vedette**
the witness	the victim	the (film) star

c) the following nouns change meaning according to gender:

	MASCULINE	FEMININE
aide	male assistant	assistance, female assistant
crêpe	mourning band	pancake
critique	critic	criticism
faux	forgery	scythe
livre	book	pound
manche	handle	sleeve
manœuvre	labourer	manoeuvre
mémoire	memorandum	memory
mode	method, way	fashion
mort	dead man	death
moule	mould	mussel
page	pageboy	page
pendule	pendulum	clock
physique	physique	physics
poêle	stove	frying pan
poste	post (*job*), set	post office

somme	nap	sum
tour	trick, tour	tower
trompette	trumpeter	trumpet
vapeur	steamer	steam
vase	vase	silt
voile	veil	sail

d) **gens** is regarded as feminine when it follows an adjective, and masculine when it precedes it:

de bonnes gens   **des gens ennuyeux**
good people   bores

B. THE FORMATION OF FEMININES

The feminine of nouns may be formed in the following ways:

1. Add an 'e' to the masculine

un ami   **une amie**
a (male) friend   a (female) friend

un Hollandais   **une Hollandaise**
a Dutchman   a Dutch woman

a) nouns which end in **e** in the masculine do not change:

un élève   **une élève**
a (male) pupil   a (female) pupil

b) the addition of **e** often entails an alteration of the masculine form:

i) nouns ending in **t** and **n** double the final consonant:

le chien   **la chienne** (dog/ bitch)

le chat   **la chatte** (cat)

ii) nouns ending in **-er** add a grave accent to the **e** before the silent **e**:

un ouvrier   **une ouvrière** (workman/ female worker)

iii) nouns ending in **-eur** change into **-euse**:

le vendeur   **la vendeuse** (male/female shop assistant)

a few nouns ending in **-eur** change into **-eresse**:

le pécheur   **la pécheresse** (sinner)

iv) nouns ending in **-teur** change into **-teuse** or **-trice** according to the following guidelines:

if the stem of the word is also that of a present participle the feminine form is in **-euse**:

le chanteur   **la chanteuse** (male/female singer)

but if the stem is not that of a present participle, the feminine form is in **-trice**:

le lecteur   **la lectrice** (male/female reader)

v) nouns ending in **f** change to **-ve**:

le veuf   **la veuve** (widower/widow)

vi) nouns ending in **x** change to **-se**:

un époux   **une épouse** (husband/wife)

vii) nouns ending in **-eau** change to **-elle** :

le jumeau   **la jumelle** (male/female twin)

2. Use a different word (as in English)

le beau-fils	**la belle-fille** (son/daughter-in-law)
le beau-père	**la belle-mère** (father/mother-in-law)
le bélier	**la brebis** (ram/ewe)
le bœuf	**la vache** (ox/cow)
le canard	**la cane** (drake/duck)
le cheval	**la jument** (horse/mare)
le cerf	**la biche** (stag/hind)
le coq	**la poule** (cock/hen)
le fils	**la fille** (son/daughter)
le frère	**la sœur** (brother/sister)
un homme	**une femme** (man/woman)
un jars	**une oie** (gander/goose)
le mâle	**la femelle** (male/female)
le neveu	**la nièce** (nephew/niece)
un oncle	**une tante** (uncle/aunt)
le parrain	**la marraine** (godfather/godmother)
le père	**la mère** (father/mother)
le porc	**la truie** (pig/sow)
le roi	**la reine** (king/queen)

3. Add the word `femme` (or `femelle` for animals)

une femme poète (poetess)
un perroquet femelle (female parrot)

4. Irregular feminines

un abbé	**une abbesse** (abbot/abbess)
un âne	**une ânesse** (donkey)
le comte	**la comtesse** (count/countess)
le dieu	**la déesse** (god/goddess)
le duc	**la duchesse** (duke/duchess)
un Esquimau	**une Esquimaude** (Eskimo)
le fou	**la folle** (madman/mad woman)
un héros	**une héroïne** (hero/heroine)
un hôte	**une hôtesse** (host/hostess)
le maître	**la maîtresse** (master/mistress)
le prêtre	**la prêtresse** (priest/priestess)
le prince	**la princesse** (prince/princess)
le tigre	**la tigresse** (tiger/tigress)
le Turc	**la Turque** (Turk)
le vieux	**la vieille** (old man/ old woman)

C.   THE FORMATION OF PLURALS

1.   Most nouns form their plural by adding **s** to the singular:

| le vin | les vins | wine |
| un étudiant | des étudiants | student |

2.   Nouns ending in 's', 'x' or 'z' remain unchanged:

le bras	les bras	arm
la voix	les voix	voice
le nez	les nez	nose

3.   Nouns ending in **-au**, **-eau** and **-eu** add **x** to the singular:

le tuyau	les tuyaux	drain-pipe
le bateau	les bateaux	boat
le jeu	les jeux	game

But:

le landau	les landaus	pram
le bleu	les bleus	bruise
le pneu	les pneus	tyre

4. Nouns ending in **-al** change to **-aux**:

| le journal | les journaux | newspaper |

But:

le bal	les bals	dance
le carnaval	les carnavals	carnival
le festival	les festivals	festival

5.   Nouns ending in **-ail** change to **-aux**:

le bail	les baux	lease
le travail	les travaux	work
le vitrail	les vitraux	stained-glass window

Common exceptions in which the plural is formed in **-ail**:

le chandail	les chandails	sweater
le détail	les détails	detail
l'épouvantail	les épouvantails	scarecrow
l'éventail	les éventails	fan
le rail	les rails	rail

6.   Nouns ending in *-ou*:

a)   seven nouns ending in **-ou** add **x** in the plural:

le bijou	les bijoux	jewel
le caillou	les cailloux	pebble
le chou	les choux	cabbage
le genou	les genoux	knee
le hibou	les hiboux	owl
le joujou	les joujoux	toy
le pou	les poux	louse

b)   other nouns ending in **-ou** add **s**:

le clou	les clous	nail

7. Plural of compound nouns

Each noun ought to be checked individually in a dictionary:

eg	le chou-fleur	les choux-fleurs	cauliflower
	le beau-père	les beaux-pères	father-in-law
But:	un essuie-glace	des essuie-glaces	windscreen wiper
	le tire-bouchon	les tire-bouchons	corkscrew

8. Irregular plurals:

un œil	des yeux	eye
le ciel	les cieux	sky
Monsieur	Messieurs	Mr
Madame	Mesdames	Mrs
Mademoiselle	Mesdemoiselles	Miss

9. Collective nouns

a)   *singular in French but plural in English*

le bétail	cattle
la famille	family
la police	police

la police *a* arrêté certains grévistes
the police *have* arrested some strikers

b)   *plural in French but singular in English*

les nouvelles sont bonnes
the news is good

10. Proper nouns

a)   Ordinary family names are invariable:

j'ai rencontré les Leblanc
I met the Leblancs

b)   Historical names add **- s**:

les Stuarts	**les Bourbons**	**les Tudors**
the Stuarts	the Bourbons	the Tudors

4. ADJECTIVES

Adjectives are describing words which usually accompany a noun (or a pronoun) and tell us what someone or something is like:

une *grande* ville
a *large* city

un passe-temps *intéressant*
an *interesting* pastime

elle est *espagnole*
she is *Spanish*

c'était *ennuyeux*
it was *boring*

A. AGREEMENT OF ADJECTIVES

In French, adjectives agree in number and gender with the noun or pronoun they refer to. This means that, unlike English adjectives, which don't change, French adjectives have four different forms which are determined by the noun they go with:

– **masculine singular** for masculine singular words (basic form, found in the dictionary)
– **feminine singular** for feminine singular words
– **masculine plural** for masculine plural words
– **feminine plural** for feminine plural words

un passeport *vert*
a green passport

une voiture *verte*
a green car

des gants *verts*
green gloves

des chaussettes *vertes*
green socks

Note: If two singular words share the same adjective, the adjective will be in the plural:

un foulard et un bonnet *rouges*
a red scarf and (a red) hat

If one of these words is feminine, one masculine, the adjective will be masculine plural:

une robe et un manteau *noirs*
a black dress and (a black) coat

B. FEMININE FORMS OF ADJECTIVES

1. General rule

Add the letter **e** to the masculine singular form:

MASCULINE	FEMININE
grand	**grande**
amusant	**amusante**
anglais	**anglaise**

bronzé	**bronzée**
un livre amusant	**une histoire amusante**
an amusing book	an amusing story
il est bronzé	**elle est bronzée**
he is suntanned	she is suntanned

2. Adjectives already ending in 'e'

These do not change:

MASCULINE	FEMININE
rouge	**rouge**
jeune	**jeune**
malade	**malade**
mon père est malade	**ma mère est malade**
my father is ill	my mother is ill

3. Others

The spelling of some adjectives changes when the **e** is added:

a) The following masculine endings generally double the final consonant before adding **e**:

MASCULINE ENDING	FEMININE ENDING
-el	-elle
-eil	-eille
-en	-enne
-on	-onne
-as	-asse
-et	-ette

MASCULINE		FEMININE
réel	(real)	**réelle**
cruel	(cruel)	**cruelle**
pareil	(similar)	**pareille**
ancien	(old)	**ancienne**
italien	(Italian)	**italienne**
bon	(good)	**bonne**
gras	(greasy)	**grasse**
bas	(low)	**basse**
muet	(dumb)	**muette**
net	(clear)	**nette**

un problème actuel	**la vie actuelle**
a topical problem	present-day life
un bon conseil	**c'est une bonne recette**
good advice	it's a good recipe

But: the feminine ending of some common adjectives in **-et** is **-ète** instead of **-ette**:

MASCULINE		FEMININE
complet	(complete)	**complète**
incomplet	(incomplete)	**incomplète**
concret	(concrete)	**concrète**
discret	(discreet)	**discrète**
inquiet	(worried)	**inquiète**
secret	(secret)	**secrète**

b)
MASCULINE IN **-er**		FEMININE IN **-ère**
cher	(dear)	**chère**
fier	(proud)	**fière**
dernier	(last)	**dernière**

c)
MASCULINE IN **-x**		FEMININE IN **-se**
heureux	(happy)	**heureuse**
malheureux	(unhappy)	**malheureuse**
sérieux	(serious)	**sérieuse**
jaloux	(jealous)	**jalouse**

But:
doux	(soft)	**douce**
faux	(false)	**fausse**
roux	(red-haired)	**rousse**
vieux	(old)	**vieille**

d)
MASCULINE IN **-eur**		FEMININE IN **-euse**
menteur	(lying)	**menteuse**
trompeur	(deceitful)	**trompeuse**

But: This rule applies only when the stem of the adjective is also the stem of a present participle (eg **mentant**, **trompant**). The following five adjectives simply add an **e** to the feminine, **-eur** becoming **- eure**:

MASCULINE		FEMININE
extérieur	(external)	**extérieure**
intérieur	(internal)	**intérieure**
inférieur	(inferior)	**inférieure**
supérieur	(superior)	**supérieure**
meilleur	(better)	**meilleure**

The feminine ending of the remaining adjectives in **-teur** is **-trice**:

MASCULINE		FEMININE
protecteur	(protective)	**protectrice**
destructeur	(destructive)	**destructrice**

e)

MASCULINE IN -f		FEMININE IN -ve
neuf	(new)	neuve
vif	(lively)	vive
naïf	(naive)	naïve
actif	(active)	active
passif	(passive)	passive
positif	(positive)	positive
bref	(brief)	brève (note the è!)

f)

MASCULINE IN -c		FEMININE IN -che or -que
blanc	(white)	blanche
franc	(frank)	franche
sec	(dry)	sèche (note the è!)
public	(public)	publique
turc	(Turkish)	turque
grec	(Greek)	grecque (note the c!)

g) The following five common adjectives have an irregular feminine form and two forms for the masculine singular; the second masculine form, based on the feminine form, is used before words starting with a vowel or a silent h:

MASCULINE	FEMININE	MASCULINE 2
beau (beautiful)	belle	bel
nouveau (new)	nouvelle	nouvel
vieux (old)	vieille	vieil
fou (mad)	folle	fol
mou (soft)	molle	mol

un beau lac a beautiful lake	une belle vue a beautiful view	un bel enfant a beautiful child
un nouveau disque a new record	la nouvelle année the new year	un nouvel ami a new friend
un vieux tableau an old painting	la vieille ville the old town	un vieil homme an old man

h) Other irregular feminines:

MASCULINE		FEMININE
favori	(favourite)	favorite
gentil	(nice)	gentille
nul	(no)	nulle
frais	(fresh)	fraîche
malin	(shrewd)	maligne

sot	(foolish)	**sotte**
long	(long)	**longue**
aigu	(sharp)	**aiguë**
ambigu	(ambiguous)	**ambiguë**
chic	(elegant)	**chic**
châtain	(chestnut)	**châtain**

C.   PLURALS OF ADJECTIVES

1.   General rule

The masculine and feminine plural of adjectives is formed by adding an **s** to the singular form:

un vélo neuf	**des vélos neufs**
a new bike	new bikes
une belle fleur	**de belles fleurs**
a beautiful flower	beautiful flowers

2.   Adjectives ending in 's' or 'x'

If the masculine singular ends in **s** or **x**, there is obviously no need to add the **s**:

il est heureux	**ils sont heureux**
he's happy	they are happy
un touriste anglais	**des touristes anglais**
an English tourist	English tourists

3.   Others

A few masculine plurals are irregular (the feminine plurals are all regular):

a)

SINGULAR IN -al		PLURAL IN -aux
normal	(normal)	**normaux**
brutal	(brutal)	**brutaux**
loyal	(loyal)	**loyaux**

But:

fatal	(fatal)	**fatals**
final	(final)	**finals**
natal	(native)	**natals**
naval	(naval)	**navals**

b)

SINGULAR IN -eau		PLURAL IN -eaux
beau	(beautiful)	**beaux**
nouveau	(new)	**nouveaux**

D. POSITION OF ADJECTIVES

1. Unlike English adjectives, French adjectives usually follow the noun:

un métier intéressant	**des parents modernes**
an interesting job	modern parents

Adjectives of colour and nationality always follow the noun:

des chaussures rouges	**le drapeau britannique**
red shoes	the British flag

2. However the following common adjectives generally come before the noun:

beau	beautiful
bon	good
court	short
gentil	nice
grand	big, tall
gros	fat
haut	high
jeune	young
joli	pretty
long	long
mauvais	bad
méchant	nasty, naughty (*child*)
meilleur	better
moindre	lesser, least
petit	small
pire	worse
vieux	old
vilain	nasty, ugly

3. Some adjectives have a different meaning according to their position:

	BEFORE NOUN	AFTER NOUN
ancien	former	ancient
brave	good	brave
certain	some	sure
cher	dear	expensive
dernier	last	last (= *latest*)
grand	great (*people only*)	big, tall
même	same	very
pauvre	poor (*pitiable*)	poor (*not rich*)
propre	own	clean
seul	single, only	alone, lonely
simple	mere	simple
vrai	real	true

mon ancien métier	**un tableau ancien**
my former job	an old painting
un brave type	**un homme brave**
a nice fellow	a brave man
un certain charme	**un fait certain**
a certain charm	a definite fact
chère Brigitte	**un cadeau cher**
dear Brigitte	an expensive present
la dernière séance	**le mois dernier**
the last performance	last month
une grande vedette	**un homme assez grand**
a great star	a fairly tall man
le même endroit	**la vérité même**
the same place	the truth itself
mon pauvre ami !	**des gens pauvres**
my poor friend!	poor people
mon propre frère	**une chambre propre**
my own brother	a clean room
mon seul espoir	**un homme seul**
my only hope	a lonely man
un simple employé	**des goûts simples**
an ordinary employee	simple tastes
un vrai casse-pieds	**une histoire vraie**
a real bore	a true story

4. If a noun is accompanied by several adjectives, the same rules apply to each of them:

> **le bon vieux temps**
> the good old days

> **un joli foulard rouge**
> a pretty red scarf

E. COMPARATIVE AND SUPERLATIVE OF ADJECTIVES

Persons or things can be compared by using:

1. *the comparative form of the adjective:*

> **more ... than, ...er than, less ... than, as ... as**

2. *the superlative form of the adjective:*

> **the most ... , the ...est, the least ...**

1. The comparative

The comparative is formed as follows:

plus ... (que)	plus long	plus cher
more ...,	longer	more expensive
...er (than)		

moins ... (que)	moins long	moins récent
less ... than	less long	less recent

aussi ... (que)	aussi bon	aussi important
as ... (as)	as good	as important

une plus grande maison   **un village plus ancien**
a larger house   an older village

le football est-il plus populaire que le rugby ?
is football more popular than rugby?

ces gants sont moins chauds que les autres
these gloves are less warm than the other ones

elle est beaucoup/bien moins patiente que lui
she's far less patient than he is

le problème de la pollution est tout aussi grave
the pollution problem is just as serious

2. The superlative

a) *Formation*

le/la/les plus ...	the most ..., the ...est
le/la/les moins ...	the least ...

le plus grand pays	la plus grande ville
the largest country	the largest city

les plus grands acteurs	les plus grandes voitures
the greatest actors	the largest cars

b) *Word order*

i) The normal rules governing word order of adjectives apply. When a superlative adjective comes after the noun, the article is used twice, before the noun and before the adjective:

le plat le plus délicieux	l'histoire la plus passionnante
the most delicious dish	the most exciting story

ii) When a possessive adjective is used, there are two possible constructions, depending on the position of the adjective:

ma plus forte matière
my best subject

or:

son besoin le plus urgent est de trouver un emploi
his most urgent need is to find a job

c) *'in' is normally translated by* **de**:

> **la plus jolie maison du quartier/de la ville**
> the prettiest house in the area/town

> **le restaurant le plus cher de France**
> the most expensive restaurant in France

Note: Verbs following the superlative usually take the subjunctive (see p 91).

3. Irregular comparatives and superlatives

ADJECTIVE	COMPARATIVE	SUPERLATIVE
bon good	**meilleur** better	**le meilleur** best
mauvais bad	**pire** **plus mauvais** worse	**le pire** **le plus mauvais** the worst
petit small	**moindre** **plus petit** smaller, lesser	**le moindre** **le plus petit** the smallest, the least

Note: – **plus mauvais** is used in the sense of worse in quality, taste etc
– **moindre** usually means 'less in importance', and **plus petit** means 'less in size':

> **le moindre de mes soucis**
> the least of my worries

> **elle est plus petite que moi**
> she is smaller than I (am)

5. ADVERBS

Adverbs are normally used with a verb to express:

		ADVERBS OF
how		manner
when		time
where	an action is done	place
with how much intensity		intensity
to what extent		quantity

A. ADVERBS OF MANNER

These are usually formed by adding **-ment** to the adjective (like **-ly** in English):

1. If the adjective ends in a consonant, **-ment** is added to its feminine form:

ADJECTIVE (masc, fem)	ADVERB
doux, douce (soft)	**doucement** (softly)
franc, franche (frank)	**franchement** (frankly)
final, finale (final)	**finalement** (finally)

2. If the adjective ends in a vowel, **-ment** is added to its masculine form:

ADJECTIVE	ADVERB
absolu (absolute)	**absolument** (absolutely)
désespéré (desperate)	**désespérément** (desperately)
vrai (true)	**vraiment** (truly)
simple (simple)	**simplement** (simply)

But:	**gai** (cheerful)	**gaiement** or **gaîment** (cheerfully)
	nouveau (new)	**nouvellement** (newly)
	fou (mad)	**follement** (madly)

3. Many adverbs have irregular forms:

a) Some change the **e** of the feminine form of the adjective to **é** before adding **-ment**:

ADJECTIVE	ADVERB
commun (common)	**communément** (commonly)
précis (precise)	**précisément** (precisely)
profond (deep)	**profondément** (deeply)
énorme (enormous)	**énormément** (enormously)
aveugle (blind)	**aveuglément** (blindly)

b) Adjectives which end in **-ent** and **-ant** change to **-emment** and **-amment** (*Note:* both endings are pronounced **-amant**):

ADJECTIVE	ADVERB
prudent (careful)	**prudemment** (carefully)
évident (obvious)	**évidemment** (obviously)
brillant (brilliant)	**brillamment** (brilliantly)

But: **lent** (slow)   **lentement** (slowly)

4. Some adverbs are completely irregular, including some of the most commonly used ones:

ADJECTIVE	ADVERB
bon (good)	**bien** (well)
bref (brief)	**brièvement** (briefly)
gentil (kind)	**gentiment** (kindly)
mauvais (bad)	**mal** (badly)
meilleur (better)	**mieux** (better)

5. Some adjectives are also used as adverbs in certain set expressions, eg:

parler bas/ haut or **fort**	to speak softly/ loudly
coûter/ payer cher	to cost/ pay a lot
s'arrêter court	to stop short
couper court	to cut short
voir clair	to see clearly
marcher droit	to walk straight
travailler dur	to work hard
chanter faux/ juste	to sing off key/ in tune
sentir mauvais/ bon	to smell bad/ good
refuser net	to refuse point blank

6. After verbs of saying and looking in French an adverbial phrase is often preferred to an adverb, eg:

> **"tu m'écriras ?" dit-il** *d'une voix triste*
> "will you write to me?" he said *sadly*

> **elle nous a regardés** *d'un air dédaigneux*
> she looked at us *disdainfully*

7. English adverbs may be expressed in French by a preposition followed by a noun, eg:

sans soin	carelessly
avec fierté	proudly
avec amour	lovingly

B.   ADVERBS OF TIME

These are not usually formed from adjectives. Here are the commonest ones:

alors	then
après	afterwards
aujourd'hui	today
aussitôt	at once
bientôt	soon
d'abord	first
déjà	already
demain	tomorrow
encore	still, again
pas encore	not yet
enfin	at last, finally
hier	yesterday
parfois	sometimes
rarement	seldom
souvent	often
tard	late
tôt	early
toujours	always
tout de suite	immediately

c'est déjà Noël !
it's Christmas already!

tu as déjà essayé ?
have you tried before?

il mange encore !
he's still eating!

elle n'est pas encore arrivée
she hasn't arrived yet

C.   ADVERBS OF PLACE

Here are the commonest ones:

ailleurs	somewhere else
ici	here
là	there
loin	far away
dessus	on top, on it
au-dessus	over, above
dessous	underneath
au-dessous	below
dedans	inside
dehors	outside
devant	in front, ahead
derrière	behind
partout	everywhere

ne restez pas dehors !
don't stay outside!

mon nom est marqué dessus
my name is written on it

qu'est-ce qu'il y a dedans ?
what's inside?

passez devant
go in front

D. ADVERBS OF INTENSITY AND QUANTITY

These may be used with a verb, an adjective or another adverb. Here are the commonest ones:

à peine	hardly
assez	enough, quite
autant	as much/ many
beaucoup	a lot, much/ many
combien	how much/ many
comme	how
moins	less
plus	more
presque	nearly
peu	little
seulement	only
si	so
tant	so much/ many
tellement	so much/ many
très	very
trop	too, too much/ many
un peu	a little

vous avez assez bu !
you've had enough to drink!

il ne fait pas assez chaud
it's not warm enough

nous avons beaucoup ri
we laughed a lot

comme c'est amusant !
how funny!

je vais un peu mieux
I'm feeling a little better

c'est si fatigant !
it's so tiring!

elle parle trop
she talks too much

il est très timide
he's very shy

Note: All of these adverbs, except **à peine, comme, presque, si, très, seulement,** may be followed by **de** and a noun to express a quantity (see p 168-70).

E. POSITION OF ADVERBS

1. Adverbs usually follow verbs:

je vais rarement au théâtre
I seldom go to the theatre

comme vous conduisez prudemment !
you do drive carefully!

2. With compound tenses, shorter adverbs usually come between the auxiliary and the past participle:

j'ai enfin terminé
I have finished at last

nous y sommes souvent allés
we've often gone there

il me l'a déjà dit
he's already told me

elle avait beaucoup souffert
she had suffered a lot

3. But adverbs of place and many adverbs of time follow the past participle:

je l'ai rencontré hier
I met him yesterday

elle avait cherché partout
she had looked everywhere

mettez-le dehors
put it outside

tu t'es couché tard ?
did you go to bed late?

4. Adverbs usually come before adjectives or other adverbs:

très rarement
very seldom

trop vite
too quickly

elle est vraiment belle
she is really beautiful

F. COMPARATIVE AND SUPERLATIVE OF ADVERBS

1. The comparative and superlative of adverbs are formed in the same way as adjectives:

ADVERB	COMPARATIVE	SUPERLATIVE
souvent often	**plus souvent (que)** more often (than)	**le plus souvent** (the) most often
	moins souvent (que) less often (than)	**le moins souvent** (the) least often
	aussi souvent (que) as often (as)	

Note: The superlative of the adverb always takes the masculine singular article **le**:

je le vois plus souvent qu'avant
I see him more often than I used to

il conduit moins prudemment que moi
he drives less carefully than I do

c'est lui qui conduit le moins prudemment
he's the one who drives the least carefully

je sais cuisiner aussi bien que toi !
I can cook as well as you!

Note:

a) **as ... as possible** is translated either by **aussi ... que possible** or by **le plus ... possible**:

as far as possible   **aussi loin que possible**
                             le plus loin possible

b) after a negative, **aussi** is often replaced by **si**:

pas si vite !
not so fast!

c) In French, the idea of **not so**, **not as** is often expressed by **moins** (less):

> **parle moins fort** !
> don't talk so loud!

2. Irregular comparatives and superlatives

ADVERB	COMPARATIVE	SUPERLATIVE
beaucoup	**plus**	**le plus**
much, a lot	more	(the) most
bien	**mieux**	**le mieux**
well	better	(the) best
mal	**pis** or **plus mal**	**le pis** or **le plus mal**
badly	worse	(the) worst
peu	**moins**	**le moins**
little	less	(the) least

Note:

i) **mieux/le mieux** must not be confused with **meilleur/le meilleur**, which are adjectives, used in front of a noun.

ii) **pis/le pis** are only found in certain set expressions:

> **tant pis**   **de mal en pis**
> so much the worse, too bad   from bad to worse

6. PRONOUNS AND CORRESPONDING ADJECTIVES

A. DEMONSTRATIVES

1. Demonstrative adjectives

a) *CE*

ce is often used to point out a particular person or thing, or persons or things. It is followed by the noun it refers to and agrees in number and gender with that noun.

- with a masculine singular noun: **ce (cet)**   this/that
- with a feminine singular noun: **cette**   this/that
- with a plural noun (masc or fem): **ces**   these/those

ce roman m'a beaucoup plu   **il a neigé ce matin**
I really liked this novel   it snowed this morning

cette chanson m'énerve   **cette fois, c'est fini !**
that song gets on my nerves   this time, it's over!

tu trouves que ces lunettes me vont bien ?
do you think these glasses suit me?

cet is used instead of **ce** in front of a word that begins with a vowel or a silent **h**:

cet après-midi   **cet hôtel**
this afternoon   that hotel

b) *-CI and -LA*

French does not have separate words to distinguish between 'this' and 'that'. However, when a particular emphasis is being placed on a person or object, or when a contrast is being made between persons or objects, **-ci** and **-là** are added to the noun:

-ci translates the idea of   this/these
-là translates the idea of   that/those

je suis très occupé ces jours-ci
I'm very busy these days

que faisiez-vous ce soir-là ?
what were you doing that evening?

d'où vient ce fromage-là ? – ce fromage-ci, Monsieur ?
where does that cheese come from? – this cheese, sir?

2. Demonstrative pronouns

Demonstrative pronouns are used instead of a noun with **ce/cette/ces**. They are:

    a)   **celui, celle, ceux, celles**
    b)   **ce**
    c)   **ceci, cela, ça**

a) *CELUI*

    i)   **celui** agrees in number and gender with the noun it refers to. It has four different forms:

	MASCULINE	FEMININE
SINGULAR	celui	celle
PLURAL	ceux	celles

    ii)   use of **celui**

        celui, celle, ceux and **celles** cannot be used on their own. They are used:

★   with **-ci** or **-là**, for emphasis or for contrast:

celui-ci	**celle-ci**	this (one)
celui-là	**celle-là**	that (one)
ceux-ci	**celles-ci**	these (ones)
ceux-là	**celles-là**	those (ones)

        j'aime bien ce maillot, mais celui-là est moins cher
        I like this swimsuit, but that one is cheaper

        je voudrais ces fleurs – lesquelles ? celles-ci ou celles-là ?
        I'd like these flowers – which ones? these or those?

★   with **de** + noun, to express possession:

        je préfère mon ordinateur à celui de Jean-Claude
        I prefer my computer to Jean-Claude's

        range ta chambre plutôt que celle de ta sœur
        tidy your own bedroom rather than your sister's

        mes parents sont moins sévères que ceux de Nicole
        my parents aren't as strict as Nicole's

        les douches municipales sont mieux que celles du camping
        the public showers are better than those at the campsite

★   with the relative pronouns **qui, que, dont** to introduce a relative clause (for use of these relative pronouns, see pp 60-64).

celui/celle/ ceux/ celles qui	the one(s) who/which
celui/ celle/ ceux/ celles que	the one(s) whom/which
celui/ celle/ ceux/ celles dont	the one(s) of which/whose

        lequel est ton père ? celui qui a une moustache ?
        which one is your father? the one with the moustache?

        regarde cette voiture ! celle qui est garée au coin
        look at that car! the one which is parked at the corner

deux filles, celles qu'il avait rencontrées la veille
two girls, the ones he had met the day before

voilà mon copain, celui dont je t'ai parlé l'autre jour
here's my friend, the one I told you about the other day

b) *CE*

i) **ce** (meaning 'it', 'that') is mostly found with the verb **être**:

c'est	**ce serait**	**c'était**
it's/that's	it/that would be	it/that was

Note: ce changes to **c'** before an **e** or an **é**.

ii) use of **ce**

★ with a noun or pronoun, **ce** is used to identify people or things, or to emphasize them; it is translated in a variety of ways:

qu'est-ce que c'est ? – c'est mon billet d'avion
what's that? – it's my plane ticket

qui est-ce ? – c'est moi	**ce doit être lui**
who is it? – it's me	that must be him

c'est un artiste bien connu	**c'était une bonne idée**
he's a well-known artist	it was a good idea

ce sont mes amis	**c'est la dernière fois !**
they're my friends	it's the last time!

c'est elle qui l'a fait	**c'est celui que j'ai vu**
she's the one who did it	he's the one I saw

★ before an adjective, **ce** is used to refer to an idea, an event or a fact which has already been mentioned; it does not refer to any specific noun:

c'était formidable	**ce serait amusant**
it was great	it would be funny

oui, c'est vrai	**c'est sûr ?**
yes, that's true	is that definite?

ce n'est pas grave	**c'est bon à entendre**
it doesn't matter	that's good to hear
or it's not serious	

Note: the translation of **it** is an area of some difficulty for students of French, as it is sometimes translated by **ce** and sometimes by **il/elle**; see the section on pp 186-7.

3. CECI, CELA, ÇA

ceci (this), **cela** (that) and **ça** (that) are used to refer to an idea, an event, a fact or an object. They never refer to a particular noun already mentioned.

non, je n'aime pas ça !	**ah, bon ? cela m'étonne**
no, I don't like that!	really? that surprises me

ça, c'est un acteur !	**souvenez-vous de ceci**
that's what I call an actor!	remember this

ça m'est égal I don't mind	**cela ne vous regarde pas** that's none of your business
buvez ceci, ça vous fera du bien drink this, it'll do you good	**ça alors !** well, really!
cela s'appelle comment, en anglais ? what do you call this in English?	

Note: **ceci** is not very common in French; **cela** and **ça** are often used to translate 'this' as well as 'that'; **ça** is used far more frequently than **cela** in spoken French.

B.   INDEFINITE ADJECTIVES AND PRONOUNS

1.   Indefinite adjectives

They are:

MASCULINE	FEMININE	
autre(s)	**autre(s)**	other
certain(s)	**certaine(s)**	certain
chaque	**chaque**	each, every
même(s)	**même(s)**	same
plusieurs	**plusieurs**	several
quelque(s)	**quelque(s)**	some
tel(s)	**telle(s)**	such
tout (tous)	**toute(s)**	all, every

a)   *CHAQUE and PLUSIEURS*

chaque (each) is always singular, **plusieurs** (several) always plural; the feminine form is the same as the masculine form:

j'y vais chaque jour I go there every day	**chaque personne** each person
plusieurs années several years	**il a plusieurs amis** he's got several friends

b)   *AUTRE, MEME and QUELQUE*

autre (other), **même** (same) and **quelque** (some) agree in number with the noun that follows; the feminine is the same as the masculine:

je voudrais un autre café I'd like another coffee	**d'autres couleurs** other colours
la même taille the same size	**les mêmes touristes** the same tourists
quelque temps après some time later	**à quelques kilomètres** a few kilometres away

Note: **même** has a different meaning when placed after the noun (see pp 29-30).

c) *CERTAIN, TEL and TOUT*

certain (certain, some), **tel** (such) and **tout** (all) agree in number and gender with the noun; they have four different forms:

un certain charme	**une certaine dame**
a certain charm	a certain lady
à certains moments	**certaines personnes**
at (certain) times	some people
un tel homme	**une telle aventure**
such a man	such an adventure
de tels avantages	**de telles difficultés**
such advantages	such difficulties

quoi ! tu as mangé tout le fromage et tous les fruits ?
what! you've eaten all the cheese and all the fruit?

toute la journée	**toutes mes matières**
all day long	all my subjects

Note:

i) **tel**: the position of the article **un/une** with **tel** is not the same as in English: **un tel homme** = such a man.

ii) **tel** cannot qualify another adjective; when it is used as an adverb, 'such' is translated by **si** or **tellement** (so):

c'était un si bon repas/ un repas tellement bon !
it was such a good meal!

iii) **tous les/ toutes les** are often translated by 'every':

tous les jours	**toutes les places**
every day	all seats, every seat

2. Indefinite pronouns

a) These are:

MASC	FEM	
aucun	aucune	none, not any
autre(s)	autre(s)	another one, other ones
certains	certaine(s)	certain, some
chacun	chacune	each one, everyone
on		one, someone, you, they, people, we
personne		nobody
plusieurs	plusieurs	several (ones)
quelque chose		something, anything
quelqu'un		someone
quelques-uns	quelques-unes	some, a few
rien		nothing
tout (tous)	toute(s)	everything, every one, all

pas celui-là, l'autre
not that one, the other one

où sont les autres ?
where are the others?

certains disent que ...
some say that...

personne n'est venu
no one came

qui est là ? – personne
who's there? – nobody

qu'as-tu ? – rien
what's wrong? – nothing

plusieurs d'entre eux
several of them

chacun pour soi !
every man for himself!

il manque quelque chose ?
is anything missing?

dis quelque chose !
say something!

quelqu'un l'a averti
someone warned him

il y a quelqu'un ?
is anyone in?

j'ai tout oublié
I've forgotten everything

c'est tout, merci
that's all, thanks

elles sont toutes arrivées
they've all arrived

allons-y tous ensemble
let's all go together

b) *Points to note*

i) **aucun(e)**, **personne** and **rien**: these can be used on their own, but they are more often used with a verb and the negative word **ne** (see negative expressions, pp 176-8):

personne n'habite ici
no one lives here

il n'y a rien à manger
there's nothing to eat

ii) **aucun(e)**, **un(e) autre**, **d'autres**, **certain(e)s**, **plusieurs** and **quelques-un(e)s**: when these pronouns are used as direct objects, the pronoun **en** must be used before the verb:

je n'en ai lu aucun
I haven't read any (of them)

donne-m'en une autre
give me another one

j'en ai vu d'autres qui étaient moins chers
I saw other ones which were cheaper

j'en connais certains
I know some of them

il y en a plusieurs
there are several

tu m'en donnes quelques-uns
will you give me a few?

achètes-en quelques-unes
buy a few

iii) **personne**, **quelque chose**, **rien**, **plusieurs**: when these are followed by an adjective, the preposition **de** (**d'**) must be used in front of the adjective:

il n'y a personne de libre
there's no one available

quelque chose de mieux
something better

il y en avait plusieurs de cassés
several of them were broken

rien de grave
nothing serious

iv) **autre** is commonly used in the following expressions:

quelqu'un d'autre
someone else

quelque chose d'autre
something else

rien d'autre
nothing else

c) *ON*

This pronoun is used in a variety of ways in French. It can mean:

i) *one/you/they/people* in a general sense:

en France, on roule à droite
in France, they drive on the right

on ne sait jamais   **on ne doit pas mentir**
you/one never know(s)   you shouldn't lie

ii) *someone* (an undefined person)

In this sense, **on** is often translated by the passive (see p 107):

on me l'a déjà dit   **on vous l'apportera**
someone's already told me   someone will bring you it
I've already been told   it will be brought to you

iii) *we*

In spoken French, **on** is increasingly used instead of **nous**; although it refers to a plural subject, it is followed by the third person singular:

qu'est-ce qu'on fait ?   **fais vite, on t'attend !**
what shall we do?   hurry up, we're waiting for you!

Note: in compound tenses with the auxiliary **être**, the agreement of the past participle with **on** is optional:

on est allé au cinéma   **on est rentré en taxi**
on est allés au cinéma   **on est rentrées en taxi**
we went to the pictures   we got home by taxi

C. INTERROGATIVE AND EXCLAMATORY ADJECTIVES AND PRONOUNS

1. The interrogative adjective QUEL ?

a) *Forms*

quel (which, what) agrees in number and gender with the noun it refers to. It has four forms:

– with a masc sing noun: **quel ?**
– with a fem sing noun: **quelle ?**
– with a masc plur noun: **quels ?**
– with a fem plur noun: **quelles ?**

b) *Direct questions*

quel est votre passe-temps favori ?
what's your favourite pastime?

quelle heure est-il ?   **quels jours as-tu de libres ?**
what time is it?   which days have you got free?

quelles affaires comptes-tu prendre avec toi ?
what/which things do you intend to take with you?

c) *Indirect questions:*

> **je ne sais pas quel disque choisir**
> I don't know which record to choose

> **il se demande quelle veste lui va le mieux**
> he's wondering which jacket suits him best

2.   The exclamatory adjective QUEL !

quel ! has the same forms as the interrogative adjective **quel** ?:

quel dommage !   **quelle belle maison !**
what a pity!   what a beautiful house!

quels imbéciles !
what idiots!

3.   Interrogative pronouns

These are:

lequel/ laquelle/	which (one)?
lesquel(le)s ?	
qui ?	who?, whom?
que ?	what?
quoi ?	what?
ce qui	what
ce que	what

ce qui and **ce que** are used only in indirect questions; all other
interrogative pronouns can be used both in direct and indirect questions.

a)   *LEQUEL ?*

i)   forms

lequel (which., which one?) agrees in gender and in number with the noun
it stands for:

– with a masc sing noun: **lequel ?**   which (one)?
– with a fem sing noun: **laquelle ?**   which (one)?
– with a masc plur noun: **lesquels ?**   which (ones)?
– with a fem plur noun: **lesquelles ?**   which (ones)?

after the prepositions **à** and **de**, the following changes occur:

à + lequel ?	→	**auquel ?**
à + lesquels ?	→	**auxquels ?**
à + lesquelles ?	→	**auxquelles ?**
de + lequel ?	→	**duquel ?**
de + lesquels ?	→	**desquels ?**
de + lesquelles ?	→	**desquelles ?**

à/de + laquelle? do not change

ii)   direct questions:

je cherche un hôtel; lequel recommandez-vous ?
I'm looking for a hotel; which one do you recommend?

nous avons plusieurs couleurs; vous préférez laquelle ?
we have several colours; which one do you prefer?

lesquels de ces livres sont à toi ?
which of these books are yours?

je voudrais essayer ces chaussures – lesquelles ?
I would like to try these shoes on – which ones?

iii)   indirect questions

demande-lui lequel de ces ordinateurs est le moins cher
ask him which (one) of these computers is the cheapest

c'est dans une de ces rues, mais je ne sais plus laquelle
it's in one of these streets, but I can't remember which one

b)   *QUI ?*

qui (who?, whom?) is used to refer to people; it can be both subject and object and can be used after a preposition:

qui t'a accompagné ?	**qui as-tu appelé ?**
who accompanied you?	who did you call?
tu y vas avec qui ?	**c'est pour qui ?**
who are you going with?	who is it for?
pour qui vous prenez-vous ?	**à qui l'as-tu donné ?**
who do you think you are?	who did you give it to?

Note: **que** (not **qui**!) changes to **qu'** before a vowel or a silent **h**:

qui est-ce qu'elle attend ?
who is she waiting for?

qui ? can be replaced by **qui est-ce qui ?** (subject) or **qui est-ce que ?** (object) in direct questions:

qui est-ce qui veut du café ?	**qui est-ce que tu as vu ?**
who wants coffee?	who did you see?

avec qui est-ce que tu sors ce soir ?
who are you going out with tonight?

But: **qui** cannot be replaced by **qui est-ce qui** or **qui est-ce que** in indirect questions:

j'aimerais savoir qui vous a dit ça
I'd like to know who told you that

elle se demandait de qui étaient les fleurs
she was wondering who the flowers were from

For more details on the use of **qui/que** as relative pronouns, see pp 60-4.

c) *QUE ?*

que (what?) is used to refer to things; it is only used in direct questions; it is always a direct object and cannot be used after prepositions:

> **que désirez-vous ?**   **qu'a-t-il dit ?**
> what do you wish?   what did he say?

que ? is rather formal and is usually replaced by **qu'est-ce qui ?** or **qu'est-ce que ?** in spoken French.

Note: **que** becomes **qu'** before a vowel or a silent **h**.

d) *QU'EST-CE QUI ?*

qu'est-ce qui ? (what?) is used as the subject of a verb; it cannot refer to a person:

> **qu'est-ce qui lui est arrivé ?**   **qu'est-ce qui la fait rire ?**
> what happened to him?   what makes her laugh?

e) *QU'EST-CE QUE ?*

qu'est-ce que ? (what?) replaces **que ?** as the object of a verb; it becomes **qu'est-ce qu'** before a vowel or a silent **h**:

> **qu'est-ce que tu aimes lire ?**
> what do you like reading?

> **qu'est-ce qu'il va faire pendant les vacances ?**
> what's he going to do during the holidays?

f) *QUOI ?*

quoi ? (what?) refers to things; it is used:

i) instead of **que** or **qu'est-ce que** after a preposition:

> **à quoi penses-tu ?**   **dans quoi l'as-tu mis ?**
> what are you thinking about?   what did you put it in?

ii) in indirect questions:

> **demandez-lui de quoi il a besoin**
> ask him what he needs

> **je ne sais pas à quoi ça sert**
> I don't know what it's for

g) *CE QUI, CE QUE*

ce qui and **ce que** (what) are only used in indirect questions; they replace **qu'est-ce qui** and **(qu'est- ce) que**.
They are used in the same way as the relative pronouns **ce qui** and **ce que** (see pp 63-4).

i) **ce qui** is used as the subject of the verb in the indirect question (**ce qui** is the subject of **s'est passé** in the following example):

> **nous ne saurons jamais ce qui s'est passé**
> we'll never know what happened

ii) **ce que**

ce que (**ce qu'** before a vowel or a silent **h**) is used as the object of the verb in the indirect question (**ce que** is the object of **il faisait** in the following example):

je n'ai pas remarqué ce qu'il faisait
I didn't notice what he was doing

D. PERSONAL PRONOUNS

There are four categories of personal pronouns:

– **subject** pronouns
– **object** pronouns
– **disjunctive** pronouns
– **reflexive** pronouns

For reflexive pronouns, see pp 77-9.

1. Subject pronouns

PERSON	SINGULAR		PLURAL	
1st	**je (j')**	I	**nous**	we
2nd	**tu**	you	**vous**	you
3rd	**il**	he, it	**ils**	they
	elle	she, it	**elles**	they
	on	one, we, they		

Note:

a) **je** changes to **j'** before a vowel or a silent **h**:

j'ai honte   **j'adore les frites**
I'm ashamed   I love chips

j'habite en Ecosse
I live in Scotland

b) **tu** and **vous**

vous can be plural or singular; it is used when speaking to more than one person (plural), or to a stranger or an older person (singular):

vous venez, les gars ?   **vous parlez l'anglais,
                                     Monsieur ?**
are you coming, lads?   do you speak English(, sir)?

tu is used when speaking to a friend, a relative, a younger person, or someone you know well:

tu viens, Marc ?
are you coming, Marc?

c) **il/ils, elle/elles** may refer to people, animals or things, and must be of the same gender as the noun they replace:

ton stylo ? *il* **est là**   **ta montre ?** *elle* **est là**
your pen? there *it* is   your watch? there *it* is

tes gants ? *ils* sont là   tes lunettes ? *elles* sont là
your gloves? there *they* are   your glasses? there *they* are

When referring to several nouns of different genders, French uses the masculine plural **ils**:

tu as vu *le* stylo et *la* montre de Marie. – oui, *ils* sont dans son sac
have you seen Marie's pen and watch. – yes, *they*'re in her bag

d)   on: see p 45.

2.   Object pronouns

These include: – direct object pronouns
                          – indirect object pronouns
                          – the pronouns **en** and **y**

a)   *Forms*

	PERSON	DIRECT	INDIRECT
SING	1st	**me (m')**	**me (m')**
		me	(to) me
	2nd	**te (t')**	**te (t')**
		you	(to) you
	3rd	**le (l')**	**lui**
		him, it	(to) him
		la (l')	**lui**
		her, it	(to) her
PLUR	1st	**nous**	**nous**
		us	(to) us
	2nd	**vous**	**vous**
		you	(to) you
	3rd	**les**	**leur**
		them	(to) them

Note:

i) **me**, **te**, **le** and **la** change to **m'**, **t'** and **l'** before a vowel or a silent **h**:

il m'énerve !   **je m'habituerai à lui**
he gets on my nerves!   I'll get used to him

ii) **te** and **vous**: the same distinction should be made as between the subject pronouns **tu** and **vous** (see p 49).

iii) **le**: is sometimes used in an impersonal sense, when it refers to a fact, a statement or an idea which has already been expressed; it is usually not translated in English:

j'irai en Amérique un jour ;   en tout cas je *l'*espère
I'll go to America one day; I hope so anyway

elle a eu un bébé – je *le* sais, elle me *l'*a dit
she's had a baby – I know, she told me

iv) **moi** and **toi** are used instead of **me** and **te**, except when **en** follows:

écris-*moi* bientôt   **donne *m'*en**
write to me soon   give me some

b) *Position*

In French, object pronouns come immediately before the verb they refer to. With a compound tense, they come before the auxiliary:

on *t*'attendra ici	we'll wait for you here
je *l*'ai rencontrée en ville	I met her in town

Note: When there are two verbs, the pronoun comes immediately before the verb it refers to:

j'aimerais lui demander	I'd like to ask him
tu *l*'as entendu chanter ?	have you heard him sing?

In positive commands (affirmative imperative) the pronoun follows the verb and is joined to it by a hyphen:

regarde-*les* !	look at them!
parle-*lui* !	speak to him!
dis-*nous* ce qui s'est passé	tell us what happened

c) *Direct pronouns and indirect pronouns*

i) Direct object pronouns replace a noun which follows the verb directly. They answer the question 'who(m)?' or 'what?':

WHO(M) did you see?	qui as-tu vu ?
I saw my friend; I saw him	j'ai vu mon ami ; je *l*'ai vu
you know me	tu *me* connais
I like to see him dance	j'aime *le* voir danser
I found them	je *les* ai trouvés
don't bother us!	ne *nous* ennuie pas !

ii) Indirect object pronouns replace a noun which follows the verb with a linking preposition (usually à = 'to'). They answer the question 'who(m) to?':

WHO did you speak to?	à qui as-tu parlé ?
I spoke to Marc; I spoke to him	j'ai parlé à Marc ; je *lui* ai parlé
she lied to him	elle *lui* a menti
I'm giving this record to you	je *te* donne ce disque
I'm not talking to them any more	je ne *leur* parle plus

iii) le/la/les or lui/leur?

Direct pronouns differ from indirect pronouns only in the 3rd person and great care must be taken here:

★ English indirect object pronouns often look like direct objects; this becomes obvious when the object is placed at the end of the sentence:

I showed him your photo =	I showed your photo to him
je *lui* ai montré ta photo	

This is particularly the case with the following verbs:

acheter	to buy	offrir	to offer
donner	to give	prêter	to lend
montrer	to show	vendre	to sell

je lui ai acheté un livre = I bought him a book
= I bought a book for him

ne leur prête pas mes affaires = don't lend them my things
= don't lend my things to them

★ Some verbs take a direct object in English and an indirect object in French (see p 148):

je ne lui ai rien dit I didn't tell him anything
je leur demanderai I'll ask them
tu lui ressembles you look like him
téléphone-leur phone them

★ Some verbs take a direct object in French and an indirect object in English (see p 148):

j'attends I'm waiting for him
écoutez-les! listen to them!

(d) *Order of object pronouns*

When several object pronouns are used together, they come in the following order:

(i) Before the verb:

1	me	te		nous	vous
2	le	la	les		
3	lui	leur			

il me l'a donné he gave me it
je vais vous les envoyer I'll send them to you
ne la leur vends pas don't sell it to them
je le lui ai acheté I bought it for him

(ii) After the verb:

With a positive command (affirmative imperative), the order is as follows:

1	le	la	les		
2	moi (m')	toi (t')	lui	nous	vous
3	leur				

apporte-les-moi! bring them to me!
prête-la-nous! lend us it!
dites-le-lui! tell him!
rends-la-leur! give it back to them!

3.   The pronoun *EN*

a)   *Use*

en is used instead of **de** + noun. Since **de** has a variety of meanings, **en** can be used in a number of ways:

i)   It means 'of it/them', but also 'with it/them', 'about it/them', 'from it/there', 'out of it/there':

tu es sûr *du prix* ? – j'*en* suis sûr
are you sure of the price? – I'm sure *of it*

je suis content *de ce cadeau* ; j'*en* suis content
I'm pleased with this present; I'm pleased *with it*

elle est folle *des animaux* ; elle *en* est folle
she's crazy about animals; she's crazy *about them*

il est descendu *du train* ; il *en* est descendu
he got off the train; he got *off it*

il revient *de Paris* ; il *en* revient
he's coming back from Paris; he's coming *from there*

ii)   Verb constructions

Particular care should be taken with verbs and expressions which are followed by **de** + noun. Since **de** is not always translated in the same way, **en** may have a number of meanings:

il a envie *de ce livre* ; il *en* a envie
he wants this book; he wants *it*

je te remercie *de ta carte* ; je t'*en* remercie
I thank you for your card; I thank you *for it*

tu as besoin *de ces papiers* ? tu *en* as besoin ?
do you need these papers? do you need *them*?

elle a peur *des chiens* ; elle *en* a peur
she's afraid of dogs; she's afraid *of them*

tu te souviens *de ce film* ? tu t'*en* souviens ?
do you remember this film? do you remember *it*?

iii)   'some'/'any'

en replaces the partitive article (**du, de la, des**) + noun; it means 'some'/'any':

tu veux *du café* ? – non, je n'*en* veux pas
do you want (any) coffee? – no, I don't want *any*

j'achète *des fruits* ? – non, j'*en* ai chez moi
shall I buy fruit. – no, I've got *some* at home

il y a *de la place* ? – *en* voilà là-bas
is there any room? – there's *some* over there

iv)   Expressions of quantity

en must be used with expressions of quantity not followed by a noun. It replaces **de** + noun and means 'of it/them', but is seldom translated in English:

tu as pris assez *d'argent* ? tu *en* as pris assez ?
did you take enough money? did you take enough?

vous avez *combien de frères* ? – j'*en* ai deux
how many brothers do you have? – I've got two

j'ai fini *mes cigarettes* ; je vais *en* acheter un paquet
I've finished my cigarettes; I'm going to buy a packet

b)   *Position*

Like object pronouns, **en** comes immediately before the verb, except with positive commands (affirmative imperative), where it comes after the verb and is linked to it by a hyphen:

j'en veux un kilo I want a kilo (of it/them)	**j'en ai marre !** I'm fed up (with it)!
prends-en assez ! take enough (of it/them)!	**laisses-en aux autres !** leave some for the others!

When used in conjunction with other object pronouns, it always comes last:

ne *m'en* parlez pas ! don't tell me about it!	**je *vous en* donnerai** I'll give you some
prête-*lui-en* ! lend him some!	**gardez-*nous-en* !** keep some for us!

4.   The pronoun Y

a)   *Use*

y is used instead of **à** + noun (not referring to a person). It is used:

i)   As the indirect object of a verb. Since the preposition **à** is translated in a variety of ways in English, **y** may have various meanings (it, of it/them, about it/them etc):

tu joues *au tennis* ? – non, j'*y* joue rarement
do you play tennis? – no, I seldom play (*it*)

je pense *à mes examens* ; j'*y* pense souvent
I'm thinking *about* my exams; I often think *about them*

il s'intéresse *à la photo* ; il s'*y* intéresse
he's interested in photography; he's interested *in it*

ii)   Meaning 'there':

j'ai passé deux jours *à Londres* ; j'*y* ai passé deux jours
I spent two days in London; I spent two days there

il est allé *en Grèce* ; il *y* est allé
he went to Greece; he went there

Note: y must always be used with the verb **aller** (to go) when the place is not mentioned in the clause. It is often not translated in English:

comment vas-tu *à l'école* ? – j'*y* vais en bus
how do you go to school? – I go (there) by bus

allons-y!   **on *y* va demain**
let's go!   we're going (there) tomorrow

iii) Replacing the prepositions **en**, **dans**, **sur** + noun; y then means 'there', 'in it/them', 'on it/them':

je voudrais vivre *en France* ;   **je voudrais *y* vivre**
I'd like to live in France; I'd like to live *there*

je les ai mis *dans ma poche* ;   **je les *y* ai mis**
I put them in my pocket; I put them *there*

***sur la table* ? non, je ne l'*y* vois pas**
on the table? no, I don't see it *there*

b) *Position*

Like other object pronouns, **y** comes immediately before the verb, except with a positive command (affirmative imperative), where it must follow the verb:

j'*y* réfléchirai   **il s'*y* est habitué**
I'll think about it   he got used to it

pensez-*y* !   **n'*y* allez pas !**
think about it!   don't go!

When used with other object pronouns, **y** comes last:

il va *nous y* rencontrer   **je *l'y* ai vu hier**
he'll meet us there   I saw him there yesterday

5. Disjunctive pronouns

a) *Forms*

PERSON		SINGULAR	PLURAL
1st		**moi**	**nous**
		me	us
2nd		**toi**	**vous**
		you	you
3rd	(masc)	**lui**	**eux**
		him	them
	(fem)	**elle**	**elles**
		her	them
	(impersonal)	**soi**	
		oneself	

Note:

i) **toi/vous**: the same difference should be made as between **tu** and **vous** (see p 49).

ii)   **soi** is used in an impersonal, general sense to refer to indefinite pronouns and adjectives (**on, chacun, tout le monde, personne, chaque** etc); it is mainly found in set phrases, such as:

   chacun pour soi
   every man for himself

b)   *Use*

Disjunctive pronouns, also called emphatic pronouns, are used instead of object pronouns (only when referring to persons) in the following cases:

i)   In answer to a question, alone or in a phrase without a verb:

   qui est là ? – moi   **j'aime les pommes ; et toi ?**
   who's there? – me   I like apples; do you?

   qui préfères-tu, lui ou elle ? – elle, bien sûr
   who do you prefer, him or her? – her, of course

ii)   After **c'est/ce sont, c'était/étaient** etc:

   ouvrez, c'est moi !   **non, ce n'était pas lui**
   open up, it's me!   no, it wasn't him

iii)   After a preposition:

   vous allez chez lui ?   **tu y vas avec elle ?**
   are you going to his place?   are you going with her?

   regarde devant toi !   **oh, c'est pour moi ?**
   look in front of you!   oh, is that for me?

iv)   Verb constructions: special care should be taken with verbs followed by a preposition:

   tu peux compter sur moi   **quoi ! tu as peur de lui ?**
   you can count on me   what! you're afraid of him?

   il m'a parlé de toi   **je pense souvent à vous**
   he told me about you   I often think about you

Note: Emphatic pronouns are only used when referring to persons. Otherwise, use **y** or **en**.

v)   For emphasis, particularly when two pronouns are contrasted. The unstressed subject pronoun is usually included:

   vous, vous m'énervez !   **lui, il joue bien ; elle, non**
   you get on my nerves!   *he* plays well; *she* doesn't

   moi, je n'aime pas l'hiver   **eux, ils sont partis**
   I don't like winter   *they*'ve left

vi)   In the case of multiple subjects (two pronouns or one pronoun and one noun):

   lui et son frère sont dans l'équipe
   he and his brother are in the team

   ma famille et moi allons très bien
   my family and I are very well

vii) As the second term of comparisons:

il est plus sympa que toi
he is nicer than you

elle chante mieux que lui
she sings better than he does

viii) Before a relative pronoun:

c'est lui que j'aime
he's the one I love

c'est toi qui l'as dit
you're the one who said it

lui qui n'aime pas le vin blanc en a bu six verres
he, who doesn't like white wine, had six glasses

ix) With **-même(s)** (-self, -selves), **aussi** (too), **seul** (alone):

faites-le vous-mêmes
do it yourselves

j'irai moi-même
I'll go myself

lui aussi est parti
he too went away

elle seule le sait
she alone knows

x) To replace a possessive pronoun (see p 59):

c'est *le mien* ;   il est à moi
it's mine; it belongs to me

E. POSSESSIVE ADJECTIVES AND PRONOUNS

1. Possessive adjectives

a) *Forms*

Possessive adjectives always come before a noun. Like other adjectives, they agree in gender and number with the noun; the masculine and feminine plural are identical:

SINGULAR		PLURAL	
MASC	FEM		
mon	**ma**	**mes**	my
ton	**ta**	**tes**	your
son	**sa**	**ses**	his/her its/one's
notre	**notre**	**nos**	our
votre	**votre**	**vos**	your
leur	**leur**	**leurs**	their

j'ai mis mon argent et mes affaires dans mon sac
I've put my money and my things in my bag

comment va ton frère ? et ta sœur ? et tes parents ?
how's your brother? and your sister? and your parents?

notre rue est assez calme
our street is fairly quiet

ce sont vos amis
they're your friends

Note: **mon/ton/son** are used instead of **ma/ta/sa** when the next word starts with a vowel or silent **h**:

mon ancienne maison   **ton amie Christine**
my old house   your friend Christine

son haleine sentait l'alcool
his breath smelled of alcohol

b)   *Use*

   i)   The possessive adjective is repeated before each noun and agrees with it:

mon père et ma mère sont sortis
my mother and father have gone out

   ii) **son/sa/ses**

son, **sa** and **ses** can all mean 'his', 'her' or 'its'. In French, the form of the adjective is determined by the gender and number of the noun that follows, and not by the possessor:

il m'a prêté sa mobylette et son casque
he lent me his moped and his helmet

elle s'entend bien avec sa mère, mais pas avec son père
she gets on well with her mother, but not with her father

il cire ses chaussures ; elle repasse ses chemisiers
he's polishing his shoes; she's ironing her shirts

   iii) **ton/ta/tes** and **votre/vos**

The two sets of words for 'your', **ton/ta/tes** and **votre/vos**, correspond to the two different forms **tu** and **vous**; they must not be used together with the same person:

Papa, tu as parlé à ton patron ?
have you spoken to your boss, Dad?

Monsieur ! votre brochure ! vous ne la prenez pas ?
Sir! your brochure! aren't you taking it?

   iv) In French, the possessive adjective is replaced by the definite article (**le/la/les**) with the following:

★   parts of the body:

il s'est essuyé les mains   **elle a haussé les épaules**
he wiped his hands   she shrugged (her shoulders)

★   descriptive phrases tagged on to the end of a clause, where English adds 'with':

il marchait lentement, les mains dans les poches
he was walking slowly, with his hands in his pockets

elle l'a regardé partir les larmes aux yeux
she watched him leave with tears in her eyes

2. Possessive pronouns

MASC	FEM	PLURAL (MASC AND FEM)	
le mien	la mienne	les mien(ne)s	mine
le tien	la tienne	les tien(ne)s	yours
le sien	la sienne	les sien(ne)s	his/hers/its
le nôtre	la nôtre	les nôtres	ours
le vôtre	la vôtre	les vôtres	yours
le leur	la leur	les leurs	theirs

Possessive pronouns are used intead of a possessive adjective + noun. They agree in gender and in number with the noun they stand for, and not with the possessor (it is particularly important to remember this when translating 'his' and 'hers'):

j'aime bien ton chapeau, mais je préfère le mien
I quite like your hat, but I prefer mine

on prend quelle voiture ? la mienne ou la tienne ?
which car shall we take? mine or yours?

comment sont vos profs ? les nôtres sont sympas
what are your teachers like? ours are nice

j'ai pris mon passeport, mais Brigitte a oublié le sien
I brought my passport, but Brigitte forgot hers

j'ai gardé ma moto, mais Paul a vendu la sienne
I've kept my motorbike but Paul has sold his

à or de + possessive pronoun

The prepositions **à** or **de** combine with the articles **le** and **les** in the usual way:

à + le mien	→	au mien
à + les miens	→	aux miens
à + les miennes	→	aux miennes
de + le mien	→	du mien
de + les miens	→	des miens
de + les miennes	→	des miennes

demande à tes parents, j'ai déjà parlé aux miens
ask your parents, I've already spoken to mine

leur appartement ressemble beaucoup au nôtre
their flat is very similar to ours

j'aime bien les chiens, mais j'ai peur du tien
I like dogs, but I'm afraid of yours

Note: after the verb **être**, the possessive pronoun is often replaced by **à** + emphatic (disjunctive) pronoun (see p 57):

à qui est cette écharpe ? – elle est à moi
whose scarf is this? – it's mine

ce livre est à toi ? – non, il est à elle
is this book yours? – no, it's hers

c'est à qui ? à vous ou à lui ?
whose is this? yours or his?

F.   RELATIVE PRONOUNS

1.   Definition

Relative pronouns are words which introduce a relative clause. In the
following sentence:

> I bought the book which you recommended

'which' is the relative pronoun, 'which you recommended' is the relative
clause and 'the book' is the antecedent (ie the noun the relative pronoun
refers to).

2.   Forms

Relative pronouns are:

qui	who, which	lequel	which
que	who(m), which	dont	of which, whose
quoi	what	ce qui	what
où	where	ce que	what

qui, que, quoi, lequel, ce qui and ce que can also be used as interrogative
pronouns (see p 46-9) and must not be confused with them.

3.   Use

a)   QUI

qui is used as the subject of a relative clause; it means:

i)   'who', 'that' (referring to people):

connaissez-vous le monsieur qui habite ici ?
do you know the man who lives here?

ce n'est pas lui qui a menti
he's not the one who lied

ii)   'which', 'that' (referring to things):

tu as pris le journal qui était sur la télé ?
did you take the paper which/that was on the telly?

b)   QUE

que (written qu' before a vowel or a silent h) is used as the object of a
relative clause; it is often not translated and means:

i)   'who(m)', 'that' (referring to people):

la fille que j'aime ne m'aime pas
the girl (that) I love doesn't love me

ii)   'which', 'that' (referring to things):

j'ai perdu le briquet qu'il m'a offert
I've lost the lighter (which/that) he gave me

c) *qui or que?*

qui (subject) and **que** (object) are translated by the same words in English (who, which, that). To use the correct pronoun in French, it is essential to know whether a relative pronoun is the object or the subject of the relative clause:

i) when the verb of the relative clause has its own subject, the object pronoun **que** must be used:

c'est un passe-temps que *j'*adore
it's a pastime (that) *I* love (*the subject of 'adore' is 'je'*)

ii) otherwise the relative pronoun is the subject of the verb in the relative clause and the subject pronoun **qui** must be used:

j'ai trouvé un manteau qui me plaît
I found a coat that I like (*the subject of 'plaît' is 'qui'*)

d) *LEQUEL*

i) forms

lequel (which) has four different forms, as it must agree with the noun it refers to:

	SINGULAR	PLURAL	
MASCULINE	**lequel**	**lesquels**	which
FEMININE	**laquelle**	**lesquelles**	

lequel etc combines with the prepositions **à** and **de** as follows:

à + lequel	→	**auquel**
à + lesquels	→	**auxquels**
à + lesquelles	→	**auxquelles**
de + lequel	→	**duquel**
de + lesquels	→	**desquels**
de + lesquelles	→	**desquelles**

à + **laquelle** and **de** + **laquelle** do not change.

quels sont les sports auxquels tu t'intéresses ?
what are the sports (which) you are interested *in*?

voilà le village près duquel on campait
here's the village near which we camped

ii) **qui** or **lequel** with a preposition?

When a relative pronoun follows a preposition, the pronoun used is either **qui** or **lequel**. In English, the relative pronoun is seldom used and the preposition is frequently placed after the verb or at the end of the sentence.

qui is generally used after a preposition when referring to people:

où est la fille *avec* qui je dansais ?
where's the girl I was dancing *with*?

montre-moi la personne *à* qui tu as vendu ton vélo
show me the person you sold your bike *to*

lequel is often used after a preposition when referring to things:

l'immeuble *dans* lequel j'habite est très moderne
the building (which) I live *in* is very modern

je ne reconnais pas la voiture *avec* laquelle il est venu
I don't recognize the car (which) he came *in*

lequel is also used when referring to persons after the prepositions
entre (between) and **parmi** (among):

des touristes, parmi lesquels il y avait des Japonais
tourists, among whom were (some) Japanese people

il aimait deux filles, entre lesquelles il hésitait
he loved two girls, between whom he was torn

e)   *DONT*

dont (of which, of whom, whose) is frequently used instead of **de qui**,
duquel etc. It means:

i)   *of which, of whom:*

un métier dont il est fier
a job (which) he is proud of

Care must be taken with verbs that are normally followed by **de** +
object: **de** is not always translated by 'of' in English, and is sometimes
not translated at all (see section on verb constructions p 148-9):

voilà les choses *dont* j'ai besoin
here are the things (*which*) I need

les gens *dont* tu parles ne m'intéressent pas
I'm not interested in the people you're talking about

l'enfant *dont* elle s'occupe n'est pas le sien
the child she is looking *after* is not hers

ii)   *whose*

dont is also used to translate the English pronoun 'whose'. In French,
the construction of the clause that follows **dont** differs from English in
two ways:

★   the noun which follows **dont** is used with the definite article (**le, la,
les, l'**):

mon copain, dont *le* père a eu un accident
my friend, whose father had an accident

★   the word order in French is **dont** + subject + verb + object:

je te présente Hélène, dont tu connais déjà le frère
this is Helen, whose brother you already know

c'était dans une petite rue dont j'ai oublié le nom
it was in a small street the name of which I've forgotten

Note: **dont** cannot be used after a preposition:

> **une jolie maison,** *près* **de laquelle il y a un petit lac**
> a pretty house, *next* to which there is a small lake

f)   *OU*

i)   **où** generally means 'where':

> **l'hôtel où on a logé était très confortable**
> the hotel where we stayed was very comfortable

ii)   **où** often replaces a preposition + **lequel**, meaning 'in/to/on/at which' etc:

> **c'est la maison où je suis né**
> that's the house in which/where I was born

> **une surprise-partie où il a invité tous ses amis**
> a party to which he invited all his friends

iii)   **où** is also used to translate 'when' after a noun referring to time:

> **le jour où**   **la fois où**   **le moment où**
> the day when   the time when   the moment when

> **tu te rappelles le soir où on a raté le dernier métro ?**
> do you remember the evening when we missed the last train?

g)   *CE QUI, CE QUE*

ce is used before **qui** and **que** when the relative pronoun does not refer to a specific noun. Both **ce qui** and **ce que** mean 'that which', 'the thing which', and are usually translated by 'what':

i)   **ce qui**

ce qui is followed by a verb without a subject (**qui** is the subject):

> **ce qui s'est passé ne vous regarde pas**
> what happened is none of your business

> **ce qui m'étonne, c'est sa patience**
> what surprises me is his patience

Note the comma and the **c'**

ii)   **ce que**

ce que (**ce qu'** before a vowel or a silent **h**) is followed by a verb with its own subject (**que** is the object):

> **fais ce que tu veux**   **c'est ce qu'il a dit?**
> do what you want   is that what he said?

> **ce que vous me demandez est impossible**
> what you're asking me is impossible

iii)   **tout ce qui/que**

   tout is used in front of **ce qui/que** in the sense of 'all that', 'everything that':

   c'est tout ce que je veux   **tout ce que tu as fait**
   that's all I want   everything you did

   tu n'as pas eu de mal ; c'est tout ce qui compte
   you weren't hurt; that's all that matters

iv)   **ce qui/que** are often used in indirect questions (see p 48-9):

   je ne sais pas ce qu'ils vont dire
   I don't know what they'll say

v)   when referring to a previous clause, **ce qui** and **ce que** are translated by 'which':

   elle est en retard, ce qui arrive souvent
   she's late, which happens often

vi)   **ce que/qui** are used with a preposition (when the preposition refers to **ce**):

   ce n'est pas étonnant, après ce qui lui est arrivé
   it's not surprising, after what happened to him

   il y a du vrai dans ce que vous dites
   there is some truth in what you say

But: **QUOI** is used instead of **ce que** after a preposition when the preposition refers to **que**, and not to **ce**:

   c'est ce à quoi je pensais
   that's what I was thinking about

vii)   **ce que** is used with the preposition **de** when **de** refers to **ce**:

   je suis fier de ce qu'il a fait
   I'm proud of what he did

But: **ce dont** is used instead of **de + ce que** when **de** refers to **que**, and not to **ce**:

   c'est ce dont j'avais peur
   that's what I was afraid of

   tu as trouvé ce dont tu avais besoin ?
   did you find what you needed?

7. VERBS

A. REGULAR CONJUGATIONS

1. Conjugations

There are three main conjugations in French, which are determined by the infinitive endings. The first conjugation verbs, by far the largest category, end in **-er** (eg aim**er**) and will be referred to as **-er** verbs; the second conjugation verbs end in **-ir** (eg fin**ir**) and will be referred to as **-ir** verbs; the third conjugation verbs, the smallest category, end in **-re** (eg vend**re**) and will be referred to as **-re** verbs.

2. Simple tenses

The simple tenses in French are:

a) present
b) imperfect
c) future
d) conditional
e) past historic
f) present subjunctive
e) imperfect subjunctive

For the use of the different tenses, see pp 82-96.

3. Formation of tenses

The tenses are formed by adding the following endings to the stem of the verb (mainly the stem of the infinitive) as set out in the following section:

a) *PRESENT:* stem of the infinitive + the following endings:

-er VERBS	-ir VERBS	-re VERBS
-e, -es, -e, -ons, -ez, -ent	-is, -is, -it, -issons, -issez, -issent	-s, -s, -, -ons, -ez, -ent

AIMER	FINIR	VENDRE
j'aime	je finis	je vends
tu aimes	tu finis	tu vends
il aime	il finit	il vend
elle aime	elle finit	elle vend
nous aimons	nous finissons	nous vendons
vous aimez	vous finissez	vous vendez
ils aiment	ils finissent	ils vendent
elles aiment	elles finissent	elles vendent

b) *IMPERFECT:* stem of the first person plural of the present tense (ie the 'nous' form minus **-ons**) + the following endings:

-ais, -ais, -ait, -ions, -iez, -aient

j'aimais	je finissais	je vendais
tu aimais	tu finissais	tu vendais
il aimait	il finissait	il vendait
elle aimait	elle finissait	elle vendait
nous aimions	nous finissions	nous vendions
vous aimiez	vous finissiez	vous vendiez
ils aimaient	ils finissaient	ils vendaient
elles aimaient	elles finissaient	elles vendaient

Note: the only irregular imperfect is **être: j'étais** etc.

c) *FUTURE:* infinitive + the following endings:

-ai, -as, -a, -ons, -ez, -ont

Note: Verbs ending in -re drop the final e of the infinitive

j'aimerai	je finirai	je vendrai
tu aimeras	tu finiras	tu vendras
il aimera	il finira	il vendra
elle aimera	elle finira	elle vendra
nous aimerons	nous finirons	nous vendrons
vous aimerez	vous finirez	vous vendrez
ils aimeront	ils finiront	ils vendront
elles aimeront	elles finiront	elles vendront

d) *CONDITIONAL:* infinitive + the following endings:

-ais, -ais, -ait, -ions, -iez, -aient

Note: Verbs ending in -re drop the final e of the infinitive

j'aimerais	je finirais	je vendrais
tu aimerais	tu finirais	tu vendrais
il aimerait	il finirait	il vendrait
elle aimerait	elle finirait	elle vendrait
nous aimerions	nous finirions	nous vendrions
vous aimeriez	vous finiriez	vous vendriez
ils aimeraient	ils finiraient	ils vendraient
elles aimeraient	elles finiraient	elles vendraient

e) *PAST HISTORIC:* stem of the infinitive + the following endings:

-er VERBS	-ir VERBS	-re VERBS
-ai, -as, -a, -âmes, -âtes, -èrent	-is, -is, -it, -îmes, -îtes, -irent	-is, -is, -it, -îmes, -îtes, -irent
j'aimai	je finis	je vendis
tu aimas	tu finis	tu vendis
il aima	il finit	il vendit
elle aima	elle finit	elle vendit
nous aimâmes	nous finîmes	nous vendîmes
vous aimâtes	vous finîtes	vous vendîtes
ils aimèrent	ils finirent	ils vendirent
elles aimèrent	elles finirent	elles vendirent

f) *PRESENT SUBJUNCTIVE:* stem of the first person plural of the present indicative + the following endings:

-e, -es, -e, -ions, -iez, -ent

j'aime	je finisse	je vende
tu aimes	tu finisses	tu vendes
il aime	il finisse	il vende
elle aime	elle finisse	elle vende
nous aimions	nous finissions	nous vendions
vous aimiez	vous finissiez	vous vendiez
ils aiment	ils finissent	ils vendent
elles aiment	elles finissent	elles vendent

g) *IMPERFECT SUBJUNCTIVE:* stem of the first person singular of the past historic + the following endings:

-er VERBS	**-ir VERBS**	**-re VERBS**
-asse, -asses, -ât, -assions, -assiez, -assent	**-isse, -isses, -ît, -issions, -issiez, -issent**	**-isse, -isses, -ît, -issions, -issiez, -issent**
j'aimasse	je finisse	je vendisse
tu aimasses	tu finisses	tu vendisses
il aimât	il finît	il vendît
elle aimât	elle finît	elle vendît
nous aimassions	nous finissions	nous vendissions
vous aimassiez	vous finissiez	vous vendissiez
ils aimassent	ils finissent	ils vendissent
elles aimassent	elles finissent	elles vendissent

B. STANDARD SPELLING IRREGULARITIES

Spelling irregularities only affect **-er** verbs.

1. Verbs ending in *-cer* and *-ger*

a) Verbs ending in **-cer** require a cedilla under the c (ç) before an **a** or an **o** to preserve the soft sound of the **c**: eg **commencer** (to begin).

b) Verbs ending in **-ger** require an **-e** after the g before an **a** or an **o** to preserve the soft sound of the **g**: eg **manger** (to eat).

Changes to **-cer** and **-ger** verbs occur in the following tenses: present, imperfect, past historic, imperfect subjunctive and present participle.

COMMENCER	MANGER

PRESENT

je commence	je mange
tu commences	tu manges
il commence	il mange
elle commence	elle mange
nous **commençons**	nous **mangeons**
vous commencez	vous mangez
ils commencent	ils mangent
elles commencent	elles mangent

IMPERFECT

je **commençais**	je **mangeais**
tu **commençais**	tu **mangeais**
il **commençait**	il **mangeait**
elle **commençait**	elle **mangeait**
nous commencions	nous mangions
vous commenciez	vous mangiez
ils **commençaient**	ils **mangeaient**
elles **commençaient**	elles **mangeaient**

PAST HISTORIC

je **commençai**	je **mangeai**
tu **commenças**	tu **mangeas**
il **commença**	il **mangea**
elle **commença**	elle **mangea**
nous **commençâmes**	nous **mangeâmes**
vous **commençâtes**	vous **mangeâtes**
ils commencèrent	ils mangèrent
elles commencèrent	elles mangèrent

IMPERFECT SUBJUNCTIVE

je **commençasse**	je **mangeasse**
tu **commençasses**	tu **mangeasses**
il **commençât**	il **mangeât**
elle **commençât**	elle **mangeât**
nous **commençassions**	nous **mangeassions**
vous **commençassiez**	vous **mangeassiez**
ils **commençassent**	ils **mangeassent**
elles **commençassent**	elles **mangeassent**

PRESENT PARTICIPLE

commençant	**mangeant**

2. Verbs ending in *-eler* and *-eter*

a) Verbs ending in *-eler*

Verbs ending in **-eler** double the **l** before a silent **e** (ie before **-e, -es, -ent** of the present indicative and subjunctive, and throughout the future and conditional): eg **appeler** (to call).

PRESENT INDICATIVE	PRESENT SUBJUNCTIVE
j'appelle	j'appelle
tu appelles	tu appelles
il appelle	il appelle
elle appelle	elle appelle
nous appelons	nous appelions
vous appelez	vous appeliez
ils appellent	ils appellent
elles appellent	elles appellent

FUTURE	CONDITIONAL
j'appellerai	j'appellerais
tu appelleras	tu appellerais
il appellera	il appellerait
elle appellera	elle appellerait
nous appellerons	nous appellerions
vous appellerez	vous appelleriez
ils appelleront	ils appelleraient
elles appelleront	elles appelleraient

But: some verbs in **-eler** including the following are conjugated like **acheter** (see p 71):

celer	to conceal
congeler	to (deep-)freeze
déceler	to detect, reveal
dégeler	to defrost
geler	to freeze
harceler	to harass
marteler	to hammer
modeler	to model
peler	to peel

b) Verbs ending in *-eter*

Verbs ending in **-eter** double the **t** before a silent **e** (ie before **-e, -es, -ent** of the present indicative and subjunctive, and throughout the future and conditional): eg **jeter** (to throw).

PRESENT INDICATIVE	PRESENT SUBJUNCTIVE
je jette	je jette
tu jettes	tu jettes
il jette	il jette
elle jette	elle jette

nous jetons	nous jetions
vous jetez	vous jetiez
ils **jettent**	ils **jettent**
elles **jettent**	elles **jettent**

FUTURE	*CONDITIONAL*
je **jetterai**	je **jetterais**
tu **jetteras**	tu **jetterais**
il **jettera**	il **jetterait**
elle **jettera**	elle **jetterait**
nous **jetterons**	nous **jetterions**
vous **jetterez**	vous **jetteriez**
ils **jetteront**	ils **jetteraient**
elles **jetteront**	elles **jetteraient**

But: some verbs in -eter including the following are conjugated like **acheter** (see p 71):

crocheter	to pick (*lock*)
fureter	to ferret about
haleter	to pant
racheter	to buy back

c)   Verbs ending in **-oyer** and **-uyer**

In verbs ending in **-oyer** and **-uyer** the **y** changes to **i** before a silent **e** (ie before **-e, -es, -ent** of the present indicative and subjunctive, and throughout the future and conditional): eg **employer** (to use) and **ennuyer** (to bore).

PRESENT INDICATIVE	*PRESENT SUBJUNCTIVE*
j'**emploie**	j'**emploie**
tu **emploies**	tu **emploies**
il **emploie**	il **emploie**
elle **emploie**	elle **emploie**
nous employons	nous employions
vous employez	vous employiez
ils **emploient**	ils **emploient**
elles **emploient**	elles **emploient**

FUTURE	*CONDITIONAL*
j'**emploierai**	j'**emploierais**
tu **emploieras**	tu **emploierais**
il **emploiera**	il **emploierait**
elle **emploiera**	elle **emploierait**
nous **emploierons**	nous **emploierions**
vous **emploierez**	vous **emploieriez**
ils **emploieront**	ils **emploieraient**
elles **emploieront**	elles **emploieraient**

Note: **envoyer** (to send) and **renvoyer** (to dismiss) have an irregular future and conditional: **j'enverrai, j'enverrais; je renverrai, je renverrais**.

d) Verbs ending in **-ayer**

In verbs ending in **-ayer**, eg **balayer** (to sweep), **payer** (to pay), **essayer** (to try), the change from **y** to **i** is optional:

eg je **balaie**	*or*	je **balaye**
je **paie**	*or*	je **paye**
j'**essaie**	*or*	j'**essaye**

e) Verbs in **e** + consonant + **er**

Verbs like **acheter**, **enlever**, **mener**, **peser** change the (last) **e** of the stem to **è** before a silent **e** (ie before **-e**, **-es**, **-ent** of the present indicative and subjunctive and throughout the future and conditional):

PRESENT INDICATIVE	*PRESENT SUBJUNCTIVE*
j'**achète**	j'**achète**
tu **achètes**	tu **achètes**
il **achète**	il **achète**
elle **achète**	elle **achète**
nous achetons	nous achetions
vous achetez	vous achetiez
ils **achètent**	ils **achètent**
elles **achètent**	elles **achètent**

FUTURE	*CONDITIONAL*
j'**achèterai**	j'**achèterais**
tu **achèteras**	tu **achèterais**
il **achètera**	il **achèterait**
elle **achètera**	elle **achèterait**
nous **achèterons**	nous **achèterions**
vous **achèterez**	vous **achèteriez**
ils **achèteront**	ils **achèteraient**
elles **achèteront**	elles **achèteraient**

Verbs conjugated like **acheter** include:

achever to complete	**haleter** to pant
amener to bring	**harceler** to harass
celer to conceal	**lever** to lift
crever to burst	**marteler** to hammer
crocheter to pick (*lock*)	**mener** to lead
élever to raise	**modeler** to model
emmener to take away	**peler** to peel
enlever to remove	**peser** to weigh
étiqueter to label	**se promener** to go for a walk
fureter to ferret about	**semer** to sow
geler to freeze	**soulever** to lift

f) Verbs in **é** + consonant + **er**

Verbs like **espérer** (to hope) change **é** to **è** before a silent **e** in the present indicative and subjunctive. BUT in the future and conditional **é** is retained.

PRESENT INDICATIVE	PRESENT SUBJUNCTIVE
j'espère	j'espère
tu espères	tu espères
il espère	il espère
elle espère	elle espère
nous espérons	nous espérions
vous espérez	vous espériez
ils espèrent	ils espèrent
elles espèrent	elles espèrent

FUTURE	CONDITIONAL
j'espérerai	j'espérerais
tu espéreras	tu espérerais
il espérera	il espérerait
elle espérera	elle espérerait
nous espérerons	nous espérerions
vous espérerez	vous espéreriez
ils espéreront	ils espéreraient
elles espéreront	elles espéreraient

Verbs conjugated like **espérer** include verbs in **-éder, -érer, -éter** etc:

accéder	to accede to
céder	to yield
célébrer	to celebrate
compléter	to complete
considérer	to consider
décéder	to die
digérer	to digest
gérer	to manage
inquiéter	to worry
libérer	to free
opérer	to operate
pénétrer	to penetrate
persévérer	to persevere
posséder	to possess
précéder	to precede
préférer	to prefer
protéger	to protect
récupérer	to recover
refréner	to curb
régler	to rule
régner	to reign
répéter	to repeat, to rehearse
révéler	to reveal
sécher	to dry
succéder	to succeed
suggérer	to suggest
tolérer	to tolerate

C. AUXILIARIES AND THE FORMATION OF COMPOUND TENSES

1. Formation

a) The two auxiliary verbs **AVOIR** and **ETRE** are used with the past participle of a verb to form compound tenses.

b) *The past participle*

The regular past participle is formed by taking the stem of the infinitive and adding the following endings:

-er	-ir	-re
aim(**er**) + **é**	fin(**ir**) + **i**	vend(**re**) + **u**
aimé	fini	vendu

For the agreement of past participles see pp 105-7.

c) *Compound tenses*

In French there are seven compound tenses: perfect, pluperfect, future perfect, past conditional (conditional perfect), past anterior, perfect subjunctive, pluperfect subjunctive.

2. Verbs conjugated with AVOIR

a) *PERFECT*

present of **avoir** +
past participle

j'ai aimé
tu as aimé
il a aimé
elle a aimé
nous avons aimé
vous avez aimé
ils ont aimé
elles ont aimé

b) *PLUPERFECT*

imperfect of **avoir** +
past participle

j'avais aimé
tu avais aimé
il avait aimé
elle avait aimé
nous avions aimé
vous aviez aimé
ils avaient aimé
elles avaient aimé

c) *FUTURE PERFECT*

future of **avoir** +
past participle

j'aurai aimé
tu auras aimé
il aura aimé
elle aura aimé
nous aurons aimé
vous aurez aimé
ils auront aimé
elles auront aimé

d) *PAST CONDITIONAL*

conditional of **avoir** +
past participle

j' aurais aimé
tu aurais aimé
il aurait aimé
elle aurait aimé
nous aurions aimé
vous auriez aimé
ils auraient aimé
elles auraient aimé

e) PAST ANTERIOR

past historic of **avoir** +
past participle

j'eus aimé
tu eus aimé
il eut aimé
elle eut aimé
nous eûmes aimé
vous eûtes aimé
ils eurent aimé
elles eurent aimé

f) PERFECT SUBJUNCTIVE

present subjunctive of
avoir + past participle

j'aie aimé
tu aies aimé
il ait aimé
elle ait aimé
nous ayons aimé
vous ayez aimé
ils aient aimé
elles aient aimé

g) PLUPERFECT SUBJUNCTIVE

pluperfect subjunctive of
avoir + past participle

j'eusse aimé
tu eusses aimé
il eût aimé
elle eût aimé
nous eussions aimé
vous eussiez aimé
ils eussent aimé
elles eussent aimé

3. Verbs conjugated with *ETRE*

a) PERFECT

present of **être** +
past participle

je suis arrivé(e)
tu es arrivé(e)
il est arrivé
elle est arrivée
nous sommes arrivé(e)s
vous êtes arrivé(e)(s)
ils sont arrivés
elles sont arrivées

b) PLUPERFECT

imperfect of **être** +
past participle

j'étais arrivé(e)
tu étais arrivé(e)
il était arrivé
elle était arrivée
nous étions arrivé(e)s
vous étiez arrivé(e)(s)
ils étaient arrivés
elles étaient arrivées

c) FUTURE PERFECT

future of **être** +
past participle

je serai arrivé(e)
tu seras arrivé(e)
il sera arrivé
elle sera arrivée
nous serons arrivé(e)s
vous serez arrivé(e)(s)
ils seront arrivés
elles seront arrivées

d) PAST CONDITIONAL

conditional of **être** +
past participle

je serais arrivé(e)
tu serais arrivé(e)
il serait arrivé
elle serait arrivée
nous serions arrivé(e)s
vous seriez arrivé(e)(s)
ils seraient arrivés
elles seraient arrivées

e) PAST ANTERIOR

past historic of **être** +
past participle

je fus arrivé(e)
tu fus arrivé(e)
il fut arrivé
elle fut arrivée
nous fûmes arrivé(e)s
vous fûtes arrivé(e)(s)
ils furent arrivés
elles furent arrivées

f) PERFECT SUBJUNCTIVE

present subjunctive of **être**
+ past participle

je sois arrivé(e)
tu sois arrivé(e)
il soit arrivé
elle soit arrivée
nous soyons arrivé(e)s
vous soyez arrivé(e)(s)
ils soient arrivés
elles soient arrivées

g) PLUPERFECT SUBJUNCTIVE

imperfect subjunctive of
être + past participle

je fusse arrivé(e)
tu fusses arrivé(e)
il fût arrivé
elle fût arrivée
nous fussions arrivé(e)s
vous fussiez arrivé(e)(s)
ils fussent arrivés
elles fussent arrivées

4. AVOIR or ETRE?

a) *Verbs conjugated with* **avoir**

The compound tenses of most verbs are formed with **avoir**.

j'ai marqué un but	**elle a dansé toute la nuit**
I scored a goal	she danced all night

b) *Verbs conjugated with* **être**

i) all reflexive verbs (see p 78):

je me suis baigné
I had a bath

ii) the following verbs (mainly of motion):

aller	to go
arriver	to arrive
descendre	to go/come down
entrer	to go/come in
monter	to go/come up
mourir	to die
naître	to be born
partir	to leave
passer	to go through, to drop in
rester	to remain

retourner	to return
sortir	to go/come out
tomber	to fall
venir	to come

and most of their compounds:

revenir	to come back
devenir	to become
parvenir	to reach, to manage to
rentrer	to return home
remonter	to go up again
redescendre	to go down again

But: **prévenir** (to warn) and **subvenir** (to provide for) take a direct object and are conjugated with **avoir**.

Note: **passer** can also be conjugated with **avoir**:

> **il a passé par Paris**
> he went via Paris

Some of the verbs listed above can take a direct object. In such cases they are conjugated with **avoir** and can take on a different meaning:

descendre	to take/bring down, to go down (*the stairs, a slope*)
monter	to take/bring up, to go up (*the stairs, a slope*)
rentrer	to take/bring/put in
retourner	to turn over
sortir	to take/bring out

les élèves sont sortis à midi
the pupils came out at midday

es élèves ont sorti leurs livres
the pupils took out their books

elle n'est pas encore descendue
she hasn't come down yet

elle a descendu un vieux tableau de l'atelier
she brought an old painting down from the loft

elle a descendu l'escalier
she came down the stairs

les prisonniers sont montés sur le toit
the prisoners climbed on to the roof

le garçon a monté les bouteilles de vin de la cave
the waiter brought the bottles of wine up from the cellar

nous sommes rentrés tard
we returned home late

j'ai rentré la voiture dans le garage
I put the car in the garage

je serais retourné à Paris
I would have returned to Paris

le jardinier a retourné le sol
the gardener turned over the soil

ils sont sortis de la piscine
they got out of the swimming pool

le gangster a sorti un revolver
the gangster pulled out a revolver

D. REFLEXIVE VERBS

1. Definition

Reflexive verbs are so called because they 'reflect' the action back onto the subject. Reflexive verbs are always accompanied by a reflexive pronoun; eg in the following sentence:

I looked at myself in the mirror

'myself' is the reflexive pronoun.

je lave la voiture
I'm washing the car

je *me* lave
I'm washing *myself*

j'ai couché le bébé
I put the baby to bed

je *me* suis couché
I went to bed (I put *myself* to bed)

2. Reflexive pronouns

They are:

PERSON	SINGULAR	PLURAL
1st	**me (m')** myself	**nous** ourselves
2nd	**te (t')** yourself	**vous** yourself/selves
3rd	**se (s')** himself, herself, itself, oneself	**se (s')** themselves

Note:

a) **m', t'** and **s'** are used instead of **me, te** and **se** in front of a vowel or a silent **h**:

   tu t'amuses ? – non, je m'ennuie
   are you enjoying yourself? – no, I'm bored

   il s'habille à la salle de bain
   he gets dressed in the bathroom

b) French reflexive pronouns are often not translated in English:

   je me demande si ...
   I wonder if ...

   ils se moquent de moi
   they're making fun of me

c) Plural reflexive pronouns can also be used to express reciprocal actions; in this case they are translated by 'each other' or 'one another':

   nous nous détestons
   we hate one another

   ils ne se parlent pas
   they're not talking to each other

d) **se** can mean 'ourselves' or 'each other' when it is used with the pronoun **on** meaning 'we' (see p 45):

   on s'est perdu
   we got lost

   on se connaît
   we know each other

3. Position of reflexive pronouns

Reflexive pronouns are placed immediately before the verb, except in positive commands, where they follow the verb and are linked to it by a hyphen:

tu te dépêches ?
will you hurry up?

dépêchons-nous !
let's hurry!

ne t'inquiète pas
don't worry

ne vous fiez pas à lui
don't trust him

Note: reflexive pronouns change to emphatic (disjunctive) pronouns in positive commands:

elle doit se reposer
she needs to rest

repose-toi
have a rest

4. Conjugation of reflexive verbs

a) *Simple tenses*

These are formed in the same way as for non-reflexive verbs, except that a reflexive pronoun is used.

b) *Compound tenses*

These are formed with the auxiliary **être** followed by the past participle of the verb.

A full conjugation table is given on p 132.

5. Agreement of the past participle

a) In most cases, the reflexive pronoun is a direct object and the past participle of the verb agrees in number and in gender with the reflexive pronoun:

il s'est trompé
he made a mistake

elle s'est endormie
she fell asleep

ils se sont excusés
they apologised

elles se sont assises
they sat down

b) When the reflexive pronoun is used as an indirect object, the past participle does not change:

nous nous sommes écrit
we wrote to each other

elle se l'est acheté
she bought it for herself

When the reflexive verb has a direct object, the reflexive pronoun is the indirect object of the reflexive verb and the past participle does not agree with it:

Caroline s'est tordu la cheville
Caroline sprained her ankle

vous vous êtes lavé les mains, les filles ?
did you wash your hands, girls?

6. Common reflexive verbs

s'en aller to go away	**s'éloigner (de)** to move away (from)	**se moquer de** to laugh at
s'amuser to have fun	**s'endormir** to fall asleep	**s'occuper de** to take care of
s'appeler to be called	**s'ennuyer** to be bored	**se passer** to happen
s'approcher (de) to come near	**s'étonner (de)** to be surprised (at)	**se passer de** to do without
s'arrêter to stop	**s'excuser (de)** to apologize (for)	**se promener** to go for a walk
s'asseoir to sit down	**se fâcher** to get angry/fall out	**se rappeler** to remember
s'attendre à to expect	**s'écrier** to cry out/exclaim	**se raser** to shave
se baigner to have a bath	**s'habiller** to get dressed	**se renseigner** to make enquiries
se battre to fight	**se hâter** to hurry	**se ressembler** to look alike
se blesser to hurt oneself	**s'inquiéter** to worry	**se retourner** to turn round
se coucher to go to bed	**s'installer** to settle down	**se réveiller** to wake up
se débarrasser de to get rid of	**se laver** to wash	**se sauver** to run away
se demander to wonder	**se lever** to get up	**se souvenir (de)** to remember
se dépêcher to hurry	**se mêler de** to meddle with	**se taire** to be/keep quiet
se déshabiller to undress	**se mettre à** to start	**se tromper** to be mistaken
se diriger vers to move towards	**se mettre en route** to set off	**se trouver** to be (situated)

E. IMPERSONAL VERBS

1. Conjugation

Impersonal verbs are used only in the third person singular and in the infinitive. The subject is always the impersonal pronoun **il** = it.

il neige
it's snowing

il y a du brouillard
it's foggy

2.   List of impersonal verbs

a)   *verbs describing the weather:*

i)   **faire** + adjective:

il fait beau/chaud	**il fait frais/froid**
it's fine/warm	it's cool/cold

il fera beau demain	**il va faire très froid**
the weather will be good tomorrow	it will be very cold

ii)   **faire** + noun:

il fait beau temps	**il fait mauvais temps**
the weather is nice	the weather is bad

Note:
il fait jour	**il fait nuit**
it's day(light)	it's dark

iii)   other impersonal verbs and verbs used impersonally to describe the weather:

il gèle	**(geler)**	it's freezing
il grêle	**(grêler)**	it's hailing
il neige	**(neiger)**	it's snowing
il pleut	**(pleuvoir)**	it's raining
il tonne	**(tonner)**	it's thundering

Note: some of these verbs may be used personally:

je gèle	I am freezing

iv)   **il y a** + noun:

il y a des nuages	it's cloudy
il y a du brouillard	it's foggy
il y a du verglas	it's icy

b)   *être*

i)   **il est** + noun:

il est cinq heures	it's five o'clock
il était une fois un géant	there was once a giant

ii)   **il est** + adjective + **de** + infinitive:

il est difficile de	it's difficult to
il est facile de	it's easy to
il est nécessaire de	it's necessary to
il est inutile de	it's useless to
il est possible de	it's possible to

il est difficile d'en parler
it is difficult to speak about it

Note: the indirect object pronoun in French corresponds to the English 'for me, for him' etc:

il m'est difficile d'en parler
it is difficult for me to speak about it

iii)   **il est** + adjective + **que**:

il est douteux que	it's doubtful that
il est évident que	it's clear that
il est possible que	it's possible that
il est probable que	it's probable that
il est peu probable que	it's unlikely that
il est vrai que	it's true that

Note: **que** may be followed by the indicative or the subjunctive (see p 89):

il est probable qu'il ne viendra pas	**il est peu probable qu'il vienne**
he probably won't come	it's unlikely that he'll come

c)   *arriver, se passer (to happen)*

il est arrivé une chose curieuse	**que se passe-t-il ?**
a strange thing happened	what's happening

d)   *exister (to exist), rester (to remain), manquer (to be missing)*

il existe trois exemplaires de ce livre
there are three copies of this book

il me restait six francs	**il me manque vingt francs**
I had six francs left	I am twenty francs short

e)   *paraître, sembler (to seem)*

il paraîtrait/semblerait qu'il ait changé d'avis
it would appear that he has changed his mind

il paraît qu'il va se marier
it seems he's going to get married

il me semble que le professeur s'est trompé
it seems to me that the teacher has made a mistake

f)   *other common impersonal verbs*

i)   **s'agir** (to be a matter of):

may be followed by a noun, a pronoun or an infinitive:

il s'agit de ton avenir	**de quoi s'agit-il ?**
it's about your future	what is it about?

il s'agit de trouver le coupable
we must find the culprit

ii)   **falloir** (to be necessary):

may be followed by a noun, an infinitive or the subjunctive:

il faut deux heures pour aller à Paris	**il me faut plus de temps**
it takes two hours to get to Paris	I need more time

il faudra rentrer plus tôt ce soir
we'll have to come home earlier tonight

il faut que tu parles à Papa
you'll have to speak to your Dad

iii) **suffire** (to be enough):

may be followed by a noun, an infinitive or the subjunctive:

il suffit de peu de chose pour être heureux
it takes little to be happy

il suffit de passer le pont
you only have to cross the bridge

il suffira qu'ils te donnent le numéro de téléphone
they will only have to give you the telephone number

iv) **valoir mieux** (to be better):

may be followed by an infinitive or the subjunctive:

il vaudrait mieux prendre le car
it would be better to take the coach

il vaut mieux que vous ne sortiez pas seule le soir
you'd better not go out alone at night

F. TENSES

For the formation of the different tenses, see pp 65-7 and 73-6.

Note: French has no continuous tenses (as in 'I am eating', 'I was going', 'I will be arriving'). The 'be' and '-ing' parts of English continuous tenses are not translated as separate words. Instead, the equivalent tense is used in French:

ENGLISH	FRENCH
I am eating	**je mange**
I will be eating	**je mangerai**

1. PRESENT

The present is used to describe what someone does/ something that happens regularly, or what someone is doing/ something that is happening at the time of speaking.

a) *regular actions*

il travaille dans un bureau   **je lis rarement le journal**
he works in an office   I seldom read the paper

b) *continuous actions*

ne le dérangez pas, il travaille
don't disturb him, he's working

je ne peux pas venir, je garde mon petit frère
I can't come, I'm looking after my little brother

Note: the continuous nature of the action can also be expressed by using the phrase **être en train de** (to be in the process of) + infinitive:

je suis en train de cuisiner
I'm (busy) cooking

c) *immediate future*

> **je pars demain**
> I'm leaving tomorrow

But: the present cannot be used after **quand** and other conjunctions of time when the future is implied (see pp 87-8):

> **je le ferai quand j'aurai le temps**
> I'll do it when I have the time

d) *general truths*

> **la vie est dure**
> life is hard

2. IMPERFECT

The imperfect is a past tense used to express what someone was doing or what someone used to do or to describe something in the past. The imperfect refers particularly to something that *continued* over a period of time, as opposed to something that happened at a specific point in time.

a) *continuous actions*

the imperfect describes an action that was happening eg when something else took place (imperfect means unfinished):

> **il prenait un bain quand le téléphone a sonné**
> he was having a bath when the phone rang

> **excuse-moi, je pensais à autre chose**
> I'm sorry, I was thinking of something else

Note: the continuous nature of the action can be emphasised by using **être en train de** + infinitive:

> **j'étais en train de faire le ménage**
> I was (busy) doing the housework

b) *regular actions in the past*

> **je le voyais souvent quand il habitait dans le quartier**
> I used to see him often when he lived in this area

> **quand il était plus jeune il voyageait beaucoup**
> when he was younger he used to travel a lot

c) *description in the past*

> **il faisait beau ce jour-là**
> the weather was fine that day

> **elle portait une robe bleue**
> she wore a blue dress

> **c'était formidable !**
> it was great!

> **elle donnait sur la rue**
> it looked onto the street

3. PERFECT

The perfect tense is a compound past tense, used to express *single* actions which have been completed, ie what someone did or what someone has done/has been doing or something that has happened or has been happening:

je l'ai envoyé lundi I sent it on Monday	**on est sorti hier soir** we went out last night
tu t'es bien amusé ? did you have a good time	**je ne l'ai pas vu** I didn't see him
j'ai lu toute la journée I've been reading all day	**tu as déjà mangé ?** have you eaten?

Note: Perfect or imperfect?

In English, the simple past ('did', 'went', 'prepared') is used to describe both single and repeated actions in the past. In French, the perfect only describes single actions in the past, while repeated actions are expressed by the imperfect (they are sometimes signposted by 'used to'). Thus 'I went' should be translated 'j'allais' or 'je suis allé' depending on the nature of the action:

après dîner, je suis allé en ville
after dinner I went to town

l'an dernier, j'allais plus souvent au théâtre
last year, I went to the theatre more often

4. PAST HISTORIC

This tense is used in the same way as the perfect tense, to describe a single, completed action in the past (what someone did or something that happened). It is a literary tense, not common in everyday spoken French; it is found mainly as a narrative tense in written form:

le piéton ne vit pas arriver la voiture
the pedestrian didn't see the car coming

5. PLUPERFECT

This compound tense is used to express what someone had done/had been doing or something that had happened or had been happening:

il n'avait pas voulu aller avec eux
he hadn't wanted to go with them

elle était essoufflée parce qu'elle avait couru
she was out of breath because she'd been running

However, the pluperfect is not used as in English with **depuis** (for, since), or with **venir de** + infinitive (to have just done something). For details see p 87.

il neigeait depuis une semaine
it had been snowing for a week

les pompiers venaient d'arriver
the firemen had just arrived

6. FUTURE

This tense is used to express what someone will do or will be doing or something that will happen or will be happening:

je ferai la vaisselle demain   **j'arriverai tard**
I'll do the dishes tomorrow   I'll be arriving late

Note: the future and not the present as in English is used in time clauses introduced by **quand** (when) or other conjunctions of time where the future is implied (see p 87):

il viendra quand il le pourra
he'll come when he can

French makes frequent use of **aller** + infinitive (to be about to do something) to express the immediate future:

je vais vous expliquer ce qui s'est passé
I'll explain (to you) what happened

il va déménager la semaine prochaine
he's moving house next week

7. FUTURE PERFECT

This compound tense is used to describe what someone will have done/will have been doing in the future or to describe something that will have happened in the future:

j'aurai bientôt fini
I will soon have finished

In particular, it is used instead of the English perfect in time clauses introduced by **quand** or other conjunctions of time where the future is implied (see p 88):

appelle-moi quand tu auras fini
call me when you've finished

on rentrera dès qu'on aura fait les courses
we'll come back as soon as we've done our shopping

8. PAST ANTERIOR

This tense is used instead of the pluperfect to express an action that preceded another action in the past (ie a past in the past). It is usually introduced by a conjunction of time (translated by 'when', 'as soon as', 'after' etc) and the main verb is in the past historic:

il se coucha dès qu'ils furent partis
he went to bed as soon as they'd left

à peine eut-elle raccroché que le téléphone sonna
she'd hardly hung up when the telephone rang

9. Use of tenses with 'depuis' (for, since)

a) The present must be used instead of the perfect to describe actions which started in the past and have continued until the present:

il habite ici depuis trois ans
he's been living here for three years

elle l'attend depuis ce matin
she's been waiting for him since this morning

But: The perfect, not the present, is used when the clause is negative or when the action has been completed:

il n'a pas pris de vacances depuis longtemps
he hasn't taken any holidays for a long time

j'ai fini depuis un bon moment
I've been finished for quite a while

Note:

i) **il y a ... que** or **voilà ... que** are also used with the present tense to translate 'for':

it's been ringing for ten minutes
ça sonne depuis dix minutes
il y a dix minutes que ça sonne
voilà dix minutes que ça sonne

ii) **depuis que** is used when 'since' introduces a clause, ie when there is a verb following **depuis**:

elle dort depuis que vous êtes partis
she's been sleeping since you left

iii) do not confuse **depuis** (for, since) and **pendant** (for, during): **depuis** refers to the starting point of an action which is still going on and **pendant** refers to the duration of an action which is over and is used with the perfect:

il vit ici depuis deux mois   **il a vécu ici pendant deux mois**
he's been living here for two months   he lived here for two months

b) the imperfect must be used instead of the pluperfect to describe an action which had started in the past and was still going on at a given time:

elle le connaissait depuis son enfance
she had known him since her childhood

il attendait depuis trois heures quand on est arrivé
he had been waiting for three hours when we arrived

But: if the sentence is negative or if the action has been completed, the pluperfect and not the imperfect is used:

je n'étais pas allé au théâtre depuis des années
I hadn't been to the theatre for years

il était parti depuis peu
he'd been gone for a short while

Note:

i) **il y avait ... que** + imperfect is also used to translate 'for':

she'd been living alone for a long time
elle habitait seule depuis longtemps
il y avait longtemps qu'elle habitait seule

ii) **depuis que** is used when 'since' introduces a clause; if it describes an action which was still going on at the time, it can be followed by the imperfect, otherwise it is followed by the pluperfect:

il pleuvait depuis que nous étions en vacances
it had been raining since we had been on holiday

il pleuvait depuis que nous étions arrivés
it had been raining since we arrived

iii) do not confuse **depuis** and **pendant**: **depuis** refers to the starting point of an action which is still going on and **pendant** refers to the duration of an action which is over; **pendant** is used with the pluperfect:

j'y travaillais depuis un an
I had been working there for a year

j'y avais travaillé pendant un an
I had worked there for a year

10. Use of tenses with 'venir de'

venir de + infinitive means 'to have just done'.

a) if it describes something that has just happened, it is used in the present instead of the perfect:

l'avion vient d'arriver   **je viens de te le dire !**
the plane has just arrived   I've just told you!

b) if it describes something that had just happened, it is used in the imperfect instead of the pluperfect:

le film venait de commencer   **je venais de rentrer**
the film had just started   I'd just got home

11. Use of tenses after conjunctions of time

quand	when
tant que	as long as
dès/aussitôt que	as soon as
lorsque	when
pendant que	while

Verbs which follow these conjunctions must be used in the following tenses:

a) *future instead of present:*

je te téléphonerai quand je serai prêt
I'll phone you when I am ready

on ira dès qu'il fera beau
we'll go as soon as the weather is fine

b) *future perfect instead of perfect* when the future is implied:

on rentrera dès qu'on aura fini les courses
we'll come back as soon as we've done our shopping

je t'appellerai dès qu'il sera arrivé
I'll call you as soon as he has arrived

c) *conditional present/perfect instead of perfect/pluperfect* in indirect speech:

il a dit qu'il sortirait quand il aurait fini
he said that he would come out when he had finished

For the tenses of the subjunctive and conditional, see pp 88-91 and 93-4.

G. MOODS

1. THE SUBJUNCTIVE

In spoken everyday French, the only two subjunctive tenses that are used are the present and the perfect. The imperfect and the pluperfect subjunctive are found mainly in literature or in texts of a formal nature.

The subjunctive is always preceded by the conjunction **que** and is used in subordinate clauses when the subject of the subordinate clause is different from the subject of the main verb.

Some clauses introduced by **que** take the indicative. But the subjunctive must be used after the following:

a) *Verbs of emotion*

être content que	to be pleased that
être déçu que	to be disappointed that
être désolé que	to be sorry that
être étonné que	to be surprised that
être fâché que	to be annoyed that
être heureux que	to be happy that
être surpris que	to be surprised that
être triste que	to be sad that
avoir peur que ... ne	to be afraid/to fear that
craindre que ... ne	to be afraid/to fear that
regretter que	to be sorry that

ils étaient contents que j'aille les voir
they were pleased (that) I went to visit them

je serais très étonné qu'il mente
I would be very surprised if he was lying

on regrette beaucoup que tu n'aies pas pu vendre ta voiture
we're very sorry (that) you couldn't sell your car

Note: **ne** is used after **craindre que** or **avoir peur que**, but does not have a negative meaning in itself and is not translated in English:

je crains que l'avion *ne* soit en retard
I'm afraid (that) the plane will be late

b) *Verbs of wishing and willing:*

aimer que	to like
désirer que	to wish (that)
préférer que	to prefer (that)
souhaiter que	to wish (that)
vouloir que	to want

Note: In English, such verbs are often used in the following type of construction: verb of willing + object + infinitive (eg I'd like you to listen); this type of construction is impossible in French, where a subjunctive clause has to be used:

je souhaite que tu réussisses
I hope you will succeed

il aimerait que je lui écrive plus souvent
he'd like me to write to him more often

voulez-vous que je vous y amène en voiture ?
would you like me to drive you there?

préférez-vous que je rappelle demain ?
would you rather I called back tomorrow?

c) *Impersonal constructions* (expressing necessity, possibility, doubt, denial, preference):

il faut que	it is necessary (that) (*must*)
il est nécessaire que	it is necessary (*must*)
il est important que	it is important (that)
il est possible que	it is possible that (*may*)
il se peut que	it is possible that (*may*)
il est impossible que	it is impossible (that) (*can't*)
il est douteux que	it is doubtful whether
il est peu probable que	it is unlikely that
il semble que	it seems (that)
il est préférable que	it is preferable (that)
il vaut mieux que	it is better (that) (*had better*)
c'est dommage que	it is a pity (that)

Note: these expressions may be used in any appropriate tense:

il faut qu'on se dépêche
we must hurry

il était important que tu le saches
it was important that you should know

il se pourrait qu'elle change d'avis
she might change her mind

il est peu probable qu'ils s'y intéressent
they're unlikely to be interested in that

il semble qu'elle ait raison
she appears to be right

il vaudrait mieux que tu ne promettes rien
you'd better not promise anything

c'est dommage que vous vous soyez manqués
it's a pity you missed each other

d) *Some verbs and impersonal constructions expressing doubt or uncertainty*
(mainly used negatively or interrogatively):

douter que	to doubt (that)
(ne pas) croire que	(not) to believe (that)
(ne pas) penser que	(not) to think (that)
(ne pas) être sûr que	(not) to be sure that
il n'est pas certain que	it isn't certain that
il n'est pas évident que	it isn't obvious that
il n'est pas sûr que	it isn't certain that
il n'est pas vrai que	it isn't true that

je doute fort qu'il veuille t'aider
I very much doubt whether he'll want to help you

croyez-vous qu'il y ait des places de libres ?
do you think there are any seats available?

on n'était pas sûr que ce soit le bon endroit
we weren't sure that it was the right place

il n'était pas certain qu'elle puisse gagner
it wasn't certain whether she could win

e) *attendre que* (to wait until, to wait for someone to do something):

attendons qu'il revienne
let's wait until he comes back

f) *Some subordinating conjunctions:*

bien que	although
quoique	although
sans que	without
pour que	so that
afin que	so that
à condition que	provided that
pourvu que	provided that
jusqu'à ce que	until
en attendant que	until
avant que ... (ne)	before
à moins que ... (ne)	unless
de peur que ... ne	for fear that
de crainte que ... ne	for fear that
de sorte que	so that
de façon que	so that
de manière que	so that

Note: When ne is shown in brackets, it may follow the conjunction, although
it is seldom used in spoken French; it does not have a negative
meaning, and is not translated in English.

il est allé travailler bien qu'il soit malade
he went to work although he was ill

elle est entrée sans que je la voie
she came in without me seeing her

voilà de l'argent pour que tu puisses aller au cinéma
here's some money so that you can go to the pictures

d'accord, pourvu que tu me promettes de ne pas le répéter
all right, as long as you promise not to tell anyone

tu l'as revu avant qu'il (ne) parte ?
did you see him again before he left?

je le ferai demain, à moins que ce (ne) soit urgent
I'll do it tomorrow, unless it's urgent

elle n'a pas fait de bruit de peur qu'il ne se réveille
she didn't make any noise, in case he would wake up

parle moins fort de sorte qu'elle ne nous entende pas
talk more quietly so that she doesn't hear us

Note: when **de façon/manière que** (so that) express a result, as opposed to a purpose, the indicative is used instead of the subjunctive:

il a fait du bruit, de sorte qu'elle l'*a entendu*
he made some noise, so that she heard him

g) *A superlative or adjectives like* **premier** *(first),* **dernier** *(last),* **seul** *(only) followed by* **qui** *or* **que:**

c'était le coureur le plus rapide que j'aie jamais vu
he was the fastest runner I ever saw

But: the indicative is used with a statement of fact rather than the expression of an opinion:

c'est le coureur le plus rapide qui a gagné
it was the fastest runner who won

h) *Negative and indefinite pronouns (eg* **rien***,* **personne***,* **quelqu'un***) followed by* **qui** *or* **que:**

je ne connais personne qui sache aussi bien chanter
I don't know anyone who can sing so well

il n'y a aucune chance qu'il réussisse
he hasn't got a chance of succeeding

ils cherchent quelqu'un qui puisse garder le bébé
they're looking for someone who can look after the baby

2. Avoiding the subjunctive

The subjunctive can be avoided, as is the tendency with modern spoken French, provided that both verbs in the sentence have the same subject. It is replaced by an infinitive introduced by the preposition **de**, the preposition **à** or by no preposition at all (see pp 96-100).

a) *de + infinitive replaces the subjunctive after:*

   i)   verbs of emotion:

j'ai été étonné d'apprendre la nouvelle
I was surprised to hear the news

il regrette de ne pas avoir vu cette émission
he's sorry he didn't see this programme

tu as peur de ne pas avoir assez d'argent ?
are you worried you won't have enough money?

ii)   **attendre** (to wait) and **douter** (to doubt):

j'attendrai d'avoir bu mon café
I'll wait until I've drunk my coffee

iii) most impersonal constructions:

il serait préférable de déclarer ces objets
it would be better to declare these things

il est important de garder votre billet
it's important that you should keep your ticket

iv)   most conjunctions:

il est resté dans la voiture afin de ne pas se mouiller
he stayed in the car so as not to get wet

j'ai lu avant de m'endormir
I read before falling asleep

tu peux sortir, à condition de rentrer avant minuit
you can go out, as long as you're back before midnight

b)   **à** + *infinitive replaces the subjunctive after:*

i)   **de façon/manière**

mets la liste sur la table, de manière à ne pas l'oublier
put the list on the table so that you won't forget it

ii)   **premier, seul, dernier**

il a été le seul à s'excuser
he was the only one who apologised

c)   the infinitive without any linking preposition replaces the
      subjunctive after:

i)   verbs of wishing and willing:

je voudrais sortir avec toi
I'd like to go out with you

ii)   **il faut, il vaut mieux:**

il vous faudra prendre des chèques de voyage
you'll have to take some traveller's cheques

il lui a fallu recommencer à zéro
he had to start all over again

il vaudrait mieux lui apporter des fleurs que des bonbons
it would be better to take her flowers than sweets

Note: an indirect object pronoun is often used with **il faut** to indicate the
subject (who has to do something)

iii) verbs of thinking:

je ne crois pas le connaître
I don't think I know him

tu penses être chez toi à cinq heures ?
do you think you'll be home at five?

iv) **pour** and **sans**:

le car est reparti sans nous attendre
the coach left without waiting for us

j'économise pour pouvoir acheter une moto
I'm saving up to buy a motorbike

3. THE CONDITIONAL

a) *The conditional present*

i) The conditional present is used to describe what someone would do or would be doing or what would happen (if something else were to happen):

si j'étais riche, j'*achèterais* un château
if I were rich, I *would buy* a castle

Note: when the main verb is in the conditional present, the verb after **si** is in the imperfect.

ii) It is also used in indirect questions or reported speech instead of the future:

il ne m'a pas dit s'il *viendrait*
he didn't tell me whether he *would come*

b) *The conditional perfect (or past conditional)*

The conditional perfect or past conditional is used to express what someone would have done or would have been doing or what would have happened:

si j'avais su, je n'aurais rien dit
if I had known, I wouldn't have said anything

qu'aurais-je fait sans toi ?
what would I have done without you?

Note: if the main verb is in the conditional perfect, the verb introduced by **si** is in the pluperfect.

c) *Tenses after si:*

The tense of the verb introduced by **si** is determined by the tense of the verb in the main clause:

MAIN VERB	VERB FOLLOWING 'SI'
conditional present →	imperfect
conditional perfect →	pluperfect

je te le dirais si je le savais
I would tell you if I knew

je te l'aurais dit si je l'avais su
I would have told you if I had known

Note: never use the conditional (or the future) with **si** unless **si** means whether
(ie when it introduces an indirect question):

je me demande si j'y serais arrivé sans toi
I wonder if (= *whether*) I would have managed without you

4.   THE IMPERATIVE

a)   *Definition*

The imperative is used to give commands, or polite
instructions, or to make requests or suggestions; these can
be positive (affirmative imperative: 'do!') or negative ('don't!'):

mange ta soupe !	**n'aie pas peur !**
eat your soup	don't be afraid!
partons !	**entrez !**
let's go!	come in!
faites attention !	**n'hésitez pas !**
be careful!	don't hesitate!
tournez à droite à la poste	
turn right at the post office	

b)   *Forms*

The imperative has only three forms, which are the same as the **tu, nous**
and **vous** forms of the present tense, but without the subject pronoun:

	-ER VERBS	-IR VERBS	-RE VERBS
'TU' FORM:	**regarde**	**choisis**	**attends**
	watch	choose	wait
'NOUS' FORM:	**regardons**	**choisissons**	**attendons**
	let's watch	let's choose	let's wait
'VOUS' FORM:	**regardez**	**choisissez**	**attendez**
	watch	choose	wait

Note:

i)   the **-s** of the **tu** form of **-er** verbs is dropped, except when **y** or **en** follow
the verb:

parle-lui !	*But*	**parles-en avec lui**
speak to him!		speak to him about it
achète du sucre !	*But*	**achètes-en un kilo**
buy some sugar!		buy a kilo (of it)

ii)   the distinction between the subject pronouns **tu** and **vous** (see p 49) applies to the **tu** and **vous** forms of the imperative:

prends ta sœur avec toi, Alain
take your sister with you, Alain

prenez le plat du jour, Monsieur ; c'est du poulet rôti
have today's set menu, sir; it's roast chicken

les enfants, prenez vos imperméables ; il va pleuvoir
take your raincoats, children; it's going to rain

c)   *Negative commands*

In negative commands, the verb is placed between **ne** and **pas** (or the second part of other negative expressions):

ne fais pas ça !   **ne dites rien !**
don't do that!   don't say anything!

d)   *Imperative with object pronouns*

In positive commands, object pronouns come after the verb and are attached to it by a hyphen. In negative commands, they come before the verb (see pp 51, 52, 54 and 55):

dites-moi ce qui s'est passé   **attendons-les !**
tell me what happened   let's wait for them

prends-en bien soin, ne l'abîme pas !
take good care of it, don't damage it!

ne le leur dis pas !   **ne les écoutez pas**
don't tell them (that)!   don't listen to them

e)   *Imperative of reflexive verbs*

The position of the reflexive pronoun of reflexive verbs is the same as that of object pronouns:

tais-toi !   **levez-vous !**
be quiet!   get up!

méfiez-vous de lui   **arrêtons-nous ici**
don't trust him   let's stop here

ne nous plaignons pas   **ne t'approche pas plus !**
let's not complain   don't come any closer!

f)   *Alternatives to the imperative*

i)   infinitive

the infinitive is often used instead of the imperative in written instructions and in recipes:

s'adresser au concierge   **ne pas fumer**
see the caretaker   no smoking

verser le lait et bien mélanger
pour in the milk and stir well

ii)   subjunctive

as the imperative has no third person (singular or plural), que +
subjunctive is used for giving orders in the third person:

que personne ne me dérange !   **qu'il entre !**
don't let anyone disturb me!   let him (come) in!

qu'elle parte, je m'en fiche !
I don't care if she goes!

g)   *Idiomatic usage*

The imperative is used in spoken French in many set phrases. Here are
some of the most common ones:

allons donc !   **dis/ dites donc !**
you don't say!   by the way!
                                          hey! (*protest*)

tiens/tenez !   **tiens ! voilà le facteur**
here you are!   ah! here comes the postman

tiens (donc) !   **tiens ! tiens !**
(oh) really?   well, well! (fancy that!)

voyons !   **voyons donc !**
come (on) now!   let's see now

H.   THE INFINITIVE

1.   The infinitive is the basic form of the verb. It is recognized by its ending,
which is found in three forms corresponding to the three conjugations:
-er, -ir, -re.

These endings give the verb the meaning 'to ...':

acheter   **choisir**   **vendre**
to buy   to choose   to sell

Note: although this applies as a general rule, the French infinitive will often
be translated by a verb form in *-ing* (see p 185).

2.   Uses of the infinitive

The infinitive can follow a preposition, a verb, a noun, a pronoun, an
adverb or an adjective.

a)   *After a preposition*

The infinitive can be used after some prepositions (**pour, avant de, sans, au
lieu de, afin de** etc):

sans attendre   **avant de partir**
without waiting   before leaving

b) *After a verb*

There are three main constructions when a verb is followed by an infinitive:

> i) with no linking preposition
> ii) with the linking preposition **à**
> iii) with the linking preposition **de**

i) Verbs followed by the infinitive with no linking preposition:

★ verbs of wishing and willing, eg:

vouloir	to want
souhaiter	to wish
désirer	to wish, to want
espérer	to hope

voulez-vous manger maintenant ou plus tard ?
do you want to eat now or later?

je souhaite parler au directeur
I wish to speak to the manager

★ verbs of seeing, hearing and feeling, eg:

voir	to see
écouter	to listen to
regarder	to watch
sentir	to feel, to smell
entendre	to hear

je l'ai vu jouer	**tu m'as regardé danser ?**
I've seen him play	did you watch me dance?

j'ai entendu quelqu'un crier
I heard someone shout

★ verbs of motion, eg:

aller	to go
monter	to go/come up
venir	to come
entrer	to go/come in
rentrer	to go/come home
sortir	to go/come out
descendre	to go/come down

je viendrai te voir demain
I'll come and see you tomorrow

il est descendu laver la voiture
he went down to wash the car

va acheter le journal
go and buy the paper

Note: in English, 'to come' and 'to go' may be linked to the verb that follows by 'and'; 'and' is not translated in French.

aller + infinitive can be used to express a future action, eg what someone is going to do:

qu'est-ce que tu vas faire demain ?
what are you going to do tomorrow?

★   modal auxiliary verbs (see pp 109-11)

★   verbs of liking and disliking, eg:

aimer	to like
adorer	to love
aimer mieux	to prefer
détester	to hate
préférer	to prefer

tu aimes voyager ?   **j'aime mieux attendre**
do you like travelling?   I'd rather wait

je déteste aller à la campagne
I hate going to the country

j'adore faire la grasse matinée
I love having a long lie in

★   some impersonal verbs (see pp 80-2)

★   a few other verbs, eg:

compter	to intend to
sembler	to seem
laisser	to let, to allow
faillir	'to nearly' (do)
oser	to dare

ils l'ont laissé partir
they let him go

je n'ose pas le lui demander
I daren't ask him

tu sembles être malade
you seem to be ill

je compte partir demain
I intend to leave tomorrow

j'ai failli manquer l'avion
I nearly missed the plane

★   in the following set expressions:

aller chercher	to go and get, to fetch
envoyer chercher	to send for
entendre dire (que)	to hear (that)
entendre parler de	to hear about
laisser tomber	to drop
venir chercher	to come and get
vouloir dire	to mean

va chercher ton argent
go and get your money

j'ai entendu dire qu'il était journaliste
I've heard that he is a journalist

tu as entendu parler de ce film ?
have you heard about this film?

ne le laisse pas tomber !
don't drop it!

ça veut dire "demain"
it means 'tomorrow'

ii) Verbs followed by **à** + infinitive:

A list of these is given on p 153:

je dois aider ma mère à préparer le déjeuner
I must help my mother prepare lunch

il commence à faire nuit
it's beginning to get dark

alors, tu t'es décidé à y aller ?
so you've made up your mind to go?

je t'invite à venir chez moi pour les vacances de Noël
I invite you to come to my house for the Christmas holidays

je passe mon temps à lire et à regarder la télé
I spend my time reading and watching TV

cela sert à nettoyer les disques
this is used for cleaning records

iii) Verbs followed by **de** + infinitive:

A list of these is given on pp 146-7:

je crois qu'il s'est arrêté de pleuvoir
I think it's stopped raining

tu as envie de sortir ?
do you feel like going out?

le médecin a conseillé à Serge de rester au lit
the doctor advised Serge to stay in bed

j'ai décidé de rester chez moi
I decided to stay at home

essayons de faire du stop
let's try and hitch-hike

tu as fini de m'ennuyer ?
will you stop annoying me?

demande à Papa de t'aider
ask your Dad to help you

je t'interdis d'y aller
I forbid you to go

n'oublie pas d'en acheter !
don't forget to buy some!

j'ai refusé de le faire
I refused to do it

je vous prie de m'excuser
please forgive me

il vient de téléphoner
he's just phoned

c) *After a noun, a pronoun, an adverb or an adjective*

There are two possible constructions: with **à** or with **de**.

i) with the linking preposition **à**:

il avait plusieurs clients à voir
he had several customers to see

c'est difficile à dire
it's difficult to say

ii) with the linking preposition **de**:

je suis content de te voir
I am pleased to see you

iii) **à** or **de** with pronouns, adverbs or nouns?

★ **à** conveys the idea of something to do or to be done after the following:

beaucoup	a lot
plus	more
tant	so much
trop	too much
assez	enough
moins	less
rien	nothing
tout	everything
quelque chose	something

une maison à vendre   **j'ai des examens à préparer**
a house for sale   I've got exams to prepare

il nous a indiqué la route à suivre
he showed us the road to follow

il y a trop de livres à lire
there are too many books to read

il n'y a pas de temps à perdre
there's no time to lose

c'était une occasion à ne pas manquer
it was an opportunity not to be missed

★ **de** is used after nouns of an abstract nature, usually with the definite article, eg:

l'habitude de	the habit of
l'occasion de	the opportunity to
le temps de	the time to
le courage de	the courage to
l'envie de	the desire to
le besoin de	the need to
le plaisir de	the pleasure of
le moment de	the time to

il n'avait pas l'habitude d'être seul
he wasn't used to being alone

je n'ai pas le temps de lui parler
I don't have time to talk to him

avez-vous eu l'occasion de la rencontrer ?
did you have the opportunity to meet her?

ce n'est pas le moment de le déranger
now is not the time to disturb him

je n'ai pas eu le courage de le lui dire
I didn't have the courage to tell him

iv) **à** or **de** with adjectives?

★ **à** is used in a passive sense (something to be done) and after **c'est**:

un livre agréable à lire
a pleasant book to read

il est facile à satisfaire
he is easily satisfied

c'est intéressant à savoir
that's interesting to know

c'était impossible à faire
it was impossible to do

★ **de** is used after **il est** in an impersonal sense (see pp 80-1):

il est intéressant de savoir que ...
it is interesting to know that ...

Note: for the use of **c'est** and **il est**, see pp 186-7.

★ **de** is used after many adjectives, in particular those where the idea of 'of' is present in English, eg:

certain/sûr de	certain of/to
capable de	capable of
incapable de	incapable of
coupable de	guilty of

j'étais sûr de réussir
I was sure of succeeding

il est incapable d'y arriver seul
he is incapable of managing on his own

de is also used with adjectives of emotion, feeling and generally with adjectives denoting a state of mind, eg:

content de	pleased/happy to
surpris/étonné de	surprised to
fier de	proud to
heureux de	happy to
fâché de	annoyed to/at
triste de	sad to
gêné de	embarrassed to
désolé de	sorry for/to

j'ai été très content de recevoir ta lettre
I was very pleased to get your letter

elle sera surprise de vous voir
she will be surprised to see you

nous avons été très tristes d'apprendre la nouvelle
we were very sad to hear the news

But: **à** is used with **prêt à** (ready to) and **disposé à** (willing to):

es-tu prête à partir ?
are you ready to go?

je suis tout disposé à vous aider
I'm very willing to help you

d) *faire* + infinitive

faire is followed by an infinitive without any linking preposition to express the sense of 'having someone do something' or 'having something done'; two constructions are possible:

i) with one object
ii) with two objects

i) when only one object is used, it is a direct object:

je dois le faire réparer
I must have it fixed

il veut faire repeindre sa voiture
he wants to have his car resprayed

je ferai nettoyer cette veste ; je la ferai nettoyer
I'll have this jacket cleaned; I'll have it cleaned

tu m'as fait attendre !	**je le ferai parler**
you made me wait!	I'll make him talk

Note: the following set expressions:

faire entrer	to show in
faire venir	to send for
faites entrer ce monsieur	**je vais faire venir le docteur**
show this gentleman in	I'll send for the doctor

ii) when both **faire** and the following infinitive have an object, the object
of **faire** is indirect:

elle lui a fait prendre une douche
she made him take a shower

je leur ai fait ranger leur chambre
I made them tidy their room

e) *Infinitive used as subject of another verb:*

trouver un emploi n'est pas facile
finding a job isn't easy

3. The perfect infinitive

a) *Form*

The perfect or past infinitive is formed with the infinitive of the auxiliary
avoir or **être** as appropriate (see pp 75-6), followed by the past participle
of the verb, eg:

avoir mangé	**être allé**	**s'être levé**
to have eaten	to have gone	to have got up

b) *Use*

i) after the preposition **après** (after):

après avoir attendu une heure, il est rentré chez lui
after waiting for an hour, he went back home

il s'en est souvenu après s'être couché
he remembered after going to bed

ii) after certain verbs:

se souvenir de	to remember
remercier de	to thank for
regretter de	to regret, to be sorry for
être désolé de	to be sorry for

je vous remercie de m'avoir invité
I thank you for inviting me

il regrettait de leur avoir menti
he was sorry for lying to them

tu te souviens d'avoir fait cela ?
do you remember doing this ?

I. PARTICIPLES

1. The present participle

a) *Formation*

Like the imperfect, the present participle is formed by using the stem of the first person plural of the present tense (the **nous** form less the **-ons** ending):

-ons is replaced by **-ant** (= English *-ing*)

Exceptions:

INFINITIVE	PRESENT PARTICIPLE
avoir to have	**ayant** having
être to be	**étant** being
savoir to know	**sachant** knowing

b) *Use as an adjective*

Used as an adjective, the present participle agrees in number and in gender with its noun or pronoun:

un travail fatigant
tiring work

la semaine suivante
the following week

ils sont très exigeants
they're very demanding

des nouvelles surprenantes
surprising news

c) *Use as a verb*

The present participle is used far less frequently in French than in English, and English present participles in *-ing* are often not translated by a participle in French (see pp 184-6).

i) used on its own, the present participle corresponds to the English present participle:

ne voulant plus attendre, ils sont partis sans moi
not wanting to wait any longer, they left without me

pensant bien faire, j'ai insisté
thinking I was doing the right thing, I insisted

ii) **en** + present participle

When the subject of the present participle is the same as that of the main verb, this structure is often used to express simultaneity (ie 'while doing something'), manner (ie 'by doing something') or to translate English phrasal verbs.

★ simultaneous actions

In English this structure is translated by:

- while/when/on + present participle (eg 'on arriving')
- while/when/as + subject + verb (eg 'as he arrived')

il est tombé en descendant l'escalier
he fell as he was going down the stairs

en le voyant, j'ai éclaté de rire
when I saw him, I burst out laughing

elle lisait le journal en attendant l'autobus
she was reading the paper while waiting for the bus

Note: the adverb **tout** is often used before **en** to emphasize the fact that both actions are simultaneous, especially when there is an element of contradiction:

elle écoutait la radio tout en faisant ses devoirs
she was listening to the radio while doing her homework

tout en protestant, je les ai suivis
under protest, I followed them

★ manner

when expressing how an action is done, **en** + participle is translated by: 'by' + participle, eg:

il gagne sa vie en vendant des voitures d'occasion
he earns his living (by) selling second-hand cars

j'ai trouvé du travail en lisant les petites annonces
I found a job by reading the classified ads

★ phrasal verbs of motion

en + present participle is often used to translate English phrasal verbs expressing motion, where the verb expresses the means of motion and a preposition expresses the direction of movement (eg 'to run out', 'to swim across').

In French, the English preposition is translated by a verb, while the English verb is translated by **en** + present participle:

il est sorti du magasin *en courant*
he *ran* out of the shop

elle a traversé la route *en titubant*
she *staggered* across the road

2. The past participle

a) *Forms*

For the formation of the past participle see p 73.

b) *Use*

The past participle is mostly used as a verb in compound tenses or in the passive, but it can also be used as an adjective. In either case, there are strict rules of agreement to be followed.

c) *Rules of agreement of the past participle*

i) When it is used as an adjective, the past participle always agrees with the noun or pronoun it refers to:

un pneu crevé   **une pomme pourrie**
a burst tyre   a rotten apple

ils étaient épuisés	trois assiettes cassées !
they were exhausted	three broken plates!

Note: in French, the past participle is used as an adjective to describe postures or attitudes of the body, where English uses the present participle. The most common of these are:

accoudé	leaning on one's elbows
accroupi	squatting
agenouillé	kneeling
allongé	lying (down)
appuyé (contre)	leaning (against)
couché	lying (down)
étendu	lying (down)
penché	leaning (over)
(sus)pendu	hanging

il est allongé sur le lit	une femme assise devant moi
he's lying on the bed	a woman sitting in front of me

ii)   In compound tenses:

★   with the auxiliary **avoir**:

the past participle only agrees in number and gender with the direct object when the direct object comes before the participle, ie in the following cases:

– in a clause introduced by the relative pronoun **que**:

le jeu-vidéo que j'ai acheté	la valise qu'il a perdue
the video-game I bought	the suitcase he lost

– with a direct object pronoun:

ta carte ? je l'ai reçue hier
your card? I got it yesterday

zut, mes lunettes ! je les ai laissées chez moi
blast, my glasses! I've left them at home

– in a clause introduced by **combien de, quel (quelle, quels, quelles)** or **lequel (laquelle, lesquels, lesquelles)**:

combien de pays as-tu visités ?
how many countries have you visited?

laquelle avez-vous choisie ?
which one did you choose?

Note: if the direct object comes after the past participle, the participle remains in the masculine singular form:

on a rencontré des gens très sympathiques
we met some very nice people

★   with the auxiliary **être**

– the past participle agrees with the subject of the verb:

quand est-elle revenue ?	elle était déjà partie
when did she come back?	she'd already left

ils sont passés te voir ?
did they come to see you?

elles sont restées là
they stayed here

Note: this rule also applies when the verb is in the passive:

elle a été arrêtée
she's been arrested

– reflexive verbs

in most cases, the past participle of reflexive verbs agrees with the
reflexive pronoun if the pronoun is a direct object; since the reflexive
pronoun refers to the subject, the number and gender of the past
participle are determined by the subject:

Jacques s'est trompé
Jacques made a mistake

Marie s'était levée tard
Marie had got up late

ils se sont disputés ?
did they have an argument?

elles se sont vues
they saw each other

Michèle et Marie, vous vous êtes habillées?
Michèle and Marie, have you got dressed yet?

But: the past participle does not agree when the reflexive pronoun is an
indirect object:

elles se sont écrit
they wrote *to* each other

This is the case in particular where parts of the body are mentioned:

elle s'est lavé les cheveux
she washed her hair

ils se sont serré la main
they shook hands

J. THE PASSIVE

1. Formation

The passive is used when the subject does not perform the
action, but is subjected to it, eg:

the house has been sold   he was made redundant

Passive tenses are formed with the corresponding tense of the verb 'être'
('to be', as in English), followed by the past participle of the verb, eg:

j'ai été invité
I was invited

The past participle must agree with its subject, eg:

elle a été renvoyée
she has been dismissed

ils seront déçus
they will be disappointed

elles ont été vues
they were seen

2. Avoidance of the passive

The passive is far less common in French than in English. In particular, an indirect object cannot become the subject of a sentence in French, ie the following sentence where 'he' is an indirect object has no equivalent in French:

he was given a book (*ie a book was given to him*)

In general, French tries to avoid the passive wherever possible. This can be done in several ways:

a) *Use of the pronoun on:*

on m'a volé mon portefeuille
my wallet has been stolen

on construit une nouvelle piscine
a new swimming pool is being built

en France, on boit beaucoup de vin
a lot of wine is drunk in France

b) *Agent becomes subject of the verb*

If the agent, ie the real subject, is mentioned in English, it can become the subject of the French verb:

la nouvelle va les surprendre
they will be surprised by *the news*

mon correspondent m'a invité
I've been invited by *my penfriend*

mon cadeau te plaît ?
are you pleased with *my present?*

c) *Use of a reflexive verb*

Reflexive forms can be created for a large number of verbs, particularly in the third person:

elle s'appelle Anne she is called Anne	**ton absence va se remarquer** your absence will be noticed
ce plat se mange froid this dish is eaten cold	**cela ne se fait pas ici** that isn't done here

d) *Use of se faire* + infinitive (when the subject is a person):

il s'est fait renverser par une voiture
he was run over by a car

je me suis fait voler (tout mon argent)
I've been robbed (of all my money)

3. Conjugation

For a complete conjugation table of a verb in the passive, see **être aimé** (to be loved) p 115.

K. MODAL AUXILIARY VERBS

The modal auxiliary verbs are always followed by the infinitive. They express an obligation, a probability, an intention, a possibility or a wish rather than a fact.

The five modal auxiliary verbs are: **DEVOIR, POUVOIR, SAVOIR, VOULOIR** and **FALLOIR**.

1. Devoir (conjugation see p 123)

Expresses: a) obligation, necessity
b) probability
c) intention, expectation

a) *obligation*

nous devons arriver à temps
we must arrive in time

demain tu devras prendre le bus
tomorrow you'll have to take the bus

nous avions dû partir
we had (had) to go

j'ai dû avouer que j'avais tort
I had to admit that I was wrong

In the conditional, **devoir** may be used for advice, ie to express what should be done (conditional present) or should have been done (past conditional):

vous devriez travailler davantage
you ought to/should work harder

tu ne devrais pas marcher sur l'herbe
you shouldn't walk on the grass

tu aurais dû tout avouer
you should have admitted everything

tu n'aurais pas dû manger ces champignons
you shouldn't have eaten those mushrooms

Note: the French infinitive is translated by a past participle in English:
manger = eat*en*.

b) *probability*

il doit être en train de dormir
he must be sleeping (he's probably sleeping)

j'ai dû me tromper de chemin
I must have taken the wrong road

Note: in a past narrative sequence in the distant past 'must have' is translated by a pluperfect in French:

il dit qu'il avait dû se tromper de chemin
he said he must have taken the wrong road

c)   *intention, expectation*

> **je dois aller chez le dentiste**
> I am supposed to go to the dentist's

> **le train doit arriver à 19h30**
> the train is due to arrive at 7.30 p.m.

2.   Pouvoir (conjugation see p 135)

Expresses: a) capacity, ability
              b) permission
              c) possibility

a)   *capacity/ability*

> **Superman peut soulever une maison**
> Superman can lift a house

> **cette voiture peut faire du 150**
> this car can go up to 93 mph

> **il était si faible qu'il ne pouvait pas sortir de son lit**
> he was so weak that he couldn't get out of bed

b)   *permission*

> **puis-je entrer ?**   **puis-je vous offrir du thé ?**
> may I come in?   may I offer you some tea?

c)   *possibility*

> **cela peut arriver**
> it can happen

Note: **pouvoir** + the infinitive is usually replaced by **peut-être** and the finite
tense: eg **il s'est peut-être trompé de livres** (he may have taken the wrong
books).

In the conditional, **pouvoir** is used to express something that could or
might be (conditional present) or that could or might have been (past
conditional):

> **tu pourrais t'excuser**
> you might apologize

> **j'aurais pu vous prêter mon magnétophone**
> I could have lent you my tape-recorder

Note: with verbs of perception (eg **entendre** to hear, **sentir** to feel, to smell,
voir to see), **pouvoir** is often omitted:

> **j'entendais le bruit des vagues**
> I could hear the sound of the waves

3.   Savoir (conjugation see p 138)

Means: 'to know how to'

> **je sais/savais conduire une moto**
> I can/used to be able to ride a motorbike

4. Voiloir (conjugation see p 144)

Expresses: a) desire
b) wish
c) intention

a) *desire*

je veux partir
I want to go

voulez-vous danser avec moi ?
will you dance with me?

b) *wish*

je voudrais être un lapin
I wish I were a rabbit

je voudrais trouver un travail intéressant
I should like to find an interesting job

j'aurais voulu lui donner un coup de poing
I would have liked to punch him

c) *intention*

il a voulu sauter par la fenêtre
he tried to jump out of the window

Note: **veuillez**, the imperative of **vouloir**, is used as a polite form to express a
request ('would you please'):

veuillez ne pas déranger
please do not disturb

5. Falloir (conjugation see p 130)

Expresses: necessity

il faut manger pour vivre
you must eat to live

il faudrait manger plus tôt ce soir
we should eat earlier tonight

il aurait fallu apporter des sandwichs
we should have brought sandwiches

Note: some of the above verbs can also be used without infinitive
constructions. They then take on a different meaning (eg **devoir** = to
owe, **savoir** = to know).

L.   CONJUGATION TABLES

The following verbs provided the main patterns of conjugation including the conjugation of the most common irregular verbs. They are arranged in alphabetical order.

-er verb (*see p 65*)	AIMER
-ir verb (*see p 65*)	*FINIR*
-re verb (*see p 65*)	VENDRE
Reflexive verb (*see p 77-9*)	SE MEFIER
Verb with auxiliary être (*see p 74-6*)	ARRIVER
Verb in the passive (*see p 107-8*)	*ETRE AIME*
Auxiliaries (*see p 73-6*)	AVOIR
	ETRE
Verb in -eler/-eter (*see p 69-70*)	APPELER
Verb in e + consonant + er (*see p 71*)	ACHETER
Verb in é + consonant + er (*see p 71-2*)	ESPERER
Modal auxiliaries (*see p 109-11*)	DEVOIR
	POUVOIR
	SAVOIR
	VOULOIR
	FALLOIR

Irregular verbs	ALLER	METTRE
	CONDUIRE	OUVRIR
	CONNAITRE	PRENDRE
	CROIRE	RECEVOIR
	DIRE	TENIR
	DORMIR	VENIR
	ECRIRE	VIVRE
	FAIRE	VOIR

ACHETER
to buy

PRESENT
j'achète
tu achètes
il achète
nous achetons
vous achetez
ils achètent

PAST HISTORIC
j'achetai
tu achetas
il acheta
nous achetâmes
vous achetâtes
ils achetèrent

IMPERFECT
j'achetais
tu achetais
il achetait
nous achetions
vous achetiez
ils achetaient

PERFECT
j'ai acheté
tu as acheté
il a acheté
nous avons acheté
vous avez acheté
ils ont acheté

FUTURE
j'achèterai
tu achèteras
il achètera
nous achèterons
vous achèterez
ils achèteront

PLUPERFECT
j'avais acheté
tu avais acheté
il avait acheté
nous avions acheté
vous aviez acheté
ils avaient acheté

CONDITIONAL

PAST ANTERIOR
j'eus acheté etc

FUTURE PERFECT
j'aurai acheté etc

PRESENT
j'achèterais
tu achèterais
il achèterait
nous achèterions
vous achèteriez
ils achèteraient

PAST
j'aurais acheté
tu aurais acheté
il aurait acheté
nous aurions acheté
vous auriez acheté
ils auraient acheté

SUBJUNCTIVE

PRESENT
j'achète
tu achètes
il achète
nous achetions
vous achetiez
ils achètent

IMPERFECT
j'achetasse
tu achetasses
il achetât
nous achetassions
vous achetassiez
ils achetassent

PLUPERFECT
j'aie acheté
tu aies acheté
il ait acheté
nous ayons acheté
vous ayez acheté
ils aient acheté

IMPERATIVE
achète
achetons
achetez

INFINITIVE
PRESENT
acheter
PAST
avoir acheté

PARTICIPLE
PRESENT
achetant
PAST
acheté

AIMER
to like, to love

PRESENT	IMPERFECT	FUTURE
j'aime	j'aimais	j'aimerai
tu aimes	tu aimais	tu aimeras
il aime	il aimait	il aimera
nous aimons	nous aimions	nous aimerons
vous aimez	vous aimiez	vous aimerez
ils aiment	ils aimaient	ils aimeront

PAST HISTORIC	PERFECT	PLUPERFECT
j'aimai	j'ai aimé	j'avais aimé
tu aimas	tu as aimé	tu avais aimé
il aima	il a aimé	il avait aimé
nous aimâmes	nous avons aimé	nous avions aimé
vous aimâtes	vous avez aimé	vous aviez aimé
ils aimèrent	ils ont aimé	ils avaient aimé

CONDITIONAL

PAST ANTERIOR	PRESENT	PAST
j'eus aimé etc	j'aimerais	j'aurais aimé
	tu aimerais	tu aurais aimé
	il aimerait	il aurait aimé
	nous aimerions	nous aurions aimé
FUTURE PERFECT	vous aimeriez	vous auriez aimé
j'aurai aimé etc	ils aimeraient	ils auraient aimé

SUBJUNCTIVE

PRESENT	IMPERFECT	PLUPERFECT
j'aime	j'aimasse	j'aie aimé
tu aimes	tu aimasses	tu aies aimé
il aime	il aimât	il ait aimé
nous aimions	nous aimassions	nous ayons aimé
vous aimiez	vous aimassiez	vous ayez aimé
ils aiment	ils aimassent	ils aient aimé

IMPERATIVE	INFINITIVE	PARTICIPLE
aime	**PRESENT**	**PRESENT**
aimons	aimer	aimant
aimez		
	PAST	**PAST**
	avoir aimé	aimé

VERBS 115

ETRE AIME
to be loved

PRESENT	IMPERFECT	FUTURE
je suis aimé(e)	j'étais aimé(e)	je serai aimé(e)
tu es aimé(e)	tu étais aimé(e)	tu seras aimé(e)
il (elle) est aimé(e)	il (elle) était aimé(e)	il (elle) sera aimé(e)
nous sommes aimé(e)s	nous étions aimé(e)s	nous serons aimé(e)s
vous êtes aimé(e)(s)	vous étiez aimé(e)(s)	vous serez aimé(e)(s)
ils (elles) sont aimé(e)s	ils (elles) étaient aimé(e)s	ils (elles) seront aimé(e)s

PAST HISTORIC	PERFECT	PLUPERFECT
je fus aimé(e)	j'ai été aimé(e)	j'avais été aimé(e)
tu fus aimé(e)	tu as été aimé(e)	tu avais été aimé(e)
il (elle) fut aimé(e)	il a (elle) été aimé(e)	il (elle) avait été aimé(e)
nous fûmes aimé(e)s	nous avons été aimé(e)s	nous avions été aimé(e)s
vous fûtes aimé(e)(s)	vous avez été aimé(e)(s)	vous aviez été aimé(e)(s)
ils (elles) furent aimé(e)s	ils (elles) ont été aimé(e)s	ils (elles) avaient été aimé(e)s

CONDITIONAL

PAST ANTERIOR	PRESENT	PAST
j'eus été etc aimé(e)	je serais aimé(e)	j'aurais été aimé(e)
	tu aurais aimé(e)	tu aurais été aimé(e)
	il (elle) serait aimé(e)	il (elle) aurait été aimé(e)
	nous serions aimé(e)s	nous aurions été aimé(e)s
FUTURE PERFECT	vous seriez aimé(e)(s)	vous auriez été aimé(e)(s)
j'aurai été aimé(e) etc	ils (elles) seraient aimé(e)s	ils (elles) auraient été aimé(e)s

SUBJUNCTIVE

PRESENT	IMPERFECT	PLUPERFECT
je sois aimé(e)	je fusse aimé(e)	j'aie été aimé(e)
tu sois aimé(e)	tu fusses aimé(e)	tu aies été aimé(e)
il (elle) soit aimé(e)	il (elle) fût aimé(e)	il (elle) ait été aimé(e)
nous soyons aimé(e)s	nous fussions aimé(e)s	nous ayons été aimé(e)s
vous soyez aimé(e)(s)	vous fussiez aimé(e)(s)	vous ayez été aimé(e)(s)
ils (elles) soient aimé(e)s	ils (elles) fussent aimé(e)s	ils (elles) aient été aimé(e)s

IMPERATIVE	INFINITIVE	PARTICIPLE
sois aimé(e)	**PRESENT**	**PRESENT**
soyons aimé(e)s	être aimé(e)(s)	étant aimé(e)(s)
soyez aimé(e)(s)		
	PAST	**PAST**
	avoir été aimé(e)(s)	été aimé(e)(s)

ALLER
to go

PRESENT	IMPERFECT	FUTURE
je vais	j'allais	j'irai
tu vas	tu allais	tu iras
il va	il allait	il ira
nous allons	nous allions	nous irons
vous allez	vous alliez	vous irez
ils vont	ils allaient	ils iront

PAST HISTORIC	PERFECT	PLUPERFECT
j'allai	je suis allé(e)	j'étais allé(e)
tu allas	tu es allé(e)	tu étais allé(e)
il alla	il (elle) est allé(e)	il (elle) était allé(e)
nous allâmes	nous sommes allé(e)s	nous étiez allé(e)s
vous allâtes	vous êtes allé(e)(s)	vous étiez allé(e)(s)
ils allèrent	ils (elles) sont allé(e)s	ils (elles) étaient allé(e)s

CONDITIONAL

PAST ANTERIOR	PRESENT	PAST
je fus allé(e) etc	j'irais	je serais allé(e)
	tu irais	tu serais allé(e)
	il irait	il (elle) serait allé(e)
	nous irions	nous serions allé(e)s
FUTURE PERFECT	vous iriez	vous seriez allé(e)(s)
je serai allé(e) etc	ils iraient	ils (elles) seraient allé(e)s

SUBJUNCTIVE

PRESENT	IMPERFECT	PLUPERFECT
j'aille	j'allasse	je sois allé(e)
tu ailles	tu allasses	tu sois allé(e)
il aille	il allât	il (elle) soit allé(e)
nous allions	nous allassions	nous soyons allé(e)s
vous alliez	vous allassiez	vous soyez allé(e)(s)
ils aillent	ils allassent	ils (elles) soient allé(e)s

IMPERATIVE	INFINITIVE	PARTICIPLE
va	**PRESENT**	**PRESENT**
allons	aller	allant
allez		
	PAST	**PAST**
	être allé(e)(s)	allé

APPELER
to call

PRESENT	IMPERFECT	FUTURE
j'appelle	j'appelais	j'appellerai
tu appelles	tu appelais	tu appelleras
il appelle	il appelait	il appellera
nous appelons	nous appelions	nous appellerons
vous appelez	vous appeliez	vous appellerez
ils appellent	ils appelaient	ils appelleront

PAST HISTORIC	PERFECT	PLUPERFECT
j'appelai	j'ai appelé	j'avais appelé
tu appelas	tu as appelé	tu avais appelé
il appela	il a appelé	il avait appelé
nous appelâmes	nous avons appelé	nous avions appelé
vous appelâtes	vous avez appelé	vous aviez appelé
ils appelèrent	ils ont appelé	ils avaient appelé

CONDITIONAL

PAST ANTERIOR	PRESENT	PAST
j'eus appelé etc	j'appellerais	j'aurais appelé
	tu appellerais	tu aurais appelé
	il appellerait	il aurait appelé
	nous appellerions	nous aurions appelé
FUTURE PERFECT	vous appelleriez	vous auriez appelé
j'aurai appelé etc	ils appelleraient	ils auraient appelé

SUBJUNCTIVE

PRESENT	IMPERFECT	PLUPERFECT
j'appelle	j'appelasse	j'aie appelé
tu appelles	tu appelasses	tu aies appelé
il appelle	il appelât	il ait appelé
nous appelions	nous appelassions	nous ayons appelé
vous appeliez	vous appelassiez	vous ayez appelé
ils appellent	ils appelassent	ils aient appelé

IMPERATIVE	INFINITIVE	PARTICIPLE
appelle	**PRESENT**	**PRESENT**
appelons	appeler	appelant
appelez		
	PAST	**PAST**
	avoir appelé	appelé

ARRIVER
to arrive, to happen

PRESENT	IMPERFECT	FUTURE
j'arrive	j'arrivais	j'arriverai
tu arrives	tu arrivais	tu arriveras
il arrive	il arrivait	il arrivera
nous arrivons	nous arrivions	nous arriverons
vous arrivez	vous arriviez	vous arriverez
ils arrivent	ils arrivaient	ils arriveront

PAST HISTORIC	PERFECT	PLUPERFECT
j'arrivai	je suis arrivé(e)	j'étais arrivé(e)
tu arrivas	tu es arrivé(e)	tu étais arrivé(e)
il arriva	il (elle) est arrivé(e)	il (elle) était arrivé(e)
nous arrivâmes	nous sommes arrivé(e)s	nous étiez arrivé(e)s
vous arrivâtes	vous êtes arrivé(e)(s)	vous étiez arrivé(e)(s)
ils arrivèrent	ils (elles) sont arrivé(e)s	ils (elles) étaient arrivé(e)s

CONDITIONAL

PAST ANTERIOR	PRESENT	PAST
je fus arrivé(e) etc	j'arriverais	je serais arrivé(e)
	tu arriverais	tu serais arrivé(e)
	il arriverait	il (elle) serait arrivé(e)
	nous arriverions	nous serions arrivé(e)s
FUTURE PERFECT	vous arriveriez	vous seriez arrivé(e)(s)
je serai arrivé(e) etc	ils arriveraient	ils (elles) seraient arrivé(e)s

SUBJUNCTIVE

PRESENT	IMPERFECT	PLUPERFECT
j'arrive	j'arrivasse	je sois arrivé(e)
tu arrives	tu arrivasses	tu sois arrivé(e)
il arrive	il arrivât	il (elle) soit arrivé(e)
nous arrivions	nous arrivassions	nous soyons arrivé(e)s
vous arriviez	vous arrivassiez	vous soyez arrivé(e)(s)
ils arrivent	ils arrivassent	ils (elle) soient arrivé(e)s

IMPERATIVE	INFINITIVE	PARTICIPLE
arrive	PRESENT	PRESENT
arrivons	arriver	arrivant
arrivez		
	PAST	PAST
	être arrivé(e)(s)	arrivé

AVOIR
to have

PRESENT	IMPERFECT	FUTURE
j'ai	j'avais	j'aurai
tu as	tu avais	tu auras
il a	il avait	il aura
nous avons	nous avions	nous aurons
vous avez	vous aviez	vous aurez
ils ont	ils avaient	ils auront

PAST HISTORIC	PERFECT	PLUPERFECT
j'eus	j'ai eu	j'avais eu
tu eus	tu as eu	tu avais eu
il eut	il a eu	il avait eu
nous eûmes	nous avons eu	nous avions eu
vous eûtes	vous avez eu	vous aviez eu
ils eurent	ils ont eu	ils avaient eu

CONDITIONAL

PAST ANTERIOR	PRESENT	PAST
j'eus eu etc	j'aurais	j'aurais eu
	tu aurais	tu aurais eu
	il aurait	il aurait eu
	nous aurions	nous aurions eu
FUTURE PERFECT	vous auriez	vous auriez eu
j'aurai eu etc	ils auraient	ils auraient eu

SUBJUNCTIVE

PRESENT	IMPERFECT	PLUPERFECT
j'aie	j'eusse	j'aie eu
tu aies	tu eusses	tu aies eu
il ait	il eût	il ait eu
nous ayons	nous eussions	nous ayons eu
vous ayez	vous eussiez	vous ayez eu
ils aient	ils eussent	ils aient eu

IMPERATIVE	INFINITIVE	PARTICIPLE
aie	PRESENT	PRESENT
ayons	avoir	ayant
ayez		
	PAST	PAST
	avoir eu	eu

CONDUIRE
to lead, to drive

PRESENT	IMPERFECT	FUTURE
je conduis	je conduisais	je conduirai
tu conduis	tu conduisais	tu conduiras
il conduit	il conduisait	il conduira
nous conduisons	nous conduisions	nous conduirons
vous conduisez	vous conduisiez	vous conduirez
ils conduisent	ils conduisaient	ils conduiront

PAST HISTORIC	PERFECT	PLUPERFECT
je conduisis	j'ai conduit	j'avais conduit
tu conduisis	tu as conduit	tu avais conduit
il conduisit	il a conduit	il avait conduit
nous conduisîmes	nous avons conduit	nous avions conduit
vous conduisîtes	vous avez conduit	vous aviez conduit
ils conduisirent	ils ont conduit	ils avaient conduit

CONDITIONAL

PAST ANTERIOR	PRESENT	PAST
j'eus conduit etc	je conduirais	j'aurais conduit
	tu conduirais	tu aurais conduit
	il conduirait	il aurait conduit
	nous conduirions	nous aurions conduit
FUTURE PERFECT	vous conduiriez	vous auriez conduit
j'aurai conduit etc	ils conduiraient	ils auraient conduit

SUBJUNCTIVE

PRESENT	IMPERFECT	PLUPERFECT
je conduise	je conduisisse	j'aie conduit
tu conduises	tu conduisisses	tu aies conduit
il conduise	il conduisît	il ait conduit
nous conduisions	nous conduisissions	nous ayons conduit
vous conduisiez	vous conduisissiez	vous ayez conduit
ils conduisent	ils conduisissent	ils aient conduit

IMPERATIVE	INFINITIVE	PARTICIPLE
conduis	PRESENT	PRESENT
conduisons	conduire	conduisant
conduisez		
	PAST	PAST
	avoir conduit	conduit

CONNAITRE
to know

PRESENT	IMPERFECT	FUTURE
je connais	je connaissais	je connaîtrai
tu connais	tu connaissais	tu connaîtras
il connaît	il connaissait	il connaîtra
nous connaissons	nous connaissions	nous connaîtrons
vous connaissez	vous connaissiez	vous connaîtrez
ils connaissent	ils connaissaient	ils connaîtront

PAST HISTORIC	PERFECT	PLUPERFECT
je connus	j'ai connu	j'avais connu
tu connus	tu as connu	tu avais connu
il connut	il a connu	il avait connu
nous connûmes	nous avons connu	nous avions connu
vous connûtes	vous avez connu	vous aviez connu
ils connurent	ils ont connu	ils avaient connu

CONDITIONAL

PAST ANTERIOR	PRESENT	PAST
j'eus connu etc	je connaîtrais	j'aurais connu
	tu connaîtrais	tu aurais connu
	il connaîtrait	il aurait connu
	nous connaîtrions	nous aurions connu
FUTURE PERFECT	vous connaîtriez	vous auriez connu
j'aurai connu etc	ils connaîtraient	ils auraient connu

SUBJUNCTIVE

PRESENT	IMPERFECT	PLUPERFECT
je connaisse	je connusse	j'aie connu
tu connaisses	tu connusses	tu aies connu
il connaisse	il connût	il ait connu
nous connaissions	nous connussions	nous ayons connu
vous connaissiez	vous connussiez	vous ayez connu
ils connaissent	ils connussent	ils aient connu

IMPERATIVE	INFINITIVE	PARTICIPLE
connais	**PRESENT**	**PRESENT**
connaissons	connaître	connaissant
connaissez		
	PAST	**PAST**
	avoir connu	connu

CROIRE
to believe

PRESENT	IMPERFECT	FUTURE
je crois	je croyais	je croirai
tu crois	tu croyais	tu croiras
il croit	il croyait	il croira
nous croyons	nous croyions	nous croirons
vous croyez	vous croyiez	vous croirez
ils croient	ils croyaient	ils croiront

PAST HISTORIC	PERFECT	PLUPERFECT
je crus	j'ai cru	j'avais cru
tu crus	tu as cru	tu avais cru
il crut	il a cru	il avait cru
nous crûmes	nous avons cru	nous aviez cru
vous crûtes	vous avez cru	vous aviez cru
ils crurent	ils ont cru	ils avaient cru

CONDITIONAL

PAST ANTERIOR	PRESENT	PAST
j'eus cru etc	je croirais	j'aurais cru
	tu croirais	tu aurais cru
	il croirait	il aurait cru
	nous croirions	nous aurions cru
FUTURE PERFECT	vous croiriez	vous auriez cru
j'aurai cru etc	ils croiraient	ilsauraient cru

SUBJUNCTIVE

PRESENT	IMPERFECT	PLUPERFECT
je croie	je crusse	j'aie cru
tu croies	tu crusses	tu aies cru
il croie	il crût	il ait cru
nous croyions	nous crussions	nous ayons cru
vous croyiez	vous crussiez	vous ayez cru
ils croient	ils crussent	ils aient cru

IMPERATIVE	INFINITIVE	PARTICIPLE
crois	PRESENT	PRESENT
croyons	croire	croyant
croyez		
	PAST	PAST
	avoir cru	cru

DEVOIR
to have to

PRESENT	IMPERFECT	FUTURE
je dois	je devais	je devrai
tu dois	tu devais	tu devras
il doit	il devait	il devra
nous devons	nous devions	nous devrons
vous devez	vous deviez	vous devrez
ils doivent	ils devaient	ils devront

PAST HISTORIC	PERFECT	PLUPERFECT
je dus	j'ai dû	j'avais dû
tu dus	tu as dû	tu avais dû
il dut	il a dû	il avait dû
nous dûmes	nous avons dû	nous avions dû
vous dûtes	vous avez dû	vous aviez dû
ils durent	ils ont dû	ils avaient dû

CONDITIONAL

PAST ANTERIOR	PRESENT	PAST
j'eus dû etc	je devrais	j'aurais dû
	tu devrais	tu aurais dû
	il devrait	il aurait dû
	nous devrions	nous aurions dû
FUTURE PERFECT	vous devriez	vous auriez dû
j'aurai dû etc	ils devraient	ils auraient dû

SUBJUNCTIVE

PRESENT	IMPERFECT	PLUPERFECT
je doive	je dusse	j'aie dû
tu doives	tu dusses	tu aies dû
il doive	il dût	il ait dû
nous devions	nous dussions	nous ayons dû
vous deviez	vous dussiez	vous ayez dû
ils doivent	ils dussent	ils aient dû

IMPERATIVE	INFINITIVE	PARTICIPLE
dois	PRESENT	PRESENT
devons	devoir	devant
devez		
	PAST	PAST
	avoir dû	dû

DIRE
to say

PRESENT	IMPERFECT	FUTURE
je dis	je disais	je dirai
tu dis	tu disais	tu diras
il dit	il disait	il dira
nous disons	nous disions	nous dirons
vous disez	vous disiez	vous direz
ils disent	ils disaient	ils diront

PAST HISTORIC	PERFECT	PLUPERFECT
je dis	j'ai dit	j'avais dit
tu dis	tu as dit	tu avais dit
il dit	il a dit	il avait dit
nous dîmes	nous avons dit	nous avions dit
vous dîtes	vous avez dit	vous aviez dit
ils dirent	ils ont dit	ils avaient dit

CONDITIONAL

PAST ANTERIOR	PRESENT	PAST
j'eus dit etc	je dirais	j'aurais dit
	tu dirais	tu aurais dit
	il dirait	il aurait dit
	nous dirions	nous aurions dit
FUTURE PERFECT	vous diriez	vous auriez dit
j'aurai dit etc	ils diraient	ils auraient dit

SUBJUNCTIVE

PRESENT	IMPERFECT	PLUPERFECT
je dise	je disse	j'aie dit
tu dises	tu disses	tu aies dit
il dise	il dît	il ait dit
nous disions	nous dissions	nous ayons dit
vous disiez	vous dissiez	vous ayez dit
ils disent	ils dissent	ils aient dit

IMPERATIVE	INFINITIVE	PARTICIPLE
dis	**PRESENT**	**PRESENT**
disons	dire	disant
dîtes		
	PAST	**PAST**
	avoir dit	dit

DORMIR
to sleep

PRESENT	IMPERFECT	FUTURE
je dors	je dormais	je dormirai
tu dors	tu dormais	tu dormiras
il dort	il dormait	il dormira
nous dormons	nous dormions	nous dormirons
vous dormez	vous dormiez	vous dormirez
ils dorment	ils dormaient	ils dormiront

PAST HISTORIC	PERFECT	PLUPERFECT
je dormis	j'ai dormi	j'avais dormi
tu dormis	tu as dormi	tu avais dormi
il dormit	il a dormi	il avait dormi
nous dormîmes	nous avons dormi	nous avions dormi
vous dormîtes	vous avez dormi	vous aviez dormi
ils dormirent	ils ont dormi	ils avaient dormi

CONDITIONAL

PAST ANTERIOR	PRESENT	PAST
j'eus dormi etc	je dormirais	j'aurais dormi
	tu dormirais	tu aurais dormi
	il dormirait	il aurait dormi
	nous dormirions	nous aurions dormi
FUTURE PERFECT	vous dormiriez	vous auriez dormi
j'aurai dormi etc	ils dormiraient	ils auraient dormi

SUBJUNCTIVE

PRESENT	IMPERFECT	PLUPERFECT
je dorme	je dormisse	j'aie dormi
tu dormes	tu dormisses	tu aies dormi
il dorme	il dormît	il ait dormi
nous dormions	nous dormissions	nous ayons dormi
vous dormiez	vous dormissiez	vous ayez dormi
ils dorment	ils dormissent	ils aient dormi

IMPERATIVE	INFINITIVE	PARTICIPLE
dors	PRESENT	PRESENT
dormons	dormir	dormant
dormez		
	PAST	PAST
	avoir dormi	dormi

ECRIRE
to write

PRESENT	IMPERFECT	FUTURE
j'écris	j'écrivais	j'écrirai
tu écris	tu écrivais	tu écriras
il écrit	il écrivait	il écrira
nous écrivons	nous écrivions	nous écrirons
vous écrivez	vous écriviez	vous écrirez
ils écrivent	ils écrivaient	ils écriront

PAST HISTORIC	PERFECT	PLUPERFECT
j'écrivis	j'ai écrit	j'avais écrit
tu écrivis	tu as écrit	tu avais écrit
il écrivit	il a écrit	il avait écrit
nous écrivîmes	nous avons écrit	nous avions écrit
vous écrivîtes	vous avez écrit	vous aviez écrit
ils écrivirent	ils ont écrit	ils avaient écrit

CONDITIONAL

PAST ANTERIOR	PRESENT	PAST
j'eus écrit etc	j'écrirais	j'aurais écrit
	tu écrirais	tu aurais écrit
	il écrirait	il aurait écrit
	nous écririons	nous aurions écrit
FUTURE PERFECT	vous écririez	vous auriez écrit
j'aurai écrit etc	ils écriraient	ils auraient écrit

SUBJUNCTIVE

PRESENT	IMPERFECT	PLUPERFECT
j'écrive	j'écrivisse	j'aie écrit
tu écrives	tu écrivisses	tu aies écrit
il écrive	il écrivît	il ait écrit
nous écrivions	nous écrivissions	nous ayons écrit
vous écriviez	vous écrivissiez	vous ayez écrit
ils écrivent	ils écrivissent	ils aient écrit

IMPERATIVE	INFINITIVE	PARTICIPLE
écris	PRESENT	PRESENT
écrivons	écrire	écrivant
écrivez		
	PAST	PAST
	avoir écrit	écrit

ESPERER
to hope

PRESENT	IMPERFECT	FUTURE
j'espère	j'espérais	j'espérerai
tu espères	tu espérais	tu espéreras
il espère	il espérait	il espérera
nous espérons	nous espérions	nous espérerons
vous espérez	vous espériez	vous espérerez
ils espèrent	ils espéraient	ils espéreront

PAST HISTORIC	PERFECT	PLUPERFECT
j'espérai	j'ai espéré	j'avais espéré
tu espéras	tu as espéré	tu avais espéré
il espéra	il a espéré	il avait espéré
nous espérâmes	nous avons espéré	nous avions espéré
vous espérâtes	vous avez espéré	vous aviez espéré
ils espérèrent	ils ont espéré	ils avaient espéré

CONDITIONAL

PAST ANTERIOR	PRESENT	PAST
j'eus espéré etc	j'espérerais	j'aurais espéré
	tu espérerais	tu aurais espéré
	il espérerait	il aurait espéré
	nous espérerions	nous aurions espéré
FUTURE PERFECT	vous espéreriez	vous auriez espéré
j'aurai espéré etc	ils espéreraient	ils auraient espéré

SUBJUNCTIVE

PRESENT	IMPERFECT	PLUPERFECT
j'espère	j'espérasse	j'aie espéré
tu espères	tu espérasses	tu aies espéré
il espère	il espérât	il ait espéré
nous espérions	nous espérassions	nous ayons espéré
vous espériez	vous espérassiez	vous ayez espéré
ils espèrent	ils espérassent	ils aient espéré

IMPERATIVE	INFINITIVE	PARTICIPLE
espère	PRESENT	PRESENT
espérons	espérer	espérant
espérez		
	PAST	PAST
	avoir espéré	espéré

ETRE
to be

PRESENT	IMPERFECT	FUTURE
je suis	j'étais	je serai
tu es	tu étais	tu seras
il est	il était	il sera
nous sommes	nous étions	nous serons
vous êtes	vous étiez	vous serez
ils sont	ils étaient	ils seront

PAST HISTORIC	PERFECT	PLUPERFECT
je fus	j'ai été	j'avais été
tu fus	tu as été	tu avais été
il fut	il a été	il avait été
nous fûmes	nous avons été	nous avions été
vous fûtes	vous avez été	vous aviez été
ils furent	ils ont été	ils avaient été

CONDITIONAL

PAST ANTERIOR	PRESENT	PAST
j'eus été etc	je serais	j'aurais été
	tu serais	tu aurais été
	il serait	il aurait été
	nous serions	nous aurions été
FUTURE PERFECT	vous seriez	vous auriez été
j'aurai été etc	ils seraient	ils auraient été

SUBJUNCTIVE

PRESENT	IMPERFECT	PLUPERFECT
je sois	je fusse	j'aie été
tu sois	tu fusses	tu aies été
il soit	il fût	il ait été
nous soyons	nous fussions	nous ayons été
vous soyez	vous fussiez	vous ayez été
ils soient	ils fussent	ils aient été

IMPERATIVE	INFINITIVE	PARTICIPLE
sois	PRESENT	PRESENT
soyons	être	étant
soyez		
	PAST	PAST
	avoir été	été

FAIRE
to do, to make

PRESENT	IMPERFECT	FUTURE
je fais	je faisais	je ferai
tu fais	tu faisais	tu feras
il fait	il faisait	il fera
nous faisons	nous faisions	nous ferons
vous faites	vous faisiez	vous ferez
ils font	ils faisaient	ils feront

PAST HISTORIC	PERFECT	PLUPERFECT
je fis	j'ai fait	j'avais fait
tu fis	tu as fait	tu avais fait
il fit	il a fait	il avait fait
nous fîmes	nous avons fait	nous avions fait
vous fîtes	vous avez fait	vous aviez fait
ils firent	ils ont fait	ils avaient fait

CONDITIONAL

PAST ANTERIOR	PRESENT	PAST
j'eus fait etc	je ferais	j'aurais fait
	tu ferais	tu aurais fait
	il ferait	il aurait fait
	nous ferions	nous aurions fait
FUTURE PERFECT	vous feriez	vous auriez fait
j'aurai fait etc	ils feraient	ils auraient fait

SUBJUNCTIVE

PRESENT	IMPERFECT	PLUPERFECT
je fasse	je fisse	j'aie fait
tu fasses	tu fisses	tu aies fait
il fasse	il fît	il ait fait
nous fassions	nous fissions	nous ayons fait
vous fassiez	vous fissiez	vous ayez fait
ils fassent	ils fissent	ils aient fait

IMPERATIVE	INFINITIVE	PARTICIPLE
fais	PRESENT	PRESENT
faisons	faire	faisant
faites		
	PAST	PAST
	avoir fait	fait

FALLOIR
to be necessary

PRESENT	IMPERFECT	FUTURE
il faut	il fallait	il faudra

PAST HISTORIC	PERFECT	PLUPERFECT
il fallut	il a fallu	il avait fallu

CONDITIONAL

PAST ANTERIOR	PRESENT	PAST
il eut fallu	il faudrait	il aurait fallu

FUTURE PERFECT
il aura fallu

SUBJUNCTIVE

PRESENT	IMPERFECT	PLUPERFECT
il faille	il fallût	il ait fallu

IMPERATIVE	INFINITIVE	PARTICIPLE
	PRESENT	PRESENT
	falloir	
	PAST	PAST
	avoir fallu	fallu

FINIR
to finish

PRESENT	IMPERFECT	FUTURE
je finis	je finissais	je finirai
tu finis	tu finissais	tu finiras
il finit	il finissait	il finira
nous finissons	nous finissions	nous finirons
vous finissez	vous finissiez	vous finirez
ils finissent	ils finissaient	ils finiront

PAST HISTORIC	PERFECT	PLUPERFECT
je finis	j'ai fini	j'avais fini
tu finis	tu as fini	tu avais fini
il finit	il a fini	il avait fini
nous finîmes	nous avons fini	nous avions fini
vous finîtes	vous avez fini	vous aviez fini
ils finirent	ils ont fini	ils avaient fini

CONDITIONAL

PAST ANTERIOR	PRESENT	PAST
j'eus fini etc	je finirais	j'aurais fini
	tu finirais	tu aurais fini
	il finirait	il aurait fini
	nous finirions	nous aurions fini
FUTURE PERFECT	vous finiriez	vous auriez fini
j'aurai fini etc	ils finiraient	ils auraient fini

SUBJUNCTIVE

PRESENT	IMPERFECT	PLUPERFECT
je finisse	je finisse	j'aie fini
tu finisses	tu finisses	tu aies fini
il finisse	il finît	il ait fini
nous finissions	nous finissions	nous ayons fini
vous finissiez	vous finissiez	vous ayez fini
ils finissent	ils finissent	ils aient fini

IMPERATIVE	INFINITIVE	PARTICIPLE
finis	PRESENT	PRESENT
finissons	finir	finissant
finissez		
	PAST	PAST
	avoir fini	fini

SE MEFIER
to be suspicious

PRESENT	IMPERFECT	FUTURE
je me méfie	je me méfiais	je me méfierai
tu te méfies	tu te méfiais	tu te méfieras
il se méfie	il se méfiait	il se méfiera
nous nous méfions	nous nous méfiions	nous nous méfierons
vous vous méfiez	vous vous méfiiez	vous vous méfierez
ils se méfient	ils se méfiaient	ils se méfieront

PAST HISTORIC	PERFECT	PLUPERFECT
je me méfiai	je me suis méfié(e)	je m'étais méfié(e)
tu te méfias	tu t'es méfié(e)	tu t'étais méfié(e)
il se méfia	il (elle) s'est méfié(e)	il (elle) s'était méfié(e)
nous nous méfiâmes	nous nous sommes méfié(e)s	nous nous étions méfié(e)s
vous vous méfiâtes	vous vous êtes méfié(e)(s)	vous vous étiez méfié(e)(s)
ils se méfièrent	ils (elles) se sont méfié(e)s	ils (elles) s'étaient méfié(e)s

CONDITIONAL

PAST ANTERIOR	PRESENT	PAST
je me fus méfié(e) etc	je me méfierais	je me serais méfié(e)
	tu te méfierais	tu te serais méfié(e)
	il se méfierait	il (elle) se serait méfié(e)
	nous nous méfierions	nous nous serions méfié(e)s
FUTURE PERFECT	vous vous méfieriez	vous vous seriez méfié(e)(s)
je me serai méfié(e) etc	ils (elles) se méfieraient	ils (elles) se seraient méfié(e)s

SUBJUNCTIVE

PRESENT	IMPERFECT	PLUPERFECT
je me méfie	je me méfiasse	je me sois méfié(e)
tu te méfies	tu te méfiasses	tu te sois méfié(e)
il se méfie	il se méfiât	il (elle) se soit méfié(e)
nous nous méfiions	nous nous méfiassions	nous nous soyons méfié(e)s
vous vous méfiiez	vous vous méfiassiez	vous vous soyez méfié(e)(s)
ils se méfient	ils se méfiassent	ils (elles) se soient méfié(e)s

IMPERATIVE	INFINITIVE	PARTICIPLE
méfie-toi	**PRESENT**	**PRESENT**
méfions-nous	se méfier	se méfiant
méfiez-vous		
	PAST	**PAST**
	s'être méfié(e)(s)	méfié

METTRE
to put

PRESENT	IMPERFECT	FUTURE
je mets	je mettais	je mettrai
tu mets	tu mettais	tu mettras
il met	il mettait	il mettra
nous mettons	nous mettions	nous mettrons
vous mettez	vous mettiez	vous mettrez
ils mettent	ils mettaient	ils mettront

PAST HISTORIC	PERFECT	PLUPERFECT
je mis	j'ai mis	j'avais mis
tu mis	tu as mis	tu avais mis
il mit	il a mis	il avait mis
nous mîmes	nous avons mis	nous avions mis
vous mîtes	vous avez mis	vous aviez mis
ils mirent	ils ont mis	ils avaient mis

CONDITIONAL

PAST ANTERIOR	PRESENT	PAST
j'eus mis etc	je mettrais	j'aurais mis
	tu mettrais	tu aurais mis
	il mettrait	il aurait mis
	nous mettrions	nous aurions mis
FUTURE PERFECT	vous mettriez	vous auriez mis
j'aurai mis etc	ils mettraient	ils auraient mis

SUBJUNCTIVE

PRESENT	IMPERFECT	PLUPERFECT
je mette	je misse	j'aie mis
tu mettes	tu misses	tu aies mis
il mette	il mît	il ait mis
nous mettions	nous missions	nous ayons mis
vous mettiez	vous missiez	vous ayez mis
ils mettent	ils missent	ils aient mis

IMPERATIVE	INFINITIVE	PARTICIPLE
mets	**PRESENT**	**PRESENT**
mettons	mettre	mettant
mettez		
	PAST	**PAST**
	avoir mis	mis

OUVRIR
to open

PRESENT	IMPERFECT	FUTURE
j'ouvre	j'ouvrais	j'ouvrirai
tu ouvres	tu ouvrais	tu ouvriras
il ouvre	il ouvrait	il ouvrira
nous ouvrons	nous ouvrions	nous ouvrirons
vous ouvrez	vous ouvriez	vous ouvrirez
ils ouvrent	ils ouvraient	ils ouvriront

PAST HISTORIC	PERFECT	PLUPERFECT
j'ouvris	j'ai ouvert	j'avais ouvert
tu ouvris	tu as ouvert	tu avais ouvert
il ouvrit	il a ouvert	il avait ouvert
nous ouvrîmes	nous avons ouvert	nous avions ouvert
vous ouvrîtes	vous avez ouvert	vous aviez ouvert
ils ouvrirent	ils ont ouvert	ils avaient ouvert

CONDITIONAL

PAST ANTERIOR	PRESENT	PAST
j'eus ouvert etc	j'ouvrirais	j'aurais ouvert
	tu ouvrirais	tu aurais ouvert
	il ouvrirait	il aurait ouvert
	nous ouvririons	nous aurions ouvert
FUTURE PERFECT	vous ouvririez	vous auriez ouvert
j'aurai ouvert etc	ils ouvriraient	ils auraient ouvert

SUBJUNCTIVE

PRESENT	IMPERFECT	PLUPERFECT
j'ouvre	j'ouvrisse	j'aie ouvert
tu ouvres	tu ouvrisses	tu aies ouvert
il ouvre	il ouvrît	il ait ouvert
nous ouvrions	nous ouvrissions	nous ayons ouvert
vous ouvriez	vous ouvrissiez	vous ayez ouvert
ils ouvrent	ils ouvrissent	ils aient ouvert

IMPERATIVE	INFINITIVE	PARTICIPLE
ouvre	PRESENT	PRESENT
ouvrons	ouvrir	ouvrant
ouvrez		
	PAST	PAST
	avoir ouvert	ouvert

POUVOIR
to be able to

PRESENT	IMPERFECT	FUTURE
je peux	je pouvais	je pourrai
tu peux	tu pouvais	tu pourras
il peut	il pouvait	il pourra
nous pouvons	nous pouvions	nous pourrons
vous pouvez	vous pouviez	vous pourrez
ils peuvent	ils pouvaient	ils pourront

PAST HISTORIC	PERFECT	PLUPERFECT
je pus	j'ai pu	j'avais pu
tu pus	tu as pu	tu avais pu
il put	il a pu	il avait pu
nous pûmes	nous avons pu	nous avions pu
vous pûtes	vous avez pu	vous aviez pu
ils purent	ils ont pu	ils avaient pu

CONDITIONAL

PAST ANTERIOR	PRESENT	PAST
j'eus pu etc	je pourrais	j'aurais pu
	tu pourrais	tu aurais pu
	il pourrait	il aurait pu
	nous pourrions	nous aurions pu
FUTURE PERFECT	vous pourriez	vous auriez pu
j'aurai pu etc	ils pourraient	ils auraient pu

SUBJUNCTIVE

PRESENT	IMPERFECT	PLUPERFECT
je puisse	je pusse	j'aie pu
tu puisses	tu pusses	tu aies pu
il puisse	il pût	il ait pu
nous puissions	nous pussions	nous ayons pu
vous puissiez	vous pussiez	vous ayez pu
ils puissent	ils pussent	ils aient pu

IMPERATIVE	INFINITIVE	PARTICIPLE
	PRESENT	PRESENT
	pouvoir	pouvant
pouvez		
	PAST	PAST
	avoir pu	pu

PRENDRE
to take

PRESENT	IMPERFECT	FUTURE
je prends	je prenais	je prendrai
tu prends	tu prenais	tu prendras
il prend	il prenait	il prendra
nous prenons	nous prenions	nous prendrons
vous prenez	vous preniez	vous prendrez
ils prennent	ils prenaient	ils prendront

PAST HISTORIC	PERFECT	PLUPERFECT
je pris	j'ai pris	j'avais pris
tu pris	tu as pris	tu avais pris
il prit	il a pris	il avait pris
nous prîmes	nous avons pris	nous avions pris
vous prîtes	vous avez pris	vous aviez pris
ils prirent	ils ont pris	ils avaient pris

CONDITIONAL

PAST ANTERIOR	PRESENT	PAST
j'eus pris etc	je prendrais	j'aurais pris
	tu prendrais	tu aurais pris
	il prendrait	il aurait pris
	nous prendrions	nous aurions pris
FUTURE PERFECT	vous prendriez	vous auriez pris
j'aurai pris etc	ils prendraient	ils auraient pris

SUBJUNCTIVE

PRESENT	IMPERFECT	PLUPERFECT
je prenne	je prisse	j'aie pris
tu prennes	tu prisses	tu aies pris
il prenne	il prît	il ait pris
nous prenions	nous prissions	nous ayons pris
vous preniez	vous prissiez	vous ayez pris
ils prennent	ils prissent	ils aient pris

IMPERATIVE	INFINITIVE	PARTICIPLE
prends	**PRESENT**	**PRESENT**
prenons	prendre	prenant
prenez		
	PAST	**PAST**
	avoir pris	pris

RECEVOIR
to receive

PRESENT	IMPERFECT	FUTURE
je reçois	je recevais	je recevrai
tu reçois	tu recevais	tu recevras
il reçoit	il recevait	il recevra
nous recevons	nous recevions	nous recevrons
vous recevez	vous receviez	vous recevrez
ils reçoivent	ils recevaient	ils recevront

PAST HISTORIC	PERFECT	PLUPERFECT
je reçus	j'ai reçu	j'avais reçu
tu reçus	tu as reçu	tu avais reçu
il reçut	il a reçu	il avait reçu
nous reçûmes	nous avons reçu	nous avions reçu
vous reçûtes	vous avez reçu	vous aviez reçu
ils reçurent	ils ont reçu	ils avaient reçu

	CONDITIONAL	
PAST ANTERIOR	**PRESENT**	**PAST**
j'eus reçu etc	je recevrais	j'aurais reçu
	tu recevrais	tu aurais reçu
	il recevrait	il aurait reçu
	nous recevrions	nous aurions reçu
FUTURE PERFECT	vous recevriez	vous auriez reçu
j'aurai reçu etc	ils recevraient	ils auraient reçu

SUBJUNCTIVE

PRESENT	IMPERFECT	PLUPERFECT
je reçoive	je reçusse	j'aie reçu
tu reçoives	tu reçusses	tu aies reçu
il reçoive	il reçût	il ait reçu
nous recevions	nous reçussions	nous ayons reçu
vous receviez	vous reçussiez	vous ayez reçu
ils reçoivent	ils reçussent	ils aient reçu

IMPERATIVE	*INFINITIVE*	*PARTICIPLE*
reçois	**PRESENT**	**PRESENT**
recevons	recevoir	recevant
recevez		
	PAST	**PAST**
	avoir reçu	reçu

SAVOIR
to know

PRESENT	IMPERFECT	FUTURE
je sais	je savais	je saurai
tu sais	tu savais	tu sauras
il sait	il savait	il saura
nous savons	nous savions	nous saurons
vous savez	vous saviez	vous saurez
ils savent	ils savaient	ils sauront

PAST HISTORIC	PERFECT	PLUPERFECT
je sus	j'ai su	j'avais su
tu sus	tu as su	tu avais su
il sut	il a su	il avait su
nous sûmes	nous avons su	nous avions su
vous sûtes	vous avez su	vous aviez su
ils surent	ils ont su	ils avaient su

CONDITIONAL

	PRESENT	PAST
PAST ANTERIOR	je saurais	j'aurais su
j'eus su etc	tu saurais	tu aurais su
	il saurait	il aurait su
	nous saurions	nous aurions su
FUTURE PERFECT	vous sauriez	vous auriez su
j'aurai su etc	ils sauraient	ils auraient su

SUBJUNCTIVE

PRESENT	IMPERFECT	PLUPERFECT
je sache	je susse	j'aie su
tu saches	tu susses	tu aies su
il sache	il sût	il ait su
nous sachions	nous sussions	nous ayons su
vous sachiez	vous sussiez	vous ayez su
ils sachent	ils sussent	ils aient su

IMPERATIVE	INFINITIVE	PARTICIPLE
sache	PRESENT	PRESENT
sachons	savoir	sachant
sachez		
	PAST	PAST
	avoir su	su

TENIR
to hold

PRESENT	IMPERFECT	FUTURE
je tiens	je tenais	je tiendrai
tu tiens	tu tenais	tu tiendras
il tient	il tenait	il tiendra
nous tenons	nous tenions	nous tiendrons
vous tenez	vous teniez	vous tiendrez
ils tiennent	ils tenaient	ils tiendront

PAST HISTORIC	PERFECT	PLUPERFECT
je tins	j'ai tenu	j'avais tenu
tu tins	tu as tenu	tu avais tenu
il tint	il a tenu	il avait tenu
nous tînmes	nous avons tenu	nous avions tenu
vous tîntes	vous avez tenu	vous aviez tenu
ils tinrent	ils ont tenu	ils avaient tenu

CONDITIONAL

PAST ANTERIOR	PRESENT	PAST
j'eus tenu etc	je tiendrais	j'aurais tenu
	tu tiendrais	tu aurais tenu
	il tiendrait	il aurait tenu
	nous tiendrions	nous aurions tenu
FUTURE PERFECT	vous tiendriez	vous auriez tenu
j'aurai tenu etc	ils tiendraient	ils auraient tenu

SUBJUNCTIVE

PRESENT	IMPERFECT	PLUPERFECT
je tienne	je tinsse	j'aie tenu
tu tiennes	tu tinsses	tu aies tenu
il tienne	il tînt	il ait tenu
nous tenions	nous tinssions	nous ayons tenu
vous teniez	vous tinssiez	vous ayez tenu
ils tiennent	ils tinssent	ils aient tenu

IMPERATIVE	INFINITIVE	PARTICIPLE
tiens	**PRESENT**	**PRESENT**
tenons	tenir	tenant
tenez	**PAST**	**PAST**
	avoir tenu	tenu

VENDRE
to sell

PRESENT	IMPERFECT	FUTURE
je vends	je vendais	je vendrai
tu vends	tu vendais	tu vendras
il vend	il vendait	il vendra
nous vendons	nous vendions	nous vendrons
vous vendez	vous vendiez	vous vendrez
ils vendent	ils vendaient	ils vendront

PAST HISTORIC	PERFECT	PLUPERFECT
je vendis	j'ai vendu	j'avais vendu
tu vendis	tu as vendu	tu avais vendu
il vendit	il a vendu	il avait vendu
nous vendîmes	nous avons vendu	nous avions vendu
vous vendîtes	vous avez vendu	vous aviez vendu
ils vendirent	ils ont vendu	ils avaient vendu

CONDITIONAL

PAST ANTERIOR	PRESENT	PAST
j'eus vendu etc	je vendrais	j'aurais vendu
	tu vendrais	tu aurais vendu
	il vendrait	il aurait vendu
	nous vendrions	nous aurions vendu
FUTURE PERFECT	vous vendriez	vous auriez vendu
j'aurai vendu etc	ils vendraient	ils auraient vendu

SUBJUNCTIVE

PRESENT	IMPERFECT	PLUPERFECT
je vende	je vendisse	j'aie vendu
tu vendes	tu vendisses	tu aies vendu
il vende	il vendît	il ait vendu
nous vendions	nous vendissions	nous ayons vendu
vous vendiez	vous vendissiez	vous ayez vendu
ils vendent	ils vendissent	ils aient vendu

IMPERATIVE	INFINITIVE	PARTICIPLE
vends	PRESENT	PRESENT
vendons	vendre	vendant
vendez		
	PAST	PAST
	avoir vendu	vendu

VENIR
to come

PRESENT	IMPERFECT	FUTURE
je viens	je venais	je viendrai
tu viens	tu venais	tu viendras
il vient	il venait	il viendra
nous venons	nous venions	nous viendrons
vous venez	vous veniez	vous viendrez
ils viennent	ils venaient	ils viendront

PAST HISTORIC	PERFECT	PLUPERFECT
je vins	je suis venu(e)	j'étais venu(e)
tu vins	tu es venu(e)	tu étais venu(e)
il vint	il (elle) est venu(e)	il (elle) était venu(e)
nous vînmes	nous sommes venu(e)s	nous étions venu(e)s
vous vîntes	vous êtes venu(e)(s)	vous étiez venu(e)(s)
ils vinrent	ils (elles) sont venu(e)s	ils (elles) étaient venu(e)s

CONDITIONAL

PAST ANTERIOR	PRESENT	PAST
je fus venu(e) etc	je viendrais	je serais venu(e)
	tu viendrais	tu serais venu(e)
	il viendrait	il (elle) serait venu(e)
	nous viendrions	nous serions venu(e)s
FUTURE PERFECT	vous viendriez	vous seriez venu(e)(s)
je serai venu(e) etc	ils viendraient	ils (elles) seraient venu(e)s

SUBJUNCTIVE

PRESENT	IMPERFECT	PLUPERFECT
je vienne	je vinsse	je sois venu(e)
tu viennes	tu vinsses	tu sois venu(e)
il vienne	il vînt	il (elle) soit venu(e)
nous venions	nous vinssions	nous soyons venu(e)s
vous veniez	vous vinssiez	vous soyez venu(e)(s)
ils viennent	ils vinssent	ils (elles) soient venu(e)s

IMPERATIVE	INFINITIVE	PARTICIPLE
viens	PRESENT	PRESENT
venons	venir	venant
venez		
	PAST	PAST
	être venu(e)(s)	venu

VIVRE
to live

PRESENT	IMPERFECT	FUTURE
je vis	je vivais	je vivrai
tu vis	tu vivais	tu vivras
il vit	il vivait	il vivra
nous vivons	nous vivions	nous vivrons
vous vivez	vous viviez	vous vivrez
ils vivent	ils vivaient	ils vivront

PAST HISTORIC	PERFECT	PLUPERFECT
je vécus	j'ai vécu	j'avais vécu
tu vécus	tu as vécu	tu avais vécu
il vécut	il a vécu	il avait vécu
nous vécûmes	nous avons vécu	nous avions vécu
vous vécûtes	vous avez vécu	vous aviez vécu
ils vécurent	ils ont vécu	ils avaient vécu

CONDITIONAL

	PRESENT	PAST
PAST ANTERIOR	je vivrais	j'aurais vécu
j'eus vécu etc	tu vivrais	tu aurais vécu
	il vivrait	il aurait vécu
	nous vivrions	nous aurions vécu
FUTURE PERFECT	vous vivriez	vous auriez vécu
j'aurai vécu etc	ils vivraient	ils auraient vécu

SUBJUNCTIVE

PRESENT	IMPERFECT	PLUPERFECT
je vive	je vécusse	j'aie vécu
tu vives	tu vécusses	tu aies vécu
il vive	il vécût	il ait vécu
nous vivions	nous vécussions	nous ayons vécu
vous viviez	vous vécussiez	vous ayez vécu
ils vivent	ils vécussent	ils aient vécu

IMPERATIVE	INFINITIVE	PARTICIPLE
vis	**PRESENT**	**PRESENT**
vivons	vivre	vivant
vivez		
	PAST	**PAST**
	avoir vécu	vécu

VOIR
to see

PRESENT	IMPERFECT	FUTURE
je vois	je voyais	je verrai
tu vois	tu voyais	tu verras
il voit	il voyait	il verra
nous voyons	nous voyions	nous verrons
vous voyez	vous voyiez	vous verrez
ils voient	ils voyaient	ils verront

PAST HISTORIC	PERFECT	PLUPERFECT
je vis	j'ai vu	j'avais vu
tu vis	tu as vu	tu avais vu
il vit	il a vu	il avait vu
nous vîmes	nous avons vu	nous avions vu
vous vîtes	vous avez vu	vous aviez vu
ils virent	ils ont vu	ils avaient vu

CONDITIONAL

PAST ANTERIOR	PRESENT	PAST
j'eus vu etc	je verrais	j'aurais vu
	tu verrais	tu aurais vu
	il verrait	il aurait vu
	nous verrions	nous aurions vu
FUTURE PERFECT	vous verriez	vous auriez vu
j'aurai vu etc	ils verraient	ils auraient vu

SUBJUNCTIVE

PRESENT	IMPERFECT	PLUPERFECT
je voie	je visse	j'aie vu
tu voies	tu visses	tu aies vu
il voie	il vît	il ait vu
nous voyions	nous vissions	nous ayons vu
vous voyiez	vous vissiez	vous ayez vu
ils voient	ils vissent	ils aient vu

IMPERATIVE	INFINITIVE	PARTICIPLE
vois	**PRESENT**	**PRESENT**
voyons	voir	voyant
voyez		
	PAST	**PAST**
	avoir vu	vu

VOULOIR
to want

PRESENT	IMPERFECT	FUTURE
je veux	je voulais	je voudrai
tu veux	tu voulais	tu voudras
il veut	il voulait	il voudra
nous voulons	nous voulions	nous voudrons
vous voulez	vous vouliez	vous voudrez
ils veulent	ils voulaient	ils voudront

PAST HISTORIC	PERFECT	PLUPERFECT
je voulus	j'ai voulu	j'avais voulu
tu voulus	tu as voulu	tu avais voulu
il voulut	il a voulu	il avait voulu
nous voulûmes	nous avons voulu	nous avions voulu
vous voulûtes	vous avez voulu	vous aviez voulu
ils voulurent	ils ont voulu	ils avaient voulu

CONDITIONAL

PAST ANTERIOR	PRESENT	PAST
j'eus voulu etc	je voudrais	j'aurais voulu
	tu voudrais	tu aurais voulu
	il voudrait	il aurait voulu
	nous voudrions	nous aurions voulu
FUTURE PERFECT	vous voudriez	vous auriez voulu
j'aurai voulu etc	ils voudraient	ils auraient voulu

SUBJUNCTIVE

PRESENT	IMPERFECT	PLUPERFECT
je veuille	je voulusse	j'aie voulu
tu veuilles	tu voulusses	tu aies voulu
il veuille	il voulût	il ait voulu
nous voulions	nous voulussions	nous ayons voulu
vous vouliez	vous voulussiez	vous ayez voulu
ils veuillent	ils voulussent	ils aient voulu

IMPERATIVE	INFINITIVE	PARTICIPLE
veuille	**PRESENT**	**PRESENT**
veuillons	vouloir	voulant
veuilez		
	PAST	**PAST**
	avoir voulu	voulu

M.   VERB CONSTRUCTIONS

There are two main types of verb constructions: verbs can be followed:

    1. by another verb in the infinitive
    2. by an object (a noun or a pronoun)

1.   Verbs followed by an infinitive

There are three main constructions when a verb is followed by an infinitive:
    a) verb + infinitive (without any linking preposition)
    b) verb + **à** + infinitive
    c) verb + **de** + infinitive

For examples of these three types of constructions, see pp 96-100 and 102-3.

a)   *Verbs followed by an infinitive without preposition*

These include verbs of wishing and willing, of movement and of perception:

adorer to love	**aimer** to like	**aimer mieux** to prefer
aller to go (and)	**compter** to intend to	**descendre** to go down (and)
désirer to wish	**détester** to hate	**devoir** to have to
écouter to listen to	**entendre** to hear	**entrer** to go in (and)
envoyer to send	**espérer** to hope to	**faire** to make
falloir to have to	**laisser** to let	**monter** to go up (and)
oser to dare	**pouvoir** to be able to	**préférer** to prefer to
regarder to watch	**rentrer** to go in/back (and)	**savoir** to know how to
sembler to seem to	**sentir** to feel	**sortir** to go out (and)
souhaiter to wish to	**valoir mieux** to be better to	**venir** to come (and)
voir to see	**vouloir** to want to	

c) *Verbs followed by à* + infinitive

aider à	to help (to do)
s'amuser à	to enjoy (doing)
apprendre à	to learn (to do)
s'apprêter à	to get ready (to do)
arriver à	to manage (to do)
s'attendre à	to expect (to do)
autoriser à	to allow (to do)
chercher à	to try (to do)
commencer à	to start (doing)
consentir à	to agree (to do)
consister à	to consist in (doing)
continuer à	to continue (to do)
se décider à	to make up one's mind (to do)
encourager à	to encourage (to do)
enseigner à	to teach how (to do)
forcer à	to force (to do)
s'habituer à	to get used (to doing)
hésiter à	to hesitate (to do)
inciter à	to prompt (to do)
s'intéresser à	to be interested in (doing)
inviter à	to invite (to do)
se mettre à	to start (doing)
obliger à	to force (to do)
parvenir à	to succeed (in doing)
passer son temps à	to spend one's time (doing)
perdre son temps à	to waste one's time (doing)
persister à	to persist in (doing)
pousser à	to urge (to do)
se préparer à	to get ready (to do)
renoncer à	to give up (doing)
rester à	to be left (to do)
réussir à	to manage (to do)
servir à	to be used for (doing)
songer à	to think of (doing)
tarder à	to delay/be late in (doing)
tenir à	to be keen (to do)

c) *Verbs followed by de* + infinitive:

accepter de	to agree (to do)
accuser de	to accuse of (doing)
achever de	to finish (doing)
s'arrêter de	to stop (doing)
avoir besoin de	to need (to do)
avoir envie de	to feel like (doing)
avoir peur de	to be afraid (to do)
cesser de	to stop (doing)
se charger de	to undertake (to do)
commander de	to order (to do)
conseiller de	to advise (to do)
se contenter de	to make do with (doing)

craindre de	to be afraid (to do)
décider de	to decide (to do)
déconseiller de	to advise against (doing)
défendre de	to forbid (to do)
demander de	to ask (to do)
se dépêcher de	to hasten (to do)
dire de	to tell (to do)
dissuader de	to dissuade from (doing)
s'efforcer de	to strive (to do)
empêcher de	to prevent (from doing)
s'empresser de	to hasten (to do)
entreprendre de	to undertake (to do)
essayer de	to try (to do)
s'étonner de	to be surprised (at doing)
éviter de	to avoid (doing)
s'excuser de	to apologize for (doing)
faire semblant de	to pretend (to do)
feindre de	to pretend (to do)
finir de	to finish (doing)
se garder de	to be careful not to (do)
se hâter de	to hasten (to do)
interdire de	to forbid (to do)
jurer de	to swear (to do)
manquer de	'to nearly' (do)
menacer de	to threaten (to do)
mériter de	to deserve (to do)
négliger de	to fail (to do)
s'occuper de	to undertake (to do)
offrir de	to offer (to do)
omettre de	to omit (to do)
ordonner de	to order (to do)
oublier de	to forget (to do)
permettre de	to allow (to do)
persuader de	to persuade (to do)
prier de	to ask (to do)
promettre de	to promise (to do)
proposer de	to offer (to do)
recommander de	to recommend (to do)
refuser de	to refuse (to do)
regretter de	to be sorry (to do)
remercier de	to thank for (doing)
résoudre de	to resolve (to do)
risquer de	to risk (doing)
se souvenir de	to remember (doing)
suggérer de	to suggest (doing)
supplier de	to implore (to do)
tâcher de	to try (to do)
tenter de	to try (to do)
venir de	to have just (done)

2. Verbs followed by an object

In general, verbs which take a direct object in French also take a direct object in English, and verbs which take an indirect object in French (ie verb + preposition + object) also take an indirect object in English.

There are however some exceptions:

a) *Verbs followed by an indirect object in English but not in French* (the English preposition is not translated):

attendre	to wait for
chercher	to look for
demander	to ask for
écouter	to listen to
espérer	to hope for
payer	to pay for
regarder	to look at
reprocher	to blame for

on a demandé l'addition
we asked for the bill

je cherche mon frère
I'm looking for my brother

j'attendais l'autobus
I was waiting for the bus

tu écoutes la radio ?
are you listening to the radio?

b) *Verbs which take a direct object in English, but an indirect object in French:*

convenir à	to suit
se fier à	to trust
jouer à	to play (*game, sport*)
jouer de	to play (*musical instrument*)
obéir à	to obey
désobéir à	to disobey
pardonner à	to forgive
renoncer à	to give up
répondre à	to answer
résister à	to resist
ressembler à	to resemble (to look like)
téléphoner à	to phone

tu peux te fier à moi
you can trust me

il joue bien de la guitare
he plays the guitar well

téléphonons au médecin
let's phone the doctor

tu joues souvent au tennis ?
do you often play tennis?

tu as répondu à sa lettre ?
did you answer his letter?

obéis à ton père !
obey your father!

c) *Verbs which take a direct object in English but* **de** *+ indirect object in French:*

s'apercevoir de	to notice
s'approcher de	to come near
avoir besoin de	to need
changer de	to change
douter de	to doubt

se douter de	to suspect
s'emparer de	to seize, to grab
jouir de	to enjoy
manquer de	to lack, to miss
se méfier de	to mistrust
se servir de	to use
se souvenir de	to remember
se tromper de ...	to get the wrong ...

je dois changer de train ?
do I have to change trains?

il ne s'est aperçu de rien
he didn't notice anything

méfiez-vous de lui
don't trust him

je me servirai de ton vélo
I'll use your bike

tu te souviens de Jean ?
do you remember Jean?

il s'est trompé de numéro
he got the wrong number

d) *Some verbs take à or de before an object, whereas their English equivalent uses a different preposition:*

i) Verb + **à** + object:

croire à	to believe in
s'intéresser à	to be interested in
penser à	to think of/about
songer à	to think of
rêver à	to dream of/about
servir à	to be used for

je m'intéresse au football et à la course automobile
I'm interested in football and in motor-racing

à quoi penses-tu ?
what are you thinking about?

ça sert à quoi ?
what is this used for?

ii) Verb + **de** + object:

dépendre de	to depend on
être fâché de	to be annoyed at
féliciter de	to congratulate for
parler de	to speak of/about
remercier de	to thank for
rire de	to laugh at
traiter de	to deal with, to be about
vivre de	to live on

cela dépendra du temps
it'll depend on the weather

il m'a parlé de toi
he told me about you

tu l'as remercié du cadeau qu'il t'a fait ?
did you thank him for the present he gave you?

3.   Verbs followed by one direct object and one indirect object

a)   In general, these are verbs of giving or lending, and their English equivalents are constructed in the same way, eg:

donner quelque chose à quelqu'un
to give something to someone

il a vendu son ordinateur à son voisin
he sold his computer to his neighbour

Note: After such verbs, the preposition 'to' is often omitted in English but **à** cannot be omitted in French, and particular care must be taken when object pronouns are used with these verbs (see p 51).

b)   With verbs expressing 'taking away', **à** is translated by 'from' (**qn** stands for 'quelqu'un' and **sb** for 'somebody'):

acheter à qn	to buy from sb
cacher à qn	to hide from sb
demander à qn	to ask sb for
emprunter à qn	to borrow from sb
enlever à qn	to take away from sb
ôter à qn	to take away from sb
prendre à qn	to take from sb
voler à qn	to steal from sb

à qui as-tu emprunté cela ?   **il l'a volé à son frère**
who did you borrow this from?   he stole it from his brother

4.   Verb + indirect object + *de* + infinitive

Some verbs which take a direct object in English are followed by **à** + object + **de** + infinitive in French (**qn** stands for 'quelqu'un' and **sb** for 'somebody'):

commander à qn de faire	to order sb to do
conseiller à qn de faire	to advise sb to do
défendre à qn de faire	to forbid sb to do
demander à qn de faire	to ask sb to do
dire à qn de faire	to tell sb to do
ordonner à qn de faire	to order sb to do
permettre à qn de faire	to allow sb to do
promettre à qn de faire	to promise sb to do
proposer à qn de faire	to offer to do for sb,
	to suggest to sb to do

je lui ai conseillé de ne pas essayer
I advised him not to try

demande à ton fils de t'aider
ask your son to help you

j'ai promis à mes parents de ne jamais recommencer
I promised my parents never to do this again

8. PREPOSITIONS

Prepositions in both French and English can have many different meanings, which presents considerable difficulties for the translator. The following guide to the most common prepositions sets out the generally accepted meanings on the left, with a description of their use in brackets, and an illustration. The main meanings are given first. Prepositions are listed in alphabetical order.

à

at	(place)	**au troisième arrêt** at the third stop
	(date)	**à Noël** at Christmas
	(time)	**à trois heures** at three o'clock
	(idiom)	**au hasard, au travail** at random, at work
in	(place)	**à Montmartre** in Montmartre **à Lyon** in Lyons **au supermarché** in the supermarket **à la campagne** in the country **au lit** in bed **au loin** in the distance
	(manner)	**à la française** in the French way **à ma façon** (in) my way
to	(place)	**aller au théâtre** to go to the theatre **aller à Londres** to go to London
	(+ infinitive)	**c'est facile à faire** it is easy to do (*see p 102*)
away from	(distance)	**à 3 km d'ici** three kms away

by	(means)	**aller à bicyclette/ à vélo**
		to go by bike
		je l'ai reconnu à ses habits
		I recognized him by his clothing
	(manner)	**fait à la main**
		made by hand
	(rate)	**à la centaine**
		by the hundred
		100 km à l'heure
		60 mph
for/ up to	(+ pronoun)	**c'est à vous de jouer**
		it's your turn
		c'est à nous de le lui dire
		it's up to us to tell him
	(purpose)	**une tasse à café**
		a coffee cup
his/her/my etc	(possessive)	**son sac à elle**
		her bag
on	(means)	**aller à cheval/ à pied**
		to go on horseback/ on foot
	(place)	**à la page 12**
		on page 12
		à droite/à gauche
		on/to the right/left
	(time)	**à cette occasion**
		on this occasion
with	(descriptive)	**une maison à cinq pièces**
		a house with five rooms
		un homme aux cheveux blonds
		a man with blond hair
		l'homme à la valise
		the man with the case
	(idiom)	**à bras ouverts**
		with open arms

For the use of the preposition à with the infinitive see verb constructions p 146.

---

après

after	(time)	**après votre arrivée**
		after your arrival
	(sequence)	**24 ans après la mort du président**
		24 years after the death of the President
		après avoir/être *(see p 103)*

auprès de

near	**assieds-toi auprès de moi** sit down near me
compared to	**ce n'est rien auprès de ce que tu as fait** it's nothing compared to what you've done

avant

before	(time)	**avant cet après-midi** before this afternoon **avant ce soir** before tonight **avant de s'asseoir** before sitting down
	(preference)	**la famille avant tout** the family first (before everything)

avec

with	(association)	**aller avec lui** to go with him
	(means)	**il a tondu le gazon avec une tondeuse** he cut the lawn with a lawnmower

chez

at	(place)	**chez moi/toi** at/to my/your house **chez mon oncle** at my uncle's **chez le pharmacien** at the chemist's
among		**chez les Ecossais** among the Scots
about		**ce qui m'énerve chez toi, c'est …** what annoys me about you is …
in		**chez Sartre** in Sartre's work

contre

against	(place)	**contre le mur** against the wall
with	(after verb)	**je suis fâché contre elle** I'm angry with her
for		**échanger des gants contre un foulard** to exchange gloves for a scarf

dans

in	(position)	**dans ma serviette** in my briefcase	
	(time)	**je pars dans deux jours** I'm leaving in two days' time	
	(idiom)	**dans l'attente de vous voir** looking forward to seeing you	
from	(idiom)	**prendre quelque chose dans l'armoire** to take something from the cupboard	
on	(idiom)	**dans le train** on the train	
out of	(idiom)	**boire dans un verre** to drink out of a glass	

de

from	(place)	**je suis venu de Glasgow** I have come from Glasgow
	(date)	**du 5 février au 10 mars** from February 5th to March 10th **d'un weekend à l'autre** from one weekend to another
of	(adjectival)	**un cri de triomphe** a shout of triumph
	(contents)	**une tasse de café** a cup of coffee
	(cause)	**mourir de faim** to die of hunger
	(measurement)	**long de 3 mètres** 3 metres long
	(time)	**ma montre retarde de 10 minutes** my watch is 10 minutes slow
	(price)	**le montant est de 200 francs** the total is 200 francs
	(possessive)	**la mini-jupe de ma sœur** my sister's miniskirt
	(adjectival)	**les vacances de Pâques** the Easter holidays
	(after 'quelque chose')	**quelque chose de bon** something good
	(after 'rien')	**rien de nouveau** nothing new

	(after 'personne')	**personne d'autre**	nobody else
	(quantity)	**beaucoup de, peu de**	many, few
by	(idiom)	**je le connais de vue**	I know him by sight
in	(manner)	**de cette façon**	in this way
	(after superlatives)	**la plus haute montagne d'Ecosse**	the highest mountain in Scotland
on		**de ce côté**	on this side
than	(comparative)	**moins de 5 francs**	less than 5 francs
		plus de trois litres	more than three litres
to	(after adjectives)	**ravi de vous voir**	delighted to see you
		il est facile de le faire	it is easy to do it
	(after verbs)	**s'efforcer de**	to try to
with	(cause)	**tomber de fatigue**	to drop with exhaustion

depuis

for	(time)	**j'étudie le français depuis 3 ans**	I have been studying French for 3 years
		j'étudiais le français depuis 3 ans	I had been studying French for 3 years
		je n'ai pas vu de lapins depuis des années	I haven't seen a rabbit for years
from	(place)	**depuis ma fenêtre, je vois la mer**	from my window I can see the sea
	(time)	**depuis le matin jusqu'au soir**	from morning till evening
since		**depuis dimanche**	since Sunday

derrière

behind	(place)	**derrière la maison**	behind the house

dès

from	(time)	**dès six heures** from six o'clock onwards **dès 1934** as far back as 1934 **dès le début** from the beginning **dès maintenant** from now on
	(place)	**dès Edimbourg** from (the moment of leaving) Edinburgh

---

devant

before/in front of	(place)	**devant l'école** in front of the school

---

en

in	(place)	**être en ville** to be in town **en Angleterre** in England
	(colour)	**un mur peint en jaune** a wall painted yellow
	(material)	**une montre en or** a gold watch
	(dates etc)	**en quelle année ?** in what year? **en 1986** in 1986 **en été, en juillet** in the summer, in July
	(dress)	**en bikini** in a bikini
	(language)	**en chinois** in Chinese
	(time)	**j'ai fait mes devoirs en 20 minutes** I did my homework in 20 minutes
by	(means)	**en auto/en avion** by car/by plane
like, as		**il s'est habillé en femme** he dressed as a woman

on	(idiom)	**en vacances**
		on holiday
		en moyenne
		on average
	(+ present	**en faisant**
	participle)	on/while/by doing

Note: **en** *is not used with the definite article except in certain expressions:* **en l'an 2000** *(in the year 2000),* **en l'honneur de** *(in honour of) and* **en la présence de** *(in the presence of).*

en tant que

| *as/in (my) capacity as* | **en tant que professeur** |
| | as a teacher |

entre

among		**être entre amis**
		to be among friends
between	(place)	**entre Londres et Douvres**
		between London and Dover
	(time)	**entre 6 et 10 heures**
		between 6 and 10
	(idiom)	**entre toi et moi**
		between you and me
in	(punctuation)	**entre guillemets**
		in inverted commas
		entre parenthèses
		in brackets

d'entre

| *of/from among* | **certains d'entre eux** |
| | some of them |

envers

| *to/towards* | **être bien disposé envers quelqu'un** |
| | to be well-disposed towards someone |

hors de

| *out of* | **hors de danger** |
| | out of danger |

jusque

| *up to/ as far as* | (place) | **jusqu'à la frontière espagnole** |
| | | as far as the Spanish border |

	(time)	**jusqu'ici/ jusque-là** up to now/up till then
till		**jusqu'à demain** till tomorrow

malgré

in spite of		**malgré la chaleur** in spite of the heat

par

by	(agent)	**la lettre a été envoyée par mon ami** the letter was sent by my friend
	(means of transport)	**par le train** by train
	(distributive)	**trois fois par semaine** three times a week
by		**deux par deux** two by two
	(place)	**par ici/là** this/that way
in/on	(weather)	**par un temps pareil** in such weather **par un beau jour d'hiver** on a beautiful winter's day
out of	(place)	**regarder par la fenêtre** to look out of the window **jeter du pain par la fenêtre** to throw bread out of the window
to/on		**tomber par terre** to fall to the ground **étendu par terre** lying on the ground
	(+ infinitive)	**commencer/finir par faire** to begin/end by doing

parmi

among		**parmi ses ennemis** among his enemies

pendant

for	(time)	**il l'avait fait pendant 5 années** he had done it for 5 years
during		**pendant l'été** during the summer

pour

for		**ce livre est pour vous** this book is for you **mourir pour la patrie** to die for one's country
	(purpose)	**c'est pour cela que je suis venu** that's why I have come
	(emphatic) ·	**pour moi, je crois que** personally, I think that
	(time)	**j'en ai pour une heure** it'll take me an hour **je serai là pour 2 semaines** I'll be here for 2 weeks

(**pour** stresses intention and future time: see **depuis** and **pendant** p 155 and above)

	(idiom)	**c'est bon pour la santé** it's good for your health
to	(+ infinitive)	**il était trop paresseux pour réussir aux examens** he was too lazy to pass the exams

près de

near	(place)	**près du marché** near the market
nearly	(time)	**il est près de minuit** it's nearly midnight
	(quantity)	**près de cinquante** nearly fifty

quant à

as for		**quant à moi** as for me

sans

without	(+ noun)	**sans espoir** without hope
	(+ pronoun)	**je n'irai pas sans vous** I'll not go without you
	(+ infinitive)	**sans parler** without speaking **sans s'arrêter** without stopping

sauf

except for		**ils sont tous partis, sauf John** everyone left except John
barring		**sauf accidents/ sauf imprévu** barring accidents/ the unexpected

selon

according to		**selon le président** according to the President **selon moi** in my opinion

sous

under	(physical)	**sous la table** under the table
	(historical)	**sous Elisabeth II** under Elizabeth II
in	(weather)	**sous la pluie** in the rain
	(idiom)	**sous peu** shortly/before long **sous la main** to hand **sous tous les rapports** in all respects **sous mes yeux** before my eyes

sur

on/upon	(place)	**le bol est sur la table** the bowl is on the table
off		**prendre sur le rayon** to take off the shelf
out of	(proportion)	**neuf sur dix** nine out of ten **une semaine sur trois** one week in three
over	(place)	**le pont sur la Loire** the bridge over the Loire
about	(idiom)	**une enquête sur ...** an enquiry about ...

at		**sur ces paroles** at these words
		sur ce, il est sorti at this /whereupon he went out
by		**quatre mètres sur cinq** four metres by five
in		**sur un ton amer** in a bitter tone (of voice)
over		**l'emporter sur quelqu'un** to prevail over someone

vers

towards	(place)	**vers le nord** towards the north
	(time)	**vers la fin du match** towards the end of the match
about	(time)	**vers 10 heures** about 10 o'clock

voici/voilà

here	(is)	**le voici qui vient** here he comes
there	(is)	**voilà où il demeure** that is where he lives

9. CONJUNCTIONS

Conjunctions are words or expressions which link words, phrases or clauses. They fall into two categories:

A. coordinating
B. subordinating

A. COORDINATING CONJUNCTIONS

1. Definition

These link two similar words or groups of words (eg nouns, pronouns, adjectives, adverbs, prepositions, phrases or clauses). The principal coordinating conjunctions (or adverbs used as conjunctions) are:

et and	**mais** but	**ou** or
ou bien or (else)	**soit** or (either)	**ni** neither
alors then	**aussi** therefore	**donc** then, therefore
puis then (next)	**car** for (because)	**or** now
cependant however	**néanmoins** nevertheless	**pourtant** yet, however
toutefois however		

il est malade, mais il ne veut pas aller au lit
he's ill but he won't go to bed

il faisait beau, alors il est allé se promener
it was fine so he went for a walk

2. Repetition

a) Some co-ordinating conjunctions are repeated:

soit ... soit   either ... or

prenez soit l'un soit l'autre
take one or the other

ni ... ni   neither ... nor

le vieillard n'avait ni amis ni argent
the old man had neither friends nor money

b)   **et** and **ou** can be repeated in texts of a literary nature:

    et ... et   both ... and
    ou ... ou   whether ... or

3.   aussi

aussi means 'therefore' only when placed before the verb. The subject pronoun is placed after the verb (see p 176).

    il pleuvait, aussi Pascal n'est-il pas sorti
    it was raining, so Pascal didn't go out

when **aussi** follows the verb it means 'also':

    j'ai aussi mis mon imperméable
    I also put my raincoat on

B.   SUBORDINATING CONJUNCTIONS

These join a subordinate clause to another clause, usually a main clause. The principal subordinating conjunctions are:

comme	as	**parce que**	because
puisque	since	**ainsi que**	(just) as
à mesure que	as	**tant que**	as long as
avant que	before	**après que**	after
jusqu'à ce que	until	**depuis que**	since
si	if	**à moins que**	unless
pourvu que	provided that	**quoique**	although
bien que	although	**quand**	when
lorsque	when	**dès que**	as soon as
aussitôt que	as soon as	**pour que**	in order that
afin que	so that	**de sorte que**	so that
de façon que	so that	**de peur que** (+ **ne**)	for fear that, lest

Note: some subordinating conjunctions require the subjunctive (see pp 90-1).

C.   QUE

que can be coordinating or subordinating

1.   coordinating in comparisons (see pp 30-2 and 37-8)

    il est plus fort que moi
    he is stronger than I

2. subordinating

a) *meaning 'that':*

> **elle dit qu'elle l'a vu**
> she says she has seen him
>
> **je pense que tu as raison**
> I think you're right
>
> **il faut que tu viennes**
> you'll have to come

b) *replacing another conjunction:*

When a conjunction introduces more than one verb, **que** usually replaces the second (and subsequent) subordinating conjunctions to avoid repetition:

> **comme il était tard et que j'étais fatigué, je suis rentré**
> as it was late and I was tired, I went home

Note: the mood after **que** is the same as that taken by the conjunction it replaces, except in the case of **si** in which **que** requires the subjunctive:

> **s'il fait beau et que tu sois libre, nous irons à la piscine**
> if it's fine, and you are free, we'll go to the swimming pool

10. NUMBERS AND QUANTITY

A. CARDINAL NUMBERS

0	zéro	40	quarante
1	un (une)	50	cinquante
2	deux	60	soixante
3	trois	70	soixante-dix
4	quatre	71	soixante et onze
5	cinq	72	soixante-douze
6	six	80	quatre-vingt(s)
7	sept	90	quatre-vingt-dix
8	huit	99	quatre-vingt-dix-neuf
9	neuf	100	cent
10	dix	101	cent un(e)
11	onze	102	cent deux
12	douze	121	cent vingt et un(e)
13	treize	122	cent vingt-deux
14	quatorze	200	deux cents
15	quinze	201	deux cent un(e)
16	seize	1000	mille
17	dix-sept	1988	mille neuf cent
18	dix-huit		quatre-vingt-huit
19	dix-neuf	2000	deux mille
20	vingt	10,000	dix mille
30	trente	1,000,000	un million

Note:

a) **un** is the only cardinal number which agrees with the noun in gender:

un kilo	**une pomme**
a kilo	an apple

b) hyphens are used in compound numbers between 17 and 99 except where **et** is used (this also applies to compound numbers after 100: **cent vingt-trois** 123).

c) **cent** and **mille** are not preceded by **un** as in English (one hundred).

d) **vingt** and **cent** multiplied by a number take an **s** when they are not followed by another number.

e) **mille** is invariable.

B.   ORDINAL NUMBERS

		abbreviation
1st	**premier/ première**	**1er/1ère**
2nd	**deuxième/ second**	**2e**
3rd	**troisième**	**3e**
4th	**quatrième**	**4e**
5th	**cinquième**	**5e**
6th	**sixième**	**6e**
7th	**septième**	**7e**
8th	**huitième**	**8e**
9th	**neuvième**	**9e**
10th	**dixième**	**10e**
11th	**onzième**	**11e**
12th	**douzième**	**12e**
13th	**treizième**	**13e**
14th	**quatorzième**	**14e**
15th	**quinzième**	**15e**
16th	**seizième**	**16e**
17th	**dix-septième**	**17e**
18th	**dix-huitième**	**18e**
19th	**dix-neuvième**	**19e**
20th	**vingtième**	**20e**
21st	**vingt et unième**	**21e**
22nd	**vingt-deuxième**	**22e**
30th	**trentième**	**30e**
100th	**centième**	**100e**
101st	**cent unième**	**101e**
200th	**deux centième**	**200e**
1000th	**millième**	**1000e**
10,000th	**dix millième**	**10 000e**

Note:

a) ordinal numbers are formed by adding **-ième** to cardinal numbers, except for **premier** and **second**; **cinq**, **neuf** and numbers ending in **e** undergo slight changes: **cinquième**, **neuvième**, **onzième**, **douzième** etc.

b) ordinal numbers agree with the noun in gender and number:

le premier ministre   **la première fleur du printemps**
the Prime Minister   the first flower of spring

c) there is no elision with **huitième** and **onzième**:

le huitième jour   **du onzième candidat**
the eighthth day   of the eleventh candidate

d) cardinal numbers are used for monarchs, except for 'first':

Charles deux   **Charles premier**
Charles II   Charles I

C. FRACTIONS AND PROPORTIONS

1. Fractions

Fractions are expressed as in English: cardinal followed by ordinal:

deux cinquièmes
two fifths

But: ¹/₄   **un quart**   ¹/₂   **un demi, une demie; la moitié**
         ¹/₃   **un tiers**   ³/₄   **trois quarts**

2. Decimals

The English decimal point is conveyed by a comma in French:

un virgule huit (1,8)
one point eight (1.8)

3. Approximate numbers

une huitaine   **une dizaine**
about eight   about ten

une trentaine   **une centaine**
some thirty   about a hundred

But: **un millier**
         about a thousand

Note: **de** is used when the approximate number is followed by a noun:

une vingtaine d'enfants
about twenty children

4. Arithmetic

Addition	**deux plus quatre**	2 + 4
Subtraction	**cinq moins deux**	5 − 2
Multiplication	**trois fois cinq**	3 × 5
Division	**six divisé par deux**	6 ÷ 2
Square	**deux au carré**	2²

D. MEASUREMENTS AND PRICES

1. Measurements

a) *Dimensions*

la salle de classe est longue de 12 mètres
la salle de classe a/fait 12 mètres de longueur/de long
the classroom is 12 metres long

Similarly:

profond(e)/de profondeur/de profond	deep
épais(se)/d'épaisseur	thick
haut(e)/de hauteur/de haut	high

ma chambre fait quatre mètres sur trois
my bedroom is about 4 metres by three

b) *Distance*

à quelle distance sommes-nous du lycée ?
how far are we from the secondary school?

nous sommes à deux kilomètres du lycée
we are 2 kilometres from the secondary school

combien y a-t-il d'ici à Blois ?
how far is it to Blois?

2. Price

ce chandail m'a coûté 110 francs
this sweater cost me 110 francs

j'ai payé ce chandail 110 francs
I paid 110 francs for this sweater

des pommes à 10 francs le kilo
apples at 10 francs a kilo

du vin blanc à 12 francs la bouteille
white wine at 12 francs a bottle

cela fait/revient à 42 francs
that comes to 42 francs

ils coûtent 25 francs pièce
they cost 25 francs each

E. EXPRESSIONS OF QUANTITY

Quantity may be expressed by an adverb of quantity (eg 'a lot', 'too much') or by a noun which names the actual quantity involved (eg 'a bottle', 'a dozen').

1. Expression of quantity + 'de' + noun

Before a noun, expressions of quantity are followed by **de** (**d'** before a vowel or a silent **h**) and never by **du**, **de la** or **des**, except for **bien des** and **la plupart du/des**:

assez de	**autant de**
enough	as much/many
beaucoup de	**combien de**
a lot of, much, many	how much/many

moins de
less, fewer

plus de
more

peu de
little, few

un peu de
a little

tant de
so much/many

tellement de
so much/many

trop de
too much/many

bien du/de la/des
many, a lot of

la plupart du/de la/des
most

il y a assez de fromage ?
is there enough cheese?

j'ai beaucoup d'amis
I've got a lot of friends

**je n'ai pas beaucoup
de temps**
I haven't got much time

il y a combien de pièces ?
how many rooms are there?

tu as combien d'argent ?
how much money have
you got?

mange plus de légumes !
eat more vegetables!

il y avait peu de choix
there was little choice

peu de gens le savent
not many people know that

tu veux un peu de pain ?
would you like a little
bread?

il y a tant d'années
so many years ago

j'ai trop de travail
I've got too much work

il y a trop de voitures
there are too many cars

bien des gens
a good many people

la plupart des Français
most French people

2. Noun expressing quantity + 'de' + noun

une boîte de
a box/tin/jar of

une bouteille de
a bottle of

une bouchée de
a mouthful of (*food*)

une cuillerée de
a spoonful of

une douzaine de
a dozen

une gorgée de
a mouthful of (*drink*)

un kilo de
a kilo of

un litre de
a litre of

une livre de
a pound of

un morceau de
a piece of

un paquet de
a packet of

une paire de
a pair of

une part de a share/helping of	**une tasse de** a cup of
une tranche de a slice of	**un verre de** a glass of

je voudrais une boîte de thon et un litre de lait
I'd like a tin of tuna fish and a litre of milk

il a mangé une douzaine d'œufs et six morceaux de poulet
he ate a dozen eggs and six pieces of chicken

3. Expressions of quantity used without a noun

When an expression of quantity is not followed by a noun, **de** is replaced by the pronoun **en** (see p 53-4):

il y avait beaucoup de neige ; il y en avait beaucoup
there was a lot of snow; there was a lot (of it)

elle a mangé trop de chocolats ; elle en a trop mangé
she's eaten too many chocolates; she's eaten too many (of them)

11. EXPRESSIONS OF TIME

A. THE TIME

quelle heure est-il?   what time is it?

a) *full hours*

il est midi/minuit   **il est une heure**
it is 12 noon midday/midnight   it is 1 o'clock

b) *half-hours*

il est minuit et demi(e)   **il est midi et demi(e)**
it is 12.30 a.m.   it is 12.30 p.m.

il est une heure et demie
it is 1.30

c) *quarter-hours*

il est deux heures un/et quart **il est deux heures moins le/un quart**

it is a quarter past two   it is a quarter to two

d) *minutes*

il est quatre heures vingt-trois **il est cinq heures moins vingt**
it 23 minutes past 4   it is 20 to 5

Note: **minutes** is usually omitted; **heures** is never omitted.

e) *a.m. and p.m.*
du matin   **de l'après-midi/du soir**
a.m.   p.m.

il est sept heures moins dix du **il est sept heures dix du soir**
matin
it is 6.50 a.m.   it is 7.10 p.m.

The 24 hour clock is commonly used:

dix heures trente   **quatorze heures trente-cinq**
10.30 a.m.   2.35 p.m.

dix-neuf heures dix
7.10 p.m.

Note: times are often abbreviated as follows:

dix-neuf heures dix   **19h10**

B.   THE DATE

1.   Names of months, days and seasons

a)   *Months (les mois)*

janvier	January
février	February
mars	March
avril	April
mai	May
juin	June
juillet	July
août	August
septembre	September
octobre	October
novembre	November
décembre	December

b)   *Days of the week (les jours de la semaine)*

dimanche	Sunday
lundi	Monday
mardi	Tuesday
mercredi	Wednesday
jeudi	Thursday
vendredi	Friday
samedi	Saturday
dimanche	Sunday

c)   *Seasons (les saisons)*

le printemp (spring)	**l'été** (summer)
l'automne (autumn)	**l'hiver** (winter)

For prepositions used with the seasons see p 12.

Note: in French the months and days are masculine and do not have a capital
letter, unless they begin a sentence.

2.   Dates

a)   cardinals (eg **deux, trois**) are used for the dates of the month except the
first:

le quatorze juillet   **le deux novembre**
the fourteenth of July   the second of November

But: **le premier février**
the first of February

The definite article is used as in English; French does not use prepositions
('on' and 'of' in English):

je vous ai écrit le trois mars
I wrote to you on the third of March

b) **mil** (a thousand) is used instead of **mille** in dates from 1001 onwards:

> **mil neuf cent quatre-vingt sept**
> nineteen hundred and eighty-seven

3. Année, journée, matinée, soirée

Année, journée, matinée, soirée (the feminine forms of **an, jour, matin** and **soir**) are usually found in the following cases:

a) *when duration is implied* (eg the whole day):

pendant une année	for a (whole) year
toute la journée	all day long
dans la matinée	in the (course of the) morning
passer une soirée	to spend an evening
l'année scolaire/universitaire	the school/academic year

b) *with an ordinal number (eg première) or an indefinite expression*

la deuxième année	the second year
dans sa vingtième année	in his twentieth year
plusieurs/quelques années	several/a few years
bien des/de nombreuses années	many years
environ une année	about a year

c) *with an adjective:*

de bonnes/mauvaises années	good/bad years

C. IDIOMATIC EXPRESSIONS

à cinq heures	at 5 o'clock
à onze heures environ	about 11 o'clock
vers minuit	about midnight
vers (les) dix heures	about 10 o'clock
il est six heures passées	it is past 6 o'clock
à quatre heures précises/pile	at exactly 4 o'clock
il est neuf heures sonnées	it has struck nine
sur le coup de trois heures	on the stroke of three
à partir de neuf heures	from 9 o'clock onwards
peu avant sept heures	shortly before seven
peu après sept heures	shortly after seven
tôt ou tard	sooner or later
au plus tôt	at the earliest
au plus tard	at the latest
il est tard	it is late
il est en retard	he is late
il se lève tard	he gets up late
il est arrivé en retard	he arrived late
le train a vingt minutes de retard	the train is twenty minutes late

ma montre retarde de six minutes	my watch is six minutes slow
ma montre avance de six minutes	my watch is six minutes fast
ce soir	tonight
demain soir	tomorrow night
hier soir	yesterday evening, last night
demain matin	tomorrow morning
demain en huit	tomorrow week
le lendemain	the next day
le lendemain matin	the next morning
hier matin	yesterday morning
la semaine dernière	last week
la semaine prochaine	next week
lundi	on Monday
le lundi	on Mondays
il y a trois semaines	three weeks ago
une demi-heure	a half-hour, half an hour
un quart d'heure	a quarter of an hour
trois quarts d'heure	three quarters of an hour
passer son temps (à faire)	to spend one's time (doing)
perdre son temps	to waste one's time
de temps en temps	from time to time
tous les samedis	every Saturday
tous les samedis soirs	every Saturday evening/night
le combien sommes-nous aujourd'hui	what's the date today?
nous sommes/c'est le trois avril	it is the third of April
le vendredi treize juillet	Friday the thirteenth of July
en février/au mois de février	in February/in the month of February
en 1970	in 1970
dans les années soixante	in the sixties
au dix-septième siècle	in the seventeenth century
au XVIIᵉ	in the 17th Century
le jour de l'An	New Year's Day
avoir treize ans	to be thirteen years old
être âgé de quatorze ans	to be fourteen years old
elle fête ses vingt ans	she's celebrating her twentieth birthday
un plan quinquennal	a five-year plan
une année bissextile	a leap year
une année civile	a calendar year
une année-lumière	a light year

12. THE SENTENCE

A. WORD ORDER

Word order is usually the same in French as in English, except in the following cases:

1. Adjectives

Many French adjectives follow the noun (see pp 29-30):

de l'argent *italien*
(some) *Italian* money

j'ai les yeux *bleus*
I've got *blue* eyes

2. Adverbs

In simple tenses, adverbs usually follow the verb (see pp 36-7):

j'y vais *rarement*
I *seldom* go there

il fera *bientôt* nuit
it will *soon* be dark

3. Object pronouns

Object pronouns usually come before the verb (see p 51):

je *t'*attendrai
I'll wait *for you*

il *la* lui a vendue
he sold *it* to him

4. Noun phrases

Noun phrases are formed differently in French (see pp 190-1):

une chemise en coton
a cotton shirt

le père de mon copain
my friend's father

5. Exclamations

The word order is not affected after **que** or **comme** (unlike after 'how' in English):

que tu es bête !
you are silly!
(how silly you are!)

qu'il fait froid !
it's so cold!

comme il chante mal !
he sings so badly!

comme c'est beau !
that's so beautiful!

6. DONT

dont must be followed by the subject of the clause it introduces; compare:

l'agence d'emploi dont j'ai perdu la lettre
the employment agency whose letter I lost

l'agence d'emploi dont la lettre est arrivée hier
the employment agency whose letter arrived yesterday

7. Inversion

In certain cases, the subject of a French clause is placed after the verb.
Word order is effectively that of an interrogative sentence (see p 180).
This occurs:

a) *after the following, but only when they start a clause:*

à peine	**aussi**	**peut-être**
hardly	therefore	maybe, perhaps

à peine Alain était-il sorti qu'il a commencé à pleuvoir
Alain had hardly gone out when it started raining

il y avait une grève du métro, aussi a-t-il pris un taxi
there was an underground strike, so he took a taxi

peut-être vont-ils téléphoner plus tard
maybe they'll phone later

But: **Alain était à peine sorti qu'il a commencé à pleuvoir**

ils vont peut-être téléphoner plus tard

b) *when a verb of saying follows direct speech:*

"si tu veux", a répondu Marie	**"attention !" a-t-elle crié**
'if you want', Marie replied	'watch out!', she shouted
"j'espère que non", dit-il	**"répondez !" ordonna-t-il**
'I hope not', he said	'answer!', he ordered

B. NEGATIVE EXPRESSIONS

1. Main negative words

a)

ne ... pas	not
ne ... point	not (*literary*)
ne ... plus	no more/longer, not ... any more
ne ... jamais	never
ne ... rien	nothing, not ... anything
ne ... guère	hardly

b)

ne ... personne	nobody, no one, not ... anyone
ne ... que	only
ne ... ni	neither ... nor
(ni ... ni)	
ne ... aucun(e)	no, not any, none
ne ... nul(le)	no
ne ... nulle part	nowhere, not ... anywhere

Note:

i)   **ne** becomes **n'** before a vowel or a silent **h**

ii) **aucun** and **nul**, like other adjectives and pronouns, agree with the word
     they refer to; they are only used in the singular.

2. Position of negative expressions

a) *with simple tenses and with the imperative*

negative words enclose the verb: **ne** comes before the verb, and the second part of the negative expression comes after the verb:

je ne la connais pas I don't know her	**n'insistez pas !** don't insist!
je n'ai plus d'argent I haven't any money left	**tu ne le sauras jamais** you'll never know
ne dis rien don't say anything	**il n'y a personne** no one's here
je n'avais que dix francs I only had ten francs	**il n'est nulle part** it isn't anywhere
tu n'as aucun sens de l'humour you have no sense of humour	**ce n'est ni noir ni bleu** it's neither black nor blue

b) *with compound tenses*

with **ne ... pas** and the other expressions in list **1a**, the word order is: **ne** + auxiliary + **pas** + past participle:

il n'est pas revenu he didn't come back	**je n'ai plus essayé** I didn't try any more
je n'avais jamais vu Paris I had never seen Paris	**on n'a rien fait** we haven't done anything

with **ne ... personne** and the other expressions in list **1b**, the word order is: **ne** + auxiliary + past participle + **personne/que/ni** etc:

il ne l'a dit à personne he didn't tell anyone	**tu n'en as acheté qu'un ?** did you only buy one?
je n'en ai aimé aucun I didn't like any of them	**il n'est allé nulle part** he hasn't gone anywhere

c) *with the infinitive*

i) **ne ... pas** and the other expressions in list **1a** are placed together before the verb:

je préfère ne pas y aller I'd rather not go	**essaye de ne rien perdre** try not to lose anything

ii) **ne ... personne** and the other expressions in list (**1b**) enclose the infinitive:

il a été surpris de ne voir personne
he was surprised not to see anybody

j'ai décidé de n'en acheter aucun
I decided not to buy any of them

d) *at the beginning of a sentence*

when **personne**, **rien**, **aucun** and **ni ... ni** begin a sentence, they are followed by **ne**:

personne ne le sait
nobody knows

rien n'a changé
nothing has changed

ni Paul ni Simone ne sont venus
neither Paul nor Simon came

aucun secours n'est arrivé
no help arrived

3. Combination of negative expressions

Negative expressions can be combined:

ne ... plus jamais
ne ... plus rien
ne ... plus personne
ne ... plus ni ... ni
ne ... plus que

ne ... jamais rien
ne ... jamais personne
ne ... jamais ni... ni
ne ... jamais que

on ne l'a plus jamais revu
we never saw him again

il n'y a plus rien
there isn't anything left

plus personne ne viendra
no one will come any more

tu ne dis jamais rien
you never say anything

je ne bois jamais que
  de l'eau
I only ever drink water

je ne vois jamais personne
I never see anybody

4. Negative expressions without a verb

a) *PAS*

pas (not) is the most common of all negatives; it is frequently used without a verb:

tu l'aimes ? – pas beaucoup
do you like it? – not much

ah non, pas lui !
oh no, not him!

non merci, pas pour moi
no thanks, not for me

un roman pas très long
not a very long novel

lui, il viendra, mais pas moi
he will come, but I won't

j'aime ça ; pas toi ?
I like that; don't you?

b) *NE*

ne is not used when there is no verb:

qui a crié ? – personne
who shouted? – nobody

jamais de la vie !
not on your life!

rien ! je ne veux rien !
nothing! I want nothing!

rien du tout
nothing at all

c) *NON*

non (no) is always used without a verb:

> **tu aimes la natation ? – non, pas du tout**
> do you like swimming? – no, no at all

> **tu viens, oui ou non ?**   **je crois que non**
> are you coming, yes or no?   I don't think so

Note: **non plus** = 'neither':

> **je ne le crois pas – moi non plus**
> I don't believe him – neither do I

> **je n'ai rien mangé – nous non plus**
> I haven't eaten anything – neither have we

C. DIRECT AND INDIRECT QUESTIONS

1. Direct questions

There are three ways of forming direct questions in French:

   a) subject + verb (+ question word)
   b) (question word) + **est-ce que** + subject + verb
   c) (question word) + verb + subject = inversion

a) *subject + verb (+ question word)*

The word order remains the same as in statements (subject + verb) but the intonation changes: the voice is raised at the end of the sentence. This is by far the most common question form in conversational French:

> **tu l'as acheté où ?**   **je peux téléphoner d'ici ?**
> where did you buy it?   can I phone from here?

> **vous prendrez quel train ?**   **tu lui fais confiance ?**
> which train will you take?   do you trust him?

> **c'était comment ?**   **la gare est près d'ici ?**
> what was it like?   is the station near here?

> **le train part à quelle heure ?**   **cette robe me va ?**
> what time does the train   does this dress suit me?
> leave?

b) *(question word) + **est-ce que** + subject + verb*

This question form is also very common in conversation:

> **qu'est-ce que tu as ?**   **est-ce qu'il est là ?**
> what's the matter with you?   is he in?

> **est-ce que ton ami s'est amusé ?**
> did your friend have a good time?

> **où est-ce que vous avez mal ?**
> where does it hurt?

c) *inversion*

This question form is the most formal of the three, and the least commonly used in conversation.

i) if the subject is a pronoun, word order is as follows:

(question word) + verb + hyphen + subject

où allez-vous ?
where are you going?

voulez-vous commander ?
do you wish to order?

quand est-il arrivé ?
when did he arrive?

avez-vous bien dormi ?
did you sleep well?

ii) if the subject is a noun, a pronoun referring to the noun is inserted after the verb, and linked to it with a hyphen:

(question word) + noun subject + verb + hyphen + pronoun

où ton père travaillait-il ?
where did your father work?

Nicole en veut-elle ?
does Nicole want any?

iii) **-t-** is inserted before **il** and **elle** when the verb ends in a vowel:

comment va-t-il voyager ?
how will he travel?

aime-t-elle le café ?
does she like coffee?

pourquoi a-t-il refusé ?
why did he refuse?

Marie viendra-t-elle ?
will Marie be coming?

Note: when a question word is used, modern French will often just invert verb and noun subject, without adding a pronoun; no hyphen is then necessary:

où travaille ton père ?
where does your father work?

2. Indirect questions

a) *Definition*

Indirect questions follow a verb and are introduced by an interrogative (question) word, eg:

ask him when he will arrive   I don't know why he did it

b) *Word order*

i) The word order is usually the same as in statements: question word + subject + verb:

je ne sais pas s'il voudra
I don't know if he'll want to

dis-moi où tu l'as mis
tell me where you put it

il n'a pas dit quand il appellerait
he didn't say when he would phone

ii) If the subject is a noun, verb and subject are sometimes inverted:

demande-leur où est le camping
ask them where the campsite is

But: **je ne comprends pas comment l'accident s'est produit**
I don't understand how the accident happened

il ne savait pas pourquoi les magasins étaient fermés
he didn't know why the shops were closed

3. Translation of English question tags

a) Examples of question tags are: isn't it? aren't you? doesn't he? won't they? haven't you? is it? did you? etc.

b) French doesn't use question tags as often as English. Some of them can however be translated in the following ways:

i) **n'est-ce pas ?**

n'est-ce pas ? is used at the end of a sentence when confirmation of a statement is expected:

c'était très intéressant, n'est-ce pas ?
it was very interesting, wasn't it?

tu voudrais trouver un emploi stable, n'est-ce pas ?
you would like to find a secure job, wouldn't you?

vous n'arriverez pas trop tard, n'est-ce pas ?
you won't be arriving too late, will you?

ii) **hein ?** and **non ?**

In conversation **hein ?** and **non ?** are often used after affirmative statements instead of **n'est-ce pas** :

il fait beau, hein ?   **il est amusant, non ?**
it's nice weather, isn't it?   he's funny, isn't he?

D. ANSWERS ('YES' AND 'NO')

1. OUI, SI and NON

a) **oui** and **si** mean 'yes' and are equivalent to longer positive answers such as: 'yes, it is', 'yes, I will', 'yes, he has' etc:

tu m'écriras ? – oui, bien sûr !
will you write to me? – (yes) of course I will

b) **non** means 'no' and is equivalent to longer negative answers such as: 'no, it isn't', 'no, I didn't' etc:

c'était bien ? – non, on s'est ennuyé(s)
was it good? – no, it wasn't; we were bored

2.   OUI or SI ?

oui and si both mean 'yes', but oui is used to answer an affirmative question, and si to contradict a negative question:

> **cette place est libre ? – oui**
> is this seat free? – yes (it is)

> **tu n'aimes pas lire ? – si, bien sûr !**
> don't you like reading? – yes, of course (I do)

13. TRANSLATION PROBLEMS

A. GENERAL TRANSLATION PROBLEMS

1. French words not translated in English

Some French words are not translated in English, particularly:

a) *Articles*

Definite and indefinite articles are not always translated (see pp 11-4):

> **dans *la* société moderne, *les* prix sont élevés**
> in modern society, prices are high

> **ah non ! encore *du* riz ! je déteste *le* riz !**
> oh no! rice again! I hate rice!

b) *que*

que meaning 'that' as a conjunction (see pp 163-4) or 'that'/'which'/'whom' as a relative pronoun (see pp 60-1) cannot be omitted in French:

> **j'espère *que* tu vas mieux** **elle pense *que* c'est vrai**
> I hope you're better   she thinks it's true

> **celui *que* j'ai vu**   **c'est un pays *que* j'aime**
> the one I saw   it's a country I like

c) *Prepositions*

Some French verbs are followed by a preposition (+ indirect object) when their English equivalent takes a direct object (without preposition) (see pp 148-50):

> **elle a téléphoné *au* médecin** **tu l'as dit *à* ton père ?**
> she phoned the doctor   did you tell your father?

d) *le*

When **le** (it) is used in an impersonal sense (see p 50), it is not translated:

> **oui, je *le* sais**   **dis-*le*-lui**
> yes, I know   tell him

2. English words not translated in French

Some English words are not translated in French, for example:

a) *Prepositions*

i) with verbs which take an indirect object in English, but a direct object in French (see p 148):

> **tu l'as payé combien ?**   **écoutez cette chanson**
> how much did you pay *for* it?   listen *to* this song

ii)   in certain expressions (see p 173-4):

> **je viendrai te voir lundi soir**
> I'll come and see you *on* Monday night

b)   *'can'*

'can' + verb of hearing or seeing (see p 110):

je ne vois rien !	**tu entends la musique ?**
I can't see anything	can you hear the music?

3.   Other differences

a)   *English phrasal verbs*

Phrasal verbs are verbs which, when followed by a preposition, take on a different meaning, eg 'to give up', 'to walk out'. They do not exist in French and are translated by simple verbs or by expressions:

to give up	to run away	to run across
abandonner	**s'enfuir**	**traverser en courant**

b)   *English possessive adjectives*

English possessive adjectives (my, your etc) are translated by the French definite article (**le/la/les**) when parts of the body are mentioned (see p 58):

brush *your* teeth	he hurt *his* foot
brosse-toi *les* dents	**il s'est fait mal *au* pied**

c)   *'from'*

'from' is translated by à with verbs of 'taking away' (see p 150):

he hid it *from* his parents	borrow some *from* your dad
il l'a caché *à* ses parents	**empruntes-en *à* ton père**

B.   SPECIFIC TRANSLATION PROBLEMS

1.   Words in -ing

The English verb form ending in **-ing** is translated in a number of ways in French:

a)   *by the appropriate French tense (see pp 82-3):*

he's speaking (present tense)	**il parle**
he was speaking (imperfect)	**il parlait**
he will be speaking (future)	**il parlera**
he has been speaking (perfect)	**il a parlé**
he had been speaking (pluperfect)	**il avait parlé**
he would be speaking (conditional)	**il parlerait**

b) *by a French present participle (see p 104)*

   i) as an adjective:

      un livre amusant   **c'est effrayant**
      a funny book   it's frightening

   ii) as a verb, with **en** (while/on/by doing something; see pp 104-5):

      "ça ne fait rien", dit-il en souriant
      'it doesn't matter', he said smiling

      j'ai vu mes copains en sortant du lycée
      I saw my friends while I (was) coming out of school

But: **en** + present participle cannot be used when the two verbs have different subjects, eg:

      I saw my brother coming out of school
      j'ai vu mon frère sortir du lycée/qui sortait du lycée

c) *by a present infinitive (see pp 96-103):*

   i) after a preposition:

      au lieu de rire   **avant de traverser**
      instead of laughing   before crossing

   ii) after verbs of perception:

      je l'ai entendu appeler   **je l'ai vue entrer**
      I heard him calling   I saw her going in

   iii) after verbs of liking and disliking:

      j'adore faire du camping   **tu aimes lire ?**
      I love camping   do you like reading?

   iv) after verbs followed by **à** or **de**:

      tu passes tout ton temps à ne rien faire
      you spend all your time doing nothing

      il a commencé à neiger   **continuez à travailler**
      it started snowing   go on working

      tu as envie de sortir ?   **il doit finir de manger**
      do you feel like going out?   he must finish eating

   v) when an English verb in **-ing** is the subject of another verb:

      attendre serait inutile   **écrire est une corvée !**
      waiting would be pointless   writing is a real chore!

   vi) when an English verb in **-ing** follows 'is' or 'was' etc:

      mon passe-temps favori, c'est d'aller à la discothèque
      my favourite pastime is going to the disco

d) *by a perfect infinitive (see p 103)*

   i) after **après** (after):

      j'ai pris une douche après avoir nettoyé ma chambre
      I had a shower after cleaning my room

ii)   after certain verbs:

regretter	**remercier de**	**se souvenir de**
to regret	to thank for	to remember

e)   *by a noun*

particularly when referring to sports, activities, hobbies etc:

le ski	**la natation**	**l'équitation**
skiing	swimming	horse-riding
la voile	**le patinage**	**le canoë**
sailing	skating	canoeing
la lecture	**la planche à voile**	**la cuisine**
reading	wind-surfing	cooking
la boxe	**la lutte**	**la marche à pied**
boxing	wrestling	walking

2.   IT IS (IT'S)

'it is' (it's) can be translated in three ways in French:

a) **il/elle + être**
b) **ce + être**
c) **il + être**

a)   *il or elle (see pp 49-50)*

il or **elle** are used with the verb **être** to translate 'it is', 'it was' etc (+ adjective) when referring to a particular masculine or feminine noun (a thing, a place etc):

merci de ta carte ; elle était très amusante
thanks for your card; it was very funny

regarde ce blouson ; il n'est vraiment pas cher
look at that bomber jacket; it really isn't expensive

b)   *ce (see p 41)*

ce (**c'** before a vowel) is used with the verb **être** to translate 'it is', 'it was' etc in two cases:

i)   if **être** is followed by a word which is not an adjective on its own, ie by a noun, a pronoun, an expression of place etc:

c'était sa voix	**c'est une grande maison**
it was his voice	it's a big house
c'est moi ! c'est Claude !	**c'est le tien ?**
it's me! it's Claude!	is it yours?
c'est en France que tu vas ?	**c'est pour lundi**
is it France you're going to?	it's for Monday

ii) if **être** is followed by an adjective which refers to something previously mentioned, an idea, an event, a fact, but not to a specific noun:

l'homme n'ira jamais sur Saturne ; ce n'est pas possible
man will never go to Saturn; it's not possible

j'ai passé mes vacances en Italie ; c'était formidable !
I spent my holidays in Italy; it was great!

oh, je m'excuse ! – ce n'est pas grave
oh, I'm sorry! – it's all right

c) *il (see pp 79-82)*

il is used to translate 'it is', 'it was' etc in three cases:

i) with **être** followed by an adjective + **de** or **que** (ie referring to something that follows, but not to a specific noun):

il est impossible de connaître l'avenir
it's impossible to know the future

il est évident que tu ne me crois pas
it's obvious you don't believe me

ii) to describe the weather (see pp 79-80):

il y a du vent	**il faisait très froid**
it's windy	it was very cold

iii) with **être** to tell the time and in phrases relating to the time of day, or in such expressions as **il est temps de** (it's time to):

il est deux heures du matin	**ah bon ! il est tard !**
it's two a.m.	really! it's late!

il est temps de partir
it's time to go

Note: with other expressions of time, **c'est** is used:

c'est lundi ou mardi ?	**c'était l'été**
is it Monday or Tuesday?	it was summer

3. TO BE

Although 'to be' is usually translated by **être**, it can also be translated in the following ways:

a) *avoir*

i) **avoir** is used instead of **être** in many set expressions:

avoir faim/soif	to be hungry/thirsty
avoir chaud/froid	to be warm/cold
avoir peur/honte	to be afraid/ashamed
avoir tort/raison	to be right/wrong

ii) **avoir** is also used for age:

quel âge as-tu ?	**j'ai vingt- cinq ans**
how old are you?	I'm twenty five

b) *aller*

aller is used for describing health:

je vais mieux
I am/feel better

tout le monde va bien
everyone's fine

c) *faire*

faire is used in many expressions to describe the weather (see p 80):

il fait beau
it's fine

il fera chaud
it will be hot

Note: **il y a** can also be used to describe the weather, but only before **du/de la/des**:

il y a du vent/des nuages/de la tempête
it's windy/cloudy/stormy

d) *untranslated*

"to be" is not translated when it is the first part of an English continuous tense; instead, the appropriate tense is used in French (see pp 82-3):

I'm having a bath
je prends un bain

he was driving slowly
il conduisait lentement

4. ANY

'any' can be translated in three different ways:

a) *du/de la/des* or *de (see pp 14-5)*

the partitive article is used with a noun in negative and interrogative sentences:

il ne mange jamais de viande
he never eats any meat

tu veux du pain ?
do you want any bread?

b) *en (see p 53)*

en is used to translate 'any' without a noun in negative and interrogative sentences:

je n'en ai pas
I haven't got any

il en reste ?
is there any left?

c) *n'importe quel(le)/quel(le)s or tout(e)/tou(te)s*

these are used to translate "any" (and "every") when they mean "no matter which":

il pourrait arriver à n'importe quel moment
he could be arriving any time

prends n'importe quelle couleur, je les aime toutes
take any colour, I like them all

5. ANYONE, ANYTHING, ANYWHERE

Like 'any', these can be translated in different ways:

a) *in interrogative sentences:*

il y a quelqu'un ?
is anyone in?

tu l'as vu quelque part ?
did you see it anywhere?

il a dit quelque chose ?
did he say anything?

b) *in negative sentences:*

il n'y a personne
there isn't anyone

je ne le vois nulle part
I can't see it anywhere

je n'ai rien fait
I didn't do anything

c) *in the sense of 'any' (and 'every'), 'no matter which':*

n'importe qui peut le faire
anyone can do that

il croit n'importe quoi
he believes anything

j'irai n'importe où
I'll go anywhere

n'importe quand
anytime

6. YOU, YOUR, YOURS, YOURSELF

French has two separate sets of words to translate 'you', 'your', 'yours', 'yourself':

a) tu, te (t'), toi, ton/ta/tes, le tien etc
b) vous, votre/vos, le vôtre etc

For their respective meanings and uses, see pp 49-51, 55, 57-9.

a) *tu etc*

tu, te, ton etc correspond to the **tu** form of the verb (second person singular) and are used when speaking to one person you know well (a friend, a relative) or to someone younger. They represent the familiar form of address:

tu **viens au concert avec** *ton* **copain, Annie ? alors, je** *t'***achète deux places : une pour** *toi* **et une pour lui**
are *you* coming to the concert with *your* boyfriend, Annie. well, then, I'll get *you* two seats: one for *you* and one for him

b) *vous etc*

vous, vos etc correspond to the **vous** form of the verb (second person plural) and are used:

i) when speaking to more than one person:

dépêchez-*vous*, les gars ! *vous* allez manquer le train
hurry up, boys! *you*'ll miss the train

ii) when speaking to one person you do not know well or to someone older. They represent the formal or polite form of address:

je regrette, Monsieur, mais *vous* ne pouvez pas garder *votre* chien avec *vous* dans ce restaurant
I'm sorry, sir, but *you* can't keep *your* dog with you in this restaurant

c) when speaking or writing to one person, you must not mix words from both sets, but decide whether you are being formal or familiar, and use the same form of address throughout:

Cher Michel,
Merci de *ta* lettre. Comment vas-*tu* ? ...
Dear Michel,
Thanks for *your* letter. How are *you*? ...

Monsieur,
Pourriez-*vous* me réserver une chambre dans *votre* hôtel pour le huit juin ?
Dear Sir,
Could *you* book a room for me in *your* hotel for the eighth of June?

vous etc and **tu** etc can only be used together when **vous** is plural (ie when it refers to more than one person):

tu sais, Jean, *toi* et *ta* sœur, *vous vous* ressemblez
you know, Jean, *you* and *your* sister look like *each other*

7. Noun phrases

A noun phrase is a combination of two nouns used together to name things or people. In English, the first of these nouns is used to describe the second one, eg 'a love story'. In French, however, the position of the two nouns is reversed, so that the describing noun comes second and is linked to the first one by the preposition **de** (or **d'**):

une histoire d'amour
a love story

un magasin de disques
a record shop

un arrêt d'autobus
a bus stop

un coup de soleil
sunstroke

un roman de science-fiction
a science fiction novel

le château d'Edimbourg
Edinburgh castle

un joueur de rugby
a rugby player

un acteur de cinéma
a film actor

un film d'aventure
an adventure film

une boule de neige
a snowball

un match de football
a football game

un conte de fées
a fairy tale

un employé de bureau
an office clerk

Note: when the describing noun refers to a material, the preposition **en** is often used instead of **de**:

un pull en laine
a woollen jumper

un pantalon en cuir
leather trousers

une bague en or
a gold ring

un sac en plastique
a plastic bag

8. Possession

In English, possession is often expressed by using a noun phrase and tagging **'s** at the end of the first word, eg:

my friend's cat

This is translated in French by: object + **de** + possessor:

le chat de mon ami

Note the use of the article **le/la/les**.

le fiancé de ma sœur
my sister's fiancé

les amis de Chantal
Chantal's friends

les événements de la semaine dernière
last week's events

When **'s** is used in the sense of "someone's house" or "shop" etc, it is translated by the preposition **chez**:

je téléphone de chez Paul
I'm telephoning from Paul's

chez le dentiste
at/to the dentist's

INDEX